PARALLEL CLASSIC COMMENTARY

on the

NEW TESTAMENT

PARALLEL CLASSIC COMMENTARY
on the
NEW TESTAMENT

COMPILED AND EDITED BY

MARK WATER

Advancing the Ministries of the Gospel

AMG *Publishers*

God's Word to you is our highest calling.

AMG Publishers
6815 Shallowford Road
Chattanooga, Tennessee 37421

Copyright © 2004 John Hunt Publishing Ltd

Text: © 2004 Editor Mark Water

Text design: Jim Weaver Design, Basingstoke, UK

ISBN 0-89957-452-1

Unless otherwise stated Scripture quotations are taken from
The Holy Bible, New International Version. Copyright © 1973,
1978, 1984 by the International Bible Society.

King James Version/Authorised (KJV, AV): Oxford University
Press

Printed by Maple-Vail Book Manufacturing Group, USA

All Scripture is God-breathed and useful for teaching, rebuking, correcting and training in righteousness ...

2 Timothy 3: 16 (NIV)

Contents

Introduction

Commentary plan

There are two columns on the left hand pages in which the Bible text for the New Testament in the *King James Version* (*Authorized Version*) is set out in one column, next to John Calvin's commentary in the adjacent column.

Calvin did not write commentaries on 2 John, 3 John, or Revelation, so for these three books A.R. Faussett commentaries are substituted.

On the right hand pages there are also two columns of commentary. These consist of Bible commentary by biblical scholars other than Calvin.

John Calvin

Calvin is universally acknowledged as the greatest biblical commentator of all time.

Spurgeon quotes a Roman Catholic whom he calls Father Simon, "Calvin possessed a sublime genius."

Spurgeon himself calls Calvin the "prince" of Bible commentators: "Of all commentators I believe John Calvin to be the most candid." Dr King has added, "No writer ever dealt more fairly and honestly by the Word of God."

The text of Calvin's commentaries has been taken from John Owen's translation of his commentary on Hebrews, and for the other New Testament books from the Rev. William

Pringle's translation from the Latin, which he collated with Calvin's French version.

In his introduction Pringle explains the similarity between Calvin's translation of the New Testament text and that of the *King James Version*. Pringle states, "It may be proper to state that, throughout this work, Calvin's own version of THE THREE EVANGELISTS is adopted, as nearly as the difference of the languages would allow, in preference to our Authorized Version, which would not have rendered equal assistance to the reader in understanding the expositions. Yet the singular coincidence between the two Versions, interrupted chiefly by verbal differences which do not affect the sense, lends countenance to the suggestion of an esteemed friend and fellow-laborer, that King James's translators have been more deeply indebted to the labors of Calvin than is generally believed."

Insight

Isaac Newton famously said, "If I have seen farther than others, it is because I was standing on the shoulders of giants." The great benefit of good biblical commentaries is that they are written by godly people who have read scores of other commentaries before they present their distilled wisdom to us.

Contributors

All the contributors are well-known for their conservative, evangelical theological position and their incisive Bible commentaries.

Adam Clarke

Over the past 150 years Adam Clarke's commentary on the Bible has become one of the most highly respected interdenominational commentaries of all time. In this present commentary Clarke's writings on Matthew, Mark, Luke, and 1 and 2 Peter, and Jude's short letter, are included.

David Brown

David Brown, one of the three contributors to the giant one-volume Bible commentary, *A Commentary, Critical, Explanatory, and Practical, on the Old and New Testament* (Jamieson, Fausset, and Brown) writes on the Gospel of John.

Albert Barnes

C. H. Spurgeon rated Albert Barnes' *Notes on the New Testament* very highly and wrote of them, "Everybody has this work, and therefore can judge for himself, or we would commend." The book of Acts, 1 and 2 Thessalonians, the letter of James, and the book of Revelation are taken from Barnes' *Notes on the New Testament*.

Robert Haldane

Martyn Lloyd-Jones wrote of Robert Haldane's commentary on Romans, the one included in this volume: "It is with particular pleasure that I recommend this commentary on the Epistle to the Romans. First and foremost is the fact that I have derived much profit and pleasure from it myself. While Hodge excels in accurate scholarship, there is greater warmth and practical application in Haldane."

Charles Hodge

Charles Hodge, the renowned Princetown theologian, wrote lengthy commentaries on 1 and 2 Corinthians which still come at the top of the list of most people's choice for a classic commentary on these two Pauline letters. Edited versions of Hodge's commentaries on 1 and 2 Corinthians are included in this volume.

Martin Luther

Martin Luther's commentary on Galatians follows. When John Bunyan first discovered Martin Luther's commentary on Galatians he declared that "that book was most fit for a wounded conscience." Bunyan also said, "I do prefer this book of Martin Luther upon the Galatians (excepting the Holy Bible) before all the books that ever I have seen."

John Gill

John Gill, 1697–1771, acquired a scope of biblical knowledge seldom attained by most other biblical scholars. Writing of him, C. H. Spurgeon believed that: "In some respects, he has no superior. For good, sound, massive, sober sense in commenting who can excel Gill?" Gill's commentaries on Ephesians, Philippians, Colossians, and Philemon, and 1, 2, and 3 John are included in this volume.

A. R. Fausset

Another scholarly expositor and major contributor to *A Commentary, Critical, Explanatory, and Practical, on the Old and New Testament*, A. R. Faussett has his commentaries on 1 and 2 Timothy and Titus in this volume.

F. B. Meyer

F. B. Meyer wrote his commentary on the

letter to the Hebrews, which is included in this volume, under the title of: "The Way into the Holiest," and in his Preface writes: "There are two strong tendencies flowing around us in the present day: the one, to minimize the substitutionary aspect of the death of Christ; the other, to exaggerate the importance of mere outward rite. To each of these the study of this great Epistle is corrective. We are taught that our Lord's death was a Sacrifice. We are taught also that we have passed from the realm of shadows into that of realities."

List of commentaries on non John Calvin commentary pages

Synoptics

Calvin did not write separate commentaries on Matthew, Mark, and Luke. Instead he wrote one combined commentary on the Synoptics called the *Harmony of the Gospels*.

This has the great advantage of grouping similar material in the first three Gospels and commentating on all three passages in one place.

The order in which Calvin comments on passages from the first three Gospels is as follows.

Luke 1: 1–4
Luke 1: 5–13
Luke 1: 14–17
Luke 1: 18–20
Luke 1: 21–25
Luke 1: 26–33
Luke 1: 34–38
Luke 1: 39–45
Luke 1: 46–50
Luke 1: 51–55
Luke 1: 56–66
Luke 1: 67–75
Luke 1: 76–80
Matthew 1: 1–17; Luke 3: 23–38
Matthew 1: 18–25
Luke 2: 1–7
Luke 2: 8–14
Luke 2: 15–21
Matthew 2: 1–6
Matthew 2: 7–12
Luke 2: 22–32
Luke 2: 33–39
Matthew 2: 13–18
Matthew 2: 19–23
Luke 2: 40–47
Luke 2: 48–52
Matthew 3: 1–6; Mark 1: 1–6; Luke 3: 1–6

Matthew 3: 7–10; Luke 3: 7–14
Matthew 3: 11–12; Mark 1: 7–8; Luke 3: 15–18
Matthew 3: 13–17; Mark 1: 9–11; Luke 3: 21–23
Matthew 4: 1–4; Mark 1: 12–13a; Luke 4: 1–4
Matthew 4: 5–11; Mark 1: 13b; Luke 4: 5–13
Matthew 4: 12,17; Mark 1: 14–15; Luke 3: 19–20; 4: 14–15
Luke 4: 16–22
Luke 4: 23–30
Matthew 4: 13–16
Matthew 4: 18–25; Mark 1: 16–20; Luke 5: 1–11
Mark 1: 21–28; Luke 4: 31–37
Matthew 8: 14–18; Mark 1: 29–39; Luke 4: 38–44
Mark 3: 13–19; Luke 6: 12–19
Matthew 5: 1–12; Luke 6: 20–26
Matthew 5: 13–16; Mark 9: 49–50; 4: 21; Luke 14: 34–35; 8: 16; 11: 33
Matthew 5: 17–19; Luke 16: 16–17
Matthew 5: 20–22
Matthew 5: 23–26; Luke 12: 58–59
Matthew 5: 27–30
Matthew 5: 31–32; Luke 16: 18
Matthew 5: 33–37
Matthew 5: 38–41; Luke 6: 29–30
Matthew 5: 42; Luke 6: 34–35a
Matthew 5: 43–48; Luke 6: 27–28,32–33,35b–36
Matthew 6: 1–4
Matthew 6: 5–8
Matthew 6: 9–13; Luke 11: 1–4
Matthew 6: 14–15; Mark 11: 25–26
Matthew 6: 16–18
Matthew 6: 19–21; Luke 12: 33–34
Matthew 6: 22–24; Luke 11: 34–36; 16: 13
Matthew 6: 25–30; Luke 12: 22–28
Matthew 6: 31–34; Luke 12: 29–32
Matthew 7: 1–5; Mark 4: 24; Luke 6: 37–42

Adam Clarke's commentaries on the facing pages of Calvin's commentary on the Synoptics follow the same order of Gospel passages as Calvin.

The Commentaries

Matthew, Mark, and Luke

Introduction by John Calvin

The argument on the Gospel of Jesus Christ according to Matthew, Mark, and Luke

IN order to read with profit the Evangelical history, it is of great importance to understand the meaning of the word Gospel.[1] We shall thus be enabled to ascertain what design those heavenly witnesses had in writing, and to what object the events related by them must be referred. That their histories did not receive this name from others, but were so denominated by the Authors, is evident from Mark, who expressly says (1: 1) that he relates the beginning of the Gospel of Jesus Christ. There is one passage in the writings of Paul, from which above all others a clear and certain definition of the word Gospel may be obtained, where he tells us that it ... "was promised by God in the Scriptures, through the prophets, concerning his Son Jesus Christ our Lord, who was made of the seed of David according to the flesh, and declared to be the Son of God with power, according to the Spirit of sanctification, by the resurrection from the dead" (Romans 1: 2–4).

First, this passage shows that the Gospel is a testimony of the revealed salvation, which had been formerly promised to the Fathers in an uninterrupted succession of ages. It points out, at the same time, a distinction between the promises which kept the hope of the people in suspense, and this joyful message, by which God declares that he has accomplished those things which he had formerly required them to expect. In the same manner he states a little afterwards, that in the Gospel "the righteousness of God is openly manifested, which was testified by the Law and the Prophets" (Romans 3: 21).

The same apostle calls it, in another passage, an Embassy by which the reconciliation of the world to God, once accomplished by the death of Christ, is daily offered to men, (2 Corinthians 5: 20).

Secondly, Paul means not only that Christ is the pledge of all the blessings that God has ever promised, but that we have in him a full and complete exhibition of them; as he elsewhere declares that all the promises of God in him are yea, and in him amen, (2 Corinthians 1: 20). And, indeed, the freely bestowed adoption, by which we are made sons of God, as it proceeds from the good pleasure which the Father had from eternity, has been revealed to us in this respect, that Christ (who alone is the Son of God by nature) has clothed himself with our flesh, and made us his brethren. That satisfaction by which sins are blotted out, so that we are no longer under the curse and the sentence of, death, is to be found nowhere else than in the sacrifice of his death. Righteousness, and salvation, and perfect happiness, are founded on his resurrection.

The Gospel, therefore, is a public exhibition of the Son of God manifested in the flesh, (1 Timothy 3: 16), to deliver a ruined world, and to restore men from death to life. It is justly called a good and joyful message, for it contains perfect happiness. Its object is to commence the reign of God, and by means of our deliverance from the corruption of the flesh, and of our renewal by the Spirit, to conduct us to the heavenly glory. For this reason it is often called the kingdom of heaven, and the restoration to a blessed life, which is brought to us by Christ, is sometimes called the kingdom of God: as when Mark says that Joseph waited for the kingdom of God, (Mark 15: 43), he undoubtedly refers to the coming of the Messiah.

Hence it is evident that the word Gospel applies properly to the New Testament, and that those writers are chargeable with a want of precision, who say that it was common to all ages, and who suppose that the Prophets, equally with the Apostles, were ministers of the Gospel. Widely different is the account which Christ gives us, when he says, that "the law and the prophets were till John, and that since that time the kingdom of God began to be preached" (Luke 16: 16).

Mark, too, declares that the preaching of John was the beginning of the Gospel, (John 1: 1). Again, the four histories, which relate how Christ discharged the office of Mediator, have with great propriety received this designation. As the birth, death, and resurrection of Christ contain the whole of our salvation, and are therefore the peculiar subject of the Gospel, the name of Evangelists is justly and suitably applied to those who place before our eyes Christ who has been sent by the Father, that our faith may acknowledge him to be the Author of a blessed life.

The power and results of his coming are still more fully expressed in other books of the New Testament. And even in this respect John differs widely from the other three Evangelists: for he is almost wholly occupied in explaining the power of Christ, and the advantages which we derive from him; while they insist more fully on one point, that our Christ is that Son of God who had been promised to be the Redeemer of the world. They interweave, no doubt, the doctrine which relates to the office of Christ, and inform us what is the nature of his grace, and for what purpose he has been given to us; but they are principally employed, as I have said, in showing that in the person of Jesus Christ has been fulfilled what God had promised from the beginning. They had no intention or design to abolish by their writings the law and the prophets; as some fanatics dream that the Old Testament is superfluous, now that the truth of heavenly wisdom has been revealed to us by Christ and his Apostles. On the contrary, they point with the finger to Christ, and admonish us to seek from him whatever is ascribed to him by the law and the prophets. The full profit and advantage, therefore, to be derived from the reading of the Gospel will only be obtained when we learn to connect it with the ancient promises.

With regard to the three writers of the Evangelical history, whom I undertake to expound, Matthew is sufficiently known. Mark is generally supposed to have been the private friend and disciple of Peter. It is even believed that he wrote the Gospel, as it was dictated to him by Peter, and thus merely performed the office of an amanuensis or clerk. But on this subject we need not give ourselves much trouble, for it is of little importance to us, provided only we believe that he is a properly qualified and divinely appointed witness, who committed nothing to writing, but as the Holy Spirit directed him and guided his pen. There is no ground whatever for the statement of Jerome, that his Gospel is an abridgment of the Gospel by Matthew. He does not everywhere adhere to the order which Matthew observed, and from the very commencement handles the subjects in a different manner. Some things, too, are related by him which the other had omitted, and his narrative of the same event is sometimes more detailed. It is more probable, in my opinion – and the nature of the case warrants the conjecture – that he had not seen Matthew's book when he wrote his own; so far is he from having expressly intended to make an abridgment.

I have the same observation to make respecting Luke: for we will not say that the diversity which we perceive in the three Evangelists was the object of express arrangement, but as they intended to give an honest narrative of what they knew to be certain and undoubted, each followed that method which he reckoned best. Now as this did not happen by chance, but by the direction of Divine Providence, so under this diversity in the manner of writing the Holy Spirit suggested to them an astonishing harmony, which would almost be sufficient of itself to secure credit to them, if there were not other and stronger evidences to support their authority.

Luke asserts plainly enough that he is the person who attended Paul. But it is a childish statement which Eusebius makes, that Paul is the Author of the Gospel which bears the name of Luke, because in one passage he mentions "his Gospel" (2 Timothy 2: 8). As if what follows did not make it clear that Paul is speaking of his whole preaching, and not of a single book: for he adds, "for which I suffer trouble, even to bonds" (2 Timothy 2: 9). Now, it is certain that he was not held guilty of having written a book, but of having administered and preached with the living voice the doctrine of Christ. Eusebius, whose industry was great, discovers here a singular want of judgment in collecting without discrimination such gross absurdities. On this head I have thought it necessary to warn my readers, that they may not be shocked at fooleries of the same description which occur in every part of his history.

Of that method of interpretation which I have chosen to adopt, and which it may be many persons, at first sight, will not approve, it will be proper to give some account for the satisfaction of pious and candid readers. First, it is beyond all dispute, that it is impossible to expound, in a proper and successful manner, any one of the Evangelists, without comparing him with the other two; and, accordingly, faithful and learned commentators spend a very great portion of their labor on reconciling the narratives of the three Evangelists. But as it frequently happens that persons of ordinary abilities find the comparison to be no easy matter, when it is necessary to pass at every turn from the one to the other, I thought that it might prove to be a seasonable and useful abridgment of their labor, if I were to arrange the three histories in one unbroken chain, or in a single picture, in which the reader may perceive at a glance the resemblance or diversity that exists. In this way I shall leave out nothing that has been written by any of the three Evangelists; and whatever may be found in more than one of them will be collected into one place.

Notes.

1. *Evangelium* in Latin, *Evangile* in French, and *Evangell* in old English, are derived, with little alteration, from the Greek word *euangelion*, which is compounded of *eu*, well, and *angelia*, a message, and signifies glad news. The English word Gospel is of Saxon derivation, and is determined by its etymology to signify God's word; but must have acquired, at a very early period, the meaning of the Greek word for which it has been adopted as a translation. In the margin of the celebrated Geneva Testament, printed AD 1557, Gospel is thus defined: "This worde signifieth good tidinges, and is taken here for the storie which conteineth the joyful message of the comming of the Sonne of God."

The commentaries on the harmony of Matthew, Mark, and Luke are by John Calvin and Adam Clarke.

LUKE 1: 1–4

1 Forasmuch as many have taken in hand to set forth in order a declaration of those things which are most surely believed among us,

2 Even as they delivered them unto us, which from the beginning were eyewitnesses, and ministers of the word;

3 It seemed good to me also, having had perfect understanding of all things from the very first, to write unto thee in order, most excellent Theophilus,

4 That thou mightest know the certainty of those things, wherein thou hast been instructed.

LUKE 1: 5–13

5 There was in the days of Herod, the king of Judaea, a certain priest named Zacharias, of the course of Abia: and his wife was of the daughters of Aaron, and her name was Elisabeth.

6 And they were both righteous before God, walking in all the commandments and ordinances of the Lord blameless.

7 And they had no child, because that Elisabeth was barren, and they both were now well stricken in years.

8 And it came to pass, that while he executed the priest's office before God in the order of his course,

9 According to the custom of the priest's office, his lot was to burn incense when he went into the temple of the Lord.

10 And the whole multitude of the people were praying without at the time of incense.

11 And there appeared unto him an angel of the Lord standing on the right side of the altar of incense.

12 And when Zacharias saw him, he was troubled, and fear fell upon him.

13 But the angel said unto him, Fear not, Zacharias: for thy prayer is heard; and thy wife Elisabeth shall bear thee a son, and thou shalt call his name John.

LUKE 1: 14–17

14 And thou shalt have joy and gladness; and many shall rejoice at his birth.

15 For he shall be great in the sight of the Lord, and shall drink neither wine nor

LUKE 1: 1–4

Luke is the only Evangelist who makes a preface to his Gospel, for the purpose of explaining briefly the motive which induced him to write. By addressing a single individual he may appear to have acted foolishly, instead of sounding the trumpet aloud, as was his duty, and inviting all men to believe. It appears, therefore, to be unsuitable that the doctrine which does not peculiarly belong to one person or to another, but is common to all, should be privately sent to his friend Theophilus. Hence some have been led to think that Theophilus is an appellative noun, and is applied to all godly people on account of their love of God; but the epithet which is joined to it is inconsistent with that opinion. Nor is there any reason for dreading the absurdity which drove them to adopt such an expedient. For it is not less true that Paul's doctrine belongs to all, though some of his Epistles were addressed to certain cities, and others to certain men.

LUKE 1: 5–13

Luke very properly begins his Gospel with John the Baptist, just as a person who was going to speak about the daylight would commence with the dawn. For, like the dawn, he went before the Sun of Righteousness, which was shortly to arise. Others also mention him, but they bring him forward as already discharging his office. Luke secures our respect for him, while he is yet unborn, by announcing the miracles of divine power which took place at the earliest period of his existence, and by showing that he had a commission from heaven to be a prophet, before it was possible for men to know his character. His object was that John might afterwards be heard with more profound veneration, when he should come invested with a public office to exhibit the glory of Christ.

7. And they had no child

By an extraordinary purpose of God it was appointed that John should be born out of the common and ordinary course of nature. The same thing happened with Isaac (Genesis 17: 17; Genesis 21: 1–3), in whom God had determined to give an uncommon and remarkable demonstration of his favor. Elisabeth had been barren in the prime of life, and now she is in old age, which of itself shuts up the womb. By two hinderances, therefore, the Lord gives a twofold, surprising exhibition of his power, in order to testify, by stretching out his hand, as it were, from heaven, that the Prophet was sent by himself (Malachi 3: 1; John 1: 6). He is indeed a mortal man, born of earthly parents; but a supernatural method, so to speak, recommends him strongly as if he had fallen from heaven.

LUKE 1: 1–4

1. Many have taken in hand – Great and remarkable characters have always many biographers. So it appears it was with our Lord: but as most of these accounts were inaccurate, recording as facts things which had not happened; and through ignorance or design mistaking others, especially in the place where St. Luke wrote; it seemed good to the Holy Spirit to inspire this holy man with the most correct knowledge of the whole history of our Lord's birth, preaching, miracles, sufferings, death, resurrection, and ascension, that the sincere, upright followers of God might have a sure foundation, on which they might safely build their faith.

Most surely believed among us – Every thing that had been done or said by Jesus Christ was so public, so plain, and so accredited by thousands of witnesses, who could have had no interest in supporting an imposture, as to carry the fullest conviction, to the hearts of those who heard and saw him, of the divinity of his doctrine, and the truth of his miracles.

3. Having had perfect understanding – Having accurately traced up – entered into the very spirit of the work, and examined every thing to the bottom; in consequence of which investigation, I am completely convinced of the truth of the whole. Though God gives his Holy Spirit to all them who ask him, yet this gift was never designed to set aside the use of those faculties with which he has already endued the soul, and which are as truly his gifts as the Holy Spirit itself is. The nature of inspiration, in the case of St. Luke, we at once discover: he set himself, by impartial inquiry and diligent investigation, to find the whole truth, and to relate nothing but the truth; and the Spirit of God presided over and directed his inquiries, so that he discovered the whole truth, and was preserved from every particle of error.

Theophilus – Theophilus appears to have been some very reputable Greek or Roman, who was one of St. Luke's disciples. The first four verses seem a private epistle, sent by the evangelist with this history, which, having been carefully preserved by Theophilus, was afterwards found and published with this Gospel.

4. Wherein thou hast been instructed – It appears that Theophilus had already received the first elements of the Christian doctrine, but had not as yet been completely grounded in them. That he might know the certainty of the things in which he had been thus catechized, by having all the facts and their proofs brought before him in order, the evangelist sent him this faithful and Divinely inspired narrative.

LUKE 1: 5–13

5. In the days of Herod, the king – For the first time, the throne of Judah was filled by a person not of Jewish extraction, who had been forced upon the people by the Roman government. Hence it appears plain that the prophecy of Jacob, Genesis 49: 10, was now fulfilled; for the scepter had departed from Judah: and now was the time, according to another prophecy, to look for the governor from Bethlehem, who should rule and feed the people of Israel: Micah 5: 1–2.

Of the daughters of Aaron – That is, she was of one of the sacerdotal families. This shows that John was most nobly descended: his father was a priest and his mother the daughter of a priest; and thus, both by father and mother, he descended from the family of Amram, of whom came Moses, Aaron, and Miriam, the most illustrious characters in the whole Jewish history.

6. They were both righteous – Upright and holy in all their outward conduct in civil life.

10. The whole multitude – were praying – The incense was itself an emblem of the prayers and praises of the people of God: see Psalm 141: 2; Revelation 8: 1.

12. Zacharias – was troubled – Or, confounded at his sudden and unexpected appearance; and fear fell upon him, lest this heavenly messenger were come to denounce the judgments of

strong drink; and he shall be filled with the Holy Ghost, even from his mother's womb.

16 And many of the children of Israel shall he turn to the Lord their God.

17 And he shall go before him in the spirit and power of Elias, to turn the hearts of the fathers to the children, and the disobedient to the wisdom of the just; to make ready a people prepared for the Lord.

LUKE 1: 18–20

18 And Zacharias said unto the angel, Whereby shall I know this? for I am an old man, and my wife well stricken in years.

19 And the angel answering said unto him, I am Gabriel, that stand in the presence of God; and am sent to speak unto thee, and to shew thee these glad tidings.

20 And, behold, thou shalt be dumb, and not able to speak, until the day that these things shall be performed, because thou believest not my words, which shall be fulfilled in their season.

LUKE 1: 21–25

21 And the people waited for Zacharias, and marveled that he tarried so long in the temple.

22 And when he came out, he could not speak unto them: and they perceived that he had seen a vision in the temple: for he beckoned unto them, and remained speechless.

23 And it came to pass, that, as soon as the days of his ministration were accomplished, he departed to his own house.

24 And after those days his wife Elisabeth conceived, and hid herself five months, saying,

25 Thus hath the Lord dealt with me in the days wherein he looked on me, to take away my reproach among men.

LUKE 1: 26–33

26 And in the sixth month the angel Gabriel was sent from God unto a city of Galilee, named Nazareth,

27 To a virgin espoused to a man whose name was Joseph, of the house of

LUKE 1: 14–17

17. And he shall go before him

By these words he points out what would be John's office, and distinguishes him by this mark from the other prophets, who received a certain and peculiar commission, while John was sent for the sole object of going before Christ, as a herald before a king. Thus also the Lord speaks by Malachi, Malachi 3: 1.

LUKE 1: 18–20

18. And Zacharias said to the angel

Next follows the doubt of Zacharias, and the punishment which the Lord inflicted on his unbelief. He had prayed that he might obtain offspring, and now that it is promised, he distrusts, as if he had forgotten his own prayers and faith. It might, at first sight, appear harsh that God is so much offended by his reply. He brings forward his old age as an objection. Abraham did the same; and yet his faith is so highly applauded that Paul declares, he "considered not his own body now dead, neither yet the deadness of Sarah's womb" (Romans 4: 19), but unhesitatingly relied on the truth and power of God.

LUKE 1: 21–25

21. And the people were waiting

Luke now relates that the people were witnesses of this vision. Zacharias had stayed in the temple longer than usual. This leads to the supposition that something unusual has happened to him. When he comes out, he makes known, by looks and gestures, that he has been struck dumb. There is reason to believe, also, that there were traces of alarm in his countenance. Hence they conclude that God has appeared to him. True, there were few or no visions in that age, but the people remembered that formerly, in the time of their fathers, they were of frequent occurrence. It is not without reason, therefore, that they draw this conclusion from obvious symptoms: for it was not an ordinary occurrence, that he became suddenly dumb, and after a long delay came out of the temple in a state of amazement.

LUKE 1: 26–33

26. Now in the sixth month

It was a wonderful dispensation of the divine purpose, and far removed from the ordinary judgment of men, that God determined to make the beginning of the generation of the herald more illustrious than that of his own Son. The prophecy respecting John was published in the temple and universally known: Christ is promised to a virgin in an obscure town of Judea, and this prophecy remains buried in

God against a faithless and disobedient people, who had too long and too well merited them.

LUKE 1: 14–17

14. Many shall rejoice at his birth – He shall be the minister of God for good to multitudes, who shall, through his preaching, be turned from the error of their ways, and converted to God their Savior.

16. Many of the children of Israel shall he turn – See this prediction fulfilled, Luke 3: 10–18.

17. He shall go before him – Jesus Christ, in the spirit and power of Elijah; he shall resemble Elijah in his retired and austere manner of life, and in his zeal for the truth, reproving even princes for their crimes; compare 1 Kings 21: 17–24, with Matthew 14: 4. It was on these accounts that the Prophet Malachi, 4: 6, had likened John to this prophet. See also Isaiah 40: 3; and Malachi 4: 5–6.

LUKE 1: 18–20

18. Whereby shall I know this? – All things are possible to God: no natural impediment can have any power when God has declared he will accomplish his purpose. He has a right to be believed on his own word alone; and it is impious, when we are convinced that it is his word, to demand a sign or pledge for its fulfillment.

20. Thou shalt be dumb – Silent; this translation is literal; the angel immediately explains it, thou shalt not be able to speak.

LUKE 1: 21–25

21. The people waited – The time spent in burning the incense was probably about half an hour, during which there was a profound silence, as the people stood without engaged in mental prayer. To this there is an allusion in Revelation 8: 1–5. Zacharias had spent not only the time necessary for burning the incense,

but also that which the discourse between him and the angel took up.

22. They perceived that he had seen a vision – As the sanctuary was separated from the court by a great veil, the people could not see what passed, but they understood this from Zacharias himself, who, made signs, or nodded unto them to that purpose. Signs are the only means by which a dumb man can convey his ideas to others.

23. As soon as the days of his ministration were accomplished – Each family of the priesthood officiated one whole week, 2 Kings 11: 17.

There is something very instructive in the conduct of this priest; had he not loved the service he was engaged in, he might have made the loss of his speech a pretext for immediately quitting it. But as he was not thereby disabled from fulfilling the sacerdotal function, so he saw he was bound to continue till his ministry was ended; or till God had given him a positive dismission. Preachers who give up their labor in the vineyard because of some trifling bodily disorder by which they are afflicted, or through some inconvenience in outward circumstances, which the follower of a cross-bearing, crucified Lord should not mention, show that they either never had a proper concern for the honor of their Master or for the salvation of men, or else that they have lost the spirit of their Master, and the spirit of their work. Again, Zacharias did not hasten to his house to tell his wife the good news that he had received from heaven, in which she was certainly very much interested: the angel had promised that all his words should be fulfilled in their season, and for this season he patiently waited in the path of duty. He had engaged in the work of the Lord, and must pay no attention to any thing that was likely to mar or interrupt his religious service. Preachers who profess to be called of God to labor in the word and doctrine, and who abandon their work for filthy lucre's sake, are the most contemptible of mortals, and traitors to their God.

David; and the virgin's name was Mary.

28 And the angel came in unto her, and said, Hail, thou that art highly favored, the Lord is with thee: blessed art thou among women.

29 And when she saw him, she was troubled at his saying, and cast in her mind what manner of salutation this should be.

30 And the angel said unto her, Fear not, Mary: for thou hast found favor with God.

31 And, behold, thou shalt conceive in thy womb, and bring forth a son, and shalt call his name JESUS.

32 He shall be great, and shall be called the Son of the Highest: and the Lord God shall give unto him the throne of his father David:

33 And he shall reign over the house of Jacob for ever; and of his kingdom there shall be no end.

LUKE 1: 34–38

34 Then said Mary unto the angel, How shall this be, seeing I know not a man?

35 And the angel answered and said unto her, The Holy Ghost shall come upon thee, and the power of the Highest shall overshadow thee: therefore also that holy thing which shall be born of thee shall be called the Son of God.

36 And, behold, thy cousin Elisabeth, she hath also conceived a son in her old age: and this is the sixth month with her, who was called barren.

37 For with God nothing shall be impossible.

38 And Mary said, Behold the handmaid of the Lord; be it unto me according to thy word. And the angel departed from her.

LUKE 1: 39–45

39 And Mary arose in those days, and went into the hill country with haste, into a city of Juda;

40 And entered into the house of Zacharias, and saluted Elisabeth.

41 And it came to pass, that, when Elisabeth heard the salutation of Mary, the babe leaped in her womb; and Elisabeth was filled with the Holy Ghost:

the breast of a young woman. But it was proper that, even from the birth of Christ, that saying should be fulfilled, "it pleased God by foolishness to save them that believe" (1 Corinthians 1: 21).

31. Behold, thou shalt conceive in thy womb

The reason for the name is given by Matthew: "for he shall save his people from their sins" (Matthew 1: 21). And so the name contains a promise of salvation, and points out the object for which Christ was sent by the Father into the world, as he tells us that he "came not to judge the world, but to save the world" (John 12: 47). Let us remember that not by the will of men, but by the command of God, was this name given to him by the angel, that our faith may have its foundation, not in earth, but in heaven.

LUKE 1: 34–38

35. The Holy Ghost shall come upon thee

The angel does not explain the manner, so as to satisfy curiosity, which there was no necessity for doing. He only leads the virgin to contemplate the power of the Holy Spirit, and to surrender herself silently and calmly to his guidance. The word *epeleusetai*, "shall come upon" denotes that this would be an extraordinary work, in which natural means have no place.

LUKE 1: 39–45

39. And Mary arising

This departure mentioned by Luke proves that Mary's faith was not of a transitory nature: for the promise of God does not fade away with the presence of the angel, but is impressed upon her mind. The haste indicates a sincere and strong affection. We may infer from it that the Virgin disregarded every thing else and formed a just estimate of this grace of God.

LUKE 1: 46–50

Now follows a remarkable and interesting song of the holy virgin, which plainly shows how eminent were her attainments in the grace of the Spirit. There are three clauses in this song.

First, Mary offers solemn thanksgiving for that mercy of God which she had experienced in her own person.

Next, she celebrates in general terms God's power and judgments.

Lastly, she applies these to the matter in hand, treating of the redemption formerly promised, and now granted to the church.

LUKE 1: 26–33

26. A city of Galilee – As Joseph and Mary were both of the family of David, the patrimonial estate of which lay in Bethlehem, it seems as if the family residence should have been in that city, and not in Nazareth; for we find that, even after the return from the captivity, the several families went to reside in those cities to which they originally belonged. See Nehemiah 11: 3. But it is probable that the holy family removed to Galilee for fear of exciting the jealousy of Herod, who had usurped that throne to which they had an indisputable right.

28. And the angel came in unto her – Some think that all this business was transacted in a vision; and that there was no personal appearance of the angel. When Divine visions were given, they are announced as such, in the sacred writings; nor can we with safety attribute any thing to a vision, where a Divine communication is made, unless it be specified as such in the text.

Hail – Analogous to, Peace be to thee – May thou enjoy all possible blessings!

Highly favored – As being chosen in preference to all the women upon earth, to be the mother of the Messiah. Not the mother of God, for that is blasphemy.

The Lord is with thee – Thou art about to receive the most convincing proofs of God's peculiar favor towards thee.

Blessed art thou among women – That is, thou art favored beyond all others.

33. The house of Jacob – All who belong to the twelve tribes, the whole Israelitish people.

LUKE 1: 34–38

34. Seeing I know not a man – Or, husband. As she was only contracted to Joseph, and not as yet married, she knew that this conception could not have yet taken place; and she modestly inquires by what means the promise of the angel is to be fulfilled in order to regulate her conduct accordingly.

35. The Holy Ghost shall come upon thee – This conception shall take place suddenly, and the Holy Spirit himself shall be the grand operator. The power, the miracle-working power, of the Most High shall overshadow thee, to accomplish this purpose, and to protect thee from danger. As there is a plain allusion to the Spirit of God brooding over the face of the waters, to render them prolific, Genesis 1: 2, I am the more firmly established in the opinion advanced on Matthew 1: 20, that the rudiments of the human nature of Christ was a real creation in the womb of the virgin, by the energy of the Spirit of God.

36. Thy cousin Elisabeth – Thy kinswoman. As Elisabeth was of the tribe of Levi, Luke 1: 5, and Mary of the tribe of Judah, they could not be relatives but by the mother's side.

She hath also conceived – And this is wrought by the same power and energy through which thou shalt conceive. Thus God has given thee a proof and pledge, in what he has done for Elisabeth, of what he will do for thyself; therefore, have faith in God.

Who was called barren – It is probable that Elisabeth got this appellative by way of reproach; or to distinguish her from some other Elisabeth also well known, who had been blessed with children. Perhaps this is the reproach which Elisabeth speaks of, Luke 1: 25, her common name among men, among the people who knew her, being Elisabeth the barren.

37. For with God nothing shall be impossible – Words of the very same import with those spoken by the Lord to Sarah, when he foretold the birth of Isaac, Genesis 18: 14, Is any thing too hard for the Lord? As there can be no doubt that Mary perceived this allusion to the promise and birth of Isaac, so she must have had her faith considerably strengthened by reflecting on the intervention of God in that case.

LUKE 1: 39–45

41. Elisabeth was filled with the Holy Ghost – This seems to have been the accomplishment of the promise made by the angel, Luke 1: 15, He shall be filled with the Holy Ghost, even

42 And she spake out with a loud voice, and said, Blessed art thou among women, and blessed is the fruit of thy womb.

43 And whence is this to me, that the mother of my Lord should come to me?

44 For, lo, as soon as the voice of thy salutation sounded in mine ears, the babe leaped in my womb for joy.

45 And blessed is she that believed: for there shall be a performance of those things which were told her from the Lord.

LUKE 1: 46–50

46 And Mary said, My soul doth magnify the Lord,

47 And my spirit hath rejoiced in God my Savior.

48 For he hath regarded the low estate of his handmaiden: for, behold, from henceforth all generations shall call me blessed.

49 For he that is mighty hath done to me great things; and holy is his name.

50 And his mercy is on them that fear him from generation to generation.

LUKE 1: 51–55

51 He hath shewed strength with his arm; he hath scattered the proud in the imagination of their hearts.

52 He hath put down the mighty from their seats, and exalted them of low degree.

53 He hath filled the hungry with good things; and the rich he hath sent empty away.

54 He hath holpen his servant Israel, in remembrance of his mercy;

55 As he spake to our fathers, to Abraham, and to his seed for ever.

LUKE 1: 56–66

56 And Mary abode with her about three months, and returned to her own house.

57 Now Elisabeth's full time came that she should be delivered; and she brought forth a son.

58 And her neighbours and her cousins heard how the Lord had shewed great mercy upon her; and they rejoiced with her.

59 And it came to pass, that on the

46. My soul magnifieth

Here Mary testifies her gratitude. But as hypocrites, for the most part, sing the praises of God with open mouth, unaccompanied by any affection of the heart, Mary says that she praises God from an inward feeling of the mind. And certainly those who pronounce his glory, not from the mind, but with the tongue alone, do nothing more than profane his holy name.

LUKE 1: 51–55

51. the proud in the thought of their heart

This expression is worth noting: for as their pride and ambition are outrageous, as their covetousness is insatiable, they pile up their deliberations to form an immense heap, and, to say all in a single word, they build the tower of Babel (Genesis 11: 9). Not satisfied with having made one or another foolish attempt beyond their strength, or with their former schemes of mad presumption, they still add to their amount. When God has for a time looked down from heaven, in silent mockery, on their splendid preparations, he unexpectedly scatters the whole mass: just as when a building is overturned, and its parts, which had formerly been bound together by a strong and firm union, are widely scattered in every direction.

LUKE 1: 56–66

This narrative indicates that the birth of John was marked by various miracles, which gave reason to expect, that something great and remarkable would appear in the child himself at a future time. For the Lord determined to confer on him from the womb remarkable tokens, that he might not afterwards come forward, as an obscure and unknown person, from the crowd, to carry out the office of a Prophet.

64. And his mouth was instantly opened

God puts honor on the birth of his prophet by restoring speech to his father: for there can be no doubt that this benefit was delayed till that day with the express object and design of fixing the eyes of men upon John.

Zacharias spake, blessing God

He did so, not only for the purpose of testifying his gratitude, but to inform his relatives and neighbors, that this punishment had been inflicted on him, because he had been too slow to believe: for he was not ashamed to unite with his own dishonor the praises of the divine glory. Thus it became universally known, that the birth of the child was not an accidental or ordinary event, but had been promised by an announcement from heaven.

from his mother's womb. The mother is filled with the Holy Spirit, and the child in her womb becomes sensible of the Divine influence.

42. Blessed art thou among women – Repeating the words of the angel, Luke 1: 28, of which she had probably been informed by the holy virgin, in the present interview.

43. The mother of my Lord – The prophetic spirit, which appears to have overshadowed Elisabeth, gave her a clear understanding in the mystery of the birth of the promised Messiah.

LUKE 1: 46–50

47. My spirit hath rejoiced – Exulted. These words are uncommonly emphatic – they show that Mary's whole soul was filled with the Divine influence, and wrapped up in God.

48. He hath regarded – Looked favorably. In the most tender and compassionate manner he has visited me in my humiliation, drawing the reasons of his conduct, not from any excellence in me, but from his own eternal kindness and love.

All generations shall call me blessed – This was the character by which alone she wished to be known; viz. The blessed or happy virgin. What dishonor do those do to this holy woman, who give her names and characters which her pure soul would abhor; and which properly belong to GOD her Savior! By her votaries she is addressed as Queen of Heaven, Mother of God, etc., titles both absurd and blasphemous.

49. He that is mighty hath done to me great things – As God fills her with his goodness, she empties herself to him in praises; and, sinking into her own nothingness, she ever confesses that God alone is all in all.

50. His mercy is on them that fear him – His exuberant kindness manifests itself in acts of mercy to all those who fear or reverence his name; and this is continued from generation to generation, because he is abundant in goodness, and because he delighteth in mercy. This is a noble, becoming, and just character

of the God of the Christians; a being who delights in the salvation and happiness of all his creatures, because his name is mercy, and his nature love.

LUKE 1: 51–55

51. With his arm – Grotius has well observed, that God's efficacy is represented by his finger, his great power by his hand, and his omnipotence by his arm. The plague of lice was the finger of God, Exodus 7: 18. The plagues in general were wrought by his hand, Exodus 3: 20, and the destruction of Pharaoh's host in the Red Sea, which was effected by the omnipotence of God, is called the act of his arm, Exodus 15: 16.

In the imagination of their hearts – While they are forming their insolent, proud, and oppressive projects – laying their plans, and imagining that accomplishment and success are waiting at their right hand, the whirlwind of God's displeasure blows, and they and their machinations are dissipated together.

53. Filled the hungry – the rich he hath sent empty away – God is here represented under the notion of a person of unbounded benevolence, who is daily feeding multitudes at his gates. The poor and the rich are equally dependent upon him; to the one he gives his affluence for a season, and to the other his daily bread. The poor man comes through a sense of his want to get his daily support, and God feeds him; the rich man comes through the lust of gain, to get more added to his abundance, and, God sends him empty away – not only gives him nothing more, but often deprives him of that which he has, because he has not improved it to the honor of the giver. There is an allusion here, as in several other parts of this song, to the case of Hannah and Peninah, as related 1 Samuel 1: 2, etc.; 2: 1–10.

LUKE 1: 56–66

58. And her neighbors and her cousins – rejoiced with her – Because sterility was a reproach; and they now rejoiced with their

eighth day they came to circumcise the child; and they called him Zacharias, after the name of his father.

60 And his mother answered and said, Not so; but he shall be called John.

61 And they said unto her, There is none of thy kindred that is called by this name.

62 And they made signs to his father, how he would have him called.

63 And he asked for a writing table, and wrote, saying, His name is John. And they marveled all.

64 And his mouth was opened immediately, and his tongue loosed, and he spake, and praised God.

65 And fear came on all that dwelt round about them: and all these sayings were noised abroad throughout all the hill country of Judaea.

66 And all they that heard them laid them up in their hearts, saying, What manner of child shall this be! And the hand of the Lord was with him.

LUKE 1: 67–75

67 And his father Zacharias was filled with the Holy Ghost, and prophesied, saying,

68 Blessed be the Lord God of Israel; for he hath visited and redeemed his people,

69 And hath raised up an horn of salvation for us in the house of his servant David;

70 As he spake by the mouth of his holy prophets, which have been since the world began:

71 That we should be saved from our enemies, and from the hand of all that hate us;

72 To perform the mercy promised to our fathers, and to remember his holy covenant;

73 The oath which he sware to our father Abraham,

74 That he would grant unto us, that we being delivered out of the hand of our enemies might serve him without fear,

75 In holiness and righteousness before him, all the days of our life.

65. And fear fell upon all

This fear mentioned by Luke proceeded from a feeling of the divine power: for the works of God ought to be contemplated by us with such reverence as to affect our minds with seriousness. God does not

LUKE 1: 67–75

67. Zacharias was filled with the Holy Ghost

This phrase means that God's servants received more abundantly the grace of the Spirit, of which, at other times, they were not destitute. Thus we read, that the Spirit was given to the prophets: not that on other occasions they lacked it, but that the power of the Spirit was more fully exerted in them, when the hand of God, as it were, brought them into public view, for the discharge of their office.

We must observe, therefore, the manner in which Luke connects the two clauses: he **was filled with the Holy Ghost, and prophesied**. This implies that divine inspiration, at that time, rested upon him in an extraordinary measure, in consequence of which he did not speak like a man or private person, but all that he uttered was heavenly instruction. Thus also Paul connects prophecy with the Spirit. "Quench not the Spirit: despise not prophesyings" (1 Thessalonians 5: 19–20). This teaches us that to despise instruction is to "quench" the light of "the Spirit." This was a remarkable instance of the goodness of God, that not only did Zacharias recover the power of speech, which he had not enjoyed for nine months, but his tongue became the organ of the Holy Spirit.

LUKE 1: 76–80

76. And thou, child

Zacharias again returns to commend the grace of Christ, but does this, as it were, in the person of his son, by describing briefly the office to which he had been appointed as an instructor. Though in a little infant eight days old he does not yet observe prophetical endowments, yet turning his eyes to the purpose of God, he speaks of it as a thing already known.

79. That he might give light to those who were sitting in darkness

These words show, that out of Christ there is no life-giving light in the world, but every thing is covered by the appalling darkness of death. Thus, in another passage, Isaiah testifies that this privilege belongs peculiarly to the church alone. "Behold, the darkness shall cover the earth, and gross darkness the people: but the Lord shall arise upon thee, and his glory shall be seen upon thee" (Isaiah 60: 2).

relative, from whom that reproach was now rolled away. To rejoice with those whom God has favored, and to congratulate them on the advantages which he has granted to them, is a duty which humanity, charity, and religion call upon us to fulfill.

59. On the eighth day they came to circumcise – Had circumcision been essential to an infant's salvation, God would not have ordered it to be delayed to the eighth day, because, in all countries, multitudes die before they arrive at that age. Baptism, which is generally allowed to have been substituted for circumcision, is no more necessary to the salvation of an infant than circumcision was. Both are signs of the covenant – circumcision, of the putting away the impurity of the flesh; and baptism, of the washing of regeneration, and renewing of the Holy Ghost, producing the answer of a good conscience towards God. Confer 1 Peter 3: 21, with Titus 3: 5. This should never be neglected: it is a sign and token of the spiritual grace.

They called him Zacharias – Among the Jews, the child was named when it was circumcised, and ordinarily the name of the father was given to the first-born son.

60. Not so; but he shall be called John – This is the name which the angel desired should be given him, Luke 1: 13, and of which Zacharias by writing had informed his wife.

64. And he spake, and praised God – In his nine months' silence, he had learned the proper use of his tongue; and God, whose power was discredited by it, is now magnified. Happy they who, in religious matters, only break silence in order to speak of the loving-kindness of the Lord!

65. And fear came – The inhabitants of Hebron and its environs, who were well acquainted with the circumstances of Zacharias and Elisabeth, perceived that God had in a remarkable manner visited them; and this begot in their minds a more than ordinary reverence for the Supreme Being. Thus the salvation of one often becomes an instrument of good to the souls of many.

66. What manner of child shall this be! – As there have been so many extraordinary things in his conception and birth, surely God has designed him for some extraordinary purpose. These things they laid up in their heart, patiently waiting to see what God would work.

The hand of the Lord was with him – God defended and prospered him in all things, and the prophetic spirit began to rest upon him.

LUKE 1: 67–75

67. Zacharias – prophesied – The word prophesy is to be taken here in its proper acceptation, for the predicting or foretelling future events.

Zacharias speaks, not only of what God had already done, but also of what he was about to do, in order to save a lost world.

68. Blessed be the Lord God of Israel; for, etc. – Zacharias praises God for two grand benefits which he had granted to his people. 1. He has visited them. 2. He has ransomed them.

69. And hath raised up a horn of salvation – That is, a mighty and glorious Savior: a quotation from Psalm 18: 2. Horns are the well-known emblems of strength, glory, and power, both in the sacred and profane writers, because the strength and beauty of horned animals consist in their horns. Horns have also been considered as emblems of light; therefore the heathen god Apollo is represented with horns, to point out the power, glory, and excellence of the solar light.

71. That we should be saved (literally, a salvation) from our enemies – As Zacharias spoke by the inspiration of the Holy Spirit, the salvation which he mentions here must necessarily be understood in a spiritual sense. Satan, death, and sin are the enemies from whom Jesus came to deliver us. Sin is the most dangerous of all, and is properly the only enemy we have to fear. Satan is without us, and can have no power over us, but what he gets through sin. Death is only in our flesh, and shall be finally destroyed (as it affects us)

LUKE 1: 76–80

76 And thou, child, shalt be called the prophet of the Highest: for thou shalt go before the face of the Lord to prepare his ways;

77 To give knowledge of salvation unto his people by the remission of their sins,

78 Through the tender mercy of our God; whereby the dayspring from on high hath visited us,

79 To give light to them that sit in darkness and in the shadow of death, to guide our feet into the way of peace.

80 And the child grew, and waxed strong in spirit, and was in the deserts till the day of his showing unto Israel.

MATTHEW 1: 1–17; LUKE 3: 23–38

Matthew 1: 1–17

1 The book of the generation of Jesus Christ, the son of David, the son of Abraham.

2 Abraham begat Isaac; and Isaac begat Jacob; and Jacob begat Judas and his brethren;

3 And Judas begat Phares and Zara of Thamar; and Phares begat Esrom; and Esrom begat Aram;

4 And Aram begat Aminadab; and Aminadab begat Naasson; and Naasson begat Salmon;

5 And Salmon begat Booz of Rachab; and Booz begat Obed of Ruth; and Obed begat Jesse;

6 And Jesse begat David the king; and David the king begat Solomon of her that had been the wife of Urias;

7 And Solomon begat Roboam; and Roboam begat Abia; and Abia begat Asa;

8 And Asa begat Josaphat; and Josaphat begat Joram; and Joram begat Ozias;

9 And Ozias begat Joatham; and Joatham begat Achaz; and Achaz begat Ezekias;

10 And Ezekias begat Manasses; and Manasses begat Amon; and Amon begat Josias;

11 And Josias begat Jechonias and his brethren, about the time they were carried away to Babylon:

12 And after they were brought to Babylon, Jechonias begat Salathiel; and

MATTHEW 1: 1–17; LUKE 3: 23–38

Matthew 1: 1–17

These two genealogies agree substantially with each other, but we must note four points of difference.

The first is; Luke ascends by a retrograde order, from the last to the first, while Matthew begins with the source of the genealogy.

The second is; Matthew does not carry his narrative beyond the holy and elect race of Abraham, while Luke proceeds as far as Adam.

The third is; Matthew treats of his legal descent, and allows himself to make some omissions in the line of ancestors, choosing to assist the reader's memory by arranging them under three fourteens; while Luke follows the natural descent with greater exactness.

The fourth and last is; when they are speaking of the same people, they sometimes give them different names.

Many look on this fourth point as a great difficulty: for from David till Joseph, with the exception of Salathiel and Zerubbabel, none of the names are alike in the two Evangelists. The excuse commonly offered, that the diversity arose from its being very customary among the Jews to have two names, appears to many people not quite satisfactory. But as we are now unacquainted with the method, which was followed by Matthew in drawing up and arranging the genealogy, there is no reason to wonder, if we are unable to determine how far both of them agree or differ as to individual names.

It cannot be doubted that, after the Babylonian captivity, the same people are mentioned under different names. In the case of Salathiel and Zerubbabel, the same names, I think, were purposely retained, on account of the change which had taken place in the nation: because the royal authority was then extinguished.

Also, note that the additional number in Luke's catalogue to that of Matthew is nothing strange; for the number of people in the natural line of descent is usually greater than in the legal line. Besides, Matthew chose to divide the genealogy of Christ into three groups, and to make each group to contain fourteen people. In this way, he felt himself at liberty to pass by some names, which Luke could not with propriety omit, not having restricted himself by that rule.

It now remains to inquire why Matthew included the whole genealogy of Christ in three classes, and assigned to each class fourteen people. Those who think that he did so, in order to aid the memory of his readers, state a part of the reason, but not the whole. It is true, indeed, that a catalogue, divided into three equal numbers, is more easily remembered. But it is also evident that this division is intended to point out a threefold condition of the nation, from the time

on the morning of the resurrection.

Jesus redeems from sin; this is the grand, the glorious, the important victory. Let us get sin cast out, and then we need, fear neither death, nor the devil.

LUKE 1: 76–80

76. And thou, child, etc. – Zacharias proclaims the dignity, employment, doctrine, and success of his son; and the ruin and recovery of the Jews and the Gentiles.

80. The child grew – Increased in stature and bodily vigor. And waxed strong in spirit – had his understanding Divinely illuminated and confirmed in the truths of God. And was in the deserts till he was thirty years old, before which time the law did not permit a man to enter into the public ministry, Numbers 4: 3. See also Luke 3: 23.

MATTHEW 1: 1–17; LUKE 3: 23–38

The genealogy of Christ divided into three classes of fourteen generations each: The first fourteen, from Abraham to David, vv. 2–6. The second fourteen, from Solomon to Jechonias, vv. 7–10. The third fourteen, from Jechonias to Christ, vv. 11–16. The sum of these generations, v. 17.

1. The book of the generation of Jesus Christ – I suppose these words to have been the original title to this Gospel; and that they signify, according to the Hebrew Phraseology, not only the account of the genealogy of Christ, as detailed below, hut the history of his birth, acts, sufferings, death, resurrection, and ascension.

2. Abraham begat Isaac – In this genealogy, those persons only, among the ancestors of Christ, which formed the direct line, as specified: hence no mention is made of Ishmael, the son of Abraham, nor of Esau, the son of Isaac; and of all the twelve patriarchs, or sons of Jacob, Judah alone is mentioned.

3. Phares and Zara – The remarkable history of these twins may be seen, Genesis 38: Some

of the ancients were of opinion, that the evangelist refers to the mystery of the youngest being preferred to the eldest, as prefiguring the exaltation of the Christian Church over the synagogue.

8. Joram begat Ozias – This is the Uzziah, king of Judah, who was struck with the leprosy for his presumption in entering the temple to offer incense before the Lord. See 2 Chronicles 26: 16.

Luke 3: 23–38

23. Being (as was supposed) the son of Joseph – This same phrase is used by Herodotus to signify one who was only reputed to be the son of a particular person. He was SUPPOSED to be this man's son.

Much learned labor has been used to reconcile this genealogy with that in St. Matthew, Matthew 1: 1–17, and there are several ways of doing it; the following, which appears to me to be the best, is also the most simple and easy. MATTHEW, in descending from Abraham to Joseph, the spouse of the blessed virgin, speaks of SONS properly such, by way of natural generation: Abraham begat Isaac, and Isaac begat Jacob, etc. But Luke, in ascending from the Savior of the world to GOD himself, speaks of sons either properly or improperly such: on this account he uses an indeterminate mode of expression, which may be applied to sons either putatively or really such. And Jesus himself began to be about thirty years of age, being, as was SUPPOSED the son of Joseph – of Heli – of Matthat, etc. That St. Luke does not always speak of sons properly such, is evident from the first and last person which he names: Jesus Christ was only the supposed son of Joseph, because Joseph was the husband of his mother Mary: and Adam, who is said to be the son of God, was such only by creation. After this observation it is next necessary to consider, that, in the genealogy described by St. Luke, there are two sons improperly such: i.e. two sons-in-law, instead of two sons. As the Hebrews never permitted women to enter into their genealogical tables, whenever a family happened to end with a daughter, instead

Salathiel begat Zorobabel;

13 And Zorobabel begat Abiud; and Abiud begat Eliakim; and Eliakim begat Azor;

14 And Azor begat Sadoc; and Sadoc begat Achim; and Achim begat Eliud;

15 And Eliud begat Eleazar; and Eleazar begat Matthan; and Matthan begat Jacob;

16 And Jacob begat Joseph the husband of Mary, of whom was born Jesus, who is called Christ.

17 So all the generations from Abraham to David are fourteen generations; and from David until the carrying away into Babylon are fourteen generations; and from the carrying away into Babylon unto Christ are fourteen generations.

Luke 3: 23–38

23 And Jesus himself began to be about thirty years of age, being (as was supposed) the son of Joseph, which was the son of Heli,

24 Which was the son of Matthat, which was the son of Levi, which was the son of Melchi, which was the son of Janna, which was the son of Joseph,

25 Which was the son of Mattathias, which was the son of Amos, which was the son of Naum, which was the son of Esli, which was the son of Nagge,

26 Which was the son of Maath, which was the son of Mattathias, which was the son of Semei, which was the son of Joseph, which was the son of Juda,

27 Which was the son of Joanna, which was the son of Rhesa, which was the son of Zorobabel, which was the son of Salathiel, which was the son of Neri,

28 Which was the son of Melchi, which was the son of Addi, which was the son of Cosam, which was the son of Elmodam, which was the son of Er,

29 Which was the son of Jose, which was the son of Eliezer, which was the son of Jorim, which was the son of Matthat, which was the son of Levi,

30 Which was the son of Simeon, which was the son of Juda, which was the son of Joseph, which was the son of Jonan, which was the son of Eliakim,

31 Which was the son of Melea, which was the son of Menan, which was the son of Mattatha, which was the son of Nathan,

when Christ was promised to Abraham, to "the fullness of the time" (Galatians 4: 4) when he was "manifested in the flesh" (2 Corinthians 4: 11). Before the time of David, the tribe of Judah, though it occupied a higher rank than the other tribes, held no power. In David the royal authority burst upon the eyes of all with unexpected splendor, and remained till the time of Jeconiah. After that period, there still lingered in the tribe of Judah a portion of rank and government, which sustained the expectations of the godly till the coming of the Messiah.

6. Begat David the King

In this genealogy, the designation of **King** is bestowed on David alone, because in his person God exhibited a type of the future leader of his people, the Messiah. The kingly office had been formerly held by Saul; but, as he reached it through tumult and the ungodly wishes of the people, the lawful possession of the office is supposed to have commenced with David, more especially in reference to the covenant of God, who promised that "his throne should be established for ever" (2 Samuel 7: 16). When the people shook off the yoke of God, and unhappily and wickedly asked a king, saying, "Give us a king to judge us" (1 Samuel 8: 5), Saul was granted for short time. But his kingdom was shortly afterwards established by God, as a pledge of true prosperity, in the hand of David. Let this expression, **David the King** be understood by us as pointing out the prosperous condition of the people, which the Lord had appointed.

Meanwhile, the Evangelist adds a human disgrace, which might almost bring a stain on the glory of this divine blessing. **David the King begat Solomon by her that had been the wife of Uriah**; by Bathsheba, whom he wickedly tore from her husband, and for the sake of enjoying whom, he basely surrendered an innocent man to be murdered by the swords of the enemy (2 Samuel 11: 15). This taint, at the commencement of the kingdom, ought to have taught the Jews not to glory in the flesh. It was the design of God to show that, in establishing this kingdom, nothing depended on human merits.

16. Jesus, who is called Christ

By the surname **Christ,** Anointed, Matthew points out his office, to inform the readers that this was not a private person, but one divinely anointed to perform the office of Redeemer.

So long as any splendor of royalty continued in the family of David, the kings were wont to be called *christoi*, anointed. But that the fearful desolation which followed might not throw the minds of the godly into despair, it pleased God to appropriate the name of Messiah, Anointed, to the Redeemer alone: as is evident from Daniel (9: 25,26).

of naming her in the genealogy, they inserted her husband, as the son of him who was, in reality, but his father-in-law. Jesus was considered according to law, or allowed custom, to be the son of Joseph, as he was of Heli. The two sons-in-law who are to be noticed in this genealogy are Joseph the son-in-law of Heli, whose own father was Jacob, Matthew 1: 16; and Salathiel, the son-in-law of Neri, whose own father was Jechonias: 1 Chronicles 3: 17, and Matthew 1: 12. This remark alone is sufficient to remove every difficulty. Thus it appears that Joseph, son of Jacob, according to St. Matthew, was son-in-law of Heli, according to St. Luke. And Salathiel, son of Jechonias, according to the former, was son-in-law of Neri, according to the latter. Mary therefore appears to have been the daughter of Heli; so called by abbreviation for Heliachim, which is the same in Hebrew with Joachim. Joseph, son of Jacob, and Mary; daughter of Heli, were of the same family: both came from Zerubbabel; Joseph from Abiud, his eldest son, Matthew 1: 13, and Mary by Rhesa, the youngest. See Luke 3: 27. Salathiel and Zorobabel, from whom St. Matthew and St. Luke cause Christ to proceed, were themselves descended from Solomon in a direct line: and though St. Luke says that Salathiel was son of Neri, who was descended from Nathan, Solomon's eldest brother, 1 Chronicles 3: 5, this is only to be understood of his having espoused Nathan's daughter, and that Neri dying, probably, without male issues the two branches of the family of David, that of Nathan and that of Solomon, were both united in the person of Zerubbabel, by the marriage of Salathiel, chief of the regal family of Solomon, with the daughter of Neri, chief and heretrix of the family of Nathan. Thus it appears that Jesus, son of Mary, reunited in himself all the blood, privileges, and rights of the whole family of David; in consequence of which he is emphatically called, The son of David. It is worthy of being remarked that St. Matthew, who wrote principally for the Jews, extends his genealogy to Abraham through whom the promise of the Messiah was given to the Jews; but St. Luke, who wrote his history for the instruction of the Gentiles, extends his genealogy to Adam, to whom the promise of the Redeemer was given in behalf of himself and of all his posterity.

36. Of Cainan – This Cainan, the son of Arphaxad, and father of Sala, is not found in any other Scripture genealogy. See Genesis 10: 24; 11: 12; 1 Chronicles 1: 18,24, where Arphaxad is made the father of Sala, and no mention at all made of Cainan. Some suppose that Cainan was a surname of Sala, and that the names should be read together thus, The son of Heber, the son of Salacainan, the son of Arphaxad, etc. If this does not untie the knot, it certainly cuts it; and the reader may pass on without any great scruple or embarrassment.

MATTHEW 1: 18–25

18. Before they came together – The woman was espoused at her own, or her father's house; and, generally, some time elapsed before she was taken home to the house of her husband: Deuteronomy 20: 7; Judges 14: 7–8. This custom has been immemorially observed among the inhabitants of Ireland, who have not only this, but many Asiatic customs, which, added to various authentic historic proofs, are collateral evidences that they received the Christian religion, not from the popes of Rome, but through the means of Asiatic missionaries.

Among the Jews, the espousal, though the marriage had not been consummated, was considered as perfectly legal and binding on both sides; and hence a breach of this contract was considered as a case of adultery, and punished exactly in the same way. See Deuteronomy 22: 25,28.

She was found with child – Her situation was the most distressing and humiliating that can be conceived. Nothing but the fullest consciousness of her own integrity, and the strongest confidence in God, could have supported her in such trying circumstances, where her reputation, her honor, and her life were at stake. What conversation passed between her and Joseph, on this discovery, we are not informed; but the issue proves that it was not satisfactory to him: nor could he resolve to

which was the son of David,

32 Which was the son of Jesse, which was the son of Obed, which was the son of Booz, which was the son of Salmon, which was the son of Naasson,

33 Which was the son of Aminadab, which was the son of Aram, which was the son of Esrom, which was the son of Phares, which was the son of Juda,

34 Which was the son of Jacob, which was the son of Isaac, which was the son of Abraham, which was the son of Thara, which was the son of Nachor,

35 Which was the son of Saruch, which was the son of Ragau, which was the son of Phalec, which was the son of Heber, which was the son of Sala,

36 Which was the son of Cainan, which was the son of Arphaxad, which was the son of Sem, which was the son of Noe, which was the son of Lamech,

37 Which was the son of Mathusala, which was the son of Enoch, which was the son of Jared, which was the son of Maleleel, which was the son of Cainan,

38 Which was the son of Enos, which was the son of Seth, which was the son of Adam, which was the son of God.

MATTHEW 1: 18–25

18 Now the birth of Jesus Christ was on this wise: When as his mother Mary was espoused to Joseph, before they came together, she was found with child of the Holy Ghost.

19 Then Joseph her husband, being a just man, and not willing to make her a publick example, was minded to put her away privily.

20 But while he thought on these things, behold, the angel of the Lord appeared unto him in a dream, saying, Joseph, thou son of David, fear not to take unto thee Mary thy wife: for that which is conceived in her is of the Holy Ghost.

21 And she shall bring forth a son, and thou shalt call his name JESUS: for he shall save his people from their sins.

22 Now all this was done, that it might be fulfilled which was spoken of the Lord by the prophet, saying,

23 Behold, a virgin shall be with child, and shall bring forth a son, and they shall call his name Emmanuel, which being

The evangelical history everywhere shows that this was an ordinary way of speaking, at the time when the Son of God was "manifested in the flesh" (1 Timothy 3: 16).

MATTHEW 1: 18–25

18. Now the birth of Jesus Christ

Matthew does not as yet relate the place or manner of Christ's birth, but the way in which his heavenly generation was made known to Joseph. First, he says that Mary **was found to be with child by the Holy Spirit**.

The phrase employed by the Evangelist, **before they came together**, is either a modest appellation for conjugal intercourse, or simply means, "before they came to dwell together as husband and wife, and to make one home and family." The meaning will thus be, that the virgin had not yet been delivered by her parents into the hands of her husband, but still remained under their roof.

20. And while he was considering these things

We see here how seasonably, and, as we would say, at the very point, the Lord usually aids his people. Hence too we infer that, when he appears not to observe our cares and distresses, we are still under his eye. He may, indeed, hide himself, and remain silent; but, when our patience has been subjected to the trial, he will aid us at the time which his own wisdom has selected. However slow or late his assistance may be thought to be, it is for our advantage that it is thus delayed.

The angel of the Lord appeared to him in a dream

This is one of two ordinary kinds of revelations mentioned in the book of Numbers, where the Lord thus speaks: "If there be a prophet among you, I the Lord will make myself known unto him in a vision, and will speak unto him in a dream. My servant Moses is not so. With him will I speak mouth to mouth, even apparently, and not in dark speeches" (Numbers 12: 6–8).

But we must understand that dreams of this sort differ widely from natural dreams; for they have a character of certainty engraven on them, and are impressed with a divine seal, so that there is not the slightest doubt of their truth.

21. And thou shalt call his name JESUS

The words of the angel explain why the Son of God is so called, **Because he shall SAVE his people**.

LUKE 2: 1–7

Luke relates how it happened, that Christ was born in the city of Bethlehem, as his mother was living at a distance from her home, when she was approaching to her confinement. And first he sets aside the idea of human contrivance,

consider her as his wife, till God had sent his angel to bear the most unequivocal testimony to the virgin's innocence. His whole conduct, on this occasion, was exceedingly benevolent and humane. He might at once have taken the advantage of the law, Deuteronomy 22: 23–24, and had her stoned to death.

21. JESUS – The same as Joshua, he saved, delivered, put in a state of safety.

He shall save his people from their sins – This shall be his great business in the world: the great errand on which he is come, viz. to make an atonement for, and to destroy, sin: deliverance from all the power, guilt, and pollution of sin, is the privilege of every believer in Christ Jesus. Less than this is not spoken of in the Gospel; and less than this would be unbecoming the Gospel. The perfection of the Gospel system is not that it makes allowances for sin, but that it makes an atonement for it: not that it tolerates sin, but that it destroys it. In Matthew 1: 1, he is called Jesus Christ, on which Dr. Lightfoot properly remarks, "That the name of Jesus, so often added to the name of Christ in the New Testament, is not only that Christ might be thereby pointed out as the Savior, but also that Jesus might be pointed out as the true Christ or Messiah, against the unbelief of the Jews." This observation will be of great use in numberless places of the New Testament. See Acts 2: 36; 8: 35; 1 Corinthians 16: 22; 1 John 2: 22; 1 John 4: 15, etc.

22. Behold, a virgin shall be with child – In what sense could this name Immanuel be applied to Jesus Christ, if he be not truly and properly GOD? Could the Spirit of truth ever design that Christians should receive him as an angel or a mere man, and yet, in the very beginning of the Gospel history, apply a character to him which belongs only to the most high God? Surely no. In what sense, then, is Christ GOD WITH US? Jesus is called Immanuel, or God with us, in his incarnation. – God united to our nature – God with man – God in man. – God with us, by his continual protection. – God with us, by the influences of his Holy Spirit – in the holy sacrament – in the preaching of his word – in private prayer. And

God with us, through every action of our life, that we begin, continue, and end in his name. He is God with us, to comfort, enlighten, protect, and defend us in every time of temptation and trial, in the hour of death, in the day of judgment; and God with us, and in us, and we with and in him, to all eternity.

25. Her first-born son – Literally, That son of hers, the first-born one. That Mary might have had other children, any person may reasonably and piously believe; that she had others, many think exceedingly probable, and that this text is at least an indirect proof of it. However this may be, the perpetual virginity of Mary should not be made an article of faith. God has not made it one: indeed it can hardly bear the light of several texts in the Gospels.

He knew her not – Had no matrimonial intercourse with her – TILL she had brought forth that son of hers, of whom the evangelist had been just speaking, the first-born, the eldest of the family, to whom the birthright belonged, and who was miraculously born before she knew any man, being yet in a state of virginity. The virginity of Mary, previously to the birth of Christ, is an article of the utmost consequence to the Christian system; and therefore it is an article of faith: her perpetual virginity is of no consequence; and the learned labor spent to prove it has produced a mere castle in the air. The thing is possible; but it never has been, and never can be proved.

He called his name JESUS – This name was given by the command of God, see Matthew 1: 16, and was imposed on Christ when eight days old; for then, according to the Jewish law, he was circumcised: thus he had the name of Savior given when he first began to shed that blood without which there could be no remission of sins.

The goodness of God is manifested, not only in his giving his Son to save a lost world, but also in the choice of the persons who were his progenitors: among whom we find, First, SAINTS, to excite our courage: Abraham, remarkable for his faith; Isaac, for his obedience; and Jacob, for his fervor and constancy. Secondly, Penitent SINNERS, to excite our

interpreted is, God with us.

24 Then Joseph being raised from sleep did as the angel of the Lord had bidden him, and took unto him his wife:

25 And knew her not till she had brought forth her firstborn son: and he called his name JESUS.

LUKE 2: 1–7

1 And it came to pass in those days, that there went out a decree from Caesar Augustus, that all the world should be taxed.

2 (And this taxing was first made when Cyrenius was governor of Syria.)

3 And all went to be taxed, every one into his own city.

4 And Joseph also went up from Galilee, out of the city of Nazareth, into Judaea, unto the city of David, which is called Bethlehem; (because he was of the house and lineage of David:)

5 To be taxed with Mary his espoused wife, being great with child.

6 And so it was, that, while they were there, the days were accomplished that she should be delivered.

7 And she brought forth her firstborn son, and wrapped him in swaddling clothes, and laid him in a manger; because there was no room for them in the inn.

LUKE 2: 8–14

8 And there were in the same country shepherds abiding in the field, keeping watch over their flock by night.

9 And, lo, the angel of the Lord came upon them, and the glory of the Lord shone round about them: and they were sore afraid.

10 And the angel said unto them, Fear not: for, behold, I bring you good tidings of great joy, which shall be to all people.

11 For unto you is born this day in the city of David a Savior, which is Christ the Lord.

12 And this shall be a sign unto you; Ye shall find the babe wrapped in swaddling clothes, lying in a manger.

13 And suddenly there was with the angel a multitude of the heavenly host praising God, and saying,

by saying, that Joseph and Mary had left home, and came to that place to make the return according to their family and tribe. If they had intentionally changed their residence that Mary might bring forth her child in Bethlehem, we would have looked only at the human beings concerned. But as they have no other reason than to obey the edict of Augustus, we readily acknowledge, that they were led like blind people, by the hand of God, to the place where Christ must be born.

This may appear to be accidental, as everything else, which does not proceed from a direct human intention, is ascribed by irreligious men to Fortune. But we must not attend merely to the events themselves. We must remember also the prediction which was uttered by the prophet many centuries before. A comparison will clearly show it to have been accomplished by the wonderful Providence of God, that a registration was then enacted by Augustus Caesar, and that Joseph and Mary set out from home, so as to arrive in Bethlehem at the very point of time.

LUKE 2: 8–14

8. And there were shepherds

It would have been to no purpose that Christ was born in Bethlehem, if it had not been made known to the world. But the method of doing so, which is described by Luke, appears to the view of men very unsuitable. First, Christ is revealed to only a few witnesses, and that too amidst the darkness of night. Again, though God had, at his command, many honorable and distinguished witnesses, he passed over them, and chose shepherds, people of humble rank, and of no account among men. Here the reason and wisdom of the flesh must prove to be foolishness; and we must acknowledge, that "the foolishness of God" (1 Corinthians 1: 25) excels all the wisdom that exists, or appears to exist, in the world. But this too was a part of the "emptying of himself" (Philippians 2: 6): not that any part of Christ's glory should be taken away by it, but that it should lie in concealment for a time. Again, as Paul reminds us, that the gospel is mean according to the flesh, "that our faith should stand" in the power of the Spirit, not in the "lofty words of human wisdom," or in any worldly splendor (1 Corinthians 2: 4,5); so this inestimable "treasure" has been deposited by God, from the beginning, "in earthen vessels" (2 Corinthians 4: 7), that he might more fully try the obedience of our faith. If then we desire to come to Christ, let us not be ashamed to follow those whom the Lord, in order to cast down the pride of the world, has taken, from among the dung of cattle, to be our instructors.

confidence: such as David, Manasses, etc.

Thirdly, Sinners, of whose repentance and salvation we hear nothing; to put us on our guard. Who can read the account of idolatrous Solomon, who, from the whole evidence of the sacred history, died In his sins, without trembling?

Four WOMEN are mentioned in this genealogy: two of these were adulteresses, Tamar and Bathsheba; and two were Gentiles, Rahab and Ruth, and strangers to the covenant of promise; to teach us that Jesus Christ came to save sinners, and that, though strangers to his people, we are not on that account excluded from a salvation which God has designed for all men. He is not the God of the Jews only; he is also the God of the Gentiles.

The state of the royal family of David, the circumstances of the holy virgin and her spouse Joseph, the very remarkable prophecy of Isaiah, the literal and circumstantial fulfillment of it, the names given to our blessed Lord, the genealogical scroll of the family, etc., etc., are all so many proofs of the wisdom, goodness, and providence of God. Every occurrence seems, at first view, to be abandoned to fortuitous influence, and yet the result of each shows that God managed the whole. These circumstances are of the greatest importance; nor can the Christian reader reflect on them without an increase of his faith and his piety.

LUKE 2: 1–7

1. **Caesar Augustus** – This was Caius Caesar Octavianus Augustus, who was proclaimed emperor of Rome in the 29th year before our Lord, and died ad 14.

That all the world should be taxed – the whole of that empire. It is agreed, on all hands, that this cannot mean the whole world, as in the common translation; for this very sufficient reason, that the Romans had not the dominion of the whole earth, and therefore could have no right to raise levies or taxes in those places to which their dominion did not extend.

It is probable that the reason why this enrolment, or census, is said to have been throughout the whole Jewish nation, was to distinguish it from that partial one, made ten years after, mentioned Acts 5: 37.

5. **With Mary his espoused wife** – There was no necessity for Mary to have gone to Bethlehem, as Joseph's presence could have answered the end proposed in the census as well without Mary as with her; but God so ordered it, that the prophecy of Micah should be thus fulfilled, and that Jesus should be born in the city of David; Micah 5: 2.

7. **Laid him in a manger** – This means not merely the manger, but the whole stable, and this I think is its proper meaning in this place.

LUKE 2: 8–14

9. **The angel of the Lord came upon them** – It is likely that the angel appeared in the air at some little distance above them, and that from him the rays of the glory of the Lord shone round about them, as the rays of light are projected from the sun.

They were sore afraid – Terrified with the appearance of so glorious a being, and probably fearing that he was a messenger of justice, coming to denounce Divine judgments, or punish them immediately, for sins with which their consciences would not fail, on such an occasion, to reproach them.

12. **This shall be a sign (or token) unto you** – You shall find this glorious person, however strange it may appear, wrapped in swaddling clothes, lying in a stable! It is by humility that Christ comes to reign; and this is the only way into his kingdom! Pride is the character of all the children of Adam: humility the mark of the Son of God, and of all his followers. Christ came in the way of humility to destroy that pride which is the root of evil in the souls of men. And thus, according to the old medical aphorism, "Opposites are destroyed by their opposites."

13. **Suddenly there was with the angel, etc.** – this multitude of the heavenly host had just now descended from on high, to honor the

14 Glory to God in the highest, and on earth peace, good will toward men.

LUKE 2: 15–21

15 And it came to pass, as the angels were gone away from them into heaven, the shepherds said one to another, Let us now go even unto Bethlehem, and see this thing which is come to pass, which the Lord hath made known unto us.

16 And they came with haste, and found Mary, and Joseph, and the babe lying in a manger.

17 And when they had seen it, they made known abroad the saying which was told them concerning this child.

18 And all they that heard it wondered at those things which were told them by the shepherds.

19 But Mary kept all these things, and pondered them in her heart.

20 And the shepherds returned, glorifying and praising God for all the things that they had heard and seen, as it was told unto them.

21 And when eight days were accomplished for the circumcising of the child, his name was called JESUS, which was so named of the angel before he was conceived in the womb.

MATTHEW 2: 1–6

1 Now when Jesus was born in Bethlehem of Judaea in the days of Herod the king, behold, there came wise men from the east to Jerusalem,

2 Saying, Where is he that is born King of the Jews? for we have seen his star in the east, and are come to worship him.

3 When Herod the king had heard these things, he was troubled, and all Jerusalem with him.

4 And when he had gathered all the chief priests and scribes of the people together, he demanded of them where Christ should be born.

5 And they said unto him, In Bethlehem of Judaea: for thus it is written by the prophet,

6 And thou Bethlehem, in the land of Juda, art not the least among the princes of Juda: for out of thee shall come a Governor, that shall rule my people Israel.

LUKE 2: 15–21

15. After that the angels departed

Here the obedience of the shepherds is described. The Lord had made them the witnesses of his Son to the whole world. What he had spoken to them by his angels was efficacious, and was not allowed to pass away. They were not plainly and expressly commanded to come to Bethlehem; but, being sufficiently aware that such was the design of God, they hasten to see Christ. In the same manner, we know that Christ is held out to us, in order that our hearts may approach him by faith; and our delay in coming admits of no excuse.

MATTHEW 2: 1–6

1. Now when Jesus had been born

How it came about that Jesus was born in Bethlehem, Matthew does not say. The Spirit of God, who had appointed the Evangelists to be his clerks, appears purposely to have regulated their style in such a manner, that they all wrote one and the same history, with the most perfect agreement, but in different ways. It was intended, that the truth of God should more clearly and strikingly appear, when it was manifest that his witnesses did not speak by jointly conceived plan, but that each of them separately, without paying any attention to another, wrote freely and honestly what the Holy Spirit dictated.

This is a very remarkable narrative. God brought Magi from Chaldea, to come to the land of Judea, for the purpose of adoring Christ, in the stable where he lay, amidst the tokens, not of honor, but of contempt. It was a truly wonderful purpose of God, that he caused the entrance of his Son into the world to be attended by deep meanness, and yet bestowed upon him illustrious ornaments, both of commendation and of other outward signs, that our faith might be supplied with everything necessary to prove his Divine Majesty.

MATTHEW 2: 7–12

7. Then Herod, having secretly called the Magi

The tyrant did not dare to reveal his fear, lest he might give fresh courage to a people, by whom he knew that he was hated. In public, therefore, he pretends that this matter does not concern him.

Let us learn, that a miracle was effected, in rescuing the Son of God from the jaws of the lion. Not less at the present day does God infatuate his enemies, so that a thousand schemes of injuring and ruining his Church do not occur to their minds, and even the opportunities which are at hand are not embraced. The trick which Herod practiced on the

new-born Prince of peace, to give his parents the fullest conviction of his glory and excellence, and to teach the shepherds, who were about to be the first proclaimers of the Gospel, what to think and what to speak of him, who, while he appeared as a helpless infant, was the object of worship to the angels of God.

14. Glory to God in the highest – The design of God, in the incarnation, was to manifest the hidden glories of his nature, and to reconcile men to each other and to himself. The angels therefore declare that this incarnation shall manifest and promote the glory of God, not only in the highest heavens, among the highest orders of beings, but in the highest and most exalted degrees. For in this astonishing display of God's mercy, attributes of the Divine nature which had not been and could not be known in any other way should be now exhibited in the fullness of their glory, that even the angels should have fresh objects to contemplate, and new glories to exult in. These things the angels desire to look into, 1 Peter 1: 12, and they desire it because they feel they are thus interested in it. The incarnation of Jesus Christ is an infinite and eternal benefit. Heaven and earth both partake of the fruits of it, and through it angels and men become one family, Ephesians 3: 15.

Peace, good will toward men – Men are in a state of hostility with Heaven and with each other.

LUKE 2: 15–21

17. They made known abroad the saying – These shepherds were the first preachers of the Gospel of Christ: and what was their text? Why, Glory to God in the highest heavens, and on earth peace and good will among men. This is the elegant and energetic saying which comprises the sum and substance of the Gospel of God. This, and this only, is the message which all Christ's true pastors or shepherds bring to men. He who, while he professes the religion of Christ, disturbs society by his preachings or writings, who excludes from the salvation of God all who hold not his religious or

political creed, never knew the nature of the Gospel, and never felt its power or influence. How can religious contentions, civil broils, or open wars, look that Gospel in the face which publishes nothing but glory to God, and peace and good will among men? Crusades for the recovery of a holy land so called, (by the way, latterly, the most unholy in the map of the world), and wars for the support of religion, are an insult to the Gospel, and blasphemy against God!

19. And pondered them in her heart – Every detail about her son's birth, Mary treasured up in her memory; and every new circumstance she weighed, or compared with those which had already taken place, in order to acquire the fullest information concerning the nature and mission of her son.

21. When eight days were accomplished – The law had appointed that every male should be circumcised at eight days old, or on the eighth day after its birth, Genesis 17: 12; and our blessed Lord received circumcision in token of his subjection to the law, Galatians 4: 4; 5: 3.

MATTHEW 2: 1–6

1. There came wise men from the east – Or, Magi came from the eastern countries. It is very probable that the persons mentioned by the evangelist were a sort of astrologers, probably of Jewish extraction.

2. We have seen his star – Having discovered an unusual luminous appearance or meteor in the heavens, supposing these persons to have been Jews, and knowing the prophecies relative to the redemption of Israel, they probably considered this to be the star mentioned by Balaam, Numbers 24: 17.

3. When Herod – heard these things, he was troubled – Herod's consternation was probably occasioned by the agreement of the account of the magi, with an opinion predominant throughout the east, and particularly in Judea, that some great personage would soon make his appearance, for the deliverance of

MATTHEW 2: 7–12

7 Then Herod, when he had privily called the wise men, inquired of them diligently what time the star appeared.

8 And he sent them to Bethlehem, and said, Go and search diligently for the young child; and when ye have found him, bring me word again, that I may come and worship him also.

9 When they had heard the king, they departed; and, lo, the star, which they saw in the east, went before them, till it came and stood over where the young child was.

10 When they saw the star, they rejoiced with exceeding great joy.

11 And when they were come into the house, they saw the young child with Mary his mother, and fell down, and worshipped him: and when they had opened their treasures, they presented unto him gifts; gold, and frankincense, and myrrh.

12 And being warned of God in a dream that they should not return to Herod, they departed into their own country another way.

LUKE 2: 22–32

22 And when the days of her purification according to the law of Moses were accomplished, they brought him to Jerusalem, to present him to the Lord;

23 (As it is written in the law of the Lord, Every male that openeth the womb shall be called holy to the Lord;)

24 And to offer a sacrifice according to that which is said in the law of the Lord, A pair of turtledoves, or two young pigeons.

25 And, behold, there was a man in Jerusalem, whose name was Simeon; and the same man was just and devout, waiting for the consolation of Israel: and the Holy Ghost was upon him.

26 And it was revealed unto him by the Holy Ghost, that he should not see death, before he had seen the Lord's Christ.

27 And he came by the Spirit into the temple: and when the parents brought in the child Jesus, to do for him after the custom of the law,

28 Then took he him up in his arms, and blessed God, and said,

29 Lord, now lettest thou thy servant

Magi by pretending that he also would come for the purpose of worshipping Christ, was avoided by the Lord.

LUKE 2: 22–32

22. And after that the days were fulfilled

On the fortieth day after the birth (Leviticus 12: 2,4), the rite of purification had to be performed. But Mary and Joseph come to Jerusalem for another reason, to present Christ to the Lord, because he was the first-born.

25. And, lo, there was a man in Jerusalem

The purpose of this narrative is to inform us that, though nearly the whole nation was profane and irreligious, and despised God, yet that a few worshippers of God remained, and that Christ was known to such people from his earliest infancy. These were "the remnant" of whom Paul says, that they were preserved "according to the election of grace" (Romans 11: 5). Within this small band lay the Church of God; though the priests and scribes, with as much pride as falsehood, claimed for themselves the title of the Church. The Evangelist mentions no more than two, who recognised Christ at Jerusalem, when he was brought into the temple. These were Simeon and Anna. We must speak first of Simeon.

As to his condition in life we are not informed: he may have been a person of humble rank and of no reputation. Luke bestows on him the commendation of being just and devout; and adds, that he had the gift of prophecy: for **the Holy Spirit was upon him**. Devotion and righteousness related to the two tables of the law, and are the two parts of an upright life. It was a proof of his being **a devout man** that he **waited for the consolation of Israel** for no true worship of God can exist without the hope of salvation, which depends on the faith of his promises, and particularly on the restoration promised through Christ. Now, since an expectation of this sort is commended in Simeon as an uncommon attainment, we may conclude, that there were few in that age, who actually cherished in their hearts the hope of redemption. All had on their lips the name of the Messiah, and of prosperity under the reign of David: but hardly any one was to be found, who patiently endured present afflictions, relying on the consolatory assurance, that the redemption of the Church was at hand. As the eminence of Simeon's piety was manifested by its supporting his mind in the hope of the promised salvation, so those who wish to prove themselves the children of God, will breathe out unceasing prayers for the promised redemption. For we, "have need of patience" (Hebrews 10: 36) till the last coming of Christ.

Israel from their enemies; and would take upon himself universal empire.

6. And thou Bethlehem, in the land of Juda – To distinguish it from Bethlehem, in the tribe of Zebulon. Joshua 19: 15.

That shall rule my people Israel – Who shall FEED my people. That is as a shepherd feeds his flock.

MATTHEW 2: 7–12

8. That I may come and worship him also – What exquisite hypocrisy was here! he only wished to find out the child that he might murder him; but see how that God who searches the heart prevents the designs of wicked men from being accomplished!

9. In the east – Or, at its rise. See Matthew 2: 2.

11. They presented unto him gifts – The people of the east never approach the presence of kings and great personages, without a present in their hands. This custom is often noticed in the Old Testament, and still prevails in the east, and in some of the newly discovered South Sea Islands.

Gold, and frankincense, and myrrh – Some will have these gifts to be emblematic of the Divinity, regal office, and manhood of Christ. "They offered him incense as their God; gold as their king; and myrrh, as united to a human body, subject to suffering and death."

LUKE 2: 22–32

22. Days of her purification – That is, thirty-three days after what was termed the seven days of her uncleanness – forty days in all: for that was the time appointed by the law, after the birth of a male child. See Leviticus 12: 2,6.

The purification of every mother and child, which the law enjoined, is a powerful argument in proof of that original corruption and depravity which every human being brings into the world. The woman to be purified was placed in the east gate of the court, called Nicanor's gate, and was there sprinkled with blood: thus she received the atonement.

24. And to offer a sacrifice – Neither mother nor child was considered as in the Lord's covenant, or under the Divine protection, till these ceremonies, prescribed by the law, had been performed.

A pair of turtle doves, etc. – One was for a burnt-offering, and the other for a sin-offering: see Leviticus 12: 8. The rich were required to bring a lamb, but the poor and middling classes were required to bring either two turtle doves, or two pigeons. This is a proof that the holy family were not in affluence. Jesus sanctified the state of poverty, which is the general state of man, by passing through it. Therefore the poor have the Gospel preached unto them; and the poor are they who principally receive it.

Though neither Mary nor her son needed any of these purifications, for she was immaculate, and He was the Holy One, yet, had she not gone through the days of purification according to the law, she could not have appeared in the public worship of the Most High, and would have been considered as an apostate from the faith of the Israel of God; and had not He been circumcised and publicly presented in the temple, he could not have been permitted to enter either synagogue or temple, and no Jew would have heard him preach, or had any intercourse or connection with him. These reasons are sufficient to account for the purification of the holy virgin, and for the circumcision of the most holy Jesus.

25. And, behold, there was a man in Jerusalem – This man is distinguished because of his singular piety. There can be no doubt that there were many persons in Jerusalem named Simeon, besides this man; but there was none of the name who merited the attention of God so much as he in the text.

The same man was just – He steadily regulated all his conduct by the law of his God: and **devout** – he had fully consecrated himself to God, so that he added a pious heart to a righteous conduct.

Waiting for the consolation of Israel – That is, the Messiah, who was known among the pious Jews by this character: he was to be

depart in peace, according to thy word:

30 For mine eyes have seen thy salvation,

31 Which thou hast prepared before the face of all people;

32 A light to lighten the Gentiles, and the glory of thy people Israel.

LUKE 2: 33–39

33 And Joseph and his mother marveled at those things which were spoken of him.

34 And Simeon blessed them, and said unto Mary his mother, Behold, this child is set for the fall and rising again of many in Israel; and for a sign which shall be spoken against;

35 (Yea, a sword shall pierce through thy own soul also,) that the thoughts of many hearts may be revealed.

36 And there was one Anna, a prophetess, the daughter of Phanuel, of the tribe of Aser: she was of a great age, and had lived with an husband seven years from her virginity;

37 And she was a widow of about fourscore and four years, which departed not from the temple, but served God with fastings and prayers night and day.

38 And she coming in that instant gave thanks likewise unto the Lord, and spake of him to all them that looked for redemption in Jerusalem.

39 And when they had performed all things according to the law of the Lord, they returned into Galilee, to their own city Nazareth.

MATTHEW 2: 13–18

13 And when they were departed, behold, the angel of the Lord appeareth to Joseph in a dream, saying, Arise, and take the young child and his mother, and flee into Egypt, and be thou there until I bring thee word: for Herod will seek the young child to destroy him.

14 When he arose, he took the young child and his mother by night, and departed into Egypt:

15 And was there until the death of Herod: that it might be fulfilled which was spoken of the Lord by the prophet, saying, Out of Egypt have I called my son.

LUKE 2: 33–39

33. And his father and mother were wondering

Luke does not say, that they were astonished at it as a new thing, but that they contemplated with reverence, and embraced with becoming admiration, this prediction of the Spirit uttered by the lips of Simeon, so that they continued to make progress in the knowledge of Christ. We learn from this example that, when we have once come to possess a right faith, we ought to collect, on every hand, whatever may aid in giving to it additional strength. That man has made great proficiency in the word of God, who does not fail to admire whatever he reads or hears every day, that contributes to his unceasing progress in faith.

36. And there was Anna, a prophetess

Luke mentions not more than two people who received Christ; and this is intended to teach us, that whatever belongs to God, however small it may be, ought to be preferred by us to the whole world.

She had lived with her husband seven years from her virginity

This is intended to inform us, that she was a widow in the very prime of life. She had married young, and shortly afterwards lost her husband; and the circumstance of her not entering into a second marriage while she was in the rigor of her bodily frame, is mentioned with the view of heightening the commendation of her chastity.

38. Made acknowledgment also to God

The holy melody, which proceeded from the lips of Simeon and Anna, is praised by Luke, in order that believers may exhort each other to sing with one mouth the praises of God.

MATTHEW 2: 13–18

13. And when they had departed

We are here taught, that God has more than one way of preserving his own people. Sometimes he makes astonishing displays of his power; while at other times he employs dark coverings or shadows, from which feeble rays of it escape. This wonderful method of preserving the Son of God under the cross teaches us, that they act improperly who prescribe to God a fixed plan of action. Let us permit him to advance our salvation by a diversity of methods; and let us not refuse to be humbled, that he may more abundantly display his glory. Above all, let us never avoid the cross, by which the Son of God himself was trained from his earliest infancy. This flight is a part of the foolishness of the cross, but it surpasses all the wisdom of the world.

the consolation of Israel, because he was to be its redemption. This consolation of Israel was so universally expected that the Jews swore by it.

The Holy Ghost was upon him – He was a man divinely inspired, overshadowed, and protected by the power and influence of the Most High.

26. He should not see death – They that seek shall find: it is impossible that a man who is earnestly seeking the salvation of God, should be permitted to die without finding it.

The Lord's Christ – Rather, the Lord's anointed. That prophet, priest, and king, who was typified by so many anointed persons under the old covenant; and who was appointed to come in the fullness of time, to accomplish all that was written in the law, in the prophets, and in the Psalms, concerning him.

27. After the custom of the law – To present him to the Lord, and then redeem him by paying five shekels, Numbers 18: 15–16, and to offer those sacrifices appointed by the law. See Luke 2: 24.

28. Then took he him up in his arms – What must the holy soul of this man have felt in this moment! O inestimable privilege! And yet ours need not be inferior: If a man love me, says Christ, he will keep my word; and I and the Father will come in unto him, and make our abode with him. And indeed even Christ in the arms could not avail a man, if he were not formed in his heart.

30. Thy salvation – That Savior which it became the goodness of God to bestow upon man, and which the necessities of the human race required. Christ is called our salvation, as he is called our life, our peace, our hope; i.e. he is the author of all these, to them who believe.

32. A light to lighten the Gentiles – A light of the Gentiles, for revelation. By Moses and the prophets, a light of revelation was given to the Jews, in the blessedness of which the Gentiles did not partake. By Christ and his

apostles, a luminous revelation is about to be given unto the Gentiles, from the blessedness of which the Jews in general, by their obstinacy and unbelief, shall be long excluded. But to all true Israelites it shall be a glory, an evident fulfillment of all the predictions of the prophets, relative to the salvation of a lost world; and the first offers of it shall be made to the Jewish people, who may see in it the truth of their own Scriptures indisputably evinced.

LUKE 2: 33–39

33. Joseph and his mother marveled – For they did not as yet fully know the counsels of God, relative to the salvation which Christ was to procure; nor the way in which the purchase was to be made: but to this Simeon refers in the following verses.

34. This child is set for the fall – This seems an allusion to Isaiah 8: 14–15: Jehovah, God of hosts, shall be – for a stone of stumbling and rock of offense to both houses of Israel; and many among them shall stumble and fall, etc. As Christ did not come as a temporal deliverer, in which character alone the Jews expected him, the consequence should be, they would reject him, and so fall by the Romans. See Romans 11: 11–12, and Matthew 24. But in the fullness of time there shall be a rising again of many in Israel. See Romans 11: 26.

35. Yea, a sword shall pierce through thy own soul also – As this is a metaphor used by the most respectable Greek writers to express the most pungent sorrow, it may here refer to the anguish Mary must have felt when standing beside the cross of her tortured son: John 19: 25.

36. Anna, a prophetess – It does not appear that this person was a prophetess in the strict sense of the word, i.e. one who could foretell future events; but rather a holy woman; who, from her extensive knowledge and deep experience in Divine things.

The tribe of Asher – This was one of the ten tribes of the kingdom of Israel, several families of which had returned from their idolatry unto

16 Then Herod, when he saw that he was mocked of the wise men, was exceeding wroth, and sent forth, and slew all the children that were in Bethlehem, and in all the coasts thereof, from two years old and under, according to the time which he had diligently inquired of the wise men.

17 Then was fulfilled that which was spoken by Jeremy the prophet, saying,

18 In Rama was there a voice heard, lamentation, and weeping, and great mourning, Rachel weeping for her children, and would not be comforted, because they are not.

MATTHEW 2: 19–23

19 But when Herod was dead, behold, an angel of the Lord appeareth in a dream to Joseph in Egypt,

20 Saying, Arise, and take the young child and his mother, and go into the land of Israel: for they are dead which sought the young child's life.

21 And he arose, and took the young child and his mother, and came into the land of Israel.

22 But when he heard that Archelaus did reign in Judaea in the room of his father Herod, he was afraid to go thither: notwithstanding, being warned of God in a dream, he turned aside into the parts of Galilee:

23 And he came and dwelt in a city called Nazareth: that it might be fulfilled which was spoken by the prophets, He shall be called a Nazarene.

LUKE 2: 40–47

40 And the child grew, and waxed strong in spirit, filled with wisdom: and the grace of God was upon him.

41 Now his parents went to Jerusalem every year at the feast of the passover.

42 And when he was twelve years old, they went up to Jerusalem after the custom of the feast.

43 And when they had fulfilled the days, as they returned, the child Jesus tarried behind in Jerusalem; and Joseph and his mother knew not of it.

44 But they, supposing him to have been in the company, went a day's jour-

MATTHEW 2: 19–23

19. But when Herod was dead

These words show the perseverance of Joseph's faith. He kept his feet firm in Egypt, till he was recalled to his native country by a command of God. We see, at the same time, that the Lord never disappoints his own people, but renders them seasonable aid. It is probable that Joseph returned from Egypt immediately after the death of Herod, before Augustus Caesar had issued his decree, appointing Archelaus to be governor of Judea. Having been declared by his father's will to be successor to the throne, he undertook the whole charge of the government, but abstained from taking the title of king, saying that this depended on the will and pleasure of Caesar. He afterwards went to Rome, and obtained confirmation; only the name of king was refused, until he had merited it by his actions. The governor of Galilee was Philip, a man of gentle disposition, and almost like a private individual. Joseph complied with the suggestion of the angel, because, under a prince who had no delight in shedding blood, and who treated his subjects with mildness, there was less danger.

We must always bear in mind the purpose of God, in training his Son, from the commencement, under the discipline of the cross, because this was the way in which he was to redeem his Church. He bore our infirmities, and was exposed to dangers and to fears, that he might deliver his Church from them by his divine power, and might bestow upon it everlasting peace. His danger was our safety: his fear was our confidence. Not that he ever in his life felt alarm; but as he was surrounded, on every hand, by the fear of Joseph and Mary, he may be justly said to have taken upon him our fears, that he might procure for us assured confidence.

LUKE 2: 40–47

40. And the child grew

From the infancy of Christ Matthew passes immediately to his manifestation. Luke relates here a single fact, which well deserved to be recorded. In the midst of his boyhood, Christ gave a specimen of his future office, or at least indicated, by a single attempt, what he would afterwards be.

The child grew, and was invigorated in spirit

These words show, that the endowments of his mind grew with his age. Hence we infer, that this progress, or advancement, relates to his human nature: for the Divine nature could receive no increase.

God, in the time that Hezekiah proclaimed the passover in Jerusalem, which is mentioned 2 Chronicles 30: 1–11.

Seven years – She was a pure virgin when married, was favored with her husband but seven years, and was now in all, taking in the time of her virginity, marriage, and widowhood, eighty-four years of age. At such an age, it might be supposed she was reasonably exempted from performing the severer duties of religion; but her spirit of piety continued still to burn with a steady and undiminished fame.

37. Departed not from the temple – Attended constantly at the hours of prayer, which were nine in the morning and three in the afternoon. See Acts 2: 15; 3: 1. It does not appear that women had any other functions to perform in that holy place.

With fastings – She accompanied her devotion with frequent fastings, probably not oftener than twice in the week; for this was the custom of the most rigid Pharisees: see Luke 18: 12.

39. They returned into Galilee – But not immediately: for the coming of the wise men, and the retreat of Joseph with his family into Egypt, happened between this period of time, and his going to Nazareth in Galilee.

MATTHEW 2: 13–18

13. Flee into Egypt – Many Jews had settled in Egypt; not only those who had fled thither in the time of Jeremiah, see Jeremiah 48; but many others who had settled there also, on account of the temple which Onias IV had built at Heliopolis. Those who could speak the Greek tongue enjoyed many advantages in that country: besides, they had the Greek version of the Septuagint, which had been translated nearly 300 years before this time. Egypt was now a Roman province, and the rage of Herod could not pursue the holy family to this place. There is an apocryphal work in Arabic, called the Gospel of the infancy, which pretends to relate all the acts of Jesus and Mary while in Egypt. I have taken the pains to read this

through, and have found it to be a piece of gross superstition, having nothing to entitle it to a shadow of credibility.

15. Out of Egypt have I called my son – This is quoted from Hosea 11: 1, where the deliverance of Israel, and that only, is referred to. But as that deliverance was extraordinary, it is very likely that it had passed into a proverb, so that "Out of Egypt have I called my son," might have been used to express any signal deliverance.

16. Slew all the children – This cruelty of Herod seems alluded to in very decisive terms by Macrobius, who flourished toward the conclusion of the fourth Century.

18. In Rama was there a voice heard – These words, quoted from Jeremiah 31: 15, were originally spoken concerning the captivity of the ten tribes; but are here elegantly applied to the murder of the innocents at Bethlehem. As if he had said, Bethlehem at this time resembled Rama; for as Rachel might be said to weep over her children, which were slaughtered or gone into captivity; so in Bethlehem, the mothers lamented bitterly their children, because they were slain.

MATTHEW 2: 19–23

20. They are dead – Both Herod and Antipater his son.

22. He turned aside into the parts of Galilee – Here Antipas governed, who had a comparatively mild disposition.

LUKE 2: 40–47

40. The child grew – As to his body – being in perfect health.

Waxed strong in spirit – His rational soul became strong and vigorous.

Filled with wisdom – The divinity continuing to communicate itself more and more, in proportion to the increase of the rational principle. The reader should never forget that Jesus was perfect man, as well as God.

And the grace of God was upon him – Even

ney; and they sought him among their kinsfolk and acquaintance.

45 And when they found him not, they turned back again to Jerusalem, seeking him.

46 And it came to pass, that after three days they found him in the temple, sitting in the midst of the doctors, both hearing them, and asking them questions.

47 And all that heard him were astonished at his understanding and answers.

LUKE 2: 48–52

48 And when they saw him, they were amazed: and his mother said unto him, Son, why hast thou thus dealt with us? behold, thy father and I have sought thee sorrowing.

49 And he said unto them, How is it that ye sought me? wist ye not that I must be about my Father's business?

50 And they understood not the saying which he spake unto them.

51 And he went down with them, and came to Nazareth, and was subject unto them: but his mother kept all these sayings in her heart.

52 And Jesus increased in wisdom and stature, and in favor with God and man.

MATTHEW 3: 1–6; MARK 1: 1–6; LUKE 3: 1–6

Matthew 3: 1–6

1 In those days came John the Baptist, preaching in the wilderness of Judaea,

2 And saying, Repent ye: for the kingdom of heaven is at hand.

3 For this is he that was spoken of by the prophet Esaias, saying, The voice of one crying in the wilderness, Prepare ye the way of the Lord, make his paths straight.

4 And the same John had his raiment of camel's hair, and a leathern girdle about his loins; and his meat was locusts and wild honey.

5 Then went out to him Jerusalem, and all Judaea, and all the region round about Jordan,

6 And were baptized of him in Jordan, confessing their sins.

Mark 1: 1–6

1 The beginning of the gospel of Jesus

LUKE 2: 48–52

48. And his mother said to him

Those who think that the holy virgin spake in this manner, for the purpose of showing her authority, are, in my opinion, mistaken. This complaint was not the result of ambition, but was the expression of grief, which had lasted three days. Yet the manner of her complaint, as if she had received an injury, shows how ready we are by nature to defend our own rights, even without paying regard to God. The holy virgin would a thousand times rather have died, than deliberately preferred herself to God: but, in the indulgence of a mother's grief, she inadvertently falls into it. And undoubtedly this example warns us, how jealous we ought to be of all the affections of the flesh, and what care we ought to exercise, lest, by following our own desires, we defraud God of his honor.

MATTHEW 3: 1–6; MARK 1: 1–6; LUKE 3: 1–6

Mark 1: 1. The beginning of the Gospel

Though what we have hitherto taken out of Matthew and Luke is a part of the Gospel, yet it is not without reason that Mark makes the beginning of the Gospel to be the preaching of John the Baptist. For the Law and the Prophets then came to an end (John 1: 17). "The Law and the Prophets were until John: since that time the kingdom of God is preached" (Luke 16: 16). And with this agrees most fully the quotation which he makes from the Prophet Malachi (3: 1). In order to inflame the minds of his people with a stronger desire of the promised salvation, the Lord had determined to leave them, for a time, without new prophecies. We know that the last of the true and lawful prophets was Malachi.

That the Jews, in the meantime, may not faint with hunger, he exhorts them to continue under the Law of Moses, until the promised redemption appear. He mentions the law only (John 1: 17), because the doctrine of the Prophets was not separate from the law, but was merely an appendage and fuller exposition of it, that the form of government in the Church might depend entirely on the Law. It is no new or uncommon thing in Scripture, to include the Prophets under the name of the Law: for they were all related to it as their fountain or design. The Gospel was not an inferior appendage to the Law, but a new form of instruction, by which the former was set aside.

Malachi, distinguishing the two conditions of the Church, places the one under the Law, and commences the other with the preaching of John. He unquestionably describes the Baptist, when he says, "Behold, I send my messenger" (Malachi 3: 1): for, as we have already said, that passage lays down an express distinction between the Law and the new order and condition of the Church. With the same view he

Christ himself, who knew no sin, grew in the favor of God; and, as to his human nature, increased in the graces of the Holy Spirit. From this we learn that, if a man were as pure and as perfect as the man Jesus Christ himself was, yet he might nevertheless increase in the image, and consequently in the favor, of God. God loves every thing and person, in proportion to the nearness of the approaches made to his own perfections.

41. His parents went – every year – This was their constant custom, because positively enjoined by the law, Exodus 23: 17. But it does not appear that infants were obliged to be present; and yet all the men-children are positively ordered to make their appearance at Jerusalem thrice in the year, Exodus 34: 23. And our Lord, being now twelve years old, Luke 2: 42, accompanies his parents to the feast. Probably this was the very age at which the male children were obliged to appear before the Lord at the three public festivals – the feast of unleavened bread, of weeks, and of tabernacles. According to the Jewish canons, it was the age at which they were obliged to begin to learn a trade.

43. Had fulfilled the days – Eight days in the whole: one was the passover, and the other seven, the days of unleavened bread.

44. Supposing him to have been in the company – Some have supposed that the men and women marched in separate companies on these occasions, which is very likely; and that sometimes the children kept company with the men, sometimes with the women. This might have led to what otherwise seems to have been inexcusable carelessness in Joseph and Mary. Joseph, not seeing Jesus in the men's company, might suppose he was with his mother in the women's company; and Mary, not seeing him with her, might imagine he was with Joseph.

46. Sitting in the midst of the doctors – The rabbins, who were explaining the law and the ceremonies of the Jewish religion to their disciples.

Asking them questions – Not as a scholar asks his teacher, to be informed; but as a teacher, who proposes questions to his scholars in order to take an occasion to instruct them.

LUKE 2: 48–52

48. Why hast thou thus dealt with us? – It certainly was not his fault, but theirs. Men are very apt to lay on others the blame of their own misconduct.

49. How is it that ye sought me? – Is not this intended as a gentle reproof? Why had ye me to seek? Ye should not have left my company, when ye knew I am constantly employed in performing the will of the Most High.

My Father's business? – My Father's concerns.

51. Was subject unto them – Behaved towards them with all dutiful submission.

MATTHEW 3: 1–6; MARK 1: 1–6; LUKE 3: 1–6

Matthew 3: 1–6

1. John the Baptist – John, surnamed The Baptist, because he required those to be baptized who professed to be contrite because of their sins, was the son of a priest named Zacharias, and his wife Elisabeth, and was born about six months before our blessed Lord. For his fidelity in reproving Herod for his incest with his brother Philip's wife, he was cast into prison, no doubt at the suggestion of Herodias, the profligate woman in question. He was at last beheaded at her instigation, and his head given as a present to Salome, her daughter, who, by her elegant dancing, had highly gratified Herod, the paramour of her incestuous mother.

Came – preaching – proclaiming, as a herald, a matter of great and solemn importance to men; the subject not his own, nor of himself, but from that God from whom alone he had received his commission.

The wilderness of Judea – That is, the country parts, as distinguished from the city; for in this sense the word wilderness.

Christ, the Son of God;

2 As it is written in the prophets, Behold, I send my messenger before thy face, which shall prepare thy way before thee.

3 The voice of one crying in the wilderness, Prepare ye the way of the Lord, make his paths straight.

4 John did baptize in the wilderness, and preach the baptism of repentance for the remission of sins.

5 And there went out unto him all the land of Judaea, and they of Jerusalem, and were all baptized of him in the river of Jordan, confessing their sins.

6 And John was clothed with camel's hair, and with a girdle of a skin about his loins; and he did eat locusts and wild honey;

Luke 3: 1–6

1 Now in the fifteenth year of the reign of Tiberius Caesar, Pontius Pilate being governor of Judaea, and Herod being tetrarch of Galilee, and his brother Philip tetrarch of Ituraea and of the region of Trachonitis, and Lysanias the tetrarch of Abilene,

2 Annas and Caiaphas being the high priests, the word of God came unto John the son of Zacharias in the wilderness.

3 And he came into all the country about Jordan, preaching the baptism of repentance for the remission of sins;

4 As it is written in the book of the words of Esaias the prophet, saying, The voice of one crying in the wilderness, Prepare ye the way of the Lord, make his paths straight.

5 Every valley shall be filled, and every mountain and hill shall be brought low; and the crooked shall be made straight, and the rough ways shall be made smooth;

6 And all flesh shall see the salvation of God.

MATTHEW 3: 7–10; LUKE 3: 7–14

Matthew 3: 7–10

7 But when he saw many of the Pharisees and Sadducees come to his baptism, he said unto them, O generation of vipers, who hath warned you to flee from the wrath to come?

had said a little before, (which is quoted by Mark [9: 13]; for the passages are quite similar), "Behold, I send you Elijah the Prophet, before the coming of the great and dreadful day of the Lord" (Malachi 4: 5). Again,

"Behold, I send my messenger, and he shall prepare the way before me: and the Lord, whom ye seek, shall suddenly come to his temple" (Malachi 3: 1).

In both passages, the Lord promises a better condition of his Church than had existed under the Law, and this unquestionably points out **the beginning of the Gospel**. But **before the Lord came** to restore the Church, a forerunner or herald was to come, and announce that he was at hand. Hence we infer, that the abrogation of the Law, and **the beginning of the Gospel**, strictly speaking, took place when John began to preach.

The Evangelist John presents to us Christ clothed in flesh, "the Word made flesh" (John 1: 14); so that his birth and the whole history of his appearance are included in the Gospel. But here Mark inquires, when the Gospel began to be published, and, therefore, properly begins with John, who was its first minister. And with this view the Heavenly Father chose that the life of his Son should be buried, as it were, in silence, until the time of the full revelation arrived. Under God's providence the Evangelists pass at once from his earliest infancy to his thirtieth year, when he was openly exhibited to the world, invested with his public character as a Redeemer; Luke excepted, who slightly touches one indication of his future calling, which occurred about his twelfth year (Luke 2: 42).

MATTHEW 3: 7–10; LUKE 3: 7–14

Matthew 3: 7. And when he saw many of the Pharisees

It is here related by Matthew and Luke, that John did not merely preach repentance in a general manner, but that he also applied his discourse to individuals. And the manner of teaching will, in point of fact, be very unprofitable, if instructors do not judiciously inquire what the season demands, and what belongs to individuals. Nothing can be more unequal, in this respect, than a constant equality. For this reason John, we are told, addressed the Pharisees and Sadducees with greater severity: because he saw that their hypocrisy, and swelling pride, rendered them liable to be more severely censured than the common people. To comprehend more fully his design, we must understand, that none are more stupid than hypocrites, who deceive themselves and others by the outward mask of holiness. While God thunders, on all sides, against the whole world, they construct a refuge for themselves in their own deceitful fancy; for they are convinced that they

2. Repent – This was the matter of the preaching.

The kingdom of heaven is at hand – Referring to the prophecy of Daniel, Daniel 7: 13–4, where the reign of Christ among men is expressly foretold. This phrase, and the kingdom of God, mean the same thing, viz. the dispensation of infinite mercy, and manifestation of eternal truth, by Christ Jesus, producing the true knowledge of God, accompanied with that worship which is pure and holy, worthy of that God who is its institutor and its object. But why is this called a kingdom? Because it has its laws, all the moral precepts of the Gospel: its subjects, all who believe in Christ Jesus: and its king, the Sovereign of heaven and earth. Jesus Christ never saved a soul which he did not govern; nor is this Christ precious or estimable to any man who does not feel a spirit of subjection to the Divine will.

But why is it called the kingdom of HEAVEN? Because God designed that his kingdom of grace here should resemble the kingdom of glory above. And hence our Lord teaches us to pray, Thy will be done on earth, as it is in heaven. The kingdom of heaven is not meat and drink, says St. Paul, Romans 14: 17; does not consist in the gratification of sensual passions, or worldly ambition; but is righteousness, peace, and joy, in the Holy Ghost. Now what can there be more than this in glory? Righteousness, without mixture of sin; peace, without strife or contention; joy, in the Holy Ghost, spiritual joy, without mixture of misery! And all this, it is possible, by the grace of the Lord Jesus Christ, to enjoy here below. How then does heaven itself differ from this state? Answer. It makes the righteousness eternal, the peace eternal, and the joy eternal. This is the heaven of heavens!

3. The voice of one crying in the wilderness – Or, A voice of a crier in the wilderness. This is quoted from Isaiah 40: 3, which clearly proves that John the Baptist was the person of whom the prophet spoke.

The idea is taken from the practice of eastern monarchs, who, whenever they entered upon an expedition, or took a journey through a desert country, sent harbingers before them, to prepare all things for their passage; and pioneers to open the passes, to level the ways, and to remove all impediments.

4. His raiment of camel's hair – A sort of coarse or rough covering, which, it appears, was common to the prophets, Zechariah 13: 4. In such a garment we find Elijah clothed, 2 Kings 1: 8. And as John had been designed under the name of this prophet, Malachi 4: 5, whose spirit and qualifications he was to possess, Luke 1: 17, he took the same habit and lived in the same state of self-denial.

His meat was locusts – may either signify the insect called the locust, which still makes a part of the food in the land of Judea; or the top of a plant. Many eminent commentators are of the latter opinion; but the first is the most likely. The Saxon translator has grasshoppers.

Wild honey – Such as he got in the rocks and hollows of trees, and which abounded in Judea: see 1 Samuel 14: 26. It is most likely that the dried locusts, which are an article of food in Asiatic countries to the present day, were fried in the honey, or compounded in some manner with it.

6. Were baptized – In what form baptism was originally administered, has been deemed a subject worthy of serious dispute. Were the people dipped or sprinkled? They were all dipped, say some. Can any man suppose that it was possible for John to dip all the inhabitants of Jerusalem and Judea, and of all the country round about the Jordan? Were both men and women dipped, for certainly both came to his baptism? This could never have comported either with safety or with decency. Were they dipped in their clothes? This would have endangered their lives, if they had not with them change of raiment: and as such a baptism as John's (however administered) was, in several respects, a new thing in Judea, it is not at all likely that the people would come thus provided. But suppose these were dipped, which I think it would be impossible to prove, does it follow that, in all regions of the world, men and women must be dipped, in order

8 Bring forth therefore fruits meet for repentance:

9 And think not to say within yourselves, We have Abraham to our father: for I say unto you, that God is able of these stones to raise up children unto Abraham.

10 And now also the axe is laid unto the root of the trees: therefore every tree which bringeth not forth good fruit is hewn down, and cast into the fire.

Luke 3: 7–14

7 Then said he to the multitude that came forth to be baptized of him, O generation of vipers, who hath warned you to flee from the wrath to come?

8 Bring forth therefore fruits worthy of repentance, and begin not to say within yourselves, We have Abraham to our father: for I say unto you, That God is able of these stones to raise up children unto Abraham.

9 And now also the axe is laid unto the root of the trees: every tree therefore which bringeth not forth good fruit is hewn down, and cast into the fire.

10 And the people asked him, saying, What shall we do then?

11 He answereth and saith unto them, He that hath two coats, let him impart to him that hath none; and he that hath meat, let him do likewise.

12 Then came also publicans to be baptized, and said unto him, Master, what shall we do?

13 And he said unto them, Exact no more than that which is appointed you.

14 And the soldiers likewise demanded of him, saying, And what shall we do? And he said unto them, Do violence to no man, neither accuse any falsely; and be content with your wages.

MATTHEW 3: 11–12; MARK 1: 7–8; LUKE 3: 15–18

Matthew 3: 11–12

11 I indeed baptize you with water unto repentance: but he that cometh after me is mightier than I, whose shoes I am not worthy to bear: he shall baptize you with the Holy Ghost, and with fire:

12 Whose fan is in his hand, and he will throughly purge his floor, and gather

have nothing to do with the judgment of God. Does any one suppose, that John acted improperly, in treating them with so much harshness at the first interview? I reply: They were not unknown to him, and the knowledge he had of them was derived, not from acquaintance or experience, but, on the contrary, from a secret revelation of the Spirit. It was therefore necessary that he should not spare them, lest they might return home more inflated with pride. Is it again objected, that they ought not to have been terrified by such severity of reproof, because they made a profession, in baptism, that they would afterwards be different people from what they had formerly been? The reply is still easy. Those whose habits of uttering falsehood to God, and of deceiving themselves, lead them to hold out hypocrisy and pretension, instead of the reality, ought to be urged, with greater sharpness than other men, to true repentance. There is an astonishing pertinacity, as I have said, in hypocrites; and, until they have been flayed by violence, they obstinately keep their skin.

As to the loud and open rebuke, which was administered to them in presence of all, it was for the sake of others; and that is the reason why Luke mentions, that it was addressed to multitudes (Luke 3: 7). Though the people whom John reproved were few in number, his design was to strike terror on all; as Paul enjoins us to regard it as the advantage of public rebukes, "that others also may fear" (1 Timothy 5: 20). He addresses directly the Pharisees and Sadducees, and at the same time, addresses, through them, a warning to all, not to hold out a hypocritical appearance of repentance, instead of a true affection of the heart. Besides, it was of great importance to the whole nation to know what sort of people the Pharisees and Sadducees were, who had miserably corrupted the worship of God, wasted the church, and overturned the whole of religion – in a word, who had extinguished the light of God by their corruptions, and infected every thing by their crimes.

It is probable, therefore, that John publicly attacked the Pharisees, for the benefit of the whole church of God, that they might no longer dazzle the eyes of simple men by empty show, or hold the body of the people under oppression by wicked tyranny.

MATTHEW 3: 11–12; MARK 1: 7–8; LUKE 3: 15–18

The three Evangelists relate the Baptist's discourse in the same words. In one respect, Luke's account is more full: for he opens it by explaining the occasion on which this discourse was delivered. It arose from the people being in danger of being led, by a false opinion, to convey to him the honor which was due to Christ. To remove, as soon as

to be evangelically baptized? In the eastern countries, bathings were frequent, because of the heat of the climate, it being there so necessary to cleanliness and health; but could our climate, or a more northerly one, admit of this with safety, for at least three-fourths of the year? We may rest assured that it could not. And may we not presume, that if John had opened his commission in the north of Great Britain, for many months of the year, he would have dipped neither man nor woman, unless he could have procured a tepid bath? Those who are dipped or immersed in water, in the name of the Holy Trinity, I believe to be evangelically baptized – those who are washed or sprinkled with water in the name of the Father, and of the Son, and of the Holy Ghost, I believe to be equally so; and the repetition of such a baptism I believe to be profane. Others have a right to believe the contrary, if they see good. After all, it is the thing signified, and not the mode, which is the essential part of the sacrament.

Confessing their sins – earnestly acknowledging that their sins were their own. And thus taking the whole blame upon themselves, and laying nothing to the charge of GOD or man. This is essential to true repentance; and, till a man take the whole blame on himself, he cannot feel the absolute need he has of casting his soul on the mercy of God, that he may be saved.

MATTHEW 3: 7–10; LUKE 3: 7–14

Matthew 3: 7–10

7. Pharisees – A very numerous sect among the Jews, who, in their origin, were, very probably, a pure and holy people. It is likely that they got the name of Pharisees, i.e. Separatists, from their separating themselves from the pollution of the Jewish national worship; and hence, the word in the Anglo-Saxon version is, holy persons who stand apart, or by themselves: but, in process of time, like all religious sects and parties, they degenerated: they lost the spirit of their institution, they ceased to recur to first principles, and had only the form of godliness, when Jesus Christ preached in

Judea; for he bore witness, that they did make the outside of the cup and platter clean – they observed the rules of their institution, but the spirit was gone.

Sadducees – A sect who denied the existence of angels and spirits, consequently all Divine influence and inspiration, and also the resurrection of the dead. The Sadducees of that time were the Materialists and Deists of the Jewish nation. When the sect of the Pharisees arose cannot be distinctly ascertained; but it is supposed to have been some time after the Babylonish captivity. The sect of the Sadducees were the followers of one Sadok, a disciple of Antigonus Sochaeus, who flourished about three centuries before Christ.

O generation of vipers – A terribly expressive speech. A serpentine brood, from a serpentine stock. As their fathers were, so were they, children of the wicked one. This is God's estimate of a SINNER, whether he wade in wealth, or soar in fame. The Jews were the seed of the serpent, who should bruise the heel of the woman's seed, and whose head should be bruised by him.

Who hath warned you – Or, privately shown you. They came privately: and John may be supposed to address them thus: "Did any person give you a private warning? No, you received your convictions under the public ministry of the word. The multitudes of the poor and wretched, who have been convinced of sin, have publicly acknowledged their crimes, and sought mercy – God will unmask you – you have deceived the people – you have deceived yourselves – you must appear just what you are; and, if you expect mercy from God, act like the penitent multitude, and bring forth FRUIT worthy of repentance. Do not begin to trifle with your convictions, by thinking, that because you are descendants of Abraham, therefore you are entitled to God's favor; God can, out of these stones (pointing probably to those scattered about in the desert, which he appears to have considered as an emblem of the Gentiles) raise up a faithful seed, who, though not natural descendants of your excellent patriarch, yet shall be his worthy children, as being partakers of his faith,

his wheat into the garner; but he will burn up the chaff with unquenchable fire.

Mark 1: 7–8

7 And preached, saying, There cometh one mightier than I after me, the latchet of whose shoes I am not worthy to stoop down and unloose.

8 I indeed have baptized you with water: but he shall baptize you with the Holy Ghost.

Luke 3: 15–18

15 And as the people were in expectation, and all men mused in their hearts of John, whether he were the Christ, or not;

16 John answered, saying unto them all, I indeed baptize you with water; but one mightier than I cometh, the latchet of whose shoes I am not worthy to unloose: he shall baptize you with the Holy Ghost and with fire:

17 Whose fan is in his hand, and he will throughly purge his floor, and will gather the wheat into his garner; but the chaff he will burn with fire unquenchable.

18 And many other things in his exhortation preached he unto the people.

MATTHEW 3: 13–17; MARK 1: 9–11; LUKE 3: 21–23

Matthew 3: 13–17

13 Then cometh Jesus from Galilee to Jordan unto John, to be baptized of him.

14 But John forbad him, saying, I have need to be baptized of thee, and comest thou to me?

15 And Jesus answering said unto him, Suffer it to be so now: for thus it becometh us to fulfil all righteousness. Then he suffered him.

16 And Jesus, when he was baptized, went up straightway out of the water: and, lo, the heavens were opened unto him, and he saw the Spirit of God descending like a dove, and lighting upon him:

17 And lo a voice from heaven, saying, This is my beloved Son, in whom I am well pleased.

Mark 1: 9–11

9 And it came to pass in those days, that Jesus came from Nazareth of Galilee, and was baptized of John in Jordan.

10 And straightway coming up out of

possible, every occasion of such a mistake, he expressly declares, that he is not the Christ, and draws such a distinction between Christ and himself as to maintain Christ's prerogative.

Scripture does sometimes, though not in a literal sense, ascribe to men what John here declares not to belong to men, but claims exclusively for Christ. In such cases, however, the design is not to inquire, what man has separately and by himself, but merely to show, what is the effect and advantage of signs, and in what manner God makes use of them, as instruments, by his Spirit. Here also is laid down a distinction between Christ and his ministers, that the world may not fall into the mistake, of giving to them what is justly due to him alone: for there is nothing to which they are more prone, than to adorn creatures with what has been taken from God by robbery. A careful attention to this observation will rid us of many difficulties. We know what disputes have arisen, in our own age, about the advantage and efficacy of signs, all of which may be disposed of in a single word. The ordinance of our Lord, viewed as a whole, includes himself as its Author, and the power of the Spirit, together with the figure and the minister: but where a comparison is made between our Lord and the minister, the former must have all the honor, and the latter must be reduced to nothing.

MATTHEW 3: 13–17; MARK 1: 9–11; LUKE 3: 21–23

Matthew 3: 13. That he might be baptized by him

For what purpose did the Son of God wish to be baptized? This may be learned, in some measure, from his answer. We have already assigned a special reason. He received the same baptism with us, in order to assure believers, that they are ingrafted into his body, and that they are "buried with him in baptism," that they may rise to "newness of life" (Romans 6: 4). But the end, which he here proposes, is more extensive: **for thus it became him to fulfill all righteousness** (verse 15).

The word righteousness frequently signifies, in Scripture, the observation of the law: and in that sense we may explain this passage to mean that, since Christ had voluntarily subjected himself to the law, it was necessary that he should keep it in every part. But I prefer a more simple interpretation. "Say nothing for the present," said our Lord, "about my rank: for the question before us is not, which of us deserves to be placed above the other. Let us rather consider what our calling demands, and what has been enjoined on us by God the Father." The general reason why Christ received baptism was, that he might render full obedience to the Father; and the special reason was, that he

and friends of his God." It should be added, that the Greek word also signifies plain or ample information.

The wrath to come? – The desolation which was about to fall on the Jewish nation for their wickedness, and threatened in the last words of their own Scriptures. See Malachi 4: 6. Lest I come and smite the earth with a curse. This wrath or curse was coming: they did not prevent it by turning to God, and receiving the Messiah, and therefore the wrath of God came upon them to the uttermost.

10. And now also the axe is laid – Or, Even now the axe lieth. As if he had said, There is not a moment to spare – God is about to cut off every impenitent soul – you must therefore either turn to God immediately, or be utterly and finally ruined. It was customary with the prophets to represent the kingdoms, nations, and individuals, whose ruin they predicted, under the notion of forests and trees, doomed to be cut down. See Jeremiah 46: 22–23; Ezekiel 31: 3,11–12. The Baptist follows the same metaphor: the Jewish nation is the tree, and the Romans the axe, which, by the just judgment of God, was speedily to cut it down. It has been well observed, that there is an allusion here to a woodman, who, having marked a tree for excision, lays his axe at its root, and strips off his outer garment, that he may wield his blows more powerfully, and that his work may be quickly performed. For about sixty years before the coming of Christ, this axe had been lying at the root of the Jewish tree, Judea having been made a province to the Roman empire, from the time that Pompey took the city of Jerusalem, during the contentions of the two brothers Hyrcanus and Aristobulus, which was about sixty-three years before the coming of Christ. But as the country might be still considered as in the hands of the Jews, though subject to the Romans, and God had waited on them now nearly ninety years from the above time, expecting them to bring forth fruit, and none was yet produced; he kept the Romans as an axe, lying at the root of this tree, who were ready to cut it down the moment God gave them the commission.

MATTHEW 3: 11–12; MARK 1: 7–8; LUKE 3: 15–18

Matthew 3: 11–12

11. But he that cometh after me – Or, I coming after me, who is now on his way, and will shortly make his appearance. Jesus Christ began his ministry when he was thirty years of age, Luke 3: 23, which was the age appointed by the law, Numbers 4: 3. John the Baptist was born about six months before Christ; and, as he began his public ministry when thirty years of age, then this coming after refers to six months after the commencement of John's public preaching, at which time Christ entered upon his.

Whose shoes I am not worthy to bear – This saying is expressive of the most profound humility and reverence. To put on, take off, and carry the shoes of their masters, was, not only among the Jews, but also among the Greeks and Romans, the work of the vilest slaves.

With the Holy Ghost, and with fire – That the influences of the Spirit of God are here designed, needs but little proof. Christ's religion was to be a spiritual religion, and was to have its seat in the heart. Outward precepts, however well they might describe, could not produce inward spirituality. This was the province of the Spirit of God, and of it alone; therefore he is represented here under the similitude of fire, because he was to illuminate and invigorate the soul, penetrate every part, and assimilate the whole to the image of the God of glory.

12. Whose fan is in his hand – The Romans are here termed God's fan, as, in Matthew 3: 10, they were called his axe, and, in Matthew 22: 7, they are termed his troops or armies.

His floor – Does not this mean the land of Judea, which had been long, as it were, the threshing-floor of the Lord? God says, he will now, by the winnowing fan (viz. the Romans) thoroughly cleanse this floor – the wheat, those who believe in the Lord Jesus, he will gather into his garner, either take to heaven from the evil to come, or put in a place of

the water, he saw the heavens opened, and the Spirit like a dove descending upon him:

11 And there came a voice from heaven, saying, Thou art my beloved Son, in whom I am well pleased.

Luke 3: 21–23

21 Now when all the people were baptized, it came to pass, that Jesus also being baptized, and praying, the heaven was opened,

22 And the Holy Ghost descended in a bodily shape like a dove upon him, and a voice came from heaven, which said, Thou art my beloved Son; in thee I am well pleased.

MATTHEW 4: 1–4; MARK 1: 12–13A; LUKE 4: 1–4

Matthew 4: 1–4

1 Then was Jesus led up of the Spirit into the wilderness to be tempted of the devil.

2 And when he had fasted forty days and forty nights, he was afterward an hungered.

3 And when the tempter came to him, he said, If thou be the Son of God, command that these stones be made bread.

4 But he answered and said, It is written, Man shall not live by bread alone, but by every word that proceedeth out of the mouth of God.

Mark 1: 12–13a

12 And immediately the Spirit driveth him into the wilderness.

13 And he was there in the wilderness forty days, tempted of Satan; and was with the wild beasts;

Luke 4: 1–4

1 And Jesus being full of the Holy Ghost returned from Jordan, and was led by the Spirit into the wilderness,

2 Being forty days tempted of the devil. And in those days he did eat nothing: and when they were ended, he afterward hungered.

3 And the devil said unto him, If thou be the Son of God, command this stone that it be made bread.

4 And Jesus answered him, saying, It

might consecrate baptism in his own body, that we might have it in common with him.

MATTHEW 4: 1–4; MARK 1: 12–13; LUKE 4: 1–4

Matthew 4: 1. Then Jesus was led

There were two reasons why Christ withdrew into the wilderness. The first was, that, after a fast of forty days, he might come forth as a new man, or rather a heavenly man, to the discharge of his office. The next was, that he might be tried by temptation and undergo an apprenticeship, before he undertook an office so arduous, and so elevated. Let us therefore learn that, by the guidance of the Spirit, Christ withdrew from the crowd of men, in order that he might come forth as the highest teacher of the church, as the ambassador of God – rather as sent from heaven, than as taken from some town, and from among the common people.

In the same way Moses, when God was about to employ him as his agent in publishing his law, was carried into Mount Sinai, withdrawn from the view of the people, and admitted, as it were, into a heavenly sanctuary (Exodus 24: 12). It was proper that Christ should be surrounded by marks of divine grace and power – at least equally illustrious with those which were bestowed on Moses, that the majesty of the Gospel might not be inferior to that of the Law. If God bestowed singular honor on a doctrine which was "the ministration of death" (2 Corinthians 3: 7), how much more honor is due to the doctrine of life? And if a shadowy portrait of God had so much brightness, ought not his face, which appears in the Gospel, to shine with full splendor?

Such also was the design of the fasting: for Christ abstained from eating and drinking, not to give an example of temperance, but to acquire greater authority, by being separated from the ordinary condition of men, and coming forth, as an angel from heaven, not as a man from the earth. For what, pray, would have been that virtue of abstinence, in not tasting food, for which he had no more appetite than if he had not been clothed with flesh? It is mere folly, therefore, to appoint a forty days' fast (as it is called), in imitation of Christ. There is no more reason why we should follow the example of Christ in this matter, than there formerly was for the holy Prophets, and other Fathers under the law, to imitate the fast of Moses. But we are aware, that none of them thought of doing so; with the single exception of Elijah, who was employed by God in restoring the law, and who, for nearly the same reason with Moses, was kept in the mount fasting.

safety. But he will burn up the chaff – the diso-bedient and rebellions Jews, who would not come unto Christ, that they might have life.

Unquenchable fire – That cannot be extinguished by man.

MATTHEW 3: 13–17; MARK 1: 9–11; LUKE 3: 21–23

Matthew 3: 13–17

14. John forbad him – Earnestly and pressingly opposed him.

15. To fulfill all righteousness – That is, Every righteous ordinance. The following passage, quoted from Justin Martyr, will doubtless appear a strong vindication of this translation. "Christ was circumcised, and observed all the other ordinances of the law of Moses, not with a view to his own justification; but to fulfill the dispensation committed to him by the Lord, the God and Creator of all things." – Wakefield.

But was this an ordinance? Undoubtedly: it was the initiatory ordinance of the Baptist's dispensation. Now, as Christ had submitted to circumcision, which was the initiatory ordinance of the Mosaic dispensation, it was necessary that he should submit to this, which was instituted by no less an authority, and was the introduction to his own dispensation of eternal mercy and truth. But it was necessary on another account: Our Lord represented the high priest, and was to be the high priest over the house of God: now, as the high priest was initiated into his office by washing and anointing, so must Christ: and hence he was baptized, washed, and anointed by the Holy Ghost. Thus he fulfilled the righteous ordinance of his initiation into the office of high priest, and thus was prepared to make an atonement for the sins of mankind.

16. The heavens were opened unto him – That is, to John the Baptist – and he, John, saw the Spirit of God – lighting upon him, i.e. Jesus. There has been some controversy about the manner and form in which the Spirit of God rendered itself visible on this occasion.

St. Luke, Luke 3: 22, says it was in a bodily shape like to a dove: and this likeness to a dove some refer to a hovering motion, like to that of a dove, and not to the form of the dove itself: but the terms of the text are too precise to admit of this far-fetched interpretation.

This passage affords no mean proof of the doctrine of the Trinity. That three distinct persons are here, represented, there can be no dispute.

1. The person of Jesus Christ, baptized by John in Jordan.

2. The person of the Holy Ghost in a bodily shape, (Luke 3: 22) like a dove.

3. The person of the Father; a voice came out of heaven, saying, This is my beloved Son, etc. The voice is here represented as proceeding from a different place to that in which the persons of the Son and Holy Spirit were manifested; and merely, I think, more forcibly to mark this Divine personality.

17. In whom I am well pleased – in whom I have delighted. By this voice, and overshadowing of the Spirit, the mission of the Lord Jesus was publicly and solemnly accredited; God intimating that he had before delighted in him: the law, in all its ordinances, having pointed him out, for they could not be pleasing to God, but as they were fulfilled in, and showed forth, the Son of man, till, he came.

MATTHEW 4: 1–4; MARK 1: 12–13A; LUKE 4: 1–4

Matthew 4: 1–4

1. Then was Jesus led up of the Spirit – This transaction appears to have taken place immediately after Christ's baptism; and this bringing up of Christ was through the influence of the Spirit of God; that Spirit which had rested upon him in his baptism.

To be tempted – The first act of the ministry of Jesus Christ was a combat with Satan. Does not this receive light from Genesis 3: 17. I will put enmity between the woman's seed and thy seed: it shall bruise thy head, and thou shalt bruise his heel.

is written, That man shall not live by bread alone, but by every word of God.

MATTHEW 4: 5–11; MARK 1: 13B; LUKE 4: 5–13

Matthew 4: 5–11

5 Then the devil taketh him up into the holy city, and setteth him on a pinnacle of the temple,

6 And saith unto him, If thou be the Son of God, cast thyself down: for it is written, He shall give his angels charge concerning thee: and in their hands they shall bear thee up, lest at any time thou dash thy foot against a stone.

7 Jesus said unto him, It is written again, Thou shalt not tempt the Lord thy God.

8 Again, the devil taketh him up into an exceeding high mountain, and sheweth him all the kingdoms of the world, and the glory of them;

9 And saith unto him, All these things will I give thee, if thou wilt fall down and worship me.

10 Then saith Jesus unto him, Get thee hence, Satan: for it is written, Thou shalt worship the Lord thy God, and him only shalt thou serve.

11 Then the devil leaveth him, and, behold, angels came and ministered unto him.

Mark 1: 13b

and the angels ministered unto him.

Luke 4: 5–13

5 And the devil, taking him up into an high mountain, shewed unto him all the kingdoms of the world in a moment of time.

6 And the devil said unto him, All this power will I give thee, and the glory of them: for that is delivered unto me; and to whomsoever I will I give it.

7 If thou therefore wilt worship me, all shall be thine.

8 And Jesus answered and said unto him, Get thee behind me, Satan: for it is written, Thou shalt worship the Lord thy God, and him only shalt thou serve.

9 And he brought him to Jerusalem, and set him on a pinnacle of the temple, and said unto him, If thou be the Son of God, cast thyself down from hence:

MATTHEW 4: 5–11; MARK 1: 13; LUKE 4: 5–13

Matthew 4: 5. Then the devil taketh him

It is not of great importance, that Luke's narrative makes that temptation to be the second, which Matthew places as the third: for it was not the intention of the Evangelists to arrange the history in such a manner, as to preserve on all occasions, the exact order of time, but to draw up an abridged narrative of the events, so as to present, as in a mirror or picture, those things which are most necessary to be known concerning Christ. Let it suffice for us to know that Christ was tempted in three ways. The question, which of these contests was the second, and which was the third, need not give us much trouble or uneasiness.

Christ is said to have been placed on the pinnacle of the temple. It is asked, was he actually carried to this elevated spot, or was it done in vision? There are many, who obstinately assert, that the body was really and actually conveyed: for they consider it to be unworthy of Christ, that he should be supposed to be liable to the delusions of Satan. But it is easy to dispose of that objection. There is no absurdity in supposing, that this took place by the permission of God and the voluntary subjection of Christ; provided we hold that within – that is, in his mind and souls – he suffered no delusion. What is next added, that all the kingdoms of the world were placed in the view of Christ – as well as what Luke relates, that he was carried to a great distance in one moment – agrees better with the idea of a vision, than with any other supposition. In a matter that is doubtful, and where ignorance brings no risk, I choose rather to suspend my judgment, than to furnish contentious people with an occasion of debate. It is also possible, that the second temptation did not follow the first, nor the third the second, in immediate succession, but that some interval of time elapsed. This is even more probable, though the words of Luke might lead to the conclusion, that there was no long interval: for he says, that Christ obtained repose for a time.

But the main question for our consideration is, what was Satan's object in this kind of temptation? That will be best determined by our Lord's reply to Satan. To meet the stratagem of the enemy, and to repel his attack, Christ interposes, as a shield, these words: **Thou shalt not tempt the Lord thy God**. Hence it is evident, that the stratagems of the enemy were intended to induce Christ to exalt himself unduly, and to rise, in a daring manner, against God. Satan had formerly attempted to drive Christ to despair, because he was destitute of food, and of the ordinary means of life. Now, he exhorts him to indulge a foolish and vain confidences – to neglect the means which are in his powers – to throw himself, without necessity, into manifest

2. And when he had fasted forty days – It is remarkable that Moses, the great lawgiver of the Jews, previously to his receiving the law from God, fasted forty days in the mount; that Elijah, the chief of the prophets, fasted also forty days; and that Christ, the giver of the New Covenant, should act in the same way. Was not all this intended to show, that God's kingdom on earth was to be spiritual and Divine? – that it should not consist in meat and drink, but in righteousness, peace, and joy in the Holy Ghost? Romans 14: 17. Relative to the forty days' fast of Moses, there is a beautiful saying in the Talmud. "Is it possible that any man can fast forty days and forty nights?" To which Rabbi Meir answered, "When thou takest up thy abode in any particular city, thou must live according to its customs. Moses ascended to heaven, where they neither eat nor drink therefore he became assimilated to them. We are accustomed to eat and drink; and, when angels descend to us, they eat and drink also."

Moses, Elijah, and our blessed Lord could fast forty days and forty nights, because they were in communion with God, and living a heavenly life.

3. And when the tempter – This onset of Satan was made (speaking after the manner of men) judiciously: he came when Jesus, after having fasted forty days and forty nights, was hungry: now, as hunger naturally diminishes the strength of the body, the mind gets enfeebled, and becomes easily irritated; and if much watching and prayer be not employed, the uneasiness which is occasioned by a lack of food may soon produce impatience, and in this state of mind the tempter has great advantages. The following advice of an Arabian philosopher to his son is worthy of attention. "My son, never go out of the house in the morning, till thou hast eaten something: by so doing, thy mind will be more firm; and, shouldest thou be insulted by any person, thou wilt find thyself more disposed to suffer patiently: for hunger dries up and disorders the brain." The state of our bodily health and worldly circumstances may afford our adversary many opportunities of doing us immense mischief. In such cases, the sin to which we are tempted may be justly termed, as in Hebrews 12: 1, the well circumstanced sin, because all the circumstances of time, place, and state of body and mind, are favorable to it.

If thou be the Son of God – Or, a son of God, is here, and in Luke 4: 3, written without the article; and therefore should not be translated THE Son.

Command that these stones – The meaning of this temptation is: "Distrust the Divine providence and support, and make use of illicit means to supply thy necessities."

4. But by (or, upon,) every word – Our Lord's meaning seems to be this: God purposes the welfare of his creatures – all his appointments are calculated to promote this end. Some of them may appear to man to have a contrary tendency; but even fasting itself, when used in consequence of a Divine injunction, becomes a mean of supporting that life which it seems naturally calculated to impair or destroy.

MATTHEW 4: 5–11; MARK 1: 13B; LUKE 4: 5–13

Matthew 4: 5–11

5. Pinnacle of the temple – It is very likely that this was what was called the king's gallery; which, as Josephus says, "deserves to be mentioned among the most magnificent things under the sun: for upon a stupendous depth of a valley, scarcely to be fathomed by the eye of him that stands above, Herod erected a gallery of a vast height, from the top of which if any looked down, he would grow dizzy, his eyes not being able to reach so vast a depth."

6. Cast thyself down – Our Lord had repelled the first temptation by an act of confidence in the power and goodness of God; and now Satan solicits him to make trial of it. Through the unparalleled subtlety of Satan, the very means we make use of to repel one temptation may he used by him as the groundwork of another. This method he often uses, in order

10 For it is written, He shall give his angels charge over thee, to keep thee:

11 And in their hands they shall bear thee up, lest at any time thou dash thy foot against a stone.

12 And Jesus answering said unto him, It is said, Thou shalt not tempt the Lord thy God.

13 And when the devil had ended all the temptation, he departed from him for a season.

MATTHEW 4: 12,17; MARK 1: 14–15; LUKE 3: 19–20; LUKE 4: 14–15

Matthew 4: 12,17

12 Now when Jesus had heard that John was cast into prison, he departed into Galilee;

17 From that time Jesus began to preach, and to say, Repent: for the kingdom of heaven is at hand.

Mark 1: 14–15

14 Now after that John was put in prison, Jesus came into Galilee, preaching the gospel of the kingdom of God,

15 And saying, The time is fulfilled, and the kingdom of God is at hand: repent ye, and believe the gospel.

Luke 3: 19–20

19 But Herod the tetrarch, being reproved by him for Herodias his brother Philip's wife, and for all the evils which Herod had done,

20 Added yet this above all, that he shut up John in prison.

Luke 4: 14–15

14 And Jesus returned in the power of the Spirit into Galilee: and there went out a fame of him through all the region round about.

15 And he taught in their synagogues, being glorified of all.

LUKE 4: 16–22

16 And he came to Nazareth, where he had been brought up: and, as his custom was, he went into the synagogue on the sabbath day, and stood up for to read.

17 And there was delivered unto him the book of the prophet Esaias. And when he had opened the book, he found the place where it was written,

danger – and, as we might say, to overleap all bounds. As it is not proper for us to be discouraged, when we are pressed by "the want of all things" (Deuteronomy 28: 57), but to rely with confidence on God, neither are we at liberty to raise our crests, or ascend higher than God permits us. The design of Satan, we have now ascertained, was to induce Christ to make trial of his divinity, and to rise up, in foolish and wicked rashness, against God.

MATTHEW 4: 12,17; MARK 1: 14–15; LUKE 3: 19–20; 4: 14

Luke 3: 19. Now Herod the tetrarch

Luke alone explains the reason why Herod threw John into prison: though we shall afterwards find it mentioned by Matthew 14: 3, and Mark 6: 17. Josephus says (Ant. 18, v. 2), that Herod, dreading a popular insurrection and a change of the government, shut up John in the castle of Macherus (because he dreaded the man's influence); and that Herodias was married, not to Philip, who was Salome's husband, but to another Herod. But as his recollection appears to have failed him in this matter, and as he mentions also Philip's death out of its proper place, the truth of the history will be obtained, with greater certainty, from the Evangelists, and we must abide by their testimony. It is well known, that Herod, though he had been married to a daughter of Aretas, King of Arabia, fell in love with Herodias, his niece, and carried her off by fraud. This injury might possibly enough remain unrevenged by his brother Philip, to whom the same Josephus bears testimony, that he was a person of a mild and gentle disposition (18: 4: 6).

This history shows clearly, what sort of reward awaits the faithful and honest ministers of the truth, particularly when they reprove vices: for scarcely one in a hundred bears reproof, and if it is at all severe, they break out into fury.

LUKE 4: 16–22

16. And he came to Nazareth

The Evangelists are very careful to show by what sort of proofs Christ became known, a striking instance of which is here related by Luke. By explaining a passage in Isaiah, and applying it to the instruction which was immediately required, he turned upon him the eyes of all.

He entered, according to his custom, into the synagogue

Hence we conclude, that not only did he address the people in the open streets and highways, but, as far as he had opportunity, observed the usual order of the church. We see also that, though the Jews were become very degenerate, though every thing was in a state of confusion, and the condition of the church was miserably corrupted, one

to confound us in our confidence.

He shall give his angels charge, etc. – This is a mutilated quotation of Psalm 91: 11. The clause, to keep thee in all thy ways, Satan chose to leave out, as quite unsuitable to his design. That God has promised to protect and support his servants, admits of no dispute; but, as the path of duty is the way of safety, they are entitled to no good when they walk out of it.

In their hands they shall bear thee up – This quotation from Psalm 91: 11, is a metaphor taken from a nurse's management of her child: in teaching it to walk, she guides it along plain ground; but, when stones or other obstacles occur, she lifts up the child, and carries it over them, and then sets it down to walk again. Thus she keeps it in all its ways, watching over, and guarding every step it takes. To this St. Paul seems also to allude, 1 Thessalonians 2: 7. We were gentle among you, even as a nurse cherisheth her children. Thus the most merciful God deals with the children of men, ever guarding them by his eye, and defending them by his power.

7. Thou shalt not tempt – To expose myself to any danger naturally destructive, with the vain presumption that God will protect and defend me from the ruinous consequences of my imprudent conduct, is to tempt God.

8. An exceeding high mountain, and showeth him – If the words, all the kingdoms of the world, be taken in a literal sense, then this must have been a visionary representation, as the highest mountain on the face of the globe could not suffice to make evident even one hemisphere of the earth, and the other must of necessity be in darkness.

But if we take the world to mean only the land of Judea, and some of the surrounding nations, as it appears sometimes to signify, then the mountain described by the Abbe Mariti could have afforded the prospect in question.

11. Behold, angels came and ministered unto him – That is, brought that food which was necessary to support nature.

MATTHEW 4: 12,17; MARK 1: 14–15; LUKE 3: 19–20; 4: 4–15

Matthew 4: 12,17

17. Jesus began to preach, and to say, Repent – Every preacher commissioned by God to proclaim salvation to a lost world, begins his work with preaching the doctrine of repentance. This was the case with all the prophets, John the Baptist, Jesus Christ, all the apostles, and all their genuine successors in the Christian ministry.

LUKE 4: 16–22

16. To Nazareth, where he had been brought up – It is likely that our Lord lived principally in this city till the 30th year of his age; but, after he entered on his public ministry, his usual place of residence was at the house of Peter, in Capernaum.

As his custom was – Our Lord regularly attended the public worship of God in the synagogues; for there the Scriptures were read: other parts of the worship were very corrupt; but it was the best at that time to be found in the land. To worship God publicly is the duty of every man, and no man can be guiltless who neglects it. If a person cannot get such public worship as he likes, let him frequent such as he can get. Better to attend the most indifferent than to stay at home, especially on the Lord's day. The place and the time are set apart for the worship of the true God: if others do not conduct themselves well in it, that is not your fault, and need not be any hinderance to you. You come to worship GOD – do not forget your errand – and God will supply the lack in the service by the teachings of his Spirit. Hear the saying of old Mr. Herbert: "The worst speak something good: should all want sense, God takes the text, and preacheth p-a-t-i-e-n-c-e." A man may always profit where the word of God is read.

Stood up for to read – The Jews, in general, sat while they taught or commented on the Sacred Writings, or the traditions of the elders; but when they read either the law or the prophets they invariably stood up: it was

18 The Spirit of the Lord is upon me, because he hath anointed me to preach the gospel to the poor; he hath sent me to heal the brokenhearted, to preach deliverance to the captives, and recovering of sight to the blind, to set at liberty them that are bruised,

19 To preach the acceptable year of the Lord.

20 And he closed the book, and he gave it again to the minister, and sat down. And the eyes of all them that were in the synagogue were fastened on him.

21 And he began to say unto them, This day is this scripture fulfilled in your ears.

22 And all bare him witness, and wondered at the gracious words which proceeded out of his mouth. And they said, Is not this Joseph's son?

LUKE 4: 23–30

23 And he said unto them, Ye will surely say unto me this proverb, Physician, heal thyself: whatsoever we have heard done in Capernaum, do also here in thy country.

24 And he said, Verily I say unto you, No prophet is accepted in his own country.

25 But I tell you of a truth, many widows were in Israel in the days of Elias, when the heaven was shut up three years and six months, when great famine was throughout all the land;

26 But unto none of them was Elias sent, save unto Sarepta, a city of Sidon, unto a woman that was a widow.

27 And many lepers were in Israel in the time of Eliseus the prophet; and none of them was cleansed, saving Naaman the Syrian.

28 And all they in the synagogue, when they heard these things, were filled with wrath,

29 And rose up, and thrust him out of the city, and led him unto the brow of the hill whereon their city was built, that they might cast him down headlong.

30 But he passing through the midst of them went his way,

good thing still remained: they read the Scriptures publicly, and took occasion from them to teach and admonish the people.

LUKE 4: 23–30

23. Physician, heal thyself

From the words of Christ it may be easily inferred, that he was treated with contempt by the inhabitants of Nazareth: for he states publicly those thoughts, which he knew to exist in their minds. He afterwards imputes to them the blame of his declining to work miracles among them, and charges them with malice, in bestowing no honor on a prophet of God. The objection, which he anticipates, is this: "There is no reason to wonder, if his countrymen hold him in little estimation, since he does not dignify his own country, as he does other places, by working miracles; and, consequently, it is but a just revenge, if his own countrymen, whom he treats with less respect than all others, are found to reject him." Such is the meaning of the common proverb, that a physician ought to begin with himself, and those immediately connected with him, before he exhibits his skill in healing others. The amount of the objection is, that Christ acts improperly, in paying no respect to his own country, while he renders other cities of Galilee illustrious by his miracles. And this was regarded by the inhabitants of Nazareth as a fair excuse for rejecting him in their turn.

MATTHEW 4: 13–16

13. And having left Nazareth

I have thought it proper to introduce this passage of Matthew, immediately after Luke's narrative, which we have just examined; because we may gather from the context that, as Christ had hitherto been wont to frequent the town of Nazareth, so, in order to avoid danger, he now bade a final adieu to it, and dwelt in Capernaum and the neighboring towns. There would be no difficulty in this history, were it not that there is some appearance, as if Matthew had put a wrong meaning on the quotation from the prophet. But if we attend to the true meaning of the prophet, it will appear to be properly and naturally accommodated to the present occasion. Isaiah, after having described a very heavy calamity of the nation, soothes their grief by a promise that, when the nation shall be reduced to extremity, a deliverance will immediately follow, which shall dispel the darkness, and restore the light of life.

not lawful for them even to lean against any thing while employed in reading.

17. And when he had opened the book – When he had unrolled it. The Sacred Writings used to this day, in all the Jewish synagogues, are written on skins of basil, parchment, or vellum, sewed end to end, and rolled on two rollers, beginning at each end; so that, in reading from right to left, they roll off with the left, while they roll on with the right. Probably the place in the Prophet Isaiah, here referred to, was the lesson for that day; and Jesus unrolled the manuscript till he came to the place: then, after having read, he rolled it up again, and returned it to the officer, Luke 4: 20, the ruler of the synagogue, or his servant, whose business it was to take care of it. The place that he opened was probably the section for the day. See the table at the end of Deuteronomy, and the note at the end of that table.

18. The Spirit of the Lord – This is found in Isaiah 61: 1; but our Lord immediately adds to it Isaiah 42: 7. The proclaiming of liberty to the captives, and the acceptable year (or year of acceptance) of the Lord, is a manifest allusion to the proclaiming of the year of jubilee by sound of trumpet: see Leviticus 25: 8. This was a year of general release of debts and obligations; of bond-men and women; of lands and possessions, which had been sold from the families and tribes to which they belonged. Our Savior, by applying this text to himself, a text so manifestly relating to the institution above mentioned, plainly declares the typical design of that institution.

He hath anointed me – I have been designed and set apart for this very purpose; my sole business among men is to proclaim glad tidings to the poor, etc. All the functions of this new prophet are exercised on the hearts of men; and the grace by which he works in the heart is a grace of healing, deliverance, and illumination; which, by an admirable virtue, causes them to pass from sickness to health, from slavery to liberty, from darkness to light, and from the lowest degrees of misery to supreme eternal happiness. To those who feel their spiritual poverty, whose hearts are broken through a sense of their sins, who see themselves tied and bound with the chains of many evil habits, who sit in the darkness of guilt and misery, without a friendly hand to lead them in the way in which they should go – to these, the Gospel of the grace of Christ is a pleasing sound, because a present and full salvation is proclaimed by it; and the present is shown to be the acceptable year of the Lord; the year, the time, in which he saves to the uttermost all who come unto him in the name of his Son Jesus. Reader! what dost thou feel? Sin-wretchedness-misery of every description? Then come to Jesus – He will save THEE – he came into the world for this very purpose. Cast thy soul upon him, and thou shalt not perish, but have everlasting life.

20. Were fastened on him – Were attentively fixed on him.

22. At the gracious words – To the words of grace, or the doctrines of grace, which he then preached. It is very strange that none of the evangelists give us any account of this sermon! There was certainly more of it than is related in Luke 4: 21. To-day is this scripture fulfilled in your ears; which seems to have been no more than the first sentence he spoke on the occasion. Had it been necessary for our salvation, it would have been recorded. It was a demonstration to those Jews, that Jesus, who preached to them, was the person of whom the prophet there spoke: it was not designed for general edification. Let us make a good use of what we have got, and we shalt not regret that this sermon is lost. The ear is never satisfied with hearing: we wish for another and another revelation, while sadly unacquainted with the nature and design of that which God's mercy has already given us.

LUKE 4: 23–30

23. Physician, heal thyself – That is, heal the broken-hearted in thy own country, as the latter clause of the verse explains it; but they were far from being in a proper spirit to receive the salvation which he was ready to communicate; and therefore they were not healed.

MATTHEW 4: 13–16

13 And leaving Nazareth, he came and dwelt in Capernaum, which is upon the sea coast, in the borders of Zabulon and Nephthalim:

14 That it might be fulfilled which was spoken by Esaias the prophet, saying,

15 The land of Zabulon, and the land of Nephthalim, by the way of the sea, beyond Jordan, Galilee of the Gentiles;

16 The people which sat in darkness saw great light; and to them which sat in the region and shadow of death light is sprung up.

MATTHEW 4: 18–25; MARK 1: 16–20; LUKE 5: 1–11

Matthew 4: 18–25

18 And Jesus, walking by the sea of Galilee, saw two brethren, Simon called Peter, and Andrew his brother, casting a net into the sea: for they were fishers.

19 And he saith unto them, Follow me, and I will make you fishers of men.

20 And they straightway left their nets, and followed him.

21 And going on from thence, he saw other two brethren, James the son of Zebedee, and John his brother, in a ship with Zebedee their father, mending their nets; and he called them.

22 And they immediately left the ship and their father, and followed him.

23 And Jesus went about all Galilee, teaching in their synagogues, and preaching the gospel of the kingdom, and healing all manner of sickness and all manner of disease among the people.

24 And his fame went throughout all Syria: and they brought unto him all sick people that were taken with divers diseases and torments, and those which were possessed with devils, and those which were lunatick, and those that had the palsy; and he healed them.

25 And there followed him great multitudes of people from Galilee, and from Decapolis, and from Jerusalem, and from Judaea, and from beyond Jordan.

Mark 1: 16–20

16 Now as he walked by the sea of Galilee, he saw Simon and Andrew his

MATTHEW 4: 18–25; MARK 1: 16–20; LUKE 5: 1–11

Luke 5: 1–11

5. Master, toiling all the night, we have taken nothing

The reason why Peter calls him Master unquestionably is, that he knows Christ to be accustomed to discharge the office of a Teacher, and is moved with reverence toward him. But he has not yet made such progress as to deserve to be ranked among his disciples: for our sentiments concerning Christ do not render him sufficient honor, unless we embrace his doctrine by the obedience of faith, and know what he requires from us. He has but a slender perception – if he has any at all – of the value of the Gospel; but the deference which he pays to Christ is manifested by this, that, when worn out by fruitless toil, he commences anew what he had already attempted in vain. Yet it cannot be denied, that he highly esteemed Christ, and had the highest respect for his authority. But a particular instance of faith, rendered to a single command of Christ, would not have made Peter a Christian, or given him a place among the sons of God, if he had not been led on, from this first act of submission, to a full obedience. But, as Peter yielded so readily to the command of Christ, whom he did not yet know to be a Prophet or the Son of God, no apology can be offered for our disgraceful conduct, if, while we call him our Lord, and King, and Judge (Isaiah 33: 22), we do not move a finger to perform our duty, to which we have ten times received his commands.

6. They inclosed a great multitude of fishes

The design of the miracle undoubtedly was, to make known Christ's divinity, and thus to induce Peter and others to become his disciples. But we may draw from this instance a general instruction, that we have no reason to be afraid lest our labor should not be attended by the blessing of God and desirable success, when it is undertaken by the authority and guidance of Christ. Such was the multitude of fishes, that the ships were sinking, and the minds of the spectators were thus excited to admiration: for it must have been in consequence of the divine glory of Christ manifested by this miracle, that his authority was fully acknowledged.

8. Depart from me, O Lord

Although men are earnest in seeking the presence of God, yet, as soon as God appears, they must be struck with terror, and almost rendered lifeless by dread and alarm, until he administers consolation. They have the best reason for calling earnestly on God, because they cannot avoid feeling that they are miserable, while he is absent from them: and, on the other hand, his presence is appalling, because they begin to feel that they are nothing, and that they are

25. In the days of Elias – See this history, 1 Kings 17: 1–9, compared with 1 Kings 18: 1–45. This was evidently a miraculous interference, as no rain fell for three years and six months, even in the rainy seasons. There were two of these in Judea, called the first and the latter rains; the first fell in October, the latter in April: the first prepared the ground for the seed, the latter ripened the harvest. As both these rains were withheld, consequently there was a great famine throughout all the land.

26. Unto none of them was Elias sent, save unto Sarepta – The sentence is elliptical, and means this: To none of them was Elias sent; he was not sent except to Sarepta; for the widow at Sarepta was a Sidonian, not a widow of Israel. Sarepta was a pagan city in the country of Sidon, in the vicinity of Galilee.

27. None of them was cleansed – This verse is to be understood as the 26th; for Naaman, being a Syrian, was no leper in Israel. The meaning of these verses is, God dispenses his benefits when, where, and to whom he pleases. No person can complain of his conduct in these respects, because no person deserves any good from his hand. God never punishes any but those who deserve it; but he blesses incessantly those who deserve it not. The reason is evident: justice depends on certain rules; but beneficence is free. Beneficence can bless both the good and the evil; justice can punish the latter only. Those who do not make this distinction must have a very confused notion of the conduct of Divine Providence among men.

28. Were filled with wrath – They seem to have drawn the following conclusion from what our Lord spoke: "The Gentiles are more precious in the sight of God than the Jews; and to them his miracles of mercy and kindness shall be principally confined." This was pretty near the truth, as the event proved. Those who profit not by the light of God, while it is among them, shall have their candle extinguished.

29. The brow of the hill – Mr. Maundrel tells us that this is still called "the Mountain of the Precipitation, and is half a league southward of Nazareth. In going to it, you cross first over the vale in which Nazareth stands; and then going down two or three furlongs, in a narrow cleft between the rocks, you there clamber up a short but difficult way on the right hand; at the top of which you find a great stone standing on the brink of a precipice, which is said to be the very place where our Lord was destined to be thrown down by his enraged neighbors."

30. Passing through the midst of them – Either he shut their eyes so that they could not see him; or he so overawed them by his power as to leave them no strength to perform their murderous purpose. The man Christ Jesus was immortal till his time came; and all his messengers are immortal till their work is done.

MATTHEW 4: 13–16

13. And leaving Nazareth – It seems that, from this time, our blessed Lord made Capernaum his ordinary place of residence; and utterly forsook Nazareth, because they had wholly rejected his word, and even attempted to take away his life. See Luke 4: 29.

15. Galilee of the Gentiles – Or of the nations. So called, because it was inhabited by Egyptians, Arabians, and Phoenicians.

16. The people which sat in darkness – This is quoted from Isaiah 9: 2, where, instead of sitting, the prophet used the word walked. The evangelist might on purpose change the term, to point out the increased misery of the state of these persons. Sitting in darkness expresses a greater degree of intellectual blindness, than walking in darkness does. In the time of Christ's appearing, the people were in a much worse state than in the time of the prophet, which was nearly 700 years before; as, during all this period, they were growing more ignorant and sinful.

The region and shadow of death – These words are amazingly descriptive. A region of death – DEATH'S country, where, in a peculiar manner, Death lived, reigned, and triumphed, subjecting all the people to his sway.

brother casting a net into the sea: for they were fishers.

17 And Jesus said unto them, Come ye after me, and I will make you to become fishers of men.

18 And straightway they forsook their nets, and followed him.

19 And when he had gone a little further thence, he saw James the son of Zebedee, and John his brother, who also were in the ship mending their nets.

20 And straightway he called them: and they left their father Zebedee in the ship with the hired servants, and went after him.

Luke 5: 1–11

1 And it came to pass, that, as the people pressed upon him to hear the word of God, he stood by the lake of Gennesaret,

2 And saw two ships standing by the lake: but the fishermen were gone out of them, and were washing their nets.

3 And he entered into one of the ships, which was Simon's, and prayed him that he would thrust out a little from the land. And he sat down, and taught the people out of the ship.

4 Now when he had left speaking, he said unto Simon, Launch out into the deep, and let down your nets for a draught.

5 And Simon answering said unto him, Master, we have toiled all the night, and have taken nothing: nevertheless at thy word I will let down the net.

6 And when they had this done, they inclosed a great multitude of fishes: and their net brake.

7 And they beckoned unto their partners, which were in the other ship, that they should come and help them. And they came, and filled both the ships, so that they began to sink.

8 When Simon Peter saw it, he fell down at Jesus' knees, saying, Depart from me; for I am a sinful man, O Lord.

9 For he was astonished, and all that were with him, at the draught of the fishes which they had taken:

10 And so was also James, and John, the sons of Zebedee, which were partners with Simon. And Jesus said unto Simon, Fear not; from henceforth thou shalt catch men.

11 And when they had brought their

overpowered by an immense mass of evils. In this manner, Peter views Christ with reverence in the miracle, and yet is so overawed by his majesty, that he does all he can to avoid his presence. Nor was this the case with Peter alone: for we learn, from the context, that astonishment had overpowered all who were with him. Hence we see, that it is natural to all men to tremble at the presence of God. And this is of advantage to us, in order to humble any foolish confidence or pride that may be in us, provided it is immediately followed by soothing consolation. And so Christ relieves the mind of Peter by a mild and friendly reply, saying to him, Fear not. Thus Christ sinks his own people in the grave, that he may afterwards raise them to life.

10. For afterwards thou shalt catch men

The words of Matthew are, **I will make you fishers of men**; and those of Mark are, **I will cause that you may become fishers of men**. They teach us, that Peter, and the other three, were not only gathered by Christ to be his disciples, but were made apostles, or, at least, chosen with a view to the apostleship. It is, therefore, not merely a general call to faith, but a special call to a particular office, that is here described. The duties of instruction, I do admit, are not yet enjoined upon them; but still it is to prepare them for being instructors, that Christ receives and admits them into his family. This ought to be carefully weighed; for all are not commanded to leave their parents and their former occupation, and literally to follow Christ. There are some whom the Lord is satisfied with having in his flock and his Church, while he assigns to others their own station. Those who have received from him a public office ought to know, that something more is required from them than from private individuals. In the case of others, our Lord makes no change as to the ordinary way of life; but he withdraws those four disciples from the employment from which they had hitherto derived their subsistence, that he may employ their labors in a nobler office.

MARK 1: 21–28; LUKE 4: 31–36

Mark 1: 21–28

This demoniac was probably one of that multitude, which was mentioned, a little before, by Matthew 4: 24. Yet the narrative of Mark and Luke is not superfluous: for they relate some circumstances, which not only present the miracle in a more striking light, but also contain useful instruction. The devil dexterously acknowledges, that Christ is **the Holy One of God**, in order to insinuate into the minds of men a suspicion, that there was some secret understanding between him and Christ. By such a trick he has since endeavored to make the Gospel suspected, and, in

Shadow of death – used only here and in Luke 1: 79, but often in the Old Covenant.

MATTHEW 4: 18–25; MARK 1: 16–20; LUKE 5: 1–11

Matthew 4: 18–25

18. Simon called Peter, and Andrew his brother – Why did not Jesus Christ call some of the eminent Scribes or Pharisees to publish his Gospel, and not poor unlearned fishermen, without credit or authority? Because it was the kingdom of heaven they were to preach, and their teaching must come from above: besides, the conversion of sinners, though it be effected instrumentally by the preaching of the Gospel, yet the grand agent in it is the Spirit of God. As the instruments were comparatively mean, and, the work which was accomplished by them was grand and glorious, the excellency of the power at once appeared to be of GOD, and not of man; and thus the glory, due alone to his name, was secured, and the great Operator of all good had the deserved praise. Seminaries of learning, in the order of God's providence and grace, have great and important uses; and, in reference to such uses, they should be treated with great respect: but to make preachers of the Gospel is a matter to which they are utterly inadequate; it is a, prerogative that God never did, and never will, delegate to man.

Where the seed of the kingdom of God is sowed, and a dispensation of the Gospel is committed to a man, a good education may be of great and general use: but it no more follows, because a man has had a good education, that therefore he is qualified to preach the Gospel, than it does, that because he has not had that, therefore he is unqualified; for there may be much ignorance of Divine things where there is much human learning; and a man may be well taught in the things of God, and be able to teach others, who has not had the advantages of a liberal education.

Men-made ministers have almost ruined the heritage of God. To prevent this, our Church requires that a man be inwardly moved to take upon himself this ministry, before he can be ordained to it. And he who cannot say, that he trusts (has rational and Scriptural conviction) that he is moved by the Holy Ghost to take upon himself this office, is an intruder into the heritage of God, and his ordination, ipso facto, vitiated and of none effect.

Fishers – Persons employed in a lawful and profitable avocation, and faithfully discharging their duty in it. It was a tradition of the elders, that one of Joshua's ten precepts was, that all men should have an equal right to spread their nets and fish in the sea of Tiberias, or Galilee. The persons mentioned here were doubtless men of pure morals; for the minister of God should have a good report from them that are without.

19. Follow me – Come after me. Receive my doctrines, imitate me in my conduct – in every respect be my disciples. We may observe that most of the calls of God to man are expressed in a few solemn words, which alarm, the conscience, and deeply impress the heart.

I will make you fishers of men – Ezekiel 47: 8–10, casts much light on this place; and to this prophet our Lord probably alludes. To follow Christ, and be admitted into a partnership of his ministry, is a great honor; but those only who are by himself fitted for it, God calls. Miserable are those who do not wait fur this call – who presume to take the name of fishers of men, and know not how to cast the net of the Divine word, because not brought to an acquaintance with the saving power of the God who bought them. Such persons, having only their secular interest in view, study not to catch men, but to catch money: and though, for charity's sake, it may be said of a pastor of this spirit, he does not enter the sheepfold as a thief, yet he certainly lives as a hireling.

20. They straightway left their nets – A change, as far as it respected secular things, every way to their disadvantage. The proud and the profane may exult and say, "Such preachers as these cannot be much injured by their sacrifices of secular property – they have nothing but nets, etc., to leave." Let such carpers at the institution of Christ know, that

ships to land, they forsook all, and followed him.

MARK 1: 21–28; LUKE 4: 31–37

Mark 1: 21–28

21 And they went into Capernaum; and straightway on the sabbath day he entered into the synagogue, and taught.

22 And they were astonished at his doctrine: for he taught them as one that had authority, and not as the scribes.

23 And there was in their synagogue a man with an unclean spirit; and he cried out,

24 Saying, Let us alone; what have we to do with thee, thou Jesus of Nazareth? art thou come to destroy us? I know thee who thou art, the Holy One of God.

25 And Jesus rebuked him, saying, Hold thy peace, and come out of him.

26 And when the unclean spirit had torn him, and cried with a loud voice, he came out of him.

27 And they were all amazed, insomuch that they questioned among themselves, saying, What thing is this? what new doctrine is this? for with authority commandeth he even the unclean spirits, and they do obey him.

28 And immediately his fame spread abroad throughout all the region round about Galilee.

Luke 4: 31–37

31 And came down to Capernaum, a city of Galilee, and taught them on the sabbath days.

32 And they were astonished at his doctrine: for his word was with power.

33 And in the synagogue there was a man, which had a spirit of an unclean devil, and cried out with a loud voice,

34 Saying, Let us alone; what have we to do with thee, thou Jesus of Nazareth? art thou come to destroy us? I know thee who thou art; the Holy One of God.

35 And Jesus rebuked him, saying, Hold thy peace, and come out of him. And when the devil had thrown him in the midst, he came out of him, and hurt him not.

36 And they were all amazed, and spake among themselves, saying, What a word is this! for with authority and power

the present day, he is continually making similar attempts. That is the reason why Christ rebukes him. It is, no doubt, possible, that this confession was violently extorted from him: but there is no inconsistency between the two suppositions, that he is forced to yield to the power of Christ, **and therefore cries out that he is the Holy One of God** – and yet that he cunningly attempts to shroud in his own darkness the glory of Christ. At the same time, we must observe that, while he flatters Christ in this manner, he indirectly withdraws himself from his power, and in this way contradicts himself. For why was Christ sanctified by the Father, but that he might deliver men from the tyranny of the devil, and overturn his kingdom? But as Satan cannot endure that power, which he feels to be destructive to himself, he would desire that Christ should satisfy himself with an empty title, without exercising it on the present occasion.

27. What new doctrine is this?

They call it new doctrine, not by way of reproach, but as an acknowledgment, that there was something in it unusual and extraordinary. It is not for the sake of blame, or to lessen its credit, that they speak of it as new. This is rather a part of their admiration, that they pronounce it to be not common or ordinary. Their only fault lies in this, that they remain in their state of hesitation, whereas the children of God ought to make increasing progress.

MATTHEW 8: 14–18; MARK 1: 29–39; LUKE 4: 38–44

Mark 1: 29. They came, with James and John, into the house of Simon and Andrew

There is reason to conjecture, that Matthew does not relate this history in its proper order: for Mark expressly states, that there were only four disciples who attended Christ. Besides, when he left the synagogue, he went straight to Peter's house; which also shows clearly, that Matthew did not observe, with exactness, the order of time. The Evangelists appear to have taken particular notice of this miracle; not that, in itself, it was more remarkable, or more worthy of being recorded, than other miracles – but because, by means of it, Christ gave to his disciples a private and familiar illustration of his grace. Another reason was, that the healing of one woman gave occasion to many miracles, so that they came to him in great numbers, from every direction, to implore his assistance.

Luke 4: 39. He rebuked the fever

To a person not well acquainted with Scripture this kind of expression may appear harsh; but there were good reasons for employing it. Fevers and other diseases, famine, pesti-

he who has nothing but a net, and leaves that for the sake of doing good to the souls of men, leaves his ALL: besides, he lived comfortably by his net before; but, in becoming the servant of all for Christ's sake, he often exposes himself to the want of even a morsel of bread.

22. Left the ship and their father – By the ship, we are to understand the mere fishing-boat, used for extending their nets in the water and bringing the hawser or rope of the farther end to shore, by which the net was pulled to land. But why should these be called to leave their employment and their father, probably now aged? To this I answer, that to be obedient to, provide for, and comfort our parents, is the highest duty we owe or can discharge, except that to God. But, when God calls to the work of the ministry, father and mother and all must be left. Were we necessary to their comfort and support before? Then God, if he call us into another work or state, will take care to supply to them our lack of service some other way; and, if this be not done, it is a proof we have mistaken our call. Again, were our parents necessary to us, and in leaving them for the sake of the Gospel, or in obedience to a Divine command, do we deprive ourselves of the comforts of life? No matter: we should prefer the honor of serving the Most High, even in poverty and humility, to all the comforts of a father's house. But what an honor was the vocation of James and John, to old Zebedee their father! His sons are called to be heralds of the God of heaven! Allowing him to have been a pious man, this must have given him unutterable delight.

23. Teaching in their synagogues – Synagogues, among the Jews, were not probably older than the return from the Babylonish captivity. They were erected not only in cities and towns, but in the country, and especially by rivers, that they might have water for the convenience of their frequent washings.

Not less than ten persons of respectability composed a synagogue; as the rabbins supposed that this number of persons, of independent property, and well skilled in the law, were necessary to conduct the affairs of the place, and keep up the Divine worship. Therefore, where this number could not be found, no synagogue was built; but there might be many synagogues in one city or town, provided it were populous. Jerusalem is said to have contained 480. This need not be wondered at, when it is considered that every Jew was obliged to worship God in public, either in a synagogue or in the temple.

The synagogue was governed by a council or assembly, over whom was a president, called in the Gospels, the ruler of the synagogue. These are sometimes called chiefs of the Jews, the rulers, the priests or elders, the governors, the overseers, the fathers of the synagogue. Service was performed in them three times a day – morning, afternoon, and night. Synagogue, among the Jews, had often the same meaning as congregation among us, or place of judicature, see James 2: 2.

Preaching the Gospel of the kingdom – Or, proclaiming the glad tidings of the kingdom. See the preceding notes. Behold here the perfect pattern of an evangelical preacher.

24. He healed them – Either with a word or a touch; and thus proved that all nature was under his control.

25. Great multitudes – This, even according to the Jews, was one proof of the days of the Messiah: for they acknowledged that in his time there should be a great famine of the word of God; and thus they understood Amos, Amos 8: 11. Behold, the days come – that I will send a famine in the land, not a famine of bread – but of hearing the words of the Lord. And as the Messiah was to dispense this word, the bread of life, hence they believed that vast multitudes from all parts should be gathered together to him.

MARK 1: 21–28; LUKE 4: 31–37

Mark 1: 21–28

21. As one that had authority – From God, to do what he was doing; and to teach a pure and beneficent system of truth.

And not as the scribes – Who had no such

he commandeth the unclean spirits, and they come out.

37 And the fame of him went out into every place of the country round about.

MATTHEW 8: 14–18; MARK 1: 29–39; LUKE 4: 38–44

Matthew 8: 14–18

14 And when Jesus was come into Peter's house, he saw his wife's mother laid, and sick of a fever.

15 And he touched her hand, and the fever left her: and she arose, and ministered unto them.

16 When the even was come, they brought unto him many that were possessed with devils: and he cast out the spirits with his word, and healed all that were sick:

17 That it might be fulfilled which was spoken by Esaias the prophet, saying, Himself took our infirmities, and bare our sicknesses.

18 Now when Jesus saw great multitudes about him, he gave commandment to depart unto the other side.

Mark 1: 29–39

29 And forthwith, when they were come out of the synagogue, they entered into the house of Simon and Andrew, with James and John.

30 But Simon's wife's mother lay sick of a fever, and anon they tell him of her.

31 And he came and took her by the hand, and lifted her up; and immediately the fever left her, and she ministered unto them.

32 And at even, when the sun did set, they brought unto him all that were diseased, and them that were possessed with devils.

33 And all the city was gathered together at the door.

34 And he healed many that were sick of divers diseases, and cast out many devils; and suffered not the devils to speak, because they knew him.

35 And in the morning, rising up a great while before day, he went out, and departed into a solitary place, and there prayed.

36 And Simon and they that were with him followed after him.

lence, and calamities of every description, are God's heralds, by whom he executes his judgments. Now, as he is said to send such messengers by his command and pleasure, so he also restrains and recalls them whenever he pleases.

The manner in which he healed them is not mentioned by Matthew and Mark: but Luke says, that it was by **laying hands on each of them**. Under the Law, this was a sign of reconciliation; and, therefore, it was not improperly, or unseasonably, that Christ laid hands on those whom he freed from the curse of God. It was also a solemn rite of consecration, as will afterwards be more fully explained. But I interpret Christ's laying hands on the sick, as meaning simply, that he recommended them to the Father, and thus obtained for them grace and deliverance from their diseases.

Matthew 8: 17. That it might be fulfilled which was spoken by Isaiah the prophet

This prediction has the appearance of being inappropriate, and even of being tortured into a meaning which it does not bear: for Isaiah does not there speak of miracles, but of the death of Christ – and not of temporal benefits, but of spiritual and eternal grace. Now, what is undoubtedly spoken about the impurities of the soul, Matthew applies to bodily diseases. The solution is not difficult, if the reader will only observe, that the Evangelist states not merely the benefit conferred by Christ on those sick people, but the purpose for which he healed their diseases. They experienced in their bodies the grace of Christ, but we must look at the design: for it would be idle to confine our view to a transitory advantage, as if the Son of God were a physician of bodies. What then? He gave sight to the blind, in order to show that he is "the light of the world" (John 8: 12). He restored life to the dead, to prove that he is "the resurrection and the life" (John 11: 25). Similar observations might be made as to those who were lame, or had palsy. Following out this analogy, let us connect those benefits, which Christ bestowed on men in the flesh, with the design which is stated to us by Matthew, that he was sent by the Father, to relieve us from all evils and miseries.

Mark 1: 34. He did not permit the devils to speak

There might be two reasons why he did not permit them: a general reason, because the time of the full revelation was not yet come; and a special reason, which we hinted at a little ago, that he refused to have, as heralds and witnesses of his divinity, those whose praise could have no other effect than to soil and injure his character. This latter reason is undoubtedly true: for he must have known, that the prince of death, and his agents, are in a state of irreconcileable enmity with the Author of eternal salvation and life.

authority, and whose teaching was not accompanied by the power of God to the souls of the people.

23. A man with an unclean spirit – By giving way to the first attacks of such a spirit, he may soon get in, and take full possession of the whole soul.

24. What have we to do with thee – Or, What is it to us and to thee? or, What business hast thou with us?

Art thou come to destroy us? – We may suppose this spirit to have felt and spoken thus: "Is this the time of which it hath been predicted, that in it the Messiah should destroy all that power which we have usurped and exercised over the bodies and souls of men? Alas! it is so. I now plainly see who thou art – the Holy One of God, who art come to destroy unholiness, in which we have our residence, and through which we have our reign in the souls of men." An unholy spirit is the only place where Satan can have his full operation, and show forth the plenitude of his destroying power.

25. And Jesus rebuked him – A spirit of this cast will only yield to the sovereign power of the Son of God. All watchings, fasting, and mortifications, considered in themselves, will do little or no good. Uncleanness, of every description, will only yield to the rebuke of God.

26. And when the unclean spirit had torn him – Never was there a person possessed by an unclean spirit who did not suffer a convulsion, perhaps a total ruin of nature by it. Sins of uncleanness, as the apostle intimates, are against the body; they sap the foundation of life, so that there are very few of this class, whether male or female, that live out half their days: they generally die martyrs to their lusts. When the propensities of the flesh are most violent in a person who is determined to serve God, it is often a proof that these are the last efforts of the impure spirit, who has great rages because he knows his time is but short.

27. What thing is this? – Words of surprise and astonishment.

For with authority – They had never heard such a gracious doctrine, and never saw any teaching supported by miracles before. How much must this person be superior to men! – they are brought into subjection by unclean spirits; this person subjects unclean spirits to himself.

28. And immediately his fame spread abroad – The miracle which he had performed was – great; evidenced much benevolence in the worker of it; and was very public, being wrought in the synagogue.

The many who saw it published it wherever they went; and thus the fame of Christ, as an incomparable teacher, and unparalleled worker of miracles, became soon spread abroad through the land.

The word immediately, occurs more frequently in this evangelist than in any other writer of the new covenant: it is very often superfluous, and may often be omitted in the translation, without any prejudice to the sense of the passage in which it is found.

MATTHEW 8: 14–18; MARK 1: 29–39; LUKE 4: 38–44

Matthew 8: 14–18

14. Peter's house – That Peter lived at Capernaum, and that Christ lodged with him, is fully evident from this verse compared with Matthew 17: 24.

Peter's – wife's mother – Learn hence, says Theophylact, that marriage is no hinderance to virtue, since the chief of the apostles had his wife. Marriage is one of the first of Divine institutions, and is a positive command of God. He says, the state of celibacy is not GOOD, Genesis 2: 18. Those who pretend to say that the single state is more holy than the other slander their Maker, and say in effect, "We are too holy to keep the commandments of God."

15. He touched her hand – Can any thing on this side the unlimited power of God effect such a cure with only a touch? If the Scriptures had not spoken of the divinity of Christ, these

37 And when they had found him, they said unto him, All men seek for thee.

38 And he said unto them, Let us go into the next towns, that I may preach there also: for therefore came I forth.

39 And he preached in their synagogues throughout all Galilee, and cast out devils.

Luke 4: 38–44

38 And he arose out of the synagogue, and entered into Simon's house. And Simon's wife's mother was taken with a great fever; and they besought him for her.

39 And he stood over her, and rebuked the fever; and it left her: and immediately she arose and ministered unto them.

40 Now when the sun was setting, all they that had any sick with divers diseases brought them unto him; and he laid his hands on every one of them, and healed them.

41 And devils also came out of many, crying out, and saying, Thou art Christ the Son of God. And he rebuking them suffered them not to speak: for they knew that he was Christ.

42 And when it was day, he departed and went into a desert place: and the people sought him, and came unto him, and stayed him, that he should not depart from them.

43 And he said unto them, I must preach the kingdom of God to other cities also: for therefore am I sent.

44 And he preached in the synagogues of Galilee.

MARK 3: 13–19; LUKE 6: 12–19

Mark 3: 13–19

13 And he goeth up into a mountain, and calleth unto him whom he would: and they came unto him.

14 And he ordained twelve, that they should be with him, and that he might send them forth to preach,

15 And to have power to heal sicknesses, and to cast out devils:

16 And Simon he surnamed Peter;

17 And James the son of Zebedee, and John the brother of James; and he surnamed them Boanerges, which is, The sons of thunder:

Matthew 8: 18. And when Jesus had seen great multitudes about him

Matthew, I have no doubt, touches briefly what the others explain in a more ample and copious narrative. The other two state a circumstance, which is not noticed by Matthew, that Christ withdrew privately, for the sake of retirement, into a desert place, before it was daylight. Mark afterwards says, that Peter informed him, all seek, thee; and Luke says, that multitudes came to that place. Again, Matthew says, that he passed over to the other side, while the other two say, that he passed through all Galilee, to preach in every place. But the other side, or, the farther bank, does not, I think, denote what was strictly the opposite side, but refers to that curvature of the lake, which was below Capernaum. In this way, he crossed over to another part of the lake, and yet did not go out of Galilee.

MARK 3: 13–19; LUKE 6: 12–19

Mark 3: 13. And he went up into a mountain

By this election he does not yet ordain them to be Apostles, to enter immediately into the discharge of their office, but merely admits them to enjoy his private instructions with a view to the apostleship. Commentators have fallen into a mistake here, by confounding those passages with the tenth chapter of the Gospel by Matthew. For the plain meaning of the words is, that they are only destined to a future commission, the bestowal of which is recorded by Matthew; and Mark and Luke will be found afterwards relating, in its proper place, the mission which Matthew there describes. And we need not wonder, if their heavenly Master chose to train and accustom them gradually to so arduous an employment: for, even by a long course of instruction, their ignorance could not be corrected.

Both the Evangelists say, that Christ went up into a mountain. Luke explains the cause to have been, that he might pray with greater freedom in his retirement, which he was accustomed to do frequently, as is evident from other passages. Now, this example ought to be regarded by us as a perpetual rule, to begin with prayer, when we are about to choose pastors to churches: otherwise, what we attempt will not succeed well. And certainly our Lord prayed, not so much on his own account, as to lay down a rule for us. We are deficient in prudence and skill; and though our sagacity were of the highest order, nothing is more easy than to be deceived in this matter. Granting that we were in no danger of mistake, if the Lord does not regulate our affections, with what force, or rather violence, shall we be carried away by favor and prepossession, or hatred or ambition? Besides, though the election were conducted in the very best manner, all will be unsuccessful, unless the Lord take under his

proofs of his power must have demonstrated it to the common sense of every man whose creed had not previously blinded him.

Ministered unto them – Serving Christ in his ordinances and in his members is the best proof we can give to others of our being soundly restored to spiritual health.

16. When the even was come – The Jews kept their sabbath from evening to evening, according to the law, Leviticus 23: 32, From evening to evening shall ye celebrate your sabbath. And the rabbins say, The sabbath doth not enter but when the sun is set. Hence it was that the sick were not brought out to our Lord till after sun-set, because then the sabbath was ended.

Many that were possessed with devils – Dr. Lightfoot gives two sound reasons why Judea, in our Lord's time, abounded with demoniacs. First, Because they were then advanced to the very height of impiety. See what Josephus, their own historian, says of them: There was not (said he) a nation under heaven more wicked than they were. Secondly, Because they were then strongly addicted to magic, and so, as it were, invited evil spirits to be familiar with them. It seems strange to find men at this distance of time questioning the truth of that which neither scribes nor Pharisees then doubted; nor did they ever object against the pretensions of Christ and his apostles to cast them out. And, if the whole business of demonism had been only a vulgar error, (as wise men now tell us), what a fine opportunity had the wise men then, to unmask the whole matter, and thus pour contempt on the pretensions of our blessed Lord and his followers, who held it to be one proof of their Divine mission, that demons were subject to them!

And healed all that were sick – Not a soul did the Lord Jesus ever reject, who came to him soliciting his aid. Need any sinner despair who comes to him, conscious of his spiritual malady, to be healed by his merciful hand?

17. Himself took our infirmities – The quotation is taken from Isaiah 53: 4, where the verb signifies to bear sin, so as to make atonement for it. And the rabbins understand this place to speak of the sufferings of the Messiah for the sins of Israel; and say that all the diseases, all the griefs, and all the punishments due to Israel shall be borne by him. Christ fulfils the prophecies in all respects, and is himself the completion and truth of them, as being the lamb and victim of God, which, bears and takes away the sin of the world. The text in Isaiah refers properly to the taking away of sin; and this in the evangelist, to the removal of corporeal afflictions: but, as the diseases of the body are the emblems of the sin of the soul, Matthew, referring to the prediction of the prophet, considered the miraculous healing of the body as an emblem of the soul's salvation by Christ Jesus.

18. Unto the other side – Viz. of the lake of Genesareth, whence he proceeded to the country of the Gergesenes, Matthew 8: 28.

MARK 3: 13–19; LUKE 6: 12–19

Mark 3: 13–19

14. He ordained twelve – Here is nothing of what we call ordaining. Christ simply appointed them to be with him; and that he might send them occasionally to preach, etc.

15. To have power to heal – and to cast out devils – The business of a minister of Christ is,

1st. To preach the Gospel.
2dly. To be the physician of souls. And,
3dly. To wage war with the devil, and destroy his kingdom.

17. Sons of thunder – A Hebraism for thunderers; probably so named because of their zeal and power in preaching the Gospel.

19. Into a house – As Christ was now returned to Capernaum, this was probably the house of Peter, mentioned Mark 2: 1.

MATTHEW 5: 1–12; LUKE 6: 20–26

Matthew 5: 1–12

1. And seeing the multitudes – These multitudes are mentioned in the preceding verse,

18 And Andrew, and Philip, and Bartholomew, and Matthew, and Thomas, and James the son of Alphaeus, and Thaddaeus, and Simon the Canaanite,

19 And Judas Iscariot, which also betrayed him: and they went into an house.

Luke 6: 12–19

12 And it came to pass in those days, that he went out into a mountain to pray, and continued all night in prayer to God.

13 And when it was day, he called unto him his disciples: and of them he chose twelve, whom also he named apostles;

14 Simon, (whom he also named Peter,) and Andrew his brother, James and John, Philip and Bartholomew,

15 Matthew and Thomas, James the son of Alphaeus, and Simon called Zelotes,

16 And Judas the brother of James, and Judas Iscariot, which also was the traitor.

17 And he came down with them, and stood in the plain, and the company of his disciples, and a great multitude of people out of all Judaea and Jerusalem, and from the sea coast of Tyre and Sidon, which came to hear him, and to be healed of their diseases;

18 And they that were vexed with unclean spirits: and they were healed.

19 And the whole multitude sought to touch him: for there went virtue out of him, and healed them all.

MATTHEW 5: 1–12; LUKE 6: 20–26

Matthew 5: 1–12

1 And seeing the multitudes, he went up into a mountain: and when he was set, his disciples came unto him:

2 And he opened his mouth, and taught them, saying,

3 Blessed are the poor in spirit: for theirs is the kingdom of heaven.

4 Blessed are they that mourn: for they shall be comforted.

5 Blessed are the meek: for they shall inherit the earth.

6 Blessed are they which do hunger and thirst after righteousness: for they shall be filled.

7 Blessed are the merciful: for they shall obtain mercy.

guidance those who are elected, and furnish them with the necessary gifts. "What then?" it will be said, "did not Christ earnestly implore the Father to preside in the election?" This I readily acknowledge, and I have also to state, that this was a declaration and acknowledgment of his care for his Church. Accordingly, he did not pray to the Father in the ordinary manner, but spent the whole night in prayer. But if he, who was full of the Holy Spirit, (John 3: 34,) implored the Father, with such ardor and earnestness, to preside in the election, how much greater need have we to do so?

He called to him whom he would

By this expression, I have no doubt, Mark conveys to us the instruction, that it was to the unmixed grace of Christ, and not to any excellence of their own, that they were indebted for receiving so honorable an office: for, if you understand him to say, that those were chosen, who were more excellent than others, this will not apply to Judas. The meaning is the apostle-ship was not bestowed on account of any human merits; but, by the free mercy of God.

MATTHEW 5: 1–12; LUKE 6: 20–26

Matthew 5: 1. He went up into a mountain

Those who think that Christ's sermon, which is here related, is different from the sermon contained in the sixth chapter of Luke's Gospel, rest their opinion on a very light and frivolous argument. Matthew states, that Christ spoke to his disciples on a mountain, while Luke seems to say, that the discourse was delivered on a plain. But it is a mistake to read the words of Luke, he went down with them, and stood in the plain (Luke 6: 17), as immediately connected with the statement that, lifting up his eyes on the disciples, he spoke thus. For the design of both Evangelists was, to collect into one place the leading points of the doctrine of Christ, which related to a devout and holy life. Although Luke had previously mentioned a plain, he does not observe the immediate succession of events in the history, but passes from miracles to doctrine, without pointing out either time or place: just as Matthew takes no notice of the time, but only mentions the place. It is probable, that this discourse was not delivered until Christ had chosen the twelve: but in attending to the order of time, which I saw that the Spirit of God had disregarded, I did not wish to be too precise. Pious and modest readers ought to be satisfied with having a brief summary of the doctrine of Christ placed before their eyes, collected out of his many and various discourses, the first of which was that in which he spoke to his disciples about true happiness.

2. Opening his mouth

This redundancy of expression (*pleonasmos*) partakes of the Hebrew idiom: for what would be faulty in other languages is frequent among the Hebrews, to say, He opened

which should make the first verse of this chapter.

He went up into a mountain – That he might have the greater advantage of speaking, so as to be heard by that great concourse of people which followed him. It is very probable that nothing more is meant here than a small hill or eminence. Had he been on a high mountain they could not have heard; and, had he been at a great distance, he would not have sat down. See the note on Matthew 5: 14.

And when he was set – The usual posture of public teachers among the Jews, and among many other people. Hence sitting was a synonymous term for teaching among the rabbins.

His disciples – Those who originally followed Christ, considered him in the light of a Divine teacher; and conscious of their ignorance, and the importance of his teaching, they put themselves under his tuition, that they might be instructed in heavenly things. Having been taught the mysteries of the kingdom of God, they became closely attached to their Divine Master, imitating his life and manners; and recommending his salvation to all the circle of their acquaintance. This is still the characteristic of a genuine disciple of Christ.

3. Blessed are the poor in spirit, etc. – Or, happy. The person whom Christ terms happy is one who is not under the influence of fate or chance, but is governed by an all-wise providence, having every step directed to the attainment of immortal glory, being transformed by the power into the likeness of the ever-blessed God. Though some of the persons, whose states are mentioned in these verses, cannot be said to be as yet blessed or happy, in being made partakers of the Divine nature; yet they are termed happy by our Lord, because they are on the straight way to this blessedness.

Poor in spirit – One who is deeply sensible of his spiritual poverty and wretchedness. Such Christ pronounces happy, because there is but a step between them and that kingdom which is here promised. Our Lord seems to have the humiliation of the spirit particularly in view.

Kingdom of heaven – A participation of all

the blessings of the new covenant here, and the blessings of glory above. Blessed are the poor! This is God's word; but who believes it? Do we not say, Yea, rather, Blessed is the rich?

4. Blessed are they that mourn – That is, those who, feeling their spiritual poverty, mourn after God, lamenting the iniquity that separated them from the fountain of blessedness. Every one flies from sorrow, and seeks after joy, and yet true joy must necessarily be the fruit of sorrow. The whole need not (do not feel the need of) the physician, but they that are sick do; i.e. they who are sensible of their disease. Only such persons as are deeply convinced of the sinfulness of sin, feel the plague of their own heart, and turn with disgust from all worldly consolations, because of their insufficiency to render them happy, have God's promise of solid comfort.

5. Blessed are the meek – Happy are those who are of a quiet, gentle spirit, in opposition to the proud and supercilious Scribes and Pharisees and their disciples. He who is of a meek or gentle spirit, is ever ready to associate with the meanest of those who fear God, feeling himself superior to none; and well knowing that he has nothing of spiritual or temporal good but what he has received from the mere bounty of God, having never deserved any favor from his hand.

For they shall inherit the earth – Under this expression, which was commonly used by the prophets to signify the land of Canaan, in which all temporal good abounded, Judges 18: 9, 10, Jesus Christ points out that abundance of spiritual good, which was provided for men in the Gospel.

6. They which do hunger and thirst – As the body has its natural appetites of hunger and thirst for the food and drink suited to its nourishment, so has the soul. No being is indestructible or unfailing in its nature but GOD; no being is independent but him: as the body depends for its nourishment, health, and strength upon the earth, so does the soul upon heaven. Heavenly things cannot support the body; they are not suited to its nature:

8 Blessed are the pure in heart: for they shall see God.

9 Blessed are the peacemakers: for they shall be called the children of God.

10 Blessed are they which are persecuted for righteousness' sake: for theirs is the kingdom of heaven.

11 Blessed are ye, when men shall revile you, and persecute you, and shall say all manner of evil against you falsely, for my sake.

12 Rejoice, and be exceeding glad: for great is your reward in heaven: for so persecuted they the prophets which were before you.

Luke 6: 20–26

20 And he lifted up his eyes on his disciples, and said, Blessed be ye poor: for yours is the kingdom of God.

21 Blessed are ye that hunger now: for ye shall be filled. Blessed are ye that weep now: for ye shall laugh.

22 Blessed are ye, when men shall hate you, and when they shall separate you from their company, and shall reproach you, and cast out your name as evil, for the Son of man's sake.

23 Rejoice ye in that day, and leap for joy: for, behold, your reward is great in heaven: for in the like manner did their fathers unto the prophets.

24 But woe unto you that are rich! for ye have received your consolation.

25 Woe unto you that are full! for ye shall hunger. Woe unto you that laugh now! for ye shall mourn and weep.

26 Woe unto you, when all men shall speak well of you! for so did their fathers to the false prophets.

MATTHEW 5: 13–16; MARK 9: 49–50; MARK 4: 21; LUKE 14: 34–35; 8: 16; 11: 33

Matthew 5: 13–16

13 Ye are the salt of the earth: but if the salt have lost his savor, wherewith shall it be salted? it is thenceforth good for nothing, but to be cast out, and to be trodden under foot of men.

14 Ye are the light of the world. A city that is set on an hill cannot be hid.

15 Neither do men light a candle, and put it under a bushel, but on a candle-

his mouth, instead of, He began to speak. Many look upon it as an emphatic mode of expression, employed to draw attention to any thing important and remarkable, either in a good or bad sense, which has been uttered: but as some passages of Scripture countenance an opposite view, I prefer the former exposition. I shall also dismiss the ingenious speculation of those, who give an allegorical turn to the fact of our Lord teaching his disciples on a mountain, as if it had been intended to teach them to elevate their minds far above worldly cares and employments. In ascending the mountain, his design rather was to seek a retreat, where he might obtain relaxation for himself and his disciples at a distance from the multitude.

Now let us see, in the first place, why Christ spoke to his disciples about true happiness. We know that not only the great body of the people, but even the learned themselves, hold this error, that he is the happy man who is free from annoyance, attains all his wishes, and leads a joyful and easy life. At least it is the general opinion, that happiness ought to be estimated from the present state. Christ, therefore, in order to accustom his own people to bear the cross, exposes this mistaken opinion, that those are happy who lead an easy and prosperous life according to the flesh. For it is impossible that men should mildly bend the neck to bear calamities and reproaches, so long as they think that patience is at variance with a happy life. The only consolation which mitigates and even sweetens the bitterness of the cross and of all afflictions, is the conviction, that we are happy in the midst of miseries: for our patience is blessed by the Lord, and will soon be followed by a happy result.

MATTHEW 5: 13–16; MARK 9: 49–50; 4: 21; LUKE 14: 34–35; 8: 16; 11: 33

Matthew 5: 13. Ye are the salt of the earth

What belongs to doctrine is applied to the people to whom the administration of it has been committed. When Christ calls the apostles the salt of the earth, he means, that it is their office to salt the earth: because men have nothing in them but what is tasteless, till they have been seasoned with the salt of heavenly doctrine. After having reminded them to what they are called, he pronounces against them a heavy and dreadful judgment, if they do not fulfill their duty. The doctrine, which has been entrusted to them, is shown to be so closely connected with a good conscience and a devout and upright life, that the corruption, which might be tolerated in others, would in them be detestable and monstrous. "If other men are tasteless in the sight of God, to you shall be given the salt which imparts a relish to them: but if you have lost your taste, where shall you obtain the remedy which you ought to supply to others?"

earthly things cannot support the soul, for the same reason.

7. The merciful – The word mercy, among the Jews, signified two things: the pardon of injuries, and almsgiving. Our Lord undoubtedly takes it in its fullest latitude here. This virtue is no other than a lively emotion of the heart, which is excited by the discovery of any creature's misery; and such an emotion as manifests itself outwardly, by effects suited to its nature.

They shall obtain mercy – Mercy is not purchased but at the price of mercy itself; and even this price is a gift of the mercy of God.

8. Pure in heart – In opposition to the Pharisees, who affected outward purity, while their hearts were full of corruption and defilement. A principal part of the Jewish religion consisted in outward washings and cleansings: on this ground they expected to see God, to enjoy eternal glory: but Christ here shows that a purification of the heart, from all vile affections and desires, is essentially requisite in order to enter into the kingdom of God. He whose soul is not delivered from all sin, through the blood of the covenant, can have no Scriptural hope of ever being with God.

Shall see God – This is a Hebraism, which signifies, possess God, enjoy his felicity: as seeing a thing, was used among the Hebrews for possessing it. See Psalm 16: 10.

Probably our Lord alludes to the advantages those had, who were legally pure, of entering into the sanctuary, into the presence of God, while those who had contracted any legal defilement were excluded from it. This also was obviously typical.

9. The peace-makers – A peace-maker is a man who, being endowed with a generous public spirit, labors for the public good, and feels his own interest promoted in promoting that of others: therefore, instead of fanning the fire of strife, he uses his influence and wisdom to reconcile the contending parties, adjust their differences, and restore them to a state of unity. As all men are represented to be in a state of hostility to God and each other, the Gospel is called the Gospel of peace, because it tends to reconcile men to God and to each other. Hence our Lord here terms peace-makers the children of God: for as he is the Father of peace, those who promote it are reputed his children. But whose children are they who foment divisions in the Church, the state, or among families? Surely they are not of that GOD, who is the Father of peace, and lover of concord; of that CHRIST, who is the sacrifice and mediator of it; of that SPIRIT, who is the nourisher and bond of peace; nor of that CHURCH of the Most High, which is the kingdom and family of peace.

10. They which are persecuted – They are happy who suffer, seems a strange saying: and that the righteous should suffer, merely because they are such, seems as strange. But such is the enmity of the human heart to every thing of God and goodness, that all those who live godly in Christ Jesus shall suffer persecution in one form or other. As the religion of Christ gives no quarter to vice, so the vicious will give no quarter to this religion, or to its professors.

For theirs is the kingdom of heaven – That spiritual kingdom and that kingdom of glory which is its counterpart and consequence.

11. When men shall revile you, and persecute – The persecution mentioned in the preceding verse comprehends all outward acts of violence – all that the hand can do. This comprehends all calumny, slander, etc., all that the tongue can effect. But persecute is a forensic term, and signifies legal persecutions and public accusations, which, though totally unsubstantiated, were the means of destroying multitudes of the primitive Christians, our Lord probably refers to such.

12. Rejoice – In the testimony of a good conscience; for, without this, suffering has nothing but misery in it.

Be exceeding glad – Leap for joy.

Great is your reward in heaven – The followers of Christ are encouraged to suffer joyfully on two considerations.

1. They are thereby conformed to the prophets who went before.

stick; and it giveth light unto all that are in the house.

16 Let your light so shine before men, that they may see your good works, and glorify your Father which is in heaven.

Mark 9: 49–50

49 For every one shall be salted with fire, and every sacrifice shall be salted with salt.

50 Salt is good: but if the salt have lost his saltness, wherewith will ye season it? Have salt in yourselves, and have peace one with another.

Mark 4: 21

21 And he said unto them, Is a candle brought to be put under a bushel, or under a bed? and not to be set on a candlestick?

Luke 14: 34–35

34 Salt is good: but if the salt have lost his savor, wherewith shall it be seasoned?

35 It is neither fit for the land, nor yet for the dunghill; but men cast it out. He that hath ears to hear, let him hear.

Luke 8: 16

16 No man, when he hath lighted a candle, covereth it with a vessel, or putteth it under a bed; but setteth it on a candlestick, that they which enter in may see the light.

Luke 11: 33

33 No man, when he hath lighted a candle, putteth it in a secret place, neither under a bushel, but on a candlestick, that they which come in may see the light.

MATTHEW 5: 17–19; LUKE 16: 16–17

Matthew 5: 17–19

17 Think not that I am come to destroy the law, or the prophets: I am not come to destroy, but to fulfil.

18 For verily I say unto you, Till heaven and earth pass, one jot or one tittle shall in no wise pass from the law, till all be fulfilled.

19 Whosoever therefore shall break one of these least commandments, and shall teach men so, he shall be called the least in the kingdom of heaven: but whosoever shall do and teach them, the

Our Lord skillfully pursues his metaphor, by saying, that other things when they lose their original qualities, are still useful after they have become corrupted: but that salt becomes even hurtful, and communicates barrenness even to dunghills. The amount of his statement is, that it is an incurable disease, when the ministers and teachers of the word corrupt and render themselves tasteless: for they ought to season the rest of the world with their salt. This warning is useful, not only to ministers, but to the whole flock of Christ. Since it is the will of God that the earth shall be salted by his own word, it follows, that whatever is destitute of this salt is, in his estimation, tasteless, how much soever it may be relished by men. There is nothing better, therefore, than to receive the seasoning, by which alone our tastelessness is corrected. But, at the same time, let those whose business is to salt it beware lest they encourage the world in their own folly, and still more, that they do not infect it with a depraved and vicious taste.

MATTHEW 5: 17–19; LUKE 16: 17

Matthew 5: 17. Think not

With regard to the perfection of his life, Christ might justly have maintained that he came to fulfill the law: but here he treats of doctrine, not of life. As he afterwards exclaimed, that "the kingdom of God is come" (Matthew 12: 28), and raised the minds of men with unusual expectation, and even admitted disciples by baptism, it is probable, that the minds of many were in a state of suspense and doubt, and were eagerly inquiring, what was the design of that novelty. Christ, therefore, now declares, that his doctrine is so far from being at variance with the law, that it agrees perfectly with the law and the prophets, and not only so, but brings the complete fulfillment of them.

I am not come to destroy

God had, indeed, promised a new covenant at the coming of Christ; but had, at the same time, showed, that it would not be different from the first, but that, on the contrary, its design was, to give a perpetual sanction to the covenant, which he had made from the beginning, with his own people.

MATTHEW 5: 20–22

Matthew 5: 21. You have heard that it was said

It is a mistake to suppose that this is a correction of the Law here, and that Christ raises his disciples to a higher degree of perfection, than Christ could raise a gross and carnal nation, which was scarcely able to learn first principles. It has been a prevailing opinion, that the beginning of righteousness was laid down in the ancient law, but that the perfection of it is pointed out in the Gospel. But nothing

2. Their reward in heaven is a great one.

God gives the grace to suffer, and then crowns that grace with glory; hence it is plain, the reward is not of debt, but of grace: Romans 6: 23.

MATTHEW 5: 13–16; MARK 9: 49–50; 4: 21; LUKE 14: 4–35; 8: 16; 11: 33

Matthew 5: 13–16

13. Ye are the salt of the earth – Our Lord shows here what the preachers of the Gospel, and what all who profess to follow him, should be; the salt of the earth, to preserve the world from putrefaction and destruction.

But if the salt have lost his savor – A preacher, or private Christian, who has lost the life of Christ, and the witness of his Spirit, out of his soul, may be likened to this salt. He may have the sparks and glittering particles of true wisdom, but without its unction or comfort. Only that which is connected with the rock, the soul that is in union with Christ Jesus by the Holy Spirit, can preserve its savor, and be instrumental of good to others.

To be trodden underfoot – There was a species of salt in Judea, which was generated at the lake Asphaltites, and hence called bituminous salt, easily rendered vapid, and of no other use but to be spread in a part of the temple, to prevent slipping in wet weather. This is probably what our Lord alludes to in this place.

14. Ye are the light of the world – That is, the instruments which God chooses to make use of to illuminate the minds of men; as he uses the sun (to which probably he pointed) to enlighten the world. Light of the world was a title applied to the most eminent rabbins. Christ transfers the title from these, and gives it to his own disciples, who, by the doctrines that he taught them, were to be the means of diffusing the light of life throughout the universe.

16. Let your light so shine – Or more literally, Thus let your light shine. As the sun is lighted up in the firmament of heaven to diffuse its light and heat freely to every inhabitant of the earth; and as the lamp is not set under the bushel, but placed upon the lamp-stand that it may give light to all in the house; THUS let every follower of Christ, and especially every preacher of the Gospel, diffuse the light of heavenly knowledge, and the warmth of Divine love through the whole circle of their acquaintance.

That they may see your good works – It is not sufficient to have light – we must walk in the light, and by the light. Our whole conduct should be a perpetual comment on the doctrine we have received, and a constant exemplification of its power and truth.

And glorify your Father – Real Christians are the children of God – they are partakers of his holy and happy nature: they should ever be concerned for their Father's honor, and endeavor so to recommend him, and his salvation, that others may be prevailed on to come to the light, and walk in it. Then God is said to be glorified, when the glorious power of his grace is manifested in the salvation of men.

MATTHEW 5: 17–19; LUKE 16: 16–17

Matthew 5: 17–19

17. Think not that I am come to destroy the law – Do not imagine that I am come to violate the law. In a word, Christ completed the law: 1st. In itself, it was only the shadow, the typical representation, of good things to come; and he added to it that which was necessary to make it perfect, HIS OWN SACRIFICE, without which it could neither satisfy God, nor sanctify men.

2dly. He completed it in himself by submitting to its types with an exact obedience, and verifying them by his death upon the cross.

3dly. He completes this law, and the sayings of his prophets, in his members, by giving them grace to love the Lord with all their heart, soul, mind, and strength, and their neighbor as themselves; for this is all the law and the prophets.

18. For verily I say unto you, Till heaven

same shall be called great in the kingdom of heaven.

Luke 16: 16–17

16 The law and the prophets were until John: since that time the kingdom of God is preached, and every man presseth into it.

17 And it is easier for heaven and earth to pass, than one tittle of the law to fail.

MATTHEW 5: 20–22

20 For I say unto you, That except your righteousness shall exceed the righteousness of the scribes and Pharisees, ye shall in no case enter into the kingdom of heaven.

21 Ye have heard that it was said by them of old time, Thou shalt not kill; and whosoever shall kill shall be in danger of the judgment:

22 But I say unto you, That whosoever is angry with his brother without a cause shall be in danger of the judgment: and whosoever shall say to his brother, Raca, shall be in danger of the council: but whosoever shall say, Thou fool, shall be in danger of hell fire.

MATTHEW 5: 23–26; LUKE 12: 58–59

Matthew 5: 23–26

23 Therefore if thou bring thy gift to the altar, and there rememberest that thy brother hath ought against thee;

24 Leave there thy gift before the altar, and go thy way; first be reconciled to thy brother, and then come and offer thy gift.

25 Agree with thine adversary quickly, whiles thou art in the way with him; lest at any time the adversary deliver thee to the judge, and the judge deliver thee to the officer, and thou be cast into prison.

26 Verily I say unto thee, Thou shalt by no means come out thence, till thou hast paid the uttermost farthing.

Luke 12: 58–59

58 When thou goest with thine adversary to the magistrate, as thou art in the way, give diligence that thou mayest be delivered from him; lest he hale thee to the judge, and the judge deliver thee to the officer, and the officer cast thee into prison.

was farther from the design of Christ, than to alter or innovate any thing in the commandments of the law. There God has once fixed the rule of life which he will never retract. But as the law had been corrupted by false expositions, and turned to a profane meaning, Christ vindicates it against such corruptions, and points out its true meaning, from which the Jews had departed.

MATTHEW 5: 23–26; LUKE 12: 58–59

Matthew 5: 23. Therefore, if thou shalt bring thy gift

This clause confirms, and at the same time explains, the preceding doctrine. It amounts to this, that the precept of the law, which forbids murder (Exodus 20: 13), is obeyed, when we maintain agreement and brotherly kindness, with our neighbor. To impress this more strongly upon us, Christ declares, that even the duties of religion are displeasing to God, and are rejected by him, if we are at variance with each other.

Here a question may be put. Is it not absurd, that the duties of charity should be esteemed more highly than the worship of God? We shall then be forced to say, that the order of the law is improper, or that the first table of the law must be preferred to the second. The answer is easy: for the words of Christ mean nothing more than this, that it is a false and empty profession of worshipping God, which is made by those who, after acting unjustly towards their brethren, treat them with haughty disdain. By a synecdoche he takes a single class to express the outward exercises of divine worship, which in many men are rather the pretenses, than the true expressions, of godliness. It ought to be observed that Christ, adapting his discourse to that age, speaks of sacrifices. Our condition is now different: but the doctrine remains the same, that whatever we offer to God is polluted, unless, at least as much as lieth in us (Romans 12: 18), we are at peace with our brethren.

MATTHEW 5: 27–30

27. Thou shalt not commit adultery

Christ proceeds with his subject, and shows, that the law of God not only has authority over the life, in a political view, to form the outward manners, but that it requires pure and holy affections of the heart.

28. Whoever shall look upon a woman

The design of Christ was to condemn generally the lust of the flesh. He says, that not only those who have seduced their neighbors' wives, but those who have polluted their eyes by an immodest look, are adulterers before God. This is a synecdoche: for not only the eyes, but even the concealed flames of the heart, render men guilty of adultery.

– In the very commencement of his ministry, Jesus Christ teaches the instability of all visible things.

One jot or one tittle – One jot was the smallest letter in the Hebrew alphabet. One tittle or point, either meaning those points which serve for vowels in this language, if they then existed; or the seraphs, or points of certain letters.

Till all be fulfilled – Or, accomplished. Though all earth and hell should join together to hinder the accomplishment of the great designs of the Most High, yet it shall all be in vain – even the sense of a single letter shall not be lost. The words of God, which point out his designs, are as unchangeable as his nature itself. Every sinner, who perseveres in his iniquity, shall surely be punished with separation from God and the glory of his power; and every soul that turns to God, through Christ, shall as surely be saved, as that Jesus himself hath died.

19. Whosoever – shall break one of these least commandments – The Pharisees were remarkable for making a distinction between weightier and lighter matters in the law, and between what has been called, in a corrupt part of the Christian Church, mortal and venial sins.

Whosoever shall break. What an awful consideration is this! He who, by his mode of acting, speaking, or explaining the words of God, sets the holy precept aside, or explains away its force and meaning, shall be called least – shall have no place in the kingdom of Christ here, nor in the kingdom of glory above. That this is the meaning of these words is evident enough from the following verse.

MATTHEW 5: 20–22

20. Except your righteousness shall exceed – Unless your righteousness abound more – unless it take in, not only the letter, but the spirit and design of the moral and ritual precept; the one directing you how to walk so as to please God; the other pointing out Christ, the great Atonement, through and by which

a sinner is enabled to do so – more than that of the scribes and Pharisees, who only attend to the letter of the law, and had indeed made even that of no effect by their traditions – ye shall not enter into the kingdom of heaven.

21. Ye have heard that it was said by them of old time – to or by the ancients. By the ancients, we may understand those who lived before the law, and those who lived under it; for murder was, in the most solemn manner, forbidden before, as well as under, the law, Genesis 9: 5–6.

But it is very likely that our Lord refers here merely to traditions and glosses relative to the ancient Mosaic ordinance; and such as, by their operation, rendered the primitive command of little or no effect.

22. Whosoever is angry with his brother without a cause – who is vainly incensed. What our Lord seems here to prohibit, is not merely that miserable facility which some have of being angry at every trifle, continually taking offense against their best friends; but that anger which leads a man to commit outrages against another, thereby subjecting himself to that punishment which was to be inflicted on those who break the peace.

Shall be in danger of the judgment – shall be liable to the judgment. That is, to have the matter brought before a senate, composed of twenty-three magistrates, whose business it was to judge in cases of murder and other capital crimes. It punished criminals by strangling or beheading; but Dr. Lightfoot supposes the judgment of God to be intended.

Raca – to be empty. It signifies a vain, empty, worthless fellow, shallow brains, a term of great contempt.

The council – the famous council, known among the Jews by the name of Sanhedrin. It was composed of seventy-two elders, six chosen out of each tribe. This grand Sanhedrin not only received appeals from the inferior Sanhedrins, or court of twenty-three mentioned above; but could alone take cognizance, in the first instance, of the highest crimes, and alone inflict the punishment of stoning.

Thou fool – to rebel, a rebel against God,

59 I tell thee, thou shalt not depart thence, till thou hast paid the very last mite.

MATTHEW 5: 27–30

27 Ye have heard that it was said by them of old time, Thou shalt not commit adultery:

28 But I say unto you, That whosoever looketh on a woman to lust after her hath committed adultery with her already in his heart.

29 And if thy right eye offend thee, pluck it out, and cast it from thee: for it is profitable for thee that one of thy members should perish, and not that thy whole body should be cast into hell.

30 And if thy right hand offend thee, cut if off, and cast it from thee: for it is profitable for thee that one of thy members should perish, and not that thy whole body should be cast into hell.

MATTHEW 5: 31–32; LUKE 16: 18

Matthew 5: 31–32

31 It hath been said, Whosoever shall put away his wife, let him give her a writing of divorcement:

32 But I say unto you, That whosoever shall put away his wife, saving for the cause of fornication, causeth her to commit adultery: and whosoever shall marry her that is divorced committeth adultery.

Luke 16: 18

18 Whosoever putteth away his wife, and marrieth another, committeth adultery: and whosoever marrieth her that is put away from her husband committeth adultery.

MATTHEW 5: 33–37

33 Again, ye have heard that it hath been said by them of old time, Thou shalt not forswear thyself, but shalt perform unto the Lord thine oaths:

34 But I say unto you, Swear not at all; neither by heaven; for it is God's throne:

35 Nor by the earth; for it is his footstool: neither by Jerusalem; for it is the city of the great King.

36 Neither shalt thou swear by thy head, because thou canst not make one hair white or black.

MATTHEW 5: 31–32; LUKE 16: 18

Matthew 5: 31. Whosoever shall put away his wife

As a more suitable occasion for discussing and explaining this doctrine at greater length will afterwards occur (Matthew 19: 9), I shall now state briefly what Christ says in this passage. As the Jews falsely imagined that they discharged their whole duty toward God, when they kept the law in a national manner, so whatever the national law did not forbid, they foolishly supposed to be lawful. Divorces, which husbands were wont to give to their wives, had not been prohibited by Moses as to external order, but only, for the sake of restraining lewdness, he had ordered that "a bill of divorcement" should be given to the wives who were put away (Deuteronomy 24: 1). It was a sort of testimonial of freedom, so that the woman was afterwards free from the yoke and power of the husband; while the husband at the same time acknowledged, that he did not send her away on account of any crime, but because she did not please him. Hence proceeded the error, that there was nothing wrong in such putting away, provided that the forms of law were observed.

MATTHEW 5: 33–37

33. Thou shalt not perjure thyself

This also is not a correction of the law, but a true interpretation of it. For God condemned in the law not only acts of perjury, but lightness in swearing, which lessens the reverence for his name. The man who **perjures himself** is not the only person who takes the name of God in vain (Exodus 20: 7). He does so, who idly and contemptuously pronounces the name of God on trivial occasions, or in ordinary conversation. While the law condemns every kind of profanation of the name of God the Jews imagined, that the guilt of it lay entirely in acts of perjury. Christ reproves this gross error of supposing that they might, without danger, abuse the name of God, provided they did not swear falsely.

MATTHEW 5: 38–41; LUKE 6: 29–30

Matthew 5: 38. An eye for an eye

Here another error is corrected. God had enjoined, by his law (Leviticus 24: 20), that judges and magistrates should punish those who had done injuries, by making them endure as much as they had inflicted. The consequence was, that every one seized on this as a pretext for taking private revenge. They thought that they did no wrong, provided they were not the first to make the attack, but only, when injured, returned like for like. Christ informs them, on the contrary, that, though judges were entrusted with the de-

apostate from all good. This term implied, among the Jews, the highest enormity, and most aggravated guilt.

Shall be in danger of hell fire – shall be liable to the hell of fire. Our Lord here alludes to the valley of the son of Hinnom. This place was near Jerusalem, and had been formerly used for those abominable sacrifices, in which the idolatrous Jews had caused their children to pass through the fire to Molech. A particular place in this valley was called Tophet, the fire stove, in which some supposed they burnt their children alive to the above idol. See 2 Kings 23: 10; 2 Chronicles 28: 3; Jeremiah 7: 31–32. From the circumstances of this valley having been the scene of those infernal sacrifices, the Jews, in our Savior's time, used the word for hell, the place of the damned.

It is very probable that our Lord means no more here than this: if a man charge another with apostasy from the Jewish religion, or rebellion against God, and cannot prove his charge, then he is exposed to that punishment (burning alive) which the other must have suffered, if the charge had been substantiated.

MATTHEW 5: 23–26; LUKE 12: 58–59

Matthew 5: 23–26

23. Therefore if thou bring thy gift – Evil must be nipped in the bud. An unkind thought of another may be the foundation of that which leads to actual murder. A Christian, properly speaking, cannot be an enemy to any man; nor is he to consider any man his enemy, without the fullest evidence: for surmises to the prejudice of another can never rest in the bosom of him who has the love of God in his heart, for to him all men are brethren. He sees all men as children of God, and members of Christ, or at least capable of becoming such. If a tender forgiving spirit was required, even in a Jew, when he approached God's altar with a bullock or a lamb, how much more necessary is this in a man who professes to be a follower of the Lamb of God; especially when he receives the symbols of that Sacrifice which was offered

for the life of the world, in what is commonly called the sacrament of the Lord's supper!

24. Leave there thy gift before the altar – This is as much as to say, "Do not attempt to bring any offering to God while thou art in a spirit of enmity against any person; or hast any difference with thy neighbor, which thou hast not used thy diligence to get adjusted."

Then come and offer thy gift – Then, when either thy brother is reconciled to thee, or thou hast done all in thy power to effect this reconciliation. My own obstinacy and uncharitableness must render me utterly unfit to receive any good from God's hands, or to worship him in an acceptable manner; bat the wickedness of another can be no hinderance to me, when I have endeavored earnestly to get it removed, though without effect.

25. Agree with thine adversary quickly – Adversary properly a plaintiff in law – a perfect law term. Our Lord enforces the exhortation given in the preceding verses, from the consideration of what was deemed prudent in ordinary law-suits. In such cases, men should make up matters with the utmost speed.

Those who make the adversary, God; the judge, Christ; the officer, Death; and the prison, Hell, abuse the passage, and highly dishonor God.

26. The uttermost farthing – If the matter issue in law, strict justice will be done, and your creditor be allowed the fullness of his just claim; but if; while you are on the way, going to the magistrate, you come to a friendly agreement with him, he will relax in his claims, take a part for the whole, and the composition be, in the end, both to his and your profit.

This text has been considered a proper foundation on which to build not only the doctrine of a purgatory, but also that of universal restoration. But the most unwarrantable violence must be used before it can be pressed into the service of either of the above antiscriptural doctrines. At the most, the text can only be considered as a metaphorical representation of the procedure of the great Judge; and let it ever be remembered, that by the general

37 But let your communication be, Yea, yea; Nay, nay: for whatsoever is more than these cometh of evil.

MATTHEW 5: 38–41; LUKE 6: 29–30

Matthew 5: 38–41

38 Ye have heard that it hath been said, An eye for an eye, and a tooth for a tooth:

39 But I say unto you, That ye resist not evil: but whosoever shall smite thee on thy right cheek, turn to him the other also.

40 And if any man will sue thee at the law, and take away thy coat, let him have thy cloke also.

41 And whosoever shall compel thee to go a mile, go with him twain.

Luke 6: 29–30

29 And unto him that smiteth thee on the one cheek offer also the other; and him that taketh away thy cloke forbid not to take thy coat also.

30 Give to every man that asketh of thee; and of him that taketh away thy goods ask them not again.

MATTHEW 5: 42; LUKE 6: 34–35A

Matthew 5: 42

42 Give to him that asketh thee, and from him that would borrow of thee turn not thou away.

Luke 6: 34–35a

34 And if ye lend to them of whom ye hope to receive, what thank have ye? for sinners also lend to sinners, to receive as much again.

35 But love ye your enemies, and do good, and lend, hoping for nothing again; and your reward shall be great,

MATTHEW 5: 43–48; LUKE 6: 27–28, 32–33,35B-36

Matthew 5: 43–48

43 Ye have heard that it hath been said, Thou shalt love thy neighbour, and hate thine enemy.

44 But I say unto you, Love your enemies, bless you that curse you, do good to them that hate you, and pray for them which despitefully use you, and persecute you;

fense of the community, and were invested with authority to restrain the wicked and repress their violence, yet it is the duty of every man to bear patiently the injuries which he receives.

MATTHEW 5: 42; LUKE 6: 34–35

Matthew 5: 42. Give to him that asketh of thee

Though the words of Christ, which are related by Matthew, appear to command us to give to all without discrimination, yet we gather a different meaning from Luke, who explains the whole matter more fully. First, it is certain, that it was the design of Christ to make his disciples generous, but not prodigals and it would be a foolish prodigality to scatter at random what the Lord has given us. Again, we see the rule which the Spirit lays down in another passage for liberality. Let us therefore hold, first, that Christ exhorts his disciples to be liberal and generous; and next, that the way of doing it is, not to think that they have discharged their duty when they have aided a few people, but to study to be kind to all.

MATTHEW 5: 43–48; LUKE 6: 27–36

Matthew 5: 43. Thou shalt love thy neighbor

It is astonishing, that the Scribes fell into so great an absurdity, as to limit the word neighbor to benevolent people: for nothing is more obvious or certain than that God, in speaking of our neighbors, includes the whole human race. Every man is devoted to himself; and whenever a regard to personal convenience occasions an interruption of acts of kindness, there is a departure from that mutual intercourse, which nature itself dictates. To keep up the exercise of brotherly love, God assures us, that all men are our brethren, because they are related to us by a common nature. Whenever I see a man, I must, of necessity, behold myself as in a mirror: for he is my bone and my flesh (Genesis 29: 14). Now, though the greater part of men break off, in most instances, from this holy society, yet their depravity does not violate the order of nature; for we ought to regard God as the author of the union.

Hence we conclude, that the precept of the law, by which we are commanded to love our neighbor, is general. But the Scribes, judging of neighborhood from the disposition of the individual, affirmed that no man ought to be reckoned a neighbor, unless he were worthy of esteem on account of his own excellencies, or, at least, unless he acted the part of a friend. This is, no doubt, supported by the common opinion; and therefore the children of the world are not ashamed to acknowledge their resentments, when they have any reason to assign for them. But the charity, which God requires in his law, looks not at what a man has

consent of all (except the basely interested) no metaphor is ever to be produced in proof of any doctrine. In the things that concern our eternal salvation, we need the most pointed and express evidence on which to establish the faith of our souls.

MATTHEW 5: 27–30

28. Whosoever looketh on a woman to lust after her – Earnestly to covet her. The verb is undoubtedly used here by our Lord, in the sense of coveting through the influence of impure desire. In all these cases, our blessed Lord points out the spirituality of the law; which was a matter to which the Jews paid very little attention. Indeed it is the property of a Pharisee to abstain only from the outward crime. Men are very often less inquisitive to know how far the will of God extends, that they may please him in performing it, than they are to know how far they may satisfy their lusts without destroying their bodies and souls, utterly, by an open violation of his law.

Hath committed adultery with her already in his heart – It is the earnest wish or desire of the soul, which, in a variety of cases, constitutes the good or evil of an act. If a man earnestly wish to commit an evil, but cannot, because God puts time, place, and opportunity out of his power, he is fully chargeable with the iniquity of the act, by that God who searches and judges the heart. So, if a man earnestly wish to do some kindness, which it is out of his power to perform, the act is considered as his; because God, in this case, as in that above, takes the will for the deed. If voluntary and deliberate looks and desires make adulterers and adulteresses, how many persons are there whose whole life is one continued crime! whose eyes being full of adultery, they cannot cease from sin, 2 Peter 2: 14. Many would abhor to commit one external act before the eyes of men, in a temple of stone; and yet they are not afraid to commit a multitude of such acts in the temple of their hearts, and in the sight of God!

29–30. Pluck it out – cut it off – We must shut our senses against dangerous objects, to avoid the occasions of sin, and deprive ourselves of all that is most dear and profitable to us, in order to save our souls, when we find that these dear and profitable things, however innocent in themselves, cause us to sin against God.

It is profitable for thee that one of thy members – Men often part with some members of the body, at the discretion of a surgeon, that they may preserve the trunk, and die a little later; and yet they will not deprive themselves of a look, a touch, a small pleasure, which endanger the eternal death of the soul.

MATTHEW 5: 31–32; LUKE 16: 18

Matthew 5: 31–32

31. Whosoever shall put away his wife – The Jewish doctors gave great license in the matter of divorce. Among them, a man might divorce his wife if she displeased him even in the dressing of his victuals!

32. Saving for the cause of fornication – A real Christian ought rather to beg of God the grace to bear patiently and quietly the imperfections of his wife, than to think of the means of being parted from her.

MATTHEW 5: 33–37

33. Thou shalt not forswear thyself – They dishonor the great God, and break this commandment, who use frequent oaths and imprecations, even in reference to things that are true; and those who make vows and promises, which they either cannot perform, or do not design to fulfill, are not less criminal.

37. Let your communication be, Yea, yea; Nay, nay – That is, a positive affirmation, or negation, according to your knowledge of the matter concerning which you are called to testify. Do not equivocate; mean what you assert, and adhere to your assertion.

45 That ye may be the children of your Father which is in heaven: for he maketh his sun to rise on the evil and on the good, and sendeth rain on the just and on the unjust.

46 For if ye love them which love you, what reward have ye? do not even the publicans the same?

47 And if ye salute your brethren only, what do ye more than others? do not even the publicans so?

48 Be ye therefore perfect, even as your Father which is in heaven is perfect.

Luke 6: 27–28,32–33,35b-36

27 But I say unto you which hear, Love your enemies, do good to them which hate you,

28 Bless them that curse you, and pray for them which despitefully use you.

32 For if ye love them which love you, what thank have ye? for sinners also love those that love them.

33 And if ye do good to them which do good to you, what thank have ye? for sinners also do even the same.

35b and ye shall be the children of the Highest: for he is kind unto the unthankful and to the evil.

36 Be ye therefore merciful, as your Father also is merciful.

MATTHEW 6: 1–4

1 Take heed that ye do not your alms before men, to be seen of them: otherwise ye have no reward of your Father which is in heaven.

2 Therefore when thou doest thine alms, do not sound a trumpet before thee, as the hypocrites do in the synagogues and in the streets, that they may have glory of men. Verily I say unto you, They have their reward.

3 But when thou doest alms, let not thy left hand know what thy right hand doeth:

4 That thine alms may be in secret: and thy Father which seeth in secret himself shall reward thee openly.

MATTHEW 6: 5–8

5 And when thou prayest, thou shalt not be as the hypocrites are: for they love to pray standing in the synagogues and in

deserved, but extends itself to the unworthy, the wicked, and the ungrateful. Now, this is the true meaning which Christ restores, and vindicates from calumny; and hence it is obvious that Christ does not introduce new laws, but corrects the wicked glosses of the Scribes.

MATTHEW 6: 1–4

1. Beware

In this passage, Christ exhorts his people to devote themselves sincerely to good works; that is, to endeavor, with simplicity, to do what is right before God, and not to make a parade before men. A very necessary admonition; for in all virtues the entrance of ambition is to be dreaded, and there is no work so laudable, as not to be in many instances corrupted and polluted by it.

2. When thou doest alms

He expressly reproves a long established custom, in which the desire of fame might not only be perceived by the eye, but felt by the hands. In places where streets or roads met, and in public situations, where large assemblies were wont to be held, they distributed alms to the poor. There was evident ostentation in that practice: for they sought crowded places, that they might be seen by multitudes, and, not satisfied with this, added even the sound of trumpets.

MATTHEW 6: 5–8

5. When thou shalt pray

He now gives the same instruction as to prayer, which he had formerly given as to alms. It is a gross and shameful profanation of the name of God, when hypocrites, in order to obtain glory from men, pray in public, or at least make a pretense of praying. But, as hypocrisy is always ambitious, we need not wonder that it is also blind. Christ, therefore, commands his disciples, if they wish to pray in a right manner, to **enter into their closet**.

We must not interpret these words literally. He speaks comparatively, and means, that we ought rather to seek retirement than desire a crowd of men to see us praying.

MATTHEW 6: 9–13; LUKE 11: 1–4

Matthew 6: 9

This form of prayer consists, as I have said, of six petitions. The first three, it ought to be known, relate to the glory of God, without any regard to ourselves; and the remaining three relate to those things which are necessary for our salvation. As the law of God is divided into two tables, of which the former contains the duties of piety, and the latter the duties of charity, so in prayer Christ enjoins us to consider and seek the glory of God, and, at the same time,

MATTHEW 5: 38–41; LUKE 6: 29–30

Matthew 5: 38–41

38. An eye for an eye – Our Lord refers here to the law of retaliation mentioned See Exodus 21: 24, which obliged the offender to suffer the same injury he had committed. The Greeks and Romans had the same law. It seems that the Jews had made this law (the execution of which belonged to the civil magistrate) a ground for authorizing private resentments, and all the excesses committed by a vindictive spirit. Revenge was often carried to the utmost extremity, and more evil returned than what had been received. This is often the case among those who are called Christians.

39. Resist not evil – Or, the evil person. Our Lord's meaning is, "Do not repel one outrage by another." He that does so makes himself precisely what the other is, a wicked person.

Turn to him the other also – That is, rather than avenge thyself, be ready to suffer patiently a repetition of the same injury. But these exhortations belong to those principally who are persecuted for righteousness' sake. Let such leave the judgment of their cause to Him for whose sake they suffer. The Jews always thought that every outrage should be resented; and thus the spirit of hatred and strife was fostered.

40. And if any man will sue thee at the law – Everywhere our blessed Lord shows the utmost disapprobation of such litigations as tended to destroy brotherly kindness and charity. It is evident he would have his followers to suffer rather the loss of all their property than to have recourse to such modes of redress, at so great a risk. Having the mind averse from contentions, and preferring peace and concord to temporal advantages, is most solemnly recommended to all Christians. We are great gainers when we lose only our money, or other property, and risk not the loss of our souls, by losing the love of God and man.

41. Shall compel thee to go a mile, go with him twain.
We are here exhorted to patience and forgive-ness:
First, When we receive in our persons all sorts of insults and affronts, Matthew 5: 39.
Secondly, When we are despoiled of our goods, Matthew 5: 40.
Thirdly, When our bodies are forced to undergo all kinds of toils, vexations, and torments, Matthew 5: 41.

The way to improve the injustice of man to our own advantage, is to exercise under it meekness, gentleness, and long-suffering, without which disposition of mind, no man can either be happy here or hereafter; for he that avenges himself must lose the mind of Christ, and thus suffer an injury ten thousand times greater than he can ever receive from man. Revenge, at such an expense, is dear indeed.

MATTHEW 5: 42; LUKE 6: 34–35A

Matthew 5: 42

Give to him that asketh thee, and from him that would borrow – To give and to lend, are two duties of charity which Christ joins together, and which he sets on equal footing. A rich man is one of God's stewards: God has given him money for the poor, and he cannot deny it without an act of injustice.

MATTHEW 5: 43–48; LUKE 6: 27–28, 32–33, 35B–36

Matthew 5: 43–48

44. Love your enemies – This is the most sublime piece of morality ever given to man. Has it appeared unreasonable and absurd to some? It has. And why? Because it is natural to man to avenge himself, and plague those who plague him; and he will ever find abundant excuse for his conduct, in the repeated evils he receives from others; for men are naturally hostile to each other. Jesus Christ design's to make men happy. Now he is necessarily miserable who hates another. Our Lord prohibits that only which, from its nature, is opposed to man's happiness. This is therefore one of the most reasonable precepts in the universe. But who

the corners of the streets, that they may be seen of men. Verily I say unto you, They have their reward.

6 But thou, when thou prayest, enter into thy closet, and when thou hast shut thy door, pray to thy Father which is in secret; and thy Father which seeth in secret shall reward thee openly.

7 But when ye pray, use not vain repetitions, as the heathen do: for they think that they shall be heard for their much speaking.

8 Be not ye therefore like unto them: for your Father knoweth what things ye have need of, before ye ask him.

MATTHEW 6: 9–13; LUKE 11: 1–4

Matthew 6: 9–13

9 After this manner therefore pray ye: Our Father which art in heaven, Hallowed be thy name.

10 Thy kingdom come. Thy will be done in earth, as it is in heaven.

11 Give us this day our daily bread.

12 And forgive us our debts, as we forgive our debtors.

13 And lead us not into temptation, but deliver us from evil: For thine is the kingdom, and the power, and the glory, for ever. Amen.

Luke 11: 1–4

1 And it came to pass, that, as he was praying in a certain place, when he ceased, one of his disciples said unto him, Lord, teach us to pray, as John also taught his disciples.

2 And he said unto them, When ye pray, say, Our Father which art in heaven, Hallowed be thy name. Thy kingdom come. Thy will be done, as in heaven, so in earth.

3 Give us day by day our daily bread.

4 And forgive us our sins; for we also forgive every one that is indebted to us. And lead us not into temptation; but deliver us from evil.

MATTHEW 6: 14–15; MARK 11: 25–26

Matthew 6: 14–15

14 For if ye forgive men their trespasses, your heavenly Father will also forgive you:

permits us to consult our own interests. Let us therefore know, that we shall be in a state of mind for praying in a right manner, if we not only are in earnest about ourselves and our own advantage, but assign the first place to the glory of God: for it would be altogether preposterous to mind only what belongs to ourselves, and to disregard the kingdom of God, which is of far greater importance.

Our Father who art in heaven

Whenever we engage in prayer, there are two things to be considered, both that we may have access to God, and that we may rely on Him with full and unshaken confidence: his fatherly love toward us, and his boundless power. Let us therefore entertain no doubt, that God is willing to receive us graciously, that he is ready to listen to our prayers – in a word, that of Himself he is disposed to aid us.

May thy name be sanctified

It is of unspeakable advantage to us that God reigns, and that he receives the honor which is due to him: but no man has a sufficiently earnest desire to promote the glory of God, unless (so to speak) he forgets himself, and raises his mind to seek God's exalted greatness. There is a close connection and resemblance between those three petitions. The sanctification of the name of God is always connected with his kingdom; and the most important part of his kingdom lies in his will being done.

MATTHEW 6: 14–15; MARK 11: 25–26

Here Christ only explains the reason why that condition was added, **Forgive us, as we forgive**. The reason is, that God will not be ready to hear us, unless we also show ourselves ready to grant forgiveness to those who have offended us. If we are not harder than iron, this exhortation ought to soften us, and render us disposed to forgive offenses. Unless God pardon us every day many sins, we know that we are ruined in innumerable ways: and on no other condition does he admit us to pardon, but that we pardon our brethren whatever offenses they have committed against us. Those who refuse to forget the injuries which have been done to them, devote themselves willingly and deliberately to destruction, and knowingly prevent God from forgiving them.

MATTHEW 6: 16–19

He again returns to the former doctrine: for, having begun to rebuke vain ostentation in alms and prayer, he laid down, before proceeding farther, the rule for praying in a right manner. The same injunction is now given to his disciples about **fasting** which he had formerly given about prayers and alms not to be too solicitous to obtain the applause of spectators, but to have God as the witness of their actions.

can obey it? None but he who has the mind of Christ. But I have it not. Seek it from God; it is that kingdom of heaven which Christ came to establish upon earth. This one precept is a sufficient proof of the holiness of the Gospel, and of the truth of the Christian religion.

Do good to them that hate you – Give your enemy every proof that you love him. We must not love in tongue, but in deed and in truth.

Pray for them which despitefully use you – Those who are making continual war upon you, and constantly harassing and calumniating you. Pray for them – This is another exquisitely reasonable precept.

45. That ye may be the children of your Father – As a man's child is called his, because a partaker of his own nature, so a holy person is said to be a child of God, because he is a partaker of the Divine nature.

46. For if ye love them which love you – He who loves only his friends, does nothing for God's sake. He who loves for the sake of pleasure or interest, pays himself. God has no enemy which he hates but sin; we should have no other.

The publicans – This class of men was detestable among the Romans, the Greeks, and the Jews, for their intolerable rapacity and avarice. They were abhorred in an especial manner by the Jews, to whom the Roman government was odious: these, assisting in collecting the Roman tribute, were considered as betrayers of the liberties of their country, and abettors of those who enslaved it.

48. Be ye therefore perfect – as your Father – God himself is the grand law, sole giver, and only pattern of the perfection which he recommends to his children. The words are very emphatic, Ye shall be therefore perfect – ye shall be filled with the spirit of that God whose name is Mercy, and whose nature is love. God has many imitators of his power, independence, justice, etc., but few of his love, condescension, and kindness. He calls himself LOVE, to teach us that in this consists that perfection, the attainment of which he has

made both our duty and privilege: for these words of our Lord include both a command and a promise.

MATTHEW 6: 1–4

1. Before men – Our Lord does not forbid public alms-giving, fasting, and prayer, but simply censures those vain and hypocritical persons who do these things publicly that they may be seen of men, and receive from them the reputation of saints, etc.

2. Therefore when thou doest thine alms – In the first verse the exhortation is general: Take YE heed. In this verse the address is pointed – and THOU – man – woman – who readest – hearest.

Do not sound a trumpet – It is very likely that this was literally practiced among the Pharisees, who seemed to live on the public esteem, and were excessively self-righteous and vain.

They have their reward – That is, the honor and esteem of men which they sought. God is under no obligation to them – they did nothing with an eye to his glory, and from HIM they can expect no recompense. They had their recompense in this life; and could expect none in the world to come.

3. Let not thy left hand know – In many cases, works of charity must be hidden from even our nearest relatives, who, if they knew, would hinder us from doing what God has given us power and inclination to perform.

4. Which seeth in secret – We should ever remember that the eye of the Lord is upon us, and that he sees not only the act, but also every motive that led to it.

Shall reward thee openly – Will give thee the fullest proofs of his acceptance of thy work of faith, and labor of love, by increasing that substance which, for his sake, thou sharest with the poor; and will manifest his approbation in thy own heart, by the witness of his Spirit.

15 But if ye forgive not men their trespasses, neither will your Father forgive your trespasses.

Mark 11: 25–26

25 And when ye stand praying, forgive, if ye have ought against any: that your Father also which is in heaven may forgive you your trespasses.

26 But if ye do not forgive, neither will your Father which is in heaven forgive your trespasses.

MATTHEW 6: 16–18

16 Moreover when ye fast, be not, as the hypocrites, of a sad countenance: for they disfigure their faces, that they may appear unto men to fast. Verily I say unto you, They have their reward.

17 But thou, when thou fastest, anoint thine head, and wash thy face;

18 That thou appear not unto men to fast, but unto thy Father which is in secret: and thy Father, which seeth in secret, shall reward thee openly.

MATTHEW 6: 19–21; LUKE 12: 33–34

Matthew 6: 19–21

19 Lay not up for yourselves treasures upon earth, where moth and rust doth corrupt, and where thieves break through and steal:

20 But lay up for yourselves treasures in heaven, where neither moth nor rust doth corrupt, and where thieves do not break through nor steal:

21 For where your treasure is, there will your heart be also.

Luke 12: 33–34

33 Sell that ye have, and give alms; provide yourselves bags which wax not old, a treasure in the heavens that faileth not, where no thief approacheth, neither moth corrupteth.

34 For where your treasure is, there will your heart be also.

MATTHEW 6: 22–24; LUKE 11: 34–36; 16: 13

Matthew 6: 22–24

22 The light of the body is the eye: if therefore thine eye be single, thy whole body shall be full of light.

23 But if thine eye be evil, thy whole

MATTHEW 6: 19–21; LUKE 12: 33–34

Matthew 6: 19. Lay not up

This deadly plague reigns everywhere throughout the world. Men are grown mad with an insatiable desire of gain. Christ charges them with folly, in collecting wealth with great care, and then giving up their happiness to moths and to **rust**, or exposing it as a prey to thieves. What is more unreasonable than to place their property, where it may perish of itself, or be carried off by men? Covetous men, indeed, take no thought of this. They lock up their riches in well-secured chests, but cannot prevent them from being exposed to thieves or to moths. They are blind and destitute of sound judgment, who give themselves so much toil and uneasiness in amassing wealth, which is liable to putrefaction, or robbery, or a thousand other accidents: particularly, when God allows us a place **in heaven for laying up a treasure**, and kindly invites us to enjoy riches which never perish.

MATTHEW 6: 22–24; LUKE 11: 34–36; 16: 13

Matthew 6: 22. The light of the body is the eye

We must bear in mind that what we find here are detached sentences, and not a continued discourse. The substance of the present statement is, that men go wrong through carelessness, because they do not keep their eye fixed, as they ought to do, on the proper object. For whence comes it, that they so shamefully wander, or dash themselves, or stumble, but because, having corrupted their judgment by choosing rather to follow their own lusts than the righteousness of God, they not only extinguish the light of reason, which ought to have regulated their life, but change it altogether into darkness.

When Christ calls the eye the light of the body, he employs a comparison which means, that neither the hands, nor the feet, nor the belly, serves to direct men in walking, but that the eye alone is a sufficient guide to the rest of the members. If the hands and feet are foolishly and improperly directed, the blame of the mistake ought to be charged on the eyes, which do not perform their duty. We must now apply this comparison to the mind. The affections may be regarded individually as its members: but as they are blind in themselves, they need direction. Now, God has given reason to guide them, and to act the part of a lantern in showing them the way.

A simple eye means an eye that has no speck, or diseased humor, or any other defect. An evil eye (*poneron*) means a diseased eye. A luminous body means one that is enlightened, so as to have all its actions properly regulated. A dark body is one which is led into numerous mistakes by a confused movement. We see, then, that these words reprove

MATTHEW 6: 5–8

5. And when thou prayest – A proper idea of prayer is, a pouring out of the soul unto God, as a free-will offering, solemnly and eternally dedicated to him, accompanied with the most earnest desire that it may know, love, and serve him alone. He that comes thus to God will ever be heard and blessed. Prayer is the language of dependence; he who prays not, is endeavoring to live independently of God.

Thou shalt not be as the hypocrites – properly a stage-player, who acts under a mask, personating a character different from his own; a counterfeit, a dissembler; one who would be thought to be different from what he really is. A person who wishes to be taken for a follower of God, but who has nothing of religion except the outside.

Love to pray standing in the synagogues and in the corners of the streets – The Jewish phylacterical prayers were long, and the canonical hours obliged them to repeat these prayers wherever they happened to be; and the Pharisees, who were full of vain glory, contrived to be overtaken in the streets by the canonical hour, that they might be seen by the people, and applauded for their great and conscientious piety.

6. But thou, when thou prayest – This is a very impressive and emphatic address. But THOU! whosoever thou art, Jew, Pharisee, Christian – enter into thy closet. Prayer is the most secret intercourse of the soul with God, and as it were the conversation of one heart with another.

Reward thee openly – What goodness is there equal to this of God to give, not only what we ask, and more than we ask, but to reward even prayer itself!

7. Use not vain repetitions – Prayer requires more of the heart than of the tongue. The eloquence of prayer consists in the fervency of desire, and the simplicity of faith.

8. Your Father knoweth what things ye have need of – Prayer is not designed to inform God, but to give man a sight of his misery; to humble his heart, to excite his desire, to inflame his faith, to animate his hope, to raise his soul from earth to heaven, and to put him in mind that THERE is his Father, his country, and inheritance.

MATTHEW 6: 9–13; LUKE 11: 1–4

Matthew 6: 9–13

9. After this manner therefore pray ye – Forms of prayer were frequent among the Jews; and every public teacher gave one to his disciples.

Our Father – It was a maxim of the Jews, that a man should not pray alone, but join with the Church; by which they particularly meant that he should, whether alone or with the synagogue, use the plural number as comprehending all the followers of God.

This prayer was evidently made in a peculiar manner for the children of God. And hence we are taught to say, not MY Father, but OUR Father.

All the petitions in this prayer stand in strictest reference to the word Father; the first three referring to the love we have for God; and the three last, to that confidence which we have in the love he bears to us.

Thy name – That is, GOD himself, with all the attributes of his Divine nature – his power, wisdom, justice, mercy, etc.

10. Thy kingdom come – The ancient Jews scrupled not to say: He prays not at all, in whose prayers there is no mention of the kingdom of God. The universal sway of the scepter of Christ: God has promised that the kingdom of Christ shall be exalted above all kingdoms.

11. Give us this day our daily bread – We must ask only that which is essential to our support, God having promised neither luxuries nor superfluities.

12. And forgive us our debts – Sin is represented here under the notion of a debt, and as our sins are many, they are called here debts.

As we forgive our debtors – It was a maxim among the ancient Jews, that no man should lie down in his bed, without forgiving those who had offended him.

body shall be full of darkness. If therefore the light that is in thee be darkness, how great is that darkness!

24 No man can serve two masters: for either he will hate the one, and love the other; or else he will hold to the one, and despise the other. Ye cannot serve God and mammon.

Luke 11: 34–36

34 The light of the body is the eye: therefore when thine eye is single, thy whole body also is full of light; but when thine eye is evil, thy body also is full of darkness.

35 Take heed therefore that the light which is in thee be not darkness.

36 If thy whole body therefore be full of light, having no part dark, the whole shall be full of light, as when the bright shining of a candle doth give thee light.

Luke 16: 13

13 No servant can serve two masters: for either he will hate the one, and love the other; or else he will hold to the one, and despise the other. Ye cannot serve God and mammon.

MATTHEW 6: 25–30; LUKE 12: 22–28

Matthew 6: 25–30

25 Therefore I say unto you, Take no thought for your life, what ye shall eat, or what ye shall drink; nor yet for your body, what ye shall put on. Is not the life more than meat, and the body than raiment?

26 Behold the fowls of the air: for they sow not, neither do they reap, nor gather into barns; yet your heavenly Father feedeth them. Are ye not much better than they?

27 Which of you by taking thought can add one cubit unto his stature?

28 And why take ye thought for raiment? Consider the lilies of the field, how they grow; they toil not, neither do they spin:

29 And yet I say unto you, That even Solomon in all his glory was not arrayed like one of these.

30 Wherefore, if God so clothe the grass of the field, which to day is, and to morrow is cast into the oven, shall he not much more clothe you, O ye of little faith?

the indolence of men, who neglect to open their eyes for the guidance of their affections.

MATTHEW 6: 25–30; LUKE 12: 22–28

Throughout the whole of this discourse, Christ reproves that *excessive* anxiety, with which men torment themselves, about food and clothing, and, at the same time, applies a remedy for curing this disease. When he forbids them to be **anxious**, this is not to be taken literally, as if he intended to take away from his people all care. We know that men are born on the condition of having some care; and, indeed, this is not the least portion of the miseries, which the Lord has laid upon us as a punishment, in order to humble us. But immoderate care is condemned for two reasons: either because in so doing men tease and vex themselves to no purpose, by carrying their anxiety farther than is proper or than their calling demands; or because they claim more for themselves than they have a right to do, and place such a reliance on their own industry, that they neglect to call upon God. We ought to remember this promise: though unbelievers shall "rise up early, and sit up late, and eat the bread of sorrows," yet believers will obtain, through the kindness of God, rest and sleep (Psalm 127: 2). Though the children of God are not free from toil and anxiety, yet, properly speaking, we do not say that they are anxious about life: because, through their reliance on the providence of God, they enjoy calm repose.

Hence it is easy to learn, how far we ought to be **anxious about food**. Each of us ought to labor, as far as his calling requires and the Lord commands; and each of us ought to be led by his own wants to call upon God. Such anxiety holds an intermediate place between indolent carelessness and the unnecessary torments by which unbelievers kill themselves. But if we give proper attention to the words of Christ, we shall find, that he does not forbid every kind of care, but only what arises from distrust.

Matthew 6: 25. Is not the life of more value than food? He argues from the greater to the less. He had forbidden them to be excessively anxious about the way in which life might be supported; and he now assigns the reason. The Lord, who has given life itself, will not suffer us to want what is necessary for its support. And certainly we do no small dishonor to God, when we fail to trust that he will give us necessary food or clothing; as if he had thrown us on the earth at random. He who is fully convinced, that the Author of our life has an intimate knowledge of our condition, will entertain no doubt that he will make abundant provision for our wants. Whenever we are seized by any fear or anxiety about food, let us remember, that God will take care of the life which he gave us.

13. And lead us not into temptation – That is, bring us not in to sore trial.

Deliver us – a very expressive word – break our chains, and loose our bands – snatch, pluck us from the evil, and its calamitous issue.

MATTHEW 6: 14–15; MARK 11: 25–26

Matthew 6: 14–15

14. If ye forgive men – He who shows mercy to men receives mercy from God.

15. But if ye forgive not – He who does not awake at the sound of so loud a voice, is not asleep but dead.

MATTHEW 6: 16–18

16. As the hypocrites – of a sad countenance – A hypocrite has always a difficult part to act: when he wishes to appear as a penitent, not having any godly sorrow at heart, he is obliged to counterfeit it the best way he can, by a gloomy and austere look.

17. Anoint thine head and wash thy face – These were forbidden in the Jewish canon on days of fasting and humiliation; and hypocrites availed themselves of this ordinance, that they might appear to fast. Our Lord, therefore, cautions us against this: as if he had said, Affect nothing – dress in thy ordinary manner, and let the whole of thy deportment prove that thou desirest to recommend my soul to God, and not thy face to men.

18. Thy father which seeth in secret – Let us not be afraid that our hearts can be concealed from God; but let us fear lest he perceive them to be more desirous of the praise of men than they are of that glory which comes from Him.

MATTHEW 6: 19–21; LUKE 12: 33–34

Matthew 6: 19–21

19. Lay not up for yourselves treasures upon earth – What blindness is it for a man to lay up that as a treasure which must necessarily perish! A heart designed for God and eternity is terribly degraded by being fixed on those things which are subject to corruption.

Where thieves do not break through – literally dig through, i.e. the wall, in order to get into the house. This was not a difficult matter, as the house was generally made of mud and straw.

20. Lay up – treasures in heaven – "The only way to render perishing goods eternal, to secure stately furniture from moths, and the richest metals from canker, and precious stones from thieves, is to transmit them to heaven by acts of charity. This is a kind of bill of exchange which cannot fail of acceptance, but through our own fault." Quesnel.

21. Where your treasure is – If God be the treasure of our souls, our hearts, i.e. our affections and desires will be placed on things above. An earthly minded man proves that his treasure is below; a heavenly minded man shows that his treasure is above.

MATTHEW 6: 22–24; LUKE 11: 34–36; 16: 13

Matthew 6: 22–24

22. The light of the body is the eye – That is, the eye is to the body what the sun is to the universe in the day time, or a lamp or candle to a house at night.

If – thine eye be single – simple, uncompounded; i.e. so perfect in its structure as to see objects distinctly and clearly, and not confusedly, or in different places to what they are, as is often the case in certain disorders of the eye; one object appearing two or more – or else in a different situation, and of a different color to what it really is.

24. No man can serve two masters – The master of our heart may be fitly termed the love that reigns in it. We serve that only which we love supremely. A man cannot be in perfect indifference betwixt two objects which are incompatible: he is inclined to despise and hate whatever he does not love supremely, when the necessity of a choice presents itself.

He will hate the one and love the other – The word hate has the same sense here as

Luke 12: 22–28

22 And he said unto his disciples, Therefore I say unto you, Take no thought for your life, what ye shall eat; neither for the body, what ye shall put on.

23 The life is more than meat, and the body is more than raiment.

24 Consider the ravens: for they neither sow nor reap; which neither have storehouse nor barn; and God feedeth them: how much more are ye better than the fowls?

25 And which of you with taking thought can add to his stature one cubit?

26 If ye then be not able to do that thing which is least, why take ye thought for the rest?

27 Consider the lilies how they grow: they toil not, they spin not; and yet I say unto you, that Solomon in all his glory was not arrayed like one of these.

28 If then God so clothe the grass, which is to day in the field, and to morrow is cast into the oven; how much more will he clothe you, O ye of little faith?

MATTHEW 6: 31–34; LUKE 12: 29–32

Matthew 6: 31–34

31 Therefore take no thought, saying, What shall we eat? or, What shall we drink? or, Wherewithal we be clothed?

32 (For after all these things do the Gentiles seek:) for your heavenly Father knoweth that ye have need of all these things.

33 But seek ye first the kingdom of God, and his righteousness; and all these things shall be added unto you.

34 Take therefore no thought for the morrow: for the morrow shall take thought for the things of itself. Sufficient unto the day is the evil thereof.

Luke 12: 29–32

29 And seek not ye what ye shall eat, or what ye shall drink, neither be ye of doubtful mind.

30 For all these things do the nations of the world seek after: and your Father knoweth that ye have need of these things.

31 But rather seek ye the kingdom of God; and all these things shall be added

26. Look at the fowls of the air

This is the remedy for teaching us to rely on the providence of God: for of all cares, which go beyond bounds, unbelief is the mother. The only cure for covetousness is to embrace the promises of God, by which he assures us that he will take care of us.

MATTHEW 6: 31–34; LUKE 12: 29–32

Matthew 6: 32. For all those things the Gentiles seek

This is a reproof of the gross ignorance, in which all such anxieties originate. For how comes it, that unbelievers never remain in a state of tranquillity, but because they imagine that God is unemployed, or asleep, in heaven, or, at least, that he does not take charge of the affairs of men, or feed, as members of his family, those whom he has admitted to his friendship. By this comparison he intimates, that they have made little proficiency, and have not yet learned the first lessons of godliness, who do not behold, with the eyes of faith, the hand of God filled with a hidden abundance of all good things, so as to expect their food with quietness and composure.

Your heavenly Father knoweth that you have need of those things: that is, "All those people who are so anxious about food, give no more honor, than unbelievers do, to the fatherly goodness and secret providence of God."

MATTHEW 7: 1–5; MARK 4: 24; LUKE 6: 37–42

Matthew 7: 1. Judge not

These words of Christ do not contain an absolute prohibition from judging, but are intended to cure a disease, which appears to be natural to us all. We see how all flatter themselves, and every man passes a severe censure on others. This vice is attended by some strange enjoyment: for there is hardly any person who is not tickled with the desire of inquiring into other people's faults. All acknowledge, indeed, that it is an intolerable evil, that those who overlook their own vices are so inveterate against their brethren. The Heathens, too, in ancient times, condemned it in many proverbs. Yet it has existed in all ages, and exists, too, in the present day. Nay, it is accompanied by another and a worse plague: for the greater part of men think that, when they condemn others, they acquire a greater liberty of sinning.

This depraved eagerness for biting, censuring, and slandering, is restrained by Christ, when he says, Judge not. It is not necessary that believers should become blind, and perceive nothing, but only that they should refrain from an undue eagerness to judge: for otherwise the proper bounds of rigor will be exceeded by every man who desires to pass sentence on his brethren. There is a similar expression in

it has in many places of Scripture; it merely signifies to love less – so Jacob loved Rachel, but hated Leah; i.e. he loved Leah much less than he loved Rachel.

God himself uses it precisely in the same sense: Jacob have I loved, but Esau have I hated; i.e. I have loved the posterity of Esau less than I have loved the posterity of Jacob: which means no more than that God, in the course of his providence, gave to the Jews greater earthly privileges than he gave to the Edomites, and chose to make them the progenitors of the Messiah, though they ultimately, through their own obstinacy, derived no more benefit from this privilege than the Edomites did. How strange is it, that with such evidence before their eyes, men will apply this loving and hating to degrees of inclusion and exclusion, in which neither the justice nor mercy of God are honored!

Ye cannot serve God and mammon – The word mammon plainly denotes riches, Luke 16: 9,11, in which latter verse mention is made not only of the deceitful mammon, but also of the true.

Our blessed Lord shows here the utter impossibility of loving the world and loving God at the same time; or, in other words, that a man of the world cannot be a truly religious character. He who gives his heart to the world robs God of it, and, in snatching at the shadow of earthly good, loses substantial and eternal blessedness. How dangerous is it to set our hearts upon riches, seeing it is so easy to make them our God!

MATTHEW 6: 25–30; LUKE 12: 22–28

Matthew 6: 25–30

25. Take no thought – Be not anxiously careful. Prudent care is never forbidden by our Lord, but only that anxious distracting solicitude, which, by dividing the mind, and drawing it different ways, renders it utterly incapable of attending to any solemn or important concern. To be anxiously careful concerning the means of subsistence is to lose all satisfaction and comfort in the things which God gives,

and to act as a mere infidel. On the other hand, to rely so much upon providence as not to use the very powers and faculties with which the Divine Being has endowed us, is to tempt God. If we labor without placing our confidence in our labor, but expect all from the blessing of God, we obey his will, co-operate with his providence, set the springs of it a-going on our behalf, and thus imitate Christ and his followers by a sedate care and an industrious confidence.

26. Behold the fowls of the air – The second reason why we should not be anxiously concerned about the future, is the example of the smaller animals, which the providence of God feeds without their own labor; though he be not their father. We never knew an earthly father take care of his fowls, and neglect his children; and shall we fear this from our heavenly Father? God forbid! That man is utterly unworthy to have God for his father, who depends less upon his goodness, wisdom, and power, than upon a crop of corn, which may be spoiled either in the field or in the barn. If our great Creator have made us capable of knowing, loving, and enjoying himself eternally, what may we not expect from him, after so great a gift?

They sow not, neither do they reap – There is a saying among the rabbins almost similar to this – "Hast thou ever seen a beast or a fowl that had a workshop? yet they are fed without labor and without anxiety. They were created for the service of man, and man was created that he might serve his Creator. Man also would have been supported without labor and anxiety, had he not corrupted his ways.

27. Which of you by taking thought can add one cubit unto his stature? – The third reason against these carking cares is the unprofitableness of human solicitude, unless God vouchsafe to bless it. What can our uneasiness do but render us still more unworthy of the Divine care? The passage from distrust to apostasy is very short and easy; and a man is not far from murmuring against Providence, who is dissatisfied with its conduct. We should depend as fully upon God for the preservation

unto you.

32 Fear not, little flock; for it is your Father's good pleasure to give you the kingdom.

MATTHEW 7: 1–5; MARK 4: 24; LUKE 6: 37–42

Matthew 7: 1–5

1 Judge not, that ye be not judged.

2 For with what judgment ye judge, ye shall be judged: and with what measure ye mete, it shall be measured to you again.

3 And why beholdest thou the mote that is in thy brother's eye, but considerest not the beam that is in thine own eye?

4 Or how wilt thou say to thy brother, Let me pull out the mote out of thine eye; and, behold, a beam is in thine own eye?

5 Thou hypocrite, first cast out the beam out of thine own eye; and then shalt thou see clearly to cast out the mote out of thy brother's eye.

MARK 4: 24

24 And he said unto them, Take heed what ye hear: with what measure ye mete, it shall be measured to you: and unto you that hear shall more be given.

Luke 6: 37–42

37 Judge not, and ye shall not be judged: condemn not, and ye shall not be condemned: forgive, and ye shall be forgiven:

38 Give, and it shall be given unto you; good measure, pressed down, and shaken together, and running over, shall men give into your bosom. For with the same measure that ye mete withal it shall be measured to you again.

39 And he spake a parable unto them, Can the blind lead the blind? shall they not both fall into the ditch?

40 The disciple is not above his master: but every one that is perfect shall be as his master.

41 And why beholdest thou the mote that is in thy brother's eye, but perceivest not the beam that is in thine own eye?

42 Either how canst thou say to thy brother, Brother, let me pull out the mote that is in thine eye, when thou thyself beholdest not the beam that is in thine own

the Apostle James, Be not many masters (James 3: 1). for he does not discourage or withdraw believers from discharging the office of teachers, but forbids them to desire the honor from motives of ambition. To judge, therefore, means here, to be influenced by curiosity in inquiring into the actions of others. This disease, in the first place, draws continually along with it the injustice of condemning any trivial fault, as if it had been a very heinous crime; and next breaks out into the insolent presumption of looking disdainfully at every action, and passing an unfavourable judgment on it, even when it might be viewed in a good light.

We now see, that the design of Christ was to guard us against indulging excessive eagerness, or peevishness, or malignity, or even curiosity, in judging our neighbors. He who judges according to the word and law of the Lord, and forms his judgment by the rule of charity, always begins with subjecting himself to examination.

MATTHEW 7: 6

Give not that which is holy

Matthew gives us here detached sentences, which ought not to be viewed as a continued discourse. The present instruction is not at all connected with what came immediately before, but is entirely separate from it. Christ reminds the Apostles, and, through them, all the teachers of the Gospel, to reserve the treasure of heavenly wisdom for the children of God alone, and not to expose it to unworthy and profane despisers of his word.

MATTHEW 7: 7–11; LUKE 11: 5–13

Matthew 7: 7. Ask, and it shall be given you

It is an exhortation to prayer: and as in this exercise of religion, which ought to be our first concern, we are so careless and sluggish, Christ presses the same thing upon us under three forms of expression. There is no superfluity of language, when he says, Ask, seek, knock: but lest the simple doctrine should be unimpressive, he perseveres in order to rouse us from our inactivity. Such is also the design of the promises that are added, Ye shall find, it shall be given to you, and it shall be opened. Nothing is better adapted to excite us to prayer than a full conviction that we shall be heard. Those who doubt can only pray in an indifferent manner; and prayer, unaccompanied by faith, is an idle and unmeaning ceremony. Accordingly, Christ, in order to excite us powerfully to this part of our duty, not only enjoins what we ought to do, but promises that our prayers shall not be fruitless.

This ought to be carefully observed. First, we learn from it, that this rule of prayer is laid down and prescribed to us, that we may be fully convinced, that God will be gracious

of his gifts as for the gifts themselves.

Cubit unto his stature? – It is evident that the phrase of adding one cubit is proverbial, denoting something minute; and is therefore applicable to the smallest possible portion of time; but, in a literal acceptation, the addition of a cubit to the stature, would be a great and extraordinary accession of height.

28. And why take ye thought for raiment? – Or, why are ye anxiously careful about raiment? The fourth reason against such inquietudes is the example of inanimate creatures: The herbs and flowers of the field have their being, nourishment, exquisite flavors, and beautiful hues from God himself. They are not only without anxious care, but also without care or thought of every kind. Your being, its excellence and usefulness, do not depend on your anxious concern: they spring as truly from the beneficence and continual superintendence of God, as the flowers of the field do; and were you brought into such a situation, as to be as utterly incapable of contributing to your own preservation and support as the lilies of the field are to theirs, your heavenly Father could augment your substance, and preserve your being, when for his glory and your own advantage.

Consider – Diligently consider this, lay it earnestly to heart, and let your confidence be unshaken in the God of infinite bounty and love.

29. Solomon in all his glory – Some suppose that as the robes of state worn by the eastern kings were usually white, as were those of the nobles among the Jews, that therefore the lily was chosen for the comparison.

30. If God so clothe the grass of the field – Christ confounds both the luxury of the rich in their superfluities, and the distrust of the poor as to the necessaries of life. Let man, who is made for God and eternity, learn from a flower of the field how low the care of Providence stoops. All our inquietudes and distrusts proceed from lack of faith: that supplies all wants. The poor are not really such, but because they are destitute of faith.

To-morrow is cast into the oven – The inhabitants of the east, to this day, make use of dry straw, withered herbs, and stubble, to heat their ovens.

If God covers with so much glory things of no farther value than to serve the meanest uses, will he not take care of his servants, who are so precious in his sight, and designed for such important services in the world?

MATTHEW 6: 31–34; LUKE 12: 29–32

Matthew 6: 31–34

31. What shall we eat? or, What shall we drink? etc. – These three inquiries engross the whole attention of those who are living without God in the world. The belly and back of a worldling are his compound god; and these he worships in the lust of the flesh, in the lust of the eye, and in the pride of life.

32. For after all these things do the Gentiles seek – The fifth reason against solicitude about the future is – that to concern ourselves about these wants with anxiety, as if there was no such thing as a providence in the world; with great affection towards earthly enjoyments, as if we expected no other; and without praying to God or consulting his will, as if we could do any thing without him: this is to imitate the worst kind of heathens, who live without hope, and without God in the world.

Seek – to seek intensely, earnestly, again and again: the true characteristic of the worldly man; his soul is never satisfied – give! give! is the ceaseless language of his earth-born heart.

Your heavenly Father knoweth, etc. – The sixth reason against this anxiety about the future is – because God, our heavenly Father, is infinite in wisdom, and knows all our wants. It is the property of a wise and tender father to provide necessaries, and not superfluities, for his children.

33. His righteousness – That holiness of heart and purity of life which God requires of those who profess to be subjects of that spiritual kingdom mentioned above.

eye? Thou hypocrite, cast out first the beam out of thine own eye, and then shalt thou see clearly to pull out the mote that is in thy brother's eye.

MATTHEW 7: 6

6 Give not that which is holy unto the dogs, neither cast ye your pearls before swine, lest they trample them under their feet, and turn again and rend you.

MATTHEW 7: 7–11; LUKE 11: 5–13

Matthew 7: 7–11

7 Ask, and it shall be given you; seek, and ye shall find; knock, and it shall be opened unto you:

8 For every one that asketh receiveth; and he that seeketh findeth; and to him that knocketh it shall be opened.

9 Or what man is there of you, whom if his son ask bread, will he give him a stone?

10 Or if he ask a fish, will he give him a serpent?

11 If ye then, being evil, know how to give good gifts unto your children, how much more shall your Father which is in heaven give good things to them that ask him?

Luke 11: 5–13

5 And he said unto them, Which of you shall have a friend, and shall go unto him at midnight, and say unto him, Friend, lend me three loaves;

6 For a friend of mine in his journey is come to me, and I have nothing to set before him?

7 And he from within shall answer and say, Trouble me not: the door is now shut, and my children are with me in bed; I cannot rise and give thee.

8 I say unto you, Though he will not rise and give him, because he is his friend, yet because of his importunity he will rise and give him as many as he needeth.

9 And I say unto you, Ask, and it shall be given you; seek, and ye shall find; knock, and it shall be opened unto you.

10 For every one that asketh receiveth; and he that seeketh findeth; and to him that knocketh it shall be opened.

11 If a son shall ask bread of any of you that is a father, will he give him a

to us, and will listen to our requests. Again, whenever we engage in prayer, or whenever we feel that our ardor in prayer is not sufficiently strong, we ought to remember the gentle invitation, by which Christ assures us of God's fatherly kindness. Each of us, trusting to the grace of Christ, will thus attain confidence in prayer, and will venture freely to call upon God "through Jesus Christ our Lord, in whom (as Paul says) we have boldness and access with confidence by the faith of him" (Ephesians 3: 11–12).

But, as we are too prone to distrust, Christ, in order to correct this fault also, repeats the promise in a variety of words. He uses the metaphor **seek** because we think, that those things which our wants and necessities require are far distant from us – and **knock**, because our carnal senses imagine, that those things which are not immediately at hand are shut up.

8. For every one that asketh receiveth

Some think that this is a proverbial saying taken from common life: but I am more inclined to a different view. Christ presents the grace of his Father to those who pray. He tells us, that God is of himself prepared to listen to us, provided we pray to him, and that his riches are at our command, provided we ask them. These words imply, that those who are destitute of what is necessary, and yet do not resort to this remedy for their poverty, are justly punished for their slothfulness. It is certain, indeed, that often, when believers are asleep, God keeps watch over their salvation, and anticipates their wishes.

MATTHEW 7: 12–14; LUKE 6: 31

Matthew 7: 12. For this is the law and the prophets

Our Lord does not intend to say, that this is the only point of doctrine laid down in the law and the prophets, but that all the precepts which they contain about charity, and all the laws and exhortations found in them about maintaining justice, have a reference to this object. The meaning is, that the second table of the law is fulfilled, when every man conducts himself in the same manner towards others, as he wishes them to conduct themselves towards him.

LUKE 13: 23–24

Although Matthew relates this answer, as if it were immediately connected with other sentences taken out of our Lord's sermons, yet I rather think that the occasion of its being spoken arose out of the present question. The reason why the question was put appears to have been, that Christ, who declared himself to be the author of life, could with difficulty collect a small number of disciples. It might appear, that a small band of men was to be saved, and that

The seventh reason against these worldly cares and fears is – because the business of our salvation ought to engross us entirely: hither all our desires, cares, and inquiries ought to tend. Grace is the way to glory – holiness the way to happiness.

34. Take therefore no thought – That is, Be not therefore anxiously careful.

How much good is omitted, how many evils caused, how many duties neglected, how many innocent persons deserted, how many good works destroyed, how many truths suppressed, and how many acts of injustice authorized by those timorous forecasts of what may happen; and those faithless apprehensions concerning the future!

Sufficient unto the day is the evil thereof – Sufficient for each day is its own calamity.

MATTHEW 7: 1–5; MARK 4: 24; LUKE 6: 37–42

Matthew 7: 1–5

1. Judge not, that ye be not judged – These exhortations are pointed against rash, harsh, and uncharitable judgments, the thinking evil, where no evil seems, and speaking of it accordingly.

2. For with what judgment – He who is severe on others will naturally excite their severity against himself. The censures and calumnies which we have suffered are probably the just reward of those which we have dealt out to others.

3. And why beholdest thou the mote – It often happens that the faults which we consider as of the first enormity in others are, to our own iniquities, as a chip is, when compared to a large beam. When we shall have as much zeal to correct ourselves, as we have inclination to reprove and correct others, we shall know our own defects better than now we know those of our neighbor.

There is a caution very similar to this of our Lord given by a heathen: "When you can so readily overlook your own wickedness, why

are you more clear-sighted than the eagle or serpent of Epidaurus, in spying out the failings of your friends?"

4. Or how wilt thou say – That man is utterly unfit to show the way of life to others who is himself walking in the way of death.

5. Thou hypocrite – A hypocrite, who professes to be what he is not, (viz. a true Christian), is obliged, for the support of the character he has assumed, to imitate all the dispositions and actions of a Christian; consequently he must reprove sin, and endeavor to show an uncommon affection for the glory of God. Our Lord unmasks this vile pretender to saintship, and shows him that his hidden hypocrisy, covered with the garb of external sanctity, is more abominable in the sight of God than the openly professed and practiced iniquity of the profligate.

In later times, the Jews made a very bad use of this saying: "I wonder," said Rabbi Zarphon, "whether there be any in this age that will suffer reproof? If one say to another, Cast out the mote out of thine eye, he is immediately ready to answer, Cast out the beam that is in thine own eye."

MATTHEW 7: 6

6. Give not that which is holy – the holy or sacred thing; i.e. any thing, especially, of the sacrificial kind, which had been consecrated to God.

As a general meaning of this passage, we may just say: "The sacrament of the Lord's supper, and other holy ordinances which are only instituted for the genuine followers of Christ, are not to be dispensed to those who are continually returning like the snarling ill-natured dog to their easily predominant sins of rash judgment, barking at and tearing the characters of others by evil speaking, back biting and slandering; nor to him who, like the swine, is frequently returning to wallow in the mud of sensual gratifications and impurities."

stone? or if he ask a fish, will he for a fish give him a serpent?

12 Or if he shall ask an egg, will he offer him a scorpion?

13 If ye then, being evil, know how to give good gifts unto your children: how much more shall your heavenly Father give the Holy Spirit to them that ask him?

MATTHEW 7: 12–14; LUKE 6: 31

Matthew 7: 12–14

12 Therefore all things whatsoever ye would that men should do to you, do ye even so to them: for this is the law and the prophets.

13 Enter ye in at the strait gate: for wide is the gate, and broad is the way, that leadeth to destruction, and many there be which go in thereat:

14 Because strait is the gate, and narrow is the way, which leadeth unto life, and few there be that find it.

Luke 6: 31

31 And as ye would that men should do to you, do ye also to them likewise.

LUKE 13: 23–24

23 Then said one unto him, Lord, are there few that be saved? And he said unto them,

24 Strive to enter in at the strait gate: for many, I say unto you, will seek to enter in, and shall not be able.

LUKE 13: 25–30

25 When once the master of the house is risen up, and hath shut to the door, and ye begin to stand without, and to knock at the door, saying, Lord, Lord, open unto us; and he shall answer and say unto you, I know you not whence ye are:

26 Then shall ye begin to say, We have eaten and drunk in thy presence, and thou hast taught in our streets.

27 But he shall say, I tell you, I know you not whence ye are; depart from me, all ye workers of iniquity.

28 There shall be weeping and gnashing of teeth, when ye shall see Abraham, and Isaac, and Jacob, and all the prophets, in the kingdom of God, and you yourselves thrust out.

the whole church was going to ruin: for the whole of that nation, among whom the doctrine of Christ made no great progress, and by whom it was universally rejected, had been adopted by God as the heir of life.

LUKE 13: 25–30

25. And when the master of the house shall have arisen

Though these words were spoken on a different and later occasion, I have chosen to pay more regard to the doctrine than to the time: for it is no slight assistance to the understanding to read, in immediate connection, those passages which are closely related in meaning. As Christ had declared that to many, who shall desire to enter into heaven, the door will not be open, he now asserts, that they gain nothing by occupying a place in the church because God will at length arise in judgment, and shut out from his kingdom those who now lay claim to a place in his family. He employs the comparison of the **master of a house**, who, having learned that some wicked and dissolute people among his own domestics steal out unperceived during the night, and expose the house to thieves, **rises and shuts the door** and does not allow those night-prowlers to enter, who have been wandering through the public streets at unseasonable hours. By these words he warns us, that we must avail ourselves of the opportunity, while it is offered: for so long as the Lord invites us to himself, the **door** is, as it were, open, that we may enter into the kingdom of heaven: but the greater part do not deign to move a step. Christ therefore threatens, that the door will at length be shut, and that those who are looking for companions are in danger of being refused admission.

MATTHEW 7: 15–20; LUKE 6: 43–45

Matthew 7: 15. But beware of false prophets

These words were intended to teach, that the Church would be exposed to various impositions, and that consequently many would be in danger of falling from the faith, if they were not carefully on their guard. We know what a strong propensity men have to falsehood, so that they not only have a natural desire to be deceived, but each individual appears to be ingenious in deceiving himself. Satan, who is a wonderful contriver of delusions, is constantly laying snares to entrap ignorant and heedless people. It was a general expectation among the Jews that, under the reign of Christ, their condition would be delightful, and free from all contest or uneasiness. He therefore warns his disciples that, if they desire to persevere, they must prepare themselves to avoid the snares of Satan. It is the will of the Lord (as has been already said), that his Church shall be engaged

MATTHEW 7: 7–11; LUKE 11: 5–13

Matthew 7: 7–11

7. Ask – seek – knock – These three words include the ideas of want, loss, and earnestness.

Ask: turn, beggar at, the door of mercy; thou art destitute of all spiritual good, and it is God alone who can give it to thee; and thou hast no claim but what his mercy has given thee on itself.

Seek: Thou hast lost thy God, thy paradise, thy soul. – Look about thee – leave no stone unturned there is no peace, no final salvation for thee till thou get thy soul restored to the favor and image of God.

Knock: Be in earnest – be importunate: Eternity is at hand! and, if thou die in thy sins, where God is thou shalt never come.

Ask with confidence and humility.

Seek with care and application.

Knock with earnestness and perseverance.

8. For every one that asketh receiveth – Prayer is always heard after one manner or other. No soul can pray in vain that prays as directed above. The truth and faithfulness of the Lord Jesus are pledged for its success. – Ye SHALL receive – ye SHALL find – it SHALL be opened. These words are as strongly binding on the side of God, as thou shalt do no murder is on the side of man. Bring Christ's word, and Christ's sacrifice with thee, and not one of Heaven's blessings can be denied thee.

9. Or what man is there – whom if his son – Men are exhorted to come unto God, with the persuasion that he is a most gracious and compassionate Parent, who possesses all heavenly and earthly good, knows what is necessary for each of his creatures, and is infinitely ready to communicate that which they need most.

Will he give him a stone? – Will he not readily give him bread if he have it?

MATTHEW 7: 12–14; LUKE 6: 31

Matthew 7: 12–14

11. If ye, then, being evil – who are radically and diabolically depraved, yet feel yourselves led, by natural affection, to give those things to your children which are necessary to support their lives, how much more will your Father who is in heaven, whose nature is infinite goodness, mercy, and grace, give good things – his grace and Spirit (the Holy Ghost, Luke 11: 13), to them who ask him? What a picture is here given of the goodness of God! Reader, ask thy soul, could this heavenly Father reprobate to unconditional eternal damnation any creature he has made? He who can believe that he has, may believe any thing: but still GOD IS LOVE.

12. Therefore all things whatsoever ye would that men – This is a most sublime precept, and highly worthy of the grandeur and beneficence of the just God who gave it. The general meaning of it is this: "Guided by justice and mercy, do unto all men as you would have them to do to you, were your circumstances and theirs reversed." Yet this saying may be misunderstood. "If the prisoner should ask the judge, 'whether he would be content to be hanged, were he in his case,' he would answer, 'No.' Then, says the prisoner, do as you would be done to. – Neither of them must do as private men; but the judge must do by him as they have publicly agreed: that is, both judge and prisoner have consented to a law, that if either of them steal he shall be hanged." – Selden. None but he whose heart is filled with love to God and all mankind can keep this precept, either in its spirit or letter. Self-love will feel itself sadly cramped when brought within the limits of this precept; but God hath spoken it: it is the spirit and design of the law and the prophets; the sum of all that is laid down in the Sacred Writings, relative to men's conduct toward each other. It seems as if God had written it upon the hearts of all men, for sayings of this kind may be found among all nations, Jewish, Christian, and Heathen.

13. Enter ye in at the strait gate – Our Savior seems to allude here to the distinction between the public and private ways mentioned by the Jewish lawyers. The public roads were allowed to be sixteen cubits broad, the private ways only four. The words in the original are very

29 And they shall come from the east, and from the west, and from the north, and from the south, and shall sit down in the kingdom of God.

30 And, behold, there are last which shall be first, and there are first which shall be last.

MATTHEW 7: 15–20; LUKE 6: 43–45

Matthew 7: 15–20

15 Beware of false prophets, which come to you in sheep's clothing, but inwardly they are ravening wolves.

16 Ye shall know them by their fruits. Do men gather grapes of thorns, or figs of thistles?

17 Even so every good tree bringeth forth good fruit; but a corrupt tree bringeth forth evil fruit.

18 A good tree cannot bring forth evil fruit, neither can a corrupt tree bring forth good fruit.

19 Every tree that bringeth not forth good fruit is hewn down, and cast into the fire.

20 Wherefore by their fruits ye shall know them.

Luke 6: 43–45

43 For a good tree bringeth not forth corrupt fruit; neither doth a corrupt tree bring forth good fruit.

44 For every tree is known by his own fruit. For of thorns men do not gather figs, nor of a bramble bush gather they grapes.

45 A good man out of the good treasure of his heart bringeth forth that which is good; and an evil man out of the evil treasure of his heart bringeth forth that which is evil: for of the abundance of the heart his mouth speaketh.

MATTHEW 7: 21–23; LUKE 6: 46

Matthew 7: 21–23

21 Not every one that saith unto me, Lord, Lord, shall enter into the kingdom of heaven; but he that doeth the will of my Father which is in heaven.

22 Many will say to me in that day, Lord, Lord, have we not prophesied in thy name? and in thy name have cast out devils? and in thy name done many wonderful works?

in uninterrupted war in this world. That we may continue to be his disciples to the end, it is not enough that we are merely submissive, and allow ourselves to be governed by his Word. Our faith, which is constantly attacked by Satan, must be prepared to resist.

MATTHEW 7: 21–23; LUKE 6: 46

Matthew 7: 21. Not every one that saith to me, Lord, Lord

Christ extends his discourse farther: for he speaks not only of false prophets, who rush upon the flock to tear and devour, but of hirelings, who insinuate themselves, under fair appearances, as pastors, though they have no feeling of piety. This doctrine embraces all hypocrites, whatever may be their rank or station, but at present he refers particularly to pretended teachers, who seem to excel others. He not only directs his discourse to them, to rouse them from the indifference, in which they lie asleep like drunk people, but also warns believers, not to estimate such masks beyond their proper value. In a word, he declares that, so soon as the doctrine of the Gospel shall have begun to bear fruit by obtaining many disciples, there will not only be very many of the common people who falsely and hypocritically submit to it, but even in the rank of pastors there will be the same treachery, so that they will deny by their actions and life what they profess with the mouth. Whoever then desires to be reckoned among the disciples, must labor to devote himself, sincerely and honestly, to the exercises of a new life.

MATTHEW 7: 24–29; LUKE 6: 47–49

Matthew 7: 24. Every one, therefore, who heareth

As it is often difficult to distinguish the true professors of the Gospel from the false, Christ shows, by a beautiful comparison, where the main difference lies. He represents two houses, one of which was built without a foundation, while the other was well-founded. Both have the same external appearance: but, when the wind and storms blow, and the floods dash against them, the former will immediately fall, while the latter will be sustained by its strength against every assault. Christ therefore compares a vain and empty profession of the Gospel to a beautiful, but not solid, building, which, however elevated, is exposed every moment to downfall, because it wants a foundation. Accordingly, Paul enjoins us to be well and thoroughly founded on Christ, and to have deep roots (Colossians 2: 7), "that we may not be tossed and driven about by every wind of doctrine" (Ephesians 4: 14), that we may not give way at every attack. The general meaning of the passage is, that true piety is not fully distinguished from its counterfeit, till it comes to the emphatic: Enter in (to the kingdom of heaven) through THIS strait gate, i.e. of doing to every one as you would he should do unto you; for this alone seems to be the strait gate which our Lord alludes to.

For wide is the gate – And very broad, a spacious roomy place, that leadeth forward, into THAT destruction, meaning eternal misery; intimating, that it is much more congenial, to the revengeful, covetous heart of fallen man, to take every advantage of another, and to enrich himself at his expense, rather than to walk according to the rule laid down before, by our blessed Lord, and that acting contrary to it is the way to everlasting misery. With those who say it means repentance, and forsaking sin, I can have no controversy. That is certainly a gate, and a strait one too, through which every sinner must turn to God, in order to find salvation. But the doing to every one as we would they should do unto us, is a gate extremely strait, and very difficult, to every unregenerate mind.

14. Because strait is the gate – How strange is it that men should be unwilling to give up their worldly interests to secure their everlasting salvation! And yet no interest need be abandoned, but that which is produced by injustice and unkindness. Reason, as well as God, says, such people should be excluded from a place of blessedness. He who shows no mercy (and much more he who shows no justice) shall have judgment without mercy. James 2: 13.

Few there be that find it – The strait gate, signifies literally what we call a wicket, i.e. a little door in a large gate. Gate, among the Jews, signifies, metaphorically, the entrance, introduction, or means of acquiring any thing. So they talk of the gate of repentance, the gate of prayers, and the gate of tears. When God, say they, shut the gate of paradise against Adam, He opened to him the gate of repentance. The way to the kingdom of God is made sufficiently manifest – the completest assistance is promised in the way, and the greatest encouragement to persevere to the end is held out in the everlasting Gospel. But men are so wedded to their own passions,

and so determined to follow the imaginations of their own hearts, that still it may be said: There are few who find the way to heaven; fewer yet who abide any time in it; fewer still who walk in it; and fewest of all who persevere unto the end. Nothing renders this way either narrow or difficult to any person, but sin. Let all the world leave their sins, and all the world may walk abreast in this good way.

LUKE 13: 23–24

23. Are there few that be saved? – A question either of impertinence or curiosity, the answer to which can profit no man. The grand question is, Can I be saved? Yes. How? Strive earnestly to enter in through the strait gate – agonize – exert every power of body and soul – let your salvation be the grand business of your whole life.

24. Many – will seek – They seek – wish and desire; but they do not strive; therefore, because they will not agonize – will not be in earnest, they shall not get in.

LUKE 13: 25–30

29. They shall come – That is, the Gentiles, in every part of the world, shall receive the Gospel of the grace of God, when the Jews shall have rejected it.

MATTHEW 7: 15–20; LUKE 6: 43–45

Matthew 7: 15–20

15. Beware of false prophets – By false prophets we are to understand teachers of erroneous doctrines, who come professing a commission from God, but whose aim is not to bring the heavenly treasure to the people, but rather to rob them of their earthly good. Teachers who preach for hire, having no motive to enter into the ministry but to get a living, as it is ominously called by some, however they may bear the garb and appearance of the innocent useful sheep, the true pastors commissioned by the Lord Jesus, or to whatever name, class or party they may

23 And then will I profess unto them, I never knew you: depart from me, ye that work iniquity.

Luke 6: 46

46 And why call ye me, Lord, Lord, and do not the things which I say?

MATTHEW 7: 24–29; LUKE 6: 47–49

Matthew 7: 24–29

24 Therefore whosoever heareth these sayings of mine, and doeth them, I will liken him unto a wise man, which built his house upon a rock:

25 And the rain descended, and the floods came, and the winds blew, and beat upon that house; and it fell not: for it was founded upon a rock.

26 And every one that heareth these sayings of mine, and doeth them not, shall be likened unto a foolish man, which built his house upon the sand:

27 And the rain descended, and the floods came, and the winds blew, and beat upon that house; and it fell: and great was the fall of it.

28 And it came to pass, when Jesus had ended these sayings, the people were astonished at his doctrine:

29 For he taught them as one having authority, and not as the scribes.

Luke 6: 47–49

47 Whosoever cometh to me, and heareth my sayings, and doeth them, I will shew you to whom he is like:

48 He is like a man which built an house, and digged deep, and laid the foundation on a rock: and when the flood arose, the stream beat vehemently upon that house, and could not shake it: for it was founded upon a rock.

49 But he that heareth, and doeth not, is like a man that without a foundation built an house upon the earth; against which the stream did beat vehemently, and immediately it fell; and the ruin of that house was great.

MATTHEW 8: 1–4; MARK 1: 40–45; LUKE 5: 12–16

Matthew 8: 1–4

1 When he was come down from the mountain, great multitudes followed him.

trial. For the temptations, by which we are tried, are like billows and storms, which easily overwhelm unsteady minds, whose lightness is not perceived during the season of prosperity.

Who heareth these sayings

He means, that the Gospel, if it be not deeply rooted in the mind, is like a wall, which has been raised to a great height, but does not rest on any foundation. "That faith (he says) is true, which has its roots deep in the heart, and rests on an earnest and steady affection as its foundation, that it may not give way to temptations." For such is the vanity of the human mind, that all build upon the sand, who do not dig so deep as to deny themselves.

MATTHEW 8: 1–4; MARK 1: 40–45; LUKE 5: 12–16

Matthew 8: 1. And when he had come down from the mountain

Matthew now returns to the course of the history. He had formerly said, that Christ went up into a mountain (verse 1), then he threw, as it were, into one heap, many leading points of the doctrine of Christ; and now he adds that, about the time when he preached on the mountain, he healed a certain leper. The same event is related by Mark and Luke, though they do not mention the time. It was a striking display of the divine power of Christ, that, by his word alone and a touch of his hand, he suddenly cleansed the man's leprosy. It is manifest that there was nothing human about this miracle.

2. Approaching, worshipped

What is the meaning of the verb *proskunein*, which is rendered in the Latin version, *adorare*, to adore or worship, may be easily learned from this passage. For the exposition of it we may rely on the other two Evangelists, of whom Mark says, that he **fell on his knees**, and Luke, that **he fell down on his face**.

The outward gesture of kneeling was exhibited by the leper as a token of reverence. Now we know, that such marks of respect were in general use among the Jews, as the people of the East are more addicted to that kind of ceremonies. Many people accordingly think, that the leper did not intend to render to Christ divine worship, but gave him a respectful salutation as a distinguished prophet of God.

I enter into no dispute as to the feelings which moved the leper to pay reverence to Christ. But I look at what he attributed to him, that he was able to cleanse him, if he were willing. By these words he declared, that he acknowledged a divine power in Christ: and when Christ replies, **I am willing**, he shows that he claimed more for himself than

belong, are, in the sight of the heart-searching God, no other than ravenous wolves, whose design is to feed themselves with the fat, and clothe themselves with the fleece, and thus ruin, instead of save, the flock.

16. Ye shall know them by their fruits – Fruits, in the Scripture and Jewish phraseology, are taken for works of any kind. "A man's works," says one, "are the tongue of his heart, and tell honestly whether he is inwardly corrupt or pure." By these works you may distinguish these ravenous wolves from true pastors. The judgment formed of a man by his general conduct is a safe one: if the judgment be not favorable to the person, that is his fault, as you have your opinion of him from his works, i.e. the confession of his own heart.

17. So every good tree – As the thorn can only produce thorns, not grapes; and the thistle, not figs, but prickles; so an unregenerate heart will produce fruits of degeneracy. As we perfectly know that a good tree will not produce bad fruit, and the bad tree will not, cannot produce good fruit, so we know that the profession of godliness, while the life is ungodly, is imposture, hypocrisy, and deceit. A man cannot be a saint and a sinner at the same time. Let us remember, that as the good tree means a good heart, and the good fruit, a holy life, and that every heart is naturally vicious; so there is none but God who can pluck up the vicious tree, create a good heart, plant, cultivate, water, and make it continually fruitful in righteousness and true holiness.

18. A good tree cannot bring forth evil fruit – Love to God and man is the root of the good tree; and from this principle all its fruit is found. To teach, as some have done, that a state of salvation may be consistent with the greatest crimes, (such as murder and adultery in David), or that the righteous necessarily sin in all their best works, is really to make the good tree bring forth bad fruit, and to give the lie to the Author of eternal truth.

19. Every tree that bringeth not forth good fruit – What a terrible sentence is this against Christless pastors, and Christless hearers!

Every tree that produceth not good fruit, ἄἐἐἴὄᾶὄᾶέ, is to be now cut down; the act of excision is now taking place: the curse of the Lord is even now on the head and the heart of every false teacher, and impenitent hearer.

20. Wherefore by their fruits, etc. – This truth is often repeated, because our eternal interests depend so much upon it. Not to have good fruit is to have evil: there can be no innocent sterility in the invisible tree of the heart. He that brings forth no fruit, and he that brings forth bad fruit, are both only fit for the fire.

MATTHEW 7: 21–23; LUKE 6: 46

21. Not every one – The sense of this verse seems to be this: No person, by merely acknowledging my authority, believing in the Divinity of my nature, professing faith in the perfection of my righteousness, and infinite merit of my atonement, shall enter into the kingdom of heaven – shall have any part with God in glory; but he who doeth the will of my Father – he who gets the bad tree rooted up, the good tree planted, and continues to bring forth fruit to the glory and praise of God. There is a good saying among the rabbins on this subject. "A man should be as vigorous as a panther, as swift as an eagle, as fleet as a stag, and as strong as a lion, to do the will of his Creator."

22. Many will say to me in that day – in that very day, viz. the day of judgment – have we not prophesied, taught, publicly preached, in thy name; acknowledging thee to be the only Savior, and proclaiming thee as such to others; cast out demons, impure spirits, who had taken possession of the bodies of men; done many miracles, being assisted by supernatural agency to invert even the course of nature, and thus prove the truth of the doctrine we preached?

23. Will I profess – I will fully and plainly tell them, I never knew you – I never approved of you; for so the word is used in many places, both in the Old and New Testaments. You

2 And, behold, there came a leper and worshipped him, saying, Lord, if thou wilt, thou canst make me clean.

3 And Jesus put forth his hand, and touched him, saying, I will; be thou clean. And immediately his leprosy was cleansed.

4 And Jesus saith unto him, See thou tell no man; but go thy way, shew thyself to the priest, and offer the gift that Moses commanded, for a testimony unto them.

Mark 1: 40–45

40 And there came a leper to him, beseeching him, and kneeling down to him, and saying unto him, If thou wilt, thou canst make me clean.

41 And Jesus, moved with compassion, put forth his hand, and touched him, and saith unto him, I will; be thou clean.

42 And as soon as he had spoken, immediately the leprosy departed from him, and he was cleansed.

43 And he straitly charged him, and forthwith sent him away;

44 And saith unto him, See thou say nothing to any man: but go thy way, shew thyself to the priest, and offer for thy cleansing those things which Moses commanded, for a testimony unto them.

45 But he went out, and began to publish it much, and to blaze abroad the matter, insomuch that Jesus could no more openly enter into the city, but was without in desert places: and they came to him from every quarter.

Luke 5: 12–16

12 And it came to pass, when he was in a certain city, behold a man full of leprosy: who seeing Jesus fell on his face, and besought him, saying, Lord, if thou wilt, thou canst make me clean.

13 And he put forth his hand, and touched him, saying, I will: be thou clean. And immediately the leprosy departed from him.

14 And he charged him to tell no man: but go, and shew thyself to the priest, and offer for thy cleansing, according as Moses commanded, for a testimony unto them.

15 But so much the more went there a fame abroad of him: and great multitudes came together to hear, and to be healed by him of their infirmities.

belongs to man. He who, by the mere expression of his will, restores health to men, must possess supreme authority.

3. Having stretched out his hand, he touched

Under the Law, the touch of a leper was infectious; but as Christ possesses such purity as to repel all filth and defilement, he does not, by touching, either pollute himself with leprosy, or become a transgressor of the law. When he took upon him our flesh, he did not only deign to touch as with his hand, but was united to one and the same body with ourselves, that we might be flesh of his flesh (Genesis 2: 23). Nor did he only stretch out his arm to us, but descended from heaven even to hell, and yet contracted no stain from it, but, retaining his innocence, took away all our impurities, and sprinkled us with his holiness. By his word alone he might have healed the leper; but he applied, at the same time, the touch of his hand, to express the feeling of compassion. Nor ought this to excite our wonder, since he chose to take upon him our flesh, that he might cleanse us from our sins. The stretching out of his hand was therefore an expression and token of infinite grace and goodness. What we indolently read, and coldly pass by, cannot be duly weighed without great astonishment. The Son of God was so far from disdaining to talk to a leper, that he even stretched out his hand to touch that uncleanness.

MATTHEW 8: 5–13; LUKE 7: 1–10

Matthew 8: 5. And when Jesus had entered

Those who think that Matthew and Luke give different narratives, are led into a mistake by a mere trifle. The only difference in the words is, that Matthew says that **the centurion came to him,** while Luke says that he sent some of the Jews to plead in his name. But there is no impropriety in Matthew saying, that the centurion did what was done in his name and at his request. There is such a perfect agreement between the two Evangelists in all the circumstances, that it is absurd to make two miracles instead of one.

The band of soldiers, which the centurion had under his command, was stationed, I have no doubt, in the town of Capernaum, in the same manner as garrisons were usually appointed for the protection of the towns. Though he perceived the morals of the people to be very vicious and depraved, (for we know that Capernaum, being on the seacoast, must have been more dissolute than other towns), yet this did not prevent him from condemning the superstitions of his country, and acquiring a taste for true and sincere piety. He had not built a synagogue for the Jews without exposing himself to some hatred and to some risk: and the only reason why **he loved that nation** was, that he had embraced the worship of one God. Before Christ healed his servant, he had been healed by the Lord.

held the truth in unrighteousness, while you preached my pure and holy doctrine; and for the sake of my own truth, and through my love to the souls of men, I blessed your preaching; but yourselves I could never esteem, because you were destitute of the spirit of my Gospel, unholy in your hearts, and unrighteous in your conduct. Alas! alas! how many preachers are there who appear prophets in their pulpits; how many writers, and other evangelical workmen, the miracles of whose labor, learning, and doctrine, we admire, who are nothing, and worse than nothing, before God, because they perform not his will, but their own? What an awful consideration, that a man of eminent gifts, whose talents are a source of public utility, should be only as a way-mark or finger-post in the way to eternal bliss, pointing out the road to others, without walking in it himself!

Depart from me – What a terrible word! What a dreadful separation! Depart from ME! from the very Jesus whom you have proclaimed in union with whom alone eternal life is to be found. For, united to Christ, all is heaven; separated from him, all is hell.

MATTHEW 7: 24–29; LUKE 6: 47–49

Matthew 7: 24–29

24. Therefore whosoever heareth these sayings of mine – That is, the excellent doctrines laid down before in this and the two preceding chapters.

I will liken him unto a wise man – To a prudent man – to a prudent man, a man of sense and understanding, who, foreseeing the evil hideth himself, who proposes to himself the best end, and makes use of the proper means to accomplish it. True wisdom consists in getting the building of our salvation completed: to this end we must build on the Rock, CHRIST JESUS, and make the building firm, by keeping close to the maxims of his Gospel, and having our tempers and lives conformed to its word and spirit; and when, in order to this, we lean on nothing but the grace of Christ, we then build upon a solid rock.

25. And the rain descended – floods came – winds blew – In Judea, and in all countries in the neighborhood of the tropics, the rain sometimes falls in great torrents, producing rivers, which sweep away the soil from the rocky hills; and the houses, which are built of brick only dried in the sun, of which there are whole villages in the east, literally melt away before those rains, and the land-floods occasioned by them. There are three general kinds of trials to which the followers of God are exposed; and to which, some think, our Lord alludes here: First, those of temporal afflictions, coming in the course of Divine Providence: these may be likened to the torrents of rain. Secondly, those which come from the passions of men, and which may be likened to the impetuous rivers. Thirdly, those which come from Satan and his angels, and which, like tempestuous whirlwinds, threaten to carry every thing before them. He alone, whose soul is built on the Rock of ages, stands all these shocks; and not only stands in, but profits by them.

26. And every one that heareth – and doeth them not – Was there ever a stricter system of morality delivered by God to man, than in this sermon? He who reads or hears it, and does not look to God to conform his soul and life to it, and notwithstanding is hoping to enter into the kingdom of heaven, is like the fool who built his house on the sand. When the rain, the rivers, and the winds come, his building must fall, and his soul be crushed into the nethermost pit by its ruins. Talking about Christ, his righteousness, merits, and atonement, while the person is not conformed to his word and spirit, is no other than solemn self-deception.

Let it be observed, that it is not the man who hears or believes these sayings of Christ, whose building shall stand, when the earth and its works are burnt up; but the man who DOES them.

Many suppose that the law of Moses is abolished, merely because it is too strict, and impossible to be observed; and that the Gospel was brought in to liberate us from its obliga-

16 And he withdrew himself into the wilderness, and prayed.

MATTHEW 8: 5–13; LUKE 7: 1–10

Matthew 8: 5–13

5 And when Jesus was entered into Capernaum, there came unto him a centurion, beseeching him,

6 And saying, Lord, my servant lieth at home sick of the palsy, grievously tormented.

7 And Jesus saith unto him, I will come and heal him.

8 The centurion answered and said, Lord, I am not worthy that thou shouldest come under my roof: but speak the word only, and my servant shall be healed.

9 For I am a man under authority, having soldiers under me: and I say to this man, Go, and he goeth; and to another, Come, and he cometh; and to my servant, Do this, and he doeth it.

10 When Jesus heard it, he marveled, and said to them that followed, Verily I say unto you, I have not found so great faith, no, not in Israel.

11 And I say unto you, That many shall come from the east and west, and shall sit down with Abraham, and Isaac, and Jacob, in the kingdom of heaven.

12 But the children of the kingdom shall be cast out into outer darkness: there shall be weeping and gnashing of teeth.

13 And Jesus said unto the centurion, Go thy way; and as thou hast believed, so be it done unto thee. And his servant was healed in the selfsame hour.

Luke 7: 1–10

1 Now when he had ended all his sayings in the audience of the people, he entered into Capernaum.

2 And a certain centurion's servant, who was dear unto him, was sick, and ready to die.

3 And when he heard of Jesus, he sent unto him the elders of the Jews, beseeching him that he would come and heal his servant.

4 And when they came to Jesus, they besought him instantly, saying, That he was worthy for whom he should do this:

This was itself a miracle. One who belonged to the military profession, and who had crossed the sea with a band of soldiers, for the purpose of accustoming the Jews to endure the yoke of Roman tyranny, submits willingly, and yields obedience to the God of Israel. Luke says that this **servant was very dear to him;** and thus anticipates a doubt which might have arisen in the mind of the reader: for we know that slaves were not held in such estimation, as to make their masters so solicitous about their life, unless by extraordinary industry, or fidelity, or some other virtue, they had secured their favor. By this statement Luke means, that this was not a low or ordinary slave, but a faithful servant, distinguished by many excellencies, and very highly esteemed by his master; and that this was the reason why he was so anxious about his life, and recommended him so earnestly. From both Evangelists it is evident that it was a sudden palsy, which, from the first attack, took away all hope of life: for slow palsies are not attended by severe pain. Matthew says, that he was **grievously tormented**, and Luke, that he was **near death**. Both descriptions – pain or agony, and extreme danger – serve to enhance the glory of the miracle: and for this reason I am the more unwilling to hazard any absolute assertion as to the nature of the disease.

8. Lord, I do not deserve that thou shouldest come under my roof

Matthew's narrative is more concise, and represents the man as saying this; while Luke explains more fully, that this was a message sent by his friends: but the meaning of both is the same. There are two leading points in this discourse. The centurion, sparing Christ by way of honoring him, requests that Christ will not trouble himself, because he reckons himself unworthy to receive a visit from him. The next point is, that he ascribes to Christ such power as to believe, that by the mere expression of his will, and by a word, his servant may recover and live. There was astonishing humility in exalting so highly above himself a man who belonged to a conquered and enslaved nation. It is possible, too, that he had become accustomed to the haughty pretensions of the Jews, and, being a modest man, did not take it ill to be reckoned a heathen, and therefore feared that he would dishonor a Prophet of God, if he pressed him to enter the house of a polluted Gentile. However that may be, it is certain that he speaks sincerely, and entertains such reverence for Christ, that he does not venture to invite him to his house, nay, as is afterwards stated by Luke, he reckoned himself unworthy to converse with him.

tions; but let all such know, that in the whole of the old covenant nothing can be found so exceedingly strict and holy as this sermon, which Christ lays down as the rule by which we are to walk. "Then, the fulfilling of these precepts is the purchase of glory." No, it is the WAY only to that glory which has already been purchased by the blood of the Lamb. To him that believes, all things are possible.

27. And the rain descended, and the floods came, etc. – A fine illustration of this may be seen in the case of the fishermen in Bengal, who, in the dry season, build their huts on the beds of sand from which the rivers had retired: but when the rain sets in suddenly; as it often does, accompanied with violent northwest winds, and the waters pour down in torrents from the mountains; in one night, multitudes of these buildings are swept away, and the place where they stood is on the next morning indiscoverable.

28. The people were astonished – the multitudes; for vast crowds attended the ministry of this most popular and faithful of all preachers. They were astonished at his doctrine. They heard the law defined in such a manner as they had never thought of before; and this sacred system of morality urged home on their consciences with such clearness and authority as they had never felt under the teaching of their scribes and Pharisees. Here is the grand difference between the teaching of scribes and Pharisees, the self-created or men-made ministers, and those whom GOD sends. The first may preach what is called very good and very sound doctrine; but it comes with no authority from God to the souls of the people: therefore, the unholy is unholy still; because preaching can only be effectual to the conversion of men, when the unction of the Holy Spirit is in it; and as these are not sent by the Lord, therefore they shall not profit the people at all. Jeremiah 23: 32.

29. Having authority – They felt a commanding power and authority in his word, i.e. his doctrine. His statements were perspicuous; his exhortations persuasive; his doctrine sound

and rational; and his arguments irresistible. These they never felt in the trifling teachings of their most celebrated doctors, who consumed their own time, and that of their disciples and hearers, with frivolous cases of conscience, ridiculous distinctions, and puerile splittings of controversial hairs – questions not calculated to minister grace to the hearers.

MATTHEW 8: 1–4; MARK 1: 40–45; LUKE 5: 12–16

Matthew 8: 1–4

1. From the mountain – That mountain on which he had delivered the preceding inimitable sermon.

Great multitudes followed him – Having been deeply impressed with the glorious doctrines which they had just heard.

2. And, behold, there came a leper – The leprosy was an inveterate cutaneous disease, appearing in dry, thin, white scurfy scales or scabs, either on the whole body, or on some part of it, usually attended with violent itching, and often with great pain. The eastern leprosy was a distemper of the most loathsome kind, highly contagious, so as to infect garments, (Leviticus 13: 47, etc)., and houses, (Leviticus 14: 34, etc)., and was deemed incurable by any human means. Among the Jews, GOD alone was applied to for its removal; and the cure was ever attributed to his sovereign power.

Lord, if thou wilt, thou canst make me clean – As this leper may be considered as a fit emblem of the corruption of man by sin; so may his cure, of the redemption of the soul by Christ. A sinner, truly penitent, seeks God with a respectful faith; approaches him in the spirit of adoration; humbles himself under his mighty hand, acknowledging the greatness of his fall, and the vileness of his sin; his prayer, like that of the leper, should be humble, plain, and full of confidence in that God who can do all things, and of dependence upon his will or mercy, from which all good must be derived. It is peculiar to God that he need only will what he intends to perform. His power is his

5 For he loveth our nation, and he hath built us a synagogue.

6 Then Jesus went with them. And when he was now not far from the house, the centurion sent friends to him, saying unto him, Lord, trouble not thyself: for I am not worthy that thou shouldest enter under my roof:

7 Wherefore neither thought I myself worthy to come unto thee: but say in a word, and my servant shall be healed.

8 For I also am a man set under authority, having under me soldiers, and I say unto one, Go, and he goeth; and to another, Come, and he cometh; and to my servant, Do this, and he doeth it.

9 When Jesus heard these things, he marveled at him, and turned him about, and said unto the people that followed him, I say unto you, I have not found so great faith, no, not in Israel.

10 And they that were sent, returning to the house, found the servant whole that had been sick.

LUKE 7: 11–17

11 And it came to pass the day after, that he went into a city called Nain; and many of his disciples went with him, and much people.

12 Now when he came nigh to the gate of the city, behold, there was a dead man carried out, the only son of his mother, and she was a widow: and much people of the city was with her.

13 And when the Lord saw her, he had compassion on her, and said unto her, Weep not.

14 And he came and touched the bier: and they that bare him stood still. And he said, Young man, I say unto thee, Arise.

15 And he that was dead sat up, and began to speak. And he delivered him to his mother.

16 And there came a fear on all: and they glorified God, saying, That a great prophet is risen up among us; and, That God hath visited his people.

17 And this rumor of him went forth throughout all Judaea, and throughout all the region round about.

LUKE 7: 11–17

11. And it happened, that he went into a city

In all the miracles of Christ, we must attend to the rule which Matthew lays down. We ought to know, therefore, that this young man, whom Christ raised from the dead, is an emblem of the spiritual life which he restores to us. The name of the city contributes to the certainty of the history. The same purpose is served by what Luke says, that **a great multitude** from every direction followed him: for Christ had many attendants along with him, and many people accompanied the woman, as a mark of respect, to the interment of her son. The resurrection of the young man was beheld by so many witnesses, that no doubt could be entertained as to its truth. There was the additional circumstance of its being a crowded place: for we know that public assemblies were held at the gates. That the dead man was carried out of the city was in accordance with a very ancient custom among all nations. Jerome says that, in his time, the city of Nain was still in existence, two miles below Mount Tabor, in a southerly direction.

MATTHEW 8: 19–22; LUKE 9: 57–62

Matthew 8: 19. And a scribe approaching

Two men are here presented to us by Matthew, and three by Luke, all of whom were prepared to become disciples of Christ, but who, having been prevented by a diversity of vices from following the right course, receive a corresponding variety of replies. It might at first sight appear strange, that Christ sends back, and does not admit into his family, one who offers to follow him immediately and without delay: while he detains another along with him who, by asking leave for a time, showed himself to be slower and less willing. But there are the best reasons for both. Whence arose the great readiness of the scribe to prepare himself immediately to accompany Christ, but from his not having at all considered the hard and wretched condition of his followers? We must bear in mind that he was a scribe, who had been accustomed to a quiet and easy life, had enjoyed honor, and was ill-fitted to endure reproaches, poverty, persecutions, and the cross. He wishes indeed to follow Christ, but dreams of an easy and agreeable life, and of dwellings filled with every convenience; whereas the disciples of Christ must walk among thorns, and march to the cross amidst uninterrupted afflictions. The more eager he is, the less he is prepared. He seems as if he wished to fight in the shade and at ease, neither annoyed by sweat nor by dust, and beyond the reach of the weapons of war. There is no reason to wonder that Christ rejects such people: for, as they rush on without consideration, they are distressed by the first uneasiness of any kind that occurs, lose cour-

will. The ability of God to do what is necessary to be done, and his willingness to make his creatures happy, should be deeply considered by all those who approach him in prayer. The leper had no doubt of the former, but he was far from being equally satisfied in respect of the latter.

3. Jesus put forth his hand – I will; be thou clean – The most sovereign authority is assumed in this speech of our blessed Lord – I WILL: there is here no supplication of any power superior to his own; and the event proved to the fullest conviction, and by the clearest demonstration, that his authority was absolute, and his power unlimited.

And immediately his leprosy was cleansed – What an astonishing sight! A man whose whole body was covered over with the most loathsome disease, cleansed from it in a moment of time! Was it possible for any soul to resist the evidence of this fact? This action of Christ is a representation of that invisible hand which makes itself felt by the most insensible heart; of that internal word which makes itself heard by the most deaf; and of that supreme will which works every thing according to its own counsel.

4. Jesus saith – See thou tell no man – Had our Lord, at this early period, fully manifested himself as the Messiah, the people in all likelihood would have proclaimed him King; this, however, refused by him, must have excited the hatred of the Jewish rulers, and the jealousy of the Roman government; and, speaking after the manner of men, his farther preachings and miracles must have been impeded. This alone seems to be the reason why he said to the leper, See thou tell no man.

Show thyself to the priest – This was to conform to the law instituted in this case, Leviticus 14: 1, etc.

Offer the gift – This gift was two living, clean birds, some cedar wood, with scarlet and hyssop, Leviticus 14: 4, which were to be brought for his cleansing; and, when clean, two he lambs, one ewe lamb, three tenth deals of flour, and one log of oil, Leviticus 14: 10; but if the person was poor, then he was to bring

one lamb, one tenth deal of flour, one log of oil and two turtle doves, or young pigeons, Leviticus 14: 21–22.

Now all this was to be done for a testimony to them; to prove that this leper, who was doubtless well known in the land, had been thoroughly cleansed; and thus, in this private way, to give full proof to the priesthood that Jesus was the true Messiah.

MATTHEW 8: 5–13; LUKE 7: 1–10

Matthew 8: 5–13

5. A centurion – A Roman military officer who had the command of one hundred men.

6. Lieth at home – lieth all along; intimating that the disease had reduced him to a state of the utmost impotence, through the grievous torments with which it was accompanied.

Sick of the palsy – Or paralytic. See Matthew 4: 24. This centurion did not act as many masters do when their servants are afflicted, have them immediately removed to an infirmary, often to a work-house; or sent home to friends or relatives, who probably either care nothing for them, or are unable to afford them any of the comforts of life. In case of a contagious disorder, it may be necessary to remove an infected person to such places as are best calculated to cure the distemper, and prevent the spread of the contagion. But, in all common cases, the servant should be considered as a child, and receive the same friendly attention. If, by a hasty, unkind, and unnecessary removal, the servant die, are not the master and mistress murderers before God?

7. I will come and heal him – I am coming, and will heal him. This saying is worthy of observation. Jesus did not positively say, I will came and heal him; this could not have been strictly true, because our Lord healed him without going to the house: and the issue shows that the words ought to be taken in the most literal sense: thus understood, they contained a promise which it seems none of them distinctly comprehended. Foreseeing the exercise of the centurion's faith, he promises that

MATTHEW 8: 19–22; LUKE 9: 57–62

Matthew 8: 19–22

19 And a certain scribe came, and said unto him, Master, I will follow thee whithersoever thou goest.

20 And Jesus saith unto him, The foxes have holes, and the birds of the air have nests; but the Son of man hath not where to lay his head.

21 And another of his disciples said unto him, Lord, suffer me first to go and bury my father.

22 But Jesus said unto him, Follow me; and let the dead bury their dead.

Luke 9: 57–62

57 And it came to pass, that, as they went in the way, a certain man said unto him, Lord, I will follow thee whithersoever thou goest.

58 And Jesus said unto him, Foxes have holes, and birds of the air have nests; but the Son of man hath not where to lay his head.

59 And he said unto another, Follow me. But he said, Lord, suffer me first to go and bury my father.

60 Jesus said unto him, Let the dead bury their dead: but go thou and preach the kingdom of God.

61 And another also said, Lord, I will follow thee; but let me first go bid them farewell, which are at home at my house.

62 And Jesus said unto him, No man, having put his hand to the plough, and looking back, is fit for the kingdom of God.

MATTHEW 9: 1–8; MARK 2: 1–12; LUKE 5: 17–26

Matthew 9: 1–8

1 And he entered into a ship, and passed over, and came into his own city.

2 And, behold, they brought to him a man sick of the palsy, lying on a bed: and Jesus seeing their faith said unto the sick of the palsy; Son, be of good cheer; thy sins be forgiven thee.

3 And, behold, certain of the scribes said within themselves, This man blasphemeth.

4 And Jesus knowing their thoughts said, Wherefore think ye evil in your hearts?

age at the first attack, give way, and basely desert their post. Besides, this scribe might have sought a place in the family of Christ, in order to live at his table without expense, and to feed luxuriously without toil. Let us therefore look upon ourselves as warned, in his person, not to boast lightly and at ease, that we will be the disciples of Christ, while we are taking no thought of the cross, or of afflictions; but, on the contrary, to consider early what sort of condition awaits us. The first lesson which he gives us, on entering his school, is to deny ourselves, and take up his cross (Matthew 16: 24).

MATTHEW 9: 1–8; MARK 2: 1–12; LUKE 5: 17–26

Matthew 9: 1. And came into his own city

This passage shows, that Capernaum was generally believed to be the birth-place of Christ, because his visits to it were frequent: for there is no room to doubt, that it is the same history which is related by the three Evangelists, though some circumstances may be more exactly related by one of them than by another. Luke says that scribes had come from various parts of Judea, who were spectators when Christ healed the paralytic; and at the same time states indirectly, that there were others who also received healing through the grace of Christ. For, before he comes to the paralytic, he speaks in the plural number, and says, that the power of God was displayed for healing their diseases; the power of the Lord was present to heal them. The glory of this miracle was very remarkable. A man destitute of the use of all his limbs, lying on a bed, and lowered by cords, suddenly rises up in health, vigor, and agility. Another special reason why the Evangelists dwell more on this miracle than on others is, that the scribes were offended at Christ for claiming power and authority to forgive sins; while Christ intended to confirm and seal that authority by a visible sign.

2. And when Jesus saw their faith

It is God alone, indeed, who knows faith: but they had given evidence of faith by the laboriousness of that attempt: for they would never have submitted to so much trouble, nor contended with such formidable hindrances, if they had not derived courage from entire confidence of success. The fruit of their faith appeared in their not being wearied out, when they found the entrance closed up on all sides.

Thy sins are forgiven thee

Christ appears here to promise to the paralytic something different from what he had requested: but, as he intends to bestow health of body, he begins with removing the cause of the disease, and at the same time reminds the paralytic of the origin of his disease, and of the manner in which he ought to arrange his prayers. As men usually do not consider that the afflictions which they endure are God's

while he is coming, ere he arrives at the house, he will heal him, and this was literally done, Matthew 8: 13. There is much beauty in this passage.

8. But speak the word only – See here the pattern of that living faith and genuine humility which ought always to accompany the prayer of a sinner: Jesus can will away the palsy, and speak away the most grievous torments. The first degree of humility is to acknowledge the necessity of God's mercy, and our own inability to help ourselves: the second, to confess the freeness of his grace, and our own utter unworthiness. Ignorance, unbelief, and presumption will ever retard our spiritual cure.

9. For I am a man under authority – That is, under the authority of others. The argument of the centurion seems to run thus. If I, who am a person subject to the control of others, yet have some so completely subject to myself, that I can say to one, Come, and he cometh, to another, Go, and he goeth, and to my slave Do this, and he doeth it; how much more then canst thou accomplish whatsoever thou willest, being under no control, and having all things under thy command: He makes a proper use of his authority, who, by it, raises his mind to the contemplation of the sovereign power of God, taking occasion from it to humble himself before Him who has all power in heaven and earth, and to expect all good from him.

10. I have not found so great faith, no, not in Israel – That is, I have not found so great an instance of confidence and faith in my power, even among the Jews, as this Roman, a Gentile, has shown himself to possess.

From Luke 7: 5, where it is said of this centurion, "he loved our nation, and has built us a synagogue," we may infer that this man was like the centurion mentioned Acts 10: 1; a devout Gentile, a proselyte of the gate, one who believed in the God of Israel, without conforming to the Jewish ritual or receiving circumcision.

11. Many shall come from the east and west – Men of every description, of all countries, and of all professions; and shall sit down, that is, to meat. The rabbins represent the blessedness of the kingdom of God under the notion of a banquet.

With Abraham, and Isaac, and Jacob – In the closest communion with the most eminent followers of God. But if we desire to inherit the promises, we must be followers of them who through faith and patience enjoy them. Let us therefore imitate Abraham in his faith, Isaac in his obedience unto death, and Jacob in his hope and expectation of good things to come, amidst all the evils of this life, if we desire to reign with them.

12. Shall be cast out into outer darkness – As the enjoyment of that salvation which Jesus Christ calls the kingdom of heaven is here represented under the notion of a nuptial festival, at which the guests sat down in a reclining posture, with the master of the feast; so the state of those who were excluded from the banquet is represented as deep darkness; because the nuptial solemnities took place at night.

13. As thou hast believed; so be it done – Let the mercy thou requestest be equal to the faith thou hast brought to receive it by. ACCORDING to thy faith be it done unto thee, is a general measure of God's dealings with mankind. To get an increase of faith is to get an increase of every grace which constitutes the mind that was in Jesus, and prepares fully for the enjoyment of the kingdom of God. God is the same in the present time which he was in ancient days; and miracles of healing may be wrought on our own bodies and souls, and on those of others, by the instrumentality of our faith. But, alas! where is faith to be found!

And his servant was healed in the self-same hour – in that very hour. Faith is never exercised in the power and goodness of God till it is needed; and, when it is exercised, God works the miracle of healing.

LUKE 7: 11–17

11. Nain – A small city of Galilee, in the tribe of Issachar.

5 For whether is easier, to say, Thy sins be forgiven thee; or to say, Arise, and walk?

6 But that ye may know that the Son of man hath power on earth to forgive sins, (then saith he to the sick of the palsy,) Arise, take up thy bed, and go unto thine house.

7 And he arose, and departed to his house.

8 But when the multitudes saw it, they marveled, and glorified God, which had given such power unto men.

Mark 2: 1–12

1 And again he entered into Capernaum, after some days; and it was noised that he was in the house.

2 And straightway many were gathered together, insomuch that there was no room to receive them, no, not so much as about the door: and he preached the word unto them.

3 And they come unto him, bringing one sick of the palsy, which was borne of four.

4 And when they could not come nigh unto him for the press, they uncovered the roof where he was: and when they had broken it up, they let down the bed wherein the sick of the palsy lay.

5 When Jesus saw their faith, he said unto the sick of the palsy, Son, thy sins be forgiven thee.

6 But there were certain of the scribes sitting there, and reasoning in their hearts,

7 Why doth this man thus speak blasphemies? who can forgive sins but God only?

8 And immediately when Jesus perceived in his spirit that they so reasoned within themselves, he said unto them, Why reason ye these things in your hearts?

9 Whether is it easier to say to the sick of the palsy, Thy sins be forgiven thee; or to say, Arise, and take up thy bed, and walk?

10 But that ye may know that the Son of man hath power on earth to forgive sins, (he saith to the sick of the palsy,)

11 I say unto thee, Arise, and take up thy bed, and go thy way into thine house.

12 And immediately he arose, took up

chastisements, they desire nothing more than some alleviation in the flesh, and, in the meantime, feel no concern about their sins: just as if a sick man were to disregard his disease, and to seek only relief from present pain. But the only way of obtaining deliverance from all evils is to have God reconciled to us.

Thus it appears that this is a frequent and ordinary way of speaking in the Scriptures, to promise the pardon of sins, when the mitigation of punishments is sought. It is proper to attend to this order in our prayers. When the feeling of afflictions reminds us of our sins, let us first of all be careful to obtain pardon, that, when God is reconciled to us, he may withdraw his hand from punishing.

3. And, lo, some of the scribes

They accuse Christ of blasphemy and sacrilege, because he claims for himself what is God's prerogative. The other two Evangelists tell us also that they said, **Who can forgive sins but God alone?** It is beyond all question, that their eagerness to slander drove them to this wicked conclusion. If they think that there is any thing which deserves blame, why do they not inquire into it? Besides, as the expression admits of more than one meaning, and as Christ said nothing more than what the Prophets frequently say when they announce the grace of God, why do they take in a bad sense what admits of a favorable interpretation? They must have been already poisoned by malice and envy, otherwise they would not so eagerly have seized an occasion of blaming Christ. They remain silent, but **think in their hearts**, that they may slander him when absent among people of their own class. It is no doubt true, that God alone has power and authority to forgive sins : but they are wrong in concluding that it does not belong to Christ, for he is God manifested in the flesh (1 Timothy 3: 16). They had a right to inquire on what grounds Christ laid claim to such authority: but, without any inquiry, they suppose him to be one of the common rank of men, and proceed rashly to condemn him.

4. And when Jesus saw their thoughts

He now gives a proof of his Divinity in bringing to light their secret thoughts: "for who knoweth the things of a man but the spirit of man which is in him?" (1 Corinthians 2: 11). And so Mark adds, that **Jesus knew by his Spirit**: which means, that what was concealed in their hearts could not be perceived by man, but that Christ by his Divine Spirit knew it thoroughly.

Why do you think evil?

This does not imply that it gave them pain to see a mortal man assuming what God claims as his own prerogative, but that they proudly and wickedly rejected God, who was openly manifested to them.

According to Eusebius, it was two miles from Mount Tabor, southward; and near to Endor.

12. Carried out – The Jews always buried their dead without the city, except those of the family of David. No burying places should be tolerated within cities or towns; much less in or about churches and chapels. This custom is excessively injurious to the inhabitants; and especially to those who frequent public worship in such chapels and churches. God, decency, and health forbid this shocking abomination.

From long observation I can attest that churches and chapels situated in grave-yards, and those especially within whose walls the dead are interred, are perfectly unwholesome; and many, by attending such places, are shortening their passage to the house appointed for the living. What increases the iniquity of this abominable and deadly work is, that the burying grounds attached to many churches and chapels are made a source of private gain. The whole of this preposterous conduct is as indecorous and unhealthy as it is profane. Every man should know that the gas which is disengaged from putrid flesh, and particularly from a human body, is not only unfriendly to, but destructive of, animal life. Superstition first introduced a practice which self-interest and covetousness continue to maintain.

16. God hath visited his people – Sometimes God visited his people in the way of judgment, to consume them in their transgressions; but it was now plain that he had visited them in the most tender compassion and mercy. This seems to have been added by some ancient copyist, by way of explanation.

MATTHEW 8: 19–22; LUKE 9: 57–62

Matthew 8: 19–22

19. I will follow thee whithersoever thou goest – A man who is not illuminated by the Spirit of God thinks himself capable of any thing: he alone who is divinely taught knows he can do nothing but through Christ strengthening him. Every teacher among the Jews had disciples, and some especially that followed or accompanied them wherever they went, that they might have some person at hand with whom they might converse concerning the Divine law.

20. The foxes have holes, etc. – Reader! art thou a poor man? and dost thou fear God? Then, what comfort must thou derive from the thought, that thou so nearly resemblest the Lord Jesus! But how unlike is the rich man, who is the votary of pleasure and slave of sin, to this heavenly pattern!

Son of man – A Hebrew phrase, expressive of humiliation and debasement; and, on that account, applied emphatically to himself, by the meek and lowly Jesus. Besides, it seems here to be used to point out the incarnation of the Son of God, according to the predictions of the prophets, Psalm 8: 5; Daniel 7: 13. And as our Lord was now showing forth his eternal Divinity in the miracles he wrought, he seems studious to prove to them the certainty of his incarnation, because on this depended the atonement for sin. Indeed our Lord seems more intent on giving the proofs of his humanity, than of his divinity, the latter being necessarily manifested by the miracles which he was continually working.

21. Another of his disciples – This does not mean any of the twelve, but one of those who were constant hearers of our Lord's preaching; the name of disciple being common to all those who professed to believe in him, John 6: 66. Bury my father: probably his father was old, and apparently near death; but it was a maxim among the Jews, that, if a man had any duty to perform to the dead, he was, for that time, free from the observance of any other precept or duty. The children of Adam are always in extremes; some will rush into the ministry of the Gospel without a call, others will delay long after they are called; the middle way is the only safe one: not to move a finger in the work till the call be given, and not to delay a moment after.

the bed, and went forth before them all; insomuch that they were all amazed, and glorified God, saying, We never saw it on this fashion.

Luke 5: 17–26

17 And it came to pass on a certain day, as he was teaching, that there were Pharisees and doctors of the law sitting by, which were come out of every town of Galilee, and Judaea, and Jerusalem: and the power of the Lord was present to heal them.

18 And, behold, men brought in a bed a man which was taken with a palsy: and they sought means to bring him in, and to lay him before him.

19 And when they could not find by what way they might bring him in because of the multitude, they went upon the housetop, and let him down through the tiling with his couch into the midst before Jesus.

20 And when he saw their faith, he said unto him, Man, thy sins are forgiven thee.

21 And the scribes and the Pharisees began to reason, saying, Who is this which speaketh blasphemies? Who can forgive sins, but God alone?

22 But when Jesus perceived their thoughts, he answering said unto them, What reason ye in your hearts?

23 Whether is easier, to say, Thy sins be forgiven thee; or to say, Rise up and walk?

24 But that ye may know that the Son of man hath power upon earth to forgive sins, (he said unto the sick of the palsy,) I say unto thee, Arise, and take up thy couch, and go into thine house.

25 And immediately he rose up before them, and took up that whereon he lay, and departed to his own house, glorifying God.

26 And they were all amazed, and they glorified God, and were filled with fear, saying, We have seen strange things to day.

MATTHEW 9: 9–13; MARK 2: 13–17; LUKE 5: 27–32

Matthew 9: 9–13

9 And as Jesus passed forth from

5. Whether is it easier to say?

The meaning is, that, as it is not easier to quicken by a word a body which is nearly dead than to forgive **sins**, there is no reason to wonder that he forgives sins, when he has accomplished the other. The argument which our Lord uses may appear to be not well-founded: for, in proportion as the soul is more excellent than the body, the forgiveness of sins is a greater work than the healing of the body. But the reply is easy. Christ adapts his discourse to their capacity: for, being carnal, they were more powerfully affected by outward signs, than by all the spiritual power of Christ, which related to eternal salvation. Thus he proves the efficacy of the Gospel for quickening men from the fact, that at the last day he will raise the dead by his voice out of their graves.

Wonder not at this: for the hour is coming, in which all who are in the graves shall hear his voice, and shall come forth (John 5: 28,29).

MATTHEW 9: 9–13; MARK 2: 13–17; LUKE 5: 27–32

Matthew 9: 9. Jesus saw a man sitting at the custom-house

The custom-house has usually been a place noted for plundering and for unjust exactions, and was at that time particularly infamous. In the choice of Matthew out of that place, not only to be admitted into the family of Christ, but even to be called to the office of Apostle, we have a striking instance of the grace of God. It was the intention of Christ to choose simple and ignorant people to that rank, in order to cast down the wisdom of the world (1 Corinthians 2: 6). But this publican, who followed an occupation little esteemed and involved in many abuses, was selected for additional reasons, that he might be an example of Christ's undeserved goodness, and might show in his person that the calling of all of us depends, not on the merits of our own righteousness, but on his pure kindness. Matthew, therefore, was not only a witness and preacher, but was also a proof and illustration of the grace exhibited in Christ. he gives evidence of his gratitude in not being ashamed to hand down for perpetual remembrance the record of what he formerly was, and whence he was taken, that he might more fully illustrate in his person the grace of Christ. In the same manner Paul says: "This is a faithful saying, that Christ Jesus came into the world to save sinners, of whom I am chief" (1 Timothy 1: 15).

As to Mark and Luke calling him Levi, it appears that this was his ordinary name: but that his being a publican was the reason why he took a foreign name.

MATTHEW 9: 1–8; MARK 2: 1–12; LUKE 5: 17–26

Matthew 9: 1–8

1. He came into his own city – Viz. Capernaum, where he seems to have had his common residence at the house of Peter. See Matthew 4: 13, and Matthew 8: 14. This verse properly belongs to the preceding chapter.

2. Sick of the palsy – See Matthew 4: 24.

Lying on a bed – a couch or sofa, such as they reclined on at meals.

Seeing their faith – The faith of the paralytic person, and the faith of those who brought him.

Be of good cheer – Son, take courage! Probably he began to despond, and Christ spoke thus to support his faith.

Thy sins be forgiven thee – Moral evil has been the cause of all the natural evil in the world. Christ goes to the source of the malady, which is sin; and to that as the procuring cause we should refer in all our afflictions. It is probable that this paralytic person had, in the earnest desires of his heart, entreated the cure of his soul, leaving his body to the care of others, as the first miracle of healing is wrought on his soul. In a state of helplessness, when we seek above all things to please God, by giving him our hearts, he often inspires others with the care of our temporal necessities. It may be necessary to be observed, that it was a maxim among the Jews that no diseased person could be healed till all his sins were blotted out.

3. This man blasphemeth – Whenever this is used in reference to GOD, it simply signifies, to speak impiously of his nature, or attributes, or works. Injurious speaking is its proper translation when referred to man.

The scribes were the literati of that time; and their learning, because not used in dependence on God, rendered them proud, envious, and obstinate. Unsanctified knowledge has still the same effect: that light serves only to blind and lead men out of the way which is not joined with uprightness of heart. The most sacred truths often become an occasion of delusion, where men are under the government of their evil passions.

4. Jesus knowing (seeing) their thoughts – In telling them what the thoughts of their hearts were, (for they had expressed nothing publicly), he gave them the fullest proof of his power to forgive sins; because God only can forgive sins, and God only can search and know the heart. Jesus pronounced the man's sins forgiven; and gave the scribes the fullest proof of his power to do so, by telling them what, in the secret of their souls, they thought on the subject.

God sounds the secrets of all hearts – no sin escapes his notice; how senseless then is the sinner to think he sins securely when unseen by men! Let us take heed to our hearts, as well as to our conduct, for God searches out and condemns all that does not spring from, and leads not to himself.

5. For whether is easier, to say, Thy sins be forgiven thee; or to say, Arise, and walk? – Both are equally easy, and equally difficult; for both require unlimited power to produce them. And every thing is equally easy to that power which is unlimited. A universe can be as easily produced by a single act of the Divine will as the smallest elementary part of matter.

The common punctuation of the above passage almost destroys the sense: the comma should be placed after easier, and to say, made the first part of the question.

6. But that ye may know, etc. – External miracles are the proofs of internal ones. Three miracles are wrought in this case. (I mean, by miracle, something produced or known that no power is capable of but that which is omnipotent, and no knowledge adequate to but that which is omniscient). The miracles are these:

1st. The remission of the poor man's sins.

2d. The discernment of the secret thoughts of the scribes.

3d. The restoring of the paralytic, in an instant, to perfect soundness.

Thus one miracle becomes the proof and

thence, he saw a man, named MATTHEW, sitting at the receipt of custom: and he saith unto him, Follow me. And he arose, and followed him.

10 And it came to pass, as Jesus sat at meat in the house, behold, many publicans and sinners came and sat down with him and his disciples.

11 And when the Pharisees saw it, they said unto his disciples, Why eateth your Master with publicans and sinners?

12 But when Jesus heard that, he said unto them, They that be whole need not a physician, but they that are sick.

13 But go ye and learn what that meaneth, I will have mercy, and not sacrifice: for I am not come to call the righteous, but sinners to repentance.

Mark 2: 13–17

13 And he went forth again by the sea side; and all the multitude resorted unto him, and he taught them.

14 And as he passed by, he saw Levi the son of Alphaeus sitting at the receipt of custom, and said unto him, Follow me. And he arose and followed him.

15 And it came to pass, that, as Jesus sat at meat in his house, many publicans and sinners sat also together with Jesus and his disciples: for there were many, and they followed him.

16 And when the scribes and Pharisees saw him eat with publicans and sinners, they said unto his disciples, How is it that he eateth and drinketh with publicans and sinners?

17 When Jesus heard it, he saith unto them, They that are whole have no need of the physician, but they that are sick: I came not to call the righteous, but sinners to repentance.

Luke 5: 27–32

27 And after these things he went forth, and saw a publican, named Levi, sitting at the receipt of custom: and he said unto him, Follow me.

28 And he left all, rose up, and followed him.

29 And Levi made him a great feast in his own house: and there was a great company of publicans and of others that sat down with them.

30 But their scribes and Pharisees

Follow me

There is no reason to doubt that Christ explained in many words why he was called, and on what conditions. This is more fully ascertained from Luke, who says, **that he left all, rose up, and followed** Christ: for it would not have been necessary for him to leave all, if he had not been a private disciple of Christ, and called in expectation of the Apostleship. In the great readiness and eagerness of Matthew to obey, we see the Divine power of the word of Christ. Not that all in whose ears he utters his voice are equally affected in their hearts: but in this man Christ intended to give a remarkable example, that we might know that his calling was not from man.

Luke 5: 29. And Levi made him a great banquet

This appears to be at variance with what Luke relates, that **he left all**: but the solution is easy. Matthew disregarded every hinderance, and gave up himself entirely to Christ, but yet did not abandon the charge of his own domestic affairs. When Paul, referring to the example of soldiers, exhorts the ministers of the word to be free and disentangled from every hinderance, and to devote their labors to the church, he says: "No man that warreth entangleth himself with the affairs of life, that he may please the commander" (2 Timothy 2: 4).

He certainly does not mean, that those who enroll themselves in the military profession divorce their wives, forsake their children, and entirely desert their homes; but that they quit their homes for a time, and leave behind them every care, that they may be wholly employed in war. In the same manner, nothing kept Matthew from following where Christ called; and yet he freely used both his house and his property, as far as the nature of his calling allowed. It was necessary, indeed, that he should leave the **custom-house**: for, had he been detained there, he would not have been a follower of Christ.

MATTHEW 9: 14–17; MARK 2: 18–22; LUKE 5: 33–39

Matthew 9: 14. Then come to him the disciples of John

Luke represents the Pharisees as speaking: Mark appears to connect both. And, indeed, there is no room to doubt that the Pharisees maliciously endeavored, by this stratagem, to draw the disciples of John to their party, and to produce a quarrel between them and the disciples of Christ. A resemblance in prayers and fastings was a plausible pretext for associating at this time: while the different manner in which Christ acted was an occasion of enmity and dislike to men whose temper was unamiable, and who were excessively devoted to themselves.

establishment of another. Never was a clearer proof of omnipotent energy and mercy brought under the senses of man. Here is an absolutely perfect miracle wrought; and here are absolute incontestable proofs that the miracle was wrought; and the conclusion is the fullest demonstration of the Divinity of the ever-blessed Jesus.

Arise, take up thy bed – Being enabled to obey this command was the public proof that the man was made whole. Such a circumstance should not pass without improvement. A man gives proof of his conversion from sin to God who imitates this paralytic person. He who does not rise and stand upright, but either continues grovelling on the earth, or falls back as soon as he is got up, is not yet cured of his spiritual palsy. When we see a penitent enabled to rejoice in hope of God's glory, and to walk in the way of his commandments, he affords us all the proof which we can reasonably require, that his conversion is real: the proof sufficient to satisfy himself is the witness of the Holy Spirit in his own heart; but this is a matter of which those who are without cannot judge: they must form their opinion from his conduct, and judge of the tree by its fruits.

8. When the multitudes saw it, they marveled – And the multitudes seeing it, wondered and feared, and glorified God. Wondered at the miracle; feared to offend against such power and goodness; and glorified God for the works of mercy which he had wrought.

That which to the doctors of the law, the worldly-wise and prudent, is a matter of scandal, is to the humble an occasion of glorifying the Most High. Divine things make a deeper impression on the hearts of the simple multitude than on those of the doctors, who, puffed up with a sense of their own wisdom, refuse to receive the truth as it is in Jesus. The conversion of one rebellious soul is a greater miracle, and more to be admired than all that can be wrought on inanimate creatures. He who sees a sinner converted from the error of his way sees a miracle wrought by eternal power and goodness. May such miracles be multiplied!

MATTHEW 9: 9–13; MARK 2: 13–17; LUKE 5: 27–32

Matthew 9: 14–17

9. Named Matthew – Generally supposed to be the same who wrote this history of our blessed Lord. Mathai signifies a gift in Syriac; probably so named by his parents as implying a gift from God.

The receipt of custom – The custom-house, – the place where the taxes levied by the Romans of the Jews, were collected.

Follow me – That is, become my disciple.

And he arose, and followed him – How blessed it is to be obedient to the first call of Christ – how much happiness and glory are lost by delays, though conversion at last may have taken place!

10. Sat at meat in the house – Viz. of Matthew, who it appears, from Luke 5: 29, made a great feast on the occasion, thus testifying his gratitude for the honor done him; and that his friends and acquaintances might profit by the teaching of his new master, he invites them to the entertainment that was honored by the presence of Christ. His companions, it appears, were not of the most creditable kind. They were tax-gatherers (see Matthew 5: 46) and sinners.

11. When the Pharisees saw it – He who, like a Pharisee, never felt himself indebted to infinite mercy for his own salvation, is rarely solicitous about the salvation of others. The grace of Christ alone inspires the soul with true benevolence. The self-righteous Pharisees considered it equal to legal defilement to sit in company with tax-gatherers and heathens. It is certain that those who fear God should not associate, through choice, with the workers of iniquity, and should only be found with them when transacting their secular business requires it, or when they have the prospect of doing good to their souls.

12. They that be whole need not a physician – A common proverb, which none could either misunderstand or misapply. Of it the reader may make the following use:

murmured against his disciples, saying,
Why do ye eat and drink with publicans
and sinners?

31 And Jesus answering said unto
them, They that are whole need not a
physician; but they that are sick.

32 I came not to call the righteous, but
sinners to repentance.

MATTHEW 9: 14–17; MARK 2: 18–22; LUKE 5: 33–39

Matthew 9: 14–17

14 Then came to him the disciples of
John, saying, Why do we and the Pharisees fast oft, but thy disciples fast not?

15 And Jesus said unto them, Can the
children of the bridechamber mourn, as
long as the bridegroom is with them? but
the days will come, when the bridegroom
shall be taken from them, and then shall
they fast.

16 No man putteth a piece of new cloth
unto an old garment, for that which is put
in to fill it up taketh from the garment, and
the rent is made worse.

17 Neither do men put new wine into
old bottles: else the bottles break, and the
wine runneth out, and the bottles perish:
but they put new wine into new bottles,
and both are preserved.

Mark 2: 18–22

18 And the disciples of John and of
the Pharisees used to fast: and they come
and say unto him, Why do the disciples
of John and of the Pharisees fast, but thy
disciples fast not?

19 And Jesus said unto them, Can the
children of the bridechamber fast, while
the bridegroom is with them? as long as
they have the bridegroom with them, they
cannot fast.

20 But the days will come, when the
bridegroom shall be taken away from
them, and then shall they fast in those
days.

21 No man also seweth a piece of new
cloth on an old garment: else the new
piece that filled it up taketh away from
the old, and the rent is made worse.

22 And no man putteth new wine into
old bottles: else the new wine doth burst
the bottles, and the wine is spilled, and

This example reminds us, that prudence and caution are necessary to prevent wicked and cunning men from sowing divisions among us on any slight grounds. Satan has a wonderful dexterity, no doubt, in laying those snares; and it is an easy matter to distress us about a trifle. But we ought especially to beware lest the unity of faith be destroyed, or the bond of charity broken, on account of outward ceremonies. Almost all labor under the disease of attaching undue importance to the ceremonies and elements of the world, as Paul calls them (Galatians 4: 3; Colossians 2: 8); and accordingly they do not hesitate, for the most part, to prefer the merest rudiments to the highest perfection. This is followed by another evil arising out of fastidiousness and pride, when every man would willingly compel the whole world to copy his example. If any thing pleases us, we forthwith desire to make it a law, that others may live according to our pleasure.

When we read that the disciples of John were caught by these snares of Satan, let us first learn not to place holiness in outward and indifferent matters, and at the same time to restrain ourselves by moderation and equity, that we may not desire to restrict others to what we approve, but may allow every one to retain his freedom. As to fasting and prayers, it ought to be understood, that John gave his disciples a particular training, and that for this purpose they had stated days for fastings, a settled form, and fixed hours of prayer. Now, I reckon those prayers among outward observances. For, though calling on God holds the first rank in spiritual worship, yet that method of doing it was adapted to the unskilfulness of men, and is justly reckoned among ceremonies and indifferent matters, the observance of which ought not to be too strictly enjoined. Of the reason why John's discipline was more severe than that of Christ we have already spoken, and a more convenient opportunity for treating of it will again occur.

15. Can the children of the bridegroom mourn?

Christ apologizes for his disciples on the score of the season, alleging that God was still pleased to indulge them in joyous feelings, as if they were present at a marriage: for he compares himself to the bridegroom, who enlivens his friends by his presence. Chrysostom thinks that this comparison was taken from the testimony of John the Baptist, He that hath the bride is the bridegroom (John 3: 29). I have no objection to that view, though I do not think that it rests on solid grounds. Let us be satisfied with Christ's declaration, that he spares his disciples, and treats them with gentleness, so long as he is with them. That none may envy them advantages which are of short duration, he gives warning that they will very soon be treated with greater harshness and severity.

1. Jesus Christ represents himself here as the sovereign Physician of souls.

2. That all stand in need of his healing power.

3. That men must acknowledge their spiritual maladies, and the need they have of his mercy, in order to be healed by him.

4. That it is the most inveterate and dangerous disease the soul can be afflicted with to imagine itself whole, when the sting of death, which is sin, has pierced it through in every part, infusing its poison every where.

13. I will have mercy, and not sacrifice – Quoted from 1 Samuel 15: 22. These are remarkable words. We may understand them as implying,

1st. That God prefers an act of mercy, shown to the necessitous, to any act of religious worship to which the person might be called at that time. Both are good; but the former is the greater good, and should be done in preference to the other.

2dly. That the whole sacrificial system was intended only to point out the infinite mercy of God to fallen man, in his redemption by the blood of the new covenant. And

3dly. That we should not rest in the sacrifices, but look for the mercy and salvation prefigured by them. This saying was nervously translated by our ancestors, I will mild-heartedness, and not sacrifice.

Go ye and learn – a form of speech in frequent use among the rabbins, when they referred to any fact or example in the Sacred Writings. Nothing tends more to humble pretenders to devotion than to show them that they understand neither Scripture nor religion, when, relying on external performances, they neglect love to God and man, which is the very soul and substance of true religion. True holiness has ever consisted in faith working by love.

MATTHEW 9: 14–17; MARK 2: 18–22; LUKE 5: 33–39

Matthew 9: 14–17

14. Thy disciples fast not? – Probably meaning that they did not fast so frequently as the others did, or for the same purposes, which is very likely, for the Pharisees had many superstitious fasts. They fasted in order to have lucky dreams, to obtain the interpretation of a dream, or to avert the evil import of a dream. They also fasted often, in order to obtain the things they wished for. The tract, Taanith is full of these fasts, and of the wonders performed thus by the Jewish doctors.

15. Can the children of the bride-chamber – These persons were the companions of the bridegroom, who accompanied him to the house of his father-in-law when he went to bring the bride to his own home. The marriage-feast among the Jews lasted seven days; but the new married woman was considered to be a bride for thirty days. Marriage feasts were times of extraordinary festivity, and even of riot, among several people of the east.

When the bridegroom shall be taken from them, etc. – There was one annual fast observed in the primitive Church, called by our ancestors the spring fast, and, by us, LENT. This fast is pretended to be kept by many, in the present day, in commemoration of our Lord's forty days' fast in the wilderness; but it does not appear that, in the purest ages of the primitive Church, genuine Christians ever pretended that their quadrigessimal fast was kept for the above purpose. Their fast was kept merely to commemorate the time during which Jesus Christ lay under the power of death, which was about FORTY HOURS; and it was in this sense they understood the words of this text: the days will come, etc. With them, the bridegroom meant Christ: the time in which he was taken away, his crucifixion, death, and the time he lay in the grave. Suppose him dying about twelve o'clock on what is called Friday, and that he rose about four on the morning of his own day, (St. John says, Early, while it was yet dark, Matthew 20: 1), the interim makes forty hours, which was the true primitive Lent, or quadrigessimal fast. It is true that many in the primitive Church were not agreed on this subject, as Socrates, in his Church History, book v. chap. 22, says, "Some

the bottles will be marred: but new wine must be put into new bottles.

Luke 5: 33–39

33 And they said unto him, Why do the disciples of John fast often, and make prayers, and likewise the disciples of the Pharisees; but thine eat and drink?

34 And he said unto them, Can ye make the children of the bridechamber fast, while the bridegroom is with them?

35 But the days will come, when the bridegroom shall be taken away from them, and then shall they fast in those days.

36 And he spake also a parable unto them; No man putteth a piece of a new garment upon an old; if otherwise, then both the new maketh a rent, and the piece that was taken out of the new agreeth not with the old.

37 And no man putteth new wine into old bottles; else the new wine will burst the bottles, and be spilled, and the bottles shall perish.

38 But new wine must be put into new bottles; and both are preserved.

39 No man also having drunk old wine straightway desireth new: for he saith, The old is better.

MATTHEW 9: 18–22; MARK 5: 21–34; LUKE 8: 40–48

Matthew 9: 18–22

18 While he spake these things unto them, behold, there came a certain ruler, and worshipped him, saying, My daughter is even now dead: but come and lay thy hand upon her, and she shall live.

19 And Jesus arose, and followed him, and so did his disciples.

20 And, behold, a woman, which was diseased with an issue of blood twelve years, came behind him, and touched the hem of his garment:

21 For she said within herself, If I may but touch his garment, I shall be whole.

22 But Jesus turned him about, and when he saw her, he said, Daughter, be of good comfort; thy faith hath made thee whole. And the woman was made whole from that hour.

Mark 5: 21–34

21 And when Jesus was passed over

MATTHEW 9: 18–22; MARK 5: 22–34; LUKE 8: 40–48

Matthew 9: 18. While he was speaking these things to them

Those who imagine that the narrative, which is here given by Mark and Luke, is different from that of Matthew, are so clearly refuted by the passage itself, that there is no necessity for a lengthened debate. All the three agree in saying that Christ was requested by a ruler of the synagogue to enter his house for the purpose of curing his daughter. The only difference is, that the name of Jairus, which is withheld by Matthew, is mentioned by Mark and Luke; and that he represents the father as saying, **My daughter is dead**, while the other two say that she was in her last moments, and that, while he was bringing Christ, her death was announced to him on the road. But there is no absurdity in saying that Matthew, studying brevity, merely glances at those particulars which the other two give in minute detail. But since all the other points agree with such exactness, since so many circumstances conspire as to give it the appearance of three fingers stretched out at the same time to point out a single object, there is no argument that would justify us in dividing this history into various dates. The Evangelists agree in relating, that while Christ, at the request of a ruler of the synagogue, was coming to his house, a woman on the road was secretly cured of a bloody flux by touching his cloak; and that afterwards Christ came into the ruler's house, and raised a dead young woman to life. There is no necessity, I think, for circuitous language to prove that all the three relate the same event. Let us now come to details.

Lo, a certain ruler

Though it is evident from the other two, that his confidence had not advanced so far as to hope that his daughter's life could be restored, there is no room to doubt that, after having been reproved by Christ, he entertained a stronger hope than when he left his house. But Matthew, as we have said, studies brevity, and puts down at the very beginning of his narrative what took place at various times. The manner in which the history must be arranged is this: Jairus first requested that his daughter might be cured of her disease, and afterwards that she might be restored from death to life; that is, after that Christ had given him courage to do so. Worship, or adoration, is here put for kneeling, as is evident from the words of Mark and Luke: for Jairus did not render divine honor to Christ, but treated him with respect as a prophet of God; and we all know how common a practice kneeling was among eastern nations.

Come and lay thy hand

We have here a bright mirror in which the divine condescension towards us is beheld. If you compare

thought they should fast one day; others two; others more." Different Churches also were divided concerning the length of the time, some keeping it three, others five, and others seven weeks; and the historian himself is puzzled to know why they all agreed in calling these fasts, differing so much in their duration, by the name of Quadrigessima, or forty days' fast: the plain obvious reason appears to me to have been simply this: They put DAYS in the place of HOURS; and this absurdity continues in some Christian Churches to the present day.

16. No man putteth a piece of new cloth – No man putteth a patch of unscoured cloth upon an old garment. This is the most literal translation I can give of this verse, to convey its meaning to those who cannot consult the original.

It – **taketh from the garment** – Instead of closing up the rent, it makes a larger, by tearing away with it the whole breadth of the cloth over which it was laid; – it taketh its fullness or whole breadth from the garment; this I am persuaded is the meaning of the original.

17. New wine into old bottles – It is still the custom, in the eastern countries, to make their bottles of goat skins: if these happened to be old, and new wine were put into them, the violence of the fermentation must necessarily burst them; and therefore newly made bottles were employed for the purpose of putting that wine in which had not yet gone through its state of fermentation. The institutes of Christ, and those of the Pharisees, could never be brought to accord: an attempt to combine the two systems would be as absurd as it would be destructive. The old covenant made way for the new, which was its completion and its end; but with that old covenant the new cannot be incorporated.

Christian prudence requires that the weak, and newly converted, should be managed with care and tenderness. To impose such duties and mortifications as are not absolutely necessary to salvation, before God has properly prepared the heart by his grace for them, is a conduct as absurd and ruinous as putting a piece of raw, unscoured cloth on an old garment; it is, in a word, requiring the person to do the work of a man, while as yet he is but a little child. Preachers of the Gospel, and especially those who are instruments in God's hand of many conversions, have need of much heavenly wisdom, that they may know to watch over, guide, and advise those who are brought to a sense of their sin and danger. How many auspicious beginnings have been ruined by men's proceeding too hastily, endeavoring to make their own designs take place, and to have the honor of that success themselves which is due only to God.

MATTHEW 9: 18–22; MARK 5: 21–34; LUKE 8: 40–48

18. A certain ruler – There were two officers in the synagogue, the bishop or overseer of the congregation; and the head or ruler of the congregation.

My daughter is even now dead – Or, my daughter was just now dying; or, is by this time dead: i.e. as Mr. Wakefield properly observes, She was so ill when I left home that she must be dead by this time. This turn of the expression reconciles the account given here with that in Mark and Luke.

To be successful in our applications to God by prayer, four things are requisite; and this ruler teaches us what they are.

First, A man should place himself in the presence of God – he came unto him.

Secondly, He should humble himself sincerely before God – he fell down before him – at his feet. Mark 5: 22.

Thirdly, He should lay open his wants with a holy earnestness – he besought him greatly. Mark 5: 23.

Fourthly, he should have unbounded confidence in the power and goodness of Christ that his request shall be granted – put thy hand upon her, and she shall live.

He who comes in this way to God, for salvation, is sure to be heard. Imposition of hands was a rite anciently used by the servants of God, through which heavenly influences were conveyed to the bodies and souls of men.

again by ship unto the other side, much people gathered unto him: and he was nigh unto the sea.

22 And, behold, there cometh one of the rulers of the synagogue, Jairus by name; and when he saw him, he fell at his feet,

23 And besought him greatly, saying, My little daughter lieth at the point of death: I pray thee, come and lay thy hands on her, that she may be healed; and she shall live.

24 And Jesus went with him; and much people followed him, and thronged him.

25 And a certain woman, which had an issue of blood twelve years,

26 And had suffered many things of many physicians, and had spent all that she had, and was nothing bettered, but rather grew worse,

27 When she had heard of Jesus, came in the press behind, and touched his garment.

28 For she said, If I may touch but his clothes, I shall be whole.

29 And straightway the fountain of her blood was dried up; and she felt in her body that she was healed of that plague.

30 And Jesus, immediately knowing in himself that virtue had gone out of him, turned him about in the press, and said, Who touched my clothes?

31 And his disciples said unto him, Thou seest the multitude thronging thee, and sayest thou, Who touched me?

32 And he looked round about to see her that had done this thing.

33 But the woman fearing and trembling, knowing what was done in her, came and fell down before him, and told him all the truth.

34 And he said unto her, Daughter, thy faith hath made thee whole; go in peace, and be whole of thy plague.

Luke 8: 40–48

40 And it came to pass, that, when Jesus was returned, the people gladly received him: for they were all waiting for him.

41 And, behold, there came a man named Jairus, and he was a ruler of the synagogue: and he fell down at Jesus'

the ruler of the synagogue with the centurion, who was a heathen (Matthew 8: 5–10), you will say that the full brightness of faith shone in the centurion, while scarcely the smallest portion of it was visible in the ruler. He ascribes to Christ no power except through his touching the person; and, when he has received information of her death, he trembles as if there were no farther remedy. We see, then, that his faith was feeble and nearly exhausted. Yet Christ yields to his prayers, and encourages him to expect a favorable result, and thus proves to us that his faith, however small it might be, was not wholly rejected. Though we have not such abundance of faith as might be desired, there is no reason why our weakness should drive away or discourage us from prayer.

20. And, lo, a woman who had been afflicted with a bloody flux

For twelve successive years the bloody flux had lasted, and the woman was so far from being negligent in seeking remedies, that **she had spent all her substance on physicians**. All this is expressly stated by the Evangelists, that the miracle may shine with brighter glory. When an incurable disease was removed so suddenly, and by the mere touch of a garment, it is perfectly obvious that it was not accomplished by human power. The thought of the woman that, **if she only touched** Christ's garment, she would immediately be cured, arose from an extraordinary impulse of the Holy Spirit, and ought not to be regarded as a general rule. We know how eagerly superstition is wont to sport in foolish and thoughtless attempts to copy the saints; but they are apes, and not imitators, who take up some remarkable example without the command of God, and are led rather by their own senses than by the direction of the Spirit.

It is even possible that there was a mixture of sin and error in the woman's faith, which Christ graciously bears and forgives. Certainly, when she afterwards thinks that she has done wrong, and fears and trembles, there is no apology for that kind of doubt: for it is opposed to faith. Why did she not rather go straight to Christ? If her reverence for him prevented, from what other source than from his mercy did she expect aid? How comes it, then, that she is afraid of offending him, if she was convinced of his favorable regard?

Yet Christ bestows high commendation on her faith. This agrees with what I have lately noticed, that God deals kindly and gently with his people – accepts their faith, though imperfect and weak – and does not lay to their charge the faults and imperfections with which it is connected. It was by the guidance of faith, therefore, that the woman approached to Christ.

This rite is still used in certain Churches; but, as there is no Holy Ghost communicated by it, some suppose it may be as well omitted. But why is this? Is it not because there is an unfaithfulness in the person who lays on hands, or an unfitness in him on whom they are laid? Let the rite be restored to its primitive simplicity, and God will own it as he formerly did. But, however this may be, where is the man or number of men who have authority to abrogate a rite of God's own appointment? In the appointment of men to the sacred ministry it should never be omitted: even in these degenerate days, it may still serve as a sign of the necessity of the gifts and graces of that Holy Spirit without which no man can fulfill the work of the ministry, or be the instrument of saving the souls of them that hear him. When the inventions of men are put in the place of the ordinances of God, the true Church of Christ is in great danger.

19. Jesus arose, and followed him – Our blessed Lord could have acted as well at a distance as present; but he goes to the place, to teach his ministers not to spare either their steps or their pains when the salvation of a soul is in question. Let them not think it sufficient to pray for the sick in their closets; but let them go to their bed-sides, that they may instruct and comfort them. He can have little unction in private, who does not also give himself up to public duties.

20. A woman which was diseased with an issue of blood – It would be easy to explain the nature and properties of the disease here mentioned; but, when it is said that prudence forbids it, the intimation itself may be thought sufficiently explanatory of the disorder in question. There are some remarkable circumstances relative to this case mentioned by St. Mark, Mark 5: 25, etc., which shall be properly noticed in the notes on that place.

The hem of his garment – The fringes, which the Jews were commanded to wear on their garments. See Numbers 15: 38.

21. She said within herself, If I may but touch his garment – Her disorder was of that delicate nature that modesty forbade her to make any public acknowledgment of it; and therefore she endeavored to transact the whole business in private. Besides, the touch of such a person was by the law reputed unclean. By faith in Christ Jesus, little things are often rendered efficacious to our salvation. What more simple than a morsel of bread, and a few drops of wine, in the Lord's Supper! And yet, they who receive them by faith in the sacrifice they represent, are made partakers of the blessings purchased by the crucified body and spilled blood of the Lord Jesus!

22. Daughter, be of good comfort – Take courage, daughter. The reason of this kind speech was – Jesus, finding that virtue had proceeded from him; made inquiry who had touched him. The woman, finding that she could not be hid, came fearing and trembling, (Mark 5: 33), and confessed the truth: to dispel these fears and to comfort her mind, Jesus said, Daughter, take courage.

Thy faith hath made thee whole – This thy faith hath saved thee: i.e. thy faith in my power has interested that power in thy behalf, so that thou art saved from thy disorder, and from all its consequences.

MATTHEW 9: 23–26; MARK 5: 35–43; LUKE 8: 49–56

Matthew 9: 23–26

23. Saw the minstrels and the people making a noise – pipers; Anglo-Saxon the whistlers; Gothic, the horn-blowers blowing with their horns. Nearly the same as the pipe-blowers of the Islandic: for among all those nations funeral lamentations accompanied with such rude instruments, were made at the death of relatives. That pipes were in use among the Jews, in times of calamity or death, is evident from Jeremiah 48: 36. And among the Greeks, and Romans, as well as among the Jews, persons were hired on purpose to follow the funeral processions with lamentations. See Jeremiah 9: 17–21; Amos 5: 16. Even the poorest among the Jews were required to have two pipers, and one mourning woman. At these

feet, and besought him that he would come into his house:

42 For he had one only daughter, about twelve years of age, and she lay a dying. But as he went the people thronged him.

43 And a woman having an issue of blood twelve years, which had spent all her living upon physicians, neither could be healed of any,

44 Came behind him, and touched the border of his garment: and immediately her issue of blood stanched.

45 And Jesus said, Who touched me? When all denied, Peter and they that were with him said, Master, the multitude throng thee and press thee, and sayest thou, Who touched me?

46 And Jesus said, Somebody hath touched me: for I perceive that virtue is gone out of me.

47 And when the woman saw that she was not hid, she came trembling, and falling down before him, she declared unto him before all the people for what cause she had touched him and how she was healed immediately.

48 And he said unto her, Daughter, be of good comfort: thy faith hath made thee whole; go in peace.

MATTHEW 9: 23–26; MARK 5: 35–43; LUKE 8: 49–56

Matthew 9: 23–26

23 And when Jesus came into the ruler's house, and saw the minstrels and the people making a noise,

24 He said unto them, Give place: for the maid is not dead, but sleepeth. And they laughed him to scorn.

25 But when the people were put forth, he went in, and took her by the hand, and the maid arose.

26 And the fame hereof went abroad into all that land.

Mark 5: 35–43

35 While he yet spake, there came from the ruler of the synagogue's house certain which said, Thy daughter is dead: why troublest thou the Master any further?

36 As soon as Jesus heard the word that was spoken, he saith unto the ruler of the synagogue, Be not afraid, only believe.

37 And he suffered no man to follow

MATTHEW 9: 23–26; MARK 5: 35–43; LUKE 8: 49–56

Mark 5: 36. Fear not, only believe

The message about her death had induced despair: for he had asked nothing from Christ but relief to the diseased young woman. Christ therefore bids him take care lest, by fear or distrust, he shut out that grace, to which death will be no hindrance. By this expression, only believe, he means that he will not want power, provided Jairus will allow him; and, at the same time, exhorts him to enlarge his heart with confidence, because there is no room to fear that his faith will be more extensive than the boundless power of God. And truly this is the case with us all: for God would be much more liberal in his communications to us, if we were not so close; but our own scanty desires hinder him from pouring out his gifts upon us in greater abundance. In general, we are taught by this passage, that we cannot go beyond bounds in believing: because our faith, however large, will never embrace the hundredth part of the divine goodness.

37. And did not permit any one to follow him

He forbade that they should be allowed to enter, either because they were unworthy to be his witnesses of the miracle, or because he did not choose that the miracle should be overpowered by a noisy crowd around him. It was better that the young woman, whose dead body they had beheld, should suddenly go out before the eyes of men, alive and full of rigor. Mark and Luke tell us that not more than three of the disciples were admitted, and both mention also the parents. Mark alone states that those who had accompanied Jairus when he came to supplicate Christ were admitted. Matthew, who is more concise, takes no notice of this circumstance.

Luke 8: 52. And all were weeping

The Evangelists mention the lamentation, that the resurrection may be more fully believed. Matthew expressly states that musicians were present, which was not usually the case till the death had been ascertained, and while the preparations for the funeral were going forward. The flute, he tells us, was heard in plaintive airs. Now, though their intention was to bestow this sort of honor on their dead, and as it were to adorn their grave, we see how strongly inclined the world is not only to indulge but to promote its faults. It was their duty to employ every method for allaying grief; but as if they had not sinned enough in disorderly lamentation, they are eager to heighten it by fresh excitements. The Gentiles even thought that this was a way of soothing departed spirits; and hence we see how many corruptions were at that time spread throughout Judea.

funeral solemnities it was usual with them to drink considerably; even ten cups of wine each, where it could be got. See Lightfoot. This custom is observed among the native Irish to this day, in what is called their Caoinan. The body of the deceased, dressed in grave-clothes and ornamented with flowers, is placed in some eminent place; the relations and caoiners range themselves in two divisions, one at the head and the other at the feet of the corpse. Anciently, where the deceased was a great personage, the bards and croteries prepared the caoinan. The chief bard of the head chorus began by singing the first stanza in a low doleful tone; which was softly accompanied by the harp. At the conclusion, the foot semichorus began the lamentation, or Ullaloo, from the final note of the preceding stanza, in which they were answered by the head semichorus; then both united in one general chorus.

The chorus of the first stanza being ended, the chief bard of the foot semichorus sung the second stanza, the strain of which was taken from the concluding note of the preceding chorus, which ended, the head semichorus began the Gol, or lamentation, in which they were answered by that of the foot, and then, as before, both united in the general full chorus. Thus alternately were the song and choruses performed during the night. I have seen a number of women, sometimes fourteen, twenty-four, or more, accompany the deceased from his late house to the graveyard, divided into two parties on each side the corpse, singing the Ullaloo, alternately, all the way. That drinking, in what is called the wake, or watching with the body of the deceased, is practiced, and often carried to a shameful excess, needs little proof. This kind of intemperance proceeded to such great lengths among the Jews that the Sanhedrin were obliged to make a decree, to restrain the drinking to ten cups each. I mention these things more particularly, because I have often observed that the customs of the aboriginal Irish bear, a very striking resemblance to those of the ancient Jews, and other Asiatic nations. The application of these observations I leave to others.

It was a custom with the Greeks to make a great noise with brazen vessels; and the Romans made a general outcry, hoping either to stop the soul which was now taking its flight, or to awaken the person, if only in a state of torpor. This they did for eight days together, calling the person incessantly by his name; at the expiration of which term the phrase, – all is over – there is no hope – was used. In all probability this was the violent outcry, mentioned here by the evangelist. How often, on the death of relatives, do men incumber and perplex themselves with vain, worldly, and tumultuous ceremonies, instead of making profitable reflections on death!

24. The maid is not dead, but sleepeth – That is, she is not dead so as to continue under the power of death; but shall be raised from it as a, person is from natural sleep.

They laughed him to scorn – they ridiculed him; they grinned a ghastly smile, expressive of the contempt they felt for his person and knowledge. People of the world generally ridicule those truths which they neither comprehend nor love, and deride those who publish them; but a faithful minister of God, (copying the example of Christ), keeps on his way, and does the work of his Lord and Master.

25. He – took her by the hand, and the maid arose – The fountain of life thus communicating its vital energy to the dead body. Where death has already taken place, no power but that of the great God can restore to life; in such a case, vain is the help of man. So the soul that is dead in trespasses and sins – that is, sentenced to death because of transgression – and is thus dead in law, can only be restored to spiritual life by the mighty power of the Lord Jesus; because HE alone has made the atonement, and HE alone can pardon transgression. If the spiritually dead person be utterly unconcerned about the state and fate of his soul, let a converted relative either bring him to Christ by leading him to hear the unadulterated Gospel of the kingdom; or bring Christ to him by fervent, faithful, and persevering prayer.

him, save Peter, and James, and John the brother of James.

38 And he cometh to the house of the ruler of the synagogue, and seeth the tumult, and them that wept and wailed greatly.

39 And when he was come in, he saith unto them, Why make ye this ado, and weep? the damsel is not dead, but sleepeth.

40 And they laughed him to scorn. But when he had put them all out, he taketh the father and the mother of the damsel, and them that were with him, and entereth in where the damsel was lying.

41 And he took the damsel by the hand, and said unto her, Talitha cumi; which is, being interpreted, Damsel, I say unto thee, arise.

42 And straightway the damsel arose, and walked; for she was of the age of twelve years. And they were astonished with a great astonishment.

43 And he charged them straitly that no man should know it; and commanded that something should be given her to eat.

Luke 8: 49–56

49 While he yet spake, there cometh one from the ruler of the synagogue's house, saying to him, Thy daughter is dead; trouble not the Master.

50 But when Jesus heard it, he answered him, saying, Fear not: believe only, and she shall be made whole.

51 And when he came into the house, he suffered no man to go in, save Peter, and James, and John, and the father and the mother of the maiden.

52 And all wept, and bewailed her: but he said, Weep not; she is not dead, but sleepeth.

53 And they laughed him to scorn, knowing that she was dead.

54 And he put them all out, and took her by the hand, and called, saying, Maid, arise.

55 And her spirit came again, and she arose straightway: and he commanded to give her meat.

56 And her parents were astonished: but he charged them that they should tell no man what was done.

Mark 5: 39. The girl sleepeth

Sleep is everywhere in Scripture employed to denote death; and there is no doubt but this comparison, taken from temporal rest, points out a future resurrection. But here Christ expressly makes a distinction between sleep and death, so as to excite an expectation of life. His meaning is, "You will presently see her raised up whom you suppose to be dead." That he was ridiculed by thoughtless and ignorant people, who were wholly engrossed with profane lamentation, and who did not comprehend his design, ought not to awaken surprise. And yet this very circumstance was an additional confirmation of the miracle, that those people entertained no doubt whatever as to her death.

41. And he took hold of her hand, and said to her
Luke 8: 54. And he took hold of her hand, and cried

Though naturally this cry was of no avail for recalling the senses of the deceased young woman, yet Christ intended to give a magnificent display of the power of his voice, that he might more fully accustom men to listen to his doctrine. It is easy to learn from this the great efficacy of the voice of Christ, which reaches even to the dead, and exerts a quickening influence on death itself. Accordingly, Luke says that her spirit returned, or, in other words, that immediately on being called, it obeyed the command of Christ.

MATTHEW 9: 27–34

27. And while Jesus was departing

The other Evangelists say nothing about these two miracles; for, as we have already said, and as John expressly affirms (21: 25), they did not intend to record every action of Christ, but only to prove, by a brief summary, that he is the Messiah. Now Matthew relates that sight was restored to two blind men, but not so speedily as Christ was wont, on many other occasions, to grant relief to the wretched. While they cry to him on the road, he makes no reply, but, as if he appeared not to notice them, allows them to follow him to his lodging. There he at length asks them what they believe as to his power. Both by action and by words he intended to make trial of their faith; for he holds them in suspense – nay, passes by as if he did not hear them – tries their patience, and what root faith had in their heads. When he afterwards inquires if they believe, he pursues the same investigation. But it may be asked, if a man is convinced of the power of God and of Christ, is that enough to make him a believer? for such appears to be the meaning of the words in verse 28: **Do you believe that I can do this?**

But from other passages of Scripture, it is evident that our knowledge of his power will be cold and unprofitable, if we are not convinced of his willingness. And yet Christ is satisfied with their reply, and applauds their faith, as if it

26. **And the fame hereof went abroad** – In this business Jesus himself scarcely appears, but the work effected by his sovereign power is fully manifested; to teach us that it is the business of a successful preacher of the Gospel to conceal himself as much as possible, that God alone may have the glory of his own grace. This is a proper miracle, and a full exemplification of the unlimited power of Christ.

MATTHEW 9: 27–34

27. **Son of David** – This was the same as if they had called him Messiah. Two things here are worthy of remark:

1st. That it was a generally received opinion at this time in Judea, that the Messiah should be son of David. (John 7: 42)

2dly. That Jesus Christ was generally and incontestably acknowledged as coming from this stock. (Matthew 12: 23)

Have mercy on us – That man has already a measure of heavenly light who knows that he has no merit; that his cry should be a cry for mercy; that he must be fervent, and that in praying he must follow Jesus Christ as the true Messiah, the son of David, expected from heaven.

28. **When he was come unto the house** – That is, the house of Peter at Capernaum, where he ordinarily lodged.

Believe ye that I am able to do this? – Without faith Jesus does nothing to men's souls now, no more than he did to their bodies in the days of his flesh.

They said unto him, Yea, Lord – Under a sense of our spiritual blindness we should have,

1st. A lively faith in the almighty grace of Christ.

2dly. A fervent, incessant cry for the communication of this grace.

3dly. A proper view of his incarnation, because it is through his union with our nature, and by his sufferings and death, we are to expect salvation.

30. **Straitly charged them** – He charged them severely.

31. **But they – spread abroad his fame** – They should have held their peace; for to obey is better than sacrifice, 1 Samuel 15: 22; but man must always be wiser than God, however, it may be profitable to remark,

1st. That honor pursues those who fly from it.

2dly. He who is thoroughly sensible of God's mercy cannot long contain his acknowledgments.

3dly. That God in general requires that what a man has received, for his own salvation, shall become subservient to that of others – Let your light so shine, etc.

God chooses to help man by man, that all may be firmly knit together in brotherly love.

32. **A dumb man possessed with a devil** – Some demons rendered the persons they possessed paralytic, some blind, others dumb, etc. It was the interest of Satan to hide his influences under the appearance of natural disorders. A man who does not acknowledge his sin to God, who prays not for salvation, who returns no praises for the mercies he is continually receiving, may well be said to be possessed with a dumb demon.

33. **And when the devil was cast out, the dumb spake** – The very miracle which was now wrought was to be the demonstrative proof of the Messiah's being manifested in the flesh. See Isaiah 35: 5–6.

It was never so seen in Israel – The greatest of the prophets has never been able to do such miracles as these. This was the remark of the people; and thus we find that the poor and the simple were more ready to acknowledge the hand of God than the rich and the learned. Many miracles had been wrought in the course of this one day, and this excited their surprise.

34. **He casteth out devils through the prince of the devils** – It is a consummate piece of malice to attribute the works of God to the devil. Envy cannot suffer the approbation which is given to the excellencies of others. Those whose hearts are possessed by this vice speak the very language of the devil. Calumny is but a little distance from envy. Though all persons

MATTHEW 9: 27–34

27 And when Jesus departed thence, two blind men followed him, crying, and saying, Thou Son of David, have mercy on us.

28 And when he was come into the house, the blind men came to him: and Jesus saith unto them, Believe ye that I am able to do this? They said unto him, Yea, Lord.

29 Then touched he their eyes, saying, According to your faith be it unto you.

30 And their eyes were opened; and Jesus straitly charged them, saying, See that no man know it.

31 But they, when they were departed, spread abroad his fame in all that country.

32 As they went out, behold, they brought to him a dumb man possessed with a devil.

33 And when the devil was cast out, the dumb spake: and the multitudes marveled, saying, It was never so seen in Israel.

34 But the Pharisees said, He casteth out devils through the prince of the devils.

MATTHEW 9: 35–38

35 And Jesus went about all the cities and villages, teaching in their synagogues, and preaching the gospel of the kingdom, and healing every sickness and every disease among the people.

36 But when he saw the multitudes, he was moved with compassion on them, because they fainted, and were scattered abroad, as sheep having no shepherd.

37 Then saith he unto his disciples, The harvest truly is plenteous, but the labourers are few;

38 Pray ye therefore the Lord of the harvest, that he will send forth labourers into his harvest.

MATTHEW 8: 23–27; MARK 4: 35–41; LUKE 8: 22–25

Matthew 8: 23–27

23 And when he was entered into a ship, his disciples followed him.

24 And, behold, there arose a great tempest in the sea, insomuch that the

had been all that could be wished. I answer, they had some perception of his grace; for they had already acknowledged him to be the Son of David; bestowing upon him this title as Redeemer of their nation and author of all blessings. He questions them, therefore, as to his power, and proceeds farther to inquire if they believe in good earnest. Faith embraces the mercy and fatherly love of God along with his power, and the generous design of Christ along with his ability to save.

MATTHEW 9: 35–38

35. And Jesus went about

This statement is made by way of anticipating an objection, and is intended to inform us that the whole ministry of Christ is not minutely described: for he was constantly employed in the discharge of his office; that is, in proclaiming the doctrine of salvation, and in confirming it by the addition of miracles.

MATTHEW 8: 23–27; MARK 4: 35–41; LUKE 8: 22–25

Though Christ's sleep was natural, yet it served the additional purpose of making the disciples better acquainted with their weakness. I will not say, as many do, that Christ pretended sleep, in order to try them. On the contrary, I think that he was asleep in such a manner as the condition and necessity of human nature required.

And yet his divinity watched over him, so that the apostles had no reason to fear that consolation would not be immediately provided, or that assistance would not be obtained from heaven. Let us therefore conclude, that all this was arranged by the secret providence of God – that Christ was asleep, that a violent tempest arose, and that the waves covered the ship, which was in imminent danger of perishing. And let us learn hence that, whenever any adverse occurrence takes place, the Lord tries our faith. If the distresses grow to such a height as almost to overwhelm us, let us believe that God does it with the same design of exercising our patience, or of bringing to light in this way our hidden weakness; as we see that, when the apostles were covered by the billows, their weakness, which formerly lay concealed, was discovered.

25. Lord, save us

A pious prayer, one would think: for what else had they to do when they were lost than to implore safety from Christ? But as Christ charges them with unbelief, we must inquire in what respect they sinned. Certainly, I have no doubt that they attached too much importance to the bodily presence of their Master: for, according to Mark, they do not merely

may not have as much envy as the Pharisees, yet they should fear having some degree of it, as all have the principle from whence it proceeds, viz. sin.

MATTHEW 9: 35–38

35. Jesus went about all the cities and villages – Of Galilee. A real minister of Jesus Christ, after his example, is neither detained in one place by a comfortable provision made by some, nor discouraged from pursuing his work by the calumny and persecution of others. It is proper to remark, that, wherever Christ comes, the proofs of his presence evidently appear: he works none but salutary and beneficial miracles, because his ministry is a ministry of salvation.

36. Moved with compassion – The Jews esteemed the bowels to be the seat of sympathy and the tender passions, and so applied the organ to the sense.

And were scattered abroad – thrown down, or, all along. They were utterly neglected as to the interests of their souls, and rejected by the proud and disdained Pharisees. This people (this mob) that knoweth not the law, is accursed, John 7: 49. Thus those execrable men spoke of the souls that God had made, and of whom they should have been the instructors.

Those teachers, in name, have left their successors behind them; but, as in the days of Christ, so now, God has in his mercy rescued the flock out of the hands of those who only fed upon their flesh, and clothed themselves with their wool. The days in which a man was obliged to give his property to what was called THE Church, for the salvation of his soul, Christ being left out of the question, are, thank God, nearly over and gone. Jesus is the true Shepherd; without him there is nothing but fainting, fatigue, vexation, and dispersion. O that we may be led out and in by him, and find pasture!

37. The harvest – The souls who are ready to receive the truth are very numerous; but the laborers are few. There are multitudes of scribes, Pharisees, and priests, of reverend and right reverend men; but there are few that work. Jesus wishes for laborers, not gentlemen, who are either idle drones, or slaves to pleasure and sin, and "Born to consume the produce of the soil."

It was customary with the Jews to call their rabbins and students reapers; and their work of instruction, the harvest. So in Idra Rabba, s. 2. "The days are few; the creditor is urgent; the crier calls out incessantly; and the reapers are few." And in Pirkey Aboth: "The day is short, the work great, the workmen idle, the reward abundant, and the master of the household is urgent." In all worldly concerns, if there be the prospect of much gain, most men are willing enough to labor; but if it be to save their own souls, or the souls of others, what indolence, backwardness, and carelessness! While their adversary, the devil, is going about as a roaring lion, seeking whom he may devour; and a careless soul, and especially a careless minister is his especial prey.

The place of the harvest is the whole earth: it signifies little where a man works, provided it be by the appointment, in the Spirit, and with the blessing of God.

38. That he will send forth laborers – that he would thrust forth laborers. Those who are fittest for the work are generally most backward to the employment. The man who is forward to become a preacher knows little of God, of human nature, or of his own heart. It is, God's province to thrust out such preachers as shall labor; and it is our duty to entreat him to do so. A minister of Christ is represented as a day-laborer: he comes into the harvest, not to become lord of it, not to live on the labor of others, but to work, and to labor his day. Though the work may be very severe, yet, to use a familiar expression, there is good wages in the harvest-home; and the day, though hot, is but a short one.

How earnestly should the flock of Christ pray to the good Shepherd to send them pastors after his own heart, who will feed them with knowledge, and who shall be the means of spreading the knowledge of his truth and the savor of his grace over the face of the

ship was covered with the waves: but he was asleep.

25 And his disciples came to him, and awoke him, saying, Lord, save us: we perish.

26 And he saith unto them, Why are ye fearful, O ye of little faith? Then he arose, and rebuked the winds and the sea; and there was a great calm.

27 But the men marveled, saying, What manner of man is this, that even the winds and the sea obey him!

Mark 4: 35–41

35 And the same day, when the even was come, he saith unto them, Let us pass over unto the other side.

36 And when they had sent away the multitude, they took him even as he was in the ship. And there were also with him other little ships.

37 And there arose a great storm of wind, and the waves beat into the ship, so that it was now full.

38 And he was in the hinder part of the ship, asleep on a pillow: and they awake him, and say unto him, Master, carest thou not that we perish?

39 And he arose, and rebuked the wind, and said unto the sea, Peace, be still. And the wind ceased, and there was a great calm.

40 And he said unto them, Why are ye so fearful? how is it that ye have no faith?

41 And they feared exceedingly, and said one to another, What manner of man is this, that even the wind and the sea obey him?

Luke 8: 22–25

22 Now it came to pass on a certain day, that he went into a ship with his disciples: and he said unto them, Let us go over unto the other side of the lake. And they launched forth.

23 But as they sailed he fell asleep: and there came down a storm of wind on the lake; and they were filled with water, and were in jeopardy.

24 And they came to him, and awoke him, saying, Master, master, we perish. Then he arose, and rebuked the wind and the raging of the water: and they ceased, and there was a calm.

pray, but expostulate with him, **Master, hast thou no care that we perish**? Luke describes also confusion and trembling: **Master, Master, we perish**. They ought to have believed that the Divinity of Christ was not oppressed by carnal sleep, and to his Divinity they ought to have had recourse. But they do nothing till they are urged by extreme danger; and then they are overwhelmed with such unreasonable fear that they do not think they will be safe till Christ is awakened. This is the reason why he accuses them of unbelief for their entreaty that he would assist them was rather a proof of their faith, if, in confident reliance on his divine power, they had calmly, and without so much alarm, expected the assistance which they asked.

And here we obtain an answer to a question which might be put, and which arises out of his reproof. Is every kind of fear sinful and contrary to faith? First, he does not blame them simply because they fear, but because they are **timid**. Mark adds the word *houto* – **Why are you so timid?** and by this term indicates that their alarm goes beyond proper bounds. Besides, he contrasts **faith** with their **fear** , and thus shows that he is speaking about immoderate dread, the tendency of which is not to exercise their faith, but to banish it from their minds. It is not every kind of fear that is opposed to faith. This is evident from the consideration that, if we fear nothing, an indolent and carnal security steals upon us; and thus faith languishes, the desire to pray becomes sluggish, and the remembrance of God is at length extinguished.

MATTHEW 8: 28–34; MARK 5: 1–20; LUKE 8: 26–39

Matthew 8: 28. Two demoniacs met him

Commentators have been led into the error of separating Matthew's narrative from that of the others by this single difference, that he mentions **two**, while the others mention but one. There is probability in the conjecture of Augustine, who thinks that there were two, but accounts for not more than one being mentioned here by saying, that this one was more generally known, and that the aggravation of his disease made the miracle performed on him the more remarkable. And, indeed, we see that Luke and Mark employ many words in describing the extraordinary rage of the devil, so as to make it evident that the wretched man, of whom they speak, was grievously fomented. The circumstance of their holding up to commendation one singular instance of Christ's divine power is not inconsistent with the narrative of Matthew, in which another, though less known man, is also mentioned.

Mark 5: 6. Worshipped him

The arrangement of the narrative may be thus stated. When

whole earth!

The subject of fasting, already slightly noticed in the preceding notes, should be farther considered.

In all countries, and under all religions, fasting has not only been considered a duty, but also of extraordinary virtue to procure blessings, and to avert evils. Hence it has often been practiced with extraordinary rigor, and abused to the most superstitious purposes. There are twelve kinds of fasts among the Hindoos:

1. The person neither eats nor drinks for a day and night. This fast is indispensable, and occurs twenty-nine times in the year.

2. The person fasts during the day, and eats at night.

3. The person eats nothing but fruits, and drinks milk or water.

4. He eats once during the day and night.

5. Eats one particular kind of food during the day and night, but as often as he pleases.

6. Called Chanderaym, which is, to eat on the first day, only one mouthful; two on the second; and thus continue increasing one mouthful every day for a month, and then decreasing a mouthful every day, till he leaves off where he began.

7. The person neither eats nor drinks for twelve days.

8. Lasts twelve days: the first three days he eats a little once in the day; the next three, he eats only once in the night; the next three, he eats nothing, unless it be brought to him; and, during the last three days, he neither eats nor drinks.

9. Lasts fifteen days. For three days and three nights, he eats only one handful at night; the next three days and nights, he eats one handful if it be brought him, if not, he takes nothing. Then he eats nothing for three days and three nights. The next three days and nights he takes only a handful of warm water each day. The next three days and nights he takes a handful of warm milk each day.

10. For three days and nights he neither eats nor drinks. He lights a fire, and sits at a door where there enters a hot wind, which he draws in with his breath.

11. Lasts fifteen days. Three, days and three nights he eats nothing but leaves; three days and three nights, nothing but the Indian fig; three days and three nights, nothing but the seed of the lotus; three days and three nights, nothing but peepul leaves; three days and three nights, the expressed juice of a particular kind of grass called doobah.

12. Lasts a week. First day he eats milk; second, milk-curds; third, ghee, i.e. clarified butter; fourth, cow's urine; fifth, cow's dung; sixth, water; seventh, nothing.

It is worthy of remark, that these children of the Bridegroom, the disciples, did not mourn, were exposed to no persecution, while the Bridegroom, the Lord Jesus, was with them, but after he had been taken from them, by death and his ascension, they did fast and mourn; they were exposed to all manner of hardships, persecutions, and even death itself, in some of its worst forms.

MATTHEW 8: 23–27; MARK 4: 35–41; LUKE 8: 22–25

Matthew 8: 23–27

24. Arose a great tempest in the sea – Probably excited by Satan, the prince of the power of the air, who, having got the author and all the preachers of the Gospel together in a small vessel, thought by drowning it, to defeat the purposes of God, and thus to prevent the salvation of a ruined world. What a noble opportunity must this have appeared to the enemy of the human race!

25. Lord, save us: we perish – One advantage of trials is to make us know our weakness, so as to oblige us to have recourse to God by faith in Christ. It is by faith alone that we may be said to approach him; by love we are united to him, and by prayer we awake him. All good perishes in us without Christ: without his grace, there is not so much as one moment in which we are not in danger of utter ruin. How proper, then, is this short prayer for us, and how familiar should it be to us! Taken in the extensive Christian sense it is exceedingly expressive: it comprehends all the power of our Lord's

25 And he said unto them, Where is your faith? And they being afraid wondered, saying one to another, What manner of man is this! for he commandeth even the winds and water, and they obey him.

MATTHEW 8: 28–34; MARK 5: 1–20; LUKE 8: 26–39

Matthew 8: 28–34

28 And when he was come to the other side into the country of the Gergesenes, there met him two possessed with devils, coming out of the tombs, exceeding fierce, so that no man might pass by that way.

29 And, behold, they cried out, saying, What have we to do with thee, Jesus, thou Son of God? art thou come hither to torment us before the time?

30 And there was a good way off from them an herd of many swine feeding.

31 So the devils besought him, saying, If thou cast us out, suffer us to go away into the herd of swine.

32 And he said unto them, Go. And when they were come out, they went into the herd of swine: and, behold, the whole herd of swine ran violently down a steep place into the sea, and perished in the waters.

33 And they that kept them fled, and went their ways into the city, and told every thing, and what was befallen to the possessed of the devils.

34 And, behold, the whole city came out to meet Jesus: and when they saw him, they besought him that he would depart out of their coasts.

Mark 5: 1–20

1 And they came over unto the other side of the sea, into the country of the Gadarenes.

2 And when he was come out of the ship, immediately there met him out of the tombs a man with an unclean spirit,

3 Who had his dwelling among the tombs; and no man could bind him, no, not with chains:

4 Because that he had been often bound with fetters and chains, and the chains had been plucked asunder by him,

the demoniacs came to meet him, Christ ordered the unclean spirits to go out of them, and then they prayed and entreated that he would not **torment them before the time**. The worship, therefore, did not precede Christ's words: nor did they complain that Christ gave them uneasiness, till he urged them to go out. We ought to be aware that they did not come of their own accord into the presence of Christ, but were drawn by a secret exercise of his authority. As they had formerly been accustomed to carry men off, in furious violence, to **the tombs**, so now a superior power compels them to appear reluctantly at the tribunal of their judge.

Hence we infer, that the whole of Satan's kingdom is subject to the authority of Christ. For the devils, when Christ summons them to appear before him, are not more at their own disposal than were the wretched men whom their tyranny was wont to drive about in every direction. At length, by the secret power of Christ, they are dragged before him, that, by casting them out, he may prove himself to be the deliverer of men. Reluctantly too they **worship** him, and their rebellious complaints testify that their confession was not made from choice, but was drawn from them by force.

Matthew 8: 29. What have we to do with thee?

Willingly would they, by this word, drive him far from them. But when they see that they are held under restraint, and that it is in vain for them to decline his authority, they complain that they are **tormented before the time**, and likewise mingle entreaty. Thus we see that the devils breathe nothing but rebellion against God; and yet, with all their swelling pride, they are crushed and fall in a moment: for their malice and obstinacy, which is never subdued, ceases not to struggle against the government of God, and yet it is compelled to yield.

Christ does not openly reject, as he did on other occasions, the confession of the devil; and the reason appears to be, that their enmity towards him was so manifest, as to remove every opportunity of unfavorable or calumnious imputation. Besides, Christ paid regard to the spectators. Accordingly, when malicious and wicked men were present, he was more eager to repress calumnies, and more inclined to put a severe restraint on devils. On the present occasion, it was quite enough that the devils, while they were offering a prayer and entreaty, raged and stormed against him.

Mark 5: 9. My name is Legion

The devil was compelled by Christ to pronounce this word, that he might more fully display the greatness and excellence of his grace. There must have been good reasons why this man should have endured so severe a punishment as to have an army of devils, so to speak, dwelling within him. What compassion then was it, to rescue from so many

might, all the merit of his atonement, and all the depth of our misery and danger.

26. Why are ye fearful, O ye of little faith? – Faith is ever bold – incredulity always timid. When faith fails in temptation, there is the utmost danger of shipwreck. Lord, increase our faith! is a necessary prayer for all who desire to be saved.

Then he arose and rebuked the winds, etc. – As the agitation of the sea was only the effect of the wind, it was necessary to remove the cause of the disturbance, that the effect might cease.

There was a great calm – One word of Christ can change the face of nature; one word of his can restore calm and peace to the most troubled and disconsolate soul. Prayer and faith, if sincere, shall be heard, though they may be weak.

1. That our imperfections may not hinder us from praying to God.

2. That we may be persuaded it is not our merits which make our prayers effectual.

3. That we may offer them up with great humility: and,

4. That we may be fully united to Christ, without which union there is no salvation.

There was at first a great agitation; then a great calm. Thus God ever proportions the comfort to the affliction.

27. The men marveled – Every part of the creation (man excepted) hears and obeys the Creator's voice. Sinners have an ear for the world, the devil, and the flesh: till this ear is shut, God's voice is not discerned; for when it is shut to its enemies it is open to its friends.

What manner of man is this – How great is this person! Here was God fully manifest; but it was in the flesh – there were the hidings of his power.

MATTHEW 8: 28–34; MARK 5: 1–20; LUKE 8: 26–39

Matthew 8: 28–34

28. Two possessed with devils – Persons possessed by evil demons. Mark and Luke mention only one demoniac, probably the fiercer of the two.

Coming out of the tombs – It is pretty evident that cupolas were generally builded over the graves among the Jews, and that these demoniacs had their dwellings under such: the evil spirits which were in them delighting more in these abodes of desolation and ruin, as being more congenial to their fierce and diabolic nature, and therefore would drive the possessed into them.

29. What have we to do with thee – The literal translation is, What is it to us and to thee; which perhaps might be understood to imply their disclaiming any design to interfere with the work of Christ, and that he should not therefore meddle with them; for it appears they exceedingly dreaded his power.

What have we to do with thee, is a Jewish phrase, which often occurs in the Old Testament, signifying an abrupt refusal of some request, or a wish not to be troubled with the company or importunity of others. Jehu said to the messenger who was sent by Joram to meet him, What hast thou to do with peace? David said, What have I to do with you, ye sons of Zeruiah? Compare Judges 11: 12; 2 Samuel 16: 10; 2 Kings 9: 18; Ezra 4: 3; John 2: 4.

Art thou come hither to torment us before the time? – From this it appears that a greater degree of punishment awaited these demons than they at that time endured; and that they knew there was a time determined by the Divine Judge, when they should be sent into greater torments.

30. A herd of many swine – These were in all probability Jewish property, and kept and used in express violation of the law of God; and therefore their destruction, in the next verse, was no more than a proper manifestation of the justice of God.

31. Suffer us to go away – Send us away seems to express more fully the absolute power Jesus Christ had over them – permission alone was not sufficient; the very power by which they were to go away, must come from Christ himself! How vain was the boast of Satan, Mat-

and the fetters broken in pieces: neither could any man tame him.

5 And always, night and day, he was in the mountains, and in the tombs, crying, and cutting himself with stones.

6 But when he saw Jesus afar off, he ran and worshipped him,

7 And cried with a loud voice, and said, What have I to do with thee, Jesus, thou Son of the most high God? I adjure thee by God, that thou torment me not.

8 For he said unto him, Come out of the man, thou unclean spirit.

9 And he asked him, What is thy name? And he answered, saying, My name is Legion: for we are many.

10 And he besought him much that he would not send them away out of the country.

11 Now there was there nigh unto the mountains a great herd of swine feeding.

12 And all the devils besought him, saying, Send us into the swine, that we may enter into them.

13 And forthwith Jesus gave them leave. And the unclean spirits went out, and entered into the swine: and the herd ran violently down a steep place into the sea, (they were about two thousand;) and were choked in the sea.

14 And they that fed the swine fled, and told it in the city, and in the country. And they went out to see what it was that was done.

15 And they come to Jesus, and see him that was possessed with the devil, and had the legion, sitting, and clothed, and in his right mind: and they were afraid.

16 And they that saw it told them how it befell to him that was possessed with the devil, and also concerning the swine.

17 And they began to pray him to depart out of their coasts.

18 And when he was come into the ship, he that had been possessed with the devil prayed him that he might be with him.

19 Howbeit Jesus suffered him not, but saith unto him, Go home to thy friends, and tell them how great things the Lord hath done for thee, and hath had compassion on thee.

20 And he departed, and began to

deaths a man who was more than a thousand times ruined! It was a magnificent display of the power of Christ., that by his voice not one devil, but a great multitude of devils, were suddenly driven out. **Legion** denotes here not a definite number of men, but merely a great multitude.

Hence it is evident what a wretched creature man is, when he is deprived of the divine protection. Every man is not only exposed to a single devil, but becomes the retreat of vast numbers. This passage refutes also the common error, which has been borrowed by Jews and Christians from the heathens, that every man is attacked by his own particular devil? On the contrary, Scripture plainly declares, that, just as it pleases God, one devil is sometimes sent to punish a whole nation, and at other times many devils are permitted to punish one man: as, on the other hand, one angel sometimes protects a whole nation, and every man has many angels to act as his guardians. There is the greater necessity for keeping diligent watch, lest so great a multitude of enemies should take us by surprise.

Mark 5: 10. And entreated him earnestly

Luke says, they requested that they might not be sent **into the deep**. Some explain these words to mean that they wished to avoid uninhabited places. I rather view it as referring to their rage for doing mischief. As the devils have no other object than to prowl among men, like lions in search of prey, they are grieved at being plunged into the deep, where they will have no opportunity of injuring and ruining men. That this is the true meaning may be inferred from the words of Mark, who says that they requested that they might not be compelled to go **out of the country**. In a word, they manifest their disposition to be such, that there is nothing which they more eagerly desire than the destruction of mankind.

Matthew 8: 31. Permit us to depart into the herd of swine

Some conjecture that they wished to attack the swine, because they are filled with enmity to all God's creatures. I do admit it to be true, that they are entirely bent on confounding and overthrowing the whole order of nature which God has appointed. But it is certain that they had a more remote object in view, to excite the inhabitants of that country to curse God on account of the loss of the swine. When the devil thunders against Job's house, he does so not from any hatred he bears to timber or stones, but in order that the good man, through impatience at suffering loss, may break out against God. Again, when Christ consents, he does not listen to their prayers, but chooses to try in this manner what sort of people the Gadarenes are. Perhaps, too, it is to punish their crimes that he grants to the devils so much power over their swine. While the reason of it is not known

thew 4: 9, when we find he could not possess the body of one of the vilest animals that God has made, without immediate authority from the Most High! Since a demon cannot enter even into a swine without being sent by God himself, how little is the power or malice of any of them to be dreaded by those who have God for their portion and protector!

32. Ran violently down a steep place, etc. – The prayer of these demons is heard and answered! Strange! But let it be noted, that God only hears demons and certain sinners when their prayer is the echo of his own justice. Here is an emblem of the final impenitence and ruin into which the swinish sinners, the habitually unpure, more commonly fall than other sinners. Christ permits the demons to do that in the swine which he did not permit them to do in the possessed, on purpose to show us what rage they would exercise on us if left to their liberty and malice. Many are the Divine favors which we do not consider, or know only in general. "But the owners of the swine lost their property." Yes; and learn from this of how small value temporal riches, are in the estimation of God. He suffers them to be lost, sometimes to disengage us from them through mercy; sometimes out of justice, to punish us for having acquired or preserved them either by covetousness or injustice.

33. And they that kept them fled – Terrified at what had happened to the swine.

34. The whole city came out – Probably with the intention to destroy Jesus for having destroyed their swine; but, having seen him, they were awed by his presence; and only besought him to depart from their borders. Many rather chose to lose Jesus Christ than those temporal goods by which they gratify their passions at the expense of their souls. They love even their swine better than their salvation.

Certain doctors in both sciences, divinity and physic, gravely tell us that these demoniacs were only common madmen, and that the disease was supposed, by the superstitious Jews, to be occasioned by demons. But, with

due deference to great characters, may not a plain man be permitted to ask, by what figure of speech can it be said that "two diseases besought – went out – filled a herd of swine – rushed down a precipice?" etc. What silly trifling is this! Some people's creeds will neither permit God nor the devil to work; and, in several respects, hardly to exist. For he who denies Divine inspiration, will scarcely acknowledge diabolic influence.

It is said, The whole city came out to meet Jesus. This means no more than all the inhabitants of that place, which, most probably, was no more than a small country village; or perhaps but a few houses. I have observed that the inhabitants of the Zetland Isles, in the North Seas, denominate any collection of houses a town, even where there are but three or four: and thus I think that the Jews denominated their villages, often calling them cities.

MATTHEW 10: 1–8; MARK 6: 7; LUKE 9: 1–2

Matthew 10: 1–8

1. Twelve disciples – Our Lord seems to have had the twelve patriarchs, heads of the congregation of Israel, in view, in his choosing twelve disciples. That he had the plan of the ancient Jewish Church in his eye is sufficiently evident from Matthew 19: 28; and from Luke 10: 1; 22: 30; John 17: 1, etc., and Revelation 21: 12–14.

He gave them power against unclean spirits – Here we find the first call to the Christian ministry, and the end proposed by the commission given. To call persons to the ministry belongs only to Him who can give them power to cast out unclean spirits. He whose ministry is not accompanied with healing to diseased souls, was never called of God. But let it be observed, that, though the spiritual gifts requisite for the ministry must be supplied by God himself, yet this does not preclude the importance of human learning. No man can have his mind too well cultivated, to whom a dispensation of the Gospel is committed. The influence of the Spirit of God was no more designed to render human learning

publish in Decapolis how great things Jesus had done for him: and all men did marvel.

Luke 8: 26–39

26 And they arrived at the country of the Gadarenes, which is over against Galilee.

27 And when he went forth to land, there met him out of the city a certain man, which had devils long time, and ware no clothes, neither abode in any house, but in the tombs.

28 When he saw Jesus, he cried out, and fell down before him, and with a loud voice said, What have I to do with thee, Jesus, thou Son of God most high? I beseech thee, torment me not.

29 (For he had commanded the unclean spirit to come out of the man. For oftentimes it had caught him: and he was kept bound with chains and in fetters; and he brake the bands, and was driven of the devil into the wilderness.)

30 And Jesus asked him, saying, What is thy name? And he said, Legion: because many devils were entered into him.

31 And they besought him that he would not command them to go out into the deep.

32 And there was there an herd of many swine feeding on the mountain: and they besought him that he would suffer them to enter into them. And he suffered them.

33 Then went the devils out of the man, and entered into the swine: and the herd ran violently down a steep place into the lake, and were choked.

34 When they that fed them saw what was done, they fled, and went and told it in the city and in the country.

35 Then they went out to see what was done; and came to Jesus, and found the man, out of whom the devils were departed, sitting at the feet of Jesus, clothed, and in his right mind: and they were afraid.

36 They also which saw it told them by what means he that was possessed of the devils was healed.

37 Then the whole multitude of the country of the Gadarenes round about besought him to depart from them; for they were taken with great fear: and he

by us with certainty, it is proper for us to behold with reverence and to adore with devout humility, the hidden judgment of God. This passage shows also the foolish trifling of some irreligious men, who imagine that the devils are not actually existing spirits, but merely the depraved affections of men: for how could covetousness, ambition, cruelty, and deceit, enter into the swine? Let us learn also, that **unclean spirits** (as they are devoted to destruction) are the enemies of mankind; so that they plunge all whom they can into the same destruction with themselves.

Mark 5: 15. And they come to Jesus

We have here a striking proof that not all who perceive the hand of God profit as they ought to do by yielding themselves to him in sincere godliness. Having seen the miracle, the Gadarenes were afraid, because the majesty of God shone brightly in Christ. So far they did right but now that they send him out of their territories, what could have been done worse than this? They too were scattered, and here is a shepherd to collect them or rather, it is God who stretches out his arms, through his Son, to embrace and carry to heaven those who were overwhelmed by the darkness of death. They choose rather to be deprived of the salvation which is offered to them, than to endure any longer the presence of Christ.

MATTHEW 10: 1–8; MARK 6: 7; LUKE 9: 1–2

The calling of the Apostles is here described to us, not as on a former occasion, when the Lord Jesus Christ, intending to prepare them for their office, selected them for admission into his private circle. They are now called to immediate performance, are ordered to prepare themselves for the work, receive injunctions, and, that there may be no want of authority, are endued with the power of the Holy Spirit. Formerly, they were held in expectation of future labor: now, Christ announces that the hour is come when they must put their hands to the work. It is proper to observe, however, that he does not as yet speak of perpetual apostleship, but only of temporary preaching, which was fitted to awaken and excite the minds of men, that they might be more attentive to hear Christ. So then they are now sent to proclaim throughout Judea that the time of the promised restoration and salvation is at hand at a future period, Christ will appoint them to spread the Gospel through the whole world. Here, he employs them as assistants only, to secure attention to him where his voice could not reach afterwards, he will commit into their hands the office of teaching which he had discharged. It is of great importance to observe this, that we may not suppose it to be a certain and fixed rule laid down for all ministers of the word, when our Lord gives instructions to the preachers of his doctrine

useless, than that learning should be considered as superseding the necessity of Divine inspiration.

2. Apostles – This is the first place where the word is used. he word was anciently used to signify a person commissioned by a king to negotiate any affair between him and any other power or people.

It is worthy of notice, that those who were Christ's apostles were first his disciples; to intimate, that men must be first taught of God, before they be sent of God. Jesus Christ never made an apostle of any man who was not first his scholar or disciple. These twelve apostles were chosen.

1. That they might be with our Lord, to see and witness his miracles, and hear his doctrine.

2. That they might bear testimony of the former, and preach his truth to mankind.

The first, Simon, who is called Peter, and Andrew his brother; etc. – A pious man remarks: "God here unites by grace those who were before united by nature." Though nature cannot be deemed a step towards grace, yet it is not to be considered as always a hinderance to it. Happy the brothers who are joint envoys of Heaven, and the parents who have two or more children employed as ambassadors for God! But this is a very rare case; and family compacts in the work of the ministry are dangerous and should be avoided.

3. Bartholomew – Many are of opinion that this was Nathanael, mentioned John 1: 46, whose name was probably Nathanael bar Talmai, Nathanael, the son of Talmai: here, his own name is repressed, and he is called Bar Talmai, or Bartholomew, from his father.

Matthew the publican – The writer of this history.

James the son of Alpheus – This person was also called Cleopas, or Clopas, Luke 24: 18; John 19: 25. He had married Mary, sister to the blessed Virgin, John 19: 25.

4. Simon – He was third son of Alpheus, and brother of James and Jude, or Judas, Matthew 13: 55.

Judas Iscariot – a man of Kerioth, which was a city in the tribe of Judah, Joshua 15: 25, where it is likely this man was born.

Who also betrayed him – Rather, even he who betrayed him, or delivered him up.

5. These twelve Jesus sent forth, and commanded – To be properly qualified for a minister of Christ, a man must be,

1. filled with the spirit of holiness;

2. called to this particular work;

3. instructed in its nature, etc.; and,

4. commissioned to go forth, and testify the Gospel of the grace of God.

These are four different gifts which a man must receive from God by Christ Jesus. To these let him add all the human qualifications he can possibly attain; as in his arduous work he will require every gift and every grace.

Go not into the way of the Gentiles – Our Lord only intended that the first offers of salvation should be made to the Jewish people; and that the heathen should not be noticed in this first mission, that no stumbling-block might be cast in the way of the Jews.

Into any city of the Samaritans enter ye not – The Samaritans had afterwards the Gospel preached to them by Christ himself, John 4: 4, etc., for the reason assigned above. Such as God seems at first to pass by are often those for whom he has designed his greatest benefits, (witness the Samaritans, and the Gentiles in general), but he has his own proper time to discover and reveal them.

The history of the Samaritans is sufficiently known from the Old Testament. Properly speaking, the inhabitants of the city of Samaria should be termed Samaritans; but this epithet belongs chiefly to the people sent into that part of the promised land by Salmanezer, king of Assyria, when he carried the Israelites that dwelt there captives beyond the Euphrates, and sent a mixed people, principally Cuthites, to dwell in their place. These were altogether heathens at first; but they afterwards incorporated the worship of the true God with that of their idols. See the whole account, 2 Kings 17: 5, etc. From this time they feared Jehovah, and served other

went up into the ship, and returned back again.

38 Now the man out of whom the devils were departed besought him that he might be with him: but Jesus sent him away, saying,

39 Return to thine own house, and shew how great things God hath done unto thee. And he went his way, and published throughout the whole city how great things Jesus had done unto him.

MATTHEW 10: 1–8; MARK 6: 7; LUKE 9: 1–2

Matthew 10: 1–8

1 And when he had called unto him his twelve disciples, he gave them power against unclean spirits, to cast them out, and to heal all manner of sickness and all manner of disease.

2 Now the names of the twelve apostles are these; The first, Simon, who is called Peter, and Andrew his brother; James the son of Zebedee, and John his brother;

3 Philip, and Bartholomew; Thomas, and MATTHEW the publican; James the son of Alphaeus, and Lebbaeus, whose surname was Thaddaeus;

4 Simon the Canaanite, and Judas Iscariot, who also betrayed him.

5 These twelve Jesus sent forth, and commanded them, saying, Go not into the way of the Gentiles, and into any city of the Samaritans enter ye not:

6 But go rather to the lost sheep of the house of Israel.

7 And as ye go, preach, saying, The kingdom of heaven is at hand.

8 Heal the sick, cleanse the lepers, raise the dead, cast out devils: freely ye have received, freely give.

Mark 6: 7

7 And he called unto him the twelve, and began to send them forth by two and two; and gave them power over unclean spirits;

Luke 9: 1–2

1 Then he called his twelve disciples together, and gave them power and authority over all devils, and to cure diseases.

as to what he wishes them to do for a short time. From inattention to this point many have been led astray, so as to demand from all ministers of the word, without distinction, conformity to this rule.

Matthew 10: 1. And having called the twelve disciples

The number, **twelve**, was intended to point out the future restoration of the Church. As the nation was descended from twelve patriarchs, so its scattered remains are now reminded by Christ of their origin, that they may entertain a fixed hope of being restored. Although the kingdom of God was not in so flourishing a state in Judea, as to preserve the nation entire, but, on the contrary, that people, which already had miserably fallen, deserved doubly to die on account of ingratitude in despising the grace which had been offered to them, yet this did not prevent a new nation from afterwards springing up. At a future period, God extended far beyond Zion the scepter of the power of his Son, and caused rivers to flow from that fountain, to water abundantly the four quarters of the world. Then God assembled his Israel from every direction, and united into one body not only the scattered and torn members, but men who had formerly been entirely alienated from the people of God.

MATTHEW 10: 9–15; MARK 6: 8–11; LUKE 9: 3–5

Matthew 10: 9. Do not provide

Christ wanted the disciples to travel across the whole of Judea within a few days, and immediately to return to him, he forbids to carry luggage with them, by which this speed may be retarded. Some have ignorantly supposed that the rule here laid down for the ministers of the word, or for the apostles, is perpetual. We shall presently meet with a few sentences which have a more extensive reference: but the present injunctions not to carry baggage must undoubtedly be restricted to that temporary commission of which I have already spoken. The whole of the prohibition of gold, silver, a scrip, and two coats, which is given by Matthew, must be read in immediate connection, as is evident from the other two Evangelists.

I have therefore chosen to translate *ue ktesesthe*, **do not provide**: for our Lord simply intended to forbid them to take any thing for the journey. They might have scrips, and shoes, and a change of coats, at home; but that they may be better prepared for the journey, he orders them to leave every thing that would be burdensome. Such too is the import of what Mark says, to be shod with sandals. There is an appearance of contradiction as to the staff, or stick for, according to Mark, the staff is allowed, while according to Matthew and Luke it is refused.

gods till after the Babylonish captivity. From Alexander the Great, Sanballat, their governor, obtained permission to build a temple upon Mount Gerizim, which the Jews conceiving to be in opposition to their temple at Jerusalem, hated them with a perfect hatred, and would have no fellowship with them. The Samaritans acknowledge the Divine authority of the law of Moses, and carefully preserve it in their own characters, which are probably the genuine ancient Hebrew; the character which is now called Hebrew being that of the Chaldeans. The Samaritan Pentateuch is printed in the London Polyglott, and is an undeniable record. A poor remnant of this people is found still at Naplouse, the ancient Shechem; but they exist in a state of very great poverty and distress, and probably will soon become extinct.

6. But go rather to the lost sheep, etc. – The Jewish Church was the ancient fold of God; but the sheep had wandered from their Shepherd, and were lost. Our blessed Lord sends these under-shepherds to seek, find, and bring them back to the Shepherd and Overseer of their souls.

7. And as ye go, preach – and as you proceed, proclaim like heralds – make this proclamation wherever ye go, and while ye are journeying. Preach and travel; and, as ye travel, preach – proclaim salvation to all you meet. Wherever the ministers of Christ go, they find lost, ruined souls; and, wherever they find them, they should proclaim Jesus, and his power to save.

From this commission we learn what the grand subject of apostolic preaching was – THE KINGDOM OF HEAVEN IS AT HAND! This was the great message. "They preached," says Quesnel, "to establish the faith; the kingdom, to animate the hope; of heaven, to inspire the love of heavenly things, and the contempt of earthly; which is at hand, that men may prepare for it without delay."

8. Freely ye have received, freely give – A rule very necessary, and of great extent. A minister or laborer in the Gospel vineyard, though worthy of his comfortable support while in the work, should never preach for hire, or make a secular traffic of a spiritual work. What a scandal is it for a man to traffic with gifts which he pretends, at least, to have received from the Holy Ghost, of which he is not the master, but the dispenser. He who preaches to get a living, or to make a fortune, is guilty of the most infamous sacrilege.

MATTHEW 10: 9–15; MARK 6: 8–11; LUKE 9: 3–5

Matthew 10: 9–15

9. Provide neither gold, nor silver, nor brass, in your purses – In a thousand instances an apostolic preacher, who goes to the wilderness to seek the lost sheep, will be exposed to hunger and cold, and other inconveniences; he must therefore resign himself to God, depending on his providence for the necessaries of life. If God have sent him, he is bound to support him, and will do it: anxiety therefore, in him, is a double crime, as it insinuates a bad opinion of the Master who has employed him. Every missionary should make himself master of this subject.

Have no money in your purse, is a command, obedience to which was secured by the narrow circumstances of most of the primitive genuine preachers of the Gospel. Whole herds of friars mendicants have professed the same principle, and abandoned themselves to voluntary poverty; but if the money be in the heart it is a worse evil. In the former case, it may be a temptation to sin; in the latter, it must be ruinous.

10. Nor scrip for your journey – To carry provisions. This was a leather pouch hung about their necks, in which they put their victuals. This was properly, the shepherd's bag.

Neither two coats, etc. – Nothing to encumber you.

Nor yet staves – As if he had said: "Ye shall take nothing to defend yourselves with, because ye are the servants of the Lord, and are to be supported by his bounty, and defended by his power. In a word, be like men in haste, and eager to begin the important work of the

2 And he sent them to preach the kingdom of God, and to heal the sick.

MATTHEW 10: 9–15; MARK 6: 8–11; LUKE 9: 3–5

Matthew 10: 9–15

9 Provide neither gold, nor silver, nor brass in your purses,

10 Nor scrip for your journey, neither two coats, neither shoes, nor yet staves: for the workman is worthy of his meat.

11 And into whatsoever city or town ye shall enter, inquire who in it is worthy; and there abide till ye go thence.

12 And when ye come into an house, salute it.

13 And if the house be worthy, let your peace come upon it: but if it be not worthy, let your peace return to you.

14 And whosoever shall not receive you, nor hear your words, when ye depart out of that house or city, shake off the dust of your feet.

15 Verily I say unto you, It shall be more tolerable for the land of Sodom and Gomorrha in the day of judgment, than for that city.

Mark 6: 8–11

8 And commanded them that they should take nothing for their journey, save a staff only; no scrip, no bread, no money in their purse:

9 But be shod with sandals; and not put on two coats.

10 And he said unto them, In what place soever ye enter into an house, there abide till ye depart from that place.

11 And whosoever shall not receive you, nor hear you, when ye depart thence, shake off the dust under your feet for a testimony against them. Verily I say unto you, It shall be more tolerable for Sodom and Gomorrha in the day of judgment, than for that city.

Luke 9: 3–5

3 And he said unto them, Take nothing for your journey, neither staves, nor scrip, neither bread, neither money; neither have two coats apiece.

4 And whatsoever house ye enter into, there abide, and thence depart.

5 And whosoever will not receive you, when ye go out of that city, shake off the

10. For the laborer is worthy of his food

Christ anticipates an objection that might be made: for it might appear to be a harsh condition to travel through the whole of Judea without any provisions. Accordingly, Christ tells them, that they have no reason to dread that they will suffer hunger; because, wherever they come, they will at least be worthy of their food. He calls them laborers, not that they resembled ordinary ministers, who labor in the Lord's vineyard, and who, by planting and watering, bring it into a state of cultivation; but merely because they were the heralds of a richer and more complete doctrine. They did not at that time receive the office of preaching any farther than to render the Jews attentive to the preaching of the Gospel.

14. Shake off the dust

As the Lord here recommends the doctrine of the gospel, that all may receive it with reverence, and terrifies rebels by threatening severe punishment, so he enjoins the apostles to proclaim the vengeance which he threatens. But this they cannot do, unless they burn with very ardent zeal to make known the doctrines which they preach. We must therefore hold that no man is qualified to become a teacher of heavenly doctrine, unless his feelings respecting it be such, that he is distressed and agonized when it is treated with contempt.

MATTHEW 10: 16–20; LUKE 12: 11–12

Matthew 10: 16. wise as serpents, and harmless as doves

Serpents, being aware that they are hated, carefully avoid and shrink from every thing that is hostile to them. In this manner he enjoins believers to take care of their life, so as not to rush heedlessly into danger, or lay themselves open to any kind of injury.

Doves, on the other hand, though naturally timid, and liable to innumerable attacks, fly in their simplicity, imagine themselves safe till they are struck, and in most cases place themselves within the reach of the fowler's snares. To such simplicity Christ exhorts his disciples, that no excess of terror may hinder them from pursuing their course. There are some who carry their ingenious reasonings still farther as to the nature of the serpent and of the dove, but this is the utmost extent of the resemblance. We see that Christ condemns that carnal wisdom, or rather that trickery, in which the greater part of men are too fond of indulging, while they look around them on every hand to discover how far it will be safe for them to proceed; and thus, from an unwillingness to encounter danger, they renounce the call of Christ.

ministry. The sheep are lost-ruined: Satan is devouring them: give all diligence to pluck them out of the jaws of the destroyer."

The workman is worthy of his meat – of his maintenance. It is a maintenance, and that only, which a minister of God is to expect, and that he has a Divine right to; but not to make a fortune, or lay up wealth: besides, it is the workman, he that labors in the word and doctrine, that is to get even this. How contrary to Christ is it for a man to have vast revenues, as a minister of the Gospel, who ministers no Gospel, and who spends the revenues of the Church to its disgrace and ruin!

11. Into whatsoever city or town ye shall enter – In the commencement of Christianity, Christ and his preachers were all itinerant.

Inquire who in it is worthy – That is, of a good character; for a preacher of the Gospel should be careful of his reputation, and lodge only with those who are of a regular life.

There abide till ye go thence – Go not about from house to house, Luke 10: 7. Acting contrary to this precept has often brought a great disgrace on the Gospel of God. Stay in your own lodging as much as possible, that you may have time for prayer and study. Seldom frequent the tables of the rich and great; if you do, it will unavoidably prove a snare to you. The unction of God will perish from your mind, and your preaching be only a dry barren repetition of old things; the bread of God in your hands will be like the dry, mouldy, Gibeonitish crusts, mentioned Joshua 9: 5. He who knows the value of time, and will redeem it from useless chit-chat, and trifling visits, will find enough for all the purposes of his own salvation, the cultivation of his mind, and the work of the ministry. He to whom time is not precious, and who lives not by rule, never finds time sufficient for any thing, is always embarrassed, always in a hurry, and never capable of bringing one good purpose to proper effect.

12. Salute it – saying, "Peace be to this house." Great is PEACE, for all other blessings are comprehended in it. To wish peace to a family, in the name and by the authority of Christ, was in effect a positive promise, on the Lord's side, of all the good implied in the wish. This was paying largely even beforehand. Whoever receives the messengers of God into his house confers the highest honor upon himself, and not upon the preacher, whose honor is from God, and who comes with the blessings of life eternal to that man and his family who receives him.

In India, it is customary for a way-faring man, when night draws on, to enter a house, and simply say, "Sir, I am a guest with you this night." If the owner cannot lodge him, he makes an apology, and the traveler proceeds to another house.

13. If that house be worthy – If that family be proper for a preacher to lodge in, and the master be ready to embrace the message of salvation.

Your peace – The blessings you have prayed for shall come upon the family: God will prosper them in their bodies, souls, and substance.

But if it be not worthy – As above explained.

Let your peace – The blessings prayed for, return to you: it shall turn back upon yourselves. They shall get nothing, and you shall have an increase.

The trials, disappointments, insults, and wants of the followers of Christ become, in the hand of the all-wise God, subservient to their best interests: hence, nothing can happen to them without their deriving profit from it, unless it be their own fault.

14. Shake off the dust of your feet – The Jews considered themselves defiled by the dust of a heathen country, when was represented by the prophets as a polluted laud, Amos 7: 17, when compared with the land of Israel, which was considered as a holy land, Ezekiel 45: 1; therefore, to shake the dust of any city of Israel from off one's clothes or feet was an emblematical action, signifying a renunciation of all farther connection with them, and placing them on a level with the cities of the Heathen. See Amos 9: 7.

15. In the day of judgment – Or, punishment. Perhaps not meaning the day of general

very dust from your feet for a testimony against them.

MATTHEW 10: 16–20; LUKE 12: 11–12

Matthew 10: 16–20

16 Behold, I send you forth as sheep in the midst of wolves: be ye therefore wise as serpents, and harmless as doves.

17 But beware of men: for they will deliver you up to the councils, and they will scourge you in their synagogues;

18 And ye shall be brought before governors and kings for my sake, for a testimony against them and the Gentiles.

19 But when they deliver you up, take no thought how or what ye shall speak: for it shall be given you in that same hour what ye shall speak.

20 For it is not ye that speak, but the Spirit of your Father which speaketh in you.

Luke 12: 11–12

11 And when they bring you unto the synagogues, and unto magistrates, and powers, take ye no thought how or what thing ye shall answer, or what ye shall say:

12 For the Holy Ghost shall teach you in the same hour what ye ought to say.

MATTHEW 10: 21–25; LUKE 6: 40

Matthew 10: 21–25

21 And the brother shall deliver up the brother to death, and the father the child: and the children shall rise up against their parents, and cause them to be put to death.

22 And ye shall be hated of all men for my name's sake: but he that endureth to the end shall be saved.

23 But when they persecute you in this city, flee ye into another: for verily I say unto you, Ye shall not have gone over the cities of Israel, till the Son of man be come.

24 The disciple is not above his master, nor the servant above his lord.

25 It is enough for the disciple that he be as his master, and the servant as his lord. If they have called the master of the house Beelzebub, how much more shall they call them of his household?

MATTHEW 10: 21–25; LUKE 6: 40

Matthew 10: 21. And the brother will deliver up the brother to death

He first gives warning what heavy calamities await them, and then adds a remarkable consideration, which sweetens all their bitterness. First, he announces that those circumstances which other men find to be the means of protection, or from which they obtain some relief, will prove to the disciples a fresh addition to their misery. Brothers, who ought to assist them when oppressed, to stretch out their hand to them amidst their distresses, and to watch over their safety, will be their mortal enemies.

It is a mistake however, to suppose that it happens to none but believers to be **delivered up to death by their brethren:** for it is possible that a father may pursue his son with holy zeal, if he perceives him to have apostatized from the true worship of God; nay, the Lord enjoins us in such a case (Deuteronomy 13: 9) to forget flesh and blood, and to bestow all our care on vindicating the glory of his name. Whoever has fear and reverence for God will not spare his own relatives, but will rather choose that all of them should perish, if it be found necessary, than that the kingdom of Christ should be scattered, the doctrine of salvation extinguished, and the worship of God abolished. If our affections were properly regulated, there would be no other cause of just hatred among us.

MATTHEW 10: 26–31; MARK 4: 22–23; LUKE 8: 17; 12: 2–7

Matthew 10: 26. Fear them not therefore

When the apostles saw the gospel so greatly despised, and recollected the small number of believers, they might be apt to throw away hope even for the future. Christ now meets this doubt, by declaring that the gospel would be widely spread, would at length rise superior to all the hindrances which might arise from men, and would become generally known. The saying, nothing is covered that shall not be revealed, has some appearance of being a proverb: but we restrict it in a special manner to the doctrine of salvation, which Christ promises will be victorious, whatsoever may be the contrivances of men to oppose it. Though he sometimes preached openly in the temple, yet, as his doctrine was rejected, it was still concealed in dark comers: but he declares that the time for proclaiming it will come; which, we know, happened shortly afterwards. In no part of the earth was there ever such thunder heard as the voice of the gospel, which resounded through the whole world. As this promise ought to fill them with courage, Christ exhorts them to devote themselves to it with boldness and perseverance, and not to be alarmed, though they see the gospel

judgment, nor the day of the destruction of the Jewish state by the Romans; but a day in which God should send punishment on that particular city, or on that person, for their crimes. So the day of judgment of Sodom and Gomorrah, was the time in which the Lord destroyed them by fire and brimstone, from the Lord out of heaven.

If men are thus treated for not receiving the preachers of the Gospel, what will it be to despise the Gospel itself, to decry it, to preach the contrary, to hinder the preaching of it, to abuse those who do preach it in its purity, or to render it fruitless by calumnies and lies! Their punishment, our Lord intimates, shall be greater than that inflicted on the inhabitants of Sodom and Gomorrah!

MATTHEW 10: 16–20; LUKE 12: 11–12

Matthew 10: 16–20

16. Behold, I send you forth as sheep in the midst of wolves – He who is called to preach the Gospel is called to embrace a state of constant labor, and frequent suffering. He who gets ease and pleasure, in consequence of embracing the ministerial office, neither preaches the Gospel, nor is sent of God. If he did the work of an evangelist, wicked men and demons would both oppose him.

Wise (prudent) as serpents, and harmless as doves – This is a proverbial saying: so in Shir hashirim Rabba, fol. 16, "The holy blessed God said to the Israelites, Ye shall be towards me as upright as the doves; but, towards the Gentiles, as cunning as serpents."

There is a beauty in this saying which is seldom observed. The serpent is represented as prudent to excess, being full of cunning, Genesis 3: 1; 2 Corinthians 11: 3; and the dove is simple, even to stupidity, Hosea 7: 11; but Jesus Christ corrects here the cunning of the serpent, by the simplicity of the dove; and the too great simplicity of the dove, by the cunning of the serpent.

17. But beware of men – Or, be on your guard against men, THESE men; i.e. your countrymen; those from whom you might have rea-

sonably expected comfort and support; and especially those in power, who will abuse that power to oppress you.

Councils – sanhedrins and synagogues. "By synagogues we may understand here, not the places of public worship, but assemblies where three magistrates, chosen out of the principal members of the synagogue, presided to adjust differences among the people: these had power, in certain cases, to condemn to the scourge, but not to death. See Acts 22: 19; 2 Corinthians 11: 24, compared with Luke 12: 11."

18. Ye shall be brought before governors, etc. – "This affords a striking proof of the prescience of Christ. Who could have thought, at that time, that these despised and illiterate men could excite so much attention, and be called upon to apologize for the profession of their faith before the tribunals of the most illustrious personages of the earth?" Wakefield.

By governors and kings we may understand, the Roman proconsuls, governors of provinces, and the kings who were tributary to the Roman government, and the emperors themselves, before whom many of the primitive Christians were brought.

For a testimony against them and the Gentiles – That is, to render testimony, both to Jews and Gentiles, of the truth and power of my Gospel.

19. Take no thought how or what ye shall speak – Be not anxiously careful, because such anxiety argues distrust in God, and infallibly produces a confused mind. In such a state, no person is fit to proclaim or vindicate the truth. This promise, It shall be given you, etc., banishes all distrust and inquietude on dangerous occasions; but without encouraging sloth and negligence, and without dispensing with the obligation we are under to prepare ourselves by the meditation of sacred truths, by the study of the Holy Scriptures, and by prayer.

20. For it is – the Spirit of your Father, etc. – This was an extraordinary promise, and was literally fulfilled to those first preachers of the Gospel; and to them it was essentially neces-

Luke 6: 40

40 And they sat down in ranks, by hundreds, and by fifties.

MATTHEW 10: 26–31; MARK 4: 22–23; LUKE 8: 17; 12: 2–7

Matthew 10: 26–31

26 Fear them not therefore: for there is nothing covered, that shall not be revealed; and hid, that shall not be known.

27 What I tell you in darkness, that speak ye in light: and what ye hear in the ear, that preach ye upon the housetops.

28 And fear not them which kill the body, but are not able to kill the soul: but rather fear him which is able to destroy both soul and body in hell.

29 Are not two sparrows sold for a farthing? and one of them shall not fall on the ground without your Father.

30 But the very hairs of your head are all numbered.

31 Fear ye not therefore, ye are of more value than many sparrows.

Mark 4: 22–23

22 For there is nothing hid, which shall not be manifested; neither was any thing kept secret, but that it should come abroad.

23 If any man have ears to hear, let him hear.

Luke 8: 17

17 For nothing is secret, that shall not be made manifest; neither any thing hid, that shall not be known and come abroad.

Luke 12: 2–7

2 For there is nothing covered, that shall not be revealed; neither hid, that shall not be known.

3 Therefore whatsoever ye have spoken in darkness shall be heard in the light; and that which ye have spoken in the ear in closets shall be proclaimed upon the housetops.

4 And I say unto you my friends, Be not afraid of them that kill the body, and after that have no more that they can do.

5 But I will forewarn you whom ye shall fear: Fear him, which after he hath killed hath power to cast into hell; yea, I say unto you, Fear him.

hitherto despised, but, on the contrary, to become its zealous preachers.

The passage which I have taken from Mark was, perhaps, spoken at a different time, and in a different sense: but as the sentences in that place are concise, I have followed the meaning which appeared to me the most probable. After having commanded the apostles to assemble burning lamps by sending out a bright light to a great distance, he immediately afterwards adds, nothing is hidden which shall not be revealed. Now the lamp of the gospel was kindled by the apostles, as it were in the midst of darkness, that by their agency it might be raised on high, and shine throughout the whole world. The passage in the eighth chapter of Luke's Gospel is precisely alike. As to the passage in the twelfth chapter, there is no room to doubt that it has the same meaning, though there is a difference in the words: for Christ there commands the apostles to bring to light what they had spoken in darkness. This means, that hitherto they had only spoken in whispers about the gospel, but that their future preaching would be so public, that it would spread to the most distant parts of the world.

MATTHEW 10: 32–35; MARK 8: 38; LUKE 9: 26; 12: 8–9,51–53

Matthew 10: 32. Whosoever therefore shall confess me

He now applies to his present subject what he formerly said in a general manner about contempt of death: for we must struggle against the dread of death, that it may not keep us back from an open confession of faith, which God strictly demands, and which the world cannot endure. For this purpose the disciples of Christ must be bold and courageous, that they may be always ready for martyrdom. Now confession of Christ, though it is regarded by the greater part of men as a trifling matter, is here represented to be a main part of divine worship, and a distinguished exercise of godliness. And justly is it so represented: for if earthly princes, in order to enlarge and protect their glory, and to increase their wealth, call their subjects to arms, why should not believers maintain, at least in language, the glory of their heavenly King?

It is therefore certain that those people extinguish faith (as far as lies in their powers), who inwardly suppress it, as if the outward profession of it were unnecessary. With good reason does Christ here call us his witnesses, by whose mouth his name shall be celebrated in the world. In other words, he intends that the profession of his name shall be set in opposition to false religions: and as it is a revolting matter, he enjoins the testimony which we must bear, that the faith of each person may not remain concealed in the

sary, because the New Testament dispensation was to be fully opened by their extraordinary inspiration. In a certain measure, it may be truly said, that the Holy Spirit animates the true disciples of Christ, and enables them to speak. The Head speaks in his members, by his Spirit; and it is the province of the Spirit of God to speak for God. Neither surprise, defect of talents, nor even ignorance itself, could hurt the cause of God, in the primitive times, when the hearts and minds of those Divine men were influenced by the Holy Spirit.

Your Father – This is added to excite and increase their confidence in God.

MATTHEW 10: 21–25; LUKE 6: 40

Matthew 10: 21–25

21. And the brother shall deliver up the brother, etc. – What an astonishing enmity is there in the soul of man against God and goodness!

That men should think they did God service, in putting to death those who differ from them in their political or religious creed, is a thing that cannot be accounted for but on the principle of an indescribable depravity.

22. Ye shall be hated of all men for my name's sake – Because ye are attached to me, and saved from the corruption that is in the world; therefore the world will hate you. "The laws of Christ condemn a vicious world, and gall it to revenge."

He that endureth to the end shall be saved – He who holds fast faith and a good conscience to the end, till the punishment threatened against this wicked people be poured out, he shall be saved, preserved from the destruction that shall fall upon the workers of iniquity. This verse is commonly understood to refer to the destruction of Jerusalem. It is also true that they who do not hold fast faith and a good conscience till death have no room to hope for an admission into the kingdom of God.

23. But when they persecute you – It is prudence and humility (when charity or righteousness obliges us not to the contrary) to avoid persecution. To deprive those who are disposed to do evil of the opportunities of doing it; to convey the grace which they despise to others; to accomplish God's designs of justice on the former, and of mercy on the latter, are consequences of the flight of a persecuted preacher. This flight is a precept to those who are highly necessary to the Church of Christ, an advice to those who might imprudently draw upon themselves persecution, and of indulgence for those who are weak. But this flight is highly criminal in those mercenary preachers who, through love to their flesh and their property, abandon the flock of Christ to the wolf.

24. The disciple is not above his master – Or in plainer terms, A scholar is not above his teacher. The saying itself requires no comment, its truth and reasonableness are self-evident, but to the spirit and design we should carefully attend. Jesus is the great teacher: we profess to be his scholars. He who keeps the above saying in his heart will never complain of what he suffers. How many irregular thoughts and affections is this maxim capable of restraining! A man is not a scholar of Christ unless he learn his doctrine; and he does not learn it as he ought unless he put it in practice.

25. It is enough for the disciple that he be as his master – Can any man who pretends to be a scholar or disciple of Jesus Christ, expect to be treated well by the world? Will not the world love its own, and them only? Why, then, so much impatience under sufferings, such an excessive sense of injuries, such delicacy? Can you expect any thing from the world better than you receive? If you want the honor that comes from it, abandon Jesus Christ, and it will again receive you into its bosom. But you will, no doubt, count the cost before you do this. Take the converse, abandon the love of the world, etc., and God will receive you.

MATTHEW 10: 26–31; MARK 4: 22–23; LUKE 8: 17; 12: 2–7

Matthew 10: 26–31

26. Fear them not – A general direction to all the persecuted followers of Christ. Fear them not, for they can make you suffer noth-

6 Are not five sparrows sold for two farthings, and not one of them is forgotten before God?

7 But even the very hairs of your head are all numbered. Fear not therefore: ye are of more value than many sparrows.

MATTHEW 10: 32–36; MARK 8: 38; LUKE 9: 26; 12: 8–9, 51–53

Matthew 10: 32–36

32 Whosoever therefore shall confess me before men, him will I confess also before my Father which is in heaven.

33 But whosoever shall deny me before men, him will I also deny before my Father which is in heaven.

34 Think not that I am come to send peace on earth: I came not to send peace, but a sword.

35 For I am come to set a man at variance against his father, and the daughter against her mother, and the daughter in law against her mother in law.

36 And a man's foes shall be they of his own household.

Mark 8: 38

38 Whosoever therefore shall be ashamed of me and of my words in this adulterous and sinful generation; of him also shall the Son of man be ashamed, when he cometh in the glory of his Father with the holy angels.

Luke 9: 26

26 For whosoever shall be ashamed of me and of my words, of him shall the Son of man be ashamed, when he shall come in his own glory, and in his Father's, and of the holy angels.

Luke 12: 8–9

8 Also I say unto you, Whosoever shall confess me before men, him shall the Son of man also confess before the angels of God:

9 But he that denieth me before men shall be denied before the angels of God.

Luke 12: 51–53

51 Suppose ye that I am come to give peace on earth? I tell you, Nay; but rather division:

52 For from henceforth there shall be five in one house divided, three against two, and two against three.

heart, but may be openly professed before men. And does not he who refuses or is silent deny the Son of God, and thus banish himself from the heavenly family?

A more public confession of faith, no doubt, is demanded from teachers than from people in a private station. Besides, all are not endued with an equal measure of faith, and in proportion as any one excels in the gifts of the Spirit, he ought to go before others by his example. But there is no believer whom the Son of God does not require to be his witness. In what place, at what time, with what degree of frequency, in what manner, and to what extent, we ought to profess our faith, cannot easily be determined by a fixed rule: but we must consider the occasion, that not one of us may fail to discharge his duty at the proper time. We must also ask from the Lord the spirit of wisdom and courage, that under his direction we may know what is proper, and may boldly follow whatever we shall have ascertained that he commands us.

Him will I also confess

A promise is added to inflame our zeal in this matter. But we must attend to the points of contrast. If we draw a comparison between ourselves and the Son of God, how base is it to refuse our testimony to him, when on his part he offers his testimony to us by way of reward? If mortals, and men who are of no worth, are brought into comparison with God and the angels and all the heavenly glory, how much more valuable is that which Christ promises than that which he requires? Although men are unbelieving and rebellious, yet the testimony which we deliver to them is estimated by Christ as if it had been made in the presence of God and of the angels.

MATTHEW 10: 37–42; MARK 9: 41; LUKE 14: 25–33

Matthew 10: 37. He who loveth father or mother

As it is exceedingly harsh, and is contrary to natural feelings, to make enemies of those who ought to have been in closest alliance with us, so Christ now says that we cannot be his disciples on any other condition. He does not indeed enjoin us to lay aside human affections, or forbid us to discharge the duties of relationship, but only desires that all the mutual love which exists among men should be so regulated as to assign the highest rank to piety. Let the husband then love his wife, the father his son, and, on the other hand, let the son love his father, provided that the reverence which is due to Christ be not overpowered by human affection. For if even among men, in proportion to the closeness of the tie that mutually binds us, some have stronger claims than others, it is shameful that all should not be deemed inferior to Christ alone. And certainly we do not consider

ing worse than they have made Christ suffer; and under all trials he has promised the most ample support.

For there is nothing covered, etc. – God sees every thing; this is consolation to the upright and dismay to the wicked; and he will bring into judgment every work, and every secret thing, whether good or bad, Ecclesiastes 12: 14.

27. What I tell you in darkness – A man ought to preach that only which he has learned from God's Spirit, and his testimonies; but let him not pretend to bring forth any thing new, or mysterious. There is nothing that concerns our salvation that is newer than the new covenant; and in that there are, properly speaking, no mysteries: what was secret before is now made manifest in the Gospel of the ever-blessed God. See Ephesians 3: 1–12.

What ye hear in the ear – The doctor who explained the law in Hebrew had an interpreter always by him, in whose ears he softly whispered what he said; this interpreter spoke aloud what had been thus whispered to him.

28. Fear not them which kill the body – Those who slay with acts of cruelty, alluding probably to the cruelties which persecutors should exercise on his followers in their martyrdom. But are not able to kill the soul. Hence we find that the body and the soul are distinct principles, for the body may be slain and the soul escape; and, secondly, that the soul is immaterial, for the murderers of the body are not able, have it not in their power, to injure it.

Fear him – It is, not hell-fire we are to fear, but it is God; without the stroke of whose justice hell itself would be no punishment, and whose frown would render heaven itself insupportable. What strange blindness is it to expose our souls to endless ruin, which should enjoy God eternally; and to save and pamper the body, by which we enjoy nothing but the creatures, and them only for a moment!

29. Are not two sparrows sold for a farthing? – The doctrine intended to be inculcated is this: The providence of God extends to the minutest things; every thing is continually under the government and care of God, and nothing occurs without his will or permission; if then he regards sparrows, how much more man, and how much more still the soul that trusts in him!

All things are ordered by the counsel of God. This is a great consolation to those who are tried and afflicted. The belief of an all-wise, all-directing Providence, is a powerful support under the most grievous accidents of life. Nothing escapes his merciful regards, not even the smallest things of which he may be said to be only the creator and preserver; how much less those of whom he is the Father, Savior, and endless felicity!

30. But the very hairs of your head are all numbered – Nothing is more astonishing than the care and concern of God for his followers. The least circumstances of their life are regulated, not merely by that general providence which extends to all things, but by a particular providence, which fits and directs all things to the design of their salvation, causing them all to co-operate for their present and eternal good. Romans 5: 1–5.

31. Fear ye not – ye are of more value – None can estimate the value of a soul, for which Christ has given his blood and life! Have confidence in his goodness; for he who so dearly purchased thee will miraculously preserve and save thee.

MATTHEW 10: 32–36; MARK 8: 38; LUKE 9: 26; 12: 8–9, 51–53

Matthew 10: 32–36

32. Whosoever therefore shall confess me before men – That is, whosoever shall acknowledge me to be the Messiah, and have his heart and life regulated by my spirit and doctrine. It is not merely sufficient to have the heart right before God; there must be a firm, manly, and public profession of Christ before men. "I am no hypocrite," says one; neither should you be. "I will keep my religion to myself" i.e. you will not confess Christ before men; then he will renounce you before God.

53 The father shall be divided against the son, and the son against the father; the mother against the daughter, and the daughter against the mother; the mother in law against her daughter in law, and the daughter in law against her mother in law.

MATTHEW 10: 37–42; MARK 9: 41; LUKE 14: 25–33

Matthew 10: 37–42

37 He that loveth father or mother more than me is not worthy of me: and he that loveth son or daughter more than me is not worthy of me.

38 And he that taketh not his cross, and followeth after me, is not worthy of me.

39 He that findeth his life shall lose it: and he that loseth his life for my sake shall find it.

40 He that receiveth you receiveth me, and he that receiveth me receiveth him that sent me.

41 He that receiveth a prophet in the name of a prophet shall receive a prophet's reward; and he that receiveth a righteous man in the name of a righteous man shall receive a righteous man's reward.

42 And whosoever shall give to drink unto one of these little ones a cup of cold water only in the name of a disciple, verily I say unto you, he shall in no wise lose his reward.

Mark 9: 41

41 For whosoever shall give you a cup of water to drink in my name, because ye belong to Christ, verily I say unto you, he shall not lose his reward.

Luke 14: 25–33

25 And there went great multitudes with him: and he turned, and said unto them,

26 If any man come to me, and hate not his father, and mother, and wife, and children, and brethren, and sisters, yea, and his own life also, he cannot be my disciple.

27 And whosoever doth not bear his cross, and come after me, cannot be my disciple.

28 For which of you, intending to build a tower, sitteth not down first, and coun-

sufficiently, or with due gratitude, what it is to be a disciple of Christ, if the excellence of this rank be not sufficient to subdue all the affections of the flesh. The phrase employed by Luke is harsher, **if any man doth not hate his father and mother,** but the meaning is the same, "If the love of ourselves hinder us from following Christ, we must resist it, courageously": as Paul says, "what things were gain to me, those I counted loss for Christ, for whom I suffered the loss of all things" (Philippians 3: 7–8).

38. He who doth not take up his cross

From particular cases he proceeds to general views, and informs us that we cannot be reckoned his disciples unless we are prepared to endure many afflictions. If we are vexed and tormented by the thought, that the gospel should set us at variance with our father, or our wife, or our children, let us remember this condition, that Christ subjects all his disciples to **the cross.** Yet let us also bear in mind this consolation, that, in **bearing the cross**, we are the companions of Christ – which will speedily have the effect of allaying all its bitterness.

Matthew 10: 40. He who receiveth you, receiveth me

A considerable portion of the world may be opposed to the disciples of Christ, and the confession of their faith may draw upon them universal hatred. Yet here is another consolation tending to excite a very great number of people to treat them with kindness. Whatever is done to them, Christ does not hesitate to reckon as done to himself. This shows how dearly he loves them, when he places to his own account the kind offices which they have received. He is not speaking here about receiving the doctrine, but about receiving the men.

MARK 6: 12–13; LUKE 9: 6

Mark 6: 12. And they departed, and preached

Matthew silently passes over what the Apostles did. Mark and Luke relate that they proceeded to execute the commission which they had received; and from their statements it appears more clearly, that the office which Christ at that time bestowed upon them, as I have formerly mentioned, was temporary, and indeed lasted but a few days. They tell us that the Apostles went through the cities and villages: and they unquestionably returned in a short time to their Master, as we shall find to be stated in another passage.

The only matter that requires exposition here is the fact related by Mark, that they **anointed with oil many diseased people**. Christ having conferred on them the power of healing, it is asked, why did they apply oil? I think that this anointing was a visible token of spiritual grace, by which the healing that was administered by them was declared to

We confess or own Christ when we own his doctrine, his ministers, his servants, and when no fear hinders us from supporting and assisting them in times of necessity.

33. Whosoever shall deny me – Whosoever prefers his worldly interest to his duty to God, sets a greater value on earthly than on heavenly things, and prefers the friendship of men to the approbation of GOD.

Let it be remembered, that to be renounced by Christ is to have him neither for a Mediator nor Savior. To appear before the tribunal of God without having Christ for our Advocate, and, on the contrary, to have him there as our Judge, and a witness against us, – how can a man think of this and not die with horror!

34. Think not that I am come to send peace, etc. – The meaning of this difficult passage will be plain, when we consider the import of the word peace, and the expectation of the Jews. The word peace was used among the Hebrews to express all possible blessings, temporal and spiritual; but especially the former. The expectation of the Jews was, that, when the Messiah should come, all temporal prosperity should be accumulated on the land of Judea. The import of our Lord's teaching here is this, Do not imagine, as the Jews in general vainly do, that I am come to send forth, by forcing out the Roman power, that temporal prosperity which they long for; I am not come for this purpose, but to send forth the Roman sword, to cut off a disobedient and rebellious nation, the cup of whose iniquity is already full, and whose crimes cry aloud for speedy vengeance. From the time they rejected the Messiah, they were a prey to the most cruel and destructive factions; they employed their time in butchering one another, till the Roman sword was unsheathed against them, and desolated the land.

35. I am come to set a man at variance – The spirit of Christ can have no union with the spirit of the world. Even a father, while unconverted, will oppose a godly child. Thus the spirit that is in those who sin against God is opposed to that spirit which is in the followers

of the Most High. It is the spirits then that are in opposition, and not the persons.

36. A man's foes shall be they of his own household – Our Lord refers here to their own traditions. So Sota, fol. 49. "A little before the coming of the Messiah, the son shall insult the father, the daughter rebel against her mother, the daughter-in-law against her mother-in-law; and each man shall have his own household fur his enemies." Again, in Sanhedrin, fol. 97, it is said: "In the age in which the Messiah shall come, the young men shall turn the elders into ridicule; the elders shall rise up against the youth, the daughter against her mother, the daughter-in-law against her mother-in-law; and the man of that age shall be excessively impudent; nor shall the son reverence his father." These are most remarkable sayings, and, by them, our Lord shows them that he was the Messiah, for all these things literally took place shortly after their final rejection of Christ. See the terrible account, given by Josephus, relative to the desolations of those times. Through the just judgment of God, they who rejected the Lord that bought them became abandoned to every species of iniquity; they rejected the salvation of God, and fell into the condemnation of the devil.

MATTHEW 10: 37–42; MARK 9: 41; LUKE 14: 25–33

Matthew 10: 37–42

37. He that loveth father or mother more than me – He whom we love the most is he whom we study most to please, and whose will and interests we prefer in all cases. If, in order to please a father or mother who are opposed to vital godliness, we abandon God's ordinances and followers, we are unworthy of any thing but hell.

38. He that taketh not his cross – i.e. He who is not ready, after my example, to suffer death in the cause of my religion, is not worthy of me, does not deserve to be called my disciple.

This alludes to the custom of causing the criminal to bear his own cross to the place of

teth the cost, whether he have sufficient to finish it?

29 Lest haply, after he hath laid the foundation, and is not able to finish it, all that behold it begin to mock him,

30 Saying, This man began to build, and was not able to finish.

31 Or what king, going to make war against another king, sitteth not down first, and consulteth whether he be able with ten thousand to meet him that cometh against him with twenty thousand?

32 Or else, while the other is yet a great way off, he sendeth an ambassage, and desireth conditions of peace.

33 So likewise, whosoever he be of you that forsaketh not all that he hath, he cannot be my disciple.

MARK 6: 12–13; LUKE 9: 6

Mark 6: 12–13

12 And they went out, and preached that men should repent.

13 And they cast out many devils, and anointed with oil many that were sick, and healed them.

Luke 9: 6

6 And they departed, and went through the towns, preaching the gospel, and healing every where.

MATTHEW 11: 1–6; LUKE 7: 18–23

Matthew 11: 1–6

1 And it came to pass, when Jesus had made an end of commanding his twelve disciples, he departed thence to teach and to preach in their cities.

2 Now when John had heard in the prison the works of Christ, he sent two of his disciples,

3 And said unto him, Art thou he that should come, or do we look for another?

4 Jesus answered and said unto them, Go and shew John again those things which ye do hear and see:

5 The blind receive their sight, and the lame walk, the lepers are cleansed, and the deaf hear, the dead are raised up, and the poor have the gospel preached to them.

6 And blessed is he, whosoever shall not be offended in me.

proceed from the secret power of God; for under the Law oil was employed to represent the grace of the Spirit.

MATTHEW 11: 1–6; LUKE 7: 18–23

Matthew 11: 1. And it happened that when Jesus had made an end

In this passage Matthew means nothing more than that Christ did not desist from the exercise of his office, while the Apostles were laboring in another direction. As soon, therefore, as he sent them away, with the necessary instructions, to perambulate Judea, he performed the duties of a teacher in Galilee. The word commanding, which Matthew employs, is emphatic; for he means that they did not receive a commission to do what they pleased, but were restricted and enjoined as to the statements which they should make, and the manner in which they should conduct themselves.

2. Now when John had heard

The Evangelists do not mean that John was excited by the miracles to acknowledge Christ at that time as Mediator; but, perceiving that Christ had acquired great reputation, and concluding that this was a fit and seasonable time for putting to the test his own declaration concerning him, he sent to him his disciples. The opinion entertained by some, that he sent them partly on his own account, is exceedingly foolish; as if he had not been fully convinced, or obtained distinct information, that Jesus is the Christ. Equally absurd is the speculation of those who imagine that the Baptist was near death, and therefore inquired what message he should carry, from Christ's mouth as it were, to the deceased fathers. It is very evident that the holy herald of Christ, perceiving that he was not far from the end of his journey, and that his disciples, though he had bestowed great pains in instructing them, still remained in a state of hesitation, resorted to this last expedient for curing their weakness. He had faithfully labored, as I have said, that his disciples should embrace Christ without delay. His continued entreaties had produced so little effect, that he had good reason for dreading that, after his death, they would entirely fall away; and therefore he earnestly attempted to arouse them from their sloth by sending them to Christ. Besides, the pastors of the Church are here reminded of their duty. They ought not to endeavor to bind and attach disciples to themselves, but to direct them to Christ, who is the only Teacher. From the beginning, John had openly avowed that he was not the bridegroom (John 3: 29). As the faithful friend of the bridegroom he presents the bride chaste and uncontaminated to Christ, who alone is the bridegroom of the Church. Paul tells us that he kept the same object in view (2 Corinthians 11: 2), and the example of both is held out for imitation to all the ministers of the Gospel.

execution; so Plutarch, "Each of the malefactors carries on his own cross." See John 19: 17.

39. He that findeth his life, etc. – i.e. He who, for the sake of his temporal interest, abandons his spiritual concerns, shall lose his soul; and he who, in order to avoid martyrdom, abjures the pure religion of Christ, shall lose his soul, and perhaps his life too. He that findeth his life shall lose it, was literally fulfilled in Archbishop Cranmer. He confessed Christ against the devil, and his eldest son, the pope. He was ordered to be burnt; to save his life he recanted, and was, notwithstanding, burnt. Whatever a man sacrifices to God is never lost, for he finds it again in God.

40. He that receiveth you – Treats you kindly, receiveth me; I will consider the kindness as shown to myself; for he who receiveth me, as the true Messiah, receiveth that God by whose counsels and through whose love I am come.

41. He that receiveth a prophet – a teacher, not a foreteller of future events, for this is not always the meaning of the word; but one commissioned by God to teach the doctrines of eternal life. It is no small honor to receive into one's house a minister of Jesus Christ. Every person is not admitted to exercise the sacred ministry; but none are excluded from partaking of its grace, its spirit, and its reward. If the teacher should be weak, or even if he should be found afterwards to have been worthless, yet the person who has received him in the name, under the sacred character, of an evangelist, shall not lose his reward; because what he did he did for the sake of Christ, and through love for his Church. Many sayings of this kind are found among the rabbins, and this one is common: "He who receives a learned man, or an elder, into his house, is the same as if he had received the Shekinah." And again: "He who speaks against a faithful pastor, it is the same as if he had spoken against God himself."

42. Little ones – My apparently mean and generally despised disciples.

But a cup of water in the eastern countries was not a matter of small worth. In India, the Hindoos go sometimes a great way to fetch it, and then boil it that it may do the less hurt to travelers when they are hot; and, after that, they stand from morning to night in some great road, where there is neither pit nor rivulet, and offer it, in honor of their god, to be drunk by all passengers. This necessary work of charity, in these hot countries, seems to have been practiced by the more pious and humane Jews; and our Lord assures them that, if they do this in his name, they shall not lose their reward.

Verily – he shall in no wise lose his reward – The rabbins have a similar saying: "He that gives food to one that studies in the law, God will bless him in this world, and give him a lot in the world to come." Syn. Sohar.

Love heightens the smallest actions, and gives a worth to them which they cannot possess without it. Under a just and merciful God every sin is either punished or pardoned, and every good action rewarded. The most indigent may exercise the works of mercy and charity; seeing even a cup of cold water, given in the name of Jesus, shall not lose its reward. How astonishing is God's kindness! It is not the rich merely whom he calls on to be charitable; but even the poor, and the most impoverished of the poor! God gives the power and inclination to be charitable, and then rewards the work which, it may be truly said, God himself hath wrought.

It is the name of Jesus that sanctifies every thing, and renders services, in themselves comparatively contemptible, of high worth in the sight of God.

MARK 6: 12–13; LUKE 9: 6

Mark 6: 12–13

13. Anointed with oil many that were sick – This is only spoken of here, and in James 5: 14. This ceremony was in great use among the Jews; and in certain cases it might be profitable. But in the cases mentioned here, which were merely miraculous, it could avail no more of itself than the imposition of hands. It was used symbolically, as an emblem of that ease, comfort, and joy, which they prayed God to impart to the sick.

Luke 7: 18–23

18 And the disciples of John shewed him of all these things.

19 And John calling unto him two of his disciples sent them to Jesus, saying, Art thou he that should come? or look we for another?

20 When the men were come unto him, they said, John Baptist hath sent us unto thee, saying, Art thou he that should come? or look we for another?

21 And in that same hour he cured many of their infirmities and plagues, and of evil spirits; and unto many that were blind he gave sight.

22 Then Jesus answering said unto them, Go your way, and tell John what things ye have seen and heard; how that the blind see, the lame walk, the lepers are cleansed, the deaf hear, the dead are raised, to the poor the gospel is preached.

23 And blessed is he, whosoever shall not be offended in me.

MATTHEW 11: 7–15; LUKE 7: 24–28

Matthew 11: 7–15

7 And as they departed, Jesus began to say unto the multitudes concerning John, What went ye out into the wilderness to see? A reed shaken with the wind?

8 But what went ye out for to see? A man clothed in soft raiment? behold, they that wear soft clothing are in kings' houses.

9 But what went ye out for to see? A prophet? yea, I say unto you, and more than a prophet.

10 For this is he, of whom it is written, Behold, I send my messenger before thy face, which shall prepare thy way before thee.

11 Verily I say unto you, Among them that are born of women there hath not risen a greater than John the Baptist: notwithstanding he that is least in the kingdom of heaven is greater than he.

12 And from the days of John the Baptist until now the kingdom of heaven suffereth violence, and the violent take it by force.

13 For all the prophets and the law prophesied until John.

14 And if ye will receive it, this is Elias,

MATTHEW 11: 7–15; LUKE 7: 24–28

Matthew 11: 7. And while they were departing

Christ praises John before the people, in order that they may state from recollection what they have heard from him, and may give credit to his testimony. For his name was widely celebrated, and men spoke of him in lofty terms: but his doctrine was held in less estimation, and there were even few that waited on his ministrations.

8. Clothed with soft garments

Those who think that Christ here condemns the extravagance of a court are mistaken. There are many other passages in which luxury of dress, and excessive attention to outward appearance, are censured. But this passage simply means, that there was nothing in the wilderness to attract the people from every quarter; that every thing there was rude and unpolished, and fitted only to inspire disgust; and that such elegance of dress as delights the eyes is rather to be looked for in the courts of kings.

11. Verily I say to you

These words not only maintain the authority of John, but elevate his doctrine above the ancient prophets, that the people may keep in view the right end of his ministry; for they mistook the design of his mission, and, in consequence of this, derived almost no advantage from his discourses. Accordingly, Christ extols and places him above the rank of the prophets, and gives the people to understand that he had received a special and more excellent commission. When he elsewhere says respecting himself that he was not a Prophet (John 1: 21), this is not inconsistent with the designation here bestowed upon him by Christ. He was, no doubt, a Prophet, like others whom God had appointed in his Church to be expounders of the Law, and messengers of his will; but he was more excellent than the Prophets in this respect, that he did not, like them, make known redemption at a distance and obscurely under shadows, but proclaimed that the time of redemption was now manifest and at hand. Such too is the import of Malachi's prediction (Malachi 3: 1), which is immediately added, that the pre-eminence of John consisted in his being the herald and forerunner of Christ; for although the ancient Prophets spoke of his kingdom, they were not, like John, placed before his face, to point him out as present. As to the other parts of the passage, the reader may consult what has been said on the first chapter of Luke's Gospel.

MATTHEW 11: 16–19; LUKE 7: 29–35

Luke 7: 29. And all the people hearing

This part is left out by Matthew, though it throws no small light on the connection of the words; for it was this circum-

MATTHEW 11: 1–6; LUKE 7: 18–23

Matthew 11: 1–6

1. This verse properly belongs to the preceding chapter, from which it should on no account be separated; as with that it has the strictest connection, but with this it has none.

To teach and to preach – To teach, to give private instructions to as many as came unto him; and to preach, to proclaim publicly, that the kingdom of God is at hand; two grand parts of the duty of a Gospel minister.

Their cities – The cities of the Jews.

2. John had heard in the prison – John was cast into prison by order of Herod Antipas, Matthew 14: 3, etc., (where see the notes), a little after our Lord began his public ministry, Matthew 4: 12; and after the first passover, John 3: 24.

3. Art thou he that should come – he that cometh, seems to have been a proper name of the Messiah; to save or deliver is necessarily implied.

There is some difficulty in what is here spoken of John. Some have thought he was utterly ignorant of our Lord's Divine mission, and that he sent merely for his own information; but this is certainly inconsistent with his own declaration, Luke 3: 15, etc.; John 1: 15, 26,33; 3: 28, etc. Others suppose he sent the message merely for the instruction of his disciples; that, as he saw his end approaching, he wished them to have the fullest conviction that Jesus was the Messiah, that they might attach themselves to him.

A third opinion takes a middle course between the two former, and states that, though John was at first perfectly convinced that Jesus was the Christ, yet, entertaining some hopes that he would erect a secular kingdom in Judea, wished to know whether this was likely to take place speedily. It is very probable that John now began, through the length of his confinement, to entertain doubts, relative to his kingdom, which perplexed and harassed his mind; and he took the most reasonable way to get rid of them at once, viz. by applying to Christ himself.

4. Go and show John the things – ye do hear and see – Christ would have men to judge only of him and of others by their works. This is the only safe way of judging. A man is not to be credited because he professes to know such and such things; but because he demonstrates by his conduct that his pretensions are not vain.

5. The blind receive their sight, etc. – The blind look upwards, contemplating the heavens which their Lord hath made.

The lame walk – they walk about; to give the fullest proof to the multitude that their cure was real. These miracles were not only the most convincing proofs of the supreme power of Christ, but were also emblematic of that work of salvation which he effects in the souls of men.

1. Sinners are blind; their understanding is so darkened by sin that they see not the way of truth and salvation.

2. They are lame – not able to walk in the path of righteousness.

3. They are leprous, their souls are defiled with sin, the most loathsome and inveterate disease; deepening in themselves, and infecting others.

4. They are deaf to the voice of God, his word, and their own conscience.

5. They are dead in trespasses and sins; God, who is the life of the soul, being separated from it by iniquity.

Nothing less than the power of Christ can redeem from all this; and, from all this, that power of Christ actually does redeem every penitent believing soul. Giving sight to the blind, and raising the dead, are allowed by the ancient rabbins to be works which the Messiah should perform, when he should manifest himself in Israel.

The poor have the Gospel preached to them – And what was this Gospel? Why, the glad tidings that Jesus Christ came into the world to save sinners: that he opens the eyes of the blind; enables the lame to walk with an even, steady, and constant pace in the way of holiness; cleanses the lepers from all the defilement of their sins; opens the ears of the

which was for to come.

15 He that hath ears to hear, let him hear.

Luke 7: 24–28

24 And when the messengers of John were departed, he began to speak unto the people concerning John, What went ye out into the wilderness for to see? A reed shaken with the wind?

25 But what went ye out for to see? A man clothed in soft raiment? Behold, they which are gorgeously apparelled, and live delicately, are in kings' courts.

26 But what went ye out for to see? A prophet? Yea, I say unto you, and much more than a prophet.

27 This is he, of whom it is written, Behold, I send my messenger before thy face, which shall prepare thy way before thee.

28 For I say unto you, Among those that are born of women there is not a greater prophet than John the Baptist: but he that is least in the kingdom of God is greater than he.

MATTHEW 11: 16–19; LUKE 7: 29–35

Matthew 11: 16–19

16 But whereunto shall I liken this generation? It is like unto children sitting in the markets, and calling unto their fellows,

17 And saying, We have piped unto you, and ye have not danced; we have mourned unto you, and ye have not lamented.

18 For John came neither eating nor drinking, and they say, He hath a devil.

19 The Son of man came eating and drinking, and they say, Behold a man gluttonous, and a winebibber, a friend of publicans and sinners. But wisdom is justified of her children.

Luke 7: 29–35

29 And all the people that heard him, and the publicans, justified God, being baptized with the baptism of John.

30 But the Pharisees and lawyers rejected the counsel of God against themselves, being not baptized of him.

31 And the Lord said, Whereunto then shall I liken the men of this generation? and to what are they like?

stance which gave rise to Christ's expostulation, when he perceived that the scribes persisted so obstinately in despising God. The substance of this passage is, that the common people and the publicans gave glory to God; while the Scribes, flattering themselves with confidence in their own knowledge, cared little for what Christ said. At first sight, this tends only to obscure, and even to disfigure, the glory of the Gospel, that Christ could not gather disciples to himself, except from the dregs and offscourings of the people; while he was rejected by those who had any reputation for holiness or learning. But the Lord intended, from the beginning, to hold out this example, that neither the men of that age, nor even posterity, might judge of the Gospel by the approbation of men; for we are all by nature inclined to this vice. And yet nothing is more unreasonable than to submit the truth of God to the judgment of men, whose acuteness and sagacity amounts to nothing more than mere vanity. Accordingly, as Paul says, "God hath chosen that part which is weak and foolish in the eyes of the world, that he may cast down from its height whatever appears to be mighty and wise" (1 Corinthians 1: 27). Our duty is to prefer this foolishness of God, to use Paul's expression (1 Corinthians 1: 25), to all the display of human wisdom.

Justified God

This is a very remarkable expression. Those who respectfully embrace the Son of God, and assent to the doctrine which he has brought, are said to ascribe righteousness to God. We need not therefore wonder, if the Holy Spirit everywhere honors faith with remarkable commendations, assigns to it the highest rank in the worship of God, and declares that it is a very acceptable service. For what duty can be deemed more sacred than to vindicate God's righteousness?

LUKE 10: 1–12

1. And after these things the Lord appointed

That the Apostles had returned to Christ before these seventy were substituted in their room, may be inferred from many circumstances. The twelve, therefore, were sent to awaken in the Jews the hope of an approaching salvation. After their return, as it was necessary that higher expectation should be excited, others were sent in greater numbers, as secondary heralds, to spread universally in every place the report of Christ's coming. Strictly speaking, they received no commission, but were only sent by Christ as heralds, to prepare the minds of the people for receiving his doctrine. As to the number seventy, he appears to have followed that order to which the people had already been long accustomed. We must bear in mind what has been already said about the twelve Apostles, that as this was the number

deaf to hear his pardoning words; and raises those who were dead in trespasses and sins to live in union with himself to all eternity.

6. Blessed is he whosoever shall not be offended in me – Or, Happy is he who will not be stumbled at me. The Jews expected a temporal deliverer. Many might he tempted to reject Christ, because of his mean appearance, etc., and so lose the benefit of salvation through him. To instruct and caution such, our blessed Lord spoke these words. By his poverty and meanness he condemns the pride and pomp of this world. He who will not humble himself, and become base, and poor, and vile in his own eyes, cannot enter into the kingdom of God. It is the poor, in general, who hear the Gospel; the rich and the great are either too busy, or too much gratified with temporal things, to pay any attention to the voice of God.

MATTHEW 11: 7–15; LUKE 7: 24–28

Matthew 11: 7–15

7. What went ye out into the wilderness to see? – The purport of our Lord's design, in this and the following verses, is to convince the scribes and Pharisees of the inconsistency of their conduct in acknowledging John Baptist for a divinely authorized teacher, and not believing in the very Christ which he pointed out to them. He also shows, from the excellencies of John's character, that their confidence in him was not misplaced, and that this was a farther argument why they should have believed in him, whom the Baptist proclaimed as being far superior to himself.

A reed shaken with the wind? – An emblem of an irresolute, unsteady mind, which believes and speaks one thing to-day, and another to-morrow. Christ asks these Jews if they had ever found any thing in John like this: Was he not ever steady and uniform in the testimony he bore to me? The first excellency which Christ notices in John was his steadiness; convinced once of the truth, he continued to believe and assert it. This is essentially necessary to every preacher, and to every private Christian. He who changes about from opinion to opinion,

and from one sect or party to another, is never to be depended on; there is much reason to believe that such a person is either mentally weak, or has never been rationally and divinely convinced of the truth.

8. A man clothed in soft raiment? – A second excellency in John was, his sober and mortified life. A preacher of the Gospel should have nothing about him which savors of effeminacy and worldly pomp: he is awfully mistaken who thinks to prevail on the world to hear him and receive the truth, by conforming himself to its fashions and manners. Excepting the mere color of his clothes, we can scarcely now distinguish a preacher of the Gospel, whether in the establishment of the country, or out of it, from the merest worldly man. Ruffles, powder, and fribble seem universally to prevail. Thus the Church and the world begin to shake hands, the latter still retaining its enmity to God. How can those who profess to preach the doctrine of the cross act in this way? Is not a worldly-minded preacher, in the most peculiar sense, an abomination in the eyes of the Lord?

Are in kings' houses – A third excellency in John was, he did not affect high things. He was contented to live in the desert, and to announce the solemn and severe truths of his doctrine to the simple inhabitants of the country. Let it be well observed, that the preacher who conforms to the world in his clothing, is never in his element but when he is frequenting the houses and tables of the rich and great.

9. A prophet? yea – and more than a prophet – That is, one more excellent than a prophet; one greatly beyond all who had come before him, being the immediate forerunner of Christ, (see below), and who was especially commissioned to prepare the way of the Lord.

This was a fourth excellency: he was a prophet, a teacher, a man divinely commissioned to point out Jesus and his salvation; and more excellent than any of the old prophets, because he not only pointed out this Christ, but saw him, and had the honor of dying for that sacred truth which he steadily believed and boldly proclaimed.

32 They are like unto children sitting in the marketplace, and calling one to another, and saying, We have piped unto you, and ye have not danced; we have mourned to you, and ye have not wept.

33 For John the Baptist came neither eating bread nor drinking wine; and ye say, He hath a devil.

34 The Son of man is come eating and drinking; and ye say, Behold a gluttonous man, and a winebibber, a friend of publicans and sinners!

35 But wisdom is justified of all her children.

LUKE 10: 1–12

1 After these things the Lord appointed other seventy also, and sent them two and two before his face into every city and place, whither he himself would come.

2 Therefore said he unto them, The harvest truly is great, but the labourers are few: pray ye therefore the Lord of the harvest, that he would send forth labourers into his harvest.

3 Go your ways: behold, I send you forth as lambs among wolves.

4 Carry neither purse, nor scrip, nor shoes: and salute no man by the way.

5 And into whatsoever house ye enter, first say, Peace be to this house.

6 And if the son of peace be there, your peace shall rest upon it: if not, it shall turn to you again.

7 And in the same house remain, eating and drinking such things as they give: for the labourer is worthy of his hire. Go not from house to house.

8 And into whatsoever city ye enter, and they receive you, eat such things as are set before you:

9 And heal the sick that are therein, and say unto them, The kingdom of God is come nigh unto you.

10 But into whatsoever city ye enter, and they receive you not, go your ways out into the streets of the same, and say,

11 Even the very dust of your city, which cleaveth on us, we do wipe off against you: notwithstanding be ye sure of this, that the kingdom of God is come nigh unto you.

12 But I say unto you, that it shall be

of the tribes when the people were in a flourishing condition, so an equal number of apostles or patriarchs was chosen, to reassemble the members of the lacerated body, that the restoration of the Church might thus be complete.

7. Eating and drinking those things which they shall give you

This is another circumstance expressly mentioned by Luke. By these words Christ not only enjoins them to be satisfied with ordinary and plain food, but allows them to eat at another man's table. Their plain and natural meaning is: "you will be at liberty to live at the expense of others, so long as you shall be on this journey; for it is proper that those for whose benefit you labor should supply you with food." Some think that they were intended to remove scruples of conscience, that the disciples might not find fault with any kind of food. But nothing of this kind was intended, and it was not even his object to enjoin frugality, but merely to permit them to accept of a reward, by living, during this commission, at the expense of those by whom they were entertained.

MATTHEW 11: 20–24; LUKE 10: 13–16

Matthew 11: 20. Then he began to upbraid.

Luke states the time when, and the reason why, Christ uttered such invectives against those cities. It was while he was sending the disciples away into various parts of Judea, to proclaim, as they passed along, that the kingdom of God was at hand. Reflecting on the ingratitude of those among whom he had long discharged the office of a prophet, and performed many wonderful works, without any good result, he broke out into these words, announcing that the time was now come, when he should depart to other cities, having learned, by experience, that the inhabitants of the country adjoining that lake, among whom he had begun to preach the Gospel and perform miracles, were full of obstinacy and of desperate malice. But he says nothing about the doctrine, and reproaches them that his miracles had not led them to repent. The object which our Lord had in view, in exhibiting those manifestations of his power, undoubtedly was to invite men to himself; but as all are by nature averse to him, it is necessary to begin with repentance.

As a considerable portion of the world foolishly estimates the Gospel according to the rank of men, and despises it because it is professed by people of mean and despicable condition, our Lord here contradicts so perverse a judgment. Again, almost all are so proud, that they do not willingly submit to their equals, or to those whom they look down upon as inferior to them. God has determined, on the other hand, to govern his Church by the ministry of men, and indeed frequently selects the ministers of the

10. Behold, I send my messenger – A fifth excellency of the Baptist was, his preparing the way of the Lord; being the instrument, in God's hand, of preparing the people's hearts to receive the Lord Jesus; and it was probably through his preaching that so many thousands attached themselves to Christ, immediately on his appearing as a public teacher.

11. A greater than John the Baptist – A sixth excellency of the Baptist – he was greater than any prophet from the beginning of the world till that time:

1st. Because he was prophesied of by them, Isaiah 40: 3, and Malachi 3: 1, where Jesus Christ himself seems to be the speaker.

2ndly. Because he had the privilege of showing the fulfillment of their predictions, by pointing out that Christ has now come, which they foretold should come. And

3dly. Because he saw and enjoyed that salvation which they could only foretell.

Notwithstanding, he that is least in the kingdom of heaven – By the kingdom of heaven in this verse is meant, the fullness of the blessings of the Gospel of peace; which fullness was not known till after Christ had been crucified, and had risen from the dead. Now the least in this kingdom, the meanest preacher of a crucified, risen, and glorified Savior, was greater than John, who was not permitted to live to see the plenitude of Gospel grace, in the pouring out of the Holy Spirit.

12. The kingdom of heaven suffereth violence – The tax-gatherers and heathens, whom the scribes and Pharisees think have no right to the kingdom of the Messiah, filled with holy zeal and earnestness, seize at once on the proffered mercy of the Gospel, and so take the kingdom as by force from those learned doctors who claimed for themselves the chiefest places in that kingdom. Christ himself said, The tax-gatherers and harlots go before you into the kingdom of God.

14. This is Elias, which was for to come – This should always be written Elijah, that as strict a conformity as possible might be kept up between the names in the Old Testament

and the New. The Prophet Malachi, who predicted the coming of the Baptist in the spirit and power of Elijah, gave the three following distinct characteristics of him. First, That he should be the forerunner and messenger of the Messiah: Behold I send my messenger before me, Malachi 3: 1. Secondly, That he should appear before the destruction of the second temple: Even the Lord whom ye seek shall suddenly come to his temple, ibid. Thirdly, That he should preach repentance to the Jews; and that, some time after, the great and terrible day of the Lord should come, and the Jewish land be smitten with a curse, Malachi 4: 5–6. Now these three characters agree perfectly with the conduct of the Baptist.

MATTHEW 11: 16–19; LUKE 7: 29–35

Matthew 11: 16–19

16. But whereunto shall I liken this generation? – That is, the Jewish people – this race.

17. We have piped unto you, and ye have not danced – We have begun the music, which should have been followed by the dance, but ye have not attended to it.

We have mourned – and ye have not lamented – There is an allusion here to those funeral lamentations explained in Matthew 9: 23.

18. For John came neither eating nor drinking – Leading a very austere and mortified life: and yet, he did not receive him. A sinner will not be persuaded that what he has no mind to imitate can come from God. There are some who will rather blame holiness itself, than esteem it in those whom they do not like.

He hath a devil – He is a vile hypocrite, influenced by a demon to deceive and destroy the simple.

19. The Son of man came eating and drinking – That is, went wheresoever he was invited to eat a morsel of bread, and observed no rigid fasts: how could he, who had no corrupt appetites to mortify or subdue?

They say, Behold a man gluttonous, etc. – Whatever measures the followers of God may

more tolerable in that day for Sodom, than for that city.

MATTHEW 11: 20–24; LUKE 10: 13–16

Matthew 11: 20–24

20 Then began he to upbraid the cities wherein most of his mighty works were done, because they repented not:

21 Woe unto thee, Chorazin! woe unto thee, Bethsaida! for if the mighty works, which were done in you, had been done in Tyre and Sidon, they would have repented long ago in sackcloth and ashes.

22 But I say unto you, It shall be more tolerable for Tyre and Sidon at the day of judgment, than for you.

23 And thou, Capernaum, which art exalted unto heaven, shalt be brought down to hell: for if the mighty works, which have been done in thee, had been done in Sodom, it would have remained until this day.

24 But I say unto you, That it shall be more tolerable for the land of Sodom in the day of judgment, than for thee.

Luke 10: 13–16

13 Woe unto thee, Chorazin! woe unto thee, Bethsaida! for if the mighty works had been done in Tyre and Sidon, which have been done in you, they had a great while ago repented, sitting in sackcloth and ashes.

14 But it shall be more tolerable for Tyre and Sidon at the judgment, than for you.

15 And thou, Capernaum, which art exalted to heaven, shalt be thrust down to hell.

16 He that heareth you heareth me; and he that despiseth you despiseth me; and he that despiseth me despiseth him that sent me.

LUKE 10: 17–20

17 And the seventy returned again with joy, saying, Lord, even the devils are subject unto us through thy name.

18 And he said unto them, I beheld Satan as lightning fall from heaven.

19 Behold, I give unto you power to tread on serpents and scorpions, and over all the power of the enemy: and nothing shall by any means hurt you.

Word from among the lowest dregs of the people. It was, therefore, necessary to support the majesty of the Gospel, that it might not appear to be degraded by proceeding from the lips of men.

LUKE 10: 17–20

18. I beheld Satan

From one instance Christ leads them to the whole class; for he commanded his Gospel to be published for the very purpose of overturning Satan's kingdom. So then, while the disciples rested solely on that demonstration which they had obtained from experience, Christ reminds them, that the power and efficacy of their doctrine extends farther, and that its tendency is to extirpate the tyranny which Satan exercises over the whole human race. We have now ascertained the meaning of the words. When Christ commanded that his Gospel should be preached, he did not at all attempt a matter of doubtful result, but foresaw the approaching ruin of Satan. Now since the Son of God cannot be deceived, and this exercise of his foresight relates to the whole course of the Gospel, we have no reason to doubt, that whenever he raises up faithful teachers, he will crown their labor with prosperous success.

MATTHEW 11: 25–29; LUKE 10: 21–22

Matthew 11: 26. Undoubtedly, O Father

This expression removes every pretense for that licentiousness of inquiry, to which we are continually excited. There is nothing which we yield to God with greater difficulty, than that his will shall be regarded by us as the highest reason and justice. He frequently repeats, that his judgments are a deep abyss (Psalm 36: 6); but we plunge with headlong violence into that depth, and if there is any thing that does not please us, we gnash our teeth, or murmur against him, and many even break out into open blasphemies. On the contrary, our Lord lays down to us this rule, that whatever God has determined must be regarded by us as right. This is sober wisdom, to acquiesce in the good pleasure of God as alone equal to a thousand arguments. Christ might indeed have brought forward the causes of that distinction, if there were any; but he is satisfied with the good pleasure of God, and inquires no farther why he calls to salvation little children rather than others, and composes his kingdom out of an obscure flock. Hence it is evident, that men direct their fury against Christ, when, on learning that some are freely chosen, and others are reprobated, by the will of God, they storm because they find it unpleasant to yield to God.

27. All things have been delivered to me

The connection of this sentence with the preceding one

take, they will not escape the censure of the world: the best way is not to be concerned at them. Iniquity, being always ready to oppose and contradict the Divine conduct, often contradicts and exposes itself.

But wisdom is justified of her children – Those who follow the dictates of true wisdom ever justify, point out as excellent, the holy maxims by which they are guided, for they find the way pleasantness, and the path, peace.

The children of true wisdom can justify all God's ways in their salvation; as they know that all the dispensations of Providence work together for the good of those who love and fear God.

LUKE 10: 1–12

1. The Lord appointed other seventy – Rather, seventy others, not other seventy, as our translation has it, which seems to intimate that he had appointed seventy before this time, though, probably, the word other has a reference to the twelve chosen first: he not only chose twelve disciples to be constantly with him; but he chose seventy others to go before him. Our blessed Lord formed every thing in his Church on the model of the Jewish Church; and why? Because it was the pattern shown by God himself, the Divine form, which pointed out the heavenly substance which now began to be established in its place. As he before had chosen twelve apostles, in reference to the twelve patriarchs, who were the chiefs of the twelve tribes, and the heads of the Jewish Church, he now publicly appointed seventy others, as Moses did the seventy elders whom he associated with himself to assist him in the government of the people. Exodus 18: 19; 24: 1–9. These Christ sent by two and two:

1. To teach them the necessity of concord among the ministers of righteousness.

2. That in the mouths of two witnesses every thing might be established. And,

3. That they might comfort and support each other in their difficult labor.

2. That he would send forth – There seems to be an allusion here to the case of reapers, who, though the harvest was perfectly ripe, yet were in no hurry to cut it down. News of this is brought to the Lord of the harvest the farmer, and he is entreated to exert his authority, and hurry them out; and this he does because the harvest is spoiling for want of being reaped and gathered in.

4. Salute no man by the way – According to a canon of the Jews, a man who was about any sacred work was exempted from all civil obligations for the time; forasmuch as obedience to God was of infinitely greater consequence than the cultivation of private friendships, or the returning of civil compliments.

6. The son of peace – In the Jewish style, a man who has any good or bad quality is called the son of it. Thus, wise men are called the children of wisdom, Matthew 11: 19; Luke 7: 35. So, likewise, what a man is doomed to, he is called the son of, as in Ephesians 2: 3, wicked men are styled the children of wrath: so Judas is called the son of perdition, John 17: 12; and a man who deserves to die is called, 2 Samuel 12: 5, a son of death. Son of peace in the text not only means a peaceable, quiet man, but one also of good report for his uprightness and benevolence. It would have been a dishonor to this mission, had the missionaries taken up their lodgings with those who had not a good report among them who were without.

9. The kingdom of God is come nigh unto you – is just upon you. This was the general text on which they were to preach all their sermons.

MATTHEW 11: 20–24; LUKE 10: 13–16

Matthew 11: 20–24

20. Then began he to upbraid the cities – The more God has done to draw men unto himself, the less excusable are they if they continue in iniquity. If our blessed Lord had not done every thing that was necessary for the salvation of these people, he could not have reproached them for their impenitence.

20 Notwithstanding in this rejoice not, that the spirits are subject unto you; but rather rejoice, because your names are written in heaven.

MATTHEW 11: 25–30; LUKE 10: 21–22

Matthew 11: 25–30

25 At that time Jesus answered and said, I thank thee, O Father, Lord of heaven and earth, because thou hast hid these things from the wise and prudent, and hast revealed them unto babes.

26 Even so, Father: for so it seemed good in thy sight.

27 All things are delivered unto me of my Father: and no man knoweth the Son, but the Father; neither knoweth any man the Father, save the Son, and he to whomsoever the Son will reveal him.

28 Come unto me, all ye that labour and are heavy laden, and I will give you rest.

29 Take my yoke upon you, and learn of me; for I am meek and lowly in heart: and ye shall find rest unto your souls.

30 For my yoke is easy, and my burden is light.

Luke 10: 21–22

21 In that hour Jesus rejoiced in spirit, and said, I thank thee, O Father, Lord of heaven and earth, that thou hast hid these things from the wise and prudent, and hast revealed them unto babes: even so, Father; for so it seemed good in thy sight.

22 All things are delivered to me of my Father: and no man knoweth who the Son is, but the Father; and who the Father is, but the Son, and he to whom the Son will reveal him.

MATTHEW 12: 1–8; MARK 2: 23–28; LUKE 6: 1–5

Matthew 12: 1–8

1 At that time Jesus went on the sabbath day through the corn; and his disciples were an hungred, and began to pluck the ears of corn, and to eat.

2 But when the Pharisees saw it, they said unto him, Behold, thy disciples do that which is not lawful to do upon the sabbath day.

3 But he said unto them, Have ye not read what David did, when he was an

is not correctly understood by those commentators who think that Christ intends nothing more than to strengthen the confidence of his disciples for preaching the Gospel. My opinion is, that Christ spoke these words for another reason, and with another object in view. Having formerly asserted that the Church proceeds from the secret source of God's free election, he now shows in what manner the grace of salvation comes to men. Many people, as soon as they learn that none are heirs of eternal life but those whom God chose before the foundation of the world (Ephesians 1: 4), begin to inquire anxiously how they may be assured of God's secret purpose, and thus plunge into a labyrinth, from which they will find no escape. Christ enjoins them to come direct to himself, in order to obtain certainty of salvation. The meaning therefore is, that life is exhibited to us in Christ himself, and that no man will partake of it who does not enter by the gate of faith. We now see that he connects faith with the eternal predestination of God – two things which men foolishly and wickedly hold to be inconsistent with each other. Though our salvation was always hidden with God, yet Christ is the channel through which it flows to us, and we receive it by faith, that it may be secure and ratified in our hearts. We are not at liberty then to turn away from Christ, unless we choose to reject the salvation which he offers to us.

MATTHEW 12: 1–8; MARK 2: 23–28; LUKE 6: 1–5

Matthew 12: 1. Jesus was walking on the Sabbath

It was the design of the Evangelists, in this history, to show partly what a malicious disposition the Pharisees had, and partly how superstitiously they were attached to outward and slight matters, so as to make holiness to consist in them entirely. They blame the disciples of Christ for **plucking the ears of corn on the Sabbath**, during their journey, when they were pressed with hunger, as if, by so doing, they were violating the Sabbath. The keeping of the Sabbath was, indeed, a holy thing, but not such a manner of keeping it as they imagined, so that one could scarcely move a finger without making the conscience to tremble. It was hypocrisy, therefore, that made them so exact in trifling matters, while they spared themselves in gross superstitions; as Christ elsewhere upbraids them with paying tithe of mint and anise, and neglecting the important matters of the Law (Matthew 23: 23).

It is the invariable practice of hypocrites to allow themselves liberty in matters of the greatest consequence, and to pay close attention to ceremonial observances. Another reason why they demand that outward rites should be more rigorously observed is, that they wish to make their

21. Wo unto thee, Chorazin – Bethsaida! – Though the people in these cities were (generally) impenitent, yet there is little doubt that several received the word of life. Indeed, Bethsaida itself furnished not less than three of the twelve apostles, Philip, Andrew, and Peter. See John 1: 44.

Tyre and Sidon – Were two heathen cities, situated on the shore of the Mediterranean Sea, into which it does not appear that Christ ever went, though he was often very nigh to them; see Matthew 15: 21.

They would have repented long ago – Our Lord intimates that, if Ezekiel had done as many miracles in those cities as himself had in Chorazin and Bethsaida, the inhabitants would have repented in sackcloth and ashes, with the deepest and most genuine sorrow.

22. But – it shall be more tolerable – Every thing will help to overwhelm the impenitent at the tribunal of God – the benefits and favors which they have received, as well as the sins which they have committed.

23 Thou, Capernaum – exalted unto heaven – A Hebrew metaphor, expressive of the utmost prosperity, and the enjoyment of the greatest privileges. This was properly spoken of this city, because that in it our Lord dwelt, and wrought many of his miraculous works.

24. But – it shall be more tolerable for the land of Sodom – the land of the Sodomites; i.e. the ancient inhabitants of that city and its neighborhood.

In Jude, Jude 7, we are told that these persons are suffering the vengeance of eternal fire.

Day of judgment – May either refer to that particular time in which God visits for iniquity, or to that great day in which he will judge the world by the Lord Jesus Christ. The day of Sodom's judgment was that in which it was destroyed by fire and brimstone from heaven, Genesis 19: 24; and the day of judgment to Chorazin, Bethsaida, and Capernaum, was the time in which they were destroyed by the Romans, Matthew 11: 23. But there is a day of final judgment, when Hades itself, (sinners

in a state of partial punishment in the invisible world) shall be cast into the lake of fire and brimstone, which is the second death. See Revelation 20: 14.

LUKE 10: 17–20

18. I beheld Satan – Or, Satan himself, the very Satan, the supreme adversary, falling as lightning, with the utmost suddenness, as a flash of lightning falls from the clouds, and at the same time in the most observable manner. The fall was both very sudden and very apparent. Thus should the fall of the corrupt Jewish state be, and thus was the fall of idolatry in the Gentile world.

19. To tread on serpents, etc. – It is possible that by serpents and scorpions our Lord means the scribes and Pharisees, whom he calls serpents and a brood of vipers, Matthew 23: 33, because, through the subtilty and venom of the old serpent, the devil, they opposed him and his doctrine; and, by trampling on these, it is likely that he means, they should get a complete victory over such: as it was an ancient custom to trample on the kings and generals who had been taken in battle, to signify the complete conquest which had been gained over them. See Joshua 10: 24. See also Romans 16: 20.

20. Because your names are written in heaven – This form of speech is taken from the ancient custom of writing the names of all the citizens in a public register, that the several families might be known, and the inheritances properly preserved. This custom is still observed even in these kingdoms, though not particularly noticed. Every child that is born in the land is ordered to be registered, with the names of its parents, and the time when born, baptized, or registered; and this register is generally kept in the parish church, or in some public place of safety. Such a register as this is called in Philippians 4: 3; Revelation 3: 5, etc., the book of life, i.e. the book or register where the persons were enrolled as they came into life. It appears also probable, that when any person died, or behaved improperly, his name

hungred, and they that were with him;

4 How he entered into the house of God, and did eat the shewbread, which was not lawful for him to eat, neither for them which were with him, but only for the priests?

5 Or have ye not read in the law, how that on the sabbath days the priests in the temple profane the sabbath, and are blameless?

6 But I say unto you, That in this place is one greater than the temple.

7 But if ye had known what this meaneth, I will have mercy, and not sacrifice, ye would not have condemned the guiltless.

8 For the Son of man is Lord even of the sabbath day.

Mark 2: 23–28

23 And it came to pass, that he went through the corn fields on the sabbath day; and his disciples began, as they went, to pluck the ears of corn.

24 And the Pharisees said unto him, Behold, why do they on the sabbath day that which is not lawful?

25 And he said unto them, Have ye never read what David did, when he had need, and was an hungred, he, and they that were with him?

26 How he went into the house of God in the days of Abiathar the high priest, and did eat the shewbread, which is not lawful to eat but for the priests, and gave also to them which were with him?

27 And he said unto them, The sabbath was made for man, and not man for the sabbath:

28 Therefore the Son of man is Lord also of the sabbath.

Luke 6: 1–5

1 And it came to pass on the second sabbath after the first, that he went through the corn fields; and his disciples plucked the ears of corn, and did eat, rubbing them in their hands.

2 And certain of the Pharisees said unto them, Why do ye that which is not lawful to do on the sabbath days?

3 And Jesus answering them said, Have ye not read so much as this, what David did, when himself was an hungred, and they which were with him;

4 How he went into the house of God,

duty toward God to consist only in carnal worship. But it was malevolence and envy, still more than superstition, that led them to this act of censure; for towards others they would not have been equally stern. It is proper for us to observe the feelings by which they were animated, lest any one should be distressed by the fact, that the very Doctors of the Law were so hostile to Christ.

Mark 2: 27. The Sabbath was made for man

The general meaning is, that those people judge amiss who turn to man's destruction, the Sabbath which God appointed for his benefit. The Pharisees saw the disciples of Christ employed in a holy work; they saw them worn out with the fatigue of the journey, and partly with want of food; and yet are offended that, when they are hungry, they take a few grains of corn for the support of their wearied bodies. Is not this a foolish attempt to overturn the purpose of God, when they demand to the injury of men that observation of the Sabbath which he intended to be advantageous? But they are mistaken, I think, who suppose that in this passage the Sabbath is entirely abolished; for Christ simply informs us what is the proper use of it. Though he asserted, a little before, that he is **Lord of the Sabbath**, yet the full time for its abolition was not yet come, because the veil of the temple was not yet rent (Matthew 27: 51).

MATTHEW 12: 9–13; MARK 3: 1–5; LUKE 6: 6–10

Matthew 12: 9. And having departed thence

This narrative and that which immediately precedes it have the same object; which is to show, that the scribes watched with a malicious eye for the purpose of turning into slander every thing that Christ did, and consequently that we need not wonder if men, whose minds were so depraved, were his implacable enemies. We see also, that it is usual with hypocrites to pursue what is nothing more than a shadow of the righteousness of the Law, and as the common saying is, to stickle more about the form than about the substance. First, then, let us learn from this passage to keep our minds pure, and free from every wicked disposition, when we are about to form a decision on any question; for if hatred, or pride, or anything of that description, reign within us, we will not only do injury to men, but will insult God himself, and turn light into darkness. No man, who was free from malice, would have refused to acknowledge that it was a Divine work, which those good teachers do not scruple to condemn. Whence comes such fury, but because all their senses are affected by a wicked hatred of Christ, so that they are blind amidst the full brightness of the sun? We learn also, that we ought to beware lest, by attaching undue importance to ceremonial observances, we allow

was sought out and erased from the book, to prevent any confusion that might happen in consequence of improper persons laying claim to an estate, and to cut off the unworthy from the rights and privileges of the peaceable, upright citizens. To this custom of blotting the names of deceased and disorderly persons out of the public registers, there appear to be allusions, Exodus 32: 32, where see the note; and Revelation 3: 5; Deuteronomy 9: 14; 25: 19; 29: 20; 2 Kings 14: 27; Psalm 69: 28; 109: 13.

MATTHEW 11: 25–30; LUKE 10: 21–22

Matthew 11: 25–30

25. Wise and prudent – The scribes and Pharisees, vainly puffed up by their fleshly minds, and having their foolish hearts darkened, refusing to submit to the righteousness of God (God's method of saving man by Christ) and going about to establish their own righteousness, (their own method of saving themselves), they rejected God's counsel, and God sent the peace and salvation of the Gospel to others, called here babes, (his disciples), simple-hearted persons, who submitted to be instructed and saved in God's own way. Let it be observed, that our Lord does not thank the Father that he had hidden these things from the wise and prudent, but that, seeing they were hidden from them, he had revealed them to the others.

26. Even so, Father – An emphatic ratification of the preceding address.

It was right that the heavenly wisdom, despised, rejected, and persecuted by the scribes and Pharisees, should be offered to the simple people, and afterwards to the foolish people, the Gentiles, who are the children of wisdom, and justify God in his ways, by bringing forth that fruit of the Gospel of which the Pharisees refused to receive even the seed.

27. All things are delivered unto me of my Father – This is a great truth, and the key of the science of salvation. The man Christ Jesus receives from the Father, and in consequence of his union with the eternal Godhead becomes the Lord and sovereign Dispenser of all things. All the springs of the Divine favor are in the hands of Christ, as Priest of God, and atoning Sacrifice for men: all good proceeds from him, as Savior, Mediator, Head, Pattern, Pastor, and sovereign Judge of the whole world.

No man knoweth the Son, but the Father; neither knoweth any man, etc. – None can fully comprehend the nature and attributes of God, but Christ; and none can fully comprehend the nature, incarnation, etc., of Christ, but the Father. The full comprehension and acknowledgment of the Godhead, and the mystery of the Trinity, belong to God alone.

28. Come unto me – This phrase in the new covenant implies simply, believing in Christ, and becoming his disciple, or follower.

All ye that labor and are heavy laden – The metaphor here appears to be taken from a man who has a great load laid upon him, which he must carry to a certain place: every step he takes reduces his strength, and renders his load the more oppressive. However, it must be carried on; and he labors, uses his utmost exertions, to reach the place where it is to be laid down. A kind person passing by, and, seeing his distress, offers to ease him of his load, that he may enjoy rest.

All are invited to come, and all are promised rest. If few find rest from sin and vile affections, it is because few come to Christ to receive it.

29. Take my yoke upon you – Strange paradox! that a man already weary and overloaded must take a new weight upon him, in order to be eased and find rest! But this advice is similar to that saying, Psalm 55: 22. Cast thy burden upon the Lord, and he will sustain thee; i.e. trust thy soul and concerns to him, and he will carry both thyself and thy load.

I am meek and lowly in heart – Wherever pride and anger dwell, there is nothing but mental labor and agony; but, where the meekness and humility of Christ dwell, all is smooth, even, peaceable, and quiet; for the work of righteousness is peace, and the effect of righteousness, quietness and assurance for ever. Isaiah 32: 17.

and did take and eat the shewbread, and gave also to them that were with him; which it is not lawful to eat but for the priests alone?

5 And he said unto them, That the Son of man is Lord also of the sabbath.

MATTHEW 12: 9–13; MARK 3: 1–5; LUKE 6: 6–10

Matthew 12:9–13

9 And when he was departed thence, he went into their synagogue:

10 And, behold, there was a man which had his hand withered. And they asked him, saying, Is it lawful to heal on the sabbath days? that they might accuse him.

11 And he said unto them, What man shall there be among you, that shall have one sheep, and if it fall into a pit on the sabbath day, will he not lay hold on it, and lift it out?

12 How much then is a man better than a sheep? Wherefore it is lawful to do well on the sabbath days.

13 Then saith he to the man, Stretch forth thine hand. And he stretched it forth; and it was restored whole, like as the other.

Mark 3: 1–5

1 And he entered again into the synagogue; and there was a man there which had a withered hand.

2 And they watched him, whether he would heal him on the sabbath day; that they might accuse him.

3 And he saith unto the man which had the withered hand, Stand forth.

4 And he saith unto them, Is it lawful to do good on the sabbath days, or to do evil? to save life, or to kill? But they held their peace.

5 And when he had looked round about on them with anger, being grieved for the hardness of their hearts, he saith unto the man, Stretch forth thine hand. And he stretched it out: and his hand was restored whole as the other.

Luke 6: 6–10

6 And it came to pass also on another sabbath, that he entered into the synagogue and taught: and there was a man whose right hand was withered.

other things to be neglected, which are of far higher value in the sight of God, and which Christ in another passage calls the more important matters of the Law (Matthew 23: 23). For so strongly are we inclined to outward rites, that we shall never preserve moderation in this respect, unless we constantly remember, that whatever is enjoined respecting the worship of God is, in the first place, spiritual; and, secondly, ought to be regulated by the rule which Christ has laid down to us in this passage.

Mark 3: 5. And when he had looked around upon them with indignation

To convince us that this was a just and holy anger, Mark explains the reason of it to be, that he was **grieved on account of the blindness of their hearts**.

First, then, Christ is grieved, because men who have been instructed in the Law of God are so grossly blind; but as it was malice that blinded them, his grief is accompanied by indignation. This is the true moderation of zeal, to be distressed about the destruction of wicked men, and, at the same time, to be filled with wrath at their ungodliness. Again, as this passage assures us, that Christ was not free from human passions, we infer from it, that the passions themselves are not sinful, provided there be no excess. In consequence of the corruption of our nature, we do not preserve moderation; and our anger, even when it rests on proper grounds, is never free from sin. With Christ the case was different; for not only did his nature retain its original purity, but he was a perfect pattern of righteousness. We ought therefore to implore from heaven the Spirit of God to correct our excesses.

MATTHEW 12: 14–21; MARK 3: 6–12; LUKE 6: 11

Matthew 12: 14. Then the Pharisees took counsel

How obstinate is the rage which drives the wicked to oppose God! Even after having been convinced, they pour out their venom more and more. It is truly monstrous and shocking, that the most distinguished teachers of the Law, who were entrusted with the government of the Church, are engaged, like robbers, in contriving murder. But this must happen, whenever the malice of men reaches such a height, that they wish to destroy every thing that is opposed to their fancy, even though it may be from God.

The circumstance of Christ's making his escape by flight must not be ascribed to fear; for he did not become more courageous by the lapse of time, but was endued with the same fortitude of the Spirit at the time when he fled, as when, at a later period, he voluntarily presented himself to die. And this was a part of that emptying of himself which Paul mentions (Philippians 2: 7), that when he could eas-

30. For my yoke is easy – My Gospel imposes nothing that is difficult; on the contrary, it provides for the complete removal of all that which oppresses and renders man miserable, viz. sin.

Christ's yoke means, the obligation to receive him as the Messiah, to believe his doctrine, and to be in all things conformed to his Word and to his Spirit.

MATTHEW 12: 1–8; MARK 2: 23–28; LUKE 6: 1–5

Matthew 12: 1–8

1. His disciples were an hungered – Were hungry. The Healer went on rest-day over acres: truly his learning disciples were hungry, and they began to pluck the ear and eat. We may well wonder at the extreme poverty of Christ and his disciples. He was himself present with them, and yet permitted them to lack bread! A man, therefore, is not forsaken of God because he is in want. It is more honorable to suffer the want of all temporal things in fellowship with Christ and his followers, than to have all things in abundance in connection with the world.

2. Thy disciples do that which is not lawful to do – The Jews were so superstitious, concerning the observance of the Sabbath, that in their wars with Antiochus Epiphanes, and the Romans, they thought it a crime even to attempt to defend themselves on the Sabbath: when their enemies observed this, they deterred their operations to that day. It was through this, that Pompey was enabled to take Jerusalem.

Those who know not the spirit and design of the divine law are often superstitious to inhumanity, and indulgent to impiety. An intolerant and censorious spirit in religion is one of the greatest curses a man can well fall under.

3–4. Have ye not read what David did – The original history is in 1 Samuel 21: 1–6.

He entered into the house of God – Viz. the house of Ahimelech the priest, who dwelt at Nob, with whom the tabernacle then was, in which the Divine presence was manifested.

And did eat the shew – bread – bread of the presence, or faces, because this bread was to be set continually before the face of Jehovah.

5. The priests – profane the Sabbath – Profane, i.e. put it to what might be called a common use, by slaying and offering up sacrifices, and by doing the services of the temple, as on common days, Exodus 29: 38; Numbers 28: 9.

6. In this place is one greater than the temple – Does not our Lord refer here to Malachi 3: 1? Compare this with Hebrews 3: 3. The Jews esteemed nothing greater than the temple, except that God who was worshipped in it. Christ, by asserting he was greater than the temple, asserts that he was God; and this he does, in still more direct terms, Matthew 12: 8, The Son of man is Lord of the Sabbath – is Institutor and Governor of it.

7. There are four ways in which positive laws may cease to oblige.
First, by the natural law of necessity.
Secondly, by a particular law, which is superior.
Thirdly, by the law of charity and mercy.
Fourthly, by the dispensation and authority of the Lawgiver.
These cases are all exemplified from Matthew 12: 4–8.

8. The Son of man is Lord even of the Sabbath-day – The change of the Jewish into the Christian Sabbath, called the Lord's day, Revelation 1: 10, shows that Christ is not only the Lord, but also the truth and completion of it. For it seems to have been by an especial providence that this change has been made and acknowledged all over the Christian world.

MATTHEW 12: 9–13; MARK 3: 1–5; LUKE 6: 6–10

Matthew 12: 9–13

10. A man which had his hand withered – Probably through a partial paralysis. The man's hand was withered; but God's mercy

7 And the scribes and Pharisees watched him, whether he would heal on the sabbath day; that they might find an accusation against him.

8 But he knew their thoughts, and said to the man which had the withered hand, Rise up, and stand forth in the midst. And he arose and stood forth.

9 Then said Jesus unto them, I will ask you one thing; Is it lawful on the sabbath days to do good, or to do evil? to save life, or to destroy it?

10 And looking round about upon them all, he said unto the man, Stretch forth thy hand. And he did so: and his hand was restored whole as the other.

MATTHEW 12: 14–21; MARK 3: 6–12; LUKE 6: 11

Matthew 12: 14–21

14 Then the Pharisees went out, and held a council against him, how they might destroy him.

15 But when Jesus knew it, he withdrew himself from thence: and great multitudes followed him, and he healed them all;

16 And charged them that they should not make him known:

17 That it might be fulfilled which was spoken by Esaias the prophet, saying,

18 Behold my servant, whom I have chosen; my beloved, in whom my soul is well pleased: I will put my spirit upon him, and he shall shew judgment to the Gentiles.

19 He shall not strive, nor cry; neither shall any man hear his voice in the streets.

20 A bruised reed shall he not break, and smoking flax shall he not quench, till he send forth judgment unto victory.

21 And in his name shall the Gentiles trust.

Mark 3: 6–12

6 And the Pharisees went forth, and straightway took counsel with the Herodians against him, how they might destroy him.

7 But Jesus withdrew himself with his disciples to the sea: and a great multitude from Galilee followed him, and from Judaea,

ily have protected his life by a miracle, he chose rather to submit to our weakness by taking flight. The only reason why he delayed to die was, that the seasonable time, which had been appointed by the Father, was not yet come (John 7: 30; 8: 20). And yet it is manifest, that he was preserved by heavenly power rather than by flight; for it would not have been difficult for his enemies to find out the place to which he had retired, and so far was he from shrouding himself in darkness, that he carried a great company along with him, and rendered that place illustrious by his miracles. He withdrew from their presence for the sole purpose of not aggravating their rage.

Mark 3: 6. The Pharisees took counsel with the Herodians

Now they regarded the Herodians with the fiercest hatred; for their eagerness to be considered the guardians and protectors of public liberty made it necessary for them to make an open profession of mortal hatred to the ministers of that tyrant. And yet this aversion is counteracted by their hatred and fury against Christ, which makes them not only enter into a conspiracy with foreigners, but insinuate themselves into the good graces of those with whom, on other occasions, they would have shrunk from intercourse. While ungodliness hurries men in various directions, and drives them to different courses, it engages them, with one consent, in a contest with God. No hostilities prevent them from giving their hand to each other for opposing the truth of God.

17. That it might be fulfilled which was spoken

Matthew does not mean that this prediction was entirely fulfilled by Christ's prohibiting loud and general reports to be circulated respecting his power, but that this was an exhibition of that mildness which Isaiah describes in the person of the Messiah. Those wonderful works which Christ performed in presence of a few, and which he did not wish to be announced in pompous terms, were fitted to shake heaven and earth (Hebrews 12: 26). It was, therefore, no ordinary proof, how widely he was removed from the pomp and ostentation of the world.

MATTHEW 12: 22–24; MARK 3: 20–22; LUKE 11: 14–15

Mark 3: 20. And they come into the house

Mark undoubtedly takes in a somewhat extended period of time, when he passes from the miracles to that wicked conspiracy which the relatives of Christ formed with each other, to bind him as if he had been a madman. Matthew and Luke mention not more than a single miracle, as having given to the Pharisees an opportunity of slander; but as

had still preserved to him the use of his feet: He uses them to bring him to the public worship of God, and Jesus meets and heals him there. How true is the proverb – It is never so ill with us, but it might be much worse!

11. If it fall into a pit on the Sabbath – day, etc. – It was a canon among the Jews: "We must take a tender care of the goods of an Israelite." Hence:

"If a beast fall into a ditch, or into a pool of water, let (the owner) bring him food in that place if he can; but, if he cannot, let him bring clothes and litter, and bear up the beast; whence, if he can come up, let him come up, etc."

"If a beast or its foal fall into a ditch on a holy day, R. Lazar saith, Let him lift up the former to kill him, and let him kill him; but let him give fodder to the other, lest he die in that place. R. Joshua saith, Let him lift up the former with the intention of killing him, although he kill him not; let him lift up the other also, although it be not in his mind to kill him." To these canons our Lord seems here very properly to appeal, in vindication of his intention to heal the distressed man.

Self-interest is a very decisive casuist, and removes abundance of scruples in a moment. It is always the first consulted, and the must readily obeyed. It is not sinful to hearken to it, but it must not govern nor determine by itself.

12. How much then is a man better than a sheep? – Our Lord's argument is what is called *argumentum ad hominem*; they are taken on their own ground, and confuted on their own maxims and conduct. There are many persons who call themselves Christians, who do more for a beast of burden or pleasure than they do for a man for whom Christ died! Many spend that on coursers, spaniels, and hounds, of which multitudes of the followers of Christ are destitute: but this also shall come to judgment.

Wherefore, it is lawful to do well, etc. – This was allowed by a multitude of Jewish canons.

13. Stretch forth thine hand – The bare command of God is a sufficient reason of obedience. This man might have reasoned thus: "Lord, my hand is withered; how then can I stretch it out? Make it whole first, and afterwards I will do as thou commandest." This may appear reasonable, but in his case it would have been foolishness. At the command of the Lord he made the effort, and in making it the cure was effected! Faith disregards apparent impossibilities, where there is a command and promise of God. The effort to believe is, often, that faith by which the soul is healed.

A little before (vv. 6,8) Jesus Christ had asserted his Godhead, in this verse he proves it. What but the omnipotence of the living God could have, in a moment, restored this withered hand? There could be no collusion here; the man who had a real disease was instantaneously and therefore miraculously cured; and the mercy and power of God were both amply manifested in this business.

It is worthy of remark, that as the man was healed with a word, without even a touch, the Sabbath was unbroken, even according to their most rigid interpretation of the letter of the law.

MATTHEW 12: 14–21; MARK 3: 6–12; LUKE 6: 11

Matthew 12: 14–21

14. Held a council against him – Nothing sooner leads to utter blindness, and hardness of heart, than envy. There are many who abandon themselves to pleasure-taking and debauchery on the Sabbath, who condemn a poor man whom necessity obliges to work on what is termed a holiday, or a national fast.

15. Jesus – withdrew himself from thence – It is the part of prudence and Christian charity not to provoke, if possible, the blind and the hardened; and to take from them the occasion of sin. A man of God is not afraid of persecution; but, as his aim is only to do good, by proclaiming every where the grace of the Lord Jesus, he departs from any place when he finds the obstacles to the accomplishment

8 And from Jerusalem, and from Idumaea, and from beyond Jordan; and they about Tyre and Sidon, a great multitude, when they had heard what great things he did, came unto him.

9 And he spake to his disciples, that a small ship should wait on him because of the multitude, lest they should throng him.

10 For he had healed many; insomuch that they pressed upon him for to touch him, as many as had plagues.

11 And unclean spirits, when they saw him, fell down before him, and cried, saying, Thou art the Son of God.

12 And he straitly charged them that they should not make him known.

Luke 6: 11

11 And they were filled with madness; and communed one with another what they might do to Jesus.

MATTHEW 12: 22–24; MARK 3: 20–22; LUKE 11: 14–15

Matthew 12: 22–24

22 Then was brought unto him one possessed with a devil, blind, and dumb: and he healed him, insomuch that the blind and dumb both spake and saw.

23 And all the people were amazed, and said, Is not this the son of David?

24 But when the Pharisees heard it, they said, This fellow doth not cast out devils, but by Beelzebub the prince of the devils.

Mark 3: 20–22

20 And the multitude cometh together again, so that they could not so much as eat bread.

21 And when his friends heard of it, they went out to lay hold on him: for they said, He is beside himself.

22 And the scribes which came down from Jerusalem said, He hath Beelzebub, and by the prince of the devils casteth he out devils.

Luke 11: 14–15

14 And he was casting out a devil, and it was dumb. And it came to pass, when the devil was gone out, the dumb spake; and the people wondered.

15 But some of them said, He casteth

all the three agree in this last clause which is contained in Mark's narrative, I have thought it proper to insert it here.

It is dreadful that such wickedness should have been found among the relatives of Christ, who ought to have been the first to aid him in advancing the kingdom of God. When they see that he has already obtained some reputation, their ambition leads them to desire that he should be admired in Jerusalem; for they exhort him to go up to that city, "that he may show himself more openly" (John 7: 3–4).

But now that they perceive him to be hated on one side by the rulers, exposed on another to numerous slanders, and even despised by the great body of the people – to prevent any injury, or envy, or dishonor, from arising to the whole family, they form the design of laying hands on him, and binding him at home, as if he had been a person who labored under mental derangement; and, as appears from the words of the Evangelist, such was their actual belief.

MATTHEW 12: 25–32; MARK 3: 23–30; LUKE 11: 16–23; 12: 10

Matthew 12: 25. But as Jesus knew their thoughts

Though Christ knew sufficiently well, and had often learned by experience, that the scribes, in the exercise of their malice were in the habit of putting an unfavorable construction on every thing that he did, yet Matthew and Luke, I have no doubt, mean that Christ was a discerner of their hearts. And indeed it is probable, that they spoke so openly against Christ, that their calumnies reached his ears; but Christ knew by his Divine Spirit the dispositions which led them to slander him. For it frequently happens that erroneous judgments are formed by men who do not intentionally, after all, oppose what is right, but err through ignorance; who do not cherish a hidden and concealed venom, but whose rashness carries them headlong. The meaning therefore is, that Christ reproved them with the greater severity, because he was a witness and judge of their inward malice.

Every kingdom divided against itself

In refuting the calumny alleged against him, he first quotes a common proverb. This refutation may appear to be not quite satisfactory. We know what subtle methods Satan sometimes employs, presenting all the while an appearance of discord, in order to entrap the minds of men by superstitions. Thus, for example, the exorcisms of Popery are nothing else than feats of dexterity, in which Satan pretends to fight with himself. But no suspicion of this nature fell on Christ; for he cast out devils in such a manner, as to restore to God the men in whom they dwelt sound and whole. Whenever Satan enters into a collusion with him-

of his end are, humanly speaking, invincible, and that he can not do good without being the means of much evil. Yield to the stream when you cannot stem it.

Great multitudes followed him, and he healed them all – The rejection of the Gospel in one place has often been the means of sending it to and establishing it in another. Jesus healed all that followed him, i.e. all who had need of healing, and who desired to be healed; for thus the passage must be understood: and is he not still the same? No soul shall ever implore his healing power in vain; but let it be remembered, that only those who follow Christ, and apply to him, are healed of their spiritual maladies.

16. Charged them that they should not make him known – See Matthew 8: 4. Jesus Christ, as GOD, could have easily concealed himself, but he chooses to do it as man, and to use no other than human means, as these were quite sufficient for the purpose, to teach us not to neglect them in our necessity. Indeed, he always used his power less on his own account, than on that of men.

18. Behold my servant – This title was given to our blessed Lord in several prophecies. See Isaiah 42: 1; 53: 2. Christ assumes it, Psalm 40: 7–9. Compare these with John 17: 4, and Philippians 2: 7. God required an acceptable and perfect service from man; but man, being sinful, could not perform it. Jesus, taking upon him the nature of man, fully performed the whole will of God, and communicates grace to all his followers, to enable them perfectly to love and worthily to magnify their Maker.

And he shall show judgment to the Gentiles – That is, He will publish the Gospel to the heathens.

19. He shall not strive, nor cry – The spirit of Christ is not a spirit of contention, murmuring, clamor, or litigiousness. He who loves these does not belong to him. Christ therefore fulfilled a prophecy by withdrawing from this place, on account of the rage of the Pharisees.

20. A bruised reed shall he not break – A reed is, in Scripture, the emblem of weakness,

Ezekiel 29: 6; and a bruised reed must signify that state of weakness that borders on dissolution and death.

And smoking flax shall he not quench – Some suppose the Jewish state, as to ecclesiastical matters, is here intended, the prophecy declaring that Christ would not destroy it, but leave it to expire of itself, as it already contained the principles of its own destruction. Others have considered it as implying that great tenderness with which the blessed Jesus should treat the weak and the ignorant, whose good desires must not be stifled, but encouraged. The bruised reed may recover itself, if permitted to vegetate under the genial influences of heaven; and the life and light of the expiring lamp may be supported by the addition of fresh oil. Jesus therefore quenches not faint desires after salvation, even in the worst and most undeserving of men; for even such desires may lead to the fullness of the blessing of the Gospel of peace.

Judgment unto victory – See Matthew 12: 18. By judgment, understand the Gospel, and by victory its complete triumph over Jewish opposition, and Gentile impiety. He will continue by these mild and gentle means to work till the whole world is Christianized, and the universe filled with his glory.

21. And in his name shall the Gentiles trust – they shall hope. Jesus Christ is the sole hope and trust of mankind; to trust and hope in his name, JESUS, is to expect salvation and all things necessary from him alone, to despise, comparatively, all earthly promises, to esteem, love, and desire heavenly things only, and to bear with patience and tranquility all the losses and evils of this life, upon the prospect and hope of that felicity which he has purchased for us.

MATTHEW 12: 22–24; MARK 3: 20–22; LUKE 11: 14–15

Matthew 12: 22–24

22. One possessed with a devil, blind and dumb – A person from whom the indwelling demon took away both sight and hearing.

out devils through Beelzebub the chief of the devils.

MATTHEW 12: 25–32; MARK 3: 23–30; LUKE 11: 16–23; 12: 10

Matthew 12: 25–32

25 And Jesus knew their thoughts, and said unto them, Every kingdom divided against itself is brought to desolation; and every city or house divided against itself shall not stand:

26 And if Satan cast out Satan, he is divided against himself; how shall then his kingdom stand?

27 And if I by Beelzebub cast out devils, by whom do your children cast them out? therefore they shall be your judges.

28 But if I cast out devils by the Spirit of God, then the kingdom of God is come unto you.

29 Or else how can one enter into a strong man's house, and spoil his goods, except he first bind the strong man? and then he will spoil his house.

30 He that is not with me is against me; and he that gathereth not with me scattereth abroad.

31 Wherefore I say unto you, All manner of sin and blasphemy shall be forgiven unto men: but the blasphemy against the Holy Ghost shall not be forgiven unto men.

32 And whosoever speaketh a word against the Son of man, it shall be forgiven him: but whosoever speaketh against the Holy Ghost, it shall not be forgiven him, neither in this world, neither in the world to come.

Mark 3: 23–30

23 And he called them unto him, and said unto them in parables, How can Satan cast out Satan?

24 And if a kingdom be divided against itself, that kingdom cannot stand.

25 And if a house be divided against itself, that house cannot stand.

26 And if Satan rise up against himself, and be divided, he cannot stand, but hath an end.

27 No man can enter into a strong man's house, and spoil his goods, except he will first bind the strong man; and then he will spoil his house.

self, he pretends to be vanquished, and yet it is himself that triumphs. But Christ attacked Satan in open combat, threw him down, and left him nothing remaining. He did not lay him low in one respect, that he might give him greater stability in another, but stripped him completely of all his armor. Christ therefore reasons justly, that there is no community of interest between him and Satan, because that father of cunning keeps one object in view – the preservation of his kingdom.

But perhaps it will be objected, that the devils are often hurried along, by giddiness and blind madness, to destroy themselves. The answer is easy. The words of Christ mean nothing more than that it was absurd in the scribes to maintain, that the devil, who endeavors by every method to make men his slaves, should, of his own accord, destroy the power which he possessed over them. Besides, it ought to be remembered, that common proverbs were employed by Christ in such a manner, as to be merely probable conjectures, and not solid arguments; and that, when he speaks of what is known and well attested, he finds it easier to reach the conscience of his adversaries. Everybody knew that Christ had driven Satan from his possession, and nothing was plainer than that all his miracles tended to this object; and hence it was easy to conclude, that his power, which was so much opposed to Satan, was divine.

27. By whom do your children cast them out?

He charges them with passing an unjust and malicious decision, because in the same case they did not decide in a similar manner, but as they were affected towards the people. Now this inequality shows, that their prevailing motive was not a regard to what is just and right, but blind love or hatred; and that it was even an evidence of wicked self-love and envy, to condemn in Christ what they praised in their own **children**. By your **children** some understand the children of the whole nation; and some think that the Apostles are so called, because they were acknowledged to be **children**, while Christ was treated as if he had been a foreigner. Others refer it to the ancient Prophets. I have no doubt that he means the Exorcists, who were at that time generally employed among the Jews, as is evident from the Acts of the Apostles (19: 19). There is reason to believe, that no greater kindness would be exercised in judging of the disciples of Christ than of their Master; and to apply these words to the dead is a forced construction, when they manifestly denote a comparison of the present time.

30. He that is not with me

There are two ways of explaining this passage. Some suppose that it is an argument drawn from contraries, and that Christ's meaning is: "I cannot reign till the devil is overthrown; for the object of all his attempts is, to scatter

Satan makes himself master of the heart, the eyes, and the tongue of the sinner. His heart he fills with the love of sin; his eyes he blinds that he may not see his guilt, and the perdition which awaits him; and his tongue he hinders from prayer and supplication, though he gives it increasing liberty in blasphemies, lies, slanders, etc. None but Jesus can redeem from this threefold captivity.

23. Is not this the son of David? – Is not this the true Messiah? Do not these miracles sufficiently prove it? See Isaiah 35: 5.

MATTHEW 12: 25–32; MARK 3: 23–30; LUKE 11: 16–23; 12: 10

Matthew 12: 25–32

25. Every kingdom divided against itself is brought to desolation – Our Lord's argument was thus: "The welfare of any kingdom, city, or family, depends on its concord and unanimity; Satan, like every other potentate, must wish to rule his empire in peace and security; how then can he be in league with me, who oppose his authority, and am destroying his kingdom?"

The reasoning of the Pharisees, Matthew 12: 24, was not expressed, and Jesus, knowing their thoughts, gave them ample proof or his omniscience. This, with our Lord's masterly confutation of their reasonings, by a conclusion drawn from their own premises, one would have supposed might have humbled and convinced these men; but the most conclusive reasoning, and the most astonishing miracles, were lost upon a people who were obstinately determined to disbelieve every thing good, relative to Christ. How true the saying – He came unto his own, and his own received him not!

26. If Satan cast out Satan – A good cause will produce a good effect, and an evil cause an evil effect. Were I on Satan's side, I would act for his interest and confirm his influence among you; but I oppose his maxims by my doctrine, and his influence by my power.

27. By whom do your children cast them out? – Children, or sons of the prophets, means the disciples of the prophets; and children or sons of the Pharisees, disciples of the Pharisees. From Acts 19: 13–14, it is evident there were exorcists among the Jews, and, from our Lord's saying here, it is also evident that the disciples of the Pharisees did east out demons, or, at least, those who educated them wished to have it believed that they had such a power. Our Lord's argument here is extremely conclusive: If the man who casts out demons proves himself thereby to be in league with and influenced by Satan, then your disciples, and you who taught them, are all of you in league with the devil: ye must either give up your assertion, that I cast out demons by Beelzebul, or else admit this conclusion, in its fullest force and latitude, that ye are all children of the devil, and leagued with him against God.

Envy causes persons often to condemn in one, what they approve in another.

28. But if I cast out devils by the Spirit of God – Perhaps the Spirit of God is here mentioned by way of opposition to the magical incantations of the Jews; for it is well known that by fumigations and magical washings, they professed to cast out devils.

Then the kingdom of God – For the destruction of the kingdom of Satan plainly implies the setting up of the kingdom of God.

Is come unto you – Is come unexpectedly upon you.

They pretended to be in expectation of the kingdom of God, and consequently of the destruction of the kingdom of Satan. But, by being not prepared to receive Christ in these proofs of his Divine mission, they showed that their expectation was but pretended. They were too carnal to mind spiritual things.

29. Else how can one enter into a strong man's house – Men, through sin, are become the very house and dwelling place of Satan, having of their own accord surrendered themselves to this unjust possessor; for whoever gives up his soul to sin gives it up to the devil. It is Jesus, and Jesus alone, who can deliver from the power of this bondage. When Satan

28 Verily I say unto you, All sins shall be forgiven unto the sons of men, and blasphemies wherewith soever they shall blaspheme:

29 But he that shall blaspheme against the Holy Ghost hath never forgiveness, but is in danger of eternal damnation:

30 Because they said, He hath an unclean spirit.

Luke 11: 16–23

16 And others, tempting him, sought of him a sign from heaven.

17 But he, knowing their thoughts, said unto them, Every kingdom divided against itself is brought to desolation; and a house divided against a house falleth.

18 If Satan also be divided against himself, how shall his kingdom stand? because ye say that I cast out devils through Beelzebub.

19 And if I by Beelzebub cast out devils, by whom do your sons cast them out? therefore shall they be your judges.

20 But if I with the finger of God cast out devils, no doubt the kingdom of God is come upon you.

21 When a strong man armed keepeth his palace, his goods are in peace:

22 But when a stronger than he shall come upon him, and overcome him, he taketh from him all his Armour wherein he trusted, and divideth his spoils.

23 He that is not with me is against me: and he that gathereth not with me scattereth.

Luke 12: 10

10 And whosoever shall speak a word against the Son of man, it shall be forgiven him: but unto him that blasphemeth against the Holy Ghost it shall not be forgiven.

MATTHEW 12: 33–37

33 Either make the tree good, and his fruit good; or else make the tree corrupt, and his fruit corrupt: for the tree is known by his fruit.

34 O generation of vipers, how can ye, being evil, speak good things? for out of the abundance of the heart the mouth speaketh.

35 A good man out of the good treasure of the heart bringeth forth good

whatever I gather." And certainly we see abundant evidence of the earnestness with which that enemy labors to destroy the kingdom of Christ. But I rather agree in opinion with those who explain it to denote, that the scribes are declared to be, in two respects, opposed to the kingdom of God, because they intentionally hinder its progress. "It was your duty to assist me, and to give me your hand in establishing the kingdom of God; for whoever does not assist is, in some measure, opposed to me, or, at least, deserves to be reckoned among enemies. What then shall be said of you, whose furious rage drives you into avowed opposition?"

MATTHEW 12: 33–37

33. Either make the tree good

It might look like absurdity, that men should be allowed a choice of being **either good or bad**; but if we consider what sort of people Christ is addressing, the difficulty will be speedily resolved. We know what opinion was generally entertained about the Pharisees; for their pretended sanctity had so blinded the minds of the common people, that no one ventured to pass sentence on their vices. Wishing to remove this mask, Christ desires them to be **either good or bad**; or, in other words, declares that nothing is more inconsistent with honesty than hypocrisy, and that it is in vain for men to boast of pretensions to righteousness who are not sincere and upright.

MATTHEW 12: 43–45; LUKE 11: 24–26

43. But when the unclean spirit hath gone out

He speaks of scribes and hypocrites of a similar character, who, despising the grace of God, enter into a conspiracy with the devil. Against such people he pronounces that punishment which their ingratitude deserves. To make his doctrine more extensively useful, he points out, in a general manner, the condemnation that awaits those who, despising the grace offered to them, again open the door to the devil. But as almost every particle has great weight, there are some points that must be noticed in their order, before we come to treat the substance of the parable.

What Christ says about the going out of the devil is intended to magnify the power and efficacy of the grace of God. Whenever God draws near to us, and, above all, when he approaches us in the person of his Son, the design is, to rescue us from the tyranny of the devil, and to receive us into his favor. This had been openly declared by Christ in the miracle which he had lately performed. As it is the peculiar office of Christ to banish wicked spirits, that they may no longer reign over men, the devil is justly said to go out of those men to whom Christ exhibits himself as a Redeemer.

is cast out, Jesus purifies and dwells in the heart.

30. He that is not with me is against me – In vain do men seek for methods to reconcile God and mammon. There is no medium between loving the Lord and being his enemy – between belonging to Christ or to Satan. If we be on the side of the devil, we must expect to go to the devil's hell; if we be on the side of Christ, we may expect to go to his heaven. When Christ, his truth, and his servants are assaulted, he who does not espouse their cause is not on Christ's side, but incurs the guilt of deserting and betraying him. There are many, (it is to be feared), in the world who are really against Christ, and scatter abroad, who flatter themselves that they are workers together with him, and of the number of his friends!

Scattereth abroad – This seems to have been a proverbial form of speech, and may be a metaphor taken from shepherds. He who does not help the true shepherd to gather his flock into the fold is, most likely, one who wishes to scatter them, that he may have the opportunity of stealing and destroying them.

31. All manner of sin and blasphemy – injurious or impious speaking, mocking and deriding speech, Anglo-Saxon. See Matthew 9: 3.

But the blasphemy against the Holy Ghost – Even personal reproaches, revilings, persecutions against Christ, were remissible; but blasphemy, or impious speaking against the Holy Spirit was to have no forgiveness: i.e. when the person obstinately attributed those works to the devil, which he had the fullest evidence could be wrought only by the Spirit of God. That this, and nothing else, is the sin against the Holy Spirit, is evident from the connection in this place, and more particularly from Mark 3: 28–30. "All sins shall be forgiven unto the sons of men, and blasphemies wherewith soever they shall blaspheme; but he that shall blaspheme against the Holy Ghost hath never forgiveness, but is in danger of eternal damnation; BECAUSE they said, He hath an unclean spirit."

Here the matter is made clear beyond the smallest doubt – the unpardonable sin, as some term it, is neither less nor more than ascribing the miracles Christ wrought, by the power of God, to the spirit of the devil. Many sincere people have been grievously troubled with apprehensions that they had committed the unpardonable sin; but let it be observed that no man who believes the Divine mission of Jesus Christ, ever can commit this sin: therefore let no man's heart fail because of it, from henceforth and for ever, Amen.

32. Neither in this world, neither in the world to come – The sin here spoken of by our Lord ranks high in the catalogue of presumptuous sins, for which there was no forgiveness under the Mosaic dispensation. See Numbers 15: 30–31; 35: 31; Leviticus 20: 10; 1 Samuel 2: 25. When our Lord says that such a sin hath no forgiveness, is he not to be understood as meaning that the crime shall be punished under the Christian dispensation as it was under the Jewish, viz. by the destruction of the body? And is not this the same mentioned 1 John 1: 7, called there the sin unto death; i.e. a sin that was to be punished by the death of the body, while mercy might be extended to the soul? The punishment for presumptuous sins, under the Jewish law, to which our Lord evidently alludes, certainly did not extend to the damnation of the soul, though the body was destroyed: therefore I think that, though there was no such forgiveness to be extended to this crime as to absolve the man from the punishment of temporal death, yet, on repentance, mercy might be extended to the soul; and every sin may be repented of under the Gospel dispensation.

Dr. Lightfoot has sufficiently vindicated this passage from all false interpretation. "They that endeavor hence to prove the remission of some sins after death, seem little to understand to what Christ had respect when he spake these words. Weigh well this common and, most known doctrine of the Jewish schools, and judge.

"He that transgresses an affirmative precept, if he presently repent, is not moved until the Lord pardon him; and of such it is said, Be ye converted, O back sliding children! and I will

things: and an evil man out of the evil treasure bringeth forth evil things.

36 But I say unto you, That every idle word that men shall speak, they shall give account thereof in the day of judgment.

37 For by thy words thou shalt be justified, and by thy words thou shalt be condemned.

MATTHEW 12: 43–45; LUKE 11: 24–26

Matthew 12: 43–45

43 When the unclean spirit is gone out of a man, he walketh through dry places, seeking rest, and findeth none.

44 Then he saith, I will return into my house from whence I came out; and when he is come, he findeth it empty, swept, and garnished.

45 Then goeth he, and taketh with himself seven other spirits more wicked than himself, and they enter in and dwell there: and the last state of that man is worse than the first. Even so shall it be also unto this wicked generation.

Luke 11: 24–26

24 When the unclean spirit is gone out of a man, he walketh through dry places, seeking rest; and finding none, he saith, I will return unto my house whence I came out.

25 And when he cometh, he findeth it swept and garnished.

26 Then goeth he, and taketh to him seven other spirits more wicked than himself; and they enter in, and dwell there: and the last state of that man is worse than the first.

MATTHEW 12: 46–50; MARK 3: 31–35; LUKE 11: 27–28; 8: 19–21

Matthew 12: 46–50

46 While he yet talked to the people, behold, his mother and his brethren stood without, desiring to speak with him.

47 Then one said unto him, Behold, thy mother and thy brethren stand without, desiring to speak with thee.

48 But he answered and said unto him that told him, Who is my mother? and who are my brethren?

49 And he stretched forth his hand toward his disciples, and said, Behold my mother and my brethren!

MATTHEW 12: 46–50; MARK 3: 31–35; LUKE 11: 27–28; 8: 19–21

Luke 11: 27. Blessed is the womb

By this eulogium the woman intended to magnify the excellence of Christ; for she had no reference to Mary, whom, perhaps, she had never seen. And yet it tends in a high degree to illustrate the glory of Christ, that she pronounces **the womb that bore him** to be noble and blessed. Nor was the blessing inappropriate, but in strict accordance with the manner of Scripture; for we know that offspring, and particularly when endued with distinguished virtues, is declared to be a remarkable gift of God, preferable to all others. It cannot even be denied that God conferred the highest honor on Mary, by choosing and appointing her to be the mother of his Son. And yet Christ's reply is so far from assenting to this female voice, that it contains an indirect reproof.

Nay, rather, blessed are they that hear the word of God

We see that Christ treats almost as a matter of indifference that point on which the woman had set a high value. And undoubtedly what she supposed to be Mary's highest honor was far inferior to the other favors which she had received; for it was of vastly greater importance to be regenerated by the Spirit of God than to conceive Christ, according to the flesh, in her womb; to have Christ living spiritually within her than to suckle him with her breasts. In a word, the highest happiness and glory of the holy Virgin consisted in her being a member of his Son, so that the heavenly Father reckoned her in the number of new creatures.

In my opinion, however, it was for another reason, and with a view to another object, that Christ now corrected the saying of the woman. It was because men are commonly chargeable with neglecting even those gifts of God, on which they gaze with astonishment, and bestow the highest praise. This woman, in applauding Christ, had left out what was of the very highest consequence, that in him salvation is exhibited to all; and, therefore, it was a feeble commendation, that made no mention of his grace and power, which is extended to all. Christ justly claims for himself another kind of praise, not that his mother alone is reckoned blessed, but that he brings to us all perfect and eternal happiness. We never form a just estimate of the excellence of Christ, till we consider for what purpose he was given to us by the Father, and perceive the benefits which he has brought to us, so that we who are wretched in ourselves may become happy in him. But why does he say nothing about himself, and mention only the word of God? It is because in this way he opens to us all his treasures; for without the word he has no intercourse with us, nor

heal your backslidings. He that transgresses a negative precept, and repents, his repentance suspends judgment, and the day of expiation expiates him; as it is said, This day shall all your uncleannesses be expiated to you. He that transgresses to cutting off (by the stroke of God) or to death by the Sanhedrin, and repents, repentance and the day of expiation do suspend judgment, and the strokes that are laid upon him wipe off sin, as it is said, And I will visit their transgression with a rod, and their iniquity with scourges. But he by whom the name of God is profaned (or blasphemed) repentance is of no avail to him to suspend judgment, nor the day of expiation to expiate it, nor scourges (or corrections inflicted) to wipe it off, but all suspend judgment, and death wipes it off. Thus the Babylonian Gemara writes; but the Jerusalem thus: Repentance and the day of expiation expiate as to the third part, and corrections as to the third part, and death wipes it off, as it is said, And your iniquities shall not be expiated to you until ye die: behold, we learn that death wipes off. Note this, which Christ contradicts, concerning blasphemy against the Holy Ghost. It shall not be forgiven, saith he, neither in this world, nor in the world to come; that is, neither before death, nor, as you dream, by death.

MATTHEW 12: 33–37

33. Either make the tree good – That is, the effect will be always similar to the cause; a bad tree will produce bad fruit, and a good tree, good fruit.

The works will resemble the heart: nothing good can proceed from an evil spirit; no good fruit can proceed from a corrupt heart. Before the heart of man can produce any good, it must be renewed and influenced by the Spirit of God.

34. O generation of vipers – These are apparently severe words; but they were extremely proper in reference to that execrable people to whom they were addressed: the whole verse is an inference from what was spoken before.

Out of the abundance (the overflow-

ings) of the heart – Wicked words and sinful actions may be considered as the overflowings of a heart that is more than full of the spirit of wickedness; and holy words and righteous deeds may be considered as the overflowings of a heart that is filled with the Holy Spirit, and running over with love to God and man.

35. A good man out of the good treasure of the heart – The good heart is the good treasury, and the treasure that is in it is the love of God, and of all mankind. The bad heart is the bad treasury, and its treasure is the carnal mind, which is enmity against God, and ill-will to man.

36. Every idle word – a word that does nothing, that neither ministers grace nor instruction to them who hear it. Our Lord must be understood here as condemning all false and injurious words: the scope of the place necessarily requires this meaning.

37. By thy words thou shalt be justified – That is, the whole tenor of thy conversation will be an evidence for or against thee, in the great day. How many are there who count words for nothing! and yet eternity often depends on them. Lord, put a watch before the door of my lips! is a prayer proper for all men.

MATTHEW 12: 43–45; LUKE 11: 24–26

Matthew 12: 43–45

43. When the unclean spirit – If there had been no reality in demoniacal possessions, our Lord would have scarcely appealed to a case of this kind here, to point out the real state of the Jewish people, and the desolation which was coming upon them. Had this been only a vulgar error, of the nonsense of which the learned scribes and the wise Pharisees must have been convinced, the case not being one in point, because not true, must have been treated by that very people with contempt for whose conviction it was alone designed.

He walketh through dry places – There seems to be a reference here to the Orphic demonology, in which evil spirits were divided into various classes, according to the different

50 For whosoever shall do the will of my Father which is in heaven, the same is my brother, and sister, and mother.

Mark 3: 31–35

31 There came then his brethren and his mother, and, standing without, sent unto him, calling him.

32 And the multitude sat about him, and they said unto him, Behold, thy mother and thy brethren without seek for thee.

33 And he answered them, saying, Who is my mother, or my brethren?

34 And he looked round about on them which sat about him, and said, Behold my mother and my brethren!

35 For whosoever shall do the will of God, the same is my brother, and my sister, and mother.

Luke 11: 27–28

27 And it came to pass, as he spake these things, a certain woman of the company lifted up her voice, and said unto him, Blessed is the womb that bare thee, and the paps which thou hast sucked.

28 But he said, Yea rather, blessed are they that hear the word of God, and keep it.

Luke 8: 19–21

19 Then came to him his mother and his brethren, and could not come at him for the press.

20 And it was told him by certain which said, Thy mother and thy brethren stand without, desiring to see thee.

21 And he answered and said unto them, My mother and my brethren are these which hear the word of God, and do it.

MATTHEW 12: 38–42; LUKE 11: 29–32

Matthew 12: 38–42

38 Then certain of the scribes and of the Pharisees answered, saying, Master, we would see a sign from thee.

39 But he answered and said unto them, An evil and adulterous generation seeketh after a sign; and there shall no sign be given to it, but the sign of the prophet Jonas:

40 For as Jonas was three days and three nights in the whale's belly; so shall the Son of man be three days and three

we with him. Communicating himself to us by the word, he rightly and properly calls us to hear and keep it, that by faith he may become ours.

We now see the difference between Christ's reply and the woman's commendation; for the blessedness, which she had limited to his own relatives, is a favor which he offers freely to all. He shows that we ought to entertain no ordinary esteem for him, because he has all the treasures of life, blessedness, and glory, hidden in him (Colossians 2: 3), which he dispenses by the word, that they may be communicated to those who embrace the word by faith; for God's free adoption of us, which we obtain by faith, is the key to the kingdom of heaven.

MATTHEW 12: 38–42; LUKE 11: 16,29–32

Luke 11: 16. And others tempting sought from him a sign

Something similar to this is afterwards related by Matthew (16: 4), and by Mark (8: 11–12). Hence it is evident, that Christ repeatedly attacked them on this subject, so that there was no end to the wickedness of those men who had once resolved to oppose the truth. There can be no doubt that they ask a sign, in order to plead, as a plausible pretense for their unbelief, that Christ's calling has not been duly attested. They do not express such submissiveness as to be prepared to yield to two or three miracles, and still less to be satisfied with a single miracle; but as I hinted a little before, they apologize for not believing the Gospel on this pretense, that Christ shows no sign of it from heaven. He had already performed miracles before their eyes sufficiently numerous and manifest; but as if these were not enough for the confirmation of doctrine, they wish to have something exhibited from heaven, by which God will, as it were, make a visible appearance. They call him Master, according to custom; for such was the appellation given at that time to all scribes and expounders of the law. But they do not acknowledge him to be a prophet of God, till he produce a testimony from heaven. The meaning therefore is: "Since thou professest to be a teacher and Master, if thou desirest that we should be thy disciples, let God declare from heaven that He is the Author of thy teaching, and let Him confirm thy calling by a miracle."

Luke 11: 30. As Jonah was a sign to the Ninevites

He declares that he will be a sign to them, as Jonah was to the inhabitants of Nineveh. But the word sign is not taken in its ordinary sense, as pointing out something, but as denoting what is widely removed from the ordinary course of nature. In this sense Jonah's mission was miraculous, when he was brought out of the belly of the fish, as if from the grave, to call the Ninevites to repentance. **Three days**

regions of their abode, or places in which they delighted.

Seeking rest – Or refreshment. Strange! a fallen corrupt spirit can have no rest but in the polluted human heart: the corruption of the one is suited to the pollution of the other, and thus like cleaves to like.

44. Into my house – The soul of that person from whom he had been expelled by the power of Christ, and out of which he was to have been kept by continual prayer, faith, and watchfulness.

He findeth it empty – Unoccupied, empty of the former inhabitant, and ready to receive a new one: denoting a soul that has lost the life and power of godliness, and the testimony of the Holy Spirit.

Swept and garnished – Swept, from love, meekness, and all the fruits of the Spirit; and garnished, or adorned, decorated, with the vain showy trifles of folly and fashion. This may comprise also smart speeches, cunning repartees, etc., for which many who have lost the life of God are very remarkable.

45. Seven other spirits more wicked – Seven was a favorite number with the Jews, implying frequently, with them, something perfect, completed, filled up, for such is the proper import of the Hebrew word. And perhaps this meaning of it refers to the seventh day, when God rested from his work, having filled up, or completed the whole of his creative design. Seven demons – as many as could occupy his soul, harassing it with pride, anger, self-will, lust, etc., and torturing the body with disease.

The last state of that man is worse than the first – His soul, before influenced by the Spirit of God, dilated and expanded under its heavenly influences, becomes more capable of refinement in iniquity, as its powers are more capacious than formerly. Evil habits are formed and strengthened by relapses; and relapses are multiplied, and become more incurable, through new habits.

So shall it be also unto this wicked generation – And so it was: for they grew worse and worse, as if totally abandoned to diabolic influence; till at last the besom of destruction swept them and their privileges, national and religious, utterly away. What a terrible description of a state of apostasy is contained in these verses! May he who readeth understand!

MATTHEW 12: 46–50; MARK 3: 31–35; LUKE 11: 27–28; 8: 19–21

Matthew 12: 46–50

46. His mother and his brethren – These are supposed to have been the cousins of our Lord, as the word brother is frequently used among the Hebrews in this sense. But there are others who believe Mary had other children beside our Lord and that these were literally his brothers, who are spoken of here. And, although it be possible that these were the sons of Mary, the wife of Cleopas or Alpheus, his mother's sister, called his relations, Mark 3: 31; yet it is as likely that they were the children of Joseph and Mary, and brethren of our Lord, in the strictest sense of the word.

48. Who is my mother? and who are my brethren? – The reason of this seeming disregard of his relatives was this: they came to seize upon him, for they thought he was distracted. See Mark 3: 33.

50. Whosoever shall do the will of my Father, etc. – Those are the best acknowledged relatives of Christ who are united to him by spiritual ties, and who are become one with him by the indwelling of his Spirit. We generally suppose that Christ's relatives must have shared much of his affectionate attention; and doubtless they did: but here we find that whosoever does the will of God is equally esteemed by Christ, as his brother, sister, or even his virgin mother. What an encouragement for fervent attachment to God!

1. From various facts related in this chapter, we see the nature and design of the revelation of God, and of all the ordinances and precepts contained in it – they are all calculated to do man good: to improve his understanding, to soften and change his nature, that he may love his neighbor as himself. That religion

nights in the heart of the earth.

41 The men of Nineveh shall rise in judgment with this generation, and shall condemn it: because they repented at the preaching of Jonas; and, behold, a greater than Jonas is here.

42 The queen of the south shall rise up in the judgment with this generation, and shall condemn it: for she came from the uttermost parts of the earth to hear the wisdom of Solomon; and, behold, a greater than Solomon is here.

Luke 11: 29–32

29 And when the people were gathered thick together, he began to say, This is an evil generation: they seek a sign; and there shall no sign be given it, but the sign of Jonas the prophet.

30 For as Jonas was a sign unto the Ninevites, so shall also the Son of man be to this generation.

31 The queen of the south shall rise up in the judgment with the men of this generation, and condemn them: for she came from the utmost parts of the earth to hear the wisdom of Solomon; and, behold, a greater than Solomon is here.

32 The men of Nineve shall rise up in the judgment with this generation, and shall condemn it: for they repented at the preaching of Jonas; and, behold, a greater than Jonas is here.

MATTHEW 13: 1–17; MARK 4: 1–12,25; LUKE 8: 1–10,18; 10: 23–24

Matthew 13: 1–17

1 The same day went Jesus out of the house, and sat by the sea side.

2 And great multitudes were gathered together unto him, so that he went into a ship, and sat; and the whole multitude stood on the shore.

3 And he spake many things unto them in parables, saying, Behold, a sower went forth to sow;

4 And when he sowed, some seeds fell by the way side, and the fowls came and devoured them up:

5 Some fell upon stony places, where they had not much earth: and forthwith they sprung up, because they had no deepness of earth:

6 And when the sun was up, they were

and three nights. This is in accordance with a well-known figure of speech. As the night is an appendage to the day, or rather, as the day consists of two parts, light and darkness, he expresses a day by a day and a night, and where there was half a day, he puts down a whole day.

MATTHEW 13: 1–17; MARK 4: 1–12,24–25; LUKE 8: 1–10,18; 10: 23–24

Matthew 13: 2. And great multitudes were gathered together to him

It is not without good reason that the Evangelists begin with informing us that, a vast multitude had assembled, and that when Christ beheld them, he was led to compare his doctrine to **seed.** That **multitude** had been collected from various places: all were held in suspense; all were alike eager to hear, but not equally desirous to receive instruction. The design of the parable was to inform them, that the **seed** of doctrine, which is scattered far and wide, is not everywhere productive; because it does not always find a fertile and well cultivated soil. Christ declared that he was there in the capacity of a husbandman, who was going out **to sow seed,** but that many of his hearers resembled an uncultivated and parched soil, while others resembled a thorny soil; so that the labor and the very seed were thrown away. If those who ran from distant places to Christ, like hungry people, are compared to an unproductive and barren soil, we need not wonder if, in our own day, the Gospel does not yield fruit in many, of whom some are lazy and sluggish, others hear with indifference, and others are scarcely drawn even to hear.

9. He that hath ears to hear, let him hear

These words were intended partly to show that all were not endued with true understanding to comprehend what he said, and partly to arouse his disciples to consider attentively that doctrine which is not readily and easily understood by all. Indeed, he makes a distinction among the hearers, by pronouncing some to have ears, and others to be deaf. If it is next inquired, how it comes to pass that the former have ears, Scripture testifies in other passages, that it is the Lord who pierces the ears (Psalm 40: 7), and that no man obtains or accomplishes this by his own industry.

10. The disciples approaching said to him

From the words of Matthew it is evident, that the disciples did not merely look to themselves, but wished also to consult the benefit of others. Being unable to comprehend the parable, they concluded that it would be as little understood by the people; and, therefore, they complain that Christ employed language from which his hearers could derive no profit. Now though parables are generally found

that does not inculcate and produce humanity never came from heaven.

2. We have already seen what the sin against the Holy Ghost is: no soul that fears God can commit it: perhaps it would be impossible for any but Jews to be guilty of it, and they only in the circumstances mentioned in the text; and in such circumstances, it is impossible that any person should now be found.

MATTHEW 12: 38–42; LUKE 11: 29–32

Matthew 12: 38–42

38. We would see a sign from thee – That is, we wish now to see thee work a miracle. Pride, vain curiosity, and incredulity, have never proof sufficient of the truth: for they will not be satisfied.

39. An evil and adulterous generation – Or, race of people. This translation is a key to unlock some very obscure passages in the evangelists.

 Seeketh after a sign – Or, seeketh another sign, , so I think this word should be translated. Our Lord had already given the Jews several signs; and here they desire sign upon sign.

 Our Lord terms the Jews an adulterous race. Under the old covenant, the Jewish nation was represented as in a marriage contract with the Lord of hosts; as believers, in the new covenant, are represented as the spouse of Christ. All unfaithfulness and disobedience was considered as a breach of this marriage contract; hence the persons who were thus guilty are denominated adulterers and adulteresses.

40. Three days and three nights – Our Lord rose from the grave on the day but one after his crucifixion: so that, in the computation in this verse, the part of the day on which he was crucified, and the part of that on which he rose again, are severally estimated as an entire day; and this, no doubt, exactly corresponded to the time in which Jonah was in the belly of the fish. Our Lord says, As Jonah was, so shall the Son of man be, etc. Evening and morning, or night and day, is the Hebrew phrase for a natural day. The very same quan-

tity of time which is here termed three days and three nights, and which, in reality, was only one whole day, a part of two others, and two whole nights, is termed three days and three nights, in the book of Esther: Go; neither eat nor drink THREE DAYS, NIGHT or DAY, and so I will go in unto the king: Esther 4: 16. Afterwards it follows, Esther 5: 1. On the THIRD DAY, Esther stood in the inner court of the king's house. For farther satisfaction, the reader, if he please, may take the following from Lightfoot.

 "I. The Jewish writers extend that memorable station of the unmoving sun, at Joshua's prayer, to six and thirty hours; for so Kimchi upon that place: 'According to more exact interpretation, the sun and moon stood still for six and thirty hours: for when the fight was on the eve of the Sabbath, Joshua feared lest the Israelites might break the Sabbath; therefore he spread abroad his hands, that the sun might stand still on the sixth day, according to the measure of the day of the Sabbath, and the moon according to the measure of the night of the Sabbath, and of the going out of the Sabbath, which amounts to six and thirty hours.'

 "II. If you number the hours that pass from our Savior's giving up the ghost upon the cross to his resurrection, you shall find almost the same number of hours; and yet that space is called by him three days and three nights, whereas two nights only came between, and one complete day. Nevertheless, while he speaks these words, he is not without the consent both of the Jewish schools and their computation. Three days and three nights, according to this Jewish method of reckoning, included any part of the first day; the whole of the following night; the next day and its night; and any part of the succeeding or third day.

 In the whale's belly – That a fish of the shark kind, and not a whale, is here meant. It is well known that the throat of a whale is capable of admitting little more than the arm of an ordinary man; but many of the shark species can swallow a man whole, and men have been found whole in the stomachs of several. Every natural history abounds with facts of this kind.

scorched; and because they had no root, they withered away.

7 And some fell among thorns; and the thorns sprung up, and choked them:

8 But other fell into good ground, and brought forth fruit, some an hundredfold, some sixtyfold, some thirtyfold.

9 Who hath ears to hear, let him hear.

10 And the disciples came, and said unto him, Why speakest thou unto them in parables?

11 He answered and said unto them, Because it is given unto you to know the mysteries of the kingdom of heaven, but to them it is not given.

12 For whosoever hath, to him shall be given, and he shall have more abundance: but whosoever hath not, from him shall be taken away even that he hath.

13 Therefore speak I to them in parables: because they seeing see not; and hearing they hear not, neither do they understand.

14 And in them is fulfilled the prophecy of Esaias, which saith, By hearing ye shall hear, and shall not understand; and seeing ye shall see, and shall not perceive:

15 For this people's heart is waxed gross, and their ears are dull of hearing, and their eyes they have closed; lest at any time they should see with their eyes, and hear with their ears, and should understand with their heart, and should be converted, and I should heal them.

16 But blessed are your eyes, for they see: and your ears, for they hear.

17 For verily I say unto you, That many prophets and righteous men have desired to see those things which ye see, and have not seen them; and to hear those things which ye hear, and have not heard them.

Mark 4: 1–12,25

1 And he began again to teach by the sea side: and there was gathered unto him a great multitude, so that he entered into a ship, and sat in the sea; and the whole multitude was by the sea on the land.

2 And he taught them many things by parables, and said unto them in his doctrine,

3 Hearken; Behold, there went out a sower to sow:

4 And it came to pass, as he sowed,

to illustrate the subject of which they treat, yet the uninterrupted course of a metaphor may lead to obscurity. So then Christ, in delivering this parable, intended to wrap up, in an allegory, what he might have said more plainly and fully, without a figure. But now that the exposition is added, the figurative discourse has greater energy and force than if it had been simple: by which is meant, that it is not only fitted to produce a more powerful impression on the mind, but is also more clear. So highly important is the manner in which any thing is said.

12. For whosoever hath, it shall be given to him

Christ reminds his disciples how kindly God acts towards them, that they may more highly prize his grace, and may acknowledge themselves to be under deeper obligations to his kindness. The same words he afterwards repeats, but in a different sense (Matthew 25: 29); for on that occasion the discourse relates to the lawful use of gifts. But here he simply teaches, that more is given to the apostles than to the generality of men, because the heavenly Father is pleased to display in perfection his kindness towards them. " He does not forsake the work of his own hand" (Psalm 138: 8).

Those whom he has once begun to form are continually polished more and more, till they are at length brought to the highest perfection. The multiplied favors which are continually flowing from him to us, and the joyful progress which we make, spring from God's contemplation of his own liberality, which prompts him to an uninterrupted course of bounty. And as his riches are inexhaustible, so he is never wearied with enriching his children. Whenever he advances us to a higher degree, let us remember that every increase of the favors which we daily receive from him flows from this source, that it is his purpose to complete the work, of our salvation already commenced. On the other hand, Christ declares that the reprobate are continually proceeding from bad to worse, till, at length exhausted, they waste away in their own poverty.

And he that hath not, even that which he hath shall be taken from him

This may appear to be a harsh expression; but instead of saying, that what the ungodly have not is taken from them, Luke softens the harshness and removes the ambiguity by a slight change of the words: **and whosoever hath not, even that which he thinketh that he hath shall be taken from him**.

And indeed it frequently happens, that the reprobate are endued with eminent gifts, and appear to resemble the children of God: but there is nothing of real value about them; for their mind is destitute of piety, and has only the glitter of an empty show. Matthew is therefore justified in saying that they have nothing; for what they have is of no

41. The men of Nineveh shell rise in judgment – The voice of God, threatening temporal judgments, caused a whole people to repent, who had neither Moses nor Christ, neither the law nor the prophets; and who perhaps never had but this one preacher among them. What judgment may not we expect, if we continue impenitent, after all that God has bestowed upon us?

A greater than Jonas is here – something more. The evidence offered by Jonah sufficed to convince and lead the Ninevites to repentance; but here was more evidence, and a greater person; and yet so obstinate are the Jews that all is ineffectual.

1. Christ, who preached to the Jews, was infinitely greater than Jonah, in his nature, person, and mission.

2. Jonah preached repentance in Nineveh only forty days, and Christ preached among the Jews for several years.

3. Jonah wrought no miracles to authorize his preaching; but Christ wrought miracles every day, in every place where he went, and of every kind. And

4. Notwithstanding all this, the people of Judea did not repent, though the people of Nineveh did.

42. The queen of the south – In 1 Kings 10: 1, this queen is said to be of Saba, which was a city and province of Arabia Felix, to the south, or south-east, of Judea.

Uttermost parts of the earth – – a form of speech which merely signifies, a great distance. See Deuteronomy 28: 49.

MATTHEW 13: 1–17; MARK 4: 1–12,25; LUKE 8: 1–10,18; 10: 23–24

Matthew 13: 1–17

1. The same day – Our Lord scarcely ever appears to take any rest: he is incessant in his labors, and instant in season and out of season; and in this he has left all his successors in the ministry an example, that they should follow his steps: for he who wishes to save souls will find few opportunities to rest. As Satan is going about as a roaring lion seeking whom he may devour, the messenger of God should imitate his diligence, that he may counteract his work. The gospels are journals of our Lord's life.

Went Jesus out of the house – This was the house of Peter. See Matthew 17: 24.

Sat by the sea side – The sea of Galilee, on the borders of which the city of Capernaum was situated.

2. Into a ship – THE vessel or boat. Mr. Wakefield supposes (which is very likely) that a particular vessel is uniformly specified, which seems to have been kept on the lake for the use of Christ and his apostles: it probably belonged to some of the fishermen, (see Matthew 4: 22), who, he thinks, occasionally, at least, followed their former occupation. See John 21: 3.

The thought of pious Quesnel on this verse should not be neglected. We see here a representation of the Church, which consists of the people united to their pastors. These, being more exposed to violent tossings and storms, are, as it were, in a ship, while those continue at ease on the shore.

3. He spake many things unto them in parables – A comparison or similitude, in which one thing is compared with another, especially spiritual things with natural, by which means these spiritual things are better understood, and make a deeper impression on an attentive mind. Or, a parable is a representation of any matter accommodated, in the way of similitude, to the real subject, in order to delineate it with the greater force and perspicuity. See more on this subject at the conclusion of this chapter. No scheme, says Dr. Lightfoot, of Jewish rhetoric was more familiarly used than that of parables; which, perhaps, creeping in from thence among the heathens, ended in fables.

Under the parable of the sower, our Lord intimates,

1. That of all the multitudes then attending his ministry, few would bring forth fruit to perfection. And

2. That this would be a general case in preaching the Gospel among men.

some fell by the way side, and the fowls of the air came and devoured it up.

5 And some fell on stony ground, where it had not much earth; and immediately it sprang up, because it had no depth of earth:

6 But when the sun was up, it was scorched; and because it had no root, it withered away.

7 And some fell among thorns, and the thorns grew up, and choked it, and it yielded no fruit.

8 And other fell on good ground, and did yield fruit that sprang up and increased; and brought forth, some thirty, and some sixty, and some an hundred.

9 And he said unto them, He that hath ears to hear, let him hear.

10 And when he was alone, they that were about him with the twelve asked of him the parable.

11 And he said unto them, Unto you it is given to know the mystery of the kingdom of God: but unto them that are without, all these things are done in parables:

12 That seeing they may see, and not perceive; and hearing they may hear, and not understand; lest at any time they should be converted, and their sins should be forgiven them.

25 For he that hath, to him shall be given: and he that hath not, from him shall be taken even that which he hath.

Luke 8: 1–10,18

1 And it came to pass afterward, that he went throughout every city and village, preaching and showing the glad tidings of the kingdom of God: and the twelve were with him,

2 And certain women, which had been healed of evil spirits and infirmities, Mary called Magdalene, out of whom went seven devils,

3 And Joanna the wife of Chuza Herod's steward, and Susanna, and many others, which ministered unto him of their substance.

4 And when much people were gathered together, and were come to him out of every city, he spake by a parable:

5 A sower went out to sow his seed: and as he sowed, some fell by the way side; and it was trodden down, and the fowls of the air devoured it.

value in the sight of God, and has no permanency within. Equally appropriate is the statement of Luke, that the gifts, with which they have been endued, are corrupted by them, so that they shine only in the eyes of men, but have nothing more than splendor and empty display. Hence, also let us learn to aim at progress throughout our whole life; for God grants to us the taste of his heavenly doctrine on the express condition, that we feed on it abundantly from day to day, till we come to be fully satiated with it.

13. For this reason I speak by parables

He says that he speaks to the multitude in an obscure manner, because they are not partakers of the true light. And yet, while he declares that a veil is spread over the blind, that they may remain in their darkness, he does not ascribe the blame of this to themselves, but takes occasion to commend more highly the grace bestowed on the Apostles, because it is not equally communicated to all. He assigns no cause for it, except the secret purpose of God; for which, as we shall afterwards see more fully, there is a good reason, though it has been concealed from us. It is not the only design of a parable to state, in an obscure manner, what God is not pleased to reveal clearly; but we have said that the parable now under our consideration was delivered by Christ, in order that the form of an allegory might present a doubtful riddle.

14. And in them is fulfilled the prophecy of Isaiah

He confirms his statement by a prediction of Isaiah, that it is far from being a new thing, if many people derive no advantage from the word of God, which was formerly appointed to the ancient people, for the purpose of inducing greater blindness. This passage of the Prophet is quoted, in a variety of ways, in the New Testament. Paul quotes it (Acts 28: 26) to charge the Jews with obstinate malice, and says that they were blinded by the light of the Gospel, because they were bitter and rebellious against God. There he points out the immediate cause which appeared in the men themselves. But in the Epistle to the Romans (11: 7) he draws the distinction from a deeper and more hidden source; for he tells us, that the remnant was saved according to the election of grace, and that the rest were blinded, according as it is written. The contrast must there be observed; for if it is the election of God, and an undeserved election, which alone saves any remnant of the people, it follows that all others perish by a hidden, though just, judgment of God. Who are the rest, whom Paul contrasts with the elect remnant, but those on whom God has not bestowed a special salvation?

Similar reasoning may be applied to the passage in John (12: 38); for he says that many believed not, because no man believes, except he to whom God reveals his arm, and

4. Some seeds fell by the way side – The hard beaten path, where no plough had broken up the ground.

5. Stony places – Where there was a thin surface of earth, and a rock at the bottom.

7. Among thorns – Where the earth was ploughed up, but the brambles and weeds had not been cleared away.

8. Good ground – Where the earth was deep, the field well ploughed, and the brambles and weeds all removed.

Some a hundred-fold – Who can help admiring the wisdom and providence of God in this single grain of corn! He has, in some sort, impressed on it an idea of his own infinity; and an idea which, like the subject to which it refers, confounds our imagination and reason. How infinitely great is God, even in his minor works.

9. Who hath ears to hear, etc. – Let every person who feels the necessity of being instructed in the things which concern his soul's welfare pay attention to what is spoken, and he shall become wise unto salvation.

11. It is given unto you to know the mysteries, etc. – By mysteries, here, we may understand not only things concerning the scheme of salvation, which had not yet been revealed; but also the prophetic declarations concerning the future state of the Christian Church, expressed in the ensuing parables. It is not given to them to know the purport and design of these things – they are gross of heart, earthly and sensual, and do not improve the light they have received: but to you it is given, because I have appointed you not only to be the first preachers of my Gospel to sinners, but also the persons who shall transmit accounts of all these things to posterity. The knowledge of these mysteries, in the first instance, can be given only to a few; but when these faithfully write and publish what they have heard and seen, unto the world, then the science of salvation is revealed and addressed to all. From Matthew 13: 17, we learn, that many prophets and righteous men had desired to see and hear these things, but had not that privilege – to them it was not given; not because God designed to exclude them from salvation, but because HE who knew all things knew, either that they were not proper persons, or that that was not the proper time: for the choice of the PERSONS by whom, and the choice of the TIME in which it is most proper to reveal Divine things, must ever rest with the all-wise God.

12. Whosoever hath, to him shall be given – This is an allusion to a common custom in all countries: he who possesses much or is rich, to such a person, presents are ordinarily given.

Whosoever hath not, from him shall be taken away even that he hath – That is, the poor man: he that has little may be easily made a prey of, and so lose his little.

13. Therefore speak I to them in parables – On this account, viz. to lead them into a proper knowledge of God. I speak to them in parables, natural representations of spiritual truths, that they may be allured to inquire, and to find out the spirit, which is hidden under the letter; because, seeing the miracles which I have wrought, they see not, i.e. the end for which I have wrought them; and hearing my doctrines, they hear not, so as to profit by what is spoken; neither do they understand, they do not lay their hearts to it. Is not this obviously our Lord's meaning? Who can suppose that he would employ his time in speaking enigmatically to them, on purpose that they might not understand what was spoken? Could the God of truth and sincerity act thus? If he had designed to act otherwise, he might have saved his time and labor, and not spoken at all, which would have answered the same end, viz. to leave them in gross ignorance.

14. In them is fulfilled – Is AGAIN fulfilled: this proper meaning of the Greek word has been generally overlooked. The evangelist means, that as these words were fulfilled in the Jews, in the time of the Prophet Isaiah, so they are now again fulfilled in these their posterity, who exactly copy their fathers example. These awful words may be again fulfilled in us,

6 And some fell upon a rock; and as soon as it was sprung up, it withered away, because it lacked moisture.

7 And some fell among thorns; and the thorns sprang up with it, and choked it.

8 And other fell on good ground, and sprang up, and bare fruit an hundredfold. And when he had said these things, he cried, He that hath ears to hear, let him hear.

9 And his disciples asked him, saying, What might this parable be?

10 And he said, Unto you it is given to know the mysteries of the kingdom of God: but to others in parables; that seeing they might not see, and hearing they might not understand.

18 Take heed therefore how ye hear: for whosoever hath, to him shall be given; and whosoever hath not, from him shall be taken even that which he seemeth to have.

Luke 10: 23–24

23 And he turned him unto his disciples, and said privately, Blessed are the eyes which see the things that ye see:

24 For I tell you, that many prophets and kings have desired to see those things which ye see, and have not seen them; and to hear those things which ye hear, and have not heard them.

MATTHEW 13: 18–23; MARK 4: 13–20; LUKE 8: 11–15

Matthew 13: 18–23

18 Hear ye therefore the parable of the sower.

19 When any one heareth the word of the kingdom, and understandeth it not, then cometh the wicked one, and catcheth away that which was sown in his heart. This is he which received seed by the way side.

20 But he that received the seed into stony places, the same is he that heareth the word, and anon with joy receiveth it;

21 Yet hath he not root in himself, but dureth for a while: for when tribulation or persecution ariseth because of the word, by and by he is offended.

22 He also that received seed among the thorns is he that heareth the word; and the care of this world, and the deceit-

immediately adds, that they could not believe, because it is again written, Blind the heart of this people. Such, too is the object which Christ has in view, when he ascribes it to the secret purpose of God, that the truth of the Gospel is not revealed indiscriminately to all, but is exhibited at a distance under obscure forms, so as to have no other effect than to overspread the minds of the people with grosser darkness. In all cases, I admit, those whom God blinds will be found to deserve this condemnation; but as the immediate cause is not always obvious in the people of men, let it be held as a fixed principle, that God enlightens to salvation, and that by a peculiar gift, those whom He has freely chosen; and that all the reprobate are deprived of the light of life, whether God withholds his word from them, or keeps their eyes and ears closed, that they do not hear or see.

MATTHEW 13: 18–23; MARK 4: 13–20; LUKE 8: 11–15

According to Matthew and Luke, Christ explains the parable to his disciples simply, and unaccompanied by a reproof; but according to Mark, he indirectly blames them for being slow of apprehension, because those who were to be the teachers of all did not run before others. The general truth conveyed is, that the doctrine of the Gospel, when it is scattered like seed, is not everywhere fruitful; because it does not always meet with a fertile and well cultivated soil. He enumerates four kinds of hearers: the first of which do not receive the seed; the second appear, indeed, to receive it, but in such a manner that it does not take deep root; in the third, the corn is choked; and so there remains a fourth part, which produces fruit. Not that one hearer only out of four, or ten out of forty, embrace the doctrine, and yield fruit; for Christ did not intend here to fix down an exact number, or to arrange the people, of whom he speaks, in equal divisions; and, indeed, where the word is sown, the produce of faith is not always alike, but is sometimes more abundant, and at other times more scanty. He only intended to warn us, that, in many people, the seed of life is lost on account of various defects, in consequence of which it is either destroyed immediately, or it withers, or it gradually degenerates. That we may derive the greater advantage from this warning, we ought to bear in mind, that he makes no mention of despisers who openly reject the word of God, but describes those only in whom there is some appearance of docility. But if the greater part of such men perish, what shall become of the rest of the world, by whom the doctrine of salvation is openly rejected? I now come down to each class.

if we take not warning by the things which these disobedient people have suffered.

By hearing ye shall hear – Jesus Christ shall be sent to you, his miracles ye shall fully see, and his doctrines ye shall distinctly hear; but God will not force you to receive the salvation which is offered.

15. Heart is waxed gross – is become fat – inattentive stupid, insensible. They hear heavily with their ears – are half asleep while the salvation of God is preached unto them.

Their eyes they have closed – Totally and obstinately resisted the truth of God, and shut their eyes against the light.

Lest – they should see, etc. – Lest they should see their lost estate, and be obliged to turn unto God, and seek his salvation. His state is truly deplorable who is sick unto death, and yet is afraid of being cured. The fault is here totally in the people, and not at all in that God whose name is Mercy and whose nature is love.

16. But blessed are your eyes – Ye improve the light which God has given you; and you receive an increase of heavenly wisdom by every miracle and by every sermon.

17. Many prophets and righteous men – These lived by and died in the faith of the promised Messiah: the fullness of the time was not then come for his manifestation in the flesh.

MATTHEW 13: 18–23; MARK 4: 13–20; LUKE 8: 11–15

Matthew 13: 18–23

19. When any one heareth the word of the kingdom – Viz. the preaching of the Gospel of Christ.

And understandeth it not – perhaps more properly, regardeth it not, does not lay his heart to it.

The wicked one – It is worthy of remark, that the three evangelists should use each a different appellative of this mortal enemy of mankind; probably to show that the devil, with all his powers and properties, opposes

every thing that tends to the salvation of the soul.

Catcheth away – Makes the utmost haste to pick up the good seed, lest it should take root in the heart.

A careless inattentive hearer is compared to the way side – his heart is an open road, where evil affections, and foolish and hurtful desires, continually pass and repass, without either notice or restraint. "A heart where Satan has" (as one terms it) "ingress, egress, regress, and progress: in a word, the devil's thoroughfare."

20. But he that received the seed into stony places – is he – That is, is a fit emblem of that man who, hearing the Gospel, is affected with its beauty and excellency, and immediately receiveth it with joy – is glad to hear what God has done to make man happy.

21. Yet hath he not root in himself – His soul is not deeply convinced of its guilt and depravity; the fallow ground is not properly ploughed up, nor the rock broken. When persecution, etc., ariseth, which he did not expect, he is soon stumbled – seeks some pretext to abandon both the doctrine and followers of Christ. Having not felt his own sore, and the plague of his heart, he has not properly discovered that this salvation is the only remedy for his soul: thus he has no motive in his heart strong enough to counteract the outward scandal of the cross; so he endureth only for the time in which there is no difficulty to encounter, no cross to bear.

22. The deceitfulness of riches – Which promise peace and pleasure, but can never give them.

Choke the word – Or, together choke the word, meaning, either that these grow up together with the word, overtop, and choke it; or that these united together, viz. worldly cares, with the delusive hopes and promises of riches, cause the man to abandon the great concerns of his soul, and seek, in their place, what he shall eat, drink, and wherewithal he shall be clothed. Dreadful stupidity of man, thus to barter spiritual for temporal good – a heavenly inheritance for an earthly portion! The seed of

fulness of riches, choke the word, and he becometh unfruitful.

23 But he that received seed into the good ground is he that heareth the word, and understandeth it; which also beareth fruit, and bringeth forth, some an hundredfold, some sixty, some thirty.

Mark 4: 13–20

13 And he said unto them, Know ye not this parable? and how then will ye know all parables?

14 The sower soweth the word.

15 And these are they by the way side, where the word is sown; but when they have heard, Satan cometh immediately, and taketh away the word that was sown in their hearts.

16 And these are they likewise which are sown on stony ground; who, when they have heard the word, immediately receive it with gladness;

17 And have no root in themselves, and so endure but for a time: afterward, when affliction or persecution ariseth for the word's sake, immediately they are offended.

18 And these are they which are sown among thorns; such as hear the word,

19 And the cares of this world, and the deceitfulness of riches, and the lusts of other things entering in, choke the word, and it becometh unfruitful.

20 And these are they which are sown on good ground; such as hear the word, and receive it, and bring forth fruit, some thirtyfold, some sixty, and some an hundred.

Luke 8: 11–15

11 Now the parable is this: The seed is the word of God.

12 Those by the way side are they that hear; then cometh the devil, and taketh away the word out of their hearts, lest they should believe and be saved.

13 They on the rock are they, which, when they hear, receive the word with joy; and these have no root, which for a while believe, and in time of temptation fall away.

14 And that which fell among thorns are they, which, when they have heard, go forth, and are choked with cares and riches and pleasures of this life, and bring

Matthew 13: 19. When any one heareth the word of the kingdom, and understandeth it not

He mentions, in the first place, the barren and uncultivated, who do not receive the seed within, because there is no preparation in their hearts. Such people he compares to a stiff and dry soil, like what we find on a public road, which is trodden down, and becomes hard, like a pavement. I wish that we had not occasion to see so many of this class at the present day, who come forward to hear, but remain in a state of amazement, and acquire no relish for the word, and in the end differ little from blocks or stones. Need we wonder that they utterly vanish away?

That which was sown in their heart

This expression, which Christ employs, is not strictly accurate, and yet it is not without meaning; for the wickedness and depravity of men do not make the word to lose its own nature, or to cease to have the character of seed. This must be carefully observed, that we may not suppose the favors of God to cease to be what they are, though the good effect of them does not reach us. With respect to God, the word **is sown in the hearts,** but it is far from being true, that the hearts of all receive with meekness what is planted in them, as James (1: 21) exhorts us to receive the word. So then the Gospel is always a fruitful seed as to its power, but not as to its produce.

MATTHEW 13: 24–30, 36–43

In order to reap the advantage of this parable, we must appreciate Christ's objective in telling it. Some think that, to guard a mixed multitude against satisfying themselves with an outward profession of the Gospel, he told them, that in his own field bad seed is often mixed with the good, but that a day is coming, when the tares shall be separated from the wheat. They accordingly connect this parable with the one immediately preceding, as if the design of both had been the same.

For my own part, I take a different view. He speaks of a separation, in order to prevent the minds of the godly from giving way to uneasiness or despondency, when they perceive a confused mixture of the good along with the bad. Although Christ has cleansed the Church with his own blood, that it may be without spot or blemish, yet hitherto he suffers it to be polluted by many stains. I speak not of the remaining infirmities of the flesh, to which every believer is liable, even after that he has been renewed by the Holy Spirit. But as soon as Christ has gathered a small flock for himself, many hypocrites mingle with it, people of immoral lives creep in, nay, many wicked men insinuate themselves; in consequence of which, numerous stains pollute that holy assembly, which Christ has separated for

the kingdom can never produce much fruit in any heart, till the thorns and thistles of vicious affections and impure desires be plucked up by the roots and burned.

23. Good ground – That which had depth of mould, was well ploughed, and well weeded.

Is he that heareth – Who diligently attends the ministry of the word.

And understandeth it – Lays the subject to heart, deeply weighing its nature, design, and importance.

Which also beareth fruit – His fruitfulness being an almost necessary consequence of his thus laying the Divine message to heart. Let it be observed, that to hear, to understand, and to bring forth fruit, are the three grand evidences of a genuine believer. He who does not hear the word of wisdom cannot understand what makes for his peace; and he who does not understand what the Gospel requires him to be and to perform, cannot bring forth fruit; and he who is not fruitful, very fruitful, cannot be a disciple of Christ – see John 15: 8; and he who is not Christ's disciple cannot enter into the kingdom of God.

From the different portions of fruit produced by the good ground, a hundred, sixty, and thirty, we may learn that all sound believers are not equally fruitful; all hear, understand, and bring forth fruit, but not in the same degrees-occasioned, partly, by their situation and circumstances not allowing them such extensive opportunities of receiving and doing good; and, partly, by lack of mental capacity – for every mind is not equally improvable.

Let it be farther observed that the unfruitfulness of the different lands was not owing to bad seed or an unskillful sower – the same sower sows the same seed in all, and with the same gracious design – but it is unfruitful in many because they are careless, inattentive, and worldly-minded.

But is not the ground naturally bad in every heart? Undoubtedly. And can any but God make it good? None. But it is your business, when you hear of the justice and mercy of God, to implore him to work in you that which

is pleasing in his sight. No man shall be condemned because he did not change his own heart, but because he did not cry to God to change it, who gave him his Holy Spirit for this very purpose, and which he, by his worldly-mindedness and impiety, quenched. Whoso hath ears to hear let him hear: and may the Lord save the reader from an impenitent and unfruitful heart!

MATTHEW 13: 24–30, 36–43

24. The kingdom of heaven – God's method of managing the affairs of the world, and the concerns of his Church.

Is likened unto a man which sowed good seed in his field – In general, the world may be termed the field of God; and in particular, those who profess to believe in God through Christ are his field or farm; among whom God sows nothing but the pure unadulterated word of his truth.

25. But while men slept – When the professors were lukewarm, and the pastors indolent, his enemy came and sowed tares, degenerate wheat. The righteous and the wicked are often mingled in the visible Church. Every Christian society, how pure soever its principles may be, has its bastard wheat – those who bear a resemblance to the good, but whose hearts are not right with God. He who sows this bastard wheat among God's people is here styled God's enemy; and he may be considered also as a sower of them who permits them to be sown and to spring up through his negligence. Wo to the indolent pastors, who permit the souls under their care to be corrupted by error and sin!

The righteous and the wicked shall be permitted to grow together, till God comes to make a full and final separation.

26. When the blade was sprung up – **then appeared the tares also** – Satan has a shoot of iniquity for every shoot of grace; and, when God revives his work, Satan revives his also. No marvel, therefore, if we find scandals arising suddenly to discredit a work of grace, where God has begun to pour out his Spirit.

no fruit to perfection.

15 But that on the good ground are they, which in an honest and good heart, having heard the word, keep it, and bring forth fruit with patience.

MATTHEW 13: 24–30,36–43

Matthew 13: 24–30

24 Another parable put he forth unto them, saying, The kingdom of heaven is likened unto a man which sowed good seed in his field:

25 But while men slept, his enemy came and sowed tares among the wheat, and went his way.

26 But when the blade was sprung up, and brought forth fruit, then appeared the tares also.

27 So the servants of the householder came and said unto him, Sir, didst not thou sow good seed in thy field? from whence then hath it tares?

28 He said unto them, An enemy hath done this. The servants said unto him, Wilt thou then that we go and gather them up?

29 But he said, Nay; lest while ye gather up the tares, ye root up also the wheat with them.

30 Let both grow together until the harvest: and in the time of harvest I will say to the reapers, Gather ye together first the tares, and bind them in bundles to burn them: but gather the wheat into my barn.

Matthew 13: 36–43

36 Then Jesus sent the multitude away, and went into the house: and his disciples came unto him, saying, Declare unto us the parable of the tares of the field.

37 He answered and said unto them, He that soweth the good seed is the Son of man;

38 The field is the world; the good seed are the children of the kingdom; but the tares are the children of the wicked one;

39 The enemy that sowed them is the devil; the harvest is the end of the world; and the reapers are the angels.

40 As therefore the tares are gathered and burned in the fire; so shall it be in the

himself. Many people, too, look upon it as exceedingly absurd, that ungodly, or profane or unprincipled men should be cherished within the bosom of the Church. Add to this, that very many, under the pretense of zeal, are excessively displeased, when every thing is not conducted to their wish, and, because absolute purity is nowhere to be found, withdraw from the Church in a disorderly manner, or subvert and destroy it by unreasonable severity.

In my opinion, the design of the parable is simply this: So long as the pilgrimage of the Church in this world continues, bad men and hypocrites will mingle in it with those who are good and upright, that the children of God may be armed with patience and, in the midst of offenses which are fitted to disturb them, may preserve unbroken stedfastness of faith. It is an appropriate comparison, when the Lord calls the Church **his field**, for believers are the seed of it; and though Christ afterwards adds that **the field is the world**, yet he undoubtedly intended to apply this designation, in a peculiar manner, to the Church, about which he had commenced the discourse. But as he was about to drive his plough through every country of the world, so as to cultivate fields, and scatter the seed of life, throughout the whole world, he has employed a synecdoche, to make the world denote what more strictly belonged only to a part of it.

We must now inquire what he means by the **wheat**, and what by the **tares**. These terms cannot be explained as referring to doctrine, as if the meaning had been that, when the Gospel **is sown**, it is immediately corrupted and adulterated by wicked inventions; for Christ would never have forbidden them to labor strenuously to purge out that kind of corruption. With respect to morals, those faults of men which cannot be corrected must be endured; but we are not at liberty to extend such a toleration to wicked errors, which corrupt the purity of faith. Besides, Christ removes all doubt, by saying expressly, that **the tares are the children of the wicked one**. And yet it must also be remarked, that this cannot be understood simply of the people of men, as if by creation God sowed good men and the devil sowed bad men. As it is not by creation that God makes his elect, who have been tainted with original sin, to become a good seed, but by regenerating them through the grace of his Spirit; so wicked men are not created by the devil, but, having been created by God, are corrupted by the devil, and thrown into the Lord's field, in order to corrupt the pure seed.

MATTHEW 13: 31–35; MARK 4: 26–34; LUKE 13: 18–22

By these parables Christ encourages his disciples not to be

27. So the servants – said unto him, Sir, didst not thou sow – A faithful and vigilant minister of Christ fails not to discover the evil, to lament it, and to address himself to God by prayer, in order to find out the cause of it, and to receive from him proper information how to behave on the occasion.

28. An enemy hath done this – It is the interest of Satan to introduce hypocrites and wicked persons into religious societies, in order to discredit the work of God, and to favor his own designs.

Wilt thou then that we go and gather them up? – A zeal which is rash and precipitate is as much to be feared as the total lack of strict discipline.

29. But he said, Nay – God judges quite otherwise than men of this mixture of good and evil in the world; he knows the good which he intends to produce from it, and how far his patience towards the wicked should extend, in order to their conversion, or the farther sanctification of the righteous. Men often persecute a true Christian, while they intend only to prosecute an impious person. The zeal which leads persons to persecute others for religious opinions is not less a seed of the devil than a bad opinion itself is.

30. Let both grow together – Though every minister of God should separate from the Church of Christ every incorrigible sinner, yet he should proceed no farther: the man is not to be persecuted in his body or goods, because he is not sound in the faith – GOD tolerates him; so should men. False doctrines are against God – he alone is the judge and punisher of them – man has no right to interfere in this matter.

36. Jesus – went into the house: and his disciples came – Circumstances of this kind should not pass unnoticed: they are instructive and important. Those who attend only to the public preaching of the Gospel of God are not likely to understand fully the mysteries of the kingdom of heaven. To understand clearly the purport of the Divine message, a man must come to God by frequent, fervent, secret prayer. It is thus that the word of God sinks into the heart, is watered, and brings forth much fruit.

Declare (explain) unto us the parable of the tares of the field. – To what has already been spoken on this parable, the following general exposition may be deemed a necessary appendage:

I. What is the cause of EVIL in the world?

1. We must allow that God, who is infinite in holiness, purity, and goodness, could not have done it. Nothing can produce what is not in itself. This is a maxim which every man subscribes to: God then could not have produced sin, forasmuch as his nature is infinite goodness and holiness. He made man at first in his own image, a transcript of his own purity: and, since sin entered into the world, He has done every thing consistent with his own perfections, and the freedom of the human mind, to drive it out, and to make and keep man holy.

2. After a thousand volumes are written on the origin of evil, we shall just know as much of it as Christ has told us here – An enemy hath done it, and this enemy is the devil, Matthew 13: 39.

1. This enemy is represented as a deceitful enemy: a friend in appearance, soliciting to sin, by pleasure, honor, riches, etc.

2. A vigilant enemy. While men sleep he watches, Matthew 13: 25.

3. A hidden or secret enemy. After having sown his seed, he disappears, Matthew 13: 25. Did he appear as himself, few would receive solicitations to sin; but he is seldom discovered in evil thoughts, unholy desires, flattering discourses, bad books, etc.

II. Why was evil permitted to enter into the world?

1. There are doubtless sufficient reasons in the Divine Mind for its permission; which, connected with his infinite essence, and extending to eternity, are not only unfathomable by us, but also, from their nature, incommunicable to men.

2. But it may be justly said, that hereby many attributes of the Divine Nature become mani-

end of this world.

41 The Son of man shall send forth his angels, and they shall gather out of his kingdom all things that offend, and them which do iniquity;

42 And shall cast them into a furnace of fire: there shall be wailing and gnashing of teeth.

43 Then shall the righteous shine forth as the sun in the kingdom of their Father. Who hath ears to hear, let him hear.

MATTHEW 13: 31–35; MARK 4: 26–34; LUKE 13: 18–22

Matthew 13: 31–35

31 Another parable put he forth unto them, saying, The kingdom of heaven is like to a grain of mustard seed, which a man took, and sowed in his field:

32 Which indeed is the least of all seeds: but when it is grown, it is the greatest among herbs, and becometh a tree, so that the birds of the air come and lodge in the branches thereof.

33 Another parable spake he unto them; The kingdom of heaven is like unto leaven, which a woman took, and hid in three measures of meal, till the whole was leavened.

34 All these things spake Jesus unto the multitude in parables; and without a parable spake he not unto them:

35 That it might be fulfilled which was spoken by the prophet, saying, I will open my mouth in parables; I will utter things which have been kept secret from the foundation of the world.

Mark 4: 26–34

26 And he said, So is the kingdom of God, as if a man should cast seed into the ground;

27 And should sleep, and rise night and day, and the seed should spring and grow up, he knoweth not how.

28 For the earth bringeth forth fruit of herself; first the blade, then the ear, after that the full corn in the ear.

29 But when the fruit is brought forth, immediately he putteth in the sickle, because the harvest is come.

30 And he said, Whereunto shall we liken the kingdom of God? or with what comparison shall we compare it?

offended and turn back on account of the mean beginnings of the Gospel. We see how haughtily profane men despise the Gospel, and even turn it into ridicule, because the ministers by whom it is preached are men of slender reputation and of low rank; because it is not instantly received with applause by the whole world; and because the few disciples whom it does obtain are, for the most part, men of no weight or consideration, and belong to the common people. This leads weak minds to despair of its success, which they are apt to estimate from the manner of its commencement. On the contrary, the Lord opens his reign with a feeble and despicable commencement, for the express purpose, that his power may be more fully illustrated by its unexpected progress.

The kingdom of God is compared to a **grain of mustard, which is the smallest among the seeds**, but grows to such a height that it becomes a shrub, **in which the birds build their nests**.

It is also compared to leaven, which, though it may be small in amount, spreads its influence in such a manner, as to impart its bitterness to a large quantity of meal. If the aspect of Christ's kingdom be despicable in the eyes of the flesh, let us learn to raise our minds to the boundless and incalculable power of God, which at once created all things out of nothing, and every day raises up things that are not (1 Corinthians 1: 28), in a manner which exceeds the capacity of the human senses. Let us leave to proud men their disdainful laugh, till the Lord, at an unexpected hour, shall strike them with amazement. Meanwhile, let us not despond, but rise by faith against the pride of the world, till the Lord give us that astonishing display of his power, of which he speaks in this passage.

Mark 4: 26. So is the kingdom of God

Though this comparison has the same object with the two immediately preceding, yet Christ appears to direct his discourse purposely to the ministers of the word, that they may not grow indifferent about the discharge of their duty, because the fruit of their labor does not immediately appear. He holds out for their imitation the example of husbandmen, who **throw seed into the ground** with the expectation of reaping, and do not torment themselves with uneasiness and anxiety, but go to bed and rise again; or, in other words, pursue their ordinary and daily toil, till the corn arrive at maturity in due season. In like manner, though the seed of the word be concealed and choked for a time, Christ enjoins pious teachers to be of good courage, and not to allow their alacrity to be slackened through distrust.

ADAM CLARKE

fest, which otherwise could not have been known; such as mercy, compassion, long-suffering, etc. All of which endear the Deity to men, and perfect the felicity of those who are saved.

III. But why does he suffer this mixture of the good and bad seed now?

1. Because of the necessary dependence of one part of the creation on the other. Were the wicked all rooted up, society must fail, the earth be nearly desolated, noxious things greatly multiplied, and the small remnant of the godly, not being able to stand against the onsets of wild beasts, etc., must soon be extirpated; and then adieu to the economy of grace!

2. Did not the wicked exist, there would be no room for the exercise of many of the graces of the Spirit, on which our spiritual perfection greatly depends.

3. Nor could the grace of God be so manifest in supporting and saving the righteous; and consequently could not have that honor which now it justly claims.

4. Were not this evil tolerated, how could the wicked be converted? The bastard wheat, by being transplanted to a better soil, may become good wheat; so sinners may be engrafted in Christ, and become sons of God through faith in his name; for the longsuffering of God leads multitudes to repentance.

IV. Observe the end of the present state of things:

1. The wicked shall be punished, and the righteous rewarded.

The wicked are termed bastard-wheat – the children of the wicked one, Matthew 13: 38, the very seed of the serpent.

Observe the place in which the wicked shall be punished, – a Furnace. The instrument of this punishment, FIRE. This is an allusion to the punishment inflicted only on those supposed to be the very worst of criminals. See Daniel 3: 6. They were cast into a burning fiery furnace. The effect of it, DESPAIR; weeping, wailing, and gnashing of teeth, Matthew 13: 42.

2. Observe the character and state of the righteous:

1. They are the children of the kingdom, a seed of God's sowing, Matthew 13: 38.

2. As to their persons, they shall be like the sun.

3. The place of their felicity shall be the kingdom of heaven: and,

4. The object of it, GOD In the relation of FATHER, Matthew 13: 43. This is a reference to Daniel 12: 2–3.

MATTHEW 13: 31–35; MARK 4: 26–34; LUKE 13: 18–22

Matthew 13: 31–35

31. The kingdom of heaven is like to a grain of mustard seed – This parable is a representation of the progress of the Gospel in the world; and of the growth of grace in the soul. That grace which leads the soul to the fullness of glory may begin, and often does, in a single good desire – a wish to escape hell, or a desire to enjoy God in heaven.

32. Which indeed is the least of all seeds – That is, of all those seeds which produce plants, whose stems and branches, according to the saying of the botanists, are apt to grow into a ligneous or woody substance.

Becometh a tree – That is, it is not only the largest of plants which are produced from such small seeds, but partakes, in its substance, the close woody texture, especially in warm climates, where we are informed it grows to an almost incredible size. The Jerusalem Talmud, tract Peah. fol. 20, says, "There was a stalk of mustard in Sichin, from which sprang out three boughs; one of which, being broken off, served to cover the tent of a potter, and produced three cabes of mustard seed. Rabbi Simeon ben Chalapha said, A stalk of mustard seed was in my field, into which I was wont to climb, as men are wont to climb into a fig tree." This may appear to be extravagant; and it is probable that, in the case of the three cabes of seed, there is considerable exaggeration; but, if it had not been usual for this plant to grow to a very large size, such relations as these would not have appeared even in the Talmud; and the parable of our Lord sufficiently attests

31 It is like a grain of mustard seed, which, when it is sown in the earth, is less than all the seeds that be in the earth:

32 But when it is sown, it groweth up, and becometh greater than all herbs, and shooteth out great branches; so that the fowls of the air may lodge under the shadow of it.

33 And with many such parables spake he the word unto them, as they were able to hear it.

34 But without a parable spake he not unto them: and when they were alone, he expounded all things to his disciples.

Luke 13: 18–22

18 Then said he, Unto what is the kingdom of God like? and whereunto shall I resemble it?

19 It is like a grain of mustard seed, which a man took, and cast into his garden; and it grew, and waxed a great tree; and the fowls of the air lodged in the branches of it.

20 And again he said, Whereunto shall I liken the kingdom of God?

21 It is like leaven, which a woman took and hid in three measures of meal, till the whole was leavened.

22 And he went through the cities and villages, teaching, and journeying toward Jerusalem.

MATTHEW 13: 44–52

44 Again, the kingdom of heaven is like unto treasure hid in a field; the which when a man hath found, he hideth, and for joy thereof goeth and selleth all that he hath, and buyeth that field.

45 Again, the kingdom of heaven is like unto a merchant man, seeking goodly pearls:

46 Who, when he had found one pearl of great price, went and sold all that he had, and bought it.

47 Again, the kingdom of heaven is like unto a net, that was cast into the sea, and gathered of every kind:

48 Which, when it was full, they drew to shore, and sat down, and gathered the good into vessels, but cast the bad away.

49 So shall it be at the end of the world: the angels shall come forth, and sever the wicked from among the just,

MATTHEW 13: 44–52

The first two of these parables are intended to instruct believers to prefer **the Kingdom of heaven** to the whole world, and therefore to deny themselves and all the desires of the flesh, that nothing may prevent them from obtaining so valuable a possession. We are greatly in need of such a warning; for we are so captivated by the allurements of the world, that eternal life fades from our view; and in consequence of our carnality, the spiritual graces of God are far from being held by us in the estimation which they deserve. Justly, therefore, does Christ speak in such lofty terms of the excellence of eternal life, that we ought not to feel uneasiness at relinquishing, on account of it, whatever we reckon in other respects to be valuable.

First, he says, that the **kingdom of heaven is like a hidden treasure**.

We commonly set a high value on what is visible, and therefore the new and spiritual life, which is held out to us in the Gospel, is little esteemed by us, because it is **hidden**, and lies in hope. There is the highest appropriateness in comparing it to a **treasure**, the value of which is in no degree diminished, though it may be buried in the earth, and withdrawn from the eyes of men. These words teach us, that we ought not to estimate the riches of the grace of God according to the views of our flesh, or according to their outward display, but in the same manner as a **treasure**, though it be **hidden**, is preferred to a vain appearance of wealth.

46. And bought it

By the word buy Christ does not mean, that men bring any price, with which they may purchase for themselves the heavenly life; for we know on what condition the Lord invites believers in the book of Isaiah (55: 1), Come and buy wine and milk without money and without price. But though the heavenly life, and every thing that belongs to it, is the free gift of God, yet we are said to buy it, when we cheerfully relinquish the desires of the flesh, that nothing may prevent us from obtaining it; as Paul says, that he "reckoned all things to be loss and dung, that he might gain Christ" (Philippians 3: 8).

LUKE 7: 36–50

36. And one of the Pharisees requested him

This narrative shows the captious disposition, not only to take, but to seek out, offenses, which was manifested by those who did not know the office of Christ. A **Pharisee** invites Christ; from which we infer, that he was not one of those who furiously and violently opposed, nor of those who haughtily despised his doctrine. But whatever might

the fact. Some soils being more luxuriant than others, and the climate much warmer, raise the same plant to a size and perfection far beyond what a poorer soil, or a colder climate, can possibly do.

33. The kingdom of heaven is like unto leaven – On the nature and effects of leaven, see the note on Exodus 12: 8. As the property of leaven is to change, or assimulate to its own nature, the meal or dough with which it is mixed, so the property of the grace of Christ is to change the whole soul into its own likeness; and God intends that this principle should continue in the soul till all is leavened – till the whole bear the image of the heavenly, as it before bore the image of the earthly. Both these parables are prophetic, and were intended to show, principally, how, from very small beginnings, the Gospel of Christ should pervade all the nations of the world, and fill them with righteousness and true holiness.

34. All these things spoke Jesus – in parables – Christ descends from Divine mysteries to parables, in order to excite us to raise our minds, from and through natural things, to the great God, and the operations of his grace and Spirit. Divine things cannot be taught to man but through the medium of earthly things. If God should speak to us in that language which is peculiar to heaven, clothing those ideas which angelic minds form, how little should we comprehend of the things thus described! How great is our privilege in being thus taught! Heavenly things, in the parables of Christ, assume to themselves a body, and thus render themselves palpable.

35. By the prophet – As the quotation is taken from Psalm 78: 2, which is attributed to Asaph, he must be the prophet who is meant in the text; and, indeed, he is expressly called a prophet, 1 Chronicles 25: 2.

MATTHEW 13: 44–52

44. The kingdom of heaven is like unto treasure hid in a field – to a hidden treasure. We are not to imagine that the treasure here

mentioned, and to which the Gospel salvation is likened, means a pot or chest of money hidden in the field, but rather a gold or silver mine, which he who found out could not get at, or work, without turning up the field, and for this purpose he bought it. Mr. Wakefield's observation is very just: "There is no sense in the purchase of a field for a pot of money, which he might have carried away with him very readily, and as honestly, too, as by overreaching the owner by an unjust purchase."

He hideth – i.e. he kept secret, told the discovery to no person, till he had bought the field.

45. A merchant man, seeking goodly pearls – Those merchants who compass sea and land for temporal gain, condemn the slothfulness of the majority of those called Christians, who, though they confess that this salvation is the most certain and the most excellent of all treasures, yet seek worldly possessions in preference to it! Alas, for him who expects to find any thing more amiable than God, more worthy to fill his heart, and more capable of making him happy!

47. Is like unto a net – A drag-net.

By the net may be understood the preaching of the Gospel of the kingdom, which keeps drawing men into the profession of Christianity, and into the fellowship of the visible Church of Christ. By the sea may be represented that abyss of sin, error, ignorance, and wickedness in which men live, and out of which they are drawn, by the truth and Spirit of God, who cordially close in with the offers of salvation made to them in the preaching of the Gospel.

51. Have ye understood all these things? – Divine truths must not be lightly passed over. – Our Lord's question here shows them to be matters of the utmost weight and importance; and that they should be considered again and again, till they be thoroughly understood.

52. Every scribe – Minister of Christ: who is instructed – taught of God; in the kingdom of heaven – in the mysteries of the Gospel of Christ: out of his treasury – his granary or store-

50 And shall cast them into the furnace of fire: there shall be wailing and gnashing of teeth.

51 Jesus saith unto them, Have ye understood all these things? They say unto him, Yea, Lord.

52 Then said he unto them, Therefore every scribe which is instructed unto the kingdom of heaven is like unto a man that is an householder, which bringeth forth out of his treasure things new and old.

LUKE 7: 36–50

36 And one of the Pharisees desired him that he would eat with him. And he went into the Pharisee's house, and sat down to meat.

37 And, behold, a woman in the city, which was a sinner, when she knew that Jesus sat at meat in the Pharisee's house, brought an alabaster box of ointment,

38 And stood at his feet behind him weeping, and began to wash his feet with tears, and did wipe them with the hairs of her head, and kissed his feet, and anointed them with the ointment.

39 Now when the Pharisee which had bidden him saw it, he spake within himself, saying, This man, if he were a prophet, would have known who and what manner of woman this is that toucheth him: for she is a sinner.

40 And Jesus answering said unto him, Simon, I have somewhat to say unto thee. And he saith, Master, say on.

41 There was a certain creditor which had two debtors: the one owed five hundred pence, and the other fifty.

42 And when they had nothing to pay, he frankly forgave them both. Tell me therefore, which of them will love him most?

43 Simon answered and said, I suppose that he, to whom he forgave most. And he said unto him, Thou hast rightly judged.

44 And he turned to the woman, and said unto Simon, Seest thou this woman? I entered into thine house, thou gavest me no water for my feet: but she hath washed my feet with tears, and wiped them with the hairs of her head.

45 Thou gavest me no kiss: but this woman since the time I came in hath not

be his mildness, he is presently offended when he sees Christ bestow a gracious reception on a woman who, in his opinion, ought not to have been permitted to approach or to converse with him; and, accordingly, disowns him as a prophet, because he does not acknowledge him to be the Mediator, whose peculiar office it was to bring miserable sinners into a state of reconciliation with God. It was something, no doubt, to bestow on Christ the honor due to a prophet; but he ought also to have inquired for what purpose he was sent, what he brought, and what commission he had received from the Father. Overlooking the grace of reconciliation, which was the main feature to be looked for in Christ, the Pharisee concluded that he was **not a prophet**. And, certainly, had it not been that through the grace of Christ this woman had obtained the forgiveness of her sins, and a new righteousness, she ought to have been rejected.

Simon's mistake lies only in this: Not considering that Christ came to save what was lost, he rashly concludes that Christ does not distinguish between the worthy and the unworthy. That we may not share in this dislike, let us learn, first, that Christ was given as a Deliverer to miserable and lost men, and to restore them from death to life.

Secondly, let every man examine himself and his life, and then we will not wonder that others are admitted along with us, for no one will dare to place himself above others. It is hypocrisy alone that leads men to be careless about themselves, and haughtily to despise others.

41. A certain creditor had two debtors

The scope of this parable is to demonstrate, that Simon is wrong in condemning the woman who is acquitted by the heavenly judge. He proves that she is righteous, not because she pleased God, but because her **sins were forgiven**; for otherwise her case would not correspond to the parable, in which Christ expressly states, that the creditor **freely forgave the debtors who were not able to pay**.

We cannot avoid wondering, therefore, that the greater part of commentators have fallen into so gross a blunder as to imagine that this woman, by her tears, and her anointing, and her **kissing his feet**, deserved the pardon of her sins. The argument which Christ employs was taken, not from the cause, but from the effect; for, until a favor has been received, it cannot awaken gratitude, and the cause of reciprocal love is here declared to be a free forgiveness. In a word, Christ argues from the fruits or effects that follow it, that this woman has been reconciled to God.

LUKE 10: 38–42

38. And it happened that he entered into a certain village

This narrative shows, that Christ, wherever he came, did

house; things new and old – a Jewish phrase for great plenty. A small degree of knowledge is not sufficient for a preacher of the Gospel. The sacred writings should be his treasure, and he should properly understand them.

LUKE 7: 36–50

36. One of the Pharisees – Called Simon, Luke 7: 40. This account is considered by many critics and commentators to be the same with that in Matthew 26: 6, etc., Mark 14: 3; and John 12: 3. This subject is considered pretty much at large in the notes on Matthew 26: 6, etc., to which the reader is requested to refer.

37. A woman – which was a sinner – Many suppose that this woman had been a notorious public prostitute; but this is taking the subject by the very worst handle. My own opinion is, that she had been a mere heathen who dwelt in this city, (probably Capernaum), who, through the ministry of Christ, had been before this converted to God, and came now to give this public testimony of her gratitude to her gracious deliverer from the darkness and guilt of sin.

38. Stood at his feet behind him – In taking their meals, the eastern people reclined on one side; the loins and knees being bent to make the more room, the feet of each person were turned outwards behind him. This is the meaning of standing BEHIND at his FEET.

Began to wash his feet with tears – She began to water his feet – to let a shower of tears fall on them. As the Jews wore nothing like our shoes, (theirs being a mere sole, bound about the foot and ankle with thongs), their feet being so much exposed had frequent need of washing, and this they ordinarily did before taking their meals.

Kissed his feet – With affectionate tenderness, or kissed them again and again.

The kiss was used in ancient times as the emblem of love, religious reverence, subjection, and supplication. Kissing the feet is a farther proof that this person had been educated a heathen. This was no part of a Jew's practice.

41. A certain creditor, etc. – It is plain that in this parable our Lord means, by the creditor, GOD, and, by the two debtors, Simon and the woman who was present.

42. Which of them will love him most? – Which is under the greater obligation and should love him most?

43. He to whom he forgave most – By this acknowledgment he was, unknowingly to himself, prepared to receive our Lord's reproof.

44. Thou gavest me no water – In this respect Simon was sadly deficient in civil respect, whether this proceeded from forgetfulness or contempt. The custom of giving water to wash the guest's feet was very ancient. See instances in Genesis 18: 4; 24: 32; Judges 19: 21; 1 Samuel 25: 41.

46. My head with oil thou didst not anoint – Anointing the head with oil was as common among the Jews as washing the face with water is among us. See Ruth 3: 3; 2 Samuel 12: 20; 14: 2; 2 Kings 4: 2; and Psalm 23: 5.

47. For she loved much – Or, THEREFORE she loved much. It appears to have been a consciousness of God's forgiving love that brought her at this time to the Pharisee's house.

Loved much – loveth little – That is, A man's love to God will be in proportion to the obligations he feels himself under to the bounty of his Maker.

48. Thy sins are forgiven – He gave her the fullest assurance of what he had said before to Simon, (Luke 7: 47), Thy sins are forgiven. While the Pharisee murmured, the poor penitent rejoiced.

50. Thy faith hath saved thee – Thy faith hath been the instrument of receiving the salvation which is promised to those who repent. Go in peace. Though peace of conscience be the inseparable consequence of the pardon of sin, yet here it seems to be used as a valediction or farewell: as if he had said, May goodness and mercy continue to follow thee! In this sense it is certainly used Judges 18: 6; 1 Samuel 1: 17; 20: 42; 29: 7; 2 Samuel 15: 9; James 2: 16.

ceased to kiss my feet.

46 My head with oil thou didst not anoint: but this woman hath anointed my feet with ointment.

47 Wherefore I say unto thee, Her sins, which are many, are forgiven; for she loved much: but to whom little is forgiven, the same loveth little.

48 And he said unto her, Thy sins are forgiven.

49 And they that sat at meat with him began to say within themselves, Who is this that forgiveth sins also?

50 And he said to the woman, Thy faith hath saved thee; go in peace.

LUKE 10: 38–42

38 Now it came to pass, as they went, that he entered into a certain village: and a certain woman named Martha received him into her house.

39 And she had a sister called Mary, which also sat at Jesus' feet, and heard his word.

40 But Martha was cumbered about much serving, and came to him, and said, Lord, dost thou not care that my sister hath left me to serve alone? bid her therefore that she help me.

41 And Jesus answered and said unto her, Martha, Martha, thou art careful and troubled about many things:

42 But one thing is needful: and Mary hath chosen that good part, which shall not be taken away from her.

LUKE 12: 13–21

13 And one of the company said unto him, Master, speak to my brother, that he divide the inheritance with me.

14 And he said unto him, Man, who made me a judge or a divider over you?

15 And he said unto them, Take heed, and beware of covetousness: for a man's life consisteth not in the abundance of the things which he possesseth.

16 And he spake a parable unto them, saying, The ground of a certain rich man brought forth plentifully:

17 And he thought within himself, saying, What shall I do, because I have no room where to bestow my fruits?

18 And he said, This will I do: I will pull

not devote himself to his private concerns, or consult his own ease or comfort; but that the single object which he kept in view was, to do good to others, and to discharge the office which had been committed to him by the Father. Luke relates that, having been hospitably received by Martha, as soon as he entered the house, he began to teach and exhort.

Though the hospitality of Martha deserved commendation, and is commended, yet there were two faults in it which are pointed out by Christ. The first is, that Martha carried her activity beyond proper bounds; for Christ would rather have chosen to be entertained in a frugal manner, and at moderate expense, than that the holy woman should have submitted to so much toil. The second fault was, that Martha, by distracting her attention, and undertaking more labor than was necessary, deprived herself of the advantage of Christ's visit.

LUKE 12: 13–21

13. Bid my brother divide

Our Lord, when requested to undertake the office of **dividing an inheritance**, refuses to do so. Now as this tended to promote brotherly harmony, and as Christ's office was, not only to reconcile men to God, but to bring them into a state of agreement with one another, what hindered him from settling the dispute between the two brothers?

There appear to have been chiefly two reasons why he declined the office of a judge. First, as the Jews imagined that the Messiah would have an earthly kingdom, he wished to guard against doing any thing that might countenance this error. If they had seen him divide inheritances, the report of that proceeding would immediately have been circulated. Many would have been led to expect a carnal redemption, which they too ardently desired; and wicked men would have loudly declared, that he was effecting a revolution in the state, and overturning the Roman Empire.

Secondly, our Lord intended to draw a distinction between the political kingdoms of this world and the government of his Church.

LUKE 13: 1–9

2. Do you imagine? etc

This passage is highly useful, were it for no other reason than that this disease is almost natural to us, to be too rigorous and severe in judging of others, and too much disposed to flatter our own faults. The consequence is, that we not only censure with excessive severity the offenses of our brethren; but whenever they meet with any calamity, we condemn them as wicked and reprobate people. On the other hand, every man that is not sorely pressed by the

LUKE 10: 38–42

38. Received him – Kindly received, she received him in a friendly manner, under her roof; and entertained him hospitably.

39. Sat at Jesus' feet – This was the posture of the Jewish scholars, while listening to the instructions of the rabbins. It is in this sense that St. Paul says he was brought up at the FEET of Gamaliel, Acts 22: 3.

40. Martha was cumbered – She was harassed with different cares and employments at the same time; one drawing one way, and another, another: a proper description of a worldly mind. But in Martha's favor it may be justly said, that all her anxiety was to provide suitable and timely entertainment for our Lord and his disciples.

Dost thou not care – Dost thou not think it wrong, that my sister thus leaves me to provide and prepare this supper, alone?

41. Thou art careful and troubled – Thou art distracted, thy mind is divided, in consequence of which, thou art disturbed, thy spirit is thrown into a tumult.

About many things – Getting a variety of things ready for this entertainment, much more than are necessary on such an occasion.

42. Mary hath chosen that good part – That is, of hearing my word, of which she shall not be deprived; it being at present of infinitely greater importance to attend to my teaching than to attend to any domestic concerns.

LUKE 12: 13–21

13. Speak to my brother, that he divide – Among the Jews, the children had the inheritance of their fathers divided among them; the eldest had a double portion, but all the rest had equal parts. It is likely the person complained of in the text was the elder brother; and he wished to keep the whole to himself – a case which is far from being uncommon. The spirit of covetousness cancels all bonds and obligations, makes wrong right, and cares nothing for father or brother.

14. A judge – Without some judgment given in the case, no division could be made; therefore Jesus added the word judge.

15. Beware of covetousness – Or rather, Beware of all inordinate desires.

Consisteth not in the abundance – That is, dependeth not on the abundance. It is not superfluities that support man's life, but necessaries. What is necessary, God gives liberally; what is superfluous, he has not promised. Nor can a man's life be preserved by the abundance of his possessions: to prove this he spoke the following parable.

16. The ground of a certain rich man, etc. – He had generally what is called good luck in his farm, and this was a remarkably plentiful year.

17. He thought within himself – Began to be puzzled in consequence of the increase of his goods. Riches, though ever so well acquired, produce nothing but vexation and embarrassment.

18. I will pull down, etc. – The rich are full of designs concerning this life, but in general take no thought about eternity till the time that their goods and their lives are both taken away.

19. Soul, thou hast much goods – Great possessions are generally accompanied with pride, idleness, and luxury; and these are the greatest enemies to salvation. Moderate poverty, as one justly observes, is a great talent in order to salvation; but it is one which nobody desires.

20. Thou fool! – To imagine that a man's comfort and peace can depend upon temporal things; or to suppose that these can satisfy the wishes of an immortal spirit!

This night – How awful was this saying! He had just made the necessary arrangements for the gratification of his sensual appetites; and, in the very night in which he had finally settled all his plans, his soul was called into the eternal world!

21. So is he – That is, thus will it be. This is not an individual case; all who make this life their

down my barns, and build greater; and there will I bestow all my fruits and my goods.

19 And I will say to my soul, Soul, thou hast much goods laid up for many years; take thine ease, eat, drink, and be merry.

20 But God said unto him, Thou fool, this night thy soul shall be required of thee: then whose shall those things be, which thou hast provided?

21 So is he that layeth up treasure for himself, and is not rich toward God.

LUKE 13: 1–9

1 There were present at that season some that told him of the Galilaeans, whose blood Pilate had mingled with their sacrifices.

2 And Jesus answering said unto them, Suppose ye that these Galilaeans were sinners above all the Galilaeans, because they suffered such things?

3 I tell you, Nay: but, except ye repent, ye shall all likewise perish.

4 Or those eighteen, upon whom the tower in Siloam fell, and slew them, think ye that they were sinners above all men that dwelt in Jerusalem?

5 I tell you, Nay: but, except ye repent, ye shall all likewise perish.

6 He spake also this parable; A certain man had a fig tree planted in his vineyard; and he came and sought fruit thereon, and found none.

7 Then said he unto the dresser of his vineyard, Behold, these three years I come seeking fruit on this fig tree, and find none: cut it down; why cumbereth it the ground?

8 And he answering said unto him, Lord, let it alone this year also, till I shall dig about it, and dung it:

9 And if it bear fruit, well: and if not, then after that thou shalt cut it down.

LUKE 13: 10–17

10 And he was teaching in one of the synagogues on the sabbath.

11 And, behold, there was a woman which had a spirit of infirmity eighteen years, and was bowed together, and could in no wise lift up herself.

12 And when Jesus saw her, he called

hand of God slumbers at ease in the midst of his sins, as if God were favorable and reconciled to him. This involves a double fault; for when God chastises any one before our eyes, he warns us of his judgments, that each of us may examine himself, and consider what he deserves. If he spares us for a time, we are so far from having a right to take such kindness and forbearance as an opportunity for slumber, that we ought to regard it as an invitation to repentance.

To correct the false and cruel judgment which we are accustomed to pass on wretched sufferers, and, at the same time, to shake off the indulgence which every man cherishes towards himself, he shows, first, that those who are treated with severity are not the most wicked of all men; because God administers his judgments in such a manner, that some are instantly seized and punished, and others are permitted to remain long in the enjoyment of ease and luxury, Secondly, he declares that all the calamities which happen in the world are so many demonstrations of the wrath of God; and hence we learn what an awful destruction awaits us, if we do not avert it.

LUKE 13: 10–17

I have resolved to place in immediate connection some events which are detailed by Luke alone, without a direct reference to dates; for on that point, as we have formerly mentioned, the Evangelists did not care much about exactness.

11. And, lo, a woman

Here is related a miracle performed on a woman who was cured, and the offense which the malignity of the Jews led them to take up, because our Lord had cured her on a Sabbath-day. Luke says that the woman was held by a **spirit of infirmity**, so that her body was bent by the contraction of her nerves. As the nature of the disease is no farther described, it is probable that it was not one of an ordinary kind, or which was understood by physicians; and, therefore, he calls it a spirit of infirmity. We know that diseases of an unusual and extraordinary kind are, for the most part, inflicted on men through the agency of the devil; and this gave the more striking display of the divine power of Christ, which triumphed over Satan. Not that Satan rules over men according to his pleasure, but only so far as God grants to him permission to injure them. Besides, as the Lord, from whom alone all our blessings flow, makes his glory to shine with peculiar brightness in those blessings which are more remarkable, and of rare occurrence; so, on the other hand, it is his will that the power and tyranny of Satan should be chiefly regarded in extraordinary chastisements, though his agency is likewise employed in those more gentle applications of the rod, which we experience from day to day.

portion, and who are destitute of the peace and salvation of God, shall, sooner or later, be surprised in the same way.

Layeth up treasure for himself – This is the essential characteristic of a covetous man: he desires riches; he gets them; he lays them up, not for the necessary uses to which they might be devoted, but for himself; to please himself, and to gratify his avaricious soul. Such a person is commonly called a miser, i.e. literally, a wretched, miserable man.

LUKE 13: 1–9

1. At that season – At what time this happened is not easy to determine; but it appears that it was now a piece of news which was told to Christ and his disciples for the first time.

Whose blood Pilate had mingled – This piece of history is not recorded (as far as I can find) by Josephus.

4. The tower in Siloam – This tower was probably built over one of the porticoes near the pool, which is mentioned John 9: 7. See also Nehemiah 3: 15.

5. Ye shall all likewise perish – This prediction of our Lord was literally fulfilled. When the city was taken by the Romans, multitudes of the priests, etc., who were going on with their sacrifices, were slain, and their blood mingled with the blood of their victims; and multitudes were buried under the ruins of the walls, houses, and temple.

6. A certain man – Many meanings are given to this parable, and divines may abound in them; the sense which our Lord designed to convey by it appears to be the following:

1. A person, God Almighty.
2. Had a fig tree, the Jewish Church.
3. Planted in his vineyard – established in the land of Judea.
4. He came seeking fruit – he required that the Jewish people should walk in righteousness, in proportion to the spiritual culture he bestowed on them.
5. The vine-dresser – the Lord Jesus, for God hath committed all judgment to the Son, John

5: 22.

6. Cut it down – let the Roman sword be unsheathed against it.

7. Let it alone – Christ is represented as intercessor for sinners, for whose sake the day of their probation is often lengthened; during which time he is constantly employed in doing every thing that has a tendency to promote their salvation.

8. Thou shalt cut it down – a time will come, that those who have not turned at God's invitations and reproofs shall be cut off, and numbered with the transgressors.

7. Behold these three years – From this circumstance in the parable, it may be reasonably concluded that Jesus had been, at the time of saying this, exercising his ministry for three years past; and, from what is said in Luke 13: 8, of letting it alone this year also, it may be concluded likewise that this parable was spoken about a year before Christ's crucifixion.

LUKE 13: 10–17

11. A woman which had a spirit of infirmity – Relative to this subject three things may be considered:

I. The woman's infirmity.

II. Her cure.

I. The woman's infirmity.

1. What was its origin? SIN. Had this never entered into the world, there had not been either pain, distortion, or death.

2. Who was the agent in it? Satan; Luke 13: 16. God has often permitted demons to act on and in the bodies of men and women; and it is not improbable that the principal part of unaccountable and inexplicable disorders still come from the same source.

II. The woman's cure.

1. Jesus saw her, Luke 13: 12. Notwithstanding her infirmity was great, painful, and shameful, she took care to attend the synagogue. While she hoped for help from God, she saw it was her duty to wait in the appointed way, in order to receive it. Jesus saw her distress, and the desire she had both to worship her Maker and

her to him, and said unto her, Woman, thou art loosed from thine infirmity.

13 And he laid his hands on her: and immediately she was made straight, and glorified God.

14 And the ruler of the synagogue answered with indignation, because that Jesus had healed on the sabbath day, and said unto the people, There are six days in which men ought to work: in them therefore come and be healed, and not on the sabbath day.

15 The Lord then answered him, and said, Thou hypocrite, doth not each one of you on the sabbath loose his ox or his ass from the stall, and lead him away to watering?

16 And ought not this woman, being a daughter of Abraham, whom Satan hath bound, lo, these eighteen years, be loosed from this bond on the sabbath day?

17 And when he had said these things, all his adversaries were ashamed: and all the people rejoiced for all the glorious things that were done by him.

LUKE 13: 31–33

31 The same day there came certain of the Pharisees, saying unto him, Get thee out, and depart hence: for Herod will kill thee.

32 And he said unto them, Go ye, and tell that fox, Behold, I cast out devils, and I do cures to day and to morrow, and the third day I shall be perfected.

33 Nevertheless I must walk to day, and to morrow, and the day following: for it cannot be that a prophet perish out of Jerusalem.

LUKE 11: 37–41

37 And as he spake, a certain Pharisee besought him to dine with him: and he went in, and sat down to meat.

38 And when the Pharisee saw it, he marveled that he had not first washed before dinner.

39 And the Lord said unto him, Now do ye Pharisees make clean the outside of the cup and the platter; but your inward part is full of ravening and wickedness.

40 Ye fools, did not he that made that which is without make that which is

LUKE 13: 31–33

It deserves our attention, that Christ gives the designation, **daughter of Abraham**, to one whose body had been **enslaved by Satan during eighteen years**.

She was so called, not only in reference to her lineage, as all the Jews without exception gloried in this title, but because she was one of the true and actual members of the Church. Here we perceive also what Paul tells us, that some are "delivered to Satan for the destruction of the flesh, that the spirit may be saved in the day of the Lord Jesus" (1 Corinthians 5: 5).

LUKE 11: 37–41

This narrative agrees in some respects, but not entirely, with the doctrine laid down by Matthew (10: 1–20), that Christ, in order to correct the superstition of the people, and particularly of the scribes, intentionally disregarded outward ceremonies of human invention, which the Jews were too solicitous to observe. God had prescribed in his Law certain kinds of washings, that by means of them he might train his people usefully to the consideration of true purity. The Jews, not satisfied with this moderate portion had added many other washings, and more especially, that no person should partake of food till he had been washed with the water of purification, as Mark relates more minutely (12: 3–4), and as is also evident from John (2: 6). This fault was accompanied by wicked confidence; for they cared little about the spiritual worship of God, and thought that they had perfectly discharged their duty, when the figure was substituted in the place of God. Christ is fully aware that his neglect of this ceremony will give offense, but he declines to observe it, in order to show that God sets very little value on outward cleanness, but demands spiritual righteousness of the heart.

LUKE 14: 1–6

This narrative contains nothing more than a miracle which Christ performed, in order to correct the superstitious observance of the Sabbath. For he did not, intend, as some imagine, absolutely to abolish the Sabbath, but only to point out, that neither the works of God, nor the duties of charity, violate the holy rest which is enjoined by the law. It is probable that he was placed there with the concealed design of tempting Christ, which, on their part, was as foolish an action as it was wicked; for they had already known by experience what Christ was accustomed to do, whenever a similar occasion presented itself.

to get her health restored, and his eye affected his heart.

2. He called her to him. Her heart and her distress spoke loudly, though her lips were silent; and, as she was thus calling for help, Jesus calls her to himself that she may receive help.

3. Jesus laid his hands on her. The hand of his holiness terrifies, and the hand of his power expels, the demon. Ordinances, however excellent, will be of no avail to a sinner, unless he apprehend Christ in them.

4. Immediately she was made straight, Luke 13: 13. This cure was –

1. A speedy one – it was done in an instant.

2. It was a perfect one – she was made completely whole.

3. It was a public one – there were many to attest and render it credible.

4. It was a stable and permanent one – she was loosed, for ever loosed from her infirmity.

5. Her soul partook of the good done to her body – she glorified God. As she knew before that it was Satan who had bound her, she knew also that it was God only that could loose her; and now, feeling that she is loosed, she gives God that honor which is due to his name.

LUKE 13: 31–33

31. Depart hence, etc. – It is probable that the place from which Christ was desired to depart was Galilee or Perea; for beyond this Herod had no jurisdiction. It can scarcely mean Jerusalem, though it appears from Luke 23: 7, that Herod Antipas was there at the time of our Lord's crucifixion.

Herod will kill thee – Lactantius says that this Herod was the person who chiefly instigated the Jewish rulers to put our Lord to death.

32. Tell that fox – Herod was a very vicious prince, and lived in public incest with his sister-in-law, Mark 6: 17: if our Lord meant him here, it is hard to say why the character of fox, which implies cunning, design, and artifice, to

hide evil intentions, should be attributed to him, who never seemed studious to conceal his vices. But we may suppose that Christ, who knew his heart, saw that he covered his desire for the destruction of our Lord, under the pretense of zeal for the law and welfare of the Jewish people. A fox among the Jews appears to have been the emblem of a wicked ruler, who united cunning with cruelty, and was always plotting how he might aggrandize himself by spoiling the people.

To-day and to-morrow – I am to work miracles for two days more, and on the third day I shall be put to death. But it is probable that this phrase only means, that he had but a short time to live, without specifying its duration.

Perfected – Or finished. I shall then have accomplished the purpose for which I came into the world, leaving nothing undone which the counsel of God designed me to complete.

33. I must walk, etc. – I must continue to work miracles and teach for a short time yet, and then I shall die in Jerusalem.

Perish out of Jerusalem – A man who professes to be a prophet can be tried on that ground only by the grand Sanhedrin, which always resides at Jerusalem; and as the Jews are about to put me to death, under the pretense of my being a false prophet, therefore my sentence must come from this city, and my death take place in it.

LUKE 11: 37–41

37. To dine – The Jews made but two meals in the day. Their chief meal was their supper, after the heat of the day was over; and the same was the principal meal among the Greeks and Romans.

40. Did not he that made that which is without – Did not the maker of the dish form it so, both outwardly and inwardly, as to answer the purpose for which it was made? And can it answer this purpose without being clean in the inside as well as on the outside? God has made you such, both as to your bodies and souls, as he intended should show forth his praise; but

within also?

41　But rather give alms of such things as ye have; and, behold, all things are clean unto you.

LUKE 14: 1–6

1　And it came to pass, as he went into the house of one of the chief Pharisees to eat bread on the sabbath day, that they watched him.

2　And, behold, there was a certain man before him which had the dropsy.

3　And Jesus answering spake unto the lawyers and Pharisees, saying, Is it lawful to heal on the sabbath day?

4　And they held their peace. And he took him, and healed him, and let him go;

5　And answered them, saying, Which of you shall have an ass or an ox fallen into a pit, and will not straightway pull him out on the sabbath day?

6　And they could not answer him again to these things.

LUKE 14: 7–14

7　And he put forth a parable to those which were bidden, when he marked how they chose out the chief rooms; saying unto them,

8　When thou art bidden of any man to a wedding, sit not down in the highest room; lest a more honorable man than thou be bidden of him;

9　And he that bade thee and him come and say to thee, Give this man place; and thou begin with shame to take the lowest room.

10　But when thou art bidden, go and sit down in the lowest room; that when he that bade thee cometh, he may say unto thee, Friend, go up higher: then shalt thou have worship in the presence of them that sit at meat with thee.

11　For whosoever exalteth himself shall be abased; and he that humbleth himself shall be exalted.

12　Then said he also to him that bade him, When thou makest a dinner or a supper, call not thy friends, nor thy brethren, neither thy kinsmen, nor thy rich neighbours; lest they also bid thee again, and a recompence be made thee.

13　But when thou makest a feast, call

LUKE 14: 7–14

7. And he spoke a parable to those who were invited

We know to what an extent ambition prevailed among the Pharisees and all the scribes. While they desired to exercise a haughty dominion over all other men, the superiority among themselves was likewise an object of emulation. It is constantly the case with men who are desirous of empty applause, that they cherish envy towards each other, every one endeavoring to draw to himself what others imagine to be due to them. Thus the Pharisees and scribes, while they were all equally disposed, in presence of the people, to glory in the title of holy order, are now disputing among themselves about the degree of honor, because every one claims for himself the highest place.

This ambition of theirs Christ exposes to ridicule by an appropriate parable. If any one sitting at another man's table were to occupy the highest place, and were afterwards compelled to give way to a **more honorable** person, it would not be without shame and dishonor that he was ordered by the master of the feast to take a different place. But the same thing must happen to all who proudly give themselves out as superior to others; for God will bring upon them disgrace and contempt. It must be observed, that Christ is not now speaking of outward and civil modesty; for we often see that the haughtiest men excel in this respect, and civilly, as the phrase is, profess great modesty. But by a comparison taken from men, he describes what we ought to be inwardly before God. "Were it to happen that a guest should foolishly take possession of the highest place, and should, on that account, be put down to the lowest, he would be so completely overpowered with shame as to wish that he had never gone higher. Lest the same thing should happen to you, that God would punish your arrogance with the deepest disgrace, resolve, of your own accord, to be humble and modest."

MATTHEW 22: 1–14; LUKE 14: 15–24

Matthew 22: 1. And Jesus answering

Though Matthew relates this parable among other discourses which were delivered by Christ about the time of the last Passover, yet as he does not specify any particular time, and as Luke expressly affirms that Christ delivered this discourse **while he sat at table in the house of a Pharisee,** I have thought it better to follow this order. The design which Matthew had in view was, to point out the reasons why the scribes were excited to the highest pitch of fury; and therefore he properly placed it in the midst of those discourses which were hateful to them, and interwove it with those discourses, without attending to the order of time. But we must attend to Luke's narrative, who

can you think that the purpose of God can be accomplished by you while you only attend to external legal purifications, your hearts being full of rapine and wickedness? How unthinking are you to imagine that God can be pleased with this outward purification, when all within is unholy!

41. Give alms of such things as ye have – Meaning either what was within the dishes spoken of before; or what was within their houses or power: or what they had at hand.

LUKE 14: 1–6

1. Chief Pharisees – Or, one of the rulers of the Pharisees. A man who was of the sect of the Pharisees, and one of the rulers of the people.

To eat bread on the Sabbath day – But why is it that there should be an invitation or dinner given on the Sabbath day? Answer: The Jews purchased and prepared the best viands they could procure for the Sabbath day, in order to do it honor. As the Sabbath is intended for the benefit both of the body and soul of man, it should not be a day of austerity or fasting, especially among the laboring poor.

They watched him – Or, were maliciously watching. The conduct of this Pharisee was most execrable.

2. The dropsy – Probably the insidious Pharisee had brought this dropsical man to the place, not doubting that our Lord's eye would affect his heart, and that he would instantly cure him; and then he could most plausibly accuse him for a breach of the Sabbath.

4. They held their peace – They could not answer the question but in the affirmative; and as they were determined to accuse him if he did heal the man, they could not give an answer but such as would condemn themselves, and therefore they were silent.

LUKE 14: 7–14

7. They chose out the chief rooms – When custom and law have regulated and settled

places in public assemblies, a man who is obliged to attend may take the place which belongs to him, without injury to himself or to others: when nothing of this nature is settled, the law of humility, and the love of order, are the only judges of what is proper. To take the highest place when it is not our due is public vanity: obstinately to refuse it when offered is another instance of the same vice; though private and concealed. Humility takes as much care to avoid the ostentation of an affected refusal, as the open seeking of a superior place. In this parable our Lord only repeats advices which the rabbins had given to their pupils, but were too proud to conform to themselves. Rabbi Akiba said, Go two or three seats lower than the place that belongs to thee, and sit there till they say unto thee, Go up higher; but do not take the uppermost seat, lest they say unto thee, Come down: for it is better that they should say unto thee, Go up, than that they should say, Come down, come down.

11. For whosoever exalteth himself, etc. – This is the unchangeable conduct of God: he is ever abasing the proud, and giving grace, honor, and glory to the humble.

12. Call not thy friends, etc. – Our Lord certainly does not mean that a man should not entertain at particular times, his friends, etc.; but what he inculcates here is charity to the poor; and what he condemns is those entertainments which are given to the rich, either to flatter them, or to procure a similar return; because the money that is thus criminally laid out properly belongs to the poor.

14. For they cannot recompense thee – Because you have done it for God's sake only, and they cannot make you a recompense, therefore God will consider himself your debtor, and will recompense you in the resurrection of the righteous. There are many very excellent sayings among the rabbins on the excellence of charity. They produce both Job and Abraham as examples of a very merciful disposition. "Job, say they, had an open door on each of the four quarters of his house, that

the poor, the maimed, the lame, the blind:

14 And thou shalt be blessed; for they cannot recompense thee: for thou shalt be recompensed at the resurrection of the just.

MATTHEW 22: 1–14; LUKE 14: 15–24

Matthew 22: 1–14

1 And Jesus answered and spake unto them again by parables, and said,

2 The kingdom of heaven is like unto a certain king, which made a marriage for his son,

3 And sent forth his servants to call them that were bidden to the wedding: and they would not come.

4 Again, he sent forth other servants, saying, Tell them which are bidden, Behold, I have prepared my dinner: my oxen and my fatlings are killed, and all things are ready: come unto the marriage.

5 But they made light of it, and went their ways, one to his farm, another to his merchandise:

6 And the remnant took his servants, and entreated them spitefully, and slew them.

7 But when the king heard thereof, he was wroth: and he sent forth his armies, and destroyed those murderers, and burned up their city.

8 Then saith he to his servants, The wedding is ready, but they which were bidden were not worthy.

9 Go ye therefore into the highways, and as many as ye shall find, bid to the marriage.

10 So those servants went out into the highways, and gathered together all as many as they found, both bad and good: and the wedding was furnished with guests.

11 And when the king came in to see the guests, he saw there a man which had not on a wedding garment:

12 And he saith unto him, Friend, how camest thou in hither not having a wedding garment? And he was speechless.

13 Then said the king to the servants, Bind him hand and foot, and take him away, and cast him into outer darkness; there shall be weeping and gnashing of teeth.

says that, **when one of those who sat at table with him said, Blessed is he that eateth bread in the kingdom of God**, Christ used that occasion it to reprimand the Jews for thier ingratitude. It is by no means probable, that the guest and friend of a Pharisee broke out into this exclamation from any sincere feeling of piety. Still, I do not look upon it as having been spoken in derision; but, as people who have a moderate knowledge of the faith, and are not openly wicked, are in the habit of indulging, amidst their cups, in idle talk about eternal life, I think that this man threw out a remark about future blessedness, in order to draw out some observation in return from Christ. And his words make it manifest, that he had nothing in view beyond what was gross and earthly; for he did not employ the phrase, eat bread, as a metaphor for **enjoy eternal life**, but appears to have dreamed of I know not what state, filled with prosperity and abundance of all things. The meaning is, Blessed shall they be who shall eat the bread of God, after that he has collected his children into his kingdom.

2. The kingdom of heaven is like a human king

As it was long ago said by a Spartan, that the Athenians knew what was right, but did not choose to practice it; so Christ now brings it as a reproach against the Jews, that they gave utterance to beautiful expressions about the kingdom of God, but, when God kindly and gently invited them, they rejected his grace with disdain. There is no room to doubt that the discourse is expressly levelled against the Jews, as will more plainly appear a little afterwards.

7. But when the king heard it

This punishment is mentioned by Matthew alone; for Luke makes no mention of any outrage committed on the servants. Both concur in stating, that those who did not come at the appointed time were shut out, and deprived of the honor of being present at the banquet. But this doctrine applies equally to us; for the same destruction which Christ denounces against the Jews awaits all the ungodly, who violently oppose the ministers of the Gospel. Those who are so entirely occupied with earthly cares, as to set no value on the divine invitation, will at length perish miserably in famine and want; and therefore, whenever God calls us, let us be prepared and ready to follow.

9. Go therefore to the highways

Having shown that they are unworthy of the grace of God who disdainfully reject it when offered to them, he now says that their place is supplied by others, by the mean and despised common people. And here is described the calling of the Gentiles, which is to excite the Jews to jealousy, as we have it in the Song of Moses; "They have provoked me by those who are not gods, and I will provoke them by that

the poor, from whatever direction they might come, might find the door of hospitality open to receive them. But Abraham was more charitable than Job, for he traveled over the whole land in order to find out the poor, that he might conduct them to his house."

MATTHEW 22: 1–24; LUKE 14: 15–24

Matthew 22: 1–24

2. The kingdom of heaven – It appears from Luke, Luke 14: 15; etc., that it was at an entertainment that this parable was originally spoken. It was a constant practice of our Lord to take the subjects of his discourses from persons present, or from the circumstances of times, persons, and places. See Matthew 16: 6; John 4: 7–10; John 6: 26, 27; 7: 37. A preacher that can do so can never be at a loss for text or sermon.

A marriage for his son – A marriage feast, or a feast of inauguration, when his son was put in possession of the government, and thus he and his new subjects became married together.

From this parable it appears plain,

1. That the KING means the great God.

2. His SON, the Lord Jesus.

3. The MARRIAGE, his incarnation, or espousing human nature, by taking it into union with himself.

4. The MARRIAGE FEAST, the economy of the Gospel, during which men are invited to partake of the blessings purchased by, and consequent on, the incarnation and death of our blessed Lord.

5. By those who HAD BEEN bidden, or invited, Matthew 22: 3, are meant the Jews in general, who had this union of Christ with human nature, and his sacrifice for sin, pointed out by various rites, ceremonies, and sacrifices under the law; and who, by all the prophets, had been constantly invited to believe in and receive the promised Messiah.

6. By the SERVANTS, we are to understand the first preachers of the Gospel, proclaiming salvation to the Jews. JOHN the Baptist and the seventy disciples (Luke 10: 1), may be here

particularly intended.

7. By the OTHER SERVANTS, Matthew 22: 4, the apostles seem to be meant, who, though they were to preach the Gospel to the whole world, yet were to begin at JERUSALEM (Luke 24: 47) with the first offers of mercy.

8. By their making light of it, etc., Matthew 22: 5, is pointed out their neglect of this salvation, and their preferring secular enjoyments, etc., to the kingdom of Christ.

9. By injuriously using some, and slaying others, of his servants, Matthew 22: 6, is pointed out the persecution raised against the apostles by the Jews, in which some of them were martyred.

10. By sending forth his troops, Matthew 22: 7, is meant the commission given to the Romans against Judea; and, burning up their city, the total destruction of Jerusalem by Titus, the son of Vespasian, which happened about forty-one years after.

On this parable it is necessary to remark,

1. That man was made at first in union with God.

2. That sin entered in, and separated between God and man.

3. That as there can be no holiness but in union with God, and no heaven without holiness, therefore he provided a way to reconcile and reunite man to himself.

4. This was effected by Christ's uniting himself to human nature, and giving his Spirit to those who believe.

5. That as the marriage union is the closest, the most intimate, solemn, and excellent, of all the connections formed among mortals, and that they who are thus united in the Lord are one flesh; so that mystical union which is formed between God and the soul through Jesus Christ, by the Eternal Spirit, is the closest, most intimate, solemn, and excellent, that can be conceived; for he who is thus joined unto the Lord is one spirit.

6. This contract is made freely: no man can be forced to it, for it is a union of will to will, heart to heart; and it is by willing and consenting that we come unto God through his Son.

7. That if this marriage do not take place here,

14 For many are called, but few are chosen.

Luke 14: 15–24

15 And when one of them that sat at meat with him heard these things, he said unto him, Blessed is he that shall eat bread in the kingdom of God.

16 Then said he unto him, A certain man made a great supper, and bade many:

17 And sent his servant at supper time to say to them that were bidden, Come; for all things are now ready.

18 And they all with one consent began to make excuse. The first said unto him, I have bought a piece of ground, and I must needs go and see it: I pray thee have me excused.

19 And another said, I have bought five yoke of oxen, and I go to prove them: I pray thee have me excused.

20 And another said, I have married a wife, and therefore I cannot come.

21 So that servant came, and shewed his lord these things. Then the master of the house being angry said to his servant, Go out quickly into the streets and lanes of the city, and bring in hither the poor, and the maimed, and the halt, and the blind.

22 And the servant said, Lord, it is done as thou hast commanded, and yet there is room.

23 And the lord said unto the servant, Go out into the highways and hedges, and compel them to come in, that my house may be filled.

24 For I say unto you, That none of those men which were bidden shall taste of my supper.

LUKE 16: 1–15

1 And he said also unto his disciples, There was a certain rich man, which had a steward; and the same was accused unto him that he had wasted his goods.

2 And he called him, and said unto him, How is it that I hear this of thee? give an account of thy stewardship; for thou mayest be no longer steward.

3 Then the steward said within himself, What shall I do? for my lord taketh away from me the stewardship: I cannot

which is not a people, and by a foolish nation will I enrage them" (Deuteronomy 32: 21).

LUKE 16: 1–15

The main object of this parable is, to show that we ought to deal kindly and generously with our neighbors; that, when we come to the judgment seat of God, we may reap the fruit of our liberality. Though the parable appears to be harsh and far-fetched, yet the conclusion makes it evident, that the design of Christ was nothing else than what I have stated. And hence we see, that to inquire with great exactness into every minute part of a parable is an absurd mode of philosophizing. Christ does not advise us to purchase by large donations the forgiveness of fraud, and of extortion, and of wasteful expenditure, and of the other crimes associated with unfaithful administration. But as all the blessings which God confers upon us are committed by Him to our administration, our Lord now lays down a method of procedure, which will protect us against being treated with rigor, when we come to render our account.

Those who imagine that alms are a sufficient compensation for sensuality and debauchery, do not sufficiently consider, that the first injunction given us is, to live in sobriety and temperance; and that the next is, that the streams which flow to us come from a pure fountain. It is certain that no man is so frugal, as not sometimes to waste the property which has been entrusted to him; and that even those who practice the most rigid economy are not entirely free from the charge of unfaithful stewardship. Add to this, that there are so many ways of abusing the gifts of God, that some incur guilt in one way, and some in another. I do not even deny, that the very consciousness of our own faulty stewardship ought to be felt by us as an additional excitement to kind actions.

But we ought to have quite another object in view, than to escape the judgment of God by paying a price for our redemption; and that object is, first, that seasonable and well-judged liberality may have the effect of restraining and moderating unnecessary expenses; and, secondly, that our kindness to our brethren may draw down upon us the mercy of God. It is very far from being the intention of Christ to point out to his disciples a way of escape, when the heavenly Judge shall require them to give their account; but he warns them to lose no time in guarding against the punishment which will await their cruelty, if they are found to have swallowed up the gifts of God, and to have paid no attention to acts of beneficence. We must always attend to this maxim, that "with what measure a man measures, it shall be recompensed to him again" (Matthew 7: 2).

an eternal separation from God, and from the glory of his power, shall be the fearful consequence.

8. That there are three states in which men run the risk of living without God and losing their souls.

1st. That of a soft, idle, voluptuous life, wherein a man thinks of nothing but quietly to enjoy life, conveniences, riches, private pleasures, and public diversions. They made light of it.

2dly. That of a man wholly taken up with agricultural or commercial employments, in which the love of riches, and application to the means of acquiring them, generally stifle all thoughts of salvation. One went to his own field, and another to his traffic.

3dly. That of a man who is openly unjust, violent, and outrageously wicked, who is a sinner by profession, and not only neglects his salvation, but injuriously treats all those who bring him the Gospel of reconciliation. Seizing his servants, they treated them injuriously, etc.

21. They say unto him, Caesars – The image was the head of the emperor; the superscription, his titles. Julius Caesar was the first who caused his image to be struck on the Roman coin. Tiberius was emperor at this time.

Render therefore unto Caesar – The conclusion is drawn from their own premises. You acknowledge this to be Caesar's coin; this coin is current, in your land; the currency of this coin shows the country to be under the Roman government; and your acknowledgment that it is Caesar's proves you have submitted. Don't therefore be unjust; but render to Caesar the things which you acknowledge to be his; at the same time, be not impious, but render unto God the thing's which belong to God.

This answer is full of consummate wisdom. It establishes the limits, regulates the rights, and distinguishes the jurisdiction of the two empires of heaven and earth. The image of princes stamped on their coin denotes that temporal things belong all to their government. The image of God stamped on the soul denotes that all its faculties and powers belong

to the Most High, and should be employed in his service.

LUKE 16: 1–15

1. A steward – One who superintends domestic concerns, and ministers to the support of the family, having the products of the field, business, etc., put into his hands for this very purpose.

Wasted his goods – Had been profuse and profligate; and had embezzled his master's substance.

2. Give an account of thy, etc. – Produce thy books of receipts and disbursements, that I may see whether the accusation against thee be true or false.

3. I cannot dig – He could not submit to become a common day-laborer, which was both a severe and base employment.

4. They may receive me – That is, the debtors and tenants, who paid their debts and rents, not in money, but in kind; such as wheat, oil, and other produce of their lands.

6. Take thy bill – Thy account. The writing in which the debt was specified, together with the obligation to pay so much, at such and such times.

8. The lord commended – Viz. the master of this unjust steward. He spoke highly of the address and cunning of his iniquitous servant. He had, on his own principles, made a very prudent provision for his support; but his master no more approved of his conduct in this, than he did in his wasting his substance before. From the ambiguous and improper manner in which this is expressed in the common English translation, it has been supposed that our blessed Lord commended the conduct of this wicked man: but the word there translated lord, simply means the master of the unjust steward.

The children of this world – Such as mind worldly things only, without regarding God or their souls. A phrase by which the Jews always designate the Gentiles.

dig; to beg I am ashamed.

4 I am resolved what to do, that, when I am put out of the stewardship, they may receive me into their houses.

5 So he called every one of his lord's debtors unto him, and said unto the first, How much owest thou unto my lord?

6 And he said, An hundred measures of oil. And he said unto him, Take thy bill, and sit down quickly, and write fifty.

7 Then said he to another, And how much owest thou? And he said, An hundred measures of wheat. And he said unto him, Take thy bill, and write fourscore.

8 And the lord commended the unjust steward, because he had done wisely: for the children of this world are in their generation wiser than the children of light.

9 And I say unto you, Make to yourselves friends of the mammon of unrighteousness; that, when ye fail, they may receive you into everlasting habitations.

10 He that is faithful in that which is least is faithful also in much: and he that is unjust in the least is unjust also in much.

11 If therefore ye have not been faithful in the unrighteous mammon, who will commit to your trust the true riches?

12 And if ye have not been faithful in that which is another man's, who shall give you that which is your own?

14 And the Pharisees also, who were covetous, heard all these things: and they derided him.

15 And he said unto them, Ye are they which justify yourselves before men; but God knoweth your hearts: for that which is highly esteemed among men is abomination in the sight of God.

LUKE 16: 19–31

19 There was a certain rich man, which was clothed in purple and fine linen, and fared sumptuously every day:

20 And there was a certain beggar named Lazarus, which was laid at his gate, full of sores,

21 And desiring to be fed with the crumbs which fell from the rich man's table: moreover the dogs came and licked his sores.

22 And it came to pass, that the beggar died, and was carried by the angels

LUKE 16: 19–31

Though Luke introduces some things between them, there can be no doubt that this example was intended by Christ to confirm the discourse which we have last examined. He points out what condition awaits those who neglect the care of the poor, and indulge in all manner of gluttony; who give themselves up to drunkenness and other pleasures, and allow their neighbors to pine with hunger; nay, who cruelly kill with famine those whom they ought to have relieved, when the means of doing so were in their power. Some look upon it as a simple parable; but, as the name Lazarus occurs in it, I rather consider it to be the narrative of an actual fact. But that is of little consequence, provided that the reader comprehends the doctrine which it contains.

19. There was a certain rich man

He is, first of all, described as clothed in purple and fine linen, and enjoying every day splendor and luxury. This denotes a life spent amidst delicacies, and superfluity, and pomp. Not that all elegance and ornaments of dress are in themselves displeasing to God, or that all the care bestowed on preparing victuals ought to be condemned; but because it seldom happens that such things are kept in moderation. He who has a liking for fine dress will constantly increase his luxury by fresh additions; and it is scarcely possible that he who indulges in sumptuous and well garnished tables shall avoid falling into intemperance. But the chief accusation brought against this man is his cruelty in suffering Lazarus, poor and full of sores, to lie out of doors at his gate.

These two clauses Christ has exhibited in contrast. The rich man, devoted to the pleasures of the table and to display, swallowed up, like an unsatiable gulf, his enormous wealth, but remained unmoved by the poverty and distresses of Lazarus, and knowingly and willingly suffered him to pine away with hunger, cold, and the offensive smell of his sores. In this manner Ezekiel (16: 49) accuses Sodom of not stretching out her hand to the poor amidst fullness of bread and wine. The fine linen, which is a peculiarly delicate fabric, is well-known to have been used by the inhabitants of eastern countries for elegance and splendor; a fashion which the Popish priests have imitated in what they call their surplices.

LUKE 17: 7–10

The object of this parable is to show that God claims all that belongs to us as his property, and possesses an entire control over our people and services; and, therefore, that all the zeal that may be manifested by us in discharging our duty does not lay him under obligation to us by any sort

Children of light – Such as are illuminated by the Spirit of God, and regard worldly things only as far as they may subserve the great purposes of their salvation, and become the instruments of good to others. But ordinarily the former evidence more carefulness and prudence, in providing for the support and comfort of this life, than the latter do in providing for another world.

9. The mammon of unrighteousness – Riches promise MUCH, and perform NOTHING: they excite hope and confidence, and deceive both: in making a man depend on them for happiness, they rob him of the salvation of God and of eternal glory. For these reasons, they are represented as unjust and deceitful.

When ye fail – That is, when ye die.

They may receive you – That is, say some, the angels. Others, the poor whom ye have relieved will welcome you into glory. It does not appear that the poor are meant:

1. Because those who have relieved them may die a long time before them; and therefore they could not be in heaven to receive them on their arrival.

2. Many poor persons may be relieved, who will live and die in their sins, and consequently never enter into heaven themselves.

The expression seems to be a mere Hebraism: they may receive you, for ye shall be received; i.e. God shall admit you, if you make a faithful use of his gifts and graces. He who does not make a faithful use of what he has received from his Maker has no reason to hope for eternal felicity.

10. He that is faithful in that which is least, etc. – He who has the genuine principles of fidelity in him will make a point of conscience of carefully attending to even the smallest things; and it is by habituating himself to act uprightly in little things that he acquires the gracious habit of acting with propriety fidelity, honor, and conscience, in matters of the greatest concern. On the contrary, he who does not act uprightly in small matters will seldom feel himself bound to pay much attention to the dictates of honor and conscience, in cases of high importance. Can we reasonably expect

that a man who is continually falling by little things has power to resist temptations to great evils?

12. That which is your own? – Grace and glory, which God has particularly designed for you; which are the only proper satisfying portion for the soul, and which no man can enjoy in their plenitude, unless he be faithful to the first small motions and influences of the Divine Spirit.

13. No servant can serve two masters – The heart will be either wholly taken up with God, or wholly engrossed with the world.

14. They derided him – Or rather, They treated him with the utmost contempt.

15. Ye – justify yourselves – Ye declare yourselves to be just.

LUKE 16: 19–31

19. There was a certain rich man – Let us carefully observe all the circumstances offered hereto our notice, and we shall see:

The CRIME of this man.

1. There was a certain rich man in Jerusalem. Provided this be a real history, there is no doubt our Lord could have mentioned his name; but, as this might have given great offense, he chose to suppress it. His being rich is, in Christ's account, the first part of his sin. To this circumstance our Lord adds nothing: he does not say that he was born to a large estate; or that he acquired one by improper methods; or that he was haughty or insolent in the possession of it. Yet here is the first degree of his reprobation – he got all he could, and kept all to himself.

2. He was clothed with purple and fine linen. Purple was a very precious and costly stuff; but our Lord does not say that in the use of it he exceeded the bounds of his income, nor of his rank in life; nor is it said that he used his superb dress to be an agent to his crimes, by corrupting the hearts of others. Yet our Lord lays this down as a second cause of his perdition.

3. He fared sumptuously every day. Now let

into Abraham's bosom: the rich man also died, and was buried;

23 And in hell he lift up his eyes, being in torments, and seeth Abraham afar off, and Lazarus in his bosom.

24 And he cried and said, Father Abraham, have mercy on me, and send Lazarus, that he may dip the tip of his finger in water, and cool my tongue; for I am tormented in this flame.

25 But Abraham said, Son, remember that thou in thy lifetime receivedst thy good things, and likewise Lazarus evil things: but now he is comforted, and thou art tormented.

26 And beside all this, between us and you there is a great gulf fixed: so that they which would pass from hence to you cannot; neither can they pass to us, that would come from thence.

27 Then he said, I pray thee therefore, father, that thou wouldest send him to my father's house:

28 For I have five brethren; that he may testify unto them, lest they also come into this place of torment.

29 Abraham saith unto him, They have Moses and the prophets; let them hear them.

30 And he said, Nay, father Abraham: but if one went unto them from the dead, they will repent.

31 And he said unto him, If they hear not Moses and the prophets, neither will they be persuaded, though one rose from the dead.

LUKE 17: 7–10

7 But which of you, having a servant plowing or feeding cattle, will say unto him by and by, when he is come from the field, Go and sit down to meat?

8 And will not rather say unto him, Make ready wherewith I may sup, and gird thyself, and serve me, till I have eaten and drunken; and afterward thou shalt eat and drink?

9 Doth he thank that servant because he did the things that were commanded him? I trow not.

10 So likewise ye, when ye shall have done all those things which are commanded you, say, We are unprofitable

of merit; for, as we are his property, so he on his part can owe us nothing. He adduces the comparison of **a servant**, who, after having spent the day in severe toil, returns home in the evening, and continues his labors till his master is pleased to relieve him. Christ speaks not of such servants as we have in the present day, who work for hire, but of the slaves that lived in ancient times, whose condition in society was such, that they gained nothing for themselves, but all that belonged to them – their toil, and application, and industry, even to their very blood – was the property of their masters. Christ now shows that a bond of servitude not less rigorous binds and obliges us to serve God; from which he infers, that we have no means of laying Him under obligations to us.

LUKE 18: 1–8

We know that perseverance in prayer is a rare and difficult attainment; and it is a manifestation of our unbelief that, when our first prayers are not successful, we immediately throw away not only hope, but all the ardor of prayer. But it is an undoubted evidence of our Faith, if we are disappointed of our wish, and yet do not lose courage. Most properly, therefore, does Christ recommend to his disciples to persevere in praying.

The parable which he employs, though apparently harsh, was admirably fitted to instruct his disciples, that they ought to be importunate in their prayers to God the Father, till they at length draw from him what He would otherwise appear to be unwilling to give. Not that by our prayers we gain a victory over God, and bend him slowly and reluctantly to compassion, but because the actual facts do not all at once make it evident that he graciously listens to our prayers. In the parable Christ describes to us a widow, who obtained what she wanted from an unjust and cruel judge, because she did not cease to make earnest demands. The leading truth conveyed is, that God does not all at once grant assistance to his people, because he chooses to be, as it were, wearied out by prayers; and that, however wretched and despicable may be the condition of those who pray to him, yet if they do not desist from the uninterrupted exercise of prayer, he will at length regard them and relieve their necessities.

LUKE 18: 9–14

Christ now gives directions about another virtue, which is necessary to acceptable prayer. Believers must not come into the presence of God but with humility and abasement. No disease is more dangerous than arrogance; and yet all have it so deeply fixed in the marrow of their bones, that it can scarcely be removed or extirpated by any remedy. It is

it be observed that the law of Moses, under which this man lived, forbade nothing on this point, but excess in eating and drinking; indeed, it seems as if a person was authorized to taste the sweets of an abundance, which that law promised as a reward of fidelity. Besides, this rich man is not accused of having eaten food which was prohibited by the law, or of having neglected the abstinences and fasts prescribed by it. It is true, he is said to have feasted sumptuously every day; but our Lord does not intimate that this was carried to excess, or that it ministered to debauch. He is not accused of licentious discourse, of gaming, of frequenting any thing like our modern plays, balls, masquerades, or other impure and unholy assemblies; of speaking an irreverent word against Divine revelation, or the ordinances of God. In a word, his probity is not attacked, nor is he accused of any of those crimes which pervert the soul or injure civil society. As Christ has described this man, does he appear culpable? What are his crimes? Why,

1. He was rich.

2. He was finely clothed. And

3. He feasted well.

No other evil is spoken of him. In comparison of thousands, he was not only blameless, but he was a virtuous man.

4. But it is intimated by many that "he was an uncharitable, hard-hearted, unfeeling wretch." Yet of this there is not a word spoken by Christ. Let us consider all the circumstances, and we shall see that our blessed Lord has not represented this man as a monster of inhumanity, but merely as an indolent man, who sought and had his portion in this life, and was not at all concerned about another.

Therefore we do not find that when Abraham addressed him on the cause of his reprobation, Luke 16: 25, that he reproached him with hard-heartedness, saying, "Lazarus was hungry, and thou gavest him no meat; he was thirsty, and thou gavest him no drink, etc.;" but he said simply, Son, remember that thou didst receive thy good things in thy lifetime, Luke 16: 25. "Thou hast sought thy consolation upon the earth, thou hast borne no cross, mortified

no desire of the flesh, received not the salvation God had provided for thee; thou didst not belong to the people of God upon earth, and thou canst not dwell with them in glory."

There are few who consider that it is a crime for those called Christians to live without Christ, when their lives are not stained with transgression. If Christianity only required men to live without gross outward sin, paganism could furnish us with many bright examples of this sort. But the religion of Christ requires a conformity, not only in a man's conduct, to the principles of the Gospel; but also a conformity in his heart to the spirit and mind of Christ.

LUKE 17: 7–10

7–9. **Which of you, having a servant** – It is never supposed that the master waits on the servant – the servant is bound to wait on his master, and to do every thing for him to the uttermost of his power: nor does the former expect thanks for it, for he is bound by his agreement to act thus, because of the stipulated reward, which is considered as being equal in value to all the service that he can perform.

10. **We are unprofitable servants** – When ages, beyond the power of arithmetic to sum up, have elapsed, it may be said of the most pure and perfect creatures, "Ye are unprofitable servants." Ye have derived your being from the infinite fountain of life: ye are upheld by the continued energy of the Almighty: his glories are infinite and eternal, and your obedience and services, however excellent in themselves, and profitable to you, have added nothing, and can add nothing, to the absolute excellencies and glories of your God.

LUKE 18: 1–8

1. **Men ought always to pray** – Therefore the plain meaning and moral of the parable are evident; viz. that as afflictions and desolations were coming on the land, and they should have need of much patience and continual

servants: we have done that which was our duty to do.

LUKE 18: 1–8

1 And he spake a parable unto them to this end, that men ought always to pray, and not to faint;

2 Saying, There was in a city a judge, which feared not God, neither regarded man:

3 And there was a widow in that city; and she came unto him, saying, Avenge me of mine adversary.

4 And he would not for a while: but afterward he said within himself, Though I fear not God, nor regard man;

5 Yet because this widow troubleth me, I will avenge her, lest by her continual coming she weary me.

6 And the Lord said, Hear what the unjust judge saith.

7 And shall not God avenge his own elect, which cry day and night unto him, though he bear long with them?

8 I tell you that he will avenge them speedily. Nevertheless when the Son of man cometh, shall he find faith on the earth?

LUKE 18: 9–14

9 And he spake this parable unto certain which trusted in themselves that they were righteous, and despised others:

10 Two men went up into the temple to pray; the one a Pharisee, and the other a publican.

11 The Pharisee stood and prayed thus with himself, God, I thank thee, that I am not as other men are, extortioners, unjust, adulterers, or even as this publican.

12 I fast twice in the week, I give tithes of all that I possess.

13 And the publican, standing afar off, would not lift up so much as his eyes unto heaven, but smote upon his breast, saying, God be merciful to me a sinner.

14 I tell you, this man went down to his house justified rather than the other: for every one that exalteth himself shall be abased; and he that humbleth himself shall be exalted.

no doubt strange that men should be so mad as to venture to raise their crests against God, and to plead their own merits before him. Though men are carried away by their ambition, yet when we come into the presence of God, all presumption ought to be laid aside; and yet every man thinks that he has sufficiently humbled himself, if he only presents a hypocritical prayer for forgiveness. Hence we infer that this warning which our Lord gives was far from being unnecessary.

There are two faults at which Christ glances, and which he intended to condemn – wicked confidence in ourselves, and the pride of despising brethren, the one of which springs out of the other. It is impossible that he who deceives himself with vain confidence should not lift himself up above his brethren. Nor is it wonderful that it should be so; for how should that man not despise his equals, who vaunts against God himself? Every man that is puffed up with self-confidence carries on open war with God, to whom we cannot be reconciled in any other way than by denial of ourselves; that is, by laying aside all confidence in our own virtue and righteousness, and relying on his mercy alone.

LUKE 17: 11–21

13. Jesus, Master
It is evident that all of them possessed some measure of faith, not only because they implore Christ's assistance, but because they honor him with the title of **Master**. That they made use of that expression sincerely, and not in hypocrisy, may be inferred from their ready obedience; for, although they perceive that the filthy scab still remains in their flesh, yet as soon as they are commanded to **show themselves to the priests,** they do not refuse to obey. Add to this that, but for the influence of faith, they would never have set out to **show themselves to the priests**; for it would have been absurd to present themselves to the judges of leprosy, for the purpose of attesting that they had been cleansed, if the promise of Christ had been regarded by them as of no more value than a mere inspection of the disease. They bear a visible leprosy in their flesh; and yet, trusting to Christ's word alone, they have no scruple about declaring that they are clean. It cannot therefore be denied, that some seed of faith had been implanted in their hearts. Now though it is certain that they were not regenerated by the Spirit of adoption, yet there is no absurdity in supposing that they had some beginnings of piety. There is the greater reason to fear that sparks of faith, which make their appearance in us, may be extinguished; for, although lively faith, which has its roots deeply fixed by the Spirit of regeneration, never dies, yet we have seen formerly that many conceive a temporary faith, which immediately disappears. Above all, it is too common

fortitude, and the constant influence and protection of the Almighty, therefore they should be instant in prayer. It states, farther, that men should never cease praying for that the necessity of which God has given them to feel, till they receive a full answer to their prayers. No other meaning need be searched for in this parable: St. Luke, who perfectly knew his Master's meaning, has explained it as above.

2. A judge, which feared not God, neither regarded man – It is no wonder that our Lord calls this person an unrighteous judge, Luke 18: 6. Even among the heathens this was the character of a man totally abandoned to all evil.

3. Avenge me of mine adversary – She desired to have justice, and that only; and by her importunity she got that which the unrighteous judge had no inclination to give, but merely for his own ease.

4. He said within himself – How many actions which appear good have neither the love of God, nor that of our neighbor, but only self-love of the basest kind, for their principle and motive!

5. She weary me – Stun me. A metaphor taken from boxers, who bruise each other, and by beating each other about the face blacken the eyes. See 1 Corinthians 9: 27.

6. Hear what the unjust judge saith – Our blessed Lord intimates that we should reason thus with ourselves: "If a person of such an infamous character as this judge was could yield to the pressing and continual solicitations of a poor widow, for whom he felt nothing but contempt, how much more ready must God be, who is infinitely good and merciful, and who loves his creatures in the tenderest manner, to give his utmost salvation to all them who diligently seek it!"

7. And shall not God avenge his own elect – And will not God the righteous Judge do justice for his chosen?

8. Shall he find faith on the earth? – Or rather, Shall he find fidelity in this land? Shall

he find that the soil has brought forth a harvest proportioned to the culture bestowed on it? No! And therefore he destroyed that land.

LUKE 18: 9–14

9. Despised – Disdained, made nothing of others, treated them with sovereign contempt. Our Lord grants that the Pharisees made clean the outside: but, alas! what pride, vain glory, and contempt for others, were lodged within!

10. Publican – Both these persons went to the temple to pray, i.e. to worship God: they were probably both Jews, and felt themselves led by different motives to attend at the temple, at the hour of prayer: the one to return thanks for the mercies he had received; the other to implore that grace which alone could redeem him from his sins.

11. Stood and prayed thus with himself – He probably supposed it disgraceful to appear to have any connection with this penitent publican.

God, I thank thee, etc. – In Matthew 5: 20, our Lord says, Unless your righteousness abound more than that of the scribes and Pharisees, ye shall not enter into the kingdom of God.

13. The publican, standing afar off – Not because he was a heathen, and dared not approach the holy place; (for it is likely he was a Jew); but because he was a true penitent, and felt himself utterly unworthy to appear before God.

14. Went down to his house justified – His sin blotted out; and himself accepted.

LUKE 17: 11–21

11. He passed through the midst of Samaria and Galilee – He first went through Galilee, whence he set out on his journey; and then through Samaria, of which mention is made, Luke 9: 51–52.

12. Which stood afar off – They kept at a distance, because forbidden by law and custom to

LUKE 17: 11–21

11 And it came to pass, as he went to Jerusalem, that he passed through the midst of Samaria and Galilee.

12 And as he entered into a certain village, there met him ten men that were lepers, which stood afar off:

13 And they lifted up their voices, and said, Jesus, Master, have mercy on us.

14 And when he saw them, he said unto them, Go shew yourselves unto the priests. And it came to pass, that, as they went, they were cleansed.

15 And one of them, when he saw that he was healed, turned back, and with a loud voice glorified God,

16 And fell down on his face at his feet, giving him thanks: and he was a Samaritan.

17 And Jesus answering said, Were there not ten cleansed? but where are the nine?

18 There are not found that returned to give glory to God, save this stranger.

19 And he said unto him, Arise, go thy way: thy faith hath made thee whole.

20 And when he was demanded of the Pharisees, when the kingdom of God should come, he answered them and said, The kingdom of God cometh not with observation:

21 Neither shall they say, Lo here! or, lo there! for, behold, the kingdom of God is within you.

MATTHEW 13: 53–58; MARK 6: 1–6

Matthew 13: 53–58

53 And it came to pass, that when Jesus had finished these parables, he departed thence.

54 And when he was come into his own country, he taught them in their synagogue, insomuch that they were astonished, and said, Whence hath this man this wisdom, and these mighty works?

55 Is not this the carpenter's son? is not his mother called Mary? and his brethren, James, and Joses, and Simon, and Judas?

56 And his sisters, are they not all with us? Whence then hath this man all these things?

57 And they were offended in him. But

a disease that, when we are urged by strong necessity, and when the Lord himself prompts us by a secret movement of the Spirit, we seek God, but, when we have obtained our wishes, ungrateful forgetfulness swallows up that feeling of piety. Thus poverty and hunger beget faith, but abundance kills it.

MATTHEW 13: 53–58; MARK 6: 1–6

Matthew 13: 53. When Jesus had concluded

Matthew does not mean, that immediately after delivering these discourses, he came into his own country; for it is evident from Mark, that some interval of time elapsed. But the meaning is, that after having taught for some time in Judea, he returned again to the Galileans, but did not receive from them kind treatment. A narrative which Luke gives (4: 22) is nearly similar, but is not the same. Nor ought we to wonder that Christ's countrymen, when they perceived that his family was mean and despised, and that he had been poorly educated, were at first so much offended as to murmur at his doctrine, and afterwards persevered in the same malice to such an extent, that they did not cease to slander him, when he chose to discharge the office of a prophet amongst them. This second rejection of Christ shows that the space of time which had intervened had not effected a reformation on the inhabitants of Nazareth, but that the same contempt was constantly thrown as an obstacle in the way, to prevent them from hearing Christ.

54. So that they were amazed

They are struck with amazement at the novelty of the occurrence, that Christ, who had not learned letters, but had been employed from youth to manhood in a mechanical occupation, is so eminent a teacher, and is filled with divine wisdom. In this miracle they ought to have perceived the hand of God; but their ingratitude made them cover themselves with darkness. They are compelled to admire him, whether they will or not; and yet they treat him with contempt. And what is this but to reject a prophet whom God has taught, because he has not been educated by men? They cut their throat by means of their own acknowledgment, when they render so honorable a testimony to the doctrine of Christ, which after all has no influence on them, because it does not take its origin, in the usual way, from the earth. Why do they not rather lift their eyes to heaven, and learn that what exceeds human reason must have come from God?

MATTHEW 14: 1–2; MARK 6: 14–16; LUKE 9: 7–9

The reason why the Evangelists relate this occurrence is,

come near to those who were sound, for fear of infecting them. See Leviticus 13: 46; Numbers 5: 2; 2 Kings 15: 5.

13. They lifted up their voices – They cried with one accord – they were all equally necessitous, and there was but one voice among them all, though ten were engaged in crying at the same time. As they were companions in suffering, they were also companions in prayer.

14. Show yourselves unto the priests – According to the direction, Leviticus 13: 2, etc.; Leviticus 14: 2, etc. Our Lord intended that their cure should be received by faith: they depended on his goodness and power; and though they had no promise, yet they went at his command to do that which those only were required by the law to do who were already healed.

And – **as they went** – In this spirit of implicit faith; they were cleansed.

15. One of them, when he saw that he was healed, etc. – It seems that he did not wait to go first to the priest, but turned immediately back, and gave public praise to the kind hand from which he had received his cure.

16. He was a Samaritan – One who professed a very corrupt religion; and from whom much less was to be expected than from the other nine, who probably were Jews.

17. Where are the nine? – Where are the numbers that from time to time have been converted to God?

18. This stranger – Often God receives more praise and affectionate obedience from those who had long lived without his knowledge and fear, than from those who were bred up among his people, and who profess to be called by his name.

19. Thy faith hath made thee whole – Thy faith hath been the means of receiving that influence by which thou hast been cleansed.

20. Cometh not with observation – With scrupulous observation. As if he had said: "The kingdom of God, the glorious religion of the Messiah, does not come in such a way as

to be discerned only by sagacious critics, or is only to be seen by those who are scrupulously watching for it; it is not of such a nature as to be confined to one place, so that men might say of it, Behold it is only here, or only there: for this kingdom of God is publicly revealed; and behold it is among you; I proclaim it publicly, and work those miracles which prove the kingdom of God is come; and none of these things are done in a corner."

21. Lo here! or, lo there! – Perhaps those Pharisees thought that the Messiah was kept secret, in some private place, known only to some of their rulers; and that by and by he should be proclaimed in a similar way to that in which Joash was by Jehoiada the priest. See the account, 2 Chronicles 23: 1–11.

MATTHEW 13: 53–58; MARK 6: 1–6

Matthew 13: 53–58

54. And when he was come into his own country – Probably Nazareth, where his parents lived, and where he had continued till his thirtieth year, though it appears he had a lodging in Peter's house at Capernaum.

They were astonished – It appears, hence, that our blessed Lord had lived in obscurity all the time above specified; for his countrymen appear not to have heard his doctrines, nor seen his miracles, until now. It is a melancholy truth, that those who should know Christ best are often the most ignorant of himself, the doctrines of his word, and the operations of his Spirit.

55. Is not this the carpenter's son? – An honest trade is no discredit to any man.

Is not his mother – Mary, and his brethren, James, etc. – This insulting question seems to intimate that our Lord's family was a very obscure one; and that they were of small repute among their neighbors, except for their piety.

It is possible that brethren and sisters may mean here near relations, as the words are used among the Hebrews in this latitude of meaning; but I confess it does not appear to

Jesus said unto them, A prophet is not without honor, save in his own country, and in his own house.

58 And he did not many mighty works there because of their unbelief.

Mark 6: 1–6

1 And he went out from thence, and came into his own country; and his disciples follow him.

2 And when the sabbath day was come, he began to teach in the synagogue: and many hearing him were astonished, saying, From whence hath this man these things? and what wisdom is this which is given unto him, that even such mighty works are wrought by his hands?

3 Is not this the carpenter, the son of Mary, the brother of James, and Joses, and of Juda, and Simon? and are not his sisters here with us? And they were offended at him.

4 But Jesus said unto them, A prophet is not without honor, but in his own country, and among his own kin, and in his own house.

5 And he could there do no mighty work, save that he laid his hands upon a few sick folk, and healed them.

6 And he marveled because of their unbelief. And he went round about the villages, teaching.

MATTHEW 14: 1–2; MARK 6: 14–16; LUKE 9: 7–9

Matthew 14: 1–2

1 At that time Herod the tetrarch heard of the fame of Jesus,

2 And said unto his servants, This is John the Baptist; he is risen from the dead; and therefore mighty works do shew forth themselves in him.

Mark 6: 14–16

14 And king Herod heard of him; (for his name was spread abroad:) and he said, That John the Baptist was risen from the dead, and therefore mighty works do shew forth themselves in him.

15 Others said, That it is Elias. And others said, That it is a prophet, or as one of the prophets.

16 But when Herod heard thereof, he said, It is John, whom I beheaded: he is risen from the dead.

to inform us that the name of Christ was universally celebrated, and, therefore, the Jews could not be excused on the plea of ignorance. Many might otherwise have been perplexed by this question, "How came it that, while Christ dwelt on the earth, Judea remained in a profound sleep, as if he had withdrawn into some corner, and had displayed to none his divine power?" The Evangelists accordingly state, that the report concerning him was everywhere spread abroad, and penetrated even into the court of Herod.

Matthew 14: 2. And said to his servants

From the words of Luke it may be inferred, that Herod did not of his own accord adopt this conjecture, but that it was suggested to him by a report which was current among the people. And, indeed, I have no doubt that the hatred which they bore to the tyrant, and their detestation of so shocking a murder, gave rise, as is commonly the ease, to those rumors. It was a superstition deeply rooted, as we have formerly mentioned, in the minds of men, that the dead return to life in a different person. Nearly akin to this is the opinion which they now adopt, that Herod, when he cruelly put to death the holy man, was far from obtaining what he expected; because he had suddenly risen from the dead by the miraculous power of God, and would oppose and attack his enemies with greater severity than ever.

MATTHEW 14: 3–12; MARK 6: 17–29

The Evangelists relate that John was seized, because he had openly condemned **Herod** for carrying off Herodias, and for his incestuous marriage with her. Josephus assigns a different reason, namely, that Herod, dreading on his own account a change of affairs, regarded John with suspicion (Ant. 18. 5: 2); and it is possible that this may have been the pretext on which the tyrant excused his crime, or that such a report may have been in circulation; for it frequently happens that various motives are assigned for unjust violence and cruelty. The true state of the fact, however, is pointed out by the Evangelists: Herod was offended at the holy man, because he had been reproved by him.

Josephus is mistaken in supposing that Herodias was carried off, not from his brother Philip, but from Herod, King of Chalcis, his uncle (Ant. 18: 5: 4). For not only was the crime still recent when the Evangelists wrote, but it was committed before the eyes of all. What is elsewhere stated by Josephus (Ant. 18: 4: 6), that Philip was a person of amiable dispositions, emboldened Herod, I have no doubt, to expect that an outrage committed on a mild, gentle, and peaceable man, would pass with impunity. Another probable conjecture may be mentioned. There is greater reason to suppose that Herodias was married to her uncle Philip than to her grand-uncle, her grandfather's brother, who

me likely. Why should the children of another family be brought in here to share a reproach which it is evident was designed for Joseph the carpenter, Mary his wife, Jesus their son, and their other children? Prejudice apart, would not any person of plain common sense suppose, from this account, that these were the children of Joseph and Mary, and the brothers and sisters of our Lord, according to the flesh? It seems odd that this should be doubted; but, through an unaccountable prejudice, Papists and Protestants are determined to maintain as a doctrine, that on which the Scriptures are totally silent, viz. the perpetual virginity of the mother of our Lord. See Matthew 1: 25.

57. And they were offended in him – They took offense at him, making the meanness of his family the reason why they would not receive him as a prophet, though they were astonished at his wisdom, and at his miracles, Matthew 13: 54. So their pride and their envy were the causes of their destruction.

A prophet is not without honor – This seems to have been a proverbial mode of speech, generally true, but not without some exceptions. The apparent meanness of our Lord was one pretense why they rejected him; and yet, God manifested in the flesh, humbling himself to the condition of a servant, and to the death of the cross, is the only foundation for the salvation of a lost world. Perhaps our Lord means, by prophet, in this place, himself alone, as if he had said, My ministry is more generally reputed, and my doctrine better received, in any other part of the land than in my own country, among my own relatives; because, knowing the obscurity of my birth, they can scarcely suppose that I have these things from heaven.

58. And he did not many mighty works there because of their unbelief – Unbelief and contempt drive Christ out of the heart, as they did out of his own country. Faith seems to put the almighty power of God into the hands of men; whereas unbelief appears to tie up even the hands of the Almighty. A man, generally speaking, can do but little good among his

relatives, because it is difficult for them to look with the eyes of faith upon one whom they have been accustomed to behold with the eyes of the flesh.

MATTHEW 14: 1–2; MARK 6: 14–16; LUKE 9: 7–9

Matthew 14: 1–2

1. Herod the tetrarch – This was Herod Antipas, the son of Herod the Great. See the notes on Matthew 2: 1, where an account is given of the Herod family. The word tetrarch properly signifies a person who rules over the fourth part of a country; but it is taken in a more general sense by the Jewish writers, meaning sometimes a governor simply, or a king; see Matthew 14: 9. The estates of Herod the Great were not, at his death, divided into four tetrarchies, but only into three: one was given by the Emperor Augustus to Archelaus; the second to Herod Antipas, the person in the text; and the third to Philip: all three, sons of Herod the Great.

2. This is John the Baptist – See the power of conscience! Herod is miserable because he is guilty; being continually under the dominion of self-accusation, reproach, and remorse. No need for the Baptist now: conscience performs the office of ten thousand accusers! But, to complete the misery, a guilty conscience offers no relief from God – points out no salvation from sin.

He is risen from the dead – From this we may observe:

1. That the resurrection of the dead was a common opinion among the Jews; and

2. That the materiality of the soul made no part of Herod's creed.

Bad and profligate as he was, it was not deemed by him a thing impossible with God to raise the dead; and the spirit of the murdered Baptist had a permanent resurrection in his guilty conscience.

Luke 9: 7–9

7 Now Herod the tetrarch heard of all that was done by him: and he was perplexed, because that it was said of some, that John was risen from the dead;

8 And of some, that Elias had appeared; and of others, that one of the old prophets was risen again.

9 And Herod said, John have I beheaded: but who is this, of whom I hear such things? And he desired to see him.

MATTHEW 14: 3–12; MARK 6: 17–29

Matthew 14: 3–12

3 For Herod had laid hold on John, and bound him, and put him in prison for Herodias' sake, his brother Philip's wife.

4 For John said unto him, It is not lawful for thee to have her.

5 And when he would have put him to death, he feared the multitude, because they counted him as a prophet.

6 But when Herod's birthday was kept, the daughter of Herodias danced before them, and pleased Herod.

7 Whereupon he promised with an oath to give her whatsoever she would ask.

8 And she, being before instructed of her mother, said, Give me here John Baptist's head in a charger.

9 And the king was sorry: nevertheless for the oath's sake, and them which sat with him at meat, he commanded it to be given her.

10 And he sent, and beheaded John in the prison.

11 And his head was brought in a charger, and given to the damsel: and she brought it to her mother.

12 And his disciples came, and took up the body, and buried it, and went and told Jesus.

Mark 6: 17–29

17 For Herod himself had sent forth and laid hold upon John, and bound him in prison for Herodias' sake, his brother Philip's wife: for he had married her.

18 For John had said unto Herod, It is not lawful for thee to have thy brother's wife.

19 Therefore Herodias had a quarrel against him, and would have killed him; but she could not:

must have been at that time in the decrepitude of old age. Now Herod Antipas (who is here mentioned) and Philip were not brothers by the same mother; for Herod was the son of Marthaca, third wife of Herod the Great, and Philip was the son of Cleopatra.

To return to the Evangelists, they tell us that John was thrown into prison, because he had reproved Herod's crime with greater freedom than the ferocity of the tyrant would endure. The atrocious character of the deed was in itself sufficiently detestable and infamous; for not only did he keep in his own house another man's wife, whom he had torn away from lawful wedlock, but the person on whom he had committed this outrage was his own brother. When, in addition to this, he is freely reproved by John, Herod has some reason to fear that sedition will suddenly break out. His lust did not allow him to correct his fault; but having imprisoned the prophet of God, he promises to himself repose and liberty.

Ignorance of history has led many people into a fruitless debate; "Have I a right to marry the woman who was formerly married to my brother?" Though the modesty of nature recoils from such a marriage, yet John condemns the rape still more than the incest; for it was by violence or by stratagem that Herod had deprived his brother of his lawful wife: and otherwise it would have been less lawful for him to marry his niece than to marry his brother's widow. There cannot be a doubt, that a crime so flagrant was universally blamed. But others loaded Herod with their curses in his absence. John alone comes into his presence, and reproves him boldly to his face, if by any means he may be brought to repentance. Hence we learn with what unshaken fortitude the servants of God ought to be armed when they have to do with princes; for in almost every court hypocrisy and servile flattery are prevalent; and the ears of princes, having been accustomed to this smooth language, do not tolerate any voice which reproves their vices with any severity. But as a prophet of God ought not to overlook so shocking a crime, John steps forward, though a disagreeable and unwelcome adviser, and, rather than fail in his duty, scruples not to incur the frown of the tyrant, even though he knew Herod to be so strongly held by the snares of the prostitute, that he could scarcely be moved from his purpose.

5. And though he wished to put him to death

There is some appearance of contradiction between the words of Matthew and Mark: for the former says that Herod was desirous to commit this shocking murder, but was restrained by the fear of the people; while the latter charges Herodias alone with this cruelty. But the difficulty is soon removed. At first Herod would have been unwilling, if a

ADAM CLARKE

MATTHEW 14: 3–12; MARK 6: 17–29

Matthew 14: 3–12

3. **For Herodias' sake** – This infamous woman was the daughter of Aristobulus and Bernice, and grand-daughter of Herod the Great. Her first marriage was with Herod Philip, her uncle, by whom she had Salome: some time after, she left her husband, and lived publicly with Herod Antipas, her brother-in-law, who had been before married to the daughter of Aretas, king of Arabia Petraea. As soon as Aretas understood that Herod had determined to put away his daughter, he prepared to make war on him: the two armies met, and that of Herod was cut to pieces by the Arabians; and this, Josephus says, was supposed to be a judgment of God on him for the murder of John the Baptist.

4. **For John said unto him, It is not lawful for thee to have her.** – Here is an instance of zeal, fidelity, and courage, highly worthy of imitation. Plainness, mildness, and modesty, are qualifications necessary to be observed when we reprove the great. The best service a subject can render his prince is to lay before him, in the plainest but most respectful manner, what the law of God requires of him, and what it forbids. How unutterable must the punishment of those be who are chaplains to princes, or great men, and who either flatter them in their vices, or wink at their sins!

5. **He feared the multitude** – Miserable prince! who fears more to offend his people, than to sin against his God, by shedding innocent blood. When a man resists sin only by the help of human motives, he cannot long defend himself.

6. **Herod's birth-day** – Either the day in which he was born, or the day on which he began to reign; for both were termed birth-days. See 1 Samuel 13: 1, and Hosea 7: 5. The kings of Persia were accustomed to reject no petition that was preferred to them during the entertainment.

The daughter – danced – This was Salome, mentioned before.

8. **Give me here John Baptist's head in a**

charger – The word charger formerly signified a large dish, bowl, or drinking cup: the Saxon has *a dish*, Tindal, *a platter*; any thing is better than charger, which never conveyed much meaning, and now conveys none. The evangelist says she was instructed before, by her mother, to ask the Baptist's head! What a most infernal mother, to give such instructions to her child! and what a promising daughter to receive them! What a present for a young lady! – the bloody head of the murdered forerunner of Jesus! and what a gratification for an adulterous wife, and incestuous mother! The disturber of her illicit pleasures, and the troubler of her brother-husband's conscience, is no more! Short, however, was their glorying!

9. **The king was sorry** – He knew John to be a righteous man, and at first did many things gladly which John told him it was his duty to perform: Mark 6: 20.

And them which sat with him at meat – Who were probably such as himself, and would have considered it a breach of honor if he had not fulfilled his sworn promise: he therefore commanded it to be given!

11. **His head was given to the damsel: and she brought it to her mother** – There is no person so revengeful as a lascivious woman when reproved and blamed. A preacher of the Gospel has most to fear from this quarter: the first of this profession lost his life for the sake of truth and chastity; and others, especially those who have any thing to do with men in power who are profligates, may learn what they are to expect in return for a faithful discharge of their duty.

12. **His disciples came, and took up the BODY** – The HEAD was in the possession of Herodias, who, 'tis probable, took a diabolic pleasure in viewing that speechless mouth which had often been the cause of planting thorns in her criminal bed; and in offering indignities to that tongue from which she could no longer dread a reproof. Her character justifies every bad conjecture that can well be formed on this head: and St. Jerome positively says that, when she got it, she drew out the tongue,

20 For Herod feared John, knowing that he was a just man and an holy, and observed him; and when he heard him, he did many things, and heard him gladly.

21 And when a convenient day was come, that Herod on his birthday made a supper to his lords, high captains, and chief estates of Galilee;

22 And when the daughter of the said Herodias came in, and danced, and pleased Herod and them that sat with him, the king said unto the damsel, Ask of me whatsoever thou wilt, and I will give it thee.

23 And he sware unto her, Whatsoever thou shalt ask of me, I will give it thee, unto the half of my kingdom.

24 And she went forth, and said unto her mother, What shall I ask? And she said, The head of John the Baptist.

25 And she came in straightway with haste unto the king, and asked, saying, I will that thou give me by and by in a charger the head of John the Baptist.

26 And the king was exceeding sorry; yet for his oath's sake, and for their sakes which sat with him, he would not reject her.

27 And immediately the king sent an executioner, and commanded his head to be brought: and he went and beheaded him in the prison,

28 And brought his head in a charger, and gave it to the damsel: and the damsel gave it to her mother.

29 And when his disciples heard of it, they came and took up his corpse, and laid it in a tomb.

MATTHEW 14: 13–21; MARK 6: 30–44; LUKE 9: 10–17

Matthew 14: 13–21

13 When Jesus heard of it, he departed thence by ship into a desert place apart: and when the people had heard thereof, they followed him on foot out of the cities.

14 And Jesus went forth, and saw a great multitude, and was moved with compassion toward them, and he healed their sick.

15 And when it was evening, his disciples came to him, saying, This is a desert place, and the time is now past; send the

stronger necessity had not compelled him reluctantly to do so, to put to death the holy man; because he regarded him with reverence, and, indeed, was prevented by religious scruples from practising such atrocious cruelty against a prophet of God; and that he afterwards shook off this fear of God, in consequence of the incessant urgency of Herodias; but that afterwards, when infuriated by that demon he longed for the death of the holy man, he was withheld by a new restraint, because he dreaded on his own account a popular commotion.

MATTHEW 14: 13–21; MARK 6: 30–44; LUKE 9: 10–17

Matthew 14: 13. When Jesus heard it

John, who relates the same narrative, does not mention the reason why Jesus crossed over to the opposite bank (6: 5). Mark and Luke differ somewhat from Matthew; for they describe the occasion of the journey to have been to give some repose to his disciples, after that they had returned from their embassy. But there is no contradiction here; for it is possible that he intended to withdraw his disciples into a desert place, in order that he might be more at leisure to train them for higher labors, and that, about the same time, an additional reason arose out of the death of John. Minds which were still feeble might have been terrified by the death of John, learning from the melancholy end of that eminent prophet what condition awaited them all. Certainly, as it was formerly related that, when John was imprisoned, Christ removed from Herod's territory, in order to avoid his fury for the time, so we may now infer that Christ, in order to keep his trembling disciples at a distance from the flame, **withdrew into a desert place**.

How long the Apostles were employed in their first embassy it is not in our power to determine; for the Evangelists, as we have formerly remarked, either did not attend to dates, or did not observe them with great exactness. I think it highly probable that their commission to proclaim the kingdom of Christ was not confined to a single occasion, but that, as opportunities were offered, they either repeated their visit to some places, or went to others after a lapse of time. The words, **they came together to him**, I look upon as meaning that ever afterwards they were his constant attendants; as if the Evangelist had said, that they did not leave their Master so as to be individually and constantly employed in the ordinary office of teaching, but that, having discharged a temporary commission, they went back to school to make greater advances in learning.

They followed him on foot out of the cities

Though Christ, who foresaw all things before they happened, was in no respect ignorant of what would take place,

and thrust it through with her bodkin. On the whole we may observe:

That the diversions of the world, feasting and dancing, are but too commonly the occasions of sin. After so fatal an example as this, can we doubt whether balls are not snares for souls; destructive of chastity, modesty, and sometimes even of humanity itself; and a pernicious invention to excite the most criminal passions! How many on such occasions have sacrificed their chastity, and then, to hide their shame, have stifled the feelings of the human being and the parent, and, by direct or indirect means, have put a period to the innocent offspring of their connections! Unhappy mother, who exposes her daughter to the same shipwreck herself has suffered, and makes her own child the instrument of her lust and revenge! Behold here, ye professedly religious parents, the fruits of what was doubtless called in those times, elegant breeding and accomplished dancing! Fix your eyes on that vicious mother, that prostituted daughter, and especially on that murdered ambassador of God, and then send your children to genteel boarding-schools, to learn the accomplishment of DANCING! where the fear of God makes no part of the education.

MATTHEW 14: 13–21; MARK 6: 30–44; LUKE 9: 10–17

Matthew 14: 13–21

13. When Jesus heard of it, he departed thence – Had the blessed Jesus continued in that place, it is probable the hand of this impure female murderer would have been stretched out against him also: he withdrew, therefore, not through fear, but to teach his messengers rather to yield to the storm than expose themselves to destruction, where, from circumstances, the case is evidently hopeless.

14. Jesus – was moved with compassion – he was moved with tender compassion, so I think the word should in general be translated: see the note on Matthew 9: 36. As a verb, it does not appear to have been used by any

but ecclesiastical writers. It always intimates that motion of the bowels, accompanied with extreme tenderness and concern, which is felt at the sight of the miseries of another.

15. Send the multitude away, that they may go – and buy – The disciples of Christ are solicitous for the people's temporal as well a spiritual welfare: and he is not worthy to be called a minister of Christ, who dues not endeavor to promote both to the uttermost of his power. The preaching of Christ must have been accompanied with uncommon power to these people's souls, to have induced them to leave their homes to follow him from village to village, for they could never hear enough; and to neglect to make use of any means for the support of their lives, so that they might still have the privilege of hearing him. When a soul is either well replenished with the bread of life, or hungry after it, the necessities of the body are, for the time, little regarded.

16. They need not depart – He that seeks first the kingdom of heaven is sure to have every temporal requisite. When a man ensures the first, God always takes care to throw the other into the bargain. He who has an interest in Jesus has in him an inexhaustible treasure of spiritual and temporal good. Though the means by which man may help his fellows have failed, we are not to suppose that the bounty of God is exhausted. When we are about to give up all hope of farther supply, the gracious word of Christ still holds good – They need not depart; give ye them to eat.

Give ye them to eat – Should we say, Lord, how shall thy poor, feeble ministering servants feed so many hungry souls as attend thy word! Begin at the command of Jesus – make the attempt – divide what you have – and the bread of God shall be multiplied in your hands, and all shall eat and be satisfied.

17. We have here but five loaves and two fishes – When we are deeply conscious of our own necessities, we shall be led to depend on Jesus with a firmer faith. God often permits his servants to be brought low, that they may have repeated opportunities of proving the

multitude away, that they may go into the villages, and buy themselves victuals.

16 But Jesus said unto them, They need not depart; give ye them to eat.

17 And they say unto him, We have here but five loaves, and two fishes.

18 He said, Bring them hither to me.

19 And he commanded the multitude to sit down on the grass, and took the five loaves, and the two fishes, and looking up to heaven, he blessed, and brake, and gave the loaves to his disciples, and the disciples to the multitude.

20 And they did all eat, and were filled: and they took up of the fragments that remained twelve baskets full.

21 And they that had eaten were about five thousand men, beside women and children.

Mark 6: 30–44

30 And the apostles gathered themselves together unto Jesus, and told him all things, both what they had done, and what they had taught.

31 And he said unto them, Come ye yourselves apart into a desert place, and rest a while: for there were many coming and going, and they had no leisure so much as to eat.

32 And they departed into a desert place by ship privately.

33 And the people saw them departing, and many knew him, and ran afoot thither out of all cities, and outwent them, and came together unto him.

34 And Jesus, when he came out, saw much people, and was moved with compassion toward them, because they were as sheep not having a shepherd: and he began to teach them many things.

35 And when the day was now far spent, his disciples came unto him, and said, This is a desert place, and now the time is far passed:

36 Send them away, that they may go into the country round about, and into the villages, and buy themselves bread: for they have nothing to eat.

37 He answered and said unto them, Give ye them to eat. And they say unto him, Shall we go and buy two hundred pennyworth of bread, and give them to eat?

38 He saith unto them, How many

yet he wished, as a man, to forewarn his disciples, that the fact might testify the anxiety which he had about them. The vast crowd that had assembled shows how widely his fame was spread in every direction: and this left the Jews without excuse in depriving themselves, by their own carelessness, of the salvation which was offered to them; for even out of this great multitude, which was inflamed by a sudden zeal to follow Christ, it is evident from what is stated by John (6: 66; 12: 37) that not more than a very small number yielded a true and steady adherence to his doctrine.

14. He was moved with compassion towards them

The other two Evangelists, and particularly Mark, state more clearly the reason why this **compassion** was awakened in the mind of Christ. It was because he saw famishing souls, whom the warmth of zeal had carried away from their homes and led into a **desert place**. This scarcity of teaching indicated a wretched state of disorder; and accordingly Mark says **that Jesus was moved with compassion towards them, because they were as sheep not having a shepherd**. Not that, as to his Divine nature, he looked upon them all as sheep, but that, as man, he judged according to the present aspect of the case. It was no small manifestation of piety that they left their own homes, and flocked in crowds to the Prophet of God, though he purposely concealed himself from them. Besides, it ought to be remarked, that Christ was mindful of the character which he sustained; for he had been commanded to discharge the duties of a public teacher, and was therefore bound to look upon all the Jews, for the time being, as belonging to the flock of God and to the Church, till they withdrew from it.

So strongly was Christ moved by this feeling of **compassion**, that though, in common with his disciples, he was fatigued and almost worn out by uninterrupted toil, he did not spare himself. He had endeavored to obtain some relaxation, and that on his own account as well as for the sake of his disciples; but when urgent duty calls him to additional labor, he willingly lays aside that private consideration, and devotes himself to teaching the multitudes. Although he has now laid aside those feelings which belonged to him as a mortal man, yet there is no reason to doubt that he looks down from heaven on poor sheep that have no shepherd, provided they ask relief of their wants. Mark says, that **he began to teach them MANY things**; that is, he spent a long time in preaching, that they might reap some lasting advantage. Luke says, that he **spoke to them concerning the Kingdom of God**, which amounts to the same thing. Matthew makes no mention of any thing but miracles, because they were of great importance in establishing Christ's reputation; but it may naturally be concluded that he did not leave out doctrine, which was a matter of the highest importance.

kindness and mercy of their gracious Lord and Master.

18. Bring them hither to me – No creature of God should be considered as good or safe without the blessing of God in it. If thou have but even a handful of meal and a few herbs, bring them to Christ by prayer and faith, and he will make them a sufficiency for thy body, and a sacrament to thy soul. Let the minister of the Gospel attend also to this – let him bring all his gifts and graces to his Maker – let him ever know that his word can be of no use, unless the blessing of Christ be in it.

19. And took the five loaves, etc. – This was the act of the father of a family among the Jews – his business it was to take the bread into his hands, and render thanks to God, before any of the family was permitted to taste of it.

Looking up to heaven – To teach us to acknowledge GOD as the Supreme Good, and fountain of all excellence.

He blessed – The word God should, I think, be rather inserted here than the word them, because it does not appear that it was the loaves which Christ blessed, but that God who had provided them; and this indeed was the Jewish custom, not to bless the food, but the God who gave it.

However, there are others who believe the loaves are meant, and that he blessed them in order to multiply them. The Jewish form of blessing, or what we term grace, before and after meat, was as follows:

BEFORE MEAT

Blessed art thou, our God, King of the universe, who bringest bread out of the earth!

AFTER MEAT

Blessed art thou, our God, King of the universe, the Creator of the fruit of the vine!

And brake – We read often in the Scriptures of breaking bread, never of cutting it: because the Jews made their bread broad and thin like cakes, and to divide such, being very brittle, there was no need of a knife.

20. They did all eat, and were filled – Little or much is the same in the hands of Jesus Christ.

Here was an incontestable miracle – five thousand men, besides women and children, fed with five cakes and two fishes! Here must have been a manifest creation of substance – the parts of the bread were not dilated to make them appear large, nor was there any delusion in the eating – for they all ate, and were all filled. Here then is one miracle of our Lord attested by at least five thousand persons! But did not this creation of bread prove the unlimited power of Jesus? Undoubtedly: and nothing less than eternal power and Godhead could have effected it.

They took up – twelve baskets – It was customary for many of the Jews to carry a basket with them at all times: and Mr. Wakefield's conjecture here is very reasonable: "By the number here particularized, it should seem that each apostle filled his own bread basket." Some think that the Jews carried baskets in commemoration of their Egyptian bondage, when they were accustomed to carry the clay and stubble to make the bricks, in a basket that was hung about their necks.

It appears that a basket about the neck, and a bunch of hay, were the general characteristic of this long enslaved and oppressed people in the different countries where they sojourned.

The simple reason why the Jews carried baskets with them appears to be this: When they went into Gentile countries, they carried their own provision with them, as they were afraid of being polluted by partaking of the meat of heathens.

After five thousand were fed, twelve times as much, at least, remained, as the whole multitude at first sat down to! See the note on Luke 9: 16.

MATTHEW 14: 22–33; MARK 6: 45–52

Matthew 14: 22–33

22. Jesus constrained his disciples to get into a ship – Either they were afraid to return into the jurisdiction of Herod, or they were unwilling to embark without their Lord and Protector, and would not enter their boat till Christ had commanded them to embark.

loaves have ye? go and see. And when they knew, they say, Five, and two fishes.

39 And he commanded them to make all sit down by companies upon the green grass.

41 And when he had taken the five loaves and the two fishes, he looked up to heaven, and blessed, and brake the loaves, and gave them to his disciples to set before them; and the two fishes divided he among them all.

42 And they did all eat, and were filled.

43 And they took up twelve baskets full of the fragments, and of the fishes.

44 And they that did eat of the loaves were about five thousand men.

Luke 9: 10–17

10 And the apostles, when they were returned, told him all that they had done. And he took them, and went aside privately into a desert place belonging to the city called Bethsaida.

11 And the people, when they knew it, followed him: and he received them, and spake unto them of the kingdom of God, and healed them that had need of healing.

12 And when the day began to wear away, then came the twelve, and said unto him, Send the multitude away, that they may go into the towns and country round about, and lodge, and get victuals: for we are here in a desert place.

13 But he said unto them, Give ye them to eat. And they said, We have no more but five loaves and two fishes; except we should go and buy meat for all this people.

14 For they were about five thousand men. And he said to his disciples, Make them sit down by fifties in a company.

15 And they did so, and made them all sit down.

16 Then he took the five loaves and the two fishes, and looking up to heaven, he blessed them, and brake, and gave to the disciples to set before the multitude.

17 And they did eat, and were all filled: and there was taken up of fragments that remained to them twelve baskets.

20. And carried away what was left

The fragments that remained after satisfying so vast a multitude of men were more than twelve times larger in quantity than what was at first put into their hands, and this contributed not a little to the splendor of the miracle. In this way all came to know that the power of Christ had not only created out of nothing the food that was necessary for immediate use, but that, if it should be required, there was also provision for future wants; and, in a word, Christ intended that, after the miracle had been wrought, a striking proof of it should still remain, which, after being refreshed by food, they might contemplate at leisure.

MATTHEW 14: 22–33; MARK 6: 45–52

Matthew 14: 22. And immediately Jesus constrained his disciples

They must have been **constrained**; for they would never, of their own accord, have left him, and gone to the other side. Now in this they testify their great veneration for him, when, contrary to their own opinions, they yield to his command and obey it. And, indeed, it had an appearance of absurdity, that he should remain alone **in a desert place**, when night was approaching. But so much the greater commendation is due to the submissiveness of those who set a higher value on the authority of their heavenly teacher than on all that could be pleaded on the other side. And, indeed, we do not truly and perfectly obey God, unless we implicitly follow whatever he commands, though our feelings may be opposed to it. There is always the best reason, no doubt, for every thing that God does; but he often conceals it from us for a time, in order to instruct us not to be wise in ourselves, but to depend entirely on the expression of his will. And thus Christ **constrained his disciples** to cross over, in order to train them to that rule of obedience which I have mentioned; though there cannot be a doubt that he intended to prepare the way for the miracle which will immediately come under our consideration.

23. He went up into a mountain alone

It is probable that the Son of God, who was fully aware of the tempest that was coming on, did not neglect the safety of his disciples in his prayers; and yet we naturally wonder that he did not rather prevent the danger than employ himself in prayer. But in discharging all the parts of his office as Mediator, he showed himself to be God and man, and exhibited proofs of both natures, as opportunities occurred. Though he had all things at his disposal, he showed himself to be a man by praying; and this he did not hypocritically, but manifested sincere and human affection towards us. In this manner his divine majesty was for a time concealed, but was afterwards displayed at the proper time.

From this verse it appears that Christ gave some advices to the multitudes after the departure of his disciples, which he did not wish them to hear.

Unto the other side – Towards Capernaum, Matthew 14: 34. John 6: 16–17, or Bethsaida, see on Mark 6: 45.

23. He went up into a mountain apart, to pray – He whom God has employed in a work of mercy had need to return, by prayer, as speedily, to his Maker, as he can, lest he should be tempted to value himself on account of that in which he has no merit – for the good that is done upon earth, the Lord doth it alone. Some make this part of our Lord's conduct emblematic of the spirit and practice of prayer, and observe that the proper dispositions and circumstances for praying well are:

1. Retirement from the world.
2. Elevation of the heart to God.
3. Solitude.
4. The silence and quiet of the night.

It is certain that in this also Christ has left us an example that we should follow his steps. Retirement from the world is often a means of animating, supporting, and spiritualizing prayer. Other society should be shut out, when a soul comes to converse with God.

24. Tossed with waves – Grievously agitated.

25. The fourth watch – Anciently the Jews divided the night into three watches, consisting of four hours each. The first watch is mentioned, Lamentations 2: 19: the second, Judges 7: 19; and the third, Exodus 14: 24; but a fourth watch is not mentioned in any part of the OLD Testament. This division the Romans had introduced in Judea, as also the custom of dividing the day into twelve hours: see John 11: 9. The first watch began at six o'clock in the evening, and continued till nine; the second began at nine, and continued till twelve; the third began at twelve, and continued till three next morning; and the fourth began at three, and continued till six. It was therefore between the hours of three and six in the morning that Jesus made his appearance to his disciples.

Walking on the sea – Thus suspending the laws of gravitation was a proper manifestation of unlimited power. Jesus did this by his own power; therefore Jesus showed forth his Godhead. In this one miracle we may discover three:

1. Though at a distance from his disciples, he knew their distress.

2. He found them out on the lake, and probably in the midst of darkness.

3. He walked upon the water.

Job, speaking of those things whereby the omnipotence of God was demonstrated, says particularly, Job 9: 8, He walketh upon the waves of the sea: intimating that this was impossible to any thing but Omnipotence.

26. It is a spirit – That the spirits of the dead might and did appear, was a doctrine held by the greatest and holiest of men that ever existed; and a doctrine which the free-thinkers and bound-thinkers, of different ages, have never been able to disprove.

27. It is I; be not afraid – Nothing but this voice of Christ could, in such circumstances, have given courage and comfort to his disciples: those who are grievously tossed with difficulties and temptations require a similar manifestation of his power and goodness. When he proclaims himself in the soul, all sorrow, and fear, and sin are at an end.

28. Bid me come unto thee on the water – A weak faith is always wishing for signs and miracles. To take Christ at his word, argues not only the perfection of faith, but also the highest exercise of sound reason. He is to be credited on his own word, because he is the TRUTH, and therefore can neither lie nor deceive.

29. Peter – walked on the water – However impossible the thing commanded by Christ may appear, it is certain he will give power to accomplish it to those who receive his word by faith; but we must take care never to put Christ's power to the proof for the gratification of a vain curiosity; or even for the strengthening of our faith, when the ordinary means for doing that are within our reach.

MATTHEW 14: 22–33; MARK 6: 45–52

Matthew 14: 22–33

22 And straightway Jesus constrained his disciples to get into a ship, and to go before him unto the other side, while he sent the multitudes away.

23 And when he had sent the multitudes away, he went up into a mountain apart to pray: and when the evening was come, he was there alone.

24 But the ship was now in the midst of the sea, tossed with waves: for the wind was contrary.

25 And in the fourth watch of the night Jesus went unto them, walking on the sea.

26 And when the disciples saw him walking on the sea, they were troubled, saying, It is a spirit; and they cried out for fear.

27 But straightway Jesus spake unto them, saying, Be of good cheer; it is I; be not afraid.

28 And Peter answered him and said, Lord, if it be thou, bid me come unto thee on the water.

29 And he said, Come. And when Peter was come down out of the ship, he walked on the water, to go to Jesus.

30 But when he saw the wind boisterous, he was afraid; and beginning to sink, he cried, saying, Lord, save me.

31 And immediately Jesus stretched forth his hand, and caught him, and said unto him, O thou of little faith, wherefore didst thou doubt?

32 And when they were come into the ship, the wind ceased.

33 Then they that were in the ship came and worshipped him, saying, Of a truth thou art the Son of God.

Mark 6: 45–52

45 And straightway he constrained his disciples to get into the ship, and to go to the other side before unto Bethsaida, while he sent away the people.

46 And when he had sent them away, he departed into a mountain to pray.

47 And when even was come, the ship was in the midst of the sea, and he alone on the land.

48 And he saw them toiling in rowing; for the wind was contrary unto them: and

27. But immediately Jesus spake to them

As Christ is not known to be a Deliverer till he actually makes his appearance, he speaks, and desires his disciples to recognize him. That confidence, to which he exhorts them, is represented by him as founded on his presence; plainly implying that, since they perceive him to be present with them, there are abundant grounds of hope. But as terror had already overpowered their minds, he corrects that terror, lest it should hinder or abate their confidence: not that they could all at once lay aside fear and experience unmingled joy, but because it was necessary that the fear which had seized them should be allayed, that it might not destroy their confidence. Although to the reprobate the voice of the Son of God is deadly, and his presence appalling, yet the effect which they produce on believers is here described to us as widely different. They cause inward peace and strong confidence to hold the sway over our hearts, that we may not yield to carnal fears. But the reason why we are disturbed by unfounded and sudden alarms is, that our ingratitude and wickedness prevent us from employing as shields the innumerable gifts of God, which, if they were turned to proper account, would give us all necessary support. Now though Christ appeared at the proper time for rendering assistance, yet the storm did not immediately cease, till the disciples were more fully aroused both to desire and to expect his grace. And this deserves our attention, as conveying the instruction, that there are good reasons why the Lord frequently delays to bestow that deliverance which he has ready at hand.

MATTHEW 14: 34–36; MARK 6: 53–56

Matthew 14: 34. They came into the country of Gennesareth

The Evangelists give that designation to the country which borrowed its name from the lake, though it is uncertain if it was not rather the name of the country that was bestowed on the lake; but that is a matter of little consequence. Our chief business is, to attend to the object which the Evangelists have in view. It is, to show that the glory of Christ was attested not by one or by another miracle, but that this part of Judea was filled with innumerable proofs of it, the report of which might easily be carried to Jerusalem and to other towns in every direction. Hence we infer, that singularly base and wicked must have been the ingratitude of that nation which wickedly shut its eyes from perceiving, and even endeavored, as far as lay in its power, to extinguish the brightness of the divine glory which was exhibited before them. Our present business is, to perceive, amidst so large an assemblage of miracles, the reason why Christ came, which was, that he might offer himself as a physician to

ADAM CLARKE

30. When he saw the wind boisterous, he was afraid – It was by faith in the power of Christ he was upheld; when that faith failed, by which the laws of gravitation were suspended, no wonder that those laws returned to their wonted action, and that he began to sink. It was not the violence of the winds, nor the raging of the waves, which endangered his life, but his littleness of faith.

31. Jesus stretched forth his hand – Every moment we stand in need of Christ: while we stand – we are upheld by his power only; and when we are falling, or have fallen, we can be saved only by his mercy. Let us always take care that we do not consider so much the danger to which we are exposed, as the power of Christ by which we are to be upheld; and then our mountain is likely to stand strong.

32. The wind ceased – Jesus is the Prince of peace, and all is peace and calm where he condescends to enter and abide.

33. Thou art the Son of God – It is probable that these words were spoken either by the sailors or passengers, and not by the disciples. It would have been a strange thing indeed, if the disciples, after all the miracles they had seen Jesus work – after their having left all to follow him, etc., were only now persuaded that he was the promised Messiah. That they had not as yet clear conceptions concerning his kingdom, is evident enough; but that they had any doubts concerning his being the promised Messiah is far from being clear.

MATTHEW 14: 34–36; MARK 6: 53–56

Matthew 14: 34–36

34. The land of Gennesaret – It was from this country that the sea or lake of Gennesaret had its name. In this district, on the western side of the lake, were the cities of Capernaum and Tiberias.

35. The men of that place had knowledge of him – i.e. They knew him again. They had already seen his miracles; and now they collect all the diseased people they can find, that he

may have the same opportunity of showing forth his marvelous power, and they of being the instruments of relieving their friends and neighbors.

They brought unto him all that were diseased – And Jesus received and healed every man and woman of them. And is not the soul, in the sight of God, of more value than the body? and will he withhold his healing power from the former, and grant it so freely to the latter? This cannot be. Let a man come himself to Jesus, and he shall be saved and afterwards let him recommend this Christ to the whole circle of his acquaintance, and they, if they come, shall also find mercy.

36. That they might only touch the hem of his garment – What mighty influence must the grace and Spirit of Christ have in the soul, when even the border or hem of his garment produced such wonders in the bodies of those who touched it! Here is a man who has turned from sin to God through Christ, and the healing hand of Jesus is laid upon him. Then, no wonder that he knows and feels his sins forgiven, his soul purified, and his heart filled with the fullness of his Maker. Lord, increase our faith! and we shall see greater manifestations of thy power and glory! Amen.

MATTHEW 15: 1–9; MARK 7: 1–13

Matthew 15: 1–9

1. The scribes and Pharisees – of Jerusalem – Our Lord was now in Galilee, Matthew 14: 34.

2. Elders – Rulers and magistrates among the Jews. For they wash not their hands – What frivolous nonsense! These Pharisees had nothing which their malice could fasten on in the conduct or doctrine of our blessed Lord and his disciples, and therefore they must dispute about washing of hands! All sorts of Pharisees are troublesome people in religious society; and the reason is, they take more pleasure in blaming others than in amending themselves.

The tradition of the elders – The word tradition, has occupied a most distinguished place,

about the fourth watch of the night he cometh unto them, walking upon the sea, and would have passed by them.

49 But when they saw him walking upon the sea, they supposed it had been a spirit, and cried out:

50 For they all saw him, and were troubled. And immediately he talked with them, and saith unto them, Be of good cheer: it is I; be not afraid.

51 And he went up unto them into the ship; and the wind ceased: and they were sore amazed in themselves beyond measure, and wondered.

52 For they considered not the miracle of the loaves: for their heart was hardened.

MATTHEW 14: 34–36; MARK 6: 53–56

Matthew 14: 34–36

34 And when they were gone over, they came into the land of Gennesaret.

35 And when the men of that place had knowledge of him, they sent out into all that country round about, and brought unto him all that were diseased;

36 And besought him that they might only touch the hem of his garment: and as many as touched were made perfectly whole.

Mark 6: 53–56

53 And when they had passed over, they came into the land of Gennesaret, and drew to the shore.

54 And when they were come out of the ship, straightway they knew him,

55 And ran through that whole region round about, and began to carry about in beds those that were sick, where they heard he was.

56 And whithersoever he entered, into villages, or cities, or country, they laid the sick in the streets, and besought him that they might touch if it were but the border of his garment: and as many as touched him were made whole.

MATTHEW 15: 1–9; MARK 7: 1–13

Matthew 15: 1–9

1 Then came to Jesus scribes and Pharisees, which were of Jerusalem, saying,

2 Why do thy disciples transgress the

heal all the diseases of all men. For we must bear in mind what Matthew had formerly quoted from the Prophet Isaiah (53: 4), that in healing bodies he shadowed out something greater, namely, that he restores our souls to health, and that it is his peculiar office to remove spiritual diseases. He is not now an inhabitant of the earth; but it is certain that, now that he is in heaven, he is authorized to bestow those favors of which he then exhibited a visible proof. Now as we labor under every kind of diseases till he heal us, let each of us not only present himself to him, but endeavor to bring others who need the same remedy.

MATTHEW 15: 1–9; MARK 7: 1–13

Matthew 15: 1. Then scribes and Pharisees

As the fault that is here corrected is not only common but highly dangerous, the passage is particularly worthy of our attention. We see the extraordinary insolence that is displayed by men as to the form and manner of worshipping God; for they are perpetually contriving new modes of worship, and when any one wishes to be thought wiser than others, he displays his ingenuity on this subject. I speak not of foreigners, but of the very domestics of the Church, on whom God has conferred the peculiar honor of declaring with their lips the rule of godliness. God has laid down the manner in which he wishes that we should worship him, and has included in his law the perfection of holiness. Yet a vast number of men, as if it were a light and trivial matter to obey God and to keep what he enjoins, collect for themselves, on every hand, many additions. Those who occupy places of authority bring forward their inventions for this purpose, as if they were in possession of something more perfect than the word of the Lord. This is followed by the slow growth of tyranny; for, when men have once assumed to themselves the right to issue commands, they demand a rigid adherence to their laws, and do not allow the smallest iota to be left out, either through contempt or through forgetfulness. The world cannot endure lawful authority, and most violently rebels against enduring the Lord's yoke, and yet easily and willingly becomes entangled in the snares of vain traditions; nay, such bondage appears to be, in the case of many, an object of desire. Meanwhile, the worship of God is corrupted, of which the first and leading principle is obedience. The authority of men is preferred to the command of God. Sternly, and therefore tyrannically, are the common people compelled to give their whole attention to trifles. This passage teaches us, first, that all modes of worship invented by men are displeasing to God, because he chooses that he alone shall be heard, in order to train and instruct us in true godliness according to his own pleasure; secondly, that those who are not satisfied with the only law

both in the Jewish and Christian Church. Man is ever fond of mending the work of his Maker; and hence he has been led to put his finishing hand even to Divine revelation! Among the Jews TRADITION signifies what is also called the oral law, which they distinguish from the written law: this last contains the Mosaic precepts, as found in the Pentateuch: the former, the traditions of the elders, i.e. traditions, or doctrines, that had been successively handed down from Moses through every generation, but not committed to writing. The Jews feign that, when GOD gave Moses the written law, he gave him also the oral law, which is the interpretation of the former. This law, Moses at first delivered to Aaron then to his sons Eleazar and Ithamar; and, after these to the seventy-two elders, who were six of the most eminent men chosen out of each of the twelve tribes. These seventy-two, with Moses and Aaron, delivered it again to all the heads of the people, and afterwards to the congregation at large. They say also that, before Moses died, he delivered this oral law, or system of traditions, to JOSHUA, and Joshua to the ELDERS which succeeded him, THEY to the Prophets, and the PROPHETS to each other, till it came to JEREMIAH, who delivered it to BARUCH his scribe, who repeated it to EZRA, who delivered it to the men of the great synagogue, the last of whom was SIMON the Just. By Simon the Just it was delivered to ANTIGONUS of Socho; by him to JOSE the son of Jochanan; by him to JOSE, the son of Joezer; by him to NATHAN the Arbelite, and Joshua the son of Perachiah; and by them to JUDAH the son of Tabbai, and Simeon, the son of Shatah; and by them to SHEMAIAH and ABTALION; and by them to HILLEL; and by Hillel to SIMEON his son, the same who took Christ in his arms when brought to the temple to be presented to the Lord: by SIMEON it was delivered to GAMALIEL his son, the preceptor of St. Paul, who delivered it to SIMEON his son, and he to Rab. JUDAH HAKKODESH his son, who compiled and digested it into the book which is called the MISHNA; to explain which the two Talmuds, called the Jerusalem and Babylonish Talmuds, were compiled, which are also called the Gemera or complement, because by these the oral law or Mishnah is fully explained. The Jerusalem Talmud was completed about A.D. 300; and the Babylonish Talmud about the beginning of the sixth century. This Talmud was printed at Amsterdam in 12 vols. folio. These contain the whole of the traditions of the elders, and have so explained, or rather frittered away, the words of God, that our Lord might well say, Ye have made the word of God of no effect by your traditions. In what estimation these are held by the Jews, the following examples will prove: "The words of the scribes are lovely beyond the words of the law: for the words of the law are weighty and light, but the words of the scribes are all weighty."

They wash not their hands – On washing of hands, before and after meat, the Jews laid great stress: they considered eating with unwashed hands to be no ordinary crime. They consider the person who undervalues this rite to be no better than a heathen, and consequently excommunicate him.

3. Why do ye – transgress the commandment – Ye accuse my disciples of transgressing the traditions of the elders – I accuse you of transgressing the commands of God, and that too in favor of your own tradition; thus preferring the inventions of men to the positive precepts of God. Pretenders to zeal often prefer superstitious usages to the Divine law, and human inventions to the positive duties of Christianity.

4. Honor thy father and mother – This word was taken in great latitude of meaning among the Jews: it not only meant respect and submission, but also to take care of a person, to nourish and support him, to enrich. See Numbers 22: 17; Judges 13: 17; 1 Timothy 5: 17. And that this was the sense of the law, as it respected parents, see Deuteronomy 27: 16, and see the note on Exodus 20: 12.

5. It is a gift – Mark 7: 11, an offering of approach; something consecrated to the service of God in the temple, by which a man had the privilege of approaching his Maker. This conduct was similar to the custom of certain

tradition of the elders? for they wash not their hands when they eat bread.

3 But he answered and said unto them, Why do ye also transgress the commandment of God by your tradition?

4 For God commanded, saying, Honor thy father and mother: and, He that curseth father or mother, let him die the death.

5 But ye say, Whosoever shall say to his father or his mother, It is a gift, by whatsoever thou mightest be profited by me;

6 And honor not his father or his mother, he shall be free. Thus have ye made the commandment of God of none effect by your tradition.

7 Ye hypocrites, well did Esaias prophesy of you, saying,

8 This people draweth nigh unto me with their mouth, and honored me with their lips; but their heart is far from me.

9 But in vain they do worship me, teaching for doctrines the commandments of men.

Mark 7: 1–13

1 Then came together unto him the Pharisees, and certain of the scribes, which came from Jerusalem.

2 And when they saw some of his disciples eat bread with defiled, that is to say, with unwashen, hands, they found fault.

3 For the Pharisees, and all the Jews, except they wash their hands oft, eat not, holding the tradition of the elders.

4 And when they come from the market, except they wash, they eat not. And many other things there be, which they have received to hold, as the washing of cups, and pots, brasen vessels, and of tables.

5 Then the Pharisees and scribes asked him, Why walk not thy disciples according to the tradition of the elders, but eat bread with unwashen hands?

6 He answered and said unto them, Well hath Esaias prophesied of you hypocrites, as it is written, This people honored me with their lips, but their heart is far from me.

7 Howbeit in vain do they worship me, teaching for doctrines the commandments of men.

of God, and weary themselves by attending to the traditions of men, are uselessly employed; thirdly, that an outrage is committed against God, when the inventions of men are so highly extolled, that the majesty of his law is almost lowered, or at least the reverence for it is abated.

Scribes who had come from Jerusalem

With what design those scribes came to Jesus is not stated; but I think it probable that their attention was excited by his fame, and that they came with the desire of receiving instruction, provided that they should approve of him as a competent teacher; though it is possible that they were sent to spy. However that may be, as they had brought their haughty disdain along with them, they are easily provoked by the slightest offense to bite or snarl at Christ. Hence we see with what difficulty those who are influenced by ambition and the lust of power are brought to submit to sound doctrine. Those especially whose attachment to ceremonies has been strengthened by long practice cannot endure any novelty, but loudly condemn every thing to which they have not been accustomed. In short, any thing more haughty or more disdainful than this class of men cannot be imagined.

9. But in vain do they worship me

The words of the prophet run literally thus: their fear toward me has been taught by the precept of men. But Christ has faithfully and accurately given the meaning, that in **vain is God worshipped**, when the will of men is substituted in the room of doctrine. By these words, all kinds of will-worship (*ethelothzeskeia*), as Paul calls it (Colossians 2: 23), are plainly condemned.

MATTHEW 15: 10–20; MARK 7: 14–23; LUKE 6: 39

Matthew 15: 10. And having called the multitudes to him

Here Christ turns to those who are ready to receive instruction, and explains more fully the truth at which he had formerly glanced, that the kingdom of God does not consist in meat and drink, as Paul also teaches us (Romans 14: 17); for, since outward things are by nature pure, the use of them is free and pure, and uncleanness is not contracted from the good creatures of God. It is therefore a general statement, that pollution does not come from without into a man, but that the fountain is concealed within him. Now when he says that all the evil actions which any man performs come **out of the mouth of man**, he employs a synecdoche; for he says so by way of allusion to the subject in hand, and conveys this instruction, that we do not draw uncleanness into our mouth along with **meat and drink**, but that every kind of defilement proceeds from ourselves.

persons who bequeath the inheritance of their children to Churches or religious uses; either through terror of conscience, thus striving to purchase the kingdom of glory; or through the persuasion of interested hireling priests. It was in this way that, in the days of popish influence, the principal lands in the nation had fallen into the hands of the Church.

It is sacrilege to dedicate that to God which is taken away from the necessities of our parents and children; and the good that this pretends to will doubtless be found in the catalogue of that unnatural man's crimes, in the judgment of the great day, who has thus deprived his own family of its due. To assist our poor relatives, is our first duty; and this is a work infinitely preferable to all pious legacies and endowments.

7. Hypocrites, well did Isaiah prophesy of you – In every place where the proper names of the Old Testament occur, in the New, the same mode of orthography should be followed: I therefore write Isaiah with the Hebrew, not Esaias, with the Greek. This prophecy is found Isaiah 29: 13. Our blessed Lord unmasks these hypocrites; and we may observe that, when a hypocrite is found out, he should be exposed to all; this may lead to his salvation: if he be permitted to retain his falsely acquired character, how can he escape perdition!

8. Their heart is far from me – The true worship of God consists in the union of the heart to him – where this exists not, a particle of the spirit of devotion cannot be found.

9. In vain they do worship me, etc. – By the traditions of the elders, not only the word of God was perverted, but his worship also was greatly corrupted. But the Jews were not the only people who have acted thus: whole Christian Churches, as well as sects and parties, have acted in the same way. Men must not mould the worship of God according to their fancy – it is not what they think will do – is proper, innocent, etc., but what God himself has prescribed, that he will acknowledge as his worship. However sincere a man may be in a worship of his own invention, or of man's

commandment, yet it profits him nothing. Christ himself says it is in vain. To condemn such, may appear to some illiberal; but whatever may be said in behalf of sincere heathens, and others who have not had the advantages of Divine Revelation, there is no excuse for the man who has the BIBLE before him.

MATTHEW 15: 10–20; MARK 7: 14–23

Matthew 15: 10–20

10. Hear and understand – A most important command. Hear – make it a point of conscience to attend to the ministry of the word. Understand – be not satisfied with attending places of public worship merely; see that the teaching be of God, and that you lay it to heart.

11. Not that which goeth into the mouth defileth – This is an answer to the carping question of the Pharisees, mentioned Matthew 15: 2, Why do thy disciples eat with unwashed hands? To which our Lord here replies, That what goes into the mouth defiles not the man; i.e. that if, in eating with unwashed hands, any particles of dust, etc., cleaving to the hands, might happen to be taken into the mouth with the food, this did not defile, did not constitute a man a sinner; for it is on this alone the question hinges: thy disciples eat with unwashed hands; therefore they are sinners; for they transgress the tradition of the elders, i.e. the oral law, which they considered equal in authority to the written law; and, indeed, often preferred the former to the latter, so as to make it of none effect, totally to destroy its nature and design.

That which cometh out of the mouth – That is, what springs from a corrupt unregenerate heart – a perverse will and impure passions – these defile, i.e. make him a sinner.

12. The Pharisees were offended – None so liable to take offense as formalists and hypocrites, when you attempt to take away the false props from the one, and question the sincerity of the other. Besides, a Pharisee must never be suspected of ignorance, for they are the men, and wisdom must die with them!

8 For laying aside the commandment of God, ye hold the tradition of men, as the washing of pots and cups: and many other such like things ye do.

9 And he said unto them, Full well ye reject the commandment of God, that ye may keep your own tradition.

10 For Moses said, Honor thy father and thy mother; and, Whoso curseth father or mother, let him die the death:

11 But ye say, If a man shall say to his father or mother, It is Corban, that is to say, a gift, by whatsoever thou mightest be profited by me; he shall be free.

12 And ye suffer him no more to do ought for his father or his mother;

13 Making the word of God of none effect through your tradition, which ye have delivered: and many such like things do ye.

MATTHEW 15: 10–20; MARK 7: 14–23

Matthew 15: 10–20

10 And he called the multitude, and said unto them, Hear, and understand:

11 Not that which goeth into the mouth defileth a man; but that which cometh out of the mouth, this defileth a man.

12 Then came his disciples, and said unto him, Knowest thou that the Pharisees were offended, after they heard this saying?

13 But he answered and said, Every plant, which my heavenly Father hath not planted, shall be rooted up.

14 Let them alone: they be blind leaders of the blind. And if the blind lead the blind, both shall fall into the ditch.

15 Then answered Peter and said unto him, Declare unto us this parable.

16 And Jesus said, Are ye also yet without understanding?

17 Do not ye yet understand, that whatsoever entereth in at the mouth goeth into the belly, and is cast out into the draught?

18 But those things which proceed out of the mouth come forth from the heart; and they defile the man.

19 For out of the heart proceed evil thoughts, murders, adulteries, fornications, thefts, false witness, blasphemies:

20 These are the things which defile

Knowest thou that the Pharisees were offended? As the scribes were presumptuous and rebellious, Christ did not take great pains to pacify them, but satisfied himself with repelling their hypocrisy and pride. The offense which they had formerly taken up was doubled, when they perceived that – not through oversight, but seemingly on purpose – Christ despised their washings as trifles. Now when Christ did not hesitate to inflame still more, by keen provocation, wicked and malicious people, let us learn from his example, that we ought not to be exceedingly solicitous to please every one by what we say and do. His disciples, however – as is usually the case with ignorant and unlearned people – no sooner perceive the result to be unfavorable, than they conclude that Christ's reply had been unseasonable and improper. For the object of their advice was, to persuade Christ to soothe the rage of the Pharisees by softening the harsh expression which he had employed.

It almost always happens with weak people, that they form an unfavorable judgment about a doctrine, as soon as they find that it is regarded with doubt or meets with opposition. And certainly it were to be wished, that it should give no offense, but receive the calm approbation of all; but, as the minds of many are blinded, and even their hearts are kindled into rage, by Satan, and as many souls are held under the benumbing influence of brutal stupidity, it is impossible that all should relish the true doctrine of salvation. Above all, we ought not to be surprised to behold the rage of those who inwardly nourish the venom of malice and obstinacy. Yet we ought to take care that, so far as may be in our power, our manner of teaching shall give no offense; but it would be the height of madness to think of exercising greater moderation than we have been taught to do by our heavenly Master. We see how his discourse was made an occasion of offense by wicked and obstinate men; and we see at the same time, how that kind of offense which arose from malignity was treated by him with contempt.

MATTHEW 15: 21–28; MARK 7: 24–30

In this miracle we are informed in what manner the grace of Christ began to flow to the Gentiles; for, though the full time was not yet come when Christ would make himself known to the whole world, yet he intended to give some early manifestations of the common mercy which was at length offered indiscriminately to Jews and Gentiles after his resurrection. A remarkable picture of faith is presented to us in the woman of Canaan, for the purpose of instructing us by means of comparison, that the Jews were justly deprived of the promised redemption, since their impiety was so shameful.

14. Let them alone – These words have been sadly misunderstood. Some have quoted them to prove that blind and deceitful teachers should not be pointed out to the people, nor the people warned against them; and that men should abide in the communion of a corrupt Church, because that Church had once been the Church of God, and in it they had been brought up; and to prove this they bring Scripture, for, in our present translation, the words are rendered, let them alone: but the whole connection of the place evidently proves that our blessed Lord meant, give them up, have no kind of religious connection with them, and the strong reason for which he immediately adds, because they are blind leaders. This passage does not at all mean that blind leaders should not be pointed out to the people, that they may avoid being deceived by them; for this our Lord does frequently, and warns his disciples, and the people in general, against all such false teachers as the scribes and Pharisees were; and though he bids men do that they heard those say, while they sat in the chair of Moses, yet he certainly meant no more than that they should be observant of the moral law when read to them out of the sacred book: yet neither does he tell them to do all these false teachers said; for he testifies in Matthew 15: 6, that they had put such false glosses on the law, that, if followed, would endanger the salvation of their souls.

Probably the words may be understood as a sort of proverbial expression for – Don't mind them: pay no regard to them. – "They are altogether unworthy of notice."

And if the blind lead the blind – This was so self-evident a case that an apter parallel could not be found – if the blind lead the blind, both must fall into the ditch. Alas, for the blind teachers, who not only destroy their own souls, but those also of their flocks! Like priest, like people. If the minister be ignorant, he cannot teach what he does not know; and the people cannot become wise unto salvation under such a ministry – he is ignorant and wicked, and they are profligate. They who even wish such God speed; are partakers of their evil deeds. But shall not the poor deceived people escape? No: both shall fall into the pit of perdition together; for they should have searched the Scriptures, and not trusted to the ignorant sayings of corrupt men, no matter of what sect or party. He who has the Bible in his hand, or within his reach, and can read it, has no excuse.

15. Declare unto us this parable – Is it not strange to hear the disciples asking for the explanation of such a parable as this! The true knowledge of the spirit of the Gospel is a thing more uncommon than we imagine, among the generality of Christians, and even of the learned.

16. Are ye also yet without understanding? – Are ye still void of understanding?

19. Out of the heart – In the heart of an unregenerate man, the principles and seeds of all sin are found. And iniquity is always conceived in the heart before it be spoken or acted. Is there any hope that a man can abstain from outward sin till his heart, that abominable fountain of corruption, be thoroughly cleansed? I trow not.

Evil thoughts – wicked dialogues – for in all evil surmisings the heart holds a conversation, or dialogue, with itself. Envy and murder are nearly allied: the former has often led to the latter.

20. These – defile a man – Our Lord's argument is very plain. What goes into the mouth descends into the stomach and other intestines; – part is retained for the nourishment of the body, and part is ejected, as being improper to afford nourishment. Nothing of this kind defiles the soul, because it does not enter into it; but the evil principles that are in it, producing evil thoughts, murders, etc., these defile the soul, because they have their seat and operation in it.

MATTHEW 15: 21–28; MARK 7: 24–30

Matthew 15: 21–28

22. A woman of Canaan – Matthew gives her this name because of the people from whom

a man: but to eat with unwashen hands defileth not a man.

Mark 7: 14–23

14 And when he had called all the people unto him, he said unto them, Hearken unto me every one of you, and understand:

15 There is nothing from without a man, that entering into him can defile him: but the things which come out of him, those are they that defile the man.

16 If any man have ears to hear, let him hear.

17 And when he was entered into the house from the people, his disciples asked him concerning the parable.

18 And he saith unto them, Are ye so without understanding also? Do ye not perceive, that whatsoever thing from without entereth into the man, it cannot defile him;

19 Because it entereth not into his heart, but into the belly, and goeth out into the draught, purging all meats?

20 And he said, That which cometh out of the man, that defileth the man.

21 For from within, out of the heart of men, proceed evil thoughts, adulteries, fornications, murders,

22 Thefts, covetousness, wickedness, deceit, lasciviousness, an evil eye, blasphemy, pride, foolishness:

23 All these evil things come from within, and defile the man.

MATTHEW 15: 21–28; MARK 7: 24–30

Matthew 15: 21–28

21 Then Jesus went thence, and departed into the coasts of Tyre and Sidon.

22 And, behold, a woman of Canaan came out of the same coasts, and cried unto him, saying, Have mercy on me, O Lord, thou Son of David; my daughter is grievously vexed with a devil.

23 But he answered her not a word. And his disciples came and besought him, saying, Send her away; for she crieth after us.

24 But he answered and said, I am not sent but unto the lost sheep of the house of Israel.

25 Then came she and worshipped him, saying, Lord, help me.

Mark 7: 24. He wished that no man should know it

We must attend to this circumstance, which is mentioned by Mark, that when Christ came to that place, he did not erect his banner, but endeavored to remain concealed for a time, in that obscure situation, like a private individual. Mark speaks according to the ordinary perception of the flesh; for, although Christ by his divine Spirit foresaw what would happen, yet so far as he was the minister and ambassador of the Father, he kept himself, as his human nature might have led us to expect, within the limits of that calling which God had given him; and in that respect it is said that what he wished, as man, he was unable to accomplish. Meanwhile, this occurrence, as I have said, tends powerfully to condemn the Jews, who – though they boasted that they were the heirs of the covenant of the Lord, his peculiar people, and a royal priesthood – were blind and deaf when Christ, with a loud voice and with the addition of miracles, offered to them the promised redemption; while this woman, who had no relationship with the children of Abraham, and to whom, at first sight, the covenant did not at all belong, came of her own accord to Christ, without having heard his voice or seen his miracles.

Matthew 15: 22. Have compassion on me, O Lord

Though this woman was an alien, and did not belong to the Lord's flock, yet she had acquired some taste of piety; for, without some knowledge of the promises, she would not have called Christ the **Son of David**. The Jews indeed had almost entirely departed, or at least had greatly turned aside, from the pure and sound doctrine of the Gospel; but a report of the promised redemption was extensively prevalent. As the restoration of the Church depended on the reign of David, whenever they spoke of the Messiah, it was customary for them to employ the name, **Son of David**; and indeed this confession was heard from the lips of all. But when the true faith had died out amongst them, it was an amazing and incredible display of the goodness of God that the sweet savor of the promises reached the neighboring nations. Though this woman had not been regularly educated by any teacher, yet her faith in Christ was not a notion adopted by her at random, but was formed out of the law and the prophets. It was therefore not less absurd than wicked in that dog, Servetus, to abuse this example for the purpose of proving that faith may exist without promises. I do not deny that, in this sense, there may sometimes be a sort of implicit faith, that is, a faith which is not accompanied by a full and distinct knowledge of sound doctrine; provided we also hold that faith always springs from the word of God, and takes its origin from true principles, and therefore is always found in connection with some light of knowledge.

she sprung – the descendants of Canaan, Judges 1: 31, 32; but Mark calls her a Syrophenician, because of the country where she dwelt.

The state of this woman is a proper emblem of the state of a sinner, deeply conscious of the misery of his soul.

Have mercy on me, etc. – How proper is this prayer for a penitent! There are many excellencies contained in it;

1. It is short;
2. humble;
3. full of faith;
4. fervent;
5. modest;
6. respectful;
7. rational;
8. relying only on the mercy of God;
9. persevering.

Can one who sees himself a slave of the devil, beg with too much earnestness to be delivered from his thraldom?

Son of David – An essential character of the true Messiah.

23. He answered her not a word – Seemed to take time to consider her request, and to give her the opportunity of exercising her faith, and manifesting her fervor.

24. I am not sent but unto the lost sheep – By the Divine appointment, I am come to preach the Gospel to the Jews only. There are certain preachers who should learn a lesson of important instruction from this part of our Lord's conduct. As soon as they hear of a lost sheep being found by other ministers, they give all diligence to get that one into their fold: but display little earnestness in seeking in the wilderness for those that are lost. This conduct, perhaps, proceeds from a consciousness of their inability to perform the work of an evangelist; and leads them to sit down in the labors of others, rather than submit to the reproach of presiding over empty chapels. Such persons should either dig or beg immediately, as they are a reproach to the pastoral office; for, not being sent of God, they cannot profit the people.

The wilderness of this world is sufficiently wide and uncultivated. Sinners abound every where; and there is ample room for all truly religious people, who have zeal for God, and love for their perishing follow creatures, to put forth all their strength, employ all their time, and exercise all their talents, in proclaiming the Gospel of God; not only to the lost sheep of the house of Israel, but to a lost WORLD. Nor can such exertions be unsuccessful. There the pure truth of God is preached, many will be converted. Where that truth is preached, though with a mixture of error, some will be converted, for God will bless his own truth. But where nothing but false doctrine is preached, no soul is converted: for God will never sanction error by a miracle of his mercy.

25. Lord, help me – Let me also share in the deliverance afforded to Israel.

26. The children's bread – The salvation provided for the Jews, who were termed the children of the kingdom. And cast it to the little dogs – to the curs; such the Gentiles were reputed by the Jewish people, and our Lord uses that form of speech which was common among his countrymen. What terrible repulses! and yet she still perseveres!

27. Truth, Lord – Yes, Lord. This appears to be not so much an assent, as a bold reply to our Lord's reason for apparently rejecting her suit.

The little dogs share with the children, for they eat the crumbs which fall from their masters' table. I do not desire what is provided for these highly favored children, only what they leave: a single exertion of thy almighty power, in the healing of my afflicted daughter, is all that I wish for; and this the highly favored Jews can well spare, without lessening the provision made for themselves. Is not this the sense of this noble woman's reply?

28. O woman, great is thy faith – The hinderances thrown in this woman's way only tended to increase her faith. Her faith resembles a river, which becomes enlarged by the dykes opposed to it, till at last it sweeps them entirely away with it.

Her daughter was made whole – Persever-

26 But he answered and said, It is not meet to take the children's bread, and to cast it to dogs.

27 And she said, Truth, Lord: yet the dogs eat of the crumbs which fall from their masters' table.

28 Then Jesus answered and said unto her, O woman, great is thy faith: be it unto thee even as thou wilt. And her daughter was made whole from that very hour.

Mark 7: 24–30

24 And from thence he arose, and went into the borders of Tyre and Sidon, and entered into an house, and would have no man know it: but he could not be hid.

25 For a certain woman, whose young daughter had an unclean spirit, heard of him, and came and fell at his feet:

26 The woman was a Greek, a Syrophenician by nation; and she besought him that he would cast forth the devil out of her daughter.

27 But Jesus said unto her, Let the children first be filled: for it is not meet to take the children's bread, and to cast it unto the dogs.

28 And she answered and said unto him, Yes, Lord: yet the dogs under the table eat of the children's crumbs.

29 And he said unto her, For this saying go thy way; the devil is gone out of thy daughter.

30 And when she was come to her house, she found the devil gone out, and her daughter laid upon the bed.

MATTHEW 15: 29–39; MARK 7: 31–37; 8: 1–10

Matthew 15: 29–39

29 And Jesus departed from thence, and came nigh unto the sea of Galilee; and went up into a mountain, and sat down there.

30 And great multitudes came unto him, having with them those that were lame, blind, dumb, maimed, and many others, and cast them down at Jesus' feet; and he healed them:

31 Insomuch that the multitude wondered, when they saw the dumb to speak, the maimed to be whole, the lame to walk, and the blind to see: and they glorified the God of Israel.

MATTHEW 15: 29–39; MARK 7: 31–37, 8: 1–10

Mark 7: 33. And when he had taken him aside from the multitude

This was done, partly to afford to those who were ignorant, and not yet sufficiently qualified for becoming witnesses, an opportunity of perceiving at a distance the glory of his Divine nature, and partly that he might have a better opportunity of pouring out earnest prayer. When he **looked up to heaven and sighed**, it was an expression of strong feeling; and this enables us to perceive the vehemence of his love towards men, for whose miseries he feels so much compassion. Nor can it be doubted, that by conveying the spittle from his own mouth to the mouth of another, and by **putting his fingers into his ears**, he intended to manifest and express the same feeling of kindness. Yet that he has supreme power to remove all our defects, and restore us to health, is proclaimed by him when he simply orders the tongue and ears **to be opened**; for it was not without a good reason that Mark inserted that Chaldaic word, (*ephphatha*) Ephphatha, be opened, but to testify the divine power of Christ. Among other fooleries with which baptism has been debased by foolish men, the ceremony used by our Lord is turned into a piece of buffoonery; and this instance shows us that there is no end to licentiousness, when men wantonly change at their own pleasure the mysteries of God.

36. Then he enjoined them not to tell it to any person

Many commentators torture these injunctions to an opposite meaning, as if Christ had purposely excited them to spread abroad the fame of the miracle; but I prefer a more natural interpretation which I have formerly stated, that Christ only intended to delay the publication of it till a more proper and convenient time. I have no doubt, therefore, that their zeal was unseasonable, when, though enjoined to be silent, they were in haste to speak. We need not wonder that men unaccustomed to the doctrine of Christ are carried away by immoderate zeal, when it is not called for. Yet what they unwisely attempted to do, was made by Christ to promote his own glory; for not only was the miracle made known, but the whole of that district, in despising the Author of heavenly gifts, was rendered inexcusable.

37. He hath done all things well

Matthew, after collecting many miracles, concludes by saying that **the multitudes wondered, and glorified the God of Israel**; that is, because God, taking unusual methods of illustrating his power, had called up the remembrance of his covenant. But the words of Mark contain perhaps an implied contrast; for the reports concerning Christ

ing faith and prayer are next to omnipotent. No person can thus pray and believe, without receiving all his soul requires. This is one of the finest lessons in the book of God for a penitent, or for a discouraged believer. Look to Jesus! As sure as God is in heaven, so surely will he hear and answer thee to the eternal salvation of thy soul! Be not discouraged at a little delay: when thou art properly prepared to receive the blessing, then thou shalt have it. Look up; thy salvation is at hand. Jesus admires this faith, to the end that we may admire and imitate it, and may reap the same fruits and advantages from it.

MATTHEW 15: 29–39; MARK 7: 31–37; 8: 1–10

Matthew 15: 29–39

29. Went up into a mountain – THE mountain. "Meaning," says Wakefield, "some particular mountain which he was accustomed to frequent; for, whenever it is spoken of at a time when Jesus is in Galilee, it is always discriminated by the article. Compare Matthew 4: 18, with Matthew 5: 1; and Matthew 13: 54, with Matthew 14: 23; and Matthew 28: 16. I suppose it was mount Tabor."

31. The multitude wondered – And well they might, when they had such proofs of the miraculous power and love of God before their eyes. Blessed be God! the same miracles are continued in their spiritual reference. All the disorders of the soul are still cured by the power of Jesus.

32. I have compassion, etc. – See a similar transaction explained, Matthew 14: 14–22.

33. Whence should we have so much bread in the wilderness, etc. – Human foresight, even in the followers of Christ, is very short. In a thousand instances, if we supply not its deficiency by faith, we shall be always embarrassed, and often miserable. This world is a desert, where nothing can be found to satisfy the soul of man, but the salvation which Christ has procured.

37. They did all eat, and were filled – they were satisfied. The husks of worldly pleasures may fill the man, but cannot satisfy the soul. A man may eat, and not be satisfied: it is the interest therefore of every follower of Christ to follow him till he be fed, and to feed on him till he be satisfied.

38. Four thousand – Let the poor learn from these miracles to trust in God for support. Whatever his ordinary providence denies, his miraculous power will supply.

39. He sent away the multitude – But not before he had instructed their souls, and fed and healed their bodies.

The coasts of Magdala – In the parallel place, Mark 8: 10, this place is called Dalmanutha. Either Magdala was formed by a transposition of letters from Dalman, to which the Syriac termination atha had been added, or the one of these names refers to the country, and the other to a town in that neighborhood. Jesus went into the country, and proceeded till he came to the chief town or village in that district. Whitby says, "Magdala was a city and territory beyond Jordan, on the banks of Gadara. It readied to the bridge above Jordan, which joined it to the other side of Galilee, and contained within its precincts Dalmanutha."

In this chapter a number of interesting and instructive particulars are contained.

1. We see the extreme superstition, envy, and incurable ill nature of the Jews. While totally lost to a proper sense of the spirituality of God's law, they are ceremonious in the extreme. They will not eat without washing their hands, because this would be a transgression of one of the traditions of their elders; but they can harbor the worst temper and passions, and thus break the law of God! The word of man weighs more with them than the testimony of Jehovah; and yet they pretend the highest respect for their God and sacred things, and will let their parents perish for lack of the necessaries of life, that they may have goods to vow to the service of the sanctuary! Pride and envy blind the hearts of men, and cause them often to act not only the most wicked, but the most ridiculous, parts. He who

32 Then Jesus called his disciples unto him, and said, I have compassion on the multitude, because they continue with me now three days, and have nothing to eat: and I will not send them away fasting, lest they faint in the way.

33 And his disciples say unto him, Whence should we have so much bread in the wilderness, as to fill so great a multitude?

34 And Jesus saith unto them, How many loaves have ye? And they said, Seven, and a few little fishes.

35 And he commanded the multitude to sit down on the ground.

36 And he took the seven loaves and the fishes, and gave thanks, and brake them, and gave to his disciples, and the disciples to the multitude.

37 And they did all eat, and were filled: and they took up of the broken meat that was left seven baskets full.

38 And they that did eat were four thousand men, beside women and children.

39 And he sent away the multitude, and took ship, and came into the coasts of Magdala,

Mark 7: 31–37

31 And again, departing from the coasts of Tyre and Sidon, he came unto the sea of Galilee, through the midst of the coasts of Decapolis.

32 And they bring unto him one that was deaf, and had an impediment in his speech; and they beseech him to put his hand upon him.

33 And he took him aside from the multitude, and put his fingers into his ears, and he spit, and touched his tongue;

34 And looking up to heaven, he sighed, and saith unto him, Ephphatha, that is, Be opened.

35 And straightway his ears were opened, and the string of his tongue was loosed, and he spake plain.

36 And he charged them that they should tell no man: but the more he charged them, so much the more a great deal they published it;

37 And were beyond measure astonished, saying, He hath done all things well: he maketh both the deaf to hear, and the dumb to speak.

were various, and the word multitude or crowd (*ochlos*) may be intended to mean that it was only wicked and malicious people who slandered his actions, since all that he did was so far from exposing him to calumny that it deserved the highest praise. But we know, and it is what nature teaches us, that nothing is more unjust than to make the bestowal of favors an occasion of envy and ill-will.

Matthew 15: 32. I have compassion on the multitude

As the blessing of God can make one loaf suffice as well as twenty for satisfying a great multitude, so, if that be wanting, a hundred loaves will not be a sufficient meal for ten men; for when the staff of bread is broken (Leviticus 26: 26), though the flour should come in full weight from the mill, and the bread from the oven, it will serve no purpose to stuff the belly. The **three days' fasting,** of which Christ speaks, must not be understood to mean that they had eaten nothing for three days; but that in desert places they had few conveniences, and must have wanted their ordinary food. Besides, in those warm countries, hunger is less keen than in our thick and cold atmosphere; and, therefore, we need not wonder that they should abstain longer from food.

33. Whence shall we obtain so many loaves in a solitary place?

The disciples manifest excessive stupidity in not remembering, at least, that earlier proof of the power and grace of Christ, which they might have applied to the case in hand. As if they had never seen any thing of the same sort, they forget to apply to him for relief. There is not a day on which a similar indifference does not steal upon us; and we ought to be the more careful not to allow our minds to be drawn away from the contemplation of divine benefits, that the experience of the past may lead us to expect for the future the same assistance which God has already on one or more occasions bestowed upon us.

MATTHEW 16: 1–4; MARK 8: 11–13; LUKE 12: 54–57

Matthew 16: 1. And the Pharisees came

Mark says that they began to dispute, from which we may conjecture that, when they had been vanquished in argument, this was their last resource; as obstinate men, whenever they are reduced to extremities, to avoid being compelled to yield to the truth, are accustomed to introduce something which is foreign to the subject. Though the nature of the dispute is not expressed, yet I think it probable that they debated about the calling of Christ, why he ventured to make any innovation, and why he made such lofty pretensions, as if by his coming he had fully restored the kingdom of God. Having nothing farther to object against

takes the book of God for the rule of his faith and practice can never go astray: but to the mazes and perplexities produced by the traditions of elders, human creeds, and confessions of faith, there is no end. These evils existed in the Christian as well as in the Jewish Church; but the Reformation, thank God! has liberated us from this endless system of uncertainty and absurdity, and the Sun of righteousness shines now unclouded! The plantation, which God did not plant, in the course of his judgments, he has now swept nearly away from the face of the earth! Babylon is fallen!

2. We wonder at the dullness of the disciples, when we find that they did not fully understand our Lord's meaning, in the very obvious parable about the blind leading the blind. But should we not be equally struck with their prying, inquisitive temper? They did not understand, but they could not rest till they did. They knew that their Lord could say nothing that had not the most important meaning in it: this meaning, in the preceding parable, they had not apprehended, and therefore they wished to have it farther explained by himself. Do we imitate their docility and eagerness to comprehend the truth of God? Christ presses every occurrence into a means of instruction. The dullness of the disciples in the present case, has been the means of affording us the fullest instruction on a point of the utmost importance – the state of a sinful heart, and how the thoughts and passions conceived in it defile and pollute it; and how necessary it is to have the fountain purified, that it may cease to send forth those streams of death.

3. The case of the Canaanitish woman is, in itself, a thousand sermons. Her faith – her prayers – her perseverance – her success – the honor she received from her Lord, etc., etc. How instructively – how powerfully do these speak and plead! What a profusion of light does this single case throw upon the manner in which Christ sometimes exercises the faith and patience of his followers! They that seek shall find, is the great lesson inculcated in this short history: God is ever the same. Reader, follow on after God – cry, pray, plead – all in Him is for thee! – Thou canst not perish, if

thou continuest to believe and pray. The Lord will help THEE.

MATTHEW 16: 1–4; MARK 8: 11–13; LUKE 12: 54–57

Matthew 16: 1–4

1. The Pharisees also with the Sadducees – The PHARISEES were the most considerable sect among the Jews, for they had not only the scribes, and all the learned men of the law of their party, but they also drew after them the bulk of the people. When this sect arose is uncertain. Josephus speaks of them as existing about 144 years before the Christian era. They had their appellation of Pharisees, from the word meaning to separate, and were probably, in their rise, the most holy people among the Jews, having separated themselves from the national corruption, with a design to restore and practice the pure worship of the most High. That they were greatly degenerated in our Lord's time is sufficiently evident; but still we may learn, from their external purity and exactness, that their principles in the beginning were holy. Our Lord testifies that they had cleansed the outside of the cup and the platter, but within they were full of abomination. They still kept up the outward regulations of the institution, but they had utterly lost its spirit; and hypocrisy was the only substitute now in their power for that spirit of piety which I suppose, and not unreasonably, characterized the origin of this sect.

The SADDUCEES had their origin and name from one Sadoc, a disciple of Antigonus of Socho, president of the Sanhedrin, and teacher of the law in one of the great divinity schools in Jerusalem, about 264 years before the incarnation.

This Antigonus having often in his lectures informed his scholars, that they should not serve God through expectation of a reward, but through love and filial reverence only, Sadoc inferred from this teaching that there were neither rewards nor punishments after this life, and, by consequence, that there was no resurrection of the dead, nor angel, nor

Mark 8: 1–10

1 In those days the multitude being very great, and having nothing to eat, Jesus called his disciples unto him, and saith unto them,

2 I have compassion on the multitude, because they have now been with me three days, and have nothing to eat:

3 And if I send them away fasting to their own houses, they will faint by the way: for divers of them came from far.

4 And his disciples answered him, From whence can a man satisfy these men with bread here in the wilderness?

5 And he asked them, How many loaves have ye? And they said, Seven.

6 And he commanded the people to sit down on the ground: and he took the seven loaves, and gave thanks, and brake, and gave to his disciples to set before them; and they did set them before the people.

7 And they had a few small fishes: and he blessed, and commanded to set them also before them.

8 So they did eat, and were filled: and they took up of the broken meat that was left seven baskets.

9 And they that had eaten were about four thousand: and he sent them away.

10 And straightway he entered into a ship with his disciples, and came into the parts of Dalmanutha.

MATTHEW 16: 1–4; MARK 8: 11–13; LUKE 12: 54–57

Matthew 16: 1–4

1 The Pharisees also with the Sadducees came, and tempting desired him that he would shew them a sign from heaven.

2 He answered and said unto them, When it is evening, ye say, It will be fair weather: for the sky is red.

3 And in the morning, It will be foul weather to day: for the sky is red and lowring. O ye hypocrites, ye can discern the face of the sky; but can ye not discern the signs of the times?

4 A wicked and adulterous generation seeketh after a sign; and there shall no sign be given unto it, but the sign of the prophet Jonas. And he left them, and departed.

his doctrine, they demand that he **shall give them a sign from heaven**.

But it is certain that a hundred signs would have no greater effect than the testimonies of Scripture. Besides, many miracles already performed had placed before their eyes the power of Christ, and had almost enabled them to touch it with their hands. Signs, by which Christ made himself familiarly known, are despised by them; and how much less will they derive advantage from a distant and obscure sign? Thus the Papists of our own day, as if the doctrine of the Gospel had not yet been proved, demand that it be ascertained by means of new miracles.

The Pharisees, together with the Sadducees

It deserves our attention that, though the Sadducees and the Pharisees looked upon each other as enemies, and not only cherished bitter hatred, but were continually engaged in hostilities, yet they enter into a mutual league against Christ. In like manner, though ungodly men quarrel among themselves, their internal broils never prevent them from conspiring against God, and entering into a compact for joining their hands in persecuting the truth.

Tempting

By this word the Evangelists mean that it was not with honest intentions, nor from a desire of instruction, but by cunning and deceit, that they demanded what they thought that Christ would refuse, or at least what they imagined was not in his power. Regarding him as utterly mean and despicable, they had no other design than to expose his weakness, and to destroy all the applause which he had hitherto obtained among the people. In this manner unbelievers are said to tempt God, when they murmur at being denied what their fancy prompted them to ask, and charge God with want of power.

3. Hypocrites, you can judge

He calls them hypocrites, because they pretend to ask that which, if it were exhibited to them, they are resolved not to observe. The same reproof applies nearly to the whole world; for men direct their ingenuity, and apply their senses, to immediate advantage; and therefore there is scarcely any man who is not sufficiently well qualified in this respect, or at least who is not tolerably acquainted with the means of gaining his object. How comes it then that we feel no concern about the signs by which God invites us to himself? Is it not because every man gives himself up to willing indifference, and extinguishes the light which is offered to him?

MATTHEW 16: 5–12; MARK 8: 14–21; LUKE 12: 1

Matthew 16: 5. And when his disciples came

Here Christ takes occasion from the circumstance that

spirit, in the invisible world; and that man is to be rewarded or punished here for the good or evil he does.

They received only the five books of Moses, and rejected all unwritten traditions.

In Matthew 22: 16, we shall meet with a third sect, called HERODIANS, of whom a few words may be spoken here, It is allowed on all hands that these did not exist before the time of Herod the Great, who died only three years after the incarnation of our Lord. What the opinions of these were is not agreed among the learned. Many of the primitive fathers believed that their distinguishing doctrine was, that they held Herod to be the Messiah; but it is not likely that such an opinion could prevail in our Savior's time, thirty years after Herod's death, when not one characteristic of Messiahship had appeared in him during his life. Others suppose that they were Herod's courtiers, who flattered the passions of their master, and, being endowed with a convenient conscience, changed with the times; but, as Herod was now dead upwards of thirty years, such a sect could not exist in reference to him; and yet all allow that they derived their origin from Herod the Great.

Our Lord says, Mark 8: 15, that they had the leaven of Herod, i.e. a bad doctrine, which they received from him. What this was may be easily discovered:

1. Herod subjected himself and his people to the dominion of the Romans, in opposition to that law, Deuteronomy 17: 15, Thou shalt not set a king over thee – which is not thy brother, i.e. one out of the twelve tribes.

2. He built temples, sat up images, and joined in heathenish worship, though he professed the Jewish religion; and this was in opposition to all the law and the prophets.

From this we may learn that the Herodians were such as, first, held it lawful to transfer the Divine government to a heathen ruler; and, secondly, to conform occasionally to heathenish rites in their religious worship. In short, they appear to have been persons who trimmed between God and the world – who endeavored to reconcile his service with that

of mammon – and who were religious just as far as it tended to secure their secular interests.

Show them a sign – These sects, however opposed among themselves, most cordially unite in their opposition to Christ and his truth. That the kingdom of Satan may not fall, all his subjects must fight against the doctrine and maxims of the kingdom of Christ.

Tempting – him – Feigning a desire to have his doctrine fully proved to them, that they might credit it, and become his disciples; but having no other design than to betray and ruin him.

2. When it is evening – There are certain signs of fair and foul weather, which ye are in the constant habit of observing, and which do not fail. – The signs of the times: the doctrine which I preach, and the miracles which I work among you, are as sure signs that the day-spring from on high has visited you for your salvation; but if ye refute to hear, and continue in darkness, the red and gloomy cloud of vindictive justice shall pour out such a storm of wrath upon you as shalt sweep you from the face of the earth.

3. The sky is red and lowering – The signs of fair and foul weather were observed in a similar manner among the Romans, and indeed among most other people.

4. Wicked and adulterous generation – The Jewish people are represented in the Sacred Writings as married to the Most High; but, like a disloyal wife, forsaking their true husband, and uniting themselves to Satan and sin. Seeketh after a sign, seeketh sign upon sign, or, still another sign. Our blessed Lord had already wrought miracles sufficient to demonstrate both his Divine mission and his divinity; only one was farther necessary to take away the scandal of his cross and death, to fulfill the Scriptures, and to establish the Christian religion; and that was, his resurrection from the dead, which, he here states, was typified in the case of Jonah.

Mark 8: 11–13

11 And the Pharisees came forth, and began to question with him, seeking of him a sign from heaven, tempting him.

12 And he sighed deeply in his spirit, and saith, Why doth this generation seek after a sign? verily I say unto you, There shall no sign be given unto this generation.

13 And he left them, and entering into the ship again departed to the other side.

Luke 12: 54–57

54 And he said also to the people, When ye see a cloud rise out of the west, straightway ye say, There cometh a shower; and so it is.

55 And when ye see the south wind blow, ye say, There will be heat; and it cometh to pass.

56 Ye hypocrites, ye can discern the face of the sky and of the earth; but how is it that ye do not discern this time?

57 Yea, and why even of yourselves judge ye not what is right?

MATTHEW 16: 5–12; MARK 8: 14–21; LUKE 12: 1

Matthew 16: 5–12

5 And when his disciples were come to the other side, they had forgotten to take bread.

6 Then Jesus said unto them, Take heed and beware of the leaven of the Pharisees and of the Sadducees.

7 And they reasoned among themselves, saying, It is because we have taken no bread.

8 Which when Jesus perceived, he said unto them, O ye of little faith, why reason ye among yourselves, because ye have brought no bread?

9 Do ye not yet understand, neither remember the five loaves of the five thousand, and how many baskets ye took up?

10 Neither the seven loaves of the four thousand, and how many baskets ye took up?

11 How is it that ye do not understand that I spake it not to you concerning bread, that ye should beware of the leaven of the Pharisees and of the Sadducees?

12 Then understood they how that he bade them not beware of the leaven of

had just occurred to exhort his disciples to beware of every abuse that makes an inroad on sincere piety. The Pharisees had come a little before; the Sadducees joined them; and apart from them stood Herod, a very wicked man, and an opponent and corrupter of sound doctrine. In the midst of these dangers it was very necessary to warn his disciples to be on their guard; for, since the human mind has a natural inclination towards vanity and errors, when we are surrounded by wicked inventions, spurious doctrines, and other plagues of the same sort, nothing is more easy than to depart from the true and simple purity of the word of God; and if we once become entangled in these things, it will never be possible for the true religion to hold an entire sway over us. But to make the matter more clear, let us examine closely the words of Christ.

Beware of the leaven of the Pharisees. Along with the **Pharisees** Matthew mentions **the Sadducees.** Instead of the latter, Mark speaks of **Herod.** Luke takes no notice of any but the **Pharisees,** (though it is not absolutely certain that it is the same discourse of Christ which Luke relates,) and explains **the leaven to be hypocrisy.** In short, he glances briefly at this sentence, as if there were no ambiguity in the words.

Now the metaphor of leaven, which is here applied to false doctrine, might have been employed, at another time, to denote the hypocrisy of life and conduct, or the same words might even have been repeated a second time. But there is no absurdity in saying, that those circumstances which are more copiously detailed by the other two Evangelists, in the order in which they took place, are slightly noticed by Luke in a manner somewhat different, and out of their proper place or order, but without any real contradiction. If we choose to adopt this conjecture, **hypocrisy** will denote here something different from a pretended and false appearance of wisdom. It will denote the very source and occasion of empty display, which, though it holds out an imposing aspect to the eyes of men, is of no estimation in the sight of God. For, as Jeremiah (5: 3) tells us that the eyes of the Lord behold the truth, so they that believe in his word are instructed to maintain true godliness in such a manner as to cleave to righteousness with an honest and perfect heart; as in these words, "An now, O Israel, what doth the Lord require from thee, but that thou shouldst cleave to him with all thy heart, and with all thy soul?" (Deuteronomy 10: 12).

On the other hand, the traditions of men, while they set aside spiritual worship, wear a temporary disguise, as if God could be imposed upon by such deceptions; for to whatever extent outward ceremonies may be carried, they are, in the sight of God, nothing more than childish trifles, unless so far as they assist us in the exercise of true piety.

ADAM CLARKE

MATTHEW 16: 5–12; MARK 8: 14–21; LUKE 12: 1

Matthew 16: 5–12

5. Come to the other side – Viz. the coast of Bethsaida, by which our Lord passed, going to Caesarea, for he was now on his journey thither. See Matthew 16: 13, and Mark 8: 22,27.

6. Beware of the leaven – What the leaven of Pharisees and Sadducees was has been already explained, see Matthew 16: 1. Bad doctrines act in the soul as leaven does in meal; they assimulate the whole Spirit to their own nature. A man's particular creed has a greater influence on his tempers and conduct than most are aware of. Pride, hypocrisy, and worldly-mindedness, which constituted the leaven of the Pharisees and Sadducees, ruin the major part of the world.

7. They reasoned – For, as Lightfoot observes, the term leaven was very rarely used among the Jews to signify doctrine, and therefore the disciples did not immediately apprehend his meaning. In what a lamentable state of blindness is the human mind? Bodily wants are perceived with the utmost readiness, and a supply is sought with all speed. But the necessities of the soul are rarely discovered, though they are more pressing than those of the body, and the supply of them of infinitely more importance.

8. O ye of little faith – There are degrees in faith, as well as in the other graces of the Spirit. Little faith may be the seed of great faith, and therefore is not to be despised. But many who should be strong in faith have but a small measure of it, because they either give way to sin, or are not careful to improve what God has already given.

9–10. Do ye not yet understand – **the five loaves** – **neither the seven** – How astonishing is it that these men should have any fear of lacking bread, after having seen the two miracles which our blessed Lord alludes to above! Though men quickly perceive their bodily wants, and are querulous enough till they get them supplied, yet they as quickly forget the mercy which they had received; and thus God gets few returns of gratitude for his kindnesses. To make men, therefore, deeply sensible of his favors, he is induced to suffer them often to be in want, and then to supply them in such a way as to prove that their supply has come immediately from the hand of their bountiful Father.

11. How is it that ye do not understand – We are not deficient in spiritual knowledge, because we have not had sufficient opportunities of acquainting ourselves with God; but because we did not improve the advantages we had. How deep and ruinous must our ignorance be, if God did not give line upon line, precept upon precept, here a little and there a little! They now perceived that he warned them against the superstition of the Pharisees, which produced hypocrisy, pride, envy, etc., and the false doctrine of the Sadducees, which denied the existence of a spiritual world, the immortality of the soul, the resurrection of the body, and the providence of God.

MARK 8: 22–26

22. They bring a blind man unto him – Christ went about to do good, and wherever he came he found some good to be done; and so should we, if we had a proper measure of the same zeal and love for the welfare of the bodies and souls of men.

23. And he took the blind man by the hand – Giving him a proof of his readiness to help him, and thus preparing him for the cure which he was about to work.

Led him out of the town – Thus showing the inhabitants that he considered them unworthy of having another miracle wrought among them. He had already deeply deplored their ingratitude and obstinacy. When a people do not make a proper improvement of the light and grace which they receive from God, their candlestick is removed – even the visible Church becomes there extinct; and the candle is put out – no more means of spiritual illumination are afforded to the unfaithful inhabitants: Revelation 2: 5.

bread, but of the doctrine of the Pharisees and of the Sadducees.

Mark 8: 14–21

14 Now the disciples had forgotten to take bread, neither had they in the ship with them more than one loaf.

15 And he charged them, saying, Take heed, beware of the leaven of the Pharisees, and of the leaven of Herod.

16 And they reasoned among themselves, saying, It is because we have no bread.

17 And when Jesus knew it, he saith unto them, Why reason ye, because ye have no bread? perceive ye not yet, neither understand? have ye your heart yet hardened?

18 Having eyes, see ye not? and having ears, hear ye not? and do ye not remember?

19 When I brake the five loaves among five thousand, how many baskets full of fragments took ye up? They say unto him, Twelve.

20 And when the seven among four thousand, how many baskets full of fragments took ye up? And they said, Seven.

21 And he said unto them, How is it that ye do not understand?

Luke 12: 1

1 In the mean time, when there were gathered together an innumerable multitude of people, insomuch that they trode one upon another, he began to say unto his disciples first of all, Beware ye of the leaven of the Pharisees, which is hypocrisy.

MARK 8: 22–26

22 And he cometh to Bethsaida; and they bring a blind man unto him, and besought him to touch him.

23 And he took the blind man by the hand, and led him out of the town; and when he had spit on his eyes, and put his hands upon him, he asked him if he saw ought.

24 And he looked up, and said, I see men as trees, walking.

25 After that he put his hands again upon his eyes, and made him look up: and he was restored, and saw every man clearly.

We now perceive the reason why hypocrisy was viewed by Luke as equivalent to doctrines invented by men, and why he included under this name the leavens of men, which only puff up, and in the sight of God contain nothing solid, and which even draw aside the minds of men from the right study of piety to empty and insignificant ceremonies.

MARK 8: 22–26

This miracle, which is omitted by the other two Evangelists, appears to have been related by Mark chiefly on account of this circumstance, that Christ **restored sight to the blind man**, not in an instant, as he was generally accustomed to do, but in a gradual manner. He did so most probably for the purpose of proving, in the case of this man, that he had full liberty as to his method of proceeding, and was not restricted to a fixed rule, so as not to resort to a variety of methods in exercising his power. On this account, he does not all at once enlighten the eyes of **the blind man**, and fit them for performing their office, but communicates to them at first a dark and confused perception, and afterwards, by laying on his hands a second time, enables them to see perfectly. And so the grace of Christ, which had formerly been poured out suddenly on others, flowed by drops, as it were, on this man.

MATTHEW 16: 13–19; MARK 8: 27–29; LUKE 9: 18–20

Matthew 16: 13. And when Jesus came to the coasts of Cesarea Philippi

Mark says that this conversation took place during the journey. Luke says that it took place while he was praying, and while there were none in company with him but his disciples. Matthew is not so exact in mentioning the time. All the three unquestionably relate the same narrative; and it is possible that Christ may have stopped at a certain place during that journey to pray, and that afterwards he may have put the question to his disciples. There were two towns called Cesarea, of which the former was more celebrated, and had been anciently called The Tower of Strato; while the latter, which is mentioned here, was situated at the foot of Mount Lebanon, not far from the river Jordan. It is for the sake of distinguishing between these two towns that Philippi is added to the name; for though it is conjectured by some to have been built on the same spot where the town of Dan formerly stood, yet, as it had lately been rebuilt by Philip the Tetrarch, it was called Philippi.

Who do men say that I am?

This might be supposed to mean, What was the current rumor about the Redeemer, who became **the Son of man**? But the question is quite different, What do men think

When he had spit on his eyes – There is a similar transaction to this mentioned by John, 9: 6. It is likely this was done merely to separate the eyelids; as, in certain cases of blindness, they are found always gummed together. It required a miracle to restore the sight, and this was done in consequence of Christ having laid his hands upon the blind man: it required no miracle to separate the eyelids, and, therefore, natural means only were employed – this was done by rubbing them with spittle; but whether by Christ, or by the blind man, is not absolutely certain. It has always been evident that false miracles have been wrought without reason or necessity, and without any obvious advantage; and they have thereby been detected: on the contrary, true miracles have always vindicated themselves by their obvious utility and importance; nothing ever being effected by them that could be performed by natural means.

24. I see men as trees, walking – His sight was so imperfect that he could not distinguish between men and trees, only by the motion of the former.

25. And saw every man clearly – Our Lord could have restored this man to sight in a moment; but he chose to do it in the way mentioned in the text, to show that he is sovereign of his own graces; and to point out that, however insignificant means may appear in themselves, they are divinely efficacious when he chooses to work by them; and that, however small the first manifestations of mercy may be, they are nevertheless the beginnings of the fullness of the blessings of the Gospel of peace. Reader, art thou in this man's state? Art thou blind? Then come to Jesus that he may restore thee. Hast thou a measure of light? Then pray that he may lay his hands again on thee, that thou mayest be enabled to read thy title clear to the heavenly inheritance.

26. He sent him away to his house – So it appears that this person did not belong to Bethsaida, for, in going to his house, he was not to enter into the village.

This miracle is not mentioned by any other of the evangelists. It affords another proof that Mark did not abridge Matthew's Gospel.

MATTHEW 16: 13–19; MARK 8: 27–29; LUKE 9: 18–20

Matthew 16: 13–19

13. Caesarea Philippi – A city, in the tribe of Naphtali, near to Mount Libanus, in the province of Iturea. Its ancient name was Dan, Genesis 14: 14; afterwards it was called Lais, Judges 18: 7. But Philip the tetrarch, having rebuilt and beautified it, gave it the name of Caesarea, in honor of Tiberius Caesar, the reigning emperor: but to distinguish it from another Caesarea, which was on the coast of the Mediterranean Sea, and to perpetuate the fame of him who rebuilt it, it was called Caesarea Philippi, or Caesarea of Philip.

When Jesus came – when Jesus was coming. Not, when Jesus came, or was come, for Mark expressly mentions that it happened in the way to Caesarea Philippi, Mark 8: 27, and he is Matthew's best interpreter.

Whom do men say – He asked his disciples this question, not because he was ignorant what the people thought and spoke of him; but to have the opportunity, in getting an express declaration of their faith from themselves, to confirm and strengthen them in it. Some, John the Baptist, etc. By this and other passages we learn, that the Pharisaic doctrine of the Metempsychosis, or transmigration of souls, was pretty general; for it was upon this ground that they believed that the soul of the Baptist, or of Elijah, Jeremiah, or some of the prophets, had come to a new life in the body of Jesus.

16. Thou art the Christ, the Son of the living God – Every word here is emphatic – a most concise, and yet comprehensive, confession of faith.

The Christ, or Messiah, points out his divinity, and shows his office; the Son – designates his person: on this account it is that both are joined together so frequently in the new covenant. Of the living God literally, of God the Living One.

26 And he sent him away to his house, saying, Neither go into the town, nor tell it to any in the town.

MATTHEW 16: 13–19; MARK 8: 27–29; LUKE 9: 18–20

Matthew 16: 13–19

13 When Jesus came into the coasts of Caesarea Philippi, he asked his disciples, saying, Whom do men say that I the Son of man am?

14 And they said, Some say that thou art John the Baptist: some, Elias; and others, Jeremias, or one of the prophets.

15 He saith unto them, But whom say ye that I am?

16 And Simon Peter answered and said, Thou art the Christ, the Son of the living God.

17 And Jesus answered and said unto him, Blessed art thou, Simon Barjona: for flesh and blood hath not revealed it unto thee, but my Father which is in heaven.

18 And I say also unto thee, That thou art Peter, and upon this rock I will build my church; and the gates of hell shall not prevail against it.

19 And I will give unto thee the keys of the kingdom of heaven: and whatsoever thou shalt bind on earth shall be bound in heaven: and whatsoever thou shalt loose on earth shall be loosed in heaven.

Mark 8: 27–29

27 And Jesus went out, and his disciples, into the towns of Caesarea Philippi: and by the way he asked his disciples, saying unto them, Whom do men say that I am?

28 And they answered, John the Baptist: but some say, Elias; and others, One of the prophets.

29 And he saith unto them, But whom say ye that I am? And Peter answereth and saith unto him, Thou art the Christ.

Luke 9: 18–20

18 And it came to pass, as he was alone praying, his disciples were with him: and he asked them, saying, Whom say the people that I am?

19 They answering said, John the Baptist; but some say, Elias; and others say, that one of the old prophets is risen again.

about Jesus the Son of Mary? He calls himself, according to custom, **the Son of man**, as much as to say, Now that clothed in flesh I inhabit the earth like other men, what is the opinion entertained respecting me? The design of Christ was, to confirm his disciples fully in the true faith, that they might not be tossed about amidst various reports, as we shall presently see.

16. Thou art the Christ

The confession is short, but it embraces all that is contained in our salvation; for the designation **Christ**, or **Anointed**, includes both an everlasting Kingdom and an everlasting Priesthood, to reconcile us to God, and, by expiating our sins through his sacrifice, to obtain for us a perfect righteousness, and, having received us under his protection, to uphold and supply and enrich us with every description of blessings. Mark says only, **Thou art the Christ.** Luke says, **Thou art the Christ of God.** But the meaning is the same; for the **Christs** (*christoi*) **of God** was the appellation anciently bestowed on kings, who had been anointed by the divine command.

MATTHEW 16: 20–28; MARK 8: 30–38; 9: 1; LUKE 9: 21–27

Having given a proof of his future glory, Christ reminds his disciples of what **he must suffer**, that they also may be prepared to **bear the cross;** for the time was at hand when they must enter into the contest, to which he knew them to be altogether unequal, if they had not been fortified by fresh courage. And first of all, it was necessary to inform them that Christ must commence his reign, not with gaudy display, not with the magnificence of riches, not with the loud applause of the world, but with an ignominious death. But nothing was harder than to rise superior to such an offense; particularly if we consider the opinion which they firmly entertained respecting their Master; for they imagined that he would procure for them earthly happiness. This unfounded expectation held them in suspense, and they eagerly looked forward to the hour when Christ would suddenly reveal the glory of his reign. So far were they from having ever adverted to the ignominy of the cross, that they considered it to be utterly unsuitable that he should be placed in any circumstances from which he did not receive honor. To them it was a distressing occurrence that he should **be rejected by the elders and the scribes**, who held the government of the Church; and hence we may readily conclude that this admonition was highly necessary. But as the bare mention of the cross must, of necessity, have occasioned heavy distress to their weak minds, he presently heals the wound by saying, that **on the third day he will rise again from the dead.** And

Living – a character applied to the Supreme Being, not only to distinguish him from the dead idols of paganism, but also to point him out as the source of life, present, spiritual, and eternal.

17. Blessed art thou, Simon Bar-jona – Or Simon, son of Jonah; so Bar-jonah should be translated, and so it is rendered by our Lord, John 1: 42. Flesh and blood – i.e. MAN; – no human being hath revealed this; and though the text is literal enough, yet every body should know that this is a Hebrew periphrasis for man; and the literal translation of it here, and in Galatians 1: 16, has misled thousands, who suppose that flesh and blood signify carnal reason, as it is termed, or the unregenerate principle in man. Is it not evident, from our Lord's observation, that it requires an express revelation of God in a man's soul, to give him a saving acquaintance with Jesus Christ; and that not even the miracles of our Lord, wrought before the eyes, will effect this? The darkness must be removed from the heart by the Holy Spirit, before a man can become wise unto salvation.

18. Thou art Peter – This was the same as if he had said, I acknowledge thee for one of my disciples – for this name was given him by our Lord when he first called him to the apostleship. See John 1: 42.

Peter, signifies a stone, or fragment of a rock; and our Lord, whose constant custom it was to rise to heavenly things through the medium of earthly, takes occasion from the name, the metaphorical meaning of which was strength and stability, to point out the solidity of the confession, and the stability of that cause which should be founded on THE CHRIST, the SON of the LIVING GOD.

Upon this very rock – this true confession of thine – that I am THE MESSIAH, that am come to reveal and communicate THE LIVING GOD, that the dead, lost world may be saved – upon this very rock, myself, thus confessed (alluding probably to Psalm 118: 22, The STONE which the builders rejected is become the HEAD-STONE of the CORNER: and to Isaiah 28: 16, Behold I lay a STONE in Zion for a FOUNDATION) – will I build my Church, my assembly, or congregation, i.e. of persons who are made partakers of this precious faith. That Peter is not designed in our Lord's words must be evident to all who are not blinded by prejudice. Peter was only one of the builders in this sacred edifice, Ephesians 2: 20 who himself tells us, (with the rest of the believers), was built on this living foundation stone: 1 Peter 2: 4–5, therefore Jesus Christ did not say, on thee, Peter, will I build my Church, but changes immediately the expression, and says, upon that very rock, to show that he neither addressed Peter, nor any other of the apostles.

The gates of hell, i.e, the machinations and powers of the invisible world. In ancient times the gates of fortified cities were used to hold councils in, and were usually places of great strength. Our Lord's expression means, that neither the plots, stratagems, nor strength of Satan and his angels, should ever so far prevail as to destroy the sacred truths in the above confession. Sometimes the gates are taken for the troops which issue out from them: we may firmly believe, that though hell should open her gates, and vomit out her devil and all his angels, to fight against Christ and his saints, ruin and discomfiture must be the consequence on their part; as the arm of the Omnipotent must prevail.

19. The keys of the kingdom – By the kingdom of heaven, we may consider the true Church, that house of God, to be meant; and by the keys, the power of admitting into that house, or of preventing any improper person from coming in. In other words, the doctrine of salvation, and the full declaration of the way in which God will save sinners; and who they are that shall be finally excluded from heaven; and on what account. When the Jews made a man a doctor of the law, they put into his hand the key of the closet in the temple where the sacred books were kept, and also tablets to write upon; signifying, by this, that they gave him authority to teach, and to explain the Scriptures to the people. – Martin. This prophetic declaration of our Lord was

20 He said unto them, But whom say ye that I am? Peter answering said, The Christ of God.

MATTHEW 16: 20–28; MARK 8: 30–37, 9: 1; LUKE 9: 21–27

Matthew 16: 20–28

20 Then charged he his disciples that they should tell no man that he was Jesus the Christ.

21 From that time forth began Jesus to shew unto his disciples, how that he must go unto Jerusalem, and suffer many things of the elders and chief priests and scribes, and be killed, and be raised again the third day.

22 Then Peter took him, and began to rebuke him, saying, Be it far from thee, Lord: this shall not be unto thee.

23 But he turned, and said unto Peter, Get thee behind me, Satan: thou art an offence unto me: for thou savourest not the things that be of God, but those that be of men.

24 Then said Jesus unto his disciples, If any man will come after me, let him deny himself, and take up his cross, and follow me.

25 For whosoever will save his life shall lose it: and whosoever will lose his life for my sake shall find it.

26 For what is a man profited, if he shall gain the whole world, and lose his own soul? or what shall a man give in exchange for his soul?

27 For the Son of man shall come in the glory of his Father with his angels; and then he shall reward every man according to his works.

28 Verily I say unto you, There be some standing here, which shall not taste of death, till they see the Son of man coming in his kingdom.

Mark 8: 30–37

30 And he charged them that they should tell no man of him.

31 And he began to teach them, that the Son of man must suffer many things, and be rejected of the elders, and of the chief priests, and scribes, and be killed, and after three days rise again.

32 And he spake that saying openly. And Peter took him, and began to rebuke him.

certainly, as there is nothing to be seen in the cross but the weakness of the flesh, till we come to his resurrection, in which the power of the Spirit shines brightly, our faith will find no encouragement or support. In like manner, all ministers of the Word, who desire that their preaching may be profitable, ought to be exceedingly careful that the glory of his resurrection should be always exhibited by them in connection with the ignominy of his death.

But we naturally wonder why Christ refuses to accept as witnesses the Apostles, whom he had already appointed to that office; for why were they sent but to be the heralds of that redemption which depended on the coming of Christ? The answer is not difficult, if we keep in mind the explanations which I have given on this subject: first, that they were not appointed teachers for the purpose of bearing full and certain testimony to Christ, but only to procure disciples for their Master; that is, to induce those who were too much the victims of sloth to become teachable and attentive; and; secondly, that their commission was temporary, for it ended when Christ himself began to preach. As the time of his death was now at hand, and as they were not yet fully prepared to testify their faith, but, on the contrary, were so weak in faith, that their confession of it would have exposed them to ridicule, the Lord enjoins them to remain silent till others shall have acknowledged him to be the conqueror of death, and till he shall have endued them with increased firmness.

Matthew 16: 22. And Peter, taking him aside, began to rebuke him

It is a proof of the excessive zeal of Peter, that he reproves his Master; though it would appear that the respect he entertained for him was his reason for **taking him aside,** because he did not venture to reprove him in presence of others. Still, it was highly presumptuous in Peter to advise our Lord to spare himself, as if he had been deficient in prudence or self-command. But so completely are men hurried on and driven headlong by inconsiderate zeal, that they do not hesitate to pass judgment on God himself, according to their own fancy. Peter views it as absurd, that the Son of God, who was to be the Redeemer of the nation, should be **crucified by the elders**, and that he who was the Author of life should be condemned to die. He therefore endeavors to restrain Christ from exposing himself to death. The reasoning is plausible; but we ought without hesitation to yield greater deference to the opinion of Christ than to the zeal of Peter, whatever excuse he may plead.

And here we learn what estimation in the sight of God belongs to what are called good intentions. So deeply is pride rooted in the hearts of men, that they think wrong is done them, and complain, if God does not comply with

literally fulfilled to Peter, as he was made the first instrument of opening, i.e. preaching the doctrines of the kingdom of heaven to the Jews, Acts 2: 41; and to the Gentiles, Acts 10: 44–47; 11: 1; 15: 7.

Whatsoever thou shalt bind on earth – This mode of expression was frequent among the Jews: they considered that every thing that was done upon earth, according to the order of God, was at the same time done in heaven: hence they were accustomed to say, that when the priest, on the day of atonement, offered the two goats upon earth, the same were offered in heaven. As one goat therefore is permitted to escape on earth, one is permitted to escape in heaven; and when the priests cast the lots on earth, the priest also casts the lots in heaven.

The disciples of our Lord, from having the keys, i.e. the true knowledge of the doctrine of the kingdom of heaven, should be able at all times to distinguish between the clean and the unclean, and pronounce infallible judgment; and this binding and loosing, or pronouncing fit or unfit for fellowship with the members of Christ, being always according to the doctrine of the Gospel of God, should be considered as proceeding immediately from heaven, and consequently as Divinely ratified.

That binding and loosing were terms in frequent use among the Jews, and that they meant bidding and forbidding, granting and refusing, declaring lawful or unlawful, etc.. Dr. Lightfoot writes: "Let the words be applied by way of paraphrase to the matter that was transacted at present with Peter: 'I am about to build a Gentile Church,' saith Christ, and to thee, O Peter, do I give the keys of the kingdom of heaven, that thou mayest first open the door of faith to them; but if thou askest by what rule that Church is to be governed, when the Mosaic rule may seem so improper for it, thou shalt be so guided by the Holy Spirit, that whatsoever of the law of Moses thou shalt forbid them shall be forbidden; whatsoever thou grantest them shall be granted; and that under a sanction made in heaven.' Hence, in that instant, when he should use his keys, that is, when he was now ready to open the gate

of the Gospel to the Gentiles, Acts 10, he was taught from heaven that the consorting of the Jew with the Gentile, which before had been bound, was now loosed; and the eating of any creature convenient for food was now loosed, which before had been bound; and he in like manner looses both these. Those words of our Savior, John 20: 23, Whose sins ye remit, they are remitted to them, for the most part are forced to the same sense with these before us, when they carry quite another sense. Here the business is of doctrine only, not of persons; there of persons, not of doctrine. Here of things lawful or unlawful in religion, to be determined by the apostles; there of persons obstinate or not obstinate, to be punished by them, or not to be punished. As to doctrine, the apostles were doubly instructed.

1. So long sitting at the feet of their Master, they had imbibed the evangelical doctrine.

"2. The Holy Spirit directing them, they were to determine concerning the legal doctrine and practice, being completely instructed and enabled in both by the Holy Spirit descending upon them. As to the persons, they were endowed with a peculiar gift, so that, the same Spirit directing them, if they would retain and punish the sins of any, a power was delivered into their hands of delivering to Satan, of punishing with diseases, plagues, yea, death itself, which Peter did to Ananias and Sapphira; Paul to Elymas, Hymeneus, and Philetus, etc."

After all these evidences and proofs of the proper use of these terms, to attempt to press the word, into the service long assigned them by the Church of Rome, would, to use the words of Dr. Lightfoot, be "a matter of laughter or of madness." No Church can use them in the sense thus imposed upon them, which was done merely to serve secular ends; and least of all can that very Church that thus abuses them.

MATTHEW 16: 20–28; MARK 8: 30–37; 9: 1; LUKE 9: 21–27

Matthew 16: 20–28

20. The Christ – Who is this Jesus? Peter answers, He is, the Messiah. The word Jesus is

33 But when he had turned about and looked on his disciples, he rebuked Peter, saying, Get thee behind me, Satan: for thou savourest not the things that be of God, but the things that be of men.

34 And when he had called the people unto him with his disciples also, he said unto them, Whosoever will come after me, let him deny himself, and take up his cross, and follow me.

35 For whosoever will save his life shall lose it; but whosoever shall lose his life for my sake and the gospel's, the same shall save it.

36 For what shall it profit a man, if he shall gain the whole world, and lose his own soul?

37 Or what shall a man give in exchange for his soul?

Mark 9: 1

1 And he said unto them, Verily I say unto you, That there be some of them that stand here, which shall not taste of death, till they have seen the kingdom of God come with power.

Luke 9: 21–27

21 And he straitly charged them, and commanded them to tell no man that thing;

22 Saying, The Son of man must suffer many things, and be rejected of the elders and chief priests and scribes, and be slain, and be raised the third day.

23 And he said to them all, If any man will come after me, let him deny himself, and take up his cross daily, and follow me.

24 For whosoever will save his life shall lose it: but whosoever will lose his life for my sake, the same shall save it.

25 For what is a man advantaged, if he gain the whole world, and lose himself, or be cast away?

27 But I tell you of a truth, there be some standing here, which shall not taste of death, till they see the kingdom of God.

MATTHEW 17: 1–8; MARK 9: 2–8; LUKE 9: 28–36A

Matthew 17: 1–8

1 And after six days Jesus taketh Peter,

every thing that they consider to be right. With what obstinacy do we see the Papists boasting of their devotions! But while they applaud themselves in this daring manner, God not only rejects what they believe to be worthy of the highest praise, but even pronounces a severe censure on its folly and wickedness. Certainly, if the feeling and judgment of the flesh be admitted, Peter's intention was pious, or at least it looked well. And yet Christ could not have conveyed his censure in harsher or more disdainful language. Tell me, what is the meaning of that stern reply? How comes it that he who so mildly on all occasions guarded against breaking even a bruised reed (Isaiah 42: 3), thunders so dismally against a chosen disciple? The reason is obvious, that in the person of one man he intended to restrain all from gratifying their own passions. Though the lusts of the flesh, as they resemble wild beasts, are difficult to be restrained, yet there is no beast more furious than the wisdom of the flesh. It is on this account that Christ reproves it so sharply, and bruises it, as it were, with an iron hammer, to teach us that it is only from the word of God that we ought to be wise.

MATTHEW 17: 1–8; MARK 9: 2–8; LUKE 9: 28–36

Matthew 17: 1. And after six days

We must first inquire for what purpose Christ clothed himself with heavenly glory for a short time, and why he did not admit more than three of his disciples to be spectators. Some think that he did so, in order to fortify them against the trial which they were soon to meet with, arising from his death. That does not appear to me to be a probable reason; for why should he have deprived the rest of the same remedy, or rather, why does he expressly forbid them to make known what they had seen till after his resurrection, but because the result of the vision would be later than his death? I have no doubt whatever that Christ intended to show that he was not dragged unwillingly to death, but that he came forward of his own accord, to offer to the Father the sacrifice of obedience. The disciples were not made aware of this till Christ rose; nor was it even necessary that, at the very moment of his death, they should perceive the divine power of Christ, so as to acknowledge it to be victorious on the cross; but the instruction which they now received was intended to be useful at a future period both to themselves and to us, that no man might take offense at the weakness of Christ, as if it were by force and necessity that he had suffered. It would manifestly have been quite as easy for Christ to protect his body from death as to clothe it with heavenly glory.

We are thus taught that he was subjected to death, because he wished it to be so; that he was crucified, because

obviously improper. What our Lord says here refers to Peter's testimony in Matthew 16: 16: Thou art the Christ – Jesus here says, Tell no man that I am the Christ, i.e. the MESSIAH; as the time for his full manifestation was not yet come; and he was not willing to provoke the Jewish malice, or the Roman envy, by permitting his disciples to announce him as the Savior of a lost world. He chose rather to wait, till his resurrection and ascension had set this truth in the clearest light, and beyond the power of successful contradiction.

21. From that time forth began Jesus, etc. – Before this time our Lord had only spoken of his death in a vague and obscure manner, see Matthew 12: 40, because he would not afflict his disciples with this matter sooner than necessity required; but now, as the time of his crucifixion drew nigh, he spoke of his sufferings and death in the most express and clear terms. Three sorts of persons, our Lord intimates, should be the cause of his death and passion: the elders, the chief priests, and the scribes.

22. Then Peter took him – took him up – suddenly interrupted him, as it were calling him to order. A man like Peter, who is of an impetuous spirit, and decides without consideration upon every subject, must of necessity be often in the wrong.

Be it far from thee Lord – Be merciful to thyself Lord.

23. Get thee behind me, Satan – Get behind me, thou adversary. Our blessed Lord certainly never designed that men should believe he called Peter, DEVIL, because he, through erring affection, had wished him to avoid that death which he predicted to himself. This translation, which is literal, takes away that harshness which before appeared in our Lord's words.

Thou art an offense unto me – Thou art a stumbling-block in my way, to impede me in the accomplishment of the great design.

Thou savourest not – That is, dost not relish, or, thou dost not understand or discern the things of God – thou art wholly taken up with the vain thought that my kingdom is of this world. He who opposes the doctrine of the atonement is an adversary and offense to Christ, though he be as sincere in his profession as Peter himself was. Let us beware of false friendships. Carnal relatives, when listened to, may prove the ruin of those whom, through their mistaken tenderness, they wish to save. When a man is intent on saving his own soul, his adversaries are often those of his own household.

24. Will come after me – i.e. to be my disciple. This discourse was intended to show Peter and the rest of the disciples the nature of his kingdom; and that the honor that cometh from the world was not to be expected by those who followed Christ.

The principles of the Christian life are:
First. To have a sincere desire to belong to Christ – If any man be WILLING to be my disciple, etc.
Secondly. To renounce self-dependence, and selfish pursuits – Let him deny HIMSELF.
Thirdly. To embrace the condition which God has appointed, and bear the troubles and difficulties he may meet with in walking the Christian road – Let him take up HIS CROSS.
Fourthly. To imitate Jesus, and do and suffer all in his spirit – Let him FOLLOW ME.

Let him deny himself – Let him deny, or renounce, himself fully – in all respects – perseveringly. A man's self is to him the prime cause of most of his miseries.

25. For whosoever will save his life – That is, shall wish to save his life – at the expense of his conscience, and casting aside the cross, he shall lose it – the very evil he wishes to avoid shall overtake him; and he shall lose his soul into the bargain. See then how necessary it is to renounce one's self! But whatsoever a man loses in this world, for his steady attachment to Christ and his cause, he shall have amply made up to him in the eternal world.

26. Lose his own soul – The soul was made for God, and can never be united to him, nor be happy, till saved from sin: therefore it is necessary. He who is saved from his sin, and

James, and John his brother, and bringeth them up into an high mountain apart,

2 And was transfigured before them: and his face did shine as the sun, and his raiment was white as the light.

3 And, behold, there appeared unto them Moses and Elias talking with him.

4 Then answered Peter, and said unto Jesus, Lord, it is good for us to be here: if thou wilt, let us make here three tabernacles; one for thee, and one for Moses, and one for Elias.

5 While he yet spake, behold, a bright cloud overshadowed them: and behold a voice out of the cloud, which said, This is my beloved Son, in whom I am well pleased; hear ye him.

6 And when the disciples heard it, they fell on their face, and were sore afraid.

7 And Jesus came and touched them, and said, Arise, and be not afraid.

8 And when they had lifted up their eyes, they saw no man, save Jesus only.

Mark 9: 2–8

2 And after six days Jesus taketh with him Peter, and James, and John, and leadeth them up into an high mountain apart by themselves: and he was transfigured before them.

3 And his raiment became shining, exceeding white as snow; so as no fuller on earth can white them.

4 And there appeared unto them Elias with Moses: and they were talking with Jesus.

5 And Peter answered and said to Jesus, Master, it is good for us to be here: and let us make three tabernacles; one for thee, and one for Moses, and one for Elias.

6 For he wist not what to say; for they were sore afraid.

7 And there was a cloud that overshadowed them: and a voice came out of the cloud, saying, This is my beloved Son: hear him.

8 And suddenly, when they had looked round about, they saw no man any more, save Jesus only with themselves.

Luke 9: 28–36a

28 And it came to pass about an eight days after these sayings, he took Peter and John and James, and went up into a

he offered himself. That same flesh, which was sacrificed on the cross and lay in the grave, might have been exempted from death and the grave; for it had already partaken of the heavenly glory. We are also taught that, so long as Christ remained in the world, bearing the form of a servant, and so long as his majesty was concealed under the weakness of the flesh, nothing had been taken from him, for it was of his own accord that he emptied himself (Philippians 2: 7); but now his resurrection has drawn aside that veil by which his power had been concealed for a time.

2. And was transfigured before them

Luke says that this happened **while he was praying** and from the circumstances of time and place, we may infer that he had prayed for what he now obtained, that in the brightness of an unusual form his Godhead might become visible; not that he needed to ask by prayer from another what he did not possess, or that he doubted his Father's willingness, but because, during the whole course of his humiliation, he always ascribed to the Father whatever he did as a divine Person, and because he intended to excite us to prayer by his example.

His transfiguration did not altogether enable his disciples to see Christ, as he now is in heaven, but gave them a taste of his boundless glory, such as they were able to comprehend. Then **his face shone as the sun;** but now he is far beyond the sun in brightness. In his raiment an unusual and dazzling whiteness appeared; but now without raiment a divine majesty shines in his whole body. Thus in ancient times God appeared to the holy fathers, not as He was in Himself, but so far as they could endure the rays of His infinite brightness; for John declares that not until "they are like him will they see him as he is" (1 John 3: 2).

5. Lo, a bright cloud overshadowed them

Their eyes were covered by a cloud, in order to inform them, that they were not yet prepared for beholding the brightness of the heavenly glory. For, when the Lord gave tokens of his presence, he employed, at the same time, some coverings to restrain the arrogance of the human mind. So now, with the view of teaching his disciples a lesson of humility, he withdraws from their eyes the sight of the heavenly glory. This admonition is likewise addressed to us, that we may not seek to pry into the secrets which lie beyond our senses, but, on the contrary, that every man may keep within the limits of sobriety, according to the measure of his faith. In a word, this cloud ought to serve us as a bridle, that our curiosity may not indulge in undue wantonness. The disciples, too, were warned that they must return to their former warfare, and therefore must not expect a triumph before the time.

united to God, possesses the utmost felicity that the human soul can enjoy, either in this or the coming world: therefore, this salvation is important.

27. For the Son of man shall come in the glory of his Father – This seems to refer to Daniel 7: 13–14. It is very likely that the words do not apply to the final judgment, to which they are generally referred; but to the wonderful display of God's grace and power after the day of pentecost.

28. There be some – which shall not taste of death – This verse seems to confirm the above explanation, as our Lord evidently speaks of the establishment of the Christian Church after the day of pentecost, and its final triumph after the destruction of the Jewish polity; as if he had said, "Some of you, my disciples, shall continue to live until these things take place." The destruction of Jerusalem, and the Jewish economy, which our Lord here predicts, took place about forty-three years after this: and some of the persons now with him doubtless survived that period, and witnessed the extension of the Messiah's kingdom; and our Lord told them these things before, that when they came to pass they might be confirmed in the faith, and expect an exact fulfillment of all the other promises and prophecies which concerned the extension and support of the kingdom of Christ.

MATTHEW 17: 1–8; MARK 9: 2–8; LUKE 9: 28–36A

Matthew 17: 1–8

1. After six days – Mark 9: 2, has the same number; but Luke says, Luke 9: 28, after eight days. The reason of this difference seems to be the following: Matthew and Mark reckon the days from that mentioned in the preceding chapter, to that mentioned in this; Luke includes both days, as well as the six intermediate: hence, the one makes eight, the other six, without any contradiction.

Peter, James, and John – He chose those that they might be witnesses of his transfigu-

ration: two or three witnesses being required by the Scripture to substantiate any fact. Eminent communications of the Divine favor prepare for, and entitle to, great services and great conflicts. The same three were made witnesses of his agony in the garden, Matthew 26: 37.

A high mountain – This was one of the mountains of Galilee; but whether Mount Tabor or not, is uncertain. Some think it was Mount Hermon. St. Luke says, Christ and his disciples went up into the mountain to pray, Luke 9: 28.

2. Was transfigured – That fullness of the Godhead, which dwelt bodily in Christ, now shone forth through the human nature, and manifested to his disciples not only that Divinity which Peter had before confessed, Matthew 16: 16, but also the glorious resurrection body, in which they should exist in the presence of God to eternity.

3. Moses and Elias – Elijah came from heaven in the same body which he had upon earth, for he was translated, and did not see death, 2 Kings 2: 11. And the body of Moses was probably raised again, as a pledge of the resurrection; and as Christ is to come to judge the quick and the dead, for we shall not all die, but all shall be changed, 1 Corinthians 15: 51, he probably gave the full representation of this in the person of Moses, who died, and was thus raised to life, (or appeared now as he shall appear when raised from the dead in the last day), and in the person of Elijah, who never tasted death. Both their bodies exhibit the same appearance, to show that the bodies of glorified saints are the same, whether the person had been translated, or whether he had died. It was a constant and prevalent tradition among the Jews, that both Moses and Elijah should appear in the times of the Messiah, and to this very tradition the disciples refer, Matthew 17: 10.

We may conceive that the law in the person of Moses, the great Jewish legislator, and the prophets in the person of Elijah, the chief of the prophets, came now to do homage to Jesus Christ, and to render up their authority

mountain to pray.

29 And as he prayed, the fashion of his countenance was altered, and his raiment was white and glistering.

30 And, behold, there talked with him two men, which were Moses and Elias:

31 Who appeared in glory, and spake of his decease which he should accomplish at Jerusalem.

32 But Peter and they that were with him were heavy with sleep: and when they were awake, they saw his glory, and the two men that stood with him.

33 And it came to pass, as they departed from him, Peter said unto Jesus, Master, it is good for us to be here: and let us make three tabernacles; one for thee, and one for Moses, and one for Elias: not knowing what he said.

34 While he thus spake, there came a cloud, and overshadowed them: and they feared as they entered into the cloud.

35 And there came a voice out of the cloud, saying, This is my beloved Son: hear him.

36a And when the voice was past, Jesus was found alone.

MATTHEW 17: 9–13; MARK 9: 9–13; LUKE 9: 36B

Matthew 17: 9–13

9 And as they came down from the mountain, Jesus charged them, saying, Tell the vision to no man, until the Son of man be risen again from the dead.

10 And his disciples asked him, saying, Why then say the scribes that Elias must first come?

11 And Jesus answered and said unto them, Elias truly shall first come, and restore all things.

12 But I say unto you, That Elias is come already, and they knew him not, but have done unto him whatsoever they listed. Likewise shall also the Son of man suffer of them.

13 Then the disciples understood that he spake unto them of John the Baptist.

Mark 9: 9–13

9 And as they came down from the mountain, he charged them that they should tell no man what things they had seen, till the Son of man were risen from

MATTHEW 17: 9–13; MARK 9: 9–13; LUKE 9: 36

Matthew 17: 9. And as they were going down from the mountain

We have said that the time for making known the vision was not yet fully come; and, indeed, the disciples would not have believed it, if Christ had not given a more striking proof of his glory in his resurrection. But after that his divine power had been openly displayed, that temporary exhibition of his glory began to be admitted, so as to make it fully evident that, even during the time that he emptied himself (Philippians 2: 7), he continued to retain his divinity entire, though it was concealed under the veil of the flesh. There are good reasons, therefore, why he enjoins his disciples to keep silence, till he be risen from the dead.

10. And his disciples asked him, saying

No sooner is the resurrection mentioned than the disciples imagine that the reign of Christ is commenced; for they explain this word to mean that the world would acknowledge him to be the Messiah. That they imagined the resurrection to be something totally different from what Christ meant, is evident from what is stated by Mark, that they disputed with each other what was the meaning of that expression which he had used, To rise from the dead.

11. And will restore all things

This does not mean that John the Baptist restored them perfectly, but that he conveyed and handed them over to Christ, who would complete the work which he had begun. Now as the scribes had shamefully rejected John, Christ reminds his disciples that the impostures of such men ought not to give them uneasiness, and that it ought not to be reckoned strange, if, after having rejected the servant, they should, with equal disdain, reject his Master. And that no one might be distressed by a proceeding so strange, our Lord mentions that the Scripture contained predictions of both events, that the Redeemer of the world, and Elijah his forerunner, would be rejected by false and wicked teachers.

MATTHEW 17: 14–18; MARK 9: 14–27; LUKE 9: 37–43

As Mark is more full, and explains the circumstances very minutely, we shall follow the order of his narrative. And first he points out clearly the reason why Christ uses a harshness so unusual with him, when he exclaims that the Jews, on account of their perverse malice, do not deserve to be any longer endured. We know how gently he was wont to receive them, even when their requests were excessively importunate. A father here entreats in behalf of an

into his hands; as he was the END of the law, and the grand subject of the predictions of the prophets. This appears more particularly from what St. Luke says, Luke 9: 31, that Moses and Elijah conversed with our Lord on his death, which he was about to accomplish, (to fulfill), because in it, all the rites, ceremonies, and sacrifices of the law, as well as the predictions of the prophets, were fulfilled.

4. Peter said – let us make, etc. – That is, when he saw Moses and Elijah ready to depart from the mount, Luke 9: 33, he wished to detain them, that he might always enjoy their company with that of his Lord and Master, still supposing that Christ would set up a temporal kingdom upon earth.

5. A bright cloud overshadowed them – This might be designed as emblematical of the old covenant, which was but the shadow of the good things which were to come, Hebrews 10: 1; and the cloud of light mentioned here, the emblem of that glorious display of God, in his Gospel, by which life and immortality were brought to light, 2 Timothy 1: 10.

This is my beloved Son – This is my Son, the beloved one, in who I have delighted, or, been well pleased. God adds his testimony of approbation to what was spoken of the sufferings of Christ by Moses and Elijah; thus showing that the sacrificial economy of the old covenant was in itself of no worth, but as it referred to the grand atonement which Jesus was about to make; therefore he says, In him HAVE I delighted, intimating that it was in him alone, as typified by those sacrifices, that he HAD delighted through the whole course of the legal administration; and that it was only in reference to the death of his Son that he accepted the offerings and oblations made to him under the old covenant. Hear HIM. The disciples wished to detain Moses and Elijah that they might hear them: but God shows that the law which had been in force, and the prophets which had prophesied, until now, must all give place to Jesus; and he alone must now be attended to, as the way, the truth, and the life; for no man could now come unto the Father but through him. This voice seems also to refer to that prediction in Deuteronomy 18: 15. The Lord shall raise up a Prophet like unto me: HIM SHALL YE HEAR. Go no more to the law, nor to the prophets, to seek for a coming Messiah; for behold he IS come! Hear and obey him, and him only.

6. Fell on their face – Dismayed by the voice, and dazzled by the glory of the cloud. So Daniel, Daniel 8: 17, and Saul of Tarsus, Acts 9: 4.

7. Jesus came and touched them – Exactly parallel to this account is Daniel 8: 18, I was in a deep sleep, i.e. (a trance) on my face towards the ground; but he TOUCHED me, and set me upright. From Jesus alone are we to expect Divine communications, and by his power only are we able to bear and improve them. It is very likely that this transfiguration took place in the night, which was a more proper season to show forth its glory than the day time, in which a part of the splendor must necessarily be lost by the presence of the solar light. Besides, St. Luke, Luke 9: 37, expressly says, that it was on the next day after the transfiguration that our Lord came down from the mount.

MATTHEW 17: 9–13; MARK 9: 9–13; LUKE 9: 36B

Matthew 17: 14–18

9. Tell the vision to no man – Observe that as this transfiguration was intended to show forth the final abolition of the whole ceremonial law, it was necessary that a matter which could not fail to irritate the Jewish rulers and people should be kept secret, till Jesus had accomplished vision and prophecy by his death and resurrection.

The whole of this emblematic transaction appears to me to be intended to prove,

1st. The reality of the world of spirits, and the immortality of the soul.

2dly. The resurrection of the body, and the doctrine of future rewards and punishments, see Matthew 16: 27.

3dly. The abolition of the Mosaic institutions, and, the fulfillment of the predictions of the

the dead.

10 And they kept that saying with themselves, questioning one with another what the rising from the dead should mean.

11 And they asked him, saying, Why say the scribes that Elias must first come?

12 And he answered and told them, Elias verily cometh first, and restoreth all things; and how it is written of the Son of man, that he must suffer many things, and be set at nought.

13 But I say unto you, That Elias is indeed come, and they have done unto him whatsoever they listed, as it is written of him.

Luke 9: 36b

36b And they kept it close, and told no man in those days any of those things which they had seen.

MATTHEW 17: 14–18; MARK 9: 14–27; LUKE 9: 37–43A

Matthew 17: 14–18

14 And when they were come to the multitude, there came to him a certain man, kneeling down to him, and saying,

15 Lord, have mercy on my son: for he is lunatick, and sore vexed: for ofttimes he falleth into the fire, and oft into the water.

16 And I brought him to thy disciples, and they could not cure him.

17 Then Jesus answered and said, O faithless and perverse generation, how long shall I be with you? how long shall I suffer you? bring him hither to me.

18 And Jesus rebuked the devil; and he departed out of him: and the child was cured from that very hour.

Mark 9: 14–27

14 And when he came to his disciples, he saw a great multitude about them, and the scribes questioning with them.

15 And straightway all the people, when they beheld him, were greatly amazed, and running to him saluted him.

16 And he asked the scribes, What question ye with them?

17 And one of the multitude answered and said, Master, I have brought unto thee my son, which hath a dumb spirit;

18 And wheresoever he taketh him,

only son, the necessity is extremely urgent, and a modest and humble appeal is made to the compassion of Christ. Why then does he, contrary to his custom, break out suddenly into passion, and declare that they can be endured no longer? As the narrative of Matthew and Luke does not enable us to discover the reason of this great severity, some commentators have fallen into the mistake of supposing that this rebuke was directed either against the disciples, or against the father of the afflicted child. But if we duly consider all the circumstances of the case, as they are related by Mark, there will be no difficulty in arriving at the conclusion, that the indignation of Christ was directed against the malice of the scribes, and that he did not intend to treat the ignorant and weak with such harshness.

During Christ's absence, a **lunatic** child had been brought forward. The scribes, regarding this as a plausible occasion for giving annoyance, seized upon it eagerly, and entreated the disciples that, if they had any power, they would exercise it in curing the child. It is probable that the disciples made an attempt, and that their efforts were unavailing; upon which the scribes raise the shout of victory, and not only ridicule the disciples, but break out against Christ, as if in their person his power had been baffled. It was an extraordinary display of outrageous impiety united with equally base ingratitude, maliciously to keep out of view so many miracles, from which they had learned the amazing power of Christ; for they manifestly endeavored to extinguish the light which was placed before their eyes. With good reason, therefore, does Christ exclaim that they could no longer be endured, and pronounce them to be **an unbelieving and perverse nation**; for the numerous proofs which they had formerly beheld ought at least to have had the effect of preventing them from seeking occasion of disparagement.

Mark 9: 14. He saw a great multitude around them

The disciples were, no doubt, held up to public gaze, as the enemies of the truth are wont, on occasions of triumph, to assemble a crowd about a trifle. The scribes had made such a noise about it, as to draw down on the disciples the ridicule of many people. And yet it appears that there were some who were not ill disposed; for, as soon as they see Jesus, they salute him; and even the insolence of the scribes is restrained by his presence, for, when they are asked what is the matter in dispute, they have not a word to say.

17. Master, I have brought to thee my son

Matthew describes a different sort of disease from what is described by Mark, for he says that the man was **lunatic**. But both agree as to these two points, that he was **dumb**, and that at certain intervals he became furious. The term **lunatic** is applied to those who, about the waning of the moon, are seized with epilepsy, or afflicted with giddiness.

prophets relative to the person, nature, sufferings, death, and resurrection of Christ, and the glory that should follow.

4thly. The establishment of the mild, light-bringing, and life-giving Gospel of the Son of God. And

5thly. That as the old Jewish covenant and Mediatorship had ended, Jesus was now to be considered as the sole Teacher, the only availing offering for sin, and the grand Mediator between God and man.

10. His disciples – THE disciples, i.e. those only who had been with him on the mount, Peter, James, and John.

Why then say the scribes that Elias must first come? – As the disciples saw that Elijah returned to heaven, knowing the tradition of the elders, and the prophecy on which the tradition was founded, Malachi 4: 5, 6, Behold I send you Elijah the prophet, before the great and terrible day of the Lord shall come; and he shall turn the hearts, etc., it was natural enough for them to inquire what the meaning of the tradition, and the intention of the prophecy, were.

11. Elias – shall first come, and restore all things – No fanciful restoration of all men, devils and damned spirits, is spoken of as either being done, or begun, by the ministry of John; but merely that he should preach a doctrine tending to universal reformation of manners, and should be greatly successful: see Matthew 3: 1–7, and especially Luke 3: 3–15, where we find that a general reformation had taken place,

1. among the common people;
2. among the tax-gatherers; and
3. among the soldiers.

And as John announced the coming Christ, who was to baptize with the Holy Ghost, i.e. to enlighten, change, and purify the heart, that the reform might be complete, both outward and inward, he may be said, in the strictest sense of the word, to have fulfilled the prophecy: and that he was the Elijah mentioned by Malachi, the words of Gabriel to the virgin Mary prove; Luke 1: 17. And he (John) shall go before him (Christ) in the spirit and power of Elijah, to turn the hearts of the fathers to the children, and the disobedient to the wisdom of the just, etc.; and that his ministry was powerfully effectual for this purpose, we have already seen.

12. Knew him not – They have not acknowledged him. That is, the Jewish rulers have not acknowledged him, did not receive him as the forerunner of the Messiah. But it appears that all the rest acknowledged him as such; and some, from the power and demonstration of his preaching, were inclined to think he was more, even the Messiah himself: see Luke 3: 15.

13. Then the disciples understood – When he spoke of the sufferings of this prophetic Elijah, and also of his own, which had been the subject of the conversation on the mount, during the transfiguration, they clearly apprehended that he spoke of John the Baptist.

MATTHEW 17: 14–18; MARK 9: 14–27; LUKE 9: 37–43A

Matthew 17: 14–18

14. When they were come to the multitude – It appears that a congregation had been collected during our Lord's stay on the mount: how great must have been the desire of these people to hear the words of Christ! The assembly is self-collected, and no delay on the preacher's side discourages them – they continue to wait for him. In the present day how rare is this zeal! How few by the most pathetic invitation can be brought together, even at the most convenient times, to hear the same doctrines, and to get their souls healed by the same wonder-working Christ!

Kneeling down to him – Or falling at his knees. The ancients consecrated the EAR to memory; the FOREHEAD to genius; the RIGHT HAND to faith; and the KNEES to mercy: hence those who entreated favor fell at and touched the knees of the person whose kindness they supplicated.

15. My son – is lunatic – One who was most affected with this disorder at the change and

he teareth him: and he foameth, and gnasheth with his teeth, and pineth away: and I spake to thy disciples that they should cast him out; and they could not.

19 He answereth him, and saith, O faithless generation, how long shall I be with you? how long shall I suffer you? bring him unto me.

20 And they brought him unto him: and when he saw him, straightway the spirit tare him; and he fell on the ground, and wallowed foaming.

21 And he asked his father, How long is it ago since this came unto him? And he said, Of a child.

22 And ofttimes it hath cast him into the fire, and into the waters, to destroy him: but if thou canst do any thing, have compassion on us, and help us.

23 Jesus said unto him, If thou canst believe, all things are possible to him that believeth.

24 And straightway the father of the child cried out, and said with tears, Lord, I believe; help thou mine unbelief.

25 When Jesus saw that the people came running together, he rebuked the foul spirit, saying unto him, Thou dumb and deaf spirit, I charge thee, come out of him, and enter no more into him.

26 And the spirit cried, and rent him sore, and came out of him: and he was as one dead; insomuch that many said, He is dead.

27 But Jesus took him by the hand, and lifted him up; and he arose.

Luke 9: 37–43a

37 And it came to pass, that on the next day, when they were come down from the hill, much people met him.

38 And, behold, a man of the company cried out, saying, Master, I beseech thee, look upon my son: for he is mine only child.

39 And, lo, a spirit taketh him, and he suddenly crieth out; and it teareth him that he foameth again, and bruising him hardly departeth from him.

40 And I besought thy disciples to cast him out; and they could not.

41 And Jesus answering said, O faithless and perverse generation, how long shall I be with you, and suffer you? Bring thy son hither.

I am of opinion that the man was not naturally deaf and dumb, but that Satan had taken possession of his tongue and ears; and that, as the weakness of his brain and nerves made him liable to epilepsy, Satan availed himself of this for aggravating the disease. The consequence was, that he was exposed to danger on every hand, and was thrown into violent convulsions, which left him lying on the ground, in a fainting state, and like a dead man.

Let us learn from this how many ways Satan has of injuring us, were it not that he is restrained by the hand of God. Our infirmities both of soul and body, which we feel to be innumerable, are so many darts with which Satan is supplied for wounding us. We are worse than stupid, if a condition so wretched does not, arouse us to prayer. But in this we see also an amazing display of the goodness of God, that, though we are liable to such a variety of dangers, he surrounds us with his protection; particularly if we consider with what eagerness our enemy is bent on our destruction. We ought also to call to remembrance the consoling truth, that Christ has come to bridle his rage, and that we are safe in the midst of so many dangers, because our diseases are effectually counteracted by heavenly medicine.

MATTHEW 17: 19–21; MARK 9: 28–29; LUKE 17: 5–6

Matthew 17: 19. Then the disciples coming

The disciples wonder that the power which they once possessed has been taken from them; but they had lost it by their own fault. Christ therefore attributes this want of ability to their unbelief, and repeats and illustrates more largely the statement which he had previously made, that nothing is impossible to faith. It is a hyperbolical mode of expression, no doubt, when he declares that faith removes trees and mountains; but the meaning amounts to this, that God will never forsake us, if we keep the door open for receiving his grace. He does not mean that God will give us every thing that we may mention, or that may strike our minds at random. On the contrary, as nothing is more at variance with faith than the foolish and irregular desires of our flesh, it follows that those in whom faith reigns do not desire every thing without discrimination, but only that which the Lord promises to give. Let us therefore maintain such moderation as to desire nothing beyond what he has promised to us, and to confine our prayers within that rule which he has laid down.

MATTHEW 17: 22–23; 18: 1–5; MARK 9: 30–37; LUKE 9: 43–48

Matthew 17: 22. And while they remained in Galilee

The nearer that the time of his death approached, the more

full of the moon. But this lunacy was occasioned by a demon, see Matthew 17: 18, and Mark 9: 17; Luke 9: 38. In this case, the devil intended to hide himself under the appearance of a natural disorder, that no supernatural means might be resorted to for his expulsion.

Falleth ofttimes into the fire, and oft into the water – The paroxysms of his disorder frequently recurred; and among his numerous falls, some were into the fire and some into the water: so that, on this account, his life was in continual danger. Those who are under the influence of the devil are often driven to extremes in every thing. Such are often driven into the fire of presumption, or the waters of despair. Satan takes advantage of our natural temper, state of health, and outward circumstances, to plague and ruin our souls.

16. **Thy disciples could not cure him** – No wonder, when the cure must be effected by supernatural agency, and they had not faith enough to interest the power of God in their behalf, Matthew 17: 20. A spiritual disorder must have a spiritual remedy: natural means, in such cases, signify just – nothing. 17. **O faithless and perverse generation!** – These and the following words may be considered as spoken:

1. To the disciples, because of their unbelief, Matthew 17: 20.

2. To the father of the possessed, who should have brought his son to Christ.

3. To the whole multitude, who were slow of heart to believe in him as the Messiah, notwithstanding the miracles which he wrought.

Perverse signifies –

1. Such as are influenced by perverse opinions, which hinder them from receiving the truth: and,

2. Such as are profligate in their manners.

This last expression could not have been addressed to the disciples, who were certainly saved from the corruption of the world, and whose minds had been lately divinely illuminated by what passed at and after the transfiguration: but at all times the expression was applicable to the Jewish people.

18. **Jesus rebuked the devil** – Deprived him

of all power to torment the child; and obliged him to abandon his present usurped habitation.

There are some souls whose cure God reserves to himself alone, and to whom all the applications of his ministers appear to be utterly ineffectual. He sometimes does all without them, that they may know they can never do any good without him.

MATTHEW 17: 19–21; MARK 9: 28–29; LUKE 17: 5–6

Matthew 17: 19–21

19. **Why could not we cast him out?** – They were confounded at their want of success – but not at their want of faith, which was the cause of their miscarriage! When the ministers of the Gospel find their endeavors, with respect to some places or persons, ineffectual, they should come, by private prayer, to Christ, humble themselves before him, and beg to be informed whether some evil in themselves have not been the cause of the unfruitfulness of their labors.

20. **Because of your unbelief** – Are we preachers of the Gospel? Do the things of God rest upon our minds with a deep and steady conviction? Can we expect that a doctrine which we do not, from conviction, credit ourselves, can be instrumental in our hands of begetting faith in others? So we preached, end so ye believed. The word preached generally begets in the people the same spirit which the preacher possesses. The disciples had some faith, but not enough – they believed, but not fully.

As a grain of mustard seed – Some eminent critics think this a proverbial expression, intimating a GREAT DEGREE of faith, because removing mountains, which St. Paul, 1 Corinthians 13: 2, attributes to ALL FAITH; i.e. the greatest possible degree of faith, is attributed here, by our Lord, to that faith which is as a grain of mustard seed. However this may be, there can be no doubt that our Lord means a thriving and increasing faith; which like the grain of mustard seed, from being the least of

42 And as he was yet a coming, the devil threw him down, and tare him. And Jesus rebuked the unclean spirit, and healed the child, and delivered him again to his father.

43a And they were all amazed at the mighty power of God.

MATTHEW 17: 19–21; MARK 9: 28–29; LUKE 17: 5–6

Matthew 17: 19–21

19 Then came the disciples to Jesus apart, and said, Why could not we cast him out?

20 And Jesus said unto them, Because of your unbelief: for verily I say unto you, If ye have faith as a grain of mustard seed, ye shall say unto this mountain, Remove hence to yonder place; and it shall remove; and nothing shall be impossible unto you.

21 Howbeit this kind goeth not out but by prayer and fasting.

Mark 9: 28–29

28 And when he was come into the house, his disciples asked him privately, Why could not we cast him out?

29 And he said unto them, This kind can come forth by nothing, but by prayer and fasting.

Luke 17: 5–6

5 And the apostles said unto the Lord, Increase our faith.

6 And the Lord said, If ye had faith as a grain of mustard seed, ye might say unto this sycamine tree, Be thou plucked up by the root, and be thou planted in the sea; and it should obey you.

MATTHEW 17: 22–23, 18: 1–5; MARK 9: 30–37; LUKE 9: 43B–48

Matthew 17: 22–23

22 And while they abode in Galilee, Jesus said unto them, The Son of man shall be betrayed into the hands of men:

23 And they shall kill him, and the third day he shall be raised again. And they were exceeding sorry.

Matthew 18: 1–5

1 At the same time came the disciples unto Jesus, saying, Who is the greatest in the kingdom of heaven?

frequently did Christ warn his disciples, lest that melancholy spectacle might give a violent shock to their faith. It was shortly after the miracle had been performed that this discourse was delivered; for Mark says that he went from that place to Galilee, in order to spend there the intervening time in privacy; for he had resolved to come to Jerusalem on the day of the annual sacrifice, because he was to be sacrificed at the approaching Passover.

The disciples had previously received several intimations on this subject, and yet they are as much alarmed as if nothing relating to it had ever reached their ears. So great is the influence of preconceived opinion, that it brings darkness over the mind in the midst of the clearest light. The apostles had imagined that the state of Christ's kingdom would be prosperous and delightful, and that, as soon as he made himself known, he would be universally received with the highest approbation. They never thought it possible that the priests, and scribes, and other rulers of the Church, would oppose him. Under the influence of this prejudice, they admit nothing that is said on the other side; for Mark says that they understood not what our Lord meant. Whence came it that a discourse so clear and distinct was not understood, but because their minds were covered by the thick veil of a foolish imagination?

They did not venture to make any farther inquiry. This must have been owing, in part, to their reverence for their Master; but I have no doubt that their grief and astonishment at what they had heard kept them silent. Such bashfulness was not altogether commendable; for it kept them in doubt, and hesitation, and sinful grief. In the meantime, a confused principle of piety, rather than a clear knowledge of the truth, kept them attached to Christ, and prevented them from leaving his school. A certain commencement of faith and right understanding had been implanted in their hearts, which made their zeal in following Christ not very different from the implicit faith of the Papists; but as they had not yet made such progress as to become acquainted with the nature of the kingdom of God and of the renewal which had been promised in Christ, I say that they were guided by zeal for piety rather than by distinct knowledge.

In this way we come to see what there was in them that deserved praise or blame. But though their stupidity could not entirely be excused, we have no reason to wonder that a plain and distinct announcement of the cross of their Master, and of the ignominy to which he would be subjected, appeared to them a riddle; not only because they reckoned it to be inconsistent with the glory of the Son of God that he should be rejected and condemned, but because it appeared to them to be highly improbable that the grace which was promised in a peculiar manner to the Jews should be set at naught by the rulers of the nation. But as the immoderate

seeds, becomes the greatest of all herbs; even a tree in whose branches the fowls of the air take shelter.

21. This kind goeth not out but by prayer, etc. – this kind, some apply to the faith which should be exercised on the occasion, which goeth not out, doth not exert itself, but by prayer and fasting; but this interpretation is, in my opinion, far from solid. However, there is great difficulty in the text. The whole verse is wanting in the famous Vatican MS., one of the most ancient and most authentic perhaps in the world; and in another one of Colbert's, written in the 11th or 12th century. It is wanting also in the Coptic, Ethiopic, Syriac, Hieros., and in one copy of the Itala. But all the MSS. acknowledge it in the parallel place, Mark 9: 29, only the Vatican MS. leaves out fasting. I strongly suspect it to be an interpolation; but, if it be, it is very ancient, as Origen, Chrysostom, and others of the primitive fathers, acknowledged it. But while candor obliges me to acknowledge that I cannot account for the fact here alleged, that a certain class or genus of demons cannot be expelled but by prayer and fasting, while others may be ejected without them, I can give a sense to the passage which all my readers will easily understand: viz. that there are certain evil propensities, in some persons, which pampering the flesh tends to nourish and strengthen; and that self-denial and fasting, accompanied by prayer to God, are the most likely means, not only to mortify such propensities, but also to destroy them.

MATTHEW 17: 22–23; 18: 1–5; MARK 9: 30–37; LUKE 9: 43B–48

Matthew 17: 22–23

22. They abode in Galilee – Lower Galilee, where the city of Capernaum was.

The Son of man shall be betrayed into the hands of men – The Son of man is about to be delivered into the hands, etc. Jesus was delivered up, by the counsel of God, to be an atonement for the sin of the world. See Acts 4: 27–28.

Against thy holy child Jesus, whom thou hast anointed to do what thy hand and thy counsel determined before to be done, Herod and Pontius Pilate were gathered together.

23. They were exceeding sorry – Since the conversation on the mount, with Moses and Elijah; Peter, James, and John could have no doubt that their Lord and Master must suffer, and that it was for this end he came into the world; but, while they submitted to the counsel of God, their affection for him caused them to feel exquisite distress.

MATTHEW 18: 6–10; MARK 9: 42–48; LUKE 17: 1–2

Matthew 18: 6–10

6. But whoso shall offend one of these little ones – But, on the contrary, whosoever shall cause one of the least of those who believe in me to be stumbled – to go into the spirit of the world, or give way to sin – such a one shall meet with the most exemplary punishment.

Let those who act the part of the devil, in tempting others to sin, hear this declaration of our Lord, and tremble.

A millstone – an ass's millstone, because in ancient times, before the invention of wind and water mills, the stones were turned sometimes by slaves, but commonly by asses or mules. The most ancient kind of mills among the inhabitants of the northern nations, was the quern, or hand-mill.

Drowned in the depth of the sea – It is supposed that in Syria, as well as in Greece, this mode of punishing criminals was practiced; especially in cases of parricide; and when a person was devoted to destruction for the public safety, as in cases of plague, famine, etc. When a person was drowned, they hung a weight, a vast stone about his neck.

7. Wo! – Or, alas! It is the opinion of some eminent critics, that this word is ever used by our Lord to express sympathy and concern.

Because of offenses – Scandals, stumbling-blocks, persecutions, etc.

For it must needs be that offenses come

2 And Jesus called a little child unto him, and set him in the midst of them,

3 And said, Verily I say unto you, Except ye be converted, and become as little children, ye shall not enter into the kingdom of heaven.

4 Whosoever therefore shall humble himself as this little child, the same is greatest in the kingdom of heaven.

5 And whoso shall receive one such little child in my name receiveth me.

Mark 9: 30–37

30 And they departed thence, and passed through Galilee; and he would not that any man should know it.

31 For he taught his disciples, and said unto them, The Son of man is delivered into the hands of men, and they shall kill him; and after that he is killed, he shall rise the third day.

32 But they understood not that saying, and were afraid to ask him.

33 And he came to Capernaum: and being in the house he asked them, What was it that ye disputed among yourselves by the way?

34 But they held their peace: for by the way they had disputed among themselves, who should be the greatest.

35 And he sat down, and called the twelve, and saith unto them, If any man desire to be first, the same shall be last of all, and servant of all.

36 And he took a child, and set him in the midst of them: and when he had taken him in his arms, he said unto them,

37 Whosoever shall receive one of such children in my name, receiveth me: and whosoever shall receive me, receiveth not me, but him that sent me.

Luke 9: 43b–48

43b But while they wondered every one at all things which Jesus did, he said unto his disciples,

44 Let these sayings sink down into your ears: for the Son of man shall be delivered into the hands of men.

45 But they understood not this saying, and it was hid from them, that they perceived it not: and they feared to ask him of that saying.

46 Then there arose a reasoning among them, which of them should be greatest.

dread of the cross, which had suddenly seized upon them, shut the door against the consolation which was immediately added, arising out of the hope of the resurrection, let us learn that, when the death of Christ is mentioned, we ought always to take into view at once the whole of the three days, that his death and burial may lead us to a blessed triumph and to a new life.

Matthew 18: 1. At that time the disciples came to Jesus

It is evident from the other two Evangelists, that the disciples did not come to Christ of their own accord, but that, having secretly **disputed on the road**, they were brought out of their lurking-places, and dragged forth to light. There is nothing inconsistent with this in the account given by Matthew, who hastens to Christ's reply, and does not relate all the circumstances of the case, but passes over the commencement, and relates in a summary manner the reason why Christ rebuked the foolish ambition of his disciples for the highest rank. When Christ makes inquiry about a secret conversation, and forces the disciples to acknowledge what they would willingly have kept back, this teaches us that we ought to beware of all ambition, however carefully it may be concealed. We must also attend to the time at which this occurred. The prediction of his death had made them sad and perplexed; but as if they had received from it unmingled delight, as if they had tasted of the nectar which the poets feign, they immediately enter into a dispute about the highest rank. How was it possible that their distress of mind vanished in a moment, but because the minds of men are so devoted to ambition, that, forgetful of their present state of warfare, they continually rush forward, under the delusive influence of a false imagination, to obtain a triumph? And if the apostles so soon forgot a discourse which they had lately heard, what will become of us if, dismissing for a long period meditation on the cross, we give ourselves up to indifference and sloth, or to idle speculations?

MATTHEW 18: 6–10; MARK 9: 42–48; LUKE 17: 1–2

Matthew 18: 6. But whosoever shall offend one of those little ones

This appears to be added for the consolation of the godly, that they may not be rendered uneasy by their condition, if they are despised by the world. It is a powerful obstruction to the voluntary exercise of modesty, when they imagine, that by so doing they expose themselves to contempt; and it is hard to be not only treated disdainfully, but almost trodden under foot, by haughty men. Christ therefore encourages his disciples by the consoling truth, that, if their mean condition draws upon them the insults of the world,

– for the coming of offenses is unavoidable. Such is the wickedness of men, such their obstinacy, that they will not come unto Christ that they may have life, but desperately continue deceiving and being deceived. In such a state of things, offenses, stumbling-blocks, persecutions, etc., are unavoidable.

Wo to that man – He who gives the offense, and he who receives it, are both exposed to ruin.

10. One of these little ones – One of my simple, loving, humble disciples.

Their angels – always behold – Our Lord here not only alludes to, but, in my opinion, establishes the notion received by almost all nations, viz. That every person has a guardian angel; and that these have always access to God, to receive orders relative to the management of their charge. See Psalm 34: 8; Hebrews 1: 14.

Always behold the face – Hence, among the Jews, the angels were styled angels of the face, and Michael is said to be the prince of the face. This is an allusion to the privilege granted by eastern monarchs to their chief favorites; a privilege which others were never permitted to enjoy. The seven princes of Media and Persia, who were the chief favorites and privy-counsellors of Ahasuerus, are said to see the king's face. Esther 1: 14; see also 2 Kings 25: 19, and Jeremiah 51: 25. Our Lord's words give us to understand that humble-hearted, child-like disciples, are objects of his peculiar care, and constant attention.

MATTHEW 18: 11–14; LUKE 15: 1–10

Matthew 18: 11–14

11. For the Son of man, etc. – This is added as a second reason, why no injury should be done to his followers. "The Son of man has so loved them as to come into the world to lay down his life for them."

That which was lost – In Revelation 9: 11, Satan is called the destroyer, or him who lays waste. This name bears a near relation to that state in which our Lord tells us he finds

all mankind – lost, desolated, ruined. So it appears that Satan and men have the nearest affinity to each other – as the destroyer and the destroyed – the desolator and the desolated – the loser and the lost. But the Son of man came to save the lost. Glorious news! May every lost soul feel it!

12. Doth he not leave the ninety and nine, and goeth into the mountains – So our common translation reads the verse; others, Doth he not leave the ninety and nine UPON THE MOUNTAINS, and go, etc. This latter reading appears to me to be the best; because, in Luke 15: 4, it is said, he leaveth the ninety and nine IN THE DESERT. The allusion, therefore, is to a shepherd feeding his sheep on the mountains, in the desert; not seeking the lost one ON the mountains.

Leaving the ninety and nine, and seeking the ONE strayed sheep: This was a very common form of speech among the Jews, and includes no mystery, though there are some who imagine that our Lord refers to the angels who kept not their first estate, and that they are in number, to men, as NINETY are to ONE. But it is likely that our Lord in this place only alludes to his constant solicitude to instruct, heal, and save those simple people of the sea coasts, country villages, etc., who were scattered abroad, as sheep without a shepherd, (Matthew 9: 36), the scribes and Pharisees paying no attention to their present or eternal well-being. This may be also considered as a lesson of instruction and comfort to backsliders. How hardly does Christ give them up!

13. He rejoiceth more – It is justly observed by one, on this verse, that it is natural for a person to express unusual joy at the fortunate accomplishment of an unexpected event.

14. It is not the will of your Father – If any soul be finally lost, it is not because God's will or counsel was against its salvation, or that a proper provision had not been made for it; but that, though light came into the world, it preferred darkness to light, because of its attachment to its evil deeds.

47 And Jesus, perceiving the thought of their heart, took a child, and set him by him,

48 And said unto them, Whosoever shall receive this child in my name receiveth me: and whosoever shall receive me receiveth him that sent me: for he that is least among you all, the same shall be great.

MATTHEW 18: 6–10; MARK 9: 42–48; LUKE 17: 1–2

Matthew 18: 6–10

6 But whoso shall offend one of these little ones which believe in me, it were better for him that a millstone were hanged about his neck, and that he were drowned in the depth of the sea.

7 Woe unto the world because of offences! for it must needs be that offences come; but woe to that man by whom the offence cometh!

8 Wherefore if thy hand or thy foot offend thee, cut them off, and cast them from thee: it is better for thee to enter into life halt or maimed, rather than having two hands or two feet to be cast into everlasting fire.

9 And if thine eye offend thee, pluck it out, and cast it from thee: it is better for thee to enter into life with one eye, rather than having two eyes to be cast into hell fire.

10 Take heed that ye despise not one of these little ones; for I say unto you, That in heaven their angels do always behold the face of my Father which is in heaven.

Mark 9: 42–48

42 And whosoever shall offend one of these little ones that believe in me, it is better for him that a millstone were hanged about his neck, and he were cast into the sea.

43 And if thy hand offend thee, cut it off: it is better for thee to enter into life maimed, than having two hands to go into hell, into the fire that never shall be quenched:

44 Where their worm dieth not, and the fire is not quenched.

45 And if thy foot offend thee, cut it off: it is better for thee to enter halt

God does not despise them.

But he appears to have had likewise another object in view; for a dispute had arisen amongst them as to the first place of honor, from which it might naturally have been inferred that the Apostles were tainted with sinful ambition. Every man who thinks too highly of himself, or desires to be preferred to others, must necessarily treat his brethren with disdain. To cure this disease, Christ threatens a dreadful punishment, if any man in his pride shall throw down those who are oppressed with poverty, or who in heart are already humbled.

Under the word **offend** he includes more than if he had forbidden them to despise their brethren; though the man who gives himself no concern about **offending** the weak, does so for no other reason, than because he does not render to them the honor to which they are entitled. Now as there are various kinds of **offenses**, it will be proper to explain generally what is meant by **offending**. If any man through our fault either stumbles, or is drawn aside from the right course, or retarded in it, we are said to **offend** him. Whoever then desires to escape that fearful punishment which Christ denounces, let him stretch out his hand to the **little ones** who are despised by the world, and let him kindly assist them in keeping the path of duty; for Christ recommends them to our notice, that they may lead us to exercise voluntary humility; as Paul enjoins the children of God to "condescend to men of low estate," (Romans 12: 16,) and again says that "we ought not to please ourselves" (Romans 15: 1).

To **hang a millstone** about a man's neck, and drown him in the sea, was the punishment then reckoned the most appalling, and which was inflicted on the most atrocious malefactors. When our Lord alludes to this punishment, we are enabled to perceive how dear and precious those people are in the sight of God, who are mean and despised in the eyes of the world.

MATTHEW 18: 11–14; LUKE 15: 1–10

Matthew 18: 11. For the Son of man cometh

Christ now employs his own example in persuading his disciples to honor even weak and despised brethren; for he came down from heaven to save not them only, but even the dead who were lost. It is in the highest degree unreasonable that we should disdainfully reject those whom the Son of God has so highly esteemed. And even if the weak labor under imperfections which may expose them to contempt, our pride is not on that account to be excused; for we ought to esteem them not for the value of their virtues, but for the sake of Christ; and he who will not conform himself to Christ's example is too saucy and proud.

LUKE 15 11–24

12. Give me the portion of goods – It may seem strange that such a demand should be made, and that the parent should have acceded to it, when he knew that it was to minister to his debauches that his profligate son made the demand here specified. But the matter will appear plain, when it is considered, that it has been an immemorial custom in the east for sons to demand and receive their portion of the inheritance during their father's lifetime; and the parent, however aware of the dissipated inclinations of the child, could not legally refuse to comply with the application. It appears indeed that the spirit of this law was to provide for the child in case of ill treatment by the father: yet the demand must first be acceded to, before the matter could be legally inquired into; and then, "if it was found that the father was irreproachable in his character, and had given no just cause for the son to separate from him, in that case, the civil magistrate fined the son in two hundred puns of cowries."

13. Not many days after – He probably hastened his departure for fear of the fine which he must have paid, and the reproach to which he must have been subjected, had the matter come before the civil magistrate.

Riotous living – in a course of life that led him to spend all. And this we are informed, Luke 15: 30, was among harlots; the readiest way in the world to exhaust the body, debase the mind, ruin the soul, and destroy the substance.

14. A mighty famine in that land – As he was of a profligate turn of mind himself, it is likely he sought out a place where riot and excess were the ruling characteristics of the inhabitants; and, as poverty is the sure consequence of prodigality, it is no wonder that famine preyed on the whole country.

15. To feed swine – The basest and vilest of all employments; and, to a Jew, peculiarly degrading. Shame, contempt, and distress are wedded to sin, and can never be divorced. No character could be meaner in the sight of

a Jew than that of a swineherd: and Herodotus informs us, that in Egypt they were not permitted to mingle with civil society, nor to appear in the worship of the gods, nor would the very dregs of the people have any matrimonial connections with them.

17. When he came to himself – A state of sin is represented in the sacred writings as a course of folly and madness; and repentance is represented as a restoration to sound sense.

I perish with hunger! – Or, I perish HERE.

18. Against heaven – that is, against God. The Jews often make use of this periphrasis in order to avoid mentioning the name of God, which they have ever treated with the utmost reverence. But some contend that it should be translated, even unto heaven; a Hebraism for, I have sinned exceedingly – beyond all description.

20. And kissed him – Or, kissed him again and again. The father thus showed his great tenderness towards him, and his great affection for him.

21. The design of the inspired penman is to show, not merely the depth of the profligate son's repentance, and the sincerity of his conversion, but to show the great affection of the father, and his readiness to forgive his disobedient son. His tenderness of heart cannot wait till the son has made his confession; his bowels yearn over him, and he cuts short his tale of contrition and self-reproach, by giving him the most plenary assurances of his pardoning love.

21. Bring forth the best robe – Bring out that chief garment the garment which was laid by, to be used only on birth-days or festival times. Such as that which Rebecca had laid by for Esau, and which she put on Jacob when she made him personate his brother.

Put a ring on his hand – Giving a ring was in ancient times a mark of honor and dignity. See Genesis 41: 42; 1 Kings 21: 8; Esther 8: 2; Daniel 6: 17; James 2: 2.

Shoes on his feet – Formerly those who were captivated had their shoes taken off, Isaiah 20:

into life, than having two feet to be cast into hell, into the fire that never shall be quenched:

46 Where their worm dieth not, and the fire is not quenched.

47 And if thine eye offend thee, pluck it out: it is better for thee to enter into the kingdom of God with one eye, than having two eyes to be cast into hell fire:

48 Where their worm dieth not, and the fire is not quenched.

Luke 17: 1–2

1 Then said he unto the disciples, It is impossible but that offences will come: but woe unto him, through whom they come!

2 It were better for him that a millstone were hanged about his neck, and he cast into the sea, than that he should offend one of these little ones.

MATTHEW 18: 11–14; LUKE 15: 1–10

Matthew 18: 11–14

11 For the Son of man is come to save that which was lost.

12 How think ye? if a man have an hundred sheep, and one of them be gone astray, doth he not leave the ninety and nine, and goeth into the mountains, and seeketh that which is gone astray?

13 And if so be that he find it, verily I say unto you, he rejoiceth more of that sheep, than of the ninety and nine which went not astray.

14 Even so it is not the will of your Father which is in heaven, that one of these little ones should perish.

Luke 15: 1–10

1 Then drew near unto him all the publicans and sinners for to hear him.

2 And the Pharisees and scribes murmured, saying, This man receiveth sinners, and eateth with them.

3 And he spake this parable unto them, saying,

4 What man of you, having an hundred sheep, if he lose one of them, doth not leave the ninety and nine in the wilderness, and go after that which is lost, until he find it?

5 And when he hath found it, he layeth it on his shoulders, rejoicing.

6 And when he cometh home, he cal-

12. What think you?

Luke carries the occasion of this parable still farther back, as having arisen from the murmurings of the Pharisees and scribes against our Lord, whom they saw conversing daily with sinners. Christ therefore intended to show that a good teacher ought not to labor less to recover those that are lost, than to preserve those which are in his possession; though according to Matthew the comparison proceeds farther, and teaches us not only that we ought to treat with kindness the disciples of Christ, but that we ought to bear with their imperfections, and endeavor, when they wander, to bring them back to the road. For, though they happen sometimes to wander, yet as they are sheep over which God has appointed his Son to be shepherd, so far are we from having a right to chase or drive them away roughly, that we ought to gather them from their wanderings; for the object of the discourse is to lead us to beware of losing what God wishes to be saved. The narrative of Luke presents to us a somewhat different object. It is, that the whole human race belongs to God, and that therefore we ought to gather those that have gone astray, and that we ought to rejoice as much, when they that are lost return to the path of duty, as a man would do who, beyond his expectation, recovered something the loss of which had grieved him.

Luke 15: 10. There will be joy in the presence of the angels

If angels mutually rejoice with each other in heaven, when they see that what had wandered is restored to the fold, we too, who have the same cause in common with them, ought to be partakers of the same joy. But. how does he say that the repentance of one ungodly man yields greater joy than the perseverance of many righteous men to angels, whose highest delight is in a continued and uninterrupted course of righteousness? I reply, though it would be more agreeable to the wishes of angels (as it is also more desirable) that men should always remain in perfect integrity, yet as in the deliverance of a sinner, who had been already devoted to destruction, and had been cut off as a rotten member from the body, the mercy of God shines more brightly, he attributes to angels, after the manner of men, a greater joy arising out of an unexpected good.

LUKE 15: 11–24

This parable is nothing else than a confirmation of the preceding doctrine. In the first part is shown how readily God is disposed to pardon our sins, and in the second part (which we shall afterwards treat in the proper place) is shown the great malignity and obstinacy of those who murmur at his compassion. In the person of a young prodigal who, after

1; and when they were restored to liberty their shoes were restored. See 2 Chronicles 28: 15. In Bengal, shoes of a superior quality make one of the distinguishing parts of a person's dress.

23. The fatted calf, and kill it – Sacrifice it. In ancient times the animals provided for public feasts were first sacrificed to God. The blood of the beast being poured out before God, by way of atonement for sin, the flesh was considered as consecrated, and the guests were considered as feeding on Divine food.

24. Was dead – Lost to all good – given up to all evil. In this figurative sense the word is used by the best Greek writers.

LUKE 15: 25–32

25. His elder son – Meaning probably persons of a regular moral life, who needed no repentance in comparison of the prodigal already described.

In the field – Attending the concerns of the farm.

He heard music – a number of sounds mingled together, as in a concert.

28. He was angry – This refers to the indignation of the scribes and Pharisees, mentioned Luke 15: 1–2. In every point of view, the anger of the older son was improper and unreasonable. He had already received his part of the inheritance, see Luke 15: 12, and his profligate brother had received no more than what was his just dividend. Besides, what the father had acquired since that division he had a right to dispose of as he pleased, even to give it all to one son; nor did the ancient customs of the Asiatic countries permit the other children to claim any share in such property thus disposed of. The following is an institute of the GENTOO law on this subject: "If a father gives, by his own choice, land, houses, orchards, and the earning of his own industry, to one of his sons, the other sons shall not receive any share of it." Besides, whatever property the father had acquired after the above division, the son or sons, as the prodigal in the text, could have no

claim at all on, according to another institute in the above Asiatic laws, but the father might divide it among those who remained with him: therefore is it said in the text, "Son, thou art ALWAYS with me, and ALL that I have is THINE," Luke 15: 31.

29. Never – a kid – It is evident from Luke 15: 12, that the father gave him his portion when his profligate brother claimed his; for he divided his whole substance between them. And though he had not claimed it, so as to separate from, and live independently of, his father, yet he might have done so whenever he chose; and therefore his complaining was both undutiful and unjust.

30. This thy son – THIS son of THINE – words expressive of supreme contempt: THIS son – he would not condescend to call him by his name, or to acknowledge him for his brother; and at the same time, bitterly reproaches his amiable father for his affectionate tenderness, and readiness to receive his once undutiful, but now penitent, child!

For HIM – I have marked those words in small capitals which should be strongly accented in the pronunciation: this last word shows how supremely he despised his poor unfortunate brother.

32. This thy brother – Or, THIS brother of THINE. To awaken this ill-natured, angry, inhumane man to a proper sense of his duty, both to his parent and brother, this amiable father returns him his own unkind words, but in a widely different spirit. This son of mine to whom I show mercy is THY brother, to whom thou shouldst show bowels of tenderness and affection; especially as he is no longer the person he was: he was dead in sin – he is quickened by the power of God: he was lost to thee, to me, to himself, and to our God; but now he is found: and he will be a comfort to me, a help to thee, and a standing proof, to the honor of the Most High, that God receiveth sinners. This, as well as the two preceding parables, was designed to vindicate the conduct of our blessed Lord in receiving tax-gatherers and heathens; and as the Jews, to whom it was

leth together his friends and neighbours, saying unto them, Rejoice with me; for I have found my sheep which was lost.

7 I say unto you, that likewise joy shall be in heaven over one sinner that repenteth, more than over ninety and nine just persons, which need no repentance.

8 Either what woman having ten pieces of silver, if she lose one piece, doth not light a candle, and sweep the house, and seek diligently till she find it?

9 And when she hath found it, she calleth her friends and her neighbours together, saying, Rejoice with me; for I have found the piece which I had lost.

10 Likewise, I say unto you, there is joy in the presence of the angels of God over one sinner that repenteth.

LUKE 15: 11–24

11 And he said, A certain man had two sons:

12 And the younger of them said to his father, Father, give me the portion of goods that falleth to me. And he divided unto them his living.

13 And not many days after the younger son gathered all together, and took his journey into a far country, and there wasted his substance with riotous living.

14 And when he had spent all, there arose a mighty famine in that land; and he began to be in want.

15 And he went and joined himself to a citizen of that country; and he sent him into his fields to feed swine.

16 And he would fain have filled his belly with the husks that the swine did eat: and no man gave unto him.

17 And when he came to himself, he said, How many hired servants of my father's have bread enough and to spare, and I perish with hunger!

18 I will arise and go to my father, and will say unto him, Father, I have sinned against heaven, and before thee,

19 And am no more worthy to be called thy son: make me as one of thy hired servants.

20 And he arose, and came to his father. But when he was yet a great way off, his father saw him, and had compassion, and ran, and fell on his neck, and kissed him.

having been reduced to the deepest poverty by luxury and extravagance, returns as a suppliant to his father, to whom he had been disobedient and rebellious, Christ describes all sinners who, wearied of their folly, apply to the grace of God. To the kind father, on the other hand, who not only pardons the crimes of his son, but of his own accord meets him when returning, he compares God, who is not satisfied with pardoning those who pray to him, but even advances to meet them with the compassion of a father. Let us now examine the parable in detail.

12. And the younger of them said to his father

The parable opens by describing a mark of wicked arrogance in the youth, which appears in his being desirous to leave his father, and in thinking that he cannot be right without being permitted to indulge in debauchery, free from his father's control. There is also ingratitude in leaving the old man, and not only withholding the performance of the duties which be owed to him, but crippling and diminishing the wealth of his house. This is at length followed by wasteful luxury and wicked extravagance, by which he squanders all that he had. After so many offenses he deserved to find his father implacable.

Under this image our Lord unquestionably depicts to us the boundless goodness and inestimable forbearance of God, that no crimes, however aggravated, may deter us from the hope of obtaining pardon, There would be some foundation for the analogy, if we were to say that this foolish and insolent youth resembles those people who, enjoying at the hand of God a great abundance of good things, are moved by a blind and mad ambition to be separated from Him, that they may enjoy perfect freedom; as if it were not more desirable than all the kingdoms of the world to live under the fatherly care and government of God. But as I am afraid that this allusion may be thought overstrained, I shall satisfy myself with the literal meaning; not that I disapprove of the opinion, that under this figure is reproved the madness of those who imagine that it will be advantageous for them to have something of their own, and to be rich apart from the heavenly Father.

LUKE 15: 25–32

This latter portion of the parable charges those people with cruelty, who would wickedly choose to set limits to the grace of God, as if they envied the salvation of wretched sinners. For we know that this is pointed at the haughtiness of the scribes, who did not think that they received the reward due to their merits, if Christ admitted publicans and the common people to the hope of the eternal inheritance. The substance of it therefore is, that, if we are desirous to be reckoned the children of God, we must forgive in a broth-

addressed, could not but approve of the conduct of this benevolent father, and reprobate that of his elder son, so they could not but justify the conduct of Christ towards those outcasts of men, and, at least in the silence of their hearts, pass sentence of condemnation upon themselves. For the sublime, the beautiful, the pathetic, and the instructive, the history of Joseph in the Old Testament, and the parable of the prodigal son in the New, have no parallels either in sacred or profane history.

Three points may be considered here:
I. The degrees of his fall.
II. The degrees of his restoration; and,
III. The consequences of his conversion.

I. The prodigal son is the emblem of a sinner who refuses to depend on and be governed by the Lord. How dangerous is it for us to desire to be at our own disposal, to live in a state of independency, and to be our own governors! God cannot give to wretched man a greater proof of his wrath than to abandon him to the corruption of his own heart.

Not many days, etc., Luke 15: 13. The misery of a sinner has its degrees; and he soon arrives, step by step, at the highest pitch of his wretchedness.

The first degree of his misery is, that he loses sight of God, and removes at a distance from him. There is a boundless distance between the love of God, and impure self-love; and yet, strange to tell, we pass in a moment from the one to the other!

The second degree of a sinner's misery is, that the love of God being no longer retained in the heart, carnal love and impure desires necessarily enter in, reign there, and corrupt all his actions.

The third degree is, that he squanders away all spiritual riches, and wastes the substance of his gracious Father in riot and debauch.

When he had spent all, etc., Luke 15: 14. The fourth degree of an apostate sinner's misery is, that having forsaken God, and lost his grace and love, he can now find nothing but poverty, misery, and want. How empty is that soul which God does not fill! What a famine is there in that heart which is no longer nour-

ished by the bread of life!

In this state, he joined himself—he cemented, closely united himself, and fervently cleaved to a citizen of that country, Luke 15: 15.

The fifth degree of a sinner's misery is, that he renders himself a slave to the devil, is made partaker of his nature, and incorporated into the infernal family. The farther a sinner goes from God, the nearer he comes to eternal ruin.

The sixth degree of his misery is, that he soon finds by experience the hardship and rigor of his slavery. There is no master so cruel as the devil; no yoke so heavy as that of sin; and no slavery so mean and vile as for a man to be the drudge of his own carnal, shameful, and brutish passions.

The seventh degree of a sinner's misery is, that he has an insatiable hunger and thirst after happiness; and as this can be had only in God, and he seeks it in the creature, his misery must be extreme. He desired to fill his belly with the husks, Luke 15: 16. The pleasures of sense and appetite are the pleasures of swine, and to such creatures is he resembled who has frequent recourse to them, 2 Peter 2: 22.

II. Let us observe, in the next place, the several degrees of a sinner's conversion and salvation.

The first is, he begins to know and feel his misery, the guilt of his conscience, and the corruption of his heart. He comes to himself, because the Spirit of God first comes to him, Luke 15: 17.

The second is, that he resolves to forsake sin and all the occasions of it; and firmly purposes in his soul to return immediately to his God. I will arise, etc., Luke 15: 18.

The third is, when, under the influence of the spirit of faith, he is enabled to look towards God as a compassionate and tender-hearted father. I will arise and go to my father.

The fourth is, when he makes confession of his sin, and feels himself utterly unworthy of all God's favors, Luke 15: 19.

The fifth is, when he comes in the spirit of obedience, determined through grace to submit to the authority of God; and to take his

21 And the son said unto him, Father, I have sinned against heaven, and in thy sight, and am no more worthy to be called thy son.

22 But the father said to his servants, Bring forth the best robe, and put it on him; and put a ring on his hand, and shoes on his feet:

23 And bring hither the fatted calf, and kill it; and let us eat, and be merry:

24 For this my son was dead, and is alive again; he was lost, and is found. And they began to be merry.

LUKE 15: 25–32

25 Now his elder son was in the field: and as he came and drew nigh to the house, he heard musick and dancing.

26 And he called one of the servants, and asked what these things meant.

27 And he said unto him, Thy brother is come; and thy father hath killed the fatted calf, because he hath received him safe and sound.

28 And he was angry, and would not go in: therefore came his father out, and intreated him.

29 And he answering said to his father, Lo, these many years do I serve thee, neither transgressed I at any time thy commandment: and yet thou never gavest me a kid, that I might make merry with my friends:

30 But as soon as this thy son was come, which hath devoured thy living with harlots, thou hast killed for him the fatted calf.

31 And he said unto him, Son, thou art ever with me, and all that I have is thine.

32 It was meet that we should make merry, and be glad: for this thy brother was dead, and is alive again; and was lost, and is found.

MATTHEW 18: 15–20; LUKE 17: 3

Matthew 18: 15–20

15 Moreover if thy brother shall trespass against thee, go and tell him his fault between thee and him alone: if he shall hear thee, thou hast gained thy brother.

16 But if he will not hear thee, then take with thee one or two more, that in the mouth of two or three witnesses every

erly manner the faults of brethren, which He forgives with fatherly kindness.

28. Therefore his father went out

By these words he reproaches hypocrites with intolerable pride, which makes it necessary that the Father should entreat them not to envy the compassion manifested to their brethren. Now though God does not entreat, yet by his example he exhorts us to bear with the faults of our brethren.

MATTHEW 18: 15–20; LUKE 17: 3

Matthew 18: 15. But if thy brother shall sin against thee

As he had discoursed about bearing the infirmities of brethren, he now shows more clearly in what manner, and for what purpose, and to what extent, we ought to bear with them. For otherwise it would have been easy to reply, that there is no other way of avoiding offenses, than by every man winking at the faults of others, and thus what is evil would be encouraged by forbearance. Christ therefore prescribes a middle course, which does not give too great offense to the weak, and yet is adapted to cure their diseases; for that severity which is employed as a medicine is profitable and worthy of praise. In short, Christ enjoins his disciples to forgive one another, but to do so in such a manner as to endeavor to correct their faults. It is necessary that this be wisely observed; for nothing is more difficult than to exercise forbearance towards men, and, at the same time, not to neglect the freedom necessary in reproving them. Almost all lean to the one side or to the other, either to deceive themselves mutually by deadly flatteries, or to pursue with excessive bitterness those whom they ought to cure. But Christ recommends to his disciples a mutual love, which is widely distant from flattery; only he enjoins them to season their admonitions with moderation, lest, by excessive severity and harshness, they discourage the weak.

Now he distinctly lays down three steps of brotherly correction. The first is, to give a private advice to the person who has offended. The second is, if he shall give any sign of obstinacy, to advise him again in presence of witnesses. The third is, if no advantage shall be obtained in that way, to deliver him up to the public decision of the Church. The design of this is, to hinder charity from being violated under the pretence of fervent zeal. As the greater part of men are driven by ambition to publish with excessive eagerness the faults of their brethren, Christ seasonably meets this fault by enjoining us to cover the faults of brethren, as far as lies in our power; for those who take pleasure in the disgrace and infamy of brethren are unquestionably carried away by hatred and malice, since, if they were under the influence of

word for the rule of all his actions, and his Spirit for the guide of all his affections and desires.

The sixth is, his putting his holy resolutions into practice without delay; using the light and power already mercifully restored to him, and seeking God in his appointed ways. And he arose and came, etc., Luke 15: 20.

The seventh is, God tenderly receives him with the kiss of peace and love, blots out all his sins, and restores him to, and reinstates him in, the heavenly family. His father – fell on his neck, and kissed him, Luke 15: 20.

The eighth is, his being clothed with holiness, united to God, married as it were to Christ Jesus, 2 Corinthians 11: 2, and having his feet shod with the shoes of the preparation of the Gospel of peace, Ephesians 6: 15, so that he may run the ways of God's commandments with alacrity and joy. Bring the best robe – put a ring – and shoes, etc., Luke 15: 22.

III. The consequences of the sinner's restoration to the favor and image of God are,

First, the sacrifice of thanksgiving is offered to God in his behalf; he enters into a covenant with his Maker, and feasts on the fatness of the house of the Most High.

Secondly, The whole heavenly family are called upon to share in the general joy; the Church above and the Church below both triumph; for there is joy (peculiar joy) in the presence of the angels of God over one sinner that repenteth. See Luke 15: 10.

Thirdly, God publicly acknowledges him for his son, not only by enabling him to abstain from every appearance of evil, but to walk before him in newness of life, Luke 15: 24. The tender-hearted father repeats these words at Luke 15: 32, to show more particularly that the soul is dead when separated from God; and that it can only be said to be alive when united to him through the Son of his love. A Christian's sin is a brother's death; and in proportion to our concern for this will our joy be at his restoration to spiritual life. Let us have a brotherly heart towards our brethren, as God has that of a father towards his children, and seems to be afflicted at their loss, and to

rejoice at their being found again, as if they were necessary to his happiness.

In this parable, the younger profligate son may represent the Gentile world; and the elder son, who so long served his father, Luke 15: 20, the Jewish people. The anger of the elder son explains itself at once – it means the indignation evidenced by the Jews at the Gentiles being received into the favor of God, and made, with them, fellow heirs of the kingdom of heaven.

It may also be remarked, that those who were since called Jews and Gentiles, were at first one family, and children of the same father: that the descendants of Ham and Japhet, from whom the principal part of the Gentile world was formed, were, in their progenitors, of the primitive great family, but had afterwards fallen off from the true religion: and that the parable of the prodigal son may well represent the conversion of the Gentile world, in order that, in the fullness of time, both Jews and Gentiles may become one fold, under one Shepherd and Bishop of all souls.

MATTHEW 18: 15–20; LUKE 17: 3

Matthew 18: 15–20

15. If thy brother – Any who is a member of the same religious society, sin against thee,

Go and reprove him alone, – it may be in person; if that cannot be so well done, by thy messenger, or in writing, (which in many cases is likely to be the most effectual). Observe, our Lord gives no liberty to omit this, or to exchange it for either of the following steps. If this do not succeed,

16. Take with thee one or two more – Men whom he esteems, who may then confirm and enforce what thou sayest; and afterwards, if need require, bear witness of what was spoken.

17. Tell it unto the Church – Lay the whole matter before the congregation of Christian believers, in that place of which he is a member, or before the minister and elders, as the representatives of the Church or assembly. If

word may be established.

17 And if he shall neglect to hear them, tell it unto the church: but if he neglect to hear the church, let him be unto thee as an heathen man and a publican.

18 Verily I say unto you, Whatsoever ye shall bind on earth shall be bound in heaven: and whatsoever ye shall loose on earth shall be loosed in heaven.

19 Again I say unto you, That if two of you shall agree on earth as touching any thing that they shall ask, it shall be done for them of my Father which is in heaven.

20 For where two or three are gathered together in my name, there am I in the midst of them.

Luke 17: 3

3 Take heed to yourselves: If thy brother trespass against thee, rebuke him; and if he repent, forgive him.

MATTHEW 18: 21–35; LUKE 17: 4

Matthew 18: 21–35

21 Then came Peter to him, and said, Lord, how oft shall my brother sin against me, and I forgive him? till seven times?

22 Jesus saith unto him, I say not unto thee, Until seven times: but, Until seventy times seven.

23 Therefore is the kingdom of heaven likened unto a certain king, which would take account of his servants.

24 And when he had begun to reckon, one was brought unto him, which owed him ten thousand talents.

25 But forasmuch as he had not to pay, his lord commanded him to be sold, and his wife, and children, and all that he had, and payment to be made.

26 The servant therefore fell down, and worshipped him, saying, Lord, have patience with me, and I will pay thee all.

27 Then the lord of that servant was moved with compassion, and loosed him, and forgave him the debt.

28 But the same servant went out, and found one of his fellowservants, which owed him an hundred pence: and he laid hands on him, and took him by the throat, saying, Pay me that thou owest.

29 And his fellowservant fell down at his feet, and besought him, saying, Have patience with me, and I will pay thee all.

charity, they would endeavor to prevent the shame of their brethren.

MATTHEW 18: 21–35 LUKE 17: 4

Matthew 18: 21. Lord, how often shall my brother offend against me?

Peter made this objection according to the natural feelings and disposition of the flesh. It is natural to all men to wish to be forgiven; and, therefore, if any man does not immediately obtain forgiveness, he complains that he is treated with sternness and cruelty. But those who demand to be treated gently are far from being equally gentle towards others; and therefore, when our Lord exhorted his disciples to meekness, this doubt occurred to Peter: "If we be so strongly disposed to grant forgiveness, what will be the consequence, but that our lenity shall be an inducement to offend?" He asks, therefore, if it be proper frequently to forgive offenders; for, since the number seven is taken for a large number, the force of the adverb (*heptakis*) **seven times**, is the same as if he had said, "How long, Lord, dost thou wish that offenders be received into favor? for it is unreasonable, and by no means advantageous, that they should, in every case, find us willing to be reconciled." But Christ is so far from yielding to this objection, that he expressly declares that there ought to be no limit to forgiving; for he did not intend to lay down a fixed number, but rather to enjoin us never to become wearied.

Luke differs somewhat from Matthew; for he states the command of Christ to be simply, that we should be prepared to **forgive seven times**; but the meaning is the same, that we ought to be ready and prepared to grant forgiveness not once or twice, but as often as the sinner shall repent. There is only this difference between them, that, according to Matthew, our Lord, in reproving Peter for taking too limited a view, employs hyperbolically a larger number, which of itself is sufficient to point out the substance of what is intended. For when Peter asked if he should **forgive seven times,** it was not because he did not choose to go any farther, but, by presenting the appearance of a great absurdity, to withdraw Christ from his opinion, as I have lately hinted. So then he who shall be prepared to **forgive seven times** will be willing to be reconciled as far as to the seventieth offense.

MATTHEW 17: 24–27

24. And when they came to Capernaum

We must attend, first of all, to the design of this narrative; which is, that Christ, by paying tribute of his own accord, declared his subjection, as he had taken upon him the form of a servant (Philippians 2: 7), but at the same time showed,

all this avail not, then,

Let him be unto thee as a heathen man and a publican – To whom thou art, as a Christian, to owe earnest and persevering good will, and acts of kindness; but have no religious communion with him, till, if he have been convicted, he acknowledge his fault. Whosoever follows this threefold rule will seldom offend others, and never be offended himself. – Rev. J. WESLEY.

Reproving a brother who had sinned was a positive command under the law. See Leviticus 19: 17. And the Jews have a saying, that one of the causes of the ruin of their nation was, "No man reproved another."

18. Whatsoever ye shall bind, etc. – Whatever determinations ye make, in conformity to these directions for your conduct to an offending brother, will be accounted just, and ratified by the Lord.

Binding and loosing, in this place, and in Matthew 16: 19, is generally restricted, by Christian interpreters, to matters of discipline and authority. Our Savior spoke to his disciples in a language which they understood, so that they were not in the least at a loss to comprehend his meaning; and its being obsolete to us is no manner of reason why we should conclude that it was obscure to them. The words, bind and loose, are used in both places in a declaratory sense, of things, not of persons. Whatsoever thing or things ye shall bind or loose. Consequently, the same commission which was given at first to St. Peter alone, (Matthew 16: 19), was afterwards enlarged to all the apostles. St. Peter had made a confession that Jesus was the Christ, the Son of God. His confession of the Divinity of our Lord was the first that ever was made by man; to him, therefore, were given the keys of the kingdom of heaven: i.e. God made choice of him among all the apostles, that the Gentiles should first, by his mouth, hear the word of the Gospel, and believe. He first opened the kingdom of heaven to the Gentiles, when he preached to Cornelius. It was open to the Jews all along before; but if we should suppose that it was not, yet to them also did St. Peter open the

kingdom of heaven, in his sermon at the great pentecost. Thus, then, St. Peter exercised his two keys: that for the Jews at the great pentecost; and that for the Gentiles, when he admitted Cornelius into the Church. And this was the reward of his first confession, in which he owned Jesus to be the promised Messiah. And what St. Peter loosed, i.e. declared as necessary to be believed and practiced by the disciples here, was ratified above. And what he declared unlawful to be believed and practiced, (i.e. what he bound), was actually forbidden by God himself.

I own myself obliged to Dr. Lightfoot for this interpretation of the true notion of binding and loosing. It is a noble one, and perfectly agrees with the ways of speaking then in use among the Jews. It is observable that these phrases, of binding and loosing, occur no where in the New Testament but in St. Matthew.

"The phrases to bind and to loose were Jewish, and most frequent in their writers. It belonged only to the teachers among the Jews to bind and to loose. When the Jews set any apart to be a preacher, they used these words, 'Take thou liberty to teach what is BOUND and what is LOOSE.'" Strype's preface to the Posthumous Remains of Dr. Lightfoot, p. 38.

19. If two of you shall agree – symphonize, or harmonize. It is a metaphor taken from a number of musical instruments set to the same key, and playing the same tune: here, it means a perfect agreement of the hearts, desires, wishes, and voices, of two or more persons praying to God. It also intimates that as a number of musical instruments, skillfully played, in a good concert, are pleasing to the ears of men, so a number of persons united together in warm, earnest, cordial prayer, is highly pleasing in the sight and ears of the Lord. Now this conjoint prayer refers, in all probability, to the binding and loosing in the preceding verse; and thus we see what power faithful prayer has with God!

It shall be done for them – What an encouragement to pray! even to two, if there be no more disposed to join in this heavenly work.

30 And he would not: but went and cast him into prison, till he should pay the debt.

31 So when his fellowservants saw what was done, they were very sorry, and came and told unto their lord all that was done.

32 Then his lord, after that he had called him, said unto him, O thou wicked servant, I forgave thee all that debt, because thou desiredst me:

33 Shouldest not thou also have had compassion on thy fellowservant, even as I had pity on thee?

34 And his lord was wroth, and delivered him to the tormentors, till he should pay all that was due unto him.

35 So likewise shall my heavenly Father do also unto you, if ye from your hearts forgive not every one his brother their trespasses.

Luke 17: 4

4 And if he trespass against thee seven times in a day, and seven times in a day turn again to thee, saying, I repent; thou shalt forgive him.

MATTHEW 17: 24–27

24 And when they were come to Capernaum, they that received tribute money came to Peter, and said, Doth not your master pay tribute?

25 He saith, Yes. And when he was come into the house, Jesus prevented him, saying, What thinkest thou, Simon? of whom do the kings of the earth take custom or tribute? of their own children, or of strangers?

26 Peter saith unto him, Of strangers. Jesus saith unto him, Then are the children free.

27 Notwithstanding, lest we should offend them, go thou to the sea, and cast an hook, and take up the fish that first cometh up; and when thou hast opened his mouth, thou shalt find a piece of money: that take, and give unto them for me and thee.

MATTHEW 19: 1–2; MARK 9: 38–40; 10: 1; LUKE 9: 49–56

Matthew 19: 1–2

1 And it came to pass, that when Jesus

both by words and by the miracle, that it was not by obligation or necessity, but by a free and voluntary submission, that he had reduced himself so low that the world looked upon him as nothing more than one of the common people. This was not a tax which was wont to be demanded on crossing the sea, but an annual tribute laid individually on every man among the Jews, so that they paid to tyrants what they were formerly in the habit of paying to God alone. For we know that this tax was imposed on them by the Law, that, by paying every year half a stater (Exodus 30: 13), they might acknowledge that God, by whom they had been redeemed, was their supreme King. When the kings of Asia appropriated this to themselves, the Romans followed their example. Thus the Jews, as if they had disowned the government of God, paid to profane tyrants the sacred tax required by the Law. But it might appear unreasonable that Christ, when he appeared as the Redeemer of his people, should not himself be exempted from paying tribute. To remove that offense, he taught by words, that it was only by his will that he was bound; and he proved the same thing by a miracle, for he who had dominion over the sea and the fishes might have released himself from earthly government.

MATTHEW 19: 1–2; MARK 9: 38–40, 10: 1; LUKE 9: 49–56

Mark 9: 38. Master, we saw one

Hence it is evident that the name of Christ was at that time so celebrated, that people who were not of the number of his intimate disciples used that name, or perhaps even abused it, for I will not venture to avouch any thing on this point as certain. It is possible that he who is here mentioned had embraced the doctrine of Christ, and betaken himself to the performance of miracles with no bad intention; but as Christ bestowed this power on none but those whom he had chosen to be heralds of his Gospel, I think that he had rashly taken, or rather seized upon, this office. Now though he was wrong in making this attempt, and in venturing to imitate the disciples without receiving a command to do so, yet his boldness was not without success: for the Lord was pleased, in this way also, to throw luster around his name, as he sometimes does by means of those of whose ministry he does not approve as lawful. It is not inconsistent with this to say, that one who was endued with special faith followed a blind impulse, and thus proceeded inconsiderately to work miracles.

I now come to John and his companions. They say that they **forbade a man to work miracles**. Why did they not first ask whether or not he was authorized? For now being in a state of doubt and suspense, they ask the opinion of

20. **For where two – are gathered together in thy name** – There are many sayings among the Jews almost exactly similar to this, such as, Wherever even two persons are sitting in discourse concerning the law, the Divine presence is among them.

In my name – Seems to refer particularly to a public profession of Christ and his Gospel.

There am I in the midst – None but God could say these words, to say them with truth, because God alone is every where present, and these words refer to his omnipresence. Wherever – suppose millions of assemblies were collected in the same moment, in different places of the creation, (which is a very possible case), this promise states that Jesus is in each of them. Can any, therefore, say these words, except that God who fills both heaven and earth? But Jesus says these words: ergo – Jesus is God. Let it be observed, that Jesus is not among them to spy out their sins; or to mark down the imperfections of their worship; but to enlighten, strengthen, comfort, and save them.

MATTHEW 18: 21–35 LUKE 17: 4

Matthew 18: 21–35

21. **Till seven times?** – Though seven was a number of perfection among the Hebrews, and often meant much more than the units in it imply, yet it is evident that Peter uses it here in its plain literal sense, as our Lord's words sufficiently testify. It was a maxim among the Jews never to forgive more than thrice. Revenge is natural to man, i.e. man is naturally a vindictive being, and, in consequence, nothing is more difficult to him than forgiveness of injuries.

22. **Seventy times seven** – There is something very remarkable in these words, especially if collated with Genesis 4: 24.

23. **Therefore is the kingdom** – In respect to sin, cruelty, and oppression, God will proceed in the kingdom of heaven (the dispensation of the Gospel) as he did in former times; and every person shall give an account of himself

to God. Every sin is a debt contracted with the justice of God; men are all God's own servants; and the day is at hand in which their Master will settle accounts with them, inquire into their work, and pay them their wages. Great Judge! what an awful time must this be, when with multitudes nothing shall be found but sin and insolvency!

24. **Ten thousand talents** – a myriad of talents, the highest number known in Greek arithmetical notation.

25. **He had not to pay** – That is not being able to pay.

Commanded him to be sold – his wife – children, etc. – Our Lord here alludes to an ancient custom among the Hebrews, of selling a man and his family to make payment of contracted debts. See Exodus 22: 3; Leviticus 25: 30,47; 2 Kings 4: 1.

26. **Fell down and worshipped him** – crouched as a dog before him, with the greatest deference, submission, and anxiety.

Have patience with me – be long-minded towards me – give me longer space.

27. **Moved with compassion** – Or with tender pity. This is the source of salvation to a lost world, the tender pity, the eternal mercy of God.

28. **A hundred pence** – Rather denarii.

Took him by the throat – it signified to half choke a person, by seizing his throat.

30. **And he would not, etc.** – To the unmerciful, God will show no mercy; this is an eternal purpose of the Lord, which never can be changed. God teaches us what to do to a fellow-sinner, by what HE does to us. Our fellow-servant's debt to us, and ours to God, are as one hundred denarii to ten thousand talents! When we humble ourselves before him, God freely forgives us all this mighty sum! And shall we exact from our brother recompense for the most trifling faults? Reader, if thou art of this unmerciful, unforgiving cast, read out the chapter.

31. **His fellow-servants saw what was done**

had finished these sayings, he departed from Galilee, and came into the coasts of Judaea beyond Jordan;

2 And great multitudes followed him; and he healed them there.

Mark 9: 38–40

38 And John answered him, saying, Master, we saw one casting out devils in thy name, and he followeth not us: and we forbad him, because he followeth not us.

39 But Jesus said, Forbid him not: for there is no man which shall do a miracle in my name, that can lightly speak evil of me.

40 For he that is not against us is on our part.

Mark 10: 1

1 And he arose from thence, and cometh into the coasts of Judaea by the farther side of Jordan: and the people resort unto him again; and, as he was wont, he taught them again.

Luke 9: 49–56

49 And John answered and said, Master, we saw one casting out devils in thy name; and we forbad him, because he followeth not with us.

50 And Jesus said unto him, Forbid him not: for he that is not against us is for us.

51 And it came to pass, when the time was come that he should be received up, he stedfastly set his face to go to Jerusalem,

52 And sent messengers before his face: and they went, and entered into a village of the Samaritans, to make ready for him.

53 And they did not receive him, because his face was as though he would go to Jerusalem.

54 And when his disciples James and John saw this, they said, Lord, wilt thou that we command fire to come down from heaven, and consume them, even as Elias did?

55 But he turned, and rebuked them, and said, Ye know not what manner of spirit ye are of.

56 For the Son of man is not come to destroy men's lives, but to save them. And they went to another village.

their Master. Hence it follows, that they had rashly taken on themselves the right to forbid; and therefore every man who undertakes more than he knows that he is permitted to do by the word of God is chargeable with rashness. Besides, there is reason to suspect the disciples of Christ of ambition, because they are anxious to maintain their privilege and honor. For how comes it that they all at once forbid a man who is unknown to them to work miracles, but because they wish to be the sole possessors of this right? For they assign the reason, that he followeth not Christ; as much as to say, "He is not one of thy associates, as we are: why then shall he possess equal honor?"

39. Forbid him not

Christ did not wish that he should be forbidden; not that he had given him authority, or approved of what he did, or even wished his disciples to approve of it, but because, when by any occurrence God is glorified, we ought to bear with it and rejoice. Thus Paul (Philippians 1: 18), though he disapproves of the dispositions of those who used the Gospel as a pretense for aggrandizing themselves, yet rejoices that by this occurrence the glory of Christ is advanced. We must attend also to the reason which is added, that it is impossible for any man who works miracles in the name of Christ to speak evil of Christ.

MATTHEW 19: 3–9; MARK 10: 2–12

Matthew 19: 3. And the Pharisees came to him, tempting him

Though the Pharisees lay snares for Christ, and cunningly endeavor to impose upon him, yet their malice proves to be highly useful to us; as the Lord knows how to turn, in a wonderful manner, to the advantage of his people all the contrivances of wicked men to overthrow sound doctrine. For, by means of this occurrence, a question arising out of the liberty of divorce was settled, and a fixed law was laid down as to the sacred and indissoluble bond of marriage. The occasion of this quibbling was, that the reply, in whatever way it were given, could not, as they thought, fail to be offensive.

They ask, **Is it lawful for a man to divorce his wife for any cause whatever?** If Christ reply in the negative, they will exclaim that he wickedly abolishes the Law; and if in the affirmative, they will give out that he is not a prophet of God, but rather a pander, who lends such countenance to the lust of men. Such were the calculations which they had made in their own minds; but the Son of God, who knew how to take the wise in their own craftiness, (Job 5: 13,) disappointed them, sternly opposing unlawful divorces, and at the same time showing that he brings forward nothing which is inconsistent with the Law. For he includes the

– An act of this kind is so dishonorable to all the followers of Christ, and to the spirit of his Gospel, that through the respect they owe to their Lord and Master, and through the concern they feel for the prosperity of his cause, they are obliged to plead against it at the throne of God.

32. His lord, after that he had called him – Alas! how shall he appear! Confounded. What shall he answer? He is speechless!

33. Shouldest not thou also have had compassion – Did it not become thee also? What a cutting reproach! It became ME to show mercy, when thou didst earnestly entreat me, because I am MERCIFUL, It became thee also to have shown mercy, because thou wert so deep in debt thyself, and hadst obtained mercy.

34. Delivered him to the tormentors – Not only continued captivity is here intended, but the tortures to be endured in it.

35. So likewise shall my heavenly Father do also unto you – The goodness and indulgence of God towards us is the pattern we should follow in our dealings with others. If we take man for our exemplar we shall err, because our copy is a bad one; and our lives are not likely to be better than the copy we imitate. Follow Christ; be merciful as your Father who is in heaven is merciful.

The unbridled and extravagant appetites of men sometimes require a rigour even beyond the law to suppress them. While, then, we learn lessons of humanity from what is before us, let us also learn lessons of prudence, sobriety, and moderation. The parable of the two debtors is blessedly calculated to give this information.

MATTHEW 17: 24–27

24. They that received tribute – This was not a tax to be paid to the Roman government; but a tax for the support of the temple. The law, Exodus 30: 13, obliged every male among the Jews to pay half a shekel yearly; for the support of the temple; and this was continued by them wherever dispersed, till after the time

of Vespasian, who ordered it afterwards to be paid into the Roman treasury.

25. He saith, Yes – From this reply of Peter, it is evident that our Lord customarily paid all taxes, tributes, etc., which were common among the people wherever he came. The children of God are subject to all civil laws in the places where they live – and should pay the taxes levied on them by public authority; and though any of these should be found unjust, THEY rebel not, as their business is not to reform the politics of nations, but the morals of the world.

26. Then are the children free – As this money is levied for the support of that temple of which I am the Lord, then I am not obliged to pay the tax; and my disciples, like the priests that minister, should be exempted from the necessity of paying.

27. Lest we – offend them – Be a stumbling-block to the priests, or rulers of the Jews, I will pay the tribute – go thou to the sea – cast a hook, and take the first fish – thou shalt find a piece of money, a stater. This piece of money was equal in value to four drachms, or two shekels, and consequently was sufficient to pay the tribute for our Lord and Peter, which amounted to about half-a-crown each. If the stater was in the mouth or belly of the fish before, who can help admiring the wisdom of Christ, that discovered it there? If it was not before in the mouth of the fish, who can help admiring the power of Christ, that impelled the fish to go where the stater had been lost in the bottom of the sea, take it up, come towards the shore where Peter was fishing, and, with the stater in its mouth or stomach, catch hold of the hook that was to draw it out of the water? But suppose there was no stater there, which is as likely as otherwise, then Jesus created it for the purpose, and here his omnipotence was shown; for to make a thing exist that did not exist before is an act of unlimited power, however small the thing itself may be.

Our Lord seems to have wrought this miracle for the following purposes:

MATTHEW 19: 3–9; MARK 10: 2–12

Matthew 19: 3–9

3 The Pharisees also came unto him, tempting him, and saying unto him, Is it lawful for a man to put away his wife for every cause?

4 And he answered and said unto them, Have ye not read, that he which made them at the beginning made them male and female,

5 And said, For this cause shall a man leave father and mother, and shall cleave to his wife: and they twain shall be one flesh?

6 Wherefore they are no more twain, but one flesh. What therefore God hath joined together, let not man put asunder.

7 They say unto him, Why did Moses then command to give a writing of divorcement, and to put her away?

8 He saith unto them, Moses because of the hardness of your hearts suffered you to put away your wives: but from the beginning it was not so.

9 And I say unto you, Whosoever shall put away his wife, except it be for fornication, and shall marry another, committeth adultery: and whoso marrieth her which is put away doth commit adultery.

Mark 10: 2–12

2 And the Pharisees came to him, and asked him, Is it lawful for a man to put away his wife? tempting him.

3 And he answered and said unto them, What did Moses command you?

4 And they said, Moses suffered to write a bill of divorcement, and to put her away.

5 And Jesus answered and said unto them, For the hardness of your heart he wrote you this precept.

6 But from the beginning of the creation God made them male and female.

7 For this cause shall a man leave his father and mother, and cleave to his wife;

8 And they twain shall be one flesh: so then they are no more twain, but one flesh.

9 What therefore God hath joined together, let not man put asunder.

10 And in the house his disciples asked him again of the same matter.

11 And he saith unto them, Whosoever

whole question under two heads: that the order of creation ought to serve for a law, that the husband should maintain conjugal fidelity during the whole of life; and that divorces were permitted, not because they were lawful, but because Moses had to deal with a rebellious and intractable nation.

4. Have you not read?

Christ does not indeed reply directly to what was asked, but he fully meets the question which was proposed; just as if a person now interrogated about the Mass were to explain faithfully the mystery of the Holy Supper, and at length to conclude, that they are guilty of sacrilege and forgery who venture either to add or to take away any thing from the pure institution of the Lord, he would plainly overturn the pretended sacrifice of the Mass. Now Christ assumes as an admitted principle, that at the beginning God **joined the male to the female**, so that the two made an entire man; and therefore he who **divorces his wife** tears from him, as it were, the half of himself. But nature does not allow any man to tear in pieces his own body.

He adds another argument drawn from the less to the greater. The bond of marriage is more sacred than that which binds children to their parents. But piety binds children to their parents by a link which cannot be broken. Much less then can the husband renounce his wife. Hence it follows, that a chain which God made is burst asunder, if the husband divorce his wife.

MATTHEW 19: 10–12

10. His disciples say to him

As if it were a hard condition for husbands to be so bound to their wives, that, so long as they remain chaste, they are compelled to endure every thing rather than leave them, the disciples, roused by this answer of Christ, reply, that it is better to want wives than to submit to a knot of this kind. But why do they not, on the other hand, consider how hard is the bondage of wives, but because, devoted to themselves and their own convenience, they are driven by the feeling of the flesh to disregard others, and to think only of what is advantageous for themselves? Meanwhile, it is a display of base ingratitude that, from the dread or dislike of a single inconvenience, they reject a wonderful gift of God. It is better, according to them, to avoid marriage than to bind one's self by the bond of living always together. But if God has ordained marriage for the general advantage of mankind, though it may be attended by some things that are disagreeable, it is not on that account to be despised. Let us therefore learn to use with reverence the gifts of God, even if there be something in them that does not please us.

ADAM CLARKE

1. More forcibly to impress the minds of his disciples, and his followers in general, with the necessity and propriety of being subject to all the laws of the different states, kingdoms, etc., wheresoever the providence of God might cast their lot.

2. To show forth his own unlimited power and knowledge, that they might be fully convinced that he knew all things, even to the most minute; and could do whatsoever he pleased; and that both his wisdom and power were continually interested in behalf of his true disciples.

3. To teach all believers a firm trust and reliance on Divine Providence, the sources of which can never be exhausted; and which, directed by infinite wisdom and love, will make every provision essentially requisite for the comfort and support, of life. How many of the poor followers of Christ have been enabled to discern his kind hand, even in the means furnished them to discharge the taxes laid on them by the state! The profane and the unprincipled may deride, and mock on, but the people of God know it to be their duty, and their interest, to be subject to every ordinance of man for the Lord's sake; and, while his grace and providence render this obedience, in things both spiritual and secular, possible, his love, which their hearts feel, renders their duty their delight. The accomplishment of such ends as these is worthy both of the wisdom and benevolence of Christ.

MATTHEW 19: 1–2; MARK 9: 38–40; 10: 1; LUKE 9: 49–56

Matthew 19: 1–2

1. **Beyond Jordan** – Or, by the side of Jordan. Matthew begins here to give an account of Christ's journey (the only one he mentions) to Jerusalem, a little before the passover, at which he was crucified. See Mark 10: 1; Luke 9: 51.

2. **Great multitudes followed him** – Some to be instructed – some to be healed – some through curiosity – and some to ensnare him.

MATTHEW 19: 3–9; MARK 10: 2–12

Matthew 19: 3–9

3. **Tempting him** – Trying what answer he would give to a question, which, however decided by him, would expose him to censure.

Is it lawful – for every cause? – What made our Lord's situation at present so critical in respect to this question was: At this time there were two famous divinity and philosophical schools among the Jews, that of SHAMMAI, and that of HILLEL. On the question of divorce, the school of Shammai maintained, that a man could not legally put away his wife, except for whoredom. The school of Hillel taught that a man might put away his wife for a multitude of other causes, and when she did not find grace in his sight; i.e. when he saw any other woman that pleased him better.

4. **He which made them at the beginning** – When Adam and Eve were the first of human kind.

Made them male and female – Merely through the design of matrimonial union, that the earth might be thus peopled. To answer a case of conscience, a man should act as Christ does here; pay no regard to that which the corruption of manners has introduced into Divine ordinances, but go back to the original will, purpose, and institution of God. Christ will never accommodate his morality to the times, nor to the inclinations of men. What was done at the beginning is what God judged most worthy of his glory, most profitable for man, and most suitable to nature.

5. **For this cause** – Being created for this very purpose; that they might glorify their Maker in a matrimonial connection. A man shall leave (wholly give up) both father and mother – the matrimonial union being more intimate and binding than even paternal or filial affection; – and shall be closely united, shall be firmly cemented to his wife. A beautiful metaphor, which most forcibly intimates that nothing but death can separate them: as a well-glued board will break sooner in the whole wood, than in the glued joint.

And they twain shall be one flesh? – Not

shall put away his wife, and marry another, committeth adultery against her.

12 And if a woman shall put away her
husband, and be married to another, she
committeth adultery.

MATTHEW 19: 10–12

10 His disciples say unto him, If the
case of the man be so with his wife, it is
not good to marry.

11 But he said unto them, All men
cannot receive this saying, save they to
whom it is given.

12 For there are some eunuchs, which
were so born from their mother's womb:
and there are some eunuchs, which were
made eunuchs of men: and there be
eunuchs, which have made themselves
eunuchs for the kingdom of heaven's
sake. He that is able to receive it, let him
receive it.

**MATTHEW 19: 13–15; MARK 10: 13–16;
LUKE 18: 15–17**

Matthew 19: 13–15

13 Then were there brought unto him
little children, that he should put his hands
on them, and pray: and the disciples rebuked them.

14 But Jesus said, Suffer little children,
and forbid them not, to come unto me: for
of such is the kingdom of heaven.

15 And he laid his hands on them, and
departed thence.

Mark 10: 13–16

13 And they brought young children
to him, that he should touch them: and
his disciples rebuked those that brought
them.

14 But when Jesus saw it, he was
much displeased, and said unto them,
Suffer the little children to come unto me,
and forbid them not: for of such is the
kingdom of God.

15 Verily I say unto you, Whosoever
shall not receive the kingdom of God as a
little child, he shall not enter therein.

16 And he took them up in his arms,
put his hands upon them, and blessed
them.

Luke 18: 15–17

15 And they brought unto him also in-

MATTHEW 19: 13–15; MARK 10: 13–16; LUKE 18: 15–17

This narrative is highly useful; for it shows that Christ receives not only those who, moved by holy desire and faith,
freely approach to him, but those who are not yet of age to
know how much they need his grace. Those **little children**
have not yet any understanding to desire his blessing; but
when they are presented to him, he gently and kindly receives them, and dedicates them to the Father by a solemn
act of blessing. We must observe the intention of those who
present the children; for if there had not been a deep-rooted
conviction in their minds, that the power of the Spirit was at
his disposal, that he might pour it out on the people of God,
it would have been unreasonable to present their children.
There is no room, therefore, to doubt that they ask for them
a participation of his grace; and so, by way of amplification,
Luke adds the particle also; as if he had said that, after they
had experienced the various ways in which he assisted adults,
they formed an expectation likewise in regard to children,
that, if he **laid hands on them**, they would not leave him
without having received some of the gifts of the Spirit. The
laying on of hands was an ancient and well known sign of
blessing; and so there is no reason to wonder, if they desire
that Christ, while employing that solemn ceremony, should
pray for the children. At the same time, as the inferior are
blessed by the better (Hebrews 7: 7), they ascribe to him the
power and honor of the highest Prophet.

MATTHEW 19: 16–22; MARK 10: 17–22; LUKE 18: 18–23

Matthew 19: 16. And, lo, one
Luke says that he was a **ruler** (*archon*), that is, a man of
very high authority, not one of the common people. And
though riches procure respect, yet he appears to be here
represented to have been held in high estimation as a good
man. For my own part, after weighing all the circumstances, I have no doubt that, though he is called a young man,
he belonged to the class of those who upheld the integrity
of the Elders, by a sober and regular life. He did not come
treacherously, as the scribes were wont to do, but from a
desire of instruction; and, accordingly, both by words and
by kneeling, he testifies his reverence for Christ as a faithful
teacher. But, on the other hand, a blind confidence in his
works hindered him from profiting under Christ, to whom,
in other respects, he wished to be submissive. Thus, in our
own day, we find some who are not ill-disposed, but who,
under the influence of I know not what shadowy holiness,
hardly relish the doctrine of the Gospel.

But, in order to form a more correct judgment of the
meaning of the answer, we must attend to the form of the

only meaning, that they should be considered as one body, but also as two souls in one body, with a complete union of interests, and an indissoluble partnership of life and fortune, comfort and support, desires and inclinations, joys and sorrows.

6. What therefore God hath joined together – yoked together, as oxen in the plough, where each must pull equally, in order to bring it on. Among the ancients, when persons were newly married, they put a yoke upon their necks, or chains upon their arms, to show that they were to be one, closely united, and pulling equally together in all the concerns of life.

7. Why did Moses then command to give a writing of divorcement? – It is not an unusual case for the impure and unholy to seek for a justification of their conduct from the law of God itself, and to wrest Scripture to their own destruction. I knew a gentleman, so called, who professed deep reverence for the sacred writings, and, strange as it may appear, was outwardly irreproachable in every respect but one; that was, he kept more women than his wife. This man frequently read the Bible, and was particularly conversant with those places that spoke of or seemed to legalize the polygamy of the patriarchs!

8. Moses, because of the hardness of your hearts – It is dangerous to tolerate the least evil, though prudence itself may require it: because toleration, in this case, raises itself insensibly into permission, and permission soon sets up for command. Moses perceived that if divorce were not permitted, in many cases, the women would be exposed to great hardships through the cruelty of their husbands.

From the beginning it was not so – There was no divorce between Eve and Adam; nor did he or his family practice polygamy. But our Lord, by the beginning, may mean the original intention or design.

9. Except it be for fornication – The decision of our Lord must be very unpleasant to these men: the reason why they wished to put away their wives was, that they might take others

whom they liked better; but our Lord here declares that they could not be remarried while the divorced person was alive, and that those who did marry, during the life of the divorced, were adulterers; and heavy judgments were, denounced, in their law, against such: and as the question was not settled by the schools of Shammai and Hillel, so as to ground national practice on it therefore they were obliged to abide by the positive declaration of the law, as it was popularly understood, till these eminent schools had proved the word had another meaning.

MATTHEW 19: 10–12

10. If the case of the man – of a husband, so I think the word should be translated here.

It is not good to marry – That is, if a man have not the liberty to put away his wife when she is displeasing to him. God had said, Genesis 2: 18, It is not good for man to be alone, i.e. unmarried. The disciples seem to say, that if the husband have not the power to divorce his wife when she is displeasing to him, it is not good for him to marry. Here was a flat contradiction to the decision of the Creator. There are difficulties and trials in all states; but let marriage and celibacy be weighed fairly, and I am persuaded the former will be found to have fewer than the latter. However, before we enter into an engagement which nothing but death can dissolve, we had need to act cautiously, carefully consulting the will and word of God. Where an unbridled passion, or a base love of money, lead the way, marriage is sure to be miserable.

11. All – cannot receive this saying – A very wise answer, and well suited to the present circumstances of the disciples. Neither of the states is condemned. If thou marry, thou dost well – this is according to the order, will, and commandment of God. But if thou do not marry, (because of the present necessity, persecution, worldly embarrassments, or bodily infirmity), thou dost better. See 1 Corinthians 7: 25.

fants, that he would touch them: but when his disciples saw it, they rebuked them.

16 But Jesus called them unto him, and said, Suffer little children to come unto me, and forbid them not: for of such is the kingdom of God.

17 Verily I say unto you, Whosoever shall not receive the kingdom of God as a little child shall in no wise enter therein.

MATTHEW 19: 16–22; MARK 10: 17–22; LUKE 18: 18–23

Matthew 19: 16–22

16 And, behold, one came and said unto him, Good Master, what good thing shall I do, that I may have eternal life?

17 And he said unto him, Why callest thou me good? there is none good but one, that is, God: but if thou wilt enter into life, keep the commandments.

18 He saith unto him, Which? Jesus said, Thou shalt do no murder, Thou shalt not commit adultery, Thou shalt not steal, Thou shalt not bear false witness,

19 Honor thy father and thy mother: and, Thou shalt love thy neighbour as thyself.

20 The young man saith unto him, All these things have I kept from my youth up: what lack I yet?

21 Jesus said unto him, If thou wilt be perfect, go and sell that thou hast, and give to the poor, and thou shalt have treasure in heaven: and come and follow me.

22 But when the young man heard that saying, he went away sorrowful: for he had great possessions.

Mark 10: 17–22

17 And when he was gone forth into the way, there came one running, and kneeled to him, and asked him, Good Master, what shall I do that I may inherit eternal life?

18 And Jesus said unto him, Why callest thou me good? there is none good but one, that is, God.

19 Thou knowest the commandments, Do not commit adultery, Do not kill, Do not steal, Do not bear false witness, Defraud not, Honor thy father and mother.

20 And he answered and said unto him, Master, all these have I observed from my youth.

question. He does not simply ask how and by what means he shall reach life, but what good thing he shall do, in order to obtain it. He therefore dreams of merits, on account of which he may receive eternal life as a reward due; and therefore Christ appropriately sends him to the keeping of the law, which unquestionably is the way of life.

17. Why callest thou me good?

I do not understand this correction in so refined a sense as is given by a good part of interpreters, as if Christ intended to suggest his Divinity; for they imagine that these words mean, "If thou perceivest in me nothing more exalted than human nature, thou falsely appliest to me the epithet good, which belongs to God alone." I do acknowledge that, strictly speaking, men and even angels do not deserve so honorable a title; because they have not a drop of goodness in themselves, but borrowed from God; and because in the former, goodness is only begun, and is not perfect. But Christ had no other intention than to maintain the truth of his doctrine; as if he had said, "Thou falsely **callest me a good Master**, unless thou acknowledgest that I have come from God." The essence of his Godhead, therefore, is not here maintained, but the **young man** is directed to admit the truth of the doctrine. He had already felt some disposition to obey; but Christ wishes him to rise higher, that he may hear God speaking. For – as it is customary with men to make angels of those who are devils – they indiscriminately give the appellation of good teachers to those in whom they perceive nothing divine; but those modes of speaking are only profanations of the gifts of God. We need not wonder, therefore, if Christ, in order to maintain the authority of his doctrine, directs the young man to God.

Keep the commandments

This passage was erroneously interpreted by some of the ancients, as if Christ taught that, by beeping the law, we may merit eternal life. On the contrary, Christ did not take into consideration what men can do, but replied to the question, What is the righteousness of works? or, What does the Law require? And certainly we ought to believe that God comprehended in his law the way of living holily and righteously, in which righteousness is included; for not without reason did Moses make this statement,

He that does these things shall live in them (Leviticus 18: 5); and again, "I call heaven and earth to witness that I have this day showed you life" (Deuteronomy 30: 19).

We have no right, therefore, to deny that the keeping of the law is righteousness, by which any man who kept the law perfectly – if there were such a man – would obtain life for himself. But as we are all destitute of the glory of God (Romans 3: 23), nothing but cursing will be found in the law; and nothing remains for us but to betake ourselves to the

12. So born from their mother's womb – Such as are naturally incapable of marriage, and consequently should not contract any.

He that is able to receive – The meaning seems to be, Let the man who feels himself capable of embracing this way of life, embrace it; but none can do it but he to whom it is given, who has it as a gift from his mother's womb.

MATTHEW 19: 13–15; MARK 10: 13–16; LUKE 18: 15–17

Matthew 19: 13–15

13. Then were there brought unto him little children – These are termed by Luke, 18: 15, infants, very young children; and it was on this account, probably, that the disciples rebuked the parents, thinking them too young to receive good.

That he should put his hands – It was a common custom among the Jews to lay their hands on the heads of those whom they blessed, or for whom they prayed. This seems to have been done by way of dedication or consecration to God – the person being considered as the sacred property of God ever after. Often God added a testimony of his approbation, by communicating some extraordinary influence of the Holy Spirit. This rite has been long practiced among Christians, when persons are appointed to any sacred office. But this consecration of children to God seems to have grown out of use. It is no wonder that the great mass of children are so wicked, when so few, are put under the care of Christ by humble, praying, believing parents. Let every parent that fears God bring up his children in that fear; and, by baptism, let each be dedicated to the holy trinity. Whatever is solemnly consecrated to God abides under his protection and blessing.

14. Of such is the kingdom of heaven – Or, the kingdom of heaven is composed of such. This appears to be the best sense of the passage, and utterly ruins the whole inhuman diabolic system of what is called non-elect infants' damnation; a doctrine which must have sprung from Moloch, and can only be defended by a heart in which he dwells. A great part of God's kingdom is composed of such literally; and those only who resemble little children shall be received into it. Christ loves little children because he loves simplicity and innocence; he has sanctified their very age by passing through it himself – the holy Jesus was once a little child.

15. He – departed thence – That is, from that part of Judea which was beyond Jordan, Matthew 19: 1; and then went to Jericho. See Matthew 20: 29.

MATTHEW 19: 16–22; MARK 10: 17–22; LUKE 18: 18–23

Matthew 19: 16–22

16. Good, etc. – Much instruction may be had from seriously attending to the conduct, spirit, and question of this person.

1. He came running, (Mark 10: 17), for he was deeply convinced of the importance of his business, and seriously determined to seek so as to find.

2. He kneeled, or caught him by the knees, thus evidencing his humility, and addressing himself only to mercy. See Matthew 17: 14.

3. He came in the spirit of a disciple, or scholar, desiring to be taught a matter of the utmost importance to him – Good teacher.

4. He came in the spirit of obedience; he had worked hard to no purpose, and he is still willing to work, provided he can have a prospect of succeeding – What good thing shall I do?

5. His question was the most interesting and important that any soul can ask of God – How shall I be saved?

17. Why callest thou me good? – Or, Why dost thou question me concerning that good thing?

Keep the commandments – From this we may learn that God's great design, in giving his law to the Jews, was to lead them to the expectation and enjoyment of eternal life. But as all the law referred to Christ, and he became the end of the law for righteousness (justification) to all that believe, so he is to be received,

21 Then Jesus beholding him loved him, and said unto him, One thing thou lackest: go thy way, sell whatsoever thou hast, and give to the poor, and thou shalt have treasure in heaven: and come, take up the cross, and follow me.

22 And he was sad at that saying, and went away grieved: for he had great possessions.

Luke 18: 18–23

18 And a certain ruler asked him, saying, Good Master, what shall I do to inherit eternal life?

19 And Jesus said unto him, Why callest thou me good? none is good, save one, that is, God.

20 Thou knowest the commandments, Do not commit adultery, Do not kill, Do not steal, Do not bear false witness, Honor thy father and thy mother.

21 And he said, All these have I kept from my youth up.

22 Now when Jesus heard these things, he said unto him, Yet lackest thou one thing: sell all that thou hast, and distribute unto the poor, and thou shalt have treasure in heaven: and come, follow me.

23 And when he heard this, he was very sorrowful: for he was very rich.

MATTHEW 19: 23–26; MARK 10: 23–27; LUKE 18: 24–27

Matthew 19: 23–26

23 Then said Jesus unto his disciples, Verily I say unto you, That a rich man shall hardly enter into the kingdom of heaven.

24 And again I say unto you, It is easier for a camel to go through the eye of a needle, than for a rich man to enter into the kingdom of God.

25 When his disciples heard it, they were exceedingly amazed, saying, Who then can be saved?

26 But Jesus beheld them, and said unto them, With men this is impossible; but with God all things are possible.

Mark 10: 23–27

23 And Jesus looked round about, and saith unto his disciples, How hardly shall they that have riches enter into the kingdom of God!

24 And the disciples were astonished at his words. But Jesus answereth again,

undeserved gift of righteousness. And therefore Paul lays down a twofold righteousness, the righteousness of the law (Romans 10: 5), and the righteousness of faith (Romans 10: 6). He makes the first to consist in works, and the second, in the free grace of Christ.

MATTHEW 19: 23–26; MARK 10: 23–27; LUKE 18: 24–27

Matthew 19: 23. A rich man will with difficulty enter
Christ warns them, not only how dangerous and how deadly a plague avarice is, but also how great an obstacle is presented by riches. In Mark, indeed, he mitigates the harshness of his expression, by restricting it to those only who place confidence in riches. But these words are, I think, intended to confirm, rather than correct, the former statement, as if he had affirmed that they ought not to think it strange, that he made the entrance into the kingdom of heaven so difficult for the rich, because it is an evil almost common to all to trust in their riches. Yet this doctrine is highly useful to all; to the rich, that, being warned of their danger, they may be on their guard; to the poor, that, satisfied with their lot, they may not so eagerly desire what would bring more damage than gain. It is true indeed, that riches do not, in their own nature, hinder us from following God; but, in consequence of the depravity of the human mind, it is scarcely possible for those who have a great abundance to avoid being intoxicated by them. So they who are exceedingly rich are held by Satan bound, as it were, in chains, that they may not raise their thoughts to heaven; nay more, they bury and entangle themselves, and became utter slaves to the earth. The comparison of the camel., which is soon after added, is intended to amplify the difficulty; for it means that the rich are so swelled with pride and presumption, that they cannot endure to be reduced to the straits through which God makes his people to pass. The word camel denotes, I think, a rope used by sailors, rather than the animal so named.

25. And his disciples, when they heard these things, were greatly amazed
The disciples are astonished, because it ought to awaken in us no little anxiety, that riches obstruct the entrance into the kingdom of God; for, wherever we turn our eyes, a thousand obstacles will present themselves. But let us observe that, while they were struck with astonishment, they did not shrink from the doctrines of Christ.

in order to have the end accomplished which the law proposed.

18. Thou shalt do no murder, etc. – But some say these commandments are not binding on us. Vain, deceived men! Can a murderer, an adulterer, a thief, and a liar enter into eternal life? No. The God of purity and justice has forbidden it. But we are not to keep these commandments in order to purchase eternal life. Right. Neither Jesus Christ, nor his genuine messengers, say you are. To save your souls, Christ must save you from your sins, and enable you to walk before him in newness of life.

19. Thou shalt love thy neighbor as thyself – Self-love, as it is generally called, has been grievously declaimed against, even by religious people, as a most pernicious and dreadful evil. But they have not understood the subject on which they spoke. They have denominated that intense propensity which unregenerate men feel to gratify their carnal appetites and vicious passions, self-love; whereas it might be more properly termed self-hatred or self-murder. If I am to love my neighbor as myself and this "love worketh no ill to its neighbor," then self-love, in the sense in which our Lord uses it, is something excellent. It is properly a disposition essential to our nature, and inseparable from our being, by which we desire to be happy, by which we seek the happiness we have not, and rejoice in it when we possess it. In a word, it is a uniform wish of the soul to avoid all evil, and to enjoy all good. Therefore, he who is wholly governed by self-love, properly and Scripturally speaking, will devote his whole soul to God, and earnestly and constantly seek all his peace, happiness, and salvation in the enjoyment of God. But self-love cannot make me happy. I am only the subject which receives the happiness, but am not the object that constitutes this happiness; for it is that object, properly speaking, that I love, and love not only for its own sake, but also for the sake of the happiness which I enjoy through it. "No man," saith the apostle, "ever hated his own flesh." But he that sinneth against God wrongeth his own soul, both of present and eternal salvation, and is so far

from being governed by self-love that he is the implacable enemy of his best and dearest interests in both worlds.

20. All these have I kept – I have made these precepts the rule of my life. There is a difference worthy of notice between this and our Lord's word.

From my youth – Perhaps the young man meant no more than that he had in general observed them, and considered them of continual obligation.

What lack I yet? – He felt a troubled conscience, and a mind unassured of the approbation of God; and he clearly perceived that something was wanting to make him truly happy.

21. If thou wilt be perfect – To be complete, to have the business finished, and all hinderances to thy salvation removed, go and sell that thou hast – go and dispose of thy possessions, to which it is evident his heart was too much attached, and give to the poor – for thy goods will be a continual snare to thee if thou keep them; and thou shalt have treasure in heaven – the loss, if it can be called such, shall be made amply up to thee in that eternal life about which thou inquirest; and come and follow me – be my disciple, and I will appoint thee to preach the kingdom of God to others.

22. Went away sorrowful – Men undergo great agony of mind while they are in suspense between the love of the world and the love of their souls. When the first absolutely predominates, then they enjoy a factitious rest through a false peace: when the latter has the upper hand, then they possess true tranquility of mind, through that peace of God that passeth knowledge.

He had great possessions – And what were these in comparison of peace of conscience, and mental rest? Besides, he had unequivocal proof that these contributed nothing to his comfort, for he is now miserable even while he possesses them! And so will every soul be, who puts worldly goods in the place of the supreme God.

and saith unto them, Children, how hard is it for them that trust in riches to enter into the kingdom of God!

25 It is easier for a camel to go through the eye of a needle, than for a rich man to enter into the kingdom of God.

26 And they were astonished out of measure, saying among themselves, Who then can be saved?

27 And Jesus looking upon them saith, With men it is impossible, but not with God: for with God all things are possible.

Luke 18: 24–27

24 And when Jesus saw that he was very sorrowful, he said, How hardly shall they that have riches enter into the kingdom of God!

25 For it is easier for a camel to go through a needle's eye, than for a rich man to enter into the kingdom of God.

26 And they that heard it said, Who then can be saved?

27 And he said, The things which are impossible with men are possible with God.

MATTHEW 19: 27–30; MARK 10: 28–31; LUKE 18: 28–30; 22: 28–30

Matthew 19: 27–30

27 Then answered Peter and said unto him, Behold, we have forsaken all, and followed thee; what shall we have therefore?

28 And Jesus said unto them, Verily I say unto you, That ye which have followed me, in the regeneration when the Son of man shall sit in the throne of his glory, ye also shall sit upon twelve thrones, judging the twelve tribes of Israel.

29 And every one that hath forsaken houses, or brethren, or sisters, or father, or mother, or wife, or children, or lands, for my name's sake, shall receive an hundredfold, and shall inherit everlasting life.

30 But many that are first shall be last; and the last shall be first.

Mark 10: 28–31

28 Then Peter began to say unto him, Lo, we have left all, and have followed thee.

29 And Jesus answered and said, Verily I say unto you, There is no man that hath left house, or brethren, or sisters, or

MATTHEW 19: 27–30; MARK 10: 28–31; LUKE 18: 28–30; 22: 28–30

Matthew 19: 27. Then Peter answering said to him

Peter tacitly compares himself and the other disciples to the rich man, whom the world had turned aside from Christ. As they had led a poor and wandering life, which was not unaccompanied by disgrace and by annoyances, and as no better condition for the future presented itself, he properly inquires if it be to no purpose that they have left all their property, and devoted themselves to Christ; for it would be unreasonable if, after having been stripped of their property by the Lord, they should not be restored to a better condition.

Lo, we have left all

But what were those all things? for, being mean and very poor men, they scarcely had a home to leave, and therefore this boasting might appear to be ridiculous. And certainly experience shows how large an estimate men commonly form of their duties towards God, as at this day, among the Papists, those who were little else than beggars make it a subject of haughty reproach that they have sustained great damage for the sake of the Gospel. But the disciples may be excused on this ground, that, though their wealth was not magnificent, they subsisted at home, by their manual labors, not less cheerfully than the richest man. And we know that men of humble condition, who have been accustomed to a quiet and modest life, reckon it a greater hardship to be torn from their wives and children than those who are led by ambition, or who are carried in various directions by the gale of prosperity. Certainly, if some reward had not been reserved for the disciples, it would have been foolish in them to have changed their course of life.

But though on that ground they might be excused, they err in this respect, that they demand a triumph to be given them, before they have finished their warfare. If we ever experience such uneasiness at delay, and if we are tempted by impatience, let us learn first to reflect on the comforts by which the Lord soothes the bitterness of the cup in this world, and next elevate our minds to the hope of the heavenly life; for these two points embrace the answer of Christ.

Matthew 19: 29. And whosoever shall forsake

After having raised the expectation of his followers to the hope of a future life, he supports them by immediate consolations, and strengthens them for bearing the cross. For though God permit his people to be severely afflicted, he never abandons them, so as not to recompense their distresses by his assistance. And here he does not merely address the apostles, but takes occasion to direct his discourse generally to all the godly. The substance of it is this:

ADAM CLARKE

MATTHEW 19: 23–26; MARK 10: 23–27; LUKE 18: 24–27

Matthew 19: 23–26

23. A rich man shall hardly enter – That is, into the spirit and privileges of the Gospel in this world, and through them into the kingdom of glory. Earthly riches are a great obstacle to salvation; because it is almost impossible to possess them, and not to set the heart upon them; and they who love the world have not the love of the Father in them. 1 John 2: 15. To be rich, therefore, is in general a great misfortune: but what rich man can be convinced of this? It is only God himself who, by a miracle of mercy, can do this. Christ himself affirms the difficulty of the salvation of a rich man, with an oath, verily; but who of the rich either hears or believes him!

25. Who can be saved? – The question of the disciples seemed to intimate that most people were rich, and that therefore scarcely any could be saved. They certainly must have attached a different meaning to what constitutes a rich man, to what we in general do. Who is a rich man in our Lord's sense of the word? This is a very important question, and has not, that I know of, been explicitly answered. A rich man, in my opinion, is not one who has so many hundreds or thousands more than some of his neighbors; but is one who gets more than is necessary to supply all his own wants, and those of his household, and keeps the residue still to himself, though the poor are starving through lack of the necessaries of life. In a word, he is a man who gets all he can, saves all he can, and keeps all he has gotten. Speak, reason! Speak, conscience! (for God has already spoken) Can such a person enter into the kingdom of God? ALL, NO!!!

26. With men this is impossible – God alone can take the love of the world out of the human heart. Therefore the salvation of the rich is represented as possible only to him: and indeed the words seem to intimate, that it requires more than common exertions of Omnipotence to save a rich man.

MATTHEW 19: 27–30; MARK 10: 28–31; LUKE 18: 28–30; 22: 28–30

Matthew 19: 27–30

27. We have forsaken all – To forsake all, without following Christ, is the virtue of a philosopher. To follow Christ in profession, without forsaking all, is the state of the generality of Christians. But to follow Christ and forsake all, is the perfection of a Christian.

28. Judging the twelve tribes – From the parallel place, Luke 22: 28–30, it is evident that sitting on thrones, and judging the twelve tribes, means simply obtaining eternal salvation, and the distinguishing privileges of the kingdom of glory, by those who continued faithful to Christ in his sufferings and death.

29. Shall receive a hundredfold – Viz. in this life, in value, though perhaps not in kind; and in the world to come everlasting life. A glorious portion for a persevering believer! The fullness of GRACE here, and the fullness of GLORY hereafter!

30. But many that are first, etc. – The Jews, who have been the first and most distinguished people of God, will in general reject the Gospel of my grace, and be consequently rejected by me. The Gentiles, who have had no name among the living, shall be brought to the knowledge of the truth, and become the first, the chief, and most exalted people of God. That this prediction of our Lord has been literally fulfilled, the present state of the Christian and Jewish Churches sufficiently proves. To illustrate this fully, and to demonstrate that the Jews and Gentiles were now put on an equal footing by the Gospel, our Lord speaks the following parable, which has been unhappily divided from its connection by making it the beginning of a new chapter.

MATTHEW 20: 1–16

1. For the kingdom of heaven is like unto a man – a householder – The very commencement of this chapter shows it to be connected with the preceding. The manner of God's

father, or mother, or wife, or children, or lands, for my sake, and the gospel's,

30 But he shall receive an hundredfold now in this time, houses, and brethren, and sisters, and mothers, and children, and lands, with persecutions; and in the world to come eternal life.

31 But many that are first shall be last; and the last first.

Luke 18: 28–30

28 Then Peter said, Lo, we have left all, and followed thee.

29 And he said unto them, Verily I say unto you, There is no man that hath left house, or parents, or brethren, or wife, or children, for the kingdom of God's sake,

30 Who shall not receive manifold more in this present time, and in the world to come life everlasting.

Luke 22: 28–30

28 Ye are they which have continued with me in my temptations.

29 And I appoint unto you a kingdom, as my Father hath appointed unto me;

30 That ye may eat and drink at my table in my kingdom, and sit on thrones judging the twelve tribes of Israel.

MATTHEW 20: 1–16

1 For the kingdom of heaven is like unto a man that is an householder, which went out early in the morning to hire labourers into his vineyard.

2 And when he had agreed with the labourers for a penny a day, he sent them into his vineyard.

3 And he went out about the third hour, and saw others standing idle in the marketplace,

4 And said unto them; Go ye also into the vineyard, and whatsoever is right I will give you. And they went their way.

5 Again he went out about the sixth and ninth hour, and did likewise.

6 And about the eleventh hour he went out, and found others standing idle, and saith unto them, Why stand ye here all the day idle?

7 They say unto him, Because no man hath hired us. He saith unto them, Go ye also into the vineyard; and whatsoever is right, that shall ye receive.

8 So when even was come, the lord of

Those who shall willingly lose all for the sake of Christ, will be more happy even in this life than if they had retained the full possession of them; but the chief reward is laid up for them in heaven.

But what he promises about recompensing them a hundredfold appears not at all to agree with experience; for in the greater number of cases, those who have been deprived of their parents, or children, and other relatives – who have been reduced to widowhood, and stripped of their wealth, for the testimony of Christ – are so far from recovering their property, that in exile, solitude and desertion, they have a hard struggle with severe poverty. I reply, if any man estimate aright the immediate grace of God, by which he relieves the sorrows of his people, he will acknowledge that it is justly preferred to all the riches of the world.

MATTHEW 20: 1–16

As this parable is nothing else than a confirmation of the preceding sentence, the **last shall be first**, it now remains to see in what manner it ought to be applied. Some commentators reduce it to this general proposition, that the glory of all; will be equal, because the heavenly inheritance is not obtained by the merits of works, but is bestowed freely. But Christ does not here argue either about the equality of the heavenly glory, or about the future condition of the godly. He only declares that those who were first in point of time have no right to boast or to insult others; because the Lord, whenever he pleases, may call those whom he appeared for a time to disregard, and may make them equal, or even superior, to the first. If any man should resolve to sift out with exactness every portion of this parable, his curiosity would be useless; and therefore we have nothing more to inquire than what was the design of Christ to teach. Now we have already said that he had no other object in view than to excite his people by continual spurs to make progress. We know that indolence almost always springs from excessive confidence; and this is the reason why many, as if they had reached the goal, stop short in the middle of the course. Thus Paul enjoins us to forget the things which are behind (Philippians 3: 13), that, reflecting on what yet remains for us, we may arouse ourselves to persevere in running. But there will be no harm in examining the words, that the doctrine may be more clearly evinced.

Matthew 20: 1. For the kingdom of heaven is like a householder

The meaning is, that such is the nature of the divine calling, as if a man were, early in the morning, to hire laborers for the cultivation of his vineyard at a fixed price, and were afterwards to employ others without an agreement, but to give them an equal hire. He uses the phrase, **kingdom**

proceeding under the Gospel dispensation resembles a householder, who went out at day break, together with the morning; as the light began to go out of its chambers in the east, so he went out of his bed-room to employ laborers, that they might cultivate his vineyard. This was what was called, among the Jews and Romans, the first hour; answering to six o'clock in the morning.

To hire laborers – Some workmen – for he had not got all that was necessary, because we find him going out at other hours to hire more.

2. A penny – A Roman coin, as noted before, Matthew 18: 28, worth about seven-pence halfpenny or seven-pence three farthings of our money, and equal to the Greek drachma. This appears to have been the ordinary price of a day's labor at that time.

3. The third hour – Nine o'clock in the morning.

Market-place – Where laborers usually stood till they were hired. I have often seen laborers standing in the market places of large towns in these countries, waiting to be employed.

5. The sixth hour – Twelve o'clock. Ninth hour – three o'clock in the afternoon.

6. Eleventh – Five o'clock in the evening, when there was only one hour before the end of the Jewish day, which, in matters of labor, closed at six.

7. No man hath hired us – This was the reason why they were all the day idle.

And whatsoever is right, that shall ye receive – Ye may expect payment in proportion to your labor, and the time ye spend in it.

8. When the even was come – Six o'clock, the time they ceased from labor, and the workmen came to receive their wages.

Steward – A manager of the household concerns under the master.

11. They murmured – The Jews made the preaching of the Gospel to the Gentiles, a pretense why they should reject that Gospel;

as they fondly imagined they were, and should be, the sole objects of the Divine approbation. How they murmured because the Gentiles were made partakers of the kingdom of God; see Acts 11: 1, etc., and Acts 15: 1, etc.

13. Friend, I do thee no wrong – The salvation of the Gentiles can in itself become no impediment to the Jews; there is the same Jesus both for the Jew and for the Greek. Eternal life is offered to both through the blood of the cross; and there is room enough in heaven for all.

15. Is it not lawful for me – As eternal life is the free gift of God, he has a right to give it in whatever proportions, at whatever times, and on whatever conditions he pleases.

Is thine eye evil – An evil eye among the Jews meant a malicious, covetous, or envious person.

Most commentators have different methods of interpreting this parable. Something was undoubtedly designed by its principal parts, besides the scope and design mentioned at the conclusion of the last chapter. The following, which is taken principally from the very pious Quesnel, may render it as useful to the reader as any thing else that has been written on it.

The Church is a vineyard, because it is a place of labor, where no man should be idle. Each of us is engaged to labor in this vineyard – to work out our salvation through him who worketh in us to will and to perform. Life is but a day, whereof childhood, or the first use of reason, is the day-break or first hour, Matthew 20: 1, in which we receive the first CALL.

The promise of the kingdom of glory is given to all those who are workers together with him, Matthew 20: 2.

The second call is in the time of youth, which is most commonly idle, or only employed in dissipation and worldly cares, Matthew 20: 3.

The third call is at the age of manhood.

The fourth, in the decline of life, Matthew 20: 5.

The fifth, when sickness and the infirmities of life press upon us. How many are there in the world who are just ready to leave it, before they properly consider for what end they were brought into it! Still idle, still unemployed in

the vineyard saith unto his steward, Call the labourers, and give them their hire, beginning from the last unto the first.

9 And when they came that were hired about the eleventh hour, they received every man a penny.

10 But when the first came, they supposed that they should have received more; and they likewise received every man a penny.

11 And when they had received it, they murmured against the goodman of the house,

12 Saying, These last have wrought but one hour, and thou hast made them equal unto us, which have borne the burden and heat of the day.

13 But he answered one of them, and said, Friend, I do thee no wrong: didst not thou agree with me for a penny?

14 Take that thine is, and go thy way: I will give unto this last, even as unto thee.

15 Is it not lawful for me to do what I will with mine own? Is thine eye evil, because I am good?

16 So the last shall be first, and the first last: for many be called, but few chosen.

MATTHEW 20: 17–19; MARK 10: 32–34; LUKE 18: 31–34

Matthew 20: 17–19

17 And Jesus going up to Jerusalem took the twelve disciples apart in the way, and said unto them,

18 Behold, we go up to Jerusalem; and the Son of man shall be betrayed unto the chief priests and unto the scribes, and they shall condemn him to death,

19 And shall deliver him to the Gentiles to mock, and to scourge, and to crucify him: and the third day he shall rise again.

Mark 10: 32–34

32 And they were in the way going up to Jerusalem; and Jesus went before them: and they were amazed; and as they followed, they were afraid. And he took again the twelve, and began to tell them what things should happen unto him,

33 Saying, Behold, we go up to Jerusalem; and the Son of man shall be delivered unto the chief priests, and unto the scribes; and they shall condemn him

of heaven, because he compares the spiritual life to the earthly life, and the reward of eternal life to money which men pay in return for work that has been done for them. There are some who give an ingenious interpretation to this passage, as if Christ were distinguishing between Jews and Gentiles. The Jews, they tell us, were called **at the first hour**, with an agreement as to the hire; for the Lord promised to them eternal life, on the condition that they should fulfill the law; while, in calling the Gentiles, no bargain was made at least as to works, for salvation was freely offered to them in Christ. But all subtleties of that sort are unseasonable; for the Lord makes no distinction in the bargain, but only in the time; because those who entered last, and in the evening, into the vineyard, receive the same hire with the first. Though, in the Law, God formerly promised to the Jews the hire of works (Leviticus 18: 5), yet we know that this was without effect, because no man ever obtained salvation by his merits.

MATTHEW 20: 17–19; MARK 10: 32–34; LUKE 18: 31–34

Though the apostles had been previously informed what kind of death awaited our Lord, yet as they had not sufficiently profited by it, he now repeats anew what he had frequently said. He sees that the day of his death is at hand; nay more, he is already in a state of readiness to offer himself to be sacrificed; and, on the other hand, he sees the disciples not only afraid, but overwhelmed by blind alarm. He therefore exhorts them to steadiness, that they may not immediately yield to temptation. Now there are two methods by which he confirms them; for, by foretelling what would happen, he not only fortifies them, that they may not give way, when a calamity, which has arisen suddenly and contrary to expectation, takes them by surprise, but meets the offense of the cross by a proof of his Divinity, that they may not lose courage at beholding his short abasement, when they are convinced that he is the Son of God, and therefore will be victorious over death. The second method of confirmation is taken from his approaching resurrection.

But it will be proper to look more closely at the words. Mark states – what is omitted by the other two Evangelists – that, before our Lord explained to his disciples in private that he was going straight to the sacrifice of death, not only they, but also the rest of his followers, were sorrowful and trembling. Now why they were seized with this fear it is not easy to say, if it was not because they had already learned that they had dangerous adversaries at Jerusalem, and would therefore have wished that Christ should remain in some quiet retreat beyond the reach of the darts, rather than voluntarily expose himself to such inveterate enemies.

the things which concern their souls; though eternal life is offered to them, and hell moving from beneath to meet them! Matthew 20: 6.

Others consider the morning the first dawn of the Gospel; and the first call to be the preaching of John Baptist.

The second call, the public preaching of our LORD; and that of the apostles when they got an especial commission to the Jews, Matthew 10: 5–6, together with that of the seventy disciples mentioned Luke 10: 1.

The third call, which was at mid-day, represents the preaching of the fullness of the Gospel after the ascension of Christ, which was the meridian of evangelic glory and excellence.

The fourth call represents the mission of the apostles to the various synagogues of the Jews, in every part of the world where they were scattered; the history of which is particularly given in the Acts of the Apostles.

The fifth call, or eleventh hour, represents the general call of the Gentiles into the Church of Christ, when the unbelieving Jews were finally rejected.

What makes this interpretation the more likely is, that the persons who are addressed at Matthew 20: 7, say, No man hath hired us, i.e. We never heard the voice of a prophet announcing the true God, nor of an apostle preaching the Lord Jesus, until now. The Jews could not use this as an argument for their carelessness about their eternal interests.

16. So the last shall be first, and the first last – The GENTILES, who have been long without the true God, shall now enjoy all the privileges of the new covenant; and the Jews, who have enjoyed these from the beginning, shall now be dispossessed of them; for, because they here rejected the Lord, he also hath rejected them.

Many are called, etc. – The simple meaning seems to be: As those who did not come at the invitation of the householder to work in the vineyard did not receive the denarius, or wages, so those who do not obey the call of the Gospel, and believe in Christ Jesus, shall not inherit eternal life.

Many are called by the preaching of the Gospel, but few are found who use their advantages in such a way as to become extensively useful in the Church – and many in the Church militant behave so ill as never to be admitted into the Church triumphant. But what a mercy that those who appear now to be rejected may be called in another muster, enrolled, serve in the field, or work in the vineyard? How many millions does the long-suffering of God lead to repentance!

MATTHEW 20: 17–19; MARK 10: 32–34; LUKE 18: 31–34

Matthew 20: 17–19

17. And Jesus going up – From Jericho to Jerusalem, See Matthew 19: 15.

18. The Son of man shall be betrayed – Or, will be delivered up. This is the third time that our Lord informed his disciples of his approaching sufferings and death. This was a subject of the utmost importance, and it was necessary they should be well prepared for such an awful event.

19. Deliver him to the Gentiles to mock – This was done by Herod and his Roman soldiers. See Luke 23: 11.

To scourge, and to crucify – This was done by Pilate, the Roman governor. The punishment of the cross was Roman not Jewish; but the chief priests condemned him to it, and the Romans executed the sentence. How little did they know that they were, by this process, jointly offering up that sacrifice which was to make an atonement for the Gentiles and for the Jews; an atonement for the sin of the whole world? How often may it be literally said, The wrath of man shall praise thee!

MATTHEW 20: 20–23; MARK 10: 35–40

Matthew 20: 20–23

20. The mother of Zebedee's children – This was Salome.

to death, and shall deliver him to the Gentiles:

34 And they shall mock him, and shall scourge him, and shall spit upon him, and shall kill him: and the third day he shall rise again.

Luke 18: 31–34

31 Then he took unto him the twelve, and said unto them, Behold, we go up to Jerusalem, and all things that are written by the prophets concerning the Son of man shall be accomplished.

32 For he shall be delivered unto the Gentiles, and shall be mocked, and spitefully entreated, and spitted on:

33 And they shall scourge him, and put him to death: and the third day he shall rise again.

34 And they understood none of these things: and this saying was hid from them, neither knew they the things which were spoken.

MATTHEW 20: 20–23; MARK 10: 35–40

Matthew 20: 20–23

20 Then came to him the mother of Zebedee's children with her sons, worshipping him, and desiring a certain thing of him.

21 And he said unto her, What wilt thou? She saith unto him, Grant that these my two sons may sit, the one on thy right hand, and the other on the left, in thy kingdom.

22 But Jesus answered and said, Ye know not what ye ask. Are ye able to drink of the cup that I shall drink of, and to be baptized with the baptism that I am baptized with? They say unto him, We are able.

23 And he saith unto them, Ye shall drink indeed of my cup, and be baptized with the baptism that I am baptized with: but to sit on my right hand, and on my left, is not mine to give, but it shall be given to them for whom it is prepared of my Father.

Mark 10: 35–40

35 And James and John, the sons of Zebedee, come unto him, saying, Master, we would that thou shouldest do for us whatsoever we shall desire.

36 And he said unto them, What would

Although this fear was in many respects improper, yet the circumstance of their following Christ is a proof of no ordinary respect and obedience. It would indeed have been far better to hasten cheerfully and without regret, wheresoever the Son of God chose to lead them; but commendation is due to their reverence for his person, which appears in choosing to do violence to their own feelings rather than to forsake him.

MATTHEW 20: 20–23; MARK 10: 35–40

Matthew 20: 20. Then came to him the mother of Zebedee's children

This narrative contains a bright mirror of human vanity; for it shows that proper and holy zeal is often accompanied by ambition, or some other vice of the flesh, so that they who follow Christ have a different object in view from what they ought to have. They who are not satisfied with himself alone, but seek this or the other thing apart from him and his promises, wander egregiously from the right path. Nor is it enough that, at the commencement, we sincerely apply our minds to Christ, if we do not stead-lastly maintain the same purity; for frequently, in the midst of the course, there spring up sinful affections by which we are led astray. In this way it is probable that the two sons of Zebedee were, at first, sincere in their adherence to Christ; but when they see that they have no ordinary share of his favor, and hear his reign spoken of as near at hand, their minds are immediately led to wicked ambition, and they are greatly distressed at the thought of remaining in their present situation. If this happens to two excellent disciples, with what care ought we to walk, if we do not wish to turn aside from the right path! More especially, when any plausible occasion presents itself, we ought to be on our guard, lest the desire of honors corrupt the feeling of piety.

Though Matthew and Mark differ somewhat in the words, yet they agree as to the substance of the matter. Matthew says that the wife of Zebedee came, and **asked for her sons** that they might hold the highest places **in the kingdom** of Christ. Mark represents themselves as making the request. But it is probable that, being restrained by bashfulness, they had the dexterity to employ their mother, who would present the request with greater boldness. That the wish came originally from themselves may be inferred from this circumstance, that Christ replied to them, and not to their mother. Besides, when their mother, **bowing down**, states that she has something to ask, and when themselves, according to Mark, apply for a general engagement, **that whatever they ask shall be granted to them**, this timid insinuation proves that they were conscious of something wrong.

ADAM CLARKE

21. Grant that these my two sons – James and John. See Mark 15: 40. In the preceding chapter, Matthew 19: 28, our Lord had promised his disciples, that they should sit on twelve thrones, judging the twelve tribes. Salome, probably hearing of this, and understanding it literally, came to request the chief dignities in this new government for her sons; and it appears it was at their instigation that she made this request, for Mark, Mark 10: 35, informs us that these brethren themselves made the request, i.e. they made it through the medium of their mother.

One on thy right hand, and the other on (THY) left – I have added the pronoun in the latter clause on the authority of almost every MS. and version of repute.

That the sons of Zebedee wished for ecclesiastical, rather than secular honors, may be thought probable, from the allusion that is made here to the supreme dignities in the great Sanhedrin. The prince of the Sanhedrin sat in the midst of two rows of senators or elders; on his right hand sat the father of the Sanhedrin; and on his left hand the sage. These persons transacted all business in the absence of the president. The authority of this council was at some periods very great, and extended to a multitude of matters both ecclesiastical and civil. These appear to have been the honors which James and John sought. They seem to have strangely forgot the lesson they had learned from the transfiguration.

22. Ye know not what ye ask – How strange is the infatuation, in some parents, which leads them to desire worldly or ecclesiastical honors for their children! He must be much in love with the cross who wishes to have his child a minister of the Gospel; for, if he be such as God approves of in the work, his life will be a life of toil and suffering; he will be obliged to sip, at least, if not to drink largely, of the cup of Christ. We know not what we ask, when, in getting our children into the CHURCH, we take upon ourselves to answer for their CALL to the sacred office, and for the salvation of the souls that are put under their care. Blind parents! rather let your children beg their bread than thrust them into an office to which God has not called them; and in which they will not only ruin their souls, but be the means of damnation to hundreds; for if God has not sent them, they shall not profit the people at all.

And to be baptized with the baptism that I am baptized, etc. – Baptism among the Jews, as it was performed in the coldest weather, and the persons were kept under water for some time, was used not only to express death, but the most cruel kind of death. See Lightfoot. As to the term cup, it was a common figure, by which they expressed calamities, judgments, desolation, etc.

They say unto him, We are able – Strange blindness! You can? No: one drop of this cup would sink you into utter ruin, unless upheld by the power of God. However, the man whom God has appointed to the work he will preserve in it.

23. Is not mine to give, but it shall be given to them for whom it is prepared of my Father – The common translation, in which the words, it shall be given to them; are interpolated by our translators, utterly changes and destroys the meaning of the passage. It represents Christ (in opposition to the whole Scriptures) as having nothing to do in the dispensing of rewards and punishments; whereas, our Lord only intimates that, however partial he may be to these two brethren, yet seats in glory can only be given to those who are fitted for them. No favor can prevail here; the elevated seat is for him who is filled with the fullness of God. The true construction of the words is this: To sit on my right hand and on my left, is not mine to give, except to them for whom it is prepared of my Father. According to the prediction of Christ, these brethren did partake of his afflictions: James was martyred by Herod, Acts 12: 2; and John was banished to Patmos, for the testimony of Christ, Revelation 1: 9.

ye that I should do for you?

37 They said unto him, Grant unto us that we may sit, one on thy right hand, and the other on thy left hand, in thy glory.

38 But Jesus said unto them, Ye know not what ye ask: can ye drink of the cup that I drink of? and be baptized with the baptism that I am baptized with?

39 And they said unto him, We can. And Jesus said unto them, Ye shall indeed drink of the cup that I drink of; and with the baptism that I am baptized withal shall ye be baptized:

40 But to sit on my right hand and on my left hand is not mine to give; but it shall be given to them for whom it is prepared.

MATTHEW 20: 24–28; MARK 10: 41–45; LUKE 22: 24–27

Matthew 20: 24–28

24 And when the ten heard it, they were moved with indignation against the two brethren.

25 But Jesus called them unto him, and said, Ye know that the princes of the Gentiles exercise dominion over them, and they that are great exercise authority upon them.

26 But it shall not be so among you: but whosoever will be great among you, let him be your minister;

27 And whosoever will be chief among you, let him be your servant:

28 Even as the Son of man came not to be ministered unto, but to minister, and to give his life a ransom for many.

Mark 10: 41–45

41 And when the ten heard it, they began to be much displeased with James and John.

42 But Jesus called them to him, and saith unto them, Ye know that they which are accounted to rule over the Gentiles exercise lordship over them; and their great ones exercise authority upon them.

43 But so shall it not be among you: but whosoever will be great among you, shall be your minister:

44 And whosoever of you will be the chiefest, shall be servant of all.

45 For even the Son of man came not

MATTHEW 20: 24–28; MARK 10: 41–45; LUKE 22: 24–27

Matthew 20: 24. And when the ten heard it

Luke appears to refer this dispute to a different time. But any one who shall carefully examine that twenty-second chapter will plainly see that discourses delivered at different times are there brought together, without any regard to order. The dispute about the primacy, therefore which Luke mentions, flowed from this source, that **the sons of Zebedee** aspired to the first places in the kingdom of Christ. And yet the displeasure of the rest was far from being well-founded; for, while the foolish ambition of the two disciples was so severely blamed, that they retired from Christ with disgrace, what injury was it to the other ten, that those disciples foolishly wished what they did not obtain? For though they had a good right to be offended at the ambition of those disciples, yet when it was put down they ought to have been satisfied. But our Lord intended to seize on this occasion for laying open a disease which was lurking within them; for there was not one of them who would willingly yield to others, but every one secretly cherished within himself the expectation of the primacy; in consequence of which, they envy and dispute with one another, and yet in all there reigns wicked ambition. And if this fault was found to be natural to uneducated men of ordinary rank, and if it broke out on a slight occasion, and almost without any occasion at all, how much more ought we to be on our guard, when there is abundance of fuel to feed a concealed flame? We see then how ambition springs up in any man who has great power and honors, and sends out its flames far and wide, unless the spirit of modesty, coming from heaven, extinguish the pride which has a firm hold of the nature of man.

25. You know that the princes of the Gentiles rule over them

It is first said that Christ **called them to him**, that he might reprove them in private; and next we learn from it that, being ashamed of their ambition, they did not openly complain, but that a sort of hollow murmur arose, and every one secretly preferred himself to the rest. He does not explain generally how deadly a plague ambition is, but simply warns them, that nothing is more foolish than to fight about nothing. He shows that the primacy, which was the occasion of dispute among them, has no existence in his kingdom.

MATTHEW 20: 24–28; MARK 10: 41–45; LUKE 22: 24–27

Matthew 20: 24–28

24. When the ten heard it, they were moved – The ambition which leads to spiritual lordship is one great cause of murmurings and animosities in religious societies, and has proved the ruin of the most flourishing Churches in the universe.

25. Exercise dominion – and – exercise authority upon them – They tyrannized and exercised arbitrary power over the people. This was certainly true of the governments in our Lord's time, both in the east and in the west.

The government of the Church of Christ is widely different from secular governments. It is founded in humility and brotherly love: it is derived from Christ, the great Head of the Church, and is ever conducted by his maxims and spirit. When political matters are brought into the Church of Christ, both are ruined. The Church has more than once ruined the State; the State has often corrupted the Church: it is certainly for the interests of both to be kept separate. This has already been abundantly exemplified in both cases, and will continue so to be, over the whole world, wherever the Church and State are united in secular matters.

26. It shall not be so among you – Every kind of lordship and spiritual domination over the Church of Christ, like that exercised by the Church of Rome, is destructive and anti-christian.

Your minister – Or, deacon. I know no other word which could at once convey the meaning of the original, and make a proper distinction between it and servant, in Matthew 20: 27. The office of a deacon, in the primitive Church, was to serve in the love feasts, to distribute the bread and wine to the communicants; to proclaim different parts and times of worship in the churches; and to take care of the widows, orphans, prisoners, and sick, who were provided for out of the revenues of the Church. Thus we find it was the very lowest ecclesiastical office. Deacons were first appointed by the apostles, Acts 6: 1–6; they had the care of the poor, and preached occasionally.

27. Your servant – the lowest secular office, as deacon was the lowest ecclesiastical office: is often put for slave.

From these directions of our Lord, we may easily discern what sort of a spirit his ministers should be of.

1. A minister of Christ is not to consider himself a lord over Christ's flock.

2. He is not to conduct the concerns of the Church with an imperious spirit.

3. He is to reform the weak, after Christ's example, more by loving instruction than by reproof or censure.

4. He should consider that true apostolic greatness consists in serving the followers of Christ with all the powers and talents he possesses.

5. That he should be ready, if required, to give up his life unto death, to promote the salvation of men.

28. A ransom for many – a ransom instead of many, – one ransom, or atonement, instead of the many prescribed in the Jewish law. Mr. Wakefield contends for the above translation, and with considerable show of reason and probability.

The whole Gentile world, as well as the Jews, believed in vicarious sacrifices. One man must be given for many. Jesus Christ laid down his life as a ransom for the lives and souls of the children of men. In the Codex Bezae, and in most of the Itala, the Saxon, and one of the Syriac, Hilary, Leo Magnus, and Juvencus, the following remarkable addition is found; "But seek ye to increase from a little, and to be lessened from that which is great. Moreover, when ye enter into a house, and are invited to sup, do not recline in the most eminent places, lest a more honorable than thou come after, and he who invited thee to supper come up to thee and say, Get down yet lower; and thou be put to confusion. But if thou sit down in the lowest place, and one inferior to thee come after, he who invited thee to supper will say unto thee, Go and sit higher: now this will be advantageous to thee." This is the largest addi-

to be ministered unto, but to minister, and to give his life a ransom for many.

Luke 22: 24–27

24 And there was also a strife among them, which of them should be accounted the greatest.

25 And he said unto them, The kings of the Gentiles exercise lordship over them; and they that exercise authority upon them are called benefactors.

26 But ye shall not be so: but he that is greatest among you, let him be as the younger; and he that is chief, as he that doth serve.

27 For whether is greater, he that sitteth at meat, or he that serveth? is not he that sitteth at meat? but I am among you as he that serveth.

MATTHEW 20: 29–34; MARK 10: 46–52; LUKE 18: 35–43

Matthew 20: 29–34

29 And as they departed from Jericho, a great multitude followed him.

30 And, behold, two blind men sitting by the way side, when they heard that Jesus passed by, cried out, saying, Have mercy on us, O Lord, thou Son of David.

31 And the multitude rebuked them, because they should hold their peace: but they cried the more, saying, Have mercy on us, O Lord, thou Son of David.

32 And Jesus stood still, and called them, and said, What will ye that I shall do unto you?

33 They say unto him, Lord, that our eyes may be opened.

34 So Jesus had compassion on them, and touched their eyes: and immediately their eyes received sight, and they followed him.

Mark 10: 46–52

46 And they came to Jericho: and as he went out of Jericho with his disciples and a great number of people, blind Bartimaeus, the son of Timaeus, sat by the highway side begging.

47 And when he heard that it was Jesus of Nazareth, he began to cry out, and say, Jesus, thou Son of David, have mercy on me.

48 And many charged him that he should hold his peace: but he cried the

MATTHEW 20: 29–34; MARK 10: 46–52; LUKE 18: 35–43

Matthew 20: 29. And while they were departing from Jericho

Osiander has resolved to display his ingenuity by making four blind men out of one. But nothing can be more frivolous than this supposition. Having observed that the Evangelists differ in a few expressions, he imagined that one blind man received sight when they were entering into the city, and that the second, and other two, received sight when Christ was departing from it. But all the circumstances agree so completely, that no person of sound judgment will believe them to be different narratives. Not to mention other matters, when Christ's followers had endeavored to put the first to silence, and saw him cured contrary to their expectation, would they immediately have made the same attempt with the other three? But it is unnecessary to go into particulars, from which any man may easily infer that it is one and the same event which is related.

But there is a puzzling contradiction in this respect, that Matthew and Mark say that the miracle was performed on one or on two blind men, when Christ had already departed from the city; while Luke relates that it was done before he came to the city. Besides, Mark and Luke speak of not more than one blind man, while Matthew mentions two. But as we know that it frequently occurs in the Evangelists, that in the same narrative one passes by what is mentioned by the others, and, on the other hand, states more clearly what they have omitted, it ought not to be looked upon as strange or unusual in the present passage. My conjecture is, that, while Christ was approaching to the city, the blind man cried out, but that, as he was not heard on account of the noise, he placed himself in the way, as they were departing from the city, and then was at length called by Christ. And so Luke, commencing with what was true, does not follow out the whole narrative, but passes over Christ's stay in the city; while the other Evangelists attend only to the time which was nearer to the miracle. There is probability in the conjecture that, as Christ frequently, when he wished to try the faith of men, delayed for a short time to relieve them, so he subjected this blind man to the same scrutiny.

The second difficulty may be speedily removed; for we have seen, on a former occasion, that Mark and Luke speak of one demoniac as having been cured, while Matthew, as in the present instance, mentions two (Matthew 8: 28; Mark 5: 2; Luke 8: 27). And yet this involves no contradiction between them; but it may rather be conjectured with probability, that at first one blind man implored the favor of Christ, and that another was excited by his example, and that in this way two people received sight. Mark and Luke

ADAM CLARKE

tion found in any of the MSS., and contains not less than sixty words In the original, and eighty-three in the Anglo-Saxon.

MATTHEW 20: 29–34; MARK 10: 46–52; LUKE 18: 35–43

Matthew 20: 29–34

30. Two blind men – Mark 10: 46, and Luke 18: 35, mention only one blind man, Bartimeus. Probably he was mentioned by the other evangelists, as being a person well known before and after his cure. Blindness of heart is a disorder of which, men seldom complain, or from which they desire to be delivered; and it is one property of this blindness, to keep the person from perceiving it, and to persuade him that his sight is good.

Sitting by the way side – In the likeliest place to receive alms, because of the multitudes going and coming between Jerusalem and Jericho.

Cried out – In the midst of judgments God remembers mercy. Though God had deprived them, for wise reasons, of their eyes, he left them the use of their speech. It is never so ill with us, but it might be much worse: let us, therefore, be submissive and thankful.

Have mercy on us – Hearing that Jesus passed by, and not knowing whether they should ever again have so good an opportunity of addressing him, they are determined to call, and call earnestly. They ask for mercy, conscious that they deserve nothing, and they ask with faith – Son of David, acknowledging him as the promised Messiah.

31. The multitude rebuked them – Whenever a soul begins to cry after Jesus for light and salvation, the world and the devil join together to drown its cries, or force it to be silent. But let all such remember, Jesus is now passing by; that their souls must perish everlastingly, if not saved by him, and they may never have so good an opportunity again. While there is a broken and a contrite heart, let it sigh its complaints to God, till he hear and answer.

They cried the more – When the world and the devil begin to rebuke, in this case, it is a proof that the salvation of God is nigh; therefore, let such cry out a great deal the more.

32. Jesus stood – "The cry of a believing penitent," says one, "is sufficient to stop the most merciful Jesus, were he going to make a new heaven and a new earth; for what is all the irrational part of God's creation in worth, when compared with the value of one immortal soul!"

What will ye that I shall do – Christ is at all times infinitely willing to save sinners: when the desire of the heart is turned towards him, there can be little delay in the salvation. What is thy wish? If it be a good one, God will surely fulfill it.

33. That our eyes may be opened – He who feels his own sore, and the plague of his heart, has no great need of a prompter in prayer. A hungry man can easily ask bread; he has no need to go to a book to get expressions to state his wants in; his hunger tells him he wants food, and he tells this to the person from whom he expects relief. Helps to devotion, in all ordinary cases, may be of great use; in extraordinary cases they can be of little importance; the afflicted heart alone can tell its own sorrows, with appropriate pleadings.

34. So Jesus had compassion on them – He was moved with tender pity. The tender pity of Christ met the earnest cry of the blind men, and their immediate cure was the result.

They followed him – As a proof of the miracle that was wrought, and of the gratitude which they felt to their benefactor. For other particulars of this miraculous cure, see the notes on Mark 10: 46, etc.

Reader, whosoever thou art, act in behalf of thy soul as these blind men did in behalf of their sight, and thy salvation is sure. Apply to the Son of David; lose not a moment; he is passing by, and thou art passing into eternity, and probably wilt never have a more favorable opportunity than the present. The Lord increase thy earnestness and faith!

more a great deal, Thou Son of David, have mercy on me.

49 And Jesus stood still, and commanded him to be called. And they call the blind man, saying unto him, Be of good comfort, rise; he calleth thee.

50 And he, casting away his garment, rose, and came to Jesus.

51 And Jesus answered and said unto him, What wilt thou that I should do unto thee? The blind man said unto him, Lord, that I might receive my sight.

52 And Jesus said unto him, Go thy way; thy faith hath made thee whole. And immediately he received his sight, and followed Jesus in the way.

Luke 18: 35–43

35 And it came to pass, that as he was come nigh unto Jericho, a certain blind man sat by the way side begging:

36 And hearing the multitude pass by, he asked what it meant.

37 And they told him, that Jesus of Nazareth passeth by.

38 And he cried, saying, Jesus, thou Son of David, have mercy on me.

39 And they which went before rebuked him, that he should hold his peace: but he cried so much the more, Thou Son of David, have mercy on me.

40 And Jesus stood, and commanded him to be brought unto him: and when he was come near, he asked him,

41 Saying, What wilt thou that I shall do unto thee? And he said, Lord, that I may receive my sight.

42 And Jesus said unto him, Receive thy sight: thy faith hath saved thee.

43 And immediately he received his sight, and followed him, glorifying God: and all the people, when they saw it, gave praise unto God.

LUKE 19: 1–10

1 And Jesus entered and passed through Jericho.

2 And, behold, there was a man named Zacchaeus, which was the chief among the publicans, and he was rich.

3 And he sought to see Jesus who he was; and could not for the press, because he was little of stature.

4 And he ran before, and climbed up

speak of one only, either because he was better known, or because in him the demonstration of Christ's power was not less remarkable than it was in both. It certainly appears to have been on account of his having been extensively known that he was selected by Mark, who gives both his own name and that of his father: **Bartimeus, son of Timeus**. By doing so, he does not claim for him either illustrious descent or wealth; for he was a beggar of the lowest class. Hence it appears that the miracle was more remarkable in his person, because his calamity had been generally known. This appears to me to be the reason why Mark and Luke mention him only, and say nothing about the other, who was a sort of inferior appendage. But Matthew, who was an eye-witness, did not choose to pass by even this person, though less known.

31. And the multitude reproved them

It is surprising that the disciples of Christ, who follow him through a sense of duty and of respect, should wish to drive wretched men from the favor of Christ, and, so far as lies in them, to prevent the exercise of his power. But it frequently happens that the greater part of those who profess the name of Christ, instead of inviting us to him, rather hinder or delay our approach. If Satan endeavored to throw obstacles in the way of **two blind men**, by means of pious and simple people, who were induced by some sentiments of religion to follow Christ, how much more will he succeed in accomplishing it by means of hypocrites and traitors, if we be not strictly on our guard. Perseverance is therefore necessary to overcome every difficulty, and the more numerous the obstacles are which Satan throws in the way, the more powerfully ought we to be excited to earnestness in prayer, as we see that the blind men redoubled their cry.

LUKE 19: 1–10

This shows how little attention Luke paid to observing the order of dates; for, after having detailed the miracle, he now relates what happened in the city of **Jericho**. He tells us that, while Christ presented himself to the view of all, as he went along the streets, **Zaccheus** alone was very desirous to see him. For it was an evidence of intense desire that he **climbed up a tree**; since rich men are, for the most part, haughty, and plume themselves on affected gravity. It is possible, indeed, that others entertained the same wish, but this man was most properly singled out by Luke, both on account of his rank, and on account of his wonderful conversion, which took place suddenly. Now, though faith was not yet formed in Zaccheus, yet this was a sort of preparation for it; for it was not without a heavenly inspiration that he desired so earnestly to get a sight of Christ; I mean, in reference to that design which immediately ap-

LUKE 19: 1–10

1. Entered and passed through – Was passing through. Our Lord had not as yet passed through Jericho – he was only passing through it; for the house of Zaccheus, in which he was to lodge, Luke 19: 5, was in it.

2. Zaccheus – It is not unlikely that this person was a Jew by birth, see Luke 19: 9; but because he had engaged in a business so infamous, in the eyes of the Jews, he was considered as a mere heathen, Luke 19: 7.

Chief among the publicans – Either a farmer-general of the taxes, who had subordinate collectors under him: or else the most respectable and honorable man among that class at Jericho.

He was rich – And therefore the more unlikely to pay attention to an impoverished Messiah, preaching a doctrine of universal mortification and self-denial.

3. And he sought to see Jesus who he was – So the mere principle of curiosity in him led to his conversion and salvation, and to that of his whole family, Luke 19: 9.

4. He ran before – The shortness of his stature was amply compensated by his agility and invention. Had he been as tall as the generality of the crowd, he might have been equally unnoticed with the rest. His getting into the tree made him conspicuous: had he not been so low of stature he would not have done so. Even the imperfections of our persons may become subservient to the grace of God in our eternal salvation. As the passover was at hand, the road was probably crowded with people going to Jerusalem; but the fame of the cure of the blind man was probably the cause of the concourse at this time.

5. Make haste, and come down – With this invitation, our blessed Lord conveyed heavenly influence to his heart; hence he was disposed to pay the most implicit and cheerful obedience to the call, and thus he received not the grace of God in vain.

6. Received him joyfully – He had now seen WHO he was, and he wished to hear WHAT he was; and therefore he rejoiced in the honor that God had now conferred upon him. How often does Christ make the proposal of lodging, not only in our house, but in our heart, without its being accepted! We lose much because we do not attend to the visitations of Christ: he passes by – he blesses our neighbors and our friends; but, often, neither curiosity nor any other motive is sufficient to induce us to go even to the house of God, to hear of the miracles of mercy which he works in behalf of those who seek him.

7. To be guest with a man that is a sinner – Meaning either that he was a heathen, or, though by birth a Jew, yet as bad as a heathen, because of his unholy and oppressive office. See the note on Luke 7: 37.

8. The half of my goods I give to the poor – Probably he had already done so for some time past; though it is generally understood that the expressions only refer to what he now purposed to do.

If I have taken any thing – by false accusation – from a fig, and I show or declare; for among the primitive Athenians, when the use of that fruit was first found out, or in the time of a dearth, when all sorts of provisions were exceedingly scarce, it was enacted that no figs should be exported from Attica; and this law (not being actually repealed, when a plentiful harvest had rendered it useless, by taking away the reason of it) gave occasion to ill-natured and malicious fellows to accuse all persons they found breaking the letter of it; and from them all busy informers have ever since been branded with the name of sycophants.

I restore him fourfold – This restitution the Roman laws obliged the tax-gatherers to make, when it was proved they had abused their power by oppressing the people. But here was no such proof: the man, to show the sincerity of his conversion, does it of his own accord. He who has wronged his fellow must make restitution, if he have it in his power. He that does not do so cannot expect the mercy of God.

9. To this house – To this very house or family.

into a sycomore tree to see him: for he was to pass that way.

5 And when Jesus came to the place, he looked up, and saw him, and said unto him, Zacchaeus, make haste, and come down; for to day I must abide at thy house.

6 And he made haste, and came down, and received him joyfully.

7 And when they saw it, they all murmured, saying, That he was gone to be guest with a man that is a sinner.

8 And Zacchaeus stood, and said unto the Lord; Behold, Lord, the half of my goods I give to the poor; and if I have taken any thing from any man by false accusation, I restore him fourfold.

9 And Jesus said unto him, This day is salvation come to this house, forsomuch as he also is a son of Abraham.

10 For the Son of man is come to seek and to save that which was lost.

MATTHEW 25: 14–30; LUKE 19: 11–28

Matthew 25: 14–30

14 For the kingdom of heaven is as a man traveling into a far country, who called his own servants, and delivered unto them his goods.

15 And unto one he gave five talents, to another two, and to another one; to every man according to his several ability; and straightway took his journey.

16 Then he that had received the five talents went and traded with the same, and made them other five talents.

17 And likewise he that had received two, he also gained other two.

18 But he that had received one went and digged in the earth, and hid his lord's money.

19 After a long time the lord of those servants cometh, and reckoneth with them.

20 And so he that had received five talents came and brought other five talents, saying, Lord, thou deliveredst unto me five talents: behold, I have gained beside them five talents more.

21 His lord said unto him, Well done, thou good and faithful servant: thou hast been faithful over a few things, I will make thee ruler over many things: enter thou into the joy of thy lord.

peared. Some were led, no doubt, by vain curiosity to run even from distant places, for the purpose of seeing Christ, but the event showed that the mind of Zaccheus contained some seed of piety. In this manner, before revealing himself to men, the Lord frequently communicates to them a secret desire, by which they are led to Him, while he is still concealed and unknown; and, though they have no fixed object in view, He does not disappoint them, but manifests himself in due time.

5. Zaccheus, make haste, and come down

It is a remarkable instance of favor, that the Lord anticipates Zaccheus, and does not wait for his invitation, but of his own accord asks lodging at his house. We know how hateful, nay, how detestable the name of publican at that time was; and we shall find that this is shortly afterwards mentioned by Luke. It is therefore astonishing kindness in the Son of God to approach a man, from whom the great body of men recoil, and that before he is requested to do so. But we need not wonder, if he bestows this honor on one who was already drawn to him by a secret movement of the Spirit; for it was a more valuable gift to dwell in his heart than to enter his house. But by this expression he made it evident, that he is never sought in vain by those who sincerely desire to know him; for Zaccheus obtained vastly more than he had expected. Besides, the great readiness of Zaccheus to obey, his hastening to come down from the tree, and his joy in receiving Christ, exhibit still more clearly the power and guidance of the Holy Spirit; for, though he did not yet possess a pure faith, yet this submissiveness and obedience must be regarded as the beginning of faith.

MATTHEW 25: 14–30; LUKE 19: 11–28

Luke 19: 11. While they were hearing these things

It was next to a prodigy that the disciples, after having been so frequently warned as to the approaching death of Christ, flew aside from it to think of his kingdom. There were two mistakes; first, that they pictured to themselves rest and happiness without the cross; secondly, that they judged of the kingdom of God according to their own carnal sense. Hence it appears how slight and obscure their faith was; for though they had entertained a hope of the resurrection, yet the taste was too slight for forming a fixed and decided opinion about Christ. They believe him to be the Redeemer who had been formerly promised, and hence they conceive a hope that the Church will be renewed; but that knowledge immediately degenerates into vain imaginations, which either overturn or obscure the power of his kingdom. But the strangest thing of all was, that so many warnings should have passed away from their recollection without yielding any advantage. At least, it was brutal stupidity that, though

ADAM CLARKE

As if he had said: "If he be a sinner, he stands in the greater need of salvation, and the Son of man is come to seek and save what was lost, Luke 19: 10; and therefore to save this lost soul is a part of my errand into the world."

MATTHEW 25: 14–30; LUKE 19: 11–28

Matthew 25: 14–30

14. Called his own servants – God never makes the children of men proprietors of his goods. They are formed by his power, and upheld by his bounty; and they hold their lives and their goods.

15. Unto one he gave five talents – to every man according to his several ability – The duties men are called to perform are suited to their situations, and the talents they receive. The good that any man has he has received from God, as also the ability to improve that good. God's graces and temporal mercies are suited to the power which a man has of improving them. To give eminent gifts to persons incapable of properly improving them, would be only to lead into a snare. The talent which each man has suits his own state best; and it is only pride and insanity which lead him to desire and envy the graces and talents of another. Five talents would be too much for some men: one talent would be too little. He who receives much, must make proportionate improvement; and, from him who has received little, the improvement only of that little will be required. As five talents, in one case, are sufficient to answer the purpose for which they were given; so also are two and one. The man who improves the grace he has received, however small, will as surely get to the kingdom of God, as he who has received most from his master, and improved all.

In this parable of our Lord, four things may be considered:

I. The master who distributes the talents.
II. The servants who improved their talents.
III. The servant who buried his talent. And
IV. His punishment.

I. The master who distributes the talents.

1. The master's kindness. The servants had nothing – deserved nothing – had no claim on their master, yet he, in his KINDNESS, delivers unto them his goods, not for his advantage, but for their comfort and salvation.

2. The master distributes these goods diversely; – giving to one five, to another, two, and to another one. No person can complain that he has been forgotten; the master gives to each. None can complain of the diversity of the gifts; it is the master who has done it. The master has an absolute right over his own goods, and the servants cannot find fault with the distribution. He who has little should not envy him who has received much, for he has the greater labor, and the greater account to give. He who has much should not despise him who has little, for the sovereign master has made the distinction; and his little, suited to the ability which God has given him, and fitted to the place in which God's providence has fixed him, is sufficiently calculated to answer the purpose of the master, in the salvation of the servant's soul.

3. The master distributes his talents with WISDOM. He gave to each according to his several ability, i.e. to the power he had to improve what was given. It would not be just to make a servant responsible for what he is naturally incapable of managing; and it would not be proper to give more than could be improved. The powers which men have, God has given; and as he best knows the extent of these powers, so he suits his graces and blessings to them in the most wise, and effectual way. Though he may make one vessel for honor, (i.e. a more honorable place or office), and another for dishonor, (a less honorable office), yet both are for the master's use – both are appointed and capacitated to show forth his glory.

II. The servants who improved their talents. These persons are termed slaves, such as were the property of the master, who might dispose of them as he pleased. Then he that had received the five talents went and traded, Matthew 25: 16.

1. The work was speedily begun – as soon as the master gave the talents and departed,

22 He also that had received two talents came and said, Lord, thou deliveredst unto me two talents: behold, I have gained two other talents beside them.

23 His lord said unto him, Well done, good and faithful servant; thou hast been faithful over a few things, I will make thee ruler over many things: enter thou into the joy of thy lord.

24 Then he which had received the one talent came and said, Lord, I knew thee that thou art an hard man, reaping where thou hast not sown, and gathering where thou hast not strawed:

25 And I was afraid, and went and hid thy talent in the earth: lo, there thou hast that is thine.

26 His lord answered and said unto him, Thou wicked and slothful servant, thou knewest that I reap where I sowed not, and gather where I have not strawed:

27 Thou oughtest therefore to have put my money to the exchangers, and then at my coming I should have received mine own with usury.

28 Take therefore the talent from him, and give it unto him which hath ten talents.

29 For unto every one that hath shall be given, and he shall have abundance: but from him that hath not shall be taken away even that which he hath.

30 And cast ye the unprofitable servant into outer darkness: there shall be weeping and gnashing of teeth.

Luke 19: 11–28

11 And as they heard these things, he added and spake a parable, because he was nigh to Jerusalem, and because they thought that the kingdom of God should immediately appear.

12 He said therefore, A certain nobleman went into a far country to receive for himself a kingdom, and to return.

13 And he called his ten servants, and delivered them ten pounds, and said unto them, Occupy till I come.

14 But his citizens hated him, and sent a message after him, saying, We will not have this man to reign over us.

15 And it came to pass, that when he was returned, having received the kingdom, then he commanded these servants

Christ had lately declared, in express terms, that he was just about to undergo a bitter and ignominious death, they not only remained unconcerned, but rushed forward, as if to a joyful triumph.

12. A certain nobleman

Matthew interweaves this parable with others, without attending to the order of time; but, as his intention was, in the twenty-second chapter, to make a collection of Christ's latest discourses, readers ought not to trouble themselves greatly with the inquiry which of them was delivered on the first, or the second, or the third day within that short period. But it is proper to observe the difference between Matthew and Luke; for, while the former touches only on one point, the latter embraces two. This point is common to both, that Christ resembles a nobleman, who, undertaking a long journey for the sake of obtaining a kingdom, has entrusted his money to the management of his servants, and so on. The other point is peculiar to Luke, that the subjects abused the absence of the prince, and raised a tumult in order to shake off his yoke. In both parts Christ intended to show, that the disciples were greatly mistaken in supposing that his royal authority was already established, and that he was coming to Jerusalem, in order to commence immediately a course of prosperity. Thus by taking away the expectation of an immediate kingdom, he exhorts them to hope and patience; for he tells them that they must long and steadily endure many toils, before they enjoy that glory for which they pant too earnestly.

Into a distant country

As the disciples thought that Christ was now about to enter into the possession of his kingdom, he first corrects this mistake by informing them, that he must undertake a long journey, in order to obtain the kingdom. As to what is meant by the distant country, I leave it to the ingenious expositions of those who are fond of subtleties. For my own part, I think that Christ expresses nothing more than his long absence, which would extend from the time of his death to his last coming. For, though he sits at the right hand of the Father, and holds the government of heaven and earth, and though, from the time that he ascended to heaven, all power was given to him, (Matthew 28: 18), that every knee might bow before him (Philippians 2: 10); yet as he has not yet subdued his enemies – has not yet appeared as Judge of the world, or revealed his majesty – it is not without propriety that he is said to be absent from his people, till he return again, clothed with his new sovereignty. It is true, indeed, that he now reigns, while he regenerates his people to the heavenly life, forms them anew to the image of God, and associates them with angels; while he governs the Church by his word, guards it by his protection, enriches

so soon they began to labor. There is not a moment to be lost – every moment has its grace, and every grace has its employment, and every thing is to be done for eternity.

2. The work was perseveringly carried on; after a long time the lord of those servants cometh, Matthew 25: 19. The master was long before he returned, but they did not relax. The longer time, the greater improvement. God gives every man just time enough to live, in this world, to glorify his Maker, and to get his soul saved. Many begin well, and continue faithful for a time – but how few persevere to the end! Are there none who seem to have outlived their glory, their character, their usefulness?

3. Their work was crowned with success. They doubled the sum which they had received. Every grace of God is capable of great improvement. Jesus himself, the pure, immaculate Jesus, grew in wisdom and favor with God, Luke 2: 52.

4. They were ready to give in a joyful account when their master came and called for them.

1st. They come without delay: they expected his coming; and it was with an eye to this that they continued their labor – they endured as seeing him who is invisible.

2d. They come without fear; the master before whom they appear has always loved them, and given them the fullest proofs of his affection for them: his love to them has begotten in them love to him; and their obedience to his orders sprung from the love they bore to him. He that loveth me, says Jesus, will keep my words.

3d. They render up their accounts without confusion: he who received five brought five others; and he who had received two brought two more: nothing was to be done when their master called; all their business was fully prepared.

4th. They gave up every thing to their master, without attempting to appropriate any thing. Their ability was his, the talents his, and the continued power to improve them, his. All is of God, and all must be returned to him.

5. Their recompense from their gracious master.

1st. They receive praise. Well done, good and faithful servants, Matthew 25: 21. What a glorious thing to have the approbation of God, and the testimony of a good conscience! They were good, pure and upright within – faithful, using to God's glory the blessings he had given.

2d. They receive gracious promises. Ye have been faithful over a little, I will set you over much. These promises refer not only to a future glory, but to an increase of God's grace and mercy here; for the more faithfully a man improves what God has already given him, the more he shall have from his gracious Master: for he giveth more grace, till he fills the faithful soul with his own fullness.

3d. They receive GLORY. Enter into the joy of your Lord. As ye were partakers of my nature on earth, be ye sharers of my glory in heaven. The joy, the happiness wherewith I am happy, shall be your eternal portion! O, what is all we can do, all we can suffer, even the most lingering and cruel martyrdom, in comparison of this unbounded, eternal joy!

III. Of the servant who buried his talent. He that had received one went and digged in the earth, and hid his Lord's money, Matthew 25: 18.

1. See the ingratitude of this servant. His master gave him a talent, capable of being improved to his own present and eternal advantage; but he slights the mercy of his lord.

2. See his idleness. Rather than exert himself to improve what he has received, he goes and hides it.

3. See his gross error. He DIGS to hide it – puts himself to more trouble to render the mercy of God to him of none effect, than he would have had in combating and conquering the world, the devil, and the flesh.

4. See his injustice. He takes his master's money, and neither improves nor designs to improve it, even while he is living on and

to be called unto him, to whom he had given the money, that he might know how much every man had gained by trading.

16 Then came the first, saying, Lord, thy pound hath gained ten pounds.

17 And he said unto him, Well, thou good servant: because thou hast been faithful in a very little, have thou authority over ten cities.

18 And the second came, saying, Lord, thy pound hath gained five pounds.

19 And he said likewise to him, Be thou also over five cities.

20 And another came, saying, Lord, behold, here is thy pound, which I have kept laid up in a napkin:

21 For I feared thee, because thou art an austere man: thou takest up that thou layedst not down, and reapest that thou didst not sow.

22 And he saith unto him, Out of thine own mouth will I judge thee, thou wicked servant. Thou knewest that I was an austere man, taking up that I laid not down, and reaping that I did not sow:

23 Wherefore then gavest not thou my money into the bank, that at my coming I might have required mine own with usury?

24 And he said unto them that stood by, Take from him the pound, and give it to him that hath ten pounds.

25 (And they said unto him, Lord, he hath ten pounds.)

26 For I say unto you, That unto every one which hath shall be given; and from him that hath not, even that he hath shall be taken away from him.

27 But those mine enemies, which would not that I should reign over them, bring hither, and slay them before me.

28 And when he had thus spoken, he went before, ascending up to Jerusalem.

MATTHEW 21: 1–9; MARK 11: 1–10; LUKE 19: 29–38

Matthew 21: 1–9

1 And when they drew nigh unto Jerusalem, and were come to Bethphage, unto the mount of Olives, then sent Jesus two disciples,

2 Saying unto them, Go into the village over against you, and straightway ye shall find an ass tied, and a colt with her: loose

it with the gifts of the Spirit, nourishes it by his grace, and maintains it by his power, and, in short, supplies it with all that is necessary for salvation; while he restrains the fury of Satan and of all the ungodly, and defeats all their schemes. But as this way of reigning is concealed from the flesh, his manifestation is properly said to be delayed till the last day. Since, therefore, the apostles foolishly aimed at the shadow of a kingdom, our Lord declares that he must go to seek a distant kingdom, that, they may learn to endure delay.

24. I knew thee, that thou art a harsh man

This harshness has nothing to do with the substance of the parable; and it is an idle speculation in which those indulge, who reason from this passage, how severely and rigorously God deals with his own people. For Christ did not intend to describe such rigor, any more than to applaud usury, when he represents the master of the house as saying, that the money ought to have been deposited with a banker, that it might, at least, gain interest. Christ only means, that there will be no excuse for the indolence of those who both conceal the gifts of God, and waste their time in idleness. Hence also we infer that no manner of life is more praiseworthy in the sight of God, than that which yields some advantage to human society.

Luke 19: 27. But those my enemies

Christ here appears to glance principally at the Jews, but includes all who in the absence of their master, determine to revolt. Now Christ's intention was, not only to terrify such people by threatening an awful punishment, but also to keep his own people in faithful subjection; for it was no small temptation to see the kingdom of God scattered by the treachery and rebellion of many. In order then that we may preserve our composure in the midst of troubles, Christ informs us that he will return, and that at his coming he will punish wicked rebellion.

MATTHEW 21: 1–9; MARK 11: 1–10; LUKE 19: 29–38

Matthew 21: 1. Then Jesus sent two disciples

Jesus sends his disciples to bring an ass to him, not because he was wearied with the journey, but for a different reason; for, in consequence of the time of his death being at hand, he intended to show, by a solemn performance, what was the nature of his kingdom. He had begun, indeed, to do this at his baptism, but it remained that this demonstration should be given by him towards the end of his calling: for why did he hitherto refrain from the title of King, and now at length openly declare himself to be a King, but because he is not far from the end of his course? So then, as his removal to heaven was at hand, he intended to commence his

consuming that bounty which would have been sufficient for a faithful servant. How much of this useless lumber is to be found in the Church of Christ! But suppose the man be a preacher – what a terrible account will he have to give to God – consuming the provision made for a faithful pastor, and so burying, or misusing his talent, as to do no good, to immortal souls!

5. Hear the absurdity of his reasoning. Lord, I knew thee that thou art a hard (or avaricious) man, reaping where thou hast not sown, etc., Matthew 25: 24. The wicked excuse of this faithless servant confuted itself and condemned him. Nevertheless it is on this very model that sinners in general seek to justify themselves; and the conclusion turns always against them. I knew thee to be a hard man. How awfully deceived and deeply depraved must that person be, who not only attempts to excuse his follies, but to charge his crimes on GOD himself!

I was afraid – Why? Because thou wert an enemy to thy soul, and to thy God. – I was afraid – of what? that he would require more than he did give. How could this be? Did he not give thee the talent freely, to show thee his benevolence? And did he not suit it to thy ability, that he might show thee his wisdom, justice, and goodness, in not making thee responsible for more than thou couldst improve?

IV. Behold the awful punishment of this faithless servant.

1.He is reproached. Thou wicked and slothful servant! Wicked – in thy heart: slothful – in thy work. THOU knewest that I reap where I sowed not. Thou art condemned by thy own mouth – whose is the unemployed talent? Did I not give thee this? And did I require the improvement of two when I gave thee but one? – Thou knowest I did not.

2. He is stripped of what he possessed. Take – the talent from him. O terrible word! – Remove the candlestick from that slothful, worldly-minded Church: take away the inspirations of the Holy Spirit from that lukewarm, Christless Christian, who only lives to resist

them and render them of none effect. Dispossess that base, man-pleasing minister of his ministerial gifts; let his silver become brass, and his fine gold, dross. He loved the present world more than the eternal world, and the praise of men more than the approbation of God. Take away the talent from him!

3. He is punished with an everlasting separation from God and the glory of his power. Cast forth the unprofitable servant, Matthew 25: 30. Let him have nothing but darkness, who refused to walk in the light: let him have nothing but misery – weeping and gnashing of teeth, who has refused the happiness which God provided for him.

Reader, if the careless virgin, and the unprofitable servant, against whom no flagrant iniquity is charged, be punished with an outer darkness, with a hell of fire: of what sorer punishment must he be judged worthy, who is a murderer, an adulterer, a fornicator, a blasphemer, a thief, a liar, or in any respect an open violater of the laws of God? The careless virgins, and the unprofitable servants, were saints in comparison of millions, who are, notwithstanding, dreaming of an endless heaven, when fitted only for an endless hell!

27. With usury – with its produce – not usury; for that is unlawful interest, more than the money can properly produce.

MATTHEW 21: 1–9; MARK 11: 1–10; LUKE 19: 29–38

Matthew 21: 1–9

1. Bethphage – A place on the west declivity of Mount Olivet, from which it is thought the whole declivity and part of the valley took their name. It is supposed to have derived its name from the fig-trees which grew there.

2. Ye shall find an ass tied, and a colt – Asses and mules were in common use in Palestine: horses were seldom to be met with. Our blessed Lord takes every opportunity to convince his disciples that nothing was hidden from him: he informs them of the most minute occurrence; and manifested his power over the

them, and bring them unto me.

3 And if any man say ought unto you, ye shall say, The Lord hath need of them; and straightway he will send them.

4 All this was done, that it might be fulfilled which was spoken by the prophet, saying,

5 Tell ye the daughter of Sion, Behold, thy King cometh unto thee, meek, and sitting upon an ass, and a colt the foal of an ass.

6 And the disciples went, and did as Jesus commanded them,

7 And brought the ass, and the colt, and put on them their clothes, and they set him thereon.

8 And a very great multitude spread their garments in the way; others cut down branches from the trees, and strawed them in the way.

9 And the multitudes that went before, and that followed, cried, saying, Hosanna to the Son of David: Blessed is he that cometh in the name of the Lord; Hosanna in the highest.

Mark 11: 1–10

1 And when they came nigh to Jerusalem, unto Bethphage and Bethany, at the mount of Olives, he sendeth forth two of his disciples,

2 And saith unto them, Go your way into the village over against you: and as soon as ye be entered into it, ye shall find a colt tied, whereon never man sat; loose him, and bring him.

3 And if any man say unto you, Why do ye this? say ye that the Lord hath need of him; and straightway he will send him hither.

4 And they went their way, and found the colt tied by the door without in a place where two ways met; and they loose him.

5 And certain of them that stood there said unto them, What do ye, loosing the colt?

6 And they said unto them even as Jesus had commanded: and they let them go.

7 And they brought the colt to Jesus, and cast their garments on him; and he sat upon him.

8 And many spread their garments in the way: and others cut down branches

reign openly on earth.

This would have been a ridiculous display, if it had not been in accordance with the prediction of Zechariah (9: 9). In order to lay claim to the honors of royalty, he enters Jerusalem, **riding an ass**. A magnificent display, truly! more especially when the ass was borrowed from some person, and when the want of a saddle and of accouterments compelled the disciples to **throw their garments on it**, which was mark of mean and disgraceful poverty. He is attended, I admit, by a large retinue; but of what sort of people? Of those who had hastily assembled from the neighboring villages. Sounds of loud and joyful welcome are heard; but from whom? From the very poorest, and from those who belong to the despised multitude. One might think, therefore, that he intentionally exposed himself to the ridicule of all. But as he had two things to do at the same time – as he had to exhibit some proof of his kingdom, and to show that it does not resemble earthly kingdoms, and does not consist of the fading riches of this world, it was altogether necessary for him to take this method.

To wicked men, no doubt, this might be very unacceptable, had not God long before testified by his Prophet that such would be the king who would come to restore the salvation of his people. In order, therefore, that the mean aspect of Christ may not hinder us from perceiving in this exhibition, his spiritual kingdom, let us keep before our eyes the heavenly prediction, by which God conferred more honor on his Son under the revolting aspect of a beggar, than if he had been decorated with all the dazzling ornaments of kings. Without this seasoning, we shall never have any relish for this history; and therefore there is great weight in the words of Matthew, when he says, that **the prediction of the Prophet was fulfilled**. Perceiving that it was hardly possible that men, who are too much devoted to wealth and splendor, should derive any advantage from this narrative, when viewed according to the feeling of the flesh, he leads them away from the simple contemplation of the fact to the consideration of the prophecy.

2. Go into the village

As he was at Bethany, he did not ask for an ass to relieve the fatigue of traveling; for he could easily have performed the rest of the journey on foot. But as kings are wont to ascend their chariots, from which they may be easily seen, so the Lord intended to turn the eyes of the people on himself, and to place some mark of approbation on the applauses of his followers, lest any might think that he unwillingly received the honor of a king.

From what place he ordered the ass to be brought is uncertain, except, what may naturally be inferred, that it was some village adjoining to the city; for the allegorical

heart in disposing the owner to permit the ass to be taken away.

3. The Lord (the proprietor of all things) hath need of them – Jesus is continually humbling himself, to show us how odious pride is in the sight of God: but in his humility he is ever giving proofs of his almighty power, that the belief of his divinity may be established.

4. Which was spoken – The Spirit of God, which predicted those things that concerned the Messiah, took care to have them literally fulfilled:

1. To show the truth of prophecy in general; and,

2. To designate Christ as the person intended by that prophecy.

5. Tell ye the daughter of Sion – The quotation is taken from Zechariah 9: 9, but not in the precise words of the prophet.

This entry into Jerusalem has been termed the triumph of Christ. It was indeed the triumph of humility over pride and worldly grandeur; of poverty over affluence; and of meekness and gentleness over rage and malice.

He is coming now meek, full of kindness and compassion to those who were plotting his destruction! He comes to deliver up himself into their hands; their king comes to be murdered by his subjects, and to make his death a ransom price for their souls!

7. And put on them their clothes – Thus acknowledging him to be their king, for this was a custom observed by the people when they found that God had appointed a man to the kingdom. When Jehu sat with the captains of the army, and Elisha the prophet came, by the order of God, to anoint him king over Israel, as soon as he came out of the inner chamber into which the prophet had taken him to anoint him, and they knew what was done, every man took his garment, and spread it under him on the top of the steps, and blew the trumpets, saying, "Jehu is king." 2 Kings 9: 13.

8. Cut down branches from the trees – Carrying palm and other branches was emblematical of victory and success. See 1 Maccabees 13: 51; 2 Maccabees 10: 7; and Revelation 7: 9.

The rabbins acknowledge that the prophecy in Zechariah refers to the Messiah; so Rab. Tancum, and Yalcut Rubeni has a strange story about the ass. "This ass is the colt of that ass which was created in the twilight of the sixth day. This is the ass which Abraham found when he went to sacrifice his son. This is the ass on which Moses rode when he went to Egypt; and this is the ass on which the Messiah shall ride."

9. Hosanna to the son of David – When persons applied to the king for help, or for a redress of grievances, they used the word hosanna. Save now! or, Save, we beseech thee! – redress our grievances, and give us help from oppression! Thus both the words and actions of the people prove that they acknowledged Christ as their king, and looked to him for deliverance. How easily might he have assumed the sovereignty at this time, had he been so disposed! For instances of the use of this form of speech, see 2 Samuel 14: 4; 2 Kings 6: 26; Psalm 118: 25.

Son of David – A well-known epithet of the Messiah. He who cometh in the name, etc. He who comes in the name and authority of the Most High.

Hosanna in the highest – Either meaning, Let the heavenly hosts join with us in magnifying this august Being! – or, Let the utmost degrees of hosanna, of salvation, and deliverance, be communicated to thy people! Probably there is an allusion here to the custom of the Jews in the feast of tabernacles. During the first seven days of that feast, they went once round the altar, each day, with palm and other branches in their hands, singing HOSANNA: but on the eighth day of that feast they walked seven times round the altar, singing the hosanna; and this was termed the GREAT hosanna: i.e. Assist with the greatest succor.

off the trees, and strawed them in the way.

9 And they that went before, and they that followed, cried, saying, Hosanna; Blessed is he that cometh in the name of the Lord:

10 Blessed be the kingdom of our father David, that cometh in the name of the Lord: Hosanna in the highest.

Luke 19: 29–38

29 And it came to pass, when he was come nigh to Bethphage and Bethany, at the mount called the mount of Olives, he sent two of his disciples,

30 Saying, Go ye into the village over against you; in the which at your entering ye shall find a colt tied, whereon yet never man sat: loose him, and bring him hither.

31 And if any man ask you, Why do ye loose him? thus shall ye say unto him, Because the Lord hath need of him.

32 And they that were sent went their way, and found even as he had said unto them.

33 And as they were loosing the colt, the owners thereof said unto them, Why loose ye the colt?

34 And they said, The Lord hath need of him.

35 And they brought him to Jesus: and they cast their garments upon the colt, and they set Jesus thereon.

36 And as he went, they spread their clothes in the way.

37 And when he was come nigh, even now at the descent of the mount of Olives, the whole multitude of the disciples began to rejoice and praise God with a loud voice for all the mighty works that they had seen;

38 Saying, Blessed be the King that cometh in the name of the Lord: peace in heaven, and glory in the highest.

LUKE 19: 41–44

41 And when he was come near, he beheld the city, and wept over it,

42 Saying, If thou hadst known, even thou, at least in this thy day, the things which belong unto thy peace! but now they are hid from thine eyes.

43 For the days shall come upon thee, that thine enemies shall cast a trench

exposition of it, which some give, as applying to Jerusalem, is ridiculous. Not a whit more admissible is the allegory which certain people have contrived about the ass and the colt. "The she-ass," they tell us, "is a figure of the Jewish nation, which had been long subdued, and accustomed to the yoke of the Law. The Gentiles, again, are represented by **the colt, on which no man ever sat**.

Christ sat first on the ass for this reason, that it was proper for him to begin with the Jews; and afterwards he passed over to the colt, because he was appointed to govern the Gentiles also in the second place." And indeed Matthew appears to say that he rode on both of them; but as instances of Synecdoche occur frequently in Scripture, we need not wonder if he mentions two instead of one. From the other Evangelists it appears manifestly that the colt only was used by Christ; and all doubt is removed by Zechariah (9: 9), who twice repeats the same thing, according to the ordinary custom of the Hebrew language. **And immediately you will find**. That the disciples may feel no hesitation about immediate compliance, our Lord anticipates and replies to their questions. First, he explains that he does not send them away at random, and this he does by saying that, at the very entrance into the village, they will find an **ass-colt with its mother**; and, secondly, that nobody will hinder them from leading him away, if they only reply that He **hath need of him**. In this way he proved his Divinity; for both to know absent matters, and to bend the hearts of men to compliance, belonged to God alone. It was, no doubt, possible that the owner of the ass, entertaining no unfavorable opinion of Christ, would cheerfully grant it; but to foresee if he would be at home, if it would then be convenient for him, or if he would place confidence in unknown people, was not in the power of a mortal man. Again, as Christ strengthens the disciples, that they may be more ready to obey, so we see how they, on the other hand, yield submission. The result shows that the whole of this affair was directed by God.

LUKE 19: 41–44

41. And wept over it

As there was nothing which Christ more ardently desired than to execute the office which the Father had committed to him, and as he knew that the end of his calling was to gather "the lost sheep of the house of Israel" (Matthew 15: 24), he wished that his coming might bring salvation to all. This was the reason why he was moved with compassion, and wept over the approaching destruction of the city of Jerusalem.

LUKE 19: 41–44

41. And wept over it – See Matthew 23: 37.

42. The things which belong unto thy peace! – It is very likely that our Lord here alludes to the meaning of the word Jerusalem: peace or prosperity. Now, because the inhabitants of it had not seen this peace and salvation, because they had refused to open their eyes, and behold this glorious light of heaven which shone among them, therefore he said, Now they are hidden from thine eyes, still alluding to the import of the name.

43. Cast a trench about thee – This was literally fulfilled when this city was besieged by Titus. Josephus gives a very particular account of the building of this wall, which he says was effected in three days, though it was not less than thirty-nine furlongs in circumference; and that, when this wall and trench were completed, the Jews were so enclosed on every side that no person could escape out of the city, and no provision could be brought in, so that they were reduced to the most terrible distress by the famine which ensued.

44. The time of thy visitation – That is, the time of God's gracious offers of mercy to thee. This took in all the time which elapsed from the preaching of John the Baptist to the coming of the Roman armies, which included a period of above forty years.

MATTHEW 21: 10–22; MARK 11: 11–24; LUKE 19: 39–48

Matthew 21: 10–22

10. All the city was moved – Or, the whole city was in motion, was in a tumult – they saw and heard plainly that the multitude had proclaimed Christ king, and Messiah. Who is this? Who is accounted worthy of this honor?

11. This is Jesus THE PROPHET – THAT prophet whom Moses spoke of, Deuteronomy 18: 18. I will raise them up a prophet – like unto thee, etc. Every expression of the multitude plainly intimated that they fully received our blessed Lord as the promised Messiah.

– How strange is it that these same people (if the creatures of the high priest be not only intended) should, about five days after, change their hosannas for, Away with him! crucify him! crucify him! How fickle is the multitude! Even when they get right, there is but little hope that they will continue so long.

12. Jesus went into the temple of God, etc. – "Avarice," says one, "covered with the veil of religion, is one of those things on which Christ looks with the greatest indignation in his Church. Merchandize of holy things, simoniacal presentations, fraudulent exchanges, a mercenary spirit in sacred functions; ecclesiastical employments obtained by flattery, service, or attendance, or by any thing which is instead of money; collations, nominations, and elections made through any other motive than the glory of God; these are all fatal and damnable profanations, of which those in the temple were only a shadow." QUESNEL.

Money-changers – Persons who furnished the Jews and proselytes who came from other countries, with the current coin of Judea, in exchange for their own.

13. My house shall be called the house of prayer – This is taken from Isaiah 56: 7.
But ye have made it a den of thieves – This is taken from Jeremiah 7: 11.

Our Lord alludes here to those dens and caves in Judea, in which the public robbers either hid or kept themselves fortified.

They who are placed in the Church of Christ to serve souls, and do it not, and they who enjoy the revenues of the Church, and neglect the service of it, are thieves and robbers in more senses than one.

Our Lord is represented here as purifying his temple; and this we may judge he did in reference to his true temple, the Church, to show that nothing that was worldly or unholy should have any place among his followers, or in that heart in which he should condescend to dwell. It is marvelous that these interested, vile men did not raise a mob against him: but it is probable they were overawed by the Divine power, or, seeing the multitudes on the side of Christ, they were afraid to molest him. I knew

about thee, and compass thee round, and keep thee in on every side,

44 And shall lay thee even with the ground, and thy children within thee; and they shall not leave in thee one stone upon another; because thou knewest not the time of thy visitation.

MATTHEW 21: 10–22; MARK 11: 11–24; LUKE 19: 39–48

Matthew 21: 10–22

10 And when he was come into Jerusalem, all the city was moved, saying, Who is this?

11 And the multitude said, This is Jesus the prophet of Nazareth of Galilee.

12 And Jesus went into the temple of God, and cast out all them that sold and bought in the temple, and overthrew the tables of the moneychangers, and the seats of them that sold doves,

13 And said unto them, It is written, My house shall be called the house of prayer; but ye have made it a den of thieves.

14 And the blind and the lame came to him in the temple; and he healed them.

15 And when the chief priests and scribes saw the wonderful things that he did, and the children crying in the temple, and saying, Hosanna to the Son of David; they were sore displeased,

16 And said unto him, Hearest thou what these say? And Jesus saith unto them, Yea; have ye never read, Out of the mouth of babes and sucklings thou hast perfected praise?

17 And he left them, and went out of the city into Bethany; and he lodged there.

18 Now in the morning as he returned into the city, he hungered.

19 And when he saw a fig tree in the way, he came to it, and found nothing thereon, but leaves only, and said unto it, Let no fruit grow on thee henceforward for ever. And presently the fig tree withered away.

20 And when the disciples saw it, they marveled, saying, How soon is the fig tree withered away!

21 Jesus answered and said unto them, Verily I say unto you, If ye have faith, and doubt not, ye shall not only do this which is done to the fig tree, but also if

MATTHEW 21: 10–22; MARK 11: 11–24; LUKE 19: 39–48

Matthew 21: 10. When he entered into Jerusalem

Matthew says that **the city was moved**, in order to inform us that the transaction did not take place secretly, or by stealth, but in the presence of all the people, and that the priests and scribes were not ignorant of it. Under this despicable aspect of the flesh the majesty of the Spirit was apparent; for how would they have endured that Christ should be conducted into the city, attended by the splendor of royalty, with so great danger to themselves, if they had not been seized with astonishment? The substance of it therefore is, that Christ's entrance was not made in a private manner, and that his enemies abstained from opposing it, not because they treated him with contempt, but rather because they were restrained by secret fear; for God had struck them with such alarm, that they dare not make any attempt. At the same time, the Evangelist glances at the careless indifference of the city, and commends the piety of those who have just reached it; for when the inhabitants, on hearing the noise, inquire, Who is this? it is manifest that they do not belong to the number of Christ's followers.

12. And Jesus entered into the temple

Though Christ frequently ascended into the temple, and though this abuse continually met his eye, twice only did he stretch out his hand to correct it; once, at the commencement of his embassy, and now again, when he was near the end of his course. But though disgraceful and ungodly confusion reigned throughout, and though the temple, with its sacrifices, was devoted to destruction, Christ reckoned it enough to administer twice an open reproof of the profanation of it. Accordingly, when he made himself known as a Teacher and Prophet sent by God, he took upon himself the office of purifying the temple, in order to arouse the Jews, and make them more attentive; and this first narrative is given by John only in the second chapter of his Gospel. But now, towards the end of his course, claiming again for himself the same power, he warns the Jews of the pollutions of the temple, and at the same time points out that a new restoration is at hand.

And yet there is no reason to doubt that he declared himself to be both King and High Priest, who presided over the temple and the worship of God. This ought to be observed, lest any private individual should think himself entitled to act in the same manner. That zeal, indeed, by which Christ was animated to do this, ought to be held in common by all the godly; but lest any one, under the pretense of imitation, should rush forward without authority, we ought to see what our calling demands, and how far we may proceed according to the commandment of God. If the Church of

a case something similar to this, which did not succeed so well. A very pious clergyman of my acquaintance, observing a woman keeping a public standing to sell nuts, gingerbread, etc., at the very porch of his Church, on the Lord's day, "desired her to remove thence, and not defile the house of God, while she profaned the Sabbath of the Lord." She paid no attention to him. He warned her the next Sabbath, but still to no purpose. Going in one Lord's day to preach, and finding her still in the very entrance, with her stall, he overthrew the stall, and scattered the stuff into the street. He was shortly after summoned to appear before the royal court, which, to its eternal reproach, condemned the action, and fined the man of God in a considerable sum of money!

14. The blind and the lame came – Having condemned the profane use of the temple, he now shows the proper use of it. It is a house of prayer, where God is to manifest his goodness and power in giving sight to the spiritually blind, and feet to the lame. The Church or chapel in which the blind and the lame are not healed has no Christ in it, and is not worthy of attendance.

15. The chief priests – were sore displeased – Or, were incensed. Incensed at what! At the purification of the profaned temple! This was a work they should have done themselves, but for which they had neither grace nor influence; and their pride and jealousy will not suffer them to permit others to do it. Strange as it may appear, the priesthood itself, in all corrupt times, has been ever the most forward to prevent a reform in the Church. Was it because they were conscious that a reformer would find them no better than money-changers in, and profaners of, the house of God, and that they and their system must be overturned, if the true worship of God were restored! Let him who is concerned answer this to his conscience.

16. Out of the mouth of babes – The eighth Psalm, out of which these words are quoted, is applied to Jesus Christ in three other places in the new covenant, 1 Corinthians 15: 27;

Ephesians 1: 22; Hebrews 2: 6. Which proves it to be merely a prophetic psalm, relating to the Messiah.

It was a common thing among the Jews for the children to be employed in public acclamations; and thus they were accustomed to hail their celebrated rabbins. This shouting of the children was therefore no strange thing in the land: only they were exasperated, because a person was celebrated against whom they had a rooted hatred. As to the prophecy that foretold this, they regarded it not. Some imagine that babes and sucklings in the prophecy have a much more extensive meaning, and refer also to the first preachers of the Gospel of Christ.

17. And he left them (finally leaving them) and went – into Bethany; and he lodged there – Bethany was a village about two miles distant from Jerusalem, by Mount Olivet, John 11: 18; and it is remarkable that from this day till his death, which happened about six days after, he spent not one night in Jerusalem, but went every evening to Bethany, and returned to the city each morning. See Luke 21: 37; 22: 39; John 8: 1–2. They were about to murder the Lord of glory; and the true light, which they had rejected, is now departing from them.

Lodged there – Not merely to avoid the snares laid for him by those bad men, but to take away all suspicion of his affecting the regal power.

18. Now in the morning, as he returned into the city – Which was his custom from the time he wholly left Jerusalem, spending only the day time teaching in the temple; see Matthew 21: 17. This was probably on Thursday, the 12th day of the month Nisan.

He hungered – Probably neither he, nor his disciples, had any thing but what they got from public charity; and the hand of that seems to have been cold at this time.

19. He saw a fig tree in the way – By the road side. As this fig tree was by the way side, it was no private property; and on this account our Lord, or any other traveler, had a right to take of its fruit.

Let no fruit grow on thee – Can a professor,

ye shall say unto this mountain, Be thou removed, and be thou cast into the sea; it shall be done.

22 And all things, whatsoever ye shall ask in prayer, believing, ye shall receive.

Mark 11: 11–24

11 And Jesus entered into Jerusalem, and into the temple: and when he had looked round about upon all things, and now the eventide was come, he went out unto Bethany with the twelve.

12 And on the morrow, when they were come from Bethany, he was hungry:

13 And seeing a fig tree afar off having leaves, he came, if haply he might find any thing thereon: and when he came to it, he found nothing but leaves; for the time of figs was not yet.

14 And Jesus answered and said unto it, No man eat fruit of thee hereafter for ever. And his disciples heard it.

15 And they come to Jerusalem: and Jesus went into the temple, and began to cast out them that sold and bought in the temple, and overthrew the tables of the moneychangers, and the seats of them that sold doves;

16 And would not suffer that any man should carry any vessel through the temple.

17 And he taught, saying unto them, Is it not written, My house shall be called of all nations the house of prayer? but ye have made it a den of thieves.

18 And the scribes and chief priests heard it, and sought how they might destroy him: for they feared him, because all the people was astonished at his doctrine.

19 And when even was come, he went out of the city.

20 And in the morning, as they passed by, they saw the fig tree dried up from the roots.

21 And Peter calling to remembrance saith unto him, Master, behold, the fig tree which thou cursedst is withered away.

22 And Jesus answering saith unto them, Have faith in God.

23 For verily I say unto you, That whosoever shall say unto this mountain, Be thou removed, and be thou cast into the sea; and shall not doubt in his heart, but shall believe that those things which he

God have contracted any pollutions, all the children of God ought to burn with grief; but as God has not put arms into the hands of all, let private individuals groan, till God bring the remedy. I do acknowledge that they are worse than stupid who are not displeased at the pollution of the temple of God, and that it is not enough for them to be inwardly distressed, if they do not avoid the contagion, and testify with their mouth, whenever an opportunity presents itself, that they desire to see a change for the better. But let those who do not possess public authority oppose by their tongue, which they have at liberty, those vices which they cannot remedy with their hands.

But it is asked, Since Christ saw the temple filled with gross superstitions, why did he only correct one that was light, or, at least, more tolerable than others? I reply, Christ did not intend to restore to the ancient custom all the sacred rites, and did not select greater or smaller abuses for correction, but had only this object in view, to show by one visible token, that God had committed to him the office of purifying the temple, and, at the same time, to point out that the worship of God had been corrupted by a disgraceful and manifest abuse. Pretexts, indeed, were not wanting for that custom of keeping a market, which relieved the people from trouble, that they might not have far to go to find sacrifices; and next, that they might have at hand those pieces of money which any man might choose to offer. Nor was it within the holy place that the **money-changers** sat, or that animals intended for sacrifice were exposed to sale, but only within the court, to which the designation of **the temple** is sometimes applied; but as nothing was more at variance with the majesty of **the temple,** than that a market should be erected there for selling goods, or that bankers should sit there for matters connected with exchange, this profanation was not to be endured. And Christ inveighed against it the more sharply, because it was well known that this custom had been introduced by the avarice of the priests for the sake of dishonest gain. For as one who enters a market well-stocked with various kinds of merchandise, though he does not intend to make a purchase, yet, in consequence of being attracted by what he sees, changes his mind, so the priests spread nets in order to obtain offerings, that they might trick every person out of some gain.

13. It is written

Christ quotes two passages taken out of two Prophets; the one from Isaiah 56: 7, and the other from Jeremiah 7: 11. What **was written** by Isaiah agreed with the circumstances of the time; for in that passage is predicted the calling of the Gentiles. Isaiah, therefore, promises that God will grant, not only that the temple shall recover its original splendor, but likewise that all nations shall flow to it, and

who affords Christ nothing but barren words and wishes, expect any thing but his malediction? When the soul continues in unfruitfulness, the influences of grace are removed, and then the tree speedily withers from the very root.

20. How soon is the fig tree withered away! – We often say to our neighbors, "How suddenly this man died! Who could have expected it so soon?" But who takes warning by these examples? What we say to-day of OTHERS, may be said to-morrow of OURSELVES. Be ye also ready! Lord, increase our faith!

21. If ye have faith, and doubt not – Removing mountains, and rooting up of mountains, are phrases very generally used to signify the removing or conquering great difficulties – getting through perplexities. So, many of the rabbins are termed rooters up of mountains, because they were dexterous in removing difficulties, solving cases of conscience, etc. In this sense our Lord's words are to be understood. He that has faith will get through every difficulty and perplexity; mountains shall become molehills or plains before him. The saying is neither to be taken in its literal sense, nor is it hyperbolical: it is a proverbial form of speech, which no Jew could misunderstand, and with which no Christian ought to be puzzled.

22. All things – ye shall ask in prayer, believing – In order to get salvation, there must be,
1. a conviction of the want of it: this begets,
2. prayer, or warm desires, in the heart: then
3. the person asks, i.e. makes use of words expressive of his wants and wishes:
4. believes the word of promise, relative to the fulfillment of his wants: and
5. receives, according to the merciful promise of God, the salvation which his soul requires.

MATTHEW 21: 23–27; MARK 11: 27–33; LUKE 20: 1–8

Matthew 21: 23–37

23. By what authority doest thou these things? – The things which the chief priests allude to, were his receiving the acclamations of the people as the promised Messiah, his casting the traders out of the temple, and his teaching the people publicly in it.

Who gave thee this authority? – Not them: for, like many of their successors, they were neither teachers nor cleansers; though they had the name and the profits of the place.

24. I also will ask you one thing – Our Lord was certainly under no obligation to answer their question: he had already given them such proofs of his Divine mission as could not possibly be exceeded, in the miracles which he wrought before their eyes, and before all Judea; and, as they would not credit him on this evidence, it would have been in vain to have expected their acknowledgment of him on any profession he would make.

25. The baptism of John – Had John a Divine commission or not, for his baptism and preaching? Our Lord here takes the wise in their own cunning. He knew the estimation John was in among the people; and he plainly saw that, if they gave any answer at all, they must convict themselves: and so they saw, when they came to examine the question. See Matthew 21: 25–26.

27. We cannot tell – Simplicity gives a wonderful confidence and peace of mind; but double dealing causes a thousand inquietudes and troubles. Let a man do his utmost to conceal in his own heart the evidence he has of truth and innocence, to countenance his not yielding to it; God, who sees the heart, will, in the light of the last day, produce it as a witness against him, and make it his judge.

We cannot tell, said they; which, in the words of truth, should have been, We will not tell, for we will not have this man for the Messiah: because, if we acknowledge John as his forerunner, we must, of necessity, receive Jesus as the Christ.

They who are engaged against the truth are abandoned to the spirit of falsity, and scruple not at a lie. Pharisaical pride, according to its different interests, either pretends to know every thing, or affects to know nothing. Among such, we may meet with numerous

saith shall come to pass; he shall have whatsoever he saith.

24 Therefore I say unto you, What things soever ye desire, when ye pray, believe that ye receive them, and ye shall have them.

Luke 19: 39–48

39 And some of the Pharisees from among the multitude said unto him, Master, rebuke thy disciples.

40 And he answered and said unto them, I tell you that, if these should hold their peace, the stones would immediately cry out.

45 And he went into the temple, and began to cast out them that sold therein, and them that bought;

46 Saying unto them, It is written, My house is the house of prayer: but ye have made it a den of thieves.

47 And he taught daily in the temple. But the chief priests and the scribes and the chief of the people sought to destroy him,

48 And could not find what they might do: for all the people were very attentive to hear him.

MATTHEW 21: 23–27; MARK 11: 27–33; LUKE 20: 1–8

Matthew 21: 23–27

23 And when he was come into the temple, the chief priests and the elders of the people came unto him as he was teaching, and said, By what authority doest thou these things? and who gave thee this authority?

24 And Jesus answered and said unto them, I also will ask you one thing, which if ye tell me, I in like wise will tell you by what authority I do these things.

25 The baptism of John, whence was it? from heaven, or of men? And they reasoned with themselves, saying, If we shall say, From heaven; he will say unto us, Why did ye not then believe him?

26 But if we shall say, Of men; we fear the people; for all hold John as a prophet.

27 And they answered Jesus, and said, We cannot tell. And he said unto them, Neither tell I you by what authority I do these things.

that the whole world shall agree in true and sincere piety. He speaks, no doubt, metaphorically; for the spiritual worship of God, which was to exist under the reign of Christ, is shadowed out by the prophets under the figures of the law. Certainly this was never fulfilled, that all nations went up to Jerusalem to worship God; and therefore, when he declares that the temple will be **a place of prayer for all nations**, this mode of expression is equivalent to saying, that the nations must be gathered into the Church of God, that with one voice they may worship the true God, along with the children of Abraham. But since he mentions **the temple**, so far as it then was the visible abode of religion, Christ justly reproaches the Jews with having applied it to totally different purposes from those to which it had been dedicated. The meaning therefore is: God intended that this temple should exist till no as a sign on which all his worshippers should fix their eyes; and how base and wicked is it to profane it by thus turning it into a market?

MATTHEW 21: 23–27; MARK 11: 27–33; LUKE 20: 1–8

Matthew 21: 23. By what authority doest thou these things

As the other schemes and open attempts to attack Christ had not succeeded, the **priests and scribes** now attempt, by indirect methods, if they may possibly cause him to desist from the practice of teaching. They do not debate with him as to the doctrine itself, whether it was true or not – for already had they often enough attacked him in vain on that question – but they raise a dispute as to his calling and commission. And, indeed, there were plausible grounds; for since a man ought not, of his own accord, to intermeddle either with the honor of priesthood, or with the prophetical office, but ought to wait for the calling of God, much less would any man be at liberty to claim for himself the title of Messiah, unless it were evident that he had been chosen by God; for he must have been appointed, not only by the voice of God, but likewise by *an oath* as it is written (Psalm 110: 4; Hebrews 7: 21).

But when the divine majesty of Christ had been attested by so many miracles, they act maliciously and wickedly in inquiring whence he came, as if they had been ignorant of all that he had done. For what could be more unreasonable than that., after seeing the hand of God openly displayed in curing the lame and blind, they should doubt if he were a private individual who had rashly assumed this authority? Besides, more than enough of evidence had been already laid before them., that Christ was sent from heaven., so that nothing was farther from their wish than to approve of the performances of Christ, after having learned that God was

instances of arrogance and affected humility. God often hides from the wise and prudent what he reveals unto babes; for, when they use their wisdom only to invent the most plausible excuses for rejecting the truth when it comes to them, it is but just that they should be punished with that ignorance to which, in their own defense, they are obliged to have recourse.

MATTHEW 21: 28–32

28. A certain man had two sons – Under the emblem of these two sons, one of whom was a libertine, disobedient, and insolent, but who afterwards thought on his ways, and returned to his duty; and the second, a hypocrite, who promised all, and did nothing; our Lord points out, on the one hand, the tax-gatherers and sinners of all descriptions, who, convicted by the preaching of John and that of Christ, turned away from their iniquities and embraced the Gospel; and, on the other hand, the scribes, Pharisees, and self-righteous people, who, pretending a zeal for the law, would not receive the salvation of the Gospel.

29. I will not – This is the general reply of every sinner to the invitations of God; and, in it, the Most High is treated without ceremony or respect. They only are safe who persist not in the denial.

30. I go, sir – This is all respect, complaisance, and professed, obedience; but he went not: he promised well, but did not perform. What a multitude of such are in the world, professing to know God, but denying him in their works! Alas! what will such professions avail, when God comes to take away the soul?

31. The publicans and the harlots – In all their former conduct they had said NO. Now they yield to the voice of truth when they hear it, and enter into the kingdom, embracing the salvation brought to them in the Gospel. The others, who had been always professing the most ready and willing obedience, and who pretended to be waiting for the kingdom of God, did not receive it when it came, but

rather chose, while making the best professions, to continue members of the synagogue of Satan.

32. John came unto you in the way of righteousness – Proclaiming the truth, and living agreeably to it. Or, John came unto you, who are in the way of righteousness. This seems rather to be the true meaning and construction of this passage. The Jews are here distinguished from the Gentiles. The former were in the way of righteousness, had the revelation of God, and the ordinances of justice established among them; the latter were in the way of unrighteousness, without the Divine revelation, and iniquitous in all their conduct: John came to both, preaching the doctrine of repentance, and proclaiming Jesus the Christ. To say that it was John who came in the way of righteousness, and that to him the words refer, is, in my opinion, saying nothing; for this was necessarily implied: as he professed to come from God, he must not only preach righteousness, but walk in it.

It is very difficult to get a worldly minded and self-righteous man brought to Christ. Examples signify little to him. Urge the example of an eminent saint, he is discouraged at it. Show him a profligate sinner converted to God, him he is ashamed to own and follow; and, as to the conduct of the generality of the followers of Christ, it is not striking enough to impress him. John, and Christ, and the apostles preach; but, to multitudes, all is in vain.

MATTHEW 21: 33–46; MARK 12: 1–12; LUKE 20: 9–19

Matthew 21: 33–46

33. There was a certain householder – Let us endeavor to find out a general and practical meaning for this parable. A householder – the Supreme Being. The family – the Jewish nation. The vineyard – the city of Jerusalem. The fence – the Divine protection. The winepress – the law and sacrificial rites. The tower – the temple, in which the Divine presence was manifested. The husbandmen – the priests and doctors of the law. Went from home

Mark 11: 27–33

27 And they come again to Jerusalem: and as he was walking in the temple, there come to him the chief priests, and the scribes, and the elders,

28 And say unto him, By what authority doest thou these things? and who gave thee this authority to do these things?

29 And Jesus answered and said unto them, I will also ask of you one question, and answer me, and I will tell you by what authority I do these things.

30 The baptism of John, was it from heaven, or of men? answer me.

31 And they reasoned with themselves, saying, If we shall say, From heaven; he will say, Why then did ye not believe him?

32 But if we shall say, Of men; they feared the people: for all men counted John, that he was a prophet indeed.

33 And they answered and said unto Jesus, We cannot tell. And Jesus answering saith unto them, Neither do I tell you by what authority I do these things.

Luke 20: 1–8

1 And it came to pass, that on one of those days, as he taught the people in the temple, and preached the gospel, the chief priests and the scribes came upon him with the elders,

2 And spake unto him, saying, Tell us, by what authority doest thou these things? or who is he that gave thee this authority?

3 And he answered and said unto them, I will also ask you one thing; and answer me:

4 The baptism of John, was it from heaven, or of men?

5 And they reasoned with themselves, saying, If we shall say, From heaven; he will say, Why then believed ye him not?

6 But and if we say, Of men; all the people will stone us: for they be persuaded that John was a prophet.

7 And they answered, that they could not tell whence it was.

8 And Jesus said unto them, Neither tell I you by what authority I do these things.

MATTHEW 21: 28–32

28 But what think ye? A certain man had two sons; and he came to the first,

the Author of them. They therefore insist on this, that he is not a lawful minister of God, because he had not been chosen by their votes, as if the power had dwelt solely with them. But though they had been the lawful guardians of the Church, still it was monstrous to rise up against God. We now understand why Christ did not make a direct reply to them. It was because they wickedly and shamelessly interrogated him about a matter which was well known.

25. Whence was the baptism of John?

Christ questions them about **the baptism of John**, not only to show that they were unworthy of any authority, because they had despised a holy prophet of God, but also to convict them, by their own reply, of having impudently pretended ignorance of a matter with which they were well acquainted. For we must bear in mind why **John** was sent, what was his commission, and on what subject he most of all insisted. He had been sent as Christ's herald. He was not deficient in his duty, and claims nothing more for himself than to prepare the way of the Lord. (Malachi 3: 1; Luke 7: 27.)

In short, he had pointed out Christ with the finger, and had declared him to be the only Son of God. From what source then do the scribes mean that the new authority of Christ should be proved, since it had been fully attested by the preaching **of John**? We now see that Christ employed no cunning stratagem in order to escape, but fully and perfectly answered the question which had been proposed; for it was impossible to acknowledge that **John** was a servant of God, without acknowledging that he was Himself the Lord. He did not therefore shelter arrogant men, who without any commission, but out of their own hardihood, take upon themselves a public office; nor did he countenance, by his example, the art of suppressing the truth, as many crafty men falsely plead his authority. I do acknowledge that, if wicked men lay snares for us, we ought not always to reply in the same way, but ought to be prudently on our guard against their malice, yet in such a manner that truth may not be left without a proper defense.

MATTHEW 21: 28–32

This conclusion shows what is the object of the parable, when Christ prefers to the scribes and priests those who were generally accounted infamous and held in detestation; for he unmasks those hypocrites, that they may no longer boast of being the ministers of God, or hold out a pretended zeal for godliness. Though their ambition, and pride, and cruelty, and avarice, were known to all, yet they wished to be reckoned quite different persons. And when, but a little ago, they attacked Christ, they falsely alleged that they were anxious about the order of the Church, as if they

– entrusted the cultivation of the vineyard to the priests, etc., with the utmost confidence; as a man would do who had the most trusty servants, and was obliged to absent himself from home for a certain time. Our Lord takes this parable from Isaiah 5: 1, etc.; but whether our blessed Redeemer quote from the law, the prophets, or the rabbins, he reserves the liberty to himself to beautify the whole, and render it more pertinent.

Some apply this parable also to Christianity, thus: The master or father – our blessed Lord. The family – professing Christians in general. The vineyard – the true Church, or assembly of the faithful. The hedge – the true faith, which keeps the sacred assembly enclosed and defended from the errors of heathenism and false Christianity. The wine-press – the atonement made by the sacrifice of Christ, typified by the sacrifices under the law. The tower – the promises of the Divine presence and protection. The husbandmen – the apostles and all their successors in the ministry. The going from home – the ascension to heaven. But this parable cannot go on all fours in the Christian cause, as any one may see. In the ease of the husbandmen, especially it is applicable; unless we suppose our Lord intended such as those inquisitorial Bonners, who always persecuted the true ministers of Christ, and consequently Christ himself in his members; and to these may be added the whole train of St. Bartholomew EJECTORS, and all the fire and faggot men of a certain Church, who think they do God service by murdering his saints. But let the persecuted take courage: Jesus Christ will come back shortly; and then he will miserably destroy those wicked men: indeed, he has done so already to several, and let out his vineyard to more faithful husbandmen.

Digged a wine-press – St. Mark has the pit under the press, into which the liquor ran, when squeezed out of the fruit by the press.

34. He sent his servants – Prophets, which, from time to time, he sent to the Jewish nation to call both priests and people back to the purity of his holy religion.

Receive the fruits of it – Alluding to the ancient custom of paying the rent of a farm in kind; that is, by a part of the produce of the farm. This custom anciently prevailed in most nations; and still prevails in the highlands of Scotland, and in some other places. The Boldon book, a survey made of the state of the bishopric of Durham in 1183, shows how much of the rents was paid in cows, sheep, pigs, fowls, eggs, etc., the remaining part being made up chiefly by manual labor.

35. Beat one – took his skin off, flayed him: probably alluding to some who had been excessively scourged.

Killed another, etc. – Rid themselves of the true witnesses of God by a variety of persecutions.

36. Other servants – There is not a moment in which God does not shower down his gifts upon men, and require the fruit of them. Various instruments are used to bring sinners to God. There are prophets, apostles, pastors, teachers: some with his gift after this manner, and some after that. The true disciples of Christ have been persecuted in all ages, and the greatest share of the persecution has fallen upon the ministers of his religion; for there have always been good and bad husbandmen, and the latter have persecuted the former.

More than the first – Or, more honorable. For, as the fullness of the time approached, each prophet more clearly and fully pointed out the coming of Christ.

37. Last of all he sent – his son – This requires no comment. Our Lord plainly means himself.

They will reverence – they will reflect upon their conduct and blush for shame because of it, when they see my son.

38. Said among themselves – Alluding to the conspiracies which were then forming against the life of our blessed Lord, in the councils of the Jewish elders and chief priests. See Matthew 27: 1.

39. Cast him out of the vineyard – Utterly rejected the counsel of God against themselves; and would neither acknowledge the

and said, Son, go work to day in my vineyard.

29 He answered and said, I will not: but afterward he repented, and went.

30 And he came to the second, and said likewise. And he answered and said, I go, sir: and went not.

31 Whether of them twain did the will of his father? They say unto him, The first. Jesus saith unto them, Verily I say unto you, That the publicans and the harlots go into the kingdom of God before you.

32 For John came unto you in the way of righteousness, and ye believed him not: but the publicans and the harlots believed him: and ye, when ye had seen it, repented not afterward, that ye might believe him.

MATTHEW 21: 33–46; MARK 12: 1–12; LUKE 20: 9–19

Matthew 21: 33–46

33 Hear another parable: There was a certain householder, which planted a vineyard, and hedged it round about, and digged a winepress in it, and built a tower, and let it out to husbandmen, and went into a far country:

34 And when the time of the fruit drew near, he sent his servants to the husbandmen, that they might receive the fruits of it.

35 And the husbandmen took his servants, and beat one, and killed another, and stoned another.

36 Again, he sent other servants more than the first: and they did unto them likewise.

37 But last of all he sent unto them his son, saying, They will reverence my son.

38 But when the husbandmen saw the son, they said among themselves, This is the heir; come, let us kill him, and let us seize on his inheritance.

39 And they caught him, and cast him out of the vineyard, and slew him.

40 When the lord therefore of the vineyard cometh, what will he do unto those husbandmen?

41 They say unto him, He will miserably destroy those wicked men, and will let out his vineyard unto other husbandmen, which shall render him the fruits in their seasons.

were its faithful and honest guardians. Since they attempt to practice such gross imposition on God and men, Christ rebukes their impudence by showing that they were at the greatest possible distance from what they boasted, and were so far from deserving that elevation with which they flattered themselves, that they ranked below **the publicans and the harlots**.

MATTHEW 21: 33–46; MARK 12: 1–12; LUKE 20: 9–19

Matthew 21: 33. Hear another parable

The words of Luke are somewhat different; for he says that Christ **spoke to the people**, while here the discourse is addressed to the priests and scribes. But the solution is easy; for, though Christ **spoke against them**, he exposed their baseness in the presence of all the people. Mark says that Christ **began to speak by parables**, but leaves out what was first in order, as also in other passages he gives only a part of the whole. The substance of this parable is, that it is no new thing, if the priests and the other rulers of the Church wickedly endeavor to defraud God of his right; for long ago they practiced the same kind of robbery towards the prophets, and now they are ready to **slay his Son**; but they will not go unpunished, for God will arise to defend his right. The object is two-fold; first, to reproach the priests with base and wicked ingratitude; and, secondly, to remove the offense which would be occasioned by his approaching death. For, by means of a false title, they had gained such influence over simple persons and the ignorant multitude, that the religion of the Jews depended on their will and decision. Christ therefore forewarns the weak, and shows that, as so many prophets, one after another, had formerly been slain by the priests, no one ought to be distressed, if a similar instance were exhibited in his own person. But let us now examine it in detail.

A man planted a vineyard

This comparison frequently occurs in Scripture. With respect to the present passage, Christ only means that, while God appoints pastors over his Church, he does not convey his right to others, but acts in the same manner as if a **proprietor** were to **let a vineyard** or **field** to a **husbandman**, who would labor in the cultivation of it, and make an annual return. As he complains by Isaiah (5: 4) and Jeremiah (2: 21), that he had received no fruit from the **vine** on the cultivation of which he had bestowed so much labor and expense; so in this passage he accuses the vine-dressers themselves, who, like base swindlers, appropriate to themselves the produce of the **vineyard**. Christ says that the **vineyard** was well furnished, and in excellent condition,

authority of Christ, nor submit to his teaching. What a strange and unaccountable case is this! – a sinner, to enjoy a little longer his false peace, and the gratification of his sinful appetites, rejects Jesus, and persecutes that Gospel which troubles his sinful repose.

41. He will miserably destroy those wicked men – So, according to this evangelist, our Lord caused them to pass that sentence of destruction upon themselves which was literally executed about forty years after.

42. The stone – This seems to have been originally spoken of David who was at first rejected by the Jewish rulers, but was afterwards chosen by the Lord to be the great ruler of his people Israel. The quotation is taken from Psalm 118: 22.

As the Church is represented in Scripture under the name of the temple and house of God, in allusion to the temple of Jerusalem, which was a type of it, 1 Corinthians 3: 16; Hebrews 3: 6; 1 Peter 2: 5; so Jesus Christ is represented as the foundation on which this edifice is laid, 1 Corinthians 3: 11; Ephesians 2: 20–21.

The builders – The chief priests and elders of the people, with the doctors of the law.

Rejected – An expression borrowed from masons, who, finding a stone, which being tried in a particular place, and appearing improper for it, is thrown aside, and another taken; however, at last, it may happen that the very stone which had been before rejected, may be found the most suitable as the head stone of the corner.

This passage, as applied by our Lord to himself, contains an abridgment of the whole doctrine of the Gospel.

1. The Lord's peculiar work is astonishingly manifested in the mission of Jesus Christ.

2. He, being rejected and crucified by the Jews, became an atonement for the sin of the world.

3. He was raised again from the dead, a proof of his conquest over death and sin, and a pledge of immortality to his followers.

4. He was constituted the foundation on which the salvation of mankind rests, and the corner stone which unites Jews and Gentiles, beautifies, strengthens, and completes the whole building, as the head stone, or uppermost stone in the corner does the whole edifice.

5. He is hereby rendered the object of the joy and admiration of all his followers and the glory of man. This was done by the Lord, and is marvelous in our eyes.

44. The 44th verse should certainly come before v. 43, otherwise the narration is not consecutive.

Verse 42. The stone which the builders rejected, is become the head of the corner, etc. **Verse 44.** Whosoever shall fall on this stone shall be broken, etc. This is an allusion to the punishment of stoning among the Jews. The place of stoning was twice as high as a man; while standing on this, one of the witnesses struck the culprit on the loins, so that he fell over this scaffold; if he died by the stroke and fall, well; if not, the other witness threw a stone upon his heart, and despatched him. That stone thrown on the culprit was, in some cases, as much as two men could lift up.

He, whether Jew or Gentile, who shall not believe in the Son of God, shall suffer grievously in consequence; but on whomsoever the stone (Jesus Christ) falls in the way of judgment, he shall be ground to powder, it shall make him so small as to render him capable of being dispersed as chaff by the wind. This seems to allude, not only to the dreadful crushing of the Jewish state by the Romans, but also to that general dispersion of the Jews through all the nations of the world, which continues to the present day.

43. Therefore say I – Thus showing them, that to them alone the parable belonged. The kingdom of God shall be taken from you – the Gospel shall be taken from you, and given to the Gentiles, who will receive it, and bring forth fruit to the glory of God.

Bringing forth the fruits – As in Matthew 21: 34 an allusion is made to paying the landlord in kind, so here the Gentiles are represented as paying God thus. The returns which He expects for his grace are the fruits of grace;

42 Jesus saith unto them, Did ye never read in the scriptures, The stone which the builders rejected, the same is become the head of the corner: this is the Lord's doing, and it is marvelous in our eyes?

43 Therefore say I unto you, The kingdom of God shall be taken from you, and given to a nation bringing forth the fruits thereof.

44 And whosoever shall fall on this stone shall be broken: but on whomsoever it shall fall, it will grind him to powder.

45 And when the chief priests and Pharisees had heard his parables, they perceived that he spake of them.

46 But when they sought to lay hands on him, they feared the multitude, because they took him for a prophet.

Mark 12: 1–12

1 And he began to speak unto them by parables. A certain man planted a vineyard, and set an hedge about it, and digged a place for the winefat, and built a tower, and let it out to husbandmen, and went into a far country.

2 And at the season he sent to the husbandmen a servant, that he might receive from the husbandmen of the fruit of the vineyard.

3 And they caught him, and beat him, and sent him away empty.

4 And again he sent unto them another servant; and at him they cast stones, and wounded him in the head, and sent him away shamefully handled.

5 And again he sent another; and him they killed, and many others; beating some, and killing some.

6 Having yet therefore one son, his wellbeloved, he sent him also last unto them, saying, They will reverence my son.

7 But those husbandmen said among themselves, This is the heir; come, let us kill him, and the inheritance shall be ours.

8 And they took him, and killed him, and cast him out of the vineyard.

9 What shall therefore the lord of the vineyard do? he will come and destroy the husbandmen, and will give the vineyard unto others.

10 And have ye not read this scripture; The stone which the builders rejected is

when the **husbandmen** received it from the hands of the **proprietor**.

By this statement he presents no slight aggravation of their crime; for the more generously he had acted toward them, the more detestable was their ingratitude. Paul employs the same argument, when he wishes to exhort pastors to be diligent in the discharge of their duty, that they are stewards, chosen to govern the house of God, which is the "pillar and round of truth" (1 Timothy 3: 16).

And properly; for the more honorable and illustrious their condition is, they lie under so much the deeper obligations to God, not to be indolent in their work. So much the more detestable (as we have already said) is the baseness of those who pour contempt on the great kindness of God, and on the great honor which they have already received from Him.

God **planted a vineyard**, when, remembering his gratuitous adoption, he brought the people out of Egypt, separated them anew to be his inheritance, and called them to the hope of eternal salvation, promising to be their God and Father; for this is the **planting** of which Isaiah speaks (60: 21; 61: 3). By the **wine-press** and the **tower** are meant the aids which were added for strengthening the faith of the people in the doctrine of the Law, such as, sacrifices and other ritual observances; for God, like a careful and provident head of a family, has left no means untried for granting to his Church all necessary protection.

And let it to husbandmen

God might indeed of himself, without the agency of men, preserve his Church in good order; but he takes men for his ministers, and makes use of their hands. Thus, of old, he appointed priests to be, as it were, cultivators of the **vineyard**.

But the wonder is, that Christ compares the prophets to servants, who are sent, after the vintage, to demand the fruit; for we know that they too were **vine-dressers**, and that they held a charge in common with the priests. I reply, it was not necessary for Christ to be careful or exact in describing the resemblance or contrariety between those two orders. The priests were certainly appointed at first on the condition of thoroughly cultivating the Church by sound doctrine; but as they neglected the work assigned them, either through carelessness or ignorance, the prophets were sent as an extraordinary supply, to clear the vine from weeds, to lop off the superfluous wood, and in other ways to make up for the neglect of the priests; and, at the same time, severely to reprove the people, to raise up decayed piety, to awaken drowsy souls, and to bring back the worship of God and a new life. And what else was this than to demand the revenue which was due to God from his vineyard? All this Christ applies justly and truly to his

nothing can ever be acceptable in the sight of God that does not spring from himself.

45. The chief priests – perceived that he spoke of them – The most wholesome advice passes for an affront with those who have shut their hearts against the truth. When that which should lead to repentance only kindles the flame of malice and revenge, there is but little hope of the salvation of such persons.

46. They sought to lay hands on him, they feared the multitude – Restraining and preventing grace is an excellent blessing, particularly where it leads to repentance and salvation; but he who abstains from certain evils, only through fear of scandal or punishment, has already committed them in his heart, and is guilty before God. The intrepidity of our Lord is worthy of admiration and imitation; in the very face of his most inveterate enemies, he bears a noble testimony to the truth, reproves their iniquities, denounces the Divine judgments, and, in the very teeth of destruction, braves danger and death! A true minister of Christ fears nothing but God, when his glory is concerned: a hireling fears every thing, except Him whom he ought to fear.

This last journey of our Lord to Jerusalem is a subject of great importance; it is mentioned by all the four evangelists, and has been a subject of criticism and cavil to some unsanctified minds. He has been accused of "attempting, by this method, to feel how far the populace were disposed to favor his pretensions in establishing himself as a king in the land; or, at least, by his conduct in this business, he gave much cause for popular seditions." Every circumstance in the case refutes this calumny.

1. His whole conduct had proved that his kingdom was not of this world, and that he sought not the honor that cometh from man.

2. He had in a very explicit manner foretold his own premature death, and particularly at this time.

3. It is evident, from what he had said to his disciples, that he went up to Jerusalem at this time for the express purpose of being sacrificed, and not of erecting a secular kingdom.

4. What he did at this time was to fulfill a declaration of God delivered by two prophets, upwards of 700 years before, relative to his lowliness, poverty, and total deadness to all secular rule and pomp. See Isaiah 62: 11; Zechariah 9: 9.

5. All the time he spent now in Jerusalem, which was about five days, he spent in teaching, precisely in the same way he had done for three years past; nor do we find that he uttered one maxim dissimilar to what he formerly taught, or said a word calculated to produce any sensation on the hearts of the populace, but that of piety towards God; and in the parable of the man and his two sons, the husbandmen and the vineyard, he spoke in such a way to the rulers of the people as to show that he knew they were plotting his destruction; and that, far from fleeing from the face of danger, or strengthening his party against his enemies, he was come to wait at the foot of the altar till his blood should be poured out for the sin of the world!

6. Had he affected any thing of a secular kind, he had now the fairest opportunity to accomplish his designs. The people had already received him as Jesus the prophet; now they acknowledge him as the Christ or MESSIAH, and sing the hosannah to him, as immediately appointed by Heaven to be their deliverer.

7. Though, with the character of the Messiah, the Jews had connected that of secular royalty, and they now, by spreading their clothes in the way, strewing branches, etc., treat him as a royal person, and one appointed to govern the kingdom; yet of this he appears to take no notice, farther than to show that an important prophecy was thus fulfilled: he went as usual into the temple, taught the people pure and spiritual truths, withdrew at night from the city, lodged in private at Mount Olivet; and thus most studiously and unequivocally showed that his sole aim was to call the people back to purity and holiness, and prepare them for that kingdom of righteousness, peace, and joy in the Holy Ghost, which he was about, by his passion, death, resurrection, ascension, and the mission of the Holy Spirit, to set up in the earth.

8. Could a person who worked such miracles

become the head of the corner:

11 This was the Lord's doing, and it is marvelous in our eyes?

12 And they sought to lay hold on him, but feared the people: for they knew that he had spoken the parable against them: and they left him, and went their way.

Luke 20: 9–19

9 Then began he to speak to the people this parable; A certain man planted a vineyard, and let it forth to husbandmen, and went into a far country for a long time.

10 And at the season he sent a servant to the husbandmen, that they should give him of the fruit of the vineyard: but the husbandmen beat him, and sent him away empty.

11 And again he sent another servant: and they beat him also, and entreated him shamefully, and sent him away empty.

12 And again he sent a third: and they wounded him also, and cast him out.

13 Then said the lord of the vineyard, What shall I do? I will send my beloved son: it may be they will reverence him when they see him.

14 But when the husbandmen saw him, they reasoned among themselves, saying, This is the heir: come, let us kill him, that the inheritance may be ours.

15 So they cast him out of the vineyard, and killed him. What therefore shall the lord of the vineyard do unto them?

16 He shall come and destroy these husbandmen, and shall give the vineyard to others. And when they heard it, they said, God forbid.

17 And he beheld them, and said, What is this then that is written, The stone which the builders rejected, the same is become the head of the corner?

18 Whosoever shall fall upon that stone shall be broken; but on whomsoever it shall fall, it will grind him to powder.

19 And the chief priests and the scribes the same hour sought to lay hands on him; and they feared the people: for they perceived that he had spoken this parable against them.

purpose; for the regular and permanent government of his Church was not in the hands of the prophets, but was always held by the priests; just as if lazy **husbandman**, while he neglected cultivation, claimed the place to which he had been once appointed, under the plea of possession.

35. And wounded one, and killed another

Here Mark andLuke differ a little from Matthew; for while Matthew mentions many servants, all of whom were ill-treated and insulted, and says that afterwards other servants were sent more numerous than the first, Mark and Luke mention but one at a time, as if the **servants** had been sent, not two or three together, but one after another. But though all the three Evangelists have the same object in view, namely, to show that the Jews will dare to act towards the Son in the same manner as they have repeatedly done towards the prophets, Matthew explains the matter more at large, namely, that God, by sending a multitude of prophets, contended with the malice of the priests. Hence it appears how obstinate their malice was, for the correction of which no remedies were of any avail.

37. They will reverence my son

Strictly speaking, indeed, this thought does not apply to God; for He knew what would happen, and was not deceived by the expectation of a more agreeable result; but it is customary, especially in parables, to ascribe to Him human feelings. And yet this was not added without reason; for Christ intended to represent, as in a mirror, how deplorable their impiety was, of which it was too certain a proof, that they rose in diabolical rage against the Son of God, who had come to bring them back to a sound mind. As they had formerly, as far as lay in their power, driven God from his inheritance by the cruel murder of the prophets, so it was the crowning point of all their crimes to **slay the Son**, that they might reign, as in a house which wanted an heir. Certainly the chief reason why the priests raged against Christ was, that, they might not lose their tyranny, which might be said to be their prey; for he it is by whom God chooses to govern, and to whom He has given all authority.

MATTHEW 22: 15–22; MARK 12: 13–17; LUKE 20: 20–26

Matthew 22: 15. That they might entrap him in his words

The Pharisees, perceiving that all their other attempts against Christ had been fruitless, at length concluded that the best and most expeditious method of destroying him was, to deliver him to the governor, as a seditious person and a disturber of the peace. There was at that time, as we have seen under another passage, a great disputing among

ADAM CLARKE

as he was in the daily habit of working-miracles which proved he possessed unlimited power and unerring wisdom, need subterfuges, or a coloring for any design he wished to accomplish? He had only to put forth that power essentially resident in himself, and all resistance to his will must be annihilated. In short, every circumstance of the case shows at once the calumny and absurdity of the charge. But, instead of lessening, or tendering suspicious this or any other part of our Lord's conduct, it shows the whole in a more luminous and glorious point of view; and thus the wrath of man praises him.

9. That he was a king, that he was born of a woman and came into the world for this very purpose, he took every occasion to declare; but all these declarations showed that his kingdom was spiritual: he would not even interfere with the duty of the civil magistrate to induce an avaricious brother to do justice to the rest of the family, Luke 12: 13, when probably a few words from such an authority would have been sufficient to have settled the business; yet to prevent all suspicion, and to remove every cause for offense, he absolutely refused to interfere, and took occasion from the very circumstance to declaim against secular views, covetousness, and worldly ambition! O how groundless does every part of his conduct prove this charge of secular ambition to be! Such was the spirit of the Master: such must be the spirit of the disciple. He that will reign with Christ, must be humbled and suffer with him. This is the royal road. The love of the world, in its power and honors, is as inconsistent with the spirit of the Gospel as the love of the grossest vice. If any man love the world, the love of the Father is not in him. Reader, take occasion from this refuted calumny, to imitate thy Lord in the spirituality of his life, to pass through things temporal so as not to lose those that are eternal, that thou mayest reign with him in the glory of his kingdom. Amen.

MATTHEW 22: 15–22; MARK 12: 13–17; LUKE 20: 20–26

Matthew 22: 15–22

15. **In his talk** – by discourse: intending to ask him subtle and ensnaring questions; his answers to which might involve him either with the Roman government, or with the great Sanhedrin.

16. **The Herodians** – For an account of this sect, see the note on Matthew 16: 1. The preceding parable had covered the Pharisees with confusion: when it was ended they went out, not to humble themselves before God, and deprecate the judgments with which they were threatened; but to plot afresh the destruction of their teacher. The depth of their malice appears,

1. In their mode of attack. They had often questioned our Lord on matters concerning religion; and his answers only served to increase his reputation, and their confusion. They now shift their ground, and question him concerning state affairs, and the question is such as must be answered; and yet the answer, to all human appearance, can be none other than what may be construed into a crime against the people, or against the Roman government.

2. Their profound malice appears farther in the choice of their companions in this business, viz. the Herodians. Herod was at this very time at Jerusalem, whither he had come to hold the passover. Jesus, being of Nazareth, which was in Herod's jurisdiction, was considered as his subject. Herod himself was extremely attached to the Roman emperor, and made a public profession of it: all these considerations engaged the Pharisees to unite the Herodians, who, as the Syriac intimates, were the domestics of Herod, in this infernal plot.

3. Their profound malice appears, farther, in the praises they gave our Lord. Teacher, we know that thou art true, and teachest the way of God. This was indeed the real character of our blessed Lord; and now they bear testimony to the truth, merely with the design to

|

MATTHEW 22: 15–22; MARK 12: 13–17; LUKE 20: 20–26

Matthew 22: 15–22

15 Then went the Pharisees, and took counsel how they might entangle him in his talk.

16 And they sent out unto him their disciples with the Herodians, saying, Master, we know that thou art true, and teachest the way of God in truth, neither carest thou for any man: for thou regardest not the person of men.

17 Tell us therefore, What thinkest thou? Is it lawful to give tribute unto Caesar, or not?

18 But Jesus perceived their wickedness, and said, Why tempt ye me, ye hypocrites?

19 Shew me the tribute money. And they brought unto him a penny.

20 And he saith unto them, Whose is this image and superscription?

21 They say unto him, Caesar's. Then saith he unto them, Render therefore unto Caesar the things which are Caesar's; and unto God the things that are God's.

22 When they had heard these words, they marveled, and left him, and went their way.

Mark 12: 13–17

13 And they send unto him certain of the Pharisees and of the Herodians, to catch him in his words.

14 And when they were come, they say unto him, Master, we know that thou art true, and carest for no man: for thou regardest not the person of men, but teachest the way of God in truth: Is it lawful to give tribute to Caesar, or not?

15 Shall we give, or shall we not give? But he, knowing their hypocrisy, said unto them, Why tempt ye me? bring me a penny, that I may see it.

16 And they brought it. And he saith unto them, Whose is this image and superscription? And they said unto him, Caesar's.

17 And Jesus answering said unto them, Render to Caesar the things that are Caesar's, and to God the things that are God's. And they marveled at him.

Luke 20: 20–26

20 And they watched him, and sent

the Jews about the tribute-money; for, since the Romans had claimed for themselves the tribute-money, which God commanded to be paid to Himself under the Law of Moses, (Exodus 30: 13,) the Jews everywhere complained that it was a shameful and intolerable crime for profane men to lay claim, in this manner, to a divine prerogative; besides that, as this payment of tribute, which was enjoined on them by the Law, was a testimony of their adoption, they looked upon themselves as deprived of an honor to which they had a just claim. Now the deeper any man's poverty was, the bolder did it render him to raise sedition.

This trick of taking Christ by surprise is therefore continued by **the Pharisees,** that, in whatever way he reply as to the tribute money, they may lay snares for him. If he affirm that they ought not to pay, he will be convicted of sedition. If, on the contrary, he acknowledge it to be justly due, he will be held to be an enemy of his nation, and a betrayer of the liberty of his country. Their principal object is, to lead the people to dislike him. This is the entrapping to which the Evangelists refer; for they suppose that Christ is surrounded on all sides by **nets,** so that he can no longer escape. Having avowed themselves to be his enemies, and knowing that they would, on that account, be suspected, they put forward – as Matthew states – **some of their disciples.**

Luke, again, calls them **spies, who pretended to be righteous men**; that is, persons who deceitfully professed an honest and proper desire to learn: for the pretense of righteousness is not here used in a general sense, but is limited to the present occasion, because they would not have been received, had they not made a pretense of docility and of genuine zeal.

With **the Herodians.** They take along with them **the Herodians,** because they were more favorable to the Roman government, and therefore would be more disposed to raise an accusation. It is worthy of attention that, though those sects had fierce contentions with each other, so bitter was their hatred against Christ, that they conspired to destroy him. What the sect of **the Herodions** was, Herod being only half a Jew, or a spurious and corrupt professor of the Law, those who desired that the Law should be kept with exactness and in every part, condemned him and his impure worship; but he had his flatterers, who gave plausible excuses for his false doctrine.

18. Knowing their malice

They had opened the conversation in such a manner that they did not appear to differ at all from excellent scholars. Whence then had Christ this knowledge, but because his Spirit was a discerner of hearts? It was not by human conjecture that he perceived their cunning, but because he

make it subserve their bloody purposes. Those whose hearts are influenced by the spirit of the wicked one never do good, but when they hope to accomplish evil by it. Men who praise you to your face are ever to be suspected. The Italians have a very expressive proverb on this subject:

He who caresses thee more than he was wont to do, has either DECEIVED thee, or is ABOUT TO DO IT.

I have never known the sentiment in this proverb to fail; and it was notoriously exemplified in the present instance. Flatterers, though they speak the truth, ever carry about with them a base or malicious soul.

4. Their malice appears still farther in the question they propose. Is it lawful to give tribute to Caesar, or not? – Matthew 22: 17.

The constitution of the Jewish republic, the expectations which they had of future glory and excellence, and the diversity of opinions which divided the Jews on this subject, rendered an answer to this question extremely difficult:

1. In the presence of the people, who professed to have no other king but God, and looked on their independence as an essential point of their religion.

2. In the presence of the Pharisees, who were ready to stir up the people against him, if his decision could be at all construed to be contrary to their prejudices, or to their religious rights.

3. In the presence of the Herodians, who, if the answer should appear to be against Caesar's rights, were ready to inflame their master to avenge, by the death of our Lord, the affront offered to his master the emperor.

4. The answer was difficult, because of the different sentiments of the Jews on this subject; some maintaining that they could not lawfully pay tribute to a heathen governor: while others held that as they were now under this strange government, and had no power to free themselves from it, it was lawful for them to pay what they had not power to refuse.

5. The answer was difficult, when it is considered that multitudes of the people had begun now to receive Jesus as the promised Messiah,

who was to be the deliverer of their nation from spiritual and temporal oppression, and therefore had lately sung to him the Hosanna Rabba: see Matthew 21: 9. If then he should decide the question in Caesar's favor, what idea must the people have of him, either as zealous for the law, or as the expected Messiah? If against Caesar, he is ruined. Who that loved Jesus, and was not convinced of his sovereign wisdom, could help trembling for him in these circumstances?

Jesus opposes the depth of his wisdom to the depth of their malice, and manifests it:

1. By unmasking them, and showing that he knew the very secrets of their hearts. Ye HYPOCRITES! why tempt ye me? i.e. why do ye try me thus? This must cover them with confusion, when they saw their motives thus discovered; and tend much to lessen their influence in the sight of the people, when it was manifest that they acted not through a desire to receive information, by which to regulate their conduct, but merely to ensnare and ruin him.

2. Christ shows his profound wisdom in not attempting to discuss the question at large; but settled the business by seizing a maxim that was common among all people, and acknowledged among the Jews, That the prince who causes his image and titles to be stamped on the current coin of a country, is virtually acknowledged thereby as the governor.

19. They brought unto him a penny – A denarius: probably the ordinary capitation tax, though the poll tax in the law, Exodus 30: 13, 14, was half a shekel, about twice as much as the denarius. The Roman denarius had the emperor's image with a proper legend stamped on one side of it. It was not therefore the sacred shekel which was to be paid for the repairs of the temple which was now demanded, but the regular tribute required by the Roman government.

20. Whose is this image and superscription? – He knew well enough whose they were; but he showed the excellency of his wisdom, 3dly, in making them answer to their own confusion. They came to ensnare our Lord in his

forth spies, which should feign them-selves just men, that they might take hold of his words, that so they might deliver him unto the power and authority of the governor.

21 And they asked him, saying, Master, we know that thou sayest and teachest rightly, neither acceptest thou the person of any, but teachest the way of God truly:

22 Is it lawful for us to give tribute unto Caesar, or no?

23 But he perceived their craftiness, and said unto them, Why tempt ye me?

24 Shew me a penny. Whose image and superscription hath it? They an-swered and said, Caesar's.

25 And he said unto them, Render therefore unto Caesar the things which be Caesar's, and unto God the things which be God's.

26 And they could not take hold of his words before the people: and they mar-veled at his answer, and held their peace.

MATTHEW 22: 23–33; MARK 12: 18–27; LUKE 20: 27–40

Matthew 22: 23–33

23 The same day came to him the Sadducees, which say that there is no resurrection, and asked him,

24 Saying, Master, Moses said, If a man die, having no children, his brother shall marry his wife, and raise up seed unto his brother.

25 Now there were with us seven brethren: and the first, when he had mar-ried a wife, deceased, and, having no is-sue, left his wife unto his brother:

26 Likewise the second also, and the third, unto the seventh.

27 And last of all the woman died also.

28 Therefore in the resurrection whose wife shall she be of the seven? for they all had her.

29 Jesus answered and said unto them, Ye do err, not knowing the scrip-tures, nor the power of God.

30 For in the resurrection they neither marry, nor are given in marriage, but are as the angels of God in heaven.

31 But as touching the resurrection of the dead, have ye not read that which was spoken unto you by God, saying,

was God he penetrated into their hearts, and therefore they gained nothing by attempting the concealment of flattery and of pretended righteousness

Accordingly, before giving a reply, he exhibited a proof of his Divinity by laying open their concealed malice. Now since wicked men every day employ snares of the same kind, while their inward malice is concealed from us, we ought to pray to Christ to bestow upon us the spirit of dis-cernment, and that what he had by nature and by his own right he may grant to us by a free gift. How much we need this prudence, is evident from the consideration that, if we do not guard against the snares of the wicked, we shall con-stantly expose the doctrine of God to their calumnies.

19. Show me the tribute-money

When Christ orders them to bring forward a coin, though at first sight it appears to be of no great importance, yet it is sufficient for breaking their snares. In this way they had already made an acknowledgment of subjection, so that Christ did not find it necessary to enjoin upon them any thing new. The coin was stamped with **Caesar's likeness**; and thus the authority of the Roman government had been approved and admitted by the general practice. Hence it was evident that the Jews themselves had voluntarily come under obligation to pay tribute for they had given up to the Romans the power of the sword; and there was no propri-ety in making a separate dispute about **the tribute-money**, for that question depended on the general arrangements of the government.

MATTHEW 22: 23–33; MARK 12: 18–27; LUKE 20: 27–40

Matthew 22: 23. The same day came to him the Sadducees

We see here how Satan brings together all the ungodly, who in other respects differ widely from each other, to attack the truth of God. For, though deadly strife existed between these two sects, yet they conspire together against Christ; so that the Pharisees are not displeased to have their own doctrine attacked in the person of Christ. Thus in the pres-ent day, we see all the forces of Satan, though in other re-spects they are opposed to each other, rising on every hand against Christ. And so fierce is the hatred with which the Papists burn against the Gospel, that they willingly support Epicureans, Libertines, and other monsters of that descrip-tion, provided that they can avail themselves of their aid for accomplishing its destruction. In short, we see that they come out of various camps to make an attack on Christ; and that this was done, because all of them alike hated the light of sound doctrine. Now **the Sadducees** propose a question to Christ, that by the appearance of absurdity

discourse, and now they are ensnared in their own. He who digs a pit for his neighbor ordinarily falls into it himself.

21. They say unto him, Caesars – The image was the head of the emperor; the superscription, his titles. JULIUS CAESAR was the first who caused his image to be struck on the Roman coin. Tiberius was emperor at this time.

Render therefore unto Caesar – The conclusion is drawn from their own premises. You acknowledge this to be Caesar's coin; this coin is current, in your land; the currency of this coin shows the country to be under the Roman government; and your acknowledgment that it is Caesar's proves you have submitted. Don't therefore be unjust; but render to Caesar the things which you acknowledge to be his; at the same time, be not impious, but render unto God the thing's which belong to God.

This answer is full of consummate wisdom. It establishes the limits, regulates the rights, and distinguishes the jurisdiction of the two empires of heaven and earth. The image of princes stamped on their coin denotes that temporal things belong all to their government. The image of God stamped on the soul denotes that all its faculties and powers belong to the Most High, and should be employed in his service.

But while the earth is agitated and distracted with the question of political rights and wrongs, the reader will naturally ask, What does a man owe to Caesar? – to the civil government under which he lives? Our Lord has answered the question – That which IS Caesar's. But what is it that is Caesar's? 1. Honor. 2. Obedience. And 3. Tribute.

1. The civil government under which a man lives, and by which he is protected, demands his honor and reverence.

2. The laws which are made for the suppression of evil doers, and the maintenance of good order, which are calculated to promote the benefit of the whole, and the comfort of the individual should be religiously obeyed.

3. The government that charges itself with the support and defense of the whole, should have its unavoidable expenses, however great, repaid by the people, in whose behalf they are incurred; therefore we should pay tribute.

But remember, if Caesar should intrude into the things of God, coin a new creed, or broach a new Gospel, and affect to rule the conscience, while he rules the state, in these things Caesar is not to be obeyed; he is taking the things of God, and he must not get them. Give not therefore God's things to Caesar, and give not Caesar's things to God. That which belongs to the commonwealth should, on no account whatever, be devoted to religious uses; and let no man think he has pleased God, by giving that to charitable or sacred uses which he has purloined from the state. The tribute of half a shekel, which the law, (Exodus 30: 13, 14), required every person above twenty years of age to pay to the temple, was, after the destruction of the temple, in the time of Vespasian, paid into the emperor's exchequer. This sum, Melancthon supposes, amounted annually to THREE TONS OF GOLD.

22. When they had heard these words, they marveled – And well they might – never man spake like this man. By this decision, CAESAR is satisfied – he gets his own to the uttermost farthing. GOD is glorified – his honor is in every respect secured. And the PEOPLE are edified – one of the most difficult questions that could possibly come before them is answered in such a way as to relieve their consciences, and direct their conduct.

MATTHEW 22: 23–33; MARK 12: 18–27; LUKE 20: 27–40

Matthew 22: 23–33

23. The same day – Malice is ever active; let it be defeated ever so often, it returns to the charge. Jesus and his Gospel give no quarter to vice; the vicious will give no quarter to him or it.

24. Raise up seed unto his brother – This law is mentioned Deuteronomy 25: 5. The meaning of the expression is, that the children produced by this marriage should be reckoned

32 I am the God of Abraham, and the God of Isaac, and the God of Jacob? God is not the God of the dead, but of the living.

33 And when the multitude heard this, they were astonished at his doctrine.

Mark 12: 18–27

18 Then come unto him the Sadducees, which say there is no resurrection; and they asked him, saying,

19 Master, Moses wrote unto us, If a man's brother die, and leave his wife behind him, and leave no children, that his brother should take his wife, and raise up seed unto his brother.

20 Now there were seven brethren: and the first took a wife, and dying left no seed.

21 And the second took her, and died, neither left he any seed: and the third likewise.

22 And the seven had her, and left no seed: last of all the woman died also.

23 In the resurrection therefore, when they shall rise, whose wife shall she be of them? for the seven had her to wife.

24 And Jesus answering said unto them, Do ye not therefore err, because ye know not the scriptures, neither the power of God?

25 For when they shall rise from the dead, they neither marry, nor are given in marriage; but are as the angels which are in heaven.

26 And as touching the dead, that they rise: have ye not read in the book of Moses, how in the bush God spake unto him, saying, I am the God of Abraham, and the God of Isaac, and the God of Jacob?

27 He is not the God of the dead, but the God of the living: ye therefore do greatly err.

Luke 20: 27–40

27 Then came to him certain of the Sadducees, which deny that there is any resurrection; and they asked him,

28 Saying, Master, Moses wrote unto us, If any man's brother die, having a wife, and he die without children, that his brother should take his wife, and raise up seed unto his brother.

29 There were therefore seven brethren: and the first took a wife, and died

they may either lead him to take part in their error, or, if he disagree with them, that they may hold him up to disgrace and ridicule among an uneducated and ignorant multitude. It is no doubt possible, that they had been formerly accustomed to employ this sophistry for harassing the Pharisees, but now they attempt to take Christ in the same snare.

Who say that there is no resurrection

How the sect of the Sadducees originated we have explained under another passage. Luke assures us that they denied not only the final **resurrection** of the body, but also the immortality of the soul (Acts 23: 8). And, indeed, if we consider properly the doctrine of Scripture, the life of the soul, apart from the hope of the resurrection, will be a mere dream; for God does not declare that, immediately after the death of the body, souls live – as if their glory and happiness were already enjoyed by them in perfections – but delays the expectation of them till the last day. I readily acknowledge that the philosophers, who were ignorant of the resurrection of the body, have many discussions about the immortal essence of the soul; but they talk so foolishly about the state of the future life that their opinions have no weight. But since the Scriptures inform us that the spiritual life depends on the hope of the resurrection, and that souls, when separated from the bodies, look forward to it, whoever destroys the resurrection deprives souls also of their immortality.

Now this enables us to perceive the dreadful confusion of the Jewish Church, that their rulers in religious matters took away the expectation of a future life, so that, after the death of the body, men differed in no respect from brute beasts. They did not indeed deny that our lives ought to be holy and righteous, and were not so profane as to consider the worship of God to be superfluous; on the contrary, they maintained that God is the Judge of the world, and that the affairs of men are directed by His providence. But as the reward of the godly, and likewise the punishment due to the wicked, were limited by them to the present life, even though there had been truth in their assertion, that every man is now treated impartially according to his merit, yet it was excessively absurd to restrict the promises of God within such narrow limits. Now experience plainly shows that they were chargeable with the grossest stupidity, since it is manifest that the reward which is laid up for the good is left incomplete till another life, and likewise that the punishment of the wicked is not wholly inflicted in this world.

In short, it is impossible to conceive any thing more absurd than this dream, that men formed after the image of God are extinguished by death like the beasts. But how disgraceful and monstrous was it that while, among the profane and blind idolaters of all nations, some notion, at least, of a future life still lingered, among the Jews, the peculiar people of God, this seed of piety was destroyed. I

ADAM CLARKE

in the genealogy of the deceased brother, and enjoy his estates. The word seed should be always translated children or posterity.

25. Seven brethren – It is very likely that the Sadducees increased the number, merely to make the question the more difficult.

Whose wife shall she be of the seven? – The rabbins have said, That if a woman have two husbands in this world, she shall have the first only restored to her in the world to come. The question put by these bad men is well suited to the mouth of a libertine. Those who live without God in the world have no other god than the world; and those who have not that happiness which comes from the enjoyment of God have no other pleasure than that which comes from the gratification of sensual appetites. The stream cannot rise higher than the spring: these men, and their younger brethren, atheists, deists, and libertines of all sorts, can form no idea of heaven as a place of blessedness, unless they can hope to find in it the gratification of their sensual desires. On this very ground Mohammed built his paradise.

29. Ye do err – Or, Ye are deceived – by your impure passions: not knowing the scriptures, which assert the resurrection: nor the miraculous power of God by which it is to be effected. In Avoda Sara, fol. 18, Sanhedrin, fol. 90, it is said: "These are they which shall have no part in the world to come: Those who say, the Lord did not come from heaven; and those who say, the resurrection cannot be proved out of the law."

Their deception appeared in their supposing, that if there were a resurrection, men and women were to marry and be given in marriage as in this life; which our Lord shows is not the case: for men and women there shall be like the angels of God, immortal, and free from all human passions, and from those propensities which were to continue with them only during this present state of existence. There shall be no death; and consequently no need of marriage to maintain the population of the spiritual world.

31. Have ye not read – This quotation is taken from Exodus 3: 6,16; and as the five books of Moses were the only part of Scripture which the Sadducees acknowledged as Divine, our Lord, by confuting them from those books, proved the second part of his assertion, "Ye are ignorant of those very scriptures which ye profess to hold sacred."

32. I am the God of Abraham – Let it be observed, that Abraham was dead upwards of 300 years before these words were spoken to Moses: yet still God calls himself the God of Abraham, etc. Now Christ properly observes that God is not the God of the dead, (that word being equal, in the sense of the Sadducees, to an eternal annihilation), but of the living; it therefore follows, that, if he be the God of Abraham, Isaac, and Jacob, these are not dead, but alive; alive with God, though they had ceased, for some hundreds of years, to exist among mortals. We may see, from this, that our Lord combats and confutes another opinion of the Sadducees, viz. that there is neither angel nor spirit; by showing that the soul is not only immortal, but lives with God, even while the body is detained in the dust of the earth, which body is afterwards to be raised to life, and united with its soul by the miraculous power of God, of which power they showed themselves to be ignorant when they denied the possibility of a resurrection.

33. The multitude were astonished at his doctrine – God uses the infidelity of some for the edification of others. Had no false doctrine been broached in the world, we had not seen the full evidence of the true teaching. The opposition of deists and infidels has only served to raise up men in behalf of the truth of God, who not only have refuted them, but shown, at the same time, that the sacred testimonies are infinitely amiable in themselves, and worthy of all acceptation. Truth always gains by being opposed.

without children.

30 And the second took her to wife, and he died childless.

31 And the third took her; and in like manner the seven also: and they left no children, and died.

32 Last of all the woman died also.

33 Therefore in the resurrection whose wife of them is she? for seven had her to wife.

34 And Jesus answering said unto them, The children of this world marry, and are given in marriage:

35 But they which shall be accounted worthy to obtain that world, and the resurrection from the dead, neither marry, nor are given in marriage:

36 Neither can they die any more: for they are equal unto the angels; and are the children of God, being the children of the resurrection.

37 Now that the dead are raised, even Moses shewed at the bush, when he calleth the Lord the God of Abraham, and the God of Isaac, and the God of Jacob.

38 For he is not a God of the dead, but of the living: for all live unto him.

39 Then certain of the scribes answering said, Master, thou hast well said.

40 And after that they durst not ask him any question at all.

MATTHEW 22: 34–40; MARK 12: 28–34; LUKE 10: 25–37

Matthew 22: 34–40

34 But when the Pharisees had heard that he had put the Sadducees to silence, they were gathered together.

35 Then one of them, which was a lawyer, asked him a question, tempting him, and saying,

36 Master, which is the great commandment in the law?

37 Jesus said unto him, Thou shalt love the Lord thy God with all thy heart, and with all thy soul, and with all thy mind.

38 This is the first and great commandment.

39 And the second is like unto it, Thou shalt love thy neighbour as thyself.

40 On these two commandments hang all the law and the prophets.

do not mention that, when they saw that the holy fathers earnestly aspired to the heavenly life, and that the covenant which God had made with them was spiritual and eternal, they must have been worse than stupid who remained blind in the midst of such clear light. But, first, this was the just reward of those who had split the Church of God into sects; and, secondly, in this manner the Lord avenged the wicked contempt of His doctrine.

29. You err, not knowing the Scriptures

Though Christ addresses the Sadducees, yet this reproof applies generally to all inventors of false doctrines. For, since God makes known His will clearly in the Scriptures, the want of acquaintance with them is the source and cause of all errors. But this is no ordinary consolation to the godly, that they will be safe from the danger of erring, so long as they humbly, modestly, and submissively inquire from the Scriptures what is right and true. As to the power of God being connected by Christ with the word, it refers to the present occasion. For, since the resurrection far exceeds the capacity of the human senses, it will be incredible to us, till our minds rise to the contemplation of the boundless power of God, by which, as Paul tells us, "he is able to subdue all things to himself" (Philippians 3: 21).

MATTHEW 22: 34–40; MARK 12: 28–34; LUKE 10: 25–37

30. And Jesus answering said

Christ might have stated simply, that the word **neighbor** extends indiscriminately to every man, because the whole human race is united by a sacred bond of fellowship. And, indeed, the Lord employed this word in the Law, for no other reason than to draw us sweetly to mutual kindness. The commandment would have run more clearly thus: **Love every man as thyself**.

But as men are blinded by their pride, so that every man is satisfied with himself, scarcely deigns to admit others to an equal rank, and withholds from them the duties he owes them, the Lord purposely declares that all are neighbors that the very relationship may produce mutual love. To make any person our neighbor, therefore, it is enough that he be, a man; for it is not in our power to blot out our common nature.

But Christ intended to draw the reply from the Pharisee, that he might condemn himself. For in consequence of the authoritative decision being generally received among them, that no man is our neighbor unless he is our friend, if Christ had put a direct question to him, he would never have made an explicit acknowledgment, that under the word neighbor all men are included, which the comparison brought forward forces him to confess. The general truth

MATTHEW 22: 34–40; MARK 12: 28–34; LUKE 10: 25–37

Matthew 22: 34–40

34. They were gathered together – they came together with one accord, or, for the same purpose; i.e. of ensnaring him in his discourse, as the Sadducees had done, Matthew 22: 23.

35. A lawyer – a teacher of the law. What is called lawyer, in the common translation, conveys a wrong idea to most readers. These teachers of the law were the same as the scribes, or what Dr. Wotton calls letter-men, whom he supposes to be the same as the Karaites, a sect of the Jews who rejected all the traditions of the elders, and admitted nothing but the written word. These are allowed to have kept more closely to the spiritual meaning of the law and prophets than the Pharisees did; and hence the question proposed by the lawyer, (Mark, 12: 28, calls him one of the scribes), or Karaite, was of a more spiritual or refined nature than any of the preceding.

36. Which is the great commandment – We see here three kinds of enemies and false accusers of Christ and his disciples; and three sorts of accusations brought against them.

1. The Herodians, or politicians and courtiers, who form their questions and accusations on the rights of the prince, and matters of state, Matthew 22: 16.

2. The Sadducees, or libertines, who found theirs upon matters of religion, and articles of faith, which they did not credit, Matthew 22: 23.

3. The Pharisees, lawyers, scribes, or Karaites, hypocritical pretenders to devotion, who found theirs on that vital and practical godliness (the love of God and man) of which they wished themselves to be thought the sole proprietors, Matthew 22: 36.

37. Thou shalt love the Lord – This is a subject of the greatest importance, and should be well understood, as our Lord shows that the whole of true religion is comprised in thus loving God and our neighbor.

One thing will be evident to all those who know what love means, that they throw much light upon the subject, and manifest it in a variety of striking points of view. The ancient author of a MS. Lexicon in the late French king's library, has the following definition: "A pleasing surrender of friendship to a friend: an identity or sameness of soul." A sovereign preference given to one above all others, present or absent: a concentration of all the thoughts and desires in a single object, which a man prefers to all others. Apply this definition to the love which God requires of his creatures, and you will have the most correct view of the subject. Hence it appears that, by this love, the soul eagerly cleaves to, affectionately admires, and constantly rests in God, supremely pleased and satisfied with him as its portion: that it acts from him, as its author; for him, as its master; and to him, as its end. That, by it, all the powers and faculties of the mind are concentrated in the Lord of the universe. That, by it, the whole man is willingly surrendered to the Most High: and that, through it, an identity, or sameness of spirit with the Lord is acquired – the man being made a partaker of the Divine nature, having the mind in him which was in Christ, and thus dwelling in God, and God in him.

But what is implied in loving God with all the heart, soul, mind, strength, etc., and when may a man be said to do this?

1. He loves God with all his heart, who loves nothing in comparison of him, and nothing but in reference to him: who is ready to give up, do, or suffer any thing in order to please and glorify him: who has in his heart neither love nor hatred, hope nor fear, inclination, nor aversion, desire, nor delight, but as they relate to God, and are regulated by him.

2. He loves God with all his soul, or rather, with all his life, who is ready to give up life for his sake – to endure all sorts of torments, and to be deprived of all kinds of comforts, rather than dishonor God: who employs life with all its comforts, and conveniences, to glorify God in, by, and through all: to whom life and death are nothing, but as they come from and lead to God, From this Divine principle sprang the blood of the martyrs, which became the seed

Mark 12: 28–34

28 And one of the scribes came, and having heard them reasoning together, and perceiving that he had answered them well, asked him, Which is the first commandment of all?

29 And Jesus answered him, The first of all the commandments is, Hear, O Israel; The Lord our God is one Lord:

30 And thou shalt love the Lord thy God with all thy heart, and with all thy soul, and with all thy mind, and with all thy strength: this is the first commandment.

31 And the second is like, namely this, Thou shalt love thy neighbour as thyself. There is none other commandment greater than these.

32 And the scribe said unto him, Well, Master, thou hast said the truth: for there is one God; and there is none other but he:

33 And to love him with all the heart, and with all the understanding, and with all the soul, and with all the strength, and to love his neighbour as himself, is more than all whole burnt offerings and sacrifices.

34 And when Jesus saw that he answered discreetly, he said unto him, Thou art not far from the kingdom of God. And no man after that durst ask him any question.

Luke 10: 25–37

25 And, behold, a certain lawyer stood up, and tempted him, saying, Master, what shall I do to inherit eternal life?

26 He said unto him, What is written in the law? how readest thou?

27 And he answering said, Thou shalt love the Lord thy God with all thy heart, and with all thy soul, and with all thy strength, and with all thy mind; and thy neighbour as thyself.

28 And he said unto him, Thou hast answered right: this do, and thou shalt live.

29 But he, willing to justify himself, said unto Jesus, And who is my neighbour?

30 And Jesus answering said, A certain man went down from Jerusalem to Jericho, and fell among thieves, which stripped him of his raiment, and wounded him, and departed, leaving him half dead.

conveyed is, that the greatest stranger is our neighbor, because God has bound all men together, for the purpose of assisting each other. He glances briefly, however, at the Jews, and especially at the priests; because, while they boasted of being the children of the same Father, and of being separated by the privilege of adoption from the rest of the nations, so as to be God's sacred heritage, yet, with barbarous and unfeeling contempt, they despised each other, as if no relationship had subsisted between them. For there is no doubt that Christ describes the cruel neglect of brotherly kindness, with which they knew that they were chargeable. But here, as I have said, the chief design is to show that the neighborhood, which lays us under obligation to mutual offices of kindness, is not confined to friends or relatives, but extends to the whole human race.

To prove this, Christ compares a **Samaritan** to a **priest** and a **Levite**. It is well known what deadly hatred the Jews bore to the Samaritans, so that, notwithstanding their living close beside them, they were always at the greatest variance. Christ now says, that a Jew, an inhabitant of Jericho, on his journey from Jerusalem, having been wounded by robbers, received no assistance either from a Levite or from a priest, both of whom met with him lying on the road, and half-dead, but that a Samaritan showed him great kindness, and then asks, Which of these three was neighbor to the Jew? This subtle doctor could not escape from preferring the Samaritan to the other two. For here, as in a mirror, we behold that common relationship of men, which the scribes endeavored to blot out by their wicked sophistry; and the compassion, which an enemy showed to a Jew, demonstrates that the guidance and teaching of nature are sufficient to show that man was created for the sake of man. Hence it is inferred that there is a mutual obligation between all men.

The allegory which is here contrived by the advocates of free will is too absurd to deserve refutation. According to them, under the figure of a wounded man is described the condition of Adam after the fall; from which they infer that the power of acting well was not wholly extinguished in him; because he is said to be only **half-dead**. As if it had been the design of Christ, in this passage, to speak of the corruption of human nature, and to inquire whether the wound which Satan inflicted on Adam were deadly or curable; nay, as if he had not plainly, and without a figure, declared in another passage, that all are **dead**, but those whom he quickens by *his voice* (John 5: 25).

As little plausibility belongs to another allegory, which, however, has been so highly satisfactory, that it has been admitted by almost universal consent, as if it had been a revelation from heaven. This Samaritan they imagine to be Christ, because he is our guardian; and they tell us that

of the Church. They overcame through the blood of the Lamb, and loved not their lives unto the death. See Revelation 12: 11.

3. He loves God with all his strength (Mark 12: 30; Luke 10: 27) who exerts all the powers of his body and soul in the service of God: who, for the glory of his Maker, spares neither labor nor cost – who sacrifices his time, body, health, ease, for the honor of God his Divine Master: who employs in his service all his goods, his talents, his power, credit, authority, and influence.

4. He loves God with all his mind (intellect) who applies himself only to know God, and his holy will: who receives with submission, gratitude, and pleasure, the sacred truths which God has revealed to man: who studies no art nor science but as far as it is necessary for the service of God, and uses it at all times to promote his glory – who forms no projects nor designs but in reference to God and the interests of mankind: who banishes from his understanding and memory every useless, foolish, and dangerous thought, together with every idea which has any tendency to defile his soul, or turn it for a moment from the center of eternal repose. In a word, he who sees God in all things – thinks of him at all times – having his mind continually fixed upon God, acknowledging him in all his ways – who begins, continues, and ends all his thoughts, words, and works, to the glory of his name: this is the person who loves God with all his heart, life, strength, and intellect. He is crucified to the world, and the world to him: he lives, yet not he, but Christ lives in him. He beholds as in a glass the glory of the Lord, and is changed into the same image from glory to glory. Simply and constantly looking unto Jesus, the author and perfecter of his faith, he receives continual supplies of enlightening and sanctifying grace, and is thus fitted for every good word and work. O glorious state! far, far, beyond this description! which comprises an ineffable communion between the ever-blessed Trinity and the soul of man!

38. This is the first and great commandment – It is so,

1. In its antiquity, being as old as the world, and engraven originally on our very nature.

2. In dignity; as directly and immediately proceeding front and referring to God.

3. In excellence; being the commandment of the new covenant, and the very spirit of the Divine adoption.

4. In justice; because it alone renders to God his due, prefers him before all things, and secures to him his proper rank in relation to them.

5. In sufficiency; being in itself capable of making men holy in this life, and happy in the other.

6. In fruitfulness; because it is the root of all commandments, and the fulfilling of the law.

7. In virtue and efficacy; because by this alone God reigns in the heart of man, and man is united to God.

8. In extent; leaving nothing to the creature, which it does not refer to the Creator.

9. In necessity; being absolutely indispensable.

10. In duration; being ever to be continued on earth, and never to be discontinued in heaven.

39. Thou shalt love thy neighbor – The love of our neighbor springs from the love of God as its source; is found in the love of God as its principle, pattern, and end; and the love of God is found in the love of our neighbor, as its effect, representation, and infallible mark. This love of our neighbor is a love of equity, charity, succor, and benevolence. We owe to our neighbor what we have a right to expect from him – "Do unto all men as ye would they should do unto you," is a positive command of our blessed Savior. By this rule, therefore, we should speak, think, and write, concerning every soul of man: put the best construction upon all the words and actions of our neighbor that they can possibly bear. By this rule we are taught to bear with, love, and forgive him; to rejoice in his felicity, mourn in his adversity, desire and delight in his prosperity, and promote it to the utmost of our power: instruct his ignorance, help him in his weakness, and risk even our life for his sake, and for the pub-

31 And by chance there came down a certain priest that way: and when he saw him, he passed by on the other side.

32 And likewise a Levite, when he was at the place, came and looked on him, and passed by on the other side.

33 But a certain Samaritan, as he journeyed, came where he was: and when he saw him, he had compassion on him,

34 And went to him, and bound up his wounds, pouring in oil and wine, and set him on his own beast, and brought him to an inn, and took care of him.

35 And on the morrow when he departed, he took out two pence, and gave them to the host, and said unto him, Take care of him; and whatsoever thou spendest more, when I come again, I will repay thee.

36 Which now of these three, thinkest thou, was neighbour unto him that fell among the thieves?

37 And he said, He that shewed mercy on him. Then said Jesus unto him, Go, and do thou likewise.

MATTHEW 22: 41–46; MARK 12: 35–37; LUKE 20: 41–44

Matthew 22: 41–46

41 While the Pharisees were gathered together, Jesus asked them,

42 Saying, What think ye of Christ? whose son is he? They say unto him, The Son of David.

43 He saith unto them, How then doth David in spirit call him Lord, saying,

44 The LORD said unto my Lord, Sit thou on my right hand, till I make thine enemies thy footstool?

45 If David then call him Lord, how is he his son?

46 And no man was able to answer him a word, neither durst any man from that day forth ask him any more questions.

Mark 12: 35–37

35 And Jesus answered and said, while he taught in the temple, How say the scribes that Christ is the Son of David?

36 For David himself said by the Holy Ghost, The Lord said to my Lord, Sit thou

wine was poured, along with **oil**, into the wound, because Christ cures us by repentance and by a promise of grace. They have contrived a third subtlety, that Christ does not immediately restore health, but sends us to the Church, as **an innkeeper**, to be gradually cured. I acknowledge that I have no liking for any of these interpretations; but we ought to have a deeper reverence for Scripture than to reckon ourselves at liberty to disguise its natural meaning. And, indeed, any one may see that the curiosity of certain men has led them to contrive these speculations, contrary to the intention of Christ.

40. On these two commandments

I now return to Matthew, where Christ says that **all the Law and the prophets depend on these two commandments**; not that he intends to limit to them all the doctrine of Scripture, but because all that is anywhere taught as to the manner of living a holy and righteous life must be referred to these two leading points. For Christ does not treat generally of what **the Law and the Prophets** contain, but, in drawing up his reply, states that nothing else is required in the Law and the prophets than that every man should **love God** and his **neighbors**; as if he had said, that the sum of a holy and upright life consists in the worship of God and in charity to men, as Paul states that charity is "the fulfilling of the law" (Romans 13: 10).

MATTHEW 22: 41–46; MARK 12: 35–37; LUKE 20: 41–44

43. How then does David by the Spirit call him Lord

The assertion made by Christ, that David spoke by the Spirit, is emphatic; for he contrasts the prediction of a future event with the testimony of a present event. By this phrase he anticipates the sophistry by which the Jews of the present day attempt to escape. They allege that this prediction celebrates the reign of David, as if, representing God to be the Author of his reign, David would rise above the mad attempts of his enemies, and affirmed that they would gain nothing by opposing the will of God. That the scribes might not shelter themselves under such an objection, Christ began with stating that the psalm was not composed in reference to the person of David, but was dictated by the prophetic Spirit to describe the future reign of Christ; as it may easily be learned even from the passage itself, that what we read there does not apply either to David, or to any other earthly king; for there David introduces a king clothed with a new priesthood, by which the ancient shadows of the Law must be abolished (Psalm 110: 4).

lic good. In a word, we must do every thing in our power, through all the possible varieties of circumstances, for our neighbors, which we would wish them to do for us, were our situations reversed.

This is the religion of Jesus! How happy would Society be, were these two plain, rational precepts properly observed! Love ME, and love thy FELLOWS! Be unutterably happy in me, and be in perfect peace, unanimity, and love, among yourselves. Great fountain and dispenser of love! fill thy creation with this sacred principle, for his sake who died for the salvation of mankind!

On the nature of self-love, see Matthew 19: 19.

40. On these two – hang all the law and the prophets – They are like the first and last links of a chain, all the intermediate ones depend on them. True religion begins and ends in love to God and man. These are the two grand links that unite God to man, man to his fellows, and men again to God.

Love is the fulfilling of the law, says St. Paul, Romans 13: 10; for he who has the love of God in him delights to obey the Divine precepts, and to do all manner of kindness to men for God's sake.

MATTHEW 22: 41–46; MARK 12: 35–37; LUKE 20: 41–44

Matthew 22: 41–46

41. While the Pharisees were gathered together – Jesus asks a question in his turn, utterly to confound them, and to show the people that the source of all the captious questions of his opponents was their ignorance of the prophecies relative to the Messiah.

42. What think ye of Christ? – Or, What are your thoughts concerning THE CHRIST – the Messiah; for to this title the emphatic article should always be added.

Whose son is he? – From what family is he to spring?

They say unto him, The son of David – This was a thing well known among the Jews, and

universally acknowledged, see John 7: 42; and is a most powerful proof against them that the Messiah is come. Their families are now so perfectly confounded that they cannot trace back any of their genealogies with any degree of certainty: nor have they been capable of ascertaining the different families of their tribes for more than sixteen hundred years. Why, then, should the spirit of prophecy assert so often, and in such express terms, that Jesus was to come from the family of David; if he should only make his appearance when the public registers were all demolished, and it would be impossible to ascertain the family? Is it not evident that God designed that the Messiah should come at a time when the public genealogies might be inspected, to prove that it was he who was prophesied of, and that no other was to be expected? The evangelists, Matthew and Luke, were so fully convinced of the conclusiveness of this proof that they had recourse to the public registers; and thus proved to the Jews, from their own records, that Jesus was born of the family mentioned by the prophets. Nor do we find that a scribe, Pharisee, or any other, ever attempted to invalidate this proof, though it would have essentially subserved their cause, could they have done it. But as this has not been done, we may fairly conclude it was impossible to do it.

43. How then doth David in spirit (or by the Spirit – by the inspiration of the Spirit of God) **call him Lord?** saying,

44. The Lord said unto my Lord, Sit thou on my right hand – Take the place of the greatest eminence and authority. Till I make thine enemies thy footstool – till I subdue both Jews and Gentiles under thee, and cause them to acknowledge thee as their sovereign and Lord. This quotation is taken from Psalm 110: 1; and, from it, these two points are clear:

1. That David wrote it by the inspiration of God; and

2. That it is a prophetic declaration of the Messiah.

45. How is he his son? – As the Jews did not attempt to deny the conclusion of our Lord's

on my right hand, till I make thine enemies thy footstool.

37 David therefore himself calleth him Lord; and whence is he then his son? And the common people heard him gladly.

Luke 20: 41–44

41 And he said unto them, How say they that Christ is David's son?

42 And David himself saith in the book of Psalms, The LORD said unto my Lord, Sit thou on my right hand,

43 Till I make thine enemies thy footstool.

44 David therefore calleth him Lord, how is he then his son?

MATTHEW 23: 1–12; MARK 12: 38–39; LUKE 11: 43,45–46; 20: 45–46

Matthew 23: 1–12

1 Then spake Jesus to the multitude, and to his disciples,

2 Saying, The scribes and the Pharisees sit in Moses' seat:

3 All therefore whatsoever they bid you observe, that observe and do; but do not ye after their works: for they say, and do not.

4 For they bind heavy burdens and grievous to be borne, and lay them on men's shoulders; but they themselves will not move them with one of their fingers.

5 But all their works they do for to be seen of men: they make broad their phylacteries, and enlarge the borders of their garments,

6 And love the uppermost rooms at feasts, and the chief seats in the synagogues,

7 And greetings in the markets, and to be called of men, Rabbi, Rabbi.

8 But be not ye called Rabbi: for one is your Master, even Christ; and all ye are brethren.

9 And call no man your father upon the earth: for one is your Father, which is in heaven.

10 Neither be ye called masters: for one is your Master, even Christ.

11 But he that is greatest among you shall be your servant.

12 And whosoever shall exalt himself shall be abased; and he that shall humble himself shall be exalted.

MATTHEW 23: 1–12; MARK 12: 38–39; LUKE 11: 43,45–46; 20: 45–46

Matthew 23: 1. Then Jesus spoke to the multitudes

This warning was highly useful, that, amidst contentions and the noise of combats, amidst the trouble and confusion of public affairs, amidst the destruction of proper and lawful order, the authority of the word of God might remain entire. The design of Christ was, that the people might not, in consequence of being offended at the vices of **the scribes**, throw away reverence for the Law. For we know how prone the minds of men are to entertain dislike of the Law; and more especially when the life of their pastors is dissolute, and does not correspond to their words, almost all grow wanton through their example, as if they had received permission to sin with impunity. The same thing happens – and something worse – when contentions arise; for the greater part of men, having thrown off the yoke, give utterance to their wicked desires, and break out into extreme contempt.

At that time **the scribes** burned with covetousness and swelled with ambition; their extortions were notorious; their cruelty was formidable; and such was their corruption of manners, that one would think they had conspired for the destruction of the Law. Besides, they had perverted by their false opinions the pure and natural meaning of the Law, so that Christ was constrained to enter into a sharp conflict with them; because their amazing rage hurried them on to extinguish the light of truth. So then, because there was danger that many persons, partly on account of such abuses, and partly on account of the din of controversies, would come to despise all religion, Christ seasonably meets them, and declares that it would be unreasonable if, on account of the vices of men, true religion were to perish, or reverence for the Law to be in any degree diminished. As **the scribes** were obstinate and inveterate enemies, and as they held the Church oppressed through their tyranny, Christ was compelled to expose their wickedness; for if good and simple men had not been withdrawn from bondage to them, the door would have been shut against the Gospel. There was also another reason; for the common people think themselves at liberty to do whatever they see done by their rulers, whose corrupt manners they form into a law.

But that no man might put a different interpretation on what he was about to say, he begins by stating, that whatever sort of men the teachers were it was altogether unreasonable, either that on account of their filth the word of God should receive any stain, or that on account of their wicked examples men should hold themselves at liberty to commit sin. And this wisdom ought to be carefully observed; for many persons, having no other object in view than to bring

question, which was, the Messiah is not only the son of David according to the flesh, but he is the Lord of David according to his Divine nature, then it is evident they could not. Indeed, there was no other way of invalidating the argument, but by denying that the prophecy in question related to Christ: but it seems the prophecy was so fully and so generally understood to belong to the Messiah that they did not attempt to do this; for it is immediately added, No man was able to answer him a word – they were completely nonplussed and confounded.

46. Neither durst any – ask him any more questions – "Thus," says Dr. Wotton, "our Lord put the four great sects of the Jews to silence, in one day, successively. The Herodians and Pharisees wanted to know whether they might lawfully pay tribute to Caesar or not. The Sadducees were inquisitive to know whose wife the woman should be of the seven brethren, in the resurrection, who had her to wife. Then comes the scribe, (or karaite), who owned no authority beyond or besides the written law, and asked which was the great commandment in the law. This lawyer deserves to be mentioned here, because he not only acquiesced in, but commended, what our Lord had said in answer to his question."

The Pharisees and Herodians were defeated, Matthew 22: 15–22. The Sadducees were confounded, Matthew 22: 29–33. The lawyers or karaites nonplussed, Matthew 22: 37–40. And the Pharisees, etc., finally routed, Matthew 22: 41–46. Thus did the wisdom of God triumph over the cunning of men.

From this time, we do not find that our Lord was any more troubled with their captious questions: their whole stock, it appears, was expended, and now they coolly deliberate on the most effectual way to get him murdered. He that resists the truth of God is capable of effecting the worst purpose of Satan.

The very important subjects of this chapter have been so amply discussed in the notes, and applied so particularly to their spiritual uses, that it does not appear necessary to add any thing by way of practical improvement.

The explanation of the great command of the law is particularly recommended to the reader's notice.

MATTHEW 23: 1–12; MARK 12: 38–39; LUKE 11: 43,45–46; 20: 45–46

Matthew 23: 1–12

2. The scribes and the Pharisees sit in Moses' seat. – They sat there formerly by Divine appointment: they sit there now by Divine permission. What our Lord says here refers to their expounding the Scriptures, for it was the custom of the Jewish doctors to sit while they expounded the law and prophets, (Matthew 5: 1; Luke 4: 20–22), and to stand up when they read them.

By the seat of Moses, we are to understand authority to teach the law. Moses was the great teacher of the Jewish people; and the scribes, etc., are here represented as his successors.

3. All therefore whatsoever – That is, all those things which they read out of the law and prophets, and all things which they teach consistently with them. This must be our Lord's meaning: he could not have desired them to do every thing, without restriction, which the Jewish doctors taught; because himself warns his disciples against their false teaching, and testifies that they had made the word of God of none effect by their traditions. See Matthew 15: 6, etc. Besides, as our Lord speaks here in the past tense – whatsoever they HAVE commanded, he may refer to the teaching of a former period, when they taught the way of God in truth, or were much less corrupted than they were now.

4. They bind heavy burdens – They are now so corrupt that they have added to the ceremonies of the law others of their own invention, which are not only burdensome and oppressive, but have neither reason, expediency, nor revelation, to countenance them. In a word, like all their successors in spirit to the present day, they were severe to others, but very indulgent to themselves.

5. All their works they do for to be seen of

Mark 12: 38–39

38 And he said unto them in his doctrine, Beware of the scribes, which love to go in long clothing, and love salutations in the marketplaces,

39 And the chief seats in the synagogues, and the uppermost rooms at feasts:

Luke 11: 43,45–46

43 Woe unto you, Pharisees! for ye love the uppermost seats in the synagogues, and greetings in the markets.

45 Then answered one of the lawyers, and said unto him, Master, thus saying thou reproachest us also.

46 And he said, Woe unto you also, ye lawyers! for ye lade men with burdens grievous to be borne, and ye yourselves touch not the burdens with one of your fingers.

Luke 20: 45–46

45 Then in the audience of all the people he said unto his disciples,

46 Beware of the scribes, which desire to walk in long robes, and love greetings in the markets, and the highest seats in the synagogues, and the chief rooms at feasts;

MATTHEW 23: 13–15; MARK 12: 40; LUKE 11: 52; 20: 47

Matthew 23: 13–15

13 But woe unto you, scribes and Pharisees, hypocrites! for ye shut up the kingdom of heaven against men: for ye neither go in yourselves, neither suffer ye them that are entering to go in.

14 Woe unto you, scribes and Pharisees, hypocrites! for ye devour widows' houses, and for a pretence make long prayer: therefore ye shall receive the greater damnation.

15 Woe unto you, scribes and Pharisees, hypocrites! for ye compass sea and land to make one proselyte, and when he is made, ye make him twofold more the child of hell than yourselves.

Mark 12: 40

40 Which devour widows' houses, and for a pretence make long prayers: these shall receive greater damnation.

hatred and detestation on the wicked and ungodly, mix and confound every thing through their inconsiderate zeal. All discipline is despised, and shame is trampled under foot; in short, there remains no respect for what is honorable, and, what is more, many are emboldened by it, and intentionally blazon the sins of priests, that they may have a pretext for sinning with less restraint. But in attacking the scribes, Christ proceeds in such a manner, that he first vindicates the Law of God from contempt. We must attend to this caution also if we desire that our reproofs should be of any service. But, on the other hand, we ought to observe, that no dread of giving offense prevented Christ from exposing ungodly teachers as they deserved; only he preserved such moderation, that the doctrine of God might not come to be despised on account of the wickedness of men.

MATTHEW 23: 13–15; MARK 12: 40; LUKE 11: 52; 20: 47

He breaks out into still stronger language of condemnation, and he does so not so much on their account, as for the purpose of withdrawing the common people and simple-minded men from their sect. For though we see frequently in Scripture the judgment of God pronounced against the reprobate, so as to render them the more inexcusable, yet in their person the children of God receive a useful warning, not to involve themselves in the snares of the same crimes, but to guard against falling into similar destruction. Certainly, when the scribes, after overturning the worship of God and corrupting the doctrine of godliness, would endure no correction, and with desperate madness, to their own destruction and that of the whole nation, opposed the redemption which was offered to them, it was proper that they should be held up to the hatred and detestation of all. And yet Christ did not so much consider what they deserved, as what would be useful to the uneducated and ignorant; for he intended, towards the close of his life, to leave a solemn testimony, that no man might, except knowingly and willingly, be deceived by persons so base and wicked.

We know how powerfully a foolish reverence for false teachers hinders simple people from getting clear of their erroneous views. The Jews were at that time deeply imbued with false doctrine, and had even imbibed from their earliest years many superstitions. While it was hard and difficult in itself to bring them back to the right path, the chief obstacle lay in the foolish opinion which they had formed about the false teachers, whom they regarded as the lawful prelates of the Church, the rulers of divine worship, and the pillars of religion. Besides, they were so strongly fascinated, that they could scarcely be drawn away from those teach-

men – In pointing out the corruptions of these men, our Lord gives us the distinguishing characteristics of all false teachers, whether Jewish or Christian.

1. They live not according to the truths they preach. They say, and do not, Matthew 23: 3.

2. They are severe to others, point out the narrowest road to heaven, and walk in the broad road themselves. They bind on burdens, etc., Matthew 23: 4.

3. They affect to appear righteous, and are strict observers of certain rites, etc., while destitute of the power of godliness. They make broad their phylacteries, etc., Matthew 23: 5.

4. They love worldly entertainments, go to feast wherever they are asked, and seek Church preferments. They love the chief places at feasts, and chief seats in the synagogues, Matthew 23: 6.

5. They love and seek public respect and high titles, salutations in the market-place, (for they are seldom in their studies), and to be called of men rabbi – eminent teacher, though they have no title to it, either from the excellence or fruit of their teaching. When these marks are found in a man who professes to be a minister of Christ, charity itself will assert he is a thief and a robber – he has climbed over the wall of the sheepfold, or broken it down in order to get in.

Phylacteries – These were small slips of parchment or vellum, on which certain portions of the law were written. The Jews tied these about their foreheads and arms, for three different purposes.

1. To put them in mind of those precepts which they should constantly observe.

2. To procure them reverence and respect in the sight of the heathen. And

3. To act as amulets or charms to drive away evil spirits.

An original phylactery lies now before me. It is a piece of fine vellum, about eighteen inches long, and an inch and quarter broad. It is divided into four unequal compartments: in the first is written, in a very fair character, with many apices, after the mode of the German Jews, the first ten verses of Ex. 13; in the second compartment is written, from the eleventh to the sixteenth verse of the same chapter, inclusive in the third, from fourth to the ninth verse, inclusive, of Deut. 6., beginning with, Hear, O Israel, etc.; in the fourth, from the thirteenth to the twenty-first verse, inclusive, of Deut. 11.

These passages seem to be chosen in vindication of the use of the phylactery itself, as the reader will see on consulting them: Bind them for a SIGN upon thy HAND – and for FRONTLETS between thy EYES – write them upon the POSTS of thy HOUSE, and upon thy GATES; all which commands the Jews took in the most literal sense.

Even the phylactery became an important appendage to a Pharisee's character, insomuch that some of them wore them very broad, either that they might have the more written on them, or that, the characters being larger, they might be the more visible, and that they might hereby acquire greater esteem among the common people, as being more than ordinarily religious. For the same reason, they wore the fringes of their garments of an unusual length. Moses had commanded (Numbers 15: 38, 39) the children of Israel to put fringes to the borders of their garments, that, when they looked upon even these distinct threads, they might remember, not only the law in general, but also the very minutiae, or smaller parts of all the precepts, rites, and ceremonies, belonging to it. As these hypocrites were destitute of all the life and power of religion within, they endeavored to supply its place by phylacteries and fringes without. See the note on Exodus 13: 9.

7. To be called of men, Rabbi, Rabbi – i.e. My teacher! my teacher!

There are three words used among the Jews as titles of dignity, which they apply to their doctors – Rabh, Rabbi, and Rabban; each of these terms has its particular meaning: rabban implies much more than rabbi, and rabbi much more than rabh.

They may be considered as three degrees of comparison: rabh great, rabbi greater, and rabban greatest. These rabbins were looked up to as infallible oracles in religious matters, and

Luke 11: 52

52 Woe unto you, lawyers! for ye have taken away the key of knowledge: ye entered not in yourselves, and them that were entering in ye hindered.

Luke 20: 47

47 Which devour widows' houses, and for a shew make long prayers: the same shall receive greater damnation.

MATTHEW 23: 16–22

16 Woe unto you, ye blind guides, which say, Whosoever shall swear by the temple, it is nothing; but whosoever shall swear by the gold of the temple, he is a debtor!

17 Ye fools and blind: for whether is greater, the gold, or the temple that sanctifieth the gold?

18 And, Whosoever shall swear by the altar, it is nothing; but whosoever sweareth by the gift that is upon it, he is guilty.

19 Ye fools and blind: for whether is greater, the gift, or the altar that sanctifieth the gift?

20 Whoso therefore shall swear by the altar, sweareth by it, and by all things thereon.

21 And whoso shall swear by the temple, sweareth by it, and by him that dwelleth therein.

22 And he that shall swear by heaven, sweareth by the throne of God, and by him that sitteth thereon.

MATTHEW 23: 23–28; LUKE 11: 42,44

Matthew 23: 23–28

23 Woe unto you, scribes and Pharisees, hypocrites! for ye pay tithe of mint and anise and cummin, and have omitted the weightier matters of the law, judgment, mercy, and faith: these ought ye to have done, and not to leave the other undone.

24 Ye blind guides, which strain at a gnat, and swallow a camel.

25 Woe unto you, scribes and Pharisees, hypocrites! for ye make clean the outside of the cup and of the platter, but within they are full of extortion and excess.

26 Thou blind Pharisee, cleanse first

ers but by violent fear. It is not therefore for the purpose of cursing the scribes that Christ pronounces against them the dreadful vengeance of God, but to withdraw others from their impostures. In like manner, we are compelled at the present day to thunder loudly against the Popish clergy, for no other reason than that those who are tractable, and not quite desperate, may direct their minds to their salvation, and, moved by the judgment of God, may break the deadly snares of superstitions by which they are held captive.

MATTHEW 23: 16–22

16. Woe to you, blind guides

As ambition is almost always connected with hypocrisy, so the superstitions of the people are usually encouraged by the covetousness and rapacity of pastors. The world has, indeed, a natural propensity to errors, and even draws down upon itself, as if on purpose, every kind of deceit and imposture; but improper modes of worship come to gain a footing only when they are confirmed by the rulers themselves. And it generally happens, that those who possess authority not only, by their connivance, fawn upon errors, because they perceive that they are a source of gain to them, but even assist in fanning the flame.

MATTHEW 23: 23–28; LUKE 11: 42,44

Christ charges the scribes with a fault which is found in all hypocrites, that they are exceedingly diligent and careful in small matters, but disregard **the principal points of the Law.** This disease has prevailed in almost all ages, and among all nations; so that men have, in most cases, endeavored to please God by observing with exactness some trivial matters. Finding that they cannot entirely release themselves from all obedience to God, they have recourse to this second remedy of expiating any heinous offenses by satisfactions which are of no value. Thus we see that the Papists, while they transgress the chief commandments of God, are extremely zealous in the performance of trifling ceremonies. Hypocrisy of the same kind is now reproved by God in the scribes, who, while they were very diligent and careful in **paying tithes,** cared little about **the principal points of the Law.**

To expose more fully to ridicule their offensive ostentation, he does not say generally that they **paid tithes,** but **tithes of mint, and anise, and** (as Luke has it) of **every kind of herb,** so as to make a display of extraordinary zeal for piety at the least possible expense.

But as Christ makes the chief righteousness of the Law to consist in **mercy, judgment, and faith,** we must first, see what he means by these words; and, secondly why he left out the commandments of the first table, which strictly

usurped not only the place of the law, but of God himself.

8. But be not ye called Rabbi – As our Lord probably spoke in Hebrew, the latter word rabbi, in this verse, must have been in the plural; but as the contracted form of the plural sounds almost exactly like the singular, the Greek writer would naturally express them both in the same letters.

None of the prophets had ever received this title, nor any of the Jewish doctors before the time of Hillel and Shammai, which was about the time of our Lord; and, as disputes on several subjects had run high between these two schools, the people were of course divided; some acknowledging Hillel as rabbi, – infallible teacher, and others giving this title to Shammai. The Pharisees, who always sought the honor that comes from men, assumed the title, and got their followers to address them by it.

Ye are brethren – No one among you is higher than another, or can possibly have from me any jurisdiction over the rest. Ye are, in this respect, perfectly equal.

10. Neither be ye called masters – leaders. God is in all these respects jealous of his honor. To him alone it belongs to guide and lead his Church, as well as to govern and defend it. Jesus is the sole teacher of righteousness. It is he alone, (who is the word, light, and eternal truth), that can illuminate every created mind; and who, as Savior and Redeemer, speaks to every heart by his Spirit.

12. Whosoever shall exalt himself, etc. – The way to arrive at the highest degree of dignity, in the sight of God, is by being willing to become the servant of all. Nothing is more hateful in his sight than pride; to bring it into everlasting contempt, God was manifest in the flesh. He who was in the likeness of God took upon him the form of a servant, and was made in the likeness of man, and humbled himself unto death. After this, can God look upon any proud man without abasing him? Spiritual lordship and domination, ecclesiastical luxury, pomp, and pride, must be an abhorrence in the sight of that God who gave the above advices to his followers.

MATTHEW 23: 13–15; MARK 12: 40 LUKE 11: 52; 20: 47

Matthew 23: 13–15

13. Ye shut up the kingdom – As a key by opening a lock gives entrance into a house, etc., so knowledge of the sacred testimonies, manifested in expounding them to the people, may be said to open the way into the kingdom of heaven. But where men who are termed teachers are destitute of this knowledge themselves, they may be said to shut this kingdom; because they occupy the place of those who should teach, and thus prevent the people from acquiring heavenly knowledge.

The kingdom of heaven here means the Gospel of Christ; the Pharisees would not receive it themselves, and hindered the common people as far as they could.

15. Compass sea and land – A proverbial expression, similar to ours, You leave no stone unturned; intimating that they did all in their power to gain converts, not to God, but to their sect. These we may suppose were principally sought for among the Gentiles, for the bulk of the Jewish nation was already on the side of the Pharisees.

Proselyte – a stranger, or foreigner; one who is come from his own people and country, to sojourn with another.

The child of hell – A Hebraism for an excessively wicked person, such as might claim hell for his mother, and the devil for his father.

Dr. Lightfoot, and others, observe, that the proselytes were considered by the Jewish nation as the scabs of the Church, and hindered the coming of the Messiah; and Justin Martyr observes, that "the proselytes did not only disbelieve Christ's doctrine, but were abundantly more blasphemous against him than the Jews themselves, endeavoring to torment and cut off the Christians wherever they could; they being in this the instruments of the scribes and Pharisees."

that which is within the cup and platter, that the outside of them may be clean also.

27 Woe unto you, scribes and Pharisees, hypocrites! for ye are like unto whited sepulchers, which indeed appear beautiful outward, but are within full of dead men's bones, and of all uncleanness.

28 Even so ye also outwardly appear righteous unto men, but within ye are full of hypocrisy and iniquity.

Luke 11: 42,44

42 But woe unto you, Pharisees! for ye tithe mint and rue and all manner of herbs, and pass over judgment and the love of God: these ought ye to have done, and not to leave the other undone.

44 Woe unto you, scribes and Pharisees, hypocrites! for ye are as graves which appear not, and the men that walk over them are not aware of them.

MATTHEW 23: 29–39; LUKE 11: 47–51; 13: 34–35; 11: 53–54

Matthew 23: 29–39

29 Woe unto you, scribes and Pharisees, hypocrites! because ye build the tombs of the prophets, and garnish the sepulchers of the righteous,

30 And say, If we had been in the days of our fathers, we would not have been partakers with them in the blood of the prophets.

31 Wherefore ye be witnesses unto yourselves, that ye are the children of them which killed the prophets.

32 Fill ye up then the measure of your fathers.

33 Ye serpents, ye generation of vipers, how can ye escape the damnation of hell?

34 Wherefore, behold, I send unto you prophets, and wise men, and scribes: and some of them ye shall kill and crucify; and some of them shall ye scourge in your synagogues, and persecute them from city to city:

35 That upon you may come all the righteous blood shed upon the earth, from the blood of righteous Abel unto the blood of Zacharias son of Barachias, whom ye slew between the temple and the altar.

relate to the worship of God, as if godliness were of less value than the duties of charity.

Judgment is taken for **equity,** or **uprightness,** the effect of which is, that we render to every man what belongs to him, and that no man deceives or injures others.

Mercy proceeds farther, and leads a man to endeavor to assist his brethren with his property, to relieve the wretched by advice or by money, to protect those who are unjustly oppressed, and to employ liberally for the common good the means which God has put into his hands.

Faith is nothing else than strict integrity; not to attempt any thing by cunning, or malice, or deceit, but to cultivate towards all that mutual sincerity which every man wishes to be pursued towards himself. The sum of the Law, therefore, relates to charity.

MARK 12: 41–44; LUKE 21: 1–4

Mark 12: 43. Verily I say to you

This reply of Christ contains a highly useful doctrine that whatever men offer to God ought to be estimated not by its apparent value, but only by the feeling of the heart, and that the holy affection of him who according to his small means, offers to God the little that he has, is more worthy of esteem than that of him who offers a hundred times more **out of his abundance**.

In two ways this doctrine is useful, for the poor who appear not to have the power of doing good, are encouraged by our Lord not to hesitate to express their affection cheerfully out of their slender means; for if they consecrate themselves, their offering, which appears to be mean and worthless, will not be less valuable than if they had presented all the treasures of Crœsus.

On the other hand, those who possess greater abundance, and who have received from God larger communications, are reminded that it is not enough if in the amount of their beneficence they greatly surpass the poor and common people; because it is of less value in the sight of God that a rich man, out of a vast heap, should bestow a moderate sum, than that a poor man, by giving very little, should exhaust his store.

This widow must have been a person of no ordinary piety, who, rather than come empty into the presence of God, chose to part with **her own living**. And our Lord applauds this sincerity, because, forgetting herself, she wished to testify that she and all that she possessed belonged to God. In like manner, the chief sacrifice which God requires from us is self-denial. As to **the sacred offerings**, it is probable that they were not at that time applied properly, or to lawful purposes; but as the service of the Law was still in force, Christ does not reject them. And certainly

MATTHEW 23: 16–22

16. Whosoever shall swear by the gold – The covetous man, says one, still gives preference to the object of his lust; gold has still the first place in his heart. A man is to be suspected when he recommends those good works most from which he receives most advantage.

Is bound thereby, i.e. to fulfill his oath.

20. Whoso – shall swear by the altar – As an oath always supposes a person who witnesses it, and will punish perjury; therefore, whether they swore by the temple or the gold, (Matthew 23: 16), or by the altar or the gift laid on it, (Matthew 23: 18), the oath necessarily supposes the God of the temple, of the altar, and of the gifts, who witnessed the whole, and would, even in their exempt cases, punish the perjury.

21. Common swearing, and the shocking frequency and multiplication of oaths in civil cases, have destroyed all respect for an oath; so that men seldom feel themselves bound by it; and thus it is useless in many cases to require it as a confirmation, in order to end strife or ascertain truth.

MATTHEW 23: 23–28; LUKE 11: 42,44

Matthew 23: 23–28

23. Ye pay tithe of mint, etc. – They were remarkably scrupulous in the performance of all the rites and ceremonies of religion, but totally neglected the soul, spirit, and practice of godliness.

Judgment – Acting according to justice and equity towards all mankind. Mercy – to the distressed and miserable. And faith in God as the fountain of all righteousness, mercy, and truth. The scribes and Pharisees neither began nor ended their works in God, nor had they any respect unto his name in doing them. They did them to be seen of men, and they had their reward – human applause.

These ought ye to have done, etc. – Our Lord did not object to their paying tithe even of common pot-herbs – this did not affect the spirit of religion; but while they did this and

such like, to the utter neglect of justice, mercy, and faith, they showed that they had no religion, and knew nothing of its nature.

25. Ye make clean the outside – The Pharisees were exceedingly exact in observing all the washings and purifications prescribed by the law; but paid no attention to that inward purity which was typified by them. A man may appear clean without, who is unclean within; but outward purity will not avail in the sight of God, where inward holiness is wanting.

27. For ye are like – ye exactly resemble – the parallel is complete.

Whited sepulchers – White-washed tombs. As the law considered those unclean who had touched any thing belonging to the dead, the Jews took care to have their tombs whitewashed each year, that, being easily discovered, they might be consequently avoided.

28. Even so ye also – appear righteous unto men – But what will this appearance avail a man, when God sits in judgment upon his soul? Will the fair reputation which he had acquired among men, while his heart was the seat of unrighteousness, screen him from the stroke of that justice which impartially sends all impurity and unholiness into the pit of destruction? No. In the sin that he hath sinned, and in which he hath died, and according to that, shall he be judged and punished; and his profession of holiness only tends to sink him deeper into the lake which burns with unquenchable fire. Reader! see that thy heart be right with God.

MATTHEW 23: 29–39; LUKE 11: 47–51; 13: 34–35; 11: 53–54

Matthew 23: 29–39

29. Ye build the tombs of the prophets – It appears that, through respect to their memory, they often repaired, and sometimes beautified, the tombs of the prophets. M. De la Valle, in his Journey to the Holy Land, says, that when he visited the cave of Machpelah, he saw some Jews honoring a sepulcher, for which they have a great veneration, with light-

36 Verily I say unto you, All these things shall come upon this generation.

37 O Jerusalem, Jerusalem, thou that killest the prophets, and stonest them which are sent unto thee, how often would I have gathered thy children together, even as a hen gathereth her chickens under her wings, and ye would not!

38 Behold, your house is left unto you desolate.

39 For I say unto you, Ye shall not see me henceforth, till ye shall say, Blessed is he that cometh in the name of the Lord.

Luke 11: 47–51

47 Woe unto you! for ye build the sepulchers of the prophets, and your fathers killed them.

48 Truly ye bear witness that ye allow the deeds of your fathers: for they indeed killed them, and ye build their sepulchers.

49 Therefore also said the wisdom of God, I will send them prophets and apostles, and some of them they shall slay and persecute:

50 That the blood of all the prophets, which was shed from the foundation of the world, may be required of this generation;

51 From the blood of Abel unto the blood of Zacharias, which perished between the altar and the temple: verily I say unto you, It shall be required of this generation.

Luke 13: 34–35

34 O Jerusalem, Jerusalem, which killest the prophets, and stonest them that are sent unto thee; how often would I have gathered thy children together, as a hen doth gather her brood under her wings, and ye would not!

35 Behold, your house is left unto you desolate: and verily I say unto you, Ye shall not see me, until the time come when ye shall say, Blessed is he that cometh in the name of the Lord.

Luke 11: 53–54

53 And as he said these things unto them, the scribes and the Pharisees began to urge him vehemently, and to provoke him to speak of many things:

54 Laying wait for him, and seeking to catch something out of his mouth, that they might accuse him.

the abuses of men could not prevent the sincere worshippers of God from doing what was holy, and in accordance with the command of God, when they offered for sacrifices and other pious uses.

MATTHEW 24: 1–8; MARK 13: 1–8; LUKE 21: 5–11

Matthew 24: 2. Verily I say to you

As the vast size and wealth of the temple, like a veil hung before the eyes of the disciples, did not permit them to elevate their faith to the true reign of Christ, which was still future, so he affirms with an oath, that those things which occupy their attention will quickly perish. This prediction of the destruction of the temple, therefore, opened up a path for the ignorant and weak. Now, though it was advantageous that the temple should be destroyed, lest its services and shadows might exercise an undue influence on the Jews, who were already too much attached to earthly elements, yet the chief reason was, that God determined, by this dreadful example, to take vengeance on that nation, for having rejected his Son, and despised the grace which was brought by him. And, therefore, this threatening must have intimidated the disciples from taking part with a rebellious people; as the punishments which Scripture denounces against the wicked ought now to deter us from those crimes which provoke the wrath of God. Every thing that it tells us, even about the fading and transitory aspect of the world, ought to correct the vanity of our senses, which too eagerly follow pomp, and luxury, and pleasure. But more especially, what it declares respecting the fearful destruction of Antichrist and his followers, ought to remove every obstacle which hinders us from pursuing the right course of faith.

3. And while he was sitting

Mark mentions four disciples, Peter, James, John, and Andrew. But neither he nor Luke states the matter so fully as Matthew; for they only say that the disciples inquired about the time of the destruction of **the temple**, and – as it was a thing difficult to be believed – what outward **sign** of it God would give from heaven. Matthew tells us that they inquired about the time of **Christ's coming, and of the end of the world**.

But it must be observed that, having believed from their infancy that the temple would stand till the end of time, and having this opinion deeply rooted in their minds, they did not suppose that, while the building **of the world** stood, the **temple** could fall to ruins. Accordingly, as soon as Christ said that the temple would be destroyed, their thoughts immediately turned to the end of the world; and – as one error leads to another – having been convinced

ing at it wax candles and burning perfumes.

30. We would not have been partakers – They imagined themselves much better than their ancestors; but our Lord, who knew what they would do, uncovers their hearts, and shows them that they are about to be more abundantly vile than all who had ever preceded them.

31. Ye be witnesses – Ye acknowledge that ye are the children of those murderers, and ye are about to give full proof that ye are not degenerated.

There are many who think that, had they lived in the time of our Lord, they would not have acted towards him as the Jews did. But we can scarcely believe that they who reject his Gospel, trample under foot his precepts, do despite to the Spirit of his grace, love sin, and hate his followers, would have acted otherwise to him than the murdering Jews, had they lived in the same times.

32. Fill ye up then – Notwithstanding the profession you make, ye will fill up the measure of your fathers – will continue to walk in their way, accomplish the fullness of every evil purpose by murdering me; and then, when the measure of your iniquity is full, vengeance shall come upon you to the uttermost, as it did on your rebellious ancestors.

33. Ye serpents, ye generation of vipers – What a terrible stroke! – Ye are serpents, and the offspring of serpents. This refers to Matthew 23: 31: they confessed that they were the children of those who murdered the prophets; and they are now going to murder Christ and his followers, to show that they have not degenerated – an accursed seed, of an accursed breed.

34. Wherefore – To show how my prediction, Ye will fill up the measure of your fathers, shall be verified, Behold, I send (I am just going to commission them) prophets, etc. and some ye will kill, (with legal process), and some ye will crucify, pretend to try and find guilty, and deliver them into the hands of the Romans, who shall, through you, thus put them to

death. By prophets, wise men, and scribes, our Lord intends the evangelists, apostles, deacons, etc., who should be employed in proclaiming his Gospel: men who should equal the ancient prophets, their wise men, and scribes, in all the gifts and graces of the Holy Spirit.

35. Upon the earth – upon this land, meaning probably the land of Judea; for thus the word is often to be understood. The national punishment of all the innocent blood which had been shed in the land, shall speedily come upon you, from the blood of Abel the just, the first prophet and preacher of righteousness, Hebrews 11: 4; 2 Peter 2: 5, to the blood of Zachariah, the son of Barachiah.

Between the temple and the altar – That is, between the sanctuary and the altar of burnt-offerings.

36. Shall come upon this generation – upon this race of men, viz. the Jews. This phrase often occurs in this sense in the evangelists.

37. O Jerusalem, Jerusalem –

1. It is evident that our blessed Lord seriously and earnestly wished the salvation of the Jews.

2. That he did every thing that could be done, consistently with his own perfections, and the liberty of his creatures, to effect this.

3. That his tears over the city, Luke 19: 41, sufficiently evince his sincerity.

4. That these persons nevertheless perished. And

5. That the reason was, they would not be gathered together under his protection: therefore wrath, i.e. punishment, came upon them to the uttermost.

From this it is evident that there have been persons whom Christ wished to save, and bled to save, who notwithstanding perished, because they would not come unto him, John 5: 40. The metaphor which our Lord uses here is a very beautiful one. When the hen sees a beast of prey coming, she makes a noise to assemble her chickens, that she may cover them with her wings from the danger. The Roman eagle is about to fall upon the Jewish state – nothing can prevent this but their

MARK 12: 41–44; LUKE 21: 1–4

Mark 12: 41–44

41 And Jesus sat over against the treasury, and beheld how the people cast money into the treasury: and many that were rich cast in much.

42 And there came a certain poor widow, and she threw in two mites, which make a farthing.

43 And he called unto him his disciples, and saith unto them, Verily I say unto you, That this poor widow hath cast more in, than all they which have cast into the treasury:

44 For all they did cast in of their abundance; but she of her want did cast in all that she had, even all her living.

Luke 21: 1–4

1 And he looked up, and saw the rich men casting their gifts into the treasury.

2 And he saw also a certain poor widow casting in thither two mites.

3 And he said, Of a truth I say unto you, that this poor widow hath cast in more than they all:

4 For all these have of their abundance cast in unto the offerings of God: but she of her penury hath cast in all the living that she had.

MATTHEW 24: 1–8; MARK 13: 1–8; LUKE 21: 5–11

Matthew 24: 1–8

1 And Jesus went out, and departed from the temple: and his disciples came to him for to shew him the buildings of the temple.

2 And Jesus said unto them, See ye not all these things? verily I say unto you, There shall not be left here one stone upon another, that shall not be thrown down.

3 And as he sat upon the mount of Olives, the disciples came unto him privately, saying, Tell us, when shall these things be? and what shall be the sign of thy coming, and of the end of the world?

4 And Jesus answered and said unto them, Take heed that no man deceive you.

5 For many shall come in my name, saying, I am Christ; and shall deceive many.

6 And ye shall hear of wars and rumors

that, as soon as the reign of Christ should commence, they would be in every respect happy, they leave warfare out of the account, and fly all at once to a triumph. They associate the coming of Christ and the end of the world as things inseparable from each other; and by the end of the world they mean the restoration of all things, so that nothing may be wanting to complete the happiness of the godly.

We now perceive that they leap at once to various questions, because they had given way to these foolish imaginations, that the temple could not fall without shaking the whole world; that the termination of the shadows of the Law, and of the whole world, would be the same; that it would be immediately followed by the exhibition of the glory of Christ's kingdom, which would make the children of God perfectly happy; that a visible renovation of the world was at hand, which would instantly bring order out of a state of confusion. But above all, a foolish hope which they entertained, as to the immediate reign of Christ, drove them to hasten to the attainment of happiness and rest, without attending to the means. Just as, when they see that Christ is risen from the dead (Acts 1: 6), they rush forward to grasp at that happiness, which is laid up for us in heaven, and which must be attained through faith and patience.

Now though our condition is different, because we have not been educated among the shadows of the Law, so as to be infatuated by that superstition of an earthly kingdom of Christ, yet scarcely one person in a hundred is to be found who does not labor under a very similar disease. For since all men naturally shrink from annoyances, combats, and every kind of cross, the dislike of these things urges them, without moderation and without hope, to rush forward unseasonably to the fruit of hope. Thus no man wishes to sow the seed, but all wish to reap the harvest before the season arrives. To return to the disciples, they had indeed formed in their minds some good seed of faith, but they do not wait till it arrive at maturity; and holding, at the same time, erroneous views, they confound the perfection of Christ's reign with the commencement of it, and wish to enjoy on earth what they ought to seek for in heaven.

4. And Jesus answering said to them

They received an answer very different from what they had expected; for whereas they were eager for a triumph, as if they had already finished their warfare, Christ exhorts them to long patience. As if he had said, "You wish to seize the prize at the very outset, but you must first finish the course. You would draw down to earth the kingdom of God, which no man can obtain till he ascend to heaven." Now while this chapter contains admonitions highly useful for regulating the course of our life, we see that, by a wonderful purpose of God, the mistake into which the apostles fell is made to

conversion to God through Christ-Jesus cries throughout the land, publishing the Gospel of reconciliation – they would not assemble, and the Roman eagle came and destroyed them. The hen's affection to her brood is so very strong as to become proverbial.

38. Behold, your house – the temple: this is certainly what is meant. It was once the Lord's temple, God's OWN house; but now he says, YOUR temple or house – to intimate that God had abandoned it.

39. Ye shall not see me – I will remove my Gospel from you, and withdraw my protection.

Till ye shall say, Blessed – Till after the fullness of the Gentiles is brought in, when the word of life shall again be sent unto you; then will ye rejoice, and bless, and praise him that cometh in the name of the Lord, with full and final salvation for the lost sheep of the house of Israel. See Romans 11: 26, 27.

MARK 12: 41–44; LUKE 21: 1–4

Mark 12: 41–44

41. Cast money into the treasury – In the preceding account, Mark 12: 41, it is said Jesus beheld how the people cast money into the treasury. To make this relation the more profitable, let us consider Christ the observer and judge of human actions.

I. Christ the observer.

1. Christ observes all men and all things: all our actions are before his eyes, what we do in public and what we do in private are equally known unto him.

2. He observes the state and situation we are in: his eye was upon the abundance of the rich who had given much; and he was well acquainted with the poverty and desolate state of the widow who had given her all, though that was but little in itself. What an awful thought for the rich!

"God sees every penny I possess, and constantly observes how I lay it out." What a comfortable thought for the poor and desolate! The eye of the most merciful and bountiful Jesus continually beholds my poverty and distress, and will cause them to work for my good.

3. Christ sees all the motives which lead men to perform their respective actions; and the different motives which lead them to perform the same action: he knows whether they act through vanity, self-love, interest, ambition, hypocrisy, or whether through love, charity, zeal for his glory, and a hearty desire to please him.

4. He observes the circumstances which accompany our actions; whether we act with care or negligence, with a ready mind or with reluctance.

5. He observes the judgment which we form of that which we do in his name; whether we esteem ourselves more on account of what we have done, speak of it to others, dwell on our labors, sufferings, expenses, success, etc., or whether we humble ourselves because we have done so little good, and even that little in so imperfect a way.

II. See the judgment Christ forms of our actions.

1. He appears surprised that so much piety should be found with so much poverty, in this poor widow.

2. He shows that works of charity, etc., should be estimated, not by their appearance, but by the spirit which produces them.

3. He shows by this that all men are properly in a state of equality; for though there is and ought to be a difference in outward things, yet God looks upon the heart, and the poorest person has it in his power to make his mite as acceptable to the Lord, by simplicity of intention, and purity of affection, as the millions given by the affluent. It is just in God to rate the value of an action by the spirit in which it is done.

4. He shows that men should judge impartially in cases of this kind, and not permit themselves to be carried away to decide for a person by the largeness of the gift on the one hand, or against him by the smallness of the bounty on the other. Of the poor widow it is said, She has cast in more than all the rich. Because: 1. She gave more; she gave her all, and they gave only a part. 2. She did this in a

of wars: see that ye be not troubled: for all these things must come to pass, but the end is not yet.

7 For nation shall rise against nation, and kingdom against kingdom: and there shall be famines, and pestilences, and earthquakes, in divers places.

8 All these are the beginning of sorrows.

Mark 13: 1–8

1 And as he went out of the temple, one of his disciples saith unto him, Master, see what manner of stones and what buildings are here!

2 And Jesus answering said unto him, Seest thou these great buildings? there shall not be left one stone upon another, that shall not be thrown down.

3 And as he sat upon the mount of Olives over against the temple, Peter and James and John and Andrew asked him privately,

4 Tell us, when shall these things be? and what shall be the sign when all these things shall be fulfilled?

5 And Jesus answering them began to say, Take heed lest any man deceive you:

6 For many shall come in my name, saying, I am Christ; and shall deceive many.

7 And when ye shall hear of wars and rumors of wars, be ye not troubled: for such things must needs be; but the end shall not be yet.

8 For nation shall rise against nation, and kingdom against kingdom: and there shall be earthquakes in divers places, and there shall be famines and troubles: these are the beginnings of sorrows.

Luke 21: 5–11

5 And as some spake of the temple, how it was adorned with goodly stones and gifts, he said,

6 As for these things which ye behold, the days will come, in the which there shall not be left one stone upon another, that shall not be thrown down.

7 And they asked him, saying, Master, but when shall these things be? and what sign will there be when these things shall come to pass?

8 And he said, Take heed that ye be not deceived: for many shall come in my

turn to our advantage. The amount of the present instruction is, that the preaching of the Gospel is like sowing the seed, and therefore we ought to wait patiently for the time of reaping; and that it arises from improper delicacy or effeminacy, if we lose courage on account of the frost, or snow, or clouds of winter or other unpleasant seasons.

Take heed lest any man deceive you

There are two charges which Christ expressly gives to the disciples, to beware of false teachers, and not to be terrified by scandals. By these words he gives warning that his Church, so long as its pilgrimage in the world shall last, will be exposed to these evils. But they might be apt to think that this was inconsistent, since the prophets gave a widely different description of the future reign of Christ. Isaiah predicts that all will then be taught of God (54: 13). The words of God are: "I will pour out my Spirit on all flesh; and your sons and your daughters shall prophesy; your young men shall see visions, and your old men shall dream dreams" (Joel 2: 28).

A still more abundant light of understanding is promised by Jeremiah. "No longer shall any man teach his neighbor, nor a man his brother, saying, Know the Lord; for all shall know me from the least to the greatest" (Jeremiah 31: 34).

And, therefore, we need not wonder if the Jews expected, that when the Sun of righteousness had arisen, as Malachi (4: 2) had predicted, they would be entirely free from every cloud of error. Hence, also, the woman of Samaria said, "When the Messiah cometh, he will teach us all things" (John 4: 25).

Now we know what splendid promises of peace, righteousness, joy, and abundance of all blessings, are to be found everywhere in Scripture. We need not, therefore, wonder if they expected that, at the coming of Christ, they would be delivered from commotions of war, from extortions and every kind of injustice, and, in short, from famine and pestilence.

But Christ warns them, that false teachers will henceforth give no less annoyance to the godly than false prophets gave to the ancient people; and that disturbances will be not less frequent under the Gospel than they formerly were under the Law. Not that those prophecies which I have just mentioned will fail to be accomplished, but because the full accomplishment of them does not immediately appear in one day; for it is enough that believers now obtain a taste of those blessings, so as to cherish the hope of the full enjoyment of them at a future period. And, therefore, they were greatly mistaken, who wished to hay at the commencement of the Gospel, an immediate and perfect exhibition of those things which we see accomplished from day to day. Besides, that happiness which the prophets ascribe to the reign of Christ, though it cannot be altogether annihilated

better spirit, having a simple desire to please God. Never did any king come near the liberality of this widow; she gave all that she had, her whole life, i.e. all that she had to provide for one day's sustenance, and could have no more till by her labor she had acquired it. What trust must there be in the Divine Providence to perform such an act as this!

Two important lessons may be learned from her conduct. 1. A lesson of humiliation to the rich, who, by reason of covetousness on the one hand, and luxury on the other, give but little to GOD and the poor. A lesson of reproof to the poor, who, through distrust of God's providence, give nothing at all. Our possessions can only be sanctified by giving a portion to God. There will be infallibly a blessing in the remainder, when a part has been given to God and the poor. If the rich and the poor reflect seriously on this, the one will learn pity, the other liberality, and both be blessed in their deed. He must be a poor man indeed who cannot find one poorer than himself.

This chapter contains a prediction of the utter destruction of the city and temple of Jerusalem, and the subversion of the whole political constitution of the Jews; and is one of the most valuable portions of the new covenant Scriptures, with respect to the evidence which it furnishes of the truth of Christianity. Every thing which our Lord foretold should come on the temple, city, and people of the Jews, has been fulfilled in the most correct and astonishing manner; and witnessed by a writer who was present during the whole, who was himself a Jew, and is acknowledged to be an historian of indisputable veracity in all those transactions which concern the destruction of Jerusalem.

MATTHEW 24: 1–8; MARK 13: 1–8; LUKE 21: 5–11

Matthew 24: 1–8

1. And Jesus went out, and departed from, the temple – Or, And Jesus, going out of the temple, was going away. This is the arrangement of the words in several eminent manuscripts, versions, and fathers; and is much clearer than that in the common translation. The Jews say the temple was built of white and green-spotted marble. Josephus says the stones were white and strong; fifty feet long, twenty-four broad, and sixteen thick.

2. There shall not be left here one stone – These seem to have been the last words he spoke as he left the temple, into which he never afterwards entered; and, when he got to the mount of Olives, he renewed the discourse. From this mount, on which our Lord and his disciples now sat, the whole of the city, and particularly the temple, were clearly seen. This part of our Lord's prediction was fulfilled in the most literal manner. Josephus says, "Caesar gave orders that they should now demolish the whole city and temple, except the three towers, Phaselus, Hippicus, and Mariamne, and a part of the western wall, and these were spared; but, for all the rest of the wall, it was laid so completely even with the ground, by those who dug it up to the foundation, that there was left nothing to make those that came thither believe it had ever been inhabited."

The temple was destroyed,

1st. Justly; because of the sins of the Jews.

2dly. Mercifully; to take away from them the occasion of continuing in Judaism: and

3dly. Mysteriously; to show that the ancient sacrifices were abolished, and that the whole Jewish economy was brought to an end, and the Christian dispensation introduced.

3. Tell us, when shall these things be? – There appear to be three questions asked here by the disciples.

1st. When shall these things be? viz. the destruction of the city, temple, and Jewish state.

2dly. What shall be the sign of thy coming? viz. to execute these judgments upon them, and to establish thy own Church: and

3dly. When shall this world end? When wilt thou come to judge the quick and the dead?

But there are some who maintain that these are but three parts of the same question, and that our Lord's answers only refer to

name, saying, I am Christ; and the time draweth near: go ye not therefore after them.

9 But when ye shall hear of wars and commotions, be not terrified: for these things must first come to pass; but the end is not by and by.

10 Then said he unto them, Nation shall rise against nation, and kingdom against kingdom:

11 And great earthquakes shall be in divers places, and famines, and pestilences; and fearful sights and great signs shall there be from heaven.

MATTHEW 24: 9–14; MARK 13: 9–13; LUKE 21: 12–19

Matthew 24: 9–14

9 Then shall they deliver you up to be afflicted, and shall kill you: and ye shall be hated of all nations for my name's sake.

10 And then shall many be offended, and shall betray one another, and shall hate one another.

11 And many false prophets shall rise, and shall deceive many.

12 And because iniquity shall abound, the love of many shall wax cold.

13 But he that shall endure unto the end, the same shall be saved.

14 And this gospel of the kingdom shall be preached in all the world for a witness unto all nations; and then shall the end come.

Mark 13: 9–13

9 But take heed to yourselves: for they shall deliver you up to councils; and in the synagogues ye shall be beaten: and ye shall be brought before rulers and kings for my sake, for a testimony against them.

10 And the gospel must first be published among all nations.

11 But when they shall lead you, and deliver you up, take no thought beforehand what ye shall speak, neither do ye premeditate: but whatsoever shall be given you in that hour, that speak ye: for it is not ye that speak, but the Holy Ghost.

12 Now the brother shall betray the brother to death, and the father the son; and children shall rise up against their

by the depravity of man, is retarded or delayed by it. It is true that the Lord, in contending with the malice of men, opens up a way for his blessings through every obstacle; and, indeed, it would be unreasonable to suppose that what is founded on the undeserved goodness of God, and does not depend on the will of man, should be set aside through their fault.

MATTHEW 24: 9–14; MARK 13: 9–13; LUKE 21: 12–19

Matthew 24: 9. Then will they deliver you up to be afflicted

Christ now foretells to the disciples another kind of temptation, by which, in addition to ordinary afflictions, their faith must be tried; and that is, that they **will be hated** and detested **by the whole world**. It is painful and distressing enough in itself that the children of God should be afflicted in such a manner as not to be distinguished from the reprobate and the despisers of God, and should be subjected to the same punishments which those men endure on account of their crimes; and it appears to be still more unjust that they should be severely oppressed by grievous calamities from which the ungodly are exempted. But as wheat, after having been beaten by the flail along with the chaff, is pressed down and bruised by the millstone, so God not only afflicts his children in common with the ungodly, but subdues them by the cross even beyond others, so that we might be apt to think them more unhappy than the rest of mankind.

But Christ treats here strictly of the afflictions which the disciples had to endure on account of the gospel. For, though what Paul stays is true, that those whom God hath elected are likewise appointed by him to bear the cross, "that they may be conformed to the image of his Son" (Romans 8: 29), yet he does not distinguish all by this special Mark of enduring persecution from the enemies of the gospel. It is of this species of the cross that Christ now speaks, when it becomes necessary that believers should incur the hatred, meet the reproaches, and provoke the fury, of the ungodly for the testimony of the gospel. For he intended to warn his disciples that the doctrine of the gospel, of which they were to be witnesses and messengers, would never be pleasant or agreeable to the world, as he had formerly explained to them. He foretells not only that they will have to contend with a few enemies, but that, wherever they come, all nations will oppose them.

But it was monstrous and incredible, and was fitted to astonish and shake even the strongest minds, that the name of the Son of God should be so infamous and hateful, that all who professed it would be everywhere disliked.

the destruction of the Jewish state, and that nothing is spoken here concerning the LAST or judgment day.

End of the world – or, of the age, viz. the Jewish economy.

4. Take heed that no man deceive you – The world is full of deceivers, and it is only by taking heed to the counsel of Christ that even his followers can escape being ruined by them. From this to Matthew 24: 31, our Lord mentions the signs which should precede his coming.

The FIRST sign is false Christs.

5. For many shall come in my name – The SECOND sign, wars and commotions.

6. The next signs given by our Lord are wars and rumors of wars, etc. – The THIRD sign, pestilence and famine.

It is farther added, that There shall be famines, and pestilences. – The FOURTH sign, earthquakes or popular commotions.

Earthquakes, in divers places. – The FIFTH sign, fearful portents.

To these St. Luke adds that there shall be fearful sights and great signs from heaven (Luke 21: 11).

8. All these are the beginning of sorrows – travailing pains. The whole land of Judea is represented under the notion of a woman in grievous travail; but our Lord intimates, that all that had already been mentioned were only the first pangs and throes, and nothing in comparison of that hard and death-bringing labor, which should afterwards take place.

From the calamities of the nation in general, our Lord passes to those of the Christians; and, indeed, the sufferings of his followers were often occasioned by the judgments sent upon the land, as the poor Christians were charged with being the cause of these national calamities, and were cruelly persecuted on that account.

MATTHEW 24: 9–14; MARK 13: 9–13; LUKE 21: 12–19

Matthew 24: 9–14

9. Then shall they deliver you up to be afflicted – Rather, Then they will deliver you up to affliction. By a bold figure of speech, affliction is here personified. They are to be delivered into affliction's own hand, to be harassed by all the modes of inventive torture.

Ye shall be hated of all nations – Both Jew and Gentile will unite in persecuting and tormenting you.

10. Then shall many be offended, and shall betray one another – To illustrate this point, one sentence out of Tacitus. will be sufficient, who, speaking of the persecution under Nero, says, At first several were seized, who confessed, and then by THEIR DISCOVERY a great multitude of others were convicted and executed.

11. False prophets – Also were to be raised up; such as Simon Magus and his followers; and the false apostles complained of by St. Paul, 2 Corinthians 11: 13, who were deceitful workers, transforming themselves into the apostles of Christ. Such also were Hymeneus and Philetus, 2 Timothy 2: 17–18.

12. The love of many shall wax cold – By reason of these trials and persecutions from without, and those apostasies and false prophets from within, the love of many to Christ and his doctrine, and to one another, shall grow cold. Some openly deserting the faith, as Matthew 24: 10; others corrupting it, as Matthew 24: 11; and others growing indifferent about it, Matthew 24: 12. Even at this early period there seems to have been a very considerable defection in several Christian Churches; see Galatians 3: 1–4; 2 Thessalonians 3: 1, etc.; 2 Timothy 1: 15.

13. But he that shall endure – The persecutions that shall come – unto the end; to the destruction of the Jewish polity, without growing cold or apostatizing – shall be saved, shall be delivered in all imminent dangers, and have his soul at last brought to an eternal

parents, and shall cause them to be put to death.

13 And ye shall be hated of all men for my name's sake: but he that shall endure unto the end, the same shall be saved.

Luke 21: 12–19

12 But before all these, they shall lay their hands on you, and persecute you, delivering you up to the synagogues, and into prisons, being brought before kings and rulers for my name's sake.

13 And it shall turn to you for a testimony.

14 Settle it therefore in your hearts, not to meditate before what ye shall answer:

15 For I will give you a mouth and wisdom, which all your adversaries shall not be able to gainsay nor resist.

16 And ye shall be betrayed both by parents, and brethren, and kinsfolks, and friends; and some of you shall they cause to be put to death.

17 And ye shall be hated of all men for my name's sake.

18 But there shall not an hair of your head perish.

19 In your patience possess ye your souls.

MATTHEW 24: 15–28; MARK 13: 14–23; LUKE 21: 20–24; 17: 22–25

Matthew 24: 15–28

15 When ye therefore shall see the abomination of desolation, spoken of by Daniel the prophet, stand in the holy place, (whoso readeth, let him understand:)

16 Then let them which be in Judaea flee into the mountains:

17 Let him which is on the housetop not come down to take any thing out of his house:

18 Neither let him which is in the field return back to take his clothes.

19 And woe unto them that are with child, and to them that give suck in those days!

20 But pray ye that your flight be not in the winter, neither on the sabbath day:

21 For then shall be great tribulation, such as was not since the beginning of the world to this time, no, nor ever shall be.

22 And except those days should be shortened, there should no flesh be

Accordingly, the words of Mark are, **take heed to yourselves**. By this expression he points out the end and use of the warning, which is, that they ought to be prepared for endurance, lest, through want of caution, they might be overwhelmed by temptation. The same Mark adds, that **this will be for a testimony to kings and rulers**, when the disciples of Christ shall be brought before their tribunal. Luke expresses it a little differently, **this will happen to you for a testimony**, but the sense is quite the same; for Christ means that his gospel will be so much the more fully attested, when they have defended it at the risk of their lives.

If the apostles had only given their attention to preaching the gospel, and had not stood so firmly in defending it against the furious attacks of enemies, the confirmation of it would not have been so complete. But when they did not hesitate to expose their lives, and were not driven from their purpose by any terrors of death, their unshaken constancy made it manifest, how firmly they were convinced of the goodness of their cause. It was therefore an authentic seal of the gospel, when the apostles advanced without terror to the tribunals of kings, and there made an open profession of the name of Christ. Accordingly, Peter calls himself "a witness of the sufferings of Christ" (1 Peter 5: 1), whose badges he wore; and Paul boasts that he was "placed for the defense of the gospel" (Philippians 1: 17).

MATTHEW 24: 15–28; MARK 13: 14–23; LUKE 21: 20–24; 17: 22–25

Matthew 24: 15. When you shall see the abomination of desolation

Because the destruction of the temple and city of Jerusalem, together with the overthrow of the whole Jewish government, was (as we have already said) a thing incredible, and because it might be thought strange, that the disciples could not be saved without being torn from that nation, to which had been committed the adoption and the covenant (Romans 9: 4) of eternal salvation, Christ confirms both by the testimony of **Daniel**.

As if he had said, That you may not be too strongly attached to the temple and to the ceremonies of the Law, God has limited them to a fixed time, and has long ago declared, that when the Redeemer should come, sacrifices would cease; and that it may not give you uneasiness to be cut off from your own nation, God has also forewarned his people, that in due time it would be rejected. Such a prediction was not only well adapted for removing ground of offense, but likewise for animating the minds of the godly, that amidst the sorest calamities – knowing that God was looking upon them, and was taking care of their salva-

glory. It is very remarkable that not a single Christian perished in the destruction of Jerusalem, though there were many there when Cestius Gallus invested the city; and, had he persevered in the siege, he would soon have rendered himself master of it; but, when he unexpectedly and unaccountably raised the siege, the Christians took that opportunity to escape.

14. And this Gospel of the kingdom shall be preached in all the world – But, notwithstanding these persecutions, there should be a universal publication of the glad tidings of the kingdom, for a testimony to all nations. God would have the iniquity of the Jews published every where, before the heavy stroke of his judgments should fall upon them; that all mankind, as it were, might be brought as witnesses against their cruelty and obstinacy in crucifying and rejecting the Lord Jesus.

Then shall the end come – When this general publication of the Gospel shall have taken place, then a period shall be put to the whole Jewish economy, by the utter destruction of their city and temple.

MATTHEW 24: 15–28; MARK 13: 14–23; LUKE 21: 20–24; 17: 22–25

Matthew 24: 15–28

15. The abomination of desolation, spoken of by Daniel – This abomination of desolation, St. Luke, (Luke 21: 20, 21), refers to the Roman army; and this abomination standing in the holy place is the Roman army besieging Jerusalem; this, our Lord says, is what was spoken of by Daniel the prophet, in the ninth and eleventh chapters of his prophecy; and so let every one who reads these prophecies understand them; and in reference to this very event they are understood by the rabbins. The Roman army is called an abomination, for its ensigns and images, which were so to the Jews. Josephus says, (War, b. vi. chap. 6), the Romans brought their ensigns into the temple, and placed them over against the eastern gate, and sacrificed to them there. The Roman army is therefore fitly called the abomination,

and the abomination which maketh desolate, as it was to desolate and lay waste Jerusalem; and this army besieging Jerusalem is called by St. Mark, 13: 14, standing where it ought not, that is, as in the text here, the holy place; as not only the city, but a considerable compass of ground about it, was deemed holy, and consequently no profane persons should stand on it.

16. Then let them which be in Judea flee into the mountains – This counsel was remembered and wisely followed by the Christians afterwards. Eusebius and Epiphanius say, that at this juncture, after Cestius Gallus had raised the siege, and Vespasian was approaching with his army, all who believed in Christ left Jerusalem and fled to Pella, and other places beyond the river Jordan; and so they all marvelously escaped the general shipwreck of their country: not one of them perished.

17. Let him which is on the house top – The houses of the Jews, as well as those of the ancient Greeks and Romans, were flat-roofed, and had stairs on the outside, by which persons might ascend and descend without coming into the house. In the eastern walled cities, these flat-roofed houses usually formed continued terraces from one end of the city to the other; which terraces terminated at the gates. He, therefore, who is walking on the house top, let him not come down to take any thing out of his house; but let him instantly pursue his course along the tops of the houses, and escape out at the city gate as fast as he can.

18. Neither let him which is in the field return back – Because when once the army of the Romans sits down before the city, there shall be no more any possibility of escape, as they shall never remove till Jerusalem be destroyed.

19. And wo unto them (alas! for them) that are with child, etc. – For such persons are not in a condition to make their escape; neither can they bear the miseries of the siege. Josephus says the houses were full of women and children that perished by the famine; and that the mothers snatched the food even out

saved: but for the elect's sake those days shall be shortened.

23 Then if any man shall say unto you, Lo, here is Christ, or there; believe it not.

24 For there shall arise false Christs, and false prophets, and shall shew great signs and wonders; insomuch that, if it were possible, they shall deceive the very elect.

25 Behold, I have told you before.

26 Wherefore if they shall say unto you, Behold, he is in the desert; go not forth: behold, he is in the secret chambers; believe it not.

27 For as the lightning cometh out of the east, and shineth even unto the west; so shall also the coming of the Son of man be.

28 For wheresoever the carcase is, there will the eagles be gathered together.

Mark 13: 14–23

14 But when ye shall see the abomination of desolation, spoken of by Daniel the prophet, standing where it ought not, (let him that readeth understand,) then let them that be in Judaea flee to the mountains:

15 And let him that is on the housetop not go down into the house, neither enter therein, to take any thing out of his house:

16 And let him that is in the field not turn back again for to take up his garment.

17 But woe to them that are with child, and to them that give suck in those days!

18 And pray ye that your flight be not in the winter.

19 For in those days shall be affliction, such as was not from the beginning of the creation which God created unto this time, neither shall be.

20 And except that the Lord had shortened those days, no flesh should be saved: but for the elect's sake, whom he hath chosen, he hath shortened the days.

21 And then if any man shall say to you, Lo, here is Christ; or, lo, he is there; believe him not:

22 For false Christs and false prophets shall rise, and shall shew signs and wonders, to seduce, if it were possible, even the elect.

tion – they might betake themselves to the sacred anchor, where, amidst the most dreadful heavings of the billows, their condition would be firm and secure.

But before I proceed farther, I must examine the passage which is quoted by Christ. Those commentators are, I think, mistaken, who think that this quotation is made from the ninth chapter of the Book of Daniel.

For there we do not literally find the words, **abomination, of desolation**; and it is certain that the angel does not there speak of the final destruction which Christ now mentions, but of the temporary dispersion which was brought about by the tyranny of Antiochus. But in the twelfth chapter the angel predicts what is called the final abrogation of the services of the Law, which was to take place at the coming of Christ. For, after having exhorted believers to unshaken constancy, he fixes absolutely the time both of the ruin and of the restoration.

"From the time, says he, that the daily sacrifices shall be taken away, and the abomination of desolation set up, there will be a thousand two hundred and ninety days. Blessed is he who shall wait till he come to the thousand three hundred and thirty-five days" (Daniel 12: 11–12).

I consider the natural meaning of this passage to be that the angel declares that, after the temple has been once purified from the pollutions and idols of Antiochus, another period will arrive when it will be exposed to a new profanation, and when all its sacredness and majesty will be for ever lost. And as that message was sad and melancholy, he again recalls the prophet to one year, and two years, and six months. These words denote both the duration and the close of the calamities; for, in an interrupted succession of calamities, the course of one year appears to us very long, but when that space of time is doubled, the distress is greatly increased. The Spirit therefore exhorts believers to prepare themselves for the exercise of patience, not only for a single year, that is, for a long period, but to lay their account with enduring tribulations through an uninterrupted succession of many ages. There is no small consolation also in the phrase, half a time (Daniel 12: 7), for though the tribulations be of long continuance, yet the Spirit shows that they will not be perpetual. And, indeed, he had formerly used this form of expression: The calamity of the Church shall last through a time, times, and half a time (Daniel 7: 25). But now he reckons the period of three years and six months by days, that believers may be more and more hardened by a very long continuance of calamities; for it is customary with men in adversity to compute time, not by years or months, but by days, a single day being, in their estimation, equal to a year. He says that those will be happy who bear up to the end of that period; that is, who with invincible patience persevere to the end.

of their own children's mouths.

20. But pray ye that your flight be not in the winter – For the hardness of the season, the badness of the roads, the shortness of the days, and the length of the nights, will all be great impediments to your flight. Rabbi Tanchum observes, "that the favor of God was particularly manifested in the destruction of the first temple, in not obliging the Jews to go out in the winter, but in the summer."

Neither on the Sabbath-day – That you may not raise the indignation of the Jews by traveling on that day, and so suffer that death out of the city which you had endeavored to escape from within. Besides, on the Sabbath-days the Jews not only kept within doors, but the gates of all the cities and towns in every place were kept shut and barred; so that their flight should be on a Sabbath, they could not expect admission into any place of security in the land.

21. For then shall be great tribulation – No history can furnish us with a parallel to the calamities and miseries of the Jews: rapine, murder, famine, and pestilence within: fire and sword, and all the horrors of war, without. Our Lord wept at the foresight of these calamities; and it is almost impossible for any humane person to read the relation of them in Josephus without weeping also. St. Luke, Luke 21: 22, calls these the days of vengeance, that all things which were written might be fulfilled.

22. Except those days should be shortened – Josephus computes the number of those who perished in the siege at eleven hundred thousand, besides those who were slain in other places. When Titus was viewing the fortifications after the taking of the city, he could not help ascribing his success to God. "We have fought," said he, "with God on our side; and it is God who pulled the Jews out of these strong holds: for what could machines or the hands of men avail against such towers as these?"

23. Then if any man shall say unto you, Lo here is Christ – Our Lord had cautioned his disciples against false Christs and prophets before, Matthew 24: 11; but he seems here to intimate that there would be especial need to attend to this caution about the time of the siege. And in fact many such impostors did arise about that time, promising deliverance from God; and the lower the Jews were reduced, the more disposed they were to listen to such deceivers. Like a man drowning, they were willing to catch even at a straw, while there was any prospect of being saved.

25. Behold, I have told you before – That is, I have forewarned you.

27. For as the lightning cometh out of the east, and shineth even unto the west – It is worthy of remark that our Lord, in the most particular manner, points out the very march of the Roman army: they entered into Judea on the EAST, and carried on their conquest WESTWARD, as if not only the extensiveness of the ruin, but the very route which the army would take, were intended in the comparison of the lightning issuing from the east, and shining to the west.

28. For wheresoever the carcass is – the dead carcass. The Jewish nation, which was morally and judicially dead.

There will the eagles – The Roman armies, called so partly from their strength and fierceness, and partly from the figure of these animals which was always wrought on their ensigns, or even in brass, placed on the tops of their ensign-staves. It is remarkable that the Roman fury pursued these wretched men wheresoever they were found. They were a dead carcass doomed to be devoured; and the Roman eagles were the commissioned devourers.

MATTHEW 24: 29–31; MARK 13: 24–27; LUKE 21: 25–28

Matthew 24: 29–31

29. Immediately after the tribulation, etc. – Commentators generally understand this, and what follows, of the end of the world and Christ's coming to judgment: but the word

23 But take ye heed: behold, I have foretold you all things.

Luke 21: 20–24

20 And when ye shall see Jerusalem compassed with armies, then know that the desolation thereof is nigh.

21 Then let them which are in Judaea flee to the mountains; and let them which are in the midst of it depart out; and let not them that are in the countries enter thereinto.

22 For these be the days of vengeance, that all things which are written may be fulfilled.

23 But woe unto them that are with child, and to them that give suck, in those days! for there shall be great distress in the land, and wrath upon this people.

24 And they shall fall by the edge of the sword, and shall be led away captive into all nations: and Jerusalem shall be trodden down of the Gentiles, until the times of the Gentiles be fulfilled.

Luke 17: 22–25

22 And he said unto the disciples, The days will come, when ye shall desire to see one of the days of the Son of man, and ye shall not see it.

23 And they shall say to you, See here; or, see there: go not after them, nor follow them.

24 For as the lightning, that lighteneth out of the one part under heaven, shineth unto the other part under heaven; so shall also the Son of man be in his day.

25 But first must he suffer many things, and be rejected of this generation.

MATTHEW 24: 29–31; MARK 13: 24–27; LUKE 21: 25–28

Matthew 24: 29–31

29 Immediately after the tribulation of those days shall the sun be darkened, and the moon shall not give her light, and the stars shall fall from heaven, and the powers of the heavens shall be shaken:

30 And then shall appear the sign of the Son of man in heaven: and then shall all the tribes of the earth mourn, and they shall see the Son of man coming in the clouds of heaven with power and great glory.

31 And he shall send his angels with a

Now Christ selects only what suited his purpose, namely, that the termination of sacrifices was at hand, and that the **abomination,** which was the sign of the final **desolation,** would be placed in the temple. But as the Jews were too strongly attached to their present condition, and therefore paid little attention to the prophecies which foretold the abolition of it, Christ, as if endeavoring to gain their ear, bids them read attentively that passage, where they would learn that what appeared to them difficult to be believed was plainly declared by the Prophets.

Abomination means *profanation;* for this word denotes uncleanness, which corrupts or overturns the pure worship of God. It is called **desolation,** because it drew along with it the destruction of the temple and of the government; as he had formerly said (Daniel 9: 27), that the pollution introduced by Antiochus was, as it were, the standard of temporary **desolation;** for such I conceive to be the meaning of the wing, or, "spreading out."

MATTHEW 24: 29–31; MARK 13: 24–27; LUKE 21: 25–28

Matthew 24: 29. And immediately after the tribulation of those days

Christ comes now to speak of the full manifestation of his kingdom, about which he was at first interrogated by the disciples, and promises that, after they have been tried by so many distressing events, the redemption will arrive in due time. The principal object of his reply was, to confirm his disciples in good hope, that they might not be dismayed on account of the troubles and confusion that would arise. For this reason, he does not speak of **his coming** in simple terms, but employs those modes of expression which were common among the prophets, by which, the more attentively they were considered, so much the more severe would be the contest of temptation experienced by the reader, in consequence of the opposite character of the event. For what could be more strange than to see the kingdom of Christ not only despised, but oppressed by the cross, loaded with many reproaches, and overwhelmed by every kind of **tribulation, that** kingdom which the prophets had frequently described in such magnificent language? Might it not be asked, where was that majesty which would darken **the sun, and moon, and stars**, shake the whole frame of the world, and change the ordinary course of nature? Our Lord now meets these temptations, declaring that, though these predictions are not immediately fulfilled, they will at length be fully justified by the event. The meaning therefore is, that the predictions which had been formerly made about the miraculous **shaking of heaven and earth**, ought not to be restricted to the commencement of

immediately shows that our Lord is not speaking of any distant event, but of something immediately consequent on calamities already predicted: and that must be the destruction of Jerusalem. "The Jewish heaven shall perish, and the sun and moon of its glory and happiness shall be darkened – brought to nothing. The sun is the religion of the Church; the moon is the government of the state; and the stars are the judges and doctors of both. Compare Isaiah 13: 10; Ezekiel 32: 7–8, etc." Lightfoot.

In the prophetic language, great commotions upon earth are often represented under the notion of commotions and changes in the heavens:

The fall of Babylon is represented by the stars and constellations of heaven withdrawing their light, and the sun and moon being darkened. See Isaiah 13: 9–10.

The destruction of Egypt, by the heaven being covered, the sun enveloped with a cloud, and the moon withholding her light. Ezekiel 32: 7–8.

The destruction of the Jews by Antiochus Epiphanes is represented by casting down some of the host of heaven, and the stars to the ground. See Daniel 8: 10.

And this very destruction of Jerusalem is represented by the Prophet Joel, Joel 2: 30–31, by showing wonders in heaven and in earth – darkening the sun, and turning the moon into blood. This general mode of describing these judgments leaves no room to doubt the propriety of its application in the present case.

The falling of stars, i.e. those meteors which are called falling stars by the common people, was deemed an omen of evil times.

30. Then shall appear the sign of the Son of man – The plain meaning of this is, that the destruction of Jerusalem will be such a remarkable instance of Divine vengeance, such a signal manifestation of Christ's power and glory, that all the Jewish tribes shall mourn, and many will, in consequence of this manifestation of God, be led to acknowledge Christ and his religion. By, of the land, in the text, is evidently meant here, as in several other places, the land of Judea and its tribes,

either its then inhabitants, or the Jewish people wherever found.

31. He shall send his angels – his messengers, the apostles, and their successors in the Christian ministry.

With a great sound of a trumpet – Or, a loud-sounding trumpet – the earnest affectionate call of the Gospel of peace, life, and salvation.

Shall gather together his elect – The Gentiles, who were now chosen or elected, in place of the rebellious, obstinate Jews, according to Our Lord's prediction, Matthew 8: 11–12, and Luke 13: 28–29. For the children of the kingdom, (the Jews who were born with a legal right to it, but had now finally forfeited that right by their iniquities) should be thrust out. It is worth serious observation, that the Christian religion spread and prevailed mightily after this period: and nothing contributed more to the success of the Gospel than the destruction of Jerusalem happening in the very time and manner, and with the very circumstances, so particularly foretold by our Lord. It was after this period that the kingdom of Christ began, and his reign was established in almost every part of the world.

The prophecy of Christ was most literally and terribly fulfilled, on a people who are still preserved as continued monuments of the truth of our Lord's prediction, and of the truth of the Christian religion.

MATTHEW 24: 32–36; MARK 13: 28–32; LUKE 21: 29–33

Matthew 24: 32–36

32. Learn a parable of the fig-tree – That is, These signs which I have given you will be as infallible a proof of the approaching ruin of the Jewish state as the budding of the trees is a proof of the coming summer.

34. This generation shall not pass – this race; i.e. the Jews shall not cease from being a distinct people, till all the counsels of God relative to them and the Gentiles be fulfilled. Some translate, this generation, meaning the

great sound of a trumpet, and they shall gather together his elect from the four winds, from one end of heaven to the other.

Mark 13: 24–27

24 But in those days, after that tribulation, the sun shall be darkened, and the moon shall not give her light,

25 And the stars of heaven shall fall, and the powers that are in heaven shall be shaken.

26 And then shall they see the Son of man coming in the clouds with great power and glory.

27 And then shall he send his angels, and shall gather together his elect from the four winds, from the uttermost part of the earth to the uttermost part of heaven.

Luke 21: 25–28

25 And there shall be signs in the sun, and in the moon, and in the stars; and upon the earth distress of nations, with perplexity; the sea and the waves roaring;

26 Men's hearts failing them for fear, and for looking after those things which are coming on the earth: for the powers of heaven shall be shaken.

27 And then shall they see the Son of man coming in a cloud with power and great glory.

28 And when these things begin to come to pass, then look up, and lift up your heads; for your redemption draweth nigh.

MATTHEW 24: 32–36; MARK 13: 28–32; LUKE 21: 29–33

Matthew 24: 32–36

32 Now learn a parable of the fig tree; When his branch is yet tender, and putteth forth leaves, ye know that summer is nigh:

33 So likewise ye, when ye shall see all these things, know that it is near, even at the doors.

34 Verily I say unto you, This generation shall not pass, till all these things be fulfilled.

35 Heaven and earth shall pass away, but my words shall not pass away.

36 But of that day and hour knoweth no man, no, not the angels of heaven, but my Father only.

redemption, because the prophets had embraced the whole course of it, till it should arrive at perfection.

Having now ascertained Christ's intention, we shall have no difficulty in perceiving the meaning of the words to be, that **heaven** will not be **darkened** immediately, but after that the Church shall have passed through the whole course of its **tribulations**. Not that the glory and majesty of the kingdom of Christ will not appear till his last coming, but because till that time is delayed the accomplishment of those things which began to take place after his resurrection, and of which God gave to his people nothing more than a taste, that he might lead them farther on in the path of hope and patience. According to this argument, Christ keeps the minds of believers in a state of suspense till the last day, that they may not imagine those declarations which the prophets made, about the future restoration, to have failed of their accomplishment, because they lie buried for a long period under the thick **darkness** of **tribulations**.

MATTHEW 24: 32–36; MARK 13: 28–32; LUKE 21: 29–33

Matthew 24: 32. Now learn a similitude from the fig-tree

I do not suppose the meaning of this to be merely that, during the state of confusion which has been mentioned, there will be as evident a sign that the coming of Christ is nigh, as that by which we know with certainty that the summer is at hand, when the trees begin to grow green; but, in my opinion, Christ expresses something else. For as in winter the trees, contracted by the severity of the cold, show greater vigor, but in spring lose their toughness, and appear more feeble, and are even cleft asunder to open up passage for fresh twigs, so the afflictions by which, according to the perception of the flesh, the Church is softened, do not in any way impair its vigor. As the inward sap diffused through the whole tree, after having produced this softness, collects strength to throw itself out for renovating what was dead, so the Lord draws from the corruption of the outward man the perfect restoration of his people. The general instruction conveyed is, that the weak and frail condition of the Church ought not to lead us to conclude that it is dying, but rather to expect the immortal glory for which the Lord prepares his people by the cross and by afflictions; for what Paul maintains in reference to each of the members must be fulfilled in the whole body, that "if the outward man is decayed the inward man is renewed day by day" (2 Corinthians 4: 16).

What Matthew and Mark had stated more obscurely, **know you that it is nigh at the door**, is more fully

ADAM CLARKE

persons who were then living, that they should not die before these signs, etc., took place: but though this was true, as to the calamities that fell upon the Jews, and the destruction of their government, temple, etc., yet as our Lord mentions Jerusalem's continuing to be under the power of the Gentiles till the fullness of the Gentiles should come in, i.e. till all the nations of the world should receive the Gospel of Christ, after which the Jews themselves should be converted unto God, Romans 11: 25, etc., I think it more proper not to restrain its meaning to the few years which preceded the destruction of Jerusalem; but to understand it of the care taken by Divine providence to preserve them as a distinct people, and yet to keep them out of their own land, and from their temple service. But still it is literally true in reference to the destruction of Jerusalem. John probably lived to see these things come to pass; compare Matthew 16: 28, with John 21: 22; and there were some rabbins alive at the time when Christ spoke these words who lived till the city was destroyed, viz. Rabban Simeon, who perished with the city; R. Jochanan ben Zaccai, who outlived it; R. Zadoch, R. Ismael, and others.

The war began, as Josephus says, in the second year of the government of Gessius Florus, who succeeded Albinus, successor of Porcius Festus, mentioned Acts 24: 27, in the month of May, in the twelfth year of Nero, and the seventeenth of Agrippa, mentioned Acts 25 and 26, that is, in May, ad 66.

The temple was burnt August 10, ad 70, the same day and month on which it had been burnt by the king of Babylon: Josephus, Ant. b. xx. c. 11. s. 8.

The city was taken September 8, in the second year of the reign of Vespasian, or the year of Christ 70. Ant. b. vi. c. 10.

That was the end of the siege of Jerusalem, which began, as Josephus several times observes, about the fourteenth day of the month Nisan, or our April.

For this complete conquest of Jerusalem, Titus had a triumphal arch erected to his honor, which still exists. It stand on the Via Sacra, leading from the forum to the amphi-theatre. On it are represented the spoils of the temple of God, such as the golden table of the show-bread, the golden candlestick with its seven branches, the ark of the covenant, the two golden trumpets, etc., etc.; for a particular account see the note on Exodus 25: 31. On this arch, a correct model of which, taken on the spot, now stands before me, is the following inscription: "The Senate and People of Rome, to the Divine Titus, son of the Divine Vespasian; and to Vespasian the Emperor."

On this occasion, a medal was struck with the following inscription round a laureated head of the emperor. On the obverse are represented a palm tree, the emblem of the land of Judaea; the emperor with a trophy standing on the left; Judea, under the figure of a distressed woman, sitting at the foot of the tree weeping, with her head bowed down, supported by her left hand. This is not only an extraordinary fulfillment of our Lord's prediction, but a literal accomplishment of a prophecy delivered about 800 years before, Isaiah 3: 26, And she, desolate, shall sit upon the ground.

36. But of that day and hour – here, is translated season by many eminent critics, and is used in this sense by both sacred and profane authors. As the day was not known, in which Jerusalem should be invested by the Romans, therefore our Lord advised his disciples to pray that it might not be on a Sabbath; and as the season was not known, therefore they were to pray that it might not be in the winter; Matthew 24: 20.

MATTHEW 24: 37–42; MARK 13: 33; LUKE 17: 26–37; 21: 34–36

Matthew 24: 37–42

37–38. As the days of Noah – they were eating and drinking – That is, they spent their time in rapine, luxury, and riot. The design of these verses seems to be, that the desolation should be as general as it should be unexpected.

39. And knew not – They considered not – did not lay Noah's warning to heart, till it was too late to profit by it: so shall it be – and so it was in this coming of the Son of man.

Mark 13: 28–32

28 Now learn a parable of the fig tree; When her branch is yet tender, and putteth forth leaves, ye know that summer is near:

29 So ye in like manner, when ye shall see these things come to pass, know that it is nigh, even at the doors.

30 Verily I say unto you, that this generation shall not pass, till all these things be done.

31 Heaven and earth shall pass away: but my words shall not pass away.

32 But of that day and that hour knoweth no man, no, not the angels which are in heaven, neither the Son, but the Father.

Luke 21: 29–33

29 And he spake to them a parable; Behold the fig tree, and all the trees;

30 When they now shoot forth, ye see and know of your own selves that summer is now nigh at hand.

31 So likewise ye, when ye see these things come to pass, know ye that the kingdom of God is nigh at hand.

32 Verily I say unto you, This generation shall not pass away, till all be fulfilled.

33 Heaven and earth shall pass away: but my words shall not pass away.

MATTHEW 24: 37–42; MARK 13: 33; LUKE 17: 26–37; 21: 34–36

Matthew 24: 37–42

37 But as the days of Noe were, so shall also the coming of the Son of man be.

38 For as in the days that were before the flood they were eating and drinking, marrying and giving in marriage, until the day that Noe entered into the ark,

39 And knew not until the flood came, and took them all away; so shall also the coming of the Son of man be.

40 Then shall two be in the field; the one shall be taken, and the other left.

41 Two women shall be grinding at the mill; the one shall be taken, and the other left.

42 Watch therefore: for ye know not what hour your Lord doth come.

explained by Luke, know you that **the kingdom of God is at hand**; and in this passage **the kingdom of God** is not represented – as in many other passages – at its commencement, but at its perfection, and that according to the views of those whom Christ was teaching. For they did not view **the kingdom of God** in the Gospel as consisting in the **peace** and **joy** of faith and in spiritual righteousness (Romans 14: 17), but sought that blessed rest and glory which is concealed under hope till the last day.

34. This generation shall not pass away

Though Christ employs a general expression, yet he does not extend the discourses to all the miseries which would befall the Church, but merely informs them, that before a single **generation** shall have been completed, they will learn by experience the truth of what he has said. For within fifty years the city was destroyed and the temple was razed, the whole country was reduced to a hideous desert, and the obstinacy of the world rose up against God. Nay more, their rage was inflamed to exterminate the doctrine of salvation, false teachers arose to corrupt the pure gospel by their impostures, religion sustained amazing shocks, and the whole company of the godly was miserably distressed. Now though the same evils were perpetrated in uninterrupted succession for many ages afterwards, yet what Christ said was true, that, before the close of a single **generation**, believers would feel in reality, and by undoubted experience, the truth of his prediction; for the apostles endured the same things which we see in the present day. And yet it was not the design of Christ to promise to his followers that their calamities would be terminated within a short time, (for then he would have contradicted himself, having previously warned them that **the end was not yet**;) but, in order to encourage them to perseverance, he expressly foretold that those things related to their own age. The meaning therefore is: "This prophecy does not relate to evils that are distant, and which posterity will see after the lapse of many centuries, but which are now hanging over you, and ready to fall in one mass, so that there is no part of it which the present **generation** will not experience." So then, while our Lord heaps upon a, single **generation** every kind of calamities, he does not by any means exempt future ages from the same kind of sufferings, but only enjoins the disciples to be prepared for enduring them all with firmness.

MATTHEW 24: 37–42; MARK 13: 33; LUKE 17: 26–37; 21: 34–36

Matthew 24: 37. But as the days of Noah were

Although Christ lately expressed his desire to keep the minds of his followers in suspense, that they might not

ADAM CLARKE

40–41. Then shall two men – two women – one shall be taken, and the other left – The meaning seems to be, that so general should these calamities be, that no two persons, wheresoever found, or about whatsoever employed, should be both able to effect their escape; and that captivity and the sword should have a complete triumph over this unhappy people.

Two women shall be grinding – Women alone are still employed in grinding the corn in the east; and it is only when despatch is required, or the uppermost millstone is heavy, that a second woman is added.

42. Watch therefore – Be always on your guard, that you may not be taken unawares, and that you may be properly prepared to meet God in the way either of judgment or mercy, whensoever he may come. This advice the followers of Christ took, and therefore they escaped; the miserable Jews rejected it, and were destroyed. Let us learn wisdom by the things which they suffered.

MATTHEW 24: 43–51; MARK 13: 34–37; LUKE 12: 35–50

Matthew 24: 43–51

43. If the good man of the house had known – "As a master of a family who expected a thief at any time of the night, would take care to be awake, and ready to protect his house; so do ye, who know that the Son of man will come. Though the day and hour be uncertain, continue always in a state of watchfulness, that he may not come upon you unawares." WAKEFIELD.

45. Who then is a faithful and wise servant – All should live in the same expectation of the coming of Christ, which a servant has with respect to the return of his master, who, in departing for a season, left the management of his affairs to him; and of which management he is to give an exact account on his master's return.

Here is an abstract of the duties of a minister of Christ.

1. He is appointed, not by himself, but by the vocation and mission of his Master.

2. He must look on himself, not as the master of the family, but as the servant.

3. He must be scrupulously faithful and exact in fulfilling the commands of his Master.

4. His fidelity must be ever accompanied by wisdom and prudence.

5. He must give the domestics – the sacred family, their food; and this food must be such as to afford them true nourishment. And

6. This must be done in its season. There are certain portions of the bread of life which lose their effect by being administered out of proper season, or to improper persons.

46. Blessed is that servant – His blessedness consists in his master's approbation.

47. He shall make him ruler over all his goods – O heavenly privilege of a faithful minister of Christ! He shall receive from God a power to dispense all the blessings of the new covenant; and his word shall ever be accompanied with the demonstration of the Holy Ghost to the hearts of all that hear it. Much of a preacher's usefulness may be lost by his unfaithfulness.

48. But, and if that evil servant – Here are three characters of a bad minister.

1. He has little or no faith in the speedy coming of Christ, either to punish for wickedness, or to pardon and sanctify those who believe. It may be, he does not outwardly profess this, but he says it in his heart, and God searches his heart, and knows that he professes to teach what he does not believe.

2. He governs with an absolute dominion, oppressing his colleagues and doing violence to the followers of Christ. And shall begin to smite, etc.

3. He leads an irregular life does not love the company of the children of God, but eats and drinks with the drunkards, preferring the tables of the great and the rich, whose god is their belly, and thus feeds himself without fear.

Great God! save thine inheritance from being ravaged by such wolves!

50. The lord of that servant – Here are three

Mark 13: 33

33 Take ye heed, watch and pray: for ye know not when the time is.

Luke 17: 26–37

26 And as it was in the days of Noe, so shall it be also in the days of the Son of man.

27 They did eat, they drank, they married wives, they were given in marriage, until the day that Noe entered into the ark, and the flood came, and destroyed them all.

28 Likewise also as it was in the days of Lot; they did eat, they drank, they bought, they sold, they planted, they builded;

29 But the same day that Lot went out of Sodom it rained fire and brimstone from heaven, and destroyed them all.

30 Even thus shall it be in the day when the Son of man is revealed.

31 In that day, he which shall be upon the housetop, and his stuff in the house, let him not come down to take it away: and he that is in the field, let him likewise not return back.

32 Remember Lot's wife.

33 Whosoever shall seek to save his life shall lose it; and whosoever shall lose his life shall preserve it.

34 I tell you, in that night there shall be two men in one bed; the one shall be taken, and the other shall be left.

35 Two women shall be grinding together; the one shall be taken, and the other left.

36 Two men shall be in the field; the one shall be taken, and the other left.

37 And they answered and said unto him, Where, Lord? And he said unto them, Wheresoever the body is, thither will the eagles be gathered together.

Luke 21: 34–36

34 And take heed to yourselves, lest at any time your hearts be overcharged with surfeiting, and drunkenness, and cares of this life, and so that day come upon you unawares.

35 For as a snare shall it come on all them that dwell on the face of the whole earth.

36 Watch ye therefore, and pray always, that ye may be accounted worthy

inquire too anxiously about the last day; yet, lest the indifference arising out of the enjoyments of the world should lull them to sleep, he now exhorts them to solicitude. He wished them to be uncertain as to his coming, but yet to be prepared to expect him every day, or rather every moment. To shake off their sloth, and to excite them more powerfully to be on their guard, he foretells that the end will come, while the world is sunk in brutal indifference; just as **in the days of Noah** all the nations were swallowed up by **the deluge**, when they had no expectation of it, but rioted in gluttony and voluptuousness, and shortly afterwards, the inhabitants of Sodom, while they were abandoning themselves without fear to sensuality, were consumed by fire from heaven. Since indifference of this sort will exist about the time of the last day, believers ought not to indulge themselves after the example of the multitude.

We have now ascertained the design of Christ, which was, to inform believers that, in order to prevent themselves from being suddenly overtaken, they ought always to keep watch, because the day of the last judgment will come when it is not expected. Luke alone mentions **Sodom**, and that in the seventeenth chapter, where he takes occasion, without attending to the order of time, to relate this discourse of Christ. But it would not have been improper that the two Evangelists should have satisfied themselves with a single example, though Christ mentioned two, more especially when those examples perfectly agreed with each other in this respect, that at one time the whole human race, in the midst of unbroken indolence and pleasure, was suddenly swallowed up, with the exception of a few individuals. When he says that men were giving their whole attention to **eating, drinking, marriage**, and other worldly employments, at the time when God destroyed the whole world by a deluge, **and Sodom** by thunder; these words mean that they were as fully occupied with the conveniences and enjoyments of the present life, as if there had been no reason to dread any change. And though we shall immediately find him commanding the disciples to guard against surfeiting and earthly cares, yet in this passage he does not directly condemn the intemperance, but rather the obstinacy, of those times, in consequence of which, they despised the threatenings of God, and awaited with indifference their awful destruction. Promising to themselves that the condition in which they then were would remain unchanged, they did not scruple to follow without concern their ordinary pursuits. And in itself it would not have been improper, or worthy of condemnation, to make provision for their wants, if they had not with gross stupidity opposed the judgment of God, and rushed, with closed eyes, to unbridled iniquity, as if there had been no Judge in heaven. So now Christ declares that the last age of the

punishments which answer to the three characteristics of the bad minister.

1. A sudden death, and the weight of God's judgments falling upon him, without a moment to avert it: this answers to his infidelity and forgetfulness. He shall come in a day in which he looked not for him.

2. A separation from the communion of saints, and from all the gifts which he has abused: this answers to the abuse of his authority in the Church of Christ.

3. He shall have tears and eternal pains, in company with all such hypocrites as himself: and this answers to his voluptuous life, pampering the flesh at the expense of his soul.

51. Cut him asunder – This refers to an ancient mode of punishment used in several countries. Isaiah is reported to have been sawed ASUNDER. That it was an ancient mode of punishment is evident from what Herodotus says: that Sabacus, king of Ethiopia, had a vision, in which he was commanded to cut in two, all the Egyptian priests, lib. ii. And in lib. vii. where Xerxes ordered one of the sons of Pythius to be cut in two, and one half placed on each side of the way, that his army might pass through between them. This kind of punishment was used among the Persians: see Daniel 2: 5; 3: 29. Story of Susanna, v. 55,59. See also 2 Samuel 12: 31, and 1 Chronicles 20: 3. It may also have reference to that mode of punishment in which the different members were chopped off first the feet, then the hands, next the legs, then the arms, and lastly the head. This mode of punishment is still in use among the Chinese. But we find an exact parallel among the Turks, in the following passage from W. Lithgow's Travels, "If a Turk should happen to kill another Turk, his punishment is thus: After he is adjudged to death, he is brought forth to the market place; and a blocke being brought hither of four foot high, the malifactor is stript naked, and then laid thereon with his belly downward; they draw in his middle together so small with running cords that they strike his body a-two with one blow: his hinder parts they cast to be eaten by hungry dogs kept for the same purpose; and the fore-quarters and head they throw into a grievous fire, made there for the same end. And this is the punishment for manslaughter."

This is the very same punishment, and for the same offense, as that mentioned by our Lord, the killing of a fellow servant – one of the same nation, and of the same religion.

THE reader has no doubt observed, in the preceding chapter, a series of the most striking and solemn predictions, fulfilled in the most literal, awful, and dreadful manner. Christ has foretold the ruin of the Jewish people, and the destruction of their polity; and in such a circumstantial manner as none else could do, but He, under whose eye are all events, and in whose hands are the government and direction of all things. Indeed he rather declared what he would do, than predicted what should come to pass. And the fulfillment has been as circumstantial as the prediction. Does it not appear that the predicted point was so literally referred to by the occurring fact, by which it was to have its accomplishment, as to leave no room to doubt the truth of the prediction, or the certainty of the event by which it was fulfilled? Thus the wisdom of God, as also his justice and providence, have had a plenary manifestation.

But this wisdom appears, farther, in preserving such a record of the prediction, and such evidence of its accomplishment, as cannot possibly be doubted. The New Testament, given by the inspiration of God, and handed down uncorrupted from father to son, by both friends and enemies, perfect in its credibility and truth, inexpungable in its evidences, and astonishingly circumstantial in details of future occurrences, which the wisdom of God alone could foreknow – that New Testament is the record of these predictions. The history of the Romans, written by so many hands; the history of the Jews, written by one of themselves; triumphal arches, coins, medals, and public monuments of different kinds, are the evidence by which the fulfillment of the record is demonstrated. Add to this the preservation of the Jewish people; a people scattered through all nations, yet subsisting as a distinct body, without temple, sacrifices, or political

to escape all these things that shall come to pass, and to stand before the Son of man.

MATTHEW 24: 43–51; MARK 13: 34–37; LUKE 12: 35–50

Matthew 24: 43–51

43 But know this, that if the goodman of the house had known in what watch the thief would come, he would have watched, and would not have suffered his house to be broken up.

44 Therefore be ye also ready: for in such an hour as ye think not the Son of man cometh.

45 Who then is a faithful and wise servant, whom his lord hath made ruler over his household, to give them meat in due season?

46 Blessed is that servant, whom his lord when he cometh shall find so doing.

47 Verily I say unto you, That he shall make him ruler over all his goods.

48 But and if that evil servant shall say in his heart, My lord delayeth his coming;

49 And shall begin to smite his fellowservants, and to eat and drink with the drunken;

50 The lord of that servant shall come in a day when he looketh not for him, and in an hour that he is not aware of,

51 And shall cut him asunder, and appoint him his portion with the hypocrites: there shall be weeping and gnashing of teeth.

Mark 13: 34–37

34 For the Son of man is as a man taking a far journey, who left his house, and gave authority to his servants, and to every man his work, and commanded the porter to watch.

35 Watch ye therefore: for ye know not when the master of the house cometh, at even, or at midnight, or at the cockcrowing, or in the morning:

36 Lest coming suddenly he find you sleeping.

37 And what I say unto you I say unto all, Watch.

Luke 12: 35–50

35 Let your loins be girded about, and your lights burning;

36 And ye yourselves like unto men

world will be in a state of stupid indifference, so that men will think of nothing but the present life, and will extend their cares to a long period, pursuing their ordinary course of life, as if the world were always to remain in the same condition. The comparisons are highly appropriate; for if we consider what then happened, we shall no longer be deceived by the belief that the uniform order of events which we see in the world will always continue. For within three days of the time, when every man was conducting his affairs in the utmost tranquillity, the world was swallowed up by a deluge, and five cities were consumed by fire.

MATTHEW 24: 43–51; MARK 13: 34–37; LUKE 12: 35–50

Matthew 24: 43. If the householder had known

Luke relates this discourse of Christ at a different place from Matthew; and we need not wonder at this, for in the twelfth chapter, where (as we have formerly explained) he collects out of various discourses a summary of doctrine, he inserts also this parable. Besides, he introduces a general preface that the disciples should **wait for their master**, with their **loins girt**, and carrying **burning lamps** in their hands. To this statement corresponds the parable, which we shall soon afterwards find in Matthew 25: 1–12 about the **wise and foolish virgins**.

In a few words Christ glances rapidly at the manner in which believers ought to conduct their pilgrimage in the world; for first he contrasts the **girding of the loins** with sloth, and **burning lamps** with the darkness of ignorance. First, then, Christ enjoins the disciples to be ready and equipped for the journey, that they may pass rapidly through the world, and may seek no fixed abode or resting-place but in heaven. The warning is highly useful; for though ungodly men have likewise in their mouth this form of expression, "the course of life," yet we see how they lay themselves down in the world, and remain unmoved in their attachment to it. But God does not bestow the honorable title of his children on any but those who acknowledge that they are strangers on the earth, and who not only are at all times prepared to leave it, but likewise move forward, in an uninterrupted "course," towards the heavenly life. Again, as they are surrounded on all sides by darkness, so long as they remain in the world, he furnishes them with **lamps**, as persons who are to perform a journey during the night. The first recommendation is, to run vigorously; and the next is, to have clear information as to the road, that believers may not weary themselves to no purpose by going astray; for otherwise it would be better to stumble in the way, than to perform a journey in uncertainty and mistake. As to the expression, **girding the loins**, it is borrowed

government; and who, while they attempt to suppress the truth, yet reluctantly stand forth as an unimpeachable collateral evidence, that the solemn record, already alluded to, is strictly and literally true! Who that has ever consulted the Roman historians of the reigns of Vespasian and Titus, the history of Josephus, and the 24th chapter of St. Matthew's Gospel, and who knows any thing of the present state of the Jews over the face of the earth, or even of those who sojourn in England, can doubt for a moment the truth of this Gospel, or the infinite and all-comprehensive knowledge of Him who is its author! Here then is one portion of Divine Revelation that is incontrovertibly and absolutely proved to be the truth of God. Reader! if he, who, while he predicted the ruin of this disobedient and refractory people, wept over their city and its inhabitants, has so, minutely fulfilled the threatenings of his justice on the unbelieving and disobedient, will he not as circumstantially fulfill the promises of his grace to all them that believe? The existence of his revelation, the continuance of a Christian Church upon earth, the certainty that there is one individual saved from his sins by the grace of the Gospel, and walking worthy of his vocation are continued proofs and evidences that he is still the same; that he will fulfill every jot and tittle of that word on which he has caused thee to trust; and save to the uttermost all that come unto the Father by him. The word of the Lord endureth for ever; and they who trust in him shall never be confounded.

MATTHEW 25: 1–13

1. **Then shall the kingdom of heaven** – The state of Jews and professing Christians – the state of the visible Church at the time of the destruction of Jerusalem, and in the day of judgment: for the parable appears to relate to both those periods. And particularly at the time in which Christ shall come to judge the world, it shall appear what kind of reception his Gospel has met with. This parable, or something very like it, is found in the Jewish records: so in a treatise entitled RESHITH CHOCMAH, the

beginning of wisdom, we read thus: "Our wise men of blessed memory say, Repent whilst thou hast strength to do it, whilst thy lamp burns, and thy oil is not extinguished; for if thy lamp be gone out, thy oil will profit thee nothing." Our doctors add, in MEDRASH: "The holy blessed God said to Israel, My sons, repent whilst the gates of repentance stand open; for I receive a gift at present, but when I shall sit in judgment, in the age to come, I will receive none." Another parable, mentioned by Kimchi, on Isaiah 65: 13. "Rabbi Yuchanan, the son of Zachai, spoke a parable concerning a king, who invited his servants, but set them no time to come: the prudent and wary among them adorned themselves and, standing at the door of the king's house, said, Is any thing wanting in the house of the king? (i.e. Is there any work to be done?) But the foolish ones that were among them went away, and working said, When shall the feast be in which there is no labor? Suddenly the king sought out his servants: those who were adorned entered in, and they who were still polluted entered in also. The king was glad when he met the prudent, but he was angry when he met the foolish: he said, Let the prudent sit down and eat – let the others stand and look on." Rabbi Eliezer said, "Turn to God one day before your death." His disciples said, "How can a man know the day of his death?" He answered them, "Therefore you should turn to God to-day, perhaps you may die to-morrow; thus every day will be employed in returning."

Virgins – Denoting the purity of the Christian doctrine and character. In this parable, the bridegroom is generally understood to mean Jesus Christ. The feast, that state of felicity to which he has promised to raise his genuine followers. The wise, or prudent, and foolish virgins, those who truly enjoy, and those who only profess the purity and holiness of his religion. The oil, the grace and salvation of God, or that faith which works by love. The vessel, the heart in which this oil is contained. The lamp, the profession of enjoying the burning and shining light of the Gospel of Christ. Going forth; the whole of their sojourning upon earth.

that wait for their lord, when he will return from the wedding; that when he cometh and knocketh, they may open unto him immediately.

37 Blessed are those servants, whom the lord when he cometh shall find watching: verily I say unto you, that he shall gird himself, and make them to sit down to meat, and will come forth and serve them.

38 And if he shall come in the second watch, or come in the third watch, and find them so, blessed are those servants.

39 And this know, that if the goodman of the house had known what hour the thief would come, he would have watched, and not have suffered his house to be broken through.

40 Be ye therefore ready also: for the Son of man cometh at an hour when ye think not.

41 Then Peter said unto him, Lord, speakest thou this parable unto us, or even to all?

42 And the Lord said, Who then is that faithful and wise steward, whom his lord shall make ruler over his household, to give them their portion of meat in due season?

43 Blessed is that servant, whom his lord when he cometh shall find so doing.

44 Of a truth I say unto you, that he will make him ruler over all that he hath.

45 But and if that servant say in his heart, My lord delayeth his coming; and shall begin to beat the menservants and maidens, and to eat and drink, and to be drunken;

46 The lord of that servant will come in a day when he looketh not for him, and at an hour when he is not aware, and will cut him in sunder, and will appoint him his portion with the unbelievers.

47 And that servant, which knew his lord's will, and prepared not himself, neither did according to his will, shall be beaten with many stripes.

48 But he that knew not, and did commit things worthy of stripes, shall be beaten with few stripes. For unto whomsoever much is given, of him shall be much required: and to whom men have committed much, of him they will ask the more.

from the ordinary custom of Eastern nations in wearing long garments.

Luke 12: 36. And you yourselves like men that wait for their master

He uses another parable not mentioned by Matthew, who writes more briefly on this subject; for he compares himself to **a householder** who, while he is joining in the festivities of the marriage feast, or in other respects indulging in pleasure, out of his own house, wishes **his servants** to conduct themselves with modesty and sobriety at home, attending to their lawful occupations, and diligently waiting for his return. Now though the Son of God has departed to the blessed rest of heaven, and is absent from us, yet as he has assigned to every one his duty, it would be improper for us to give way to indolent repose. Besides, as he has promised that he will return to us, we ought to hold ourselves prepared, at every moment, to receive him, that he may not find **us sleeping.** For if a mortal man looks upon it as a duty which **his servants** owe him, that, **at whatever hour he returns home**, they shall be prepared to receive him, how much more has he a right to demand from his followers that they shall be sober and vigilant, and always wait for his coming? To excite them to greater alacrity, he mentions that earthly masters are so delighted with such promptitude on the part of their servants, that they even **serve them**; not that all **masters** are accustomed to act in this manner, but because it does sometimes happen that a **master**, who is kind and gentle, admits his **servants** to his own table, as if they were his companions.

MATTHEW 25: 1–13

Though this exhortation – as will appear from the conclusion of it – has nearly the same object with the former, yet it is properly added, in order to confirm believers in perseverance. Our Lord knew how strongly the nature of men is inclined to idleness, and how, for the most part, they not only grow weary after a great lapse of time, but give way through sudden dislike. To remedy this disease, he taught his disciples that they were not duly fortified, unless they had sufficient perseverance for a long period. When this is ascertained to be the design of the parable, we ought not to trouble ourselves much with minute investigations, which have nothing to do with what Christ intended. Some people give themselves a good deal of uneasiness about **the lamps, the vessels, and the oil**; but the plain and natural meaning of the whole is, that it is not enough to have ardent zeal for a short time, if we have not also a constancy that never tires. And Christ employs a very appropriate parable to express this. A little before, he had exhorted the disciples, that as they had a journey to perform through dark and dreary

2. Five of them were wise – Or, provident, they took care to make a proper provision beforehand, and left nothing to be done in the last moment.

Five were foolish – which might be translated careless, is generally rendered foolish; but this does not agree so well with provident, or prudent, in the first clause, which is the proper meaning of the word. These did not see that it was necessary to have oil in their vessels, (the salvation of God in their souls), as well as a burning lamp of religious profession, Matthew 25: 3–4.

4. Took oil in their vessels – They not only had a sufficiency of oil in their lamps, but they carried a vessel with oil to recruit their lamps, when it should be found expedient. This the foolish or improvident neglected to do: hence, when the oil that was in their lamps burned out, they had none to pour into the lamp to maintain the flame.

5. The bridegroom tarried – The coming of the bridegroom to an individual may imply his death: his coming to the world – the final judgment. The delay – the time from a man's birth till his death, in the first case; in the second, the time from the beginning to the end of the world.

Slumbered and slept – Or, they became drowsy and fell asleep. As sleep is frequently used in the sacred writings for death, so drowsiness, which precedes sleep, may be considered as pointing out the decays of the constitution, and the sicknesses which precede death. The other explanations which are given of this place must be unsatisfactory to every man who is not warped by some point in his creed, which must be supported at every expense. Carelessness disposed them to drowsiness, drowsiness to sleep, deep sleep, which rendered them as unconscious of their danger as they were before inattentive to their duty. The Anglo-Saxon has hit the meaning of the original well – of which my old MS. Bible gives a literal version, in the English of the 14th century: *forsothe-alle nappeden and sleptyn.*

6. At midnight there was a cry – The Jewish weddings were generally celebrated in the night; yet they usually began at the rising of the evening star; but in this case there was a more than ordinary delay.

Behold, the bridegroom cometh – What an awful thing to be summoned to appear before the Judge of quick and dead!

7. Trimmed their lamps – adorned them. I have seen some of the eastern lamps or lanthorns, the body of which was a skeleton of wood and threads, covered with a very thin transparent membrane, or very fine gauze, and decorated with flowers painted on it. It is probable that the nuptial lamps were highly decorated in this way; though the act mentioned here may mean no more than preparing the lamps for burning.

There are certain preparations which most persons believe they must make at the approach of death; but, alas! it is often too late. The lamp is defiled, the light almost out, and the oil expended; and what adorning is a wretched sinner, struggling in the agonies of death, capable of preparing for his guilty soul!

8. Our lamps are gone out – are going out. So then it is evident that they were once lighted. They had once hearts illuminated and warmed by faith and love; but they had backslidden from the salvation of God, and now they are excluded from heaven, because, through their carelessness, they have let the light that was in them become darkness, and have not applied in time for a fresh supply of the salvation of God.

A Jewish rabbin supposes God addressing man thus: I give thee my lamp, give thou me thy lamp; if thou keep my lamp I will keep thy lamp; but if thou extinguish my lamp I will extinguish thy lamp. That is, I give thee my WORD and testimonies to be a light unto thy feet and a lanthorn to thy steps, to guide thee safely through life; give me thy SOUL and all its concerns, that I may defend and save thee from all evil: keep my WORD, walk in my ways, and I will keep thy SOUL that nothing shall injure it; but if thou trample under foot my laws, I will cast thy soul into outer darkness.

49 I am come to send fire on the earth; and what will I if it be already kindled?

50 But I have a baptism to be baptized with; and how am I straitened till it be accomplished!

MATTHEW 25: 1–13

1 Then shall the kingdom of heaven be likened unto ten virgins, which took their lamps, and went forth to meet the bridegroom.

2 And five of them were wise, and five were foolish.

3 They that were foolish took their lamps, and took no oil with them:

4 But the wise took oil in their vessels with their lamps.

5 While the bridegroom tarried, they all slumbered and slept.

6 And at midnight there was a cry made, Behold, the bridegroom cometh; go ye out to meet him.

7 Then all those virgins arose, and trimmed their lamps.

8 And the foolish said unto the wise, Give us of your oil; for our lamps are gone out.

9 But the wise answered, saying, Not so; lest there be not enough for us and you: but go ye rather to them that sell, and buy for yourselves.

10 And while they went to buy, the bridegroom came; and they that were ready went in with him to the marriage: and the door was shut.

11 Afterward came also the other virgins, saying, Lord, Lord, open to us.

12 But he answered and said, Verily I say unto you, I know you not.

13 Watch therefore, for ye know neither the day nor the hour wherein the Son of man cometh.

MATTHEW 25: 31–46; LUKE 21: 37–38

Matthew 25: 31–46

31 When the Son of man shall come in his glory, and all the holy angels with him, then shall he sit upon the throne of his glory:

32 And before him shall be gathered all nations: and he shall separate them one from another, as a shepherd divideth his sheep from the goats:

places, they should provide themselves with **lamps**; but as the wick of the lamp, if it be not supplied with oil, gradually dries up, and loses its brightness, Christ now says, that believers need to have incessant supplies of courage, to support the flame which is kindled in their hearts, otherwise their zeal will fail ere they have completed the journey.

1. Then shall the kingdom of heaven

By this term is meant the condition of the future Church, which was to be collected by the authority and direction of Christ. He employs this remarkable title, that believers may not deceive themselves by an erroneous opinion that they have arrived at absolute perfection. The parable is borrowed from the ordinary custom of life; for it was a childish speculation of Jerome and others, to adduce this passage in praise of virginity; while Christ had no other object in view than to lessen the uneasiness which they might be apt to feel in consequence of the delay of his coming. He says, therefore, that he asks nothing more from us than is usually done for friends at a marriage-feast. The custom was, that **virgins**, who are tender and delicate – should, by way of respect, accompany **the bridegroom** to his chamber. But the general instruction of the parable consists in this, that it is not enough to have been once ready and prepared for the discharge of duty, if we do not persevere to the end.

MATTHEW 25: 31–46; LUKE 21: 37–38

Matthew 25: 31. Now when the Son of man shall come in his glory

Christ follows out the same doctrine, and what he formerly described under parables, he now explains clearly and without figures. The sum of what is said is, that believers, in order to encourage themselves to a holy and upright conduct, ought to contemplate with the eyes of faith the heavenly life, which, though it is now concealed, will at length be manifested at the last coming of Christ. For, when he declares that, **when he shall come with the angels, then will he sit on the throne of his glory**, he contrasts this last revelation with the disorders and agitations of earthly warfare; as if he had said, that he did not appear for the purpose of immediately setting up his kingdom, and therefore that there was need of hope and patience, lest the disciples might be discouraged by long delay. Hence we infer that this was again added, in order that the disciples, being freed from mistake about immediate and sudden happiness, might keep their minds in warfare till Christ's second coming, and might not give way, or be discouraged, on account of his absence.

This is the reason why he says that he will then assume the title of King; for though he commenced his reign on the earth, and now sits at the right hand of the Father, so as to

9. Lest there be not enough for us and you – These had all been companions in the Christian course, and there was a time when they might have been helpful to each other; but that time is now past for ever – none has a particle of grace to spare, not even to help the soul of the dearest relative! The grace which every man receives is just enough to save his own soul; he has no merits to bequeath to the Church; no work of supererogation which can be placed to the account of another.

10. While they went to buy, the bridegroom came – What a dismal thing it is, not to discover the emptiness of one's heart of all that is good, till it is too late to make any successful application for relief! God alone knows how many are thus deceived.

And they that were ready – They who were prepared – who had not only a burning lamp of an evangelical profession, but had oil in their vessels, the faith that works by love in their hearts, and their lives adorned with all the fruits of the Spirit.

The door was shut – Sinners on a death-bed too often meet with those deceitful merchants, who promise them salvation for a price which is of no value in the sight of God. Come unto me, says Jesus, and buy: there is no salvation but through his blood – no hope for the sinner but that which is founded upon his sacrifice and death. The door was shut – dreadful and fatal words! No hope remains. Nothing but death can shut this door; but death may surprise us in our sins, and then despair is our only portion.

11. Afterwards came also the other virgins, saying, Lord, Lord – Earnest prayer, when used in time, may do much good: but it appears, from this parable, that there may come a time when prayer even to Jesus may be too late! – viz. when the door is shut – when death has separated the body and the soul.

12. I know you not – As if he had said, Ye are not of my company – ye were neither with the bride nor the bridegroom: ye slept while the others were in procession. I do not acknowledge you for my disciples – ye are not like him

who is love – ye refused to receive his grace – ye sinned it away when ye had it; now you are necessarily excluded from that kingdom where nothing but love and purity can dwell.

13. Watch therefore – If to watch be to employ ourselves chiefly about the business of our salvation, alas! how few of those who are called Christians are there who do watch! How many who slumber! How many who are asleep! How many seized with a lethargy! How many quite dead!

MATTHEW 25: 31–46; LUKE 21: 37–38

Matthew 25: 31–46

31. When the Son of man shall come – This must be understood of Christ's coming at the last day, to judge mankind: though all the preceding part of the chapter may be applied also to the destruction of Jerusalem.

The throne of his glory – That glorious throne on which his glorified human nature is seated, at the right hand of the Father.

32. All nations – Literally, all the nations – all the Gentile world; the Jews are necessarily included, but they were spoken of in a particular manner in the preceding chapter.

He shall separate them – Set each kind apart by themselves.

As a shepherd divideth, etc. – It does not appear that sheep and goats were ever penned or housed together, though they might feed in the same pasture.

33. He shall set the sheep, etc. – The right hand signifies, among the rabbins, approbation and eminence: the left hand, rejection, and disapprobation. Hence in Sohar Chadash it is said, "The right hand is given, the left also is given – to the Israelites and the Gentiles are given paradise and hell – this world, and the world to come." The right and left were emblematical of endless beatitude and endless misery among the Romans.

Of the good and faithful servants he approves, and therefore exalts them to his glory; of the slothful and wicked he disapproves, and casts them into hell.

33 And he shall set the sheep on his right hand, but the goats on the left.

34 Then shall the King say unto them on his right hand, Come, ye blessed of my Father, inherit the kingdom prepared for you from the foundation of the world:

35 For I was an hungred, and ye gave me meat: I was thirsty, and ye gave me drink: I was a stranger, and ye took me in:

36 Naked, and ye clothed me: I was sick, and ye visited me: I was in prison, and ye came unto me.

37 Then shall the righteous answer him, saying, Lord, when saw we thee an hungred, and fed thee? or thirsty, and gave thee drink?

38 When saw we thee a stranger, and took thee in? or naked, and clothed thee?

39 Or when saw we thee sick, or in prison, and came unto thee?

40 And the King shall answer and say unto them, Verily I say unto you, Inasmuch as ye have done it unto one of the least of these my brethren, ye have done it unto me.

41 Then shall he say also unto them on the left hand, Depart from me, ye cursed, into everlasting fire, prepared for the devil and his angels:

42 For I was an hungred, and ye gave me no meat: I was thirsty, and ye gave me no drink:

43 I was a stranger, and ye took me not in: naked, and ye clothed me not: sick, and in prison, and ye visited me not.

44 Then shall they also answer him, saying, Lord, when saw we thee an hungred, or athirst, or a stranger, or naked, or sick, or in prison, and did not minister unto thee?

45 Then shall he answer them, saying, Verily I say unto you, Inasmuch as ye did it not to one of the least of these, ye did it not to me.

46 And these shall go away into everlasting punishment: but the righteous into life eternal.

Luke 21: 37–38

37 And in the day time he was teaching in the temple; and at night he went out, and abode in the mount that is called the mount of Olives.

38 And all the people came early in

exercise the supreme government of heaven and earth; yet he has not yet erected before the eyes of men that throne, from which his divine majesty will be far more fully displayed than it now is at the last day; for that, of which we now obtain by faith nothing more than a taste, will then have its full effect. So then Christ now sits on his heavenly throne, as fir as it is necessary that he shall reign for restraining his enemies and protecting the Church; but then he will appear openly, to establish perfect order in heaven and earth, to crush his enemies under his feet, to assemble his believing people to partake of an everlasting and blessed life, to ascend his judgment-seat; and, in a word, there will be a visible manifestation of the reason why the kingdom was given to him by the Father. He says that he will come in his glory; because, while he dwelt in this world as a mortal man, he appeared in the despised form of a servant. And he calls it his glory, though he elsewhere ascribes it to his Father, but the meaning is the same; for he means simply the divine glory, which at that time shone in the Father only, for in himself it was concealed.

32. And all nations shall be assembled before him
He employs large and splendid titles for extolling his kingdom, that the disciples may learn to expect a different kind of happiness from what they had imagined. For they were satisfied with this single consideration, that their nation was delivered from the miseries with which it was then oppressed, so that it would be manifest that God had not in vain established his covenant with Abraham and his posterity. But Christ extends much farther the benefit of the redemption brought by him, for he will be the Judge of the whole world. Again, in **order** to persuade believers to holiness of life, he assures them that the good and the bad will not share alike; because he will bring with him the reward which is laid up for both. In short, he declares that his kingdom will be fully established, when the righteous shall have obtained a crown of glory, and when the wicked shall have received the reward which they deserved.

MATTHEW 26: 1–13; MARK 14: 1–9; LUKE 22: 1–2

Christ now confirms again what we have seen that he had sometimes predicted to his disciples; but this last prediction clearly shows how willingly he offered himself to die; and it was necessary that he should do so, because God could not be appeased but by a sacrifice of obedience. He intended, at the same time, to prevent the disciples from taking offense, lest they might be altogether discouraged by the thought that he was dragged to death by necessity. Two purposes were thus served by this statement: to testify, first, that the Son of God willingly surrendered himself to

SHEEP, which have ever been considered as the emblems of mildness, simplicity, patience, and usefulness, represent here the genuine disciples of Christ.

GOATS, which are naturally quarrelsome, lascivious, and excessively ill-scented, were considered as the symbols of riotous, profane, and impure men. They here represent all who have lived and died in their sins. See Ezekiel 34: 17, and Zechariah 10: 3.

34. Ye blessed of my Father – This is the king's address to his followers; and contains the reason why they were found in the practice of all righteousness, and were now brought to this state of glory – they were blessed – came as children, and received the benediction of the Father, and became, and continued to be, members of the heavenly family.

Inherit – The inheritance is only for the children of the family – if sons, then heirs, Galatians 4: 7, but not otherwise. The sons only shall enjoy the father's estate.

Prepared for you – That is, the kingdom of glory is designed for such as you – you who have received the blessing of the Father, and were holy, harmless, undefiled, and separated from sinners.

From the foundation of the world – It was God's purpose and determination to admit none into his heaven but those who were made partakers of his holiness, Hebrews 12: 14.

35. I was an hungered, and ye gave me meat – Every thing which is done to a follower of Christ, whether it be good or evil, he considers as done to himself, see Matthew 25: 40; Acts 9: 4–5; Hebrews 6: 10.

A stranger, and ye took me in – ye entertained me: Strangers are sometimes so destitute as to be ready to perish for lack of food and raiment: a supply of these things keeps their souls and bodies together, which were about to be separated through lack of the necessaries of life. The word may also allude to a provision made for a poor family, which were scattered abroad, perhaps begging their bread, and who by the ministry of benevolent people are collected, relieved, and put in a way of getting their bread. O blessed work! to be

the instruments of preserving human life, and bringing comfort and peace into the habitations of the wretched!

36. I was sick, and ye visited me – Relieving the strangers, and visiting the sick, were in high estimation among the Jews. One of their sayings on this head is worthy of notice: "He who neglects to visit the sick is like him who has shed blood." That is, as he has neglected, when it was in his power, to preserve life, he is as guilty in the sight of the Lord as he is who has committed murder

37. Lord, when saw we thee an hungered, etc. – This barbarous expression, an hungered, should be banished out of the text, wheresoever it occurs, and the simple word hungry substituted for it. Whatever is done for Christ's sake, is done through Christ's grace; and he who does the work attributes to Jesus both the will and the power by which the work was done, and seeks and expects the kingdom of heaven not as a reward, but as a gift of pure unmerited mercy. Yet, while workers together with his grace, God attributes to them that which they do through his influence, as if they had done it independently of him. God has a right to form what estimate he pleases of the works wrought through himself: but man is never safe except when he attributes all to his Maker.

40. Inasmuch as ye have done it unto one of the least of these my brethren – The meanest follower of Christ is acknowledged by him as his brother! What infinite condescension! Those, whom many would scorn to set with the dogs of their flock, are brothers and sisters of the blessed Jesus, and shall soon be set among the princes of his people.

41. Depart from me, ye cursed – Or, Ye cursed! depart. – These words are the address of the king to the sinners; and contain the reason why they are to be separated from blessedness: Ye are cursed, because ye have sinned, and would not come unto me that ye might have life. – No work of piety has proceeded from your hand, because the carnal mind, which is enmity against me, reigned in your heart;

the morning to him in the temple, for to hear him.

MATTHEW 26: 1–13; MARK 14: 1–9; LUKE 22: 1–2

Matthew 26: 1–13

1 And it came to pass, when Jesus had finished all these sayings, he said unto his disciples,

2 Ye know that after two days is the feast of the passover, and the Son of man is betrayed to be crucified.

3 Then assembled together the chief priests, and the scribes, and the elders of the people, unto the palace of the high priest, who was called Caiaphas,

4 And consulted that they might take Jesus by subtilty, and kill him.

5 But they said, Not on the feast day, lest there be an uproar among the people.

6 Now when Jesus was in Bethany, in the house of Simon the leper,

7 There came unto him a woman having an alabaster box of very precious ointment, and poured it on his head, as he sat at meat.

8 But when his disciples saw it, they had indignation, saying, To what purpose is this waste?

9 For this ointment might have been sold for much, and given to the poor.

10 When Jesus understood it, he said unto them, Why trouble ye the woman? for she hath wrought a good work upon me.

11 For ye have the poor always with you; but me ye have not always.

12 For in that she hath poured this ointment on my body, she did it for my burial.

13 Verily I say unto you, Wheresoever this gospel shall be preached in the whole world, there shall also this, that this woman hath done, be told for a memorial of her.

Mark 14: 1–9

1 After two days was the feast of the passover, and of unleavened bread: and the chief priests and the scribes sought how they might take him by craft, and put him to death.

2 But they said, Not on the feast day,

die, in order to reconcile the world to the Father, (for in no other way could the guilt of sins have been expiated, or righteousness obtained for us;) and, secondly, that he did not die like one oppressed by violence which he could not escape, but because he voluntarily offered himself to die. He therefore declares that he comes to Jerusalem with the express intention of suffering death there; for while he was at liberty to withdraw and to dwell in a safe retreat till that time was come, he knowingly and willfully comes forward at the exact time. And though it was of no advantage to the disciples to be informed, at that time, of the obedience which he was rendering to the Father, yet afterwards this doctrine tended in no small degree to the edification of their faith. In like manner, it is of singular utility to us at the present day, because we behold, as in a bright mirror, the voluntary sacrifice, by which all the transgressions of the world were blotted out, and, contemplating the Son of God advancing with cheerfulness and courage to death, we already behold him victorious over death.

Matthew 26: 3. Then were assembled the chief priests

Matthew does not mean that they assembled during the **two days**, but introduces this narrative to show, that Christ was not led by any opinion of man to fix the day of his death; for by what conjectures could he have been led to it, since his enemies themselves had resolved to delay for a time? The meaning therefore is, that by the spirit of prophecy he spoke of his own death, which no man could have suspected to be so near at hand. John explains the reason why the scribes and priests held this meeting: it was because, from day to day, the people flocked to Christ in greater multitudes, (John 11: 48.) And at that time it was decided, at the instigation of **Caiaphas**, that he should be put to death, because they could not succeed against him in any other way.

5. But they said, Not during the festival

They did not think it a fit season, till the festival was past, and the crowd was dispersed. Hence we infer that, although those hungry dogs eagerly opened their mouths to devour Christ, or rather, rushed furiously upon him, still God withheld them, by a secret restraint, from doing any thing by their deliberation or at their pleasure. So far as lies in their power, they delay till another time; but, contrary to their wish, God hastens the hour. And it is of great importance for us to hold, that Christ was not unexpectedly dragged to death by the violence of his enemies, but was led to it by the providence of God; for our confidence in the propitiation is founded on the conviction that he was offered to God as that sacrifice which God had appointed from the beginning. And therefore he determined that; his Son should be sacrificed on the very day of **the passover**,

and ye would not have me to reign over you. Depart! this includes what some have termed the punishment of loss or privation. Ye cannot, ye, shall not be united to me – Depart! O terrible word! and yet a worse is to come.

Into everlasting fire – This is the punishment of sense. Ye shall not only be separated from me, but ye shall be tormented, awfully, everlastingly tormented in that place of separation.

Prepared for the devil and his angels – The devil and his angels sinned before the creation of the world, and the place of torment was then prepared for them: it never was designed for human souls; but as the wicked are partakers with the devil and his angels in their iniquities, in their rebellion against God, so it is right that they should be sharers with them in their punishment.

42. I was an hungered, and ye gave me no meat – I put it in your power to do good, and ye would not. A variety of occasions offered themselves to you, but ye neglected them all, so that my blessings in your hands, not being improved, according to my order, became a curse to you.

43. I was a stranger – If men were sure that Jesus Christ was actually somewhere in the land, in great personal distress, hungry, thirsty, naked, and confined, they would doubtless run unto and relieve him. Now Christ assures us that a man who is hungry, thirsty, naked, etc., is his representative, and that whatever we do to such a one he will consider as done to himself; yet this testimony of Christ is not regarded! Well, he will be just when he judges, and righteous when he punishes.

44. Lord, when saw we thee an hungered, etc. – It is want of faith which in general produces hard-heartedness to the poor. The man who only sees with eyes of flesh is never likely to discover Christ in the person of a man destitute of the necessaries of life. Some pretend not to know the distressed; because they have no desire to relieve them; but we find that this ignorance will not avail them at the bar of God.

46. And these shall go away into everlasting punishment – No appeal, no remedy, to all eternity! No end to the punishment of those whose final impenitence manifests in them an eternal will and desire to sin. By dying in a settled opposition to God, they cast themselves into a necessity of continuing in an eternal aversion from him.

MATTHEW 26: 1–13; MARK 14: 1–9; LUKE 22: 1–2

Matthew 26: 1–13

1. When Jesus had finished all these sayings – He began these sayings on Mount Olivet, Matthew 24: 1, and continued them till he entered into Bethany, whither he was going.

2. The passover – A feast instituted in Egypt, to commemorate the destroying angel's passing over the houses of the Israelites, when he slew the firstborn of the Egyptians. This feast began on the fourteenth day of the first moon, in the first month, Nisan, and it lasted only one day; but it was immediately followed by the days of unleavened bread, which were seven, so that the whole lasted eight days, and all the eight days are sometimes called the feast of the passover, and sometimes the feast or days of unleavened bread. See Luke 22: 1–7.

The Son of man is betrayed, (rather delivered up), to be crucified – With what amazing calmness and precision does our blessed Lord speak of this awful event! What a proof does he here give of his prescience in so correctly predicting it; and of his love in so cheerfully undergoing it! Having instructed his disciples and the Jews by his discourses, edified them by his example, convinced them by his miracles, he now prepares to redeem them by his blood! These two verses have no proper connection with this chapter, and should be joined to the preceding.

3. Then assembled together the chief priests – That is, during the two days that preceded the passover.

4. And consulted that they might take Jesus by subtilty – The providence of God frustrated

lest there be an uproar of the people.

3 And being in Bethany in the house of Simon the leper, as he sat at meat, there came a woman having an alabaster box of ointment of spikenard very precious; and she brake the box, and poured it on his head.

4 And there were some that had indignation within themselves, and said, Why was this waste of the ointment made?

5 For it might have been sold for more than three hundred pence, and have been given to the poor. And they murmured against her.

6 And Jesus said, Let her alone; why trouble ye her? she hath wrought a good work on me.

7 For ye have the poor with you always, and whensoever ye will ye may do them good: but me ye have not always.

8 She hath done what she could: she is come aforehand to anoint my body to the burying.

9 Verily I say unto you, Wheresoever this gospel shall be preached throughout the whole world, this also that she hath done shall be spoken of for a memorial of her.

Luke 22: 1–2

1 Now the feast of unleavened bread drew nigh, which is called the Passover.

2 And the chief priests and scribes sought how they might kill him; for they feared the people.

MATTHEW 26: 14–20; MARK 14: 10–17; LUKE 22: 3–14

Matthew 26: 14–20

14 Then one of the twelve, called Judas Iscariot, went unto the chief priests,

15 And said unto them, What will ye give me, and I will deliver him unto you? And they covenanted with him for thirty pieces of silver.

16 And from that time he sought opportunity to betray him.

17 Now the first day of the feast of unleavened bread the disciples came to Jesus, saying unto him, Where wilt thou that we prepare for thee to eat the passover?

18 And he said, Go into the city to such a man, and say unto him, The Master

that the ancient figure might give place to the only sacrifice of eternal redemption. Those who had no other design in view than to ruin Christ thought that another time would be more appropriate; but God, who had appointed him to be a sacrifice for the expiation of sins, selected a suitable day for contrasting the body with its shadow, by placing them together. Hence also we obtain a brighter display of the fruit of Christ's suffering.

MATTHEW 26: 14–20; MARK 14: 10–17; LUKE 22: 3–14

Matthew 26: 14. Then one of the twelve, who was called Judas Iscariot

Christ's admonition was so far from being of any avail for softening the heart of Judas, or producing any change in it for the better, that he immediately went away, without any concern, to transact an infamous bargain with his enemies. It was amazing and prodigious stupidity, that he considered himself to have found, in the expense of the ointment, a fair excuse for so heinous a crime; and next, that, after having been warned by the words of Christ, he did not perceive what he was doing. The bare mention of the burying ought to have softened a heart of iron; for it would have been easy to infer from it, that Christ offered himself as a sacrifice for the salvation of the human race. But we see in this mirror how great is the blindness of wicked desires, and how powerfully they fascinate the mind. Judas was inflamed with the desire to steal; long practice had hardened him in wickedness; and now when he meets with no other prey, he does not scruple to betray basely to death the Son of God, the Author of life, and, though restrained by a holy admonition, rushes violently forward.

With good reason, therefore, does Luke expressly say that **Satan entered into him**; not that the Spirit of God formerly directed him, for he would not have been addicted to theft and robbery, if he had not been the slave of Satan. But Luke means, that he was at that time wholly given up to Satan, so that, like a desperate man, he violently sought his destruction. For though Satan drives us every day to crimes, and reigns in us, when he hurries us into a course of extraordinary wickedness; yet he is said to enter into the reprobate, when he takes possession of all their senses, overthrows the fear of God, extinguishes the light of reason, and destroys every feeling of shame. This extremity of vengeance God does not execute on any but those who are already devoted to destruction. Let us therefore learn to repent early, lest our long-continued harshness should confirm the reign of Satan within us; for as soon as we have been abandoned to this tyranny, his rage will have no bounds. It is particularly worthy of notice, that the cause

their artful machinations; and that event which they wished to conduct with the greatest privacy and silence was transacted with all possible celebrity, amidst the thousands who resorted to Jerusalem, at this season, for the keeping of the passover. It was, doubtless, of the very first importance that the crucifixion of Christ, which was preparatory to the most essential achievement of Christianity, viz. his resurrection from the grave, should be exhibited before many witnesses, and in the most open manner, that infidelity might not attempt, in future, to invalidate the evidences of the Christian religion, by alleging that these things were done in a corner.

5. Not on the feast day, lest there be an uproar – It was usual for the Jews to punish criminals at the public festivals; but in this case they were afraid of an insurrection, as our Lord had become very popular. The providence of God directed it thus, for the reason given in the preceding note.

He who observes a festival on motives purely human violates it in his heart, and is a hypocrite before God. It is likely they feared the Galileans, as being the countrymen of our Lord, more than they feared the people of Jerusalem.

7. There came unto him a woman – There is much contention among commentators about the transaction mentioned here, and in John 12: 3; some supposing them to be different, others to be the same.

Some think that the woman mentioned here was Mary, the sister of Lazarus; others Mary Magdalene; but against the former opinion it is argued that it is not likely, had this been Mary the sister of Lazarus, that Matthew and Mark would have suppressed her name. Besides, say they, we should not confound the repast which is mentioned here, with that mentioned by John, 12: 3. This one was made only two days before the passover, and that one six days before: the one was made at the house of Simon the leper, the other at the house of Lazarus, John 12: 1–2. At this, the woman poured the oil on the head of Christ; at the other, Mary anointed Christ's feet with it.

8. His disciples – One of them, viz. Judas. This mode of speaking was common among the Hebrews. So, Matthew 27: 44, the thieves also, i.e. one of them. So, Matthew 28: 17, some doubted, i.e. one, Thomas. See also Genesis 8: 4; Judges 12: 7; Nehemiah 6: 7, etc. Among rhetoricians the plural is put for the singular; it is, however, possible that Judas, who made the objection, was followed in the sentiment by the rest of the disciples.

9. And given to the poor – How often does charity serve as a cloak for covetousness! God is sometimes robbed of his right under the pretense of devoting what is withheld to some charitable purpose, to which there was no intention ever to give it.

10. Why trouble ye the woman? – Or, Why do ye put the woman to pain? A generous mind is ever pained when it is denied the opportunity of doing good, or when its proffered kindness is refused.

11. Ye have the poor always with you – And, consequently, have the opportunity of doing them good at any time; but me ye have not always; my bodily presence is about to be removed from you for ever. The woman, under a presentiment of my death is preparing me for my burial.

12. She did it for my burial – Or, She hath done it to embalm me. Our Lord took this opportunity to tell them, once more, that he was shortly to die.

13. Wheresoever this Gospel shall be preached – Another remarkable proof of the prescience of Christ. Such a matter as this, humanly speaking, depended on mere fortuitous circumstances, yet so has God disposed matters, that the thing has continued, hitherto, as firm and regular as the ordinances of heaven.

For a memorial of her – As embalming preserves the body from corruption, and she has done this good work to embalm and preserve this body, so will I order every thing concerning this transaction to be carefully recorded, to preserve her memory to the latest ages. The

saith, My time is at hand; I will keep the passover at thy house with my disciples.

19 And the disciples did as Jesus had appointed them; and they made ready the passover.

20 Now when the even was come, he sat down with the twelve.

Mark 14: 10–17

10 And Judas Iscariot, one of the twelve, went unto the chief priests, to betray him unto them.

11 And when they heard it, they were glad, and promised to give him money. And he sought how he might conveniently betray him.

12 And the first day of unleavened bread, when they killed the passover, his disciples said unto him, Where wilt thou that we go and prepare that thou mayest eat the passover?

13 And he sendeth forth two of his disciples, and saith unto them, Go ye into the city, and there shall meet you a man bearing a pitcher of water: follow him.

14 And wheresoever he shall go in, say ye to the goodman of the house, The Master saith, Where is the guestchamber, where I shall eat the passover with my disciples?

15 And he will shew you a large upper room furnished and prepared: there make ready for us.

16 And his disciples went forth, and came into the city, and found as he had said unto them: and they made ready the passover.

17 And in the evening he cometh with the twelve.

Luke 22: 3–14

3 Then entered Satan into Judas surnamed Iscariot, being of the number of the twelve.

4 And he went his way, and communed with the chief priests and captains, how he might betray him unto them.

5 And they were glad, and covenanted to give him money.

6 And he promised, and sought opportunity to betray him unto them in the absence of the multitude.

7 Then came the day of unleavened bread, when the passover must be killed.

8 And he sent Peter and John, saying,

and source of so great blindness in Judas was avarice, which makes it evident that it is justly denominated by Paul the root of all evils (1 Timothy 6: 10).

To inquire here whether or not Satan entered into Judas bodily is an idle speculation. We ought rather to consider how fearfully monstrous it is, that men formed after the image of God, and appointed to be temples for the Holy Spirit, should not only be turned into filthy stables or sinks, but should become the wretched abodes of Satan.

17. Now on the first day of unleavened bread, the disciples came to Jesus

It is first inquired, Why does the day which preceded the sacrificing of the lamb receive the name of the day of unleavened bread? For the Law did not forbid the use of leaven till the lamb was eaten (Exodus 12: 18). But this difficulty may be speedily removed, for the phrase refers to the following day, as is sufficiently evident from Mark and Luke. Since, therefore, the day of killing and eating the passover was at hand, the disciples ask Christ where **he wishes them to eat the passover**. But hence arises a more difficult question. How did Christ observe that ceremony on the day before the whole nation celebrated the public passover? For John plainly affirms that the day on which Christ was crucified was, among the Jews, **the preparation**, not of the Sabbath, but of **the passover** (John 19: 14); and that "they did not enter into the hall of judgment, lest they should be defiled, because next day they were to eat the passover" (John 18: 28).

I am aware that there are some who resort to evasions, which do not, however, give them any relief; for no sophistry can set aside the fact; that, on the day they crucified Christ, they did not keep the feast, (when it would not have been lawful to have any public executions) and that they had, at that the a solemn **preparation**, so that they ate the passover after that Christ had been buried.

It comes now to be inquired, Why did Christ anticipate? For it must not be supposed that, in this ceremony, he took any liberty which was at variance with the prescriptions of the Law. As to the notion entertained by some, that the Jews, through their eagerness to put Christ to death, delayed the passover, it is ably refuted by Bucer, and, indeed, falls to the ground by its own absurdity. I have no doubt, therefore, that Christ observed the day appointed by the Law, and that the Jews followed a custom which had been long in use. First, it is beyond a doubt that Christ was put to death on the day before the Sabbath; for he was hastily buried before sunset in a sepulcher which was at hand, (John 19: 42,) because it was necessary to abstain from work after the commencement of the evening. Now it is universally admitted that, by an ancient custom, when **the passover**

actions which the world blames, through the spirit of envy, covetousness, or malice, God takes delight to distinguish and record.

MATTHEW 26: 14–20; MARK 14: 10–17; LUKE 22: 3–14

Matthew 26: 14–20

14. **Then – Judas –** After this supper at Bethany, Judas returned to Jerusalem, and made his contract with the chief priests.

16. **He sought opportunity –** a convenient or fit opportunity. Men seldom leave a crime imperfect: when once sin is conceived, it meets, in general, with few obstacles, till it brings forth death. How deceitful, how deeply damning, is the love of money!

Judas is deservedly considered as one of the most infamous of men, his conduct base beyond description, and his motives vile. But how many, since his time, have walked in the same way! How many, for the sake of worldly wealth, have renounced the religion of their Lord and Master, and sold Jesus, and their interest in heaven, for a short-lived portion of secular good! From John 12: 6, we learn that Judas, who was treasurer to our Lord and his disciples, (for he carried the bag), was a thief, and frequently purloined a portion of what was given for the support of this holy family. Being disappointed of the prey he hoped to have from the sale of the precious ointment, Matthew 26: 9, he sold his Master to make up the sum. A thorough Jew!

17. **Now the first day of the feast of unleavened bread –** As the feast of unleavened bread did not begin till the day after the passover, the fifteenth day of the month, Leviticus 23: 5, 6; Numbers 28: 16, 17, this could not have been, properly, the first day of that feast; but as the Jews began to eat unleavened bread on the fourteenth, Exodus 12: 18, this day was often termed the first of unleavened bread. The evangelists use it in this sense, and call even the paschal day by this name. See Mark 14: 12; Luke 22: 7.

Where wilt thou that we prepare – How astonishing is this, that HE who created all things, whether visible or invisible, and by whom all things were upheld, should so empty himself as not to be proprietor of a single house in his whole creation, to eat the last passover with his disciples! This is certainly a mystery, and so, less or more is every thing that God does. But how inveterate and destructive must the nature of sin be, when such emptying and humiliation were necessary to its destruction! It is worthy of note what the Talmudists say, that the inhabitants of Jerusalem did not let out their houses to those who came to the annual feasts; but afforded all accommodations of this kind gratis. A man might therefore go and request the use of any room, on such an occasion, which was as yet unoccupied. The earthen jug, and the skin of the sacrifice, were left with the host.

18. **Go – to such a man –** It is probable that this means some person with whom Christ was well acquainted, and who was known to the disciples. Grotius observes that the Greeks use this form when they mean some particular person who is so well known that there is no need to specify him by name. The circumstances are more particularly marked in Luke 22: 8, etc.

My time is at hand – That is, the time of my crucifixion.

19. **And the disciples did –** The disciples that were sent on this errand were Peter and John. See Luke 22: 8.

They made ready the passover – That is, they provided the lamb, etc., which were appointed by the law for this solemnity. Mr. Wakefield justly observes, "that the Jews considered the passover as a sacrificial rite. It was highly necessary that this should be considered as an expiatory sacrifice, as it typified that Lamb of God who takes away the sin of the world.

20. **Now when the even was come, he sat down with the twelve. –** It is a common opinion that our Lord ate the passover some hours before the Jews ate it; for the Jews, according to custom, ate theirs at the end of the four-

Go and prepare us the passover, that we may eat.

9 And they said unto him, Where wilt thou that we prepare?

10 And he said unto them, Behold, when ye are entered into the city, there shall a man meet you, bearing a pitcher of water; follow him into the house where he entereth in.

11 And ye shall say unto the goodman of the house, The Master saith unto thee, Where is the guestchamber, where I shall eat the passover with my disciples?

12 And he shall shew you a large upper room furnished: there make ready.

13 And they went, and found as he had said unto them: and they made ready the passover.

14 And when the hour was come, he sat down, and the twelve apostles with him.

MATTHEW 26: 21–25; MARK 14: 18–21; LUKE 22: 15–16,21–23

Matthew 26: 21–25

21 And as they did eat, he said, Verily I say unto you, that one of you shall betray me.

22 And they were exceeding sorrowful, and began every one of them to say unto him, Lord, is it I?

23 And he answered and said, He that dippeth his hand with me in the dish, the same shall betray me.

24 The Son of man goeth as it is written of him: but woe unto that man by whom the Son of man is betrayed! it had been good for that man if he had not been born.

25 Then Judas, which betrayed him, answered and said, Master, is it I? He said unto him, Thou hast said.

Mark 14: 18–21

18 And as they sat and did eat, Jesus said, Verily I say unto you, One of you which eateth with me shall betray me.

19 And they began to be sorrowful, and to say unto him one by one, Is it I? and another said, Is it I?

20 And he answered and said unto them, It is one of the twelve, that dippeth with me in the dish.

21 The Son of man indeed goeth, as it

and other festivals happened on Friday, they were delayed till the following day, because the people would have reckoned it hard to abstain from work on two successive days. The Jews maintain that this law was laid down immediately after the return of the people from the Babylonian captivity, and that it was done by a revelation from heaven, that they may not be thought to have made any change, of their own accord, in the commandments of God.

MATTHEW 26: 21–25; MARK 14: 18–21; LUKE 22: 15–16, 21–23

Matthew 26: 21. One of you will betray me

To render the treachery of Judas more detestable, he points out the aggravated baseness of it by this circumstance, that he was meditating the act of betraying him while he sat with him at the holy table. For if a stranger had done this, it would have been more easily endured; but that one of his intimate friends should form such a design, and – what is more – that, after having entered into an infamous bargain, he should be present at the sacred banquet, was incredibly monstrous. And therefore Luke employs a connecting particle which marks a contrast: but yet, **lo, the hand of him that betrayeth me.** And though Luke adds this saying of Christ after the supper was finished, we cannot obtain from it any certainty as to the order of time, which, we know, was often disregarded by the Evangelists. Yet I do not deny that it is probable that Judas was present, when Christ distributed to his disciples the symbols of his flesh and blood.

22. They began every one of them to say to him

I do not think that the disciples were alarmed, as persons struck with terror are wont to give themselves uneasiness without any reason; but, abhorring the crime, they are desirous to clear themselves from the suspicion of it. It is, indeed, a mark of reverence, that when indirectly blamed, they do not reply angrily to their Master, but each person constitutes himself his own judge (as the object which we ought chiefly to aim at is, to be acquitted by his own mouth); but, relying on a good conscience, they wish to declare frankly how far they are from meditating such a crime.

MATTHEW 26: 26–30; MARK 14: 22–26; LUKE 22: 17–20

As Luke mentions that **the cup** was twice presented by Christ, we must inquire, in the first place, if it be a repetition, (as the Evangelists are wont frequently to say the same thing twice,) or if Christ, after having tasted the cup, repeated the same thing a second time. This latter conjecture

teenth day, but Christ ate his the preceding even, which was the beginning of the same sixth day, or Friday; the Jews begin their day at sunsetting, we at midnight. Thus Christ ate the passover on the same day with the Jews, but not on the same hour. Christ kept this passover the beginning of the fourteenth day, the precise day and hour in which the Jews had eaten their first passover in Egypt. See Exodus 12: 6–12. And in the same part of the same day in which the Jews had sacrificed their first paschal lamb, viz. between the two evenings, about the ninth hour, or 3 o'clock, Jesus Christ our passover was sacrificed for us: for it was at this hour that he yielded up his last breath; and then it was that, the sacrifice being completed, Jesus said, IT IS FINISHED. See Exodus 12: 6, etc., and Deuteronomy 16: 6, etc.

MATTHEW 26: 21–25; MARK 14: 18–21; LUKE 22: 15–16,21–23

Matthew 26: 21–25

21. One of you shall betray me – Or, will deliver me up. Judas had already betrayed him, Matthew 26: 15, and he was now about to deliver him into the hands of the chief priests, according to the agreement he had made with them.

22. They were exceeding sorrowful – That is, the eleven who were innocent; and the hypocritical traitor, Judas, endeavored to put on the appearance of sorrow. Strange! Did he not know that Christ knew the secrets of his soul! Or had his love of money so far blinded him, as to render him incapable of discerning even this, with which he had been before so well acquainted?

23. He that dippeth his hand – As the Jews ate the passover a whole family together, it was not convenient for them all to dip their bread in the same dish; they therefore had several little dishes or plates, in which was the juice of the bitter herbs, mentioned Exodus 12: 8, on different parts of the table; and those who were nigh one of these, dipped their bread in it. As Judas is represented as dipping

in the same dish with Christ, it shows that he was either near or opposite to him. If this man's heart had not been hardened, and his conscience seared beyond all precedent, by the deceitfulness of his sin, would he have showed his face in this sacred assembly, or have thus put the seal to his own perdition, by eating of this sacrificial lamb? Is it possible that he could feel no compunction? Alas! having delivered himself up into the hands of the devil, he was capable of delivering up his Master into the hands of the chief priests; and thus, when men are completely hardened by the deceitfulness of sin, they can outwardly perform the most solemn acts of devotion, without feeling any sort of inward concern about the matter.

24. The Son of man goeth – That is, is about to die. Going, going away, departing, etc., are frequently used in the best Greek and Latin writers, for death, or dying. The same words are often used in the Scriptures in the same sense.

It had been good for that man – Can this be said of any sinner, in the common sense in which it is understood, if there be any redemption from hell's torments? If a sinner should suffer millions of millions of years in them, and get out at last to the enjoyment of heaven, then it was well for him that he had been born, for still he has an eternity of blessedness before him. Can the doctrine of the non-eternity of hell's torments stand in the presence of this saying? Or can the doctrine of the annihilation of the wicked consist with this declaration? It would have been well for that man if he had never been born! Then he must be in some state of conscious existence, as non-existence is said to be better than that state in which he is now found. It was common for the Jews to say of any flagrant transgressor, It would have been better for him had he never been born.

25. Judas – said, Master, is it I? – What excessive impudence! He knew, in his conscience, that he had already betrayed his Master, and was waiting now for the servants of the chief priests, that he might deliver him into their hands; and yet he says, (hoping that he had

is written of him: but woe to that man by whom the Son of man is betrayed! good were it for that man if he had never been born.

Luke 22: 15–16,21–23

15 And he said unto them, With desire I have desired to eat this passover with you before I suffer:

16 For I say unto you, I will not any more eat thereof, until it be fulfilled in the kingdom of God.

21 But, behold, the hand of him that betrayeth me is with me on the table.

22 And truly the Son of man goeth, as it was determined: but woe unto that man by whom he is betrayed!

23 And they began to inquire among themselves, which of them it was that should do this thing.

MATTHEW 26: 26–30; MARK 14: 22–26; LUKE 22: 17–20

Matthew 26: 26–30

26 And as they were eating, Jesus took bread, and blessed it, and brake it, and gave it to the disciples, and said, Take, eat; this is my body.

27 And he took the cup, and gave thanks, and gave it to them, saying, Drink ye all of it;

28 For this is my blood of the new testament, which is shed for many for the remission of sins.

29 But I say unto you, I will not drink henceforth of this fruit of the vine, until that day when I drink it new with you in my Father's kingdom.

30 And when they had sung an hymn, they went out into the mount of Olives.

Mark 14: 22–26

22 And as they did eat, Jesus took bread, and blessed, and brake it, and gave to them, and said, Take, eat: this is my body.

23 And he took the cup, and when he had given thanks, he gave it to them: and they all drank of it.

24 And he said unto them, This is my blood of the new testament, which is shed for many.

25 Verily I say unto you, I will drink no more of the fruit of the vine, until that day that I drink it new in the kingdom of God.

appears to me to be probable; for we know that the holy fathers, during sacrifices, observed the solemn rite of tasting the cup; and hence those words of the Psalmist, **I will take the cup of salvation**, and will call on the name of the Lord (Psalm 116: 13).

I have no doubt, therefore, that Christ, according to the ancient custom, tasted the cup in the holy feast, which otherwise could not have been correctly observed; and Luke expressly mentions this, before coming to give an account of the new mystery, which was a totally different institution from the paschal lamb. It was in compliance also with received and ordinary custom, that he is expressly said to have **given thanks,** after having **taken the cup.** For at the commencement of the supper, I have no doubt, he prayed, as he was accustomed never to sit down at table without calling on God; but now he wished to discharge once more the same duty, that he might not leave out a ceremony which, I have just now shown, was connected with the sacred act of taking the cup and tasting it.

Matthew 26: 26. And while they were eating, Jesus took bread

I do not understand these words to mean that with the paschal supper was mixed this new and more excellent supper, but rather that an end was then put to the former banquet. This is still more clearly expressed by Luke, when he says that, Christ **gave the cup after that he had supped;** for it would have been absurd that one and the same mystery should be broken off by an interval of time. And therefore I have no doubt that, in immediate succession, after having distributed the bread, he added the cup; and what Luke relates particularly respecting the cup, I regard as including also the bread. **While they were eating**, therefore, Christ took bread, to invite them to partake of a new supper. The **thanksgiving** was a sort of preparation and transition to consider the mystery. Thus when the supper was ended, they tasted the sacred **bread** and **wine;** because Christ had previously aroused them from their indifference, that they might be all alive to so lofty a mystery. And, indeed, the nature of the case demands that this clear testimony of the spiritual life should be distinguished from the ancient shadow.

Jesus took bread

It is uncertain if the custom which is now observed among the Jews was at that time in use: for the master of the house breaks off a portion of a common loaf, hides it under the table-cloth, and afterwards distributes a part of it to, each member of the family. But as this is a human tradition not founded on any commandment of God, we need not toil with excessive eagerness to investigate its origin; and it is possible that it may have been afterwards contrived, by a

transacted his business so privately that it had not yet transpired), Master, is it I? It is worthy of remark, that each of the other disciples said, LORD, is it I? But Judas dares not, or will not, use this august title, but simply says, TEACHER, is it I?

Thou hast said – "Ye have said," was a common form of expression for YES. IT IS so.

MATTHEW 26: 26–30; MARK 14: 22–26; LUKE 22: 17–20

Matthew 26: 26–30

26. As they were eating – Either an ordinary supper, or the paschal lamb, as some think. See the observations at the end of this chapter.

Jesus took bread – Of what kind? Unleavened bread, certainly, because there was no other kind to be had in all Judea at this time; for this was the first day of unleavened bread, (Matthew 26: 17), i.e. the 14th of the month Nisan, when the Jews, according to the command of God, (Exodus 12: 15–20; 23: 15; 34: 25), were to purge away all leaven from their houses; for he who sacrificed the passover, having leaven in his dwelling, was considered to be such a transgressor of the Divine law as could no longer be tolerated among the people of God; and therefore was to be cut off from the congregation of Israel.

Let those, therefore, who consider that man shall live by every word which proceeds from the mouth of God, and who are conscientiously solicitous that each Divine institution be not only preserved, but observed in all its original integrity, attend to this circumstance. The Lutheran Church makes use of unleavened bread to the present day.

And blessed it – Both St. Matthew and St. Mark use the word blessed, instead of gave thanks, which is the word used by St. Luke and St. Paul.

No blessing of the elements is here intended; they were already blessed, in being sent as a gift of mercy from the bountiful Lord; but God the sender is blessed, because of the liberal provision he has made for his worthless creatures. Blessing and touching the bread are merely Popish ceremonies, unauthorized either by Scripture or the practice of the pure Church of God; necessary of course to those who pretend to transmute, by a kind of spiritual incantation, the bread and wine into the real body and blood of Jesus Christ; a measure the grossest in folly, and most stupid in nonsense, to which God in judgment ever abandoned the fallen spirit of man.

And brake it – We often read in the Scriptures of breaking bread, but never of cutting it. The Jewish people had nothing similar to our high-raised loaf: their bread was made broad and thin, and was consequently very brittle, and, to divide it, there was no need of a knife.

And gave it to the disciples – Not only the breaking, but also the DISTRIBUTION, of the bread are necessary parts of this rite.

This is my body – Here it must be observed that Christ had nothing in his hands, at this time, but part of that unleavened bread which he and his disciples had been eating at supper, and therefore he could mean no more than this, viz. that the bread which he was now breaking represented his body, which, in the course of a few hours, was to be crucified for them.

In this solemn transaction we must weigh every word, as there is none without its appropriate and deeply emphatic meaning. So it is written, Ephesians 5: 2. Christ hath loved us, and given himself, on our account, or in our stead, an offering and a SACRIFICE to God for a sweet-smelling savor.

27. And he took the cup – after having supped, Luke 22: 20, and 1 Corinthians 11: 25. How strange is it, that the very men who plead so much for the bare literal meaning of this is my body, in the preceding verse, should deny all meaning to drink YE ALL of this cup, in this verse! And though Christ has in the most positive manner enjoined it, they will not permit one of the laity to taste it! O, what a thing is man – a constant contradiction to reason and to himself.

28. For this is my blood of the New Testament – In this place, our Lord terms his blood

26 And when they had sung an hymn, they went out into the mount of Olives.

Luke 22: 17–20
17 And he took the cup, and gave thanks, and said, Take this, and divide it among yourselves:
18 For I say unto you, I will not drink of the fruit of the vine, until the kingdom of God shall come.
19 And he took bread, and gave thanks, and brake it, and gave unto them, saying, This is my body which is given for you: this do in remembrance of me.
20 Likewise also the cup after supper, saying, This cup is the new testament in my blood, which is shed for you.

MATTHEW 26: 31–35; MARK 14: 27–31; LUKE 22: 31–34

Matthew 26: 31–35
31 Then saith Jesus unto them, All ye shall be offended because of me this night: for it is written, I will smite the shepherd, and the sheep of the flock shall be scattered abroad.
32 But after I am risen again, I will go before you into Galilee.
33 Peter answered and said unto him, Though all men shall be offended because of thee, yet will I never be offended.
34 Jesus said unto him, Verily I say unto thee, That this night, before the cock crow, thou shalt deny me thrice.
35 Peter said unto him, Though I should die with thee, yet will I not deny thee. Likewise also said all the disciples.

Mark 14: 27–31
27 And Jesus saith unto them, All ye shall be offended because of me this night: for it is written, I will smite the shepherd, and the sheep shall be scattered.
28 But after that I am risen, I will go before you into Galilee.
29 But Peter said unto him, Although all shall be offended, yet will not I.
30 And Jesus saith unto him, Verily I say unto thee, That this day, even in this night, before the cock crow twice, thou shalt deny me thrice.
31 But he spake the more vehemently, If I should die with thee, I will not deny thee in any wise. Likewise also said they all.

trick of Satan, for the purpose of obscuring the mystery of the Lord's Supper. And even if this ceremony was at that time in use among the Jews, Christ followed the ordinary custom in such a manner as to draw away the minds of his followers to another object, by changing the use of the **bread** for a different purpose. This, at least, ought to be considered as beyond all controversy, that Christ, at this time, abolished the figures of the Law, and instituted a new Sacrament.

MATTHEW 26: 31–35; MARK 14: 27–31; LUKE 22: 31–34

Matthew 26: 31. You will all be offended at me
What Matthew and Mark extend to all the disciples alike is related by Luke as having been spoken to Peter only. But though the statement was equally addressed to all, yet it is probable that Christ spoke to them in the person of one man, who was to be admonished more than all the rest, and who needed extraordinary consolation, that, after having denied Christ, he might not be altogether overwhelmed with despair.

Luke 22: 31. Lo, Satan hath desired
The other two Evangelists relate more briefly and simply, that our Lord foretold to his disciples their fall. But the words of Luke contain more abundant instruction; for Christ does not speak of the future trouble in the way of narrative, but expressly declares, that they will have a contest with Satan, and, at the same time, promises to them victory. It is a highly useful admonition, whenever we meet with any thing that gives us offense, to have always before our eyes the snares of Satan; as Paul also teaches, that "we wrestle not with flesh and blood, but with spiritual armies" (Ephesians 6: 12).

The meaning of the words therefore is: "When, a short time hence, you shall see me oppressed, know that Satan employs these arms to fight against you, and that this is a convenient opportunity for destroying your faith." I have said that this is a useful doctrine, because it frequently happens that, from want of consideration, we are overcome by disregarding temptations, which we would regard as formidable, if we reflected that they are "the fiery darts" (Ephesians 6: 16) of a vigorous and powerful enemy. And though he now speaks of that singularly fierce attack, by which the disciples, at one time, received dreadful shocks, so that their faith was well nigh extinguished, yet he manifestly conveys a more extensive doctrine, that Satan continually goes about, roaring for his prey. As he is impelled by such furious madness to destroy us, nothing is more unreasonable than that we should give ourselves up to drowsiness. Before there is apparent necessity for fighting,

the blood of the NEW covenant; by which he means that grand plan of agreement, or reconciliation, which God was now establishing between himself and mankind, by the passion and death of his Son, through whom alone men could draw nigh to God; and this NEW covenant is mentioned in contradistinction from the OLD covenant.

Which is shed (poured out) for many – The blood of the new covenant sacrifice poured out for the multitudes, that there might be but one fold, as there is but one Shepherd; and that God might be ALL and in ALL.

For the remission of sins – for (or, in reference to) the taking away of sins. For, although the blood is shed, and the atonement made, no man's sins are taken away until, as a true penitent, he returns to God, and, feeling his utter incapacity to save himself, believes in Christ Jesus, who is the justifier of the ungodly.

29. I will not drink henceforth of this fruit of the vine – These words seem to intimate no more than this: We shall not have another opportunity of eating this bread and drinking this wine together; as in a few hours my crucifixion shall take place.

Until that day when I drink it new with you – That is, I shall no more drink of the produce of the vine with you; but shall drink new wine – wine of a widely different nature from this – a wine which the kingdom of God alone can afford. The term new in Scripture is often taken in this sense. So the NEW heaven, the NEW earth, the NEW covenant, the NEW man – mean a heaven, earth, covenant, man, of a very different nature from the former.

30. And when they had sung a hymn – means, probably, no more than a kind of recitative reading or chanting. As to the hymn itself, we know, from the universal consent of Jewish antiquity, that it was composed of Psalms 113, 114, 115, 116, 117, and 118. These six Psalms were always sung at every paschal solemnity. They sung this great hillel on account of the five great benefits referred to in it; viz.

1. The Exodus from Egypt, Psalm 114: 1. When Israel went out of Egypt, etc.

2. The miraculous division of the Red Sea, Psalm 114: 3. The sea saw it and fled.

3. The promulgation of the law, Psalm 114: 4. The mountains skipped like lambs.

4. The resurrection of the dead, Psalm 116: 9. I will walk before the Lord in the land of the living.

5. The passion of the Messiah, Psalm 115: 1. Not unto us, O Lord, not unto us, etc.

MATTHEW 26: 31–35; MARK 14: 27–31; LUKE 22: 31–34

Matthew 26: 31–35

31. All ye shall be offended – Or rather, Ye will all be stumbled – ye will all forsake me, and lose in a great measure your confidence in me.

This night – The time of trial is just at hand.

I will smite the shepherd – It will happen to you as to a flock of sheep, whose shepherd has been slain – the leader and guardian being removed, the whole flock shall be scattered, and be on the point of becoming a prey to ravenous beasts.

32. But after I am risen again – Don't lose your confidence; for though I shall appear for a time to be wholly left to wicked men, and be brought under the power of death, yet I will rise again, and triumph over all your enemies and mine.

I will go before you – Still alluding to the case of the shepherd and his sheep. Though the shepherd has been smitten and the sheep scattered, the shepherd shall revive again, collect the scattered flock, and go before them, and lead them to peace, security, and happiness.

33. Peter – **said unto him, Though all men shall be offended** – **yet will I never** – The presumptuous person imagines he can do every thing, and can do nothing: thinks he can excel all, and excels in nothing: promises every thing, and performs nothing. The humble man acts a quite contrary part. There is nothing we know so little of as ourselves – nothing we see less of than our own weakness and poverty. The strength of pride is only for a moment.

Luke 22: 31–34

31 And the Lord said, Simon, Simon, behold, Satan hath desired to have you, that he may sift you as wheat:

32 But I have prayed for thee, that thy faith fail not: and when thou art converted, strengthen thy brethren.

33 And he said unto him, Lord, I am ready to go with thee, both into prison, and to death.

34 And he said, I tell thee, Peter, the cock shall not crow this day, before that thou shalt thrice deny that thou knowest me.

LUKE 22: 35–38

35 And he said unto them, When I sent you without purse, and scrip, and shoes, lacked ye any thing? And they said, Nothing.

36 Then said he unto them, But now, he that hath a purse, let him take it, and likewise his scrip: and he that hath no sword, let him sell his garment, and buy one.

37 For I say unto you, that this that is written must yet be accomplished in me, And he was reckoned among the transgressors: for the things concerning me have an end.

38 And they said, Lord, behold, here are two swords. And he said unto them, It is enough.

MATTHEW 26: 36–44; MARK 14: 32–40; LUKE 22: 39–46

Matthew 26: 36–44

36 Then cometh Jesus with them unto a place called Gethsemane, and saith unto the disciples, Sit ye here, while I go and pray yonder.

37 And he took with him Peter and the two sons of Zebedee, and began to be sorrowful and very heavy.

38 Then saith he unto them, My soul is exceeding sorrowful, even unto death: tarry ye here, and watch with me.

39 And he went a little further, and fell on his face, and prayed, saying, O my Father, if it be possible, let this cup pass from me: nevertheless not as I will, but as thou wilt.

40 And he cometh unto the disciples,

let us already prepare ourselves; for we know that Satan desires our destruction, and with great skill and assiduity seizes on every method of injuring us. And when we come to the conflict, let us know that all temptations, from whatever quarter they come, were forged in the workshop of that enemy.

LUKE 22: 35–38

35. And he said to them

The whole object of this discourse of Christ is to show, that hitherto he spared his disciples, so as to lay on them no heavier burden than they were able to bear. He reminds them of the indulgence exercised during the past time, that they may now prepare themselves with greater alacrity for severer warfare. For why did he, while they were altogether destitute of skill and training, keep them in the shade and in repose, at a distance from the darts of the enemy, except that, by gradually gathering courage and strength during the interval of leisure, they might be better prepared for fighting? The meaning is: "Hitherto you have had an easy and prosperous condition, because I wished to treat you gently, like children; the full time is now come, when I must employ you in labor, like men."

MATTHEW 26: 36–44; MARK 14: 32–40; LUKE 22: 39–46

Matthew 26: 36. Then Jesus cometh with them

Luke mentions **the mountain of Olives** only. Mark and Matthew add a more minute description of the place. But Luke expresses what is still more to the purpose, that Christ came there **according to his custom**. Hence we infer, that he did not seek retirement for the purpose of concealing himself, but, as if he had made an assignation with his enemies, he presented himself to death. On this account John says (18: 2) that the place was known to the traitor, **because Jesus was wont to come there frequently**. In this passage, therefore, his obedience is again described to us, because he could not have appeased the Father but by a voluntary death. **Sit here**. By leaving the disciples at a distance, he spares their weakness; as if a man, perceiving that he would soon be in extreme danger in battle, were to leave his wife and children in a situation of safety. But though he intended to place them all beyond arrow-shot, yet he took three of them who accompanied him more closely than the rest, and these were the flower and choice, in which there was greater rigor. And yet he did not take them, as if he believed that they would be able to sustain the attack, but that they might afford a proof of the defect which was common to them all.

Peter, though vainly confident, was certainly sincere – he had never been put to a sore trial, and did not know his own strength. Had this resolution of his been formed in the strength of God, he would have been enabled to maintain it against earth and hell. This most awful denial of Christ, and his abandoning him in the time of trial, was sufficient to have disqualified him for ever from being, in any sense, head of the Church, had such a supremacy been ever designed him. Such a supremacy was never given him by Christ; but the fable of it is in the Church of Rome, and the mock Peter, not Peter the apostle, is there and there only to be found.

34. Jesus said – Our Lord's answer to Peter is very emphatic and impressive. Verily – I speak a solemn weighty truth, thou wilt not only be stumbled, fall off, and forsake thy Master, but thou wilt even deny that thou hast, or ever had, any knowledge of or connection with me; and this thou wilt do, not by little and little, through a long process of time, till the apostasy, daily gathering strength, shall be complete; but thou wilt do it this very night, and that not once only, but thrice; and this thou wilt do also in the earlier part of the night, before even a cock shall crow. Was not this warning enough to him not to trust in his own strength, but to depend on God?

35. Though I should die with thee, yet will I not deny thee – He does not take the warning which his Lord gave him – he trusts in the warm, sincere attachment to Christ which he now feels, not considering that this must speedily fail, unless supported by the power of God.

LUKE 22: 35–38

36. He that hath no sword – Judea was at this time much infested by robbers: while our Lord was with his disciples, they were perfectly safe, being shielded by his miraculous power. Shortly they must go into every part of the land, and will need weapons to defend themselves against wild beasts, and to intimidate wicked men, who, if they found them totally defenceless, would not hesitate to make them their prey, or take away their life. However the matter may be understood, we may rest satisfied that these swords were neither to be considered as offensive weapons, nor instruments to propagate the truth. The genius and spirit of the Christian religion is equally against both. Perhaps, in this counsel of our Lord, he refers to the contention about supremacy: as if he had said, Instead of contending among yourselves about who shall be the greatest, ye have more need to unite yourselves against the common enemy, who are now at hand: this counsel was calculated to show them the necessity of union among themselves, as their enemies were both numerous and powerful.

37. Must yet be accomplished – Probably meaning that, though this prophecy did refer to some particular matter in the time of the prophet, yet it farther related to Christ, and could not have its complete accomplishment but in his crucifixion as a criminal.

For the things concerning me have an end – As if he had said, My work is now almost done; yours is only beginning; I am now about to be crucified and numbered with the transgressors; think what will be done to you, and what ought to be done by you; and then think if this be a time for you to be contending with each other.

38. Lord, behold, here are two swords. And he said unto them, It is enough – I must here confess that the matter about the swords appear to me very obscure. I am afraid I do not understand it, and I know of none who does.

36. A place called Gethsemane – A garden at the foot of the mount of Olives. The garden of the oil-press, or olive-press.

Sit ye here – Or, stay in this place, while I go and pray yonder: and employ ye the time as I shall employ it – in watching unto prayer.

37. And he took with him Peter and the two sons of Zebedee – That is, James and John; the same persons who had beheld his transfiguration on the mount – that they might contemplate this agony in the light of that glory which they had there seen; and so be

and findeth them asleep, and saith unto Peter, What, could ye not watch with me one hour?

41 Watch and pray, that ye enter not into temptation: the spirit indeed is willing, but the flesh is weak.

42 He went away again the second time, and prayed, saying, O my Father, if this cup may not pass away from me, except I drink it, thy will be done.

43 And he came and found them asleep again: for their eyes were heavy.

44 And he left them, and went away again, and prayed the third time, saying the same words.

Mark 14: 32–40

32 And they came to a place which was named Gethsemane: and he saith to his disciples, Sit ye here, while I shall pray.

33 And he taketh with him Peter and James and John, and began to be sore amazed, and to be very heavy;

34 And saith unto them, My soul is exceeding sorrowful unto death: tarry ye here, and watch.

35 And he went forward a little, and fell on the ground, and prayed that, if it were possible, the hour might pass from him.

36 And he said, Abba, Father, all things are possible unto thee; take away this cup from me: nevertheless not what I will, but what thou wilt.

37 And he cometh, and findeth them sleeping, and saith unto Peter, Simon, sleepest thou? couldest not thou watch one hour?

38 Watch ye and pray, lest ye enter into temptation. The spirit truly is ready, but the flesh is weak.

39 And again he went away, and prayed, and spake the same words.

40 And when he returned, he found them asleep again, (for their eyes were heavy,) neither wist they what to answer him.

Luke 22: 39–46

39 And he came out, and went, as he was wont, to the mount of Olives; and his disciples also followed him.

40 And when he was at the place, he said unto them, Pray that ye enter not into

37. He began to be affected with grief

We have seen that our Lord formerly contended with the fear of death; but as he now fights face to face with temptation, such an attack is called the **beginning** of **grief** and **sorrow**.

Hence we infer that the true test of virtue is only to be found when the contest begins; for then the weakness of the flesh, which was formerly concealed, shows itself, and the secret feelings are abundantly displayed. Thus, though God had already tried his Son by certain preparatory exercises, he now wounds him more sharply by a nearer prospect of death, and strikes his mind with a terror to which he had not been accustomed. But as it appears to be inconsistent with the divine glory of Christ, that he was seized with trembling and sadness, many commentators have labored with toil and anxiety to find some way of evading the difficulty. But their labor has been ill-judged and of no use; for if we are ashamed that Christ should experience fear and sorrow, our redemption will perish and be lost.

Ambrose justly says: "I not only do not think that there is any need of excuse, but there is no instance in which I admire more his kindness and his majesty; for he would not have done so much for me, if he had not taken upon him my feelings. He grieved for me, who had no cause of grief for himself; and, laying aside the delights of the eternal Godhead, he experiences the affliction of my weakness. I boldly call it **sorrow**, because I preach the cross. For he took upon him not the appearance, but the reality, of incarnation. It was therefore necessary that he should experience grief, that he might overcome sorrow, and not shut it out; for the praise of fortitude is not bestowed on those who are rather stupefied than pained by wounds." Thus far Ambrose.

Certainly those who imagine that the Son of God was exempt from human passions do not truly and sincerely acknowledge him to be a man. And when it is even said that the divine power of Christ rested and was concealed for a time, that by his sufferings he might discharge all that belonged to the Redeemer, this was so far from being absurd, that in no other way could the mystery of our salvation have been accomplished. For Cyril has properly said: "That the suffering of Christ on the cross was not in every respect voluntary, but that it was voluntary on account of the will of the Father, and on account of our salvation, you may easily learn from his prayer, **Father, if it be possible, let this cup pass from me**. For the same reason that the Word of God is God (John 1: 1), and is naturally life itself (John 11: 25), nobody doubts that he had no dread of death; but, having been made flesh (John 1: 14), he allows the flesh to feel what belongs to it, and, therefore, being truly a man, he trembles at death, when it is now at the door, and says, **Father, if it be possible, let this cup pass from me; but**

kept from being stumbled by a view of his present humiliation.

Began to be sorrowful – exquisite sorrow, such as dissolves the natural vigor, and threatens to separate soul and body.

And very heavy – Overwhelmed with anguish. This word is used by the Greeks to denote the most extreme anguish which the soul can feel – excruciating anxiety and torture of spirit.

38. My soul is exceeding sorrowful, (or, is surrounded with exceeding sorrow), even unto death – This latter word explains the two former: My soul is so dissolved in sorrow, my spirit is filled with such agony and anguish, that, if speedy succor be not given to my body, death must be the speedy consequence.

Now, the grand expiatory sacrifice begins to be offered: in this garden Jesus enters fully into the sacerdotal office; and now, on the altar of his immaculate divinity, begins to offer his own body – his own life – a lamb without spot, for the sin of the world. St. Luke observes, Luke 22: 43–44, that there appeared unto him an angel from heaven strengthening him; and that, being in an agony, his sweat was like great drops of blood falling to the ground. How exquisite must this anguish have been, when it forced the very blood through the coats of the veins, and enlarged the pores in such a preternatural manner as to cause them to empty it out in large successive drops! In my opinion, the principal part of the redemption price was paid in this unprecedented and indescribable agony.

Bloody sweats are mentioned by many authors; but none was ever such as this – where a person in perfect health, (having never had any predisposing sickness to induce a debility of the system), and in the full vigor of life, about thirty-three years of age, suddenly, through mental pressure, without any fear of death, sweat great drops of blood; and these continued, during his wrestling with God to fall to the ground.

To say that all this was occasioned by the fear he had of the ignominious death which he was about to die confutes itself – for this would not only rob him of his divinity, for which purpose it is brought, but it deprives him of all excellency, and even of manhood itself. The prospect of death could not cause him to suffer thus, when he knew that in less than three days he was to be restored to life, and be brought into an eternity of blessedness. His agony and distress can receive no consistent explication but on this ground – He SUFFERED, the JUST for the UNJUST, that he might BRING us to GOD. O glorious truth! O infinitely meritorious suffering! And O! above all, the eternal love, that caused him to undergo such sufferings for the sake of SINNERS!

MATTHEW 26: 36–44; MARK 14: 32–40; LUKE 22: 39–46

Matthew 26: 36–44

39. Fell on his face – This was the ordinary posture of the supplicant when the favor was great which was asked, and deep humiliation required. The head was put between the knees, and the forehead brought to touch the earth – this was not only a humiliating, but a very painful posture also.

This cup – The word cup is frequently used in the Sacred Writings to point out sorrow, anguish, terror, death.

Pass from me – Perhaps there is an allusion here to several criminals standing in a row, who are all to drink of the same cup; but, the judge extending favor to a certain one, the cup passes by him to the next.

40. He – saith unto Peter – He addressed himself more particularly to this apostle, because of the profession he had made, Matthew 26: 33; as if he had said: "Is this the way you testify your affectionate attachment to me? Ye all said you were ready to die with me; what, then, cannot you watch ONE hour?"

41. That ye enter not into temptation – If ye cannot endure a little fatigue when there is no suffering, how will ye do when the temptation, the great trial of your fidelity and courage, cometh? Watch – that ye be not taken una-

temptation.

41 And he was withdrawn from them about a stone's cast, and kneeled down, and prayed,

42 Saying, Father, if thou be willing, remove this cup from me: nevertheless not my will, but thine, be done.

43 And there appeared an angel unto him from heaven, strengthening him.

44 And being in an agony he prayed more earnestly: and his sweat was as it were great drops of blood falling down to the ground.

45 And when he rose up from prayer, and was come to his disciples, he found them sleeping for sorrow,

46 And said unto them, Why sleep ye? rise and pray, lest ye enter into temptation.

MATTHEW 26: 45–50; MARK 14: 41–46; LUKE 22: 47–48

Matthew 26: 45–50

45 Then cometh he to his disciples, and saith unto them, Sleep on now, and take your rest: behold, the hour is at hand, and the Son of man is betrayed into the hands of sinners.

46 Rise, let us be going: behold, he is at hand that doth betray me.

47 And while he yet spake, lo, Judas, one of the twelve, came, and with him a great multitude with swords and staves, from the chief priests and elders of the people.

48 Now he that betrayed him gave them a sign, saying, Whomsoever I shall kiss, that same is he: hold him fast.

49 And forthwith he came to Jesus, and said, Hail, master; and kissed him.

50 And Jesus said unto him, Friend, wherefore art thou come? Then came they, and laid hands on Jesus, and took him.

Mark 14: 41–46

41 And he cometh the third time, and saith unto them, Sleep on now, and take your rest: it is enough, the hour is come; behold, the Son of man is betrayed into the hands of sinners.

42 Rise up, let us go; lo, he that betrayeth me is at hand.

43 And immediately, while he yet

since it cannot be otherwise, let it be not as I will, but as thou wilt. You see how human nature, even in Christ himself, has the sufferings and fears which belong to it, but that the Word, who is united to it, raises it to a fortitude which is worthy of God.

MATTHEW 26: 45–50; MARK 14: 41–46; LUKE 22: 47–48

Matthew 26: 45. Sleep on now, and take your rest

It is plain enough, that Christ now speaks ironically, but we must, at the same time, attend to the object of the irony. For Christ, having gained nothing by warning his disciples, not only gives an indirect reproof of their indifference, but threatens, that how indolent so ever they may choose to be, no longer delay will be allowed them. The meaning therefore is, "Having hitherto wasted my words on you, I shall now come to exhort you; but whatever permission I may give you to sleep, the enemies will not allow it to you, but will compel you to watch against your will." In Mark, it is accordingly added, **It is enough**; as if he had said, that there is no more time for **sleeping**.

And this is the way in which the Lord usually chastises the indolence of men, that those who wax deaf to words may at length be compelled, by their sufferings, to arouse themselves. Let us, therefore, learn to give immediate attention to the words of the Lord, lest what he wishes to draw from us voluntarily may be too late forced from us by necessity.

46. Arise, let us go

By these words he declares that, after having prayed, he was furnished with new arms. He had formerly, indeed, been sufficiently voluntary as to dying; but, when he came to the point, he had a hard struggle with the weakness of the flesh, so that he would willingly have withdrawn from dying, provided that he had been permitted to do so with the good-will of his Father. He, therefore, obtained by prayers and tears (Hebrews 5: 7) new strength from heaven; not that he ever hesitated through want of strength, but because under the weakness of the flesh, which he had voluntarily undertaken, he wished to labor anxiously, and with painful and difficult exertion, to gain a victory for us in his own person. But now, when the trembling is allayed, and the fear is subdued, that he may again present a voluntary sacrifice to the Father, he not only does not retire or conceal himself, but cheerfully advances to death.

47. While he was still speaking

The Evangelists are careful to state that our Lord foresaw what happened; from which it might be inferred, that he was not dragged to death by external violence, except so far

wares; and pray – that when it comes ye may be enabled to bear it.

The spirit – is willing, but the flesh is weak – Your inclinations are good – ye are truly sincere; but your good purposes will be overpowered by your timidity. Ye wish to continue steadfast in your adherence to your Master; but your fears will lead you to desert him.

42. O my Father, if this cup may not pass away from me – If it be not possible – to redeem fallen man, unless I drink this cup, unless I suffer death for them; thy will be done – I am content to suffer whatever may be requisite to accomplish the great design. In this address the humanity of Christ most evidently appears; for it was his humanity alone that could suffer; and if it did not appear that he had felt these sufferings, it would have been a presumption that he had not suffered, and consequently made no atonement. And had he not appeared to have been perfectly resigned in these sufferings, his sacrifice could not have been a free-will but a constrained offering, and therefore of no use to the salvation of mankind.

43. Their eyes were heavy – That is, they could not keep them open. Was there nothing preternatural in this? Was there no influence here from the powers of darkness?

44. Prayed the third time – So St. Paul – I besought the Lord THRICE that it might depart from me, 2 Corinthians 12: 8. This thrice repeating the same petition argues deep earnestness of soul.

MATTHEW 26: 45–50; MARK 14: 41–46; LUKE 22: 47–48

Matthew 26: 45–50

45. Sleep on now, and take your rest – Perhaps it might be better to read these words interrogatively, and paraphrase them thus: Do ye sleep on still? Will no warnings avail? Will no danger excite you to watchfulness and prayer? My hour – in which I am to be delivered up, is at hand; therefore now think of your own personal safety.

The Son of man is betrayed into the hands of sinners – viz. the Gentiles or heathens, who were generally distinguished by this appellation from the Jews. Here it probably means the Roman cohort that was stationed on festivals for the defense of the temple. By the Romans he was adjudged to death; for the Jews acknowledged that they had no power in capital cases.

46. Rise, let us be going – That is, to meet them, giving thereby the fullest proof that I know all their designs, and might have, by flight or otherwise, provided for my own safety; but I go willingly to meet that death which their malice designs me, and, through it, provide for the life of the world.

47. Judas, one of the twelve – More deeply to mark his base ingratitude and desperate wickedness – HE was ONE of the TWELVE – and he is a TRAITOR, and one of the vilest too that ever disgraced human nature.

A great multitude with swords and staves – They did not come as officers of justice, but as a desperate mob. Justice had nothing to do in this business. He who a little before had been one of the leaders of the flock of Christ is now become the leader of ruffians and murderers! What a terrible fall!

48. Gave them a sign – How coolly deliberate is this dire apostate! The man whom I shall kiss – how deeply hypocritical! That is he, hold him fast, seize him – how diabolically malicious!

Hail, Master – A usual compliment among the Jews. Judas pretends to wish our Lord continued health while he is meditating his destruction!

How many compliments of this kind are there in the world! Judas had a pattern in Joab, who, while he pretends to inquire tenderly for the health of Amasa, thrust him through with his sword; but the disciple here vastly outdoes his master, and through a motive, if possible, still more base. Let all those who use unmeaning or insidious compliments rank for ever with Joab and Judas.

And kissed him – And tenderly kissed him – this is the proper meaning of the original

spake, cometh Judas, one of the twelve, and with him a great multitude with swords and staves, from the chief priests and the scribes and the elders.

44 And he that betrayed him had given them a token, saying, Whomsoever I shall kiss, that same is he; take him, and lead him away safely.

45 And as soon as he was come, he goeth straightway to him, and saith, Master, master; and kissed him.

46 And they laid their hands on him, and took him.

Luke 22: 47–48

47 And while he yet spake, behold a multitude, and he that was called Judas, one of the twelve, went before them, and drew near unto Jesus to kiss him.

48 But Jesus said unto him, Judas, betrayest thou the Son of man with a kiss?

MATTHEW 26: 51–56; MARK 14: 47–52; LUKE 22: 49–53

Matthew 26: 51–56

51 And, behold, one of them which were with Jesus stretched out his hand, and drew his sword, and struck a servant of the high priest's, and smote off his ear.

52 Then said Jesus unto him, Put up again thy sword into his place: for all they that take the sword shall perish with the sword.

53 Thinkest thou that I cannot now pray to my Father, and he shall presently give me more than twelve legions of angels?

54 But how then shall the scriptures be fulfilled, that thus it must be?

55 In that same hour said Jesus to the multitudes, Are ye come out as against a thief with swords and staves for to take me? I sat daily with you teaching in the temple, and ye laid no hold on me.

56 But all this was done, that the scriptures of the prophets might be fulfilled. Then all the disciples forsook him, and fled.

Mark 14: 47–52

47 And one of them that stood by drew a sword, and smote a servant of the high priest, and cut off his ear.

48 And Jesus answered and said unto them, Are ye come out, as against a thief,

as wicked men carried into execution the secret purpose of God. Although, therefore, a melancholy and frightful spectacle was exhibited to the disciples, yet they received, at the same time, grounds of confidence to confirm them, since the event itself showed that nothing occurred by chance; and since Christ's prediction directed them to contemplate the glory of his divinity.

MATTHEW 26: 51–56; MARK 14: 47–52; LUKE 22: 49–53

Matthew 26: 51. And, lo, one of those who were with Jesus

Luke says, that all the disciples made an agreement together to fight for their Master. Hence it is again evident, that we are much more courageous and ready for fighting than for bearing the cross; and, therefore, we ought always to deliberate wisely what the Lord commands, and what he requires from every one of us, lest the fervor of our zeal exceed the bounds of reason and moderation. When the disciples asked Christ, **Shall we strike with the sword?** they did so, not with the intention of obeying his injunction; but by these words they declared that they were prepared and ready to repel the violence of enemies. And, indeed, Peter did not wait till he was commanded or permitted to strike, but inconsiderately proceeded to unlawful violence. It appears, at first view, to be praiseworthy valor in the disciples, that, forgetting their own weakness, though they are unable to make resistance, they do not hesitate to present their bodies before their Master, and to encounter certain death; for they choose rather to perish with the Lord than to survive and look on while he is oppressed. But as they improperly attempt more than the calling of God commands or permits, their rashness is justly condemned; and therefore let us learn, that in order that our obedience may be acceptable to the Lord, we must depend on his will, so that no man shall move a finger, except so far as God commands. One reason ought, above all, to lead us to be zealous in cultivating this modesty; which is, that instead of a proper and well-regulated zeal, confused irregularity for the most part reigns in us.

Peter's name is not mentioned here by the Evangelists; but John (18: 10) assures us – and from what occurs shortly afterwards in the narrative it is evident – that it was Peter who is here described, though the name is suppressed.

52. Put thy sword again into its place

By these words, Christ confirms the precept of the Law, which forbids private individuals to use the sword. And above all, we ought to attend to the threatening of punishment which is immediately added; for men did not, at their own pleasure, appoint this punishment for avenging their

word, he kissed him again and again – still pretending the most affectionate attachment to him, though our Lord had before unmasked him.

50. Jesus said – Friend – Rather, companion, (not FRIEND), wherefore, art thou come? How must these words have cut his very soul, if he had any sensibility left! Surely, thou, who hast so long been my companion, art not come against me, thy Lord, Teacher and Friend! What is the human heart not capable of, when abandoned by God, and influenced by Satan and the love of money!

Laid hands on Jesus – But not before they had felt that proof of his sovereign power by which they had all been struck down to the earth, John 18: 6. It is strange that, after this, they should dare to approach him; but the Scriptures must be fulfilled.

MATTHEW 26: 51–56; MARK 14: 47–52; LUKE 22: 49–53

Matthew 26: 51–56

51. One of them which were with Jesus – This was Peter – struck a servant of the high priest's, the servant's name was Malchus, John 18: 10, and smote off his ear. In Luke 22: 51, it is said, Jesus touched and healed it. Here was another miracle, and striking proof of the Divinity of Christ. Peter did not cut the ear, merely, he cut it OFF. Now to heal it, Jesus must either take up the ear and put it on again, or else create a new one – either of these was a miracle, which nothing less than unlimited power could produce.

52. Put up again thy sword into his place – Neither Christ nor his religion is to be defended by the secular arm. God is sufficiently able to support his ark: Uzzah need not stretch out his hand on the occasion. Even the shadow of public justice is not to be resisted by a private person, when coming from those in public authority. The cause of a Christian is the cause of God: sufferings belong to one, and vengeance to the other. Let the cause, there-

fore, rest in his hands, who will do it ample justice.

Shall perish with the sword – The general meaning of this verse is, they who contend in battle are likely, on both sides, to become the sacrifices of their mutual animosities. But it is probably a prophetic declaration of the Jewish and Roman states. The Jews put our Lord to death under the sanction of the Romans – both took the sword against Christ, and both perished by it. The Jews by the sword of the Romans, and the Romans by that of the Goths, Vandals, etc. The event has verified the prediction – the Jewish government has been destroyed upwards of 1700 years, and the Roman upwards of 1000. Confer with this passage, Psalm 2: 4,9; 110: 1,5–6. But how came Peter to have a sword? Judea was at this time so infested with robbers and cut-throats that it was not deemed safe for any person to go unarmed. He probably carried one for his mere personal safety.

53. More than twelve legions of angels? – As if he had said, Instead of you twelve, one of whom is a traitor, my Father can give me more than twelve legions of angels to defend me. A legion, at different times, contained different numbers; 4,200, 5,000, and frequently 6,000 men; and from this saying, taking the latter number, which is the common rate, may we not-safely believe that the angels of God amount to more than 72,000?

54. But how then – Had I such a defense – shall the Scriptures be fulfilled, which say, that thus it must be? That is, that I am to suffer and die for the sin of the world. Probably the Scriptures to which our Lord principally refers are Psalm 22, 69, and especially Isaiah 53, and Daniel 9: 24–27. Christ shows that they had no power against him but what he permitted; and that he willingly gave up himself into their hands.

55. Are ye come out as against a thief – At this time Judea was much infested by robbers, so that armed men were obliged to be employed against them – to this our Lord seems to allude.

with swords and with staves to take me?

49 I was daily with you in the temple teaching, and ye took me not: but the scriptures must be fulfilled.

50 And they all forsook him, and fled.

51 And there followed him a certain young man, having a linen cloth cast about his naked body; and the young men laid hold on him:

52 And he left the linen cloth, and fled from them naked.

Luke 22: 49–53

49 When they which were about him saw what would follow, they said unto him, Lord, shall we smite with the sword?

50 And one of them smote the servant of the high priest, and cut off his right ear.

51 And Jesus answered and said, Suffer ye thus far. And he touched his ear, and healed him.

52 Then Jesus said unto the chief priests, and captains of the temple, and the elders, which were come to him, Be ye come out, as against a thief, with swords and staves?

53 When I was daily with you in the temple, ye stretched forth no hands against me: but this is your hour, and the power of darkness.

MATTHEW 26: 57–61; MARK 14: 53–59; LUKE 22: 54

Matthew 26: 57–61

57 And they that had laid hold on Jesus led him away to Caiaphas the high priest, where the scribes and the elders were assembled.

58 But Peter followed him afar off unto the high priest's palace, and went in, and sat with the servants, to see the end.

59 Now the chief priests, and elders, and all the council, sought false witness against Jesus, to put him to death;

60 But found none: yea, though many false witnesses came, yet found they none. At the last came two false witnesses,

61 And said, This fellow said, I am able to destroy the temple of God, and to build it in three days.

own blood; but God himself, by severely prohibiting murder, has declared how dearly he loves mankind. First, then, he does not choose to be defended by force and violence, because God in the Law forbade men to strike. This is a general reason; and he immediately descends to a special reason.

But here a question arises. Is it never lawful to use violence in repelling unjust violence? For though Peter had to deal with wicked and base robbers, still he is condemned for having drawn his sword.

If, in such a case of moderate defense, an exception was not allowed, Christ appears to tie up the hands of all. Though we have treated this question more copiously under Matthew 5: 39, yet I shall now state my opinion again in a few words. First, we must make a distinction between a civil court and the court of conscience; or if any man resist a robber, he will not be liable to public punishment, because the laws arm him against one who is the common enemy of mankind. Thus, in every case when defense is made against unjust violence, the punishment which God enjoins earthly judges to carry into execution ceases. And yet it is not the mere goodness of the cause that acquits the conscience from guilt, unless there be also pure affection. So then, in order that a man may properly and lawfully defend himself, he must first lay aside excessive wrath, and hatred, and desire of revenge, and all irregular sallies of passion, that nothing tempestuous may mingle with the defense. As this is of rare occurrence, or rather, as it scarcely ever happens, Christ properly reminds his people of the general rule, that they should entirely abstain from using **the sword**.

MATTHEW 26: 57–61; MARK 14: 53–59; LUKE 22: 54

Luke follows a different order from Matthew and Mark in the narrative; but when we come to the proper place, we will endeavor to reconcile the points in which they differ. It will be proper, in the meantime, to glance briefly at those things which claim our attention in the words of Matthew and Mark. First, in order to remove the offense of the cross, we ought to consider the advantage which we have derived from Christ's emptying of himself (Philippians 2: 7); for thus will the inestimable goodness of God, and the efficacy of his grace, be found to remove by its brightness every thing in it that was disagreeable or shameful. According to the flesh, it was disgraceful that the Son of God should be seized, bound, and made a prisoner; but when we reflect that by his chains we are loosed from the tyranny of the devil, and from the condemnation in which we were involved before God, not only is the stumbling-block, on which our faith might have struck, removed out of the way, but in place of it

I sat daily with you – Why come in this hostile manner? Every day, for four days past, ye might have met with me in the temple, whither I went to teach you the way of salvation.

56. **But all this was done** – This is probably the observation of the evangelist.

Then all the disciples forsook him and fled – O what is man! How little is even his utmost sincerity to be depended on! Jesus is abandoned by all! – even zealous Peter and loving John are among the fugitives! Was ever master so served by his scholars? Was ever parent so treated by his children? Is there not as much zeal and love among them all as might make one martyr for God and truth? Alas! no. He had but twelve who professed inviolable attachment to him; one of these betrayed him, another denied him with oaths, and the rest run away and utterly abandon him to his implacable enemies! Are there not found among his disciples still,

1st. Persons who betray him and his cause?

2dly. Persons who deny him and his people?

3dly. Persons who abandon him, his people, his cause, and his truth?

Reader! dost thou belong to any of these classes?

MATTHEW 26: 57–61; MARK 14: 53–59; LUKE 22: 54

Matthew 26: 57–61

57. **They – led him away to Caiaphas** – John says, John 18: 13, that they led him first to Annas; but this appears to have been done merely to do him honor as the father-in-law of Caiaphas, and his colleague in the high priesthood. But as the Sanhedrin was assembled at the house of Caiaphas, it was there he must be brought to undergo his mock trial.

58. **Peter followed him afar off** – Poor Peter! this is the beginning of his dreadful fall. His fear kept him from joining the company, and publicly acknowledging his Lord; and his affection obliged him to follow at a distance that he might see the end.

And sat with the servants, to see the end – When a man is weak in faith, and can as yet only follow Christ at a distance, he should avoid all dangerous places, and the company of those who are most likely to prove a snare to him. Had not Peter got to the high priest's palace, and sat down with the servants, he would not thus have denied his Lord and Master.

59. **All the council sought false witness** – What a prostitution of justice! – they first resolve to ruin him, and then seek the proper means of effecting it: they declare him criminal, and after that do all they can to fix some crime upon him, that they may appear to have some shadow of justice on their side when they put him to death. It seems to have been a common custom of this vile court to employ false witness, on any occasion, to answer their own ends. See this exemplified in the case of Stephen, Acts 6: 11–13.

60. **Though many false witnesses came** – I shall give that which I believe to be the genuine sense of the evangelist. Then the chief priests and elders, and all the council, sought false witness against Jesus, to put him to death; but they found it not, though many false witnesses came up. At last two false witnesses came up, saying; This man said, etc. It is the property of falsity to be ever inconsistent, and to contradict itself; therefore they could not find two consistent testimonies, without which the Jewish law did not permit any person to be put to death. However, the hand of God was in this business: for the credit of Jesus, and the honor of the Christian religion, he would not permit him to be condemned on a false accusation; and, therefore, at last they were obliged to change their ground, and, to the eternal confusion of the unrighteous council, he is condemned on the very evidence of his own innocence, purity, and truth!

61. **I am able to destroy the temple of God** – 1st. These words were not fairly quoted. Jesus had said, John 2: 19, Destroy this temple, and I will build it again in three days.

2dly. The innuendo which they produce, applying these words to a pretended design to destroy the temple at Jerusalem, was utterly

Mark 14: 53–59

53 And they led Jesus away to the high priest: and with him were assembled all the chief priests and the elders and the scribes.

54 And Peter followed him afar off, even into the palace of the high priest: and he sat with the servants, and warmed himself at the fire.

55 And the chief priests and all the council sought for witness against Jesus to put him to death; and found none.

56 For many bare false witness against him, but their witness agreed not together.

57 And there arose certain, and bare false witness against him, saying,

58 We heard him say, I will destroy this temple that is made with hands, and within three days I will build another made without hands.

59 But neither so did their witness agree together.

Luke 22: 54

54 Then took they him, and led him, and brought him into the high priest's house. And Peter followed afar off.

MATTHEW 26: 62–68; MARK 14: 60–65; LUKE 22: 63–71

Matthew 26: 62–68

62 And the high priest arose, and said unto him, Answerest thou nothing? what is it which these witness against thee?

63 But Jesus held his peace. And the high priest answered and said unto him, I adjure thee by the living God, that thou tell us whether thou be the Christ, the Son of God.

64 Jesus saith unto him, Thou hast said: nevertheless I say unto you, Hereafter shall ye see the Son of man sitting on the right hand of power, and coming in the clouds of heaven.

65 Then the high priest rent his clothes, saying, He hath spoken blasphemy; what further need have we of witnesses? behold, now ye have heard his blasphemy.

66 What think ye? They answered and said, He is guilty of death.

67 Then did they spit in his face, and buffeted him; and others smote him with the palms of their hands,

there comes an admiration of the boundless grace of God, who set so high a value on our deliverance, as to give up his only-begotten Son to be bound by wicked men. This will also be a pledge of the astonishing love of Christ towards us, that he spared not himself, but willingly submitted to wear fetters on his flesh, that our souls might be freed from fetters of a far worse description.

Matthew 26: 57. But they who had seized Jesus led him to Caiaphas

Though the Jews had been deprived of what is called, the higher jurisdiction, there still lingered among them some vestiges of that judicial authority which the Law confers on the high priest (Deuteronomy 1: 8); so that, while they had lost the absolute authority, they retained the power of administering moderate correction. This is the reason why Christ is brought before to be interrogated; not that a final sentence may be pronounced on him by theft tribunal, but that the priests may afterwards present him before the governor, under the aggravating influence of their decision.

MATTHEW 26: 62–68; MARK 14: 60–65; LUKE 22: 63–71

Matthew 26: 62. And the high priest, rising up

It is certain that Christ was **silent** when **false witnesses** pressed hard upon him, not only because they did not deserve a reply, but because he did not seek to be now acquitted, knowing that his hour was come. But Caiaphas triumphs over him on account of his silence, as if he was struck dumb by being vanquished; which is usually the case with men who are conscious of having done wrong. But it is an instance of extreme wickedness that he insinuates that Christ is not free from blame, because **witnesses** speak against him. The question, **What is it that those men testify against thee?** amounts to this: "How comes it that those men oppose thee, but because they are urged by conscientious views? For they would not have appeared against thee without a good reason." As if he did not know that those **witnesses** had been procured by fraud: but this is the way in which wicked men, when they find themselves in the possession of authority and power, throw off sham and indulge in arrogance. Christ was again silent, not only because the objection was frivolous, but because, having been appointed to be a sacrifice, he had thrown aside all anxiety about defending himself.

63. I adjure thee by the living God

The high priest thought that this alone was a crime sufficient to condemn Christ, if he professed that he was **the Christ**. But since they all boasted of expecting redemption from Christ, he ought first to have inquired if such was the

unfair; for these words he spoke of the temple of his body.

It is very easy, by means of a few small alterations, to render the most holy things and innocent persons odious to the world, and even to take away the life of the innocent.

MATTHEW 26: 62–68; MARK 14: 60–65; LUKE 22: 63–71

62. Answerest thou nothing? – The accusation was so completely frivolous that it merited no notice: besides, Jesus knew that they were determined to put him to death, and that his hour was come; and that therefore remonstrance or defense would be of no use: he had often before borne sufficient testimony to the truth.

63. I adjure thee by the living God – I put thee to thy oath. To this solemn adjuration Christ immediately replies, because he is now called on, in the name of God, to bear another testimony to the truth. The authority of God in the most worthless magistrate should be properly respected. However necessary our Lord saw it to be silent, when the accusations were frivolous, and the evidence contradictory, he felt no disposition to continue this silence, when questioned concerning a truth, for which he came into the world to shed his blood.

64. Thou hast said – That is, I am the Christ, the promised Messiah, and you and this whole nation shall shortly have the fullest proof of it: for hereafter, in a few years, ye shall see the Son of man sitting on the right hand of power, fully invested with absolute dominion, and coming in the clouds of heaven, to execute judgment upon this wicked race. See Matthew 24: 30. Our Lord appears to refer to Daniel 7: 13: One like the Son of man came with the clouds of heaven, etc. This may also refer to the final judgment.

65. The high priest rent his clothes – This rending of the high priest's garments was expressly contrary to the law, Leviticus 10: 6: 21: 10. But it was a common method of expressing violent grief, Genesis 37: 29,34; Job

1: 20, and horror at what was deemed blasphemous or impious. 2 Kings 18: 37; 19: 1; Acts 14: 14. All that heard a blasphemous speech were obliged to rend their clothes, and never to sew them up again.

He hath spoken blasphemy – Quesnel's note on this is worthy of notice. "See here a false zeal, a mask of religion, and a passionate and seditious way of proceeding, tending only to incense and stir up others, all which are common to those who would oppress truth by cabal, and without proof. By crying out, 'heresy, blasphemy, and faction,' though contrary to all appearance, men fail not to stir up those in power, to gain the simple, to give some shadow of authority to the ill-disposed, to cast devout but ignorant people into scruples, and thereby to advance the mystery of iniquity, which is the mystery of all ages." This was the very plan his Catholic brethren adopted in this country, in the reign of Queen Mary, called the bloody queen, because of the many murders of righteous men which she sanctioned at the mouth of her Catholic priesthood.

66. He is guilty of death – he is liable to death. All the forms of justice are here violated. The judge becomes a party and accuser, and proceeds to the verdict without examining whether all the prophecies concerning the Messiah, and the innumerable miracles which he wrought, did not justify him. Examination and proof are the ruin of all calumnies, and of the authors of them, and therefore they take care to keep off from these two things.

67. Then did they spit in his face – This was done as a mark of the most profound contempt. See Job 16: 10; 30: 10; Isaiah 50: 6; Micah 5: 1. The judges now delivered him into the hands of the mob.

And buffeted him – Smote him with their fists.

Smote him with the palms of their hands – Thus they offered him indignity in all its various and vexatious forms. Insults of this kind are never forgiven by the world: Jesus not only takes no revenge, (though it be completely in his power), but bears all with meekness, without even one word of reply.

68 Saying, Prophesy unto us, thou Christ, Who is he that smote thee?

Mark 14: 60–65

60 And the high priest stood up in the midst, and asked Jesus, saying, Answerest thou nothing? what is it which these witness against thee?

61 But he held his peace, and answered nothing. Again the high priest asked him, and said unto him, Art thou the Christ, the Son of the Blessed?

62 And Jesus said, I am: and ye shall see the Son of man sitting on the right hand of power, and coming in the clouds of heaven.

63 Then the high priest rent his clothes, and saith, What need we any further witnesses?

64 Ye have heard the blasphemy: what think ye? And they all condemned him to be guilty of death.

65 And some began to spit on him, and to cover his face, and to buffet him, and to say unto him, Prophesy: and the servants did strike him with the palms of their hands.

Luke 22: 63–71

63 And the men that held Jesus mocked him, and smote him.

64 And when they had blindfolded him, they struck him on the face, and asked him, saying, Prophesy, who is it that smote thee?

65 And many other things blasphemously spake they against him.

66 And as soon as it was day, the elders of the people and the chief priests and the scribes came together, and led him into their council, saying,

67 Art thou the Christ? tell us. And he said unto them, If I tell you, ye will not believe:

68 And if I also ask you, ye will not answer me, nor let me go.

69 Hereafter shall the Son of man sit on the right hand of the power of God.

70 Then said they all, Art thou then the Son of God? And he said unto them, Ye say that I am.

71 And they said, What need we any further witness? for we ourselves have heard of his own mouth.

fact. That there would be a **Christ**, by whose hands the people were to be delivered, they would not have ventured to deny. Jesus came publicly forward, bearing the title of **the Christ**. Why do they not consider the fact itself? Why do they not examine the signs, by means of which a correct decision might have been formed? But, having already determined to put Christ to death, they are satisfied with this pretense of sacrilege, that he claimed for himself the glory of Divinity. And yet Caiaphas examines the matter on oath, as if he had been prepared to yield as soon as it was fully ascertained; but all the while his whole mind is filled with a malicious hatred and contempt of Christ, and is so blinded by pride and ambition, that he takes for granted, that as soon as the fact has been ascertained, without inquiring whether it is right or wrong, he will have just grounds for condemning him. **If thou art the Christ, the Son of God**.

From the words of Caiaphas we may infer, that it was at that time common among the Jews to bestow on the Messiah the title of **the Son of God**; for this form of interrogation could not have originated in any other way than from the ordinary custom; and, indeed, they had learned from the predictions of Scripture that he was not less **the Son of God** than **the Son of David**. It appears, too, that Caiaphas employed this epithet, with the view either of terrifying Christ, or of exciting a prejudice against him; as if he had said, "See where you are going; for you cannot call yourself **the Christ,** without claiming, at the same time, the appellation of **Son of God**, with which Scripture honors him."

Such is also his reason for using the word **Blessed**, which Mark gives instead of **God**; for this pretended reverence for God was intended to bring a heavier charge against Christ than that of profaning the holy name of God.

MATTHEW 26: 69–75; MARK 14: 66–72; LUKE 22: 55–62

Peter's fall, which is here related, is a bright mirror of our weakness. In his repentance, also, a striking instance of the goodness and mercy of God is held out to us. This narrative, therefore, which relates to a single individual, contains a doctrine which may be applied to the whole Church, and which indeed is highly useful, both to instruct those who are standing to cherish anxiety and fear, and to comfort those who have fallen, by holding out to them the hope of pardon. And first it ought to be observed, that Peter acted inconsiderately, when he entered into the hall of the high priest. It was his duty, no doubt, to follow his Master; but having been warned that he would revolt, he ought rather to have concealed himself in some corner, so as not to expose himself to an occasion of sinning. Thus it frequently

68. Prophesy unto us, thou Christ – Their conduct toward him now was expressly prophesied of, by a man whose Divine mission they did not pretend to deny; see Isaiah 50: 6. It appears that, before they buffeted him, they bound up his eyes, See Mark 14: 65.

MATTHEW 26: 69-75; MARK 14: 66-72; LUKE 22: 55-62

Matthew 26: 69-75

69. A damsel came unto him – A maid servant.

Thou also wast with Jesus – What a noble opportunity had Peter now to show his zeal for the insulted cause of truth, and his attachment to his Master. But, alas! he is shorn of his strength. Constables and maid servants are no company for an apostle, except when he is delivering to them the message of salvation. Evil communications corrupt good manners. Had Peter been in better company, he would not have had so foul a fall.

70. But he denied before them all – So the evil principle gains ground. Before, he followed at a distance, now he denies; this is the second gradation in his fall.

72. And again he denied with an oath – This is a third gradation of his iniquity. He has told a lie, and he swears to support it. A liar has always some suspicion that his testimony is not credited, for he is conscious to his own falsity, and is therefore naturally led to support his assertions by oaths.

73. Thy speech – Thy manner of speech, that dialect of thine – his accent being different from that of Jerusalem. The Galileans had a very corrupt pronunciation.

Bewrayeth thee – maketh thee manifest.

74. Then began he to curse and to swear – Rather, Then he began positively to affirm – In Matthew 26: 72, Peter is said to deny with an oath; here, he positively affirms and swears, probably by the name of God, for this is the import of the word "swear" This makes the fourth and final gradation in the climax of

Peter's fall. From these awful beginnings it is not unfair to conclude that Peter might have gone almost as far as Judas himself, had not the traitorous business been effected before. Yet all this evil sprung simply from the fear of man. How many denials of Christ and his truth have sprung since, from the same cause!

The cock crew – This animal becomes, in the hand of God, the instrument of awaking the fallen apostle, at last, to a sense of his fall, danger, and duty. When abandoned of God, the smallest thing may become the occasion of a fall; and, when in the hand of God, the smallest matter may become the instrument of our restoration. Let us never think lightly of what are termed little sins: the smallest one has the seed of eternal ruin in it. Let us never think contemptibly of the feeblest means of grace: each may have the seed of eternal salvation in it. Let us ever remember that the great Apostle Peter fell through fear of a servant maid, and rose through the crowing of a cock.

75. Peter remembered the word of Jesus – St. Luke says, Luke 22: 61, The Lord turned and looked upon Peter. So it appears he was nigh to our Lord, either at the time when the cock crew, or shortly after. The delicacy of this reproof was great – he must be reproved and alarmed, otherwise he will proceed yet farther in his iniquity; Christ is in bonds, and cannot go and speak to him; if he call aloud, the disciple is discovered, and falls a victim to Jewish malice and Roman jealousy; he therefore does the whole by a look. In the hand of Omnipotence every thing is easy, and he can save by a few, as well as by many.

He went out – He left the place where he had sinned, and the company which had been the occasion of his transgression.

And wept bitterly – Felt bitter anguish of soul, which evidenced itself by the tears of contrition which flowed plentifully from his eyes. Let him that standeth take heed lest he fall! Where the mighty have been slain, what shall support the feeble? Only the grace of the ALMIGHTY God.

This transaction is recorded by the inspired penmen,

MATTHEW 26: 69–75; MARK 14: 66–72; LUKE 22: 55–62

Matthew 26: 69–75

69 Now Peter sat without in the palace: and a damsel came unto him, saying, Thou also wast with Jesus of Galilee.

70 But he denied before them all, saying, I know not what thou sayest.

71 And when he was gone out into the porch, another maid saw him, and said unto them that were there, This fellow was also with Jesus of Nazareth.

72 And again he denied with an oath, I do not know the man.

73 And after a while came unto him they that stood by, and said to Peter, Surely thou also art one of them; for thy speech bewrayeth thee.

74 Then began he to curse and to swear, saying, I know not the man. And immediately the cock crew.

75 And Peter remembered the word of Jesus, which said unto him, Before the cock crow, thou shalt deny me thrice. And he went out, and wept bitterly.

Mark 14: 66–72

66 And as Peter was beneath in the palace, there cometh one of the maids of the high priest:

67 And when she saw Peter warming himself, she looked upon him, and said, And thou also wast with Jesus of Nazareth.

68 But he denied, saying, I know not, neither understand I what thou sayest. And he went out into the porch; and the cock crew.

69 And a maid saw him again, and began to say to them that stood by, This is one of them.

70 And he denied it again. And a little after, they that stood by said again to Peter, Surely thou art one of them: for thou art a Galilaean, and thy speech agreeth thereto.

71 But he began to curse and to swear, saying, I know not this man of whom ye speak.

72 And the second time the cock crew. And Peter called to mind the word that Jesus said unto him, Before the cock crow twice, thou shalt deny me thrice. And when he thought thereon, he wept.

happens that believers, under an appearance of virtue, throw themselves within the reach of temptation.

It is therefore our duty to pray to the Lord to restrain and keep us by his Spirit, lest, going beyond our measure, we be immediately punished. We ought also to pray, whenever we commence any undertaking, that he may not permit us to fail in the midst of our efforts, or at the beginning of the work, but may supply us with strength from heaven till the end. Conviction of our weakness ought not, indeed, to be a reason for indolence, to prevent us from going wherever God calls us; but it ought to restrain our rashness, that we may not attempt any thing beyond our calling; and it ought also to stimulate us to prayer, that God, who has given us grace to begin well, may also continue to give us grace to persevere.

Matthew 26: 69. A maid came to him

Here we see that there is no necessity for a severe contest, or for many forces or implements of war, to overpower a man; for any man, who is not supported by the hand of God, will instantly fall by a slight gale or the rustling of a falling leaf. Peter undoubtedly was not less courageous than any of us, and he had already given no ordinary proof of his valor, though it was exercised in a rash and improper manner; and yet he does not wait until he is dragged before the tribunal of the high priest, or until his enemies attempt to put him to death by violence, but, terrified by a woman's voice, immediately denies his Master. And yet but lately he thought himself a valiant soldier even to death. Let us therefore remember that our strength is so far from being sufficient to resist powerful attacks, that it will give way, when there is the mere shadow of a battle. But in this way God gives us the just reward of our treachery, when he disarms and strips us of all power, so that, when we have thrown off the fear of him, we tremble for a mere nothing. For if a deep fear of God had dwelt in Peter's heart, it would have been an invincible fortress; but now, naked and defenseless, he trembles while he is still far from danger.

70. But he denied before them all

This circumstance aggravates the criminality of Peter, that, in denying his Master, he did not even dread a multitude of witnesses. And the Spirit intended expressly to state this, that even the presence of men may excite us to hold fast the confession of faith. For if we deny Christ before the weak, they are shaken by our example, and give way; and thus we destroy as many souls as we can; but if, in presence of those who wickedly despise God and oppose the Gospel, we withhold from Christ the testimony which is due to him, we expose his sacred name to the ridicule of all. In short, as a bold and open confession edifies all the godly, and puts unbelievers to shame, so apostasy draws along with it the public ruin

1st. That all may watch unto prayer, and shun the occasions of sin.

2dly. That if a man be unhappily overtaken in a fault, he may not despair, but cast himself immediately with a contrite heart on the infinite tenderness and compassion of God.

MATTHEW 27: 1–10; MARK 15: 1; LUKE 23: 1

Matthew 27: 1–10

1. When the morning was come – As soon as it was light – took counsel against Jesus. They had begun this counsel the preceding evening, see Matthew 26: 59. But as it was contrary to all forms of law to proceed against a person's life by night, they seem to have separated for a few hours, and then, at the break of day, came together again, pretending to conduct the business according to the forms of law.

To put him to death – They had already determined his death, and pronounced the sentence of death on him; Matthew 26: 66. And now they assemble under the pretense of reconsidering the evidence, and deliberating on it, to give the greater appearance of justice to their conduct. They wished to make it appear that "they had taken ample time to consider of it, and, from the fullest conviction, by the most satisfactory and conclusive evidence, they had now delivered him into the hands of the Romans, to meet that death to which they had adjudged him."

2. They – delivered him to Pontius Pilate – The Sanhedrin had the power of life and death in their own hands in every thing that concerned religion; but as they had not evidence to put Christ to death because of false doctrine, they wished to give countenance to their conduct by bringing in the civil power, and therefore they delivered him up to Pilate as one who aspired to regal dignities, and whom he must put to death, if he professed to be Caesar's friend. Pontius Pilate governed Judea ten years under the Emperor Tiberius; but, having exercised great cruelties against the Samaritans, they complained of him to the emperor, in consequence of which he was deposed, and sent in exile to Vienna, in Dauphiny, where he killed himself two years after.

3. Judas – when he saw that he was condemned, repented – There is much of the wisdom and goodness of God to be seen in this part of Judas's conduct. Had our Lord been condemned to death on the evidence of one of his own disciples, it would have furnished infidels with a strong argument against Christ and the Christian religion. "One of his own disciples, knowing the whole imposture, declared it to the Jewish rulers, in consequence of which he was put to death as an impostor and deceiver." But the traitor, being stung with remorse, came and acknowledged his crime, and solemnly declared the innocence of his Master, threw back the money which they gave him to induce him to do this villainous act; and, to establish the evidence which he now gave against them and himself, in behalf of the innocence of Christ, hanged himself, or died through excessive grief and contrition. Thus the character of Christ was rescued from all reproach; infidelity deprived of the power to cry "imposture!" and the Jewish rulers overwhelmed with eternal infamy. If it should ever be said, "One who knew him best delivered him up as an impostor," – to this it may be immediately answered, "The same person, struck with remorse, came and declared his own guilt, and Christ's innocence; accused and convicted the Jewish rulers, in the open council, of having hired him to do this iniquitous action, threw them back the bribe they had given him, and then hanged himself through distress and despair, concluding his iniquity in this business was too great to be forgiven." Let him who chooses, after this plenary evidence to the innocence of Christ, continue the objection, and cry out imposture! take heed that he go not and do LIKEWISE. Caiaphas, Pilate, and Judas have done so already, and I have known several, who have called Christ an impostor, who have cut their own throats, shot, drowned, or hanged themselves. God is a jealous God, and highly resents every thing that is done and said against that eternal truth that came to man through Jesus Christ,

Luke 22: 55–62

55 And when they had kindled a fire in the midst of the hall, and were set down together, Peter sat down among them.

56 But a certain maid beheld him as he sat by the fire, and earnestly looked upon him, and said, This man was also with him.

57 And he denied him, saying, Woman, I know him not.

58 And after a little while another saw him, and said, Thou art also of them. And Peter said, Man, I am not.

59 And about the space of one hour after another confidently affirmed, saying, Of a truth this fellow also was with him: for he is a Galilaean.

60 And Peter said, Man, I know not what thou sayest. And immediately, while he yet spake, the cock crew.

61 And the Lord turned, and looked upon Peter. And Peter remembered the word of the Lord, how he had said unto him, Before the cock crow, thou shalt deny me thrice.

62 And Peter went out, and wept bitterly.

MATTHEW 27: 1–10; MARK 15: 1; LUKE 23: 1

Matthew 27: 1–10

1 When the morning was come, all the chief priests and elders of the people took counsel against Jesus to put him to death:

2 And when they had bound him, they led him away, and delivered him to Pontius Pilate the governor.

3 Then Judas, which had betrayed him, when he saw that he was condemned, repented himself, and brought again the thirty pieces of silver to the chief priests and elders,

4 Saying, I have sinned in that I have betrayed the innocent blood. And they said, What is that to us? see thou to that.

5 And he cast down the pieces of silver in the temple, and departed, and went and hanged himself.

6 And the chief priests took the silver pieces, and said, It is not lawful for to put them into the treasury, because it is the price of blood.

7 And they took counsel, and bought

of faith in the Church, and the reproach of sound doctrine. The more eminent a man is, therefore, he ought to be the more careful to be on his guard; for his elevation makes it impossible for him to fall from it without doing greater harm. **I know not what thou sayest.** The form of denial, which is here set down, shows sufficiently that the wretched sophists, who endeavor to escape by ambiguous expressions, which they turn to a. variety of meanings, when they are called to give an account of their faith, gain nothing by their dexterity in fraud. **Peter** does not absolutely **deny** the whole doctrine of the Gospel; he only **denies** that he **knew the man**; but, because in the person of Christ he indirectly buries the light of the promised redemption, he is charged with base and shameful treachery. But lately he had heard from the mouth of the Lord, that the confession of faith is a sacrifice acceptable to God; and therefore a mode of **denying**, which withholds from God his lawful worship, and from Christ the honor that is due to him, admits of no excuse. Let us therefore hold: , that as soon as we depart from a plain and candid profession of Christ, we deprive him of the testimony to which he has a lawful claim.

MATTHEW 27: 1–10; MARK 15: 1; LUKE 23: 1

Matthew 27: 1. But when it was morning
The high priest, with his council, after having examined him at an unseasonable hour of the night, finally resolve, at sunrise, to place him at the bar of the governor. By so doing, they observe the form of judicial proceedings, that they may not be suspected of undue haste, when they run to Pilate at an unusually early hour, as usually happens in cases of tumult. But it is probable, that when Christ had been led away from their council, they immediately held a consultation, and, without long delay, resolved what they would do; for we have been already told at what time Christ went out from them and met Peter, which was after the **cock-crowing**, and just as day was breaking. The Evangelists, therefore, do not mean that they removed from the place, but only relate, that as soon as it was daylight, they condemned Christ to death, and did not lose a moment in earnestly putting into execution their wicked design. What Luke formerly stated (22: 66), that **they assembled in the morning**, ought not to be explained as referring to the very beginning, but to the last act, which is immediately added: as if he had said, that as soon as it was day, our Lord having acknowledged that he was the Son of God, they pronounced their sentence of his death. Now if they had been permitted to decide in taking away life, they would all have been eager, in their fury, to murder him with their own hands; but as Pilate had cognizance of capital crimes, they are constrained to refer the matter to his jurisdiction;

by the Holy Spirit. Indeed, there is one class of Deists, viz. those who are vicious in their lives, and virulent in their opposition to Christianity, who generally bring themselves to an untimely end.

4. Innocent blood – a Hebraism, for an innocent man.

What is that to us? – What is it? – A great deal. You should immediately go and reverse the sentence you have pronounced, and liberate the innocent person. But this would have been justice, and that would have been a stranger at their tribunal.

5. In the temple – signifies, properly, the temple itself, into which none but the priests were permitted to enter; therefore this phrase must signify, near the temple, by the temple door, where the boxes stood to receive the free-will offerings of the people, for the support and repairs of the sacred edifice.

Hanged himself – Or was strangled –

6. The treasury – the place whither the people brought their free-will offerings for the service of the temple. It is from this idea that the phrase to draw nigh to God is taken, which is so frequently used in the sacred writings.

Because it is the price of blood – "What hypocrites, as one justly exclaims, to adjudge an innocent man to death, and break the eternal laws of justice and mercy without scruple, and to be, at the same time, so very nice in their attention to a ceremonial direction of the law of Moses! Thus it is that the devil often deludes many, even among the priests, by a false and superstitious tenderness or conscience in things indifferent, while calumny, envy, oppression of the innocent, and a conformity to the world, give them no manner of trouble or disturbance."

7. To bury strangers in – the strangers, probably meaning, as some learned men conjecture, the Jewish strangers who might have come to Jerusalem, either to worship, or on some other business, and died there during their stay. See here, the very money for which the blessed Jesus was sold becomes subservient to the purpose of mercy and kindness! The

bodies of strangers have a place of rest in the field purchased by the price at which his life was valued, and the souls of strangers and foreigners have a place of rest and refuge in his blood which was shed as a ransom price for the salvation of the whole world.

8. The field of blood – In vain do the wicked attempt to conceal themselves; God makes them instrumental in discovering their own wickedness. Judas, by returning the money, and the priests, by laying it out, raise to themselves an eternal monument – the one of his treachery, the others of their perfidiousness, and both of the innocence of Jesus Christ. As, long as the Jewish polity continued, it might be said, "This is the field that was bought from the potter with the money which Judas got from the high priests for betraying his Master; which he, in deep compunction of spirit, brought back to them, and they bought this ground for a burial-place for strangers: for as it was the price of the blood of an innocent man, they did not think proper to let it rest in the treasury of the temple where the traitor had thrown it, who afterwards, in despair, went and hanged himself." What a standing proof must this have been of the innocence of Christ, and of their perfidy!

9. Jeremy the prophet – The words quoted here are not found in the Prophet Jeremiah, but in Zechariah 11: 13. But St. Jerome says that a Hebrew of the sect of the Nazarenes showed him this prophecy in a Hebrew apocryphal copy of Jeremiah; but probably they were inserted there only to countenance the quotation here.

It was an ancient custom among the Jews, says Dr. Lightfoot, to divide the Old Testament into three parts: the first beginning with the law was called THE LAW; the second beginning with the Psalms was called THE PSALMS; the third beginning with the prophet in question was called JEREMIAH: thus, then, the writings of Zechariah and the other prophets being included in that division that began with Jeremiah, all quotations from it would go under the name of this prophet. If this be admitted, it solves the difficulty at

with them the potter's field, to bury strangers in.

8 Wherefore that field was called, The field of blood, unto this day.

9 Then was fulfilled that which was spoken by Jeremy the prophet, saying, And they took the thirty pieces of silver, the price of him that was valued, whom they of the children of Israel did value;

10 And gave them for the potter's field, as the Lord appointed me.

Mark 15: 1

1 And straightway in the morning the chief priests held a consultation with the elders and scribes and the whole council, and bound Jesus, and carried him away, and delivered him to Pilate.

Luke 23: 1

1 And the whole multitude of them arose, and led him unto Pilate.

MATTHEW 27: 11–14; MARK 15: 2–5; LUKE 23: 2–12

Matthew 27: 11–14

11 And Jesus stood before the governor: and the governor asked him, saying, Art thou the King of the Jews? And Jesus said unto him, Thou sayest.

12 And when he was accused of the chief priests and elders, he answered nothing.

13 Then said Pilate unto him, Hearest thou not how many things they witness against thee?

14 And he answered him to never a word; insomuch that the governor marveled greatly.

Mark 15: 2–5

2 And Pilate asked him, Art thou the King of the Jews? And he answering said unto him, Thou sayest it.

3 And the chief priests accused him of many things: but he answered nothing.

4 And Pilate asked him again, saying, Answerest thou nothing? behold how many things they witness against thee.

5 But Jesus yet answered nothing; so that Pilate marveled.

Luke 23: 2–12

2 And they began to accuse him, saying, We found this fellow perverting the nation, and forbidding to give tribute to

only they entangle him by their own previous decision. For the stoning of Stephen (Acts 7: 59) took place in a seditious manner, as happens in cases of tumult; but it was proper that the Son of God should be solemnly condemned by an earthly judge, that he might efface our condemnation in heaven.

3. Then Judas, perceiving that he was condemned

By this adverb (*tote*) **then**, Matthew does not fix the exact point of time; for we shall find him shortly afterwards adding, that Judas, when he saw that the priests disdainfully refused to take back the reward of his treason, threw it down in the temple. But from the house of Caiaphas they came straight to the Pretorium, and stood there until Christ was condemned. It can scarcely be supposed that they were found in the temple on that day; but as the Evangelist was speaking of the rage and madness of the council, he inserted also the death of Judas, by which their blind obstinacy, and the hardness of their hearts like iron, were more fully displayed.

MATTHEW 27: 11–14; MARK 15: 2–5; LUKE 23: 2–12

Matthew 27: 11. Now Jesus stood before the governor

Though it was a shocking exhibition, and highly incompatible with the majesty of the Son of God, to be dragged before the judgment-seat of a profane man, to be tried on the charge of a capital offense, as a malefactor in chains; yet we ought to remember that; our salvation consists in the doctrine of the cross, which is "folly to the Greeks, and an offense to the Jews" (1 Corinthians 1: 23).

For the Son of God chose to stand bound before an earthly judge, and there to receive sentence of death, in order that we, delivered from condemnation, may not fear to approach freely to the heavenly throne of God. If, therefore, we consider what advantage we reap from Christ having been tried before Pilate, the disgrace of so unworthy a subjection will be immediately washed away. And certainly none are offended at the condemnation of Christ, but those who are either proud hypocrites, or stupid and gross despisers of God, who are not ashamed of their own iniquity.

So then, the Son of God **stood**, as a criminal, before a mortal man, and there permitted himself to be accused and condemned, that we may stand boldly before God. His enemies, indeed, endeavored to fasten upon him everlasting infamy; but we ought rather to look at the end to which the providence of God directs us. For if we recollect how dreadful is the judgment-seat of God, and that we could never have been acquitted there, unless Christ had been pronounced to be guilty on earth, we shall never be

once. Dr. Lightfoot quotes Baba Bathra, and Rabbi David Kimchi's preface to the prophet Jeremiah, as his authorities; and insists that the word Jeremiah is perfectly correct as standing at the head of that division from which the evangelist quoted, and which gave its denomination to all the rest.

MATTHEW 27: 11–14; MARK 15: 2–5; LUKE 23: 2–12

Matthew 27: 11–14

11. Art thou the King of the Jews? – The Jews had undoubtedly delivered him to Pilate as one who was rising up against the imperial authority, and assuming the regal office.

12. He answered nothing – An answer to such accusations was not necessary: they sufficiently confuted themselves.

14. Marveled greatly – Silence under calumny manifests the utmost magnanimity. The chief priests did not admire this because it confounded them; but Pilate, who had no interest to serve by it, was deeply affected. This very silence was predicted. Isaiah 53: 7.

MATTHEW 27: 15–23; MARK 15: 6–14; LUKE 23: 13–23

Matthew 27: 15–23

15. The governor was wont to release – Whence this custom originated among the Jews is not known, – probably it was introduced by the Romans themselves, or by Pilate, merely to oblige the Jews, by showing them this public token of respect; but if it originated with him, he must have had the authority of Augustus; for the Roman laws never gave such discretionary power to any governor.

16. A notable prisoner – Barabbas – This person had, a short time before, raised an insurrection in Jerusalem, in which it appears, from Mark 15: 7, some lives were lost. Which of the two do ye wish me to release unto you, Jesus Barabbas, or Jesus who is called Christ? As Jesus, or Joshua, was a very common name among the Jews, and as the name of the father

was often joined to that of the son, as Simon Barjonah, Simon, son of Jonah; so it is probable it was the case here, Jesus Barabba, Jesus, son of Abba, or Abbiah. If this name were originally written as above, which I am inclined to believe, the general omission of JESUS in the MSS. may be accounted for from the over zealous scrupulosity of Christian copyists, who were unwilling that a murderer should, in the same verse, be honored with the name of the Redeemer of the world.

18. For envy – through malice. Then it was his business, as an upright judge, to have dispersed this mob, and immediately released Jesus.

Seeing malice is capable of putting even Christ himself to death, how careful should we be not to let the least spark of it harbor in our breast. Let it be remembered that malice as often originates from envy as it does from anger.

19. I have suffered many things – in a dream – There is no doubt that God had appeared unto this woman, testifying the innocence of Christ, and showing the evils which should pursue Pilate if this innocent blood should be shed by his authority. See Matthew 27: 2.

20. Ask Barabbas – Who had raised an insurrection and committed murder – and to destroy Jesus, whose voice was never heard in their streets, and who had, during the space of three years and a half, gone about unweariedly, from village to village, instructing the ignorant, healing the diseased, and raising the dead.

21. They said, Barabbas – What a fickle crowd! A little before they all hailed him as the Son of David, and acknowledged him as a gift from God; now they prefer a murderer to him! But this it appears they did at the instigation of the chief priests. We see here how dangerous wicked priests are in the Church of Christ; when pastors are corrupt, they are capable of inducing their flock to prefer Barabbas to Jesus, the world to God, and the pleasures of sense to the salvation of their souls. The invidious epithet which a certain statesman

Caesar, saying that he himself is Christ a King.

3 And Pilate asked him, saying, Art thou the King of the Jews? And he answered him and said, Thou sayest it.

4 Then said Pilate to the chief priests and to the people, I find no fault in this man.

5 And they were the more fierce, saying, He stirreth up the people, teaching throughout all Jewry, beginning from Galilee to this place.

6 When Pilate heard of Galilee, he asked whether the man were a Galilaean.

7 And as soon as he knew that he belonged unto Herod's jurisdiction, he sent him to Herod, who himself also was at Jerusalem at that time.

8 And when Herod saw Jesus, he was exceeding glad: for he was desirous to see him of a long season, because he had heard many things of him; and he hoped to have seen some miracle done by him.

9 Then he questioned with him in many words; but he answered him nothing.

10 And the chief priests and scribes stood and vehemently accused him.

11 And Herod with his men of war set him at nought, and mocked him, and arrayed him in a gorgeous robe, and sent him again to Pilate.

12 And the same day Pilate and Herod were made friends together: for before they were at enmity between themselves.

MATTHEW 27: 15–23; MARK 15: 6–14; LUKE 23: 13–23

Matthew 27: 15–23

15 Now at that feast the governor was wont to release unto the people a prisoner, whom they would.

16 And they had then a notable prisoner, called Barabbas.

17 Therefore when they were gathered together, Pilate said unto them, Whom will ye that I release unto you? Barabbas, or Jesus which is called Christ?

18 For he knew that for envy they had delivered him.

19 When he was set down on the judgment seat, his wife sent unto him, saying, Have thou nothing to do with that just man: for I have suffered many things this

ashamed of glorying in his chains. Again, whenever we hear that Christ **stood before** Pilate with a sad and dejected countenance, let us draw from it grounds of confidence, that, relying on him as our intercessor, we may come into the presence of God with joy and alacrity. To the same purpose is what immediately follows: **he did not answer him a single word.** Christ was silent, while the priests were pressing upon him on every hand; and it was, in order that he might open our mouth by his silence. For hence arises that distinguished privilege of which Paul speaks in such magnificent terms (Romans 8: 15), that we can boldly cry, Abba, Father.

Art thou the King of the Jews?

Although they attempted to overwhelm Christ by many and various accusations, still it is probable that they maliciously seized on the title of **King,** in order to excite greater odium against him on the part of Pilate. For this reason Luke expressly represents them as **saying, we have found him subverting the nation,** and forbidding to give tribute to Caesar, saying that he is the Christ.

MATTHEW 27: 15–23; MARK 15: 6–14; LUKE 23: 13–23

Matthew 27: 15. Now the governor was wont at the festival

Here is described to us, on the one hand, the insatiable cruelty of the priests, and, on the other, the furious obstinacy of the people; for both must have been seized with astonishing madness, when they were not satisfied with conspiring to put to death an innocent man, if they did not also, through hatred of him, release **a robber.** Thus wicked men after having once begun to fall, are driven headlong by Satan, so that they shrink from no crime, however detestable, but, blinded and stupefied, add sin to sin. There can be no doubt that **Pilate,** in order to prevail upon them through shame, selected a very wicked man, by contrast with whom Christ might be set free; and the very atrocity of the crime of which **Barabbas** was guilty ought justly to have made the resentment of the people to fall on him, that by comparison with him, at least, Christ might be released. But no disgrace makes either the priests, or the whole nation, afraid to ask that a seditious man and a murderer should be granted to them.

Meanwhile, we ought to consider the purpose of God, by which Christ was appointed to be crucified, as if he had been the basest of men. The Jews, indeed, rage against him with blinded fury; but as God had appointed him to be a sacrifice (*katharma*) to atone for the sins of the world, he permitted him to be placed even below a **robber** and **murderer.** That the Son of God was reduced so low none

gave to the people at large was, in its utmost latitude, applicable to these Jews, – they were a SWINISH MULTITUDE.

22. What shall I do then with Jesus? – Showing, hereby, that it was his wish to release him.

23. What evil hath he done? – Pilate plainly saw that there was nothing laid to his charge for which, consistently with the Roman laws, he could condemn him.

But they cried out the more – What strange fury and injustice! They could not answer Pilate's question, What evil hath he done? He had done none, and they knew he had done none; but they are determined on his death.

MATTHEW 27: 24–32; MARK 15: 15–21; LUKE 23: 24–32

Matthew 27: 24–32

24. Pilate – took water, and washed his hands – Thus signifying his innocence. It was a custom among the Hebrews, Greeks, and Latins, to wash the hands in token of innocence, and to show that they were pure from any imputed guilt. In case of an undiscovered murder, the elders of that city which was nearest to the place where the dead body was found, were required by the law, Deuteronomy 21: 1–10, to wash their hands over the victim which was offered to expiate the crime, and thus make public protestation of their own innocence. David says, I will wash my hands in innocence, so shall I compass thine altar, Psalm 26: 6. As Pilate knew Christ was innocent, he should have prevented his death: he had the armed force at his command, and should have dispersed this infamous mob. Had he been charged with countenancing a seditious person, he could have easily cleared himself, had the matter been brought before the emperor. He, therefore, was inexcusable.

25. His blood be on us and on our children – If this man be innocent, and we put him to death as a guilty person, may the punishment due to such a crime be visited upon us, and upon our children after us! What a dreadful imprecation! and how literally fulfilled! They were visited with the same kind of punishment; for the Romans crucified them in such numbers when Jerusalem was taken, that there was found a deficiency of crosses for the condemned, and of places for the crosses. Their children or descendants have had the same curse entailed upon them, and continue to this day a proof of the innocence of Christ, the truth of his religion, and of the justice of God.

26. Scourged Jesus – This is allowed to have been a very severe punishment of itself among the Romans, the flesh being generally cut by the whips used for this purpose: so the poet: "To be cut by the horrible whip." And sometimes it seems, they were whipped to death. It has been thought that Pilate might have spared this additional cruelty of whipping; but it appears that it was a common custom to scourge those criminals which were to be crucified, and lenity in Christ's case is not to be allowed; he must take all the misery in full.

Delivered him to be crucified – Tacitus, the Roman historian, mentions the death of Christ in very remarkable terms:

"Nero put those who commonly went by the name of Christians to the most exquisite tortures. The author of this name was CHRIST, who was capitally punished in the reign of TIBERIUS, by PONTIUS PILATE the PROCURATOR."

28. Stripped him – Took off his mantle, or upper garment.

A scarlet robe – Or, according to Mark and John, a purple robe, such as emperors and kings wore.

29. A crown of thorns – It does not appear that this crown was intended to be an instrument of punishment or torture to his head, but rather to render him ridiculous; for which cause also they put a reed in his hand, by way of scepter, and bowed their knees, pretending to do him homage. The crown was not probably of thorns, in our sense of the word: there are eminently learned men who think that the crown was formed of the herb acanthus.

day in a dream because of him.

20 But the chief priests and elders persuaded the multitude that they should ask Barabbas, and destroy Jesus.

21 The governor answered and said unto them, Whether of the twain will ye that I release unto you? They said, Barabbas.

22 Pilate saith unto them, What shall I do then with Jesus which is called Christ? They all say unto him, Let him be crucified.

23 And the governor said, Why, what evil hath he done? But they cried out the more, saying, Let him be crucified.

Mark 15: 6–14

6 Now at that feast he released unto them one prisoner, whomsoever they desired.

7 And there was one named Barabbas, which lay bound with them that had made insurrection with him, who had committed murder in the insurrection.

8 And the multitude crying aloud began to desire him to do as he had ever done unto them.

9 But Pilate answered them, saying, Will ye that I release unto you the King of the Jews?

10 For he knew that the chief priests had delivered him for envy.

11 But the chief priests moved the people, that he should rather release Barabbas unto them.

12 And Pilate answered and said again unto them, What will ye then that I shall do unto him whom ye call the King of the Jews?

13 And they cried out again, Crucify him.

14 Then Pilate said unto them, Why, what evil hath he done? And they cried out the more exceedingly, Crucify him.

Luke 23: 13–23

13 And Pilate, when he had called together the chief priests and the rulers and the people,

14 Said unto them, Ye have brought this man unto me, as one that perverteth the people: and, behold, I, having examined him before you, have found no fault in this man touching those things whereof ye accuse him:

can properly remember without the deepest horror, and displeasure with themselves, and detestation of their own crimes. But hence also arises no ordinary ground of confidence; for Christ was sunk into the depths of ignominy, that he might obtain for us, by his humiliation, an ascent to the heavenly glory: he was reckoned worse than **a robber,** that he might admit us to the society of the angels of God. If this advantage be justly estimated, it will be more than sufficient to remove the offense of the cross.

The custom of having **one of the prisoners released by the governor on the festival,** to gratify the people, was a foolish and improper practice, and, indeed, was an open abuse of the worship of God; for nothing could be more unreasonable than that festivals should be honored by allowing crimes to go unpunished. God has armed magistrates with the sword, that they may punish with severity those crimes which cannot be tolerated without public injury; and hence it is evident that lie does not wish to be worshipped by a violation of laws and punishments. But since nothing ought to be attempted but by the rule of his word, all that men gain by methods of worshipping God which have been rashly contrived by themselves is, that under the pretense of honoring, they often throw dishonor upon Him. We ought therefore to preserve such moderation, as not to offer to God any thing but what he requires; for he is so far from taking pleasure in profane gift that they provoke his anger the more.

19. While he was sitting on the judgment-seat
Although the thoughts which had passed through the mind of Pilate's wife during the day might be the cause of her **dream,** yet there can be no doubt that she suffered these torments, not in a natural way, (such as happens to us every day,) but by an extraordinary inspiration of God. It has been commonly supposed that the devil stirred up this woman, in order to retard the redemption of mankind; which is in the highest degree improbable, since it was he who excited and inflamed, to such a degree, the priests and scribes to put Christ to death. We ought to conclude, on the contrary, that God the Father took many methods of attesting the innocence of Christ, that it might evidently appear that he suffered death in the room of others – that is, in our room. God intended that Pilate should so frequently acquit him with his own mouth before condemning him, that in his undeserved condemnation the true satisfaction for our sins might be the more brightly displayed. Matthew expressly mentions this, that none may wonder at the extreme solicitude of Pilate, when he debates with the people, in the midst of a tumult, for the purpose of saving the life of a man whom he despised. And, indeed, by the terrors which his wife, had suffered during the night, God

Mark, Mark 15: 17, and John, John 19: 5, term it, a *crown* or wreath, formed out of the branches of the herb acanthus, or bear's foot. This, however, is a prickly plant, though nothing like thorns, in the common meaning of that word. Many Christians have gone astray in magnifying the sufferings of Christ from this circumstance; and painters, the worst of all commentators, frequently represent Christ with a crown of long thorns, which one standing by is striking into his head with a stick. These representations engender ideas both false and absurd.

There is a passage produced from Philo by Dr. Lardner, which casts much light on these indignities offered to our blessed Lord.

"Caligula, the successor of Tiberius, gave Agrippa the tetrarchy of his uncle Philip, with the right of wearing a diadem or crown. When he came to Alexandria, on his way to his tetrarchate, the inhabitants of that place, filled with envy at the thoughts of a Jew having the title of king, showed their indignation in the following way. They brought one Carabus (a sort of an idiot) into the theater; and, having placed him on a lofty seat, that he might be seen by all, they put a diadem upon his head, made of the herb which made the ancient papyrus, or paper flag; his body they covered with a mat or carpet, instead of a royal cloak. One seeing a piece of reed, (the stem, probably, of the aforesaid herb) lying on the ground, picked it up, and put it in his hand in place of a scepter. Having thus given him a mock royal dress, several young fellows, with poles on their shoulders, came and stood on each side of him as his guards. Then there came people, some to pay their homage to him, some to ask justice, and some to consult him on affairs of state and the crowd that stood round about made a confused noise, crying, Mario, that being, as they say, the Syriac word for LORD; thereby showing that they intended to ridicule Agrippa, who was a Syrian." Philo.

There is the most remarkable coincidence between this account and that given by the evangelists; and the conjecture concerning the acanthus will probably find no inconsiderable support from the byblos and papyrus of Philo. This plant, Pliny says, grows to ten cubits long in the stem and the flowers were used for CROWNING THE GODS.

The reflections of pious Quesnel on these insults offered to our blessed Lord merit serious attention. "Let the crown of thorns make those Christians blush who throw away so much time, pains, and money, in beautifying and adorning a sinful head. Let the world do what it will to render the royalty and mysteries of Christ contemptible, it is my glory to serve a King thus debased; my salvation, to adore that which the world despises; and my redemption, to go unto God through the merits of him who was crowned with thorns."

30. And they spit upon him – "Let us pay our adoration," says the same pious writer, "and humble ourselves in silence at the sight of a spectacle which faith alone renders credible, and which our senses would hardly endure. Jesus Christ, in this condition, preaches to the kings of the earth this truth – that their scepters are but reeds, with which themselves shall be smitten, bruised, and crushed at his tribunal, if they do not use them here to the advancement of his kingdom."

32. A man of Cyrene – him they compelled to bear his cross – In John, John 19: 16–17, we are told Christ himself bore the cross, and this, it is likely, he did for a part of the way; but, being exhausted with the scourging and other cruel usage which he had received, he was found incapable of bearing it alone; therefore they obliged Simon, not, I think, to bear it entirely, but to assist Christ, by bearing a part of it. It was a constant practice among the Romans, to oblige criminal to bear their cross to the place of execution: insomuch that Plutarch makes use of it as an illustration of the misery of vice. "Every kind of wickedness produces its own particular torment, just as every malefactor, when he is brought forth to execution, carries his own cross."

15 No, nor yet Herod: for I sent you to him; and, lo, nothing worthy of death is done unto him.

16 I will therefore chastise him, and release him.

17 (For of necessity he must release one unto them at the feast.)

18 And they cried out all at once, saying, Away with this man, and release unto us Barabbas:

19 (Who for a certain sedition made in the city, and for murder, was cast into prison.)

20 Pilate therefore, willing to release Jesus, spake again to them.

21 But they cried, saying, Crucify him, crucify him.

22 And he said unto them the third time, Why, what evil hath he done? I have found no cause of death in him: I will therefore chastise him, and let him go.

23 And they were instant with loud voices, requiring that he might be crucified. And the voices of them and of the chief priests prevailed.

MATTHEW 27: 24–32; MARK 15: 15–21; LUKE 23: 24–32

Matthew 27: 24–32

24 When Pilate saw that he could prevail nothing, but that rather a tumult was made, he took water, and washed his hands before the multitude, saying, I am innocent of the blood of this just person: see ye to it.

25 Then answered all the people, and said, His blood be on us, and on our children.

26 Then released he Barabbas unto them: and when he had scourged Jesus, he delivered him to be crucified.

27 Then the soldiers of the governor took Jesus into the common hall, and gathered unto him the whole band of soldiers.

28 And they stripped him, and put on him a scarlet robe.

29 And when they had platted a crown of thorns, they put it upon his head, and a reed in his right hand: and they bowed the knee before him, and mocked him, saying, Hail, King of the Jews!

30 And they spit upon him, and took the reed, and smote him on the head.

compelled him to defend the innocence of his own Son; not to rescue him from death, but only to make it manifest, that in the room of others he endured that punishment which he had not deserved.

20. But the chief priests and elders persuaded the multitude

The Evangelist points out the chief instigators of the wicked proceedings; not that the foolish credulity of the people, who were influenced by others, admits of any excuse; but for the purpose of informing us that they were not, of their own accord, hostile to Christ, but that, having sold themselves to gratify the priests, they forget all justice and modesty, as well as their own salvation. Hence we learn how pernicious is the influence of wicked men, who can easily turn in every direction, to all kind of wickedness, the giddy and changeful multitude. Yet we must attend to the design of the Evangelist, which was to show, that the death of Christ was so eagerly demanded by the voice of the people, not because he was universally hated, but because the greater part of them, ambitiously desirous to follow the inclination of their rulers, threw aside all regard to justice, and might be said to have sold and enslaved their tongue to the wicked conspiracy of a few.

MATTHEW 27: 24–32; MARK 15: 15–21; LUKE 23: 24–32

Matthew 27: 24. But Pilate, perceiving that he gained nothing by it

As sailors, who have experienced a violent tempest, at last give way, and permit themselves to be carried out of the proper course; so Pilate, finding himself unable to restrain the commotion of the people, lays aside his authority as a judge, and yields to their furious outcry. And though he had long attempted to hold out, still the necessity does not excuse him; for he ought rather to have submitted to any amount of suffering than to have swerved from his duty. Nor is his guilt alleviated by the childish ceremony which he uses; for how could a few drops of water wash away the stain of a crime which no satisfaction of any kind could obliterate? His principal object in doing so was not to wash out his stains before God, but to exhibit to the people a mark of abhorrence, to try if perhaps he might lead them to repent of their fury; as if he had employed such a preface as this, "Lo, you compel me to an unrighteous murder, to which I cannot come but with trembling and horror. What then shall become of you, and what dreadful vengeance of God awaits you, who are the chief actors in the deed?" But whatever might be the design of Pilate, God intended to testify, in this manner, the innocence of his Son, that it might be more manifest that in him our sins were condemned.

MATTHEW 27: 33–38; MARK 15: 22–28; LUKE 23: 33–34,38

Matthew 27: 33–38

33. **A place called Golgotha** – From the Hebrew for a skull, probably so called from the many skulls of these who had suffered crucifixion and other capital punishments scattered up and down in the place. It is the same as Calvary, the place of bare skulls. Some think the place was thus called, because it was in the form of a human skull.

34. **They gave him vinegar – mingled with gall** – Perhaps, commonly translated gall, signifies no more than bitters of any kind. It was a common custom to administer a stupefying potion compounded of sour wine, which is the same as vinegar, to condemned persons, to help to alleviate their sufferings, or so disturb their intellect that they might not be sensible of them. The rabbins say that they put a grain of frankincense into a cup of strong wine; and they ground this on Proverbs 31: 6: Give strong drink unto him that is ready to perish, i.e. who is condemned to death. Some person, out of kindness, appears to have administered this to our blessed Lord; but he, as in all other cases, determining to endure the fullness of pain, refused to take what was thus offered to him, choosing to tread the winepress alone. This custom of giving stupefying potions to condemned malefactors is alluded to in Proverbs 31: 6: Give strong drink, inebriating drink, to him who is ready to PERISH, and wine to him who is BITTER of soul – because he is just going to suffer the punishment of death. And thus the rabbins, as we have seen above, understand it.

35. **And they crucified him** – Crucifixion properly means the act of nailing or tying to a cross. The cross was made of two beams, either crossing at the top at right angles, like a T, or in the middle of their length, like an X. There was, besides, a piece on the center of the transverse beam, to which the accusation or statement of the crime of the culprit was attached, and a piece of wood which projected from the middle, on which the person sat, as on a sort of saddle; and by which the whole body was supported. Tertullian mentions this particularly. Justin Martyr, in his dialogue with Trypho the Jew, gives precisely the same description of the cross; and it is worthy of observation that both he and Tertullian flourished before the punishment of the cross had been abolished. The cross on which our Lord suffered was of the former kind; being thus represented in all old monuments, coins, and crosses. St. Jerome compares it to a bird flying, a man swimming, or praying with his arms extended. The punishment of the cross was inflicted among the ancient Hindoos from time immemorial for various species of theft, and was common among the Syrians, Egyptians, Persians, Africans, Greeks, and Romans: it is also still in use among the Chinese, who do not nail, but tie the criminal to it. It was probably the Romans who introduced it among the Jews. Before they became subject to the Romans, they used hanging or gibbeting, but not the cross. This punishment was the most dreadful of all others, both for the shame and pain of it: and so scandalous, that it was inflicted as the last mark of detestation upon the vilest of people. It was the punishment of robbers and murderers, provided they were slaves; but if they were free, it was thought too infamous a punishment for such, let their crimes be what they might.

The body of the criminal was fastened to the upright beam, by nailing or tying the feet to it, and on the transverse piece by nailing, and sometimes tying the hands to it. As the hands and feet are the grand instruments of motion, they are provided with a greater quantity of nerves; and the nerves in those places, especially the hands, are peculiarly sensible. Now, as the nerves are the instruments of all sensation or feeling, wounds in the parts where they abound must be peculiarly painful; especially when inflicted with such rude instruments as large nails, forced through the places by the violence of a hammer; thus tearing asunder the nervous fibrillae, delicate tendons, and small bones of those parts. This punishment will appear dreadful enough, when it is considered that the person was permitted to hang

31 And after that they had mocked him, they took the robe off from him, and put his own raiment on him, and led him away to crucify him.

32 And as they came out, they found a man of Cyrene, Simon by name: him they compelled to bear his cross.

Mark 15: 15–21

15 And so Pilate, willing to content the people, released Barabbas unto them, and delivered Jesus, when he had scourged him, to be crucified.

16 And the soldiers led him away into the hall, called Praetorium; and they call together the whole band.

17 And they clothed him with purple, and platted a crown of thorns, and put it about his head,

18 And began to salute him, Hail, King of the Jews!

19 And they smote him on the head with a reed, and did spit upon him, and bowing their knees worshipped him.

20 And when they had mocked him, they took off the purple from him, and put his own clothes on him, and led him out to crucify him.

21 And they compel one Simon a Cyrenian, who passed by, coming out of the country, the father of Alexander and Rufus, to bear his cross.

Luke 23: 24–32

24 And Pilate gave sentence that it should be as they required.

25 And he released unto them him that for sedition and murder was cast into prison, whom they had desired; but he delivered Jesus to their will.

26 And as they led him away, they laid hold upon one Simon, a Cyrenian, coming out of the country, and on him they laid the cross, that he might bear it after Jesus.

27 And there followed him a great company of people, and of women, which also bewailed and lamented him.

28 But Jesus turning unto them said, Daughters of Jerusalem, weep not for me, but weep for yourselves, and for your children.

29 For, behold, the days are coming, in the which they shall say, Blessed are the barren, and the wombs that never bare,

The supreme and sole Judge of the world is placed at the bar of an earthly judge, is condemned to crucifixion as a malefactor, and – what is more – is placed between two robbers, as if he had been the prince of robbers. A spectacle so revolting might, at first sight, greatly disturb the senses of men, were it not met by this argument, that the punishment which had been due to us was laid on Christ, so that, our guilt having now been removed, we do not hesitate to come into the presence of the Heavenly Judge. Accordingly, the water, which was of no avail for washing away the filth of Pilate, ought to be efficacious, in the present day, for a different purpose, to cleanse our eyes from every obstruction, that, in the midst of condemnation, they may clearly perceive the righteousness of Christ.

25. His blood be on us

There can be no doubt that the Jews pronounced this curse on themselves without any concern, as if they had been fully convinced that they had a righteous cause before God; but their inconsiderate zeal carries them headlong, so that, while they commit an irreparable crime, they add to it a solemn imprecation, by which they cut themselves off from the hope of pardon. Hence we infer how carefully we ought to guard against headlong rashness in all our judgments. For when men refuse to make inquiry, and venture to decide in this or the other matter according to their own fancy, blind impulse must at length carry them to rage. And this is the righteous vengeance of God with which he visits the pride of those who do not deign to take the trouble of distinguishing between right and wrong. The Jews thought that, in slaying Christ, they were performing a service acceptable to God; but whence arose this wicked error, unless from wicked obstinacy, and from despising God himself? Justly, therefore, were they abandoned to this rashness of drawing upon themselves final ruin. But when the question relates to the worship of God and his holy mysteries, let us learn to open our eyes, and to inquire into the matter with reverence and sobriety, lest through hypocrisy and presumption we become stupefied and enraged.

Now as God would never have permitted this execrable word to proceed from the mouth of the people, if their impiety had not been already desperate, so afterwards he justly revenged it by dreadful and unusual methods; and yet by an incredible miracle he reserved for himself some remnant, that his covenant might not be abolished by the destruction of the whole nation. He had adopted for himself the seed of Abraham, that it might be "a chosen nation, a royal priesthood, his peculiar people and inheritance" (1 Peter 2: 9).

The Jews now conspire, as with one voice, to renounce a favor so distinguished. Who would not say that the whole

(the whole weight of his body being borne up by his nailed hands and the projecting piece which passed between the thighs) till he perished through agony and lack of food. Some, we are informed, have lived three whole days in this state. It is true that, in some cases, there was a kind of mercy shown to the sufferer, which will appear sufficiently horrid, when it is known that it consisted in breaking the bones of their legs and thighs to pieces with a large hammer, in order to put them the sooner out of pain! Such a coup de grace as this could only spring from those tender mercies of the wicked which God represents as cruelty itself. Some were permitted to hang on the cross till eaten up by birds of prey, which often began to tear them before life was extinct. Horace alludes to this punishment, and from what he says, it seems to have been inflicted on slaves, etc., not on trifling occasions, but for the most horrible crimes.

> If a poor slave who takes away your plate,
> Lick the warm sauce, or half cold frag-
> ments eat,
> Yet should you crucify the wretch!
> "I have not committed murder:
> Then thou shalt not be nailed to the cross,
> to feed the ravens."

The anguish occasioned by crucifixion was so intense, that a cruce, among the Romans, was the common word by which they expressed suffering and torment in general.

And parted his garments, casting lots – These were the Roman soldiers, who had crucified him: and it appears from this circumstance, that in those ancient times the spoils of the criminal were claimed by the executioners, as they are to the present day. It appears that they divided a part, and cast lots for the rest: viz. for his seamless coat, John 19: 23–24.

36. They watched him – To prevent his disciples or relatives from taking away the body or affording any relief to the sufferer.

37. His accusation – It was a common custom to affix a label to the cross, giving a statement of the crime for which the person suffered. This is still the case in China, when a person is crucified. Sometimes a person was employed to carry this before the criminal, while going to the place of punishment.

It is with much propriety that Matthew calls this accusation; for it was false that ever Christ pretended to be KING OF THE JEWS, in the sense the inscription held forth: he was accused of this, but there was no proof of the accusation; however it was affixed to the cross. From John 19: 21, we find that the Jews wished this to be a little altered: Write, said they, that HE said, l am king of the Jews; thus endeavoring, by the addition of a vile lie, to countenance their own conduct in putting him to death. But this Pilate refused to do. Both Luke, Luke 23: 38, and John, John 19: 20, say that this accusation was written in Greek, Latin, and Hebrew. In those three languages, we may conceive the label to stand thus, according to the account given by St. John; the Hebrew being the mixed dialect then spoken.

It is only necessary to observe, that all the letters, both of the Greek and Roman alphabets, were those now called square or uncial.

38. Two thieves – robbers, or cutthroats: men who had committed robbery and murder; for it does not appear that persons were crucified for robbery only. Thus was our Lord numbered (his name enrolled, placed as it were in the death warrant) with transgressors, according to the prophetic declaration, Isaiah 53: 12; and the Jews placed him between these two, perhaps to intimate that he was the worst felon of the three.

MATTHEW 27: 39–44; MARK 15: 29–32; LUKE 23: 35–37,39–43

Matthew 27: 39–44

39. Wagging their heads – In token of contempt.

40. Thou that destroyest – Who didst pretend that thou couldst have destroyed the temple, and built it up again in three days. This malicious torturing of our Lord's words has been noticed before. Cruelty is obliged to take refuge in lies, in order to vindicate its infamous proceedings.

and the paps which never gave suck.

30 Then shall they begin to say to the mountains, Fall on us; and to the hills, Cover us.

31 For if they do these things in a green tree, what shall be done in the dry?

32 And there were also two other, malefactors, led with him to be put to death.

MATTHEW 27: 33–38; MARK 15: 22–28; LUKE 23: 33–34,38

Matthew 27: 33–38

33 And when they were come unto a place called Golgotha, that is to say, a place of a skull,

34 They gave him vinegar to drink mingled with gall: and when he had tasted thereof, he would not drink.

35 And they crucified him, and parted his garments, casting lots: that it might be fulfilled which was spoken by the prophet, They parted my garments among them, and upon my vesture did they cast lots.

36 And sitting down they watched him there;

37 And set up over his head his accusation written, THIS IS JESUS THE KING OF THE JEWS.

38 Then were there two thieves crucified with him, one on the right hand, and another on the left.

Mark 15: 22–28

22 And they bring him unto the place Golgotha, which is, being interpreted, The place of a skull.

23 And they gave him to drink wine mingled with myrrh: but he received it not.

24 And when they had crucified him, they parted his garments, casting lots upon them, what every man should take.

25 And it was the third hour, and they crucified him.

26 And the superscription of his accusation was written over, THE KING OF THE JEWS.

27 And with him they crucify two thieves; the one on his right hand, and the other on his left.

28 And the scripture was fulfilled, which saith, And he was numbered with the transgressors.

nation was utterly rooted out from the kingdom of God? But God, through their treachery, renders more illustrious the fidelity of his promise, and, to show that he did not in vain make a covenant with Abraham, he rescues from the general destruction those whom he has elected by free grace. Thus the truth of God always rises superior to all the obstacles raised by human unbelief.

MATTHEW 27: 33–38; MARK 15: 22–28; LUKE 23: 33–34,38

Matthew 27: 33. And they came to the place

Jesus was **brought to the place** where it was customary to execute criminals, that his death might be more ignominious. Now though this was done according to custom, still we ought to consider the loftier purpose of God; for he determined that his Son should be cast out of the city as unworthy of human intercourse, that he might admit us into his heavenly kingdom with the angels. For this reason the apostle, in the Epistle to the Hebrews (13: 12), refers it to an ancient figure of the law. For as God commanded his people to "burn without the camp" the bodies of those animals, the blood of which was carried into the sanctuary to make atonement for sins (Exodus 29: 14; Leviticus 16: 27); so he says that Christ went out of the gate of the city, that, by taking upon him the curse which pressed us down, he might be regarded as accursed, and might in this manner atone for our sins. Now the greater the ignominy and disgrace which he endured before the world, so much the more acceptable and noble a spectacle did he exhibit in his death to God and to the angels. For the infamy of the place did not hinder him from erecting there a splendid trophy of his victory; nor did the offensive smell of the carcasses which lay there hinder the sweet savor of his sacrifice from diffusing itself throughout the whole world, and penetrating even to heaven.

34. And they gave him vinegar

Although the Evangelists are not so exact in placing each matter in its due order, as to enable us to fix the precise moment at which the events occurred; yet I look upon it as a probable conjecture that, before our Lord was elevated on the cross, there was offered to him in a cup, according to custom, **wine mingled with myrrh**, or some other mixture, which appears to have been compounded of **gall and vinegar**. It is sufficiently agreed, indeed, among nearly all interpreters, that this draught was different from that which is mentioned by John (14: 29). I consider the cup to have been offered to our Lord when he was about to be crucified; but that after the cross was lifted up, **a sponge** was then dipped and given to him. At what time he began to ask something to drink, I am not very anxious to inquire;

If thou be the Son of God – Or rather, A son of God, i.e. a peculiar favorite of the Most-High; not, THE Son of God. "It is not to be conceived," says a learned man, "that every passenger who was going to the city had a competent knowledge of Christ's supernatural conception by the Holy Spirit, or an adequate comprehension of his character as the Messiah, and THE SON OF GOD. There is not a single passage where Jesus is designed to be pointed out as the MESSIAH, THE SON OF GOD, where the article is omitted: nor, on the other hand, is this designation ever specified without the article. See Matthew 16: 16; 26: 63; 28: 19."

41. Chief priests – scribes and elders – To these, several ancient MSS. and versions add, and Pharisees. But though the authority for this reading is respectable, yet it does not appear that the Pharisees joined in with the others in the condemnation of our Lord. Probably his discourses and parables, related in some of the preceding chapters, which were spoken directly to them, had so far convinced them that they would at least have no hand in putting him to death. All the infamy of this seems to fall upon the PRIESTS, scribes, and elders.

42. He saved others; himself he cannot save – Or, Cannot he save himself? Several MSS. read this with the mark of interrogation as above; and this makes the sarcasm still more keen.

A high priest who designs to destroy the temple of God: a Savior who saves not himself; and the Son of God crucified: these are the contradictions which give offense to Jews and libertines. But a high priest who dispels the types and shadows, only that he may disclose the substance of religion, and become the minister of a heavenly sanctuary; a Savior who dies only to be the victim of salvation; and the Son of God who confines his power within the bounds of the cross to establish the righteousness of faith: this is what a Christian adores; this is the foundation of his hope, and the fountain of his present comfort and final blessedness. See Quesnel.

We will believe him – Instead of him, many excellent MSS. have IN him: this is a reading which Griesbach and other eminent critics have adopted.

43. If he will have him – Or, if he delight in him – The verbs are used by the Septuagint in more than forty places for the Hebrew, which signifies, earnestly to desire, or delight in. Now as this is a quotation from Psalm 22: 8, He trusted in the Lord, that he would deliver him; let him deliver him, for he HATH DELIGHTED IN HIM. This will sufficiently vindicate the above translation; as the evangelist quotes the words from that version, with the simple change of if, for because.

44. The thieves also – cast the same in his teeth – That is, one of the robbers; for one, we find, was a penitent, Luke 23: 39–40.

MATTHEW 27: 45–56; MARK 15: 33–41; LUKE 23: 44–49

Matthew 27: 45–56

45. There was darkness over all the land – I am of opinion that "over all the land" does not mean all the world, but only the land of Judea. So the word is used Matthew 24: 30; Luke 4: 25, and in other places. Several eminent critics are of this opinion. Besides, it is evident that the evangelists speak of things that happened in Judea, the place of their residence. It is plain enough there was a darkness in Jerusalem, and over all Judea; and probably over all the people among whom Christ had for more than three years preached the everlasting Gospel; and that this darkness was supernatural is evident from this, that it happened during the passover, which was celebrated only at the full moon, a time in which it was impossible for the sun to be eclipsed. But many suppose the darkness was over the whole world, and think there is sufficient evidence of this in ancient authors. PHLEGON and THALLUS, who flourished in the beginning of the second century, are supposed to speak of this. The former says: "In the fourth year of the 202nd Olympiad, there was an extraordinary eclipse of the sun:

Luke 23: 33–34,38

33 And when they were come to the place, which is called Calvary, there they crucified him, and the malefactors, one on the right hand, and the other on the left.

34 Then said Jesus, Father, forgive them; for they know not what they do. And they parted his raiment, and cast lots.

38 And a superscription also was written over him in letters of Greek, and Latin, and Hebrew, THIS IS THE KING OF THE JEWS.

MATTHEW 27: 39–44; MARK 15: 29–32; LUKE 23: 35–37,39–43

Matthew 27: 39–44

39 And they that passed by reviled him, wagging their heads,

40 And saying, Thou that destroyest the temple, and buildest it in three days, save thyself. If thou be the Son of God, come down from the cross.

41 Likewise also the chief priests mocking him, with the scribes and elders, said,

42 He saved others; himself he cannot save. If he be the King of Israel, let him now come down from the cross, and we will believe him.

43 He trusted in God; let him deliver him now, if he will have him: for he said, I am the Son of God.

44 The thieves also, which were crucified with him, cast the same in his teeth.

Mark 15: 29–32

29 And they that passed by railed on him, wagging their heads, and saying, Ah, thou that destroyest the temple, and buildest it in three days,

30 Save thyself, and come down from the cross.

31 Likewise also the chief priests mocking said among themselves with the scribes, He saved others; himself he cannot save.

32 Let Christ the King of Israel descend now from the cross, that we may see and believe. And they that were crucified with him reviled him.

Luke 23: 35–37,39–43

35 And the people stood beholding. And the rulers also with them derided him, saying, He saved others; let him

but when we compare all the circumstances, it is not unreasonable to suppose that, after he had refused that bitter mixture, it was frequently in derision presented to his lips. For we shall find Matthew afterwards adding that the soldiers, while they were giving him to drink, upbraided him for not being able to rescue himself from death. Hence we infer that, while the remedy was offered, they ridiculed the weakness of Christ, because he had complained that he was forsaken by God (Matthew 27: 49).

MATTHEW 27: 39–44; MARK 15: 29–32; LUKE 23: 35–37,39–43

Matthew 27: 39. And they that passed by

These circumstances carry great weight; for they place before us the extreme abasement of the Son of God, that we may see more clearly how much our salvation cost him, and that, reflecting that we justly deserved all the punishments which he endured, we may be more and more excited to repentance. For in this exhibition God hath plainly showed to us how wretched our condition would have been, if we had not a Redeemer. But all that Christ endured in himself ought to be applied for our consolation. This certainly was more cruel than all the other tortures, that they upbraided, and reviled, and tormented him as one that had been cast off and forsaken by God (Isaiah 53: 4). And, therefore, David, as the representative of Christ, complains chiefly of this among the distresses which he suffered (Psalm 22: 7). And, indeed, there is nothing that inflicts a more painful wound on pious minds than when ungodly men, in order to shake their faith, upbraid them with being deprived of the assistance and favor of God. This is the harsh persecution with which, Paul tells us, Isaac was tormented by Ishmael (Galatians 4: 29); not that he attacked him with the sword, and with outward violence, but that, by turning the grace of God into ridicule, he endeavored to overthrow his faith. These temptations were endured, first by David, and afterwards by Christ him-self, that they might not at the present day strike us with excessive alarm, as if they had been unusual; for there never will be wanting wicked men who are disposed to insult our distresses. And whenever God does not assist us according to our wish, but conceals his aid for a little time, it is a frequent stratagem of Satan, to allege that our hope was to no purpose, as if his promise had failed.

40. Thou who destroyedst the temple

They charge Christ with teaching falsehood, because, now that it is called for, he does not actually display the power to which he laid claim. But if their unbridled propensity to cursing had not deprived them of sense and reason, they would shortly afterwards have perceived clearly the truth of his statement. Christ had said, **Destroy this temple,**

at the sixth hour, the day was turned into dark night, so that the stars in heaven were seen; and there was an earthquake in Bithynia, which overthrew many houses in the city of Nice." This is the substance of what Phlegon is reputed to have said on this subject: but

1. All the authors who quote him differ, and often very materially, in what they say was found in him.

2. Phlegon says nothing of Judea: what he says is, that in such an Olympiad, (some say the 102nd, others the 202nd), there was an eclipse in Bithynia, and an earthquake at Nice.

3. Phlegon does not say that the earthquake happened at the time of the eclipse.

4. Phlegon does not intimate that this darkness was extraordinary, or that the eclipse happened at the full of the moon, or that it lasted three hours. These circumstances could not have been omitted by him, if he had known them.

5. Phlegon speaks merely of an ordinary, though perhaps total, eclipse of the sun, and cannot mean the darkness mentioned by the evangelists.

6. Phlegon speaks of an eclipse that happened in some year of the 102nd, or 202nd Olympiad; and therefore little stress can be laid on what he says as applying to this event.

The quotation from THALLUS, made by AFRICANUS, found in the Chronicle of SYNCELLUS, of the eighth century, is allowed by eminent critics to be of little importance. This speaks "of a darkness over all the world, and an earthquake which threw down many houses in Judea and in other parts of the earth." It may be necessary to observe, that THALLUS is quoted by several of the ancient ecclesiastical writers for other matters, but never for this; and that the time in which he lived is so very uncertain, that Dr. Lardner supposes there is room to think he lived rather before than after Christ.

DIONYSIUS the Areopagite is supposed to have mentioned this event in the most decided manner: for being at Heliopolis in Egypt, with his friend Apollophanes, when our Savior suffered, they there saw a wonderful eclipse of the sun, whereupon Dionysius said to his friend, "Either God himself suffers, or sympathizes with the sufferer." It is enough to say of this man, that all the writings attributed to him are known to be spurious, and are proved to be forgeries of the fifth or sixth century. Whoever desires to see more on this subject, may consult Dr. Lardner, (vol. vii. p. 371, ed. 1788), a man whose name should never be mentioned but with respect, notwithstanding the peculiarities of his religious creed; who has done more in the service of Divine revelation than most divines in Christendom; and who has raised a monument to the perpetuity of the Christian religion, which all the infidels in creation shall never be able to pull down or deface.

This miraculous darkness should have caused the enemies of Christ to understand that he was the light of the world, and that because they did not walk in it, it was now taken away from them.

46. My God! My God! why hast thou forsaken me! – These words are quoted by our Lord from Psalm 22: 1; they are of very great importance, and should be carefully considered.

Some suppose "that the divinity had now departed from Christ, and that his human nature was left unsupported to bear the punishment due to men for their sins." But this is by no means to be admitted, as it would deprive his sacrifice of its infinite merit, and consequently leave the sin of the world without an atonement. Take deity away from any redeeming act of Christ, and redemption is ruined. Others imagine that our Lord spoke these words to the Jews only, to prove to them that he was the Messiah. "The Jews," say they, "believed this psalm to speak of the Messiah: they quoted the eighth verse of it against Christ – He trusted in God that he would deliver him; let him deliver him, seeing he delighted in him. (See Matthew 27: 43). To which our Lord immediately answers, My God! my God! etc , thus showing that he was the person of whom the psalmist prophesied." I have doubts concerning the propriety of this interpretation.

save himself, if he be Christ, the chosen of God.

36 And the soldiers also mocked him, coming to him, and offering him vinegar,

37 And saying, If thou be the king of the Jews, save thyself.

39 And one of the malefactors which were hanged railed on him, saying, If thou be Christ, save thyself and us.

40 But the other answering rebuked him, saying, Dost not thou fear God, seeing thou art in the same condemnation?

41 And we indeed justly; for we receive the due reward of our deeds: but this man hath done nothing amiss.

42 And he said unto Jesus, Lord, remember me when thou comest into thy kingdom.

43 And Jesus said unto him, Verily I say unto thee, To day shalt thou be with me in paradise.

MATTHEW 27: 45–56; MARK 15: 33–41; LUKE 23: 44–49

Matthew 27: 45–56

45 Now from the sixth hour there was darkness over all the land unto the ninth hour.

46 And about the ninth hour Jesus cried with a loud voice, saying, Eli, Eli, lama sabachthani? that is to say, My God, my God, why hast thou forsaken me?

47 Some of them that stood there, when they heard that, said, This man calleth for Elias.

48 And straightway one of them ran, and took a spunge, and filled it with vinegar, and put it on a reed, and gave him to drink.

49 The rest said, Let be, let us see whether Elias will come to save him.

50 Jesus, when he had cried again with a loud voice, yielded up the ghost.

51 And, behold, the veil of the temple was rent in twain from the top to the bottom; and the earth did quake, and the rocks rent;

52 And the graves were opened; and many bodies of the saints which slept arose,

53 And came out of the graves after his resurrection, and went into the holy city, and appeared unto many.

54 Now when the centurion, and they

and after three days I will raise it up, (John 2: 19); but now they indulge in a premature triumph, and do not wait for the **three days** that would elapse from the commencement of its destruction. Such is the daring presumption of wicked men, when, under the pretense of the cross, they endeavor to cut them off from the hope of the future life. "Where," say they, "is that immortal glory of which weak and credulous men are accustomed to boast? while the greater part of them are mean and despised, some are slenderly provided with food, others drag out a wretched life, amidst uninterrupted disease; others are driven about in flight, or in banishment; others pine away in prisons, and others are burnt and reduced to ashes?" Thus are they blinded by the present corruption of our outward man, so as to imagine that the hope of the future restoration of life is vain and foolish but our duty is to wait for the proper season of the promised building, and not to take it ill if we are now crucified with Christ "that we may afterwards be partakers of his resurrection" (Romans 6: 5–6).

MATTHEW 27: 45–56; MARK 15: 33–41; LUKE 23: 44–49

Matthew 27: 45. Now from the sixth hour

Although in the death of Christ the weakness of the flesh concealed for a short time the glory of the Godhead, and though the Son of God himself was disfigured by shame and contempt, and, as Paul says, "was emptied" (Philippians 2: 7), yet the heavenly Father did not cease to distinguish him by some marks, and during his lowest humiliation prepared some indications of his future glory, in order to fortify the minds of the godly against the offense of the cross. Thus the majesty of Christ was attested by the **obscuration of the sun,** by the **earthquake,** by the **splitting** of the **rocks,** and the **rending** of **the veil,** as if heaven and earth were rendering the homage which they owed to their Creator.

But we inquire, in the first place, what was the design of the eclipse of **the sun?** For the fiction of the ancient poets in their tragedies, that the light of the sun is withdrawn from the earth whenever any shocking crime is perpetrated, was intended to express the alarming effects of the anger of God; and this invention unquestionably had its origin in the ordinary feelings of mankind. In accordance with this view, some commentators think that, at the death of Christ, God sent darkness as a Mark of detestation, as if God, by bringing darkness over the sun, hid his face from beholding the blackest of all crimes. Others say that, when the visible sun was extinguished, it pointed out the death of the Sun of righteousness. Others choose to refer it to the blinding of the nation, which followed shortly afterwards. For the Jews, by rejecting Christ, as soon as he was removed from among

It has been asked, What language is it that our Lord spoke? *Eli, Eli, lama sabachthani.* Some say it is Hebrew – others Syriac. I say, as the evangelists quote it, it is neither. St. Matthew comes nearest the Hebrew. And St. Mark comes nearest the Syriac, Mark 15: 34.

Some have taken occasion from these words to depreciate the character of our blessed Lord. "They are unworthy," say they, "of a man who suffers, conscious of his innocence, and argue imbecility, impatience, and despair." This is by no means fairly deducible from the passage. However, some think that the words, as they stand in the Hebrew and Syriac, are capable of a translation which destroys all objections, and obviates every difficulty. They translate it: My God! my God! to what sort of persons hast thou left me? The words thus understood are rather to be referred to the wicked Jews than to our Lord, and are an exclamation indicative of the obstinate wickedness of his crucifiers, who steeled their hearts against every operation of the Spirit and power of God.

Through the whole of the Sacred Writings, God is represented as doing those things which, in the course of his providence, he only permits to be done; therefore, the words, to whom hast thou left or given me up, are only a form of expression for, "How astonishing is the wickedness of those persons into whose hands I am fallen!" If this interpretation be admitted, it will free this celebrated passage from much embarrassment, and make it speak a sense consistent with itself, and with the dignity of the Son of God.

47. This man calleth for Elias – Probably these were Hellenistic Jews, who did not fully understand the meaning of our Lord's words. Elijah was daily expected to appear as the forerunner of the Messiah, whose arrival, under the character of a mighty prince, was generally supposed to be at hand throughout the east. See Malachi 4: 5; Matthew 2: 2–4; 17: 10–12.

48. Took a sponge – This being the most convenient way to reach a liquid to his mouth; tied it on a reed, that they might be able to reach his lips with it. This reed, as we learn from St. John, was a stalk of hyssop, which,

in that country, must have grown to a considerable magnitude. This appears also to have been done in mercy, to alleviate his sufferings. See Matthew 27: 34.

50. Yielded up the ghost – He dismissed the spirit. He himself willingly gave up that life which it was impossible for man to take away. It is not said that he hung on the cross till he died through pain and agony; nor is it said that his bones were broken, the sooner to put him out of pain, and to hasten his death; but that himself dismissed the soul, that he might thus become, not a forced sacrifice, but a free-will offering for sin.

Now, as our English word ghost, an inmate, inhabitant, guest, (a casual visitant), also a spirit, is now restricted among us to the latter meaning, always signifying the immortal spirit or soul of man, the guest of the body and as giving up the spirit, ghost, or soul, is an act not proper to man, though commending it to God, in our last moments, is both an act of faith and piety; and as giving up the ghost, i.e. dismissing his spirit from his body, is attributed to Jesus Christ, to whom alone it is proper; I therefore object against its use in every other case.

Every man, since the fall, has not only been liable to death, but has deserved it; as all have forfeited their lives because of sin. Jesus Christ, as born immaculate, and having never sinned, had not forfeited his life, and therefore may be considered as naturally and properly immortal. No man, says he, taketh it, my life, from me, but I lay it down of myself: I have power to lay it down, and I have power to take it again; therefore doth the Father love me, because I lay down my life that I might take it again, John 10: 17–18. Hence we rightly translate Matthew 27: 50, he gave up the ghost; i.e. he dismissed his spirit, that he might die for the sin of the world. The Evangelist St. John (John 19: 30) makes use of an expression to the same import, which we translate in the same way: he delivered up his spirit. We translate Mark 15: 37, and Luke 23: 46, he gave up the ghost, but not correctly, because the word in both these places is very different – he breathed

that were with him, watching Jesus, saw the earthquake, and those things that were done, they feared greatly, saying, Truly this was the Son of God.

55 And many women were there beholding afar off, which followed Jesus from Galilee, ministering unto him:

56 Among which was Mary Magdalene, and Mary the mother of James and Joses, and the mother of Zebedee's children.

Mark 15: 33–41

33 And when the sixth hour was come, there was darkness over the whole land until the ninth hour.

34 And at the ninth hour Jesus cried with a loud voice, saying, Eloi, Eloi, lama sabachthani? which is, being interpreted, My God, my God, why hast thou forsaken me?

35 And some of them that stood by, when they heard it, said, Behold, he calleth Elias.

36 And one ran and filled a spunge full of vinegar, and put it on a reed, and gave him to drink, saying, Let alone; let us see whether Elias will come to take him down.

37 And Jesus cried with a loud voice, and gave up the ghost.

38 And the veil of the temple was rent in twain from the top to the bottom.

39 And when the centurion, which stood over against him, saw that he so cried out, and gave up the ghost, he said, Truly this man was the Son of God.

40 There were also women looking on afar off: among whom was Mary Magdalene, and Mary the mother of James the less and of Joses, and Salome;

41 (Who also, when he was in Galilee, followed him, and ministered unto him;) and many other women which came up with him unto Jerusalem.

Luke 23: 44–49

44 And it was about the sixth hour, and there was a darkness over all the earth until the ninth hour.

45 And the sun was darkened, and the veil of the temple was rent in the midst.

46 And when Jesus had cried with a loud voice, he said, Father, into thy hands I commend my spirit: and having said thus,

them, were deprived of the light of heavenly doctrine, and nothing was left to them but the darkness of despair.

I rather think that, as stupidity had shut the eyes of that people against the light, the **darkness** was intended to arouse them to consider the astonishing design of God in the death of Christ. For if they were not altogether hardened, an unusual change of the order of nature must have made a deep impression on their senses, so as to look forward to an approaching renewal of the world. Yet it was a terrific spectacle which was exhibited to them, that they might tremble at the judgment of God. And, indeed, it was an astonishing display of the wrath of God that he did not spare even his only begotten Son, and was not appeased in any other way than by that price of expiation.

As to the scribes and priests, and a great part of the nation, who paid no attention to the eclipse of the sun, but passed it by with closed eyes, their amazing madness ought to strike us with horror; for they must have been more stupid than brute beasts, who when plainly warned of the severity of the judgment of heaven by such a miracle, did not cease to indulge in mockery. But this is the spirit of stupidity and of giddiness with which God intoxicates the reprobate, after having long contended with their malice. Meanwhile, let us learn that, when they were bewitched by the enchantments of Satan, the glory of God, however manifest, was afterwards hidden from them, or, at least, that their minds were darkened, so that, "seeing they did not see" (Matthew 13: 14). But as it was a general admonition, it ought also to be of advantage to us, by informing us that the sacrifice by which we are redeemed was of as much importance as if the sun had fallen from heaven, or if the whole fabric of the world had fallen to pieces; for this will excite in us deeper horror at our sins.

As to the opinion entertained by some who make this eclipse of the sun extend to every quarter of the world, I do not consider it to be probable. For though it was related by one or two authors, still the history of those times attracted so much attention, that it was impossible for so remarkable a miracle to be passed over in silence by many other authors, who have described minutely events which were not so worthy of being recorded. Besides, if the eclipse had been universal throughout the world, it would have been regarded as natural, and would more easily have escaped the notice of men. But when the sun was shining elsewhere, it was a more striking miracle that Judea was covered with **darkness**.

MATTHEW 27: 57–61; MARK 15: 42–47; LUKE 23: 50–56

The burial of Christ is now added, as an intermediate transition from the ignominy of the cross to the glory of the

his last, or expired; though in the latter place, Luke 23: 46, there is an equivalent expression – O Father, into thy hands, I commit my spirit; i.e. I place my soul in thy hand: proving that the act was his own; that no man could take his life away from him; that he did not die by the perfidy of his disciple, or the malice of the Jews, but by his own free act. Thus HE LAID DOWN his life for the sheep. Of Ananias and Sapphira, Acts 5: 5,10, and of Herod, Acts 12: 23, our translation says, they gave up the ghost; but the word in both places simply means to breathe out, to expire, or die. But in no case, either by the Septuagint in the Old, or any of the sacred writers in the New Testament, is he dismissed his spirit, or delivered up his spirit, spoken of any person but Christ. Abraham, Isaac, Ishmael, Jacob, etc., breathed their last; Ananias, Sapphira, and Herod, expired; but none, Jesus Christ excepted, gave up the ghost, dismissed, or delivered up his own spirit, and was, consequently, free among the dead. Of the patriarchs, etc., the Septuagint use the word, failing; or, he ceased, or rested.

51. The veil of the temple was rent – That is, the veil which separated the holy place, where the priests ministered, from the holy of holies, into which the high priest only entered, and that once a year, to make a general expiation for the sins of the people. This rending of the veil was emblematical, and pointed out that the separation between Jews and Gentiles was now abolished, and that the privilege of the high priest was now communicated to all mankind: ALL might henceforth have access to the throne of grace, through the one great atonement and mediator, the Lord Jesus. See this beautifully illustrated in Hebrews 10: 19–22.

52. And the graves were opened – By the earthquake; and many bodies of saints which slept, i.e. were dead, sleep being a common expression for death in the Scriptures.

53. And came out of the graves after his resurrection – Not BEFORE, as some have thought, for Christ was himself the FIRST FRUITS of them who slept, 1 Corinthians 15: 20. The graves were opened at his death, by

the earthquake, and the bodies came out at his resurrection.

And appeared unto many – Thus establishing the truth of our Lord's resurrection in particular, and of the resurrection of the body in general, by many witnesses. Quesnel's reflections on these passages may be very useful. "1. The veil being rent shows that his death is to put an end to the figurative worship, and to establish the true religion.

2. The earthquake, that this dispensation of the Gospel is to make known through the earth the judgments of God against sin and sinners.

3. The rocks being rent declare that the sacrifice of Christ is to make way for the grace of repentance.

4. The graves being opened, that it is to destroy the death of sin, and confer the life grace on sinners.

5. The rising of the bodies of the saints shows that this death of Christ is to merit, and his Gospel publish, the eternal happiness of body and soul for all that believe in his name."

It is difficult to account for the transaction mentioned Matthew 27: 52–53. Some have thought that these two verses have been introduced into the text of Matthew from the gospel of the Nazarenes; others think that the simple meaning is this: by the earthquake several bodies that had been buried were thrown up and exposed to view, and continued above ground till after Christ's resurrection, and were seen by many persons in the city. Why the graves should be opened on Friday, and the bodies not be raised to life till the following Sunday, is difficult to be conceived. The place is extremely obscure.

54. The centurion – The Roman officer who superintended the execution, had the command of one hundred men.

Truly this was the Son of God – An innocent, holy, and Divine person; and God thus shows his disapprobation of this bloody tragedy. It is not likely that this centurion had any knowledge of the expectation of the Jews relative to the Messiah, and did not use the words in this sense. A son of God, as the Romans

he gave up the ghost.

47 Now when the centurion saw what was done, he glorified God, saying, Certainly this was a righteous man.

48 And all the people that came together to that sight, beholding the things which were done, smote their breasts, and returned.

49 And all his acquaintance, and the women that followed him from Galilee, stood afar off, beholding these things.

MATTHEW 27: 57–61; MARK 15: 42–47; LUKE 23: 50–56

Matthew 27: 57–61

57 When the even was come, there came a rich man of Arimathaea, named Joseph, who also himself was Jesus' disciple:

58 He went to Pilate, and begged the body of Jesus. Then Pilate commanded the body to be delivered.

59 And when Joseph had taken the body, he wrapped it in a clean linen cloth,

60 And laid it in his own new tomb, which he had hewn out in the rock: and he rolled a great stone to the door of the sepulcher, and departed.

61 And there was Mary Magdalene, and the other Mary, sitting over against the sepulcher.

Mark 15: 42–47

42 And now when the even was come, because it was the preparation, that is, the day before the sabbath,

43 Joseph of Arimathaea, and honorable counselor, which also waited for the kingdom of God, came, and went in boldly unto Pilate, and craved the body of Jesus.

44 And Pilate marveled if he were already dead: and calling unto him the centurion, he asked him whether he had been any while dead.

45 And when he knew it of the centurion, he gave the body to Joseph.

46 And he bought fine linen, and took him down, and wrapped him in the linen, and laid him in a sepulcher which was hewn out of a rock, and rolled a stone unto the door of the sepulcher.

47 And Mary Magdalene and Mary the

resurrection. True, indeed, God determined, for another reason, that Christ should be buried, that it might be more fully attested that he suffered real death on our account. But yet it ought to be regarded as the principal design, that in this manner the cursing, which he had endured for a short time, began to be removed; for his body was not thrown into a ditch in the ordinary way, but honorably laid in a **hewn sepulcher**. Although at that time the weakness of the flesh was still visible, and the divine power of the Spirit was not clearly seen before his resurrection; yet God determined by this, as a sort of preparation, to shadow out what he was shortly afterwards to do, that he might exalt gloriously above the heavens his Son, the conqueror of death.

Matthew 27: 57. And when the evening was come

Now though this affection of **Joseph** deserved uncommon praise, still we ought first to consider the providence of God, in subduing a man of high and honorable rank among his countrymen, to wipe away the reproach of the cross by the honor of burial. And, indeed, as he exposed himself to the dislike and hatred of the whole nation, and to great dangers, there can be no doubt that this singular courage arose from a secret movement of the Spirit; for though he had formerly been one of Christ's **disciples**, yet he had never ventured to make a frank and open profession of his faith. When the death of Christ now presents to him a spectacle full of despair, and fitted to break the strongest minds, how comes he suddenly to acquire such noble courage that, amidst the greatest terrors, he feels no dread, and hesitates not to advance farther than he had ever done, when all was in peace? Let us know then that, when the Son of God was buried by the hand of Joseph, it was the work of God.

To the same purpose must also be referred the circumstances which are here detailed. **Joseph's** piety and integrity of life are commended, that in the servant of God we may learn to recognize the work of God. The Evangelists relate that he was **rich**, in order to inform us that his amazing magnanimity of mind enabled him to rise superior to the obstruction which would otherwise have compelled him to retire. For rich men, being naturally proud, find nothing more difficult than to expose themselves voluntarily to the contempt of the people. Now we know how mean and disgraceful an act it was to receive from the hand of the executioner the body of a crucified man. Besides, as men devoted to riches are wont to avoid everything fitted to excite prejudice, the more eminent he was for wealth, the more cautious and timid he would have been, unless a holy boldness had been imparted to him from heaven. The dignity of his rank is likewise mentioned, that he was a **counselor**, or **senator**, that in this respect also the power of God may be displayed; for it was not one of the lowest of the people that was employed to bury the body of Christ in

used the term, would signify no more than a very eminent or Divine person; a hero.

55. Many women – To their everlasting honor, these women evidenced more courage, and affectionate attachment to their Lord and Master, than the disciples did, who had promised to die with him rather than forsake him.

Beholding afar off – At a distance. Though this expression may be understood to refer, rather to the distance from which they came, (viz. from Galilee), than the distance they stood from the cross; yet, as all malefactors were crucified naked, perhaps this may account for the distance at which these modest women stood.

56. Mary Magdalene – She probably had her name from Magdala, a village or district in Lower Galilee. See Matthew 15: 39.

Mary the mother of James – She was mother of him called James the lesser, or junior, who was son of Alpheus or Cleopas – see Matthew 10: 3; Mark 15: 40; John 19: 25; and she was sister to the holy virgin. Thus it appears that there were four remarkable Marys mentioned in the Gospels.

1. MARY the Virgin, wife of JOSEPH.

2. MARY SALOME, her sister, wife of Cleopas, John 19: 25.

3. MARY MAGDALENE, or MARY of Magdala; and,

4. MARY, the sister of Martha and Lazarus, John 11: 1.

Though Baronius asserts, and Lightfoot is of the same opinion, that Mary Magdalene, and Mary, the sister of Martha and Lazarus, was one and the same person. It is difficult to ascertain and distinguish these women where their names occur in the Gospels, so many being called by the name of Mary.

MATTHEW 27: 57–61; MARK 15: 42–47; LUKE 23: 50–56

Matthew 27: 57–61

57. When the even – This must have been about three o'clock, or a little after; for our Lord having expired about three o'clock, Matthew 27:

46, and the Jewish passover beginning about four, it was necessary that Joseph, who would not fail to eat the passover at the usual time, should have obtained and buried the body of Christ some time before four o'clock. But such was the general consternation, occasioned by the prodigies that took place on this most awful occasion, that we may safely conjecture that nothing was done in order, and perhaps the passover itself was not eaten at the usual hour, if at all, that day. See at the end of the preceding chapter.

A rich man – He was a counselor of the great Sanhedrin, Luke 23: 50; and, from the accounts given of him by the evangelists we learn that he was a man of the greatest respectability. He now acted a more honorable part than all the disciples of our Lord. He was of Arimathea, or Rama, in the tribe of Benjamin, Matthew 2: 18, but lived ordinarily in Jerusalem, as being a member of the great council.

58. Begged the body – That he might bury it honorably otherwise, by the Jewish customs, he would have either been burned, or buried in the common place appointed for executed criminals.

59. Wrapped it in a clean linen cloth – The Jews, as well as the Egyptians, added spices to keep the body from putrefaction, and the linen was wrapped about every part to keep the aromatics in contact with the flesh. From John 19: 39–40, we learn that a mixture of myrrh and aloes of one hundred pounds' weight had been applied to the body of Jesus when he was buried. And that a second embalmment was intended, we learn from Luke 23: 56; 24: 1, as the hurry to get the body interred before the Sabbath did not permit them to complete, the embalming in the first instance.

60. Laid it in his own new tomb – To all human appearance the body of Christ must have had the same burial-place with those of the two robbers, as he was numbered with the transgressors, and suffered with them; for then he was a sacrifice, bearing the sin of the world in his own body on the tree; but now the sacrifice is offered, the atonement made and

mother of Joses beheld where he was laid.

Luke 23: 50–56

50 And, behold, there was a man named Joseph, a counselor; and he was a good man, and a just:

51 (The same had not consented to the counsel and deed of them;) he was of Arimathaea, a city of the Jews: who also himself waited for the kingdom of God.

52 This man went unto Pilate, and begged the body of Jesus.

53 And he took it down, and wrapped it in linen, and laid it in a sepulcher that was hewn in stone, wherein never man before was laid.

54 And that day was the preparation, and the sabbath drew on.

55 And the women also, which came with him from Galilee, followed after, and beheld the sepulcher, and how his body was laid.

56 And they returned, and prepared spices and ointments; and rested the sabbath day according to the command-ment.

MATTHEW 27: 62–66

62 Now the next day, that followed the day of the preparation, the chief priests and Pharisees came together unto Pilate,

63 Saying, Sir, we remember that that deceiver said, while he was yet alive, After three days I will rise again.

64 Command therefore that the sepul-cher be made sure until the third day, lest his disciples come by night, and steal him away, and say unto the people, He is risen from the dead: so the last error shall be worse than the first.

65 Pilate said unto them, Ye have a watch: go your way, make it as sure as ye can.

66 So they went, and made the sepul-cher sure, sealing the stone, and setting a watch.

MATTHEW 28: 1–7; MARK 16: 1–7; LUKE 24: 1–8

Matthew 28: 1–7

1 In the end of the sabbath, as it began to dawn toward the first day of the week, came Mary Magdalene and the other

haste and in concealment, but from a high rank of honor he was raised up to discharge this office. For the less credible it was that such an office of kindness should be performed towards Christ, the more clearly did it appear that the whole of this transaction was regulated by the purpose and hand of God.

We are taught by this example, that the rich are so far from being excusable, when they deprive Christ of the honor due to him: that they must be held to be doubly criminal, for turning into obstructions those circumstances which ought to have been excitements to activity. It is too frequent and customary, I acknowledge, for those who think themselves superior to others, to withdraw from the yoke, and to become soft and effeminate through excessive timidity and solicitude about their affairs. But we ought to view it in a totally different light; for if riches and honors do not aid us in the worship of God, we utterly abuse them. The present occurrence shows how easy it is for God to correct wicked fears by hindering us from doing our duty; since formerly Jobseph did not venture to make an open profession of being a disciple of Christ, when matters were doubtful, but now, when the rage of enemies is at its height, and when their cruelty abounds, he gathers courage, and does not hesitate to incur manifest danger. We see then how the Lord in a moment forms the hearts to new feelings, and raises up by a spirit of fortitude those who had previously fainted. But if, through a holy desire to honor Christ, Joseph assumed such courage, while Christ was hanging on the cross, woe to our slothfulness, if, now that he has risen from the dead, an equal zeal, at least, to glorify him do not burn in our hearts.

MATTHEW 27: 62–66

62. And the next day

In this narrative Matthew did not so much intend to show with what determined rage the scribes and priests pur-sued Christ, as to exhibit to us, as in a mirror, the amazing providence of God in proving the resurrection of his Son. Cunning men, practiced at least in fraud and treachery, plot among themselves, and contrive a method by which they may extinguish the memory of a dead man; for they see that they have gained nothing, if they do not destroy the certainty of the resurrection. But while they are attempting to do this, they appear rather as if they had expressly in-tended to bring it forth to the light, that it might be known. The resurrection of Christ would undoubtedly have been less manifest, or, at least, they would have had more plau-sible grounds for denying it, if they had not taken pains to station witnesses at the sepulcher.

accepted, he is no longer to be enrolled with the transgressors, and, according to a prophecy delivered nearly seven hundred years before that time, he is to have the burying-place of a rich man. See Isaiah 53: 9–10. Had our Lord been buried in the common burial-ground of the malefactors, his resurrection could not have been so distinctly remarked, as the chief priests would never have thought of sealing the stone there, or setting a watch; but now that the body is got into the hands of a friend, they judge it necessary to make use of these precautions, in order, as they said, to prevent imposture; and from this very circumstance the resurrection of Christ had its fullest evidence, and was put beyond the power of successful contradiction. What a number of objections would not human prudence have made to Joseph's conduct, had he consulted it on this occasion! It would have represented to him that, "this was to expose himself, to bring himself into trouble, to render himself suspected, to put himself out of all capacity of doing good, to ruin himself irrecoverably; and now it could do no good to his teacher – he is now dead, and needs no longer any office of kindness from men." There is, sometimes in our whole life, but one opportunity in which God designs signally to employ us; and, through our general backwardness to every good work, we are for reserving ourselves to other opportunities, in which God neither requires nor will accept our services.

Rolled a great stone to the door – Some are of opinion that this tomb was cut down into the rock, perpendicularly from the surface; and that the great stone spoken of here covered over the entrance to it. The stone, no doubt, was intended to secure the place as much as possible.

61. Mary Magdalene, and the other Mary – The mother of James and Joses, Matthew 27: 56. The mother of our Lord had probably, by this time, been taken home to the house of John. See John 19: 26–27.

Sitting over against the sepulcher – These holy women, filled with that love to their Lord which death cannot destroy, cleaved to him in life, and in death were not divided. They came to the grave to see the end, and overwhelmed with sorrow and anguish, sat down to mourn.

MATTHEW 27: 62–66

62. The next day – This was the seventh, or Saturday, and might be what we should term the evening of the sixth, or Friday, because the Jews always ended their day when the sun set, and then began the next.

That followed the day of the preparation – That is, of the Sabbath. The victuals, etc., which were to be used on the Sabbath by the Jews, were always prepared the preceding evening before the sun set. It is of this preparation that the evangelist speaks here; and it is the same which is mentioned by Mark, 15: 42; by Luke, 23: 54; and by John, 19: 31. But there was another preparation which happened in the same day: viz. The preparation of the passover; this began about twelve o'clock, and continued till four, the time in which they ate the paschal lamb. See John 19: 14.

63. Sir, we remember, etc. – While these wicked men are fulfilling their own vicious counsels, they are subserving the great cause of Christianity. Every thing depended on the resurrection of Christ; if it did not appear that he rose from the dead, then the whole system was false, and no atonement was made. It was necessary therefore that the chief priests, etc., should make use of every precaution to prevent an imposture, that the resurrection of Christ might have the fullest evidence to support it.

After three days I will rise again – This they probably took from his saying, Destroy this temple, and in three days I will build it up. If so, they destroyed, by their own words, the false accusation they brought against him to put him to death; then they perverted the meaning, now they declare it. Thus the wise are taken in their own craftiness. Neither the devil nor his servants ever speak truth, but when they expect to accomplish some bad purpose by it.

Mary to see the sepulcher.

2 And, behold, there was a great earthquake: for the angel of the Lord descended from heaven, and came and rolled back the stone from the door, and sat upon it.

3 His countenance was like lightning, and his raiment white as snow:

4 And for fear of him the keepers did shake, and became as dead men.

5 And the angel answered and said unto the women, Fear not ye: for I know that ye seek Jesus, which was crucified.

6 He is not here: for he is risen, as he said. Come, see the place where the Lord lay.

7 And go quickly, and tell his disciples that he is risen from the dead; and, behold, he goeth before you into Galilee; there shall ye see him: lo, I have told you.

Mark 16: 1–7

1 And when the sabbath was past, Mary Magdalene, and Mary the mother of James, and Salome, had bought sweet spices, that they might come and anoint him.

2 And very early in the morning the first day of the week, they came unto the sepulcher at the rising of the sun.

3 And they said among themselves, Who shall roll us away the stone from the door of the sepulcher?

4 And when they looked, they saw that the stone was rolled away: for it was very great.

5 And entering into the sepulcher, they saw a young man sitting on the right side, clothed in a long white garment; and they were affrighted.

6 And he saith unto them, Be not affrighted: Ye seek Jesus of Nazareth, which was crucified: he is risen; he is not here: behold the place where they laid him.

7 But go your way, tell his disciples and Peter that he goeth before you into Galilee: there shall ye see him, as he said unto you.

Luke 24: 1–8

1 Now upon the first day of the week, very early in the morning, they came unto the sepulcher, bringing the spices which they had prepared, and certain others with them.

MATTHEW 28: 1–7; MARK 16: 1–7; LUKE 24: 1–8

We now come to the closing scene of our redemption. For the lively assurance of our reconciliation with God arises from Christ having come from hell as the conqueror of death, in order to show that he had the power of a new life at his disposal. Justly, therefore, does Paul say that there will be no gospel, and that the hope of salvation will be vain and fruitless, unless we believe that Christ is risen from the dead (1 Corinthians 15: 14). For then did Christ obtain righteousness for us, and open up our entrance into heaven; and, in short, then was our adoption ratified, when Christ, by rising from the dead, exerted the power of his Spirit, and proved himself to be the Son of God. No though he manifested his resurrection in a different manner from what the sense of our flesh would have desired, still the method of which he approved ought to be regarded by us also as the best. he went out of the grave without a witness, that the emptiness of the place might be the earliest indication; next, he chose to have it announced to the women by the angels that he was alive; and shortly afterwards he appeared to the women, and, finally, to the apostles, and on various occasions.

Thus he gradually brought his followers, according to their capacity, to a larger measure of knowledge. He began with **the women**, and not only presented himself to be seen by them, but even gave them a commission to announce the gospel to the apostles, so as to become their instructors. This was intended, first, to chastise the indifference of the apostles, who were like persons half-dead with fear, while the women ran with alacrity to the sepulcher, and likewise obtained no ordinary reward. For though their design to anoint Christ, as if Ire were still dead, was not free from blame, still he forgave their weakness, and bestowed on them distinguished honor, by taking away from men the apostolic office, and committing it to them for a short time. In this manner also he exhibited an instance of what Paul tells us, that he chooses those things which are foolish and weak in the world to abase the loftiness of the flesh. And never shall we be duly prepared to learn this article of our faith in any other manner than by laying aside all pride, and submitting to receive the testimony of the women. Not that our faith ought to be confined within such narrow limits, but because the Lord, in order to make trial of our faith, determines that we shall become fools, before he admits us to a more ample knowledge of his mysteries.

As for the narrative, Matthew says only that **the two Marys came to see the sepulcher**; Mark adds a third, **Salome**, and says that they **bought spices to anoint the body**; and from Luke we infer, that not two or three only,

65. Ye have a watch – The Jews had a corps of Roman troops, consisting of several companies, as a guard for the temple, Acts 4: 1. These companies mounted guard by turns, see Luke 22: 4. Some of these companies, which were not then on duty, Pilate gave them leave to employ to watch the tomb.

66. Made the sepulcher sure, sealing the stone, and setting a watch – Or rather, made the tomb secure by the guard, and by sealing the stone. The guard was to take care that the disciples should not steal him away; and the seal, which was probably the seal of the governor, was to prevent the guards from being corrupted so as to permit the theft. So every thing was done which human policy and prudence could, to prevent a resurrection, which these very precautions had the most direct tendency to authenticate and establish. How wonderful are the wisdom and goodness of God! – and how true is it, that there is neither might nor counsel against him!

1. The death of Christ was ordered, so as to be witnessed by thousands; and if his resurrection take place, it must be demonstrated; and it cannot take place without being incontestable, such are the precautions used here to prevent all imposture.

2. The more the circumstances of the death of Christ are examined, the more astonishing the whole will appear. The death is uncommon – the person uncommon – and the object uncommon; and the whole is grand, majestic, and awful. Nature itself is thrown into unusual action, and by means and causes wholly supernatural. In every part, the finger of God most evidently appears.

3. How glorious does Christ appear in his death! Were it not for his thirst, his exclamation on the cross, and the piercing of his side, we should have found it difficult to believe that such a person could ever have entered the empire of death; but the divinity and the manhood equally appear, and thus the certainty of the atonement is indubitably established.

4. But who can reflect on the state of the poor disciples, during the whole of the time in which our blessed Lord lay under the empire of death, without sharing their sorrows! When he expired on the cross their expectation was cut off; and when his body was laid in the grave their hopes were buried; and nothing but the resurrection of Christ from the dead could have given a resurrection to their hopes. It is true they had heard him say that he would rise again the third day; but in this it is evident their faith was very imperfect; and the uncertainty, perplexity, anxiety, and distress which they in consequence must have suffered, can neither be described nor imagined. Though we know the glorious result, yet who can help sympathizing with the pious father, the virgin mother, and the disconsolate disciples!

MATTHEW 28: 1–7; MARK 16: 1–7; LUKE 24: 1–8

Matthew 28: 1–7

1. In the end of the Sabbath – In general the Jews divided their natural day, which consisted of twenty-four hours, into day and night. Their artificial day began at the rising and ended at the setting of the sun; all the rest of the time, from the setting to the rising of the sun, they termed night: hence the same word, in Hebrew, signifies both evening and night. Genesis 1: 5; Mark 6: 47. Matthew has employed the word in this extensive sense here, pointing out the latter part of the Jewish night, that which immediately preceded the rising of the sun, and not that first part which we call the evening. The transaction mentioned here evidently took place early on the morning of the third day after our Lord's crucifixion; what is called our Sunday morning, or first day of the next week.

Came – to see the sepulcher – That is, they set out at this time in order to visit the tomb of our Lord, and also to weep there, John 11: 31, and to embalm the body of our Lord, Luke 24: 1. St. Matthew omits Mary Salome, mentioned by Mark; and Joanna, the wife of Chuza, Herod's steward, mentioned by Luke. The other Mary was the wife of Cleopas, and mother of James and Joses, mentioned before, Matthew

2 And they found the stone rolled away from the sepulcher.

3 And they entered in, and found not the body of the Lord Jesus.

4 And it came to pass, as they were much perplexed thereabout, behold, two men stood by them in shining garments:

5 And as they were afraid, and bowed down their faces to the earth, they said unto them, Why seek ye the living among the dead?

6 He is not here, but is risen: remember how he spake unto you when he was yet in Galilee,

7 Saying, The Son of man must be delivered into the hands of sinful men, and be crucified, and the third day rise again.

8 And they remembered his words,

MATTHEW 28: 8–10; MARK 16: 8–11; LUKE 24: 9–12

Matthew 28: 8–10

8 And they departed quickly from the sepulcher with fear and great joy; and did run to bring his disciples word.

9 And as they went to tell his disciples, behold, Jesus met them, saying, All hail. And they came and held him by the feet, and worshipped him.

10 Then said Jesus unto them, Be not afraid: go tell my brethren that they go into Galilee, and there shall they see me.

Mark 16: 8–11

8 And they went out quickly, and fled from the sepulcher; for they trembled and were amazed: neither said they any thing to any man; for they were afraid.

9 Now when Jesus was risen early the first day of the week, he appeared first to Mary Magdalene, out of whom he had cast seven devils.

10 And she went and told them that had been with him, as they mourned and wept.

11 And they, when they had heard that he was alive, and had been seen of her, believed not.

Luke 24: 9–12

9 And returned from the sepulcher, and told all these things unto the eleven, and to all the rest.

10 It was Mary Magdalene, and Joanna, and Mary the mother of James, and

but many women came. But we know that it is customary with the sacred writers, when speaking of a great number, to name but a few of them. It may also be conjectured with probability, that **Mary Magdalene**, with another companion – whether she was sent before, or ran forward of her own accord arrived at the grave before the rest of the women. And this appears to be conveyed by the words of Matthew, that those two women **came for the purpose of seeing**; for without **seeing** Christ: , they had no means of anointing him. He says nothing, in the meantime, about the purpose which they had formed of doing honor to him; for the principal object which he had in view was, to testify of the resurrection.

MATTHEW 28: 8–10; MARK 16: 8–11; LUKE 24: 9–12

Matthew 28: 8. And they departed quickly

The three Evangelists pass by what John relates about Mary Magdalene (20: 2), that she returned into the city before she had seen the angels, and complained with tears that the body of Christ had been taken away. Here they mention only the second return to the city, when she, and other women who accompanied her, **told the disciples that Christ was risen**; which they had learned both from the words and testimony of the angel, and from seeing Christ himself. Now before Christ showed himself, they already **ran to the disciples**, as they had been commanded by the angel. On the road they received a second confirmation, that they might with greater certainty assert the resurrection of the Lord. **With fear and great joy.** By these words Matthew means that they were indeed gladdened by what the angel told them, but, at the same the were struck with fear, so that they were held in suspense between joy and perplexity. For there are sometimes opposite feelings in the hearts of the godly, which move them alternately in opposite directions, until at length the peace of the Spirit brings them into a settled condition. For if their faith had been strong, it would have given them entire composure by subduing fear; but now fear, mingled with joy, shows that they had not yet fully relied on the testimony of the angel. And here Christ exhibited a remarkable instance of compassion, in meeting them while they thus doubted and trembled, so as to remove all remaining doubt.

10. Then Jesus saith to them

We conclude, that it was an improper fear, from which Christ again delivers them; for though it arose out of admiration, still it was opposed to the tranquillity of faith. That they may raise themselves to Christ, the Conqueror of death, they are commanded to be cheerful. But by those words we are taught that we never know aright our Lord's

27: 56. Were not Mary and Salome two distinct persons?

2. A great earthquake – a shaking or commotion of any kind: probably the word means no more than the confusion caused among the guards by the angel's appearance. All this had taken place before the women reached the sepulcher.

The angel of the Lord descended from heaven – Matthew is very particular in this, to show that the word angel is not to be taken in the sense of an ordinary messenger, who might have come from Joseph of Arimathea, or from any other; but in the sense of an extraordinary messenger, who descended from GOD, out of heaven, for this very purpose. It is likely that the angel had descended, rolled away the stone, and was sitting on it, before the women reached the tomb.

3. His countenance – His appearance, or, his face, for so the word is used in some of the best Greek writers. It seems, from Mark 16: 5, that this angel had assumed the appearance of a young man.

Like lightning – Coruscations of glory continually flaming from his face. This might produce the confusion mentioned Matthew 28: 2.

His raiment white as snow – He was clothed in garments emblematical of the glad tidings which he came to announce. It would have been inconsistent with the message he brought, had the angel appeared in black robes, such as those preposterously wear who call themselves his successors in the ministry of a once suffering, but now risen and highly exalted, Savior. But the world is as full of nonsense as of sin; and who can correct and bring it to reason and piety?

4. The keepers – became as dead men – God can, by one and the same means, comfort his servants, and terrify his enemies. The resurrection of Christ is a subject of terror to the servants of sin, and a subject of consolation to the sons of God; because it is a proof of the resurrection of both, the one to shame and everlasting contempt – the other to eternal glory and joy.

5. I know that ye seek Jesus – Speaking after the manner of men, these women deserved to be the first witnesses of the resurrection of Christ: during life they ministered to him, and in death they were not divided. They attended him to the CROSS, notwithstanding their attachment to him exposed them to the most imminent danger; and now they come to watch and weep at his TOMB. The common opinion is, that women are more fickle and less courageous than men. The reverse of this I believe to be the truth, in those who are thoroughly converted to God; and who, previously to conversion, whether man or woman, can be trusted in any case?

6. Come, see the place – The tomb in which our Lord was laid was no doubt like the rest of the Jewish burying places, a receptacle for the several dead of a whole family, divided into separate niches, where each had his place. Come and see the place – was tantamount to, Come and see the niche in which he was laid – it is now empty; nor was there any other body in the place, for the tomb was a new one, in which no man had ever been laid, John 19: 41; so there could be no deception in the case.

7. Go quickly and tell his disciples – Thus these faithful women proclaim the Gospel to those who were afterwards to be the teachers of the whole human race! Behold what honor God puts upon those who persevere in his truth, and continue to acknowledge him before men!

That he is risen from the dead – There is a remarkable saying of R. Judah Hakkodesh, which some critics quote on this subject: "After THREE DAYS the SOUL of the Messiah shall RETURN to its body, and he shall GO OUT of that STONE in which he shall be BURIED."

Goeth before you into Galilee – As himself promised, Matthew 26: 32.

MATTHEW 28: 8–10; MARK 16: 8–11; LUKE 24: 9–12

Matthew 28: 8–10

8. They departed quickly from the sepulcher

other women that were with them, which told these things unto the apostles.

11 And their words seemed to them as idle tales, and they believed them not.

12 Then arose Peter, and ran unto the sepulcher; and stooping down, he beheld the linen clothes laid by themselves, and departed, wondering in himself at that which was come to pass.

MATTHEW 28: 11–15

11 Now when they were going, behold, some of the watch came into the city, and shewed unto the chief priests all the things that were done.

12 And when they were assembled with the elders, and had taken counsel, they gave large money unto the soldiers,

13 Saying, Say ye, His disciples came by night, and stole him away while we slept.

14 And if this come to the governor's ears, we will persuade him, and secure you.

15 So they took the money, and did as they were taught: and this saying is commonly reported among the Jews until this day.

MARK 16: 12; LUKE 24: 13–30

Mark 16: 12

12 After that he appeared in another form unto two of them, as they walked, and went into the country.

Luke 24: 13–30

13 And, behold, two of them went that same day to a village called Emmaus, which was from Jerusalem about three-score furlongs.

14 And they talked together of all these things which had happened.

15 And it came to pass, that, while they communed together and reasoned, Jesus himself drew near, and went with them.

16 But their eyes were holden that they should not know him.

17 And he said unto them, What manner of communications are these that ye have one to another, as ye walk, and are sad?

18 And the one of them, whose name was Cleopas, answering said unto him,

resurrection, until, through the firm assurance which we have conceived in our hearts, we venture to rejoice that we have been made partakers of the same life. Our faith ought, at least, to proceed so far that fear shall not predominate.

MATTHEW 28: 11–15

11. And while they were departing

It is not only credible, but the fact is manifest, that the soldiers, to whom had been entrusted the charge of the sepulcher, were corrupted by a bribe, so that they were prepared to tell a lie at the bidding of the priests. They knew well that there was nothing which the priests dreaded more than that a report should gain credit that Christ rose on the third day after his death; and they knew that they had been sent there, that, by guarding the body, they might suppress that report. Those men, therefore, being addicted to making gain, and seizing on opportunities of making it from every quarter, after having found that their diligence was of no service to them, contrive a new method of cheating their employers out of their money. The words of Matthew – **some of them came** – leave it uncertain if a few cunning men adopted this resolution without communicating with the rest, or if they were sent, by a general agreement, in the name of all. The latter supposition appears to be more probable; for Matthew afterwards says that **money was given**, not to one or two, but generally **to the soldiers**, to induce them to commit perjury. It is at all events certain that, whether they all plotted together, or only a part of them, they sought to make profit of the cruel and implacable hatred which the priests bore towards Christ; and that, looking upon them as convicted of a crime. they abused their evil conscience to extort money from them. For, as usually happens with all wicked men, the priests, conscious of having done wrong, in order to cover their disgrace, were compelled to bribe the soldiers by a **large reward**.

MARK 16: 12; LUKE 24: 13–30

Luke 24:13. And lo, two of them

Although Mark touches slightly and briefly on this narrative, and Matthew and John say not a single word respecting it; yet as it is highly useful to be known and worthy of being remembered, it is not without reason that Luke treats it with so much exactness. But I have already mentioned on various occasions, that each of the Evangelists had his portion so appropriately assigned to him by the Spirit of God, that what is not to be found in one or two of them may be learned from the others. For there are also many appearances which are mentioned by John, but are passed over in silence by our three Evangelists.

Two chosen witnesses, by whom the Lord intended, not

– At the desire of the angel they went into the tomb, to have the fullest certainty of the resurrection.

Fear and great joy – Fear, produced by the appearance of this glorious messenger of God; and great joy occasioned by the glad tidings of the resurrection of their Lord and Master. At the mention of unexpected good news, fear and joy are generally intermingled.

9. **Jesus met them** – Christ bestows his graces and consolations by degrees, first by his angels, and then by himself. He does not reveal himself to incredulous and disobedient souls; he appears not even to these women till he has tried their faith and obedience by his ministering angels.

All hail – Anglo-Saxon, Health be to you! Be ye safe, rejoice.

And they held him by the feet, and worshipped him – This kind of reverence is in daily use among the Hindoos: when a disciple meets his religious guide in the public streets, he prostrates himself before him, and, taking the dust from his teacher's feet, rubs it on his forehead, breast, etc.

10. **Be not afraid** – They were seized with fear at the sight of the angel; and this was now renewed by this unexpected appearance of Christ.

Go, tell my brethren – This is the first time our Lord called his disciples by this endearing name: they no doubt thought that their Lord would reproach them with their past cowardice and infidelity; but, in speaking thus, he gives them a full assurance, in the most tender terms, that all that was passed was as buried for ever.

MATTHEW 28: 11–15

11. **Some of the watch** – Or guards. Probably the rest still remained at the tomb, waiting for orders to depart, and had sent these to intimate to their employers the things that had taken place.

12. **With the elders** – That is, the senators of the great Sanhedrin or Jewish council of state,

elsewhere called the elders of the people; they could now meet, as the Sabbath was over.

13. **His disciples came by night** – This was as absurd as it was false. On one hand, the terror of the disciples, the smallness of their number (only eleven); and their almost total want of faith; on the other, the great danger of such a bold enterprise, the number of armed men who guarded the tomb, the authority of Pilate and of the Sanhedrin, must render such an imposture as this utterly devoid of credit.

Stole him away while we slept – Here is a whole heap of absurdities.

1st. Is it likely that so many men would all fall asleep, in the open air, at once?

2dly. Is it at all probable that a Roman guard should be found off their watch, much less asleep, when it was instant death, according to the Roman military laws, to be found in this state?

3dly. Could they be so sound asleep as not to awake with all the noise which must be necessarily made by removing the great stone, and taking away the body?

4thly. Is it at all likely that these disciples could have had time sufficient to do all this, and to come and return, without being perceived by any person? And

5thly. If they were asleep, how could they possibly know that it was the disciples that stole him, or indeed that any person or persons stole him? – for, being asleep, they could see no person. From their own testimony, therefore, the resurrection may be as fully proved as the theft.

14. **If this came to the governor's ears** – Pilate – we will persuade him that it is for his own interest and honor to join in the deception; and we will render you secure – we will take care that you shalt not suffer that punishment for this pretended breach of duty which otherwise you might expect.

15. **Until this day** – That is to say, the time in which Matthew wrote his Gospel; which is supposed by some to have been eight, by others eighteen, and by others thirty years after our Lord's resurrection.

Art thou only a stranger in Jerusalem, and hast not known the things which are come to pass therein these days?

19 And he said unto them, What things? And they said unto him, Concerning Jesus of Nazareth, which was a prophet mighty in deed and word before God and all the people:

20 And how the chief priests and our rulers delivered him to be condemned to death, and have crucified him.

21 But we trusted that it had been he which should have redeemed Israel: and beside all this, to day is the third day since these things were done.

22 Yea, and certain women also of our company made us astonished, which were early at the sepulcher;

23 And when they found not his body, they came, saying, that they had also seen a vision of angels, which said that he was alive.

24 And certain of them which were with us went to the sepulcher, and found it even so as the women had said: but him they saw not.

25 Then he said unto them, O fools, and slow of heart to believe all that the prophets have spoken:

26 Ought not Christ to have suffered these things, and to enter into his glory?

27 And beginning at Moses and all the prophets, he expounded unto them in all the scriptures the things concerning himself.

28 And they drew nigh unto the village, whither they went: and he made as though he would have gone further.

29 But they constrained him, saying, Abide with us: for it is toward evening, and the day is far spent. And he went in to tarry with them.

30 And it came to pass, as he sat at meat with them, he took bread, and blessed it, and brake, and gave to them.

MARK 16: 13–14 LUKE 24: 31–40

Mark 16: 13–14

13 And they went and told it unto the residue: neither believed they them.

14 Afterward he appeared unto the eleven as they sat at meat, and upbraided them with their unbelief and hardness of heart, because they believed not them

to convince the apostles that he was risen, but to reprove their slowness; for though at first; they were of no service, yet their testimony, strengthened by other aids, had at length its due weight with the apostles. Who they were is uncertain, except that from the name of one of them, whom we shah find that Luke shortly afterwards calls **Cleopas**, we may conjecture that they did not belong; to the eleven. Emmaus was an ancient, and by no means inconsiderable, town, which the Romans afterwards called Nicopolis and was not at a great distance **from Jerusalem**, for **sixty furlongs** are not more than seven thousand and four hundred paces. But the place is named by Luke, not so much on account of its celebrity, as to add certainty to the narrative.

16. But their eyes were restrained

The Evangelist expressly states this, lest any one should think that the aspect of Christ's body was changed, and that the features of his countenance were different from what they had formerly been. For though Christ remained like himself, he was not recognized, because the eyes of beholders were held; and this takes away all suspicion of a phantom or false imagination. But hence we learn how great is the weakness of all our senses, since neither eyes nor ears discharge their office, unless so far as power is incessantly communicated to them from heaven. Our members do indeed possess their natural properties; but to make us more fully sensible that they are held by us at the will of another, God retains in his own hand the use of them, so that we ought ever to reckon it to be one of his daily favors, that our ears hear and our eyes see; for if he does not every hour quicken our senses, all their power will immediately give way. I readily acknowledge that our senses are not frequently held in the same manner as happened at that time, so as to make so gross a mistake about an object presented to us; but by a single example God shows that it is in his power to direct the faculties which he has. bestowed, so as to assure us that nature is subject to his will. Now if the bodily eyes, to which peculiarly belongs the power of seeing, are held, whenever it pleases the Lord, so as not to perceive the objects presented to them, our understandings would possess no greater acuteness, even though their original condition remained unimpaired; but no in this wretched corruption, after having been deprived of their light, they are liable to innumerable deceptions, and are sunk into such gross stupidity, that they can do nothing but commit mistakes, as happens to us incessantly. The proper discrimination between truth and falsehood, therefore, does not arise from the sagacity of our own mind, but comes to us from the Spirit of wisdom. But it is chiefly in the contemplation of heavenly things that our stupidity is

MARK 16: 12; LUKE 24: 13-30

12. He appeared – unto two of them – These were the two who were going to Emmaus. The whole account is given by Luke, 24: 13-34.

MARK 16: 13-14 LUKE 24: 31-40

Mark 16: 13-14

14. And upbraided them with their unbelief – Never were there a people so difficult to be persuaded of the truth of spiritual things as the disciples. It may be justly asserted, that people of so skeptical a turn of mind would never credit any thing till they had the fullest evidence of its truth. The unbelief of the disciples is a strong proof of the truth of the Gospel of God.

LUKE 24: 41-49

41. They – believed not for joy – They were so overcome with the joy of his resurrection, that they did not, for some time, properly receive the evidence that was before them – as we phrase it, they thought the news too good to be true.

44. The law – the prophets – the psalms – This was the Jewish division of the whole old covenant. The LAW contained the five books of Moses; the PROPHETS, the Jews divided into former and latter; they were, according to Josephus, thirteen. "The PSALMS included not only the book still so named, but also three other books, Proverbs, Job, and Canticles. "These all," says the above author, "contain hymns to God, and rules for the conduct of the lives of men." This account is imperfect: the common Jewish division of the writings of the old covenant is the following, and indeed seems to be the same to which our Lord alludes:
I. The LAW, including Genesis, Exodus, Leviticus, Numbers, and Deuteronomy.
II. The PROPHETS, or teachers, including Joshua, Judges, the two books of Samuel, and the two books of Kings: these were termed the former prophets. Isaiah, Jeremiah, Ezekiel,

Hosea, Joel, Amos, Obadiah, Jonah, Micah, Nahum, Habakkuk, Zephaniah, Haggai, Zechariah, and Malachi: these were termed the latter prophets.
III. The HAGIOGRAPHA, (holy writings), which comprehended the Psalms, Proverbs, Job, Canticles, Ruth, Lamentations, Ecclesiastes, Esther, Daniel, Ezra, Nehemiah, and the two books of Chronicles. The Jews made anciently only twenty-two books of the whole, to bring them to the number of the letters in the Hebrew alphabet; and this they did by joining Ruth to Judges, making the two books of Samuel only one; and so of Kings and Chronicles; joining the Lamentations to Jeremiah, and making the twelve minor prophets only one book.

45. Then opened he their understanding – He fully opened. They had a measure of light before, so that they discerned the Scriptures to be the true word of God, and to speak of the Messiah; but they had not light sufficient to enable them to apply these Scriptures to their Lord and Master; but now, by the influence of Christ, they see, not only, the prophecies which pointed out the Messiah, but also the Messiah who was pointed out by these prophecies. The book of God may be received in general as a Divine revelation, but the proper meaning, reference, and application of the Scriptures can only be discerned by the light of Christ. Even the very plain word of God is a dead letter to those who are not enlightened by the grace of Christ; and why? because this word speaks of spiritual and heavenly things; and the carnal mind of man cannot discern them. They who receive not this inward teaching continue dark and dead while they live.

47. Remission of sins – The taking away – removal of sins, in general every thing that relates to the destruction of the power, the pardoning of the guilt, and the purification of the heart from the very nature of sin.
Should be preached in his name – In his name – On his authority, and in virtue of the atonement made by him: for on what other ground could the inhabitants of the earth expect remission of sins?

which had seen him after he was risen.

Luke 24: 31–40

31 And their eyes were opened, and they knew him; and he vanished out of their sight.

32 And they said one to another, Did not our heart burn within us, while he talked with us by the way, and while he opened to us the scriptures?

33 And they rose up the same hour, and returned to Jerusalem, and found the eleven gathered together, and them that were with them,

34 Saying, The Lord is risen indeed, and hath appeared to Simon.

35 And they told what things were done in the way, and how he was known of them in breaking of bread.

36 And as they thus spake, Jesus himself stood in the midst of them, and saith unto them, Peace be unto you.

37 But they were terrified and affrighted, and supposed that they had seen a spirit.

38 And he said unto them, Why are ye troubled? and why do thoughts arise in your hearts?

39 Behold my hands and my feet, that it is I myself: handle me, and see; for a spirit hath not flesh and bones, as ye see me have.

40 And when he had thus spoken, he shewed them his hands and his feet.

LUKE 24: 41–49

41 And while they yet believed not for joy, and wondered, he said unto them, Have ye here any meat?

42 And they gave him a piece of a broiled fish, and of an honeycomb.

43 And he took it, and did eat before them.

44 And he said unto them, These are the words which I spake unto you, while I was yet with you, that all things must be fulfilled, which were written in the law of Moses, and in the prophets, and in the psalms, concerning me.

45 Then opened he their understanding, that they might understand the scriptures,

46 And said unto them, Thus it is written, and thus it behoved Christ to suffer,

discovered; for not only do we imagine false appearances to be true, but we turn the clear light into darkness.

MARK 16: 13–14; LUKE 24: 31–40

Luke 24: 31. And their eyes were opened

By these words, we are taught that there was not in Christ any metamorphosis, or variety of forms, by which he might impose on the eyes of men (as the poets feign their Proteus), but that, on the contrary, the eyes of beholders were mistaken, because they were covered; just as, shortly afterwards, **he vanished from the eyes** of those very persons, not because his body was in itself invisible, but because God, by withdrawing their rigor, blunted their acuteness. Nor ought we to wonder that Christ, as soon as he was recognized, immediately disappeared; for it was not advantageous that they should any longer behold him, lest, as they were naturally too much addicted to the earth, they might desire again to bring him back to an earthly life. So far, then, as it was necessary to assure them of his resurrection, he made himself visible to them; but by the sudden departure, he taught them that they must seek him elsewhere than in the world, because the completion of the new life was his ascension to heaven.

32. Did not our heart burn within us?

Their recognition of Christ led the disciples to a lively perception of the secret and hidden grace of the Spirit, which he had formerly bestowed upon them. For God sometimes works in his people in such a manner, that for a time they are not aware of the power of the Spirit (of which, however, they are not destitute), or, at least, that they do not perceive it distinctly, but only feel it by a secret movement. Thus the disciples had formerly indeed felt an ardor, which they now remember, but which they had not then observed: now that Christ has made himself known to them, they at length begin to consider the grace which they had formerly, as it were, swallowed without tasting it, and perceive that they were stupid.

LUKE 24: 41–49

41. But while they yet believed not for joy

This passage shows also that they were not purposely incredulous, like persons who deliberately resolve not to believe; but while their will led them to believe eagerly, they were held bound by the vehemence of their feelings, so that they could not rest satisfied. For certainly the joy which Luke mentions arose from nothing but faith; and yet it hindered their faith from gaining the victory. Let us therefore observe with what suspicion we ought to regard the vehemence of our feelings, which, though it may have

Among all nations – Because God wills the salvation of ALL; and Jesus Christ by his grace has tasted death for EVERY man. Hebrews 2: 9.

Beginning at Jerusalem – Making the first overtures of mercy to my murderers! If, then, the sinners of Jerusalem might repent, believe, and be saved, none, on this side hell, need despair.

48. **Ye are witnesses of these things** – He gave them a full commission to proclaim these glad tidings of peace and salvation to a lost world. The disciples were witnesses not only that Christ had suffered and rose again from the dead; but also that he opens the understanding by the inspiration of his Spirit, that he gives repentance, that he pardons sin, and purifies from all unrighteousness, and that he is not willing that any should perish, but that all should come unto the knowledge of the truth and be saved. And these are the things of which their successors in the Gospel ministry must bear witness. As far as a man steadily and affectionately proclaims these doctrines, so far God will bless his labor to the salvation of those who hear him. But no man can with any propriety bear witness of that grace that saves the soul, whose own soul is not saved by that grace.

49. **The promise of my Father** – That is, the Holy Ghost, promised, John 15: 26. See Acts 1: 4; 2: 33.

Until ye be endued with power – The energy of the Holy Ghost was to be communicated to them for three particular purposes.

1. That he might be in them, a sanctifying comforter, fortifying their souls and bringing to their remembrance whatever Jesus had before spoken to them.

2. That their preaching might be accompanied by his demonstration and power to the hearts of their hearers, so that they might believe and be saved.

3. That they might be able to work miracles to confirm their pretensions to a Divine mission, and to establish the truth of the doctrines they preached.

MATTHEW 28: 16–20; MARK 16: 15–18

Matthew 28: 16–20

16. **Then the eleven disciples went** – When the women went and told them that they had seen the Lord, and that he had promised to meet them in Galilee. From the eleventh to the fifteenth verse inclusive, should be read in a parenthesis, as the sixteenth verse is the continuation of the subject mentioned in the tenth.

17. **But some doubted** – That is, Thomas only at first doubted. The expression simply intimates, that they did not all believe at that time.

18. **And Jesus came and spake unto them** – It is supposed by some that the reason why any doubted was, that when they saw Jesus at first, he was at a distance; but when he came up, drew near to them, they were fully persuaded of the identity of his person.

All power is given unto me – Or, All authority in heaven and upon earth is given unto me. One fruit of the sufferings and resurrection of Christ is represented to be, his having authority or right in heaven to send down the Holy Spirit – to raise up his followers thither – and to crown them in the kingdom of an endless glory: in earth, to convert sinners; to sanctify, protect, and perfect his Church; to subdue all nations to himself; and, finally, to judge all mankind. If Jesus Christ were not equal with the Father, could he have claimed this equality of power, without being guilty of impiety and blasphemy? Surely not; and does he not, in the fullest manner, assert his Godhead, and his equality with the Father, by claiming and possessing all the authority in heaven and earth? – i.e. all the power and authority by which both empires are governed?

19. **Go ye therefore** – Because I have the authority aforesaid, and can send whomsoever I will to do whatsoever I please: teach, make disciples of all nations, bring them to an acquaintance with God who bought them, and then baptize them in the name of the Father. It

and to rise from the dead the third day:

47 And that repentance and remission of sins should be preached in his name among all nations, beginning at Jerusalem.

48 And ye are witnesses of these things.

49 And, behold, I send the promise of my Father upon you: but tarry ye in the city of Jerusalem, until ye be endued with power from on high.

MATTHEW 28: 16–20; MARK 16: 15–18

Matthew 28: 16–20

16 Then the eleven disciples went away into Galilee, into a mountain where Jesus had appointed them.

17 And when they saw him, they worshipped him: but some doubted.

18 And Jesus came and spake unto them, saying, All power is given unto me in heaven and in earth.

19 Go ye therefore, and teach all nations, baptizing them in the name of the Father, and of the Son, and of the Holy Ghost:

20 Teaching them to observe all things whatsoever I have commanded you: and, lo, I am with you alway, even unto the end of the world. Amen.

Mark 16: 15–18

15 And he said unto them, Go ye into all the world, and preach the gospel to every creature.

16 He that believeth and is baptized shall be saved; but he that believeth not shall be damned.

17 And these signs shall follow them that believe; In my name shall they cast out devils; they shall speak with new tongues;

18 They shall take up serpents; and if they drink any deadly thing, it shall not hurt them; they shall lay hands on the sick, and they shall recover.

MARK 16: 19–20; LUKE 24: 50–53

Mark 16: 19–20

19 So then after the Lord had spoken unto them, he was received up into heaven, and sat on the right hand of God.

20 And they went forth, and preached everywhere, the Lord working with them,

good beginnings, hurries us out of the right path. We are also reminded how earnestly we ought to struggle against every thing that retards faith, since the joy which sprung up in the minds of the apostles from the presence of Christ was the cause of their unbelief.

43. And he took, and ate it in their presence

Here we perceive, on the other hand, how kindly and gently Christ bears with the weakness of his followers, since he does not fail to give them this new support when they are falling. And, indeed, though he has obtained a new and heavenly life, and has no more need of meat and drink than angels have, still he voluntarily condescends to join in the common usages of mortals.

MATTHEW 28: 16–20; MARK 16: 15–18

Matthew 28: 16. And the eleven disciples went into Galilee

Matthew, passing by those occurrences which we have taken out of the other three Evangelists, mentions only in what place the eleven disciples were appointed to the apostolic office. For – as we have already had frequent opportunities of perceiving – it was not the intention of the Evangelists to embrace every part of the history; because the Holy Spirit, who guided their pen, has thought fit to compose such a summary as we see out of their united testimonies. Matthew has therefore selected what was of the greatest importance to us, namely, that when Christ appeared to the disciples, he likewise commissioned them to be apostles, to convey into every part of the world the message of eternal life. **To the mountain where Jesus had appointed them**. Though the mountain is not mentioned any where else, yet we con-elude that this spot in Galilee was known to Mary.

MARK 16: 19–20; LUKE 24: 50–53

Mark 16: 19. And after the Lord had thus spoken to them

The Evangelist Matthew, having extolled in magnificent language the reign of Christ over the whole world, says nothing about his ascension to heaven. Mark, too, takes no notice of the place and the manner, both of which are described by Luke; for he says that **the disciples were led out to Bethany**, that from the Mount of Olives, (Matthew 24: 3,) whence he had descended to undergo the ignominy of the cross, he might ascend the heavenly throne. Now as he did not, after his resurrection, appear indiscriminately to all, so he did not permit all to be the witnesses of his ascension to heaven; for he intended that this mystery of faith should be known by the preaching of the gospel rather than beheld by the eyes.

ADAM CLARKE

is natural to suppose that adults were the first subjects of baptism; for as the Gospel was, in a peculiar manner, sent to the Gentiles, they must hear and receive it, before they could be expected to renounce their old prejudices and idolatries, and come into the bonds of the Christian covenant. But, certainly, no argument can be drawn from this concession against the baptism of children. When the Gentiles and Jews had received the faith and blessings of the Gospel, it is natural enough to suppose they should wish to get their children incorporated with the visible Church of Christ; especially if, as many pious and learned men have believed, baptism succeeded to circumcision, which I think has never yet been disproved. The apostles knew well that the Jews not only circumcised the children of proselytes, but also baptized them; and as they now received a commission to teach and proselyte all the nations, and baptize them in the name of the holy Trinity, they must necessarily understand that infants were included: nor could they, the custom of their country being considered, have understood our Lord differently, unless he had, in the most express terms, said that they were not to baptize children, which neither he nor his apostles ever did. And as to the objection, that the baptized were obliged to profess their faith, and that, therefore, only adults should be baptized, there is no weight at all in it; because what is spoken of such refers to those who, only at that period of life, heard the Gospel, and were not born of parents who had been Christians; therefore they could not have been baptized into the Christian faith, forasmuch as no such faith was at their infancy preached in the world. That the children and even infants, of proselytes, were baptized among the Jews, and reputed, in consequence, clean, and partakers of the blessings of the covenant.

In the name of the Father, etc. – Baptism, properly speaking, whether administered by dipping or sprinkling, signifies a full and eternal consecration of the person to the service and honor of that Being in whose name it is administered; but this consecration can never be made to a creature; therefore the Father, and the Son, and the Holy Spirit, are not creatures. Again, baptism is not made in the name of a quality or attribute of the Divine nature; therefore the Father, and the Son, and the Holy Spirit, are not qualities or attributes of the Divine nature. The orthodox, as they are termed, have generally considered this text as a decisive proof of the doctrine of the holy Trinity.

20. Teaching them to observe all things – Men are ignorant of Divine things, and must be taught. Only those can be considered as proper teachers of the ignorant who are thoroughly instructed in whatsoever Christ has commanded. Persons who are entrusted with the public ministry of the word should take care that they teach not human creeds and confessions of faith, in place of the Sacred Writings; but those things, and those only, which Jesus has commanded.

And, lo, I am with you alway – literally, Behold, I am with you every day. A minister of Christ should consider, that while his soul simply and uniformly follows Jesus, he shall be made a constant instrument of bringing many sons and daughters to glory. The dark, it is true, must be enlightened, the ignorant instructed, the profligate reclaimed, the guilty justified, and the unholy sanctified; and who is sufficient for this work? He with whom the Son of God is EVERY DAY, and none other.

Unto the end of the world – Some translate this, to the end of this age; meaning the apostolic age, or Jewish dispensation; and then they refer the promise of Christ's presence to the working of miracles, and explain this by Mark 16: 17–19. By my name they shall cast out demons, etc., etc. But though the words are used in this sense in several places, see Matthew 13: 39–40, Matthew 13: 49; 24: 3, yet it is certain they were repeatedly used among the primitive ecclesiastical writers to denote the consummation of all things; and it is likely that this is the sense in which they are used here, which the Anglo-Saxon has happily expressed: *And I, be with you all days, until world ending*; and this is indispensably necessary, because the presence and influence of

and confirming the word with signs following. Amen.

Luke 24: 50–53

50 And he led them out as far as to Bethany, and he lifted up his hands, and blessed them.

51 And it came to pass, while he blessed them, he was parted from them, and carried up into heaven.

52 And they worshipped him, and returned to Jerusalem with great joy:

53 And were continually in the temple, praising and blessing God. Amen.

Luke 24: 50. And lifted up his hands, and blessed them

By which he showed that the office of blessing, which was enjoined on the priests under the law, belonged truly and properly to himself. When men bless one another it is nothing else than praying in behalf of their brethren; but with God it is otherwise, for he does not merely befriend us by wishes, but by a simple act of his will grants what is desirable for us. But while He is the only Author of all blessing, yet that men might obtain a familiar view of his grace, he chose that at first the priests should bless in his name as mediators. Thus Melchizedek blessed Abraham (Genesis 14: 19), and in Numbers 6: 23–27, a perpetual law is laid down in reference to this matter. To this purport also is what we read in Psalm 118: 26, We bless you out of the house of the Lord

In short, the apostle has told us that to bless others is a Mark of superiority; for the less, he says, is blessed by the greater (Hebrews 7: 7). Now when Christ, the true Melchizedek and eternal Priest, was manifested, it was necessary that in him should be fulfilled what had been shadowed out by the figures of the law; as Paul also shows that we are blessed in him by God the Father, that we may be rich in all heavenly blessings (Ephesians 1: 3). Openly and solemnly he once blessed the apostles, that believers may go direct to himself, if they desire to be partakers of his grace. In **the lifting up of the hands** is described an ancient ceremony which, we know, was formerly used by the priests.

52. And having worshipped him, they returned

By the word worship, Luke means, first, that the apostles were relieved from all doubt, because at that time the majesty of Christ shone on all sides, so that there was no longer any room for doubting of his resurrection; and, secondly, that for the same reason they began to honor him with greater reverence than when they enjoyed his society on earth. For the worship which is here mentioned was rendered to him not only as Master or Prophet, nor even as the Messiah, whose character had been but half known, but as the King of glory and the Judge of the world.

Jesus Christ are essentially requisite in every age of the world, to enlighten, instruct, and save the lost. The promise takes in not only the primitive apostles, but also all their successors in the Christian ministry, as long as the earth shall endure.

MARK 16: 19–20; LUKE 24: 50–53

Mark 16: 19–20

19. After the Lord had spoken – These things, and conversed with them for forty days, he was taken up into heaven, there to appear in the presence of God for us.

20. The Lord working with them – This co-operation was twofold, internal and external. Internal, illuminating their minds, convincing them of the truth, and establishing them in it. External, conveying their word to the souls that heard it, by the demonstration of the Holy Ghost; convincing them of sin, righteousness, and judgment; justifying them by his blood, and sanctifying them by his Spirit. Though miraculous powers are not now requisite, because the truth of the Gospel has been sufficiently confirmed, yet this co-operation of God is indispensably necessary, without which no man can be a successful preacher; and without which no soul can be saved.

With signs following – the accompanying signs: viz. those mentioned in the 17th and 18th verses, and those others just now spoken of, which still continue to be produced by the energy of God, accompanying the faithful preaching of his unadulterated word.

Amen – This is added here by many MSS. and versions; but is supposed not to have made a part of the text originally.

The Gospel according to Mark, if not an abridgment of the Gospel according to Matthew, contains a neat, perspicuous abridgment of the history of our Lord; and, taken in this point of view, is very satisfactory; and is the most proper of all the four Gospels to be put into the hands of young persons, in order to bring them to an acquaintance with the great facts of evangelical history. But as a substitute for the Gospel by Matthew, it should never be used. It is very likely that it was written originally for the use of the Gentiles, and probably for those of Rome. Of this, there seem to be several evidences in the work itself. Of the other Gospels it is not only a grand corroborating evidence, but contains many valuable hints for completing the history of our Lord, which have been omitted by the others; and thus, in the mouths of FOUR witnesses, all these glorious and interesting facts are established.

One thing may be observed, that this Gospel has suffered more by the carelessness and inaccuracy of transcribers than any of the others: and hence the various readings in the MSS. are much more numerous, in proportion, than in the other evangelists. However this may be, the Gospel according to Mark is a very important portion of Divine revelation, which God has preserved by a chain of providences, from the time of its promulgation until now; and for which no truly pious reader will hesitate to render due praise to that God whose work is ever perfect. Amen.

John

Introduction by John Calvin

THE meaning of the Greek word, *euangelion* (Gospel) is well known. In Scripture it denotes, by way of eminence, the glad and delightful message of the grace exhibited to us in Christ, in order to instruct us, by despising the world and its fading riches and pleasures, to desire with our whole heart, and to embrace when offered to us, this invaluable blessing. The conduct which we perceive in irreligious men, who take an extravagant delight in the empty enjoyments of the world, while they are little if at all, affected by a relish for spiritual blessings, is natural to us all. For the purpose of correcting this fault, God expressly bestows the name *Gospel* on the message which he orders to be proclaimed concerning Christ; for thus he reminds us that nowhere else can true and solid happiness be obtained, and that in him we have all that is necessary for the perfection of a happy life.

Some consider the word *Gospel* as extending to all the gracious promises of God which are found scattered even in the Law and the Prophets. Nor can it be denied that, whenever God declares that he will be reconciled to men, and forgives their sins, he at the same time exhibits Christ, whose peculiar office it is, wherever he shines, to spread abroad the rays of joy. I acknowledge, therefore, that the Fathers were partakers of the same *Gospel* with ourselves, so far as relates to the faith of a gratuitous salvation. But as it is the ordinary declaration made by the Holy Spirit in the Scriptures, that the *Gospel* was first proclaimed when Christ came, let us also adhere to this mode of expression; and let us keep by that definition of the *Gospel* which I have given, that it is a solemn publica-

tion of the grace revealed in Christ. On this account the *Gospel* is called the power of God to salvation to every one who believeth (Romans 1: 16), because in it God displays his righteousness. It is called also an embassy, by which he reconciles men to himself (2 Corinthians 5: 20), and as Christ is the pledge of the mercy of God, and of his fatherly love towards us, so he is, in a peculiar manner, the subject of the Gospel.

Hence it came that the histories which relate that Christ appeared in the flesh and died, and was raised from the dead, and at length was taken up into heaven, have peculiarly obtained the name *Gospel*. For although, for the reason already stated, this word means the New Testament, yet the name which denote, the whole has come, by general practice, to stand for that part of it which declares that Christ was manifested to us in the flesh, and died, and rose from the dead. But as the bare history would not be enough, and, indeed, would be of no advantage for salvation, the Evangelists do not merely relate that Christ was born, and that he died and vanquished death, but also explain for what purpose he was born, and died, and rose again, and what benefit we derive from those events.

Yet there is also this difference between them, that the other three are more copious in their narrative of the life and death of Christ, but John dwells more largely on the doctrine by which the office of Christ, together with the power of his death and resurrection, is unfolded. They do not, indeed, omit to mention that Christ came to bring salvation to the world, to atone for the sins of the world by the

John 425

sacrifice of his death, and, in short, to perform every thing that was required from the Mediator, (as John also devotes a portion of his work to historical details); but the doctrine, which points out to us the power and benefit of the coming of Christ, is far more clearly exhibited by him than by the rest. And as all of them had the same object in view, to point out Christ, the three former exhibit his body, if we may be permitted to use the expression, but John exhibits his soul. On this account, I am accustomed to say that this Gospel is a key to open the door for understanding the rest; for whoever shall understand the power of Christ, as it is here strikingly portrayed, will afterwards read with advantage what the others relate about the Redeemer who was manifested.

John is believed to have written chiefly with the intention of maintaining the Divinity of Christ, in opposition to the wicked blasphemies of Ebion and Cerinthus; and this is asserted by Eusebius and Jerome, in accordance with the general opinion of the ancients. But whatever might be his motive for writing at that time, there can be no doubt whatever that God intended a far higher benefit for his Church. He therefore dictated to the Four Evangelists what they should write, in such a manner that, while each had his own part assigned him, the whole might be collected into one body; and it is our duty now to blend the Four by a mutual relation, so that we may permit ourselves to be taught by all of them, as by one mouth. As to John being placed the fourth in order, it was done on account of the time when he wrote, but in reading them, a different order would be more advantageous, which is, that when we wish to read in Matthew and the others, that Christ was given to us by the Father, we should first learn from John the purpose for which he was manifested.

The commentaries on John are by John Calvin and David Brown.

JOHN 1

1 In the beginning was the Word, and the Word was with God, and the Word was God.

2 The same was in the beginning with God.

3 All things were made by him; and without him was not any thing made that was made.

4 In him was life; and the life was the light of men.

5 And the light shineth in darkness; and the darkness comprehended it not.

6 There was a man sent from God, whose name was John.

7 The same came for a witness, to bear witness of the Light, that all men through him might believe.

8 He was not that Light, but was sent to bear witness of that Light.

9 That was the true Light, which lighteth every man that cometh into the world.

10 He was in the world, and the world was made by him, and the world knew him not.

11 He came unto his own, and his own received him not.

12 But as many as received him, to them gave he power to become the sons of God, even to them that believe on his name:

13 Which were born, not of blood, nor of the will of the flesh, nor of the will of man, but of God.

14 And the Word was made flesh, and dwelt among us, (and we beheld his glory, the glory as of the only begotten of the Father,) full of grace and truth.

15 John bare witness of him, and cried, saying, This was he of whom I spake, He that cometh after me is preferred before me: for he was before me.

16 And of his fullness have all we received, and grace for grace.

17 For the law was given by Moses, but grace and truth came by Jesus Christ.

18 No man hath seen God at any time; the only begotten Son, which is in the bosom of the Father, he hath declared him.

19 And this is the record of John, when the Jews sent priests and Levites from Jerusalem to ask him, Who art thou?

20 And he confessed, and denied not;

JOHN 1

1. In the beginning was the Speech

In this introduction he asserts the eternal Divinity of Christ, in order to inform us that he is the eternal God, who *was manifested in the flesh* (1 Timothy 4:16). The design is, to show it to have been necessary that the restoration of mankind should be accomplished by the Son of God, since by his power all things were created, since he alone breathes into all the creatures life and energy, so that they remain in their condition; and since in man himself he has given a remarkable display both of his power and of his grace, and even subsequently to the fall of man has not ceased to show liberality and kindness towards his posterity. And this doctrine is highly necessary to be known; for since apart from God we ought not at all to seek life and salvation, how could our faith rest on Christ, if we did not know with certainty what is here taught? By these words, therefore, the Evangelist assures us that we do not withdraw from the only and eternal God, when we believe in Christ, and likewise that life is now restored to the dead through the kindness of him who was the source and cause of life, when the nature of man was still uncorrupted.

6. There was a man

The Evangelist now begins to discourse about the manner in which the Son of God was manifested in flesh; and that none may doubt that Christ is the eternal Son of God, he relates that Christ was announced by John the Baptist, as his herald. For not only did Christ exhibit himself to be seen by men, but he chose also to be made known by the testimony and doctrine of John; or rather, God the Father sent this witness before his Christ, that they might more willingly receive the salvation offered by him.

14. And the Speech was made flesh

The Evangelist shows what was that coming of Christ which he had mentioned; namely, that having been clothed with our flesh, he showed himself openly to the world. Although the Evangelist touches briefly the unutterable mystery, that the Son of God was clothed with human nature, yet this brevity is wonderfully perspicuous.

15. John testifieth

He now relates what was the preaching of John. By using the verb *testifieth* (*marturei*) in the present tense, he denotes a continued act, and certainly this doctrine must be continually in force, as if the voice of John were continually resounding in the ears of men.

20. And he confessed, and denied not

That is, *he confessed* openly, and without any ambiguity or

DAVID BROWN

JOHN 1

John 1: 1–5

1. In the beginning – of all time and created existence, for this Word gave it being (John 1: 3,10); therefore, "before the world was" (John 17: 5,24); or, from all eternity.

was the Word – He *who is to God what man's word is to himself, the manifestation or expression of himself to those without him.* (See on John 1: 18). On the *origin* of this most lofty and now for ever consecrated title of Christ, this is not the place to speak. It occurs only in the writings of this seraphic apostle.

was with God – having a conscious personal existence *distinct from God* (as one is from the person he is "with"), but *inseparable from Him* and *associated with Him* (John 1: 18; John 17: 5; 1 John 1: 2), where "THE FATHER" is used in the same sense as "GOD" here.

was God – in substance and essence GOD; or was possessed of essential or proper divinity.

2. The same, &c – See what property of the Word the stress is laid upon – His *eternal distinctness*, in unity, from God – the Father (John 1: 2).

3. All things, &c – all things *absolutely* (as is evident from John 1: 10; 1 Cor. 8: 6; Col. 1: 16–17; but put beyond question by what follows).

without Him was not any thing – *not one thing.*

made – brought into being.

that was made – This is a denial of the *eternity* and *non-creation* of matter, which was held by the whole thinking world *outside of Judaism and Christianity:* or rather, its proper *creation* was never so much as dreamt of save by the children of *revealed religion.*

4. In Him was life – *essentially* and *originally*, as the previous verses show to be the meaning. Thus He is *the Living Word*, or, as He is called in 1 John 1: 1–2, "the Word of Life."

the life ... the light of men – All that in men which is *true light* – knowledge, integrity, intelligent, willing subjection to God, love to Him and to their fellow creatures, wisdom, purity, holy joy, rational happiness – all this "light of men" has its fountain in the essential original "life" of "the Word" (1 John 1: 5–7; Ps. 36: 9).

5. shineth in darkness, &c – in this dark, fallen world, or in mankind "sitting in darkness and the shadow of death," *with no ability to find the way either of truth or of holiness.* In this thick darkness, and consequent intellectual and moral obliquity, "the light of the Word" shineth – *by all the rays whether of natural or revealed teaching which men* (apart from the Incarnation of the Word) *are favored with.*

the darkness comprehended it not – *did not take it in*, a brief summary of the effect of all the strivings of this *unincarnate* Word throughout this wide world from the beginning, and a hint of the necessity of His putting on *flesh*, if any recovery of men was to be effected (1 Cor. 1: 21).

John 1: 6–9

The Evangelist here *approaches* his grand thesis, so paving his way for the full statement of it in John 1: 14, that we may be able to bear the bright light of it, and take in its length and breadth and depth and height.

7. through him – John.

8. not that Light – (See on John 5: 35). What a testimony to John to have to explain that "he was *not* that Light!" Yet was he but a foil to set it off, his night-taper dwindling before the Dayspring from on high (John 3: 30).

9. lighteth every man, &c. – rather, "which, coming into the world, enlighteneth every man"; or, is "the Light of the world" (John 9: 5). "Coming into the world" is a superfluous and quite unusual description of "every man"; but it is of all descriptions of Christ amongst the most familiar, especially in the writings of this Evangelist (John 12: 46; 16: 28; 18: 37; 1 John 4: 9; 1 Tim. 1: 15, &c.).

John 1: 10–15

He was in the world, &. – The language here is nearly as wonderful as the thought. Observe its compact simplicity, its sonorousness – "the world" resounding in each of its three members – and the enigmatic form in which it is couched, startling the reader and setting his ingenuity a-working to solve the stupendous enigma of *Christ ignored in His own world.*

11. his own – "His own" (property or possession), for the word is in the *neuter* gender. It

but confessed, I am not the Christ.

21 And they asked him, What then? Art thou Elias? And he saith, I am not. Art thou that prophet? And he answered, No.

22 Then said they unto him, Who art thou? that we may give an answer to them that sent us. What sayest thou of thyself?

23 He said, I am the voice of one crying in the wilderness, Make straight the way of the Lord, as said the prophet Esaias.

24 And they which were sent were of the Pharisees.

25 And they asked him, and said unto him, Why baptizest thou then, if thou be not that Christ, nor Elias, neither that prophet?

26 John answered them, saying, I baptize with water: but there standeth one among you, whom ye know not;

27 He it is, who coming after me is preferred before me, whose shoe's latchet I am not worthy to unloose.

28 These things were done in Bethabara beyond Jordan, where John was baptizing.

29 The next day John seeth Jesus coming unto him, and saith, Behold the Lamb of God, which taketh away the sin of the world.

30 This is he of whom I said, After me cometh a man which is preferred before me: for he was before me.

31 And I knew him not: but that he should be made manifest to Israel, therefore am I come baptizing with water.

32 And John bare record, saying, I saw the Spirit descending from heaven like a dove, and it abode upon him.

33 And I knew him not: but he that sent me to baptize with water, the same said unto me, Upon whom thou shalt see the Spirit descending, and remaining on him, the same is he which baptizeth with the Holy Ghost.

34 And I saw, and bare record that this is the Son of God.

35 Again the next day after John stood, and two of his disciples;

36 And looking upon Jesus as he walked, he saith, Behold the Lamb of God!

37 And the two disciples heard him speak, and they followed Jesus.

38 Then Jesus turned, and saw them

hypocrisy. The word *confess*, in the first instance, means generally, that he stated the fact as it really was. In the second instance, it is repeated in order to express the form of the confession. He replied expressly, *that he was not the Christ.*

26. I baptize with water

This ought to have been abundantly sufficient for the correction of their mistake, but a reproof otherwise clear is of no advantage to the deaf; for, when he sends them to Christ, and declares that Christ is present, this is a clear proof not only that he was divinely appointed to be a minister of Christ, but that he is the true *Elijah*, who is sent to testify that the time is come for the renovation of the Church. There is a contrast here which is not fully stated; for the spiritual *baptism* of Christ is not expressly contrasted with the external *baptism* of John, but that latter clause about the *baptism* of the Spirit might easily be supplied, and shortly afterwards both are set down by the Evangelist.

29. Behold the Lamb of God

The principal office of Christ is briefly but clearly stated; that he *takes away the sins of the world* by the sacrifice of his death, and reconciles men to God. There are other favors, indeed, which Christ bestows upon us, but this is the chief favor, and the rest depend on it; that, by appeasing the wrath of God, he makes us to be reckoned holy and righteous. For from this source flow all the streams of blessings, that, by not imputing our sins, he receives us into favor. Accordingly, John, in order to conduct us to Christ, commences with the gratuitous forgiveness of sins which we obtain through him.

32. I saw the Spirit, descending like a dove

This is not a literal but a figurative mode of expression; for with what eyes could he *see the Spirit?* But as the *dove* was a certain and infallible sign of the presence of *the Spirit*, it is called *the Spirit,* by a figure of speech in which one name is substituted for another; not that he is in reality *the Spirit*, but that he points him out, as far as human capacity can admit.

36. Behold the Lamb of God!

Hence appears more clearly that when John perceived that he was approaching the end of his course, he labored incessantly to resign his office to Christ. His firmness too gives greater credit to his testimony. But by insisting so earnestly, during many successive days, in repeating the commendation of Christ, he shows that his own course was nearly finished. Here we see also how small and low the beginning of the Church was. John, indeed, prepared disciples for Christ, but it is only now that Christ begins to collect a Church.

means His own land, city, temple, Messianic rights and possessions.

received him not – *nationally*, as God's chosen witnesses.

12. But as many – *individuals*, of the "disobedient and gainsaying people."

gave he power – The word signifies both *authority* and *ability*, and both are certainly meant here.

to become – Mark these words: Jesus is the Son of God; He is never said to have become such.

the sons – or more simply, "sons of God," in *name* and in *nature*.

believe on his name – *a phrase never used in Scripture of any mere creature*, to express the credit given to human testimony, even of prophets or apostles, inasmuch it carries with it the idea of *trust* proper only towards GOD. In this sense of *supreme faith*, as due to Him who "gives those that *believe in Himself* power to become sons of God," it is manifestly used here.

13. Which were born – a sonship therefore not of mere title and privilege, but of *nature*, the soul being made conscious of the vital capacities, perceptions, and emotions of *a child of God*, before unknown.

not of blood, &c – not of superior human descent, not of human generation at all, not of man in any manner of way. By this elaborate threefold denial of the *human* source of this sonship, immense force is given to what follows,

but of God – Right royal gift, and He who confers must be absolutely divine. For who would not worship Him who can bring him into the family, and evoke within him the very life, of the sons of God?

14. And the Word, &c – To raise the reader to the altitude of this climax were the thirteen foregoing verses written.

was made flesh – BECAME MAN, in man's present frail, mortal condition, denoted by the word "flesh" (Is. 40: 6; 1 Pet. 1: 24).

and dwelt – tabernacled or pitched his tent; a word peculiar to John, who uses it four times, all in the sense of *a permanent stay* (Rev. 7: 15; 12: 12; 13: 6; 21: 3).

full of grace and truth – So it should read: "He dwelt among us full of grace and truth"; or,

in Old Testament phrase, "Mercy and truth," denoting the whole fruit of God's purposes of love towards sinners of mankind, which until now existed only in *promise*, and the *fulfilment* at length of that promise in Christ; in one great word, "*the* SURE MERCIES *of David*" (Is. 55: 3; Acts 13: 34; compare 2 Sam. 23: 5).

and we beheld his glory – not by the eye of *sense*, which saw in Him only "the carpenter." His glory was "spiritually discerned" (1 Cor. 2: 7–15; 2 Cor. 3: 18; 4: 4, 6; 5: 16) – the glory of surpassing grace, love, tenderness, wisdom, purity, spirituality; majesty and meekness, richness and poverty, power and weakness, meeting together in unique contrast; ever attracting and at times ravishing the "babes" that followed and forsook all for Him.

the glory as of the only begotten of the Father – (See on Luke 1: 35); not *like*, but "such as (belongs to)," such as *became* or was *befitting* the only begotten of the Father [CHRYSOSTOM in LUCKE, CALVIN, &c.], according to a well-known use of the word "as."

15. after me – in *official manifestation*.

before me – in *rank and dignity*.

John 1: 16–18

SAME SUBJECT CONTINUED.

16. of his fulness – of "grace and truth," resuming the thread of John 1: 14.

grace for grace – that is, grace upon grace (so all the best interpreters), in successive communications and larger measures, as each was able to take it in. Observe, the word "truth" is here dropped. "Grace" being the chosen New Testament word for the whole fulness of the new covenant, all that dwells in Christ for men.

18. No man – "No one," in the widest sense.

hath seen God – by immediate gaze, or direct intuition.

he – emphatic; As if he should say, "He and He only hath declared Him," because He only *can*.

John 1: 19–36

THE BAPTIST'S TESTIMONY TO CHRIST.

19. record – testimony.

the Jews – that is, the heads of the nation, the members of the Sanhedrim. *In this pecu-*

following, and saith unto them, What seek ye? They said unto him, Rabbi, (which is to say, being interpreted, Master,) where dwellest thou?

39 He saith unto them, Come and see. They came and saw where he dwelt, and abode with him that day: for it was about the tenth hour.

40 One of the two which heard John speak, and followed him, was Andrew, Simon Peter's brother.

41 He first findeth his own brother Simon, and saith unto him, We have found the Messias, which is, being interpreted, the Christ.

42 And he brought him to Jesus. And when Jesus beheld him, he said, Thou art Simon the son of Jona: thou shalt be called Cephas, which is by interpretation, A stone.

43 The day following Jesus would go forth into Galilee, and findeth Philip, and saith unto him, Follow me.

44 Now Philip was of Bethsaida, the city of Andrew and Peter.

45 Philip findeth Nathanael, and saith unto him, We have found him, of whom Moses in the law, and the prophets, did write, Jesus of Nazareth, the son of Joseph.

46 And Nathanael said unto him, Can there any good thing come out of Nazareth? Philip saith unto him, Come and see.

47 Jesus saw Nathanael coming to him, and saith of him, Behold an Israelite indeed, in whom is no guile!

48 Nathanael saith unto him, Whence knowest thou me? Jesus answered and said unto him, Before that Philip called thee, when thou wast under the fig tree, I saw thee.

49 Nathanael answered and saith unto him, Rabbi, thou art the Son of God; thou art the King of Israel.

50 Jesus answered and said unto him, Because I said unto thee, I saw thee under the fig tree, believest thou? thou shalt see greater things than these.

51 And he saith unto him, Verily, verily, I say unto you, Hereafter ye shall see heaven open, and the angels of God ascending and descending upon the Son of man.

43. Follow me

When *Philip* was inflamed by this single word to follow Christ, we infer from it how great is the efficacy of the word of God; but it does not appear indiscriminately in all, for God addresses many without any advantage, just as if he struck their ears with a sound which vanished into air. So then the external preaching of the word is in itself unfruitful, except that it inflicts a deadly wound on the reprobate, so as to render them inexcusable before God. But when the secret grace of God quickens it, all the senses must be affected in such a manner that men will be prepared to *follow* wherever God calls them. We ought, therefore, to pray to Christ that he may display in us the same power of the Gospel. In the case of *Philip*, there was no doubt a peculiarity about his *following* Christ; for he is commanded to follow, not like one of us, but as a domestic, and as a familiar companion. But still the calling of all of us is illustrated by this calling of *Philip*.

51. You shall see heaven opened

They are greatly mistaken, in my opinion, who anxiously inquire into the place where, and the time when, Nathanael and others *saw heaven opened*; for he rather points out something perpetual which was always to exist in his kingdom. I acknowledge indeed, that the disciples sometimes *saw angels*, who are not seen in the present day; and I acknowledge also that the manifestation of the heavenly glory, when Christ ascended to heaven, was different from what we now behold. But if we duly consider what took place at that time, it is of perpetual duration; for the kingdom of God, which was formerly closed against us, is actually opened in Christ. A visible instance of this was shown to Stephen (Acts 7: 55), to the three disciples on the mountain (Matthew 17: 5), and to the other disciples at Christ's ascension (Luke 24: 51; Acts 1: 9). But all the signs by which God shows himself present with us depend on this *opening of heaven*, more especially when God communicates himself to us to be our life. *Ascending and descending on the Son of man*. This second clause refers to *angels*.

JOHN 2

1. There was a marriage in Cana of Galilee

This narrative contains the first miracle which Christ performed.

11. This beginning of miracles

The meaning is, that this was the first of Christ's miracles; for when the angels announced to the shepherds that he was born in Bethlehem (Luke 2: 8), when the *star* appeared to *the Magi* (Matthew 2: 2), when *the Holy Spirit descended on*

DAVID BROWN

liar sense our Evangelist seems always to use the term.

20. confessed, &c – that is, While many were ready to hail him as the Christ, he neither gave the slightest ground for such views, nor the least entertainment to them.

21. Elias – in His own proper person.
that prophet – announced in Deut. 18: 15, &c., about whom they seem not to have been agreed whether he were the same with the Messiah or no.

25. Why baptizest thou, if not, &c – Thinking he disclaimed any special connection with Messiah's kingdom, they demand his right to gather disciples by baptism.

26. there standeth – This must have been spoken after the baptism of Christ, and possibly just after His temptation (see on John 1: 29).

29. seeth Jesus – fresh, probably, from the scene of the temptation.
coming unto him – as to congenial company (Acts 4: 23), and to receive from him His first greeting.
and saith – catching a sublime inspiration at the sight of Him approaching.
the Lamb of God – the one God-ordained, God-gifted sacrificial offering.
the sin – The *singular* number being used to mark the *collective burden* and *all-embracing efficacy.*

35. John stood – "was standing," at his accustomed place.

36. looking – having fixed his eyes, with significant gaze, on Jesus.
as he walked – but not now *to him.* To have done this once (see on John 1: 29) was humility enough [BENGEL].
Behold, &c – The repetition of that wonderful proclamation, in identical terms and without another word, could only have been meant as a gentle hint to go after Him – as they did.

John 1: 37–51

FIRST GATHERING OF DISCIPLES – JOHN ANDREW, SIMON, PHILIP, NATHANAEL.

38. What seek ye – gentle, winning question, remarkable as the Redeemer's *first public utterance.* (See on Matt. 12: 18–20.)

where dwellest thou – that is, "That is a question we cannot answer in a moment; but had we Thy company for a calm hour in private, gladly should we open our burden."

39. Come and see – His *second utterance,* more winning still.

40. Peter's brother – and the elder of the two.

41. have found the Messias – The previous preparation of their simple hearts under the Baptist's ministry, made quick work of this blessed conviction, while others hesitated till doubt settled into obduracy. *So it is still.*

42. brought him to Jesus – Happy brothers that thus do to each other!
beheld him – fixed his eyes on him, with significant gaze (as John 1: 36).

43. would go ... into Galilee – for from His baptism He had sojourned in *Judea* (showing that the calling at the Sea of Galilee [Matt. 4: 18] was a *subsequent* one, see on Luke 5: 1).
Follow me – the first express call given, the former three having come to Him spontaneously.

44. the city of Andrew and Peter – of their *birth* probably, for they seem to have *lived* at Capernaum (Mark 1: 29).

45. son of Joseph – the current way of speaking. (See Luke 3: 23).

46. any good out of Nazareth – remembering Bethlehem, perhaps, as Messiah's predicted birthplace, and Nazareth having no *express* prophetic place at all, besides being in no repute. The question sprang from mere dread of mistake in a matter so vital.

47. an Israelite indeed ... no guile – not only no hypocrite, but with a guileless simplicity not always found even in God's own people, ready to follow wherever truth might lead him, saying, Samuel-like, "Speak, Lord, for Thy servant heareth" (1 Sam. 3: 10).

48. Whence knowest thou me – conscious that his very heart had been read, and at this critical moment more than ever before.
Before Philip called thee – showing He knew all that passed between Philip and him at a distance.

JOHN 2

1 And the third day there was a marriage in Cana of Galilee; and the mother of Jesus was there:

2 And both Jesus was called, and his disciples, to the marriage.

3 And when they wanted wine, the mother of Jesus saith unto him, They have no wine.

4 Jesus saith unto her, Woman, what have I to do with thee? mine hour is not yet come.

5 His mother saith unto the servants, Whatsoever he saith unto you, do it.

6 And there were set there six waterpots of stone, after the manner of the purifying of the Jews, containing two or three firkins apiece.

7 Jesus saith unto them, Fill the waterpots with water. And they filled them up to the brim.

8 And he saith unto them, Draw out now, and bear unto the governor of the feast. And they bare it.

9 When the ruler of the feast had tasted the water that was made wine, and knew not whence it was: (but the servants which drew the water knew;) the governor of the feast called the bridegroom,

10 And saith unto him, Every man at the beginning doth set forth good wine; and when men have well drunk, then that which is worse: but thou hast kept the good wine until now.

11 This beginning of miracles did Jesus in Cana of Galilee, and manifested forth his glory; and his disciples believed on him.

12 After this he went down to Capernaum, he, and his mother, and his brethren, and his disciples: and they continued there not many days.

13 And the Jews' passover was at hand, and Jesus went up to Jerusalem,

14 And found in the temple those that sold oxen and sheep and doves, and the changers of money sitting:

15 And when he had made a scourge of small cords, he drove them all out of the temple, and the sheep, and the oxen; and poured out the changers' money, and overthrew the tables;

16 And said unto them that sold doves, Take these things hence; make not my

him in the shape of a dove (Matthew 3: 16; Mark 1: 10; John 1: 32), though these were *miracles*, yet, strictly speaking, they were not performed by him; but the Evangelist now speaks of the *miracles* of which he was himself the Author. For it is a frivolous and absurd interpretation which some give, that this is reckoned the first among; the miracles which Christ performed in Cana of Galilee; as if a place, in which we do not read that he ever was more than twice, had been selected by him for a display of his power. It was rather the design of the Evangelist to mark the order of time which Christ followed in the exercise of his power. For until he was thirty years of age, he kept himself concealed at home, like one who held no public office. Having been consecrated, at his baptism, to the discharge of his office, he then began to appear in public, and to show by clear proofs for what purpose he was sent by the Father. We need not wonder, therefore, if he delayed till this time the first proof of his Divinity. It is a high honor given to marriage, that Christ not only deigned to be present at a nuptial banquet, but honored it with his first miracle. There are some ancient Canons which forbid the clergy to attend a marriage. The reason of the prohibition was, that by being the spectators of the wickedness which was usually practiced on such occasions, they might in some measure be regarded as approving of it. But it would have been far better to carry to such places so much gravity as to restrain the licentiousness in which unprincipled and abandoned men indulge, when they are withdrawn from the eyes of others. Let us, on the contrary, take Christ's example for our rule; and let us not suppose that any thing else than what we read that he did can be profitable to us.

16. Make not my Father's house a house of merchandise

At the second time that he drove the traders out of the Temple, the Evangelists relate that he used sharper and more severe language; for he said, that they *had made* the Temple of God *a den of robbers* (Matthew 21: 13); and this was proper to be done, when a milder chastisement was of no avail. At present, he merely warns them not to profane the Temple of God by applying it to improper uses. The Temple was called *the house of God*; because it was the will of God that there He should be peculiarly invoked; because there He displayed his power; because, finally, he had set it apart to spiritual and holy services.

19. Destroy this temple

This is an allegorical mode of expression; and Christ intentionally spoke with that degree of obscurity, because he reckoned them unworthy of a direct reply;

DAVID BROWN

50–51. Because I said, &c – "So quickly convinced, and on this evidence only?" – an expression of admiration.

JOHN 2

John 2: 1–12

FIRST MIRACLE, WATER MADE WINE – BRIEF VISIT TO CAPERNAUM.

1. third day – He would take two days to reach Galilee, and this was the third.

mother there – it being probably some relative's marriage. *John never names her* [BENGEL].

3. no wine – evidently expecting some display of His glory, and hinting that now was His time.

4–5. Woman – no term of disrespect in the language of that day (John 19: 26).

what ... to do with thee – that is, "In my Father's business I have to do with Him only." It was a gentle rebuke for *officious interference,* entering a region from which all creatures were excluded (compare Acts 4: 19–20).

mine hour, &c – hinting that He *would* do something, but at His own time; and so she understood it (John 2: 5).

6. firkins – about seven and a half gallons in Jewish, or nine in Attic measure; each of these huge water jars, therefore, holding some twenty or more gallons, for washings at such feasts (Mark 7: 4).

7–8. Fill ... draw ... bear – directing all, but Himself touching nothing, to prevent all appearance of collusion.

9–10. well drunk – "drunk abundantly" (as Song 5: 1), speaking of the general practice.

10. the good wine ... until now – thus testifying, while ignorant of the source of supply, not only that it was real wine, but better than any at the feast.

11. manifested forth his glory – Nothing in the least like this is said of the miracles of prophet or apostle, nor could without manifest blasphemy be said of any mere creature.

12. Capernaum – on the Sea of Galilee. (See on Matt. 9: 1).

his mother and his brethren – (See on Luke 2: 51, and Matt. 13: 54–56).

John 2: 13–25

CHRIST'S FIRST PASSOVER – FIRST CLEANSING OF THE TEMPLE.

14–17. in the temple – not the temple itself, as John 2: 19–21, but the *temple-court.*

sold oxen, &c – for the convenience of those who had to offer them in sacrifice.

changers of money – of Roman into Jewish money, in which the temple dues (see on Matt. 17: 24) had to be paid.

15. small cords – likely some of the rushes spread for bedding, and when twisted used to tie up the cattle there collected. "Not by this slender whip but by divine majesty was the ejection accomplished, the whip being but a sign of the scourge of divine anger" [GROTIUS].

poured out ... overthrew – thus expressing the mingled indignation and authority of the impulse.

16. house of merchandise – There was nothing wrong in the merchandise; but to bring it, for their own and others' convenience, into that most sacred place, was a high-handed profanation which the eye of Jesus could not endure.

17. eaten me up – a glorious feature in the predicted character of the suffering Messiah (Ps. 69: 9), and rising high even in some not worthy to loose the latchet of His shoes. (Ex. 32: 19, &c.).

18–22. What sign showest thou unto us, seeing that thou doest these things? – Though the *act* and the *words* of Christ, taken together, were sign enough, they were unconvinced: yet they were *awed,* and though at His very next appearance at Jerusalem they "sought to kill Him" for speaking of "His Father" just as He did now (John 5: 18), they, at this early stage, only ask a sign.

20. Forty and six years – From the eighteenth year of Herod till then was just forty-six years [JOSEPHUS, *Antiquities,* 15.11.1].

21. temple of his body – in which was enshrined the glory of the eternal Word. (See

Father's house an house of merchandise.

17 And his disciples remembered that it was written, The zeal of thine house hath eaten me up.

18 Then answered the Jews and said unto him, What sign shewest thou unto us, seeing that thou doest these things?

19 Jesus answered and said unto them, Destroy this temple, and in three days I will raise it up.

20 Then said the Jews, Forty and six years was this temple in building, and wilt thou rear it up in three days?

21 But he spake of the temple of his body.

22 When therefore he was risen from the dead, his disciples remembered that he had said this unto them; and they believed the scripture, and the word which Jesus had said.

23 Now when he was in Jerusalem at the passover, in the feast day, many believed in his name, when they saw the miracles which he did.

24 But Jesus did not commit himself unto them, because he knew all men,

25 And needed not that any should testify of man: for he knew what was in man.

JOHN 3

1 There was a man of the Pharisees, named Nicodemus, a ruler of the Jews:

2 The same came to Jesus by night, and said unto him, Rabbi, we know that thou art a teacher come from God: for no man can do these miracles that thou doest, except God be with him.

3 Jesus answered and said unto him, Verily, verily, I say unto thee, Except a man be born again, he cannot see the kingdom of God.

4 Nicodemus saith unto him, How can a man be born when he is old? can he enter the second time into his mother's womb, and be born?

5 Jesus answered, Verily, verily, I say unto thee, Except a man be born of water and of the Spirit, he cannot enter into the kingdom of God.

6 That which is born of the flesh is flesh; and that which is born of the Spirit is spirit.

7 Marvel not that I said unto thee, Ye

as he elsewhere declares that *he speaks to them in parables*, because they are unable to comprehend the mysteries of the heavenly kingdom (Matthew 13: 13). But first he refuses to them the sign which they demanded, either because it would have been of no advantage, or because he knew that it was not the proper time. Some compliances he occasionally made even with their unreasonable requests, and there must have been a strong reason why he now refused. Yet that they may not seize on this as a pretense for excusing themselves, he declares that his power will be approved and confirmed by a *sign* of no ordinary value; for no greater approbation of the divine power in Christ could be desired than his resurrection from the dead. But he conveys this information figuratively, because he does not reckon them worthy of an explicit promise. In short, he treats unbelievers as they deserve, and at the same time protects himself against all contempt. It was not yet made evident, indeed, that they were obstinate, but Christ knew well what was the state of their feelings.

JOHN 3

1. Now there was a man of the Pharisees

In the person of Nicodemus the Evangelist now exhibits to our view how vain and fleeting was the faith of those who, having been excited by miracles, suddenly professed to be the disciples of Christ. For since this man was of the order of the Pharisees, and held the rank of a ruler in his nation, he must have been far more excellent than others. The common people, for the most part, are light and unsteady; but who would not have thought that he who had learning and experience was also a wise and prudent man? Yet from Christ's reply it is evident, that nothing was farther from his design in coming than a desire to learn the first principles of religion. If he who was *a ruler* among men is less than a child, what ought we to think of the multitude at large? Now though the design of the Evangelist was, to exhibit, as in a mirror, how few there were in Jerusalem who were properly disposed to receive the Gospel, yet, for other reasons, this narrative is highly useful to us; and especially because it instructs us concerning the depraved nature of mankind, what is the proper entrance into the school of Christ, and what must be the commencement of our training to make progress in the heavenly doctrine. For the sum of Christ's discourse is, that, in order that we may be his true disciples, we must become new men. But, before proceeding farther, we must ascertain from the circumstances which are here detailed by the Evangelist, what were the obstacles which

on John 1: 14). By its resurrection the true Temple of God upon earth was reared up, of which the stone one was but a shadow; so that the allusion is not *quite* exclusively to Himself, but takes in that Temple of which He is the foundation, and all believers are the "lively stones." (1 Pet. 2: 4–5).

22. believed the scripture – on this subject; that is, what was meant, which was hid from them till then.

23–25. in the feast day – the foregoing things occurring probably before the feast began.

many believed – superficially, struck merely by "the miracles He did." Of these we have no record.

24. did not commit – "entrust," or let Himself down familiarly to them, as to His genuine disciples.

25. knew what was in man – It is impossible for language more clearly to assert of Christ what in Jer. 17: 9–10, and elsewhere, is denied of all mere creatures.

JOHN 3

John 3: 1–21

Night Interview of Nicodemus with Jesus.

1– 2. Nicodemus – In this member of the Sanhedrim sincerity and timidity are seen struggling together.

2. came to Jesus by night – One of those superficial "believers" mentioned in John 2: 23–24, yet inwardly craving further satisfaction, Nicodemus comes to Jesus in quest of it, but comes "by night" (see John 19: 38–39; 12: 42); he avows his conviction that He was

come from God – *an expression never applied to a merely human messenger,* and probably meaning more here – but only as "a *teacher,*" and in His miracles he sees a proof merely that "God is with Him." Thus, while unable to repress his convictions, he is afraid of committing himself too far.

3. be born again – or, as it were, *begin life anew* in relation to God; his manner of thinking, feeling, and acting, with reference to spiritual things, undergoing *a fundamental and permanent revolution.*

cannot see – can have no part in (just as one is said to "see life," "see death," &c.).

the kingdom of God – whether in its beginnings here (Luke 16: 16), or its consummation hereafter (Matt. 25: 34; Eph. 5: 5).

4. How, &c – The figure of the new birth, if it had been meant only of *Gentile proselytes* to the Jewish religion, would have been intelligible enough to Nicodemus, being quite in keeping with the language of that day; but that *Jews themselves* should need a new birth was to him incomprehensible.

5. of water and of the Spirit – A twofold explanation of the "new birth," so startling to Nicodemus.

6–8. That which is born, &c – A great universal proposition; "That which is begotten carries within itself the nature of that which begat it" [Olshausen].

flesh – Not the mere material body, but all that comes into the world by birth, *the entire man;* yet not humanity simply, but in its corrupted, depraved condition, *in complete subjection to the law of the fall* (Rom. 8: 1–9). So that though a man "could enter a second time into his mother's womb and be born," he would be no nearer this "new birth" than before (Job 14: 4; Ps. 51: 5).

is spirit – "partakes of and possesses His spiritual nature."

7. Marvel not, &c – If a spiritual nature only can see and enter the kingdom of God; if all we bring into the world with us be the reverse of spiritual; and if this spirituality be solely of the Holy Ghost, no wonder a new birth is indispensable.

Ye must – "*Ye,* says Jesus, not *we*" [Bengel]. After those universal propositions, about what "*a man*" must be, to "enter the kingdom of God" (John 3: 5) – this is remarkable, showing that our Lord meant to hold Himself forth as "*separate from sinners.*"

8. The wind, &c – *Breath* and *spirit* (one word both in *Hebrew* and *Greek*) are constantly brought together in Scripture as analogous (Job 27: 3; 33: 4; Ezek. 37: 9–14).

canst not tell, &c – The laws which govern the motion of the *winds* are even yet but partially discovered; but the risings, failings, and change in direction many times in a day, of

must be born again.

8 The wind bloweth where it listeth, and thou hearest the sound thereof, but canst not tell whence it cometh, and whither it goeth: so is every one that is born of the Spirit.

9 Nicodemus answered and said unto him, How can these things be?

10 Jesus answered and said unto him, Art thou a master of Israel, and knowest not these things?

11 Verily, verily, I say unto thee, We speak that we do know, and testify that we have seen; and ye receive not our witness.

12 If I have told you earthly things, and ye believe not, how shall ye believe, if I tell you of heavenly things?

13 And no man hath ascended up to heaven, but he that came down from heaven, even the Son of man which is in heaven.

14 And as Moses lifted up the serpent in the wilderness, even so must the Son of man be lifted up:

15 That whosoever believeth in him should not perish, but have eternal life.

16 For God so loved the world, that he gave his only begotten Son, that whosoever believeth in him should not perish, but have everlasting life.

17 For God sent not his Son into the world to condemn the world; but that the world through him might be saved.

18 He that believeth on him is not condemned: but he that believeth not is condemned already, because he hath not believed in the name of the only begotten Son of God.

19 And this is the condemnation, that light is come into the world, and men loved darkness rather than light, because their deeds were evil.

20 For every one that doeth evil hateth the light, neither cometh to the light, lest his deeds should be reproved.

21 But he that doeth truth cometh to the light, that his deeds may be made manifest, that they are wrought in God.

22 After these things came Jesus and his disciples into the land of Judaea; and there he tarried with them, and baptized.

23 And John also was baptizing in Aenon near to Salim, because there was much water there: and they came, and

prevented Nicodemus from giving himself unreservedly to Christ.

16. For God so loved the world

Christ opens up the first cause, and, as it were, the source of our salvation, and he does so, that no doubt may remain; for our minds cannot find calm repose, until we arrive at the unmerited love of God. As the whole matter of our salvation must not be sought any where else than in Christ, so we must see whence Christ came to us, and why he was offered to be our Savior. Both points are distinctly stated to us: namely, that faith in Christ brings life to all, and that Christ brought life, because the Heavenly Father loves the human race, and wishes that they should not perish. And this order ought to be carefully observed; for such is the wicked ambition which belongs to our nature, that when the question relates to the origin of our salvation, we quickly form diabolical imaginations about our own merits. Accordingly, we imagine that God is reconciled to us, because he has reckoned us worthy that he should look upon us. But Scripture everywhere extols his pure and unmingled mercy, which sets aside all merits.

27. A man cannot receive any thing

Some refer these words to Christ, as if John accused the disciples of wicked presumption in opposition to God, by endeavoring to deprive Christ of what the Father had given to him. They suppose the meaning to be this: "That within so short a time he has risen to so great honor, is the work of God; and therefore it is in vain for you to attempt to degrade him whom God with his own hand has raised on high." Others think that it is an exclamation into which he indignantly breaks forth, because his disciples had hitherto made so little progress. And certainly it was excessively absurd that they should still endeavor to reduce to the rank of ordinary men him who, they had so often heard, was the Christ, that he might not rise above his own servants; and, therefore, John might justly have said that it is useless to spend time in instructing men, because they are dull and stupid, until they are renewed in mind.

But I rather agree with the opinion of those who explain it as applying to John, as asserting that it is not in his power, or in theirs, to make him great, because the measure of us all is to be what God intended us to be. For if even the Son of God *took not that honour to himself* (Hebrews 5: 4), what man of the ordinary rank would venture to desire more than what the Lord has given him? This single thought, if it were duly impressed on the minds of us all, would be abundantly sufficient for restraining ambition; and were ambition corrected and destroyed, the plague of conten-

those *gentle breezes* here referred to, will probably ever be a mystery to us: So of the operation of the Holy Ghost in the new birth.

9–10. How, &c – Though the subject still confounds Nicodemus, the necessity and possibility of the new birth is no longer the point with him, but the nature of it and how it is brought about [LUTHARDT]. "From this moment Nicodemus *says nothing more,* but has sunk unto a disciple who has found his true teacher. Therefore the Saviour now graciously advances in His communications of truth, and once more solemnly brings to the mind of this teacher in Israel, now become a learner, his own not guiltless *ignorance,* that He may then proceed to utter, out of the fulness of His divine knowledge, such farther testimonies both of earthly and heavenly things as his docile scholar may to his own profit receive" [STIER].

10. master – "teacher." The question clearly implies that *the doctrine of regeneration is so far disclosed in the Old Testament that Nicodemus was culpable in being ignorant of it.* Nor is it merely as something that should be experienced *under the Gospel* that the Old Testament holds it forth – as many distinguished critics allege, denying that there was any such thing as regeneration before Christ. For our Lord's proposition is universal, that no fallen man is or can be spiritual without a regenerating operation of the Holy Ghost, and the necessity of a *spiritual obedience* under whatever name, in opposition to mere mechanical services, is proclaimed throughout all the Old Testament.

11–13. We speak that we know, and ... have seen – that is, by *absolute* knowledge and *immediate* vision of God, which "the only-begotten Son in the bosom of the Father" claims as exclusively His own (John 1: 18). The "we" and "our" are here used, though Himself only is intended, in emphatic contrast, probably, with the opening words of Nicodemus, "Rabbi, *we know*.", &c.

ye receive not, &c – referring to the *class* to which Nicodemus belonged, but from which he was beginning to be separated in spirit.

12. earthly things – such as *regeneration,* the gate of entrance to the kingdom of God *on earth,* and which Nicodemus should have understood better, as a truth even of that more *earthly* economy to which he belonged.

heavenly things – the things of the new and more heavenly evangelical economy, only to be fully understood after the effusion of the Spirit from heaven through the exalted Saviour.

13. no man hath ascended, &c – There is something paradoxical in this language – "No one has gone up but He that came down, even He who is at once both up and down." Doubtless it was intended to startle and constrain His auditor to think that there must be mysterious elements in His Person. The old Socinians, to subvert the doctrine of the pre-existence of Christ, seized upon this passage as teaching that the man Jesus was secretly caught up to heaven to receive His instructions, and then "came down from heaven" to deliver them. But the sense manifestly is this: "The perfect knowledge of God is not obtained by any man's going up from earth to heaven to receive it – no man hath so ascended – but He whose *proper habitation,* in His essential and eternal nature, is heaven, hath, by taking human flesh, descended as the Son of man to disclose the Father, whom He knows by immediate gaze alike in the flesh as before He assumed it, being essentially and unchangeably 'in the bosom of the Father'" (John 1: 18).

14–16. And as Moses, &c – Here now we have the "heavenly things," as before the "earthly," but under a veil, for the reason mentioned in John 3: 12. The crucifixion of Messiah is twice after this veiled under the same lively term – *"uplifting,"* John 8: 28; 12: 32, 33. Here it is still further veiled – though to us who know what it means, rendered vastly more instructive – by reference to the brazen serpent. The venom of the fiery serpents, shooting through the veins of the rebellious Israelites, was spreading death through the camp – lively emblem of the perishing condition of men by reason of sin. In both cases the remedy was divinely provided. In both the way of cure strikingly resembled that of the disease. Stung by serpents, by a serpent they are healed. By "fiery serpents" bitten – serpents, probably, with skin spotted fiery red [KURTZ] – the instrument of cure is a serpent of brass or copper, having at a distance *the same appearance.* So in redemption, as by man

were baptized.

24 For John was not yet cast into prison.

25 Then there arose a question between some of John's disciples and the Jews about purifying.

26 And they came unto John, and said unto him, Rabbi, he that was with thee beyond Jordan, to whom thou barest witness, behold, the same baptizeth, and all men come to him.

27 John answered and said, A man can receive nothing, except it be given him from heaven.

28 Ye yourselves bear me witness, that I said, I am not the Christ, but that I am sent before him.

29 He that hath the bride is the bridegroom: but the friend of the bridegroom, which standeth and heareth him, rejoiceth greatly because of the bridegroom's voice: this my joy therefore is fulfilled.

30 He must increase, but I must decrease.

31 He that cometh from above is above all: he that is of the earth is earthly, and speaketh of the earth: he that cometh from heaven is above all.

32 And what he hath seen and heard, that he testifieth; and no man receiveth his testimony.

33 He that hath received his testimony hath set to his seal that God is true.

34 For he whom God hath sent speaketh the words of God: for God giveth not the Spirit by measure unto him.

35 The Father loveth the Son, and hath given all things into his hand.

36 He that believeth on the Son hath everlasting life: and he that believeth not the Son shall not see life; but the wrath of God abideth on him.

JOHN 4

1 When therefore the Lord knew how the Pharisees had heard that Jesus made and baptized more disciples than John,

2 (Though Jesus himself baptized not, but his disciples,)

3 He left Judaea, and departed again into Galilee.

4 And he must needs go through Samaria.

5 Then cometh he to a city of Samaria,

tions would likewise be removed. How comes it then, that every man exalts himself more than is proper, but because we do not depend on the Lord, so as to be satisfied with the rank which he assigns to us?

36. He who believeth in the Son

This was added, not only to inform us that we ought to ask all good things from Christ, but likewise to make us, acquainted with the manner in which they are enjoyed. He shows that enjoyment consists in faith; and not without reason, since by means of it we possess Christ, who brings along with him both righteousness and *life,* which is the fruit of righteousness. When faith in Christ is declared to be the cause of *life,* we learn from it that *life* is to be found in Christ alone, and that in no other way do we become partakers of it than by the grace of Christ himself. But all are not agreed as to the way in which the *life* of Christ comes to us. Some understand it thus: "as by believing we receive the Spirit, who regenerates us in order to justification, by that very regeneration we obtain salvation." For my own part, though I acknowledge it to be true, that we are renewed by faith, so that the Spirit of Christ governs us, yet I say that we ought first to take into consideration the free forgiveness of sins, through which we are accepted by God. Again, I say that on this all our confidence of salvation is founded, and in this it consists; because justification before God cannot be reckoned to us in any other way than when he does not impute to us our sins.

JOHN 4

15. Give me this water

This woman undoubtedly is sufficiently aware that Christ is speaking of spiritual water; but because she despises him, she sets at naught all his promises; for so long as the authority of him who speaks is not acknowledged by us, his doctrine is not permitted to enter. Indirectly, therefore, the woman taunted Christ, saying, "Thou boastest much, but I see nothing: show it in reality, if thou canst."

21. Woman, believe me

In the first part of this reply, he briefly sets aside the ceremonial worship which had been appointed under the Law; for when he says that the hour is at hand when there shall be no peculiar and fixed place for worship, he means that what Moses delivered was only for a time, and that the time was now approaching when the partition-wall (Ephesians 2:14) should be thrown down. In this manner he extends the worship of God far beyond its former narrow limits, that the Samaritans might become partakers of it.

came death, by Man also comes life – Man, too, "*in the likeness of sinful flesh*" (Rom. 8: 3), differing in nothing *outward* and *apparent* from those who, pervaded by the poison of the serpent, were ready to perish. But as the uplifted serpent had none of the venom of which the serpent-bitten people were dying, so while the whole human family were perishing of the deadly wound inflicted on it by the old serpent, "the Second Man," who arose over humanity with healing in His wings, was without spot or wrinkle, or any such thing. In both cases the remedy is *conspicuously displayed;* in the one case on a pole, in the other on the cross, to "draw all men unto Him" (John 12: 32). In both cases it is by *directing the eye to the uplifted Remedy* that the cure is effected; in the one case the bodily eye, in the other the gaze of the soul by "believing in Him," as in that glorious ancient proclamation – "*Look* unto me and be ye saved, all the ends of the earth," &c. (Is. 45: 22). Both methods are stumbling to human reason. What, to any thinking Israelite, could seem more unlikely than that a deadly poison should be dried up in his body by simply looking on a reptile of brass? Such a stumbling-block to the Jews and to the Greeks foolishness was faith in the crucified Nazarene as a way of deliverance from eternal perdition. Yet was the warrant in both cases to expect a cure equally rational and well grounded. As the serpent was *God's ordinance* for the cure of every bitten Israelite, so is Christ for the salvation of every perishing sinner – the one however a purely *arbitrary* ordinance, the other divinely *adapted* to man's complicated maladies. In both cases the efficacy is the same. As one simple look at the serpent, however distant and however weak, brought an instantaneous cure, even so, real faith in the Lord Jesus, however tremulous, however distant – be it but *real* faith – brings certain and instant healing to the perishing soul. In a word, the consequences of disobedience are the same in both. Doubtless many bitten Israelites, galling as their case was, would *reason* rather than *obey*, would *speculate* on the absurdity of expecting the bite of a living serpent to be cured by looking at a piece of dead metal in the shape of one – speculate thus *till they died.* Alas! is not salvation by a crucified Redeemer subjected to like treatment? Has the offense of the cross" yet ceased? (Compare 2 Kgs. 5: 12).

16. For God so loved, &c – What proclamation of the Gospel has been so oft on the lips of missionaries and preachers in every age since it was first uttered? What has sent such thrilling sensations through millions of mankind? What has been honored to bring such multitudes to the feet of Christ? What to kindle in the cold and selfish breasts of mortals the fires of self-sacrificing love to mankind, as these words of transparent simplicity, yet overpowering majesty? The picture embraces several distinct compartments: "THE WORLD" – in its widest sense – *ready* "*to perish*"; the immense "LOVE OF GOD" *to that perishing world,* measurable only, and conceivable only, by the gift which it drew forth from Him; THE GIFT itself – "He *so* loved the world that He *gave* His only begotten Son," or, in the language of Paul, "*spared not* His own Son" (Rom. 8: 32), or in that addressed to Abraham when ready to offer IsaActs on the altar, "*withheld not* His Son, His only Son, whom He loved" (Gen. 22: 16); the FRUIT of this stupendous gift – not only *deliverance from* impending "*perdition*," but *the bestowal of everlasting life;* the MODE in which all takes effect – by "*believing*" on the Son. How would Nicodemus' narrow Judaism become invisible in the blaze of this Sun of righteousness seen rising on "the world" with healing in His wings! (Mal. 4: 2).

17–21. not to condemn, &c – A statement of vast importance. Though "condemnation" is to many the *issue* of Christ's mission (John 3: 19), it is not the *object* of His mission, which is purely a *saving* one.

18. is not condemned – Having, immediately on his believing, "passed from death unto life" (John 5: 24).

condemned already – Rejecting the one way of deliverance from that "condemnation" which God gave His Son to *remove,* and so wilfully *remaining* condemned.

19. this is the condemnation, &c – emphatically so, *revealing* the condemnation already existing, and *sealing up* under it those who will not be delivered from it.

light is come into the world – in the Person of Him to whom Nicodemus was listening.

loved darkness, &c – This can only be known by the deliberate rejection of Christ, but that *does* fearfully reveal it.

which is called Sychar, near to the parcel of ground that Jacob gave to his son Joseph.

6 Now Jacob's well was there. Jesus therefore, being wearied with his journey, sat thus on the well: and it was about the sixth hour.

7 There cometh a woman of Samaria to draw water: Jesus saith unto her, Give me to drink.

8 (For his disciples were gone away unto the city to buy meat.)

9 Then saith the woman of Samaria unto him, How is it that thou, being a Jew, askest drink of me, which am a woman of Samaria? for the Jews have no dealings with the Samaritans.

10 Jesus answered and said unto her, If thou knewest the gift of God, and who it is that saith to thee, Give me to drink; thou wouldest have asked of him, and he would have given thee living water.

11 The woman saith unto him, Sir, thou hast nothing to draw with, and the well is deep: from whence then hast thou that living water?

12 Art thou greater than our father Jacob, which gave us the well, and drank thereof himself, and his children, and his cattle?

13 Jesus answered and said unto her, Whosoever drinketh of this water shall thirst again:

14 But whosoever drinketh of the water that I shall give him shall never thirst; but the water that I shall give him shall be in him a well of water springing up into everlasting life.

15 The woman saith unto him, Sir, give me this water, that I thirst not, neither come hither to draw.

16 Jesus saith unto her, Go, call thy husband, and come hither.

17 The woman answered and said, I have no husband. Jesus said unto her, Thou hast well said, I have no husband:

18 For thou hast had five husbands; and he whom thou now hast is not thy husband: in that saidst thou truly.

19 The woman saith unto him, Sir, I perceive that thou art a prophet.

20 Our fathers worshipped in this mountain; and ye say, that in Jerusalem is the place where men ought to worship.

21 Jesus saith unto her, Woman, be-

The hour cometh

He uses the present tense instead of the future; but the meaning is, that the repeal of the Law is already at hand, so far as relates to the Temple, and Priesthood, and other outward ceremonies. By calling God Father, he seems indirectly to contrast Him with the Fathers whom the woman had mentioned, and to convey this instruction, that God will be a common Father to all, so that he will be generally worshipped without distinction of places or nations.

24. God is a Spirit

This is a confirmation drawn from the very nature of God. Since men are flesh, we ought not to wonder, if they take delight in those things which correspond to their own disposition. Hence it arises, that they contrive many things in the worship of God which are full of display, but have no solidity. But they ought first of all to consider that they have to do with God, who can no more agree with the flesh than fire with water. This single consideration, when the inquiry relates to the worship of God, ought to be sufficient for restraining the wantonness of our mind, that God is so far from being like us, that those things which please us most are the objects of his loathing and abhorrence. And if hypocrites are so blinded by their own pride, that they are not afraid to subject God to their opinion, or rather to their unlawful desires, let us know that this modesty does not hold the lowest place in the true worship of God, to regard with suspicion whatever is gratifying according to the flesh. Besides, as we cannot ascend to the height of God, let us remember that we ought to seek from His word the rule by which we are governed. This passage is frequently quoted by the Fathers against the Arians, to prove the Divinity of the Holy Spirit, but it is improper to strain it for such a purpose; for Christ simply declares here that his Father is of a spiritual nature, and, therefore, is not moved by frivolous matters, as men, through the lightness and unsteadiness of their character, are wont to be.

25. The Messiah is about to come

Although religion among the Samaritans was corrupted and mixed up with many errors, yet some principles taken from the Law were impressed on their minds, such as that which related to the Messiah. Now it is probable that, when the woman ascertained from Christ's discourse that a very extraordinary change was about to take place in the Church of God, her mind instantly recurred to the recollection of Christ, under whom she hoped that all things would be fully restored. When she says that *the Messiah is about to come*, she seems to speak of the time as near at hand; and, indeed, it is sufficiently evident from many arguments, that the minds

20. reproved – by detection.

21. doeth truth – whose only object in life is to be and do what will bear the light. Therefore he loves and "comes to the light," that all he is and does, being thus thoroughly tested, may be seen to have nothing in it but what is divinely wrought and divinely approved. This is the "Israelite, indeed, in whom is no guile."

John 3: 22–36

JESUS IN THE NEIGHBORHOOD OF THE BAPTIST – HIS NOBLE TESTIMONY TO HIS MASTER.

22–24. land of Judea – the rural parts of that province, the foregoing conversation being held in the capital.

baptized – in the sense explained in John 4: 2.

23. Ænon … Salim – on the west of Jordan. (Compare John 3: 26 with John 1: 28).

24. John not yet cast into prison – Hence it is plain that our Lord's ministry did not *commence* with the imprisonment of John, though, but for this, we should have drawn that inference from Matt. 4: 12 and Mark's (Mark 1: 14) express statement.

25–26. between some of – rather, "on the part of."

and the Jews – rather (according to the best manuscripts), "and a Jew,"

about purifying – that is, baptizing, the symbolical meaning of washing with water being put (as in John 2: 6) for the act itself. As John and Jesus were the only teachers who baptized Jews, discussions might easily arise between the Baptist's disciples and such Jews as declined to submit to that rite.

26. Rabbi, &c – "Master, this man tells us that He to whom thou barest such generous witness beyond Jordan is requiting thy generosity by drawing all the people away to Himself. At this rate, thou shalt soon have no disciples at all." The reply to this is one of the noblest and most affecting utterances that ever came from the lips of man.

27–30. A man, &c – "I do my heaven-prescribed work, and that is enough for me. Would you have me mount into my Master's place? Said I not unto you, I am not the Christ? The Bride is not mine, why should the people stay with me?? Mine it is to point the burdened to the Lamb of God that taketh away the sin of the world, to tell them there is Balm in Gilead, and a Physician there. And shall I grudge to see them, in obedience to the call, flying as a cloud, and as doves to their windows? Whose is the Bride but the Bridegroom's? Enough for me to be the Bridegroom's *friend*, sent by Him to negotiate the match, privileged to bring together the Saviour and those He is come to seek and to save, and rejoicing with joy unspeakable if I may but 'stand and hear the Bridegroom's voice,' witnessing the blessed espousals. Say ye, then, they go from me to Him? Ye bring me glad tidings of great joy. He must increase, but I must decrease; this, my joy, therefore is fulfilled."

A man can receive, &c – assume nothing, that is, lawfully and with any success; that is, Every man has his work and sphere appointed him from above, Even Christ Himself came under this law (Heb. 5: 4).

31–34. He that, &c – Here is the reason why He must increase while all human teachers must decrease. The Master "cometh from above" – descending from *His proper element,* the region of those "heavenly things" which He came to reveal, and so, although mingling with men and things on the earth, is not "of the earth," either in Person or Word. The servants, on the contrary, springing of earth, are of the earth, and their testimony, even though divine in authority, partakes necessarily of their own earthiness. (So strongly did the Baptist feel this contrast that the last clause just repeats the first). It is impossible for a sharper line of distinction to be drawn between Christ and all human teachers, even when divinely commissioned and speaking by the power of the Holy Ghost. And who does not perceive it? The words of prophets and apostles are undeniable and most precious truth; but in the words of Christ we hear a voice as from the excellent Glory, the Eternal Word making Himself heard in our own flesh.

32. what he hath seen and heard – (See on John 3: 11 and John 1: 18).

and no man receiveth, &c – John's disciples had said, "*All* come to Him" (John 3: 26). The Baptist here virtually says, Would it were so,

lieve me, the hour cometh, when ye shall neither in this mountain, nor yet at Jerusalem, worship the Father.

22 Ye worship ye know not what: we know what we worship: for salvation is of the Jews.

23 But the hour cometh, and now is, when the true worshippers shall worship the Father in spirit and in truth: for the Father seeketh such to worship him.

24 God is a Spirit: and they that worship him must worship him in spirit and in truth.

25 The woman saith unto him, I know that Messias cometh, which is called Christ: when he is come, he will tell us all things.

26 Jesus saith unto her, I that speak unto thee am he.

27 And upon this came his disciples, and marveled that he talked with the woman: yet no man said, What seekest thou? or, Why talkest thou with her?

28 The woman then left her waterpot, and went her way into the city, and saith to the men,

29 Come, see a man, which told me all things that ever I did: is not this the Christ?

30 Then they went out of the city, and came unto him.

31 In the mean while his disciples prayed him, saying, Master, eat.

32 But he said unto them, I have meat to eat that ye know not of.

33 Therefore said the disciples one to another, Hath any man brought him ought to eat?

34 Jesus saith unto them, My meat is to do the will of him that sent me, and to finish his work.

35 Say not ye, There are yet four months, and then cometh harvest? behold, I say unto you, Lift up your eyes, and look on the fields; for they are white already to harvest.

36 And he that reapeth receiveth wages, and gathereth fruit unto life eternal: that both he that soweth and he that reapeth may rejoice together.

37 And herein is that saying true, One soweth, and another reapeth.

38 I sent you to reap that whereon ye bestowed no labour: other men laboured, and ye are entered into their labours.

of men were everywhere aroused by the expectation of the Messiah, who would restore the affairs which were wretchedly decayed, or rather, which were utterly ruined.

34. My food is to do the will of him who sent me

He means not only that he esteems it very highly, but that there is nothing in which he takes greater delight, or in which he is more cheerfully or more eagerly employed; as David, in order to magnify the Law of God, says not only that he values it highly, but that it is *sweeter than honey* (Psalm 19: 10). If, therefore, we would follow Christ, it is proper not only that we devote ourselves diligently to the service of God, but that we be so cheerful in complying with its injunctions that the labor shall not be at all oppressive or disagreeable.

39. And many Samaritans out of that city believed

The Evangelist here relates what was the success of the woman's announcement to her citizens, from which it is evident that the expectation and desire of the promised Messiah had no small vigor among them. Now, the word *believe* is here used inaccurately, and means that they were induced by the woman's statement to acknowledge Christ to be a Prophet. It is, in some respects, a commencement of *faith*, when minds are prepared to receive the doctrine. Such an entrance to *faith* receives here the honorable appellation of *faith*, in order to inform us how highly God esteems reverence for his word, when he confers so great honor on the docility of those who have not yet been taught. Now, their *faith* manifests itself in this respect, that they are seized with a desire to profit, and, for that reason, desire that Christ *should remain with them.*

41. And many more believed

From what followed it is evident that Christ's compliance with their wish was highly proper; for we see how much fruit was reaped from the *two days* which he granted to their request. By this example we are taught that we ought never to refrain from working, when we have it in our power to advance the kingdom of God; and if we are afraid that our readiness in complying may be liable to unfavorable reports, or may often prove to be useless, let us ask from Christ the Spirit of counsel to direct us. The word *believe* is now used in a different sense; for it means not only that they were prepared for *faith*, but that they actually had a proper *faith.*

42. On account of thy speech

Though I have followed Erasmus in rendering this word by *oratio* (*speech*), because *loquela*, which the ancient interpreter uses, is a barbarous term; yet I wish to warn my readers

DAVID BROWN

but alas! they are next to *"none"* [BENGEL]. They were far readier to receive himself, and obliged him to say, I am not the Christ, and he seems pained at this.

33. **hath set to His seal, &c** – gives glory to God whose words Christ speaks, not as prophets and apostles by a partial communication of the Spirit to them.

34. **for God giveth not the Spirit by measure** – Here, again, the sharpest conceivable line of distinction is drawn between Christ and all human-inspired teachers: "They have the Spirit in a *limited* degree; but God giveth not [to Him] the Spirit by *measure*." It means the entire fulness of divine life and divine power. The present tense *"giveth,"* very aptly points out the permanent communication of the Spirit by the Father to the Son, so that a constant flow and reflow of living power is to be understood (Compare John 1: 15) [OLSHAUSEN].

35–36. **The Father loveth, &c** – See on Matt. 11: 27, where we have the *"delivering over* of all things into the hands of the Son,"* while here we have the deep spring of that august act in the Father's ineffable *"love of the Son."*

36. **hath everlasting life** – already has it. (See on John 3: 18 and John 5: 24).

shall not see life – The contrast here is striking: The one has already a life that will endure for ever – the other not only has it not now, but shall never have it – never see it.

abideth on him – It was on Him before, and not being *removed* in the only possible way, by "believing on the Son," it necessarily *remaineth* on him! *Note.* – How flatly does this contradict the teaching of many in our day, that there neither was, nor is, anything *in God* against sinners which needed to be removed by Christ, but only *in men* against God!

JOHN 4

John 4: 1–42

CHRIST AND THE WOMAN OF SAMARIA – THE SAMARITANS OF SYCHAR.

1–4. **the Lord knew** – not by report, but in the sense of John 2: 25, for which reason He is here styled "the Lord."

2. **Jesus baptized not** – John being a servant baptized with his own hand; Christ as the Master, "baptizing with the Holy Ghost," administered the outward symbol only through His disciples.

3. **left Judea** – to avoid persecution, which at that early stage would have marred His work.

departed into Galilee – by which time John had been cast into prison (Mark 1: 14).

4. **must needs go through Samaria** – for a geographical reason, no doubt, as it lay straight in his way, but certainly not without a higher design.

5. **cometh ... to** – that is, as far as: for He remained at some distance from it.

Sychar – the "Shechem" of the Old Testament, about thirty-four miles from Jerusalem, afterwards called "Neapolis," and now "Nablous."

6–8. **wearied ... sat thus** – that is, "as you might fancy a weary man would"; an instance of the graphic style of St. John [WEBSTER and WILKINSON]. In fact, this is perhaps the most *human* of all the scenes of our Lord's earthly history. We seem to be beside Him, overhearing all that is here recorded, nor could any painting of the scene on canvas, however perfect, do other than lower the conception which this exquisite narrative conveys to the devout and intelligent reader. But with all that is *human,* how much also of the *divine* have we here, both blended in one glorious manifestation of the majesty, grace, pity, patience with which "the Lord" imparts light and life to this unlikeliest of strangers, standing midway between Jews and heathens.

the sixth hour – noonday, reckoning from six A.M. From Song 1: 7 we know, as from other sources, that the very flocks "rested at noon." But Jesus, whose maxim was, "I must work the works of Him that sent Me while it is day" (John 9: 4), seems to have denied Himself that repose, at least on this occasion, probably that He might reach this well when He knew the woman would be there. Once there, however, He accepts ... the grateful ease of a seat on the patriarchal stone. But what music is that which I hear from His lips, "Come unto Me, all ye that labor and are heavy laden, and I will give you rest" (Matt. 11: 28).

7. **Give me to drink** – for the heat of a noon-

39 And many of the Samaritans of that city believed on him for the saying of the woman, which testified, He told me all that ever I did.

40 So when the Samaritans were come unto him, they besought him that he would tarry with them: and he abode there two days.

41 And many more believed because of his own word;

42 And said unto the woman, Now we believe, not because of thy saying: for we have heard him ourselves, and know that this is indeed the Christ, the Savior of the world.

43 Now after two days he departed thence, and went into Galilee.

44 For Jesus himself testified, that a prophet hath no honor in his own country.

45 Then when he was come into Galilee, the Galilaeans received him, having seen all the things that he did at Jerusalem at the feast: for they also went unto the feast.

46 So Jesus came again into Cana of Galilee, where he made the water wine. And there was a certain nobleman, whose son was sick at Capernaum.

47 When he heard that Jesus was come out of Judaea into Galilee, he went unto him, and besought him that he would come down, and heal his son: for he was at the point of death.

48 Then said Jesus unto him, Except ye see signs and wonders, ye will not believe.

49 The nobleman saith unto him, Sir, come down ere my child die.

50 Jesus saith unto him, Go thy way; thy son liveth. And the man believed the word that Jesus had spoken unto him, and he went his way.

51 And as he was now going down, his servants met him, and told him, saying, Thy son liveth.

52 Then inquired he of them the hour when he began to amend. And they said unto him, Yesterday at the seventh hour the fever left him.

53 So the father knew that it was at the same hour, in the which Jesus said unto him, Thy son liveth: and himself believed, and his whole house.

54 This is again the second miracle

that the Greek word lalia has the same meaning with the Latin word *loquentia*, that is, *talk*, or *talkativeness*; and the Samaritans appear to boast that they have now a stronger foundation than a woman's tongue, which is, for the most part, light and trivial.

We believe

This expresses more fully the nature of their faith, that it has been drawn from the word of God itself, so that they can boast of having the Son of God as their Teacher; as, indeed, it is on his authority alone that we can safely rely. True, indeed, he is not now visibly present, so as to speak to us mouth to mouth; but, by whomsoever we happen to hear him, our faith cannot rest on any other than on himself. And from no other source proceeds that *knowledge* which is likewise mentioned; for the speech which comes from the mouth of a mortal man may indeed fill and satisfy the ears, but will never confirm the soul in calm confidence of salvation, so that he who has heard may be entitled to boast that he *knows*. In *faith*, therefore, the first thing necessary is, to *know* that it is Christ who speaks by his ministers; and the next is, to give him the honor which is due; that is, not to doubt that he is true and faithful, so that, relying on so undoubted a guarantee, we may rely safely on his doctrine.

53. And he believed, and his whole house

It may appear absurd that the Evangelist should mention this as the commencement of faith in that man, whose faith he has already commended. Nor can it be supposed that the word *believe* – at least in this passage – relates to the progress of faith. But it must be understood that this man, being a Jew and educated in the doctrine of the Law, had already obtained some taste of faith when he came to Christ; and that he afterwards *believed in the saying of Christ* was a particular faith, which extended no farther than to expect the life of his son. But now he began to *believe* in a different manner; that is, because, embracing the doctrine of Christ, he openly professed to be one of his disciples. Thus not only does he now *believe* that his son will be cured through the kindness of Christ, but he acknowledges Christ to be the Son of God, and makes a profession of faith in his Gospel. His whole family joins him, which was an evidence of the miracle; nor can it be doubted that he did his utmost to bring others along with him to embrace the Christian religion.

JOHN 5

14. After these things Jesus found him

These words show still more clearly that, when Christ

day sun had parched His lips. But "in the last, that great day of the feast," Jesus stood and cried, saying, "If any man thirst let him come unto Me and *drink*" (John 7: 37).

9–12. How is it that thou – not altogether refusing, yet wondering at so unusual a request from a Jew, as His dress and dialect would at once discover Him to be, to a Samaritan.

for, &c – It is this national antipathy that gives point to the parable of the good Samaritan (Luke 10: 30–37), and the thankfulness of the Samaritan leper (Luke 17: 16,18).

10. If thou knewest, &c – that is, "In Me thou seest only a petitioner to thee but if thou knewest who that Petitioner is, and the Gift that God is giving to men, thou wouldst have changed places with Him, gladly suing of Him living water – nor shouldst thou have sued in vain" (gently reflecting on her for not immediately meeting His request).

12. Art thou greater, &c. – already perceiving in this Stranger a claim to some mysterious greatness.

our father Jacob – for when it went well with the Jews, they claimed kindred with them, as being descended from Joseph; but when misfortunes befell the Jews, they disowned all connection with them [JOSEPHUS, *Antiquities*, 9.14,3].

13–14. thirst again ... never thirst, &c – The contrast here is fundamental and all comprehensive. "This water" plainly means "this natural water and *all satisfactions of a like earthly and perishable nature.*" Coming to us *from without*, and reaching only the *superficial* parts of our nature, they are soon spent, and need to be anew supplied as much as if we had never experienced them before, while the deeper wants of our being are not reached by them at all; whereas the "water" that Christ gives – *spiritual life* – is struck out of the very depths of our being, making the soul not a *cistern*, for holding water *poured into* it *from without*, but a *fountain* (the word had been better so rendered, to distinguish it from the word rendered "well" in John 4: 11), springing, gushing, bubbling up and flowing forth *within* us, ever fresh, ever living. *The indwelling of the Holy Ghost as the Spirit of Christ* is the secret of this life with all its enduring energies and sat-

isfactions, as is expressly said (John 7: 37–39). "Never thirsting," then, means simply that such souls have the supplies *at home*.

into everlasting life – carrying the thoughts up from the eternal freshness and vitality of these waters to the great ocean in which they have their confluence. "Thither may I arrive!" [BENGEL].

15–18. give me this water, &c – This is not obtuseness – that is giving way – it expresses a wondering desire after she scarce knew what from this mysterious Stranger.

16. call thy husband – now proceeding to arouse her slumbering conscience by laying bare the guilty life she was leading, and by the minute details which that life furnished, not only bringing her sin vividly up before her, but preparing her to receive in His true character that wonderful Stranger to whom her whole life, in its minutest particulars, evidently lay open.

19–20. Sir, I perceive, &c – Seeing herself all revealed, does she now break down and ask what hopes there might be for one so guilty? Nay, her convictions have not reached that point yet. She ingeniously shifts the subject from a personal to a public question. It is not, "Alas, what a wicked life am I leading!" but "Lo, what a wonderful prophet I got into conversation with! He will be able to settle that interminable dispute between us and the Jews. Sir, you must know all about such matters – our fathers hold to this mountain here," pointing to *Gerizim* in Samaria, "as the divinely consecrated place of worship, but ye Jews say that *Jerusalem* is the proper place – which of us is right?" How slowly does the human heart submit to *thorough* humiliation! (Compare the *prodigal*; see on Luke 15: 15). Doubtless our Lord saw through the fetch; but does He say, "That question is not the point just now, but have you been living in the way described, yea or nay? Till this is disposed of I cannot be drawn into theological controversies." The Prince of preachers takes another method: He humors the poor woman, letting her take her own way, allowing her to lead while He follows – but thus only the more effectually gaining His object. He answers her question, pours light into her mind on the *spirituality* of all true worship, as of its glorious Object, and so

that Jesus did, when he was come out of Judaea into Galilee.

JOHN 5

1 After this there was a feast of the Jews; and Jesus went up to Jerusalem.

2 Now there is at Jerusalem by the sheep market a pool, which is called in the Hebrew tongue Bethesda, having five porches.

3 In these lay a great multitude of impotent folk, of blind, halt, withered, waiting for the moving of the water.

4 For an angel went down at a certain season into the pool, and troubled the water: whosoever then first after the troubling of the water stepped in was made whole of whatsoever disease he had.

5 And a certain man was there, which had an infirmity thirty and eight years.

6 When Jesus saw him lie, and knew that he had been now a long time in that case, he saith unto him, Wilt thou be made whole?

7 The impotent man answered him, Sir, I have no man, when the water is troubled, to put me into the pool: but while I am coming, another steppeth down before me.

8 Jesus saith unto him, Rise, take up thy bed, and walk.

9 And immediately the man was made whole, and took up his bed, and walked: and on the same day was the sabbath.

10 The Jews therefore said unto him that was cured, It is the sabbath day: it is not lawful for thee to carry thy bed.

11 He answered them, He that made me whole, the same said unto me, Take up thy bed, and walk.

12 Then asked they him, What man is that which said unto thee, Take up thy bed, and walk?

13 And he that was healed wist not who it was: for Jesus had conveyed himself away, a multitude being in that place.

14 Afterward Jesus findeth him in the temple, and said unto him, Behold, thou art made whole: sin no more, lest a worse thing come unto thee.

15 The man departed, and told the Jews that it was Jesus, which had made him whole.

16 And therefore did the Jews per-

concealed himself for a time, it was not in order that the remembrance of the kindness which he had conferred might perish, for he now appears in public of his own accord; only he intended that the work should first be known, and that he should afterwards be declared to be the Author of it. This passage contains a highly useful doctrine; for when Christ says, *lo, thou art made whole,* his meaning is, that we make an improper use of the gifts of God, if we are not excited to gratitude. Christ does not reproach the man with what he had given him, but only reminds him that he had been cured in order that, remembering the favor which he had received, he might all his life serve God his Deliverer. Thus, as God by stripes instructs and spurs us on to repentance, so he invites us to it by his goodness and forbearance; and, indeed, it is the universal design both of our redemption and of all the gifts of God, to keep us entirely devoted to Him. Now this cannot be done, unless the remembrance of the past punishment remain impressed on the mind, and unless he who has obtained pardon be employed in this meditation throughout his whole life.

This admonition teaches us also, that all the evils which we endure ought to be imputed to our sins; for the afflictions of men are not accidental, but are so many stripes for our chastisement. First, then, we ought to acknowledge the hand of God which strikes us, and not to imagine that our distresses arise from a blind impetuosity of fortune; and next we ascribe this honor to God, that, since He is a Father full of goodness, He does not take pleasure in our sufferings, and therefore does not treat us more harshly than he has been offended by our sins. When he charges him, *sin no more,* he does not enjoin him to be free from all sin, but speaks comparatively as to his former life; for Christ exhorts him henceforth to repent, and not to do as he had done before.

18. For this reason, therefore, the Jews sought the more to slay him

This defense was so far from allaying their fury that it even enraged them the more. Nor was he unacquainted with their malignity and wickedness and hardened obstinacy, but he intended first to profit a few of his disciples who were then present, and next to make a public display of their incurable malice. By his example he has taught us that we ought never to yield to the fury of wicked men, but should endeavor to maintain the truth of God, so far as necessity demands it, though the whole world should oppose and murmur. Nor is there any reason why the servants of Christ should take it ill that they do not profit all men according to their wish, since Christ himself did not always succeed; and we need not wonder if, in proportion as the glory of God is

brings her insensibly to the point at which He could disclose to her wondering mind whom she was all the while speaking to.

21–24. Woman, &c – Here are three weighty pieces of information: (1) The point raised will very soon cease to be of any moment, for a total change of dispensation is about to come over the Church. (2) The Samaritans are wrong, not only as to the *place,* but the whole *grounds* and *nature* of their worship, while in all these respects the truth lies with the Jews. (3) As God is a *Spirit,* so He both *invites* and *demands* a *spiritual worship,* and already all is in preparation for a *spiritual economy,* more in harmony with the true nature of acceptable service than the ceremonial worship by consecrated *persons, place,* and *times,* which God for a time has seen meet to keep up till fulness of the time should come.

neither in this mountain nor yet at Jerusalem – that is, *exclusively* (Mal. 1: 11; 1 Tim. 2: 8).

worship the Father – She had talked simply of "worship"; our Lord brings up before her the great OBJECT of all acceptable worship – "THE FATHER."

22. Ye worship ye know not what – without any *revealed authority,* and so very much in the dark. In this sense, the Jews *knew what they were about.* But the most glorious thing here is the reason assigned,

for salvation is of the Jews – intimating to her that *Salvation* was not a thing left to be reached by any one who might vaguely desire it of a God of mercy, but something that had been *revealed, prepared, deposited with a particular people,* and must be sought *in connection with, and as issuing from them*; and that people, "the Jews."

23. hour cometh, and now is – evidently meaning her to understand that this new economy was in some sense being set up while He was talking to her, a sense which would in a few minutes so far appear, when He told her plainly He was *the Christ.*

25–26. I know Messias cometh … when He is come, &c – If we take our Lord's immediate disclosure of Himself, in answer to this, as the proper key to its meaning to *His ear,* we can hardly doubt that the woman was already *all*

but prepared for even this startling announcement, which indeed she seems (from John 4: 29) to have already begun to suspect by His revealing her to herself. Thus quickly, under so matchless a Teacher, was she brought up from her sunken condition to a frame of mind and heart capable of the noblest revelations.

tell us all things – an expectation founded probably on Deut. 18: 15.

26. I that speak … am he – He scarce ever said anything like this to His own people, the Jews. He had magnified them to the woman, and yet to themselves He is to the last far more reserved than to her – *proving* rather than plainly *telling* them He was the Christ. But what would not have been *safe* among them was safe enough with her, whose *simplicity* at this stage of the conversation appears from the sequel to have become perfect. What now will the woman say? We listen, the scene has changed, a new party arrives, the disciples have been to Sychar, at some distance, to buy bread, and on their return are astonished at the company their Lord has been holding in their absence.

27. marvelled that he talked with the woman – It never probably occurred to them to marvel that He talked with *themselves*; yet in His eye, as the sequel shows, He was quite as nobly employed. How poor, if not false, are many of our most plausible estimates!

no man said … What? … Why? – awed by the spectacle, and thinking there must be something under it.

28–30. left her water-pot – How exquisitely natural! The presence of strangers made her feel that it was time for her to withdraw, and He who knew what was in her heart, and what she was going to the city to do, let her go without exchanging a word with her in the hearing of others. Their interview was too sacred, and the effect on the woman too overpowering (not to speak of His own deep emotion) to allow of its being continued. But this one artless touch – that she "left her water-pot" – speaks volumes. The living water was already beginning to spring up within her; she found that man doth not live by bread nor by water only, and that there was a water of wondrous virtue that raised people above meat and drink, and the vessels that held them, and all

secute Jesus, and sought to slay him, because he had done these things on the sabbath day.

17 But Jesus answered them, My Father worketh hitherto, and I work.

18 Therefore the Jews sought the more to kill him, because he not only had broken the sabbath, but said also that God was his Father, making himself equal with God.

19 Then answered Jesus and said unto them, Verily, verily, I say unto you, The Son can do nothing of himself, but what he seeth the Father do: for what things soever he doeth, these also doeth the Son likewise.

20 For the Father loveth the Son, and sheweth him all things that himself doeth: and he will shew him greater works than these, that ye may marvel.

21 For as the Father raiseth up the dead, and quickeneth them; even so the Son quickeneth whom he will.

22 For the Father judgeth no man, but hath committed all judgment unto the Son:

23 That all men should honor the Son, even as they honor the Father. He that honored not the Son honored not the Father which hath sent him.

24 Verily, verily, I say unto you, He that heareth my word, and believeth on him that sent me, hath everlasting life, and shall not come into condemnation; but is passed from death unto life.

25 Verily, verily, I say unto you, The hour is coming, and now is, when the dead shall hear the voice of the Son of God: and they that hear shall live.

26 For as the Father hath life in himself; so hath he given to the Son to have life in himself;

27 And hath given him authority to execute judgment also, because he is the Son of man.

28 Marvel not at this: for the hour is coming, in the which all that are in the graves shall hear his voice,

29 And shall come forth; they that have done good, unto the resurrection of life; and they that have done evil, unto the resurrection of damnation.

30 I can of mine own self do nothing: as I hear, I judge: and my judgment is just; because I seek not mine own will, but the

more fully displayed, Satan rages the more violently in his members and instruments.

Because he not only had broken the Sabbath

When the Evangelist says that the Jews were hostile to Christ, *because he had broken the Sabbath* , he speaks according to the opinion which they had formed; for I have already showed that the state of the case was quite the contrary. The principal cause of their wrath was, that *he called God his Father.*

20. For the Father loveth the Son

Every body sees how harsh and far-fetched is the exposition of this passage which is given by the Fathers. "God," they say, "loves himself in the Son." But this statement applies beautifully to Christ as clothed with flesh, that he is beloved by the Father. What is more, we know that it is by this excellent title that he is distinguished both from angels and from men, *This is my beloved Son* (Matthew 3: 17). For we know that Christ was chosen, that the whole love of God might dwell in him, and might flow from him to us as from a full fountain. Christ is loved by the Father, as he is the Head of the Church. He shows that this love is the cause why the Father does all things by his hand. For when he says that the Father SHOWTH *to him* this word must be understood to denote communication, as if he had said, "As the Father hath given to me his heart, so he hath poured out his power on me, that the Divine glory may shine in my works, and – what is more – that men may seek nothing Divine but what they find in me." And, indeed, out of Christ it will be in vain to seek the power of God.

30. I can do nothing of myself

It would be superfluous here to enter into abstruse reasonings, whether the Son of God *can do any thing of himself* or otherwise, so far as relates to his eternal Divinity; for he did not intend to keep our minds employed about such trifles. Consequently there was no reason why the ancients should have given themselves so much anxiety and distress about refuting the calumny of Arius. That scoundrel gave out that the Son is not equal to the Father because *he can do nothing of himself* The holy men reply, that the Son justly claims for himself all that can be ascribed to the Father, from whom he takes his commencement. with respect to his person. But, in the first place, Christ does not speak of his Divinity simply, but warns us that, so far as he is clothed with our flesh, we ought not to judge of him from the outward appearance, because he has something higher than man. Again, we ought to consider with whom he has to deal. His intention was, to refute the Jews who were endeavoring to contrast him with God. He therefore affirms that he does

human things. In short, she was transported, forgot everything but One, and her heart running over with the tale she had to tell, she hastens home and pours it out.

29. is not this the Christ – The *form* of the question (in the *Greek*) is a distant, modest way of only half *insinuating* what it seemed hardly fitting for her to *affirm*; nor does she refer to what He said of Himself, but solely to His disclosure to her of the particulars of her own life.

30. Then they went out, &c – How different from the Jews! and richly was their openness to conviction rewarded.

31–38. meantime – that is, while the woman was away.

Master, eat – *Fatigue* and *thirst* we saw He felt; here is revealed another of our common infirmities to which the Lord was subject – *hunger*.

32. meat ye know not of – What spirituality of mind! "I *have* been eating all the while, and such food as ye dream not of." What can that be? they ask each other; have any supplies been brought Him in our absence? He knows what they are saying though He hears it not.

34. My meat is, &c – "A Servant here to fulfil a prescribed work, to *do* and to *finish,* that is 'meat' to Me; and of this, while you were away, I have had My fill." And of what does He speak thus? Of the condescension, pity, patience, wisdom He had been laying out upon *one soul* – a very humble woman, and in some respects repulsive too! But He had gained her, and through her was going to gain more, and lay perhaps the foundations of a great work in the country of Samaria; and this filled His whole soul and raised Him above the sense of natural hunger (Matt. 4: 4).

35. yet four months, and then harvest – that is, "In current speech, ye say thus at this season; but lift up your eyes and look upon those fields in the light of *another* husbandry, for lo! *in that sense,* they are even now white to harvest, ready for the sickle." The simple beauty of this language is only surpassed by the glow of holy emotion in the Redeemer's own soul which it expresses. It refers to the *ripeness* of these Sycharites for accession to

Him, and the joy of this great Lord of the reapers over the anticipated ingathering. Oh, could we but *so,* "lift up our eyes and look" upon many fields abroad and at home, which to dull sense appear unpromising, as *He* beheld those of Samaria, what movements, as yet scarce in embryo, and accessions to Christ, as yet seemingly far distant, might we not discern as quite near at hand, and thus, amidst difficulties and discouragements too much for nature to sustain, be cheered – *as our Lord Himself was* in circumstances far more overwhelming – with "songs in the night!"

36. he that reapeth, &c – As our Lord could not mean that the reaper only, and not the sower, received "wages," in the sense of *personal reward* for his work, the "wages" here can be no other than the joy of having such a harvest to gather in – the joy of "gathering fruit unto life eternal."

rejoice together – The blessed issue of the whole ingathering is the interest alike of the sower as of the reaper; it is no more the fruit of the last operation than of the first; and just as there can be no reaping without previous sowing, so have those servants of Christ, to whom is assigned the pleasant task of merely reaping the spiritual harvest, no work to do, and no joy to taste, that has not been prepared to their hand by the toilsome and often thankless work of their predecessors in the field. *The joy, therefore, of the great harvest festivity will be the common joy of all who have taken any part in the work from the first operation to the last.* (See Deut. 16: 11,14; Ps. 126: 6; Is. 9: 3). What encouragement is here for those "fishers of men" who "have toiled all the night" of their official life, and, to human appearance, "have taken nothing!"

38. I sent you, &c – The *I* is emphatic – I, the Lord of the whole harvest: "sent you," points to their *past* appointment to the apostleship, though it has reference only to their *future* discharge of it, for they had nothing to do with the present ingathering of the Sycharites.

ye bestowed no labour – meaning that much of their future success would arise from the *preparation already made* for them. (See on John 4: 42).

others laboured – Referring to the Old Testament laborers, the Baptist, and *by impli-*

will of the Father which hath sent me.

31 If I bear witness of myself, my witness is not true.

32 There is another that beareth witness of me; and I know that the witness which he witnesseth of me is true.

33 Ye sent unto John, and he bare witness unto the truth.

34 But I receive not testimony from man: but these things I say, that ye might be saved.

35 He was a burning and a shining light: and ye were willing for a season to rejoice in his light.

36 But I have greater witness than that of John: for the works which the Father hath given me to finish, the same works that I do, bear witness of me, that the Father hath sent me.

37 And the Father himself, which hath sent me, hath borne witness of me. Ye have neither heard his voice at any time, nor seen his shape.

38 And ye have not his word abiding in you: for whom he hath sent, him ye believe not.

39 Search the scriptures; for in them ye think ye have eternal life: and they are they which testify of me.

40 And ye will not come to me, that ye might have life.

41 I receive not honor from men.

42 But I know you, that ye have not the love of God in you.

43 I am come in my Father's name, and ye receive me not: if another shall come in his own name, him ye will receive.

44 How can ye believe, which receive honor one of another, and seek not the honor that cometh from God only?

45 Do not think that I will accuse you to the Father: there is one that accuseth you, even Moses, in whom ye trust.

46 For had ye believed Moses, ye would have believed me: for he wrote of me.

47 But if ye believe not his writings, how shall ye believe my words?

JOHN 6

1 After these things Jesus went over the sea of Galilee, which is the sea of Tiberias.

2 And a great multitude followed him,

nothing by human power, because he has for his guide and director God who dwells in him.

40. And you will not come to me

He again reproaches them that it is nothing but their own malice that hinders them from becoming partakers of the life offered in the Scriptures; for when he says that they *will not* , he imputes the cause of their ignorance and blindness to wickedness and obstinacy. And, indeed, since he offered himself to them so graciously, they must have been willfully blind; but when they intentionally fled from the light, and even desired to extinguish the sun by the darkness of their unbelief, Christ justly reproves them with greater severity.

41. I receive not glory from men

He proceeds in his reproof; but that he may not be suspected of pleading his own cause, he begins by saying that he does not care for *the glory of men*, and that it gives him no concern or uneasiness to see himself despised; and, indeed, he is too great to depend on the opinions of men, for the malignity of the whole world can take nothing from him, or make the slightest infringement on his high rank. He is so eager to refute their calumny that he exalts himself above men. Afterwards, he enters freely into invectives against them, and charges them with contempt and hatred of God. And though, in regard to honorable rank, there is an immense distance between Christ and us, still we ought boldly to despise the opinions of men. We ought, at least, to guard most zealously against being excited to anger, when we are, despised; but, on the contrary, let us learn never to kindle into indignation, except when men do not render to God the honor due to Him. Let our souls be burned and tortured by this holy jealousy, whenever we see that the world is so ungrateful as to reject God.

JOHN 6

10. Make the men sit down

That the disciples were not sooner prepared to cherish the hope which their Master held out, and did not remember to ascribe to his power all that was proper, was a degree of stupidity worthy of blame; but no small praise is due to their cheerful obedience in now complying with his injunction, though they know not what is his intention, or what advantage they will derive from what they are doing. The same readiness to obey is manifested by the people; for, while they are uncertain about the result, they all sit down as soon as a single word of command has been pronounced. And this is the trial of true faith, when God commands men to walk, as it were, in darkness. For this purpose let us learn not to be wise in ourselves, but, amidst

DAVID BROWN

cation Himself, though He studiously keeps this in the background, *that the line of distinction between Himself and all His servants might not be lost sight of.* "Christ represents Himself as the Husbandman [rather the Lord of the laborers], who has the direction both of the sowing and of the harvest, who commissions *all* the agents – those of the Old Testament as well as of the New – and therefore does not stand on a level with either the sowers or the reapers" [OLSHAUSEN].

39–42. many … believed, &c. – The truth of John 4: 35 begins to appear. These Samaritans were the foundation of the Church afterwards built up there. No miracle appears to have been wrought there (but unparalleled supernatural knowledge displayed): "*we have heard Him ourselves*" (John 4: 42) sufficed to raise their faith to a point never attained by the Jews, and hardly as yet by the disciples – that He was "the Saviour of *the world*" [ALFORD]. "This incident is further remarkable as a rare instance of the Lord's ministry producing *an awakening on a large scale*" [OLSHAUSEN].

40. abode two days – Two precious days, surely, to the Redeemer Himself! Unsought, He had come to His own, yet His own received Him not: now those who were not His own had come to Him, been won by Him, and invited Him to their town that others might share with them in the benefit of His wonderful ministry. Here, then, would He solace His already wounded spirit and have in this outfield village triumph of His grace, a sublime foretaste of the inbringing of the whole Gentile world into the Church.

John 4: 43–54

SECOND GALILEAN MIRACLE – HEALING OF THE COURTIER'S SON.

43–44. after two days – literally, the two days of His stay at Sychar.

44. For Jesus testified, &c – This verse had occasioned much discussion. For it seems strange, if "His own country" here means *Nazareth*, which was in Galilee, that it should be said He came to Galilee *because* in one of its towns He expected no good reception. But all will be simple and natural if we fill up the statement thus: "He went into the region of

Galilee, but not, as might have been expected, to that part of it called 'His own country,' Nazareth (see Mark 6: 4; Luke 4: 24), *for* He acted on the maxim which He oft repeated, that 'a prophet,'" &c.

45. received – welcomed Him.

having seen … at the feast – proud, perhaps, of their Countryman's wonderful works at Jerusalem, and possibly won by this circumstance to regard His claims as at least worthy of respectful investigation. Even this our Lord did not despise, for saving conversion often begins in less than this (so Zaccheus, Luke 19: 3–10).

for they also went – that is, it was their practice to go up to the feast.

46–47. nobleman – courtier, king's servant, or one connected with a royal household; such as Chuza (Luke 8: 3), or Manaen (Acts 13: 1).

heard that Jesus was come out of Judea – "where he had doubtless seen or heard what things Jesus had done at Jerusalem" (John 4: 45), [BENGEL].

come down – for Capernaum was down on the northwest shore of the Sea of Galilee.

48–54. Except ye see signs, &c – He *did* believe, both as his coming and his urgent entreaty show; but how imperfectly we shall see; and our Lord would deepen his faith by such a blunt and seemingly rough answer as He made to Nicodemus.

49. come down ere my child die – "While we talk, the case is at its crisis, and if Thou come not instantly, all is over." This was faith, but partial, and our Lord would perfect it. The man cannot believe the cure could be wrought without the Physician coming to the patient – the thought of such a thing evidently never occurred to him. But Jesus will in a moment bring him up to this.

50. Go thy way; thy son liveth – Both effects instantaneously followed: "The man believed the word," and the cure, shooting quicker than lightning from Cana to Capernaum, was felt by the dying youth. In token of faith, the father takes his leave of Christ – in the circumstances this evidenced full faith. The servants hasten to convey the joyful tidings to the anxious parents, whose faith now only wants one confirmation. "*When* began he to amend?

because they saw his miracles which he did on them that were diseased.

3 And Jesus went up into a mountain, and there he sat with his disciples.

4 And the passover, a feast of the Jews, was nigh.

5 When Jesus then lifted up his eyes, and saw a great company come unto him, he saith unto Philip, Whence shall we buy bread, that these may eat?

6 And this he said to prove him: for he himself knew what he would do.

7 Philip answered him, Two hundred pennyworth of bread is not sufficient for them, that every one of them may take a little.

8 One of his disciples, Andrew, Simon Peter's brother, saith unto him,

9 There is a lad here, which hath five barley loaves, and two small fishes: but what are they among so many?

10 And Jesus said, Make the men sit down. Now there was much grass in the place. So the men sat down, in number about five thousand.

11 And Jesus took the loaves; and when he had given thanks, he distributed to the disciples, and the disciples to them that were set down; and likewise of the fishes as much as they would.

12 When they were filled, he said unto his disciples, Gather up the fragments that remain, that nothing be lost.

13 Therefore they gathered them together, and filled twelve baskets with the fragments of the five barley loaves, which remained over and above unto them that had eaten.

14 Then those men, when they had seen the miracle that Jesus did, said, This is of a truth that prophet that should come into the world.

15 When Jesus therefore perceived that they would come and take him by force, to make him a king, he departed again into a mountain himself alone.

16 And when even was now come, his disciples went down unto the sea,

17 And entered into a ship, and went over the sea toward Capernaum. And it was now dark, and Jesus was not come to them.

18 And the sea arose by reason of a great wind that blew.

19 So when they had rowed about five

great confusion, still to hope for a prosperous issue, when we follow the guidance of God, who never disappoints his own people.

11. After having given thanks

Christ has oftener than once instructed us by his example that, whenever we take food, we ought to begin with prayer. For those things which God has appointed for our use, being evidences of his infinite goodness and fatherly love towards us, call on us to offer praise to Him; and *thanksgiving*, as Paul informs us, is a kind of solemn *sanctification*, by means of which the use of them begins to be pure to us, (1 Timothy 4: 4.) Hence it follows, that they who swallow them down without thinking of God, are guilty of sacrilege, and of profaning the gifts of God. And this instruction is the more worthy of attention, because we daily see a great part of the world feeding themselves like brute beasts. When Christ determined that the bread given to the disciples should grow among their hands, we are taught by it that God blesses our labor when we are serviceable to each other.

Let us now sum up the meaning of the whole miracle. It has this in common with the other miracles, that Christ displayed in it his Divine power in union with beneficence, It is also a confirmation to us of that statement by which he exhorts us to *seek the kingdom of God*, promising that *all other things shall be added to us* (Matthew 6: 33). For if he took care of those who were led to him only by a sudden impulse, how would he desert us, if we seek him with a firm and steady purpose? True, indeed, he will sometimes allow his own people, as I have said, to suffer hunger; but he will never deprive them of his aid; and, in the meantime, he has very good reasons for not assisting us till matters come to an extremity.

27. Labor for food, not that which perisheth

He shows to what object our desires ought to be directed, namely, to eternal life; but because, in proportion as our understandings are gross, we are always devoted to earthly things, for this reason he corrects that disease which is natural to us, before he points out what we ought to do. The simple doctrine would have been, "Labor to have the incorruptible food;" but, knowing that the senses of men are held bound by earthly cares, he first enjoins them to be loosed and freed from those cords, that they may rise to heaven. Not that he forbids his followers to labor that they may procure daily food; but he shows that the heavenly life ought to be preferred to this earthly life, because the godly have no other reason for living here than that, being sojourners in the world, they may travel rapidly towards

... Yesterday, at the seventh hour, the fever left him" – the very hour in which was uttered that great word, "Thy son liveth!" So "himself believed and his whole house." He *had* believed before this, first very imperfectly; then with assured confidence of Christ's word; but now with a faith crowned by "sight." And the wave rolled from the head to the members of his household. "To-day is salvation come to this *house*" (Luke 19: 9); and no mean house this!

second miracle Jesus did – that is, in Cana; done "after He came out of Judea," as the former before.

JOHN 5

John 5: 1–47

The Impotent Man Healed – Discourse Occasioned by the Persecution Arising Thereupon.

1. a feast of the Jews – *What feast?* No question has more divided the Harmonists of the Gospels, and the duration of our Lord's ministry may be said to hinge on it. For if, as the majority have thought (until of late years) it was a *Passover*, His ministry lasted three and a half years; if not, probably a year less. Those who are dissatisfied with the Passover-view all differ among themselves what other feast it was, and some of the most acute think there are no grounds for deciding. In our judgment the evidence is in favor of its being a *Passover*, but the reasons cannot be stated here.

2–3. sheep *market* – The supplement should be (as in *Margin*) "sheep [gate]," mentioned in Neh. 3: 1, 32.

Bethesda – that is, "house (place) of mercy," from the cures wrought there.

five porches – for shelter to the patients.

3. impotent – infirm.

4. an angel, &c – This miracle differed in two points from all other miracles recorded in Scripture: (1) It was not one, but a succession of miracles periodically wrought: (2) As it was only wrought "when the waters were troubled," so only upon one patient at a time, and that the patient "who first stepped in after the troubling of the waters." But this only the more undeniably fixed its miraculous character. We have heard of many waters having a medicinal virtue; but what water was ever known to cure *instantaneously* a single disease? And who ever heard of any water curing all, even the most diverse diseases – "blind, halt, withered" – alike? Above all, who ever heard of such a thing being done "only at a certain season," and most singularly of all, doing it only to the first person who stepped in after the moving of the waters? Any of these peculiarities – much more all taken together – must have proclaimed the supernatural character of the cures wrought. (If the text here be genuine, there can be no doubt of the miracle, as there were multitudes living when this Gospel was published who, from their own knowledge of Jerusalem, could have exposed the falsehood of the Evangelist, if no such cure had been known there. The want of John 5: 4 and part of John 5: 3 in some good manuscripts, and the use of some unusual words in the passage, are more easily accounted for than the evidence in their favor if they were not originally in the text. Indeed John 5: 7 is unintelligible without John 5: 4. The *internal* evidence brought against it is merely the *unlikelihood* of such a miracle – a principle which will carry us a great deal farther if we allow it to weigh against positive evidence).

5–9. thirty and eight years – but not all that time at the pool. This was probably the most pitiable of all the cases, and *therefore selected*.

6. saw him lie, and knew, &c – As He doubtless visited the spot just to perform this cure, so He knows where to find His patient, and the whole previous history of his case (John 2: 25).

Wilt thou be made whole? – Could anyone doubt that a sick man would like to be made whole, or that the patients came thither, and this man had returned again and again, just in hope of a cure? But our Lord asked the question. (1) To fasten attention upon Himself; (2) By making him detail his case to deepen in him the feeling of entire helplessness; (3) By so singular a question to beget in his desponding heart the hope of a cure. (Compare Mark 10: 51).

7. Sir, I have no man, &c – Instead of *saying* he wished to be cured, he just tells with piteous simplicity how fruitless had been all his efforts to obtain it, and how *helpless* and all

and twenty or thirty furlongs, they see Jesus walking on the sea, and drawing nigh unto the ship: and they were afraid.

20 But he saith unto them, It is I; be not afraid.

21 Then they willingly received him into the ship: and immediately the ship was at the land whither they went.

22 The day following, when the people which stood on the other side of the sea saw that there was none other boat there, save that one whereinto his disciples were entered, and that Jesus went not with his disciples into the boat, but that his disciples were gone away alone;

23 (Howbeit there came other boats from Tiberias nigh unto the place where they did eat bread, after that the Lord had given thanks:)

24 When the people therefore saw that Jesus was not there, neither his disciples, they also took shipping, and came to Capernaum, seeking for Jesus.

25 And when they had found him on the other side of the sea, they said unto him, Rabbi, when camest thou hither?

26 Jesus answered them and said, Verily, verily, I say unto you, Ye seek me, not because ye saw the miracles, but because ye did eat of the loaves, and were filled.

27 Labour not for the meat which perisheth, but for that meat which endureth unto everlasting life, which the Son of man shall give unto you: for him hath God the Father sealed.

28 Then said they unto him, What shall we do, that we might work the works of God?

29 Jesus answered and said unto them, This is the work of God, that ye believe on him whom he hath sent.

30 They said therefore unto him, What sign shewest thou then, that we may see, and believe thee? what dost thou work?

31 Our fathers did eat manna in the desert; as it is written, He gave them bread from heaven to eat.

32 Then Jesus said unto them, Verily, verily, I say unto you, Moses gave you not that bread from heaven; but my Father giveth you the true bread from heaven.

33 For the bread of God is he which cometh down from heaven, and giveth life unto the world.

their heavenly country.

Next, we ought to see what is the present question; for, since the power of Christ is debased by those who are devoted to the belly and to earthly things, he argues what we ought to seek in him, and why we ought to seek it. He employs metaphors adapted to the circumstances in which his sermon was delivered. If food had not been mentioned, he would have said, without a figure, "You ought to lay aside anxiety about the world, and strive to obtain the heavenly life." But as those men were running to their fodder like cattle, without looking to anything better, Christ presents his sermon in a metaphorical dress, and gives the name of *food* to everything that belongs to newness of life. We know that our souls are fed by the doctrine of the gospel, when it is efficacious in us by the power of the Spirit; and, therefore, as faith is the life of the soul, all that nourishes and promotes faith is compared to *food which endureth to eternal life.*

This kind of food he calls incorruptible, and says that it *endureth to eternal life*, in order to inform us that our souls are not fed for a day, but are nourished in the expectation of a blessed immortality; because the Lord commences the work of our salvation, that he may perform it till the day of Christ (Philippians 1: 6).

For this reason we must receive the gifts of the Spirit, that they may be earnests and pledges of eternal life. For, though the reprobate, after having tasted this food, frequently reject it, so that it is not permanent in them, yet believing souls feel that enduring power, when they are made partakers of the power of the Holy Spirit in his gifts, which is not of short duration, but, on the contrary, never fails. It is a frivolous exercise of ingenuity to infer, as some do, from the word [?text missing?]

30. What sign doest thou?

This wickedness abundantly proves how truly it is said elsewhere, *This wicked generation seeketh a sign* (Matthew 12: 39). They had been at first drawn to Christ by the admiration of his miracles or *signs*, and afterwards, through amazement at a new *sign*, they acknowledged Christ to be the Messiah, and, with that conviction, *wished to make him a king*; but now they demand *a sign* from him, as if he were a man unknown to them. Whence came such sudden forgetfulness, but because they are ungrateful to God, and, through their own malice, are blind to his power, which is before their eyes? Nor can it be doubted that they treat disdainfully all the miracles which they had already beheld, because Christ does not comply with their wishes, and because they do not find him to be what they imagined him to be. If he had given them expectation of earthly happiness, he would have been highly applauded by them; they

but *hopeless* he was. Yet not quite. For here he is at the pool, waiting on. It seemed of no use; nay, only tantalizing, **while I am coming, another steppeth down before me** – the fruit was snatched from his lips. Yet he will not go away. He may get nothing by staying, he may drop into his grave ere he get into the pool; but by going from the appointed, divine way of healing, he can get nothing. Wait therefore he will, wait he does, and when Christ comes to heal him, lo! he is waiting his turn. *What an attitude for a sinner at Mercy's gate!* The man's hopes seemed low enough ere Christ came to him. He might have said, just before "Jesus passed by that way," "This is no use; I shall never get in; let me die at home." Then all had been lost. But he *held on,* and his perseverance was rewarded with a glorious cure. Probably some rays of hope darted into his heart as he told his tale before those Eyes whose glance measured his whole case. But the word of command consummates his preparation to receive the cure, and instantaneously works it.

8. Rise, take up thy bed, &c – "Immediately" he did so. "He *spake* and it was *done.*" The slinging of his portable couch over his shoulders was designed to show the perfection of the cure.

9. the same day was the sabbath – Beyond all doubt this was intentional, as in so many other healings, in order that when opposition arose on this account men might be compelled to listen to His claims and His teaching.

10–16. The Jews – that is, *those in authority.* (See on John 1: 19.)

it is not lawful to carry thy bed – a glorious testimony to the cure, as *instantaneous* and *complete,* from the lips of the most prejudiced! (And what a contrast does it, as all our Lord's miracles, present to the bungling miracles of the Church of Rome!) In *ordinary* circumstances, the rulers had the law on their side (Neh. 13: 15; Jer. 17: 21). But when the man referred them to "Him that had made him whole" (John 5: 11) as his authority, the argument was resistless. Yet they ingeniously parried the thrust, asking him, not who had "made him whole" – that would have condemned themselves and defeated their purpose – but who had bidden him "take up his

bed and walk," in other words, who had dared to order a breach of the sabbath? It is time we were looking after Him – thus hoping to shake the man's faith in his Healer.

13. he that was healed wist not, &c – That some one, with unparalleled generosity, tenderness and power, had done it, the man knew well enough: but as he had never heard of Him before, so he disappeared too quickly for any inquiries.

conveyed himself away – slipped out of the crowd that had gathered, to avoid both hasty popularity and precipitate hatred (Matt. 12: 14–19).

14. findeth him in the temple – saying, perhaps, "I will go into Thy house with burnt offerings, I will pay my vows which my lips have uttered and my mouth hath spoken when I was in trouble" (Ps. 66: 13, 14). Jesus, there Himself for His own ends, "findeth him there" – *not all accidentally,* be assured.

sin no more, &c – a glimpse this of the reckless life he had probably led *before* his thirty-eight years' infirmity had come upon him, and which not improbably had brought on, in the just judgment of God, his chronic complaint. Fearful illustration this of "the severity of God," but glorious manifestation of our Lord's insight into "what was in man."

15. The man departed, and told, &c – little thinking how unwelcome his grateful and eager testimony would be. "The darkness received not the light which was pouring its rays upon it" (John 1: 5,11) [OLSHAUSEN].

16. because he had done these things on the sabbath day – What to these hypocritical religionists was the doing of the most glorious and beneficent miracles, compared with the atrocity of doing them on the sabbath day! Having given them this handle, on purpose to raise the first public controversy with them, and thus open a fitting opportunity of laying His claims before them, He rises at once to the whole height of them, in a statement which for grandeur and terseness exceeds almost anything that ever afterwards fell from Him, at least to His enemies.

17–18. My Father worketh hitherto and I work – The "*I*" is emphatic; "The creative and conservative activity of My Father has known

34 Then said they unto him, Lord, evermore give us this bread.

35 And Jesus said unto them, I am the bread of life: he that cometh to me shall never hunger; and he that believeth on me shall never thirst.

36 But I said unto you, That ye also have seen me, and believe not.

37 All that the Father giveth me shall come to me; and him that cometh to me I will in no wise cast out.

38 For I came down from heaven, not to do mine own will, but the will of him that sent me.

39 And this is the Father's will which hath sent me, that of all which he hath given me I should lose nothing, but should raise it up again at the last day.

40 And this is the will of him that sent me, that every one which seeth the Son, and believeth on him, may have everlasting life: and I will raise him up at the last day.

41 The Jews then murmured at him, because he said, I am the bread which came down from heaven.

42 And they said, Is not this Jesus, the son of Joseph, whose father and mother we know? how is it then that he saith, I came down from heaven?

43 Jesus therefore answered and said unto them, Murmur not among yourselves.

44 No man can come to me, except the Father which hath sent me draw him: and I will raise him up at the last day.

45 It is written in the prophets, And they shall be all taught of God. Every man therefore that hath heard, and hath learned of the Father, cometh unto me.

46 Not that any man hath seen the Father, save he which is of God, he hath seen the Father.

47 Verily, verily, I say unto you, He that believeth on me hath everlasting life.

48 I am that bread of life.

49 Your fathers did eat manna in the wilderness, and are dead.

50 This is the bread which cometh down from heaven, that a man may eat thereof, and not die.

51 I am the living bread which came down from heaven: if any man eat of this bread, he shall live for ever: and the bread that I will give is my flesh, which I will give

would undoubtedly have hailed him as a Prophet, and the Messiah, and the Son of God; but now, because he blames them for being too much addicted to the flesh, they think that they ought not to listen to him any more. And in the present day, how many are there who resemble them! At first, because they promise to themselves that Christ will flatter their vices, they eagerly embrace the gospel, and call for no proof of it; but when they are called to deny the flesh and to bear the cross, then do they begin to renounce Christ and ask whence the gospel came. In short, as soon as Christ does not grant their prayers, he is no longer their Master.

35. I am the bread of life

First, he shows that *the bread* , which they asked in mockery, is before their eyes; and, next, he reproves them. He begins with doctrine, to make it more evident that they were guilty of ingratitude. There are two parts of the doctrine; for he shows whence we ought to seek *life,* and how we may enjoy it. We know what gave occasion to Christ to use those metaphors; it was because *manna* and daily food had been mentioned. But still this figure is better adapted to teach ignorant persons than a simple style. When we eat *bread* for the nourishment of the body, we see more clearly not only our own weakness, but also the power of divine grace, than if, without, *bread,* God were to impart a secret power to nourish the body itself. Thus, the analogy which is traced between the body and the soul, enables us to perceive more clearly the grace of Christ. For when we learn that Christ *is the bread* by which our souls must be fed, this penetrates more deeply into our hearts than if Christ simply said that *he is our life.*

It ought to be observed, however, that the word *bread* does not express the quickening power of Christ so fully as we feel it; for *bread* does not commence *life,* but nourishes and upholds that *life* which we already possess. But, through the kindness of Christ, we not only continue to possess life, but have the beginning of life, and therefore the comparison is partly inappropriate; but there is no inconsistency in this, for Christ adapts his style to the circumstances of the discourse which he formerly delivered. Now the question had been raised, Which of the two was more eminent in feeding men, Moses or Christ himself? This is also the reason why he calls it *bread* only, for it was only the *manna* that they objected to him, and, therefore, he reckoned it enough to contrast with it a different kind of *bread* The simple doctrine is, "Our souls do not *live* by an intrinsic power, so to speak, that is, by a power which they have naturally in themselves, but borrow *life* from Christ."

no sabbath-cessation from the beginning until now, *and that is the law of My working."*

18. God was his Father – literally, "His own [or peculiar] Father," (as in Rom. 8: 32). The addition is their own, but a very proper one.

making himself equal with God – rightly gathering this to be His meaning, not from the mere words "My Father," but from His claim of right to act as His Father did in the like high sphere, and by the same law of ceaseless activity in that sphere. And as, instead of instantly disclaiming any such meaning – as He must have done if it was false – He positively sets His seal to it in the following verses, merely explaining how consistent such claim was with the prerogatives of His Father, it is beyond all doubt that we have here an assumption of *peculiar personal Sonship*, or participation in the Father's essential nature.

19–20. the Son can do nothing of himself – that is, *apart from* and *in rivalry of* the Father, as they supposed. The meaning is, "The Son can have no separate *interest* or *action* from the Father."

for what things, &c – On the contrary, "whatever the Father doeth that same doeth the Son,"

likewise – "in the like manner." What claim to absolute equality with the Father could exceed this: not only to do "the same things," but to do them *as the Father does them*?

20. Father loveth ... and showeth him all, &c – As love has no concealments, so it results from the perfect fellowship and mutual endearment of the Father and the Son (see on John 1: 1; John 1: 18), whose interests are one, even as their nature, that the Father communicates to the Son all His counsels, and what has been thus shown to the Son is by Him executed in His mediatorial character. "With the Father, *doing* is *willing*; it is only the Son who *acts in Time*" [ALFORD]. Three things here are clear: (1) The *personal distinctions* in the Godhead. (2) Unity of *action* among the Persons results from unity of *nature*. (3) Their oneness of interest is no unconscious or involuntary thing, but a thing of glorious *consciousness, will,* and *love,* of which the Persons themselves are the proper Objects.

show him greater things, &c – referring to what He goes on to mention (John 5: 21–31),

comprised in two great words, LIFE and JUDGMENT, which STIER beautifully calls God's *Regalia*. Yet these, Christ says, the Father and He do in common.

21–23. raiseth the dead and quickeneth *them* – one act in two stages. This is His absolute prerogative as God.

so the Son quickeneth them – that is, raiseth up and quickeneth.

whom he will – not only *doing the same divine act*, but doing it *as the result of His own will*, even as the Father does it. This statement is of immense importance in relation to the miracles of Christ, distinguishing them from similar miracles of prophets and apostles, who as *human instruments* were employed to perform super-natural actions, while Christ did all as the Father's *commissioned Servant* indeed, but *in the exercise of His own absolute right of action*.

22. For the Father judgeth no man, &c – rather, "For neither doth the Father judge any man," implying that the same "thing was meant in the former verse of the quickening of the dead" – both acts being done, not by the Father *and* the Son, as though twice done, but by the Father *through* the Son as His voluntary Agent.

all judgment – judgment in its most comprehensive sense, or as we should say, all *administration*.

23. honour the Son as ... the Father – As he who believes that Christ in the foregoing verses has given a true account of His relation to the Father must of necessity hold Him entitled to the same *honor* as the Father, so He here adds that it was the Father's express intention in making over all judgment to the Son, that men *should* thus honor Him.

honoureth not the Father – does not do it in fact, whatever he may imagine, and will be held as not doing it by the Father Himself, who will accept no homage which is not accorded to His own Son.

24. believeth on him that sent me – that is, believeth in Him as having sent Me. I have spoken of the Son's right not only to heal the sick but to raise from the dead, and quicken whom He will: And now I say unto you, *That life-giving operation has already passed upon all*

for the life of the world.

52 The Jews therefore strove among themselves, saying, How can this man give us his flesh to eat?

53 Then Jesus said unto them, Verily, verily, I say unto you, Except ye eat the flesh of the Son of man, and drink his blood, ye have no life in you.

54 Whoso eateth my flesh, and drinketh my blood, hath eternal life; and I will raise him up at the last day.

55 For my flesh is meat indeed, and my blood is drink indeed.

56 He that eateth my flesh, and drinketh my blood, dwelleth in me, and I in him.

57 As the living Father hath sent me, and I live by the Father: so he that eateth me, even he shall live by me.

58 This is that bread which came down from heaven: not as your fathers did eat manna, and are dead: he that eateth of this bread shall live for ever.

59 These things said he in the synagogue, as he taught in Capernaum.

60 Many therefore of his disciples, when they had heard this, said, This is an hard saying; who can hear it?

61 When Jesus knew in himself that his disciples murmured at it, he said unto them, Doth this offend you?

62 What and if ye shall see the Son of man ascend up where he was before?

63 It is the spirit that quickeneth; the flesh profiteth nothing: the words that I speak unto you, they are spirit, and they are life.

64 But there are some of you that believe not. For Jesus knew from the beginning who they were that believed not, and who should betray him.

65 And he said, Therefore said I unto you, that no man can come unto me, except it were given unto him of my Father.

66 From that time many of his disciples went back, and walked no more with him.

67 Then said Jesus unto the twelve, Will ye also go away?

68 Then Simon Peter answered him, Lord, to whom shall we go? thou hast the words of eternal life.

69 And we believe and are sure that thou art that Christ, the Son of the living God.

55. For my flesh is truly food

He confirms the same statement by other words, "As the body is weakened and consumed by the want of food, so the soul, if it be not fed with heavenly bread, will soon perish with hunger." For when he declares that *his flesh is truly food,*he means that souls are famished, if they want that food. Then only wilt thou find life in Christ, when thou shalt seek the nourishment of life in his flesh. Thus we ought to boast, with Paul, that we reckon nothing to be excellent but Christ crucified; because, as soon as we have departed from the sacrifice of his death, we meet with nothing but death; nor is there any other road that conducts us to a perception of his Divine power than through his death and resurrection. Embrace Christ, therefore, as *the Servant of the Father* (Isaiah 42: 1), that he may show himself to thee to be *the Prince of life* (Acts 3: 15). For when *he emptied himself* (Philippians 2: 7), in this manner we were enriched with abundance of all blessings; his humiliation and descent into hell raised us to heaven; and, by enduring the curse of his cross, he erected the banner of our righteousness as a splendid memorial of his victory. Consequently, they are false expounders of the mystery of the Lord's Supper, who draw away souls from the flesh of Christ.

65. Therefore have I told you

He again states that faith is an uncommon and remarkable gift of the Spirit of God, that we may not be astonished that the Gospel is not received in every place and by all. For, being ill qualified to turn to our advantage the course of events, we think more meanly of the Gospel, because the whole world does not assent to it. The thought arises in our mind, How is it possible that the greater part of men shall deliberately reject their salvation? Christ therefore assigns a reason why there are so few believers, namely, because no man, whatever may be his acuteness, can arrive at faith by his own sagacity; for all are blind, until they are illuminated by the Spirit of God, and therefore they only partake of so great a blessing whom the Father deigns to make partakers of it. If this grace were bestowed on all without exception, it would have been unseasonable and inappropriate to have mentioned it in this passage; for we must understand that it was Christ's design to show that not many believe the Gospel, because faith proceeds only from the secret revelation of the Spirit.

JOHN 7

5. For even his brethren did not believe in him

Hence we infer how small is the value of carnal relationship; for the Holy Spirit stamps with a perpetual mark of

who receive My words as the Sent of the Father on the great errand of mercy.

hath everlasting life – immediately on his believing (compare John 3: 18; 1 John 5: 12, 13).

is passed – "hath passed over" **from death unto life** – What a transition! (Compare 1 John 3: 14.)

25–29. The hour cometh – in its whole fulness, at Pentecost.

and now is – in its beginnings.

the dead – the *spiritually* dead, as is clear from John 5: 28. Here He rises from the calmer phrase "hearing *his word*" (John 5: 24), to the grander expression, "hearing *the voice of the Son of God*," to signify that as it finds men in a *dead* condition, so it carries with it a *resurrection-power*.

shall live – in the sense of John 5: 24.

26. given to the Son, &c – Does this refer to the essential life of the Son before all time (John 1: 4) (as most of the Fathers, and OLSHAUSEN, STIER, ALFORD, &c., among the moderns), or to the purpose of God that this essential life should reside in the Person of the Incarnate Son, and be manifested thus to the world? [CALVIN, LUCKE, LUTHARDT, &c.] The question is as difficult as the subject is high. But as all that Christ says of His *essential* relation to the Father is intended to explain and exalt His *mediatorial* functions, so the one seems in our Lord's own mind and language mainly the starting-point of the other.

27. because he is the Son of man – This seems to confirm the last remark, that what Christ had properly in view was the indwelling of the Son's essential life in *humanity* as the great *theater* and *medium* of divine display, in both the great departments of His work – *life-giving and judgment*. The appointment of a Judge in our *own nature* is one of the most beautiful arrangements of divine wisdom in redemption.

28. Marvel not at this – this committal of all judgment to *the Son of man*.

for the hour is coming – He adds not in this case (as in John 5: 25), "and now is," because this was not to be till the close of the whole dispensation of mercy.

29. resurrection of life – that is, to life ever-

lasting (Matt. 25: 46).

of damnation – It would have been harsh to say "the resurrection of death," though that is meant, for sinners rise *from death to death* [BENGEL]. The resurrection of both classes is an exercise of *sovereign authority*; but in the one case it is an act of *grace*, in the other of *justice*. (Compare Dan. 12: 2, from which the language is taken). How awfully grand are these unfoldings of His dignity and authority from the mouth of Christ Himself! And they are all in the *third person*; in what follows He resumes the *first person*.

30–32. of mine own self do nothing – that is, apart from the Father, or in any interest than My own. (See on John 5: 19.)

as I hear – that is, "My judgments are all *anticipated* in the bosom of My Father, to which I have immediate access, and by Me only *responded to* and *reflected*. They cannot therefore err, as I live for one end only, to carry into effect the will of Him that sent Me."

31. If I ... witness of myself – standing alone, and setting up any separate interest.

32. There is another – that is, *the Father*, as is plain from the connection. How brightly the distinction of the Persons shines out here!

and I know that the witness, &c – "This is the Son's testimony to the Father's truth (see John 7: 28; 8: 26,55). It testifies to the full consciousness on the part of the Son, even in the days of His humiliation, of the righteousness of the Father" [ALFORD]. And thus He cheered His spirit under the cloud of human opposition which was already gathering over His head.

33–35. Ye sent unto John – (See John 1: 19, &c.)

receive not testimony ... from man – that is, depend not on human testimony.

but ... that ye might be saved – "I refer to him merely to aid your salvation."

35. He was a burning and a shining light – literally, "*the* burning and shining lamp" (or torch): that is, "the great light of his day." Christ is never called by the humble word here applied to John – a *light-bearer* – studiously used to distinguish him from his Master, but ever *the Light* in the most absolute sense. (See on John 1: 6.)

70 Jesus answered them, Have not I chosen you twelve, and one of you is a devil?

71 He spake of Judas Iscariot the son of Simon: for he it was that should betray him, being one of the twelve.

JOHN 7

1 After these things Jesus walked in Galilee: for he would not walk in Jewry, because the Jews sought to kill him.

2 Now the Jews' feast of tabernacles was at hand.

3 His brethren therefore said unto him, Depart hence, and go into Judaea, that thy disciples also may see the works that thou doest.

4 For there is no man that doeth any thing in secret, and he himself seeketh to be known openly. If thou do these things, shew thyself to the world.

5 For neither did his brethren believe in him.

6 Then Jesus said unto them, My time is not yet come: but your time is alway ready.

7 The world cannot hate you; but me it hateth, because I testify of it, that the works thereof are evil.

8 Go ye up unto this feast: I go not up yet unto this feast; for my time is not yet full come.

9 When he had said these words unto them, he abode still in Galilee.

10 But when his brethren were gone up, then went he also up unto the feast, not openly, but as it were in secret.

11 Then the Jews sought him at the feast, and said, Where is he?

12 And there was much murmuring among the people concerning him: for some said, He is a good man: others said, Nay; but he deceiveth the people.

13 Howbeit no man spake openly of him for fear of the Jews.

14 Now about the midst of the feast Jesus went up into the temple, and taught.

15 And the Jews marveled, saying, How knoweth this man letters, having never learned?

16 Jesus answered them, and said, My doctrine is not mine, but his that sent me.

infamy the relations of Christ, because, though convinced by the testimonies of so many works, they did not even then believe. *Therefore, whosoever wishes to be thought to be in Christ,* as Paul says, *let him be a new creature* (2 Corinthians 5: 17; Galatians 6: 15); for they who dedicate themselves wholly to God obtain the place of father, and mother, and brethren to Christ, and all others he utterly disavows (Matthew 12: 50).

11. The Jews therefore sought him

Here we ought to consider what was the condition of the Church. For the Jews, at that time, gaped for the promised redemption like hungry men; yet, when Christ appears to them, they remain in suspense. Hence arose that murmuring and that variety of opinions. That they whisper secretly is an indication of the tyranny which the priests and scribes exercised over them. It is a shocking exhibition, indeed, that this Church, which was at that time the only Church on earth, is here represented to us as a confused and shapeless chaos. They who rule, instead of pastors, hold the people oppressed by fear and terror, and throughout the whole body there is shameful desolation and lamentable disorder. By *the Jews* he means the common people, who, having been accustomed for two years to hear Christ, inquire about him, because he does not appear according to his custom. For when they say, *Where is he?* they describe a man whom they knew, and yet that word shows that they had not yet been earnestly moved, and that they always remained in doubt and suspense.

16. My doctrine is not mine

Christ shows that this circumstance, which was an offense to the Jews, was rather a ladder by which they ought to have risen higher to perceive the glory of God; as if he had said, "When you see a teacher not trained in the school of men, know that I have been taught by God." For the reason why the Heavenly Father determined that his Son should go out of a mechanic's workshop, rather than from the schools of the scribes, was, that the origin of the Gospel might be more manifest, that none might think that it had been fabricated on the earth, or imagine that any human being was the author of it. Thus also Christ chose ignorant and uneducated men to be his apostles, and permitted them to remain three years in gross ignorance, that, having instructed them in a single instant, he might bring them forward as new men, and even as angels who had just come down from heaven.

24. Judge not according to the appearance

Having concluded his defense, he likewise administers a reproof on this ground, that they are carried away by wicked dispositions, and do not form *a judgment* according to the fact and the matter in hand. *Circumcision* was properly

willing for a season – that is, till they saw that it pointed whither they were not prepared to go.

to rejoice in his light – There is a play of irony here, referring to the hollow delight with which his testimony tickled them.

36–38. I have greater witness – rather, "The witness which I have is greater."

the works ... bear witness of me – not simply as *miracles* nor even as a miracle of *mercy*, but these miracles, *as He did them*, with a *will* and a *power*, a *majesty* and a *grace* manifestly *His own*.

37. the Father himself ... hath borne witness of me – not referring, probably, to the voice of His baptism, but (as seems from what follows) to the testimony of the Old Testament Scripture [CALVIN, LUCKE, MEYER, LUTHARDT, &c.].

neither heard his voice, &c – never recognized Him in this character. The words are "designedly mysterious, like many others which our Lord uttered" [STIER].

38. not his word abiding in you – passing now from the *Witness* to the *testimony* borne by Him in "the lively oracles" (Acts 7: 38): both were alike strangers to their breasts, as was evidenced by their rejecting Him to whom all that witness was borne.

39–42. Search the scriptures, &c – "In the Scriptures ye find your charter of eternal life; go search them then, and you will find that I am the Great Burden of their testimony; yet ye will not come to Me for that life eternal which you profess to find there, and of which they tell you I am the appointed Dispenser." (Compare Acts 17: 11, 12). How touching and gracious are these last words! Observe here (1) The honor which Christ gives to the Scriptures, as a record which all *have a right* and *are bound* to search – the reverse of which the Church of Rome teaches; (2) The opposite extreme is, resting in the mere *Book* without *the living Christ*, to direct the soul to whom is its main use and chiefest glory.

41. I receive not honour from men – contrasting His own end with theirs, which was to obtain *human applause*.

42. not the love of God in you – which would

inspire you with a single desire to know His mind and will, and yield yourselves to it, in spite of prejudice and regardless of consequences.

43–47. if another shall come, &c – How strikingly has this been verified in the history of the Jews! "From the time of the true Christ to our time, sixty-four false Christs have been reckoned by whom they have been deceived" [BENGEL].

44. How can ye believe, &c – (See on John 5: 40–41). The "*will not*" of John 5: 40, and "*cannot*" here are just different features of the same awful state of the human heart.

45. Do not think I will accuse you to the Father – "My errand hither is not to collect evidence to condemn you at God's bar."

one that accuseth you, even Moses, &c. – "Alas! that will be too well done by another, and him the object of all your religious boastings – Moses," here put for "*the Law*," the basis of the Old Testament Scriptures.

46. he wrote of me – "an important testimony to the subject of the whole Pentateuch – 'of Me'" [ALFORD].

47. If ye believe not – (See Luke 16: 31).

his writings ... my words – a remarkable contrast, not *absolutely* exalting Old Testament Scripture above His own words, but pointing to the office of those venerable documents to *prepare* Christ's way, to the necessity universally felt for *documentary* testimony in revealed religion, and perhaps (as STIER adds) to the relation which the comparative "*letter*" of the Old Testament holds to the more flowing "words" of "spirit and life" which characterize the New Testament.

JOHN 6

John 6: 1–13

FIVE THOUSAND MIRACULOUSLY FED.

3. a mountain – somewhere in that hilly range which skirts the east side of the lake.

4. passover ... was nigh – but for the reason mentioned (John 7: 1), Jesus kept away from it, remaining in Galilee.

17 If any man will do his will, he shall know of the doctrine, whether it be of God, or whether I speak of myself.

18 He that speaketh of himself seeketh his own glory: but he that seeketh his glory that sent him, the same is true, and no unrighteousness is in him.

19 Did not Moses give you the law, and yet none of you keepeth the law? Why go ye about to kill me?

20 The people answered and said, Thou hast a devil: who goeth about to kill thee?

21 Jesus answered and said unto them, I have done one work, and ye all marvel.

22 Moses therefore gave unto you circumcision; (not because it is of Moses, but of the fathers;) and ye on the sabbath day circumcise a man.

23 If a man on the sabbath day receive circumcision, that the law of Moses should not be broken; are ye angry at me, because I have made a man every whit whole on the sabbath day?

24 Judge not according to the appearance, but judge righteous judgment.

25 Then said some of them of Jerusalem, Is not this he, whom they seek to kill?

26 But, lo, he speaketh boldly, and they say nothing unto him. Do the rulers know indeed that this is the very Christ?

27 Howbeit we know this man whence he is: but when Christ cometh, no man knoweth whence he is.

28 Then cried Jesus in the temple as he taught, saying, Ye both know me, and ye know whence I am: and I am not come of myself, but he that sent me is true, whom ye know not.

29 But I know him: for I am from him, and he hath sent me.

30 Then they sought to take him: but no man laid hands on him, because his hour was not yet come.

31 And many of the people believed on him, and said, When Christ cometh, will he do more miracles than these which this man hath done?

32 The Pharisees heard that the people murmured such things concerning him; and the Pharisees and the chief priests sent officers to take him.

33 Then said Jesus unto them, Yet a

held by them in reverence; and when it was performed on the Sabbath-day, they knew that the Law was not violated by it, because *the works of God* agree well with each other. Why do they not arrive at the same conclusion as to the *work* of Christ, but because their minds are preoccupied by a prejudice which they have formed against his person?

30. Therefore they sought to seize him

They had no want of will to do him mischief; they even made the attempt, and they had strength to do it. Why, then, amidst so much ardor, are they benumbed, as if they had their hands and feet bound? The Evangelist replies, *because Christ's hour was not yet come*; by which he means that, against all their violence and furious attacks, Christ was guarded by the protection of God. And at the same time he meets the offense of the cross; for we have no reason to be alarmed when we learn that Christ was dragged to death, not through the caprice of men, but because he was destined for such a sacrifice by the decree of the Father. And hence we ought to infer a general doctrine; for though we live from day to day, still the time of every man's death has been fixed by God. It is difficult to believe that, while we are subject to so many accidents, exposed to so many open and concealed attacks both from men and beasts, and liable to so many diseases, we are safe from all risk until God is pleased to call us away. But we ought to struggle against our own distrust; and we ought to attend first to the doctrine itself which is here taught, and next, to the object at which it aims, and the exhortation which is drawn from it, namely, that each of us, *casting all his cares on God* (Psalm 55: 22; 1 Peter 5: 7), should follow his own calling, and not be led away from the performance of his duty by any fears. Yet let no man go beyond his own bounds; for confidence in the providence of God must not go farther than God himself commands.

40. Many of the multitude

The Evangelist now relates what fruit followed from this last sermon of our Lord Jesus Christ; namely, that some thought one thing and some another, so that *a difference of opinion arose among the people*. It ought to be observed that John does not speak of the open enemies of Christ, or of those who were already filled with deadly hatred against sound doctrine, but of the common people, among whom there ought to have been greater integrity. He enumerates three classes of them. *He is truly a Prophet.* The first acknowledged that Jesus *was truly a Prophet*, from which we infer that they did not dislike his doctrine. But, on the other hand, how light and trifling this confession was, is evident from the fact, that, while they approve of the Teacher, they nei-

John 6: 14–21

JESUS WALKS ON THE SEA.

15. departed … to a mountain himself alone – (1) to *rest*, which He came to this "desert place" on purpose to do before the miracle of the loaves, but could not for the multitude that followed Him (see Mark 6: 31); and (2) "*to pray*" (Matt. 14: 23; Mark 6: 46). But from His mountain-top He kept watching the ship (see on John 6: 18), and doubtless prayed both for them, and with a view to the new manifestation which He was to give them of His glory.

18–19. sea arose, &c – and they were "now in the midst of it" (Matt. 14: 24). Mark adds the graphic and touching particular, "He saw them toiling in rowing" (Mark 6: 48), putting forth all their strength to buffet the waves and bear on against a head wind, but to little effect. He *saw* this from His mountain-top, and through the darkness of the night, for His heart was all with them; yet would He not go to their relief till His own time came.

19. they see Jesus – "about the fourth watch of the night" (Matt. 14: 25; Mark 6: 48), or between three and six in the morning.

20. It is I; be not afraid – Matthew (Matt. 14: 27) and Mark (Mark 6: 50) give before these exhilarating words, that to them well-known one, "Be of good cheer!"

21. willingly received him into the ship – their first fears being now converted into wonder and delight.

John 6: 22–71

JESUS FOLLOWED BY THE MULTITUDES TO CAPERNAUM, DISCOURSES TO THEM IN THE SYNAGOGUE OF THE BREAD OF LIFE – EFFECT OF THIS ON TWO CLASSES OF THE DISCIPLES.

23. Howbeit, &c – "Howbeit," adds the Evangelist, in a lively parenthesis, "there came other boats from Tiberias" (which lay near the southwest coast of the lake), whose passengers were part of the multitude that had followed Jesus to the east side, and been miraculously fed; these boats were fastened somewhere (says the Evangelist).

25. when they had found him on the other side – at Capernaum.

27. which the Son of man – taking that title of Himself which denoted His incarnate life.

shall give unto you – in the sense of John 6: 51.

him hath God the Father sealed – marked out and authenticated for that transcendent office, to impart to the world the bread of an everlasting life, and this in the character of "the Son of *man*."

28–31. What shall we do … the works of God – such works as God will approve. Different answers may be given to such a question, according to the *spirit* which prompts the inquiry. (See Hos. 6: 6–8; Luke 3: 12–14). Here our Lord, knowing whom He had to deal with, shapes His reply accordingly.

29. This is the work of God – That lies at the threshold of all acceptable obedience, being not only the prerequisite to it, but the proper spring of it – in that sense, the work of works, emphatically "*the* work of God."

31. Our fathers did eat manna, &c – insinuating the inferiority of Christ's miracle of the loaves to those of Moses: "When Moses claimed the confidence of the fathers, 'he gave them bread from heaven to eat' – not for a few thousands, but for millions, and not once only, but daily throughout their wilderness journey."

33. For the bread of God is he, &c – This verse is perhaps best left in its own transparent grandeur – holding up the Bread Itself as *divine, spiritual*, and *eternal*; its ordained Fountain and essential Substance, "*Him who came down from heaven to give it*" (that Eternal Life which was with the Father and was manifested unto us, 1 John 1: 2); and its designed objects, "*the world*."

34. Lord, evermore give us this bread – speaking now with a certain reverence (as at John 6: 25), the perpetuity of the manna floating perhaps in their minds, and much like the Samaritan woman, when her eyes were but half opened, "Sir, give Me this water," &c. (John 4: 15).

35. I am the bread of life – Henceforth the discourse is all *in the first person*, "I," "Me," which

little while am I with you, and then I go unto him that sent me.

34 Ye shall seek me, and shall not find me: and where I am, thither ye cannot come.

35 Then said the Jews among themselves, Whither will he go, that we shall not find him? will he go unto the dispersed among the Gentiles, and teach the Gentiles?

36 What manner of saying is this that he said, Ye shall seek me, and shall not find me: and where I am, thither ye cannot come?

37 In the last day, that great day of the feast, Jesus stood and cried, saying, If any man thirst, let him come unto me, and drink.

38 He that believeth on me, as the scripture hath said, out of his belly shall flow rivers of living water.

39 (But this spake he of the Spirit, which they that believe on him should receive: for the Holy Ghost was not yet given; because that Jesus was not yet glorified.)

40 Many of the people therefore, when they heard this saying, said, Of a truth this is the Prophet.

41 Others said, This is the Christ. But some said, Shall Christ come out of Galilee?

42 Hath not the scripture said, That Christ cometh of the seed of David, and out of the town of Bethlehem, where David was?

43 So there was a division among the people because of him.

44 And some of them would have taken him; but no man laid hands on him.

45 Then came the officers to the chief priests and Pharisees; and they said unto them, Why have ye not brought him?

46 The officers answered, Never man spake like this man.

47 Then answered them the Pharisees, Are ye also deceived?

48 Have any of the rulers or of the Pharisees believed on him?

49 But this people who knoweth not the law are cursed.

50 Nicodemus saith unto them, (he that came to Jesus by night, being one of them,)

51 Doth our law judge any man, before

ther understand what he means, nor relish what he says; for they could not truly receive him *as a Prophet*, without, at the same time, acknowledging that he is the Son of God and the Author of their salvation. Yet this is good in them, that they perceive in Christ something Divine, which leads them to regard him with reverence; for this willingness to learn might afterwards give an easy opening to faith.

41. Others said, He is the Christ

The second have a more correct opinion than the first; for they plainly acknowledge that he is the Christ; but the third rise up against them, and hence proceeds the debate. By this example we are warned that we ought not to think it strange in the present day, if men are divided among themselves by various controversies. We learn that Christ's sermon produced a schism, and that not among Gentiles who were strangers to the faith, but in the midst of the Church of Christ, and even in the chief seat of the Church. Shall the doctrine of Christ be blamed on that account, as if it were the cause of disturbances? Nay rather, though the whole world were in commotion, the word of God is so precious, that we ought to wish that it were received, at least by a few. There is no reason, therefore, why our consciences should be distressed, when we see those who wish to be accounted the people of God fighting with each other by contrary opinions.

50. Nicodemus said to them

The Evangelist describes *Nicodemus* as a neutral man, who does not venture to undertake in good earnest the defense of sound doctrine, and yet cannot endure to have the truth oppressed. *He who came to Jesus by night.* This circumstance is mentioned by the Evangelist, partly to the praise, and partly to the disgrace, of *Nicodemus.*

If he had not loved the doctrine of Christ, he would never have dared to meet the rage of wicked men; for he knew that, if any of them but opened his mouth, he would be immediately exposed to dislike and to danger. When, therefore, he ventures to throw out one word, however feeble it may be, some small spark of godliness shines from his heart; but in not defending Christ openly, he manifests excessive timidity. Thus the Evangelist means that he has still a hankering after the concealment of the night, and is not a true disciple of Christ. He says that he once *came to Jesus by night,* but remained openly among his enemies, and kept his place in their camp.

JOHN 8

7. He who is without sin among you

He said this according to the custom of the Law; for God

occur in one form or other, as STIER reckons, thirty-five times.

36. But ... ye have seen me, and believe not – seen Him not in His mere bodily presence, but in all the majesty of His life, His teaching, His works.

37–40. All that, &c – This comprehensive and very grand passage is expressed with a peculiar artistic precision. The opening general statement (John 6: 37) consists of two members: (1) "ALL THAT THE FATHER GIVETH ME SHALL COME TO ME" – that is, "Though ye, as I told you, have no faith in Me, My errand into the world shall in no wise be defeated; for all that the Father giveth Me shall infallibly come to Me." (2) "AND HIM THAT COMETH TO ME I WILL IN NO WISE CAST OUT." As the former was the *divine*, this is just the *human* side of the same thing.

38. For I came down from heaven not to do Mine own will – to play an independent part.
   but – in respect to both the foregoing things, the *divine* and the *human* side of salvation.

39. And this – in the *first* place.
   is the will of Him that sent me, that of all – everything.
   which He hath given Me – (taking up the identical words of John 6: 37).

40. And this – in the *second* place.

41–46. Jews murmured – muttered, not in our Lord's hearing, but He knew it (John 6: 43; John 2: 25).

43–44. Murmur not ... No man – that is, Be not either startled or stumbled at these sayings; for it needs divine teaching to understand them, divine drawing to submit to them.

44. can come to me – in the sense of John 6: 35.
   except the Father which hath sent me – that is, the Father *as the Sender of Me* and *to carry out the design of My mission.*

45. written in the prophets – in Is. 54: 13; Jer. 31: 33–34; other similar passages may also have been in view. Our Lord thus falls back upon Scripture authority for this seemingly hard saying.

46. Not that any man hath seen, &c – Lest they should confound that "hearing and learning of the Father," to which believers are admitted by divine *teaching,* with His own immediate access to Him, He here throws in a parenthetical explanation; stating, as explicitly as words could do it, how totally different the two cases were, and that only He who is "from God" hath this naked, immediate access to the Father. (See John 1: 18.)

48. I am the bread of life – "As he that believeth in Me hath everlasting life, so I am Myself the everlasting *Sustenance* of that life." (Repeated from John 6: 35.)

49. Your fathers – of whom ye spake (John 6: 31); not *"ours,"* by which He would hint that *He* had a higher descent, of which they dreamt not [BENGEL].

51. I am, &c – Understand, it is of MYSELF I now speak as the Bread from heaven; of ME if a man eat he shall live for ever; and "THE BREAD WHICH I WILL GIVE IS MY FLESH, WHICH I WILL GIVE FOR THE LIFE OF THE WORLD."

52. Jews strove among themselves – arguing the point together.

53–58. Except ye eat the flesh ... and drink the blood ... no life, &c – The harshest word He had yet uttered in their ears. They asked how it was *possible* to eat His flesh. He answers, with great solemnity, "It is *indispensable.*"

54. Whoso eateth ... hath, &c – The former verse said that *unless* they partook of Him they had no life; this adds, that *whoever* does so "hath eternal life."

56. He that eateth ... dwelleth in me and I in him – As our food becomes incorporated with ourselves, so Christ and those who eat His flesh and drink His blood become spiritually *one life,* though *personally* distinct.

57. As the living Father hath sent me – to communicate His own life.
   and I live by the Father – literally, "because of the Father"; My life and His being one, but Mine that of a *Son,* whose it is to be *"of the Father."* (See John 1: 18; 5: 26.)
   he that eateth me, ... shall live by me – literally, "because of Me." So that though *one spiritual life* with Him, "the Head of every man

it hear him, and know what he doeth?

52 They answered and said unto him, Art thou also of Galilee? Search, and look: for out of Galilee ariseth no prophet.

53 And every man went unto his own house.

JOHN 8

1 Jesus went unto the mount of Olives.

2 And early in the morning he came again into the temple, and all the people came unto him; and he sat down, and taught them.

3 And the scribes and Pharisees brought unto him a woman taken in adultery; and when they had set her in the midst,

4 They say unto him, Master, this woman was taken in adultery, in the very act.

5 Now Moses in the law commanded us, that such should be stoned: but what sayest thou?

6 This they said, tempting him, that they might have to accuse him. But Jesus stooped down, and with his finger wrote on the ground, as though he heard them not.

7 So when they continued asking him, he lifted up himself, and said unto them, He that is without sin among you, let him first cast a stone at her.

8 And again he stooped down, and wrote on the ground.

9 And they which heard it, being convicted by their own conscience, went out one by one, beginning at the eldest, even unto the last: and Jesus was left alone, and the woman standing in the midst.

10 When Jesus had lifted up himself, and saw none but the woman, he said unto her, Woman, where are those thine accusers? hath no man condemned thee?

11 She said, No man, Lord. And Jesus said unto her, Neither do I condemn thee: go, and sin no more.

12 Then spake Jesus again unto them, saying, I am the light of the world: he that followeth me shall not walk in darkness, but shall have the light of life.

13 The Pharisees therefore said unto him, Thou bearest record of thyself; thy

commanded that the witnesses should, with their own hands, put malefactors to death, according to the sentence which had been pronounced on them; that greater caution might be used in bearing testimony (Deuteronomy 17: 7). There are many who proceed rashly to overwhelm their brother by perjury, because they do not think that they inflict a deadly wound by their tongue. And this very argument, had weight with those slanderers, desperate as they were; for no sooner do they obtain a sight of it, than they lay aside those fierce passions with which they were swelled when they came. Yet there is this difference between the injunction of the Law and the words of Christ, that in the Law God merely enjoined that they should not condemn a man with the tongue, unless they were permitted to put him to death with their own hands; but here Christ demands from the witnesses perfect innocence, so that no man ought to accuse another of crime, unless he be pure, and free from every fault. Now what he said, at that time, to a few persons, we ought to view as spoken to all, that whoever accuses another, ought to impose on himself a law of innocence; otherwise, we do not pursue wicked actions, but rather are hostile to the persons of men.

12. I am the light of the world

Those who leave out the former narrative, which relates to the adulteress, connect this discourse of Christ with the sermon which he delivered on the last day of the assembly. It is a beautiful commendation of Christ, when he is called *the light of the world;* for, since we are all blind by nature, a remedy is offered, by which we may be freed and rescued from darkness and made partakers of the true *light* Nor is it only to one person or to another that this benefit is offered, for Christ declares that he is *the light of the whole world* ; for by this universal statement he intended to remove the distinction, not only between Jews and Gentiles, but between the learned and ignorant, between persons of distinction and the common people.

23. You are from beneath, I am from above

As they did not deserve that he should teach them, he wished only to strike them with reproofs conveyed in few words, as in this passage he declares that they do not receive his doctrine, because they have an utter dislike of the kingdom of God. Under the words, *world* and *beneath,* he includes all that men naturally possess, and thus points out the disagreement which exists between his Gospel and the ingenuity and sagacity of the human mind; for the Gospel is heavenly wisdom, but our mind grovels on the earth. No man, therefore, will ever be qualified to become a disciple of Christ, till Christ has formed him by his Spirit. And

DAVID BROWN

is Christ, as the head of Christ is God" (1 Cor. 11: 3; 3: 23).

58. This is that bread, &c – a sort of summing up of the whole discourse.

59. These things said he in the synagogue – which seems to imply that what follows took place after the congregation had broken up.

60–65. Many ... of his disciples – His pretty constant followers, though an outer circle of them.

63. the flesh profiteth nothing – Much of His discourse was *about* "flesh"; but flesh as such, mere flesh, could profit nothing, much less impart that *life* which the Holy Spirit alone communicates to the soul.

64. But there are some, &c – that is, "But it matters little to some of you in what sense I speak, for ye believe not." This was said, adds the Evangelist, not merely of the outer but of the inner circle of His disciples; for He knew the traitor, though it was not yet time to expose him.

65. Therefore said I, &c – that is, "That was why I spoke to you of the necessity of divine teaching which some of you are strangers to."

except it were given him - plainly showing that by the Father's "drawing" (John 6:44) was meant an internal and efficacious operation, for in recalling the statement here He says, it must b [e "*given* to a man to come" to Christ.]

67. the twelve – the first time they are thus mentioned in this Gospel.

68. Then Simon Peter – whose forwardness in this case was noble, and to the wounded spirit of His Lord doubtless very grateful.

70. Have not I chosen ... and one of you is a devil: "Well said, Simon-Barjonas, but that 'we' embraces not so wide a circle as in the simplicity of thine heart thou thinkest; for though I have chosen you but twelve, one even of these is a 'devil'" (the temple, the tool of that wicked one).

JOHN 7

John 7: 1–53

CHRIST AT THE FEAST OF TABERNACLES.

1–2. After these things – that is, *all that is recorded after* John 5: 18.

walked in Galilee – continuing His labors there, instead of going to Judea, as might have been expected.

sought to kill him – referring back to John 5: 18. *Hence it appears that our Lord did not attend the Passover mentioned in* John 6: 4 – being the *third* since His ministry began, if the feast mentioned in John 5: 1 was a Passover.

2. feast of tabernacles ... at hand – This was the last of the three annual festivals, celebrated on the fifteenth of the seventh month (September). (See Lev. 23: 33, &c.; Deut. 16: 13, &c.; Neh. 8: 14–18).

10. then went he ... not openly – not "in the (caravan) company" [MEYER]. See on Luke 2: 44.

as it were in secret – rather, "in a manner secretly"; perhaps by some other route, and in a way not to attract notice.

11–13. Jews – the rulers.

sought him – for no good end.

Where is He? – He had not been at Jerusalem for probably *a year and a half.*

12. much murmuring – buzzing.

among the people – the multitudes; the natural expression of a Jewish writer, indicating without design the crowded state of Jerusalem at this festival [WEBSTER and WILKINSON].

13. none spake openly of him – that is, in His favor, "for fear of the [*ruling*] Jews."

14–15. about the midst of the feast – the fourth or fifth day of the eight, during which it lasted.

15. How knoweth ... letters – learning (Acts 26: 24).

16–18. doctrine ... not mine, &c – that is, from Myself unauthorized; I am here by commission.

17. If any man will do his will, &c – "is willing," or "wishes to do."

record is not true.

14 Jesus answered and said unto them, Though I bear record of myself, yet my record is true: for I know whence I came, and whither I go; but ye cannot tell whence I come, and whither I go.

15 Ye judge after the flesh; I judge no man.

16 And yet if I judge, my judgment is true: for I am not alone, but I and the Father that sent me.

17 It is also written in your law, that the testimony of two men is true.

18 I am one that bear witness of myself, and the Father that sent me beareth witness of me.

19 Then said they unto him, Where is thy Father? Jesus answered, Ye neither know me, nor my Father: if ye had known me, ye should have known my Father also.

20 These words spake Jesus in the treasury, as he taught in the temple: and no man laid hands on him; for his hour was not yet come.

21 Then said Jesus again unto them, I go my way, and ye shall seek me, and shall die in your sins: whither I go, ye cannot come.

22 Then said the Jews, Will he kill himself? because he saith, Whither I go, ye cannot come.

23 And he said unto them, Ye are from beneath; I am from above: ye are of this world; I am not of this world.

24 I said therefore unto you, that ye shall die in your sins: for if ye believe not that I am he, ye shall die in your sins.

25 Then said they unto him, Who art thou? And Jesus saith unto them, Even the same that I said unto you from the beginning.

26 I have many things to say and to judge of you: but he that sent me is true; and I speak to the world those things which I have heard of him.

27 They understood not that he spake to them of the Father.

28 Then said Jesus unto them, When ye have lifted up the Son of man, then shall ye know that I am he, and that I do nothing of myself; but as my Father hath taught me, I speak these things.

29 And he that sent me is with me: the Father hath not left me alone; for I do

hence it arises that faith is so seldom found in the world, because all mankind are naturally opposed and averse to Christ, except those whom he elevates by the special grace of his Holy Spirit.

24. You shall die in your sins

Having formerly employed the singular number, *in your sin*, he now resorts to the plural number, *in your sins;* but the meaning is the same, except that in the former passage he intended to point out that unbelief is the source and cause of all evils. Not that there are no other sins but unbelief, or that it is unbelief alone which subjects us to the condemnation of eternal death before God, as some men too extravagantly talk; but because it drives us away from Christ, and deprives us of his grace, from which we ought to expect deliverance from all our sins. That the Jews reject the medicine with obstinate malice, is their mortal disease; and hence it arises that the slaves of Satan do not cease to heap up sins on sins, and continually to bring down upon themselves fresh condemnations. And, therefore, he immediately adds – *If you do not believe that I am.* For there is no other way for lost men to recover salvation, but to betake themselves to Christ. The phrase, *that I am*, is emphatic; for, in order to make the meaning complete, we must supply all that the Scripture ascribes to the Messiah, and all that it bids us expect from him. But the sum and substance is – the restoration of the Church, the commencement of which is the light of faith, from which proceed righteousness and a new life. Some of the ancient writers have deduced from this passage the Divine essence of Christ; but that is a mistake, for he speaks of his office towards us. This statement is worthy of observation; for men never consider sufficiently the evils in which they are plunged; and though they are constrained to acknowledge their destruction, yet they neglect Christ, and look around them, in every direction, for useless remedies. Wherefore we ought to believe that, until the grace of Christ be manifested to deliver us, nothing but a boundless mass of all evils reigns perpetually in us.

26. I have many things to say and judge of you

Perceiving that he is in the position of one who sings to the deaf, he pursues his discourse no farther, but only declares that God will defend that doctrine, which they despise, because he is the Author of it. "If I wished to accuse you," says he, "your malice and wickedness supply me with ample materials; but I leave you for the present. But my Father, who committed to me the office of a teacher, will not fail to fulfill his promise; for he will always vindicate his word against the wicked and sacrilegious contempt of men." This saying of Christ is of the same import with that of Paul, If

whether ... of God, or ... of myself – from above or from beneath; is divine or an imposture of Mine. A principle of immense importance, showing, on the one hand, that *singleness of desire to please God is the grand inlet to light on all questions vitally affecting one's eternal interests,* and on the other, that *the want of his,* whether perceived or not, *is the chief cause of infidelity amidst the light of revealed religion.*

19-20. Did not Moses, &c – that is, In opposing Me ye pretend zeal for Moses, but to the spirit and end of that law which he gave ye are total strangers, and in "going about to kill Me" ye are its greatest enemies.

20. The people answered, Thou hast a devil: who goeth about to kill thee? – This was said by *the multitude,* who as yet had no bad feeling to Jesus, and were not in the secret of the plot hatching, as our Lord knew, against Him.

21-24. I have done one work, &c – Taking no notice of the popular appeal, as there were those there who knew well enough what He meant, He recalls His cure of the impotent man, and the murderous rage it had kindled (John 5: 9,16,18). It may seem strange that He should refer to an event a year and a half old, as if but newly done. But their present attempt "to kill Him" brought up the past scene vividly, not only to Him, but without doubt to them, too, if indeed they had ever forgotten it; and by this fearless reference to it, exposing their hypocrisy and dark designs, He gave His position great moral strength.

25-27. some of them of Jerusalem – the citizens, who, knowing the long-formed purpose of the rulers to put Jesus to death, wondered that they were now letting Him teach openly.

28-29. cried Jesus – in a louder tone, and more solemn, witnessing style than usual.

30-32. sought to take ... none laid hands – their *impotence* being equal to their *malignity.*

31. When Christ cometh, will he, &c – that is, If this be not the Christ, what can the Christ do, when He does come, which has not been anticipated and eclipsed by this man? This was evidently the language of friendly persons, overborne by their spiteful superiors, but unable to keep quite silent.

32. heard that the people murmured – that mutterings to this effect were going about, and thought it high time to stop Him if He was not to be allowed to carry away the people.

33-34. Yet a little while, &c – that is, "Your desire to be rid of Me will be for you all too soon fulfilled. Yet a little while and we part company – for ever; for I go whither ye cannot come: nor, even when ye at length seek Him whom ye now despise, shall ye be able to find Him" – referring not to any penitential, but to purely selfish cries in their time of desperation.

35-36. Whither will he go, &c – They cannot comprehend Him, but seem awed by the solemn grandeur of His warning. He takes no notice, however, of their questions.

37-39. the last day, that great day of the feast – the eighth (Lev. 23: 39). It was a sabbath, the last feast day of the year, and distinguished by very remarkable ceremonies. "The generally joyous character of this feast broke out on this day into loud jubilation, particularly at the solemn moment when the priest, as was done on every day of this festival, brought forth, in golden vessels, water from the stream of Siloah, which flowed under the temple-mountain, and solemnly poured it upon the altar. Then the words of Is. 12: 3 were sung, *With joy shall ye draw water out of the wells of Salvation,* and thus the symbolical reference of this act, intimated in John 7: 39, was expressed" [OLSHAUSEN]. So ecstatic was the joy with which this ceremony was performed – accompanied with sound of trumpets – that it used to be said, "Whoever had not witnessed it had never seen rejoicing at all" [LIGHTFOOT].

38. as the scripture hath said – These words belong to what follows, "Out of his belly, as the scripture hath said, shall flow," &c. referring not to any particular passage, but to such as Is. 58: 11; Joel 3: 18; Zech. 14: 8; Ezek. 47: 1-12; in most of which the idea is that of waters issuing from beneath the temple, to which our Lord compares Himself and those who believe in Him.

out of his belly – that is, his inner man, his soul, as in Prov. 20: 27.

39. this spake he of the Spirit – who, by His direct personal agency, opens up this spring

always those things that please him.

30 As he spake these words, many believed on him.

31 Then said Jesus to those Jews which believed on him, If ye continue in my word, then are ye my disciples indeed;

32 And ye shall know the truth, and the truth shall make you free.

33 They answered him, We be Abraham's seed, and were never in bondage to any man: how sayest thou, Ye shall be made free?

34 Jesus answered them, Verily, verily, I say unto you, Whosoever committeth sin is the servant of sin.

35 And the servant abideth not in the house for ever: but the Son abideth ever.

36 If the Son therefore shall make you free, ye shall be free indeed.

37 I know that ye are Abraham's seed; but ye seek to kill me, because my word hath no place in you.

38 I speak that which I have seen with my Father: and ye do that which ye have seen with your father.

39 They answered and said unto him, Abraham is our father. Jesus saith unto them, If ye were Abraham's children, ye would do the works of Abraham.

40 But now ye seek to kill me, a man that hath told you the truth, which I have heard of God: this did not Abraham.

41 Ye do the deeds of your father. Then said they to him, We be not born of fornication; we have one Father, even God.

42 Jesus said unto them, If God were your Father, ye would love me: for I proceeded forth and came from God; neither came I of myself, but he sent me.

43 Why do ye not understand my speech? even because ye cannot hear my word.

44 Ye are of your father the devil, and the lusts of your father ye will do. He was a murderer from the beginning, and abode not in the truth, because there is no truth in him. When he speaketh a lie, he speaketh of his own: for he is a liar, and the father of it.

45 And because I tell you the truth, ye believe me not.

46 Which of you convinceth me of sin? And if I say the truth, why do ye not believe me?

we deny him, he remaineth faithful, he cannot deny himself (2 Timothy 2:13).

In short, he threatens the judgment of God against unbelievers, who refuse to give credit to his word; and he does so on this ground, that God must inevitably defend his truth. Now this is the true firmness of faith, when we believe that God is alone sufficient to establish the authority of his doctrine, though the world should reject it. All who, relying on this doctrine, serve Christ faithfully, may fearlessly accuse the whole world of falsehood.

And I speak to the world those things which I have heard from him

He says that he utters nothing which he has not received from the Father; and this is the only confirmation of a doctrine, when the minister shows that what he speaks has proceeded from the Father. Now we know that Christ sustained, at that time, the office of a minister; and, therefore, we need not wonder, if he demands that men listen to him, because he brings to them the commandments of God. Besides, by his example he lays down a general law for the whole Church, that no man ought to be heard, unless he speak from the mouth of God. But while he lays low the wicked arrogance of those men who take upon themselves to speak without the word of God, faithful teachers, who know well the nature of their calling, are fortified and armed by him with unshaken firmness, that, under the guidance of God, they may boldly bid defiance to all mortals.

27. They did not know that he spoke to them about the Father

Hence we see how stupid those men are whose understandings are possessed by Satan. Nothing could be more plain than that they were summoned to the judgment-seat of God. But what then? They are altogether blind. This happens daily to other enemies of the Gospel; and such blindness ought to instruct us to walk with fear.

28. When you shall have exalted the Son of man

Offended at that stupidity which the Evangelist has described, Christ again declares that they do not deserve that he should open his mouth to speak to them any more. "You now," says he, "have all your senses – as it were – fascinated, and, therefore, you understand nothing of all that I say; but the time will yet come, when you shall know that a Prophet of God has lived among you, and has spoken to you." This is the manner in which we ought to deal with wicked men; we ought expressly to summon them to the judgment-seat of God. But this knowledge, which Christ speaks of, comes too late, when the reprobate and unbelievers, dragged to punishment, reluctantly acknowledge that God, to whom

of living waters in the human spirit (John 3: 6), and by His indwelling in the renewed soul ensures their *unfailing flow*.

for the Holy Ghost was not yet *given* – Beyond all doubt the word "given," or some similar word, is the right supplement. In John 16: 7 the Holy Ghost is represented not only as the *gift of Christ*, but a gift the communication of which was *dependent upon His own departure to the Father*. Now as Christ was *not yet gone*, so the Holy Ghost *was not yet given*.

Jesus not yet glorified – The word "*glorified*" is here used advisedly, to teach the reader not only that the *departure* of Christ to the Father was *indispensable* to the giving of the Spirit, but that this illustrious Gift, direct from the hands of the ascended Saviour, was God's intimation to the world that He whom it had cast out, crucified, and slain, was "His Elect, in whom His soul delighted," and that it was through the smiting of that Rock that the waters of the Spirit – for which the Church was waiting, and with pomp at the feast of tabernacles proclaiming its expectation – had gushed forth upon a thirsty world.

40–43. Many ... when they heard this ... said, Of a truth, &c – The only wonder is they did not all say it. "But their minds were blinded."

42. scripture said ... of the seed of David, and out of ... Bethlehem, &c. – We accept this spontaneous testimony to our David-descended, Bethlehem-born Savior. Had those who gave it made the inquiry which the case demanded, they would have found that Jesus "came out of Galilee" (John 7: 41) and "out of Bethlehem" both, alike in fulfilment of prophecy as in point of fact. (Matt. 2: 23; 4: 13–16).

45. Then came the officers – "sent to take him" (John 7: 32).

46. Never man spake like this man – Noble testimony of unsophisticated men! Doubtless they were strangers to the profound intent of Christ's teaching, but there was that in it which by its mysterious grandeur and transparent purity and grace, held them spellbound. No doubt it was of God that they should so feel, that their arm might be paralyzed, as Christ's hour was not yet come; but even in human teaching there has sometimes been felt such a divine power, that men who came to kill them

(for example, ROWLAND HISS) have confessed to all that they were unmanned.

47. ye also deceived – In their own servants this seemed intolerable.

48. any of the rulers or ... Pharisees believed – "Many of them" did, including Nicodemus and Joseph, but not one of these had openly "confessed Him" (John 12: 42), and this appeal must have stung such of them as heard it to the quick.

49. But this people – literally, "multitude," meaning the *ignorant rabble*. (Pity these important distinctions, so marked in the original of this Gospel, should not be also in our version.)

50–53. Nicodemus – reappearing to us after nearly three years' absence from the history, as a member of the council, probably then sitting.

51. Doth our law, &c – a very proper, but all too tame rejoinder, and evidently more from pressure of conscience than any design to pronounce *positively* in the case. "The feebleness of his defense of Jesus has a strong contrast in the fierceness of the rejoinders of the Pharisees" [WEBSTER and WILKINSON].

52. thou of Galilee – in this taunt expressing their scorn of the party. Even a word of caution, or the gentlest proposal to inquire before condemning, was with them equivalent to an espousal of the hated One.

53. every man went unto his own home – *finding their plot could not at that time be carried into effect*. Is your rage thus impotent, ye chief priests?

JOHN 8

John 8: 1–11

THE WOMAN TAKEN IN ADULTERY.

1–2. Jesus went unto the Mount of Olives – This should have formed the last verse of the foregoing chapter. "The return of the people to the inert quiet and security of their *dwellings* (John 7: 53), at the close of the feast, is designedly contrasted with our Lord's *homeless* way, so to speak, of spending the short night, who is early in the morning on the scene again. One

47 He that is of God heareth God's words: ye therefore hear them not, because ye are not of God.

48 Then answered the Jews, and said unto him, Say we not well that thou art a Samaritan, and hast a devil?

49 Jesus answered, I have not a devil; but I honor my Father, and ye do dishonor me.

50 And I seek not mine own glory: there is one that seeketh and judgeth.

51 Verily, verily, I say unto you, If a man keep my saying, he shall never see death.

52 Then said the Jews unto him, Now we know that thou hast a devil. Abraham is dead, and the prophets; and thou sayest, If a man keep my saying, he shall never taste of death.

53 Art thou greater than our father Abraham, which is dead? and the prophets are dead: whom makest thou thyself?

54 Jesus answered, If I honor myself, my honor is nothing: it is my Father that honored me; of whom ye say, that he is your God:

55 Yet ye have not known him; but I know him: and if I should say, I know him not, I shall be a liar like unto you: but I know him, and keep his saying.

56 Your father Abraham rejoiced to see my day: and he saw it, and was glad.

57 Then said the Jews unto him, Thou art not yet fifty years old, and hast thou seen Abraham?

58 Jesus said unto them, Verily, verily, I say unto you, Before Abraham was, I am.

59 Then took they up stones to cast at him: but Jesus hid himself, and went out of the temple, going through the midst of them, and so passed by.

JOHN 9

1 And as Jesus passed by, he saw a man which was blind from his birth.

2 And his disciples asked him, saying, Master, who did sin, this man, or his parents, that he was born blind?

3 Jesus answered, Neither hath this man sinned, nor his parents: but that the works of God should be made manifest in him.

4 I must work the works of him that sent me, while it is day: the night cometh,

they ought mildly to have given honor and reverence, is their Judge. For he does not promise them repentance, but declares that, after they have been struck with new and unexpressed horror at the wrath of God, they will be aroused from that sleep in which they now repose. Thus Adam's eyes were opened, so that, overwhelmed with shame, he sought in vain for places of concealment, and ultimately was convinced that he was ruined. Yet that knowledge of Adam, which was in itself useless, turned to his advantage through the grace of God; but the reprobate, being overwhelmed with despair, have their eyes opened only for this purpose, that they may perceive their destruction. To this kind of knowledge God conducts them in a variety of ways. Sometimes it happens that, constrained by heavy afflictions, they learn that God is angry with them; sometimes, without any outward punishment, he inwardly torments them; and, at other times, he permits them to sleep until he call them out of the world.

59. Then they took up stones

There is reason to believe that they did this, as if Christ ought to be stoned according to the injunction of the Law (Leviticus 24: 16). Hence we infer how great is the madness of inconsiderate zeal; for they have no ears to know the cause, but they have hands ready to commit murder. I have no doubt that Christ rescued himself by his secret power, but yet under the appearance of a low condition; for he did not intend to make a clear display of his Divinity without leaving something for human infirmity. Some copies have the words, *And so Jesus passed through the midst of them*; which Erasmus justly considers to have been borrowed from the Gospel by Luke 4: 30. It deserves notice also, that the wicked priests and scribes, after having banished Christ, in whom dwelleth all the fullness of the Godhead (Colossians 2: 9), retain possession of the outward temple; but they are greatly deceived, when they think that they have a temple in which God does not dwell. Such is the course now pursued by the Pope and his followers. After having banished Christ, and in this manner profaned the Church, they foolishly glory in the false disguise of a Church.

JOHN 9

1. Jesus saw a man blind

In this chapter, the Evangelist describes the restoration of sight to the blind man, at the same time mingling doctrine, to point out the fruit of the miracle.

3. Neither did this man sin, nor his parents. Christ does not absolutely say that the blind man, and his parents, were free from all blame; but he declares that we ought not to seek

cannot well see why what is recorded in Luke 21: 37–38 may not even thus early have taken place; it might have been the Lord's ordinary custom from the beginning to leave the brilliant misery of the city every night, that so He might compose His sorrowful and interceding heart, and collect His energies for new labors of love; preferring for His resting-place Bethany, and the *Mount of Olives*, the scene thus consecrated by many preparatory prayers for His final humiliation and exaltation" [STIER].

3–6. scribes and Pharisees – foiled in their yesterday's attempt, and hoping to succeed better in this.

4–5. woman ... in adultery ... Moses ... commanded ... should be stoned – simply put to death (Deut. 22: 22), but in aggravated cases, at least in later times, this was probably by stoning (Ezek. 16: 40).

6. stooped down – It will be observed He was *sitting* when they came to Him.

with his finger wrote on the ground – The words of our translators in italics ("as though He heard them not") have hardly improved the sense, for it is scarcely probable He could wish that to be thought. Rather He wished to show them His aversion to enter on the subject. But as this did not suit them, they "continue asking Him," pressing for an answer. At last, raising Himself He said.

7. He that is without sin – not meaning sinless altogether; nor yet, guiltless of a literal breach of the Seventh Commandment; but probably, he whose conscience acquits him of *any such* sin.

8. again he stooped down and wrote – The design of this second stooping and writing on the ground was evidently to give her accusers an opportunity to slink away unobserved *by Him*, and so avoid an exposure to His eye which they could ill have stood. Accordingly it is added.

9. they ... convicted ... went out one by one ... Jesus was left alone – that is, without one of her accusers remaining; for it is added.

10. Woman, &c – What inimitable tenderness and grace! Conscious of her own guilt, and till now in the hands of men who had talked of stoning her, wondering at the *skill* with which

her accusers had been dispersed, and the *grace* of the few words addressed to herself, she would be disposed to listen, with a reverence and teachableness before unknown, to our Lord's admonition. "And Jesus said unto her, Neither do I condemn thee, go and sin no more." He pronounces no pardon upon the woman (such as, "Thy sins are forgiven thee" [compare Luke 5: 28; 7: 48] – "Go in peace" [compare Mark 5: 34; Luke 7: 50; 8: 48]), much less does He say that she had done nothing condemnable; He simply leaves the matter where it was.

John 8: 12–59

FURTHER DISCOURSES OF JESUS – ATTEMPT TO STONE HIM.

12. I am the light of the world – As the former references to *water* (John 4: 13–14; 7: 37–39) and to *bread* (John 6: 35) were occasioned by outward occurrences, so this one to *light*. In "the treasury" where it was spoken (see on John 8: 20) stood two colossal golden lampstands, on which hung a multitude of lamps, lighted after the evening sacrifice (probably every evening during the feast of tabernacles), diffusing their brilliancy, it is said, over all the city. Around these the people danced with great rejoicing.

13–19. bearest record of thyself; thy record is not true – How does He meet this specious cavil? Not by disputing the wholesome human maxim that "self-praise is no praise," but by affirming that He was *an exception to the rule*, or rather, that it *had no application to Him*.

15. Ye judge after the flesh – with no spiritual apprehension.

I judge no man.

16. And yet if I judge, my judgment is true, &c – Ye not only *form* your carnal and warped judgments of Me, but are bent on carrying them into effect; I, though I form and utter My judgment of you, am not here to carry this into execution – that is reserved to a future day; yet the judgment I now pronounce and the witness I now bear is not Mine only as ye suppose, but His also that sent Me.

20. These words spake Jesus in the treasury – a division, so called, of the fore court of

when no man can work.

5 As long as I am in the world, I am the light of the world.

6 When he had thus spoken, he spat on the ground, and made clay of the spittle, and he anointed the eyes of the blind man with the clay,

7 And said unto him, Go, wash in the pool of Siloam, (which is by interpretation, Sent.) He went his way therefore, and washed, and came seeing.

8 The neighbours therefore, and they which before had seen him that he was blind, said, Is not this he that sat and begged?

9 Some said, This is he: others said, He is like him: but he said, I am he.

10 Therefore said they unto him, How were thine eyes opened?

11 He answered and said, A man that is called Jesus made clay, and anointed mine eyes, and said unto me, Go to the pool of Siloam, and wash: and I went and washed, and I received sight.

12 Then said they unto him, Where is he? He said, I know not.

13 They brought to the Pharisees him that aforetime was blind.

14 And it was the sabbath day when Jesus made the clay, and opened his eyes.

15 Then again the Pharisees also asked him how he had received his sight. He said unto them, He put clay upon mine eyes, and I washed, and do see.

16 Therefore said some of the Pharisees, This man is not of God, because he keepeth not the sabbath day. Others said, How can a man that is a sinner do such miracles? And there was a division among them.

17 They say unto the blind man again, What sayest thou of him, that he hath opened thine eyes? He said, He is a prophet.

18 But the Jews did not believe concerning him, that he had been blind, and received his sight, until they called the parents of him that had received his sight.

19 And they asked them, saying, Is this your son, who ye say was born blind? how then doth he now see?

20 His parents answered them and said, We know that this is our son, and

the cause of the blindness in sin. And this is what I have already said, that God has sometimes another object in view than to punish the sins of men, when he sends afflictions to them. Consequently, when the causes of afflictions are concealed, we ought to restrain curiosity, that we may neither dishonor God nor be malicious towards our brethren. Wherefore, Christ assigns another reason. This man, he says, was born blind — *That the works of God might be manifested in him.* He does not, say a single work, but uses the plural number, *works*; for, so long as he was blind, there was exhibited in him a proof of the severity of God, from which others might learn to fear and to humble themselves.

18. But the Jews did not believe

There are two things here which ought to be observed; that *they do not believe* that a miracle has been performed, and that, being wilfully blinded through a perverse hatred of Christ, they do not perceive what is manifest. The Evangelist tells us that *they did not believe.* If the reason be asked, there can be no doubt that their blindness was voluntary. For what prevents them from seeing an obvious work of God placed before their eyes; or, after having been fully convinced, what prevents them from believing what they already know, except that the inward malice of their heart keeps their eyes shut? Paul informs us that the same thing takes place in the doctrine of the Gospel; for he says that it is not *hidden* or obscure, except to the reprobate, whose understandings the god of this world hath blinded (2 Corinthians 4: 3–4).

Warned by such examples, let us learn not to bring upon ourselves those obstacles which drive us away from the faith. By *the Jews,* the Evangelist means that part of them which held the government of the people.

24. A second time, therefore, they called the man who had been blind

There can be no doubt that they were constrained by shame to call the blind man, whom they had previously found to be too firm and steady. In this way, the more fiercely they struggle against God, the more numerous are the cords which they put about their neck, and the more strongly do they bind themselves. Besides, they put the questions in such a manner as to endeavor to make the man say what they wish. It is a plausible preface, indeed, when they exhort him to *give glory to God;* but immediately afterwards they strictly forbid him to answer according to the conviction of his mind; and therefore, under the pretense of the name of God, they demand from him servile obedience.

34. Thou wast altogether born in sins

They alluded, I doubt not, to his blindness; as proud men

DAVID BROWN

the temple, part of the court of the women [JOSEPHUS, *Antiquities*, 19.6.2, &c.], which may confirm the genuineness of John 8: 2–11, as the place where the woman was brought.

22. Then said the Jews, Will he kill himself? – seeing something more in His words than before (John 7: 35), but their question more malignant and scornful.

23. Ye are from beneath; I am from above – contrasting Himself, not as in John 3: 31, simply with *earthborn messengers of God,* but *with men sprung from and breathing an opposite element* from His, which rendered it impossible that He and they should have any present fellowship, or dwell eternally together.

24. if ye believe not that I am he, ye shall die in your sins – They knew well enough what He meant (Mark 13: 6, *Greek;* compare Matt. 24: 5). But He would not, by speaking it out, give them the materials for a charge for which they were watching. At the same time, one is irresistibly reminded by such language, so far transcending what is becoming in *men,* of those ancient declarations of the God of Israel, "I AM HE" (Deut. 32: 39; Is. 43: 10,13; 46: 4; 48: 12).

25. Who art thou? – hoping thus to extort an explicit answer; but they are disappointed.

26–27. I have many things to say and to judge of you; but he that sent me is true, &c – that is, I could, and at the fitting time, will say and judge many things of you (referring perhaps to the work of the Spirit which is for *judgment* as well as *salvation,* John 16: 8), but what I do say is just the message My Father hath given Me to deliver.

28–30. When ye have lifted up the Son of man – The plainest intimation He had yet given *in public* of *the manner and the authors* of His death.

29. the Father hath not left me alone; for I do always those things that please him, &c – that is, To you, who gnash upon Me with your teeth, and frown down all open appearance for Me, I seem to stand uncountenanced and alone; but I have a sympathy and support transcending all human applause; I came hither to do My Father's will, and in the doing of it have not ceased to please Him; therefore is He ever by Me with His approving smile, His cheering words, His supporting arm.

30. As he spake these words, many believed on him – Instead of wondering at this, the wonder would be if words of such unearthly, surpassing grandeur *could* be uttered without captivating *some* that heard them.

31–33. Then said Jesus to those Jews who believed, If ye continue in my word, then are ye my disciples indeed, &c – The impression produced by the last words of our Lord may have become visible by some decisive movement, and here He takes advantage of it to press on them *"continuance"* in the faith, since then only were they His real disciples (compare John 15: 3–8), and then should they *experimentally* "know the truth," and "by the truth be made (*spiritually*) free."

34–35. Whosoever committeth sin – that is, *liveth in the commission* of it – (Compare 1 John 3: 8; Matt. 7: 23.)

   is the servant of sin – that is, the *bond-servant,* or *slave* of it; for the question is not about free service, but who are in *bondage.* (Compare 2 Pet. 2: 19; Rev. 6: 16.)

35. And the servant abideth not in the house for ever, but the Son abideth ever – that is, "And if your connection with the family of God be that of BOND-SERVANTS, ye have no *natural tie* to the house; your tie is essentially *uncertain and precarious.*

37–41. ye seek to kill me – He had said this to their face before: He now repeats it, and they do not deny it; yet are they held back, as by some marvellous spell – it was the awe which His combined dignity, courage, and benignity struck into them.

39. If ye were Abraham's children, ye would do the works of Abraham – He had just said He "knew they were Abraham's children," that is, according to the *flesh;* but the children of his *faith and holiness* they were not, but the reverse.

40. this did not Abraham – In so doing ye act in direct opposition to him.

41. We be not born of fornication ... we have one Father, God – meaning, as is generally allowed, that they were not an illegitimate

that he was born blind:

21 But by what means he now seeth, we know not; or who hath opened his eyes, we know not: he is of age; ask him: he shall speak for himself.

22 These words spake his parents, because they feared the Jews: for the Jews had agreed already, that if any man did confess that he was Christ, he should be put out of the synagogue.

23 Therefore said his parents, He is of age; ask him.

24 Then again called they the man that was blind, and said unto him, Give God the praise: we know that this man is a sinner.

25 He answered and said, Whether he be a sinner or no, I know not: one thing I know, that, whereas I was blind, now I see.

26 Then said they to him again, What did he to thee? how opened he thine eyes?

27 He answered them, I have told you already, and ye did not hear: wherefore would ye hear it again? will ye also be his disciples?

28 Then they reviled him, and said, Thou art his disciple; but we are Moses' disciples.

29 We know that God spake unto Moses: as for this fellow, we know not from whence he is.

30 The man answered and said unto them, Why herein is a marvelous thing, that ye know not from whence he is, and yet he hath opened mine eyes.

31 Now we know that God heareth not sinners: but if any man be a worshipper of God, and doeth his will, him he heareth.

32 Since the world began was it not heard that any man opened the eyes of one that was born blind.

33 If this man were not of God, he could do nothing.

34 They answered and said unto him, Thou wast altogether born in sins, and dost thou teach us? And they cast him out.

35 Jesus heard that they had cast him out; and when he had found him, he said unto him, Dost thou believe on the Son of God?

36 He answered and said, Who is he, Lord, that I might believe on him?

37 And Jesus said unto him, Thou hast

are wont to teaze those who have any distress or calamity; and, therefore, they continually insult him, as if he had come out of his mother's womb, bearing the mark of his *sins* For all the scribes were convinced in their hearts, that souls, after having finished one life, entered into new bodies, and there suffered the punishment of their former crimes. Hence they conclude that he who was born blind was, at that very time, covered and polluted by his sins.

This undeserved censure ought to instruct us to be exceedingly cautious, not always to estimate the sins of any person by the chastisements of God; for, as we have already seen, God has various ends to accomplish, by inflicting calamities on men. But not only do those hypocrites insult the wretched man; they likewise reject disdainfully his warnings, though they are holy and good; as indeed it very frequently happens that one cannot endure to be taught by him whom he despises. Now, since we ought always to hear God, by whomsoever he may talk to us, let us learn not to despise any man, that God may find us always mild and submissive, even though he employ a person altogether mean and despicable to instruct us. For there is not a more dangerous plague than when pride stops our ears, so that we do not deign to hear those who warn us for our profit; and it frequently happens that God purposely selects vile and worthless persons to instruct and warn us, in order to subdue our pride.

41. If you were blind

These words may be explained in two ways; either, that ignorance would, in some degree, alleviate their guilt, if they were not fully convinced, and did not deliberately fight against the truth; or, that there was reason to hope that their disease of ignorance might be cured, if they would only acknowledge it. The former view is supported by the words of Christ, If I had not come and spoken to them, they would have no sin (John 15: 22).

But as it is added in this passage, *but now you say you see,* in order that the points of contrast may correspond to each other, it appears to be more consistent to explain them to mean, that he is *blind* who, aware of his own blindness, seeks a remedy to cure his disease. In this way the meaning will be, "If you would acknowledge your disease, it would not be altogether incurable; but now because you think that you are in perfect health, you continue in a desperate state." When he says that *they who are blind have no sin,* this does not excuse ignorance, as if it were harmless, and were placed beyond the reach of condemnation. He only means that the disease may easily be cured, when it is truly felt; because, when a *blind* man is desirous to obtain deliverance, God is ready to assist him; but they who, insensible to their diseases, despise the grace of God, are incurable.

DAVID BROWN

race in point of *religion*, pretending only to be God's people, but were descended from His own chosen Abraham.

42–43. If God were your Father, ye would love me – "If ye had anything of His moral image, as children have their father's likeness, ye would love Me, for I am immediately of Him and directly from Him." But "My speech" (meaning His peculiar style of expressing Himself on these subjects) is unintelligible to you because ye cannot take in the truth which it conveys.

44. Ye are of your father the devil – "This is one of the most decisive testimonies to the *objective* (outward) *personality* of the devil. It is quite impossible to suppose an accommodation to Jewish views, or a metaphorical form of speech, in so solemn an assertion as this" [ALFORD].

45–47. And because I tell you the truth, ye believe me not – not *although*, but just *because* He did so, for the reason given in the former verse. Had He been *less* true they would have hailed Him more readily.

46. Which of you convinceth me of sin – "Convicteth," bringeth home a charge of sin. Glorious dilemma! "Convict Me of sin, and reject Me: If not, why stand ye out against My claims?" Of course, they could only be supposed to impeach His *life;* but in One who had already passed through unparalleled complications, and had continually to deal with friends and foes of every sort and degree, such a challenge thrown wide among His bitterest enemies, can amount to nothing short of a claim to *absolute sinlessness.*

48–51. Say we not well that thou art a Samaritan, and hast a devil? – What intense and virulent scorn! (See Heb. 12: 3). The "say we not well!" refers to John 7: 20. "A Samaritan" means more than "no Israelite at all"; it means one who *pretended, but had no manner of claim* to the title – retorting perhaps, this denial of their *true* descent from Abraham.

51. If a man keep my saying, he shall never see death – Partly thus vindicating His lofty claims as Lord of the kingdom of life everlasting, and, at the same time, holding out even to His revilers the scepter of grace. The word

"keep" is in harmony with John 8: 31, "If ye *continue* in My word," expressing the permanency, as a living and paramount principle, of that faith to which He referred: *"never see death,"* though virtually uttered before (John 5: 24; 6: 40,47,51), is the strongest and most naked statement of a very glorious truth yet given. (In John 11: 26 it is repeated in nearly identical terms.)

52–53. Then said the Jews unto him, Now we know that thou hast a devil, &c – "Thou art now self-convicted; only a demoniActs could speak so; the most illustrious of our fathers are dead, and Thou promisest exemption from death to anyone who will keep *Thy saying!* pray, who art Thou?"

55. I shall be a liar like unto you – now rising to the summit of holy, naked severity, thereby to draw this long dialogue to a head.

56. Abraham rejoiced to see my day, &c – exulted, or exceedingly rejoiced that he should see, he exulted to see it, that is, by *anticipation.* Nay,

57–59. Then said the Jews unto him, Thou art not yet fifty years old – "No inference can be drawn from this as to the age of our Lord at the time as man. Fifty years was with the Jews the completion of manhood" [ALFORD].

JOHN 9

John 9: 1–41

THE OPENING OF THE EYES OF ONE BORN BLIND, AND WHAT FOLLOWED ON IT.

1–5. as Jesus passed by, he saw a man which was blind from birth – and who "sat begging" (John 9: 8).

2. who did sin, this man or his parents, that he was born blind – not in a former state of existence, in which, as respects the wicked, the Jews did not believe; but, perhaps, expressing loosely that sin *somewhere* had surely been the cause of this calamity.

3. Neither ... this man, &c – The cause was neither in himself nor his parents, but, in order to the manifestation of "the works of God," in his cure.

4. I must work the works of him that sent

both seen him, and it is he that talketh with thee.

38 And he said, Lord, I believe. And he worshipped him.

39 And Jesus said, For judgment I am come into this world, that they which see not might see; and that they which see might be made blind.

40 And some of the Pharisees which were with him heard these words, and said unto him, Are we blind also?

41 Jesus said unto them, If ye were blind, ye should have no sin: but now ye say, We see; therefore your sin remaineth.

JOHN 10

1 Verily, verily, I say unto you, He that entereth not by the door into the sheepfold, but climbeth up some other way, the same is a thief and a robber.

2 But he that entereth in by the door is the shepherd of the sheep.

3 To him the porter openeth; and the sheep hear his voice: and he calleth his own sheep by name, and leadeth them out.

4 And when he putteth forth his own sheep, he goeth before them, and the sheep follow him: for they know his voice.

5 And a stranger will they not follow, but will flee from him: for they know not the voice of strangers.

6 This parable spake Jesus unto them: but they understood not what things they were which he spake unto them.

7 Then said Jesus unto them again, Verily, verily, I say unto you, I am the door of the sheep.

8 All that ever came before me are thieves and robbers: but the sheep did not hear them.

9 I am the door: by me if any man enter in, he shall be saved, and shall go in and out, and find pasture.

10 The thief cometh not, but for to steal, and to kill, and to destroy: I am come that they might have life, and that they might have it more abundantly.

11 I am the good shepherd: the good shepherd giveth his life for the sheep.

12 But he that is an hireling, and not the shepherd, whose own the sheep are

JOHN 10

7. I am the door

If this explanation had not been added, the whole discourse would have been allegorical. He now explains more clearly what was the chief part of the parable when he declares that *he is the door* The amount of what is stated is, that the principal point of all spiritual doctrine, on which souls are fed, consists in Christ. Hence also Paul, one of the shepherds, says: I reckon nothing to be worth knowing but Jesus Christ (1 Corinthians 2: 2). And this mode of expression conveys the same meaning as if Christ had testified that to him alone we must all be gathered together. Therefore, he invokes and exhorts all who desire salvation to come to him. By these words, he means that in vain do they wander about who leave him to go to God, because there is but one open *door* , and all approach in any other way is prohibited.

11. The good shepherd giveth his life for the sheep

From the extraordinary affection which he bears towards the *sheep,* he shows how truly he acts towards them as a *shepherd;* for he is so anxious about their salvation, that he does not even spare his own life. Hence it follows, that they who reject the guardianship of so kind and amiable a *shepherd* are exceedingly ungrateful, and deserve a hundred deaths, and are exposed to every kind of harm. The remark of Augustine is exceedingly just, that this passage informs us what we ought to desire, what we ought to avoid, and what we ought to endure, in the government of the Church. Nothing is more desirable than that the Church should be governed by good and diligent *shepherds.* Christ declares that *he is the good shepherd,* who keeps his Church safe and sound, first, by himself, and, next, by his agents. Whenever there is good order, and fit men hold the government, then Christ shows that he is actually *the shepherd.* But there are many wolves and thieves who, wearing the garb of *shepherds,* wickedly scatter the Church. Whatever name such persons may assume, Christ threatens that we must avoid them.

12. But the hireling

By *hirelings* we are to understand those who retain the pure doctrine, and who proclaim the truth, as Paul says, to serve a purpose rather than from pure zeal. Though such persons do not serve Christ faithfully, yet we ought to hear them; for Christ wished that *the Pharisees* should be heard, *because they sat in Moses' seat* (Matthew 23: 2); and, in like manner, we ought to give such honor to the Gospel, as not to shrink from its ministers, though they be not good men. And as even the slightest offenses render the Gospel distasteful to us, that we may not be hindered by such false delicacy, let us always remember what I have formerly suggested,

DAVID BROWN

me, &c – a most interesting statement from the mouth of Christ; intimating, (1) that He had a precise work to do upon earth, with every particular of it arranged and laid out to Him; (2) that all He did upon earth was just "the works of God" – particularly "going about *doing good*," though not exclusively by miracles; (3) that each work had its precise *time* and *place* in His program of instructions, so to speak; hence, (4) that as His period for work had definite termination, so by letting any one service pass by its allotted time, the whole would be disarranged, marred, and driven beyond its destined period for completion; (5) that He acted ever under the impulse of these considerations, as man – "the night cometh when no man (or no one) can work." What lessons are here for others, and what encouragement from such Example!

5. As long as I am in the world, I am the light of the world – not as if He would cease, after that, to be so; but that He must make full proof of His fidelity while His earthly career lasted by displaying His glory. "As before the raising of Lazarus (John 11: 25), He announces Himself as *the Resurrection and the Life*, so now He sets Himself forth as the source of the archetypal spiritual light, of which the natural, now about to be conferred, is only a derivation and symbol" [ALFORD].

6–7. he spat on the ground, and made clay ... and he anointed the eyes of the blind man – These operations were not so incongruous in their nature as might appear, though it were absurd to imagine that they contributed in the least degree to the effect which followed.

7. Go, wash in the pool of Siloam, ... Sent, &c – (See 2 Kgs. 5: 10,14). As the prescribed action was purely symbolical in its design, so in connection with it the Evangelist notices the symbolical name of the pool as in this case bearing testimony to him who was *sent* to do what it only *symbolized*. (See Is. 8: 6, where this same pool is used figuratively to denote "the streams that make glad the city of God," and which, humble though they be, betoken *a present God of Israel*.)

8–15. The neighbours therefore ... said, Is

not this he that sat and begged – Here are a number of details to identify the newly seeing with the long-known blind beggar.

13. They brought to the Pharisees – sitting probably in council, and chiefly of that sect (John 7: 47–48).

Others said, &c – such as Nicodemus and Joseph.

17. the blind man ... said, He is a prophet – rightly viewing the miracle as but a "sign" of His prophetic commission.

18–23. the Jews did not believe ... he had been born blind ... till they called the parents of him that had received his sight – Foiled by the testimony of the young man himself, they hope to throw doubt on the fact by close questioning his parents, who, perceiving the snare laid for them, ingeniously escape it by testifying simply to the identity of their son, and his birth-blindness, leaving it to himself, as a competent witness, to speak as to the cure.

24–34. Give God the praise; we know that this man is a sinner – not wishing him to own, even to the praise of God, that a miracle had been wrought upon him, but to show more regard to the honor of God than ascribe any such act to one who was a sinner.

25. He answered and said, Whether he be a sinner *or no*, &c – Not that the man meant to insinuate any doubt in his own mind on the point of His being "a sinner," but as his *opinion* on such a point would be of no consequence to others, he would speak only to what he *knew* as *fact* in his *own case*.

26. Then said they ... again, What did he to thee? &c – hoping by repeated questions to ensnare him, but the youth is more than a match for them.

27. I have told you already ... will ye also be his disciples? – In a vein of keen irony he treats their questions as those of anxious inquirers, almost ready for discipleship! Stung by this, they retort upon *him* as the disciple (and here they plainly were not wrong); for themselves, they fall back upon Moses; about *him* there could be no doubt; but who knew about this upstart?

30. He had no need to say another word; but

not, seeth the wolf coming, and leaveth the sheep, and fleeth: and the wolf catcheth them, and scattereth the sheep.

13 The hireling fleeth, because he is an hireling, and careth not for the sheep.

14 I am the good shepherd, and know my sheep, and am known of mine.

15 As the Father knoweth me, even so know I the Father: and I lay down my life for the sheep.

16 And other sheep I have, which are not of this fold: them also I must bring, and they shall hear my voice; and there shall be one fold, and one shepherd.

17 Therefore doth my Father love me, because I lay down my life, that I might take it again.

18 No man taketh it from me, but I lay it down of myself. I have power to lay it down, and I have power to take it again. This commandment have I received of my Father.

19 There was a division therefore again among the Jews for these sayings.

20 And many of them said, He hath a devil, and is mad; why hear ye him?

21 Others said, These are not the words of him that hath a devil. Can a devil open the eyes of the blind?

22 And it was at Jerusalem the feast of the dedication, and it was winter.

23 And Jesus walked in the temple in Solomon's porch.

24. Then came the Jews round about him, and said unto him, How long dost thou make us to doubt? If thou be the Christ, tell us plainly.

25 Jesus answered them, I told you, and ye believed not: the works that I do in my Father's name, they bear witness of me.

26 But ye believe not, because ye are not of my sheep, as I said unto you.

27 My sheep hear my voice, and I know them, and they follow me:

28 And I give unto them eternal life; and they shall never perish, neither shall any man pluck them out of my hand.

29 My Father, which gave them me, is greater than all; and no man is able to pluck them out of my Father's hand.

30 I and my Father are one.

31 Then the Jews took up stones again to stone him.

32 Jesus answered them, Many good

that if the Spirit of Christ does not operate so powerfully in ministers, as to make it plainly evident that he is their *shepherd*, we suffer the punishment of our sins, and yet our obedience is proved.

20. He hath a devil

They employ the most offensive reproach which they can devise, in slandering Christ, that all may shudder at the thought of hearing him. For wicked men, that they may not be forced to yield to God, in a furious manner, and with closed eyes, break out into proud contempt of him, and excite others to the same rage, so that not a single word of Christ is heard in silence. But the doctrine of Christ has sufficient power in itself to defend it against slanders.

39. Therefore they sought again to seize him

This was undoubtedly that they might drive him out of the temple, and immediately stone him; for their rage was not at all abated by the words of Christ. As to what the Evangelist says, that *he escaped out of their hands,* this could not be accomplished in any other way than by a wonderful exertion of Divine power. This reminds us that we are not exposed to the lawless passions of wicked men, which God restrains by his bridle, whenever he thinks fit.

40. He went away beyond Jordan

Christ passed *beyond Jordan* that he might not have to fight continually without any advantage. He has therefore taught us, by his example, that we ought to avail ourselves of opportunities, when they occur. As to the place of his retreat, the reader may consult the observations which I have made at Chapter 1, verse 28.

41. And many came to him

This large assembly shows that Christ did not seek solitude, in order to cease from the discharge of his duty, but to erect a sanctuary of God in the wilderness, when Jerusalem, which was his own abode and dwelling-place, had obstinately driven him out. And indeed this was a dreadful vengeance of God, that, while the temple chosen by God was *a den of robbers* (Jeremiah 7: 11; Matthew 21: 13), the Church of God was collected in a despised place.

John indeed did no miracle

They infer that Christ is more excellent than *John,* because he has distinguished himself by so many miracles, while *John did not perform a single miracle.* Not that we ought always to judge from *miracles,* but that *miracles,* when united with doctrine, have no small weight, as has already been repeatedly mentioned. Their argument is defective; for they compare Christ with John, but they express only one part of the comparison. Besides, they take for granted, that John

waxing bolder in defense of his Benefactor, and his views brightening by the very courage which it demanded, he puts it to them how they could pretend inability to tell whether one who opened the eyes of a man born blind was "of God" or "a sinner" – from above or from beneath – and proceeds to argue the case with remarkable power. So irresistible was his argument that their rage burst forth in a speech of intense Pharisaism, "Thou wast altogether born in sins, and dost thou teach us?" – thou, a base-born, uneducated, impudent youth, teach us, the trained, constituted, recognized guides of the people in the things of God! Out upon thee!

31. they cast him out – judicially, no doubt, as well in fact. The allusion to his being "born in sins" seems a tacit admission of his being blind from birth – the very thing they had been so unwilling to own. But rage and enmity to truth are seldom consistent in their outbreaks. The friends of this excommunicated youth, crowding around him with their sympathy, would probably express surprise that One who could work such a cure should be unable to protect his patient from the persecution it had raised against him, or should possess the power without using it. Nor would it be strange if such thoughts should arise in the youth's own mind. But if they did, it is certain, from what follows, that they made no lodgment there, conscious as he was that "whereas he was blind, now he saw," and satisfied that if his Benefactor "were not of God, He could do nothing" (John 9: 33). There was a word for him too, which, if whispered in his ear from the oracles of God, would seem expressly designed to describe his case, and prepare him for the coming interview with his gracious Friend.

35–38. Jesus heard – that is, by intelligence brought Him.

that they had cast him out; and when he had found him – by accident? Not very likely. Sympathy in that breast could not long keep aloof from its object.

he said unto him, Dost thou believe on the Son of God? – A question stretching purposely beyond his present attainments, in order the more quickly to lead him – in his present teachable frame – into the highest truth.

36. He answered and said, Who is he, Lord, that I may believe on him? – "His reply is affirmative, and believing by anticipation, promising faith as soon as Jesus shall say who He is" [STIER].

37. Jesus said unto him, Thou hast both seen him – the new sense of sight having at that moment its highest exercise, in gazing upon "the Light of the world."

38. he said, Lord, I believe: and he worshipped him – a *faith* and a *worship*, beyond doubt, meant to express far more than he would think proper to any human "prophet" (John 9: 17) – the unstudied, resistless expression, probably of SUPREME faith and adoration, though without the full understanding of what that implied.

39–41. Jesus said – perhaps at the same time, but after a crowd, including some of the skeptical and scornful rulers, had, on seeing Jesus talking with the healed youth, hastened to the spot.

that they which see not might see, &c – rising to that *sight* of which the natural vision communicated to the youth was but the symbol.

that they which see might be made blind – judicially incapable of apprehending and receiving the truth, to which they have wilfully shut their eyes.

40. Are we blind also? – We, the constituted, recognized guides of the people in spiritual things? pride and rage prompting the question.

41. If ye were blind – wanted light to discern My claims, and only waited to receive it.

ye should have no sin – none of the guilt of shutting out the light.

ye say, We see; therefore your sin remaineth – Your claim to possess light, while rejecting Me, is that which seals you up in the guilt of unbelief.

JOHN 10

John 10: 1–21

THE GOOD SHEPHERD.

This discourse seems plainly to be a continuation of the closing verses of the ninth chapter.

works have I shewed you from my Father; for which of those works do ye stone me?

33 The Jews answered him, saying, For a good work we stone thee not; but for blasphemy; and because that thou, being a man, makest thyself God.

34 Jesus answered them, Is it not written in your law, I said, Ye are gods?

35 If he called them gods, unto whom the word of God came, and the scripture cannot be broken;

36 Say ye of him, whom the Father hath sanctified, and sent into the world, Thou blasphemest; because I said, I am the Son of God?

37 If I do not the works of my Father, believe me not.

38 But if I do, though ye believe not me, believe the works: that ye may know, and believe, that the Father is in me, and I in him.

39 Therefore they sought again to take him: but he escaped out of their hand,

40 And went away again beyond Jordan into the place where John at first baptized; and there he abode.

41 And many resorted unto him, and said, John did no miracle: but all things that John spake of this man were true.

42 And many believed on him there.

JOHN 11

1 Now a certain man was sick, named Lazarus, of Bethany, the town of Mary and her sister Martha.

2 (It was that Mary which anointed the Lord with ointment, and wiped his feet with her hair, whose brother Lazarus was sick.)

3 Therefore his sisters sent unto him, saying, Lord, behold, he whom thou lovest is sick.

4 When Jesus heard that, he said, This sickness is not unto death, but for the glory of God, that the Son of God might be glorified thereby.

5 Now Jesus loved Martha, and her sister, and Lazarus.

6 When he had heard therefore that he was sick, he abode two days still in the same place where he was.

7 Then after that saith he to his disciples, Let us go into Judaea again.

was an eminent prophet of God, and that he was endued with extraordinary grace of the Holy Spirit. They justly argue, therefore, that Christ ought to be preferred to John, because it was only by the fixed Providence of God that it was brought about that *John,* though in other respects a very great prophet, yet was not honored by performing any miracle. Hence they conclude, that this was done on Christ's account, that he might be more highly esteemed.

JOHN 11

1. And one named Lazarus was sick

The Evangelist passes on to another narrative, which contains a miracle eminently worthy of being recorded. For not only did Christ give a remarkable proof of his Divine power in raising Lazarus, but he likewise placed before our eyes a lively image of our future resurrection. This might indeed be said to be the latest and concluding action of his life, for the time of his death was already at hand. We need not wonder, therefore, if he illustrated his own glory, in an extraordinary manner, in that work, the remembrance of which he wished to be deeply impressed on their minds, that it might seal, in some respects, all that had gone before. There were others whom Christ had raised from the dead, but he now displays his power on a rotting corpse.

5. And Jesus loved Martha and her sister, and Lazarus

These two things appear to be inconsistent with each other, that Christ *remains two days* beyond Jordan, as if he did not care about the life of Lazarus, and yet the Evangelist says, that Christ *loved him and his sisters;* for, since *love* produces anxiety, he ought to have hastened immediately. As Christ is the only mirror of the grace of God, we are taught by this delay on his part, that we ought not to judge of the love of God from the condition which we see before our eyes. When we have prayed to him, he often delays his assistance, either that he may increase still more our ardor in prayer, or that he may exercise our patience, and, at the same time, accustom us to obedience. Let believers then implore the assistance of God, but let them also learn to suspend their desires, if he does not stretch out his hand for their assistance as soon as they may think that necessity requires; for, whatever may be his delay, he never sleeps, and never forgets his people. Yet let us also be fully assured that he wishes all whom he loves to be saved.

25. I am the resurrection and the life

Christ first declares that *he is the resurrection and the life,* and then he explains, separately and distinctly, each clause of this sentence. His first statement is, that *he is the resurrection,* because the restoration from death to life naturally

The figure was familiar to the Jewish ear (from Jer. 23: 1–40; Ezek. 34: 1–31; Zech. 11: 1–17, &c.). "This simple creature [the sheep] has this special note among all animals, that it quickly hears the voice of the shepherd, follows no one else, depends entirely on him, and seeks help from him alone – cannot help itself, but is shut up to another's aid" [LUTHER in STIER].

1-2. He that entereth not by the door – the legitimate way (without saying what that was, as yet).

into the sheepfold – the sacred enclosure of God's true people.

climbeth up some other way – not referring to the assumption of ecclesiastical office without an external call, for those Jewish rulers, specially aimed at, had this (Matt. 23: 2), but to the want of a true spiritual commission, the seal of heaven going along with the outward authority; it is the assumption of spiritual guidance of the people *without this* that is meant.

2. he that entereth in by the door is the shepherd of the sheep – a true, divinely recognized shepherd.

3. To him the porter openeth – that is, *right of free access* is given, by order of Him to whom the sheep belong; for it is better not to give the allusion a more specific interpretation [CALVIN, MEYER, LUTHARDT].

7-14. I am the door of the sheep – that is, *the way in* to the fold, with all blessed privileges, both for shepherds and sheep (compare John 14: 6; Eph. 2: 18).

8. All that ever came before me – the false prophets; not as claiming the prerogatives of Messiah, but as perverters of the people from the way of life, all pointing to Him [OLSHAUSEN].

9. shall be saved – the great object of the pastoral office, as of all the divine arrangements towards mankind.

10. I am come that they might have life, and ... more abundantly – not merely to *preserve* but *impart* LIFE, and communicate it in rich and unfailing exuberance. What a claim! Yet it is only an echo of all His teaching; and He who uttered these and like words must be either a blasphemer, all worthy of the death He died,

or "God with us" – there can be no middle course.

11. I am the good shepherd – emphatically, and, in the sense intended, exclusively so (Is. 40: 11; Ezek. 34: 23; 37: 24; Zech. 13: 7).

12. an hireling ... whose own the sheep are not – who has no *property*, in them. By this He points to His own peculiar relation to the sheep, the same as His Father's, the great Proprietor and Lord of the flock, who styles Him "My Shepherd, *the Man that is My Fellow*" (Zech. 13: 7), and though faithful under-shepherds are so in their Master's interest, that they feel a measure of His own concern for their charge, the language is strictly applicable only to "the Son over His own house" (Heb. 3: 6).

14. I am the good shepherd, and know my sheep – in the peculiar sense of 2 Tim. 2: 19.

16. other sheep I have ... not of this fold: them also I must bring – He means the perishing Gentiles, *already His "sheep"* in the love of His heart and the purpose of His grace to "*bring* them" in due time.

and there shall be one fold – rather "one flock" (for the word for "fold," as in the foregoing verses, is quite different).

17. Therefore doth my Father love me, because I lay down my life, &c – As the highest act of the Son's love to the Father was the laying down of His life for the sheep at His "commandment," so the Father's love to Him as His *incarnate* Son reaches its consummation, and finds its highest justification, in that sublimest and most affecting of all acts.

18. It is impossible for language more plainly and emphatically to express the *absolute voluntariness* of Christ's death, such a voluntariness as it would be manifest presumption in any mere *creature* to affirm of his own death. It is beyond all doubt the language of One who was conscious that *His life was His own* (which no creature's is), and therefore His to surrender or retain *at will*. Here lay the glory of His sacrifice, that it was *purely* voluntary. The claim of "power to take it again" is no less important, as showing that His resurrection, though ascribed to the Father, in the sense we shall presently see, was nevertheless *His own*

8 His disciples say unto him, Master, the Jews of late sought to stone thee; and goest thou thither again?

9 Jesus answered, Are there not twelve hours in the day? If any man walk in the day, he stumbleth not, because he seeth the light of this world.

10 But if a man walk in the night, he stumbleth, because there is no light in him.

11 These things said he: and after that he saith unto them, Our friend Lazarus sleepeth; but I go, that I may awake him out of sleep.

12 Then said his disciples, Lord, if he sleep, he shall do well.

13 Howbeit Jesus spake of his death: but they thought that he had spoken of taking of rest in sleep.

14 Then said Jesus unto them plainly, Lazarus is dead.

15 And I am glad for your sakes that I was not there, to the intent ye may believe; nevertheless let us go unto him.

16 Then said Thomas, which is called Didymus, unto his fellowdisciples, Let us also go, that we may die with him.

17 Then when Jesus came, he found that he had lain in the grave four days already.

18 Now Bethany was nigh unto Jerusalem, about fifteen furlongs off:

19 And many of the Jews came to Martha and Mary, to comfort them concerning their brother.

20 Then Martha, as soon as she heard that Jesus was coming, went and met him: but Mary sat still in the house.

21 Then said Martha unto Jesus, Lord, if thou hadst been here, my brother had not died.

22 But I know, that even now, whatsoever thou wilt ask of God, God will give it thee.

23 Jesus saith unto her, Thy brother shall rise again.

24 Martha saith unto him, I know that he shall rise again in the resurrection at the last day.

25 Jesus said unto her, I am the resurrection, and the life: he that believeth in me, though he were dead, yet shall he live:

26 And whosoever liveth and believeth in me shall never die. Believest thou this?

comes before the state of life. Now the whole human race is plunged in death; and, therefore, no man will be a partaker of life until he is risen from the dead. Thus Christ shows that he is the commencement of life, and he afterwards adds, that the continuance of life is also a work of his grace. That he is speaking about spiritual life, is plainly shown by the exposition which immediately follows,

He who believeth in me, though, he were dead, shall live

Why then is Christ *the resurrection?* Because by his Spirit he regenerates the children of Adam, who had been alienated from God by sin, so that they begin to live a new life. On this subject, I have spoken more fully under John 5: 21 and 24; and Paul is an excellent interpreter of this passage (Ephesians 2: 5 and Ephesians 5: 8). Away now with those who idly talk that men are prepared for receiving the grace of God by the movement of nature. They might as well say that the dead walk. For that men live and breathe, and are endued with sense, understanding, and will, all this tends to their destruction, because there is no part or faculty of the soul that is not corrupted and turned aside from what is right. Thus it is that death everywhere holds dominion, for the death of the soul is nothing else than its being estranged and turned aside from God. Accordingly, they who believe in Christ, though they were formerly dead, begin to live, because faith is a spiritual resurrection of the soul, and – so to speak – animates the soul itself that it may live to God; according to that passage, The dead shall hear the voice of the Son of God, and they who hear shall live (John 5: 25). This is truly a remarkable commendation of faith, that it conveys to us the life of Christ, and thus frees us from death.

36. Behold, how he loved him!

The Evangelist John here describes to us two different opinions which were formed about Christ. As to the former, who said, *Behold, how he loved him* though they think less highly of Christ than they ought to have done, since they ascribe to him nothing but what may belong to a man, yet they speak of him with greater candor and modesty than the latter, who maliciously slander him for not having hindered Lazarus from dying. For, though they applaud the power of Christ, of which the former said nothing, yet they do so, not without bringing against him some reproach. It is evident enough from their words, that the miracles which Christ had performed were not unknown to them; but so much the more base is their ingratitude, that they do not scruple to complain, because now, in a single instance, he abstained from working. Men have always been ungrateful to God in the same manner, and continue to be so. If he does not grant all our wishes, we immediately launch into

assertion of His own right to life as soon as the purposes of His voluntary death were accomplished.

19–21. There was a division ... again among the Jews for these sayings – the light and the darkness revealing themselves with increasing clearness in the separation of the teachable from the obstinately prejudiced. The one saw in Him only "a devil and a madman"; the other revolted at the thought that *such words* could come from one possessed, and sight be given to the blind by a demoniac; showing clearly that a deeper impression had been made upon them than their words expressed.

John 10: 22–42

DISCOURSE AT THE FEAST OF DEDICATION – FROM THE FURY OF HIS ENEMIES JESUS ESCAPES BEYOND JORDAN, WHERE MANY BELIEVE ON HIM.

22. it was ... the feast of the dedication – celebrated rather more than *two months* after the feast of tabernacles, during which intermediate period our Lord seems to have remained in the neighborhood of Jerusalem. It was instituted by Jude Maccabeus, to commemorate the purification of the temple from the profanations to which it had been subjected by Antiochus Epiphanes 165 BC, and kept for eight days, from the twenty-fifth Chisleu (December), the day on which Judas began the first joyous celebration of it (1 Maccabees 4: 52,56,59; and JOSEPHUS, *Antiquities*, 7.7.7).

it was winter – implying some *inclemency*. Therefore,

23. Jesus walked ... in Solomon's porch – for shelter. This portico was on the east side of the temple, and JOSEPHUS says it was part of the original structure of Solomon [*Antiquities*, 20.9.7].

24. If thou be the Christ, tell us plainly – But when the plainest *evidence* of it was resisted, what weight could a mere *assertion* of it have?

25–26. Jesus answered them, I told you – that is, in substance, what I am (for example John 7: 37–38; 8: 12,35–36,58).

29. is greater than all – with whom no adverse power can contend. It is a general expression of an admitted truth, and what follows shows

for what purpose it was uttered, "and none is able to pluck them out of My Father's hand."

31. Then the Jews took up stones again to stone Him – and for precisely the same thing as before (John 8: 58–59).

32. Many good works have I showed you – that is, works of pure benevolence (as in Acts 10: 38, "Who went about doing good," &c.; see Mark 7: 37).

33. for a blasphemy – whose legal punishment was stoning (Lev. 24: 11–16).

thou, being a man – that is, a man only.

makest thyself God – Twice before they understood Him to advance the same claim, and both times they prepared themselves to avenge what they took to be the insulted honor of God, as here, in the way directed by their law (John 5: 18; 8: 59).

35–36. If he called them gods unto whom the word of God came ... Say ye of him whom the Father hath sanctified and sent into the world, Thou blasphemest – The whole force of this reasoning, which has been but in part seized by the commentators, lies in what is said of the two parties compared. The *comparison* of Himself with mere men, divinely commissioned, is intended to show (as NEANDER well expresses it) that the idea of a communication of the Divine Majesty to human nature was by no means foreign to the revelations of the Old Testament; but there is also a *contrast* between Himself and all merely human representatives of God – the one "*sanctified by the Father and sent into the world*"; the other, "*to whom the word of God* (merely) *came*," which is expressly designed to prevent His being massed up with them as only one of many human officials of God. *It is never said of Christ* that "the word of the Lord came to Him"; whereas this is the well-known formula by which the divine commission, even to the highest of *mere men*, is expressed, as John the Baptist (Luke 3: 2). The reason is that given by the Baptist himself (see on John 3: 31). The contrast is between those "to whom the word of God came" – men of the earth, earthy, who were merely privileged to get a divine *message* to utter (if prophets), or a divine *office* to discharge (if judges) – and "Him whom (not being of the earth at all) the *Father sanctified* (or set apart), and *sent into*

27 She saith unto him, Yea, Lord: I believe that thou art the Christ, the Son of God, which should come into the world.

28 And when she had so said, she went her way, and called Mary her sister secretly, saying, The Master is come, and calleth for thee.

29 As soon as she heard that, she arose quickly, and came unto him.

30 Now Jesus was not yet come into the town, but was in that place where Martha met him.

31 The Jews then which were with her in the house, and comforted her, when they saw Mary, that she rose up hastily and went out, followed her, saying, She goeth unto the grave to weep there.

32 Then when Mary was come where Jesus was, and saw him, she fell down at his feet, saying unto him, Lord, if thou hadst been here, my brother had not died.

33 When Jesus therefore saw her weeping, and the Jews also weeping which came with her, he groaned in the spirit, and was troubled,

34 And said, Where have ye laid him? They said unto him, Lord, come and see.

35 Jesus wept.

36 Then said the Jews, Behold how he loved him!

37 And some of them said, Could not this man, which opened the eyes of the blind, have caused that even this man should not have died?

38 Jesus therefore again groaning in himself cometh to the grave. It was a cave, and a stone lay upon it.

39 Jesus said, Take ye away the stone. Martha, the sister of him that was dead, saith unto him, Lord, by this time he stinketh: for he hath been dead four days.

40 Jesus saith unto her, Said I not unto thee, that, if thou wouldest believe, thou shouldest see the glory of God?

41 Then they took away the stone from the place where the dead was laid. And Jesus lifted up his eyes, and said, Father, I thank thee that thou hast heard me.

42 And I knew that thou hearest me always: but because of the people which stand by I said it, that they may believe that thou hast sent me.

43 And when he thus had spoken, he cried with a loud voice, Lazarus, come forth.

complaints: "Since he has been accustomed to aid us hitherto, why does he now forsake and disappoint us?" There is here a twofold disease. First, though we rashly desire what is not expedient for us, yet we wish to subject God to the perverse desires of the flesh. Secondly, we are rude in our demands, and the ardor of impatience hurries us before the time.

43. He cried with a loud voice

By not touching with the hand, but only *crying with the voice*, his Divine power is more fully demonstrated. At the same time, he holds out to our view the secret and astonishing efficacy of his word. For how did Christ restore life to the dead but by the word? And therefore, in raising Lazarus, he exhibited a visible token of his spiritual grace, which we experience every day by the perception of faith, when he shows that his voice gives life.

44. Bound hand and foot with bandages

The Evangelist is careful to mention the *napkin* and *bandages,* in order to inform us that Lazarus went out of the tomb, in the same manner that he was laid in it. This mode of burying is retained to the present day by the Jews, who cover the body with a shroud, and wrap the head separately in a handkerchief.

Loose him, and let him go

To magnify the glory of the miracle, it only remained that the Jews should even touch with their hands that Divine work which they had beheld with their eyes. For Christ might have removed the *bandages* with which Lazarus was bound, or made them to give way of themselves; but Christ intended to employ the hands of the spectators as his witnesses.

53. They consulted to put him to death

The Evangelist relates that Christ again fled, knowing that his enemies sought him with so great rage. Yet let us remember that he did not fly in order to withdraw from his Father's calling; for he had no other intention than to present himself to undergo voluntary death at the time which God had appointed. This *consultation,* which the Evangelist mentions, related not so much to slaying Christ as to find out some method of crushing him. They had already determined to put him to death; it only remained to advise in what way they could carry their resolution into effect.

56. They therefore sought Jesus

The design of the Evangelist is, to show how extensively the fame of Christ was diffused through the whole of Judea; for they who assemble in the temple, from whatever quarter they come, are eager to seek Christ, and are employed in

DAVID BROWN

the world," an expression *never used of any merely human messenger of God,* and *used only of Himself.*

37–39. though ye believe not me, believe the works – There was in Christ's words, independently of any miracles, a self-evidencing truth, majesty and grace, which those who had any spiritual susceptibility were unable to resist (John 7: 46; 8: 30). But, for those who wanted this, "the works" were a mighty help. When these failed, the case was desperate indeed.

that ye may know and believe that the Father is in me, and I in him – thus reiterating His claim to essential *oneness with the Father,* which He had only *seemed* to soften down, that He might calm their rage and get their ear again for a moment.

39. Therefore they sought again to take him – true to their original understanding of His words, for they saw perfectly well that He *meant* to "make Himself God" throughout all this dialogue.

41. many resorted to him – on whom the ministry of the Baptist had left permanent impressions.

John did no miracle, but all things John spake of this man were true – what they now heard and saw in Jesus only confirming in their minds the divinity of His forerunner's mission, though unaccompanied by any of His Master's miracles. And thus, "many believed on Him there."

JOHN 11

John 11: 1–46

LAZARUS RAISED FROM THE DEAD – THE CONSEQUENCES OF THIS.

1. of Bethany – at the east side of Mount Olivet.

the town of Mary and her sister Martha – thus distinguishing it from the other Bethany, "beyond Jordan." (See on John 1: 28; John 10: 40.)

2. It was that Mary who anointed the Lord with ointment, &c – This, though not recorded by our Evangelist till John 12: 3, was so well known in the teaching of all the churches, according to our Lord's prediction (Matt. 26: 13), that it is here alluded to by anticipation,

as the most natural way of identifying her; and she is first named, though the younger, as the more distinguished of the two. She "anointed THE LORD," says the Evangelist – led doubtless to the use of this term here, as he was about to exhibit Him illustriously as the *Lord of Life.*

3–5. his sisters sent unto him, saying, Lord, he whom thou lovest is sick – a most womanly appeal, yet how reverential, to the known affection of her Lord for the patient. (See John 11: 5,11). "Those whom Christ loves are no more exempt than others from their share of earthly trouble and anguish: rather are they bound over to it more surely" [TRENCH].

5. Jesus loved Martha and her sister and Lazarus – what a picture! – one that in every age has attracted the admiration of the whole Christian Church. No wonder that those miserable skeptics who have carped at the ethical system of the Gospel, as not embracing private friendships in the list of its virtues, have been referred to the Saviour's peculiar regard for this family as a triumphant refutation, if such were needed.

6. When he heard he was sick, he abode two days still ... where he was – at least twenty-five miles off. Beyond all doubt this was just to let things come to their worst, in order to display His glory.

7–10. Let us go into Judea again – He was now in Perea, "beyond Jordan."

9. Jesus answered, Are there not twelve hours in the day? Our Lord's day had now reached its eleventh hour, and having till now "walked in the day," He would not *mistime* the remaining and more critical part of His work, which would be as fatal, He says, as omitting it altogether; for "if *a man* (so He speaks, putting Himself under the same great law of duty as all other men – if a man) walk in the night, he stumbleth, because there is no light in him."

12. if he sleep, he shall do well – literally, "be preserved"; that is, recover. "Why then go to Judea?"

14. Then said Jesus unto them plainly, Lazarus is dead – Says BENGEL beautifully, "Sleep is the death of the saints, in the language of heaven; but this language the disciples here understood not; incomparable is the generos-

44 And he that was dead came forth, bound hand and foot with graveclothes: and his face was bound about with a napkin. Jesus saith unto them, Loose him, and let him go.

45 Then many of the Jews which came to Mary, and had seen the things which Jesus did, believed on him.

46 But some of them went their ways to the Pharisees, and told them what things Jesus had done.

47 Then gathered the chief priests and the Pharisees a council, and said, What do we? for this man doeth many miracles.

48 If we let him thus alone, all men will believe on him: and the Romans shall come and take away both our place and nation.

49 And one of them, named Caiaphas, being the high priest that same year, said unto them, Ye know nothing at all,

50 Nor consider that it is expedient for us, that one man should die for the people, and that the whole nation perish not.

51 And this spake he not of himself: but being high priest that year, he prophesied that Jesus should die for that nation;

52 And not for that nation only, but that also he should gather together in one the children of God that were scattered abroad.

53 Then from that day forth they took counsel together for to put him to death.

54 Jesus therefore walked no more openly among the Jews; but went thence unto a country near to the wilderness, into a city called Ephraim, and there continued with his disciples.

55 And the Jews' passover was nigh at hand: and many went out of the country up to Jerusalem before the passover, to purify themselves.

56 Then sought they for Jesus, and spake among themselves, as they stood in the temple, What think ye, that he will not come to the feast?

57 Now both the chief priests and the Pharisees had given a commandment, that, if any man knew where he were, he should shew it, that they might take him.

JOHN 12

1 Then Jesus six days before the passover came to Bethany, where Lazarus was

holding conversations among themselves concerning him. It is true that they *seek* him after a human fashion, but yet, in *seeking* him, they discover that it is the tyranny of the priests which prevents him from appearing openly.

JOHN 12

2. There therefore they made him a banquet

Matthew (Matthew 26: 7) and Mark (Mark 14: 3) say that he then supped at the house of Simon the leper. John does not mention the house, but shows plainly enough, that it was in some other place than the house of Lazarus and Martha that he supped; for he says that **Lazarus was one of those who sat at table with him**, that is, one who had been invited along with Christ. Nor does it involve any contradiction, that Matthew and Mark relate that the **head** of Christ was anointed, while John relates that his **feet** were anointed. The usual practice was the anointing of **the head**, and on this account Pliny reckons it an instance of excessive luxury, that some anointed the ankles. The three Evangelists agree in this; that Mary did not anoint Christ sparingly, but poured on him a large quantity of ointment. What John speaks, about **the feet**, amounts to this, that the whole body of Christ, down to the feet, was anointed. There is an amplification in the word **feet**, which appears more fully from what follows, when he adds, that Mary **wiped his feet with her hair.**

8. For the poor you have always with you

We must observe what I have already pointed out, that a distinction is here drawn expressly between the extraordinary action of Mary, and the daily service which is due to Christ. Those persons, therefore, are apes, and not imitators, who are desirous to serve Christ by costly and splendid display; as if Christ approved of what was done once, and did not rather forbid that it should be done afterwards. **But me you have not always.**

When he says, that he will not always be with his disciples, this ought to be referred to that kind of presence to which carnal worship and costly honors are suitable. For as to his presence with us by the grace and power of his Spirit, his dwelling in us, and also feeding us with his flesh and blood, this has nothing to do with bodily observances. Of all the pompous ceremonies which the Papists have contrived for the worship of Christ, in vain do they tell us, that they have bestowed them upon him, for he openly rejects them. When he says, **that the poor will always be with us**, though, by this saying, he reproves the hypocrisy of the Jews, yet we may learn from it a profitable doctrine; namely, that alms, by which the wants of the poor are

ity of the divine manner of discoursing, but such is the slowness of men's apprehension that Scripture often has to descend to the more miserable style of human discourse; compare Matt. 16: 11."

15. I am glad for your sakes I was not there – This certainly implies that if He had been present, Lazarus would not have died; not because He could not have resisted the importunities of the sisters, but because, in presence of the personal Life, death could not have reached His friend [LUTHARDT]. "It is beautifully congruous to the divine decorum that in presence of the Prince of Life no one is ever said to have died" [BENGEL].

16. Thomas, ... called Didymus – or "the twin."

Let us also go, that we may die with him – lovely spirit, though tinged with some sadness, such as reappears at John 14: 5, showing the tendency of this disciple to take the *dark* view of things.

17–19. when Jesus came, he found that he had lain in the grave four days – If he died on the day the tidings came of his illness – and was, according to the Jewish custom, buried the same day (see JAHN'S *Archæology*, and John 11: 39; Acts 5: 5–6,10) – and if Jesus, after two days' further stay in Perea, set out on the day following for Bethany, some ten hours' journey, that would make out the four days; the first and last being incomplete [MEYER].

18. Bethany was nigh Jerusalem, about fifteen furlongs – rather less than two miles; mentioned to explain the visits of sympathy noticed in the following words, which the proximity of the two places facilitated.

19. many of the Jews came to Martha and Mary to comfort them – Thus were provided, in a most natural way, so many witnesses of the glorious miracle that was to follow, as to put the fact beyond possible question.

21. Then said Martha ... Lord, if thou hadst been here, my brother had not died – As Mary afterwards said the same thing (John 11: 32), it is plain they had made this very natural remark to each other, perhaps many times during these four sad days, and not without having their confidence in His love at times

overclouded. Such trials of faith, however, are not peculiar to them.

22. But I know that even now, &c – Energetic characters are usually sanguine, the rainbow of hope peering through the drenching cloud.

23–27. Jesus saith unto her, Thy brother shall rise again – purposely expressing Himself in general terms, to draw her out.

24. Martha said, ... I know that he shall rise again ... at the last day – "But are we never to see him in life till then?"

25. Jesus said, I am the resurrection and the life – "*The whole power to restore, impart, and maintain* life, resides in Me." What higher claim to supreme divinity than this grand saying can be conceived?

27. Yea, ... I believe that thou art the Christ, the Son of God, &c – that is, And having *such* faith in Thee, I can believe all which that comprehends. While she had a glimmering perception that Resurrection, in every sense of the word, belonged to the Messianic office and Sonship of Jesus, she means, by this way of expressing herself, to cover much that she felt her ignorance of – as no doubt belonging to Him.

28–32. The Master is come and calleth for thee – The narrative does not give us this interesting detail, but Martha's words do.

29. As soon as she heard that, she arose quickly – affection for her Lord, assurance of His sympathy, and His hope of interposition, putting a spring into her distressed spirit.

31. The Jews ... followed her ... to the grave – Thus *casually* were provided witnesses of the glorious miracle that followed, *not prejudiced*, certainly, *in favor* of Him who wrought it.

to weep there – according to Jewish practice, for some days after burial.

fell at his feet – more impassioned than her sister, though her words were fewer.

33–38. When Jesus ... saw her weeping, and the Jews ... weeping ... he groaned in the spirit – the tears of Mary and her friends acting sympathetically upon Jesus, and drawing forth His emotions. What a vivid and beautiful outcoming of His "real" humanity! The

which had been dead, whom he raised from the dead.

2 There they made him a supper; and Martha served: but Lazarus was one of them that sat at the table with him.

3 Then took Mary a pound of ointment of spikenard, very costly, and anointed the feet of Jesus, and wiped his feet with her hair: and the house was filled with the odor of the ointment.

4 Then saith one of his disciples, Judas Iscariot, Simon's son, which should betray him,

5 Why was not this ointment sold for three hundred pence, and given to the poor?

6 This he said, not that he cared for the poor; but because he was a thief, and had the bag, and bare what was put therein.

7 Then said Jesus, Let her alone: against the day of my burying hath she kept this.

8 For the poor always ye have with you; but me ye have not always.

9 Much people of the Jews therefore knew that he was there: and they came not for Jesus' sake only, but that they might see Lazarus also, whom he had raised from the dead.

10 But the chief priests consulted that they might put Lazarus also to death;

11 Because that by reason of him many of the Jews went away, and believed on Jesus.

12 On the next day much people that were come to the feast, when they heard that Jesus was coming to Jerusalem,

13 Took branches of palm trees, and went forth to meet him, and cried, Hosanna: Blessed is the King of Israel that cometh in the name of the Lord.

14 And Jesus, when he had found a young ass, sat thereon; as it is written,

15 Fear not, daughter of Sion: behold, thy King cometh, sitting on an ass's colt.

16 These things understood not his disciples at the first: but when Jesus was glorified, then remembered they that these things were written of him, and that they had done these things unto him.

17 The people therefore that was with him when he called Lazarus out of his grave, and raised him from the dead, bare record.

18 For this cause the people also met

relieved, are sacrifices acceptable, and of sweet savor, to God, and that any other kind of expense in the worship of God is improperly bestowed.

14. And Jesus having found a young ass

This part of the history is more minutely related by the other Evangelists, who tell us, that Christ **sent two of his disciples** to bring an ass (Matthew 21: 1; Mark 11: 1; Luke 19: 29). John, who was the latest writer of all the Evangelists, reckoned it enough to notice briefly the substance of what had been stated by the rest; and, on this account, he leaves out many circumstances. An apparent contradiction, by which many persons are perplexed, is very easily removed. When Matthew says, that Christ sat upon a **she-ass and her colt**, we ought to view it as a synecdoche. Some imagine that he sat first on the she-ass, and afterwards on her colt; and out of this conjecture they frame an allegory, that he first sat on the Jewish people, who had been long accustomed to bear the yoke of the Law, and afterwards. subdued the Gentiles, like an untrained **young ass** which had never carried a rider. But the plain truth is, that Christ rode on an ass which had been brought along with its mother; and to this agree the words of the Prophet, who, by a repetition very frequent among the Hebrews, expresses the same thing twice by different words. **On an ass,** he says, **and on the colt of an ass which was under the yoke**, (*hupozugiou*). Our Evangelist, who studies brevity, leaves out the former clause, and quotes only the latter.

24. Unless a grain of wheat having fallen into the ground, die, it remaineth alone

If a grain of wheat do not die or putrefy, it continues to be dry and unfruitful; but the death of the seed has the beneficial effect of quickening it, that it may yield fruit. In short, Christ compares his death to sowing, which appears to tend to the destruction of the **wheat,** but yet is the cause of far more abundant increase. Though this admonition was especially necessary at that time, yet it is of continual use in the Church. And, first, we ought to begin with the Head. That dreadful appearance of disgrace and cursing, which appears in the death of Christ, not only obscures his glory, but removes it altogether from our view. We must not, therefore, confine our attention to his death alone, but must likewise consider the fruit which has been yielded by his glorious resurrection. Thus there will be nothing to prevent his glory from being every where displayed. From him we must next come to the members; for not only do we think that we perish in death, but our life also is a sort of continual death (Colossians 3: 3). We shall therefore be undone, unless we be supported by that consolation which

word here rendered "groaned" does not mean "sighed" or "grieved," but rather "powerfully checked his emotion" – made a visible effort to restrain those tears which were ready to gush from His eyes.

34. Where have ye laid him? ... Lord, come and see – Perhaps it was to retain composure enough to ask this question, and on receiving the answer to proceed with them to the spot, that He checked Himself.

35. Jesus wept – This beautifully conveys the sublime brevity of the two original words; else *"shed tears"* might have better conveyed the difference between the word here used and that twice employed in John 11: 33, and there properly rendered "weeping," denoting the loud wail for the dead, while that of Jesus consisted of *silent tears*.

36. Then said the Jews, Behold how he loved him! – We thank you, O ye visitors from Jerusalem, for this spontaneous testimony to the *human* tenderness of the Son of God.

37. And – rather, "But."

some ... said, Could not this man, which opened the eyes of the blind, have caused that this man should not have died? – The former exclamation came from the better-feeling portion of the spectators; this betokens a measure of suspicion. It hardly goes the length of attesting the miracle on the blind man; but "if (as everybody says) He did that, why could He not also have kept Lazarus alive?"

38. Jesus again groaning in himself – that is, as at John 11: 33, checked or repressed His rising feelings, in the former instance, of sorrow, here of righteous indignation at their unreasonable unbelief; (compare Mark 3: 5) [WEBSTER and WILKINSON]. But here, too, struggling emotion was deeper, now that His eye was about to rest on the spot where lay, in the still horrors of death, His "friend."

40. Jesus saith unto her, Said I not unto thee, that if thou wouldest believe, thou shouldest see the glory of God? – He had not said those very words, but this was the scope of all that He had uttered to her about His life-giving power (John 11: 23, 25, 26); a gentle yet emphatic and most instructive rebuke: "Why doth the restoration of life, even to a decom-

posing corpse, seem hopeless in the presence of the Resurrection and the Life? Hast thou yet to learn that 'if thou canst believe, all things are possible to him that believeth?'" (Mark 9: 23).

41. Jesus lifted up his eyes – an expression marking His calm solemnity. (Compare John 17: 1).

Father, I thank thee that thou hast heard me – rather, "heardest Me," referring to a specific prayer offered by Him, probably on intelligence of the case reaching Him (John 11: 3–4); for His living and loving oneness with the Father was maintained and manifested in the flesh, not merely by the spontaneous and uninterrupted outgoing of Each to Each in spirit, but by specific actings of faith and exercises of prayer about each successive case as it emerged.

42. And – rather, "Yet."

I knew that thou hearest me always, but because of the people that stand by I said it, that they might believe that thou hast sent me – Instead of praying now, He simply gives thanks for answer to prayer offered ere He left Perea, and adds that His doing even this, in the audience of the people, was not from any doubt of the prevalency of His prayers in any case, but to show the people that *He did nothing without His Father, but all by direct communication with Him.*

43–44. and when he had thus spoken, he cried with a loud voice – On one other occasion only did He this – on the *cross*. His last utterance was a "loud cry" (Matt. 27: 50). "He shall not cry," said the prophet, nor, in His ministry, did He. What a sublime contrast is this "loud cry" to the magical "whisperings" and "mutterings" of which we read in Is. 8: 19; 29: 4 (as GROTIUS remarks)! It is second only to the grandeur of that voice which shall raise all the dead (John 5: 28–29; 1 Thess. 4: 16).

44. Jesus saith unto them, Loose him and let him go – Jesus will no more do this Himself than roll away the stone. The one was the necessary *preparation* for resurrection, the other the necessary *sequel* to it. THE LIFE-GIVING ACT ALONE HE RESERVES TO HIMSELF. So *in the quickening of the dead to spiritual life, human instrumentality is employed first to prepare the*

him, for that they heard that he had done this miracle.

19 The Pharisees therefore said among themselves, Perceive ye how ye prevail nothing? behold, the world is gone after him.

20 And there were certain Greeks among them that came up to worship at the feast:

21 The same came therefore to Philip, which was of Bethsaida of Galilee, and desired him, saying, Sir, we would see Jesus.

22 Philip cometh and telleth Andrew: and again Andrew and Philip tell Jesus.

23 And Jesus answered them, saying, The hour is come, that the Son of man should be glorified.

24 Verily, verily, I say unto you, Except a corn of wheat fall into the ground and die, it abideth alone: but if it die, it bringeth forth much fruit.

25 He that loveth his life shall lose it; and he that hateth his life in this world shall keep it unto life eternal.

26 If any man serve me, let him follow me; and where I am, there shall also my servant be: if any man serve me, him will my Father honor.

27 Now is my soul troubled; and what shall I say? Father, save me from this hour: but for this cause came I unto this hour.

28 Father, glorify thy name. Then came there a voice from heaven, saying, I have both glorified it, and will glorify it again.

29 The people therefore, that stood by, and heard it, said that it thundered: others said, An angel spake to him.

30 Jesus answered and said, This voice came not because of me, but for your sakes.

31 Now is the judgment of this world: now shall the prince of this world be cast out.

32 And I, if I be lifted up from the earth, will draw all men unto me.

33 This he said, signifying what death he should die.

34 The people answered him, We have heard out of the law that Christ abideth for ever: and how sayest thou, The Son of man must be lifted up? who is this Son of man?

35 Then Jesus said unto them, Yet a

Paul holds out: if our outward man decays, the inward man is renewed from day to day (2 Corinthians 4: 16).

26. If any, man serve me

That death may not be exceedingly bitter and disagreeable to us, Christ invites us by his example to submit to it cheerfully; and certainly we shall be ashamed to refuse the honor of being his disciples. But on no other condition does he admit us into their number, except that we follow the path which he points out. He leads the way to us to suffer death. The bitterness of death is therefore mitigated, and is in some measure rendered agreeable, when we have in common with the Son of God the condition of submitting to it. So far is it from being proper that we should shrink from Christ on account of the cross, that we ought rather to desire death for his sake. To the same purpose. pose is the statement which immediately follows: *And where I am, there shall also my servant be.* For he demands that his servants should not refuse to submit to death, to which they see him go before them as an example; for it is not right that; the servant should have any thing separate from his lord. The future tense, shall be, (*estai*) is put for let him be, according to the custom of the Hebrew language. Others regard it as a consolation, as if Christ promised to those who should not be unwilling to die along with him, that they would be partakers of his resurrection. But the former view, as I have said, is more probable; for he afterwards adds the consolation, that the Father will not leave without reward the servants of Christ who shall have been his companions both in life and in death.

43. For they loved the glory of men

The Evangelist expressly states that those men were not guided by any superstition, but only endeavored to avoid disgrace among men; for if ambition had greater influence over them than the fear of God, it follows, that it was no vain scruple of conscience that gave them uneasiness. Now, let the reader observe how great ignominy is incurred before God, by the cowardice of those who, from the fear of being hated, dissemble their faith before men. Can any thing be more foolish, or rather, can any thing be more beastly, than to prefer the silly applause of men to the judgment of God? But he declares that all who shrink from the hatred of men, when the pure faith ought to be confessed, are seized with this kind of madness. And justly; for the apostle, in applauding the unshaken steadiness of Moses, says that he remained firm, as if he had seen him who is invisible (Hebrews 11: 27).

By these words he means that, when any person has fixed his eyes on God, his heart will be invincible, and utterly incapable of being moved.

way, and then to turn it to account.

45–46. many … which … had seen … believed … But some … went … to the Pharisees and told them what Jesus had done – the two classes which continually reappear in the Gospel history; nor is there ever any great work of God which does not produce both. "It is remarkable that on each of the three occasions on which our Lord raised the dead, a large number of persons was assembled. In two instances, the resurrection of the widow's son and of Lazarus, these were all witnesses of the miracle; in the third (of Jairus' daughter) they were necessarily cognizant of it. Yet this important circumstance is in each case only incidentally noticed by the historians, not put forward or appealed to as a proof of their veracity. In regard to this miracle, we observe a greater degree of preparation, both in the provident arrangement of events, and in our Lord's actions and words than in any other. The preceding miracle (cure of the man born blind) is distinguished from all others by the open and formal investigation of its facts. And both these miracles, the most public and best attested of all, are related by John, who wrote long after the other Evangelists" [WEBSTER and WILKINSON].

47–54. What do we? for this man doeth many miracles – "While we trifle, 'this man,' by His 'many miracles,' will carry all before Him; the popular enthusiasm will bring on a revolution, which will precipitate the Romans upon us, and our all will go down in one common ruin." What a testimony to the reality of our Lord's miracles, and their resistless effect, from His bitterest enemies!

51. Caiaphas … prophesied that Jesus should die for that nation – He meant nothing more than that the way to prevent the apprehended ruin of the nation was to make a sacrifice of the Disturber of their peace. But in giving utterance to this suggestion of political expediency, he was so guided as to give forth a divine prediction of deep significance; and God so ordered it that it should come from the lips of the high priest for that memorable year, the recognized head of God's visible people, whose ancient office, symbolized by the Urim and Thummim, was to decide in the last resort, all vital questions as the oracle of the

divine will.

52. and not for that nation only, &c – These are the Evangelist's words, not Caiaphas'.

53. they took council together to put him to death – Caiaphas but expressed what the party was secretly wishing, but afraid to propose.

55–57. passover … at hand … many went … up … before the passover, to purify themselves – from any legal uncleanness which would have disqualified them from keeping the feast. This is mentioned to introduce the graphic statement which follows.

56. sought they for Jesus, and spake among themselves, as they stood in the temple – giving forth the various conjectures and speculations about the probability of His coming to the feast.

57. This is mentioned to account for the conjectures whether He would come, in spite of this determination to seize Him.

JOHN 12

John 12: 1–11

THE ANOINTING AT BETHANY.

1–8. six days before the passover – that is, on the sixth day before it; probably after sunset on *Friday* evening, or the commencement of the Jewish *sabbath* preceding the passover.

2. Martha served – This, with what is afterwards said of Mary's way of honoring her Lord, is so true to the character in which those two women appear in Luke 10: 38–42, as to constitute one of the strongest and most delightful confirmations of the truth of both narratives. (See also on John 11: 20).

3. spikenard – or pure *nard*, a celebrated aromatic (Song 1: 12).

anointed the feet of Jesus – and "poured it on His head" (Matt. 26: 7; Mark 14: 3). The only use of this was to refresh and exhilarate – a grateful compliment in the East, amidst the closeness of a heated atmosphere, with many guests at a feast. Such was the form in which Mary's love to Christ, at so much cost to herself, poured itself out.

6. had the bag – the purse.

bare what was put therein – not, bare it

little while is the light with you. Walk while ye have the light, lest darkness come upon you: for he that walketh in darkness knoweth not whither he goeth.

36 While ye have light, believe in the light, that ye may be the children of light. These things spake Jesus, and departed, and did hide himself from them.

37 But though he had done so many miracles before them, yet they believed not on him:

38 That the saying of Esaias the prophet might be fulfilled, which he spake, Lord, who hath believed our report? and to whom hath the arm of the Lord been revealed?

39 Therefore they could not believe, because that Esaias said again,

40 He hath blinded their eyes, and hardened their heart; that they should not see with their eyes, nor understand with their heart, and be converted, and I should heal them.

41 These things said Esaias, when he saw his glory, and spake of him.

42 Nevertheless among the chief rulers also many believed on him; but because of the Pharisees they did not confess him, lest they should be put out of the synagogue:

43 For they loved the praise of men more than the praise of God.

44 Jesus cried and said, He that believeth on me, believeth not on me, but on him that sent me.

45 And he that seeth me seeth him that sent me.

46 I am come a light into the world, that whosoever believeth on me should not abide in darkness.

47 And if any man hear my words, and believe not, I judge him not: for I came not to judge the world, but to save the world.

48 He that rejecteth me, and receiveth not my words, hath one that judgeth him: the word that I have spoken, the same shall judge him in the last day.

49 For I have not spoken of myself; but the Father which sent me, he gave me a commandment, what I should say, and what I should speak.

50 And I know that his commandment is life everlasting: whatsoever I speak therefore, even as the Father said unto me, so I speak.

JOHN 13

1. Before the feast of the passover

John intentionally passes by many things which, he knew, had been related by Matthew and others. He undertakes to explain those circumstances which they had left out, one of which was the narrative of the **washing of feet** and though he will afterwards explain more clearly for what purpose Christ **washed the feet** of his disciples, yet, before doing so, he states, in a single word, that the Lord testified, by this visible sign, that the love with which he embraced them was firm and lasting; that, though they were deprived of his presence, they might still be convinced that death itself would not quench this love. This conviction ought now to be fixed also in our hearts.

The words are, that Christ *loved even to the end his own, who were in the world.* Why does he employ this circumlocution in describing the Apostles, but in order to inform us that, in consequence of their being engaged, as we are, in a hazardous and difficult warfare, Christ regarded them with so much the greater solicitude? And, therefore, though we think that we are at a distance from Christ, yet we ought to know that he is looking at us; for he loveth his own, who are in the world; for we, have no reason to doubt that he still bears the same affection which he retained at the very moment of his death.

To remove from this world to the Father

This phrase is worthy of notice; for it refers to the knowledge of Christ, that he knew that his death was a passage to the heavenly kingdom of God. And if, while he was hastening thither, he did not cease to regard *his own* with his wonted love, there is no reason why we should now think that his affection is changed. Now, since he is the first-born from the dead, this definition of death applies to the whole body of the Church, that it is an opening or passage to go to God, from whom believers are now absent.

2. After supper

The devil having already put it into the heart of Judas

When the Evangelist says that Judas had been impelled by the devil to form the design of betraying Christ, this tends to show the enormity of the crime; for it was dreadful and most atrocious wickedness, in which the efficacy of Satan was openly displayed. There is no wickedness, indeed, that is perpetrated by men, to which Satan does not excite them, but the more hideous and execrable any crime is, the more ought we to view in it the rage of the devil, who drives about, in all possible directions, men who have been forsaken by God. But though the lust of men is kindled into a fiercer flame by Satan's fan, still it does not cease to be a furnace;

DAVID BROWN

off by theft, though that he did; but simply, had charge of its contents, was treasurer to Jesus and the Twelve. How worthy of notice is this arrangement, by which an avaricious and dishonest person was not only taken into the number of the Twelve, but entrusted with the custody of their little property! The purposes which this served are obvious enough; but it is further noticeable, that the remotest hint was never given to the eleven of His true character, nor did the disciples most favored with the intimacy of Jesus ever suspect him, till a few minutes before he voluntarily separated himself from their company – for ever!

7. said Jesus, Let her alone, against the day of my burying hath she done this – not that she thought of His burial, much less reserved any of her nard to anoint her dead Lord. But as the time was so near at hand when that office would have to be performed, *and she was not to have that privilege even alter the spices were brought for the purpose* (Mark 16: 1), He lovingly *regards it as done now.*

8. the poor always ... with you – referring to Deut. 15: 11.

9–11. Crowds of the Jerusalem Jews hastened to Bethany, not so much to see Jesus, whom they knew to be there, as to see dead Lazarus alive; and this, issuing in their accession to Christ, led to a plot against the life of Lazarus also, as the only means of arresting the triumphs of Jesus (see John 12: 19) – to such a pitch had these chief priests come of diabolical determination to shut out the light from themselves, and quench it from the earth!

John 12: 12–19

CHRIST'S TRIUMPHAL ENTRY INTO JERUSALEM.

12. On the next day – the Lord's day, or Sunday; the tenth day of the Jewish month Nisan, on which the paschal lamb was set apart to be "kept up until the fourteenth day of the same month, when the whole assembly of the congregation of Israel were to kill it in the evening" (Ex. 12: 3, 6). Even so, from the day of this solemn entry into Jerusalem, "Christ our Passover" was virtually set apart to be "sacrificed for us" (1 Cor. 5: 7).

16. when Jesus was glorified, then remem- bered they that these things were written of him, &c – The Spirit, descending on them from the glorified Saviour at Pentecost, opened their eyes suddenly to the true sense of the Old Testament, brought vividly to their recollection this and other Messianic predictions, and to their unspeakable astonishment showed them that they, and all the actors in these scenes, had been unconsciously fulfilling those predictions.

John 12: 20–36

SOME GREEKS DESIRE TO SEE JESUS – THE DISCOURSE AND SCENE THEREUPON.

20–22. Greeks – Not Grecian Jews, but Greek proselytes to the Jewish faith, who were wont to attend the annual festivals, particularly this primary one, the Passover.

The same came therefore to Philip ... of Bethsaida – possibly as being from the same quarter.

saying, Sir, we would see Jesus – certainly in a far better sense than Zaccheus (Luke 19: 3). Perhaps He was then in that part of the temple court to which Gentile proselytes had no access. "These men from the *west* represent, at the end of Christ's life, what the wise men from the *east* represented at its beginning; but those come to the cross of the King, even as these to His manger" [STIER].

22. Philip ... telleth Andrew – As follow townsmen of Bethsaida (John 1: 44), these two seem to have drawn to each other.

23–26. Jesus answered them, The hour is come that the Son of man should be glorified – that is, They would see Jesus, would they? Yet a little moment, and they shall see Him so as now they dream not of. The middle wall of partition that keeps them out from the commonwealth of Israel is on the eve of breaking down, "and I, if I be lifted up from the earth, shall draw all men unto Me"; I see them "flying as a cloud, and as doves to their cotes" – a glorious event that will be for the Son of man, by which this is to be brought about. It is His *death* He thus sublimely and delicately alluded to. Lost in the scenes of triumph which this desire of the Greeks to see Him called up before His view, He gives no direct answer to their petition for an interview, but

JOHN 13

1 Now before the feast of the passover, when Jesus knew that his hour was come that he should depart out of this world unto the Father, having loved his own which were in the world, he loved them unto the end.

2 And supper being ended, the devil having now put into the heart of Judas Iscariot, Simon's son, to betray him;

3 Jesus knowing that the Father had given all things into his hands, and that he was come from God, and went to God;

4 He riseth from supper, and laid aside his garments; and took a towel, and girded himself.

5 After that he poureth water into a bason, and began to wash the disciples' feet, and to wipe them with the towel wherewith he was girded.

6 Then cometh he to Simon Peter: and Peter saith unto him, Lord, dost thou wash my feet?

7 Jesus answered and said unto him, What I do thou knowest not now; but thou shalt know hereafter.

8 Peter saith unto him, Thou shalt never wash my feet. Jesus answered him, If I wash thee not, thou hast no part with me.

9 Simon Peter saith unto him, Lord, not my feet only, but also my hands and my head.

10 Jesus saith to him, He that is washed needeth not save to wash his feet, but is clean every whit: and ye are clean, but not all.

11 For he knew who should betray him; therefore said he, Ye are not all clean.

12 So after he had washed their feet, and had taken his garments, and was set down again, he said unto them, Know ye what I have done to you?

13 Ye call me Master and Lord: and ye say well; for so I am.

14 If I then, your Lord and Master, have washed your feet; ye also ought to wash one another's feet.

15 For I have given you an example, that ye should do as I have done to you.

16 Verily, verily, I say unto you, The servant is not greater than his lord; neither he that is sent greater than he that sent him.

it contains the flame kindled within itself, it receives with avidity the agitation of the fan, so that no excuse is left for wicked men.

15. For I have given you an example

It deserves our attention that Christ says that he **gave an example;** for we are not at liberty to take all his actions, without reserve, as subjects of imitation. The Papists boast that, by Christ's example, they observe the forty days' fast, or Lent. But we ought first to see whether or not he intended to lay down his fast as an example that the disciples might conform to it as a rule. We read: nothing of this sort, and, therefore, the imitation of it is not less wicked than if they attempted to fly to heaven. Besides, when they ought to have followed Christ, they were not imitators, but apes. Every year they have a fashion of washing some people's feet, as if it were a farce which they were playing on the stage; and so, when they have performed this idle and unmeaning ceremony, they think that they have fully discharged their duty, and reckon themselves at liberty to despise their brethren during the rest of the year. But – what is far worse – after having washed the feet of twelve men, they subject every member of Christ to cruel torture, and thus spit in Christ's face. This display of buffoonery, therefore, is nothing else than a shameful mockery of Christ. At all events, Christ does not here enjoin an annual ceremony, but bids us be ready, throughout our whole life, to wash the feet of our brethren and neighbors.

21. When Jesus had said these words

The more sacred the apostolic office is, and the higher its dignity, the more base and detestable was the treachery of Judas. A crime so monstrous and detestable struck Christ himself with horror, when he saw how the incredible wickedness of one man had polluted that sacred order in which the majesty of God ought to have shone with brightness. To the same purpose is what the Evangelist adds, that he **testified.**

His meaning is, the action was so monstrous that the bare mention of it could not be immediately believed. *He was troubled in spirit.* The Evangelist says that Christ was troubled in spirit, in order to inform us that he did not merely, in countenance and language, assume the appearance of a man who was troubled, but that he was deeply moved in his mind.

Spirit here denotes the understanding, or, the soul; for I do not assent to the opinion of some who explain it, as if Christ had been driven by a violent impulse of the Holy Spirit to break out into these words. I readily acknowledge. that all the affections of Christ were guided by the

sees the cross which was to bring them gilded with glory.

24. Except a corn of wheat fall into the ground and die, it abideth alone; but if it die, it bringeth forth much fruit – The *necessity* of His death is here brightly expressed, and its proper operation and fruit – *life springing forth out of death* – imaged forth by a beautiful and deeply significant law of the vegetable kingdom. For a double reason, no doubt, this was uttered – to explain what he had said of His death, as the hour of His own glorification, and to sustain His own Spirit under the agitation which was mysteriously coming over it in the view of that death.

25. He that loveth his life shall lose it; and he that hateth his life in this world shall keep it unto life eternal – Did our Lord mean to exclude Himself from the operation of the great principle here expressed – *self-renunciation, the law of self-preservation*; and its converse, *self-preservation, the law of self-destruction*? On the contrary, as He became Man to exemplify this fundamental law of the Kingdom of God in its most sublime form, so the very utterance of it on this occasion served to sustain His own Spirit in the double prospect to which He had just alluded.

26. If any man serve me, let him follow me; and where I am, there shall also my servant be: If any man serve me, him will my Father honour – *Jesus here claims the same absolute subjection to Himself, as the law of men's exaltation to honor, as He yielded to the Father.*

27–28. Now is my soul troubled – He means at the prospect of His death, just alluded to. Strange view of the Cross this, immediately after representing it as the hour of His glory! (John 12: 23). But the two views naturally meet, and blend into one. It was the Greeks, one might say, that troubled Him. Ah! they shall see Jesus, but *to Him* it shall be a costly sight.

28. Father, glorify thy name – by a present testimony.

I have both glorified it – referring specially to the voice from heaven at His *baptism,* and again at His *transfiguration.*

29–33. The people therefore that stood by, said, It thundered; others, An angel spake to him – some hearing only a sound, others an articulate, but to them unintelligible voice.

30. Jesus ... said, This voice came not because of me, but for your sakes – that is, probably, to correct the unfavorable impressions which His momentary agitation and mysterious prayer for deliverance may have produced on the by-standers.

31. Now is the judgment of this world – the world that "crucified the Lord of glory" (1 Cor. 2: 8), considered as a vast and complicated kingdom of Satan, breathing his spirit, doing his work, and involved in his doom, which Christ's death by its hands irrevocably sealed.

now shall the prince of this world be cast out – How differently is that fast-approaching "hour" regarded in the kingdoms of darkness and of light! "The hour of relief; from the dread Troubler of our peace – how near it is! Yet a little moment, and the day is ours!" So it was calculated and felt in the one region. "Now shall the prince of this world be cast out," is a somewhat different view of the same event. We know who was right. Though yet under a veil, He sees the triumphs of the Cross in unclouded and transporting light.

32. And I, if I be lifted up from the earth, will draw all men unto me – The "I" here is emphatic – I, taking the place of the world's ejected prince.

33. This he said, signifying what death he should die – that is, "by being lifted up from the earth" on "the accursed tree" (John 3: 14; 8: 28).

34. We have heard out of the law – the scriptures of the Old Testament (referring to such places as Ps. 89: 28–29; 110: 4; Dan 2: 44; 7: 13–14).

that Christ – the Christ "endureth for ever."

and how sayest thou, The Son of Man must be lifted up, &c – How can that consist with this "uplifting?" They saw very well both that He was holding Himself up as *the Christ* and *a Christ to die a violent death*; and as that ran counter to all their ideas of the Messianic prophecies, they were glad to get this seeming advantage to justify their unyielding attitude.

17 If ye know these things, happy are ye if ye do them.

18 I speak not of you all: I know whom I have chosen: but that the scripture may be fulfilled, He that eateth bread with me hath lifted up his heel against me.

19 Now I tell you before it come, that, when it is come to pass, ye may believe that I am he.

20 Verily, verily, I say unto you, He that receiveth whomsoever I send receiveth me; and he that receiveth me receiveth him that sent me.

21 When Jesus had thus said, he was troubled in spirit, and testified, and said, Verily, verily, I say unto you, that one of you shall betray me.

22 Then the disciples looked one on another, doubting of whom he spake.

23 Now there was leaning on Jesus' bosom one of his disciples, whom Jesus loved.

24 Simon Peter therefore beckoned to him, that he should ask who it should be of whom he spake.

25 He then lying on Jesus' breast saith unto him, Lord, who is it?

26 Jesus answered, He it is, to whom I shall give a sop, when I have dipped it. And when he had dipped the sop, he gave it to Judas Iscariot, the son of Simon.

27 And after the sop Satan entered into him. Then said Jesus unto him, That thou doest, do quickly.

28 Now no man at the table knew for what intent he spake this unto him.

29 For some of them thought, because Judas had the bag, that Jesus had said unto him, Buy those things that we have need of against the feast; or, that he should give something to the poor.

30 He then having received the sop went immediately out: and it was night.

31 Therefore, when he was gone out, Jesus said, Now is the Son of man glorified, and God is glorified in him.

32 If God be glorified in him, God shall also glorify him in himself, and shall straightway glorify him.

33 Little children, yet a little while I am with you. Ye shall seek me: and as I said unto the Jews, Whither I go, ye cannot come; so now I say to you.

34 A new commandment I give unto you, That ye love one another; as I have

Holy Spirit; but the meaning of the Evangelist is different, namely, that this suffering of Christ was inward, and was not feigned; and it is of great importance for us to know this, because his zeal is held out for our imitation, that we may be moved with deep horror by those monsters which overturn the sacred order of God and of his Church.

27. Satan entered into him

As it is certain that it was only at the instigation of Satan that Judas formed the design of committing so heinous a crime, why is it now said, for the first time, that **Satan entered into him**, who had already held the throne in his heart? But as they who are more fully confirmed in The faith which they formerly possessed are often said to **believe**, and thus an increase of their faith is called **faith**, so now that Judas is utterly given up to Satan, so as to be hurried on, by vehement impetuosity, to every extremity of evil, **Satan** is said to have **entered into him**. For as the saints make gradual progress, and in proportion to the new gifts by which they are continually enlarged, they are said to be filled with the Holy Spirit; so, in proportion as wicked men provoke the anger of God against themselves by their ingratitude, The Lord deprives them of his Spirit, of all light of reason, and, indeed, of all human feeling, and delivers them unreservedly to **Satan**. This is a dreadful vengeance of God, when men are **given up to a reprobate mind** (Romans 1: 28), so that they scarcely differ at all from the brutes, and – what is worse – fall into horrid crimes from which the brutes themselves would shrink. We ought, therefore, to walk diligently in the fear of the Lord, lest, if we overpower his goodness by our wickedness, he at length give us up to the rage of, Satan.

JOHN 14

1. Let not your heart be troubled

Not without good reason does Christ confirm his disciples by so many words, since a contest so arduous and so terrible awaited them; for it was no ordinary temptation, that soon afterwards they would see him hanging on the cross; a spectacle in which nothing was to be seen but ground for the lowest despair. The season of so great distress being at hand, he points out the remedy, that they may not be vanquished and overwhelmed; for he does not simply exhort and encourage them to be steadfast, but likewise informs them where they must go to obtain courage; that is, by faith, when he is acknowledged to be the Son of God, who has in himself a sufficiency of strength for maintaining the safety of his followers.

We ought always to attend to the time when these words

35–36. Yet a little while is the light with you. Walk while ye have the light, &c – Instead of answering their question, He warns them, with mingled majesty and tenderness, against trifling with their last brief opportunity, and entreats them to let in the Light while they have it in the midst of them, that they themselves might be "light in the Lord."

36. These things spake Jesus, and departed, and did hide himself from them – He who spake as never man spake, and immediately after words fraught with unspeakable dignity and love, had to "hide Himself" from His auditors! What then must *they* have been? He retired, probably to Bethany. (The parallels are: Matt. 21: 17; Luke 21: 37.)

37–41. It is the manner of this Evangelist alone to record his own reflections on the scenes he describes; but here, having arrived at what was virtually the close of our Lord's public ministry, he casts an affecting glance over the fruitlessness of His whole ministry on the bulk of the now doomed people.

38. That the saying of Esaias … might be fulfilled – This unbelief did not at all set aside the purposes of God, but, on the contrary, fulfilled them.

39–40. Therefore they could not believe, because Esaias said again, He hath blinded their eyes, that they should not see, &c – That this expresses *a positive divine act*, by which those who wilfully close their eyes and harden their hearts against the truth are judicially *shut up* in their unbelief and impenitence, is admitted by all candid critics [as OLSHAUSEN], though many of them think it necessary to contend that this is in no way inconsistent with the liberty of the human will, which of course it is not.

41. These things said Esaias, when he saw his glory, and spake of him – a key of immense importance to the opening of Isaiah's vision (Is. 6: 1–13), and all similar Old Testament representations. "THE SON is the King Jehovah who rules in the Old Testament and appears to the elect, as in the New Testament THE SPIRIT, the invisible Minister of the Son, is the Director of the Church and the Revealer in the sanctuary of the heart" [OLSHAUSEN].

42–43. among the chief rulers also – rather, "even of the rulers"; such as Nicodemus and Joseph.

43. they loved the praise of men more than the praise of God – "a severe remark, considering that several at least of these persons afterwards boldly confessed Christ. It indicates the displeasure with which God regarded their conduct at this time, and with which He continues to regard similar conduct" [WEBSTER and WILKINSON].

44–50. Jesus cried – in a loud tone, and with peculiar solemnity. (Compare John 7: 37.)
    and said, He that believeth on me, &c – This seems to be a supplementary record of some weighty proclamations, for which there had been found no natural place before, and introduced here as a sort of *summary and winding up* of His whole testimony.

JOHN 13

John 13: 1–20

AT THE LAST SUPPER JESUS WASHES THE DISCIPLES' FEET – THE DISCOURSE ARISING THEREUPON.

1. having loved his own which were in the world, he loved them unto the end – The meaning is, that on the very edge of His last sufferings, when it might have been supposed that He would be absorbed in His own awful prospects, He was so far from forgetting "His own," who were to be left struggling "in the world" after He had "departed out of it to the Father" (John 17: 11), that in His care for them He seemed scarce to think of Himself save in connection with them: "Herein is love," not only "enduring to the end," but most affectingly manifested when, judging by a human standard, least to be expected.

2. supper being ended – rather, "being prepared," "being served," or, "going on"; for that it was not "ended" is plain from John 13: 26.

3. Jesus knowing that the Father had given all things into his hands, &c – This verse is very sublime, and as a preface to what follows, were we not familiar with it, would fill us with inexpressible surprise. An unclouded perception of His relation to the Father, the commission He held from Him, and His approaching

loved you, that ye also love one another.

35 By this shall all men know that ye are my disciples, if ye have love one to another.

36 Simon Peter said unto him, Lord, whither goest thou? Jesus answered him, Whither I go, thou canst not follow me now; but thou shalt follow me afterwards.

37 Peter said unto him, Lord, why cannot I follow thee now? I will lay down my life for thy sake.

38 Jesus answered him, Wilt thou lay down thy life for my sake? Verily, verily, I say unto thee, The cock shall not crow, till thou hast denied me thrice.

JOHN 14

1 Let not your heart be troubled: ye believe in God, believe also in me.

2 In my Father's house are many mansions: if it were not so, I would have told you. I go to prepare a place for you.

3 And if I go and prepare a place for you, I will come again, and receive you unto myself; that where I am, there ye may be also.

4 And whither I go ye know, and the way ye know.

5 Thomas saith unto him, Lord, we know not whither thou goest; and how can we know the way?

6 Jesus saith unto him, I am the way, the truth, and the life: no man cometh unto the Father, but by me.

7 If ye had known me, ye should have known my Father also: and from henceforth ye know him, and have seen him.

8 Philip saith unto him, Lord, shew us the Father, and it sufficeth us.

9 Jesus saith unto him, Have I been so long time with you, and yet hast thou not known me, Philip? he that hath seen me hath seen the Father; and how sayest thou then, Shew us the Father?

10 Believest thou not that I am in the Father, and the Father in me? the words that I speak unto you I speak not of myself: but the Father that dwelleth in me, he doeth the works.

11 Believe me that I am in the Father, and the Father in me: or else believe me for the very works' sake.

12 Verily, verily, I say unto you, He that

were spoken, that Christ wished his disciples to remain brave and courageous, when they might think that every thing was in the greatest confusion; and therefore we ought to employ the same shield for warding off such assaults. It is impossible for us, indeed, to avoid feeling various emotions, but though we are shaken, we must not fall down. Thus it is said of believers, that they *are not troubled*, because, relying on the word of God, though very great difficulties press hard upon them, still they remain steadfast and upright.

6. I am the way

Though Christ does not give a direct reply to the question put to him, yet he passes by nothing that is useful to be known. It was proper that Thomas' curiosity should be checked; and, therefore, Christ does not explain what would be his condition when he should have departed out of this world to go to the Father, but dwells on a subject far more necessary. Thomas would gladly have heard what Christ intended to do in heaven, as we never become weary of those intricate speculations; but it is of greater importance to us to employ our study and labor in another inquiry, how we may become partakers of the blessed resurrection. The statement amounts to this, that whoever obtains Christ is ill want of nothing; and, therefore, that whoever is not satisfied with Christ alone, strives after something beyond absolute perfection.

23. And my Father will love him

We have already explained that the love of God to us is not placed in the second rank, as if it came after our piety as the cause of that love, but that believers may be fully convinced that the obedience which they render to the Gospel is pleasing to God, and that they may continually expect from him fresh additions of gifts. *And we will come to him who loveth me;* that is, he will feel that the grace of God dwelleth in him, and will every day receive additions to the gifts of God. He therefore speaks, not of that eternal love with which he loved us, before we were born, and even before the world was created, but since the time when he seals it on our hearts by making us partakers of his adoption. Nor does he even mean the first illumination, but those degrees of faith by which believers must continually advance, according to that saying, Whosoever hath it shall be given to him (Matthew 13:12).

So it is wrong to infer from this passage that there are two kinds of love with which we love God. They falsely maintain that we naturally love God, before he regenerates us by his Spirit, and even that by this preparation we merit the grace of regeneration; as if Scripture did not everywhere teach, and as if experience also did not loudly proclaim,

return to Him, possessed His soul.

4–5. He riseth from supper, and laid aside his garments – outer garments which would have impeded the operation of washing.

5. began to wash – proceeded to wash. *Beyond all doubt the feet of Judas were washed*, as of all the rest.

7. Jesus answered and said ... What I do thou knowest not now – that is, Such condescension *does* need explanation; it *is* fitted to astonish.

8. Peter saith unto him, Thou shalt never wash, &c – more emphatically, "Never shalt Thou wash my feet": that is, "That is an incongruity to which I can never submit." How like the man!

9. Lord, not my feet only, but also my hands and my head – that is, "To be severed from Thee, Lord, is death to me: If that be the meaning of my speech, I tread upon it; and if to be washed of Thee have such significance, then not my feet only, but hands, head, and all, be washed!"

10. He that is washed – in this *thorough* sense, to express which the word is carefully changed to one meaning to wash *as in a bath*.

but not all – important, as showing that Judas, instead of being as true-hearted a disciple as the rest at first, and merely *falling away* afterwards – as many represent it – *never experienced that cleansing at all which made the others what they were.*

12–15. Know ye what I have done? – that is, its intent. The question, however, was put merely to summon their attention to His own answer.

13. Ye call me Master – Teacher.

and Lord – *learning* of Him in the one capacity, *obeying* Him in the other.

and ye say well, for so I am – The conscious dignity with which this claim is made is remarkable, following immediately on His laying aside the towel of service. Yet what is this whole history but a succession of such astonishing contrast from first to last?

14. If I then – the Lord.

ought to wash one another's feet – not in

the narrow sense of a literal washing, profanely caricatured by popes and emperors, but by the very humblest *real* services one to another.

16–17. The servant is not greater than his lord, &c – an oft-repeated saying (Matt. 10: 24, &c.).

18–19. I speak not of you all – the "happy *are* ye," of John 13: 17, being on no supposition applicable to Judas.

19. I tell you before ... that when it comes to pass, ye may believe – and it came to pass when they deeply needed such confirmation.

20. He that receiveth whomsoever I send, receiveth me, &c – (See on Matt. 10: 40). The connection here seems to be that despite the dishonor done to Him by Judas, and similar treatment awaiting themselves, they were to be cheered by the assurance that their office, even as His own, was divine.

John 13: 21–30

The Traitor Indicated – He Leaves the Supper Room.

21. When Jesus had thus said, he was troubled in spirit, and testified, and said, Verily, verily, I say unto you, One of you shall betray me – The announcement of John 13: 18 seems not to have been plain enough to be quite apprehended, save by the traitor himself. He will therefore speak it out in terms not to be misunderstood. But how much it cost Him to do this, appears from the "trouble" that came over His "spirit" – visible emotion, no doubt – before He got it uttered. What wounded susceptibility does this disclose, and what exquisite delicacy in His social intercourse with the Twelve, to whom He cannot, without an effort, break the subject!

23–26. there was leaning on Jesus' bosom one of his disciples, whom Jesus loved – Thus modestly does our Evangelist denote himself, as reclining next to Jesus at the table.

25. He then lying – rather leaning over on Jesus' bosom.

saith – *in a whisper*, "Lord, who is it?"

26. Jesus answered – *also inaudibly*, the answer being communicated to Peter perhaps from behind.

believeth on me, the works that I do shall he do also; and greater works than these shall he do; because I go unto my Father.

13 And whatsoever ye shall ask in my name, that will I do, that the Father may be glorified in the Son.

14 If ye shall ask any thing in my name, I will do it.

15 If ye love me, keep my commandments.

16 And I will pray the Father, and he shall give you another Comforter, that he may abide with you for ever;

17 Even the Spirit of truth; whom the world cannot receive, because it seeth him not, neither knoweth him: but ye know him; for he dwelleth with you, and shall be in you.

18 I will not leave you comfortless: I will come to you.

19 Yet a little while, and the world seeth me no more; but ye see me: because I live, ye shall live also.

20 At that day ye shall know that I am in my Father, and ye in me, and I in you.

21 He that hath my commandments, and keepeth them, he it is that loveth me: and he that loveth me shall be loved of my Father, and I will love him, and will manifest myself to him.

22 Judas saith unto him, not Iscariot, Lord, how is it that thou wilt manifest thyself unto us, and not unto the world?

23 Jesus answered and said unto him, If a man love me, he will keep my words: and my Father will love him, and we will come unto him, and make our abode with him.

24 He that loveth me not keepeth not my sayings: and the word which ye hear is not mine, but the Father's which sent me.

25 These things have I spoken unto you, being yet present with you.

26 But the Comforter, which is the Holy Ghost, whom the Father will send in my name, he shall teach you all things, and bring all things to your remembrance, whatsoever I have said unto you.

27 Peace I leave with you, my peace I give unto you: not as the world giveth, give I unto you. Let not your heart be troubled, neither let it be afraid.

28 Ye have heard how I said unto you, I go away, and come again unto you. If

that we are altogether alienated from God, and that we are infected and filled with hatred of him, until he change our hearts. We must therefore keep in view the design of Christ, that he *and the Father will come*, to confirm believers, in uninterrupted confidence in his grace.

27. Peace I leave with you

By the word **peace** he means prosperity, which men are wont to wish for each other when they meet or part; for such is the import of the word **peace** in the Hebrew language.

Let not your heart be troubled

He again corrects the alarm which the disciples had felt on account of his departure. It is no ground for alarm, he tells them; for they want only his bodily presence, but will enjoy his actual presence through the Spirit. Let us learn to be always satisfied with this kind of presence, and let us not give a loose reign to the flesh, which always binds God by its outward inventions.

28. For the Father is greater than I

This passage has been tortured in various ways. The Aryans, in order to prove that Christ is some sort of inferior God, argued that he is less than the Father. The orthodox Fathers, to remove all ground for such a calumny, said that this must have referred to his human nature; but as the Aryans wickedly abused this testimony, so the reply given by the Fathers to their objection was neither correct nor appropriate; for Christ does not now speak either of his human nature, or of his eternal Divinity, but, accommodating himself to our weakness, places himself between God and us; and, indeed, as it has not been granted to us to reach the height of God, Christ descended to us, that he might raise us to it. You ought to have rejoiced, he says, because I return to the Father; for this is the ultimate object at which you ought to aim. By these words he does not show in what respect he differs in himself from the Father, but why he descended to us; and that was that he might unite us to God; for until we have reached that point, we are, as it were, in the middle of the course. We too imagine to ourselves but a half-Christ, and a mutilated Christ, if he do not lead us to God.

There is a similar passage in the writings of Paul, where he says that Christ "will deliver up the Kingdom to God his Father, that God may be all in all"(1 Corinthians 15: 24).

Christ certainly reigns, not only in human nature, but as he is God manifested in the flesh. In what manner, therefore, will he lay aside the kingdom? It is, because the Divinity which is now beheld in Christ's face alone, will then be openly visible in him. The only point of difference is, that Paul there describes the highest perfection of the Divine

He ... to whom I shall give a sop when I have dipped it – a piece of the bread soaked in the wine or the sauce of the dish; one of the ancient ways of testifying peculiar regard; compare John 13: 18, "*he that eateth bread with Me.*"

And when he had dipped ... he gave it to Judas, &c – Thus the sign of Judas' treachery was an affecting expression, and the last, of the Saviour's wounded love!

28–29. no man ... knew for what intent he spake this unto him ... some thought ... Jesus ... said ... But what we need ... or, ... give ... to the poor – a very important statement, as showing how carefully. Jesus had kept the secret, and Judas his hypocrisy, to the last.

30. He then, having received the sop, went immediately out – severing himself *for ever* from that holy society with which he never had any spiritual sympathy.

and it was night – but far blacker night in the soul of Judas than in the sky over his head.

John 13: 31–38

DISCOURSE AFTER THE TRAITOR'S DEPARTURE – PETER'S SELF-CONFIDENCE – HIS FALL PREDICTED.

31. when he was gone out, Jesus said, Now is the Son of man glorified – These remarkable words plainly imply that up to this moment our Lord had spoken *under a painful restraint*, the presence of a traitor within the little circle of His holiest fellowship on earth preventing the free and full outpouring of His heart; as is evident, indeed, from those oft-recurring clauses, "Ye are not all clean," "I speak not of you all," &c.

God is glorified in him – the glory of Each reaching its zenith in the Death of the Cross!

32. If God be glorified in him, God shall also – in return and reward of this highest of all services ever rendered to Him, or capable of being rendered.

33–35. Little children – From the height of His own glory He now descends, with sweet pity, to His "little children," *all now His own.* This term of endearment, nowhere else used in the Gospels, and once only employed by Paul

(Gal. 4: 19), is appropriated by the beloved disciple himself, who no fewer than seven times employs it in his first Epistle.

34. a new commandment I give unto you, That ye love one another; as I have loved you, that ye also love one another – This was the *new* feature of it. Christ's love to His people in giving His life a ransom for them was altogether new, and consequently as a Model and Standard for theirs to one another.

35. By this shall all men know that ye are my disciples – the disciples of Him who laid down His life for those He loved.

36–38. Peter said – seeing plainly in these directions how to behave themselves, that He was indeed going from them.

37. why not ... now? I will lay down my life for thy sake – He seems now to see that it was *death* Christ referred to as what would sever Him from them, but is not staggered at following Him thither. Jesus answered,

38. Wilt thou lay down thy life for my sake? – In this repetition of Peter's words there is deep though affectionate irony, and this Peter himself would feel for many a day after his recovery, as he retraced the painful particulars.

JOHN 14

John 14: 1–31

DISCOURSE AT THE TABLE, AFTER SUPPER.

1. Let not your heart be troubled, &c – What myriads of souls have not these opening words cheered, in deepest gloom, since first they were uttered!

ye believe in God – absolutely.

believe also in me – that is, Have the *same* trust in Me. What less, and what else, can these words mean?

2. In my Father's house are many mansions – and so room for all, and a place for each.

3. I will come again and receive you unto myself – *strictly*, at His Personal appearing; but in a secondary and comforting sense, to each individually. Mark again the claim made: to come again to receive His people *to Himself*, that where *He* is there they may be also. He

ye loved me, ye would rejoice, because I said, I go unto the Father: for my Father is greater than I.

29 And now I have told you before it come to pass, that, when it is come to pass, ye might believe.

30 Hereafter I will not talk much with you: for the prince of this world cometh, and hath nothing in me.

31 But that the world may know that I love the Father; and as the Father gave me commandment, even so I do. Arise, let us go hence.

JOHN 15

1 I am the true vine, and my Father is the husbandman.

2 Every branch in me that beareth not fruit he taketh away: and every branch that beareth fruit, he purgeth it, that it may bring forth more fruit.

3 Now ye are clean through the word which I have spoken unto you.

4 Abide in me, and I in you. As the branch cannot bear fruit of itself, except it abide in the vine; no more can ye, except ye abide in me.

5 I am the vine, ye are the branches: He that abideth in me, and I in him, the same bringeth forth much fruit: for without me ye can do nothing.

6 If a man abide not in me, he is cast forth as a branch, and is withered; and men gather them, and cast them into the fire, and they are burned.

7 If ye abide in me, and my words abide in you, ye shall ask what ye will, and it shall be done unto you.

8 Herein is my Father glorified, that ye bear much fruit; so shall ye be my disciples.

9 As the Father hath loved me, so have I loved you: continue ye in my love.

10 If ye keep my commandments, ye shall abide in my love; even as I have kept my Father's commandments, and abide in his love.

11 These things have I spoken unto you, that my joy might remain in you, and that your joy might be full.

12 This is my commandment, That ye love one another, as I have loved you.

13 Greater love hath no man than this, that a man lay down his life for his friends.

brightness, the rays of which began to shine from the time when Christ ascended to heaven. To make the matter more clear, we must use still greater plainness of speech. Christ does not here make a comparison between the Divinity of the Father and his own, nor between his own human nature and the Divine essence of the Father, but rather between his present state and the heavenly glory, to which he would soon afterwards be received; as if he had said, "You wish to detain me in the world, but it is better that I should ascend to heaven." Let us therefore learn to behold Christ humbled in the flesh, so that he may conduct us to the fountain of a blessed immortality; for he was not appointed to be our guide, merely to raise us to the sphere of the moon or of the sun, but to make us one with God the Father.

JOHN 15

7. If you abide in me

Believers often feel that they are starved, and are very far from that rich fatness which is necessary for yielding abundant fruit. For this reason it is expressly added, whatever those who are in Christ may need, there is a remedy provided for their poverty, as soon as they ask it from God. This is a very useful admonition; for the Lord often suffers us to hunger, in order to train us to earnestness in prayer. But if we fly to him, we shall never want what we ask, but, out of his inexhaustible abundance, he will supply us with every thing that we need (1 Corinthians 1: 5).

17. These things I command you

This too, was appropriately added, that the Apostles might know that mutual love among ministers is demanded above all things, that they may be employed, with one accord, in building up the Church of God; for there is no greater hindrance than when every one labors apart, and when all do not direct their exertions to the common good. If, then, ministers do not maintain brotherly intercourse with each other, they may possibly erect some large heaps, but latterly disjointed and confused; and, all the while, there will be no building of a Church.

19. If you were of the world

This is another consolation, that the reason why they are **hated by the world** is, that they have been separated from it. Now, this is their true happiness and glory, for in this manner they have been rescued from destruction.

20. Remember the word

It might also be read in the indicative mood, **You remember the word**, and the meaning is not very different; but I think that it is more suitable to read it in the imperative

DAVID BROWN

thinks it ought to be enough to be assured that they shall be where He is and in His keeping.

7. from henceforth – now, or from this time, understand.

8–12. The substance of this passage is that the Son is the ordained and perfect manifestation of the Father, that His own word for this ought to His disciples to be enough; that if any doubts remained His works ought to remove them; but yet that these works of His were designed merely to aid weak faith, and would be repeated, nay exceeded, by His disciples, in virtue of the power He would confer on them after His departure. His miracles the apostles wrought, though wholly in His name and by His power, and the "greater" works – not in degree but in kind – were the conversion of thousands in a day, by His Spirit accompanying them.

13–14. whatsoever ye … ask in my name – as Mediator.

15–17. If ye love me, keep my commandments. And I will pray the Father, &c – This connection seems designed to teach that the proper temple for the indwelling Spirit of Jesus is a heart filled with that love to Him which lives actively for Him, and so this was the fitting preparation for the promised gift.

17. whom the world cannot receive, &c – (See 1 Cor. 2: 14).

he dwelleth with you, and shall be in you – Though the proper fulness of both these was yet future, our Lord, by using both the present and the future, seems plainly to say that they already had the germ of this great blessing.

18–20. I will not leave you comfortless – in a bereaved and desolate condition; or (as in Margin) "orphans."

19. world seeth – beholdeth.
me no more, but ye see – behold.

22. Judas saith … not Iscariot – Beautiful parenthesis this! The traitor being no longer present, we needed not to be told that this question came not from *him*.
how … manifest thyself to us, and not to the world – a most natural and proper question, founded on John 14: 19, though interpreters speak against it as *Jewish*.

23. we will come and make our abode with him – Astonishing statement! In the Father's "coming" He "refers to the revelation of Him *as a Father* to the soul, which does not take place till the Spirit comes into the heart, teaching it to cry, *Abba, Father*" [OLSHAUSEN]. The "abode" means a permanent, eternal stay!

27. Peace I leave with you, my peace I give unto you – If John 14: 25–26 sounded like a note of preparation for drawing the discourse to a close, this would sound like a farewell. But oh, how different from ordinary adieus! It *is* a parting word, but of richest import, the customary "peace" of a parting friend sublimed and transfigured.

30–31. Hereafter I will not talk much with you – "I have a little more to say, but My work hastens apace, and the approach of the adversary will cut it short."
cometh – with hostile intent, for a last grand attack, having failed in His first formidable assault (Luke 4: 1–13) from which he "departed [only] *for a season*" (John 14: 13).

31. But that the world may know that I love the Father, &c – The sense must be completed thus: "But to the Prince of the world, though he has nothing in Me, I shall yield Myself up even unto death, that the world may know that I love and obey the Father, whose commandment it is that I give My life a ransom for many."

JOHN 15

John 15: 1–27

DISCOURSE AT THE SUPPER TABLE CONTINUED.

1–8. *The spiritual oneness of Christ and His people, and His relation to them as the Source of all their spiritual life and fruitfulness,* are here beautifully set forth by a figure familiar to Jewish ears (Is. 5: 1, &c.).
I am the true vine – of whom the vine of *nature* is but a shadow.
my Father is the husbandman – the great Proprietor of the vineyard, the Lord of the spiritual kingdom. (It is surely unnecessary to point out the claim to *supreme divinity* involved in this).

3. Now – rather, "Already."

14 Ye are my friends, if ye do whatsoever I command you.

15 Henceforth I call you not servants; for the servant knoweth not what his lord doeth: but I have called you friends; for all things that I have heard of my Father I have made known unto you.

16 Ye have not chosen me, but I have chosen you, and ordained you, that ye should go and bring forth fruit, and that your fruit should remain: that whatsoever ye shall ask of the Father in my name, he may give it you.

17 These things I command you, that ye love one another.

18 If the world hate you, ye know that it hated me before it hated you.

19 If ye were of the world, the world would love his own: but because ye are not of the world, but I have chosen you out of the world, therefore the world hateth you.

20 Remember the word that I said unto you, The servant is not greater than his lord. If they have persecuted me, they will also persecute you; if they have kept my saying, they will keep yours also.

21 But all these things will they do unto you for my name's sake, because they know not him that sent me.

22 If I had not come and spoken unto them, they had not had sin: but now they have no cloke for their sin.

23 He that hateth me hateth my Father also.

24 If I had not done among them the works which none other man did, they had not had sin: but now have they both seen and hated both me and my Father.

25 But this cometh to pass, that the word might be fulfilled that is written in their law, They hated me without a cause.

26 But when the Comforter is come, whom I will send unto you from the Father, even the Spirit of truth, which proceedeth from the Father, he shall testify of me:

27 And ye also shall bear witness, because ye have been with me from the beginning.

JOHN 16

1 These things have I spoken unto you, that ye should not be offended.

mood, **Remember the word**. It is a confirmation of what Christ had spoken immediately before, when he said that he was hated by the world, though he was far more excellent than his disciples; for it is unreasonable that the condition of **the servant** should be better than that of **his master**. Having spoken of persons, he likewise makes mention of doctrine.

If they have heard my word, they will keep yours also
Nothing gives greater uneasiness to the godly than when they see the doctrine, which is of God, haughtily despised by men; for it is truly shocking and dreadful, and the sight of it might shake the stoutest heart. But when we remember on the other hand, that not less obstinate resistance was manifested against the Son of God himself, we need not wonder that the doctrine of God is so little reverenced among men. When he calls it his doctrine and their doctrine, this refers to the ministry. Christ is the only Teacher of the Church; but he intended that his doctrine, of which he had been the first Teacher, should be afterwards preached by the apostles.

JOHN 16

13. But when he is come, the Spirit of truth
The Spirit, whom Christ promised to the apostles, is declared to be perfect Master or Teacher **of truth**. **The Spirit** was given to them, and under his guidance and direction they discharged the office to which they had been appointed. *He will lead you into all truth*. That very Spirit had *lead them into all truth*, when they committed to writing the substance of their doctrine. Whoever imagines that anything must be added to their doctrine, as if it were imperfect and but half-finished, not only accuses the apostles of dishonesty, but blasphemes against the Spirit. If the doctrine which they committed to writing had proceeded from mere learners or persons imperfectly taught, an addition to it would not have been superfluous; but now that their writings may be regarded as perpetual records of that revelation which was promised and given to them, nothing can be added to them without doing grievous injury to the Holy Spirit.

14. He will glorify me
Christ now reminds them that the Spirit will not come to erect any new kingdom, but rather to confirm the glory which has been given to him by the Father. For many foolishly imagine that Christ taught only so as to lay down the first lessons, and then to send the disciples to a higher school. In this way they make the Gospel to be of no greater value than the Law, of which it is said that it was a schoolmaster of the ancient people (Galatians 3: 24).

ye are clean through – by reason of.

the word I have spoken to you – already in a purified, fruitful condition, in consequence of the long action upon them of that searching "word" which was "as a refiner's fire" (Mal.3: 2–3).

4. Abide in me, and I in you; as the branch cannot bear fruit of itself, except it abide in the vine, &c – As all spiritual fruitfulness had been ascribed to the mutual *inhabitation*, and living, active *interpenetration* (so to speak) of Christ and His disciples, so here the keeping up of this vital connection is made essential to continued fruitfulness.

5. without me – apart, or vitally disconnected from Me.

ye can do nothing – spiritually, acceptably.

6. If a man abide not in me, he is cast forth as a branch ... withered ... cast into the fire ... burned – The one proper use of the vine is to *bear fruit*; failing this, it is good for one other thing – *fuel*. (See Ezek. 15: 1–5.) How awfully striking the figure, in this view of it!

7. If ye abide in me, and my words ... in you – Mark the change from the inhabitation of *Himself* to that of His *words*, paving the way for the subsequent exhortations (John 15: 9–10).

ask what ye will, and it shall be done unto you – because this indwelling of His words in them would secure the harmony of their askings with the divine will.

8. glorified that ye bear much fruit – not only from His delight in it for its own sake, but as from "the juices of the Living Vine."

so shall ye be my disciples – *evidence* your discipleship.

9–11. continue ye in my love – not, "Continue to love Me," but, "Continue in the possession and enjoyment of My love to you"; as is evident from the next words.

10. If ye keep my commandments, ye shall abide in my love – the obedient spirit of true discipleship cherishing and attracting the continuance and increase of Christ's love; and this, He adds, was the secret even of His own abiding in His Father's love!

13. Greater love hath no man than this, that

a man lay down his life for his friends – The emphasis lies not on "friends," but on "*laying down his life*" for them; that is, "One can show no greater regard for those dear to him than to give his life for them, and this is the love ye shall find in Me."

14. Ye are my friends, if ye do whatsoever I command you – hold yourselves in absolute subjection to Me.

15. Henceforth I call you not servants – that is, *in the sense explained* in the next words; for servants He still calls them (John 15: 20), and they delight to call themselves so, in the sense of being "under law to Christ" (1 Cor. 9: 20).

the servant knoweth not what his lord doeth – knows nothing of his master's *plans* and *reasons*, but simply receives and executes his orders.

but ... friends, for all things that I have heard of my Father I have made known unto you – admitted you to free, unrestrained fellowship, keeping back nothing from you which I have received to communicate. (Compare Gen. 18: 17; Ps. 25: 14; Is. 50: 4.)

16. Ye have not chosen me, but I ... you – a wholesale memento after the lofty things He had just said about their mutual indwelling, and the unreservedness of the friendship they had been admitted to.

ordained – appointed.

you, that ye should go and bring forth fruit – that is, give yourselves to it.

and that your fruit should remain – showing itself to be an imperishable and ever growing principle. (Compare Prov. 4: 18; 2 John 8).

17–21. The substance of these important verses has occurred more than once before. (See Matt. 10: 34–36; Luke 12: 49–53, &c.)

22–25. If I had not come and spoken unto them, they had not had sin – *comparatively* none; all other sins being light compared with the rejection of the Son of God.

now they have no cloak for their sin – rather, "pretext."

25. that the word might be fulfilled ... They hated me without a cause – quoted from the Messianic Ps. 69: 4, applied also in the same sense in John 2: 17; Acts 1: 20; Rom. 11: 9–10; 15: 3.

2 They shall put you out of the synagogues: yea, the time cometh, that whosoever killeth you will think that he doeth God service.

3 And these things will they do unto you, because they have not known the Father, nor me.

4 But these things have I told you, that when the time shall come, ye may remember that I told you of them. And these things I said not unto you at the beginning, because I was with you.

5 But now I go my way to him that sent me; and none of you asketh me, Whither goest thou?

6 But because I have said these things unto you, sorrow hath filled your heart.

7 Nevertheless I tell you the truth; It is expedient for you that I go away: for if I go not away, the Comforter will not come unto you; but if I depart, I will send him unto you.

8 And when he is come, he will reprove the world of sin, and of righteousness, and of judgment:

9 Of sin, because they believe not on me;

10 Of righteousness, because I go to my Father, and ye see me no more;

11 Of judgment, because the prince of this world is judged.

12 I have yet many things to say unto you, but ye cannot bear them now.

13 Howbeit when he, the Spirit of truth, is come, he will guide you into all truth: for he shall not speak of himself; but whatsoever he shall hear, that shall he speak: and he will shew you things to come.

14 He shall glorify me: for he shall receive of mine, and shall shew it unto you.

15 All things that the Father hath are mine: therefore said I, that he shall take of mine, and shall shew it unto you.

16 A little while, and ye shall not see me: and again, a little while, and ye shall see me, because I go to the Father.

17 Then said some of his disciples among themselves, What is this that he saith unto us, A little while, and ye shall not see me: and again, a little while, and ye shall see me: and, Because I go to the Father?

18 They said therefore, What is this that he saith, A little while? we cannot tell what he saith.

15. All things that the Father hath are mine

As it might be thought that Christ took away from the Father what he claimed for himself, he acknowledges that he has received from the Father all that he communicates to us by the Spirit. When he says that *all things that the Father hath are his,* he speaks in the person of the Mediator, for we must draw out of his fullness (John 1: 16). He always keeps his eye on us, as we have said. We see, on the other hand, how the greater part of men deceive themselves; for they pass by Christ, and go out of the way to seek God by circuitous paths.

16. A little while, and you do not see me

Christ had often forewarned the apostles of his departure, partly that they might bear it with greater courage, partly that they might desire more ardently the grace of the Spirit, of which they had no great desire, so long as they had Christ present with them in body. We must, therefore, guard against becoming weary of reading what Christ, not without cause, repeats so frequently. First, he says that he will very soon be taken from them, that, when they are deprived of his presence, on which alone they relied, they may continue to be firm. Next, he promises what will, compensate them for his absence, and he even testifies that he will quickly be restored to them, after he has been removed, but in another manner, that is, by the presence of the Holy Spirit.

24. Hitherto you have asked nothing in my name

It is probable that the apostles kept the rule of prayer which had been laid down in the Law. Now we know that the fathers were not accustomed to pray without a Mediator; for God had trained them, by so many exercises, to such a form of prayer. They saw the high priest enter into the holy place in the name of the whole people, and they saw sacrifices offered every day, that the prayers of the Church might be acceptable before God. It was, therefore, one of the principles of faith, that prayers offered to God, when there was no Mediator, were rash and useless. Christ had already testified to his disciples plainly enough that he was the Mediator, but their knowledge was so obscure, that they were not yet able to form their prayers **in his name** in a proper manner.

Nor is there any absurdity in saying that they prayed to God, with confidence in the Mediator, according to the injunction of the Law, and yet did not clearly and fully understand what that meant. The veil of the temple was still stretched out, the majesty of God was concealed under the shadow of the cherubim, the true High Priest had not yet entered into the heavenly sanctuary to intercede for his

27. ye also shall bear witness – rather, "are witnesses"; with reference indeed to their *future* witness-bearing, but putting the emphasis upon their *present* ample opportunities for acquiring their qualifications for that great office, inasmuch as they had been "with Him from the beginning."

JOHN 16

John 16: 1–33

Discourse at the Supper Table Concluded.

1–5. **These things have I spoken unto you, that ye should not be offended** – both the *warnings* and the *encouragements* just given.

2. **They shall put you out of the synagogue** – (John 9: 22; 12: 42).
    the time cometh, that whosoever killeth you will think that he doeth God service – The words mean *religious service* – "that he is offering a service to God." (So Saul of Tarsus, Gal. 1: 13–14; Phil. 3: 6.)

4. **these things I said not … at** – from.
    the beginning – He *had* said it pretty early (Luke 6: 22), but not quite as in John 16: 2.
    because I was with you.

5. **But now I go my way to him that sent me** – While He was with them, the world's hatred was directed chiefly against Himself; but His departure would bring it down upon them as His representatives.
    and none of you asketh me, Whither goest thou? – They *had* done so in a sort (John 13: 36; 14: 5); but He wished more intelligent and eager inquiry on the subject.

6–7. **But because I have said these things … sorrow hath filled your heart** – Sorrow had too much paralyzed them, and He would rouse their energies.

8. **And when he is come, he will, &c** – This is one of the passages most pregnant with thought in the profound discourses of Christ; with a few great strokes depicting all and every part of the ministry of the Holy Ghost in the world – His operation with reference to individuals as well as the mass, on believers and unbelievers alike [Olshausen].
    he will reprove – This is too weak a word

to express what is meant. *Reproof* is indeed implied in the term employed, and doubtless the word begins with it. But *convict* or *convince* is the thing intended; and as the one expresses the work of the Spirit on the *unbelieving* portion of mankind, and the other on the *believing,* it is better not to restrict it to either.

9. **Of sin, because they believe not on me** – As all sin has its root in unbelief, so the most aggravated form of unbelief is the rejection of Christ. The Spirit, however, in fastening this truth upon the conscience, does not *extinguish,* but, on the contrary, does *consummate and intensify,* the sense of all other sins.

10. **Of righteousness, because I go to my Father, and ye see me no more** – Beyond doubt, it is *Christ's personal righteousness* which the Spirit was to bring home to the sinner's heart. The evidence of this was to lie in the great *historical fact,* that He had "gone to His Father and was no more visible to men": for if His claim to be the Son of God, the Saviour of the world, had been a lie, how should the Father, who is "a jealous God," have raised such a blasphemer from the dead and exalted him to His right hand? But if He was the "Faithful and True Witness," the Father's "Righteous Servant," "His Elect, in whom His soul delighted," then was His departure to the Father, and consequent disappearance from the view of men, but the fitting consummation, the august reward, of all that He did here below, the seal of His mission, the glorification of the testimony which He bore on earth, by the reception of its Bearer to the Father's bosom. This triumphant vindication of Christ's *rectitude* is to us divine evidence, bright as heaven, that He is indeed the Saviour of the world, God's Righteous Servant to justify many, because He bare their iniquities (Is. 53: 11). Thus the Spirit, in this clause, is seen convincing men that there is in Christ perfect relief under the sense of *sin* of which He had before convinced them; and so far from mourning over His absence from us, as an irreparable loss, we learn to glory in it, as the evidence of His perfect acceptance on our behalf, exclaiming with one who understood this point, "Who shall lay anything to the charge of God's elect? It is God that justifieth: Who is he that condemneth? It is Christ that died; *yea, rather, that is risen again, who is even*

19 Now Jesus knew that they were desirous to ask him, and said unto them, Do ye inquire among yourselves of that I said, A little while, and ye shall not see me: and again, a little while, and ye shall see me?

20 Verily, verily, I say unto you, That ye shall weep and lament, but the world shall rejoice: and ye shall be sorrowful, but your sorrow shall be turned into joy.

21 A woman when she is in travail hath sorrow, because her hour is come: but as soon as she is delivered of the child, she remembereth no more the anguish, for joy that a man is born into the world.

22 And ye now therefore have sorrow: but I will see you again, and your heart shall rejoice, and your joy no man taketh from you.

23 And in that day ye shall ask me nothing. Verily, verily, I say unto you, Whatsoever ye shall ask the Father in my name, he will give it you.

24 Hitherto have ye asked nothing in my name: ask, and ye shall receive, that your joy may be full.

25 These things have I spoken unto you in proverbs: but the time cometh, when I shall no more speak unto you in proverbs, but I shall shew you plainly of the Father.

26 At that day ye shall ask in my name: and I say not unto you, that I will pray the Father for you:

27 For the Father himself loveth you, because ye have loved me, and have believed that I came out from God.

28 I came forth from the Father, and am come into the world: again, I leave the world, and go to the Father.

29 His disciples said unto him, Lo, now speakest thou plainly, and speakest no proverb.

30 Now are we sure that thou knowest all things, and needest not that any man should ask thee: by this we believe that thou camest forth from God.

31 Jesus answered them, Do ye now believe?

32 Behold, the hour cometh, yea, is now come, that ye shall be scattered, every man to his own, and shall leave me alone: and yet I am not alone, because the Father is with me.

33 These things I have spoken unto

people, and held not yet consecrated the way by his blood. We need not wonder, therefore, if he was not acknowledged to be the Mediator as he is, now that he appears for us in heaven before the Father, reconciling Him to us by his sacrifice, that we, miserable men, may venture to appear before him with boldness; for truly Christ, after having completed the satisfaction for sin, was received into heaven, and publicly showed himself to be the Mediator.

But we ought to attend to the frequent repetition of this clause, that we must pray in the name of Christ. This teaches us that it is a wicked profanation of the name of God, when any one, leaving Christ out of view, ventures to present himself before the judgment-seat of God. And if this conviction be deeply impressed on our minds, that God will willingly and abundantly give to us *whatever we shall ask in the name* of his Son, we will not go hither and thither to call to our aid various advocates, but will be satisfied with having this single Advocate, who so frequently and so kindly offers to us his labors in our behalf. We are said to pray in the name of Christ when we take him as our Advocate, to reconcile us, and make us find favor with his Father, though we do not expressly mention his name with our lips.

JOHN 17

1. Father, the hour is come

Christ asks that his kingdom may be glorified, in order that he also may advance the glory of the Father. He says that the hour is come, because though, by miracles and by every kind of supernatural events, he had been manifested to be the Son of God, yet his spiritual kingdom was still in obscurity, but soon afterwards shone with full brightness. If it be objected, that never was there any thing less glorious than the death of Christ, which was then at hand, I reply, that in that death we behold a magnificent triumph which is concealed from wicked men; for there we perceive that, atonement having been made for sins, the world has been reconciled to God, the curse has been blotted out, and Satan has been vanquished.

It is also the object of Christ's prayer, that his death may produce, through the power of the Heavenly Spirit, such fruit as had been decreed by the eternal purpose of God; for he says that *the hour is come*, not an hour which is determined by the fancy of men, but an hour which God had appointed. And yet the prayer is not superfluous, because, while Christ depends on the good pleasure of God, he knows that he ought to desire what God promised would certainly take place. True, God will do whatever he has decreed, not only though the whole world were asleep, but though it were opposed to him; but it is our duty to ask

at the right hand of God," &c. (Rom. 8: 33–34).

11. Of judgment, because the prince of this world is judged – By supposing that the *final judgment* is here meant, the point of this clause is, even by good interpreters, quite missed. The statement, "The prince of this world is *judged,"* means, beyond all reasonable doubt, the same as that in John 12: 31, "Now shall the prince of this world be *cast out*"; and both mean that his dominion over men, or his power to enslave and so to ruin them, is destroyed. The death of Christ "judged" or judicially overthrew him, and he was thereupon "cast out" or expelled from his usurped dominion (Heb. 2: 14; 1 John 3: 8; Col. 2: 15).

12–15. when he, the Spirit of truth, is come ... he shall not speak of himself – that is, *from* Himself, but, like Christ Himself, "what He hears," what is given Him to communicate.

he will show you things to come – referring specially to those revelations which, in the Epistles partially, but most fully in the Apocalypse, open up a vista into the Future of the Kingdom of God, whose horizon is everlasting hills.

14. He shall glorify me; for he shall receive of mine and show it unto you – Thus the whole design of the Spirit's office is to glorify Christ – not in His own Person, for this was done by the Father when He exalted Him to His own right hand – but in the view and estimation of men. For this purpose He was to *"receive of Christ"* – all the truth relating to Christ – *"and show it unto them,"* or make them to discern it in its own light. The *subjective* nature of the Spirit's teaching – the discovery to the souls of men of what is Christ *outwardly* – is here very clearly expressed; and, at the same time, the vanity of looking for revelations of the Spirit which shall do anything beyond throwing light in the soul upon what Christ Himself is, and taught, and did upon earth.

15. All things that the Father hath are mine – a plainer expression than this of *absolute community* with the Father in all things cannot be conceived, though the "all things" here have reference to the things of the Kingdom of Grace, which the Spirit was to receive that He might show it to us. We have here a wonderful glimpse into the *inner relations of the Godhead.*

16–22. A little while, and ye shall not see me; and again a little while, and ye shall see me, because I go to the Father – The joy of the world at their not seeing Him seems to show that His removal from them by *death* was what He meant; and in that case, their joy at again seeing Him points to their transport at His reappearance amongst them on His *Resurrection,* when they could no longer doubt His identity. At the same time the sorrow of the widowed Church in the absence of her Lord in the heavens, and her transport at His personal return, are certainly here expressed.

23–28. In that day – of the dispensation of the Spirit (as in John 14: 20).

ye shall ask – inquire of

me nothing – by reason of the fulness of the Spirit's teaching (John 14: 26; 16: 13; and compare 1 John 2: 27).

24. Hitherto have ye asked nothing in my name – for "prayer *in the name of* Christ, and prayer to Christ, presuppose His *glorification"* [OLSHAUSEN].

ask – when I am gone, "in My name."

25. in proverbs – in obscure language, opposed to "showing plainly" – that is, by the Spirit's teaching.

26. I say not ... I will pray the Father for you – as if He were not of *Himself* disposed to aid you: Christ does pray the Father for His people, but not for the purpose of inclining an *unwilling* ear.

27. For the Father himself loveth you, because ye have loved me – This love of theirs is that which is called forth by God's eternal love in the gift of His Son *mirrored* in the hearts of those who believe, and resting on His dear Son.

28. I came forth from the Father, &c – that is, "And ye are right, for I have indeed so come forth,and shall soon return whence I came." This echo of the truth, alluded to in John 16: 27, seems like *thinking aloud,* as if it were grateful to His own spirit on such a subject and at such an hour.

29–30. His disciples said, ... now speakest thou plainly, and speakest no proverb – hardly more so than before; the time for perfect plainness was yet to come; but hav-

you, that in me ye might have peace. In the world ye shall have tribulation: but be of good cheer; I have overcome the world.

JOHN 17

1 These words spake Jesus, and lifted up his eyes to heaven, and said, Father, the hour is come; glorify thy Son, that thy Son also may glorify thee:

2 As thou hast given him power over all flesh, that he should give eternal life to as many as thou hast given him.

3 And this is life eternal, that they might know thee the only true God, and Jesus Christ, whom thou hast sent.

4 I have glorified thee on the earth: I have finished the work which thou gavest me to do.

5 And now, O Father, glorify thou me with thine own self with the glory which I had with thee before the world was.

6 I have manifested thy name unto the men which thou gavest me out of the world: thine they were, and thou gavest them me; and they have kept thy word.

7 Now they have known that all things whatsoever thou hast given me are of thee.

8 For I have given unto them the words which thou gavest me; and they have received them, and have known surely that I came out from thee, and they have believed that thou didst send me.

9 I pray for them: I pray not for the world, but for them which thou hast given me; for they are thine.

10 And all mine are thine, and thine are mine; and I am glorified in them.

11 And now I am no more in the world, but these are in the world, and I come to thee. Holy Father, keep through thine own name those whom thou hast given me, that they may be one, as we are.

12 While I was with them in the world, I kept them in thy name: those that thou gavest me I have kept, and none of them is lost, but the son of perdition; that the scripture might be fulfilled.

13 And now come I to thee; and these things I speak in the world, that they might have my joy fulfilled in themselves.

14 I have given them thy word; and the world hath hated them, because they are

from him whatever he has promised, because the end and use of promises is to excite us to prayer.

That thy Son also may glorify thee

He means that there is a mutual connection between the advancement of his glory and of the glory of his Father; for why is Christ manifested, but that he may lead us to the Father? Hence it follows, that all the honor which is bestowed on Christ is so far from diminishing the honor of the Father, that it confirms it the more. We ought always to remember under what character Christ speaks in this passage; for we must not look only at his eternal Divinity, because he speaks as God manifested in the flesh, and according to the office of Mediator.

16. They are not of the world

That the heavenly Father may be more favourably disposed to assist them, he again says that **the whole world** hates them, and, at the same time, states that this hatred does not arise from any fault of theirs, but because the world hates God and Christ.

17. Sanctify them by thy truth

This **sanctification** includes the kingdom of God and his righteousness; that is, when God renews us by his Spirit, and confirms in us the grace of renewal, and continues it to the end. He asks, first, therefore, that the Father would sanctify the disciples, or, in other words, that he would consecrate them entirely to himself, and defend them as his sacred inheritance. Next, he points out the means of **sanctification**, and not without reason; for there are fanatics who indulge in much useless prattle about **sanctification**, but who neglect **the truth of** God, by which he consecrates us to himself. Again, as there are others who chatter quite as foolishly about **the truth** and yet disregard **the word**, Christ expressly says that **the truth**, by which God sanctifies his sons, is not to be found any where else than in **the word**.

Thy word is truth; for the word here denotes the doctrine of the Gospel, which the apostles had already heard from the mouth of their Master, and which they were afterwards to preach to others. In this sense Paul says that "the Church has been cleansed with the washing of water by the word of life" (Ephesians 5: 26).

26. And I have declared to them thy name, and will declare it

Christ discharged the office of Teacher, but, in order to make known the Father, he employed the secret revelation of the Spirit, and not the sound of his voice alone. He means, therefore, that he taught the apostles efficaciously. Besides, their faith being at that time very weak, he prom-

ing caught a glimpse of His meaning (it was nothing more), they eagerly express their satisfaction, as if glad to make anything of His words. How touchingly does this show both the simplicity of their hearts and the infantile character of their faith!

31–33. Jesus answered … Do ye now believe? – that is, "It is well ye do, for it is soon to be tested, and in a way ye little expect."

the hour cometh, yea, is now come, that ye shall be scattered, every man to his own, and shall leave me alone; and yet I am not alone – A deep and awful sense of *wrong* experienced is certainly expressed here, but how lovingly! That He was not to be utterly deserted, that there was One who would not forsake Him, was to Him matter of ineffable support and consolation; but that He should be without all *human* countenance and cheer, who as Man was exquisitely sensitive to the law of sympathy, would fill themselves with as much *shame*, when they afterwards recurred to it, as the Redeemer's heart in His hour of need with pungent *sorrow*. "I looked for some to take pity, but there was none; and for comforters, but I found none" (Ps. 69: 20).

because the Father is with me – how near, and with what sustaining power, who can express?

33. These things I have spoken unto you – not the immediately preceding words, but this whole discourse, of which these were the very last words, and which He thus winds up.

that in me ye might have peace – in the sublime sense before explained.

In the world ye shall have tribulation – specially arising from its deadly opposition to those who "are not of the world, but chosen out of the world." So that the "peace" promised was far from an unruffled one.

I have overcome the world – not only *before* you, but *for* you, that ye may be able to do the same (1 John 5: 4–5).

JOHN 17

John 17: 1–26

THE INTERCESSORY PRAYER.

Had this prayer *not* been recorded, what reverential reader would not have exclaimed, Oh,

to have been within hearing of such a prayer as that must have been, which wound up the whole of His past ministry and formed the point of transition to the dark scenes which immediately followed! But here it is, and with such signature of the Lips that uttered it that we seem rather to hear it from Himself than read it from the pen of His faithful reporter.

1–3. These words spake Jesus, and lifted up his eyes – "John very seldom depicts the gestures or looks of our Lord, as here. But this was an occasion of which the impression was indelible, and the upward look could not be passed over" [ALFORD].

glorify thy Son – Put honor upon Thy Son, by countenancing, sustaining, and carrying Him through that "hour."

2. give eternal life to as many as, &c – literally, "to all that which thou hast given him."

3. this is – that.

life eternal, that they might – may.

know, &c – This life eternal, then, is not mere conscious and unending existence, but a life of acquaintance with God in Christ (Job 22: 21).

thee, the only true God – the sole personal living God; in glorious contrast equally with heathen *polytheism*, philosophic *naturalism*, and mystic *pantheism*.

and Jesus Christ whom thou hast sent – This is the only place where our Lord gives Himself this compound name, afterwards so current in apostolic preaching and writing. Here the terms are used in their strict signification – "JESUS," because He "*saves* His people from their sins"; "CHRIST," as *anointed* with the measureless fulness of the Holy Ghost for the exercise of His saving offices.

4–5. I have glorified thee on the earth – rather, "I glorified" (for the thing is conceived as now *past*).

the work which thou gavest me to do – It is very important to preserve in the translation the *past* tense, used in the original, otherwise it might be thought that the work already "*finished*" was only what He had done *before uttering that prayer;* whereas it will be observed that our Lord speaks throughout as already beyond this present scene (John 17: 12, &c.), and so must be supposed to include in His "finished

not of the world, even as I am not of the world.

15 I pray not that thou shouldest take them out of the world, but that thou shouldest keep them from the evil.

16 They are not of the world, even as I am not of the world.

17 Sanctify them through thy truth: thy word is truth.

18 As thou hast sent me into the world, even so have I also sent them into the world.

19 And for their sakes I sanctify myself, that they also might be sanctified through the truth.

20 Neither pray I for these alone, but for them also which shall believe on me through their word;

21 That they all may be one; as thou, Father, art in me, and I in thee, that they also may be one in us: that the world may believe that thou hast sent me.

22 And the glory which thou gavest me I have given them; that they may be one, even as we are one:

23 I in them, and thou in me, that they may be made perfect in one; and that the world may know that thou hast sent me, and hast loved them, as thou hast loved me.

24 Father, I will that they also, whom thou hast given me, be with me where I am; that they may behold my glory, which thou hast given me: for thou lovedst me before the foundation of the world.

25 O righteous Father, the world hath not known thee: but I have known thee, and these have known that thou hast sent me.

26 And I have declared unto them thy name, and will declare it: that the love wherewith thou hast loved me may be in them, and I in them.

JOHN 18

1 When Jesus had spoken these words, he went forth with his disciples over the brook Cedron, where was a garden, into the which he entered, and his disciples.

2 And Judas also, which betrayed him, knew the place: for Jesus ofttimes resorted thither with his disciples.

3 Judas then, having received a band

ises greater progress for the future, and thus prepares them to expect more abundant grace of the Holy Spirit. Though he speaks of the apostles, we ought to draw from this a general exhortation, to study to make constant progress, and not to think that we have run so well that we have not still a long journey before us, so long as we are surrounded by the flesh.

JOHN 18

5. It is I

He replies mildly that he is the person **whom they seek**, and yet, as if they had been struck down by a violent tempest, or rather by a thunderbolt, he lays them prostrate on the ground. There was no want of power in him, therefore, to restrain their hands, if he had thought proper; but he wished to obey his Father, by whose decree he knew that he was called to die.

We may infer from this how dreadful and alarming to the wicked the voice of Christ will be, when he shall ascend his throne to judge the world. At that time he stood as a lamb ready to be sacrificed; his majesty, so far as outward appearance was concerned, was utterly gone; and yet when he utters but a single word, his armed and courageous enemies fall down. And what was the word? He thunders no fearful excommunication against them, but only replies, It is I. What then will be the result, when he shall come, not to be judged by a man, but to be the Judge of the living and the dead; not in that mean and despicable appearance but shining in heavenly glory, and accompanied by his angels? He intended, at that time, to give a proof of that efficacy which Isaiah ascribes to his voice. Among other glorious attributes of Christ, the Prophet relates that he will strike the earth with the rod of his mouth, and will slay the wicked by the breath of his lips (Isaiah 11: 4).

True, the fulfillment of this prophecy is declared by Paul to be delayed till the end of the world (2 Thessalonians 2: 8). Yet we daily see the wicked, with all their rage and pride, struck down by the voice of Christ; and, when those men fell down who had come to bind Christ, there was exhibited a visible token of that alarm which wicked men feel within themselves, whether they will or not, when Christ speaks by his ministers. Besides, as this was in some measure accidental to the voice of Christ, to whom it peculiarly belongs to raise up men who were lying in a state of death, he will undoubtedly display toward us such power as to raise us even to heaven.

25. He denied it

How shocking the stupidity of Peter, who, after having

work" the "decease which He was to accomplish at Jerusalem."

5. And now – in return.

with the glory which I had with thee before the world was – when "in the beginning the Word was *with God*" (John 1: 1), "the only-begotten Son *in the bosom of the Father*" (John 1: 18). With this pre-existent glory, which He veiled on earth, He asks to be reinvested, the design of the veiling being accomplished – not, however, simply as before, but *now in our nature*.

6–8. From praying for Himself He now comes to pray for His disciples.

I have manifested – I manifested.

thy name – His whole character towards mankind.

9–14. I pray for them – not as individuals merely, but as representatives of all such in every succeeding age.

not for the world – for they had been given Him "*out of* the world" (John 17: 6), and had been already transformed into the very *opposite* of it. The things sought for them, indeed, are applicable only to such.

10. all mine are thine, and thine are mine – literally, "All My things are Thine and Thy things are Mine."

11. Holy Father – an expression He nowhere else uses. "*Father*" is His wonted appellation, but "*Holy*" is here prefixed, because His appeal was to that perfection of the Father's nature, to "keep" or preserve them from being tainted by the unholy atmosphere of "the world" they were still in.

12. I kept – guarded.

them in thy name – acting as Thy Representative on earth.

none of them is lost, but the son of perdition – It is not implied here that the son of perdition was one of those whom the Father had given to the Son, but rather the contrary (John 13: 18) [WEBSTER and WILKINSON]. It is just as in Luke 4: 26–27, where we are not to suppose that the woman of *Sarepta* (in Sidon) was one of the widows of *Israel*, nor Naaman the *Syrian* one of the lepers in *Israel*, though the language – the same as here – might *seem* to express it.

son of perdition – doomed to it (2 Thess. 2: 3; Mark 14: 21).

13. I speak in the world, that they might have my joy fulfilled in themselves – that is, Such a strain befits rather the upper sanctuary than the scene of conflict; but I speak so "*in the world*," that My joy, the joy I experience in knowing that such intercessions are to be made for them by their absent Lord, may be tasted by those who now hear them, and by all who shall hereafter read the record of them,

15–19. I pray not that thou shouldest take them out of the world – for that, though it would secure their own safety, would leave the world unblessed by their testimony.

but ... keep them from the evil – all evil in and of the world.

16. They are not of the world, even as I am not of the world – (See John 15: 18–19). This is reiterated here, to pave the way for the prayer which follows.

17. Sanctify them – As the former prayer, "*Keep* them," was "negative," asking *protection* for them from the poisonous element which surrounded and pressed upon their renewed nature, so this prayer, "*Sanctify* them," is positive, asking the *advancement and completion* of their begun sanctification.

through – in.

thy truth – God's revealed truth, as the medium or element of sanctification; a statement this of immense importance.

thy word is truth – (Compare John 15: 3; Col. 1: 5; Eph. 1: 13.)

18. As thou hast sent – sentest.

me into the world, even so have I also sent them – sent I also them.

into the world – As their mission was to carry into effect the purposes of their Master's mission, so our Lord speaks of the *authority* in both cases as *co-ordinate*.

19. And for their sakes I sanctify – consecrate.

myself that they also might – may.

be sanctified – consecrated.

20–23. Neither pray I for these alone – This very important explanation, uttered in condescension to the hearers and readers of this prayer in all time, is meant not merely of what

of men and officers from the chief priests and Pharisees, cometh thither with lanterns and torches and weapons.

4 Jesus therefore, knowing all things that should come upon him, went forth, and said unto them, Whom seek ye?

5 They answered him, Jesus of Nazareth. Jesus saith unto them, I am he. And Judas also, which betrayed him, stood with them.

6 As soon then as he had said unto them, I am he, they went backward, and fell to the ground.

7 Then asked he them again, Whom seek ye? And they said, Jesus of Nazareth.

8 Jesus answered, I have told you that I am he: if therefore ye seek me, let these go their way:

9 That the saying might be fulfilled, which he spake, Of them which thou gavest me have I lost none.

10 Then Simon Peter having a sword drew it, and smote the high priest's servant, and cut off his right ear. The servant's name was Malchus.

11 Then said Jesus unto Peter, Put up thy sword into the sheath: the cup which my Father hath given me, shall I not drink it?

12 Then the band and the captain and officers of the Jews took Jesus, and bound him,

13 And led him away to Annas first; for he was father in law to Caiaphas, which was the high priest that same year.

14 Now Caiaphas was he, which gave counsel to the Jews, that it was expedient that one man should die for the people.

15 And Simon Peter followed Jesus, and so did another disciple: that disciple was known unto the high priest, and went in with Jesus into the palace of the high priest.

16 But Peter stood at the door without. Then went out that other disciple, which was known unto the high priest, and spake unto her that kept the door, and brought in Peter.

17 Then saith the damsel that kept the door unto Peter, Art not thou also one of this man's disciples? He saith, I am not.

18 And the servants and officers stood there, who had made a fire of coals; for it was cold: and they warmed themselves:

denied his Master, not only has no feeling of repentance, but hardens himself by the very indulgence he takes in sinning! If each of them in his turn had asked him, he would not have hesitated to deny his Master a thousand times. Such is the manner in which Satan hurries along wretched men, after having degraded them. We must also attend to the circumstance which is related by the other Evangelists (Matthew 26: 74; Mark 14: 71), that **he began to curse and to swear, saying, that he did not know Christ.** Thus it happens to many persons every day. At first, the fault will not be very great; next, it becomes habitual, and at length, after that conscience has been laid asleep, he who has accustomed himself to despise God will think nothing unlawful for him, but will dare to commit the greatest wickedness. There is nothing better for us, therefore, than to be early on our guard, that he who is tempted by Satan, while he is yet uncorrupted, may not allow himself the smallest indulgence.

27. Immediately the cock crew

The Evangelist mentions **the crowing of the cock**, in order to inform us, that Peter was warned by God at the very time; and for this reason the other Evangelists tell us, that **he then remembered the words of the Lord,** (Matthew 26: 75; Mark 14: 72), though Luke relates that the mere **crowing of the cock** did not produce any effect on Peter, till Christ **looked at him,** (Luke 22: 61). Thus, when any person has once begun to fall through the suggestions of Satan, no voice, no sign, no warning, will bring him back, until the Lord himself cast his eyes upon him.

28. Then they lead Jesus

That trial, which the Evangelist mentions, took place before daybreak; and yet there can be no doubt, that they had their bellows at work throughout the whole of the city to inflame the people. Thus the rage of the people was suddenly kindled, as if all, with one consent, demanded that Christ should be put to death, Now, the trial was conducted by the priests, not that they had it in their power to pronounce a sentence, but that, after having excited a prejudice against him by their previous decision, they might deliver him to the governor, as if he had already been fully tried. The Romans gave the name **Praetorium** both to the governor's house or palace, and to the judgment-seat, where he was wont to decide causes.

That they might not be defiled

In abstaining from all defilement, that, being purified according to the injunction of the Law, they may eat the Lord's Passover, their religion, in this respect, deserves commendation. But there are two faults, and both of them are very

follows, but of the whole prayer.

21. that they all may be one, as thou, Father, art in me, and I in thee, that they may be one in us – *The indwelling Spirit of the Father and the Son* is the one perfect bond of union, knitting up into a living unity, first all believers amongst themselves; next, this unity into one still higher, with the Father and the Son.

that the world may believe that thou hast sent me – sentest me. So the grand impression upon the world at large, that the mission of Christ is divine, is to be made by *the unity of His disciples*. Of course, then, it must be something that shall be *visible* or perceptible to the world.

22. And the glory which thou gavest – hast given.

me I have given them, that they may be one, even as we are one – The last clause shows the meaning of the first. It is not the *future* glory of the heavenly state, but the secret of that *present* unity just before spoken of; *the glory*, therefore, *of the indwelling Spirit of Christ*; the glory of an accepted state, of a holy character, of every grace.

24–26. Father, I will – The majesty of this style of speaking is quite transparent. No petty criticism will be allowed to fritter it away in any but superficial or perverted readers.

25. O righteous Father, the world hath not known thee – knew thee not.

me – As before He said "*Holy* Father," when desiring the display of that perfection on His disciples (John 17: 11), so here He styles Him "*Righteous* Father," because He is appealing to His righteousness or justice, to make a distinction between those two diametrically opposite classes – "*the world*," on the one hand, which would not "know the Father, though brought so nigh to it in the Son of His love, and, on the other, *Himself*, who recognized and owned Him, *and even His disciples*, who owned His mission from the Father.

26. And I have declared – I made known or communicated.

me may be in them, and I in them – This eternal love of the Father, resting first on Christ, is by His Spirit imparted to and takes up its permanent abode in all that believe in Him; and "He abiding in them and they in

Him" (John 15: 5), they are "*one Spirit*." "With this lofty thought the Redeemer closes His prayer for His disciples, and in them for His Church through all ages. He has compressed into the last moments given Him for conversation with His own the most sublime and glorious sentiments ever uttered by mortal lips. But hardly has the sound of the last word died away, when He passes with the disciples over the brook Kedron to Gethsemane – and the bitter conflict draws on. The seed of the new world must be sown in Death, that thence Life may spring up" [OLSHAUSEN].

JOHN 18

John 18: 1–13

BETRAYAL AND APPREHENSION OF JESUS.

1–3. over the brook Kedron – a deep, dark ravine, to the northeast of Jerusalem, through which flowed this small storm brook or winter torrent, and which in summer is dried up.

where was a garden – at the foot of the Mount of Olives, "called Gethsemane; that is, olive press (Matt. 26: 30,36).

2. Judas ... knew the place, for Jesus oft-times – see John 8: 1; Luke 21: 37.

resorted thither with his disciples – The baseness of this abuse of knowledge in Judas, derived from admission to the closest privacies of his Master, is most touchingly conveyed here, though nothing beyond bare narrative is expressed.

3. Judas then – "He that was called Judas, one of the Twelve," says Luke (Luke 22: 47), in language which brands him with peculiar infamy, as *in* the sacred circle while in no sense *of* it.

4–9. Jesus ... knowing all things that should come – were coming.

upon him, went forth – from the shade of the trees, probably, into open view, indicating His sublime preparedness to meet His captors.

5. They answered ... Jesus of Nazareth – just the sort of blunt, straight forward reply one expects from military men, simply acting on their instructions.

Judas ... stood with them – No more is recorded here of *his* part of the scene, but we

and Peter stood with them, and warmed himself.

19 The high priest then asked Jesus of his disciples, and of his doctrine.

20 Jesus answered him, I spake openly to the world; I ever taught in the synagogue, and in the temple, whither the Jews always resort; and in secret have I said nothing.

21 Why askest thou me? ask them which heard me, what I have said unto them: behold, they know what I said.

22 And when he had thus spoken, one of the officers which stood by struck Jesus with the palm of his hand, saying, Answerest thou the high priest so?

23 Jesus answered him, If I have spoken evil, bear witness of the evil: but if well, why smitest thou me?

24 Now Annas had sent him bound unto Caiaphas the high priest.

25 And Simon Peter stood and warmed himself. They said therefore unto him, Art not thou also one of his disciples? He denied it, and said, I am not.

26 One of the servants of the high priest, being his kinsman whose ear Peter cut off, saith, Did not I see thee in the garden with him?

27 Peter then denied again: and immediately the cock crew.

28 Then led they Jesus from Caiaphas unto the hall of judgment: and it was early; and they themselves went not into the judgment hall, lest they should be defiled; but that they might eat the passover.

29 Pilate then went out unto them, and said, What accusation bring ye against this man?

30 They answered and said unto him, If he were not a malefactor, we would not have delivered him up unto thee.

31 Then said Pilate unto them, Take ye him, and judge him according to your law. The Jews therefore said unto him, It is not lawful for us to put any man to death:

32 That the saying of Jesus might be fulfilled, which he spake, signifying what death he should die.

33 Then Pilate entered into the judgment hall again, and called Jesus, and said unto him, Art thou the King of the Jews?

34 Jesus answered him, Sayest thou this thing of thyself, or did others tell it

heinous. The first is, they do not consider that they carry more pollution within their hearts, than they can contract by entering any place however profane; and the second is, they carry to excess their care about smaller matters, and neglect what is of the highest importance.

To the defiled and to unbelievers, says Paul, nothing is pure; because their minds are polluted, (Titus 1: 15).

But these hypocrites, though they are so full of malice, ambition, fraud, cruelty, and avarice, that they ahnost infect heaven and earth with their abominable smell, are only afraid of external pollutions. So then it is an intolerable mockery, that they expect to please God, provided that they do not contract defilement by touching some unclean thing, though they have disregarded true purity.

Another fault connected with hypocrisy is, that, while it is careful in performing ceremonies, it makes no scruple of neglecting matters of the highest importance; for God enjoined on the Jews those ceremonies which are contained in the Law, for no other reason, than that they might be habituated to the love and practice of true holiness. Besides, no part of the Law forbade them to enter into the house of a Gentile, but it was a precaution derived from the traditions of the fathers, that no person might, through oversight, contract any pollution from an unclean house. But those venerable expounders of the Law, while they carefully strain at a gnat, swallow the camel without any hesitation (Matthew 23: 24); and it is usual with hypocrites to reckon it a greater crime to kill a flea than to kill a man. This fault is closely allied to the other, of greatly preferring the traditions of men to the holy commandments of God. In order *that they may eat the Passover* in a proper manner, they wish to keep themselves pure; but they suppose uncleanness to be confined within the wails of the governor's house, and yet they do not hesitate, while heaven and earth are witnesses, to pursue an innocent person to death. In short, they observe the shadow of the passover with a false and pretended reverence, and yet not only do they violate the true passover by sacrilegious hands, but endeavor, as far as lies in their power, to bury it in eternal oblivion.

36. My kingdom is not of this world

By these words he acknowledges that he is **a king**, but, so far as was necessary to prove his innocence, he clears himself of the calumny; for he declares, that there is no disagreement between his kingdom and political government or order; as if he had said, "I am falsely accused, as if I had attempted to produce a dis-turbanee, or to make a revolution in public affairs. I have preached about **the kingdom of God**; but that is spiritual, and, therefore, you have no right to suspect me of aspiring to kingly power."

have found the gap painfully supplied by all the other Evangelists.

6. As soon then as he said unto them, I am He, they went backward – recoiled.

7. Then asked he them again, Whom seek ye? – Giving them a door of escape from the guilt of a deed which *now* they were able in some measure to understand.

8. I have told you that I am He: if therefore ye seek me, let these go their way – Wonderful self-possession, and consideration for others, in such circumstances!

10–11. None of the other Evangelists mention the name either of the ardent disciple or of his victim.

11. Then said Jesus – "Suffer ye thus far" (Luke 22: 51).

Put up thy sword into the sheath: the cup which my Father hath given me, shall I not drink it? – This expresses *both the feelings* which struggled in the Lord's breast during the Agony in the garden – *aversion to the cup* viewed *in itself,* but, *in the light of the Father's will,* perfect *preparedness to drink it.*

12. Then the band ... took Jesus – but not till He had made them feel that "no man took His life from Him, but that He laid it down of Himself."

John 18: 13–27

JESUS BEFORE ANNAS AND CAIAPHAS – FALL OF PETER.

15–18. Simon Peter followed Jesus – Natural though this was, and safe enough, had he only "watched and prayed that he enter not into temptation," as his Master bade him (Matt. 26: 41), it was, in his case, a fatal step.

16. But Peter stood at the door without – by preconcerted arrangement with his friend till he should get access for him.

17. Art thou not also one of this man's disciples? – that is, thou as well as "that other disciple," whom she knew to be one, but did not challenge, perceiving that he was a privileged person.

18. a fire of coals, for it was cold, and they warmed themselves – "John alone notices the

material (charcoal) of which the fire was made, and the reason for a fire – the coldness of the night" [WEBSTER and WILKINSON]. "Peter went in and sat with the servants to see the end (Matt. 26: 58), and warmed himself at the fire" (Mark 14: 54).

19–21. The high priest ... asked Jesus of his disciples, and of his doctrine – probably to entrap Him into some statements which might be used against Him at the trial. From our Lord's answer it would seem that "His disciples" were understood to be some secret party.

20. I spake – have spoken.

nothing – that is, nothing of any different nature; all His private communications with the Twelve being but explanations and developments of His public teaching.

21. Why askest thou me? ask them which heard me ... they know what I ... said – This seems to imply that He saw the attempt to draw Him into self-crimination, and resented it by falling back upon the right of every accused party to have some charge laid against Him by competent witnesses.

23. if well – He does not say "If *not*" evil, as if His reply were merely unobjectionable: "*well*" seems to challenge more than this as due to His remonstrance This shows that Matt. 5: 39 is not to be taken to the letter.

25. In Matt. 26: 71 the *second* charge was made by "another maid, when he was gone out into the porch," who "saw him, and said unto them that were there, This [fellow] was also with Jesus of Nazareth." So also Mark 14: 69. But in Luke 22: 58 it is said, "After a little while" (from the time of the first denial), "another [*man*] saw him, and said, Thou art also of them." Possibly it was thrown at him by more than one; but these circumstantial variations only confirm the truth of the narrative.

26. No doubt his relationship to Malchus drew attention to the man who smote him, and this enabled him to identify Peter.

27. the cock crew – As Mark is the only Evangelist who tells us that our Lord predicted that the cock should crow *twice* (Mark 14: 30), so he only mentions that it *did* crow twice (Mark 14: 72).

thee of me?

35 Pilate answered, Am I a Jew? Thine own nation and the chief priests have delivered thee unto me: what hast thou done?

36 Jesus answered, My kingdom is not of this world: if my kingdom were of this world, then would my servants fight, that I should not be delivered to the Jews: but now is my kingdom not from hence.

37 Pilate therefore said unto him, Art thou a king then? Jesus answered, Thou sayest that I am a king. To this end was I born, and for this cause came I into the world, that I should bear witness unto the truth. Every one that is of the truth heareth my voice.

38 Pilate saith unto him, What is truth? And when he had said this, he went out again unto the Jews, and saith unto them, I find in him no fault at all.

39 But ye have a custom, that I should release unto you one at the passover: will ye therefore that I release unto you the King of the Jews?

40 Then cried they all again, saying, Not this man, but Barabbas. Now Barabbas was a robber.

JOHN 19

1 Then Pilate therefore took Jesus, and scourged him.

2 And the soldiers platted a crown of thorns, and put it on his head, and they put on him a purple robe,

3 And said, Hail, King of the Jews! and they smote him with their hands.

4 Pilate therefore went forth again, and saith unto them, Behold, I bring him forth to you, that ye may know that I find no fault in him.

5 Then came Jesus forth, wearing the crown of thorns, and the purple robe. And Pilate saith unto them, Behold the man!

6 When the chief priests therefore and officers saw him, they cried out, saying, Crucify him, crucify him. Pilate saith unto them, Take ye him, and crucify him: for I find no fault in him.

7 The Jews answered him, We have a law, and by our law he ought to die, because he made himself the Son of God.

8 When Pilate therefore heard that saying, he was the more afraid;

JOHN 19

1. Then Pilate therefore took Jesus

Pilate adheres to his original intention; but to the former ignominy he adds a second, hoping that, when Christ shall have been scourged, the Jews will be satisfied with this light chastisement. When he labors so earnestly, and without any success, we ought to recognize in this the decree of Heaven, by which Christ was appointed to death. Yet his innocence is frequently attested by the testimony of the judge, in order to assure us that he was free from all sin, and that he was substituted as a guilty person in the room of others, and bore the punishment due to the sins of others. We see also in Pilate a remarkable example of a trembling conscience. He acquits Christ with his mouth, and acknowledges that **there is no guilt in him,** and yet inflicts punishment on him, as if he were guilty. Thus, they who have not so much courage as to defend, with unshaken constancy, what is right, must be driven hither and thither, and led to adopt opposite and conflicting opinions.

We all condemn *Pilate;* and yet, it is shameful to relate that there are so many *Pilates* in the world, who *scourge Christ,* not only in his members, but also in his doctrine. There are many who, for the purpose of saving the life of those who are persecuted for the sake of the Gospel, constrain them wickedly to deny Christ.

10. Knowest thou not that I have power to crucify thee?

This shows that the dread with which Pilate had been suddenly seized was transitory, and had no solid root; for now, forgetting all fear, he breaks out into haughty and monstrous contempt of God. He threatens Christ, as if there had not been a Judge in heaven; but this must always happen with irreligious men, that, shaking off the fear of God, they quickly return to their natural disposition. Hence also we infer, that it is not without good reason that **the heart of man** is called **deceitful,** (Jeremiah 17: 9); for, though some fear of God dwells in it, there likewise comes from it mere impiety. Whoever, then, is not regenerated by the Spirit of God, though he pretend for a time to reverence the majesty of God, will quickly show, by opposite facts, that this fear was hypocritical.

22. What I have written I have written

Pilate's firmness must be ascribed to the providence of God; for there can be no doubt that they attempted, in various ways, to change his resolution. Let us know, therefore, that he was held by a Divine hand, so that he remained unmoved. Pilate did not yield to the prayers of the priests, and did not allow himself to be corrupted by them; but God testified, by

DAVID BROWN

John 18: 28–40

JESUS BEFORE PILATE.

Note. – Our Evangelist, having given the interview with Annas, omitted by the other Evangelists, here omits the trial and condemnation before Caiaphas, which the others had recorded. (See on Mark 14: 53–65.)

Mark 14: 61–65

The high priest asked Him, Art Thou the Christ, the Son of the blessed? – Matthew says the high priest *put Him upon solemn oath,* saying, "I adjure Thee by the living God that Thou tell us whether Thou be the Christ, the Son of God" (Matt. 26: 63). This rendered an answer by our Lord legally necessary (Lev. 5: 1). Accordingly, Mark 14: 62:

Jesus said, I am – "Thou hast said" (Matt. 26: 64). In Luke 22: 67–68, some other words are given, "If I tell you, ye will not believe; and if I also ask you, ye will not answer Me, nor let Me go." This seems to have been uttered *before* giving His direct answer, as a calm remonstrance and dignified protest against the prejudgment of His case and the unfairness of their mode of procedure.

and ye shall see the Son of man, &c – This concluding part of our Lord's answer is given somewhat more fully by Matthew and Luke. "Nevertheless I say unto you, Hereafter [rather, 'From henceforth'] shall ye see the Son of man sitting on the right hand of power, and coming in the clouds of heaven" (Matt. 26: 64; Luke 22: 69).

Then the high priest rent his clothes, and saith, What need we any further witnesses? Ye have heard the blasphemy – "of his own mouth" (Luke 22: 71); an affectation of religious horror.

What think ye? – "Say, what verdict would ye pronounce."

They all condemned Him to be guilty of death – of a capital crime. (See Lev. 24: 16). Mark 14: 65:

And some began to spit on Him – "Then did they spit in His face" (Matt. 26: 67). See Is. 50: 6.

And to cover His face, and to buffet Him, and to say unto Him, Prophesy – or, "divine," "unto us, Thou Christ, who is he that smote Thee?" The sarcasm in styling Him *the Christ,* and as such demanding of Him the perpetrator of the blows inflicted upon Him, was in them as infamous as to Him it was stinging.

and the servants did strike him with the palms of their hands – "And many other things blasphemously spake they against him" (Luke 22: 65). This general statement is important, as showing that virulent and varied as were the *recorded* affronts put upon Him, they are but a *small specimen* of what He endured on that black occasion.

John 18: 28. Then led they Jesus from Caiaphas to the hall of judgment – but not till "in the morning the chief priests held a consultation with the elders and scribes and the whole council against Him to put Him to death, and bound Him."

30. If he were not a malefactor, we would not have delivered him up unto thee – They were conscious they *had no case* of which Pilate could take cognizance, and therefore insinuate that they had already found Him worthy of death by their own law; but not having the power, under the Roman government, to carry their sentence into execution, they had come merely for his sanction.

32. That the saying ... might be fulfilled which he spake, signifying what death he should die – that is, by *crucifixion* (John 12: 32–33; Matt. 20: 19); which being a Roman mode of execution, could only be carried into effect by order of the governor. (The Jewish mode in such cases as this was by *stoning.*)

33–38. Pilate ... called Jesus, and said ... Art thou the King of the Jews? – In Luke 23: 2 they charge our Lord before Pilate with "perverting the nation, and forbidding to give tribute to Cæsar, saying that He Himself is Christ a king." Perhaps this was what occasioned Pilate's question.

34. Jesus answered ... Sayest thou this of thyself, or did others tell it thee of me? – an important question for our Lord's case, to bring out whether the word "*King*" were meant in a *political* sense, with which Pilate had a right to deal, or whether he were merely *put up* to it by His accusers, who had no claims to charge Him but such as were of a purely *religious* nature, with which Pilate had nothing to do.

9 And went again into the judgment hall, and saith unto Jesus, Whence art thou? But Jesus gave him no answer.

10 Then saith Pilate unto him, Speakest thou not unto me? knowest thou not that I have power to crucify thee, and have power to release thee?

11 Jesus answered, Thou couldest have no power at all against me, except it were given thee from above: therefore he that delivered me unto thee hath the greater sin.

12 And from thenceforth Pilate sought to release him: but the Jews cried out, saying, If thou let this man go, thou art not Caesar's friend: whosoever maketh himself a king speaketh against Caesar.

13 When Pilate therefore heard that saying, he brought Jesus forth, and sat down in the judgment seat in a place that is called the Pavement, but in the Hebrew, Gabbatha.

14 And it was the preparation of the passover, and about the sixth hour: and he saith unto the Jews, Behold your King!

15 But they cried out, Away with him, away with him, crucify him. Pilate saith unto them, Shall I crucify your King? The chief priest answered, We have no king but Caesar.

16 Then delivered he him therefore unto them to be crucified. And they took Jesus, and led him away.

17 And he bearing his cross went forth into a place called the place of a skull, which is called in the Hebrew Golgotha:

18 Where they crucified him, and two other with him, on either side one, and Jesus in the midst.

19 And Pilate wrote a title, and put it on the cross. And the writing was, JESUS OF NAZARETH THE KING OF THE JEWS.

20 This title then read many of the Jews: for the place where Jesus was crucified was nigh to the city: and it was written in Hebrew, and Greek, and Latin.

21 Then said the chief priests of the Jews to Pilate, Write not, The King of the Jews; but that he said, I am King of the Jews.

22 Pilate answered, What I have written I have written.

23 Then the soldiers, when they had crucified Jesus, took his garments, and made four parts, to every soldier a part;

his mouth, the firmness and stability of the kingdom of his Son. And if, in the writing of Pilate, the kingdom of Christ was shown to be so firm that it could not be shaken by all the attacks of its enemies, what value ought we to attach to the testimonies of the Prophets, whose tongues and hands God consecrated to his service?

The example of *Pilate* reminds us, also, that it is our duty to remain steady in defending the truth. A heathen refuses to retract what he has justly and properly written concerning Christ, though he did not understand or consider what he was doing. How great, then, will be our dishonor, if, terrified by threatenigs or dangers, we withdraw from the profession of his doctrine, which God hath sealed on our hearts by his Spirit! Besides, it ought to be observed how detestable is the tyranny of the Papists, which prohibits the reading of the Gospel, and of the whole of the Scripture, by the common people. Pilate, though he was a reprobate man, and, in other respects, an instrument of Satan, was nevertheless, by a secret guidance, appointed to be a herald of the Gospel, that he might publish a short summary of it in three languages. What rank, therefore, shall we assign to those who do all that they can to suppress the knowledge of it, since they show that they are worse than Pilate?

25. Now there stood by the cross of Jesus
The Evangelist here mentions incidentally, that while Christ obeyed God the Father, he did not fail to perform the duty which he owed, as a son, towards **his mother**. True, he forgot himself, and he forgot every thing, so far as was necessary for the discharge of obedience to his Father, but, after having performed that duty, he did not neglect what he owed to **his mother**. Hence we learn in what manner we ought to discharge our duty towards God and towards men. It often happens that, when God calls us to the performance of any thing, our parents, or wife, or children, draw us in a contrary direction, so that we cannot give equal satisfaction to all. If we place men in the same rank with God, we judge amiss. We must, therefore, give the preference to the command, the worship, and the service of God; after which, as far as we are able, we must give to men what is their due.

And yet the commands of the first and second table of the Law never jar with each other, though at first sight they appear to do so; but we must begin with the worship of God, and afterwards assign to men an inferior place. Such is the import of the following statements: "He who loveth father or mother more than me, is not worthy of me" (Matthew 10: 41); and, "If any one hate not his father, and mother, and wife, and children, and brethren, and sisters, he cannot be my disciple" (Luke 14: 26).

35. Pilate answered, Am I a Jew? Thine own nation and the chief priests delivered thee to me: What hast thou done? – that is, "Jewish questions I neither understand nor meddle with; but Thou art here on a charge which, though it *seems* only Jewish, *may* yet involve treasonable matter: As *they* state it, I cannot decide the point; tell me, then, what procedure of Thine has brought Thee into this position." In modern phrase, Pilate's object in this question was merely to determine the *relevancy* of the charge.

36. Jesus answered, My kingdom is not of this world – He does not say "not *over*," but "not of this world" – that is, in its *origin* and *nature*; therefore "no such kingdom as need give thee or thy master the least alarm."

Every one that is of the truth heareth my voice – Our Lord here not only affirms that His word had in it a self-evidencing, self-recommending power, but gently insinuated the *true secret of the growth and grandeur of His kingdom* – as A KINGDOM OF TRUTH, in its highest sense, into which all souls who have learned to live and count all things but loss for the truth are, by a most heavenly attraction, drawn as into their proper element; THE KING of whom Jesus is, fetching them in and ruling them by His captivating power over their hearts.

38. Pilate saith unto him, What is truth? – that is, "Thou stirrest the question of questions, which the thoughtful of every age have asked, but never man yet answered."

I find in him no fault – no crime.

39. But ye have a custom that I should release one unto you at the passover, &c – "On the typical import of the choice of Christ to suffer, by which Barabbas was set free, see the sixteenth chapter of Leviticus, particularly Lev. 16: 5–10, where the subject is the *sin offering* on the great day of atonement" [KRAFFT in LUTHARDT].

JOHN 19

John 19: 1–16

JESUS BEFORE PILATE – SCOURGED – TREATED WITH OTHER SEVERITIES AND INSULTS – DELIVERED UP, AND LED AWAY TO BE CRUCIFIED.

1–3. Pilate took Jesus and scourged him – in hope of appeasing them. (See Mark 15: 15). "And the soldiers led Him away into the palace, and they call the whole band" (Mark 15: 16) – the body of the military cohort stationed there – to take part in the mock coronation now to be enacted.

2. the soldiers platted a crown of thorns, and put it on his head – in mockery of a regal *crown.*

and they put on him a purple robe – in mockery of the *imperial purple*; first "stripping him" (Matt. 27: 28) of His own outer garment.

3. And said, Hail, King of the Jews! – doing Him derisive homage, in the form used on approaching the emperors. "And they spit upon Him, and took the reed and smote Him on the head" (Matt. 27: 30). The best comment on these affecting details is to *cover the face.*

4–5. Pilate ... went forth again, and saith ... Behold, I bring him forth to you – am bringing, that is, going to bring him forth to you.

6–7. When the chief priests ... saw him, they cried out – their fiendish rage kindling afresh at the sight of Him.

Pilate saith unto them, Take ye him, and crucify him; for I find no fault in him – as if this would relieve *him* of the responsibility of the deed, who, by surrendering Him, incurred it all!

7. Their criminal charges having come to nothing, they give up that point, and as Pilate was throwing the whole responsibility upon them, they retreat into their own Jewish law, by which, as claiming equality with God (see John 5: 18 and John 8: 59), He ought to die; insinuating that it was Pilate's duty, even as civil governor, to protect their law from such insult.

8–11. When Pilate ... heard this saying, he was the more afraid – the name "SON OF GOD," the lofty sense evidently attached to it by His Jewish accusers, the dialogue he had already held with Him, and the dream of his wife (Matt. 27: 19), all working together in the breast of the wretched man.

9. and went again into the judgment hall, and saith to Jesus, Whence art thou? – beyond all doubt a question relating not to His *mission* but to His personal *origin.*

and also his coat: now the coat was without seam, woven from the top throughout.

24 They said therefore among themselves, Let us not rend it, but cast lots for it, whose it shall be: that the scripture might be fulfilled, which saith, They parted my raiment among them, and for my vesture they did cast lots. These things therefore the soldiers did.

25 Now there stood by the cross of Jesus his mother, and his mother's sister, Mary the wife of Cleophas, and Mary Magdalene.

26 When Jesus therefore saw his mother, and the disciple standing by, whom he loved, he saith unto his mother, Woman, behold thy son!

27 Then saith he to the disciple, Behold thy mother! And from that hour that disciple took her unto his own home.

28 After this, Jesus knowing that all things were now accomplished, that the scripture might be fulfilled, saith, I thirst.

29 Now there was set a vessel full of vinegar: and they filled a spunge with vinegar, and put it upon hyssop, and put it to his mouth.

30 When Jesus therefore had received the vinegar, he said, It is finished: and he bowed his head, and gave up the ghost.

31 The Jews therefore, because it was the preparation, that the bodies should not remain upon the cross on the sabbath day, (for that sabbath day was an high day,) besought Pilate that their legs might be broken, and that they might be taken away.

32 Then came the soldiers, and brake the legs of the first, and of the other which was crucified with him.

33 But when they came to Jesus, and saw that he was dead already, they brake not his legs:

34 But one of the soldiers with a spear pierced his side, and forthwith came there out blood and water.

35 And he that saw it bare record, and his record is true: and he knoweth that he saith true, that ye might believe.

36 For these things were done, that the scripture should be fulfilled, A bone of him shall not be broken.

37 And again another scripture saith, They shall look on him whom they pierced.

We ought, therefore, to devote ourselves to the interests of men, so as not in any degree to interfere with the worship and obedience which we owe to God. When we have obeyed God, it will then be the proper time to think about parents, and wife, and children; as Christ attends to *his mother,* but it is after that he is on the cross, to which he has been called by his Father's decree.

27. The disciple took her to his own home

It is a token of the reverence due by a **disciple** to his master, that John so readily obeys the command of Christ. Hence also it is evident, that the Apostles had their families; for John could not have exercised hospitality towards the mother of Christ, or have **taken her to his own home**, if he had not had a house and a regular way of living. Those men, therefore, are fools, who think that the Apostles relinquished their property, and came to Christ naked and empty; but they are worse than fools, who make perfection to consist in beggary.

30. It is finished

He repeats the same word which he had lately employed, Now this word, which Christ employs, well deserves our attention; for it shows that the whole accomplishment of our salvation, and all the parts of it, are contained in his death. We have already stated that his resurrection is not separated from his death, but Christ only intends to keep our faith fixed on himself alone, and not to allow it to turn aside in any direction whatever. The meaning, therefore, is, that every thing which contributes to the salvation of men is to be found in Christ, and ought not to be sought anywhere else; or – which amounts to the same thing – that the perfection of salvation is contained in him.

There is also an implied contrast; for Christ contrasts his death with the ancient sacrifices and with all the figures; as if he had said," Of all that was practiced under the *Law,* there was nothing that had any power in itself to make atonement for sins, to appease the wrath of God, and to obtain justification; but now the true salvation is exhibited and manifested to the world." On this doctrine depends the abolition of all the ceremonies of the Law; for it would be absurd to follow shadows, since we have the body in Christ.

JOHN 20

1. Now, on the first day of the week

As the resurrection of Christ is the most important article of our faith, and without it the hope of eternal life is extinguished, for this reason the Evangelists are the more careful to prove it, as John here collects many proofs, in order to assure us that Christ is risen from the dead. It may be

10. Then saith Pilate unto him, Speakest thou not to me? – The "me" is the emphatic word in the question. He falls back upon the *pride of office*, which doubtless tended to blunt the workings of his conscience.

11. have no power at all against me – neither to crucify nor to release, nor to do anything whatever against Me [BENGEL].

hath the greater sin – as having better opportunities and more knowledge of such matters.

12-16. And from thenceforth – particularly this speech, which seems to have filled him with awe, and redoubled his anxiety.

Pilate sought to release him – that is, to gain their *consent* to it, for he could have done it at once on his authority.

in a place called the Pavement – a tesselated pavement, much used by the Romans.

in the Hebrew, Gabbatha – from its being *raised*.

14. It was the preparation – that is, the day before the Jewish sabbath.

he saith to the Jews, Behold your King! – Having now made up his mind to yield to them, he takes a sort of quiet revenge on them by this irony, which he knew would sting them. This only reawakens their cry to despatch Him.

15. crucify your King? ... We have no king but Cæsar – "Some of those who thus cried died miserably in rebellion against Cæsar forty years afterwards. But it suited their present purpose" [ALFORD].

16. Then delivered he him therefore unto them to be crucified, &c – (See Mark 15: 15).

John 19: 17–30

CRUCIFIXION AND DEATH OF THE LORD JESUS.

18. they crucified him, and two others with him – "malefactors" (Luke 23: 33), "thieves" (rather "robbers," Matt. 27: 38; Mark 15: 27).

19-22. Pilate wrote a title, and put it on the cross ... Jesus of Nazareth, the King of the Jews ... and it was written in Hebrew – or *Syro-Chaldaic*, the language of the country.

and Greek – the current language.

and Latin – the official language.

23-24. Then the soldiers, when they had crucified Jesus, took his garments, and made four parts; to every soldier – the four who nailed Him to the cross, and whose perquisite they were.

a part, and also his coat – the Roman *tunic*, or close-fitting vest.

26-27. When Jesus ... saw his mother, and the disciple whom he loved, standing by, he saith to his mother, Woman, Behold Thy Son! Then saith he to the disciple, Behold Thy Mother! – What forgetfulness of self, what filial love, and to the "mother" and "son" what parting words!

from that hour ... took her to his own home – or, home with him; for his father Zebedee and his mother Salome were both alive, and the latter here present (Mark 15: 40).

that the scripture – (Ps. 69: 21.)

29. filled a sponge with vinegar, and put it upon – a stalk of **hyssop**, and put it to his mouth.

30. It is finished! and he bowed his head and gave up the ghost – What is finished? The Law is fulfilled as never before, nor since, in His "obedience unto death, even the death of the cross"; Messianic prophecy is accomplished; Redemption is completed; "He hath finished the transgression, and made reconciliation for iniquity, and brought in everlasting righteousness, and sealed up the vision and prophecy, and anointed a holy of holies"; He has inaugurated the kingdom of God and given birth to a new world.

John 19: 31–42

BURIAL OF CHRIST.

31-37. the preparation – sabbath eve.

that the bodies should not remain – over night, against the Mosaic law (Deut. 21: 22–23).

on the sabbath day, for that sabbath day was an high day – or "great" day – the first day of unleavened bread, and, as concurring with an ordinary sabbath, the most solemn season of the ecclesiastical year. Hence their peculiar jealousy lest the law should be infringed.

besought Pilate that their legs might be broken – to hasten their death, which was done in such cases with clubs.

38 And after this Joseph of Arimathaea, being a disciple of Jesus, but secretly for fear of the Jews, besought Pilate that he might take away the body of Jesus: and Pilate gave him leave. He came therefore, and took the body of Jesus.

39 And there came also Nicodemus, which at the first came to Jesus by night, and brought a mixture of myrrh and aloes, about an hundred pound weight.

40 Then took they the body of Jesus, and wound it in linen clothes with the spices, as the manner of the Jews is to bury.

41 Now in the place where he was crucified there was a garden; and in the garden a new sepulcher, wherein was never man yet laid.

42 There laid they Jesus therefore because of the Jews' preparation day; for the sepulcher was nigh at hand.

JOHN 20

1 The first day of the week cometh Mary Magdalene early, when it was yet dark, unto the sepulcher, and seeth the stone taken away from the sepulcher.

2 Then she runneth, and cometh to Simon Peter, and to the other disciple, whom Jesus loved, and saith unto them, They have taken away the Lord out of the sepulcher, and we know not where they have laid him.

3 Peter therefore went forth, and that other disciple, and came to the sepulcher.

4 So they ran both together: and the other disciple did outrun Peter, and came first to the sepulcher.

5 And he stooping down, and looking in, saw the linen clothes lying; yet went he not in.

6 Then cometh Simon Peter following him, and went into the sepulcher, and seeth the linen clothes lie,

7 And the napkin, that was about his head, not lying with the linen clothes, but wrapped together in a place by itself.

8 Then went in also that other disciple, which came first to the sepulcher, and he saw, and believed.

9 For as yet they knew not the scripture, that he must rise again from the dead.

thought strange, however, that he does not produce more competent witnesses; for he begins with a woman; but thus the saying is fulfilled, that "God chooseth what is weak, and foolish, and contemptible in the world, that he may bring to nought the wisdom, and excellence, and glory, of the flesh" (1 Corinthians 1: 27).

There certainly was nothing more of earthly grandeur in the disciples than in the women who followed Christ; but as Christ was pleased to reckon them the principal witnesses of his resurrection, on this single ground their testimony is entitled to the greatest deference, and is not liable to any objection. As to the priests, and scribes, and the whole people, and even Pilate, nothing but gross and wilful blindness prevented them from firmly believing that Christ was risen. All of them, therefore, deserved that *seeing they should not see;* yet Christ revealed himself to the little flock.

8. And he saw and believed

It is a poor exposition which some give of these words, that John **believed** what he had heard Mary say, namely, that Christ's body had been carried away; for there is no passage in which the word **believe** bears this meaning, especially when it is used simply and without any addition. Nor is this inconsistent with the fact, that **Peter and John** return home, while they are still in doubt and perplexity; for in some passages John had employed this phraseology, when lie intended to describe the increase of faith. Besides, *Luke 24: 12* relates that **Peter wondered** at seeing the sepulcher in such good order; meaning by this, that Peter thought of something greater and loftier than what Mary had told him.

9. For as yet they knew not the scripture, that he must rise again from the dead

They had often heard from the mouth of Christ what they now saw with their eyes, but this flowed from their hearts. Being now warned by the sight of a strange spectacle, they begin to think of Christ as having something Divine, though they are still far from having a clear and accurate knowledge of him. John, therefore, accuses himself, when he acknowledges that the first time that he **believed** was, when he beheld the proofs of Christ's resurrection.

Besides, he represents more strongly his own guilt and that of his brethren, by adding, that they not only had forgotten the words of Christ, but that they did not believe *the Scriptures;* for to this ignorance lie ascribes the deficiency of their faith. Hence, too, we may draw a useful instruction, that we ought, to ascribe it to our carelessness, when we are ignorant of what we ought to know about Christ, because we have not profited as we ought to have done by *the Scriptures,* which clearly reveal the excellence of Christ.

33. But when they came to Jesus, and saw that he was dead already – there being in *His* case elements of suffering, unknown to the malefactors, which might naturally hasten His death, lingering though it always was in such cases, not to speak of His *previous* sufferings.

they brake not his legs – a fact of vast importance, as showing that the *reality* of His death was visible to those whose business it was to see to it. The *other* divine purpose served by it will appear presently.

34. But one of the soldiers – to make assurance of the fact doubly sure.

with a spear pierced his side – making a wound deep and wide, as indeed is plain from John 20: 27,29. Had life still remained, it must have fled now.

and forthwith came thereout blood and water – "It is now well known that the effect of long-continued and intense agony is frequently to produce a secretion of a colorless lymph within the pericardium (the membrane enveloping the heart), amounting in many cases to a very considerable quantity" [WEBSTER and WILKINSON].

35. And he that saw it bare record – hath borne witness.

36. that the scripture should be fulfilled, A bone of him shall not be broken – The reference is to the paschal lamb, as to which this ordinance was stringent (Ex. 12: 46; Num. 9: 12. Compare 1 Cor. 5: 7). But though we are to see here the fulfilment of a very definite typical ordinance, we see in it *a remarkable divine interposition to protect the sacred body of Christ from the last indignity after He had finished the work given Him to do.*

37. And again another scripture saith, They shall look on him whom they pierced – The quotation is from Zech. 12: 10; not taken as usual from the *Septuagint* (the current *Greek* version), which here is all wrong, but direct from the *Hebrew*. And there is a remarkable nicety in the choice of the words employed both by the prophet and the Evangelist for "piercing." The word in Zechariah means to *thrust through* with spear, javelin, sword, or any such weapon.

38–40. Joseph of Arimathea – "a rich man" (Matt. 27: 57), thus fulfilling Is. 53: 9; "an honor-

able counsellor," a member of the Sanhedrim, and of good condition, "which also waited for the kingdom of God" (Mark 15: 43), a devout expectant of Messiah's kingdom; "a good man and a just, the same had not consented to the counsel and deed of them" (Luke 23: 50–51 – he had gone the length, perhaps, of dissenting and protesting in open council against the condemnation of our Lord); "who also himself was Jesus' disciple," (Matt. 27: 57).

39. also Nicodemus, which at the first came to Jesus by night – "This remark corresponds to the secrecy of Joseph's discipleship, just noticed, and calls attention to the similarity of their previous character and conduct, and the remarkable change which had now taken place" [WEBSTER and WILKINSON].

brought ... myrrh and aloes, about an hundred pounds weight – an immense quantity, betokening the greatness of their love, but part of it probably intended as a layer for the spot on which the body was to lie. (See 2 Chr. 16: 14) [MEYER].

40. Then took they the body of Jesus, and wound it in linen clothes with the spices, as the manner of the Jews is to bury – the mixed and pulverized myrrh and aloes shaken into the folds, and the entire body, thus swathed, wrapt in an outer covering of "clean linen cloth" (Matt. 27: 59).

41–42. Now in the place where he was crucified there was a garden, and in the garden a new sepulchre – The choice of this tomb was, on *their* part, dictated by the double circumstance that it was so near at hand, and by its belonging to a friend of the Lord; and as there was need of haste, even they would be struck with the providence which thus supplied it.

JOHN 20

John 20: 1–18

MARY'S VISIT TO THE SEPULCHRE, AND RETURN TO IT WITH PETER AND JOHN – HER RISEN LORD APPEARS TO HER.

3–10. Peter therefore went forth, and that other disciple, and came first to the sepulcher – These particulars have a singular air of artless truth about them. Mary, in her grief, runs to the two apostles who were soon

10 Then the disciples went away again unto their own home.

11 But Mary stood without at the sepulcher weeping: and as she wept, she stooped down, and looked into the sepulcher,

12 And seeth two angels in white sitting, the one at the head, and the other at the feet, where the body of Jesus had lain.

13 And they say unto her, Woman, why weepest thou? She saith unto them, Because they have taken away my Lord, and I know not where they have laid him.

14 And when she had thus said, she turned herself back, and saw Jesus standing, and knew not that it was Jesus.

15 Jesus saith unto her, Woman, why weepest thou? whom seekest thou? She, supposing him to be the gardener, saith unto him, Sir, if thou have borne him hence, tell me where thou hast laid him, and I will take him away.

16 Jesus saith unto her, Mary. She turned herself, and saith unto him, Rabboni; which is to say, Master.

17 Jesus saith unto her, Touch me not; for I am not yet ascended to my Father: but go to my brethren, and say unto them, I ascend unto my Father, and your Father; and to my God, and your God.

18 Mary Magdalene came and told the disciples that she had seen the Lord, and that he had spoken these things unto her.

19 Then the same day at evening, being the first day of the week, when the doors were shut where the disciples were assembled for fear of the Jews, came Jesus and stood in the midst, and saith unto them, Peace be unto you.

20 And when he had so said, he shewed unto them his hands and his side. Then were the disciples glad, when they saw the Lord.

21 Then said Jesus to them again, Peace be unto you: as my Father hath sent me, even so send I you.

22 And when he had said this, he breathed on them, and saith unto them, Receive ye the Holy Ghost:

23 Whose soever sins ye remit, they are remitted unto them; and whose soever sins ye retain, they are retained.

24 But Thomas, one of the twelve, called Didymus, was not with them when

16. Jesus saith to her, Mary!
That Christ allowed Mary, a short time, to fall into a mistake, was useful for confirming her faith; but now, by a single word, he corrects her mistake. He had formerly addressed her, but his discourse seemed to be that of an unknown person; he now assumes the character of the Master, and addresses his disciple by name, as we have formerly seen that "the good shepherd calleth to him by name every sheep of his flock" (John 10: 3).

28. My Lord and my God!
Thomas awakes at length, though late, and as persons who have been mentally deranged commonly do when they come to themselves, exclaims, in astonishment, *My Lord and my God!* For the abruptness of the language has great vehemence; nor can it be doubted that shame compelled him to break out into this expression, in order to condemn his own stupidity. Besides, so sudden an exclamation shows that faith was not wholly extinguished in him, though it had been choked; for in the side or hands of Christ he does not handle Christ's Divinity, but from those signs he infers much more than they exhibited. Whence comes this, but because, after forgetfulness and deep sleep, he suddenly comes to himself? This shows, therefore, the truth of what I said a little ago, that the faith which appeared to be destroyed was, as it were, concealed and buried in his heart.

The same thing happens sometimes with many persons; for they grow wanton for a time, as if they had cast off all fear of God, so that there appears to be no longer any faith in them; but as soon as God has chastised them with a rod, the rebellion of their flesh is subdued, and they return to their right senses. It is certain that disease would not, of itself, be sufficient to teach piety; and hence we infer, that, when the obstructions have been removed, the good seed, which had been concealed and crushed, springs up. We have a striking instance of this in David; for, so long as he is permitted to gratify his lust, we see how he indulges without restraint. Every person would have thought that, at that time, faith had been altogether banished from his mind; and yet, by a short exhortation of the Prophet, he is so suddenly recalled to life, that it may easily be inferred, that some spark, though it had been choked, still remained in his mind, and speedily burst into a flame. So far as relates to the men themselves, they are as guilty as if' they had renounced faith and all the grace of the Holy Spirit; but the infinite goodness of God prevents the elect from falling so low as to be entirely alienated from God. We ought, therefore, to be most zealously on our guard not to fall from faith; and yet we ought to believe that God restrains his elect by secret bridle, that they may not fall to their destruction, and that He always

to be so closely associated in proclaiming the Saviour's resurrection, and they, followed by Mary, hasten to see with their own eyes. The younger disciple outruns the older; love haply supplying swifter wings. He stoops, he gazes in, but enters not the open sepulchre, held back probably by a reverential fear. The bolder Peter, coming up, goes in at once, and is rewarded with bright evidence of what had happened.

6–7. seeth the linen clothes lie – lying.

And the napkin, that was about his head, not lying with the linen clothes – not loosely, as if hastily thrown down, and indicative of a hurried and disorderly removal.

but wrapped – folded.

together in a place by itself – showing with what grand tranquillity "the Living One" had walked forth from "the dead" (Luke 24: 5). "Doubtless the two attendant angels (John 20: 12) did this service for the Rising One, the one disposing of the linen clothes, the other of the napkin" [BENGEL].

8. Then went in ... that other disciple which came first to the sepulcher – The repetition of this, in connection with his not having gone in till after Peter, seems to show that at the moment of penning these words the advantage which each of these loving disciples had of the other was present to his mind.

and he saw and believed – Probably he means, though he does not say, that he believed in his Lord's resurrection more immediately and certainly than Peter.

9. For as yet they knew – that is, understood.

not the scripture that he must rise again from the dead – In other words, they believed in His resurrection at first, not because they were prepared by Scripture to expect it; but *facts* carried resistless conviction of it in the first instance to their minds, and furnished a key to the Scripture predictions of it.

11–15. But Mary stood without at the sepulchre weeping, &c – Brief was the stay of those two men. But Mary, arriving perhaps by another direction after they left, lingers at the spot, weeping for her missing Lord. As she gazes through her tears on the open tomb, she also ventures to stoop down and look into it, when lo! "two angels in white" appear to her

in a "sitting" posture, "as having finished some business, and awaiting some one to impart tidings to" [BENGEL].

12. one at the head, and the other at the feet where the body of Jesus had lain – not merely proclaiming silently the *entire* charge they had had of the body, of Christ [quoted in LUTHARDT], but rather, possibly, calling mute attention to the narrow space within which the Lord of glory had contracted Himself; as if they would say, Come, see within what limits, marked off by the interval here between us two, *the Lord* lay! But she is in tears, and these suit not the scene of so glorious an Exit. They are going to point out to her the incongruity.

13. Woman, why weepest thou? – You would think the vision too much for a lone woman. But absorbed in the one Object of her affection and pursuit, she speaks out her grief without fear.

15. Sir, if thou have borne him hence – borne *whom*? She says not. She can think only of *One*, and thinks others must understand her. It reminds one of the question of the Spouse, "Saw ye him whom my soul loveth?" (Song 3: 3).

tell me where thou hast laid him, and I will take him away – Wilt thou, dear fragile woman? But it is the language of sublime affection, that thinks itself fit for anything if once in possession of its Object. It is enough. Like Joseph, He can no longer restrain Himself (Gen. 45: 1).

16–17. Jesus saith unto her, Mary – It is not now the distant, though respectful, "Woman." It is the oft-repeated name, uttered, no doubt, with all the wonted manner, and bringing a rush of unutterable and overpowering associations with it.

She turned herself, and saith to him, Rabboni! – But that single word of transported recognition was not enough for woman's full heart. Not knowing the change which had passed upon Him, she hastens to express by her action what words failed to clothe; but she is checked.

17. Jesus saith unto her, Touch me not, for I am not yet ascended to my Father – Old familiarities must now give place to new and more awful yet sweeter approaches; but for

Jesus came.

25 The other disciples therefore said unto him, We have seen the Lord. But he said unto them, Except I shall see in his hands the print of the nails, and put my finger into the print of the nails, and thrust my hand into his side, I will not believe.

26 And after eight days again his disciples were within, and Thomas with them: then came Jesus, the doors being shut, and stood in the midst, and said, Peace be unto you.

27 Then saith he to Thomas, reach hither thy finger, and behold my hands; and reach hither thy hand, and thrust it into my side: and be not faithless, but believing.

28 And Thomas answered and said unto him, My Lord and my God.

29 Jesus saith unto him, Thomas, because thou hast seen me, thou hast believed: blessed are they that have not seen, and yet have believed.

30 And many other signs truly did Jesus in the presence of his disciples, which are not written in this book:

31 But these are written, that ye might believe that Jesus is the Christ, the Son of God; and that believing ye might have life through his name.

JOHN 21

1 After these things Jesus shewed himself again to the disciples at the sea of Tiberias; and on this wise shewed he himself.

2 There were together Simon Peter, and Thomas called Didymus, and Nathanael of Cana in Galilee, and the sons of Zebedee, and two other of his disciples.

3 Simon Peter saith unto them, I go a fishing. They say unto him, We also go with thee. They went forth, and entered into a ship immediately; and that night they caught nothing.

4 But when the morning was now come, Jesus stood on the shore: but the disciples knew not that it was Jesus.

5 Then Jesus saith unto them, Children, have ye any meat? They answered him, No.

6 And he said unto them, Cast the net on the right side of the ship, and ye shall find. They cast therefore, and now they

cherishes miraculously in their hearts some sparks of faith, which he afterwards, at the proper time, kindles anew by the breath of his Spirit.

JOHN 21

6. Cast the net on the right side of the ship

Christ does not command with authority and power as **Master** and **Lord**, but gives advice like one of the people; and the disciples, being at a loss what to do, readily obey him, though they did not know who he was. If, before the first **casting of the net**, any thing of this sort had been said to them, they would not have so quickly obeyed. I mention this, that no one may wonder that they were so submissive, for they had already been worn out by long and useless toil. Yet it was no small proof of patience and perseverance, that, though they had labored unsuccessfully during the whole night, they continue their toil after the return of daylight. And, indeed, if we wish to allow an opportunity for the blessing of God to descend on us, we ought constantly to expect it; for nothing can be more unreasonable than to withdraw the hand immediately from labor, if it do not give promise of success.

16. Feed my sheep

Christ does not give to Peter and others the office **of feeding** all sorts of persons, but only **his sheep** or **his lambs**. He elsewhere describes who they are whom he reckons to belong to his flock. "My sheep, says he, hear my voice, and follow me; they hear not the voice of a stranger" (John 10: 5, 27).

True, faithful teachers ought to endeavor to gather all to Christ; and as they cannot distinguish between *sheep* and wild beasts, they ought to try by all methods if they can tame those who resemble wolves rather than *sheep*. But after having put forth their utmost efforts, their labor will be of no avail to any but the elect *sheep;* for docility and faith arise from this, that the heavenly Father delivers to his Son, that they may obey him, those whom he elected before the creation of the world. Again, we are taught by this passage, that none can be *fed* to salvation by the doctrine of the Gospel but those who are mild and teachable; for it is not without reason that Christ compares his disciples to *lambs* and *sheep*; but it must also be observed, that the Spirit of God tames those who by nature were bears or lions.

17. Peter was grieved

Peter undoubtedly did not perceive the object which Christ had in view, in putting the same question so frequently; and therefore he thinks that he is-in-directly accused, as if he had not answered with sincerity. But we have already

these the time has not come yet. This seems the spirit, at least, of these mysterious words, on which much difference of opinion has obtained, and not much that is satisfactory said.

I ascend unto my Father and your Father, and to my God and your God – words of incomparable glory! Jesus had called God habitually His *Father,* and on one occasion, in His darkest moment, His *God.*

18. Mary Magdalene came and told the disciples that she had seen the Lord, and that he had spoken these things unto her – *To a woman was this honor given to be the first that saw the risen R edeemer, and that woman was not His mother.*

John 20: 19–23

JESUS APPEARS TO THE ASSEMBLED DISCIPLES.

19–23. the same day at evening, the first day of the week, the doors being shut where the disciples were assembled for fear of the Jews, came Jesus – plainly not by the ordinary way of entrance.

and saith unto them Peace be unto you – not the mere *wish* that even His own exalted peace might be theirs (John 14: 27), but conveying it into their hearts, even as He "opened their understandings to understand the scriptures" (Luke 24: 45).

20. And when he had so said, he showed them his hands and his side – not only as *ocular* and *tangible* evidence of the *reality* of His resurrection, but as through "the *power* of that resurrection" dispensing all His peace to men.

21. Then said Jesus – prepared now to listen to Him in a new character.

22. he breathed on them – a symbolical conveyance to them of the Spirit.

and saith, Receive ye the Holy Ghost – an earnest and first-fruits of the more copious Pentecostal effusion.

23. Whose soever sins ye remit, they are remitted unto them, &c. – In any *literal* and *authoritative* sense *this power was never exercised by one of the apostles,* and plainly *was never understood by themselves as possessed by them or conveyed to them.*

John 20: 24–29

JESUS AGAIN APPEARS TO THE ASSEMBLED DISCIPLES.

24–25. was not with them when Jesus came – why, we know not, though we are loath to think (with STIER, ALFORD and LUTHARDT) it was *intentional,* from sullen despondency. The fact merely is here stated, as a loving apology for his slowness of belief.

25. We have seen the Lord – This way of speaking of Jesus (as John 20: 20 and John 21: 7), so suited to His resurrection-state, was soon to become the prevailing style.

Except I see in his hands the print of the nails, and put my linger into the print of the nails, and thrust my hand into his side, I will not believe – The very form of this speech betokens the strength of the unbelief. "It is not, *If I shall see I shall believe,* but, *Unless I shall see I will not believe*; nor does he expect to see, although the others tell him they had" [BENGEL].

26–29. And after eight days – that is, on the eighth, or first day of the preceding week. They probably met every day during the preceding week, but their Lord designedly reserved His second appearance among them till the recurrence of His resurrection day, that He might thus inaugurate the delightful sanctities of THE LORD'S DAY (Rev. 1: 10).

27. Then saith he to Thomas, Reach hither ... behold ... put it into my side, and be not faithless, but believing – "There is something rhythmical in these words, and they are purposely couched in the words of Thomas himself, to put him to shame" [LUTHARDT]. But wish what condescension and gentleness is this done!

28. Thomas answered and said unto him, My Lord and my God – That Thomas did *not* do what Jesus invited him to do, and what he had made the condition of his believing, seems plain from John 20: 29 ("Because thou hast *seen* Me, thou hast believed"). He is overpowered, and the glory of Christ now breaks upon him in a flood. His exclamation surpasses all that had been yet uttered, nor can it be surpassed by anything that ever will be uttered in earth or heaven.

were not able to draw it for the multitude of fishes.

7 Therefore that disciple whom Jesus loved saith unto Peter, It is the Lord. Now when Simon Peter heard that it was the Lord, he girt his fisher's coat unto him, (for he was naked,) and did cast himself into the sea.

8 And the other disciples came in a little ship; (for they were not far from land, but as it were two hundred cubits,) dragging the net with fishes.

9 As soon then as they were come to land, they saw a fire of coals there, and fish laid thereon, and bread.

10 Jesus saith unto them, Bring of the fish which ye have now caught.

11 Simon Peter went up, and drew the net to land full of great fishes, and hundred and fifty and three: and for all there were so many, yet was not the net broken.

12 Jesus saith unto them, Come and dine. And none of the disciples durst ask him, Who art thou? knowing that it was the Lord.

13 Jesus then cometh, and taketh bread, and giveth them, and fish likewise.

14 This is now the third time that Jesus shewed himself to his disciples, after that he was risen from the dead.

15 So when they had dined, Jesus saith to Simon Peter, Simon, son of Jonas, lovest thou me more than these? He saith unto him, Yea, Lord; thou knowest I love thee. He saith unto him, Feed my lambs.

16 He saith to him again the second time, Simon, son of Jonas, lovest thou me? He saith unto him, Yea, Lord; thou knowest that I love thee. He saith unto him, Feed my sheep.

17 He saith unto him the third time, Simon, son of Jonas, lovest thou me? Peter was grieved because he said unto him the third time, Lovest thou me? And he said unto him, Lord, thou knowest all things; thou knowest that I love thee. Jesus saith unto him, Feed my sheep.

18 Verily, verily, I say unto thee, When thou wast young, thou girdedst thyself, and walkedst whither thou wouldest: but when thou shalt be old, thou shalt stretch forth thy hands, and another shall gird thee, and carry thee whither thou would-

showed that the repetition was not superfluous. Besides, Peter was not yet sufficiently aware how deeply the love of Christ must be engraven on the hearts of those who have to struggle against innumerable difficulties. He afterwards learned by long experience, that such a trial had not been made in vain. Those who are to undertake the charge of governing the Church are also taught, in his person, not to examine themselves slightly, but to make a thorough scrutiny what zeal they possess, that they may not shrink or faint in the middle of their course. We are likewise taught, that we ought patiently and mildly to submit, if at any time the Lord subject us to a severe trial; because he has good reasons for doing so, though they are generally unknown to us.

25. There are also many other things that Jesus did

Lest any one should view his narrative with suspicion, as if it had been written through partiality, because **Jesus loved him**, he anticipates this objection, by saying, that he has passed over more than he has written. He does not speak of Christ's actions of every kind, but of those which relate to his public office; nor ought we to think that the hyperbole is absurd, when we bear with many figures of speech of the same kind in heathen authors. Not only ought we to take into account the number of Christ's works, but we ought also to consider their importance and magnitude. The majesty of Christ, which by its infinity swallowed up, if I may so speak, not only the senses of men, but heaven and earth, gave a miraculous display of its own splendor in those works. If the Evangelist, casting his eyes on that brightness, exclaims in astonishment, that even the whole world could not contain a full narrative, ought we to wonder at it? Nor is he at all to be blamed, if he employ a frequent and ordinary figure of speech for commending the excellence of the works of Christ. For we know how God accommodates himself to the ordinary' way of speaking, on account of our ignorance, and sometimes even, if I may be allowed the expression, stammers.

Yet we ought to remember what we formerly stated, that the summary which the Evangelists have committed to writing, is sufficient both for regulating faith and for obtaining salvation. That man who has duly profited under such teachers will be truly wise. And, indeed, since they were appointed by God to be witnesses to us, as they have faithfully discharged their duty; so it is our duty, on the other hand, to depend wholly on their testimony, and to desire nothing more than what they have handed down to us; and especially, because their pens were guided by the sure providence of God, that they might not oppress us by an unlimited mass of narratives, and yet, in making a

29. because thou hast seen me, thou hast believed – words of measured commendation, but of indirect and doubtless painfully – felt rebuke: that is, 'Thou hast indeed believed; it is well: it is only on the evidence of thy senses, and after peremptorily refusing all evidence short of that.'

blessed they that have not seen, and yet have believed – "Wonderful indeed and rich in blessing for us who have not seen Him, is this closing word of the Gospel" [ALFORD].

John 20: 30–31

FIRST CLOSE OF THIS GOSPEL.

The connection of these verses with the last words of John 20: 29 is beautiful: that is, And indeed, as the Lord pronounced them blessed who not having seen Him have yet believed, so for that one end have the whole contents of this Gospel been recorded, that all who read it may believe on Him, and believing, have life in that blessed name.

31. But these are written – as sufficient specimens.

the Christ, the Son of God – the one His *official*, the other His *personal*, title.

JOHN 21

John 21: 1–23

SUPPLEMENTARY PARTICULARS.

1–2. Jesus showed himself again – manifested himself again.

and on this wise he manifested himself – This way of speaking shows that after His resurrection He appeared to them but *occasionally, unexpectedly*, and in a way quite *unearthly*, though yet *really* and *corporeally*.

5. Children – This term would not necessarily identify Him, being not unusual from any superior; but when they did recognize Him, they would feel it sweetly like Himself.

6. he said unto them, Cast the net on the right side of the ship – no doubt, by this very specific direction, intending to reveal to them His knowledge of the deep and power over it.

7–11. he was naked – his vest only on, worn next the body.

cast himself into the sea – the shallow

part, not more than a hundred yards from the water's edge (John 21: 8), not meaning therefore to swim, but to get sooner to Jesus than in the full boat which they could hardly draw to shore.

8. the other disciples came in a little ship – by ship.

9. a fire of coals, and fish laid thereon, and bread – By comparing this with 1 Kgs. 19: 6, and similar passages, the unseen agency by which Jesus made this provision will appear evident.

10. Jesus saith unto them, Bring of the fish ye have now caught – Observe the double supply thus provided – His and theirs. The meaning of this will perhaps appear presently.

11. Peter went up – into the boat; went aboard.

12–14. none … durst ask him, Who art thou, knowing it was the Lord – implying that they *would* have liked Him just to say, "It is I"; but having such convincing *evidence* they were afraid of being "upbraided for their unbelief and hardness of heart" if they ventured to put the question.

14. This is the third time that Jesus showed himself – was manifested.

to his disciples – His *assembled* disciples; for if we reckon His appearances to individual disciples, they were more.

15–17. when they had dined, Jesus saith – Silence appears to have reigned during the meal; unbroken on *His* part, that by their mute observation of Him they might have their assurance of His identity the more confirmed; and on *theirs,* from reverential shrinking to speak till He did.

Simon, son of Jonas, lovest thou me more than these? – referring lovingly to those sad words of Peter, shortly before denying his Lord, "Though *all men* shall be offended because of *Thee, yet will I never* be offended" (Matt. 26: 33), and intending by this allusion to bring the whole scene vividly before his mind and put him to shame.

Yea, Lord; thou knowest that I love thee – He adds not, "more than these," but prefixes a touching appeal to the Saviour's own omniscience for the truth of his protestation, which

est not.

19 This spake he, signifying by what death he should glorify God. And when he had spoken this, he saith unto him, Follow me.

20 Then Peter, turning about, seeth the disciple whom Jesus loved following; which also leaned on his breast at supper, and said, Lord, which is he that betrayeth thee?

21 Peter seeing him saith to Jesus, Lord, and what shall this man do?

22 Jesus saith unto him, If I will that he tarry till I come, what is that to thee? follow thou me.

23 Then went this saying abroad among the brethren, that that disciple should not die: yet Jesus said not unto him, He shall not die; but, If I will that he tarry till I come, what is that to thee?

24 This is the disciple which testifieth of these things, and wrote these things: and we know that his testimony is true.

25 And there are also many other things which Jesus did, the which, if they should be written every one, I suppose that even the world itself could not contain the books that should be written. Amen.

selection, might make known to us all that God knew to be necessary for us, who alone is wise, and the only fountain of wisdom; to whom be praise and glory for ever. Amen.

DAVID BROWN

makes it a totally different kind of speech from his former.

He saith unto him, Feed my lambs – It is surely wrong to view this term as a mere diminutive of affection, and as meaning the same thing as "the sheep" [WEBSTER and WILKINSON]. It is much more according to usage to understand by the "lambs," *young and tender* disciples, whether in age or Christian standing (Is. 40: 11; 1 John 2: 12–13), and by the "sheep" the more *mature*. Shall we say (with many) that Peter was here reinstated in office? Not exactly, since he was not actually excluded from it. But after such conduct as his, the deep wound which the honor of Christ had received, the stain brought on his office, the damage done to his high standing among his brethren, and even his own comfort, in prospect of the great work before him, required some such renewal of his call and re-establishment of his position as this.

18–19. When thou wast young – embracing the whole period of life to the verge of old age.

when … old thou shalt stretch forth thine hands – to be bound for execution, though not necessarily meaning *on a cross*. There is no reason, however, to doubt the very early tradition that Peter's death was by crucifixion.

19. This spake he, signifying by what death he should glorify God – not, therefore, a mere prediction of the manner of his *death,* but of the *honor* to be conferred upon him by dying for his Master.

21. Peter … saith to Jesus, Lord, and what shall this man do? – What of this man? or, How shall it fare with him?

22–23. Jesus saith to him, If I will that he tarry fill I come, what is that to thee? follow thou me – From the fact that John alone of the Twelve survived the destruction of Jerusalem, and so witnessed the commencement of that series of events which belongs to "the last days," many good interpreters think that this is a virtual prediction of fact, and not a mere supposition.

23. Then went this saying abroad among the brethren, that that disciple should not die – into which they the more easily fell from the prevalent expectation that Christ's second coming was then near at hand.

yet Jesus said not unto him, He shall not die – The Evangelist is jealous for His Master's honor, which his death might be thought to compromise if such a misunderstanding should not be corrected.

John 21: 24–25

FINAL CLOSE OF THIS GOSPEL.

24. This is the disciple which testifieth of these things, and wrote these things – thus identifying the author of this book with all that it says of this disciple.

25. if … written every one, I suppose – an expression used to show that what follows is not to be pressed too far.

even the world itself would not hold the books, &c – not a *mere* hyperbolical expression, unlike the sublime simplicity of this writer, but intended to let his reader know that, even now that he had done, he felt his materials so far from being exhausted, that he was still running over, and could multiply "Gospels" to almost any extent within the strict limits of what "Jesus did." But in the *limitation* of these matchless histories, in point of number, there is as much of that divine wisdom which has presided over and pervades the living oracles, as in their *variety* and *fulness.*

Acts

Introduction by John Calvin

To the intent that all godly men may, with more diligence, read this history, and also be more desirous thereof, it shall not be without profit briefly to note what commodity they shall reap thereby.

This is the chiefest praise that a profane history hath, namely, that it is the mistress of life. If that narration of famous deeds, which only teacheth men what they ought to follow, or what they ought to eschew, in their common actions, deserve such a title, of how great praise are the divine histories worthy, which do not only frame the outward life of man that he may win praise by virtue, but also (which is more) which declare unto us that God, from the beginning, hath had a special regard always of his Church (and faithful congregation), that he hath been always a most just revenger of all wrongs done unto those that have betaken themselves unto his tuition, and have committed themselves unto his custody; that he hath showed himself favorable and merciful unto most miserable and wretched sinners; and, lastly, by teaching us faith, raised us high above the heavens. I say nothing of this, that they do everywhere set forth the providence of God, that they distinguish the true worship of God from the false, and never err in the difference of vice and virtue; although I omit now also those worthy praises which used most commonly to be attributed unto the sacred histories, intending only shortly to touch those which are proper to this book which we have taken in hand.

Those things which Luke setteth before us in this place to be learned are not only great, but also of rare profit; for, first, in that he showeth that the Spirit of God was sent unto the apostles, he doth not only prove that Christ was faithful (and true) in keeping his promise made unto his apostles; but also he certifieth us, that he is always mindful of his, and a perpetual governor of his Church, because the Holy Spirit did descend from heaven to this end; whereby we learn that the distance of place doth no whit hinder Christ from being present with those that be his at all times. Now, here is most lively painted out the beginning of Christ's kingdom, and as it were the renewing of the world; for although the Son of God had gathered together, by his preaching, a certain Church, before such time as he departed out of the world, yet, nevertheless, that was the best form of the Church which began then, when as the apostles, having new power given them from above, began to preach that that only Shepherd did both die and also rise again, that through his conduct all those which were dispersed, far and wide (upon the face of the whole earth), might be gathered unto one sheepfold. Here is, therefore, set down both the beginning and also the increasing of the Church of Christ after his ascension, whereby he was declared to be King both of heaven and earth.

Furthermore, therein appeareth, as well the marvelous power of Christ, as the great force and efficacy of the gospel itself; for in that Christ, by a sort of simple souls (and of no reputation amongst men), being indued also with no eloquence at all, hath subdued the whole world so easily, by the only voice of the gospel, whereas, notwithstanding Satan did resist him with so many lets, he hath showed a most manifest token of his divine power and might therein. And also, we see in the same the incredible force of the gospel, that it did not only come forth and show itself, although the whole world did say nay, but also with great glory and majesty, make all that which did seem stubborn to be obedient unto Christ. Therefore, these few and simple creatures did more prevail against the troublesome tumults of the world, with the base and simple sound of their mouth, than if God should openly have thrown down lightnings from heaven. And, on the other side, the Spirit of God teacheth us, that the kingdom of Christ beginneth never sooner to flourish, but by and by Satan opposeth himself most furiously against the same, and useth all his engines either utterly to overthrow or sore to shake the *same*. Neither are we only taught, that Satan doth resist Christ as an enemy, but also that the whole world doth furiously rage together against him, that he may not reign over them. Yea, furthermore, that is to be set down as a thing most certain, that wicked men, whilst they do so rage against the gospel, do both fight under Satan's banner, and are pricked forward by him into so blind fury. Hereupon do arise so many uproars, so many plaguy conspiracies, so many devilish endeavors of the reprobate to overthrow the gospel (and to hinder the free passage of the same), which Luke setteth down almost in every place.

Lastly, like as the apostles have indeed tried, that the doctrine of the gospel is a fire and a sword, so may we learn by their experience that it will always come to pass, not only by the obstinate malice of Satan, but also by the fatal stubbornness of men, that the gospel shall suffer many conflicts, and that thereby many tumults shall be raised. But, on the other side, he declareth that the apostles (with a stout stomach), with a lively courage and invincible violentness [force] of mind, did, notwithstanding, execute the office which they knew was enjoined them by God; and also, what innumerable troubles they suffered with great perseverance, what wearisomeness they passed over, how patiently they sustained most cruel persecution; and, lastly, how meekly they suffered reproach, sorrow, and calamity of all sorts. And we must learn patience by such examples, seeing the Son of God hath pronounced that the

cross and tribulation shall always accompany his gospel; we must not pamper and cherish ourselves with a vain hope, as though the state and condition of the Church should be quiet (prosperous) and flourishing here upon earth. Let us, therefore, address ourselves to suffer the like things. And that is added as no small comfort for us, that as God hath marvelously delivered his Church in times past, being afflicted and oppressed so many ways, so he will at this day be present with us also. For, surely, seeing that in this book is declared how that God, by his mighty hand and outstretched arm alone, doth continually defend his Church, being amidst continual deaths: God himself, by this means, setteth before our eyes his continual providence in procuring the safety thereof.

Furthermore, here are set down certain sermons of the apostles which intreat in such sort of the great mercies of God, of the grace of Christ, of the hope of blessed immortality, of the calling upon God, of repentance and the fear of God, and also of other principal points of Christian doctrine, that we need not seek the whole sum of godliness anywhere else. But that I may now omit the declaration of sound and pure doctrine – if that be a thing most needful to be known, namely, to understand how the Church of Christ first began; how the apostles began to preach the gospel; what success they had in the same; what cruel combats they suffered; how manfully they passed through so many lets and impediments; how courageously they triumphed over all the pride of the world under the reproach of the cross; how wonderfully God was present with them: then must we highly esteem of this book, which, unless it were extant, the knowledge of so great things should either be quite buried, or greatly obscured, or wrapped in divers doubts. For we see that Satan used all his engines, that he might so bring to pass, that never any of the acts of the apostles might come to light, but such only as were mixed with lies; to the end he might bring into suspicion what thing soever was spoken of them, and so by that means might pluck out of the minds of the godly all the remembrance of that age. For he always raised up, either doting fools or crafty flouters, that they might spread abroad a sort of filthy fables under the names of other men; the blockishness whereof did much discredit even the true histories.

So in those books of Peter and Paul, which are reigned to be of Linus his doing, are contained such a sort of stinking trifles, that they cause the wicked to laugh at them, and the godly to loathe them. So that reigned disputation of Peter with Simon Magus is so ridiculous, that it doth discredit the name of a Christian. The same opinion must we have of all that mingle-mangle, which is set before the Recognitions and Councils of Clement, and recited of Gratianus in his Fragments. They beguile the unskillful under color of ancient names; the wicked boast of those as of oracles, no less boldly than impudently, when as, indeed, they are filthy toys. Satan did use such liberty to lie, that we might have no certain thing left us after Christ's ascension. So that unless this work of Luke were extant, it might seem that Christ being taken up into heaven, left no fruit of his death or resurrection upon earth. For all should have vanished away with his body. We should not know that Christ was so received into his celestial glory, that, nevertheless, he beareth rule in all the world; we should not know that the gospel was published by the apostles, and so came from them unto us, though by the means of others; we should not know that they were inspired by the Holy Ghost, lest they should teach anything but that which was divine, to the end our faith might be grounded only upon the infallible verity of God. Last of all, we should not know that that prophecy of Esaias was fulfilled, wherein he foretold that the law should come out of Sion, and the Word of the Lord out of Jerusalem.

Seeing this book proceeding, no doubt, from the Spirit of God, taketh from us all doubting of these things, we must count the same as a great treasure, as I have said before not without cause, and now again confirm the same.

The commentaries on Acts are by John Calvin and Albert Barnes.

ACTS 1

1 The former treatise have I made, O Theophilus, of all that Jesus began both to do and teach,

2 Until the day in which he was taken up, after that he through the Holy Ghost had given commandments unto the apostles whom he had chosen:

3 To whom also he shewed himself alive after his passion by many infallible proofs, being seen of them forty days, and speaking of the things pertaining to the kingdom of God:

4 And, being assembled together with them, commanded them that they should not depart from Jerusalem, but wait for the promise of the Father, which, saith he, ye have heard of me.

5 For John truly baptized with water; but ye shall be baptized with the Holy Ghost not many days hence.

6 When they therefore were come together, they asked of him, saying, Lord, wilt thou at this time restore again the kingdom to Israel?

7 And he said unto them, It is not for you to know the times or the seasons, which the Father hath put in his own power.

8 But ye shall receive power, after that the Holy Ghost is come upon you: and ye shall be witnesses unto me both in Jerusalem, and in all Judaea, and in Samaria, and unto the uttermost part of the earth.

9 And when he had spoken these things, while they beheld, he was taken up; and a cloud received him out of their sight.

10 And while they looked stedfastly toward heaven as he went up, behold, two men stood by them in white apparel;

11 Which also said, Ye men of Galilee, why stand ye gazing up into heaven? this same Jesus, which is taken up from you into heaven, shall so come in like manner as ye have seen him go into heaven.

12 Then returned they unto Jerusalem from the mount called Olivet, which is from Jerusalem a sabbath day's journey.

13 And when they were come in, they went up into an upper room, where abode both Peter, and James, and John, and Andrew, Philip, and Thomas, Bartholomew, and Matthew, James the son of Alphaeus, and Simon Zelotes, and Judas the brother

ACTS 1

2. Even until that day

The ascension of Christ is the end of the history of the gospel. For he hath ascended, saith Paul, that he might fulfill all things (Ephesians 4: 10). Our faith gathereth other fruit thereby; but it shall be sufficient to note in this place, that our redemption was fully complete and finished then when Christ did ascend unto his Father; and, therefore, that Luke did fully perform his duty in this narration, as touching the doctrine and works of Christ. And he is said to be taken up, that we may know that he is truly departed out of this world, lest we should consent unto their dotings who think that in his ascension there was no alteration of place made.

Commandment by the Holy Ghost

Luke showeth in these words, that Christ did not so depart out of the world that he did no longer care for us; for in that he hath ordained a perpetual government in his Church, he thereby declareth that he had a care to provide for our salvation; yea, he hath promised that he will be present with his to the end (Matthew 28: 20), like as, indeed, he is always present by his ministers. Luke, therefore, doth show unto us, that Christ did no sooner depart hence, but straightway he provided for the government of his Church; whence we may gather that he is careful for our salvation.

15. It was right that Matthias should be chosen into the place of Judas, lest, through the treachery of one man, all that might seem to have been made of none effect which Christ had once appointed. He did not unadvisedly choose the twelve in the beginning, as principal preachers of his gospel. For when he said that they should be judges of twelve tribes of Israel, Luke 6: 13, John 6: 70; he showeth here that it was done of set purpose, that they might gather together the tribes of Israel unto one faith. But after that the Jews had refused the grace offered unto them, it was behoveful that the Israel of God should be gathered together out of all countries.

This, therefore, was, as it were, a holy number, which, if it should have been diminished through the wickedness of Judas, then should the preaching of the gospel both have had, and also have, less credit at this day, if the beginning thereof had been imperfect. Although, therefore, Judas would (as much as in him lay) have disappointed the purpose of Christ, yet nevertheless it stood firm and stable. He perished as he was worthy, yet did the order of the apostles remain whole and sound.

16. Which the Holy Ghost foretold

Such manner of speeches bring greater reverence to the Scriptures, whilst we are taught by them that David and all the rest of the prophets did speak only as they were di-

ACTS 1

1. The former treatise. The former book. The Gospel by Luke is here evidently intended.

As this book was written to the same individual as the former, it was evidently written with the same design – to furnish an authentic and full narrative of events concerning which there would be many imperfect and exaggerated accounts given. See Luke 1: 1–4. As these events pertained to the descent of the Spirit, to the spread of the gospel, to the organization of the church by inspired authority, to the kind of preaching by which the church was collected and organized; and as those events were a full proof of the truth and power of the Christian religion, and would be a model for ministers and the church in all future times, it was of great importance that a fair and full narrative of them should be preserved. Luke was the companion of Paul in his travels, and was an eye-witness of no small part of the transactions recorded in this book. See Acts 16: 10,17; 20: 1–6; 27; 28.

As an eye-witness, he was well qualified to make a record of the leading events of the primitive church. And as he was the companion of Paul, he had every opportunity of obtaining information about the great events of the gospel of Christ.

Of all. That is, of the principal, or most important parts of the life and doctrines of Christ. It cannot mean that he recorded all that Jesus did, as he has omitted many things that have been preserved by the other evangelists. The word all is frequently thus used to denote the most important or material facts.

To do. This refers to his miracles and his acts of benevolence, including all that he did for man's salvation. It probably includes, therefore, his sufferings, death, and resurrection, as a part of what he has done to save men.

To teach. His doctrines. He had given an account of what the Lord Jesus did, so he was now about to give a narrative of what his apostles did in the same cause, that thus the world might be in possession of an inspired record respecting the redemption and establishment of the Christian church. The history of these events is one of the greatest blessings that God has conferred on mankind; and one of

the highest privileges which men can enjoy is that which has been conferred so abundantly on this age in the possession and extension of the word of God.

2. Until the day. The fortieth day after his resurrection, Acts 1: 3; Luke 24: 51.

Through the Holy Ghost. To understand this, it is necessary to call to mind the promise that Jesus made before his death, that after his departure, the Holy Ghost would descend to be a guide to his apostles. See John 16: 7–11.

3. He shewed himself. The resurrection of Jesus was the great fact on which the truth of the gospel was to be established. Hence the sacred writers so often refer to it, and establish it by so many arguments. As that truth lay at the foundation of all that Luke was about to record in his history, it was of importance that he should state clearly the sum of the evidence of it in the beginning of his work.

4. But wait for the promise of the Father. For the fulfillment of the promise respecting the descent of the Holy Spirit, made by the Father.

8. But ye shall receive power, etc. Literally, as it is translated in the margin, "ye shall receive the power of the Holy Ghost coming upon you." This was said to them to console them.

In Jerusalem. In the capital of the nation.

12. Then returned they unto Jerusalem. In Luke 24: 52, we are told that they worshipped Jesus before they returned. And it is probable that the act of worship to which he refers, was that which is mentioned in this chapter – their gazing intently on their departing Lord.

13. Were come in. To Jerusalem.
Peter, etc. All the apostles were there which Jesus had at first chosen, except Judas, Luke 6: 13–16.

14. These all continued., The word continued denotes persevering and constant attention. The main business was devotion. Acts 6: 4, "We will give ourselves continually – to the ministry of the word." Rom. 12: 12, "Continuing instant in prayer: " Rom. 13: 6, "Attending continually upon this very thing." It is their main and constant employment, Col. 4: 2.

of James.

14 These all continued with one accord in prayer and supplication, with the women, and Mary the mother of Jesus, and with his brethren.

15 And in those days Peter stood up in the midst of the disciples, and said, (the number of names together were about an hundred and twenty,)

16 Men and brethren, this scripture must needs have been fulfilled, which the Holy Ghost by the mouth of David spake before concerning Judas, which was guide to them that took Jesus.

17 For he was numbered with us, and had obtained part of this ministry.

18 Now this man purchased a field with the reward of iniquity; and falling headlong, he burst asunder in the midst, and all his bowels gushed out.

19 And it was known unto all the dwellers at Jerusalem; insomuch as that field is called in their proper tongue, Aceldama, that is to say, The field of blood.

20 For it is written in the book of Psalms, Let his habitation be desolate, and let no man dwell therein: and his bishoprick let another take.

21 Wherefore of these men which have companied with us all the time that the Lord Jesus went in and out among us,

22 Beginning from the baptism of John, unto that same day that he was taken up from us, must one be ordained to be a witness with us of his resurrection.

23 And they appointed two, Joseph called Barsabas, who was surnamed Justus, and Matthias.

24 And they prayed, and said, Thou, Lord, which knowest the hearts of all men, shew whether of these two thou hast chosen;

25 That he may take part of this ministry and apostleship, from which Judas by transgression fell, that he might go to his own place.

26 And they gave forth their lots; and the lot fell upon Matthias; and he was numbered with the eleven apostles.

ACTS 2

1 And when the day of Pentecost was fully come, they were all with one accord in one place.

rected by the Holy Ghost; so that they themselves were not the authors of their prophecies, but the Spirit which used their tongues as an instrument. Wherefore, seeing that our dullness is so great, that we ascribe less authority unto the Scriptures than we ought, we must diligently note such manner of speeches, and acquaint ourselves with them, that we may oftentimes remember the authority of God to confirm our faith withal.

17. Adopted

It is word for word reckoned. And he saith that he was one of the number, that he might signify unto them that it was needful that the empty place should be filled, to the end that the number might continue whole. And to this propose serveth that which followeth, that he had obtained a part in the ministry. For thereupon it doth follow that the body should be, as it were, lame, if that part should be wanting. Surely it was a thing which might make them greatly amazed, that he whom Christ had extolled unto so high dignity should fall headlong into such destruction.

24. In praying, they said

Word for word it is, Having prayed, they said; but there is no obscurity in the sense, because his meaning was to speak as followeth, that they prayed; and yet he doth not reckon up all the words, being content briefly to show the sum. Therefore, although they were both of honest conversation, yea, although they did excel in holiness and other virtues, yet because the integrity of the heart, whereof God is the alone knower and judge, is the chief, the disciples pray that God would bring that to light which was hidden from men. The same ought to be required even at this day in choosing pastors; for howsoever we are not to appoint two for one, yet because we may oftentimes be deceived, and the discerning of spirits cometh of the Lord, we must always pray unto God, that he will show unto us what men he will have to be ministers, that he may direct and govern our purposes. Here we may also gather what great regard we must have of integrity and innocency in choosing pastors, without which both learning and eloquence, and what excellency soever can be invented, are as nothing.

ACTS 2

11. The wonderful works of God

Luke noteth two things which caused the hearers to wonder; first, because the apostles being before ignorant and private persons, born in a base corner, did, notwithstanding, intreat profoundly of divine matters, and of heavenly wisdom. The other is, because they have new tongues given them suddenly. Both things are worth the noting, because to huddle out [utter] words unadvisedly and foolishly, should

15. In those days. On one of the days intervening between the ascension of Jesus and the day of Pentecost.

Peter stood up. Peter standing up, or rising. This is a customary expression in the Scriptures when one begins to do a thing, Luke 15: 18.

The disciples. This was the name which was given to them as being learners in the school of Christ.

16. Men and brethren. This is a customary mode of address, implying affection and respect, Acts 13: 26.

The Holy Ghost, etc. This is a strong attestation to the inspiration of David, and accords with the uniform testimony of the New Testament, that the sacred writer spake as they were moved by the Holy Ghost, 2 Pet. 1: 21.

17. He was numbered with us. He was chosen as an apostle by the Lord Jesus, Luke 6: 13–16, This does not mean that he was a true Christian, but that he was reckoned among the apostles.

20. For it is written, etc. See Ps. 69: 26. This is the prediction, doubtless, to which Peter refers in Acts 1: 16.

21, 22. Wherefore of these men. Of those who had witnessed the life and works of Christ, and who were therefore qualified to discharge the duties of the office from which Judas fell. Probably Peter refers to the seventy disciples, Luke 10: 1–2.

Went in and out. A phrase signifying that he was their constant companion. It expresses, in general, all the actions of the life, Ps. 121: 8; Deut. 28: 19; 31: 2.

23. And they appointed two. They proposed, or, as we should say, nominated two. Literally, they placed two, or made them to stand forth, as persons do who are candidates for office. These two were probably more distinguished by prudence, wisdom, piety, and age, than the others; and were so nearly equal in qualifications, that they could not determine which was the best fitted for the office.

24. And they prayed. As they could not agree on the individual, they invoked the direction

of God in their choice – an example which should be followed in every selection of an individual to exercise the duties of the sacred office of the ministry.

Which knowest the hearts of all men. This is often declared to be the peculiar prerogative of God. Jer. 17: 10, "I, Jehovah, search the heart," etc.; Ps. 139: 1,23; 1 Chr. 28: 9.

25. Ministry and apostleship. This is an instance of the figure of speech hendiadys, when two words are used to express one thing. It means the apostolic ministry. See instances in Gal. 1: 14, "Let them be for signs, and for seasons," i.e., signs of seasons. Acts 23: 6, "Hope and resurrection of the dead," i.e., hope of the resurrection of the dead.

26. And they gave forth their lots. Casting lots was common among the Jews on important and difficult occasions, and it was natural that the apostles should resort to it in this. Thus David divided the priests by lot, 1 Chr. 24: 5. The land of Canaan was divided by lot, Num. 26: 55; Josh. 15: 1–17: 18. Jonathan, son of Saul, was detected as having violated his father's command, and as bringing calamity on the Israelites, by lot, 1 Sam. 14: 41–42. Achan was detected by lot, Josh. 7: 16–18. In these cases the use of the lot was regarded as a solemn appeal to God, for his direct interference in cases which they could not themselves decide. Prov. 16: 33, "The lot is cast into the lap; but the whole disposing thereof is of the Lord." The choice of an apostle was an event of the same kind, and was regarded as a solemn appeal to God for his direction and guidance in a case which the apostles could not determine. The manner in which this was done is not certainly known.

ACTS 2

1. And when the day of Pentecost. The word Pentecost is a Greek word, signifying the fiftieth part of a thing; or the fiftieth in order. Among the Jews it was applied to one of their three great feasts which began on the fiftieth day after the Passover. The paschal lamb was slain on the fourteenth of the month at even, (Lev. 23: 5); on the fifteenth of the month was

2 And suddenly there came a sound from heaven as of a rushing mighty wind, and it filled all the house where they were sitting.

3 And there appeared unto them cloven tongues like as of fire, and it sat upon each of them.

4 And they were all filled with the Holy Ghost, and began to speak with other tongues, as the Spirit gave them utterance.

5 And there were dwelling at Jerusalem Jews, devout men, out of every nation under heaven.

6 Now when this was noised abroad, the multitude came together, and were confounded, because that every man heard them speak in his own language.

7 And they were all amazed and marveled, saying one to another, Behold, are not all these which speak Galilaeans?

8 And how hear we every man in our own tongue, wherein we were born?

9 Parthians, and Medes, and Elamites, and the dwellers in Mesopotamia, and in Judaea, and Cappadocia, in Pontus, and Asia,

10 Phrygia, and Pamphylia, in Egypt, and in the parts of Libya about Cyrene, and strangers of Rome, Jews and proselytes,

11 Cretes and Arabians, we do hear them speak in our tongues the wonderful works of God.

12 And they were all amazed, and were in doubt, saying one to another, What meaneth this?

13 Others mocking said, These men are full of new wine.

14 But Peter, standing up with the eleven, lifted up his voice, and said unto them, Ye men of Judaea, and all ye that dwell at Jerusalem, be this known unto you, and hearken to my words:

15 For these are not drunken, as ye suppose, seeing it is but the third hour of the day.

16 But this is that which was spoken by the prophet Joel;

17 And it shall come to pass in the last days, saith God, I will pour out of my Spirit upon all flesh: and your sons and your daughters shall prophesy, and your young men shall see visions, and your old men shall dream dreams:

not so much have served to move their minds; and the majesty of the things ought the more to have moved them to consider the miracle. Although they give due honor to God, in that they are astonished and amazed, yet the principal and of the miracle is expressed in this, that they inquire, and thereby declare that they are prepared to learn; for otherwise their amazedness and wondering should not have done them any great good. And certainly we must so wonder at the works of God, that there must be also a consideration, and a desire to understand.

12. Others mocking

Hereby it appeareth how monstrous as well the sluggishness, as also the ungodliness of men is, when Satan hath taken away their mind. If God should openly (and visibly) descend from heaven, his majesty could scarce more manifestly appear than in this miracle. Whosoever hath any drop of sound understanding in him must needs be stricken with the only hearing of it. How beastly, then, are those men who see it with their eyes, and yet scoff, and go about with their jests to mock the power of God? But the matter is so. There is nothing so wonderful which those men do not turn to a jest who are touched with no care of God; because they do, even upon set purposes, harden themselves in their ignorance in things most plain. And it is a just punishment of God, which he bringeth upon such pride, to deliver them to Satan, to be driven headlong into blind fury. Wherefore, there is no cause why we should marvel that there be so many at this day so blind in so great light, if they be so deaf when such manifest doctrine is delivered, yea, if they wantonly refuse salvation when it is offered unto them. For if the wonderful and strange works of God, wherein he doth wonderfully set forth his power, be subject to the mockery of men, what shall become of doctrine, which they think tasteth of nothing but of that which is common? Although Luke doth signify unto us that they were not of the worst sort, or altogether past hope, which did laugh (and mock); but he meant rather to declare how the common sort was affected when they saw this miracle. And truly it hath been always so in the world, for very few have been touched with the true feeling of God as often as he hath revealed himself. Neither is it any marvel; for religion is a rare virtue, and a virtue which few men have; which is, indeed, the beginning of understanding. Nevertheless, howsoever the more part of men, through a certain hard stiff-neckedness, doth reject the consideration of the works of God, yet are they never without fruit, as we may see in this history.

17. I will pour out my Spirit

He intendeth to prove that the Church can be repaired by no other means, saving only by the giving of the Holy

a holy convocation – the proper beginning of the feast; on the sixteenth was the offering of the first-fruits of harvest, and from that day they were to reckon seven weeks, i.e., forty-nine days to the feast called the feast of Pentecost, so that it occurred fifty days after the first day of the feast of the Passover. This feast was also called the feast of weeks, from the circumstance that it followed a succession of weeks, Ex. 34: 22; Num. 28: 26; Deut. 16: 10. It was also a harvest festival, and was accordingly called the feast of harvest. And it was for this reason that two loaves made of new meal were offered on this occasion as first-fruits, Lev. 23: 17,20; Num. 28: 27–31.

2. And suddenly. It burst upon them at once. Though they were waiting for the descent of the Spirit, yet it is not probable that they expected it in this manner.

3. And there appeared unto them. There were seen by them, or they saw. They were first seen by them in the room before they rested on the heads of the disciples. Perhaps the fire appeared at first as scintillations or coruscations, until it became fixed on their heads.

6. When this was noised abroad. When the rumor of this remarkable transaction was spread, as it naturally would be without delay. **Every man heard them speak**, etc. Though the multitude spoke different tongues, yet they now heard Galileans use the language which they had learned in foreign nations. **His own language.** His own dialect. A work of grace on the hearts of men in a revival of religion will always be noised abroad.

12. Were in doubt. This expression denotes a state of hesitancy or anxiety about an event. It is applied to those who are traveling, and are ignorant of the way, or who hesitate about the road. They were all astonished at this; they did not know how to understand it or explain it, until some of them supposed it was merely the effect of new wine.

16. This is that. This is the fulfillment of that, or this was predicted. This was the second part of Peter's argument to show that this was in accordance with the predictions in their own Scriptures.

By the prophet Joel. Joel 2: 28–32. This is not quoted literally either from the Hebrew or from the Septuagint. The substance, however, is preserved.

17. It shall come to pass. It shall happen, or shall occur.

My Spirit. The Spirit here denotes the Third Person of the Trinity, promised by the Savior, and sent to finish his work, and apply it to men. The Holy Spirit is regarded as the source, or conveyer of all the blessings which Christians experience. Hence he renews the heart, John 3: 5–6. He is the Source of all proper feelings and principles in Christians, or he produces the Christian graces, Gal. 5: 22–25; Titus 3: 5–7. The spread and success of the gospel are attributed to him, Is. 32: 15–16. Miraculous gifts are traced to him; especially the various gifts with which the early Christians were endowed, 1 Cor. 12: 4–10. The promise that he would pour out his Spirit, means that he would, in the time of the Messiah, impart a large measure of those influences, which it was his peculiar province to communicate to men. A part of them were communicated on the day of Pentecost, in the miraculous endowment of the power of speaking foreign languages, in the wisdom of the apostles, and in the conversion of the three thousand.

Upon all flesh. The word flesh here means persons, or men. The word **all**, here, does not mean every individual, but every class or rank of men.

Shall prophesy. The word prophesy is used in a great variety of senses.

(1.) It means to predict, or foretell future events, Matt. 11: 13; 15: 7.

(2.) To divine, to conjecture, to declare as a prophet might. Matt. 26: 68, "Prophesy, Who is he that smote thee."

(3.) To celebrate the praises of God, being under a Divine influence, Luke 1: 67. This seems to have been a considerable part of the employment in the ancient schools of the prophets, 1 Sam. 10: 5; 19: 20; 30: 15.

(4.) To teach – as no small part of the office of the prophets was to teach the doctrines of religion. Matt. 7: 22, "Have we not prophesied in thy name?"

(5.) It denotes then, in general, to speak

18 And on my servants and on my handmaidens I will pour out in those days of my Spirit; and they shall prophesy:

19 And I will shew wonders in heaven above, and signs in the earth beneath; blood, and fire, and vapor of smoke:

20 The sun shall be turned into darkness, and the moon into blood, before that great and notable day of the Lord come:

21 And it shall come to pass, that whosoever shall call on the name of the Lord shall be saved.

22 Ye men of Israel, hear these words; Jesus of Nazareth, a man approved of God among you by miracles and wonders and signs, which God did by him in the midst of you, as ye yourselves also know:

23 Him, being delivered by the determinate counsel and foreknowledge of God, ye have taken, and by wicked hands have crucified and slain:

24 Whom God hath raised up, having loosed the pains of death: because it was not possible that he should be holden of it.

25 For David speaketh concerning him, I foresaw the Lord always before my face, for he is on my right hand, that I should not be moved:

26 Therefore did my heart rejoice, and my tongue was glad; moreover also my flesh shall rest in hope:

27 Because thou wilt not leave my soul in hell, neither wilt thou suffer thine Holy One to see corruption.

28 Thou hast made known to me the ways of life; thou shalt make me full of joy with thy countenance.

29 Men and brethren, let me freely speak unto you of the patriarch David, that he is both dead and buried, and his sepulcher is with us unto this day.

30 Therefore being a prophet, and knowing that God had sworn with an oath to him, that of the fruit of his loins, according to the flesh, he would raise up Christ to sit on his throne;

31 He seeing this before spake of the resurrection of Christ, that his soul was not left in hell, neither his flesh did see corruption.

32 This Jesus hath God raised up, whereof we all are witnesses.

33 Therefore being by the right hand of God exalted, and having received of the

Spirit. Therefore, forasmuch as they did all hope that the restoring drew near, he accuseth them of sluggishness, because they do not once think upon the way and means thereof. And when the prophet saith, "I will pour out," it is, without all question, that he meant by this word to note the great abundance of the Spirit.

21. Whosoever shall call upon

An excellent place. For as God doth prick us forward like sluggish asses, with threatenings and terrors to seek salvation, se, after that he hath brought darkness upon the face of heaven and earth, yet doth he show a means whereby salvation may shine before our eyes, to wit, if we shall call upon him. For we must diligently note this circumstance. If God should promise salvation simply, it were a great matter; but it is a far greater when as he promiseth the same amidst manifold dungeons of death. Whilst that (saith he) all things shall be out of order, and the fear of destruction shall possess all things, only call upon me, and ye shall be saved. Therefore, howsoever man be swallowed up ill the gulf of miseries, yet is there set before him a way to escape. We must also note the universal word, whosoever. For God admitteth all men unto himself without exception, and by this means doth he invite them to salvation.

32. This Jesus

After that he had proved by the testimony of David, that it was most requisite that Christ should rise again, he saith, that he and the rest of his fellows were such witnesses as saw him with their eyes after his resurrection. For this text will not allow this word raised up to be drawn into any other sense. Whereupon it followeth that that was fulfilled in Jesus of Nazareth which David did foreshow concerning Christ. After that he intreateth of the fruit or effect. For it was requisite for him to declare that first, that Christ is alive. Otherwise it had been an absurd and incredible thing that he should be the author of so great a miracle. Notwithstanding he doth therewithal teach us, that he did not rise for his own sake alone, but that he might make the whole Church partaker of his life, having poured out the Spirit.

42. In their doctrine

Luke doth not only commend in them the constancy of faith or of godliness, but he saith, also, that they did constantly give themselves to those exercises which serve to the confirmation of faith; to wit, that they studied continually to profit by hearing the apostles; that they gave themselves much to prayer; that they did use fellowship and breaking of bread very much.

As touching prayer and doctrine the sense is plain. Communication or fellowship, and breaking of bread, may be taken diversely. Some think that breaking of bread

under a Divine influence, whether in foretelling future events; in celebrating the praises of God; in instructing others in the duties of religion; or in speaking foreign languages under that influence. In this last sense, the word is used in the New Testament to denote those who were miraculously endowed with the power of speaking foreign languages, Acts 19: 6. The word is also used to denote teaching, or speaking in intelligible language, in opposition to speaking a foreign tongue, 1 Cor. 14: 1–5. In this place it means that they should speak under a Divine influence, and is specially applied to the power of speaking in a foreign tongue.

20. The sun shall be turned into darkness. The shining of the sun is an emblem of prosperity; the withdrawing, or eclipse, or setting of the sun is an emblem of calamity. To say that the sun is darkened, or turned into darkness, is an image of calamity, and especially of the calamities of war; when the smoke of burning cities rises to heaven, and obscures his light. This is not, therefore, to be taken literally, nor does it afford any indication of what will be at the end of the world in regard to the sun.

The moon into blood. The word blood here means that obscure, sanguinary color which the moon has when the atmosphere is filled with smoke and vapor; and especially the lurid and alarming appearance which it assumes when smoke and flames are thrown up by earthquakes and fiery eruptions.

24. Whom God hath raised up. This was the main point, in this part of his argument, which Peter wished to establish. He could not but admit that the Messiah had been in an ignominious manner put to death. But he now shows them that God had also raised him up; had thus given his attestation to his doctrine; and had sent down his Spirit according to the promise which the Lord Jesus made before his death.

Having loosed the pains of death. The word loosed is opposed to bind, and is properly applied to a cord, or to anything which is bound. See Matt. 21: 2; Mark 1: 7. Hence it means to free, or to liberate, Luke 13: 16; 1 Cor.

7: 27. It is used in this sense here; though the idea of untying or loosing a band is retained, because the word translated pains often means a cord or band.

31. He seeing this before, etc. By the spirit of prophecy. From this it appears that David had distinct views of the great doctrines pertaining to the Messiah.

32. This Jesus. Peter, having shown that it was predicted that the Messiah would rise, now affirms that it was done in the case of Jesus. If it were a matter of prophecy, all objection to the truth of the doctrine was taken away, and the only question was, whether there was evidence that this had been done. The proof of this Peter now alleges, and offers his own testimony, and that of his brethren, to the truth of this great and glorious fact.

We all are witnesses. It seems probable that Peter refers here to the whole one hundred and twenty who were present, and who were ready to attest it in any manner. The matter which was to be proved was, that Jesus was seen alive after he had been put to death. The apostles were appointed to bear witness of this. And we are told by Paul (1 Cor. 15: 6), that he was seen by more than five hundred brethren, that is, Christians, at one time. The hundred and twenty assembled on this occasion were doubtless part of the number, and were ready to attest this. This was the proof that Peter alleged; and the strength of this proof was, and should have been, perfectly irresistible.

33. Therefore being by the right hand. The right hand among the Hebrews was often used to denote power; and the expression here means, not that he was exalted to the right hand of God, but by his power. He was raised from the dead by his power, and borne to heaven, triumphant over all his enemies. The use of the word right hand to denote power is common in the Scriptures. Job 40: 14, "Thine own right hand can save thee." Ps. 17: 7, "Thou savest by thy right hand them which put their trust in thee."

Exalted. Constituted King and Messiah in heaven. Raised up from his condition of humiliation to the glory which he had with the

Father the promise of the Holy Ghost, he hath shed forth this, which ye now see and hear.

34 For David is not ascended into the heavens: but he saith himself, The LORD said unto my Lord, Sit thou on my right hand,

35 Until I make thy foes thy footstool.

36 Therefore let all the house of Israel know assuredly, that God hath made that same Jesus, whom ye have crucified, both Lord and Christ.

37 Now when they heard this, they were pricked in their heart, and said unto Peter and to the rest of the apostles, Men and brethren, what shall we do?

38 Then Peter said unto them, Repent, and be baptized every one of you in the name of Jesus Christ for the remission of sins, and ye shall receive the gift of the Holy Ghost.

39 For the promise is unto you, and to your children, and to all that are afar off, even as many as the Lord our God shall call.

40 And with many other words did he testify and exhort, saying, Save yourselves from this untoward generation.

41 Then they that gladly received his word were baptized: and the same day there were added unto them about three thousand souls.

42 And they continued stedfastly in the apostles' doctrine and fellowship, and in breaking of bread, and in prayers.

43 And fear came upon every soul: and many wonders and signs were done by the apostles.

44 And all that believed were together, and had all things common;

45 And sold their possessions and goods, and parted them to all men, as every man had need.

46 And they, continuing daily with one accord in the temple, and breaking bread from house to house, did eat their meat with gladness and singleness of heart,

47 Praising God, and having favor with all the people. And the Lord added to the church daily such as should be saved.

ACTS 3

1 Now Peter and John went up together into the temple at the hour of prayer, being the ninth hour.

doth signify the Lord's Supper; other some do think that it signifieth alms; other some that the faithful did banquet together among themselves. Some do think that koin nia, doth signify the celebrating of the Holy Supper; but I do rather agree to those others who think that the same is meant by the breaking of bread. For koin nia, unless it have somewhat added unto it, is never found in this sense; therefore, I do rather refer it unto mutual society and fellowship, unto alms, and unto other duties of brotherly fellowship. And my reason why I would rather have breaking of bread to be understood of the Lord's Supper in this place is this, because Luke doth reckon up those things wherein the public estate of the Church is contained. Yea, he expresseth in this place four marks whereby the true and natural face of the Church may be judged. Do we then seek the true Church of Christ? The image thereof is lively depainted and set forth unto us in this place. And he beginneth with doctrine which is, as it were, the soul of the Church. Neither doth he name all manner of doctrine, but the doctrine of the apostles, that is, that which the Son of God had delivered by their hands. Therefore, wheresoever the pure voice of the gospel doth sound, where men continue in the profession thereof, where they exercise themselves in hearing the same ordinarily that they may profit, without all doubt there is the Church.

47. Having favor

This is the fruit of an innocent life, to find favor even amongst strangers. And yet we need not to doubt of this, but that they were hated of many. But although he speak generally of the people, yet he meaneth that part alone which was sound, neither yet infected with any poison of hatred; he signifieth briefly, that the faithful did so behave themselves, that the people did full well like of them for their innocency of life.

The Lord added daily

He showeth in these words that their diligence was not without profit; they studied so much as in them lay to gather into the Lord's sheepfold those which wandered and went astray. He saith that their labor bestowed herein was not lost; because the Lord did increase his Church daily. And surely, whereas the Church is rather diminished than increased, that is to be imputed to our slothfulness, or rather forwardness And although they did all of them stoutly labor to increase the kingdom of Christ, yet Luke ascribeth this honor to God alone, that he brought strangers into the Church. And surely this is his own proper work. For the ministers do no good by planting or watering, unless he make their labor effectual by the power of his Spirit (1 Corinthians 3).

Father before the world was, John 17: 5.

37. Now when they heard this. When they heard this declaration of Peter, and this proof that Jesus was the Messiah. There was no fanaticism in his discourse; it was cool, close, pungent reasoning. He proved to them the truth of what he was saying, and thus prepared the way for this effect.

They were pricked in their heart. The word translated were pricked is not used elsewhere in the New Testament. It properly denotes to pierce or penetrate with a needle, lancet, or sharp instrument; and then to pierce with grief, or acute pain of any kind. It answers precisely to our word compunction. It implies also the idea of sudden as well as acute grief. In this case it means that they were suddenly and deeply affected with anguish and alarm at what Peter had said. The causes of their grief may have been these:

(1.) Their sorrow that the Messiah had been put to death by his own countrymen.

(2.) Their deep sense of guilt in having done this. There would be mingled here a remembrance of ingratitude, and a consciousness that they had been guilty of murder of the most aggravated and horrid kind, that of having killed their own Messiah.

(3.) The fear of his wrath. He was still alive, exalted to be their Lord, and entrusted with all power. They were afraid of his vengeance; they were conscious that they deserved it; and they supposed that they were exposed to it.

(4.) What they had done could not be undone. The guilt remained; they could not wash it out. They had imbrued their hands in the blood of innocence; and the guilt of that oppressed their souls. This expresses the usual feelings which sinners have when they are convicted of sin.

39. For the promise. That is, the promise respecting the particular thing of which he was speaking – the influences of the Holy Ghost. This promise he had adduced in the beginning of his discourse (Acts 2: 17), and he now applies it to them. As the Spirit was promised to descend on Jews and their sons and daughters, it was applicable to them in the circumstances in which they then were. The

only hope of lost sinners is in the promises of God; and the only thing that can give comfort to a soul that is convicted of sin, is the hope that God will pardon and save.

To you. To you Jews, even though you have crucified the Messiah. The promise had especial reference to the Jewish people.

42. And they continued stedfastly. They persevered in, or they adhered to. This is the inspired record of the result. That any of these apostatized is nowhere recorded, and is not to be presumed. Though they had been suddenly converted, though suddenly admitted to the church, though exposed to much persecution and contempt, and many trials, yet the record is that they adhered to the doctrines and duties of the Christian religion.

The apostles' doctrine. This does not mean that they held or believed the doctrines of the apostles, though that was true; but it means that they adhered to, or attended on, their teaching or instruction. The word doctrine has now a technical sense, and means a collection and arrangement of abstract views supposed to be contained in the Bible. In the Scriptures the word means simply teaching; and the expression here denotes that they continued to attend on their instructions. One evidence of conversion is a desire to be instructed in the doctrines and duties of religion, and a willingness to attend on the preaching of the gospel.

And fellowship. The word rendered fellowship is often rendered communion. It properly denotes having things in common, or participation, society, friendship. It may apply to anything which may be possessed in common, or in which all may partake. Thus all Christians have the same hope of heaven; the same joys; the same hatred of sin; the same enemies to contend with. Thus they have the same subjects of conversation, of feeling, and of prayer; or they have communion in these things.

ACTS 3

1. Peter and John went up, etc. In Luke 24: 53, it is said that the apostles were continually in the temple, praising and blessing God. From Acts 2: 46, it is clear that all the disciples were

2 And a certain man lame from his mother's womb was carried, whom they laid daily at the gate of the temple which is called Beautiful, to ask alms of them that entered into the temple;

3 Who seeing Peter and John about to go into the temple asked an alms.

4 And Peter, fastening his eyes upon him with John, said, Look on us.

5 And he gave heed unto them, expecting to receive something of them.

6 Then Peter said, Silver and gold have I none; but such as I have give I thee: In the name of Jesus Christ of Nazareth rise up and walk.

7 And he took him by the right hand, and lifted him up: and immediately his feet and ancle bones received strength.

8 And he leaping up stood, and walked, and entered with them into the temple, walking, and leaping, and praising God.

9 And all the people saw him walking and praising God:

10 And they knew that it was he which sat for alms at the Beautiful gate of the temple: and they were filled with wonder and amazement at that which had happened unto him.

11 And as the lame man which was healed held Peter and John, all the people ran together unto them in the porch that is called Solomon's, greatly wondering.

12 And when Peter saw it, he answered unto the people, Ye men of Israel, why marvel ye at this? or why look ye so earnestly on us, as though by our own power or holiness we had made this man to walk?

13 The God of Abraham, and of Isaac, and of Jacob, the God of our fathers, hath glorified his Son Jesus; whom ye delivered up, and denied him in the presence of Pilate, when he was determined to let him go.

14 But ye denied the Holy One and the Just, and desired a murderer to be granted unto you;

15 And killed the Prince of life, whom God hath raised from the dead; whereof we are witnesses.

16 And his name through faith in his name hath made this man strong, whom ye see and know: yea, the faith which is by him hath given him this perfect soundness in the presence of you all.

ACTS 3

1. We saw before that many signs were showed by the hands of the apostles; now Luke reciteth one of many for example's sake, after his common custom; namely, that a lame man, which was lame of his feet from his mother's womb, was perfectly restored to his limbs. And he doth diligently gather all the circumstances which serve to set forth the miracle. If it had been that his legs had been out of joint, or if it had been some disease coming by some casualty, it might have been the more easily cured. But the default of nature could not have been so easily redressed. When as he saith that he was carried, we gather thereby that it was no light halting, but that this man did lie as if his legs had been dead. Forasmuch as he was wont daily to ask alms, hereby all the people might the better know him. In that being healed, he walked in the temple at the time of prayer, this served to spread abroad the fame of the miracle. Furthermore, this doth not a little set forth the same, that being lifted up and set upon his feet, he leapeth up therewithal, and walketh joyfully.

12. Men of Israel

He beginneth his sermon with a reproving of the people. And yet doth he not simply reprove them because they wonder; for that was altogether profitable and worthy praise; but because they do wickedly ascribe unto men that praise which is due to the work of God. As if he should say, Ye do amiss, in that you stay in us, and stand gazing upon us, whereas you ought rather to look upon God and Christ. Therefore, this is to be amazed evilly, when as our minds do stay in men. And we must note that he condemneth the respect of men; as if, saith he, we by our own power and virtue had done this. Therefore there is an error and corruption in this, if we attribute that unto the godliness and power of men which is proper to God and Christ.

26. He hath raised up his Son

He gathereth out of the words of Moses that Christ is now revealed. But the words do seem to import no such thing; yet doth he reason fitly thus, because the blessing could no otherwise be, unless the beginning thereof did flow from the Messias. For we must always remember this, that all mankind is accursed, and, therefore, there is a singular remedy promised us, which is performed by Christ alone. Wherefore, he is the only fountain and beginning of the blessing. And if so be that Christ came to this end, that he may bless the Jews first, and, secondly, us, he hath undoubtedly done that which was his duty to do; and we shall feel the force and effect of this duty in ourselves, unless our unbelief do hinder us.

This was a part of the priest's office under the law, to

accustomed daily to resort to the temple for devotion.

6. Silver and gold have I none. The man had asked for money; Peter assures him that he had not that to give; it was done, however, in such a way as to show his willingness to aid him, if he had possessed it.

Such as I have. Such as is in my power. It is not to be supposed that he meant to say that he originated this power himself, but only that it was entrusted to him. He immediately adds, that it was derived solely from the Lord Jesus Christ.

In the name. The expression means, by his authority, or in virtue of power derived from him. We are here struck with a remarkable difference between the manner in which the Lord Jesus wrought miracles, and that in which it was done by his apostles. He did it in his own name, and by virtue of his own power. He claimed dominion over disease and death. The apostles never attempted to perform a miracle by their own power. It was only in the name of Jesus; and this circumstance alone shows that there was a radical difference between Christ and all other prophets and teachers.

Of Nazareth. This was the name by which he was commonly known. By this name he had been designated among the Jews, and on the cross. It is by no means improbable that the man had heard of him by this name; and it was important that he should understand that it was by the authority of him who had been crucified as an impostor.

Rise up and walk. To do this would be evidence of signal power. It is remarkable that, in cases like this, they were commanded to do the thing at once. See similar cases in John 5: 8; Matt. 9: 6; 12: 13.

It would have been easy to allege that they had no power, that they were lame, or sick, or palsied, and could do nothing until God should give them strength. But the command was to do the thing; nor did the Savior or the apostles stop to convince them that they could do nothing. They did not doubt that, if it were done, they would ascribe the power to God.

15. And killed the Prince of life. The word rendered prince denotes, properly, a military

leader or commander. Hence, in Heb. 2: 10, it is translated captain: "It became him – to make the captain of their salvation perfect through sufferings." As a captain or commander leads on to victory, and is said to obtain it, so the word comes to denote one who is the cause, the author, the procurer, etc. In this sense it is used: Acts 5: 31, "Him hath God exalted to be a Prince and a Savior, for to give repentance to Israel," etc. In Heb. 12: 2, it is properly rendered author: "Looking unto Jesus, the author and finisher of our faith." The word author, or giver, would express the meaning of the word here. It also implies that he has dominion over life; an idea, indeed, which is essentially connected with that of his being the author of it. The word life here is used in a large sense, as denoting all manner of life. In this sense it is used in reference to Christ in John 1: 4, "In him was life," etc. Comp. John 5: 26; 1 John 5: 11; 1 Cor. 15: 45.

Jesus is here called the Prince of life in contrast with him whom the Jews demanded in his place, Barabbas. He was a murderer, Luke 23: 19; Mark 15: 7, one who had destroyed life; and yet they demanded that he whose character it was to destroy life should be released, and the Author of life be put to death.

16. Whom ye see and know. There could, therefore, be no mistake. He was well known to them. There was no doubt about the truth of the miracle, Acts 4: 16, and the only inquiry was in what way it had been done. This Peter affirms to have been accomplished only by the power of the Lord Jesus.

22. For Moses truly said. The authority of Moses among the Jews was absolute and final. It was of great importance, therefore, to show not only that they were not departing from his law, but that he had actually foretold these very things. The object of the passage is not to prove that the heavens must receive him, but that he was truly the Messiah.

Unto the fathers. To their ancestors, or the founders of the nation. See Deut. 18: 16–19.

A prophet. Literally, one who foretells future events. But it is also used to denote a religious teacher in general.

26. Unto you first. To you who are Jews. This

17 And now, brethren, I wot that through ignorance ye did it, as did also your rulers.

18 But those things, which God before had shewed by the mouth of all his prophets, that Christ should suffer, he hath so fulfilled.

19 Repent ye therefore, and be converted, that your sins may be blotted out, when the times of refreshing shall come from the presence of the Lord;

20 And he shall send Jesus Christ, which before was preached unto you:

21 Whom the heaven must receive until the times of restitution of all things, which God hath spoken by the mouth of all his holy prophets since the world began.

22 For Moses truly said unto the fathers, A prophet shall the Lord your God raise up unto you of your brethren, like unto me; him shall ye hear in all things whatsoever he shall say unto you.

23 And it shall come to pass, that every soul, which will not hear that prophet, shall be destroyed from among the people.

24 Yea, and all the prophets from Samuel and those that follow after, as many as have spoken, have likewise foretold of these days.

25 Ye are the children of the prophets, and of the covenant which God made with our fathers, saying unto Abraham, And in thy seed shall all the kindreds of the earth be blessed.

26 Unto you first God, having raised up his Son Jesus, sent him to bless you, in turning away every one of you from his iniquities.

ACTS 4

1 And as they spake unto the people, the priests, and the captain of the temple, and the Sadducees, came upon them,

2 Being grieved that they taught the people, and preached through Jesus the resurrection from the dead.

3 And they laid hands on them, and put them in hold unto the next day: for it was now eventide.

4 Howbeit many of them which heard the word believed; and the number of the men was about five thousand.

5 And it came to pass on the morrow,

bless the people; and, lest this should be only a vain ceremony, there was a promise added; as it is (Numbers 6: 27). And that which was shadowed in the old priesthood was truly performed in Christ (Hebrews 7: 1,6). Concerning which matter we have spoken more at large in the seventh chapter to the Hebrews. I like not Erasmus's translation; for he saith, *when he had raised him up,* as if he spoke of a thing which was done long ago. But Peter meaneth rather, that Christ was raised up, when he was declared to be the author of the blessing; which thing, since it was done of late and suddenly, it ought to move their minds the more. For the Scripture useth to speak thus, as in the last place, of Moses, whereunto Peter alludeth. To raise up a prophet, is to furnish him with necessary gifts to fulfill his function, and, as it were, to prefer him to the degree of prophetical honor. And Christ was raised up then, when he fulfilled the function enjoined him by his Father, but the same thing is done daily when he is offered by the gospel, that he may excel amongst us. We have said that in the adverb of order, first, is noted the right of the first-be-gotten, because it was expedient that Christ should begin with the Jews, that he might afterward pass over unto the Gentiles.

Whilst that he turneth

He doth again commend the doctrine of repentance, to the end we may learn to conclude under the blessing of Christ newness of life, as when Esaias promiseth that a "Redeemer should come to Zion," he addeth a restraint; "Those which in Jacob shall be turned from their iniquities." For Christ doth not do away the sins of the faithful, to the end they may grant liberty to themselves to sin under this color; but he maketh them therewith all new men. Although we must diligently distinguish these two benefits which are linked together, that this ground-work may continue, that we are reconciled to God by free pardon, I know that other men turn it otherwise; but this is the true meaning of Luke; for he speaketh thus word for word, "In turning every one from his wickedness."

ACTS 4

In this narration we must consider three things chiefly. That so soon as the truth of the gospel doth once appear, Satan setteth himself against the same on the other side, so much as he is able, and attempteth all things that he may smolder the same in the very first beginnings. Secondly, That God doth furnish his children with invincible force and strength, that they may stand steadfast and unmovable against all assaults of Satan, and not yield unto the violence of the wicked. And, last of all, we must note the event and end, that howsoever the adversaries seem to bear the chiefest swing, and they themselves do omit nothing which

was the direction that the gospel should be first preached to the Jews, beginning at Jerusalem, Luke 24: 47. Jesus himself also confined his ministry entirely to the Jews.

Having raised up. This expression does not refer to his having raised him from the dead, but is used in the same sense as in Acts 3: 22, where God promised that he would raise up a prophet, and send him to teach the people. Peter means that God had appointed his Son Jesus, or had commissioned him to go and preach to the people to turn them away from their sins.

To bless you. To make you happy; to fulfill the promise made to Abraham.

In turning away. That is, by his preaching, example, death, etc. The highest blessing that can be conferred on men is to be turned from sin. It is the source of all woes; and if men are turned from that, they will be happy. Christ blesses no one in sin, or while loving sin, but by turning them from sin. This was the object which he had in view in coming, Is. 59: 20; Matt. 1: 21. The design of Peter in these remarks was to show them that the Messiah had come, and that now they might look for happiness, pardon, and mercy through him. As the Jews might, so may all; and as Jesus while living sought to turn away men from their sins, so he does still, and still designs to bless all nations by the gospel which he had himself preached, and to establish which he died. All may therefore come and be blessed; and all may rejoice in the prospect that these blessings shall yet be bestowed on all the kindreds of the earth. May the happy day soon come!

ACTS 4

2. Being grieved. The word thus translated occurs but in one other place in the New Testament, Acts 16: 18. It implies more than simple sorrow; it was a mingled emotion of indignation and anger. They did not grieve because they thought it a public calamity, but because it interfered with their authority, and opposed their doctrine. It means that it was painful to them, or they could not bear it. It is often the case that bigots, and men in authority, have

this kind of grief at the zeal of men in spreading the truth, and thus undermining their influence and authority.

That they taught the people. The ground of their grief was as much the fact that they should presume to instruct the people, as the matter which they taught them. They were offended that unlearned Galileans, in no way connected with the priestly office, and unauthorized by them, should presume to set themselves up as religious teachers. They claimed the right to watch over the interests of the people, and to declare who was authorized to instruct the nation. It has been no unusual thing for men in ecclesiastical stations to take exceptions to the ministry of those who have not been commissioned by themselves. Men easily fancy that all power to instruct others is lodged in their hands; and they oppose others simply from the fact that they have not derived their authority from them. The true question in this case was, whether these Galileans gave proof that they were sent by God. The fact of the miracle in this case should have been satisfactory. We have here, also, a striking instance of the fact that men may turn away from evidence, and from most important points, and fix on something that opposes their prejudices, and which may be a matter of very little moment. No inquiry was made whether the miracle had been really wrought; but the only inquiry was, whether they had conformed to their views of doctrine and order.

And preached through Jesus, etc. The Sadducees would be particularly opposed to this. They denied the doctrine of the resurrection, and they were troubled that the apostles adduced proof of it so strong as the resurrection of Jesus. It was perceived that this doctrine was becoming established among the people; multitudes believed that he had risen; and if he had been raised up, it followed also that others would rise. The Sadducees, therefore, felt that their cause was in danger; and they joined with the priests in endeavoring to arrest its spread among the people. This is the account of the first opposition that was made to the gospel as it was preached by the apostles. It is worthy of remark, that it excited so much and so speedily the enmity of those

that their rulers, and elders, and scribes,

6 And Annas the high priest, and Caiaphas, and John, and Alexander, and as many as were of the kindred of the high priest, were gathered together at Jerusalem.

7 And when they had set them in the midst, they asked, By what power, or by what name, have ye done this?

8 Then Peter, filled with the Holy Ghost, said unto them, Ye rulers of the people, and elders of Israel,

9 If we this day be examined of the good deed done to the impotent man, by what means he is made whole;

10 Be it known unto you all, and to all the people of Israel, that by the name of Jesus Christ of Nazareth, whom ye crucified, whom God raised from the dead, even by him doth this man stand here before you whole.

11 This is the stone which was set at nought of you builders, which is become the head of the corner.

12 Neither is there salvation in any other: for there is none other name under heaven given among men, whereby we must be saved.

13 Now when they saw the boldness of Peter and John, and perceived that they were unlearned and ignorant men, they marveled; and they took knowledge of them, that they had been with Jesus.

14 And beholding the man which was healed standing with them, they could say nothing against it.

15 But when they had commanded them to go aside out of the council, they conferred among themselves,

16 Saying, What shall we do to these men? for that indeed a notable miracle hath been done by them is manifest to all them that dwell in Jerusalem; and we cannot deny it.

17 But that it spread no further among the people, let us straitly threaten them, that they speak henceforth to no man in this name.

18 And they called them, and commanded them not to speak at all nor teach in the name of Jesus.

19 But Peter and John answered and said unto them, Whether it be right in the sight of God to hearken unto you more than unto God, judge ye.

may serve to blot out the name of Christ; and, on the other side, howsoever the ministers of sound doctrine be as sheep in the mouths of wolves, yet doth God spread abroad the kingdom of his Son; he fostereth the light of the gospel which is lighted; and he is the protector of his children. Therefore, so often as the doctrine of the gospel ariseth, and divers motions do rise on the other side, and the course thereof is letted divers ways, there is no cause why godly minds should faint or quail, as at some unwonted thing; but they ought rather to remember, that these are ordinary endeavors of Satan, so that we must think upon this well before it come to pass, that it cannot otherwise be but that Satan will spew out all his might and main, so often as Christ doth come abroad with his doctrine. And therewithal let us consider that the constancy of the apostles is set forth unto us for an example, lest, being overcome either with any perils, or threatenings, or terrors, we leap back from that profession of faith which the Lord requireth at our hands. And, moreover, let us comfort ourselves with this, that we need not to doubt but that the Lord will give prosperous success when we have done our duty faithfully.

12. Neither is there salvation in any other

He passes from the species [salvation] unto the genus [or more particular], and he goeth from the corporal benefit unto perfect health [or general]. And assuredly Christ had showed this one token of his grace, to the end he might be known to be the only author of life. We must consider this in all the benefits of God, to wit, that he is the fountain of salvation. And he meant to prick and sting the priests with this sentence, when as he saith that there is salvation in none other save only in Christ, whom they went about to put quite out of remembrance. As if he should say, that they are twice damned who did not only refuse the salvation offered them by God, but endeavor to bring the same to nought, and did take from all the people the fruit and use thereof. And although he seemeth to speak unto deaf men, yet doth he preach of the grace of Christ, if peradventure some can abide to hear; if not, that they may at least be deprived of all excuse by this testimony. Neither is there any other name. He expoundeth the sentence next going before. Salvation (saith he) is in Christ alone, because God hath decreed that it should be so. For by *name* he meaneth the cause or mean, as if he should have said, forasmuch as salvation is in God's power only, he will not have the same to be common to us by any other means than if we ask it of Christ alone. Whereas he saith *under heaven* , they do commonly refer it unto creatures, as if he should say, that the force and power to save is given to Christ alone. Notwithstanding, I do rather think that this was added, because men cannot ascend into heaven, that they may come unto God.

in power; and that the apostles were so soon called to test the sincerity of their attachment to their Master. They who but a few days before had fled at the approach of danger, were called to meet this opposition, and to show their attachment to a risen Redeemer; and they did it without shrinking. They showed now that they were indeed the true friends of the crucified Savior: and this remarkable change in their conduct is one among the many proofs that they were influenced from above.

8. Ye rulers, etc. Peter addressed the Sanhedrim with perfect respect. He did not call in question their authority to propose this question. He seemed to regard this as a favorable opportunity to declare the truth, and state the evidence of the Christian religion. In this he acted on the principle of the injunction which he himself afterwards gave, 1 Pet. 3: 15, "Be ready always to give an answer to every man that asketh you a reason of the hope that is in you with meekness and fear." Innocence is willing to be questioned; and a believer in the truth will rejoice in any opportunity to state the evidence of what is believed. It is remarkable, also, that this was before the great council of the nation; the body that was clothed with the highest authority. And Peter could not have forgotten that before this very council, and these very men, his Master had been arraigned and condemned. Nor could he have forgotten that in the very room where this same council was convened to try his Lord, he had himself shrunk from an honest avowal of attachment to him, and shamefully and profanely denied him. That he was now able to stand boldly before this same tribunal evinced a remarkable change in his feelings, and was a most clear and impressive proof of the genuineness of his repentance when he went out and wept bitterly.

19. Whether it be right, etc. The apostles abated nothing of their boldness when threatened. They openly appealed to their judges whether their command could be right. And in doing this, they expressed their full conviction of the truth of what they had said, and their deliberate purpose not to regard their command, but still to proclaim to the people the truth that Jesus was the Messiah.

In the sight of God. That is, whether God will judge this to be right. The grand question was, how God would regard it. If he disapproved it, it was wrong. It was not merely a question pertaining to their reputation, safety, or life; but it was a question of conscience before God. And we have here a striking instance of the principle on which Christians act. It is to lay their safety, reputation, and life out of view, and to bring everything to this test, WHETHER IT WILL PLEASE GOD. If it will, it is right; if it will not, it is wrong.

To hearken. To hear and to hearken are often used to denote to obey, John 5: 24; 8: 47, etc.

Judge ye. This was an appeal to them directly as judges, and as men. And it may be presumed that it was an appeal which they could not resist. The Sanhedrim acknowledged itself to have been appointed by God; and to have no authority which was not derived from his appointment. Of course God could modify, supersede, or repeal their authority; and the abstract principle, that it was better to obey God than man, they could not call in question. The only inquiry was, whether they had evidence that God had issued any command in the case. Of that the apostles were satisfied; and that the rulers could not deny. It may be remarked, that this is one of the first and most bold appeals on record in favor of the right of private judgment and the liberty of conscience. That liberty was supposed in all the Jewish religion. It was admitted that the authority of God in all matters was superior to that of man. And the same spirit manifested itself thus early in the Christian church against all dominion over the conscience, and in favor of the right to follow the dictates of the conscience and the will of God. As a mere historical fact, therefore, it is interesting to contemplate this; and still more interesting in its important bearings on human liberty and human happiness. The doctrine is still more explicitly stated in Acts 5: 29 – "We ought to obey God rather than men."

20. These two verses contain an important principle in favor of religious liberty – the liberty of conscience, and of private judg-

20 For we cannot but speak the things which we have seen and heard.

21 So when they had further threatened them, they let them go, finding nothing how they might punish them, because of the people: for all men glorified God for that which was done.

22 For the man was above forty years old, on whom this miracle of healing was shewed.

23 And being let go, they went to their own company, and reported all that the chief priests and elders had said unto them.

24 And when they heard that, they lifted up their voice to God with one accord, and said, Lord, thou art God, which hast made heaven, and earth, and the sea, and all that in them is:

25 Who by the mouth of thy servant David hast said, Why did the heathen rage, and the people imagine vain things?

26 The kings of the earth stood up, and the rulers were gathered together against the Lord, and against his Christ.

27 For of a truth against thy holy child Jesus, whom thou hast anointed, both Herod, and Pontius Pilate, with the Gentiles, and the people of Israel, were gathered together,

28 For to do whatsoever thy hand and thy counsel determined before to be done.

29 And now, Lord, behold their threatenings: and grant unto thy servants, that with all boldness they may speak thy word,

30 By stretching forth thine hand to heal; and that signs and wonders may be done by the name of thy holy child Jesus.

31 And when they had prayed, the place was shaken where they were assembled together; and they were all filled with the Holy Ghost, and they spake the word of God with boldness.

32 And the multitude of them that believed were of one heart and of one soul: neither said any of them that ought of the things which he possessed was his own; but they had all things common.

33 And with great power gave the apostles witness of the resurrection of the Lord Jesus: and great grace was upon them all.

34 Neither was there any among them

Therefore, seeing we are so far from the kingdom of God, it is needful that God do not only invite us unto himself, but that reaching out his hand he offer salvation unto us, that we may enjoy the same. Peter teacheth in this place, that he hath done that in Christ, because he came down into the earth for this cause, that he might bring salvation with him, Neither is that contrary to this doctrine, that Christ is ascended above all heavens (Ephesians 4: 10). For he took upon him our flesh once for this cause, that he might be a continual pledge of our adoption. He hath reconciled the Father to us for ever by the sacrifice of his death: by his resurrection he hath purchased for us eternal life. And he is present with us now also, that he may make us partakers of the fruit of eternal redemption; but the revealing of salvation is handled in this place, and we know that the same was so revealed in Christ, that we need not any longer to say, "Who shall ascend into heaven?" (Romans 10: 6). And if so be this doctrine were deeply imprinted in the minds of all men, then should so many controversies concerning the causes of salvation be soon at an end, wherewith the Church is so much troubled. The Papists confess with us, that salvation is in God alone, but by and by they forge to themselves infinite ways to attain unto the same. But Peter calleth us back unto Christ alone. They dare not altogether deny that we have salvation given us by Christ; but whilst they feign so many helps, they leave him scarce the hundredth part of salvation. But they were to seek for salvation at the hands of Christ wholly; for when Peter excludeth plainly all other means, he placeth perfect salvation in Christ alone, and not some part thereof only. So that they are far from understanding this doctrine.

33. And with great power

Luke signifies that the zeal which the apostles had to preach the gospel was so far from being diminished, that they were rather endowed with new power. Whereas he doth only name the resurrection of Christ, it is synecdoche; for this part is put for the whole gospel. But Luke maketh mention of the resurrection alone, because it is, as it were, the furnishing or fulfilling of the gospel; and, secondly, because they had endured a sore combat for the same, and the Sadducees were sore grieved at it, who aid then bear the chief sway. And great grace was. He signifieth that this served not a little to the spreading abroad of doctrine, in that, by helping the poor so bountifully, they found favor at the hands of strangers. For he saith that they were beloved, because they were beneficial. Therefore, there is a showing of a reason in these words, No man amongst them did lack. Although we need not doubt of this, but that their honesty, and temperance, and modesty, and patience, and other virtues, did provoke many to bear them good-will. He declareth

ment. They contain the great principle of the Christian, and of the Protestant religion, that the responsibility of men for their religious opinions is direct to God, and that other men have no power of control. The opposite of this is tyranny and oppression.

26. The kings of the earth. The Psalmist specifies more particularly that kings and rulers would be opposed to the Messiah. This had occurred already by the opposition made to the Messiah by the rulers of the Jewish people; and it would be still more evinced by princes and kings, as the gospel should spread among the nations.

The rulers. This is another instance of the Hebrew parallelism. The word does not denote another class of men from kings, but expresses the same idea in another form, or in a more general manner, meaning that all classes of persons in authority would be opposed to the gospel.

Were gathered together. Hebrew, consulted together; were united in a consultation. The Greek implies that they were assembled for the purpose of consultation.

Against the Lord. In the Hebrew, "against Jehovah." This is the peculiar name which is given in the Scriptures to God. They rose against his plan of appointing a Messiah, and against the Messiah whom he had chosen.

Against his Christ. Hebrew, against his Messiah, or his Anointed.

This is one of the places where the word Messiah is used in the Old Testament. The word occurs in about forty places, and is commonly translated his anointed, and is applied to kings. The direct reference of the word to the Messiah in the Old Testament is not frequent. This passage implies that opposition to the Messiah is opposition to Jehovah. And this is uniformly supposed in the sacred Scriptures. He that is opposed to Christ is opposed to God. He that neglects him neglects God. He that despises him despises God, Matt. 10: 40; 18: 5; John 12: 44–45; Luke 10: 16, "He that despiseth me despiseth him that sent me." The reasons of this are,

(1.) that the Messiah is "the brightness of the Father's glory, and the express image of his" subsistence, Heb. 1: 3.

(2.) He is equal with the Father, possessing the same attributes, and the same power, John 1: 1; Phil. 2: 6, etc. To despise him, therefore, is to despise God.

(3.) He is appointed by God to this great work of saving men. To despise him, or to oppose him, is to despise and oppose him who appointed him to this work, to contemn his counsels, and to set him at nought.

(4.) His work is dear to God. It has engaged his thoughts. It has been approved by him. His mission has been confirmed by the miraculous power of the Father, and by every possible manifestation of his approbation and love. To oppose the Messiah is, therefore, to oppose that which is dear to the heart of God, and which has long been the object of his tender solicitude.

31. And when they had prayed. The event which followed was regarded by them as an evidence that God heard their prayer.

The place was shaken. The word which is translated "was shaken," commonly denotes violent agitation, as the raging of the sea, the convulsion of an earthquake, or trees shaken by the wind, Matt. 11: 7; Acts 16: 26; Heb. 12: 26. The language here is fitted to express the idea of an earthquake.

They were all filled, etc. Their being filled with the Holy Ghost, here, rather denotes their being inspired with confidence or boldness, than being endowed with new powers, as in Acts 2: 4.

32. One heart. This expression denotes tender union. They felt alike, or were attached to the same things, and this preserved them from jars and dissensions.

One soul. This phrase also denotes close and tender union. No expression could denote it more strikingly than to say of friends they have one soul. Plutarch cites an ancient verse in his life of Cato of Utica, with this very expression, "Two friends, one soul" (Grotius). Thus Diogenes Laertius also says respecting Aristotle, that "being asked what was a friend, answered, that it was one soul dwelling in two bodies."

35. And laid them down, etc. That is, they committed the money received for their prop-

that lacked: for as many as were possessors of lands or houses sold them, and brought the prices of the things that were sold,

35 And laid them down at the apostles' feet: and distribution was made unto every man according as he had need.

36 And Joses, who by the apostles was surnamed Barnabas, (which is, being interpreted, The son of consolation,) a Levite, and of the country of Cyprus,

37 Having land, sold it, and brought the money, and laid it at the apostles' feet.

ACTS 5

1 But a certain man named Ananias, with Sapphira his wife, sold a possession,

2 And kept back part of the price, his wife also being privy to it, and brought a certain part, and laid it at the apostles' feet.

3 But Peter said, Ananias, why hath Satan filled thine heart to lie to the Holy Ghost, and to keep back part of the price of the land?

4 Whiles it remained, was it not thine own? and after it was sold, was it not in thine own power? why hast thou conceived this thing in thine heart? thou hast not lied unto men, but unto God.

5 And Ananias hearing these words fell down, and gave up the ghost: and great fear came on all them that heard these things.

6 And the young men arose, wound him up, and carried him out, and buried him.

7 And it was about the space of three hours after, when his wife, not knowing what was done, came in.

8 And Peter answered unto her, Tell me whether ye sold the land for so much? And she said, Yea, for so much.

9 Then Peter said unto her, How is it that ye have agreed together to tempt the Spirit of the Lord? behold, the feet of them which have buried thy husband are at the door, and shall carry thee out.

10 Then fell she down straightway at his feet, and yielded up the ghost: and the young men came in, and found her dead, and, carrying her forth, buried her by her husband.

11 And great fear came upon all the

afterward, after what sort they had their goods common, which he had touched before, to wit, that the rich men sold their lands and houses, that they might relieve the poverty of the poor.

ACTS 5

1. Those things which Luke hath reported hitherto did show that that company, which was gathered together under the name of Christ, was rather a company of angels than of men, Moreover, that was incredible virtue, that the rich men did despoil themselves of their own accord, not only of their money, but also of their land, that they might relieve the poor. But now he showeth that Satan had invented a shift to get into that holy company, and that under color of such excellent virtue; for he hath wonderful wiles of hypocrisy to insinuate himself. This way doth Satan assault the Church, when as he cannot prevail by open war. But we must specially in this place have respect unto the drift of the Holy Ghost. For in this history he meant to declare, first, how acceptable singleness of heart is to God, and what an abomination hypocrisy is in his sight; secondly, how greatly he approves the holy and pure policy and govermnent of his Church. For this is the principal point, the punishment wherewith punished Ananias and his wife. As the greatness thereof did at that time terrify them all, so it is unto us a testimony that God cannot abide this unfaithfulness, when as bearing a show of holiness where there is none, we do mock him contemptibly. For if, having weighed all the circumstances, we be desirous to know the sum, Luke condemneth no other fault in Ananias than this, that he meant to deceive God and the Church with a reigned offering. Yet there were more evils packed under this dissimulation: the contempt of God, whom he feareth not, though he knew his wickedness; sacrilegious defrauding, because he keepeth back part of that which he professeth to be holy to God; perverse vanity and ambition, because he vaunteth himself in the presence of men, without having any respect unto God's judgment; want of faith, because he would never have gone this way to work, unless he had mistrusted God; the corrupting of a godly and holy order; furthermore, the hypocrisy itself was a great offense of itself. The fact of Ananias did bear a goodly show, although he had given only the half of his land. Neither is this a small virtue, for a rich man to bestow the half of his goods upon the poor; but the sacrifices of the ungodly are an abomination to God (Proverbs 15: 8); neither can any thing please him where the singleness of heart is wanting. For this cause is it that Christ maketh more account of the two mites offered by the widow, than of the great sums of others, who of their great heaps gave some part (Luke 21: 2).

erty to the disposal of the apostles, to distribute it as was necessary among the poor. This soon became a burdensome and inconvenient office, and they therefore appointed men who had especial charge of it, Acts 6: 1–2, etc. Many have been wealthy, and have devoted all to Christ; and in regard to others, it is to be remarked, that a very considerable proportion of them could have gained more wealth in some other profession than they do in the ministry. The ministry is a work of self-denial; and none should enter it who are not prepared to devote all to the service of the Lord Jesus Christ.

ACTS 5

1. **But a certain man.** In the previous chapter, the historian had given an account of the eminent liberality and sincerity of the mass of early Christians, in being willing to give up their property to provide for the poor, and had mentioned the case of Barnabas as worthy of special attention. In this chapter he proceeds to mention a case, quite as striking, of insincerity and hypocrisy, and of the just judgment of God on those who were guilty of it. The case is a remarkable instance of the nature of hypocrisy, and goes to illustrate the art and cunning of the enemy of souls in attempting to corrupt the church, and to pervert the religion of the gospel. Hypocrisy consists in an attempt to imitate the people of God, or to assume the appearance of religion, in whatever form it may be manifested. In this case religion had been manifested by great self-denial and benevolence. The hypocrisy of Ananias consisted in attempting to imitate this appearance, and to impose in this way on the early Christians and on God.

With Sapphira his wife. With her concurrence, or consent. It was a matter of agreement between them, Acts 5: 2,9.

Sold a possession. The word here used does not indicate whether this was land or some other property. In Acts 5: 3, however, we learn that it was land that was sold; and the word here translated possession, is translated in the Syriac, Arabic, and the Latin Vulgate, land. The pretence for which this was sold was doubtless

to have the appearance of religion. That it was sold could be easily known by the Christian society, but it might not be so easily known for how much it was sold. Hence the attempt to impose on the apostles. It is clear that they were not under obligation to sell their property. But having sold it for the purposes of religion, it became their duty, if they professed to devote the avails of it to God, to do it entirely, and without any reservation.

9. **Agreed together.** Conspired, or laid a plan. From this, it seems that Sapphira was as guilty as her husband.

To tempt. To try; to endeavor to impose on, or to deceive; that is, to act as if the Spirit of the Lord could not detect the crime. They did this by trying to see whether the Spirit of God could detect hypocrisy.

At the door. Are near at hand. They had not yet returned. The dead were buried without the walls of cities; and this space of three hours, it seems, had elapsed before they returned from the burial.

Shall carry thee out. This passage shows that it was by Divine interposition or judgment that their lives were taken. The judgment was in immediate connection with their crime, and was designed as an expression of the Divine displeasure.

If it be asked here, why Ananias and Sapphira were punished in this severe and awful manner, an answer may be found in the following considerations:

(1.) This was an atrocious crime, a deep and dreadful act of iniquity. It was committed knowingly, and without excuse, Acts 5: 4. It was important that sudden and exemplary punishment should follow it, because the society of Christians was just then organized, and it was designed that it should be a pure society, and be regarded as a body of holy men. Much was gained by making this impression on the people, that sin could not be allowed in this new community, but would be detected and punished.

(2.) God has often, in a most solemn manner, showed his abhorrence of hypocrisy and insincerity. By awful declarations and fearful judgments he has declared his displeasure at it. In a particular manner no small part

church, and upon as many as heard these things.

12 And by the hands of the apostles were many signs and wonders wrought among the people; (and they were all with one accord in Solomon's porch.

13 And of the rest durst no man join himself to them: but the people magnified them.

14 And believers were the more added to the Lord, multitudes both of men and women.)

15 Insomuch that they brought forth the sick into the streets, and laid them on beds and couches, that at the least the shadow of Peter passing by might overshadow some of them.

16 There came also a multitude out of the cities round about unto Jerusalem, bringing sick folks, and them which were vexed with unclean spirits: and they were healed every one.

17 Then the high priest rose up, and all they that were with him, (which is the sect of the Sadducees,) and were filled with indignation,

18 And laid their hands on the apostles, and put them in the common prison.

19 But the angel of the Lord by night opened the prison doors, and brought them forth, and said,

20 Go, stand and speak in the temple to the people all the words of this life.

21 And when they heard that, they entered into the temple early in the morning, and taught. But the high priest came, and they that were with him, and called the council together, and all the senate of the children of Israel and sent to the prison to have them brought.

22 But when the officers came, and found them not in the prison, they returned, and told,

23 Saying, The prison truly found we shut with all safety, and the keepers standing without before the doors: but when we had opened, we found no man within.

24 Now when the high priest and the captain of the temple and the chief priests heard these things, they doubted of them whereunto this would grow.

25 Then came one and told them, saying, Behold, the men whom ye put in prison are standing in the temple, and

This is the cause why God doth show an example of such sharp punishment in Ananias.

19. The angel of the Lord

The Lord brought the apostles out of prison, not because he would rid them quite out of the hands of their enemies, for he suffered them afterwards to be brought back again, and to be beaten with rods; but he meant to declare, by this miracle, that they were in his hand and tuition, to the end he might maintain the credit of the gospel; partly that the Church might have another confirmation thereby, partly that the wicked might be left without excuse wherefore we must not hope always, nay, we must not always desire that God will deliver us from death; but we must be content with this one thing, that our life is defended by his hand, so far as is expedient. In that he useth the ministry of an angel, in this he doth according to his common custom; for he testifieth every where in the Scriptures, that the angels are ministers of his goodness towards us. Neither is that a vain speculation, for this is a profitable help for our infirmity, that we know that not only God doth care for us, but also that the heavenly spirits do watch for our safety. Again, this was no small pledge of God's love towards us, that the creatures of all other most noble are appointed to have regard of our safety. The angel openeth the prison in the night, because he would not work the miracle when the wicked might see him, although he would have the same being wrought known by the event itself.

29. This is the sum of their answer, It is lawful for them, nay, they ought to prefer God before men. God commandeth us to bear witness of Christ; therefore it is in vain for you to command us to keep silence. But I have declared before in the third chapter, when this sentence taketh place, that we ought rather to obey God than men. God doth set men over us in such sort with power, that he keepeth still his own authority safe and sound. Therefore, we must obey rulers so far, that the commandment of God be not broken. Whereas power and authority is lawfully used, then it is out of season to make comparison between God and man. If a faithful pastor do command or forbid out of the Word of God, it shall be in vain for men which are stubborn to object that we ought to obey God; for God will be heard by man. Yea, man is nothing else but an instrument of God. If a magistrate do his duty as he ought, a man shall in vain say that he is contrary to God, seeing that he dissenteth in nothing; yea, rather the contrary rule is then in force. We must obey God's ministers and officers if we will obey him. But so soon as rulers do lead us away from the obedience of God, because they strive against God with sacrilegious boldness, their pride must be abated, that God may be above

of the preaching of the Savior was employed in detecting the hypocrisy of the scribes and Pharisees, and denouncing heavy judgments on them. See Matt. 23 throughout, for the most sublime and awful denunciation of hypocrisy anywhere to be found.

14. And believers. This is the name by which Christians were designated, because one of the main things that distinguished them was that they believed that Jesus was the Christ. It is also an incidental proof that none should join themselves to the church who are not believers, i.e. who do not profess to be Christians in heart and in life.

Were the more added. The effect of all things was to increase the number of converts. Their persecutions, their preaching, and the judgment of God, all tended to impress the minds of the people, and to lead them to the Lord Jesus Christ. Comp. Acts 4: 4. Though the judgment of God had the effect of deterring hypocrites from entering the church, though it produced awe and caution, yet still the number of true converts was increased. An effort to keep the church pure by wholesome discipline, by cutting off unworthy members, however rich or honored, so far from weakening its true strength, has a tendency greatly to increase its numbers as well as its purity. Men will not seek to enter a corrupt church; or regard it as worth any thought to be connected with a society that does not endeavor to be pure.

19. But the angel of the Lord. This does not denote any particular angel, but simply an angel. The article is not used in the original. The word angel denotes, properly, a messenger, and particularly it is applied to the pure spirits that are sent to this world on errands of mercy.

The case here was evidently a miracle. An angel was employed for this special purpose; and the design might have been,

(1.) to reprove the Jewish rulers, and to convince them of their guilt in resisting the gospel of God;

(2.) to convince the apostles more firmly of the protection and approbation of God;

(3.) to encourage them more and more in

their work, and in the faithful discharge of their high duty; and,

(4.) to give the people a new and impressive proof of the truth of the message which they bore. That they were imprisoned would be known to the people. That they were made as secure as possible was also known. When, therefore, the next morning, before they could have been tried or acquitted, they were found again in the temple, delivering the same message still, it was a new and striking proof that they were sent by God.

23. Found we shut. It had not been broken open; and there was therefore clear proof that they had been delivered by the interposition of God. Nor could they have been released by the guard, for they were keeping watch, as if unconscious that anything had happened, and the officers had the only means of entering the prison.

26. Without violence. Not by force; not by binding them. Comp. Matt. 27: 22. The command of the Sanhedrim was sufficient to secure their presence, as they did not intend to refuse to answer for any alleged violation of the laws. Besides, their going before the council would give them another noble opportunity to bear witness to the truth of the gospel. Christians, when charged with a violation of the laws of the land, should not refuse to answer. Acts 25: 11, "If I be an offender, or have committed anything worthy of death, I refuse not to die." It is a part of our religion to yield obedience to all the just laws of the land, and to evince respect for all that are in authority, Rom. 13: 1–7.

For they feared the people. The people were favorable to the apostles. If violence had been attempted, or they had been taken in a cruel and forcible manner, the consequence would have been a tumult and bloodshed. In this way, also, the apostles showed that they were not disposed to excite tumult. Opposition by them would have excited commotion; and though they would have been rescued, yet they resolved to show that they were not obstinate, contumacious, or rebellious, but were disposed, as far as it could be done with a clear conscience, to yield obedience to the laws of the land.

teaching the people.

26 Then went the captain with the officers, and brought them without violence: for they feared the people, lest they should have been stoned.

27 And when they had brought them, they set them before the council: and the high priest asked them,

28 Saying, Did not we straitly command you that ye should not teach in this name? and, behold, ye have filled Jerusalem with your doctrine, and intend to bring this man's blood upon us.

29 Then Peter and the other apostles answered and said, We ought to obey God rather than men.

30 The God of our fathers raised up Jesus, whom ye slew and hanged on a tree.

31 Him hath God exalted with his right hand to be a Prince and a Savior, for to give repentance to Israel, and forgiveness of sins.

32 And we are his witnesses of these things; and so is also the Holy Ghost, whom God hath given to them that obey him.

33 When they heard that, they were cut to the heart, and took counsel to slay them.

34 Then stood there up one in the council, a Pharisee, named Gamaliel, a doctor of the law, had in reputation among all the people, and commanded to put the apostles forth a little space;

35 And said unto them, Ye men of Israel, take heed to yourselves what ye intend to do as touching these men.

36 For before these days rose up Theudas, boasting himself to be somebody; to whom a number of men, about four hundred, joined themselves: who was slain; and all, as many as obeyed him, were scattered, and brought to nought.

37 After this man rose up Judas of Galilee in the days of the taxing, and drew away much people after him: he also perished; and all, even as many as obeyed him, were dispersed.

38 And now I say unto you, Refrain from these men, and let them alone: for if this counsel or this work be of men, it will come to nought:

39 But if it be of God, ye cannot overthrow it; lest haply ye be found even to

all in authority. Then all smokes of honor vanish away. For God doth not vouchsafe to bestow honorable titles upon men, to the end they may darken his glory. Therefore, if a father, being not content with his own estate, do essay to take from God the chief honor of a father, he is nothing else but a man. If a king, or ruler, or magistrate, do become so lofty that he diminisheth the honor and authority of God, he is but a man. We must thus think also of pastors. For he which goeth beyond his bounds in his office (because he setteth himself against God) must be despoiled of his honor, lest, under a color or visor, he deceive. The office of a pastor is very excellent, the authority of the Church is great, yet so that no part of God's power and Christ's mastership be diminished. Whence we may easily gather that the pride of the Pope is ridiculous, who, when as he treadeth under foot the whole kingdom of Christ, and doth set himself openly against God, will yet, nevertheless, lie hid under the name of Christ.

42. They ceased not

Constancy did also accompany their Joy. For how is it that we are discouraged with persecution, save only because none lifteth up himself unto Christ, that he may in mind lay hold upon the fruit of victory, and so be pricked forward unto patience? But that man which thinketh with himself that he is happy when he suffereth for Christ's sake, shall never faint, though he must suffer hard conflicts. Therefore the apostles are, after a sort, armed with stripes, so that they valiantly make haste unto death. Therefore, woe be to our daintiness, who, having suffered a little persecution, do by and by resign up the light to another, as if we were now old worn soldiers.

ACTS 6

1. Luke declareth here upon what occasion, and to what end, and also with what rite, deacons were first made. He saith, When there arose a murmuring amongst the disciples, it was appeased by this remedy, as it is said in the common proverb, Good laws have taken their beginning of evil manners. And it may seem to be a strange thing, seeing that this is a function so excellent and so necessary in the Church, why it came not into the apostles' minds at the first (before there was any such occasion ministered), to appoint deacons, and why the Spirit of God did not give them such counsel which they take now, being, as it were, enforced thereunto. But that which happened was both better then, and is also more profitable for us at this day, to be unto us an example. If the apostles had spoken of choosing deacons before any necessity did require the same, they should not have had the people so ready; they should have seemed

30. **Raised up Jesus.** This refers to his resurrection.

Hanged on a tree. That is, on the cross, Gal. 3: 13; 1 Pet. 2: 24; Acts 10: 39; 13: 29. This is the amount of Peter's defense. He begins with the great principle (Acts 5: 29), which they could not gainsay, that God ought to be obeyed rather than man. He then proceeds to state that they were convinced that God had raised up Jesus from the dead. And as they had such decisive evidence of that, and were commanded by the authority of the Lord Jesus to be witnesses of that, and had constant evidence that God had done it, they were not at liberty to be silent. They were bound to obey God rather than the Sanhedrim, and to make known everywhere the fact that the Lord Jesus was risen. The remark that God had raised up Jesus, whom they had slain, does not seem to have been made to irritate or to reproach them, but mainly to identify the person that had been raised. It was also a confirmation of the truth and reality of the miracle. Of his death they had no doubt, for they had been at pains to certify it, John 19: 31–34. It is certain, however, that Peter did not shrink from charging on them their guilt; nor was he at any pains to soften or mitigate the severe charge that they had murdered their own Messiah.

32. **And we are his witnesses.** For this purpose they had been appointed, Acts 1: 8,21–22; 2: 32; 3: 15; Luke 24: 48.

Of these things. Particularly of the resurrection of the Lord Jesus, and of the events which had followed it. Perhaps, however, he meant to include everything pertaining to the life, teachings, and death of the Lord Jesus.

And so is also, etc. The descent of the Holy Ghost to endow them with remarkable gifts (Acts 2: 1–4), to awaken and convert such a multitude (Acts 2: 41; 4: 4; 5: 14), was an unanswerable attestation of the truth of these doctrines, and of the Christian religion. So manifest and decided was the presence of God attending them, that they could have no doubt that what they said was true; and so open and public was this attestation, that it was an evidence to all the people of the truth of their doctrine.

33. **When they heard that.** That which the apostle Peter had said; to wit, that they were guilty of murder; that Jesus was raised up; and that he stir lived as the Messiah.

They were cut to the heart. The word used here properly denotes to cut with a saw; and as applied to the mind, it means, to be agitated with rage and indignation, as if wrath should seize upon the mind as a saw does upon wood, and tear it violently, or agitate it severely. It is commonly used in connection with the heart; and means that the heart is violently agitated, and rent with rage. See Acts 7: 54. It is not used elsewhere in the New Testament. The reasons why they were thus indignant were, doubtless, (1.) because the apostles had disregarded their command; (2.) because they charged them with murder; (3.) because they affirmed the doctrine of the resurrection of Jesus, and thus tended to overthrow the sect of the Sadducees. The effect of the doctrines of the gospel is, often, to make men enraged.

Took counsel. The word rendered took counsel denotes, commonly, to will; then, to deliberate; and, sometimes, to decree, or to determine. It doubtless implies here that their minds were made up to do it; but probably the formal decree was not passed to put them to death.

38. **Refrain from these men.** Cease to oppose them, or to threaten them. The reason why he advised this, he immediately adds: that if it were of men, it would come to nought; if of God, they could not overthrow it.

This counsel. This plan, or purpose. If the apostles had originated it for the purposes of imposture.

It will come to nought. Gamaliel inferred that from the two instances which he specified. They had been suppressed without the interference of the Sanhedrim; and he inferred that this would also die away if it was a human device. It will be remembered that this is the mere advice of Gamaliel, who was not inspired; and that this opinion should not be adduced to guide us, except as it was an instance of great shrewdness and prudence. It is, doubtless, right to oppose error in the proper way and with the proper temper – not with arms,

fight against God.

40 And to him they agreed: and when they had called the apostles, and beaten them, they commanded that they should not speak in the name of Jesus, and let them go.

41 And they departed from the presence of the council, rejoicing that they were counted worthy to suffer shame for his name.

42 And daily in the temple, and in every house, they ceased not to teach and preach Jesus Christ.

ACTS 6

1 And in those days, when the number of the disciples was multiplied, there arose a murmuring of the Grecians against the Hebrews, because their widows were neglected in the daily ministration.

2 Then the twelve called the multitude of the disciples unto them, and said, It is not reason that we should leave the word of God, and serve tables.

3 Wherefore, brethren, look ye out among you seven men of honest report, full of the Holy Ghost and wisdom, whom we may appoint over this business.

4 But we will give ourselves continually to prayer, and to the ministry of the word.

5 And the saying pleased the whole multitude: and they chose Stephen, a man full of faith and of the Holy Ghost, and Philip, and Prochorus, and Nicanor, and Timon, and Parmenas, and Nicolas a proselyte of Antioch:

6 Whom they set before the apostles: and when they had prayed, they laid their hands on them.

7 And the word of God increased; and the number of the disciples multiplied in Jerusalem greatly; and a great company of the priests were obedient to the faith.

8 And Stephen, full of faith and power, did great wonders and miracles among the people.

9 Then there arose certain of the synagogue, which is called the synagogue of the Libertines, and Cyrenians, and Alexandrians, and of them of Cilicia and of Asia, disputing with Stephen.

10 And they were not able to resist the wisdom and the spirit by which he spake.

11 Then they suborned men, which said,

to avoid labor and trouble; many would not have offered so liberally into the hands of other men. Therefore, it was requisite that the faithful should be convict [convinced] by experience that they might choose deacons willingly, whom they saw they could not want; and that through their own fault.

We learn in this history that the Church cannot be so framed by and by, but that there remain somewhat to be amended; neither can so great a building be so finished in one day, that there may not something be added to make the same perfect. Furthermore, we learn that there is no ordinance of God so holy and laudable, which is not either corrupt or made unprofitable through the fault of men. We wonder that things are never so well ordered in the world, but that there is always some evil mixed with the good; but it is the wickedness and corruption of our nature which causeth this. That was, indeed, a godly order, whereof Luke made mention before, when the goods of all men being consecrated to God, were distributed to every man as he had need; when as the apostles, being, as it were, the stewards of God and the poor, had the chief government of the alms. But shortly after there ariseth a murmuring which troubleth this order. Here appeareth that corruption of men whereof I have spoken, which doth not suffer us to use our good things. We must also mark the subtilty of Satan, who, to the end he may take from us the use of the gifts of God, goeth about this continually, that it may not remain pure and sound; but that, being mixed with other discommodities, it may, first, be suspected, secondly, loathed, and, lastly, quite taken away. But the apostles have taught us, by their example, that we must not yield unto such engines (and policies) of Satan. For they do not think it meet (being offended with the murmuring) to take away that ministry which they know pleaseth God; but rather invent a remedy whereby the offense may be taken away, and that may be retained which is God's. Thus must we do. For what offenses soever Satan raise, we must take good heed that he take not from us those ordinances which are otherwise wholesome.

12. Being overcome with the power of the Spirit, they give over disputing, but they prepare false witnesses, that with false and slanderous reports, they may oppress him; whereby it appeareth that they did strive with an evil conscience. For what can be more unmeet than in their cause to lean unto lies? Admit he were a wicked man, and guilty, yet he must not have false witness borne against him. But hypocrites, which shroud themselves under zeal, do carelessly grant themselves leave to do that. We see how the Papists at this day corrupt manifest places of Scripture, and that wittingly, whilst that they will falsely wrest testimo-

or vituperation, or with the civil power, but with argument and kind entreaty. But the sentiment of Gamaliel is full of wisdom in regard to error. For,

(1.) the very way to exalt error into notice, and to confirm men in it, is to oppose it in a harsh, authoritative, and unkind manner.

(2.) error, if left alone, will often die away itself. The interest of men in it will often cease as soon as it ceases to be opposed; and having nothing to fan the flame, it will expire. It is not so with truth.

(3.) in this respect the remark may be applied to the Christian religion. It has stood too long, and in too many circumstances of prosperity and adversity, to be of men. It has been subjected to all trials from its pretended friends and real foes; and it still lives as vigorous and flourishing as ever. Other kingdoms have changed; empires have risen and fallen since Gamaliel spoke this; systems of opinion and belief have had their day, and expired; but the preservation of the Christian religion, unchanged through so many revolutions, and in so many fiery trials, shows that it is not of men, but of God. The argument for the Divine origin of the Christian religion from its perpetuity, is one that can be applied to no other system that has been, or that now exists. For Christianity has been opposed in every form. It confers no temporal conquests, and appeals to no base and strong native passions. Mohammedanism is supported by the sword and the state; paganism relies on the arm of the civil power and the terrors of superstition, and is sustained by all the corrupt passions of men; atheism and infidelity have been short-lived, varying in their forms – dying today, and tomorrow starting up in a new form – never organized, consolidated, or pure, and never tending to promote the peace or happiness of men. Christianity, without arms or human power, has lived, holding its steady and triumphant movements among men, regardless alike of the opposition of its foes, and of the treachery of its pretended friends. If the opinion of Gamaliel was just, it is from God; and the Jews particularly should regard as important an argument derived from the opinion of one of the wisest of their ancient Rabbis.

ACTS 6

1. In those days, etc. The first part of this chapter contains an account of the appointment of deacons. It may be asked, perhaps, why the apostles did not appoint these officers at the first organization of the church? To this question we may reply, that it was better to defer the appointment until an occasion should occur when it should appear to be manifestly necessary and proper. When the church was small, its alms could be distributed by the apostles themselves without difficulty; but when it was greatly increased in when its charities would be multiplied, and when the distribution might give rise to contentions, it was necessary that this matter should be entrusted to the hands of laymen, and that the ministry should be freed from all embarrassment, and all suspicions of dishonesty and unfairness in regard to pecuniary matters. It has never been found to be wise that the temporal affairs of the church should be entrusted in any considerable degree to the clergy; and they should be freed from such sources of difficulty and embarrassment.

Was multiplied. By the accession of the three thousand on the day of Pentecost, and of those who were subsequently added, Acts 4: 4; 5: 14.

A murmuring. A complaint – as if there had been partiality in the distribution.

8. And Stephen. The remarkable death of this first Christian martyr, which soon occurred, gave occasion to the sacred writer to give a detailed account of his character, and of the causes which led to his death. Hitherto the opposition of the Jews had been confined to threats and imprisonment; but it was now to burst forth with furious rage and madness, that could be satisfied only with blood. This was the first in a series of persecutions against Christians that filled the church with blood, and that closed the lives of thousands, perhaps millions, in the great work of establishing the gospel on the earth.

Full of faith. Full of confidence in God; or trusting entirely to his promises.

15. Looking stedfastly on him. Fixing the eyes intently on him. Probably they were attracted

We have heard him speak blasphemous words against Moses, and against God.

12 And they stirred up the people, and the elders, and the scribes, and came upon him, and caught him, and brought him to the council,

13 And set up false witnesses, which said, This man ceaseth not to speak blasphemous words against this holy place, and the law:

14 For we have heard him say, that this Jesus of Nazareth shall destroy this place, and shall change the customs which Moses delivered us.

15 And all that sat in the council, looking stedfastly on him, saw his face as it had been the face of an angel.

ACTS 7

1 Then said the high priest, Are these things so?

2 And he said, Men, brethren, and fathers, hearken; The God of glory appeared unto our father Abraham, when he was in Mesopotamia, before he dwelt in Charran,

3 And said unto him, Get thee out of thy country, and from thy kindred, and come into the land which I shall shew thee.

4 Then came he out of the land of the Chaldaeans, and dwelt in Charran: and from thence, when his father was dead, he removed him into this land, wherein ye now dwell.

5 And he gave him none inheritance in it, no, not so much as to set his foot on: yet he promised that he would give it to him for a possession, and to his seed after him, when as yet he had no child.

6 And God spake on this wise, That his seed should sojourn in a strange land; and that they should bring them into bondage, and entreat them evil four hundred years.

7 And the nation to whom they shall be in bondage will I judge, said God: and after that shall they come forth, and serve me in this place.

8 And he gave him the covenant of circumcision: and so Abraham begat Isaac, and circumcised him the eighth day; and Isaac begat Jacob; and Jacob begat the twelve patriarchs.

9 And the patriarchs, moved with envy, sold Joseph into Egypt: but God was with him,

nies against us. I confess, indeed, that they offend for the most part through ignorance; yet can we find none of them which doth not grant himself liberty to corrupt both the sense and also the words of the Scripture, that they may bring our doctrine into contempt; yea, they slander us monstrously even in the pulpit.

ACTS 7

1. There appeareth as yet some color of equity in the high priest and in the council; and yet, notwithstanding, there is a most unjust prejudice in his words; for he asketh him not what cause he had to teach thus, neither doth he admit him unto the defense of right (which was, notwithstanding, the chief); but he demanded precisely whether Stephen uttered these words, whatsoever they were; as the Papists at this day will not demand what doctrine it is, and whether it can be proved out of the Scriptures; but they inquire whether any man durst mutter against their superstitions, that so soon as he is convict, they may forthwith burn him. Furthermore, Stephen's answer may seem at the first blush absurd and foolish. He beginneth first at the very first beginning; afterwards he maketh a long narration, wherein there is no mention made, in a manner, of the matter in hand; and there can be no greater fault than to utter many words which are nothing appertinent unto the matter; but whosoever shall thoroughly consider this long speech, he shall find nothing therein which is superfluous; and shall full well perceive that Stephen speaketh very appertinently, as the matter requireth. He was accused as an apostate (or revolt), which did attempt the overthrow of religion and the worship of God; therefore, he beateth in this diligently, that he retaineth that God which the fathers have always worshipped, so that he turneth away the crime of wicked backsliding; and declareth that his enemies were pricked forward with nothing less than with the zeal of the law, for they bear a show that they were wholly determined to increase the glory of God; therefore, he wringeth from them this false boasting, and because they had the fathers always in their mouths, because they were puffed up with the glory of their nation, Stephen declareth also that they have no cause to be proud of this, but rather that the corruptions of the fathers were so great and so many, that they ought to be ashamed and humbled.

As concerning the principal state of the cause, because the question was concerning the temple and the ceremonies, he affirmeth plainly that their fathers were elected of God to be a peculiar people before there was any temple, and before Moses was born; and to this end tendeth that *exordium* or beginning which is so far fet (fetched). Secondly, he telleth them that all external rites which God gave by the

by the unusual appearance of the man, his meekness, and calm and collected fearlessness, and the proofs of conscious innocence and sincerity.

The face of an angel. This expression is one evidently denoting that he manifested evidence of sincerity, gravity, fearlessness, confidence in God. It is used in the Old Testament to denote peculiar wisdom, 2 Sam. 14: 17; 19: 27. In Gen. 33: 10, it is used to denote peculiar majesty and glory, as if it were the face of God. When Moses came down from Mount Sinai from communing with God, it is said that the skin of his face shone, so that the children of Israel were afraid to come nigh to him.

ACTS 7

2. Men, brethren, and fathers. These were the usual titles by which the Sanhedrim was addressed. In all this Stephen was perfectly respectful, and showed that he was disposed to render due honor to the institutions of the nation.

The God of glory. This is a Hebrew form of expression denoting the glorious God. It properly denotes his majesty, or splendor, or magnificence; and the word glory is often applied to the splendid appearances in which God has manifested himself to men, Deut. 5: 24; Ex. 33: 18; 16: 7,10; Lev. 9: 23; Num. 14: 10.

Perhaps Stephen meant to affirm that God appeared to Abraham in some such glorious or splendid manifestation, by which he would know that he was addressed by God. Stephen, moreover, evidently uses the word glory to repel the charge of blasphemy against God, and to show that he regarded him as worthy of honor and praise.

Appeared, etc. In what manner he appeared is not said. In Gen. 12: 1, it is simply recorded that God had said unto Abraham, etc.

Unto our father. The Jews valued themselves much on being the children of Abraham. This expression was therefore well calculated to conciliate their minds.

9. Moved with envy. That is, dissatisfied with the favor which their father Jacob showed Joseph, and envious at the dreams which indi-

cated that he was to be raised to remarkable honor above his parents and brethren, Gen. 37: 3–11.

Sold Joseph into Egypt. Sold him, that he might be taken to Egypt. This was done at the suggestion of Judah, who advised it that Joseph might not be put to death by his brethren, Gen. 27: 28. It is possible that Stephen, by this fact, might have designed to prepare the way for a severe rebuke of the Jews for having dealt in a similar manner with their Messiah.

But God was with him. God protected him, and overruled all these wicked doings, so that he was raised to extraordinary honors.

10. And delivered him, etc. That is, restored him to liberty from his servitude and humiliation, and raised him up to high honors and offices in Egypt.

Favor and wisdom. The favor was the result of his wisdom. His wisdom was particularly evinced in interpreting the dreams of Pharaoh, Gen. 41.

20. In which time, etc. During this period of oppression. See Ex. 2: 2, etc.

Was exceeding fair. Greek, "was fair to God;" properly rendered, was very handsome. The word God is used in the Greek here in accordance with the Hebrew usage, by which anything that is very handsome, or lofty, or grand, is thus designated. Thus, Ps. 36: 7, mountains of God mean lofty mountains; Ps. 80: 10, (ver. 11, Heb.) cedars of God mean lofty, beautiful cedars. Thus Nineveh is called "a great city to God," (Jon. 3: 3, Greek) meaning a very great city. The expression here means simply, that Moses was very fair, or handsome. Comp. Heb. 11: 23, where he is called a "proper child," i.e., a handsome child. It would seem from this, that Moses was preserved by his mother on account of his beauty; and this is hinted at in Ex. 2: 2. And it would also seem from this, that Pharaoh had succeeded by his oppressions in what he had attempted; and that it was not unusual for parents among the Jews to expose their children, or to put them to death.

21. Was cast out. When he was exposed on the banks of the Nile, Ex. 2: 3.

And nourished him. Adopted him, and

10 And delivered him out of all his afflictions, and gave him favor and wisdom in the sight of Pharaoh king of Egypt; and he made him governor over Egypt and all his house.

11 Now there came a dearth over all the land of Egypt and Chanaan, and great affliction: and our fathers found no sustenance.

12 But when Jacob heard that there was corn in Egypt, he sent out our fathers first.

13 And at the second time Joseph was made known to his brethren; and Joseph's kindred was made known unto Pharaoh.

14 Then sent Joseph, and called his father Jacob to him, and all his kindred, threescore and fifteen souls.

15 So Jacob went down into Egypt, and died, he, and our fathers,

16 And were carried over into Sychem, and laid in the sepulcher that Abraham bought for a sum of money of the sons of Emmor the father of Sychem.

17 But when the time of the promise drew nigh, which God had sworn to Abraham, the people grew and multiplied in Egypt,

18 Till another king arose, which knew not Joseph.

19 The same dealt subtilly with our kindred, and evil entreated our fathers, so that they cast out their young children, to the end they might not live.

20 In which time Moses was born, and was exceeding fair, and nourished up in his father's house three months:

21 And when he was cast out, Pharaoh's daughter took him up, and nourished him for her own son.

22 And Moses was learned in all the wisdom of the Egyptians, and was mighty in words and in deeds.

23 And when he was full forty years old, it came into his heart to visit his brethren the children of Israel.

24 And seeing one of them suffer wrong, he defended him, and avenged him that was oppressed, and smote the Egyptian:

25 For he supposed his brethren would have understood how that God by his hand would deliver them: but they understood not.

hand of Moses were fashioned according to the heavenly pattern.

Whereupon it followeth, that the ceremonial law is referred unto another end, and that those deal foolishly and disorderly who omit the truth, and stay only in the signs. If the readers shall refer the whole oration of Stephen unto these points, they shall find nothing therein which agreeth not very well with the cause, as I shall declare again briefly in the end; nevertheless, that scope of the whole oration shall not hinder but that we may discuss all things briefly which are worth the noting.

17. Stephen passes over unto the deliverance of the people, before which went that innumerable issue which had increased beyond the ordinary manner in no long space of time. Therefore, he setteth down this as a singular gift of God, that the people was increased, to the end we may know that that came not to pass according to the common or wonted custom of nature. But, on the other side, God seemeth to take from the Jews all hope, because Pharaoh doth tyrannously afflict them, and their bondage groweth greater daily. And when as they are commanded to cast out their male infants, it seemeth that the destruction of the whole nation was present. There is another token of deliverance given, when Moses cometh abroad; but because he is by and by refused and enforced to fly into exile, there remaineth nothing but mere despair. The sum is this; that God, being mindful of his promise, did increase the people in time, that he might perform that which he had sworn to Abraham; but the Jews (as they were unthankful and froward) did refuse the grace of God, so that they did what they could to shut up the way before themselves. Furthermore, we must note the providence of God in this place, whilst that he doth so order the course of times, that his works have always their opportunity. But men who make haste disorderly in their desires cannot hope patiently, and be at rest, until such time as God showeth forth his hand; for this cause, because they take no heed to that moderation whereof I have spoken. And to the end God may exercise the faith of his children so often as he appeareth with joyful tokens of grace, he setteth other things against those on the other side, which cut off suddenly the hope of salvation. For who would not have said of the Hebrews, that they were utterly undone, when as the king's commandment appointed all the men children to be put to death? For which cause the meditating upon that doctrine is the most [more] necessary for us, that God doth kill and restore to life; he leadeth unto hell, and bringeth back again.

33. Because the place wherein

The Lord meant by this commendation which he giveth

treated him as her son, Ex. 2: 10. It is implied in this, that he was educated by her. An adopted son in the family of Pharaoh would be favored with all the advantages which the land could furnish for an education.

29. Then fled Moses, etc. Moses fled because he now ascertained that it was known. He supposed that it had been unobserved, Ex. 2: 12. But he now supposed that the knowledge of it might reach Pharaoh, and that his life might thus be endangered. Nor did he judge incorrectly; for as soon as Pharaoh heard of it, he sought to take his life, Ex. 2: 16.

Was a stranger. Or became a sojourner, one who had a temporary abode in the land. The use of this word implies that he did not expect to make that his permanent dwelling.

In the land of Madian. This was a part of Arabia. It was situated on the east side of the Red Sea. The city of Midian is placed there by the Arabian geographers; but the Midianites seem to have spread themselves along the desert east of Mount Seir, to the vicinity of the Moabites. To the west they ex, tended also to the neighborhood of Mount Sinai. This was extensively a desert region, an unknown land; and Moses expected there to be safe from Pharaoh.

34. I have seen, etc. The repetition of this word is in accordance with the usage of the Hebrew writers when they wish to represent anything emphatically.

Their groaning. Under their oppressions.

Am come down. This is spoken in accordance with human conceptions. It means that God was about to deliver them.

I will send this, etc. This is a mere summary of what is expressed at much greater length in Ex. 3: 7–10.

35. When they refused. That is, when he first presented himself to them, Ex. 2: 13–14. Stephen introduces and dwells upon this refusal in order, perhaps, to remind them that this had been the character of their nation; and to prepare the way for the charge which he intended to bring against those whom he addressed, as being stiff-necked and rebellious. See Acts 7: 51–52, etc.

A ruler. A military leader, or a governor in civil matters.

A deliverer. A Redeemer. It properly means one who redeems a captive or a prisoner by paying a price or ransom. And it is applied thus to our Lord Jesus, as having redeemed or purchased sinners by his blood as a price, Titus 2: 14; 1 Pet. 1: 18; Heb. 9: 12.

38. In the church. The word church means, literally, the people called out; and is applied with great propriety to the assembly or multitude called out of Egypt, and separated from the world. It has not, however, of necessity our idea of a church; but means the assembly, or people called out of Egypt, and placed under the con- duct of Moses,

With the angel. In this place there is undoubted reference to the giving of the law on Mount Sinai. Yet that was done by God himself, Ex. 20. It is clear, therefore, that by the angel here Stephen intends to designate him who was God. It may be observed, however, that the law is represented as having been given by the ministry of an angel (in this place), and by the ministry of angels, Acts 7: 53; Heb. 2: 2. The essential idea is, that God did it by a messenger, or by mediators. The character and rank of the messengers, or of the principal messenger, must be learned by looking at all the circumstances of the case.

The lively oracles. See Rom. 3: 2. The word oracles here means commands or laws of God, The word lively, or living stands in opposition to that which is dead, or useless, and means that which is vigorous, efficacious; and in this place it means that the commands were of such a nature, and given in such circumstances, as to secure attention; to produce obedience; to excite them to act for God – in opposition to laws which would fall powerless, and produce no effect.

39. Would not obey, etc. This refers to what they said of him when he was in the mount, Ex. 32: 1,23.

In their hearts turned, etc. They wished to return to Egypt. They regretted that they had come out of Egypt, and desired again the things which they had there, as preferable to what they had in the desert, Num. 11: 5. Perhaps, however, the expression means, not

26 And the next day he shewed himself unto them as they strove, and would have set them at one again, saying, Sirs, ye are brethren; why do ye wrong one to another?

27 But he that did his neighbour wrong thrust him away, saying, Who made thee a ruler and a judge over us?

28 Wilt thou kill me, as thou diddest the Egyptian yesterday?

29 Then fled Moses at this saying, and was a stranger in the land of Madian, where he begat two sons.

30 And when forty years were expired, there appeared to him in the wilderness of mount Sina an angel of the Lord in a flame of fire in a bush.

31 When Moses saw it, he wondered at the sight: and as he drew near to behold it, the voice of the Lord came unto him,

32 Saying, I am the God of thy fathers, the God of Abraham, and the God of Isaac, and the God of Jacob. Then Moses trembled, and durst not behold.

33 Then said the Lord to him, Put off thy shoes from thy feet: for the place where thou standest is holy ground.

34 I have seen, I have seen the affliction of my people which is in Egypt, and I have heard their groaning, and am come down to deliver them. And now come, I will send thee into Egypt.

35 This Moses whom they refused, saying, Who made thee a ruler and a judge? the same did God send to be a ruler and a deliverer by the hand of the angel which appeared to him in the bush.

36 He brought them out, after that he had shewed wonders and signs in the land of Egypt, and in the Red sea, and in the wilderness forty years.

37 This is that Moses, which said unto the children of Israel, A prophet shall the Lord your God raise up unto you of your brethren, like unto me; him shall ye hear.

38 This is he, that was in the church in the wilderness with the angel which spake to him in the mount Sina, and with our fathers: who received the lively oracles to give unto us:

39 To whom our fathers would not obey, but thrust him from them, and in their hearts turned back again into Egypt,

40 Saying unto Aaron, Make us gods to go before us: for as for this Moses, which

to the place, to lift up the mind of Moses into heaven, that he might not think upon any earthly thing. And if so be that Moses was to be pricked forward with so many pricks, that having forgotten the earth, he might hearken to God, must not we have our sides even, as it were, digged through, seeing we are an hundred times more slow than he? Notwithstanding, here may a question be asked, how this place became so holy? for it was no more holy than other places before that day. I answer, that this honor is given to the presence of God, and not to the place, and that the holiness of the place is spoken of for man's sake. For if the presence of God do make the earth holy, how much more force thereof ought men to have? Notwithstanding, we must also note, that the place was thus beautified only for a time, so that God did not fix his glory there, as Jacob erected an altar to God in Bethel, after that God had showed some token of his presence there (Genesis 35: 7). When as his posterity did imitate the same afterward, it was such worship as was reproved. Finally, the place is called holy for Moses' sake only, that he may the better address himself to fear God and to obey him. Forasmuch as God doth now show himself unto us everywhere in Christ, and that in no obscure figures, but in the full light and perfect truth, we must not only put off our shoes from our feet, but strip ourselves stark-naked of ourselves.

41. And they made a calf

We may easily gather by that which goeth before, why they were more delighted in that figure than in any other. For although Egypt did swarm with innumerable idols, yet it is well known that they made the greatest account of an ox. And whence is it that they are so desirous to have an idol, save only because they were turned back into Egypt, as Stephen hath already said? We must note the speech when he saith that they offered sacrifice to the idol. Aaron commandeth the people to assemble themselves together to worship God; they come all together. Therefore they testify that they mean nothing less [any thing rather] than to defraud God of his worship, howsoever they translate the same unto the calf; yea, rather, they are determined to worship God in the image of the calf. But because they forsook the true God, by making an idol, whatsoever followeth afterward it is judged to be given to the idol, because God refuseth all wicked worshipping. For it is not meet to account that as bestowed upon him which he hath not commanded; and because he forbids them expressly to erect any visible image unto him, that is mere sacrilege whatsoever is done afterward in honor thereof.

56. Behold, I see the heavens

God meant not only privately to provide for his servant,

that they desired literally to return to Egypt, but that their hearts inclined to the habits and morals of the Egyptians. They forsook God, and imitated the idolatries of the Egyptians.

40. Saying unto Aaron. Ex. 32: 1
Make us gods. That is, idols.

42. Then God turned. That is, turned away from them; abandoned them to their own desires.
　The host of heaven. The stars, or heavenly bodies. The word host means armies. It is applied to the heavenly bodies, because they are very numerous, and appear to be marshaled or arrayed in military order. It is from this that God is called JEHOVAH of hosts, as being the Ruler of these well-arranged heavenly bodies, Is. 1: 9. The proof that they did this, Stephen proceeds to allege by a quotation from the prophets.
　In the book of the Prophets. Amos 5: 25–26. The twelve minor prophets were commonly written in one volume, and were called the Book of the Prophets; the book containing these several prophecies, Daniel, Hosea, Micah, etc. They were small tracts separately, and were bound up together to preserve them from being lost. This passage is not quoted literally; it is evidently made from memory; and though in its main spirit it coincides with the passage in Amos, yet in some important respects it varies from it.

43. Yea, ye took up. That is, you bore, or you carried with you, for purposes of idolatrous worship.
　The tabernacle. This word properly means a tent; but it is also applied to the small tent or house in which was contained the image of the god; the house, box, or tent, in which the idol was placed. It is customary for idolatrous nations to bear their idols about with them, enclosed in cases or boxes of various sizes, usually very small, as their idols are commonly small. Probably they were made in the shape of small temples or tabernacles; and such appear to have been the silver shrines for Diana, made at Ephesus, Acts 19: 24. These shrines, or images, were borne with them as a species of amulet, or charm, or talisman, to defend them from evil. Such images the Jews

seem to have borne with them.
　Moloch. This word comes from the Hebrew word signifying king. This was a god of the Ammonites, to whom human sacrifices were offered. Moses in several places forbids the Israelites, under penalty of death, to dedicate their children to Moloch, by making them pass through the fire, Lev. 18: 21; 20: 2–5. There is great probability that the Hebrews were addicted to the worship of this deity after they entered the land of Canaan. Solomon built a temple to Moloch on the Mount of Olives, 1 Kgs. 11: 7; and Manasseh made his son pass through the fire in honor of this idol, 2 Kgs. 21: 3,6. The image of this idol was made of brass, and his arms extended so as to embrace any one; and when they offered children to him, they heated the statue, and when it was burning hot, they placed the child in his arms, where it was soon destroyed by heat. It is not certain what this god was supposed to represent. Some suppose it was in honor of the planet Saturn, others the sun, others Mercury, Venus, etc. What particular god it was, is not material. It was the most cutting reproof that could be made to the Jews, that their fathers had been guilty of worshipping this idol.

47. But Solomon, etc. Built the temple. David was not permitted to do it, because he had been a man of war, 1 Chr. 22: 8. David prepared the principal materials for the temple, but Solomon built it, 1 Chr. 22; comp. 1 Kgs. 6.

48. Howbeit. But. Why Stephen added this, is not very clear. He was charged with speaking against the temple. He had now shown that he had due veneration for it, by his declaring that it had been built by the command of God. But he now adds, that God does not need such a temple. Heaven is his throne; the universe his dwelling-place; and therefore this temple might be destroyed. A new, glorious truth was to be revealed to mankind, that God was not confined in his worship to any age, or people, or nation. In entire consistency, therefore, with all proper respect for the temple at Jerusalem, it might be maintained that the time would come when that temple would be destroyed, and when God might be worshipped by all nations.

brought us out of the land of Egypt, we wot not what is become of him.

41 And they made a calf in those days, and offered sacrifice unto the idol, and rejoiced in the works of their own hands.

42 Then God turned, and gave them up to worship the host of heaven; as it is written in the book of the prophets, O ye house of Israel, have ye offered to me slain beasts and sacrifices by the space of forty years in the wilderness?

43 Yea, ye took up the tabernacle of Moloch, and the star of your god Remphan, figures which ye made to worship them: and I will carry you away beyond Babylon.

44 Our fathers had the tabernacle of witness in the wilderness, as he had appointed, speaking unto Moses, that he should make it according to the fashion that he had seen.

45 Which also our fathers that came after brought in with Jesus into the possession of the Gentiles, whom God drave out before the face of our fathers, unto the days of David;

46 Who found favor before God, and desired to find a tabernacle for the God of Jacob.

47 But Solomon built him an house.

48 Howbeit the most High dwelleth not in temples made with hands; as saith the prophet,

49 Heaven is my throne, and earth is my footstool: what house will ye build me? saith the Lord: or what is the place of my rest?

50 Hath not my hand made all these things?

51 Ye stiffnecked and uncircumcised in heart and ears, ye do always resist the Holy Ghost: as your fathers did, so do ye.

52 Which of the prophets have not your fathers persecuted? and they have slain them which shewed before of the coming of the Just One; of whom ye have been now the betrayers and murderers:

53 Who have received the law by the disposition of angels, and have not kept it.

54 When they heard these things, they were cut to the heart, and they gnashed on him with their teeth.

55 But he, being full of the Holy Ghost, looked up stedfastly into heaven, and saw

but also to wring and torment his enemies; as Stephen doth courageously triumph over them, when he affirmeth plainly that he saw a miracle. And here may a question be moved, how the heavens were opened? For mine own part, I think that there was nothing changed in the nature of the heavens; but that Stephen had new quickness of sight granted him, which pierced through all lets, even unto the invisible glory of the kingdom of heaven. For admit we grant that there was some division or parting made in heaven, yet man's eye could never reach so far. Again, Stephen alone did see the glory of God. For that spectacle was not only hid from the wicked, who stood in the same place, but they were also so blinded within themselves, that they did not see the manifest truth. Therefore, he saith that the heavens are opened to him in this respect, because nothing keepeth him from beholding the glory of God. Whereupon it followeth that the miracle was not wrought in heaven, but in his eyes. Wherefore, there is no cause why we should dispute long about any natural vision; because it is certain that Christ appeared unto him not after some natural manner, but after a new and singular sort. And I pray you of what color was the glory of God, that it could be seen naturally with the eyes of the flesh? Therefore, we must imagine nothing in this vision but that which is divine. Moreover, this is worth the noting, that the glory of God appeared not unto Stephen wholly as it was, but according to man's capacity. For that infiniteness cannot be comprehended with the measure of any creature.

The Son of man standing

He seeth Christ reigning in that flesh wherein he was abased; so that in very deed the victory did consist in this one thing. Therefore, it is not superfluous in that Christ appeareth unto him, and for this cause doth he also call him the Son of man, as if he should say, I see that man whom ye thought ye had quite extinguished by death enjoying the government of heaven; therefore, gnash with your teeth as much as you list: there is no cause why I should fear to fight for him even unto blood, who shall not only defend his own cause, but my salvation also. Notwithstanding, here may a question be moved, why he saw him standing, who is said elsewhere to sit? Augustine, as he is sometimes more subtle than needs, saith, "that he sitteth as a judge, that he stood then as an advocate." For mine own part, I think that though these speeches be diverse, yet they signify both one thing. For neither sitting, nor yet standing, noteth out how the body of Christ was framed; but this is referred unto his power and kingdom. For where shall we erect him a throne, that he may sit at the right hand of God the Father, seeing God doth fill all things in such sort, that we ought to imagine no place for his right hand?

The Most High. God. This sentiment was expressed by Solomon when the temple was dedicated, 1 Kgs. 8: 27.

As saith the prophet. Is. 66: 1–2. The place is not literally quoted, but the sense is given.

49. What house, etc. What house or temple can be large or magnificent enough for the dwelling of Him who made all things?

The place of my rest. My home, my abode, my fixed seat or habitation. Comp. Ps. 95: 11.

51. Ye stiffnecked. The discourse of Stephen has every appearance of having been interrupted by the clamors and opposition of the Sanhedrim. This verse has no immediate connection with that which precedes; and appears to have been spoken in the midst of much opposition and clamor. If we may conjecture in this case, it would seem that the Jews saw the drift of his argument; that they interrupted him; and that when the tumult had somewhat subsided, he addressed them in the language of this verse, showing them that they sustained a character precisely similar to their rebellious fathers. The word stiff-necked is often used in the Old Testament. It is a figurative expression taken from oxen that were refractory, and that would not submit to be yoked. Applied to men, it means that they were stubborn, contumacious, and unwilling to submit to the restraints of law.

Uncircumcised in heart. Circumcision was a sign of being a Jew – of acknowledging the authority of the laws of Moses. It was also emblematic of purity, and of submission to the law of God. The expression uncircumcised in heart denotes those who were not willing to acknowledge the law, and submit to it. They had hearts filled with vicious and unsubdued affections and desires.

And ears. That is, who are unwilling to hear what God says. Comp. Lev. 26: 41; Jer. 9: 26.

Resist the Holy Ghost. You oppose the message which is brought to you by the authority of God, and the inspiration of his Spirit. The message brought by Moses, by the prophets, by the Savior, and by the apostles – all by the infallible direction of the Holy Ghost – they and their fathers opposed.

As your fathers did, etc. As he had specified in Acts 7: 27,35,39–43.

52. Which of the prophets, etc. The interrogative form here is a strong mode of saying that they had persecuted all the prophets. It was the characteristic of the nation to persecute the messengers of God. This is not to be taken as literally and universally true; but it was a general truth; it was the national characteristic.

And they have slain them, etc. That is, they have slain the prophets, whose main message was that the Messiah was to come. It was a great aggravation of their offence, that they put to death the messengers which foretold the greatest blessing that the nation could receive.

The Just One. The Messiah.

Of whom ye, etc. You thus show that you resemble those who rejected and put to death the prophets. You have even gone beyond them in guilt, because you have put the Messiah himself to death.

The betrayers. They are called betrayers here, because they employed Judas to betray him – agreeable to the maxim in law, He who does anything by another, is held to have done it himself.

54. They were cut to the heart. They were exceedingly enraged and indignant. The whole course of the speech had been such as to excite their anger, and now they could restrain themselves no longer.

They gnashed on him, etc. Expressive of the bitterness and malignity.

55. Looked up stedfastly. Fixed his eyes intently on heaven. Foreseeing his danger, and the effect his speech had produced – seeing that there was no safety in the great council of the nation, and no prospect of justice at their hands-he cast his eyes to heaven and sought protection them. When dangers threaten us, our hope of safety lies in heaven. When men threaten our persons, reputation, or lives, it becomes us to fix our eyes on the heavenly world; and we shall not look in vain.

And saw the glory of God. This phrase is commonly used to denote the visible symbols of God. It means some magnificent representation; a splendor, or light, that is the appro-

the glory of God, and Jesus standing on the right hand of God,

56 And said, Behold, I see the heavens opened, and the Son of man standing on the right hand of God.

57 Then they cried out with a loud voice, and stopped their ears, and ran upon him with one accord,

58 And cast him out of the city, and stoned him: and the witnesses laid down their clothes at a young man's feet, whose name was Saul.

59 And they stoned Stephen, calling upon God, and saying, Lord Jesus, receive my spirit.

60 And he kneeled down, and cried with a loud voice, Lord, lay not this sin to their charge. And when he had said this, he fell asleep.

ACTS 8

1 And Saul was consenting unto his death. And at that time there was a great persecution against the church which was at Jerusalem; and they were all scattered abroad throughout the regions of Judaea and Samaria, except the apostles.

2 And devout men carried Stephen to his burial, and made great lamentation over him.

3 As for Saul, he made havock of the church, entering into every house, and haling men and women committed them to prison.

4 Therefore they that were scattered abroad went every where preaching the word.

5 Then Philip went down to the city of Samaria, and preached Christ unto them.

6 And the people with one accord gave heed unto those things which Philip spake, hearing and seeing the miracles which he did.

7 For unclean spirits, crying with loud voice, came out of many that were possessed with them: and many taken with palsies, and that were lame, were healed.

8 And there was great joy in that city.

9 But there was a certain man, called Simon, which beforetime in the same city used sorcery, and bewitched the people of Samaria, giving out that himself was some great one:

10 To whom they all gave heed, from

60. Kneeling down, he cried

This is the other part of his prayer, wherein he joineth the love of men with faith in Christ; and surely if we desire to be gathered to Christ for our salvation, we must put on this affection. Whereas Stephen prayeth for his enemies, and those most deadly, and even in the very instant when their cruelty might provoke him unto desire of revenge, he declareth sufficiently what affection he beareth toward all other men.

ACTS 8

In this history we may first see the state of the godly in this world, to wit, that they are like sheep appointed to be slain, as it is in the Psalm (Psalm 44: 22); and especially when the Lord letteth loose the bridle to his enemies, that they may put that cruelty in execution which they have in mind conceived. Secondly, here is set down the end of persecutions, to wit, that they are so far from breaking off the course of the gospel, that they are rather made helps to further the same through the wonderful counsel of God. Like as it was a manifest miracle, that the scattering abroad, mentioned by Luke, gathered many unto the unity of faith who were estranged from God before. Now, let us consider every thing in order.

1. At that day

The persecution began at Stephen, after that, when their madness was thereby set on fire, it waxed hot against all, both one and other. For the wicked are like brute beasts, for when they have once tasted blood they are more desirous thereof, and become more cruel through committing murder. For Satan, who is the father of all cruelty, doth first take from them all feeling of humanity when they are once imbrued with innocent blood; that done, he stirreth up in them an unquenchable thirsting after blood, whence those violent assaults to commit murder come; so that when they have once begun, they will never make an end with their will. Moreover, when they have power once granted them to do hurt, their boldness increaseth in tract of time, so that they are carried headlong more immoderately, which thing Luke also noteth when he saith, The persecution was great. Undoubtedly the Church had but small rest before, neither was it free from the vexation of the wicked; but the Lord spared his for a time, that they might have some liberty, and now they began to be sorer set on.

These things must be applied unto our time also. If the furiousness of our enemies seem at any time to be as it were fallen on sleep, so that it casteth not out flames far, let us know that the Lord provideth for our weakness; yet, let us not in the mean season imagine that we shall have

priate exhibition of the presence of God, Matt. 16: 27; 24: 30.

In the case of Stephen there is every indication of a vision, or supernatural representation of the heavenly objects; something in advance of mere faith, such as dying Christians now have. What was its precise nature, we have no means of ascertaining. Objects were often represented to prophets by visions; and probably something similar is intended here. It was such an elevation of view, such a representation of truth, and of the glory of God, as to be denoted by the word see; though it is not to be maintained that Stephen really saw the Savior with the bodily eye.

On the right hand of God. That is, exalted to a place of honor and power in the heavens.

59. Calling upon God. This was, therefore, an act of worship; a solemn invocation of the Lord Jesus, in the most interesting circumstances in which a man can be placed – in his dying moments. And this shows that it is right to worship the Lord Jesus, and to pray to him. For if Stephen was inspired, it settles the question. The example of an inspired man, in such circumstances, is a safe and correct example. If it should be said that the inspiration of Stephen cannot be made out, yet the inspiration of Luke, who has recorded it, will not be called in question. Then the following circumstances show that he, an inspired man, regarded it as right, and as a proper example to be followed.

Receive my spirit. That is, receive it to thyself; take it to thine abode in heaven.

60. And he kneeled down. This seems to have been a voluntary kneeling; a placing himself in this position for the purpose of prayer, choosing to die in this attitude.

Lay not, etc. Forgive them. This passage strikingly resembles the dying prayer of the Lord Jesus, Luke 23: 34. Nothing but the Christian religion will enable a man to utter this passage in his dying moments.

ACTS 8

1. And Saul was consenting, etc. Was pleased with his being put to death, and approved

it. Comp. Acts 22: 20. This part of the verse should have been connected with the previous chapter.

At that time. That is, immediately following the death of Stephen. The persecution arose on account of Stephen, Acts 11: 19. The tumult did not subside when Stephen was killed. Their anger continued to be excited against all Christians. They had become so embittered by the zeal and success of the apostles, and by their frequent charges of murder in putting the Son of God to death, that they resolved at once to put a period to their progress and success. This was the first persecution against Christians; the first in a series that terminated only when the religion which they wished to destroy was fully established on the ruins of both Judaism and Paganism.

The Church. The collection of Christians which were now organized into a church. The church at Jerusalem was the first that was collected.

All scattered. That is, the great mass of Christians.

Except the apostles. Probably, the other Christians fled from fear. Why the apostles, who were particularly in danger, did not flee also, is not stated by the historian. Having been, however, more fully instructed than the others, and having been taught their duty by the example and teaching of the Savior, they resolved, it seems, to remain and brave the fury of the persecutors. For them to have fled then would have exposed them, as leaders and founders of the new religion, to the charge of timidity and weakness. They therefore resolved to remain in the midst of their persecutors; and a merciful Providence watched over them, and defended them from harm. The dispersion extended not only to Judea and Samaria, but those who fled carried the gospel also to Phenice, and Cyprus, and Antioch, Acts 11: 19. There was a reason why this was permitted. The early converts were Jews. They had strong feelings of attachment to the city of Jerusalem, to the temple, and to the land of their fathers. Yet it was the design of the Lord Jesus that the gospel should be preached everywhere. To accomplish this, he suffered a persecution to rage; and they were scattered

the least to the greatest, saying, This man is the great power of God.

11 And to him they had regard, because that of long time he had bewitched them with sorceries.

12 But when they believed Philip preaching the things concerning the kingdom of God, and the name of Jesus Christ, they were baptized, both men and women.

13 Then Simon himself believed also: and when he was baptized, he continued with Philip, and wondered, beholding the miracles and signs which were done.

14 Now when the apostles which were at Jerusalem heard that Samaria had received the word of God, they sent unto them Peter and John:

15 Who, when they were come down, prayed for them, that they might receive the Holy Ghost:

16 (For as yet he was fallen upon none of them: only they were baptized in the name of the Lord Jesus.)

17 Then laid they their hands on them, and they received the Holy Ghost.

18 And when Simon saw that through laying on of the apostles' hands the Holy Ghost was given, he offered them money,

19 Saying, Give me also this power, that on whomsoever I lay hands, he may receive the Holy Ghost.

20 But Peter said unto him, Thy money perish with thee, because thou hast thought that the gift of God may be purchased with money.

21 Thou hast neither part nor lot in this matter: for thy heart is not right in the sight of God.

22 Repent therefore of this thy wickedness, and pray God, if perhaps the thought of thine heart may be forgiven thee.

23 For I perceive that thou art in the gall of bitterness, and in the bond of iniquity.

24 Then answered Simon, and said, Pray ye to the Lord for me, that none of these things which ye have spoken come upon me.

25 And they, when they had testified and preached the word of the Lord, returned to Jerusalem, and preached the gospel in many villages of the Samaritans.

26 And the angel of the Lord spake

continual truce, but let us be in readiness to suffer sorer brunts, as often as they shall break out suddenly. Let us also remember, that if at any time the constancy of one man have whetted the cruelty of our enemies, the blame of the evil is unjustly ascribed to him. For Luke doth not defame Stephen, when as he saith, that by means of him the Church was sorer vexed than before; but he rather turneth this to his praise, because he did valiantly, as the standard-bearer, encourage others with his example to fight courageously. When he calleth it the Church which was at Jerusalem, his meaning is not that there were Churches elsewhere, but he passes over unto these things which ensued thereupon. For whereas there was but this one only body of the godly in all the world, it was rent in pieces through flight; yet there sprung up more Churches by and by of those lame members which were dispersed here and there, and so the body of Christ was spread abroad far and wide, whereas it was before shut up within the walls of Jerusalem,

They were all scattered abroad

It is certain that they were not all scattered abroad, but the Scripture useth an universal note, for that which we say, Every where or abroad. The sum is this, that not only a few were in danger; because the cruelty of the enemies raged throughout the whole Church. Many do oftentimes take themselves to their feet, through faintness of heart, even when they hear any light rumor, but these are in another case. For they fled not unadvisedly, being discouraged, but because they saw no other means to pacify the fury of the adversaries. And he saith, that they were scattered not only through divers places of Judea, but that they came even unto Samaria; so that the middle wall began to be pulled down, which made division between the Jews and the Gentiles (Ephesians 2: 14). For the conversion of Samaria was, as it were, the first fruits of the calling of the Gentiles. For although they had circumcision, as had the people of God, yet we know that there was great dissension, and that not without great cause, forasmuch as they had in Samaria only a forged worship of God, as Christ affirmeth, because it was only an unsavory emulation. Therefore God set open the gate for the gospel then, that the scepter of Christ, sent out of Jerusalem, might come unto the Gentiles. He exempteth the apostles out of this number, not that they were free from the common danger, but because it is the duty of a good pastor to set himself against the invasions of wolves for the safety of his flock.

But here may a question be asked, forasmuch as they were commanded to preach the gospel throughout the whole world (Mark 16: 16), why they stayed at Jerusalem, even when they were expelled thence with force and hand? I answer, that seeing Christ had commanded them to begin

abroad, and bore his gospel to other cities and lands. Good thus came out of evil; and the first persecution resulted, as all others have done, in advancing the cause which was intended to be destroyed.

18. Simon saw, etc. That is, he witnessed the extraordinary effects, the power of speaking in a miraculous manner, etc.

He offered them money. He had had a remarkable influence over the Samaritans, and he saw that the possession of this power would perpetuate and increase his influence. Men commonly employ the tricks of legerdemain for the purpose of making money; and it seems probable that such had been the design of Simon. He saw that if he could communicate to others this power, if he could confer on them the talent of speaking other languages, it might be turned to vast account, and he sought therefore to purchase it of the apostles. From this act of Simon we have derived our word simony, to denote the buying and selling of ecclesiastical preferment, or church offices, where religion is supported by the state. This act of Simon shows conclusively that he was influenced by improper motives in becoming connected with the church.

20. Thy money perish with thee. This is an expression of the horror and indignation of Peter at the base offer of Simon. It is not to be understood as an imprecation on Simon. The main idea is the apostle's contempt for the money, as if he regarded it as of no value. "Let your money go to destruction. We abhor your impious offer. We can freely see any amount of money destroyed, before we will be tempted to sell the gift of the Holy Ghost." But there was here also an expression of his belief that Simon also would perish. It was a declaration that he was hastening to ruin, and as if this was certain, Peter says, let your money perish too.

The gift of God. That which he has given, or conferred as a favor. The idea was absurd that that which God himself gives as a sovereign could be purchased. It was impious to think of attempting to buy with worthless gold that which was of so inestimable value. The gift of God here means the extraordinary influences

of the Holy Ghost, Acts 10: 45; 11: 17. How can we pay a price to God? All that we can give, the silver, and the gold, and the cattle on a thousand hills, belong to him already. We have nothing which we can present for his favors. And yet there are many who seek to purchase the favor of God. Some do it by alms and prayers; some by penance and fasting; some by attempting to make their own hearts better, and by self-righteousness; and some by penitence and tears. All these will not purchase his favor. Salvation, like every other blessing, will be his gift; and if ever received, we must be willing to accept it on his own terms, at his own time, and in his own way. We are without merit; and if saved, it will be by the sovereign grace of God.

26. And go, etc. Philip had been employed in Samaria. As God now intended to send the gospel to another place, he gave a special direction to Philip to go and convey it. It is evident that God designed the conversion of this eunuch; and the direction to Philip shows how he accomplishes his designs. It is not by miracle, but by the use of means. It is not by direct power without truth, but it is by a message fitted to the end. The salvation of a single sinner is an object worthy the attention of God. When such a sinner is converted, it is because God forms a plan or purpose to do it. When it is done, he inclines his servants to labor; he directs their labors; he leads his ministers; and he prepares the way Acts 8: 28 for the reception of the truth.

28. And sitting in his chariot. His carriage; his vehicle. The form of the carriage is not known. In some instances the carriages of the ancients were placed on wheels; in others, were borne on poles in the form of a litter or palanquin, by men, or mules, or horses.

Read Esaias, etc. Isaiah. Reading doubtless the translation of Isaiah called the Septuagint. This translation was made in Egypt, for the special use of the Jews in Alexandria and throughout Egypt, and was that which was commonly used. Why he was reading the Scriptures, and especially this prophet, is not certainly known. It is morally certain, however, that he was in Judea at the time of

unto Philip, saying, Arise, and go toward the south unto the way that goeth down from Jerusalem unto Gaza, which is desert.

27 And he arose and went: and, behold, a man of Ethiopia, an eunuch of great authority under Candace queen of the Ethiopians, who had the charge of all her treasure, and had come to Jerusalem for to worship,

28 Was returning, and sitting in his chariot read Esaias the prophet.

29 Then the Spirit said unto Philip, Go near, and join thyself to this chariot.

30 And Philip ran thither to him, and heard him read the prophet Esaias, and said, Understandest thou what thou readest?

31 And he said, How can I, except some man should guide me? And he desired Philip that he would come up and sit with him.

32 The place of the scripture which he read was this, He was led as a sheep to the slaughter; and like a lamb dumb before his shearer, so opened he not his mouth:

33 In his humiliation his judgment was taken away: and who shall declare his generation? for his life is taken from the earth.

34 And the eunuch answered Philip, and said, I pray thee, of whom speaketh the prophet this? of himself, or of some other man?

35 Then Philip opened his mouth, and began at the same scripture, and preached unto him Jesus.

36 And as they went on their way, they came unto a certain water: and the eunuch said, See, here is water; what doth hinder me to be baptized?

37 And Philip said, If thou believest with all thine heart, thou mayest. And he answered and said, I believe that Jesus Christ is the Son of God.

38 And he commanded the chariot to stand still: and they went down both into the water, both Philip and the eunuch; and he baptized him.

39 And when they were come up out of the water, the Spirit of the Lord caught away Philip, that the eunuch saw him no more: and he went on his way rejoicing.

40 But Philip was found at Azotus: and

at Jerusalem, they employed themselves there until such time as being brought into some other place by his hand, they might know, for a surety, that he was their guide. And we see how fearfully they proceeded to preach the gospel; not that they foreslowed [shunned] that function which was enjoined them, but because they were amazed at a new and unwonted thing. Therefore, seeing they see the gospel so mightily resisted at Jerusalem, they dare go to no other place until such time as they have broken that first huge heap of straits. Assuredly, they provide neither for their ease, nor yet for their own commodities either for being void of care by staying at Jerusalem; for they have a painful charge, they are continually amidst divers dangers they encounter with great troubles. Wherefore, undoubtedly, they are purposed to do their duty; and especially, whereas they stand to it when all the rest fly, that is an evident testimony of valiant constancy. If any man object that they might have divided the provinces amongst them, that they might not all have been occupied in one place, I answer, that Jerusalem alone had business enough for them all.

In sum, Luke reckoneth up this as a thing worthy of praise, that they followed not the rest into voluntary exile to avoid persecution; and yet he doth not reprehend the flight of those men whose state was more free. For the apostles did consider what particular thing their calling had; to wit, that they should keep their standing, seeing the wolves did invade the sheepfold. The rigor of Tertullian, and such like, was too great, who did deny indifferently that it is lawful to fly for fear of persecution. Augustine saith better, who giveth leave to fly in such sort that the churches, being destitute of their pastors, be not betrayed into the hands of the enemies. This is surely the best moderation, which beareth neither too much with the flesh, neither driveth those headlong to death who may lawfully save their lives.

ACTS 9

1. And Saul

Luke setteth down in this place a noble history, and a history full well worthy to be remembered, concerning the conversion of Paul; after what sort the Lord did not only bring him under, and make him subject to his commandment, when he raged like an untamed beast but also how he made him another and a new man. But because Luke setteth down all things in order as in a famous work of God, it shall be more convenient to follow his context, that all may come in order whatsoever is worth the noting. When as he saith, that he breathed out threatenings and slaughter as yet, his meaning is, that after that his hands were once imbued with innocent blood, he proceeded in like cruelty, and was always a furious and bloody enemy to the Church,

the crucifixion and resurrection of Jesus; that he had heard much of him; that this would be a subject of discussion; and it was natural for him, in returning, to look at the prophecies respecting the Messiah, perhaps either to meditate on them as a suitable subject of inquiry and thought, or perhaps to examine the claims of Jesus of Nazareth to this office. The prophecy in Is. 53 was so striking, and coincided so clearly with the character of Jesus, that it was natural for a candid mind to examine whether he might not be the person intended by the prophet.

30. And Philip ran, etc. Indicating his haste, and his desire to obey the suggestions of the Spirit. A thousand difficulties might have been started in the mind of Philip if he had reflected a little. The eunuch was a stranger; he had the appearance of a man of rank; he was engaged in reading; he might be indisposed to be interrupted or to converse, etc. But Philip obeyed without any hesitation the monitions of the Spirit, and ran to him. It is well to follow the first suggestions of the Spirit; to yield to the clear indications of duty, and to perform it at once. Especially in a deed of benevolence, and in conversing with others on the subject of religion, our first thoughts are commonly safest and best. If we do not follow them, the calculations of avarice, or fear, or some worldly prudence, are very apt to come in. We become alarmed; we are afraid of the rich and the great; and we suppose that our conversation and admonitions will be unacceptable.

37. And Philip said, etc. This was then stated to be the proper qualification for making a profession of religion. The terms are:

(1.) Faith, that is, a reception of Jesus as a Savior; yielding the mind to the proper influences of the truths of redemption.

(2.) There is required not merely the assent of the understanding, but a surrender of the heart, the will, the affections, to the truth of the gospel. As these were the proper qualifications then, so they are now. Nothing less is required; and nothing but this can constitute a proper qualification for the Lord's Supper.

I believe, etc. This profession is more than a professed belief that Jesus was the Messiah.

The name Christ implies that. "I believe that Jesus the Messiah" is, etc. In addition to this, he professed his belief that he was the Son of God – showing either that he had before supposed that the Messiah would be the Son of God, or that Philip had instructed him on that point. It was natural for Philip, in discoursing on the humiliation and poverty of Jesus, to add also that he sustained a higher rank of being than a man, and was the Son of God.

39. His mind was enlightened on a perplexing passage of scripture. He was satisfied respecting the Messiah. He was baptized; and he experienced that which all feel who embrace the Savior and are baptized, joy. It was joy resulting from the fact that he was reconciled to God; and a joy, the natural effect of having done his duty promptly, in making a profession of religion. If we wish happiness, if we would avoid clouds and gloom, we shall do our duty at once. If we delay till tomorrow what we ought to do today, we may expect to be troubled with melancholy thoughts. If we find peace, it will be in doing promptly: just that which God requires at our hands. This is the last that we hear of this man. From this narrative we may learn,

(1.) that God often prepares the mind to receive the truth.

(2.) That this takes place sometimes with the great and the noble, as well as the poor and obscure.

(3.) We should study the Scriptures. It is the way in which God usually directs the mind in the truths of religion.

(4.) They who read the Bible with candor and care may expect that God will, in some mode, guide them into the truth. It will often be in a way which they least expect; but they need not be afraid of being left to darkness or error.

(5.) We should be ready at all times to speak to sinners. God often prepares their minds, as he did that of the eunuch, to receive the truth.

(6.) We should not be afraid of the great, the rich, or of strangers. God often prepares their minds to receive the truth; and we may find a man willing to hear of the Savior where we least expected it.

(7.) We should do our duty in this respect, as

passing through he preached in all the cities, till he came to Caesarea.

ACTS 9

1 And Saul, yet breathing out threatenings and slaughter against the disciples of the Lord, went unto the high priest,

2 And desired of him letters to Damascus to the synagogues, that if he found any of this way, whether they were men or women, he might bring them bound unto Jerusalem.

3 And as he journeyed, he came near Damascus: and suddenly there shined round about him a light from heaven:

4 And he fell to the earth, and heard a voice saying unto him, Saul, Saul, why persecutest thou me?

5 And he said, Who art thou, Lord? And the Lord said, I am Jesus whom thou persecutest: it is hard for thee to kick against the pricks.

6 And he trembling and astonished said, Lord, what wilt thou have me to do? And the Lord said unto him, Arise, and go into the city, and it shall be told thee what thou must do.

7 And the men which journeyed with him stood speechless, hearing a voice, but seeing no man.

8 And Saul arose from the earth; and when his eyes were opened, he saw no man: but they led him by the hand, and brought him into Damascus.

9 And he was three days without sight, and neither did eat nor drink.

10 And there was a certain disciple at Damascus, named Ananias; and to him said the Lord in a vision, Ananias. And he said, Behold, I am here, Lord.

11 And the Lord said unto him, Arise, and go into the street which is called Straight, and inquire in the house of Judas for one called Saul, of Tarsus: for, behold, he prayeth,

12 And hath seen in a vision a man named Ananias coming in, and putting his hand on him, that he might receive his sight.

13 Then Ananias answered, Lord, I have heard by many of this man, how much evil he hath done to thy saints at Jerusalem:

14 And here he hath authority from the chief priests to bind all that call on

after that he had once made that entrance whereof mention is made in the death of Stephen. For which cause it was the more incredible that he could be so suddenly tamed. And whereas such a cruel wolf was not only turned into a sheep, but did also put on the nature of a shepherd, the wonderful hand of God did show itself therein manifestly.

2. And Luke describeth therewithal that he was furnished with weapons and power to do hurt, when as he saith that he had obtained letters of the highest priest, that he might bring all those bound to Jerusalem whom he should find professing the name of Christ. There is mention made of women, that it may the better appear how desirous he was to shed blood who had no respect of sex whom even armed enemies are wont to spare in the heat of war. Therefore he setteth forth before us a fierce and cruel beast who had not only liberty given him to rage, but had also his power increased to devour and destroy godly men, as if a madman had a sword put into his hand. Whereas I have translated it sect, Luke hath way, which metaphor is common enough in the Scriptures. Therefore Paul's purpose was quite to put out the name of Christ by destroying all the godly cruelly.

3. As he was in the way

In craving epistles of the high priest, he ran headlong against Christ willingly; and now he is enforced to obey whether he will or no. This is surely the most excellent mercy of God, in that that man is reclaimed unto salvation contrary to the purpose of his mind, whom so great a heat carried headlong into destruction. Whereas the Lord suffereth him to receive letters, and to come near to the city; (whereby we see how well he knoweth the very instants of times to do everything in due time); he could have prevented him sooner, if it had seemed good to him so to do, that he might deliver the godly from fear and carelessness. But he setteth out his benefits more thereby, in that he tieth the jaws of the greedy wolf, even when he was ready to enter the sheepfold. Also we know that men's stubbornness increaseth more and more by going forward. Wherefore the conversion of Paul was so much the harder, forasmuch as he was already made more obstinate by continuing his fury.

4. And therefore Luke saith that he fell to the ground. For what other thing can befall man, but that he must lie prostrate and be, as it were, brought to nothing, when he is overwhelmed with the present feeling of God's glory? And this was the first beginning of the bringing down of Paul, that he might become apt to hear the voice of Christ, which he had despised so long as he sat haughtily upon his horse. **Saul, Saul!**

Luke compared the light which shined round about Paul to lightning, though I do not doubt but that lightnings did

Philip did, promptly. We should not delay or hesitate; but should at once do that which we believe is in accordance with the will of God. See Ps. 119: 60.

ACTS 9

1. Yet breathing. Not satisfied with what he had done, Acts 8: 3. The word breathing out is expressive often of any deep, agitating emotion, as we then breathe rapidly and violently. It is thus expressive of violent anger. The emotion is absorbing, agitating, exhausting, and demands a more rapid circulation of blood to supply the exhausted vitality; and this demands an increased supply of oxygen, or vital air, which leads to the increased action of the lungs.

Threatening. Denunciation; threatening them with every breath – the action of a man violently enraged, and who was bent on vengeance. It denotes, also, intense activity and energy in persecution.

Slaughter. Murder. Intensely desiring to put to death as many Christians as possible. He rejoiced in their death, and joined in condemning them, Acts 26: 10–11. From this latter place, it seems that he had been concerned in putting many of them to death.

The disciples of the Lord. Against Christians.

Went unto the High Priest. The letters were written and signed in the name and by the authority of the Sanhedrim, or great council of the nation. The high priest did it as president of that council. See Acts 9: 14; 22: 5. The high priest of that time was Theophilus, son of Artanus, who had been appointed at the feast of Pentecost, AD 37, by Vitellius, the Roman governor. His brother Jonathan had been removed from that office the same year.

3. And as he journeyed. On his way; or while he was traveling. The place where this occurred is not known. Tradition has fixed it at the mountain now called Cocab. All that we know of it is, that it was near to Damascus.

And suddenly. Like a flash of lightning.

There shined round about him, etc. The language which is expressed here would be used in describing a flash of lightning. Many critics have supposed that God made use of a sudden flash to arrest Paul, and that he was much alarmed, and brought to reflection. That God might make use of such a means cannot be denied. But to this supposition in this case there are some unanswerable objections.

(1.) It was declared to be the appearance of the Lord Jesus: Acts 9: 27, "Barnabas declared unto them how that he had seen the Lord in the way." 1 Cor. 15: 8: "And last of all he was seen of me also." 1 Cor. 9: 1: "Have I not seen Jesus Christ our Lord?"

(2.) Those who were with Saul saw the light, but did not hear the voice, Acts 22: 9. This is incredible on the supposition that it was a flash of lightning near them.

(3.) It was manifestly regarded as a message to Saul. The light appeared, and the voice spake to him. The others did not even hear the address. Besides,

(4.) it was as easy for Jesus to appear in a supernatural manner, as to appear amidst thunder and lightning. That the Lord Jesus appeared, is distinctly affirmed. And we shall see that it is probable that he would appear in a supernatural manner.

10. A certain disciple. A Christian. Many have supposed that he was one of the seventy disciples. But nothing more is certainly known of him than is related here. He had very probably been some time a Christian, Acts 9: 13 and had heard of Saul, but was personally a stranger to him. In Acts 22: 12, it is said that he was a devout man according to the law, having a good report of all the Jews which dwelt there. There was wisdom in sending such a Christian to Saul, as it might do much to conciliate the minds of the Jews there towards him.

Said the Lord. The Lord Jesus is alone mentioned in all this transaction. And as he had commenced the work of converting Saul, it is evident that he is intended here.

In a vision. Perhaps by a dream. The main idea is, that he revealed his will to him in the case. The word vision is often used in speaking of the communications made to the prophets, and commonly means that future events were made to pass in review before the mind, as we look upon a landscape.

thy name.

15 But the Lord said unto him, Go thy way: for he is a chosen vessel unto me, to bear my name before the Gentiles, and kings, and the children of Israel:

16 For I will shew him how great things he must suffer for my name's sake.

17 And Ananias went his way, and entered into the house; and putting his hands on him said, Brother Saul, the Lord, even Jesus, that appeared unto thee in the way as thou camest, hath sent me, that thou mightest receive thy sight, and be filled with the Holy Ghost.

18 And immediately there fell from his eyes as it had been scales: and he received sight forthwith, and arose, and was baptized.

19 And when he had received meat, he was strengthened. Then was Saul certain days with the disciples which were at Damascus.

20 And straightway he preached Christ in the synagogues, that he is the Son of God.

21 But all that heard him were amazed, and said; Is not this he that destroyed them which called on this name in Jerusalem, and came hither for that intent, that he might bring them bound unto the chief priests?

22 But Saul increased the more in strength, and confounded the Jews which dwelt at Damascus, proving that this is very Christ.

23 And after that many days were fulfilled, the Jews took counsel to kill him:

24 But their laying await was known of Saul. And they watched the gates day and night to kill him.

25 Then the disciples took him by night, and let him down by the wall in a basket.

26 And when Saul was come to Jerusalem, he assayed to join himself to the disciples: but they were all afraid of him, and believed not that he was a disciple.

27 But Barnabas took him, and brought him to the apostles, and declared unto them how he had seen the Lord in the way, and that he had spoken to him, and how he had preached boldly at Damascus in the name of Jesus.

28 And he was with them coming in and going out at Jerusalem.

fly in the air. And this voice, which Christ did send out to beat down his pride, may full well be called a lightning or thunderbolt, because it did not only strike him, and make him astonished, but did quite kill him, so that he was now as nobody with himself, who did so much please himself before and did challenge to himself authority to put the gospel to flight. Luke putteth down his name in Hebrew in this place, Saul, Saul! because he repeateth the words of Christ, who spake unto him, undoubtedly, according to the common custom of the country.

27. When Barnabas had taken him

Whereas the disciples fled so fast from Paul, that was, peradventure, a point of too great fearfulness, and yet he speaketh of none of the common sort, but of the apostles themselves. But he doth either extenuate or lighten their fault, because they suspected him for just causes, whom they had found and tried to be such a deadly enemy; and, it was to be feared, lest they should rashly endanger themselves if they should have showed themselves to be so easy to entreat. Therefore, I think that they are not to be blamed for that fear which they conceived for just cause, or that they deserve to be even accused for the same. For if they had been called to give an account of their faith, they would have provoked not Paul only, but also all the furies of hell, without fear. Whence we gather that every fear is not to be condemned but such as causeth us to turn aside from our duty. The narration which Luke addeth may be referred as well unto the person of Barnabas as of Paul. Yet I think rather that Paul declareth to the apostles what had befallen him; and yet the speech may be well applied to Barnabas, especially when as mention is made of Paul's boldness.

40. When they were all put forth

When as he taketh a time to pray, he seemeth as yet to doubt what will be the end. When he healed AEneas he brake out into these words, without making any stop, AEneas, Jesus Christ make thee whole. But as the operation of the Spirit is not always alike and the same, it may be that though he knew the power of God, yet he went forward unto the miracle by degrees. Yet it seemeth to be an absurd thing, that he putteth all the saints out of the chamber, for whom it had been better to have seen it with their eyes. But because the Lord had not as yet revealed the time when, and the manner how, he would show forth his power, he desired to be alone, that he might the more fitly pray. Also it might be, that he knew some other reason which moved him to do this, which we know not. It is recorded in the Sacred History (1 Kings 17: 23), that Elias did the same. For he being alone, and not so much as the mother of the child with him, doth stretch himself thrice upon the dead corpse. For the Spirit of God

15. Go thy way. This is often the only answer that we obtain to the suggestion of our doubts and hesitations about duty. God tells us still to do what he requires, with an assurance only that his commands are just, and that there are good reasons for them.

A chosen vessel. The usual meaning of the word vessel is well known. It usually denotes a cup or basin, such as is used in a house. It then denotes any instrument which may be used to accomplish a purpose, perhaps particularly with the notion of conveying or communicating. In the Scriptures it is used to denote the instrument or agent which God employs to convey his favors to mankind; and is thus employed to represent the ministers of the gospel, or the body of the minister, 2 Cor. 4: 7; 1 Thess. 4: 4; comp. Is. 13: 5. Paul is called chosen because Christ had selected him, as he did his other apostles, for this service.

To bear my name. To communicate the knowledge of me.

Before the Gentiles. The nations; all who were not Jews. This was the principal employment of Paul. He spent his life in this, and regarded himself as peculiarly called to be the apostle of the Gentiles, Rom. 11: 13; 15: 16; Gal. 2: 8.

And kings. This was fulfilled, Acts 25: 23; 26: 1–32; 27: 24.

And the children of Israel. The Jews. This was done. He immediately began to preach to them, Acts 9: 20–22.

25. They took him by night, etc. This was done through a window in the wall, 2 Cor. 11: 33.

In a basket. This word is used to denote commonly the basket in which food was carried, Matt. 15: 37; Mark 8: 8,20.

This conduct of Saul was in accordance with the direction of the Lord Jesus, Matt. 10: 23, "When they persecute you in this city, flee ye into another," etc. Saul was certain of death if he remained; and as he could secure his life by flight without abandoning any principle of religion, or denying his Lord, it was his duty to do so. Christianity requires us to sacrifice our lives only when we cannot avoid it without denying the Savior, or abandoning the principles of our holy religion.

26. Was come to Jerusalem. It is probable that he then went immediately to Jerusalem, Gal. 1: 18. This was three years after his conversion.

He assayed. He attempted; he endeavored.

To join himself. To become connected with them as their fellow Christian.

But they were all afraid of him. Their fear, or suspicion, was excited probably on these grounds:

(1.) They remembered his former violence against Christians. They had an instinctive shrinking from him, and suspicion of the man that had been so violent a persecutor.

(2.) He had been absent three years. If they had not heard of him during that time, they would naturally retain much of their old feelings towards him. If they had, they might suspect the man who had not returned to Jerusalem; who had not before sought the society of other Christians; and who had spent that time in a distant country, and among strangers. It would seem remarkable that he had not at once returned to Jerusalem and connected himself with the apostles. But the sacred writer does not justify the fears of the apostles. He simply records the fact of their apprehension. It is not unnatural, however, to have doubts respecting an open and virulent enemy of the gospel who suddenly professes a change in favor of it. The human mind does not easily cast off suspicion of some unworthy motive, and open itself at once to entire confidence. When great and notorious sinners profess to be converted – men who have been violent, or artful, or malignant – it is natural to ask whether they have not some unworthy motive still in their professed change. Confidence is a plant of slow growth, and starts up not by a sudden profession, but by a course of life which is worthy of affection and of trust.

A disciple. A sincere Christian.

29. He spake boldly. He openly defended the doctrine that Jesus was the Messiah.

31. Then had the churches rest. That is, the persecutions against Christians ceased. Those persecutions had been excited by the opposition made to Stephen, Acts 11: 19 they had been greatly promoted by Saul, Acts 8: 3 and

29 And he spake boldly in the name of the Lord Jesus, and disputed against the Grecians: but they went about to slay him.

30 Which when the brethren knew, they brought him down to Caesarea, and sent him forth to Tarsus.

31 Then had the churches rest throughout all Judaea and Galilee and Samaria, and were edified; and walking in the fear of the Lord, and in the comfort of the Holy Ghost, were multiplied.

32 And it came to pass, as Peter passed throughout all quarters, he came down also to the saints which dwelt at Lydda.

33 And there he found a certain man named Aeneas, which had kept his bed eight years, and was sick of the palsy.

34 And Peter said unto him, Aeneas, Jesus Christ maketh thee whole: arise, and make thy bed. And he arose immediately.

35 And all that dwelt at Lydda and Saron saw him, and turned to the Lord.

36 Now there was at Joppa a certain disciple named Tabitha, which by interpretation is called Dorcas: this woman was full of good works and almsdeeds which she did.

37 And it came to pass in those days, that she was sick, and died: whom when they had washed, they laid her in an upper chamber.

38 And forasmuch as Lydda was nigh to Joppa, and the disciples had heard that Peter was there, they sent unto him two men, desiring him that he would not delay to come to them.

39 Then Peter arose and went with them. When he was come, they brought him into the upper chamber: and all the widows stood by him weeping, and showing the coats and garments which Dorcas made, while she was with them.

40 But Peter put them all forth, and kneeled down, and prayed; and turning him to the body said, Tabitha, arise. And she opened her eyes: and when she saw Peter, she sat up.

41 And he gave her his hand, and lifted her up, and when he had called the saints and widows, presented her alive.

42 And it was known throughout all Joppa; and many believed in the Lord.

hath his vehement motions, which, if any man will square out according to the common use of men, or measure by the sense of the flesh, he shall do wickedly and unjustly. We must this think, when as Peter, as it were doubting, seeketh a by place, he preventeth superstition, lest any man should ascribe to his power the work of God, whereof he was only a minister, For he which withdrew himself from company, and did pray so instantly, did plainly confess that the matter was not in his own hand. Therefore, when Peter wisheth to know what pleaseth the Lord, he confesseth that he alone was the author of the work. Kneeling in time of prayer is a token of humility, which hath a double profit, that all our members may be applied unto the worship of God, and that the external exercise of the body may help the weakness of the mind; but we must take heed so often as we kneel down, that the inward submission of the heart be answerable to the ceremony, that it be not vain and false.

41. Luke repeateth, again, in the end that she was showed openly to the disciples; whence we gather that she was raised again, rather for other men's sake than for her own. Brain-sick fellows, who dream that the soul of man is only a blast which vanisheth away until the day of the resurrection, snatch at this place to prove their doting withal. To what end was it (say they) to call back the soul of Tabitha into the prison of the body, where it should suffer such misery, if it were received into blessed rest? As if it were not lawful for God to have respect of his glory as well in death as in life; and as if this were not the true felicity of the godly to live and die to him, yea, as if Christ were not to us a vantage, as well by living as dying (Philippians 1: 21), when we dedicate ourselves to him.

ACTS 10

1. Luke passes over now unto a worthy history, to wit, that God vouchsafeth to advance a stranger, and one uncircumcised, unto singular honor above all the Jews because he doth both send his angel unto him, and for his sake bringeth Peter to Cesarea, that he may instruct him in the gospel. But first of all Luke showeth what manner of person this Cornelius was, for whose cause an angel descended from heaven, and God spake to Peter in a vision. He was a captain [centurion] of the Italian band; a cohort did consist of a thousand footmen, and he which was chief captain was called a tribune (or marshal). Again, every hundred had a captain. A legion had for the most part five bands. That band was called the Italian band, because the Romans did choose soldiers oftentimes from amongst those which dwelt in the provinces; but they had the strength of the army out of Italy; therefore, Cornelius was an Italian

had extended, doubtless, throughout the whole land of Palestine. The precise causes of this cessation of the persecution are not known. Probably they were the following:

(1.) It is not improbable that the great mass of Christians had been driven into other regions by these persecutions.

(2.) He who had been most active in exciting the persecution, who was, in a sort, its leader, and who was best adapted to carry it on, had been converted. He had ceased his opposition; and even he now was removed from Judea. All this would have some effect in causing the persecution to subside.

(3.) But it is not improbable that the civil state of things in Judea contributed much to turn the attention of the Jews to other matters.

Were edified. Were built up, increased, and strengthened. See Rom. 14: 19; 15: 2; 1 Cor. 8: 1.

And walking. Proceeding; living. The word is often used to denote Christian conduct, or manner of life, Col. 1: 10; Luke 1: 6; 1 Thess. 4: 1; 1 John 2: 6. The idea is that of travelers who are going to any place, and who walk in the right path. Christians are thus travelers to another country, an heavenly.

In the fear of the Lord. Fearing the Lord; with reverence for him and his commandments. This expression is often used to denote piety in general, 2 Chr. 19: 7; Job 28: 28; Ps. 19: 9.

In the comfort of the Holy Ghost. In the consolations which the Holy Ghost produced, John 14: 16–17; Rom. 5: 1–6.

Were multiplied. Were increased.

36. At Joppa. This was a seaport town, situated on the Mediterranean, in the tribe of Dan, about thirty miles south of Caesarea, and forty-five north-west of Jerusalem. It was the principal seaport of Palestine; and hence, though the harbor was poor, it had considerable celebrity.

Tabitha. This word is properly Syriac, and means, literally, the gazelle or antelope. The name became an appellation of a female probably on account of the beauty of its form. "It is not unusual in the East to give the names of beautiful animals to young women." (Clark.)

Dorcas. A Greek word signifying the same as Tabitha. Our word doe or roe answers to it in signification.

Full of good works. Distinguished far good works. Comp. 1 Tim. 2: 10; Titus 2: 7.

And almsdeeds. Acts of kindness to the poor.

37. Whom, when they had washed. Among most people it has been customary to wash the body before it buried or burned. They prepared her in the usual manner for interment. There is no evidence that they expected that Peter would raise her up to life.

40. But Peter put them all forth. From the room. See a similar case in Matt. 9: 25. Why this was done is not said. Perhaps because he did not wish to appear as if seeking publicity. If done in the presence of many persons, it might seem like ostentation. Others suppose it was that he might offer more fervent and agonizing prayer to God than he would be willing they should witness. Compare 2 Kgs. 4: 23.

41. He presented her alive. He exhibited, or showed her to them alive. Compare 1 Kgs. 17: 23.

42. And many believed, etc. A similar effect followed when Jesus raised up Lazarus. See John 12: 11.

This was the first miracle of this kind that was performed by the apostles. The effect was, that many believed. It was not merely a work of benevolence in restoring to life one who contributed largely to the comfort of the poor, but it was used as a means of extending and establishing, as it was designed doubtless to do, the kingdom of the Savior.

ACTS 10

This chapter commences a very important part of the history of the transactions of the apostles. Before this, they had preached the gospel to the Jews only. They seem to have retained the feelings of their countrymen on this subject, that the Jews were to be regarded as the peculiarly favored people, and that salvation was not to be offered beyond the limits of their nation. it was important, indeed, that

43 And it came to pass, that he tarried many days in Joppa with one Simon a tanner.

ACTS 10

1 There was a certain man in Caesarea called Cornelius, a centurion of the band called the Italian band,

2 A devout man, and one that feared God with all his house, which gave much alms to the people, and prayed to God alway.

3 He saw in a vision evidently about the ninth hour of the day an angel of God coming in to him, and saying unto him, Cornelius.

4 And when he looked on him, he was afraid, and said, What is it, Lord? And he said unto him, Thy prayers and thine alms are come up for a memorial before God.

5 And now send men to Joppa, and call for one Simon, whose surname is Peter:

6 He lodgeth with one Simon a tanner, whose house is by the sea side: he shall tell thee what thou oughtest to do.

7 And when the angel which spake unto Cornelius was departed, he called two of his household servants, and a devout soldier of them that waited on him continually;

8 And when he had declared all these things unto them, he sent them to Joppa.

9 On the morrow, as they went on their journey, and drew nigh unto the city, Peter went up upon the housetop to pray about the sixth hour:

10 And he became very hungry, and would have eaten: but while they made ready, he fell into a trance,

11 And saw heaven opened, and a certain vessel descending unto him, as it had been a great sheet knit at the four corners, and let down to the earth:

12 Wherein were all manner of four-footed beasts of the earth, and wild beasts, and creeping things, and fowls of the air.

13 And there came a voice to him, Rise, Peter; kill, and eat.

14 But Peter said, Not so, Lord; for I have never eaten any thing that is common or unclean.

15 And the voice spake unto him again the second time, What God hath cleansed, that call not thou common.

born; but he was at Cesarea with his hundred, to guard the city. For the Romans were wont so to distribute their places of abode, that every city of renown might have a garrison to stay sudden uproars. A rare example that a soldier was so devout towards God, so upright and courteous towards men! For at that time the Italians, when as they were carried into the provinces to live in warfare, ran to and fro like hungry wolves to get some prey; they had for the most part no more religion than beasts; they had as great care of innocency as cutthroats; for which cause the virtues of Cornelius deserve the greater commendation, in that leading a soldier's life, which was at that time most corrupt, he served God holily, and lived amongst men without doing any hurt or injury. And this is no small amplification of his praise, in that casting away superstition wherein he was born and brought up, he embraced the pure worship of God; for we know what account the Italians made of themselves, and how proudly they despised others. And the Jews were at that time in such contempt, that for their sakes pure religion was counted infamous, and almost execrable. Seeing that none of these things could hinder Cornelius, but that forsaking his idols he did embrace the true worship of the true God alone, it must needs be that he was endued with rare and singular sincerity.

2. He saith that he was a godly man, and one that feared God; secondly, that like a good householder he had a care to instruct his families; he praiseth him afterward for the offices of love, because he was beneficent toward all the people; and, lastly, that he prayed to God continually. The sum is this, that Cornelius was a man of singular virtues, wherein the integrity of the godly consisteth, so that his life was framed, in all points, according to the rule which God prescribeth unto us. And because the law is contained in two tables, Luke commendeth, in the former place, Cornelius' godliness; secondly, he descendeth unto the second part, that he exercised the offices of love toward men. This is very profitable to be marked, because we have a way to live well described in his person.

Wherefore, in ordering the life well, let faith and religion be the foundation, which being taken away, all other virtues are nothing else but smokes. Luke reckoneth up the fear of God and prayer as fruits and testimonies of godliness and of the worship of God, and that for good causes. For religion cannot be separated from the fear of God and the reverence of him, neither can any man be counted godly, save he who acknowledgeth God to be his Father and Lord, doth addict himself wholly to him. And let us know that voluntary fear is commended in this place when those men submit themselves to God willingly and from their heart, who duly consider themselves what is due to him.

the gospel should be offered to them first; but the whole tendency of the Christian religion was to enlarge and liberalize the mind; to overcome the narrow policy and prejudices of the Jewish people; and to diffuse itself over all the nations of the earth. In various ways, and by various parables, the Savior had taught the apostles, indeed, that his gospel should be spread among the Gentiles. He had commanded them to go and preach it to every creature, Mark 16: 15. But he had told them to tarry in Jerusalem until they were endued with power from on high, Luke 24: 49. It was natural, therefore, that they should receive special instructions and Divine revelation on a point so important as this; and God selected the case of Cornelius as the instance by which he would fully establish his purpose of conveying the gospel to the Gentile world. It is worthy of observation, also, that he selected Peter for the purpose of conveying the gospel first to the Gentiles. The Savior had told him, that on him he would build his church; that he would give to him first the key of the kingdom of heaven; that is, that he should be the agent in opening the doors of the church to both Jews and Gentiles.

Peter had, in accordance with these predictions, been the agent in first presenting the gospel to the Jews, Acts 2; and the prediction was now to be completely fulfilled in extending the same gospel to the Gentile world. The transaction recorded in this chapter is one, therefore, that is exceedingly important in the history of the church; and we are not to be surprised that it is recorded at length. It should be remembered, also, that this point became afterwards the source of incessant controversy in the early church. The converts from Judaism insisted on the observance of the whole of the rites of their religion; the converts from among the Gentiles claimed exemption eruption from them all. To settle these disputes, and to secure the reception of the gospel among the Gentiles, and to introduce them to the church with all the privileges of the Jews, required all the wisdom, talent, and address of the apostles. See Acts 11: 1–18; Acts 15; Rom. 14; Rom. 15; Gal. 2: 11–16.

1. Cornelius. This is a Latin name, and shows

that the man was doubtless a Roman. It has been supposed by many interpreters that this man was "a proselyte of the gate;" that is, one who had renounced idolatry, and who observed some of the Jewish rites, though not circumcised, and not called a Jew. But there is no sufficient evidence of this. The reception of the narrative of Peter, Acts 11: 1–3, shows that the other apostles regarded him as a Gentile. In Acts 10: 28, Peter evidently regards him as a foreigner; one who did not in any sense esteem himself to be a Jew. In Acts 11: 1, it is expressly said that "the Gentiles" had received the word of God; evidently alluding to Cornelius and those who were with him.

A centurion. One who was the commander of a division in the Roman army, consisting of a hundred men. A captain of a hundred.

Of the band. A division of the Roman army, consisting of from four hundred to six hundred men.

The Italian band. Probably a band or regiment that was composed of soldiers from Italy, in distinction from those which were composed of soldiers born in provinces. It is evident that many of the soldiers in the Roman army would be those who were born in other parts of the world; and it is altogether probable, that those who were born in Rome or Italy would claim pre-eminence over those enlisted in other places.

17. Doubted in himself. Doubted in his own mind. He was perplexed to understand it.

Behold, the men, etc. We see here an admirable arrangement of the events of Providence to fit each other. Every part of this transaction is made to harmonize with every other part; and it was so arranged, that, just in the moment when the mind of Peter was filled with perplexity, the very event should occur which should relieve him of his embarrassment. Such a coincidence is not uncommon. An event of Divine Providence may be as clear an expression of his will, and may as certainly serve to indicate our duty, as the most manifest revelation would do; and a state of mind may, by an arrangement of circumstances, be produced, that shall be extremely perplexing until some event shall occur, or some field of usefulness shall open, that shall exactly cor-

16 This was done thrice: and the vessel was received up again into heaven.

17 Now while Peter doubted in himself what this vision which he had seen should mean, behold, the men which were sent from Cornelius had made inquiry for Simon's house, and stood before the gate,

18 And called, and asked whether Simon, which was surnamed Peter, were lodged there.

19 While Peter thought on the vision, the Spirit said unto him, Behold, three men seek thee.

20 Arise therefore, and get thee down, and go with them, doubting nothing: for I have sent them.

21 Then Peter went down to the men which were sent unto him from Cornelius; and said, Behold, I am he whom ye seek: what is the cause wherefore ye are come?

22 And they said, Cornelius the centurion, a just man, and one that feareth God, and of good report among all the nation of the Jews, was warned from God by an holy angel to send for thee into his house, and to hear words of thee.

23 Then called he them in, and lodged them. And on the morrow Peter went away with them, and certain brethren from Joppa accompanied him.

24 And the morrow after they entered into Caesarea. And Cornelius waited for them, and had called together his kinsmen and near friends.

25 And as Peter was coming in, Cornelius met him, and fell down at his feet, and worshipped him.

26 But Peter took him up, saying, Stand up; I myself also am a man.

27 And as he talked with him, he went in, and found many that were come together.

28 And he said unto them, Ye know how that it is an unlawful thing for a man that is a Jew to keep company, or come unto one of another nation; but God hath shewed me that I should not call any man common or unclean.

29 Therefore came I unto you without gainsaying, as soon as I was sent for: I ask therefore for what intent ye have sent for me?

30 And Cornelius said, Four days ago I was fasting until this hour; and at the

Moreover, because a great part of the world doth, with reigned trifles, corrupt and deprave the worship of God, Luke added, for good causes, that Cornelius prayed continually; whereby he doth signify, that he proved not his godliness only with external ceremonies, but that he worshipped God spiritually, when as he exercised himself in prayer. We must also note the continuance of his prayer; whence we gather, that he did not pray only coldly, after the common custom, but that he was earnestly bent to prayer, as the continual benefits of God do exhort us and prick us forward thereunto, and the force of faith ought there to show itself. Wherefore let every one of us exhort himself to persevere in prayer by the example of Cornelius.

With all his house

We must not lightly pass over this commendation that Cornelius had a church in his house. And, surely, a true worshipper of God will not suffer so much as in him lieth God to be banished from his house. For how unmeet a thing is it for him to maintain his own right stoutly, that his wife, children, servants, and maids may obey him, and not to regard that God is disobeyed. It shall sometimes fall out so that a godly man cannot have even his wife to be of his mind; yet he, which ruleth others, must endeavor by all means to have God obeyed; and there is nothing more meet than that we should consecrate all ours to God as ourselves. Therefore, if a godly man have children which are unlike him, or a wife of evil conditions, or lewd and wicked servants, let him not wink, nor yet suffer his house to be polluted through his slothfulness. The diligence of Cornelius is not so much commended as the blessing of God, whereby it came to pass that he had his house obedient unto him in godliness. And we must not omit the circumstance, that he instructed his family in the fear of God, setting light by the fear of danger, which did hang over his head therefore. For the Jewish religion was in great contempt; and no citizen of Rome might freely receive any strange religion, as they called it. Wherefore, although the sincere profession of the gospel be evil spoken of in the world, yet is it too corrupt frightfulness if that unjust hatred hinder any man from offering his family to God for a sacrifice, by godly instruction.

Giving alms

There is also the figure *synecdoche* in this member [clause]. For as it was said, even now, that the worship of God was proved by prayers, so now, when Luke speaketh of love, he maketh choice of one kind; whereby he showeth that Cornelius was a liberal and bountiful man. For our godliness ought so to appear to men, that we declare that we fear God by using bountifulness and justice. The word *alms* is translated unto those external good works wherewith we help

respond to it, and shall indicate to us the will of God. We should observe then the events of God's Providence. We should mark and record the train of our own thoughts, and we should watch with interest any event that occurs, when we are perplexed and embarrassed, to obtain, if possible, an expression of the will of God.

25. Fell down at his feet. This was an act of profound regard for him as an ambassador of God. In Oriental countries it was usual to prostrate themselves at length on the ground before men of rank and honor.

Worshipped him. This does not mean religious worship, but civil respect; the homage, or profound regard, which was due to one in honor.

26. Stand up, etc. This does not imply that Peter supposed that Cornelius intended to do him religious reverence. It was practically saying to him, "I am nothing more than a man, as thou art, and pretend to no right to such profound respects as these, but am ready in civil life to show thee all the respect that is due." – Doddridge.

28. It is an unlawful thing. This was not explicitly enjoined by Moses, but it seemed to be implied in his institutions, and was at any rate the common understanding of the Jews. The design was to keep them a separate people. To do this, Moses forbade alliances by contract, or marriage, with the surrounding nations, which were idolatrous. See Lev. 18: 24–30; Deut. 7: 3–12; comp. Ezra 9: 11–12. This command the Jews perverted; and explained as referring to intercourse of an kinds, even to the exercise of friendly offices and commercial transactions. Comp. John 4: 9.

Of another nation. Greek, Another tribe. It refers here to all who were not Jews.

God hath shewed me. Comp. Acts 15: 8–9. He had showed him by the vision, Acts 10: 11–12.

Any man common or unclean.

That no man was to be regarded as excluded from the opportunity of salvation; or be despised and abhorred. The gospel was to be preached to all; the barrier between Jews and Gentiles to be broken down; and all were to be regarded as capable of being saved.

33. Thou hast well done. This is an expression of grateful feeling.

Before God. In the presence of God. It is implied that they believed that God saw them, and that they were assembled at his command, and that they were disposed to listen to his instructions.

34. Then Peter opened his mouth. Began to speak, Matt. 5: 2.

Of a truth. Truly; evidently. That is, I have evidence here that God is no respecter of persons.

Is no respecter of persons. The word used here denotes the act of showing favor to one on account of rank, family, wealth, or partiality, arising from any cause. It is explained in James 2: 1–4. A judge is a respecter of persons when he favors one of the parties on account of private friendship; or because he is a man of rank, influence, or power; or because he belongs to the same political party, etc. The Jews supposed that they were peculiarly favored by God, and that salvation was not extended to other nations, and that the fact of being a Jew entitled them to this favor. Peter here says that he has learned the error of this doctrine. That a man is not to be accepted because he is a Jew, nor is he to be excluded because he is a Gentile. The barrier is broken down, the offer is made to all, and God will save all on the same principle – not by external privileges, or rank, but according to their character. The same doctrine is elsewhere explicitly stated in the New Testament, Rom. 2: 11; Eph. 6: 9; Col. 3: 25.

It may be observed here, that this does not refer to the doctrine of Divine sovereignty or election. It simply affirms that God will not save a man because he is a Jew; nor because he is rich, or learned, or of elevated rank; nor by any external privileges. Nor will he exclude any man because he is destitute of these privileges. But this does not affirm that he will not make a difference in their character, and then treat them according to their character; nor that he will not pardon whom he pleases, which is a different question. The interpretation of this passage should be limited strictly

ninth hour I prayed in my house, and, behold, a man stood before me in bright clothing,

31 And said, Cornelius, thy prayer is heard, and thine alms are had in remembrance in the sight of God.

32 Send therefore to Joppa, and call hither Simon, whose surname is Peter; he is lodged in the house of one Simon a tanner by the sea side: who, when he cometh, shall speak unto thee.

33 Immediately therefore I sent to thee; and thou hast well done that thou art come. Now therefore are we all here present before God, to hear all things that are commanded thee of God.

34 Then Peter opened his mouth, and said, Of a truth I perceive that God is no respecter of persons:

35 But in every nation he that feareth him, and worketh righteousness, is accepted with him.

36 The word which God sent unto the children of Israel, preaching peace by Jesus Christ: (he is Lord of all:)

37 That word, I say, ye know, which was published throughout all Judaea, and began from Galilee, after the baptism which John preached;

38 How God anointed Jesus of Nazareth with the Holy Ghost and with power: who went about doing good, and healing all that were oppressed of the devil; for God was with him.

39 And we are witnesses of all things which he did both in the land of the Jews, and in Jerusalem; whom they slew and hanged on a tree:

40 Him God raised up the third day, and shewed him openly;

41 Not to all the people, but unto witnesses chosen before of God, even to us, who did eat and drink with him after he rose from the dead.

42 And he commanded us to preach unto the people, and to testify that it is he which was ordained of God to be the Judge of quick and dead.

43 To him give all the prophets witness, that through his name whosoever believeth in him shall receive remission of sins.

44 While Peter yet spake these words, the Holy Ghost fell on all them which heard the word.

the poor (Isaiah 58: 7), forasmuch as *misericordia*, or mercy, is the inward affection of the heart properly. For from this fountain springeth true and well ordered bountifulness, if the troubles and sorrows of our brethren do move us to compassion; if, considering the unity which is amongst us, we foster and cherish them as we would cherish our own flesh, and study to help them as we would help our own members. Hypocrites are, indeed, sometimes liberal, or at least bountiful; but howsoever they waste all, yet no relief which they shall bestow upon the poor shall be worthy to be called by the name of alms. For we must hold that of Paul, He which hath no love is nothing, though he give all his goods to the poor (1 Corinthians 13: 3). Let us, therefore, learn by this word, that God doth then allow our liberality, if we relieve the poverty of the poor, being moved with compassion, and if, as it were, with open bowels we bestow that which the liberality of God doth give.

41. If any man demand here, Why God did not show his Son openly to all men after his resurrection? I answer, Although there could no reason be showed, yet ought the counsel of God alone to suffice sober and modest men, that they may assure themselves without all doubt that that is best which God hath thought meet. And yet, assuredly God used this moderation to a good end. For the certainty of the resurrection was proved by many and firm testimonies, and this was profitable to exercise the faith of the godly, to believe the gospel rather than their eyes. As touching the wicked and professed enemies of Christ seeing that being so often convict they would never yield to God, they were unworthy to have Christ to admit them to behold the glow of his resurrection. Though even they were sufficiently convict with the report of the soldiers, whom they had hired to keep the sepulcher; that I may omit other reasons which we may fet out of the Harmony. Therefore, let us assure ourselves of this, that the holy apostles were chosen by the holy decree of God, that by their testimony the truth of Christ's resurrection might stand. Whosoever is not content with this approbation, let him take away and overthrow if he can that inviolable decree of God, which Peter commendeth to us in this place. And as for us, if we covet to have God the sure author of our faith let us learn to be content with the witnesses whom in due time he hath brought forth, as were, by his hand, being ordained by him before the world was made.

ACTS 11

1. And the apostles

Whereas Luke declareth that the fame of one house which was converted was spread abroad everywhere amongst the

to the case in hand – to mean that God will not accept and save a man on account of external national rank and privileges. That by receiving some, and leaving others, on other grounds, he will not make a difference, is not anywhere denied. Comp. 1 Cor. 4: 7; Rom. 12: 6. It is worthy of remark, further, that the most strenuous advocate for the doctrines of sovereignty and election in the New Testament – the apostle Paul – is also the one that labored most to establish the doctrine that God was no respecter of persons; that is, that there was no difference between the Jews and Gentiles in regard to the way of salvation; that God would not save a man because he was a Jew, nor destroy a man because he was a Gentile. Yet, in regard to the whole race viewed as lying on a level, he maintained that God had a right to exercise the prerogatives of a sovereign, and to have mercy on whom he would have mercy.

44. The Holy Ghost fell, etc. Endowing them with the power of speaking with other tongues, Acts 10: 46. Of this the apostle Peter makes much in his argument in Acts 11: 17. By this God showed that the Gentiles were to be admitted to the same privileges with the Jews, and to the blessings of salvation in the same manner. Comp. Acts 2: 1–4.

Which heard the word. The word of God; the message of the gospel.

45. And they of the circumcision. Who had been Jews.

Were astonished. Were amazed that Gentiles should be admitted to the same favor as themselves.

47. Can any man forbid water, etc. They have shown that they are favored in the same way as the Jewish converts. God has manifested himself to them, as he did to the Jews on the day of Pentecost. Is it not clear, therefore, that they are entitled to the privilege of Christian baptism? The expression here used is one that would naturally refer to water being brought; that is, to a small quantity; and would seem to imply that they were baptized, not by immersion, but by pouring or sprinkling.

48. And he commanded them, etc. Why Peter did not himself baptize them is unknown. But

it might be, perhaps, because he chose to make use of the ministry of the brethren who were with him, to prevent the possibility of future cavil. If they did it themselves, they could not so easily be led by the Jews to find fault with it. It may be added, also, that it seems not to have been the practice of the apostles themselves to baptize very extensively. This was left to be performed by others. See 1 Cor. 1: 14–17: "Christ sent me not to baptize, but to preach the gospel."

ACTS 11

1. And the apostles and brethren. The Christians who were in Judea.

Heard, etc. So extraordinary an occurrence as that at Caesarea, the descent of the Holy Spirit on the Gentiles, and their reception into the church, would excite attention, and be likely to produce much sensibility in regard to the conduct of Peter and those with him. It was so contrary to all the ideas of the Jews, that it is not to be wondered at that it led to contention.

2. They that were of the circumcision. The Christians who had been converted from among the Jews.

Contended with him. Disputed, or reproved him; charged him with being in fault. This is one of the circumstances which show conclusively that the apostles and early Christians did not regard Peter as having any particular supremacy over the church, or as being in any peculiar sense the vicar of Christ upon earth. If Peter had been regarded as having the authority which the Roman Catholics claim for him, they would have submitted at once to what he had thought proper to do. But the primitive Christians had no such idea of his authority. This claim for Peter is not only opposed to this place, but to every part of the New Testament.

4. But Peter rehearsed. Greek, Peter beginning, explained it to them in order. That is, he began with the vision which he saw, and gave a narrative of the various events in order, as they actually occurred. A simple and unvarnished statement of facts is usually the best way of

45 And they of the circumcision which believed were astonished, as many as came with Peter, because that on the Gentiles also was poured out the gift of the Holy Ghost.

46 For they heard them speak with tongues, and magnify God. Then answered Peter,

47 Can any man forbid water, that these should not be baptized, which have received the Holy Ghost as well as we?

48 And he commanded them to be baptized in the name of the Lord. Then prayed they him to tarry certain days.

ACTS 11

1 And the apostles and brethren that were in Judaea heard that the Gentiles had also received the word of God.

2 And when Peter was come up to Jerusalem, they that were of the circumcision contended with him,

3 Saying, Thou wentest in to men uncircumcised, and didst eat with them.

4 But Peter rehearsed the matter from the beginning, and expounded it by order unto them, saying,

5 I was in the city of Joppa praying: and in a trance I saw a vision, A certain vessel descend, as it had been a great sheet, let down from heaven by four corners; and it came even to me:

6 Upon the which when I had fastened mine eyes, I considered, and saw fourfooted beasts of the earth, and wild beasts, and creeping things, and fowls of the air.

7 And I heard a voice saying unto me, Arise, Peter; slay and eat.

8 But I said, Not so, Lord: for nothing common or unclean hath at any time entered into my mouth.

9 But the voice answered me again from heaven, What God hath cleansed, that call not thou common.

10 And this was done three times: and all were drawn up again into heaven.

11 And, behold, immediately there were three men already come unto the house where I was, sent from Caesarea unto me.

12 And the spirit bade me go with them, nothing doubting. Moreover these six brethren accompanied me, and we entered into the man's house:

brethren, that did arise by reason of admiration; for the Jews accounted it as a monster that the Gentiles should be gathered unto them as if they should have heard that there had been men made of stones. Again, the immoderate love of their nation did hinder them from acknowledging the work of God. For we see that through this ambition and pride the Church was troubled; because the equality which did diminish their dignity was not tolerable. For which cause they did contend stoutly to bring the necks of the Gentiles under the yoke. But forasmuch as it was foretold by so many prophecies of the prophets, that the Church should be gathered of all people after the coming of the Messiah, and forasmuch as Christ had given commandment to his apostles touching the preaching of the gospel throughout the whole world, how can it be that the conversion of a few men should move some, as some strange thing, and should terrify other some, as if it were some monster? I answer, that whatsoever was foretold touching the calling of the Gentiles, it was so taken as if the Gentiles should be made subject to the law of Moses, that they might have a place in the Church. But the manner of the calling, the beginning whereof they saw then, was not only unknown, but it seemed to be quite contrary to reason. For they did dream that it was impossible that the Gentiles could be mixed with the sons of Abraham, and be made one body with them, (the ceremonies being taken away,) but that there should be great injury done to the covenant of God; for to what end served the law save only to be the mid wall to note out the disagreement? Secondly, because they were acquainted with that difference during their whole life, the unlooked-for newness of the thing doth so pierce them, that they did forget all that which ought to have quieted their minds. Finally, they do not straightway comprehend the mystery, which, as Paul teacheth, was unknown to the angels from the creation of the world.

2. They reasoned with him

Obstinacy doth for the most part accompany error. This was now a fault having in it too gross ignorance, in that they did not quietly receive the Gentiles into their bosom, united to them by the same Spirit of faith. But they do not only leap back, but also contend with Peter contentiously, and blame him for his fact, which deserved great praise. They hear that the Gentiles have embraced the Word of God; what letteth them then from embracing them, that they may be coupled together under the government of one God? For what more holy bond can there be, than when all men, with one consent, are coupled and joined to God? And why should not those grow together into one body who make the Messiah of God their head? But because they saw the external form of the law broken, they thought that

disarming prejudice and silencing opposition. In revivals of true religion, the best way of silencing opposition, and especially among Christians, is to make a plain statement of things as they actually occurred. Opposition most commonly arises from prejudice, or from false or exaggerated statements; and those can be best removed, not by angry contention, but by an unvarnished relation of the facts. In most cases prejudice will thus be disarmed, and opposition will die away, as was the case in regard to the admission of the Gentiles to the church.

And expounded it. Explained it; stated it as it actually occurred.

By order. One event after another, as they happened. He thus showed that his own mind had been as much biased as theirs, and stated in what manner his prejudices had been removed. It often happens that those who become most zealous and devoted in any new plans for the advancement of religion, were as much opposed to them at first as others. They are led from one circumstance to another, until their prejudices die away, and the Providence and Spirit of God indicate clearly their duty.

14. And all thy house. Thy family. This is a circumstance which is omitted in the account in Acts 10. It is said, however, in Acts 10: 2, that Cornelius feared God with all his house. And it is evident, from Acts 10: 48, that the family also received the ordinance of baptism, and was received into the church.

15. And as I began to speak. Or, when I was speaking.

The Holy Ghost, etc. Acts 10: 44

17. What was I. What power or right had I to oppose the manifest will of God that the Gentiles should be received into the Christian church.

Withstand God. Oppose or resist God. He had indicated his will; he had showed his intention to save the Gentiles; and the prejudices of Peter were all overcome. One of the best means of destroying prejudice and false opinions, is a powerful revival of religion. More erroneous doctrines and unholy feelings are overcome in such scenes, than in all the angry controversies, and bigoted and fierce conten-

tions, that have ever taken place. If men wish to root error out of the church, they should strive by all means to promote everywhere revivals of pure and undefiled religion. The Holy Spirit more easily and effectually silences false doctrine, and destroys heresy, than all the denunciations of fierce theologians; all the alarms of professed zeal for truth; and all the anathemas Which professed orthodoxy and love for the purity of the church ever uttered from the icebergs on which such champions usually seek their repose and their home.

18. They held their peace. They were convinced, as Peter had been, by the manifest indications of the will of God.

Then hath God, etc. The great truth is in this manner established, that the doors of the church are opened to the entire Gentile world – a great and glorious truth, that was worthy of this remarkable interposition. It at once changed the views of the apostles and of the early Christians; gave them new, large, and liberal conceptions of the gospel; broke down all their long-cherished prejudices; taught them to look upon all men as their brethren; and impressed their hearts with the truth, never after to be eradicated, that the Christian church was founded for the wide world, and opened the same glorious pathway to life wherever man might be found, whether with the narrow prejudice of the Jew, or amidst the degradations of the pagan world. To this truth we owe our hopes; for this, we should thank the God of heaven; and impressed with it, we should seek to invite the entire world to partake with us of the rich provisions of the gospel of the blessed God.

19. Now they, etc. This verse introduces a new train of historical remark; and from this point the course of the history of the Acts of the Apostles takes a new direction. Thus far, the history had recorded chiefly the preaching of the gospel to the Jews only. From this point the history records the efforts made to convert the Gentiles. It begins with the labors put forth in the important city of Antioch, Acts 11: 19–20 and as, during the work of grace that occurred in that city, the labors of the apostle Paul were especially sought, Acts 11: 25–26, the

13 And he shewed us how he had seen an angel in his house, which stood and said unto him, Send men to Joppa, and call for Simon, whose surname is Peter;

14 Who shall tell thee words, whereby thou and all thy house shall be saved.

15 And as I began to speak, the Holy Ghost fell on them, as on us at the beginning.

16 Then remembered I the word of the Lord, how that he said, John indeed baptized with water; but ye shall be baptized with the Holy Ghost.

17 Forasmuch then as God gave them the like gift as he did unto us, who believed on the Lord Jesus Christ; what was I, that I could withstand God?

18 When they heard these things, they held their peace, and glorified God, saying, Then hath God also to the Gentiles granted repentance unto life.

19 Now they which were scattered abroad upon the persecution that arose about Stephen traveled as far as Phenice, and Cyprus, and Antioch, preaching the word to none but unto the Jews only.

20 And some of them were men of Cyprus and Cyrene, which, when they were come to Antioch, spake unto the Grecians, preaching the Lord Jesus.

21 And the hand of the Lord was with them: and a great number believed, and turned unto the Lord.

22 Then tidings of these things came unto the ears of the church which was in Jerusalem: and they sent forth Barnabas, that he should go as far as Antioch.

23 Who, when he came, and had seen the grace of God, was glad, and exhorted them all, that with purpose of heart they would cleave unto the Lord.

24 For he was a good man, and full of the Holy Ghost and of faith: and much people was added unto the Lord.

25 Then departed Barnabas to Tarsus, for to seek Saul:

26 And when he had found him, he brought him unto Antioch. And it came to pass, that a whole year they assembled themselves with the church, and taught much people. And the disciples were called Christians first in Antioch.

27 And in these days came prophets from Jerusalem unto Antioch.

28 And there stood up one of them

heaven and earth did go together.

And note, that although Luke said before that the apostles and brethren had heard this fame, yet he spake nothing of offense; but he bringeth in now, as it were, a new sect of men, which did contend with Peter. The brethren, saith he, heard, and there an end; it followeth, When Peter was come to Jerusalem, those which were of the circumcision did contend with him, who were undoubtedly unlike to the first; again, these words peritomes, do not simply signify the Jews, but those who were too much addicted to keeping the ceremonies of the law. For there were none of Jerusalem in Christ's flock at that time, save only those which were circumcised. From whom, then, could he distinguish those men? Lastly, it seemeth to be a thing unlike to be true that the apostles, and those which were moderate being of the number of the faithful, did attempt this combat. For though they had been offended, yet they might have conferred with Peter privately, and have demanded some reason of his fact. By these reasons am I moved to think that those are said to be of the circumcision who did make so great account of circumcision, that they granted no man a place in the kingdom of God, unless he took upon him the profession of the law, and, being admitted into the Church by this holy rite, did put off uncleanness.

3. Unto men being uncircumcised

This was not forbidden by the law of God, but it was a tradition which came from the fathers. And yet, notwithstanding, Peter doth not object that they dealt too hardly with him in this point, and that he was not bound by the necessity of man's law. He omitteth all this defense, and doth only answer, that they came first unto him, and that they were offered unto him, as it were, by the hand of God. And here we see the rare modesty of Peter, because whereas, trusting to the goodness of the cause, he might have justly despised unskillful men, who did trouble him unjustly, yet doth he mildly excuse himself as it becometh brethren. This was no small trial in that he was unworthily accused, because he had obeyed God faithfully. But because he knew that this law was enjoined the whole Church, that every man be ready to give an account of his doctrine and life so often as the matter requireth, and he remembered that he was one of the flock, he doth not only suffer himself to be ruled, but submitteth himself willingly to the judgment of the Church. Doctrine, indeed, if it be of God, is placed above the chance and die of man's judgment; but because the Lord will have prophecy judged, his servants must not refuse this condition, that they prove themselves to be such as they will be accounted.

sacred writer thenceforward confines the history mainly to his travels and labors.

Which were scattered abroad. See Acts 8: 1.

As far as Phenice. Phoenice, or Phoenicia, was a province of Syria, which in its largest sense comprehended a narrow strip of country lying on the eastern coast of the Mediterranean, and extending from Antioch to the borders of Egypt. But Phoenice Proper extended only from the cities of Laodicea to Tyre, and included only the territories of Tyre and Sidon. This country was called sometimes simply Canaan.

And Cyprus. An island off the coast of Asia Minor, in the Mediterranean Sea.

23. **Had seen the grace of God.** The favor or mercy of God, in converting sinners to himself.

Was glad. Approved of what had been done in preaching the gospel to the Gentiles, and rejoiced that God had poured down his Spirit on them. The effect of a revival is to produce joy in the hearts of all those who love the Savior.

And exhorted them all. Entreated them. They would be exposed to many trials and temptations, and he sought to secure their affections in the cause of religion.

That with purpose of heart. With a firm mind; with a fixed, settled resolution; that they would make this their settled plan of life, their main object.

24. **For he was a good man.** This is given as a reason why he was so eminently successful. It is not said that he was a man of distinguished talents or learning; that he was a splendid or an imposing preacher; but simply that he was a pious, humble man of God. He was honest, and devoted to his master's work. We should not undervalue talent, eloquence, or learning in the ministry; but we may remark, that humble piety will often do more in the conversion of souls than the most splendid talents. No endowments can be a substitute for this. The real power of a minister is concentrated in this; and without this his ministry will be barrenness and a curse. There is nothing on this earth so mighty as goodness. If a man

wished to make-the most of his powers, the true secret would be found in employing them for a good object, and suffering them to be wholly under the direction of benevolence. John Howard's purpose to do good has made a more permanent impression on the interests of the world than the mad ambition of Alexander or Caesar. Perhaps the expression, "he was a good man," means that he was a man of a kind, amiable, and sweet disposition.

Full of the Holy Ghost. Was entirely under the influence of the Holy Spirit. He was eminently a pious man. This is the second qualification here mentioned of a good minister. He was not merely exemplary for mildness and kindness of temper, but he was eminently a man of God. He was filled with the influences of the sacred Spirit, producing zeal, love, peace, joy, etc. See Gal. 5: 22–23.

And of faith. Confidence in the truth and promises of God. This is the third qualification mentioned; and this was another cause of his success. He confided in God. He trusted to his promises. He depended not on his own strength, but on the strength of the arm of God. With these qualifications he engaged in his work, and he was successful. These qualifications should be sought by the ministry of the gospel. Others should not indeed be neglected, but a man's ministry will usually be successful only as he seeks to possess those endowments which distinguished Barnabas – a kind, tender, benevolent heart; devoted piety; the fullness of the Spirit's influence; and strong, unwavering confidence in the promises and power of God.

And much people. Many people.

29. **Then the disciples.** The Christians at Antioch.

According to his ability. According as they had prospered. It does not imply that they were rich, but that they rendered aid as they could afford it.

Determined to send relief. This arose not merely from their general sense of their obligation to aid the poor, but they felt themselves particularly bound to aid their Jewish brethren. The obligation to aid the temporal wants of those from whom they had received so important spiritual mercies, is repeatedly

named Agabus, and signified by the spirit that there should be great dearth throughout all the world: which came to pass in the days of Claudius Caesar.

29 Then the disciples, every man according to his ability, determined to send relief unto the brethren which dwelt in Judaea:

30 Which also they did, and sent it to the elders by the hands of Barnabas and Saul.

ACTS 12

1 Now about that time Herod the king stretched forth his hands to vex certain of the church.

2 And he killed James the brother of John with the sword.

3 And because he saw it pleased the Jews, he proceeded further to take Peter also. (Then were the days of unleavened bread.)

4 And when he had apprehended him, he put him in prison, and delivered him to four quaternions of soldiers to keep him; intending after Easter to bring him forth to the people.

5 Peter therefore was kept in prison: but prayer was made without ceasing of the church unto God for him.

6 And when Herod would have brought him forth, the same night Peter was sleeping between two soldiers, bound with two chains: and the keepers before the door kept the prison.

7 And, behold, the angel of the Lord came upon him, and a light shined in the prison: and he smote Peter on the side, and raised him up, saying, Arise up quickly. And his chains fell off from his hands.

8 And the angel said unto him, Gird thyself, and bind on thy sandals. And so he did. And he saith unto him, Cast thy garment about thee, and follow me.

9 And he went out, and followed him; and wist not that it was true which was done by the angel; but thought he saw a vision.

10 When they were past the first and the second ward, they came unto the iron gate that leadeth unto the city; which opened to them of his own accord: and they went out, and passed on through one street; and forthwith the angel departed from him.

ACTS 12

1. Here followeth new persecution raised by Herod. We see that the Church had some short truce, that it might, as it were, by a short breathing, recover some courage against the time to come, and that it might then fight afresh. So at this day there is no cause why the faithful, having borne the brunt of one or two conflicts, should promise themselves rest, or should desire such a calling as old overworn soldiers use to have. Let this suffice them if the Lord grant them some time wherein they may recover their strength. This Herod was Agrippa the greater [elder], the son of Aristobulus, whom his father slew. Josephus doth no where call him Herod, it may be, because he had a brother who was king of Chalcis, whose name was Herod. This man was incensed to afflict the Church not so much for any love he had to religion, as that by this means he might flatter the common people which did otherwise not greatly favor him; or rather, he was moved hereunto with tyrannical cruelty, because he was afraid of innovation, which tyrants do always fear, lest it trouble the quiet estate of their dominion. Yet it is likely that he did shed innocent blood, that, according to the common craft of kings, he might gratify a furious people; because St. Luke will shortly after declare that Peter the apostle was put into prison that he might be a pleasant spectacle.

He killed James

Undoubtedly the cruelty of this mad man was restrained and bridled by the secret power of God. For assuredly he would never have been content with one or two murders, and so have abstained from persecuting the rest, but he would rather have piled up martyrs upon heaps, unless God had set his hand against him, and defended his flock. So when we see that the enemies of godliness, being full of fury, do not commit horrible slaughters, that they may mix and imbrue all things with blood, let us know that we need not thank their moderation and clemency for this; but because, when the Lord doth spare his sheep, he doth not suffer them to do so much hurt as they would. This Herod was not so courteous, that he would stick to win peace or the people's favor with the punishment of an hundred men or more.

Wherefore, we must think with ourselves that he was tied by one that had the rule over him, that he might not more vehemently oppress the Church. He slew James, as, when any sedition is raised, the heads and captains go first to the pot, that the common riff-raft may by their punishment be terrified. Nevertheless, the Lord suffered him whom he had furnished with constancy to be put to death, that by death he might get the victory as a strong and invincible champion. So that the attempts of tyrants notwithstanding, God

enforced in the New Testament. Comp. Rom. 15: 25–27; 1 Cor. 16: 1–2; 2 Cor. 9: 1–2; Gal. 2: 10.

ACTS 12

1. Now about that time. That is, during the time that the famine existed; or the time when Barnabas and Saul went up to Jerusalem. This was probably about the fifth or sixth year of the reign of Claudius, not far from AD 47.

Herod the king. This was Herod Agrippa.

Stretched forth his hands. A figurative expression, denoting that he laid his hands on them, or that he endeavored violently to oppress the church.

To vex. To injure, to do evil to.

Certain. Some of the church. Who they were the writer immediately specifies.

2. And he killed, etc. He caused to be put to death with a sword, either by beheading, or piercing him through. The Roman procurators were entrusted with authority over life, though in the time of Pilate the Jews had not this authority. James the brother of John. This was the son of Zebedee, Matt. 4: 21. He is commonly called James the Greater, in contradistinction from James the son of Alpheus, who is called James the Less, Matt. 10: 3. In this manner were the predictions of our Savior respecting him fulfilled. Matt. 20: 23, "Ye shall indeed drink of my cup, and be baptized with the baptism that I am baptized with."

3. And because he saw it pleased the Jews. This was the principle on which he acted. It was not from a sense of right; it was not to do justice, and protect the innocent; it was not to discharge the appropriate duties of a magistrate, and a king; but it was to promote his own popularity. It is probable that Agrippa would have acted in this way in any circumstances. He was ambitious, vain, and fawning; he sought, as his great principle, popularity; and he was willing to sacrifice, like many others, truth and justice to obtain this end. But there was also a particular reason for this in his case. He held his appointment under the Roman emperor. This foreign rule was always unpopular among the Jews. In order, there-fore, to secure a peaceful reign, and to prevent insurrection and tumult, it was necessary for him to court their favor; to indulge their wishes, and to fall in with their prejudices. Alas! how many monarchs and rulers there have been, who were governed by no better principle, and whose sole aim has been to secure popularity, even at the expense of law, and truth and justice.

9. And wist not. Knew not.

Saw a vision. That is, was a representation made to his mind, similar to that which he had seen before. Comp. Acts 10: 11–12. It was so astonishing, so unexpected, so wonderful, that he could not realize that it was true.

10. The iron gate. The outer gate, secured with iron, as the doors of prisons are now.

Of his own accord. Itself. It opened spontaneously, without the application of any force, or key, thus showing conclusively that Peter was delivered by miraculous interposition.

And passed on through one street. Till Peter was entirely safe from any danger of pursuit, and then the angel left him. God had effected his complete rescue, and now left him to his own efforts as usual.

11. And when Peter was come to himself. This expression naturally means, when he had over-come his amazement and astonishment at the unexpected deliverance, so as to be capable of reflection. He had been amazed by the whole transaction. He thought it was a vision; and in the suddenness and rapidity with which it was done, he had no time for cool reflection. The events of Divine Providence often overwhelm and amaze us; and such are their suddenness, and rapidity, and unexpected character in their development, as to confound us, and prevent calm and collected reflection.

Of a surety. Certainly; surely. He considered all the circumstances; he saw that he was actually at liberty and that it could have been effected only by Divine interposition.

The expectation of the people. From this it appears that the people earnestly desired his death; and it was to gratify that desire that Herod had imprisoned him.

15. Thou art mad. Thou art insane. They seem

11 And when Peter was come to himself, he said, Now I know of a surety, that the Lord hath sent his angel, and hath delivered me out of the hand of Herod, and from all the expectation of the people of the Jews.

12 And when he had considered the thing, he came to the house of Mary the mother of John, whose surname was Mark; where many were gathered together praying.

13 And as Peter knocked at the door of the gate, a damsel came to hearken, named Rhoda.

14 And when she knew Peter's voice, she opened not the gate for gladness, but ran in, and told how Peter stood before the gate.

15 And they said unto her, Thou art mad. But she constantly affirmed that it was even so. Then said they, It is his angel.

16 But Peter continued knocking: and when they had opened the door, and saw him, they were astonished.

17 But he, beckoning unto them with the hand to hold their peace, declared unto them how the Lord had brought him out of the prison. And he said, Go shew these things unto James, and to the brethren. And he departed, and went into another place.

18 Now as soon as it was day, there was no small stir among the soldiers, what was become of Peter.

19 And when Herod had sought for him, and found him not, he examined the keepers, and commanded that they should be put to death. And he went down from Judaea to Caesarea, and there abode.

20 And Herod was highly displeased with them of Tyre and Sidon: but they came with one accord to him, and, having made Blastus the king's chamberlain their friend, desired peace; because their country was nourished by the king's country.

21 And upon a set day Herod, arrayed in royal apparel, sat upon his throne, and made an oration unto them.

22 And the people gave a shout, saying, It is the voice of a god, and not of a man.

23 And immediately the angel of the Lord smote him, because he gave not God the glory: and he was eaten of worms,

maketh choice of sweet-smelling sacrifices to establish the faith of his gospel. Luke calleth this games which was slain the brother of John, that he may distinguish him from the son of Alpheus. For whereas some make him a third cousin of Christ's, who was only some one of the disciples, I do not like of that, because I am by strong reasons persuaded to think that there were no more. Let him that will, repair to the second to the Galatians. Therefore, I think that the apostle and the son of Alpheus were all one, whom the Jews threw down headlong from the top of the temple, whose death was so highly Commended for his singular praise of holiness.

3. Seeing that it pleased the Jews

It appeareth more plainly by this that Herod was not moved either with any zeal that he had to Moses' law or with any hatred of the gospel, thus to persecute the Church; but that he might provide for his own private affairs, for he proceedeth in his cruelty that he may win the people's favor; therefore we must know that there be diverse causes for which the Church is assaulted on every side. Oftentimes perverse zeal driveth the wicked headlong to fight for their superstitions, and that they may sacrifice an offering to their idols by shedding innocent blood; but the more part is moved with private commodities only, so in times past, at such time as Nero knew, after the burning of the city, that he was loathed and hated of the people, he sought by this subtle means to get into favor again, or, at least, he went about to stay their slanders and complaints, by putting certain thousands of the godly to death.

24. And the word of God

When the tyrant was once taken out of the way the Church was suddenly delivered, as it were, out of the jaws of the wolf. Therefore, though the faithful be accounted as sheep appointed to be slain (Psalm 44: 23), yet the Church doth always overlive her enemies; and though the word of God seem oftentimes to be oppressed with the wicked tyranny of men, yet it getteth up the head again by and by (Romans 8: 37). For Luke determined not only what had happened after that Herod was dead, but also by this example to encourage us, that we may be assured that God will do that, in all ages, which he then did, to the end the gospel may at length break through all impediments of the enemies, and that the more the Church is diminished, it may the more increase through the heavenly blessing.

ACTS 13

Here followeth an history, not only worthy to be remembered, but also very profitable to be known, how Paul was appointed the teacher of the Gentiles; for his calling was,

to have regarded his rescue as so difficult and so hopeless, that they deemed it proof of derangement that she now affirmed it. And yet this was the very thing for which they had been so earnestly praying. When it was now announced to them that the object of their prayers was granted, they deemed the messenger that announced it insane. Christians are often surprised even when their prayers are answered. They are overwhelmed and amazed at the success of their own petitions, and are slow to believe that the very thing for which they have sought could be granted. It shows, perhaps, with how little faith, after all, they pray; and how slow they are to believe that God can hear and answer prayer. In a revival of religion, in answer to prayer, Christians are often overwhelmed, and astonished when even their own petitions are granted, and when God manifests his own power in his own way and time. Prayer should be persevered in, and we should place ourselves in a waiting posture to catch the first indications that God has heard us with joy.

But she constantly affirmed it. She insisted on it. How much better it would have been to have hastened at once to the gate, than thus to have engaged in a controversy on the subject. Peter was suffered to remain knocking, while they debated the matter. Christians are often engaged in some unprofitable controversy, when they should hasten to catch the first tokens of Divine favor, and open their arms to welcome the proofs that God has heard their prayers.

Then said they. Still resolved not to be convinced.

It is his angel. Any way of accounting for it rather than to admit the simple fact, or to ascertain the simple truth. All this was produced by the little hope which they had of his release, and their earnest desire that it should be so. It was just such a state of mind as is indicated when we say, "the news is too good to be believed."

16. Were astonished. They were now convinced that it was Peter, and they were amazed that he had been rescued. As yet they were of course ignorant of the manner in which it was done.

23. And immediately the angel of the Lord. Diseases and death are, in the Scriptures, often attributed to an angel. See 2 Sam. 24: 16.

It is not intended that there was a miracle in this case, but it certainly is intended by the sacred writer, that his death was a Divine judgment on him for his receiving homage as a god.

Because he gave not God the glory. Because he was willing himself to receive the worship due to God. It was the more sinful in him as he was a Jew, and was acquainted with the true God, and with the evils of idolatry. He was proud, and willing to be flattered, and even adored. He had sought their applause; he had arrayed himself in this splendid manner to excite their admiration; and when they carried it even so far as to offer Divine homage, he did not reject the impious flattery, but listened still to their praises. Hence he was judged; and God vindicated his own insulted honor by inflicting severe pains on him, and by his most awful death.

And he was eaten of worms. The word used here is not elsewhere found in the New Testament.

ACTS 13

2. As they ministered to the Lord. It is probable that this took place on some day set apart for fasting and prayer. The expression "ministered to the Lord" denotes, as they were engaged in prayer to the Lord, or as they were engaged in Divine service.

The Holy Ghost said. Evidently by direct revelation.

Separate me. Set apart to me, or for my service. It does not mean to ordain, but simply to designate, or appoint to this specific work.

For the work whereunto I have called them. Not the apostolic office, for Saul was called to that by the express revelation of Jesus Christ, Gal. 1: 12, and Barnabas was not an apostle. The "work" to which they were now set apart was that of preaching the gospel in the regions round about Antioch. It was not any permanent office in the church, but was a temporary designation to a missionary enterprise in extending the gospel especially

and gave up the ghost.

24 But the word of God grew and multiplied.

25 And Barnabas and Saul returned from Jerusalem, when they had fulfilled their ministry, and took with them John, whose surname was Mark.

ACTS 13

1 Now there were in the church that was at Antioch certain prophets and teachers; as Barnabas, and Simeon that was called Niger, and Lucius of Cyrene, and Manaen, which had been brought up with Herod the tetrarch, and Saul.

2 As they ministered to the Lord, and fasted, the Holy Ghost said, Separate me Barnabas and Saul for the work whereunto I have called them.

3 And when they had fasted and prayed, and laid their hands on them, they sent them away.

4 So they, being sent forth by the Holy Ghost, departed unto Seleucia; and from thence they sailed to Cyprus.

5 And when they were at Salamis, they preached the word of God in the synagogues of the Jews: and they had also John to their minister.

6 And when they had gone through the isle unto Paphos, they found a certain sorcerer, a false prophet, a Jew, whose name was Bar-jesus:

7 Which was with the deputy of the country, Sergius Paulus, a prudent man; who called for Barnabas and Saul, and desired to hear the word of God.

8 But Elymas the sorcerer (for so is his name by interpretation) withstood them, seeking to turn away the deputy from the faith.

9 Then Saul, (who also is called Paul,) filled with the Holy Ghost, set his eyes on him,

10 And said, O full of all subtilty and all mischief, thou child of the devil, thou enemy of all righteousness, wilt thou not cease to pervert the right ways of the Lord?

11 And now, behold, the hand of the Lord is upon thee, and thou shalt be blind, not seeing the sun for a season. And immediately there fell on him a mist and a darkness; and he went about seeking some to lead him by the hand.

as it were, a key whereby God opened to us the kingdom of heaven. We know that the covenant of eternal life was properly concluded with the Jews, so that we had nothing to do with God's inheritance, forasmuch as we were strangers (Ephesians 2: 12); and the wall of separation was between, which did distinguish those of the household from strangers. Therefore it had profited us nothing, that Christ brought salvation unto the world, unless, the disagreement being taken away, there had been some entrance made for us into the Church. The apostles had already received commandment touching the preaching of the gospel throughout the whole world (Mark 16: 16), but they had kept themselves until this time within the borders of Judea. When Peter was sent to Cornelius, it was a thing so new and strange, that it was almost counted a prodigy.

Secondly, that might seem to be a privilege granted to a few men extraordinarily; but now, forasmuch as God doth plainly and openly appoint Paul and Barnabas to be apostles of the Gentiles, by this means he maketh them equal with the Jews; that the gospel may begin to be common as well to the one as to the other. And now the wall of separation is taken away, that both those who were far off and those which were nigh hand may be reconciled to God; and that being gathered under one head, they may grow together to be one body. Therefore Paul's calling ought to be of no less weight amongst us, than if God should cry from heaven in the hearing of all men, that the salvation, promised in times past to Abraham, and to the seed of Abraham (Genesis 22: 17) doth no less appertain unto us at this day, than if we had come out of the loins of Abraham. For this cause is it that Paul laboreth so much in defense and avouching of his calling (Galatians 1: 17, 12–24); that the Gentiles may assuredly persuade themselves that the doctrine of the gospel was not brought to them by chance, neither by man's rashness, but, first, by the wonderful counsel of God; secondly, by express commandment, whilst that he made that known to men which he had decreed with himself.

1. There were in the church

I have declared in the fourth to the Ephesians (Ephesians 4: 11) and in the twelfth of the First to the Corinthians (1 Corinthians 12: 28), what difference there is (at least in my judgment) between doctors and prophets. It may be that they are in this place synonymous (or that they signify both one thing), so that this is Luke's meaning, that there were many men in that church endowed with singular grace of the Spirit to teach. Surely I cannot see how it can hang together, to understand by prophets those which were endowed with the gift of foretelling things; but I think rather that it signifieth excellent interpreters of Scripture. And such had the office to teach and exhort, as Paul doth testify

through Asia Minor and the adjacent regions. Accordingly, when, in the fulfillment of this appointment, they had traveled through Seleucia, Cyprus, Paphos, Pamphylia, Pisidia, etc., they returned to Antioch, having fulfilled the work to which they were separated. See Acts 14: 26–27.

Whereunto I have called them. This proves that they received their commission to this work directly from God the Holy Spirit. It is possible that Paul and Barnabas had been influenced by the Spirit to engage in this work, but they were to be sent forth by the concurrence and designation of the church.

8. But Elymas the sorcerer, for so is his name by interpretation. Elymas the magician. Elymas is the interpretation, not of the name Bar-jesus, but of the word rendered the sorcerer. It is an Arabic word, and means the same as magus. It seems that he was better known by this foreign name than by his own.

Withstood them. Resisted them. He was sensible that if the influence of Saul and Barnabas should be extended over the proconsul, that he would be seen to be an impostor, and his power be at an end. His interest, therefore, led him to oppose the gospel, His own popularity was at stake; and being governed by this, he opposed the gospel of God. The love of popularity and power, the desire of retaining some political influence, is often a strong reason why men oppose the gospel.

To turn away the deputy from the faith. To prevent the influence of the truth on his mind; or to prevent his becoming the friend and patron of the Christians.

9. Then Saul, (who also is called Paul.) This is the last time that this apostle is called Saul.

Filled with the Holy Ghost. Inspired to detect his sin; to denounce Divine judgment; and to inflict punishment on him.

10. O full of all subtilty and mischief. The word subtilty denotes deceit and fraud; and implies that he was practicing an imposition, and that he knew it. The word rendered mischief denotes, properly, facility of acting, and then sleight of hand; sly, cunning arts, by which one imposes on another, and deceives him with a fraudulent intention. It is not

elsewhere used in the New Testament. The art of Elymas consisted probably in sleight of hand, legerdemain, or trick, aided by skill in the abstruse sciences, by which the ignorant might be easily imposed on.

Child of the devil. Being under his influence; practicing his arts; promoting his designs by deceit and imposture, so that he may be called your father.

Satan is here represented as the author of deceit, and the father of lies.

Enemy of all righteousness. Practicing deceit and iniquity, and thus opposed to righteousness and honesty. A man who lives by wickedness will, of course, be the foe of every form of integrity. A man who lives by fraud will be opposed to the truth; a pander to the vices of men will hate the rules of chastity and purity; a manufacturer or vender of ardent spirits will be the enemy of temperance societies.

Wilt thou not cease to pervert. In what way he had opposed Paul and Barnabas is not known. Probably it might be by misrepresenting their doctrines; by representing them as apostate Jews; and thus by retarding or hindering the progress of the gospel. The expression, "wilt thou not cease," implies that he had been engaged sedulously in doing this, probably from the commencement of their work in the city.

The right ways of the Lord. The straight paths, or doctrines of the Christian religion, in opposition to the crooked and perverse arts of deceivers and impostors. Straight paths denote integrity, sincerity, truth, Jer. 31: 9; Heb. 12: 13.

Crooked ways denote the ways of the sinner, the deceiver, the impostor, Deut. 32: 5.

16. Men of Israel. Jews. The design of this discourse of Paul was to introduce to them the doctrine that Jesus was the Messiah. To do this, he evinced his usual wisdom and address. To have commenced at once on this would have probably excited their prejudice and rage. He therefore pursued a train of argument which showed that he was a firm believer in the Scriptures; that he was acquainted with the history and promises of the Old Testament; and that he was not disposed to call

KING JAMES VERSION

12 Then the deputy, when he saw what was done, believed, being astonished at the doctrine of the Lord.

13 Now when Paul and his company loosed from Paphos, they came to Perga in Pamphylia: and John departing from them returned to Jerusalem.

14 But when they departed from Perga, they came to Antioch in Pisidia, and went into the synagogue on the sabbath day, and sat down.

15 And after the reading of the law and the prophets the rulers of the synagogue sent unto them, saying, Ye men and brethren, if ye have any word of exhortation for the people, say on.

16 Then Paul stood up, and beckoning with his hand said, Men of Israel, and ye that fear God, give audience.

17 The God of this people of Israel chose our fathers, and exalted the people when they dwelt as strangers in the land of Egypt, and with an high arm brought he them out of it.

18 And about the time of forty years suffered he their manners in the wilderness.

19 And when he had destroyed seven nations in the land of Chanaan, he divided their land to them by lot.

20 And after that he gave unto them judges about the space of four hundred and fifty years, until Samuel the prophet.

21 And afterward they desired a king: and God gave unto them Saul the son of Cis, a man of the tribe of Benjamin, by the space of forty years.

22 And when he had removed him, he raised up unto them David to be their king; to whom also he gave testimony, and said, I have found David the son of Jesse, a man after mine own heart, which shall fulfil all my will.

23 Of this man's seed hath God according to his promise raised unto Israel a Savior, Jesus:

24 When John had first preached before his coming the baptism of repentance to all the people of Israel.

25 And as John fulfilled his course, he said, Whom think ye that I am? I am not he. But, behold, there cometh one after me, whose shoes of his feet I am not worthy to loose.

26 Men and brethren, children of the

JOHN CALVIN

in the fourteenth of the First to the Corinthians (1 Corinthians 45: 37). We must mark Luke's drift: Paul and Barnabas were ministers of the church of Antioch; God calleth them thence now unto another place. Lest any man should think that that church was destitute of good and fit ministers, so that God did provide for other churches with the loss of it, Luke preventeth this, and saith, that there was such store there, that though it did help others, yet did there remain sufficient for the use thereof; whereby appeareth how plentifully God had poured out his grace upon the Church, whence rivers, as it were, might be deducted and carried into diverse places.

So even in our time God doth so enrich certain churches more than others, that they be seminaries to spread abroad the doctrine of the gospel. It must needs be that Manaen, who was brought up with Herod, came of some noble family. And this doth Luke recite of purpose that he may set forth to us his godliness who, despising worldly pomp, had coupled himself to the simple and despised flock of Christ. He might, indeed, have been a principal courtier if he had been ruled by ambition; but that he may wholly addict himself to Christ, he refuseth not to change those smokes of honor for reproach and ignominy. For if we consider in what state the Church stood then, he could not give his name to the gospel, unless he should make himself subject to common infamy. Therefore the Lord meant to teach us, by his example, to despise the world, that those may learn with a valiant and lofty mind to despise the world, who cannot otherwise be true Christians, unless they cast away those things which are precious to the flesh, as hurtful lets and hindrances.

2. And they ministered to the Lord

The word which Luke useth doth not only signify to be occupied about holy things, but also sometimes to bear public offices. And because the holy rites of the Gentiles did for the most part consist of burnt-offerings and sacrifices, it is oftentimes taken for to offer sacrifice; which sense did well like the Papists, that they might prove that the apostles did use some sacrifice. But admit it were so; yet do they foolishly pretend for defense of their mass, that the teachers of Antioch did sacrifice. First, forasmuch as the word is of the plural number, it followeth that every one of them did say mass. But letting toys pass, I say we must consider what manner of sacrifice Christ commended to his Church. The Papists feign that the office of priesthood is enjoined them, to sacrifice Christ and by sacrificing him to redeem peace with God. There is so little mention made hereof in Scripture, that the Son of God doth rather challenge this honor to himself alone. Wherefore Christ's Church hath another priesthood, to wit that every man may

in question the doctrines of their fathers. By going over, in a summary way, their history, and recounting the former dealings of God with them, he showed them that he believed the Scriptures; that a promise had been given of a Messiah; and that he had actually come according to the promise.

Ye that fear God. Probably proselytes of the gate, who had not yet been circumcised, but who had renounced idolatry, and were accustomed to worship with them in their synagogues.

Give audience. Hear.

23. Of this man's seed. Of his posterity.

24. When John had first preached, etc. After John had preached, and prepared the way, Matt. 3.

25. And as John fulfilled his course. As he was engaged in completing his work. His ministry is called a course or race; that which was to be run or completed.

He said, etc. These are not the precise words which the evangelists have recorded, but the sense is the same.

26. Men and brethren. Paul now exhorts them to embrace the Lord Jesus as the Messiah. He uses, therefore, the most respectful and fraternal language.

Children of the stock of Abraham. Descendants of Abraham; who regard Abraham as your ancestor. He means here to address particularly the native-born Jews; and appellation is used because they valued themselves highly on account of their descent from Abraham.

Is the word of this salvation sent. This message of salvation. It was sent particularly to the Jewish people. The Savior was sent to that nation, Matt. 15: 24 and the design was to offer to them first the message of life.

27. Because they knew him not. The statement in this verse is designed, not to reproach the Jews at Jerusalem, but to introduce the fact that Jesus had died, and had risen again. With great wisdom and tenderness, he speaks of his murderers in such a manner as not to exasperate, but as far as possible to mitigate their crime. There was sufficient guilt in the murder of the Son of God to overwhelm the

nation with alarm, even after all that could be said to mitigate the deed. See Acts 2: 23,36–37.

When Paul says, "They knew him not," he means, that they did not know him to be the Messiah, (see 1 Cor. 2: 8) they were ignorant of the true meaning of the prophecies of the Old Testament; they regarded him as an impostor.

Nor yet the voices of the Prophets. Neither the meaning of the predictions in the Old Testament, respecting the Messiah. They expected a prince, and a conqueror, but did not expect a Messiah poor and despised, and a man of sorrows, and that was to die on a cross.

Which are read every sabbath day. In the synagogues. Though the Scriptures were read so constantly, yet they were ignorant of their true meaning. They were blinded by pride, and prejudice, and preconceived opinions. Men may often m this way read the Bible a good part of their lives, and, for want of attention, or of a humble mind, never understand it.

They have fulfilled them, etc. By putting him to death they have accomplished what was foretold.

28. And though they found, etc. They found no crime which deserved death. This is conclusively shown by the trial itself. After all their efforts; after the treason of Judas; after their employing false witnesses; still no crime was laid to his charge. The Sanhedrim condemned him for blasphemy; and yet they knew that they could not substantiate this charge before Pilate, and they therefore endeavored to procure his condemnation on the ground of sedition.

29. They took him down, etc. That is, it was done by the Jews, Not that it was done by those who put him to death, but by Joseph of Arimathea, a Jew, and by Nicodemus, and their companions. Paul is speaking of what was done to Jesus by the Jews at Jerusalem; and he does not affirm that the same persons put him to death and laid him in a tomb, but that all this was done by Jews. See John 19: 38–39.

32. And we. We who are present. Paul and Barnabas.

Declare unto you glad tidings We preach the gospel – the good news. To a Jew, nothing

stock of Abraham, and whosoever among you feareth God, to you is the word of this salvation sent.

27 For they that dwell at Jerusalem, and their rulers, because they knew him not, nor yet the voices of the prophets which are read every sabbath day, they have fulfilled them in condemning him.

28 And though they found no cause of death in him, yet desired they Pilate that he should be slain.

29 And when they had fulfilled all that was written of him, they took him down from the tree, and laid him in a sepulcher.

30 But God raised him from the dead:

31 And he was seen many days of them which came up with him from Galilee to Jerusalem, who are his witnesses unto the people.

32 And we declare unto you glad tidings, how that the promise which was made unto the fathers,

33 God hath fulfilled the same unto us their children, in that he hath raised up Jesus again; as it is also written in the second psalm, Thou art my Son, this day have I begotten thee.

34 And as concerning that he raised him up from the dead, now no more to return to corruption, he said on this wise, I will give you the sure mercies of David.

35 Wherefore he saith also in another psalm, Thou shalt not suffer thine Holy One to see corruption.

36 For David, after he had served his own generation by the will of God, fell on sleep, and was laid unto his fathers, and saw corruption:

37 But he, whom God raised again, saw no corruption.

38 Be it known unto you therefore, men and brethren, that through this man is preached unto you the forgiveness of sins:

39 And by him all that believe are justified from all things, from which ye could not be justified by the law of Moses.

40 Beware therefore, lest that come upon you, which is spoken of in the prophets;

41 Behold, ye despisers, and wonder, and perish: for I work a work in your days, a work which ye shall in no wise believe, though a man declare it unto you.

offer himself and his to God; and that the public ministers may sacrifice to God, souls, with the spiritual sword of the gospel, as Paul teacheth (Romans 15: 16). Moreover, the prayers of all the godly are the spiritual calves of the lips (Hosea 14: 2), wherewith God is well pleased, when they are offered up upon the holy altar; that is, in Christ's name, as the thirteenth to the Hebrews (Hebrews 13: 15). Therefore, when Luke saith that the prophets and teachers ministered to God when the Spirit spake to them, I understand nothing else but that they were in the public action. He addeth fasting, that we may know that their minds were then free from all impediments, that nothing might hinder them from giving attendance to prophesying. But the question is, whether they kept a common fast, or Luke doth only signify that they were fasting then until that time. This is, without question, that these circumstances were expressed, that Paul's calling may carry the more credit amongst us.

Separate to me

God commandeth that Paul and Barnabas be sent by the consent of the Church, thither whither he had appointed them to be sent; whereby we gather that there is no lawful election of pastors, save only wherein God is chief. For whereas he hath commanded that the Church should elect pastors and bishops, he hath not therefore granted men so much liberty, but that he will bear the chief sway as the chief governor. The ordinary election of pastors differeth from this appointing of Paul and Barnabas, because it was requisite that they should be appointed by the heavenly oracle to be the apostles of the Gentiles; which is not necessary to be done daily in ordaining pastors. But they agree in this, that as God did testify that Paul and Barnabas were already appointed by his decree to preach the gospel, so none may be called unto the office of teaching save only those whom God hath already chosen to himself after a sort.

Furthermore, there is no need that the Spirit should cry to us out of heaven, that he is called of God about whom we are, because we receive those, as it were, from hand to hand (as they say). whom God hath furnished with necessary gifts, forasmuch as they are framed and made fit by his hand. But whereas Luke saith in this place, that Paul was appointed by the voices and consents of the Church; it doth seem not to agree with Paul's own words, where he doth deny that he was called of men, or by men (Galatians 1: 1). I answer, that he was made an apostle long before, before such time as he was sent unto the Gentiles; and he had now already executed the office of an apostle many years, when he was called to go unto the Gentiles by a new oracle. Wherefore, that he may have God for the author of his apostleship, it is not without cause that he excludeth men. And he doth not now command that he be ordained

could be more grateful intelligence than that the Messiah had come; to a sinner convinced of his sins, nothing can be more cheering than to hear of a Savior.

The promises, etc. The promise here refers to all that had been spoken in the Old Testament respecting the advent, sufferings, death, and resurrection of Christ.

33. **God hath fulfilled.** God has completed, or carried into effect, by the resurrection of Jesus. He does not say that all the promise had reference to his resurrection; but his being raised up completed or perfected the fulfillment of the promises which had been made respecting him.

This day have I begotten thee. It is evident that Paul uses the expression here as implying that the Lord Jesus is called the Son of God because he raised him up from the dead; and that he means to imply that it was for this reason that he is so called in the psalm. This interpretation of an inspired apostle fixes the meaning of this passage in the psalm; and proves that it is not there used with reference to the doctrine of eternal generation, or to his incarnation, but that he is here called his Son because he was raised from the dead. And this interpretation accords with the scope of the psalm. In Ps. 2: 1–3, the psalmist records the combination of the rulers of the earth against the Messiah, and their efforts to cast off his reign. This was done, and the Messiah was rejected. All this pertains, not to his previous existence, but to the Messiah on the earth. In Ps. 2: 4–5, the psalmist shows that their efforts should not be successful; that God would laugh at their designs; that is, that their plans should not succeed. In Ps. 2: 6–7, he knows that the Messiah would be established as a King; that this was the fixed decree, that he had begotten him for this. All this is represented as subsequent to the raging of the heathen, and to the counsel of the kings against him, and must, therefore, refer not to his eternal generation, or his incarnation, but to something succeeding his death; that is, to his resurrection, and establishment as King at the right hand of God. This interpretation by the apostle Paul proves, therefore, that this passage is not to be used to establish the doctrine of the eternal

generation of Christ. Christ is called the Son of God from various reasons. In Luke 1: 35, because he was begotten by the Holy Ghost. In this place, on account of his resurrection. In Rom. 1: 4, it is also said, that he was declared to be the Son of God by the resurrection from the dead.

44. **And the next sabbath day.** This was the regular day for worship, and it was natural that a greater multitude should convene on that day than on the other days of the week.

Came almost the whole city. Whether this was in the synagogue is not affirmed; but it is probable that that was the place where the multitude convened. The news of the presence of the apostles, and of their doctrines, had been circulated doubtless by the Gentiles who had heard them, and curiosity attracted the multitude to hear them.

45. **They were filled with envy.** Greek, zeal. The word here denotes wrath, indignation, that such multitudes should be disposed to hear a message which they rejected, and which threatened to overthrow their religion.

Spake against. Opposed the doctrine that Jesus was the Messiah; that the Messiah would be humble, lowly, despised, and put to death, etc.

Contradicting. Contradicting the apostles. This was evidently done in their presence, Acts 13: 46, and would cause great tumult and disorder.

47. **For so,** etc. Paul, as usual, appeals to the Scriptures in order to justify his course. He here appeals to the Old Testament, rather than to the command of the Savior, because the Jews recognized the authority of their own Scriptures, while they would have turned in scorn from the command of Jesus of Nazareth.

I have set thee, etc. I have constituted or appointed thee. This passage is found in Is. 49: 6. That it refers to the Messiah there can be no doubt. From the fortieth chapter of Isaiah to the end of the prophecies, Isaiah had a primary and main reference to the times of the Messiah.

48. **When the Gentiles heard this.** Heard

42 And when the Jews were gone out of the synagogue, the Gentiles besought that these words might be preached to them the next sabbath.

43 Now when the congregation was broken up, many of the Jews and religious proselytes followed Paul and Barnabas: who, speaking to them, persuaded them to continue in the grace of God.

44 And the next sabbath day came almost the whole city together to hear the word of God.

45 But when the Jews saw the multitudes, they were filled with envy, and spake against those things which were spoken by Paul, contradicting and blaspheming.

46 Then Paul and Barnabas waxed bold, and said, It was necessary that the word of God should first have been spoken to you: but seeing ye put it from you, and judge yourselves unworthy of everlasting life, lo, we turn to the Gentiles.

47 For so hath the Lord commanded us, saying, I have set thee to be a light of the Gentiles, that thou shouldest be for salvation unto the ends of the earth.

48 And when the Gentiles heard this, they were glad, and glorified the word of the Lord: and as many as were ordained to eternal life believed.

49 And the word of the Lord was published throughout all the region.

50 But the Jews stirred up the devout and honorable women, and the chief men of the city, and raised persecution against Paul and Barnabas, and expelled them out of their coasts.

51 But they shook off the dust of their feet against them, and came unto Iconium.

52 And the disciples were filled with joy, and with the Holy Ghost.

ACTS 14

1 And it came to pass in Iconium, that they went both together into the synagogue of the Jews, and so spake, that a great multitude both of the Jews and also of the Greeks believed.

2 But the unbelieving Jews stirred up the Gentiles, and made their minds evil affected against the brethren.

3 Long time therefore abode they speaking boldly in the Lord, which gave

by the Church therefore, that his calling may depend upon men; but God publisheth that his decree, which was as yet known to a few, and that with a public commandment, and he commandeth that it be sealed with the solemn subscription of the Church. Therefore, this is the meaning of the words, That this is the time wherein Paul must preach the gospel among the Gentiles, and the wall being pulled down, he must gather a Church of the Gentiles, who were before strangers from the kingdom of God (Ephesians 2: 14). For although God had used him hitherto at Antioch and elsewhere, this was now added as a peculiar thing, that God did intend to adopt the Gentiles into the same inheritance of life with the Jews. But and if he were thus created a teacher of the Church from the beginning, he should not then have been called at that time by men. For, seeing the Lord doth pronounce that he had called him, what doth he leave for the Church, save only that they subscribe obediently? For men's judgment is not here put as in a doubtful matter, neither have their voices and consents any freedom. But we must mark what I have already said, that Paul and Barnabas are not now only appointed teachers, but they have an extraordinary office enjoined them, that they may begin to bring the grace of God commonly unto the Gentiles.

ACTS 14

1. In the chapter last going before, Luke declared how Paul and Barnabas took in hand their embassage unto the Gentiles. Furthermore, it might seem to be an unprosperous and unlucky beginning, in that they were not only expelled out of Antioch, but also enforced by the obstinate wickedness of certain to shake off the dust from their feet. But though they had but short entertainment in one place, yet do they not yield; because they consider that the Lord had called them upon that condition, that they should do their duty though the whole world and Satan did say nay. Therefore, we see that they came not only ready to teach, but also armed to enter conflicts, that they might courageously proceed in publishing the gospel, even through the midst of combats.

And assuredly, that which was once spoken to Jeremiah is common to all the prophets and ministers of God, "They shall fight against thee, but they shall not prevail" (Jeremiah 1: 19).

Now, whithersoever they fly, they carry with them the same courage still; whereby it appeareth that they were not only furnished for one combat, but even for continual warfare; which Luke doth now prosecute. He saith first, that they came to Iconium, and therewithal he showeth that they sought not there some haven where they might

that the gospel was to be preached to them. The doctrine of the Jews had been, that salvation was confined to themselves. The Gentiles rejoiced that from the mouths of Jews they now heard a different doctrine. **They glorified the word of the Lord.** They honored it as a message from God; they recognized and received it as the word of God. The expression conveys the idea of praise on account of it, and of reverence for the message as the word of God.

And as many as were ordained. Syriac, "Who were destined," or constituted. Vulgate, "As many as were foreordained to eternal life believed."

There has been much difference of opinion in regard to this expression. One class of commentators have supposed that it refers to the doctrine of election – to God's ordaining men to eternal life; and another class, to their being disposed themselves to embrace the gospel – to those among them who did not reject and despise the gospel, but who were disposed and inclined to embrace it. The main inquiry is, what is the meaning of the word rendered ordained? The word is used but eight times in the New Testament. Matt. 28: 16, "Into a mountain where Jesus had appointed them," i.e., previously appointed, or commanded them – before his death. Luke 7: 8, "For I also am a man set under authority" – appointed, or designated, as a soldier, to be under the authority of another. Acts 15: 2, "They determined that Paul and Barnabas, etc., should go to Jerusalem." Acts 22: 10, "It shall be told thee of all things which are appointed for thee to do;" Acts 28: 23, "And when they had appointed him a day," etc. Rom. 13: 1, "The powers that be, are ordained of God." 1 Cor. 16: 15, "They have addicted themselves to the ministry of saints." The word properly means to place; to place in a certain rank or order. Its meaning is derived from arranging or disposing a body of soldiers in regular order; to arrange in military order. In the places which have been mentioned above, the word is used to denote the following things:

(1.) To command, or to designate, Matt. 28: 16; Acts 22: 10; 28: 23.

(2.) To institute, constitute, or appoint, Rom. 13: 1. Comp. 2 Sam. 7: 11; 1 Sam. 22: 7.

(3.) To determine, to take counsel, to resolve, Acts 15: 2

(4.) To subject to the authority of another, Luke 7: 8.

(5.) To addict to; to devote to, 1 Cor. 16: 15. The meaning may be thus expressed:

(1.) The word is never used to denote an internal disposition or inclination arising from one's own self. It does not mean that they disposed themselves to embrace eternal life.

(2.) It has uniformly the notion of an ordering, disposing, or arrangement from without, i.e., from some other source than the individual himself; as of a soldier, who is arranged or classified according to the will of the proper officer. In relation to these persons it means, therefore, that they were disposed or inclined to this from some other source than themselves.

(3.) It does not properly refer to an eternal decree, or directly to the doctrine of election; though that may be inferred from it; but it refers to their being THEN IN FACT disposed to embrace eternal life. They were then inclined by an influence from without themselves, or so disposed as to embrace eternal life. It refers not to an eternal decree, but that then there was such an influence as to dispose them, or incline them, to lay hold on salvation. That this was done by the influence of the Holy Spirit, is clear from all parts of the New Testament, Titus 3: 5–6; John 1: 13.

It was not a disposition or arrangement originating with themselves, but with God.

(4.) This implies the doctrine of election. It was in fact that doctrine expressed. It was nothing but God's disposing them to embrace eternal life. And that he does this according to a plan in his own mind – a plan which is unchangeable as God himself is unchangeable – is clear from the Scriptures.

The meaning may be expressed in few words: who were THEN disposed, and in good earnest determined, to embrace eternal life, by the operation of the grace of God on their hearts.

testimony unto the word of his grace, and granted signs and wonders to be done by their hands.

4 But the multitude of the city was divided: and part held with the Jews, and part with the apostles.

5 And when there was an assault made both of the Gentiles, and also of the Jews with their rulers, to use them despitefully, and to stone them,

6 They were ware of it, and fled unto Lystra and Derbe, cities of Lycaonia, and unto the region that lieth round about:

7 And there they preached the gospel.

8 And there sat a certain man at Lystra, impotent in his feet, being a cripple from his mother's womb, who never had walked:

9 The same heard Paul speak: who stedfastly beholding him, and perceiving that he had faith to be healed,

10 Said with a loud voice, Stand upright on thy feet. And he leaped and walked.

11 And when the people saw what Paul had done, they lifted up their voices, saying in the speech of Lycaonia, The gods are come down to us in the likeness of men.

12 And they called Barnabas, Jupiter; and Paul, Mercurius, because he was the chief speaker.

13 Then the priest of Jupiter, which was before their city, brought oxen and garlands unto the gates, and would have done sacrifice with the people.

14 Which when the apostles, Barnabas and Paul, heard of, they rent their clothes, and ran in among the people, crying out,

15 And saying, Sirs, why do ye these things? We also are men of like passions with you, and preach unto you that ye should turn from these vanities unto the living God, which made heaven, and earth, and the sea, and all things that are therein:

16 Who in times past suffered all nations to walk in their own ways.

17 Nevertheless he left not himself without witness, in that he did good, and gave us rain from heaven, and fruitful seasons, filling our hearts with food and gladness.

18 And with these sayings scarce restrained they the people, that they had not

rest quietly; but they entered the synagogue as if they had suffered no hurt at all.

5. Mark how far forth the holy champions of Christ did suffer. They give not back when their enemies do only set themselves against them; but when the sedition waxeth hot, and they be in danger of stoning, though they have many favorers of their doctrine, they go no further, but remembering the saying of Christ, wherein he warneth the faithful in patience to possess their souls, they avoid the fury of the enemy. And though they fly, lest they throw themselves headlong into death, yet their constancy in preaching the gospel doth sufficiently declare that they feared not danger. For Luke saith that they preached the gospel in other places also. This is the right kind of fear, when the servants of Christ do not run willfully into the hands of their enemies, of them to be murdered, and yet they do not foreslow [abandon] their duty; neither doth fear hinder them from obeying God when he calleth; and so, consequently, they can afford, if need be, to go even through death itself to do their duty.

14. Therefore, we must take good heed that we suffer not that honor to be given us which may darken the glory of God; but rather so soon as there appeareth any profaning of God's glory, let this heat break out, whereof we have an example in Paul and Barnabas. And though the teachers of the Church ought especially to be imbued with zeal, yet there is no one of the godly which ought not to be sore displeased, when he seeth the worship of God polluted or given to some other; because it is written of all, "The zeal of thine house hath eaten me up, and the rebukes of them that rebuked thee fell on me" (Psalms 69: 10).

And if so be it holy men being yet compassed about with the flesh did so greatly detest idolatry, how shall we think them to be affected now, when they are stripped out of all the affections of the flesh? When as the world abuseth their names and persons unto superstition, it thinketh it doth them a great pleasure; but it is greatly deceived. For they will stand up first against their worshippers, and will indeed declare that they never make more account of anything, than that the worship of God might remain whole and sound to him. Moreover, there can be no greater injury done to them, than when the honor which is taken from God is given to them; which must needs be when any divine thing is ascribed and given them.

Whereas Luke saith that Paul and Barnabas did tear their clothes, it appeareth by other places of Scripture that this rite and custom was used among the men of the east country, so often as they would by external gesture express either great sorrow or detesting of any thing. When Luke

ACTS 14

2. And made their minds evil affected. Irritated, or exasperated them. Against the brethren. One of the common appellations by which Christians were known.

9. Who stedfastly beholding him. Fixing his eyes intently on him.

And perceiving. How he perceived this, is not said. Perhaps it was indicated by the ardor, humility, and strong desire depicted in his countenance. He had heard Paul, and perhaps the apostle had dwelt particularly on the miracles with which the gospel had been attested. The miracles wrought also in Iconium had doubtless also been heard of in Lystra.

11. They lifted up their voices. They spoke with astonishment, such as might be expected when it was supposed that the gods had come down.

The gods, etc. All the region was idolatrous. The gods which were worshipped there were those which were worshipped throughout Greece.

Are come down. The miracle which Paul had wrought led them to suppose this. It was evidently beyond human ability, and they had no other way of accounting for it than by supposing that their gods had personally appeared.

In the likeness of men. Many of their gods were heroes, whom they worshipped after they were dead. It was common among them to suppose that the gods appeared to men in human form. The poems of Homer, of Virgil etc., are filled with accounts of such appearances; and the only way in which they supposed the gods to take knowledge of human affairs, and to aid men, was by their personally appearing in this form.

12. And they called Barnabas, Jupiter. Jupiter was represented as the most powerful of all the gods of the ancients. He was represented as the son of Saturn and Ops, and was educated in a cave on Mount Ida, in the island of Crete. The worship of Jupiter was almost universal.

And Paul, Mercarius. Mercury, called by the Greeks Hermes, was a celebrated god of antiquity. No less than five of this name are mentioned by Cicero. The most celebrated was the son of Jupiter and Maia. He was the messenger of the gods, and of Jupiter in particular; he was the patron of travelers and shepherds; he conducted the souls of the dead into the infernal regions; and he presided over orators, and declaimers, and merchants; and he was also the god of thieves, pickpockets, and all dishonest persons. He was regarded as the god of eloquence; and as light, rapid, and quick in his movements. The conjecture of Chrysostom is, that Barnabas was a large, athletic man, and was hence taken for Jupiter; and Paul was small in his person, and was hence supposed to be Mercury.

Because he was the chief speaker. The office of Mercury was to deliver the messages of the gods; and as Paul only had been discoursing, he was supposed to be Mercury.

19. And there came thither certain Jews. Not satisfied with having expelled them from Antioch and Iconium, they still pursued them. Persecutors often exhibit a zeal and perseverance in a bad cause, which it would be well if Christians evinced in a holy cause. Men will often travel farther to do evil than they will to do good; and many men show more zeal in opposing the gospel than professed Christians do in advancing it.

Who persuaded the people. That they were impostors; and who excited their rage against them.

And, having stoned Paul. Whom they were just before ready to worship as a god! What a striking instance of the fickleness and instability of idolaters! and what a striking instance of the instability and uselessness of mere popularity. Just before, they were ready to adore him; now they sought to put him to death. Nothing is more fickle than mere popular favor. The unbounded admiration of a man may soon be changed into unbounded indignation and contempt! It was well for Paul that he was not seeking this popularity, and that he did not depend on it for happiness. He had a good conscience; he was engaged in a good cause; he was under the protection of God; and his happiness was to be sought from a higher source than the applause of men, fluctuating and uncertain as the waves of the sea. To this transaction Paul referred when he

done sacrifice unto them.

19 And there came thither certain Jews from Antioch and Iconium, who persuaded the people, and, having stoned Paul, drew him out of the city, supposing he had been dead.

20 Howbeit, as the disciples stood round about him, he rose up, and came into the city: and the next day he departed with Barnabas to Derbe.

21 And when they had preached the gospel to that city, and had taught many, they returned again to Lystra, and to Iconium, and Antioch,

22 Confirming the souls of the disciples, and exhorting them to continue in the faith, and that we must through much tribulation enter into the kingdom of God.

23 And when they had ordained them elders in every church, and had prayed with fasting, they commended them to the Lord, on whom they believed.

24 And after they had passed throughout Pisidia, they came to Pamphylia.

25 And when they had preached the word in Perga, they went down into Attalia:

26 And thence sailed to Antioch, from whence they had been recommended to the grace of God for the work which they fulfilled.

27 And when they were come, and had gathered the church together, they rehearsed all that God had done with them, and how he had opened the door of faith unto the Gentiles.

28 And there they abode long time with the disciples.

ACTS 15

1 And certain men which came down from Judaea taught the brethren, and said, Except ye be circumcised after the manner of Moses, ye cannot be saved.

2 When therefore Paul and Barnabas had no small dissension and disputation with them, they determined that Paul and Barnabas, and certain other of them, should go up to Jerusalem unto the apostles and elders about this question.

3 And being brought on their way by the church, they passed through Phenice and Samaria, declaring the conversion of the Gentiles: and they caused great joy unto all the brethren.

calleth Barnabas an apostle together with Paul, he extendeth the signification of the word farther than unto the primary order which Christ appointed in his Church; like as Paul maketh Andronicus and Junias excellent among the apostles. But if we should speak properly, they were evangelists and not apostles; unless peradventure because Barnabas was made Paul's fellow in office, we place them both in like degree of office, so may he be truly called an apostle.

ACTS 15

1. When Paul and Barnabas had endured many combats against the professed enemies of the gospel, Luke doth now begin to declare that they were tried by domestic war; so that it was meet that their doctrine and ministry should be proved by all means, to the end it might the better appear that they were furnished by God, and armed against all the assaults of the world and Satan. For that was no small confirmation for their doctrine, in that being shaken and battered with so many engines, it stood nevertheless, neither could the course thereof be broken off by so many hindrances. Therefore, to this end doth Paul boast that he suffered fights without and terrors within (2 Corinthians 7: 5). This history is most worthy the noting; for though we do naturally abhor the cross and all manner of persecution, yet civil and domestic discord is more dangerous, lest haply they discourage us.

When tyrants bend their force and run violently upon men, flesh indeed is afraid; and all those who are not endued with the spirit of fortitude do tremble with all their heart; but then their consciences are not properly touched with any temptation. For this is known to be as it were the fatal estate of the Church. But when it falleth out so that the brethren go together by the ears, and that the Church is on an uproar within itself, it cannot be but that weak minds shall be troubled and also faint; and especially when the controversy is about doctrine, which alone is the holy bond of brotherly unity. Finally, there is nothing which doth more indamage the gospel than civil discord, because it doth not only pierce and wound weak conscience, but also minister occasion to the wicked to backbite.

Wherefore, we must diligently note this history, that we may know that it is no new example, if among those who profess the same gospel there arise some wranglings and strife about doctrine, when proud men can get them a name, (whereof they are so furiously desirous,) by no other means but by bringing in their own inventions. It is certain, that as there is but one God, so there is but one truth of this God. Therefore, when Paul goeth about to exhort the faithful unto mutual consent, he useth this argument, "One

enumerated his trials, in 2 Cor. 11: 26, "Once was I stoned." **Drew him out of the city.** Probably in haste, and in popular rage, as if he was unfit to be in the city, and was unworthy of a decent burial; for it does not appear that they contemplated an interment, but indignantly dragged him beyond the walls of the city to leave him there. Such sufferings and trials it cost to establish that religion in the world which has shed so many blessings on man, and which now crowns us with comfort, and saves us from the abominations and degradations of idolatry here, and from the pains of hell hereafter. **Supposing he had been dead.** The next verse shows that he was really not dead, though many commentators, as well as the Jews, have supposed that he was, and was miraculously restored to life. It is remarkable that Barnabas was not exposed to this popular fury. But it is to be remembered that Paul was the chief speaker, and it was his peculiar zeal that exposed him to this tumult.

ACTS 15

1. And certain men. These were men undoubtedly who had been Jews, but who were now converted to Christianity. The fact that they were willing to refer the matter in dispute to the apostles and elders, Acts 15: 2, shows that they had professedly embraced the Christian religion. The account which follows is a record of the first internal dissension which occurred in the Christian church. Hitherto they had been struggling against external foes. Violent persecutions had raged, and had fully occupied the attention of Christians. But now the churches were at peace. They enjoyed great external prosperity in Antioch. And the great enemy of souls took occasion then, as he has often done in similar circumstances since, to excite contentions in the church itself; so that when external violence could not destroy it, an effort was made to secure the same object by internal dissension and strife. The history, therefore, is particularly important, as it is the record of the first unhappy debate which arose in the bosom of the church. It is further important, as it shows the manner in which

such controversies were settled in apostolic times; and as it established some very important principles respecting the perpetuity of the religious rites of the Jews. **Came down from Judea.** To Antioch, and to the regions adjacent, which had been visited by the apostles, Acts 15: 23. Judea was a high and hilly region; and going from that toward the level countries adjacent to the sea, was represented to be descending or going down. **Taught the brethren.** That is, Christians. They endeavored to convince them of the necessity of keeping the laws of Moses. **Except ye be circumcised.** This was the leading or principal rite of the Jewish religion. It was indispensable to the name and privileges of a Jew. Proselytes to their religion were circumcised as well as native-born Jews, and they held it to be indispensable to salvation. It is evident, from this, that Paul and Barnabas had dispensed with this rite in regard to the Gentile converts, and that they intended to found the Christian church on the principle that the Jewish ceremonies were to cease. When, however, it was necessary to conciliate the minds of the Jews and to prevent contention, Paul did not hesitate to practice circumcision, Acts 16: 3. **After the manner of Moses.** According to the custom which Moses commanded; according to the Mosaic ritual. **Ye cannot be saved.** The Jews regarded this as indispensable to salvation.

8. And God, which knoweth the hearts, Acts 1: 24. God thus knew whether they were true converts or not, and gave a demonstration that he acknowledged them as his.

9. And put no difference, etc. Though they had not been circumcised, and though they did not conform to the law of Moses. Thus God showed that the observance of these rites was not necessary in order to the true conversion of men, and to acceptance with him. He did not give us, who are Jews, any advantage over them, but justified and purified all in the same manner. **Purifying their hearts.** Thus giving the best evidence that he had renewed them, and admitted them to favor with him.

4 And when they were come to Jerusalem, they were received of the church, and of the apostles and elders, and they declared all things that God had done with them.

5 But there rose up certain of the sect of the Pharisees which believed, saying, That it was needful to circumcise them, and to command them to keep the law of Moses.

6 And the apostles and elders came together for to consider of this matter.

7 And when there had been much disputing, Peter rose up, and said unto them, Men and brethren, ye know how that a good while ago God made choice among us, that the Gentiles by my mouth should hear the word of the gospel, and believe.

8 And God, which knoweth the hearts, bare them witness, giving them the Holy Ghost, even as he did unto us;

9 And put no difference between us and them, purifying their hearts by faith.

10 Now therefore why tempt ye God, to put a yoke upon the neck of the disciples, which neither our fathers nor we were able to bear?

11 But we believe that through the grace of the Lord Jesus Christ we shall be saved, even as they.

12 Then all the multitude kept silence, and gave audience to Barnabas and Paul, declaring what miracles and wonders God had wrought among the Gentiles by them.

13 And after they had held their peace, James answered, saying, Men and brethren, hearken unto me:

14 Simeon hath declared how God at the first did visit the Gentiles, to take out of them a people for his name.

15 And to this agree the words of the prophets; as it is written,

16 After this I will return, and will build again the tabernacle of David, which is fallen down; and I will build again the ruins thereof, and I will set it up:

17 That the residue of men might seek after the Lord, and all the Gentiles, upon whom my name is called, saith the Lord, who doeth all these things.

18 Known unto God are all his works from the beginning of the world.

19 Wherefore my sentence is, that we trouble not them, which from among the

God, one faith, one baptism," etc. (Ephesians 4: 6). But when we see wicked men arise, who go about to divide the Church by their factions, and also either to corrupt the gospel with their false and spurious inventions, or else to bring the same in suspicion, we ought to know the craftiness of Satan. Therefore, Paul saith elsewhere that heresies come abroad, that those who are tried may be made manifest (1 Corinthians 11: 19). And, assuredly, the Lord doth wonderfully make void the subtlety of Satan, in that he trieth the faith of his by such trials, and doth beautify his word with worthy and excellent victory; and causeth the truth to shine more clearly which the wicked went about to darken.

Therefore, we must beware first of this plague, that some prescribe not a law to other some after their manner, that the example of one church be not a prejudice of a common rule. Also, we must use another caution, that the persons of men do not hinder or darken the examination of the matter or cause. For if Satan transfigure himself into an angel of light (2 Corinthians 11: 14), and if, by sacrilegious boldness, he usurp the holy name of God, what marvel is it if he do like wickedly deceive men under the names of holy men? The end shall at length declare that the apostles meant nothing less than to lay the yoke of the law upon the neck of the Gentiles; and yet Satan meant under this shift to get in. So it falleth out oftentimes that those who oppose the doctrine of Christ, creep in under the title of his servants. Therefore, there is one only remedy, to come to search out the matter with sound judgments; also it behoveth us to prevent an offense, lest we think that the faithful servants of God do therefore strive among themselves, because Satan doth falsely abuse their names, that he may set certain shadows by the ears together to terrify the simple.

2. Let us, being admonished by this example, learn, so often as there ariseth any tumult in the Church, wisely to weigh through whose fault it came, lest we rashly condemn the faithful ministers of Christ, whose gravity is rather to be praised, because they can abide so valiantly such violent assaults of Satan. Secondly, let us call to mind that Satan was bridled by the wonderful providence of God, that he might not put the doctrine of Paul to the foil. For if he had been suffered to do hurt at his pleasure, so soon as the faith of the Gentiles had been pulled down and overthrown, the gospel preached by Paul should have fallen to the ground, and the gate should have [been] shut against the calling of the Gentiles. Thirdly, let us learn that we must in time prevent dissension, of what sort soever it be, lest it break out into the flame of contention; because Satan seeketh nothing else but by the fans of dissension but to kindle so many fires. But again, seeing we see the primitive Church on an uproar, and the best servants of Christ exercised with sedition, if

By faith. By believing on the Lord Jesus Christ. This showed that the plan on which God was now about to show favor to men, was not by external rites and ceremonies, but by a scheme which required faith as the only condition of acceptance. It is further implied here, that there is no true faith which does not purify the heart.

14. Simeon. This is a Hebrew name. The Greek mode of writing it commonly was Simon. It was one of the names of Peter, Matt. 4: 18.

To take out of them a people. To choose from among the Gentiles those who should be his friends.

18. Known unto God, etc. The meaning of this verse, in this connection, is this. God sees everything future; he knows what he will accomplish; he has a plan; and all his works are so arranged in his mind, that he sees all things distinctly and clearly. As he foretold these, it was a part of his plan; and as it was a part of his plan long since foretold, it should not be opposed and resisted by us.

19. My sentence. Gr., I judge, that is, I give my opinion. It is the usual language in which a judge delivers his opinion; but it does not imply here that James assumed authority to settle the case, but merely that he gave his opinion or counsel.

That we trouble not them. That we do not molest, disturb, or oppress them, by imposing on them unnecessary and burdensome rites and ceremonies.

20. That we write unto them. Expressing our judgment, or our views of the case. This verse has greatly perplexed commentators. The main grounds of difficulty have been,

(1.) why fornication – an offence against the moral law, and about which there could be no dispute – should have been included; and,

(2.) whether the prohibition to abstain from blood is still binding.

That they abstain. That they refrain from these things, or wholly avoid them.

Pollutions of idols. The word rendered pollutions means any kind of defilement. But here it is evidently used to denote the flesh of those animals that were offered in sacrifice to idols.

See Acts 15: 29. That flesh, after being offered in sacrifice, was often exposed for sale in the markets, or was served up at feasts, 1 Cor. 10: 25–29. It became a very important question whether it was right for Christians to partake of it. The Jews would contend that it was, in fact, partaking of idolatry. The Gentile converts would allege that they did not eat it as a sacrifice to idols, or lend their countenance in any way to the idolatrous worship where it had been offered. See this subject discussed at length in 1 Cor. 8: 4–13. As idolatry was forbidden to the Jews in every form, and as partaking even of the sacrifices to idols, in their feasts, might seem to countenance idolatry, the Jews would be utterly opposed to it; and for the sake of peace, James advised that they be recommended to abstain from this. To partake of that food might not be morally wrong (1 Cor. 8: 4), but it would give occasion for scandal and offence; and, therefore, as a matter of expediency, it was advised that they should abstain from it.

And from fornication, The word used here is applicable to all illicit intercourse; and may refer to adultery, incest, and licentiousness in any form.

And from things strangled. That is, from animals or birds that were killed without shedding their brood. The reason why these were considered by the Jews unlawful to be eaten was, that thus they would be under a necessity of eating blood, which was positively forbidden by the law. Hence it was commanded in the law, that when any beast or fowl was taken in a snare, the blood should be poured out before it was lawful to be eaten, Lev. 17: 13.

And from blood. The eating of blood was strictly forbidden to the Jews. The reason of this was that it contained the life, Lev. 17: 11,14.

The use of blood was common among the Gentiles. They drank it often at their sacrifices, and in making covenants or compacts. To separate the Jews from them in this respect was one design of the prohibition.

22. Then pleased it. It seemed fit and proper to them.

The apostles and elders. To whom the business had been particularly referred, Acts 15: 2.

Gentiles are turned to God:

20 But that we write unto them, that they abstain from pollutions of idols, and from fornication, and from things strangled, and from blood.

21 For Moses of old time hath in every city them that preach him, being read in the synagogues every sabbath day.

22 Then pleased it the apostles and elders, with the whole church, to send chosen men of their own company to Antioch with Paul and Barnabas; namely, Judas surnamed Barsabas, and Silas, chief men among the brethren:

23 And they wrote letters by them after this manner; The apostles and elders and brethren send greeting unto the brethren which are of the Gentiles in Antioch and Syria and Cilicia:

24 Forasmuch as we have heard, that certain which went out from us have troubled you with words, subverting your souls, saying, Ye must be circumcised, and keep the law: to whom we gave no such commandment:

25 It seemed good unto us, being assembled with one accord, to send chosen men unto you with our beloved Barnabas and Paul,

26 Men that have hazarded their lives for the name of our Lord Jesus Christ.

27 We have sent therefore Judas and Silas, who shall also tell you the same things by mouth.

28 For it seemed good to the Holy Ghost, and to us, to lay upon you no greater burden than these necessary things;

29 That ye abstain from meats offered to idols, and from blood, and from things strangled, and from fornication: from which if ye keep yourselves, ye shall do well. Fare ye well.

30 So when they were dismissed, they came to Antioch: and when they had gathered the multitude together, they delivered the epistle:

31 Which when they had read, they rejoiced for the consolation.

32 And Judas and Silas, being prophets also themselves, exhorted the brethren with many words, and confirmed them.

33 And after they had tarried there a space, they were let go in peace from the brethren unto the apostles.

34 Notwithstanding it pleased Silas to

the same thing befall us now, let us not fear as in some new and unwonted matter; but, craving at the Lord's hands such an end as he now made, let us pass through tumults with the same tenor of faith.

9. And he put no difference

This question arises: whether that purity which the fathers had in times past were unlike to that which God gave now to the Gentiles? For it seemeth that Peter distinguisheth the Gentiles from the Jews by this mark, because, being content with the cleanness of the heart alone, they need no help of the law. I answer, that the one of them differ from the other, not in substance, but in form [only]. For God had respect always unto the inward cleanness of the heart; and the ceremonies were given to the old [ancient] people only for this cause, that they might help their faith. So that cleanness, as touching figures and exercises, was only for a time, until the coming of Christ, which hath no place among us at this day; like as there remaineth from the very beginning of the world unto the end the same true worship of God, to wit, the spiritual worship; yet is there great difference in the visible form. Now, we see that the fathers did not obtain righteousness by ceremonies, neither were they therefore pure before God, but by the cleanness of the heart. For the ceremonies of themselves were of no importance to justify them; but they were only helps, which did accidentally (that I may so term it) purge them; yet so that the fathers and we had the same truth. Now, when Christ came, all that which was accidental did vanish away; and, therefore, seeing the shadows be driven away, there remaineth the bare and plain pureness of the heart.

Thus is that objection easily answered which the Jews think cannot possibly be answered. Circumcision is called the eternal covenant, or of the world (Genesis 17: 13); therefore, say they, it was not to be abolished. If any man shall say that this is not referred unto the visible sign, but rather unto the thing figured, it shall be well answered; but there is another answer besides this. Seeing that the kingdom of Christ was a certain renewing of the world, there shall no inconvenience follow if he made an end of all the shadows of the law, forasmuch as the perpetuity of the law is grounded in Christ. I come now unto the second member, where Peter placeth the cleanness [purity] of the Gentiles in faith. Why doth not he say, In perfection of virtues, or holiness of life, save only because men have righteousness from another, and not from themselves? For, if men, by living well and justly, should purchase righteousness, or if they should be clean before God by nature, this sentence of Peter should fall to the ground. Therefore, the Spirit doth in these words plainly pronounce that all mankind is polluted, and with filthiness defiled; secondly, that their blots can by

Comp. Acts 16: 4.

With the whole Church. All the Christians who were there assembled together. They concurred in the sentiment, and expressed their approbation in the letter that was sent, Acts 15: 23. Whether they were consulted, does not particularly appear. But as it is not probable that they would volunteer an opinion unless they were consulted, it seems most reasonable to suppose that the apostles and elders submitted the case to them for their approbation. It would seem that the apostles and elders deliberated on it, and decided it; but still, for the sake of peace and unity, they also took measures to ascertain that their decision agreed with the unanimous sentiment of the church.

Chosen men. Men chosen for this purpose.

Of their own company. From among themselves. Greater weight and authority would thus be attached to their message.

28. For it seemed good to the Holy Ghost. This is a strong and undoubted claim to inspiration. It was with special reference to the organization of the church that the Holy Spirit had been promised to them by the Lord Jesus, Matt. 18: 18–20; John 14: 26.

No greater burthen. To impose no greater restraints; to enjoin no other observances.

Than these necessary things. Necessary,

(1.) in order to preserve the peace of the church.

(2.) To conciliate the minds of the Jewish converts, Acts 15: 21.

(3.) Necessary in their circumstances, particularly, because the crime which is specified – licentiousness – was one to which all early converts were particularly exposed.

29. From meats offered to idols. This explains what is meant by "pollutions of idols," Acts 15: 20.

Ye shall do well. You will do what ought to be done in regard to the subjects of dispute.

31. They rejoiced for the consolation. They acquiesced in the decision of the apostles and elders, and rejoiced that they were not to be subjected to the burdensome rites and ceremonies of the Jewish religion. This closes the account of the first Christian council. It

was conducted throughout on Christian principles, in a mild, kind, conciliatory spirit; and is a model for all similar assemblages. It came together, not to promote, but to silence disputation; not to persecute the people of God, but to promote their peace; not to be a scene of harsh and angry recrimination, but to be an example of all that was mild, and tender, and kind. Those who composed it came together, not to carry a point, not to overreach their adversaries, not to be party men; but to mingle their sober counsels to inquire what was right, and to express, in a Christian manner, that which was proper to be done. Great and important principles were to be established, in regard to the Christian church; and they engaged in their work evidently with a deep sense of their responsibility, and with a just view of their dependence on the aid of the Holy Spirit. How happy would it have been if this spirit had been possessed by all professedly Christian councils! How happy, if all had really sought the peace and harmony of the churches; and if none had ever been convened to kindle the fires of persecution, to evince the spirit of party, or to rend and destroy the church of God!

ACTS 16

1. Then came he. That is, Paul, in company with Silas. Luke does not give us the history of Barnabas, but confines his narrative to the journey of Paul.

And behold a certain disciple – named Timotheus. It was to this disciple that Paul afterwards addressed the two epistles which bear his name. It is evident that he was a native of one of these places, but whether of Derbe or Lystra it is impossible to determine.

The son of a certain woman, etc. Her name was Eunice, 2 Tim. 1: 5.

And believed. And was a Christian. It is evident also that her mother was a woman of distinguished Christian piety, 2 Tim. 1: 5. It was not lawful for a Jew to marry a woman of another nation, or to give his daughter in marriage to a Gentile, Ezra 9: 12. But it is probable that this law was not regarded very strictly by the Jews who lived in the midst of heathen

abide there still.

35 Paul also and Barnabas continued in Antioch, teaching and preaching the word of the Lord, with many others also.

36 And some days after Paul said unto Barnabas, Let us go again and visit our brethren in every city where we have preached the word of the Lord, and see how they do.

37 And Barnabas determined to take with them John, whose surname was Mark.

38 But Paul thought not good to take him with them, who departed from them from Pamphylia, and went not with them to the work.

39 And the contention was so sharp between them, that they departed asunder one from the other: and so Barnabas took Mark, and sailed unto Cyprus;

40 And Paul chose Silas, and departed, being recommended by the brethren unto the grace of God.

41 And he went through Syria and Cilicia, confirming the churches.

ACTS 16

1 Then came he to Derbe and Lystra: and, behold, a certain disciple was there, named Timotheus, the son of a certain woman, which was a Jewess, and believed; but his father was a Greek:

2 Which was well reported of by the brethren that were at Lystra and Iconium.

3 Him would Paul have to go forth with him; and took and circumcised him because of the Jews which were in those quarters: for they knew all that his father was a Greek.

4 And as they went through the cities, they delivered them the decrees for to keep, that were ordained of the apostles and elders which were at Jerusalem.

5 And so were the churches established in the faith, and increased in number daily.

6 Now when they had gone throughout Phrygia and the region of Galatia, and were forbidden of the Holy Ghost to preach the word in Asia,

7 After they were come to Mysia, they assayed to go into Bithynia: but the Spirit suffered them not.

8 And they passing by Mysia came down to Troas.

no other means be wiped away than by the grace of Christ. For, seeing that faith is the remedy whereby the Lord doth freely help us, it is set as well against the common nature of all men, as against every man's own merits. When I say that all mankind is polluted, my meaning is, that we bring nothing from our mother's womb but mere filthiness, and that there is no righteousness in our nature which can reconcile us to God. Man's soul was indeed endued with singular gifts at the first; but all parts thereof are so corrupt with sin, that there remaineth in it no drop of pureness any longer; therefore we must seek for cleanness without ourselves.

ACTS 16

1. Luke doth now begin to declare what were the proceedings of Paul after that Barnabas and he were separate. And first he showeth, that he took to his company at Lystra Timothy to be his companion. But, to the end we may know that Paul did nothing rashly, or without good consideration, Luke saith plainly, that Timothy was such a man as the brethren did well like of, and that they gave testimony of his godliness; for thus doth he speak word for word. And so Paul himself observeth the like choice, which he elsewhere commandeth to be made in choosing ministers (1 Timothy 3: 7). Neither is it to be thought, that those prophecies did even then come to light wherewith Timothy was set forth and adorned by the Spirit, as Paul doth testify elsewhere (1 Timothy 1: 18). But there seemeth to be some disagreement in that, in that Luke saith that Timotheus was well reported of amongst the brethren; and Paul will have him to have a good report of those who are without, who is chosen to be a bishop. I answer, that we must principally look unto the judgment of the godly, as they be sole meet witnesses, and do alone rightly discern well and wisely according to the Spirit of God; and that we ought to attribute no more to the wicked than to blind men. Therefore it appeareth that godliness and holiness of life must be judged according to the will and consent of godly men; that he be counted worthy to be a bishop whom they commend. Notwithstanding, I confess that even this also is required in the second place, that the very infidels be enforced to commend him; lest the Church of God come in danger of their slanders and evil speaking, if it commit [permit] itself to be governed by men of evil report.

3. He circumcised him, because of the Jews

Now, the question is, whether it were lawful for Paul to use a vain sign, whose signification and force was abolished; for it seemeth a vain thing when there is a departure made from the institution of God. But circumcision was commanded by God to continue only until the coming of

nations. It is evident that Timothy, at this time, was very young; for when Paul besought him to abide at Ephesus, to take charge of the church there, 1 Tim. 1: 3, he addressed him then as a young man: 1 Tim. 4: 12, "Let no man despise thy youth."

But his father was a Greek. Evidently a man who had not been circumcised – for had he been, Timothy would have been also.

4. And as they went through the cities. The cities of Syria, Cilicia, etc.

They delivered them. Paul and Silas delivered to the Christians in those cities.

The decrees. The decrees in regard to the four things specified in Acts 15: 20,29. In this instance it was the decision of the council in a case submitted to it; and implied an obligation on the Christians to submit to that decision. The laws of the apostles would, and ought to be, in such cases, esteemed to be binding. It is probable that a correct and attested copy of the letter, Acts 15: 23–29 would be sent to the various churches of the Gentiles.

To keep. To obey, or to observe.

5. Established in the faith. Confirmed in the belief of the Gospel. The effect of the wise and conciliatory measure was to increase and strengthen the churches.

6. Throughout Phrygia. This was the largest province of Asia Minor. It had Bithynia, north; Pisidia and Lycia, south; Galatia and Cappadocia, east; and Lydia and Mysia, west.

And the region of Galatia. This province was directly east of Phrygia. The region was formerly conquered by the Gauls. They settled in it, and called it, after their own name, Galatia. The Gauls invaded the country at different times, and no less than three tribes or bodies of Gauls had possession of it. Many Jews were also settled there. It was from this cause that so many parties could be formed there, and that so much controversy would arise between the Jewish and Gentile converts.

And were forbidden. Probably by a direct revelation. The reason of this was, doubtless, that it was the intention of God to extend the gospel farther into the regions of Greece than would have been done if they had remained in Asia Minor. This prohibition was the means

of the first introduction of the gospel into Europe.

8. Came down to Troas. This was a city of Phrygia or Mysia, on the Hellespont, between Troy north, and Assos south. Sometimes the name Troas, or Troad, is used to denote the whole country of the Trojans, the province where the ancient city of Troy had stood. This region was much celebrated in the early periods of Grecian history. It was here that the events recorded in the Iliad of Homer are supposed to have occurred. The city of Troy has long since been completely destroyed.

21. And teach customs. The word customs here refers to religious rites or forms of worship.

They meant to charge the apostles with introducing a new mode of worship and a new religion, which was unauthorized by the Roman laws. This was a cunning and artful accusation. It is perfectly evident that they cared nothing either for the religion of the Romans or of the Jews. Nor were they really concerned about any change of religion. Paul had destroyed their hopes of gain; and as they could not prevent that except by securing his punishment or expulsion, and as they had no way of revenge except by endeavoring to excite indignation against him and Silas for violating the laws, they endeavored to convict them of such violation. This is one, among many instances, where wicked and unprincipled men will endeavor to make religion the means of promoting their own interest. If they can make money by it, they will become its professed friends; or if they can annoy Christians, they will at once have remarkable zeal for the laws and for the purity of religion. Many a man opposes revivals of religion and the real progress of evangelical piety, from professed zeal for truth and order.

Which are not lawful for us to receive. There were laws of the Roman Empire under which they might shield themselves in this charge, though it is evident that their zeal was not because they loved the laws more, but because they loved Christianity less. Thus Servius on Virgil says, "Care was taken among the Athenians and the Romans, that no one

9 And a vision appeared to Paul in the night; There stood a man of Macedonia, and prayed him, saying, Come over into Macedonia, and help us.

10 And after he had seen the vision, immediately we endeavored to go into Macedonia, assuredly gathering that the Lord had called us for to preach the gospel unto them.

11 Therefore loosing from Troas, we came with a straight course to Samothracia, and the next day to Neapolis;

12 And from thence to Philippi, which is the chief city of that part of Macedonia, and a colony: and we were in that city abiding certain days.

13 And on the sabbath we went out of the city by a river side, where prayer was wont to be made; and we sat down, and spake unto the women which resorted thither.

14 And a certain woman named Lydia, a seller of purple, of the city of Thyatira, which worshipped God, heard us: whose heart the Lord opened, that she attended unto the things which were spoken of Paul.

15 And when she was baptized, and her household, she besought us, saying, If ye have judged me to be faithful to the Lord, come into my house, and abide there. And she constrained us.

16 And it came to pass, as we went to prayer, a certain damsel possessed with a spirit of divination met us, which brought her masters much gain by soothsaying:

17 The same followed Paul and us, and cried, saying, These men are the servants of the most high God, which shew unto us the way of salvation.

18 And this did she many days. But Paul, being grieved, turned and said to the spirit, I command thee in the name of Jesus Christ to come out of her. And he came out the same hour.

19 And when her masters saw that the hope of their gains was gone, they caught Paul and Silas, and drew them into the marketplace unto the rulers,

20 And brought them to the magistrates, saying, These men, being Jews, do exceedingly trouble our city,

21 And teach customs, which are not lawful for us to receive, neither to observe, being Romans.

Christ. To this question I answer, that circumcision did so cease at the coming of Christ, that, notwithstanding the use thereof was not quite abolished by and by; but it continued free, until all men might know that Christ was the end of the law, by the more manifest revelation of the light of the gospel.

And here we must note three stages. The first is, that the ceremonies of the law were so abolished by the coming of Christ, that they did neither any longer appertain unto the worship of God, neither were they figures of spiritual things, neither was there any necessity to use them.

The second is, that the use thereof was free, until the truth of the gospel might more plainly appear.

The third, that it was not lawful for the faithful to retain them, save only so far forth as the use thereof served for edification, neither was there any superstition thereby fostered; though that free power to use them, whereof I have spoken, be not without exception, because there was a divers respect to be had of ceremonies. For circumcision was not in the same place wherein the sacrifices were, which were ordained for the purging of sins. Wherefore it was lawful for Paul to circumcise Timotheus; it had not been lawful for him to offer a sacrifice for sin. This is, indeed, a general thing, that all the worship of the law did cease at the coming of Christ (because it was to continue but for a time), as touching faith and conscience; but concerning the use we must know this, that it is indifferent, and left in the liberty of the godly for a short time, so far as it was not contrary to the confession of faith. We must note the shortness of time whereof I speak, to wit, until the plain manifestation of the Gospel; because some learned men are grossly deceived in this point, who think that circumcision doth yet take place among the Jews; whereas Paul teacheth, that it is superfluous when we are buried with Christ by baptism (Colossians 2: 11–12). It was better and more truly said in the old proverb, That the synagogue was to be buried with honor.

Now it resteth that we declare how far forth the use of circumcision was indifferent. That shall easily appear by the manner of the liberty. Because the calling of the Gentiles was not as yet generally known, it was meet that the Jews should have some prerogative granted them. Therefore, until it might be better known that the adoption was deducted from the lineage and kindred of Abraham unto all the Gentiles, it was lawful, so far as edification did require, to retain the sign of difference. For seeing that Paul would not circumcise Titus, and doth avouch that the same was well done (Galatians 2: 3), it followeth that it was not lawful to use this ceremony always and without choice. Therefore they were to have respect unto edification, and unto the public commodity of the Church. Because he

should introduce new religions. It was on this account that Socrates was condemned, and the Chaldeans or Jews were banished from the city." Cicero says, "No person shall have any separate gods, or new ones; nor shall he privately worship any strange gods, unless they be publicly allowed." Wetstein says, "The Romans would indeed allow foreigners to worship their own gods, but not unless it were done secretly, so that the worship of foreign gods would not interfere with the allowed worship of the Romans, and so that occasion for dissension and controversy might be avoided. Neither was it lawful among the Romans to recommend a new religion to the citizens, contrary to that which was confirmed and established by the public authority, and to call off the people from that. It was on this account that there was such a hatred of the Romans against the Jews." Tertullian says, that "there was a decree that no god should be consecrated, unless approved by the senate."

22. And the multitude, etc. It is evident that this was done in a popular tumult, and without even the form of law. Of this, Paul afterwards justly complained, as it was a violation of the privileges of a Roman citizen, and contrary to the laws.

It was one instance in which men affect great zeal for the honor of the law, and yet are among the first to disregard it.

And the magistrates. Acts 16: 20. They who should have been their protectors, until they had had a fair trial according to law.

Rent off their clothes. This was always done when one was to be scourged or whipped. The criminal was usually stripped entirely naked. Livy says, "The lictors, being sent to inflict punishment, beat them with rods, being naked." Cicero against Vetres says, "He commanded the man to be seized, and to be stripped naked in the midst of the forum, and to be bound, and rods to be brought."

And commanded to beat them. To beat them with rods. This was done by lictors, whose office it was, and was a common mode of punishment among the Romans. Probably Paul alludes to this when he says (2 Cor. 11: 25), "Thrice was I beaten with rods."

23. And when they had laid many stripes upon them. The Jews were by law prohibited from inflicting more than forty stripes, and usually inflicted but thirty-nine, 2 Cor. 11: 24. But there was no such law among the Romans. They were unrestricted in regard to the number of lashes; and probably inflicted many more. Perhaps Paul refers to this when he says (2 Cor. 11: 23), "In stripes above measure," i.e., beyond the usual measure among the Jews, or beyond moderation.

They cast them into prison. The magistrates, Acts 16: 36–37, as a punishment; and probably with a view hereafter of taking vengeance on them, more according to the forms of law.

24. Thrust them into the inner prison. Into the most retired and secure part of the prison. The cells in the interior of the prison would be regarded as more safe, being doubtless more protected, and the difficulty of escape would be greater.

And made their feet fast in the stocks. Greek, And made their feet secure to wood. The word stocks, with us, denotes a machine made of two pieces of timber, between which the feet of the criminals are placed, and in which they are thus made secure. The account here does not imply necessarily that they were secured precisely in this way, but that they were fastened or secured by the feet, probably by cords, to a piece or beam of wood, so that they could not escape. It is supposed that the legs of the prisoners were bound to large pieces of wood, which not only encumbered them, but which often were so placed as to extend their feet to a considerable distance. In this condition it might be necessary for them to lie on their backs; and if this, as is probable, was on the cold ground, after their severe scourging, their sufferings must have been very great. Yet in the midst of this they sang praises to God.

28. Do thyself no harm. This is the solemn command of religion in his case, and in all others. It enjoins on men to do themselves no harm – by self-murder, whether by the sword, the pistol, the halter; or by intemperance, and lust, and dissipation. In all cases Christianity

22 And the multitude rose up together against them: and the magistrates rent off their clothes, and commanded to beat them.

23 And when they had laid many stripes upon them, they cast them into prison, charging the jailor to keep them safely:

24 Who, having received such a charge, thrust them into the inner prison, and made their feet fast in the stocks.

25 And at midnight Paul and Silas prayed, and sang praises unto God: and the prisoners heard them.

26 And suddenly there was a great earthquake, so that the foundations of the prison were shaken: and immediately all the doors were opened, and every one's bands were loosed.

27 And the keeper of the prison awaking out of his sleep, and seeing the prison doors open, he drew out his sword, and would have killed himself, supposing that the prisoners had been fled.

28 But Paul cried with a loud voice, saying, Do thyself no harm: for we are all here.

29 Then he called for a light, and sprang in, and came trembling, and fell down before Paul and Silas,

30 And brought them out, and said, Sirs, what must I do to be saved?

31 And they said, Believe on the Lord Jesus Christ, and thou shalt be saved, and thy house.

32 And they spake unto him the word of the Lord, and to all that were in his house.

33 And he took them the same hour of the night, and washed their stripes; and was baptized, he and all his, straightway.

34 And when he had brought them into his house, he set meat before them, and rejoiced, believing in God with all his house.

35 And when it was day, the magistrates sent the serjeants, saying, Let those men go.

36 And the keeper of the prison told this saying to Paul, The magistrates have sent to let you go: now therefore depart, and go in peace.

37 But Paul said unto them, They have beaten us openly uncondemned, being Romans, and have cast us into prison;

could not circumcise Titus, unless he would betray the doctrine of the Gospel, and lay himself open to the slanders of the adversaries, he abstained from the free use of the ceremony, which he did use in Timotheus, when he saw that it was profitable for the Church. Hereby it doth easily appear what horrible confusion doth reign in Popery. There is there a huge heap of ceremonies, and to what end but that hey may have instead of one veil of the old temple an hundred. God did abrogate those ceremonies which he had commanded, that the truth of the Gospel might shine more clearly. Men durst take upon them to bring in new, and that without keeping any measure. After this came in a wicked surmise, that all these serve for the worship of God. At length followed the devilish confidence of merit. Now, forasmuch as it is evident enough that such ceremonies are neither veils nor sepulchres wherewith Christ is covered, but rather stinking dunghills wherein faith and religion are choked, those who make the use thereof generally free do ascribe more to the Pope than the Lord granteth to his law. It is to no end to speak of the mass and of such filthiness which contain in themselves manifest idolatry.

11. This history doth, as it were in a glass, show how sharply the Lord did exercise the faith and patience of his, by bringing them in great straits which they could not have overcome unless they had been endued with singular constancy; for the entrance of Paul into Macedonia is reported to be such, as that it might have cause him to give but small credence to the vision. These holy men, leaving the work which they had in hand, did cross the seas with great haste, as if the whole nation of the Macedonians would have come to meet them with earnest desire to be helped. Now, the success is so far from being answerable to their hope, that their mouths are almost quite stopped. When they enter the chief city, they find non there with whom they may take any pains; therefore they are enforced to go into the field, that they may speak in an obscure corner and wilderness. Yea, even there they cannot have one man which will hearken to their doctrine; they can only have one woman to be a disciple of Christ, and that one which was an alien. Who would not have said that this journey was taken in hand foolishly which fell out so unhappily? But the Lord doth thus bring to pass his works under a base and weak kind, that his power may shine more clearly at length; and it was most meet that the beginnings of the kingdom of Christ should be so ordered, that they might savor the humility of the cross.

ACTS 17

1. They came to Thessalonica

We know not why Paul attempted nothing at Amphipolis

seeks the true welfare of man. In all cases, if it were obeyed, men would do themselves no harm. They would promote their own best interests here, and their eternal welfare hereafter.

29. Then he called for a light. Greek, Lights, in the plural. Probably several torches were brought by his attendants.

And came trembling. Alarmed at the earthquake, and amazed that the prisoners were still there, and probably not a little confounded at the calmness of Paul and Silas, and overwhelmed at the proof of the presence of God. Comp. Jer. 5: 22, "Fear ye not me, saith the Lord? will ye not tremble at my presence?" etc.

And fell down, etc. This was an act of profound reverence. It is evident that he regarded them as the favorites of God, and was constrained to recognize them in their character as religious teachers.

30. And brought them out. From the prison.

Sirs. Lords – an address of respect; a title usually given to masters, or owners of slaves.

What must I do to be saved? Never was a more important question asked than this. It is evident that by this question he did not refer to any danger to which he might be exposed from what had happened. For,

(1.) the apostles evidently understood him as referring to his eternal salvation, as is manifest from their answer; since to believe on the Lord Jesus would have no effect in saving him from any danger of punishment to which he might be exposed from what had occurred.

(2.) He could scarcely consider himself as exposed to punishment by the Romans. The prisoners were all safe; none had escaped, or showed any disposition to escape: and besides, for the earthquake and its effects he could not be held responsible. It is not improbable that there was much confusion in his mind. There would be a rush of many thoughts; a state of agitation, and alarm, and fear; and in view of all he would naturally ask those whom he now saw to be men sent by God, and under his protection, what he should do to obtain the favor of that great Being under whose protection he saw that they manifestly were.

33. And he took them. To a convenient place for washing. It is evident from this, that though the apostles had the gift of miracles, that they did not exercise it in regard to their own sufferings, or to heal their own wounds. They restored others to health, not themselves.

And washed their stripes. The wounds which had been inflicted by the severe scourging which they had received the night before. We have here a remarkable instance of the effect of religion in producing humanity and tenderness. This same man, a few hours before, had thrust them into the inner prison, and made them fast in the stocks. He evidently had then no concern about their stripes or their wounds. But no sooner was he converted, and his heart changed, than one of his first acts was an act of humanity. He saw them suffering; he pitied them, and hastened to minister to them, and to heal their wounds. Till the time of Christianity there never had been an hospital or an almshouse. Nearly all the hospitals for the sick since have been reared by Christians. They who are most ready to minister to the sick and dying are Christians. They who are willing to encounter the pestilential damps of dungeons to aid the prisoner, are, like Howard, Christians. Who ever saw an infidel attending a dying bed, if he could help it? and where has infidelity ever reared a hospital or an almshouse, or made provision for the widow and the fatherless? Often one of the most striking changes that occurs in conversion is seen in the disposition to be kind and humane to the suffering. Comp. James 1: 27.

And was baptized. This was done straightway; that is, immediately. As it is altogether improbable that either in his house or in the prison there would be water sufficient for immersing them, there is every reason to suppose that this was performed in some other mode. All the circumstances lead us to suppose that it was not by immersion. It was at the dead of night, in a prison, amidst much agitation, and evidently performed in haste.

and now do they thrust us out privily? nay verily; but let them come themselves and fetch us out.

38 And the serjeants told these words unto the magistrates: and they feared, when they heard that they were Romans.

39 And they came and besought them, and brought them out, and desired them to depart out of the city.

40 And they went out of the prison, and entered into the house of Lydia and when they had seen the brethren, they comforted them, and departed.

ACTS 17

1 Now when they had passed through Amphipolis and Apollonia, they came to Thessalonica, where was a synagogue of the Jews:

2 And Paul, as his manner was, went in unto them, and three sabbath days reasoned with them out of the scriptures,

3 Opening and alleging, that Christ must needs have suffered, and risen again from the dead; and that this Jesus, whom I preach unto you, is Christ.

4 And some of them believed, and consorted with Paul and Silas; and of the devout Greeks a great multitude, and of the chief women not a few.

5 But the Jews which believed not, moved with envy, took unto them certain lewd fellows of the baser sort, and gathered a company, and set all the city on an uproar, and assaulted the house of Jason, and sought to bring them out to the people.

6 And when they found them not, they drew Jason and certain brethren unto the rulers of the city, crying, These that have turned the world upside down are come hither also;

7 Whom Jason hath received: and these all do contrary to the decrees of Caesar, saying that there is another king, one Jesus.

8 And they troubled the people and the rulers of the city, when they heard these things.

9 And when they had taken security of Jason, and of the other, they let them go.

10 And the brethren immediately sent away Paul and Silas by night unto Berea: who coming thither went into the synagogue of the Jews.

and Appollonia, which were, notwithstanding, famous cities, as appeareth by Pliny; save only because he followed the Spirit of God as his guide; and took occasion by the present matter, as occasion he did also essay to do some good there, but because it was without any good success, therefore Luke passes over it. And whereas being beaten at Philippos [Philippi], and scarce escaping out of great danger, he preached Christ at Thessalonica, it appeareth thereby how courageous he was to keep the course of his calling, and how bold he was ever now and then to enter into new dangers.

This so invincible fortitude of mind, and such patient enduring of the cross, do sufficiently declare, that Paul labored not after the manner of men, but that he was furnished with the heavenly power of the Spirit. And this was all so wonderful patience in him, in that, entering in unto the Jews, whose unbridled frowardness he had so often tried [experienced], he proceedeth to procure their salvation. But because he knew that Christ was given to the Jews for salvation, and that he himself was made an apostle upon this condition, that he should preach repentance and faith, first to the Jews and then to the Gentiles, committing the success of his labor to the Lord, he obeyeth his commandment (though he had no great hope to do good). He seemed before to have taken his last farewell of the Jews, when he said, It was behoveful that the kingdom of God should be first preached to you; but because ye receive it not, behold we turn to the Gentiles; but that harder sentence must be restrained to that company who had wickedly rejected the gospel when it was offered unto them, and made themselves unworthy [of] the grace of God. And toward the nation itself Paul ceaseth not to do his embassage; by which example we are taught, that we ought to make so great account of the calling of God, that no unthankfulness of men may be able to hinder us, but that we proceed to be careful for their salvation, so long as the Lord appointeth us to be their ministers. And it is to be though that even now there were some who on the first Sabbath refused sound doctrine, but their frowardness did not hinder him, but that he came again upon other Sabbaths.

2. He disputed

Luke setteth down first what was the sum of the disputation; to wit, that Jesus, the son of Mary, is Christ, who was promised in times past in the law and the prophets, who, by the sacrifice of his death, did make satisfaction for the sins of the world, and brought righteousness and life by his resurrection; secondly, how he proved that which he taught. Let us handle this second member first. Luke saith that he disputed out of the Scriptures; therefore the proofs of faith must be fet from [sought at] the mouth of God alone. If we

ACTS 17

2. His manner was. His custom was to attend on the worship of the synagogue, and to preach the gospel to his countrymen first, Acts 9: 20; 13: 5,14.
Reasoned with them. Discoursed to them, or attempted to prove that Jesus was the Messiah. The word used here means often no more than to make a public address or discourse.

3. Opening. See Luke 24: 32. The word means, to explain, or to unfold. It is usually applied to that which is shut, as to the eyes, etc. Then it means to explain that which is concealed or obscure. It means here, that he explained the Scriptures in their true sense.
And alleging. Laying down the proposition; that is, maintaining that it must be so.
That Christ must needs have suffered. That there was a fitness and necessity in his dying, as Jesus of Nazareth had done. The sense of this will be better seen by retaining the word Messiah. "That there was a fitness or necessity that the Messiah expected by the Jews, and predicted in their Scriptures, should suffer." This point the Jews were unwilling to admit; but it was essential to his argument in proving that Jesus was the Messiah, to show that it was foretold that he should die for the sins of men.
Have suffered. That he should die.
And that this Jesus. And that this Jesus of Nazareth, who has thus suffered and risen, whom, said he, I preach to you, is the Messiah.

6. These that have turned the world upside down. That have excited commotion and disturbance in other places. The charge has been often brought against the gospel, that it has been the occasion of confusion and disorder.

7. Whom Jason hath received. Has received into his house, and entertained kindly.
These all do contrary to the decrees of Caesar. The charge against them was that of sedition and rebellion against the Roman emperor. Grotius on this verse remarks, that the Roman people, and after them the emperors, would not permit the name of king to be mentioned in any of the vanquished provinces,

except by their permission.
Saying that there is another king. This was probably a charge of mere malignity. They probably understood, that when the apostles spoke of Jesus as a king, they did not do it as of a temporal prince. But it was easy to pervert their words, and to give plausibility to the accusation. The same thing had occurred in regard to the Lord Jesus himself, Luke 23: 2.

8. And they troubled the people. They excited the people to commotion and alarm. The rulers feared the tumult that was excited, and the people feared the Romans, when they heard the charge that there were rebels against the government in their city. It does not appear, that there was a disposition in the rulers or the people to persecute the apostles; but they were excited and alarmed by the representations of the Jews, and by the mob that they had collected.

11. These were more noble. This literally means more noble by birth; descended from more illustrious ancestors. But here the word is used to denote a quality of mind and heart; they were more generous, liberal, and noble in their feelings; more disposed to inquire candidly into the truth of the doctrines advanced by Paul and Silas. It is always proof of a noble, liberal, and ingenuous disposition, to be willing to examine into the truth of any doctrine presented. The writer refers here particularly to the Jews.
They received the word, etc. They listened attentively and respectfully to the gospel. They did not reject and spurn it, as unworthy of examination. This is the first particular in which they were more noble than those in Thessalonica.
And searched the Scriptures. That is, the Old Testament.
The apostles always affirmed that the doctrines which they maintained respecting the Messiah were in accordance with the Jewish Scriptures. The Bereans made diligent and earnest inquiry in respect to this, and were willing to ascertain the truth.
Daily. Not only on the Sabbath, and in the synagogue; but they made it a daily employment. It is evident from this, that they had the

11 These were more noble than those in Thessalonica, in that they received the word with all readiness of mind, and searched the scriptures daily, whether those things were so.

12 Therefore many of them believed; also of honorable women which were Greeks, and of men, not a few.

13 But when the Jews of Thessalonica had knowledge that the word of God was preached of Paul at Berea, they came thither also, and stirred up the people.

14 And then immediately the brethren sent away Paul to go as it were to the sea: but Silas and Timotheus abode there still.

15 And they that conducted Paul brought him unto Athens: and receiving a commandment unto Silas and Timotheus for to come to him with all speed, they departed.

16 Now while Paul waited for them at Athens, his spirit was stirred in him, when he saw the city wholly given to idolatry.

17 Therefore disputed he in the synagogue with the Jews, and with the devout persons, and in the market daily with them that met with him.

18 Then certain philosophers of the Epicureans, and of the Stoicks, encountered him. And some said, What will this babbler say? other some, He seemeth to be a setter forth of strange gods: because he preached unto them Jesus, and the resurrection.

19 And they took him, and brought him unto Areopagus, saying, May we know what this new doctrine, whereof thou speakest, is?

20 For thou bringest certain strange things to our ears: we would know therefore what these things mean.

21 (For all the Athenians and strangers which were there spent their time in nothing else, but either to tell, or to hear some new thing.)

22 Then Paul stood in the midst of Mars' hill, and said, Ye men of Athens, I perceive that in all things ye are too superstitious.

23 For as I passed by, and beheld your devotions, I found an altar with this inscription, TO THE UNKNOWN GOD. Whom therefore ye ignorantly worship, him declare I unto you.

24 God that made the world and all

dispute about matters which concern men, then let human reasons take place; but in the doctrine of faith, the authority of God alone must reign, and upon it must we depend.

All men confess that this is true, that we must stay ourselves upon God alone; yet there be but a few which hear him speak in the Scriptures. But and if that maxim take place among us, that the Scripture cometh of God, the rule either of teaching or of learning ought to be taken nowhere else. Whereby it doth also appear with what devilish fury the Papists are driven, when they deny that there can any certainty be gathered out of the Scriptures; and, therefore, they hold that we must stand to the decrees of men. For I demand of them whether Paul did observe a right order in disputing or no? at least, let them blush for shame, that the Word of the Lord was more reverenced in an unbelieving nation than it is at this day among them. The Jews admit Paul, and suffer him when he disputeth out of the Scriptures; the Pope and all his count it a mere mock when the Scripture is cited; as if God did speak doubtfully there, and did with vain boughts mock men. Hereunto is added, that there is at this day much more light in the Scriptures, and the truth of God shineth there more clearly than in the law and the prophets. For in the gospel, Christ, who is the Son of righteousness, doth shed out his beam with perfect brightness upon us; for which cause the blasphemy of the Papists is the more intolerable, whilst that they will make the Word of God as yet uncertain. But let us know, as faith can be grounded nowhere else than in the Word of the Lord, so we must only stand to the testimony thereof in all controversies.

3. Opening

And, surely, there is no more apt or effectual way to prove the office of Christ, than when men, being humbled with the feeling of their miseries, see that there is no hope left, unless they be reconciled by the sacrifice of Christ. Then laying away their pride, they humbly embrace his cross, whereof they were before both weary and ashamed. Therefore, we must come unto the same fountains at this day, from which Paul focuses on the evidence of the death and resurrection of Christ. And that definition brought great light to the second chapter. It had not been so easy a matter for Paul to prove, and certainly to gather, that the Son of Mary is Christ, unless the Jews had been taught before what manner of Redeemer they were to hope for. And when that doth once appear, it doth only remain that those things be applied to Christ which the Scripture doth attribute to the Mediator. But this is the sum of our faith, that we know that the Son of Mary is that Christ and Mediator which God promised from the beginning; that done, that we know and understood why he died and rose again; that we do not

Scriptures; and this is one proof that Jewish families would, if possible, obtain the oracles of God.

Whether those things were so. Whether the doctrines stated by Paul and Silas were in accordance with the Scriptures. The Old Testament they received as the standard of truth, and whatever could be shown to be in accordance with that they received.

16. Now while Paul waited. How long he was there is not intimated; but doubtless some time would elapse before they could arrive. In the mean time, Paul had ample opportunity to observe the state of the city.

His spirit was stirred in him. His mind was greatly excited. The word used here denotes any excitement, agitation, or paroxysm of mind, 1 Cor. 13: 5. It here means that the mind of Paul was greatly concerned, or agitated, doubtless with pity and distress, at their folly and danger.

The city wholly given to idolatry. It is well translated in the margin, "full of idols." The word is not elsewhere used in the New Testament. That this was the condition of the city is abundantly testified by profane writers. In this verse we may see how a splendid, idolatrous city will strike a pious mind. Athens then had more that was splendid in architecture, more that was brilliant in science, and more that was beautiful in the arts, than any other city in the world; perhaps more than all the rest of the world united. Yet there is no account that the mind of Paul was filled with admiration; there is no record that he spent his time in examining the works of art; there is no evidence that he forgot his high purpose in an idle and useless contemplation of temples and statuary. His was a Christian mind; and he contemplated all this with a Christian heart. That heart was deeply affected in view of the amazing guilt of a people that were ignorant of the true God, and that had filled their city with idols reared to the honor of imaginary divinities; and who, in the midst of all this splendor and luxury, were going down to the gates of death. So should every pious man feel who treads the streets of a splendid and guilty city. The Christian will not despise the productions of art; but he will feel, deeply feel, for the unhappy condition of those who, amidst wealth and splendor and adorning, are withholding their affections from the living God, bestowing them on the works of their own hands, or on objects degraded and polluting, and who are going unredeemed to eternal woe. Happy would it be if every Christian traveler who visits cities of wealth and splendor would, like Paul, be affected in view of their crimes and dangers; and happy if, like him, men could cease their unbounded admiration of magnificence and splendor in temples and palaces and statuary, to regard the condition of mind, not perishable like marble; and of the soul, more magnificent even in its ruins than all the works of Phidias or Praxiteles.

26. And hath made of one blood. All the families of men are descended from one origin, or stock. However different their complexion, features, language, etc., yet they are derived from a common parent. The word blood is often used to denote race, stock, kindred. This passage completely proves that all the human family are descended from the same ancestor; and that, consequently, all the variety of complexion, etc., is to be traced to some other cause than that there were originally different races created. See Gen. 1; comp. Mal. 2: 10. The design of the apostle in this affirmation was, probably, to convince the Greeks that he regarded them all as brethren; and that, although he was a Jew, yet he was not enslaved to any narrow notions or prejudices in reference to other men. It follows also from this, that no one nation, and no individual, can claim any pre-eminence over others in virtue of birth or blood. All are in this respect equal; and the whole human family, however they may differ in complexion, customs, and laws, are to be regarded and treated as brethren.

27. That they should seek the Lord. Gr., To seek the Lord. The design of thus placing them on the earth – of giving them their habitation among his works – was that they should contemplate his wisdom in his works, and thus come to a knowledge of his existence and character. All nations, though living in different regions and climates, have thus the opportunity of becoming acquainted with

things therein, seeing that he is Lord of heaven and earth, dwelleth not in temples made with hands;

25 Neither is worshipped with men's hands, as though he needed any thing, seeing he giveth to all life, and breath, and all things;

26 And hath made of one blood all nations of men for to dwell on all the face of the earth, and hath determined the times before appointed, and the bounds of their habitation;

27 That they should seek the Lord, if haply they might feel after him, and find him, though he be not far from every one of us:

28 For in him we live, and move, and have our being; as certain also of your own poets have said, For we are also his offspring.

29 Forasmuch then as we are the offspring of God, we ought not to think that the Godhead is like unto gold, or silver, or stone, graven by art and man's device.

30 And the times of this ignorance God winked at; but now commandeth all men every where to repent:

31 Because he hath appointed a day, in the which he will judge the world in righteousness by that man whom he hath ordained; whereof he hath given assurance unto all men, in that he hath raised him from the dead.

32 And when they heard of the resurrection of the dead, some mocked: and others said, We will hear thee again of this matter.

33 So Paul departed from among them.

34 Howbeit certain men clave unto him, and believed: among the which was Dionysius the Areopagite, and a woman named Damaris, and others with them.

ACTS 18

1 After these things Paul departed from Athens, and came to Corinth;

2 And found a certain Jew named Aquila, born in Pontus, lately come from Italy, with his wife Priscilla; (because that Claudius had commanded all Jews to depart from Rome:) and came unto them.

3 And because he was of the same craft, he abode with them, and wrought: for by their occupation they were tentmakers.

feign to ourselves any earthly king, but that we seek in him righteousness, and all parts of our salvation; both which things Paul is said to have proved out of the Scriptures. We must know that the Jews were not so blockish, nor so impudent, as they be at this day. Paul might have drawn arguments from the sacrifices and from all the worship of the law, whereat the Jews gnarl at this day like dogs. It is well known how unseemly they rent and corrupt other places of Scripture. At that day they had some courtesy in them; also they did somewhat reverence the Scripture, so that they were not altogether such as would not be taught; at this day the veil is laid over their hearts (2 Corinthians 3: 15), so that they can see no more in the clear light than moles.

ACTS 18

1. This history is worthy to be remembered even for this one cause, because it containeth the first beginning of the Church of Corinth, which, as it was famous for good causes, both because of the multitude of men, and also because of the excellent gifts bestowed upon them, so there were in it gross and shameful vices. Furthermore, Luke showeth in this place with what great labor, and how hardly, Paul did win the same to Christ. It is well known what a rich city Corinth was by reason of the noble mart, how populous, how greatly given to pleasure. And the old proverb doth testify that it was sumptuous and full of riot: All men cannot go to Corinth. When Paul entereth the same, what hope, I pray you, can he conceive? He is a simple man, unknown, having no eloquence or pomp, showing no wealth or power. In that that huge gulf doth not swallow up his and desire which he had to spread abroad the gospel, by this we gather that he was furnished with wonderful power of the Spirit of God; and also that God wrought by his hand after a heavenly manner, and not after any human manner. Wherefore he boasteth not without cause, that the Corinthians are the seal of his apostleship (1 Corinthians 9: 2). For they be twice blind, who do not acknowledge that the glory of God did more plainly appear in such a simple and base kind of dealing; and he himself showed no small token of invincible constancy, when, being vexed with the mocks of all men, (as the proud did contemn him,) he did notwithstanding stay himself upon God's help alone. But it is worth the labor to note all the circum-stances, as Luke setteth down the same in order.

2. A Jew called Aquila

This was no small trial, in that Paul findeth none at Corinthus to lodge him save Aquila, who had been twice exiled. For being born in Pontus, he forsook his country, and sailed over the sea, that he might dwell at Rome. He was

God, Rom. 1: 19–20. The fact, that the nations did not thus learn the character of the true God, shows their great stupidity and wickedness. The design of Paul in this was, doubtless, to reprove the idolatry of the Athenians. The argument is this: "God has given to each nation its proper opportunity to learn his character. Idolatry, therefore, is folly and wickedness; since it is possible to find out the existence of the one God from his works."

If haply. If perhaps – implying that it was possible to find God, though it might be attended with some difficulty. God has placed us here that we may make the trial; and has made it possible thus to find him.

They might feel after him. The word used here means, properly, to touch, to handle, Luke 24: 39; Heb. 12: 18; and then to ascertain the qualities of an object by the sense of touch. And as the sense of touch is regarded as a certain way of ascertaining the existence and qualities of an object, the word means to search diligently, that we may know distinctly and certainly. The word has this sense here. It means to search diligently and accurately for God, to learn his existence and perfections. The Syriac renders it, "that they may seek for God, and find him from his creatures."

And find him. Find the proofs of his existence. Become acquainted with his perfections and laws.

Though he be not far, etc. This seems to be stated by the apostle to show that it was possible to find him; and that even those who were without a revelation need not despair of becoming acquainted with his existence and perfections.

ACTS 18

2. And found a certain Jew. Aquila is elsewhere mentioned as the friend of Paul, Rom. 16: 3; 2 Tim. 4: 19; 1 Cor. 16: 19.

Though a Jew by birth, yet it is evident that he became a convert to the Christian faith.

Lately come from Italy. Though the command of Claudius extended only to Rome, yet it was probably deemed not safe to remain, or it might have been difficult to procure occupation in any part of Italy.

3. The same craft. Of the same trade, or occupation.

And wrought. And worked at that occupation. Why he did it, the historian does not affirm; but it seems pretty evident that it was because he had no other means of maintenance. He also labored for his own support in Ephesus, Acts 20: 34 and also at Thessalonica, 2 Thess. 3: 9–10. The apostle was not ashamed of honest industry for a livelihood; nor did he deem it any disparagement that a minister of the gospel should labor with his own hands.

For by their occupation. By their trade; that is, they had been brought up to this business. Paul had been designed originally for a lawyer, and had been brought up at the feet of Gamaliel. But it was a regular custom among the Jews to train up their sons to some useful employment, that they might have the means of an honest livelihood. Even though they were trained up to the liberal sciences, yet they deemed a handicraft trade, or some honorable occupation, an indispensable part of education.

10. For I am with thee. I will attend, bless, and protect you.

No man shall set on thee. No one who shall rise up against thee shall be able to hurt thee. His life was in God's hands, and he would preserve him, in order that his people might be collected into the church.

For I have. Greek, There is to me; i.e., I possess, or there belongs to me.

Much people. Many who should be regarded as his true friends, and who should be saved.

In this city. In that very city that was so voluptuous, so rich, so effeminate, and where there had been already so decided opposition shown to the gospel. This passage evidently means that God had a design or purpose to save many of that people; for it was given to Paul as all encouragement to him to labor there, evidently meaning that God would grant him success in his work. It cannot mean that the Lord meant to say that the great mass of the people, or that the moral and virtuous part, if there were any such, was then regarded as his people; but that he intended to convert many of those guilty and profligate Corinthians to himself, and to gather a people for his

4 And he reasoned in the synagogue every sabbath, and persuaded the Jews and the Greeks.

5 And when Silas and Timotheus were come from Macedonia, Paul was pressed in the spirit, and testified to the Jews that Jesus was Christ.

6 And when they opposed themselves, and blasphemed, he shook his raiment, and said unto them, Your blood be upon your own heads; I am clean: from henceforth I will go unto the Gentiles.

7 And he departed thence, and entered into a certain man's house, named Justus, one that worshipped God, whose house joined hard to the synagogue.

8 And Crispus, the chief ruler of the synagogue, believed on the Lord with all his house; and many of the Corinthians hearing believed, and were baptized.

9 Then spake the Lord to Paul in the night by a vision, Be not afraid, but speak, and hold not thy peace:

10 For I am with thee, and no man shall set on thee to hurt thee: for I have much people in this city.

11 And he continued there a year and six months, teaching the word of God among them.

12 And when Gallio was the deputy of Achaia, the Jews made insurrection with one accord against Paul, and brought him to the judgment seat,

13 Saying, This fellow persuadeth men to worship God contrary to the law.

14 And when Paul was now about to open his mouth, Gallio said unto the Jews, If it were a matter of wrong or wicked lewdness, O ye Jews, reason would that I should bear with you:

15 But if it be a question of words and names, and of your law, look ye to it; for I will be no judge of such matters.

16 And he drave them from the judgment seat.

17 Then all the Greeks took Sosthenes, the chief ruler of the synagogue, and beat him before the judgment seat. And Gallio cared for none of those things.

18 And Paul after this tarried there yet a good while, and then took his leave of the brethren, and sailed thence into Syria, and with him Priscilla and Aquila; having shorn his head in Cenchrea: for he had a vow.

compelled to depart thence again by the commandment of Claudius Caesar. Though the commodiousness of the city was such, the plenty so great, the situation so pleasant, and there were also so many Jews there, yet Paul found no more fit host than a man that had been banished out of his own country, and also out of another soil. If we compare the great fruit which ensued immediately upon his preaching with such a base entrance, the power of the Spirit of God shall [more] plainly appear. Also we may see how the Lord, by his singular counsel, turneth those things to his glory, and the salvation of the godly, which seem contrary to the flesh, and unhappy. Nothing is more miserable than exile, according to the sense of the flesh. But it was far better for Aquila to be Paul's companion, than to be in the highest office either at Rome or in his country. Therefore, this happy calamity of Aquila doth teach us, that the Lord doth often better provide for when he doth sharply punish us, than if he should most gently entreat us, and when he tosseth us to and fro in most extreme exile, that he may bring us unto the heavenly rest.

11. He continued there a year

We do not read that Paul stayed so long anywhere else save there; and yet it appeareth by his two epistles that he was not only likely to suffer much troubles, but that he had suffered many unjust and unmeet things by reason of the pride and unthankfulness of the people, so that we see that there was no part of warfare wherein the Lord did not wonderfully exercise him. Also, we gather what a hard and laborious matter the edifying of the Church is, seeing that the most excellent workmaster spent so much time about the laying of the foundation of one church only. Neither doth he boast that he had finished the work, but that the Lord had put others in his place, that they might build upon his foundation; as he saith afterwards that he had planted, and that Apollos had watered (1 Corinthians 3: 6).

12. When Gallio

Here we see what the ignorance of true godliness doth in setting in order the state of every commonwealth and dominion. All men confess that this is the principal thing that true religion be in force and flourish. Now, when the true God is known, and the certain and sure rule of worshipping him is understood, there is nothing more equal than that which God commandeth in his law, to wit, that those who bear rule with power (having abolished contrary superstitions) defend the pure worship of the true God. But seeing that the Romans did observe their rites only through pride and stubbornness, and seeing they had no certainty where there was no truth, they thought that this was the best way they could take if they should grant liberty to those who

own service there. We may learn from this,

(1.) that God has a purpose in regard to the salvation of sinners.

(2.) That that purpose is so fixed in the mind of God, that he can say that those in relation to whom it is formed are his. There is no chance; no hap-hazard; no doubt in regard to his gathering them to himself.

(3.) This is the ground of encouragement to the ministers of the gospel. Had God no purpose to save sinners, they could have no hope in their work.

(4.) This plan may have reference to the most gay, and guilty, and abandoned population; and ministers should not be deterred by the amount or the degree of wickedness from attempting to save them.

(5.) There may be more hope of success among a dissolute and profligate population, than among proud, and cold, and skeptical philosophers. Paul had little success in philosophic Athens; he had great success in dissolute Corinth. There is often more hope of converting a man openly dissolute and abandoned, than one who prides himself on his philosophy, and is confident in his own wisdom.

17. Then all the Greeks. The Greeks who had witnessed the persecution of Paul by the Jews, and who had seen the tumult which they had excited.

Took Sosthenes, etc. As he was the chief ruler of the synagogue, he had probably been a leader in the opposition to Paul, and in the prosecution. Indignant at the Jews – at their bringing such questions before the tribunal – at their bigotry, and rage, and contentious spirit – they probably fell upon him in a tumultuous and disorderly manner as he was leaving the tribunal. The Greeks would feel no small measure of indignation at these disturbers of the public peace, and they took this opportunity to express their rage.

And beat him. This word is not that which is commonly used to denote a judicial act of scourging. It probably means that they fell upon him, and beat him with their fists, or with whatever was at hand.

18. And sailed thence into Syria. Or set sail for Syria. His design was to go to Jerusalem

to the festival which was soon to occur, Acts 18: 21.

For he had a vow. A vow is a solemn promise made to God respecting anything. The use of vows is observable throughout the Scripture. Jacob, going into Mesopotamia, vowed the tenth of his estate, and promised to offer it at Bethel to the honor of God, Gen. 28: 22. Moses made many regulations in regard to vows. A man might devote himself or his children to the Lord. He might devote any part of his time or property to his service. The vow they were required sacredly to observe, (Deut. 23: 21–22) except in certain specified cases they were permitted to redeem that which had been thus devoted.

21. Keep this feast. Probably the Passover is here referred to. Why he was so anxious to celebrate that feast at Jerusalem, the historian has not informed us. It is probable, however, that he wished to meet as many of his countrymen as possible, and to remove, if practicable, the prejudices which had everywhere been raised against him, Acts 21: 20–21. Perhaps, also, he supposed that there would be many Christian converts present, whom he might meet also.

But I will return, etc. This he did, Acts 19: 1, and remained there three years, Acts 20: 31.

24. And a certain Jew named Apollos. Apollos afterwards became a distinguished and successful preacher of the gospel, 1 Cor. 1: 12; 3: 5–6; 4: 6; Titus 3: 13. Nothing more is known of him than is stated in these passages.

Born at Alexandria. Alexandria was a celebrated city in Egypt, founded by Alexander the Great. There were large numbers of Jews resident there.

An eloquent man. Alexandria was famous for its schools; and it is probable that Apollos, in addition to his natural endowments, had enjoyed the benefit of these schools.

Mighty in the Scriptures. Well instructed, or able in the Old Testament. The foundation was thus laid for future usefulness in the Christian church.

28. For he mightily convinced the Jews. He did it by strong arguments; he bore down all opposition, and effectually silenced them. And

19 And he came to Ephesus, and left them there: but he himself entered into the synagogue, and reasoned with the Jews.

20 When they desired him to tarry longer time with them, he consented not;

21 But bade them farewell, saying, I must by all means keep this feast that cometh in Jerusalem: but I will return again unto you, if God will. And he sailed from Ephesus.

22 And when he had landed at Caesarea, and gone up, and saluted the church, he went down to Antioch.

23 And after he had spent some time there, he departed, and went over all the country of Galatia and Phrygia in order, strengthening all the disciples.

24 And a certain Jew named Apollos, born at Alexandria, an eloquent man, and mighty in the scriptures, came to Ephesus.

25 This man was instructed in the way of the Lord; and being fervent in the spirit, he spake and taught diligently the things of the Lord, knowing only the baptism of John.

26 And he began to speak boldly in the synagogue: whom when Aquila and Priscilla had heard, they took him unto them, and expounded unto him the way of God more perfectly.

27 And when he was disposed to pass into Achaia, the brethren wrote, exhorting the disciples to receive him: who, when he was come, helped them much which had believed through grace:

28 For he mightily convinced the Jews, and that publickly, shewing by the scriptures that Jesus was Christ.

ACTS 19

1 And it came to pass, that, while Apollos was at Corinth, Paul having passed through the upper coasts came to Ephesus: and finding certain disciples,

2 He said unto them, Have ye received the Holy Ghost since ye believed? And they said unto him, We have not so much as heard whether there be any Holy Ghost.

3 And he said unto them, Unto what then were ye baptized? And they said, Unto John's baptism.

4 Then said Paul, John verily baptized

dwelt in the provinces to live as they listed. But nothing is more absurd than to leave the worship of God to men's choice. Wherefore, it was not without cause that God commanded by Moses that the king should cause a book of the law to be written out for himself (Deuteronomy 17: 18); to wit, that being well instructed, and certain of his faith, he might with more courage take in hand to maintain that which he knew certainly was right.

18. And when he had tarried there many days

Paul's constancy appeareth in this, in that he is not driven away with fear, lest he should trouble the disciples, who were as yet ignorant and weak, with his sudden and untimely departure. We read in many other places, that when persecution was raised against him elsewhere he fled forthwith. What is the cause then, that he stayeth at Corinth? to wit, when he saw that the enemies were provoked with his presence to rage against the whole Church, he did not doubt but that the faithful should have peace and rest by his departure; but now, when he seeth their malice bridled, so that they cannot hurt the flock of God, he had rather sting and nettle them, than by departing minister unto them any new occasion of rage. Furthermore, this was the third journey which Paul took to Jerusalem. For going from Damascus, he went once up that he might be made known to the apostles. And he was sent the second time with Barnabas, that he might handle and end the controversy about ceremonies. But Luke doth not set down for what cause he now took such a long and laborious journey, determining with all speed to return.

ACTS 19

1. Luke showeth here that the Church of Ephesus was not only confirmed and increased by Paul's return, but also that there was a miracle wrought there, because the visible graces of the Spirit were given to certain rude and new disciples. Furthermore, it is not known whether they were inhabitants of the city or strangers; neither doth it greatly skill. It is not to be doubted but that they were Jews, because they had received the baptism of John; also, it is to be thought that they dwelt at Ephesus when Paul found them there.

2. Whether they had received the Holy Ghost

The end of the history doth show that Paul doth not speak in this place of the Spirit of regeneration, but of the special gifts which God gave to divers at the beginning of the gospel, for the common edifying of the Church. But now upon this interrogation of Paul ariseth a question, whether the Spirit were common to all everywhere at that time? For if he were given only to a few, why doth he join him with faith, as if they were so linked together that they could not

that publicly. In his public preaching in the synagogue and elsewhere.

Showing by the Scriptures. Proving from the Old Testament. Showing that Jesus of Nazareth corresponded with the account of the Messiah given by the prophets.

That Jesus was Christ. That Jesus of Nazareth was the Messiah.

ACTS 19

1. While Apollos was at Corinth. It is probable that he remained there a considerable time.

Paul having passed through the upper coasts. The upper, or more elevated regions of Asia Minor. The writer refers here particularly to the provinces of Phrygia and Galatia, Acts 18: 23. These regions were called upper, because they were situated on the high table-land in the interior of Asia Minor; while Ephesus was in the low maritime regions, and called the low country.

Came to Ephesus. Agreeably to his promise, Acts 18: 21.

And finding certain disciples. Certain persons who had been baptized into John's baptism, and who had embraced John's doctrine, that the Messiah was soon to appear, Acts 19: 3–4. It is very clear that they had not yet heard that he had come, or that the Holy Ghost was given. They were evidently in the same situation as Apollos.

2. Have ye received the Holy Ghost? Have ye received the extraordinary effusions and miraculous influences of the Holy Ghost Paul would not doubt that, if they had "believed," they had received the ordinary converting influences of the Holy Spirit – for it was one of his favorite doctrines, that the Holy Spirit renews the heart. But, besides this, the miraculous influences of the Spirit were conferred on most societies of believers. The power of speaking with tongues, or of working miracles, was imparted as an evidence of the presence of God, and of their acceptance with him, Acts 10: 45–46; 1 Cor. 15. It was natural for Paul to ask whether this evidence of the Divine favor had been granted to them.

Since ye believed. Since you embraced the

doctrine of John, that the Messiah was soon to come.

We have not so much as heard, etc. This seems to be a very remarkable and strange answer. Yet we are to remember,

(1.) that these were mere disciples of John's doctrine, and that his preaching related particularly to the Messiah, and not to the Holy Ghost.

(2.) It does not even appear that they had heard that the Messiah had come, or had heard of Jesus of Nazareth, Acts 19: 4–5.

(3.) It is not remarkable, therefore, that they had no clear conceptions of the character and operations of the Holy Ghost. Yet,

(4.) they were just in that state of mind, that they were willing to embrace the doctrine when it was proclaimed to them; thus showing that they were really under the influence of the Holy Spirit. God may often produce important changes in the hearts and lives of sinners, even where they have no clear and systematic views of religious doctrines. In all such cases, however, as in this, there will be readiness of heart to embrace the truth where it is made known.

9. But when divers. When some were hardened.

Were hardened. When their hearts were hardened, and they became violently opposed to the gospel. When the truth made no impression on them. The word harden, as applied to the heart, is often used to denote insensibility and opposition to the gospel.

But spake evil of that way. Of the gospel – the way, path, or manner in which God saves men. See Acts 16: 17; 18: 26; Matt. 7: 13–14.

Separated the disciples. Removed them from the influence and society of those who were seeking to draw them away from the faith. This is often the best way to prevent the evil influence of others. Christians, if they wish to preserve their minds calm and peaceful; if they wish to avoid the agitations of conflict, and the temptations of those who would lead them astray, may often find it necessary to withdraw from their society, and should seek the fellowship of their Christian brethren.

12. So that from his body. That is, these hand-

with the baptism of repentance, saying unto the people, that they should believe on him which should come after him, that is, on Christ Jesus.

5 When they heard this, they were baptized in the name of the Lord Jesus.

6 And when Paul had laid his hands upon them, the Holy Ghost came on them; and they spake with tongues, and prophesied.

7 And all the men were about twelve.

8 And he went into the synagogue, and spake boldly for the space of three months, disputing and persuading the things concerning the kingdom of God.

9 But when divers were hardened, and believed not, but spake evil of that way before the multitude, he departed from them, and separated the disciples, disputing daily in the school of one Tyrannus.

10 And this continued by the space of two years; so that all they which dwelt in Asia heard the word of the Lord Jesus, both Jews and Greeks.

11 And God wrought special miracles by the hands of Paul:

12 So that from his body were brought unto the sick handkerchiefs or aprons, and the diseases departed from them, and the evil spirits went out of them.

13 Then certain of the vagabond Jews, exorcists, took upon them to call over them which had evil spirits the name of the Lord Jesus, saying, We adjure you by Jesus whom Paul preacheth.

14 And there were seven sons of one Sceva, a Jew, and chief of the priests, which did so.

15 And the evil spirit answered and said, Jesus I know, and Paul I know; but who are ye?

16 And the man in whom the evil spirit was leaped on them, and overcame them, and prevailed against them, so that they fled out of that house naked and wounded.

17 And this was known to all the Jews and Greeks also dwelling at Ephesus; and fear fell on them all, and the name of the Lord Jesus was magnified.

18 And many that believed came, and confessed, and shewed their deeds.

19 Many of them also which used curious arts brought their books together, and burned them before all men: and they

be separate? Peradventure, they were none of the common sort; or because they were an indifferent number, that is, twelve, Paul demandeth whether they were all without the gifts of the Spirit. Notwithstanding, I think thus, that so many Jews were offered in presence of the Gentiles, not by chance, but by the counsel of God; and that at one time being disciples, that is, of the number of the faithful, who did notwithstanding confess that they were ignorant of the principal glory of the gospel, which was apparent in spiritual gifts, that by them Paul's ministry might be beautified and set forth. For it is unlike that Apollos left so few disciples at Ephesus; and he might have taught them better, since that he learned the way of the Lord perfectly of Priscilla and Aquila.

Moreover, I do not doubt but that the brethren of whom Luke spake before were other than these. In sum, when Paul seeth that these men do profess the name of Christ, to the end he may have a more certain trial of their faith, he asketh them whether they have received the Holy Ghost. For it appeareth by Paul himself that this was a sign and token of the grace of God to establish the credit of doctrine; I would know of you whether ye received the Holy Ghost by the works of the law, or by the hearing of faith (Galatians 3: 2).

8. Going into the synagogue

From this we gather that Paul began with the company of the godly, who had already given their names to Christ. Secondly, that he came into the synagogue, that he might gather together into one body of the Church the rest of the Jews who knew not Christ as yet, or at least who had not as yet received him. And he saith that Paul behaved himself boldly, that we may know that he was not therefore heard by the space of three months, because he did craftily cover the doctrine of the gospel, or did insinuate himself by certain dark crooks. Luke doth also by and by express some token of boldness, showing that he disputed and persuaded touching the kingdom of God. And we know that by this word is oftentimes noted that restoring which was promised to the fathers, and which was to be fulfilled by the coming of Christ. For seeing that without Christ there is an evil-favored and confused scattering abroad and ruin of all things, the prophets did attribute this not in vain to the Mesas who was to come, that it should come to pass that he should establish the kingdom of God in the world. And now, because this kingdom doth bring us back from falling and sliding back, unto the obedience of God, and maketh us sons of enemies; it consisteth – First in the free forgiveness of sins, whereby God doth reconcile us to himself, and doth adopt us to be his people: Secondly, in newness of life, whereby he fashioneth and maketh us like to his own image. He saith that he disputed and persuaded, meaning that

kerchiefs which had been applied to his body, which he had used, or which he had touched. An instance somewhat similar to this occurs in the case of the woman who was healed by touching the hem of the Savior's garment, Matt. 9: 20–22.

Unto the sick. The sick who were at a distance, and who were unable to go where he was. If it be asked why this was done, it may be observed,

(1.) that the working of miracles in that region would greatly contribute to the spread of the gospel.

(2.) We are not to suppose that there was any efficacy in the aprons thus brought, or in the mere fact that they had touched the body of Paul, any more than there was in the hem of the Savior's garment which the woman touched, or in the clay which he made use of to open the eyes of the blind man, John 8: 6.

(3.) In this instance the fact, that the miracles were wrought in this manner by garments which had touched his body, was a mere sign, or an evidence to the persons concerned, that it was done by the instrumentality of Paul, as the fact that the Savior put his fingers into the ears of a deaf man, and spit and touched his tongue, Mark 7: 33, was an evidence to those who saw it, that the power of healing came from him. The bearing of these aprons to the sick was, therefore, a mere sign, or evidence to all concerned, that miraculous power was given to Paul.

Handkerchiefs. The word used here properly denotes a piece of linen with which sweat was wiped from the face; and then any piece of linen used for tying up, or containing anything, In Luke 19: 20, it denotes the "napkin" in which the talent of the unprofitable servant was concealed; in John 11: 44; 20: 7, the "napkin" which was used to bind up the face of the dead, applied to Lazarus and to our Savior.

Or aprons. This also is a Latin word, and means, literally, a half-girdle – a piece of cloth which was girded round the waist to preserve the clothes of those who were engaged in any kind of work. The word aprons expresses the idea.

And the diseases departed. The sick were healed.

It is evident that this power of working miracles would contribute greatly to Paul's success among the people.

18. Their deeds. Their actions; their evil course of life. Their deeds of iniquity in their former state. The direct reference here is to the magical arts which had been used, but the word may also be designed to denote iniquity in general. They who make a profession of religion will be willing to confess their transgressions. And no man can have evidence that he is truly renewed who is not willing to confess as well as to forsake his sins, Rom. 10: 10; Prov. 28: 13: "He that covereth his sins shall not prosper; but whoso confesseth and forsaketh them shall find mercy."

20. So mightily. So powerfully. It had such efficacy and power in this wicked city. The power must have been mighty that would thus make them willing, not only to cease to practice imposition, but to give up all hopes of future gains, and to destroy their property. On this instructive narrative, we may remark,

(1.) that religion has power to break the hold of sinners on unjust and dishonest means of living.

(2.) That those who have been engaged in an unchristian and dishonorable practice, will abandon it when they become Christians.

(3.) That their abhorrence of their former course will be, and ought to be, expressed as publicly as was the offence.

(4.) That the evil practice will be abandoned at any sacrifice, however great. The only question will be, what is right; not, what will it cost. Property, in the view of a converted man, is nothing When compared with a good conscience.

(5.) This conduct of those who had used curious arts shows us what ought to be done by those who have been engaged in any evil course of life, and who are then converted. If their conduct was right – and who can doubt it? – it settles a great principle on which young converts should act. If a man has been engaged in the slave-trade, he will abandon it; and his duty will not be to sell his ship to one who he knows will continue the traffic. His property should be withdrawn from the

counted the price of them, and found it fifty thousand pieces of silver.

20 So mightily grew the word of God and prevailed.

21 After these things were ended, Paul purposed in the spirit, when he had passed through Macedonia and Achaia, to go to Jerusalem, saying, After I have been there, I must also see Rome.

22 So he sent into Macedonia two of them that ministered unto him, Timotheus and Erastus; but he himself stayed in Asia for a season.

23 And the same time there arose no small stir about that way.

24 For a certain man named Demetrius, a silversmith, which made silver shrines for Diana, brought no small gain unto the craftsmen;

25 Whom he called together with the workmen of like occupation, and said, Sirs, ye know that by this craft we have our wealth.

26 Moreover ye see and hear, that not alone at Ephesus, but almost throughout all Asia, this Paul hath persuaded and turned away much people, saying that they be no gods, which are made with hands:

27 So that not only this our craft is in danger to be set at nought; but also that the temple of the great goddess Diana should be despised, and her magnificence should be destroyed, whom all Asia and the world worshippeth.

28 And when they heard these sayings, they were full of wrath, and cried out, saying, Great is Diana of the Ephesians.

29 And the whole city was filled with confusion: and having caught Gaius and Aristarchus, men of Macedonia, Paul's companions in travel, they rushed with one accord into the theatre.

30 And when Paul would have entered in unto the people, the disciples suffered him not.

31 And certain of the chief of Asia, which were his friends, sent unto him, desiring him that he would not adventure himself into the theatre.

32 Some therefore cried one thing, and some another: for the assembly was confused; and the more part knew not wherefore they were come together.

33 And they drew Alexander out of the

Paul did so dispute, that he proved that with sound reasons which he did allege; that done, he used the pricks of godly exhortations, whereby he pricked forward his hearers. For no profound disputations shall make us obedient to God, unless we be moved with godly admonitions.

9. Seeing their hearts were hardened

We do not read that Paul was heard so patiently and so favorably by the Jews at any place as at Ephesus at his first coming. For whereas others raising tumults did drive him away, he was requested by these to tarry longer. Now, after that he had endeavored, by the space of three months, to erect the kingdom of God among them, the ungodliness and stubbornness of many doth show itself. For Luke saith that they were hardened; and surely such is the power of the heavenly doctrine that it doth either make the reprobate mad or else more obstinate; and that not of nature, but accidentally, as they say, because, when they be urged by the truth, their secret poison breaketh out.

13. To the end it may more plainly appear that the apostleship of Paul was confirmed by those miracles whereof mention was made of late, Luke doth now teach that when certain did falsely pretend the name of Christ, such abuse was most sharply punished. Whereby we gather that such miracles were wrought by the hand of Paul, to no other end, save only that all men might know that he did faithfully preach Christ to be the power of God; forasmuch as the Lord did not only not suffer them to be separate from the pure doctrine of the gospel; but did so sharply punish those who did draw them preposterously unto their enchantments; whence we gather again, that whatsoever miracles do darken the name of Christ they be juggling casts of the devil; and that those be coziness and falsifiers who draw the true miracles of God to any other end, save only that true religion may be established.

18. Many which believed

Luke bringeth forth one token of that fear whereof he spake. For they did indeed declare that they were thoroughly touched and moved with the fear of God, who, of their own accord, did confess the faults and offenses of their former life, lest, through their dissimulation, they should nourish the wrath of God within. We know what a hard matter it is to wring true confession out of those who have offended, for seeing men count nothing more precious than their estimation, they make more account of shame than of truth; yea, so much as in them lieth, they seek to cover their shame. Therefore, this voluntary confession was a testimony of repentance and of fear. For no man, unless he be thoroughly touched, will make himself subject to the slanders and reproaches of men, and will willingly be judged upon

business publicly, either by being destroyed, or by being converted to a useful purpose. If a man has been a distiller of ardent spirits as a drink, his duty will be to forsake his evil course. Nor will it be his duty to sell his distillery to one who will continue the business; but to withdraw his property from it publicly, either by destroying it, or converting it to some useful purpose. If a man has been engaged in traffic in ardent spirits, his duty is not to sell his stock to those who will continue the sale of the poison, but to withdraw it from public use; converting it to some useful purpose, if he can; if not, by destroying it. All that has ever been said by money-loving distillers, or vendors of ardent spirits, about the loss which they would sustain by abandoning the business, might have been said by these practitioners of curious arts in Ephesus. And if the excuses of rum-selling men are valid, their conduct was folly; and they should either have continued the business of practicing "curious arts," after they were converted, or have sold their "books" to those who would have continued it. For assuredly it was not worse to practice jugglery and fortune-telling than it is to destroy the bodies and souls of men by the traffic in ardent spirits. And yet how few men there are in Christian lands who practice on the principle of these honest, but comparatively unenlightened men at Ephesus!

28. Were full of wrath. Were greatly enraged – probably at the prospect of losing their gains.

Great is Diana, etc. The term great was often applied by the Greeks to Diana. Thus in Xenophon he says, "I adjure you by your own goddess, the great Diana of the Ephesians." The design of this clamor was doubtless to produce a persecution against Paul; and thus to secure a continuance of their employment. Often, when men have no arguments, they raise a clamor; when their employments are in danger of being ruined, they are filled with rage. We may learn, also, that when men's pecuniary interests are affected, they often show great zeal for religion, and expect by clamor in behalf of some doctrine, to maintain their own interest, and to secure their own gains.

29. Confusion. Tumult; disorder.

Gaius. He had lived at Corinth, and had kindly entertained Paul at his house, 1 Cor. 1: 14; Rom. 16: 23.

Aristarchus. He attended Paul to Rome, and was there a prisoner with him, Col. 4: 10.

With one accord. Tumultuously; or with one mind, or purpose.

Into the theatre. The theatres of the Greeks were not only places for public exhibitions, but also for holding assemblies, and often for courts, elections, etc. The people, therefore, naturally rushed there, as being a suitable place to decide this matter.

38. Have a matter against any man. Have a complaint of injury; if injustice has been done them by any one.

The law is open. There are court days; days which are open, or appointed for judicial trials, where such matters can be determined in a proper manner. Perhaps the courts were then held, and the matter might be immediately determined.

Let them implead one another. Let them accuse each other in the court; i.e., let them defend their own cause, and arraign one another. The laws are equal, and impartial justice will be done.

39. But if ye enquire. If you seek to determine any other matters than that pertaining to the alleged wrong which Demetrius has suffered in his business.

Other matters. Anything respecting public affairs; anything pertaining to the government and the worship of Diana.

In a lawful assembly. In an assembly convened, not by tumult and riot, but in conformity to law. This was a tumultuous assemblage, and it was proper in the public officer to demand that they should disperse; and that, if there were any public grievances to be remedied, it should be done in an assembly properly convened.

41. Dismissed the assembly. The word usually translated church. Here it is applied to the irregular and tumultuous assemblage which had convened in a riotous manner.

multitude, the Jews putting him forward. And Alexander beckoned with the hand, and would have made his defence unto the people.

34 But when they knew that he was a Jew, all with one voice about the space of two hours cried out, Great is Diana of the Ephesians.

35 And when the townclerk had appeased the people, he said, Ye men of Ephesus, what man is there that knoweth not how that the city of the Ephesians is a worshipper of the great goddess Diana, and of the image which fell down from Jupiter?

36 Seeing then that these things cannot be spoken against, ye ought to be quiet, and to do nothing rashly.

37 For ye have brought hither these men, which are neither robbers of churches, nor yet blasphemers of your goddess.

38 Wherefore if Demetrius, and the craftsmen which are with him, have a matter against any man, the law is open, and there are deputies: let them implead one another.

39 But if ye inquire any thing concerning other matters, it shall be determined in a lawful assembly.

40 For we are in danger to be called in question for this day's uproar, there being no cause whereby we may give an account of this concourse.

41 And when he had thus spoken, he dismissed the assembly.

ACTS 20

1 And after the uproar was ceased, Paul called unto him the disciples, and embraced them, and departed for to go into Macedonia.

2 And when he had gone over those parts, and had given them much exhortation, he came into Greece,

3 And there abode three months. And when the Jews laid wait for him, as he was about to sail into Syria, he purposed to return through Macedonia.

4 And there accompanied him into Asia Sopater of Berea; and of the Thessalonians, Aristarchus and Secundus; and Gaius of Derbe, and Timotheus; and of Asia, Tychicus and Trophimus.

earth, that he may be loosed and acquitted in heaven. When he saith, Many, by this we gather that they had not all one cause, for it may be that these men had corrupt consciences a long time; as many are oftentimes infected with hidden and inward vices. Wherefore, Luke doth not prescribe all men a common law; but he setteth before them an example which those must follow who need like medicine. For why did these men confess their facts, save only that they might give testimony of their repentance, and seek counsel and ease at Paul's hands? It was otherwise with those who came unto the baptism of John, confessing their sins (Matthew 3: 6). For by this means they did confess that they did enter into repentance without dissimulation.

ACTS 20

1. Luke declareth in this chapter how Paul, loosing from Asia, did again cross the seas to go to Jerusalem. And though whatsoever is written in this narration be worthy of most diligent meditation and marking, yet doth it need no long exposition. It appeareth that the Church was preserved in safety by the wonderful power of God amidst those troublesome tumults. The church of Ephesus was as yet slender and weak: the faithful having had experience of a sudden motion [commotion] once, might for just causes fear, lest like storms should ever now and then arise. We need not doubt that Paul did with much ado depart from them; yet because greater necessity doth draw him unto another place, he is enforced to leave his sons who were lately begotten, and had as yet scarce escaped shipwreck in the midst of the raging sea. As for them, though they be very loath to forego Paul, yet, lest they do injury to other churches, they do not keep him back nor stay him. So that we see that they were not wedded to themselves, but that they were careful for the kingdom of Christ, that they might provide as well for their brethren as for themselves. We must diligently note these examples, that one of us may study to help another in this miserable dispersing; but if it so fall out at any time that we be bereft of profitable helps, let us not doubt nor waver, knowing that God doth hold the helm of our ship. And we must also note this, that Paul doth not depart until he have saluted the brethren, but doth rather strengthen them at his departure. As Luke saith straightway of the Macedonians, that Paul exhorted them with many words, that is, not overfields, as if it were sufficient to put them only in mind of their duty; but as he commandeth elsewhere that others should do, he urged importunately, and beat in [inculcated] thoroughly things which were needful to be known, that they might never be forgotten (2 Timothy 4: 2).

ACTS 20

1. The uproar. The tumult excited by Demetrius and the workmen. After it had been quieted by the town-clerk, Acts 19: 40–41.

Embraced them. Saluted them; gave them parting expressions of kindness. The Syriac translates this, "Paul called the disciples, and consoled them, and kissed them."

To go into Macedonia. On his way to Jerusalem, agreeably to his purpose – recorded in Acts 19: 21.

2. Over those parts. The parts of country in and near Macedonia. He probably went to Macedonia by Troas, where he expected to find Titus, 2 Cor. 2: 12; but not finding him there, he went by himself to Philippi, Thessalonica, etc., and then returned to Greece proper.

Into Greece. Into Greece Proper, of which Athens was the capital. While in Macedonia, he had great anxiety and trouble, but was at length comforted by the coming of Titus, who brought him intelligence of the liberal disposition of the churches of Greece in regard to the collection for the poor saints at Jerusalem, 2 Cor. 7: 5–7. It is probable that the Second Epistle to the Corinthians was written during this time in Macedonia, and sent to them by Titus.

3. And there abode. Why he remained here is unknown. It is probable, that while in Greece he wrote the Epistle to the Romans. Comp. Rom. 15: 25–27.

Laid wait. There was a design formed against him by the Jews, which they sought to execute. Why they formed this purpose, the historian has not informed us.

As he was about to sail. It would seem from this, that the design of the Jews was to attack the ship in which he was about, to sail, or to arrest him on ship-board. This fact determined him to take a much more circuitous route by land, so that the churches Of Macedonia were favored with another visit from him.

Into Syria. On his way to Jerusalem.

He purposed, etc. He resolved to avoid the snare which they had laid for him, and to return by the same way in which he had come into Greece.

4. And there accompanied him. It was usual for some of the disciples to attend the apostles in their journeys.

Into Asia. It is not meant that they attended him from Greece through Macedonia; but that they went with him to Asia, having gone before him, and joined him at Troas.

Sopater of Berea. Perhaps the same person who, in Rom. 16: 21, is called Sosipater, and who is there said to have been a kinsman of Paul.

7. And upon the first day of the week. Showing thus that this day was then observed buy Christians as holy time. Comp. 1 Cor. 16: 2; Rev. 1: 10.

To break bread. Evidently to celebrate the Lord's Supper. Comp. Acts 2: 46. So the Syriac understands it, by translating it, "to break the Eucharist," i.e. the eucharistic bread. It is probable that the apostles and early Christians celebrated the Lord's Supper on every Lord's-day.

And continued his speech until midnight. The discourse of Paul continued until the breaking of day, Acts 20: 11. But it was interrupted about midnight by the accident that occurred to Eutychus. The fact that Paul was about to leave them on the next day, probably to see them no more, was the principal reason why his discourse was so long continued. We are not to suppose, however, that it was one continued or set discourse. No small part of the time might have been passed in hearing and answering questions, though Paul was the chief speaker. The case proves that such seasons of extraordinary devotion may, in peculiar circumstances, be proper. Occasions may arise where it will be proper for Christians to spend a much longer time than usual in public worship. It is evident, however, that such seasons do not often occur.

10. And fell on him, etc. Probably stretching himself on him as Elisha did on the Shunammite's son, 2 Kgs. 4: 33–35. It was an act of tenderness and compassion, evincing a strong desire to restore him to life.

Trouble not yourselves. They would doubtless be thrown into great consternation by such an event. Paul therefore endeavored to

5 These going before tarried for us at Troas.

6 And we sailed away from Philippi after the days of unleavened bread, and came unto them to Troas in five days; where we abode seven days.

7 And upon the first day of the week, when the disciples came together to break bread, Paul preached unto them, ready to depart on the morrow; and continued his speech until midnight.

8 And there were many lights in the upper chamber, where they were gathered together.

9 And there sat in a window a certain young man named Eutychus, being fallen into a deep sleep: and as Paul was long preaching, he sunk down with sleep, and fell down from the third loft, and was taken up dead.

10 And Paul went down, and fell on him, and embracing him said, Trouble not yourselves; for his life is in him.

11 When he therefore was come up again, and had broken bread, and eaten, and talked a long while, even till break of day, so he departed.

12 And they brought the young man alive, and were not a little comforted.

13 And we went before to ship, and sailed unto Assos, there intending to take in Paul: for so had he appointed, minding himself to go afoot.

14 And when he met with us at Assos, we took him in, and came to Mitylene.

15 And we sailed thence, and came the next day over against Chios; and the next day we arrived at Samos, and tarried at Trogyllium; and the next day we came to Miletus.

16 For Paul had determined to sail by Ephesus, because he would not spend the time in Asia: for he hasted, if it were possible for him, to be at Jerusalem the day of Pentecost.

17 And from Miletus he sent to Ephesus, and called the elders of the church.

18 And when they were come to him, he said unto them, Ye know, from the first day that I came into Asia, after what manner I have been with you at all seasons,

19 Serving the Lord with all humility of mind, and with many tears, and temptations, which befell me by the lying in wait of the Jews:

3. Because the Jews laid wait for him

The Lord did exercise his servant so diversely and continually that he set before us in him an example of most excellent constancy. It is not sufficient for him to be wearied with the labor and trouble of a long and wearisome journey, unless he be also brought in danger of his life by those which lay in wait for him. Let all the servants of Christ set this mirror before their eyes, that they may never faint through the wearisomeness of straits. Notwithstanding, when Paul doth journey another way that he may avoid their laying in wait, he showeth that we must have regard of our life so far forth that we throw not ourselves headlong into the midst of dangers. And those who accompany him give no small testimony of their godliness; and we see how precious his life was to the faithful, when as a great many being chosen out of diverse countries to be his companions, do for his sake take a hard and sharp journey not without great charges. Luke saith that Paul tarried at Philippos so long as the days of unleavened bread did last, because he had at that time better opportunity offered to teach. And forasmuch as it was unknown as yet that the law was disannulled, it stood him upon to beware, lest by neglecting the feast-day he should be thought among the rude to be a contemner of God. Though, for mine own part, I think that he sought principally opportunity to teach, because the Jews were then more attentive to learn.

22. And, behold

He declareth now more fully to what end he intreated of his upright dealing; to wit, because they should never see him any more. And it was very expedient that the pattern which was set before them by God of them to be followed should be always before their eyes, and that they should remember him when he was dead. For we know how readily men degenerate from pure institution. But though he deny that he doth know what shall befall him at Jerusalem, yet because he was taught by many prophecies that bonds were prepared for him there, as if he were now ready to die, he cutteth off shortly after the hope of his return. And yet for all this he is not contrary to himself. He speaketh doubtfully at the first of set purpose, that he may soften that which was about to be more (hard and) bitter; and yet he doth truly affirm, that he knew not as yet the ends and events of things, because he had no certain and special revelation touching the whole process.

Bound in the spirit

Some expound this that he was bound to the churches, who had committed to him this function to carry alms. Notwithstanding, I do rather think that hereby is meant the inward force and motion of the Spirit, not as though he were so inspired, that he was out of his wit, but because

compose their minds by the assurance that he would live.

For his life is in him. He is restored to life. This has all the appearance of having been a miracle. Life was restored to him as Paul spoke.

16. To sail by Ephesus. The word by in our translation is ambiguous. We say to go by a place, meaning either to take it in our way, to go to it, or to go past it. Here it means the latter. He intended to sail past Ephesus, without going to it.

For he hasted, etc. Had he gone to Ephesus, he would probably have been so delayed in his journey that he could not reach Jerusalem at the time of Pentecost.

19. Serving the Lord. In the discharge of the appropriate duties of his apostolic office, and in private life. To discharge aright our duties in any vocation is serving the Lord. Religion is often represented in the Bible as a service rendered to the Lord.

With all humility. Without arrogance, pride, or a spirit of dictation; without a desire to "lord it over God's heritage;" without being elated with the authority of the apostolic office, the variety of the miracles which he was enabled to perform, or the success which attended his labors. What an admirable model for all who are in the ministry, for all who are endowed with talents and learning, and for all who meet with remarkable success in their work. The proper effect of such success, and of such talent, will be to produce true humility. Eminent success in the work of the ministry tends to produce lowliness and humbleness of mind; and the greatest endowments are usually connected with the most simple and childlike humility.

And with many tears. Paul not infrequently gives evidence of the tenderness of his heart, and his regard for the souls of men, and his deep solicitude for the salvation of sinners, Acts 20: 31; Phil. 3: 18; 2 Cor. 2: 4. The particular thing, however, here specified as producing weeping, was the opposition of the Jews. But it cannot be supposed that those tears were shed from an apprehension of personal danger. It was rather because the opposition of the Jews

impeded his work, and retarded his progress in winning souls to Christ. A minister of the gospel will

(1.) feel, and deeply feel, for the salvation of his people. He will weep over their condition when he sees them going astray, and in danger of perishing, He will

(2.) be especially affected with opposition, because it will retard his work, and prevent the progress and the triumph of the gospel. It is not because it is a personal concern, but because it is the cause of his Master.

And temptations. Trials, arising from their opposition. We use the word temptation, in a more limited sense, to denote inducements offered to one to lead him into sin. The word in the Scriptures most commonly denotes trials of any kind.

20. I kept back nothing, etc. No doctrine, no admonition, no labor. Whatever he judged would promote their salvation, he had faithfully and fearlessly delivered. A minister of the gospel must be the judge of what will be profitable to the people of his charge. His aim should be to promote their real welfare – to preach that which will be profitable. His object will not be to please their fancy, to gratify their taste, to flatter their pride, or to promote his own popularity. "All Scripture is profitable," 2 Tim. 3: 16; and it will be his aim to declare that only which will tend to promote their real welfare. Even if it be unpalatable; if it be the language of reproof and admonition; if it be doctrine to which the heart is by nature opposed; if it run counter to the native prejudices and passions of men; yet, by the grace of God, it should be, and will be delivered. No doctrine that will be profitable should be kept back; no plan, no labor, that may promote the welfare of the flock, should be withheld.

But have shewed you. Have announced or declared to you. The word here used is most commonly applied to preaching in public assemblies, or in a public manner.

Have taught you publicly. In the public assembly; by public preaching.

And from house to house. Though Paul preached in public, and though his time was much occupied in manual labor for his own support, Acts 20: 34, yet he did not esteem his

20 And how I kept back nothing that was profitable unto you, but have shewed you, and have taught you publickly, and from house to house,

21 Testifying both to the Jews, and also to the Greeks, repentance toward God, and faith toward our Lord Jesus Christ.

22 And now, behold, I go bound in the spirit unto Jerusalem, not knowing the things that shall befall me there:

23 Save that the Holy Ghost witnesseth in every city, saying that bonds and afflictions abide me.

24 But none of these things move me, neither count I my life dear unto myself, so that I might finish my course with joy, and the ministry, which I have received of the Lord Jesus, to testify the gospel of the grace of God.

25 And now, behold, I know that ye all, among whom I have gone preaching the kingdom of God, shall see my face no more.

26 Wherefore I take you to record this day, that I am pure from the blood of all men.

27 For I have not shunned to declare unto you all the counsel of God.

28 Take heed therefore unto yourselves, and to all the flock, over the which the Holy Ghost hath made you overseers, to feed the church of God, which he hath purchased with his own blood.

29 For I know this, that after my departing shall grievous wolves enter in among you, not sparing the flock.

30 Also of your own selves shall men arise, speaking perverse things, to draw away disciples after them.

31 Therefore watch, and remember, that by the space of three years I ceased not to warn every one night and day with tears.

32 And now, brethren, I commend you to God, and to the word of his grace, which is able to build you up, and to give you an inheritance among all them which are sanctified.

33 I have coveted no man's silver, or gold, or apparel.

34 Yea, ye yourselves know, that these hands have ministered unto my necessities, and to them that were with me.

35 I have shewed you all things, how

being certified of the will of God, he did meekly follow the direction and instinct of the Spirit, even of his own accord. Therefore, this speech importeth as much as if he should have said, I cannot otherwise do, unless I would be stubborn and rebellious against God, who doth as it were draw me thither, being bound by his Spirit. For to the end he may excuse himself of rashness, he saith that the Spirit is the author and guide of his journey. But would to God those brain-sick men, who boast that the Spirit doth incite to them those things which proceed from their own fantasy, did know the Spirit as familiarly as did Paul, who doth, notwithstanding, not say that all his motions and instigations are of the Spirit, but declareth that that fell out in one thing as a singular thing. For men do oftentimes foolishly and unadvisedly take in hand those things which they put in practice afterward stoutly, because they be ashamed of lightness and instability. And he doth not only mean that he took in hand his journey for a good cause, which the Spirit of God showeth him, but that it is altogether necessary for him, because it is wickedness to resist. Furthermore, let us learn, by the example of the holy man, not to kick against the Spirit of the Lord, but obediently to give over ourselves by him to be governed, that he may rule us at his pleasure after we be as it were bound to him. For if the reprobate, who are the bond-slaves of Satan, be carried not only willingly, but also greedily, through his motion, how much more ought this voluntary bondage or service to be in the children of God?

ACTS 21

1. Luke reckoneth up briefly the course of his sailing; and that not only to win credit to the history, that we may know what was done in every place, but that the readers may weigh with themselves the invincible and heroic fortitude which was in Paul, who would rather be tossed and troubled with such long, unlevel, and troublesome journeys, that he might serve Christ, than provide for his own quietness. Whereas he saith that they were drawn and pulled away, it is not simply referred unto the distance of places; but because the brethren stood on the shore, so long as they could see the ship wherein Paul and his companions were carried. He nameth the havens where the ship arrived, for this cause that we may know that they sailed quietly without trouble of tempest. Let us search the describers of countries touching the situation of the cities whereof he maketh mention; it is sufficient for me to show Luke's purpose.

7. Luke doth briefly declare that Paul was also received at Ptolemais by the brethren. This is a city of Phenicia, standing upon the sea-coast, not far from the borders of Judea,

public preaching to be all that was required of him; nor his daily occupation to be an excuse for not visiting from house to house. We may observe here,

(1.) that Paul's example is a warrant and an implied injunction for family visitation by a pastor. If proper in Ephesus, It is proper still. If practicable in that city, it is in other cities. If it was useful there, it will be elsewhere. If it furnished to him consolation in the retrospect when he came to look over his ministry, and if it was one of the things which enabled him to say, "I am pure from the blood of all men," it will be so in other cases.

(2.) The design for which ministers should visit, should be a religious design, Paul did not visit for mere ceremony, nor for idle gossip, or chit-chat; nor to converse on the mere news or politics of the day. His aim was to show the way of salvation, and to teach in private what he taught in public.

(3.) How much of this is to be done, is of course to be left to the discretion of every minister. Paul, in private visiting, did not neglect public instruction. The latter he evidently considered to be his main or chief business. His high views of the ministry are evinced in his life, and in his letters to Timothy and Titus. Yet, while public preaching is the main, the prime, the leading business of a minister, and while his first efforts should be directed to preparation for that, he may and should find time to enforce his public instructions by going from house to house; and often he will find that his most immediate and apparent success will result from such family instructions.

(4.) If it is his duty to visit, it is the duty of his people to receive him as becomes an ambassador of Christ. They should be willing to listen to his instructions; to treat him with kindness, and to aid his endeavors in bringing a family under the influence of religion.

33. I have coveted. I have not desired. I have not made it an object of my living among you to obtain your property. Thus 2 Cor. 12: 14 he says, "I seek not yours, but you." Paul had power to demand support in the ministry as the reward of his labor, 1 Cor. 9: 13–14. Yet he did not choose to exercise it, lest it should bring the charge of avarice against the min-

istry, 1 Cor. 9: 12,15. Paul also had power in another respect. He had a vast influence over the people. The early Christians were disposed to commit their property to the disposal of the apostles. See Acts 4: 34–35,37.

The heathen had been accustomed to devote their property to the support of religion. Of this propensity, if the object of Paul had been to make money, he might have availed himself, and have become enriched. Deceivers often thus impose on people for the purpose of amassing wealth; and one of the incidental but striking proofs of the Christian religion is here furnished, in the appeal which the apostle Paul made to his hearers, that this had not been his motive for action.

36. He kneeled down. The usual attitude of prayer. It is the proper posture of a suppliant. It indicates reverence and humility; and is represented in the Scriptures as the common attitude of devotion, 2 Chr. 6: 13; Dan. 6: 10; Luke 22: 41; Acts 7: 60; 9: 40; 21: 5; Rom. 11: 4; Phil. 2: 10; Eph. 3: 14; Mark 1: 40.

37. Wept sore. Wept much. Greek, "There was a great weeping of all."

And fell on, Paul's neck. Embraced him, as a token of tender affection. The same thing Joseph did when he met his aged father Jacob, Gen. 46: 29.

And kissed him. This was the common token of affection. Note, Matt. 26: 48; Luke 15: 20; Rom. 16: 16; 1 Cor. 16: 20.

38. Sorrowing most of all, etc. This was a most tender and affectionate parting scene. It can be more easily imagined than described. We may learn from it,

(1.) that the parting of ministers and people is a most solemn event, and should be one of much tenderness and affection.

(2.) The effect of true religion is to make the heart more tender; to make friendship more affectionate and sacred; and to unite more closely the bonds of love.

(3.) Ministers of the gospel should be prepared to leave their people with the same consciousness of fidelity, and the same kindness and love, which Paul evinced. They should live such lives as to be able to look back upon their whole ministry as pure and disinterested;

that so labouring ye ought to support the weak, and to remember the words of the Lord Jesus, how he said, It is more blessed to give than to receive.

36 And when he had thus spoken, he kneeled down, and prayed with them all.

37 And they all wept sore, and fell on Paul's neck, and kissed him,

38 Sorrowing most of all for the words which he spake, that they should see his face no more. And they accompanied him unto the ship.

ACTS 21

1 And it came to pass, that after we were gotten from them, and had launched, we came with a straight course unto Coos, and the day following unto Rhodes, and from thence unto Patara:

2 And finding a ship sailing over unto Phenicia, we went aboard, and set forth.

3 Now when we had discovered Cyprus, we left it on the left hand, and sailed into Syria, and landed at Tyre: for there the ship was to unlade her burden.

4 And finding disciples, we tarried there seven days: who said to Paul through the Spirit, that he should not go up to Jerusalem.

5 And when we had accomplished those days, we departed and went our way; and they all brought us on our way, with wives and children, till we were out of the city: and we kneeled down on the shore, and prayed.

6 And when we had taken our leave one of another, we took ship; and they returned home again.

7 And when we had finished our course from Tyre, we came to Ptolemais, and saluted the brethren, and abode with them one day.

8 And the next day we that were of Paul's company departed, and came unto Caesarea: and we entered into the house of Philip the evangelist, which was one of the seven; and abode with him.

9 And the same man had four daughters, virgins, which did prophesy.

10 And as we tarried there many days, there came down from Judaea a certain prophet, named Agabus.

11 And when he was come unto us, he took Paul's girdle, and bound his own hands and feet, and said, Thus saith the

from which Paul and his companions had no long journey to Cesarea. But if the readers be disposed to know farther touching the situation of regions, let them resort unto the describers of places and countries [geographers]. Furthermore, he saith, that when he came to Cesarea, they lodged with Philip, whom he calleth an Evangelist, though he were one of the seven deacons, as we may see in the sixth chapter (Acts 6: 5). By this we may easily gather, that that deaconship was an office which continued but for a time; because it had not otherwise been lawful for Philip to forsake Jerusalem, and to go to Cesarea. And in this place he is set before us, not as a voluntary forsaker of his office, but as one to whom a greater and more excellent charge was committed. The evangelists, in my judgment, were in the midst between apostles and doctors. For it was a function next to the apostles to preach the gospel in all places, and not to have any certain place of abode; only the degree of honor was inferior. For when Paul describeth the order of the Church (Ephesians 4: 11) he doth so put them after the apostles, that he showeth that they have more room given them where they may teach than the pastors, who are tied to certain places. Therefore, Philip did for a time exercise the office of a deacon at Jerusalem, whom the Church thought afterward to be a meet man to whom the treasure of the gospel should be committed.

9. By this means the Lord meant to beautify the first beginnings of the gospel, when he raised up men and women to foretell things to come. Prophecies had now almost ceased many years among the Jews, to the end they might be more attentive and desirous to hear the new voice of the gospel. Therefore, seeing that prophesying, which was in a manner quite ceased, doth now after long time return again, it was a token of a more perfect state. Notwithstanding, it seemeth that the same was the reason why it ceased shortly after; for God did support the old people with diverse foretellings, until Christ should make an end of all prophecies. Therefore, it was meet that the new kingdom of Christ should be thus furnished and beautified with this furniture, that all men might know that that promised visitation of the Lord was present; and it was also expedient that it should last but for a short time, lest the faithful should always wait for some farther thing, or lest that curious wits might have occasion given to seek or invent some new thing ever now and then. For we know that when that ability and skill was taken away, there were, notwithstanding, many brain-sick fellows, who did boast that they were prophets; and also it may be that the frowardness of men did deprive the Church of this gift. But that one cause ought to be sufficient, in that God, by taking away prophecies, did testify that the end and perfection was present in Christ; and it is uncertain

and as having been employed in guarding the flock, and in making known to them the whole counsel of God. So parting, they may part in peace. And so living, and acting, they will be prepared to give up their account with joy, and not with grief. May God grant to every minister the spirit which Paul evinced at Ephesus, and enable each one, when called to leave his people by death or otherwise, to do it with the same consciousness of fidelity which Paul evinced, when he left his people to see their face no more!

ACTS 21

1. After we were gotten from them. After we had left the elders at Miletus, Acts 20: 38. They were on their way to Jerusalem.

9. Which did prophesy. That females sometimes partook of the prophetic influence, and foretold future events, is evident from various places in the New Testament.

11. He took Paul's girdle. The loose, flowing robes, or outer garments, which were worn in eastern countries, were bound by a girdle, or sash, around the body, when they ran, or labored, or walked. Such a girdle was, therefore, an indispensable part of dress.

And bound his own hands and feet. As emblematic of what would be done by the Jews to Paul. It was common for the prophets to perform actions which were emblematic of the events which they predicted. The design was to make the prediction more forcible and impressive, by representing it to the eye. Thus Jeremiah was directed to bury his girdle by the Euphrates, to denote the approaching captivity of the Jews, Jer. 13: 4. Thus he was directed to make bands and yokes, and to put them around his neck, as a sign to Edom and Moab, etc., Jer. 27: 2–3. Thus the act of the potter was emblematic of the destruction that was coming upon the nation of the Jews, Jer. 18: 4. So Isaiah walked naked and barefoot as a sign of the captivity of Egypt and Ethiopia, Is. 20: 3–4. Comp. Ezra 4; 12, etc.

13. What mean ye. Greek, What do ye. A tender and affectionate, but firm reproach.

To weep and to break mine heart? To afflict me, and distract my mind by alarms, and by the expressions of tenderness. His mind was fixed on going to Jerusalem; and he felt that he was prepared for whatever awaited him. Expressions of tenderness among friends are proper. Tears may be inevitable at parting from those whom we love; but such expressions of tenderness and love ought not to be allowed to interfere with the convictions of duty in their minds. If they have made up their minds that a certain course is proper, and have resolved to pursue it, we ought neither to attempt to divert them from it, nor to distract their minds by our remonstrances or our tears. We should resign them to their convictions of what is demanded of them, with affection and prayer, but with cheerfulness. We should lend them all the aid in our power, and then commend them to the blessing and protection of God. These remarks apply especially to those who are engaged in the missionary enterprise. It is trying to part with a son, a daughter, or a beloved friend, in order that they may go to proclaim the gospel to the benighted and dying heathen. The act of parting – for life – and the apprehension of the perils which they may encounter on the ocean, and in heathen lands, may be painful; but if they, like Paul, have looked at it calmly, candidly, and with much prayer – if they have come to the deliberate conclusion that it is the will of God that they should devote their lives to this service – we ought not to weep, and to break their hearts. We should cheerfully and confidently commit them to the protection of the God whom they serve, and remember that they are seeking his glory, and that the parting of Christians, though for life, will be short. Soon, in a better world, they will be united again, to part no more; and the blessedness of that future meeting will be greatly heightened by all the sorrows and self-denials of separation here, and by all the benefits which such a separation may be the means of conveying to a dying world. That mother will meet with joy, in heaven, the son from whom, with many tears, she was sundered, when he entered on a missionary life; and surrounded with many ransomed heathen, heaven will be made more blessed, and all eternity more happy.

Holy Ghost, So shall the Jews at Jerusalem bind the man that owneth this girdle, and shall deliver him into the hands of the Gentiles.

12 And when we heard these things, both we, and they of that place, besought him not to go up to Jerusalem.

13 Then Paul answered, What mean ye to weep and to break mine heart? for I am ready not to be bound only, but also to die at Jerusalem for the name of the Lord Jesus.

14 And when he would not be persuaded, we ceased, saying, The will of the Lord be done.

15 And after those days we took up our carriages, and went up to Jerusalem.

16 There went with us also certain of the disciples of Caesarea, and brought with them one Mnason of Cyprus, an old disciple, with whom we should lodge.

17 And when we were come to Jerusalem, the brethren received us gladly.

18 And the day following Paul went in with us unto James; and all the elders were present.

19 And when he had saluted them, he declared particularly what things God had wrought among the Gentiles by his ministry.

20 And when they heard it, they glorified the Lord, and said unto him, Thou seest, brother, how many thousands of Jews there are which believe; and they are all zealous of the law:

21 And they are informed of thee, that thou teachest all the Jews which are among the Gentiles to forsake Moses, saying that they ought not to circumcise their children, neither to walk after the customs.

22 What is it therefore? the multitude must needs come together: for they will hear that thou art come.

23 Do therefore this that we say to thee: We have four men which have a vow on them;

24 Them take, and purify thyself with them, and be at charges with them, that they may shave their heads: and all may know that those things, whereof they were informed concerning thee, are nothing; but that thou thyself also walkest orderly, and keepest the law.

25 As touching the Gentiles which

how these maids did execute the office of prophesying, saving that the Spirit of God did so guide and govern them, that he did not overthrow the order which he himself set down. And forasmuch as he doth not suffer women to bear any public office in the Church, it is to be thought that they did prophesy at home, or in some private place, without the common assembly.

19. And now Paul showeth his modesty when he doth not make himself the author of those things which he had done, but giving the praise to God, doth call himself only the minister whose industry [agency] God had used. As we must grant, that whatsoever thing is excellent and worthy of praise, it is not done by our own power, but forasmuch as God doth work in us; and especially touching the edifying of the Church. Again, it appeareth how far off the elders were from envy, when they glorify God for the joyful success. But because mention is made of no other apostle besides James, we may conjecture that they were gone into diverse places to spread abroad and preach the gospel as their calling did require; for the Lord had not appointed them to stay still at Jerusalem; but after they had made a beginning there, he commanded them to go into Judea and other parts of the world. Moreover, the error of those men, who think that James was one of the disciples whom Paul numbereth among the three pillars of the Church, is refuted before in the fifteenth chapter. And though the same commandment was given to him which was given to the rest of his fellows in office; yet I do not doubt but that they did so divide themselves, that James stood still at Jerusalem, whither many strangers were wont daily to resort. For that was all one as if he had preached the gospel far and wide in strange places.

26. Whereas some accuse Paul of subtilty, as if he did play the hypocrite, I have before refuted this. Yet I do not deny but that he granted to do thus much at the request of the brethren, being thereunto in a manner enforced. Therefore, it hath more color, and is (as they say) more disputable, that he was too easily entreated, and too ready to obey; and yet I do not admit that which some men say, that it went not well with Paul, because, taking upon him a new and unwonted person, he did not so constantly, as he was wont, maintain the liberty purchased by Christ. I confess, indeed, that God doth oftentimes punish foolish purposes with unhappy success; but I see not why this should be applied to Paul, who through voluntary subjection sought to win the favor of the rude, and such as were not thoroughly instructed, that he might do them good; being about to do that not willingly, but because he had rather yield to the brethren than stick to his own judgment. Furthermore, when he was

But also to die. This was the true spirit of a martyr. This spirit reigned in the hearts of all the early Christians.

20. They glorified the Lord. They gave praise to the Lord for what he had done. They saw new proofs of his goodness and mercy, and they rendered him thanks for all that had been accomplished. There was no jealousy that it had been done by the instrumentality of Paul. True piety will rejoice in the spread of the gospel, and in the conversion of sinners, by whatever instrumentality it may be effected.

Thou seest, brother. The language of tenderness in this address, recognizing Paul as a fellow-laborer and fellow Christian, implies a wish that Paul would do all that could be done to avoid giving offence, and to conciliate the favor of his country-men.

How many thousands. The number of converts at this time must have been very great. Twenty-five years before this, three thousand had been converted at one time, Acts 2, and afterwards the number had swelled to some more thousands, Acts 4: 4, The assertion, that there were then "many thousands," implies that the work, so signally begun on the day of Pentecost in Jerusalem, had not ceased, and that many more had been converted to the Christian faith.

Which believe. Who are Christians. They are spoken of as believers, or as having faith in Christ, in contradistinction from those who rejected him, and whose characteristic trait it was that they were unbelievers.

And they are all zealous of the law. They still observe the law of Moses. The reference here is to the law respecting circumcision, sacrifices, distinctions of meats and days, festivals, etc. It may seem remarkable that they should still continue to observe those rites, since it was the manifest design of Christianity to abolish them. But we are to remember,

(1.) that those rites had been appointed by God, and that they were trained to their observance.

(2.) That the apostles conformed to them while they remained in Jerusalem, and did not deem it best to set themselves violently against them, Acts 3: 1 Luke 24: 53.

(3.) That the question about their observ-

ance had never been agitated at Jerusalem. It was only among the Gentile converts that the question had risen, and there it must arise, for if they were to be observed, they must have been imposed upon them by authority.

(4.) The decision of the council Acts 15 related only to the Gentile converts. It did not touch the question, whether those rites were to be observed by the Jewish converts.

(5.) It was to be presumed, that as the Christian religion became better understood – that as its large, free, and catholic nature became more and more developed, the peculiar institutions of Moses would be laid aside of course, without agitation and without tumult. Had the question been agitated at Jerusalem, it would have excited tenfold opposition to Christianity, and would have rent the Christian church into factions, and greatly retarded the advance of the Christian doctrine. We are to remember also,

(6.) that, in the arrangement of Divine Providence, the time was drawing near which was to destroy the temple, the city, and the nation; which was to put an end to sacrifices, and effectually to close for ever the observance of the Mosaic rites. As this destruction was so near, and as it would be so effectual an argument against the observance of the Mosaic rites, the Great Head of the church did not suffer the question of their obligation to be needlessly agitated among the disciples at Jerusalem.

26. Then Paul took the men. Took them to himself; united with them in observing the ceremonies connected with their vow. To transactions like this he refers in 1 Cor. 9: 20, "And unto the Jews I became as a Jew, that I might gain the Jews; to them that are under the law, as under the law." Thus, it has always been found necessary in propagating the gospel among the heathen, not to offend them needlessly, but to conform to their innocent customs in regard to dress, language, modes of traveling, sitting, eating, etc. Paul did nothing more than this. He violated none of the dictates of honesty and truth.

Purifying himself with them. Observing the ceremonies connected with the rite of purification. This means evidently that he

believe, we have written and concluded that they observe no such thing, save only that they keep themselves from things offered to idols, and from blood, and from strangled, and from fornication.

26 Then Paul took the men, and the next day purifying himself with them entered into the temple, to signify the accomplishment of the days of purifcation, until that an offering should be offered for every one of them.

27 And when the seven days were almost ended, the Jews which were of Asia, when they saw him in the temple, stirred up all the people, and laid hands on him,

28 Crying out, Men of Israel, help: This is the man, that teacheth all men every where against the people, and the law, and this place: and further brought Greeks also into the temple, and hath polluted this holy place.

29 (For they had seen before with him in the city Trophimus an Ephesian, whom they supposed that Paul had brought into the temple.)

30 And all the city was moved, and the people ran together: and they took Paul, and drew him out of the temple: and forthwith the doors were shut.

31 And as they went about to kill him, tidings came unto the chief captain of the band, that all Jerusalem was in an uproar.

32 Who immediately took soldiers and centurions, and ran down unto them: and when they saw the chief captain and the soldiers, they left beating of Paul.

33 Then the chief captain came near, and took him, and commanded him to be bound with two chains; and demanded who he was, and what he had done.

34 And some cried one thing, some another, among the multitude: and when he could not know the certainty for the tumult, he commanded him to be carried into the castle.

35 And when he came upon the stairs, so it was, that he was borne of the soldiers for the violence of the people.

36 For the multitude of the people followed after, crying, Away with him.

37 And as Paul was to be led into the castle, he said unto the chief captain, May I speak unto thee? Who said, Canst thou speak Greek?

once admitted, he might fitly have passed over to moderate that zeal. His courtesy doth rather deserve great praise, in that he doth not only gently abase himself for the unskillful people's sake, but doth also obey their foolishness who did unworthily, and against reason, suspect him. He might well have reproved them, because they had been so ready to believe reports contrary to his reputation. In that he abstaineth, he showeth great patience; in that he winneth their favor so carefully, it is singular modesty.

Moreover, he might have been more rough and round with James and his fellows in office, because they had not been more diligent to root out errors from among the people. For though it be certain that they taught faithfully, yet it may be that the sight of the temple, and the very seat of the law, did hinder them in defending the use of liberty. But Paul, whether he went from his right of his own accord, or whether he think that they see better what is expedient than he, doth follow their counsel. And whereas false Nicodemites, following this example of Paul, go about to color their treacherous dissimulation, whilst they pollute themselves with all filthiness of Popery, it needeth no long refutation. They boast that they do this to win the weak brethren (or that they follow their vein thus far) as if Paul did yield to them in all things without choice. If, being Jews, they should take upon them according to the pre-script of the law, to fulfill among the Jews a vow infected with no idolatry, then might they prove themselves to be like Paul. Now, forasmuch as they inwrap themselves in gross and altogether wicked superstitions, and that because they will escape the cross, what likelihood is that which they imagine?

ACTS 22

Though we may guess by the beginning of this speech what was Paul's drift, yet because he was interrupted, we know not certainly what he was about to say. The sum of that part which is refitted is this, that forasmuch as he was well and faithfully instructed in the doctrine of the law, he was a godly and religious worshipper of God in the sight of the world. Secondly, that he was an enemy to the gospel of Christ, so that he was counted among the priests one of the principal maintainers and defenders of the law. Thirdly, that he did not change his sect unadvisedly; but that being tamed and convict by an oracle from heaven, he gave his name to Christ. Fourthly, that he did not embrace unknown things, but that God appointed him a faithful teacher, of whom he learned all things perfectly. Lastly, that when he was returned to Jerusalem, and sought to do good to his countrymen, God did not permit him. So that he brought not the doctrine of salvation unto foreign nations without

entered on the ceremonies of the separation according to the law of the Nazarite.

To signify. Greek, Signifying or making known. That is, he announced to the priests in the temple his purpose of observing this vow with the four men, according to the law respecting the Nazarite. It was proper that such an announcement should be made beforehand, in order that the priests might know that all the ceremonies required had been observed.

The accomplishment, etc. The fulfilling; the completion. That is, he announced to them his purpose to observe all the days, and all the rites of purification required in the law, in order that an offering might be properly made. It does not mean that the days had been accomplished, but that it was his intention to observe them, so that it would be proper to offer the usual sacrifice. Paul had not, indeed, engaged with them in the beginning of their vow of separation; but he might come in with hearty intention to share with them.

30. The city was moved. Was agitated; was thrown into commotion.

Drew him out of the temple. Under the pretence that he had defiled it. The evident design was to put him to death, Acts 21: 31.

The doors were shut. The doors leading into the courts of the temple.

31. And as they were about to kill him. Gr., They seeking to kill him. This was evidently done in a popular tumult, as had been done in the case of Stephen, Acts 7. They could not pretend that they had a right to do it by law.

Tidings came. The news, or rumor came; he was told of it.

The chief captain of the band. This band or body of Roman soldiers was stationed in the tower Antonia, on the north of the temple. This tower was built by John Hyrcanus, high priest of the Jews, and was by him called Baris. It was beautified and strengthened by Herod the Great, and was called Antonia, in honor of his friend Mark Antony. Josephus describes this castle as consisting of four towers, one of which overlooked the temple, and which he says was seventy cubits high. In this tower a guard of Roman soldiers was stationed, to

secure the temple, and to maintain the peace. The commander of this cohort is here called "the chief captain." Reference is made to this guard several times in the New Testament, Matt. 27: 65–66; John 18: 12; Acts 5: 26.

38. Art not thou that Egyptian. That Egyptian was probably a Jew, who resided in Egypt.

39. A Jew of Tarsus. A Jew by birth.

Of no mean city. Not obscure, or undistinguished. He could claim an honorable birth, so far as the place of his nativity was concerned. Tarsus was much celebrated for its learning, and was at one time the rival of Alexandria and Athens. Xenophon calls it a great and flourishing city. Anabasis. Josephus says that it was the metropolis and most renowned city among them.

40. License. Liberty; permission.

Beckoned with the hand. Waving the hand as a sign that he was about to address them, and to produce silence and attention. See Acts 12: 17.

In the Hebrew tongue. The language which was spoken by the Jews, which was then a mixture of the Chaldee and Syriac, called Syro-Chaldaic. This language he doubtless used on this occasion in preference to the Greek, because it was understood better by the multitude, and would tend to conciliate them if they heard him address them in their own language. The following chapter should have been connected with this. The division here is unnatural.

ACTS 22

1. Men, brethren, and fathers. This defense was addressed to the Jews; and Paul commenced it with an expression of sincere respect for them. Stephen began his defense with the same form of address.

My defense. Against the charges brought against me. Those charges were, that he had endeavored to prejudice men everywhere against the Jews, and the law, and the temple, Acts 21: 28. In order to meet this charge, Paul stated,

(1.) that he had been born a Jew, and had

38 Art not thou that Egyptian, which before these days madest an uproar, and leddest out into the wilderness four thousand men that were murderers?

39 But Paul said, I am a man which am a Jew of Tarsus, a city in Cilicia, a citizen of no mean city: and, I beseech thee, suffer me to speak unto the people.

40 And when he had given him license, Paul stood on the stairs, and beckoned with the hand unto the people. And when there was made a great silence, he spake unto them in the Hebrew tongue, saying,

ACTS 22

1 Men, brethren, and fathers, hear ye my defence which I make now unto you.

2 (And when they heard that he spake in the Hebrew tongue to them, they kept the more silence: and he saith,)

3 I am verily a man which am a Jew, born in Tarsus, a city in Cilicia, yet brought up in this city at the feet of Gamaliel, and taught according to the perfect manner of the law of the fathers, and was zealous toward God, as ye all are this day.

4 And I persecuted this way unto the death, binding and delivering into prisons both men and women.

5 As also the high priest doth bear me witness, and all the estate of the elders: from whom also I received letters unto the brethren, and went to Damascus, to bring them which were there bound unto Jerusalem, for to be punished.

6 And it came to pass, that, as I made my journey, and was come nigh unto Damascus about noon, suddenly there shone from heaven a great light round about me.

7 And I fell unto the ground, and heard a voice saying unto me, Saul, Saul, why persecutest thou me?

8 And I answered, Who art thou, Lord? And he said unto me, I am Jesus of Nazareth, whom thou persecutest.

9 And they that were with me saw indeed the light, and were afraid; but they heard not the voice of him that spake to me.

10 And I said, What shall I do, Lord? And the Lord said unto me, Arise, and go into Damascus; and there it shall be told thee of all things which are appointed for thee to do.

good consideration, or because he hated his own nation, but being commanded by God so to do.

1. Men, brethren, and fathers

It is a wonder that he giveth so great honor yet to the desperate enemies of the gospel, for they had broken all bond of brotherly fellowship, and by oppressing the glory of God, had spoiled themselves of all titles of dignity. But because Paul speaketh in this place as some one of the people, he speaketh so lovingly unto the body itself, and useth towards the heads words honorable without dissembling. And surely because their casting off was not made known as yet, though they were unworthy of any honor, yet it was meet that Paul should reverently acknowledge in them the grace of God's adoption. Therefore, in that he calleth them brethren and fathers, he doth not so much regard what they have deserved, as into what degree of honor God had exalted them. And all his oration is so framed that he goeth about to satisfy them, freely indeed, and without flattering, yet humbly and meekly. Therefore, let us learn so to reverence and honor men that we impair not God's right. For which cause the pope's pride is the more detestable, who, seeing he hath made himself an high priest without the commandment of God and the consent of the Church, doth not only challenge to himself all titles of honor, but also such tyranny, that he goeth about to bring Christ in subjection; as if when God doth exalt men he did resign up his right and authority to them, and did stoop down to them.

2. That he spake Hebrew

This is indeed an usual thing, that when men which speak diverse languages are together, we hear those more willingly who speak our own language; but the Jews were moved with another peculiar cause, because they imagined that Paul was offended with his own kindred, so that he did even hate their tongue, or that he was some rogue which had not so much as learned the speech of that nation whereof he said he came. Now, so soon as they heard their own language, they began to have some better hope. Furthermore, it is uncertain whether Paul spake in the Hebrew or in the Syrian tongue; for we know that the speech of the Jews was corrupt and degenerate after their exile, forasmuch as they had much from the Chaldeans and Syrians. For mine own part, I think, that because he spake as well to the common sort as unto the elders, he used the common speech which was at that day usual.

3. I am a Jew

As all things were out of order at that day among the Jews, many rogues and vagabonds, to the end they might have some shroud for their wickedness, did falsely boast that

enjoyed all the advantages of a Jewish educa-tion, Acts 22: 3;

(2.) he recounted the circumstances of his conversion, and the reason why he believed that he was called to preach the gospel, Acts 22: 4–16;

(3.) he proceeded to state the reasons why he went among the Gentiles, and evidently designed to vindicate his conduct there, Acts 22: 17–21; but at this point, at the name Gentiles, his defense was interrupted by the enraged multitude, and he was not permitted to proceed. What would have been his defense, therefore, had he been suffered to finish it, it is impossible to know with certainty. On another occasion, however, he was permitted to make a similar defense, and perhaps to complete the train of thought which he had purposed to pursue here. See Acts 26.

4. And I persecuted, Acts 8: 3.

This way. Those who were of this mode of worshipping God; that is, Christians.

Unto the death. Intending to put them to death, He did not probably put any to death himself, but he committed them to prison, he sought their lives, he was the agent employed in arresting them; and when they were put to death, he tells us that he gave his voice against them, Acts 26: 10; that is, he joined in and approved of their condemnation.

Delivering into prisons, etc. Acts 8: 3

5. Unto the brethren. The Jewish brethren, who were at Damascus. Paul here speaks as a Jew, and regards his countrymen as his breth-ren.

6. As I made my journey. As I was on my jour-ney.

About noon. Acts 26: 13. "At mid-day." This cir-cumstance is omitted by Luke in account in Acts 9. Paul mentions it, as being the more remark-able since it occurred at mid-day, to show that he was not deluded by any meteoric or natural appearances, which usually occur at night.

11. The gory of that light. The splendor, the intense brilliancy of the light.

14. Shouldest know his will. His will in the plan of salvation, and in regard to your future life.

And see that Just One. The Messiah. As Paul was to be an apostle. and as it was the peculiar office of an apostle to bear witness to the person and deeds of the Lord Jesus.

Shouldest hear the voice of his mouth. Shouldest hear and obey his commands.

15. For thou shalt be his witness, etc. As an apostle to testify to all men that the Messiah has come, that he has died, that he has risen, and that he is the Savior of the world.

Of what thou hast seen and heard. Of the remarkable proof which has been furnished you of the Divine mission and character of the Lord Jesus.

16. And now, why tarriest thou? Why dost thou delay, or wait any longer? These words are not recorded by Luke in Acts 9, where he has given an account of the conversion of Paul; but there is nothing here contradictory to his statement.

And wash away thy sins. Receive baptism, as an act expressive of the washing away of sins. It cannot be intended that the external rite of baptism was sufficient to make the soul pure, but that it was an ordinance divinely appointed as expressive of the washing away of sins, or of purifying the heart. Comp. Heb. 10: 22. Sinners are represented in the Scrip-tures as defiled or polluted by sin. To wash away the sins denotes the purifying of the soul from this polluted influence, 1 Cor. 6: 11; Rev. 1: 5; 7: 14; Is. 1: 16; Ps. 51: 2,7.

Calling on the name of the Lord. For pardon and sanctification. Rom. 10: 13, "Who-soever shall call upon the name of the Lord shall be saved." It was proper that this calling on the name of the Lord should be connected with the ordinance of baptism. That ordinance was expressive of a purifying which the Lord only could produce. It is proper that the rite of baptism should be attended with extraordi-nary prayer; and that he who is to be baptized should make it the occasion of peculiar and very solemn religious exercises. The external rite will avail nothing without the pardoning mercy of God.

21. And he said unto me, Depart. Because the Christians at Jerusalem would not receive him.

11 And when I could not see for the glory of that light, being led by the hand of them that were with me, I came into Damascus.

12 And one Ananias, a devout man according to the law, having a good report of all the Jews which dwelt there,

13 Came unto me, and stood, and said unto me, Brother Saul, receive thy sight. And the same hour I looked up upon him.

14 And he said, The God of our fathers hath chosen thee, that thou shouldest know his will, and see that Just One, and shouldest hear the voice of his mouth.

15 For thou shalt be his witness unto all men of what thou hast seen and heard.

16 And now why tarriest thou? arise, and be baptized, and wash away thy sins, calling on the name of the Lord.

17 And it came to pass, that, when I was come again to Jerusalem, even while I prayed in the temple, I was in a trance;

18 And saw him saying unto me, Make haste, and get thee quickly out of Jerusalem: for they will not receive thy testimony concerning me.

19 And I said, Lord, they know that I imprisoned and beat in every synagogue them that believed on thee:

20 And when the blood of thy martyr Stephen was shed, I also was standing by, and consenting unto his death, and kept the raiment of them that slew him.

21 And he said unto me, Depart: for I will send thee far hence unto the Gentiles.

22 And they gave him audience unto this word, and then lifted up their voices, and said, Away with such a fellow from the earth: for it is not fit that he should live.

23 And as they cried out, and cast off their clothes, and threw dust into the air,

24 The chief captain commanded him to be brought into the castle, and bade that he should be examined by scourging; that he might know wherefore they cried so against him.

25 And as they bound him with thongs, Paul said unto the centurion that stood by, Is it lawful for you to scourge a man that is a Roman, and uncondemned?

26 When the centurion heard that, he went and told the chief captain, saying,

they were Jews. Therefore, to the end Paul may acquit himself of this suspicion, he beginneth at his birth; that done, he declareth that he was known in Jerusalem, because he was brought up there of [from] a child; though this latter thing seemeth to be spoken not only for certainty's sake, but because it skilled much that this should also be known how well he had been instructed.

There is nothing more bold to cause trouble than unlearned men. And at that day the government of the Church was so decayed, that religion was not only subject to sects, but also miserably mangled and torn in pieces. Therefore, Paul nameth his master, lest any man may think that he had not been nousled up in learning, and therefore had he forsaken the worship of the fathers; as many men, who are not trained up in learning, forget their nature and grow out of kind. But Paul saith chiefly that he was well taught in the law, that the Jews may understand that it was not through ignorance (as it falleth out oftentimes) that he causeth such ado, and doth counterfeit their monsters.

It is to be doubted whether this be that Gamaliel of whom mention is made before (Acts 5: 34). Scholars are said to sit at their masters' feet, because forasmuch as they be not as yet of strong and sound judgment, they must bring such modesty and aptness to be taught, that they must make all their senses subject to their masters, and must depend upon their mouth. So Mary is said to sit at Jesus' feet (Luke 10: 39) when she giveth ear to his doctrine. But and if such reverence be due to earthly masters, how much more ought we to prostrate ourselves before the feet of Christ, that we may give ear to him when he teacheth us out of his heavenly throne? This speech doth also put boys and young men in remembrance of their duty, that they be not stout nor stubborn, or that they be not puffed nor lifted up against their masters through some foolish confidence, but that they suffer themselves quietly and gently to be framed by them.

ACTS 23

1. Looking earnestly

Paul beginneth with the testimony of a good conscience, that all the whole multitude may understand that he is unjustly charged with such an heinous offense, as if he had gone about to overthrow the worship of God. It may be, indeed, that a man may offend of ignorance, who will not otherwise be a contemner either of God or of religion; but Paul meant at the first, only with this excuse, to mollify their nettled minds, that he might the better be heard; for it had been in vain for him to have defended himself, so long as that opinion did stick in the minds of the priests, that he was a wicked revolt, [apostate]. Therefore, before he enter

Far hence. Paul traveled far in the heathen nations. A large part of his time in the ministry was spent in remote countries, and in the most distant regions then known. Rom. 15: 19.

22. And they gave him audience. They heard him patiently.

Away with such a fellow. Greek, Take such a man from the earth; i.e., put him to death. It is language of strong indignation and abhorrence. The reasons of their indignation were not that they supposed that the Gentiles could not be brought into covenant with God, for they would themselves compass sea and land to make one proselyte; but they were,

(1.) that they believed that Paul taught that they might be saved without conforming to the law of Moses; and,

(2.) his speech implied that the Jews were more hardened than the Gentiles, and that he had a greater prospect of success in bringing them to God than he had in regard to the Jews.

23. Cast off their clothes. Their outer garments. Probably they did it now intending to stone him, Acts 7: 58.

And threw dust into the air. As expressive of their abhorrence and indignation. This was a striking exhibition of rage and vindictive malice. Paul was guarded by Roman soldiers, so that they could not injure him; and their only way of expressing their wrath was by menaces and threats, and by these tokens of furious indignation. Thus Shimei expressed his indignation against David by cursing him, and throwing stones at him, and casting dust, 2 Sam. 16: 13.

24. The castle. The tower of Antonia. He would be there removed entirely from the wrath of the Jews.

Should be examined. The word examine with us commonly means to inquire, to question, to search for, or to look carefully into a subject. The word here used is commonly applied to metals, whose nature is tested or examined by fire; and then it means to subject to torture or torments, in order to extort a confession, where persons were accused of crime. It was often resorted to among the

ancients. The usual mode has been by the rack; but various kinds of torments have been invented in order to extort confessions of guilt from those who were accused. The whole practice has been one of the most flagrant violations of justice, and one of the foulest blots on human nature. In this case, the tribune saw that Paul was accused violently by the Jews; he was ignorant of the Hebrew language, and had not probably understood the address of Paul; he supposed from the extraordinary excitement that Paul must have been guilty of some flagrant offence, and he therefore resolved to subject him to torture, to extort from him a confession.

29. Then straightway. Immediately. They saw that by scourging him they would have violated the Roman law, and exposed themselves to its penalty.

Which should have examined him. Who were about to torture him by scourging him, Acts 22: 24.

Because he had bound him. Preparatory to scourging him. The act of binding a Roman citizen, with such an intent, untried and uncondemned, was unlawful. Prisoners who were to be scourged were usually bound by the Romans to a pillar or post; and a similar custom prevailed among the Jews. That it was unlawful to bind a man, with this intent, who was uncondemned, appears from an express declaration in Cicero. "It is a heinous sin to bind a Roman citizen; it is wickedness to beat him; it is next to parricide to kill him; and what shall I say to crucify him?"

30. On the morrow. After he had arrested Paul. Paul was still a prisoner; and if suffered to go at liberty among the Jews, his life would have been in danger.

And commanded the chief priests, etc. Summoned a meeting of the Sanhedrim, or great council of the nation. He did this, as he was prevented from scourging Paul, in order to know what he had done, and that he might learn from the Jews themselves the nature of the charge against him. This was necessary for the safety of Paul, and for the ends of justice. This should have been done without any attempt to torture him in order to extort a

Take heed what thou doest: for this man is a Roman.

27 Then the chief captain came, and said unto him, Tell me, art thou a Roman? He said, Yea.

28 And the chief captain answered, With a great sum obtained I this freedom. And Paul said, But I was free born.

29 Then straightway they departed from him which should have examined him: and the chief captain also was afraid, after he knew that he was a Roman, and because he had bound him.

30 On the morrow, because he would have known the certainty wherefore he was accused of the Jews, he loosed him from his bands, and commanded the chief priests and all their council to appear, and brought Paul down, and set him before them.

ACTS 23

1 And Paul, earnestly beholding the council, said, Men and brethren, I have lived in all good conscience before God until this day.

2 And the high priest Ananias commanded them that stood by him to smite him on the mouth.

3 Then said Paul unto him, God shall smite thee, thou whited wall: for sittest thou to judge me after the law, and commandest me to be smitten contrary to the law?

4 And they that stood by said, Revilest thou God's high priest?

5 Then said Paul, I wist not, brethren, that he was the high priest: for it is written, Thou shalt not speak evil of the ruler of thy people.

6 But when Paul perceived that the one part were Sadducees, and the other Pharisees, he cried out in the council, Men and brethren, I am a Pharisee, the son of a Pharisee: of the hope and resurrection of the dead I am called in question.

7 And when he had so said, there arose a dissension between the Pharisees and the Sadducees: and the multitude was divided.

8 For the Sadducees say that there is no resurrection, neither angel, nor spirit: but the Pharisees confess both.

9 And there arose a great cry: and the scribes that were of the Pharisees' part

the cause, he excuseth himself of that crime, not only that he may purchase favor by that desire which he had to live godlily, but also that he may prevent false accusations, or at least that he may refute unjust prejudices which might have made against him, wherewith he saw the whole multitude infected and corrupted. We know not what he meant to say besides. Notwithstanding, this preface teacheth that no man can rightly handle the doctrine of godliness, unless the fear of God reign and bear the chief sway in him. And now, though he give not the priests so honorable a title here as he did a little before, when he stood upon the steps of the fortress, yet he calleth them brethren, giving them that honor, not because they deserve it, but that he may testify that he is not the cause of the breach of friendship.

2. And the chief priest

Luke's narration seemeth not to agree with the usual history; for Josephus writeth thus concerning the high priests of that time, that Quadratus, deputy proconsul of Syria, deposing Cumanus from the government of Judea, commanded him to answer for himself before Caesar, and sent Ananias, the highest priest, bound with him, into whose place who was chosen he maketh no mention, saving that it is likely that Jonathas had the honor given him, who, as he reporteth, was afterward slain by the subtilty and treachery of Felix, prefect of Judea, who succeeded Cumanus; for when he had oftentimes told Felix part of his mind, and he could not away with the constancy of the man, he made a compact with one Doras, that he should privily convey in murderers to slay him. Then, as the same Josephus doth witness, king Agrippa made Ismael, the son of Phebeus, priest. But when he was sent by the people to Rome about a certain suit, and was kept there by Popea, wife to Nero, Agrippa putteth in his place one Josephus, whose name was Chabus, the son of Simon. But immediately being also weary of him, he appointeth Ananus, the son of Ananus, to be high priest.

Furthermore, he saith that this last thing happened at such time as, after the death of Festus, Albinus did succeed him. And I see not why some call this Ananus Ananias. That hath indeed some color, in that he is called a Pharisee; also in that it is said that he was bold and stout, who, without any lawful authority, caused James, the Lord's brother, to be stoned. But if we give credence to Josephus, he could not be that Ananias of whom mention is made in this place by Luke, who was then made priest, when many years were past and gone, after that Felix departed out of the province.

10. We see again what a cruel mischief contention is, which so soon as it doth once wax hot, hath such violent motions,

confession.

And brought Paul down. From the elevated castle or tower of Antonia. The council assembled commonly in the house of the high priest.

And set him before them. He brought the prisoner to their bar, that they might have an opportunity to accuse him, and that thus the chief captain might learn the real nature of the charge against him.

ACTS 23

1. And Paul, earnestly beholding. Fixing his eyes intently on the council. The word denotes a fixed and earnest gazing; a close observation. See Luke 4: 20. Paul would naturally look with a keen and attentive observation on the council. He was arraigned before them, and he would naturally observe the appearance, and endeavor to ascertain the character of his judges. Besides, it was by this council that he had been formerly commissioned to persecute the Christians, Acts 9: 1–2. He had not seen them since that commission was given, he would naturally, therefore, regard them with an attentive eye. The result shows, also, that Paul looked at them to see what was the character of the men there assembled, and what was the proportion of Pharisees and Sadducees, Acts 23: 6.

The council. Greek, The Sanhedrim, Acts 22: 30. It was the great council composed of seventy elders, to whom was entrusted the affairs of the nation.

7. A dissension. A dispute or difference.

And the multitude. The council. Comp. Acts 14: 4. The Pharisees embraced, as he desired and expected, his side of the question, and became his advocates, in opposition to the Sadducees, who were arrayed against him.

8. For the Sadducees say. They believe.

No resurrection. Of the dead. By this doctrine they also understood that there was no future state, and that the soul did not exist after death.

Neither angel. That there are no angels. They deny the existence of good or bad angels.

Nor spirit. Nor soul. That there was nothing

but matter. They were materialists, and supposed that all the operations which we ascribe to mind, could be traced to some modification of matter. The Sadducees, says Josephus, "take away the belief of the immortal duration of the soul, and the punishments and rewards in Hades." "The doctrine of the Sadducees is this," says he, "that souls die with the bodies." The opinion that the soul is material, and that there is nothing but matter in the universe, has been held by many philosophers, ancient and modern, as well as by the Sadducees.

Confess both. Acknowledge, or receive both as true; i.e., that there is a future state, and that there are spirits distinct from matter, as angels, and the disembodied souls of men. The two points in dispute were,

(1.) whether the dead would be raised and exist in a future state; and,

(2.) whether mind was distinct from matter. The Sadducees denied both, and the Pharisees believed both. Their belief of the latter point was, that spirits existed in two forms – that of angels, and that of souls of men distinct from the body.

13. Which had made this conspiracy. This oath, this agreement or compact. This large number of desperate men, bound of by so solemn an oath, would be likely to be successful; and the life Paul was therefore in peculiar danger. The manner in which they purposed to accomplish their design is stated in Acts 23: 15.

14. And they came, etc. Probably by a deputation.

To the chief priests and elders. The members of the great council, or Sanhedrim. It is probable that the application was made to the party of the Sadducees, as the Pharisees had shown their determination to defend Paul. They would have had no prospect of success had they attacked the castle; and they therefore devised this ingenious mode of obtaining access to Paul, where they might easily despatch him.

Under a great curse. Greek, "We have anathematized ourselves with an anathema." We have made the vow as solemn as possible.

16. Paul's sister's son. This is all we know of

arose, and strove, saying, We find no evil in this man: but if a spirit or an angel hath spoken to him, let us not fight against God.

10 And when there arose a great dissension, the chief captain, fearing lest Paul should have been pulled in pieces of them, commanded the soldiers to go down, and to take him by force from among them, and to bring him into the castle.

11 And the night following the Lord stood by him, and said, Be of good cheer, Paul: for as thou hast testified of me in Jerusalem, so must thou bear witness also at Rome.

12 And when it was day, certain of the Jews banded together, and bound themselves under a curse, saying that they would neither eat nor drink till they had killed Paul.

13 And they were more than forty which had made this conspiracy.

14 And they came to the chief priests and elders, and said, We have bound ourselves under a great curse, that we will eat nothing until we have slain Paul.

15 Now therefore ye with the council signify to the chief captain that he bring him down unto you to morrow, as though ye would inquire something more perfectly concerning him: and we, or ever he come near, are ready to kill him.

16 And when Paul's sister's son heard of their lying in wait, he went and entered into the castle, and told Paul.

17 Then Paul called one of the centurions unto him, and said, Bring this young man unto the chief captain: for he hath a certain thing to tell him.

18 So he took him, and brought him to the chief captain, and said, Paul the prisoner called me unto him, and prayed me to bring this young man unto thee, who hath something to say unto thee.

19 Then the chief captain took him by the hand, and went with him aside privately, and asked him, What is that thou hast to tell me?

20 And he said, The Jews have agreed to desire thee that thou wouldest bring down Paul to morrow into the council, as though they would inquire somewhat of him more perfectly.

21 But do not thou yield unto them: for there lie in wait for him of them more than

that even most wise men are not well in their wits. Therefore, so soon as any beginning shall show itself, let us study to prevent it in time, lest the remedy be too late in bridling it when it is in the middle, because no fire is so swift as it. As for the chief captain, as he was appointed to be the minister of God's providence to save Paul's life, so he delivereth him now the second time by his soldiers from death. For though the chief captain defend him so diligently, for no other purpose save only that he may prevent uproars and murder; yet the Lord, who from heaven provided and appointed help for his servant, doth direct his blind hands thither.

11. And the night following

Luke declareth that Paul was strengthened with an oracle, that he might stand courageously against terrible assaults when things were so far out of order. Surely it could not be but that he was sore afraid, and that he was sore troubled with the remembrance of things to come. Wherefore, the oracle was not superfluous. Those former things whereby he was taught that God cared for him, ought to have sufficed to nourish his hope, and to have kept him from fainting; but because in great dangers Satan doth oftentimes procure new fears, that he may thereby (if he cannot altogether overwhelm God's promises in the hearts of the godly) at least darken the same with clouds, it is needful that the remembrance of them be renewed, that faith, being holpen with new props and stays, may stand more steadfastly. But the sum is, that Paul may behave himself boldly, because he must be Christ's witness at Rome also. But this seemeth to be but a cold and vain consolation, as if he should say, Fear not, because thou must abide a sorer brunt; for it had been better, according to the flesh, once to die, and with speed to end his days, than to pine away in bands, and long time to lie in prison. The Lord doth not promise to deliver him; no, he saith not so much as that he shall have a joyful end; only he saith, that those troubles and afflictions, wherewith he was too sore oppressed already, shall continue long. But by this we gather better of what great importance this confidence is, that the Lord hath respect unto us in our miseries, though he stretch not forth his hand by and by to help us.

Therefore, let us learn, even in most extreme afflictions, to stay ourselves upon the word of God alone; and let us never faint so long as he quickeneth us with the testimony of his fatherly love. And because oracles are not now sent from heaven, neither doth the Lord himself appear by visions, we must meditate upon his innumerable promises, whereby he doth testify that he will be nigh unto us continually. If it be expedient that an angel come down unto us, the Lord will not deny even this kind of confirmation. Nevertheless, we must give this honor to the word, that being content with it alone we wait patiently for that help

the family of Paul. Nor do we know for what purpose he was at Jerusalem. It is possible that Paul might have a sister residing there; though, as Paul had been sent there formerly for his education, it seems more probable that this young man was sent there for the same purpose.

Entered into the castle. Paul had the privileges of a Roman citizen; and as no well-founded charge had been laid against him, it is probable that he was not very closely confined, and that his friends might have free access to him.

17. Called one of the centurions. Who might at that time have had special charge of the castle, or been on guard. Paul had the most positive assurance that his life would be spared, and that he would yet see Rome; but he always understood the Divine promises and purposes as being consistent with his own efforts, and with all proper measures of prudence and diligence in securing his own safety. He did not rest merely on the Divine promise without any effort of his own; but he took encouragement from those promises to put forth his own exertions for security and for salvation.

19. Took him by the hand. As an expression of kindness and civility. He did it to draw him aside from the multitude, that he might communicate his message privately.

20. And he said, etc. In what way this young man had received intelligence of this, we can only conjecture. It is not improbable that he was a student under some one of the Jewish teachers, and that he might have learned it of him. It is not at all probable that the purpose of the forty men would be very closely kept. Indeed, it is evident that they were not themselves very anxious about concealing their oath, as they mentioned it fully to the chief priests and elders, Acts 23: 14.

21. Looking for a promise from thee. Waiting for you consent to bring him down to them.

23. And he called unto him two centurions, etc. Each centurion had under him one hundred men. The chief captain resolved to place Paul beyond the power of the Jews, and to protect him as became a Roman citizen.

Two hundred soldiers. These foot-soldiers were designed only to guard Paul till he was safely out of Jerusalem. The horsemen only were intended to accompany him to Caesarea. Acts 23: 32.

And horsemen. These were commonly attached to foot-soldiers. In this case, however, they were designed to attend Paul to Caesarea.

And spearmen. This word is found nowhere else in the New Testament, and occurs in no classic writer. It properly means those who take, or apprehend by the right hand; and might be applied to those who apprehend prisoners, or to those who hold a spear or dart in the right hand for the purpose of throwing it.

At the third hour of the night. At nine o'clock. This was in order that it might be done with secrecy, and to elude the band of desperadoes that had resolved to murder Paul. If it should seem that this guard was very numerous for one man, it should be remembered,

(1.) that the number of those who had conspired against him was also large; and,

(2.) that they were men accustomed to scenes of blood, of desperate characters, and who had solemnly sworn that they would take his life. In order, therefore, to deter them effectually from attacking the guard, it was made very numerous and strong, and nearly five hundred men were appointed to guard Paul as he left Jerusalem.

24. And provide them beasts. One for Paul, and one for each of his attendants. The word translated beasts may be applied either to horses, to camels, or to asses. The latter were most commonly employed in Judea.

Unto Felix the governor. The governor of Judea. His place of residence was Caesarea, about sixty miles from Jerusalem.

His name was Antonius Felix, and was a freedman of Antonia, the mother of the emperor Claudius. He was high in the favor of Claudius, and was made by him governor of Judea. Josephus calls him Claudius Felix. He had married three wives in succession that were of royal families, one of whom was Drusilla, afterwards mentioned in Acts 23: 24, who was sister to king Agrippa. Tacitus

forty men, which have bound themselves with an oath, that they will neither eat nor drink till they have killed him: and now are they ready, looking for a promise from thee.

22 So the chief captain then let the young man depart, and charged him, See thou tell no man that thou hast shewed these things to me.

23 And he called unto him two centurions, saying, Make ready two hundred soldiers to go to Caesarea, and horsemen threescore and ten, and spearmen two hundred, at the third hour of the night;

24 And provide them beasts, that they may set Paul on, and bring him safe unto Felix the governor.

25 And he wrote a letter after this manner:

26 Claudius Lysias unto the most excellent governor Felix sendeth greeting.

27 This man was taken of the Jews, and should have been killed of them: then came I with an army, and rescued him, having understood that he was a Roman.

28 And when I would have known the cause wherefore they accused him, I brought him forth into their council:

29 Whom I perceived to be accused of questions of their law, but to have nothing laid to his charge worthy of death or of bonds.

30 And when it was told me how that the Jews laid wait for the man, I sent straightway to thee, and gave commandment to his accusers also to say before thee what they had against him. Farewell.

31 Then the soldiers, as it was commanded them, took Paul, and brought him by night to Antipatris.

32 On the morrow they left the horsemen to go with him, and returned to the castle:

33 Who, when they came to Caesarea, and delivered the epistle to the governor, presented Paul also before him.

34 And when the governor had read the letter, he asked of what province he was. And when he understood that he was of Cilicia;

35 I will hear thee, said he, when thine accusers are also come. And he commanded him to be kept in Herod's judgment hall.

which it promiseth us.

Moreover, it did profit some nothing to hear angels which were sent down from heaven; but the Lord doth not in vain seal up in the hearts of the faithful by his Spirit those promises which are made by him. And as he doth not in vain beat them in and often repeat them, so let our faith exercise itself diligently in the continual remembrance of them. For if it were necessary that Paul's faith should be oftentimes set and stored up with a new help, there is none of us which needeth not many more helps. Also, our minds must be armed with patience, that they may pass through the long and troublesome circuits of troubles and afflictions.

ACTS 24

6. Who went about to pollute the temple

It was a light and almost a frivolous accusation to lay this to his charge before the Roman governor, who could have wished that the temple had been turned topsy-turvy. But because nothing was more fit for procuring uproars than the polluting of the temple, he doth craftily accuse Paul thereof, as if he should say, that it was no thanks to him that Jerusalem was not on an uproar; and that he carried such a firebrand as might have procured sore hurt if he had not been prevented. Also he includeth that other thing, that because Paul had offended in matters of religion, it did belong properly to the Jews to give judgment in that matter. And here he complaineth also of the chief captain Lysias, because he robbed them of their right. Therefore his drift is, to obtain at the hands of the ruler that he will restore to them that which Lysias had taken from them. This is also not void of subtilty, in that Tertullus doth discredit the chief captain, because he dealt more courteously towards Paul than the priests would he should; and glancingly he bringeth him in suspicion, because he dare not openly accuse him. But the question is, whether they could hope that the governor would grant them so much, seeing the Roman magistrates alone were to sit upon life and death? I answer, that he maketh in this place some semblance of equity, as if they were purposed to handle him more gently than he deserved. For though they might not condemn any man to death, yet they might use some light chastisement as was scourging. Nevertheless, Tertullus doth not cease to desire before the president to have him put to death.

8. Having made inquiry

A good request, that the governor do not give sentence before he thoroughly examine and know the matter; and that he do not condemn Paul before he be lawfully convict. But how dare they put in these conditions, seeing their own consciences do accuse them of unjust dealing? I an-

says, that he governed with all the authority of a king, and the baseness and insolence of a slave. "He was an unrighteous governor, a base, mercenary, and bad man." (Clarke.)

26. Unto the most excellent governor Felix. The most honored, etc. This was a mere title of office.

Greeting. A term of salutation in an epistle wishing health, joy, and prosperity.

27. Should have been killed of them. Was about to be killed by them. The life of Paul had been twice endangered in this manner, Acts 21: 30; 23: 10.

With an army. With a band of soldiers, Acts 23: 10.

29. Questions of their law. So he understood the whole controversy to be.

Worthy of death. By the Roman law. He had been guilty of no crime against the Roman people.

Or of bonds. Of chains, or of confinement.

32. They left the horsemen. As they were then beyond the danger of the conspirators, the soldiers who had guarded them thus far returned to Jerusalem.

34. Of what province he was. This he doubtless did in order to ascertain whether he properly belonged to his jurisdiction. Roman provinces were districts of country which were entrusted to the jurisdiction of procurators. How far the jurisdiction of Felix extended is not certainly known. It appears, however, that it included Cilicia.

Was of Cilicia. Tarsus, the birthplace of Paul, was in this province, Acts 21: 39.

35. In Herod's judgment hall. Greek, In the praetorium of Herod. The word here used denoted, formerly, the tent of the Roman praetor; and as that was the place where justice was administered, it came to be applied to halls, or courts of justice. This had been reared probably by Herod the Great as his palace, or as a place for administering justice. It is probable also that prisons, or places of security, would be attached to such places.

ACTS 24

1. And after five days. This time was occupied, doubtless, in their receiving the command to go to Caesarea, and in making the necessary arrangements. This was the twelfth day after his arrival at Jerusalem. See Acts 24: 11.

2. And when he was called forth. When Paul was called forth from prison. See Acts 23: 35.

We enjoy great quietness. This was said in the customary style of flatterers and orators, to conciliate his favor, and is strikingly in contrast with the more honest and straightforward introduction in the reply of Paul, Acts 24: 10.

5. We have found this man a pestilent fellow. This word is commonly applied to a plague, or pestilence; and then to a man who corrupts the morals of others, or who is turbulent, and an exciter of sedition.

And a mover of sedition. An exciter of tumult. This they pretended he did by preaching doctrines contrary to the laws and customs of Moses, and exciting the Jews to tumult and disorder.

Throughout the world. Throughout the Roman empire, and thus leading the Jews to violate the laws, and to produce tumults, riots, and disorder.

And a ringleader. This word occurs nowhere else in the New Testament. It is properly a military word, and denotes one who stands first in an army, a standard-bearer, a leader, or commander. The meaning is, that Paul had been so active, and so prominent in preaching the gospel, that he had been a leader, or the principal person, in extending the sect of the Nazarenes.

Of the sect. The original word here is the word from which we have derived the term heresy. It is, however, properly translated sect, or party, and should have been so translated in Acts 24: 14.

Of the Nazarenes. This was the name usually given to Christians by way of contempt. They were so called because Jesus was of Nazareth.

6. To profane the temple. This was a serious, but unfounded charge. It arose from the gross

ACTS 24

1 And after five days Ananias the high priest descended with the elders, and with a certain orator named Tertullus, who informed the governor against Paul.

2 And when he was called forth, Tertullus began to accuse him, saying, Seeing that by thee we enjoy great quietness, and that very worthy deeds are done unto this nation by thy providence,

3 We accept it always, and in all places, most noble Felix, with all thankfulness.

4 Notwithstanding, that I be not further tedious unto thee, I pray thee that thou wouldest hear us of thy clemency a few words.

5 For we have found this man a pestilent fellow, and a mover of sedition among all the Jews throughout the world, and a ringleader of the sect of the Nazarenes:

6 Who also hath gone about to profane the temple: whom we took, and would have judged according to our law.

7 But the chief captain Lysias came upon us, and with great violence took him away out of our hands,

8 Commanding his accusers to come unto thee: by examining of whom thyself mayest take knowledge of all these things, whereof we accuse him.

9 And the Jews also assented, saying that these things were so.

10 Then Paul, after that the governor had beckoned unto him to speak, answered, Forasmuch as I know that thou hast been of many years a judge unto this nation, I do the more cheerfully answer for myself:

11 Because that thou mayest understand, that there are yet but twelve days since I went up to Jerusalem for to worship.

12 And they neither found me in the temple disputing with any man, neither raising up the people, neither in the synagogues, nor in the city:

13 Neither can they prove the things whereof they now accuse me.

14 But this I confess unto thee, that after the way which they call heresy, so worship I the God of my fathers, believing all things which are written in the law and in the prophets:

15 And have hope toward God, which they themselves also allow, that there

swer, that they had witnesses in readiness; and that they do not offer themselves to prove the matter until they do call them; though there were another end. For they did hope that Felix would be so persuaded with such glorious words, that he would turn over unto them the man whom they did accuse for a condemned man, whom they might handle at their pleasure. In sum, the more fierce they be upon him, and the more they were puffed up with some affiance they had in themselves, they think they shall get the upper hand by this means, because the party arraigned shall have no license granted to defend himself. Thus do false accusers boldly boast that their matter is plain, that they may blind the eyes of the judges.

10. And Paul

The state of Paul's defense is not conversant in the quality; but he denieth the crime that was laid to his charge; not that he was ashamed of the gospel, or afraid of the cross, but because that was no place to make any full confession of faith in. Therefore, omitting the cause of the gospel, which his accuser had not touched, he answereth simply unto the crimes whereof he was accused. But before he come thither, he saith that he doth the more willingly answer for himself before Felix, because he had long time been governor of Judea; because, peradventure, some new governor would have been sore moved hearing such things laid to his charge. He doth not commend the virtues of the governor, but he saith that he is glad, because he is of great experience, that he may judge more justly. This is surely a sincere and free manner of defending, to set matter against words. Yet Paul seemeth to gather amiss, that Felix can know the time of his coming, because he had been governor many years. I answer, that this is said therefore, because it is likely that he will deal more moderately; as if he should say, Because thou hast been acquainted with their conditions long time, I have the better hope that they shall not deceive thee. For want of skill doth make judges too credulous, and doth enforce them to make too much haste.

12. Disputing with any man

Paul had no need to deny any of these things if he had done them; because he might have answered for himself that it was well done. He had been one of the scribes which disputed daily; neither were they forbidden either by the law or by custom, but that they might assemble themselves together to be taught. Yea, to this end there were in divers places of the city synagogues, wherein they met together. Moreover, he knew that both Christ and also his apostles had done the same thing. Also he might easily have retorted back upon his adversaries the crime which they did object to him, who did daily use the very same things. But

calumny of the apostle, when they pretended that he had introduced Greeks into that sacred place, Acts 21: 28. To this charge the apostle replies in Acts 24: 18.

11. Because that thou mayest understand. Greek, "Thou being able to know." That is, he could understand or know, by taking the proper evidence. Paul does not mean to say that Felix could understand the case, because he had been many years a judge of that nation. That fact would qualify him to judge correctly, or to understand the customs of the Jews. But the fact that he had been but twelve days in Jerusalem, and had been orderly and peaceable there, Felix could ascertain only by the proper testimony. The first part of Paul's defense Acts 24: 11–13 consists in an express denial of what they alleged against him.

For to worship. This farther shows that the design of Paul was not to produce sedition. He had gone up for the peaceful purpose of devotion, and not to produce riot and disorder. That this was his design in going to Jerusalem, or at least a part of his purpose, is indicated by the passage in Acts 20: 16. It should be observed, however, that our translation conveys an idea which is not necessarily in the Greek – that this was the design of his going to Jerusalem.

13. Neither can they prove the things, etc. That is, that I am a mover of sedition, or a disturber of the peace of the people. This appeal he boldly makes; he challenges investigation; and as they did not offer to specify any acts of disorder or tumult excited by him, this charge falls of course.

14. But this I confess, etc. The next specification in the charge of Tertullus was, Acts 24: 5, that he was "a ringleader of the sect of the Nazarenes." To this, Paul replies in this and the two following verses. Of this reply we may observe,

(1.) that he does not stoop to notice the contempt implied in the use of the word Nazarenes. He was engaged in a more important business than to contend about the name which they chose to give to Christians.

(2.) He admits that he belonged to that sect or class of people. That he was a Christian he neither denied, nor was disposed to deny.

(3.) He maintains that in this way he is still worshipping the God of his fathers. Of this, the fact that he was engaged in worship in the temple, was sufficient proof.

(4.) He shows them that he believed only what was written in the law and the prophets; that this involved the main doctrine of their religion – the hope of the resurrection of the dead, Acts 24: 15; and that it was his constant and earnest desire to keep a pure conscience in all things, Acts 24: 16. These are the points of his defense to this second charge, and we shall see that they fully meet and dispose of the accusation.

15. And have hope toward God. Having a hope of the resurrection of the dead, which arises from the promises of God.

Which they themselves, etc. That is, the Pharisees. Perhaps he designated in this remark the Pharisees who were present, he held nothing in this great cardinal point, which they did not also hold. For the reasons why Paul introduced this point so prominently, and the success of thus introducing it.

23. And he commanded, etc. It is evident from this verse, that Felix was disposed to show Paul all the favors that were consistent with his safe keeping. He esteemed him to be a persecuted man, and doubtless regarded the charges against him as entirely malicious. What was Felix's motive in this cannot be certainly known. It is not improbable, however, that he detained him,

(1.) to gratify the Jews by keeping him in custody as if he were guilty; and,

(2.) that he hoped the friends of Paul would give him money to release him. Perhaps it was for this purpose that he gave orders that his friends should have free access to him, that thus Paul might be furnished with the means of purchasing his freedom.

24. Felix came with his wife Drusilla. Drusilla was the daughter of Herod Agrippa the elder, and was engaged to be married to Epiphanes, the son of king Antiochus, on condition that he would embrace the Jewish religion; but as he afterwards refused to do that, the contract was broken off.

shall be a resurrection of the dead, both of the just and unjust.

16 And herein do I exercise myself, to have always a conscience void of offence toward God, and toward men.

17 Now after many years I came to bring alms to my nation, and offerings.

18 Whereupon certain Jews from Asia found me purified in the temple, neither with multitude, nor with tumult.

19 Who ought to have been here before thee, and object, if they had ought against me.

20 Or else let these same here say, if they have found any evil doing in me, while I stood before the council,

21 Except it be for this one voice, that I cried standing among them, Touching the resurrection of the dead I am called in question by you this day.

22 And when Felix heard these things, having more perfect knowledge of that way, he deferred them, and said, When Lysias the chief captain shall come down, I will know the uttermost of your matter.

23 And he commanded a centurion to keep Paul, and to let him have liberty, and that he should forbid none of his acquaintance to minister or come unto him.

24 And after certain days, when Felix came with his wife Drusilla, which was a Jewess, he sent for Paul, and heard him concerning the faith in Christ.

25 And as he reasoned of righteousness, temperance, and judgment to come, Felix trembled, and answered, Go thy way for this time; when I have a convenient season, I will call for thee.

26 He hoped also that money should have been given him of Paul, that he might loose him: wherefore he sent for him the oftener, and communed with him.

27 But after two years Porcius Festus came into Felix' room: and Felix, willing to shew the Jews a pleasure, left Paul bound.

ACTS 25

1 Now when Festus was come into the province, after three days he ascended from Caesarea to Jerusalem.

2 Then the high priest and the chief of the Jews informed him against Paul, and besought him,

3 And desired favor against him, that

because he aimeth at no other thing at this present, but to refute the false accusations of his adversaries, and to prove that importunate men had unadvisedly molested him for no cause; he intreateth not of the lawfulness of the fact, (as they say) but only of the fact. And he standeth chiefly upon this point to refute that slander, because he was burdened to be a raiser of tumults. Therefore he concludeth that he was falsely and unjustly accused; because the adversaries had never proved those things which they had alleged. This ought to have been sufficient to discharge him, seeing he was thus burdened with wicked lies, whereas there rested in him not the very least suspicion that could be devised.

ACTS 25

1. Then when Festus

The second action is described in this place, wherein Paul hath as hard a combat, and is in no less danger than in the first. Seeing he was left in bonds, Festus might suspect that the cause was doubtful, and so gather an unjust prejudice. But there was another thing which was cause of great danger. We know that new rulers, because they will win the favor of those who are in the provinces, use to grant them many things at their first coming; so that it was to be thought that the death of Paul should be to Festus a fine means to win favor with all. Therefore, the faith of the holy man is assailed afresh with a new trial, as if the promise had been vain whereto he had hitherto trusted; but the grace of God doth so much the more plainly show itself in delivering him, because, contrary to all hope, he is delivered out of the jaws of death. The Jews prevent the governor with their false accusations, yet they do not as yet seek to have him punished, but they do only desire that he may not be brought into any foreign court to plead his cause. They desire that ambitiously as a great benefit, which was to look to equal. How is it then that they do not obtain, save only because God doth hold the mind of Festus, so that he doth stoutly deny that which he was afterward ready to grant? And as the Lord did then hold his mind bound with the secret bridle of his providence, so when he granted him freedom of will he bound his hands, that he could not execute that which he would. Let this confidence support us in dangers, and let it also stir us up to call upon God; and let this make our minds quiet and calm, in that the Lord, in stretching forth his hand, and breaking such a strong conspiracy, did show an eternal example of his power in defending his.

7. Many and grievous crimes

So long as Paul lived under the law, his integrity was well known and famous. Again, when he was converted to

25. And as he reasoned. Greek, "And he discoursing." No argument should be drawn from the word that is used here, to prove that Paul particularly appealed to reason, or that his discourse was argumentative. That it was so, is indeed not improbable, from all that we know of the man, and from the topics on which he discoursed. But the word used here means simply, as he discoursed, and is applied usually to making a public address, to preaching, etc., in whatever way it is done, Acts 17: 2; 18: 4,19; 19: 8–9; 24: 12.

Of righteousness, Of justice. Not of the justice of God particularly, but of the nature and requirements of justice in the relations of life, the relations which we sustain to God and to man. This was a proper topic with which to introduce his discourse, as it was the office of Felix to dispense justice between man and man; and as his administration was not remarkable for the exercise of that virtue. It is evident that he could be influenced by a bribe (Acts 24: 26); and it was proper for Paul to dwell on this as designed to show him the guilt of his life, and his danger of meeting the justice of a Being who cannot be bribed, but who will dispense equal justice alike to the great and the mean. That Paul dwelt also on the justice of God, as the moral Governor of the world, may also be presumed. The apprehension of that justice, and the remembrance of his own guilty life, tended to produce the alarm of Felix, and to make him tremble.

Temperance. The word temperance we now use commonly to denote moderation, or restraint in regard to eating and drinking, particularly to abstinence from the use of ardent spirits. But this is not its meaning here. There is no reason to suppose that Felix was intemperate in the use of intoxicating liquors. The original word here denotes a restraint of all the passions and evil inclinations; and may be applied to prudence, chastity, and moderation in general. The particular thing in the life of Felix which Paul had probably in view, was the indulgence of licentious desires, or incontinence. He was living in adultery with Drusilla; and for this, Paul wished doubtless to bring him to repentance.

And judgment to come. The universal judg-ment; the judgment that was to come on all transgressors. On this topic Paul also dwelt when he preached before the Areopagus at Athens, Acts 17: 31. These topics were admirably adapted to excite the alarm of both Felix and Drusilla. It evinced great boldness and faithfulness in Paul to select them; and the result showed that he correctly judged of the kind of truth which was adapted to alarm the fears of his guilty auditor.

Felix trembled. In view of his past sins, and in the apprehension of the judgment to come. The Greek does not denote that his body was agitated or shaken, but only that he was alarmed, or terrified. That such fear usually shakes the frame, we know; but it is not certain that the body of Felix was thus agitated. He was alarmed and terrified; and looked with deep apprehension to the coming judgment. This was a remarkable instance of the effect of truth on the mind of a man unaccustomed to such alarms, and unused to hear such truth. It shows the power of conscience, when thus under the preaching of a prisoner the judge should be thrown into violent alarm.

ACTS 25

2. Then the High Priest. The high priest at this time was Ismael, the son of Fabi.

Informed him against Paul. Informed him of the accusation against him; and doubtless endeavored to prejudice the mind of Festus against him. They thus showed their unrelenting disposition. It might have been supposed that after two years this unjust prosecution would be abandoned and forgotten. But malice does not thus forget its object; and the spirit of persecution is not thus satisfied. It is evident that there was here every probability that injustice would be done to Paul, and that the mind of Festus would be biased against him. He was a stranger to Paul, and to the embittered feelings of the Jewish character, he would wish to conciliate their favor on entering on the duties of his office. And a strong representation therefore, made by the chief men of the nation, would be likely to prejudice him violently against Paul, and to unfit him for the exercise of impartial justice.

he would send for him to Jerusalem, laying wait in the way to kill him.

4 But Festus answered, that Paul should be kept at Caesarea, and that he himself would depart shortly thither.

5 Let them therefore, said he, which among you are able, go down with me, and accuse this man, if there be any wickedness in him.

6 And when he had tarried among them more than ten days, he went down unto Caesarea; and the next day sitting on the judgment seat commanded Paul to be brought.

7 And when he was come, the Jews which came down from Jerusalem stood round about, and laid many and grievous complaints against Paul, which they could not prove.

8 While he answered for himself, Neither against the law of the Jews, neither against the temple, nor yet against Caesar, have I offended any thing at all.

9 But Festus, willing to do the Jews a pleasure, answered Paul, and said, Wilt thou go up to Jerusalem, and there be judged of these things before me?

10 Then said Paul, I stand at Caesar's judgment seat, where I ought to be judged: to the Jews have I done no wrong, as thou very well knowest.

11 For if I be an offender, or have committed any thing worthy of death, I refuse not to die: but if there be none of these things whereof these accuse me, no man may deliver me unto them. I appeal unto Caesar.

12 Then Festus, when he had conferred with the council, answered, Hast thou appealed unto Caesar? unto Caesar shalt thou go.

13 And after certain days king Agrippa and Bernice came unto Caesarea to salute Festus.

14 And when they had been there many days, Festus declared Paul's cause unto the king, saying, There is a certain man left in bonds by Felix:

15 About whom, when I was at Jerusalem, the chief priests and the elders of the Jews informed me, desiring to have judgment against him.

16 To whom I answered, It is not the manner of the Romans to deliver any man to die, before that he which is accused

Christ, he was a singular pattern of innocence. Yet we see how he is subject to many slanders, cruel and false accusations. And this is almost always the estate of the servants of Christ, wherefore they must be the more courageous, to pass valiantly through evil report and good report; neither let them think it strange to be evil reported of where they have done good.

In the mean season, they must do their endeavor, that they may not only have a clear conscience before God, but that they may be very well able to defend themselves before men, when they have time and place. For Paul doth not fail in his cause, but courageously setteth the defense of his innocency against their false crimes. Furthermore, let us note that the wicked can never be bridled, but they will speak evil of good men, and will impudently slander them; for they resemble the nature of Satan, by whose spirit they are led. Therefore, whereas we be commanded to stop the mouth of the wicked, it must not be so taken as if he shall be free from all backbiting, whosoever shall behave himself uprightly, but that our life may answer for us, and may wipe away all blots of false infamy. So we see the adversaries of Paul, though they had a favorable judge, yet their slanders were all in vain, seeing he did defend and avouch his innocency by his deeds. And yet it is likely that they wanted not false witnesses, neither were they slack in suborning them; but because the Lord giveth his servants invincible strength, so that the brightness of honesty doth drive away their vain clouds; they are ashamed, and at length they depart from the judgment-seat with this infamy, that they were false accusers. But the defense of Paul doth show what things the Jews laid principally to his charge. The first crime was ungodliness against God, that he overthrew the law and polluted the temple; the other, rebellion against Caesar and the Roman empire, because he raised tumults everywhere. He was helped by the singular grace of God to answer and refute both, who maketh the innocence of his as bright as the morning.

9. And Festus

Whether Festus knew somewhat of their laying await (which we may well conjecture) or whether he were altogether ignorant thereof, he dealeth unjustly with Paul; and we see how soon those are drawn unto all corruption which are not guided by the Spirit of God. For Festus doth not openly contemn or hate Paul; but ambition, and peradventure also desire of gain, got the upper hand, so that, for pleasing the other part, he doth unjustly bring him in danger of death; also, it is likely that he was enticed with the smell [hope] of some reward to hearken so courteously to the priests. Notwithstanding, I marvel that he giveth Paul leave to choose, and doth not rather, according to this au-

7. Grievous complaints. Heavy accusations. Doubtless the same with which they had charged him before Felix, Acts 24: 5–6. Comp. Acts 25: 19.

Which they could not prove. Acts 24: 13,19.

9. But Festus, willing to do the Jews a pleasure. Desirous of securing their favor, as he had just entered on his administration. Comp. Acts 24: 27. In this he evinced rather a desire, of popularity than an inclination to do justice.

10. Then said Paul, etc. The reasons why Paul declined the proposal to be tried at Jerusalem are obvious. He had experienced so much violent persecution from his countrymen, and their minds were so full of prejudice, misconception, and enmity, that he had neither justice nor favor to hope at their hands. He knew, too, that they had formerly plotted against his life, and that he had been removed to Cesarea for the purpose of safety. It would be madness and folly to throw himself again into their hands, or to give them another opportunity to form a plan against his life. As he was, therefore, under no obligation to return to Jerusalem, and as Festus did not propose it because it could be supposed that justice would be promoted by it, but to gratify the Jews, Paul prudently declined the proposal, and appealed to the Roman emperor.

I stand at Caesar's judgment seat. The Roman emperors, after Julius Caesar, were all called Caesar; thus, Augustus Caesar, Claudius Caesar, etc., as all the kings of Egypt were called Pharaoh, though they had each his proper name, as Pharaoh Necho, etc. The emperor at this time (AD 60) was Nero, one of the most cruel and impious men that ever sat on a throne. It was under him that Paul was afterwards beheaded. When Paul says, "I stand at Caesar's judgment-seat, he means to say that he regarded the tribunal before which he then stood, and on which Festus sat, as really the judgment-seat of Caesar. The procurator, or governor, held his commission from the Roman emperor, and it was, in fact, his tribunal. The reason why Paul made this declaration may be thus expressed:

"I am a Roman citizen. I have a right to justice. I am under no obligation to put myself again in the hands of the Jews. I have a right to a fair and impartial trial; and I claim the protection and privileges which all Roman citizens have before their tribunals, the right of a fair and just trial."

21. But when Paul had appealed. Acts 25: 11.

To be reserved. To be kept; not to be tried at Jerusalem, but to be sent to Rome for trial.

Of Augustus. The reigning emperor at this time was Nero. The name Augustus properly denotes that which is venerable, or worthy of honor and reverence. It was first applied to Caesar Octavianus, who was the Roman emperor in the time when our Savior was born, and who is usually called Augustus Caesar. But the title continued to be used of his successors in office, as denoting the veneration or reverence which was due to the rank of emperor.

22. Then Agrippa said, etc. Agrippa doubtless had heard much of the fame of Jesus, and of the new sect of Christians; and probably he was induced by mere curiosity to hear what Paul could say in explanation and defense of the doctrine of Christianity. This wish of Agrippa gave occasion to the noblest defense which was ever made before any tribunal, and to as splendid eloquence as can be found anywhere in any language. See Acts 26.

26. Of whom. Respecting his character, opinions, manner of life, and respecting the charges against him.

No certain thing. Nothing definite, and well established. They had not accused Paul of any crime against the Roman laws; and Festus professes himself too ignorant of the customs of the Jews to inform the emperor distinctly of the nature of the charges, and the subject of trial.

Unto my lord. To the emperor; to Caesar. This name lord the emperors Augustus and Tiberius had rejected, and would not suffer it to be applied to them.

I might have somewhat to write. As Agrippa was a Jew, and was acquainted with the customs and doctrine of the Jews, Festus supposed that, after hearing Paul, he would be able to inform him of the exact nature of these charges, so that he could present the

have the accusers face to face, and have license to answer for himself concerning the crime laid against him.

17 Therefore, when they were come hither, without any delay on the morrow I sat on the judgment seat, and commanded the man to be brought forth.

18 Against whom when the accusers stood up, they brought none accusation of such things as I supposed:

19 But had certain questions against him of their own superstition, and of one Jesus, which was dead, whom Paul affirmed to be alive.

20 And because I doubted of such manner of questions, I asked him whether he would go to Jerusalem, and there be judged of these matters.

21 But when Paul had appealed to be reserved unto the hearing of Augustus, I commanded him to be kept till I might send him to Caesar.

22 Then Agrippa said unto Festus, I would also hear the man myself. To morrow, said he, thou shalt hear him.

23 And on the morrow, when Agrippa was come, and Bernice, with great pomp, and was entered into the place of hearing, with the chief captains, and principal men of the city, at Festus' commandment Paul was brought forth.

24 And Festus said, King Agrippa, and all men which are here present with us, ye see this man, about whom all the multitude of the Jews have dealt with me, both at Jerusalem, and also here, crying that he ought not to live any longer.

25 But when I found that he had committed nothing worthy of death, and that he himself hath appealed to Augustus, I have determined to send him.

26 Of whom I have no certain thing to write unto my lord. Wherefore I have brought him forth before you, and specially before thee, O king Agrippa, that, after examination had, I might have somewhat to write.

27 For it seemeth to me unreasonable to send a prisoner, and not withal to signify the crimes laid against him.

ACTS 26

1 Then Agrippa said unto Paul, Thou art permitted to speak for thyself. Then Paul stretched forth the hand, and answered

thority, command them to carry him whether he would or no. Surely we gather that he was kept back with fear, lest he should infringe the privilege of the city of Rome, which was a very odious crime. Notwithstanding, he studied craftily to persuade Paul not to refuse to be judged at Jerusalem. For he was not ignorant of that which indeed came to pass, that a citizen of Rome might lawfully appeal, so that he could then go no farther. Nevertheless, it was no thank to him that he was not delivered into the hands of murderers.

10. I stand at Caesar's judgment-seat

Because Paul seeth that he is betrayed into the hands of the Jews through the ambition of the governor, he objecteth the privilege of the city of Rome. He had submitted himself modestly, if he had commanded him to do that which was just and equal. Now, because the governor doth not his duty willingly, necessity compelleth the holy man to defend himself by law; and by this means the Lord delivereth him now again, even when he was almost given over into the hands of the enemies. And whereas he desireth to have his matter handled before Caesar's judgment-seat, he doth not, therefore, make the doctrine of the gospel subject to the judgment of a profane and wicked man; but being ready to give an account of his faith everywhere, he appealeth from that court where he could no longer hope for equity. Furthermore, though the citizens of Rome did retain their privilege, yet the order was then altered, because the Caesars had taken into their own hands the judging of the people, as if they would be good maintainers and patrons of common liberty.

2. We have declared to what end Paul was brought before that assembly, to wit, that Festus might write unto Caesar as he should be counseled by Agrippa and the rest. Therefore, he doth not use any plain or usual form of defense, but doth rather apply his speech unto doctrine. Luke useth indeed a word of excusing; yet such a one as is nothing inconvenient whensoever there is any account given of doctrine. Furthermore, because Paul knew well that Festus did set light by all that which should be taken out of the law and prophets, he turneth himself unto the king, who he hoped would be more attentive, seeing he was no stranger to the Jewish religion. And because he had hitherto spoken to deaf men, he rejoiceth now that he hath gotten a man who, for his skill and experience, can judge aright. But as he commendeth the skill and knowledge which is in Agrippa, because he is a lawful judge in those matters whereof he is to speak, so he desireth him on the other side to hear him patiently; for otherwise contempt and loathsomeness should have been less excusable in him. He calleth those points of doctrine, which were handled among the scribes,

case intelligibly to the emperor.

27. For it seemeth to me unreasonable, Festus felt that he was placed in an embarrassing situation, he was about to send a prisoner to Rome to be tried, who had been tried by himself, and who had appealed from his jurisdiction; and yet he was ignorant of the charges against him, and of the nature of his offences, if any had been committed. When prisoners were thus sent to Rome to be tried before the emperor, it would be proper that the charges should be all specified, and the evidence stated by which they were supported. Yet Festus could do neither; and it is not wonderful that he felt himself perplexed and embarrassed; and that he was glad to avail himself of the desire which Agrippa had expressed to hear Paul, that he might be able to specify the charges against him.

In concluding this chapter, we may observe: (1.) That in the case of Agrippa, we have an instance of the reasons which induce many men to hear the gospel, he had no belief in it; he had no concern for its truth or its promises; but he was led by curiosity to desire to hear the minister of the gospel of Christ. Curiosity thus draws multitudes to the sanctuary. In many instances they remain unaffected and unconcerned in regard to its provisions of mercy. They listen, and are unmoved, and die in their sins. In many instances, like Agrippa, they are almost persuaded to be Christians, Acts 26: 28. But, like him, they resist the appeals; and die uninterested in the plan of salvation. In some instances, they are converted; and their curiosity, like that of Zaccheus, is made the means of their embracing the Savior, Luke 19: 1–9. Whatever may be the motive which induces men to desire to hear, it is the duty of the ministry cheerfully and thankfully, like Paul, to state the truth, and to defend the Christian religion.

(2.) In Festus we have a specimen of the manner in which the great men, and the rich, and the proud, usually regard Christianity. They esteem it to be a subject of inquiry in which they have no interest; a question about "one dead Jesus," whom Christians affirm to be alive. Whether he be alive or not, whether Christianity be true or false, they suppose, is an inquiry which does not pertain to them. Strange that it did not occur to Festus that if he was alive, his religion was true; and that it was possible that it might be from God. And strange that the men of this world regard the Christian religion as a subject in which they have no personal interest, but as one concerning which Christians only should inquire, and in which they alone should feel any concern.

(3.) In Paul we have the example of a man unlike both Festus and Agrippa. He felt a deep interest in the subject – a subject which pertained as much to them as to him. He was willing not only to look at it with curiosity, but to stake his life, his reputation, his all, on its truth, he was willing to defend it everywhere, and before any class of men. At the same time that he urged his rights as a Roman citizen, yet it was mainly that he might preach the gospel. At the same time that he was anxious to secure justice to himself, yet his chief anxiety was to declare the truth of God. Before any tribunal, before any class of men, in the presence of princes, nobles, and kings, of Romans and of Jews, he was ready to pour forth irresistible eloquence and argument in defense of the truth. Who would not rather be Paul than either Festus or Agrippa? Who would not rather be a prisoner like him, than invested with authority like Festus, or clothed in splendor like Agrippa? And who would not rather be an honest and cordial believer of the gospel like Paul, than, like them, to be cold contemners or neglecters of the God that made them, and of the Savior that died, and rose again?

ACTS 26

6. And now I stand. I stand before the tribunal. I am arraigned.

And am judged. Am tried with reference to being judged. I am undergoing a trial on the point in which all my nation are agreed.

For the hope. On account of the hope; or because, in common with my countrymen, I had entertained this hope, and now believe in its fulfillment.

Of the promise, etc. The promises had been made to the fathers of a Messiah to come, and that embraced the promise of a future state,

for himself:

2 I think myself happy, king Agrippa, because I shall answer for myself this day before thee touching all the things whereof I am accused of the Jews:

3 Especially because I know thee to be expert in all customs and questions which are among the Jews: wherefore I beseech thee to hear me patiently.

4 My manner of life from my youth, which was at the first among mine own nation at Jerusalem, know all the Jews;

5 Which knew me from the beginning, if they would testify, that after the most straitest sect of our religion I lived a Pharisee.

6 And now I stand and am judged for the hope of the promise made of God unto our fathers:

7 Unto which promise our twelve tribes, instantly serving God day and night, hope to come. For which hope's sake, king Agrippa, I am accused of the Jews.

8 Why should it be thought a thing incredible with you, that God should raise the dead?

9 I verily thought with myself, that I ought to do many things contrary to the name of Jesus of Nazareth.

10 Which thing I also did in Jerusalem: and many of the saints did I shut up in prison, having received authority from the chief priests; and when they were put to death, I gave my voice against them.

11 And I punished them oft in every synagogue, and compelled them to blaspheme; and being exceedingly mad against them, I persecuted them even unto strange cities.

12 Whereupon as I went to Damascus with authority and commission from the chief priests,

13 At midday, O king, I saw in the way a light from heaven, above the brightness of the sun, shining round about me and them which journeyed with me.

14 And when we were all fallen to the earth, I heard a voice speaking unto me, and saying in the Hebrew tongue, Saul, Saul, why persecutest thou me? it is hard for thee to kick against the pricks.

15 And I said, Who art thou, Lord? And he said, I am Jesus whom thou persecutest.

questions, who were wont to discuss religion more subtilely. By the word *customs*, he meaneth those rites which were common to the whole nation. Therefore, the sum is this, that king Agrippa was not ignorant either in doctrine, either in the ceremonies of the law. That which he bringeth in or concludeth, wherefore I pray thee hear me patiently (as I said even now), doth signify that the more expert a man is in the Scripture, the more attentive must he be when the question is about religion. For that which we understand doth not trouble us so much. And it is meet that we be so careful for the worship of God, that it do not grieve us to hear those things which belong to the defining thereof, and chiefly when we have learned the principle, so that we may readily judge, if we list to take heed.

4. My life which I have led

He doth not as yet enter into the state of the cause; but because he was wrongfully accused and burdened with many crimes, lest king Agrippa should envy the cause through hatred of the person, he doth first avouch his innocency. For we know that when a sinister suspicion hath once possessed the minds of men, all their senses are so shut up that they can admit nothing. Therefore, Paul doth first drive away the clouds of an evil opinion which were gathered of false reports, that he may be heard of pure and well purged ears. By this we see that Paul was enforced by the necessity of the cause to commend his life which he had led before. But he standeth not long upon that point, but passes over straightway unto the resurrection of the dead, when he saith that he is a Pharisee. And I think that that is called the most strait sect, not in respect of holiness of life, but because there was in it more natural sincerity of doctrine, and greater learning. For they did boast that they knew the secret meaning of the Scripture. And surely forasmuch as the Sadducees did vaunt that they did stick to the letter, they fell into filthy and gross ignorance after they had darkened the light of the Scripture. The Essenes, contenting themselves with an austere and strait kind of life, did not greatly care for doctrine. Neither doth that any whit hinder, because Christ inveigheth principally against the Pharisees, as being the worst corrupters of the Scripture (Matthew 23: 13). For seeing they did challenge to themselves authority to interpret the Scripture according to the hidden and secret meaning, hence came that boldness to change and innovate, wherewith the Lord is displeased. But Paul doth not touch those inventions which they had rashly invented, and which they urged with tyrannous rigor. For it was his purpose to speak only of the resurrection of the dead. For though they had corrupted the law in many points, yet it was meet that the authority of that sect should be of more estimation in defending the sound and true faith, than of

or of the resurrection of the dead. It will help us to understand the stress which Paul and the other apostles laid on the doctrine of the resurrection of the dead, to remember that it involved the whole doctrine of the separate existence of the soul, and of a future state. The Sadducees denied all this; and when the Pharisees, the Savior, and the apostles opposed them, they did it by showing that there would be a future state of rewards and punishments.

10. Which thing I also did, etc. Acts 8: 3.

And many of the saints, etc. Many Christians, Acts 8: 3.

And when they were put to death. In the history of those transactions there is no account of any Christian being put to death, except Stephen, Acts 7. But there is no improbability in supposing that the same thing which had happened to Stephen, had occurred in other cases. Stephen was the first martyr; and as he was a prominent man, his case is particularly recorded.

I gave my voice. Paul was not a member of the Sanhedrim, and this does not mean that he voted, but simply that he joined in the persecution; he approved it; he assented to the putting of the saints to death. Comp. Acts 22: 20. The Syriac renders it, "I joined with those who condemned them." It is evident also that Paul instigated them in this persecution, and urged them on to deeds of blood and cruelty.

16. But rise, etc. The particulars mentioned in this verse and the two following are not recorded in the account of Paul's conversion in Acts 9. But it is not improbable that many circumstances may have occurred which are not recorded. Paul dwells on them here at length, in order particularly to show his authority for doing what he had done in preaching to the Gentiles.

To make thee a minister. A minister of the gospel; a preacher of the truth.

Which thou hast seen. On the road to Damascus; that is, of the Lord Jesus, and of the fact that he was risen from the dead.

18. To open their eyes. To enlighten or instruct them. Ignorance is represented by the eyes being closed, and the instruction of the gospel by the opening of the eyes. See Eph. 1: 18.

And to turn them from darkness to light. From the darkness of heathenism and sin, to the light and purity of the gospel. Darkness in an emblem of ignorance and of sin; and the heathen nations are often represented as sitting in darkness.

And from the power of Satan. From the dominion of Satan. Comp. Col. 1: 13; 1 Pet. 2: 9.

Satan is thus represented as the prince of this world; the ruler of the darkness of this world; the prince of the power of the air, etc. The heathen world, lying in sin and superstition, is represented as under his control; and this passage teaches, doubtless, that the great mass of the people of this world are the subjects of the kingdom of Satan, and are led captive by him at his will.

Unto God. To the obedience of the one living and true God.

That they may receive forgiveness of sins. Through the merits of that Savior who died; that thus the partition wall between the Jews and the Gentiles might be broken down, and all might be admitted to the same precious privileges of the favor and mercy of God.

26. For the king. King Agrippa.

Knoweth. He had been many years in that region, and the fame of Jesus and of Paul's conversion were probably well known to him.

These things. The things pertaining to the early persecutions of Christians; the spread of the gospel; and the remarkable conversion of Paul. Though Agrippa might not have been fully informed respecting these things, yet he had an acquaintance with Moses and the prophets; he knew the Jewish expectation respecting the Messiah; and he could not be ignorant respecting the remarkable public events in the life of Jesus of Nazareth, and of his having been put to death by order of Pontius Pilate on the cross.

I speak freely. I speak openly, boldly. I use no disguise; and I speak the more confidently before him, because, from his situation, he must be acquainted with the truth of what I say. Truth is always bold and free; and it is an evidence of honesty when a man is willing to declare everything without reserve before those who are qualified to detect him if he is

16 But rise, and stand upon thy feet: for I have appeared unto thee for this purpose, to make thee a minister and a witness both of these things which thou hast seen, and of those things in the which I will appear unto thee;

17 Delivering thee from the people, and from the Gentiles, unto whom now I send thee,

18 To open their eyes, and to turn them from darkness to light, and from the power of Satan unto God, that they may receive forgiveness of sins, and inheritance among them which are sanctified by faith that is in me.

19 Whereupon, O king Agrippa, I was not disobedient unto the heavenly vision:

20 But shewed first unto them of Damascus, and at Jerusalem, and throughout all the coasts of Judaea, and then to the Gentiles, that they should repent and turn to God, and do works meet for repentance.

21 For these causes the Jews caught me in the temple, and went about to kill me.

22 Having therefore obtained help of God, I continue unto this day, witnessing both to small and great, saying none other things than those which the prophets and Moses did say should come:

23 That Christ should suffer, and that he should be the first that should rise from the dead, and should shew light unto the people, and to the Gentiles.

24 And as he thus spake for himself, Festus said with a loud voice, Paul, thou art beside thyself; much learning doth make thee mad.

25 But he said, I am not mad, most noble Festus; but speak forth the words of truth and soberness.

26 For the king knoweth of these things, before whom also I speak freely: for I am persuaded that none of these things are hidden from him; for this thing was not done in a corner.

27 King Agrippa, believest thou the prophets? I know that thou believest.

28 Then Agrippa said unto Paul, Almost thou persuadest me to be a Christian.

29 And Paul said, I would to God, that not only thou, but also all that hear me this day, were both almost, and altogether such as I am, except these bonds.

the other, which were departed farther from natural purity. Moreover, Paul speaketh only of the common judgment, which did respect the color of more subtile knowledge.

18. That thou mayest open their eyes

Paul, in taking to himself that which is proper to God, doth seem to exalt himself too high. For we know that it is the Holy Ghost alone which doth lighten the eyes. We know that Christ is the only Redeemer which doth deliver us from the tyranny of Satan. We know that it is God alone who, having put away our sins, doth adopt us unto the inheritance of the saints. But this is a common thing, that God doth translate unto his ministers that honor which is due to himself alone, not that he may take any thing from himself, but that he may commend that mighty working of his Spirit which he doth show forth in them. For he doth not send them to work, that they may be dead instruments, or, as it were, stage-players; but that he may work mightily by their hand. But it dependeth upon the secret power of his Spirit that their preaching is effectual, who worketh all things in all men, and which only giveth the increase.

Therefore, teachers are sent, not to utter their words in vain in the air, or to beat the ears only with a vain sound, but to bring lively light to the blind, to fashion again men's hearts unto the righteousness of God, and to ratify the grace of salvation which is gotten by the death of Christ. But they do none of all these, save only inasmuch as God worketh by them, that their labor may not be in vain, that all the praise may be his, as the effect cometh from him.

ACTS 27

1. Luke recounts Paul's sea voyage so that we may know that he was brought to Rome by God's hand. He is delivered to be carried with other prisoners; but the Lord doth afterward put great difference between him and the evildoers, who were in bonds as well as he. Yea, moreover, we shall see how the captain doth loose him, and let him be at liberty, when the rest lie bound. I know not what band that was which Luke calleth the band of Augustus, unless, peradventure, it be that which was commonly called the praetor's band, before the monarchy of the Caesars. And Luke setteth down in plain words, that they were put in a ship of Adramyttium; because they should sail by the coast of Asia. For Adramyttium is a city of Aeolia. I cannot tell out of what haven they launched. Because they could not sail with a straight course to Sidon, unless the maps do greatly deceive me, we may well guess that they were brought thither, either because they could find a ship nowhere else, or else because they were to take the other prisoners, of whom mention is made, out of that region.

an impostor. Such evidence of truth and honesty was given by Paul.

For I am persuaded. I am convinced; I doubt not that he is well acquainted with these things.

Are hidden from him. That he is unacquainted with them.

For this thing. The thing to which Paul had mainly referred in this defense, his own conversion to the Christian religion.

Was not done in a corner. Did not occur secretly and obscurely; but was public, and was of such a character as to attract attention. The conversion of a leading persecutor, such as Paul had been, and in the manner in which that conversion had taken place, could not but attract attention and remark. And although the Jews would endeavor as much as possible to conceal it, yet Paul might presume that it could not be entirely unknown to Agrippa.

27. King Agrippa. This bland personal address is an instance of Paul's happy manner of appeal. He does it to bring in the testimony of Agrippa to meet the charge of Festus that he was deranged.

Believest thou the prophets? The prophecies respecting the character, the sufferings, and the death of the Messiah.

I know that thou believest. Agrippa was a Jew; and, as such, he of course believed the prophets. Perhaps, too, from what Paul knew of his personal character, he might confidently affirm that he professed to be a believer. Instead, therefore, of waiting for his answer, Paul anticipates it, and says that he knows that Agrippa professes to believe all these prophecies respecting the Messiah.

28. Then Agrippa said unto Paul. He could not deny that he believed the prophets. He could not deny that the argument was a strong one, that they had been fulfilled in Jesus of Nazareth. He could not deny that the evidence of the miraculous interposition of God in the conversion of Paul was overwhelming. And instead, therefore, of charging him as Festus had done with derangement, he candidly and honestly avows the impression which the proof had made on his mind.

Almost. Except a very little. Thou hast

nearly convinced me that Christianity is true, and persuaded me to embrace it. The arguments of Paul had been so rational; the appeal which he had made to his belief of the prophets had been so irresistible, that he had been nearly convinced of the truth of Christianity.

ACTS 27

1. And when it was determined. By Festus, Acts 25: 12 and when the time was come when it was convenient to send him.

That we should sail. The use of the term "we" here shows that the author of this book, Luke, was with Paul. He had been the companion of Paul; and though he had not been accused, yet it was resolved that he should still accompany him.

Into Italy. The country still bearing the same name, of which Rome was the capital.

6. A ship of Alexandria. A ship belonging to Alexandria. Alexandria was in Egypt, and was founded by Alexander the Great. It appears, from Acts 27: 38, that the ship was laden with wheat. It is well known that great quantities of wheat were imported from Egypt to Rome; and it appears that this was one of the large ships which were employed for that purpose. Why the ship was on the coast of Asia Minor, is not known. But it is probable that it had been driven out of its way by adverse winds or tempests.

7. Had sailed slowly. By reason of the prevalence of the western winds, Acts 27: 4.

Over against Cnidus. This was a city standing on a promontory of the same name in Asia Minor, in the part of the province of Cans called Doris, and a little north-west of the island of Rhodes.

The wind not suffering us. The wind repelling us in that direction; not permitting us to hold on a direct course, we were driven off near to Crete.

9. When much time was spent. In sailing along the coast of Asia; in contending with the contrary winds. It is evident that, when they started, they had hoped to reach Italy before the dangerous time of navigating the Medi-

30 And when he had thus spoken, the king rose up, and the governor, and Bernice, and they that sat with them:

31 And when they were gone aside, they talked between themselves, saying, This man doeth nothing worthy of death or of bonds.

32 Then said Agrippa unto Festus, This man might have been set at liberty, if he had not appealed unto Caesar.

ACTS 27

1 And when it was determined that we should sail into Italy, they delivered Paul and certain other prisoners unto one named Julius, a centurion of Augustus' band.

2 And entering into a ship of Adramyttium, we launched, meaning to sail by the coasts of Asia; one Aristarchus, a Macedonian of Thessalonica, being with us.

3 And the next day we touched at Sidon. And Julius courteously entreated Paul, and gave him liberty to go unto his friends to refresh himself.

4 And when we had launched from thence, we sailed under Cyprus, because the winds were contrary.

5 And when we had sailed over the sea of Cilicia and Pamphylia, we came to Myra, a city of Lycia.

6 And there the centurion found a ship of Alexandria sailing into Italy; and he put us therein.

7 And when we had sailed slowly many days, and scarce were come over against Cnidus, the wind not suffering us, we sailed under Crete, over against Salmone;

8 And, hardly passing it, came unto a place which is called The fair havens; nigh whereunto was the city of Lasea.

9 Now when much time was spent, and when sailing was now dangerous, because the fast was now already past, Paul admonished them,

10 And said unto them, Sirs, I perceive that this voyage will be with hurt and much damage, not only of the lading and ship, but also of our lives.

11 Nevertheless the centurion believed the master and the owner of the ship, more than those things which were spoken by Paul.

12 And because the haven was not

2. And there continued with us

Luke seemeth so to commend one man's constancy, that he nippeth the rest. For there were more which did accompany him to Jerusalem; whereof we see two only which remained with him. But because it may be that the rest were letted with some just causes, or that Paul refused to have them to minister unto him, I will say nothing either way. Neither is it an unmeet thing to say that Luke had some special reason for which he doth commend this man above the rest, albeit he was but one of many. Surely, it is likely that he was a rich man, seeing he was able to bear the charges whereat he was by the space of three years, having left his house. For we heard before (Acts 17: 11) that many of the chief families in Thessalonica did receive Christ, and Luke saith, for honor's sake, that Aristarchus and Secundus came with Paul into Asia (Acts 20: 4). Therefore, let it suffice us to hold that which is certain and good to be known, that there is set before us an example of holy patience, because Aristarchus is not wearied with any trouble, but doth willingly take part with Paul in his trouble, and after that he had been in prison with him two years, he doth now cross the seas, that he may likewise minister to him at Rome, not without the reproachings of many, besides the loss of his goods at home, and so great charges.

9. When sailing was now jeopardous

He doth not only mean that the winds were contrary then, but also that the time of the year was not then commodious, which he expresseth more plainly afterward, when he saith that the fast was passed; for I think that this word was added by way of exposition, to note the end of harvest. Neither do I pass for that, that that solemn time of fasting, whereof Luke speaketh, was strange to the centurion and the rest of the mariners; for he noteth out the times of the year according to the custom of the Jews. Furthermore, we need not doubt but that it was the harvest [autumnal] fast. Though I am not of their mind who think that it was one of the four fasts which the Jews did appoint after the carrying away into Babylon. For Luke would not have put down simply, without adding any distinction, the third fast, which was in the seventh month, seeing it was not more famous than the rest, being commanded to be kept because of the death of Godolia, and because of the destruction of the rest of the people. Again, I cannot tell whether that custom were retained by the people after their return. It is more likely that he meaneth the feast of the atonement, wherein the Lord commanded them to humble their souls seven days. And they began the tenth day of the seventh month; whereto partly September and partly October doth now agree (Leviticus 16: 29). Therefore, seeing they were now entered into October, it is said, not without cause,

terranean should arrive. But they had been detained and embarrassed contrary to their expectation, so that they were now sailing in the most dangerous and tempestuous time of the year.

Because the fast was now already past. By "the fast," here is evidently intended the fast which occurred among the Jews on the great day of atonement.

Paul admonished them. Paul exhorted, entreated, or persuaded them. He was somewhat accustomed to the navigation of that sea; and endeavored to persuade them not to risk the danger of sailing at that season of the year.

10. Sirs. Greek, Men.

I perceive. It is not certain that Paul understood this by direct inspiration. He might have perceived it from his own knowledge of the danger of navigation at the autumnal equinox, and from what he saw of the ship as unfitted to a dangerous navigation. But there is nothing that should prevent our believing also that he was guided to this conclusion by the inspiration of the Spirit of God. Comp. Acts 27: 23–24.

Will be with hurt. With injury, or hazard. It is not meant that their lives would be lost, but that they would put into jeopardy.

The lading. The freight of the ship. It was laden with wheat, Acts 27: 38. Paul evidently, by this, intended to suggest the propriety of remaining where they were, until the time of dangerous navigation was past.

13. The south wind. The wind before had probably been a headwind, blowing from the west. When it veered round to the south, and when it blew gently, though not entirely favorable, yet it was so that they supposed they could sail along the coast of Crete.

Had obtained their purpose. The object of their desire; that is, to sail safely along the coast of Crete.

Loosing thence. Setting sail for the fair havens.

Close by Crete. Near the shore. It is evident that they designed, if possible, to make the harbor of Phenice, to winter there.

14. Arose. Beat violently.

Against it. Against the island of Crete.

A tempestuous wind. Turbulent, violent, strong.

Called Euroclydon. Interpreters have been much perplexed about the meaning of this word, which occurs nowhere else in the New Testament. The most probable supposition is, that it denotes a wind not blowing steadily from any quarter, but a hurricane, or wind veering about to different quarters. Such hurricanes are known to abound in the Mediterranean, and are now called Levanters, deriving their name from blowing chiefly in the Levant, or eastern part of the Mediterranean.

15. The ship was caught. By the wind. It came suddenly upon them as a tempest.

Could not bear up, etc. Could not resist its violence, or could not direct the ship. It was seized by the wind, and driven with such violence that it became unmanageable.

We let her drive. We suffered the ship to be borne along by the wind, without attempting to control it.

17. They used helps. They used ropes, cables, stays, or chains, for the purpose of securing the ship. The danger was, that the ship would be destroyed; and they, therefore, made use of such aids as should prevent the loss of the ship.

Undergirding the ship. The ancients were accustomed to pass cables or strong ropes from one side of the ship to another, to keep the planks from springing or starting by the action of the sea. The rope was slipped under the prow, and passed along to any part of the keel which they pleased, and made fast on the deck.

22. There shall be no loss. This must have been cheering news those who had given up all for lost. As Paul had manifested great wisdom in former advice to them, they might now be more disposed to listen to him. The reason why he believed they would be safe, he immediately states.

23. There stood by me. There appeared to me.

The angel of God. The message of God were often communicated by angels. See Heb. 1: 14. This does not mean that there was any par-

commodious to winter in, the more part advised to depart thence also, if by any means they might attain to Phenice, and there to winter; which is an haven of Crete, and lieth toward the south west and north west.

13 And when the south wind blew softly, supposing that they had obtained their purpose, loosing thence, they sailed close by Crete.

14 But not long after there arose against it a tempestuous wind, called Euroclydon.

15 And when the ship was caught, and could not bear up into the wind, we let her drive.

16 And running under a certain island which is called Clauda, we had much work to come by the boat:

17 Which when they had taken up, they used helps, undergirding the ship; and, fearing lest they should fall into the quicksands, strake sail, and so were driven.

18 And we being exceedingly tossed with a tempest, the next day they lightened the ship;

19 And the third day we cast out with our own hands the tackling of the ship.

20 And when neither sun nor stars in many days appeared, and no small tempest lay on us, all hope that we should be saved was then taken away.

21 But after long abstinence Paul stood forth in the midst of them, and said, Sirs, ye should have hearkened unto me, and not have loosed from Crete, and to have gained this harm and loss.

22 And now I exhort you to be of good cheer: for there shall be no loss of any man's life among you, but of the ship.

23 For there stood by me this night the angel of God, whose I am, and whom I serve,

24 Saying, Fear not, Paul; thou must be brought before Caesar: and, lo, God hath given thee all them that sail with thee.

25 Wherefore, sirs, be of good cheer: for I believe God, that it shall be even as it was told me.

26 Howbeit we must be cast upon a certain island.

27 But when the fourteenth night was come, as we were driven up and down in Adria, about midnight the shipmen

that sailing was jeopardous at that time. But and if you refer it unto hunger (as some do) I do not see what sense can be gathered thence; for they had as yet store of wheat in the ship, so that they needed not to be hunger starved. And why should he say that the time of the voluntary fast was passed? Moreover, it shall hereafter appear by the text, that they were, therefore, exhorted by Paul to stay because winter was at hand, whose sharpness [severity] useth to shut up the seas. For though he were assured that God would govern the ship, yet he would not tempt him rashly by making too great haste.

11. But the centurion

The centurion is not reproved because he hearkened rather to the master and governor of the ship than to Paul. For what should he have done? For though he did well like Paul's counsel in other matters, yet he knew that he was unskillful in sailing. Therefore he suffered himself to be governed by those which were expert, which was a point of a wise and modest man. Yea, very necessity did almost compel him to do this; for the haven was not commodious to winter in. Neither did the governor give counsel to commit the ship to the main sea, but to thrust into the next haven, which was almost in view. So that, with taking a little pains, they might commodiously pass the winter. Luke reciteth this not in vain; but that we may know that Paul was from the beginning furnished with the sense of the Spirit, so that he did better see what things were profitable than did the masters. We know not whether he were taught by oracles, or whether he gave this counsel through secret inspiration. This is certain, that it served afterward to his commendation. Furthermore, in that he saith that they sailed beyond the coast of Candia, until they were caught and carried away; our friend Beza doth justly reprove the error of interpreters in this word asson, who make of an adverb the name of a city.

15. When the ship was caught

Luke saith that that fell out here, which useth to fall out in extreme danger; namely, they suffered themselves to be carried of the winds. Seeing they were first gone some space, and the mariners thought that all things fell out as they would have it, undoubtedly they did deride Paul's admonition; as rash men use commonly to wax proud if fortune favor them. Being now caught, they are grievously punished for their boldness; yea, when they drew near to an haven, they were no less afraid lest they should break the ship, than they were before of overturning the same. Luke doth diligently note all these things, out of which we may gather, that the storm was so vehement and fierce, and that it continued still at one stay, that they were still in dan-

ticular angel, but simply an angel.

Whose I am. Of the God to whom I belong. This is an expression of Paul's entire devotedness to him.

Whom I serve. In the gospel. To whom and to whose cause I am entirely devoted.

24. Fear not, Paul. Do not be alarmed with the danger of the loss of life.

Thou must be brought, etc. And therefore thy life will be spared.

God hath given thee all, etc. That is, they shall all be preserved with thee. None of their lives shall be lost. It does not mean that they should be converted; but that their lives should be preserved. It is implied here that it was for the sake of Paul, or that the leading purpose of the Divine interposition to rescue them from danger was to save his life. The wicked often derive important benefits from being connected with Christians; and God often confers important favors on them in his general purposes to benefit his own people. The lives of impenitent men are often spared because God interposes to save his own people.

27. The fourteenth night. From the time when the tempest commenced.

In Adria. In the Adriatic Sea. This sea is properly situated between Italy and Dalmatia, now called the Adriatic Gulf. But, among the ancients, the name was given not only to that gulf, but to the whole sea lying between Greece, Italy, and Africa, including the Sicilian and Ionian Sea. It is evident, from the narrative, that they were not in the Adriatic Gulf, but somewhere in the vicinity of Malta.

28. And sounded. To sound is to make use of a line and lead to ascertain the depth of water.

Twenty fathoms. A fathom is six feet, or the distance from the extremity of the middle finger on one hand to the extremity of the other, when the arms are extended. The depth, therefore, was about one hundred and twenty feet.

Fifteen fathoms. They knew, therefore, that they were drawing near to shore.

31. Paul said to the centurion and to the soldiers. The centurion had, it appears, the general direction of the ship, Acts 27: 11. Prob-

ably it had been pressed into the service of the government.

Except these. These seamen. The soldiers and the centurion were unqualified to manage the ship, and the presence of the sailors was therefore indispensable to the preservation of any.

Abide in the ship. Remain on board.

Ye cannot be saved. You cannot be preserved from death. You will have no hope of managing the ship so as to be secure from death. It will be remembered that Paul had been informed by the angel, and had assured then, Acts 27: 22-24, that no lives should be lost. But it was only in the use of the proper means that their lives would be safe, yet this did not, in his view, prevent the use of the proper means to secure it. From this we lay learn,

(1.) that the certainty of an event does not render it improper to use means to obtain it.

(2.) That though the event may be determined, yet the use of the means may be indispensable. The event is rendered no more certain than the means requisite to accomplish it.

(3.) That the doctrine of the Divine purposes or decrees, making certain future events, does not make the use of man's agency unnecessary or improper. The means are determined as well as the end; and the one will not be secured without the other.

(4.) The same is true in regard to the decrees respecting salvation. The end is not determined without the means; and as God has resolved that his people shall be saved, so he has also determined the means. He has ordained that they shall repent, shall believe, shall be holy, and shall thus be saved.

(5.) We have in this case a full answer to the objection that a belief in the decrees of God will make men neglect the means of salvation, and lead to licentiousness. It has just the contrary tendency. Here is a case in which Paul certainly believed in the purpose of God to save these men; in which he was assured that it was fully determined; and yet the effect was not to produce inattention and unconcern, but to prompt him to use strenuous efforts to accomplish the very effect which God had determined should take

deemed that they drew near to some country;

28 And sounded, and found it twenty fathoms: and when they had gone a little further, they sounded again, and found it fifteen fathoms.

29 Then fearing lest we should have fallen upon rocks, they cast four anchors out of the stern, and wished for the day.

30 And as the shipmen were about to flee out of the ship, when they had let down the boat into the sea, under color as though they would have cast anchors out of the foreship,

31 Paul said to the centurion and to the soldiers, Except these abide in the ship, ye cannot be saved.

32 Then the soldiers cut off the ropes of the boat, and let her fall off.

33 And while the day was coming on, Paul besought them all to take meat, saying, This day is the fourteenth day that ye have tarried and continued fasting, having taken nothing.

34 Wherefore I pray you to take some meat: for this is for your health: for there shall not an hair fall from the head of any of you.

35 And when he had thus spoken, he took bread, and gave thanks to God in presence of them all: and when he had broken it, he began to eat.

36 Then were they all of good cheer, and they also took some meat.

37 And we were in all in the ship two hundred threescore and sixteen souls.

38 And when they had eaten enough, they lightened the ship, and cast out the wheat into the sea.

39 And when it was day, they knew not the land: but they discovered a certain creek with a shore, into the which they were minded, if it were possible, to thrust in the ship.

40 And when they had taken up the anchors, they committed themselves unto the sea, and loosed the rudder bands, and hoised up the mainsail to the wind, and made toward shore.

41 And falling into a place where two seas met, they ran the ship aground; and the forepart stuck fast, and remained unmoveable, but the hinder part was broken with the violence of the waves.

42 And the soldiers' counsel was to

ger of death. Also he declareth, that they did courageously use all remedies which might save them from suffering shipwreck, and that they spared not the merchandise and tackling; whence we gather that they were enforced, with a lively feeling of danger, to do what they were able. And Luke addeth, that when they had essayed all things, they despaired of their safety. And surely the very darkness of heaven was as it were a grave. Neither need we doubt but that the Lord meant by this means to commend and make more notable the grace of their deliverance which ensued shortly after. Nevertheless, he suffered his servant to labor with the rest, until he thought he should die. For he did not appear unto him by his angel, before it might seem that he was past hope of recovery. Wherefore his body was not only tossed amidst many storms, but his soul was also shaken with violent tentations. Notwithstanding the end doth show, that he stood upright by faith, so that he did not faint. Luke speaketh nothing of his prayers; but because he himself saith afterward that the angel of God, whom he served, appeared to him, it is likely that when others did curse both heaven and earth, he made his prayers to God, and so was quiet, and did patiently tarry the Lord's leisure. And whereas he saith that all hope of safety was taken away, it must not be referred unto his sense, but only unto the means which men could use; as if he should say, that things were so far out of order, that there was no safety to be looked for at men's hands.

ACTS 28

1. That doleful spectacle is described in the beginning of the chapter, when so many men being wet, and also all berayed with the foam and filth of the sea, and stiff with cold, did with much ado crawl to the shore; for that was all one as if they had been cast up by the sea to die some other death. After that, Luke declareth that they were courteously entertained of the barbarians, that they kindled a fire that they might dry their clothes, and refresh their joints, which were stiff with cold, and at length that they were saved from the shower. Therefore, in that Paul commendeth these duties, he showeth his thankfulness; and so great liberality toward strangers is for good causes advanced, whereof there be rare examples in the world. And though common nature doth wring out of the barbarous Gentiles some affection of mercy in so great necessity; yet undoubtedly it was God which caused the men of Melita to handle these men so courteously, that his promise might be sure and certain, which might seem imperfect if the shipwreck had caused the loss of any man's life.

6. let us learn by this history, with patient and quiet minds,

place. So it is always. A belief that God has purposes of mercy; that he designs, and has always designed, to save some, will prompt to the use of all proper means to secure it. If we had no evidence that God had any such purpose, effort would be vain. We should have no inducement in exertion. Where we have such evidence, it operates as it did in the case of Paul, to produce great and strenuous endeavors to secure the object.

41. And falling. Being carried by the wind and waves.

Into a place where two seas met. Gr., Into a place of a double sea. That is, a place which is washed on both sides by the sea. It refers properly to an isthmus, tongue of land, or a sand-bar, stretching out from the main land, and which was washed on both sides by the waves. It is evident that this was not properly an isthmus that was above the waves, but was probably a long sandbank that stretched far out into the sea, and which they did not perceive. In endeavoring to make the harbor, they ran on this bar or sand-bank.

They ran the ship aground. Not designedly, but in endeavoring to reach the harbor, Acts 27: 39.

The hinder part was broken. The stern was broken or staved in. By this means the company was furnished with boards, etc., on which they were safely conveyed to the shore, Acts 27: 44.

42. And the soldiers' counsel, etc. Why they gave this advice is not known. It was probably, however, because the Roman military discipline was very strict, and if they escaped, it would probably be charged on them that it had been done by the negligence and unfaithfulness of the soldiers. They therefore proposed, in a most cruel and bloodthirsty manner, to kill them, though contrary to all humanity, justice, and laws; presuming probably that it would be supposed that they had perished in the wreck. This is a remarkable proof that men can be cruel even when experiencing the tender mercy of God; and that the most affecting scenes of Divine goodness will not mitigate the natural ferocity and cruelty of those who delight in blood.

ACTS 28

1. They knew. Either from their former acquaintance with the island, or from the information of the inhabitants.

Was called Melita. Now called Malta. It was celebrated formerly for producing large quantities of honey, and is supposed to have been called Melita from the Greek word signifying honey.

3. Had gathered a bundle of sticks. For the purpose of making a fire.

There came a viper. A poisonous serpent. It is not expressly affirmed that Paul was bitten by the viper, yet it is evidently implied; and it is wholly incredible that a viper, unless miraculously prevented, should fasten himself to the hand without biting.

4. The venomous beast. The fact that the viper had fastened on him, and that, as they supposed, he must now certainly die, was the proof from which they inferred his guilt.

Is a murderer. Why they thought he was a murderer rather than guilty of some other crime, is not known. It might have been,

(1.) because they inferred that he must have been guilty of some very atrocious crime; and as murder was the highest crime that man could commit, they inferred that he had been guilty of this. Or,

(2.) more probably, they had an opinion that when Divine vengeance overtook a man, he would be punished in a manner similar to the offence; and as murder is committed usually with the hand, and as the viper had fastened on the hand of Paul, they inferred that he had been guilty of taking life. It was supposed among the ancients, that persons were often punished by Divine vengeance in that part of the body which had been the instrument of the sin.

5. And he shook off, etc. In this was remarkably fulfilled the promise of the Savior; "They shall take up serpents," etc. Mark 16: 18.

8. A bloody flux. Gr. Dysentery.

And laid his hand on him, In accordance with the promise of the Savior, Mark 16: 18. This miracle was a suitable return for the hospitality of Publius, and would serve to con-

kill the prisoners, lest any of them should swim out, and escape.

43 But the centurion, willing to save Paul, kept them from their purpose; and commanded that they which could swim should cast themselves first into the sea, and get to land:

44 And the rest, some on boards, and some on broken pieces of the ship. And so it came to pass, that they escaped all safe to land.

ACTS 28

1 And when they were escaped, then they knew that the island was called Melita.

2 And the barbarous people shewed us no little kindness: for they kindled a fire, and received us every one, because of the present rain, and because of the cold.

3 And when Paul had gathered a bundle of sticks, and laid them on the fire, there came a viper out of the heat, and fastened on his hand.

4 And when the barbarians saw the venomous beast hang on his hand, they said among themselves, No doubt this man is a murderer, whom, though he hath escaped the sea, yet vengeance suffereth not to live.

5 And he shook off the beast into the fire, and felt no harm.

6 Howbeit they looked when he should have swollen, or fallen down dead suddenly: but after they had looked a great while, and saw no harm come to him, they changed their minds, and said that he was a god.

7 In the same quarters were possessions of the chief man of the island, whose name was Publius; who received us, and lodged us three days courteously.

8 And it came to pass, that the father of Publius lay sick of a fever and of a bloody flux: to whom Paul entered in, and prayed, and laid his hands on him, and healed him.

9 So when this was done, others also, which had diseases in the island, came, and were healed:

10 Who also honored us with many honors; and when we departed, they laded us with such things as were necessary.

11 And after three months we de-

to wait for the prosperous event of things, which seem at the first to tend toward the robbing of God of his honor. Which of us would not have been terrified with this spectacle which did arm the wicked to slander with all manner of slanderous speeches the glory of the gospel? Yet we see how God did in good time prevent this inconvenience; therefore, let us not doubt but that after he hath suffered his to be darkened with clouds of slanders, he will send remedy in his good time, and will turn their darkness into light. In the mean season, let us remember that we must beware of the judgment of the flesh. And because men do always forget themselves, let us beg of God the Spirit of moderation, that he may keep us always in the right mean. Furthermore, let us learn by this how ready the world is to fall to superstition. Yea, this wickedness is in a manner born with us, to be desirous to adorn creatures with that which we take from God.

Wherefore, no marvel if new errors have come abroad in all ages, seeing every one of us is, even from his mother's womb, expert in inventing idols. But lest men excuse themselves therewithal, this history doth witness that this is the fountain of superstitions, because men are unthankful to God, and do give his glory to some other.

15. When the brethren heard

God did comfort Paul by the coming of the brethren who came forth to meet him, that he might the more joyfully make haste to defend the gospel. And the zeal and godly care of the brethren appeareth therein, in that they inquire for Paul's coming, and go out to meet him. For it was at that time not only an odious thing to profess the Christian faith, but it might also bring them in hazard of their life. Neither did a few men only put themselves in private danger, because the envy redounded to the whole Church. But nothing is more dear to them than their duty wherein they could not be negligent, unless they would be counted sluggish and unthankful. It had been a cruel fact to neglect so great an apostle of Jesus Christ, especially seeing he labored for the common salvation.

And now forasmuch as he had written to them before, and had of his own accord offered his service to them, it had been an unseemly thing not to repay to him brotherly goodwill and courtesy. Therefore, the brethren did, by this their dutifulness, testify their godliness toward Christ; and Paul's desire was more inflamed, because he saw fruit prepared for his constancy. For though he were endued with invincible strength, so that he did not depend upon man's help; yet God, who useth to strengthen his by means of men, did minister to him new strength by this means. Though he were afterward forsaken when he was in prison, as he complaineth in a certain place (2 Timothy 4: 16) yet he

ciliate further the kindness of the people, and prepare the way for the usefulness of Paul.

10. Who also honored us. As men who were favored of heaven, and who had been the means of conferring important benefits on them in healing the sick, etc. Probably the word "honors" here means gifts, or marks of favor.

They laded us. They gave us, or conferred on us. They furnished us with such things as were necessary for us on our journey.

11. And after three months. Probably they remained there so long, because there was no favorable opportunity for them to go to Rome. If they arrived there, as is commonly supposed, in October, they left for Rome in January.

Whose sign. Which was ornamented with an image of Castor and Pollux. It was common to place on the prow of the ship the image Of some person, or god, whose name the ship bore. This custom is still observed.

Castor and Pollux. These were two semi-deities. They were reputed to be twin brothers, sons of Jupiter and Leda, the wife of Tyndarus, king of Sparta. After their death, they are fabled to have been translated to heaven, and made constellations under the name of gemini, or the twins. They then received divine honors, and were called the sons of Jupiter. They were supposed to preside over sailors, and to be their protectors; hence it was not uncommon to place their image on ships.

12. And landing at Syracuse. Syracuse was the capital of the island of Sicily, on the eastern coast. It was in the direct course from Malta to Rome.

14. Brethren. Christian brethren. But by whom the gospel had been preached there is unknown.

15. And from thence. From Puteoli.

When the brethren heard of us. The Christians who were at Rome.

As far as Appii forum. This was a city about fifty-six miles from Rome. The remains of an ancient city are still seen there. It is on the borders of the Pontine marshes. The city was built on the celebrated Appian way, or road

from Rome to Capua. The road was made by Appius Claudius, and probably the city also. It was called the forum or market-place of Appius, because it was a convenient place for travelers on the Appian way to stop for purposes of refreshment.

He thanked God. He had long ardently desired to see the Christians of Rome, Rom. 1: 9–11; 15: 23,32.

He was now grateful to God that the object of his long desire was at last granted to him, and that he was permitted to see them, though in bonds.

And took courage. From their society and counsel. The presence and counsel of Christian brethren is often of inestimable value in encouraging and strengthening us in the toils and trials of life.

17. Paul called the chief of the Jews. He probably had two objects in this: one was to vindicate himself from the suspicion of crime, or to convince them that the charges alleged against him were false; and the other, to explain to them the gospel of Christ. In accordance with his custom everywhere, he seized the excellent opportunity of making the gospel known to his own countrymen; and he naturally supposed that charges highly unfavorable to his character had been sent forward against him to the Jews at Rome by those in Judea.

Against the people. Against the Jews, Acts 24: 12.

Or customs, etc. The religious rites of the nation.

Was I delivered prisoner, etc. By the Jews, Acts 21: 33, etc.

19. Not that I had ought, etc. I did it for my own preservation and safety; not that I wished to accuse my own countrymen. It was not from motives of revenge, but for safety. Paul had been unjustly accused and injured; yet, with the true spirit of the Christian religion, he here says that he cherished no unkind feelings towards them.

20. Because that for the hope of Israel. On account of the hope which the Jews cherished of the coming of the Messiah; of the resurrection; and of the future state through him.

I am bound with this chain. Probably

parted in a ship of Alexandria, which had wintered in the isle, whose sign was Castor and Pollux.

12 And landing at Syracuse, we tarried there three days.

13 And from thence we fetched a compass, and came to Rhegium: and after one day the south wind blew, and we came the next day to Puteoli:

14 Where we found brethren, and were desired to tarry with them seven days: and so we went toward Rome.

15 And from thence, when the brethren heard of us, they came to meet us as far as Appiiforum, and The three taverns: whom when Paul saw, he thanked God, and took courage.

16 And when we came to Rome, the centurion delivered the prisoners to the captain of the guard: but Paul was suffered to dwell by himself with a soldier that kept him.

17 And it came to pass, that after three days Paul called the chief of the Jews together: and when they were come together, he said unto them, Men and brethren, though I have committed nothing against the people, or customs of our fathers, yet was I delivered prisoner from Jerusalem into the hands of the Romans.

18 Who, when they had examined me, would have let me go, because there was no cause of death in me.

19 But when the Jews spake against it, I was constrained to appeal unto Caesar; not that I had ought to accuse my nation of.

20 For this cause therefore have I called for you, to see you, and to speak with you: because that for the hope of Israel I am bound with this chain.

21 And they said unto him, We neither received letters out of Judaea concerning thee, neither any of the brethren that came shewed or spake any harm of thee.

22 But we desire to hear of thee what thou thinkest: for as concerning this sect, we know that every where it is spoken against.

23 And when they had appointed him a day, there came many to him into his lodging; to whom he expounded and testified the kingdom of God, persuading them concerning Jesus, both out of the law of Moses, and out of the prophets,

did not despair; but did fight no less valiantly and manfully under Christ's banner, than if he had been guarded with a great army. But the remembrance of this meeting did serve even then to encourage him, seeing he did consider with himself that there were many godly brethren at Rome, but they were weak, and that he was sent to strengthen them. And there is no cause why we should marvel that Paul was emboldened at this present when he saw the brethren, because he did hope that the confession his faith would yield no small fruit. For so often as God showeth to his servants any fruit of their labor, he doth, as it were, prick them forward with a goad, that they may proceed more courageously in their work.

25. And when they could not

The malice of the unfaithful is the cause of this, that Christ, who is our peace, and the only bond of holy unity, is an occasion of dissension, and doth cause those to go together by the ears who were friends before. For, behold, when the Jews come together to hear Paul, they think all one thing; and speak all one thing; they do all profess that they embrace the law of Moses. So soon as they hear the doctrine of reconciliation, there ariseth dissension among them, so that they are divided. And yet for all this we must not think that the preaching of the gospel is the cause of discord; but that privy displeasure, which lurked before in their malicious minds, doth then break out; and as the brightness of the sun doth not color things otherwise than they were, but doth plainly show the difference, which was none so long as it was dark. Therefore, seeing God doth illuminate his elect peculiarly, and faith is not common to all men, let us remember that it cannot be but that, so soon as Christ cometh abroad, there will be a division among men. But then let us call to mind that which Simon foretold of him, that he shall be a sign which shall be spoken against, that the thoughts of many hearts may be disclosed (Luke 2: 34–35) and that unbelief which striveth against God is the mother of dissension.

30. He received all

The apostle showed an excellent example of constancy, in that he offered himself so willingly to all those which were desirous to hear him. Surely he was not ignorant what great hatred he did purchase; and that this was his best way, if by holding his peace he might appease the hatred of his adversaries. For a man being desirous to provide for himself alone would not have done thus; but because he remembered that he was no less the servant of Christ, and a preacher of the gospel, when he was in prison, than if he had been at liberty, he thought it was not lawful for him to withdraw himself from any which was ready to learn, lest he should

he was attached constantly to a soldier by a chain.

21. We neither received letters, etc. Why the Jews in Judea had not forwarded the accusation against Paul to their brethren at Rome, that they might continue the prosecution before the emperor, is not known. It is probable that they regarded their cause as hopeless, and chose to abandon the prosecution. Paul had been acquitted successively by Lysias, Felix, Festus, Agrippa; and as they had not succeeded in procuring his condemnation before them, they saw no prospect of doing it at Rome, and chose therefore not to press the prosecution any farther.

Neither any of the brethren that came. Any of the Jews. There was a very constant intercourse between Judea and Rome; but it seems that the Jews, who had come before Paul had arrived, had not mentioned his case, so as to prejudice them against him.

22. What thou thinkest. What your belief is; or what are the doctrines of Christians respecting the Messiah.

This sect. The sect of Christians.

Spoken against. Particularly by Jews. This was the case then, and, to a great extent, is the case still. It has been the common lot of the followers of Christ to be spoken of with contempt. Comp. Acts 24: 5.

23. Appointed him a day. A day when they would hear him.

To his lodging. To the house where he resided, Acts 28: 30.

He expounded. He explained or declared the principles of the Christian religion.

And testified the kingdom of God. Bore witness to, or declared the principles and doctrines of the reign of the Messiah.

Persuading them concerning Jesus. Endeavoring to convince them that Jesus was the Messiah.

Both out of the law of Moses. Endeavoring to convince them that he corresponded with the predictions respecting the Messiah in the books of Moses, Gen. 49: 10; Deut. 18: 18, and with the types which Moses had instituted to prefigure the Messiah.

And out of the prophets. Showing that he corresponded with the predictions of the prophets.

From morning till evening. An instance of Paul's indefatigable toil in endeavoring to win his own countrymen to Jesus as the Messiah.

25. Had spoken one word. One declaration of solemn prophecy, reminding them that it was the characteristic of the nation to reject the testimony of God, and that it was to be expected. It was the last solemn warning which we know Paul to have delivered to his countrymen the Jews.

28. The salvation of God. The knowledge of God's mode of saving men.

Is sent unto the Gentiles. Since you have rejected it, it will be offered to them.

And that they will hear it. They will embrace it. Paul was never discouraged. If the gospel was rejected by one class of people, he was ready to offer it to another. If his own countrymen rejected and despised it, he never allowed himself to suppose that Christ had died in vain, but believed that others would be inclined to embrace its saving benefits. How happy would it be if all Christians had the same unwavering faith and zeal as Paul!

29. And had great reasoning. Great discussion or debates. That is, the part which believed that Jesus was the Messiah, Acts 28: 24, discussed the subject warmly with those who did not believe.

30. Paul dwelt two whole years. Doubtless in the custody of the soldiers. Why he was not prosecuted before the emperor during this time is not known. It is evident, however, Acts 28: 21, that the Jews were not disposed to carry the case before Nero; and the matter, during this time, was suffered quietly to sleep. There is great probability that the Jews durst not prosecute him before the emperor. It is clear that they had never been in favor of the appeal to Rome, and that they had no hope of gaining their cause.

In his own hired house. In a house which he was permitted to hire, and occupy as his own. Probably in this he was assisted by the kindness of his Roman friends.

And received all, etc. Received all hospita-

from morning till evening.

24 And some believed the things which were spoken, and some believed not.

25 And when they agreed not among themselves, they departed, after that Paul had spoken one word, Well spake the Holy Ghost by Esaias the prophet unto our fathers,

26 Saying, Go unto this people, and say, Hearing ye shall hear, and shall not understand; and seeing ye shall see, and not perceive:

27 For the heart of this people is waxed gross, and their ears are dull of hearing, and their eyes have they closed; lest they should see with their eyes, and hear with their ears, and understand with their heart, and should be converted, and I should heal them.

28 Be it known therefore unto you, that the salvation of God is sent unto the Gentiles, and that they will hear it.

29 And when he had said these words, the Jews departed, and had great reasoning among themselves.

30 And Paul dwelt two whole years in his own hired house, and received all that came in unto him,

31 Preaching the kingdom of God, and teaching those things which concern the Lord Jesus Christ, with all confidence, no man forbidding him.

foreslow [neglect] the occasion which was offered him by God, and therefore he did more regard the holy calling of God than his own life. And that we may know that he did incur danger willingly, Luke doth shortly after expressly commend his boldness, as if he should say, that setting all fear aside, he did faithfully obey the commandment of God, neither was he terrified with any danger, but did proceed to take pains with whomsoever he met.

Preaching the kingdom of God

He doth not separate the kingdom of God, and those things which belong to Christ, as diverse things, but doth rather add the second thing by way of exposition, that we may know that the kingdom of God is grounded and contained in the knowledge of the redemption purchased by Christ. Therefore, Paul taught that men are strangers and foreigners from the kingdom of God, until having their sins done away they be reconciled to God, and be renewed into holiness of life by the Spirit; and that the kingdom of God is then erected, and doth then flourish among them, when Christ the Mediator doth join them to the Father, having both their sins freely forgiven them, and being also regenerate unto righteousness, that beginning the heavenly life upon earth, they may always have a longing desire to come to heaven, where they shall fully and perfectly enjoy glory. Also, Luke setteth forth a singular benefit of God, in that Paul had so great liberty granted him. For that came not to pass through the winking and dissimulation of those who could hinder it, seeing they did detest religion, but because the Lord did shut their eyes. Wherefore, it is not without cause that Paul himself doth boast that the Word of God was not bound with his bonds (2 Timothy 2: 9).

bly and kindly who came to him to show him kindness, or to listen to his instructions. It is evident from this, that he was still a prisoner, and was not permitted to go at large.

31. With all confidence. Openly and boldly, without any one to hinder him. It is known, also, that Paul was not unsuccessful even when a prisoner at Rome. Several persons were converted by his preaching even in the court of the emperor. The things which had happened to him, he says, Phil. 1: 12–14, had fallen out rather to the furtherance of the gospel, so that his bonds in Christ were manifested in all the palace, and in all other places; and many brethren in the Lord, says he, waxing confident by my bonds, are much more bold to speak the word without fear.

Romans

Introduction by John Calvin

WITH regard to the excellency of this Epistle, I know not whether it would be well for me to dwell long on the subject; for I fear, lest through my recommendations falling far short of what they ought to be, I should do nothing but obscure its merits: besides, the Epistle itself, at its very beginning, explains itself in a much better way than can be done by any words which I can use. It will then be better for me to pass on to the Argument, or the contents of the Epistle; and it will hence appear beyond all controversy, that besides other excellencies, and those remarkable, this can with truth be said of it, and it is what can never be sufficiently appreciated – that when any one gains a knowledge of this Epistle, he has an entrance opened to him to all the most hidden treasures of Scripture.

The whole Epistle is so methodical, that even its very beginning is framed according to the rules of art. As contrivance appears in many parts, which shall be noticed as we proceed, so also especially in the way in which the main argument is deduced: for having begun with the proof of his Apostleship, he then comes to the Gospel with the view of recommending it; and as this necessarily draws with it the subject of faith, he glides into that, being led by the chain of words as by the hand: and thus he enters on the main subject of the whole Epistle justification by faith; in treating which he is engaged to the end of the fifth chapter.

The subject then of these chapters may be stated thus – man's only righteousness is through the mercy of God in Christ, which being offered by the Gospel is apprehended by faith.

But as men are asleep in their sins, and flatter and delude themselves with a false notion about righteousness, so that they think not that they need the righteousness of faith, except they be cast down from all self-confidence – and further, as they are inebriated with the sweetness of lusts, and sunk in deep self-security, so that they are not-easily roused to seek righteousness, except they are struck down by the terror of divine judgment – the Apostle proceeds to do two things – to convince men of iniquity, and to shake off the torpor of those whom he proves guilty.

He *first* condemns all mankind from the beginning of the world for ingratitude, because they recognized not the workman in his extraordinary work: nay, when they were constrained to acknowledge him, they did not duly honor his majesty, but in their vanity profaned and dishonored it. Thus all became guilty of impiety, a wickedness more detestable than any thing else. And that he might more clearly show that all had departed from the Lord, he recounts the filthy and horrible crimes of which men everywhere became guilty: and this is a manifest proof, that they had degenerated from God, since these sins are evidences of divine wrath, which appear not except in the ungodly. And as the Jews and some of the Gentiles, while they covered their inward depravity by the veil of outward holiness, seemed to be in no way chargeable with such crimes, and hence thought themselves exempt from the common sentence of condemnation, the Apostle directs his discourse against this fictitious holiness; and as this mask before men cannot be taken away from saintlings (sanctulis – petty saints), he summons them to the tribunal of God, whose eyes no latent evils can escape. Having afterwards divided his subject, he places apart both the Jews and the Gentiles before the tribunal of God. He cuts off from the Gentiles the excuse which they pleaded from ignorance, because conscience was to them a law, and by this they were abundantly convicted as guilty. He chiefly urges on the Jews that from which they took their defense, even the written law; and as they were proved to have transgressed it, they could not free themselves from the charge of iniquity, and a sentence against them had already been pronounced by the mouth of God himself. He at the same time obviates any objection which might have been made by them – that the covenant of God, which was the symbol of holiness, would have been violated, if they were not to be distinguished from others. Here he first shows, that they excelled not others by the right of the covenant, for they had by their unfaithfulness departed from it: and then, that he might not derogate from the perpetuity of the divine promise, he concedes to them some privilege as arising from the covenant; but it proceeded from the mercy of God, and not from their merits. So that with regard to their own qualifications they were on a level with the Gentiles. He then proves by the authority of Scripture, that both Jews and Gentiles were all sinners; and he also slightly refers to the use of the law.

Having wholly deprived all mankind of their confidence in their own virtue and of their boast of righteousness, and laid them prostrate by the severity of God's judgment, he returns to what he had before laid down as his subject – that we are justified by faith; and he explains what faith is, and how the righteousness of Christ is by it attained by us. To these things he adds at the end of the third chapter a remarkable conclusion, with the view of beating down the fierceness of human pride, that it might not dare to raise up itself against the grace of God: and lest the Jews should confine so great a favor of God to their own nation, he also by the way claims it in behalf of the Gentiles.

In the fourth chapter he reasons from example; which he adduces as being evident, and hence not liable to be cavilled at; and it is that of Abraham, who, being the father of the faithful ought to be deemed a pattern and a kind of universal example. Having then proved that he was justified by faith, the Apostle teaches us that we ought to maintain no other way of justification. And here he shows, that it follows from the rule of contraries, that the righteousness of works ceases to exist, since the righteousness of faith is introduced. And he confirms this by the declaration of David, who, by making the blessedness of man to depend on the mercy of God, takes it away from works, as they are incapable of making a man blessed. He then treats more fully what he had before shortly referred to – that the Jews had no reason to raise themselves above the Gentiles, as this felicity is equally common to them both, since Scripture declares that Abraham obtained this righteousness in an uncircumcised state: and here he takes the opportunity of adding some remarks on the use of circumcision. He afterwards subjoins, that the promise of salvation depends on God's goodness alone: for were it to depend on the law, it could not bring peace to consciences, which it ought to confirm, nor could it attain its own fulfillment. Hence, that it may be sure and certain, we must, in embracing it, regard the truth of God alone, and not ourselves, and follow the example of Abraham, who, turning away from himself, had regard only to the power of God. At the end of the chapter, in order to make a more general application of the adduced example, he introduces several comparisons.

In the fifth chapter, after having touched on the fruit and effects of the righteousness of faith, he is almost wholly taken up with illustrations, in order to make the point clearer. For, deducing an argument from one greater, he shows how much we, who have been redeemed and reconciled to God, ought to expect from his love; which was so abundantly poured forth towards us, when we were sinners and lost, that he gave for us his only-begotten and beloved Son. He afterwards makes comparisons between sin and free righteousness, between Christ and Adam, between death and life, between the law and grace: it hence appears that our evils, however vast they are, are swallowed up by the infinite mercy of God.

He proceeds in the sixth chapter to mention the sanctification which we obtain in Christ. It is indeed natural to our flesh, as soon as it has had some slight knowledge of grace, to indulge quietly in its own vices and lusts, as though it had become free from all danger: but Paul, on the contrary, contends here, that we cannot partake of the righteousness of Christ, except we also lay hold on sanctification. He reasons from baptism, by which we are initiated into a participation of Christ (*per quem in Christi participationem initiamur*); and in it we are buried together with Christ, so that being dead in ourselves, we may through his life be raised to a newness of life. It then follows, that without regeneration no one can put on his righteousness. He hence deduces exhortations as to purity and holiness of life, which must necessarily appear in those who have been removed from the kingdom of sin to the kingdom of righteousness, the sinful indulgence of the flesh, which seeks in Christ a greater liberty in sinning, being cast aside. He makes also a brief mention of the law as being abrogated; and in the abrogation of this the New Testament shines forth eminently; for together with the remission of sins, it contains the promise of the Holy Spirit.

In the *seventh* chapter he enters on a full discussion on the use of the law, which he had pointed out before as it were by the finger, while he had another subject in hand: he assigns a reason why we are loosed from the law, and that is, because it serves only for condemnation. Lest, however, he should expose the law to reproach, he clears it in the strongest terms from any imputation of this kind; for he shows that through our fault it is that the law, which was given for life, turns to be an occasion of death. He also explains how sin is by it increased. He then proceeds to describe the contest between the Spirit and the flesh, which the children of God find in themselves, as long as they are surrounded by the prison of a mortal body; for they carry with them the relics of lust, by which they are continually prevented from yielding full obedience to the law.

The *eighth* chapter contains abundance of consolations, in order that the consciences of the faithful, having heard of the disobedience which he had before proved, or rather imperfect obedience, might not be terrified and dejected. But that the ungodly might not hence flatter themselves, he first testifies that this privilege belongs to none but to the regenerated, in whom the Spirit of God lives and prevails. He unfolds then two things – that all who are planted by the Spirit in the Lord Jesus Christ, are beyond the danger or the chance of condemnation, however burdened they may yet be with sins; and, also, that all who remain in the flesh, being without the sanctification of the Spirit, are by no means partakers of this great benefit. He afterwards explains how great is the certainty of our confidence, since the Spirit of God by his own testimony drives away all doubts and fears. He further shows, for the purpose of anticipating objections, that the certainty of eternal life cannot be intercepted or disturbed by present evils, to which we are subject in this life; but that, on the contrary, our salvation is promoted by such trials, and that the value of it, when compared with our present miseries, renders them as nothing. He confirms this by the example of Christ, who, being the first-begotten and holding the highest station in the family of God, is the pattern to which we must all be conformed. And, in the last place, as though all things were made secure, he concludes in a most exulting strain, and boldly triumphs over all the power and artifices of Satan.

But as most were much concerned on seeing the Jews, the first guardians and heirs of the covenant, rejecting Christ, for they hence concluded, that either the covenant was transferred from the posterity of Abraham, who disregarded the fulfilling of the covenant, or that he, who made no better provision for the people of Israel, was not the promised Redeemer – he meets this objection at the beginning of the *ninth* chapter. Having then spoken of his love towards his own nation, that he might not appear to speak from hatred, and having also duly mentioned those privileges by which they excelled others, he gently glides to the point he had in view, that is, to remove the offence, which arose from their own blindness. And he divides the children of Abraham into two classes, that he might show that not all who descended from him according to the flesh, are to be counted for seed and become partakers of the grace of the covenant; but that, on the contrary, aliens become his children, when they possess his faith. He brings forward

Jacob and Esau as examples. He then refers us back here to the election of God, on which the whole matter necessarily depends. Besides, as election rests on the mercy of God alone, it is in vain to seek the cause of it in the worthiness of man. There is, on the other hand, rejection (*rejectio*), the justice of which is indubitable, and yet there is no higher cause for it than the will of God. Near the end of the chapter, he sets forth the calling of the Gentiles and the rejection of the Jews as proved by the predictions of the Prophets.

Having again begun, in the *tenth* chapter, by testifying his love towards the Jews, he declares that a vain confidence in their own works was the cause of their ruin; and lest they should pretend the law, he obviates their objection, and says, that we are even by the law itself led as it were by the hand to the righteousness of faith. He adds that this righteousness is through God's bountiful goodness offered indiscriminately to all nations, but that it is only apprehended by those, whom the Lord through special favor illuminates. And he states, that more from the Gentiles than from the Jews would obtain this benefit, as predicted both by Moses and by Isaiah; the one having plainly prophesied of the calling of the Gentiles, and the other of the hardening of the Jews.

The question still remained, "Is there not a difference between the seed of Abraham and other nations according to the covenant of God?" Proceeding to answer this question, he first reminds us, that the work of God is not to be limited to what is seen by our eyes, since the elect often escape our observation; for Elias was formerly mistaken, when he thought that religion had become wholly extinct among the Israelites, when there were still remaining seven thousand; and, further, that we must not be perplexed by the number of unbelievers, who, as we see, hate the gospel. He at length alleges, that the covenant of God continues even to the posterity of Abraham according to the flesh, but to those only whom the Lord by a free election hath predestinated. He then turns to the Gentiles, and speaks to them, lest they should become insolent on account of their adoption, and exult over the Jews as having been rejected since they excel them in nothing, except in the free favor of the Lord, which ought to make them the more humble; and that this has not wholly departed from the seed of Abraham, for the Jews were at length to be provoked to emulation by the faith of the Gentiles, so that God would gather all Israel to himself.

The *three* chapters which follow are admonitory, but they are various in their contents. The *twelfth* chapter contains general precepts on Christian life. The *thirteenth*, for the; most part, speaks of the authority of magistrates. We may hence undoubtedly gather that there were then some unruly persons, who thought Christian liberty could not exist without overturning the civil power. But that Paul might not appear to impose on the Church any duties but those of love, he declares that this obedience is included in what love requires. He afterwards adds those precepts, which he had before mentioned, for the guidance of our conduct. In the *next* chapter he gives an exhortation, especially necessary in that age: for as there were those who through obstinate superstition insisted on the observance of Mosaic rites, and could not endure the neglect of them without being most grievously offended; so there were others, who, being convinced of their abrogation, and anxious to pull down superstition, designedly showed their contempt of such things. Both parties offended through being too intemperate; for the superstitious condemned the others as being despisers of God's law; and the latter in their turn unreasonably ridiculed the simplicity of the former. Therefore the Apostle recommends to both a befitting moderation, deporting the one from superciliousness and insult, and the other from excessive moroseness: and he also prescribes the best way of exercising Christian liberty, by keeping within the boundaries of love and edification; and he faithfully provides for the weak, while he forbids them to do any thing in opposition to conscience.

The *fifteenth* chapter begins with a repetition of the general argument, as a conclusion of the whole subject – that the strong should use their strength in endeavors to confirm the weak. And as there was a perpetual discord, with regard to the Mosaic ceremonies, between the Jews and the Gentiles, he allays all emulation between them by removing the cause of contention; for he shows, that the salvation of both rested on the mercy of God alone; on which relying, they ought to lay aside all high thoughts of themselves and being thereby connected together in the hope of the same inheritance, they ought mutually to embrace one another. And being anxious, in the last place, to turn aside for the purpose of commending his own apostleship, which secured no small authority to his doctrine, he takes occasion to defend himself, and to deprecate presumption in having assumed with so much confidence the office of teacher among them. He further gives them some hope of his coming to them, which he had mentioned at the beginning, but had hitherto in vain looked for and tried to effect; and he states the reason which at that time hindered him, and that was, because the churches of Macedonia and Achaia had committed to him the care of conveying to Jerusalem those alms which they had given to relieve the wants of the faithful in that city.

The *last* chapter is almost entirely taken up with salutations, though scattered with some precepts worthy of all attention; and concludes with a remarkable prayer.

The commentaries on Romans are by John Calvin and Robert Haldane.

ROMANS 1

1 Paul, a servant of Jesus Christ, called to be an apostle, separated unto the gospel of God,

2 (Which he had promised afore by his prophets in the holy scriptures,)

3 Concerning his Son Jesus Christ our Lord, which was made of the seed of David according to the flesh;

4 And declared to be the Son of God with power, according to the spirit of holiness, by the resurrection from the dead:

5 By whom we have received grace and apostleship, for obedience to the faith among all nations, for his name:

6 Among whom are ye also the called of Jesus Christ:

7 To all that be in Rome, beloved of God, called to be saints: Grace to you and peace from God our Father, and the Lord Jesus Christ.

8 First, I thank my God through Jesus Christ for you all, that your faith is spoken of throughout the whole world.

9 For God is my witness, whom I serve with my spirit in the gospel of his Son, that without ceasing I make mention of you always in my prayers;

10 Making request, if by any means now at length I might have a prosperous journey by the will of God to come unto you.

11 For I long to see you, that I may impart unto you some spiritual gift, to the end ye may be established;

12 That is, that I may be comforted together with you by the mutual faith both of you and me.

13 Now I would not have you ignorant, brethren, that oftentimes I purposed to come unto you, (but was let hitherto,) that I might have some fruit among you also, even as among other Gentiles.

14 I am debtor both to the Greeks, and to the Barbarians; both to the wise, and to the unwise.

15 So, as much as in me is, I am ready to preach the gospel to you that are at Rome also.

16 For I am not ashamed of the gospel of Christ: for it is the power of God unto salvation to every one that believeth; to the Jew first, and also to the Greek.

17 For therein is the righteousness of

ROMANS 1

1. Paul

Those who think that the Apostle attained this name as a trophy for having brought Sergius, the proconsul, to the faith of Christ, are confuted by the testimony of Luke, who shows that he was so called before that time (Acts 13: 7,9). Nor does it seem probable to me, that it was given him when he was converted to Christ; though this idea so pleased Augustine, that he took occasion refinedly to philosophize on the subject; for he says, that from a proud Saul he was made a very little (*parvulum*) disciple of Christ. More probable is the opinion of Origen, who thought that he had two names; for it is not unlikely to be true, that his name, Saul, derived from his kindred, was given him by his parents to indicate his religion and his descent; and that his other name, Paul, was added, to show his right to Roman citizenship; they would not have this honor, then highly valued, to be otherwise than made evident; but they did not so much value it as to withhold a proof of his Israelitic descent. But he has commonly taken the name Paul in his Epistles, and it may be for the following reasons: because in the churches to which he wrote, it was more known and more common, more acceptable in the Roman empire, and less known among his own nation. It was indeed his duty to avoid the foolish suspicion and hatred under which the name of a Jew then labored among the Romans and in their provinces, and to abstain from inflaming the rage of his own countrymen, and to take care of himself.

A servant of Jesus Christ, etc

He signalizes himself with these distinctions for the purpose of securing more authority to his doctrine; and this he seeks to secure by two things – first, by asserting his call to the Apostleship; and secondly, by showing that his call was not unconnected with the Church of Rome: for it was of great importance that he should be deemed an Apostle through God's call, and that he should be known as one destined for the Roman Church. He therefore says, that he was a *servant* of Christ, and called to the office of an Apostle, thereby intimating that he had not presumptuously intruded into that office. He then adds, that he was *chosen*, by which he more fully confirms the fact, that he was not one of the people, but a particular Apostle of the Lord. Consistently with this, he had before proceeded from what was general to what was particular, as the Apostleship was an especial service; for all who sustain the office of teaching are to be deemed Christ's servants, but Apostles, in point of honor, far exceed all others. But the *choosing* for the gospel, etc., which he afterwards mentions, expresses the end as well as the use of the Apostleship; for he intended briefly to show for what purpose he was called to that function.

ROMANS 1:1–15

1. **Paul, a servant of Jesus Christ, called to be an apostle, separated unto the Gospel of God.** Conformably to the practice of antiquity, Paul commences his Epistle by prefixing his name, title, and designation. He had, as was usual among his countrymen, two names: by the first, as a Jew, he was known in his own land; by the second, among the Gentiles. Formerly his name was SAUL, but after the occurrence related of him, Acts 13: 9, he was called PAUL. Paul was of unmingled Jewish descent, a Hebrew of the Hebrews, born at Tarsus in Cilicia, but educated at Jerusalem; a Pharisee by profession, and distinguished among the disciples of Gamaliel, one of the most celebrated teachers of his age and nation. Before his conversion, he was an ardent and bigoted supporter of the traditions of his fathers, violently opposed to the humbling doctrines of Christianity, and a cruel persecutor of the Church.

Separated unto the Gospel of God. This may regard either God's eternal purpose concerning Paul, or His pre-ordination of him to be a preacher of the Gospel, to which he was separated from his mother's womb, as it was said to Jeremiah, 1: 5.

2. **Which He had promised afore by His prophets in the Holy Scriptures.** By declaring that the Gospel had been before promised, Paul tacitly repels the accusation that it was a novel doctrine. At the same time, he states its Divine origin as a reason why nothing new is to be admitted in religion. He further shows in what respect the Old and New Testaments differ – not as containing two religions essentially dissimilar, but as exhibiting the same grand truth – predicted, prefigured, and fulfilled.

3. **Concerning His Son Jesus Christ our Lord, which was made of the seed of David according to the flesh.** The Gospel of God concerns His Son. The whole of it is comprised in the knowledge of Jesus Christ; so that whoever departs one step from Him, departs from the Gospel. For as Jesus Christ is the Divine image of the Father, He is set before us as the real object of our faith.

4. **And declared to be the Son of God with power, according to the Spirit of holiness, by the resurrection from the dead.** Declared to be the Son of God.

With power. Some explain the meaning of this to be, that by His resurrection Jesus Christ was powerfully declared to be the Son of God. But He was not merely powerfully declared – which would intimate the high degree of the evidence – but, according to the Apostle, He was absolutely declared to be the Son of God. Some, again, suppose that He was declared to be the Son of God by the power of the Father who raised Him up.

5 **By whom we have received grace and apostleship, for obedience to the faith among all nations, for His name.** One of the first acts of the power of Jesus Christ, after His resurrection, was to bestow His Spirit and His grace on those who were chosen by Him, to qualify them to be His witnesses and the heralds of His Gospel.

6. **Among whom are ye also the called of Jesus Christ.** Those to whom Paul wrote, were included among the nations to whom his commission extended.

10. **Making request, if by any means now at length I might have a prosperous journey, by the will of God, to come unto you.** Making request. Paul's affection for those to whom he wrote impelled him, not once or twice with a passing wish, but at all times, to desire to be present with them, notwithstanding the inconveniences of so long and perilous a journey. He asks of God that, by some means now at length, he might be permitted to visit them. Thus Christian love searches out new objects on which to exercise itself, and extends itself even to those who are personally unknown.

15. **So, as much as in me, I am ready to preach the gospel to you that are at Rome also.**

Paul was always zealous to do his duty; at the same time, he always acknowledged his dependence on God. This is an example which Christians ought to imitate on all occasions, never to deviate from the path of duty, but to leave events in the hands of God. The contrary

God revealed from faith to faith: as it is written, The just shall live by faith.

18 For the wrath of God is revealed from heaven against all ungodliness and unrighteousness of men, who hold the truth in unrighteousness;

19 Because that which may be known of God is manifest in them; for God hath shewed it unto them.

20 For the invisible things of him from the creation of the world are clearly seen, being understood by the things that are made, even his eternal power and Godhead; so that they are without excuse:

21 Because that, when they knew God, they glorified him not as God, neither were thankful; but became vain in their imaginations, and their foolish heart was darkened.

22 Professing themselves to be wise, they became fools,

23 And changed the glory of the uncorruptible God into an image made like to corruptible man, and to birds, and four-footed beasts, and creeping things.

24 Wherefore God also gave them up to uncleanness through the lusts of their own hearts, to dishonor their own bodies between themselves:

25 Who changed the truth of God into a lie, and worshipped and served the creature more than the Creator, who is blessed for ever. Amen.

26 For this cause God gave them up unto vile affections: for even their women did change the natural use into that which is against nature:

27 And likewise also the men, leaving the natural use of the woman, burned in their lust one toward another; men with men working that which is unseemly, and receiving in themselves that recompence of their error which was meet.

28 And even as they did not like to retain God in their knowledge, God gave them over to a reprobate mind, to do those things which are not convenient;

29 Being filled with all unrighteousness, fornication, wickedness, covetousness, maliciousness; full of envy, murder, debate, deceit, malignity; whisperers,

30 Backbiters, haters of God, despiteful, proud, boasters, inventors of evil things, disobedient to parents,

31 Without understanding, covenant-

By saying then that he was servant of Christ, he declared what he had in common with other teachers; by claiming to himself the title of an Apostle, he put himself before others; but as no authority is due to him who willfully intrudes himself, he reminds us, that he was appointed by God.

Then the meaning is – that Paul was a servant of Christ, not any kind of servant, but an Apostle, and that by the call of God, and not by presumptuous intrusion: then follows a clearer explanation of the Apostolic office – it was ordained for the preaching of the Gospel. For I cannot agree with those who refer this call of which he speaks to the eternal election of God; and who understand the separation, either that from his mother's womb, which he mentions in Galatians 1: 15, or that which Luke refers to, when Paul was appointed for the Gentiles: but I consider that he simply glories in having God as the author of his call, lest any one should think that he had through his own rashness taken this honor to himself.

We must here observe, that all are not fitted for the ministry of the word; for a special call is necessary: and even those who seem particularly fitted ought to take heed lest they thrust themselves in without a call. But as to the character of the Apostolic and of the Episcopal call, we shall consider it in another place. We must further observe, that the office of an Apostle is the preaching of the gospel. It hence appears what just objects of ridicule are those dumb dogs, who render themselves conspicuous only by their mitre and their crook, and boast themselves to be the successors of the Apostles!

The word, servant, imports nothing else but a minister, for it refers to what is official. I mention this to remove the mistake of those who too much refine on this expression and think that there is here to be understood a contrast between the service of Moses and that of Christ.

2. Which he had before promised

As the suspicion of being new subtracts much from the authority of a doctrine, he confirms the faith of the gospel by antiquity; as though he said, "Christ came not on the earth unexpectedly, nor did he introduce a doctrine of a new kind and not heard of before, inasmuch as he, and his gospel too, had been promised and expected from the beginning of the world." But as antiquity is often fabulous, he brings witnesses, and those approved, even the Prophets of God, that he might remove every suspicion. He in the third place adds, that their testimonies were duly recorded, that is, in the Holy Scriptures.

We may learn from this passage what the gospel is: he teaches us, not that it was promulgated by the Prophets but only promised. If then the Prophets promised the gospel, it follows, that it was revealed, when our Lord was at

of this is generally the case. Christians are often more anxious and perplexed about their success, than with respect to their duty.

ROMANS 1:16–32

The Apostle now announces, in brief but comprehensive terms, the grand subject which occupies the first five chapters of this Epistle, namely, the doctrine of justification by faith.

16. For I am not ashamed of the Gospel of Christ; for it is the power of God unto salvation to every one that believeth; to the Jew first, and also to the Greek.

I am not ashamed. – Paul here follows up what he had just said of his readiness to preach the Gospel at Rome, by declaring that he was not ashamed of it. This would also convey a caution to those whom he addressed against giving way to a strong temptation to which they were exposed, and which was no doubt a means of deterring many from embracing the Gospel, to whom it was preached. He knew from personal experience the opposition which the Gospel everywhere encountered.

17. For therein is the righteousness of God revealed from faith to faith; as it is written, The just shall live by faith.

The righteousness of God. – This phrase may, according to circumstances, mean either the personal attribute of God, or, as in this place, the righteousness which God has provided, which He has effected, and which He imputes for justification to all His elect. It is through this righteousness, revealed in the Gospel, that the Gospel is the power of God unto salvation.

22. Professing themselves to be wise, they became fools.

It appears that, by the term **wise,** the Apostle intended to point out the philosophers, – that is to say, in general, those who were most esteemed for their knowledge, like those among the Greeks who were celebrated by the titles either of men wise or philosophers.

28. And even as they did not like to retain God in their knowledge, God gave them

over to a reprobate mind, to do those things which are not convenient.

The Apostle shows here how justly the Pagan idolaters were abandoned since they had so far departed from the right knowledge of God. In the 18th verse he had declared that the wrath of God was revealed against all ungodliness and unrighteousness of men. He had now conclusively established the first charge of **ungodliness** against the Gentiles, adding to it their consequent abandonment to the vilest affections; he next proceeds to demonstrate their **unrighteousness.**

God also gave them up to a **reprobate mind.** It denotes a mind judicially blinded, so as not to discern the difference between things distinguished even by the light of nature. Thus the dark eclipse of their understanding concerning Divine things, which they had despised and rejected, had been followed by another general eclipse respecting things human, to which they had applied themselves, and in this consisted the proportion which God observed in their punishment. They did not act according to right reason and judgment towards God, – this is their crime; they did not act according to it among themselves in society, – this was the effect of the abandonment of God, and became their punishment. This passage clearly shows that all that remains of moral uprightness among men is from God, who restrains and sets bounds to the force of their perversity.

32. Who, knowing the judgment of God, that they which commit such things are worthy of death, not only do the same, but have pleasure in them that do them.

Knowing the judgment of God. – Sentence or ordinance of God. This the heathens knew, from the work of the law written in their hearts. Although they had almost entirely stifled in themselves the dictates of conscience, it did not cease, in some measure, to remonstrate against the unworthiness of their conduct, and to threaten the wrath of God, which their sins deserved. They recognized it by some remains they had of right notions of the Godhead, and by which they still understood that God was judge of the world; and this was confirmed to

breakers, without natural affection, implacable, unmerciful:

32 Who knowing the judgment of God, that they which commit such things are worthy of death, not only do the same, but have pleasure in them that do them.

ROMANS 2

1 Therefore thou art inexcusable, O man, whosoever thou art that judgest: for wherein thou judgest another, thou condemnest thyself; for thou that judgest doest the same things.

2 But we are sure that the judgment of God is according to truth against them which commit such things.

3 And thinkest thou this, O man, that judgest them which do such things, and doest the same, that thou shalt escape the judgment of God?

4 Or despisest thou the riches of his goodness and forbearance and longsuffering; not knowing that the goodness of God leadeth thee to repentance?

5 But after thy hardness and impenitent heart treasurest up unto thyself wrath against the day of wrath and revelation of the righteous judgment of God;

6 Who will render to every man according to his deeds:

7 To them who by patient continuance in well doing seek for glory and honor and immortality, eternal life:

8 But unto them that are contentious, and do not obey the truth, but obey unrighteousness, indignation and wrath,

9 Tribulation and anguish, upon every soul of man that doeth evil, of the Jew first, and also of the Gentile;

10 But glory, honor, and peace, to every man that worketh good, to the Jew first, and also to the Gentile:

11 For there is no respect of persons with God.

12 For as many as have sinned without law shall also perish without law: and as many as have sinned in the law shall be judged by the law;

13 (For not the hearers of the law are just before God, but the doers of the law shall be justified.

14 For when the Gentiles, which have not the law, do by nature the things contained in the law, these, having not the

length manifested in the flesh. They are then mistaken who confound the promises with the gospel, since the gospel is properly the appointed preaching of Christ as manifested, in whom the promises themselves are exhibited.

3. Concerning his own Son

This is a remarkable passage, by which we are taught that the whole gospel is included in Christ, so that if any removes one step from Christ, he withdraws himself from the gospel. For since he is the living and express image of the Father, it is no wonder, that he alone is set before us as one to whom our whole faith is to be directed and in whom it is to center. It is then a definition of the gospel, by which Paul expresses what is summarily comprehended in it. I have rendered the words which follow, Jesus Christ our Lord, in the same case; which seems to me to be most agreeable with the context. We hence learn, that he who has made a due proficiency in the knowledge of Christ, has acquired every thing which can be learned from the gospel; and, on the other hand, that those who seek to be wise without Christ, are not only foolish, but even completely insane.

ROMANS 2

1. Therefore inexcusable art thou, O man

This reproof is directed against hypocrites, who dazzle the eyes of men by displays of outward sanctity, and even think themselves to be accepted before God, as though they had given him full satisfaction.

2. But we know that the judgment of God

The design of Paul is to shake off from hypocrites their self-complacencies, that they may not think that they can really gain any thing, though they be applauded by the world, and though they regard themselves guiltless; for a far different trial awaits them in heaven. But as he charges them with inward impurity, which, being hid from the eyes of men, cannot be proved and convicted by human testimonies, he summons them to the tribunal of God, to whom darkness itself is not hid, and by whose judgment the case of sinners, be they willing or unwilling, must be determined.

3. And thinkest thou, O man

As rhetoricians teach us, that we ought not to proceed to give strong reproof before the crime be proved, Paul may seem to some to have acted unwisely here for having passed so severe a censure, when he had not yet proved the accusation which he had brought forward. But the fact is otherwise; for he adduced not his accusation before men, but appealed to the judgment of conscience; and thus he deemed that proved which he had in view – that they could

them by examples of Divine vengeance which sometimes passed before their eyes.

ROMANS 2

1. Therefore thou art inexcusable, O man, whosoever thou art that judges: for wherein thou judgest another, thou condemnest thyself; for thou that judgest doest the same things.

Therefore. – This particle introduces a conclusion, not from anything in the preceding chapter, but to establish a truth from what follows. The Apostle had proved the guilt of the Gentiles, who, since they had a revelation vouchsafed to them in the works of God, though they did not possess His word, were inexcusable. The Jews, who had His word, yet practiced the same things for which the former were condemned, must therefore also be inexcusable. In the sequel, he specifies and unfolds the charge thus generally preferred.

2. But we are sure that the judgment of God is according to truth against them which commit such things.

Paul proceeds here to preclude a thought that might present itself, and to stifle it as it were, before its birth. It might be suggested that the judgment of God – that is, the sentence of condemnation with respect to transgressors – is not uniform; that He condemns some and acquits others, as it pleases Him; and therefore, although the Jew does the same things as the Gentile, it does not follow that he will be held equally culpable, – God having extended indulgence to the one, which He has not vouchsafed to the other. The Jew, then, does not hold himself guilty when he condemns the Gentile, although he does the same things. This is the odious and perverse imagination which the Apostle here repels.

11. For there is no respect of persons with God.

Whatever difference of order there may be between the Jew and the Gentile, that difference does not change the foundation and substance of the judgment. To have respect to the appearance of persons, or to accept of persons,

is the vice of an iniquitous judge, who in some way violates justice; but the Divine judgment cannot commit such a fault. Besides, we must never lose sight of the train of the Apostle's reasoning. His design is to show that the Jews, being, as they really are, sinners equally with the Gentiles, are involved with them in the same condemnation.

The declaration that God has no respect of persons is frequently quoted as militating against the doctrine of election; but it has no bearing on the subject. It relates to men's character, and God's judgment according to character. Every man will be judged according to his works. This, however, does not say that God may not choose some eternally to life, and give them faith, and create them unto good works, according to which, as evidences that they belong to Christ, they shall be judged. God's sovereign love to the elect is manifested in a way that not only shows Him to be just in their justification, but also true to His declaration with respect to the future judgment.

12. For as many as have sinned without law shall also perish without law: and as many as have sinned in (or under) law shall be judged by law.

Here Paul explains the equality of the judgment, both with respect to the Gentiles and the Jews.

22. Thou that sayest a man should not commit adultery? thou that abhorrest idols, dost thou commit sacrilege?

Oppression of the poor, and adultery, are the crimes with which the Jews were chiefly charged by our Lord. **Abhorrest idols.** – The Jews now generally abhorred the idolatry to which in the former ages of their history they were so prone, even in its grossest forms. The word in the original signifies to abominate, alluding to things most disagreeable to the senses. This is according to God's account of the sin of idolatry. According to human standards of morality, idolatry appears a very innocent thing, or at least not very sinful; but in Scripture it is classed among the works of the flesh, Galatians 5:20, and is called "abominable," 1 Peter 4:3. It robs God of His glory,

law, are a law unto themselves:

15 Which shew the work of the law written in their hearts, their conscience also bearing witness, and their thoughts the mean while accusing or else excusing one another;)

16 In the day when God shall judge the secrets of men by Jesus Christ according to my gospel.

17 Behold, thou art called a Jew, and restest in the law, and makest thy boast of God,

18 And knowest his will, and approvest the things that are more excellent, being instructed out of the law;

19 And art confident that thou thyself art a guide of the blind, a light of them which are in darkness,

20 An instructor of the foolish, a teacher of babes, which hast the form of knowledge and of the truth in the law.

21 Thou therefore which teachest another, teachest thou not thyself? thou that preachest a man should not steal, dost thou steal?

22 Thou that sayest a man should not commit adultery, dost thou commit adultery? thou that abhorrest idols, dost thou commit sacrilege?

23 Thou that makest thy boast of the law, through breaking the law dishonorest thou God?

24 For the name of God is blasphemed among the Gentiles through you, as it is written.

25 For circumcision verily profiteth, if thou keep the law: but if thou be a breaker of the law, thy circumcision is made uncircumcision.

26 Therefore if the. uncircumcision keep the righteousness of the law, shall not his uncircumcision be counted for circumcision?

27 And shall not uncircumcision which is by nature, if it fulfil the law, judge thee, who by the letter and circumcision dost transgress the law?

28 For he is not a Jew, which is one outwardly; neither is that circumcision, which is outward in the flesh:

29 But he is a Jew, which is one inwardly; and circumcision is that of the heart, in the spirit, and not in the letter; whose praise is not of men, but of God.

not deny their iniquity, if they examined themselves and submitted to the scrutiny of God's tribunal. And it was not without urgent necessity, that he with so much sharpness and severity rebuked their fictitious sanctity; for men of this class will with astonishing security trust in themselves, except their vain confidence be forcibly shaken from them. Let us then remember, that this is the best mode of dealing with hypocrisy, in order to awaken it from its inebriety, that is, to draw it forth to the light of God's judgment.

9. To the Jew first

He simply places, I have no doubt, the Jew in opposition to the Gentile; for those whom he calls Greeks he will presently call Gentiles. But the Jews take the precedence in this case, for they had, in preference to others, both the promises and the threatenings of the law; as though he had said, "This is the universal rule of the divine judgment; it shall begin with the Jews, and it shall include the whole world."

11. There is no respect of persons

He has hitherto generally arraigned all mortals as guilty; but now he begins to bring home his accusation to the Jews and to the Gentiles separately: and at the same time he teaches us, that it is no objection that there is a difference between them, but that they are both without any distinction exposed to eternal death. The Gentiles pretended ignorance as their defense; the Jews gloried in the honor of having the law: from the former he takes away their subterfuge, and he deprives the latter of their false and empty boasting.

14. For when the Gentiles

He now states what proves the former clause; for he did not think it enough to condemn us by mere assertion, and only to pronounce on us the just judgment of God; but he proceeds to prove this by reasons, in order to excite us to a greater desire for Christ, and to a greater love towards him. He indeed shows that ignorance is in vain pretended as an excuse by the Gentiles, since they prove by their own deeds that they have some rule of righteousness: for there is no nation so lost to every thing human, that it does not keep within the limits of some laws. Since then all nations, of themselves and without a monitor, are disposed to make laws for themselves, it is beyond all question evident that they have some notions of justice and rectitude, which the Greeks call preconceptions, and which are implanted by nature in the hearts of men. They have then a law, though they are without law: for though they have not a written law, they are yet by no means wholly destitute of the knowledge of what is right and just; as they could not otherwise distinguish between vice and virtue; the first of which they restrain by punishment, and the latter they commend, and manifest their approbation of it by honoring it with re-

transferring it to the creature. **Commit sacrilege.** – The word here used literally applies to the robbery of temples, for which the Jews and many opportunities, as well as of appropriating to themselves what was devoted to religion, as is complained of, Nehemiah 13:10; and of robbing God in tithes and offerings, Malachi 3:8; also of violating and profaning things sacred.

24. For the name of God is blasphemed among the Gentiles through you, as it is written.

The charge alleged here against the Jews, is not that they themselves blasphemed the name of God as some understand it, but that they gave occasion to the heathen to blaspheme. The Apostle is not charging the Jews with speaking evil of God, or with one particular sin, but with the breach of their law in general. He here confirms what he had just said to this purpose in the foregoing verse, by the authority of Scripture. Many suppose that he refers to a passage of Isaiah 52:5, where the Prophet says, "And my name continually every day is blasphemed." But there the Prophet does not charge the Jews as having, by their bad conduct, occasioned the injury which the name of God received. He ascribes it, on the contrary, to the Assyrians, by whom they had been subjected. In the passage before us, the reference is to Ezekiel 36:17–20, where it is evident that the Jews, by the greatness and the number of their sins, had given occasion to the Gentiles to insult and blaspheme the holy name of God, which is precisely the meaning of the Apostle.

26. Therefore, if the uncircumcision keep the righteousness of the law, shall not his uncircumcision be counted for circumcision?

The Apostle does not mean to affirm that an uncircumcised Gentile can fulfill the righteousness of the law, nor does he here retract what he had said in the first chapter respecting the corruption and guilt of the Gentiles, but he supposes a case in regard to them like that concerning the Jews in the preceding verse. This hypothetical mode of reasoning is common with Paul, of which we have an example

in this same chapter, where he says that **the doers of the law shall be justified;** of whom, however, in the conclusion of his argument, ch. 3:19, he affirms that none can be found. The supposition, then, as to the obedience of the Gentile, though in itself impossible, is made in order to prove that, before the judgment seat of God, neither circumcision nor uncircumcision enters at all into consideration for justification or condemnation. If an uncircumcised Gentile kept the law, his uncircumcision would avail as much as the circumcision of the Jew. The reason of this is, that the judgment of God regards only the observance or the violation of the law, and not extraneous advantages or disadvantages, and, as is said above, with God there is no respect of persons. In reality, then, the Jews and Gentiles were on a level as to the impossibility of salvation by the law; in confirmation of which truth, the inquiry here introduced is for the conviction of the Jew on this important point.

29. The object of the whole of this chapter is to show that the Jews are sinners, violators of the law as well as the Gentiles, and consequently that they cannot be justified before God by their works; but that, on the contrary, however superior their advantages are to those of the Gentiles, they can only expect from His strict justice, condemnation. The Jews esteemed it the highest honor to belong to their nation, and they gloried over all other nations. An uncircumcised person was by them regarded with abhorrence. They did not look to character, but to circumcision or uncircumcision. Nothing, then, could be more cogent, or more calculated to arrest the attention of the Jews, than this argument respecting the name in which they gloried, and circumcision, their distinguishing national rite, with which Paul here follows up what he had said concerning the demands of the law, and of their outward transgressions of its precepts. He had dwelt, in the preceding part of this chapter, on their more glaring and atrocious outward violations of the law, as theft, adultery, and sacrilege, by which they openly dishonored God. Now he enters into the recesses of the heart, of which, even if their outward conduct had been blame-

ROMANS 3

1 What advantage then hath the Jew? or what profit is there of circumcision?

2 Much every way: chiefly, because that unto them were committed the oracles of God.

3 For what if some did not believe? shall their unbelief make the faith of God without effect?

4 God forbid: yea, let God be true, but every man a liar; as it is written, That thou mightest be justified in thy sayings, and mightest overcome when thou art judged.

5 But if our unrighteousness commend the righteousness of God, what shall we say? Is God unrighteous who taketh vengeance? (I speak as a man)

6 God forbid: for then how shall God judge the world?

7 For if the truth of God hath more abounded through my lie unto his glory; why yet am I also judged as a sinner?

8 And not rather, (as we be slanderously reported, and as some affirm that we say,) Let us do evil, that good may come? whose damnation is just.

9 What then? are we better than they? No, in no wise: for we have before proved both Jews and Gentiles, that they are all under sin;

10 As it is written, There is none righteous, no, not one:

11 There is none that understandeth, there is none that seeketh after God.

12 They are all gone out of the way, they are together become unprofitable; there is none that doeth good, no, not one.

13 Their throat is an open sepulcher; with their tongues they have used deceit; the poison of asps is under their lips:

14 Whose mouth is full of cursing and bitterness:

15 Their feet are swift to shed blood:

16 Destruction and misery are in their ways:

17 And the way of peace have they not known:

18 There is no fear of God before their eyes.

19 Now we know that what things soever the law saith, it saith to them who are under the law: that every mouth may

wards. He sets nature in opposition to a written law, meaning that the Gentiles had the natural light of righteousness, which supplied the place of that law by which the Jews were instructed, so that they were a law to themselves.

ROMANS 3

5. But if our unrighteousness

Though this is a digression from the main subject, it was yet necessary for the Apostle to introduce it, lest he should seem to give to the ill-disposed an occasion to speak evil, which he knew would be readily laid hold on by them. For since they were watching for every opportunity to defame the gospel, they had, in the testimony of David, what they might have taken for the purpose of founding a calumny – "If God seeks nothing else, but to be glorified by men, why does he punish them, when they offend, since by offending they glorify him? Without cause then surely is he offended, if he derives the reason of his displeasure from that by which he is glorified." There is, indeed, no doubt, but that this was an ordinary, and everywhere a common calumny, as it will presently appear. Hence Paul could not have covertly passed it by; but that no one should think that he expressed the sentiments of his own mind, he premises that he assumes the person of the ungodly; and at the same time, he sharply, touches, by a single expression, on human reason; whose work, as he intimates, is ever to bark against the wisdom of God; for he says not, "according to the ungodly," but "according to man," or as man. And thus indeed it is, for all the mysteries of God are paradoxes to the flesh: and at the same tine it possesses so much audacity, that it fears not to oppose them and insolently to assail what it cannot comprehend. We are hence reminded, that if we desire to become capable of understanding them, we must especially labor to become freed from our own reason (*proprio sensu*) and to give up ourselves, and unreservedly to submit to his word. The word *wrath*, taken here for judgment, refers to punishment; as though he said, "Is God unjust, who punishes those sins which set forth his righteousness?"

21. But now without the law

It is not certain for what distinct reason he calls that the righteousness of God, which we obtain by faith; whether it be, because it can alone stand before God, or because the Lord in his mercy confers it on us. As both interpretations are suitable, we contend for neither. This righteousness then, which God communicates to man, and accepts alone, and owns as righteousness, has been revealed, he says, *without the law*, that is without the aid of the law; and the law is to be understood as meaning works; for it is not

less, and the subject of the praise of men, its want of inward conformity to that law, which was manifest in the sight of God, could not obtain his praise.

ROMANS 3: 1–20

This chapter consists of three parts. The first part extends to the 8th verse inclusively, and is designed to answer and remove some objections to the doctrine previously advanced by the Apostle. In the second part, from the 9th to the 20th verses, it is proved, by the testimonies of various scriptures, that the Jews, as well as the Gentiles, are involved in sin and guilt, and consequently that none can be justified by the law. The third part commences at verse 21, where the Apostle reverts to the declaration, ch. 1:17, with which his discussion commenced, and exhibits the true and only way of justification for all men, by the righteousness of God imputed through faith in Jesus Christ.

1. What advantage then hath the Jew? or what profit is there of circumcision?

If the preceding doctrine be true, it may be asked, What advantage hath the Jew over the Gentile; and what profit is there in circumcision, if it does not save from sin? If, on the contrary, the Jews, on account of their superior privileges, will be held more culpable before the tribunal of Divine justice, as the Apostle had just shown, it appears obviously improper to allege that God has favored them more than the Gentiles. This objection it was necessary to obviate, not only because it is specious, but because it is important, and might, in regard to the Jews, arrest the course of the Gospel.

2. Much every way; chiefly, because that unto them were committed the oracles of God.

Paul here repels the foregoing objection as false and unfounded. Although the privileges of the Jews cannot come into consideration for their justification before the judgment-seat of God, it does not follow that they were as nothing, or of no advantage; on the contrary, they were marks of the peculiar care of God for that

people, while He had, as it were, abandoned all the other nations.

Chiefly, because that unto them were committed the oracles of God. – The original denotes **primarily**, which is not a priority of order, but a priority in dignity and advantage; that is to say, that of all the advantages God had vouchsafed to them, the most estimable and most excellent was that of having entrusted to them His oracles.

9. What then? are we better than they? No, in no wise: for we have before proved both Jew and Gentiles, that they are all under sin.

Here commences the second part of the chapter, in which, having proposed and replied to the above objections to his doctrine, Paul now resumes the thread of his discourse. In the two preceding chapters he had asserted the guilt of the Gentiles and of the Jews separately; in what follows he takes them together, and proves by express testimonies from Scripture that all men are sinners, and that there is none righteous, no, not one. In this manner he follows up and completes his argument to support the conclusion at which he is about to arrive in the 20th verse, which all along he had in view, namely, that by works of law no man can be justified, and with the purpose of fully unfolding, in verses 21, 22, 23, and 24, the means that God has provided for our justification, which he had briefly announced, ch. 1:17.

10. As it is written, There is none righteous, no, not one.

After having proceeded in his discussion, appealing to the natural sentiments of conscience and undeniable fact, Paul now employs the authority of Scripture, and alleges several passages drawn from the books of the Old Testament, written at different times, more clearly to establish the universal guilt both of Jews and Gentiles, in order that he might prove them all under condemnation before the tribunal of God.

There is none righteous. – This passage may be regarded as the leading proposition, the truth of which the Apostle is about to establish by the following quotations. None could

be stopped, and all the world may become guilty before God.

20 Therefore by the deeds of the law there shall no flesh be justified in his sight: for by the law is the knowledge of sin.

21 But now the righteousness of God without the law is manifested, being witnessed by the law and the prophets;

22 Even the righteousness of God which is by faith of Jesus Christ unto all and upon all them that believe: for there is no difference:

23 For all have sinned, and come short of the glory of God;

24 Being justified freely by his grace through the redemption that is in Christ Jesus:

25 Whom God hath set forth to be a propitiation through faith in his blood, to declare his righteousness for the remission of sins that are past, through the forbearance of God;

26 To declare, I say, at this time his righteousness: that he might be just, and the justifier of him which believeth in Jesus.

27 Where is boasting then? It is excluded. By what law? of works? Nay: but by the law of faith.

28 Therefore we conclude that a man is justified by faith without the deeds of the law.

29 Is he the God of the Jews only? is he not also of the Gentiles? Yes, of the Gentiles also:

30 Seeing it is one God, which shall justify the circumcision by faith, and uncircumcision through faith.

31 Do we then make void the law through faith? God forbid: yea, we establish the law.

ROMANS 4

1 What shall we say then that Abraham our father, as pertaining to the flesh, hath found?

2 For if Abraham were justified by works, he hath whereof to glory; but not before God.

3 For what saith the scripture? Abraham believed God, and it was counted unto him for righteousness.

4 Now to him that worketh is the reward not reckoned of grace, but of debt.

proper to refer this to its teaching, which he immediately adduces as bearing witness to the gratuitous righteousness of faith. Some confine it to ceremonies; but this view I shall presently show to be unsound and frigid. We ought then to know, that the merits of works are excluded. We also see that he blends not works with the mercy of God; but having taken away and wholly removed all confidence in works, he sets up mercy alone.

22. Even the righteousness of God

He shows in few words what this justification is, even that which is found in Christ and is apprehended by faith. At the same time, by introducing again the name of God, he seems to make God the founder (*autorem*, the author), and not only the approver of the righteousness of which he speaks; as though he had said, that it flows from him alone, or that its origin is from heaven, but that it is made manifest to us in Christ.

When therefore we discuss this subject, we ought to proceed in this way:

First, the question respecting our justification is to be referred, not to the judgment of men, but to the judgment of God, before whom nothing is counted righteousness, but perfect and absolute obedience to the law; which appears clear from its promises and threatenings: if no one is found who has attained to such a perfect measure of holiness, it follows that all are in themselves destitute of righteousness.

Secondly, it is necessary that Christ should come to our aid; who, being alone just, can render us just by transferring to us his own righteousness. You now see how the righteousness of faith is the righteousness of Christ. When therefore we are justified, the efficient cause is the mercy of God, the meritorious is Christ, the instrumental is the word in connection with faith. Hence faith is said to justify, because it is the instrument by which we receive Christ, in whom righteousness is conveyed to us. Having been made partakers of Christ, we ourselves are not only just, but our works also are counted just before God, and for this reason, because whatever imperfections there may be in them, are obliterated by the blood of Christ; the promises, which are conditional, are also by the same grace fulfilled to us; for God rewards our works as perfect, inasmuch as their defects are covered by free pardon.

ROMANS 4

1. What then

This is a confirmation by example; and it is a very strong one, since all things are alike with regard to the subject and the person; for he was the father of the faithful, to

be more appropriate or better adapted to his purpose, which was to show that every man is in himself entirely divested of righteousness. There is none righteous, no, not one. Not one possessed of a righteousness that can meet the demands of God's holy law. The words in this verse, and those contained in verses 11 and 12, are taken from Psalms 14: and 53, which are the same as to the sense, although they do not follow the exact expressions. But does it seem proper that Paul should draw a consequence in relation to all, from what David has only said of the wicked of his time? The answer is, That the terms which David employs are too strong not to contemplate the universal sinfulness of the human race. "The Lord looked down from heaven upon the children of men, to see if there were any that did understand, and seek God. They are all gone aside; they are altogether become filthy; there is none that doeth good, no, not one." This notifies universal depravity, so that, according to the Prophet, the application is just. It is not that David denies that God had sanctified some men by His Spirit; for, on the contrary, in the same Psalm, he speaks of the afflicted, of whom God is the refuge; but the intention is to say that, in their natural condition, without the grace of regeneration, which God vouchsafes only to His people, who are a small number, the whole human race is in a state of universal guilt and condemnation. This is also what is meant by Paul, and it is the use, as is clear from the context, that he designed to make of this passage of David, according to which none are excepted in such a way as that, if God examined them by their obedience to the law, they could stand before Him; and, besides this, whatever holiness is found in any man, it is not by the efficacy of the law, but by that of the Gospel, and if they are now sanctified, they were formerly under sin as well as others; so that it remains a truth, that all who are under the law, to which the Apostle is exclusively referring, are under **sin** that is, guilty before God.

12. They are all gone out of the way, they are together become unprofitable; there is none that doeth good, no, not one.

Sin is a wandering or departure from the right way; that is to say, out of the way of duty and obligation, out of the way of the means which conduct to felicity. These are the ways open before the eyes of men to walk in them; he who turns from there wanders out of the way. The Prophet here teaches what is the nature of sin; he also shows us what are its consequences; for as the man who loses his way cannot have any rest in his mind, nor any security, it is the same with the sinner; and as a wanderer cannot restore himself to the right way without the help of a guide, in the same manner the sinner cannot restore himself, if the Holy Spirit comes not to his aid.

They are together become unprofitable. – They have become corrupted, or have rendered themselves useless; for everything that is corrupted loses its use. They are become unfit for that for which God made them; unprofitable to God, to themselves, and to their neighbor.

16. Destruction and misery are in their ways.

This declaration, taken also from Isaiah 59:7, must be understood in an active sense, – that is to say, men labor to destroy and to ruin one another; proceeding in their perverse ways, they cause destruction and misery.

17. And the way of peace have they not known.

They have not known peace to follow and approve of it; and are not acquainted with its ways, in which they do not walk in order to procure the good of their neighbor, – for peace imports prosperity, or the way to maintain concord and friendship. Such is a just description of man's ferocity, which fills the world with animosities, quarrels, hatred in the private connections of families and neighborhoods; and with revolutions, and wars, and murders, among nations. The most savage animals do not destroy so many of their own species to appease their hunger, as man destroys of his fellows; to satiate his ambition, his revenge, or cupidity.

ROMANS 3: 21–31

At the opening of his discussion, ch. 1:16, 17, Paul had announced that the Gospel is the power of God unto salvation to every one

5 But to him that worketh not, but believeth on him that justifieth the ungodly, his faith is counted for righteousness.

6 Even as David also describeth the blessedness of the man, unto whom God imputeth righteousness without works,

7 Saying, Blessed are they whose iniquities are forgiven, and whose sins are covered.

8 Blessed is the man to whom the Lord will not impute sin.

9 Cometh this blessedness then upon the circumcision only, or upon the uncircumcision also? for we say that faith was reckoned to Abraham for righteousness.

10 How was it then reckoned? when he was in circumcision, or in uncircumcision? Not in circumcision, but in uncircumcision.

11 And he received the sign of circumcision, a seal of the righteousness of the faith which he had yet being uncircumcised: that he might be the father of all them that believe, though they be not circumcised; that righteousness might be imputed unto them also:

12 And the father of circumcision to them who are not of the circumcision only, but who also walk in the steps of that faith of our father Abraham, which he had being yet uncircumcised.

13 For the promise, that he should be the heir of the world, was not to Abraham, or to his seed, through the law, but through the righteousness of faith.

14 For if they which are of the law be heirs, faith is made void, and the promise made of none effect:

15 Because the law worketh wrath: for where no law is, there is no transgression.

16 Therefore it is of faith, that it might be by grace; to the end the promise might be sure to all the seed; not to that only which is of the law, but to that also which is of the faith of Abraham; who is the father of us all,

17 (As it is written, I have made thee a father of many nations,) before him whom he believed, even God, who quickeneth the dead, and calleth those things which be not as though they were.

18 Who against hope believed in hope, that he might become the father of many nations; according to that which was spo-

whom we ought all to be conformed; and there is also but one way and not many ways by which righteousness may be obtained by all. In many other things one example would not be sufficient to make a common rule; but as in the person of Abraham there was exhibited a mirror and pattern of righteousness, which belongs in common to the whole Church, rightly does Paul apply what has been written of him alone to the whole body of the Church, and at the same time he gives a check to the Jews, who had nothing more plausible to glory in than that they were the children of Abraham; and they could not have dared to claim to themselves more holiness than what they ascribed to the holy patriarch. Since it is then evident that he was justified freely, his posterity, who claimed a righteousness of their own by the law, ought to have been made silent even through shame.

5. But believes on him

This is a very important sentence, in which he expresses the substance and nature both of faith and of righteousness. He indeed clearly shews that faith brings us righteousness, not because it is a meritorious act, but because it obtains for us the favor of God. Nor does he declare only that God is the giver of righteousness, but he also arraigns us of unrighteousness, in order that the bounty of God may come to aid our necessity: in short, no one will seek the righteousness of faith except he who feels that he is ungodly; for this sentence is to be applied to what is said in this passage – that faith adorns us with the righteousness of another, which it seeks as a gift from God. And here again, God is said to justify us when he freely forgives sinners, and favors those, with whom he might justly be angry, with his love, that is, when his mercy obliterates our unrighteousness.

13. For the promise

He now more clearly sets the law and faith in opposition, the one to the other, which he had before in some measure done; and this ought to be carefully observed: for if faith borrows nothing from the law in order to justify, we hence understand, that it has respect to nothing else but to the mercy of God. And further, the romance of those who would have this to have been said of ceremonies, may be easily disproved; for if works contributed anything towards justification, it ought not to have been said, through the written law, but rather, through the law of nature. But Paul does not oppose spiritual holiness of life to ceremonies, but faith and its righteousness. The meaning then is, that heirship was promised to Abraham, not because he deserved it by keeping the law, but because he had obtained righteousness by faith. And doubtless (as Paul will presently show) consciences can then only enjoy solid peace, when they know that what is not justly due is freely given them.

that believeth, **because therein is the right-eousness of God revealed.** He had said that the righteous by faith shall live, intimating that there is no other way of obtaining life. In proof of this, he had declared that the wrath of God is revealed from heaven against all ungodliness and unrighteousness of men, and had shown at large that both Jews and Gentiles are all under sin, and that, therefore, by obedience to law no flesh shall be justified. He now proceeds to speak more particularly of the righteousness of God provided for man's justification, describing the manner in which it is conferred, and the character of those by whom it is received. To this subject, therefore, he here reverts.

ROMANS 4

This chapter beautifully connects with all that precedes it. In the first chapter the Apostle had announced that "the righteousness of God" was revealed in the Gospel, which is on that account the power of God unto salvation to every one that believeth. He had shown at great length that this way of salvation was necessary for man, proving by an appeal to fact, and then to Scripture, that both Jews and Gentiles were guilty before God, and that, consequently, no one could be justified by his own obedience. He had afterwards reverted to this righteousness which God had provided in His Son. In this fourth chapter he strikingly illustrates these truths, by first obviating the objection that might be offered by the Jews respecting their great progenitor Abraham, whose character they held in such veneration. This would lead them to suppose that he must be an exception to the Apostle's doctrine, by furnishing an example of one justified by works. Having refuted this objection in the particular case of Abraham, and confirmed the truth of what he had advanced by the testimony of David, Paul makes use of the history of Abraham himself to prove what he had previously asserted, and to show that in the matter of justification before God there was no exception, and no difference between Jews and Gentiles. The chapter consists of four parts. In the first, the Apostle, by referring, as has just

been observed, to the history of Abraham and the authority of David, illustrates his doctrine of justification by faith. Nothing could be so well calculated to convince both Jewish and Gentile believers, especially the former, how vain is the expectation of those who look for justification by their own works. Abraham was a patriarch eminently holy, the head of the nation of Israel, the friend of God, the father of all who believe, in whose seed all the nations of the world were to be blessed. David was a man according to God's own heart, the progenitor of the Messiah, His great personal type, and a chosen and anointed king of Israel. If, then, Abraham had not been justified by his works, but by the righteousness of God imputed to him through faith, and David, speaking by the Spirit of God, had declared that the only way in which a man can receive justification is by his sin being covered by the imputation of that righteousness, who could suppose that it was to be obtained by any other means? By these two references, the Apostle likewise shows that the way of justification was the same from the beginning, both under the old and the new dispensation. This he had before intimated, in saying that both the law and the Prophets bore witness to the righteousness of God, which is now manifested, and which is upon all them that believe.

In the other three parts of this chapter, Paul shows, first, that circumcision, to which the Jews ascribed so much efficacy, contrib-uted nothing to Abraham's justification, and that the righteousness imputed to him was bestowed before his circumcision, with the express intention of proving that righteous-ness should be imputed to all who believe though they be not circumcised. In the next place, he proves that the promise of the inher-itance made to Abraham was not through obe-dience to law, but through that righteousness which is received by faith; and that the whole plan of justification was arranged in this manner, in order that the blessing conveyed through faith by the free favor of God might be made sure to all the seed of Abraham, – that is, to "the children of the promise," Romans 9:8, whether Jews or Gentiles. And, lastly Paul describes Abraham's faith, and states the ben-

ken, So shall thy seed be.

19 And being not weak in faith, he considered not his own body now dead, when he was about an hundred years old, neither yet the deadness of Sara's womb:

20 He staggered not at the promise of God through unbelief; but was strong in faith, giving glory to God;

21 And being fully persuaded that, what he had promised, he was able also to perform.

22 And therefore it was imputed to him for righteousness.

23 Now it was not written for his sake alone, that it was imputed to him;

24 But for us also, to whom it shall be imputed, if we believe on him that raised up Jesus our Lord from the dead;

25 Who was delivered for our offences, and was raised again for our justification.

ROMANS 5

1 Therefore being justified by faith, we have peace with God through our Lord Jesus Christ:

2 By whom also we have access by faith into this grace wherein we stand, and rejoice in hope of the glory of God.

3 And not only so, but we glory in tribulations also: knowing that tribulation worketh patience;

4 And patience, experience; and experience, hope:

5 And hope maketh not ashamed; because the love of God is shed abroad in our hearts by the Holy Ghost which is given unto us.

6 For when we were yet without strength, in due time Christ died for the ungodly.

7 For scarcely for a righteous man will one die: yet peradventure for a good man some would even dare to die.

8 But God commendeth his love toward us, in that, while we were yet sinners, Christ died for us.

9 Much more then, being now justified by his blood, we shall be saved from wrath through him.

10 For if, when we were enemies, we were reconciled to God by the death of his Son, much more, being reconciled, we shall be saved by his life.

11 And not only so, but we also joy

Hence also it follows, that this benefit, the reason for which applies equally to both, belongs to the Gentiles no less than to the Jews; for if the salvation of men is based on the goodness of God alone, they check and hinder its course, as much as they can, who exclude from it the Gentiles.

19. In faith

If you prefer to omit one of the negatives you may render it thus, "Being weak in faith, he considered not his own body," etc.; but this makes no sense. He indeed shows now more fully what might have hindered, yea, and wholly turned Abraham aside from receiving the promise. A seed from Sarah was promised to him at a time when he was not by nature fit for generating, nor Sarah for conceiving. Whatever he could see as to himself was opposed to the accomplishment of the promise. Hence, that he might yield to the truth of God, he withdrew his mind from those things which presented themselves to his own view, and as it were forgot himself.

ROMANS 5

1. Being then justified

The Apostle begins to illustrate by the effects, what he has hitherto said of the righteousness of faith: and hence the whole of this chapter is taken up with amplifications, which are no less calculated to explain than to confirm. He had said before, that faith is abolished, if righteousness is sought by works; and in this case perpetual inquietude would disturb miserable souls, as they can find nothing substantial in themselves: but he teaches us now, that they are rendered quiet and tranquil, when we have obtained righteousness by faith, we have peace with God; and this is the peculiar fruit of the righteousness of faith. When any one strives to seek tranquillity of conscience by works (which is the case with profane and ignorant men), he labors for it in vain; for either his heart is asleep through his disregard or forgetfulness of God's judgment, or else it is full of trembling and dread, until it reposes on Christ, who is alone our peace.

Then peace means tranquillity of conscience, which arises from this – that it feels itself to be reconciled to God. This the Pharisee has not, who swells with false confidence in his own works; nor the stupid sinner, who is not disquieted, because he is inebriated with the sweetness of vices: for though neither of these seems to have a manifest disquietude, as he is who is smitten with a consciousness of sin; yet as they do not really approach the tribunal of God, they have no reconciliation with him; for insensibility of conscience is, as it were, a sort of retreating from God.

efit resulting from its exhibition to believers, for whose sake chiefly his faith was recorded. It is particularly to be noticed that not a word is said respecting Abraham's sanctification, although his whole history, after leaving his own country, furnishes so remarkable an example of a holy walk and conversation. All that is brought into view is his faith.

It is thus shown that neither moral nor ceremonial, neither evangelical nor legal works, are of any account whatever in the act of justification, or contribute in any degree to procure that blessing. The whole of this chapter is particularly calculated to make a deep impression on the Jews; and no doubt the day is approaching, and probably near at hand, when they will read it with much interest, and derive from it signal benefit.

1. What shall we then say that Abraham, our father as pertaining to the flesh, hath found?

In the third chapter the Apostle had replied to the objections which might be offered to what he had before advanced respecting the Jews. First, it might be inquired if, as appeared from his doctrine, the Jew could not be saved by their distinguished privileges connected with the law, or by observing the rite of circumcision, what **advantage** did they possess over others, and what **profit** had they from circumcision? Second, on the supposition of their being transgressors, it was asked, if their sin was the means of **condemning** the righteousness of God, was it not unjust to punish them as sinners? Lastly, if all that had been said was true, what were they **better** than others? After obviating all these objections, and proving from the character of the Jews, and of all other men as delineated in the Scriptures, the impossibility of their justification by the works of law, Paul had exhibited the only way in which sinners could be justified before God, and had shown that it was effected in such a way that all boasting on the part of man is excluded. Another objection might now naturally present itself to the Jews in connection with the case of Abraham, who had received the ordinance of circumcision from God Himself, and whose eminent piety they held in such

veneration. It might be asked what, according to the Apostle's doctrine, could be said regarding him: what had he found, or obtained? Did not he obtain justification in these ways? Such is the objection which the Apostle introduces in this and the following verse, and answers fully in both its parts.

10. How was it then reckoned? when he was in circumcision, or in uncircumcision? Not in circumcision, but in uncircumcision.

How was it? or in what circumstances was righteousness counted to him? – This question, with the affirmation which follows, determines that Abraham's justification by faith was previous to circumcision, and therefore circumcision could not be its cause. If righteousness was imputed to him before he was circumcised, then circumcision is not necessary to justification. It may come on Gentiles as well as on Jews. This is founded on the history of Abraham, recorded in the Old Testament, who was in a state of justification before Ishmael's birth, many years antecedent to the appointment of circumcision.

ROMANS 5

The apostle describes in this chapter the blessed accompaniments, the security, and the foundation of justification. This last branch of the subject is interwoven with an account of the entrance of sin and death into the world; while a parallel is drawn between the first and the second Adam in their opposite tendencies and influences. By the first came sin, condemnation, and death; by the second, righteousness, justification, and life. From this comparison, occasion is taken to show why God had made the promulgation of the written law to intervene betwixt the author of condemnation and the author of justification. On the one hand, the extent, the evil, and the demerit of sin, and the obstructions raised up by law and justice to man's recovery, were thus made fully manifest; while, on the other hand, the superabundant riches of Divine grace, in its complete ascendancy and victory over them in the way of righteousness, were

in God through our Lord Jesus Christ, by whom we have now received the atonement.

12 Wherefore, as by one man sin entered into the world, and death by sin; and so death passed upon all men, for that all have sinned:

13 (For until the law sin was in the world: but sin is not imputed when there is no law.

14 Nevertheless death reigned from Adam to Moses, even over them that had not sinned after the similitude of Adam's transgression, who is the figure of him that was to come.

15 But not as the offence, so also is the free gift. For if through the offence of one many be dead, much more the grace of God, and the gift by grace, which is by one man, Jesus Christ, hath abounded unto many.

16 And not as it was by one that sinned, so is the gift: for the judgment was by one to condemnation, but the free gift is of many offences unto justification.

17 For if by one man's offence death reigned by one; much more they which receive abundance of grace and of the gift of righteousness shall reign in life by one, Jesus Christ.)

18 Therefore as by the offence of one judgment came upon all men to condemnation; even so by the righteousness of one the free gift came upon all men unto justification of life.

19 For as by one man's disobedience many were made sinners, so by the obedience of one shall many be made righteous.

20 Moreover the law entered, that the offence might abound. But where sin abounded, grace did much more abound:

21 That as sin hath reigned unto death, even so might grace reign through righteousness unto eternal life by Jesus Christ our Lord.

ROMANS 6

1 What shall we say then? Shall we continue in sin, that grace may abound?

2 God forbid. How shall we, that are dead to sin, live any longer therein?

3 Know ye not, that so many of us as were baptized into Jesus Christ were

Peace with God is opposed to the dead security of the flesh, and for this reason – because the first thing is, that every one should become awakened as to the account he must render of his life; and no one can stand boldly before God, but he who relies on a gratuitous reconciliation; for as long as he is God, all must otherwise tremble and be confounded. And this is the strongest of proofs, that our opponents do nothing but prate to no purpose, when they ascribe righteousness to works; for this conclusion of Paul is derived from this fact – that miserable souls always tremble, except they repose on the grace of Christ.

19. This is no tautology, but a necessary explanation of the former verse. For he shows that we are guilty through the offense of one man, in such a manner as not to be ourselves innocent. He had said before, that we are condemned; but that no one might claim for himself innocence, he also subjoined, that every one is condemned because he is a sinner. And then, as he declares that we are made righteous through the obedience of Christ, we hence conclude that Christ, in satisfying the Father, has provided a righteousness for us. It then follows, that righteousness is in Christ, and that it is to be received by us as what peculiarly belongs to him. He at the same time shows what sort of righteousness it is, by calling it obedience. And here let us especially observe what we must bring into God's presence, if we seek to be justified by works, even obedience to the law, not to this or to that part, but in every respect perfect; for when a just man falls, all his former righteousness will not be remembered. We may also hence learn, how false are the schemes which they take to pacify God, who of themselves devise what they obtrude on him. For then only we truly worship him when we follow what he has commanded us, and render obedience to his word. Away then with those who confidently lay claim to the righteousness of works, which cannot otherwise exist than when there is a full and complete observance of the law; and it is certain that this is nowhere to be found. We also learn, that they are madly foolish who vaunt before God of works invented by themselves, which he regards as the filthiest things; for obedience is better than sacrifices.

ROMANS 6

3. Know ye not

What he intimated in the last verse – that Christ destroys sin in his people, he proves here by mentioning the effect of baptism, by which we are initiated into his faith; for it is beyond any question, that we put on Christ in baptism, and that we are baptized for this end – that we may be one with him. But Paul takes up another principle – that we are then really united to the body of Christ, when his death brings

displayed to the greatest advantage, and with the fullest effect.

1. Therefore, being justified by faith, we have peace with God, through our Lord Jesus Christ.

Therefore. – This particle of inference draws its conclusion from the whole foregoing discussion concerning justification by faith, though it may have a more immediate reference to the nearest preceding context. The Apostle having fully proved that salvation is by grace, and that it is by faith, now shows the consequences of this doctrine.

Justified by faith. – This expression is elliptical; faith must be understood as inclusive of its object. This is very usual in all cases where the thing elliptically expressed is frequently spoken of, and therefore sufficiently explained by the elliptical expression. It is not by faith, abstractly considered, that we are justified, nor even by faith in everything that God reveals. It is by faith in the Lord Jesus Christ. Even this phrase itself, namely, faith in the Lord Jesus Christ, is still elliptical, and supposes the knowledge of what is to be believed with respect to Christ. It is not believing in His existence, but believing on Him as revealed in the Scriptures, in His person and work. In the same manner as we have the phrase, "justified by faith," we have the phrase, justified by the blood of Christ. As, in the former case, faith implies its object, so, in the latter, it is implied that we are justified by faith in the blood of Christ. The blood of Christ justifies by being the object of belief and of trust.

We have peace with God. – This shows that all men, till they are justified, are at war with God, and that He is at war with them. But when they are justified by faith, the wrath of God, which **abideth** on those who believe not on His Son, John 3:36, is turned away, and they cease to be enemies to God. Thus peace, succeeding hostility, brings with it every blessing; for there is no middle place for the creature between the love and the wrath of God. This peace, then, arises from righteousness, – the imputation of the righteousness of God by which the believer is justified, – and is followed by a sense of peace obtained. While guilt remains in the conscience, enmity will also rankle in the heart; for so long as men look upon their sins as unpardoned, and on God as the avenger of their transgressions, they must regard Him as being to them a consuming fire. But when they view God in Christ reconciling them to Himself, not imputing their iniquities to them, peace, according to the measure of faith, is established in the conscience.

This never can be experienced by going about to establish our own righteousness. If any man have peace in his conscience, it must flow from Christ's righteousness – it must be the effect of that righteousness which God has "created," Isaiah 45:8; and of which the Spirit, when He comes, brings with Him the conviction, John 16:8. Resting on this righteousness, the believer beholds God at peace with him, perfectly reconciled. The belief of this satisfies his conscience, which, being purged by blood, Hebrews 9:14, he is freed from guilty fears, and reconciled to God. Through this sense of the pardon of sin, and of friendship with God, the peace of God, which passeth all understanding, keeps his heart and mind through Christ Jesus. The maintenance of this peace, by preserving the conscience free from guilt by continual application to the blood of Christ, is the main point in the believer's walk with God and the powerful spring of His obedience. In the New Testament God is frequently denominated "the God of peace." The Apostle prays that the Lord Himself may give His people peace by all means, and enjoins that the peace of God should rule in the hearts of believers, to which they are also called in one body, and that they should be thankful. Peace is the fruit of the Spirit; and the kingdom of God is righteousness, and peace, and joy in the Holy Ghost.

Through our Lord Jesus Christ. – Peace comes through the death of Jesus Christ. The faith, therefore, by which it is obtained, must refer to Him who made peace through the blood of His cross. He alone, as the one Mediator, can make peace between God, who is holy, and man, who is sinful. God has established three covenants, or three ways of communication with man. The first was the covenant of nature; the second, the covenant of the law; the third, the covenant of the Gospel.

baptized into his death?

4 Therefore we are buried with him by baptism into death: that like as Christ was raised up from the dead by the glory of the Father, even so we also should walk in newness of life.

5 For if we have been planted together in the likeness of his death, we shall be also in the likeness of his resurrection:

6 Knowing this, that our old man is crucified with him, that the body of sin might be destroyed, that henceforth we should not serve sin.

7 For he that is dead is freed from sin.

8 Now if we be dead with Christ, we believe that we shall also live with him:

9 Knowing that Christ being raised from the dead dieth no more; death hath no more dominion over him.

10 For in that he died, he died unto sin once: but in that he liveth, he liveth unto God.

11 Likewise reckon ye also yourselves to be dead indeed unto sin, but alive unto God through Jesus Christ our Lord.

12 Let not sin therefore reign in your mortal body, that ye should obey it in the lusts thereof.

13 Neither yield ye your members as instruments of unrighteousness unto sin: but yield yourselves unto God, as those that are alive from the dead, and your members as instruments of righteousness unto God.

14 For sin shall not have dominion over you: for ye are not under the law, but under grace.

15 What then? shall we sin, because we are not under the law, but under grace? God forbid.

16 Know ye not, that to whom ye yield yourselves servants to obey, his servants ye are to whom ye obey; whether of sin unto death, or of obedience unto righteousness?

17 But God be thanked, that ye were the servants of sin, but ye have obeyed from the heart that form of doctrine which was delivered you.

18 Being then made free from sin, ye became the servants of righteousness.

19 I speak after the manner of men because of the infirmity of your flesh: for as ye have yielded your members servants to uncleanness and to iniquity unto

forth in us its fruit; yea, he teaches us, that this fellowship as to death is what is to be mainly regarded in baptism; for not washing alone is set forth in it, but also the putting to death and the dying of the old man. It is hence evident, that when we become partakers of the grace of Christ, immediately the efficacy of his death appears. But the benefit of this fellowship as to the death of Christ is described in what follows.

20. For when ye were

He still repeats the difference, which he had before mentioned, between the yoke of righteousness and that of sin; for these two things, sin and righteousness, are so contrary, that he who devotes himself to the one, necessarily departs from the other. And he thus represents both, that by viewing them apart we may see more clearly what is to be expected from each; for to set things thus apart enables us to understand better their distinctive character. He then sets sin on one side, and righteousness on the other; and having stated this distinction, he afterwards shows what results from each of them.

Let us then remember that the Apostle still reasons on the principle of contraries, and in this manner, "While ye were the servants of sin, ye were freed from righteousness; but now a change having taken place, it behoves you to serve righteousness; for you have been liberated from the yoke of sin. He calls those free from righteousness who are held by no bridle to obey righteousness. This is the liberty of the flesh, which so frees us from obedience to God, that it makes us slaves to the devil. Wretched then and accursed is this liberty, which with unbridled or rather mad frenzy, leads us exultingly to our destruction.

21. What fruit, then

He could not more strikingly express what he intended than by appealing to their conscience, and by confessing shame as it were in their person. Indeed the godly, as soon as they begin to be illuminated by the Spirit of Christ and the preaching of the gospel, do freely acknowledge their past life, which they have lived without Christ, to have been worthy of condemnation; and so far are they from endeavouring to excuse it, that, on the contrary, they feel ashamed of themselves. Yea, further, they call to mind the remembrance of their own disgrace, that being thus ashamed, they may more truly and more readily be humbled before God.

Nor is what he says insignificant, Of which ye are now ashamed; for he intimates that we are possessed with extreme blind love for ourselves, when we are involved in the darkness of our sins, and think not that there is so much filth in us. The light of the Lord alone can open our eyes to behold the filthiness which lies hid in our flesh.

Under the first covenant, man, being in a state of innocence, needed no mediator. Under the second, there was a mediator simply of communication, and not of reconciliation, – a mediator as to the exterior, or a messenger who goes between two parties, a simple depository of words spoken on the one side of the other, without having any part in the interior or essence of the covenant, of which he was neither the founder nor the bond. Under the third covenant, Jesus Christ is a true mediator of reconciliation, who has produced a real peace between God and man, and is the founder of their mutual communion. "He is our peace." It is established by the new covenant in His hands, and is everlasting, being made through the blood of that everlasting covenant. "The Lord is well pleased for His righteousness' sake," Isaiah 42:21. "The work of righteousness shall be **peace,** and the effect of righteousness, quietness and assurance for ever," Isaiah 32:17. This peace, then, is through Jesus Christ and His righteousness, which brings this quietness and assurance. He is the King of righteousness and Prince of Peace. In parting from His disciples before His death, He said, "These things have I spoken unto you, that in Me ye might have peace;" and this peace He bequeathed to them. "Peace I leave with you, My peace I give unto you." When He met them again after His resurrection, His first salutation to them was, "Peace be unto you."

ROMANS 6

In the preceding part of the Epistle the universal depravity and guilt of man, and the free salvation through the blood of the Lord Jesus Christ, had been fully exhibited. Paul now proceeds to prove the intimate connection between the justification of believers and their sanctification. He commences by stating an objection which has in all ages been advanced as an unanswerable argument against salvation by grace. He asks, What is the consequence of the doctrine he has been inculcating? If justification be bestowed through faith, without works, and if, where sin abounded, grace has much more abounded, may we not continue in sin that grace may abound? No objection could be more plausible. It is such as will forcibly strike every natural man, and is as common now as it was in the days of the Apostle. Paul repels this charge by declaring the union of believers with Jesus Christ, by whom, as is represented in baptism, His people are dead to sin, and risen with Him to walk in newness of life. Having established these important truths, he urges (11) on those whom he addresses the duty of being convinced that such is their actual state. In verses 12 and 13, he warns them not to abuse this conviction; and for their encouragement in fighting the good fight of faith, to which they are called, assures them, in the 14th verse, that sin shall not have dominion over them, because they are not under the law but under grace. Thus the Apostle proves that, by the gracious provision of the covenant of God, ratified by the blood of Him with whom they are inseparably united, they who are justified cannot continue to live in sin; but though sin shall not have dominion over them, still, as their sanctification is not yet perfect, he goes on to address them as liable to temptation. What he had said, therefore, concerning their state as being in Christ, did not preclude the duty of watchfulness; nor, since they had formerly been the servants of sin, of now proving that they were the servants of God, by walking in holiness of life. Paul concludes by an animated appeal to their own experience of the past, and to their prospects for the future. He asks, what fruit had they in their former ways, which could only conduct to shame and death? On the other hand, he exhorts them to press onwards in the course of holiness, at the end of which they would receive the crown of everlasting life. But, along with this assurance, he reminds them of the important truth, that while the just **recompense** of sin is death, eternal life is the **gift** of God, through Jesus Christ our Lord.

10. For in that he died, He died unto sin once; but in that He liveth, He liveth unto God.

In that – or with respect to that – **He died, He died unto sin.** – Here we have the same

iniquity; even so now yield your members servants to righteousness unto holiness.

20 For when ye were the servants of sin, ye were free from righteousness.

21 What fruit had ye then in those things whereof ye are now ashamed? for the end of those things is death.

22 But now being made free from sin, and become servants to God, ye have your fruit unto holiness, and the end everlasting life.

23 For the wages of sin is death; but the gift of God is eternal life through Jesus Christ our Lord.

ROMANS 7

1 Know ye not, brethren, (for I speak to them that know the law,) how that the law hath dominion over a man as long as he liveth?

2 For the woman which hath an husband is bound by the law to her husband so long as he liveth; but if the husband be dead, she is loosed from the law of her husband.

3 So then if, while her husband liveth, she be married to another man, she shall be called an adulteress: but if her husband be dead, she is free from that law; so that she is no adulteress, though she be married to another man.

4 Wherefore, my brethren, ye also are become dead to the law by the body of Christ; that ye should be married to another, even to him who is raised from the dead, that we should bring forth fruit unto God.

5 For when we were in the flesh, the motions of sins, which were by the law, did work in our members to bring forth fruit unto death.

6 But now we are delivered from the law, that being dead wherein we were held; that we should serve in newness of spirit, and not in the oldness of the letter.

7 What shall we say then? Is the law sin? God forbid. Nay, I had not known sin, but by the law: for I had not known lust, except the law had said, Thou shalt not covet.

8 But sin, taking occasion by the commandment, wrought in me all manner of concupiscence. For without the law sin was dead.

ROMANS 7

Though he had, in a brief manner, sufficiently explained the question respecting the abrogation of the law; yet as it was a difficult one, and might have given rise to many other questions, he now shows more at large how the law, with regard to us, is become abrogated; and then he sets forth what good is thereby done to us: for while it holds us separated from Christ and bound to itself, it can do nothing but condemn us. And lest any one should on this account blame the law itself, he takes up and confutes the objections of the flesh, and handles, in a striking manner, the great question respecting the use of the law.

1. Know ye not

Let the general proposition be that the law was given to men for no other end but to regulate the present life, and that it belongs not to those who are dead: to this he afterwards subjoins this truth – that we are dead to it through the body of Christ. Some understand, that the dominion of the law continues so long to bind us as it remains in force. But as this view is rather obscure, and does not harmonize so well with the proposition which immediately follows, I prefer to follow those who regard what is said as referring to the life of man, and not to the law. The question has indeed a peculiar force, as it affirms the certainty of what is spoken; for it shows that it was not a thing new or unknown to any of them, but acknowledged equally by them all.

(For to those who know the law I speak.) This parenthesis is to be taken in the same sense with the question, as though he had said – that he knew that they were not so unskilful in the law as to entertain any doubt on the subject. And though both sentences might be understood of all laws, it is yet better to take them as referring to the law of God, which is the subject that is discussed. There are some who think that he ascribes knowledge of the law to the Romans, because the largest part of the world was under their power and government; but this is puerile: for he addressed in part the Jews or other strangers, and in part common and obscure individuals; nay, he mainly regarded the Jews, with whom he had to do respecting the abrogation of the law: and lest they should think that he was dealing captiously with them, he declares that he took up a common principle, known to them all, of which they could by no means be ignorant, who had from their childhood been brought up in the teaching of the law.

24. Miserable

He closes his argument with a vehement exclamation, by which he teaches us that we are not only to struggle with our flesh, but also with continual groaning to bewail within ourselves and before God our unhappy condition. But he

declaration concerning our Lord and Savior as in the 2nd verse concerning believers, of whom the Apostle says that they are **dead to sin.** Whatever, then, the expression signifies in the one case, it must also be understood to signify in the other. But those who attach a wrong interpretation to the phrase in the first occurrence, are necessitated to attribute to it a different one in the second. Accordingly Calvin remarks on this 10th verse, – "The very form of expression, as applied to Christ, shows that He did not, like us, die to sin for the purpose of ceasing to commit it." Here are two misinterpretations, – first, of the 2nd verse, and next, as a natural consequence, of this 10th. A similar difference of interpretation will be found in the other commentators. Having mistaken the meaning of the one, they are compelled to vary it in the other. In the first, they introduce the idea of death to the **power** of sin, but in the last this is impossible. Our Lord never felt the power of sin, and therefore could not die to it. But He died to the **guilt** of sin – to the guilt of His people's sins, which He had taken upon Him; and they, dying with Him, as is above declared, die to sin precisely in the same sense in which He died to it. This declaration, then, that Christ **died to sin,** explains in the clearest manner the meaning of the expression "dead to sin," verse 2, proving that it signifies exclusively dying to the guilt of sin; for in no other sense could our Lord Jesus Christ die to sin.

23. For the wages of sin is death; but the gift of God is eternal life through Jesus Christ our Lord.

The wages of sin is death. – Here, as in the conclusion of the preceding chapter, death is contrasted with eternal life. Sin is a service or slavery, and its reward is death, or eternal misery. As death is the greatest evil in this world, so the future punishment of the wicked is called death figuratively, or the second death. In this sense death is frequently spoken of in Scripture; as when our Lord says, "Whosoever believeth on Me shall never die." Death is the just recompense of sin. The Apostle does not add, But the wages of obedience is eternal life. This is not the doctrine of Scripture.

He adds, **But the gift of God is eternal life.** The gift that God bestows is eternal life. He bestows no less upon any of His people; and it is the greatest gift that can be bestowed.

Life after death are set before us in the Scriptures. On the one hand, indignation and wrath, tribulation and anguish; on the other, glory, and honor, and peace. To one or other of these states every child of Adam will finally be consigned. To both of them, in the concluding verse of this chapter, our attention is directed; and the grounds on which never-ending misery or everlasting blessedness will be awarded, are expressly declared. "The wages of sin is **death;** but the gift of God is **eternal life,** through **Jesus Christ our Lord.**"

ROMANS 7

In the preceding chapter the Apostle had answered the chief objection against the doctrine of justification by faith without works. He had proved that, by union with Christ in His death and resurrection, believers who are thereby justified are also sanctified; he had exhibited and enforced the motives to holiness furnished by the consideration of that union; he had, moreover, affirmed that sin shall not have dominion over them, for this specific reason, that they are not under the law, but under grace. To the import of this declaration he now reverts, both to explain its meaning, and to state the ground of deliverance from the law. This, again, rendered it proper to vindicate the holiness of the law, as well as to demonstrate its use in convincing of sin; while at the same time he proves that all its light and all its authority, so far from being sufficient to subdue sin, on the contrary, only tend, by the strictness of its precepts and the awful nature of its sanctions, the more to excite and bring into action the corruptions of the human heart.

Paul next proceeds plainly to show what might be inferred from the preceding chapter. Although he had there described believers as dead to the guilt of sin, he had, notwithstanding, by his earnest exhortations to watchfulness and holiness, clearly intimated that they

9 For I was alive without the law once: but when the commandment came, sin revived, and I died.

10 And the commandment, which was ordained to life, I found to be unto death.

11 For sin, taking occasion by the commandment, deceived me, and by it slew me.

12 Wherefore the law is holy, and the commandment holy, and just, and good.

13 Was then that which is good made death unto me? God forbid. But sin, that it might appear sin, working death in me by that which is good; that sin by the commandment might become exceeding sinful.

14 For we know that the law is spiritual: but I am carnal, sold under sin.

15 For that which I do I allow not: for what I would, that do I not; but what I hate, that do I.

16 If then I do that which I would not, I consent unto the law that it is good.

17 Now then it is no more I that do it, but sin that dwelleth in me.

18 For I know that in me (that is, in my flesh,) dwelleth no good thing: for to will is present with me; but how to perform that which is good I find not.

19 For the good that I would I do not: but the evil which I would not, that I do.

20 Now if I do that I would not, it is no more I that do it, but sin that dwelleth in me.

21 I find then a law, that, when I would do good, evil is present with me.

22 For I delight in the law of God after the inward man:

23 But I see another law in my members, warring against the law of my mind, and bringing me into captivity to the law of sin which is in my members.

24 O wretched man that I am! who shall deliver me from the body of this death?

25 I thank God through Jesus Christ our Lord. So then with the mind I myself serve the law of God; but with the flesh the law of sin.

ROMANS 8

1 There is therefore now no condemnation to them which are in Christ Jesus, who walk not after the flesh, but after the Spirit.

asks not by whom he was to be delivered, as one in doubt, like unbelievers, who understand not that there is but one real deliverer: but it is the voice of one panting and almost fainting, because he does not find immediate help, as he longs for. And he mentions the word rescue, in order that he might show, that for his liberation no ordinary exercise of divine power was necessary.

By the *body of death* he means the whole mass of sin, or those ingredients of which the whole man is composed; except that in him there remained only relics, by the captive bonds of which he was held. The pronoun toutou *this*, which I apply, as Erasmus does, to the body, may also be fitly referred to death, and almost in the same sense; for Paul meant to teach us, that the eyes of God's children are opened, so that through the law of God they wisely discern the corruption of their nature and the death which from it proceeds. But the word *body* means the same as the *external man* and *members*; for Paul points out this as the origin of evil, that man has departed from the law of his creation, and has become thus carnal and earthly. For though he still excels brute beasts, yet his true excellency has departed from him, and what remains in him is full of numberless corruptions so that his soul, being degenerated, may be justly said to have passed into a body. So God says by Moses, "No more shall my Spirit contend with man, for he is even flesh" (Genesis 6: 3): thus stripping man of his spiritual excellency, he compares him, by way of reproach, to the brute creation.

This passage is indeed remarkably fitted for the purpose of beating down all the glory of the flesh; for Paul teaches us, that the most perfect, as long as they dwell in the flesh, are exposed to misery, for they are subject to death; nay, when they thoroughly examine themselves, they find in their own nature nothing but misery.

But it must be added, that though the faithful level at the true mark, they are not yet carried away by an unbridled desire in wishing for death, but submit themselves to the will of God, to whom it behoves us both to live and to die: hence they clamor not with displeasure against God, but humbly deposit their anxieties in his bosom; for they do not so dwell on the thoughts of their misery, but that being mindful of grace received, they blend their grief with joy.

ROMANS 8

1. There is then

After having described the contest which the godly have perpetually with their own flesh, he returns to the consolation, which was very needful for them, and which he had before mentioned; and it was this, – that though they were still beset by sin, they were yet exempt fiom the power of

were still exposed to its seductions.

He now exhibits this fact, by relating his own experience since he became dead to the law and was united to Christ By thus describing his inward conflict with sin, and showing how far short he came of the demands of the law, he proves the necessity of being dead to the law as a covenant, since, in the highest attainments of grace during this mortal life, the old nature, which he calls flesh, still remains in believers. At the same time he represents himself as delighting in the law of God, as hating sin, and looking forward with confidence to future deliverance from its power. In this manner he illustrates not only the believer's real character, but the important fact that the obedience of the most eminent Christian, which is always imperfect, cannot have the smallest influence in procuring his justification. He had proved that men cannot be justified by their works in their natural state.

He now shows, by a reference to himself, that as little can they be justified by their works in their regenerated state. And thus he confirms his assertion in the 3rd chapter, that by the deeds of the law there shall no flesh be justified. He might have described more generally the incessant combat between the old and new natures in the believer; but he does this more practically, as well as more efficiently, by laying open the secrets of his own heart, and exhibiting it in his own person.

7. What shall we say then? Is the law sin? God forbid. Nay, I had not known sin, but by the law: for I had not known lust, except the law had said, Thou shalt not covet.

What Shall we say then! Is the law sin! – In the 5th verse Paul had described the effect of the law on himself and those whom he addressed before conversion, while he and they were under its dominion. In the 6th verse he had spoken of their deliverance and his own from the law; here and in the four following verses he illustrates what were the effects of the law on himself. While he peremptorily rejects the supposition that there was anything evil in the law, he shows that, by the strictness of its precepts exciting the corruptions of his

heart, it was the means of convincing him that he was a sinner, and under its condemnation, and was thus the instrument to him of much good, for he would not have known sin to be sin but by the law.

12. Wherefore the law is holy, and the commandment holy, and just, and good.

Having now shown that the law is not the cause, but only the occasion of sin, Paul here draws the conclusion as to its character and excellence.

Wherefore. – In the 7th verse he had strongly denied that there was anything sinful in the law; and, in the intermediate verses, had shown, by its effects, that, so far from being the cause of sin, it had been the means of enlightening his mind, in giving him to discover the evil nature of sin, and its deceitful workings in himself. From these effects he now draws the conclusion here stated, which fully illustrates the above assertion, proving how far the law is removed from sin, namely, that it is holy, and just, and good. The two words, law and commandment, appear to be used to give the greater force to his declaration, – thus meaning the law and every precept it enjoins. It is **holy,** in opposition to whatever is sinful, holy, as embodying the perfect rule of what is right and conformable to the character of God, and a transcript of His perfections. It is just. Can anything be more just than that we should abstain from all that God prohibits? It is highly just that we should not only abstain from all that God forbids, but that we should not even desire what is forbidden. The law demands what is equitable, and due to God, and nothing more, – and what is just and equitable in regard to man; and a just law could demand no less.

And good. – It is not only just, it is also good. It is good in itself, and its whole tendency is adapted to maintain perfect order, and to establish in the highest degree the happiness of all who are under its authority. Every commandment of the Decalogue tends to promote human happiness. This is the glory of the law, and shows that it proceeds from the Giver of every good and perfect gift – from Him who alone is good. But this is not the ground of

2 For the law of the Spirit of life in Christ Jesus hath made me free from the law of sin and death.

3 For what the law could not do, in that it was weak through the flesh, God sending his own Son in the likeness of sinful flesh, and for sin, condemned sin in the flesh:

4 That the righteousness of the law might be fulfilled in us, who walk not after the flesh, but after the Spirit.

5 For they that are after the flesh do mind the things of the flesh; but they that are after the Spirit the things of the Spirit.

6 For to be carnally minded is death; but to be spiritually minded is life and peace.

7 Because the carnal mind is enmity against God: for it is not subject to the law of God, neither indeed can be.

8 So then they that are in the flesh cannot please God.

9 But ye are not in the flesh, but in the Spirit, if so be that the Spirit of God dwell in you. Now if any man have not the Spirit of Christ, he is none of his.

10 And if Christ be in you, the body is dead because of sin; but the Spirit is life because of righteousness.

11 But if the Spirit of him that raised up Jesus from the dead dwell in you, he that raised up Christ from the dead shall also quicken your mortal bodies by his Spirit that dwelleth in you.

12 Therefore, brethren, we are debtors, not to the flesh, to live after the flesh.

13 For if ye live after the flesh, ye shall die: but if ye through the Spirit do mortify the deeds of the body, ye shall live.

14 For as many as are led by the Spirit of God, they are the sons of God.

15 For ye have not received the spirit of bondage again to fear; but ye have received the Spirit of adoption, whereby we cry, Abba, Father.

16 The Spirit itself beareth witness with our spirit, that we are the children of God:

17 And if children, then heirs; heirs of God, and joint-heirs with Christ; if so be that we suffer with him, that we may be also glorified together.

18 For I reckon that the sufferings of this present time are not worthy to be compared with the glory which shall be

death, and from every curse, provided they lived not in the flesh but in the Spirit: for he joins together these three things – the imperfection under which the faithful always labor – the mercy of God in pardoning and forgiving it – and the regeneration of the Spirit; and this indeed in the last place, that no one should flatter himself with a vain notion, as though he were freed from the curse, while securely indulging in the meantime his own flesh. As then the carnal man flatters himself in vain, when in no way solicitous to reform his life, he promises to himself impunity under the pretense of having this grace; so the trembling consciences of the godly have an invincible fortress, for they know that while they abide in Christ they are beyond every danger of condemnation.

We shall now examine the words. After the Spirit. Those who walk after the Spirit are not such as have wholly put off all the emotions of the flesh, so that their whole life is redolent with nothing but celestial perfection; but they are those who sedulously labor to subdue and mortify the flesh, so that the love of true religion seems to reign in them. He declares that such walk not after the flesh; for wherever the real fear of God is vigorous, it takes away from the flesh its sovereignty, though it does not abolish all its corruptions.

2. For the law of the Spirit of life

This is a confirmation of the former sentence; and that it may be understood, the meaning of the words must be noticed. Using a language not strictly correct, by the *law of the Spirit* he designates the Spirit of God, who sprinkles our souls with the blood of Christ, not only to cleanse us from the stain of sin with respect to its guilt, but also to sanctify us that we may be really purified. He adds that it is life-giving (for the genitive case, after the manner of the Hebrew, is to be taken as an adjective), it hence follows, that those who detain man in the letter of the law, expose him to death. On the other hand, he gives the name of the *law of sin* and *death* to the dominion of the flesh and to the tyranny of death, which thence follows: the law of God is set as it were in the middle, which by teaching righteousness cannot confer it, but on the contrary binds us with the strongest chains in bondage to sin and to death.

The meaning then is – that the law of God condemns men, and that this happens, because as long as they remain under the bond of the law, they are oppressed with the bondage of sin, and are thus exposed to death; but that the Spirit of Christ, while it abolishes the law of sin in us by destroying the prevailing desires of the flesh, does at the same time deliver us from the peril of death. If any one objects and says, that then pardon, by which our transgressions are buried, depends on regeneration; to this it may be easily answered, that the reason is not here assigned by

obedience; and those who have endeavored to place the foundation of morals on the principle of utility, or of the happiness of the many, have only proved their shortsighted ignorance, and verified the declaration of Scripture, "professing themselves to be wise, they become fools."

From the nature of the Apostle's description of the glory and excellence of the law, it is clear that he is speaking of the Decalogue, and not of the ceremonial law or the Mosaic institutions.

ROMANS 8

This chapter presents a glorious display of the power of Divine grace, and of the provision which God has made for the consolation of His people. While the Apostle had proved, in the sixth, that his previous doctrine gave no license to believers to continue in sin, he had still kept in view his main purpose of establishing their free justification. In the seventh he had prosecuted the same object, declaring that by their marriage with Christ they were delivered from the law as a covenant of life or death, while he vindicated its character, use, and authority. In this chapter, he continues the subject of justification, and resumes that of the believer's assurance of his salvation, of which he had spoken in the fifth, establishing it on new grounds; and from the whole train of his argument from the commencement of the Epistle, he now draws the general conclusion, that to them who are in Christ Jesus there is no condemnation. While this could not have been accomplished by the law, he shows that it had been effected by the incarnation of the Son of God, by whom the law has been fulfilled for all who are one with Him as members of His body. Paul next points out the difference of character between those who, being in their natural state under the law and under sin, are carnally-minded; and those who, being renewed by grace, in whom the law has been fulfilled, are spiritually-minded. The condition of the former is death, that of the latter life and peace. Of these last he proceeds, through the remainder of the chapter, to assert the high privileges and absolute security.

Those who are spiritually-minded have the Spirit of Christ, and possess spiritual life. Although their bodies must return to the dust, they shall be raised up again. They are led by the Spirit; they are the sons of God, and in His service are delivered from a spirit of bondage. They look to Him as their Father; are heirs of God and joint-heirs with Jesus Christ. To encourage believers to sustain the sufferings to which, while in this world, they are exposed, the most varied and abundant consolations are exhibited. Their salvation is declared to have taken its rise in the eternal counsels of God, by whom, through all its steps, it is carried into effect. Their condemnation, then, is impossible; for who shall condemn those whom God justifieth, – for whom Christ died, and rose, and intercedes? The Apostle concludes by defying the whole universe to separate believers from the love of God in Christ Jesus our Lord. In this manner he follows out, in this chapter, what had been his grand object through all the preceding part of the Epistle.

1. There is therefore now no condemnation to them which are in Christ Jews who walk not after the flesh, but after the Spirit.

Therefore. – This is an inference from the general strain of the doctrine which the Apostle had been teaching in the preceding part of the Epistle; especially it follows from what he had asserted, in the sixth and seventh chapters, with respect to believers dying with Christ, and consequently being dead to sin and to the law.

Now no condemnation. – This implies that there would have been condemnation to those to whom he wrote, had they remained under the law; but **now,** since they have died with Christ, and thereby given complete satisfaction to the law, both in its penalty and precept, it is not possible that by it they can be condemned. And, to mark the completeness of this exemption, he says, there is now **no** condemnation to them; the reason of which he fully explains in the 2nd, 3rd, and 4th verses. This **now,** then, distinguishes two conditions of a man, namely, his condition under the law, and his condition under grace, – that is, his

revealed in us.

19 For the earnest expectation of the creature waiteth for the manifestation of the sons of God.

20 For the creature was made subject to vanity, not willingly, but by reason of him who hath subjected the same in hope,

21 Because the creature itself also shall be delivered from the bondage of corruption into the glorious liberty of the children of God.

22 For we know that the whole creation groaneth and travaileth in pain together until now.

23 And not only they, but ourselves also, which have the firstfruits of the Spirit, even we ourselves groan within ourselves, waiting for the adoption, to wit, the redemption of our body.

24 For we are saved by hope: but hope that is seen is not hope: for what a man seeth, why doth he yet hope for?

25 But if we hope for that we see not, then do we with patience wait for it.

26 Likewise the Spirit also helpeth our infirmities: for we know not what we should pray for as we ought: but the Spirit itself maketh intercession for us with groanings which cannot be uttered.

27 And he that searcheth the hearts knoweth what is the mind of the Spirit, because he maketh intercession for the saints according to the will of God.

28 And we know that all things work together for good to them that love God, to them who are the called according to his purpose.

29 For whom he did foreknow, he also did predestinate to be conformed to the image of his Son, that he might be the firstborn among many brethren.

30 Moreover whom he did predestinate, them he also called: and whom he called, them he also justified: and whom he justified, them he also glorified.

31 What shall we then say to these things? If God be for us, who can be against us?

32 He that spared not his own Son, but delivered him up for us all, how shall he not with him also freely give us all things?

33 Who shall lay any thing to the charge of God's elect? It is God that justifieth.

Paul, but that the manner only is specified, in which we are delivered from guilt; and Paul denies that we obtain deliverance by the external teaching of the law, but intimates that when we are renewed by the Spirit of God, we are at the same time justified by a gratuitous pardon, that the curse of sin may no longer abide on us. The sentence then has the same meaning, as though Paul had said, that the grace of regeneration is never disjoined from the imputation of righteousness.

37. We do more than conquer

That is, we always struggle and emerge. I have retained the word used by Paul, though not commonly used by the Latins. It indeed sometimes happens that the faithful seem to succumb and to lie forlorn; and thus the Lord not only tries, but also humbles them. This issue is however given to them – that they obtain the victory.

That they might at the same time remember whence this invincible power proceeds, he again repeats what he had said before: for he not only teaches us that God, because he loves us, supports us by his hand; but he also confirms the same truth by mentioning the love of Christ. And this one sentence sufficiently proves, that the Apostle speaks not here of the fervency of that love which we have towards God, but of the paternal kindness of God and of Christ towards us, the assurance of which, being thoroughly fixed in our hearts, will always draw us from the gates of hell into the light of life, and will sufficiently avail for our support.

38. He is now carried away into hyperbolic expressions, that he might confirm us more fully in those things which are to be experienced. Whatever, he says, there is in life or in death, which seems capable of tearing us away from God, shall effect nothing; nay, the very angels, were they to attempt to overturn this foundation, shall do us no harm. It is no objection, that angels are ministering spirits, appointed for the salvation of the elect, (Hebrews 1:14:) for Paul reasons here on what is impossible, as he does in Galatians 1:8; and we may hence observe, that all things ought to be deemed of no worth, compared with the glory of God, since it is lawful to dishonor even angels in vindicating his truth. Angels are also meant by principalities and powers, and they are so called, because they are the primary instruments of the Divine power: and these two words were added, that if the word angels sounded too insignificant, something more might be expressed. But you would, perhaps, prefer this meaning, "Nor angels, and whatever powers there may be;" which is a mode of speaking that is used, when we refer to things unknown to us, and exceeding our capacities.

Nor present things, nor future things. Though he speaks hyperbolically, yet he declares, that by no length of time can it be effected, that we should be separated from the Lord's

natural and his supernatural conditions. For by nature we are children of wrath, but now God has rendered us accepted in the Beloved. Being now in Christ, we are not under the curse of the law, because He has borne it for us in the moment in which we believed in Him, we were redeemed from its curse; we entered into another covenant, in which there is nothing but grace and pardon. That there is now no condemnation to them that are in Him is according to our Lord's declaration, "Verily, verily, I say unto you, he that heareth My word, and believeth on Him that sent Me, hath everlasting life," and "shall not come into condemnation."

6. For to be carnally minded is death; but to be spiritually minded is life and peace.

In the preceding verse the Apostle contrasts the dispositions and practices of believers and unbelievers; here he contrasts their opposite states and conditions. These two states of carnal and spiritual mindedness include and divide the whole world. All men belong either to the one or the other.

They are either in the flesh or in the Spirit; in a state of nature or in a state of grace. **For to be carnally minded is death.** – This is the awful state of the carnal mind – the mind of the flesh without faith in Christ, and renovation of the Spirit of God. It is death spiritual and eternal. All the works of those who are in this state are "dead works," Hebrews 9:14. "The sacrifice of the wicked is an abomination to the Lord," although the Lord commanded to offer sacrifices, which therefore was in itself a good work. "She that liveth in pleasure is dead while she liveth." All by nature being in this carnal state, are "dead in trespasses and sins." Let those whose minds are set on the things of the world consider this fearful saying, that to be carnally minded is death, and let them look to Jesus the Savior of the guilty, through whom alone they can escape condemnation.

17. And if children, then heirs; heirs of God, and joint heirs with Christ: if so be that we suffer with Him, that we may be also, glorified together.

If children, then heirs. – The Apostle, hav-ing proved the adoption of believers from the confirmation of the double and concurrent testimony of their own spirit and of the Spirit of God, here infers from it the certainty of their possessing the eternal inheritance. The fact of their being heirs he deduces from their being children. In this world children are, in all nations, heirs of their parents' possessions. This is the law of nature. As such, it not only illustrates but confirms the fact that believers are heirs as being children. By the declaration that they are heirs, we are reminded that it is not by purchase, or by any work of their own, that they obtain the inheritance to which they are predestinated, Ephesians 1:11, and begot-ten, 1 Peter 1:3. It is solely in virtue of their sonship. The inheritance, which is a kingdom, was provided for them from the foundation of the world, Matthew 25:34, before they existed; and as inheritances were under the law inal-ienable, so this inheritance is eternal. They are heirs according to the promise, Galatians 3:29; heirs of promise, Hebrews 6:17, – that is, of all the blessings contained in the promise of God, which He confirmed by an oath; heirs of salvation, Hebrews 1:14; heirs of the grace of life, 1 Peter 3:7; heirs according to the hope of eternal life, Titus 3:7; heirs of righteousness, Hebrews 11:7; heirs of the kingdom which God hath promised, James 2:5. All things are theirs: for they are Christ's and Christ is God's, 1 Corinthians 3:23.

Heirs of God. – Here, in one word, the Apostle states what is the inheritance of those who are the children of God. It is God Him-self. "If a son, then an heir of God through Christ," Galatians 4:7. This expression, "heirs of God," has a manifest relation to the title of "son," which is acquired by adoption, on which account the Apostle here joins them together. This teaches that believers have not only a right to the good things of God, but that they have this right by their adoption, and not by merit. As the birthright of a child confers a title to the property of its father, and so dis-tinguishes such property from what the child may acquire by industry and labor, so also is the case with adoption.

Here we see the difference between the law and the Gospel. The law treats men as merce-

34 Who is he that condemneth? It is Christ that died, yea rather, that is risen again, who is even at the right hand of God, who also maketh intercession for us.

35 Who shall separate us from the love of Christ? shall tribulation, or distress, or persecution, or famine, or nakedness, or peril, or sword?

36 As it is written, For thy sake we are killed all the day long; we are accounted as sheep for the slaughter.

37 Nay, in all these things we are more than conquerors through him that loved us.

38 For I am persuaded, that neither death, nor life, nor angels, nor principalities, nor powers, nor things present, nor things to come,

39 Nor height, nor depth, nor any other creature, shall be able to separate us from the love of God, which is in Christ Jesus our Lord.

ROMANS 9

1 I say the truth in Christ, I lie not, my conscience also bearing me witness in the Holy Ghost,

2 That I have great heaviness and continual sorrow in my heart.

3 For I could wish that myself were accursed from Christ for my brethren, my kinsmen according to the flesh:

4 Who are Israelites; to whom pertaineth the adoption, and the glory, and the covenants, and the giving of the law, and the service of God, and the promises;

5 Whose are the fathers, and of whom as concerning the flesh Christ came, who is over all, God blessed for ever. Amen.

6 Not as though the word of God hath taken none effect. For they are not all Israel, which are of Israel:

7 Neither, because they are the seed of Abraham, are they all children: but, In Isaac shall thy seed be called.

8 That is, They which are the children of the flesh, these are not the children of God: but the children of the promise are counted for the seed.

9 For this is the word of promise, At this time will I come, and Sara shall have a son.

favor: and it was needful to add this; for we have not only to struggle with the sorrow which we feel from present evils, but also with the fear and the anxiety with which impending dangers may harass us. The meaning then is – that we ought not to fear, lest the continuance of evils, however long, should obliterate the faith of adoption.

ROMANS 9

In this chapter he begins to remove the offences which might have diverted the minds of men from Christ: for the Jews, for whom he was appointed according to the covenant of the law, not only rejected him, but regarded him with contempt, and for the most part bated him. Hence one of two things seemed to follow – either that there was no truth in the Divine promise – or that Jesus, whom Paul preached, was not the Lord's anointed, who had been especially promised to the Jews. This twofold knot Paul fully unties in what follows. He, however, so handles this subject, as to abstain from all bitterness against the Jews, that he might not exasperate their minds; and yet he concedes to them nothing to the injury of the gospel; for he allows to them their privileges in such a way, as not to detract anything from Christ. But he passes, as it were abruptly, to the mention of this subject, so that there appears to be no connection in the discourse. He, however, so enters on this new subject, as though he had before referred to it. It so happened in this way – Having finished the doctrine he discussed, he turned his attention to the Jews, and being astonished at their unbelief as at something monstrous, he burst forth into this sudden protestation, in the same way as though it was a subject which he had previously handled; for there was no one to whom this thought would not of itself immediately *occur* – "If this be the doctrine of the law and the Prophets, how comes it that the Jews so pertinaciously reject it?" And further, it was everywhere known, that all that he had hitherto spoken of the law of Moses, and of the grace of Christ, was more disliked by the Jews, than that the faith of the Gentiles should be assisted by their consent. It was therefore necessary to remove this obstacle, lest it should impede the course of the gospel.

1. The truth I say in Christ

As it was an opinion entertained by most that Paul was, as it were, a sworn enemy to his own nation, and as it was suspected somewhat even by the household of faith, as though he had taught them to forsake Moses, he adopts a preface to prepare the minds of his readers, before he proceeds to his subject, and in this preface he frees himself from the false suspicion of evil will towards the Jews. And as the matter was not unworthy of an oath, and as he perceived

naries, and says, Do, and live; the Gospel treats them as children, and says, Live, and do. God is the portion of His people; and in Him, who is "the possessor of heaven and" earth, they are heirs of all things. "He that overcometh shall inherit all things: and I will be his God, and he shall be My son," Revelation 21:7. God is all sufficient; and this is an all-sufficient inheritance. God is eternal and unchangeable; and therefore it is an eternal inheritance, – an inheritance incorruptible, undefiled, and that fadeth not away. They cannot be dispossessed of it, for the omnipotence of God secures against all opposition. It is reserved for them in heaven, which is the throne of God, and where He manifests His glory. It is God Himself, then, who is the inheritance of His children. This shows that He communicates Himself to them by His grace, His light, His holiness, His life. They possess God as their inheritance in two degrees, namely, in possessing in this life His grace, and in the life to come His glory. "Thou shalt guide me with Thy counsel, and afterward receive me to glory. Whom have I in heaven but Thee? and there is none upon earth that I desire besides Thee!" Psalms 73:24. And what is the inheritance in glory, if it be not God, who is all in all! Here we have the life of grace, "The grace of the Lord Jesus Christ, and the love of God, and the communion of the Holy Ghost, be with you all." In the life to come, it is the enjoyment or the vision of God which, in the seventeenth Psalm, the Prophet opposes to the inheritance of the men of this world, – "Deliver me, O Lord, from men of the world, which have their portion in this life. As for me, I will behold Thy face in righteousness; I shall be satisfied when I awake with Thy likeness." Into this inheritance Moses – that is to say, the law – cannot introduce us. He alone can do it who is the great Joshua – Jesus Christ, the Mediator of a better covenant.

ROMANS 9

Through the whole of the doctrinal part of this Epistle, Paul has an eye to the state and character of the Jewish nation, and the aspect which the Gospel bears towards them. In the preceding chapters, he had exhibited that righteous-

ness which God has provided for men, all of whom are entirely divested of any righteousness of their own, "none being righteous, no, not one." He had discoursed largely on the justification and sanctification of believers, and now he proceeds to treat particularly of the doctrine of predestination, and to exhibit the sovereignty of God in His dealings both towards Jews and Gentiles. The way in which, in the ninth, tenth, and eleventh chapters, he so particularly adverts to the present state and future destination of the Jews, in connection with what regards the Gentiles, furnishes the most ample opportunity for the illustration of this highly important subject.

In the eighth chapter, the Apostle had declared the glorious and exalted privileges of the people of God. But it was impossible for one so ardently attached to his own nation, and so zealously concerned for the welfare of his countrymen, not to be touched with the melancholy contrast which naturally arose to his mind, as he turned from these lofty and cheering contemplations to consider the deplorable state of apostate Israel. If there was a people upon earth to whom, more than to another, the blessings of the Gospel belonged as a birthright, it was assuredly to the descendants, according to the flesh, of Abraham, of Isaac, and of Jacob. But they had willfully rebelled against their God; they had rejected the Messiah, and consequently forfeited the rights and immunities secured to their forefathers by covenant. Their condition was therefore itself well calculated to awaken the sympathies of Paul; while at the same time it was necessary to vindicate the faithfulness of God, and to prove that the rejection of the Jews was by no means opposed to the absolute security of God's elect, on which he had been so largely expatiating. This subject is therefore discussed in the three following chapters; and as it is one of the greatest importance, so also it is introduced in a manner the most appropriate and the most affecting.

Scarcely has his sublime conclusion to the eighth chapter terminated, when, at the beginning of the ninth, the triumphant language of victory is exchanged by the Apostle for the voice of commiseration, in which he

10 And not only this; but when Rebecca also had conceived by one, even by our father Isaac;

11 (For the children being not yet born, neither having done any good or evil, that the purpose of God according to election might stand, not of works, but of him that calleth;)

12 It was said unto her, The elder shall serve the younger.

13 As it is written, Jacob have I loved, but Esau have I hated.

14 What shall we say then? Is there unrighteousness with God? God forbid.

15 For he saith to Moses, I will have mercy on whom I will have mercy, and I will have compassion on whom I will have compassion.

16 So then it is not of him that willeth, nor of him that runneth, but of God that sheweth mercy.

17 For the scripture saith unto Pharaoh, Even for this same purpose have I raised thee up, that I might shew my power in thee, and that my name might be declared throughout all the earth.

18 Therefore hath he mercy on whom he will have mercy, and whom he will he hardeneth.

19 Thou wilt say then unto me, Why doth he yet find fault? For who hath resisted his will?

20 Nay but, O man, who art thou that repliest against God? Shall the thing formed say to him that formed it, Why hast thou made me thus?

21 Hath not the potter power over the clay, of the same lump to make one vessel unto honor, and another unto dishonor?

22 What if God, willing to shew his wrath, and to make his power known, endured with much longsuffering the vessels of wrath fitted to destruction:

23 And that he might make known the riches of his glory on the vessels of mercy, which he had afore prepared unto glory,

24 Even us, whom he hath called, not of the Jews only, but also of the Gentiles?

25 As he saith also in Osee, I will call them my people, which were not my people; and her beloved, which was not beloved.

26 And it shall come to pass, that in the place where it was said unto them, Ye are not my people; there shall they be

that his affirmation would hardly be otherwise believed against a prejudice already entertained, he declares by an oath that he speaks the truth. By this example and the like (as I reminded you in the first chapter), we ought to learn that oaths are lawful, that is, when they render that truth credible which is necessary to be known, and which would not be otherwise believed.

The expression, *In Christ,* means "according to Christ." By adding *I lie not,* he signifies that he speaks without fiction or disguise. *My conscience testifying to me* By these words he calls his own conscience before the tribunal of God, for he brings in the Spirit as a witness to his feeling. He adduced the Spirit for this end, that he might more fully testify that he was free and pure from an evil disposition, and that he pleaded the cause of Christ under the guidance and direction of the Spirit of God. It often happens that a person, blinded by the passions of the flesh (though not purposing to deceive), knowingly and wilfully obscures the light of truth. But to swear by the name of God, in a proper sense of the word, is to call him as a witness for the purpose of confirming what is doubtful, and at the same time to bind ourselves over to his judgment, in case we say what is false.

2. That I have great sorrow

He dexterously manages so to cut short his sentence as not yet to express what he was going to say; for it was not as yet seasonable openly to mention the destruction of the Jewish nation. It may be added, that he thus intimates a greater measure of sorrow, as imperfect sentences are for the most part full of pathos. But he will presently express the cause of his sorrow, after having more fully testified his sincerity.

But the perdition of the Jews caused very great anguish to Paul, though he knew that it happened through the will and providence of God. We hence learn that the obedience we render to God's providence does not prevent us from grieving at the destruction of lost men, though we know that they are thus doomed by the just judgment of God; for the same mind is capable of being influenced by these two feelings: that when it looks to God it can willingly bear the ruin of those whom he has decreed to destroy; and that when it turns its thoughts to men, it condoles with their evils. They are then much deceived, who say that godly men ought: to have apathy and insensibility (*apatheian kai analgesian*), lest they should resist the decree of God.

3. For I could wish

He could not have expressed a greater ardour of love than by what he testifies here; for that is surely perfect love which refuses not to die for the salvation of a friend. But there is another word added, *anathema,* which proves that he speaks not only of temporal but of eternal death; and he

bewails the apostasy of his countrymen. He does not dwell so much upon the magnitude of their guilt, as he does upon the memory of their ancestral glory and ancient privileges. He strongly affirms the ardor of his affection for them as his brethren, and feelingly deplores the misery of their rejected condition. Finally, he turns from this scene of ruin and degradation, to declare that their apostasy, though general, was not universal, and to predict the dawn of a brighter day, which shall yet make manifest the truth and faithfulness of their covenant God, whose purposes concerning Israel had evidently alike included their present rejection and future restoration. The rejection of Israel, Paul proves to have been from the earliest periods of their history prefigured by God's dealing towards them as a nation. For, after declaring that "they are not all Israel which are of Israel," he adduces various and conclusive testimonies in confirmation of this truth, and thus forcibly illustrates the conduct of God towards the natural descendants of Abraham. In following this course of argument, he draws a solemn and most impressive picture of the sovereignty of God in the general administration of His government, and asserts the distinction which God makes between vessels of wrath and vessels of mercy, in order "that He might make known the riches of His glory on the vessels of mercy, which He had afore prepared unto glory." He further affirms the calling of a portion both of Jews and Gentiles, with whom in combination he classes himself as one of those "called of God," concerning whom he had, in the preceding chapter, so largely discoursed. The introduction of the Gentiles into the Church of Christ, as well as of a remnant or portion of the Jews, being thus clearly intimated, he shows that both of these events had been expressly foretold by the Prophets, who had also affirmed that except the Lord of Sabbath had left them a seed, the national ruin of Israel would have been as complete as that of Sodom and Gomorrah.

The Apostle had thus two great objects in view. In the first place, he illustrates the sovereignty of God as exhibited in the infallible accomplishment of the Divine purposes predicted by the Prophets, which led to the national rejection of the Jews, with the exception of a remnant who were saved by grace. In the second place, he proves that the poses of God were equally fulfilled in bringing in the Gentiles; and this he does in such a way as to cut off, on their part, all pretensions to everything like merit, desert, or worthiness, since, without seeking for it, they attained to the righteousness which is of faith.

Having established these two important truths with great force and clearness, Paul accounts for the fact of the Jews having stumbled at and rejected the Messiah. He shows that the Messiah had been characterized by the Prophets as "that stumbling stone" which God had laid in Zion; and that the Jews stumbled in consequence of their ignorance of the righteousness which God had provided in the fulfillment of His violated law, and of their vain attempt to establish a righteousness of their own.

His discussion of this topic is thus most appropriately introduced. It is also in the last degree important, as furnishing additional confirmation of the sovereignty of God, which is here exhibited in the certainty of the accomplishment of His purposes; while it is testified how well merited was that punishment of rejecting and casting off the great body of the Jews. Paul sums up the whole, by appealing, at the end of the tenth chapter, to the testimonies of Moses and Isaiah, in confirmation of what he had advanced. But still, as the apostasy was so general, it might be concluded that God had for ever cast off the Jewish nation, and had thus made void the promises made to the fathers. This error he once more encounters and largely confutes in the eleventh chapter, where he shows most conclusively that, in whatever form it presents itself, it cannot abide the test of truth. So far is this from being the case, that, in the infallible dispensations of God, a period will arrive when the Redeemer shall come out of Zion, and turn away ungodliness from Jacob; when the whole of Israel shall, as one people, be brought within the bond of that new covenant established with the house of Israel, and with the house of Judah, of the blessings of which

called the children of the living God.

27 Esaias also crieth concerning Israel, Though the number of the children of Israel be as the sand of the sea, a remnant shall be saved:

28 For he will finish the work, and cut it short in righteousness: because a short work will the Lord make upon the earth.

29 And as Esaias said before, Except the Lord of Sabaoth had left us a seed, we had been as Sodoma, and been made like unto Gomorrha.

30 What shall we say then? That the Gentiles, which followed not after righteousness, have attained to righteousness, even the righteousness which is of faith.

31 But Israel, which followed after the law of righteousness, hath not attained to the law of righteousness.

32 Wherefore? Because they sought it not by faith, but as it were by the works of the law. For they stumbled at that stumblingstone;

33 As it is written, Behold, I lay in Sion a stumblingstone and rock of offence: and whosoever believeth on him shall not be ashamed.

ROMANS 10

1 Brethren, my heart's desire and prayer to God for Israel is, that they might be saved.

2 For I bear them record that they have a zeal of God, but not according to knowledge.

3 For they being ignorant of God's righteousness, and going about to establish their own righteousness, have not submitted themselves unto the righteousness of God.

4 For Christ is the end of the law for righteousness to every one that believeth.

5 For Moses describeth the righteousness which is of the law, That the man which doeth those things shall live by them.

6 But the righteousness which is of faith speaketh on this wise, Say not in thine heart, Who shall ascend into heaven? (that is, to bring Christ down from above:)

7 Or, Who shall descend into the deep?

explains its meaning when he says, from Christ, for it signifies a separation. And what is to be separated from Christ, but to be excluded from the hope of salvation? It was then a proof of the most ardent love, that Paul hesitated not to wish for himself that condemnation which he saw impending over the Jews, in order that he might deliver them. It is no objection that he knew that his salvation was based on the election of God, which could by no means fail; for as those ardent feelings hurry us on impetuously, so they see and regard nothing but the object in view. So Paul did not connect God's election with his wish, but the remembrance of that being passed by, he was wholly intent on the salvation of the Jews.

ROMANS 10

1. We here see with what solicitude the holy man obviated offenses; for in order to soften whatever sharpness there may have been in his manner of explaining the rejection of the Jews, he still testifies, as before, his goodwill towards them, and proves it by the effect; for their salvation was an object of concern to him before the Lord, and such a feeling arises only from genuine love. It may be at the same time that he was also induced by another reason to testify his love towards the nation from which he had sprung; for his doctrine would have never been received by the Jews had they thought that he was avowedly inimical to them; and his defection would have been also suspected by the Gentiles, for they would have thought, as we have said in the last chapter, that he became an apostate from the law through his hatred of men.

2. For I bear to them a testimony,

This was intended to secure credit to his love. There was indeed a just cause why he should regard them with compassion rather than hatred, since he perceived that they had fallen only through ignorance, and not through malignancy of mind, and especially as he saw that they were not led except by some regard for God to persecute the kingdom of Christ. Let us hence learn where our good intentions may guide us, if we yield to them. It is commonly thought a good and a very fit excuse, when he who is reproved pretends that he meant no harm. And this pretext is held good by many at this day, so that they apply not their minds to find out the truth of God, because they think that whatever they do amiss through ignorance, without any designed maliciousness, but with good intention, is excusable. But no one of us would excuse the Jews for having crucified Christ, for having cruelly raged against the Apostles, and for having attempted to destroy and extinguish the gospel; and yet they had the same defense as that in which we

they shall all partake. The three following chapters thus hold a very distinguished place in this most instructive Epistle, and exhibit in a manner the most comprehensive, as well as conspicuous and edifying, the sovereignty of God in the government of the world, and the character of His dealings towards men in the whole of the Divine administration.

As the nation of Israel were types of the true Israel, and as their rejection might seem, as has been observed, to militate against the security of the people of God, it was necessary in this ninth chapter to enter fully upon the subject. It was, however, one sure to be highly offensive to the Jews; and therefore Paul introduces it in a manner calculated, as far as possible, to allay their prejudices against him, while at the same time he does not in this matter shun to declare the whole counsel of God, for the instruction of those to whom he wrote.

9. For this is the word of promise, At this time will I come, and Sarah shall have a son. The birth of Isaac was by promise, and without a miracle it would never have taken place. But the birth of Ishmael was not by promise, but in the ordinary course of nature. Thus the children of God specially promised to Abraham were those who, according to the election of God (who had chosen Isaac in preference to Ishmael), were to come into a spiritual relation with Christ, who is emphatically the promised seed in the line of Isaac, Galatians 3:16. To them the spiritual blessings were restricted, while only the temporal advantages of the national covenant belonged to the whole of Israel. This was intimated in God's dealings with Abraham.

ROMANS 10

Paul was fully aware that the doctrine of the sovereignty of God in the rejection of the Jews and the preaching of salvation to the Gentiles, would greatly offend his countrymen. He accordingly begins this chapter with an acknowledgment of their sincerity as actuated by a zeal of God; but before prosecuting the subject of God's sovereignty further, he more particularly recurs to their unbelief, to

which in the preceding chapter he had already alluded. This leads him to remark the contrast between the righteousness of the law and the righteousness of faith. He next insists on the free invitations of the Gospel, which proclaims salvation to all of every nation who believe, and from this takes occasion to point out the necessity of preaching it to the Gentiles. The Gentiles, as he had before proved, were among the children of the promise made to Abraham, and it was only by means of the Gospel that they could be brought to the knowledge of Christ, through which alone the promise to them could be fulfilled. This duty, notwithstanding the objections of the Jews, he therefore urges, and enforces it by referring to the Scriptures, while he answers the objection, that the Gospel had not been generally received. In the last place, he proves, by the testimony of the Prophets, that the rejection of Israel and the in gathering of the Gentiles had been long before predicted, and concludes the chapter by showing that the Jews had both heard and rejected the gracious and long continued invitations to reconciliation with God. In the whole of this chapter, Paul treats in a practical way what in the preceding one he had chiefly referred to the sovereignty of God, to which he afterwards revert.

We here see a beautiful example in Paul of the meekness and gentleness of the Lord Jesus Christ, who prayed for His murderers. The Jews considered Paul as one of their greatest enemies. They had persecuted him from city to city, again and again they had attempted his life, and had succeeded in depriving him of his liberty, yet his affection for them was not diminished. He prayed for them, he accommodated himself to their prejudices as far as his obedience to God permitted, and thus he labored by all means to save some. He here assures those to whom he writes of his cordial good will towards Israel, and of his prayers to God that they might be saved.

1. Brethren, my heart's desire and prayer to God for Israel is, that they might be saved.

Brethren. – Those here addressed are the brethren in Christ to whom Paul wrote, and not the Jews in general, who were his brethren

(that is, to bring up Christ again from the dead.)

8 But what saith it? The word is nigh thee, even in thy mouth, and in thy heart: that is, the word of faith, which we preach;

9 That if thou shalt confess with thy mouth the Lord Jesus, and shalt believe in thine heart that God hath raised him from the dead, thou shalt be saved.

10 For with the heart man believeth unto righteousness; and with the mouth confession is made unto salvation.

11 For the scripture saith, Whosoever believeth on him shall not be ashamed.

12 For there is no difference between the Jew and the Greek: for the same Lord over all is rich unto all that call upon him.

13 For whosoever shall call upon the name of the Lord shall be saved.

14 How then shall they call on him in whom they have not believed? and how shall they believe in him of whom they have not heard? and how shall they hear without a preacher?

15 And how shall they preach, except they be sent? as it is written, How beautiful are the feet of them that preach the gospel of peace, and bring glad tidings of good things!

16 But they have not all obeyed the gospel. For Esaias saith, Lord, who hath believed our report?

17 So then faith cometh by hearing, and hearing by the word of God.

18 But I say, Have they not heard? Yes verily, their sound went into all the earth, and their words unto the ends of the world.

19 But I say, Did not Israel know? First Moses saith, I will provoke you to jealousy by them that are no people, and by a foolish nation I will anger you.

20 But Esaias is very bold, and saith, I was found of them that sought me not; I was made manifest unto them that asked not after me.

21 But to Israel he saith, All day long I have stretched forth my hands unto a disobedient and gainsaying people.

ROMANS 11

1 I say then, Hath God cast away his people? God forbid. For I also am an Isra-

confidently glory. Away then with these vain evasions as to good intention; if we seek God sincerely, let us follow the way by which alone we can come to him. For it is better, as Augustine says, even to go limping in the right way than to run with all our might out of the way. If we would be really religious, let us remember that what Lactantius teaches is true, that true religion is alone that which is connected with the word of God.

And further, since we see that they perish, who with good intention wander in darkness, let us bear in mind, that we are worthy of thousand deaths, if after having been illuminated by God, we wander knowingly and willfully from the right way.

3. For being ignorant of the righteousness of God

See how they went astray through inconsiderate zeal! for they sought to set up a righteousness of their own; and this foolish confidence proceeded from their ignorance of God's righteousness. Notice the contrast between the righteousness of God and that of men. We first see, that they are opposed to one another, as things wholly contrary, and cannot stand together. It hence follows, that God's righteousness is subverted, as soon as men set up their own. And again, as there is a correspondence between the things contrasted, the righteousness of God is no doubt his gift; and in like manner, the righteousness of men is that which they derive from themselves, or believe that they bring before God. Then he who seeks to be justified through himself, submits not to God's righteousness; for the first step towards obtaining the righteousness of God is to renounce our own righteousness.

ROMANS 11

1. I say then

What he has hitherto said of the blindness and obstinacy of the Jews, might seem to import that Christ at his coming had transferred elsewhere the promises of God, and deprived the Jews of every hope of salvation. This objection is what he anticipates in this passage, and he so modifies what he had previously said respecting the repudiation of the Jews, that no one might think that the covenant formerly made with Abraham is now abrogated, or that God had so forgotten it that the Jews were now so entirely alienated from his kingdom, as the Gentiles were before the coming of Christ. All this he denies, and he will presently show that it is altogether false. But the question is not whether God had justly or unjustly rejected the people; for it was proved in the last chapter that when the people, through false zeal, had rejected the righteousness of God, they suffered a just punishment for their presumption, were deservedly

in the flesh. There is no doubt but by apostrophe he might address the unbelieving Jews; but there is nothing like an apostrophe here, nor is there any need of such a supposition. Whoever was addressed, the sentiment would be equally well understood by the unbelieving Jews who should read or hear the Epistle.

My heart's desire and prayer to God. – It is of great importance to remove prejudices as far as possible, and to show good will to those whom we wish to benefit by the publication of Divine truth. We see here the love of a Christian to his bitterest enemies. Paul was abused, reviled, and persecuted by his countrymen, yet he not only forgave them, but constantly prayed for their conversion. Unbelievers often accuse Christians, though very falsely, as haters of mankind, because they faithfully declare that there is no salvation but through faith in Christ.

Here we should especially remark, that while the salvation of his countrymen was the desire of Paul's heart, and while he was endeavoring in every way possible to call their attention to the Gospel, he did not neglect to offer up prayer for them to God. Other means, as we have opportunity, should not be left untried; but prayer is at all times in our power, and in this we should ever persevere. When we are shut out from access to man, we have always access to God, and with Him is the residue of the Spirit. In this duty, we learn from the Epistles that Paul was ever much engaged for his brethren in Christ, and here we see that he did not neglect it in behalf of those by whom he was hated and persecuted. He thus obeyed the injunctions, and imitated the example, of our blessed Lord.

In this verse, too, standing in connection with what immediately precedes it, we learn that Paul's faithful annunciation of these doctrines, which by so many are most erroneously considered as harsh towards men, and unfavorable to the character of God, so far from being opposed to feelings of the warmest affection for others, is closely and intimately conjoined with them.

We should never cease to pray for, and to use all proper means for the conversion of, those who either oppose the Gospel with violence, or from some preconceived opinion. Secret things belong to God, and none can tell whether or not they are among the number of the elect. No one among the Jews was more opposed to the Gospel than Paul himself had been; and every Christian who knows his own heart, and who recollects the state of his mind before his conversion, should consider the repugnance he once felt to the doctrine of grace. We ought not, indeed, to treat those as Christians who do not appear to be such. This would be directly opposed to the dictates of charity, and would tend to lull them into a false security. But assuredly none can have such powerful inducements to exercise patience towards any who reject the Gospel, as they who know who it is that has made them to differ from others, and that by the grace of God they are what they are. These considerations have a direct tendency to make them humble and gentle. Those who are elected shall indeed be finally saved, but this will-take place through the means which God has appointed. It is on this ground that Paul says, "Therefore I endure all things for the elect's sake, that they may also obtain the salvation which is in Christ Jesus with eternal glory."

ROMANS 11

In this chapter the Apostle first denies that the whole of the nation of Israel was indiscriminately rejected, for, as he had already intimated, there was to be a remnant saved, and of that remnant he holds himself forth as a noted example. He then brings again into view the sovereignty of God, in reserving this "remnant according to the election of grace." In the next place, he affirms that, though blindness in part, as had been expressly foretold, had happened to Israel, yet, seeing that the gifts and calling of God are without repentance, the period must arrive when, according to the repeated promises of Scripture, all Israel shall be saved. They shall be brought in with the fullness of the Gentiles, when the wisdom and the goodness of God, in His dealings towards both, will be finally unfolded, and the assembled universe shall with one voice acknowledge that God is all in all, and that of Him,

elite, of the seed of Abraham, of the tribe of Benjamin.

2 God hath not cast away his people which he foreknew. Wot ye not what the scripture saith of Elias? how he maketh intercession to God against Israel, saying,

3 Lord, they have killed thy prophets, and digged down thine altars; and I am left alone, and they seek my life.

4 But what saith the answer of God unto him? I have reserved to myself seven thousand men, who have not bowed the knee to the image of Baal.

5 Even so then at this present time also there is a remnant according to the election of grace.

6 And if by grace, then is it no more of works: otherwise grace is no more grace. But if it be of works, then is it no more grace: otherwise work is no more work.

7 What then? Israel hath not obtained that which he seeketh for; but the election hath obtained it, and the rest were blinded

8 (According as it is written, God hath given them the spirit of slumber, eyes that they should not see, and ears that they should not hear;) unto this day.

9 And David saith, Let their table be made a snare, and a trap, and a stumbling block, and a recompence unto them:

10 Let their eyes be darkened, that they may not see, and bow down their back alway.

11 I say then, Have they stumbled that they should fall? God forbid: but rather through their fall salvation is come unto the Gentiles, for to provoke them to jealousy.

12 Now if the fall of them be the riches of the world, and the diminishing of them the riches of the Gentiles; how much more their fullness?

13 For I speak to you Gentiles, inasmuch as I am the apostle of the Gentiles, I magnify mine office:

14 If by any means I may provoke to emulation them which are my flesh, and might save some of them.

15 For if the casting away of them be the reconciling of the world, what shall the receiving of them be, but life from the dead?

16 For if the firstfruit be holy, the lump is also holy: and if the root be holy, so are

blinded, and were at last cut off from the covenant. The reason then for their rejection is not now under consideration; but the dispute is concerning another thing, which is this, That though they deserved such a punishment from God, whether yet the covenant which God made formerly with the fathers was abolished. That it should fail through any perfidiousness of men, was wholly unreasonable; for Paul holds this as a fixed principle, that since adoption is gratuitous and based on God alone and not on men, it stands firm and inviolable, howsoever great the unfaithfulness of men may be, which may tend to abolish it. It was necessary that this knot should be untied, lest the truth and election of God should be thought to be dependent on the worthiness of men.

For I am also an Israelite. Before he proceeds to the subject, he proves, in passing, by his own example, how unreasonable it was to think that the nation was utterly forsaken by God; for he himself was in his origin an Israelite, not a proselyte, or one lately introduced into the commonwealth of Israel. As then he was justly deemed to be one of God's special servants, it was an evidence that God's favor rested on Israel. He then assumes the conclusion as proved, which yet he will hereafter explain in a satisfactory manner.

That in addition to the title of an Israelite, he called himself the seed of Abraham, and mentioned also his own tribe; this he did that he might be counted a genuine Israelite, and he did the same in his Epistle to the Philippians, Philippians 3: 4. But what some think, that it was done to commend God's mercy, inasmuch as Paul sprung from that tribe which had been almost destroyed, seems forced and far-fetched.

33. Oh! the depth

Here first the Apostle bursts into an exclamation, which arose spontaneously from a devout consideration of God's dealings with the faithful; then in passing he checks the boldness of impiety, which is wont to clamor against the judgments of God. When therefore we hear, Oh! the depth, this expression of wonder ought greatly to avail to the beating down of the presumption of our flesh; for after having spoken from the word and by the Spirit of the Lord, being at length overcome by the sublimity of so great a mystery, he could not do otherwise than wonder and exclaim, that, the riches of God's wisdom are deeper than our reason can penetrate to. Whenever then we enter on a discourse respecting the eternal counsels of God, let a bridle be always set on our thoughts and tongue, so that after having spoken soberly and within the limits of God's word, our reasoning may at last end in admiration. Nor ought we to be ashamed, that if we are not wiser than he, who, having been taken into the third heaven, saw mysteries to man ineffable, and

and through Him, and to Him are all things, to whom the glory shall be ascribed through the endless ages of eternity.

1. I say then, Hath God cast away His people? God forbid. For I also am an Israelite, of the seed of Abraham, of the tribe of Benjamin.

Dr. Macknight imagines that a Jew, and Mr. Stuart that an objector, is here and in other places in this Epistle introduced as disputing with the Apostle. Such a supposition is not only unnecessary but groundless.

When Paul begins with the words, **I say then,** he states in a manner familiar to the best writers, a very obvious and probable objection which he was about to remove.

Hath God cast away His people? God forbid. – Some might conclude, from the previous declarations of the Apostle, that the whole Jewish nation was now rejected of God, and for ever excluded from the blessings of the Gospel. This inference he strongly disclaims, and shows that God designed even now to reserve for Himself a people out of the Jews as well as out of the Gentiles, while, hereafter, it is the Divine purpose to recall the whole nation to Himself. Paul therefore answers his own pointed interrogatory, by rejecting the thought with his usual energy, while, to strengthen his denial, he further exhibits himself as a signal example of one not cast away. Had his doctrine involved the total rejection of the Jews, he would have pronounced his own condemnation.

For I also am an Israelite of the seed of Abraham, of the tribe of Benjamin. – Besides being an Israelite, Paul here states that he was of the seed of Abraham. This was implied in his being an Israelite, but it is not needless tautology. A charge is often brought of tautology when the reiteration of an important truth is made for the purpose of giving it redoubled force. Although, in declaring himself an Israelite, he virtually claimed a direct descent from Abraham, yet it was a fact of no ordinary moment, and one therefore on which he emphatically dwells. It is his object to impress on the minds of his readers a sense of its intrinsic importance, as well as to recall to their recollection the covenant of God with Abraham, which confirmed the promises made to him respecting his descendants. This was much to the Apostle's purpose, in affirming that God had not cast away the children of him who was called the friend of God. Paul likewise adds that he was of the tribe of Benjamin. It was doubtless an honor to deduce his lineage through a tribe which adhered to the true worship of God, and had not revolted from the house of David. The fact, too, of his being enabled with certainty to trace his pedigree from Benjamin was sufficient to establish the purity of his origin, and to prove that he was not merely found mingled with the nation, but was, in the expressive language which he elsewhere adopts, "a Hebrew of the Hebrews," an Israelite by birth, parentage, and unbroken hereditary descent. The design of the Apostle is evidently to magnify his privileges, that he may produce the conviction that he has no interest in teaching anything derogatory to the just pretensions of his countrymen.

6. And if by grace, then is it no more of works; otherwise grace is no more grace. But if it be of works, then it is no more grace; otherwise work is no more work.

The opponents of the doctrine of election maintain that men are chosen on account of their good works **foreseen.** But here it is expressly declared by the Apostle that it is not on account of works at all, whether past, present, or future. What, then, is the source of election?

Grace. – It is an election of grace, or free favor; that is, a gratuitous election, not by the merit of works of any kind, but purely from the favor of God. Grace and works are here stated as diametrically opposite and totally irreconcilable. If, then, election is by grace, it is not of works; for this would imply a contradiction. Grace would not then be grace. Here we have the warrant of Scripture for asserting that a contradiction is necessarily untrue, and that no authority is sufficient to establish two propositions which actually contradict each other.

28. As concerning the Apostle, they are enemies for your sakes; but as touching the

the branches.

17 And if some of the branches be broken off, and thou, being a wild olive tree, wert graffed in among them, and with them partakest of the root and fatness of the olive tree;

18 Boast not against the branches. But if thou boast, thou bearest not the root, but the root thee.

19 Thou wilt say then, The branches were broken off, that I might be graffed in.

20 Well; because of unbelief they were broken off, and thou standest by faith. Be not highminded, but fear:

21 For if God spared not the natural branches, take heed lest he also spare not thee.

22 Behold therefore the goodness and severity of God: on them which fell, severity; but toward thee, goodness, if thou continue in his goodness: otherwise thou also shalt be cut off.

23 And they also, if they abide not still in unbelief, shall be graffed in: for God is able to graff them in again.

24 For if thou wert cut out of the olive tree which is wild by nature, and wert graffed contrary to nature into a good olive tree: how much more shall these, which be the natural branches, be graffed into their own olive tree?

25 For I would not, brethren, that ye should be ignorant of this mystery, lest ye should be wise in your own conceits; that blindness in part is happened to Israel, until the fullness of the Gentiles be come in.

26 And so all Israel shall be saved: as it is written, There shall come out of Sion the Deliverer, and shall turn away ungodliness from Jacob:

27 For this is my covenant unto them, when I shall take away their sins.

28 As concerning the gospel, they are enemies for your sakes: but as touching the election, they are beloved for the fathers' sakes.

29 For the gifts and calling of God are without repentance.

30 For as ye in times past have not believed God, yet have now obtained mercy through their unbelief:

31 Even so have these also now not believed, that through your mercy they

who yet could find in this instance no other end designed but that he should thus humble himself.

Some render the words of Paul thus, "Oh! the deep riches, and wisdom, and knowledge of God!" as though the word bathos was an adjective; and they take *riches* for abundance, but this seems to me strained, and I have therefore no doubt but that he extols God's deep riches of wisdom and knowledge.

How incomprehensible. By different words, according to a practice common in Hebrew, he expresses the same thing. For he speaks of judgments , then he subjoins ways, which mean appointments or the mode of acting, or the manner of ruling. But he still continues his exclamation, and thus the more he elevates the height of the divine mystery, the more he deters us from the curiosity of investigating it. Let us then learn to make no searchings respecting the Lord, except as far as he has revealed himself in the Scriptures; for otherwise we shall enter a labyrinth, from which the retreat is not easy. It must however be noticed, that he speaks not here of all God's mysteries, but of those which are hid with God himself, and ought to be only admired and adored by us.

36. For from him and through him

A confirmation of the last verse. He shows, that it is very far from being the case, that we can glory in any good thing of our own against God, since we have been created by him from nothing, and now exist through him. He hence infers, that our being should be employed for his glory: for how unreasonable would it be for creatures, whom he has formed and whom he sustains, to live for any other purpose than for making his glory known? It has not escaped my notice, that the phrase, eis auton, to him, is sometimes taken for en aut , in or by him, but improperly: and as its proper meaning is more suitable to the present subject, it is better to retain it, than to adopt that which is improper. The import of what is said is – that the whole order of nature would be strangely subverted, were not God, who is the beginning of all things, the end also.

ROMANS 12

After having handled those things necessary for the erection of the kingdom of God – that righteousness is to be sought from God alone, that salvation is to come to us alone from his mercy, that all blessings are laid up and daily offered to us in Christ only – Paul now passes on, according to the best order, to show how the life is to be formed. If it be, that through the saving knowledge of God and of Christ, the soul is, as it were, regenerated into a celestial life, and that the life is in a manner formed and regulated by holy exhortations and precepts; it is then in vain that you

election, they are beloved for the fathers' sakes.

The Apostle next obviates an objection that might be brought against the future recall of the Jews. The great body of the nation – all whom the Apostle declared to be judicially blinded – were now the enemies of God with respect – to the Gospel. They had rejected God's message by His Son, and thus proved themselves His enemies while they called Him their God. The Gentiles, then, might object, How can the Jewish nation ever be grafted in again, seeing they have thus refused to listen to God's message of reconciliation? This the Apostle answers: first, he grants that they were indeed enemies to God, and were dealt with as enemies for their contempt and disbelief of the Gospel. In the next place, he says that this was for the sake of the Gentiles, or on their account. The rejection of the Jews was, in the inscrutable counsels of Jehovah, connected with and overruled for the salvation of the Gentiles. Some understand the words, "for your sakes," as importing that the Jews were enemies to God because of His sending the Gospel to the Gentiles. This no doubt gave the Jews great offense; but it was before this event that they rejected and crucified Christ.

29. For the gifts and calling of God are to without repentance.

The Apostle here announces a general truth applicable to the case before him. The purposes of God are unchangeable, and His gifts and callings irrevocable, so that the nation of Israel cannot be deprived of what He engaged to do for them. What He has given them He will not withdraw, and His choice of them as His special people never can be altered. Calling is in this verse equivalent to election in the preceding. This election or calling as a nation cannot be revoked, and that national election was connected with and subservient to the election to eternal life of multitudes of their descendants, at the period when all Israel shall be saved. For this purpose it was, that in the destruction of Jerusalem the whole Jewish nation was not exterminated: "Except," said our blessed Lord, "those days should be shortened, there should no flesh be saved: but for

the elect's sake those days shall be shortened," Matthew 24:22. The term elect here cannot be applicable to those Jews who had then embraced the Gospel, for the tribulations of those days, even had they not been shortened, would not have caused their destruction, scattered as they were through many countries. It must refer to the elect of God in that future age, when all Israel shall be saved. It was for their sakes, who were to descend from the Jewish people, that the destruction of that people was limited, and for which God was pleased to preserve a part of them, and continues to preserve them to this day. The same reason, then, for this miraculous preservation, had likewise been given by the Prophet Isaiah, "thus saith the Lord, as the new wine is found in the cluster, and one saith, Destroy it not; for a blessing is in it: so will I do for My servants' sakes, that I may not destroy them all. And I will bring forth a seed out of Jacob, and out of Judah an inheritor of My mountains: and Mine elect shall inherit it, and My servants shall dwell there," Isaiah 65:8.

ROMANS 12

Here we enter on the second division of this Epistle, where Paul, according to his accustomed method, enforces the duties of believers, by arguments dependent on his previous exhibition of the grand and influential doctrines of the Gospel. These doctrines, as well as all the commandments of God, may be summed up in one word, namely, in love. By the view which they present of the goodness, the forbearance, and the long-suffering of God, believers are daily led to repentance, while the contemplation of the Divine compassion and philanthropy is calculated to beget reciprocal confidence and child-like affection. "We have known and believed," says the Apostle John, "the love that God hath to us." "We love Him because He first loved us." This love of God does not exclude reverential fear and filial devotion; of which, on the contrary, it is the principle and the foundation – while both together unite in the spirit of adoption to inspire the cry, "Abba, Father!"

also may obtain mercy.

32 For God hath concluded them all in unbelief, that he might have mercy upon all.

33 O the depth of the riches both of the wisdom and knowledge of God! how unsearchable are his judgments, and his ways past finding out!

34 For who hath known the mind of the Lord? or who hath been his counselor?

35 Or who hath first given to him, and it shall be recompensed unto him again?

36 For of him, and through him, and to him, are all things: to whom be glory for ever. Amen.

ROMANS 12

1 I beseech you therefore, brethren, by the mercies of God, that ye present your bodies a living sacrifice, holy, acceptable unto God, which is your reasonable service.

2 And be not conformed to this world: but be ye transformed by the renewing of your mind, that ye may prove what is that good, and acceptable, and perfect, will of God.

3 For I say, through the grace given unto me, to every man that is among you, not to think of himself more highly than he ought to think; but to think soberly, according as God hath dealt to every man the measure of faith.

4 For as we have many members in one body, and all members have not the same office:

5 So we, being many, are one body in Christ, and every one members one of another.

6 Having then gifts differing according to the grace that is given to us, whether prophecy, let us prophesy according to the proportion of faith;

7 Or ministry, let us wait on our ministering: or he that teacheth, on teaching;

8 Or he that exhorteth, on exhortation: he that giveth, let him do it with simplicity; he that ruleth, with diligence; he that sheweth mercy, with cheerfulness.

9 Let love be without dissimulation. Abhor that which is evil; cleave to that which is good.

10 Be kindly affectioned one to another with brotherly love; in honor preferring

show a desire to form the life aright, except you prove first, that the origin of all righteousness in men is in God and Christ; for this is to raise them from the dead.

And this is the main difference between the gospel and philosophy: for though the philosophers speak excellently and with great judgment on the subject of morals, yet whatever *excellency* shines forth in their precepts, it is, as it were, a beautiful superstructure without a foundation; for by omitting principles, they offer a mutilated doctrine, like a body without a head. Not very unlike this is the mode of teaching under the Papacy: for though they mention, by the way, faith in Christ and the grace of the Holy Spirit, it yet appears quite evident, that they approach heathen philosophers far nearer than Christ and his Apostles.

But as philosophers, before they lay down laws respecting morals, discourse first of the end of what is good, and inquire into the sources of virtues, from which afterwards they draw and derive all duties; so Paul lays down here the principle from which all the duties of holiness flow, even this – that we are redeemed by the Lord for this end – that we may consecrate to him ourselves and all our members. But it may be useful to examine *every* part.

1. I therefore beseech you by the mercies of God

We know that unholy men, in order to gratify the flesh, anxiously lay hold on whatever is set forth in Scripture respecting the infinite goodness of God; and hypocrites also, as far as they can, maliciously darken the knowledge of it, as though the grace of God extinguished the desire for a godly life, and opened to audacity the door of sin. But this exhortation teaches us, that until men really apprehend how much they owe to the mercy of God, they will never with a right feeling worship him, nor be effectually stimulated to fear and obey him. It is enough for the Papists, if they can extort by terror some sort of forced obedience, I know not what. But Paul, that he might bind us to God, not by servile fear, but by the voluntary and cheerful love of righteousness, allures us by the sweetness of that favor, by which our salvation is effected; and at the same time he reproaches us with ingratitude, except we, after having found a Father so kind and bountiful, do strive in our turn to dedicate ourselves wholly to him.

21. Be not overcome by evil

This sentence is laid down as a confirmation; for in this case our contest is altogether with perverseness, if we try to retaliate it, we confess that we are overcome by it; if, on the contrary, we return good for evil, by that very deed we show the invincible firmness of our mind. This is truly a most glorious kind of victory, the fruit of which is not only apprehended by the mind, but really perceived, while the Lord is giving success to their patience, than which they can

1. I beseech you therefore, brethren, by the mercy of God, that ye present your bodies a living sacrifice, holy, acceptable unto God, which is your reasonable service.

Brethren. – The Apostle addresses the believers at Rome as his brethren, as standing on the same level with himself regarding acceptance with God.

I beseech you. – We may here remark the difference between the endearing manner of address often used by inspired Apostles, and the haughty, overbearing tone of Popish antichristian tyranny. Those whose authority was avouched by mighty signs and wonders, whose very word was command, strive frequently to express commands as entreaties.

Therefore. – This may have reference to what had been said in the foregoing chapter respecting the Gentiles and the Jewish nation in general, to whom, as being part of the elect remnants, some of those addressed belonged; or rather, as he now enters on the second division of the Epistle, Paul here refers to those grand doctrines of the Gospel which, in the preceding part of it, he had been unfolding, denominating the whole of them, as forming together the great plan of salvation, the **mercies** of God.

By the mercies of God. – The word mercies or compassions is here used in the plural number, because it refers to the different instances before enumerated of Divine compassion. In the foregoing chapter, the Apostle had been declaring the mercies of God in the calling and restoration both of the Gentiles and the Jews, verse 31. But the whole of his preceding discourse contained a most striking and encouraging display of the mercies of God to all believers, in their election and predestination to eternal life, their calling, their deliverance from condemnation, their justification, their union with the Lord Jesus Christ, and communion with God, with the enjoyment of all the unspeakable blessings of the new covenant. Christians are here urged to devote themselves to the service of God by the consideration of these mercies because they present the strongest motives to obedience. How different is the mind of the Apostle from the mind of the world on this subject!

The wisdom of this world rejects the grace of the Gospel, because it is thought to lead to licentiousness. The interests of morality are supposed to be better secured when salvation is suspended on men's good works, than when it is represented as flowing from the Divine compassion. But Paul presents the mercies of God to the mind of believers, as the most powerful incitement to devote themselves to His service. In the remainder of the Epistle, we find him as strenuous in pressing the duty of holiness and personal obedience, as in the previous part of it, in insisting on those truths on which obedience is founded. This ought to convince of their error those who, misunderstanding the doctrine which the Apostle teaches, imagine that it is inconsistent with attention to the peculiar duties of Christianity. It will, however, be seen that the persons who seem to fear that his doctrine tends to licentiousness, are equally opposed to the strictness of his precepts, the observance of which they speak of as impracticable.

7. Or ministry, let us wait on our ministering; or he that teacheth, on teaching.

Or ministry. – The word in the original is that which appropriately designates the office of the deacon. If it refers to office, it must refer to this officer. For though ministry equally applies to Apostles, and all who serve in the Gospel, yet appropriately it refers to one office; and when it is applied to others, it is with circumstances that make the reference obvious. Indeed, what is here said applies to all offices as well as to that of the deacon; but this should not influence us so as to prevent our ascertaining its immediate reference. There is no necessity here to restrict the word to an official meaning, for it will apply to every one who devotes himself to the interests of the body of Christ. As Howard, the philanthropist, was to humanity, so may many Christians be to the Church of Christ, – at least, to that part of it with which they are more immediately connected.

He that teacheth, on teaching. – Fitness to teach is a gift of the Head of the Church, which all who teach ought to possess, and without which no appointment of any one

one another;

11 Not slothful in business; fervent in spirit; serving the Lord;

12 Rejoicing in hope; patient in tribulation; continuing instant in prayer;

13 Distributing to the necessity of saints; given to hospitality.

14 Bless them which persecute you: bless, and curse not.

15 Rejoice with them that do rejoice, and weep with them that weep.

16 Be of the same mind one toward another. Mind not high things, but condescend to men of low estate. Be not wise in your own conceits.

17 Recompense to no man evil for evil. Provide things honest in the sight of all men.

18 If it be possible, as much as lieth in you, live peaceably with all men.

19 Dearly beloved, avenge not yourselves, but rather give place unto wrath: for it is written, Vengeance is mine; I will repay, saith the Lord.

20 Therefore if thine enemy hunger, feed him; if he thirst, give him drink: for in so doing thou shalt heap coals of fire on his head.

21 Be not overcome of evil, but overcome evil with good.

ROMANS 13

1 Let every soul be subject unto the higher powers. For there is no power but of God: the powers that be are ordained of God.

2 Whosoever therefore resisteth the power, resisteth the ordinance of God: and they that resist shall receive to themselves damnation.

3 For rulers are not a terror to good works, but to the evil. Wilt thou then not be afraid of the power? do that which is good, and thou shalt have praise of the same:

4 For he is the minister of God to thee for good. But if thou do that which is evil, be afraid; for he beareth not the sword in vain: for he is the minister of God, a revenger to execute wrath upon him that doeth evil.

5 Wherefore ye must needs be subject, not only for wrath, but also for conscience sake.

wish nothing better. On the other hand, he who attempts to overcome evil with evil, may perhaps surpass his enemy in doing injury, but it is to his own ruin; for by acting thus he carries on war for the devil.

ROMANS 13

1. Let every soul

Inasmuch as he so carefully handles this subject in connection with what forms the Christian life, it appears that he was constrained to do so by some great necessity which existed especially in that age, though the preaching of the gospel at all times renders this necessary. There are indeed always some tumultuous spirits who believe that the kingdom of Christ cannot be sufficiently elevated, unless all earthly powers be abolished, and that they cannot enjoy the liberty given by him, except they shake off every yoke of human subjection. This error, however, possessed the minds of the Jews above all others; for it seemed to them disgraceful that the offspring of Abraham, whose kingdom flourished before the Redeemer's coming, should now, after his appearance, continue in submission to another power. There was also another thing which alienated the Jews no less than the Gentiles from their rulers, because they all not only hated piety, but also persecuted religion with the most hostile feelings. Hence it seemed unreasonable to acknowledge them for legitimate princes and rulers, who were attempting to take away the kingdom from Christ, the only Lord of heaven and earth.

By these reasons, as it is probable, Paul was induced to establish, with greater care than usual, the authority of magistrates, and first he lays down a general precept, which briefly includes what he afterwards says: secondly, he subjoins an exposition and a proof of his precept.

He calls them the higher powers, not the supreme, who possess the chief authority, but such as excel other men. Magistrates are then thus called with regard to their subjects, and not as compared with each other. And it seems indeed to me, that the Apostle intended by this word to take away the frivolous curiosity of men, who are wont often to inquire by what right those who rule have obtained their authority; but it ought to be enough for us, that they *do rule*; for they have not ascended by their own power into this high station, but have been placed there by the Lord's hand. And by mentioning every soul, he removes every exception, lest any one should claim an immunity from the common duty of obedience.

ROMANS 14

1. Him indeed

He passes on now to lay down a precept especially neces-

can make Him a minister of Christ. They who possess the gift of teaching ought to employ it diligently.

21. Be not overcome of evil, but overcome evil with good.

Be not overcome of evil. – Christians are here exhorted not to suffer themselves to indulge a spirit of wrath or resentment from the provocations of their enemies. In the world they will experience evil on the part of others, but they ought never to allow themselves to be drawn into the commission of evil and to be overcome by it. To yield to anger is to be conquered by an enemy. Men in general suppose that to resent an injury is only to show a proper spirit. But in the estimation of God it is the opposite, and manifests defeat. He acts as the Christian, who yields not to anger, but remains without wrath under insult and ill treatment. When the Lord commanded the disciples to forgive their offending brethren, perceiving the difficulty of acting in this manner, they immediately prayed, "Lord, increase our faith." No prayer could be more suitable, and nothing more necessary for the performance of this duty.

Overcome evil with good. – This implies that the injurious person may, by repeated acts of kindness, be won over from his enmity.

ROMANS 13

Christians having become the subjects of a kingdom which is not of this world, might be led to suppose that they were released from the ties of obedience to human authorities, especially such as were not Christians. Far different is the doctrine here taught by the Apostle. He commands "every soul," both Jew and Gentile, to be subject to the existing powers. He makes no exception as to the nature or constitution of any government. He speaks neither of monarchies, nor of republics, nor of mixed constitutions. But he applies all his precepts to every form that government may assume. As there is nothing from which political partisans in the present day more widely differ than from the apostolic doctrine laid down in this chapter, Christians ought to give

to it the more earnest heed, lest they be led away on this subject by the opinions of the world, or of those who "despise government." They ought to examine carefully what is here taught by the Apostle, without attempting to accommodate it to their preconceived views of civil liberty. This is the more necessary, as many have lately embarked in politics with a keenness that will be of no service to their spiritual life, and will rather tend to make them cleave more closely to the dust.

In considering the duties enjoined in the apostolic Epistles, it is constantly to be kept in view that, while written on particular occasions, and addressed to particular churches, they are equally adapted, in the wisdom of God, to all times and circumstances. They are intended for the instruction and guidance of Christians in every country and every age, just as the Decalogue, though delivered to only one nation, and that only once, is binding on every nation under heaven, in every period, till the end of time. Christians learn at present from this passage the will of God respecting their duty to evil government, just as those to whom this Epistle was addressed. It is true that there is an innumerable variety of differences in circumstances; but this is nothing to the purpose.

The things taught in these Epistles are in all circumstances duty. The Roman Christians were under a despotism, and those who read this Epistle may live under a free government. But the duty of obedience is in both cases the same. The powers are under both equally to be obeyed. It is of the utmost moment that Christians, under all forms of government, should have a rule concerning their duty to civil government clear and precise. Such a rule we have here laid down. No practical subject is more fully or more explicitly treated in the word of God. The weakest Christian cannot be at a loss to discover the will of his Lord with respect to obedience to civil government. It is presented to us in the Scriptures in two different aspects, – the one as the ordinance of God, the other as the ordinance of man; and in both these characters obedience is enjoined by the same authority.

6 For for this cause pay ye tribute also: for they are God's ministers, attending continually upon this very thing.

7 Render therefore to all their dues: tribute to whom tribute is due; custom to whom custom; fear to whom fear; honor to whom honor.

8 Owe no man any thing, but to love one another: for he that loveth another hath fulfilled the law.

9 For this, Thou shalt not commit adultery, Thou shalt not kill, Thou shalt not steal, Thou shalt not bear false witness, Thou shalt not covet; and if there be any other commandment, it is briefly comprehended in this saying, namely, Thou shalt love thy neighbour as thyself.

10 Love worketh no ill to his neighbour: therefore love is the fulfilling of the law.

11 And that, knowing the time, that now it is high time to awake out of sleep: for now is our salvation nearer than when we believed.

12 The night is far spent, the day is at hand: let us therefore cast off the works of darkness, and let us put on the Armour of light.

13 Let us walk honestly, as in the day; not in rioting and drunkenness, not in chambering and wantonness, not in strife and envying.

14 But put ye on the Lord Jesus Christ, and make not provision for the flesh, to fulfil the lusts thereof.

ROMANS 14

1 Him that is weak in the faith receive ye, but not to doubtful disputations.

2 For one believeth that he may eat all things: another, who is weak, eateth herbs.

3 Let not him that eateth despise him that eateth not; and let not him which eateth not judge him that eateth: for God hath received him.

4 Who art thou that judgest another man's servant? to his own master he standeth or falleth. Yea, he shall be holden up: for God is able to make him stand.

5 One man esteemeth one day above another: another esteemeth every day alike. Let every man be fully persuaded in his own mind.

6 He that regardeth the day, regardeth

sary for the instruction of the Church – that those who have made the most progress in Christian doctrine should accommodate themselves to the more ignorant, and employ their own strength to sustain their weakness; for among the people of God there are some weaker than others, and who, except they are treated with great tenderness and kindness, will be discouraged, and become at length alienated from religion. And it is very probable that this happened especially at that time; for the Churches were formed of both Jews and Gentiles; some of whom, having been long accustomed to the rites of the Mosaic law, having been brought up in them from childhood, were not easily drawn away from them; and there were others who, having never learnt such things, refused a yoke to which they had not been accustomed.

Now, as man's disposition is to slide from a difference in opinion to quarrels and contentions, the Apostle shows how those who thus vary in their opinions may live together without any discord; and he prescribes this as the best mode – that those who are strong should spend their labor in assisting the weak, and that those who have made the greatest advances should bear with the more ignorant. For God, by making us stronger than others, does not bestow strength that we may oppress the weak; nor is it the part of Christian wisdom to be above measure insolent, and to despise others. The import then of what he addresses to the more intelligent and the already confirmed, is this – that the ampler the grace which they had received from the Lord, the more bound they were to help their neighbors.

17. For the kingdom of God

He now, on the other hand, teaches us, that we can without loss abstain from the use of our liberty, because the kingdom of God does not consist in such things. Those things indeed, which are necessary either to build up or preserve the kingdom of God, are by no means to be neglected, whatever offenses may hence follow: but if for love's sake it be lawful to abstain from meat, while God's honor is uninjured, while Christ's kingdom suffers no harm, while religion is not hindered, then they are not to be borne with, who for meat's sake disturb the Church. He uses similar arguments in his first Epistle to the Corinthians:

"Meat," he says, "for the stomach, and the stomach for meat; but God will destroy both" (1 Corinthians 6: 13): again, "If we eat, we shall not abound" (1 Corinthians 8: 8). By these words he meant briefly to show, that meat and drink were things too worthless, that on their account the course of the gospel should be impeded.

But righteousness and peace. He, in passing, has set these in opposition to meat and drink; not for the purpose of enumerating all the things which constitute the kingdom

1. Let every soul be subject unto the higher powers. For there is no power but of God; the powers that be are ordained of God.

In this verse the Apostle first states the duty he enjoins on Christians towards civil rulers. Next he states the ground on which the command rests as the reason why he gives the injunction: every government is to be obeyed, because there is no government but of God. Lastly, he brings it home to the existing government under which the servants of God are placed.

Let every soul. – This most comprehensive expression shows that to every Christian, in every country, in all variety of situations, and on all occasions, the doctrine which the Apostle is about to teach is applicable.

Be subject unto the higher powers. – By this expression is meant the persons who possess the supreme authority, who are in the 3rd verse denominated **rulers**. Government, in our language, is a term of similar import. No phrase could more clearly and definitely express the duty of subjection to the civil rulers whom God has placed over us, than that which the Apostle here employs.

ROMANS 14

1. Him that is weak in the faith receive ye, but not to doubtful disputations.

Him that is weak in the faith receive ye. – In this verse, and onwards to the 13th of the following chapter, the Apostle, as in the 8th and 10th chapters of First Corinthians, establishes the duty of mutual forbearance among Christians. The subjects of dispute often vary, but the principles here laid down are always the same. The discussion in this chapter regards things in themselves indifferent, as the observance of certain days, and the abstinence from certain kinds of food; the errors, however, into which we may fall respecting them, are represented as springing from weakness of faith, to which every evil that appears among Christians may be traced. We may here remark that, though faith is the gift of God, yet it is on that account no less a duty.

Repentance and every good work are also gifts of God, Acts 5:31; 2 Timothy 2:25;

Ephesians 2:10. All men, notwithstanding, are bound to believe, to repent, and to obey, under pain of God's most awful displeasure. Many of the Jews might be fully instructed in the points which are here treated, and many of the Gentiles might be weak with respect to the defilement of meats offered in sacrifice to idols. Why should it be thought that the Jewish believers in general should be uninstructed, and that every Gentile believer should be fully acquainted with his duty respecting meats? Some of them might in this easily adopt the prejudices of the Jews, and others might have prejudices of their own. To confine what is left general by the Apostle, must be useless, and in some cases very hurtful.

Faith. – Faith here regards the doctrine of the Gospel as a whole. Improper views of any part of it always imply something defective with respect to its nature. But partial ignorance may be consistent with so much knowledge as is connected with salvation.

Receive ye. – That is, into the Church, to the fellowship of the brethren, in all the ordinances of Christ's house.

Doubtful disputations. – The phrase in the original is variously rendered and explained. The meaning seems to be, that when they should receive a weak brother, they should not press him to receive their views by harassing discussions on the points on which he is ignorant. Such conduct would either tend to wound his mind, or induce him to acquiesce without enlightened conviction. Disputation seldom begets unanimity. If a statement of the will of Christ from the Scriptures has not the effect of producing conviction, lengthened discussions are more likely to increase prejudice than to resolve doubts. While, therefore, it is greatly important that believers, who have inadequate views of any part of Divine truth, should be taught more fully the way of the Lord, it is also true that the most likely way to effect this is to avoid disputations with them on the points in which they are weak. This observation is founded on experience, and it is warranted by the command of God. To push them forward faster than they are taught by the word and Spirit of God, will stumble and injure instead of making them strong. Christians seldom

it unto the Lord; and he that regardeth not the day, to the Lord he doth not regard it. He that eateth, eateth to the Lord, for he giveth God thanks; and he that eateth not, to the Lord he eateth not, and giveth God thanks.

7 For none of us liveth to himself, and no man dieth to himself.

8 For whether we live, we live unto the Lord; and whether we die, we die unto the Lord: whether we live therefore, or die, we are the Lord's.

9 For to this end Christ both died, and rose, and revived, that he might be Lord both of the dead and living.

10 But why dost thou judge thy brother? or why dost thou set at nought thy brother? for we shall all stand before the judgment seat of Christ.

11 For it is written, As I live, saith the Lord, every knee shall bow to me, and every tongue shall confess to God.

12 So then every one of us shall give account of himself to God.

13 Let us not therefore judge one another any more: but judge this rather, that no man put a stumblingblock or an occasion to fall in his brother's way.

14 I know, and am persuaded by the Lord Jesus, that there is nothing unclean of itself: but to him that esteemeth any thing to be unclean, to him it is unclean.

15 But if thy brother be grieved with thy meat, now walkest thou not charitably. Destroy not him with thy meat, for whom Christ died.

16 Let not then your good be evil spoken of:

17 For the kingdom of God is not meat and drink; but righteousness, and peace, and joy in the Holy Ghost.

18 For he that in these things serveth Christ is acceptable to God, and approved of men.

19 Let us therefore follow after the things which make for peace, and things wherewith one may edify another.

20 For meat destroy not the work of God. All things indeed are pure; but it is evil for that man who eateth with offence.

21 It is good neither to eat flesh, nor to drink wine, nor any thing whereby thy brother stumbleth, or is offended, or is made weak.

of Christ, but of showing, that it consists of spiritual things. He has at the same time no doubt included in few words a summary of what it is; namely, that we, being well assured, have peace with God, and possess real joy of heart through the Holy Spirit dwelling in us. But as I have said, these few things he has accommodated to his present subject. He indeed who is become partaker of true righteousness, enjoys a great and an invaluable good, even a calm joy of conscience; and he who has peace with God, what can he desire more?

By connecting peace and joy together, he seems to me to express the character of this joy; for however torpid the reprobate may be, or however they may elevate themselves, yet the conscience is not rendered calm and joyful, except when it feels God to be pacified and propitious to it; and there is no solid joy but what proceeds from this peace. And though it was necessary, when mention was made of these things, that the Spirit should have been declared as the author; yet he meant in this place indirectly to oppose the Spirit to external things, that we might know, that the things which belong to the kingdom of God continue complete to us without the use of meats.

ROMANS 15

1. We then who are strong

Lest those who had made more advances than others in the knowledge of God should think it unreasonable, that more burden was to be laid on them than on others, he shows for what purpose this strength, by which they excelled others, was bestowed on them, even that they might so sustain the weak as to prevent them to fall. For as God has destined those to whom he has granted superior knowledge to convey instruction to the ignorant, so to those whom he makes strong he commits the duty of supporting the weak by their strength; thus ought all gifts to be communicated among all the members of Christ. The stronger then any one is in Christ, the more bound he is to bear with the weak.

By saying that a Christian ought not to please himself, he intimates, that he ought not to be bent on satisfying himself, as they are wont to be, who are content with their own judgment, and heedlessly neglect others: and this is indeed an admonition most suitable on the present subject; for nothing impedes and checks acts of kindness more than when any one is too much swallowed up with himself, so that he has no care for others, and follows only his own counsels and feelings.

4. For whatsoever things

This is an application of the example, lest any one should think, that to exhort us to imitate Christ was foreign to his purpose; "Nay," he says, "there is nothing in Scripture

argue one another into their views, and more frequently each is more confirmed in his own opinion. When it is necessary to show the weak brother his errors, it is best to exhibit the truth in its evidences, to leave him to the general use of the means of edification, and to give him affectionate instructions, for the purpose of his becoming stronger in the faith, and riper in his judgment, by the internal influences and teaching of the Holy Spirit. The principles on which the Apostle proceeds are not, that the views of those who differ among themselves are equally well founded, but that they are all brethren, having in view the glory of God and obedience to His will, and that, as their heavenly Father is so indulgent to His children, that, notwithstanding their defects in knowledge, and the consequent difference in their conduct, they ought not to be less forbearing to one another.

8. For whether we live, we live unto the Lord; and whether we die, we die unto the Lord: whether we live, therefore, or die, we are the Lord's.

For whether we live, we live unto the Lord. – The former verse denies that we live or die to ourselves; by inference, therefore, we live or die to Christ. But this verse makes the assertion directly which was implied in the other. Both in life and death we ought to serve God, and endeavor to promote His glory. The end of the verse draws the conclusion.

Whether we live, therefore, or die, we are the Lord's. – Not only are we the Lord's in giving our life at His command, but we are the Lord's in the state of separation between soul and body. Our bodies are the Lord's, and will be preserved by Him till the resurrection, when in glory they shall be given back to us; and our souls, in the presence of God, will have happiness and glory till that period shall arrive.

17. For the kingdom of God is not meat and drink; but righteousness, and peace, and joy in the Holy Ghost.

For the kingdom of God is not meat and drink. – This imports that the service which belongs to the kingdom of God, and which He requires from all His subjects, does not consist in abstaining from, or in using, any kind of meats. The typical dispensation of the Old Testament enjoined a distinction of meats. Men are peculiarly prone to cling to externals in religious worship. It is, then, of great importance to attend to this decision of the Holy Ghost by the Apostle Paul. The distinction of meats has nothing to do in the service of God under the New Testament. This settles the question as to blood. If the eating of blood is still prohibited, it cannot be said that the kingdom of God is not meat and drink.

But righteousness. – This is not the righteousness of God which is imputed to the believer, as is evident from the following verse, but the righteousness of which he is the subject.

ROMANS 15

1. We then that are strong ought to bear the infirmities of the weak, and not to please ourselves.

We then that are strong. – The Apostle continues here to treat of the subject of mutual forbearance among Christians, raking himself with those who are strong in the faith, and who know that under the new covenant there is no longer any distinction in the sight of God between different kinds of meat, or any sanctity in the feast days enjoined to be observed under the Jewish dispensation.

To know the mind of God, as revealed in the Scriptures, is to be strong; to be ignorant of it, is to be weak. It is not the man of the greatest intellectual vigor who is strong, nor the imbecile in understanding who is weak. Many of those who possess the greatest talents, and are most distinguished for mental acquirements, even although Christians, may be weak in respect to the things of God. And many who are of feeble intellect, may be strong in knowledge of Divine things.

Ought to bear the infirmities of the weak. The allusion is to travelers assisting a weak companion, by taking a part of his burden and carrying it for him. The strong believer is to carry the weak believer's burden, by acting as

22 Hast thou faith? have it to thyself before God. Happy is he that condemneth not himself in that thing which he alloweth.

23 And he that doubteth is damned if he eat, because he eateth not of faith: for whatsoever is not of faith is sin.

ROMANS 15

1 We then that are strong ought to bear the infirmities of the weak, and not to please ourselves.

2 Let every one of us please his neighbour for his good to edification.

3 For even Christ pleased not himself; but, as it is written, The reproaches of them that reproached thee fell on me.

4 For whatsoever things were written aforetime were written for our learning, that we through patience and comfort of the scriptures might have hope.

5 Now the God of patience and consolation grant you to be likeminded one toward another according to Christ Jesus:

6 That ye may with one mind and one mouth glorify God, even the Father of our Lord Jesus Christ.

7 Wherefore receive ye one another, as Christ also received us to the glory of God.

8 Now I say that Jesus Christ was a minister of the circumcision for the truth of God, to confirm the promises made unto the fathers:

9 And that the Gentiles might glorify God for his mercy; as it is written, For this cause I will confess to thee among the Gentiles, and sing unto thy name.

10 And again he saith, Rejoice, ye Gentiles, with his people.

11 And again, Praise the Lord, all ye Gentiles; and laud him, all ye people.

12 And again, Esaias saith, There shall be a root of Jesse, and he that shall rise to reign over the Gentiles; in him shall the Gentiles trust.

13 Now the God of hope fill you with all joy and peace in believing, that ye may abound in hope, through the power of the Holy Ghost.

14 And I myself also am persuaded of you, my brethren, that ye also are full of goodness, filled with all knowledge, able also to admonish one another.

which is not useful for your instruction, and for the direction of your life."

This is an interesting passage, by which we understand that there is nothing vain and unprofitable contained in the oracles of God; and we are at the same time taught that it is by the reading of the Scripture that we make progress in piety and holiness of life. Whatever then is delivered in Scripture we ought to strive to learn; for it were a reproach offered to the Holy Spirit to think, that he has taught anything which it does not concern us to know; let us also know, that whatever is taught us conduces to the advancement of religion. And though he speaks of the Old Testament, the same thing is also true of the writings of the Apostles; for since the Spirit of Christ is everywhere like itself, there is no doubt but that he has adapted his teaching by the Apostles, as formerly by the Prophets, to the edification of his people. Moreover, we find here a most striking condemnation of those fanatics who vaunt that the Old Testament is abolished, and that it belongs not in any degree to Christians; for with what front can they turn away Christians from those things which, as Paul testifies, have been appointed by God for their salvation?

But when he adds, that through the patience and the consolation of the Scriptures we might have hope, he does not include the whole of that benefit which is to be derived from God's word; but he briefly points out the main end; for the Scriptures are especially serviceable for this purpose – to raise up those who are prepared by patience, and strengthened by consolations, to the hope of eternal life, and to keep them in the contemplation of it. The word *consolation* some render exhortation; and of this I do not disapprove, only that consolation is more suitable to patience, for this arises from it; because then only we are prepared to bear adversities with patience, when God blends them with consolation. The patience of the faithful is not indeed that hardihood which philosophers recommend, but that meekness, by which we willingly submit to God, while a taste of his goodness and paternal love renders all things sweet to us: this nourishes and sustains hope in us, so that it fails not.

5. And the God of patience

God is so called from what he produces; the same thing has been before very fitly ascribed to the Scriptures, but in a different sense: God alone is doubtless the author of patience and of consolation; for he conveys both to our hearts by his Spirit: yet he employs his word as the instrument; for he first teaches us what is true consolation, and what is true patience; and then he instills and plants this doctrine in our hearts.

But after having admonished and exhorted the Romans

if he had the same weakness, and abstaining from whatever would cause the weak brother to sin. Strictly speaking, it is improper to speak of one believer **bearing with, enduring,** or **tolerating** the opinions of another, for over these he has no control. God only is the Lord of the conscience. The man who speaks of tolerating the belief of another speaks improperly.

And not to please ourselves. – If there be not a spirit of love, there will be a proneness in men to bring forward, and to urge with vehemence anything in which they have received more light than their brethren. This is not for the good of their weak brethren, but to please themselves, and discover their own superior acquirements.

8. Now I say that Jesus Christ was a minister of the circumcision for the truth of God to confirm the promises made unto the fathers:

Now I say. – The Apostle proceeds to reconcile the Jews and Gentiles to each other, by showing them the reason why Jesus Christ, who was equally the Lord of the Jews and the Gentiles, was born a Jew, as a **minister of the circumcision.** Jesus Christ was made under the law and ministered among the Jews; and though He gave some examples of His purpose of mercy to the Gentiles, yet He did not go out to preach to the nations. But this exclusive service among the Jews is not to be understood as indicating an exclusion of His mercy from the nations. It was **for the truth of God.** It was to fulfill the predictions and promises of Scripture, **to confirm the promises made to the fathers.** His ministry was the fulfillment of the promises that God had made to His ancient servants.

27. It hath pleased them verily, and their debtors they are. For if the Gentiles have been made partakers of their spiritual things, their duty is also to minister unto them in carnal things.

It hath pleased them verily. – Paul repeats this expression, in order to show the grounds on which he used it. They thought it good to act so, and good reason they had for it. It was,

indeed, a matter of their own free will; yet it was one to which they were called by the voice of duty. They were debtors to the Jews for the Gospel. Not only did the kingdom of God first originate with the Jews, but it was through the instrumentality of Jews that the Gentiles received it. They carried it to their doors, and besought them to receive the blessing. From this we may learn the extent of the obligation, and the unity of the body of Christ. The services of any one of the Lord's people lays those who receive them under obligations to the whole family to which they belong. If the Gentiles were under obligation to the Jewish brethren on account of being made partakers of the Gospel through their means, how much more are converts under obligation to those who are personally the means of their conversion.

Spiritual things. – This phrase denotes the blessings of the Gospel, and communion with God, and everything that concerns the soul and body in their future state, as distinguished from those things that concern the wants of the body, and relate only to this world, which are called carnal things.

30. Now I beseech you, brethren, for the Lord Jesus Christ's sake and for the love of the Spirit, that ye strive together with me in your prayers to God for me; Now I beseech you, brethren, for the Lord Jesus Christ's sake. – To do everything for the sake of Christ, implies that the thing is agreeable to Christ. It must show love or obedience to Him. We could not be properly required to do anything for Christ's sake which was contrary, or rather which we did not know to be agreeable, to the will of Christ. To pray for one another in our mutual difficulties, is a thing most pleasing and honorable to Christ. But when we are called upon for Christ's sake to assist in the promotion or maintenance of superstition or false religion or in any way to support or countenance it, we ought to resist and not comply.

For **Christ's sake** implies also that those addressed are the people of Christ. They who are not such can do nothing for His sake.

Love of the Spirit. – Some understand this of the love which the Spirit has for Christ's

15 Nevertheless, brethren, I have written the more boldly unto you in some sort, as putting you in mind, because of the grace that is given to me of God,

16 That I should be the minister of Jesus Christ to the Gentiles, ministering the gospel of God, that the offering up of the Gentiles might be acceptable, being sanctified by the Holy Ghost.

17 I have therefore whereof I may glory through Jesus Christ in those things which pertain to God.

18 For I will not dare to speak of any of those things which Christ hath not wrought by me, to make the Gentiles obedient, by word and deed,

19 Through mighty signs and wonders, by the power of the Spirit of God; so that from Jerusalem, and round about unto Illyricum, I have fully preached the gospel of Christ.

20 Yea, so have I strived to preach the gospel, not where Christ was named, lest I should build upon another man's foundation:

21 But as it is written, To whom he was not spoken of, they shall see: and they that have not heard shall understand.

22 For which cause also I have been much hindered from coming to you.

23 But now having no more place in these parts, and having a great desire these many years to come unto you;

24 Whensoever I take my journey into Spain, I will come to you: for I trust to see you in my journey, and to be brought on my way thitherward by you, if first I be somewhat filled with your company.

25 But now I go unto Jerusalem to minister unto the saints.

26 For it hath pleased them of Macedonia and Achaia to make a certain contribution for the poor saints which are at Jerusalem.

27 It hath pleased them verily; and their debtors they are. For if the Gentiles have been made partakers of their spiritual things, their duty is also to minister unto them in carnal things.

28 When therefore I have performed this, and have sealed to them this fruit, I will come by you into Spain.

29 And I am sure that, when I come unto you, I shall come in the fullness of the blessing of the gospel of Christ.

as to what they were to do, he turns to pray for them: for he fully understood, that to speak of duty was to no purpose, except God inwardly effected by his Spirit what he spoke by the mouth of man. The sum of his prayer is – that he would bring their minds to real unanimity, and make them united among themselves: he also shows at the same time what is the bond of unity, for he wished them to agree together according to Christ Jesus. Miserable indeed is the union which is unconnected with God, and that is unconnected with him, which alienates us from his truth.

And that he might recommend to us an agreement in Christ, he teaches us how necessary it is: for God is not truly glorified by us, unless the hearts of all agree in giving him praise, and their tongues also join in harmony. There is then no reason for any to boast that he will give glory to God after his own manner; for the unity of his servants is so much esteemed by God, that he will not have his glory sounded forth amidst discords and contentions. This one thought ought to be sufficient to check the wanton rage for contention and quarreling, which at this day too much possesses the minds of many.

ROMANS 16

1. I commend to you

The greater part of this chapter is taken up with salutations; and as they contain no difficulties, it would be useless to dwell long on them. I shall only touch on those things which require some light by an explanation.

He first commends to them Phoebe, to whom he gave this Epistle to be brought to them; and, in the first place, he commends her on account of her office, for she performed a most honorable and a most holy function in the Church; and then he adduces another reason why they ought to receive her and to show her every kindness, for she had always been a helper to all the godly. As then she was an assistant of the Cenchrean Church, he bids that on that account she should be received in the Lord; and by adding as it is meet for saints, he intimates that it would be unbecoming the servants of Christ not to show her honor and kindness. And since it behooves us to embrace in love all the members of Christ, we ought surely to regard and especially to love and honor those who perform a public office in the Church. And besides, as she had always been full of kindness to all, so he bids that help and assistance should now be given to her in all her concerns; for it is what courtesy requires, that he who is naturally disposed to kindness should not be forsaken when in need of aid, and to incline their minds the more, he numbers himself among those whom she had assisted.

people, and others of the love to one another which the Spirit works in them. The expression is capable in itself of either sense; and other considerations must determine the preference. Some unite both opinions, which is the most mischievous of all methods of interpretation, as it tends to encourage us in slothfulness with respect to the meaning of Scripture, and to a prostitution of Scripture as implying a sense which it does not truly bear. No passage unites two different senses at once. Yet those who, in interpreting Scripture, attach to it only one meaning, when, according to the best of their judgment, it is the true one, are often loudly accused of dogmatism.

The love of God may be either God's love to us, or our love to God; and accordingly, in Scripture, it is sometimes used in the one sense, and sometimes in the other. But it never at the same time signifies both. It is always the connection and other circumstances that must determine the meaning. The love of the Spirit here is most probably the love which the Spirit works in His people, which disposes them to love one another.

Now, from this principle of pure love, Paul entreats their prayers for himself. Love is not the fruit of the natural heart of man. Men are by nature hateful and hating one another. When sinners believe in Christ, the Holy Spirit produces in their hearts love to one another. This phrase, also, whether it refers to the love which the Spirit produces in believers, or which He has for them, clearly implies His Godhead.

That ye strive together with me in your prayers. – The word here employed signifies the strongest exertion, alluding to the struggle of wrestlers in the games. Prayer, then, is not a formal exercise. This shows the great importance at all times, to the Lord's people, of an ardent spirit of prayer.

ROMANS 16

1. I commend unto you Phebe our sister, which is a servant of the church which is at Cenchrea:

I commend unto you Phebe. – Paul here introduces Phebe to the brethren at Rome. Letters of recommendation were unnecessary for those who derived their credentials specially from the Lord, and who were officially well known to the churches. Paul disclaims the necessity of such letters for himself to the church at Corinth, though at his first visit he needed the introduction of Barnabas to the brethren at Jerusalem. There might be doubts respecting Phebe at Rome, as there were doubts at Jerusalem with respect to Paul, and these could not be removed by mere profession, unsupported by sufficient evidence, whether of her faith, or of his apostleship.

Phebe. – This was the name of the moon, one of the objects of the worship of the heathens. The moon was reverenced by females in honor of the goddess Diana. This person retaining that name shows that there is no necessity to renounce names that have been adopted under heathenish in honor of false gods. There is no necessity to give other names, as Christian names.

Sister. – The terms brother and sister, taken from human relations, are given to express the new and spiritual relationship which subsists among believers, who by a new nature have become the sons of God and the brethren of Christ. This shows how nearly Christians are related, and how affectionately they ought to love one another. If Christians be all really brethren and sisters, nothing should disunite them in affection.

Which is a servant, or deaconess. – As deacons were appointed to attend to the poor, so deaconesses were specially set apart in the churches in order to attend to the wants of their own sex.

2. That ye receive her in the Lord, as becometh Saints, and that ye assist her in whatsoever business she hath need of you: for she hath, been a succorer of many, and of myself also.

That ye receive her. – The purpose of Paul's recommendation was, that Phebe should be received by the church.

In the Lord. – That is, that they would receive her as a member of the body of Christ. This shows that none ought to be received

30 Now I beseech you, brethren, for the Lord Jesus Christ's sake, and for the love of the Spirit, that ye strive together with me in your prayers to God for me;

31 That I may be delivered from them that do not believe in Judaea; and that my service which I have for Jerusalem may be accepted of the saints;

32 That I may come unto you with joy by the will of God, and may with you be refreshed.

33 Now the God of peace be with you all. Amen.

ROMANS 16

1 I commend unto you Phebe our sister, which is a servant of the church which is at Cenchrea:

2 That ye receive her in the Lord, as becometh saints, and that ye assist her in whatsoever business she hath need of you: for she hath been a succorer of many, and of myself also.

3 Greet Priscilla and Aquila my helpers in Christ Jesus:

4 Who have for my life laid down their own necks: unto whom not only I give thanks, but also all the churches of the Gentiles.

5 Likewise greet the church that is in their house. Salute my wellbeloved Epaenetus, who is the firstfruits of Achaia unto Christ.

6 Greet Mary, who bestowed much labour on us.

7 Salute Andronicus and Junia, my kinsmen, and my fellowprisoners, who are of note among the apostles, who also were in Christ before me.

8 Greet Amplias my beloved in the Lord.

9 Salute Urbane, our helper in Christ, and Stachys my beloved.

10 Salute Apelles approved in Christ. Salute them which are of Aristobulus' household.

11 Salute Herodion my kinsman. Greet them that be of the household of Narcissus, which are in the Lord.

12 Salute Tryphena and Tryphosa, who labour in the Lord. Salute the beloved Persis, which laboured much in the Lord.

13 Salute Rufus chosen in the Lord, and his mother and mine.

17. And I beseech you

He now adds an exhortation, by which all Churches have often need of being stirred up; for the ministers of Satan are ever ready to take occasion to disturb the kingdom of Christ: and they attempt to make disturbances in two ways; for they either sow discord, by which the minds of men are drawn away from the unity of truth, or they occasion offenses, by which men are alienated from the love of the gospel. The former evil is done when the truth of God is mixed with new dogmas devised by men; and the latter takes place, when by various arts it is made odious and contemptible. He therefore bids all, who did either of these two things, to be observed, lest they should deceive and catch the unwary; and also to be shunned, for they were injurious. Nor was it without reason that he required this attention from the faithful; for it often happens through our neglect or want of care, that such wicked men do great harm to the Church, before they are opposed; and they also creep in, with astonishing subtlety, for the purpose of doing mischief, except they be carefully watched.

21. Timothy

The salutations which he records, served in part to foster union between those who were far asunder, and in part to make the Romans know that their brethren subscribed to the Epistle; not that Paul had need of the testimony of others, but because the consent of the godly is not of small importance.

The Epistle closes, as we see, with praise and thanksgiving to God. It indeed records the remarkable kindness of God in favoring the Gentiles with the light of the gospel, by which his infinite and unspeakable goodness has been made evident. The conclusion has, at the same time, this to recommend it – that it serves to raise up and strengthen the confidence of the godly, so that with hearts lifted up to God they may fully expect all those things which are here ascribed to him, and may also confirm their hope as to what is to come by considering his former benefits. But as he has made a long period, by collecting many things into one passage, the different clauses, implicated by being transposed, must be considered apart.

He ascribes first all the glory to God alone; and then, in order to show that it is rightly due to him, he by the way mentions some of his attributes; whence it appears that he alone is worthy of all praise. He says that he *only is wise;* which praise, being claimed for him alone, is taken away from all creatures. Paul, at the same time, after having spoken of the secret counsel of God, seems to have designedly annexed this eulogy, in order that he might draw all men to reverence and adore the wisdom of God: for we know how inclined men are to raise a clamor, when they can find out

into communion by a church but those who are considered as being in the Lord. It shows also that all who are in the Lord ought to be received. The ground of Christian fellowship is union with Christ.

As becometh saints. – Literally, worthily of the saints; that is, in a manner worthy of the saints. This is usually understood as respecting the receivers, – "in a manner that becomes saints to receive such persons."

But it may respect the received, and signify, "in a manner worthy of those who are received, viz., the saints." The latter appears to be the meaning.

The word **worthily** applies best to this reference. The saints may be poor and despised, but they belong to the family in heaven; they are the brethren of the Lord Jesus Christ, and the sons of God. They are therefore worthy of honorable reception by their brethren.

And that ye assist her. – The saints are not only to receive one another into fellowship and to hospitality, but also they are to pay attention to strangers thus received, assisting them in the business which may have brought them to their place of residence.

For she hath been a succorer of many. – In addition to the general claim, the Apostle enhances the particular claims of Phebe by a reference to her own character. She was a most devoted person, and had exerted herself in assisting the brethren in distress.

Myself also. – In what way Phebe had ministered to the assistance of the Apostle we are not informed. But she might have many opportunities of relieving him, either by contributing to his support or ministering personally to his comfort. Here we see that, while the Apostle often shows the obligation of the churches and individuals to himself, yet he acknowledges with gratitude the services of all who contributed to his relief.

25. Now to Him that is of power to establish you according to my Gospel, and the preaching of Jesus Christ, according to the revelation of the mystery, which was kept secret since the world began.

Now to Him that is of power to establish **you.** – From this we learn that establishment

in the faith is not of ourselves, but of God. It requires the power of Jehovah to stablish His people in the truth. So far from being able to bring themselves into the faith of the Gospel, they are not able to continue in it without God. What blindness, then, is it to boast of the power of man to believe and to keep himself in the truth! Power to do anything in the service of God must be communicated from above.

According to my Gospel. – Here we see in what a Christian is to be established, namely, in the faith according to the Gospel. Men may be established in error, they may die for human traditions, and have a zeal of God, but not according to knowledge; but this is of no value. Paul calls the Gospel his Gospel, to intimate that different doctrines would be preached by false teachers as the Gospel. But all other gospels, except that of Paul and the other Apostles, are false. Believers must be established in Paul's Gospel. How many other gospels are now preached as the Gospel of Christ! yet none of them can avail for the salvation of the soul.

And the preaching of Jesus Christ – This phrase is not the mere repetition of the same thing. It is indeed the same truth, but in a different point of view. In the one it is considered as the Gospel or good news, and this according to the doctrine of Paul. In the other it is considered as the publication of the truth about Jesus Christ. We are to be established according to what the Apostles preached concerning Jesus Christ. Believers have nothing to do with the vain speculations and opinions of men about the way of salvation. They must believe, and ought to be confirmed, in the truth, according as it was originally preached by the Apostles. The preaching of the Gospel is called preaching Jesus Christ, Acts 5:42, who is the subject of the Gospel.

According to the revelation of the mystery. – This is another view of the same truth, but not a mere synonymous expression. The Gospel is here considered as the revelation of a mystery. It was couched in dark figures under the Old Testament dispensation, but is now developed by the Apostles of the Lord. It is first considered as the Gospel, or good news, characterized as the Gospel of Paul; secondly

14 Salute Asyncritus, Phlegon, Hermas, Patrobas, Hermes, and the brethren which are with them.

15 Salute Philologus, and Julia, Nereus, and his sister, and Olympas, and all the saints which are with them.

16 Salute one another with an holy kiss. The churches of Christ salute you.

17 Now I beseech you, brethren, mark them which cause divisions and offences contrary to the doctrine which ye have learned; and avoid them.

18 For they that are such serve not our Lord Jesus Christ, but their own belly; and by good words and fair speeches deceive the hearts of the simple.

19 For your obedience is come abroad unto all men. I am glad therefore on your behalf: but yet I would have you wise unto that which is good, and simple concerning evil.

20 And the God of peace shall bruise Satan under your feet shortly. The grace of our Lord Jesus Christ be with you. Amen.

21 Timotheus my workfellow, and Lucius, and Jason, and Sosipater, my kinsmen, salute you.

22 I Tertius, who wrote this epistle, salute you in the Lord.

23 Gaius mine host, and of the whole church, saluteth you. Erastus the chamberlain of the city saluteth you, and Quartus a brother.

24 The grace of our Lord Jesus Christ be with you all. Amen.

25 Now to him that is of power to stablish you according to my gospel, and the preaching of Jesus Christ, according to the revelation of the mystery, which was kept secret since the world began,

26 But now is made manifest, and by the scriptures of the prophets, according to the commandment of the everlasting God, made known to all nations for the obedience of faith:

27 To God only wise, be glory through Jesus Christ for ever. Amen.

no reason for the works of God.

By adding, that God was *able* to confirm the Romans, he made them more certain of their final perseverance. And that they might acquiesce more fully in his power, he adds, that a testimony is borne to it in the gospel. Here you see, that the gospel not only promises to us present grace, but also brings to us an assurance of that grace which is to endure for ever; for God declares in it that he is our Father, not only at present, but that he will be so to the end: nay, his adoption extends beyond death, for it will conduct us to an eternal inheritance.

as the doctrine preached concerning Jesus Christ by those whom He had inspired to reveal and publish it; and, lastly, it is considered as a mystery revealed. In this there is no tautology. It is designed to present the same thing in several different aspects. The word mystery here refers to the Gospel itself, which was obscurely revealed in the Old Testament. It is the Gospel itself which is called a mystery in Ephesians 3:9. The thing hid in God from the beginning of the world, was the plan of salvation through the death of His Son; and the revelation of it by Christ and His Apostles, was making known the manifold wisdom of God in the redemption of His people. In Colossians 1:26, it is the Gospel as the word of God that is the mystery. In 27, this mystery is said, by the preaching of the Gospel, to be made known among the Gentiles, just as in the verse before us. The calling of the Gentiles is not called a mystery.

1 Corinthians

Introduction by John Calvin

THE advantages of this Epistle are various and manifold; for it contains many special topics, the handling of which successively in their order, will show how necessary they are to be known. Nay, it will appear in part from the argument itself, in the recital of which I shall study to be brief, yet in such a way as to take in the whole, without omitting any of the leading points.

Corinth, as every one knows, was a wealthy and celebrated city of Achaia. While it was destroyed by L. Mummius for no other reason than that the advantageousness of its situation excited his suspicions, posterity afterwards rebuilt it for the same reason that Mummius had for destroying it. The convenience of the situation, too, occasioned its being restored again in a short time. For as it had the Aegean Sea contiguous on the one side, and the Ionian on the other, and as it was a thoroughfare between Attica and the Peloponnesus, it was very conveniently situated for imports and exports. Paul, after teaching there for a year and a half, as Luke mentions in the Acts, constrained at length by the wickedness of the Jews, sailed thence into Syria (Acts 18: 11,18). During Paul's absence false apostles had crept in, not, in my opinion, to disturb the Church openly with wicked doctrines, or designedly to undermine sound doctrine; but, priding themselves in the splendor and magnificence of their address, or rather, being puffed up with an empty loftiness of speech, they looked upon Paul's simplicity, and even the Gospel itself, with contempt. They afterwards, by their ambition, gave occasion for the Church being split into various parties; and, last of all, reck-

less as to every thing, provided only they were themselves held in estimation, made it their aim to promote their own honor, rather than Christ's kingdom and the people's welfare.

On the other hand, as those vices prevailed at Corinth with which mercantile cities are wont to be particularly infested – luxury, pride, vanity, effeminacy, insatiable covetousness, and ambition; so they had found their way even into the Church itself, so that discipline was greatly relaxed. Nay more, purity of doctrine had already begun to decline, so that the main article of religion – the resurrection of the dead – was called in question. Yet amidst this great corruption in every department, they were satisfied with themselves, equally as though every thing had been on the best possible footing. Such are Satan's usual artifices. If he cannot prevent the progress of doctrine, he creeps forward secretly to make an attack upon it: if he cannot by direct falsehoods suppress it, so as to prevent it from coming forth to light, he digs secret mines for its overthrow; and in fine, if he cannot alienate men's minds from it, he leads them by little and little to deviate from it.

As to those worthless persons, however, who had disturbed the Corinthian Church, it is not without good ground that I conclude that they were not open enemies of the truth. We see that Paul nowhere else spares false doctrines. The Epistles to the Galatians, to the Colossians, to the Philippians, and to Timothy, are short; yet in all of them he does not merely censure the false apostles, but also points out at the same time in what respects they injured the Church. Nor is it without good reason; for believers must not merely be admonished as

744

to the persons whom they ought to shun, they must also be shown the evil against which they should be on their guard. I cannot therefore believe that, in this comparatively long Epistle, he was prepared to pass over in silence what he carefully insists upon in others that are much shorter. In addition to this, he makes mention of many faults of the Corinthians, and even some that are apparently trivial, so that he appears to have had no intention of passing over any thing in them that was deserving of reproof. Besides, he must, in any other view, be regarded as wasting many words in disputing against those absurd teachers and prating orators. He censures their ambition; he reproves them for transforming the gospel into human philosophy; he shows that they are destitute of the efficacy of the Spirit, inasmuch as they are taken up with mere ornaments of speech, and seek after a mere dead letter; but not a word is there as to a single false doctrine. Hence I conclude that they were persons who did not openly take away any thing from the substance of the gospel, but, as they burned with a misdirected eagerness for distinction, I am of opinion that, with the view of making themselves admired, they contrived a new method of teaching, at variance with the simplicity of Christ. This must necessarily be the case with all that have not as yet thrown off self, that they may engage unreservedly in the Lord's work. The first step towards serving Christ is to lose sight of ourselves, and think only of the Lord's glory and the salvation of men. Farther, no one will ever be qualified for teaching that has not first himself tasted the influence of the gospel, so as to speak not so much with the mouth, as with the dispositions of the heart. Hence, those that are not regenerated by the Spirit of God – not having felt inwardly the influence of the gospel, and know not what is meant when it is said that we must become new creatures (John 3: 7), have a dead preaching, whereas it ought to be lively and efficacious; and, with the view of playing off their part, they disfigure the gospel by painting it over, so as to make it a sort of worldly philosophy.

Nor was it difficult for those of whom we are now speaking to accomplish this at Corinth. For merchants are usually led away with outward disguises, and they do not merely allow themselves to be imposed upon by the empty show with which they deceive others, but in a manner take delight in this. Besides, as they have delicate ears, so that they cannot bear to be rudely taken to task, so if they meet with teachers of the milder sort, that will handle them gently, they give them, as it were, a reward in turn by caressing them. It is so, I grant, everywhere; but it is more especially common in wealthy and mercantile cities. Paul, who was in other respects a god-like man, and distinguished by admirable virtues, was, nevertheless, not adorned with outward elegance, and was not puffed up with show, with the view of setting himself off to advantage. In fine, as he was inwardly replenished with the genuine excellence of the Spirit, so he had nothing of outward show. He knew not to flatter, and was not concerned to please men (Galatians 1: 10). The one object that he had in view was, that Christ might reign, himself and all others being brought under subjection to him. As the Corinthians were desirous of doctrine that was ingenious, rather than useful, the gospel had no relish for them. As they were eager for new things, Christ had now become stale. Or if they had not as yet fallen into these vices, they were, nevertheless, already of their own accord predisposed to corruptions of that nature. Such were the facilities afforded to the false apostles for adulterating the doctrine of Christ among them; for *adulterated* it is, when its native simplicity is stained, and in a manner painted over, so as to differ nothing from worldly philosophy. Hence, to suit the taste of the Corinthians, they seasoned their preaching in such a way that the true savor of the gospel was destroyed. We are now in possession of the design that Paul had in view in writing this Epistle. I shall now take in the sum of the argument, by noting down briefly the particular heads of discourse.

He begins with an ascription of praise, that is in effect an exhortation, that they should go on as they have begun, and in this way he soothes them beforehand, that he may make them the more docile. Immediately afterwards, however, he proceeds to chide them, making mention of the dissensions with which their Church was infested. Being desirous to cure this evil, he calls upon them to exchange haughtiness for humility. For he overthrows all the wisdom of the world, that the preaching of the Cross may alone be exalted. He also at the same time abases them as individuals, in exhorting them to look around and see what class of persons chiefly the Lord has adopted as members of his flock.

In the *second chapter* he brings forward, by way of example, his own preaching, which, in the account of men, was base and contemptible, but had nevertheless been signalized by the influence of the Spirit. And in the meantime he unfolds at greater length the sentiment, that there is a heavenly and secret wisdom that is contained in the gospel, which cannot be apprehended by any acuteness or perspicacity of intellect, or by any perception of sense, and is not influenced by human reasonings, and needs no meretricious ornament of words or embellishment, but simply by the revelation of the Spirit comes to be known by the understandings of men, and is sealed upon their hearts. He at length comes to this conclusion, that the preaching of the gospel does not merely differ widely from the wisdom of the flesh, and consists in the abasement of the Cross, but cannot be estimated as to its true nature by the judgment of the flesh; and this he does, with the view of drawing them off from a mistaken confidence in their own judgment, by which they measured every thing amiss.

The beginning of the *third chapter* contains the application of this last department of the subject to their case. For Paul complains, that, being carnal, they were scarcely capable of learning the first rudiments of the gospel. He intimates in this way, that the distaste which they had contracted for the word, arose from no fault in the word itself, but from their ignorance; and at the same time he indirectly admonishes them, that they need to have their minds renewed, before they will begin to judge aright. He afterwards shows in what estimation the ministers of the gospel ought to be held – that it ought to be in such a way, that the honor given to them does not in any degree detract from the glory that is due to God – as there is one Lord, and all are his servants: all are mere instruments; he alone imparts efficacy, and from him proceeds the entire result. He shows them, at the same time, what they ought to have as their aim – to build up the Church.

He takes occasion from this to point out the true and proper method of building aright. It is to have Christ alone as the foundation, and the entire structure harmonizing with the foundation. And here, having stated in passing that he is a wise master-builder, he admonishes those that come after him to make the end correspond with the beginning. He exhorts also the Corinthians not to allow their souls to be desecrated by corrupt doctrines, inasmuch as they are temples of God. Here he again brings to naught proud fleshly wisdom, that the knowledge of Christ may alone be in estimation among believers.

In the beginning of the *fourth chapter* he points out what is the office of a true apostle. And as it was their corrupt judgment that prevented them from recognizing him as such, putting it aside, he appeals to the day of the Lord. Farther, as he was contemptible in their view from an appearance of abasement, he teaches them that this ought to be regarded as an honor to him rather than a disgrace. He afterwards brings forward tokens, from which it might in reality appear that he had not consulted his own glory, or his own belly (Romans 16: 18), but had with faithfulness devoted himself exclusively to Christ's work. He comes at length to infer what honor is due to him from the Corinthians. In the close of the chapter he recommends Timothy to them, until he shall come to them himself; and at the same time he forewarns them that, on his coming, he will openly discover how little account he makes of those empty boastings by which the false apostles endeavored to recommend themselves.

In the *fifth chapter* he takes them to task, for silently tolerating an incestuous connection between a son-in-law and a mother-in-law, and instructs them that in connection with a crime of such enormity, there was good reason why they should be covered with shame, instead of being elated with pride. From this he passes on to lay down a general doctrine to this effect, that crimes of that nature ought to be punished with excommunication, that indulgence in sin may be repressed, and that the infection may not spread from one individual to the others.

The *sixth chapter* consists chiefly of two parts. In the *first* he inveighs against law-suits, with which they harassed one another, before unbelievers, to the great dishonor of the gospel. In the *second* he reproves indulgence in fornication, which had come to such a pitch, that it was almost looked upon as a lawful thing. He sets out with a heavy threatening, and afterwards enforces that threatening with arguments.

The *seventh chapter* contains a discussion in reference to virginity, marriage, and celibacy. So far as we may conjecture from Paul's words, a superstitious notion had become prevalent among the Corinthians of this nature – that virginity was a distinguished, and in a manner angelic virtue, so that marriage was held by them in contempt, as though it had been a profane thing. With the view of removing this error, he teaches that every one must consider what his gift is, and not strive in this matter beyond his ability, inasmuch as all have not the same calling. Accordingly he shows who they are that may abstain from marriage, and what ought to be the design of abstaining from it; and on the other hand, who they are that ought to enter into the married state, and what is the true principle of Christian marriage.

In the *eighth chapter* he prohibits them from having fellowship with idolaters in their impure sacrifices, or giving countenance to anything of such a nature as might injure weak consciences. And as they excused themselves on this pretext, that they did not by any means connect themselves with idolaters in any corrupt sentiment, inasmuch as they acknowledged in their heart *one* God, and regarded idols as empty contrivances, he sets aside this excuse, on this principle that every one ought to have a regard to his brethren, and that there are many weak persons whose faith might be staggered by such dissimulation.

In the *ninth chapter* he shows that he requires from them nothing more than he himself practiced, that he may not be reckoned so unreasonable as to impose upon others a law that he did not himself observe. For he puts them in mind how he had voluntarily refrained from availing himself of the liberty granted him by the Lord, lest he should give occasion of offense to any one, and how he had, in things indifferent, put on as it were various appearances, with the view of accommodating himself to all, that they may learn from his example that no one should be so devoted to self as not to endeavor

to accommodate himself to his brethren for their edification.

Now as the Corinthians were highly satisfied with themselves, as we said in the outset, in the beginning of the *tenth chapter* he admonishes them, from the example of the Jews, not to deceive themselves by a mistaken confidence; for if they are puffed up on account of outward things and gifts of God, he shows that the Jews were not without similar ground of glorying, and yet all this availed them nothing, because they abused their privileges. After alarming them by this threatening he returns immediately to the subject on which he had previously entered, and shows how unseemly it is for those who partake of the Lord's Supper to be participants in the "table of devils," that being a shameful and insufferable pollution. He at length draws this conclusion, that all our actions should be regulated in such a manner as not to be an occasion of offense to any one.

In the *eleventh chapter* he clears the public assemblies from certain corrupt observances, which were at variance with Christian decorum and propriety, and shows what gravity and modesty ought to be exercised when we stand in the view of God and angels. He takes them to task, however, chiefly for their corrupt administration of the Supper. He subjoins the method of correcting the abuse that had crept in, which is by calling them back to our Lord's original institution, as the only sure rule and permanent law of right acting.

As, however, many abused spiritual gifts for purposes of ambition, he enters into a discussion, in the *twelfth chapter*, as to the purpose for which they are conferred by God, and also as to what is the proper and genuine use of them, which is, that by contributing mutually to each other's advantage, we may be united together in one body, that of Christ. This doctrine he illustrates by drawing a similitude from the human body, in which, although there are different members and various faculties, there is nevertheless such a symmetry and fellow-feeling, that what has been conferred on the members severally contributes to the advantage of the whole body – and hence love is the best directress in this matter.

The subject he follows out at greater length, and illustrates it more fully in the *thirteenth chapter*. The sum is this – that all things must be viewed in relation to love. He takes occasion from this to make a digression for the purpose of commending that virtue, that he may the more strongly recommend the pursuit of it, and may encourage the Corinthians the more to cultivate it.

In the *fourteenth chapter* he begins to point out more particularly in what respect the Corinthians had erred in the use of spiritual gifts; and as mere show bulked so much in their estimation, he teaches them that in all things edification alone should be looked to. For this reason he prefers prophecy to all other gifts, as being more useful, while the Corinthians set a higher value on tongues, purely from empty show. In addition to this, he lays down the right order of procedure, and at the same time reproves the fault of sounding forth in unknown tongues without any advantage, while in the meantime the doctrine and exhortations, which ought ever to hold the foremost place, were left in the background. He afterwards forbids women to teach publicly, as being a thing unseemly.

In the *fifteenth chapter* he inveighs against a very pernicious error, which, although we can scarcely suppose it to have spread generally among the Corinthians, had nevertheless taken possession of the minds of some of them to such a degree, that it was necessary that a remedy should be openly administered. He appears, however, to have intentionally delayed mentioning this matter until the close of the Epistle, for this reason – that if he had set out with this, or had entered upon it immediately after commencing, they might have thought that they were all reckoned to be in fault. The hope of a resurrection, accordingly, he shows to be so necessary, that, if it is taken away, the whole gospel falls to pieces. Having established the doctrine itself by powerful arguments, he subjoins also the principle and manner of it. In fine, he carefully draws out a full discussion of this point.

The *sixteenth chapter* consists of two parts. In the first of these he exhorts them to relieve the necessity of the brethren at Jerusalem. They were at that time pinched with famine, and they were cruelly treated by the wicked. The apostles had assigned to Paul the charge of stirring up the Churches of the Gentiles to afford them help. He accordingly exhorts them to lay up in store whatever they were inclined to contribute, that it might be transmitted to Jerusalem without delay. He at length concludes the Epistle with a friendly exhortation and congratulations.

Hence we may gather, as I stated in the outset, that the Epistle is replete with most profitable doctrine, containing, as it does, a variety of discussions on many important topics.

The commentaries on 1 Corinthians are by John Calvin and Charles Hodge.

1 CORINTHIANS 1

1 Paul, called to be an apostle of Jesus Christ through the will of God, and Sosthenes our brother,

2 Unto the church of God which is at Corinth, to them that are sanctified in Christ Jesus, called to be saints, with all that in every place call upon the name of Jesus Christ our Lord, both theirs and ours:

3 Grace be unto you, and peace, from God our Father, and from the Lord Jesus Christ.

4 I thank my God always on your behalf, for the grace of God which is given you by Jesus Christ;

5 That in every thing ye are enriched by him, in all utterance, and in all knowledge;

6 Even as the testimony of Christ was confirmed in you:

7 So that ye come behind in no gift; waiting for the coming of our Lord Jesus Christ:

8 Who shall also confirm you unto the end, that ye may be blameless in the day of our Lord Jesus Christ.

9 God is faithful, by whom ye were called unto the fellowship of his Son Jesus Christ our Lord.

10 Now I beseech you, brethren, by the name of our Lord Jesus Christ, that ye all speak the same thing, and that there be no divisions among you; but that ye be perfectly joined together in the same mind and in the same judgment.

11 For it hath been declared unto me of you, my brethren, by them which are of the house of Chloe, that there are contentions among you.

12 Now this I say, that every one of you saith, I am of Paul; and I of Apollos; and I of Cephas; and I of Christ.

13 Is Christ divided? was Paul crucified for you? or were ye baptized in the name of Paul?

14 I thank God that I baptized none of you, but Crispus and Gaius;

15 Lest any should say that I had baptized in mine own name.

16 And I baptized also the household of Stephanas: besides, I know not whether I baptized any other.

17 For Christ sent me not to baptize, but to preach the gospel: not with wisdom of words, lest the cross of Christ should

1 CORINTHIANS 1

1. Paul, called to be an Apostle

In this manner does Paul proceed, in almost all the introductions to his Epistles, with the view of procuring for his doctrine authority and favor. The former he secures to himself from the station that had been assigned to him by God, as being an Apostle of Christ sent by God; the latter by testifying his affection towards those to whom he writes. We believe much more readily the man whom we look upon as regarding us with affection, and as faithfully endeavoring to promote our welfare. In this salutation, therefore, he claims for himself authority, when he speaks of himself as *an Apostle of Christ*, and that, too, as *called by God*, that is, set apart by the will of God. Now, two things are requisite in any one that would be listened to in the Church, and would occupy the place of a teacher; for he must be *called* by God to that office, and he must faithfully employ himself in the discharge of its duties. Paul here lays claim to both. For the name, *Apostle*, implies that the individual conscientiously acts the part of an ambassador for Christ (2 Corinthians 5: 19), and proclaims the pure doctrine of the gospel. But as no one ought to assume this honor to himself, unless he be *called* to it, he adds, that he had not rashly intruded into it, but had been appointed to it by God.

Let us learn, therefore, to take these two things together when we wish to ascertain what kind of persons we ought to esteem as ministers of Christ – a call to the office, and faithfulness in the discharge of its duties. For as no man can lawfully assume the designation and rank of a minister, unless he be called, so it were not enough for any one to be called, if he does not also fulfill the duties of his office. For the Lord does not choose ministers that they may be dumb idols, or exercise tyranny under pretext of their calling, or make their own caprice their law; but at the same time marks out what kind of persons they ought to be, and binds them by his laws, and in fine chooses them for the ministry, or, in other words, that in the first place they may not be idle, and, secondly, that they may confine themselves within the limits of their office. Hence, as the apostleship depends on the *calling*, so the man who would be reckoned an apostle, must show himself to be really such: nay more, so must every one who demands that credit be given him, or that his doctrine be listened to. For since Paul rests on these arguments for establishing his authority, worse than impudent were the conduct of that man who would think to have any standing without such proofs.

It ought, however, to be observed, that it is not enough for any one to hold out to view the title to a call to the office, along with faithfulness in discharging its duties, if he does not in reality give proof of both. For it often happens that

1 CORINTHIANS 1

Salutation, vs. 1–3. Introduction, vs. 4–9. The divisions which existed in the Church at Corinth, vs. 10–16. Defense of the Apostle's mode of preaching, vs. 17–31.

Introduction to the epistle. vs. 1–9.

Paul declares himself to be a divinely appointed messenger of Christ, v. 1.

In this character he addresses the church at Corinth, as those who were sanctified in Christ, and called to be saints. He includes in his salutation all the worshippers of Christ in that vicinity, v. 2; and invokes upon them the blessings of grace and peace, v. 3.

The introduction is as usual commendatory. He thanks God for the favor shown to the Corinthians; for the various gifts by which the gospel had been confirmed among them, and by which they were placed on a full equality with the most favored churches, vs. 4–7. He expresses his confidence, founded on the fidelity of God, that they would be preserved from apostasy until the day of the Lord, vs. 8–9.

1. Paul, called (to be) an apostle of Jesus Christ through the will of God, and Sosthenes (our) brother.

Paul, so called after his conversion and the commencement of his labors among the Gentiles. His Jewish name was Saul. It was common for the Jews to bear one name among their own people, and another among foreigners.

Called (to be) an apostle, that is, appointed an apostle. The apostleship being an office, it could not be assumed at pleasure. Appointment by competent authority was absolutely indispensable. The word **apostle** means literally **a messenger**, and then **a missionary**, or one sent to preach the gospel. In its strict official sense it is applied only to the immediate messengers of Christ, the infallible teachers of his religion and founders of his church. In calling himself an apostle Paul claims divine authority derived immediately from Christ. **By the will of God**, that is, by divine author-

ity. Paul was made an apostle neither by popular election, nor by consecration by those who were apostles before him; but by immediate appointment from God. On this point, see his explicit declaration, Galatians 1: 1.

And Sosthenes (our) brother. In the Greek it is **the** brother. He was a brother well known to the Corinthians, and probably one of the messengers sent by them to the apostle, or whom they knew to be with him. In Acts 18: 17 a man by this name is mentioned as the ruler of the synagogue in Corinth, and a leader of those who arraigned Paul before the judgment seat of Gallio. This identity of name is not a sufficient proof that the person was the same, especially as the name was a common one. The companions of the apostles, whom he associates with himself in his salutations to the churches, are not merely placed in the position of equality of office and authority with the apostle. On the contrary, they are uniformly distinguished in these respects from the writer of the epistles.

Thus it is "Paul **the apostle**," but "Sosthenes **the brother**;" or, "Paul the apostle and Timothy the brother," Colossians 1: 1, and elsewhere. They are associated in the salutation, not in the epistle. Very probably Sosthenes was the amanuensis of Paul in this instance, and Timothy in others.

Of the divisions in the church of Corinth. vs. 10–16.

As one of the principal objects of this epistle was to correct the evils which had arisen in the church of Corinth, the apostle adverts, first, to the divisions which there existed. He exhorts the members of that church to unity, v. 10. The reason of that exhortation was the information which he had received concerning their dissensions. v. 11. These divisions arose from their ranging themselves under different religious teachers as party leaders, v. 12. The sin and folly of such divisions are manifest, in the first place, because Christ is incapable of division. As there is one head, there can be but one body. As there is but one Christ, there can

be made of none effect.

18 For the preaching of the cross is to them that perish foolishness; but unto us which are saved it is the power of God.

19 For it is written, I will destroy the wisdom of the wise, and will bring to nothing the understanding of the prudent.

20 Where is the wise? where is the scribe? where is the disputer of this world? hath not God made foolish the wisdom of this world?

21 For after that in the wisdom of God the world by wisdom knew not God, it pleased God by the foolishness of preaching to save them that believe.

22 For the Jews require a sign, and the Greeks seek after wisdom:

23 But we preach Christ crucified, unto the Jews a stumblingblock, and unto the Greeks foolishness;

24 But unto them which are called, both Jews and Greeks, Christ the power of God, and the wisdom of God.

25 Because the foolishness of God is wiser than men; and the weakness of God is stronger than men.

26 For ye see your calling, brethren, how that not many wise men after the flesh, not many mighty, not many noble, are called:

27 But God hath chosen the foolish things of the world to confound the wise; and God hath chosen the weak things of the world to confound the things which are mighty;

28 And base things of the world, and things which are despised, hath God chosen, yea, and things which are not, to bring to nought things that are:

29 That no flesh should glory in his presence.

30 But of him are ye in Christ Jesus, who of God is made unto us wisdom, and righteousness, and sanctification, and redemption:

31 That, according as it is written, He that glorieth, let him glory in the Lord.

1 CORINTHIANS 2

1 And I, brethren, when I came to you, came not with excellency of speech or of wisdom, declaring unto you the testimony of God.

2 For I determined not to know any thing among you, save Jesus Christ, and him crucified.

none boast more haughtily of their titles than those that are destitute of the reality; as of old the false prophets, with lofty disdain, boasted that they had been sent by the Lord. Nay, at the present day, what else do the Romanists make a noise about, but "ordination from God, and an inviolably sacred succession even from the Apostles themselves," while, after all, it appears that they are destitute of those things of which they vaunt? Here, therefore, it is not boasting that is required, but reality. Now, as the name is assumed by good and bad alike, we must come to the test, that we may ascertain who has a right to the name of Apostle, and who has not. As to Paul, God attested his *calling* by many revelations, and afterwards confirmed it by miracles. The *faithfulness* must be estimated by this – whether or not he proclaimed the pure doctrine of Christ.

2. To the Church of God which is at Corinth

It may perhaps appear strange that he should give the name of a Church of God to a multitude of persons that were infested with so many distempers, that Satan might be said to reign among them rather than God. Certain it is, that he did not mean to flatter the Corinthians, for he speaks under the direction of the Spirit of God, who is not accustomed to flatter. But among so many pollutions, what appearance of a Church is any longer presented? I answer, the Lord having said to him, "Fear not: I have much people in this place" (Acts 18: 9, 10); keeping this promise in mind, he conferred upon a godly few so much honor as to recognize them as a Church amidst a vast multitude of ungodly persons. Farther, notwithstanding that many vices had crept in, and various corruptions both of doctrine and manners, there were, nevertheless, certain tokens still remaining of a true Church. This is a passage that ought to be carefully observed, that we may not require that the Church, while in this world, should be free from every wrinkle and stain, or forthwith pronounce unworthy of such a title every society in which everything is not as we would wish it. For it is a dangerous temptation to think that there is no Church at all where perfect purity is not to be seen. For the man that is prepossessed with this notion, must necessarily in the end withdraw from all others, and look upon himself as the only saint in the world, or set up a peculiar sect in company with a few hypocrites.

What ground, then, had Paul for recognizing a Church at Corinth? It was this: that he saw among them the doctrine of the gospel, baptism, the Lord's Supper – tokens by which a Church ought to be judged of. For although some had begun to have doubts as to the resurrection, the error not having spread over the entire body, the name of the Church and its reality are not thereby affected. Some faults had crept in among them in the administration of

be but one church. And in the second place, because religious teachers are not centres of unity to the church. They had not redeemed it, nor did its members profess allegiance to them in baptism, v. 13. These divisions, therefore, arose, on the one hand, from a forgetfulness of the common relation which all Christians bear to Christ; and, on the other, from a misapprehension of the relation in which believers stand to their religious teachers. Paul expresses his gratitude that he had not given any occasion for such misapprehension. He had baptized so few among them, that no man could suspect him of a desire to make himself the head of the church or the leader of a party, vs. 14–16.

10. Now I beseech you, brethren, by the name of our Lord Jesus Christ, that ye all speak the same thing, and that there be no divisions among you, but (that) ye be perfectly joined together in the same mind and in the same judgment.

There is but one exhortation in this verse, which is expressed first in general terms, "that ye all say the same thing;" and is then explained in the negative form, "that there be no divisions among you;" and then positively, "that ye be perfectly joined together." **By the name of our Lord Jesus Christ,** i.e. out of regard to Christ, Romans 12: 1; 15: 30; 2 Thessalonians 4: 12. Their reverence and love of Christ, and regard for his authority as their Lord, should induce them to yield obedience to the apostle's exhortation. It was not out of respect to him, but out of regard to Christ they should obey. This renders obedience easy and elevating. **To say the same thing** (τὸ αὐτὸ λέγειν) is a phrase of frequent occurrence to express agreement. It may be so understood here, and then the following clauses are explanatory. Or, it may be understood in reference to v. 12, of outward profession. "Do not say I am of Paul, and I of Apollos, but all say the same thing." The former explanation appears the more natural.

And that there be no divisions among you,

literally, **schisms.** The word (σχίσμα) means,

1. A **rent,** as in a garment, Matthew 9: 16.
2. Difference of opinion, John 7: 43.
3. Alienation of feeling, or inward separation.
4. In its ecclesiastical sense, it is an unauthorized separation from the church.

The schisms which existed in Corinth were not of the nature of hostile sects refusing communion with each other, but such as may exist in the bosom of the same church, consisting in alienation of feeling and party strifes.

But (that) ye be perfectly joined together. The original word (καταρτίζω) means **to repair, or to mend,** Matthew 4: 21, **to reduce to place,** as a dislocated limb; **to render complete,** or **perfect** (ἄρτιος); then figuratively, **to restore** or **set right** those in error; **to prepare, to render perfect.** Hence in this place the sense may be, "That ye be perfect," as the Vulgate renders it; or, "that ye be united," as in our translation; or, "that ye be reduced to order." The context shows that the idea of union is what the apostle intended. They were not to be divided, but united. This union was to be both **in mind** and **in judgment** (νοῦς and γνώμη). The former term may refer either to the intellect or feelings. The latter in the New Testament always means judgment or opinion. When the words are united, the former is most naturally understood of feeling, a sense in which the word **mind** is often used by us. The unity which Paul desired was a union in faith and love. Considering the relation in which Christians stand to each other as the members of Christ, dissensions among them are as inconsistent with their character, as conflict between the members of the human body.

Paul's defense of his manner of preaching. vs. 17–31.

The apostle having been led to mention incidentally that he had baptized very few persons in Corinth, assigns as the reason of that fact that his great official duty was to preach the gospel. This naturally led him to speak of

3 And I was with you in weakness, and in fear, and in much trembling.

4 And my speech and my preaching was not with enticing words of man's wisdom, but in demonstration of the Spirit and of power:

5 That your faith should not stand in the wisdom of men, but in the power of God.

6 Howbeit we speak wisdom among them that are perfect: yet not the wisdom of this world, nor of the princes of this world, that come to nought:

7 But we speak the wisdom of God in a mystery, even the hidden wisdom, which God ordained before the world unto our glory:

8 Which none of the princes of this world knew: for had they known it, they would not have crucified the Lord of glory.

9 But as it is written, Eye hath not seen, nor ear heard, neither have entered into the heart of man, the things which God hath prepared for them that love him.

10 But God hath revealed them unto us by his Spirit: for the Spirit searcheth all things, yea, the deep things of God.

11 For what man knoweth the things of a man, save the spirit of man which is in him? even so the things of God knoweth no man, but the Spirit of God.

12 Now we have received, not the spirit of the world, but the spirit which is of God; that we might know the things that are freely given to us of God.

13 Which things also we speak, not in the words which man's wisdom teacheth, but which the Holy Ghost teacheth; comparing spiritual things with spiritual.

14 But the natural man receiveth not the things of the Spirit of God: for they are foolishness unto him: neither can he know them, because they are spiritually discerned.

15 But he that is spiritual judgeth all things, yet he himself is judged of no man.

16 For who hath known the mind of the Lord, that he may instruct him? But we have the mind of Christ.

1 CORINTHIANS 3

1 And I, brethren, could not speak unto you as unto spiritual, but as unto carnal, even as unto babes in Christ.

the Supper, discipline and propriety of conduct had very much declined: despising the simplicity of the gospel, they had given themselves up to show and pomp; and in consequence of the ambition of their ministers, they were split into various parties. Notwithstanding of this, however, inasmuch as they retained fundamental doctrine: as the one God was adored among them, and was invoked in the name of Christ: as they placed their dependence for salvation upon Christ, and, had a ministry not altogether corrupted: there was, on these accounts, a Church still existing among them. Accordingly, wherever the worship of God is preserved uninfringed, and that fundamental doctrine, of which I have spoken, remains, we must without hesitation conclude that in that case a Church exists.

1 CORINTHIANS 2

1. And I, when I came

Paul having begun to speak of his own method of teaching, had straightway fallen into a discussion as to the nature of gospel preaching generally. Now again he returns to speak of himself, to show that nothing in him was despised but what belonged to the nature of the gospel itself, and did in a manner adhere to it. He allows therefore that he had not had any of the aids of human eloquence or wisdom to qualify him for producing any effect, but while he acknowledges himself to be destitute of such resources, he hints at the inference to be drawn from this – that the power of God shone the more illustriously in his ministry, from its standing in no need of such helps. This latter idea, however, he will be found bringing forward shortly afterwards. For the present he simply grants that he has nothing of human wisdom, and in the meantime reserves to himself this much – that he published the testimony of God. Some interpreters, indeed, explain the testimony of God in a passive sense; but as for myself, I have no doubt that another interpretation is more in accordance with the Apostle's design, so that the testimony of God is that which has come forth from God – the doctrine of the gospel, of which he is the author and witness. He now distinguishes between speech and wisdom *He* has not been speaking of mere empty prattling, but has included the entire training of human learning.

16. For who hath known?

It is probable that Paul had an eye to what we read in the 40th chapter of Isaiah. The Prophet there asks, Who hath been God's counselor? Who hath weighed his Spirit (Isaiah 40: 13), or hath aided him both in the creation of the world and in his other works? and, in fine, who hath comprehended the reason of his works? Now, in like manner Paul, by this interrogation, designs to teach, that his secret counsel which is contained in the gospel is far removed from the

the manner of preaching. It was one of the objections urged against him that he did not preach "with the wisdom of words," that is, that he did not preach the doctrines taught by human reason, which he calls the wisdom of the world. Through the remainder of this, and the whole of the following chapter, he assigns his reasons for thus renouncing the wisdom of the world, – and resumes the subject of the divisions existing in the church of Corinth at the beginning of the third chapter.

1. His first reason for not teaching human wisdom is that God had pronounced all such wisdom to be folly, vs. 19–20.

2. Expedience had proved the insufficiency of human wisdom to lead men to a saving knowledge of God, v. 21.

3. God had ordained the gospel to be the great means of salvation, vs. 21–25.

4. The expedience of the Corinthians themselves showed that it was not wisdom nor any other human distinction that secured the salvation of men. Human wisdom could neither discover the method of salvation, nor secure compliance with its terms when revealed. They were in Christ (i.e. converted), not because they were wiser, better, or more distinguished than others, but simply because God had chosen or called them, vs. 26–30.

The design of God in all this was to humble them so that he who glories should glory in the Lord. v. 31.

1 CORINTHIANS 2

Continues his defense of his mode of preaching. In vs. 1–5 he shows that he acted on the principles set forth in the preceding paragraph. In vs. 6–9 he shows that the gospel is the true wisdom. The source of this knowledge, as externally revealed as a spiritually apprehended, is the Holy Spirit, vs. 10–16.

Continuation of his defense of his mode of preaching. vs. 1–16.

As God had determined to save men not by human wisdom but by the gospel, Paul, when he appeared in Corinth, came neither as an orator nor as a philosopher, but simply as a witness, vs. 1, 2. He had no confidence in himself, but relied for success exclusively on the demonstration of the Spirit, vs. 3, 4. The true foundation of faith is not reason, but the testimony of God, v. 5.

Though what he preached was not the wisdom of men, it was the wisdom of God, undiscoverable by human reason, vs. 6–9. The revealer of this divine wisdom is the Holy Ghost, he alone being competent to make this revelation, because he only knows the secret purposes of God, vs. 10–12.

In communicating the knowledge thus derived from the Spirit, the apostle used words taught by the Spirit, v. 13. Though the knowledge communicated was divine, and although communicated in appropriate language, it was not with excellency of speech;' or with the word **declaring**, 'I came not declaring with the spiritual,' vs. 14–16.

1. And I, brethren, when I came to you, came not with excellency of speech or of wisdom, declaring unto you the testimony of God.

And I, i.e. **Accordingly I** 'In accordance with the clearly revealed purpose of God to reject the wisdom of the world and to make the cross the means of salvation.' **Excellency of speech or of wisdom**. As speech and wisdom (λόγος and 50 σοφία) are here distinguished, the former probably refers to the manner or form, and the latter to the matter of his preaching. It was neither as a rhetorician nor as a philosopher that he appeared among them. This clause may be connected either with the word **came**, 'I came not with excellency of speech;' or with the word **declaring**, 'I came not declaring with excellency of speech, etc.' The former mode is generally preferred, not only because of the position of the words in the sentence, but also because of the sense. Paul does not mean to say merely that he did not declare the testimony of God in a rhetorical or philosophical manner; but that what he declared was not the wisdom of men, but the revelation of God.

2 I have fed you with milk, and not with meat: for hitherto ye were not able to bear it, neither yet now are ye able.

3 For ye are yet carnal: for whereas there is among you envying, and strife, and divisions, are ye not carnal, and walk as men?

4 For while one saith, I am of Paul; and another, I am of Apollos; are ye not carnal?

5 Who then is Paul, and who is Apollos, but ministers by whom ye believed, even as the Lord gave to every man?

6 I have planted, Apollos watered; but God gave the increase.

7 So then neither is he that planteth any thing, neither he that watereth; but God that giveth the increase.

8 Now he that planteth and he that watereth are one: and every man shall receive his own reward according to his own labour.

9 For we are labourers together with God: ye are God's husbandry, ye are God's building.

10 According to the grace of God which is given unto me, as a wise masterbuilder, I have laid the foundation, and another buildeth thereon. But let every man take heed how he buildeth thereupon.

11 For other foundation can no man lay than that is laid, which is Jesus Christ.

12 Now if any man build upon this foundation gold, silver, precious stones, wood, hay, stubble;

13 Every man's work shall be made manifest: for the day shall declare it, because it shall be revealed by fire; and the fire shall try every man's work of what sort it is.

14 If any man's work abide which he hath built thereupon, he shall receive a reward.

15 If any man's work shall be burned, he shall suffer loss: but he himself shall be saved; yet so as by fire.

16 Know ye not that ye are the temple of God, and that the Spirit of God dwelleth in you?

17 If any man defile the temple of God, him shall God destroy; for the temple of God is holy, which temple ye are.

18 Let no man deceive himself. If any man among you seemeth to be wise in this world, let him become a fool, that he may be wise.

19 For the wisdom of this world is

understanding of men. This then is a confirmation of the preceding statement.

1 CORINTHIANS 3

1. And I, brethren

He begins to apply to the Corinthians themselves, that he had said respecting carnal persons, that they may understand that the fault was their own – that the doctrine of the Cross had not more charms for them. It is probable, that in mercantile minds like theirs there was too much confidence and arrogance still lingering, so that it was not without much ado and great difficulty that they could bring themselves to embrace the simplicity of the gospel. Hence it was, that undervaluing the Apostle, and the divine efficacy of his preaching, they were more prepared to listen to those teachers that were subtle and showy, while destitute of the Spirit. Hence, with the view of beating down so much the better their insolence, he declares, that they belong to the company of those who, stupefied by carnal sense, are not prepared to receive the spiritual wisdom of God. He tones down, it is true, the harshness of his reproach by calling them *brethren*, but at the same time he brings it forward expressly as a matter of reproach against them, that their minds were suffocated with the darkness of the flesh to such a degree that it formed a hindrance to his preaching among them. What sort of sound judgment then must they have, when they are not fit and prepared as yet even for hearing! He does not mean, however, that they were altogether *carnal*, so as to have not one spark of the Spirit of God – but that they had still greatly too much of carnal sense, so that the flesh prevailed over the Spirit, and did as it were drown out his light. Hence, although they were not altogether destitute of grace, yet, as they had more of the flesh than of the Spirit, they are on that account termed *carnal*. This sufficiently appears from what he immediately adds – that they were *babes in Christ*; for they would not have been *babes* had they not been begotten, and that begetting is from the Spirit of God.

Babes in Christ

This term is sometimes taken in a good sense, as it is by Peter, who exhorts us to be like *new-born babes* (1 Peter 2: 2), and in that saying of Christ, Unless ye become as these little children, "ye shall not enter into the kingdom of God" (Luke 18: 17). Here, however, it is taken in a bad sense, as referring to the understanding. For we must be *children in malice, but not in understanding*, as he says afterwards in 1 Corinthians 14: 20 – a distinction which removes all occasion of doubt as to the meaning. To this also there is a corresponding passage in Ephesians 4: 14.

That we be no longer children tossed to and fro with

The testimony of God may mean either the testimony which Paul bore concerning God, or God's own testimony which Paul bore concerning God, or God's own testimony, i.e. what God had revealed and testified to be true. "The testimony of God" is, in this sense, the gospel, as in 2 Timothy 1: 8. The latter interpretation best suits the connection, as throughout these chapters Paul contrasts what reason teaches with what God teaches. He did not appear as a teacher of human wisdom, but as announcing what God had revealed.

1 CORINTHIANS 3

Transition from the defense of his mode of preaching to the subject of their divisions, vs. 1–5. The true relation of ministers to the church as servants, and not party leaders, vs. 7–23.

Reproof of the Corinthians for their dissensions about their religious teachers. vs. 1–23.

The apostle resumes the subject of the contentions in the church of Corinth. He passes to that subject from the defense of his mode of preaching by a natural association. One of the objections against him was, that his preaching was too simple. He answers, he could not make it otherwise, because they were there babes in Christ. The proof of their being in this infantile or carnal state was that strifes and divisions existed among them; one saying, I am of Paul; and another, I am of Apollos, vs. 1–4.

As their dissentions had reference to their religious teachers, the apostle endeavors to correct the evil by presenting the ministerial office in its true light:

1. Ministers were not heads of schools or rival sects as were the Grecian philosophers, but there servants, without any authority or power of their own. One may plant, and another water, but the whole increase is of God, vs. 5–7.

2. Ministers are one. They have one master and one work. They may have different depart-

ments in that great work, but they are like fellow-laborers on the same farm, or fellow-builders on the same temple, vs. 8–9.

3. In the discharge of their respective duties they incur a great responsibility. If they attempt to build up the temple of God with the rubbish of their own wisdom, they will be severely punished. If they employ the materials which God has furnished, they will be rewarded, vs. 10–15.

4. is because the church is the temple of God, that ministers will be held to this strict account for the doctrines which they preach, and for the way in which they execute their office, vs. 16–17.

5. No minister need deceive himself in this matter. He cannot preach a higher wisdom than the wisdom of God; and to learn that wisdom he must renounce his own, vs. 18–20.

6. Therefore the people should not place their confidence in ministers, who belong to the church, and not the church to them. To the interests and consummation of the church, all things, visible and invisible, are made subservient, vs. 21–23.

1. And I, brethren, could not speak unto you as unto spiritual, but as unto carnal, (even) as unto babes in Christ.

There were two classes of opponents of the apostle in Corinth. The false teachers, some of whom he denounces as anti-Christian, and others he speaks of as only errorists; and secondly, those members of the church whom these false teachers had seduced. As against the false teachers and the unconverted Jews and Greeks he upheld the simple gospel as higher man the wisdom of the world. His only answer to their objection that he did not preach with "the wisdom of words," was that the wisdom of the world was foolishness with God. To the objection, as urged by believers, that his preaching was too elementary, he answered, it was adapted to their state. He could only speak to them as to children.

They were **babes in Christ**, that is, children in Christian knowledge and experience. This

foolishness with God. For it is written, He taketh the wise in their own craftiness.

20 And again, The Lord knoweth the thoughts of the wise, that they are vain.

21 Therefore let no man glory in men. For all things are yours;

22 Whether Paul, or Apollos, or Cephas, or the world, or life, or death, or things present, or things to come; all are yours;

23 And ye are Christ's; and Christ is God's.

1 CORINTHIANS 4

1 Let a man so account of us, as of the ministers of Christ, and stewards of the mysteries of God.

2 Moreover it is required in stewards, that a man be found faithful.

3 But with me it is a very small thing that I should be judged of you, or of man's judgment: yea, I judge not mine own self.

4 For I know nothing by myself; yet am I not hereby justified: but he that judgeth me is the Lord.

5 Therefore judge nothing before the time, until the Lord come, who both will bring to light the hidden things of darkness, and will make manifest the counsels of the hearts: and then shall every man have praise of God.

6 And these things, brethren, I have in a figure transferred to myself and to Apollos for your sakes; that ye might learn in us not to think of men above that which is written, that no one of you be puffed up for one against another.

7 For who maketh thee to differ from another? and what hast thou that thou didst not receive? now if thou didst receive it, why dost thou glory, as if thou hadst not received it?

8 Now ye are full, now ye are rich, ye have reigned as kings without us: and I would to God ye did reign, that we also might reign with you.

9 For I think that God hath set forth us the apostles last, as it were appointed to death: for we are made a spectacle unto the world, and to angels, and to men.

10 We are fools for Christ's sake, but ye are wise in Christ; we are weak, but ye are strong; ye are honorable, but we are despised.

11 Even unto this present hour we both hunger, and thirst, and are naked, and are buffeted, and have no certain

every wind of doctrine, and made the sport of human fallacies, but may day by day grow up, etc.

23. Christ is God's

This subjection relates to Christ's humanity, for by taking upon him our flesh, he assumed "the form" and condition "of a servant," that he might make himself obedient to his Father in all things. (Philippians 2: 7,8). And assuredly, that we may cleave to God through him, it is necessary that he have God as his *head* (1 Corinthians 11: 3). We must observe, however, with what intention Paul has added this. For he admonishes us, that the sum of our felicity consists in this, that we are united to God who is the chief good, and this is accomplished when we are gathered together under the *head* that our heavenly Father has set over us. In the same sense Christ said to his disciples, "Ye ought to rejoice, because I go to the Father, for the Father is greater than I" (John 14: 28), for there he set himself forth as the medium, through which believers come to the original source of every blessing. It is certain, that those are left destitute of that signal blessing, who depart from the unity of the Head. Hence this order of things suits the connection of the passage – that those subject themselves to Christ alone, who desire to remain under God's jurisdiction.

1 CORINTHIANS 4

1. Let a man so account of us

As it was a matter of no little importance to see the Church in this manner torn by corrupt factions, from the likings or dislikings that were entertained towards individuals, he enters into a still more lengthened discussion as to the ministry of the word. Here there are *three* things to be considered in their order.

In the *first* place, Paul describes the office of a pastor of the Church.

Secondly, he shows, that it is not enough for any one to produce a title, or even to undertake the duty – a faithful administration of the office being requisite.

Thirdly, as the judgment formed of him by the Corinthians was preposterous, he calls both himself and them to the judgment-seat of Christ. In the first place, then, he teaches in what estimation every teacher in the Church ought to be held. In this department he modifies his discourse in such a manner as neither, on the one hand, to lower the credit of the ministry, nor, on the other, to assign to man more than is expedient. For both of these things are exceedingly dangerous, because, when ministers are lowered, contempt of the word arises, while, on the other hand, if they are extolled beyond measure, they abuse liberty, and become "wanton against the Lord." (1 Timothy 5: 11). Now the medium observed by Paul consists in this, that

idea he expresses by saying they were not **spiritual** but **carnal**. Now as all Christians are spiritual, in the sense in which that term is used in the preceding chapter, to say that men are not spiritual in that sense, would be to say they are not Christians. Here, however, the apostle tells those whom he admits to be Christians, and whom he calls brethren, that they are not spiritual. He must use the word therefore in a modified sense. This is a very common usage. When we predicate spirituality of a Christian as compared to other Christians, we mean that he is eminently spiritual. But when the distinction is between Christians and the world, then every Christian is said to be spiritual. In like manner we speak of some Christians as worldly or carnal, without intending to deny that they are Christians. It is obvious that the apostle uses the terms here in the same manner. He is not speaking of Christians as distinguished from the world, but of one class of Christians as distinguished from another.

1 CORINTHIANS 4

Deduction from the preceding discussion, teaching the proper light in which the people should regard the ministry, vs. 1–6. contrast between the apostles and the false teachers, vs. 6–21.

Ministers, as stewards, should be faithful, as Paul had proved himself to be, vs. 1–21.

It follows, from what was said in the preceding chapter, that the people should regard their ministers as the servants of Christ, and dispensers of the truths which God had revealed, v. 1. The most important qualification of a dispenser is fidelity, v. 2. It is a small matter how men may estimate the fidelity of ministers. The only competent judge is the Lord; and, therefore, to his judgment the decision of that question should be referred, vs. 3–6.

What the apostle had said of himself and of Apollos, in the foregoing exhibition of the true nature of the ministerial office, was intended to apply to all ministers, that the people should

not estimate them unduly, and that all emulous contentions might be avoided, vs. 6–7. The false teachers in Corinth, and the people under their influence, considered themselves to be in a high state of religious prosperity, and were disposed to self-indulgence, v. 8. The apostles were in a very different condition, at least as to their external circumstances. They were despised, afflicted, and persecuted; while their adversaries were honored, prosperous, and caressed, vs. 9–13. Paul presented this contrast not to mortify, but to admonish his readers, v. 14. He, if any one, had a right to admonish them, for he was their spiritual father, v. 15. They should therefore imitate him; and, to that end, he had sent Timothy to remind them of his instructions and example, vs. 16–17. He himself intended soon to visit Corinth; and it depended on them whether he should come with a rod, or in the Spirit of meekness, vs. 18–21.

1. Let a man so account of us, as of the ministers of Christ, and stewards of the mysteries of God.

This is the conclusion or deduction from the preceding discussion.

Ministers are the servants of Christ, and stewards of God. **Let a man**, i.e. every one. **Account of us**, (λογιζέσθω) let him think of us, or regard us as being. **The ministers of Christ**. Literally the word (ὑπηρέτης) means an **under-rower**, or common sailor; and men, subordinate servant of any kind.

It is generally and properly used of menials, or of those of the lower class of servants. This is not always the case, but here the idea of entire subjection is to be retained. Ministers are the mere servants of Christ; they have no authority of their own; their whole business is to do what they are commanded.

And stewards of the mysteries of God. Stewards (οἰκονόμοι) were generally slaves appointed as managers or overseers. It was their business to direct the affairs of the household, and dispense the provisions. It is as **dispensers** ministers are here called

dwellingplace;

12 And labour, working with our own hands: being reviled, we bless; being persecuted, we suffer it:

13 Being defamed, we intreat: we are made as the filth of the world, and are the offscouring of all things unto this day.

14 I write not these things to shame you, but as my beloved sons I warn you.

15 For though ye have ten thousand instructors in Christ, yet have ye not many fathers: for in Christ Jesus I have begotten you through the gospel.

16 Wherefore I beseech you, be ye followers of me.

17 For this cause have I sent unto you Timotheus, who is my beloved son, and faithful in the Lord, who shall bring you into remembrance of my ways which be in Christ, as I teach every where in every church.

18 Now some are puffed up, as though I would not come to you.

19 But I will come to you shortly, if the Lord will, and will know, not the speech of them which are puffed up, but the power.

20 For the kingdom of God is not in word, but in power.

21 What will ye? shall I come unto you with a rod, or in love, and in the spirit of meekness?

1 CORINTHIANS 5

1 It is reported commonly that there is fornication among you, and such fornication as is not so much as named among the Gentiles, that one should have his father's wife.

2 And ye are puffed up, and have not rather mourned, that he that hath done this deed might be taken away from among you.

3 For I verily, as absent in body, but present in spirit, have judged already, as though I were present, concerning him that hath so done this deed,

4 In the name of our Lord Jesus Christ, when ye are gathered together, and my spirit, with the power of our Lord Jesus Christ,

5 To deliver such an one unto Satan for the destruction of the flesh, that the spirit may be saved in the day of the Lord Jesus.

6 Your glorying is not good. Know ye not that a little leaven leaveneth the

he calls them *ministers of Christ*; by which he intimates, that they ought to apply themselves not to their own work but to that of the Lord, who has hired them as his servants, and that they are not appointed to bear rule in an authoritative manner in the Church, but are subject to Christ's authority – in short, that they are servants, not masters.

As to what he adds – *stewards of the mysteries of God*, he expresses hereby the kind of service. By this he intimates, that their office extends no farther than this, that they are *stewards of the mysteries of God*. In other words, what the Lord has committed to their charge they deliver over to men from hand to hand – as the expression is – not what they themselves might choose. "For this purpose has God chosen them as ministers of his Son, that he might through them communicate to men his heavenly wisdom, and hence they ought not to move a step beyond this." He appears, at the same time, to give a stroke indirectly to the Corinthians, who, leaving in the background the heavenly mysteries, had begun to hunt with excessive eagerness after strange inventions, and hence they valued their teachers for nothing but profane learning. It is an honorable distinction that he confers upon the gospel when he terms its contents *the mysteries of God*. But as the sacraments are connected with these mysteries as appendages, it follows, that those who have the charge of administering the word are the authorized *stewards* of them also.

21. What will ye?

The person who divided the Epistles into chapters ought to have made this the beginning of the *fifth* chapter. For having hitherto reproved the foolish pride of the Corinthians, their vain confidence, and their judgment as perverted and corrupted by ambition, he now makes mention of the vices with which they were infected, and on account of which they ought to be ashamed – "You are puffed up, as though everything were on the best possible footing among you, but it were better if you did with shame and sighing acknowledge the unhappiness of your condition, for if you persist, I shall be under the necessity of laying aside mildness, and exercising towards you a paternal severity." There is, however, still more of emphasis in this threatening in which he gives them liberty to choose, for he declares that it does not depend upon himself whether he shall show himself agreeable and mild, but that it is their own fault that he is necessitated to use severity.

1 CORINTHIANS 5

1. It is generally reported that there is among you

Those contentions having originated, as has been observed, in presumption and excessive confidence, he most appropriately proceeds to make mention of their diseases,

stewards. They are to dispense **the mysteries of God**, that is, the truths which God had revealed, and which, as being undiscoverable by human reason, are called mysteries, into the knowledge of which men must be initiated. **Mysteries** here do not mean the sacraments. The word is never used in reference to either baptism or the Lord's Supper in the New Testament. And such a reference in this case is forbidden by the whole context. In the second chapter, the mystery which Paul speaks of is declared to be the gospel considered as a revelation of God. In the Romish church, the principal function of ministers is to dispense the sacraments to which they are assumed to have the power, in virtue of the grace of orders, to give supernatural power. In the apostolic church they were regarded as the dispensers of the truth. This verse, therefore, contains two important truths: Ministers have no arbitrary or discretionary authority in the church. Neither have they any supernatural power, such as is attributed to them in the Romish church. Their authority is merely ministerial, limited by the commands of Christ, and, therefore, to be judged by the standard of those commands, which are known to the whole church. And secondly, they are not, like Aristotle or Plato, the originators of their own doctrines, or the teachers of the doctrines of other men, but simply the dispensers of the truths which God has revealed.

1 CORINTHIANS 5

The case of the incestuous member of the church, vs. 1–5. Exhortation to purity, and to fidelity in discipline, vs. 6–13.

Reproof for retaining an unworthy member in the church. vs. 1–13.

The second evil in the church of Corinth, to which Paul directs his attention, is allowing a man guilty of incest to remain in its communion. He says it was generally reported that fornication was tolerated among them, and even such fornication as was not heard of

among the heathen, v. 1. He reproves them for being inflated, instead of being humbled and penitent, and excommunicating the offender, v. 2. As they had neglected their duty, he determined, in the name of Christ, and as spiritually present in their assembly, to deliver the man guilty of incest to Satan, vs. 3–5. He exhorts to purity, in language borrowed from the Mosaic law respecting the Passover. As during the feast of the Passover all leaven was to be removed from the habitations of the Hebrews, so the Christian's life should be a perpetual paschal feast, all malice and hypocrisy being banished from the hearts and from the assemblies of believers, vs. 6–8.

He corrects or guards against a misapprehension of his command not to associate with the immoral. He shows that the command had reference to church communion, and not to social intercourse, and therefore was limited in its application to members of the church. Those out of the church, it was neither his nor their prerogative to judge. They must be left to the judgment of God, vs. 9–13.

1. It is reported commonly (that there is) fornication among you, and such fornication as is not so much as named among the Gentiles, that one should have his father's wife.

Having dismissed the subject of the divisions in the church of Corinth, he takes up the case of the incestuous member of that church. **It is reported commonly** (ὅλως ἀκούεται). This may mean what our translation expresses, viz., it was a matter of notoriety that fornication existed among them. Ὅλως may have the force of **omnino**, 'nothing is heard of among you except, etc.' Or it may mean, 'In general, fornication is heard of among you.' That is, it was a common thing that fornication was heard of; implying that the offense, in different forms, more or less prevailed. This is the less surprising, considering how little sins of that class were condemned among the heathen and how notorious Corinth was for its licentiousness. To change the moral

whole lump?

7 Purge out therefore the old leaven, that ye may be a new lump, as ye are unleavened. For even Christ our passover is sacrificed for us:

8 Therefore let us keep the feast, not with old leaven, neither with the leaven of malice and wickedness; but with the unleavened bread of sincerity and truth.

9 I wrote unto you in an epistle not to company with fornicators:

10 Yet not altogether with the fornicators of this world, or with the covetous, or extortioners, or with idolaters; for then must ye needs go out of the world.

11 But now I have written unto you not to keep company, if any man that is called a brother be a fornicator, or covetous, or an idolater, or a railer, or a drunkard, or an extortioner; with such an one no not to eat.

12 For what have I to do to judge them also that are without? do not ye judge them that are within?

13 But them that are without God judgeth. Therefore put away from among yourselves that wicked person.

1 CORINTHIANS 6

1 Dare any of you, having a matter against another, go to law before the unjust, and not before the saints?

2 Do ye not know that the saints shall judge the world? and if the world shall be judged by you, are ye unworthy to judge the smallest matters?

3 Know ye not that we shall judge angels? how much more things that pertain to this life?

4 If then ye have judgments of things pertaining to this life, set them to judge who are least esteemed in the church.

5 I speak to your shame. Is it so, that there is not a wise man among you? no, not one that shall be able to judge between his brethren?

6 But brother goeth to law with brother, and that before the unbelievers.

7 Now therefore there is utterly a fault among you, because ye go to law one with another. Why do ye not rather take wrong? why do ye not rather suffer yourselves to be defrauded?

8 Nay, ye do wrong, and defraud, and that your brethren.

9 Know ye not that the unrighteous

the knowledge of which should have the effect of humbling them. First of all, he shows them what enormous wickedness it is to allow one of their society to have an illicit connection with his mother-in-law. It is not certain, whether he had seduced her from his father as a prostitute, or whether he kept her under pretense of marriage. This, however, does not much affect, the subject in hand; for, as in the former case, there would have been an abominable and execrable whoredom, so the latter would have involved an incestuous connection, abhorrent to all propriety and natural decency. Now, that he may not seem to charge them on doubtful suspicions, he says, that the case which he brings forward is well known and in general circulation. For it is in this sense that I take the particle *holos* (generally) as intimating that it was no vague rumor, but a matter well known, and published everywhere so as to cause great scandal.

From his saying that such a kind of whoredom was *not named even among the Gentiles*, some are of opinion, that he refers to the incest of Reuben (Genesis 35: 22), who, in like manner, had an incestuous connection with his mother-in-law. They are accordingly of opinion, that Paul did not make mention of Israel, because a disgraceful instance of this kind had occurred among them, as if the annals of the Gentiles did not record many incestuous connections of that kind! This, then, is an idea that is quite foreign to Paul's intention; for in making mention of the Gentiles rather than of the Jews, he designed rather to heighten the aggravation of the crime. "You," says he, "permit, as though it were a lawful thing, an enormity, which would not be tolerated even among the Gentiles – nay more, has always been regarded by them with horror, and looked upon as a prodigy of crime." When, therefore, he affirms that it was *not named among the Gentiles*, he does not mean by this, that no such thing had ever existed among them, or was not recorded in their annals, for even tragedies have been founded upon it; but that it was held in detestation by the Gentiles, as a shameful and abominable monstrosity, for it is a beastly lust, which destroys even natural modesty. Should any one ask, "Is it just to reproach all with the sin of one individual?" I answer, that the Corinthians are accused, not because one of their number has sinned, but because, as is stated afterwards, they encouraged by connivance a crime that was deserving of the severest punishment.

1 CORINTHIANS 6

12. All things are lawful for me

It is probable, that the Corinthians even up to that time retained much of their former licentiousness, and had still a savor of the morals of their city. Now when vices stalk abroad with impunity, custom is regarded as law, and then

sentiments of a community is a difficult and gradual work. The New Testament furnishes sad evidence, that Jewish and Gentile converts brought into the church many of the errors of their former belief and practice. The word **fornication** (πορνεία) is used in a comprehensive sense, including all violations of the seventh commandment. Here a particular case is distinguished as peculiarly atrocious. The offense was that a man had married his step-mother. His **father's wife** is a Scriptural periphrase for step-mother, Leviticus 18: 8.

That it was a case of marriage is to be inferred from the uniform use of the phrase **to have a woman** in the New Testament, which always means to marry. Matthew 14: 4; 22: 28; 1 Corinthians 7: 2,29. Besides, although the connection continued, the offense is spoken of as past, vs. 2–3. Such a marriage Paul says was unheard of among the Gentiles, that is, it was regarded by them with abhorrence. Cicero, **pro Cluent**. 5–6, speaks of such a connection as an incredible crime, and as, with one exception, unheard of.

It is probable from 2 Corinthians 7: 12, that the father of the offender was still alive. The crime, however, was not adultery, but incest; for otherwise the apostle would not have spoken of it as an unheard of offense, and made the atrocity of it to arise out of the relation of the woman to the offender's father. We have here therefore a clear recognition of the perpetual obligation of the Levitical law concerning marriage. The Scriptures are a perfect rule of duty; and therefore, if they do not prohibit marriage between near relatives, such marriages are not sins in the sight of God. To deny, therefore, the permanency of the law recorded in Leviticus 18, is not only to go contrary to the authority of the apostle, but also to teach that there is for Christians no such crime as incest.

1 CORINTHIANS 6

This chapter consists of two distinct paragraphs. The first, vs. 1–11, relates to lawsuits

before heathen magistrates. The second, vs. 12–20, to the abuse which some had made of the principle, "All things are lawful."

On going to law before the heathen. vs. 1–11.

Paul expresses surprise that any Christian should prosecute a fellow Christian before a heathen judge, v. 1. If Christians are destined to judge the world, and even angels, they may surely settle among themselves their worldly affairs, vs. 2–3. If they had such suits must they appoint those whom the church could not esteem to decide them? Was there not one man among themselves able to act as a judge? vs. 4–6. It was a great evil that they had such lawsuits. It would be better to submit to injustice, v. 7.

Instead, however, of submitting to wrong, they committed it, v. 8. He solemnly assures them that the unjust, or rapacious, or corrupt should not inherit the kingdom of God, vs. 9–10. They had been such, but as Christians they were washed from these defilements, and justified through Christ and by his Spirit, v. 11.

1. **Dare any of you, having a matter against another, go to law before the unjust, and not before the saints?** The third evil in the church of Corinth which the apostle endeavors to correct, was the prosecuting legal suits before heathen judges. There was no necessity for this practice. The Roman laws allowed the Jews to settle their disputes about property by arbitration among themselves. And the early Christians, who were not distinguished as a distinct class from the Jews, had no doubt the same privilege. It is not necessary, however, to assume that the apostle has reference here to that privilege. It was enough that these civil suits might be arranged without the disgraceful spectacle of Christian suing Christian before heathen magistrates. The Rabbins say, "It is a statute which binds all Israelites, that if one Israelite has a cause against another, it must not be prosecuted before the Gentiles."

shall not inherit the kingdom of God? Be not deceived: neither fornicators, nor idolaters, nor adulterers, nor effeminate, nor abusers of themselves with mankind,

10 Nor thieves, nor covetous, nor drunkards, nor revilers, nor extortioners, shall inherit the kingdom of God.

11 And such were some of you: but ye are washed, but ye are sanctified, but ye are justified in the name of the Lord Jesus, and by the Spirit of our God.

12 All things are lawful unto me, but all things are not expedient: all things are lawful for me, but I will not be brought under the power of any.

13 Meats for the belly, and the belly for meats: but God shall destroy both it and them. Now the body is not for fornication, but for the Lord; and the Lord for the body.

14 And God hath both raised up the Lord, and will also raise up us by his own power.

15 Know ye not that your bodies are the members of Christ? shall I then take the members of Christ, and make them the members of an harlot? God forbid.

16 What? know ye not that he which is joined to an harlot is one body? for two, saith he, shall be one flesh.

17 But he that is joined unto the Lord is one spirit.

18 Flee fornication. Every sin that a man doeth is without the body; but he that committeth fornication sinneth against his own body.

19 What? know ye not that your body is the temple of the Holy Ghost which is in you, which ye have of God, and ye are not your own?

20 For ye are bought with a price: therefore glorify God in your body, and in your spirit, which are God's.

1 CORINTHIANS 7

1 Now concerning the things whereof ye wrote unto me: It is good for a man not to touch a woman.

2 Nevertheless, to avoid fornication, let every man have his own wife, and let every woman have her own husband.

3 Let the husband render unto the wife due benevolence: and likewise also the wife unto the husband.

4 The wife hath not power of her own body, but the husband: and likewise also

afterwards vain pretexts are sought for by way of excuse; an instance of which we have in their resorting to the pretext of Christian liberty, so as to make almost everything allowable for themselves to do. They reveled in excess of luxury. With this there was, as usual, much pride mixed up. As it was an outward thing, they did not think that there was any sin involved in it: nay more, it appears from Paul's words that they abused liberty so much as to extend it even to fornication. Now therefore, most appropriately, after having spoken of their vices, he discusses those base pretexts by which they flattered themselves in outward sins.

It is, indeed, certain, that he treats here of outward things, which God has left to the free choice of believers, but by making use of a term expressive of universality, he either indirectly reproves their unbridled licentiousness, or extols God's boundless liberality, which is the best directress to us of moderation. For it is a token of excessive licentiousness, when persons do not, of their own accord, restrict themselves, and set bounds to themselves, amidst such manifold abundance. And in the *first* place, he limits liberty by two exceptions; and *secondly*, he warns them, that it does not by any means extend to fornication. These words, All things are lawful for me, must be understood as spoken in name of the Corinthians (by anticipation), as though he had said, I am aware of the reply which you are accustomed to make, when desirous to avoid reproof for outward vices. You pretend that all things are lawful for you, without any reserve or limitation. *But all things are not expedient.* Here we have the *first* exception, by which he restricts the use of liberty – that they must not abandon themselves to licentiousness, because respect must be had to edification. The meaning is, "It is not enough that this or that is allowed us, to be made use of indiscriminately; for we must consider what is profitable to our brethren, whose edification it becomes us to study. For as he will afterwards point out at greater length (1 Corinthians 10: 23–24), and as he has already shown in Romans 14: 13, etc., every one has liberty inwardly in the sight of God on this condition, that all must restrict the use of their liberty with a view to mutual edification.

I will not be brought under the power of anything

Here we have a *second* restriction – that we are constituted lords of all things, in such a way, that we ought not to bring ourselves under bondage to anything; as those do who cannot control their appetites.

1 CORINTHIANS 7

As he had spoken of fornication, he now appropriately proceeds to speak of marriage which is the remedy for avoiding fornication. Now it appears, that, notwithstanding the greatly scattered state of the Corinthian Church, they still

Dare any of you? Is any one so bold as thus to shock the Christian sense of propriety? **Having a matter.** The Greek phrase (πρᾶγμα ἔχειν) means to have a suit, which is obviously the sense here intended. **To go to law before the unjust.** It is plain that by the **unjust** are meant the heathen. But why are they so called? As the terms holy and righteous are often used in a technical sense to designate the professed people of God without reference to personal character; so the terms sinners and unjust are used to designate the heathen as distinguished from the people of God. The Jews as a class were holy, and the Gentiles were unholy; though many of the latter were morally much better than many of the former. In Galatians 2: 15, Paul says to Peter, "We are by nature Jews, and not sinners of the Gentiles;" meaning thereby simply that they were not Gentiles. The reason why the heathen as such are called the unjust, or sinners, is that according to the Scriptures the denial of the true God, and the worship of idols, is the greatest unrighteousness and therefore the heathen, because heathen, are called the unrighteous. The word **unjust** is too limited a word to answer fully to the Greek term (ἄδικος), which in its scriptural sense means **wicked**, not conformed to the Law of God. In this verse the opposite term, **saints,** or **the holy**, designates Christians as a class; and, therefore, the **unjust** must mean the heathen as a class. The complaint against the Corinthians was not that they went to law before unjust judges, but that they appealed to heathen judges. It is true their being heathen proved them to be unrighteous in the scriptural sense of the term; but it was not their moral character, so much as their religious status, that was the ground of the complaint. It was indeed not to be expected that men governed by heathen laws and principles of morals, would be as fair and just as those governed by Christian principles; but what Paul complained of was, not that the Corinthians could not get justice at the hands of heathen magistrates, but that they acted unworthily of their dignity as Christians in seeking justice

from such a source. Paul himself appealed to Cesar. It was, therefore, no sin in his eyes to seek justice from a heathen judge, when it could not otherwise be obtained. But it was a sin and a disgrace in his estimation for Christians to appeal to heathen magistrates to settle disputes among themselves.

Abuse of the principle of Christian liberty. vs. 12–20.

The principle of Christian liberty, or the doctrine that "all things are lawful," is to be limited in its application to things indifferent; first, by considerations of expediency; and secondly, by regard to our own spiritual freedom, v. 12. From that principle it is legitimate to infer, because of the adaptation of the stomach to food, that all things suited for food are lawful. The one is obviously designed for the other, during the temporary condition of the present life. But no such application of the principle is allowable in the case of fornication; because the body is not designed for that end, but belongs to the Lord, with whom it stands in an indissoluble connection, so that he who raised him up will also raise up our bodies, vs. 13–14. It is because of this intimate relation of our bodies to Christ as his members, that fornication is so great a crime, inconsistent with our union to him as partakers of his Spirit, vs. 15–17. It is, in a peculiar manner, a sin against the body, destructive of its very nature, v. 18. The body is a temple in which the Spirit dwells, but it ceases to be such if profaned by licentiousness, v. 19. Believers must remember that they, even their bodies, are the objects of redemption, having been purchased by the blood of Christ, and therefore they should be devoted to his glory, v. 20.

1 CORINTHIANS 7

Instructions relative to marriage, vs. 1–17. The Gospel was not designed to interfere with the ordinary relations of men, vs. 18–24. Concerning virgins and widows, vs. 25–40.

the husband hath not power of his own body, but the wife.

5 Defraud ye not one the other, except it be with consent for a time, that ye may give yourselves to fasting and prayer; and come together again, that Satan tempt you not for your incontinency.

6 But I speak this by permission, and not of commandment.

7 For I would that all men were even as I myself. But every man hath his proper gift of God, one after this manner, and another after that.

8 I say therefore to the unmarried and widows, It is good for them if they abide even as I.

9 But if they cannot contain, let them marry: for it is better to marry than to burn.

10 And unto the married I command, yet not I, but the Lord, Let not the wife depart from her husband:

11 But and if she depart, let her remain unmarried, or be reconciled to her husband: and let not the husband put away his wife.

12 But to the rest speak I, not the Lord: If any brother hath a wife that believeth not, and she be pleased to dwell with him, let him not put her away.

13 And the woman which hath an husband that believeth not, and if he be pleased to dwell with her, let her not leave him.

14 For the unbelieving husband is sanctified by the wife, and the unbelieving wife is sanctified by the husband: else were your children unclean; but now are they holy.

15 But if the unbelieving depart, let him depart. A brother or a sister is not under bondage in such cases: but God hath called us to peace.

16 For what knowest thou, O wife, whether thou shalt save thy husband? or how knowest thou, O man, whether thou shalt save thy wife?

17 But as God hath distributed to every man, as the Lord hath called every one, so let him walk. And so ordain I in all churches.

18 Is any man called being circumcised? let him not become uncircumcised. Is any called in uncircumcision? let him not be circumcised.

19 Circumcision is nothing, and uncircumcision is nothing, but the keeping of

retained some respect for Paul, inasmuch as they consulted him on doubtful points. What their questions had been is uncertain, except in so far as we may gather them from his reply. This, however, is perfectly well known, that immediately after the first rise of the Church, there crept into it, through Satan's artifice, a superstition of such a kind, that a large proportion of them, through a foolish admiration of celibacy, despised the sacred connection of marriage; nay more, many regarded it with abhorrence, as a profane thing. This contagion had perhaps spread itself among the Corinthians also; or at least there were idly-disposed spirits, who, by immoderately extolling celibacy, endeavored to alienate the minds of the pious from marriage. At the same time, as the Apostle treats of many other subjects, he intimates that he had been consulted on a variety of points. What is chiefly of importance is, that we listen to his doctrine as to each of them.

1. It is good for a man

The answer consists of two parts. In the *first*, he teaches that it were *good* for every one to abstain from connection with a woman, provided it was in his power to do so. In the *second*, he subjoins a correction to this effect, that as many cannot do this, in consequence of the weakness of their flesh, these persons must not neglect the remedy which they have in their power, as appointed for them by the Lord. Now we must observe what he means by the word good, when he declares that it is good to abstain from marriage, that we may not conclude, on the other hand, that the marriage connection is therefore evil – a mistake which Jerome has fallen into, not so much from ignorance, in my opinion, as from the heat of controversy. For though that great man was endowed with distinguished excellences, he labored, at the same time, under one serious defect, that when disputing he allowed himself to be hurried away into great extravagancies, so that he did not keep within the bounds of truth.

The inference then which he draws is this "It is *good not to touch a woman*: it is therefore *wrong* to do so." Paul, however, does not make use of the word *good* here in such a signification as to be opposed to what is evil or vicious, but simply points out what is expedient on account of there being so many troubles, vexations, and anxieties that are incident to married persons. Besides, we must always keep in view the limitation which he subjoins. Nothing farther, therefore, can be elicited from Paul's words than this – that it is indeed expedient and profitable for a man not to be bound to a wife, provided he can do otherwise. Let us explain this by a comparison. Should any one speak in this way: "It were *good* for a man not to eat, or to drink, or to sleep" – he would not thereby condemn eating, or drinking, or

Instructions concerning marriage and other social relations. vs 1–24.

The Corinthians had written to the Apostle, seeking his advice in reference to the state of things in their church. It appears from this chapter that one of the subjects about which they were in difficulty, and respecting which they sought direction, was marriage. On this subject the Apostle tells them,

1st. That, as they were situated, marriage was inexpedient to them. But as a general law every man should have his own wife, and every woman her own husband, vs. 1–2.

2nd. That the obligation of the parties to the marriage covenant is mutual; the one therefore has no right to desert the other. Temporary separation, for the purpose of devotion, is allowable; but nothing more, vs. 3–5.

3rd. What he had said either in reference to marriage or temporary separation, was not to be considered as any thing more than advice. He could only tell them what, under the circumstances, was expedient; each one must act according to the grace given to him, vs. 6–9.

4th. With regard to the married the Lord had already taught that divorce was unlawful; the husband could not put away his wife, nor the wife her husband, vs. 10–11.

5th. As to the case not specially contemplated in our Lord's instructions, where one of the parties was a Christian and the other a Jew or Pagan, the Apostle teaches, first, that if the unbelieving party is willing to remain in the marriage relation, it should not be dissolved. Secondly, that if the unbeliever departed, and refused to continue in the marriage connection, the marriage contract was thereby dissolved, and the believing party was at liberty, vs. 12–15.

6th. Such separations, however, are, if possible, to be avoided, because the gospel is a gospel of peace. It was not designed to break up any of the lawful relations of life. As a general rule, therefore, every man should continue in the same condition in which he was called. If a man was called being circumcised, his becoming a Christian did not impose upon him the obligation to become uncircumcised; and if called being uncircumcised, he was not required to be circumcised. In like manner, if a slave is called to be a Christian, he may remain a slave, because every slave is the Lord's free man, and every free man is the Lord's slave. These social distinctions do not affect our relation to Christ. Redemption, in raising all to the relation of slaves to Christ, that is, making them all his property, has raised them into a sphere where all earthly distinctions are insignificant. Therefore, let every man abide in the relation wherein he was called, vs. 16–24.

1. Now concerning the things whereof ye wrote unto me: (It is) good for a man not to touch a woman.

It is evident that there was a diversity of opinion on the subject of marriage among the Corinthian Christians. Probably some of them of Jewish origin thought it obligatory, while other members of the church thought it undesirable, if not wrong. Paul says, It is good for a man not to marry. The word **good** (καλόν) here means expedient, profitable, as it does frequently elsewhere, Matthew 17: 4; 18: 8–9; 1 Corinthians 9: 15.

That the Apostle does not mean to teach either that marriage is morally an evil as compared with celibacy, or that as a general rule it is inexpedient, is evident.

1. Because in the following verse he declares directly the reverse.

2. Because in v. 26 he expressly states that "the present distress," or the peculiar circumstances of trial and difficulty in which the Christians of that day were placed, was the ground of his advice on this subject.

3. Because in 1 Timothy 4: 3, he specifies "forbidding to marry" as one of the signs of the great apostasy which he predicted was to occur.

4. Because marriage is a divine institution, having its foundation in the nature of man, and therefore must be a good. God accordingly declared, "It is not good for man to be alone," i.e. to be unmarried, Genesis 2: 18.

the commandments of God.

20 Let every man abide in the same calling wherein he was called.

21 Art thou called being a servant? care not for it: but if thou mayest be made free, use it rather.

22 For he that is called in the Lord, being a servant, is the Lord's freeman: likewise also he that is called, being free, is Christ's servant.

23 Ye are bought with a price; be not ye the servants of men.

24 Brethren, let every man, wherein he is called, therein abide with God.

25 Now concerning virgins I have no commandment of the Lord: yet I give my judgment, as one that hath obtained mercy of the Lord to be faithful.

26 I suppose therefore that this is good for the present distress, I say, that it is good for a man so to be.

27 Art thou bound unto a wife? seek not to be loosed. Art thou loosed from a wife? seek not a wife.

28 But and if thou marry, thou hast not sinned; and if a virgin marry, she hath not sinned. Nevertheless such shall have trouble in the flesh: but I spare you.

29 But this I say, brethren, the time is short: it remaineth, that both they that have wives be as though they had none;

30 And they that weep, as though they wept not; and they that rejoice, as though they rejoiced not; and they that buy, as though they possessed not;

31 And they that use this world, as not abusing it: for the fashion of this world passeth away.

32 But I would have you without carefulness. He that is unmarried careth for the things that belong to the Lord, how he may please the Lord:

33 But he that is married careth for the things that are of the world, how he may please his wife.

34 There is difference also between a wife and a virgin. The unmarried woman careth for the things of the Lord, that she may be holy both in body and in spirit: but she that is married careth for the things of the world, how she may please her husband.

35 And this I speak for your own profit; not that I may cast a snare upon you, but for that which is comely, and that ye may attend upon the Lord without distraction.

36 But if any man think that he beha-

sleeping, as things that were wrong – but as the time that is devoted to these things is just so much taken from the soul, his meaning would be, that we would be happier if we could be free from these hindrances, and devote ourselves wholly to meditation on heavenly things. Hence, as there are in married life many impediments which keep a man entangled, it were on that account *good* not to be connected in marriage.

But here another question presents itself, for these words of Paul have some appearance of inconsistency with the words of the Lord, in Genesis 2:18, where he declares, that *it is not good for a man* to be without a wife. What the Lord there pronounces to be *evil* Paul here declares to be *good*. I answer, that in so far as a wife is *a help* to her husband, so as to make his life happy, that is in accordance with God's institution; for in the beginning God appointed it so, that the man without the woman was, as it were, but half a man, and felt himself destitute of special and necessary assistance, and the wife is, as it were, the completing of the man. Sin afterwards came in to corrupt that institution of God; for in place of so great a blessing there has been substituted a grievous punishment, so that marriage is the source and occasion of many miseries. Hence, whatever evil or inconvenience there is in marriage, that arises from the corruption of the divine institution. Now, although there are in the meantime some remains still existing of the original blessing, so that a single life is often much more unhappy than the married life; yet, as married persons are involved in many inconveniences, it is with good reason that Paul teaches that it would be *good for a man* to abstain. In this way, there is no concealment of the troubles that are attendant upon marriage; and yet, in the meantime, there is no countenance given to those profane jests which are commonly in vogue with a view to bring it into discredit, such as the following: that a wife is a necessary evil, and that a wife is one of the greatest evils. For such sayings as these have come from Satan's workshop, and have a direct tendency to brand with disgrace God's holy institution; and farther, to lead men to regard marriage with abhorrence, as though it were a deadly evil and pest.

The sum is this, that we must remember to distinguish between the pure ordinance of God and the punishment of sin, which came in subsequently. According to this distinction, it was in the beginning *good for a man*, without any exception, to be joined to a wife, and even yet, it is *good* in such a way, that there is in the meantime a mixture of bitter and sweet, in consequence of the curse of God. To those, however, who have not the gift of continency, it is a necessary and salutary remedy in accordance with what follows.

Paul cannot be understood in a sense which would make him directly contradict the word of God.

5. Because throughout the Scriptures marriage is spoken of as honorable, Hebrews 13: 4, and is used to illustrate the relation between God and his people, and between Christ and his church.

6. Because all experience teaches that it is, as a general rule, necessary to the full development of the character of the individual, and absolutely essential to the virtue and the well-being of society. To depreciate marriage would be to go contrary both to nature and revelation, and such depreciation has never failed to be attended by the most injurious consequences to the church and to the world. If, therefore, Scripture is to be interpreted by Scripture, we must understand the Apostle as intending to say: "Considering your peculiar circumstances, it is expedient for you not to marry."

Of virgins and widows. vs. 25–40.

In this portion of the chapter the apostle treats principally of the marriage of virgins – including, however, the young of both sexes. On this subject he says he was not authorized to speak with authority, but simply to advise, v. 25. His advice was, on account of the impending troubles, that they should not marry, vs. 26–27. It was not wrong to marry, but it would expose them to greater suffering, v. 28. Besides, they should consider the transitory nature of all earthly ties. The fashion of the world was passing away, vs. 29–31. Still further, a single life was freer from worldly cares.

The unmarried could consecrate themselves without distraction to the service of the Lord, vs. 32–35. To parents he says, that, if circumstances render it desirable, they might without hesitation give their daughters in marriage, v. 36. But if they were free to act on their own judgment, his advice was to keep them unmarried, vs. 37–38. Marriage can only be dissolved by death. After the death of her husband, a woman is at liberty to marry again; but she

should intermarry only with a Christian; and in Paul's judgment, her happiness would be promoted by remaining single, vs. 39–40.

25. Now concerning virgins I have no commandment of the Lord: yet I give my judgment, as one that hath obtained mercy of the Lord to be faithful.

Now (δέ, but,) serves to resume the connection broken off by the preceding digression. "But to resume my subject," which in this chapter is marriage. Concerning virgins, (παρθένοι.) The word properly means maidens, though as an adjective it is used of both sexes, Revalation 14: 4. I have no commandment of the Lord. That is, neither Christ himself, nor the Spirit of Christ, by whom Paul was guided, had commissioned him to do any thing more than to counsel these persons. He was inspired, or led by the Spirit, in this matter, not to command, but to advise. His advice, however, was worthy of great deference. It was not merely the counsel of a wise and experienced man; but of one who had obtained mercy of the Lord to be faithful, i.e. worthy of confidence, one who could be trusted.

This is a sense the word; (πιστός) often has, as in the expressions, "faithful saying," "faithful witness." Paul felt himself indebted to the mercy of Christ for those inward graces and qualities which entitled him to the confidence of his readers. He recognized Christ as the giver of those gifts, and himself as undeserving of them. Had he been left to himself, instead of being the wise, disinterested, and faithful counselor of Christians, he would have been a blaspheming persecutor. Philosophy would teach us that moral excellence must be self-acquired. The Bible teaches us that it is the gift of God; and being the gift of Christ, Christ must be God. As such, Paul blessed him for having been so merciful to him as to convert him, and bring him to the knowledge and obedience of the truth.

26. I suppose therefore that this is good for the present distress, (I say,) that (it is) good for a man so to be.

veth himself uncomely toward his virgin, if she pass the flower of her age, and need so require, let him do what he will, he sinneth not: let them marry.

37 Nevertheless he that standeth stedfast in his heart, having no necessity, but hath power over his own will, and hath so decreed in his heart that he will keep his virgin, doeth well.

38 So then he that giveth her in marriage doeth well; but he that giveth her not in marriage doeth better.

39 The wife is bound by the law as long as her husband liveth; but if her husband be dead, she is at liberty to be married to whom she will; only in the Lord.

40 But she is happier if she so abide, after my judgment: and I think also that I have the Spirit of God.

1 CORINTHIANS 8

1 Now as touching things offered unto idols, we know that we all have knowledge. Knowledge puffeth up, but charity edifieth.

2 And if any man think that he knoweth anything, he knoweth nothing yet as he ought to know.

3 But if any man love God, the same is known of him.

4 As concerning therefore the eating of those things that are offered in sacrifice unto idols, we know that an idol is nothing in the world, and that there is none other God but one.

5 For though there be that are called gods, whether in heaven or in earth, (as there be gods many, and lords many,)

6 But to us there is but one God, the Father, of whom are all things, and we in him; and one Lord Jesus Christ, by whom are all things, and we by him.

7 Howbeit there is not in every man that knowledge: for some with conscience of the idol unto this hour eat it as a thing offered unto an idol; and their conscience being weak is defiled.

8 But meat commendeth us not to God: for neither, if we eat, are we the better; neither, if we eat not, are we the worse.

9 But take heed lest by any means this liberty of yours become a stumblingblock to them that are weak.

10 For if any man see thee which hast knowledge sit at meat in the idol's temple, shall not the conscience of him which is

2. But to avoid fornication

He now commands, that those who are liable to the vice of incontinency should have recourse to the remedy. For though it may seem that the statement is universal, it ought, nevertheless, to be restricted to those who feel themselves urged by necessity. As to this, every one must judge for himself. Whatever difficulty, therefore, is perceived to be in marriage, let all that cannot resist the promptings of their flesh, know that this commandment has been enjoined upon them by the Lord. But it is asked – "Is this the only reason for entering into matrimony, that we may cure incontinency?" I answer, that this is not Paul's meaning; for as for those that have the gift of abstinence from marriage, he leaves *them* at liberty, while he commands others to provide against their infirmity by marrying. The sum is this – that the question is not as to the reasons for which marriage has been instituted, but as to the persons for whom it is necessary. For if we look to the first institution, it could not be a remedy for a disease which had as yet no existence, but was appointed for begetting offspring; but after the fall, this second purpose was added.

This passage is also opposed to *polygamy*. For the Apostle desires that every woman have her own husband, intimating that the obligation is mutual. The man, therefore, who has once pledged his fidelity to a woman as his wife, must not separate from her, as is manifestly done in case of a second connection.

1 CORINTHIANS 8

He now passes on to another question, which he had merely touched upon in the sixth chapter, without fully discussing. For when he had spoken of the avarice of the Corinthians, and had drawn that discussion to a close with this statement – *Neither covetous, nor extortioners, nor fornicators, etc., shall inherit the kingdom of God,* he passed on to speak of the liberty of Christians – *All things are lawful for me.* He had taken occasion from this to speak of *fornication,* and from that, of *marriage.* Now, therefore, he at length follows out what he had touched upon as to things intermediate — how we ought to restrain our liberty in intermediate things. By intermediate things, I mean those that are neither good nor bad in themselves, but indifferent, which God has put in our power, but in the use of which we ought to observe moderation, that there may be a difference between liberty and licentiousness. In the outset, he selects one instance, distinguished above all the others, as to which the Corinthians grievously offended – their having been present on occasion of the sacred banquets, which were held by idolaters in honor of their gods, and eating indiscriminately of the meats that were offered to them. As this gave much occa-

I suppose therefore, (νομίζω οὖν,) i.e. I think then, The being so, i.e. as you are, unmarried, is good, in the sense of expedient. There is a slight grammatical inaccuracy, or change of construction, in this verse. 'I think then this to be expedient on account of the coming necessity; that is, I think that it is expedient for a man so to be.' Paul here expressly states the ground of his opinion that it was inexpedient for his readers to marry. It was on account of the **present distress**, (ἐνεστῶσαν ἀνάγκην,) the distress standing near, whether actually present, or impending, depends on the context, Luke 21: 23; 2 Corinthians 6: 4; 10: 12; 1 Thessalonians 3: 7. In the present case it was probably not so much the troubles in which Christians were then actually involved, as those which the apostle saw to be hanging over them, which he refers to. The Scriptures clearly predicted that the coming of Christ was to be preceded and attended by great commotions and calamities. These predictions had reference both to his first and second advent. The insight even of inspired men into the future was very imperfect. The ancient prophets searched diligently into the meaning of their own predictions, 1 Peter 1: 10–12, and the apostles knew little of the times and seasons, Acts 1: 7. They knew that great calamities were to come on the earth, but how or when it was not given to them clearly to see. The awful desolation which was soon to fall upon Jerusalem and on the whole Jewish race, and which could not but involve more or less the Christians also, and the inevitable struggles and persecution which, according to our Lord's predictions, his followers were to encounter, were surely enough to create a deep impression on the apostle's mind, and to make him solicitous to prepare his brethren for the coming storm. It is not necessary, therefore, to assume, as is so often done, that the apostle anticipated the second advent of Christ during that generation, and that he refers to the calamities which were to precede that event. Such expectation would not, indeed, be incompatible with his inspiration.

It was revealed to him that Christ was to come the second time; and that he was to come as a thief in the night. He might, therefore, naturally look for it at any time. We know, however, that in the case of Paul at least, it was revealed, that the second advent was not to occur before the national conversion of the Jews, Romans 11: 25; or before the great apostasy and rise of the man of sin, 2 Thessalonians 2: 2–3. Still, he knew not when those events might occur, and therefore he knew not when Christ would come. It was not, however, to the calamities which are to precede the second advent, to which Paul here refers, but rather to those which it was predicted should attend the introduction of the gospel.

1 CORINTHIANS 8

Eating of sacrifices offered to idols is not in itself wrong, vs. 1–7. But it should be avoided if it gave offense, vs. 8–13.

On eating of sacrifices. vs. 1–13.

The second subject on which the Corinthians had requested the advice of the apostle was the lawfulness of eating of the sacrifices offered to idols.

To the discussion of that question in its different aspects the eighth, ninth and tenth chapters of this epistle are principally devoted. At the council of Jerusalem it was decided by the apostles, elders and brethren, that the Gentile converts should abstain "from meat offered to idols, from blood, and from things strangled, and from fornication," Acts 15: 29; and this decree was referred to the Holy Ghost as its author, v. 28. Yet Paul, though present in that council, not only does not refer to it, but goes directly against it. That decree forbade the eating of meat offered to idols; Paul, in ch. 10, tells the Corinthians that when exposed for sale in the market, or found on private tables, they might eat it without scruple.

These facts do not prove any discrepancy between the apostles gathered in Jerusalem

weak be emboldened to eat those things which are offered to idols;

11 And through thy knowledge shall the weak brother perish, for whom Christ died?

12 But when ye sin so against the brethren, and wound their weak conscience, ye sin against Christ.

13 Wherefore, if meat make my brother to offend, I will eat no flesh while the world standeth, lest I make my brother to offend.

1 CORINTHIANS 9

1 Am I not an apostle? am I not free? have I not seen Jesus Christ our Lord? are not ye my work in the Lord?

2 If I be not an apostle unto others, yet doubtless I am to you: for the seal of mine apostleship are ye in the Lord.

3 Mine answer to them that do examine me is this,

4 Have we not power to eat and to drink?

5 Have we not power to lead about a sister, a wife, as well as other apostles, and as the brethren of the Lord, and Cephas?

6 Or I only and Barnabas, have not we power to forbear working?

7 Who goeth a warfare any time at his own charges? who planteth a vineyard, and eateth not of the fruit thereof? or who feedeth a flock, and eateth not of the milk of the flock?

8 Say I these things as a man? or saith not the law the same also?

9 For it is written in the law of Moses, Thou shalt not muzzle the mouth of the ox that treadeth out the corn. Doth God take care for oxen?

10 Or saith he it altogether for our sakes? For our sakes, no doubt, this is written: that he that ploweth should plow in hope; and that he that thresheth in hope should be partaker of his hope.

11 If we have sown unto you spiritual things, is it a great thing if we shall reap your carnal things?

12 If others be partakers of this power over you, are not we rather? Nevertheless we have not used this power; but suffer all things, lest we should hinder the gospel of Christ.

13 Do ye not know that they which minister about holy things live of the

sion of offense, the Apostle teaches them that they rashly perverted the liberty granted them by the Lord.

1. Concerning things offered unto idols

He begins with a concession, in which he voluntarily grants and allows to them everything that they were prepared to demand or object. "I see what your pretext is: you make Christian liberty your pretext. You hold out that *you have knowledge*, and that there is not one of you that is so ignorant as not to know that *there is but one God*.

I grant all this to be true, but of what avail is that knowledge which is ruinous to the brethren?" Thus, then, he grants them what they demand, but it is in such a way as to show that their excuses are empty and of no avail. *Knowledge puffeth up.* He shows, from the effects, how frivolous a thing it is to boast of *knowledge*, when *love* is wanting. "Of what avail is *knowledge*, that is of such a kind as *puffs us up* and elates us, while it is the part of *love* to *edify*?" This passage, which otherwise is somewhat obscure, in consequence of its brevity, may easily be understood in this way – "Whatever is devoid of *love* is of no account in the sight of God; nay more, it is displeasing to him, and much more so what is openly at variance with *love*. Now that, *knowledge* of which you boast, O ye Corinthians, is altogether opposed to *love*, for it *puffs up* men with pride, and leads to contempt of the brethren, while *love* is concerned for the welfare of brethren, and exhorts us to *edify* them. Accursed, then, be that *knowledge* which makes men proud, and is not regulated by a desire of *edifying*."

Paul, however, did not mean, that this is to be reckoned as a fault attributable to *learning* – that those who are learned are often self-complacent, and have admiration of themselves, accompanied with contempt of others. Nor did he understand this to be the natural tendency of learning – to produce arrogance, but simply meant to show what effect *knowledge* has in an individual, that has not the fear of God, and love of the brethren; for the wicked abuse all the gifts of God, so as to exalt themselves.

1 CORINTHIANS 9

26. I therefore so run

He returns to speak of himself, that his doctrine may have the more weight, on his setting himself forward by way of pattern. What. he says here some refer to *assurance of hope* – (Hebrews 6: 11) – "I do not run in vain, nor do I run the risk of losing my labor, for I have the Lord's promise, which never deceives." It rather appears to me, however, that his object is to direct the course of believers straight forward toward the goal, that it may not be wavering and devious. "The Lord exercises us here in the way of running and wrestling, but he sets before us the object at which we

and Paul; nor that the decisions of that council were not obligatory on the church. They only serve to explain the true intent and meaning of those decisions. They show,

1. That there was no permanent moral ground for the prohibition of meat offered to idols.

2. That the ground of the prohibition being expediency, it was of necessity temporary and limited. It had reference to Christians in the midst of those to whom eating such meat was an abomination. It, therefore, ceased to be binding whenever and wherever the grounds of the prohibition did not exist. It is analogous to Paul's condemnation of women appearing in church without a veil. The decisions of that council, therefore, were no barrier to Paul's discussing the question on its merits.

In this chapter the subject is viewed in two aspects; first, considered in itself; and secondly, in its bearing on the weaker or less enlightened class of Christians. Most of the questions which disturbed the early church had their origin in the conflicting prepossessions and prejudices of the Jewish and Gentile converts; or at least, of the more and less enlightened of the Christian converts. For it is probable that many of those who had been educated as heathen belonged to the class of weaker brethren. As a body, however, the Gentiles were disposed to latitudinarianism; and the Jews to superstitious scrupulousness. So far as general principles were concerned, Paul sided with the Gentile party. Their views about meats and drinks, and holy days, and ceremonies were derived from the apostle himself, and were therefore approved by him. But the spirit and practice of this party he severely condemns. Thus, in the present instance, he admits that an idol is nothing; that a sacrifice is nothing; that all enlightened Christians know this; that, consequently, eating of the heathen sacrifices was a matter of indifference, it made a man neither better nor worse; and yet eating of them might be, and in their case it was, sinful; because injurious to their weaker brethren. He begins the chapter with the admission, therefore, that all enlightened Christians have knowledge. He

reminds them, however, that there is something higher than knowledge; that knowledge without love is, after all, only another form of ignorance. The main thing to be known is not apprehended, vs. 1–3. He admits, however, that Christians know that the gods of the heathen are vanities and lies, that there is but one only, the living and true God, v. 4. For although the heathen acknowledge a whole hierarchy of deities, celestial and terrestrial, Christians acknowledge but one God and one Mediator, v. 6. All this is admitted. It is, however, nevertheless true that many Christians, though they know that there is but one God, yet are not persuaded that the heathen deities are nothing, and therefore they stand in awe of them, and could not help believing that eating of sacrifices offered to idols was an act of worship, or in some way defiling, v. 7. The apostle also admits the second principle relied upon by the Gentile converts, viz., that meat does not commend us to God, that it can have no influence on our spiritual state, v. 8. It is not enough, however, that an act should be in its own nature indifferent to justify us in performing it. If our doing what is in itself innocent be the occasion of leading others into sin, it is for that reason sinful for us, v. 9. If, therefore, a weak brother should be led, against the convictions of his own mind, to join his stronger brethren in eating such sacrifices, he would bring himself into condemnation. It was, therefore, a breach of charity and a sin against Christ, to eat of the heathen sacrifices under circumstances which emboldened others to sin, vs. 10–12. The apostle avows his own determination never to eat meat at all, if by so doing he should cause his brethren to sin, v. 13.

1 CORINTHIANS 9

The apostle illustrates the duty of foregoing the exercise of our rights for the good of others, by a reference to his giving up his undoubted right to be supported by the church, vs. 1–18. He shows that in other ways he accommo-

things of the temple? and they which wait at the alter are partakers with the alter?

14 Even so hath the Lord ordained that they which preach the gospel should live of the gospel.

15 But I have used none of these things: neither have I written these things, that it should be so done unto me: for it were better for me to die, than that any man should make my glorying void.

16 For though I preach the gospel, I have nothing to glory of: for necessity is laid upon me; yea, woe is unto me, if I preach not the gospel!

17 For if I do this thing willingly, I have a reward: but if against my will, a dispensation of the gospel is committed unto me.

18 What is my reward then? Verily that, when I preach the gospel, I may make the gospel of Christ without charge, that I abuse not my power in the gospel.

19 For though I be free from all men, yet have I made myself servant unto all, that I might gain the more.

20 And unto the Jews I became as a Jew, that I might gain the Jews; to them that are under the law, as under the law, that I might gain them that are under the law;

21 To them that are without law, as without law, (being not without law to God, but under the law to Christ,) that I might gain them that are without law.

22 To the weak became I as weak, that I might gain the weak: I am made all things to all men, that I might by all means save some.

23 And this I do for the gospel's sake, that I might be partaker thereof with you.

24 Know ye not that they which run in a race run all, but one receiveth the prize? So run, that ye may obtain.

25 And every man that striveth for the mastery is temperate in all things. Now they do it to obtain a corruptible crown; but we an incorruptible.

26 I therefore so run, not as uncertainly; so fight I, not as one that beateth the air:

27 But I keep under my body, and bring it into subjection: lest that by any means, when I have preached to others, I myself should be a castaway.

ought to aim, and prescribes a sure rule for our wrestling, that we may not weary ourselves in vain." Now he takes in both the similitudes that he had employed. "I know," says he, "*whither* I am running, and, like a skillful wrestler, I am anxious that I may not miss my aim." Those things ought to kindle up and confirm the Christian breast, so as to devote itself with greater alacrity to all the duties of piety; for it is a great matter not to wander in ignorance through uncertain windings.

27. But I keep under my body

The Apostle has employed the word *hup piazein* here, to mean **treating in a servile manner**. For he declares that he does not indulge self, but restrains his inclinations – which cannot be accomplished unless the body is tamed, and, by being held back from its inclinations, is habituated to subjection, like a wild and refractory steed. The ancient monks, with a view to yield obedience to this precept, contrived many exercises of discipline, for they slept on benches, they forced themselves to long watchings, and shunned delicacies. The main thing, however, was wanting in them, for they did not apprehend why it was that the Apostle enjoins this, because they lost sight of another injunction – to take no concern for our flesh to fulfill the lusts thereof (Romans 13: 14).

For what he says elsewhere (1 Timothy 4: 8) always holds good – that *bodily exercise profiteth little*. Let us, however, treat the body so as to make a slave of it, that it may not, by its wantonness, keep us back from the duties of piety; and farther, that we may not indulge it, so as to occasion injury, or offense, to others.

That, when I have preached to others

Some explain these words in this way – "Lest, after having taught others with propriety and faithfulness, I should incur the judgment of condemnation in the sight of God by a wicked life." But it will suit better to view this expression as referring to men, in this way – "My life ought to be a kind of rule to others. Accordingly, I strive to conduct myself in such a manner, that my character and conduct may not be inconsistent with my doctrine, and that thus I may not, with great disgrace to myself, and a grievous occasion of offense to my brethren, neglect those things which I require from others." It may also be taken in connection with a preceding statement (1 Corinthians 9: 23), in this way – "Lest I should be defrauded of the gospel, of which others are partakers through means of my labors."

1 CORINTHIANS 10

What he had previously taught by two similitudes, he now confirms by examples. The Corinthians grew wanton, and gloried, as if they had served out their time, or at least had

dated himself to the opinions and prejudices of others, 19–23. He reminds his readers that nothing good or great could be attained without self-denial, vs. 24–27.

The right of ministers to an adequate maintenance. the necessity of self-denial. vs. 1–27.

Having in the preceding chapter urged on the strong the duty of foregoing the use of their rights for the sake of their weaker brethren, the apostle shows how he had acted on that principle. He was an apostle, and therefore had all the rights of an apostle. His apostleship was abundantly clear, because he had seen the Lord Jesus and was his immediate messenger; and his divine mission had been confirmed, at least among the Corinthians, beyond dispute. They were the seal of his apostleship, vs. 1–3. Being an apostle, he had the same right to be supported and to have his family supported, had he chosen to marry, as Peter or any other apostle, vs. 4–6. This right to adequate support he proves,

First, from the principle which lies at the foundation of society, that the laborer is worthy of his reward, v. 7.

Secondly, from the fact that this principle is recognized in the Old Testament, even in its application to brutes, vs. 8–10.

Thirdly, from the principles of commutative justice, v. 11.

Fourthly, from the fact that the Corinthians recognized this right in the case of other teachers, v. 12.

Fifthly, from the universal recognition of the principle among all nations. Those who served the temple were supported from the temple, v. 13.

Sixthly, from the express ordinance of Christ, who had ordained that those who preached the gospel should live by the gospel, v. 14. This undoubted right Paul had not availed himself of, and he was determined, especially at Corinth, not to avail himself of it in the future. By so doing he cut off occasion to question his motives, and gave himself a ground of confi-

dence in resisting his opponents which he was determined not to relinquish, vs. 15–18. This was not, however, the only case in which he abstained from the exercise of his rights for the good of others. He accommodated himself to Jews and Gentiles in every thing indifferent, that he might gain the more, vs. 19–23. Such self-denial the heathen exercised to gain a corruptible crown – should not Christians do as much to gain a crown that is incorruptible? Without self-denial and effort the prize of their high calling could never be attained, vs. 24–27.

1. **Am I not an apostle? am I not free? have I not seen Jesus Christ our Lord? are not ye my work in the Lord?**
The order of the first two of these questions is reversed by most editors on satisfactory external and internal evidence. **Am I not free?** That is, am I not a Christian, invested with all the liberties wherewith Christ has made his people free? Am I not as free as any other believer to regulate my conduct according to my own convictions of what is right; free from any obligation to conform to the opinions or prejudices of other men? This, however, is a freedom which I have not availed myself of. Nay more, **Am I not an apostle?** Besides the rights which belong to all Christians, have I not all the prerogatives of an apostle? Am I not on a level with the chief of the apostles? Who of them can show a better title to the office? There were three kinds of evidence of the apostleship.

1. The immediate commission from Christ in the sight of witnesses, or otherwise confirmed.

2. Signs and wonders, and mighty deeds, 2 Corinthians 12: 12.

3. The success of their ministry. No man could be an apostle who had not seen the Lord Jesus after his resurrection, because that was one of the essential facts of which they were to be the witnesses, Acts 1: 22.

Neither could any man be an apostle who did not receive his knowledge of the gospel

1 CORINTHIANS 10

1 Moreover, brethren, I would not that ye should be ignorant, how that all our fathers were under the cloud, and all passed through the sea;

2 And were all baptized unto Moses in the cloud and in the sea;

3 And did all eat the same spiritual meat;

4 And did all drink the same spiritual drink: for they drank of that spiritual Rock that followed them: and that Rock was Christ.

5 But with many of them God was not well pleased: for they were overthrown in the wilderness.

6 Now these things were our examples, to the intent we should not lust after evil things, as they also lusted.

7 Neither be ye idolaters, as were some of them; as it is written, The people sat down to eat and drink, and rose up to play.

8 Neither let us commit fornication, as some of them committed, and fell in one day three and twenty thousand.

9 Neither let us tempt Christ, as some of them also tempted, and were destroyed of serpents.

10 Neither murmur ye, as some of them also murmured, and were destroyed of the destroyer.

11 Now all these things happened unto them for ensamples: and they are written for our admonition, upon whom the ends of the world are come.

12 Wherefore let him that thinketh he standeth take heed lest he fall.

13 There hath no temptation taken you but such as is common to man: but God is faithful, who will not suffer you to be tempted above that ye are able; but will with the temptation also make a way to escape, that ye may be able to bear it.

14 Wherefore, my dearly beloved, flee from idolatry.

15 I speak as to wise men; judge ye what I say.

16 The cup of blessing which we bless, is it not the communion of the blood of Christ? The bread which we break, is it not the communion of the body of Christ?

17 For we being many are one bread, and one body: for we are all partakers of that one bread.

18 Behold Israel after the flesh: are not

finished their course, when they had scarcely left the starting-point. This vain exultation and confidence he represses in this manner – "As I see that you are quietly taking your ease at the very outset of your course, *I would not have you ignorant* of what befell the people of Israel in consequence of this, that their example may arouse you." As, however, on examples being adduced, any point of difference destroys the force of the comparison, Paul premises, that there is no such dissimilarity between us and the Israelites, as to make our condition different from theirs. Having it, therefore, in view to threaten the Corinthians with the same vengeance as had overtaken them, he begins in this manner – "Beware of glorying in any peculiar privilege, as if you were in higher esteem than they were in the sight of God." For they were favored with the same benefits as we at this day enjoy; there was a Church of God among them, as there is at this day among us; they had the same sacraments, to be tokens to them of the grace of God; but, on their abusing their privileges, they did not escape the judgment of God. Be afraid, therefore; for the same thing is impending over *you*. Jude makes use of the same argument in his Epistle (Jude 1: 5).

1. All were under the cloud

The Apostle's object is to show, that the Israelites were no less the people of God than we are, that we may know, that we will not escape with impunity the hand of God, which punished them with so much severity. For the sum is this – "If God spared not them, neither will he spare you, for your condition is similar." That similarity he proves from this – that they had been honored with the same tokens of God's grace, for the sacraments are badges by which the Church of God is distinguished. He treats first of baptism, and teaches that the cloud, which protected the Israelites in the desert from the heat of the sun, and directed their course, and also their passage through the sea, was to them as a baptism; he says, also, that in the manna, and the water flowing from the rock, there was a sacrament which corresponded with the sacred Supper.

They were, says he, baptized in Moses, that is, under the ministry or guidance of Moses. For I take the particle *eis* to be used here instead of *en*, agreeably to the common usage of Scripture, because we are assuredly baptized in the name of Christ, and not of any mere man, as he has stated in 1 Corinthians 1: 13, and that for two reasons. These are, *first*, because we are by baptism initiated into the doctrine of Christ alone; and, *secondly*, because his name alone is invoked, inasmuch as baptism is founded on his influence alone. They were, therefore, baptized in Moses, that is, under his guidance or ministry, as has been already stated. How? In the cloud and in the sea. "They were, then, baptized twice," some one will say. I answer, that there are *two*

by immediate revelation from Christ, for the apostles were the witnesses also of his doctrines, Acts 1: 8; 10: 39; 22: 15; Galatians 1: 12. The necessity of this immediate mission and independent knowledge is insisted upon at length in the epistle to the Galatians. In proof of his apostleship Paul here appeals only to two sources of evidence; first, to his having seen the Lord Jesus; and second, to the success of his ministry. **Ye are my work in the Lord**. That is, either, you in the Lord, your being in the Lord (i.e. your conversion), is my work; or, the words (ἐν κυρίῳ) may mean **by the Lord**, i.e. by his co-operation. The former explanation is to be preferred, as the apostle's object is to state in what sense they were his work. It was as being in the Lord. The connection of this verse, and of the whole chapter, with what precedes is obvious. His design is to show that he had himself acted on the principle which he urged on others. Neither as a Christian nor as an apostle had he insisted upon his rights, without regard to the prejudices of others or the good of the church.

1 CORINTHIANS 10

A continuation of the exhortation to self-denial and caution, vs. 1–13. Express prohibition of joining in the sacrificial feasts of the heathen, vs. 14–22. Particular directions as to the use of meat sacrificed to idols, vs. 23–33.

The necessity of self-denial argued from the case of the Israelites. vs. 1–13.

At the close of the preceding chapter the apostle had exhorted his readers to self-denial and effort, in order to secure the crown of life. He here enforces that exhortation, by showing how disastrous had been the want of such self-control in the case of the Israelites. They had been highly favored as well as we. They had been miraculously guided by the pillar of cloud; they had been led through the Red Sea; they had been fed with manna from heaven, and with water from the rock; and yet the great majority of them perished, vs. 1–5. This

is a solemn warning to Christians not to give way to temptation, as the Israelites did, v. 6. That is, not to be led into idolatry, v. 7, nor into fornication, v. 8, nor into tempting Christ, v. 9, nor into murmuring, v. 10. In all these points the experience of the Israelites was a warning to Christians; and therefore those who thought themselves secure should take heed lest they fall, vs. 11–12. God is merciful, and would not suffer them to be too severely tempted, v. 13.

1. Moreover, brethren, I would not that ye should be ignorant, how that all our fathers were under the cloud, and all passed through the sea; Moreover. The true reading is not (δέ) **moreover**, but (γάρ) **for**, which marks the connection with what precedes. 'We must use self-denial and effort; **for,** brethren, our fathers, notwithstanding all they experienced, perished.' **I would not have you ignorant**, Romans 1: 10; 11: 25, a formula used when something specially important is to be presented. **That (not how that). All our fathers.** The emphasis is on **all**. 'All our fathers left Egypt; Caleb and Joshua alone entered the promised land.' All run, but one obtains the prize. The history of the church affords no incident better suited to enforce the necessity of guarding against false security, than that selected by the apostle. The Israelites doubtless felt, as they stood on the other side of the Red Sea, that all danger was over, and that their entrance into the land of promise was secured. They had however a journey beset with dangers before them, and perished because they thought there was no need of exertion. So the Corinthians, when brought to the knowledge of the gospel, thought heaven secure. Paul reminds them that they had only entered on the way, and would certainly perish unless they exercised constant self-denial. **Our fathers**. Abraham is our father, though we are not his natural descendants. And the Israelites were the fathers of the Corinthian Christians, although most of them were Gentiles. Although this is true, it is probable that the

they which eat of the sacrifices partakers of the alter?

19 What say I then? that the idol is any thing, or that which is offered in sacrifice to idols is any thing?

20 But I say, that the things which the Gentiles sacrifice, they sacrifice to devils, and not to God: and I would not that ye should have fellowship with devils.

21 Ye cannot drink the cup of the Lord, and the cup of devils: ye cannot be partakers of the Lord's table, and of the table of devils.

22 Do we provoke the Lord to jealousy? are we stronger than he?

23 All things are lawful for me, but all things are not expedient: all things are lawful for me, but all things edify not.

24 Let no man seek his own, but every man another's wealth.

25 Whatsoever is sold in the shambles, that eat, asking no question for conscience sake:

26 For the earth is the Lord's, and the fullness thereof.

27 If any of them that believe not bid you to a feast, and ye be disposed to go; whatsoever is set before you, eat, asking no question for conscience sake.

28 But if any man say unto you, This is offered in sacrifice unto idols, eat not for his sake that shewed it, and for conscience sake: for the earth is the Lord's, and the fullness thereof:

29 Conscience, I say, not thine own, but of the other: for why is my liberty judged of another man's conscience?

30 For if I by grace be a partaker, why am I evil spoken of for that for which I give thanks?

31 Whether therefore ye eat, or drink, or whatsoever ye do, do all to the glory of God.

32 Give none offence, neither to the Jews, nor to the Gentiles, nor to the church of God:

33 Even as I please all men in all things, not seeking mine own profit, but the profit of many, that they may be saved.

1 CORINTHIANS 11

1 Be ye followers of me, even as I also am of Christ.

2 Now I praise you, brethren, that ye remember me in all things, and keep the ordinances, as I delivered them to you.

signs made mention of, making, however, but *one* baptism, corresponding to ours.

Here, however, a more difficult question presents itself. For it is certain, that the advantage of those gifts, which Paul makes mention of, was temporal. The *cloud* protected them from the heat of the sun, and showed them the way: these are outward advantages of the present life. In like manner, their passage through the *sea* was attended with this effect, that they got clear off from Pharaoh's cruelty, and escaped from imminent hazard of death. The advantage of *our* baptism, on the other hand, is spiritual. Why then does Paul turn earthly benefits into sacraments, and seek to find some spiritual mystery in them? I answer, that it was not without good reason that Paul sought in miracles of this nature something more than the mere outward advantage of the flesh. For, though God designed to promote his people's advantage in respect of the present life, what he had mainly in view was, to declare and manifest himself to be their God, and under *that*, eternal salvation is comprehended.

The *cloud*, in various instances, is called the symbol of his presence. As, therefore, he declared by means of it, that he was present with them, as his peculiar and chosen people, there can be no doubt that, in addition to an earthly advantage, they had in it, besides, a token of spiritual life. Thus its use was twofold, as was also that of the passage through the sea, for a way was opened up for them through the midst of the sea, that they might escape from the hand of Pharaoh; but to what was this owing, but to the circumstance, that the Lord, having taken them under his guardianship and protection, determined by every means to defend them? Hence, they concluded from this, that they were the objects of God's care, and that he had their salvation in charge. Hence, too, the Passover, which was instituted to celebrate the remembrance of their deliverance, was nevertheless, at the same time, a sacrament of Christ. How so? Because God had, under a temporal benefit, manifested himself as a Savior. Any one that will attentively consider these things, will find that there is no absurdity in Paul's words. Nay more, he will perceive both in the spiritual substance and in the visible sign a most striking correspondence between the baptism of the Jews, and ours.

33. Even as I please all men in all this

As he speaks in a general way, and without exception, some extend it by mistake to things that are unlawful, and at variance with the word of the Lord – as if it were allowable, for the sake of our neighbor, to venture farther than the Lord permits us. It is, however, more than certain, that Paul accommodated himself to men only in things indifferent, and in things lawful in themselves. Farther, the end must be carefully observed – *that they may be saved*. Hence what is op-

apostle, although writing to a church, many, if not most, of whose members were of heathen origin, speaks as a Jew to Jews; as he often addresses a congregation as a whole, when what he says has reference only to a part.

Were under the cloud, not underneath it, but under its guidance. Exodus 13: 21. "The Lord went before them by day in a pillar of cloud, to lead them; and by night in a pillar of fire to give them light, to go by day and night." See Numbers 9: 15,23; 14: 14. Deuteronomy 1: 33. Psalms 78: 14, etc. No more decisive evidence could have been given of their election as a people, than this supernatural guidance. The symbol of the divine presence and favor was before their eyes day and night. If any people ever had reason to think their salvation secure, it was those whom God thus wonderfully guided. **They all passed through the sea**. Would God permit those to perish for whom he had wrought so signal a deliverance, and for whose sake he sacrificed the hosts of Egypt? Yet their carcasses were strewed in the wilderness. It is not enough, therefore, to be recipients of extraordinary favors; it is not enough to begin well. It is only by constant self-denial and vigilance, that the promised reward can be obtained. This is the lesson the apostle intends to inculcate.

Proof that attendance on sacrificial feasts in a heathen temple is idolatry. vs. 14–22.

This whole discussion arose out of the question whether it was lawful to eat the sacrifices offered to idols. Paul, while admitting that there was nothing wrong in eating of such meat, exhorts the Corinthians to abstain for the sake of their weaker brethren. There was another reason for this abstinence; they might be led into idolatry. By going to the verge of the allowable, they might be drawn into the sinful. There was great danger that the Corinthians, convinced that an idol was nothing, might be induced to join the sacrificial feasts within the precincts of the temples.

The danger was the greater, because such feasts, if held in a private house, lost their religious character, and might be attended without scruple. To convince his readers, that if the feast was held in a temple, attendance upon it was an act of idolatry, is the object of this section. The apostle's argument is from analogy. Attendance on the Lord's Supper is an act of communion with Christ, the object of Christian worship, and with all those who unite with us in the service. From its very nature, it brings all who partake of the bread and wine into fellowship with Christ and with one another, vs. 14–17. The same is true of Jewish sacrifices. Whoever eats of those sacrifices, is thereby brought into communion with the object of Jewish worship. The act is in its nature an act of worship, v. 18. The conclusion is too plain to need being stated – those who join in the sacrificial feasts of the heathen, join in the worship of idols. Such is the import of the act, and no denial on the part of those who perform it can alter its nature. It is not to be inferred from this mode of reasoning, that the objects of heathen worship are what the heathen suppose them to be. Because Paul argued that, as partaking of the Lord's Supper is an act of Christian worship, partaking of an idol-feast must be an act of heathen worship, it is not to be inferred that he regarded Jupiter or Juno as much real beings as Christ is.

Far from it. What the heathen sacrifice, they sacrifice to demons; and therefore, to partake of their sacrifices under circumstances which gave religious significance to the act, brought them into communion with demons, vs. 19–20. The two things are incompatible. A man cannot be a worshipper of Christ and a worshipper of demons, or in communion with the one while in communion with the other. Going to the Lord's table is a renunciation of demons; and going to the table of demons is a renunciation of Christ, v. 21. By this conduct the jealousy of the Lord would be excited against them, as of old it was excited against the Jews who turned aside after false gods, v. 22.

3 But I would have you know, that the head of every man is Christ; and the head of the woman is the man; and the head of Christ is God.

4 Every man praying or prophesying, having his head covered, dishonoreth his head.

5 But every woman that prayeth or prophesieth with her head uncovered dishonoreth her head: for that is even all one as if she were shaven.

6 For if the woman be not covered, let her also be shorn: but if it be a shame for a woman to be shorn or shaven, let her be covered.

7 For a man indeed ought not to cover his head, forasmuch as he is the image and glory of God: but the woman is the glory of the man.

8 For the man is not of the woman; but the woman of the man.

9 Neither was the man created for the woman; but the woman for the man.

10 For this cause ought the woman to have power on her head because of the angels.

11 Nevertheless neither is the man without the woman, neither the woman without the man, in the Lord.

12 For as the woman is of the man, even so is the man also by the woman; but all things of god.

13 Judge in yourselves: is it comely that a woman pray unto God uncovered?

14 Doth not even nature itself teach you, that, if a man have long hair, it is a shame unto him?

15 But if a woman have long hair, it is a glory to her: for her hair is given her for a covering.

16 But if any man seem to be contentious, we have no such custom, neither the churches of God.

17 Now in this that I declare unto you I praise you not, that ye come together not for the better, but for the worse.

18 For first of all, when ye come together in the church, I hear that there be divisions among you; and I partly believe it.

19 For there must be also heresies among you, that they which are approved may be made manifest among you.

20 When ye come together therefore into one place, this is not to eat the Lord's supper.

21 For in eating every one taketh

posed to their salvation ought not to be conceded to them, but we must use prudence, and that of a spiritual kind.

1 CORINTHIANS 11

1. Imitators of me

From this it appears, how absurdly chapters are divided, inasmuch as this sentence is disjoined from what goes before, with which it ought to have been connected, and is joined to what follows, with which it has no connection. Let us view this, then, as the close of the preceding chapter. Paul had there brought forward his own example in confirmation of his doctrine. Now, in order that the Corinthians may understand that this would be becoming in them, he exhorts them to *imitate* what he had done, *even as he had imitated Christ.*

Here there are two things to be observed – first, that he prescribes nothing to others that he had not first practiced himself; and, secondly, that he directs himself and others to Christ as the only pattern of right acting. For while it is the part of a good teacher to enjoin nothing in words but what he is prepared to practice in action, he must not, at the same time, be so austere, as straightway to require from others everything that he does himself, as is the manner of the superstitious. For everything that they contract a liking for they impose also upon others, and would have their own example to be held absolutely as a rule. The world is also, of its own accord, inclined to a misdirected imitation (*kakoz lian*) and, after the manner of apes, strive to copy whatever they see done by persons of great influence. We see, however how many evils have been introduced into the Church by this absurd desire of imitating all the actions of the saints, without exception. Let us, therefore, maintain so much the more carefully this doctrine of Paul – that we are to follow men, provided they take Christ as their grand model (*pr totupon*), that the examples of the saints may not tend to lead us away from Christ, but rather to direct us to him.

28. But let a man examine himself

An exhortation drawn from the foregoing threatening. "*If* those that *eat unworthily* are *guilty of the body and blood of the Lord,* then let no man approach who is not properly and duly prepared. Let every one, therefore, take heed to himself, that he may not fall into this sacrilege through idleness or carelessness." But now it is asked, what sort of *examination,* that ought to be to which Paul exhorts us. Papists make it consist in auricular confession. They order all that are to receive the Supper, to examine their life carefully and anxiously, that they may unburden all their sins in the ear of the priest. Such is *their* preparation! I maintain, however, that this holy *examination* of which Paul speaks, is widely

1 CORINTHIANS 11

The impropriety of women appearing unveiled in the public assemblies, vs. 2–16. The improper manner of celebrating the Lord's Supper which prevailed in the Corinthian church, vs. 11–34.

On the impropriety of women appearing in public unveiled. vs. 2–16.

Having corrected the more private abuses which prevailed among the Corinthians, the apostle begins in this chapter to consider those which relate to the mode of conducting public worship. The first of these is the habit of women appearing in public without a veil. Dress is in a great degree conventional. A costume which is proper in one country, would be indecorous in another. The principle insisted upon in this paragraph is, that women should conform in matters of dress to all those usages which the public sentiment of the community in which they live demands. The veil in all eastern countries was, and to a great extent still is, the symbol of modesty and subjection. For a woman, therefore, in Corinth to discard the veil was to renounce her claim to modesty, and to refuse to recognize her subordination to her husband. It is on the assumption of this significancy in the use of the veil, that the apostle's whole argument in this paragraph is founded.

He begins by praising the Corinthians for their obedience in general to his instructions, v. 2.

He then reminds them of the divinely constituted subordination of the woman to the man, v. 3.

Consequently it was disgraceful in the man to assume the symbol of subordination, and disgraceful in the woman to discard it, vs. 4–5.

If the veil were discarded as the symbol of subordination, it must also be discarded as the symbol of modesty. An unveiled woman, therefore, in Corinth proclaimed herself as not only insubordinate, but as immodest, v. 6.

The man ought not to wear a veil because he represents the authority of God; but the woman is the glory of the man, v. 7.

This subordination is proved by the very history of her creation. Eve was formed out of Adam, and made for him, vs. 8–9, and, therefore, women should wear, especially in the religious assemblies where angels are present, the conventional symbol of their relation, v. 10.

This subordination, however, of the woman is perfectly consistent with the essential equality and mutual dependence of the sexes. Neither is, or can be, without the other, vs. 11–12.

The apostle next appeals to their instinctive sense of propriety, which taught them that as it is disgraceful in a man to appear in the costume of a woman, so it is disgraceful in a woman to appear in the costume of a man, vs. 13–15.

Finally he appeals to authority; the custom which he censured was contrary to the universal practice of Christians, v. 16.

2. Now I praise, you, brethren, that ye remember me in all things, and keep the ordinances, as I delivered (them) to you.
Now I praise you. The particle (δέ) rendered **now**, either simply indicates the transition to a new subject, or it is adversative. 'Though I exhort you to imitate me as though you were deficient, **yet** I praise you that you remember me.' The Corinthians, although backward in following the self-denial and conciliatory conduct of the apostle, were nevertheless in general mindful of the ordinances or rules which he had delivered to them.

The word (παράδοσις) **tradition**, here rendered **ordinance**, is used not only for instructions orally transmitted from generation to generation, as in Matthew 15: 2–3,6, but for any instruction, whether relating to faith or practice, and whether delivered orally or in writing. 2 Thessalonians 2: 15; 3: 6. In reference to the rule of faith it is never used in the New Testament, except for the immediate instructions of inspired men. When used in

before other his own supper: and one is hungry, and another is drunken.

22 What? have ye not houses to eat and to drink in? or despise ye the church of God, and shame them that have not? What shall I say to you? shall I praise you in this? I praise you not.

23 For I have received of the Lord that which also I delivered unto you, That the Lord Jesus the same night in which he was betrayed took bread:

24 And when he had given thanks, he brake it, and said, Take, eat: this is my body, which is broken for you: this do in remembrance of me.

25 After the same manner also he took the cup, when he had supped, saying, This cup is the new testament in my blood: this do ye, as oft as ye drink it, in remembrance of me.

26 For as often as ye eat this bread, and drink this cup, ye do shew the Lord's death till he come.

27 Wherefore whosoever shall eat this bread, and drink this cup of the Lord, unworthily, shall be guilty of the body and blood of the Lord.

28 But let a man examine himself, and so let him eat of that bread, and drink of that cup.

29 For he that eateth and drinketh unworthily, eateth and drinketh damnation to himself, not discerning the Lord's body.

30 For this cause many are weak and sickly among you, and many sleep.

31 For if we would judge ourselves, we should not be judged.

32 But when we are judged, we are chastened of the Lord, that we should not be condemned with the world.

33 Wherefore, my brethren, when ye come together to eat, tarry one for another.

34 And if any man hunger, let him eat at home; that ye come not together unto condemnation. And the rest will I set in order when I come.

1 CORINTHIANS 12

1 Now concerning spiritual gifts, brethren, I would not have you ignorant.

2 Ye know that ye were Gentiles, carried away unto these dumb idols, even as ye were led.

different from torture. Those persons, after having *tortured* themselves with reflection for a few hours, and making the priest – such as he is – privy to their vileness, imagine that they have done their duty. It is an *examination* of another sort that Paul here requires – one of such a kind as may accord with the legitimate use of the sacred Supper.

You see here a method that is most easily apprehended. If you would wish to use aright the benefit afforded by Christ, bring faith and repentance. As to these two things, therefore, the trial must be made, if you would come duly prepared. Under repentance I include love; for the man who has learned to renounce himself, that he may give himself up wholly to Christ and his service, will also, without doubt, carefully maintain that unity which Christ has enjoined. At the same time, it is not a perfect faith or repentance that is required, as some, by urging beyond due bounds, a perfection that can nowhere be found, would shut out for ever from the Supper every individual of mankind. If, however, thou aspirest after the righteousness of God with the earnest desire of thy mind, and, trembled under a view of thy misery, dost wholly lean upon Christ's grace, and rest upon it, know that thou art a worthy guest to approach the table – *worthy* I mean in this respect, that the Lord does not exclude thee, though in another point of view there is something in thee that is not as it ought to be. For faith, when it is but begun, makes those *worthy* who were *unworthy*.

29. He who shall eat unworthily, eateth judgment to himself

He had previously pointed out in express terms the heinousness of the crime, when he said that those who should *eat unworthily* would be *guilty of the body and blood of the Lord*. Now he alarms them, by denouncing punishment; for there are many that are not affected with the sin itself; unless they are struck down by the judgment of God. This, then, he does, when he declares that this food, otherwise health-giving, will turn out to their destruction, and will be converted into poison to those that *eat unworthily*.

He adds the reasons because **they distinguish not the Lord's body**, that is, as a sacred thing from a profane. "They handle the sacred body of Christ with unwashed hands (Mark 7: 2), nay more, as if it were a thing of nought, they consider not how great is the value of it. They will therefore pay the penalty of so dreadful a profanation." Let my readers keep in mind what I stated a little ago, that the body is presented to them, though their unworthiness deprives them of a participation in it.

the modern sense of the word **tradition**, it is always in reference to what is human and untrustworthy, Galatians 1: 14. Colossians 2: 8, and frequently in the gospels of the traditions of the elders.

Celebration of the lord's supper. vs. 17–34.

This section relates to the disorders connected with the celebration of the Lord's supper. These disorders were of a kind which, according to our method of celebrating that sacrament, seems almost unaccountable. It was, however, the early custom to connect the Lord's supper in the strict sense of the words with an ordinary meal. As this sacrament was instituted by our Lord at the close of the Paschal supper, so it appears to have been customary at the beginning for the Christians to assemble for a common meal and to connect with it the commemoration of the Redeemer's death.

Intimations of this usage may be found in such passages as Acts 2: 42. "They continued steadfastly in the apostle's doctrine and fellowship, and in breaking of bread, and in prayer." In v. 46 it is said, this breaking of bread was from house to house. In Acts 20: 7, it is said, "The disciples came together on the first day of the week to break bread," which, from the narrative which follows, appears to have been an ordinary meal. Whatever may be thought of these passages, it is clear from the paragraph before us that at Corinth at least, the sacrament of the Lord's supper was connected with a regular meal. This may have arisen, not so much from the original institution of the Eucharist in connection with the Paschal supper, as from the sacred festivals both of the Jews and Greeks. Both classes had been accustomed to unite with their sacrifices a feast of a more or less public character. It is also evident that, agreeably to a familiar Grecian custom, the persons assembled brought their own provisions, which being placed on the table formed a common stock. The rich brought plentifully, the poor brought little or nothing. It was, however, essential to the very idea of a Christian feast, that it should be a communion; that all the guests at the table of their common Lord should be on the terms of equality. Instead of this fraternal union, there were divisions among the Corinthians even at the Lord's table. The rich eating by themselves the provisions which they had brought, and leaving their poorer brethren mortified and hungry. It is to the correction of these disorders that the concluding portion of this chapter is devoted.

It was no matter of praise that the assemblies of the Corinthians made them worse rather than better, v. 17.

The prominent evil was, that there were schisms even in their most sacred meetings; an evil necessary in the state in which they were, and which God permitted in order that the good might be made manifest, vs. 18–19.

The evil to which he referred was not merely that they had degraded the Lord's supper into an ordinary meal, but that in that meal they were divided into parties, some eating and drinking to excess, and others left without any thing, vs. 20–21.

This was not only making the Lord's supper a meal for satisfying hunger – contrary to its original design, but a cruel perversion of a feast of love into a means of humiliating and wounding their poorer brethren, v. 22.

In order to show how inconsistent their conduct was with the nature of the service in which they professed to engage, the apostle recounts the original institution of the Lord's supper, vs. 23–25.

From this account it follows, first, that the Lord's supper was designed not as an ordinary meal, but as a commemoration of the death of Christ; secondly, that to participate in this ordinance in an unworthy manner, was an offense against his body and blood, the symbols of which were so irreverently treated; thirdly, that no one ought to approach the Lord's table without self-examination, in order that with due preparation and with a proper understanding of the ordinance, he may receive the bread and wine as the symbols

3 Wherefore I give you to understand, that no man speaking by the Spirit of God calleth Jesus accursed: and that no man can say that Jesus is the Lord, but by the Holy Ghost.

4 Now there are diversities of gifts, but the same Spirit.

5 And there are differences of administrations, but the same Lord.

6 And there are diversities of operations, but it is the same God which worketh all in all.

7 But the manifestation of the Spirit is given to every man to profit withal.

8 For to one is given by the Spirit the word of wisdom; to another the word of knowledge by the same Spirit;

9 To another faith by the same Spirit; to another the gifts of healing by the same Spirit;

10 To another the working of miracles; to another prophecy; to another discerning of spirits; to another divers kinds of tongues; to another the interpretation of tongues:

11 But all these worketh that one and the selfsame Spirit, dividing to every man severally as he will.

12 For as the body is one, and hath many members, and all the members of that one body, being many, are one body: so also is Christ.

13 For by one Spirit are we all baptized into one body, whether we be Jews or Gentiles, whether we be bond or free; and have been all made to drink into one Spirit.

14 For the body is not one member, but many.

15 If the foot shall say, Because I am not the hand, I am not of the body; is it therefore not of the body?

16 And if the ear shall say, Because I am not the eye, I am not of the body; is it therefore not of the body?

17 If the whole body were an eye, where were the hearing? If the whole were hearing, where were the smelling?

18 But now hath God set the members every one of them in the body, as it hath pleased him.

19 And if they were all one member, where were the body?

20 But now are they many members, yet but one body.

21 And the eye cannot say unto the hand, I have no need of thee: nor again

1 CORINTHIANS 12

1. Now concerning spiritual things

He goes on to correct another fault. As the Corinthians abused the gifts of God for ostentation and show, and love was little, if at all, regarded, he shows them for what purpose believers are adorned by God with spiritual gifts – for the edification of their brethren. This proposition, however, he divides into two parts; for, in the *first* place, he teaches, that God is the author of those gifts, and, *secondly,* having established this, he reasons as to their design. He proves from their own experience, that those things in which they gloried, are bestowed upon men through the exercise of God's favor; for he reminds them how ignorant they were, and stupid, and destitute of all spiritual light, previously to God's calling them. Hence it appears, that they had been furnished with them – not by nature, but through God's unmerited benignity.

As to the words; when he says – would not that ye should be ignorant, we must supply the expression – *as to what is right,* or *as to what is your duty,* or some similar expression; and by *spiritual things* he means spiritual gifts, as to which we shall have occasion to see afterwards. In what follows there is a twofold reading; for some manuscripts have simply hoti others add hote. The former means *because* – assigning a reason: the latter means *when;* and this latter reading suits much better. But besides this diversity, the construction is in other respects confused; but still, the meaning is evident.

Literally, it is this – Ye know, that when ye were Gentiles, after dumb idols, according as ye were led, following I have, however, faithfully given Paul's meaning. By *dumb idols* he means – having neither feeling nor motion.

Let us learn from this passage how great is the blindness of the human mind: when it is without the illumination of the Holy Spirit, inasmuch as it stands in amazement at *dumb idols,* and cannot rise higher in searching after God; nay more, it is *led* by Satan as if it were a brute. He makes use of the term *Gentiles* here, in the same sense as in Ephesians 2: 12. Ye were at one time Gentiles, says he, without God, strangers to the hope of salvation, etc.

Perhaps, too, he reasons by way of contrast. What if they should now show themselves to be less submissive to God, after his having taken them under his care, to be governed by his word and Spirit, than they formerly discovered themselves to be forward and compliant, in following the suggestions of Satan!

27. But ye are the body of Christ

Hence what has been said respecting the nature and condition of the human body must be applied to us; for we are not a mere civil society, but, being ingrafted into

of Christ's body and blood, vs. 26–29.

In this way they would escape the judgments which the Lord had brought upon them on account of their profanation of his table, vs. 30–32.

In conclusion, he exhorts them to use their houses for their ordinary meals, and to make the Lord's supper a real communion, vs. 33–34.

1 CORINTHIANS 12

Of spiritual gifts. vs. 1–31.

The ancient prophets had clearly predicted that the Messianic period should be attended by a remarkable effusion of the Holy Spirit. "And it shall come to pass in those days," it is said in the prophecies of Joel, "saith God, I will pour out of my Spirit upon all flesh; and your sons and your daughters shall prophesy, and your young men shall see visions, and your old men shall dream dreams." Our Lord, before his crucifixion, promised to send the Comforter, who is the Holy Ghost, to instruct and guide his church, John 14, etc. And after his resurrection he said to his disciples, "These signs shall follow them that believe. In my name shall they cast out devils; they shall speak with new tongues; they shall take up serpents; and if they drink any deadly thing it shall not hurt them; they shall lay hands on the sick and they shall recover," Mark 16: 17–18. And immediately before his ascension he said to the disciples, "Ye shall be baptized with the Holy Ghost not many days hence," Acts 1: 5.

Accordingly, on the day of Pentecost, these promises and prophecies were literally fulfilled. The peculiarity of the new dispensation consisted, in the first place, in the general diffusion of these gifts. They were not confined to any one class of the people, but extended to all classes; male and female, young and old; and secondly, in the wonderful diversity of these supernatural endowments. Under circumstances so extraordinary it was unavoidable that many disorders should arise.

Some men would claim to be the organs of the Spirit, who were deluded or impostors, some would be dissatisfied with the gifts which they had received, and envy those whom they regarded as more highly favored; others would be inflated, and make an ostentatious display of their extraordinary powers; and in the public assemblies it might be expected that the greatest confusion would arise from so many persons being desirous to exercise their gifts at the same time. To the correction of these evils, all of which had manifested themselves in the church of Corinth, the apostle devotes this and the two following chapters. It is impossible to read these chapters without being deeply impressed by the divine wisdom with which they are pervaded.

After contrasting the condition of the Corinthians, as members of that body which was instinct with the life-giving Spirit of God, with their former condition as the senseless worshippers of dumb idols, he, First, lays down the criterion by which they might decide whether those who pretended to be the organs of the Spirit were really under his influence.

How do they speak of Christ? Do they blaspheme, or do they worship him? If they openly and sincerely recognize Jesus as the Supreme Lord, then they are under the influence of the Holy Ghost, vs. 1–3.

Secondly, these gifts, whether viewed as graces of the Spirit, or as forms of ministering to Christ, or the effects of God's power, that is, whether viewed in relation to the Spirit, to the Son, or to the Father, are but different manifestations of the Holy Ghost dwelling in his people, and are all intended for the edification of the church, vs. 4–7.

Thirdly, he arranges them under three heads,

1. The word of wisdom and the word of knowledge.

2. Faith, the gift of healing, the power of working miracles, prophesying, and the discerning of spirits.

3. The gift of tongues and the interpretation of tongues, vs. 8–10.

the head to the feet, I have no need of you.

22 Nay, much more those members of the body, which seem to be more feeble, are necessary:

23 And those members of the body, which we think to be less honorable, upon these we bestow more abundant honor; and our uncomely parts have more abundant comeliness.

24 For our comely parts have no need: but God hath tempered the body together, having given more abundant honor to that part which lacked:

25 That there should be no schism in the body; but that the members should have the same care one for another.

26 And whether one member suffer, all the members suffer with it; or one member be honored, all the members rejoice with it.

27 Now ye are the body of Christ, and members in particular.

28 And God hath set some in the church, first apostles, secondarily prophets, thirdly teachers, after that miracles, then gifts of healings, helps, governments, diversities of tongues.

29 Are all apostles? are all prophets? are all teachers? are all workers of miracles?

30 Have all the gifts of healing? do all speak with tongues? do all interpret?

31 But covet earnestly the best gifts: and yet shew I unto you a more excellent way.

1 CORINTHIANS 13

1 Though I speak with the tongues of men and of angels, and have not charity, I am become as sounding brass, or a tinkling cymbal.

2 And though I have the gift of prophecy, and understand all mysteries, and all knowledge; and though I have all faith, so that I could remove mountains, and have not charity, I am nothing.

3 And though I bestow all my goods to feed the poor, and though I give my body to be burned, and have not charity, it profiteth me nothing.

4 Charity suffereth long, and is kind; charity envieth not; charity vaunteth not itself, is not puffed up,

5 Doth not behave itself unseemly, seeketh not her own, is not easily pro-

Christ's body, are truly members one of another. Whatever, therefore, any one of us has, let him know that it has been given him for the edification of his brethren in common; and let him, accordingly, bring it forward, and not keep it back – buried, as it were, within himself, or make use of it as his own. Let not the man, who is endowed with superior gifts, be puffed up with pride, and despise others; but let him consider that there is nothing so diminutive as to be of no use – as, in truth, even the least among the pious brings forth fruit, according to his slender capacity, so that there is no useless member in the Church. Let not those who are not endowed with so much honor, envy those above them, or refuse to do their duty to them, but let them maintain the station in which they have been placed. Let there be mutual affection, mutual fellow-feeling (*sumpatheia*), mutual concern. Let us have a regard to the common advantage, in order that we may not destroy the Church by malignity, or envy, or pride, or any disagreement; but may, on the contrary, every one of us, strive to the utmost of his power to preserve it. Here is a large subject, and a magnificent one; but I content myself with having pointed out the way in which the above similitude must be applied to the Church.

31. Seek after the more excellent gifts

It might also be rendered – *value highly*; and it would not suit in with the passage, though it makes little difference as to the meaning; for Paul exhorts the Corinthians to esteem and desire those gifts especially, which are most conducive to edification. For this fault prevailed among them – that they aimed at show, rather than usefulness. Hence prophecy was neglected, while languages sounded forth among them, with great show, indeed, but with little profit. He does not, however, address individuals, as though he wished that every one should aspire at prophecy, or the office of teacher; but simply recommends to them a desire to promote edification, that they may apply themselves the more diligently to those things that are most conducive to edification.

1 CORINTHIANS 13

The division of the Chapter being so absurd, I could not refrain from changing it, especially as I could not conveniently interpret it otherwise. For what purpose did it serve to connect with what goes before a detached sentence, which agrees so well with what comes after – nay more, is thereby rendered complete? It is likely, that it happened through a mistake on the part of the transcribers. However it may be as to this, after having commanded that regard should be had chiefly to edification, he now declares that he will show them something of greater importance – that everything be regulated according to the rule of *love*. This, then, is the

Fourthly, these gifts are not only all the fruits of the Spirit, but they are distributed according to his sovereign will, v. 11.

Fifthly, there is therefore in this matter a striking analogy between the church and the human body.

For,

1. As the body is one organic whole, because animated by one spirit, so the church is one because of the indwelling of the Holy Ghost as the principle of its life.

2. As the unity of life in the body is manifested in a diversity of organs and members; so the indwelling of the Spirit in the church is manifested by a diversity of gifts and offices.

3. As the very idea of the body as an organization supposes this diversity in unity, the same is true in regard to the church.

4. As in the human body the members are mutually dependent, and no one exists for itself alone but for the body as a whole, so also in the church there is the same dependence of its members on each other, and their various gifts are not designed for the exclusive 261 benefit of those who exercise them, but for the edification of the whole church.

5. As in the body the position and function of each member are determined not by itself, but by God, so also these spiritual gifts are distributed according to the good pleasure of their author.

6. In the body the least attractive parts are those which are indispensable to its existence, and so in the church it is not the most attractive gifts which are the most useful.

Sixthly, the apostle draws from this analogy the following inferences.

1. Every one should be contented with the gift which he has received of the Lord, just as the hand and foot are contented with their position and office in the body.

2. There should be no exaltation of one member of the church over others, on the ground of the supposed superiority of his gifts.

3. There should, and must be mutual sympathy between the members of the church, as there is between the members of the body.

One cannot suffer without all the others suffering with it.

No one lives, or acts, or feels for itself alone, but each in all the rest, vs. 12–27.

In conclusion the apostle shows that what he had said with regard to these spiritual gifts, applies in all its force to the various offices of the church, which are the organs through which the gifts of the Spirit are exercised, vs. 28–31.

1 CORINTHIANS 13

Christian love. vs. 1–13.

Love is superior to all extraordinary gifts. It is better than the gift of tongues, v. 1; than the gifts of prophecy and knowledge, v. 2; and than the gift of miracles, v. 2. All outward works of charity without it are worthless, v. 3. Love has this superiority, first, because of its inherent excellence, and secondly, because of its perpetuity. As to its superior excellence, it implies or secures all other excellence.

1. It includes all the forms of kindness.

2. It is humble and modest.

3. It is unselfish.

4. It sympathizes with all good, vs. 4–7. It is perpetual – all the extraordinary gifts mentioned in the preceding chapter were designed for the present state of existence, or were temporary.

Love is never to cease, v. 8. Knowledge, as a special gift, and perhaps also in the form in which it exists in this world, is to pass away. It is now the apprehension of truth as through a mirror – hereafter it will be lost in immediate vision, vs. 9–12. The permanent graces are faith, hope, and love, and the greatest of these is Love, v. 13.

This chapter, although devoted to a single Christian grace, and therefore not to be compared with the eighth chapter of Romans, or with some chapters in the epistle to the Ephesians, as an unfolding of the mysteries of redemption, still has ever been considered as one of the jewels of Scripture. For moral

voked, thinketh no evil;

6 Rejoiceth not in iniquity, but rejoiceth in the truth;

7 Beareth all things, believeth all things, hopeth all things, endureth all things.

8 Charity never faileth: but whether there be prophecies, they shall fail; whether there be tongues, they shall cease; whether there be knowledge, it shall vanish away.

9 For we know in part, and we prophesy in part.

10 But when that which is perfect is come, then that which is in part shall be done away.

11 When I was a child, I spake as a child, I understood as a child, I thought as a child: but when I became a man, I put away childish things.

12 For now we see through a glass, darkly; but then face to face: now I know in part; but then shall I know even as also I am known.

13 And now abideth faith, hope, charity, these three; but the greatest of these is charity.

1 CORINTHIANS 14

1 Follow after charity, and desire spiritual gifts, but rather that ye may prophesy.

2 For he that speaketh in an unknown tongue speaketh not unto men, but unto God: for no man understandeth him; howbeit in the spirit he speaketh mysteries.

3 But he that prophesieth speaketh unto men to edification, and exhortation, and comfort.

4 He that speaketh in an unknown tongue edifieth himself; but he that prophesieth edifieth the church.

5 I would that ye all spake with tongues, but rather that ye prophesied: for greater is he that prophesieth than he that speaketh with tongues, except he interpret, that the church may receive edifying.

6 Now, brethren, if I come unto you speaking with tongues, what shall I profit you, except I shall speak to you either by revelation, or by knowledge, or by prophesying, or by doctrine?

7 And even things without life giving sound, whether pipe or harp, except they give a distinction in the sounds, how shall

most excellent way, when *love* is the regulating principle of all our actions. And, in the outset, he proceeds upon this – that all excellencies are of no value without *love;* for nothing is so excellent or estimable as not to be vitiated in the sight of God, if *love* is wanting. Nor does he teach anything here but what he does elsewhere, when he *declares,* that it is the *end of the law,* and the *bond of perfection* (1 Timothy 1: 5), and also when he makes the holiness of the godly consist entirely in this (Colossians 3: 14) – for what else does God require from us in the second Table of the Law? It is not then to be wondered, if all our deeds are estimated by this test – their appearing to proceed from love. It is also not to be wondered, if gifts, otherwise ex*cellent,* come to have their true value only when they are made subservient to *love.*

1. If should speak with the tongues of men

He begins with eloquence, which is, it is true, an admirable gift, considered in itself, but, when apart from *love,* does not recommend a man in the estimation of God. When he speaks of the *tongue of angels,* he uses a hyperbolical expression to denote what is singular, or distinguished. At the same time, I explain it rather as referring to the diversity of languages, which the Corinthians held in much esteem, measuring everything by ambition – not by fruit. "Make yourself master," says he, "of all the languages, not of men merely, but even of Angels. You have, in that case, no reason to think, that you are of higher estimation in the sight of God than a mere cymbal, if you have not *love.*"

1 CORINTHIANS 14

As he had previously exhorted them to *follow after the more excellent gifts* (1 Corinthians 12: 31), so he exhorts them now to *follow after love,* for that was the distinguished excellence, which he had promised that he would show them. They will, therefore, regulate themselves with propriety in the use of gifts, if *love* prevails among them. For he tacitly reproves the want of *love,* as appearing in this – that they had hitherto abused their gifts, and, inferring from what goes before, that where they do not assign to *love* the chief place, they do not take the right road to the attainment of true excellence, he shows them how foolish their ambition is, which frustrates their hopes and desires.

1. Covet spiritual gifts

Lest the Corinthians should object that they wronged God, if they despised his gifts, the Apostle anticipates this objection by declaring, that it was not his design to draw them away even from those gifts that they had abused – nay rather he commends the pursuit of them, and wishes them to have a place in the Church. And assuredly, as they had been conferred for the advantage of the Church, man's

elevation, for richness and comprehensiveness, for beauty and felicity of expression, it has been the admiration of the church in all ages. – With regard to the word **charity**, as the translation of the Greek ἀγάπη, it has already been remarked in the comment on 8: 1, that it is peculiarly unhappy. Neither in its primary signification, nor in the sense which usage has attached to it, does it properly answer to the Greek term.

The latter occurs about one hundred and sixteen times in the New Testament, and is translated **love** in all places except twenty-three; and in those the departure from the common usage is altogether arbitrary. The word charity is just as inappropriate in this chapter as it would be in such phrases as, "the Son of his charity," or, "the charity of God is shed abroad in our hearts," or, "the charity of Christ." The Greek word ἀγάπη is not of heathen origin. The heathen had no conception of the grace which in the Scriptures is expressed by that term; neither ἔρως nor φιλία answers to the Scriptural sense of ἀγάπη; nor do the Latin words **amor** or **caritas**. It was the unsuitableness of the former that induced Jerome to adopt the latter as the more elevated of the two. The one properly expresses love founded on sympathy; the latter came to mean love founded on respect.

Its English derivative (**charity**) retains more of the original force of the Latin word. Caritas (from carus, **a carendo, dear**, i.e. costly) is properly dearness or costliness; and then it came to express the feeling arising from the sight of want and suffering. And this is the common meaning still attached to the English word, which renders it unsuitable as the substitute of the comprehensive word love. Many have been led to think that almsgiving covers a multitude of sins, because charity is said to have that effect; and that kindness to the poor and the sick is the sum of all religion, because Paul exalts charity above faith and hope. It is not of charity, but of love, of which the Bible thus speaks.

1 CORINTHIANS 14

Superiority of the gift of prophecy to that of tongues, vs. 1–25. Special directions for the conduct of public worship, vs. 26–40.

Superiority of the gift of prophecy to that of tongues. vs. 1–25.

The superiority of the gift of prophecy to that of tongues is founded on the consideration that he who speaks with tongues speaks to God, whereas, he who prophesies, speaks to men, vs. 2–3.

2. That he who speaks with tongues edifies only himself, whereas, he who prophesies edifies the church, vs. 4–5. That this must be so, is proved,

1. By an appeal to their own judgment and experience. If Paul came to them speaking in a way which they could not understand, what good could it do them? But if, as a prophet, he brought them a revelation from God, or as a teacher, set before them a doctrine, they would be edified, v. 6.

2. From the analogy of musical instruments. It is only when the sounds, are understood, that they produce the desired effect. If a man does not know that a given note of the trumpet is a signal for battle, he will not prepare himself for the conflict, vs. 7–9.

3. From their experience in intercourse with strangers. If a man comes to the speaking a language which I cannot understand, no matter how polished or significant that language may be, he is a barbarian to me, and I to him, vs. 10–11. In their zeal, therefore, for spiritual gifts, they should have regard to the edification of the church, v. 12. Hence, he who had the gift of tongues should pray for the gift of interpretation; as without the latter gift, however devotional he might be, his prayers could not profit others, vs. 13–14. It was not enough that the prayers and praises should be spiritual, they must be intelligible; otherwise those who were unlearned could not join in them, vs. 15–17.

For himself, the apostle says, although more

it be known what is piped or harped?

8 For if the trumpet give an uncertain sound, who shall prepare himself to the battle?

9 So likewise ye, except ye utter by the tongue words easy to be understood, how shall it be known what is spoken? for ye shall speak into the air.

10 There are, it may be, so many kinds of voices in the world, and none of them is without signification.

11 Therefore if I know not the meaning of the voice, I shall be unto him that speaketh a barbarian, and he that speaketh shall be a barbarian unto me.

12 Even so ye, forasmuch as ye are zealous of spiritual gifts, seek that ye may excel to the edifying of the church.

13 Wherefore let him that speaketh in an unknown tongue pray that he may interpret.

14 For if I pray in an unknown tongue, my spirit prayeth, but my understanding is unfruitful.

15 What is it then? I will pray with the spirit, and I will pray with the understanding also: I will sing with the spirit, and I will sing with the understanding also.

16 Else when thou shalt bless with the spirit, how shall he that occupieth the room of the unlearned say Amen at thy giving of thanks, seeing he understandeth not what thou sayest?

17 For thou verily givest thanks well, but the other is not edified.

18 I thank my God, I speak with tongues more than ye all:

19 Yet in the church I had rather speak five words with my understanding, that by my voice I might teach others also, than ten thousand words in an unknown tongue.

20 Brethren, be not children in understanding: howbeit in malice be ye children, but in understanding be men.

21 In the law it is written, With men of other tongues and other lips will I speak unto this people; and yet for all that will they not hear me, saith the Lord.

22 Wherefore tongues are for a sign, not to them that believe, but to them that believe not: but prophesying serveth not for them that believe not, but for them which believe.

23 If therefore the whole church be come together into one place, and all speak with tongues, and there come in

abuse of them ought not to give occasion for their being thrown away as useless or injurious, but in the meantime he commends *prophecy* above all other gifts, as it was the most useful of them all. He observes, therefore, an admirable medium, by disapproving of nothing that was useful, while at the same time he exhorts them not to prefer, by an absurd zeal, things of less consequence to what was of primary importance. Now he assigns the first place to *prophecy.*

Covet, therefore, *spiritual gifts – that* is, "Neglect no gift, for I exhort you to seek after them all, provided only *prophecy* holds the first place."

18. I thank

As there are many that detract from another's excellencies, in which they cannot themselves have distinction, Paul, that he might not seem to depreciate, through malignity or envy, the gift of tongues, anticipates that suspicion, by showing that he is, in this respect, superior to them all. "See," says he, "how little occasion you have to suspect the design of my discourse, as if I depreciated what I myself lacked; for if we were to contend as to tongues, there is not one of you that could bear comparison with me. While, however, I might display myself to advantage in this department., I am more concerned for edification." Paul's doctrine derives no small weight from the circumstance, that he has not an eye to himself. Lest, however, he should appear excessively arrogant, in preferring himself before all others, he ascribes it all to God. Thus he tempers his boasting with modesty.

19. I would rather speak five words

This is spoken *hyperbolically,* unless you understand *five words,* as meaning five sentences. Now as Paul, who might otherwise have exulted loftily in his power of speaking with tongues, voluntarily abstains from it, and, without any show, aims at edification exclusively, he reproves, by this means, the empty ambition of those, that are eagerly desirous to show themselves off with empty *tinkling* (1 Corinthians 13: 1). The authority of the Apostle ought, also, to have no little weight in drawing them off from vanity of this kind.

20. Brethren, be not children in understanding

He proceeds a step farther; for he shows that the Corinthians are so infatuated, that they, of their own accord. draw down upon themselves, and eagerly desire, as though it were a singular benefit, what the Lord threatens that he will send, when he designs to inflict upon his people the severest punishment. What dreadful madness is this – to pursue eagerly with their whole desire, what, in the sight of God, is regarded as a curse! That we may, however, understand more accurately Paul's meaning, we must, observe, that this

richly endowed with the gift of tongues than any of his readers, he would rather speak five words so as to be understood, than ten thousand words in an unknown tongue, vs. 18–19. It was mere childishness in the Corinthians to be so delighted with a gift which they could not turn to any practical account, v. 20. They should learn wisdom from the experience of the Hebrews. It was as a judgment that God sent among them teachers whom they could not understand. So long as they were obedient, or there was hope of bringing them to repentance, he sent them prophets speaking their own language, vs. 21–22.

Their experience would not be dissimilar. If they came together, each speaking in an unknown tongue, the effect would be only evil. But if, when they assembled, all the speakers spoke so as to be understood, and under the influence of the Spirit, then men would be convinced and converted, and God glorified, vs. 23–25.

Every one must feel the truth of the remark of Chrysostom in his commentary on this chapter: "This whole passage is very obscure; but the obscurity arises from our ignorance of the facts described, which, though familiar to those to whom the apostle wrote, have ceased to occur." That this gift should be specially connected with prophesying, as in Acts 19: 6, "they spake with tongues and prophesied," and elsewhere, is to be explained from the fact that all speaking under divine, supernatural influence, was included under the head of prophesying; and as all who spake with tongues "spake as the Spirit gave them utterance," in the wide sense of the word they all prophesied. But it is not so easy to understand why this gift should have been so common, nor why it should so often attend on conversion; see Acts 10: 46; 19: 6.

There are many things also in this chapter which it is not easy to understand on any theory of the nature of the gift. Under these circumstances it is necessary to hold fast what is clear, and to make the certain our guide in explaining what is obscure. It is clear,

1. That the word **tongues** in this connection, as already proved, means languages.

2. That the speaker with tongues was in a state of calm self-control. He could speak, or be silent, 14: 28.

3. That what he said was intelligible to himself, and could be interpreted to others.

4. That the unintelligibleness of what was said, arose not from the sounds uttered being inarticulate, but from the ignorance of the hearer. The interpretation of particular passages must, therefore, be controlled by these facts.

Special directions as to the mode of conducting their public assemblies. vs. 26–40.

The apostle concludes this chapter with certain practical directions derived from the principles which he had laid down. He neither denied the reality of the extraordinary gifts with which the Corinthians were so richly endowed, nor forbade their exercise. He only enjoined that mutual edification should be the end aimed at, v. 26. With regard to those having the gift of tongues, he directed that not more than two, or at most three, should speak, and that in succession, while one interpreted. But in case no interpreter was present, there was to be no speaking with tongues, vs. 27–28. Of the prophets also only two or three were to speak, and the rest were to sit in judgment on what was said. In case a new revelation was made to one of the prophets, he was not to interrupt the speaker, but wait until he had concluded; or the one was to give way to the other. Both were not to speak at the same time, for God did not approve of confusion. As the influence of which the prophets were the subjects did not destroy their self-control, there could be no difficulty in obeying this injunction, vs. 29–33. Women were not to speak in public; but to seek instruction at home. This prohibition rests on the divinely established subordination of the women, and on the instinct of propriety, vs. 34–35. The Corinthians were not to act in this matter as though they were

those that are unlearned, or unbelievers, will they not say that ye are mad?

24 But if all prophesy, and there come in one that believeth not, or one unlearned, he is convinced of all, he is judged of all:

25 And thus are the secrets of his heart made manifest; and so falling down on his face he will worship God, and report that God is in you of a truth.

26 How is it then, brethren? when ye come together, everyone of you hath a psalm, hath a doctrine, hath a tongue, hath a revelation, hath an interpretation. Let all things be done unto edifying.

27 If any man speak in an unknown tongue, let it be by two, or at the most by three, and that by course; and let one interpret.

28 But if there be no interpreter, let him keep silence in the church; and let him speak to himself, and to God.

29 Let the prophets speak two or three, and let the other judge.

30 If any thing be revealed to another that sitteth by, let the first hold his peace.

31 For ye may all prophesy one by one, that all may learn, and all may be comforted.

32 And the spirits of the prophets are subject to the prophets.

33 For God is not the author of confusion, but of peace, as in all churches of the saints.

34 Let your women keep silence in the churches: for it is not permitted unto them to speak; but they are commanded to be under obedience, as also saith the law.

35 And if they will learn any thing, let them ask their husbands at home: for it is a shame for women to speak in the church.

36 What? came the word of God out from you? or came it unto you only?

37 If any man think himself to be a prophet, or spiritual, let him acknowledge that the things that I write unto you are the commandments of the Lord.

38 But if any man be ignorant, let him be ignorant.

39 Wherefore, brethren, covet to prophesy, and forbid not to speak with tongues.

40 Let all things be done decently and in order.

statement is grounded on the testimony of Isaiah, which he immediately afterwards subjoins (Isaiah 28: 11–12). And as interpreters have been misled, from not observing the connection to be of this nature, to prevent all mistake, we shall first explain the passage in Isaiah, and then we shall come to Paul's words.

In that chapter the Prophet, inveighs with severity against the ten tribes, which had abandoned themselves to every kind of wickedness. The only consolation is, that God had still a people uncorrupted in the tribe of Judah; but straightway he deplores the corruption of that tribe also; and he does so the more sharply, because there was no hope of amendment. For thus he speaks in the name of God – *Whom shall I teach knowledge? those that are weaned from their mother? those that are drawn from the breasts.* By this he means, that they are no more capable of instruction than little children but lately weaned. It is added – *Precept upon precept, instruction upon instruction, charge upon charge, direction upon direction, here a little, and there a little.* In these words he expresses, in the style of a mimic, the slowness and carelessness by which they were kept back. "In teaching them, I lose my labor, for they make no progress, because they are beyond measure uncultivated, and what they had been taught by means of long-continued labor, they in a single moment forget."

It is added still farther – *He that speaketh to that people is like one that maketh use of stammering lips, and a foreign language.* This is the passage that Paul quotes. Now the meaning is, that the people have been visited with such blindness and madness, that they no more understand God when speaking to them, than they would some barbarian or foreigner, stammering in an unknown tongue – which is a dreadful curse. He has not, however, quoted the Prophet's words with exactness, because he reckoned it enough to make a pointed reference to the passage, that the Corinthians, on being admonished, might attentively consider it. As to his saying that it was *written in the law,* this is not at variance with common usage; for the Prophets had not a ministry distinct from the law, but were the interpreters of the law, and their doctrine is, as it were, a sort of appendage to it; hence the law included the whole body of Scripture, up to the advent of Christ. Now Paul from this infers as follows – "Brethren, it is necessary to guard against that childishness, which is so severely reproved by the Prophet – that the word of God sounds in your ears without any fruit. Now, when you reject prophecy, which is placed within your reach, and prefer to stand amazed at empty sound, is not this voluntarily to incur the curse of God?

Farther, lest the Corinthians should say in reply, that to be spiritually *children,* is elsewhere commended (Matthew 18: 4), Paul anticipates this objection, and exhorts them,

the oldest or the only church, v. 36. The apostle requires all classes, no matter how highly gifted, to regard his directions as the commands of Christ, vs. 37–38. He sums up the chapter in two sentences.

1. Earnestly to seek the gift of prophecy, and not to prohibit the exercise of the gift of tongues.

2. To do all things with decency and order.

26. How is it then, brethren? when ye come together, every one of you hath a Psalm, hath a doctrine, hath a tongue, hath a revelation, hath an interpretation. Let all things be done unto edifying.

How is it then? i.e. as in v. 15, What is the conclusion from what has been said? What is the condition of things among you? How, in point of fact, do you conduct your public worship? **When ye come together**. That is, as often as ye come together. **Every one of you hath**, etc. **Every one** is used distributively; one has this and another that. **A psalm**, a song of praise to God. This can hardly mean one of the Psalms of the Old Testament but something prepared or suggested for the occasion. One was impelled by the Spirit to pour forth his heart in a song of praise. Comp. v. 15. **Hath a doctrine**, i.e. comes prepared to expound some doctrine. **Hath a tongue**, i.e. is able and impelled to deliver an address or to pray in an unknown tongue.

Hath a revelation, i.e. as a prophet he has received a revelation from God which he desires to communicate. **Hath an interpretation**, i.e. is prepared to give the interpretation of some discourse previously delivered in an unknown tongue. This passage, and indeed the whole chapter, presents a lively image of an early Christian assembly. Although there were officers in every church, appointed to conduct the services and especially to teach, yet as the extraordinary gifts of the Spirit were not confined to them or to any particular class, any member present who experienced the working of the Spirit in any of its extraordinary manifestations, was authorized to use and exercise

his gift. Under such circumstances confusion could hardly fail to ensue. That such disorder did prevail in the public assemblies in Corinth is clear enough from this chapter. To correct this evil is the apostle's design in this whole passage. It was only so long as the gifts of tongues, of prophecy, of miracles, and others of a like kind continued in the church that the state of things here described prevailed. Since those gifts have ceased, no one has the right to rise in the church under the impulse of his own mind to take part in its services. The general rule which the apostle lays down, applicable to all gifts alike, is that every thing **should be done unto edifying**. That is, that the edification of the church should be the object aimed at in the exercise of these gifts. It was not enough that a man felt himself the subject of a divine influence; or that acting under it would be agreeable or even profitable to himself, he must sit in silence unless the exercise of his gift would benefit the brethren as a worshipping assembly.

1 CORINTHIANS 15

The resurrection of the dead.

In treating this subject the apostle first proves the fact of Christ's resurrection, vs. 1–11. He thence deduces, first, the possibility, and then the certainty of the resurrection of his people, vs. 12–34. He afterwards teaches the nature of the resurrection, so far as to show that the doctrine is not liable to the objections which had been brought against it, vs. 35–58.

The resurrection of Christ as securing the resurrection of his people vs. 1–34.

That certain false teachers in Corinth denied the resurrection of the dead is plain, not only from the course of argument here adopted but from the explicit statement in v. 12. Who these persons were, and what were the grounds of their objections, can only be conjectured from the nature of the apostolic argument. The most common opinion is that the objectors were converted Sadducees. The only reason

1 CORINTHIANS 15

1 Moreover, brethren, I declare unto you the gospel which I preached unto you, which also ye have received, and wherein ye stand;

2 By which also ye are saved, if ye keep in memory what I preached unto you, unless ye have believed in vain.

3 For I delivered unto you first of all that which I also received, how that Christ died for our sins according to the scriptures;

4 And that he was buried, and that he rose again the third day according to the scriptures:

5 And that he was seen of Cephas, then of the twelve:

6 After that, he was seen of above five hundred brethren at once; of whom the greater part remain unto this present, but some are fallen asleep.

7 After that, he was seen of James; then of all the apostles.

8 And last of all he was seen of me also, as of one born out of due time.

9 For I am the least of the apostles, that am not meet to be called an apostle, because I persecuted the church of God.

10 But by the grace of God I am what I am: and his grace which was bestowed upon me was not in vain; but I laboured more abundantly than they all: yet not I, but the grace of God which was with me.

11 Therefore whether it were I or they, so we preach, and so ye believed.

12 Now if Christ be preached that he rose from the dead, how say some among you that there is no resurrection of the dead?

13 But if there be no resurrection of the dead, then is Christ not risen:

14 And if Christ be not risen, then is our preaching vain, and your faith is also vain.

15 Yea, and we are found false witnesses of God; because we have testified of God that he raised up Christ: whom he raised not up, if so be that the dead rise not.

16 For if the dead rise not, then is not Christ raised:

17 And if Christ be not raised, your faith is vain; ye are yet in your sins.

18 Then they also which are fallen asleep in Christ are perished.

19 If in this life only we have hope in

indeed, to be *children in malice,* but to beware of being *children in understanding.* Hence we infer how shameless a part those act, who make Christian simplicity consist in ignorance. Paul would have all believers to be, as far as possible, in full maturity as to *understanding.*

1 CORINTHIANS 15

10. But more abundantly

Some refer this to vain-glorious boasters, who, by detracting from Paul, endeavored to set off themselves and their goods to advantage, as, in their opinion at least, it is not likely that he wished to enter upon a contest with the Apostles. When he compares himself, however, with the Apostles, he does so merely for the sake of those wicked persons, who were accustomed to bring them forward for the purpose of detracting from his reputation, as we see in the Epistle to the Galatians (Galatians 1: 11). Hence the probability is, that it is of the Apostles that he speaks, when he represents his own labors as superior to theirs, and it is quite true, that he was superior to others, not merely in respect of his enduring many hardships, encountering many dangers, abstaining from things lawful, and perseveringly despising all perils (2 Corinthians 11: 26); but also because the Lord gave to his labors a much larger measure of success. For I take labor here to mean the fruit of his labor that appeared.

Not I, but the grace

The old translator, by leaving out the article, has given occasion of mistake to those that are not acquainted with the Greek language, for in consequence of his having rendered the words thus – not I, but the grace of God with me, they thought that only the half of the praise is ascribed to God, and that the other half is reserved for man. They, accordingly, understand the meaning to be that Paul labored not alone, inasmuch as he could do nothing without co-operating grace, but at the same time it was under the influence of his own free-will, and by means of his own strength. His words, however, have quite a different meaning, for what he had said was his own, he afterwards, correcting himself, ascribes wholly to the grace of God – **wholly,** I say, not in part, for whatever he might have seemed to do, was **wholly,** he declares, the work of grace. A remarkable passage certainly, both for laying low the pride of man, and for magnifying the operation of Divine grace in us. For Paul, as though he had improperly made himself the author of anything good, corrects what he had said, and declares the grace of God to have been the efficient cause of the whole. Let us not think that there is here a mere pretense of humility It is in good earnest that he speaks thus, and from knowing that it is so in truth. Let us learn, therefore, that we have nothing that is good, but what the Lord has graciously

for this opinion is that the Sadducees denied the doctrine of the resurrection, and that Paul, as appears from Acts 24: 6–9 and 26: 6–8, had been before brought into collision with them on this subject. The objections to this view are of no great weight. It is said that such was the hostility of the Sadducees to the gospel that it is not probable any of their number were among the converts to Christianity.

The case of Paul himself proves that the bitterest enemies could, by the grace of God, be converted into friends. It is further objected that Paul could not, in argument with Sadducees, make the resurrection of Christ the basis of his proof. But he does not assume that fact as conceded, but proves it by an array of the testimony by which it was supported. Others suppose that the opponents of the doctrine were Epicureans. There is, however, no indication of their peculiar opinions in the chapter. In v. 32 Epicurean carelessness and indulgence are represented as the consequence, not the cause, of the denial of the resurrection. Nothing more definite can be arrived at on this point than the conjecture that the false teachers in question were men of Grecian culture. In Acts 17: 32 it is said of the Athenians that "some mocked" when they heard Paul preach the doctrine of the resurrection. From the character of the objections answered in the latter part of the chapter, vs. 35–58, it is probable that the objections urged against the doctrine were founded on the assumption that a material organization was unsuited to the future state. It is not unlikely that oriental philosophy, which assumed that matter was the source and seat of evil, had produced an effect on the minds of these Corinthian skeptics as well as on the Christians of Colosse. The decision of the question as to what particular class of persons the opponents of the doctrine of the resurrection belonged, happily is of no importance in the interpretation of the apostle's argument. As in 2 Timothy 2: 17–18 he speaks of Hymeneus and Philetus as teaching that the resurrection was passed already, it is probable that these errorists in Corinth

also refused to acknowledge any other than a spiritual resurrection.

After reminding the Corinthians that the doctrine of the resurrection was a primary principle of the gospel, which he had preached to them, and on which their salvation depended, vs. 1–3, he proceeds to assert and prove the fact that Christ rose from the dead on the third day. This event had been predicted in the Old Testament. Its actual occurrence is proved,

1. By Christ appearing after his resurrection, first to Peter and then to the twelve.

2. By his appearing to upward of five hundred brethren at one time, most of whom were still alive.

3. By a separate appearance to James.

4. And then again to all the apostles.

5. Finally by his appearance to Paul himself.

There never was a historical event established on surer evidence than that of the resurrection of Christ, vs. 4–8 This fact, therefore, was included in the preaching of all the apostles, and in the faith of all Christians, v. 11. But if this be so, how can the doctrine of the resurrection be denied by any who pretend to be Christians? To deny the resurrection of the dead is to deny the resurrection of Christ; and to deny the resurrection of Christ, is to subvert the gospel, vs. 12–14; and also to make the apostles false witnesses, v. 15. If Christ be not risen, our faith is vain, we are yet in our sins, those dead in Christ are perished, and all the hopes of Christians are destroyed, vs. 16–19. But if Christ be risen, then his people will also rise, because he rose as a pledge of their resurrection.

As Adam was the cause of death, so Christ is the cause of life; Adam secured the death of all who are **in** him, and Christ secures the life of all who are **in** him, vs. 20–22.

Although the resurrection of Christ secures the resurrection of his people, the two events are not contemporaneous. Christ rose first, his people are to rise when he comes the second time. Then is to be the final consummation, when Christ shall deliver up his providential

Christ, we are of all men most miserable.

20 But now is Christ risen from the dead, and become the firstfruits of them that slept.

21 For since by man came death, by man came also the resurrection of the dead.

22 For as in Adam all die, even so in Christ shall all be made alive.

23 But every man in his own order: Christ the firstfruits; afterward they that are Christ's at his coming.

24 Then cometh the end, when he shall have delivered up the kingdom to God, even the Father; when he shall have put down all rule and all authority and power.

25 For he must reign, till he hath put all enemies under his feet.

26 The last enemy that shall be destroyed is death.

27 For he hath put all things under his feet. But when he saith, all things are put under him, it is manifest that he is excepted, which did put all things under him.

28 And when all things shall be subdued unto him, then shall the Son also himself be subject unto him that put all things under him, that God may be all in all.

29 Else what shall they do which are baptized for the dead, if the dead rise not at all? why are they then baptized for the dead?

30 And why stand we in jeopardy every hour?

31 I protest by your rejoicing which I have in Christ Jesus our Lord, I die daily.

32 If after the manner of men I have fought with beasts at Ephesus, what advantageth it me, if the dead rise not? let us eat and drink; for to morrow we die.

33 Be not deceived: evil communications corrupt good manners.

34 Awake to righteousness, and sin not; for some have not the knowledge of God: I speak this to your shame.

35 But some man will say, How are the dead raised up? and with what body do they come?

36 Thou fool, that which thou sowest is not quickened, except it die:

37 And that which thou sowest, thou sowest not that body that shall be, but bare grain, it may chance of wheat, or of some other grain:

38 But God giveth it a body as it hath

given us, that we do nothing good but what he **worketh in us** (Philippians 2: 13) – not that we do nothing ourselves, but that we do nothing without being influenced – that is, under the guidance and impulse of the Holy Spirit.

24. When he shall have abolished all rule

Some understand this as referring to the powers that are opposed to Christ himself; for they have an eye to what immediately follows, until he shall have put all his enemies. This clause, however, corresponds with what goes before, when he said, that Christ would not sooner deliver up the kingdom. Hence there is no reason why we should restrict in such a manner the statement before us. I explain it, accordingly, in a general way, and understand by it – all powers that are lawful and **ordained by God** (Romans 13: 1). In the **first** place, what we find in the Prophets (Isaiah 13: 10; Ezekiel 32: 7) as to the darkening of the sun and moon, that God alone may shine forth, while it has begun to be fulfilled under the reign of Christ, will, nevertheless, not be fully accomplished until the last day; but then **every height shall be brought low** (Luke 3: 5), that the glory of God may alone shine forth. Farther, we know that all earthly principalities and honors are connected exclusively with the keeping up of the present life, and, consequently, are a part of the world. Hence it follows that they are temporary.

Hence as the world will have an end, so also will government, and magistracy, and laws, and distinctions of ranks, and different orders of dignities, and everything of that nature. There will be no more any distinction between servant and master, between king and peasant, between magistrate and private citizen. Nay more, there will be then an end put to angelic principalities in heaven, and to ministries and superiorities in the Church, that God may exercise his power and dominion by himself alone, and not by the hands of men or angels. The angels, it is true, will continue to exist, and they will also retain their distinction. The righteous, too, will shine forth, every one according to the measure of his grace; but the angels will have to resign the dominion, which they now exercise in the name and by the commandment of God. Bishops, teachers, and Prophets will cease to hold these distinctions, and will resign the office which they now discharge. *Rule*, and *authority*, and *power* have much the same meaning in this passage; but these three terms are conjoined to bring out the meaning more fully.

43. It is sown in corruption

That there may be no doubt remaining, Paul explains himself, by unfolding the difference between their present condition, and that which will be after the resurrection. What connection, then, would there be in his discourse, if he had intended in the first instance to distinguish between

kingdom as mediator to the Father, after all his enemies are subdued, vs. 23–24. It is necessary that Christ's dominion over the universe, to which he was exalted after his resurrection, should continue until his great work of subduing or restraining evil was accomplished. When that is done, then the Son (the Theantropos, the Incarnate Logos), will be subject to the Father, and God as God, and not as Mediator, reign supreme, vs. 25–28.

Besides the arguments already urged, there are two other considerations which prove the truth or importance of the doctrine of the resurrection.

The first is, "the baptism for the dead" (whatever that means) prevailing in Corinth, assumes the truth of the doctrine, v. 29.

The other is, the intimate connection between this doctrine and that of a future state is such, that if the one be denied, the other cannot, in a Christian sense, be maintained. If there be no resurrection, there is for Christians no hereafter, and they may act on the principle, "Let us eat and drink for to-morrow we die," vs. 30–32. The apostle concludes this part of the subject by warning his readers against the corrupting influence of evil associations. Whence it is probable that the denial of the doctrine had already produced the evil effects, referred to among those who rejected it, vs. 33–34.

Nature of the resurrection body. vs. 35–58.

Having proved the fact of the resurrection, the apostle comes to illustrate its nature, or to teach with what kind of bodies the dead are to rise. It seems that the great objection against the doctrine in the minds of his readers rested on the assumption that our future bodies are to be of the same nature with those which we now have; that is, natural bodies consisting of flesh and blood, and sustained by air, food and sleep. Paul says this is a foolish assumption. Our future bodies may be material and identical with our present bodies, and yet organized in a very different way. You plant a seed; it does not come up a seek, but a flower. Why then may not the future be to the present body what the flower is to the seed? vs. 35–37.

Matter admits of indefinite varieties in organization. There is not only immense diversity in the vegetable productions of the earth, but even flesh is variously modified in the different orders of animals, vs. 38–39.

This is true not only as to the earth, for there are heavenly as well as earthly bodies. And even the sun, moon and stars differ from each other in glory; why then may not our future differ from our present bodies in glory? vs. 40–41.

Such not only may be, but will be the case. The body deposited in the grave is corruptible, mean, weak, and, in a word, natural; as raised from the grave, it will be incorruptible, glorious, powerful, and spiritual, vs. 42–44.

This is according to Scripture. Adam was created with a natural body, adapted to an earthly state of existence; Christ, as a life-giving spirit, has a spiritual body. As Adam was before Christ, so our early tabernacles are before our heavenly ones. As we have borne the image of the earthly, we shall bear the image of the heavenly, vs. 45–49.

It is freely admitted that flesh and blood, i.e. bodies organized as our now are, are unfit for heaven. Corruption cannot inherit incorruption, morality shall put on immortality, vs. 51–53.

When this is done, the original promise that death shall be swallowed up in victory, will be fully accomplished, v. 54.

Death, therefore, to the believer, has lost its sting, and the grave is conquered. Death has no sting but sin; sin has no strength but from the law; the law has no power over those who are in Christ Jesus, therefore thanks be to God, who giveth us the victory through Christ Jesus our Lord! vs. 55–57.

Seeing then that we have such a glorious hereafter, we should be steadfast, unmoveable, always abounding in the work of the Lord, v. 58.

pleased him, and to every seed his own body.

39 All flesh is not the same flesh: but there is one kind of flesh of men, another flesh of beasts, another of fishes, and another of birds.

40 There are also celestial bodies, and bodies terrestrial: but the glory of the celestial is one, and the glory of the terrestrial is another.

41 There is one glory of the sun, and another glory of the moon, and another glory of the stars: for one star differeth from another star in glory.

42 So also is the resurrection of the dead. It is sown in corruption; it is raised in incorruption:

43 It is sown in dishonor; it is raised in glory: it is sown in weakness; it is raised in power:

44 It is sown a natural body; it is raised a spiritual body. There is a natural body, and there is a spiritual body.

45 And so it is written, The first man Adam was made a living soul; the last Adam was made a quickening spirit.

46 Howbeit that was not first which is spiritual, but that which is natural; and afterward that which is spiritual.

47 The first man is of the earth, earthy: the second man is the Lord from heaven.

48 As is the earthy, such are they also that are earthy: and as is the heavenly, such are they also that are heavenly.

49 And as we have borne the image of the earthy, we shall also bear the image of the heavenly.

50 Now this I say, brethren, that flesh and blood cannot inherit the kingdom of God; neither doth corruption inherit incorruption.

51 Behold, I shew you a mystery; We shall not all sleep, but we shall all be changed,

52 In a moment, in the twinkling of an eye, at the last trump: for the trumpet shall sound, and the dead shall be raised incorruptible, and we shall be changed.

53 For this corruptible must put on incorruption, and this mortal must put on immortality.

54 So when this corruptible shall have put on incorruption, and this mortal shall have put on immortality, then shall be brought to pass the saying that is written, Death is swallowed up in victory.

55 O death, where is thy sting? O

the different degrees of future glory among the saints? There can, therefore, be no doubt, that he has been, up to this point, following out one subject. He now returns to the first similitude that he had made use of, but applies it more closely to his design. Or, if you prefer it, keeping up that similitude, he figuratively compares the time of the present life to the seed-time, and the resurrection to the harvest; and he says, that our body is now, indeed, subject to mortality and ignominy, but will then be glorious and incorruptible. He says the same thing in other words in Philippians 3: 21. Christ will change our vile body, that he may make it like to his own glorious body.

58. Wherefore, my brethren

Having satisfied himself that he had sufficiently proved the doctrine of the resurrection, he now closes his discussion with an exhortation; and this has much more force, than if he had made use of a simple conclusion with an affirmation. Since your labor *says he*, is not in vain in the Lord, be steadfast, and abound in good works.

Now he says that their labor is not in vain, for this reason, that there is a reward laid up for them with God. This is that exclusive hope which, in the first instance, encourages believers, and afterwards sustains them, so that they do not stop short in the race. Hence he exhorts them to remain steadfast, because they rest on a firm foundation, as they know that a better life is prepared for them in heaven.

He adds – abounding in the work of the Lord; for the hope of a resurrection makes us not be **weary** in well doing, as he teaches in Colossians 1: 10. For amidst so many occasions of offense as constantly present themselves to us, who is there that would not despond, or turn aside from the way, were it not that, by thinking of a better life he is by this means kept in the fear of God? Now, on the other hand, he intimates, that if the hope of a resurrection is taken away, then, the foundation (as it were) being rooted up, the whole structure of piety falls to the ground. Unquestionably, if the hope of reward is taken away and extinguished, alacrity in running will not merely grow cold, but will be altogether destroyed.

1 CORINTHIANS 16

1. But concerning the collection

Luke relates (Acts 11: 28) that the prediction of Agabus, foretelling that there would be a famine under Claudius Caesar, gave occasion for alms being collected by the saints, with the view of affording help to the brethren in Jerusalem. For though the Prophet had foretold, that this calamity would be generally prevalent almost throughout the world, yet as they were more heavily oppressed with penury at Jerusalem, and as all the Gentile Churches

35. But some (man) will say, How are the dead raised up? and with what body do they come? The discussion of the fact of the resurrection being ended, the apostle comes to consider the manner of it. He supposes some objector to ask, **How are the dead raised** up? This may mean, How can a corrupted and disorganized body be restored to life? And the next question, **With what body do they come?** may refer to the result of the process. What is to be the nature of our future bodies? Or the latter question may be merely explanatory of the former, so that only one point is presented. How, i.e. with what kind of body are the dead raised? There are, however, two distinct questions, for although the two are not connected by καί, **and,** but by the particle δέ which might be merely explanatory, yet the apostle really answers, in what follows, both questions, viz., How it is possible for life to come out of death, and, What is to be the nature of the body after the resurrection. The latter difficulty was the main one, and therefore to that the most of what follows refers. The great objection in the minds of the Corinthians to the doctrine of the resurrection was evidently the same as that of the Sadducees. Both supposed our future bodies are to be like our present ones. Our Lord's answer to the Sadducees, therefore, is the same as that which Paul gives to the Corinthian objectors. The future body is not to be like the present. To reject a plainly-revealed and most important doctrine on such grounds as these is wicked as well as foolish, and therefore the apostle says in the next verse – **36. (Thou) fool, that which thou sowest is not quickened, except it die.**

It is not, **Thou** fool, but simply, Fool! an exclamation both of disapprobation and contempt. Luke 12: 20. Romans 1: 22. Ephesians 5: 15.

It does not, however, necessarily express any bitterness of feeling; for our blessed Lord said to his doubting disciples, "O fools, and slow of heart to believe all that the prophets have spoken!" Luke 24: 25. It was the senselessness of the objection that roused the apostle's indig-nation. The body cannot live again because it dies. Fool! says Paul, a seed cannot live unless it does die. Disorganization is the necessary condition of reorganization. If the seed remain a seed there is an end of it. But if it die, it bringeth forth much fruit, John 12: 24. The seed is as much disorganized, it as really ceases to be a seed when sown in the ground, as the body when laid in the grave. If the one dies, the other dies. Death is not annihilation, but disorganization; the passing from one form or mode of existence to another. How then can the disorganization of the body in the grave be an objection to the doctrine of a resurrection? It may be said that the apostle does not pursue the objection; that the body is not only disorganized but dispersed; its elements scattered over the earth, and embraced in new combinations; whereas in the seed the germ remains, so that there is no interruption of the organic life of the plant. To those who make this objection our Savior's answer is, that they err, "not knowing the power of God." Who knows where the principle of the organic life of the body is? It may be in the soul, which when the time comes may unfold itself into a new body, gathering or regathering its materials according to its own law; just as the principle of vegetable life in the seed unfolds itself into some gorgeous flower, gathering from surrounding nature the materials for its new organization. The identity between the present and future body is implied in the apostle's illustration. But it is his object neither to assert that identity, nor to explain its nature. The latter is a very subordinate point. The Bible clearly teaches that our bodies hereafter are to be the same as those which we now have; but it nowhere teaches us wherein that sameness consists. In what sense is a sprouting acorn the same with the full-grown oak? Not in substance, not in form, not in appearance. It is, however, the same individual organism. The same is true of the human body. It is the same in old age that it was in infancy. But in what sense? The materials of which the body is composed change many times in the course of an ordinary life,

grave, where is thy victory?

56 The sting of death is sin; and the strength of sin is the law.

57 But thanks be to God, which giveth us the victory through our Lord Jesus Christ.

58 Therefore, my beloved brethren, be ye stedfast, unmoveable, always abounding in the work of the Lord, forasmuch as ye know that your labour is not in vain in the Lord.

1 CORINTHIANS 16

1 Now concerning the collection for the saints, as I have given order to the churches of Galatia, even so do ye.

2 Upon the first day of the week let every one of you lay by him in store, as God hath prospered him, that there be no gatherings when I come.

3 And when I come, whomsoever ye shall approve by your letters, them will I send to bring your liberality unto Jerusalem.

4 And if it be meet that I go also, they shall go with me.

5 Now I will come unto you, when I shall pass through Macedonia: for I do pass through Macedonia.

6 And it may be that I will abide, yea, and winter with you, that ye may bring me on my journey whithersoever I go.

7 For I will not see you now by the way; but I trust to tarry a while with you, if the Lord permit.

8 But I will tarry at Ephesus until Pentecost.

9 For a great door and effectual is opened unto me, and there are many adversaries.

10 Now if Timotheus come, see that he may be with you without fear: for he worketh the work of the Lord, as I also do.

11 Let no man therefore despise him: but conduct him forth in peace, that he may come unto me: for I look for him with the brethren.

12 As touching our brother Apollos, I greatly desired him to come unto you with the brethren: but his will was not at all to come at this time; but he will come when he shall have convenient time.

13 Watch ye, stand fast in the faith, quit you like men, be strong.

14 Let all your things be done with charity.

were bound, if they would not be held guilty of very great ingratitude, to afford aid to that place from which they had received the gospel, every one, consequently, forgetful of self, resolved to afford relief to Jerusalem. That the pressure of want was felt heavily at Jerusalem, appears from the Epistle to the Galatians (Galatians 2: 10), where Paul relates, that he had been charged by the Apostles to stir up the Gentiles to afford help. Now the Apostles would never have given such a charge, had they not been constrained by necessity. Farther, this passage is an evidence of the truth of what Paul states there also – that he had been careful to exhort the Gentiles to afford help in such a case of necessity. Now, however, he prescribes the method of relief; and that the Corinthians may accede to it the more readily, he mentions that he had already prescribed it to the Churches of Galatia; for they would necessarily be the more influenced by example, as we are wont to feel a natural backwardness to anything that is not ordinarily practiced. Now follows the method – by which he designed to cut off all hinderances and impediments.

13. Watch ye

A short exhortation, but of great weight. He exhorts them to watch, in order that Satan may not oppress them, finding them off their guard. For as the warfare is incessant, the watching requires to be incessant too. Now watchfulness of spirit is this – when, free and disentangled from earthly cares, we meditate on the things of God. For as the body is weighed down by surfeiting and drunkenness (Luke 21: 34), so as to be fit for nothing, so the cares and lusts of the world, idleness or carelessness, are like a spiritual surfeiting that overpowers the mind.

The **second** thing is that they persevere in the faith, or that they hold fast the faith, so as to **stand firm;** because that is the foundation on which we rest. It is certain, however, that he points out the means of perseverance – by resting upon God with a firm faith.

In the **third** exhortation, which is much of the same nature, he stirs them up to manly fortitude. And, as we are naturally weak, he exhorts them **fourthly** to strengthen themselves, or gather strength. For where we render it be strong. Paul makes use of only one word, which is equivalent to strengthen yourselves.

14. Let all your things be done in love

Again he repeats what is the rule in all those transactions, in which we have dealings with one another. He wishes, then, that love shall be the directress; because the Corinthians erred chiefly in this respect – that every one looked to himself without caring for others.

yet the body remains the same. We may rest assured that our future bodies will be the same with those which we now have in a high and satisfying sense, though until the time comes we may be as little able to explain the nature of that identity as we are to tell what constitutes the identity of the body in this life. The same body which is sown in tears, shall be reaped in joy. To doubt the fact of the resurrection, because we cannot understand the process, is, as the apostle says, a proof of folly.

1 CORINTHIANS 16

Treats,

1. Of the collection to be made for the saints in Jerusalem, vs. 1–9.

2. Of Timothy and Apollos, whom the apostle commends to the confidence of the Corinthians, vs. 10–14.

3. The third paragraph contains exhortations and greetings, vs. 15–20.

4. The last paragraph is the salutation written with Paul's own hand, vs. 21–24.

Concerning the collection for the saints at Jerusalem.

For some reason not now to be certainly ascertained, poverty prevailed in Jerusalem among the believers more than in any other part of the church.

Almost all the special exhortations to provide for the poor, in Paul's epistles, have primary reference to the poor in Jerusalem. He had exhorted the churches of Galatia to make a collection for their relief; and then those of Macedonia, and he now addresses the Corinthians on the subject. It is a very common opinion that the poverty of the Christians in Jerusalem arose from the community of goods introduced among them at the beginning; an error which arose from an excess of love over knowledge. In thirty years that mistake may have produced its legitimate effects.

Perfection in one thing requires perfection in all. Perfect equality in goods requires perfect freedom from selfishness and indolence.

The collection made by the Syrian churches, as recorded in Acts 11: 29, was in consequence of the death the Christian prophet Agablus warned his brethren was to come on all the world. Whatever may have been the cause, the fact is certain that the saints in Jerusalem stood in special need of the assistance of their richer brethren. Paul, therefore, undervalued and suspected as he was by the Jewish Christians, labored assiduously in their behalf. He exhorts the Corinthians to adopt the same arrangements in reference to this matter, which he had established in the churches of Galatia.

A contribution was to be made on the Lord's day every week, proportioned to their resources, so that the collection might be ready when he came, vs. 1–2.

He would either send it by persons whom they might approve to Jerusalem, or if the sum were of sufficient magnitude to make it worth while, he would himself accompany their messengers, vs. 3–4.

He announces his purpose to visit the Corinthians after having passed over Macedonia, and perhaps to pass the winter with them. His prospects of usefulness in Ephesus would detain him in that city until Pentecost, vs. 5–9.

As to Timothy and Apollos he exhorts them to treat the former in such a manner that he might be free from fear among them, for he was worthy of their confidence, vs. 10–11.

Of the latter he says he had urged him to go to Corinth with the other brethren, but that he was unwilling to do so then, but would go when a suitable occasion offered, vs. 12–14.

He exhorts them to submission to the household of Stephanas, and to every one who was laboring in the good cause, vs. 15–16.

He expresses his gratification in seeing the brethren from Corinth, and sends salutations from those around him to the Christians in Achaia, vs. 17–20.

The conclusion of the epistle was written with his own hand as an authentification of the whole, vs. 21–24.

15 I beseech you, brethren, (ye know the house of Stephanas, that it is the firstfruits of Achaia, and that they have addicted themselves to the ministry of the saints,)

16 That ye submit yourselves unto such, and to every one that helpeth with us, and laboureth.

17 I am glad of the coming of Stephanas and Fortunatus and Achaicus: for that which was lacking on your part they have supplied.

18 For they have refreshed my spirit and yours: therefore acknowledge ye them that are such.

19 The churches of Asia salute you. Aquila and Priscilla salute you much in the Lord, with the church that is in their house.

20 All the brethren greet you. Greet ye one another with an holy kiss.

21 The salutation of me Paul with mine own hand.

22 If any man love not the Lord Jesus Christ, let him be Anathema Maranatha.

23 The grace of our Lord Jesus Christ be with you.

24 My love be with you all in Christ Jesus. Amen.

20. Salute one another with a holy kiss.
The practice of kissing was very common among the Jews, as is manifest from the Scriptures. In **Greece**, though it was not so common and customary, it was by no means unknown; but the probability is, that Paul speaks here of a solemn kiss, with which they saluted each other in the sacred assembly.

22. If any man love not the Lord Jesus
Paul entreats the grace of Christ in behalf of the Corinthians: he makes a declaration of his love towards them, and, with the severest threatening, he inveighs against those that falsely took upon themselves the Lord's name, while not loving him from the heart. For he is not speaking of strangers, who avowedly hated the Christian name, but of pretenders and hypocrites, who troubled the Churches for the sake of their own belly, or from empty boasting. On such persons he denounces an anathema, and he also pronounces a curse upon them. It is not certain, however, whether he desires their destruction in the presence of God, or whether he wishes to render them odious – nay, even execrable, in the view of believers. Thus in Galatians 1: 8, when pronouncing one who corrupts the Gospel to be accursed, he does not mean that he was rejected or condemned by God, but he declares that he is to be abhorred by us. I expound it in a simple way as follows: "Let them perish and be cut off, as being the pests of the Church." And truly, there is nothing that is more pernicious, than that class of persons, who prostitute a profession of piety to their own depraved affections. Now he points out the origin of this evil, when he says, that they do not love Christ, for a sincere and earnest love to Christ will not suffer us to give occasion of offense to brethren.

1. Now concerning the collection for the saints, as I have given order to the churches of Galatia, even so do ye. But concerning the collection which is for the saints. What saints were intended was already known to the Corinthians. Instead of for the saints, in Romans 15: 26 we have the more definite expression, "for the poor of the saints who are in Jerusalem," in whose behalf, he tells the Romans, Macedonia and Achaia had made a contribution. The Greek word λογία in the sense of συλλογή, collection, is only found in this passage. As I have given orders, i.e. as I arranged or ordered. This is the language of authority.

For although these contributions were voluntary, and were required to be made cheerfully, 2 Corinthians 9: 7, yet they were a duty, and therefore both the collection itself, and the mode in which it should be accomplished, were proper subjects for apostolic direction. In the epistle to the Galatians there is no mention of this collection. It was probably ordered when Paul visited those churches. So do ye, i.e. adopt the same plan as to the mode of making the collection. What that was, is stated in the following verse.

2 Corinthians

Introduction by John Calvin

So far as we can judge from the connection of this Epistle, it appears that the *first* Epistle was not without some good effect among the Corinthians, but at the same time was not productive of so much benefit as it ought to have been; and farther, that some wicked persons, despising Paul's authority, persisted in their obstinacy. For the fact of his being so much occupied, at one time in declaring his fidelity, and at another in maintaining the dignity of his office, is itself a token that they had not as yet been thoroughly confirmed. He himself, too, complains in express terms, that there were some that made sport of his former Epistle, instead of deriving benefit from it. Understanding, then, the condition of the Church among them to be such, and being detained by other matters, so as to be prevented from coming to them so soon as he had at that time contemplated, he wrote this Epistle from Macedonia. We are now in possession of the purpose which he had in view in writing this Epistle – that he might perfect what he had already begun, in order that he might, when he came, find every thing in proper order.

He begins, as he is wont, with thanksgiving, rendering thanks to God, that he had been marvelously rescued from the most imminent dangers, and at the same time he calls them to notice, that all his afflictions and distresses tended to their benefit and welfare, that he may the better secure their favor by this farther pledge of union, while the, wicked perversely took occasion from this to lessen his influence. Farther, when wishing to apologize for delaying to come to them, he declares that he had not changed his purpose from lightness

or unsteadiness, and that he had not, for the purpose of deceiving, professed anything that he had not really had in view; for there was the same consistency to be seen by them in all his sayings, that they had had experience of in his doctrine. Here, too, he briefly notices, how stable and sure was the truth of his preaching, as being founded on Christ, by whom all the promises of God are fixed and ratified – which is a high recommendation of the gospel.

After this he declares, that the reason why he had not come was this, that he could not appear among them cheerful and agreeable. In this statement, he reproves those, who, from his change of purpose, took occasion to calumniate him. He accordingly throws the blame upon the Corinthians, as being not yet well prepared for receiving him. He shows, at the same time, with what fatherly forbearance he was actuated, inasmuch as he kept himself back from visiting their city for this reason – that he might not be under the necessity of exercising severity upon them.

Farther, lest any one should object, that he had in the mean time not at all refrained from handling the Corinthians severely in his writings, he apologizes for the vehemence that he made use of in his first Epistle, by saying that it was owing to others – they having shut him up to the necessity of this against his will. That this keenness had proceeded from a friendly disposition he satisfactorily shows, by ordering that the incestuous person himself, on whose account he had been much exasperated, should be received back into favor, having since that time given some evidence of repentance. Farther, he brings forward this additional evidence of his affection towards them, that he *had no rest in his mind* (2 Corinthians 2: 13) until he had learned through means of Titus the state of their affairs, for an anxiety of this kind originates in affection.

Having had occasion, however, to make mention here of his journey to Macedonia, he begins to speak of the glory of his ministry. As, however, those darling Apostles, who endeavored to detract from him, had obtained an easy victory over him by trumpeting their own praises, that he may have nothing in common with them, and that he may at the same time beat down their foolish boasting, he declares that he derives commendation from the work itself, and does not borrow it from men. In the same passage, he extols in magnificent terms the efficacy of his preaching, and sets off to advantage the dignity of his Apostleship by comparing the gospel with the law, declaring, however, first of all, that he claimed nothing as his own, but acknowledged everything, whatever it might be, to have come forth from God.

After this he relates again, with what fidelity and integrity he had discharged the office intrusted to him, and in this he reproves those who malignantly reproached him. Nay more, rising still higher in holy confidence, he declares, that all are blinded by the devil, who do not perceive the luster of his gospel. Perceiving, however, that the meanness of his person (as being contemptible) detracted much from the respect due to his Apostleship, embracing this favorable opportunity, he does not merely remove this occasion of offense, but turns it into an opposite direction, by saying, that the excellence of God's grace shines forth so much the more brightly, from the circumstance that so valuable a treasure was presented in earthen vessels (2 Corinthians 4: 7).

Thus he turns to his own commendation those things which the malevolent were wont to cast up to him by way of reproach, because on his being weighed down with so many distresses, he always, nevertheless, after the manner of the palm tree, rises superior to them. He treats of this subject up to the middle of the *fourth* chapter (2 Corinthians 4). As, however, the true glory of Christians lies beyond this world, he teaches that we must, by contempt of this present life and mortification of the *outward*

man, set ourselves with the whole bent of our mind to meditation on a blessed immortality.

Farther, near the beginning of the *fifth* chapter, (2 Corinthians 5), he glories in this – that being actuated by such a disposition, he has nothing else as the object of his desire, than to have his services approved unto the Lord, and he entertains a hope, that he will have the Corinthians as witnesses of his sincerity. As, however, there was a danger of his being suspected of vanity, or arrogance, he again repeats, that he is constrained to this by the unreasonableness of wicked persons, and that it was not for his own sake, as though he were eager to retain their good opinion, but for the benefit of the Corinthians, to whom it was of advantage to have this opinion and persuasion; and he declares that he is concerned for nothing but their welfare. With the view of confirming this, he subjoins a universal statement, showing what ought to be the object aimed at by the servants of Christ – that, losing sight of themselves, they should live to the honor of their Lord; and at length he concludes, that everything except newness of life ought to be reckoned of no importance, so that he alone, who has denied himself, is to be held in esteem. From this he passes on to unfold the sum of the Gospel message, that by the magnitude and excellence of it he may stir up both ministers and people to a pious solicitude. This he does in the beginning of the *sixth* chapter (2 Corinthians 6).

Here again, after having noticed how faithfully he discharged his office, he gently reproves the Corinthians, as being hindrances to themselves in the way of their reaping advantage. To this expostulation he immediately subjoins an exhortation, to *flee from idolatry* – from which it appears, that the Corinthians had not yet been brought so far as he wished. Hence it is not without good reason that he complains, that they had themselves to blame, inasmuch as they had not had their ears open to doctrine so plain. But lest he should, by pressing too severely their tender minds, dishearten or alienate them, he again assures them of his kind disposition towards them, and resuming his apology for severity, which he had left off in a manner abruptly, he brings it to a conclusion, though in a different way. For assuming greater confidence, he acknowledges that he is not dissatisfied with himself for having grieved them, inasmuch as he had done it for their good; while at the same time, by congratulating them on the happy issue, he shows them how cordially he desires their best interests. These things he treats of to the end of the *seventh* chapter (2 Corinthians 7).

From the beginning of the *eighth* chapter (2 Corinthians 8), to the end of the *ninth* (2 Corinthians 9), he stirs them up to cheerfulness in giving alms, of which he had made mention in the last chapter of the first Epistle. He commends them, it is true, for having begun well, but lest the ardor of their zeal should cool in process of time, as often happens, he encourages them by a variety of arguments to go on perseveringly in the course on which they had entered.

In the *tenth* chapter (2 Corinthians 10), he begins to defend himself, and his office as an Apostle, from the calumnies with which the wicked assailed him. And in the first place, he shows that he is admirably equipped with the armor that is requisite for maintaining Christ's warfare.

Farther, he declares, that the authority which he had exercised in the former Epistle was grounded on the assurance of a good conscience, and he shows them that he had no less power in his actions, when present, than authority in his words when absent. Lastly, by instituting a comparison between himself and them, he shows how vain their boasting is.

In the *eleventh* chapter, (2 Corinthians 11), he calls upon the Corinthians to renounce those depraved inclinations, by which they had been corrupted, showing them that nothing is more dangerous than to allow themselves to be drawn aside from the simplicity of the Gospel. The fact of his having begun to be somewhat disesteemed among them, while others had been more favorably received by them, had arisen, as he shows, not from any fault on his part, but from their being haughty or nice to please; inasmuch as those others had brought them nothing better or more excellent, while he was contemptible in their view because he

did not set himself off to advantage by elegance of speech, or because he had, by voluntary subjection, by way of humoring their weakness, given up his just claim. This irony contains in it an indirect reproach for their ingratitude, for where was the reasonableness of esteeming him the less, because he had accommodated himself to them? He declares, however, that the reason why he had refrained from taking the wages to which he was entitled, was not that he had less affection to the Corinthians, but in order that no advantage might be gained over him in any respect by the false apostles, who, he saw, laid snares for him by this stratagem.

Having reproved the unreasonable and malignant judgment of the Corinthians, he magnifies himself in a strain of pious glorying, letting them know in what magnificent terms he could boast, were he so inclined, premising however, that it is for their sakes that he acts the fool in heralding his own praises. At length, checking himself, as it were, in the middle of the course, he says that his chief ground of glorying is that abasement which was despised by the proud, for he had been admonished by the Lord, not to glory in anything but in his infirmities.

Towards the close of the *twelfth* chapter (2 Corinthians 12), he again expostulates with them for shutting him up to the necessity of thus playing the fool, while they give themselves up to ambitious men, by whom they are estranged from Christ. Farther, he inveighs keenly against those who wantonly raged against him, adding to their previous crimes this impudence of opposition.

In the *thirteenth* chapter, (2 Corinthians 13), by forewarning such persons, that he will treat them with peculiar severity, he exhorts all in general to recognize his apostleship, as it will be for their advantage to do so; while it is a dangerous thing for them to despise one, whom they had found by experience to be a trusty and faithful ambassador from the Lord.

The commentaries on 2 Corinthians are by John Calvin and Charles Hodge.

2 CORINTHIANS 1

1 Paul, an apostle of Jesus Christ by the will of God, and Timothy our brother, unto the church of God which is at Corinth, with all the saints which are in all Achaia:

2 Grace be to you and peace from God our Father, and from the Lord Jesus Christ.

3 Blessed be God, even the Father of our Lord Jesus Christ, the Father of mercies, and the God of all comfort;

4 Who comforteth us in all our tribulation, that we may be able to comfort them which are in any trouble, by the comfort wherewith we ourselves are comforted of God.

5 For as the sufferings of Christ abound in us, so our consolation also aboundeth by Christ.

6 And whether we be afflicted, it is for your consolation and salvation, which is effectual in the enduring of the same sufferings which we also suffer: or whether we be comforted, it is for your consolation and salvation.

7 And our hope of you is stedfast, knowing, that as ye are partakers of the sufferings, so shall ye be also of the consolation.

8 For we would not, brethren, have you ignorant of our trouble which came to us in Asia, that we were pressed out of measure, above strength, insomuch that we despaired even of life:

9 But we had the sentence of death in ourselves, that we should not trust in ourselves, but in God which raiseth the dead:

10 Who delivered us from so great a death, and doth deliver: in whom we trust that he will yet deliver us;

11 Ye also helping together by prayer for us, that for the gift bestowed upon us by the means of many persons thanks may be given by many on our behalf.

12 For our rejoicing is this, the testimony of our conscience, that in simplicity and godly sincerity, not with fleshly wisdom, but by the grace of God, we have had our conversation in the world, and more abundantly to you-ward.

13 For we write none other things unto you, than what ye read or acknowledge; and I trust ye shall acknowledge even to

2 CORINTHIANS 1

6. Whether we are afflicted

It is to be observed, that the word *afflicted* here refers not merely to outward misery, but also to that of the mind, so as to correspond with the opposite term *comforted*. (*parakaleisthai*). Thus the meaning is, that the person's mind is pressed down with anxiety from a feeling of misery. What we render *consolation*, is in the Greek *paraklesis* – a term which signifies also *exhortation*. If, however, you understand that kind of consolation, by which a person's mind is lightened of grief, and is raised above it, you will be in possession of Paul's meaning. For example, Paul himself would well-nigh have fallen down dead under the pressure of so many afflictions, had not God encouraged him, by raising him up by means of his consolation. Thus, too, the Corinthians derive strength and fortitude of mind from his sufferings, while they take comfort from his example. Let us now sum up the whole matter briefly. As he saw that his afflictions were made by some an occasion of holding him in contempt, with the view of calling back the Corinthians from an error of this nature, he shows in the first place that he ought to be in high esteem among them, in consideration of advantage redounding to themselves; and then afterwards he associates them with himself, that they may reckon his afflictions to be in a manner their own. "Whether I suffer afflictions, or experience consolation, it is all for your benefit, and I cherish an assured hope, that you will continue to enjoy this advantage."

For such were Paul's afflictions, and his consolations also, that they would have contributed to the edification of the Corinthians, had not the Corinthians of their own accord deprived themselves of the advantage redounding from it. He, accordingly, declares his confidence in the Corinthians to be such, that he entertains the assured hope that it will not be in vain, that he has been afflicted, and has received consolation for their advantage. The false apostles made every effort to turn to Paul's reproach everything that befell him. Had they obtained their wish, the afflictions which he endured for their salvation, had been vain and fruitless; they would have derived no advantage from the consolations with which the Lord refreshed him. To contrivances of this nature he opposes his present confidence. His afflictions tended to promote the comfort of believers, as furnishing them with occasion of confirmation, on their perceiving that he suffered willingly, and endured with fortitude so many hardships for the sake of the gospel. For however we may acknowledge that afflictions ought to be endured by us for the sake of the gospel, we, nevertheless, tremble through a consciousness of our weakness, and think ourselves not prepared for it. In that case, we should

2 CORINTHIANS 1

The Salutation, vs. 1–2. Thanksgiving to God for the deliverance and consolation which the writer had experienced, vs. 3–11. Defense of himself against the charge of inconstancy and inconsistency, vs. 12–24.

Paul's gratitude for the deliverance and consolation which he had experienced. vs. 1–11.

After the apostle had written his former letter to the Corinthians, and had sent Titus, either as the bearer of the letter or immediately after its having been sent by other hands, to ascertain the effect which it produced, he seems to have been in a state of unusual depression and anxiety. The persecutions to which he had been exposed in Asia placed him in continued danger of death, 1: 8; and his solicitude about the church in Corinth allowed him no inward peace, 7: 5. After leaving Ephesus he went to Troas; but although the most promising prospects of usefulness there presented themselves, he could not rest, but passed over into Macedonia in hopes of meeting Titus and obtaining from him intelligence from Corinth, 2: 12,23. This letter is the outpouring of his heart occasioned by the information which he received. More than any other of Paul's epistles, it bears the impress of the strong feelings under the influence of which it was written. That the Corinthians had received his former letter with a proper spirit, that it brought them to repentance, led them to excommunicate the incestuous person, and called forth, on the part of the larger portion of the congregation, the manifestation of the warmest affection for the apostle, relieved his mind from a load of anxiety, and filled his heart with gratitude to God. On the other hand, the increased boldness and influence of the false teachers, the perverting errors which they inculcated, and the frivolous and calumnious charges which they brought against himself, filled him with indignation. This accounts for the abrupt transitions from one subject to another, the

sudden changes of tone and manner which characterize this epistle. When writing to the Corinthians as a church obedient, affectionate, and penitent, there is no limit to his tenderness and love. His great desire seems to be to heal the temporary breach which had occurred between them, and to assure his readers that all was forgiven and forgotten, and that his heart was entirely theirs. But when he turns to the wicked, designing corrupters of the truth among them, there is a tone of severity to be found in no other of his writings, not even in his epistle to the Galatians. Erasmus compares this epistle to a river which sometimes flows in a gentle stream, sometimes rushes down as a torrent bearing all before it; sometimes spreading out like a placid lake; sometimes losing itself, as it were, in the sand, and breaking out in its fullness in some unexpected place. Though perhaps the least methodical of Paul's writings, it is among the most interesting of his letters as bringing out the man before the reader and revealing his intimate relations to the people for whom he labored. The remark must be borne in mind (often made before), that the full play allowed to the peculiarities of mind and feeling of the sacred writers, is in no way inconsistent with their plenary inspiration. The grace of God in conversion does not change the natural character of its subjects, but accommodates itself to all their peculiarities of disposition and temperament. And the same is true with regard to the influence of the Spirit in inspiration.

The salutation in this epistle is nearly in the same words as in the former letter, vs. 1–2.

Here also as there, the introduction is a thanksgiving. As these expressions of gratitude are not mere forms, but genuine effusions of the heart, they vary according to the circumstances under which each epistle was written. Here the thanksgiving was for consolation. Paul blesses God as the God of all mercy for the consolation which he had experienced. He associates, or rather identifies himself with the Corinthians; representing his afflictions as theirs and his consolation also as belonging to

the end;

14 As also ye have acknowledged us in part, that we are your rejoicing, even as ye also are ours in the day of the Lord Jesus.

15 And in this confidence I was minded to come unto you before, that ye might have a second benefit;

16 And to pass by you into Macedonia, and to come again out of Macedonia unto you, and of you to be brought on my way toward Judaea.

17 When I therefore was thus minded, did I use lightness? or the things that I purpose, do I purpose according to the flesh, that with me there should be yea yea, and nay nay?

18 But as God is true, our word toward you was not yea and nay.

19 For the Son of God, Jesus Christ, who was preached among you by us, even by me and Silvanus and Timotheus, was not yea and nay, but in him was yea.

20 For all the promises of God in him are yea, and in him Amen, unto the glory of God by us.

21 Now he which stablisheth us with you in Christ, and hath anointed us, is God;

22 Who hath also sealed us, and given the earnest of the Spirit in our hearts.

23 Moreover I call God for a record upon my soul, that to spare you I came not as yet unto Corinth.

24 Not for that we have dominion over your faith, but are helpers of your joy: for by faith ye stand.

2 CORINTHIANS 2

1 But I determined this with myself, that I would not come again to you in heaviness.

2 For if I make you sorry, who is he then that maketh me glad, but the same which is made sorry by me?

3 And I wrote this same unto you, lest, when I came, I should have sorrow from them of whom I ought to rejoice; having confidence in you all, that my joy is the joy of you all.

4 For out of much affliction and anguish of heart I wrote unto you with many tears; not that ye should be grieved, but that ye might know the love which I have

call to mind the examples of the saints, which should make us more courageous.

On the other hand, his personal consolation flowed out to the whole Church, inasmuch as they concluded, that God who had sustained and refreshed him in his emergency, would, in like manner, not be wanting to them. Thus their welfare was promoted in both ways, and this is what he introduces as it were by way of parenthesis, when he says – **which is made effectual in the endurance**. For he wished to add this clause, by way of explanation, that they might not think that they had nothing to do with the afflictions which he alone endured.

Paul wanted to explain in what respect everything that befell him was for their *salvation*. He says, accordingly, that he suffers, indeed, alone, but that his sufferings are of use for promoting their *salvation* – not as though they were expiations or sacrifices for sins, but as edifying them by confirming them. Hence he conjoins consolation and salvation, with the view of pointing out the way in which their salvation was to be accomplished.

20. God, indeed, is always true and steadfast in his promises, and has always his *Amen,* as often as he speaks. But as for us, such is our vanity, that we do not utter our Amen in return, except when he gives a sure testimony in our hearts by his word. This he does by his Spirit. That is what Paul means here. He had previously taught, that this is a befitting harmony – when, on the one hand, *the calling of God is without repentance* (Romans 11: 29), and we, in our turn, with an unwavering faith, accept of the blessing of adoption that is held out to us. That God remains steadfast to his promise is not surprising; but to keep pace with God in the steadfastness of our faith in return – *that* truly is not in man's power. He teaches us, also, that God cures our weakness or defect (as they term it), when, by correcting our belief, he confirms us by his Spirit. Thus it comes, that we glorify him by a firm steadfastness of faith. He associates himself, however, with the Corinthians, expressly for the purpose of conciliating their affections the better, with a view to the cultivation of unity.

2 CORINTHIANS 2

12. When I had come to Troas

By now mentioning what he had been doing in the mean time, in what places he had been, and what route he had pursued in his journeyings, he more and more confirms what he had said previously as to his coming to the Corinthians. He says that he had come to Troas from Ephesus for the sake of the gospel, for he would not have proceeded in that direction, when going into Achaia, had he not been desirous to pass through Macedonia. As, however, he did

them, vs. 3–7.

He refers to the afflictions which came upon him in Asia, so that he despaired of life, but through their prayers God who had delivered, still delivered, and he was assured, would continue to deliver him, vs. 8–11.

1–2. Paul, an apostle of Jesus Christ by the will of God, and Timothy (our) brother, unto the church of God which is at Corinth, with all the saints which are in all Achaia: Grace (be) to you, and peace, from God our Father, and (from) our Lord Jesus Christ.

The sense in which the word **apostle** is to be here taken, the force of the expression **by the will of God**, the scriptural meaning of the words **church** and **saints**, are all stated in the remarks on the first verse of the former epistle. In the first epistle Paul associates Sosthenes with himself in the salutation; here it is Timothy who is mentioned. In neither case is there any community of office or authority implied. On the contrary, a marked distinction is made between Paul the apostle and Sosthenes or Timothy the brother, i.e. the Christian companion of the apostle. From 1 Corinthians 4: 17 it appears that Timothy was in Macedonia, on his way to Corinth, when the first epistle was written. From the form of expression (if Timothy come) in 1 Corinthians 16: 10, and from the absence of any intimation in this epistle that Paul had received from him the information from Corinth which he was so desirous to obtain, it is doubtful whether Timothy had been able to reach that city. At any rate he was now with the apostle at Nicopolis or some other city in Macedonia.

With all the saints which are in all Achaia. This epistle was not intended exclusively for the Christians in Corinth, but also for all the believers scattered through the province who were connected with the church in Corinth. These believers were probably not collected into separate congregations, otherwise the apostle would have used the plural form, as when writing to the **churches** of Galatia, Galatians 1: 3. Achaia was originally the name of

the northern part of the Peloponnesus including Corinth and its isthmus. Augustus divided the whole country into the two provinces, Macedonia and Achaia; the former included Macedonia proper, Illyricum, Epirus and Thessaly; and the latter all the southern part of Greece. It is in this wide sense **Achaia** is always used in the New Testament. From this it appears that the converts to Christianity in Greece were at this time very few out of Corinth, as they were all members of the church in that city. **Grace** and **peace**, the favor of God and its fruits, comprehend all the benefits of redemption. The apostle's prayer is not only that believers may be the objects of the love of God our Father and of Jesus Christ our Lord, but that they may have the assurance of that love. He knew that the sense of the love of God would keep their hearts in perfect peace. God is our Father, Jesus Christ is our Lord. Every one feels the distinction in this relationship, whether he reduces it to clear conceptions in his own mind or not. God, as God, is our Father because he is the Father of all spirits, and because, if believers, we are born again by his adopted as his children, made the objects of his love and the heirs of his kingdom. Jesus Christ, the eternal Son of God clothed in our nature, is our Lord, for two reasons: first, because as God he is our absolute sovereign, and secondly, because as Redeemer he has purchased us by his own most precious blood. To him, therefore, as God and Redeemer, our allegiance as Christians is specially due.

The apostle's defense against the charge of inconstancy. vs. 12–24.

Paul had informed the Corinthians that it was his purpose to go direct from Ephesus to Corinth, thence into Macedonia, and back again to Corinth, v. 16. This plan he had been induced to modify before the former epistle was sent, as in 1 Corinthians 16: 5 he tells them he would not visit them until he had passed through Macedonia. On this slight ground his enemies in Corinth represented him as saying one thing and meaning another. They seem

more abundantly unto you.

5 But if any have caused grief, he hath not grieved me, but in part: that I may not overcharge you all.

6 Sufficient to such a man is this punishment, which was inflicted of many.

7 So that contrariwise ye ought rather to forgive him, and comfort him, lest perhaps such a one should be swallowed up with overmuch sorrow.

8 Wherefore I beseech you that ye would confirm your love toward him.

9 For to this end also did I write, that I might know the proof of you, whether ye be obedient in all things.

10 To whom ye forgive any thing, I forgive also: for if I forgave any thing, to whom I forgave it, for your sakes forgave I it in the person of Christ;

11 Lest Satan should get an advantage of us: for we are not ignorant of his devices.

12 Furthermore, when I came to Troas to preach Christ's gospel, and a door was opened unto me of the Lord,

13 I had no rest in my spirit, because I found not Titus my brother: but taking my leave of them, I went from thence into Macedonia.

14 Now thanks be unto God, which always causeth us to triumph in Christ, and maketh manifest the savor of his knowledge by us in every place.

15 For we are unto God a sweet savor of Christ, in them that are saved, and in them that perish:

16 To the one we are the savor of death unto death; and to the other the savor of life unto life. And who is sufficient for these things?

17 For we are not as many, which corrupt the word of God: but as of sincerity, but as of God, in the sight of God speak we in Christ.

2 CORINTHIANS 3

1 Do we begin again to commend ourselves? or need we, as some others, epistles of commendation to you, or letters of commendation from you?

2 Ye are our epistle written in our hearts, known and read of all men:

3 Forasmuch as ye are manifestly declared to be the epistle of Christ minis-

not find Titus there, whom he had sent to Corinth, and by whom he ought to have been informed respecting the state of that Church, though he might have done much good there, and though he had an opportunity presented to him, yet, he says, setting everything aside, he came to Macedonia, desirous to see Titus. Here is an evidence of a singular degree of attachment to the Corinthians, that he was so anxious respecting them, that he had no rest anywhere, even when a large prospect of usefulness presented itself, until he had learned the state of their affairs. Hence it appears why it was that he delayed his coming. He did not wish to come to them until he had learned the state of their affairs. Hence it appears, why it was that he delayed his coming. He did not wish to come to them, until he had first had a conversation with Titus. He afterwards learned from the report brought him by Titus, that matters were at that time not yet ripe for his coming to them. Hence it is evident, that Paul loved the Corinthians so much, that he accommodated all his journeyings and long circuits to their welfare, and that he had accordingly come to them later than he had promised – not from having, in forgetfulness of his promise, rashly changed his plan, or from having been carried away by some degree of fickleness (2 Corinthians 1: 17), but because delay was more profitable for them.

A door also having been opened to me

This metaphor means that an opportunity of promoting the gospel had presented itself. For as an opportunity of entering is furnished when the **door is opened**, so the servants of the Lord make advances when an opportunity is presented. The **door is shut**, when no prospect of usefulness is held out. Now as, on the door being shut, it becomes us to enter upon a new course, rather than by farther efforts to weary ourselves to no purpose by useless labor, so where an opportunity presents itself of edifying, let us consider that by the hand of God a door is opened to us for introducing Christ there, and let us not withhold compliance with so kind an indication from God.

It may seem, however, as if Paul had erred in this – that disregarding, or at least leaving unimproved, an opportunity that was placed within his reach, he betook himself to Macedonia. "Ought he not rather to have applied himself to the work that he had in hand, than, after making little more than a commencement, break away all on a sudden in another direction?" We have also observed already, that the *opening of a door* is an evidence of a divine call, and this is undoubtedly true. I answer, that, as Paul was not by any means restricted to one Church, but was bound to many at the same time, it was not his duty, in consequence of the present aspect of one of them, to leave off concern as to the others. Farther, the more connection he had with the Corinthian Church, it was his duty to be so much the more

also to have made this an occasion for charging him with like inconsistency in doctrine. If his word could not be depended on in small matters, what dependence could be placed on his preaching? Paul shows there was no levity or insincerity involved in this change of his plans, and no inconsistency in his preaching; but that to spare them he had deferred his visit to Corinth, vs. 12–24.

2 CORINTHIANS 2

The first paragraph, vs. 1–4, relates to the change of his plan of going immediately to Corinth. In vs. 5–11 he refers to the case of discipline mentioned in his former letter. In vs. 12–14 he states why he did not remain in Troas. And in vs. 14–17 he pours out his heart in gratitude to God for the continued triumph of the gospel.

The true reason why the apostle did not go immediately to corinth, and his views in reference to the offender whose excommunication he had insisted upon in his former letter.

There is no change of subject in this chapter. The apostle after defending himself from the charge of levity in conduct and inconsistency in doctrine, had said, in v. 23 of the preceding chapter, that he did not go to Corinth before giving the church time to comply with the injunctions contained in his former letter, because he did not wish to appear among them as a judge.

He here says, in amplification, that he had determined not again to visit Corinth under circumstances which could only give pain to the Corinthians and to himself. He knew that he could not give them sorrow without being himself grieved, and he was assured that if he was happy they would share in his joy, vs. 1–4.

The sorrow occasioned by the incestuous person was not confined to the apostle, but shared by the church. He was satisfied with the course which the church had pursued in reference to that case, and was willing the

offender should be restored to their fellowship if they were, vs. 5–11.

His anxiety about them was so great that not finding Titus, from whom he expected to receive intelligence, he was unable to remain at Troas, but passed over into Macedonia to meet him on his way, vs. 12–13.

The intelligence which he received from Titus being favorable, the apostle expresses in strong terms his gratitude to God who always caused him to triumph, vs. 15–17.

1. But I determined this with myself, that I would not come again to you in heaviness.

The connection is with what immediately precedes. 'I deferred my visit in order to spare you, not that I assume to be a Lord over your faith, but a helper of your joy. **But** the true reason for my not coming was that I did not wish to come with heaviness.' The words ἔκρινα ἐμαυτῷ rendered **I determined with myself**, may mean simply **I determine as to myself**. I had made up my mind; or, 'I determined **for myself**,' i.e. for my own sake. This perhaps is to be preferred. The apostle thus delicately intimates that it was not merely to spare them, but also himself, that he put off his visit.

2 CORINTHIANS 3

The apostle shows that he does not need to commend himself or to be commended by the Corinthians; that God had qualified him for the work of a minister of the new, and not of the old covenant, vs. 1–11. He exercised his ministry in accordance with the peculiar character of the new dispensation, vs. 12–18.

Proof of the apostle's fitness for his work, and its nature. vs. 1–11.

Although the concluding paragraph of the preceding chapter contained a strong assertion of the integrity and fidelity of the apostle, he says, it was not written for the purpose of self-commendation. He needed no commendation from any source, v. 1. The Corinthians themselves were his commendation. Their conversion was an epistle of Christ authenticating

tered by us, written not with ink, but with the Spirit of the living God; not in tables of stone, but in fleshy tables of the heart.

4 And such trust have we through Christ to God-ward:

5 Not that we are sufficient of ourselves to think any thing as of ourselves; but our sufficiency is of God;

6 Who also hath made us able ministers of the new testament; not of the letter, but of the spirit: for the letter killeth, but the spirit giveth life.

7 But if the ministration of death, written and engraven in stones, was glorious, so that the children of Israel could not stedfastly behold the face of Moses for the glory of his countenance; which glory was to be done away:

8 How shall not the ministration of the spirit be rather glorious?

9 For if the ministration of condemnation be glory, much more doth the ministration of righteousness exceed in glory.

10 For even that which was made glorious had no glory in this respect, by reason of the glory that excelleth.

11 For if that which is done away was glorious, much more that which remaineth is glorious.

12 Seeing then that we have such hope, we use great plainness of speech:

13 And not as Moses, which put a vail over his face, that the children of Israel could not stedfastly look to the end of that which is abolished:

14 But their minds were blinded: for until this day remaineth the same vail untaken away in the reading of the old testament; which vail is done away in Christ.

15 But even unto this day, when Moses is read, the vail is upon their heart.

16 Nevertheless when it shall turn to the Lord, the vail shall be taken away.

17 Now the Lord is that Spirit: and where the Spirit of the Lord is, there is liberty.

18 But we all, with open face beholding as in a glass the glory of the Lord, are changed into the same image from glory to glory, even as by the Spirit of the Lord.

2 CORINTHIANS 4

1 Therefore seeing we have this ministry, as we have received mercy, we faint not;

inclined to aid it; for we must consider it to be reasonable, that a Church, which he had founded by his ministry, should be regarded by him with a singular affection – just as at this day it is our duty, indeed, to promote the welfare of the whole Church, and to be concerned for the entire body of it; and yet, every one has, nevertheless, a closer and holier connection with his own Church, to whose interests he is more particularly devoted. Matters were in an unhappy state at Corinth, so that Paul was in no ordinary degree anxious as to the issue. It is not, therefore, to be wondered, if, under the influence of this motive, he left unimproved an opportunity that in other circumstances was not to be neglected; as it was not in his power to occupy every post of duty at one and the same time. It is not, however, at all likely that he left Troas, till he had first introduced some one in his place to improve the opening that had occurred.

2 CORINTHIANS 3

6. Not of the letter but of the spirit

He now follows out the comparison between the law and the gospel, which he had previously touched upon. It is uncertain, however, whether he was led into this discussion, from seeing that there were at Corinth certain perverse devotees of the law, or whether he took occasion from something else to enter upon it. For my part, as I see no evidence that the false apostles had there confounded the law and the gospel, I am rather of opinion, that, as he had to do with lifeless declaimers, who endeavored to obtain applause through mere prating, and as he saw, that the ears of the Corinthians were captivated with such glitter, he was desirous to show them what was the chief excellence of the gospel, and what was the chief praise of its ministers. Now this he makes to consist in the efficacy of the Spirit. A comparison between the law and the gospel was fitted in no ordinary degree to show this. This appears to me to be the reason why he came to enter upon it.

There is, however, no doubt, that by the term letter, he means the Old Testament, as by the term spirit he means the gospel; for, after having called himself a minister of the New Testament, he immediately adds, by way of exposition, that he is a minister of the spirit, and contrasts the letter with the spirit.

By the term spirit, on the other hand, is meant spiritual doctrine, that is, what is not merely uttered with the mouth, but effectually makes its way to the souls of men with a lively feeling. For Paul had an eye to the passage in Jeremiah, that I quoted a little ago (Jeremiah 31: 31), where the Lord says, that his law had been proclaimed merely with the mouth, and that it had, therefore, been of short duration, because the people did not embrace it in their heart, and

his mission and his fidelity, which all men could read, vs. 2–3. His fitness or sufficiency for his work was due in no measure to himself, but to God, who had endowed him with the qualifications of a minister of the new covenant, vs. 4–6. This covenant and its ministry are far superior to the old covenant and the ministry of Moses, because the one was a ministry of death, the other of life; the one was of condemnation, the other of righteousness; the glory of the one was transient, the glory of the other is abiding, vs. 7–11.

The clearness and freedom of the gospel as contrasted with the obscurity of the law. vs. 12–18.

The apostle having referred to the transient brightness of Moses's face, as a symbol of the passing glory of his ministry, here employs the fact that Moses veiled his face as a twofold illustration. In the first place, it is symbolical of the obscurity of the revelation made under the old dispensation. As the brightness of Moses's face was covered, so spiritual or evangelical truth was of old covered under the types and shadows of the Mosaic economy. In the second place, it is symbolical of the blindness which rested on the minds of the Jews, which prevented their seeing the true import of their own institutions, vs. 12–15. Nevertheless, as Moses removed the veil from his face when he turned to the Lord, so both the obscurity which rests on the law, and the blindness which rests upon the mind of the Jew, are dispelled when he turns towards Christ. The vision of his glory transforms the soul into his likeness, vs. 16–18.

2 CORINTHIANS 4

In vs. 1–6 the apostle resumes the theme of 3, 12, viz. the open and faithful manner in which he preached the gospel. In vs. 7–15 he shows that his own personal insufficiency and suffering served to manifest more clearly the power of God, who rendered such a feeble instrument the means of producing so great effects. Therefore, vs. 16–18, he was not discouraged or faint-hearted, but exultingly looked above the things seen to those unseen.

As Paul had been made a minister of the new covenant, intrusted with the ministration of righteousness and life, he acted as became his high commission. He was neither timid nor deceitful. He doubted not the truth, the power, or the success of the gospel which he preached; nor did he in any way corrupt or conceal the truth, but by its open proclamation commended himself to every man's conscience, vs. 1–2. If, notwithstanding this clear exhibition of the truth, the gospel still remained hid, that could only be accounted for by the God of this world blinding the eyes of men. Nothing short of this can account for the fact; for, says the apostle, we preach Christ and not ourselves, and Christ is the image of God. In him there is a revelation of the glory of God to which there is nothing analogous but the original creation of light out of darkness, vs. 3–6.

This treasure, however, is in earthen vessels. The gospel is the revelation of God. It is to do for the world what the creation of light did for the chaotic earth. But we ministers are to have none of the glory of the work.

We are nothing. The whole power is of God; who so orders events as to make his power apparent. I am so perplexed, persecuted, down-trodden and exposed to death, as to render it evident that a divine power is exercised in my preservation and continued efficiency. My continuing to live and labor with success is a proof that Jesus lives. This he tells the Corinthians is for their benefit. vs. 7–12.

Having the same faith that David had, he spoke with equal confidence, assured that God, who raised up Christ, would not only preserve him while in this world, but also raise him hereafter from the dead. As all Paul endured and did was for the benefit of 99 the Church, thanks would be rendered by the people of God for his preservation and success, vs. 13–15.

2 But have renounced the hidden things of dishonesty, not walking in craftiness, nor handling the word of God deceitfully; but by manifestation of the truth commending ourselves to every man's conscience in the sight of God.

3 But if our gospel be hid, it is hid to them that are lost:

4 In whom the god of this world hath blinded the minds of them which believe not, lest the light of the glorious gospel of Christ, who is the image of God, should shine unto them.

5 For we preach not ourselves, but Christ Jesus the Lord; and ourselves your servants for Jesus' sake.

6 For God, who commanded the light to shine out of darkness, hath shined in our hearts, to give the light of the knowledge of the glory of God in the face of Jesus Christ.

7 But we have this treasure in earthen vessels, that the excellency of the power may be of God, and not of us.

8 We are troubled on every side, yet not distressed; we are perplexed, but not in despair;

9 Persecuted, but not forsaken; cast down, but not destroyed;

10 Always bearing about in the body the dying of the Lord Jesus, that the life also of Jesus might be made manifest in our body.

11 For we which live are alway delivered unto death for Jesus' sake, that the life also of Jesus might be made manifest in our mortal flesh.

12 So then death worketh in us, but life in you.

13 We having the same spirit of faith, according as it is written, I believed, and therefore have I spoken; we also believe, and therefore speak;

14 Knowing that he which raised up the Lord Jesus shall raise up us also by Jesus, and shall present us with you.

15 For all things are for your sakes, that the abundant grace might through the thanksgiving of many redound to the glory of God.

16 For which cause we faint not; but though our outward man perish, yet the inward man is renewed day by day.

17 For our light affliction, which is but for a moment, worketh for us a far more

he promises the Spirit of regeneration under the reign of Christ, to write his gospel, that is, the new covenant, upon their hearts. Paul now makes it his boast, that the accomplishment of that prophecy is to be seen in his preaching, that the Corinthians may perceive, how worthless is the loquacity of those vain boasters, who make incessant noise while devoid of the efficacy of the Spirit.

2 CORINTHIANS 4

4. Whose minds the god of this world

The devil is called the *god of this world*, in no other way than as Baal is called the god of those that worship him, or as the dog is called the god of Egypt. The Manicheans contend not so much respecting the **term**, as respecting the **power**. As the **power** of **blinding** is ascribed to Satan, and dominion over unbelievers, they conclude from this that he is, from his own resources, the author of all evil, so as not to be subject to God's control – as if Scripture did not in various instances declare, that devils, no less than the angels of heaven, are servants of God, each of them severally in his own manner. For, as the latter dispense to us God's benefits for our salvation, so the former execute his wrath. Hence good angels are called **powers** and **principalities** (Ephesians 3: 10), but it is simply because they exercise the power given them by God. For the same reason Satan is **the prince of this world**, not as if he conferred dominion upon himself, or obtained it by his own right, or, in fine, exercised it at his own pleasure. On the contrary, he has only so much as the Lord allows him. Hence Scripture does not merely make mention of the good spirit of God, and good angels, but he also speaks of evil spirits of God. **An evil spirit from God came upon Saul** (1 Samuel 16: 14). Again, chastisements through means of **evil angels** (Psalm 78: 49).

With respect to the passage before us, the *blinding* is a work common to God and to Satan, for it is in many instances ascribed to God; but the *power* is not alike, nor is the *manner* the same. I shall not speak at present as to the manner. Scripture, however, teaches that Satan *blinds* men, not merely with God's permission, but even by his command, that he may execute his vengeance. Thus Ahab was deceived by Satan (1 Kings 22: 21), but could Satan have done this of himself? By no means; but having offered to God his services for inflicting injury, he was sent to be a "lying spirit in the mouth of all his prophets" (1 Kings 22: 22).

Nay more, the reason why God is said to *blind* men is, that after having deprived us of the right exercise of the understanding, and the light of his Spirit, he delivers us over to the devil, to be hurried forward by him to a *reprobate mind* (Romans 1: 28), gives him the power of deception, and by this means inflicts just vengeance upon us by the

Therefore, adds this great apostle, I do not faint; although my outward man perishes, my inward man is renewed day by day; for I know that my present afflictions are not only temporary, but that they are to be succeeded by an eternal weight of glory, vs. 16–18.

1. Therefore, seeing we have this ministry, as we have received mercy, we faint not.
Therefore, i.e. on this account. This is explained by what follows; **seeing we have this ministry,** that is, because we have it. In the former chapter he had proclaimed himself a minister of the new covenant, not of the letter, but of the spirit, 3: 6; a ministry far more glorious than that of the law, inasmuch as the law could only condemn, whereas the gospel conveys righteousness and life. The possession of such an office he assigns as the reason why he does not **faint;** οὐκ ἐγκακοῦμεν, **we do not turn out bad,** or prove recreant. That is, we do not fail in the discharge of duty, either through weariness or cowardice. **As we have received mercy.** The position of these words in the text admits of their being connected either with what precedes or with what follows. In the former case, the sense is, having through the mercy of God obtained this ministry; in the latter, the meaning would be, as we have obtained mercy we faint not. The former is almost universally preferred, both because his not fainting is referred to his having so glorious an office, and because he so often refers to his call to the apostleship as a signal manifestation of the mercy and grace of God.

3. But if our gospel be hid, it is hid to them that are lost.
Although the gospel is thus glorious in itself, and although it was clearly set forth, yet to some it remained hid. That is, its true character and excellence as a revelation from God and of God was not apprehended or recognized. The reason or cause of this fact was not to be sought either in the nature of the gospel, or in the mode of its exhibition, but in the

state and character of those who rejected it. The sun does not cease to be the sun although the blind do not see it. And if any man cannot see the sun on a clear day at noon, he must be blind. So Paul does not hesitate to say that if any man does not receive the gospel when clearly presented, he is lost. If our gospel be hid, it is hid to them that are lost, ἐν τοῖς ἀπολλυμένοις, **among,** or **before** them who are lost. See 1 Corinthians 1: 18, where it is said that the gospel is foolishness to them that perish. **The lost** are those who are in a state of perdition and who are certain (if they continue to reject the gospel) to perish forever. Nothing can be plainer than the doctrine of this passage. A man's faith is not a matter of indifference. He cannot be an atheist and yet be saved. He cannot reject the gospel and yet go to heaven when he dies. This is not an arbitrary decision. There is and must be an adequate ground for it. Atheism implies spiritual death, the absence of all that constitutes the true life of the soul, of all its highest and best aspirations, instincts and feelings. The rejection of the gospel is as clear a proof of moral depravity, as inability to see the light of the sun at noon is a proof of blindness. Such is the teaching of the Bible, and such has ever been the faith of the church. Men of the world cry out against this doctrine. They insist that a man is not accountable for his opinions. He is, however, accountable for the character by which those opinions are determined. If he has such a character, such an inward moral state, as permits and decides him to believe that there is no God, that murder, adultery, theft and violence are right and good, then that inward state which constitutes his character, and for which he is responsible, (according to the intuitive perception and universal judgment of men,) is reprobate. A good infidel is, according to the Bible, as much a contradiction as good wickedness or sweet bitterness. It is not for nothing that infinite truth and love, in the person of our Lord, said, "He that believeth not shall be damned."

exceeding and eternal weight of glory;

18 While we look not at the things which are seen, but at the things which are not seen: for the things which are seen are temporal; but the things which are not seen are eternal.

2 CORINTHIANS 5

1 For we know that if our earthly house of this tabernacle were dissolved, we have a building of God, an house not made with hands, eternal in the heavens.

2 For in this we groan, earnestly desiring to be clothed upon with our house which is from heaven:

3 If so be that being clothed we shall not be found naked.

4 For we that are in this tabernacle do groan, being burdened: not for that we would be unclothed, but clothed upon, that mortality might be swallowed up of life.

5 Now he that hath wrought us for the selfsame thing is God, who also hath given unto us the earnest of the Spirit.

6 Therefore we are always confident, knowing that, whilst we are at home in the body, we are absent from the Lord:

7 (For we walk by faith, not by sight:)

8 We are confident, I say, and willing rather to be absent from the body, and to be present with the Lord.

9 Wherefore we labour, that, whether present or absent, we may be accepted of him.

10 For we must all appear before the judgment seat of Christ; that every one may receive the things done in his body, according to that he hath done, whether it be good or bad.

11 Knowing therefore the terror of the Lord, we persuade men; but we are made manifest unto God; and I trust also are made manifest in your consciences.

12 For we commend not ourselves again unto you, but give you occasion to glory on our behalf, that ye may have somewhat to answer them which glory in appearance, and not in heart.

13 For whether we be beside ourselves, it is to God: or whether we be sober, it is for your cause.

14 For the love of Christ constraineth

minister of his wrath. Paul's meaning, therefore, is, that all are possessed by the devil, who do not acknowledge his doctrine to be the sure truth of God. For it is more severe to call them slaves of the devil, than to ascribe their blindness to the judgment of God. As, however, he had a little before adjudged such persons to destruction (2 Corinthians 4: 3), he now adds that they perish, for no other reason than that they have drawn down ruin upon themselves, as the effect of their own unbelief.

2 CORINTHIANS 5

1. For we know

We know, says he. This knowledge does not spring from the human intellect, but takes its rise from the revelation of the Holy Spirit. Hence it is peculiar to believers. Even the heathens had some idea of the immortality of the soul, but there was not one of them, that had assurance of it – not one of them could boast that he spoke of a thing that was **known** to him. Believers alone can **affirm** this, to whom it has been testified of by the word and Spirit of God.

Besides, it is to be observed, that this knowledge is not merely of a general kind, as though believers were merely in a general way persuaded, that the children of God will be in a better condition after death, and had no assurance as to themselves individually, for of how very little service this would be for affording a consolation, so difficult of attainment! On the contrary, every one must have a knowledge peculiar to himself, for this, and this only, can animate me to meet death with cheerfulness – if I am fully persuaded, that I am departing to a better life.

The body, such as we now have it, he calls a *house of tabernacle*. For as **tabernacles** are constructed, for a temporary purpose, of slight materials, and without any firm foundation, and then shortly afterwards are thrown down, or fall of their own accord, so the mortal body is given to men as a frail hut, to be inhabited by them for a few days. The same metaphor is made use of, also, by Peter in his Second Epistle (2 Peter 1: 13–14), and by Job (Job 4: 19), when he calls it a **house of clay**. He places in contrast with this a **building of perpetual duration**. It is not certain, whether he means by this term a state of blessed immortality, which awaits believers after death, or the incorruptible and glorious body, such as it will be after the resurrection. In whichever of these senses it is taken, it will not be unsuitable; though I prefer to understand it as meaning, that the blessed condition of the soul after death is the commencement of this **building**, and the glory of the final resurrection is the consummation of it. This exposition will correspond better with the Apostle's context. The epithets, which he applies to this building, tend to confirm more fully its perpetuity.

2 CORINTHIANS 5

The confidence expressed in the preceding chapter is justified by showing that the apostle was assured of a habitation in heaven, even if his earthly tabernacle should be destroyed, vs. 1–10. His object in what he had said of himself was not self-commendation.

He labored only for the good of the church, impelled by the love of Christ, whose ambassador he was, in exhorting men to be reconciled to God, vs. 11–21.

The state of believers after death. vs. 1–10.

Paul did not faint in the midst of his sufferings, because he knew that even if his earthly house should be destroyed, he had a house in heaven – not like the present perishable tabernacle, but one not made with hands, and eternal, v. 1.

He looked forward to the things unseen, because in his present tabernacle he groaned, desiring to enter his heavenly habitation. He longed to be unclothed that he might be clothed upon with his house which is from heaven, vs. 2–4.

This confidence he owed to God, who had given him the Holy Spirit as a pledge of his salvation, v. 5.

Having this indwelling of the Spirit he was always in good courage, knowing that as soon as he should be absent from the body, he would be present with the Lord, vs. 6–8.

Therefore his great desire was to please him, before whose tribunal he and all other men were to appear to receive according to their works, vs. 9–10.

Paul's defense of himself against the charge of self-commendation. vs. 11–21.

He declares that he acted under a solemn sense of his responsibility to God, v. 11.

This was not said with the view of commending himself; but rather to afford them the means of vindicating his character, v. 12.

Whether his way of speaking of himself was extravagant or moderate, sane or insane, his motive in doing as he did was a sincere regard to the glory of God and the good of his church, v. 13.

For the love of Christ constrained him to live, not for himself, but for him who died for him and rose again, vs. 14–15.

Acting under the control of this elevated principle, he was raised above the influence of external things. He did not judge of men by their external condition. He was a new creature in virtue of his union with Christ, vs. 16–17.

This great change which he had experienced was not self-wrought; it was of God, who is the author of the whole scheme of redemption. He is reconciled unto the world through Jesus Christ, and he has commissioned his ministers to proclaim this great truth to all men, vs. 18–19.

Therefore, the apostle, as an ambassador of God, exhorted men to accept of this offer of reconciliation, for which the most abundant provision had been made, in that God had made Christ to be sin for us, in order that we might be made the righteousness of God in him, vs. 20–21.

11. Knowing therefore the terror of the Lord, we persuade men; but we are made manifest unto God; and I trust also are made manifest in your consciences.

This verse is an inference from what precedes, as is indicated by the particle (οὖν) **therefore**. Paul had asserted his earnest desire to be acceptable to the Lord, and, therefore, **knowing the terror of the Lord**, etc.

In this version of the clause, τὸν φόβον τοῦ κυρίου, the genitive is taken as the genitive of the subject. It is the terror which belongs to the Lord.

'Knowing how terrible the Lord is.' But this is contrary to the constant use of the phrase. The fear of the Lord is that fear or reverence which the Lord excites, or of which he is the object. Hence it so often stands in Scripture for true religion. "The fear of the Lord is the beginning of wisdom." So in Acts 9: 31, "Walk-

us; because we thus judge, that if one died for all, then were all dead:

15 And that he died for all, that they which live should not henceforth live unto themselves, but unto him which died for them, and rose again.

16 Wherefore henceforth know we no man after the flesh: yea, though we have known Christ after the flesh, yet now henceforth know we him no more.

17 Therefore if any man be in Christ, he is a new creature: old things are passed away; behold, all things are become new.

18 And all things are of God, who hath reconciled us to himself by Jesus Christ, and hath given to us the ministry of reconciliation;

19 To wit, that God was in Christ, reconciling the world unto himself, not imputing their trespasses unto them; and hath committed unto us the word of reconciliation.

20 Now then we are ambassadors for Christ, as though God did beseech you by us: we pray you in Christ's stead, be ye reconciled to God.

21 For he hath made him to be sin for us, who knew no sin; that we might be made the righteousness of God in him.

2 CORINTHIANS 6

1 We then, as workers together with him, beseech you also that ye receive not the grace of God in vain.

2 (For he saith, I have heard thee in a time accepted, and in the day of salvation have I succored thee: behold, now is the accepted time; behold, now is the day of salvation.)

3 Giving no offence in any thing, that the ministry be not blamed:

4 But in all things approving ourselves as the ministers of God, in much patience, in afflictions, in necessities, in distresses,

5 In stripes, in imprisonments, in tumults, in labours, in watchings, in fastings;

6 By pureness, by knowledge, by longsuffering, by kindness, by the Holy Ghost, by love unfeigned,

7 By the word of truth, by the power of God, by the Armour of righteousness on the right hand and on the left,

8 By honor and dishonor, by evil report

3. Since clothed

Paul restricts to believers, what he had stated respecting the certainty of a future life, as it is a thing peculiar to them. For the wicked, too, are stripped of the body, but as they bring nothing within the view of God, but a disgraceful nakedness, they are, consequently, not clothed with a glorious body. Believers, on the other hand, who appear in the view of God, clothed with Christ, and adorned with His image, receive the glorious robe of immortality. For I am inclined to take this view that Paul simply repeats here, what he had previously said as to putting on an eternal habitation. The Apostle, therefore, mentions here of a twofold clothing, with which God invests us – the righteousness of Christ, and sanctification of the Spirit in this life; and, after death, immortality and glory. The first is the cause of the second, because "those whom God has determined to glorify, he first justifies" (Romans 8: 30).

This meaning, too, is elicited from the particle *also*, which is without doubt introduced for the purpose of amplifying – as if Paul had said, that a new robe will be prepared for believers after death, since they have been clothed in this life *also*.

2 CORINTHIANS 6

1. Assisting

Ministers are here taught, that it is not enough simply to advance doctrine. They must also labor that it may be received by the hearers, and that not once merely, but continually. For as they are messengers between God and men, the **first** duty devolving upon them is, to make offer *of the grace of God*, and the **second** is, to strive with all their might, that it may not be offered in vain.

3. Giving no offense

Paul sometimes commends the ministry of the gospel generally, and at other times his own integrity. In the present instance, then, he speaks of himself, and sets before us in his own person a living picture of a good and faithful apostle, that the Corinthians may be led to see how unfair they were in their judgment, in preferring before him empty blusterers. For as they assigned the praise to mere pretences, they held in the highest esteem persons that were effeminate and devoid of zeal, while, on the other hand, as to the best ministers, they cherished no views but such as were mean and abject. Nor is there any reason to doubt, that those very things that Paul makes mention of to his own commendation, had been brought forward by them in part as a ground of contempt; and they were so much the more deserving of reproof, inasmuch as they converted into matter of reproach, what was ground of just praise.

Paul, therefore, treats here of *three* things: In the *first* place,

ing in the fear of the Lord." Romans 3: 18, "The fear of God is not before their eyes;" and in 7: 1 of this epistle, "perfecting holiness in the fear of God." See also Ephesians 5: 21, "Submitting yourselves one to another in the fear of Christ." In all these cases (φόβος) **fear** means pious reverence. There is no reason for departing from that sense in this place. Knowing i.e. feeling or experiencing, the pious reverence for Christ, the earnest desire to meet his approbation, asserted in the context, the apostle acted under the influence of that sentiment, and not from selfish or unworthy motives, in all his conduct as a man and as a minister. As the expression "fear of the Lord" is so uniformly used to express that reverence and submission which are due only to God, it is clear from this and analogous passages that Christ was to the apostles the object of the religious affections; and that they felt themselves to be responsible to him for their moral character and conduct. The evidence of the divinity of the Lord is thus seen to pervade the New Testament, and is not confined to a few isolated passages. Influenced, says the apostle, by the fear of the Lord, **I persuade men.** What this means is somewhat doubtful. The word πείθειν expresses the endeavor to convince, as in Acts 18: 4, "He persuaded the Jews," i.e. endeavored to convince them of the truth, and in Acts 28: 23, "Persuading them concerning Jesus." The apostle therefore may here mean that he endeavored to convince men of the truth of the gospel, i.e. to convert them, or bring them to the obedience of faith. Or, he may mean that he endeavored to convince them of his integrity, or that he was really governed by the fear of Christ, and was therefore sincere and honest, which in Corinth had been so unjustly called in question. This latter explanation is generally preferred, both because it suits the context, and because the following clause seems to require this idea. 'We seek to convince men of our integrity, but God we need not convince, to him our inmost soul is manifest.' The word (πείθειν), however, also signifies **to conciliate,** to seek to please, as in

Galatians 1: 10, "Do we persuade (i.e. seek to please) men, or God." Matthew 28: 14; Acts 12: 20; 1 John 3: 19.

2 CORINTHIANS 6

The apostle continues the vindication of himself vs. 1–10. Asserts his strong love for the Corinthians, and exhorts them to keep themselves free from all contaminating alliances, vs. 11–18.

The apostle's fidelity and love. vs. 1–18.

As the occasion of writing this epistle was the false accusations of his opponents, a strain of self-vindication runs through the whole. In 5: 12 he said he spoke of himself to enable his friends in Corinth to defend him against his enemies. He was governed by the love of Christ, and acted as his ambassador; as such he was a fellow-worker with God, and exhorted men not to fail of the grace of God, vs. 1–2. In the exercise of this office he avoided all offense, v. 3, proving his sincerity and fidelity as a minister of God, by the patient endurance of all kinds of trials, vs. 4–5; by the exercise of all the graces and gifts of the Spirit, vs. 6–7; and under all circumstances, whether of honor or dishonor, prosperity or adversity, whether understood or misunderstood by his fellow men, vs. 8–10.

He thus unbosomed himself to the Corinthians, because his heart was enlarged. It was wide enough to take them all in. Whatever there was of the want of love or of due appreciation between them and him, the fault was on their side, not on his, vs. 11–12.

He begs them to be as large-hearted towards him as he was towards them, v. 13, and not to allow themselves to be involved in any intimate alliances with the wicked, vs. 13–18.

1. We then, (as) workers together (with him), beseech (you) also that ye receive not the grace of God in vain.

This verse is intimately connected with the preceding chapter by the particles δὲ καί, **but also.** He is still describing his manner of

and good report: as deceivers, and yet true;

9 As unknown, and yet well known; as dying, and, behold, we live; as chastened, and not killed;

10 As sorrowful, yet alway rejoicing; as poor, yet making many rich; as having nothing, and yet possessing all things.

11 O ye Corinthians, our mouth is open unto you, our heart is enlarged.

12 Ye are not straitened in us, but ye are straitened in your own bowels.

13 Now for a recompence in the same, (I speak as unto my children,) be ye also enlarged.

14 Be ye not unequally yoked together with unbelievers: for what fellowship hath righteousness with unrighteousness? and what communion hath light with darkness?

15 And what concord hath Christ with Belial? or what part hath he that believeth with an infidel?

16 And what agreement hath the temple of God with idols? for ye are the temple of the living God; as God hath said, I will dwell in them, and walk in them; and I will be their God, and they shall be my people.

17 Wherefore come out from among them, and be ye separate, saith the Lord, and touch not the unclean thing; and I will receive you,

18 And will be a Father unto you, and ye shall be my sons and daughters, saith the Lord Almighty.

2 CORINTHIANS 7

1 Having therefore these promises, dearly beloved, let us cleanse ourselves from all filthiness of the flesh and spirit, perfecting holiness in the fear of God.

2 Receive us; we have wronged no man, we have corrupted no man, we have defrauded no man.

3 I speak not this to condemn you: for I have said before, that ye are in our hearts to die and live with you.

4 Great is my boldness of speech toward you, great is my glorying of you: I am filled with comfort, I am exceeding joyful in all our tribulation.

5 For, when we were come into Macedonia, our flesh had no rest, but we were

he shows what are the excellences, on the ground of which preachers of the gospel ought to be esteemed; *secondly,* he shows that he is himself endowed with those excellences; *thirdly,* he admonishes the Corinthians not to acknowledge as Christ's servants those who conduct themselves otherwise than he prescribes here by his example. His design is, that he may procure authority for himself and those that were like him, with a view to the glory of God and the good of the Church, or may restore it where it has fallen into decay; and *secondly,* that he may call back the Corinthians from an unreasonable attachment to the false apostles, which was a hinderance in the way of their making so much proficiency in the gospel as was necessary. Ministers give occasion of stumbling, when by their own misconduct they hinder the progress of the gospel on the part of their hearers. *That* Paul says he does not do; for he declares that he carefully takes heed not to stain his apostleship by any spot of disgrace.

For this is the artifice of Satan – to seek some misconduct on the part of ministers, that may tend to the dishonor of the gospel. For when he has been successful in bringing the ministry into contempt, all hope of profit is at an end. Hence the man who would usefully serve Christ, must strive with his whole might to maintain the credit of his ministry. The method is – to take care that he be deserving of honor, for nothing is more ridiculous than striving to maintain your reputation before others, while you call forth upon yourself reproach by a wicked and base life. That man, therefore, will alone be honorable, who will allow himself in nothing that is unworthy of a minister of Christ.

2 CORINTHIANS 7

6. Who comforteth the lowly

This is mentioned as a reason; for he means that consolation had been offered to him, because he was borne down with evils, and almost overwhelmed, inasmuch as God is wont to comfort the lowly, that is, those that are cast down. Hence a most profitable doctrine may be inferred – that the more we have been afflicted, so much the greater consolation has been prepared for us by God. Hence, in the epithet here applied to God, there is a choice promise contained, as though he had said, that it is peculiarly the part of God to comfort those that are miserable and are abased to the dust.

7. And not by his coming only

Lest the Corinthians should object in these terms – "What is it to us if Titus has cheered you by his coming? No doubt, as you loved him, you would feel delighted to see him;" he declares, that the occasion of his joy was, that Titus had, on returning from them, communicated the most joyful intel-

discharging his apostolic duties. He not only announced that God had made Christ sin for us, that we might become the righteousness of God in him, but also, as a co-worker with God, he exhorted men not to receive the grace of God in vain. In our version the apostle is made to say, "I beseech you also." This is wrong; the **also** belongs to the verb – "I also beseech you." That the word συνεργοῦντες, **co-operating,** refers to the apostle's co-operating with God, is plain from the connection, and from the nature of the work.

He had just before, 5: 20, spoken of God's beseeching them; and now he says, we as co-workers beseech you. So in 1 Corinthians 3: 9, he says, "We are co-workers with God." In the Vulgate the word is rendered **adjuvantes,** which favors the ideal that he was co-operating with them, assisting them (i.e. the Corinthians) by his exhortations. Luther's version suggests the same meaning; Wir ermahnen aber euch, als Mithelfer, **as joint-laborers or helpers we exhort you.** Compare 1: 24, where the apostle says, "We are helpers (συνεργοί) of your joy." This view of the passage is given by many commentators. It does not, however, so well, as just remarked, agree with the context; and it would require, to prevent ambiguity, the insertion of ὑμῖν, **with you.** As an apostle or minister of the gospel, Paul was a co-worker with God.

2 CORINTHIANS 7

An exhortation founded on what is said in the preceding chapter, v. 1. Paul's consolation derived from the favorable account which he had received from Corinth, vs. 2–16.

The effect produced on the church in corinth by the apostle's former letter, and his consequent satisfaction and joy.

After in v. 1 exhorting them to live as became those to whom such precious promises had been given as he had just recited from the word of God, he in vs. 2–3 repeats his desire before expressed, 6: 13, that they would reciprocate

his ardent love. So far as he was concerned there was nothing in the way of this cordial reconciliation. He had not injured them, nor was he alienated from them. He had great confidence in them. His apprehensions and anxiety had been in a great measure removed by the account which he had received from Titus of the feelings of the Corinthians towards him, vs. 4–7. It is true that he did at one time regret having written that letter respecting the incestuous person; but he no longer regretted it, because he found that the sorrow which that letter occasioned was the sorrow of true repentance, rebounding not to their injury, but to their good, vs. 8–9. It was not the sorrow of the world, but true godly sorrow, as was evident from its effects, vs. 10–12. Therefore the apostle was comforted, and delighted to find how much Titus had been gratified by his visit to Corinth. All that the apostle had told him of the good dispositions of the Corinthians had proved to be true, vs. 13–16.

1. Having therefore these promises, dearly beloved, let us cleanse ourselves from all filthiness of the flesh and spirit, perfecting holiness in the fear of God.
The verse properly belongs to the preceding chapter. It is the appropriate conclusion of the exposition there made. The promises referred to are,

1st. Of the indwelling of God, 6: 16.

2nd. Of his favor, v. 17.

3rd. That they should be his sons and daughters. Therefore, says the apostle, having these promises of intimate association with God, and this assurance of his love, **let us purify ourselves**; i.e. not merely keep ourselves pure by avoiding contamination, but, as already defiled, let us strive to become pure. Though the work of purification is so often referred to God as its author, Acts 15: 9; Ephesians 5: 26, this does not preclude the agency of his people. They are to work out their own salvation, because it is God who worketh in them both to will and to do. If God's agency in sanctification does not arouse and direct ours; if it does not

troubled on every side; without were fightings, within were fears.

6 Nevertheless God, that comforteth those that are cast down, comforted us by the coming of Titus;

7 And not by his coming only, but by the consolation wherewith he was comforted in you, when he told us your earnest desire, your mourning, your fervent mind toward me; so that I rejoiced the more.

8 For though I made you sorry with a letter, I do not repent, though I did repent: for I perceive that the same epistle hath made you sorry, though it were but for a season.

9 Now I rejoice, not that ye were made sorry, but that ye sorrowed to repentance: for ye were made sorry after a godly manner, that ye might receive damage by us in nothing.

10 For godly sorrow worketh repentance to salvation not to be repented of: but the sorrow of the world worketh death.

11 For behold this selfsame thing, that ye sorrowed after a godly sort, what carefulness it wrought in you, yea, what clearing of yourselves, yea, what indignation, yea, what fear, yea, what vehement desire, yea, what zeal, yea, what revenge! In all things ye have approved yourselves to be clear in this matter.

12 Wherefore, though I wrote unto you, I did it not for his cause that had done the wrong, nor for his cause that suffered wrong, but that our care for you in the sight of God might appear unto you.

13 Therefore we were comforted in your comfort: yea, and exceedingly the more joyed we for the joy of Titus, because his spirit was refreshed by you all.

14 For if I have boasted any thing to him of you, I am not ashamed; but as we spake all things to you in truth, even so our boasting, which I made before Titus, is found a truth.

15 And his inward affection is more abundant toward you, whilst he remembereth the obedience of you all, how with fear and trembling ye received him.

16 I rejoice therefore that I have confidence in you in all things.

ligence. Accordingly he declares, that it was not so much the presence of one individual, as the prosperous condition of the Corinthians, that had cheered him.

Your desire

Mark, what joyful tidings were communicated to Paul respecting the Corinthians. Their *desire* originated in the circumstance, that they held Paul's doctrine in high estimation. Their *tears* were a token of respect; because, being affected with his reproof, they mourned over their sins. Their *zeal* was an evidence of good will. From these *three* things he inferred that they were penitent. This afforded him full satisfaction, because he had no other intention or anxiety, than the consulting of their welfare.

13. We received consolation

Paul was wholly intent upon persuading the Corinthians, that nothing was more eagerly desired by him than their advantage. Hence he says, that he had shared with them in their consolation. Now their consolation had been this – that, acknowledging their fault, they did not merely take the reproof in good part, but had received it joyfully. For the bitterness of a reproof is easily sweetened, so soon as we begin to taste the profitableness of it to us.

What he adds – that he rejoiced more abundantly on account of the consolation of Titus, is by way of congratulation. Titus had been overjoyed in finding them more obedient and compliant than could have been expected – nay more, in his finding a sudden change for the better. Hence we may infer, that Paul's gentleness was anything but flattery, inasmuch as he rejoiced in their joy, so as to be, at the same time, chiefly taken up with their repentance.

14. But if I have boasted any thing to him

He shows indirectly, how friendly a disposition he had always exercised towards the Corinthians, and with what sincerity and kindness he had judged of them; for at the very time that they seemed to be unworthy of commendation, he still promised much that was honorable on their behalf. Here truly we have a signal evidence of a rightly constituted and candid mind – reproving to their face those that you love, and yet hoping well, and giving others good hopes respecting them. Such sincerity ought to have induced them not to take amiss any thing that proceeded from him. In the mean time, he takes this opportunity of setting before them again, in passing, his fidelity in all other matters. "You have hitherto had opportunity of knowing my candor, so that I have shown myself to be truthful, and not by any means fickle. I rejoice, therefore, that I have now also been found truthful, when boasting of you before others."

create the desire for holiness, and strenuous efforts to attain it, we may be sure that we are not its subjects. He is leaving us undisturbed in our sins. **From all filthiness of the flesh and spirit**. All sin is a pollution. There are two classes of sin here recognized; those of the flesh, and those of the spirit. By the former we are to understand those sins which defile the body, as drunkenness and debauchery; and by the latter those which affect only the soul, as pride and malice. By filthiness of the flesh, therefore, is not to be understood mere ceremonial uncleanness, nor the participation of the body in sinful acts, such as bowing down to an idol, or offering incense to false gods, but the desecration of the body as the temple of the Holy Ghost. See 1 Corinthians 6: 19. **Perfecting holiness**. This expresses or indicates the way in which we are to purify ourselves. It is by perfecting holiness. The word ἐπιτελέω does not here mean simply **to practice**, but to complete, to carry on to perfection. Comp. 8: 6,11. Philippians 1: 6. It is only by being completely or perfectly holy that we can attain the purity required of us as the temples of God. **Holiness** (ἁγιωσύνη, Romans 1: 3; 1 Thessalonians 3: 13) includes not only the negative idea of purity, or freedom from all defilement, but also, positively, that of moral excellence.

In the fear of God. This is the motive which is to determine our endeavors to purify ourselves. It is not regard to the good of others, nor our own happiness, but reverence for God. We are to be holy, because he is holy.

2 CORINTHIANS 8

The extraordinary liberality of the Macedonians, vs. 1–6. Exhortation to the Corinthians to follow the example of their Macedonian brethren, vs. 7–16. Commendation of Titus for his zeal in promoting the collection of contributions for the poor, and of the other brethren who were to accompany him to Corinth, vs. 17–24.

Exhortation to liberality to the poor.

To this subject the apostle devotes this and the following chapter. He begins by setting before the Corinthians the liberality of the churches in Macedonia. They, in the midst of great affliction and of extreme poverty, had exceeded their ability in the contributions which they had made for the saints, vs. 1–3. And this not by constraint or in obedience to earnest entreaties on the part of the apostle; but on the contrary, it was they who besought him to receive and take charge of their alms, v. 4. Liberality to the poor was only a part of what they did; they devoted themselves to the Lord, v. 5. The conduct of the Macedonians led the apostle to exhort Titus, as he had already begun the work, to carry it on to completion in Corinth, v. 6.

He begs them, therefore, to add this to all their other graces, v. 7. This was a matter of advice, not of command. He was induced to give this exhortation because others had evinced so much zeal in this matter, and because he desired them to prove the sincerity of their love. What was all they could do for others, compared to what Christ had done for them, vs. 8–9.

The exercise of liberality was a good to them, provided their feelings found expression in corresponding acts, vs. 10–11.

The disposition, not the amount of their contributions, was the main thing, v. 12.

What the apostle wished was that there might be some approximation to equality among Christians, that the abundance of one may supply the wants of another, vs. 13–15.

He thanks God who had inspired Titus with so much zeal on this subject, vs. 16–17.

With him he had sent a brother who had not only the approbation of the churches, but had been chosen for the very purpose of taking charge of the contributions in connection with the apostle, vs. 18–19.

Paul was determined to avoid all occasion of reproach, and therefore he associated others with himself in the charge of the money

2 CORINTHIANS 8

1 Moreover, brethren, we do you to wit of the grace of God bestowed on the churches of Macedonia;

2 How that in a great trial of affliction the abundance of their joy and their deep poverty abounded unto the riches of their liberality.

3 For to their power, I bear record, yea, and beyond their power they were willing of themselves;

4 Praying us with much intreaty that we would receive the gift, and take upon us the fellowship of the ministering to the saints.

5 And this they did, not as we hoped, but first gave their own selves to the Lord, and unto us by the will of God.

6 Insomuch that we desired Titus, that as he had begun, so he would also finish in you the same grace also.

7 Therefore, as ye abound in every thing, in faith, and utterance, and knowledge, and in all diligence, and in your love to us, see that ye abound in this grace also.

8 I speak not by commandment, but by occasion of the forwardness of others, and to prove the sincerity of your love.

9 For ye know the grace of our Lord Jesus Christ, that, though he was rich, yet for your sakes he became poor, that ye through his poverty might be rich.

10 And herein I give my advice: for this is expedient for you, who have begun before, not only to do, but also to be forward a year ago.

11 Now therefore perform the doing of it; that as there was a readiness to will, so there may be a performance also out of that which ye have.

12 For if there be first a willing mind, it is accepted according to that a man hath, and not according to that he hath not.

13 For I mean not that other men be eased, and ye burdened:

14 But by an equality, that now at this time your abundance may be a supply for their want, that their abundance also may be a supply for your want: that there may be equality:

15 As it is written, He that had gathered much had nothing over; and he that had gathered little had no lack.

2 CORINTHIANS 8

As, in the event of the Corinthians retaining any feeling of offense, occasioned by the severity of the preceding Epistle, that might stand in the way of Paul's authority having influence over them, he has hitherto made it his endeavor to conciliate their affections. Now, after clearing away all occasion of offense, and regaining favor for his ministry, he recommends to them the brethren at Jerusalem, that they may furnish help to their necessities. He could not, with any great advantage, have attempted this in the commencement of the Epistle. Hence, he has prudently deferred it, until he has prepared their minds for it. Accordingly, he takes up the whole of this chapter, and the next, in exhorting the Corinthians to be active and diligent in collecting alms to be taken to Jerusalem for relieving the indigence of the brethren. For they were afflicted with a great famine, so that they could scarcely support life without being aided by other churches. The Apostles had intrusted Paul with this matter (Galatians 2: 10), and he had promised to concern himself in reference to it, and he had already done so in part, as we have seen in the former Epistle. Now, however, he presses them still farther.

1. I make known to you

He commends the Macedonians, but it is with the design of stimulating the Corinthians by their example, although he does not expressly say so; for the former had no need of commendation, but the latter had need of a stimulus. And that he may stir up the Corinthians the more to emulation, he ascribes it to the *grace of God* that the Macedonians had been so forward to give help to their brethren. For although it is acknowledged by all, that it is a commendable virtue to give help to the needy, they, nevertheless, do not reckon it to be a gain, nor do they look upon it as the *grace of God*. Nay rather, they reckon, that it is so much of what was theirs taken from them, and lost. Paul, on the other hand, declares, that we ought to ascribe it to the grace of God, when we afford aid to our brethren, and that it ought to be desired by us as a privilege of no ordinary kind.

He makes mention, however, of a twofold favor, that had been conferred upon the Macedonians. The *first* is, that they had endured afflictions with composure and cheerfulness. The *second* is, that from their slender means, equally as though they had possessed abundance, they had taken something – to be laid out upon their brethren. Each of these things, Paul affirms with good reason, is a work of the Lord, for all quickly fail, that are not upheld by the Spirit of God, who is the Author of all consolation, and distrust clings to us, deeply rooted, which keeps us back from all offices of love, until it is subdued by the grace of the same Spirit.

intrusted to him, vs. 20–21.

With those already mentioned he sent another brother of approved character and great zeal, v. 22.

Therefore if any one inquired who Titus was, they might answer, He was Paul's companion and fellow-laborer; or who those brethren were, they might say, They were the messengers of the churches, and the glory of Christ. Let the church therefore prove their love and justify his boasting of them, vs. 23–24.

1. Moreover, brethren, we do you to wit of the grace of God bestowed on the churches of Macedonia.

Moreover (δέ) marks the transition to a new subject. **We do you to wit,** (γνωρίζομεν,) 'we cause you to know.' The word to wit, (Anglo-Saxon, **Witan**; German, **Wissen**,) to know, and the cognate words, **Wis** and **Wot**, are nearly obsolete, although they occur frequently in our version. The **grace of God**, the divine favor. The liberality of the Corinthians was due to the operation of the grace of God. The sacred writers constantly recognize the fact that the freest and most spontaneous acts of men, their inward states and the outward manifestations of those states, when good, are due to the secret influence of the Spirit of God, which eludes our consciousness. The believer is most truly self-determined, when determined by the grace of God. **Bestowed on**, (δεδομένην ἐν,) "given in," i.e. given so that it is in. See 1: 22. "Given the earnest of the Spirit in our hearts." In v. 16 of this chapter, διδόντι ἐν is rendered "**put into.**" **The churches of Macedonia**. Under the Romans Macedonia included the whole of the northern provinces of Greece. The churches of that region founded by the apostle were those of Philippi, Thessalonica, and Beroea.

Of the extraordinary liberality of those churches the epistles of Paul furnish numerous intimations. 11: 9; Philippians 2: 25; 4: 15,18.

2. How that, in a great trial of affliction, the abundance of their joy, and their deep

poverty, abounded unto the riches of their liberality.

A somewhat condensed sentence, meaning, as some say, that in the midst of their afflictions their joy, and in the midst of their poverty, their liberality abounded. But this brings into view two graces, joy in affliction, and liberality in poverty, whereas the context calls for only one. The meaning rather is, that notwithstanding their afflictions, their joy and their poverty abounded to their liberality. This the grammatical structure of the passage requires. **How that** (ὅτι); the connection is with the verb in the preceding verse, 'I cause you to know that, etc.' **In a great trial of affliction**, i.e. in afflictions which were a great trial (δοκιμή) i.e. a test of their sincerity and devotion. These afflictions were either those which they shared in common with their fellow-citizens, arising out of their social condition, or they were peculiar to them as Christians, arising from persecution. In writing to the Thessalonians, Paul reminds them that they had received the word in much affliction. 1: 6; 2: 14; Comp. Acts 16: 20; 17: 5. **The abundance of their joy**; i.e. the joy arising from the pardon of their sins and the favor of God, which in 1 Thessalonians 1: 6, he calls the joy of the Holy Ghost, was abundant. That is, it rose above their sorrows, and produced in them the effect of which he afterwards speaks. **And their deep poverty**, (ἡ κατὰ βάθους πτωχεία) their abject poverty, or poverty down to the depth. **Abounded unto**, i.e. manifested itself as abundant in relation to. The same verb (ἐπερίσσευσεν) belongs to both the preceding nouns, "joy" and "poverty," but in a somewhat different sense. Their joy abounded unto their liberality, because it produced it. The effect proved the joy to be abundant. Their poverty abounded unto their liberality, because it was seen to be great in relation to it. Their liberality made their poverty, by contrast, appear the greater. **Unto the riches**, (πλοῦτος) a favorite word with Paul, which he often uses in the sense of abundance.

Romans 2: 4, "Riches of his goodness," for

16 But thanks be to God, which put the same earnest care into the heart of Titus for you.

17 For indeed he accepted the exhortation; but being more forward, of his own accord he went unto you.

18 And we have sent with him the brother, whose praise is in the gospel throughout all the churches;

19 And not that only, but who was also chosen of the churches to travel with us with this grace, which is administered by us to the glory of the same Lord, and declaration of your ready mind:

20 Avoiding this, that no man should blame us in this abundance which is administered by us:

21 Providing for honest things, not only in the sight of the Lord, but also in the sight of men.

22 And we have sent with them our brother, whom we have oftentimes proved diligent in many things, but now much more diligent, upon the great confidence which I have in you.

23 Whether any do inquire of Titus, he is my partner and fellowhelper concerning you: or our brethren be inquired of, they are the messengers of the churches, and the glory of Christ.

24 Wherefore shew ye to them, and before the churches, the proof of your love, and of our boasting on your behalf.

2 CORINTHIANS 9

1 For as touching the ministering to the saints, it is superfluous for me to write to you:

2 For I know the forwardness of your mind, for which I boast of you to them of Macedonia, that Achaia was ready a year ago; and your zeal hath provoked very many.

3 Yet have I sent the brethren, lest our boasting of you should be in vain in this behalf; that, as I said, ye may be ready:

4 Lest haply if they of Macedonia come with me, and find you unprepared, we (that we say not, ye) should be ashamed in this same confident boasting.

5 Therefore I thought it necessary to exhort the brethren, that they would go before unto you, and make up beforehand your bounty, whereof ye had notice before,

2. In much trial

In other words, while they were tried with adversity, they, nevertheless, did not cease to rejoice in the Lord: nay, this disposition rose so high, as to swallow up sorrow; for the minds of the Macedonians, which must otherwise have been straitened, required to be set free from their restraints, that they might liberally furnish aid to the brethren.

By the term **joy** he means that spiritual consolation by which believers are sustained under their afflictions; for the wicked either delude themselves with empty consolations, by avoiding a perception of the evil, and drawing off the mind to rambling thoughts, or else they wholly give way to grief, and allow themselves to be overwhelmed with it. Believers, on the other hand, seek occasions of **joy** in the affliction itself, as we see in the 8th chapter of the Romans.

And their deep poverty

Here we have a metaphor taken from exhausted vessels, as though he had said, that the Macedonians had been emptied, so that they had now reached the bottom. He says, that even in such straits they had abounded in liberality, and had been rich, so as to have enough – not merely for their own use, but also for giving assistance to others. Mark the way, in which we shall always be liberal even in the most straitened poverty – if by liberality of mind we make up for what is deficient in our coffers.

2 CORINTHIANS 9

This statement may seem at first view to suit ill, or not sufficiently well, with what goes before; for he seems to speak of a new matter, that he had not previously touched upon, while in reality he is following out the same subject. Let the *reader,* however, observe, that Paul treats of the very same matter that he had been treating of before – that it was from no want of confidence that he exhorted the Corinthians, and that his admonition is not coupled with any reproof as to the past, but that he has particular reasons that influence him. The meaning, then, of what he says now is this: "I do not teach you that it is a duty to afford relief to the saints, for what need were there of this? For that is sufficiently well known to you, and you have given practical evidence that you are not prepared to be wanting to them; but as I have, from boasting everywhere of your liberality, pledged my credit along with yours, this consideration will not allow me to refrain from speaking." But for this, such anxious concern might have been somewhat offensive to the Corinthians, because they would have thought, either that they were reproached for their indolence, or that they were suspected by Paul. By bringing forward, however, a most, suitable apology, he secures for himself the liberty of not merely exhorting them, without giving offense, but

abundant goodness. Ephesians 1: 7, "Riches of his grace," for his abundant grace; 1: 18, "Riches of his glory," for abundant glory, etc. **Of their liberality**, ἁπλότης, which is properly the opposite of duplicity, or double-mindedness, and, therefore, singleness of heart, simplicity, sincerity. Ephesians 6: 5; Colossians 3: 22.

The Scriptures, however, often use a generic term for a specific one, as glory for wisdom, or mercy, or power, which are different forms of the divine glory. So here the general term for right-mindedness is put for liberality, which is a specific form or manifestation of the generic virtue.

2 CORINTHIANS 9

An exhortation to the Corinthians not to falsify his boasting of their liberality, vs. 1–5. An exhortation to give not only liberally, but cheerfully, vs. 6–15.

Continuation of the discourse in the preceding chapter on making collections for the saints.

Although aware of their readiness, the apostle sent the brethren to bring the collection for the poor to an end, lest when the Macedonians who were to accompany him to Corinth arrived, they should find them unprepared, not so much to their disgrace, as to his mortification, vs. 1–4.

He sent the brethren, therefore, that every thing they intended to do might be done in time, and be done cheerfully, v. 5.

It was not only liberality, but cheerfulness in giving that the Lord required, vs. 6–7.

God who commanded them to give could and would supply their wants, and increase their graces. They would be the richer and the better for what they gave, vs. 8–10.

What he had at heart was not so much that the temporal sufferings of the poor should be relieved, as that God might be glorified by the gratitude and mutual love of believers, and by the exhibition of their Christian graces, vs. 10–14.

What are our gifts to the poor compared to the gift of Christ to us? v. 15.

1. For as touching the ministering to the saints, it is superfluous for me to write to you.
This is not a new paragraph, much less, as some have conjectured, a separate writing. It is intimately connected with the preceding. In the last verse of chapter 8, he exhorted them to receive the brethren with confidence, **for indeed** it is superfluous to write about the collection. He exhorted them to show their love to the brethren who were to visit them, for they needed no exhortation to liberality. This is another of those exhibitions of urbanity and rhetorical skill with which the epistles of Paul abounds. The δέ answering to the μέν of this verse is by some said to be found in verse 3. 'It is not necessary **indeed** to write, **but** I send, etc.' Or, if the connection between vs. 2 and 3 forbid this, the μέν may be taken as standing alone, as in 1 Corinthians 5: 3; 11: 18. So Deut. Wette. Concerning the **ministering** (περὶ τῆς διακονίας) The word is often used not only for the ministry of the word, but also for the service rendered in the collection and distribution of alms. Acts 6: 1; 12: 25; Romans 15: 31. **To the saints.** All believers are called ἅγιοι in the sense of **sacred,** i.e. separated from the world and consecrated to God, and as inwardly renewed and purified by the Holy Spirit. 8: 4; Acts 9: 13; Romans 1: 7; 8: 27. The saints referred to were of course the poor believers in Jerusalem for whose benefit Paul instituted this collection in the several churches which he had founded. 1 Corinthians 16: 1–3. **It is superfluous for me** (περισσόν μοι ἐστί) **to write** (τὸ γράφειν, the infinitive has the article because it is the subject of the sentence) **unto you.** Paul had written and was about to write still further on the subject; so that this is to be understood as only a polite intimation that his writing, so far as they were concerned, was not necessary. They did not need urging.

2. For I know the forwardness of your mind, for which I boast of you to them of Macedo-

that the same might be ready, as a matter of bounty, and not as of covetousness.

6 But this I say, He which soweth sparingly shall reap also sparingly; and he which soweth bountifully shall reap also bountifully.

7 Every man according as he purposeth in his heart, so let him give; not grudgingly, or of necessity: for God loveth a cheerful giver.

8 And God is able to make all grace abound toward you; that ye, always having all sufficiency in all things, may abound to every good work:

9 (As it is written, He hath dispersed abroad; he hath given to the poor: his righteousness remaineth for ever.

10 Now he that ministereth seed to the sower both minister bread for your food, and multiply your seed sown, and increase the fruits of your righteousness;)

11 Being enriched in every thing to all bountifulness, which causeth through us thanksgiving to God.

12 For the administration of this service not only supplieth the want of the saints, but is abundant also by many thanksgivings unto God;

13 Whiles by the experiment of this ministration they glorify God for your professed subjection unto the gospel of Christ, and for your liberal distribution unto them, and unto all men;

14 And by their prayer for you, which long after you for the exceeding grace of God in you.

15 Thanks be unto God for his unspeakable gift.

2 CORINTHIANS 10

1 Now I Paul myself beseech you by the meekness and gentleness of Christ, who in presence am base among you, but being absent am bold toward you:

2 But I beseech you, that I may not be bold when I am present with that confidence, wherewith I think to be bold against some, which think of us as if we walked according to the flesh.

3 For though we walk in the flesh, we do not war after the flesh:

4 (For the weapons of our warfare are not carnal, but mighty through God to the pulling down of strong holds;)

even from time to time urging them.

Some one, however, may possibly suspect, that Paul here pretends what he does not really think. This were exceedingly absurd; for if he reckons them to be sufficiently prepared for doing their duty, why does he set himself so vigorously to admonish them? and, on the other hand, if he is in doubt as to their willingness, why does he declare it to be unnecessary to admonish them? Love carries with it these two things – good hope, and anxious concern. Never would he have borne such a testimony in favor of the Corinthians, had he not been fully of the mind that he expresses. He had seen a happy commencement: he had hoped, that the farther progress of the matter would be corresponding; but as he was well aware of the unsteadiness of the human mind, he could not provide too carefully against their turning aside from their pious design.

1. Ministering

This term seems not very applicable to those that give of their substance to the poor, inasmuch as liberality is deserving of a more splendid designation. Paul, however, had in view, what believers owe to their fellowmembers. For the members of Christ ought mutually to minister to each other. In this way, when we relieve the brethren, we do nothing more than discharge a ministry that is due to them. On the other hand, to neglect the saints, when they stand in need of our aid, is worse than inhuman, inasmuch as we defraud them of what is their due.

2 CORINTHIANS 10

Having finished his exhortation, he now proceeds partly to refute the calumnies with which he had been defamed by the false apostles, and partly to repress the insolence of certain wicked persons, who could not bear to be under restraint. Both parties, with the view of destroying Paul's authority, construed the vehemence with which he thundered in his Epistles to be *thrasodeilian* – (*mere bravado*), because when present he was not equally prepared to show himself off in respect of appearance, and address, but was mean and contemptible. "See," said they, "here is a man, that, under a consciousness of his inferiority, is so very modest and timid, but now, when at a distance, makes a fierce attack! Why is he less bold in speech than in letters? Will *he* terrify us, when he is at a distance, who, when present, is the object of contempt? How comes he to have such confidence as to imagine, that he is at liberty to do anything with us?" They put speeches of this kind into circulation, with the view of disparaging his strictness, and even rendering it odious. Paul replies, that he is not *bold* except in so far as he is constrained by necessity, and that the meanness of his bodily presence, for which he was held in

nia, that Achaia was ready a year ago; and your zeal hath provoked very many. The reason why it was superfluous to write to them was that they were disposed to act spontaneously. The apostle says he knew their **forwardness of mind,** (προθυμίαν,) their readiness or disposition to give.

For which I boast (ἣν καυχῶμαι see 11, 30 for the same construction) **of you** (ὑπὲρ ὑμῶν, for you, to your advantage). Their readiness to give was a matter of which Paul at that time boasted to the Macedonians among whom he then was. This does not imply that the apostle regarded their liberal disposition an honor to himself, as though it owed its existence to his agency. We are said to boast of the good qualities of a friend when we proclaim them to his honor and not our own. **That Achaia was ready a year ago.** This was Paul's boast. All the Christians in Achaia belonged to the church in Corinth, although they did not all reside in that city. See 1: 1.

Was ready, i.e. to take part in a collection for the saints. He does not mean that the collection had already been completed, so that nothing remained to be done. The context does not justify the disparaging supposition that Paul, to excite the emulation of the Macedonian Christians, had overstated the fact as to the Corinthians, representing them as having already a year ago made their collection. **The readiness** to which he here refers is the readiness of purpose. They were fully prepared to take part in the work.

2 CORINTHIANS 10

Paul deprecates the necessity of asserting his authority and of exercising his power to punish the disobedient, vs. 1–6. He confronts his opposers with the assertion of divinely derived power, vs. 9–11. He shows that he claims authority only over those who were committed to his care, vs. 12–18.

Paul's assertion of his authority and vindication of his apostolic prerogatives.

The remarkable change in the whole tone and style of this portion of the epistle, from the beginning of the 10th chapter to near the end of the 13th, has attracted the attention of every careful reader. The contrast between this and the preceding portions of the epistle is so great, that some have concluded that they are separate letters, written at different times and under different circumstances. There is no external authority for this conjecture, and it is not only unnecessary, but inconsistent with the facts of the case. The same topics are presented, and there is in 12: 18 reference to the mission of Titus, spoken of in the earlier chapters. It is an adequate explanation of the change in question, that in chs. 1–9, Paul had in his mind, and was really addressing, the faithful and obedient portion of the church, whereas he has here in view the unreasonable and wicked false teachers and their adherents, who not only made light of his authority, but corrupted the gospel, which he was appointed to propagate and defend.

He therefore naturally assumes a tone of authority and severity. Satisfied of his divine mission, and conscious of supernatural power, he cautioned them not to rely too much on his forbearance. He was indeed as a man humble, and, if they chose, insignificant; but there was slumbering in his arm an energy which they would do well not to provoke. He had no desire to exercise in Corinth the authority with which Christ had invested him for the purpose of bringing down all opposition. He would give them a fair trial, and wait to see how far they would be obedient, before he punished their disobedience, vs. 1–6.

They should not judge by appearance, or set themselves up on the ground of their fancied advantages, because whatever they had, he had in larger measures vs. 7–8.

He had no intention to frighten them by his epistles – which they said were written in a tone he would not dare to assume when

5 Casting down imaginations, and every high thing that exalteth itself against the knowledge of God, and bringing into captivity every thought to the obedience of Christ;

6 And having in a readiness to revenge all disobedience, when your obedience is fulfilled.

7 Do ye look on things after the outward appearance? If any man trust to himself that he is Christ's, let him of himself think this again, that, as he is Christ's, even so are we Christ's.

8 For though I should boast somewhat more of our authority, which the Lord hath given us for edification, and not for your destruction, I should not be ashamed:

9 That I may not seem as if I would terrify you by letters.

10 For his letters, say they, are weighty and powerful; but his bodily presence is weak, and his speech contemptible.

11 Let such an one think this, that, such as we are in word by letters when we are absent, such will we be also in deed when we are present.

12 For we dare not make ourselves of the number, or compare ourselves with some that commend themselves: but they measuring themselves by themselves, and comparing themselves among themselves, are not wise.

13 But we will not boast of things without our measure, but according to the measure of the rule which God hath distributed to us, a measure to reach even unto you.

14 For we stretch not ourselves beyond our measure, as though we reached not unto you: for we come as far as to you also in preaching the gospel of Christ:

15 Not boasting of things without our measure, that is, of other men's labours; but having hope, when your faith is increased, that we shall be enlarged by you according to our rule abundantly,

16 To preach the gospel in the regions beyond you, and not to boast in another man's line of things made ready to our hand.

17 But he that glorieth, let him glory in the Lord.

18 For not he that commendeth himself is approved, but whom the Lord commendeth.

contempt, detracted nothing from his authority, inasmuch as he was distinguished by spiritual excellence, not by carnal show. Hence those would not pass with impunity, who derided either his exhortations, or his reproaches, or his threatenings. The words *I myself* are emphatic; as though he had said, that however the malevolent might blame him for inconstancy, he was in reality not changeable, but remained uniformly the same.

1. I exhort you

The speech is abrupt, as is frequently the case with speeches uttered under the influence of strong feeling. The meaning is this: "I beseech you, nay more, I earnestly entreat you by the *gentleness of Christ*, not to compel me, through your obstinacy, to be more severe than I would desire to be, and than I will be, towards those who despise me, on the ground of my having nothing excellent in external appearance, and do not recognize that spiritual excellence, with which the Lord has distinguished me, and by which I ought rather to be judged of."

The form of entreaty, which he makes use of, is taken from the subject in hand, when he says – by *the meekness and gentleness of Christ*. Calumniators took occasion to find fault with him, because his bodily presence was deficient in dignity, and because, on the other hand, when at a distance, he thundered forth in his Epistles. Both calumnies he befittingly refutes, as has been said, but he declares here, that nothing delights him more than *gentleness*, which becomes a minister of Christ, and of which the Master himself furnished an example. "Learn of me, says he, for I am meek and lowly. My yoke is easy and my burden is light" (Matthew 11: 29–30).

The Prophet also says of him, "His voice will not be heard in the streets: a bruised reed he shall not break, etc." (Isaiah 42: 2–3).

That gentleness, therefore, which Christ showed, he requires also from his servants. Paul, in making mention of it, intimates that he is no stranger to it. "I earnestly beseech you not to despise that *gentleness*, which Christ showed us in his own person, and shows us every day in his servants, nay more, which ye see in me."

2 CORINTHIANS 11

6. It is asked, however, whether elegance of *speech* is not also necessary for Apostles; for how will they otherwise be prepared for teaching? *Knowledge* might perhaps suffice for others, but how could a teacher be dumb? I answer, that, while Paul acknowledges himself to be *rude in speech*, it is not as though he were a mere infant, but as meaning, that he was not distinguished by such splendid eloquence as others, to whom he yields the palm as to this, retaining

present – for they would find that, when occasion called for it, he could be as bold when present as when he was absent, vs. 9–11.

They were subject to his apostolic authority. He usurped nothing in exercising the powers of his office over the churches which he had himself founded. He did not interfere with the jurisdiction of the other apostles, or undertake the special oversight of churches founded by others.

Macedonia and Achaia were within the sphere of his operations, and he hoped to preach the gospel far beyond those limits in regions where it had never been heard, vs. 12–16.

His confidence was not self-confidence, but confidence in God. His self-commendation amounted to nothing, unless the Lord commended him. Paul constantly felt that in himself he could do nothing, but in the Lord he could do all things, vs. 17–18.

1. Now I Paul myself beseech you, by the meekness and gentleness of Christ, who in presence (am) base among you, but being absent am bold toward you.

He enters without any preamble or circumlocution on his new subject, and places himself face to face with his unscrupulous opponents. He says, I Paul myself. He usually employs the first person plural when speaking of himself. Here, and throughout this context, he makes his individuality prominent in saying I. This is rendered the more emphatic by the addition of the word myself; αὐτὸς ἐγώ, I myself, the man whom you so despise and calumniate. Comp. Galatians 5: 2; Ephesians 3: 1; Philemon 19. In this case the expression is so emphatic that many suppose that Paul here began to write with his own hand; as though he were so excited, that he seized the pen from his amanuensis, and says, 'I Paul myself now write to you.' This, however, is unnecessary, and unsustained by any thing in the context. Beseech you by the meekness and gentleness of Christ. That is, the meekness and gentleness which belonged to

Christ, and which, therefore, his disciples are bound to imitate. To beseech by (διά), is to beseech on account of, or out of regard to. The request is enforced by a reference to the obligation of Christians to be meek and gentle as was their Lord.

Matthew 11: 29; Isaiah 42: 2. In Romans 12: 1, we have a similar expression, "I beseech you by the mercies of God." See Philippians 2: 1. The words πραότης and ἐπιείκεια differ very much as our words meekness and gentleness do; the former referring more to the inward virtue, the latter to its outward expression. As Christians are bound to be meek and gentle, Paul begged the Corinthians not to force him to be severe. He describes himself as his opposers described him, as craven when present, and a braggart when absent. Who in presence am base among you. In presence, κατὰ πρόσωπον, coram, before, towards the face of any one, here opposed to ἀπών, absent. The word ταπεινός, literally, low; then lowly, humble. It is commonly used in a good sense. Our Lord says of himself that he was, ταπεινὸς τῇ καρδίᾳ, lowly in heart, and his followers are always described as the lowly. But the word also means downcast, as in 7: 6, and thence it sometimes expresses depression when it is the effect of the want of courage. This is its meaning here. But being absent am bold towards you. Bold, in the sense opposite to base, or craven. This word also (θαρρέω) is commonly used in a good sense, 5: 6. It is only the context which gives it a different shade of meaning. Paul was regarded by his enemies as in heart a coward, and his boldness as merely, assumed when there was no danger to confront. No one (except Ruckert) now believes this. True heroism was never more fully exemplified than in the life of this apostle, who against numbers, wealth and power, always was true to his convictions; who encountered all manner of dangers and sufferings in the service of Christ, and whose whole conduct showed that he was ready not only to be bound, but to die for the name of the Lord Jesus. Acts 21: 13.

2 CORINTHIANS 11

1 Would to God ye could bear with me a little in my folly: and indeed bear with me.

2 For I am jealous over you with godly jealousy: for I have espoused you to one husband, that I may present you as a chaste virgin to Christ.

3 But I fear, lest by any means, as the serpent beguiled Eve through his subtilty, so your minds should be corrupted from the simplicity that is in Christ.

4 For if he that cometh preacheth another Jesus, whom we have not preached, or if ye receive another spirit, which ye have not received, or another gospel, which ye have not accepted, ye might well bear with him.

5 For I suppose I was not a whit behind the very chiefest apostles.

6 But though I be rude in speech, yet not in knowledge; but we have been throughly made manifest among you in all things.

7 Have I committed an offence in abasing myself that ye might be exalted, because I have preached to you the gospel of God freely?

8 I robbed other churches, taking wages of them, to do you service.

9 And when I was present with you, and wanted, I was chargeable to no man: for that which was lacking to me the brethren which came from Macedonia supplied: and in all things I have kept myself from being burdensome unto you, and so will I keep myself.

10 As the truth of Christ is in me, no man shall stop me of this boasting in the regions of Achaia.

11 Wherefore? because I love you not? God knoweth.

12 But what I do, that I will do, that I may cut off occasion from them which desire occasion; that wherein they glory, they may be found even as we.

13 For such are false apostles, deceitful workers, transforming themselves into the apostles of Christ.

14 And no marvel; for Satan himself is transformed into an angel of light.

15 Therefore it is no great thing if his ministers also be transformed as the ministers of righteousness; whose end shall

for himself what was the principal thing – the reality itself, while he leaves them talkativeness without gravity. If, however, any one should inquire, why it is that the Lord, who made men's tongues (Exodus 4: 11), did not also endow so eminent an apostle with eloquence, that nothing might be wanting to him, I answer, that he was furnished with a sufficiency for supplying the want of eloquence. For we see and feel, what majesty there is in his writings, what elevation appears in them, what a weight of meaning is couched under them, what power is discovered in them. In fine, they are thunderbolts, not mere words. Does not the efficacy of the Spirit appear more clearly in a naked rusticity of words (so to speak), than under the disguise of elegance and ornament? Of this matter, however, we have treated more largely in the former Epistle.

In short, he admits, as far as words are concerned, what his adversaries allege by way of objection, while he denies in reality what they hold forth. Let us also learn, from his example, to prefer deeds to words, and, to use a barbarous but common proverb – "Teneant alii quid nominis, nos autem quid rei;" – "Let others know something of the name, but let us know something of the reality." If eloquence is superadded, let it be regarded by us as something over and above; and farther, let it not be made use of for disguising doctrine, or adulterating it, but for unfolding it in its genuine simplicity.

But everywhere

As there was something magnificent in placing himself on a level with the chief Apostles, that this may not be ascribed to arrogance, he makes the Corinthians judges, provided they judge from what they have themselves experienced; for they had known sufficiently well, from many proofs, that he did not boast needlessly, or without good reason. He means, therefore, that he needs not make use of words, inasmuch as reality and experience afford clear evidence of every thing that he was about to say.

16. I say again

The Apostle has a twofold design. He has it partly in view to expose the disgusting vanity of the false Apostles, inasmuch as they were such extravagant trumpeters of their own praises; and farther, to expostulate with the Corinthians, because they shut him up to the necessity of glorying, contrary to the inclinations of his own mind. "*I say again*," says he. For he had abundantly shown previously, that there was no reason, why he should be despised. He had also shown at the same time, that he was very unlike others, and therefore ought not to have his grounds of glorying estimated according to the rule of their measure. Thus he again shows, for what purpose he had hitherto gloried – that he might clear his apostleship from contempt; for if

2 CORINTHIANS 11

The apostle apologizes for the self-commendation which was forced upon him, vs. 1–15. He contrasts himself and his labors with the assumptions of the false teachers, vs. 15–33.

Reasons for his self-commendation. vs 1–15.

He had just condemned all self-commendation, yet he was forced to do what had the appearance of self-laudation. The Corinthians were in danger of being turned away from Christ by having their confidence in Paul undermined by the misrepresentations of his enemies. It was therefore necessary for him to present the grounds which he had for claiming authority over them, and for asserting his superiority over his opponents.

Yet so repugnant was this task to his feelings, that he not only humbly apologizes for thus speaking of himself, but he finds it difficult to do what he felt must be done. He over and over begins what he calls his boasting, and immediately turns aside to something else. He begs them to bear with him while he proceeds to praise himself, v. 1, for his doing so sprang from the purest motive, love for them and anxiety for their welfare, vs. 2–3.

An anxiety justified by the readiness with which they bore with those who preached another gospel, v. 4.

He thus spoke because he was on a par with the chief apostles, and not behind those who among them claimed to be his superiors, v. 5.

They might have higher pretensions as orators, but in knowledge and in every thing that really pertained to the apostolic office he was abundantly manifest among them, v. 6.

His refusal to avail himself of his right to be supported by those to whom he preached was no offense to them, and no renunciation of his apostleship, vs. 7–9.

He was determined to refuse any pecuniary aid from the Christians in Achaia, not because he did not love them, but because he wished to cut off all occasion to question his

sincerity from those who sought such occasion, and because he desired to put the false teachers to the same test of disinterestedness, vs. 10–12.

These teachers claimed to be apostles, though they had no more right to the office, than Satan had to be regarded as an angel of light, vs. 13–15.

1. Would to God ye could bear with me a little in (my) folly: and indeed bear with me.
The self-commendation of the false teachers was the fruit of conceit and vanity; with the apostle it was self-vindication. Although so different in character and design, they had one element in common. Both included self-laudation. Both, therefore, are designated by the same word, boasting; and both, therefore, he calls ἀφροσύνη, a want of sense. **Would to God**, in the Greek simply, ὄφελον, **oh that, I would**. In fact, however, every such exclamation is, in the pious mind, a prayer; and, therefore, the rendering, 'I would to God,' is neither irreverent nor inaccurate. Oh that **ye could bear with me**, (ἀνείχεσθε, Hellenistic form, instead of ἠνείχεσθε.) The pronoun μοῦ properly belongs to the verb, and not to the following μικρόν τι, as if the sense were, **a little of my folly**. The meaning is, 'Bear with me (μικρόν τι ἀφροσύνης), as to a little of folly.' This reading is, on the authority of the majority of MSS., adopted by the later editors.

Knapp and others read, μικρὸν τῇ ἀφροσύνῃ, a little as to folly; Which amounts to the same thing. **And indeed bear with me.** So Calvin, Beza, and many others, who take ἀνέχεσθε as the imperative. This clause is then a repetition of the first, only more vehemently expressed. The former is a wish, the latter a supplication or demand. But the context does not require this vehemence. A more appropriate sense is afforded by taking the word in the indicative, "But indeed ye do bear with me"; i.e. the request is not necessary, I know you are disposed to suffer me to speak as I see fit.

be according to their works.

16 I say again, Let no man think me a fool; if otherwise, yet as a fool receive me, that I may boast myself a little.

17 That which I speak, I speak it not after the Lord, but as it were foolishly, in this confidence of boasting.

18 Seeing that many glory after the flesh, I will glory also.

19 For ye suffer fools gladly, seeing ye yourselves are wise.

20 For ye suffer, if a man bring you into bondage, if a man devour you, if a man take of you, if a man exalt himself, if a man smite you on the face.

21 I speak as concerning reproach, as though we had been weak. Howbeit whereinsoever any is bold, (I speak foolishly,) I am bold also.

22 Are they Hebrews? so am I. Are they Israelites? so am I. Are they the seed of Abraham? so am I.

23 Are they ministers of Christ? (I speak as a fool) I am more; in labours more abundant, in stripes above measure, in prisons more frequent, in deaths oft.

24 Of the Jews five times received I forty stripes save one.

25 Thrice was I beaten with rods, once was I stoned, thrice I suffered shipwreck, a night and a day I have been in the deep;

26 In journeyings often, in perils of waters, in perils of robbers, in perils by mine own countrymen, in perils by the heathen, in perils in the city, in perils in the wilderness, in perils in the sea, in perils among false brethren;

27 In weariness and painfulness, in watchings often, in hunger and thirst, in fastings often, in cold and nakedness.

28 Beside those things that are without, that which cometh upon me daily, the care of all the churches.

29 Who is weak, and I am not weak? who is offended, and I burn not?

30 If I must needs glory, I will glory of the things which concern mine infirmities.

31 The God and Father of our Lord Jesus Christ, which is blessed for evermore, knoweth that I lie not.

32 In Damascus the governor under Aretas the king kept the city of the Damascenes with a garrison, desirous to

the Corinthians had done their duty, he would not have said one word as to this matter.

Otherwise now as a fool

"If I am reckoned by you a *fool*, allow me at least to make use of my right and liberty – that is, to speak foolishly after the manner of fools." Thus he reproves the false Apostles, who, while they were exceedingly silly in this respect, were not merely borne with by the Corinthians, but were received with great applause. He afterwards explains what kind of folly it is – the publishing of his own praises. While they did so without end and without measure, he intimates that it was a thing to which he was unaccustomed; for he says, **for a little while.** For I take this clause as referring to time, so that the meaning is, that Paul did not wish to continue it long, but assumed, as it were, for the moment, the person of another, and immediately thereafter laid it aside, as we are accustomed to pass over lightly those things that are foreign to our object, while fools occupy themselves constantly (*en parergois*) in matters of inferior moment.

31. Paul proceeds to mock those ambitious men, who, while they had never had experience of any thing but applauses, favors, honorable salutations, and agreeable lodgings, wished to be held in the highest esteem. For, in opposition to this, he relates, that he was shut in, so that he could with difficulty save his life by a miserable and ignominious flight.

Some, however, ask, whether it was lawful for Paul to leap over the walls, inasmuch as it was a capital crime to do so? I answer, in the first place, that it is not certain, whether that punishment was sanctioned by law in the East; and farther, that even if it was so, Paul, nevertheless, was guilty of no crime, because he did not do this as an enemy, or for sport, but from necessity. For the law would not punish a man, that would throw himself down from the walls to save his life from the flames; and what difference is there between a fire, and a fierce attack from robbers? We must always, in connection with laws, have an eye to reason and equity. This consideration will exempt Paul entirely from blame.

2 CORINTHIANS 12

10. I take pleasure in infirmities

There can be no doubt, that he employs the term weakness in different senses; for he formerly applied this name to the punctures that he experienced in the flesh. He now employs it to denote those external qualities, which occasion contempt in the view of the world. Having spoken, however, in a general way, of *infirmities* of every kind, he now returns to that particular description of them, that had given occasion for his turning aside into this general discourse. Let us take notice, then, that infirmity is a general term, and that under

2 CORINTHIANS 12

The account of a remarkable vision granted to the apostle, vs. 1–6. The other evidences of his apostleship and his conduct and purposes in the exercise of his office, vs. 7–21.

Paul's revelations and visions.

He would give over boasting, and refer not to what he had done, but to what God had done; not to scenes in which he was the agent, but to those in which he was merely the subject – to revelations and visions. He had been caught up to the third heavens, and received communications and revelations which he was not permitted to make known. This was to him, and to all who believed his word, a more reliable evidence of the favor of God to him as an apostle than any thing he had yet mentioned, vs. 1–6.

With this extraordinary proof of the divine favor there was given him some painful bodily affection, from which he could not be delivered, in order to keep him duly humble, vs. 7–10.

This reference to his personal experience was exceedingly painful to him. He had been forced by their unreasonable opposition to speak of himself as he had done; for the external signs of his apostleship should have convinced them that he was the immediate messenger of Christ, vs. 11–12.

They themselves were a standing proof that he was truly an apostle. They were not less richly endowed than other churches founded by other apostles. If inferior at all, it was only that he had refused to be supported by them. This he could not help. He was determined to pursue in the future the course in that matter which he had hitherto adopted; neither by himself nor by others, neither mediately nor immediately, would he receive any thing at their hands, vs. 13–18.

All this self-vindication was of little account. It was a small matter what they thought of him. God is the only competent and final judge. His fear was that when he reached Cor-

inth he would be forced to appear as a judge; that not finding them what he desired them to be, he should be obliged to assume the aspect of a reprover, vs. 19–21.

1. It is not expedient for me doubtless to glory. I will come to visions and revelations of the Lord.

Boasting, the apostle says, **is not expedient for me**, either in the sense that it does not become me, is not a seemly or proper thing; or, is not profitable; does not contribute to set my apostleship in a clear light. There is a better way of proving my divine mission than by boasting. The former explanation is better suited to the apostle's mode of representation. He had repeatedly spoken of boasting as a kind of folly, something derogatory and painful. He expresses me same feeling here when he says it is not expedient. **I will come.** Our translators omit the γάρ, **for I will come.** The connection is with a thought omitted. Boasting is not expedient, (therefore I desist,) **for** I will pass to something else. What follows in the relation of the revelations made to him, was no self-laudation, but a recital of God's goodness. **Visions and revelations.** The latter term is, on the one hand, more general than the former, as there might be revelations where there were no visions; and, on the other, the latter is higher than the former, as implying a disclosure of the import of the things seen. **Of the Lord;** not visions of which the Lord was the object; it was not seeing the Lord that he here speaks of, but visions and revelations of which the Lord is the author. By **Lord** is obviously to be understood Christ, whose continued existence and divine power over the thoughts and states of the soul is hereby recognized.

2 CORINTHIANS 13

Threatening of punishment to impenitent offenders; exhortation to self-examination and amendment; conclusion of the epistle.

Paul's warnings and exhortations.

Having previously admonished and warned,

apprehend me:

33 And through a window in a basket was I let down by the wall, and escaped his hands.

2 CORINTHIANS 12

1 It is not expedient for me doubtless to glory. I will come to visions and revelations of the Lord.

2 I knew a man in Christ above fourteen years ago, (whether in the body, I cannot tell; or whether out of the body, I cannot tell: God knoweth;) such an one caught up to the third heaven.

3 And I knew such a man, (whether in the body, or out of the body, I cannot tell: God knoweth;)

4 How that he was caught up into paradise, and heard unspeakable words, which it is not lawful for a man to utter.

5 Of such an one will I glory: yet of myself I will not glory, but in mine infirmities.

6 For though I would desire to glory, I shall not be a fool; for I will say the truth: but now I forbear, lest any man should think of me above that which he seeth me to be, or that he heareth of me.

7 And lest I should be exalted above measure through the abundance of the revelations, there was given to me a thorn in the flesh, the messenger of Satan to buffet me, lest I should be exalted above measure.

8 For this thing I besought the Lord thrice, that it might depart from me.

9 And he said unto me, My grace is sufficient for thee: for my strength is made perfect in weakness. Most gladly therefore will I rather glory in my infirmities, that the power of Christ may rest upon me.

10 Therefore I take pleasure in infirmities, in reproaches, in necessities, in persecutions, in distresses for Christ's sake: for when I am weak, then am I strong.

11 I am become a fool in glorying; ye have compelled me: for I ought to have been commended of you: for in nothing am I behind the very chiefest apostles, though I be nothing.

12 Truly the signs of an apostle were wrought among you in all patience, in signs, and wonders, and mighty deeds.

it is comprehended the weakness of our nature, as well as all tokens of abasement. Now the point in question was Paul's outward abasement. He proceeded farther, for the purpose of showing, that the Lord humbled him in every way, that, in his defects, the glory of God might shine forth the more resplendently, which is, in a manner, concealed and buried, when a man is in an elevated position. He now again returns to speak of his excellences, which, at the same time, made him contemptible in public view, instead of procuring for him esteem and commendation.

For when I am weak, that is – "The more deficiency there is in me, so much the more liberally does the Lord, from his strength, supply me with whatever he sees to be needful for me." For the fortitude of philosophers is nothing else than contumacy, or rather a mad enthusiasm, such as fanatics are accustomed to have. "If a man is desirous to be truly *strong,* let him not refuse to be at the same time *weak.* Let him," I say, "*be weak* in himself that he may be *strong in the Lord*" (Ephesians 6: 10). Should any one object, that Paul speaks here, not of a failure of strength, but of poverty, and other afflictions, I answer, that all these things are exercises for discovering to us our own weakness; for if God had not exercised Paul with such trials, he would never have perceived so clearly his weakness. Hence, he has in view not merely poverty, and hardships of every kind, but also those effects that arise from them, as, for example, a feeling of our own weakness, self-distrust, and humility.

20. For I fear

He declares, in what way it tends to their edification, that his integrity should be vindicated, for, on the ground that he had come into contempt, many grew wanton, as it were, with loosened reins. Now respect for him would have been a means of leading them to repentance, for they would have listened to his admonitions. I fear, says he. This fear proceeded from love, for, unless he had been concerned as to their welfare, he would very readily have overlooked all this, from which he sought to obtain no personal advantage. For otherwise we are afraid to give occasion of offense, when we foresee that it will be hurtful to ourselves.

And I shall be found by you

Here is a second ground of fear – lest he should be constrained to act with greater severity. Now it is a token not merely of love, but even of indulgence, to shun severity, and have recourse to milder measures. "As to my striving at present to maintain my authority, and endeavoring to bring you back to obedience, I do this, lest I should find occasion to punish your obstinacy more severely, if I come, and find among you nothing of amendment." He teaches, accordingly, by his example, that mild remedies must always be resorted to by Pastors, for the correction of faults, before

he now distinctly announces his purpose to exercise his apostolic power in the punishment of offenders, vs. 1–2.

As they sought evidence of his apostleship, he would show that although weak in himself, he was invested with supernatural power by Christ. As Christ appeared as weak in dying, but was none the less imbued with divine power, as was proved by his resurrection from the dead; so the apostle in one sense was weak, in another full of power, vs. 3–4.

Instead of exposing themselves to this exercise of judicial authority, he exhorts them to try themselves, since Christ lived in them unless they were reprobates, v. 5.

He trusted that they would acknowledge him as an apostle, as he sought their good, vs. 6–7.

His power was given, and could be exercised, only for the truth. He rejoiced in his own weakness and in the prosperity of the Corinthians. The object in thus warning them was to avoid the necessity of exercising the power of judgment with which Christ had invested him, vs. 8–10.

Concluding exhortation and benediction, vs. 11–13.

1. This is the third (time) I am coming to you: In the mouth of two or three witnesses shall every word be established From this it is evident that Paul had already been twice in Corinth. He was about to make his third visit.

5. Know ye not your own selves how that Christ is in you. This version overlooks the connecting particle η"(or), the force of which indeed it is not easy to see. It may be that the apostle designed in these words to shame or to rouse them, 'Examine yourselves, **or** are you so besotted or ignorant as not to know that Christ is in you; that some thing is to be discovered by self-examination, unless ye are no Christians at all.' It may, however, be a direct appeal to the consciousness of his readers. 'Do you not recognize in yourselves, that is, are ye not conscious, that Christ is in you.' The construction in this clause is analo-

gous to that in 1 Corinthians 14: 37 and 16: 15. 'Know yourselves that, etc.,' equivalent to 'know that.' Winer 63: 3. The expression **Christ is in you,** does not mean 'Christ is among you as a people.' It refers to an indwelling of Christ in the individual believer, as is plain from such passages as Galatians 2: 20, "Christ liveth in me," and Galatians 4: 19; Romans 8: 10. Christ dwells in his people by his Spirit. The presence of the Spirit is the presence of Christ. This is not a mere figurative expression, as when we say we have a friend in our heart – but a real truth. The Spirit of Christ, the Holy Ghost, is in the people of God collectively and individually, the ever-present source of a new kind of life, so that if any man have not the Spirit of Christ he is none of his. Romans 8: 9.

Unless ye be reprobates. The word **reprobate,** in its theological sense, means one who is judicially abandoned to everlasting perdition. Such is obviously not its sense here, otherwise all those not now converted would perish forever. The word is to be taken in its ordinary meaning, **disapproved,** unworthy of approbation. Any person or thing which cannot stand the test is ἀδόκιμος. Those therefore in whom Christ does not dwell cannot stand the test, and are proved to be Christians, if at all, only in name.

6. But I trust that ye shall know that we are not reprobates.
In v. 3 Paul had said that the Corinthians sought δοκιμήν (evidence) that Christ was in him as an apostle. He exhorted them to seek evidence that he was in them as believers. If they should prove to be (ἀδόκιμος) without evidence, he was satisfied that they would find that he was not ἀδόκιμος.

The δοκιμή (or evidence) of Christ speaking in him which he proposed or threatened to give, was the exercise of the apostolic power which resulted from the indwelling of Christ, and therefore proved his presence. He was loath, however, to give that evidence; he would rather be (ἀδόκιμος) without that evidence; and he therefore adds,

13 For what is it wherein ye were inferior to other churches, except it be that I myself was not burdensome to you? forgive me this wrong.

14 Behold, the third time I am ready to come to you; and I will not be burdensome to you: for I seek not yours, but you: for the children ought not to lay up for the parents, but the parents for the children.

15 And I will very gladly spend and be spent for you; though the more abundantly I love you, the less I be loved.

16 But be it so, I did not burden you: nevertheless, being crafty, I caught you with guile.

17 Did I make a gain of you by any of them whom I sent unto you?

18 I desired Titus, and with him I sent a brother. Did Titus make a gain of you? walked we not in the same spirit? walked we not in the same steps?

19 Again, think ye that we excuse ourselves unto you? we speak before God in Christ: but we do all things, dearly beloved, for your edifying.

20 For I fear, lest, when I come, I shall not find you such as I would, and that I shall be found unto you such as ye would not: lest there be debates, envyings, wraths, strifes, backbitings, whisperings, swellings, tumults:

21 And lest, when I come again, my God will humble me among you, and that I shall bewail many which have sinned already, and have not repented of the uncleanness and fornication and lasciviousness which they have committed.

2 CORINTHIANS 13

1 This is the third time I am coming to you. In the mouth of two or three witnesses shall every word be established.

2 I told you before, and foretell you, as if I were present, the second time; and being absent now I write to them which heretofore have sinned, and to all other, that, if I come again, I will not spare:

3 Since ye seek a proof of Christ speaking in me, which to you-ward is not weak, but is mighty in you.

4 For though he was crucified through weakness, yet he liveth by the power of God. For we also are weak in him, but we shall live with him by the power of God

they have recourse to extreme severity; and, at the same time, that we must, by admonitions and reproofs, prevent the necessity of having recourse to the utmost rigor.

Lest, by any means, there be contentions

He enumerates the vices, which chiefly prevailed among the Corinthians; almost all of which proceeded from the same source. For had not every one been devoted to self, they would never have contended with each other – they would never have envied one another – there would have been no slandering among them. Thus the sum and substance of the first catalogue is want of love, because (*philautia*) self-love, and ambition prevailed.

2 CORINTHIANS 13

1. This will be the third

He goes on to reprove still farther the insolence of those of whom he had been speaking, some of whom living in profligacy and licentiousness, and others, carrying on contentions and strifes among themselves, cared nothing for his reproof. For his discourse did not apply to the entire body of the Church, but to certain diseased and half-rotten members of it. Hence he now, with greater freedom, uses sharpness, because he has to do with particular individuals, not with the whole body of the people, and besides this, it was with persons of such a stamp, that he perceived, that he would do them no good by kindness, and mild remedies. After having spent a year and a half among them (Acts 18: 11), he had visited them a second time. Now he forewarns them, that he will come to them a third time, and he says, that his three comings to them will be in the place of three witnesses. He quotes the law as to the authority of witnesses; not in the natural and literal sense, as it is termed, but by accommodation, or similitude, applying it to his particular purpose.

14. The grace of the Lord Jesus

He closes the Epistle with a prayer, which contains three clauses, in which the sum of our salvation consists. In the first place, he desires for them the grace of Christ; **secondly**, the **love of God**; and, **thirdly**, the **communion of the Spirit**. The term grace does not here mean unmerited favor, but is taken by metonymy, to denote the whole benefit of redemption. The order, however, may appear to be here inverted, because the love of God is placed **second**, while is the source of that grace, and hence it is **first** in order. I answer, that the arrangement of terms in the Scriptures is not always so very exact; but, at the same time, this order, too, corresponds with the common form of doctrine, which is *contained in the Scriptures* – that "when we were enemies to God, we were reconciled by the death of his Son" (Romans 5: 10), though the Scripture is wont to speak of this in two

7. Now I pray to God that ye do not evil; not that we should appear approved, but that ye should do that which is honest, though we be as reprobates.

Now I pray God that ye do no evil; that is, I pray that ye may not give occasion for me to give the evidence of Christ speaking in me, which I have threatened to give, in case of your continued disobedience. So far from desiring an opportunity of exhibiting my supernatural power, I earnestly desire that there may be no occasion for its exercise. The interpretation which Grotius, and after him Flatt, Billroth, and others give of this clause, 'I pray God that I may do you no evil,' is possible so far as the words are concerned, as ποιῆσαι ὑμᾶς κακὸν may mean either, to do you evil, or, that you do evil. But to do evil is not to punish. And had Paul intended to say, 'I pray God that I may not punish you,' he certainly would have chosen some more suitable expression. Besides, ποιῆσαι κακὸν is the opposite of ποιῆτε τὸ καλὸν (ye may do right) in this same verse. Not that we should appear approved, etc. This and the following clause give the reason of the prayer just uttered. The negative statement of that reason comes first. He did not desire their good estate for the selfish reason that he might appear, i.e. stand forth apparent, as δόκιμος (approved), as one concerning whom there could be no doubt that Christ dwelt in him. There were different kinds of evidence of the validity of Paul's claims as a believer and as an apostle; his holy life and multiform labors; signs and wonders; the apostolic power with which he was clothed; his success in preaching, or the number and character of his converts. The good state of the Corinthian church was therefore an evidence that he was approved, i.e. could stand the test. This, however, as he says, was not the reason why he prayed that they might do no evil. That reason, as stated positively, was, that ye should do that which is honest. That is, it was their good, and not his own recognition, that he had at heart. Do what is honest, τὸ καλὸν ποιῆτε, that ye may do me good, the beautiful, what is at once right and pleasing. Though we be as reprobates, ἀδόκιμοι, without approbation.

Paul was earnestly desirous that the Corinthians should do what was right, although the consequence was that he should have no opportunity of giving that δοκιμήν (evidence) of Christ speaking in him which he had threatened to give, and thus, in that respect, be ἀδόκιμος, without evidence. There is such a play on words in this whole connection that the sense of the passage is much plainer in the Greek than it is in the English version. This view of the passage is simple and suited to the connection, and is commonly adopted. Calvin and others interpret it more generally and without specific reference to the connection. "Concerning myself," he makes the apostle say, "I am not solicitous; I only fear lest ye should offend God. I am ready to appear as reprobate, if you are free of offense.

Reprobate, I mean, in the judgment of men, who often reject those who are worthy of special honor." This is the general sense, but the peculiar coloring of the passage is thus lost.

8. For we can do nothing against the truth, but for the truth.

This verse is connected with the last clause of the preceding. 'We shall, in one sense, be ἀδόκιμοι (without evidence) if you do what is right, for we can do nothing against the truth, but are powerful only for the truth.' That is, 'We can exercise the apostolic and supernatural power which is the evidence of Christ speaking in us, only in behalf of the truth.' By the truth is not to be understood moral excellence, or rectitude – a sense indeed which the word ἀλήθεια often has when antithetical to unrighteousness; nor does it mean judicial rectitude specifically, i.e. that standard to which a judge should be conformed, or, as Bengel explains it, "the exact authority to be exercised over the Corinthians;" but it means truth in its religious, scriptural sense; that revelation which God has made in his word as the rule of our faith and practice. This pas-

toward you.

5 Examine yourselves, whether ye be in the faith; prove your own selves. Know ye not your own selves, how that Jesus Christ is in you, except ye be reprobates?

6 But I trust that ye shall know that we are not reprobates.

7 Now I pray to God that ye do no evil; not that we should appear approved, but that ye should do that which is honest, though we be as reprobates.

8 For we can do nothing against the truth, but for the truth.

9 For we are glad, when we are weak, and ye are strong: and this also we wish, even your perfection.

10 Therefore I write these things being absent, lest being present I should use sharpness, according to the power which the Lord hath given me to edification, and not to destruction.

11 Finally, brethren, farewell. Be perfect, be of good comfort, be of one mind, live in peace; and the God of love and peace shall be with you.

12 Greet one another with an holy kiss.

13 All the saints salute you.

14 The grace of the Lord Jesus Christ, and the love of God, and the communion of the Holy Ghost, be with you all. Amen.

ways. For it sometimes declares what I have quoted from Paul — that there was enmity between us and God, before we were reconciled through Christ. On the other hand, we hear what John says — that "God so loved the world, that he gave his only-begotten Son, etc." (John 3: 16).

The statements are apparently opposite; but it is easy to reconcile them; because in the one case we look to God, and in the other to ourselves. For God, viewed in himself, loved us before the creation of the world, and redeemed us for no other reason than this — because he loved us. As for us, on the other hand, as we see in ourselves nothing but occasion of wrath, that is, sin, we cannot apprehend any love of God towards us without a Mediator. Hence it is that, with respect to us, the beginning of love is from the grace of Christ. According to the former view of the matter, Paul would have expressed himself improperly, had he put the love of God before the grace of Christ, or, in other words, the cause before the effect; but according to the latter, it were a suitable arrangement to begin with the grace of Christ, which was the procuring cause of God's adopting us into the number of his sons, and honoring us with his love, whom previously he regarded with hatred and abhorrence on account of sin.

The fellowship of the Holy Spirit is added, because it is only under his guidance, that we come to possess Christ, and all his benefits. He seems, however, at the same time, to allude to the diversity of gifts, of which he had made mention elsewhere (2 Corinthians 12: 11); because God does not give the Spirit to every one in a detached way, but distributes to each according to the measure of grace, that the members of the Church, by mutually participating, one with another, may cherish unity.

sage is of special interest as fixing the units of all ecclesiastical power, whether ordinary or miraculous. The decision of the apostle, if against the truth, availed nothing in the sight of God; the supernatural power with which he was invested forsook his arm, if raised against God's own people. The promise of our Lord, that what the church binds on earth shall be bound in heaven, is limited by the condition that her decisions be in accordance with the truth. The doctrine of the extreme Romish party that acts of discipline are effectual in cutting off from the true church and the communion of God, even **clave errante**, i.e. when the church errs in her knowledge of the facts, is utterly inconsistent with Paul's doctrine. He claimed no such power.

9. For we are glad, when we are weak, and ye are strong: and this also we wish,(even) your perfection.
If connected with the preceding clause the sense of this verse is, 'We can act only for me truth, **for** we have no desire to exercise our power to punish; we are glad when we are weak.' The meaning is better if this verse is regarded as co-ordinate with verse 8, and subordinate to v. 7. 'We desire that you should do right, though we appear as ἀδόκιμοι (without evidence), for we are glad when we are weak.' That is, we are glad when we have no occasion to exercise or manifest our power to punish. This is evidently the sense in which the word **weak is** to be here taken. It does not mean weak in the estimation of men, that is, despised as unworthy of respect. **And ye are strong,** i.e. such as cannot be overcome. They were strong when they were good. Their goodness was a sure protection from the disciplinary power of the apostle. **This also we wish,** viz. **your perfection.** That is, we are not only glad when you are strong, but we pray for your complete establishment. **Perfection,** κατάρτισις, from καταρτίζω, in the sense **to put in complete order.** Paul prayed that they might be perfectly restored from the state of confusion, contention, and evil into which they had fallen.

Galatians

Introduction by John Calvin

WHAT part of Asia was inhabited by the Galatians, and what were the boundaries of their country, is well known; but whence they originally came is not agreed among historians. It is universally admitted that they were Gauls, and, on that account, were denominated Gallo-Grecians. But from what part of Gaul they came it is more difficult to determine.

Strabo thought that the Tectosages came from Gallia Narbonensis, and that the remainder were Celtae; and this opinion has been generally adopted. But, as Pliny enumerates the Ambiani among the Tectosagi, and as it is universally agreed that they were allied to the Tolistobogi, who dwelt on the banks of the Rhine, I think it more probable that, they were Belgians, whose territory extended from a very distant part of the course of the Rhine to the English Channel. The Tolistobogi inhabited that part which receives from its present inhabitants the names of Cleves and Brabant.

The mistake originated, I think, in this way. A band of Tectosagi, who had made all irruption into Gallia Narbonensis, retained their own name, and gave it to the country which they had conquered. This is intimated by Ausonius, who says, "As far as the Teutosagi, whose original name was Belgians; for he calls them Belgians, and says that they were first called Teutosagi, and afterwards Tectosagi. Caesar, indeed, places the Tectosagi in the Hercynian forest; but I consider this to have been in consequence of their emigration, which indeed appears from that very passage.

But more than enough has now been said as to the origin of the nation, so far as relates to the present passage. Pliny informs us that the

Galatians, who inhabited that part of Asia to which they gave their name, were divided into three chief nations, Tectosagi, Tolistobogi, and Trocmi, and accordingly occupied three chief cities. So great was the power which they at one time swayed over their unwarlike neighbors, that they received tribute from a great part of Lesser Asia. Losing at length their ancient valor, and giving themselves up to pleasure and luxury, they were vanquished in war and subdued, with little difficulty, by Cneius Manlius, a Roman consul.

At the time of the Apostle Paul they were under the dominion of the Romans. He had purely and faithfully instructed them in the Gospel; but false apostles had entered, during his absence, and had corrupted the true seed by false and erroneous doctrines. They taught that the observation of ceremonies was still necessary. This might appear to be a trivial matter; but Paul very properly contends as for a fundamental article of the Christian faith. It is no small evil to quench the light of the Gospel, to lay a snare for consciences, and to remove the distinction between the Old and New Testaments. He perceived that these errors were also connected with a wicked and dangerous opinion as to the manner in which justification is obtained. This is the reason why he fights with so much earnestness and vehemence; and, having learned from him the important and serious nature of the controversy, it is our duty to read with greater attention.

One who forms his views of the subject from the Commentaries of Origen and Jerome, will be astonished that Paul should take so deep an interest in external rites; but whoever goes to the fountain will acknowledge that there was abundant reason for all this sharpness of reproof. The Galatians had allowed themselves to be drawn aside from the right course by excessive credulity, or rather by lightness and folly. He therefore censures them more severely; for I do not agree with those who attribute the harshness of his language to their slowness of apprehension. The Ephesians and Colossians had been subjected to the same temptations. If they had lent as ready an ear to the tale of the impostors, do we imagine that Paul would have treated them with greater gentleness? This boldness of rebuke was not suggested by the disposition of the people, but extorted by the baseness of their conduct.

Having ascertained what was the design of writing the Epistle, let us attend to the order in which it is treated. In the *first* and *second* Chapters (Galatians 1 and Galatians 2) he maintains the authority of his Apostleship, except that, towards the close of the second chapter, he touches incidentally on his main point, the question of Man's Justification, which, however, is avowedly and directly argued in the *third* Chapter, Galatians 3. Although he appears in those two Chapters to have many objects in view, yet his sole object is to prove that He is equal to the highest apostles, and that there is no reason why he should not be considered to hold an equally honorable rank with any of them.

But it is of importance to know why he labors so hard in establishing his own claim to respect. Provided that Christ reigns, and that the purity of doctrine remains uncontaminated, what matters it whether he is higher or lower than Peter, or whether they are all on a footing of equality? If all must "decrease," that Christ alone may "increase" (John 3: 30), it is idle to dispute about human ranks. Besides, it may be asked, why does he draw a comparison between himself and other apostles? What dispute had he with Peter, and James, and John? What good purpose did it serve to bring into collision those who were united in sentiment, and in the closest friendship?

I reply, the false apostles, who had deceived the Galatians, endeavored to obtain favor by pretending that they had received a commission from the Apostles. Their chief influence arose from insinuating the belief that they represented the Apostles, and delivered their message. To Paul, on the other hand, they refused the name and authority of an Apostle. They objected that he had not been chosen by our Lord as one of the Twelve; that he had never been acknowledged as such by the college of the Apostles; that he did not receive his doctrine from Christ, or even from the Apostles themselves. All this tended not only to lower Paul's authority, but to rank him with the ordinary members of the Church, and therefore to place him far below those persons who made these insinuations.

If this had been merely a personal matter, it would have given no uneasiness to Paul to be reckoned an ordinary disciple. But when he saw that his doctrine was beginning to lose its weight and authority, he was not entitled to be silent. It became his duty to make a bold resistance. When Satan does not venture openly to attack doctrine, his next stratagem is to diminish its influence by indirect attacks. Let us remember, then, that in the person of Paul the truth of the Gospel was assailed; for, if he had allowed himself to be stripped of the honor of apostleship, it followed that he had hitherto claimed what he had no title to enjoy; and this false boasting would have made him liable to suspicion in other matters. The estimation in which his doctrine was held depended on the question, whether it came, as some had begun to think, from an ordinary disciple, or from an apostle of Christ.

He was overwhelmed, on the other hand, by the luster of great names. Those who referred, in a boastful manner, to Peter, and James, and John, pretended to apostolical authority. If Paul had not manfully resisted this boasting, he would have given way to falsehood, and would have allowed the truth of God to suffer again in his own person. He therefore contends earnestly for both points: that he was appointed by the Lord to be an apostle, and that he was in no respect inferior to the rest, but enjoyed the same title, and was equal to them in authority and rank. He might, indeed, have denied that those men were either sent, or hold any commission from Peter and his associates. But he takes far higher ground, that he does not yield to the Apostles themselves; and if he had declined doing so, he would have been supposed to have distrusted his cause.

Jerusalem was, at that time, the Mother of all the Churches; for the Gospel had spread from it over the whole world, and it might be said to be the principal seat of the kingdom of Christ. Any one who came from it into other churches was received with due respect. But many were foolishly elated with the thought that they had enjoyed the friendship of the Apostles, or at least had been taught in their school; and therefore nothing pleased them but what they had seen at Jerusalem. Every custom that had not been practiced there was not only disliked, but unsparingly condemned by them. This peevish manner becomes highly pernicious, when the custom of a single church is attempted to be enforced as a universal law. We are sometimes so devoted to an instructor or a place, that, without exercising any judgment of our own, we make the opinion of one man the standard for all men, and the customs of one place the standard for every other place. Such attachment is ridiculous, if there be not always in it a mixture of ambition; or rather we should say, excessive peevishness is always ambitious.

To return to those false apostles, if they had only attempted, through wicked contention, to establish everywhere the use of those ceremonies, which they had seen observed at Jerusalem, that would have been no slight offense; for, when a custom is forthwith converted into a law, injustice is perpetrated. But a more serious evil was involved in the wicked and dangerous doctrine, which held consciences to be bound to them by religious considerations, which made justification to depend on the observation of them. Such were the reasons why Paul defended his Apostleship with so much earnestness, and why he contrasted himself with the rest of the Apostles.

He pursues this subject to the end of the *second* Chapter, Galatians 2, when he proceeds to argue the doctrine, that we are justified in the sight of God by Free Grace, and not by the Works of the Law. His argument is this: If Ceremonies have not the power of bestowing Justification, the observation of them is therefore unnecessary. We must remark, however, that he does not confine himself entirely to Ceremonies, but argues generally about Works, otherwise the whole discussion would be trifling.

If any person thinks that we are thus straining the matter too far, let him attend to the two following reasons. First, the question could not be settled without assuming the general principle, that we are justified by the free grace of God; and this principle sets aside not only ceremonies, but every other kind of works. Secondly, Paul did not attach so much importance to Ceremonies as to the wicked doctrine of obtaining Salvation by Works. Let it be observed, therefore, that Paul had good reasons for recurring to first principles. It was necessary to go to the fountain, and to warn his readers that the controversy related, not to some insignificant trifle, but to the most important of all matters – the method of obtaining salvation.

It is a mistake, therefore, to suppose that the Apostle confined himself wholly to the special question about Ceremonies, a subject which did not admit of being settled by itself. A similar instance occurs in history (Acts 15: 2). Strife and contention had arisen out of the question, whether or not Ceremonies were necessary to be observed. In the course of the discussion, the Apostles dwell largely on the intolerable yoke of the Law, and on the Forgiveness of Sins through Free Grace. What was the object of this? It appears to be a foolish departure from the point in hand; but the contrary is the fact, for a particular error cannot be satisfactorily refuted without assuming a universal principle. As, for instance, if I am called to dispute about, forbidding the use of flesh, I shall not speak merely about the different kinds of food, but shall arm myself with the general doctrine: What authority have the Traditions of men for binding the conscience? I shall quote the declaration, that "There is one Lawgiver, who has power to save and to destroy" (James 4: 12).

In short, Paul here argues negatively from general to particular propositions, which is the ordinary and most natural method of reasoning. By what evidences and arguments he proves this principle, that we are justified by the grace of God alone, we shall see when we come to the passage. He pursues this topic till the end of the *third* Chapter, Galatians 3.

In the commencement of the *fourth* Chapter, Galatians 4, he inquires into the proper use of Ceremonies, and the reason why they were appointed; shewing, at the same time, that they are now abolished. It became necessary to meet this silly objection, which might occur to some minds. What, then, was the purpose of Ceremonies? Were they useless? Were the Fathers idly employed in observing them? He illustrates briefly two statements, that in their own time they were not superfluous, and that they have now been abolished by the coming of Christ, because He is the truth and end of them; and therefore he shews that we must abide by Him. Glancing briefly at the difference between our condition and that of the Fathers, he infers that the doctrine of the false apostles is wicked and dangerous, because it darkens the clearness of the gospel by ancient shadows. The Apostle's doctrine is now intermingled with some affecting exhortations. Towards the close of the Chapter his argument is enlivened by a beautiful allegory.

In the *fifth* Chapter, Galatians 5, he exhorts them to hold fast the Liberty which has been obtained by the blood of Christ, that they may not surrender their consciences to be ensnared by the opinions of men. But he reminds them, at the same time, in what manner Liberty may be lawfully used. He then takes occasion to point out the proper employments of Christians, that they may not uselessly spend their time in Ceremonies, and neglect matters of real importance.

The commentaries on Galatians are by John Calvin and Martin Luther.

GALATIANS 1

1 Paul, an apostle, (not of men, neither by man, but by Jesus Christ, and God the Father, who raised him from the dead;)

2 And all the brethren which are with me, unto the churches of Galatia:

3 Grace be to you and peace from God the Father, and from our Lord Jesus Christ,

4 Who gave himself for our sins, that he might deliver us from this present evil world, according to the will of God and our Father:

5 To whom be glory for ever and ever. Amen.

6 I marvel that ye are so soon removed from him that called you into the grace of Christ unto another gospel:

7 Which is not another; but there be some that trouble you, and would pervert the gospel of Christ.

8 But though we, or an angel from heaven, preach any other gospel unto you than that which we have preached unto you, let him be accursed.

9 As we said before, so say I now again, If any man preach any other gospel unto you than that ye have received, let him be accursed.

10 For do I now persuade men, or God? or do I seek to please men? for if I yet pleased men, I should not be the servant of Christ.

11 But I certify you, brethren, that the gospel which was preached of me is not after man.

12 For I neither received it of man, neither was I taught it, but by the revelation of Jesus Christ.

13 For ye have heard of my conversation in time past in the Jews' religion, how that beyond measure I persecuted the church of God, and wasted it:

14 And profited in the Jews' religion above many my equals in mine own nation, being more exceedingly zealous of the traditions of my fathers.

15 But when it pleased God, who separated me from my mother's womb, and called me by his grace,

16 To reveal his Son in me, that I might preach him among the heathen; immediately I conferred not with flesh and blood:

17 Neither went I up to Jerusalem to them which were apostles before me; but I went into Arabia, and returned again

GALATIANS 1

1. Paul, an apostle. In the salutations with which he commenced his Epistles, Paul was accustomed to claim the title of "an Apostle." His object in doing so, as we have remarked on former occasions, was to employ the authority of his station, for the purpose of enforcing his doctrine. This authority depends not on the judgment or opinion of men, but exclusively on the calling of God; and therefore he demands a hearing on the ground of his being "an Apostle." Let us always bear this in mind, that in the church we ought to listen to God alone, and to Jesus Christ, whom he has appointed to be our teacher. Whoever assumes a right to instruct us, must speak in the name of God or of Christ.

But as the calling of Paul was more vehemently disputed among the Galatians, he asserts it more strongly in his address to that church, than in his other Epistles; for he does not simply affirm that he was called by God, but states expressly that it was *not either from men or by men*. This statement, be it observed, applies not to the office which he held in common with other pastors, but to the apostleship. The authors of the calumnies which he has in his eye did not venture to deprive him altogether of the honor of the Christian ministry. They merely refused to allow him the name and rank of an apostle.

We are now speaking of the apostleship in the strictest sense; for the word is employed in two different ways. Sometimes, it denotes preachers of the Gospel, to whatever class they might belong; but here it bears a distinct reference to the highest rank in the church; so that Paul is equal to Peter and to the other twelve.

The first clause, that he was called *not from men*, he had in common with all the true ministers of Christ. As no man ought to "take this honor unto himself" (Hebrews 5: 4), so it is not in the power of men to bestow it on whomsoever they choose. It belongs to God alone to govern his church; and therefore the calling cannot be lawful, unless it proceed from Him. So far as the church is concerned, a man who has been led to the ministry, not by a good conscience, but by ungodly motives, may happen to be regularly called. But Paul is here speaking of a call ascertained in so perfect a manner, that nothing farther can be desired.

The second clause, that he was called *not by man*, belonged in a peculiar manner to the apostles; for in an ordinary pastor, this would have implied nothing wrong. Paul himself, when travelling through various cities in company with Barnabas, "ordained elders in every church," by the votes of the people (Acts 14: 23); and he enjoins Titus and Timothy to proceed in the same work. (1 Timothy 5: 17; Titus 1: 5). Such is the ordinary method of electing pastors; for we are not entitled to wait until God shall reveal from heaven the

GALATIANS 1

1. Paul, an apostle, (not of men, neither by man, but by Jesus Christ, and God the Father, who raised him from the dead).

St. Paul wrote this epistle because, after his departure from the Galatian churches, Jewish-Christian fanatics moved in, who perverted Paul's Gospel of man's free justification by faith in Christ Jesus.

The world bears the Gospel a grudge because the Gospel condemns the religious wisdom of the world. Jealous for its own religious views, the world in turn charges the Gospel with being a subversive and licentious doctrine, offensive to God and man, a doctrine to be persecuted as the worst plague on earth.

As a result we have this paradoxical situation: The Gospel supplies the world with the salvation of Jesus Christ, peace of conscience, and every blessing. Just for that the world abhors the Gospel.

These Jewish-Christian fanatics who pushed themselves into the Galatian churches after Paul's departure, boasted that they were the descendants of Abraham, true ministers of Christ, having been trained by the apostles themselves, that they were able to perform miracles.

In every way they sought to undermine the authority of St. Paul. They said to the Galatians: "You have no right to think highly of Paul. He was the last to turn to Christ. But we have seen Christ. We heard Him preach. Paul came later and is beneath us. It is possible for us to be in error we who have received the Holy Ghost? Paul stands alone. He has not seen Christ, nor has he had much contact with the other apostles. Indeed, he persecuted the Church of Christ for a long time."

When men claiming such credentials come along, they deceive not only the naive, but also those who seemingly are well-established in the faith. This same argument is used by the papacy. "Do you suppose that God for the sake of a few Lutheran heretics would disown His entire Church? Or do you suppose that God would have left His Church floundering in error all these centuries?" The Galatians were taken in by such arguments with the result that Paul's authority and doctrine were drawn in question.

Against these boasting, false apostles, Paul boldly defends his apostolic authority and ministry. Humble man that he was, he will not now take a back seat. He reminds them of the time when he opposed Peter to his face and reproved the chief of the apostles.

Every minister should make much of his calling and impress upon others the fact that he has been delegated by God to preach the Gospel. As the ambassador of a government is honored for his office and not for his private person, so the minister of Christ should exalt his office in order to gain authority among men. This is not vain glory, but needful glorying.

Paul takes pride in his ministry, not to his own praise but to the praise of God. Writing to the Romans, he declares, "Inasmuch as I am the apostle of the Gentiles, I magnify mine office," i.e., I want to be received not as Paul of Tarsus, but as Paul the apostle and ambassador of Jesus Christ, in order that people might be more eager to hear. Paul exalts his ministry out of the desire to make known the name, the grace, and the mercy of God.

21. Afterwards I came into the regions of Syria and Cilicia.

Syria and Cilicia are adjacent countries. Paul traces his movements carefully in order to convince the Galatians that he had never been the disciple of any apostle.

22–24. And was unknown by face unto the churches of Judaea which were in Christ: But they had heard only, that he which persecuted us in times past now preacheth the faith which once he destroyed. And they glorified God in me.

In Syria and Cilicia Paul won the indorsement of all the churches of Judea, by his preaching. All the churches everywhere, even those of Judea, could testify that he had preached the same faith everywhere. "And," Paul adds, "these churches glorified God in me, not because I taught that circumcision and the law of Moses should be observed, but because I urged upon all faith in the Lord Jesus Christ."

unto Damascus.

18 Then after three years I went up to Jerusalem to see Peter, and abode with him fifteen days.

19 But other of the apostles saw I none, save James the Lord's brother.

20 Now the things which I write unto you, behold, before God, I lie not.

21 Afterwards I came into the regions of Syria and Cilicia;

22 And was unknown by face unto the churches of Judaea which were in Christ:

23 But they had heard only, That he which persecuted us in times past now preacheth the faith which once he destroyed.

24 And they glorified God in me.

GALATIANS 2

1 Then fourteen years after I went up again to Jerusalem with Barnabas, and took Titus with me also.

2 And I went up by revelation, and communicated unto them that gospel which I preach among the Gentiles, but privately to them which were of reputation, lest by any means I should run, or had run, in vain.

3 But neither Titus, who was with me, being a Greek, was compelled to be circumcised:

4 And that because of false brethren unawares brought in, who came in privily to spy out our liberty which we have in Christ Jesus, that they might bring us into bondage:

5 To whom we gave place by subjection, no, not for an hour; that the truth of the gospel might continue with you.

6 But of these who seemed to be somewhat, (whatsoever they were, it maketh no matter to me: God accepteth no man's person:) for they who seemed to be somewhat in conference added nothing to me:

7 But contrariwise, when they saw that the gospel of the uncircumcision was committed unto me, as the gospel of the circumcision was unto Peter;

8 (For he that wrought effectually in Peter to the apostleship of the circumcision, the same was mighty in me toward the Gentiles:)

9 And when James, Cephas, and John, who seemed to be pillars, perceived the grace that was given unto me, they gave

names of the persons whom he has chosen.

But if human agency was not improper, if it was even commendable, why does Paul disclaim it in reference to himself? I have already mentioned that something more was necessary to be proved than that Paul was a pastor, or that he belonged to the number of the ministers of the Gospel; for the point in dispute was the apostleship. It was necessary that the apostles should be elected, not in the same manner as other pastors, but by the direct agency of the Lord himself. Thus, Christ himself (Matthew 10: 1) called the Twelve; and when a successor was to be appointed in the room of Judas, the church does not venture to choose one by votes, but has recourse to *lot* (Acts 1: 26). We are certain that the lot was not employed in electing pastors. Why was it resorted to in the election of Matthias? To mark the express agency of God for it was proper that the apostles should be distinguished from other ministers. And thus Paul, in order to shew that he does not belong to the ordinary rank of ministers, contends that his calling proceeded immediately from God.

GALATIANS 2

1. Fourteen years after

This cannot with certainty be affirmed to be the same journey mentioned by Luke (Acts 15: 2). The connection of the history leads us rather to an opposite conclusion. We find that Paul performed four journeys to Jerusalem. Of the first we have already spoken. The second took place when, in company with Barnabas, he brought the charitable contributions of the Greek and Asiatic Churches (Acts 15: 25). My belief that this second journey is referred to in the present passage rests on various grounds. On any other supposition, the statements of Paul and Luke cannot be reconciled. Besides, there is ground for conjecturing that the rebuke was administered to Peter at Antioch while Paul was residing there. Now, this happened before he was sent to Jerusalem by the Churches to settle the dispute which had arisen about ceremonial observances (Acts 15: 2). is not reasonable to suppose that Peter would have used such dissimulation, if that controversy had been settled and the decree of the Apostles published. But Paul writes that he came to Jerusalem, and afterwards adds that he had rebuked Peter for an act of dissimulation, an act which Peter certainly would not have committed except in matters that were doubtful.

Besides, he would scarcely have alluded, at any time, to that journey undertaken with the consent of all the believers, without mentioning the occasion of it, and the memorable decision which was passed. It is not even certain at what time the Epistle was written, only that the Greeks

GALATIANS 2

1. Then fourteen years after I went up again to Jerusalem.

Paul taught justification by faith in Christ Jesus, without the deeds of the Law. He reported this to the disciples at Antioch. Among the disciples were some that had been brought up in the ancient customs of the Jews. These rose against Paul in quick indignation, accusing him of propagating a gospel of lawlessness.

Great dissension followed. Paul and Barnabas stood up for the truth. They testified: "Wherever we preached to the Gentiles, the Holy Ghost came upon those who received the Word. This happened everywhere. We preached not circumcision, we did not require observance of the Law. We preached faith in Jesus Christ. At our preaching of faith, God gave to the hearers the Holy Ghost." From this fact Paul and Barnabas inferred that the Holy Ghost approved the faith of the Gentiles without the Law and circumcision. If the faith of the Gentiles had not pleased the Holy Ghost, He would not have manifested His presence in the uncircumcised hearers of the Word.

Unconvinced, the Jews fiercely opposed Paul, asserting that the Law ought to be kept and that the Gentiles ought to be circumcised, or else they could not be saved.

When we consider the obstinacy with which Romanists cling to their traditions, we can very well understand the zealous devotion of the Jews for the Law. After all, they had received the Law from God. We can understand how impossible it was for recent converts from Judaism suddenly to break with the Law. For that matter, God did bear with them, as He bore with the infirmity of Israel when the people halted between two religions. Was not God patient with us also while we were blindfolded by the papacy? God is longsuffering and full of mercy. But we dare not abuse the patience of the Lord. We dare no longer continue in error now that the truth has been revealed in the Gospel.

The opponents of Paul had his own example to prefer against him. Paul had circumcised Timothy. Paul defended his action on the ground that he had circumcised Timothy, not from compulsion, but from Christian love, lest the weak in faith should be offended. His opponents would not accept Paul's explanation.

When Paul saw that the quarrel was getting out of hand he obeyed the direction of God and left for Jerusalem, there to confer with the other apostles. He did this not for his own sake, but for the sake of the people.

4–5. And that because of false brethren unawares brought in, who came in privily to spy out our liberty which we have in Christ Jesus, that they might bring us into bondage:

To whom we gave place by subjection, no, not for an hour; that the truth of the gospel might continue with you.

Paul here explains his motive for going up to Jerusalem. He did not go to Jerusalem to be instructed or confirmed in his Gospel by the other apostles. He went to Jerusalem in order to preserve the true Gospel for the Galatian churches and for all the churches of the Gentiles.

When Paul speaks of the truth of the Gospel he implies by contrast a false gospel. The false apostles also had a gospel, but it was an untrue gospel. "In holding out against them," says Paul, "I conserved the truth of the pure Gospel."

Now the true Gospel has it that we are justified by faith alone, without the deeds of the Law. The false gospel has it that we are justified by faith, but not without the deeds of the Law. The false apostles preached a conditional gospel.

So do the papists. They admit that faith is the foundation of salvation. But they add the conditional clause that faith can save only when it is furnished with good works. This is wrong. The true Gospel declares that good works are the embellishment of faith, but that faith itself is the gift and work of God in our hearts. Faith is able to justify, because it apprehends Christ, the Redeemer.

Human reason can think only in terms of the Law. It mumbles: "This I have done, this I have not done." But faith looks to Jesus Christ, the Son of God, given into death for the sins of the whole world. To turn one's eyes away from

to me and Barnabas the right hands of fellowship; that we should go unto the heathen, and they unto the circumcision.

10 Only they would that we should remember the poor; the same which I also was forward to do.

11 But when Peter was come to Antioch, I withstood him to the face, because he was to be blamed.

12 For before that certain came from James, he did eat with the Gentiles: but when they were come, he withdrew and separated himself, fearing them which were of the circumcision.

13 And the other Jews dissembled likewise with him; insomuch that Barnabas was carried away with their dissimulation.

14 But when I saw that they walked not uprightly according to the truth of the gospel, I said unto Peter before them all, If thou, being a Jew, livest after the manner of Gentiles, and not as do the Jews, why compellest thou the Gentiles to live as do the Jews?

15 We who are Jews by nature, and not sinners of the Gentiles,

16 Knowing that a man is not justified by the works of the law, but by the faith of Jesus Christ, even we have believed in Jesus Christ, that we might be justified by the faith of Christ, and not by the works of the law: for by the works of the law shall no flesh be justified.

17 But if, while we seek to be justified by Christ, we ourselves also are found sinners, is therefore Christ the minister of sin? God forbid.

18 For if I build again the things which I destroyed, I make myself a transgressor.

19 For I through the law am dead to the law, that I might live unto God.

20 I am crucified with Christ: nevertheless I live; yet not I, but Christ liveth in me: and the life which I now live in the flesh I live by the faith of the Son of God, who loved me, and gave himself for me.

21 I do not frustrate the grace of God: for if righteousness come by the law, then Christ is dead in vain.

GALATIANS 3

1 O foolish Galatians, who hath bewitched you, that ye should not obey the truth, before whose eyes Jesus Christ hath been evidently set forth, crucified

conjecture that it was sent from Rome, and the Latins from Ephesus. For my own part, I think that it was written, not only before Paul had seen Rome, but before that consultation had been held, and the decision of the Apostles given about ceremonial observances. While his opponents were falsely pleading the name of the apostles, and earnestly striving to ruin the reputation of Paul, what carelessness would it have angered in him to pass by the decree universally circulated among them, which struck at those very persons! Undoubtedly, this one word would have shut their mouth: "You bring against me the authority of the apostles, but who does not know their decision? and therefore I hold you convicted of unblushing falsehood. In their name, you oblige the Gentiles to keep the law, but I appeal to their own writing, which sets the consciences of men at liberty."

We may likewise observe, that, in the commencement of the Epistle, he reproved the Galatians for having so soon revolted from the gospel which had been delivered to them. But we may readily conclude, that, after they had been brought to believe the gospel, some time must have elapsed before that dispute about the ceremonial law arose. I consider, therefore, that the fourteen years are to be reckoned, not from one journey to another, but from Paul's conversion. The space of time between the two journeys was eleven years.

2. And I went up according to revelation

He now proceeds to prove his apostleship and his doctrine, not only by works, but also by a Divine revelation. Since God directed that journey, which had for its object the confirmation of his doctrine, the doctrine was confirmed, not by the concurrence of men only, but likewise by the authority of God. This ought to have been more than enough to overcome the obstinacy of those who blamed Paul by holding up the names of the apostles. For although, up to this time, there had been some room for debate, the communication of the mind of God put an end to all discussion.

3. But neither Titus

This is an additional argument to prove that the Apostles held the same views with himself; for he had brought to them an uncircumcised man, whom they did not hesitate to acknowledge as a brother. The reason is assigned why he was not circumcised; for circumcision, being a matter of indifference, might be neglected or practiced as edification required. Our invariable rule of action is, that, if "all things are lawful for us" (1 Corinthians 10: 23) we ought to inquire what is expedient. He circumcises Timothy (Acts 16: 3), in order to take away a ground of offense from weak minds; for he was at that time dealing with weak minds, which it was his duty to treat with tenderness. And he would gladly have done the same thing with Titus, for he was unwearied

Jesus means to turn them to the Law.

True faith lays hold of Christ and leans on Him alone. Our opponents cannot understand this. In their blindness they cast away the precious pearl, Christ, and hang onto their stubborn works. They have no idea what faith is. How can they teach faith to others?

Not satisfied with teaching an untrue gospel, the false apostles tried to entangle Paul. "They went about," says Paul, "to spy out our liberty which we have in Christ Jesus, that they might bring us into bondage."

When Paul saw through their scheme, he attacked the false apostles. He says, "We did not let go of the liberty which we have in Christ Jesus. We routed them by the judgment of the apostles, and we would not give in to them, no, not an inch."

We too were willing to make all kinds of concessions to the papists. Yes, we are willing to offer them more than we should. But we will not give up the liberty of conscience which we have in Christ Jesus. We refuse to have our conscience bound by any work or law, so that by doing this or that we should be righteous, or leaving this or that undone we should be damned.

GALATIANS 3

1. O foolish Galatians.

The Apostle Paul manifests his apostolic care for the Galatians. Sometimes he entreats them, then again he reproaches them, in accordance with his own advice to Timothy: "Preach the word; be instant in season, out of season; reprove, rebuke, exhort."

In the midst of his discourse on Christian righteousness Paul breaks off, and turns to address the Galatians. "O foolish Galatians," he cries. "I have brought you the true Gospel, and you received it with eagerness and gratitude. Now all of a sudden you drop the Gospel. What has got into you?"

Paul reproves the Galatians rather sharply when he calls them "fools, bewitched, and disobedient." Whether he is indignant or sorry, I cannot say. He may be both. It is the duty of a Christian pastor to reprove the people committed to his charge. Of course, his anger must not flow from malice, but from affection

and a real zeal for Christ.

There is no question that Paul is disappointed. It hurts him to think that his Galatians showed so little stability. We can hear him say: "I am sorry to hear of your troubles, and disappointed in you for the disgraceful part you played." I say rather much on this point to save Paul from the charge that he railed upon the churches, contrary to the spirit of the Gospel.

A certain distance and coolness can be noted in the title with which the Apostle addresses the Galatians. He does not now address them as his brethren, as he usually does. He addresses them as Galatians in order to remind them of their national trait to be foolish.

We have here an example of bad traits that often cling to individual Christians and entire congregations. Grace does not suddenly transform a Christian into a new and perfect creature. Dregs of the old and natural corruption remain. The Spirit of God cannot at once overcome human deficiency. Sanctification takes time.

Although the Galatians had been enlightened by the Holy Spirit through the preaching of faith, something of their national trait of foolishness plus their original depravity clung to them. Let no man think that once he has received faith, he can presently be converted into a faultless creature. The leavings of old vices will stick to him, be he ever so good a Christian.

1. Who hath bewitched you, that ye should not obey the truth?

Paul calls the Galatians foolish and bewitched. In the fifth chapter he mentions sorcery among the works of the flesh, declaring that witchcraft and sorcery are real manifestations and legitimate activities of the devil. We are all exposed to the influence of the devil, because he is the prince and god of the world in which we live.

Satan is clever. He does not only bewitch men in a crude manner, but also in a more artful fashion. He bedevils the minds of men with hideous fallacies. Not only is he able to deceive the self-assured, but even those who profess the true Christian faith. There is not one among us who is not at times seduced by

among you?

2 This only would I learn of you, Received ye the Spirit by the works of the law, or by the hearing of faith?

3 Are ye so foolish? having begun in the Spirit, are ye now made perfect by the flesh?

4 Have ye suffered so many things in vain? if it be yet in vain.

5 He therefore that ministereth to you the Spirit, and worketh miracles among you, doeth he it by the works of the law, or by the hearing of faith?

6 Even as Abraham believed God, and it was accounted to him for righteousness.

7 Know ye therefore that they which are of faith, the same are the children of Abraham.

8 And the scripture, foreseeing that God would justify the heathen through faith, preached before the gospel unto Abraham, saying, In thee shall all nations be blessed.

9 So then they which be of faith are blessed with faithful Abraham.

10 For as many as are of the works of the law are under the curse: for it is written, Cursed is every one that continueth not in all things which are written in the book of the law to do them.

11 But that no man is justified by the law in the sight of God, it is evident: for, The just shall live by faith.

12 And the law is not of faith: but, The man that doeth them shall live in them.

13 Christ hath redeemed us from the curse of the law, being made a curse for us: for it is written, Cursed is every one that hangeth on a tree:

14 That the blessing of Abraham might come on the Gentiles through Jesus Christ; that we might receive the promise of the Spirit through faith.

15 Brethren, I speak after the manner of men; Though it be but a man's covenant, yet if it be confirmed, no man disannulleth, or addeth thereto.

16 Now to Abraham and his seed were the promises made. He saith not, And to seeds, as of many; but as of one, And to thy seed, which is Christ.

17 And this I say, that the covenant, that was confirmed before of God in Christ, the law, which was four hundred and thirty years after, cannot disannul, that it should make the promise of none effect.

in his endeavors to "support (*Acts* 20: 35) the weak;" but the case was different. For some false brethren were watching for an opportunity of slandering his doctrine, and would immediately have spread the report: "See how the valiant champion of liberty, when he comes into the presence of the apostles, lays aside the bold and fierce aspect which he is wont to assume among the ignorant!" Now, as it is our duty to "bear the infirmities of the weak" (Romans 15: 1), so concealed foes, who purposely watch for our liberty, must, be vigorously resisted. The duties of love to our neighbor ought never to be injurious to faith; and therefore, in matters of indifference, the love of our neighbor will be our best guide, provided that faith shall always receive our first regard.

GALATIANS 3

1. O foolish Galatians. An expostulation is here interwoven – I should rather say, inserted – amidst his doctrinal statements. Some will wonder that he did not delay it to the close of the Epistle, but the very serious nature of the errors which he has brought forward unquestionably roused him to a burst of passion. When we hear that the Son of God, with all his benefits, is rejected, that his death is esteemed as nothing, what pious mind would not break out into indignation? He therefore declares that those who allowed themselves to be involved in so heinous a crime must have been ano toi, that is, "disordered in mind." He accuses them not only of having suffered themselves to be deceived, but of having been carried away by some sort of magical enchantment, which is a still more serious charge. He insinuates that their fall partook more of madness than of folly.

Some think that Paul refers to the temper of the nation, that, being sprung from barbarians, it was more difficult to train them; but I rather think that he refers to the subject itself. It looks like something supernatural, that, after enjoying the gospel in such clearness, they should be affected by the delusions of Satan. He does not merely say that they were "bewitched" and "disordered in mind," because they did not obey the truth; but because, after having received instruction so clear, so full, so tender, and so powerful, they immediately fell away. Erasmus has chosen to interpret the words, "that ye should not believe the truth." I am not quite prepared to set aside that rendering, but would prefer the word obey, because Paul does not charge them with having, from the outset, rejected the gospel, but with not having persevered in obedience.

Before whose eyes

This is intended to express an aggravation; for, the better opportunities they had of knowing Christ, the more heinous was the criminality of forsaking him. Such, he tells

Satan into false beliefs.

This accounts for the many new battles we have to wage nowadays. But the attacks of the old Serpent are not without profit to us, for they confirm our doctrine and strengthen our faith in Christ. Many a time we were wrestled down in these conflicts with Satan, but Christ has always triumphed and always will triumph. Do not think that the Galatians were the only ones to be bewitched by the devil. Let us realize that we too may be seduced by Satan.

1. Who hath bewitched you?

In this sentence Paul excuses the Galatians, while he blames the false apostles for the apostasy of the Galatians.

As if he were saying: "I know your defection was not willful. The devil sent the false apostles to you, and they tallied you into believing that you are justified by the Law. With this our epistle we endeavor to undo the damage which the false apostles have inflicted upon you."

Like Paul, we struggle with the Word of God against the fanatical Anabaptists of our day; and our efforts are not entirely in vain. The trouble is there are many who refuse to be instructed. They will not listen to reason; they will not listen to the Scriptures, because they are bewitched by the tricky devil who can make a lie look like the truth.

Since the devil has this uncanny ability to make us believe a lie until we would swear a thousand times it were the truth, we must not be proud, but walk in fear and humility, and call upon the Lord Jesus to save us from temptation.

Although I am a doctor of divinity, and have preached Christ and fought His battles for a long time, I know from personal experience how difficult it is to hold fast to the truth. I cannot always shake off Satan. I cannot always apprehend Christ as the Scriptures portray Him. Sometimes the devil distorts Christ to my vision. But thanks be to God, who keeps us in His Word, in faith, and in prayer.

GALATIANS 4

1–2.

The Apostle had apparently finished his discourse on justification when this illustra-

tion of the youthful heir occurred to him. He throws it in for good measure. He knows that plain people are sooner impressed by an apt illustration than by learned discussion.

"I want to give you another illustration from everyday life," he writes to the Galatians. "As long as an heir is under age he is treated very much like a servant. He is not permitted to order his own affairs. He is kept under constant surveillance. Such discipline is good for him, otherwise he would waste his inheritance in no time. This discipline, however, is not to last forever. It is to last only until 'the time appointed of the father.'"

3. Even so we, when we were children, were in bondage under the elements of the world.

As children of the Law we were treated like servants and prisoners. We were oppressed and condemned by the Law. But the tyranny of the Law is not to last forever. It is to last only until "the time appointed of the father," until Christ came and redeemed us.

3. Under the elements of the world.

By the elements of the world the Apostle does not understand the physical elements, as some have thought. In calling the Law "the elements of the world" Paul means to say that the Law is something material, mundane, earthly. It may restrain evil, but it does not deliver from sin. The Law does not justify; it does not bring a person to heaven. I do not obtain eternal life because I do not kill, commit adultery, steal, etc. Such mere outward decency does not constitute Christianity. The heathen observe the same restraints to avoid punishment or to secure the advantages of a good reputation. In the last analysis such restraint is simple hypocrisy. When the Law exercises its higher function it accuses and condemns the conscience. All these effects of the Law cannot be called divine or heavenly. These effects are elements of the world.

In calling the Law the elements of the world Paul refers to the whole Law, principally to the ceremonial law which dealt with external matters, as meat, drink, dress, places, times, feasts, cleansings, sacrifices, etc. These are mundane matters which cannot save the sinner. Ceremonial laws are like the statutes of

18 For if the inheritance be of the law, it is no more of promise: but God gave it to Abraham by promise.

19 Wherefore then serveth the law? It was added because of transgressions, till the seed should come to whom the promise was made; and it was ordained by angels in the hand of a mediator.

20 Now a mediator is not a mediator of one, but God is one.

21 Is the law then against the promises of God? God forbid: for if there had been a law given which could have given life, verily righteousness should have been by the law.

22 But the scripture hath concluded all under sin, that the promise by faith of Jesus Christ might be given to them that believe.

23 But before faith came, we were kept under the law, shut up unto the faith which should afterwards be revealed.

24 Wherefore the law was our schoolmaster to bring us unto Christ, that we might be justified by faith.

25 But after that faith is come, we are no longer under a schoolmaster.

26 For ye are all the children of God by faith in Christ Jesus.

27 For as many of you as have been baptized into Christ have put on Christ.

28 There is neither Jew nor Greek, there is neither bond nor free, there is neither male nor female: for ye are all one in Christ Jesus.

29 And if ye be Christ's, then are ye Abraham's seed, and heirs according to the promise.

GALATIANS 4

1 Now I say, That the heir, as long as he is a child, differeth nothing from a servant, though he be lord of all;

2 But is under tutors and governors until the time appointed of the father.

3 Even so we, when we were children, were in bondage under the elements of the world:

4 But when the fullness of the time was come, God sent forth his Son, made of a woman, made under the law,

5 To redeem them that were under the law, that we might receive the adoption of sons.

6 And because ye are sons, God hath

them, was the clearness of his doctrine, that it was not naked doctrine, but the express, living image of Christ. They had known Christ in such a manner, that they might be almost said to have seen him.

13. Christ hath redeemed us

The apostle had made all who are under the law subject to the curse; from which arose this great difficulty, that the Jews could not free themselves from the curse of the law. Having stated this difficulty, he meets it, by shewing that Christ hath made us free, which still farther aids his purpose. If we are saved, because we have been freed from the curse of the law, then righteousness is not by the law. He next points out the manner in which we are made free.

It is written, Cursed is every one that hangeth on a tree

Now, Christ hung upon the cross, therefore he fell under that curse. But it is certain that he did not suffer that punishment on his own account. It follows, therefore, either that he was crucified in vain, or that our curse was laid upon him, in order that we might be delivered from it. Now, he does not say that Christ was cursed, but, which is still more, that he was a curse – intimating, that the curse "of all men was laid upon him" (Isaiah 53: 6). If any man think this language harsh, let him be ashamed of the cross of Christ, in the confession of which we glory. It was not unknown to God what death his own Son would die, when he pronounced the law, "He that is hanged is accursed of God" (Deuteronomy 21: 23).

But how does it happen, it will be asked, that a beloved Son is cursed by his Father? We reply, there are two things which must be considered, not only in the person of Christ, but even in his human nature. The one is, that he was the unspotted Lamb of God, full of blessing and of grace; the other is, that he placed himself in our room, and thus became a sinner, and subject to the curse, not in himself indeed, but in us, yet in such a manner, that it became necessary for him to occupy our place. He could not cease to be the object of his Father's love, and yet he endured his wrath. For how could he reconcile the Father to us, if he had incurred his hatred and displeasure? We conclude, that he "did always those things that pleased" (John 8: 29) his Father. Again, how would he have freed us from the wrath of God, if he had not transferred it from us to himself? Thus, "he was wounded for our transgressions" (Isaiah 53: 5), and had to deal with God as an angry judge. This is the foolishness of the cross (1 Corinthians 1: 18), and the admiration of angels (1 Peter 1: 12), which not only exceeds, but swallows up, all the wisdom of the world.

governments dealing with purely civil matters, as commerce, inheritance, etc. As for the pope's church laws forbidding marriage and meats, Paul calls them elsewhere the doctrines of devils. You would not call such laws elements of heaven.

The Law of Moses deals with mundane matters. It holds the mirror to the evil which is in the world. By revealing the evil that is in us it creates a longing in the heart for the better things of God. The Law forces us into the arms of Christ, "who is the end of the law for righteousness to every one that believeth." (Romans 1: 4.) Christ relieves the conscience of the Law. In so far as the Law impels us to Christ it renders excellent service.

I do not mean to give the impression that the Law should be despised. Neither does Paul intend to leave that impression. The Law ought to be honored. But when it is a matter of justification before God, Paul had to speak disparagingly of the Law, because the Law has nothing to do with justification. If it thrusts its nose into the business of justification we must talk harshly to the Law to keep it in its place. The conscience ought not to be on speaking terms with the Law. The conscience ought to know only Christ. To say this is easy, but in times of trial, when the conscience writhes in the presence of God, it is not so easy to do. As such times we are to believe in Christ as if there were no Law or sin anywhere, but only Christ. We ought to say to the Law: "Mister Law, I do not get you. You stutter so much. I don't think that you have anything to say to me."

When it is not a question of salvation or justification with us, we are to think highly of the Law and call it "holy, just, and good." (Romans 7: 12) The Law is of no comfort to a stricken conscience. Therefore it should not be allowed to rule in our conscience, particularly in view of the fact that Christ paid so great a price to deliver the conscience from the tyranny of the Law. Let us understand that the Law and Christ are impossible bedfellows. The Law must leave the bed of the conscience, which is so narrow that it cannot hold two, as Isaiah says, chapter 28, verse 20.

Only Paul among the apostles calls the Law "the elements of the world, weak and beggarly elements, the strength of sin, the letter that killeth," etc. The other apostles do not speak so slightingly of the Law. Those who want to be first-class scholars in the school of Christ want to pick up the language of Paul. Christ called him a chosen vessel and equipped with a facility of expression far above that of the other apostles, that he as the chosen vessel should establish the doctrine of justification in clear-cut words.

4–5. But when the fullness of the time was come, God sent forth his Son, made of a woman, made under the law, to redeem them that were under the law.

"The fullness of the time" means when the time of the Law was fulfilled and Christ was revealed. Note how Paul explains Christ. "Christ," says he, "is the Son of God and the son of a woman. He submitted Himself under the Law to redeem us who were under the Law." In these words the Apostle explains the person and office of Christ. His person is divine and human. "God sent forth His Son, made of a woman." Christ therefore is true God and true man. Christ's office the Apostle describes in the words: "Made under the law, to redeem them that were under the law."

Paul calls the Virgin Mary a woman. This has been frequently deplored even by some of the ancient fathers who felt that Paul should have written "virgin" instead of woman. But Paul is now treating of faith and Christian righteousness, of the person and office of Christ, not of the virginity of Mary. The inestimable mercy of God is sufficiently set forth by the fact that His Son was born of a woman. The more general term "woman" indicates that Christ was born a true man. Paul does not say that Christ was born of man and woman, but only of woman. That he has a virgin in mind is obvious.

This passage furthermore declares that Christ's purpose in coming was the abolition of the Law, not with the intention of laying down new laws, but "to redeem them that were under the law." Christ himself declared: "I judge no man." (John 8: 15.) Again, "I came not to judge the world, but to save the world." (John 12: 47.) In other words: "I came not to

sent forth the Spirit of his Son into your hearts, crying, Abba, Father.

7 Wherefore thou art no more a servant, but a son; and if a son, then an heir of God through Christ.

8 Howbeit then, when ye knew not God, ye did service unto them which by nature are no gods.

9 But now, after that ye have known God, or rather are known of God, how turn ye again to the weak and beggarly elements, whereunto ye desire again to be in bondage?

10 Ye observe days, and months, and times, and years.

11 I am afraid of you, lest I have bestowed upon you labour in vain.

12 Brethren, I beseech you, be as I am; for I am as ye are: ye have not injured me at all.

13 Ye know how through infirmity of the flesh I preached the gospel unto you at the first.

14 And my temptation which was in my flesh ye despised not, nor rejected; but received me as an angel of God, even as Christ Jesus.

15 Where is then the blessedness ye spake of? for I bear you record, that, if it had been possible, ye would have plucked out your own eyes, and have given them to me.

16 Am I therefore become your enemy, because I tell you the truth?

17 They zealously affect you, but not well; yea, they would exclude you, that ye might affect them.

18 But it is good to be zealously affected always in a good thing, and not only when I am present with you.

19 My little children, of whom I travail in birth again until Christ be formed in you,

20 I desire to be present with you now, and to change my voice; for I stand in doubt of you.

21 Tell me, ye that desire to be under the law, do ye not hear the law?

22 For it is written, that Abraham had two sons, the one by a bondmaid, the other by a freewoman.

23 But he who was of the bondwoman was born after the flesh; but he of the freewoman was by promise.

24 Which things are an allegory: for these are the two covenants; the one from the mount Sinai, which gendereth to

GALATIANS 4

1. Now I say

Whoever made the division into chapters has improperly separated this paragraph from the preceding, as it is nothing else than the concluding section, in which Paul explains and illustrates the difference that exists between us and the ancient people. He does so by introducing a third comparison, drawn from the relation which a person under age bears to his tutor. The young man, though he is free, though he is lord of all his father's family, still resembles a slave; for he is under the government of tutors. But the period of guardianship lasts only "until the time appointed by the father" after which he enjoys his freedom. In this respect the fathers under the Old Testament, being the sons of God, were free; but they were not in possession of freedom, while the law held the place of their tutor, and kept them under its yoke. That slavery of the law lasted as long as it pleased God, who put an end to it at the coming of Christ. Lawyers enumerate various methods by which the tutelage or guardianship is brought to a close; but of all these methods, the only one adapted to this comparison is that which Paul has selected, "the appointment of the father."

Let us now examine the separate clauses. Some apply the comparison in a different manner to the case of any man whatever, whereas Paul is speaking of two nations. What they say, I acknowledge, is true; but it has nothing to do with the present passage. The elect, though they are the children of God from the womb, yet, until by faith they come to the possession of freedom, remain like slaves under the law; but, from the time that they have known Christ, they no longer require this kind of tutelage. Granting all this, I deny that Paul here treats of individuals, or draws a distinction between the time of unbelief and the calling by faith. The matters in dispute were these. Since the church of God is one, how comes it that our condition is different from that of the Israelites? Since we are free by faith, how comes it that they, who had faith in common with us, were not partakers with us of the same freedom? Since we are all equally the children of God, how comes it that we at this day are exempt from a yoke which they were forced to bear? On these points the controversy turned, and not on the manner in which the law reigns over each of us before we are freed by faith from its slavery. Let this point be first of all settled, that Paul here compares the Israelitish church, which existed under the Old Testament, with the Christian church, that thus we may perceive in what points we agree and in what we differ. This comparison furnishes most abundant and most profitable instruction.

First, we learn from it that our hope at the present day, and that of the fathers under the Old Testament, have been

bring more laws, or to judge men according to the existing Law. I have a higher and better office. I came to judge and to condemn the Law, so that it may no more judge and condemn the world."

GALATIANS 5

1. Stand fast therefore in the liberty wherewith Christ hath made us free.

"Be steadfast, not careless. Lie not down and sleep, but stand up. Be watchful. Hold fast the liberty wherewith Christ hath made you free." Those who loll cannot keep this liberty. Satan hates the light of the Gospel. When it begins to shine a little he fights against it with might and main.

What liberty does Paul mean? Not civil liberty (for which we have the government to thank), but the liberty which Christ has procured for us.

At one time the emperor was compelled to grant to the bishop of Rome certain immunities and privileges. This is civil liberty. That liberty exempts the clergy from certain public charges. Then there is also another kind of "liberty," when people obey neither the laws of God nor the laws of men, but do as they please. This carnal liberty the people want in our day. We are not now speaking of this liberty. Neither are we speaking of civil liberty.

Paul is speaking of a far better liberty, the liberty "wherewith Christ hath made us free," not from material bonds, not from the Babylonian captivity, not from the tyranny of the Turks, but from the eternal wrath of God.

Where is this liberty? In the conscience.

Our conscience is free and quiet because it no longer has to fear the wrath of God. This is real liberty, compared with which every other kind of liberty is not worth mentioning. Who can adequately express the boon that comes to a person when he has the heart-assurance that God will nevermore be angry with him, but will forever be merciful to him for Christ's sake? This is indeed a marvelous liberty, to have the sovereign God for our Friend and Father who will defend, maintain, and save us in this life and in the life to come.

As an outgrowth of this liberty, we are at the same time free from the Law, sin, death, the power of the devil, hell, etc. Since the wrath of God has been assuaged by Christ no Law, sin, or death may now accuse and condemn us. These foes of ours will continue to frighten us, but not too much. The worth of our Christian liberty cannot be exaggerated.

Our conscience must he trained to fall back on the freedom purchased for us by Christ. Though the fears of the Law, the terrors of sin, the horror of death assail us occasionally, we know that these feelings shall not endure, because the prophet quotes God as saying: "In a little wrath I hid my face from thee for a moment: but with everlasting kindness will I have mercy on thee." (Is. 54: 8.)

We shall appreciate this liberty all the more when we bear in mind that it was Jesus Christ, the Son of God, who purchased it with His own blood. Hence, Christ's liberty is given us not by the Law, or for our own righteousness, but freely for Christ's sake. In the eighth chapter of the Gospel of St. John, Jesus declares: "If the Son shall make you free, ye shall be free indeed." He only stands between us and the evils which trouble and afflict us and which He has overcome for us.

Reason cannot properly evaluate this gift. Who can fully appreciate the blessing of the forgiveness of sins and of everlasting life? Our opponents claim that they also possess this liberty. But they do not. When they are put to the test all their self-confidence slips from them. What else can they expect when they trust in works and not in the Word of God?

Our liberty is founded on Christ Himself, who sits at the right hand of God and intercedes for us. Therefore our liberty is sure and valid as long as we believe in Christ. As long as we cling to Him with a steadfast faith we possess His priceless gifts. But if we are careless and indifferent we shall lose them. It is not without good reason that Paul urges us to watch and to stand fast. He knew that the devil delights in taking this liberty away from us.

1. And be not entangled again with the yoke of bondage.

Because reason prefers the righteousness of the Law to the righteousness of faith, Paul calls the Law a yoke, a yoke of bondage. Peter

bondage, which is Agar.

25 For this Agar is mount Sinai in Arabia, and answereth to Jerusalem which now is, and is in bondage with her children.

26 But Jerusalem which is above is free, which is the mother of us all.

27 For it is written, Rejoice, thou barren that bearest not; break forth and cry, thou that travailest not: for the desolate hath many more children than she which hath an husband.

28 Now we, brethren, as Isaac was, are the children of promise.

29 But as then he that was born after the flesh persecuted him that was born after the Spirit, even so it is now.

30 Nevertheless what saith the scripture? Cast out the bondwoman and her son: for the son of the bondwoman shall not be heir with the son of the freewoman.

31 So then, brethren, we are not children of the bondwoman, but of the free.

GALATIANS 5

1 Stand fast therefore in the liberty wherewith Christ hath made us free, and be not entangled again with the yoke of bondage.

2 Behold, I Paul say unto you, that if ye be circumcised, Christ shall profit you nothing.

3 For I testify again to every man that is circumcised, that he is a debtor to do the whole law.

4 Christ is become of no effect unto you, whosoever of you are justified by the law; ye are fallen from grace.

5 For we through the Spirit wait for the hope of righteousness by faith.

6 For in Jesus Christ neither circumcision availeth anything, nor uncircumcision; but faith which worketh by love.

7 Ye did run well; who did hinder you that ye should not obey the truth?

8 This persuasion cometh not of him that calleth you.

9 A little leaven leaveneth the whole lump.

10 I have confidence in you through the Lord, that ye will be none otherwise minded: but he that troubleth you shall bear his judgment, whosoever he be.

11 And I, brethren, if I yet preach circumcision, why do I yet suffer perse-

directed to the same inheritance; for they were partakers of the same adoption. According to the dreams of some fanatics, and of Servetus among others, the fathers were divinely elected for the sole purpose of prefiguring to us a people of God. Paul, on the other hand, contends that they were elected in order to be together with us the children of God, and particularly attests that to them, not less than to us, belonged the spiritual blessing promised to Abraham.

Secondly, we learn that, notwithstanding their outward slavery, their consciences were still free. The obligation to keep the law did not hinder Moses and Daniel, all the pious kings, priests, and prophets, and the whole company of believers, from being free in spirit. They bore the yoke of the law upon their shoulders, but with a free spirit they worshipped God. More particularly, having been instructed concerning the free pardon of sin, their consciences were delivered from the tyranny of sin and death. Hence we ought to conclude that they held the same doctrine, were joined with us in the true unity of faith, placed reliance on the one Mediator, called on God as their Father, and were led by the same Spirit. All this leads to the conclusion, that the difference between us and the ancient fathers lies in accidents, not in substance. In all the leading characters of the Testament or Covenant we agree: the ceremonies and form of government, in which we differ, are mere additions. Besides, that period was the infancy of the church; but now that Christ is come, the church has arrived at the estate of manhood.

The meaning of Paul's words is clear, but has he not some appearance of contradicting himself? In the Epistle to the Ephesians he exhorts us to make daily progress "till we come to a perfect man, to the measure of the stature of the fullness of Christ" (Ephesians 4: 13). In the first Epistle to the Corinthians he says (1 Corinthians 3: 2), "I have fed you with milk, and not with meat: for hitherto ye were not able to bear it, neither yet now are ye able;" and shortly after this he compares the Galatians to children. (Galatians 4: 19) In those passages, I reply, the apostle speaks of particular men, and of their faith as individuals; but here he speaks generally of two bodies without regard to persons. This reply will assist us in resolving a much greater difficulty. When we look at the matchless faith of Abraham, and the vast intelligence of the holy prophets, with what effrontery shall we dare to talk of such men as our inferiors?

GALATIANS 5

1. Stand fast therefore

After having told them that they are the children of the free woman, he now reminds them that they ought not lightly to despise a freedom so precious. And certainly it

MARTIN LUTHER

also calls it a yoke. "Why tempt ye God, to put a yoke upon the neck of the disciples which neither our fathers nor we were able to bear?" (Acts 15: 10.)

In this passage Paul again disparages the pernicious notion that the Law is able to make men righteous before God, a notion deeply rooted in man's reason. All mankind is so wrapped up in this idea that it is hard to drag it out of people. Paul compares those who seek to be justified by the Law to oxen that are hitched to the yoke. Like oxen that toil in the yoke all day, and in the evening are turned out to graze along the dusty road, and at last are marked for slaughter when they no longer can draw the burden, so those who seek to be justified by the Law are "entangled with the yoke of bondage," and when they have grown old and broken-down in the service of the Law they have earned for their perpetual reward God's wrath and everlasting torment.

We are not now treating of an unimportant matter. It is a matter that involves everlasting liberty or everlasting slavery. For as a liberation from God's wrath through the kind office of Christ is not a passing boon, but a permanent blessing, so also the yoke of the Law is not a temporary but an everlasting affliction.

Rightly are the doors of the Law called devil's martyrs. They take more pains to earn hell than the martyrs of Christ to obtain heaven. Theirs is a double misfortune. First they torture themselves on earth with self- inflicted penances and finally when they die they gain the reward of eternal damnation.

2. Behold, I Paul say unto you, that if ye be circumcised, Christ shall profit you nothing.
Paul is incensed at the thought of the tyranny of the Law. His antagonism to the Law is a personal matter with him. "Behold, I, Paul," he says, "I who have received the Gospel not from men, but by the revelation of Jesus Christ: I who have been commissioned from above to preach the Gospel to you: I Paul say to you, If you submit to circumcision Christ will profit you nothing." Paul emphatically declares that for the Galatians to be circumcised would mean for them to lose the benefits of Christ's suffering and death. This passage may well serve as a criterion for all the religions. To teach that besides faith in Christ other devices like works, or the observance of rules, traditions, or ceremonies are necessary for the attainment of righteousness and everlasting life, is to make Christ and His salvation of no benefit to anybody.

If one can earn the forgiveness of sins and everlasting life through one's own efforts to what purpose was Christ born? What was the purpose of His suffering and death, His resurrection, His victory over sin, death, and the devil, if men may overcome these evils by their own endeavor? Tongue cannot express, nor heart conceive what a terrible thing it is to make Christ worthless.

The person who is not moved by these considerations to leave the Law and the confidence in his own righteousness for the liberty in Christ, has a heart that is harder than stone and iron.

Paul does not condemn circumcision in itself. Circumcision is not injurious to the person who does not ascribe any particular importance to it. Neither are works injurious provided a person does not attach any saving value to them. The Apostle does not say that works are objectionable, but to build one's hopes for righteousness on works is disastrous, for that makes Christ good for nothing.

Let us bear this in mind when the devil accuses our conscience. When that dragon accuses us of having done no good at all, but only evil, say to him: "You trouble me with the remembrance of my past sins; you remind me that I have done no good. But this does not bother me, because if I were to trust in my own good deeds, or despair because I have done no good deeds, Christ would profit me neither way. I am not going to make him unprofitable to me. This I would do, if I should presume to purchase for myself the favor of God and everlasting life by my good deeds, or if I should despair of my salvation because of my sins."

GALATIANS 6

1. Brethren, if a man be overtaken in a fault ye which are spiritual, restore such an one in the spirit of meekness.
If we carefully weigh the words of the Apostle

cution? then is the offence of the cross ceased.

12 I would they were even cut off which trouble you.

13 For, brethren, ye have been called unto liberty; only use not liberty for an occasion to the flesh, but by love serve one another.

14 For all the law is fulfilled in one word, even in this; Thou shalt love thy neighbour as thyself.

15 But if ye bite and devour one another, take heed that ye be not consumed one of another.

16 This I say then, Walk in the Spirit, and ye shall not fulfill the lust of the flesh.

17 For the flesh lusteth against the Spirit, and the Spirit against the flesh: and these are contrary the one to the other: so that ye cannot do the things that ye would.

18 But if ye be led of the Spirit, ye are not under the law.

19 Now the works of the flesh are manifest, which are these; Adultery, fornication, uncleanness, lasciviousness,

20 Idolatry, witchcraft, hatred, variance, emulations, wrath, strife, seditions, heresies,

21 Envyings, murders, drunkenness, revelings, and such like: of the which I tell you before, as I have also told you in time past, that they which do such things shall not inherit the kingdom of God.

22 But the fruit of the Spirit is love, joy, peace, longsuffering, gentleness, goodness, faith,

23 Meekness, temperance: against such there is no law.

24 And they that are Christ's have crucified the flesh with the affections and lusts.

25 If we live in the Spirit, let us also walk in the Spirit.

26 Let us not be desirous of vain glory, provoking one another, envying one another.

GALATIANS 6

1 Brethren, if a man be overtaken in a fault, ye which are spiritual, restore such an one in the spirit of meekness; considering thyself, lest thou also be tempted.

2 Bear ye one another's burdens, and so fulfil the law of Christ.

is an invaluable blessing, in defense of which it is our duty to fight, even to death; since not only the highest temporal considerations, but our eternal interests also, animate us to the contest. Many persons, having never viewed the subject in this light, charge us with excessive zeal, when they see us so warmly and earnestly contending for freedom of faith as to outward matters, in opposition to the tyranny of the Pope. Under this cloak, our adversaries raise a prejudice against us among ignorant people, as if the whole object of our pursuit were licentiousness, which is the relaxation of all discipline. But wise and skillful persons are aware that this is one of the most important doctrines connected with salvation. This is not a question whether you shall eat this or that food – whether you shall observe or neglect a particular day (which is the foolish notion entertained by many, and the slander uttered by some), but what is your positive duty before God, what is necessary to salvation, and what cannot be omitted without sin. In short, the controversy relates to the liberty of conscience, when placed before the tribunal of God.

The *liberty* of which Paul speaks is exemption from the ceremonies of the law, the observance of which was demanded by the false apostles as necessary. But let the reader, at the same time, remember, that such liberty is only a part of that which Christ has procured for us: for how small a matter would it be, if he had only freed us from ceremonies? This is but a stream, which must be traced to a higher source. It is because "Christ was made a curse, that he might redeem us from the curse of the law" (Galatians 3: 13); because he has revolted the power of the law" so far as it held us liable to the judgment of God under the penalty of eternal death; because, in a word, he has rescued us from the tyranny of sin, Satan, and death. Thus, under one department is included the whole class; but on this subject we shall speak more fully on the Epistle to the Colossians.

This *liberty* was procured for us by Christ on the cross: the fruit and possession of it are bestowed upon us through the Gospel. Well does Paul, then, warn the Galatians, *not to be entangled again with the yoke of bondage* – that is, not to allow a snare to be laid for their consciences. For if men lay upon our shoulders an unjust burden, it may be borne; but if they endeavor to bring our consciences into bondage, we must resist valiantly, even to death. If men be permitted to bind our consciences, we shall be deprived of an invaluable blessing, and an insult will be, at the same time, offered to Christ, the Author of our freedom. But what is the force of the word *again*, in the exhortation, "and be not entangled again with the yoke of bondage?" for the Galatians had never lived under the law. It simply means that they were not to be entangled, as if they had not been redeemed by the grace of Christ. Although the law was given to Jews, not

we perceive that he does not speak of doctrinal faults and errors, but of much lesser faults by which a person is overtaken through the weakness of his flesh. This explains why the Apostle chooses the softer term "fault." To minimize the offense still more, as if he meant to excuse it altogether and to take the whole blame away from the person who has committed the fault, he speaks of him as having been "overtaken," seduced by the devil and of the flesh. As if he meant to say, "What is more human than for a human being to fall, to be deceived and to err?" This comforting sentence at one time saved my life. Because Satan always assails both the purity of doctrine which he endeavors to take away by schisms and the purity of life which he spoils with his continual temptations to sin, Paul explains how the fallen should be treated. Those who are strong are to raise up the fallen in the spirit of meekness.

This ought to be borne in mind particularly by the ministers of the Word in order that they may not forget the parental attitude which Paul here requires of those who have the keeping of souls. Pastors and ministers must, of course, rebuke the fallen, but when they see that the fallen are sorry they are to comfort them by excusing the fault as well as they can. As unyielding as the Holy Spirit is in the matter of maintaining and defending the doctrine of faith, so mild and merciful is He toward men for their sins as long as sinners repent.

14. By whom the world is crucified unto me, and I unto the world.

"The world is crucified unto me," means that I condemn the world. "I am crucified unto the world," means that the world in turn condemns me. I detest the doctrine, the self-righteousness, and the works of the world. The world in turn detests my doctrine and condemns me as a revolutionary heretic. Thus the world is crucified unto us and we unto the world.

The monks imagined the world was crucified unto them when they entered the monastery. Not the world, but Christ, is crucified in the monasteries.

In this verse Paul expresses his hatred of the world. The hatred was mutual. As Paul, so we are to despise the world and the devil.

With Christ on our side we can defy him and say: "Satan, the more you hurt me, the more I oppose you."

15. For in Christ Jesus neither circumcision availeth anything, nor uncircumcision, but a new creature.

Since circumcision and uncircumcision are contrary matters we would expect the Apostle to say that one or the other might accomplish some good. But he denies that either of them do any good. Both are of no value because in Christ Jesus neither circumcision nor uncircumcision avail anything.

Reason fails to understand this, "for the natural man receiveth not the things of the Spirit of God." (I Cor. 2:14.) It therefore seeks righteousness in externals. However, we learn from the Word of God that there is nothing under the sun that can make us righteous before God and a new creature except Christ Jesus.

A new creature is one in whom the image of God has been renewed. Such a creature cannot be brought into life by good works, but by Christ alone. Good works may improve the outward appearance, but they cannot produce a new creature. A new creature is the work of the Holy Ghost, who imbues our hearts with faith, love, and other Christian virtues, grants us the strength to subdue the flesh and to reject the righteousness of the world.

16. And as many as walk according to this rule, peace be on them, and mercy.

This is the rule by which we ought to live, "that ye put on the new man, which after God is created in righteousness and true holiness." (Eph. 4:24.) Those who walk after this rule enjoy the favor of God, the forgiveness of their sins, and peace of conscience. Should they ever be overtaken by any sin, the mercy of God supports them.

17. From henceforth let no man trouble me.

The Apostle speaks these words with a certain amount of indignation. "I have preached the Gospel to you in conformity with the revelation which I received from Jesus Christ. If you do not care for it, very well. Trouble me no more. Trouble me no more."

17. For I bear in my body the marks of the Lord Jesus.

3 For if a man think himself to be something, when he is nothing, he deceiveth himself.

4 But let every man prove his own work, and then shall he have rejoicing in himself alone, and not in another.

5 For every man shall bear his own burden.

6 Let him that is taught in the word communicate unto him that teacheth in all good things.

7 Be not deceived; God is not mocked: for whatsoever a man soweth, that shall he also reap.

8 For he that soweth to his flesh shall of the flesh reap corruption; but he that soweth to the Spirit shall of the Spirit reap life everlasting.

9 And let us not be weary in well doing: for in due season we shall reap, if we faint not.

10 As we have therefore opportunity, let us do good unto all men, especially unto them who are of the household of faith.

11 Ye see how large a letter I have written unto you with mine own hand.

12 As many as desire to make a fair shew in the flesh, they constrain you to be circumcised; only lest they should suffer persecution for the cross of Christ.

13 For neither they themselves who are circumcised keep the law; but desire to have you circumcised, that they may glory in your flesh.

14 But God forbid that I should glory, save in the cross of our Lord Jesus Christ, by whom the world is crucified unto me, and I unto the world.

15 For in Christ Jesus neither circumcision availeth anything, nor uncircumcision, but a new creature.

16 And as many as walk according to this rule, peace be on them, and mercy, and upon the Israel of God.

17 From henceforth let no man trouble me: for I bear in my body the marks of the Lord Jesus.

18 Brethren, the grace of our Lord Jesus Christ be with your spirit. Amen.

to Gentiles, yet, apart from Christ, neither the one nor the other enjoys any freedom, but absolute bondage.

GALATIANS 6

1. Brethren, if a man be overtaken in any fault

Ambition is a serious and alarming evil. But hardly less injury is frequently done by unseasonable and excessive severity, which, under the plausible name of zeal, springs in many instances from pride, and from dislike and contempt of the brethren. Most men seize on the faults of brethren as an occasion of insulting them, and of using reproachful and cruel language. Were the pleasure they take in upbraiding equalled by their desire to produce amendment, they would act in a different manner. Reproof, and often sharp and severe reproof, must be administered to offenders. But while we must not shrink from a faithful testimony against sin, neither must we omit to mix oil with the vinegar.

We are here taught to correct the faults of brethren in a mild manner, and to consider no rebukes as partaking a religious and Christian character which do not breathe the spirit of meekness. To gain this object, he explains the design of pious reproofs, which is, to restore him who is fallen, to place him in his former condition. That design will never be accomplished by violence, or by a disposition to accuse, or by fierceness of manner or language; and consequently, we must display a gentle and meek spirit, if we intend to heal our brother. And lest any man should satisfy himself with assuming the outward form, he demands the spirit of meekness; for no man is prepared for chastising a brother till he has succeeded in acquiring a gentle spirit.

Another argument for gentleness in correcting brethren is contained in the expression, "if a man be *overtaken*." If he has been carried away through want of consideration, or through the cunning arts of a deceiver, it would be cruel to treat such a man with harshness. Now, we know that the devil is always lying in wait, and has a thousand ways of leading us astray. When we perceive a brother to have transgressed, let us consider that he has fallen into the snares of Satan; let us be moved with compassion, and prepare our minds to exercise forgiveness. But offenses and falls of this description must undoubtedly be distinguished from deep seated crimes, accompanied by deliberate and obstinate disregard of the authority of God. Such a display of wicked and perverse disobedience to God must be visited with greater severity, for what advantage would be gained by gentle treatment? The particle *if also (ea n kai)*, implies that not only the weak who have been tempted, but those who have yielded to temptation, shall receive forbearance.

"The marks on my body indicate whose servant I am. If I was anxious to please men, if I approved of circumcision and good works as factors in our salvation, if I would take delight in your flesh as the false apostles do, I would not have these marks on my body. But because I am the servant of Jesus Christ and publicly declare that no person can obtain the salvation of his soul outside of Christ, I must bear the badge of my Lord. These marks were given to me against my will as decorations from the devil and for no other merit but that I made known Jesus."

Of the marks of suffering which he bore in his body the Apostle makes frequent mention in his epistles. "I think," he says, "that God hath set forth us the apostles last, as it were appointed to death: for we are made a spectacle unto the world, and to angels, and to men." (I Cor. 4:9.) Again, "Unto this present hour we both hunger, and thirst, and are naked, and are buffeted, and have no certain dwellingplace; And labour, working with our hands: being reviled, we bless; being persecuted, we suffer it; being defamed, we intreat: we are made as the filth of the world, and are the offscouring of all things unto this day." (I Cor. 4:11–13.)

18. Brethren, the grace of our Lord Jesus Christ be with your spirit. Amen.

This is the Apostle's farewell. He ends his Epistle as he began it by wishing the Galatians the grace of God. We can hear him say: "I have presented Christ to you, I have pleaded with you, I have reproved you, I have overlooked nothing that I thought might be of benefit to you. All I can do now is to pray that our Lord Jesus Christ would bless my Epistle and grant you the guidance of the Holy Ghost."

The Lord Jesus Christ, our Savior, who gave me the strength and the grace to explain this Epistle and granted you the grace to hear it, preserve and strengthen us in faith unto the day of our redemption. To Him, the Father and the Son and the Holy Spirit, be glory, world without end. Amen.

Ephesians

Introduction by John Calvin

EPHESUS, which is familiarly known in history under a great variety of names, was a very celebrated city of Lesser Asia. The remarkable events connected with the work of God in "forming there a people for himself" (Isaiah 43: 21), through the labors of Paul, together with the commencement and progress of that church, are related by Luke in the Acts of the Apostles. At present, I shall do nothing more than glance at what bears directly on the argument of the Epistle. The Ephesians had been instructed by Paul in the pure doctrine of the gospel. At a later period, while he was a prisoner at Rome, and perceiving that they needed confirmation, he wrote to them, on that account, the present Epistle.

The first three chapters are chiefly occupied with commending the grace of God. Immediately after the salutation in the commencement of the first chapter, he treats of God's free election. This affords him an opportunity of stating that they were now called into the kingdom of God, because they had been appointed to life before they were born. And here occurs a striking display of God's wonderful mercy, when the salvation of men is traced to its true and native source, the free act of adoption. But as the minds of men are ill fitted to receive so sublime a mystery, he betakes himself to prayer, that God would enlighten the Ephesians in the full knowledge of Christ.

In the second chapter, by drawing two comparisons, he places in a strong light the riches of divine grace. 1. He reminds them how wretched they were before they were called to Christ. We never become duly sensible of our obligations to Christ, nor estimate aright his kindness towards us, till we have been led to view, on the other side, the unhappy condition in which we formerly were "without Christ" (Ephesians 2: 12). 2. The Gentiles were "aliens" from the promises of eternal life, which God had been pleased to bestow on the Jews alone.

In the third chapter, he declares that he had been appointed to be, in a peculiar manner, the Apostle of the Gentiles, because, for a long period, they were "strangers and foreigners" (Ephesians 2: 19), but are now included among the people of God. As this was an unusual event, and as its very novelty produced uneasiness in many minds, he calls it a "mystery which in other ages was not made known to the sons of men" (Ephesians 3: 4,5), but "the dispensation" (Ephesians 3: 2) of which had been intrusted to himself.

Toward the close of the chapter, he again prays that God would grant to the Ephesians such an intimate knowledge of Christ, that they would have no desire to know anything else. His object in doing so is not merely to lead them to gratitude to God for so many favors, and to the expression of that gratitude by entire devotion to his service, but still more to remove all doubt about his own calling. Paul was probably afraid that the false apostles would shake their faith by insinuating that they had been only half-instructed. They had been Gentiles, and, when they embraced pure Christianity, had been told nothing about ceremonies or circumcision. But all who enjoined on Christians the observance of the law were loud in the avowal, that those who have not been introduced into the church of God by circumcision must be held as profane persons. This was their ordinary song, that no man who is not circumcised is entitled to be reckoned among the people of God, and that all the rites prescribed by Moses ought to be observed. Accordingly, they brought it as a charge against Paul, that he exhibited Christ as equally the Savior of Gentiles and of Jews. They asserted that his apostleship was a profanation of the heavenly doctrine, because it threw open to wicked men, without discrimination, a share in the covenant of grace.

That the Ephesians, when assailed by these calumnies, might not give way, he resolved to meet them. While he argues so earnestly that they were called to the gospel because they had been chosen before the creation of the world, he charges them, on the other hand, not to imagine that the gospel had been accidentally brought to them by the will of men, or that it flew to them by chance; for the preaching of Christ among them was nothing else than the announcement of that eternal decree. While he lays before them the unhappy condition of their former life, he at the same time reminds them that the singular and astonishing mercy of God appeared in rescuing them from so

deep a gulf. While he sets before their eyes his own commission as the apostle of the Gentiles, he confirms them in the faith which they had once received, because they had been divinely admitted into the communion of the church. And yet each of the sentences to which we have now referred must be viewed as an exhortation fitted to excite the Ephesians to gratitude.

In the fourth chapter, he describes the manner in which the Lord governs and protects his church, which is, by the gospel preached by men. Hence it follows, that in no other way can its integrity be preserved, and that the object at which it aims is true perfection. The apostle's design is, to commend to the Ephesians the ministry by which God reigns amongst us. He afterwards details the fruits of this preaching – a holy life and all the duties of piety. Nor does he satisfy himself with describing in general terms how Christians ought to live, but lays down particular exhortations adapted to the various relations of society.

The commentaries on Ephesians are by John Calvin and John Gill.

EPHESIANS 1

1 Paul, an apostle of Jesus Christ by the will of God, to the saints which are at Ephesus, and to the faithful in Christ Jesus:

2 Grace be to you, and peace, from God our Father, and from the Lord Jesus Christ.

3 Blessed be the God and Father of our Lord Jesus Christ, who hath blessed us with all spiritual blessings in heavenly places in Christ:

4 According as he hath chosen us in him before the foundation of the world, that we should be holy and without blame before him in love:

5 Having predestinated us unto the adoption of children by Jesus Christ to himself, according to the good pleasure of his will,

6 To the praise of the glory of his grace, wherein he hath made us accepted in the beloved.

7 In whom we have redemption through his blood, the forgiveness of sins, according to the riches of his grace;

8 Wherein he hath abounded toward us in all wisdom and prudence;

9 Having made known unto us the mystery of his will, according to his good pleasure which he hath purposed in himself:

10 That in the dispensation of the fullness of times he might gather together in one all things in Christ, both which are in heaven, and which are on earth; even in him:

11 In whom also we have obtained an inheritance, being predestinated according to the purpose of him who worketh all things after the counsel of his own will:

12 That we should be to the praise of his glory, who first trusted in Christ.

13 In whom ye also trusted, after that ye heard the word of truth, the gospel of your salvation: in whom also after that ye believed, ye were sealed with that holy Spirit of promise,

14 Which is the earnest of our inheritance until the redemption of the purchased possession, unto the praise of his glory.

15 Wherefore I also, after I heard of your faith in the Lord Jesus, and love unto all the saints,

16 Cease not to give thanks for you,

EPHESIANS 1

1. Paul, an apostle. As the same form of salutation, or at least very little varied, is found in all the Epistles, it would be superfluous to repeat here the observations which we have formerly made. He calls himself "an apostle of Jesus Christ;" for all to whom has been given the ministry of reconciliation are his ambassadors. The word Apostle, indeed, carries something more; for it is not every minister of the gospel, as we shall afterwards see (Ephesians 4: 11), that can be called an apostle. But this subject has been explained more fully in my remarks on the Epistle to the Galatians.

He adds, *by the will of God*; for "no man ought to take this honor unto himself" (Hebrews 5: 4), but every man ought to wait for the calling of God, which alone makes lawful ministers. He thus meets the jeers of wicked men by holding out the authority of God, and removes every occasion of inconsiderate strife.

To all the saints

He gives the name of saints to those whom he afterwards denominates *faithful in Christ Jesus*. No man, therefore, is a believer who is not also a saint; and, on the other hand, no man is a saint who is not a believer. Most of the Greek copies want the word all; but I was unwilling to strike it out, because it must, at all events, be understood.

3. Blessed be the God and Father of our Lord Jesus Christ

The lofty terms in which he extolls the grace of God toward the Ephesians, are intended to rouse their hearts to gratitude, to set them all on flame, to fill them even to overflowing with this thought. They who perceive in themselves discoveries of the Divine goodness, so full and absolutely perfect, and who make them the subject of earnest meditation, will never embrace new doctrines, by which the very grace which they feel so powerfully in themselves is thrown into the shade. The design of the apostle, therefore, in asserting the riches of divine grace toward the Ephesians, was to protect them against having their faith shaken by the false apostles, as if their calling were doubtful, or salvation were to be sought in some other way. He shews, at the same time, that the full certainty of future happiness rests on the revelation of his love to us in Christ, which God makes in the gospel. But to confirm the matter more fully, he rises to the first cause, to the fountain – the eternal election of God, by which, ere we are born (Romans 9: 11), we are adopted as sons. This makes it evident that their salvation was accomplished, not by any accidental or unlooked-for occurrence, but by the eternal and unchangeable decree of God.

The word bless is here used in more than one sense, as referring to God, and as referring to men. I find in Scripture four different significations of this word. 1. We are said to

EPHESIANS 1

1. To the saints which are at Ephesus; of this place. The persons residing there, to whom the epistle is written, are described by their character, as **saints**; being separated by the grace of God the Father in eternal election; whose sins were expiated by the blood and sacrifice of Christ; and to whom he himself was made sanctification; and who were internally sanctified by the Spirit of God, and lived holy lives and conversations.

3. Blessed be the God and Father of our Lord Jesus Christ. God, the first person in the Trinity, is the God of Christ, as Christ is man and Mediator; he chose and appointed him to be the Mediator, and made a covenant with him as such; he formed and prepared an human nature for him, and anointed it with the Holy Ghost above measure, and supported it under all his trials and sufferings, and at last glorified it: and Christ, as man, prayed to him as his God, believed, hoped, and trusted in him as such, and loved him as in such a relation to him, and cheerfully obeyed his commands.

4. According as he hath chosen us in him. This choice cannot be understood of a national one, as Israel of old were chosen by the Lord; for the persons the apostle writes to were not a nation; nor does he address all the inhabitants of Ephesus, only the saints and faithful in Christ that resided there; nor are they all intended here, if any of them. However, not they only, since the apostle includes himself, and perhaps some others, who did not belong to that place, nor were of that country: nor does this choice regard them as a church; for though the saints at Ephesus were in a church state, yet the apostle does not write to them under that formal consideration, but as saints and faithful; nor are these persons said to be chosen to church privileges, but to grace and glory, to be holy and blameless: besides, from Ephesians 1: 3, the apostle seems to speak of himself, and some others, who first trusted in Christ, as distinct from the believers at Ephesus, Ephesians 1: 13, nor is this choice of persons to an office, for all that are here intended were not apostles, or pastors, or deacons: nor can it design the effectual calling, or the call of

persons in time by efficacious grace; because this was before the foundation of the world, as follows: but it intends an eternal election of particular persons to everlasting life and salvation; and which is the first blessing of grace, and the foundation one, upon which all the rest proceed, and according to which they are dispensed; for according to predestination are calling, justification, and glorification. The author of this choice is God, God the Father, who is distinguished from Christ, in whom this act is made; and it is according to his foreknowledge, and is an act of his grace, and is entirely sovereign.

5. Having predestinated us. Predestination, taken in a large sense, includes both election and reprobation, and even reaches to all affairs and occurrences in the world; to the persons, lives, and circumstances of men; to all mercies, temporal or spiritual; and to all afflictions, whether in love or in wrath: and indeed providence, or the dispensations of providence, are no other than the execution of divine predestination.

7. In whom we have redemption through his blood. Redemption supposes captivity and slavery, and is a deliverance out of it; God's elect by nature are in bondage to sin, Satan, and the law; through the grace of Christ, they are redeemed from all iniquity.

14. Which is the earnest of our inheritance. The incorruptible and never fading one in heaven, or the heavenly kingdom; this is the Father's gift, his bequest, and belongs only to children; it comes to them through the death of the testator, Christ, and is for ever; and of this the Spirit of God is the pledge and earnest.

16. Cease not to give thanks for you. On account of their faith and love; which were gifts of grace bestowed upon them, and not the produce of their own free will and power; and therefore thanks are given to God for them.

18. The eyes of your understanding being enlightened. By the Spirit of God already, to see the exceeding sinfulness of sin; the insufficiency of their own righteousness; the beauty,

making mention of you in my prayers;

17 That the God of our Lord Jesus Christ, the Father of glory, may give unto you the spirit of wisdom and revelation in the knowledge of him:

18 The eyes of your understanding being enlightened; that ye may know what is the hope of his calling, and what the riches of the glory of his inheritance in the saints,

19 And what is the exceeding greatness of his power to usward who believe, according to the working of his mighty power,

20 Which he wrought in Christ, when he raised him from the dead, and set him at his own right hand in the heavenly places,

21 Far above all principality, and power, and might, and dominion, and every name that is named, not only in this world, but also in that which is to come:

22 And hath put all things under his feet, and gave him to be the head over all things to the church,

23 Which is his body, the fullness of him that filleth all in all.

EPHESIANS 2

1 And you hath he quickened, who were dead in trespasses and sins;

2 Wherein in time past ye walked according to the course of this world, according to the prince of the power of the air, the spirit that now worketh in the children of disobedience:

3 Among whom also we all had our conversation in times past in the lusts of our flesh, fulfilling the desires of the flesh and of the mind; and were by nature the children of wrath, even as others.

4 But God, who is rich in mercy, for his great love wherewith he loved us,

5 Even when we were dead in sins, hath quickened us together with Christ, (by grace ye are saved;)

6 And hath raised us up together, and made us sit together in heavenly places in Christ Jesus:

7 That in the ages to come he might shew the exceeding riches of his grace in his kindness toward us through Christ Jesus.

8 For by grace are ye saved through faith; and that not of yourselves: it is the gift of God:

bless God when we offer praise to him for his goodness. 2. God is said to bless us, when he crowns our undertakings with success, and, in the exercise of his goodness, bestows upon us happiness and prosperity; and the reason is, that our enjoyments depend entirely upon his pleasure. Our attention is here called to the singular efficacy which dwells in the very word of God, and which Paul expresses in beautiful language. 3. Men bless each other by prayer. 4. The priest's blessing is not simply a prayer, but is likewise a testimony and pledge of the Divine blessing; for the priests received a commission to bless in the name of the Lord. Paul therefore blesses God, because he hath blessed us, that is, hath enriched us with all blessing and grace.

With all spiritual blessings

I have no objection to Chrysostom's remark, that the word spiritual conveys an implied contrast between the blessing of Moses and of Christ. The law had its blessings; but in Christ only is perfection found, because he gives us a perfect revelation of the kingdom of God, which leads us directly to heaven. When the body itself is presented to us, figures are no longer needed.

In heavenly

Whether we understand the meaning to be, in heavenly Places, or in heavenly Benefits, is of little consequence. All that was intended to be expressed is the superiority of that grace which we receive through Christ. The happiness which it bestows is not in this world, but in heaven and everlasting life. In the Christian religion, indeed, as we are elsewhere taught (1 Timothy 4: 8), is contained the "promise of the life that now is, and of that which is to come;" but its aim is spiritual happiness, for the kingdom of Christ is spiritual. A contrast is drawn between Christ and all the Jewish emblems, by which the blessing under the law was conveyed; for where Christ is, all those things are superfluous.

EPHESIANS 2

1. And you who were dead

This is an *epexergasia* of the former statements, that is, an exposition accompanied by an illustration. To bring home more effectually to the Ephesians the general doctrine of Divine grace, he reminds them of their former condition. This application consists of two parts. "Ye were formerly lost; but now God, by his grace, has rescued you from destruction." And here we must observe, that, in laboring to give an impressive view of both of these parts, the apostle makes a break in the style by (*huperbaton*) a transposition. There is some perplexity in the language; but, if we attend carefully to what the apostle says about those two parts, the meaning is clear. As to the first, he says that they **were dead**; and states, at the same time, the cause of the death

glory, fullness, and suitableness of Christ, as a Savior; the excellency, truth, and usefulness of the doctrines of the Gospel; in which their understandings were before dark, but now had light into them: wherefore these words are not to be considered as part of the apostle's petitions, but rather as what was taken for granted by him; and are to be put into a parenthesis.

20. Which he wrought in Christ, when he raised him from the dead. There are many articles of faith contained in this passage; as that Christ died, that he is raised from the dead, that he was raised from the dead by God the Father, and that his resurrection was by the power of God: the resurrection of any person is an instance of great power, but Christ's resurrection from the dead was an instance of peculiar and special power; for he was raised from the dead as a public person, representing all his people, for whom he became a surety; and he was raised again for their justification, and to great glory in himself, after he had been brought into a very low estate indeed: moreover, this passage in connection with the preceding suggests, that there is some proportion between the power put forth on Christ in raising him from the dead, and that which is exerted in the work of conversion and faith.

22. And hath put all things under his feet. These words are taken out of Psalm 8: 6. This headship of Christ is the gift of God; and it is an honorable gift to him, as Mediator; it is a glorifying of him, and a giving him in all things the pre-eminence; and it is a free grace gift to the church, and a very special, valuable, and excellent one, and of infinite benefit and advantage to it; and which is expressed in his being head "over all things" to it; to overrule all things for its good; to communicate all good things to it; and to perform all the good offices of an head for it.

23. Which is his body. That is, which church is the body of Christ; as an human body is but one, consisting of various members, united to each other, and set in an exact proportion and symmetry, and in a proper subservience to one another, and which must be neither more nor fewer than they are; so the church of Christ is but one general assembly, which con-sists of many persons, of different gifts and usefulness, and are all united together under one head, Christ, whose name they bear, and are made to drink of the same Spirit.

EPHESIANS 2

1. And you hath he quickened. The design of the apostle in this and some following verses, is to show the exceeding sinfulness of sin, and to set forth the sad estate and condition of man by nature, and to magnify the riches of the grace of God, and represent the exceeding greatness of his power in conversion.

4. But God, who is rich in mercy. Mercy is a perfection of the divine nature, and is essential to God; and may be considered with respect to the objects of it, either as general, extending to all men in a providential way; or as special, reaching only to some in a way of grace; for though mercy is his nature, yet the display and exertion of it towards any object, is the act of his will; and special mercy, with all the blessings and benefits of it, is only exhibited in Christ Jesus: and God is said to be "rich" in it, because he is free and liberal in dispensing it, and the effects of it; and that to a large number of persons, in great abundance and variety, by various ways, and in divers instances; as in the covenant of grace, in the mission of Christ, in redemption by him, in regeneration, in pardon of sin, and in eternal salvation; and yet it is inexhaustible and perpetual; and this sets forth the excellency and glory of it.

8. For by grace are ye saved. This is to be understood, not of temporal salvation, nor of preservation in Christ, nor of providential salvation in order to calling, and much less of being put in a way of salvation, or only in a salvable state; but of spiritual salvation, and that actual; for salvation was not only resolved upon, contrived and secured in the covenant of grace, for the persons here spoken to, but it was actually obtained and wrought out for them by Christ, and was actually applied unto them by the Spirit; and even as to the full enjoyment of it, they had it in faith and hope; and because of the certainty of it, they are said to be already saved; and besides, were

9 Not of works, lest any man should boast.

10 For we are his workmanship, created in Christ Jesus unto good works, which God hath before ordained that we should walk in them.

11 Wherefore remember, that ye being in time past Gentiles in the flesh, who are called Uncircumcision by that which is called the Circumcision in the flesh made by hands;

12 That at that time ye were without Christ, being aliens from the commonwealth of Israel, and strangers from the covenants of promise, having no hope, and without God in the world:

13 But now in Christ Jesus ye who sometimes were far off are made nigh by the blood of Christ.

14 For he is our peace, who hath made both one, and hath broken down the middle wall of partition between us;

15 Having abolished in his flesh the enmity, even the law of commandments contained in ordinances; for to make in himself of twain one new man, so making peace;

16 And that he might reconcile both unto God in one body by the cross, having slain the enmity thereby:

17 And came and preached peace to you which were afar off, and to them that were nigh.

18 For through him we both have access by one Spirit unto the Father.

19 Now therefore ye are no more strangers and foreigners, but fellowcitizens with the saints, and of the household of God;

20 And are built upon the foundation of the apostles and prophets, Jesus Christ himself being the chief corner stone;

21 In whom all the building fitly framed together groweth unto an holy temple in the Lord:

22 In whom ye also are builded together for an habitation of God through the Spirit.

EPHESIANS 3

1 For this cause I Paul, the prisoner of Jesus Christ for you Gentiles,

2 If ye have heard of the dispensation of the grace of God which is given me to youward:

3 How that by revelation he made

– trespasses and sins. He does not mean simply that they were in danger of death; but he declares that it was a real and present death under which they labored. As spiritual death is nothing else than the alienation of the soul from God, we are all born as dead men, and we live as dead men, until we are made partakers of the life of Christ – agreeably to the words of our Lord, "The hour is coming, and now is, when the dead shall hear the voice of the Son of God, and they that hear shall live" (John 5: 25).

We must never undervalue the grace of God and say that while we are out of Christ, we are half dead. For we are not at liberty to set aside the declarations of our Lord and of the Apostle Paul, that, while we remain in Adam, we are entirely devoid of life; and that regeneration is a new life of the soul, by which it rises from the dead. Some kind of life, I acknowledge, does remain in us, while we are still at a distance from Christ; for unbelief does not altogether destroy the outward senses, or the will, or the other faculties of the soul. But what has this to do with the kingdom of God? What has it to do with a happy life, so long as every sentiment of the mind, and every act of the will, is death? Let this, then, be held as a fixed principle, that the union of our soul with God is the true and only life; and that out of Christ we are altogether dead, because sin, the cause of death, reigns in us.

22. Through the Spirit

This is again repeated for two reasons: first, to remind them that all human exertions are of no avail without the operation of the Spirit; and secondly, to point out the superiority of the spiritual building to all Jewish and outward services.

EPHESIANS 3

7. Of which I was made a minister

Having declared the gospel to be the instrument employed in communicating grace to the Gentiles, he now adds, that he was made a minister of the Gospel; and thus applies to himself the general statements which had been made. But, to avoid claiming for himself more than is proper, he affirms that it is the gift of the grace of God, and that this gift was an exhibition of divine power. As if he had said, "Inquire not what I have deserved; for in the free exercise of kindness, the Lord made me an apostle of the Gentiles, not for any excellence of mine, but by his own grace. Inquire not what I formerly was; for it is the Lord's prerogative to 'exalt them of low degree'" (Luke 1: 52). To produce something great out of nothing, shews the effectual working of his power.

8. To me, who am the least

He labors to exhibit himself, and everything that belongs to him, in as humiliating a light as possible, in order that the

representatively possessed of it in Christ their head: those interested in this salvation, are not all mankind, but particular persons; and such who were by nature children of wrath, and sinners of the Gentiles; and it is a salvation from sin, Satan, the law, its curse and condemnation, and from eternal death, and wrath to come; and includes all the blessings of grace and glory; and is entirely owing to free grace: for by grace is not meant the Gospel, nor gifts of grace, nor grace infused; but the free favor of God, to which salvation in all its branches is ascribed; as election, redemption, justification, pardon, adoption, regeneration, and eternal glory.

9. Not of works. Of any kind, moral or ceremonial, before or after conversion, done without faith or in it, nor of these in any sense; works are neither the moving causes, nor the procuring causes, nor the helping causes, or conditions of salvation; the best works that are done by men, are not done of themselves, but by the grace of God, and therefore can never merit at his hand: and salvation is put upon such a foot, lest any man should boast; of his works before God, and unto men; wherefore he has denied works any place in justification and salvation, in order to exclude all boasting in man; and has fixed it in a way of grace, and has chosen and called poor sinful worthless creatures to enjoy it, that whoever glories, may glory in the Lord.

14. For he is our peace. The author of peace between Jew and Gentile: there was a great enmity of the Jew against the Gentile, and of the Gentile against the Jew; and chiefly on account of circumcision, the one being without it, and the other insisting on it, and branding one another with nicknames on account of it; but Christ has made peace between them by abrogating the ceremonial law, which was the occasion of the difference, and by sending the Gospel of peace to them both, by converting some of each, and by granting the like privileges to them all, as may be observed in the following verses: and Christ is the author of peace between God and his people; there is naturally in man an enmity to God; sin has separated chief friends; nor can man make his

peace with God; what he does, or can do, will not do it; and what will, he cannot do; Christ is the only fit and proper person for this work, being a middle person between both, and is only able to effect it, being God as well as man; and so could draw nigh to God, and treat with him about terms of peace, and agree to them, and perform them; and which he has brought about by his blood, his sufferings and death; and which is made on honorable terms, by a full satisfaction to the law and justice of God; and so is a lasting one, and attended with a train of blessings.

20. And are built upon the foundation of the apostles and prophets. The prophets of the Old Testament, and the apostles of the New, who agree in laying ministerially the one and only foundation, Jesus Christ; for not the persons of the apostles and prophets, nor their doctrines merely, are here meant; but Christ who is contained in them, and who is the foundation on which the church, and all true believers are built: he is the foundation of the covenant of grace, of all the blessings and promises of it, of faith and hope, of peace, joy, and comfort, of salvation and eternal happiness; on this foundation the saints are built by Father, Son, and Spirit, as the efficient causes, and by the ministers of the Gospel as instruments.

EPHESIANS 3

1. For this cause I Paul, the prisoner of Jesus Christ. Not actively, whom Christ had apprehended by his grace, and made a prisoner of hope; but passively, who was made a prisoner for Christ, on account of preaching Christ, and his Gospel: he was not a prisoner for any capital crime, as theft, murder, and therefore be was not ashamed of his bonds, but rather glories in them; and a prison has often been the portion of the best of men in this world: from hence we learn, that this epistle was written when the apostle was a prisoner at Rome; and the consideration of this his condition serves much to confirm the truths he had before delivered, seeing they were such as he could, and did suffer for; and which must engage the attention of the Ephesians to them, and

known unto me the mystery; (as I wrote afore in few words,

4 Whereby, when ye read, ye may understand my knowledge in the mystery of Christ)

5 Which in other ages was not made known unto the sons of men, as it is now revealed unto his holy apostles and prophets by the Spirit;

6 That the Gentiles should be fellow-heirs, and of the same body, and partakers of his promise in Christ by the gospel:

7 Whereof I was made a minister, according to the gift of the grace of God given unto me by the effectual working of his power.

8 Unto me, who am less than the least of all saints, is this grace given, that I should preach among the Gentiles the unsearchable riches of Christ;

9 And to make all men see what is the fellowship of the mystery, which from the beginning of the world hath been hid in God, who created all things by Jesus Christ:

10 To the intent that now unto the principalities and powers in heavenly places might be known by the church the manifold wisdom of God,

11 According to the eternal purpose which he purposed in Christ Jesus our Lord:

12 In whom we have boldness and access with confidence by the faith of him.

13 Wherefore I desire that ye faint not at my tribulations for you, which is your glory.

14 For this cause I bow my knees unto the Father of our Lord Jesus Christ,

15 Of whom the whole family in heaven and earth is named,

16 That he would grant you, according to the riches of his glory, to be strengthened with might by his Spirit in the inner man;

17 That Christ may dwell in your hearts by faith; that ye, being rooted and grounded in love,

18 May be able to comprehend with all saints what is the breadth, and length, and depth, and height;

19 And to know the love of Christ, which passeth knowledge, that ye might be filled with all the fullness of God.

20 Now unto him that is able to do exceeding abundantly above all that we ask or think, according to the power that

grace of God may be the more highly exalted. But this acknowledgment had the additional effect of anticipating the objections which his adversaries might bring against him. "Who is this man that God should have raised him above all his brethren? What superior excellence did he possess that he should be chosen in preference to all the others?" All such comparisons of personal worth are set aside by the confession, that he was the least of all the saints.

This is no hypocritical declaration. Most men are ready enough to make professions of feigned humility, while their minds are swelled with pride, and in words to acknowledge themselves inferior to every one else, while they wish to be regarded with the highest esteem, and think themselves entitled to the highest honor. Paul is perfectly sincere in admitting his unworthiness; nay, at other times he speaks of himself in far more degrading language. "For I am the least of the apostles, and am not worthy to be called an apostle, because I persecuted the church of God" (1 Corinthians 15: 9). "Christ Jesus came into the world to save sinners, of whom I am chief" (1 Timothy 1: 15).

But let us observe, that, when he speaks of himself as the meanest of all, he confines his attention to what he was in himself, apart from the grace of God. As if he had said, that his own worthlessness did not prevent him from being appointed, while others were passed by, to be the apostle of the Gentiles. *The grace of God given to me* is the expression used by him, to intimate that it was a peculiar gift, as compared with what had been bestowed on others. Not that he alone had been elected to discharge that office, but that he held the highest rank among "the teachers of the Gentiles," — a title which he employs on another occasion as peculiar to himself.

"I am ordained a preacher, and an apostle, (I speak the truth in Christ, and lie not,) a teacher of the Gentiles in faith and truth" (1 Timothy 2: 7).

By *the unsearchable riches of Christ* are meant the astonishing and boundless treasures of grace, which God had suddenly and unexpectedly bestowed on the Gentiles. The Ephesians are thus reminded how eagerly the gospel ought to be embraced, and how highly it ought to be esteemed. This subject has been treated in the Exposition of the Epistle to the Galatians (Galatians 1: 15–16; 2: 7,9). And certainly, while Paul held the office of apostleship in common with others, it was an honor peculiar to himself to be appointed apostle of the Gentiles.

EPHESIANS 4

The three remaining chapters consist entirely of practical exhortations. Mutual agreement is the first subject, in the course of which a discussion is introduced respecting the government of the church, as having been framed by our

especially since his sufferings were on their account.

7. Whereof I was made a minister. That is, of the Gospel, not by men, but by God: and he is a true minister of the Gospel who is called of God to the work of the ministry, and is qualified by him with grace and gifts for it; and who faithfully discharges it according to the ability God has given; and such a one was the apostle.

11. According to the eternal purpose. The whole of salvation, in which is displayed the great wisdom of God, is according to a purpose of his; the scheme of it is fixed in the council of peace; the thing itself is effected in pursuance of it; Christ, the Redeemer, was set forth in it; his incarnation, the time of his coming into the world, his sufferings and death, with all their circumstances, were decreed by God; and the persons for whom Christ became incarnate, suffered, and died, were appointed unto salvation by him; and the application of it to them is according to his purpose; the time when, the place where, and the means whereby souls are converted, are all settled in the decrees of God; the Gospel itself, the preaching of it by such and such persons, its use to make men see the mysteries of grace, and the fellowship of them, and to make known these things to the angels of heaven, are all according to a divine purpose.

12. In whom we have boldness and access. Into the holy of holies, to the throne of grace there, and to God the Father, as seated on it: Christ is the way of access; union to him gives right of access; through his mediation his people have audience of God, and acceptance with him, both of person and service: and this access is with boldness; which denotes liberty of coming, granted by God, and a liberty in their own souls to speak out their minds plainly and freely; and an holy courage and intrepidity of soul, being free from servile fear, or a spirit of bondage; which is owing to the heart being sprinkled from an evil conscience, to an act of faith, on the person, blood, and righteousness of Christ, and to a view of God, as a God of peace, grace and mercy: and this access may be had with confidence by the faith of him; with confidence of interest in the everlasting love of God; of relation to him, as a covenant God and Father.

17. That Christ may dwell in your hearts by faith. This is another petition put up by the apostle for the Ephesians, which is for the inhabitation of Christ in them: the inhabitant Christ is he who dwells in the highest heavens, who dwells in the Father, and the Father in him, in whom all fullness dwells, the fullness of the Godhead, and the fullness of grace; so that those in whose hearts he dwells cannot want any good thing, must be in the greatest safety, and enjoy the greatest comfort and pleasure; and this inhabitation of Christ prayed for is not to be understood in such sense, as he dwells everywhere, being the omnipresent God; or as he dwells in the human nature; nor of his dwelling merely by his Spirit, but of a personal indwelling of his; and which is an instance of his special grace: he dwells in his people, as a king in his palace, to rule and protect them, and as a master in his family to provide for them, and as their life to quicken them; it is in consequence of their union to him.

18. May be able to comprehend with all saints. This is the end of their being rooted and grounded in love, that they, together with the rest of the saints interested in it, might have a larger and more comprehensive view of what is the breadth, and length, and depth, and height.

19. And to know the love of Christ, which passeth knowledge. The love of Christ to his own, to his church and people, is special and peculiar; free and Sovereign; as early as his Father's love, and is durable and unchangeable; the greatest love that ever was heard of; it is matchless and unparalleled; it is exceeding strong and affectionate, and is wonderful and surprising: the instances of it are, his engaging as a surety for them; his espousing both their persons and their cause; his assumption of their nature; his dying in their room and stead; his payment of their debts, atoning for their sins, and bringing in for them an everlasting righteousness; his going to prepare a place for them in heaven; his intercession for

worketh in us,

21 Unto him be glory in the church by Christ Jesus throughout all ages, world without end. Amen.

EPHESIANS 4

1 I therefore, the prisoner of the Lord, beseech you that ye walk worthy of the vocation wherewith ye are called,

2 With all lowliness and meekness, with longsuffering, forbearing one another in love;

3 Endeavoring to keep the unity of the Spirit in the bond of peace.

4 There is one body, and one Spirit, even as ye are called in one hope of your calling;

5 One Lord, one faith, one baptism,

6 One God and Father of all, who is above all, and through all, and in you all.

7 But unto every one of us is given grace according to the measure of the gift of Christ.

8 Wherefore he saith, When he ascended up on high, he led captivity captive, and gave gifts unto men.

9 (Now that he ascended, what is it but that he also descended first into the lower parts of the earth?

10 He that descended is the same also that ascended up far above all heavens, that he might fill all things.)

11 And he gave some, apostles; and some, prophets; and some, evangelists; and some, pastors and teachers;

12 For the perfecting of the saints, for the work of the ministry, for the edifying of the body of Christ:

13 Till we all come in the unity of the faith, and of the knowledge of the Son of God, unto a perfect man, unto the measure of the stature of the fullness of Christ:

14 That we henceforth be no more children, tossed to and fro, and carried about with every wind of doctrine, by the sleight of men, and cunning craftiness, whereby they lie in wait to deceive;

15 But speaking the truth in love, may grow up into him in all things, which is the head, even Christ:

16 From whom the whole body fitly joined together and compacted by that which every joint supplieth, according to the effectual working in the measure of every part, maketh increase of the body unto the edifying of itself in love.

Lord for the purpose of maintaining unity among Christians.

1. I therefore, the prisoner of the Lord

His imprisonment, which might have been supposed more likely to render him despised, is appealed to, as we have already seen, for a confirmation of his authority. It was the seal of that embassy with which he had been honored. Whatever belongs to Christ, though in the eyes of men it may be attended by ignominy, ought to be viewed by us with the highest regard. The apostle's prison is more truly venerable than the splendid retinue or triumphal chariot of kings.

That ye may walk worthy

This is a general sentiment, a sort of preface, on which all the following statements are founded. He had formerly illustrated *the calling with which they were called,* and now reminds them that they must live in obedience to God, in order that they may not be unworthy of such distinguished grace.

2. With all humility

He now descends to particulars, and first of all he mentions humility. The reason is, that he was about to enter on the subject of Unity, to which humility is the first step. This again produces meekness, which disposes us to bear with our brethren, and thus to preserve that unity which would otherwise be broken a hundred times in a day. Let us remember, therefore, that, in cultivating brotherly kindness, we must begin with humility. Whence come rudeness, pride, and disdainful language towards brethren? Whence come quarrels, insults, and reproaches? Come they not from this, that every one carries his love of himself, and his regard to his own interests, to excess? By laying aside haughtiness and a desire of pleasing ourselves, we shall become meek and gentle, and acquire that moderation of temper which will overlook and forgive many things in the conduct of our brethren. Let us carefully observe the order and arrangement of these exhortations. It will be to no purpose that we inculcate forbearance till the natural fierceness has been subdued, and mildness acquired; and it will be equally vain to discourse of meekness, till we have begun with humility.

Forbearing one another in love

This agrees with what is elsewhere taught, that "love suffereth long and is kind" (1 Corinthians 13: 4). Where love is strong and prevalent, we shall perform many acts of mutual forbearance.

3. Endeavoring to keep the unity of the Spirit

With good reason does he recommend forbearance, as tending to promote the unity of the Spirit. Innumerable offenses arise daily, which might produce quarrels, par-

them there; his constant supply of all their wants, and the freedom and familiarity he uses them with.

EPHESIANS 4

1. That ye walk worthy of the calling wherewith ye are called; by which is meant, not that private and peculiar state and condition of life, that the saints are called to, and in: but that calling, by the grace of God, which is common to them all; and is not a mere outward call by the ministry of the word, with which men may be called, and not be chosen, sanctified, and saved; but that which is internal, and is of special grace, and by the Spirit of God; by whom they are called out of darkness into light, out of bondage into liberty, out of the world, and from the company and conversation of the men of it, into the fellowship of Christ, and his people, to the participation of the grace of Christ here, and to his kingdom and glory hereafter; and which call is powerful, efficacious, yea, irresistible; and being once made is unchangeable, and without repentance, and is holy, high, and heavenly.

2. With all lowliness and meekness. In the exercise of humility, which shows itself in believers, in entertaining and expressing the meanest thoughts of themselves, and the best of others; in not envying the gifts and graces of others, but rejoicing at them, and at every increase of them; in a willingness to receive instruction from the meanest saints.

3. Endeavoring to keep the unity of the Spirit. That is, a spiritual union: there is an union between God and his people, and between Christ and his members, and between saints and saints, and the bond of each union is love; and that it is which knits and cements them together; and it is the last of these which is here intended: the saints are united under one head, and are members of one and the same body, and should be of the same mind and judgment, and of one accord, heart, and affection: and this may be called **the unity of the Spirit**; because it is an union of spirits, of the spirits or souls of men; and that in spiritual affairs, in the spiritual exercises of religion; and it is effected by the Spirit of God, by

whom they are baptized into one body.

7. But unto everyone of us is given grace. Which may refer to the saints in common, and may be interpreted of justifying, pardoning, adopting, sanctifying, and persevering grace, bestowed upon them all, freely and liberally, not grudgingly, nor niggardly, and without motive and condition in them; or to the ministers of the Gospel, and so design gifts fitting for the ministry, which every one has, though differing one from another, and all of free grace.

11. And he gave some apostles. That is, he gave them gifts by which they were qualified to be apostles; who were such as were immediately called by Christ, and had their doctrine from him, and their commission to preach it; and were peculiarly and infallibly guided by the Spirit of God, and had a power to work miracles for the confirmation of their doctrine; and had authority to go everywhere and preach the Gospel, and plant churches, and were not confined to anyone particular place or church; this was the first and chief office in the church, and of an extraordinary kind, and is now ceased; and though the apostles were before Christ's ascension, yet they had not received till then the fullness of the Spirit, and his extraordinary gifts to fit them for their office; nor did they enter upon the discharge of it in its large extent till that time; for they were not only to bear witness of Christ in Jerusalem, in Judea and Samaria, but in the uttermost parts of the earth.

13. Till we all come in the unity of the faith. These words regard the continuance of the Gospel ministry in the church, until all the elect of God come in: or "to the unity of the faith"; by which is meant, not the union between the saints, the cement of which is love; nor that which is between Christ and his people, of which his love, and not their faith, is the bond; but the same with the "one faith," Ephesians 4: 5 and designs either the doctrine of faith, which is uniform, and all of a piece; and the sense is, that the ministration of the Gospel will continue until the saints entirely unite in their sentiments about it, and both watchmen and churches see eye to eye: or

17 This I say therefore, and testify in the Lord, that ye henceforth walk not as other Gentiles walk, in the vanity of their mind,

18 Having the understanding darkened, being alienated from the life of God through the ignorance that is in them, because of the blindness of their heart:

19 Who being past feeling have given themselves over unto lasciviousness, to work all uncleanness with greediness.

20 But ye have not so learned Christ;

21 If so be that ye have heard him, and have been taught by him, as the truth is in Jesus:

22 That ye put off concerning the former conversation the old man, which is corrupt according to the deceitful lusts;

23 And be renewed in the spirit of your mind;

24 And that ye put on the new man, which after God is created in righteousness and true holiness.

25 Wherefore putting away lying, speak every man truth with his neighbour: for we are members one of another.

26 Be ye angry, and sin not: let not the sun go down upon your wrath:

27 Neither give place to the devil.

28 Let him that stole steal no more: but rather let him labour, working with his hands the thing which is good, that he may have to give to him that needeth.

29 Let no corrupt communication proceed out of your mouth, but that which is good to the use of edifying, that it may minister grace unto the hearers.

30 And grieve not the holy Spirit of God, whereby ye are sealed unto the day of redemption.

31 Let all bitterness, and wrath, and anger, and clamor, and evil speaking, be put away from you, with all malice:

32 And be ye kind one to another, tenderhearted, forgiving one another, even as God for Christ's sake hath forgiven you.

EPHESIANS 5

1 Be ye therefore followers of God, as dear children;

2 And walk in love, as Christ also hath loved us, and hath given himself for us an offering and a sacrifice to God for a sweetsmelling savor.

3 But fornication, and all uncleanness, or covetousness, let it not be once named

ticularly when we consider the extreme bitterness of man's natural temper. Some consider the unity of the Spirit to mean that spiritual unity which is produced in us by the Spirit of God. There can be no doubt that He alone makes us "of one accord, of one mind" (Philippians 2: 2), and thus makes us one; but I think it more natural to understand the words as denoting harmony of views. This unity, he tells us, is maintained by the bond of peace; for disputes frequently give rise to hatred and resentment. We must live at peace, if we would wish that brotherly kindness should be permanent amongst us.

EPHESIANS 5

1. Be ye therefore followers
The same principle is followed out and enforced by the consideration that children ought to be like their father. He reminds us that we are the children of God, and that therefore we ought, as far as possible, to resemble Him in acts of kindness. It is impossible not to perceive, that the division of chapters, in the present instance, is particularly unhappy, as it has made a separation between parts of the subject which are very closely related. If, then, we are the children of God, we ought to be followers of God. Christ also declares, that, unless we shew kindness to the unworthy, we cannot be the children of our heavenly Father.

"Love your enemies, bless them that curse you, do good to them that hate you, and pray for them who despitefully use you and persecute you; that ye may be the children of your Father which is in heaven; for he maketh his sun to rise on the evil and on the good, and sendeth rain on the just and on the unjust" (Matthew 5: 44–45).

2. And walk in love as Christ also hath loved us
Having called on us to imitate God, he now calls on us to imitate Christ, who is our true model. We ought to embrace each other with that love with which Christ has embraced us, for what we perceive in Christ is our true guide.

And gave himself for us
This was a remarkable proof of the highest love. Forgetful, as it were, of himself, Christ spared not his own life, that he might redeem us from death. If we desire to be partakers of this benefit, we must cultivate similar affections toward our neighbors. Not that any of us has reached such high perfection, but all must aim and strive according to the measure of their ability.

An offering and a sacrifice to God of a sweet smelling savor
While this statement leads us to admire the grace of Christ, it bears directly on the present subject. No language, indeed, can fully represent the consequences and efficacy of Christ's death. This is the only price by which we are reconciled to

else the grace of faith, which as to its nature, object, author, spring, and cause, is the same; and it usually comes by hearing; and all God's elect shall have it; and the work and office of the ministry will remain until they are all brought to believe in Christ.

19. Who being past feeling. Their consciences being cauterized or seared as with a red hot iron, which is the consequence of judicial hardness; so that they have lost all sense of sin, and do not feel the load of its guilt upon them, and are without any concern about it; but on the contrary commit it with pleasure, boast of it and glory in it, plead for it and defend it publicly, and openly declare it, and stand in no fear of a future judgment, which they ridicule and despise.

22. That ye put off concerning the former conversation, the old man. Which is the corruption of nature. The putting him off, is not a removing him from the saints, nor a destroying him in them, nor a changing his nature; for he remains, and remains alive, and is the same old man he ever was, in regenerate persons; but it is a putting him off from his seat, and a putting him down from his government; a showing no regard to his rule and dominion, to his laws and lusts, making no provision for his support; and particularly, not squaring the life and conversation according to his dictates and directions; and therefore it is called a putting him off, concerning the former conversation.

The change lies not, in the old man, who can never be altered, but in the conversation; he is not in the same power, but he retains the same sinful nature; he is put off, but he is not put out; and though he does not reign, he rages, and often threatens to get the ascendant: these words stand either in connection with Ephesians 4: 17 and so are a continuation and an explanation of that exhortation; or else they point out what regenerate souls are taught by Christ to do, to quit the former conversation, to hate the garment spotted with the flesh, and to put it off; for the allusion is to the putting off of filthy garments, as the works of the flesh may be truly called, which flow from the vitiosity of nature, the old man.

29. Let no corrupt communication proceed out of your mouth. As unsavory speech, foolish talking, light and frothy language, that which is filthy, unprofitable, noxious, and nauseous, and all that is sinful; such as profane oaths, curses, and imprecations, unchaste words, angry ones, proud, haughty, and arrogant expressions, lies, perjury, etc.

EPHESIANS 5

1. Be ye therefore followers of God. Not in his works of infinite wisdom and almighty power, which is impossible; but in acts of righteousness and holiness, and particularly in acts of mercy, goodness, and beneficence; as in forgiving injuries and offences, and in freely distributing to the necessities of the saints; as the connection of the words with the preceding chapter, and the instance and example in the following show.

2. And walk in love. To God; to which the saints are obliged, not only by the law of God, which requires it, but by the goodness of God, and the discoveries of his love to them; and which shows itself in fearing to offend him, in a conformity to his will, in making his glory the chief end of all actions, and in loving all that belong to him: and also the saints should walk in love to Christ; who is to be loved fervently, constantly, in sincerity, with all the heart, and above all creatures and things; because of the loveliness of his person, the love he bears to them, and the things he has done for them, and the relations he stands in to them; and which is manifested in keeping his commands, in delighting in his presence, and in a concern at his absence.

They should walk in love to one another, which is chiefly designed; which is Christ's new commandment, and is an evidence of regeneration; and without which a profession of religion is in vain: and to "walk" in love, is not merely to talk of it, but to exercise it; and to do all that is done for God, and Christ, and the saints, from a principle of love; and to advance, increase, and abound in it, and to go on and continue therein.

3. But fornication, and all uncleanness, or covetousness. The apostle proceeds to dehort from several vices, which are unbecoming the

among you, as becometh saints;

4 Neither filthiness, nor foolish talking, nor jesting, which are not convenient: but rather giving of thanks.

5 For this ye know, that no whoremonger, nor unclean person, nor covetous man, who is an idolater, hath any inheritance in the kingdom of Christ and of God.

6 Let no man deceive you with vain words: for because of these things cometh the wrath of God upon the children of disobedience.

7 Be not ye therefore partakers with them.

8 For ye were sometimes darkness, but now are ye light in the Lord: walk as children of light:

9 (For the fruit of the Spirit is in all goodness and righteousness and truth;)

10 Proving what is acceptable unto the Lord.

11 And have no fellowship with the unfruitful works of darkness, but rather reprove them.

12 For it is a shame even to speak of those things which are done of them in secret.

13 But all things that are reproved are made manifest by the light: for whatsoever doth make manifest is light.

14 Wherefore he saith, Awake thou that sleepest, and arise from the dead, and Christ shall give thee light.

15 See then that ye walk circumspectly, not as fools, but as wise,

16 Redeeming the time, because the days are evil.

17 Wherefore be ye not unwise, but understanding what the will of the Lord is.

18 And be not drunk with wine, wherein is excess; but be filled with the Spirit;

19 Speaking to yourselves in psalms and hymns and spiritual songs, singing and making melody in your heart to the Lord;

20 Giving thanks always for all things unto God and the Father in the name of our Lord Jesus Christ;

21 Submitting yourselves one to another in the fear of God.

22 Wives, submit yourselves unto your own husbands, as unto the Lord.

23 For the husband is the head of the wife, even as Christ is the head of the church: and he is the savior of the body.

God. The doctrine of faith on this subject holds the highest rank. But the more extraordinary the discoveries which have reached us of the Redeemer's kindness, the more strongly are we bound to his service. Besides, we may infer from Paul's words, that, unless we love one another, none of our duties will be acceptable in the sight of God. If the reconciliation of men, effected by Christ, was a sacrifice of a sweet smelling savor, we, too, shall be "unto God a sweet savor" (2 Corinthians 2: 15), when this holy perfume is spread over us. To this applies the saying of Christ, "Leave thy gift before the altar, and go and be reconciled to thy brother" (Matthew 5: 24).

3. But fornication

This chapter, and the third of the Epistle to the Colossians, contain many parallel passages, which an intelligent reader will be at no loss to compare without my assistance. Three things are here enumerated, which the apostle desires Christians to hold in such abhorrence, that they shall not even be named, or, in other words, shall be entirely unknown among them. By uncleanness he means all base and impure lusts; so that this word differs from fornication, only as the whole class differs from a single department. The third is covetousness, which is nothing more than an immoderate desire of gain. To this precept he adds the authoritative declaration, that he demands nothing from them but that which becometh saints – manifestly excluding from the number and fellowship of the saints all fornicators, and impure and covetous persons.

4. Neither filthiness

To those three – other three are now added. By filthiness I understand all that is indecent or inconsistent with the modesty of the godly. By foolish talking I understand conversations that are either unprofitably or wickedly foolish; and as it frequently happens that idle talk is concealed under the garb of jesting or wit, he expressly mentions pleasantry – which is so agreeable as to seem worthy of commendation – and condemns it as a part of foolish talking. The Greek word eutrapelia is often used by heathen writers, in a good sense, for that ready and ingenious pleasantry in which able and intelligent men may properly indulge. But as it is exceedingly difficult to be witty without becoming satirical, and as jesting itself carries in it a portion of conceit not at all in keeping with the character of a godly man, Paul very properly dissuades from this practice. Of all the three offenses now mentioned, Paul declares that they are not convenient, or, in other words, that they are inconsistent with Christian duty.

But rather grace

Others render it *giving of thanks*; but I prefer Jerome's interpretation. With the vices which had been formerly

dear children and followers of God; and which the love of Christ should constrain them to avoid: the first of these, which is simple "fornication," is the sin which is committed between single or unmarried persons; and is contrary to the law of God, is a work of the flesh, and is against a man's own body; it renders persons unfit for church communion, brings many temporal calamities upon them, and exposes them to divine wrath, and excludes from the kingdom of heaven, without repentance; and the reason why it is so often taken notice of is, because it was very frequent among the Gentiles, and not thought criminal: "all uncleanness" takes in adultery, incest, sodomy, and every unnatural lust; and "covetousness" seems not so much to design that sin which is commonly so called, namely, an immoderate desire after worldly things, as a greedy and insatiable appetite after the above lusts.

9. For the fruit of the Spirit. Either of the spirit of man, as renewed, or rather of the Spirit of God; the allusion is to fruits of trees: the believer is a tree of righteousness; Christ is his root; the Spirit is the sap, which supports and nourishes; and good works, under the influence of his grace, are the fruit.

13. But all things that are reproved. As all sins should be, by the ministers of the Gospel, and by other saints, and will be by God; either by his Spirit convincing of them, or by his judgments, and the letting out of his wrath and fury, either here or hereafter, for the punishment of them.

15. See then that ye walk circumspectly. The Alexandrian copy and the Vulgate Latin version read, "see then, brethren," it being an exhortation to the saints at Ephesus, upon the foregoing discourse and citation, to take heed to their walk: the believer's walk is both inward and outward; his inward walk is by faith on Christ; his outward walk is his conversation among men: this supposes life; requires strength and prudence; denotes continuance and progression; with patience and courage: this walk should be seen to, and watched over; a man should see to it that he does walk, and to the way in which he walks, and how he walks; that he walks circumspectly, with his eyes

about him; that he walks with diligence, caution, accuracy, and exactness, to the uttermost of his strength and power; and with wisdom and prudence, looking well to his going.

20. Giving thanks always for all things. For things temporal, for our beings, and the preservation of them, and for all the mercies of life; for things spiritual, for Christ, and for all spiritual blessings in him; for electing, redeeming, sanctifying, adopting, pardoning, and justifying grace; for a meetness for heaven, and for eternal life itself; for the Gospel, promises, truths, ordinances, and ministry; and this is to be done always, at all times, in times of adversity, desertion, temptation, affliction, and persecution, as well as in prosperity.

21. Submitting yourselves one to another. Which may be understood either in a political sense, of giving honor, obedience, and tribute, to civil magistrates, since they are set up by God for the good of men, and it is for the credit of religion for the saints to submit to them; or in an economical sense; thus the wife should be subject to the husband, children to their parents, and servants to their masters, which several things are afterwards insisted on, as explanative of this rule; or in an ecclesiastic sense, so the Ethiopic version renders it, "subject yourselves to your brethren": thus members of churches should be subject to their pastors, not in the same sense as they are to Christ, the head, nor are they obliged to believe or do everything they say, right or wrong; yet honor and esteem are due to them, and submission and obedience should be yielded to their doctrines, precepts, and exhortations, when they are agreeably to the word of God; since God has set them in the highest place in the church, called them to the highest service, and most honorable work, and bestowed on them the greatest gifts; the younger members should also submit to the elder, and the minority to the majority; one member should submit to another, to the superior judgment of another, and to the weakness of another, and to the admonitions of others, and so as to perform all offices of love.

22. Wives, submit yourselves unto your own husbands. This is an instance, explaining

24 Therefore as the church is subject unto Christ, so let the wives be to their own husbands in every thing.

25 Husbands, love your wives, even as Christ also loved the church, and gave himself for it;

26 That he might sanctify and cleanse it with the washing of water by the word,

27 That he might present it to himself a glorious church, not having spot, or wrinkle, or any such thing; but that it should be holy and without blemish.

28 So ought men to love their wives as their own bodies. He that loveth his wife loveth himself.

29 For no man ever yet hated his own flesh; but nourisheth and cherisheth it, even as the Lord the church:

30 For we are members of his body, of his flesh, and of his bones.

31 For this cause shall a man leave his father and mother, and shall be joined unto his wife, and they two shall be one flesh.

32 This is a great mystery: but I speak concerning Christ and the church.

33 Nevertheless let every one of you in particular so love his wife even as himself; and the wife see that she reverence her husband.

EPHESIANS 6

1 Children, obey your parents in the Lord: for this is right.

2 Honor thy father and mother; (which is the first commandment with promise;)

3 That it may be well with thee, and thou mayest live long on the earth.

4 And, ye fathers, provoke not your children to wrath: but bring them up in the nurture and admonition of the Lord.

5 Servants, be obedient to them that are your masters according to the flesh, with fear and trembling, in singleness of your heart, as unto Christ;

6 Not with eyeservice, as menpleasers; but as the servants of Christ, doing the will of God from the heart;

7 With good will doing service, as to the Lord, and not to men:

8 Knowing that whatsoever good thing any man doeth, the same shall he receive of the Lord, whether he be bond or free.

9 And, ye masters, do the same things unto them, forbearing threatening: knowing that your Master also is in heaven;

mentioned it was proper that Paul should contrast something of a general character, displaying itself in all our communications with each other. If he had said, "While they take pleasure in idle or abusive talk, do you give thanks to God," the exhortation would have been too limited. The Greek word, *eucharistia*, though it usually signifies *Thanksgiving*, admits of being translated *Grace*. "All our conversations ought to be, in the true sense of the words, sweet and graceful; and this end will be gained if the useful and the agreeable are properly mingled."

5. For this ye know

If his readers were at all captivated by the allurements of those vices which have been enumerated, the consequence would be that they would lend a hesitating or careless ear to his admonitions. He determines, therefore, to alarm them by this weighty and dreadful threatening, that such vices shut against us the kingdom of God. By appealing to their own knowledge, he intimates that this was no doubtful matter. Some might think it harsh, or inconsistent with the Divine goodness, that all who have incurred the guilt of fornication or covetousness are excluded from the inheritance of the kingdom of heaven. But the answer is easy. Paul does not say that those who have fallen into those sins, and recovered from them, are not pardoned, but pronounces sentence on the sins themselves.

EPHESIANS 6

1. Children, obey

Why does the apostle use the word obey instead of honor, which has a greater extent of meaning? It is because Obedience is the evidence of that honor which children owe to their parents, and is therefore more earnestly enforced. It is likewise more difficult; for the human mind recoils from the idea of subjection, and with difficulty allows itself to be placed under the control of another. Experience shews how rare this virtue is; for do we find one among a thousand that is obedient to his parents? By a figure of speech, a part is here put for the whole, but it is the most important part, and is necessarily accompanied by all the others.

In the Lord

Besides the law of nature, which is acknowledged by all nations, the obedience of children is enforced by the authority of God. Hence it follows, that parents are to be obeyed, so far only as is consistent with piety to God, which comes first in order. If the command of God is the rule by which the submission of children is to be regulated, it would be foolish to suppose that the performance of this duty could lead away from God himself.

For this is right

This is added in order to restrain the fierceness which, we

the above general rule; which subjection lies in honor and reverence, Ephesians 5: 33, and in obedience; they should think well of their husbands, speak becomingly to them, and respectfully of them.

25. Husbands, love your wives. Which consists in a strong and cordial affection for them; in a real delight and pleasure in them; in showing respect, and doing honor to them; in seeking their contentment, satisfaction, and pleasure; in a quiet, constant, and comfortable dwelling with them; in providing all things necessary for them; in protecting them from all injuries and abuses; in concealing their faults, and covering their infirmities; in entertaining the best opinion of their persons and actions; and in endeavoring to promote their spiritual good and welfare: this love ought to be hearty and sincere, and not feigned and selfish; it should be shown in private, as well as in public: it should be chaste and single, constant and perpetual; it should exceed that which is bore to neighbors, or even to parents, and should be equal to that a man bears to himself; though not so as to hinder, and break in upon love to God and Christ: many are the reasons why husbands should love their wives; they are given to be helps unto them; they are companions of them; they are wives of covenant; they are their own wives, yea, their own bodies, their own flesh, nay, as themselves; they are their image and their glory; and especially the example of Christ, in his love to his church and people, should engage to it.

even as Christ also loved the church, and gave himself for it. The SyriActs and Ethiopic versions read, "his own church"; his bride and spouse, whom he betrothed to himself from all eternity, the Father having given her to him; and is no other than the church of the firstborn, whose names are written in heaven, even all the elect of God.

EPHESIANS 6

1. Children, obey your parents in the Lord. The persons whose duty this is, "children," are such of every sex, male and female, and of every age, and of every state and condition; and though the true, legitimate, and immedi-

ate offspring of men may be chiefly respected, yet not exclusive of spurious children, and adopted ones, and of children-in-law; and the persons to whom obedience from them is due, are not only real and immediate parents, both father and mother, but such who are in the room of parents, as step-fathers, step-mothers, guardians, nurses, etc. and all who are in the ascending line, as grandfathers, grandmothers, etc. to these, children should be subject and obedient in all things lawful, just, and good; in everything that is not sinful and unlawful, by the word of God; and in things indifferent, as much as in them lies, and even in things which are difficult to perform: and this obedience should be hearty and sincere, and not merely verbal, and in show and appearance, nor mercenary; and should be joined with gratitude and thankfulness for past favors: and it should be "in the Lord"; which may be considered either as a limitation of the obedience, that it should be in things that are agreeable to the mind and will of the Lord; or as an argument to it, because it is the command of the Lord, and is wellpleasing in his sight, and makes for his glory, and therefore should be done for his sake.

4. And ye fathers, provoke not your children to wrath. Neither by words; by unjust and, unreasonable commands; by contumelious and reproachful language; by frequent and public chidings, and by indiscreet and passionate expressions: nor by deeds; preferring one to another; by denying them the necessaries of life; by not allowing them proper recreation; by severe and cruel blows, and inhuman usage; by not giving them suitable education; by an improper disposal of them in marriage; and by profusely spending their estates, and leaving nothing to them: not but that parents may, and ought to correct and rebuke their children; nor are they accountable to them for their conduct; yet they should take care not to provoke them to wrath, because this alienates their minds from them, and renders their instructions and corrections useless, and puts them upon sinful practices; wrath lets in Satan, and leads to sin against God; and indeed it is difficult in the best of men to be angry and not sin; see Colossians 3: 21.

neither is there respect of persons with him.

10 Finally, my brethren, be strong in the Lord, and in the power of his might.

11 Put on the whole Armour of God, that ye may be able to stand against the wiles of the devil.

12 For we wrestle not against flesh and blood, but against principalities, against powers, against the rulers of the darkness of this world, against spiritual wickedness in high places.

13 Wherefore take unto you the whole Armour of God, that ye may be able to withstand in the evil day, and having done all, to stand.

14 Stand therefore, having your loins girt about with truth, and having on the breastplate of righteousness;

15 And your feet shod with the preparation of the gospel of peace;

16 Above all, taking the shield of faith, wherewith ye shall be able to quench all the fiery darts of the wicked.

17 And take the helmet of salvation, and the sword of the Spirit, which is the word of God:

18 Praying always with all prayer and supplication in the Spirit, and watching thereunto with all perseverance and supplication for all saints;

19 And for me, that utterance may be given unto me, that I may open my mouth boldly, to make known the mystery of the gospel,

20 For which I am an ambassador in bonds: that therein I may speak boldly, as I ought to speak.

21 But that ye also may know my affairs, and how I do, Tychicus, a beloved brother and faithful minister in the Lord, shall make known to you all things:

22 Whom I have sent unto you for the same purpose, that ye might know our affairs, and that he might comfort your hearts.

23 Peace be to the brethren, and love with faith, from God the Father and the Lord Jesus Christ.

24 Grace be with all them that love our Lord Jesus Christ in sincerity. Amen.

have already said, appears to be natural to almost all men. He proves it to be right, because God has commanded it; for we are not at liberty to dispute, or call in question, the appointment of him whose will is the unerring rule of goodness and righteousness. That honor should be represented as including obedience is not surprising; for mere ceremony is of no value in the sight of God. The precept, *honor thy father and mother*, comprehends all the duties by which the sincere affection and respect of children to their parents can be expressed.

2. Which is the first commandment with promise

The promises annexed to the commandments are intended to excite our hopes, and to impart a greater cheerfulness to our obedience; and therefore Paul uses this as a kind of seasoning to render the submission, which he enjoins on children, more pleasant and agreeable. He does not merely say, that God has offered a reward to him who obeys his father and mother, but that such an offer is peculiar to this commandment. If each of the commandments had its own promises, there would have been no ground for the commendation bestowed in the present instance. But this is the first commandment, Paul tells us, which God has been pleased, as it were, to seal by a remarkable promise. There is some difficulty here; for the second commandment likewise contains a promise, "I am the Lord thy God, who shew mercy unto thousands of them that love me, and keep my commandments." (Exodus 20: 5–6).

But this is universal, applying indiscriminately to the whole law, and cannot be said to be annexed to that commandment. Paul's assertion still holds true, that no other commandment but that which enjoins the obedience due by children to their parents is distinguished by a promise.

11. Put on the whole armor

God has furnished us with various defensive weapons, provided we do not indolently refuse what is offered. But we are almost all chargeable with carelessness and hesitation in using the offered grace; just as if a soldier, about to meet the enemy, should take his helmet, and neglect his shield. To correct this security, or, we should rather say, this indolence, Paul borrows a comparison from the military art, and bids us put on the whole armor of God. We ought to be prepared on all sides, so as to want nothing. The Lord offers to us arms for repelling every kind of attack. It remains for us to apply them to use, and not leave them hanging on the wall.

Fathers are particularly mentioned, they being the heads of families, and are apt to be too severe, as mothers too indulgent.

But bring them up in the nurture and admonition of the Lord; instructing them in the knowledge of divine things, setting them good examples, taking care to prevent their falling into bad company, praying with them, and for them, bringing them into the house of God, under the means of grace, to attend public worship; all which, under a divine blessing, may be very useful to them; the example of Abraham is worthy of imitation, Genesis 18: 19, and the advice of the wise man deserves attention, Proverbs 22: 6.

11. Put on the whole armor of God. Not that which God himself is sometimes clothed with, and uses against his enemies; but what he has provided for his people, and furnishes them with; the particulars of which are after mentioned: and it is called "the armor of God," because it is prepared by him for his people, and is bestowed on them by him; and because it is in its own nature divine and spiritual, and not carnal; and because it is provided for fighting the Lord's battles, and is used in them; and because the efficacy of it is from him, and the execution it does is owing to him: and it is whole, complete, and perfect; and all of it is useful, and no part to be neglected, but all to be taken and "put on"; which is not to make and provide this armor, but to take it, as in Ephesians 6: 13; as being ready made and provided, and to expect and prepare for battle, and make use of it; and this supposes saints to be in a warfare state, and that they are in the character of soldiers, and have enemies to fight with, and therefore should be accoutred with proper and suitable armor, to meet them.

that ye may be able to stand against the wiles of the devil; who is the grand enemy of Christ and his people, and a very powerful and cunning one he is; so that the whole armor of God should be put on, which is proof against all his might and craft, in order to stand against him, oppose him, and fight, and get the victory over him, which in the issue is always obtained by believers; for they not only stand their ground in the strength of Christ, and by

the use of their armor confound his schemes, and baffle all his arts and stratagems, but are more than conquerors through him that has loved them.

12. For we wrestle not against flesh and blood. The Syriac, Arabic, and Ethiopic versions, and some copies, read "you," instead of "we." This is a reason why saints should be strong in the Lord, and why they should put on the whole armor of God, and prepare for battle, since their enemies are such as here described: not **flesh and blood**; frail mortal men, such as were wrestled against in the Olympic games, to which the apostle alludes. For this wrestling, as Philo the Jew says, concerning Jacob's wrestling, is not of the body, but of the soul; see Matthew 16: 17; and the meaning is, not with men only, for otherwise the saints have a conflict with men; with profane men, and wrestle against them, by bearing a testimony against their enormities, and by patiently enduring their reproaches, and conquer them by a constant adherence to Christ, and an exercise of faith upon him, which gets the victory over the world; and with heretical men, and maintain a conflict with them, by watching and observing the first appearance of their errors and heresies, and declaring against them, and by using Scripture arguments to confute them, and by rejecting the stubborn and incorrigible from church communion: yet they wrestle not against these only, **but against principalities, against powers**; by whom are meant not civil magistrates, or the Roman governors, though these are sometimes so called, Titus 3: 1, and may be said to be the rulers of the darkness of this world, or of the dark Heathen world, and were in high places, and were of wicked and malicious spirits, against the people of Christ; yet these cannot be opposed to flesh and blood, or to men, since they were such themselves; and though they were in high, yet not in heavenly places; and the connection with the preceding shows the contrary, the enemy being the devil, and the armor spiritual; wherefore the devils are here designed, who are described from their power, rule, and government.

Philippians

Introduction by John Calvin

IT is generally known that PHILIPPI was a city of Macedonia, situated on the confines of Thrace, on the plains of which *Pompey* was conquered by *Caesar*; and *Brutus* and *Cassius* were afterwards conquered by *Antony* and *Octavius.* Thus Roman insurrections rendered this place illustrious by two memorable engagements. When PAUL was called into Macedonia by an express revelation, he first founded a Church in that city (as is related by LUKE in Acts 16: 12), which did not merely persevere steadfastly in the faith, but was also, in process of time, as this Epistle bears evidence, enlarged both in the number of individuals, and in their proficiency in respect of attainments.

The occasion of Paul's writing to the Philippians was this – As they had sent to him by Epaphroditus, their pastor, such things as were needed by him when in prison, for sustaining life, and for other more than ordinary expenses, there can be no doubt that Epaphroditus explained to him at the same time the entire condition of the Church, and acted the part of an adviser in suggesting those things, respecting which they required to be admonished. It appears, however, that attempts had been made upon them by false apostles, who wandered hither and thither, with the view of spreading corruptions of sound doctrine; but as they had remained steadfast in the truth, the Apostle commends their steadfastness. Keeping, however, in mind human frailty, and having, perhaps, been instructed by Epaphroditus that they required to be seasonably confirmed, lest they should in process of time fall away, he subjoins such admonitions as he knew to be suitable to them.

And having, first of all, with the view of securing their confidence, declared the pious attachment of his mind towards them, he proceeds to treat of himself and of his bonds, lest they should feel dismayed on seeing him a prisoner, and in danger of his life. He shews them, accordingly, that the glory of the gospel is so far from being lessened by this means, that it is rather an argument in confirmation of its truth, and he at the same time stirs them up by his own example to be prepared for every event. He at length concludes the *First Chapter* with a short exhortation to unity and patience.

As, however, ambition is almost invariably the mother of dissensions, and comes, on this account, to open a door for new and strange doctrines, he, in the commencement of the *Second Chapter*, entreats them, with great earnestness, to hold nothing more highly in esteem than humility and modesty. With this view he makes use of various arguments. And that he may the better retain them, he promises to send Timothy to them shortly, nay more, he expresses a hope of being able to visit them himself. He afterwards assigns a reason for delay on the part of Epaphroditus.

In the *Third Chapter* he inveighs against the false apostles, and sets aside both their empty boastings and the doctrine of circumcision, which they eagerly maintained. To all their contrivances he opposes the simple doctrine of Christ. To their arrogance he opposes his former life and present course of conduct, in which a true image of Christian piety shone forth. He shews, also, that the summit of perfection, at which we must aim during our whole life, is this – to have fellowship with

886

Christ in his death and resurrection; and this he establishes by his own example.

He begins the *Fourth Chapter* with particular admonitions, but proceeds afterwards to those of a general nature. He concludes the Epistle with a declaration of his gratitude to the PHILIPPIANS, that they may not think that what they had laid out for relieving his necessities had been ill bestowed.

The commentaries on Philippians are by John Calvin and John Gill.

PHILIPPIANS 1

1 Paul and Timotheus, the servants of Jesus Christ, to all the saints in Christ Jesus which are at Philippi, with the bishops and deacons:

2 Grace be unto you, and peace, from God our Father, and from the Lord Jesus Christ.

3 I thank my God upon every remembrance of you,

4 Always in every prayer of mine for you all making request with joy,

5 For your fellowship in the gospel from the first day until now;

6 Being confident of this very thing, that he which hath begun a good work in you will perform it until the day of Jesus Christ:

7 Even as it is meet for me to think this of you all, because I have you in my heart; inasmuch as both in my bonds, and in the defence and confirmation of the gospel, ye all are partakers of my grace.

8 For God is my record, how greatly I long after you all in the bowels of Jesus Christ.

9 And this I pray, that your love may abound yet more and more in knowledge and in all judgment;

10 That ye may approve things that are excellent; that ye may be sincere and without offence till the day of Christ;

11 Being filled with the fruits of righteousness, which are by Jesus Christ, unto the glory and praise of God.

12 But I would ye should understand, brethren, that the things which happened unto me have fallen out rather unto the furtherance of the gospel;

13 So that my bonds in Christ are manifest in all the palace, and in all other places;

14 And many of the brethren in the Lord, waxing confident by my bonds, are much more bold to speak the word without fear.

15 Some indeed preach Christ even of envy and strife; and some also of good will:

16 The one preach Christ of contention, not sincerely, supposing to add affliction to my bonds:

17 But the other of love, knowing that I am set for the defence of the gospel.

PHILIPPIANS 1

1. Paul and Timotheus, servants of Jesus Christ

While Paul is accustomed, in the inscription of his epistles, to employ titles of distinction, with the view of procuring credit for himself and his ministry, there was no need of lengthened commendations in writing to the Philippians, who had known him by experience as a true Apostle of Christ, and still acknowledged him as such beyond all controversy. For they had persevered in the calling of God steadfastly, and in an even tenor.

Bishops

He names the *pastors* separately, for the sake of honor. We may, however, infer from this, that the name of *bishop* is common to all the ministers of the Word, inasmuch as he assigns several *bishops* to one Church. The titles, therefore, of *bishop* and *pastor*, are synonymous.

Deacons

This term may be taken in two ways – either as meaning administrators, and curators of the poor, or for elders, who were appointed for the regulation of morals. As, however, it is more generally made use of by Paul in the former sense, I understand it rather as meaning stewards, who superintended the distributing and receiving of alms. On the other points consult the preceding commentaries.

3. I give thanks

He begins with thanksgiving on two accounts – *first*, that he may by this token shew his love to the Philippians; and secondly, that, by commending them as to the past, he may exhort them, also, to perseverance in time to come. He adduces, also, another evidence of his love – the anxiety which he exercised in supplications. It is to be observed, however, that, whenever he makes mention of things that are joyful, he immediately breaks forth into thanksgiving – a practice with which we ought also to be familiar. We must, also, take notice, what things they are for which he gives thanks to God – the fellowship of the Philippians in the gospel of Christ; for it follows from this, that it ought to be ascribed to the grace of God. When he says, *upon every remembrance of you*, he means, "As often as I remember you."

4. Always in every prayer

Connect the words in this manner: "*Always presenting prayer for you all in every prayer of mine.*" For as he had said before, that the remembrance of them was an occasion of joy to him, so he now subjoins, that they come into his mind as often as he prays. He afterwards adds, that it is *with joy* that he presents prayer in their behalf. *Joy* refers to the past; *prayer* to the future. For he rejoiced in their auspicious beginnings, and was desirous of their perfection. Thus it becomes us always to rejoice in the blessings received from God in such a man-

PHILIPPIANS 1

3. I thank my God. After the inscription and salutation follows a thanksgiving, the object of which is God; to whom thanks is to be given at the remembrance of his name, and the perfections of his nature, and for all his mercies, temporal and spiritual. The apostle expresses his propriety and interest in him, calling him **my God**; thereby distinguishing him from all others, the nominal and fictitious gods of the Gentiles, and the idols and lusts of men's hearts; he was the God whom he served in the Gospel, by whom he was sent, and from whom he received all his possessions, and to whom he was accountable. He had a special, particular, covenant interest in him, had knowledge of it, and faith in it; and therefore could draw nigh to God with freedom, use confidence, plead promises, expect favors, and do all he did, whether in a way of prayer, or praise in faith, and therefore was acceptable unto God.

5. For your fellowship in the Gospel. Or "for your communication unto the Gospel"; that is, to the support of it. These Philippians were one of the churches of Macedonia the apostle so highly commends for their liberality in 2 Corinthians 8: 1; they had been very communicative to him, and those that were with him, from the beginning of the Gospel being preached to them: as the instances of Lydia and the jailer show, and which are taken notice of in this epistle, Philippians 4: 15; And this same generous spirit still continued, of which their present by Epaphroditus was an evidence; and for this the apostle gives thanks, not only that they had an ability to support the Gospel, and assist Gospel ministers, but that they were willing to communicate, and did communicate, readily and cheerfully, largely and liberally; or this may intend their "participation in the Gospel," as the Arabic version renders it. The Gospel was in a very wonderful and providential manner brought unto them, and it was attended with mighty power to the conversion of them; they received it with joy and gladness, and cheerfully submitted to the ordinances of it; they had much light into it, and spiritual knowledge of it; and were made partakers of the blessings of grace, which are revealed and exhibited in it, and of the exceeding great and precious promises of it, for which the apostle gives thanks to God; for all this was from him, and a wonderful instance of his grace it was. Moreover, through the Gospel being thus brought unto them, and succeeded among them, they became a Gospel church, and had, through the Gospel, and the ordinances of it, fellowship one with another; yea, they had fellowship with the Father, and his Son Jesus Christ, unto which they were called by the Gospel; and in this they remained.

11. Being filled with the fruits of righteousness. Good works. Some think alms deeds, or acts of liberality and bounty, are here particularly intended; and that respect is had to the generosity of these Philippians to the apostle, and others: and true it is, that these are sometimes so called, as in 2 Corinthians 9: 10, but rather good works in general are meant, which are called "fruits," because, like fruits, they spring from a seed, even from the incorruptible seed of grace in the heart, implanted there in regeneration; and because they are owing, as the fruits of the earth are, to divine bounty and goodness, to the dews of grace, the rising and bright shining of the sun of righteousness, and to the south gale of the blessed Spirit, when brought forth aright; and also because they are pleasant and delightful, they are well pleasing to Christ, and are acceptable to God through Christ; and likewise, because they are profitable, not to God, but to men: and they are styled fruits of "righteousness," either of imputed righteousness, the righteousness of Christ imputed without works, the effects of which are good works; for nothing more strongly influences and engages men to the performance of good works, than a view of their free justification by the righteousness of Christ; hence there can be no justification by works, since these are the fruits and effects of justification, and not the cause: or of righteousness and holiness implanted in the soul by the Spirit of God.

16. The one preach Christ of contention. That is, those that preached of envy and strife, and not of good will to Christ, to the Gospel, to the souls of men, or to the apostle; and though

18 What then? notwithstanding, every way, whether in pretence, or in truth, Christ is preached; and I therein do rejoice, yea, and will rejoice.

19 For I know that this shall turn to my salvation through your prayer, and the supply of the Spirit of Jesus Christ,

20 According to my earnest expectation and my hope, that in nothing I shall be ashamed, but that with all boldness, as always, so now also Christ shall be magnified in my body, whether it be by life, or by death.

21 For to me to live is Christ, and to die is gain.

22 But if I live in the flesh, this is the fruit of my labour: yet what I shall choose I wot not.

23 For I am in a strait betwixt two, having a desire to depart, and to be with Christ; which is far better:

24 Nevertheless to abide in the flesh is more needful for you.

25 And having this confidence, I know that I shall abide and continue with you all for your furtherance and joy of faith;

26 That your rejoicing may be more abundant in Jesus Christ for me by my coming to you again.

27 Only let your conversation be as it becometh the gospel of Christ: that whether I come and see you, or else be absent, I may hear of your affairs, that ye stand fast in one spirit, with one mind striving together for the faith of the gospel;

28 And in nothing terrified by your adversaries: which is to them an evident token of perdition, but to you of salvation, and that of God.

29 For unto you it is given in the behalf of Christ, not only to believe on him, but also to suffer for his sake;

30 Having the same conflict which ye saw in me, and now hear to be in me.

PHILIPPIANS 2

1 If there be therefore any consolation in Christ, if any comfort of love, if any fellowship of the Spirit, if any bowels and mercies,

2 Fulfil ye my joy, that ye be likeminded, having the same love, being of one accord, of one mind.

ner, as to remember to ask from him those things that we are still in need of.

5. For your fellowship

He now, passing over the other clause, states the ground of his joy – that they had come into the *fellowship of the gospel*, that is, had become partakers of the gospel, which, as is well known, is accomplished by means of faith; for the gospel appears as nothing to us, in respect of any enjoyment of it, until we have received it by faith. At the same time the term *fellowship* may be viewed as referring to the common society of the saints, as though he had said that they had been associated with all the children of God in the faith of the gospel. When he says, *from the first day*, he commends their promptitude in having shewn themselves teachable immediately upon the doctrine being set before them. The phrase *until now* denotes their perseverance. Now we know how rare an excellence it is, to follow God immediately upon his calling us, and also to persevere steadfastly unto the end. For many are slow and backward to obey, while there are still more that fall short through fickleness and inconstancy.

6. Persuaded of this very thing

An additional ground of joy is furnished in his confidence in them for the time to come. But some one will say, why should men dare to assure themselves for to-morrow amidst so great an infirmity of nature, amidst so many impediments, ruggednesses, and precipices? Paul, assuredly, did not derive this confidence from the steadfastness or excellence of men, but simply from the fact, that God had manifested his love to the Philippians. And undoubtedly this is the true manner of acknowledging God's benefits – when we derive from them occasion of hoping well as to the future. For as they are tokens at once of his goodness, and of his fatherly benevolence towards us, what ingratitude were it to derive from this no confirmation of hope and good courage! In addition to this, God is not like men, so as to be wearied out or exhausted by conferring kindness. Let, therefore, believers exercise themselves in constant meditation upon the favors which God confers, that they may encourage and confirm hope as to the time to come, and always ponder in their mind this syllogism: God does not forsake the work which his own hands have begun, as the Prophet bears witness, (Psalm 138: 8; Isaiah 64: 8;) we are the work of his hands; therefore he will complete what he has begun in us. When I say that we are the work of his hands, I do not refer to mere creation, but to the calling by which we are adopted into the number of his sons. For it is a token to us of our election, that the Lord has called us effectually to himself by his Spirit.

they preached Christ, yet **not sincerely** or "purely"; not but that they delivered the sincere milk of the word, and preached the pure Gospel of Christ, without any mixture and adulteration; but then they did not preach it with a sincere heart, and a pure intention; for this respects not the doctrine they preached, but their views in it, which were not honest and upright; they did not preach Christ from a principle of love to his person, and from an inward experience of the power of his Gospel, and a zealous affection for it, and firm attachment to it, and with a view to the glory of God, the honor of Christ, and the good of immortal souls; but were influenced by avarice, ambition, and envy: they had very evil designs upon the apostle.

21. For to me to live is Christ. Christ was his life "efficiently," the efficient cause and author of his spiritual life; he spoke it into him, produced it in him, and disciplined him with it: and he was his life, objectively, the matter and object of his life, that on which he lived; yea, it was not so much he that lived, as Christ that lived in him; he lived by faith on Christ, and his spiritual life was maintained and supported by feeding on him as the bread of life: and he was his life, "finally," the end of his life; what he aimed at throughout the whole course of his life was the glory of Christ, the good of his church and people, the spread of his Gospel, the honor of his name, and the increase of his interest; and this last seems to be the true sense of the phrase here.

and to die is gain; to himself, for death is gain to believers: it is not easy to say what a believer gains by dying; he is released thereby, and delivered from all the troubles and distresses of this life, arising from diseases of body, losses and disappointments in worldly things; from the oppressions and persecutions of wicked men; from indwelling sin, unbelief, doubts, and fears, and the temptations of Satan; he as soon as dies enters into the presence of God, where is fullness of joy, and is immediately with Christ, which is far better than being here, beholding his glory and enjoying communion with him; he is at once in the company of angels and glorified saints; is possessed of perfect holiness and knowledge;

inherits a kingdom prepared from the foundation of the world, and wears a crown of life.

27. Only let your conversation be as it becometh the Gospel of Christ. Or "behave as citizens worthy of the Gospel"; for not so much their outward conversation in the world is here intended, which ought to be in wisdom towards them that are without; so as to give no offence to any, and to put to, silence, the ignorance of foolish men, and them to confusion and: shame, who falsely accuse their good conversation in Christ; though this is what is highly becoming professors of the Gospel; and a moral conversation proceeding from principles of grace, under the influence of the Spirit of God, is very ornamental to the Gospel, being what that requires and powerfully teaches; but the conversation of the saints one with another, in their church state, is here meant.

PHILIPPIANS 2

1. If [there be] therefore any consolation in Christ. Or "exhortation," as the word is sometimes rendered; that is, either if there is any exhortation of Christ to love and unity, as there is in John 13: 34, and this is of any weight and value; or if an exhortation hereunto made in the name of Christ, by any of his ministers, messengers, and ambassadors, will be regarded, as it ought to be, then fulfill ye my joy, etc. Philippians 2: 2, but as the word is frequently translated "consolation," as it is here in the Vulgate Latin, Syriac, and Arabic versions; the sense may be either, if there is any comfort to be given to them that are in Christ Jesus, as every converted man is, and as the apostle was, and especially to them that are afflicted and persecuted for the sake of Christ, are prisoners in him, and on his account, which was the apostle's case, then he desired they would attend to his following request: or if there was any consolation for them, and they had had any comfort in and from Christ; as all true, solid, strong, and everlasting consolation is only in Christ, and is founded on the greatness of his person, as God our Savior, on the fullness of his grace, the efficacy of his blood, the perfection of his righteousness and sacrifice,

3 Let nothing be done through strife or vainglory; but in lowliness of mind let each esteem other better than themselves.

4 Look not every man on his own things, but every man also on the things of others.

5 Let this mind be in you, which was also in Christ Jesus:

6 Who, being in the form of God, thought it not robbery to be equal with God:

7 But made himself of no reputation, and took upon him the form of a servant, and was made in the likeness of men:

8 And being found in fashion as a man, he humbled himself, and became obedient unto death, even the death of the cross.

9 Wherefore God also hath highly exalted him, and given him a name which is above every name:

10 That at the name of Jesus every knee should bow, of things in heaven, and things in earth, and things under the earth;

11 And that every tongue should confess that Jesus Christ is Lord, to the glory of God the Father.

12 Wherefore, my beloved, as ye have always obeyed, not as in my presence only, but now much more in my absence, work out your own salvation with fear and trembling.

13 For it is God which worketh in you both to will and to do of his good pleasure.

14 Do all things without murmurings and disputings:

15 That ye may be blameless and harmless, the sons of God, without rebuke, in the midst of a crooked and perverse nation, among whom ye shine as lights in the world;

16 Holding forth the word of life; that I may rejoice in the day of Christ, that I have not run in vain, neither laboured in vain.

17 Yea, and if I be offered upon the sacrifice and service of your faith, I joy, and rejoice with you all.

18 For the same cause also do ye joy, and rejoice with me.

19 But I trust in the Lord Jesus to send Timotheus shortly unto you, that I also may be of good comfort, when I know

PHILIPPIANS 2

1. If there is therefore any consolation

There is an extraordinary tenderness in this exhortation, in which he entreats by all means the Philippians mutually to cherish harmony among themselves, lest, in the event of their being torn asunder by intestine contentions, they should expose themselves to the impostures of the false apostles. For when there are disagreements, there is invariably a door opened for Satan to disseminate impious doctrines, while agreement is the best bulwark for repelling them.

As the term paraklses is often taken to mean **exhortation**, the commencement of the passage might be explained in this manner: "If an exhortation which is delivered in the name and by the authority of Christ, has any weight with you." The other meaning, however, corresponds better with the context: "If there is among you **any consolation of Christ**," by means of which you may alleviate my griefs, and if you would afford me **any consolation** and relief, which you assuredly owe me in the exercise of love; if you take into view that **fellowship of the Spirit**, which ought to make us all one; if any feeling of humanity and mercy resides in you, which might stir you up to alleviate my miseries, **fulfill ye my joy**, etc. From this we may infer, how great a blessing unity in the Church is, and with what eagerness pastors should endeavor to secure it. We must also at the same time take notice, how he humbles himself by beseechingly imploring their pity, while he might have availed himself of his paternal authority, so as to demand respect from them as his sons. He knew how to exercise authority when it was necessary, but at present he prefers to use entreaties, because he knew that these would be better fitted to gain an entrance into their affections, and because he was aware that he had to do with persons who were docile and compliant. In this manner the pastor must have no hesitation to assume different aspects for the sake of the Church.

2. Fulfil ye my joy

Here again we may see how little anxiety he had as to himself, provided only it went well with the Church of Christ. He was kept shut up in prison, and bound with chains; he was reckoned worthy of capital punishment – before his view were tortures – near at hand was the executioner; yet all these things do not prevent his experiencing unmingled joy, provided he sees that the Churches are in a good condition. Now what he reckons the chief indication of a prosperous condition of the Church is – when mutual agreement prevails in it, and brotherly harmony. Psalm 137 also teaches us that our crowning joy is the remembrance of Jerusalem (Psalm 137: 6). But if this were the completion

and on the great salvation he is the author of: agreeably the SyriActs version renders it, "if therefore ye have any consolation in Christ"; and the Arabic version, "if therefore ye enjoy any consolation from the grace of Christ"; which is displayed in the Gospel, as undoubtedly they did; and since then all this comfort was enjoyed by them, through the Gospel the apostle preached to them, the argument from hence must be strong upon them, to attend to what he desired of them.

8. he humbled himself: by becoming man, and by various outward actions in his life; as subjection to his parents, working at the trade of a carpenter, conversing with the meanest of men, washing his disciples' feet, etc. and the whole of his deportment both to God and man, his compliance with his Father's will, though disagreeable to flesh and blood, his behavior towards his enemies, and his forbearance of his disciples, showed him to be of a meek and humble spirit; he humbled himself both to God and man.

    and became obedient unto death, or "until death"; for he was obedient from the cradle to the cross, to God, to men, to his earthly parents, and to magistrates; he was obedient to the ceremonial law, to circumcision, the passover, etc. to the moral law, to all the precepts of it, which he punctually fulfilled; and to the penalty of it, death, which he voluntarily and cheerfully bore, in the room and stead of his people.

    even the death of the cross; which was both painful and shameful; it was an accursed one, and showed that he bore the curse of the law, and was made a curse for us: this was a punishment usually inflicted on servants, and is called a servile punishment; and such was the form which he took, when he was found in fashion as a man: this is now the great instance of humility the apostle gives, as a pattern of it to the saints, and it is a matchless and unparalleled one.

14. Do all things. Not evil things, these are to be abhorred, shunned, and avoided, even all appearance of them, they are not to be done, even the sake of good; nor all indifferent things at all times, and under all circumstances, when

the peace and edification of others are in danger of being hurt by so doing; but all good things, all that are agreeable to the righteous law and good will of God; all those good things which accompany salvation, as hearing the word, and attendance on ordinances: all church affairs relating to public worship, private conference, everything at church meetings, and which concern the discipline and laws of Christ's house; and all things that are civilly, morally, spiritually, and evangelically good; even all things that God would have done, or we would desire should be done to us by fellow creatures and fellow Christians: let all these be done without murmurings; either against God and Christ, as if anything hard and severe was enjoined, when Christ's yoke is easy, and his burden light, Matthew 11: 30.

18. For the same cause also do ye joy and rejoice with me. He would not have them be sorrowful, should they hear of his death for the sake of the Gospel, and of his blood being poured out in such a cause, since it was as a libation on their faith, and for the confirmation of it, and would be gain to Christ, and his interest, and to the apostle also: and therefore they should be so far from indulging grief and sorrow on that account, that they should rather joy and rejoice with him, who was ready to be offered up, or poured out; since he had run out his race, and that not in vain, but to so good a purpose, and especially among them.

19. But I trust in the Lord Jesus. Or "hope"; not in himself, his wisdom, will, resolutions, and purposes; nor in an arm of flesh, in any human aid and power; nor in princes, nor in Nero, the Roman emperor, as expecting a release from bonds by him, when he could the more easily part with Timothy; but in the Lord Jesus, in the Lord whom every tongue shall confess to be so; and in that Jesus, in whose name every knee shall bow; who is King of kings, and Lord of lords, and the only Savior and Deliverer of his people; who has the hearts of all men in his hands, and all power in heaven and in earth: he hoped and trusted, that through the goodness and power of Christ, opening a way for him, he should be able to send Timotheus shortly unto you; one

your state.

20 For I have no man likeminded, who will naturally care for your state.

21 For all seek their own, not the things which are Jesus Christ's.

22 But ye know the proof of him, that, as a son with the father, he hath served with me in the gospel.

23 Him therefore I hope to send presently, so soon as I shall see how it will go with me.

24 But I trust in the Lord that I also myself shall come shortly.

25 Yet I supposed it necessary to send to you Epaphroditus, my brother, and companion in labour, and fellowsoldier, but your messenger, and he that ministered to my wants.

26 For he longed after you all, and was full of heaviness, because that ye had heard that he had been sick.

27 For indeed he was sick nigh unto death: but God had mercy on him; and not on him only, but on me also, lest I should have sorrow upon sorrow.

28 I sent him therefore the more carefully, that, when ye see him again, ye may rejoice, and that I may be the less sorrowful.

29 Receive him therefore in the Lord with all gladness; and hold such in reputation:

30 Because for the work of Christ he was nigh unto death, not regarding his life, to supply your lack of service toward me.

PHILIPPIANS 3

1 Finally, my brethren, rejoice in the Lord. To write the same things to you, to me indeed is not grievous, but for you it is safe.

2 Beware of dogs, beware of evil workers, beware of the concision.

3 For we are the circumcision, which worship God in the spirit, and rejoice in Christ Jesus, and have no confidence in the flesh.

4 Though I might also have confidence in the flesh. If any other man thinketh that he hath whereof he might trust in the flesh, I more:

5 Circumcised the eighth day, of the stock of Israel, of the tribe of Benjamin,

of Paul's joy, the Philippians would have been worse than cruel if they had tortured the mind of this holy man with a twofold anguish by disagreement among themselves.

That ye think the same thing

The sum is this – that they be joined together in views and inclinations. For he makes mention of agreement in doctrine and mutual love; and afterwards, repeating the same thing, (in my opinion,) he exhorts them to be of one mind, and to have the same views. The expression *to auto*, (*the same thing*), implies that they must accommodate themselves to each other. Hence the beginning of love is harmony of views, but that is not sufficient, unless men's hearts are at the same time joined together in mutual affection. At the same time there were no inconsistency in rendering it thus: "that ye may be of the same mind – so as to have mutual love, to be one in mind and one in views;" for participles are not unfrequently made use of instead of infinitives.

3. Nothing through strife or vain-glory

These are two most dangerous pests for disturbing the peace of the Church. *Strife* is awakened when every one is prepared to maintain pertinaciously his own opinion; and when it has once begun to rage it rushes headlong in the direction from which it has entered. *Vain-glory* tickles men's minds, so that every one is delighted with his own inventions. Hence the only way of guarding against dissensions is – when we avoid strifes by deliberating and acting peacefully, especially if we are not actuated by ambition. For ambition is a means of fanning all strifes. *Vain-glory* means any glorying in the flesh; for what ground of glorying have men in themselves that is not vanity?

PHILIPPIANS 3

1. Rejoice in the Lord

This is a conclusion from what goes before, for as Satan never ceased to distress them with daily rumors, he bids them divest themselves of anxiety and be of good courage. In this way he exhorts them to constancy, that they may not fall back from the doctrine which they have once received. The phrase *henceforward* denotes a continued course, that, in the midst of many hinderances, they may not cease to exercise holy joy. It is a rare excellence when Satan endeavors to exasperate us by means of the bitterness of the cross, so as to make God's name unpleasant, to take such satisfaction in the simple tasting of God's grace, that all annoyances, sorrows, anxieties, and griefs are sweetened.

To write the same thing to you

Here he begins to speak of the false Apostles, with whom, however, he does not fight hand to hand, as in the Epistle to the Galatians, but in a few words severely exposes them, as far as was sufficient. For as they had simply made an

that had known the Scriptures from his youth, and was very early converted to the Christian faith, was an eminent preacher of the Gospel, and well known to the Philippians.

24. But I trust in the Lord. The SyriActs version reads, "in my Lord": that I also myself shall come shortly: this he adds, partly to let them see, that he still retained a secret hope and persuasion in his own mind of a deliverance, though he could not be certain of it, how things would go with him; and partly, that he might not be thought to put them off with sending Timothy to them; for notwithstanding that, his intention still was, should he be released, to pay them a visit himself.

29. Receive him therefore. Not only into their houses, where such as bring the doctrine of Christ should be admitted, and not others; but into their bosoms, into their hearts and affections, as he had reason to believe they would, and into their fellowship and communion, and to the exercise of his office among them, as their minister: and that in the Lord; or "for the Lord," as the Arabic version renders it; for his sake, because he was one that was put into the ministry by him, was called unto it, and qualified for it, and sent forth to minister in it by him; or in the name of the Lord, as an ambassador of his, as representing him, and as if he himself was present; for he that receives a minister of Christ, receives Christ himself; see Luke 10: 16.

PHILIPPIANS 3

1. Finally, my brethren, rejoice in the Lord. The SyriActs version reads, "in our Lord," i.e. Christ. The apostle seems as if he was about to conclude his epistle; and therefore, as if he was taking his farewell of this church, and giving his last advice to them, he exhorts them in a most affectionate manner, as his dear brethren in a spiritual relation, that they would make Christ their chief joy; that whatever sorrow they might have on account of his bonds, or the sickness of Epaphroditus, yet, he observes they had reason to rejoice in their Lord and Savior; and however, it might be matter of rejoicing to them to hear of his hope of coming once more to them, and of the recovery of their minister and his return to them, yet Christ should be the principal object of their joy. A believer has always reason to rejoice in Christ; in the greatness of his person, he being in the form of God, and equal to him, and therefore able to save his to the uttermost by his obedience and death.

2. Beware of dogs. By whom are meant the "judaizing" teachers, who were for imposing the works and ceremonies of the law upon the Gentiles, as necessary to salvation; and they have the name retorted on them they used to give to the Gentiles; see Matthew 15: 26. They may be styled dogs for their covetousness, being such greedy ones as in Isaiah 56: 10, with feigned words making merchandise of men; and for their love of their, bellies, which they served, and not Christ, and made a god of, Philippians 3: 19. Moreover, because they were without, as dogs are, Revelation 22: 15; having gone out from the communion of the saints, because they were not of them; or if among them, yet not true members of Christ, nor of his mystical body; all which are so many arguments why the saints should beware of them, and why their persons, conversation, and doctrine should be avoided.

Beware of evil workers: meaning the same persons, who were deceitful workers, did the work of the Lord unfaithfully, walked in craftiness, and handled the word of God deceitfully, endeavored to subvert the Gospel of Christ, and the faith of men in it; who worked from bad principles, and with evil views; and notwithstanding their large pretensions to good works, teaching that justification and salvation were by them, which notion the apostle tacitly refers to in this character; yet were of bad a character, and such as Christ will reject another day as workers of iniquity; a character they deservedly bear, if there was no other reason for it than their preaching the doctrine of salvation by men's own works of righteousness, and who, and their ministry, are by all means to be shunned.

Beware of the concision; the men of the circumcision, as the Arabic version renders it; they chose to be called so, but the apostle would not give them that name, but calls them the **concision**; or "the concision of the flesh,"

an Hebrew of the Hebrews; as touching the law, a Pharisee;

6 Concerning zeal, persecuting the church; touching the righteousness which is in the law, blameless.

7 But what things were gain to me, those I counted loss for Christ.

8 Yea doubtless, and I count all things but loss for the excellency of the knowledge of Christ Jesus my Lord: for whom I have suffered the loss of all things, and do count them but dung, that I may win Christ,

9 And be found in him, not having mine own righteousness, which is of the law, but that which is through the faith of Christ, the righteousness which is of God by faith:

10 That I may know him, and the power of his resurrection, and the fellowship of his sufferings, being made conformable unto his death;

11 If by any means I might attain unto the resurrection of the dead.

12 Not as though I had already attained, either were already perfect: but I follow after, if that I may apprehend that for which also I am apprehended of Christ Jesus.

13 Brethren, I count not myself to have apprehended: but this one thing I do, forgetting those things which are behind, and reaching forth unto those things which are before,

14 I press toward the mark for the prize of the high calling of God in Christ Jesus.

15 Let us therefore, as many as be perfect, be thus minded: and if in any thing ye be otherwise minded, God shall reveal even this unto you.

16 Nevertheless, whereto we have already attained, let us walk by the same rule, let us mind the same thing.

17 Brethren, be followers together of me, and mark them which walk so as ye have us for an ensample.

18 (For many walk, of whom I have told you often, and now tell you even weeping, that they are the enemies of the cross of Christ:

19 Whose end is destruction, whose God is their belly, and whose glory is in their shame, who mind earthly things.)

20 For our conversation is in heaven;

attempt upon the Philippians, and had not made an inroad upon them, it was not so necessary to enter into any regular disputation with the view of refuting errors, to which they had never lent an ear. Hence he simply admonishes them to be diligent and attentive in detecting impostors and guarding against them.

2. In the *first* place, however, he calls them *dogs;* the metaphor being grounded upon this – that, for the sake of filling their belly, they assailed true doctrine with their impure barking. Accordingly, it is as though he had said – impure or profane persons; for I do not agree with those who think that they are so called on the ground of envying others, or biting them.

In the *second* place, he calls them *evil workers,* meaning, that, under the pretext of building up the Church, they did nothing but ruin and destroy everything; for many are busily occupied who would do better to remain idle. As the public crier on being asked by Gracchus in mockery, on the ground of his sitting idle, what he was doing? had his answer ready, "Nay, but what are you doing?" for he was the ringleader of a ruinous sedition. Hence Paul would have a distinction made among *workers,* that believers may be on their guard against those that are *evil.*

In the *third* term employed, there is an elegant (*pros nomasia*) play upon words. They boasted that they were the *circumcision:* he turns aside this boasting by calling them the **concision,** inasmuch as they tore asunder the unity of the Church. In this we have an instance tending to shew that the Holy Spirit in his organs has not in every case avoided wit and humor, yet so as at the same time to keep at a distance from such pleasantry as were unworthy of his majesty. There are innumerable examples in the Prophets, and especially in Isaiah, so that there is no profane author that abounds more in agreeable plays upon words, and figurative forms of expression. We ought, however, more carefully still to observe the vehemence with which Paul inveighs against the false Apostles, which will assuredly break forth wherever there is the ardor of pious zeal. But in the mean time we must be on our guard lest any undue warmth or excessive bitterness should creep in under a pretext of zeal.

PHILIPPIANS 4

1. Therefore, my brethren

He concludes his doctrine, as he is wont, with most urgent exhortations, that he may fix it the more firmly in the minds of men. He also insinuates himself into their affections by endearing appellations, which at the same time are not dictated by flattery, but by sincere affection. He calls them his *joy* and *crown;* because, delighted to see those who had

as the SyriActs version renders it; referring either to the cuttings in the flesh, forbidden Leviticus 21: 5; or to the circumcision of the flesh rather, which they valued themselves upon, and were for introducing among the Gentiles, whereby they made sad divisions, and cutting work among the churches; and were some of them at least "cut" off, as the Ethiopic version renders it, from the churches; and who, as much as in them lay, cut themselves off from Christ, and rendered him unprofitable to them; see Galatians 5: 2.

7. But what things were gain to me. As circumcision, and the observance of the ceremonial law, which he thought were necessary to salvation; and his natural and lineal descent from Abraham, which he supposed entitled him to the favor of God, and eternal life, as well as to outward privileges; and his being of that strict sect of religion, a Pharisee, which he doubted not, being brought up and continued in, would secure to him everlasting happiness; and his zeal in persecuting the church of Christ, in which he thought he did God good service, and merited heaven for himself; and his legal righteousness, which he fancied was perfect, and so justified him in the sight of God, and rendered him acceptable to him: for the apostle's meaning is, not only that these things were judged by him, while in an unconverted state, good in themselves, and in some respects useful, but that they were really gainful, and meritorious of happiness in another world. But being converted, he saw all those things in a different light, and had a different opinion of them.

those I counted loss for Christ; circumcision he saw was now abolished, and was nothing, and that the circumcision of the heart was the main thing; and that the other was so far from being useful and necessary to salvation, that it was hurtful, was a yoke of bondage, bound men over to keep the whole law, and made Christ of none effect to them; and the same opinion he had of the whole ceremonial law: as for natural descent, which he once valued and trusted in, he now rejected it, well knowing it signified not whether a man was a Greek, or a Jew, a Barbarian, or Scythian, provided he was but a believer in Christ, Colossians 3: 11; and

as for any outward form or sect of religion, he knew there was no salvation in it.

14. I press toward the mark. The allusion is to the white line, or mark, which the runners in the Olympic games made up to, and to which he that came first received the prize; and by which the apostle intends the Lord Jesus Christ, who is the **mark** of all the thoughts, purposes, and counsels of God, to which they all aim, and in which they all center; and of the covenant of grace of which he is the sum and substance, the Mediator, surety, and messenger, in whom are all the blessings and promises of it; and of the Scriptures of truth, the writings of the Old and New Testament, which all testify of him, and agree in him; and of both law and Gospel, he is the end of the law, and the substance of the Gospel; and of all the graces of the Spirit, in the hearts of his people, faith looks at him, hope is concerned with him, and love has him for its object; and of all the duties believers are concerned in, they all point at him, they are done in his name and strength, through faith in him, and from a principle of love to him, and with a view to his glory; and so he is of their thoughts, affections, and desires: and to this mark they press, or "run," as the SyriActs version renders it.

17. Brethren, be followers together of me. Not that the apostle set up himself as the head of a party, which is what he always blamed in others; he did not assume a dominion over the faith of men, or seek to lord it over God's heritage; nor did he desire any to be followers of him, any further than he was a follower of Christ; and in what he was, whether in doctrine or practice, he desires to be followed in: and here he has a particular regard to what went before, concerning reckoning what was gain loss; accounting all things but dung, in comparison of the knowledge of Christ, looking to his righteousness alone for justification, Philippians 3: 9; disclaiming perfection, yet forgetting things behind; reaching towards things before, and pressing to the mark for the prize, Philippians 3: 13; and walking according to the rule of God's word; in which things he had some that followed him, who were his spiritual children, and to whom he had been

from whence also we look for the Savior, the Lord Jesus Christ:

21 Who shall change our vile body, that it may be fashioned like unto his glorious body, according to the working whereby he is able even to subdue all things unto himself.

PHILIPPIANS 4

1 Therefore, my brethren dearly beloved and longed for, my joy and crown, so stand fast in the Lord, my dearly beloved.

2 I beseech Euodias, and beseech Syntyche, that they be of the same mind in the Lord.

3 And I intreat thee also, true yokefellow, help those women which laboured with me in the gospel, with Clement also, and with other my fellowlabourers, whose names are in the book of life.

4 Rejoice in the Lord alway: and again I say, Rejoice.

5 Let your moderation be known unto all men. The Lord is at hand.

6 Be careful for nothing; but in every thing by prayer and supplication with thanksgiving let your requests be made known unto God.

7 And the peace of God, which passeth all understanding, shall keep your hearts and minds through Christ Jesus.

8 Finally, brethren, whatsoever things are true, whatsoever things are honest, whatsoever things are just, whatsoever things are pure, whatsoever things are lovely, whatsoever things are of good report; if there be any virtue, and if there be any praise, think on these things.

9 Those things, which ye have both learned, and received, and heard, and seen in me, do: and the God of peace shall be with you.

10 But I rejoiced in the Lord greatly, that now at the last your care of me hath flourished again; wherein ye were also careful, but ye lacked opportunity.

11 Not that I speak in respect of want: for I have learned, in whatsoever state I am, therewith to be content.

12 I know both how to be abased, and I know how to abound: every where and in all things I am instructed both to be full and to be hungry, both to abound and to

been gained over through his instrumentality persevering in the faith, he hoped to attain that triumph, of which we have spoken, when the Lord will reward with a *crown* those things which have been accomplished under his guidance. When he bids them *so stand fast in the Lord,* he means that their condition is approved of by him. At the same time, the particle *so* might be taken as referring to the doctrine going before; but the former view is more suitable, so that, by praising their present condition, he exhorts them to perseverance. They had already, it is true, given some evidence of their constancy. Paul, however, well knowing human weakness, reckons that they have need of confirmation for the future.

2. I exhort Euodias and Syntyche

It is an almost universally received opinion that Paul was desirous to settle a quarrel, I know not of what sort, between those two women. While I am not inclined to contend as to this, the words of Paul do not afford ground enough for such a conjecture to satisfy us that it really was so. It appears, from the testimony which he gives in their favor, that they were very excellent women; for he assigns to them so much honor as to call them fellow-soldiers in the gospel. Hence, as their agreement was a matter of great moment, and, on the other hand, there would be great danger attendant on their disagreement, he stirs them up particularly to concord.

We must take notice, however, that, whenever he speaks of agreement, he adds also the bond of it – *in the Lord.* For every combination will inevitably be accursed, if apart from the Lord, and, on the other hand, nothing is so disjoined, but that it ought to be reunited in Christ.

4. Rejoice in the Lord

It is an exhortation suited to the times; for, as the condition of the pious was exceedingly troublous, and dangers threatened them on every side, it was possible that they might give way, overcome by grief or impatience. Hence he enjoins it upon them, that, amidst circumstances of hostility and disturbance, they should nevertheless *rejoice in the Lord,* as assuredly these spiritual consolations, by means of which the Lord refreshes and gladdens us, ought *then* most of all to show their efficacy when the whole world tempts us to despair. Let us, however, in connection with the circumstances of the times, consider what efficacy there must have been in this word uttered by the mouth of Paul, who might have had special occasion of sorrow. For if they are appalled by persecutions, or imprisonments, or exile, or death, here is the Apostle setting himself forward, who, amidst imprisonments, in the very heat of persecution, and in fine, amidst apprehensions of death, is not merely himself joyful, but even stirs up others to joy. The sum, then, is this

useful in conversion and edification; see 1 Corinthians 4: 15; and he would therefore have these Philippians followers of him.

PHILIPPIANS 4

1. Therefore, my brethren. Not in a natural but spiritual relation; having the same Father, being of the same family, and household of faith: seeing that on the one hand there were false teachers, who stand described by various characters in the preceding chapter, by whom they were in danger of being carried away from the simplicity of the Gospel; and on the other hand, such were the conduct and conversation of the apostle, and other true believers, and such were their expectations of Christ from heaven, and of happiness from him as there expressed; therefore he exhorts to steadfastness in him, and that under the most tender, affectionate, and endearing appellations; given in the uprightness of his soul, without any manner of flattery, to signify his strong affection for them, and to engage them to attend the more to what he was about to exhort them to; and which arose from pure love to them, an hearty concern for their good, and the honor of Christ Jesus.

dearly beloved: as belonging to Christ, interested in him, members of him, redeemed by him, and bearing his image; and as his brethren, and so not loved with a carnal, but spiritual love.

and longed for; to see them, and impart some spiritual gift to them; being the excellent in the earth, as other saints, towards whom was his desire, and with whom was all his delight. These epithets are joined with the word "brethren," in the Vulgate Latin, Syriac, and Arabic versions, and read thus, "my dearly beloved, and longed for brethren"; and in the Ethiopic version, "our beloved brethren":

my joy and crown; they were matter of joy to him, as he had reason to hope well of them; yea, to be confident that the good work was begun, and would be carried on in them; and that they had hitherto continued in the doctrine of the Gospel, and walked worthy of it; and they were his "crown," as they were seals of his ministry; and whom he valued more, and reckoned a greater honor and ornament to him, than the richest diadem, set with the most costly jewels and precious stones, and which he hoped and believed would be his crown of rejoicing another day; when he, with them, should stand at the hand of Christ triumphing, as victors crowned, ever sin, Satan, the world, death, and hell.

so stand fast in the Lord; or "by the Lord"; by his power and strength, which is only able to make to stand fast; saints are liable to failing, and would fall, were they not upheld with his right hand, and kept by his power.

12. I know both how to be abased. Or "humbled"; to be treated with indignity and contempt, to be trampled upon by man, to suffer hardships and distress, to be in a very mean and low condition, to work with his own hands, and minister to his own and the necessities of others in that way; yea, to be in hunger and thirst, in cold and nakedness, and have no certain dwelling place; and he knew how to behave under all this; not to be depressed and cast down, or to fret, repine, and murmur.

and I know how to abound; or "to excel"; to be in the esteem of men, and to have an affluence of the things of this world, and how to behave in the midst of plenty; so as not to be lifted up, to be proud and haughty, and injurious to fellow creatures; so as not to abuse the good things of life; and so as to use them to the honor of God, the interest of religion, and the good of fellow creatures, and fellow Christians.

every where; whether among Jews or Gentiles, at Jerusalem or at Rome, or at whatsoever place; or as the Arabic version renders it, "every time": always, in every season, whether of adversity or prosperity.

and in all things; in all circumstances of life.

I am instructed; or "initiated," as he was by the Gospel; and, ever since he embraced it, was taught this lesson of contentment, and inured to the exercise of it, and was trained up and instructed how to behave himself in the different changes and vicissitudes he came into.

both to be full, and to be hungry; to know what it was to have plenty and want, to have a full meal and to want one, and be almost starved and famished, and how to conduct

suffer need.

13 I can do all things through Christ which strengtheneth me.

14 Notwithstanding ye have well done, that ye did communicate with my affliction.

15 Now ye Philippians know also, that in the beginning of the gospel, when I departed from Macedonia, no church communicated with me as concerning giving and receiving, but ye only.

16 For even in Thessalonica ye sent once and again unto my necessity.

17 Not because I desire a gift: but I desire fruit that may abound to your account.

18 But I have all, and abound: I am full, having received of Epaphroditus the things which were sent from you, an odor of a sweet smell, a sacrifice acceptable, wellpleasing to God.

19 But my God shall supply all your need according to his riches in glory by Christ Jesus.

20 Now unto God and our Father be glory for ever and ever. Amen.

21 Salute every saint in Christ Jesus. The brethren which are with me greet you.

22 All the saints salute you, chiefly they that are of Caesar's household.

23 The grace of our Lord Jesus Christ be with you all. Amen.

– that come what may, believers, having the Lord standing on their side, have amply sufficient ground of joy.

The repetition of the exhortation serves to give greater force to it: Let this be your strength and stability, to *rejoice in the Lord*, and that, too, not for a moment merely, but so that your joy in him may be perpetuated.

under such different circumstances.

both to abound and to suffer need; which the apostle repeats for confirmation sake; and the whole of what he here says is an explanation of the lesson of contentment he had learned; and the knowledge he speaks of was not speculative but experimental, and lay not merely in theory, but in practice; and now lest he should be thought guilty of arrogance, and to ascribe too much to himself, he in Philippians 4: 13 attributes all to the power and grace of Christ.

13. I can do all things. Which must not be understood in the greatest latitude, and without any limitation; for the apostle was not omnipotent, either in himself, or by the power of Christ; nor could he do all things that Christ could do; but it must be restrained to the subject matter treated of: the sense is, that he could be content in every state, and could know how to behave himself in adversity and prosperity, amidst both poverty and plenty; yea, it may be extended to all the duties incumbent on him both as a Christian and as an apostle, as to exercise a conscience void of offence towards God and men; to take the care of all the churches; to labor more abundantly than others in preaching the Gospel; and to bear all afflictions, reproaches, and persecutions for the sake of it; yea, he could willingly and cheerfully endure the most cruel and torturing death for the sake of Christ: all these things he could do, not in his own strength, for no man was more conscious of his own weakness than he was, or knew more of the impotency of human nature; and therefore always directed others to be strong in the Lord, and in, the power of his might, and in the grace that is in Christ, on which he himself always depended, and by which he did what he did; as he adds here.

through Christ which strengtheneth me. The Vulgate Latin and Ethiopic versions leave out the word "Christ," and only read "him"; and so the Alexandrian copy and others; but intend Christ as those that express it: strength to perform duty and to bear sufferings is in Christ, and which he communicates to his people; he strengthens them with strength in their souls, internally, as the word here used signifies; by virtue of which they can do whatever he enjoins them or calls them to, though without him they can do nothing.

20. Now unto God and our Father. To God, who is our Father in Christ, [be] **glory for ever and ever, Amen.** For all the grace he gives now, and for all the glory and happiness expected hereafter; for the supply of every want both temporal and spiritual; seeing every good gift comes from him, and is to be ascribed to his free grace and favor, and not to any deserts of men: and particularly he may mean for what they had sent him, and he had received from them.

21. Salute every saint in Christ Jesus. Meaning at Philippi, whether rich or poor, lesser or greater believers, common saints, as well as the officers of the church, bishops and deacons; who were in Christ by electing grace, and as their covenant head, and representative from everlasting, and which was manifested and made known by their conversion and the effectual calling.

Colossians

Introduction by John Calvin

THERE were three neighboring cities in Phrygia, as made mention of by Paul in this Epistle – Laodicea, Hierapolis, and Colosse which, as *Orosius* informs us, were overthrown by an earthquake in the times of the emperor *Nero*. Accordingly, not long after this Epistle was written, three Churches of great renown perished by a mournful as well as horrible occurrence – a bright mirror truly of divine judgment, if we had but eyes to see it. The Colossians had been, not indeed by Paul, but with fidelity and purity by Epaphras and other ministers, instructed in the gospel; but immediately afterwards, Satan had, with his *tares*, crept in (Matthew 13: 25), according to his usual and invariable manner, that he might there pervert the right faith.

Some are of opinion that there were two classes of men that endeavored to draw aside the Colossians from the purity of the gospel – that, on the one hand, the philosophers, by disputing in reference to stars, fate, and trifles of a like nature, and that the Jews, on the other hand, by urging the observance of their ceremonies, had raised up many mists with the view of throwing Christ into the shade. Those, however, who are of this opinion are influenced by a conjecture of exceedingly little weight – on the ground that PAUL makes mention of *thrones*, and *powers*, and heavenly creatures. For as to their adding also the term *elements*, it is worse than ridiculous. As, however, it is not my intention to refute the opinions of others, I shall simply state what appears to me to be the truth, and what may be inferred by sound reasoning.

In the first place, it is abundantly evident, from Paul's words, that those profligates were intent upon this – that they might mix up Christ with Moses, and might retain the shadows of the law along with the gospel. Hence it is probable that they were Jews. As, however, they colored over their fallacies with specious disguises, Paul, on this account, calls it a *vain philosophy* (Colossians 2: 8). At the same time, in employing that term, he had in his eye, in my opinion, the speculations with which they amused themselves, which were subtle, it is true, but at the same time useless and profane: for they contrived a way of access to God through means of angels, and put forth many speculations of that nature, such as are contained in the books of Dionysius on the Celestial Hierarchy, drawn from the school of the Platonists. This, therefore, is the principal object at which he aims – to teach that all things are in Christ, and that he alone ought to be reckoned amply sufficient by the Colossians.

The order, however, which he follows is this: After the inscription usually employed by him, he commends them, with the view of leading them to listen to him more attentively. He then, with the view of shutting up the way against all new and strange contrivances, bears testimony to the doctrine which they had previously received from Epaphras. Afterwards, in entreating that the Lord would increase their faith, he intimates that something is still wanting to them, that he may pave the way for imparting to them more solid instruction. On the other hand, he extols with suitable commendations the grace of God towards them, that they may not lightly esteem it. Then follows the instruction, in which he teaches that all parts of our salvation are to be found in Christ alone, that they may not seek anything elsewhere; and he puts them in mind that it was in Christ that they had obtained every blessing that they possessed, in order that they might the more carefully make it their aim to retain him to the end. And, truly, even this one article were of itself perfectly sufficient to lead us to reckon this Epistle, short as it is, to be an inestimable treasure; for what is of greater importance in the whole system of heavenly doctrine than to have Christ drawn to the life, that we may distinctly behold his excellence, his office, and all the fruits that arise to us from it.

For in this respect especially we differ from Papists, that while we are both of us called Christians, and profess to believe in Christ, they picture to themselves one that is torn, disfigured, divested of his excelience, denuded of his office, in fine, such as to be a specter rather than Christ himself: we, on the other hand, embrace him such as he is here described by Paul – loving and efficacious. This Epistle, therefore, to express it in one word, distinguishes the true Christ from a fictitious one – than which nothing better or more excellent can be desired. Towards the end of the *First Chapter* he again endeavors to secure authority for himself from the station assigned him, and in magnificent terms extols the dignity of the gospel.

In the *Second Chapter* he opens up more distinctly than he had done the reason which had induced him to write – that he might provide against the danger which he saw to be impending over them, while he touches, in passing, on the affection which he cherishes towards them, that they may know that their welfare is the object of his concern. From this he proceeds to exhortation, by which he applies the foregoing doctrine, as it were, to present use; for he bids them rest in Christ alone, and brands as vanity everything that is apart from Christ. He speaks particularly of circumcision, abstinence from food, and of other outward exercises – in which they mistakingly made the service of God to consist; and also of the absurd worship of angels, whom they put in Christ's room. Having made mention of circumcision, he takes occasion to notice also, in passing, what is the office, and what is the nature of ceremonies – from which he lays it down as a settled point that they have been abrogated by Christ. These things are treated of till the end of the *Second Chapter*.

In the *Third Chapter*, in opposition to those vain prescriptions, to the observance of which the false apostles were desirous to bind believers, he makes mention of those true offices of piety in which the Lord would have us employ ourselves; and he begins with the very *springhead* – that is, mortification of the flesh and newness of life. From this he derives the *streams* – that is, particular exhortations, some of which apply to all Christians alike, while others relate more especially to particular individuals, according to the nature of their calling.

In the beginning of the *Fourth Chapter* he follows out the same subject: afterwards, having commended himself to their prayers, he shews by many tokens how much he loves them, and is desirous to promote their welfare.

The commentaries on Colossians are by John Calvin and John Gill.

COLOSSIANS 1

1 Paul, an apostle of Jesus Christ by the will of God, and Timotheus our brother,

2 To the saints and faithful brethren in Christ which are at Colosse: Grace be unto you, and peace, from God our Father and the Lord Jesus Christ.

3 We give thanks to God and the Father of our Lord Jesus Christ, praying always for you,

4 Since we heard of your faith in Christ Jesus, and of the love which ye have to all the saints,

5 For the hope which is laid up for you in heaven, whereof ye heard before in the word of the truth of the gospel;

6 Which is come unto you, as it is in all the world; and bringeth forth fruit, as it doth also in you, since the day ye heard of it, and knew the grace of God in truth:

7 As ye also learned of Epaphras our dear fellowservant, who is for you a faithful minister of Christ;

8 Who also declared unto us your love in the Spirit.

9 For this cause we also, since the day we heard it, do not cease to pray for you, and to desire that ye might be filled with the knowledge of his will in all wisdom and spiritual understanding;

10 That ye might walk worthy of the Lord unto all pleasing, being fruitful in every good work, and increasing in the knowledge of God;

11 Strengthened with all might, according to his glorious power, unto all patience and longsuffering with joyfulness;

12 Giving thanks unto the Father, which hath made us meet to be partakers of the inheritance of the saints in light:

13 Who hath delivered us from the power of darkness, and hath translated us into the kingdom of his dear Son:

14 In whom we have redemption through his blood, even the forgiveness of sins:

15 Who is the image of the invisible God, the firstborn of every creature:

16 For by him were all things created, that are in heaven, and that are in earth, visible and invisible, whether they be

COLOSSIANS 1

1. Paul an Apostle

As the Colossians had never seen Paul, and on that account his authority was not as yet so firmly established among them as to make his private name by itself sufficient, he premises that he is an Apostle of Christ set apart by the will of God. From this it followed, that he did not act rashly in writing to persons that were not known by him, inasmuch as he was discharging an embassy with which God had intrusted him. For he was not bound to one Church merely, but his Apostleship extended to all. The term *saints* which he applies to them is more honorable, but in calling them *faithful brethren,* he allures them more willingly to listen to him. As for other things, they may be found explained in the foregoing Epistles.

3. We give thanks to God

He praises the faith and love of the Colossians, that it may encourage them the more to alacrity and constancy of perseverance. Farther, by shewing that he has a persuasion of this kind respecting them, he procures their friendly regards, that they may be the more favourably inclined and teachable for receiving his doctrine. We must always take notice that he makes use of thanksgiving in place of congratulation, by which he teaches us, that in all our joys we must readily call to remembrance the goodness of God, inasmuch as everything that is pleasant and agreeable to us is a kindness conferred by him. Besides, he admonishes us, by his example, to acknowledge with gratitude not merely those things which the Lord confers upon us, but also those things which he confers upon others.

But for what things does he give thanks to the Lord? For the *faith* and *love* of the Colossians. He acknowledges, therefore, that both are conferred by God: otherwise the gratitude were pretended. And what have we otherwise than through his liberality? If, however, even the smallest favors come to us from that source, how much more ought this same acknowledgment to be made in reference to those two gifts, in which the entire sum of our excellence consists?

4. Having heard of your faith

This was a means of stirring up his love towards them, and his concern for their welfare, when he heard it that they were distinguished by *faith* and *love.* And, unquestionably, gifts of God that are so excellent ought to have such an effect upon us as to stir us up to love them wherever they appear. He uses the expression, *faith in Christ,* that we may always bear in mind that Christ is the proper object of faith.

He employs the expression, *love towards the saints,* not with the view of excluding others, but because, in proportion as

COLOSSIANS 1

5. For the hope which is laid up for you in heaven. These words may be considered either in connection with the foregoing, and express the reason or motive which encouraged these saints to believe in Christ, and to go on believing in him, and hold fast the profession of their faith in him, and to love the saints, and show it upon all occasions, and in every case; because of the rich treasure of glory and happiness in reserve for them in heaven, which they were hoping and waiting for; this encouraged their faith in Christ, and enlarged their love and beneficence to the saints: or else with the thanksgiving of the apostle, and so contains fresh matter of it, that as thanks were given for faith and love, so for "hope"; by which is meant, not the grace of hope, for that is not in heaven, though it enters within the vail, and is conversant with heavenly things, but is in the heart; and though it supposes it, and which these persons had; they were not without it; they had a good hope through grace of eternal glory, for faith, hope, and love, always go together: nor Christ the foundation of hope; there are many things in him, which are a ground of hope of happiness, as his sufferings, and death, and redemption thereby; his resurrection from the dead, his intercessions and preparations; the promise of life in him, and the thing itself being in his gift; his righteousness and grace, which, give a title to it, and meetness for it; and he is also in heaven, but then he cannot be said to be laid up there: but the thing hoped for, everlasting happiness, is intended.

10. That ye might walk worthy of the Lord. The Vulgate Latin version reads, "of God"; to which the Ethiopic version agrees; but rather the Lord Jesus Christ seems to be designed: and to "walk worthy" of him, is to walk by faith in him; to walk after his Spirit, and according to his word, and in his ordinances; to have the conversation as becomes his Gospel, and worthy of that calling wherewith the saints are called by grace to the obtaining of his kingdom and glory. The apostle prays that their knowledge might issue in practice; for knowledge, without practice, is of no avail: he first asks for knowledge, and then practice, for how should men act according to the will of God, or Christ, unless they know it? and when they know it, they should not rest in their knowledge, but put it in practice.

unto all pleasing. The SyriActs reads it, "that ye may please God in all good works": an unregenerate man cannot please God in anything; without faith in Christ it is impossible to please him by anything man can do; Christ only could, and did always the things that pleased his Father; there are many things done by believers which are displeasing to God; nor is there anything they can do that is pleasing to God but through Christ, in whom their persons and, services are accepted; good works being done in faith, and from a principle of love, and with a view to the glory of God, are acceptable unto him through Christ; and therefore are to be carefully maintained, and studiously performed by all those that have a spiritual understanding of the will of God, and believe in Christ their Lord and Redeemer.

being fruitful in every good work; saints are trees of righteousness, the planting of the Lord; good works are the fruit, which, under the influence of divine grace, they bring forth; and this is not of one sort only, as trees usually do, but of every kind; being ingrafted into Christ the true vine, and deriving life, sap, and nourishment from him, they are filled with the fruits of righteousness by him, which they bring forth and bear, to the glory of his heavenly Father; and being such, they are pleasant plants to him, as fruit bearing trees are to the owner of them: wherefore, in order to the saints walking in their lives and conversations unto all pleasing, or pleasing in all things, the apostle prays they might be fruitful in good works, and that in everyone, in every kind of good works.

and increasing in the knowledge of God; not barely of his nature and perfections, as they are displayed in the works of creation; but of his mind, and will, and the mysteries of his grace, as they are revealed in the Gospel; of the knowledge of him in Christ, as the God of all grace, and as a covenant God and Father. The apostle had before prayed for an increase of the knowledge of the will of God, previous

thrones, or dominions, or principalities, or powers: all things were created by him, and for him:

17 And he is before all things, and by him all things consist.

18 And he is the head of the body, the church: who is the beginning, the firstborn from the dead; that in all things he might have the preeminence.

19 For it pleased the Father that in him should all fullness dwell;

20 And, having made peace through the blood of his cross, by him to reconcile all things unto himself; by him, I say, whether they be things in earth, or things in heaven.

21 And you, that were sometime alienated and enemies in your mind by wicked works, yet now hath he reconciled

22 In the body of his flesh through death, to present you holy and unblameable and unreproveable in his sight:

23 If ye continue in the faith grounded and settled, and be not moved away from the hope of the gospel, which ye have heard, and which was preached to every creature which is under heaven; whereof I Paul am made a minister;

24 Who now rejoice in my sufferings for you, and fill up that which is behind of the afflictions of Christ in my flesh for his body's sake, which is the church:

25 Whereof I am made a minister, according to the dispensation of God which is given to me for you, to fulfil the word of God;

26 Even the mystery which hath been hid from ages and from generations, but now is made manifest to his saints:

27 To whom God would make known what is the riches of the glory of this mystery among the Gentiles; which is Christ in you, the hope of glory:

28 Whom we preach, warning every man, and teaching every man in all wisdom; that we may present every man perfect in Christ Jesus:

29 Whereunto I also labour, striving according to his working, which worketh in me mightily.

any one is joined to us in God, we ought to embrace him the more closely with special affection. True love, therefore, will extend to mankind universally, because they all are our flesh, and *created in the image of God* (Genesis 9: 6); but in respect of degrees, it will begin with those who are of the *household of faith* (Galatians 6: 10).

5. For the hope which is laid up for you in heaven

For the *hope* of eternal life will never be inactive in us, so as not to produce *love* in us. For it is of necessity, that the man who is fully persuaded that a treasure of life is laid up for him in heaven will aspire thither, looking down upon this world. Meditation, however, upon the heavenly life stirs up our affections both to the worship of God, and to exercises of love. The Sophists pervert this passage for the purpose of extolling the merits of works, as if the hope of salvation depended on works. The reasoning, however, is futile. For it does not follow, that because hope stimulates us to aim at upright living, it is therefore founded upon works, inasmuch as nothing is more efficacious for this purpose than God's unmerited goodness, which utterly overthrows all confidence in works.

There is, however, an instance of *metonymy* in the use of the term *hope*, as it is taken for the thing hoped for. For the hope that is in our hearts is the glory which we hope for in heaven. At the same time, when he says, that there is a *hope* that is *laid up for us in heaven*, he means, that believers ought to feel assured as to the promise of eternal felicity, equally as though they had already a treasure laid up in a particular place.

6. As also in all the world it brings forth fruit

This has a tendency both to confirm and to comfort the pious – to see the effect of the gospel far and wide in gathering many to Christ. The faith of it does not, it is true, depend on its success, as though *we* should believe it on the ground that *many* believe it. Though the whole world should fail, though heaven itself should fall, the conscience of a pious man must not waver, because God, on whom it is founded, does nevertheless remain true. This, however, does not hinder our faith from being confirmed, whenever it perceives God's excellence, which undoubtedly shews itself with more power in proportion to the number of persons that are gained over to Christ.

COLOSSIANS 2

2. That their hearts may receive consolation

He now intimates what he desires for them, and shews that his affection is truly apostolic; for he declares that nothing else is desired by him than that they may be united together in faith and love. He shews, accordingly, that it was by no

to his request, for the putting of it in practice; and now suggests, that an increase of the knowledge of God himself may be expected in a practical use of means, an attendance on the ordinances of Christ, and a diligent performance of good works: from the whole of these petitions, it may be observed by the apostle's asking for them, that all our knowledge, and the increase of it, and all our fruitfulness in good works, are all from the Lord; and therefore we have no reason to boast of our knowledge, nor depend upon our works, but frankly to own, that notwithstanding all we know, and do, we are but unprofitable servants.

19. For it pleased [the Father]. The phrase, "the Father," is not in the original text, but is rightly supplied; since he is expressly mentioned in the context, as he who makes the saints meet to be partakers of the heavenly glory; who deliver, them from the power and dominion of sin, and translates them into the kingdom of his dear Son; and who, by Christ, reconciles all things to himself, Colossians 1: 12, and whose sovereign will and pleasure it is, **that in him should all fullness dwell**: by which is meant, not the fullness of the deity, though it is read by some the fullness of the Godhead: which seems to be transcribed from Colossians 2: 9; but though all the perfections of God are in Christ, as eternity, omnipotence, omniscience, omnipresence, immutability, independence, and necessary existence, and every other, or he would not be equal with God; nor could all the fullness of the Godhead be said to dwell in him, should anyone be wanting; yet this is a fullness possessed by him, that does not spring from, nor depend upon the Father's good will and pleasure; but what he naturally and necessarily enjoys by a participation of the same undivided nature and essence with the Father and Spirit: nor is the relative fullness of Christ intended, which is his church, so called, Ephesians 1: 23; and will be so when all the elect are gathered in, and filled with all the gifts and graces of his Spirit, and are arrived to the measure of the stature of the fullness of Christ; for though every believer dwells in Christ, and Christ in him, yet the church is not said to dwell in Christ, but Christ in the church; moreover, as

yet she is not his fullness, at least in the sense she will be, and much less can she be said to be all fullness: nor is this to be understood of Christ's fullness of fitness and abilities, as God-man and Mediator, to perform his work and office as such; though this may be taken into the sense of the text as a part, yet is not the whole; but rather chiefly that dispensatory communicative fullness, which is, of the Father's good will and pleasure, put into the hands of Christ to be distributed to others, is here designed. There is a fullness of nature in Christ; the light of nature is from him, and communicated by him to mankind; the blessings of nature are the blessings of his left hand, which he distributes to his people as he thinks fit; and all things in nature are subservient to his mediatorial kingdom and glory.

28. Whom we preach. Under the above considerations; as the riches, the glory, and the mystery of the Gospel; as the hope set before lost sinners to lay hold upon; as the only Savior and Redeemer, by whose righteousness believers are justified, through whose blood their sins are pardoned, by whose sacrifice and satisfaction atonement is made, and in whose person alone is acceptance with God: Christ and him crucified, and salvation by him, were the subjects of the ministry of the apostles; on this they dwelt, and it was this which was blessed for the conversion of sinners, the edification of saints, the planting of churches, and the setting up and establishing the kingdom and interest of Christ.

warning every man; of his lost state and condition by nature; of the wrath to come, and the danger he is in of it; of the terrors of the Lord, and of an awful judgment; showing sinners that they are unrighteous and unholy, that their nature is corrupt and impure, their best righteousness imperfect, and cannot justify them before God; that they stand guilty before him, and that destruction and misery are in all their ways; and therefore advise them to flee from the wrath to come, to the hope set before them in the Gospel.

and teaching every man in all wisdom; not natural, but spiritual and evangelical; the whole Gospel of Christ, the counsel of God, the wisdom of God in a mystery, and all the

COLOSSIANS 2

1 For I would that ye knew what great conflict I have for you, and for them at Laodicea, and for as many as have not seen my face in the flesh;

2 That their hearts might be comforted, being knit together in love, and unto all riches of the full assurance of understanding, to the acknowledgement of the mystery of God, and of the Father, and of Christ;

3 In whom are hid all the treasures of wisdom and knowledge.

4 And this I say, lest any man should beguile you with enticing words.

5 For though I be absent in the flesh, yet am I with you in the spirit, joying and beholding your order, and the stedfastness of your faith in Christ.

6 As ye have therefore received Christ Jesus the Lord, so walk ye in him:

7 Rooted and built up in him, and stablished in the faith, as ye have been taught, abounding therein with thanksgiving.

8 Beware lest any man spoil you through philosophy and vain deceit, after the tradition of men, after the rudiments of the world, and not after Christ.

9 For in him dwelleth all the fullness of the Godhead bodily.

10 And ye are complete in him, which is the head of all principality and power:

11 In whom also ye are circumcised with the circumcision made without hands, in putting off the body of the sins of the flesh by the circumcision of Christ:

12 Buried with him in baptism, wherein also ye are risen with him through the faith of the operation of God, who hath raised him from the dead.

13 And you, being dead in your sins and the uncircumcision of your flesh, hath he quickened together with him, having forgiven you all trespasses;

14 Blotting out the handwriting of ordinances that was against us, which was contrary to us, and took it out of the way, nailing it to his cross;

15 And having spoiled principalities and powers, he made a shew of them openly, triumphing over them in it.

16 Let no man therefore judge you

unreasonable affection (as happens in the case of some) that he had been led to take upon himself so great a concern for the Colossians and others, but because the duty of his office required it.

The term *consolation* is taken here to denote that true quietness in which they may repose. This he declares they will at length come to enjoy in the event of their being *united in love* and faith. From this it appears where the chief good is, and in what things it consists – when mutually agreed in one faith, we are also joined together in mutual love. This, I say, is the solid joy of a pious mind – this is the blessed life. As, however, love is here commended from its effect, because it fills the mind of the pious with true joy; so, on the other hand, the cause of it is pointed out by him, when he says, in *all fullness of understanding.* The bond also of holy unity is the truth of God, when we embrace it with one consent; for peace and agreement with men flow forth from that fountain.

Riches of the assurance of understanding

As many, contenting themselves with a slight taste, have nothing but a confused and evanescent knowledge, he makes mention expressly of the *riches of understanding.* By this phrase he means full and clear perception; and at the same time admonishes them, that according to the measure of understanding they must make progress also in love.

In the term assurance, he distinguishes between faith and mere opinion; for that man truly knows the Lord who does not vacillate or waver in doubt, but stands fast in a firm and constant persuasion. This constancy and stability Paul frequently calls (pl *rophorian*) full assurance, (which term he makes use of here also,) and always connects it with faith, as undoubtedly it can no more be separated from it than heat or light can be from the sun. The doctrine, therefore, of the schoolmen is devilish, inasmuch as it takes away assurance, and substitutes in its place moral conjecture, as they term it.

Is an acknowledgment of the mystery

This clause must be read as added by way of *apposition*, for he explains what that knowledge is, of which he has made mention – that it is nothing else than the knowledge of the gospel. For the false apostles themselves endeavor to set off their impostures under the title of wisdom, but Paul retains the sons of God within the limits of the gospel exclusively, that they may desire to *know nothing else* (1 Corinthians 2: 2). Why he uses the term *mystery* to denote the gospel, has been already explained. Let us, however, learn from this, that the gospel can be understood by faith alone – not by reason, nor by the perspicacity of the human understanding, because otherwise it is a thing that is hid from us.

The *mystery of God* I understand in a passive signification, as meaning – that in which God is revealed, for he immedi-

branches of it; teaching them to believe in Christ for salvation, to lay hold on his righteousness for justification, to deal with his blood for pardon, and with his sacrifice for the atonement of their sins; and to observe all things commanded by Christ, and to live soberly, righteously, and godly: by these two words, "warning" and "teaching," the several parts of the Gospel ministry are expressed; and which extend to all sorts of men, rich and poor, bond and free, greater and lesser sinners, Gentiles as well as Jews; and who are chiefly designed here, and elsewhere, by every man and every creature.

that we may present every man perfect in Christ Jesus; not in themselves, in which sense no man is perfect in this life; but in the grace, holiness, and righteousness of Christ, in whom all the saints are complete: or it may regard that ripeness of understanding, and perfection of knowledge, which, when arrived unto, saints become perfect men in Christ; and is the end of the Gospel ministry, and to which men are brought by it; see Ephesians 4: 13.

COLOSSIANS 2

3. In whom are hid all the treasures of wisdom and knowledge. This may be understood either of the mystery of the Gospel, which contains the rich mines and hidden treasures of all divine truths; so called, because of the richness and intrinsic value and excellency of them; and because of their variety and abundance, being the unsearchable riches of Christ: or of Christ himself; and not so much of his personal wisdom, either as God, being the all-wise God, the wisdom of God, an omniscient Being, that knows all persons and things whatever, within the whole circle of wisdom and knowledge; or as man, whose wisdom and knowledge, though created, was very large and abundant; or as Mediator, on whom the spirit of wisdom and understanding, of counsel and of knowledge, rests; but of that fullness of truth as well as grace, which dwells in him as in its subject and fountain; by whom it comes, and from whom it is derived unto us; and our highest wisdom and knowledge lies in knowing him, whom to know is life eternal; and the excellency of whose knowledge surpasses everything else; it is the greatest riches, and most valuable treasure; nor is there anything worth knowing but what is in Christ, all is laid up in him: and being said to be "hid" in him, shows the excellency of the wisdom and knowledge that is in him only valuable things being hid, or compared to hid treasure; that this cannot be had without knowing him; that it is imperfect in the present state.

12. Buried with him in baptism. The apostle goes on to observe how complete and perfect the saints are in Christ; that they are not only circumcised in him in a spiritual sense, and the body of the sins of their flesh is put off, and removed from them, in allusion to the cutting off and casting away of the foreskin in circumcision; but that they and all their sins were buried with Christ, of which their baptism in water was a lively representation: Christ having died for their sins, was laid in the grave, where he continued for a while, and then rose again; and as they were crucified with him, they were also buried with him, as their head and representative; and all their sins too, which he left behind him in the grave, signified by his grave clothes there; and baptism being performed by immersion, when the person baptized is covered with water, and as it were buried in it, is a very significant emblem of all this; it is a representation of the burial of Christ, and very fitly holds him forth to the view of faith in the state of the dead, in the grave, and points out the place where the Lord lay; and it is also a representation of our burial with him, as being dead to sin, to the law, and to the world, by him. This shows now, that baptism was performed by dipping, or covering the whole body in water, for no other form of administration of baptism, as sprinkling, or pouring water on the face, can represent a burial, or be called one.

15. [And] having spoiled principalities and powers. Principalities of hell, the infernal powers of darkness, the devil that had the power of death, the accuser of the brethren, who often objected their debts, with all his works and posse: these Christ has divested of their armor, wherein they trusted to have ruined men, as sin, the law, and death; he

in meat, or in drink, or in respect of an holyday, or of the new moon, or of the sabbath days:

17 Which are a shadow of things to come; but the body is of Christ.

18 Let no man beguile you of your reward in a voluntary humility and worshipping of angels, intruding into those things which he hath not seen, vainly puffed up by his fleshly mind,

19 And not holding the Head, from which all the body by joints and bands having nourishment ministered, and knit together, increaseth with the increase of God.

20 Wherefore if ye be dead with Christ from the rudiments of the world, why, as though living in the world, are ye subject to ordinances,

21 (Touch not; taste not; handle not;

22 Which all are to perish with the using;) after the commandments and doctrines of men?

23 Which things have indeed a shew of wisdom in will worship, and humility, and neglecting of the body; not in any honor to the satisfying of the flesh.

COLOSSIANS 3

1 If ye then be risen with Christ, seek those things which are above, where Christ sitteth on the right hand of God.

2 Set your affection on things above, not on things on the earth.

3 For ye are dead, and your life is hid with Christ in God.

4 When Christ, who is our life, shall appear, then shall ye also appear with him in glory.

5 Mortify therefore your members which are upon the earth; fornication, uncleanness, inordinate affection, evil concupiscence, and covetousness, which is idolatry:

6 For which things' sake the wrath of God cometh on the children of disobedience:

7 In the which ye also walked some time, when ye lived in them.

8 But now ye also put off all these; anger, wrath, malice, blasphemy, filthy communication out of your mouth.

ately adds – *and of the Father, and of Christ* – by which expression he means that God cannot be known otherwise than *in Christ*, as, on the other hand, the Father must necessarily be known where Christ is known. For John affirms both: "He that hath the Son, hath the Father also: he that hath not the Son, hath also not the Father" (1 John 2: 23).

Hence all that think that they know anything of God apart from Christ, contrive to themselves an idol in the place of God; as also, on the other hand, that man is ignorant of Christ, who is not led by him to the Father, and who does not in him embrace God wholly. In the mean time, it is a memorable passage for proving Christ's divinity, and the unity of his essence with the Father. For having spoken previously as to the knowledge of God, he immediately applies it to the Son, as well as to the Father, whence it follows, that the Son is God equally with the Father.

COLOSSIANS 3

To those fruitless exercises which the false apostles urged, as though perfection consisted in them, he opposes those true exercises in which it becomes Christians to employ themselves; and this has no slight bearing upon the point in hand; for when we see what God would have us do, we afterwards easily despise the inventions of men. When we perceive, too, that what God recommends to us is much more lofty and excellent than what men inculcate, our alacrity of mind increases for following God, so as to disregard men. Paul here exhorts the Colossians to meditation upon the heavenly life. And what as to his opponents? They were desirous to retain their childish rudiments. This doctrine, therefore, makes the ceremonies be the more lightly esteemed. Hence it is manifest that Paul, in this passage, exhorts in such a manner as to confirm the foregoing doctrine; for, in describing solid piety and holiness of life, his aim is, that those vain *shows* of human traditions may vanish. At the same time, he anticipates an objection with which the false apostles might assail him. What then? "Wouldst thou rather have men be idle than addict themselves to such exercises, of whatever sort they may be?" When, therefore, he bids Christians apply themselves to exercises of a greatly superior kind, he cuts off the handle for this calumny; nay more, he loads them with no small odium, on the ground that they impede the right course of the pious by worthless amusements.

1. If ye are risen with Christ

Ascension follows resurrection: hence, if we are the members of Christ we must ascend into heaven, because he, on being raised up from the dead, was *received up into heaven* (Mark 16: 19), that he might draw us up with him. Now, we *seek those things which are above*, when in our minds we are

has ransomed his people from him that was stronger than they, and taken the prey out of the hands of the mighty; he has bruised the serpent's head, demolished his works, destroyed him himself, and all his powers, and defeated all their counsels and designs against his elect.

17. Which are a shadow of things to come. By Christ, and under the Gospel dispensation; that is, they were types, figures, and representations of spiritual and evangelical things: the different "meats and drinks," clean and unclean, allowed or forbidden by the law, were emblems of the two people, the Jews and Gentiles, the one clean, the other unclean; but since these are become one in Christ, the distinction of meats is ceased, these shadows are gone; and also of the different food of regenerate and unregenerate souls, the latter feeding on impure food, the ashes and husks of sensual lusts, or their own works, the former on the milk and meat in the Gospel, the wholesome words of Christ; and likewise the clean meat was a shadow of Christ himself, whose flesh is meat indeed, and whose blood is drink indeed. The "holy days," or "feasts" of the Jews, the feasts of tabernacles, of the passover and Pentecost, were types of Christ; the feast of tabernacles, though it was in remembrance of the Israelites dwelling in tents and booths when they came out of Egypt, yet was also a representation of the people of God dwelling in the earthly houses of their tabernacles here on earth; and particularly of Christ's dwelling, or tabernacling in human nature.

COLOSSIANS 3

1. If ye then be risen with Christ. The apostle having observed in the former chapter, that the believing Colossians were dead with Christ from the rudiments of the world, were buried with him in baptism, and were risen with him through the faith of the operation of God, argues from hence how much it became them to regard a new and spiritual life, and to seek after superior and heavenly things, and treat with neglect and contempt carnal and earthly ones. For he does not here call in question their being risen with Christ, but takes it for

granted that they were, and makes use of it as an argument for his present purpose. They were risen with Christ as their head, and as members in union with him representatively, when he rose from the dead; and emblematically in their baptism, when having gone down into the water, and being baptized, they emersed from it; and spiritually in conversion, when they were raised from a death of sin, to a life of grace, by Christ, as the resurrection and the life, the efficient cause of it, and in virtue of his resurrection from the dead: wherefore being thus raised again in every sense, it highly became them to **seek those things which are above**. This refers to the better and heavenly country, the continuing city, which is above the heavens, whose builder and maker is God; Christ, who is in heaven, and salvation alone by him without the works of the law; all spiritual blessings, such as pardon, peace, righteousness, life, and glory, which are in heavenly places in him; doctrines and ordinances, which come from heaven, and are the means of supporting a spiritual and heavenly life.

8. But now you also put off all these. Intimating, that now since they were converted and delivered out of the former state in which they were once, and professed not to walk and live in sin, it became them to separate, remove, and put at a distance from them all sins, and every vice, to lay them aside as dead weights upon them, and put them off as filthy garments; for such sins are never to be put on, and cleaved to again as formerly; and that not only those, the above mentioned, fornication, uncleanness, inordinate affection, evil concupiscence, and covetousness, but the following also, **anger, wrath, malice, blasphemy**, or "evil speaking"; what vices are here intended; to which is added, **filthy communication, which comes out of** the mouth. It is to be removed and put out of it, or abstained from; and which is to be understood also of blasphemy, or evil speaking of one another, whereby the credit and reputation of each other may be hurt. **Filthy communication** is the same with that which is said to be corrupt, Ephesians 4: 29; and which, though it is applicable to all speech that is unsavory, unedifying, idle, and useless, and may be properly enough said of flattery, lying,

9 Lie not one to another, seeing that ye have put off the old man with his deeds;

10 And have put on the new man, which is renewed in knowledge after the image of him that created him:

11 Where there is neither Greek nor Jew, circumcision nor uncircumcision, Barbarian, Scythian, bond nor free: but Christ is all, and in all.

12 Put on therefore, as the elect of God, holy and beloved, bowels of mercies, kindness, humbleness of mind, meekness, longsuffering;

13 Forbearing one another, and forgiving one another, if any man have a quarrel against any: even as Christ forgave you, so also do ye.

14 And above all these things put on charity, which is the bond of perfectness.

15 And let the peace of God rule in your hearts, to the which also ye are called in one body; and be ye thankful.

16 Let the word of Christ dwell in you richly in all wisdom; teaching and admonishing one another in psalms and hymns and spiritual songs, singing with grace in your hearts to the Lord.

17 And whatsoever ye do in word or deed, do all in the name of the Lord Jesus, giving thanks to God and the Father by him.

18 Wives, submit yourselves unto your own husbands, as it is fit in the Lord.

19 Husbands, love your wives, and be not bitter against them.

20 Children, obey your parents in all things: for this is well pleasing unto the Lord.

21 Fathers, provoke not your children to anger, lest they be discouraged.

22 Servants, obey in all things your masters according to the flesh; not with eyeservice, as menpleasers; but in singleness of heart, fearing God:

23 And whatsoever ye do, do it heartily, as to the Lord, and not unto men;

24 Knowing that of the Lord ye shall receive the reward of the inheritance: for ye serve the Lord Christ.

25 But he that doeth wrong shall receive for the wrong which he hath done: and there is no respect of persons.

truly sojourners in this world, and are not bound to it. The word rendered *think upon* expresses rather assiduity and intensity of aim: "Let your whole meditation be as to this: to this apply your intellect – to this your mind." But if we ought to think of nothing but of what is heavenly, because Christ is in heaven, how much less becoming were it to seek Christ upon the earth. Let us therefore bear in mind that *that* is a true and holy *thinking* as to Christ, which forthwith bears us up into heaven, that we may there adore him, and that our minds may dwell with him.

As to the *right hand of God*, it is not confined to heaven, but fills the whole world. Paul has made mention of it here to intimate that Christ encompasses us by his power, that we may not think that distance of place is a cause of separation between us and him, and that at the same time his majesty may excite us wholly to reverence him.

2. Not the things that are on earth

He does not mean, as he does a little afterwards, depraved appetites, which reign in earthly men, nor even riches, or fields, or houses, nor any other things of the present life, which we must "use, as though we did not use them" (1 Corinthians 7: 30–31), but is still following out his discussion as to ceremonies, which he represents as resembling entanglements which constrain us to creep upon the ground. "Christ," says he, "calls us upwards to himself, while these draw us downwards." For this is the winding-up and exposition of what he had lately touched upon as to the abolition of ceremonies through the death of Christ. "The ceremonies are dead to you through the death of Christ, and you to them, in order that, being raised up to heaven with Christ, you may think only of those things that are above. Leave off therefore earthly things." I shall not contend against others who are of a different mind; but certainly the Apostle appears to me to go on step by step, so that, in the first instance, he places traditions as to trivial matters in contrast with meditation on the heavenly life, and afterwards, as we shall see, goes a step farther.

COLOSSIANS 4

5. Walk wisely

He makes mention of *those that are without*, in contrast with those that are of the *household of faith* (Galatians 6: 10). For the Church is like a city of which all believers are the inhabitants, connected with each other by a mutual relationship, while unbelievers are strangers. But why would he have regard to be had to them, rather than to believers? There are three reasons: *first*, "lest any stumblingblock be put in, the way of the blind" (Leviticus 19: 14), for nothing is more ready to occur, than that unbelievers are driven from bad to worse through our imprudence, and their minds are

cursing, and swearing; yet chiefly regards obscene language, unchaste words, and filthy talking, which tend to encourage and cherish the sin of uncleanness in any of its branches, flattery, lying, cursing, and swearing; yet chiefly regards obscene language, unchaste words, and filthy talking, which tend to encourage and cherish the sin of uncleanness in any of its branches.

12. Put on therefore. As the apostle had argued for the putting off of the members of the body, from their having put off the old man himself; so he now argues from their having put on the new man, to their putting on of his members; that is, to the exercise of the various graces of the Spirit, and the discharge of the several duties of religion; which though they would not be a robe of righteousness, or garments of salvation to them, yet would be very becoming conversation garments, such as would be adorning to themselves, to the doctrine of Christ, and their profession of it, without which they would be naked in their walk, and exposed to shame.

as the elect of God, holy and beloved; that is, "as becomes the elect of God," as the Arabic version renders it; as such who were chosen in Christ from eternity, according to the sovereign will and pleasure of God, and his free grace unto salvation and eternal life; which carries in it a strong argument to enforce the performance of good works, since men are hereby chosen unto holiness, and good works are what God has foreordained that they should walk in, and especially to mercy, and acts of it; since hereby their salvation appears to be not of man's will and works, but of God, that shows mercy; and such who are the objects of this grace are vessels of mercy. The apostle calls all the members of this church by this name, though every individual of them might not be chosen of God; but because they were all under a visible profession of faith and holiness, and the greater part of them were truly believers, he in a judgment of charity gives them all this appellation, and upon the same foot, the next, "holy"; not by birth, for they were by nature unclean and filthy, conceived in sin, and shapen in iniquity; nor by baptism, which takes away neither original

nor actual sin, but leaves men as it finds them, and who ought to be holy before they partake of that; but in Christ imputatively, as he was made of God unto them sanctification; and by him efficaciously, in virtue of his blood, righteousness, and sacrifice, by which he sanctifies his people; and by his spirit inherently and internally, who is the author of the work of sanctification in the heart; and they were likewise so externally in a professional way, and therefore it highly became them to exercise and practice the following graces and duties, to which they were still more obliged, inasmuch as they were "beloved"; that is, of God, as appeared both from their election and sanctification. God had loved them, and therefore had chosen them in his Son, and had given his Son to die for them, that he might sanctify them; and because of his great love to them, had quickened them when dead in sin, and sanctified them by his spirit.

bowels of mercies; a sympathizing spirit with saints in distress, weeping with them that weep, suffering with them that suffer, being touched, as their high priest is, with a feeling of their sorrows and weaknesses: it denotes inward pity and compassion to distressed objects, the most tender regard to persons in misery, and such compassion as is free from all hypocrisy and deceit, and therefore is expressed by "bowels"; and what is very large, and reaches to multitudes of objects, and is displayed and exerted various ways, and therefore signified by **mercies**.

kindness, which is this inward, tender, unfeigned, and abundant mercy put into act and exercise; this is doing good to all men, especially to the household of faith, distributing to the necessities of the saints, and a showing mercy with cheerfulness, and is very ornamental to a Christian professor: as is also **humbleness of mind**; which lies in the saints entertaining mean thoughts of themselves, looking upon themselves as the chief of sinners, and less than the least of all saints.

23. And whatsoever ye do. Some have thought that these words, and the two following verses, regard the Colossians in general, and the performance of any, and all good works by them; but by their connection with the

COLOSSIANS 4

1 Masters, give unto your servants that which is just and equal; knowing that ye also have a Master in heaven.

2 Continue in prayer, and watch in the same with thanksgiving;

3 Withal praying also for us, that God would open unto us a door of utterance, to speak the mystery of Christ, for which I am also in bonds:

4 That I may make it manifest, as I ought to speak.

5 Walk in wisdom toward them that are without, redeeming the time.

6 Let your speech be alway with grace, seasoned with salt, that ye may know how ye ought to answer every man.

7 All my state shall Tychicus declare unto you, who is a beloved brother, and a faithful minister and fellowservant in the Lord:

8 Whom I have sent unto you for the same purpose, that he might know your estate, and comfort your hearts;

9 With Onesimus, a faithful and beloved brother, who is one of you. They shall make known unto you all things which are done here.

10 Aristarchus my fellowprisoner saluteth you, and Marcus, sister's son to Barnabas, (touching whom ye received commandments: if he come unto you, receive him;)

11 And Jesus, which is called Justus, who are of the circumcision. These only are my fellowworkers unto the kingdom of God, which have been a comfort unto me.

12 Epaphras, who is one of you, a servant of Christ, saluteth you, always labouring fervently for you in prayers, that ye may stand perfect and complete in all the will of God.

13 For I bear him record, that he hath a great zeal for you, and them that are in Laodicea, and them in Hierapolis.

14 Luke, the beloved physician, and Demas, greet you.

15 Salute the brethren which are in Laodicea, and Nymphas, and the church which is in his house.

16 And when this epistle is read

wounded, so that they hold religion more and more in abhorrence.

Secondly, it is lest any occasion may be given for detracting from the honor of the gospel, and thus the name of Christ be exposed to derision, persons be rendered more hostile, and disturbances and persecutions be stirred up.

Lastly, it is, lest, while we are mingled together, in partaking of food, and on other occasions, we be defiled by their pollutions, and by little and little become profane.

To the same effect, also, is what follows, *redeeming the time,* that is, because intercourse with them is dangerous. For in Ephesians 5: 16, he assigns the reason, *because the days are evil.* "Amidst so great a corruption as prevails in the world we must seize opportunities of doing good, and we must struggle against impediments." The more, therefore, that our path is blocked up with occasions of offense, so much the more carefully must we take heed lest our feet should stumble, or we should stop short through indolence.

16. Let it be read in the Church of the Laodiceans

Hence, though it was addressed to the Colossians, it was, nevertheless, necessary that it should be profitable to others. The same view must also be taken of all the Epistles. They were indeed, in the first instance, addressed to particular Churches, but, as they contain doctrine that is always in force, and is common to all ages, it is of no importance what title they bear, for the subject matter belongs to us. It has been groundlessly supposed that the other Epistle of which he makes mention was written by Paul, and those labor under a double mistake who think that it was written by Paul to the Laodiceans. I have no doubt that it was an Epistle that had been sent to Paul, the perusal of which might be profitable to the Colossians, as neighboring towns have usually many things in common. There was, however, an exceedingly gross imposture in the circumstance that some worthless person, I know not who, had the audacity to forge, under this pretext, an Epistle, that is so insipid, that nothing can be conceived to be more foreign to Paul's spirit.

17. Say to Archippus

So far as I can conjecture, this Archippus was, in the mean time, discharging the office of pastor, during the absence of Epaphras; but perhaps he was not of such a disposition as to be sufficiently diligent of himself without being stirred up. Paul, accordingly, would have him be more fully encouraged by the exhortation of the whole Church. He might have admonished him in his own name individually; but he gives this charge to the Colossians that they may know that they must themselves employ incitements, if they see their pastor cold, and the pastor himself does not refuse to be admonished by the Church. For the ministers of the word are

preceding verse, and with the beginning of the next chapter, they appear to concern servants only, and what they do under that character, and under the discharge of their duty.

do it heartily, not by mere force and necessity, grudgingly, and with murmurings, but from the heart, and with good will, having a true, real, and hearty affection for their masters, having their good and interest at heart, and a delight in their service; like the Hebrew servant, that loved his master, as also his wife and children, and therefore would not depart from him, see Exodus 21: 5.

COLOSSIANS 4

2. Continue in prayer. This is not said particularly to masters, as in the foregoing verse, but to all the members of the church in general; for the apostle having taken notice of some special duties relating to persons in different stations of life, returns to such as were common to them all; as this of prayer to God is, for such prayer is intended; for though the object is not expressed here, he is in the following verse, and the Mediator Christ is supposed, and also the Holy Spirit, whose assistance is necessary to it. The things exhorted to, and required in prayer, are, first, as in this clause, continuance in it, which does not mean that men should be always formally praying to God; nor can it be thought that saints are always in praying frames of soul, though such are always desirable; but it intends frequency and constancy in prayer, in opposition to an entire restraint and omission of it, and to a performance of it but now and then, or very rarely; for though Christians are not, as the Jews were, bound to certain stated hours of prayer, so many times in a day, yet a day should not pass without prayer to God; for their daily cases call for it; their lives, their health, their daily bread, and all their temporal enjoyments, which depend on his daily goodness, providence, and power; their spiritual affairs, the renewing of the inward man day by day, fresh supplies of grace for new service; their daily trials and afflictions, their continued enemies, sin, Satan, and the world, all fully show the necessity of daily prayer: besides, God does not always immediately answer the prayers of his people,

he will be sought unto time after time, even for a blessing he intends to give; and therefore the saints should not be discouraged, but continue in prayer till they receive the mercy, and their importunity is a means of enjoying it, as in the case of the poor widow; and which is an encouraging reason why men should pray always, and not faint.

5. Walk in wisdom. Or wisely, circumspectly, not as fools, but as wise men.

Towards them that are without; so the Jews used to call the Gentiles, all that were out of their own land, that were not of their nation or religion, who were aliens from them, and strangers to their privileges; and sometimes the unbelieving. Jews bear the same character, see Mark 4: 11.

redeeming the time; as an instance of prudent walking towards them that are without.

14. Luke, the beloved physician. Luke the Evangelist, though some doubt it, is here intended, who was a constant companion of the apostle in his troubles, and went with him to Rome, as the Acts of the Apostles wrote by him show, and as from 2 Timothy 4: 11 it appears; so Jerome calls the Evangelist Luke, the physician of Antioch, for from thence he was; and being converted by the Apostle Paul, as is very probable, though some make him to be one of the seventy disciples. He became of a physician of bodies, a physician of souls: some say he was a scholar of Galen, the famous physician, and others that he was his sister's son; who having heard of Christ's miracles, set out with his master Galen for Judea, to know the truth of them, of which they doubted; Galen died by the way, Luke came to Christ, and being taught by him, became one of the seventy disciples.

The apostle calls him **beloved**, not on account of his profession, in which he might be useful to many, but as he was a brother in Christ, a minister of the Gospel, and a fellow laborer of his. This is the same person as Lucas, mentioned along with Demas, and others, as here, in Philemon 1: 24. The name perhaps is Roman, but was, however, well known among the Jews.

and Demas greet you; the same who,

among you, cause that it be read also in the church of the Laodiceans; and that ye likewise read the epistle from Laodicea.

17 And say to Archippus, Take heed to the ministry which thou hast received in the Lord, that thou fulfil it.

18 The salutation by the hand of me Paul. Remember my bonds. Grace be with you. Amen.

endowed with signal authority, but such at the same time as is not exempt from laws. Hence, it is necessary that they should shew themselves teachable if they would duly teach others. As to Paul's calling attention again to his *bonds*, he intimates by this that he was in no slight degree afflicted. For he was mindful of human infirmity, and without doubt he felt some twinges of it in himself, inasmuch as he was so very urgent that all pious persons, should be mindful of his distresses. It is, however, no evidence of distrust, that he calls in from all quarters the helps that were appointed him by the Lord.

The subscription, *with his own hand*, means that there were even then spurious epistles in circulation, so that it was necessary to provide against imposition.

through the love of the present world, forsook the apostle, 2 Timothy 4: 10 which he did either after the writing of this epistle, or if before it, he was now returned again to him.

16. And when this epistle is read amongst you, etc, Which the apostle was now writing, and sent unto them; and which was to be read publicly, before the whole church; being sent not to any particular person, or persons, but to the whole body, and for their general good and instruction.

18. The salutation by the hand of me Paul. After his amanuensis had finished the epistle, he added his usual salutation to it with his own hand, to prevent all counterfeits and impositions, and that the churches to whom he wrote might be sure of the genuineness of his epistles; but before he added it to it, he either wrote with his own hand, or ordered to be written the following words, **remember my bonds**; this he says, partly that they might be animated to abide by the Gospel, for which, as he had told them before, Colossians 4: 3 that he was in bonds; and partly to encourage them, by his example, patiently to endure what afflictions and persecutions soever they should meet with, for the sake of it; as also that they might be moved hereby, to remember him in their prayers, that, if it was the will of God, he might be released, and be yet further useful in preaching the Gospel; or however, that he might be supported in his bonds, and cheerfully bear them, and remain steadfast in his faith in Christ unto the end: and then follows the salutation, **grace be with you, Amen**; which is common to all his epistles, and well suits them; in which he so much displays the grace of God, as it is expressed in the Gospel; and which his heart was full of, and earnestly desired might be more largely manifested to, and bestowed upon the saints.

1 Thessalonians

Introduction by John Calvin

THE greater part of this Epistle consists of exhortations. Paul had instructed the Thessalonians in the right faith. On hearing, however, that persecutions were raging there, he had sent Timothy with the view of animating them for the conflict, that they might not give way through fear, as human infirmity is apt to do. Having been afterwards informed by Timothy respecting their entire condition, he employs various arguments to confirm them in steadfastness of faith, as well as in patience, should they be called to endure anything for the testimony of the gospel. These things he treats of in the *first three* Chapters.

In the beginning of the *Fourth* Chapter, he exhorts them, in general terms, to holiness of life, afterwards he recommends mutual benevolence, and all offices that flow from it. Towards the end, however, he touches upon the question of the resurrection, and explains in what way we shall all be raised up from death. From this it is manifest, that there were some wicked or light-minded persons, who endeavored to unsettle their faith by unseasonably bringing forward many frivolous things. Hence with the view of cutting off all pretext for foolish and needless disputations, he instructs them in few words as to the views which they should entertain.

In the *Fifth* Chapter he prohibits them, even more strictly, from inquiring as to *times*; but admonishes them to be ever on the watch, lest they should be taken unawares by Christ's sudden and unexpected approach. From this he proceeds to employ various exhortations, and then concludes the Epistle.

The commentaries on 1 Thessalonians are by John Calvin and Albert Barnes.

1 THESSALONIANS 1

1 Paul, and Silvanus, and Timotheus, unto the church of the Thessalonians which is in God the Father and in the Lord Jesus Christ: Grace be unto you, and peace, from God our Father, and the Lord Jesus Christ.

2 We give thanks to God always for you all, making mention of you in our prayers;

3 Remembering without ceasing your work of faith, and labour of love, and patience of hope in our Lord Jesus Christ, in the sight of God and our Father;

4 Knowing, brethren beloved, your election of God.

5 For our gospel came not unto you in word only, but also in power, and in the Holy Ghost, and in much assurance; as ye know what manner of men we were among you for your sake.

6 And ye became followers of us, and of the Lord, having received the word in much affliction, with joy of the Holy Ghost:

7 So that ye were ensamples to all that believe in Macedonia and Achaia.

8 For from you sounded out the word of the Lord not only in Macedonia and Achaia, but also in every place your faith to God-ward is spread abroad; so that we need not to speak any thing.

9 For they themselves shew of us what manner of entering in we had unto you, and how ye turned to God from idols to serve the living and true God;

10 And to wait for his Son from heaven, whom he raised from the dead, even Jesus, which delivered us from the wrath to come.

1 THESSALONIANS 2

1 For yourselves, brethren, know our entrance in unto you, that it was not in vain:

2 But even after that we had suffered before, and were shamefully entreated, as ye know, at Philippi, we were bold in our God to speak unto you the gospel of God with much contention.

3 For our exhortation was not of deceit, nor of uncleanness, nor in guile:

4 But as we were allowed of God to be put in trust with the gospel, even so

1 THESSALONIANS 1

The brevity of the inscription clearly shews that Paul's doctrine had been received with reverence among the Thessalonians, and that without controversy they all rendered to him the honor that he deserved. For when in other Epistles he designates himself an Apostle, he does this for the purpose of claiming for himself authority. Hence the circumstance, that he simply makes use of his own name without any title of honor, is an evidence that those to whom he writes voluntarily acknowledged him to be such as he was. The ministers of Satan, it is true, had endeavored to trouble this Church also, but it is evident that their machinations were fruitless. He associates, however, two others along with himself, as being, in common with himself, the authors of the Epistle. Nothing farther is stated here that has not been explained elsewhere, excepting that he says, "the Church *in God the Father, and in Christ;*" by which terms (if I mistake not) he intimates, that there is truly among the Thessalonians a Church of God. This mark, therefore, is as it were an approval of a true and lawful Church. We may, however, at the same time infer from it, that a Church is to be sought for only where God presides, and where Christ reigns, and that, in short, there is no Church but what is founded upon God, is gathered under the auspices of Christ, and is united in his name.

2. We give thanks to God

He praises, as he is wont, their faith and other virtues, not so much, however, for the purpose of praising them, as to exhort them to perseverance. For it is no small excitement to eagerness of pursuit, when we reflect that God has adorned us with signal endowments, that he may finish what he has begun, and that we have, under his guidance and direction, advanced in the right course, in order that we may reach the goal. For as a vain confidence in those virtues, which mankind foolishly arrogate to themselves, puffs them up with pride, and makes them careless and indolent for the time to come, so a recognition of the gifts of God humbles pious minds, and stirs them up to anxious concern. Hence, instead of congratulations, he makes use of *thanksgivings*, that he may put them in mind, that everything in them that he declares to be worthy of praise, is a kindness from God. He also turns immediately to the future, in making mention of his *prayers*. We thus see for what purpose he commends their previous life.

1 THESSALONIANS 2

He now, leaving out of view the testimony of other Churches, reminds the Thessalonians of what they had themselves experienced, and explains at large in what way he, and in like manner the two others, his associates, had conducted themselves among them, inasmuch as this was of the greatest importance for confirming their faith. For it is with this

1 THESSALONIANS 1

1. Paul, and Silvanus, and Timotheus. Silvanus, or Silas, and Timothy were properly united with him on this occasion, because they had been with him when the church was founded there, Acts 17, and because Timothy had been sent by the apostle to visit them after he had himself been driven away, 1 Thess. 3: 1–2. Silas is first mentioned in the New Testament as one who was sent by the church at Jerusalem with Paul to Antioch, See Barnes "Acts 15: 22"; and he afterwards became his traveling companion.

7. So that ye were ensamples to all that believe. Examples in reference to the firmness with which you embraced the gospel, the fidelity with which you adhered to it in trials, and the zeal which you showed in spreading it abroad. These things are specified in the previous and subsequent verses as characterizing their piety. The word here rendered ensamples is that from which the word type is derived. It properly denotes anything caused or produced by the means of blows, and hence a mark, print, or impression, made by a stamp, or die; and then a resemblance, figure, pattern, exemplar – a model after which anything is made. This is the meaning here. They became, as it were, a model or pattern after which the piety of others should be molded, or showed what the piety of others ought to be.

10. And to wait for his Son from heaven. It is clear from this and from other parts of these two epistles, that the return of the Lord Jesus to this world was a prominent subject of the preaching of Paul at Thessalonica. No small part of these epistles is occupied with stating the true doctrine on this point, (1 Thess. 4; 5) and in correcting the errors which prevailed in regard to it after the departure of Paul. Perhaps we are not to infer, however, that this doctrine was made more prominent there than others, or that it had been inculcated there more frequently than it had been elsewhere; but the apostle adverts to it here particularly because it was a doctrine so well fitted to impart comfort to them in their trials, 1 Thess. 4: 13–18, and because, in that connection, it was so well

calculated to rouse them to vigilance and zeal, 1 Thess. 5: 1–11. He makes it prominent in the second epistle, because material errors prevailed there in reference to it, which needed to be corrected. In the passage before us, he says that the return of the Son of God from heaven was an important point which had been insisted on when he was there, and that their conduct, as borne witness to by all, had shown with what power it had seized upon them, and what a practical influence it had exerted in their lives. They lived as if they were "waiting" for his return. They fully believed in it; they expected it. They were looking out for it, not knowing when it might occur, and as if it might occur at any moment.

1 THESSALONIANS 2

3. For our exhortation. That is, the exhortation to embrace the gospel. The word seems to be used here so as to include preaching in general. The sense is, that the means which they used to induce them to become Christians were not such as to delude them.

Was not of deceit. Was not founded on sophistry. The apostle means to say, that the Thessalonians knew that his manner of preaching was not such as was adopted by the advocates of error.

Nor of uncleanness. – Not such as to lead to an impure life. It was such as to lead to holiness and purity. The apostle appeals to what they knew to be the tendency of his doctrine as an evidence that it was true. Most of the teaching of the heathen philosophers led to a life of licentiousness and corruption. The tendency of the gospel was just the reverse.

Nor in guile. Not by the arts of deceit. There was no craftiness or trick, such as could not bear a severe scrutiny. No point was carried by art, cunning, or stratagem. Everything was done on the most honorable and fair principles. It is much when a man can say that he has never endeavored to accomplish anything by mere trick, craft, or cunning. Sagacity and shrewdness are always allowable in ministers as well as others; trick and cunning never. Yet stratagem often takes the place of sagacity, and trick is often miscalled shrewdness. Guile, craft, cunning, imply deception, and can never

we speak; not as pleasing men, but God, which trieth our hearts.

5 For neither at any time used we flattering words, as ye know, nor a cloke of covetousness; God is witness:

6 Nor of men sought we glory, neither of you, nor yet of others, when we might have been burdensome, as the apostles of Christ.

7 But we were gentle among you, even as a nurse cherisheth her children:

8 So being affectionately desirous of you, we were willing to have imparted unto you, not the gospel of God only, but also our own souls, because ye were dear unto us.

9 For ye remember, brethren, our labour and travail: for labouring night and day, because we would not be chargeable unto any of you, we preached unto you the gospel of God.

10 Ye are witnesses, and God also, how holily and justly and unblameably we behaved ourselves among you that believe:

11 As ye know how we exhorted and comforted and charged every one of you, as a father doth his children,

12 That ye would walk worthy of God, who hath called you unto his kingdom and glory.

13 For this cause also thank we God without ceasing, because, when ye received the word of God which ye heard of us, ye received it not as the word of men, but as it is in truth, the word of God, which effectually worketh also in you that believe.

14 For ye, brethren, became followers of the churches of God which in Judaea are in Christ Jesus: for ye also have suffered like things of your own countrymen, even as they have of the Jews:

15 Who both killed the Lord Jesus, and their own prophets, and have persecuted us; and they please not God, and are contrary to all men:

16 Forbidding us to speak to the Gentiles that they might be saved, to fill up their sins alway: for the wrath is come upon them to the uttermost.

17 But we, brethren, being taken from you for a short time in presence, not in heart, endeavored the more abundantly to see your face with great desire.

view that he declares his integrity – that the Thessalonians may perceive that they had been called to the faith, not so much by a mortal man, as by God himself. He says, therefore, that his *entering in unto them had not been vain*, as ambitious persons manifest much show, while they have nothing of solidity; for he employs the word *vain* here as contrasted with *efficacious*.

He proves this by *two* arguments. The *first* is, that he had suffered persecution and ignominy at Philippi; the *second* is, that there was a great conflict prepared at Thessalonica. We know that the minds of men are weakened, nay, are altogether broken down by means of ignominy and persecutions. It was therefore an evidence of a Divine work that Paul, after having been subjected to evils of various kinds and to ignominy, did, as if in a perfectly sound state, shew no hesitation in making an attempt upon a large and opulent city, with the view of subjecting the inhabitants of it to Christ. In this *entering in*, nothing is seen that savors of vain ostentation. In the *second* department the same Divine power is beheld, for he does not discharge his duty with applause and favor, but required to maintain a keen conflict. In the mean time he stood firm and undaunted, from which it appears that he was held up by the hand of God; for this is what he means when he says that he was *emboldened*. And, unquestionably, if all these circumstances are carefully considered, it cannot be denied that God there magnificently displayed his power. As to the history, it is to be found in the sixteenth and seventeenth chapters of the Acts [Acts 16, 17].

3. For our exhortation

He confirms, by another argument, the Thessalonians in the faith which they had embraced – inasmuch as they had been faithfully and purely instructed in the word of the Lord, for he maintains that his doctrine was free from all deception and uncleanness. And with the view of placing this matter beyond all doubt, he calls their conscience to witness. The three terms which he makes use of may, it would seem, be distinguished in this manner: *imposture* may refer to the substance of doctrine, *uncleanness* to the affections of the heart, *guile* to the manner of acting.

In the *first* place, therefore, he says that they had not been deluded or imposed upon by fallacies, when they embraced the kind of doctrine that had been delivered to them by him.

Secondly, he declares his integrity, inasmuch as he had not come to them under the influence of any impure desire, but actuated solely by upright disposition.

Thirdly, he says that he had done nothing fraudulently or maliciously, but had, on the contrary, manifested a simplicity befitting a minister of Christ. As these things were well known to the Thessalonians, they had a sufficiently firm foundation for their faith.

be reconciled with that entire honesty which a minister of the gospel, and all other Christians, ought to possess.

7. But we were gentle among you, etc. Instead of using authority, we used only the most kind and gentle methods to win you and to promote your peace and order. The word here rendered "nurse" may mean any one who nurses a child, whether a mother or another person. It seems here to refer to a mother, 1 Thess. 2: 11; and the idea is, that the apostle felt for them the affectionate solicitude which a mother does for the child at her breast.

12. That ye would walk worthy of God, etc. That you would live in such a manner as would honor God, who has chosen you to be his friends.

A child "walks worthy of a parent" when he lives in such way as to reflect honor on that parent for the method in which he has trained him; when he so lives as to bring no disgrace on him, so as not to pain his heart by misconduct, or so as to give no occasion to any to speak reproachfully of him. This he does, when

(1.) he keeps all his commands;

(2.) when he leads a life of purity and virtue;

(3.) when he carries out the principles of the family into his own life;

(4.) when he honors a father by evincing a profound respect for his opinions; and

(5.) when he endeavors to provide for his comfort, and to promote his welfare. In a manner similar to this, a true Christian honors God. He lives so as not to bring a reproach upon him or his cause, and so as to teach the world to honor him who has bestowed such grace upon him.

15. Who both killed the Lord Jesus. The meaning here is, that it was characteristic of the Jews to be engaged in the work of persecution, and that they should not regard it strange, that they who had put their own Messiah to death, and slain the prophets, should now be found persecuting the true children of God.

16. Forbidding us to speak to the Gentiles. See Acts 17: 5, 13. No particular instance is mentioned in the life of Paul previous to this,

when they had formally commanded him not to preach to the heathen; but no one can doubt that this was one of the leading points of difference between him and them. Paul maintained, that the Jews and Gentiles were now on a level with regard to salvation; that the wall of partition was broken down; that the Jew had no advantages over the rest of mankind in this respect, and that the heathen might be saved without becoming Jews, or being circumcised, Rom. 2: 25–29; Rom. 3: 22–31.

The Jews did not hold it unlawful **to speak to the Gentiles,** and even to offer to them eternal life, (Matt. 23: 15) but it was only on condition that they should become proselytes to their religion, and should observe the institutions of Moses. If saved, they held that it would be as Jews – either originally such, or such by becoming proselytes. Paul maintained just the opposite opinion, that heathens might be saved without becoming proselytes to the Jewish system, and that, in fact, salvation was as freely offered to them as to the children of Abraham. Though there are no express instances in which they prohibited Paul from speaking to the Gentiles recorded before the date of this epistle, yet events occurred afterwards which showed what were their feelings, and such as to make it in the highest degree probable that they had attempted to restrain him.

That they might be saved. That is, as freely as others, and on the same terms, not by conversion to Judaism, but by repentance and faith.

To fill up their sins alway. At all times, in every generation. That is, to do now as they have always done, by resisting God and exposing themselves to his wrath. The idea is, that it had been a characteristic of the nation, at all times, to oppose God, and that they did it now in this manner in conformity with their fixed character.

For the wrath is come upon them. This cannot mean that the wrath of God had been then actually poured out upon them in the extreme degree referred to, or that they had experienced the full expressions of the Divine displeasure, for this epistle was written before the destruction of their city and temple, but

18 Wherefore we would have come unto you, even I Paul, once and again; but Satan hindered us.

19 For what is our hope, or joy, or crown of rejoicing? Are not even ye in the presence of our Lord Jesus Christ at his coming?

20 For ye are our glory and joy.

1 THESSALONIANS 3

1 Wherefore when we could no longer forbear, we thought it good to be left at Athens alone;

2 And sent Timotheus, our brother, and minister of God, and our fellowlabourer in the gospel of Christ, to establish you, and to comfort you concerning your faith:

3 That no man should be moved by these afflictions: for yourselves know that we are appointed thereunto.

4 For verily, when we were with you, we told you before that we should suffer tribulation; even as it came to pass, and ye know.

5 For this cause, when I could no longer forbear, I sent to know your faith, lest by some means the tempter have tempted you, and our labour be in vain.

6 But now when Timotheus came from you unto us, and brought us good tidings of your faith and charity, and that ye have good remembrance of us always, desiring greatly to see us, as we also to see you:

7 Therefore, brethren, we were comforted over you in all our affliction and distress by your faith:

8 For now we live, if ye stand fast in the Lord.

9 For what thanks can we render to God again for you, for all the joy wherewith we joy for your sakes before our God;

10 Night and day praying exceedingly that we might see your face, and might perfect that which is lacking in your faith?

11 Now God himself and our Father, and our Lord Jesus Christ, direct our way unto you.

12 And the Lord make you to increase and abound in love one toward another, and toward all men, even as we do toward you:

13 To the end he may stablish your hearts unblameable in holiness before

4. As we have been approved

He goes even a step higher, for he appeals to God as the Author of his apostleship, and he reasons in this manner: "God, when he assigned me this office, bore witness to me as a faithful servant; there is no reason, therefore, why men should have doubts as to my fidelity, which they know to have been *approved of by God*. Paul, however, does not glory in having been *approved of*, as though he were such of himself; for he does not dispute here as to what he had by nature, nor does he place his own power in collision with the grace of God, but simply says that the Gospel had been committed to him as a faithful and *approved* servant. Now, God approves of those whom he has formed for himself according to his own pleasure. *Not as pleasing men.* What is meant by *pleasing men* has been explained in the Epistle to the Galatians (Galatians 1:10) and this passage, also, shews it admirably. For Paul contrasts *pleasing* men, and *pleasing* God, as things that are opposed to each other. Farther, when he says – *God, who trieth our hearts*, he intimates, that those who endeavor to obtain the favor of men, are not influenced by an upright conscience, and do nothing from the heart. Let us know, therefore, that true ministers of the gospel ought to make it their aim to devote to God their endeavors, and to do it from the heart, not from any outward regard to the world, but because conscience tells them that it is right and proper. Thus it will be secured that they will not make it their aim to *please men*, that is, that they will not act under the influence of ambition, with a view to the favor of men.

1 THESSALONIANS 3

1. Wherefore, when we could no longer endure

By the detail which follows, he assures them of the desire of which he had spoken. For if, on being detained elsewhere, he had sent no other to Thessalonica in his place, it might have seemed as though he were not so much concerned in regard to them; but when he substitutes Timothy in his place, he removes that suspicion, more especially when he prefers them before himself. Now that he esteemed them above himself, he shews from this, that he chose rather to be left alone than that they should be deserted: for these words, *we judged it good to be left alone*, are emphatic. Timothy was a most faithful companion to him: he had at that time no others with him; hence it was inconvenient and distressing for him to be without him. It is therefore a token of rare affection and anxious desire that he does not refuse to deprive himself of all comfort, with the view of relieving the Thessalonians. To the same effect is the word eudok samen, which expresses a prompt inclination of the mind.

2. Our brother

He assigns to him these marks of commendation, that he may shew the more clearly how much inclined he was to consult their welfare: for if he had sent them some com-

that the cup of their iniquity was full; that they were, in fact, abandoned by God; that they were the objects, even then, of his displeasure, and that their destruction was so certain, that it might be spoken of as an indubitable fact. The "wrath of God" may be said to have come upon a man when he abandons him, even though there may not be as yet any external expressions of his indignation. It is not punishment that constitutes the wrath of God. That is the mere outward expression of the Divine indignation; and the wrath of God may, in fact, have come upon a man when as yet there are no external tokens of it. The overthrow of Jerusalem and the temple, were but the outward expressions of the Divine displeasure at their conduct. Paul, inspired to speak of the feelings God, describes that wrath as already existing in the Divine mind.

1 THESSALONIANS 3

1. We could no longer forbear. That is, when I could not (1 Thess. 3: 5), for there is every evidence that Paul refers to himself only, though he uses the plural form of the word. There was no one with him at Athens after he had sent Timothy away, (Acts 17: 15; 18: 5) and this shows that when, in 1 Thess. 2: 6, he uses the term apostles in the plural number, he refers to himself only, and does not mean to give the name to Timothy and Silas. If this be so, Timothy and Silas are nowhere called "apostles" in the New Testament. The word rendered here could forbear, means, properly, to cover, to conceal; and then to hide or conceal anger, impatience, weariness, etc.; that is, to hold out as to anything, to bear with, to endure. It is rendered suffer in 1 Cor. 9: 12; beareth, 1 Thess. 3: 1, 5. It is not elsewhere used in the New Testament. It means that he could no longer bear up under, hide, or suppress his impatience in regard to them, his painful emotions, his wish to know of their state; and he therefore sent Timothy to them.

We thought it good. I was willing to suffer the inconvenience of parting with him in order to show my concern for you.

To be left at Athens alone. Paul had been conducted to Athens from Berea, where he remained until Silas and Timothy could come

to him, Acts 17: 15. It appears from the statement here, that Timothy had joined him there, but such was his solicitude for the church at Thessalonica, that he very soon after sent him there, and chose to remain himself alone at Athens.

7. We were comforted over you. The sense here is, that their steadfastness was a great source of comfort to him in his trials. It was an instance where the holy lives and the fidelity of a people did much, as will always be the case, to lighten the burdens and cheer the heart of a minister of the gospel. In the inevitable trials of the ministerial office there is no source of comfort more rich and pure than this.

8. For now we live, if ye stand fast in the Lord. This is equivalent to saying, "My life and comfort depend on your stability in the faith, and your correct Christian walk." The meaning here is, that Paul now enjoyed life; he had that which constituted real life, in the fact that they acted as became Christians, and so as to show that his labor among them had not been in vain. The same thing here affirmed is true of all faithful ministers of the gospel. They feel that they have something that may be called life, and that is worth living for, when those to whom they preach maintain a close walk with God.

9. For what thanks can we render to God again. That is, what expression of thanksgiving can we render to God that shall be an equivalent for the joy which your holy walk has furnished, or which shall suitably express our gratitude for it.

10. Night and day. Constantly.
    Praying exceeedingly. Gr., abundantly; that is, there was much more than ordinary prayer. He made this a special subject of prayer; he urged it with earnestness, and without intermission. Comp. 1 Thess. 2: 17.
    And might perfect that which is lacking in your faith. Might render it complete, or fill up anything which is wanting. The word here used, means, properly, to make fully ready, to put full in order, to make complete.

11. Now God himself. This is evidently a prayer, he earnestly sought of God that he

God, even our Father, at the coming of our Lord Jesus Christ with all his saints.

1 THESSALONIANS 4

1 Furthermore then we beseech you, brethren, and exhort you by the Lord Jesus, that as ye have received of us how ye ought to walk and to please God, so ye would abound more and more.

2 For ye know what commandments we gave you by the Lord Jesus.

3 For this is the will of God, even your sanctification, that ye should abstain from fornication:

4 That every one of you should know how to possess his vessel in sanctification and honor;

5 Not in the lust of concupiscence, even as the Gentiles which know not God:

6 That no man go beyond and defraud his brother in any matter: because that the Lord is the avenger of all such, as we also have forewarned you and testified.

7 For God hath not called us unto uncleanness, but unto holiness.

8 He therefore that despiseth, despiseth not man, but God, who hath also given unto us his holy Spirit.

9 But as touching brotherly love ye need not that I write unto you: for ye yourselves are taught of God to love one another.

10 And indeed ye do it toward all the brethren which are in all Macedonia: but we beseech you, brethren, that ye increase more and more;

11 And that ye study to be quiet, and to do your own business, and to work with your own hands, as we commanded you;

12 That ye may walk honestly toward them that are without, and that ye may have lack of nothing.

13 But I would not have you to be ignorant, brethren, concerning them which are asleep, that ye sorrow not, even as others which have no hope.

14 For if we believe that Jesus died and rose again, even so them also which sleep in Jesus will God bring with him.

15 For this we say unto you by the word of the Lord, that we which are alive and remain unto the coming of the Lord shall not prevent them which are asleep.

mon person, it could not have afforded them much assistance; and inasmuch as Paul would have done this without inconvenience to himself, he would have given no remarkable proof of his fatherly concern in regard to them. It is, on the other hand, a great thing that he deprives himself of a *brother* and *fellow-laborer*, and one to whom, as he declares in Philippians 2: 20, he found no equal, inasmuch as all aimed at the promotion of their own interests. In the mean time, he procures authority for the doctrine which they had received from Timothy, that it may remain the more deeply impressed upon their memory.

1 THESSALONIANS 4

1. Furthermore

This chapter contains various injunctions, by which he trains up the Thessalonians to a holy life, or confirms them in the exercise of it. They had previously learned what was the rule and method of a pious life: he calls this to their remembrance. *As*, says he, *ye have been taught*. Lest, however, he should seem to take away from them what he had previously assigned them, he does not simply exhort them to *walk* in such a manner, but to *abound more and more*.

When, therefore, he urges them to make progress, he intimates that they are already in the way. The sum is this, that they should be more especially careful to make progress in the doctrine which they had received, and this Paul places in contrast with frivolous and vain pursuits, in which we see that a good part of the world very generally busy themselves, so that profitable and holy meditation as to the due regulation of life scarcely obtains a place, even the most inferior. Paul, accordingly, reminds them in what manner they had been instructed, and bids them aim at this with their whole might. Now, there is a law that is here enjoined upon us – that, *forgetting the things that are behind*, we always aim at farther progress (Philippians 3: 13) and pastors ought also to make this their endeavor. Now, as to his *beseeching*, when he might rightfully enjoin – it is a token of humanity and modesty which pastors ought to imitate, that they may, if possible, allure people to kindness, rather than violently compel them.

3. For this is the will of God

This is doctrine of a general nature, from which, as from a fountain, he immediately deduces special admonitions. When he says that *this is the will of God*, he means that we have been called by God with this design. "For this end ye are Christians – this the gospel aims at – that ye may *sanctify* yourselves to *God*." The meaning of the term *sanctification* we have already explained elsewhere in repeated instances – that renouncing the world, and clearing ourselves from the pollutions of the flesh, we offer ourselves to God as if in sacrifice, for nothing can with propriety be offered to Him, but what is pure and holy. *That ye abstain.* This is one

might be permitted to visit them, and that he would so prepare the way that he might do it.

1 THESSALONIANS 4

3. For this is the will of God, even your sanctification. It is the will or command of God that you should be holy. This does not refer to the purpose or decree of God, and does not mean that he intended to make them holy; but it means that it was his command that they should be holy. It was also true that it was agreeable to the Divine will or purpose that they should be holy, and that he meant to use such an influence as to secure this; but this is not the truth taught here. This text, therefore, should not be brought as a proof that God intends to make his people holy, or that they are sanctified. It is a proof only that he requires holiness. The word here rendered sanctification is not used in the Greek classics, but is several times found in the New Testament. It is rendered holiness, Rom. 6: 19, 22; 1 Thess. 4: 7 1 Tim. 2: 15; Heb. 12: 14; and sanctification, 1 Cor. 1: 30 1 Thess. 4: 3–4; 2 Thess. 2: 13; 1 Pet. 1: 2.

7. For God hath not called us unto uncleanness. When he called us to be his followers, it was not that we should lead lives of impurity, but of holiness. We should, therefore, fulfill the purposes for which we were called into his kingdom. The word uncleanness, means, properly, impurity, filth; and then, in a moral sense, pollution, lewdness, as opposed to chastity, Rom. 1: 24; 6: 19; 2 Cor. 12: 21; Gal. 5: 19; Eph. 4: 19; 5: 3; Col. 3: 5.

9. But as touching brotherly love. The "peculiar charity and affection which one Christian owes to another." Doddridge. Ye need not that I write unto you. That is, "as I have done on the other points." They were so taught of God in regard to this duty, that they did not need any special instruction.

For ye yourselves are taught of God. The word here rendered "taught of God" *yeodidaktoi* occurs nowhere else in the New Testament. It is correctly translated, and must refer here to some direct teaching of God on their own hearts, for Paul speaks of their being so taught by him as to need no special precepts in the case. He probably refers to that influence exerted on them when they became Christians, by which they were led to love all who bear the Divine image. He calls this being "taught of God," not because it was of the nature of revelation or inspiration, but because it was, in fact, the teaching of God in this case, though it was secret and silent. God has many ways of teaching men. The lessons which we learn from his Providence are a part of his instructions. The same is true of the decisions of our own consciences, and of the secret and silent influence of his Spirit on our hearts, disposing us to love what is lovely, and to do what ought to be done. In this manner all true Christians are taught to love those who bear the image of their Savior. They feel that they are brethren; and such is their strong attachment to them, from the very nature of religion, that they do not need any express command of God to teach them to love them. It is one of the first – the elementary effects of religion on the soul, to lead us to love "the brethren;" and to do this is one of the evidences of piety about which there need be no danger of deceptions. Comp. 1 John 3: 14.

13. But I would not have you to be ignorant. I would have you fully informed on the important subject which is here referred to. It is quite probable from this, that some erroneous views prevailed among them in reference to the condition of those who were dead, which tended to prevent their enjoying the full consolation which they might otherwise have done. Of the prevalence of these views, it is probable the apostle had been informed by Timothy on his return from Thessalonica, 1 Thess. 3: 6. What they were we are not distinctly informed, and can only gather from the allusions which Paul makes to them, or from the opposite doctrines which he states, and which are evidently designed to correct those which prevailed among them. From these statements, it would appear that they supposed that those who had died, though they were true Christians, would be deprived of some important advantages which those would possess who should survive to the coming of the Lord. There seems some reason to suppose that the cause of their grief was

16 For the Lord himself shall descend from heaven with a shout, with the voice of the archangel, and with the trump of God: and the dead in Christ shall rise first:

17 Then we which are alive and remain shall be caught up together with them in the clouds, to meet the Lord in the air: and so shall we ever be with the Lord.

18 Wherefore comfort one another with these words.

1 THESSALONIANS 5

1 But of the times and the seasons, brethren, ye have no need that I write unto you.

2 For yourselves know perfectly that the day of the Lord so cometh as a thief in the night.

3 For when they shall say, Peace and safety; then sudden destruction cometh upon them, as travail upon a woman with child; and they shall not escape.

4 But ye, brethren, are not in darkness, that that day should overtake you as a thief.

5 Ye are all the children of light, and the children of the day: we are not of the night, nor of darkness.

6 Therefore let us not sleep, as do others; but let us watch and be sober.

7 For they that sleep sleep in the night; and they that be drunken are drunken in the night.

8 But let us, who are of the day, be sober, putting on the breastplate of faith and love; and for an helmet, the hope of salvation.

9 For God hath not appointed us to wrath, but to obtain salvation by our Lord Jesus Christ,

10 Who died for us, that, whether we wake or sleep, we should live together with him.

11 Wherefore comfort yourselves together, and edify one another, even as also ye do.

12 And we beseech you, brethren, to know them which labour among you, and are over you in the Lord, and admonish you;

13 And to esteem them very highly in love for their work's sake. And be at peace among yourselves.

injunction, which he derives from the fountain of which he had immediately before made mention; for nothing is more opposed to holiness than the defilement of *fornication*, which pollutes the whole man.

5. On this account he assigns the *lust of concupiscence* to the *Gentiles, who know not God.* "Where the knowledge of God reigns, lusts must be subdued."

By the *lust of concupiscence*, he means all base lusts of the flesh, but, at the same time, by this manner of expression, he brands with dishonor all desires that allure us to pleasure and carnal delights, as in Romans 13:14, he bids us *have no care for the flesh in respect of the lust thereof.* For when men give indulgence to their appetites, there are no bounds to lasciviousness. Hence the only means of maintaining temperance is to bridle all lusts.

1 THESSALONIANS 5

1. But as to times

He now, in the third place, calls them back from a curious and unprofitable inquiry as to *times*, but in the mean time admonishes them to be constantly in a state of preparation for receiving Christ. He speaks, however, by way of *anticipation*, saying, that they have no need that he should write as to those things which the curious desire to know. For it is an evidence of excessive incredulity not to believe what the Lord foretells, unless he marks out the day by certain circumstances, and as it were points it out with the finger. As, therefore, those waver between doubtful opinions who require that moments of time should be marked out for them, as if they would draw a conjecture from some plausible demonstration, he accordingly says that discussions of this nature are not necessary for the pious. There is also another reason – that believers do not desire to know more than they are permitted to learn in God's school. Now Christ designed that the day of his coming should be hid from us, that, being in suspense, we might be as it were upon watch.

2. Ye know perfectly

He places exact knowledge in contrast with an anxious desire of investigation. But what is it that he says the Thessalonians know accurately? It is, that the day of Christ will come suddenly and unexpectedly, so as to take unbelievers by surprise, as a thief does those that are asleep. This, however, is opposed to evident tokens, which might portend afar off his coming to the world. Hence it were foolish to wish to determine the time precisely from presages or prodigies.

15. See that no one render evil for evil

As it is difficult to observe this precept, in consequence of the strong bent of our nature to revenge, he on this account bids us take care to be on our guard. For the word *see* de-

two-fold: one that some among them doubted whether there would be any resurrection (comp. 1 Cor. xv. 12), and that they supposed that they who had died were thus cut off from the hope of eternal happiness, so as to leave their surviving friends to sorrow "as those who had no hope;" the other, that some of them believed that, though those who were dead would indeed rise again, yet it would be long after those who were living when the Lord Jesus would return had been taken to glory, and would always be in a condition inferior to them. The effect of such opinions as these can be readily imagined. It would be to deprive them of the consolation which they might have had, and should have had, in the loss of their pious friends. They would either mourn over them as wholly cut off from hope, or would sorrow that they were to be deprived of the highest privileges which could result from redemption. It is not to be regarded as wonderful that such views should have prevailed in Thessalonica. There were those even at Corinth who wholly denied the doctrine of the resurrection (1 Cor. 15: 12); and we are to remember that those to whom the apostle now wrote, had been recently converted from heathenism; that they had enjoyed his preaching but a short time; that they had few or no books on the subject of religion; and that they were surrounded by those who had no faith in the doctrine of the resurrection at all, and who were doubtless able – as skeptical philosophers often are now – to urge their objections to the doctrines in such a way as greatly to perplex Christians. The apostle, therefore, felt the importance of stating the exact truth on the subject, that they might not have unnecessary sorrow, and that their unavoidable grief for their departed friends might not be aggravated by painful apprehensions about their future condition.

Concerning them which are asleep. It is evident from this that they had been recently called to part with some dear and valued members of their church. The word sleep is frequently applied in the New Testament to the death of saints.

1 THESSALONIANS 5

1. But of the times and the seasons. The reference here is to the coming of the Lord Jesus, and to the events connected with his advent. See the close of 1 Thess. 4.

Ye have no need that I write unto you. That is, they had received all the information on the particular point to which he refers, which it was necessary they should have. He seems to refer to the suddenness of his coming. It is evident from this, as well as from other parts of this epistle, that this had been, from some cause, a prominent topic which he had dwelt on when he was with them.

2. For yourselves know perfectly. That is, they had been taught this. There could be no doubt in their minds respecting it.

The day of the Lord so cometh. Of the Lord Jesus – for so the word "Lord" in the New Testament commonly means. The "day of the Lord" means that day in which he will be manifested, or in which he will be the prominent object in view of the assembled universe.

As a thief in the night. Suddenly and unexpectedly, as a robber breaks into a dwelling. A thief comes without giving any warning, or any indications of his approach. He not only gives none, but he is careful that none shall be given. It is a point with him, that, it possible, the man whose house he is about to rob shall have no means of ascertaining his approach until he comes suddenly upon him.

12. And we beseech you, brethren, to know them which labor among you. Who they were is not mentioned. It is evident, however: that the church was not left without appointed persons to minister to it when its founders should be away. We know that there were presbyters ordained over the church at Ephesus, and over the churches in Crete, Acts 20: 17 Titus 1: 5; and that there were bishops and deacons at Philippi, Phil. 1: 1; and there is every reason to believe that similar officers would be appointed in every newly organized church. The word "know" seems to mean that they were not to make themselves strangers to them – to be cold and distant towards them – to be ignorant of their wants, or to be indifferent to them. While a people are not obtru-

14 Now we exhort you, brethren, warn them that are unruly, comfort the feeble-minded, support the weak, be patient toward all men.

15 See that none render evil for evil unto any man; but ever follow that which is good, both among yourselves, and to all men.

16 Rejoice evermore.

17 Pray without ceasing.

18 In every thing give thanks: for this is the will of God in Christ Jesus concerning you.

19 Quench not the Spirit.

20 Despise not prophesyings.

21 Prove all things; hold fast that which is good.

22 Abstain from all appearance of evil.

23 And the very God of peace sanctify you wholly; and I pray God your whole spirit and soul and body be preserved blameless unto the coming of our Lord Jesus Christ.

24 Faithful is he that calleth you, who also will do it.

25 Brethren, pray for us.

26 Greet all the brethren with an holy kiss.

27 I charge you by the Lord that this epistle be read unto all the holy brethren.

28 The grace of our Lord Jesus Christ be with you. Amen.

notes anxious care. Now, although he simply forbids us to strive with each other in the way of inflicting injuries, there can, nevertheless, be no doubt that he meant to condemn, at the same time, every disposition to do injury. For if it is unlawful to *render evil for evil*, every disposition to injure is culpable. This doctrine is peculiar to Christians – not to retaliate injuries, but to endure them patiently. And lest the Thessalonians should think that revenge was prohibited only towards their brethren, he expressly declares that they are to *do evil to no one*. For particular excuses are wont to be brought forward in some cases. "What! why should it be unlawful for me to avenge myself on one that is so worthless, so wicked, and so cruel?" But as vengeance is forbidden us in every case, without exception, however wicked the man that has injured us may be, we must refrain from inflicting injury.

But always follow benignity

By this last clause he teaches that we must not merely refrain from inflicting vengeance, when any one has injured us, but must cultivate beneficence towards all. For although he means that it should in the first instance be exercised among believers mutually, he afterwards extends it to all, however undeserving of it, that we may make it our aim to *overcome evil with good*, as he himself teaches elsewhere (Romans 12: 21). The first step, therefore, in the exercise of patience, is, not to revenge injuries; the second is, to bestow favors even upon enemies.

22. From every evil appearance

The phrase *appearance of evil*, or *evil appearance*, I understand to mean – when falsity of doctrine has not yet been discovered in such a manner, that it can on good grounds be rejected; but at the same time an unhappy suspicion is left upon the mind, and fears are entertained, lest there should be some poison lurking. He, accordingly, commands us to abstain from that kind of doctrine, which has an appearance of being evil, though it is not really so – not that he allows that it should be altogether rejected, but inasmuch as it ought not to be received, or to obtain belief. For why has he previously commanded that *what is good* should be *held fast*, while he now desires that we should *abstain* not simply from evil, but from *all appearance of evil*? It is for this reason, that, when truth has been brought to light by careful examination, it is assuredly becoming in that case to give credit to it. When, on the other hand, there is any fear of false doctrine, or when the mind is involved in doubt, it is proper in that case to retreat, or to suspend our step, as they say, lest we should receive anything with a doubtful and perplexed conscience. In short, he shews us in what way *prophecy* will be useful to us without any danger – in the event of our being attentive in *proving all things*, and our being free from lightness and haste.

sively to intermeddle with the business of a minister, any more than they are with that of any other man, yet there are things in regard to him with which they should be acquainted. They should seek to be personally acquainted with him, and make him their confidant and counselor in their spiritual troubles. They should seek his friendship, and endeavor to maintain all proper intercourse with him. They should not regard him as a distant man, or as a stranger among them. They should so far understand his circumstances as to know what is requisite to make him comfortable, and should be on such terms that they may readily and cheerfully furnish what he needs. And they are to "know" or regard him as their spiritual teacher and ruler; not to be strangers to the place where he preaches the word of life, and not to listen to his admonitions and reproofs as those of a stranger, but as those of a pastor and friend.

Which labor among you. There is no reason to suppose, as many have done, that the apostle here refers to different classes of ministers, he rather refers to different parts of the work which the same ministers perform. The first is, that they "labor" – that is, evidently, in preaching the gospel. For the use of the word, see John 4: 3, where it occurs twice; 1 Cor. 15: 10; 16: 16. The word is one which properly expresses wearisome toil, and implies that the office of preaching is one that demands constant industry.

And are over you in the Lord. That is, by the appointment of the Lord, or under his direction. They are not absolute sovereigns, but are themselves subject to one who is over them – the Lord Jesus.

And admonish you. The word here used is rendered admonish, and admonished, in Rom. 15: 14; Col. 3: 16; 1 Thess. 5: 12; 2 Thess. 3: 15. And warn, and warning, 1 Cor. 4: 14; Col. 1: 28; 1 Thess. 5: 14. It does not elsewhere occur in the New Testament. It means, to put in mind; and then to warn, entreat, exhort. It is a part of the duty of a minister to put his people in mind of the truth; to warn them of danger; to exhort them to perform their duty; to admonish them if they go astray.

15. See that none render evil for evil. The meaning here is, that we are not to take vengeance.

This law is positive, and is universally binding. The moment we feel ourselves acting from a desire to "return evil for evil," that moment we are acting wrong. It may be right to defend our lives, and the lives of our friends; to seek the protection of the law for our persons, reputation, or property, against those who would wrong us; to repel the assaults of calumniators and slanderers; but in no case should the motive be to do them wrong for the evil which they have done us.

But ever follow that which is good. Which is benevolent, kind, just, generous.

Both among yourselves, and to all men. The phrase **to all men** seems to have been added to avoid the possibility of misconstruction. Some might possibly suppose that this was a good rule to be observed towards those of their own number, but that a greater latitude in avenging injuries might be allowable towards their enemies out of the church. The apostle, therefore, says that the rule is universal. It relates to the heathen, to infidels, skeptics, and persecutors, as well as to the members of the church. To every man we are to do good as we are able – no matter what they do to us. This is the rule which God himself observes toward the evil and unthankful and is one of the original and beautiful laws of our holy religion.

25. Brethren pray for us. A request which the apostle often makes. He was a man of like passions as others; liable to the same temptations; engaged in an arduous work; often called to meet with opposition, and exposed to peril and want, and he peculiarly needed the prayers of the people of God. A minister, surrounded as he is by temptations, is in great danger if he has not the prayers of his people. Without those prayers, he will be likely to accomplish little in the cause of his Master.

2 Thessalonians

Introduction by John Calvin

IT does not appear to me probable that this Epistle was sent from Rome, as the Greek manuscripts commonly bear; for he would have made some mention of his bonds, as he is accustomed to do in other Epistles. Besides, about the end of the third Chapter, he intimates that he is in danger from unreasonable men. From this it may be gathered, that when he was going to Jerusalem, he wrote this Epistle in the course of the journey. It was also from an ancient date a very generally received opinion among the Latins, that it was written at Athens. The occasion, however, of his writing was this – that the Thessalonians might not reckon themselves overlooked, because Paul had not visited them, when hastening to another quarter. In the *first Chapter*, he exhorts them to patience. In the *second*, a vain and groundless fancy, which had got into circulation as to the coming of Christ being at hand, is set aside by him by means of this argument – that there must previously to that be a revolt in the Church, and a great part of the world must treacherously draw back from God, nay more, that Antichrist must reign in the temple of God. In the *third Chapter*, after having commended himself to their prayers, and having in a few words encouraged them to perseverance, he commands that those be severely chastised who live in idleness at the expense of others. If they do not obey admonitions, he teaches that they should be excommunicated.

The commentaries on 2 Thessalonians are by John Calvin and Albert Barnes.

2 THESSALONIANS 1

1 Paul, and Silvanus, and Timotheus, unto the church of the Thessalonians in God our Father and the Lord Jesus Christ:

2 Grace unto you, and peace, from God our Father and the Lord Jesus Christ.

3 We are bound to thank God always for you, brethren, as it is meet, because that your faith groweth exceedingly, and the charity of every one of you all toward each other aboundeth;

4 So that we ourselves glory in you in the churches of God for your patience and faith in all your persecutions and tribulations that ye endure:

5 Which is a manifest token of the righteous judgment of God, that ye may be counted worthy of the kingdom of God, for which ye also suffer:

6 Seeing it is a righteous thing with God to recompense tribulation to them that trouble you;

7 And to you who are troubled rest with us, when the Lord Jesus shall be revealed from heaven with his mighty angels,

8 In flaming fire taking vengeance on them that know not God, and that obey not the gospel of our Lord Jesus Christ:

9 Who shall be punished with everlasting destruction from the presence of the Lord, and from the glory of his power;

10 When he shall come to be glorified in his saints, and to be admired in all them that believe (because our testimony among you was believed) in that day.

11 Wherefore also we pray always for you, that our God would count you worthy of this calling, and fulfil all the good pleasure of his goodness, and the work of faith with power:

12 That the name of our Lord Jesus Christ may be glorified in you, and ye in him, according to the grace of our God and the Lord Jesus Christ.

2 THESSALONIANS 2

1 Now we beseech you, brethren, by the coming of our Lord Jesus Christ, and by our gathering together unto him,

2 That ye be not soon shaken in mind, or be troubled, neither by spirit, nor by

2 THESSALONIANS 1

1. To the Church of the Thessalonians which is in God

As to the form of salutation, it were superfluous to speak. This only it is necessary to notice — that by a *Church in God and Christ* is meant one that has not merely been gathered together under the banner of faith, for the purpose of worshipping one God the Father, and confiding in Christ, but is the work and building as well of the Father as of Christ, because while God adopts us to himself, and regenerates us, we from him begin to be in Christ (1 Corinthians 1: 30).

7. When the Lord shall be manifested

Here we have a confirmation of the foregoing statement. For as it is one of the articles of our faith, that Christ will come from heaven, and will not come in vain, faith ought to seek the end of his coming. Now this is – that he may come as a Redeemer to his own people; nay more, that he may judge the whole world. The description which follows has a view to this – that the pious may understand that God is so much the more concerned as to their afflictions in proportion to the dreadfulness of the judgment that awaits his enemies. For the chief occasion of grief and distress is this – that we think that God is but lightly affected with our calamities. We see into what complaints David from time to time breaks forth, while he is consumed by the pride and insolence of his enemies. Hence he has brought forward all this for the consolation of believers, while he represents the tribunal of Christ as full of horror, that they may not be disheartened by their present oppressed condition, while they see themselves proudly and disdainfully trampled upon by the wicked.

12. That the name of our Lord Jesus Christ may be glorified

He calls us back to the chief end of our whole life – that we may promote the Lord's glory. What he adds, however, is more especially worthy of notice, that those who have advanced the glory of Christ will also in their turn be glorified in him. For in this, first of all, the wonderful goodness of God shines forth – that he will have his glory be conspicuous in us who are covered over with ignominy. This, however, is a twofold miracle, that he afterwards irradiates us with his glory, as though he would do the same to us in return. On this account he adds, *according to the grace of God and Christ.* For there is nothing here that is ours either in the action itself, or in the effect or fruit, for it is solely by the guidance of the Holy Spirit that our life is made to contribute to the glory of God. And the circumstance that so much fruit arises from this ought to be ascribed to the great mercy of God. In the mean time, if we are not worse than

2 THESSALONIANS 1

5. Which is a manifest token of the righteous judgment of God. The word **which** is supplied by our translators, and there may be some doubt to what the apostle has reference as being **a manifest token of the righteous judgment of God.** The general sense seems to be, that the fact that they were thus persecuted was an evidence that there would be a future judgment, when the righteous who were persecuted would be rewarded, and the wicked who persecuted them would be punished. The manner in which they bore their trials was an indication, also, of what the result would be in regard to them. Their patience and faith under persecutions were constantly showing that they would "be counted worthy of the kingdom of God," for which they were called to suffer. It is evident that a relative must be supplied here, as our translators have done; but there has been a difference of view as to what it refers: Some suppose that it is to "patience;" others to persecutions and tribulations; and others to the whole sentence preceding. The latter is probably the true construction; and the sense is, that the endurance of affliction, in a proper manner, by the righteous, is a proof that there will be a righteous judgment of God in the last day.

7. And to you who are troubled. That is, "It will be a righteous thing for God to give to you who are persecuted rest in the last day." As it will be right and proper to punish the wicked, so it will be right to reward the good. It will not, however, be in precisely the same sense. The wicked will deserve all that they will suffer; but it cannot be said that the righteous will deserve the reward which they will receive. It will be right and proper, because

(1.) there is a fitness that they who are the friends of God should be treated as such, or it is proper that he should show himself to be their Friend; and

(2.) because in this life this is not always clearly done. They are often less prospered, and less happy in their outward circumstances, than the wicked. There is, therefore, a propriety that in the future state God should manifest himself as their Friend, and show to

assembled worlds that he is not indifferent to character, or that wickedness does not deserve his smiles, and piety incur his frown. At the same time, however, it will be owing wholly to his grace that any are ever admitted to heaven.

Rest. The future happiness of believers is often represented under the image of rest. It is rest like that of the weary laborer after his day of toil; rest, like that of the soldier after the hardships of a long and perilous march; rest, like the calm repose of one who has been racked with pain.

The word rest here means a letting loose, a remission, a relaxation; and hence composure, quiet. 2 Cor. 2: 13; 7: 5.

12. That the name of our Lord Jesus Christ. That is, that the Lord Jesus himself may be honored among you: the name often denoting the person. The idea is, that the apostle wished that the Lord Jesus might be honored among them by the fair application and development of the principles of his religion.

2 THESSALONIANS 2

2. That ye be not soon shaken in mind. The word here used signifies, properly, to be moved as a wave of the sea, or to be tossed upon the waves, as a vessel is. Then it means to be shaken in any way. See Matt. 11: 7; 24: 29; Luke 6: 38; Acts 4: 31; Heb. 12: 26.

The reference here is to the agitation or alarm felt from the belief that the day of judgment would soon occur. It is uniformly said in the Scriptures, that the approach of the Lord Jesus to judge the world, will produce a great consternation and alarm. Matt. 24: 30, "Then shall appear the sign of the Son of man in heaven: and then shall all the tribes of the earth mourn." Rev. 1: 7, "Behold, he cometh with clouds; and every eye shall see him, and they also which pierced him: and all kindreds of the earth shall wail because of him." Luke 23: 30, "Then shall they begin to say to the mountains, Fall on us; and to the hills, Cover us." Comp. Is. 2: 21–22. Of the truth of this, there can be no doubt. We may imagine something of the effects which will be produced by the alarm caused in a community when

word, nor by letter as from us, as that the day of Christ is at hand.

3 Let no man deceive you by any means: for that day shall not come, except there come a falling away first, and that man of sin be revealed, the son of perdition;

4 Who opposeth and exalteth himself above all that is called God, or that is worshipped; so that he as God sitteth in the temple of God, shewing himself that he is God.

5 Remember ye not, that, when I was yet with you, I told you these things?

6 And now ye know what withholdeth that he might be revealed in his time.

7 For the mystery of iniquity doth already work: only he who now letteth will let, until he be taken out of the way.

8 And then shall that Wicked be revealed, whom the Lord shall consume with the spirit of his mouth, and shall destroy with the brightness of his coming:

9 Even him, whose coming is after the working of Satan with all power and signs and lying wonders,

10 And with all deceivableness of unrighteousness in them that perish; because they received not the love of the truth, that they might be saved.

11 And for this cause God shall send them strong delusion, that they should believe a lie:

12 That they all might be damned who believed not the truth, but had pleasure in unrighteousness.

13 But we are bound to give thanks alway to God for you, brethren beloved of the Lord, because God hath from the beginning chosen you to salvation through sanctification of the Spirit and belief of the truth:

14 Whereunto he called you by our gospel, to the obtaining of the glory of our Lord Jesus Christ.

15 Therefore, brethren, stand fast, and hold the traditions which ye have been taught, whether by word, or our epistle.

16 Now our Lord Jesus Christ himself, and God, even our Father, which hath loved us, and hath given us everlasting consolation and good hope through grace,

stupid, we must aim with all our might at the advancement of the glory of Christ, which is connected with ours.

2 THESSALONIANS 2

1. Now I beseech you, by the coming

It may indeed be read, as I have noted on the margin, *concerning the coming*, but it suits better to view it as an earnest entreaty, taken from the subject in hand, just as in 1 Corinthians 15: 31, when discoursing as to the hope of a resurrection, he makes use of an oath by that *glory* which is to be hoped for by believers. And this has much more efficacy when he adjures believers by the coming of Christ, not to imagine rashly that his day is at hand, for he at the same time admonishes us not to think of it but with reverence and sobriety. For it is customary to adjure by those things which are regarded by us with reverence. The meaning therefore is, "As you set a high value on the coming of Christ, when he will gather us to himself, and will truly perfect that unity of the body which we cherish as yet only in part through means of faith, so I earnestly beseech you by his coming not to be too credulous, should any one affirm, on whatever pretext, that his day is at hand."

As he had in his former Epistle adverted to some extent to the resurrection, it is possible that some fickle and fanatical persons took occasion from this to mark out a near and fixed day. For it is not likely that this error had taken its rise earlier among the Thessalonians. For Timothy, on returning thence, had informed Paul as to their entire condition, and as a prudent and experienced man had omitted nothing that was of importance. Now if Paul had received notice of it, he could not have been silent as to a matter of so great consequence. Thus I am of opinion, that when Paul's Epistle had been read, which contained a lively view of the resurrection, some that were disposed to indulge curiosity philosophized unseasonably as to the time of it. This, however, was an utterly ruinous fancy, as were also other things of the same nature, which were afterwards disseminated, not without artifice on the part of Satan. For when any day is said to be *near*, if it does not quickly arrive, mankind being naturally impatient of longer delay, their spirits begin to languish, and that languishing is followed up shortly afterwards by despair.

This, therefore, was Satan's subtlety: as he could not openly overturn the hope of a resurrection with the view of secretly undermining it, as if by pits underground, he promised that the day of it would be near, and would soon arrive. Afterwards, too, he did not cease to contrive various things, with the view of effacing, by little and little, the belief of a resurrection from the minds of men, as he could not openly eradicate it. We now see how necessary Paul's

a belief prevails that the day of judgment is near. In a single year (1843) seventeen persons were admitted to the Lunatic Asylum in Worcester, Mass., who had become deranged in consequence of the expectation that the Lord Jesus was about to appear. It is easy to account for such facts; and no doubt, when the Lord Jesus shall actually come, the effect on the guilty world will be overwhelming. The apostle here says, also, that those who were Christians were "shaken in mind and troubled" by this anticipation. There are, doubtless, many true Christians who would be alarmed at such an event, as there are many who, like Hezekiah, Is. 38: 1–2, are alarmed at the prospect of death. Many real Christians might, on the sudden occurrence of such an event, feel that they were not prepared, and be alarmed at the prospect of passing through the great trial which is to determine their everlasting destiny. It is no certain evidence of a want of piety to be alarmed at the approach of death. Our nature dreads death, and though there may be a well-founded hope of heaven, it will not always preserve a delicate physical frame from trembling when it comes.

11. And for this cause. Because they chose error, or their hearts love that more than they do truth. The original reason then of their embracing and adhering to the system was not an arbitrary decree on the part of God, but that they did not love the truth. Hence he gave them up to this system of error. If a man strongly prefers error to truth, and sin to holiness, it is not wrong to allow him freely to evince his own preference.

God shall send them strong delusion. Gr., "energy of deceit;" a Hebraism, meaning strong deceit. The agency of God is here distinctly recognized, in accordance with the uniform statements of the Scriptures, respecting evil. Comp. Ex. 7: 13; 9: 12; 10: 1,20,27; 11: 10; 14: 8; Deut. 2: 30; Is. 45: 7.

That they should believe a lie. This does not affirm that God wished them to believe a lie nor that he would not have preferred that they should believe the truth; nor that he exerted any direct agency to cause them to believe a lie. It means merely that he left them, because they did not love the truth, to believe what

was false, and what would end in their destruction. Can any one doubt that this constantly occurs in the world? Men are left to believe impostors; to trust to false guides; to rely on unfounded information; to credit those who live to delude and betray the innocent; and to follow those who lead them to ruin. God does not impose by direct power to preserve them. Can any one doubt this? Yet this is not peculiarly the doctrine of revelation. The fact pertains just as much to the infidel as it does to the believer in Christianity, and he is just as much bound to explain it as the Christian is. It belongs to our world – to us all – and it should not be charged on Christianity as a doctrine pertaining peculiarly to that system.

15. Therefore. In view of the fact that you are thus chosen from eternity, and that you are to be raised up to such honor and glory.

Stand fast. Amidst all the temptations which surround you.

And hold the traditions which ye have been taught. It means properly things delivered over from one to another; then anything orally delivered – any precept, doctrine, or law. It is frequently employed to denote that which is not written, as contradistinguished from that which is written (comp. Matt. 15: 2), but not necessarily or always; for here the Apostle speaks of the "traditions which they had been taught by his epistle."

Here it means the doctrines or precepts which they had received from the apostle, whether when he was with them, or after he left them; whether communicated by preaching or by letter. This passage can furnish no authority for holding the "traditions" which have come down from ancient times, and which profess to have been derived from the apostles; for

(1.) there is no evidence that any of those traditions were given by the apostles;

(2.) many of them are manifestly so trifling, false, and contrary to the writings of the apostles, that they could not have been delivered by them;

(3.) if any of them are genuine, it is impossible to separate them from those which are false,

(4.) we have all that is necessary for salvation

17 Comfort your hearts, and stablish you in every good word and work.

2 THESSALONIANS 3

1 Finally, brethren, pray for us, that the word of the Lord may have free course, and be glorified, even as it is with you:

2 And that we may be delivered from unreasonable and wicked men: for all men have not faith.

3 But the Lord is faithful, who shall stablish you, and keep you from evil.

4 And we have confidence in the Lord touching you, that ye both do and will do the things which we command you.

5 And the Lord direct your hearts into the love of God, and into the patient waiting for Christ.

6 Now we command you, brethren, in the name of our Lord Jesus Christ, that ye withdraw yourselves from every brother that walketh disorderly, and not after the tradition which he received of us.

7 For yourselves know how ye ought to follow us: for we behaved not ourselves disorderly among you;

8 Neither did we eat any man's bread for nought; but wrought with labour and travail night and day, that we might not be chargeable to any of you:

9 Not because we have not power, but to make ourselves an ensample unto you to follow us.

10 For even when we were with you, this we commanded you, that if any would not work, neither should he eat.

11 For we hear that there are some which walk among you disorderly, working not at all, but are busybodies.

12 Now them that are such we command and exhort by our Lord Jesus Christ, that with quietness they work, and eat their own bread.

13 But ye, brethren, be not weary in well doing.

14 And if any man obey not our word by this epistle, note that man, and have no company with him, that he may be ashamed.

15 Yet count him not as an enemy, but admonish him as a brother.

admonition was, as but for this all religion would have been overturned among the Thessalonians under a specious pretext.

3. Let no man deceive you

That they may not groundlessly promise themselves the arrival in so short a time of the joyful day of redemption, he presents to them a melancholy prediction as to the future scattering of the Church. This discourse entirely corresponds with that which Christ held in the presence of his disciples, when they had asked him respecting the end of the world. For he exhorts them to prepare themselves for enduring hard conflicts, (Matthew 24: 6,) and after he has discoursed of the most grievous and previously unheard of calamities, by which the earth was to be reduced almost to a desert, he adds, that the *end is not yet*, but that *these things are the beginnings of sorrows*. In the same way, Paul declares that believers must exercise warfare for a long period, before gaining a triumph.

2 THESSALONIANS 3

1. Pray for us

Though the Lord powerfully aided him, and though he surpassed all others in earnestness of prayer, he nevertheless does not despise the prayers of believers, by which the Lord would have us aided. It becomes us, after his example, eagerly to desire this aid, and to stir up our brethren to pray for us.

When, however, he adds – *that the word of God may have its course*, he shows that he has not so much concern and regard for himself personally, as for the entire Church. For why does he desire to be recommended to the prayers of the Thessalonians? That the doctrine of the gospel may *have its course*. He does not desire, therefore, so much that regard should be had to himself individually, as to the glory of God and the common welfare of the Church. *Course* means here dissemination; *glory* means something farther – that his preaching may have its power and efficacy for renewing men after the image of God. Hence, holiness of life and uprightness on the part of Christians is the glory of the gospel; as, on the other hand, those defame the gospel who make profession of it with the mouth, while in the meantime they live in wickedness and baseness. He says – *as among you*; for this should be a stimulus to the pious, to see all others like them. Hence those that have already entered into the kingdom of God are exhorted to pray daily that it may *come* (Matthew 6: 10).

3. But God is faithful

As it was possible that their minds, influenced by unfavorable reports, might come to entertain some doubts as to

in the written word; and

(5.) there is not the least evidence that the apostle here meant to refer to any such thing. He speaks only of what had been delivered to them by himself, whether orally or by letter; not of what was delivered from one to another as from him. There is no intimation here that they were to hold anything as from him which they had not received directly from him, either by his own instructions personally or by letter. With what propriety, then, can this passage be adduced to prove that we are to hold the traditions which professedly come to us through a great number of intermediate persons? Nowhere is the evidence here that the church was to hold those unwritten traditions, and transmit them to future times?

Whether by word. By preaching, when we were with you. It does not mean that he had sent any oral message to them by a third person.

Or our epistle. The former letter which he had written to them.

2 THESSALONIANS 3

1. Finally, brethren, pray for us. That is, for Paul, Silas, and Timothy, then engaged in arduous labors at Corinth. This request for the prayers of Christians is one which Paul often makes.

That the word of the Lord may have free course. That is, the gospel. The margin is "run". So also the Greek. The idea is, that it might meet with no obstruction, but that it might be carried abroad with the rapidity of a racer out of whose way every hinderance was removed. The gospel would spread rapidly in the earth if all the obstructions which men have put in its way were removed; and that they may be removed should be one of the constant subjects of prayer.

And be glorified. Be honored; or appear to be glorious.

As it is with you. It is evident from this Paul met with some obstructions in preaching the gospel where he was then laboring. What they were, he mentions in the next verse. He was then at Corinth, (see the Introduction,) and the history in the Acts of the Apostles informs

us of the difficulties which he had to encounter there. See Acts 18.

8. Neither did we eat any man's bread for nought. We were not supported in idleness at the expense of others. We gave a fair equivalent for all that we received, and, in fact, labored for our own support.

13. But ye, brethren, be not weary in well-doing. Marg., faint not. The Greek means, properly, to turn out a coward; then to be faint-hearted, to despond. The idea is, that they were not to be discouraged from doing good to the truly worthy and deserving, by the idleness and improper conduct of some who asked their assistance. They were, indeed, shiftless and worthless. They would not labor; they spent their time in intermeddling with the concerns of their neighbors, and they depended for their support on the charity of others. The tendency of this, as all persons who have ever been applied to by such persons for aid, is, to indispose us to do good to any. We almost insensibly feel that all who ask for aid are of the same character; or, not being able to discriminate, we close our hands alike against all. Against this the apostle would guard us, and he says that though there may be many such persons, and though we may find it difficult to distinguish the worthy from the unworthy, we should not become so disheartened as not to give at all. Nor should we be weary though the applications for assistance are frequent. They are indeed frequent. God designs that they should be. But the effect should not be to dishearten us, or to make us weary in well-doing, but to fill us with gratitude – for it is a privilege to be permitted to do good. It is the great distinguishing characteristic of God that he always does good. It was that which marked the character of the Redeemer, that he "went about doing good;" and whenever God gives us the opportunity and the means of doing good, it should be to us an occasion of special thanksgiving. A man ought to become "weary" of everything else sooner than of evincing benevolence.

15. Yet count him not as an enemy, but admonish him as a brother. This shows the true spirit in which discipline is to be

16 Now the Lord of peace himself give you peace always by all means. The Lord be with you all.

17 The salutation of Paul with mine own hand, which is the token in every epistle: so I write.

18 The grace of our Lord Jesus Christ be with you all. Amen.

Paul's ministry, having taught them that faith is not always found in men, he now calls them back to God, and says that he is *faithful*, so as to confirm them against all contrivances of men, by which they will endeavor to shake them. "They, indeed, are treacherous, but there is in God a support that is abundantly secure, so as to keep you from giving way." He calls the Lord *faithful*, inasmuch as he adheres to his purpose to the end in maintaining the salvation of his people, seasonably aids them, and never forsakes them in dangers, as in 1 Corinthians 10: 13, "God is faithful, who will not suffer you to be tried above that ye are able to bear."

These words, however, themselves shew that Paul was more anxious as to others than as to himself. Malicious men directed against him the stings of their malignity; the whole violence of it fell upon him. In the mean time, he directs all his anxieties towards the Thessalonians, lest this temptation should do them any injury.

The term *evil* may refer as well to the thing, that is, malice, as to the persons of the wicked. I prefer, however, to interpret it of Satan, the head of all the wicked. For it were a small thing to be delivered from the cunning or violence of men, if the Lord did not protect us from all spiritual injury.

17. The salutation, with my own hand

Here again he provides against the danger, of which he had previously made mention – lest epistles falsely ascribed to him should find their way into the Churches. For this was an old artifice of Satan – to put forward spurious writings, that he might detract from the credit of those that are genuine; and farther, under pretended designations of the Apostles, to disseminate wicked errors with the view of corrupting sound doctrine. By a singular kindness on the part of God, it has been brought about that, his frauds being defeated, the doctrine of Christ has come down to us sound and entire through the ministry of Paul and others. The concluding prayer explains in what manner God aids his believing people – by the presence of Christ's grace.

administered in the Christian church. We are not to deal with a man as an adversary over whom we are to seek to gain a victory, but as an erring brother – a brother still, though he errs. There was necessity for this caution. There is great danger that when we undertake the work of discipline we shall forget that he who is the subject of it is a brother, and that we shall regard and treat him as an enemy. Such is human nature. We set ourselves in array against him. We cut him off as one who is unworthy to walk with us. We triumph over him, and consider him at once as an enemy of the church, and as having lost all claim to its sympathies. We abandon him to the tender mercies of a cold and unfeeling world, and let him take his course. Perhaps we follow him with anathemas, and hold him up as unworthy the confidence of mankind. Now all this is entirely unlike the method and aim of discipline as the New Testament requires. There all is kind and gentle, though firm; the offender is a man and a brother still; he is to be followed with tender sympathy and prayer, and the hearts and the arms of the Christian brotherhood are to be open to receive him again when he gives any evidence of repenting.

17. Which is the token in every epistle. Gr., sign. This signature is a sign or proof of the genuineness of the letter.

So I write. Referring to some mark or method which Paul had of signing his name which was well known, and which would easily be recognized by them.

1 Timothy

Introduction by John Calvin

THIS Epistle appears to me to have been written more for the sake of others than for the sake of Timothy, and that opinion will receive the assent of those who shall carefully consider the whole matter. I do not, indeed, deny that Paul intended also to teach and admonish him; but my view of the Epistle is, that it contains many things which it would have been superfluous to write, if he had had to deal with Timothy alone. He was a young man, not yet clothed with that authority which would have been sufficient for restraining the headstrong men that rose up against him. It is manifest, from the words used by Paul, that there were at that time some who were prodigiously inclined to ostentation, and for that reason would not willingly yield to any person, and who likewise burned with such ardent ambition, that they would never have ceased to disturb the Church, had not a greater than Timothy interposed. It is likewise manifest, that there were many things to be adjusted at Ephesus, and that needed the approbation of Paul, and the sanction of his name. Having therefore intended to give advice to Timothy on many subjects, he resolved at the same time to advise others under the name of Timothy.

In the first chapter, he attacks some ambitious persons who made their boast of discussing idle questions. It may readily be concluded that they were Jews, who, while they pretended to have zeal for the law, disregarded edification, and attended only to frivolous disputes. It is an intolerable profanation of the law of God, to draw out of it nothing that is profitable, but merely to pick up materials for talking and to abuse the pretense of it for the purpose of burdening the Church with contemptible trifles.

Longer shall enough have such corruptions prevailed in Popery; for what else was the scholastic theology than a huge chaos of empty and useless speculations? And in our own day there are many who in order to display their acuteness in handling the word of God, allow themselves to sport with it in the same manner as if it were profane philosophy. Paul undertakes to support Timothy in the correction of this vice, and points out what is the principal instruction to be derived from the Law; that it may be evident that they who use the Law in a different manner are corrupters of it.

Next, that his authority may not be despised, after having acknowledged his unworthiness he, at the same time, asserts in lofty terms what he became through the grace of God. At length he concludes the chapter by a solemn threatening, by means of which he both confirms Timothy in sound doctrine and a good conscience, and fills others with terror and alarm, by holding out to them the example of Hymenaeus and Alexander.

In the second chapter, he enjoins that public prayers be offered to God for all men, and especially for princes and magistrates; and here, in passing, he likewise makes a remark on the advantage which the world derives from civil government. He then mentions the reason why we ought to pray for all men; namely, that God, by exhibiting to all the gospel and Christ the Mediator, shews that he wishes all men to be saved; and he likewise confirms this statement by his own apostleship, which was specially appointed to the Gentiles. Next, he invites all men, whatever may be their country or place of abode, to pray to God; and takes occasion for inculcating that modesty and subjection which females ought to maintain in the holy assembly.

In the third chapter, after having declared the excellence of the bishop's office, he delineates a true bishop, and enumerates the qualifications required in him. Next, he describes the qualifications of deacons, and of the wives both of deacons and of bishops. And in order that Timothy may be more diligent and conscientious in observing all things, he reminds him what it is to be employed in the government of "the Church, which is the house of God, and the pillar of truth." Finally, he mentions the chief and fundamental point of all heavenly doctrine — that which relates to the Son of God manifested in the flesh; in comparison of which all things else, to which he perceived that ambitious men were wholly devoted, should be reckoned of no value.

As to what follows, in the beginning of *the fourth chapter*, the false doctrines about forbidding marriage and various kinds of food, and the absurd fables which are at variance with this doctrine, are severely condemned by him. Next, he adds, that he and all good men, who hold this doctrine, have none for their adversaries but those who cannot endure that men shall place their trust in the living God. At the close of the chapter, he again fortifies Timothy by a new exhortation.

In the fifth chapter, after having recommended modesty and gentleness in reproofs, he reasons about widows, who at that time were admitted into the service of the Church. He enjoins that they shall not be received indiscriminately, but only those who, having been approved throughout their whole life, are arrived at sixty years of age, and have no domestic tie. Hence he passes on to the elder's, and explains how they ought to conduct themselves, both in their manner of life and in the exercise of discipline. This doctrine the Apostle seals by a solemn oath, and again forbids him to admit any one heedlessly into the office of the eldership. He exhorts him to drink wine, instead of water, for the preservation of his health. At the close of the chapter, he exhorts him to defer pronouncing judgment on concealed transgressions.

In the sixth chapter, he gives instruction concerning the duty of servants, and takes occasion to make a vehement attack on false teachers, who, by disputing about unprofitable speculations, are more eager for gain than for edification, and shews that covetousness is a most deadly plague. He then returns to a solemn charge similar to the former, that the exhortations which he now gives to Timothy may not be ineffectual. Lastly, after having taken a passing notice of riches, he again forbids Timothy to entangle himself with useless doctrines.

As to the ordinary Greek inscription, which states that this Epistle was written from Laodicea, I do not agree with it; for since Paul, writing to the Colossians while he was a prisoner, affirms that he had never seen the Laodiceans, those who hold the opinion, which I reject, are constrained to make two Laodiceas in Asia Minor, though only one is mentioned by historians. Besides, when Paul went into Macedonia, he left Timothy at Ephesus, as he expressly declares. He wrote this Epistle either on the road, before he arrived there, or after having returned from the journey. Now Laodicea is evidently at a greater distance from Macedonia than Ephesus is; and it is not probable that Paul, on his return, went to Laodicea, passing by Ephesus, especially since there were many reasons that urged him to visit it; and therefore I rather think that he wrote it from some other place. But this is not a matter of so much importance that I should wish to debate it with those who are of an opposite opinion. Let every person follow his own judgment. I only point out what — at least in my opinion – is more probable.

The commentaries on 1 Timothy are by John Calvin and A. R. Fausset.

1 TIMOTHY 1

1 Paul, an apostle of Jesus Christ by the commandment of God our Savior, and Lord Jesus Christ, which is our hope;

2 Unto Timothy, my own son in the faith: Grace, mercy, and peace, from God our Father and Jesus Christ our Lord.

3 As I besought thee to abide still at Ephesus, when I went into Macedonia, that thou mightest charge some that they teach no other doctrine,

4 Neither give heed to fables and endless genealogies, which minister questions, rather than godly edifying which is in faith: so do.

5 Now the end of the commandment is charity out of a pure heart, and of a good conscience, and of faith unfeigned:

6 From which some having swerved have turned aside unto vain jangling;

7 Desiring to be teachers of the law; understanding neither what they say, nor whereof they affirm.

8 But we know that the law is good, if a man use it lawfully;

9 Knowing this, that the law is not made for a righteous man, but for the lawless and disobedient, for the ungodly and for sinners, for unholy and profane, for murderers of fathers and murderers of mothers, for manslayers,

10 For whoremongers, for them that defile themselves with mankind, for menstealers, for liars, for perjured persons, and if there be any other thing that is contrary to sound doctrine;

11 According to the glorious gospel of the blessed God, which was committed to my trust.

12 And I thank Christ Jesus our Lord, who hath enabled me, for that he counted me faithful, putting me into the ministry;

13 Who was before a blasphemer, and a persecutor, and injurious: but I obtained mercy, because I did it ignorantly in unbelief.

14 And the grace of our Lord was exceeding abundant with faith and love which is in Christ Jesus.

15 This is a faithful saying, and worthy of all acceptation, that Christ Jesus came into the world to save sinners; of whom I am chief.

16 Howbeit for this cause I obtained

1 TIMOTHY 1

1. Paul an apostle

If he had written to Timothy alone, it would have been unnecessary to claim this designation, and to maintain it in the manner that he does. Timothy would undoubtedly have been satisfied with having merely the name; for he knew that Paul was an Apostle of Christ, and had no need of proof to convince him of it, being perfectly willing, and having been long accustomed, to acknowledge it. He has his eye, therefore, chiefly on others, who were not so ready to listen to him, or did not so easily believe his words. For the sake of such persons, that they may not treat lightly what he writes, he affirms that he is "*an Apostle of Christ.*"

According to the Appointment of God our Savior, and of the Lord Jesus Christ. He confirms his apostleship by the appointment or command of God; for no man can make himself to be an apostle, but he whom God hath appointed is a true apostle, and worthy of the honor. Nor does he merely say, that he owes his apostleship to God the Father, but ascribes it to Christ also; and, indeed, in the government of the Church, the Father does nothing but through the Son, and therefore they both act together.

He calls God the Savior, a title which he is more frequently accustomed to assign to the Son; but it belongs to the Father also, because it is he who gave the Son to us. Justly, therefore, is the glory of our salvation ascribed to him. For how comes it that we are saved? It is because the Father loved us in such a manner that he determined to redeem and save us through the Son. He calls Christ *our hope*; and this appellation is strictly applicable to him; for then do we begin to have good hope, when we look to Christ, since in him alone dwells all that on which our salvation rests.

2. To Timothy my own son

This commendation expresses no small praise. Paul means by it, that he owns Timothy to be a true and not a bastard son, and wishes that others should acknowledge him to be such; and he even applauds Timothy in the same manner as if he were another Paul.

But how does this agree with the injunction given by Christ, (Matthew 23: 9,) "Call no man your father on the earth?" Or how does it agree with the declaration of the Apostle, "Though ye have many fathers according to the flesh, yet there is but One who is the Father of spirits" (1 Corinthians 4: 15; Hebrews 12: 9).

I reply, while Paul claims for himself the appellation of father, he does it in such a manner as not to take away or diminish the smallest portion of the honor which is due to God (Hebrews 12: 9). It is a common proverb "That which is placed below another is not at variance with it." The name father, applied to Paul, with reference to God, belongs to

1 TIMOTHY 1

2. my own son – literally, "a genuine son" (compare Acts 16: 1; 1 Cor. 4: 14–17).

4. fables – legends about the origin and propagation of angels, such as the false teachers taught at Colosse (Col. 2: 18–23). "Jewish fables" (Titus 1: 14). "Profane, and old wives' fables" (1 Tim. 4: 7; 2 Tim. 4: 4).

genealogies – not merely such civil genealogies as were common among the Jews, whereby they traced their descent from the patriarchs, to which Paul would not object, and which he would not as here class with "fables," but Gnostic genealogies of spirits and eons, as they called them.

8. law is good – in full agreement with God's holiness and goodness.

if a man – primarily, a teacher; then, every Christian.

use it lawfully – in its lawful place in the Gospel economy, namely, not as a means of a "'righteous man" attaining higher perfection than could be attained by the Gospel alone (1 Tim. 4: 8; Titus 1: 14), which was the perverted use to which the false teachers put it, but as a means of awakening the sense of sin in the ungodly (1 Tim. 1: 9–10; compare Rom. 7: 7–12; Gal. 3: 21).

9. law is not made for a righteous man – not for one standing by faith in the righteousness of Christ put on him for justification, and imparted inwardly by the Spirit for sanctification. "One not forensically amenable to the law" [ALFORD]. For sanctification, the law gives no inward power to fulfill it; but ALFORD goes too far in speaking of the righteous man as "not morally needing the law." Doubtless, in proportion as he is inwardly led by the Spirit, the justified man needs not the law, which is only an outward rule (Rom. 6: 14; Gal. 5: 18,23). But as the justified man often does not give himself up wholly to the inward leading of the Spirit, he morally needs the outward law to show him his sin and God's requirements. The reason why the ten commandments have no power to condemn the Christian, is not that they have no authority over him, but because Christ has fulfilled them as our surety (Rom.

10: 4).

disobedient – Greek, "not subject"; insubordinate; it is translated "unruly," Titus 1: 6,10; "lawless and disobedient" refer to opposers of the law, for whom it is "enacted" (so the Greek, for "is made").

ungodly and . . . sinners – Greek, he who does not reverence God, and he who openly sins against Him; the opposers of God, from the law comes.

unholy and profane – those inwardly impure, and those deserving exclusion from the outward participation in services of the sanctuary; sinners against the third and fourth commandments.

murderers – or, as the Greek may mean, "smiters" of fathers and . . . mothers; sinners against the fifth commandment.

manslayers – sinners against the sixth commandment.

14. And – Greek, "But." Not only so (was mercy shown me), but

the grace – by which "I obtained mercy" (1 Tim. 1: 13).

was exceeding abundant – Greek, "superabounded." Where sin abounded, grace did much more abound" (Rom. 5: 20).

with faith – accompanied with faith, the opposite of "unbelief" (1 Tim. 1: 13).

love – in contrast to "a blasphemer, persecutor, and injurious."

which is in Christ – as its element and home: here as its source whence it flows to us.

15. faithful – worthy of credit, because "God" who says it "is faithful" to His word (1 Cor. 1: 9; 1 Thess. 5: 24; 2 Thess. 3: 3; Rev. 21: 5; 22: 6). This seems to have become an axiomatic saying among Christians the phrase, "faithful saying," is peculiar to the Pastoral Epistles (1 Tim. 2: 11; 4: 9; Titus 3: 8). Translate as Greek, "Faithful is the saying."

all – all possible; full; to be received by all, and with all the faculties of the soul, mind, and heart. Paul, unlike the false teachers (1 Tim. 1: 7), understands what he is saying, and whereof he affirms; and by his simplicity of style and subject, setting forth the grand fundamental truth of salvation through Christ, confutes the false teachers' abstruse and unpractical

mercy, that in me first Jesus Christ might shew forth all longsuffering, for a pattern to them which should hereafter believe on him to life everlasting.

17 Now unto the King eternal, immortal, invisible, the only wise God, be honor and glory for ever and ever. Amen.

18 This charge I commit unto thee, son Timothy, according to the prophecies which went before on thee, that thou by them mightest war a good warfare;

19 Holding faith, and a good conscience; which some having put away concerning faith have made shipwreck:

20 Of whom is Hymenaeus and Alexander; whom I have delivered unto Satan, that they may learn not to blaspheme.

1 TIMOTHY 2

1 I exhort therefore, that, first of all, supplications, prayers, intercessions, and giving of thanks, be made for all men;

2 For kings, and for all that are in authority; that we may lead a quiet and peaceable life in all godliness and honesty.

3 For this is good and acceptable in the sight of God our Savior;

4 Who will have all men to be saved, and to come unto the knowledge of the truth.

5 For there is one God, and one mediator between God and men, the man Christ Jesus;

6 Who gave himself a ransom for all, to be testified in due time.

7 Whereunto I am ordained a preacher, and an apostle, (I speak the truth in Christ, and lie not;) a teacher of the Gentiles in faith and verity.

8 I will therefore that men pray every where, lifting up holy hands, without wrath and doubting.

9 In like manner also, that women adorn themselves in modest apparel, with shamefacedness and sobriety; not with broided hair, or gold, or pearls, or costly array;

10 But (which becometh women professing godliness) with good works.

11 Let the woman learn in silence with all subjection.

12 But I suffer not a woman to teach, nor to usurp authority over the man, but

this class. God alone is the Father of all in faith, because he regenerates us all by his word, and by the power of his Spirit, and because none but he bestows faith. But they whom he is graciously pleased to employ as his ministers for that purpose, are likewise allowed to share with him in his honor, while, at the same time, He parts with nothing that belongs to himself. Thus God, and God alone, strictly speaking, was Timothy's spiritual Father; but Paul, who was God's minister in begetting Timothy, lays claim to this title, by what may be called a subordinate right.

Grace, mercy, peace

So far as relates to the word mercy, he has departed from his ordinary custom in introducing it, moved, perhaps, by his extraordinary affection for Timothy. Besides, he does not observe the exact order; for he places first what ought to love been last, namely, the grace which flows from mercy. For the reason why God at first receives us into favor and why he loves us is, that he is merciful. But it is not unusual to mention the cause after the effect, for the sake of explanation. As to the words grace and peace, we have spoken on other occasions.

1 TIMOTHY 2

1. I exhort therefore

These exercises of godliness maintain and even strengthen us in the sincere worship and fear of God, and cherish the good conscience of which he had spoken. Not inappropriately does he make use of the word *therefore*, to denote an inference; for those exhortations depend on the preceding commandment.

That, above all, prayers be made

First, he speaks of public prayers, which he enjoins to be offered, not only for believers, but for all mankind. Some might reason thus with themselves: "Why should we be anxious about the salvation of unbelievers, with whom we have no connection? Is it not enough, if we, who are brethren, pray mutually for our brethren, and recommend to God the whole of his Church? for we have nothing to do with strangers." This perverse view Paul meets, and enjoins the Ephesians to include in their prayers all men, and not to limit them to the body of the Church.

2. For kings

He expressly mentions kings and other magistrates because, more than all others, they might be hated by Christians. All the magistrates who existed at that time were so many sworn enemies of Christ; and therefore this thought might occur to them, that they ought not to pray for those who devoted all their power and all their wealth to fight against the kingdom of Christ, the extension of which is above all things desirable. The apostle meets this difficulty,

speculations (1 Cor. 1: 18–28; Titus 2: 1).

acceptation – reception (as of a boon) into the heart, as well as the understanding, with all gladness; this is faith acting on the Gospel offer, and welcoming and appropriating it (Acts 2: 41).

20. **Hymenaeus** – There is no difficulty in supposing him to be the Hymenæus of 2 Tim. 2: 17. Though **delivered over to Satan**(the lord of all outside the Church, Acts 26: 18, and the executor of wrath, when judicially allowed by God, on the disobedient, 1 Cor. 5: 5; 2 Cor. 12: 7), he probably was restored to the Church subsequently, and again troubled it. Paul, as an apostle, though distant at Rome pronounced the sentence to be executed at Ephesus, involving, probably, the excommunication of the offenders (Matt. 18: 17–18). The sentence operated not only spiritually, but also physically, sickness, or some such visitation of God, falling on the person excommunicated, in order to bring him to repentance and salvation. Alexander here is probably "the coppersmith" who did Paul "much evil" when the latter visited Ephesus. The "delivering him to Satan" was probably the consequence of his withstanding the apostle (2 Tim. 4: 14–15); as the same sentence on Hymenæus was the consequence of "saying that the resurrection is past already" (2 Tim. 2: 18).

1 TIMOTHY 2

3. **this** – praying for all men.

in the sight of God – not merely before men, as if it were their favor that we sought (2 Cor. 8: 21).

our Savior – a title appropriate to the matter in hand. He who is "our Savior" is willing that all should be saved (1 Tim. 2: 4; Rom. 5: 18); therefore we should meet the will of God in behalf of others, by praying for the salvation of all men. More would be converted if we would pray more. He has actually saved us who believe, being "our Savior." He is willing that all should be saved, even those who do not as yet believe, if they will believe (compare 1 Tim. 4: 10; Titus 2: 11).

5. **For there is one God** – God's unity in essence and purpose is a proof of His compre-

hending all His human children alike (created in His image) in His offer of grace (compare the same argument from His unity, Rom. 3: 30; Gal. 3: 20); therefore all are to be prayed for. 1 Tim. 2: 4 is proved from 1 Tim. 2: 5; 1 Tim. 2: 1, from 1 Tim. 2: 4. The one God is common to all (Is. 45: 22; Acts 17: 26). The one Mediator is mediator between God and all men potentially (Rom. 3: 29; Eph. 4: 5–6; Heb. 8: 6; 9: 15; 12: 24). They who have not this one God by one Mediator, have none: literally, a "go-between." The Greek order is not "and one mediator," but "one mediator also between . . . While God will have all men to be saved by knowing God and the Mediator, there is a legitimate, holy order in the exercise of that will wherewith men ought to receive it.

8. **I will** – The active wish, or desire, is meant.

that men – rather as Greek, "that the men," as distinguished from "the women," to whom he has something different to say from what he said to the men (1 Tim. 2: 9–12; 1 Cor. 11: 14–15; 14: 34–35). The emphasis, however, is not on this, but on the precept of praying, resumed from 1 Tim. 2: 1.

everywhere – Greek, "in every place," namely, of public prayer. Fulfilling Mal. 1: 11, "In every place . . . from the rising of the sun even unto the going down of the same . . . incense shall be offered unto My name"; and Jesus' words, Matt. 18: 20; John 4: 21,23.

lifting up holy hands – The early Christians turned up their palms towards heaven, as those craving help do. So also Solomon (1 Kgs. 8: 22; Ps. 141: 2). The Jews washed their hands before prayer (Ps. 26: 6). Paul figuratively (compare Job 17: 9; James 4: 8) uses language alluding to this custom here: so Is. 1: 15–16. The Greek for "holy" means hands which have committed no impiety, and observed every sacred duty. This (or at least the contrite desire to be so) is a needful qualification for effectual prayer (Ps. 24: 3–4).

without wrath – putting it away (Matt. 5: 23–24; 6: 15).

doubting – rather, "disputing," as the Greek is translated in Phil. 2: 14. Such things hinder prayer (Luke 9: 46; Rom. 14: 1; 1 Pet. 3: 7).

15. **be saved in childbearing** – Greek, "in

to be in silence.

13 For Adam was first formed, then Eve.

14 And Adam was not deceived, but the woman being deceived was in the transgression.

15 Notwithstanding she shall be saved in childbearing, if they continue in faith and charity and holiness with sobriety.

1 TIMOTHY 3

1 This is a true saying, If a man desire the office of a bishop, he desireth a good work.

2 A bishop then must be blameless, the husband of one wife, vigilant, sober, of good behavior, given to hospitality, apt to teach;

3 Not given to wine, no striker, not greedy of filthy lucre; but patient, not a brawler, not covetous;

4 One that ruleth well his own house, having his children in subjection with all gravity;

5 (For if a man know not how to rule his own house, how shall he take care of the church of God?)

6 Not a novice, lest being lifted up with pride he fall into the condemnation of the devil.

7 Moreover he must have a good report of them which are without; lest he fall into reproach and the snare of the devil.

8 Likewise must the deacons be grave, not doubletongued, not given to much wine, not greedy of filthy lucre;

9 Holding the mystery of the faith in a pure conscience.

10 And let these also first be proved; then let them use the office of a deacon, being found blameless.

11 Even so must their wives be grave, not slanderers, sober, faithful in all things.

12 Let the deacons be the husbands of one wife, ruling their children and their own houses well.

13 For they that have used the office of a deacon well purchase to themselves a good degree, and great boldness in the faith which is in Christ Jesus.

14 These things write I unto thee, hoping to come unto thee shortly:

15 But if I tarry long, that thou may-

and expressly enjoins Christians to pray for them also. And, indeed, the depravity of men is not a reason why God's ordinance should not be loved. Accordingly, seeing that God appointed magistrates and princes for the preservation of mankind, however much they fall short of the divine appointment, still we must not on that account cease to love what belongs to God, and to desire that it may remain in force. That is the reason why believers, in whatever country they live, must not only obey the laws and the government of magistrates, but likewise in their prayers supplicate

6. Who gave himself a ransom for all

The mention of redemption in this passage is not superfluous; for there is a necessary connection between the two things, the sacrifice of the death of Christ, and his continual intercession. (Romans 8: 34.) These are the two parts of his priesthood; for, when Christ is called our priest, it is in this sense, that he once made atonement for our sins by his death, that he might reconcile us to God; and now having entered into the sanctuary of heaven, he appears in presence of the Father, in order to obtain grace for us, that we may be heard in his name (Psalm 110: 4; Hebrews 7: 17).

1 TIMOTHY 3

14. These things I write to thee

He holds out to Timothy the hope of his coming, partly in order to encourage him, and partly in order to repress the insolence of those who grew more haughty on account of his absence. And yet he does not make any feigned promise to Timothy, or terrify others through false presence; for he fully expected that he would come, as it is probable that he came, if he wrote this epistle at the time when he passed through Phrygia, as is related by Luke (Acts 18: 23). Let us look on this as a proof how great was his anxiety for the churches, when he could not endure to delay for a short time a remedy for a present evil. Yet immediately afterwards he adds, that he wrote this epistle for the purpose of informing Timothy, if it should happen that he were delayed longer than he thought.

15. How thou oughtest to conduct thyself

By this mode of expression he commends the weight and dignity of the office; because pastors may be regarded as stewards, to whom God has committed the charge of governing his house. If any person has the superintendence of a large house, he labors night and day with earnest solicitude, that nothing may go wrong through his neglect, or ignorance, or carelessness. If only for men this is done, how much more should it be done for God?

In the house of God

There are good reasons why God bestows this name on his

(literally, 'through') (her, literally, 'the') child-bearing." Through, or by, is often so used to express not the means of her salvation, but the circumstances in which it has place. Thus 1 Cor. 3: 15, "He . . . shall be saved: yet so as by (literally, 'through,' that is, amidst) fire": in spite of the fiery ordeal which he has necessarily to pass through, he shall be saved. So here, "In spite of the trial of childbearing which she passes through (as her portion of the curse, Gen. 3: 16, 'in sorrow shalt thou bring forth children'), she shall be saved." Moreover, I think it is implied indirectly that the very curse will be turned into a condition favorable to her salvation, by her faithfully performing her part in doing and suffering what God has assigned to her, namely, child-bearing and home duties, her sphere, as distinguished from public teaching, which is not hers, but man's (1 Tim. 2: 11–12).

1 TIMOTHY 3

3. Not given to wine – The Greek includes besides this, not indulging in the brawling, violent conduct towards others, which proceeds from being given to wine. The opposite of "patient" or (Greek) "forbearing," reasonable to others.

no striker – with either hand or tongue: not as some teachers pretending a holy zeal (2 Cor. 11: 20), answering to "not a brawler" or fighter (compare 1 Kgs. 22: 24; Neh. 13: 25; Is. 58: 4; Acts 23: 2; 2 Tim. 2: 24–25).

not covetous – Greek, "not a lover of money," whether he have much or little (Titus 1: 7).

4. ruleth – Greek, "presiding over."

his own house – children and servants, as contrasted with "the church" (house) of God (1 Tim. 3: 5,15) which he may be called on to preside over.

having his children – rather as Greek, "having children (who are) in subjection" (Titus 1: 6).

gravity – propriety: reverent modesty on the part of the children. The fact that he has children who are in subjection to him in all gravity, is the recommendation in his favor as one likely to rule well the Church.

7. a good report – Greek, "testimony." So Paul was influenced by the good report given of Timothy to choose him as his companion (Acts 16: 2).

of them which are without – from the as yet unconverted Gentiles around (1 Cor. 5: 12; Col. 4: 5; 1 Thess. 4: 12), that they may be the more readily won to the Gospel (1 Pet. 2: 12), and that the name of Christ may be glorified. Not even the former life of a bishop should be open to reproach [BENGEL].

reproach and the snare of the devil – reproach of men (1 Tim. 5: 14) proving the occasion of his falling into the snare of the devil (1 Tim. 6: 9; Matt. 22: 15; 2 Tim. 2: 26). The reproach continually surrounding him for former sins might lead him into the snare of becoming as bad as his reputation. Despair of recovering reputation might, in a weak moment, lead some into recklessness of living (Jer. 18: 12). The reason why only moral qualities of a general kind are specified is, he presupposes in candidates for a bishopric the special gifts of the Spirit (1 Tim. 4: 14) and true faith, which he desires to be evidenced outwardly; also he requires qualifications in a bishop not so indispensable in others.

9. the mystery of the faith – holding the faith, which to the natural man remains a mystery, but which has been revealed by the Spirit to them (Rom. 16: 25; 1 Cor. 2: 7–10), in a pure conscience (1 Tim. 1: 5,19). Though deacons were not ordinarily called on to preach (Stephen and Philip are not exceptions to this, since it was as evangelists, rather than as deacons, they preached), yet as being office-bearers in the Church, and having much intercourse with all the members, they especially needed to have this characteristic, which every Christian ought to have.

15. But if I tarry long – before coming to thee.

that – that is, I write (1 Tim. 3: 14) "that thou mayest know," etc.

behave thyself – in directing the Church at Ephesus (1 Tim. 4: 11).

the house of God – the Church (Heb. 3: 2,5–6; 10: 21; 1 Pet. 4: 17; 1 Cor. 3: 16, "the temple of God"; Eph. 2: 22).

est know how thou oughtest to behave thyself in the house of God, which is the church of the living God, the pillar and ground of the truth.

16 And without controversy great is the mystery of godliness: God was manifest in the flesh, justified in the Spirit, seen of angels, preached unto the Gentiles, believed on in the world, received up into glory.

1 TIMOTHY 4

1 Now the Spirit speaketh expressly, that in the latter times some shall depart from the faith, giving heed to seducing spirits, and doctrines of devils;

2 Speaking lies in hypocrisy; having their conscience seared with a hot iron;

3 Forbidding to marry, and commanding to abstain from meats, which God hath created to be received with thanksgiving of them which believe and know the truth.

4 For every creature of God is good, and nothing to be refused, if it be received with thanksgiving:

5 For it is sanctified by the word of God and prayer.

6 If thou put the brethren in remembrance of these things, thou shalt be a good minister of Jesus Christ, nourished up in the words of faith and of good doctrine, whereunto thou hast attained.

7 But refuse profane and old wives' fables, and exercise thyself rather unto godliness.

8 For bodily exercise profiteth little: but godliness is profitable unto all things, having promise of the life that now is, and of that which is to come.

9 This is a faithful saying and worthy of all acceptation.

10 For therefore we both labour and suffer reproach, because we trust in the living God, who is the Savior of all men, specially of those that believe.

11 These things command and teach.

12 Let no man despise thy youth; but be thou an example of the believers, in word, in conversation, in charity, in spirit, in faith, in purity.

13 Till I come, give attendance to reading, to exhortation, to doctrine.

14 Neglect not the gift that is in thee, which was given thee by prophecy, with

Church; for not only has he received us to be his children by the grace of adoption, but he also dwelleth in the midst of us.

The pillar and foundation of truth

No ordinary enhancement is derived from this appellation. Could it have been described in loftier language? Is anything more venerable, or more holy, than that everlasting truth which embraces both the glory of God and the salvation of men? Were all the praises of heathen philosophy, with which it has been adorned by its followers, collected into one heap, what is this in comparison of the dignity of this wisdom, which alone deserves to be called light and truth, and the instruction of life, and the way, and the kingdom of God? Now it is preserved on earth by the ministry of the Church alone. What a weight, therefore, rests on the pastors, who have been entrusted with the charge of so inestimable a treasure! With what impudent trifling do Papists argue from the words of Paul that all their absurdities ought to be held as oracles of God, because they are "the pillar of truth," and therefore cannot err!

First, we ought to see why Paul adorns the Church with so magnificent a title. By holding out to pastors the greatness of the office, he undoubtedly intended to remind them with what fidelity, and industry, and reverence they ought to discharge it. How dreadful is the vengeance that awaits them, if, through their fault, that truth which is the image of the Divine glory, the light of the world, and the salvation of men, shall be allowed to fall! This consideration ought undoubtedly to lead pastors to tremble continually, not to deprive them of all energy, but to excite them to greater vigilance.

Hence we may easily conclude in what sense Paul uses these words. The reason why the Church is called the "pillar of truth" is, that she defends and spreads it by her agency. God does not himself come down from heaven to us, nor does he daily send angels to make known his truth; but he employs pastors, whom he has appointed for that purpose. To express it in a more homely manner, is not the Church the mother of all believers? Does she not regenerate them by the word of God, educate and nourish them through their whole life, strengthen, and bring them at length to absolute perfection? For the same reason, also, she is called "the pillar of truth;" because the office of administering doctrine, which God hath placed in her hands, is the only instrument of preserving the truth, that it may not perish from the remembrance of men.

1 TIMOTHY 4

1. Now the Spirit plainly saith

He had industriously admonished Timothy about many

the church – "the congregation." The fact that the sphere of thy functions is "the congregation of the living God" (who is the ever living Master of the house, 2 Tim. 2: 19–21), is the strongest motive to faithfulness in this behavior as president of a department of the house." The living God forms a striking contrast to the lifeless idol, Diana of Ephesus (1 Thess. 1: 9).

1 TIMOTHY 4

1. the Spirit – speaking by the prophets in the Church (whose prophecies rested on those of the Old Testament, Dan. 7: 25; 8: 23, etc.; 11: 30, as also on those of Jesus in the New Testament, Mt 24: 11–24), and also by Paul himself, 2 Thess. 2: 3 (with whom accord 2 Pet. 3: 3; 1 John 2: 18; Jude 18).

expressly – "in plain words." This shows that he refers to prophecies of the Spirit then lying before him.

in the latter times – in the times following upon the times in which he is now writing. Not some remote future, but times immediately subsequent, the beginnings of the apostasy being already discernible (Acts 20: 29): these are the forerunners of "the last days" (2 Tim. 3: 1).

depart from the faith – The apostasy was to be within the Church, the faithful one becoming the harlot. In 2 Thess. 2: 3 (written earlier), the apostasy of the Jews from God (joining the heathen against Christianity) is the groundwork on which the prophecy rises; whereas here, in the Pastoral Epistles, the prophecy is connected with Gnostic errors, the seeds of which had already been sown in the Church [AUBERLEN] (2 Tim. 2: 18). Apollonius Tyanæus, a heretic, came to Ephesus in the lifetime of Timothy.

giving heed – (1 Tim. 1: 4; Titus 1: 14).

seducing spirits – working in the heretical teachers. 1 John 4: 2–3,6, "the spirit of error," opposed to "the spirit of truth," "the Spirit" which "speaketh" in the true prophets against them.

doctrines of devils – literally "teachings of (that is suggested by) demons." James 3: 15, "wisdom . . . devilish"; 2 Cor. 11: 15, "Satan's ministers."

3. Sensuality leads to false spiritualism. Their own inward impurity is reflected in their eyes in the world without them, and hence their asceticism (Titus 1: 14, 15) [WIESINGER]. By a spurious spiritualism (2 Tim. 2: 18), which made moral perfection consist in abstinence from outward things, they pretended to attain to a higher perfection. Matt. 19: 10–12 (compare 1 Cor. 7: 8,26,38) gave a seeming handle to their **forbidding marriage** (contrast 1 Tim. 5: 14); and the Old Testament distinction as to clean and unclean, gave a pretext for teaching to **abstain from meats** (compare Col. 2: 16–17,20–23). As these Judaizing Gnostics combined the harlot or apostate Old Testament Church with the beast (Rev. 17: 3), or Gnostic spiritualizing anti-Christianity, so Rome's Judaizing elements (1 Tim. 4: 3) shall ultimately be combined with the open worldly-wise anti-Christianity of the false prophet or beast (1 Tim. 6: 20–21; Col. 2: 8; 1 John 4: 1–3; Rev. 13: 12–15). Austerity gained for them a show of sanctity while preaching false doctrine (Col. 2: 23).

14. Neglect not the gift – by letting it lie unused. In 2 Tim. 1: 6 the gift is represented as a spark of the Spirit lying within him, and sure to smolder by neglect, the stirring up or keeping in lively exercise of which depends on the will of him on whom it is bestowed (Matt. 25: 18, 25,27–28). The charism or spiritual gift, is that of the Spirit which qualified him for "the work of an evangelist" (Eph. 4: 11; 2 Tim. 4: 5), or perhaps the gift of discerning spirits, specially needed in his function of ordaining, as overseer.

given thee – by God (1 Cor. 12: 4,6).

by prophecy – that is, by the Holy Spirit, at his general ordination, or else consecration, to the special see of Ephesus, speaking through the prophets God's will to give him the graces needed to qualify him for his work (1 Tim. 1: 18; Acts 13: 1–3).

with . . . laying on of . . . hands – So in Joshua's case (Num. 27: 18–20; Deut. 34: 9). The gift was connected with the symbolical act of laying on hands. But the Greek "with" implies that the presbyter's laying on hands was the mere accompaniment of the conferring of the gift. "By" (2 Tim. 1: 6) implies that Paul's laying

the laying on of the hands of the presbytery.

15 Meditate upon these things; give thyself wholly to them; that thy profiting may appear to all.

16 Take heed unto thyself, and unto the doctrine; continue in them: for in doing this thou shalt both save thyself, and them that hear thee.

1 TIMOTHY 5

1 Rebuke not an elder, but intreat him as a father; and the younger men as brethren;

2 The elder women as mothers; the younger as sisters, with all purity.

3 Honor widows that are widows indeed.

4 But if any widow have children or nephews, let them learn first to shew piety at home, and to requite their parents: for that is good and acceptable before God.

5 Now she that is a widow indeed, and desolate, trusteth in God, and continueth in supplications and prayers night and day.

6 But she that liveth in pleasure is dead while she liveth.

7 And these things give in charge, that they may be blameless.

8 But if any provide not for his own, and specially for those of his own house, he hath denied the faith, and is worse than an infidel.

9 Let not a widow be taken into the number under threescore years old, having been the wife of one man,

10 Well reported of for good works; if she have brought up children, if she have lodged strangers, if she have washed the saints' feet, if she have relieved the afflicted, if she have diligently followed every good work.

11 But the younger widows refuse: for when they have begun to wax wanton against Christ, they will marry;

12 Having damnation, because they have cast off their first faith.

13 And withal they learn to be idle, wandering about from house to house; and not only idle, but tattlers also and busybodies, speaking things which they ought not.

14 I will therefore that the younger

things; and now he shews the necessity, because it is proper to provide against the danger which the Holy Spirit forewarns to be fast approaching, namely, that false teachers will come, who shall hold out trifles as the doctrine of faith, and who, placing all holiness in outward exercises, shall throw into the shade the spiritual worship of God, which alone is lawful. And, indeed, the servants of God have always had to contend against such persons as Paul here describes. Men being by nature inclined to hypocrisy, Satan easily persuades them that God is worshipped aright by ceremonies and outward discipline; and, indeed, without a teacher, almost all have this conviction deeply rooted in their hearts.

Next is added the craftiness of Satan to confirm the error: the consequence is, that, in all ages, there have been impostors, who recommended false worship, by which true godliness was buried. Again, this plague produces another, namely, that, in matters indifferent, men are laid under restraint; for the world easily permits itself to be hindered from doing that which God had declared to be lawful, in order that they may have it in their power to transgress with impunity the laws of God.

Here Paul, therefore, in the person of Timothy, forewarns not only the Ephesians, but all the churches throughout the world, about hypocritical teachers, who, by setting up false worship, and by ensnaring consciences with new laws, adulterate the true worship of God, and corrupt the pure doctrine of faith. This is the real object of the passage.

1 TIMOTHY 5

1. Do not harshly rebuke an elder

He now recommends to Timothy gentleness and moderation in correcting faults. Correction is a medicine, which has always some bitterness, and consequently is disagreeable. Besides, Timothy being a young man, his severity would have been less tolerable, if it had not been somewhat moderated.

But exhort him as a father

The Apostle enjoins him to reprove elder persons as parents; and he even employs the milder term, exhort. It is impossible not to be moved with reverence, when we place before our eyes our father or our mother; in consequence of which, instead of harsher vehemence, we are immediately influenced by modesty. Yet it ought to be observed, that he does not wish old men to be spared or indulged in such a manner as to sin with impunity and without correction; he only wishes that some respect should be paid to their age, that they may more patiently bear to be admonished.

The younger as brethren

Even towards younger persons he wishes moderation to be

on his hands was the actual instrument of its being conferred.

of the presbytery – In 2 Tim. 1: 6 the apostle mentions only his own laying on of hands. But there his aim is to remind Timothy specially of the part he himself took in imparting to him the gift. Here he mentions the fact, quite consistent with the other, that the neighboring presbyters took part in the ordination or consecration, he, however, taking the foremost part. Paul, though having the general oversight of the elders everywhere, was an elder himself (1 Pet. 5: 1; 2 John 1). The Jewish council was composed of the elders of the Church (the presbytery, Luke 22: 66; Acts 22: 5), and a presiding rabbi; so the Christian Church was composed of apostles, elders, and a president (Acts 15: 16).

1 TIMOTHY 5

1. an elder – in age; probably not an elder in the ministry; these latter are not mentioned till 1 Tim. 5: 17, "the elders that rule." Compare Acts 2: 17, "your old men," literally, "elders." Contrasted with "the younger men." As Timothy was admonished so to conduct himself as to give no man reason to despise his youth (1 Tim. 4: 12); so here he is told to bear in mind his youth, and to behave with the modesty which becomes a young man in relation to his elders.

Rebuke not – literally, "Strike not hard upon"; Rebuke not sharply: a different word from "rebuke" in 2 Tim. 4: 2.

entreat – exhort.

as brethren – and therefore equals; not lording it over them (1 Pet. 5: 1–3).

2. with all purity – respectful treatment of the other sex will promote "purity."

3. Honour – by setting on the church roll, as fit objects of charitable sustenance (1 Tim. 5: 9, 17–18; Acts 6: 1). So "honor" is used for support with necessaries (Matt. 15: 4,6; Acts 28: 10).

widows indeed – (1 Tim. 5: 16). Those really desolate; not like those (1 Tim. 5: 4) having children or relations answerable for their support, nor like those (in 1 Tim. 5: 6) "who live in pleasure"; but such as, from their earthly des-

olation as to friends, are most likely to trust wholly in God, persevere in continual prayers, and carry out the religious duties assigned to Church widows (1 Tim. 5: 5). Care for widows was transferred from the Jewish economy to the Christian (Deut. 14: 29; 16: 11; 24: 17,19).

4. if any widow have children – not "a widow indeed," as having children who ought to support her.

let them – the children and descendants.

learn first – ere it falls to the Church to support them.

to show piety at home – filial piety towards their widowed mother or grandmother, by giving her sustenance. Literally, "to show piety towards their own house." "Piety is applied to the reverential discharge of filial duties; as the parental relation is the earthly representation of God our heavenly Father's relation to us. "Their own" stands in opposition to the Church, in relation to which the widow is comparatively a stranger. She has a claim on her own children, prior to her claim on the Church; let them fulfill this prior claim which she has on them, by sustaining her and not burdening the Church.

8. worse than an infidel – because even an infidel (or unbeliever) is taught by nature to provide for his own relatives, and generally recognizes the duty; the Christian who does not so, is worse (Matt. 5: 46–47). He has less excuse with his greater light than the infidel who may break the laws of nature.

20. Them that sin – whether presbyters or laymen.

rebuke before all – publicly before the Church (Matt. 18: 15–17; 1 Cor. 5: 9–13; Eph. 5: 11). Not until this "rebuke" was disregarded was the offender to be excommunicated.

others . . . fear – that other members of the Church may have a wholesome fear of offending (Deut. 13: 11; Acts 5: 11).

21. I charge thee – rather as Greek, "I adjure thee"; so it ought to be translated (2 Tim. 4: 1).

before – "in the presence of God."

elect angels – an epithet of reverence. The objects of divine electing love (1 Pet. 2: 6).

women marry, bear children, guide the house, give none occasion to the adversary to speak reproachfully.

15 For some are already turned aside after Satan.

16 If any man or woman that believeth have widows, let them relieve them, and let not the church be charged; that it may relieve them that are widows indeed.

17 Let the elders that rule well be counted worthy of double honor, especially they who labour in the word and doctrine.

18 For the scripture saith, Thou shalt not muzzle the ox that treadeth out the corn. And, The labourer is worthy of his reward.

19 Against an elder receive not an accusation, but before two or three witnesses.

20 Them that sin rebuke before all, that others also may fear.

21 I charge thee before God, and the Lord Jesus Christ, and the elect angels, that thou observe these things without preferring one before another, doing nothing by partiality.

22 Lay hands suddenly on no man, neither be partaker of other men's sins: keep thyself pure.

23 Drink no longer water, but use a little wine for thy stomach's sake and thine often infirmities.

24 Some men's sins are open beforehand, going before to judgment; and some men they follow after.

25 Likewise also the good works of some are manifest beforehand; and they that are otherwise cannot be hid.

1 TIMOTHY 6

1 Let as many servants as are under the yoke count their own masters worthy of all honor, that the name of God and his doctrine be not blasphemed.

2 And they that have believing masters, let them not despise them, because they are brethren; but rather do them service, because they are faithful and beloved, partakers of the benefit. These things teach and exhort.

3 If any man teach otherwise, and consent not to wholesome words, even the words of our Lord Jesus Christ, and to

used, though not in an equal degree; for the vinegar must always be mingled with oil, but with this difference, that reverence should always be shewn to older persons, and equals should be treated with brotherly gentleness. Hence pastors are taught, that they must not only take into account their office, but must also see particularly what is due to the age of individuals; for the same things are not applicable to all. Let it therefore be remembered, that, if dramatic performers attend to decorum on the stage, it ought not to be neglected by pastors, who occupy so lofty a station.

2. The younger as sisters, with all chastity

The phrase, with all chastity, relates to younger women; for at that age they ought always to dread every kind of suspicion. Yet Paul does not forbid Timothy to have any criminal or immodest conduct towards young women, (for there was no need of such a prohibition,) but only enjoins him to beware of giving to wicked men any handle for laughter. For this purpose, he demands a chaste gravity, which shall shine throughout all their intercourse and conversation; so that he may more freely converse with young persons, without any unfavorable reports.

3. Honor widows that are really widows

By the word **honor** he does not mean any expression of respect, but that special care of them which bishops took in the ancient Church; for widows were taken under the protection of the Church, that they might be supported out of the common funds. The meaning of this mode of expression is as if he had said, "For selecting widows that are to be taken under your care and that of the deacons, you ought to consider who they are **that are really widows**. What was their condition we shall afterwards explain more fully. But we must here attend to the reason why Paul does not admit any but those who are absolutely widows, and, at the same time, widows without children; for, in that condition, they dedicated themselves to the Church, that they might withdraw from all the private concerns of a family, and might lay aside every hindrance. Justly, therefore, does Paul forbid to receive the mothers of families, who are already bound by a charge of a different kind. When he calls them "really widows", he alludes to the Greek word ch ra, which is derived apo tou ch rousthai, from a verb which signifies to be "deprived" or "destitute."

1 TIMOTHY 6

It appears that, at the beginning of the gospel, slaves cheered their hearts, as if the signal had been given for their emancipation; for Paul labors hard, in all his writings, to repress that desire; and indeed the condition of slavery was so hard that we need not wonder that it was exceedingly hateful.

Not only "elect" (according to the everlasting purpose of God) in contradistinction to the reprobate angels (2 Pet. 2: 4), but also to mark the excellence of the angels in general (as God's chosen ministers, "holy angels," "angels of light"), and so to give more solemnity to their testimony.

23. no longer – as a habit. This injunction to drink wine occasionally is a modification of the preceding "keep thyself pure." The presbyter and deacon were enjoined to be "not given to wine" (1 Tim. 3: 3,8). Timothy seems to have had a tendency to undue ascetical strictness on this point (compare Note, see on 1 Tim. 4: 8; compare the Nazarene vow, Num. 6: 1–4; John the Baptist, Luke 1: 15; Rom. 14). Paul therefore modifies the preceding words, "keep thyself pure," virtually saying, "Not that I mean to enjoin that kind of purity which consists in asceticism, nay, be no longer a water-drinker," that is, no longer drink only water, but use a little wine, as much as is needed for thy health. Timothy was of a feeble frame (see on 1 Cor. 16: 10–11), and prone to timidity in his duties as overseer where vigorous action was needed; hence Paul exhorts him to take all proper means to raise his bodily condition above these infirmities. God hereby commands believers to use all due means for preserving health, and condemns by anticipation the human traditions which among various sects have denied the use of wine to the faithful.

1 TIMOTHY 6

3. teach otherwise – than I desire thee to "teach" (1 Tim. 6: 2). The Greek indicative implies, he puts not a merely supposed case, but one actually existing, 1 Tim. 1: 3, "Every one who teaches otherwise," that is, who teaches heterodoxy.

consent not – Greek, "accede not to."

wholesome – "sound" (1 Tim. 1: 10): opposed to the false teachers' words, unsound through profitless science and immorality.

words of our Lord Jesus Christ – Paul's inspired words are not merely his own, but are also Christ's words.

4. He is proud – literally, "wrapt in smoke"; filled with the fumes of self-conceit (1 Tim.

3: 6) while "knowing nothing," namely, of the doctrine which is according to godliness (1 Tim. 6: 3), though arrogating pre-eminent knowledge (1 Tim. 1: 7).

doting about – literally, "sick about"; the opposite of "wholesome" (1 Tim. 6: 3). Truth is not the center about which his investigations move, but mere word-strifes.

questions – of controversy.

strifes of words – rather than about realities (2 Tim. 2: 14). These stand with them instead of "godliness" and "wholesome words" (1 Tim. 6: 3; 1 Tim. 1: 4; Titus 3: 9).

evil surmisings – as to those who are of a different party from themselves.

5. Perdisputings – useless disputings. The oldest manuscripts read, "lasting contests" [WIESINGER]; "incessant collisions" [ALFORD]. "Strifes of words" had already been mentioned so that he would not be likely to repeat the same idea (as in the English Version reading) again.

corrupt minds – Greek, "of men corrupted (depraved) in mind." The inmost source of the evil is in the perverted mind (1 Tim. 6: 4; 2 Tim. 3: 8; Titus 1: 15).

destitute of the truth – (Titus 1: 14). They had had the truth, but through want of moral integrity and of love of the truth, they were misled by a pretended deeper gnosis (knowledge) and higher ascetical holiness, of which they made a trade [WIESINGER].

6. But – Though they err in this, there is a sense in which "piety is" not merely gain, but "great means of gain": not the gaining which they pursue, and which makes men to be discontented with their present possessions, and to use religion as "a cloak of covetousness" (1 Thess. 2: 5) and means of earthly gain, but the present and eternal gain which piety, whose accompaniment is contentment, secures to the soul. WIESINGER remarks that Paul observed in Timothy a tendency to indolence and shrinking from the conflict, whence he felt (1 Tim. 6: 11) that Timothy needed cautioning against such temptation; compare also the second Epistle. Not merely contentment is great gain (a sentiment of the heathen CICEROM. "the greatest and surest riches"),

the doctrine which is according to godliness;

4 He is proud, knowing nothing, but doting about questions and strifes of words, whereof cometh envy, strife, railings, evil surmisings,

5 Perverse disputings of men of corrupt minds, and destitute of the truth, supposing that gain is godliness: from such withdraw thyself.

6 But godliness with contentment is great gain.

7 For we brought nothing into this world, and it is certain we can carry nothing out.

8 And having food and raiment let us be therewith content.

9 But they that will be rich fall into temptation and a snare, and into many foolish and hurtful lusts, which drown men in destruction and perdition.

10 For the love of money is the root of all evil: which while some coveted after, they have erred from the faith, and pierced themselves through with many sorrows.

11 But thou, O man of God, flee these things; and follow after righteousness, godliness, faith, love, patience, meekness.

12 Fight the good fight of faith, lay hold on eternal life, whereunto thou art also called, and hast professed a good profession before many witnesses.

13 I give thee charge in the sight of God, who quickeneth all things, and before Christ Jesus, who before Pontius Pilate witnessed a good confession;

14 That thou keep this commandment without spot, unrebukeable, until the appearing of our Lord Jesus Christ:

15 Which in his times he shall shew, who is the blessed and only Potentate, the King of kings, and Lord of lords;

16 Who only hath immortality, dwelling in the light which no man can approach unto; whom no man hath seen, nor can see: to whom be honor and power everlasting. Amen.

17 Charge them that are rich in this world, that they be not highminded, nor trust in uncertain riches, but in the living God, who giveth us richly all things to enjoy;

18 That they do good, that they be rich

Now, it is customary to seize, for the advantage of the flesh, everything that has the slightest appearance of being in our favor. Thus when they were told that we are all brethren, they instantly concluded that it was unreasonable that they should be the slaves of brethren. But although nothing of all this had come into their mind, still wretched men are always in need of consolation, that may allay the bitterness of their afflictions. Besides, they could not without difficulty be persuaded to bend their necks, willingly and cheerfully, to so harsh a yoke. Such, then, is the object of the present doctrine.

1. They who are slaves under the yoke

Owing to the false opinion of his own excellence which every person entertains, there is no one who patiently endures that others should rule over him. They who cannot avoid the necessity do, indeed, reluctantly obey those who are above them; but inwardly they fret and rage, because they think that they suffer wrong. The Apostle cuts off, by a single word, all disputes of this kind, by demanding that all who live "under the yoke" shall submit to it willingly. He means that they must not inquire whether they deserve that lot or a better one; for it is enough that they are bound to this condition.

When he enjoins them *to esteem worthy of all honor the masters* whom they serve, he requires them not only to be faithful and diligent in performing their duties, but to regard and sincerely respect them as persons placed in a higher rank than themselves. No man renders either to a prince or to a master what he owes to them, unless, looking at the eminence to which God has raised them, he honor them, because he is subject to them; for, however unworthy of it they may often be, still that very authority which God bestows on them always entitles them to honor. Besides, no one willingly renders service or obedience to his master, unless he is convinced that he is bound to do so. Hence it follows, that subjection begins with that honor of which Paul wishes that they who rule should be accounted worthy.

That the name and doctrine of God may not be blasphemed

We are always too ingenious in our behalf. Thus slaves, who have unbelieving masters, are ready enough with the objection, that it is unreasonable that they who serve the devil should have dominion over the children of God. But Paul throws back the argument to the opposite side, that they ought to obey unbelieving masters, in order that the name of God and the gospel may not be evil spoken of; as if God, whom we worship, incited us to rebellion, and as if the gospel rendered obstinate and disobedient those who ought to be subject to others.

but "piety with contentment"; for piety not only feels no need of what it has not, but also has that which exalts it above what it has not [WIESINGER]. The Greek for contentment is translated "sufficiency" (2 Cor. 9: 8). But the adjective (Phil. 4: 11) "content"; literally, "having a sufficiency in one's self" independent of others.

9. will be rich – have more than "food and raiment." Greek, "wish to be rich"; not merely are willing, but are resolved, and earnestly desire to have riches at any cost (Prov. 28: 20,22). This wishing (not the riches themselves) is fatal to "contentment" (1 Tim. 6: 6). Rich men are not told to cast away their riches, but not to "trust" in them, and to "do good" with them (1 Tim. 6: 17–18; Ps. 62: 10).

fall into temptation – not merely "are exposed to temptation," but actually "fall into" it. The falling into it is what we are to pray against, "Lead us not into temptation" (James 1: 14); such a one is already in a sinful state, even before any overt act of sin.

snare – a further step downwards (1 Tim. 3: 7). He falls into "the snare of the devil."

foolish – irrational.

hurtful – to those who fall into the snare. Compare Eph. 4: 22, "deceitful lusts" which deceive to one's deadly hurt.

lusts – With the one evil lust ("wish to be rich") many others join themselves: the one is the "root of all evils" (1 Tim. 6: 10).

which – Greek, "whatever (lusts)."

drown – an awful descending climax from "fall into"; this is the last step in the terrible descent (James 1: 15); translated "sink," Luke 5: 7.

destruction . . . perdition – destruction in general (temporal or eternal), and perdition in particular, namely, that of body and soul in hell.

10. the love of money – not the money itself, but the love of it – the wishing to be rich (1 Tim. 6: 9) – "is a root (ELLICOTT and MIDDLETON: not as English Version, 'the root') of all evils." (So the Greek plural.) The wealthiest may be rich not in a bad sense; the poorest may covet to be so (Ps. 62: 10). Love of money is not the sole root of evils, but it is

a leading "root of bitterness" (Heb. 12: 15), for "it destroys faith, the root of all that is good" [BENGEL]; its offshoots are "temptation, a snare, lusts, destruction, perdition."

coveted after – lusted after.

erred from – literally, "have been made to err from the faith" (1 Tim. 1: 19; 4: 1).

pierced – (Luke 2: 35).

with . . . sorrows – "pains": "thorns" of the parable (Matt. 13: 22) which choke the word of "faith." "The prosperity of fools destroys them" (Pr 1: 32). BENGEL and WIESINGER make them the gnawings of conscience, producing remorse for wealth badly acquired; the harbingers of the future "perdition" (1 Tim. 6: 9).

11. But thou – in contrast to the "some" (1 Tim. 6: 10).

man of God – who hast God as thy true riches (Gen. 15: 1; Ps. 16: 5; Lam. 3: 24). Applying primarily to Timothy as a minister (compare 2 Pet. 1: 21), just as the term was used of Moses (Deut. 33: 1), Samuel (1 Sam. 9: 6), Elijah, and Elisha; but, as the exhortation is as to duties incumbent also on all Christians, the term applies secondarily to him (so 2 Tim. 3: 17) as a Christian man born of God (James 1: 18; 1 John 5: 1), no longer a man of the world raised above earthly things; therefore, God's property, not his own, bought with a price, and so having parted with all right in himself: Christ's work is to be his great work: he is to be Christ's living representative.

flee these things – namely, "the love of money" with its evil results (1 Tim. 6: 9–10).

follow after righteousness – (2 Tim. 2: 22).

godliness – "piety." Righteousness is more in relation to our fellow man; piety ("godliness") to God"; faith is the root of both (see on Titus 2: 12).

love – by which "faith worketh."

patience – enduring perseverance amidst trials.

meekness – The oldest manuscripts read, "meek-spiritedness," namely, towards the opponents of the Gospel.

14. keep this commandment – Greek, "the commandment," that is, the Gospel rule of life (1 Tim. 1: 5; John 13: 34; 2 Pet. 2: 21; 3: 2).

without spot, unrebukeable – agreeing

in good works, ready to distribute, willing to communicate;

19 Laying up in store for themselves a good foundation against the time to come, that they may lay hold on eternal life.

20 O Timothy, keep that which is committed to thy trust, avoiding profane and vain babblings, and oppositions of science falsely so called:

21 Which some professing have erred concerning the faith. Grace be with thee. Amen.

12. Fight the good fight of faith

In the next epistle he says, "He who hath become a soldier doth not entangle himself with matters inconsistent with his calling" (2 Timothy 2: 4). In like manner, in order to withdraw Timothy from excessive solicitude about earthly things, he reminds him that he must "fight;" for carelessness and self-indulgence arise from this cause, that the greater part wish to serve Christ at ease, and as if it were pastime, whereas Christ calls all his servants to warfare.

For the purpose of encouraging him to fight such a fight courageously, he calls it good; that is, successful, and therefore not to be shunned; for, if earthly soldiers do not hesitate to fight, when the result is doubtful, and when there is a risk of being killed, how much more bravely ought we to do battle under the guidance and banner of Christ, when we are certain of victory? More especially, since a reward awaits us, not such as other generals are wont to give to their soldiers, but a glorious immortality and heavenly blessedness; it would certainly be disgraceful that we, who have such a hope held out to us, should grow weary or give way. And that is what he immediately afterwards adds – *Lay hold on eternal life.* As if he had said, "God calls thee to eternal life, and therefore, despising the world, strive to obtain it." When he commands them to "lay hold on it," he forbids them to pause or slacken in the middle of their course; as if he had said, that "nothing has been done, till we have obtained the life to come, to which God invites us." In like manner, he affirms that he strives to make progress, because he has not yet laid hold (Philippians 3: 12).

with "thou." Keep the commandment and so be without spot," etc. "Pure" (1 Tim. 5: 22; Eph. 5: 27; James 1: 27; 2 Pet. 3: 14).

until the appearing of . . . Christ – His coming in person (2 Thess. 2: 8; Titus 2: 13). Believers then used in their practice to set before themselves the day of Christ as near at hand; we, the hour of death [BENGEL]. The fact has in all ages of the Church been certain, the time as uncertain to Paul, as it is to us; hence, 1 Tim. 6: 15, he says, "in HIS times": the Church's true attitude is that of continual expectation of her Lord's return (1 Cor. 1: 8; Phil. 1: 6,10).

16. Who only hath immortality – in His own essence, not merely at the will of another, as all other immortal beings [JUSTIN MARTYR, Quæst. ad Orthod., 61]. As He hath immortality, so will He give it to us who believe; to be out of Him is death. It is mere heathen philosophy that attributes to the soul indestructibility in itself, which is to be attributed solely to God's gift. As He hath life in Himself, so hath He given to the Son to have life in Himself (John 5: 26). The term used in the New Testament for "immortal," which does not occur, is "incorruptible." "Immortality" is found in 1 Cor. 15: 53–54.

20–21. Recapitulatory conclusion: the main aim of the whole Epistle being here summarily stated.

O Timothy – a personal appeal, marking at once his affection for Timothy, and his prescience of the coming heresies.

keep – from spiritual thieves, and from enemies who will, while men sleep, sow tares amidst the good seed sown by the Son of man.

that which is committed to thy trust – Greek, "the deposit" (1 Tim. 1: 18; 2 Tim. 1: 12,14; 2: 2). "The true" or "sound doctrine" to be taught, as opposed to "the science falsely so called," which leads to "error concerning the faith" (1 Tim. 6: 21). "It is not thine: it is another's property with which thou hast been entrusted: Diminish it not at all" [CHRYSOSTOM]. "That which was entrusted to thee, not found by thee; which thou hast received, not invented; a matter not of genius, but of teaching; not of private usurpation, but of public tradition; a matter brought to thee, not put forth by thee, in which thou oughtest to be not an enlarger, but a guardian; not an originator, but a disciple; not leading, but following.

2 Timothy

Introduction by John Calvin

IT cannot be absolutely ascertained from Luke's history at what time the former Epistle was written. But I have no doubt that, after that time, Paul had personal communication with Timothy; and it is even possible (if the generally received opinion be believed) that Paul had him for a companion and assistant in many places. Yet it may readily be concluded that he was at Ephesus when this Epistle was written to him; because, towards the close of the Epistle (2 Timothy 4: 19), Paul "salutes Priscilla, and Aquila, and Onesiphorus," the last of whom was an Ephesian, and Luke informs us that the other two remained at Ephesus when Paul sailed to Judea (Acts 18: 18,19).

The chief point on which it turns is to confirm Timothy, both in the faith of the gospel, and in the pure and constant preaching of it. But yet these exhortations derive no small weight from the consideration of the time when he wrote them. Paul had before his eyes the death which he was prepared to endure for the testimony of the gospel. All that we read here, therefore, concerning the kingdom of Christ, the hope of eternal life, the Christian warfare, confidence in confessing Christ, and the certainty of doctrine, ought to be viewed by us as written not with ink but with Paul's own blood; for nothing is asserted by him for which he does not offer the pledge of his death; and therefore this Epistle may be regarded as a solemn subscription and ratification of Paul's doctrine.

It is of importance to remember, however, what we stated in the exposition of the former Epistle, that the Apostle did not write it merely for the sake of one man, but that he exhibited, under the person of one man, a general doctrine, which should afterwards be transmitted from one hand to another. And first, having praised the faith of Timothy, in which he had been educated from his childhood, he exhorts him to persevere faithfully in the doctrine which he had learned, and in the office intrusted to him; and, at the same time, lest Timothy should be discouraged on account of Paul's imprisonment, or the apostasy of others, he boasts of his apostleship and of the reward laid up for him. He likewise praises Onesiphorus, in order to encourage others by his example; and because the condition of those who serve Christ is painful and difficult, he borrows comparisons both from husbandmen and from soldiers, the former of whom do not hesitate to bestow much labor on the cultivation of the soil before any fruit is seen, while the latter lay aside all cares and employments, in order to devote themselves entirely to the life of a soldier and to the command of their general.

Next, he gives a brief summary of his gospel, and commands Timothy to hand it down to others, and to take care that it shall be transmitted to posterity. Having taken occasion from this to mention again his own imprisonment, he rises to holy boldness, for the purpose of animating others by his noble courage; for he invites us all to contemplate, along with him, that crown which awaits him in heaven.

He bids him also abstain from contentious disputes and vain questions, recommending to him, on the contrary, to promote edification; and in order to shew more clearly how enormous an evil it is, he relates that some have been ruined by it, and particularly mentions two,

Hymenaeus and Philetus who, having fallen into monstrous absurdity, so as to overturn the faith of the resurrection, suffered the horrible punishment of their vanity. But because falls of that kind, especially of distinguished men and those who enjoyed some reputation are usually attended by great scandal, he shews that believers ought not to be distressed on account of them, because they who possess the name of Christ do not all belong actually to Christ, and because the Church must be exposed to the misery of dwelling among wicked and ungodly persons in this world. Yet that this may not unduly terrify weak minds, he prudently softens it, by saying that the Lord will preserve till the end his own, whom he has elected.

He afterwards returns to exhort Timothy to persevere faithfully in the discharge of his ministry; and in order to make him more careful, he foretells what dangerous times await the good and the pious, and what destructive men shall afterwards arise; but, in opposition to all this, he confirms him by the hope of a good and successful result. More especially, he recommends to him to be constantly employed in teaching sound doctrine, pointing out the proper use of Scripture, that he may know that he will find in it everything that is necessary for the solid edification of the Church.

Next, he mentions that his own death is at hand, but he does so in the manner of a conqueror hastening to a glorious triumph, which is a clear testimony of wonderful confidence. Lastly, after having besought Timothy to come to him as soon as possible, he points out the necessity arising from his present condition. This is the principal subject in the conclusion of the Epistle.

The commentaries on 2 Timothy are by John Calvin and A. R. Fausset.

2 TIMOTHY 1

1 Paul, an apostle of Jesus Christ by the will of God, according to the promise of life which is in Christ Jesus,

2 To Timothy, my dearly beloved son: Grace, mercy, and peace, from God the Father and Christ Jesus our Lord.

3 I thank God, whom I serve from my forefathers with pure conscience, that without ceasing I have remembrance of thee in my prayers night and day;

4 Greatly desiring to see thee, being mindful of thy tears, that I may be filled with joy;

5 When I call to remembrance the unfeigned faith that is in thee, which dwelt first in thy grandmother Lois, and thy mother Eunice; and I am persuaded that in thee also.

6 Wherefore I put thee in remembrance that thou stir up the gift of God, which is in thee by the putting on of my hands.

7 For God hath not given us the spirit of fear; but of power, and of love, and of a sound mind.

8 Be not thou therefore ashamed of the testimony of our Lord, nor of me his prisoner: but be thou partaker of the afflictions of the gospel according to the power of God;

9 Who hath saved us, and called us with an holy calling, not according to our works, but according to his own purpose and grace, which was given us in Christ Jesus before the world began,

10 But is now made manifest by the appearing of our Savior Jesus Christ, who hath abolished death, and hath brought life and immortality to light through the gospel:

11 Whereunto I am appointed a preacher, and an apostle, and a teacher of the Gentiles.

12 For the which cause I also suffer these things: nevertheless I am not ashamed: for I know whom I have believed, and am persuaded that he is able to keep that which I have committed unto him against that day.

13 Hold fast the form of sound words, which thou hast heard of me, in faith and love which is in Christ Jesus.

14 That good thing which was committed unto thee keep by the Holy Ghost which dwelleth in us.

15 This thou knowest, that all they which are in Asia be turned away from

2 TIMOTHY 1

1. Paul an Apostle

From the very preface we already perceive that Paul had not in view Timothy alone; other wise he would not have employed such lofty titles in asserting his apostleship; for what purpose would it have served to employ these ornaments of language in writing to one who was fully convinced of the fact? He, therefore, lays claim to that authority over all which belonged to his public character and he does this the more diligently, because, being near death, he wishes to secure the approbation of the whole course of his ministry, and to seal his doctrine which he had labored so hard to teach, that it may be held sacred by posterity, and to leave a true portrait of it in Timothy.

Of Jesus Christ by the will of God

First, according to his custom, he calls himself an "Apostle of Christ." Hence it follows, that he does not speak as a private person, and must not be heard slightly, and for form's sake, like a man, but as one who is a representative of Christ. But because the dignity of the office is too great to belong to any man, except by the special gift and election of God, he at the same time pronounces a eulogy on his calling, by adding that he was ordained by the will of God. His apostleship, therefore, having God for its author and defender, is beyond all dispute.

According to the promise of life

That his calling may be the more certain, he connects it with the promises of eternal life; as if he had said, "As from the beginning God promised eternal life in Christ, so now he has appointed me to be the minister for proclaiming that promise." Thus also he points out the design of his apostleship, namely, to bring men to Christ, that in him they may find life.

Which is in Christ Jesus

He speaks with great accuracy, when he mentions that "the promise of life" was indeed given, in ancient times, to the fathers (Acts 26: 6). But yet he declares that this life is in Christ, in order to inform us that the faith of those who lived under the Law must nevertheless have looked towards Christ; and that life, which was contained in promises, was, in some respects, suspended, till it was exhibited in Christ.

2. My beloved son

By this designation he not only testifies his love of Timothy, but procures respect and submission to him; because he wishes to be acknowledged in him, as one who may justly be called his son. The reason of the appellation is, that he had begotten him in Christ; for, although this honor belongs to God alone, yet it is also transferred to ministers, whose agency he employs for regenerating us.

Grace, mercy.

2 TIMOTHY 1

1. This Epistle is the last testament and swan-like death song of Paul [BENGEL].

according to the promise of life . . . in Christ – Paul's apostleship is in order to carry into effect this promise. Compare "according to the faith . . . in hope of eternal life . . . promise," etc. (Titus 1: 1, 2). This "promise of life in Christ" (compare 2 Tim. 1: 10; 2 Tim. 2: 8) was needed to nerve Timothy to fortitude amidst trials, and to boldness in undertaking the journey to Rome, which would be attended with much risk (2 Tim. 1: 8).

2. **my dearly beloved son** – In 1 Tim. 1: 2, and Titus 1: 4, written at an earlier period than this Epistle, the expression used is in the Greek, "my genuine son." ALFORD sees in the change of expression an intimation of an altered tone as to Timothy, more of mere love, and less of confidence, as though Paul saw m him a want of firmness, whence arose the need of his stirring up afresh the faith and grace in Him (2 Tim. 1: 6).

3. **I thank** – Greek, "I feel gratitude to God."

whom I serve from my forefathers – whom I serve (Rom. 1: 9) as did my forefathers. He does not mean to put on the same footing the Jewish and Christian service of God; but simply to assert his own conscientious service of God as he had received it from his progenitors (not Abraham, Isaac, etc., whom he calls "the fathers," not "progenitors" as the Greek is here; Rom. 9: 5). The memory of those who had gone before to whom he is about to be gathered, is now, on the eve of death, pleasant to him; hence also, he calls to mind the faith of the mother and grandmother of Timothy; as he walks in the faith of his forefathers (Acts 23: 1; 24: 14; 26: 6–7; 28: 20), so Timothy should persevere firmly in the faith of his parent and grandparent. Not only Paul, but the Jews who reject Christ, forsake the faith of their forefathers, who looked for Christ; when they accept Him, the hearts of the children shall only be returning to the faith of their forefathers (Mal. 4: 6; Luke 1: 17; Rom. 11: 23–24,28). Probably Paul had, in his recent defense, dwelt on this topic, namely, that he was, in being a

Christian, only following his hereditary faith.

5. **When I call to remembrance** – This increased his "desire to see" Timothy. The oldest manuscripts read, "When I called to remembrance"; implying that some recent incident (perhaps the contrasted cowardice of the hypocrite Demas, who forsook him) had reminded him of the sincerity of Timothy's faith.

faith that is in thee – ALFORD translates, "that was in thee." He remembers Timothy's faith in the past as a fact; its present existence in him is only matter of his confident persuasion or hope.

dwelt – "made its dwelling" or abode (John 14: 23). The past tense implies they were now dead.

first – before it dwelt in thee. She was the furthest back of the progenitors of Timothy whom Paul knew.

mother Eunice – a believing Jewess; but his father was a Greek, that is, a heathen (Acts 16: 1). The faith of the one parent sanctified the child (2 Tim. 3: 15; 1 Cor. 7: 14). She was probably converted at Paul's first visit to Lystra (Acts 14: 6). It is an undesigned coincidence, and so a mark of truth, that in Acts 16: 1 the belief of the mother alone is mentioned, just as here praise is bestowed on the faith of the mother, while no notice is taken of the father.

9. **Who . . . called us** – namely, God the Father (Gal. 1: 6). The having "saved us" in His eternal purpose of "grace, given us in Christ before the world began," precedes his actual "calling" of us in due time with a call made effective to us by the Holy Spirit; therefore, "saved us" comes before "called us" (Rom. 8: 28–30).

holy calling – the actual call to a life of holiness. The call comes wholly from God and claims us wholly for God. "Holy" implies the separation of believers from the rest of the world unto God.

not according to – not having regard to our works in His election and calling of grace (Rom. 9: 11; Eph. 2: 8–9).

his own purpose – The origination of salvation was of His own purpose, flowing from His own goodness, not for works of ours coming first, but wholly because of His own gratuitous, electing love.

me; of whom are Phygellus and Hermogenes.

16 The Lord give mercy unto the house of Onesiphorus; for he oft refreshed me, and was not ashamed of my chain:

17 But, when he was in Rome, he sought me out very diligently, and found me.

18 The Lord grant unto him that he may find mercy of the Lord in that day: and in how many things he ministered unto me at Ephesus, thou knowest very well.

2 TIMOTHY 2

1 Thou therefore, my son, be strong in the grace that is in Christ Jesus.

2 And the things that thou hast heard of me among many witnesses, the same commit thou to faithful men, who shall be able to teach others also.

3 Thou therefore endure hardness, as a good soldier of Jesus Christ.

4 No man that warreth entangleth himself with the affairs of this life; that he may please him who hath chosen him to be a soldier.

5 And if a man also strive for masteries, yet is he not crowned, except he strive lawfully.

6 The husbandman that laboureth must be first partaker of the fruits.

7 Consider what I say; and the Lord give thee understanding in all things.

8 Remember that Jesus Christ of the seed of David was raised from the dead according to my gospel:

9 Wherein I suffer trouble, as an evil doer, even unto bonds; but the word of God is not bound.

10 Therefore I endure all things for the elect's sakes, that they may also obtain the salvation which is in Christ Jesus with eternal glory.

11 It is a faithful saying: For if we be dead with him, we shall also live with him:

12 If we suffer, we shall also reign with him: if we deny him, he also will deny us:

13 If we believe not, yet he abideth faithful: he cannot deny himself.

14 Of these things put them in remembrance, charging them before the Lord that they strive not about words to no profit, but to the subverting of the hearers.

15 Study to shew thyself approved

The word mercy, which he employs here, is commonly left out by him in his ordinary salutations. I think that he introduced it, when he poured out his feelings with more than ordinary vehemence. Moreover, he appears to have inverted the order; for, since "mercy" is the cause of "grace," it ought to have come before it in this passage. But still it is not unsuitable that it should be put after "grace", in order to express more clearly what is the nature of that grace, and whence it proceeds; as if he had added, in the form of a declaration, that the reason why we are loved by God is, that he is merciful. Yet this may also be explained as relating to God's daily benefits, which are so many testimonies of his "mercy"; for, whenever he assists us, whenever he delivers us from evils, pardons our sins, and bears *with our weakness, he does so, because he has compassion on us.*

2 TIMOTHY 2

1. Be strong in the grace

As he had formerly commanded him to keep, by the Spirit, that which was committed to him, so now he likewise enjoins him "to be strengthened in grace." By this expression he intends to shake off sloth and indifference; for the flesh is so sluggish, that even those who are endued with eminent gifts are found to slacken in the midst of their course, if they be not frequently aroused.

Some will say: "Of what use is it to exhort a man to 'be strong in grace,' unless free-will have something to do in cooperation?" I reply, what God demands from us by his word he likewise bestows by his Spirit, so that we are strengthened in the grace which he has given to us. And yet the exhortations are not superfluous, because the Spirit of God, teaching us inwardly, causes that they shall not sound in our ears fruitlessly and to no purpose. Whoever, therefore, shall acknowledge that the present exhortation could not have been fruitful without the secret power of the Spirit, will never support free-will by means of it.

Which is in Christ Jesus

This is added for two reasons; to shew that the grace comes from Christ alone, and from no other, and that no Christian will be destitute of it; for, since there is one Christ common to all, it follows that all are partakers of his grace, which is said to be in Christ, because all who belong to Christ must have it.

My son

This kind appellation, which he employs, tends much to gain the affections, that the doctrine may more effectually obtain admission into the heart.

14. Remind them of these things

The expression (*tauta*) **these things**, is highly emphatic. It means that the summary of the gospel which he gave,

grace . . . given us – in His everlasting purpose, regarded as the same as when actually accomplished in due time.

in Christ – believers being regarded by God as IN HIM, with whom the Father makes the covenant of salvation (Eph. 1: 4; 3: 11).

before the world began – Greek, "before the times (periods) of ages"; the enduring ages of which no end is contemplated (1 Cor. 2: 7; Eph. 3: 11).

2 TIMOTHY 2

1. Thou therefore – following my example (2 Tim. 1: 8,12), and that of ONESIPHORUS (2 Tim. 1: 16–18), and shunning that of those who forsook me (2 Tim. 1: 15).

my son – Children ought to imitate their father.

be strong – literally, "be invested with power." Have power, and show thyself to have it; implying an abiding state of power.

in the grace – the element IN which the believer's strength has place. Compare 2 Tim. 1: 7, "God hath given us the spirit of power."

7. Consider the force of the illustrations I have given from the soldier, the contender in the games, and the husbandmen, as applying to thyself in thy ministry.

and the Lord give, etc. – The oldest manuscripts read, "for the Lord will give thee understanding." Thou canst understand my meaning so as personally to apply it to thyself; for the Lord will give thee understanding when thou seekest it from Him "in all things." Not intellectual perception, but personal appropriation of the truths metaphorically expressed, was what he needed to be given him by the Lord.

9. Wherein – in proclaiming which Gospel.

suffer trouble – literally, "evil." I am a sufferer of evil as though I were a doer of evil.

bonds – (2 Tim. 1: 16).

word . . . not bound – Though my person is bound, my tongue and my pen are not (2 Tim. 4: 17; Acts 28: 31). Or he alludes not merely to his own proclamation of the Gospel, though in chains, but to the freedom of its circulation by others, even though his power of circulating it is now prescribed (Phil. 1: 18). He also hints to Timothy that he being free ought to be the more earnest in the service of it.

10. Therefore – Because of the anxiety I feel that the Gospel should be extended; that anxiety being implied in 2 Tim. 2: 9.

endure – not merely "I passively suffer," but "I actively and perseveringly endure," and "am ready to endure patiently all things."

the elect's sakes – for the sake of the Church: all the members of Christ's spiritual body (Col. 1: 24).

they . . . also – as well as myself: both God's elect not yet converted and those already so.

salvation . . . glory – not only salvation from wrath, but glory in reigning with Him eternally (2 Tim. 2: 12). Glory is the full expansion of salvation (Acts 2: 47; Rom. 8: 21–24, 30; Heb. 9: 28). So grace and glory (Ps. 84: 12).

13. believe not – "If we are unbelievers (literally, 'unfaithful'), He remains faithful" (Deut. 7: 9–10). The oldest manuscripts read, "For He cannot (it is an impossibility that He should) deny Himself." He cannot be unfaithful to His word that He will deny those who deny Him, though we be not faithful to our profession of faith in Him (Rom. 3: 3). Three things are impossible to God, to die, to lie, and to be deceived, (Heb. 6: 18). This impossibility is not one of infirmity, but of infinite power and majesty. Also, indirectly, comfort is suggested to believers, that He is faithful to His promises to them; at the same time that apostates are shaken out of their self-deceiving fancy, that because they change, Christ similarly may change. A warning to Timothy to be steadfast in the faith.

16. shun – literally, "stand above," separate from, and superior to.

vain – opposed to "the truth" (2 Tim. 2: 15).

babblings – with loud voice: opposed to the temperate "word" (Titus 3: 9).

increase – Greek, advance"; literally, "strike forward": an image from pioneers cutting away all obstacles before an advancing army. They pretend progress; the only kind of progress they make is to a greater pitch of impiety.

more ungodliness – Greek, "a greater degree of impiety."

17. will eat – literally, "will have pasture." The

unto God, a workman that needeth not to be ashamed, rightly dividing the word of truth.

16 But shun profane and vain babblings: for they will increase unto more ungodliness.

17 And their word will eat as doth a canker: of whom is Hymenaeus and Philetus;

18 Who concerning the truth have erred, saying that the resurrection is past already; and overthrow the faith of some.

19 Nevertheless the foundation of God standeth sure, having this seal, The Lord knoweth them that are his. And, Let every one that nameth the name of Christ depart from iniquity.

20 But in a great house there are not only vessels of gold and of silver, but also of wood and of earth; and some to honor, and some to dishonor.

21 If a man therefore purge himself from these, he shall be a vessel unto honor, sanctified, and meet for the master's use, and prepared unto every good work.

22 Flee also youthful lusts: but follow righteousness, faith, charity, peace, with them that call on the Lord out of a pure heart.

23 But foolish and unlearned questions avoid, knowing that they do gender strifes.

24 And the servant of the Lord must not strive; but be gentle unto all men, apt to teach, patient,

25 In meekness instructing those that oppose themselves; if God peradventure will give them repentance to the acknowledging of the truth;

26 And that they may recover themselves out of the snare of the devil, who are taken captive by him at his will.

2 TIMOTHY 3

1 This know also, that in the last days perilous times shall come.

2 For men shall be lovers of their own selves, covetous, boasters, proud, blasphemers, disobedient to parents, unthankful, unholy,

3 Without natural affection, trucebreakers, false accusers, incontinent, fierce, despisers of those that are good,

4 Traitors, heady, highminded, lovers of pleasures more than lovers of God;

5 Having a form of godliness, but denying the power thereof: from such turn away.

and the exhortations which he added to it, are of so great importance, that a good minister ought never to be weary of exhibiting them; for they are things that deserve to be continually handled, and that cannot be too frequently repeated. "They are things" (he says) "which I wish you not only to teach once, but to take great pains to impress on the hearts of men by frequent repetition." A good teacher ought to look at nothing else than edification, and to give his whole attention to that alone. On the contrary, he enjoins him not only to abstain from useless questions, but likewise to forbid others to follow them.

24. But the servant of the Lord must not fight

Paul's argument is to this effect: "The servant of God must stand aloof from contentions; but foolish questions are contentions; therefore whoever desires to be a 'servant of God,' and to be accounted such, ought to shun them." And if superfluous questions ought to be avoided on this single ground, that it is unseemly for a servant of God to fight, how impudently do they act, who have the open effrontery of claiming applause for raising incessant controversies? Let the theology of the Papists now come forth; what else will be found in it than the art of disputing and fighting? The more progress any man has made in it, the more unfit will he be for serving, Christ. But gentle towards all, qualified for teaching. When he bids the servant of Christ be "gentle," he demands a virtue which is opposite to the disease of contentions. *To* the same purpose is what immediately follows, that he be *didaktikos,* "qualified for teaching." There will be no room for instruction, if he have not moderation and some equability of temper. What limit will be observed by a teacher, when he is warmed for fighting? The better a man is qualified for teaching, the more earnestly does he keep aloof from quarrels and disputes.

Patient to the bad

The importunity of some men may sometimes produce either irritation or weariness; and for that reason he adds, "bearing with them," at the same time pointing out the reason why it is necessary; namely, because a godly teacher ought even to try whether it be possible for him to bring back to the right path obstinate and rebellious persons, which cannot be done without the exercise of gentleness.

2 TIMOTHY 3

1. But know this

By this prediction he intended still more to sharpen his diligence; for, when matters go on to our wish, we become more careless; but necessity urges us keenly. Paul, therefore informs him, that the Church will be subject to terrible diseases, which will require in the pastors uncommon fidelity, diligence, watchfulness, prudence, and unwearied

consuming progress of mortification is the image. They pretend to give rich spiritual pasture to their disciples: the only pasture is that of a spiritual cancer feeding on their vitals.

canker – a "cancer" or "gangrene."

Hymenaeus After his excommunication he seems to have been readmitted into the Church and again to have troubled it.

18. erred – Greek, "missed the aim" (see 1 Tim. 6: 21).

is past already – has already taken place. The beginnings of the subsequent Gnostic heresy already existed. They "wrested" (2 Pet. 3: 16) Paul's own words (Rom. 6: 4; Eph. 2: 6; Col. 2: 12) "to their own destruction," as though the resurrection was merely the spiritual raising of souls from the death of sin. Compare 1 Cor. 15: 12, where he shows all our hopes of future glory rest on the literal reality of the resurrection. To believe it past is to deny it in its true sense.

overthrow – trying to subvert "the foundation" on which alone faith can rest secure (2 Tim. 2: 19; compare Titus 1: 11).

20. in a great house – that is, the visible professing Christian Church (1 Tim. 3: 15). Paul is speaking, not of those without, but of the [visible] family of God. So the parable of the sweep-net (Matt. 13: 47–49) gathering together of every kind, good and bad: as the good and bad cannot be distinguished while under the waves, but only when brought to shore, so believers and unbelievers continue in the same Church, until the judgment makes the everlasting distinction. "The ark of Noah is a type of the Church; as in the former there were together the leopard and the kid, the wolf and the lamb; so in the latter, the righteous and sinners, vessels of gold and silver, with vessels of wood and earth" [JEROME] (compare Matt. 20: 16).

vessels of gold . . . silver – precious and able to endure fire.

of wood and earth – worthless, fragile, and soon burnt (1 Cor. 3: 12–15; 15: 47).

22. Flee – There are many lusts from which our greatest safety is in flight (Gen. 39: 12). Avoid occasions of sin. From the abstemious character of Timothy (1 Tim. 5: 23) it is likely

that not animal indulgences, but the impetuosity, rash self-confidence, hastiness, strife, and vainglory of young men (1 John 2: 14–16), are what he is here warned against: though the Spirit probably intended the warning to include both in its application to the Church in general.

youthful – Timothy was a youth (1 Tim. 4: 12).

righteousness – the opposite of "iniquity," that is, unrighteousness (2 Tim. 2: 19; compare 1 Tim. 6: 11).

2 TIMOTHY 3

2. men – in the professing Church. Compare the catalogue, Rom. 1: 29, etc., where much the same sins are attributed to heathen men; it shall be a relapse into virtual heathendom, with all its beast-like propensities, whence the symbol of it is "a beast" (Rev. 13: 1,11–12, etc.; 17: 3,8,11).

covetous – Translate, "money-loving," a distinct Greek word from that for "covetous".

boasters – empty boasters [ALFORD]; boasting of having what they have not.

proud – overweening: literally, showing themselves above their fellows.

blasphemous – rather, "evil-speakers," revilers.

disobedient to parents – The character of the times is even to be gathered especially from the manners of the young [BENGEL].

unthankful – The obligation to gratitude is next to that of obedience to parents.

unholy – irreligious [ALFORD]; inobservant of the offices of piety.

7. Ever learning – some new point, for mere curiosity, to the disparagement of what they seemed to know before.

the knowledge – Greek, "the perfect knowledge"; the only safeguard against further novelties. Gnosticism laid hold especially of the female sex.

16. All scripture – Greek, "Every Scripture," that is, Scripture in its every part. However, English Version is sustained, though the Greek article be wanting, by the technical use of the term "Scripture" being so well known as not to need the article (compare Greek, Eph.

6 For of this sort are they which creep into houses, and lead captive silly women laden with sins, led away with divers lusts,

7 Ever learning, and never able to come to the knowledge of the truth.

8 Now as Jannes and Jambres withstood Moses, so do these also resist the truth: men of corrupt minds, reprobate concerning the faith.

9 But they shall proceed no further: for their folly shall be manifest unto all men, as theirs also was.

10 But thou hast fully known my doctrine, manner of life, purpose, faith, longsuffering, charity, patience,

11 Persecutions, afflictions, which came unto me at Antioch, at Iconium, at Lystra; what persecutions I endured: but out of them all the Lord delivered me.

12 Yea, and all that will live godly in Christ Jesus shall suffer persecution.

13 But evil men and seducers shall wax worse and worse, deceiving, and being deceived.

14 But continue thou in the things which thou hast learned and hast been assured of, knowing of whom thou hast learned them;

15 And that from a child thou hast known the holy scriptures, which are able to make thee wise unto salvation through faith which is in Christ Jesus.

16 All scripture is given by inspiration of God, and is profitable for doctrine, for reproof, for correction, for instruction in righteousness:

17 That the man of God may be perfect, throughly furnished unto all good works.

2 TIMOTHY 4

1 I charge thee therefore before God, and the Lord Jesus Christ, who shall judge the quick and the dead at his appearing and his kingdom;

2 Preach the word; be instant in season, out of season; reprove, rebuke, exhort with all longsuffering and doctrine.

3 For the time will come when they will not endure sound doctrine; but after their own lusts shall they heap to themselves teachers, having itching ears;

4 And they shall turn away their ears from the truth, and shall be turned unto fables.

constancy; as if he enjoined Timothy to prepare for arduous and deeply anxious contests which awaited him. And hence we learn, that, so far from giving way, or being terrified, on account of any difficulties whatsoever, we ought, on the contrary. to arouse our hearts for resistance.

In the last days

Under "the last days," he includes the universal condition of the Christian Church. Nor does he compare his own age with ours, but, on the contrary, informs Timothy what will be the future condition of the kingdom of Christ; for many imagined some sort of condition that would be absolutely peaceful, and free from any annoyance. In short, he means that there will not be, even under the gospel, such a state of perfection, that all vices shall be banished, and virtues of every kind shall flourish; and that therefore the pastors of the Christian Church will have quite as much to do with wicked and ungodly men as the prophets and godly priests had in ancient times. Hence it follows, that there is no time for idleness or for repose.

2. For men will be

It is proper to remark, first, in what he makes the hardship of those "dangerous" or "troublesome" times to consist; not in war, nor in famine, nor in diseases, nor in any calamities or inconveniences to which the body is incident, but in the wicked and depraved actions of men. And, indeed, nothing is so distressingly painful to godly men, and to those who truly fear God, as to behold such corruptions of morals; for, as there is nothing which they value more highly than the glory of God, so they cannot but suffer grievous anguish when it is attacked or despised.

Secondly, it ought to be remarked, who are the persons of whom he speaks. They whom he briefly describes are not external enemies, who openly assail the name of Christ, but domestics, who wish to be reckoned among the members of the Church; for God wishes to try his Church to such an extent as to carry within her bosom such plagues, though she abhors to entertain them. So then, if in the present day many whom we justly abhor are mingled within us, let us learn to groan patiently under that burden, when we are informed that this is the lot of the Christian Church.

Next, it is wonderful that those persons, whom Paul pronounces to be guilty of so many and so aggravated acts of wickedness, can keep up the appearance of piety, as he also declares. But daily experience shows that we ought not to regard this as so wonderful; for such is the amazing audacity and wickedness of hypocrites, that, even in excusing the grossest crimes, they are excessively impudent, after having once learned falsely to shelter themselves under the name of God. In ancient times, how many crimes abounded in the life of the Pharisees? And yet, as if they had been pure

3: 15; 2: 21). The Greek is never used of writings in general, but only of the sacred Scriptures. The position of the two Greek adjectives closely united by "and," forbids our taking the one as an epithet, the other as predicated and translated as ALFORD and ELLICOTT. "Every Scripture given by inspiration of God is also profitable." Vulgate and the best manuscripts, favor English Version. Clearly the adjectives are so closely connected that as surely as one is a predicate, the other must be so too. ALFORD admits his translation to be harsh, though legitimate. It is better with English Version to take it in a construction legitimate, and at the same time not harsh. The Greek, "God-inspired," is found nowhere else. Most of the New Testament books were written when Paul wrote this his latest Epistle: so he includes in the clause "All Scripture is God-inspired," not only the Old Testament, in which alone Timothy was taught when a child (2 Tim. 3: 15), but the New Testament books according as they were recognized in the churches which had men gifted with "discerning of spirits," and so able to distinguish really inspired utterances, persons, and so their writings from spurious. Paul means, "All Scripture is God-inspired and therefore useful"; because we see no utility in any words or portion of it, it does not follow it is not God-inspired. It is useful, because God-inspired; not God-inspired, because useful.

Knapp well defines inspiration, "An extraordinary divine agency upon teachers while giving instruction, whether oral or written, by which they were taught how and what they should speak or write" (compare 2 Sam. 23: 1; Acts 4: 25; 2 Pet. 1: 21). The inspiration gives the divine sanction to all the words of Scripture, though those words be the utterances of the individual writer, and only in special cases revealed directly by God (1 Cor. 2: 13). Inspiration is here predicated of the writings, "all Scripture," not of the persons. The question is not how God has done it; it is as to the word, not the men who wrote it. What we must believe is that He has done it, and that all the sacred writings are every where inspired, though not all alike matter of special revelation: and that even the very words are stamped with divine sanction, as Jesus used them (for example in

the temptation and John 10: 34–35), for deciding all questions of doctrine and practice.

There are degrees of revelation in Scripture, but not of inspiration. The sacred writers did not even always know the full significancy of their own God-inspired words (1 Pet. 1: 10–12). Verbal inspiration does not mean mechanical dictation, but all "Scripture is (so) inspired by God," that everything in it, its narratives, prophecies, citations, the whole – ideas, phrases, and words – are such as He saw fit to be there.

2 TIMOTHY 4

2. Preach – literally, "proclaim as a herald." JUSTIN MARTYR describes the order of public worship, "On Sunday all meet and the writings of the apostles and prophets are read; then the president delivers a discourse; after this all stand up and pray; then there is offered bread and wine and water; the president likewise prays and gives thanks, and the people solemnly assent, saying, Amen." The bishops and presbyters had the right and duty to preach, but they sometimes called on deacons, and even laymen, to preach.

be instant – that is, urgent, earnest, in the whole work of the ministry.

in season, out of season – that is, at all seasons; whether they regard your speaking as seasonable or unseasonable. "Just as the fountains, though none may draw from them, still flow on; and the rivers, though none drink of them, still run; so must we do all on our part in speaking, though none give heed to us" [CHRYSOSTOM]. I think with CHRYSOSTOM, there is included also the idea of times whether seasonable or unseasonable to Timothy himself; not merely when convenient, but when inconvenient to thee, night as well as day (Acts 20: 31), in danger as well as in safety, in prison and when doomed to death as well as when at large, not only in church, but everywhere and on all occasions, whenever and wherever the Lord's work requires it.

reprove – "convict," "confute."

8. a crown – rather as Greek, "the crown." The "henceforth" marks the decisive moment; he looks to his state in a threefold aspect: (1)

5 But watch thou in all things, endure afflictions, do the work of an evangelist, make full proof of thy ministry.

6 For I am now ready to be offered, and the time of my departure is at hand.

7 I have fought a good fight, I have finished my course, I have kept the faith:

8 Henceforth there is laid up for me a crown of righteousness, which the Lord, the righteous judge, shall give me at that day: and not to me only, but unto all them also that love his appearing.

9 Do thy diligence to come shortly unto me:

10 For Demas hath forsaken me, having loved this present world, and is departed unto Thessalonica; Crescens to Galatia, Titus unto Dalmatia.

11 Only Luke is with me. Take Mark, and bring him with thee: for he is profitable to me for the ministry.

12 And Tychicus have I sent to Ephesus.

13 The cloke that I left at Troas with Carpus, when thou comest, bring with thee, and the books, but especially the parchments.

14 Alexander the coppersmith did me much evil: the Lord reward him according to his works:

15 Of whom be thou ware also; for he hath greatly withstood our words.

16 At my first answer no man stood with me, but all men forsook me: I pray God that it may not be laid to their charge.

17 Notwithstanding the Lord stood with me, and strengthened me; that by me the preaching might be fully known, and that all the Gentiles might hear: and I was delivered out of the mouth of the lion.

18 And the Lord shall deliver me from every evil work, and will preserve me unto his heavenly kingdom: to whom be glory for ever and ever. Amen.

19 Salute Prisca and Aquila, and the household of Onesiphorus.

20 Erastus abode at Corinth: but Trophimus have I left at Miletum sick.

21 Do thy diligence to come before winter. Eubulus greeteth thee, and Pudens, and Linus, and Claudia, and all the brethren.

22 The Lord Jesus Christ be with thy spirit. Grace be with you. Amen.

from every stain, they enjoyed a reputation of eminent holiness.

2 TIMOTHY 4

2. Be instant in season, out of season

By these words he recommends not only constancy, but likewise earnestness, so as to overcome all hindrances and difficulties; for, being, by nature, exceedingly effeminate or slothful, we easily yield to the slightest opposition, and sometimes we gladly seek apologies for our slothfulness. Let us now consider how many arts Satan employs to stop our course, and how slow to follow, and how soon wearied are those who are called. Consequently the gospel will not long maintain its place, if pastors do not urge it earnestly.

Moreover, this earnestness must relate both to the pastor and to the people; to the pastor, that he may not devote himself to the office of teaching merely at his own times and according to his own convenience, but that, shrinking neither from toils nor from annoyances, he may exercise his faculties to the utmost. So far as regards the people, there is constancy and earnestness, when they arouse those who are asleep, when they lay their hands on those who are hurrying in a wrong direction, and when they correct the trivial occupations of the world. To explain more fully in what respects the pastor must "be instant," the Apostle adds – Reprove, rebuke, exhort. By these words he means, that we have need of many excitements to urge us to advance in the right course; for if we were as teachable as we ought to be, a minister of Christ would draw us along by the slightest expression of his will. But now, not even moderate exhortations, to say nothing of sound advices, are sufficient for shaking off our sluggishness, if there be not increased vehemence of reproofs and threatenings.

With all gentleness and doctrine

A very necessary exception; for reproofs either fall through their own violence, or vanish into smoke, if they do not rest on doctrine. Both exhortations and reproofs are merely aids to doctrine, and, therefore, have little weight without it. We see instances of this in those who have merely a large measure of zeal and bitterness, and are not furnished with solid doctrine. Such men toil very hard, utter loud cries, make a great noise, and all to no purpose, because they build without a foundation. I speak of men who, in other respects, are good, but with little learning, and excessive warmth; for they who employ all the energy that they possess in battling against sound doctrine, are far more dangerous, and do not deserve to be mentioned here at all.

The past "I have fought"; (2) The immediate present; "there is laid up for me." (3) The future "the Lord will give in that day" [BENGEL].

crown – a crown, or garland, used to be bestowed at the Greek national games on the successful competitor in wrestling, running, etc. (compare 1 Pet. 5: 4; Rev. 2: 10).

of righteousness – The reward is in recognition of righteousness wrought in Paul by God's Spirit; the crown is prepared for the righteous; but it is a crown which consists in righteousness. Righteousness will be its own reward (Rev. 22: 11). Compare Ex. 39: 30. A man is justified gratuitously by the merits of Christ through faith; and when he is so justified God accepts his works and honors them with a reward which is not their due, but is given of grace. "So great is God's goodness to men that He wills that their works should be merits, though they are merely His own gifts" [POPE CELESTINE I].

10. Demas – once a "fellow laborer" of Paul, along with Mark and Luke (Col. 4: 14; Phile. 24). His motive for forsaking Paul seems to have been love of worldly ease, safety, and comforts at home, and disinclination to brave danger with Paul (Matt. 13: 20–22).

11. Take – Greek, "take up" on thy journey (Acts 20: 13–14). John Mark was probably in, or near, Colosse, as in the Epistle to the Colos-

sians (Col. 4: 10), written two years before this, he is mentioned as about to visit them. Timothy was now absent from Ephesus and somewhere in the interior of Asia Minor; hence he would be sure to fall in with Mark on his journey.

he is profitable to me for the ministry – Mark had been under a cloud for having forsaken Paul at a critical moment in his missionary tour with Barnabas (Acts 15: 37–40; 13: 5,13). Timothy had subsequently occupied the same post in relation to Paul as Mark once held. Hence Paul, appropriately here, wipes out the past censure by high praise of Mark and guards against Timothy's making self-complacent comparisons between himself and Mark, as though he were superior to the latter (compare Phile. 24). Demas apostatizes. Mark returns to the right way, and is no longer unprofitable, but is profitable for the Gospel ministry (Phile. 11).

18. And the Lord shall, etc. – Hope draws its conclusions from the past to the future [BENGEL].

will preserve me – literally, "will save" (Ps. 22: 21), "will bring me safe to." Jesus is the Lord and the Deliverer (Phil. 3: 20; 1 Thess. 1: 10): He saves from evil; He gives good things.

heavenly kingdom – Greek, "His kingdom which is a heavenly one."

Titus

Introduction by John Calvin

PAUL, having only laid the foundations of the church in Crete, and hastening to go to another place (for he was not the pastor of a single island only, but the Apostle of the Gentiles), had given charge to Titus to prosecute this work as an Evangelist. It is evident from this Epistle that, immediately after Paul's departure, Satan labored not only to overthrow the government of the Church, but likewise to corrupt its doctrine.

There were some who, through ambitious motives, wished to be elevated to the rank of pastors, and who, because Titus did not comply with their wicked desires, spoke unfavorably of him to many persons. On the other hand, there were Jews who, under the pretense of supporting the Mosaic law, introduced a great number of trifles; and such persons were listened to with eagerness and with much acceptance. Paul therefore writes with this design, to arm Titus with his authority, that he may be able to bear so great a burden; for undoubtedly there were some who fearlessly despised him as being but one of the ordinary rank of pastors. It is also possible that complaints about him were in circulation, to the effect that he assumed more authority than belonged to him when he did not admit pastors till he had made trial and ascertained their fitness.

Hence we may infer, that this was not so much a private epistle of Paul to Titus, as it was a public epistle to the Cretans. It is not probable that Titus is blamed for having with too great indulgence raised unworthy persons to the office of bishop, or that, as an ignorant man and a novice, he is told what is that kind of doctrine in which he ought to instruct the people;

but because due honor was not rendered to him, Paul clothes him with his own authority, both in ordaining ministers and in the whole government of the Church. Because there were many who foolishly desired to have another form of doctrine than that which he delivered, Paul approves of this alone – rejecting all others – and exhorts him to proceed as he had begun.

First, then, he shows what sort of persons ought to be chosen for being ministers. Among other qualifications, he requires that a minister shall be well instructed in sound doctrine, that by means of it he may resist adversaries. Here he takes occasion to censure some vices of the Cretans, but especially rebukes the Jews, who made some kind of holiness to consist in a distinction of food, and in other outward ceremonies. In order to refute their fooleries, he contrasts with them the true exercises of piety and Christian life; and, with the view of pressing them more closely, he describes what are the duties which belong to every one in his calling. These duties he enjoins Titus diligently and constantly to inculcate. On the other hand, he admonishes others not to be weary of hearing them, and shows that this is the design of the redemption and salvation obtained through Christ. If any obstinate person oppose, or refuse to obey, he bids him set that person aside. We now see that Paul has no other object in view than to support the cause of Titus, and to stretch out the hand to assist him in performing the work of the Lord.

The commentaries on Titus are by John Calvin and A. R. Fausset.

TITUS 1

1 Paul, a servant of God, and an apostle of Jesus Christ, according to the faith of God's elect, and the acknowledging of the truth which is after godliness;

2 In hope of eternal life, which God, that cannot lie, promised before the world began;

3 But hath in due times manifested his word through preaching, which is committed unto me according to the commandment of God our Savior;

4 To Titus, mine own son after the common faith: Grace, mercy, and peace, from God the Father and the Lord Jesus Christ our Savior.

5 For this cause left I thee in Crete, that thou shouldest set in order the things that are wanting, and ordain elders in every city, as I had appointed thee:

6 If any be blameless, the husband of one wife, having faithful children not accused of riot or unruly.

7 For a bishop must be blameless, as the steward of God; not selfwilled, not soon angry, not given to wine, no striker, not given to filthy lucre;

8 But a lover of hospitality, a lover of good men, sober, just, holy, temperate;

9 Holding fast the faithful word as he hath been taught, that he may be able by sound doctrine both to exhort and to convince the gainsayers.

10 For there are many unruly and vain talkers and deceivers, specially they of the circumcision:

11 Whose mouths must be stopped, who subvert whole houses, teaching things which they ought not, for filthy lucre's sake.

12 One of themselves, even a prophet of their own, said, The Cretians are alway liars, evil beasts, slow bellies.

13 This witness is true. Wherefore rebuke them sharply, that they may be sound in the faith;

14 Not giving heed to Jewish fables, and commandments of men, that turn from the truth.

15 Unto the pure all things are pure: but unto them that are defiled and unbelieving is nothing pure; but even their mind and conscience is defiled.

16 They profess that they know God;

TITUS 1

4. To Titus, my own son, according to the common faith

Hence it is evident in what sense a minister of the word is said to beget spiritually those whom he brings to the obedience of Christ, that is, so that he himself is also begotten. Paul declares himself to be the father of Titus, with respect to his faith; but immediately adds, that this faith is common to both, so that both of them alike have the same Father in heaven. Accordingly, God does not diminish his own prerogative, when he pronounces those to be spiritual fathers along with himself, by whose ministry he regenerates whom he chooses; for of themselves they do nothing, but only by the efficacy of the Spirit.

5. For this reason I left thee in Crete

This preface clearly proves, that Titus is not so much admonished on his own account as recommended to others, that no one may hinder him. Paul testifies that he has appointed him in his own room; and on that account all should acknowledge and receive him with reverence as the Apostle's deputy. The apostles had no fixed place assigned to them, but were charged to spread the gospel through the whole world; and for this reason, when they left one city or district to go to another, they were wont to place fit men as their substitutes, to complete the work which they had begun. Thus Paul affirms that he founded the church of the Corinthians, but that there were other workmen, who must build on his foundation, that is, carry forward the building.

This, indeed, belongs to all pastors; for the churches will always stand in need of increase and progress, as long as the world shall endure. But in addition to the ordinary office of pastors, the care of organizing the church was committed to Titus. Till the churches have been already organized, and reduced to some order, pastors were not usually appointed over them. But Titus held some additional charge, which consisted in giving a form to churches that had not yet been properly arranged, and in appointing a fixed kind of government accompanied by discipline. Having laid the foundation, Paul departed; and then it became the duty of Titus to carry the work higher, that the building might have fair proportions.

This is what he calls correcting those things which are still wanting. The building of the Church is not a work so easy that it can be brought all at once to perfection. How long Paul was in Crete – is uncertain; but he had spent some time there, and had faithfully devoted his labors to erect the kingdom of Christ. He did not lack the most consummate skill that can be found in man; he was unwearied in toil; and yet he acknowledged that he left the work rough and incomplete. Hence we see the difficulty; and, indeed, we

TITUS 1

1. servant of God – not found elsewhere in the same connection. In Rom. 1: 1 it is "servant of Jesus Christ" (Gal. 1: 10; Phil. 1: 1; compare Acts 16: 17; Rev. 1: 1; 15: 3). In Rom. 1: 1, there follows, "called to be an apostle," which corresponds to the general designation of the office first, "servant of GOD," here, followed by the special description, "apostle of Jesus Christ." The full expression of his apostolic office answers, in both Epistles, to the design, and is a comprehensive index to the contents. The peculiar form here would never have proceeded from a forger.

according to the faith – rather, "for," "with a view to subserve the faith"; this is the object of my apostleship (compare Titus 1: 4, 9; Rom. 1: 5).

the elect – for whose sake we ought to endure all things (2 Tim. 2: 10). This election has its ground, not in anything belonging to those thus distinguished, but in the purpose and will of God from everlasting (2 Tim. 1: 9; Rom. 8: 30–33; compare Luke 18: 7; Eph. 1: 4; Col. 3: 12). Acts 13: 48 shows that all faith on the part of the elect, rests on the divine foreordination: they do not become elect by their faith, but receive faith, and so become believers, because they are elect.

and the acknowledging of the truth – "and (for promoting) the full knowledge of the truth," that is, the Christian truth (Eph. 1: 13).

after godliness – that is, which belongs to piety: opposed to the knowledge which has not for its object the truth, but error, doctrinal and practical (Titus 1: 11,16; 1 Tim. 6: 3); or even which has for its object mere earthly truth, not growth in the divine life. "Godliness," or "piety," is a term peculiar to the Pastoral Epistles: a fact explained by the apostle having in them to combat doctrine tending to "ungodliness" (2 Tim. 2: 16; compare Titus 2: 11–12).

2. In hope of eternal life – connected with the whole preceding sentence. That whereon rests my aim as an apostle to promote the elect's faith and full knowledge of the truth, is, "the hope of eternal life" (Titus 2: 13; 3: 7;

Acts 23: 6; 24: 15; 28: 20).

that cannot lie – (Rom. 3: 4; 11: 29; Heb. 6: 18).

promised before the world began – a contracted expression for "purposed before the world began (literally, 'before the ages of time'), and promised actually in time," the promise springing from the eternal purpose; as in 2 Tim. 1: 9, the gift of grace was the result of the eternal purpose "before the world began."

11. mouths . . . stopped – literally, "muzzled," "bridled" as an unruly beast (compare Ps 32: 9).

who – Greek, "(seeing that they are) such men as"; or "inasmuch as they" [ELLICOTT].

subvert . . . houses – "overthrowing" their "faith" (2 Tim. 2: 18). "They are the devil's levers by which he subverts the houses of God" [THEOPHYLACT].

for filthy lucre – (1 Tim. 3: 3,8; 6: 5).

12. One – Epimenides of Phæstus, or Gnossus, in Crete, about 600. He was sent for to purify Athens from its pollution occasioned by Cylon. He was regarded as a diviner and prophet. The words here are taken probably from his treatise "concerning oracles." Paul also quotes from two other heathen writers, ARATUS (Acts 17: 28) and MENANDER (1 Cor. 15: 33), but he does not honor them so far as even to mention their names.

of themselves . . . their own – which enhances his authority as a witness. "To Cretanize" was proverbial for to lie: as "to Corinthianize" was for to be dissolute.

alway liars – not merely at times, as every natural man is. Contrast Titus 1: 2, "God that cannot lie." They love "fables" (Titus 1: 14); even the heathen poets laughed at their lying assertion that they had in their country the sepulcher of Jupiter.

evil beasts – rude, savage, cunning, greedy. Crete was a country without wild beasts. Epimenides' sarcasm was that its human inhabitants supplied the place of wild beasts.

slow bellies – indolent through pampering their bellies. They themselves are called "bellies," for that is the member for which they live (Rom. 16: 18; Phil. 3: 19).

but in works they deny him, being abominable, and disobedient, and unto every good work reprobate.

TITUS 2

1 But speak thou the things which become sound doctrine:

2 That the aged men be sober, grave, temperate, sound in faith, in charity, in patience.

3 The aged women likewise, that they be in behavior as becometh holiness, not false accusers, not given to much wine, teachers of good things;

4 That they may teach the young women to be sober, to love their husbands, to love their children,

5 To be discreet, chaste, keepers at home, good, obedient to their own husbands, that the word of God be not blasphemed.

6 Young men likewise exhort to be sober minded.

7 In all things shewing thyself a pattern of good works: in doctrine shewing uncorruptness, gravity, sincerity,

8 Sound speech, that cannot be condemned; that he that is of the contrary part may be ashamed, having no evil thing to say of you.

9 Exhort servants to be obedient unto their own masters, and to please them well in all things; not answering again;

10 Not purloining, but shewing all good fidelity; that they may adorn the doctrine of God our Savior in all things.

11 For the grace of God that bringeth salvation hath appeared to all men,

12 Teaching us that, denying ungodliness and worldly lusts, we should live soberly, righteously, and godly, in this present world;

13 Looking for that blessed hope, and the glorious appearing of the great God and our Savior Jesus Christ;

14 Who gave himself for us, that he might redeem us from all iniquity, and purify unto himself a peculiar people, zealous of good works.

15 These things speak, and exhort, and rebuke with all authority. Let no man despise thee.

find, by experience, in the present day, that it is not the labor of one or two years to restore fallen. churches to a tolerable condition. Accordingly, those who have made diligent progress for many years – must still be attentive to correct many things.

Here it is highly proper to observe the modesty of Paul who willingly permits another person to complete the work which he had begun. And, indeed, although Titus is greatly inferior to him, he does not refuse to have him for epanorthoten a "corrector," to give the finishing hand to his work. Such ought to be the dispositions of godly teachers; not that every one should labor to make everything bend to his own ambitious views, but that they should strive to assist each other, and that, when any one has labored more successfully, he should be congratulated and not envied by all the rest.

TITUS 2

1. But speak thou the things which become sound doctrine

He points out the remedy for driving away fables, namely, that Titus should devote himself to edification. He gives the appellation of *sound doctrine* to that which may instruct men to godliness; for all trifles vanish away, when that which is solid is taught. When he enjoins him to speak those things which agree with "sound doctrine," it is as if he had said, that Titus must be continually employed in this preaching; for to mention these things once or twice would not be enough. And Paul does not speak of the discourse of a single day; but so long as Titus shall hold the office of pastor, he wishes him to be employed in teaching this doctrine.

"Sound doctrine" is so called from the effect produced by it; as, on the contrary, he says, that unskillful men dote about questions which do no good. *Sound,* therefore, means wholesome, that which actually feeds souls. Thus, by a single word, as by a solemn proclamation, he banishes from the Church all speculations which serve rather to promote ostentation than to aid godliness, as he did in both of the Epistles to Timothy.

He makes "sound doctrine" to consist of two parts. The first is that which magnifies the grace of God in Christ, from which we may learn where we ought to seek our salvation; and the second is that by which the life is framed to the fear of God, and inoffensive conduct. Although the former, which includes faith, is far more excellent, and therefore ought to be more zealously inculcated; yet Paul, in writing to Timothy, was not careful about attending to order; for he had to deal with an intelligent man, to whom he would offer an insult, if he dictated to him word by word, as is usually done to apprentices or beginners. Under the person of

13. This witness – "This testimony (though coming from a Cretan) is true."

sharply – Gentleness would not reclaim so peroffenders.

that they – that those seduced by the false teachers may be brought back to soundness in the faith. Their malady is strifes about words and questions (Titus 3: 9; 1 Tim. 6: 4).

TITUS 2

1. But . . . thou – in contrast to the reprobate seducers stigmatized in Titus 1: 11,15–16.

speak – without restraint: contrast Titus 1: 11, "mouths . . . stopped."

doctrine – "instruction" or "teaching."

2. sober – Translated "vigilant," as sober men alone can be (1 Tim. 3: 2). But "sober" here answers to "not given to wine," Titus 2: 3; Titus 1: 7.

grave – "dignified"; behaving with reverent propriety.

temperate – "self-restrained"; "discreet" [ALFORD], (Titus 1: 8; 1 Tim. 2: 9).

faith . . . charity [love] . . . patience – combined in 1 Tim. 6: 11. "Faith, hope, charity" (1 Cor. 13: 13). "Patience," Greek, "enduring perseverance," is the attendant on, and is supported by, "hope" (1 Cor. 13: 7; 1 Thess. 1: 3). It is the grace which especially becomes old men, being the fruit of ripened experience derived from trials overcome (Rom. 5: 3).

5. keepers at home – as "guardians of the house," as the Greek expresses. The oldest manuscripts read, "Workers at home": active in household duties (Prov. 7: 11; 1 Tim. 5: 13).

Be – kind, beneficent (Matt. 20: 15; Rom. 5: 7; 1 Pet. 2: 18). Not churlish and niggardly, but thrifty as housewives.

obedient – rather "submissive," as the Greek is translated; (see on Eph. 5: 21–22; Eph. 5: 24).

their own – marking the duty of subjection which they owe them, as being their own husbands (Eph. 5: 22; Col. 3: 18).

blasphemed – "evil spoken of." That no reproach may be cast on the Gospel, through the inconsistencies of its professors (Titus 2: 8,10; Rom. 2: 24; 1 Tim. 5: 14; 6: 1). "Unless we are virtuous, blasphemy will come through us

to the faith" [THEOPHYLACT].

6. Young – Greek, "The younger men."

sober-minded – self-restrained [ALFORD]. "Nothing is so hard at this age as to overcome pleasures and follies" [CHRYSOSTOM].

7. In – with respect to all things.

thyself a pattern – though but a young man thyself. All teaching is useless unless the teacher's example confirm his word.

in doctrine – in thy ministerial teaching (showing) uncorruptness, that is, untainted purity of motive on thy part (compare 2 Cor. 11: 3), so as to be "a pattern" to all. As "gravity," etc., refers to Titus himself, so "uncorruptness"; though, doubtless, uncorruptness of the doctrine will be sure to follow as a consequence of the Christian minister being of simple, uncorrupt integrity himself.

gravity – dignified seriousness in setting forth the truth.

12. Teaching – Greek, "disciplining us." Grace exercises discipline, and is imparted in connection with disciplining chastisements (1 Cor. 11: 32; Heb. 12: 6–7). The education which the Christian receives from "the grace" of God is a discipline often trying to flesh and blood: just as children need disciplining. The discipline which it exercises teaches us to deny ungodliness and worldly lusts, and to live soberly, righteously, and godly, in this present world (Greek, "age," or course of things) where such self-discipline is needed, seeing that its spirit is opposed to God (Titus 1: 12,16; 1 Cor. 1: 20; 3: 18–19): in the coming world we may gratify every desire without need of self-discipline, because all desires there will be conformable to the will of God.

that – Greek, "in order that"; the end of the "disciplining" is "in order that . . . we may live soberly," etc. This point is lost by the translation, "teaching us."

denying . . . lusts – (Luke 9: 23). The Greek aorist expresses "denying once for all." We deny "worldly lusts" when we withhold our consent from them, when we refuse the delight which they suggest, and the act to which they solicit us, nay, tear them up by the roots out of our soul and mind.

worldly lusts – The Greek article expresses,

TITUS 3

1 Put them in mind to be subject to principalities and powers, to obey magistrates, to be ready to every good work,

2 To speak evil of no man, to be no brawlers, but gentle, shewing all meekness unto all men.

3 For we ourselves also were sometimes foolish, disobedient, deceived, serving divers lusts and pleasures, living in malice and envy, hateful, and hating one another.

4 But after that the kindness and love of God our Savior toward man appeared,

5 Not by works of righteousness which we have done, but according to his mercy he saved us, by the washing of regeneration, and renewing of the Holy Ghost;

6 Which he shed on us abundantly through Jesus Christ our Savior;

7 That being justified by his grace, we should be made heirs according to the hope of eternal life.

8 This is a faithful saying, and these things I will that thou affirm constantly, that they which have believed in God might be careful to maintain good works. These things are good and profitable unto men.

9 But avoid foolish questions, and genealogies, and contentions, and strivings about the law; for they are unprofitable and vain.

10 A man that is an heretick after the first and second admonition reject;

11 Knowing that he that is such is subverted, and sinneth, being condemned of himself.

12 When I shall send Artemas unto thee, or Tychicus, be diligent to come unto me to Nicopolis: for I have determined there to winter.

13 Bring Zenas the lawyer and Apollos on their journey diligently, that nothing be wanting unto them.

14 And let ours also learn to maintain good works for necessary uses, that they be not unfruitful.

15 All that are with me salute thee. Greet them that love us in the faith. Grace be with you all. Amen.

Titus, indeed, he instructs the whole church of Crete; yet he attends to the rules of propriety, that he may not appear to distrust his prudence. Besides, the reason why he is longer in his exhortations is, that they who gave their whole attention to idle questions – needed especially to be exhorted to the practice of a good and holy life; for nothing is better fitted to restrain the wandering curiosity of men than to know in what duties they ought to be employed.

TITUS 3

5. Not by works

Let us remember that here Paul addresses his discourse to believers, and describes the manner in which they entered into the kingdom of God. He affirms that by their works they did not at all deserve that they should become partakers of salvation, or that they should be reconciled to God through faith; but he says that they obtained this blessing solely through the mercy of God. We therefore conclude from his words, that we bring nothing to God, but that he goes before us by his pure grace, without any regard to works. For when he says – "Not by works which we have done", he means, that we can do nothing but sin till we have been renewed by God. This negative statement depends on the former affirmation, by which he said that they were foolish and disobedient, and led away by various desires, till they were created anew in Christ.

He hath saved us

He speaks of faith, and shews that we have already obtained salvation. Although, so long as we are held by the entanglements of sin, we carry about a body of death, yet we are certain of our salvation, provided that we are ingrafted into Christ by faith, according to that saying – "He that believeth in the Son of God hath passed from death into life" (John 5: 24).

By the washing of regeneration

I have no doubt that he alludes, at least, to baptism, and even I will not object to have this passage expounded as relating to baptism; not that salvation is contained in the outward symbol of water, but because baptism tells to us the salvation obtained by Christ. Paul treats of the exhibition of the grace of God, which, we have said, has been made by faith. Since therefore a part of revelation consists in baptism, that is, so far as it is intended to confirm our faith, he properly makes mention of it. Besides, baptism – being the entrance into the Church and the symbol of our ingrafting into Christ – is here appropriately introduced by Paul, when he intends to shew in what manner the grace of God appeared to us; so that the strain of the passage runs thus: "God hath saved us by his mercy, the symbol and pledge of which he gave in baptism, by admitting us into his Church, and ingrafting us into the body of his Son."

"the lusts of the world," "all worldly lusts" [ALFORD], (Gal. 5: 16; Eph. 2: 3; 1 John 2: 15–17; 5: 19). The world will not come to an end when this present age or course of things shall end.

live soberly, righteously, and godly – the positive side of the Christian character; as "denying . . . lusts" was the negative. "Soberly," that is, with self-restraint, in relation to one's self: "righteously" or justly, in relation to our neighbor; "godly" or piously, in relation to God (not merely amiably and justly, but something higher, godly, with love and reverence toward God). These three comprise our "disciplining" in faith and love, from which he passes to hope (Titus 2: 13).

TITUS 3

5. Not by – Greek, "Out of"; "not as a result springing from works," etc.

of righteousness – Greek, "in righteousness," that is, wrought "in a state of righteousness": as "deeds . . . wrought in God." There was an utter absence in us of the element ("righteousness") in which alone righteous works could be done, and so necessarily an absence of the works. "We neither did works of righteousness, nor were saved in consequence of them; but His goodness did the whole" [THEOPHYLACT].

mercy – the prompting cause of our salvation individually: "In pursuance of His mercy." His kindness and love to man were manifested in redemption once for all wrought by Him for mankind generally; His mercy is the prompting cause for our individual realization of it. Faith is presupposed as the instrument of our being "saved"; our being so, then, is spoken of as an accomplished fact. Faith is not mentioned, but only God's part. as Paul's object here is not to describe man's new state, but the saving agency of God in bringing about that state, independent of all merit on the man's part.

by – Greek, "through"; by means of.

the washing – rather, "the laver," that is, the baptismal font.

of regeneration – designed to be the visible instrument of regeneration. Adult candidates for baptism are presupposed to have had repentance and faith (for Paul often assumes in faith and charity that those addressed are what they profess to be, though in fact some of them were not so, 1 Cor. 6: 11), in which case baptism would be the visible "laver or regeneration" to them, "faith being thereby confirmed, and grace increased, by virtue of prayer to God" [Article XXVII, Church of England].

and renewing – not "the laver ('washing') of renewing," but "and BY the renewing," etc., following "saved us." To make "renewing of the Holy Ghost" follow "the laver" would destroy the balance of the clauses of the sentence, and would make baptism the seal, not only of regeneration, but also of the subsequent process of progressive sanctification ("renewing of the Holy Ghost"). Regeneration is a thing once for all done; renewing is a process daily proceeding. As "the washing," or "laver," is connected with "regeneration," so the "renewing of the Holy Ghost" is connected with "shed on us abundantly" (Titus 3: 6).

10. heretic – Greek "heresy," originally meant a division resulting from individual self-will; the individual doing and teaching what he chose, independent of the teaching and practice of the Church. In course of time it came to mean definitely "heresy" in the modern sense; and in the later Epistles it has almost assumed this meaning. The heretics of Crete, when Titus was there, were in doctrine followers of their own self-willed "questions" reprobated in Titus 3: 9, and immoral in practice.

reject – decline, avoid; not formal excommunication, but, "have nothing more to do with him," either in admonition or intercourse.

Philemon

Introduction by John Gill

THIS epistle has an inscription, salutation, and preface, the same with others, which are in Philemon 1: 1, the principal view of it is to persuade Philemon to receive his servant Onesimus; the arguments used are taken from the general character he had for love to the saints, and people of God, and therefore it was hoped he would act up to it in this instance, Philemon 1: 5, from the consideration of the person who made the suit to him, who could have used authority, but chose rather to entreat him in love; and also of his age, and the condition in which he was, a prisoner of Jesus Christ, Philemon 1: 8 from the spiritual relation Onesimus was in to the apostle, who had begotten him in his bonds, Philemon 1: 10 from the present usefulness of him, both to Philemon and the apostle, who before was useless, Philemon 1: 11, from the strong affection the apostle had for him, being as his own bowels, Philemon 1: 12 from his unwillingness to do anything without his consent, though he could have detained him upon the foot of equity and justice, to have served him in his stead, Philemon 1: 13, from the overruling providence of God, which had so ordered it, that he should depart from him for a time, that he might be received for ever,

Philemon 1: 15 from the character under which he could now be received, not as a servant, but as a beloved brother, Philemon 1: 16 from the partnership and association in which the apostle and Philemon were, Philemon 1: 17 from the assurance he gave him of repaying him whatever his servant owed him, and making good whatever he had injured him in, Philemon 1: 18 and from that pleasure, delight, and refreshment he should have, should he receive him, Philemon 1: 20.

And, upon the whole, the apostle expresses his confidence that he would grant his request, obey his commands, and even do more than he had mentioned to him, Philemon 1: 21. And then gives him some hope of his being delivered from prison, through the prayers of Philemon, and others, and of seeing him shortly; and therefore desires he would prepare a lodging for him, Philemon 1: 22 and closes with the salutations of several friends to him, mentioned by name, with their characters, Philemon 1: 23 and with his own common salutation, Philemon 1: 25.

The commentaries on Philemon are by John Calvin and John Gill.

PHILEMON

1 Paul, a prisoner of Jesus Christ, and Timothy our brother, unto Philemon our dearly beloved, and fellowlabourer,

2 And to our beloved Apphia, and Archippus our fellowsoldier, and to the church in thy house:

3 Grace to you, and peace, from God our Father and the Lord Jesus Christ.

4 I thank my God, making mention of thee always in my prayers,

5 Hearing of thy love and faith, which thou hast toward the Lord Jesus, and toward all saints;

6 That the communication of thy faith may become effectual by the acknowledging of every good thing which is in you in Christ Jesus.

7 For we have great joy and consolation in thy love, because the bowels of the saints are refreshed by thee, brother.

8 Wherefore, though I might be much bold in Christ to enjoin thee that which is convenient,

9 Yet for love's sake I rather beseech thee, being such an one as Paul the aged, and now also a prisoner of Jesus Christ.

10 I beseech thee for my son Onesimus, whom I have begotten in my bonds:

11 Which in time past was to thee unprofitable, but now profitable to thee and to me:

12 Whom I have sent again: thou therefore receive him, that is, mine own bowels:

13 Whom I would have retained with me, that in thy stead he might have ministered unto me in the bonds of the gospel:

14 But without thy mind would I do nothing; that thy benefit should not be as it were of necessity, but willingly.

15 For perhaps he therefore departed for a season, that thou shouldest receive him for ever;

16 Not now as a servant, but above a servant, a brother beloved, specially to me, but how much more unto thee, both in the flesh, and in the Lord?

17 If thou count me therefore a partner, receive him as myself.

18 If he hath wronged thee, or oweth thee ought, put that on mine account;

19 I Paul have written it with mine own hand, I will repay it: albeit I do not say to

PHILEMON

The singular loftiness of the mind of Paul, though it may be seen to greater advantage in his other writings which treat of weightier matters, is also attested by this Epistle, in which, while he handles a subject otherwise low and mean, he rises to God with his wonted elevation. Sending back a runaway slave and thief, he supplicates pardon for him. But in pleading this cause, he discourses about Christian forbearance with such ability, that he appears to speak about the interests of the whole Church rather than the private affairs of a single individual. In behalf of a man of the lowest condition, he demeans himself so modestly and humbly, that nowhere else is the meekness of his temper painted in a more lively manner.

1. A prisoner of Jesus Christ

In the same sense in which he elsewhere calls himself an Apostle of Christ, or a minister of Christ, he now calls himself "a prisoner of Christ"; because the chains by which he was bound on account of the gospel, were the ornaments or badges of that embassy which he exercised for Christ. Accordingly, he mentions them for the sake of strengthening his authority; not that he was afraid of being despised, (for Philemon undoubtedly had so great reverence and esteem for him, that there was no need of assuming any title,) but because he was about to plead the cause of a runaway slave, the principal part of which was entreaty for forgiveness.

To Philemon our friend and fellow-laborer

It is probable that this "Philemon" belonged to the order of pastors; for the title with which he adorns him, when he calls him fellow-laborer, is a title which he is not accustomed to bestow on a private individual.

2. And to Archippus our fellow-soldier

He next adds "Archippus," who appears also to have been a minister of the Church; at least, if he be the same person who is mentioned towards the conclusion of the Epistle to the Colossians, (Colossians 4: 17,) which is not at all improbable; for the designation – "fellow-soldier" – which he bestows on this latter individual, belongs peculiarly to ministers. Although the condition of a soldier belongs to all Christians universally, yet because teachers may be regarded as standardbearers in the warfare, they ought to be ready more than all others to fight, and Satan usually gives them greater annoyance. It is also possible, that Archippus attended and shared in some contests which Paul maintained; and, indeed, this is the very word that Paul makes use of, whenever he mentions persecutions.

And to the Church which is in thy house

By employing these terms, he bestows the highest praise on the family of Philemon. And certainly it is no small praise

PHILEMON

1. Paul, a prisoner of Jesus Christ. Not made a prisoner by Christ, though he was apprehended, laid hold on, and detained by Christ as a prisoner of hope, at his conversion; but this is not intended here: but he was a prisoner at Rome for the sake of Christ, on account of professing him, and preaching in his name; his bonds were for the sake of the Gospel of Christ; and therefore they are in this epistle called the bonds of the Gospel. He was not a prisoner for any capital crime, and therefore had no reason to be ashamed of his chain, nor was he; but rather gloried in it, as his taking this title and character to himself, and prefixing it to this epistle shows; and which he chooses to make use of rather than that of a servant of God, or an apostle of Christ, as he elsewhere does, that he might not by constraint, or authority, but by love, move the pity and compassion of Philemon to grant his request, and receive his servant; which, should he deny, would be to add affliction to his bonds: and that this is his view in the choice of this character, is manifest from Philemon 1: 8

10. I beseech thee for my son Onesimus. Now he comes to the request itself, and mentions by name the person on whose account he makes it, and whom he calls his son; not merely because of his affection to him, but because he really was his spiritual father; he had been the happy instrument of his conversion, and he was his son according to the common faith, or in a spiritual sense.

whom I have begotten in my bonds: which is to be understood of a begetting again, or of regeneration; not as if the apostle was the efficient cause of it, as the nature of it shows, it being expressed by men's being born from above; by their being quickened, when dead in trespasses and sins; by being made new creatures, and transformed in the renewing of their minds; by Christ being formed in them, and by a partaking of the divine nature; and who is sufficient for these things? besides it is expressly denied to be of man, but is always ascribed to God, Father, Son, and Spirit; but as

being the instrument and means of it, through the preaching of the Gospel, the word of truth, by which God of his own will, and by the power of his grace, regenerated this person; and this is said to be done "in his bonds": by which it appears, that the word of God was not bound, but had a free course, and was glorified, and the bonds of the apostle were the means of the spread of it; and that it was attended with great power, to the conversion of souls: and this circumstance is mentioned to engage Philemon to regard the entreaty of the apostle; he had been the instrument of begetting many souls to Christ; but this man was begotten by him in his bonds, when he was a prisoner, and so was peculiarly dear to him.

16. Not now as a servant. That is, not only as a servant, for a servant he was, and was to be received as such; his call by grace had not dissolved the civil relation that was between him and his master, though it had added to it something that was above it, and greater than it.

but above a servant; in a higher condition, as the Arabic version renders it, than a servant; not barely considered in that relation, but as being in one much preferable to it.

a brother beloved, specially to me; a brother in Christ, and to be beloved on that account, as he was especially by the apostle, who had been the instrument of his conversion; see Colossians 4: 9.

But how much more unto thee, both in the flesh and in the Lord? both in a natural and civil sense, as being of the same nation and country, and as being part of his family, his servant, and now become an useful and profitable one; and, in a spiritual sense, being in the Lord, belonging to the Lord Jesus, to that family which is named of him, being a fellow citizen with the saints, and of the household of God, and therefore must be doubly dear to him.

17. If thou count me therefore a partner. A companion and friend, who reckon each other's affairs and interest their own: the word answers to *rbx*, a word often used in Talmudic

thee how thou owest unto me even thine own self besides.

20 Yea, brother, let me have joy of thee in the Lord: refresh my bowels in the Lord.

21 Having confidence in thy obedience I wrote unto thee, knowing that thou wilt also do more than I say.

22 But withal prepare me also a lodging: for I trust that through your prayers I shall be given unto you.

23 There salute thee Epaphras, my fellowprisoner in Christ Jesus;

24 Marcus, Aristarchus, Demas, Lucas, my fellowlabourers.

25 The grace of our Lord Jesus Christ be with your spirit. Amen.

of a householder, that he regulates his family in such a manner as to be an image of the Church, and to discharge also the duty of a pastor within the walls of his dwelling. Nor must we forget to mention that this good man had a wife of the same character; for she, too, not without reason, is commended by Paul.

10. I beseech thee for my son

Since less weight is commonly attached to those prayers which are not founded in some cause of just commendation, Paul shows that Onesimus is so closely related to him as to afford a good reason for supplicating in his behalf. Here it is of importance to consider how deep is his condescension, when he gives the name of "son" to a slave, and a runaway, and a thief.

When he says that Onesimus has been begotten by him this must be understood to mean, that it was done by his ministry, and not by his power. To renew a soul of man and form it anew to the image of God – is not a human work, and it is of this spiritual regeneration that he now speaks. Yet because the soul is regenerated by faith, and "faith is by hearing" (Romans 10: 17), on that, account he who administers the doctrine holds the place of a parent. Moreover, because the word of God preached by man is the seed of eternal life, we need not wonder that he from whose mouth we receive that seed is called a father. Yet, at the same time, we must believe that, while the ministry of a man is efficacious in regenerating the soul, yet, strictly speaking, God himself regenerates by the power of his Spirit. These modes of expression, therefore, do not imply any opposition between God and man, but only show what God does by means of men. When he says that he had *begotten him in his bonds*, this circumstance adds weight to the commendation.

12. Receive him, that is, my bowels

Nothing could have been more powerful for assuaging the wrath of Philemon; for if he had refused to forgive his slave, he would thus have used cruelty against "the bowels" of Paul. This is remarkable kindness displayed by Paul, that he did not hesitate to receive, as it were into his bowels, a contemptible slave, and thief, and runaway, so as to defend him from the indignation of his master. And, indeed, if the conversion of a man to God were estimated by us, at its proper value, we too would embrace, in the same manner, those who should give evidence that they had truly and sincerely repented.

13. Whom I was desirous to keep beside me

This is another argument for the purpose of appeasing Philemon, that Paul sends him back a slave, of whose services, in other respects, he stood greatly in need. It would have

writings, for an associate of the doctors or wise men: here it may mean also a partner both in grace, and in the ministry; one that shared in the same gifts and graces of the Spirit of God, and one that was to be a partaker of the inheritance with the saints in light: now if Philemon reckoned the apostle such an one, as he doubtless did, as being engaged in the same common cause, and a partaker of the same common faith, and interested in the same common salvation; then he entreats him on account of Onesimus, in the following manner.

receive him as myself; intimating, that he was as dear to him as himself; that he loved him as his own soul; and that he should take whatever respect and affection were shown to him as done to himself; and that he would have him receive him into his house, his heart and affections, as he would receive him the apostle himself, should he come to him.

19. I Paul have written it, with mine own hand. Meaning either this epistle, which being short, he used no amanuensis, but wrote it all himself, and which might be taken as an engagement to do what he promised; or else a bill, a promissory note, written with his own hand, which he sent along with Onesimus, by which he laid himself under obligation to give Philemon full satisfaction in every thing, in which he had been injured by his servant.

I will repay it: this was not an ironical expression, nor a piece of vanity in the apostle; he spoke seriously, and heartily, and meant what he said; and though his circumstances were often so mean, that he was forced to work with his own hands to minister to his necessities; yet such was his interest in the churches, and such their obligation to him, on account of his personal and useful ministrations to them, that he could easily raise a sum of money among them, upon any emergent occasion; so that Philemon had a good surety and paymaster of the apostle: and this shows his great humility to be a bondsman for a servant, and to make good damages and debts brought on in a scandalous manner; as also that suretyship in some cases is lawful, though it ought to be cautiously, and for very good reasons, entered into: and this engagement of the apostle for Onesimus bears some resemblance with, and may serve to illustrate the suretyship of Christ, for his people, they, and Onesimus, being much in a like condition; as he was an unprofitable and run away servant, so they are all gone out of the way, and together become unprofitable; and Christ engaged with his Father to bring them back again, and set them before him; and by his sufferings and death has brought them nigh, which were afar off; as he had wronged his master and was indebted to him, so they have injured the law of God, affronted his justice, and incurred his displeasure; and having owed to him more than ten thousand talents, and having nothing to pay, Christ engaged to satisfy law and justice, to make reconciliation for them, and pay all their debts; all which he has accordingly done; their sins have been placed to his account, imputed to him, and charged upon him; and he has bore them, and the punishment due to them, and so has satisfied for them, and restored that which he took not away.

Albeit I do not say to thee how thou owest unto me even thine own self besides; having respect to his conversion, which he was the happy instrument of the apostle was his spiritual father, and he was his son, according to the common faith; he had been the instrument of saving his soul from death; he had been the means of that in the hand of God, which all his riches, and the riches of his friends and relations, could never have procured: the salvation of his soul, his better part, was instrumentally owing to him, and so his whole self; and therefore, what favor might he not ask of him? and what was it he could, or should deny him? this the apostle introduces in a very artificial manner, and does not insist upon it, but suggests, that should he forgive the injuries and debts, he had took upon him to make satisfaction for, it would not be an equivalent to the debt he owed to him. From hence may be observed, how greatly obliged regenerated persons are to those, who have been the means and instruments of their conversion.

been extreme cruelty, to disdain so strong affection manifested by Paul. He likewise states indirectly, that it will be a
gratification to himself to have Onesimus sent back to him
rather than that he should be harshly treated at home.

**That he might minister to me instead of thee in the
bonds of the gospel**

He now mentions other circumstances: first, Onesimus will
supply the place of his master, by performing this service;
secondly, Paul himself, through modesty, was unwilling to
deprive Philemon of his right; and, thirdly, Philemon will
receive more applause, if, after having had his slave restored
to him, he shall willingly and generously send him back.
From this last consideration we infer, that we ought to aid
the martyrs of Christ by every kind office in our power,
while they are laboring for the testimony of the gospel; for
if exile, imprisonment stripes, blows, and violent seizing of
our property, are believed by us to belong to the gospel, as
Paul here calls them, whoever refuses to share and partake
of them separates himself even from Christ. Undoubtedly
the defense of the gospel belongs alike to all. Accordingly,
he who endures persecution, for the sake of the gospel,
ought not to be regarded as a private individual, but as
one who publicly represents the whole Church. Hence it
follows, that all believers ought to be united in taking care
of it, so that they may not, as is frequently done, leave the
gospel to be defended in the person of one man.

20. Yea, brother, let me have joy of thee in the Lord. Through the apostle was his spiritual father, having been the instrument of his conversion, yet he calls him his brother, as being a partaker of the same grace, and a minister of the same Gospel.

Hebrews

Introduction by John Calvin

Not only various opinions were formerly entertained as to the author of this Epistle, but it was only at a late period that it was received by the Latin Churches. They suspected that it favored Novatus in denying pardon to the fallen; but that this was a groundless opinion will be shown by various passages. I, indeed, without hesitation, class it among apostolical writings; nor do I doubt but that it has been through the craft of Satan that any have been led to dispute its authority. There is, indeed, no book in the Holy Scriptures which speaks so clearly of the priesthood of Christ, so highly exalts the virtue and dignity of that only true sacrifice which he offered by his death, so abundantly treats of the use of ceremonies as well as of their abrogation, and, in a word, so fully explains that Christ is the end of the Law. Let us not therefore suffer the Church of God nor ourselves to be deprived of so great a benefit, but firmly defend the possession of it.

Moreover, as to its author, we need not be very solicitous. Some think the author to have been Paul, others Luke, others Barnabas, and others Clement, as Jerome relates; yet Eusebius, in his sixth book of his Church History, mentions only Luke and Clement. I well know that in the time of Chrysostom it was everywhere classed by the Greeks among the Pauline Epistles; but the Latins thought otherwise, even those who were nearest to the times of the Apostles.

I indeed, can adduce no reason to show that Paul was its author; for they who say that he designedly suppressed his name because it was hateful to the Jews, bring nothing to the purpose; for why, then, did he mention the name of Timothy as by this he betrayed himself. But the manner it of teaching, and the style, sufficiently show that Paul was not the author; and the writer himself confesses in the second chapter that he was one of the disciples of the Apostles, which is wholly different from the way in which Paul spoke of himself. Besides, what is said of the practice of catechizing in the sixth chapter, does not well suit the time or age of Paul. There are other things which we shall notice in their proper places.

What excuse is usually made as to the style I well know that is, that no opinion can be hence formed, because the Greek is a translation made from the Hebrew by Luke or someone else. But this conjecture can be easily refuted: to pass by other places quoted from Scripture, on the supposition that the Epistle was written in Hebrew, there would have been no allusion to the word Testament, on which the writer so much dwells; what he says of a Testament, in the ninth chapter, could not have been drawn from any other fountain than from the Greek word; for *diath k* has two meanings in Greek, while |berit| in Hebrew means only a covenant. This reason alone is enough to convince men of sound judgment that the epistle was written in the Greek languages. Now, what is objected on the other hand, that it is more probable that the Apostle wrote to the Jews in their own language, has no weight in it; for how few then understood their ancient language? Each had learned the language of the country where he dwelt. Besides, the Greek was then more widely known than all other languages. We shall proceed now to the Argument.

The object at the beginning is not to show to the Jews that Jesus, the son of Mary, was the Christ, the Redeemer promised to them, for he wrote to those who had already made a profession of Christ; that point, then, is taken as granted. But the design of the writer was to prove what the office of Christ is. And it hence appears evident, that by his coming an end was put to ceremonies. It is necessary to draw this distinction; for as it would have been a superfluous labor for the Apostle to prove to those who were already convinced that he was the Christ who had appeared, so it was necessary for him to show what he was, for they did not as yet clearly understand the end, the effect, and the advantages of his coming; but being taken up with a false view of the Law, they laid hold on the shadow instead of the substance. Our business with the Papists is similar in the present day; for they confess with us that Christ is the Son of God, the redeemer who had been promised to the world: but when we come to the reality, we find that they rob him of more than onehalf of his power.

Now, the beginning is respecting the dignity of Christ; for it seemed strange to the Jews that the Gospel should be preferred to the Law. And first indeed he settles that point which was in dispute, that the doctrine brought by Christ had the preeminence, for it was the fulfillment of all the prophecies. But as the reverence in which they held Moses might have been a hindrance to them, he shows that Christ was far superior to all others. And after having briefly referred to those things in which he excelled others, he mentions by name the angels, that with them he might reduce all to their proper rank. Thus he advanced prudently in his course; for if he had begun with Moses, his comparison would have been more disliked. But when it appears from Scripture that celestial powers are subordinated to Christ, there is no reason why Moses or any mortal being should refuse to be classed with them, so that the Son of God may appear eminent above angels as well as men.

After having thus brought the angels under the power and dominion of Christ, the Apostle having, as it were, gained confidence, declares that Moses was so much inferior to him as a servant is to his master.

By thus setting Christ in the **three first chapters** in a supreme state of power, he intimates, that when he speaks all ought to be silent, and that nothing should prevent us from seriously attending to his doctrine. At the same time he sets him forth in the second chapter as our brother in our flesh; and thus he allures us to devote ourselves more willingly to him; and he also blends exhortations and threatening in order to lead those to obedience who are tardy or perversely resist; and he continues in this strain nearly to the end of the fourth chapter.

At the end of the **fourth chapter** he begins to explain the priesthood of Christ, which abolishes all the ceremonies of the Law. But after having briefly showed how welcome that priesthood ought to be to us, and how gladly we ought to acquiesce in it, he shortly turns aside to reprove the Jews, because they stopped at the first elements of religion like children; and he also terrifies them with a grievous and severe denunciation, that there was danger lest they, if slothful to make progress, should at length be rejected by the Lord. But he presently softens this asperity by saying, that he hoped better things of them, in order that he might encourage them, whom he had depressed, to make progress.

Then [in the **seventh** chapter] he returns to the priesthood; and first shows that it differed from the ancient priesthood under the Law; secondly, that it was more excellent, because it succeeded it, and was sanctioned by an oath – because it is eternal, and remains for ever efficacious – because he who performs its duties is superior in honor and dignity to Aaron and all the rest of the Levitical tribe; and he shows that the type which shadowed forth all things was found in the person of Melchisedec.

And in order to prove more fully that the ceremonies of the Law were abrogated he mentions that the ceremonies were appointed, and also the tabernacle, for a particular end, even that they might get forth the heavenly prototype. Hence it follows, that they were not to be rested in unless we wish to stop in the middle of our course, having no regard to the goal. On this subject he quotes a passage from Jeremiah, in which a new covenant is promised, which was nothing else than an improvement on the old. It hence follows, that the old was weak and fading.

Having spoken of the likeness and similitude between the shadows and the reality exhibited in Christ, he then concludes that all the rituals appointed by Moses have been abrogated by the one only true sacrifice of Christ, because the efficacy of this sacrifice is perpetual, and that not only the sanction of the New Testament is made by it complete, but that it is also a true and a spiritual accomplishment of that external priesthood which was in force under the Law.

To this doctrine he again connects exhortation like a goad, that putting aside all impediments they might receive Christ with due reverence.

As to the many examples he mentions in the **eleventh** chapter concerning the fathers, they seem to me to have been brought forward for this purpose – that the Jews might understand, that if they were led from Moses to Christ, they would be so far from departing from the fathers, that they would thus be especially connected with them. For if the chief thing in them

was faith, and the root of all other virtues, it follows that this is especially that by which they should be counted the children of Abraham and the Prophets; and that on the other hand all are bastards who follow not the faith of the fathers. And this is no small commendation of the Gospel, that by it we have union and fellowship with the universal Church, which has been from the beginning of the world.

The **two last** chapters contain various precepts as to the way in which we ought to live: they speak of hope, of bearing the cross, of perseverance, of gratitude towards God, of obedience, of mercy, of the duties of love, of chastity, and of such like things. And lastly, he concludes with prayer, and at the same time gives them a hope of his coming to see them.

The commentaries on Hebrews are by John Calvin and F. B. Meyer.

HEBREWS 1

1 God, who at sundry times and in divers manners spake in time past unto the fathers by the prophets,

2 Hath in these last days spoken unto us by his Son, whom he hath appointed heir of all things, by whom also he made the worlds;

3 Who being the brightness of his glory, and the express image of his person, and upholding all things by the word of his power, when he had by himself purged our sins, sat down on the right hand of the Majesty on high;

4 Being made so much better than the angels, as he hath by inheritance obtained a more excellent name than they.

5 For unto which of the angels said he at any time, Thou art my Son, this day have I begotten thee? And again, I will be to him a Father, and he shall be to me a Son?

6 And again, when he bringeth in the firstbegotten into the world, he saith, And let all the angels of God worship him.

7 And of the angels he saith, Who maketh his angels spirits, and his ministers a flame of fire.

8 But unto the Son he saith, Thy throne, O God, is for ever and ever: a scepter of righteousness is the scepter of thy kingdom.

9 Thou hast loved righteousness, and hated iniquity; therefore God, even thy God, hath anointed thee with the oil of gladness above thy fellows.

10 And, Thou, Lord, in the beginning hast laid the foundation of the earth; and the heavens are the works of thine hands:

11 They shall perish; but thou remainest; and they all shall wax old as doth a garment;

12 And as a vesture shalt thou fold them up, and they shall be changed: but thou art the same, and thy years shall not fail.

13 But to which of the angels said he at any time, Sit on my right hand, until I make thine enemies thy footstool?

14 Are they not all ministering spirits, sent forth to minister for them who shall be heirs of salvation?

HEBREWS 1

1. God formerly, *etc*

This beginning is for the purpose of commending the doctrine taught by Christ; for it shows that we ought not only reverently to receive it, but also to be satisfied with it alone. That we may understand this more clearly, we must observe the contrast between each of the clauses. First, the Son of God is set in opposition to the prophets; then we to the fathers; and, thirdly, the various and manifold modes of speaking which God had adopted as to the fathers, to the last revelation brought to us by Christ. But in this diversity he still sets before us but one God, that no one might think that the Law militates against the Gospel, or that the author of one is not the author of the other. That you may, therefore, understand the full import of this passage, the following arrangement shall be given.

This foundation being laid, the agreement between the Law and the Gospel is established; for God, who is ever like himself, and whose word is the same, and whose truth is unchangeable, has spoken as to both in common.

But we must notice the difference between us and the fathers; for God formerly addressed them in a way different from that which he adopts towards us now. And first indeed as to them he employed the prophets, but he has appointed his Son to be an ambassador to us. Our condition, then, in this respect, is superior to that of the fathers. Even Moses is to be also classed among the prophets, as he is one of the number of those who are inferior to the Son. In the manner also in which revelation was made, we have an advantage over them. For the diversity as to visions and other means adopted under the Old Testament, was an indication that it was not yet a fixed state of things, as when matters are put completely in order. Hence he says, **multifariously and in many ways**. God would have indeed followed the same mode perpetually to the end, had the mode been perfect and complete. It hence follows, that this variety was an evidence of imperfection.

The two words I thus understand: I refer *multifariously* to a diversity as to times; for the Greek word *polumer s* which we may render, "in many parts," as the case usually is, when we intend to speak more fully hereafter; but *polutrop s* points out a diversity, as I think, in the very manner itself. And when he speaks of *the last times*, he intimates that there is no longer any reason to expect any new revelation; for it was not a word in part that Christ brought, but the final conclusion. It is in this sense that the Apostles take *the last times* and *the last days*. And Paul means the same when he says, "Upon whom the ends of the world are come" (1 Corinthians 10: 11). If God then has spoken now for the last time, it is right to advance thus far; so also when you come to Christ, you

HEBREWS 1

1. God. What word could more fittingly stand at the head of the first line of the first paragraph in this noble epistle! Each structure must rest on him as foundation; each tree must spring from him as root; each design and enterprise must originate in him as source. "IN THE BEGINNING-GOD," is a worthy motto to inscribe at the commencement of every treatise, be it the ponderous volume or the ephemeral tract. And with that name we commence our attempt to gather up some of the glowing lessons which were first addressed to the persecuted and wavering Hebrews in the primitive age, but have ever been most highly prized by believing Gentiles throughout the universal Church. The feast was originally spread for the children of the race of Abraham; but who shall challenge our right to the crumbs? In our endeavor to gather them, be thou, God, Alpha and Omega, First and Last. In the original Greek, the word "God" is preceded by two other words, which describe the variety and multitudinousness of his revelation to man. And the whole verse is full of interest as detailing the origin and authority of the Word of God, and as illustrating the great law which appears in so many parts of the works of God.

2. Hath . . . spoken unto us by his Son. God has many sons, but only one Son. When, on the morning of his resurrection, our Lord met the frightened women, he said, "I ascend unto my Father and your Father, and my God and your God." But, as he used the words, they meant infinitely more of himself than they could ever mean of man, however saintly or childlike. No creature-wing shall ever avail to carry us across the abyss which separates all created from all uncreated life. But we may reverently accept the fact, so repeatedly emphasized, that Jesus is "the only begotten Son, which is in the bosom of the Father" (John 1: 18). He is Son in a sense altogether unique.

This term, as used by our Lord, and as understood by the Jews, not only signified divine relationship, but divine equality. Hence, on one occasion, the Jews sought to kill him, because he said that God was his Father, making himself equal with God (John 5: 18). And he, so far from correcting the opinion-as he must have done instantly, had it been erroneous, went on to confirm it and to substantiate its truthfulness. The impression which Jesus of Nazareth left on all who knew him was that of his extreme humility; but here was a point in which he could not abate one jot or tittle of his claims, lest he should be false to his knowledge of himself, and to the repeated voice of God. And so he died, because he affirmed, amid the assumed horror of his judges, that he was the Christ, the Son of God. "He counted it not a prize to be on an equality with God." It was his right.

3. Upholding all things by the word of his power. He is the prop which underpins creation. Christ, and not fate. Christ, and not nature. Christ, and not abstract impersonal law. Law is but the invariable method of his working. "In him all things live, and move, and have their being." "By him all things consist." He is ever at work repeating on the large scale of creation the deeds of his earthly life. And if he did not do them, they must be forever undone. At his word rainwater and dew become grape-juice; tiny handfuls of grain fill the autumn barns; storms die away into calm; fish are led through the paths of the sea; rills are sent among the mountains; and stars are maintained in their courses, so that "not one faileth."

All power is given unto him in heaven and on earth. Why, then, art thou so sad? Thy best Friend is the Lord of Providence. Thy Brother is Prime Minister of the universe, and holds the keys of the divine commissariat. Go to him with the empty sacks of thy need; he will not only fill them, but fill them freely, without money and without price; as Joseph did in the old story of the days of the Pharaohs.

purged our sins. We shall have many opportunities of dwelling on this glorious fact. Jesus is Savior, Redeemer, and the High-Priest. This is his proudest title; in this work no angel or created spirit can bear him rivalry. In the work of salvation he is alone. No angel could atone for sin, or plead our cause, or emancipate us from the thrall of evil.

But notice the finality of this act. "He made purging of sins " (see Greek). It is finished; forever complete; done irrevocably and finally. If

HEBREWS 2

1 Therefore we ought to give the more earnest heed to the things which we have heard, lest at any time we should let them slip.

2 For if the word spoken by angels was stedfast, and every transgression and disobedience received a just recompence of reward;

3 How shall we escape, if we neglect so great salvation; which at the first began to be spoken by the Lord, and was confirmed unto us by them that heard him;

4 God also bearing them witness, both with signs and wonders, and with divers miracles, and gifts of the Holy Ghost, according to his own will?

5 For unto the angels hath he not put in subjection the world to come, whereof we speak.

6 But one in a certain place testified, saying, What is man, that thou art mindful of him? or the son of man, that thou visitest him?

7 Thou madest him a little lower than the angels; thou crownedst him with glory and honor, and didst set him over the works of thy hands:

8 Thou hast put all things in subjection under his feet. For in that he put all in subjection under him, he left nothing that is not put under him. But now we see not yet all things put under him.

9 But we see Jesus, who was made a little lower than the angels for the suffering of death, crowned with glory and honor; that he by the grace of God should taste death for every man.

10 For it became him, for whom are all things, and by whom are all things, in bringing many sons unto glory, to make the captain of their salvation perfect through sufferings.

11 For both he that sanctifieth and they who are sanctified are all of one: for which cause he is not ashamed to call them brethren,

12 Saying, I will declare thy name unto my brethren, in the midst of the church will I sing praise unto thee.

13 And again, I will put my trust in him. And again, Behold I and the children which God hath given me.

ought not to go farther: and these two things it is very needful for us to know. For it was a great hindrance to the Jews that they did not consider that God had deferred a fuller revelation to another time; hence, being satisfied with their own Law, they did not hasten forward to the goal. But since Christ has appeared, an opposite evil began to prevail in the world; for men wished to advance beyond Christ. What else indeed is the whole system of Popery but the overleaping of the boundary which the Apostle has fixed? As, then, the Spirit of God in this passage invites all to come as far as Christ, so he forbids them to go beyond the last time which he mentions. In short, the limit of our wisdom is made here to be the Gospel.

HEBREWS 2

1. Therefore we ought, etc

He now declares what he had before in view, by comparing Christ with angels, even to secure the highest authority to his doctrine. For if the Law given through angels could not have been received with contempt, and if its transgression was visited with severe punishment, what is to happen, he asks, to the despisers of that gospel, which has the Son of God as its author, and was confirmed by so many miracles? The import of the whole is this, that the higher the dignity of Christ is than that of angels, the more reverence is due to the Gospel than to the Law. Thus he commends the doctrine by mentioning its author.

But should it seem strange to any one, that as the doctrine both of the Law and of the Gospel is from God, one should be preferred to the other; inasmuch as by having the Law lowered the majesty of God would be degraded; the evident answer would be this – that he ought indeed always to be heard with equal attention whenever he may speak, and yet that the fuller he reveals himself to us, it is but right that our reverence and attention to obedience should increase in proportion to the extent of his revelations; not that God is in himself less at one time than at another; but his greatness is not at all times equally made known to us.

Here also another question arises. Was not the Law also given by Christ? If so, the argument of the Apostle seems not to be well grounded. To this I reply, that in this comparison regard is had to a veiled revelation on one side, and to that which is manifest on the other. Now, as Christ in bringing the Law showed himself but obscurely or darkly, and as it were under coverings, it is nothing strange that the Law should be said to have been brought by angels without any mention being made of his name; for in that transaction he never appeared openly; but in the promulgation of the Gospel his glory was so conspicuous, that he may justly be deemed its author.

only we are one with him by a living faith, our sins, which were many, are washed out; as an inscription from a slate, as a stain from a robe, as a cloud from the azure of heaven. Gone-as a stone into the bottomless abyss! Gone-never to confront us here or hereafter!

HEBREWS 2

2. Therefore we ought to give the more earnest heed to the things which we have heard, lest at any time we should let them slip. For every one that definitely turns his back on Christ, there are hundreds who drift from him. Life's ocean is full of currents, any one of which will sweep us past the harbor-mouth even when we seem nearest to it, and carry us far out to sea.

It is the drift that ruins men. The drift of the religious world. The drift of old habits and associations; which, in the case of these Hebrew Christians, was setting so strongly toward Judaism, bearing them back to the religious system from which they had come out. The drift of one's own evil nature, always chafing to bear us from God to that which is earthly and sensuous. The drift of the pressure of temptation.

The young man coming from a pious home does not distinctly and deliberately say, "I renounce my father's God." But he finds himself in a set of business associates who have no care for religion; and, after a brief struggle, he relaxes his efforts and begins to drift, until the coastline of heaven recedes so far into the dim distance that he is doubtful if he ever really saw it.

The business man who now shamelessly follows the lowest maxims of his trade was once upright and high-minded. He would have blushed to think it possible for such things to be done by him. But he began by yielding in very trivial points to the strong pressure of competition; and when once he had allowed himself to be caught by the tide, it bore him far beyond his first intention.

The professing Christian who now scarcely pretends to open the Bible or pray came to so terrible a position, not at a single leap, but by yielding to the pressure of the constant way-wardness of the old nature, and thus drifted into an arctic region, where he is likely to perish, benumbed and frozen, unless rescued, and launched on the warm gulf-stream of the love of God.

It is so easy, and so much pleasanter, to drift. Just to lie back, and renounce effort, and let yourself go whither the waters will, as they break musically on the sides of the rocking boat. But, ah, how ineffable the remorse, how disastrous the result!

Are you drifting? You can easily tell. Are you conscious of effort, of daily, hourly resistance to the stream around you, and within? Do the things of God and heaven loom more clearly on your vision? Do the waters foam angrily at your prow as you force your way through them? If so, rejoice! but remember that only divine strength can suffice to maintain the conflict, and keep the boat's head against the stream. If not, you are drifting. Hail the strong Son of God! Ask him to come on board, and stay you, and bring you into port.

9. We see Jesus, . . . crowned with glory and honour. In the first great division of this treatise, we have seen the incomparable superiority of the Lord Jesus to angels, and archangels, and all the heavenly host. But now there arises an objection which was very keenly realized by these Hebrew Christians; and which, to a certain extent, presses upon us all; Why did the Son of God become man? How are the sorrows, sufferings, and death of the Man of Nazareth consistent with the sublime glories of the Son of God, the equal and fellow of the Eternal?

These questions are answered during the remainder of the chapter, and may be gathered up into a single sentence: he who was above all angels became lower than the angels for a little time; that he might lift men from their abasement, and set them on his own glorious level in his heavenly Father's kingdom; and that he might be a faithful and merciful High Priest for the sorrowful and tempted and dying. Here is an act worthy of a God Here are reasons which are more than sufficient to answer the old question, for which Anselm prepared so elaborate a reply in his book, *Cur Deus Homo? What is man?* Those three words in verse 6 are the fit starting point of the argument. We need not only a true philosophy of God, but a true philosophy of man, in order

14 Forasmuch then as the children are partakers of flesh and blood, he also himself likewise took part of the same; that through death he might destroy him that had the power of death, that is, the devil;

15 And deliver them who through fear of death were all their lifetime subject to bondage.

16 For verily he took not on him the nature of angels; but he took on him the seed of Abraham.

17 Wherefore in all things it behoved him to be made like unto his brethren, that he might be a merciful and faithful high priest in things pertaining to God, to make reconciliation for the sins of the people.

18 For in that he himself hath suffered being tempted, he is able to succor them that are tempted.

HEBREWS 3

1 Wherefore, holy brethren, partakers of the heavenly calling, consider the Apostle and High Priest of our profession, Christ Jesus;

2 Who was faithful to him that appointed him, as also Moses was faithful in all his house.

3 For this man was counted worthy of more glory than Moses, inasmuch as he who hath builded the house hath more honor than the house.

4 For every house is builded by some man; but he that built all things is God.

5 And Moses verily was faithful in all his house, as a servant, for a testimony of those things which were to be spoken after;

6 But Christ as a son over his own house; whose house are we, if we hold fast the confidence and the rejoicing of the hope firm unto the end.

7 Wherefore (as the Holy Ghost saith, To day if ye will hear his voice,

8 Harden not your hearts, as in the provocation, in the day of temptation in the wilderness:

9 When your fathers tempted me, proved me, and saw my works forty years.

10 Wherefore I was grieved with that generation, and said, They do alway err in their heart; and they have not known

Lest at any time we should let them slip, or, "lest we should at any time flow abroad," or, if you prefer, "let dip," though in reality there is not much difference. The true sense is to be gathered from the contrast; for to give heed, or to attend and to let slip, are opposites; the first means to hold a thing, and the other to let off like a sieve, or a perforated vessel, whatever may be poured into it. I do not indeed approve of the opinion of those who take it in the sense of dying, according to what we find **in** 2 Samuel 15:14, "We all die and slide away like water." On the contrary, we ought, as I have said, to regard the contrast between attention and flowing out; an attentive mind is like a vessel capable of holding water; but that which is roving and indolent is like a vessel with holes.

2. Steadfast, or "firm," or sure, *etc*

That is, it was the word of authority, for God required it to be believed; and that it was authoritative, was made more evident by its sanctions; for no one despised the law with impunity. Then firmness means authority; and what is added respecting punishment ought to be understood as explanatory; for it is evident the doctrine of which God shows himself to be the avenger, is by no means unprofitable.

HEBREWS 3

1. Wherefore, holy brethren, *etc*

He concludes the preceding doctrine with a necessary exhortation, that the Jews should attentively consider what sort of being and how great Christ is. As he had before, by naming him a teacher and a priest, briefly compared him with Moses and Aaron, so he now includes both clauses; for he adorns him with two titles, as he sustains a twofold character in the Church of God. Moses was a prophet and a teacher, and Aaron was a priest; but the two offices belong to Christ. If then we seek rightly to know him, we must inquire what sort of being he is; yea, he must be clothed with his own power, lest we lay hold on an empty shadow and not on him.

First, the word **consider**, is important, for it intimates that singular attention is required, as he cannot be disregarded with impunity, and that at the same time the true knowledge of Christ is sufficient to dissipate the darkness of all errors. And to encourage them the more to pursue this study, he reminds them of their **calling**; as though he had said, "God favored you with no common grace when He called you into his kingdom; it now remains that you have your eyes fixed on Christ as your leader in the way." For the calling of the godly cannot be otherwise confirmed than by a thorough surrender of themselves to Christ. We ought not therefore to regard this as said only to the Jews,

to right thinking on the Gospel. The idolater thinks man inferior to birds and beasts and creeping things, before which he prostrates himself. The materialist reckons him to be the chance product of natural forces which have evolved him; and before which he is therefore likely to pass away. The pseudo-science of the time makes him of one blood with ape and gorilla, and assigns him a common origin with the beasts. See what gigantic systems of error have developed from mistaken conceptions of the true nature and dignity of man!

HEBREWS 3

12. Take heed, brethren, lest there be in any of you an evil heart of unbelief, in departing from the living God.

The contrast between the third and fourth chapters of this epistle is very marked. The former is like a drear November day, when all the landscape is drenched by sweeping rain, and the rotting leaves fall in showers to find a grave upon the damp and muddy soil. The latter is like a still clear day in midsummer, when nature revels in reposeful bliss beneath the unstinted caresses of the sun. There is as much difference between them as between the seventh and eighth chapters of the Epistle to the Romans.

But each chapter represents an experience of the inner Christian life. Perhaps the majority of Christians live and die in the third chapter, to their infinite loss. Comparatively few pass over into the fourth. Yet why, reader, should you not pass the boundary line today, and leave behind forever the bitter, unsatisfactory experiences which have become the normal rule of your existence? Come up out of the wilderness, in which you have wandered so long. Your sojourn there has been due, not to any desire on the part of God, or to any arbitrary appointment of his, or to any natural disability of your temperament; but to certain grave failures on your part, in the regimen of the inner life.

The antipodes of your hitherto dreary experiences is Christ, the unsearchable riches of Christ; to be made a partaker of Christ: for Christ is the Promised Land that flows with milk and honey, in which we eat bread without scarceness, and gather the grapes and pomegranates and olives of rare spiritual blessedness.

Never did a nation occupy a prouder position than the children of Israel on the morning when they stood victorious on the shores of the Red Sea. The power of the tyrant had been broken by a series of marvelous miracles. The chivalry of Egypt had sunk as lead in the mighty waters of death. And as the sun rose behind the mountains of Edom, and struck a flashing pathway across the burnished mirror of the sea, it revealed long lines of corpses washed up to the water's edge. Behind, Egypt left forever. Above, the fleecy cloud, chariot of God, tabernacle for his presence. Before, the Land of Promise. Many a man was already dreaming of vineyards and olive yards, and a settled home, all of which lay within two or three months' easy march.

But of those six hundred thousand men, flushed with victory and hope, two only were destined to see the land flowing with milk and honey; and these not until forty weary years had slowly passed away. And what became of all the rest? Alas! their carcasses fell in the wilderness. Instead of reposing in some family burying-place in the Land of Promise, their bodies were taken up one by one and laid in the desert waste; the sands their winding-sheet; the solitude their mausoleum. It took forty years for them all to die. And to accomplish this there must have been a high percentage of deaths. How dreary those incessant funerals!

The wilderness experience is emblematic, amongst other things, of unrest, aimlessness, and unsatisfied longings. Unrest: the tents were constantly being struck to be erected again in much the same spot. Theirs a perpetual weariness; and they were not suffered to enter into God's rest. Aimlessness: they wandered in the wilderness in a desert way; they found no city of habitation. Unsatisfied longings: hungry and thirsty, their soul fainted in them.

But how typical of the lives of many amongst ourselves! Life is passing away so swiftly from us, but how unideal! How few Christians seem to have learned the secret of the inner rest! How many are the victims of murmuring and discontent; or are bitten by the serpents of jealousy and passion, of hatred and ill-will!

my ways.

11 So I sware in my wrath, They shall not enter into my rest.)

12 Take heed, brethren, lest there be in any of you an evil heart of unbelief, in departing from the living God.

13 But exhort one another daily, while it is called To day; lest any of you be hardened through the deceitfulness of sin.

14 For we are made partakers of Christ, if we hold the beginning of our confidence stedfast unto the end;

15 While it is said, To day if ye will hear his voice, harden not your hearts, as in the provocation.

16 For some, when they had heard, did provoke: howbeit not all that came out of Egypt by Moses.

17 But with whom was he grieved forty years? was it not with them that had sinned, whose carcases fell in the wilderness?

18 And to whom sware he that they should not enter into his rest, but to them that believed not?

19 So we see that they could not enter in because of unbelief.

HEBREWS 4

1 Let us therefore fear, lest, a promise being left us of entering into his rest, any of you should seem to come short of it.

2 For unto us was the gospel preached, as well as unto them: but the word preached did not profit them, not being mixed with faith in them that heard it.

3 For we which have believed do enter into rest, as he said, As I have sworn in my wrath, if they shall enter into my rest: although the works were finished from the foundation of the world.

4 For he spake in a certain place of the seventh day on this wise, And God did rest the seventh day from all his works.

5 And in this place again, If they shall enter into my rest.

6 Seeing therefore it remaineth that some must enter therein, and they to whom it was first preached entered not in because of unbelief:

7 Again, he limiteth a certain day, saying in David, To day, after so long a time; as it is said, To day if ye will hear his voice, harden not your hearts.

but that it is a general truth addressed to all who desire to come into the kingdom of God; they ought sedulously to attend to Christ, for he is the sole instructor of our faith, and has confirmed it by the sacrifice of himself; for **confession**, or profession, is to be taken here for faith, as thought he had said, that the faith we profess is vain and of no avail, unless Christ be its object.

2. Who was, *or is* faithful, *etc*

This is a commendation of the apostleship of Christ, in order that the faithful may securely acquiesce in him; and he commends it on two grounds, because the Father has set him to be over us as our teacher, and because Christ himself has faithfully performed the office committed to him. These two things are always necessary to secure authority to a doctrine; for God alone ought to be attended to, as the whole Scripture testifies; hence Christ declares, that the doctrine which he delivered was not his own, but the Father's (John 7: 16), and in another place he says, "He who received me, receiveth him who has sent me" (Luke 9: 48). For we say of Christ, that as he is clothed with our flesh, he is the Father's minister to execute his commands. To the calling of God is added the faithful and upright performance of duty on the part of Christ; and this is required in true ministers, in order that they may obtain credence in the Church. Since these two things are found in Christ, doubtless he cannot be disregarded without despising God in him.

HEBREWS 4

1. Let us therefore fear, *etc*

He concludes that there was reason to fear lest the Jews to whom he was writing should be deprived of the blessing offered to them; and then he says, *lest anyone,* intimating that it was his anxious desire to lead them, one and all, to God; for it is the duty of a good shepherd, in watching over the whole flock so to care for every sheep that no one may be lost; nay, we ought also so to feel for one another that every one should fear for his neighbors as well as for himself.

But the fear which is here recommended is not that which shakes the confidence of faith but such as fills us with such concern that we grow not torpid with indifference. Let us then fear, not that we ought to tremble or to entertain distrust as though uncertain as to the issue, but lest we be unfaithful to God's grace.

By saying **Lest we be disappointed of the promise left us,** he intimates that no one comes short of it except he who by rejecting grace has first renounced the promise; for God is so far from repenting to do us good that he ceases not to bestow his gifts except when we despise his calling. The illative therefore, or then means that by the fall of oth-

The almost universal experience tells of broken vows and blighted hopes, of purposeless wanderings, of a monotony of failure. Always striking and pitching the camp! Always surrounded by the same monotonous horizon, sand, with here and there a palm tree! Always fed on the same food, till the soul loathes it! Life passes away amid fret and chafing disappointment and weariness of existence, till we say with Solomon, "Vanity of vanities, all is vanity."

One of the scourges of the desert is the sandstorm, when the hot wind is laden with light powdery dust, which finds its way into eyes and mouth and lungs; penetrating the clothes, stinging the skin, and making life almost unbearable. An apt illustration of the small annoyances, the petty irritations, the perpetual swarm of gnat-like stings, which invade our most comfortable circumstances, and make us question whether life is worth living.

Then there is also the mirage. When from afar green glades seem to attract the weary traveler, who, as he reaches them, finds his hopes deceived and his thirst mocked. Emblem this of the disappointments to which they expose themselves who are ever seeking for some earthly good to mitigate the hardships and sorrows of their life, instead of seeking the fellowship and blessed help of the living Christ. They travel forward, thinking at every step that they are nearing an oasis in their desert march; but, as they approach, the fabric of their hopes fades away into the air.

"We are made partakers of Christ." These words may either mean that all believers together partake of the fullness of Jesus, or that they all partake with him of the fullness of God. "Heirs of God, and joint-heirs with Christ." But whichever be the true rendering, the thought is inexpressibly helpful. Jesus Christ is our Promised Land, and our Joshua to lead us thither. He gives us rest. In him are orchards and vineyards, and all manner of precious things. His comfort for our sorrow; his rest for our weariness; his strength for our weakness; his purity for our corruption; his ever-present help for our need. Oh, blessed Jesus, surely it is the wonder of heaven that we make so little of thee!

HEBREWS 4

9. There remaineth therefore a rest to the people of God. The keynote of this chapter is Rest. In the second verse it is spoken of as a gospel, or good news. And is there any gospel that more needs preaching in these busy, weary days, through which our age is rushing to its close, than the Gospel of Rest? On all hands we hear of strong and useful workers stricken down in early life by the exhausting effects of mental toil. The tender brain tissues were never made to sustain the tremendous wear and tear of our times. There is no machinery in human nature to repair swiftly enough the waste of nervous energy which is continually going on. It is not, therefore, to be wondered at that the symptoms of brain tiredness are becoming familiar to many workers, acting as warning signals, which, if not immediately attended to, are followed by some terrible collapse of mind or body, or both.

And yet it is not altogether that we work so much harder than our forefathers; but that there is so much more fret and chafe and worry in our lives. Competition is closer. Population is more crowded. Brains are keener and swifter in their motion. The resources of ingenuity and inventiveness, of creation and production, are more severely and constantly taxed. And the age seems so merciless and selfish. If the lonely spirit trips and falls, it is trodden down in the great onward rush, or left behind to its fate; and the dread of the swoop of the vultures, with rustling wings, from unknown heights upon us as their prey, fills us with an anguish which we know by the familiar name of care. We could better stand the strain of work if only we had rest from worry, from anxiety, and from the fret of the troubled sea that cannot rest, as it moans around us, with its yeasty waves, hungry to devour. Is such a rest possible?

This chapter states that such a rest is possible. "Let us labor therefore to enter into that rest." Rest? What rest? His rest, says the first verse; my rest, says the third verse; God's rest, says the fourth verse. And this last verse is a quotation from the earliest page of the Bible, which tells how God rested from all the work that he had made. And as we turn to that

8 For if Jesus had given them rest, then would he not afterward have spoken of another day.

9 There remaineth therefore a rest to the people of God.

10 For he that is entered into his rest, he also hath ceased from his own works, as God did from his.

11 Let us labour therefore to enter into that rest, lest any man fall after the same example of unbelief.

12 For the word of God is quick, and powerful, and sharper than any twoedged sword, piercing even to the dividing asunder of soul and spirit, and of the joints and marrow, and is a discerner of the thoughts and intents of the heart.

13 Neither is there any creature that is not manifest in his sight: but all things are naked and opened unto the eyes of him with whom we have to do.

14 Seeing then that we have a great high priest, that is passed into the heavens, Jesus the Son of God, let us hold fast our profession.

15 For we have not an high priest which cannot be touched with the feeling of our infirmities; but was in all points tempted like as we are, yet without sin.

16 Let us therefore come boldly unto the throne of grace, that we may obtain mercy, and find grace to help in time of need.

HEBREWS 5

1 For every high priest taken from among men is ordained for men in things pertaining to God, that he may offer both gifts and sacrifices for sins:

2 Who can have compassion on the ignorant, and on them that are out of the way; for that he himself also is compassed with infirmity.

3 And by reason hereof he ought, as for the people, so also for himself, to offer for sins.

4 And no man taketh this honor unto himself, but he that is called of God, as was Aaron.

5 So also Christ glorified not himself to be made an high priest; but he that said unto him, Thou art my Son, to day have I begotten thee.

6 As he saith also in another place,

ers we are taught humility and watchfulness according to what Paul also says, "These through unbelief have fallen; be not thou then high-minded, but fear" (Romans 11: 20).

10. For he that is entered into his rest, or, For he who has rested, *etc*

This is a definition of that perpetual Sabbath in which there is the highest felicity, when there will be a likeness between men and God, to whom they will be united. For whatever the philosophers may have ever said of the chief good, it was nothing but cold and vain, for they confined man to himself, while it is necessary for us to go out of ourselves to find happiness. The chief good of man is nothing else but union with God; this is attained when we are formed according to him as our exemplar.

Now this conformation the Apostle teaches us takes place when we rest from our works. It hence at length follows, that man becomes happy by self-denial. For what else is to cease from our works, but to mortify our flesh, when a man renounces himself that he may live to God? For here we must always begin, when we speak of a godly and holy life, that man being in a manner dead to himself, should allow God to live in him, that he should abstain from his own works, so as to give place to God to work. We must indeed confess, that then only is our life rightly formed when it becomes subject to God. But through inbred corruption this is never the case, until we rest from our own works; nay, such is the opposition between God's government and our corrupt affections, that he cannot work in us until we rest. But though the completion of this rest cannot be attained in this life, yet we ought ever to strive for it. Thus believers enter it but on this condition – that by running they may continually go forward.

HEBREWS 5

1. For every high priest, *etc*

He compares Christ with the Levitical priests, and he teaches us what is the likeness and the difference between them; and the object of the whole discourse is, to show what Christ's office really is, and also to prove that whatever was ordained under the law was ordained on his account. Hence the Apostle passes on at last to show that the ancient priesthood was abolished.

He first says that the priests were **taken from among men**; secondly, that they did not act a private part but for the whole people; thirdly, that they were not to come empty to appease God, but furnished with sacrifices; fourthly, that they were not to be exempt from human infirmities, that they might more readily succor the distressed; and lastly, that they were not presumptuously to rush into this office, and that then only was the honor legitimate when

marvelous apocalypse of the past, which in so many respects answers to the apocalypse of the future given us by the Apostle John, we find that, whereas we are expressly told of the evening and morning of each of the other days of creation, there is no reference to the dawn or close of God's rest-day; and we are left to infer that it is impervious to time, independent of duration, unlimited, and eternal; that the ages of human story are but hours in the rest-day of Jehovah; and that, in point of fact, we spend our years in the Sabbath-keeping of God. But, better than all, it would appear that we are invited to enter into it and share it; as a child living by the placid waters of a vast fresh water lake may dip into them its cup, and drink and drink again, without making any appreciable diminution of its volume or ripple on its expanse.

What is meant by God resting? Surely not the rest of weariness! "He fainteth not, neither is weary." Though he had spread forth the heavens, and laid the foundations of the earth, and weighed the mountains in scales, and the hills in a balance, and had invented ten thousand differing forms of being, yet his inventiveness was as fresh, his energy as vigorous as ever. Surely not the rest of inactivity. "My Father worketh hitherto," said our Lord. "In him we live, and move, and have our being." True, he is not now sending forth, so far as we know, suns, or systems, or fresh types of being. But his power is ever at work, repairing, renewing, and sustaining the fabric of the vast machinery of the universe. No sparrow falls to the ground without him. The cry of the young lion and the lowing of the oxen in the pastures attract his instant regard. "In him all things consist." It was the rest of a finished work. He girded himself to the specific work of creation, and summoned into being all that is; and when it was finished he said it was very good: and at once he rested from all his work which he had created and made. It was the rest of divine complacency, of infinite satisfaction, of perfect content. It was equivalent to saying, "This creation of mine is all that I meant it to be, finished and perfect. I am perfectly satisfied; there is nothing more to be done; it is all very good."

This, then, is the rest which we are invited to share. We are not summoned to the heavy slumber which follows over-taxing toil, nor to inaction or indolence; but to the rest which is possible amid swift activity and strenuous work; to perfect equilibrium between the outgoings and incomings of the life; to a contented heart; to peace that passeth all understanding; to the repose of the will in the will of God; and to the calm of the depths of the nature which are undisturbed by the hurricanes which sweep the surface, and urge forward the mighty waves. This rest is holding out both its hands to the weary souls of men throughout the ages, offering its shelter as a harbor from the storms of life.

HEBREWS 5

7–8. Who in the days of his flesh, when he had offered up prayers and supplications with strong crying and tears unto him that was able to save him from death, and was heard in that he feared: though he were a Son, yet learned he obedience by the things which he suffered.

Eight ancient olive trees still mark the site of Gethsemane; not improbably they witnessed that memorable and mysterious scene referred to here. And what a scene was that! It had stood alone in unique and unapproachable wonder, had it not been followed by fifteen hours of even greater mystery.

The strongest words in Greek language are used to tell of the keen anguish through which the Savior passed within those Garden walls. "He began to be sorrowful"; as if his mind were almost dazed and overwhelmed. "He was very heavy," his spirit stooped beneath the weight of his sorrows, as afterward his body stooped beneath the weight of his cross; or the word may mean that he was so distracted with sorrow, as to be almost beside himself. And the Lord himself could not have found a stronger word than he used when he said, "My soul is exceeding sorrowful, even unto death."

But the evangelist Luke gives us the most convincing proof of his anguish when he tells us that his sweat, like great beads of blood, fell upon the ground, touched by the slight frost, and in the cold night air. The finishing touch is given in these words, which tell of his "strong crying and tears."

Thou art a priest for ever after the order of Melchisedec.

7 Who in the days of his flesh, when he had offered up prayers and supplications with strong crying and tears unto him that was able to save him from death, and was heard in that he feared;

8 Though he were a Son, yet learned he obedience by the things which he suffered;

9 And being made perfect, he became the author of eternal salvation unto all them that obey him;

10 Called of God an high priest after the order of Melchisedec.

11 Of whom we have many things to say, and hard to be uttered, seeing ye are dull of hearing.

12 For when for the time ye ought to be teachers, ye have need that one teach you again which be the first principles of the oracles of God; and are become such as have need of milk, and not of strong meat.

13 For every one that useth milk is unskilful in the word of righteousness: for he is a babe.

14 But strong meat belongeth to them that are of full age, even those who by reason of use have their senses exercised to discern both good and evil.

HEBREWS 6

1 Therefore leaving the principles of the doctrine of Christ, let us go on unto perfection; not laying again the foundation of repentance from dead works, and of faith toward God,

2 Of the doctrine of baptisms, and of laying on of hands, and of resurrection of the dead, and of eternal judgment.

3 And this will we do, if God permit.

4 For it is impossible for those who were once enlightened, and have tasted of the heavenly gift, and were made partakers of the Holy Ghost,

5 And have tasted the good word of God, and the powers of the world to come,

6 If they shall fall away, to renew them again unto repentance; seeing they crucify to themselves the Son of God afresh, and put him to an open shame.

7 For the earth which drinketh in the

they were chosen and approved by God. We shall consider briefly each of these points.

We must first, however, expose the ignorance of those who apply these things to our time, as though there was at this day the same need of priests to offer sacrifices; at the same time there is no necessity for a long refutation. For what can be more evident than that the reality found in Christ is compared with its types, which, being prior in time, have now ceased? But this will appear more fully from the context. How extremely ridiculous then are they who seek by this passage to establish and support the sacrifice of the mass! I now return to the words of the Apostle.

Taken from among men, *etc*

This he says of the priests. It hence follows that it was necessary for Christ to be a real man; for as we are very far from God, we stand in a manner before him in the person of our priest, which could not be, were he not one of us. Hence, that the Son of God has a nature in common with us, does not diminish his dignity, but commends it the more to us; for he is fitted to reconcile us to God, because he is man. Therefore Paul, in order to prove that he is a Mediator, expressly calls him man; for had he been taken from among angels or any other beings, we could not by him be united to God, as he could not react down to us.

For men, *etc*

This is the *second* clause; the priest was not privately a minister for himself, but was appointed for the common good of the people. But it is of great consequence to notice this, so that we may know that the salvation of us all is connected with and revolves on the priesthood of Christ. The benefit is expressed in these words, *ordains those things which pertain to God.* They may, indeed, be explained in two ways, as the verb *kathistatai* has a passive as well as an active sense. They who take it passively give this version, "is ordained in those things," etc.; and thus they would have the preposition *in* to be understood; I approve more of the other rendering, that the high priest takes care of or ordains the things pertaining to God; for the construction flows better, and the sense is fuller. But still in either way, what the Apostle had in view is the same, namely, that we have no intercourse with God, except there be a priest; for, as we are unholy, what have we to do with holy things? We are in a word alienated from God and his service until a priest interposes and undertakes our cause.

HEBREWS 6

1. Therefore, leaving, *etc*

To his reproof he joins this exhortation – that leaving first principles they were to proceed forward to the goal. For by *the word of beginning* he understands the first rudiments,

What were the things that Christ suffered? They were not those of the Substitute. The tenor of Scripture goes to show that the work of substitution was really wrought out upon the cross. There the robe of our completed righteousness was woven from the top through-out. It was on the tree that he bare our sins in his own body. It was by his blood that he brought us nigh to God. It was by the death of God's Son that we have been reconciled to God; and the repeated references of Scripture, and especially of this epistle, to sacrifice, indicate that in the act of dying, that was done which magnifies the law, and makes it honorable, and removes every obstacle that had otherwise prevented the love of God from following out its purposes of mercy.

We shall never fully understand here how the Lord Jesus made reconciliation for the sins of the world, or how that which he bore could be an equivalent for the penalty due from a sinful race. We have no standard of comparison; we have no line long enough to let us down into the depths of that unexplored mystery; but we may thankfully accept it as a fact stated on the page of Scripture perpetually, that he did that which put away the curse, atoned for human guilt, and was more than equivalent to all those sufferings which a race of sinful men must otherwise have borne. The mystery defies our language, but it is apprehended by faith; and as she stands upon her highest pinnacles, love discerns the meaning of the death of Christ by a spiritual instinct, though as yet she has not perfectly learned the language in which to express her conceptions of the mysteries that circle around the cross. It may be that in thousands of unselfish actions, she is acquiring the terms in which some day she will be able to understand and explain all.

But all that we need insist on here, and now, is that the sufferings of the Garden are not to be included in the act of Substitution, though, as we shall see, they were closely associated with it. Gethsemane was not the altar, but the way to it.

Our Lord's suffering in Gethsemane could hardly arise from the fear of his approaching physical sufferings. Such a supposition seems wholly inconsistent with the heroic fortitude, the majestic silence, the calm ascendency over suffering with which he bore himself till he breathed out his spirit, and which drew from a hardened and worldly Roman expressions of respect.

Besides, if the mere prospect of scourging and crucifixion drew from our Lord these strong crying and tears and bloody sweat, he surely would stand on a lower level than that to which multitudes of his followers attained through faith in him. Old men like Polycarp, tender maidens like Blandina, timid boys like Attalus, have contemplated beforehand with unruffled composure, and have endured with unshrinking fortitude, deaths far more awful, more prolonged, more agonizing. Degraded criminals have climbed the scaffold without a tremor or a sob; and surely the most exalted faith ought to bear itself as bravely as the most brutal indifference in the presence of the solemnities of death and eternity. It has been truly said that there is no passion in the mind of man, however weak, which cannot master the fear of death; and it is therefore impossible to suppose that the fear of physical suffering and disgrace could have so shaken our Savior's spirit.

HEBREWS 6

4–6. It Is impossible for those who were once enlightened, and have tasted of the heavenly gift, and were made partakers of the Holy Ghost, and have tasted the good word of God, and the powers of the world to come, if they shall fall away, to renew them again unto repentance; seeing they crucify to themselves the Son of God afresh, and put him to an open shame.

The sacred writer enumerates four fundamental principles: Repentance from dead works, which in the old dispensation was symbolized by divers baptisms, or washings; Faith toward God, typified by the laying of hands on the head of the victim-sacrifices; the Resurrection of the dead; and Eternal Judgment. And then he proposes not to lay them again, but to leave them. There is no thought, however, of deserting them. The great principles on which God saves the soul are identical in every age, and indispensable.

We can only leave them as the child leaves the multiplication-table, when it is well learnt,

rain that cometh oft upon it, and bringeth forth herbs meet for them by whom it is dressed, receiveth blessing from God:

8 But that which beareth thorns and briers is rejected, and is nigh unto cursing; whose end is to be burned.

9 But, beloved, we are persuaded better things of you, and things that accompany salvation, though we thus speak.

10 For God is not unrighteous to forget your work and labour of love, which ye have shewed toward his name, in that ye have ministered to the saints, and do minister.

11 And we desire that every one of you do shew the same diligence to the full assurance of hope unto the end:

12 That ye be not slothful, but followers of them who through faith and patience inherit the promises.

13 For when God made promise to Abraham, because he could swear by no greater, he sware by himself,

14 Saying, Surely blessing I will bless thee, and multiplying I will multiply thee.

15 And so, after he had patiently endured, he obtained the promise.

16 For men verily swear by the greater: and an oath for confirmation is to them an end of all strife.

17 Wherein God, willing more abundantly to shew unto the heirs of promise the immutability of his counsel, confirmed it by an oath:

18 That by two immutable things, in which it was impossible for God to lie, we might have a strong consolation, who have fled for refuge to lay hold upon the hope set before us:

19 Which hope we have as an anchor of the soul, both sure and stedfast, and which entereth into that within the veil;

20 Whither the forerunner is for us entered, even Jesus, made an high priest for ever after the order of Melchisedec.

HEBREWS 7

1 For this Melchisedec, king of Salem, priest of the most high God, who met Abraham returning from the slaughter of the kings, and blessed him;

2 To whom also Abraham gave a tenth part of all; first being by interpretation King of righteousness, and after that also

taught to the ignorant when received into the Church. Now, he bids them to leave these rudiments, not that the faithful are ever to forget them, but that they are not to remain in them; and this idea appears more clear from what follows, the comparison of a *foundation;* for in building a house we must never leave the foundation; and yet to be always engaged in laying it, would be ridiculous. For as the foundation is laid for the sake of what is built on it, he who is occupied in laying it and proceeds not to the superstructure, wearies himself with foolish and useless labor. In short, as the builder must begin with the foundation, so must he go on with his work that the house may be built. Similar is the case as to Christianity; we have the first principles as the foundation, but the higher doctrine ought immediately to follow which is to complete the building. They then act most unreasonably who remain in the first elements, for they propose to themselves no end, as though a builder spent all his labor on the foundation, and neglected to build up the house. So then he would have our faith to be at first so founded as afterwards to rise upwards, until by daily progress it be at length completed.

Of repentance from dead works, *etc*

He here refers to a catechism commonly used. It is hence a probable conjecture that this Epistle was written, not immediately after the promulgation of the Gospel, but when they had some kind of polity established in the Churches; such as this, that the catechumen made a confession of his faith before he was admitted to baptism. And there were certain primary points on which the pastor questioned the catechumen, as it appears from the various testimonies of the fathers; there was an examination had especially on the creed called the Apostles' Creed. This was the first entrance, as it were, into the church to those who were adults and enlisted under Christ, as they were before alienated from faith in him. This custom the Apostle mentions, because there was a short time fixed for catechumens, during which they were taught the doctrine of religion, as a master instructs his children in the alphabet, in order that he may afterwards advance them to higher things.

HEBREWS 7

1. For this Melchisedec, *etc*

He has hitherto been stimulating the Jews by exhortations, that they might attentively consider the comparison between Christ and Melchisedec. At the end of the last chapter, that he might return from his digression to his subject, he quoted again the passage from the Psalms; and now he enters fully into what he had before slightly referred to; for he enumerates particularly the things connected with Melchisedec, in which he resembled Christ. It is indeed no

but which lies at the root of all after-study; as the plant leaves the root, when it towers into the majestic shrub, which draws all its life from that low origin; and as the builder leaves the foundation, that he may carry up stone on stone, and leans on the foundation most heavily, when he has left it at the furthest distance below him. And we are taught the reason why these principles are not laid afresh. It would be useless to do so; it would serve no good purpose; it would leave in the same state as it found them those who had apostatized from the faith. And so we are led to one of those passages which sensitive spirits have turned to their own torment and anguish; just as men will distil the rankest poison from some of the sweetest flowers.

These apostate disciples had been enlightened (ver. 4). They had been led to see their sin and danger, the temporary nature of Judaism, the dignity and glory of the Savior. Other Hebrews might be ignorant, the folds of the veil hanging heavily over their sight; but it could never be so with them, since they had stood in the midst of the Gospel's meridian light, and had been enlightened.

So may it be with us. Not like the savage, crouching before his fetish, or roaming over the wild; not like the follower of Confucius, Buddha, or Mahomet, groping in the twilight of nature or religious guess-work; not like myriads in our own land, whose hearts are as dark as the chaos into which God commanded the primeval beam to shine: we have been enlightened. We may know that we are sinners; we may have learnt from childhood the scheme of salvation; we may be familiar with the mysteries of the kingdom of heaven, into which angels desire to look: and yet we may fall away.

These Hebrews, here referred to, had also tasted of the heavenly gift. What gift is that? I hear a voice, which we know well, speaking from the well of Sychar, and saying: "The water that I shall give shall be in thee, springing up into everlasting life." It is the life of God in the soul; it is Christ himself; and he is willing to be in us, like a perennial spring, unstanched in drought, unfrozen in frost, leaping up, in fresh and living beauty, like some warm spring that makes a paradise in the arctic circle.

But some are content not to receive it, only to taste it. This is what these persons did. They sipped the sweetness of Christ. They had a passing superficial glimpse into his heart. Like Gideon's soldiers, they caught up a few drops in their hands from the river of God, and hastened on their way. So we may have some pleasure in thoughts of Christ. His sufferings touch; his beauty attracts; his history moves and inspires. But it is only a taste; and yet we may fall away. They had also been made partakers of the Holy Ghost. It is not said that they had been converted, regenerated, or filled by the Holy Ghost. The expression is a very peculiar one, and it is used because the sacred writer could not affirm any of these things of them, and yet was anxious to show that they had been brought under his gracious influences. For instance, he had convinced them of sin, had striven with them, had plied them with warning and entreaty, with fear and hope. And they had so far yielded to him as to give up some of their sins and assume the outward guise of Christianity.

Moreover, they had tasted the good Word of God, and the powers of the world to come. The first of these is obviously the Scriptures; and the second is the usual expression for the age in which we live, and which, with all its spiritual forces, was beginning to thrill the hearts of men when these words were penned. They liked a good sermon; the Bible was full of interest and charm; they had heard the prophets, and seen the apostles of the Pentecostal age. All these had been analyzed, weighed, and counted; and yet they were in peril of going back. Let us, therefore, beware!

HEBREWS 7

17. Thou art a Priest forever after the order of Melchizedek.

Various fancies have gathered around the person of Melchizedek, investing him with extraordinary qualities; but it is better far to think of him simply as the head or chieftain of a large family or clan, which gathered around the site to be known, in after years, as the holy city." Already its name was shadowed forth in the term "Salem," which designated the clustered rude huts or tents. Amid the almost universal lawlessness and depravity which swept

King of Salem, which is, King of peace;

3 Without father, without mother, without descent, having neither beginning of days, nor end of life; but made like unto the Son of God; abideth a priest continually.

4 Now consider how great this man was, unto whom even the patriarch Abraham gave the tenth of the spoils.

5 And verily they that are of the sons of Levi, who receive the office of the priesthood, have a commandment to take tithes of the people according to the law, that is, of their brethren, though they come out of the loins of Abraham:

6 But he whose descent is not counted from them received tithes of Abraham, and blessed him that had the promises.

7 And without all contradiction the less is blessed of the better.

8 And here men that die receive tithes; but there he receiveth them, of whom it is witnessed that he liveth.

9 And as I may so say, Levi also, who receiveth tithes, payed tithes in Abraham.

10 For he was yet in the loins of his father, when Melchisedec met him.

11 If therefore perfection were by the Levitical priesthood, (for under it the people received the law,) what further need was there that another priest should rise after the order of Melchisedec, and not be called after the order of Aaron?

12 For the priesthood being changed, there is made of necessity a change also of the law.

13 For he of whom these things are spoken pertaineth to another tribe, of which no man gave attendance at the altar.

14 For it is evident that our Lord sprang out of Juda; of which tribe Moses spake nothing concerning priesthood.

15 And it is yet far more evident: for that after the similitude of Melchisedec there ariseth another priest,

16 Who is made, not after the law of a carnal commandment, but after the power of an endless life.

17 For he testifieth, Thou art a priest for ever after the order of Melchisedec.

18 For there is verily a disannulling of the commandment going before for the weakness and unprofitableness thereof.

19 For the law made nothing perfect,

wonder that he dwells so minutely on this subject. It was doubtless no common thing that in a country abounding in the corruptions of so many superstitions, a man was found who preserved the pure worship of God; for on one side he was nigh to Sodom and Gomorrah, and on the other to the Canaanites, so that he was on every side encompassed by ungodly men. Besides, the whole world was so fallen into impiety, that it is very probable that God was nowhere faithfully worshipped except in the family of Abraham; for his father and his grandfather, who ought to have retained true religion, had long before degenerated into idolatry. It was therefore a memorable fact, that there was still a king who not only retained true religion, but also performed himself the office of a priest. And it was doubtless necessary that in him who was to be a type of the Son of God all things excellent should be found: and that Christ was shadowed forth by this type is evident from the Psalm referred to; for David did not say without reason, "Thou art a priest forever after the order Melchisedec;" no, but on the contrary, by these words a sublime mystery was recommended to the Church.

Let us now consider each of those particulars in which the Apostle makes Christ like Melchisedec.

The first likeness is in the name; for it was not without a mystery that he was called **the King of righteousness**. For though this honor is ascribed to kings who rule with moderation and in equity, yet this belongs really to Christ alone, who not only exercises authority justly as others do, but also communicates to us the righteous of God, partly when he makes us to be counted righteous by a gratuitous reconciliation, and partly when he renews us by his Spirit, that we may lead a godly and holy life. He is then called the King of righteousness, because of what he effects in diffusing righteousness on all his people. It hence follows, that out of his kingdom nothing but sin reigns among men. And therefore Zechariah, when he introduces him, as by the solemn decree of God, into the possession of his kingdom, thus extols him – "Rejoice, O daughter of Sion, Behold thy righteous King cometh to thee" (Zechariah 2: 10); intimating that the righteousness, which is otherwise wanting to us, is brought to us by the coming of Christ.

The second likeness which the Apostle states is as to the kingdom of **peace**. This peace indeed is the fruit of that righteousness which he has mentioned. It hence follows that wherever Christ's kingdom extends, there peace ought to be, as we find in Isaiah 2 and 9, and in other places. But as peace among the Hebrews means also a prosperous and happy state, it may be so taken here: yet I prefer to understand it here of that inward peace which tranquilizes the conscience and renders it confident before God. And the excellency of this blessing cannot be sufficiently estimated,

over Palestine, righteousness and peace seem to have fled for shelter to this little community, where alone due reverence was given to the Most High God, possessor of heaven and earth.

How this oasis had come into existence amid the surrounding moral desert we cannot tell; but it may have been due to the commanding personal influence of the king, who, according to patriarchal custom, as father of the family, was not only the ruler of the family life, but leader in the family devotions; and thus, while Melchizedek was king of Salem, he was also priest of the Most High. Moreover, it would appear that he bore a special commission, and was raised up for a specific purpose, as the ordained messenger between God and men; and as embodying a striking portraiture of the priesthood to be exercised for man by the Son of God.

Note the significance of the words, made like unto the Son of God (3). Christ's eternal Priesthood was the archetypal reality, after the similitude of which that of Melchizedek was fashioned. It was as if the Father could not await the day of his Son's priestly entrance within the veil but must needs anticipate the marvels of his ministry by embodying its leading features in miniature. Let us now study some of them.

History gives its unanimous judgment against the temporal and the spiritual power being vested in the same man. In Israel the two offices were kept rigorously separate; and when, on one occasion, a king passed the sacred barrier, and, snatching up a censer, strode into the inner court, he was at once followed by the remonstrances of the priestly band, whilst the white brand of leprosy wrote his doom upon his brow; "and he himself hastened to go out, because the Lord had smitten him." But the simple monarch of whom we write, living before gathering abuses forbade the union, combined in his person the royal scepter and the sacerdotal censer. And herein he foreshadowed the Christ.

Jesus is King and Priest. He is King because he is a priest. He is highly exalted, demanding homage from every knee, and confession from every lip, because he became obedient to the death of the cross. He bases his royal claims, not on hereditary descent, though the blood of David flowed in his veins; not on conquest or superior force; not on the legislation that underpins the kingdom of heaven among men: but on this, that he redeemed us to God by his blood. He is the King of glory, because he is the Lamb of God which taketh away the sin of the world. The cross was the stepping-stone to his throne.

And he cannot fulfill his office as Priest unless he be first recognized as King. Many fail to derive all the blessing offered to men through the Priesthood of Christ, because they are not willing to admit his claims as King. They do not reverence and obey him. They do not open the whole of the inner realm to his scepter. They endeavor to serve two masters; and to stand well with empires as different as light and darkness, heaven and hell, God and Satan. There must be consecration before there can be perfect faith; coronation before deliverance; the King before the Priest.

The order is invariable first King of Righteousness, and after that also King of Peace (2). "Peace, give us peace!" is the importunate demand of men; peace at any price; by all means peace. But God, in the deep waters, lays the foundation of righteousness; "and the work of righteousness shall be peace, and the effect of righteousness quietness and assurance forever." It is of no use to heal the wound slightly, saying, "Peace, peace," when there is none. Infinitely better is it to probe to the bottom, and to build up from a sound and healthy foundation to the surface of the flesh. And the King of Peace will never enter your soul until you have first acknowledged him as King of Righteousness, submitting yourself to his righteous claims, and renouncing the righteousness which is of the law for that which is by faith.

It is lamentable to find how few Christians, comparatively, are realizing the full meaning or power of Christianity. Joyless, fruitless, powerless, they are a stumbling block to the world, and a mockery to devils. And is not the reason here? They are not right. They are harboring traitors and aliens in their souls. They constantly condemn themselves in things that they allow. No doubt they excuse themselves, and invent special reasons to palliate

but the bringing in of a better hope did; by the which we draw nigh unto God.

20 And inasmuch as not without an oath he was made priest:

21 (For those priests were made without an oath; but this with an oath by him that said unto him, The Lord sware and will not repent, Thou art a priest for ever after the order of Melchisedec:)

22 By so much was Jesus made a surety of a better testament.

23 And they truly were many priests, because they were not suffered to continue by reason of death:

24 But this man, because he continueth ever, hath an unchangeable priesthood.

25 Wherefore he is able also to save them to the uttermost that come unto God by him, seeing he ever liveth to make intercession for them.

26 For such an high priest became us, who is holy, harmless, undefiled, separate from sinners, and made higher than the heavens;

27 Who needeth not daily, as those high priests, to offer up sacrifice, first for his own sins, and then for the people's: for this he did once, when he offered up himself.

28 For the law maketh men high priests which have infirmity; but the word of the oath, which was since the law, maketh the Son, who is consecrated for evermore.

HEBREWS 8

1 Now of the things which we have spoken this is the sum: We have such an high priest, who is set on the right hand of the throne of the Majesty in the heavens;

2 A minister of the sanctuary, and of the true tabernacle, which the Lord pitched, and not man.

3 For every high priest is ordained to offer gifts and sacrifices: wherefore it is of necessity that this man have somewhat also to offer.

4 For if he were on earth, he should not be a priest, seeing that there are priests that offer gifts according to the law:

5 Who serve unto the example and shadow of heavenly things, as Moses was admonished of God when he was about

unless you consider on the other hand, how miserable a thing it is to be tormented by constant inquietude; which must necessarily be the case until we have our consciences pacified by being reconciled to God through Christ.

3. Without father, *etc*

I prefer this rendering to that of "unknown father"; for the Apostle meant to express something more emphatic than that the family of Melchisedec was obscure or unknown. Nor does this objection disturb me, that the reality does not correspond with the figure or type, because Christ has a Father in heaven, and had a mother on earth; for the Apostle immediately explains his meaning by adding *without descent*, or kindred. He then exempts Melchisedec from what is common to others, a descent by birth; by which he means that he is eternal, so that his beginning from men was not to be sought after. It is indeed certain that he descended from parents; but the Apostle does not speak of him here in his private capacity; on the contrary, he sets him forth as a type of Christ.

4. Now consider, *etc*

This is the fourth comparison between Christ and Melchisedec, that Abraham presented tithes to him. But though tithes were instituted for several reasons, yet the Apostle here refers only to what serves his present purpose. One reason why tithes were paid to the Levites was, because they were the children of Abraham, to whose seed the land was promised. It was, then, by a hereditary right that a portion of the land was allotted to them; for as they were not allowed to possess land, a compensation was made to them in tithes. There was also another reason – that as they were occupied in the service of God and the public ministry of the Church, it was right that they should be supported at the public cost of the people. Then the rest of the Israelites owed them tithes as a remuneration for their work. But these reasons bear not at all on the present subject; therefore, the Apostle passes them by. The only reason now alleged is, that as the people offered the tithes as a sacred tribute to God, the Levites only received them. It hence appears that it was no small honor that God in a manner substituted them for himself. Then Abraham, being one of the chief sergeants of God and a prophet, having offered tithes to Melchisedec the priest, thereby confessed that Melchisedec excelled him in dignity. If, then, the *patriarch* Abraham owned him more honourable than himself, his dignity must have been singular and extraordinary. The word *patriarch* is mentioned for the sake of setting forth his dignity; for it was in the highest degree honourable to him to have been called a father in the Church of God.

Then the argument is this – Abraham, who excelled all others, was yet inferior to Melchisedec; then Melchisedec

their faults, so that what would be inadmissible with others is pardonable in them. What special pleading! What ingenious arguments! What gymnastic feats are theirs! But all in vain. Let any such who read these lines learn that it is peremptory to make Christ King, and King of Righteousness, before ever they can appreciate the peace which accrues from his Priesthood on our behalf.

Christ's priesthood is continual, (3). The priests of Aaron's line were not suffered to continue by reason of death. But of him "it is witnessed that he liveth" (ver. 8). Hallelujah! a Priest has arisen "after the power of an endless life" (ver. 16). "The Lord sware and will not repent, Thou art a Priest forever" (ver. 21). "Because he abideth forever, his Priesthood is unchangeable" (ver. 24). "He ever liveth to make intercession" (ver. 25). "Consecrated forevermore" (ver. 28). What explicit and abundant testimony! Our High-Priest shall never ascend Mount Hor to be stripped of his robes of office and die. The secrets confided to him need never be told again to his successor. The tender love which links him and us shall never be snapped or cut in death. No one else will ever be called in to take his place in the superintendence of our souls.

This teaching rebukes two errors. The error of those who teach sinlessness in the flesh. It is impossible to exaggerate the mischief which is being wrought just now by some who take advantage of the universal yearning for a higher experience, and are holding out to credulous souls the prospect of reaching a position in which they will no longer need to confess sin, no longer require perpetual cleansing in the blood of Christ, no longer be sensible of their sinnership.

They who speak thus confound sin and sins. They apply the term infirmity to acts and dispositions which the Word of God calls by blacker, darker names. This teaching lowers a man's standard of sin to suit the erroneous doctrine which he has imbibed. It is contrary to the distinct teaching of Scripture that the flesh in the believer may yet lust for the upper hand. It is in Opposition to all deeper experience of the Christian life, which goes to show that, even when we know nothing against ourselves, yet are we not hereby justified; because

there may be many evils of which, for want of clearer light, we are completely ignorant, but which stand out patent enough to the eye of him who judges us, the Lord who searches the heart and reins.

The error of those who teach the perplexity if sacrificing priesthood. Of course all believers are priests, in the sense of offering the sacrifice of praise and prayer, the offerings of self-denying love. But there are many among us who persist in affirming that they are called, in addition, constantly to offer the perpetual sacrifice of Calvary, in the elements of the Lord's Supper. Amid the ceremonial of the mass, as offered in too many of our English churches by professed Protestants, claiming to be priests, it is hard to see any trace of the simple institution of the Lord's Supper. And it makes one tingle with righteous indignation to see the way in which these blind leaders of the blind are deceiving the multitudes to the ruin of their soul Sometimes one longs for the withering sarcasm of an Erasmus, the sturdy common sense of a Latimer, the vehemence of a Knox, to show up the unscriptural pretensions of these men, tricked out in the gaudy finery of pagan costumes, and going through mummeries which would provoke to laughter, if the whole system were not so inexpressibly sad. "How long, Lord, how long!"

HEBREWS 8

10. I will be to them a God, and they shall be to me a people.

A new word comes into this marvelous treatise which may repel some. It is the word Covenant. We all understand pretty clearly the covenants into which men enter with each other with respect to property, or other matters of daily business. One man undertakes to do certain things, on condition that another pledges himself to do certain other things. When these respective undertakings are settled, they are engrossed on parchment, signed, and sealed; and from that moment each party is honorably bound to perform his share in the transaction.

In some such way, adapting himself to our methods of thought and practice, the eternal God has entered into covenant with faithful

to make the tabernacle: for, See, saith he, that thou make all things according to the pattern shewed to thee in the mount.

6 But now hath he obtained a more excellent ministry, by how much also he is the mediator of a better covenant, which was established upon better promises.

7 For if that first covenant had been faultless, then should no place have been sought for the second.

8 For finding fault with them, he saith, Behold, the days come, saith the Lord, when I will make a new covenant with the house of Israel and with the house of Judah:

9 Not according to the covenant that I made with their fathers in the day when I took them by the hand to lead them out of the land of Egypt; because they continued not in my covenant, and I regarded them not, saith the Lord.

10 For this is the covenant that I will make with the house of Israel after those days, saith the Lord; I will put my laws into their mind, and write them in their hearts: and I will be to them a God, and they shall be to me a people:

11 And they shall not teach every man his neighbour, and every man his brother, saying, Know the Lord: for all shall know me, from the least to the greatest.

12 For I will be merciful to their unrighteousness, and their sins and their iniquities will I remember no more.

13 In that he saith, A new covenant, he hath made the first old. Now that which decayeth and waxeth old is ready to vanish away.

HEBREWS 9

1 Then verily the first covenant had also ordinances of divine service, and a worldly sanctuary.

2 For there was a tabernacle made; the first, wherein was the candlestick, and the table, and the shewbread; which is called the sanctuary.

3 And after the second veil, the tabernacle which is called the Holiest of all;

4 Which had the golden censer, and the ark of the covenant overlaid round about with gold, wherein was the golden pot that had manna, and Aaron's rod that budded, and the tables of the covenant;

had the highest place of honor, and is to be regarded as superior to all the sons of Levi. The first part is proved, for what Abraham owed to God he gave to Melchisedec: then by paying him the tenth he confessed himself to be inferior.

HEBREWS 8

7. For if that first, *etc*

He confirms what he had said of the excellency of the covenant which God has made with us through Christ; and he confirms it on this ground, because the covenant of the Law was neither valid nor permanent; for if nothing was wanting in it, why was another substituted for it? But another has been substituted; and from this it is evident that the old covenant was not in every respect perfect. To prove this he adduces the testimony of Jeremiah.

10. For this is the covenant that I will make, *etc*

There are two main parts in this covenant; the first regards the gratuitous remission of sins; and the other, the inward renovation of the heart; there is a third which depends on the second, and that is the illumination of the mind as to the knowledge of God. There are here many things most deserving of notice.

The first is, that God calls us to himself without effect as long as he speaks to us in no other way than by the voice of man. He indeed teaches us and commands what is right but he speaks to the deaf; for when we seem to hear anything, our ears are only struck by an empty sound; and the heart, full of depravity and perverseness, rejects every wholesome doctrine. In short, the word of God never penetrates into our hearts, for they are iron and stone until they are softened by him; nay, they have engraven on them a contrary law, for perverse passions rule within, which lead us to rebellion. In vain then does God proclaim his Law by the voice of man, unless he writes it by his Spirit on our hearts, that is, unless he forms and prepares us for obedience. It hence appears of what avail is freewill and the uprightness of nature before God regenerates us. We will indeed and choose freely; but our will is carried away by a sort of insane impulse to resist God. Thus it comes that the Law is ruinous and fatal to us as long as it remains written only on tables of stone, as Paul also teaches us (2 Corinthians 3: 3). In short, we then only obediently embrace what God commands, when by his Spirit he changes and corrects the natural pravity of our hearts; otherwise he finds nothing in us but corrupt affections and a heart wholly given up to evil. The declaration indeed is clear, that a new covenant is made according to which God engraves his laws on our hearts, for otherwise it would be in vain and of no effect.

The second particular refers to the gratuitous pardon

and obedient souls. Nor is it possible to overestimate the condescension on his part, or the honor and advantage placed within our reach, by such relationship. It seems too wonderful to be true; yet it must be true, for on no other grounds than its revealed truthfulness could it ever have become a matter of human statement or debate. The covenant between a prince and a beggar, or between a man like William Penn and the rude dark skins of America, is dwarfed into utter insignificance and paltriness when mentioned in the same day as the covenant between God and the soul of man.

Verse 6 speaks of a **better** covenant. It is so much better than that of Moses, in this way: while it pledges God to even better promises (ver. 6) than those of the earlier covenant, promises which for a moment demand our attention, there is no pledge or undertaking of any kind demanded from us. There are no ifs; no injunctions of observe to do; no conditions of obedience to be fulfilled. From first to last it consists of the wills of the Most High.

"I will write my laws into their minds." That refers to the intellectual faculty, which thinks, remembers, argues. It will be of inestimable value to have them there for constant reference; so that they shall always stand inscribed on the side posts and lintels of the inner life, demanding reverence, and compelling daily attention.

"I will write them upon their hearts." That is the seat of the emotional life and of the affections. If they are written there, they must engage our love. And what a man loves, he is pretty certain to follow and obey. "A little lower," said the dying veteran, as they probed for the bullet, which had sunk deep down into his breast, "and you will find the Emperor"; and in the case of the Christian who has been taken into covenant with God, the law is inscribed on the deepest affections of his being. He obeys because he loves to obey. He stays in his Master's service, not because he must, but because he chooses it for himself, saying, as his ear is bored to the door, "I love my Master, I will not go out free."

HEBREWS 9

Chapter 9 describes the heavenly things themselves.

2. For there was a tabernacle made.

The eye is quicker than the ear. And there is therefore no language so expressive as the language of symbols. The multitude will better catch your meaning by one apt symbol than by a thousand words. The mind shrinks from the intellectual effort of grappling with the subtle essences of things, and loves to have truth wrapped up in a form which can easily be taken in by the eye, the ear, the sense of touch.

Let us for a moment study those ancient symbols.

Choose an expanse of sand; mark out an oblong space forty-five feet long by fifteen feet broad. Lay all along upon your outlines a continuous belt of silver sockets, hollowed out so as to hold the ends of the planks that form the walls of the Tabernacle. Now fetch those boards themselves, beams of acacia wood fifteen feet high, covered with the choicest gold, and fastened together by three long bars of gold, running from end to end. The entrance doorway must face the east, composed of five golden pillars, over which fall the folds of a rich and heavy curtain. Then measure thirty feet from this, and let another curtain separate the holy from the most holy place. Now fetch more curtains to make the ceiling, and to hang down on either side over the gilded acacia beams that form the outer walls; first, a gorgeous curtain wrought with brilliant hues, and covered with the forms of cherubim; next, a veil of pure white linen; third, a strong curtain of rams' skins, dyed red; and, lastly, to defend it from the weather, a common and coarse covering of badgers' skins. The court is constituted by heavy curtains that hang around and veil the movements of the priests within.

Let us cast a brief glance at each item as we briefly pass from the outer to the inner shrine.

The bronze altar, with its projecting horns, to which animals designated for sacrifice were tied (Psalm 118: 27), or on which the fugitive laid hold for sanctuary and shelter (Ex. 21: 14),

5 And over it the cherubims of glory shadowing the mercyseat; of which we cannot now speak particularly.

6 Now when these things were thus ordained, the priests went always into the first tabernacle, accomplishing the service of God.

7 But into the second went the high priest alone once every year, not without blood, which he offered for himself, and for the errors of the people:

8 The Holy Ghost this signifying, that the way into the holiest of all was not yet made manifest, while as the first tabernacle was yet standing:

9 Which was a figure for the time then present, in which were offered both gifts and sacrifices, that could not make him that did the service perfect, as pertaining to the conscience;

10 Which stood only in meats and drinks, and divers washings, and carnal ordinances, imposed on them until the time of reformation.

11 But Christ being come an high priest of good things to come, by a greater and more perfect tabernacle, not made with hands, that is to say, not of this building;

12 Neither by the blood of goats and calves, but by his own blood he entered in once into the holy place, having obtained eternal redemption for us.

13 For if the blood of bulls and of goats, and the ashes of an heifer sprinkling the unclean, sanctifieth to the purifying of the flesh:

14 How much more shall the blood of Christ, who through the eternal Spirit offered himself without spot to God, purge your conscience from dead works to serve the living God?

15 And for this cause he is the mediator of the new testament, that by means of death, for the redemption of the transgressions that were under the first testament, they which are called might receive the promise of eternal inheritance.

16 For where a testament is, there must also of necessity be the death of the testator.

17 For a testament is of force after men are dead: otherwise it is of no strength at all while the testator liveth.

18 Whereupon neither the first testament was dedicated without blood.

of sins. Though they have sinned, saith the Lord, yet I will pardon them. This part is also most necessary; for God never so forms us for obedience to his righteousness, but that many corrupt affections of the flesh still remain; nay, it is only in part that the viciousness of our nature is corrected; so that evil lusts break out now and then. And hence is that contest of which Paul complains, when the godly do not obey God as they ought, but in various ways offend (Romans 7: 13). Whatever desire then there may be in us to live righteously, we are still guilty of eternal death before God, because our life is ever very far from the perfection which the Law requires. There would then be no stability in the covenant, except God gratuitously forgave our sins. But it is the peculiar privilege of the faithful who have once embraced the covenant offered to them in Christ, that they feel assured that God is propitious to them; nor is the sin to which they are liable, a hindrance to them, for they have the promise of pardon.

HEBREWS 9

1. Then verily the first, *etc*

After having spoken generally of the abrogation of the old covenant, he now refers specially to the ceremonies. His object is to show that there was nothing practiced then to which Christ's coming has not put an end. He says first, that under the old covenant there was a specific form of divine worship, and that it was peculiarly adapted to that time. It will hereafter appear by the comparison what kind of things were those rituals prescribed under the Law.

2. For there was a tabernacle, *etc*

As the Apostle here touches but lightly on the structure of the tabernacle, that he might not be detained beyond what his subject required; so will I also designedly abstain from any refined explanation of it. It is then sufficient for our present purpose to consider the tabernacle in its three parts – the first was the court of the people; the middle was commonly called the sanctuary; and the last was the inner sanctuary, which they called, by way of eminence, *the holy of holies*.

9. Which was a figure, *etc*

The word *parathol* , used here, signifies, as I think, the same thing with *antitupos*, antitype; for he means that that tabernacle was a second pattern which corresponded with the first. For the portrait of a man ought to be so like the man himself, that when seen, it ought immediately to remind us of him whom it represents. He says further, that it was a figure, or likeness, for the time then present, that is, as long as the external observance was in force; and he says this in order to confine its use and duration to the time of the Law;

stood in the outer court. There were offered the sin offering, the burnt offering, and the peace offering. It was deemed most holy (Ex. 29: 37.) And well it might be; for it was the symbol of the cross of Calvary, that wondrous cross where Jesus offered himself as a sacrifice for sin; himself both priest and victim and altar too.

None could enter the holy place, save by passing this sacred emblem, any more than we could ever have entered into fellowship with God, unless there had been wrought for us upon the cross that one all-sufficient sacrifice and oblation for sins, which purges our heart from an evil conscience. The longer we live, and the more we know of God, the more precious and indispensable does that cross appear: our hope in sorrow, our beacon in the dark, our shelter in the storm, our refuge in hours of conviction, our trysting-place with God, our pride and joy.

"Blest cross! blest sepulcher! blest rather be The Man that there was put to death for me."

And if the brazen altar speaks of the one sacrifice, once for all, of Calvary, the laver speaks of the daily washing of the stains of our wilderness journeyings, as Jesus washed the feet of his disciples (John 13).

The seven-branched candlestick, from which the light was shed which lit up the holy place, would first arrest the eye of the priest, who might cross the threshold for the first time. Its form is familiar to us from the bas-relief upon the Arch of Titus. How eloquently does it speak of Christ! The texture of beaten gold, on every part of which the hammer strokes had fallen, tells of his bruisings for us (Ex. 25: 36). The union of the six lesser lamps, with the one tall Center one, betokens the mystery of that union in light-giving which makes the Church one with her Lord forevermore in illuminating a dark world. The golden oil, stealing through the golden pipes that needed to be kept clean and unchoked, shows our dependence on him for supplies of the daily grace of the Holy Spirit (Zech. 4: 2). And the very snuffers, all of gold, used wisely by the high-priest to trim the flame, are significant of those processes by which our dear Lord is often obliged to cut · away the unevenness of the wick, and to cause

us a momentary dimming of light that we may afterward burn more clearly and steadily. His life is the light of men. In his light we see light. He sheds light on hearts and homes and mysteries and space; and hereafter the Lamb shall be the light of heaven.

The golden shewbread table must not be over looked, with its array of twelve loaves of fine flour, sprinkled with sweet smelling frankincense, and eaten only by the priests, when replaced on the seventh day by a fresh supply. Here again, as in the last symbol, is that mysterious blending of Christ and his people. Christ is the true bread of presence. He is the bread of God. Jehovah finds in his obedience and life and death perfect satisfaction; and we too feed on him. His flesh is meat indeed. We eat his flesh and live by him. The table was portable, so as to be carried in the journeyings of the people; and we can never thrive without taking him with us wherever we go. This is the heavenly manna; our daily bread; our priestly perquisite. But the people also were represented in those twelve loaves, as they were in the twelve stones of the breastplate. And doubtless there is a sense in which all believers still stand ever before God in the purity and sweetness of Christ; "for we, being many, are one bread and one body, for we are all partakers of that one bread." Oh, is it possible for me to give aught of satisfaction to God? To believe this would surely instill a new meaning into the most trivial acts of life. Yet this may be so.

The censer, or altar of incense, is classed with the most holy place; not because it stood inside the veil, but because it was so closely associated with the worship rendered there. It was as near as possible to the ark (Ex. 30: 6). It reminds us of the golden altar which was before the throne (Rev. 8: 3). No blood ever dimmed the luster of the gold; the ashes that glowed there were brought from the altar of burnt offering; and on them were sprinkled the incense, which had been compounded by very special art (Ex. 30: 34–38). That precious incense, which it was death to imitate, speaks of his much merit, in virtue of which our prayers and praises find acceptance. Is not this his perpetual work for us, standing in heaven as our great High Priest? ever living to make

19 For when Moses had spoken every precept to all the people according to the law, he took the blood of calves and of goats, with water, and scarlet wool, and hyssop, and sprinkled both the book, and all the people,

20 Saying, This is the blood of the testament which God hath enjoined unto you.

21 Moreover he sprinkled with blood both the tabernacle, and all the vessels of the ministry.

22 And almost all things are by the law purged with blood; and without shedding of blood is no remission.

23 It was therefore necessary that the patterns of things in the heavens should be purified with these; but the heavenly things themselves with better sacrifices than these.

24 For Christ is not entered into the holy places made with hands, which are the figures of the true; but into heaven itself, now to appear in the presence of God for us:

25 Nor yet that he should offer himself often, as the high priest entereth into the holy place every year with blood of others;

26 For then must he often have suffered since the foundation of the world: but now once in the end of the world hath he appeared to put away sin by the sacrifice of himself.

27 And as it is appointed unto men once to die, but after this the judgment:

28 So Christ was once offered to bear the sins of many; and unto them that look for him shall he appear the second time without sin unto salvation.

HEBREWS 10

1 For the law having a shadow of good things to come, and not the very image of the things, can never with those sacrifices which they offered year by year continually make the comers thereunto perfect.

2 For then would they not have ceased to be offered? because that the worshippers once purged should have had no more conscience of sins.

3 But in those sacrifices there is a remembrance again made of sins every year.

for it means the same with what he afterwards adds, that all the ceremonies were imposed until the time of reformation; nor is it any objection that he uses the present tense in saying, gifts are offered; for as he had to do with the Jews, he speaks by way of concession, as though he were one of those who sacrificed. Gifts and sacrifices differ, as the first is a general term, and the other is particular.

That could not make him that did the service perfect as pertaining to the conscience

That is, they did not reach the soul so as to confer true holiness. I do not reject the words, make perfect, and yet I prefer the term sanctify, as being more suitable to the context. But that readers may better understand the meaning of the Apostle, let the contrast between the flesh and the conscience be noticed; he denies that worshippers could be spiritually and inwardly cleansed by the sacrifices of the Law. It is added as a reason, that all these rites were of the flesh or carnal. What then does he allow them to be? It is commonly supposed, that they were useful only as means of training to men, conducive to virtue and decorum. But they who thus think do not sufficiently consider the promises which are added. This gloss, therefore, ought to be wholly repudiated. Absurdly and ignorantly too do they interpret the ordinances of the flesh, as being such as cleansed or sanctified only the body; for the Apostle understands by these words that they were earthly symbols, which did not reach the soul; for though they were true testimonies of perfect holiness, yet they by no means contained it in themselves, nor could they convey it to men; for the faithful were by such helps led, as it were, by the hand to Christ, that they might obtain from him what was wanting in the symbols.

HEBREWS 10

1. For the Law having a shadow, *etc*

He has borrowed this similitude from the pictorial art; for a shadow here is in a sense different from what it has in Colossians 2: 17; where he calls the ancient rites or ceremonies shadows, because they did not possess the real substance of what they represented. But he now says that they were like rude lineaments, which shadow forth the perfect picture; for painters, before they introduce the living colors by the pencil, are wont to mark out the outlines of what they intend to represent. This indistinct representation is called by the Greeks *skiagraphia*, which you might call in Latin, "*umbratilem*", shadowy. The Greeks had also the *eik n*, the full likeness. Hence also "*eiconia*" are called images (imagines) in Latin, which represent to the life the form of men or of animals or of places.

The difference then which the Apostle makes between

intercession, catching our poor prayers, and presenting them to his Father, fragrant with the savor of his own grace and loveliness and merit?

The veil, passed through only once a year by the high-priest, carrying blood, reminded the worshipers that the way into the holiest was not yet perfect. There were degrees of fellowship with God to which those rites could give no introduction. "The way into the holiest was not yet made manifest." "The veil, that is to say, his flesh" (Heb. 10: 20). Oh, fine twined linen, in thy purity, thou wert never so pure as that body which was conceived without sin! Oh, exquisite work of curious imagery, thou canst not vie with the marvelous mysteries that gather in that human form! Yet, till Jesus died, there was a barrier, an obstacle, a veil. It was bespattered with blood, but it was a veil still. But at the hour when he breathed out his soul in death, the veil was rent by mighty unseen hands from top to bottom, disclosing all the sacred mysteries beyond to the unaccustomed eyes of any priests who at that moment may have been burning incense at the hour of prayer, while the whole multitude stood without (Luke 1: 9). It is a rent veil now, and the way into the holiest lies open. It is new and living and blood-marked; we may therefore tread it without fear or mistake, and pass in with holy boldness to stand where angels veil their faces with their wings in ceaseless adoration (10: 19–20).

The ark was a box, oblong in shape, 4 ft. 6 in. in length, by 2 ft. 8 in. in breadth and height; made of acacia wood, overlaid with gold; its lid, a golden slab, called the mercy-seat, on which cherubic forms stood or knelt, with eyes fixed on the blood stained golden slab between them; for it was on the mercy-seat that the blood was copiously sprinkled year by year, and there the Shekinah light ever shone. In the wilderness wanderings the ark contained the tables of stone, not broken but whole, the manna, and the rod. But when it came to rest, and the staves were drawn out, the manna, food for pilgrims, and the rod, which symbolized the power of life, were gone; only the law remained.

22. Without shedding of blood is no remission.

Round and round this ancient window into the past (vv. 15–28) is bound the red cord of blood. Twelve times at the very least does this solemn, this awful, word occur. The devil himself seems to admit that it is invested with some mystic potency; else why should he compel so many of his miserable followers to interlard each phrase they utter by some reference to it? Man cannot look on or speak of blood without an involuntary solemnity; unless, indeed, he has done despite to some of the deepest instincts of his being, or through familiarity has learned con-tempt. And we feel whilst reading this chapter, as if we have come into the very heart of the deepest of all mysteries, the most solemn of all solemnities, the most awful of all tragedies or martyrdoms or sacrificial rites. Take off the shoes from your feet; for the place on which we stand together now is holy ground.

Why, then, should we hesitate to speak of the blood of Christ? It was royal blood. "His own" (ver. 12); and he was a King indeed. It was voluntarily shed: " He offered himself" (ver. 14). It was pure "innocent blood," "without spot" (ver. 14). It was sacrificial. He died not as a martyr, but as a Savior (ver. 26). It flowed from his head, thorn-girt, that it might atone for sins of thought; from his hands and feet, fast nailed, that it might expiate sins of deed and walk; from his side, that it might wipe out the sins of our affections, as well as tell us of his deep and fervent love, which could not be confined within the four chambers of his heart, but must find vent in falling on the earth. Why should we be ashamed of the blood of Christ? No other phrase will so readily or sufficiently gather up all the complex thoughts which mingle in the death of Christ. Life; life shed; life shed violently; life shed violently, and as a sacrifice; life passing forth by violence, and sacrificially, to become a tide of which we must also all stoop down and drink, if we desire to have life in ourselves (John 6: 53–56).

HEBREWS 10

38. The just shall live by faith; but if any man draw back, my soul shall have no pleasure in him.

The Epistle has been for some time glowing with ever-increasing heat; and now it flames

4 For it is not possible that the blood of bulls and of goats should take away sins.

5 Wherefore when he cometh into the world, he saith, Sacrifice and offering thou wouldest not, but a body hast thou prepared me:

6 In burnt offerings and sacrifices for sin thou hast had no pleasure.

7 Then said I, Lo, I come (in the volume of the book it is written of me,) to do thy will, O God.

8 Above when he said, Sacrifice and offering and burnt offerings and offering for sin thou wouldest not, neither hadst pleasure therein; which are offered by the law;

9 Then said he, Lo, I come to do thy will, O God. He taketh away the first, that he may establish the second.

10 By the which will we are sanctified through the offering of the body of Jesus Christ once for all.

11 And every priest standeth daily ministering and offering oftentimes the same sacrifices, which can never take away sins:

12 But this man, after he had offered one sacrifice for sins for ever, sat down on the right hand of God;

13 From henceforth expecting till his enemies be made his footstool.

14 For by one offering he hath perfected for ever them that are sanctified.

15 Whereof the Holy Ghost also is a witness to us: for after that he had said before,

16 This is the covenant that I will make with them after those days, saith the Lord, I will put my laws into their hearts, and in their minds will I write them;

17 And their sins and iniquities will I remember no more.

18 Now where remission of these is, there is no more offering for sin.

19 Having therefore, brethren, boldness to enter into the holiest by the blood of Jesus,

20 By a new and living way, which he hath consecrated for us, through the veil, that is to say, his flesh;

21 And having an high priest over the house of God;

22 Let us draw near with a true heart in full assurance of faith, having our hearts sprinkled from an evil conscience,

the Law and the Gospel is this – that under the Law was shadowed forth only in rude and imperfect lines what is under the Gospel set forth in living colors and graphically distinct. He thus confirms again what he had previously said, that the Law was not useless, nor its ceremonies unprofitable. For though there was not in them the image of heavenly things, finished, as they say, by the last touch of the artist; yet the representation, such as it was, was of no small benefit to the fathers; but still our condition is much more favorable. We must however observe, that the things which were shown to them at a distance are the same with those which are now set before our eyes. Hence to both the same Christ is exhibited, the same righteousness, sanctification, and salvation; and the difference only is in the manner of painting or setting them forth.

Of good things to come, *etc*

These, I think, are eternal things. I indeed allow that the kingdom of Christ, which is now present with us, was formerly announced as future; but the Apostle's words mean that we have a lively image of future blessings. He then understands that spiritual pattern, the full fruition of which is deferred to the resurrection and the future world. At the same time I confess again that these good things began to be revealed at the beginning of the kingdom of Christ; but what he now treats of is this, that they are not only future blessings as to the Old Testament, but also with respect to us, who still hope for them.

Which they offered year by year, *etc*

He speaks especially of the yearly sacrifice, mentioned in Leviticus 16, though all the sacrifices are here included under one kind. Now he reasons thus: When there is no longer any consciousness of sin, there is then no need of sacrifice; but under the Law the offering of the same sacrifice was often repeated; then no satisfaction was given to God, nor was guilt removed nor were consciences appeased; were it otherwise there would have been made an end of sacrificing. We must further carefully observe, that he calls those the same sacrifices which were appointed for a similar purpose; for a better notion may be formed of them by the design for which God instituted them, than by the different beasts which were offered.

And this one thing is abundantly sufficient to confute and expose the subtlety of the Papists, by which they seem to themselves ingeniously to evade an absurdity in defending the sacrifice of the mass; for when it is objected to them that the repetition of the sacrifice is superfluous, since the virtue of that sacrifice which Christ offered is perpetual, they immediately reply that the sacrifice in the mass is not different but the same. This is their answer. But what, on the contrary, does the Apostle say? He expressly denies that the sacrifice which is repeatedly offered, though the same,

out into a vehement expostulation, which must have startled and terrified those Hebrew Christians who were still wavering between Judaism and Christianity. As we have had more than one occasion to remark, it had become a great question with some of them whether they should go back to the one, or go on with the other. The splendid ceremonial, venerable age, and olden associations of Judaism, were fighting hard to wean them away from the simplicity and spiritual demands of the later faith. But surely the retrograde movement would be arrested, and the impetus toward Christ accelerated, by these sublime and soul-stirring remonstrances.

We may boldly enter the holiest by the blood of Jesus. The holiest was the chamber of innermost communion with God. To enter it was to speak with God face to face. And its equivalent for us is the right to make our God our confidant and friend, into whose secret ear we may pour the whole story of sin and sorrow and need. Nor need the memory of recent sin distress us; because the blood of Jesus is the pledge of the forgiveness and acceptance of those who are penitent and believing. We may go continually, and even dwell, where Israel's high priests might tread but once each year.

Jesus has inaugurated a new and living way. The veil of the Temple was rent when Jesus died, to indicate that the way to God was henceforth free to man, without let or hindrance, and without the intervention of a human priest. Priests have tried to block it, and to compel men to pay them toll for Opening it. But their pretensions are false. They have no such power. The way stands open still for every trembling seeker. It is new, because, though myriads have trodden it, it is as fresh as ever for each new priestly foot. It is living, because it is through the living Savior that we come to God. "No man cometh unto the Father but by me." Stay here to note that the veil, with its curious workmanship, was a symbol of the body of Christ. "The veil, that is to say, his flesh." We get near to God through the death of that Son of man who, in real human sorrow, hung on the cross for us.

We have a Great priest. We belong to the household of God by faith; but we need a Priest. Priests need a Priest. And such a one

we have, who ever liveth to make intercession for us, and to offer our prayers on the golden altar, mingled with the much incense of his own precious merit. These are the three conclusions which recapitulate the positions laid down and proved up to this point.

There is a threefold exhortation founded on the previous conclusions.

"Let us draw near" (ver. 22).

"Let us hold fast" (ver. 23).

"Let us consider one an-other" (ver. 24). And each of these three exhortations revolves around one of the three words which are so often found in combination in the Epistles- Faith, Hope, and Love.

Faith consists of two parts belief, which accepts certain declarations as true; and trust in the person about whom these declarations are made. Neither will do without the other. On the one hand, we cannot trust a person without knowing something about him; on the other hand, our knowledge will not help us unless it leads to trust, any more than it avails the shivering wretch outside the Bank of England to know that the vaults are stored with gold. A mere intellectual faith is not enough. The holding of a creed will not save. We must pass from a belief in words to trust in the Word. By faith we know that Jesus lives, and by faith we also appropriate that life. By faith we know that Jesus made on the cross a propitiation for sin; and by faith we lay our hand reverently on his dear head and confess our sin. Faith is the open hand receiving Christ. Faith is the golden pipe through which his fullness comes to us. Faith is the narrow channel by which the life that pulses in the Redeemer's heart enters our souls. Faith is the attitude we assume when we turn aside from the human to the divine.

Hope is more than faith, and has special reference to the unknown future which it realizes, and brings to bear on our daily life. The veil that hides the future parts only as smitten by the prow of our advancing boat; it is natural, therefore, that we should often ask what lies beyond.

Foreboding is the prophet of ill; Hope of good. Foreboding cries, "We shall certainly fall by the hand of; Hope replies, "No weapon that is formed against us shall prosper." Foreboding cries, "Who shall roll away the stone? " Hope

and our bodies washed with pure water.

23 Let us hold fast the profession of our faith without wavering; (for he is faithful that promised;)

24 And let us consider one another to provoke unto love and to good works:

25 Not forsaking the assembling of ourselves together, as the manner of some is; but exhorting one another: and so much the more, as ye see the day approaching.

26 For if we sin wilfully after that we have received the knowledge of the truth, there remaineth no more sacrifice for sins,

27 But a certain fearful looking for of judgment and fiery indignation, which shall devour the adversaries.

28 He that despised Moses' law died without mercy under two or three witnesses:

29 Of how much sorer punishment, suppose ye, shall he be thought worthy, who hath trodden under foot the Son of God, and hath counted the blood of the covenant, wherewith he was sanctified, an unholy thing, and hath done despite unto the Spirit of grace?

30 For we know him that hath said, Vengeance belongeth unto me, I will recompense, saith the Lord. And again, The Lord shall judge his people.

31 It is a fearful thing to fall into the hands of the living God.

32 But call to remembrance the former days, in which, after ye were illuminated, ye endured a great fight of afflictions;

33 Partly, whilst ye were made a gazingstock both by reproaches and afflictions; and partly, whilst ye became companions of them that were so used.

34 For ye had compassion of me in my bonds, and took joyfully the spoiling of your goods, knowing in yourselves that ye have in heaven a better and an enduring substance.

35 Cast not away therefore your confidence, which hath great recompence of reward.

36 For ye have need of patience, that, after ye have done the will of God, ye might receive the promise.

37 For yet a little while, and he that shall come will come, and will not tarry.

38 Now the just shall live by faith: but

is efficacious or capable of making an atonement. Now, though the Papists should cry out a thousand times that the sacrifice which Christ once offered is the same with, and not different from what they make daily, I shall still always contend, according to the express words of the Apostle, that since the offerings of Christ availed to pacify God, not only an end was put to former sacrifices, but that it is also impious to repeat the sacrifice. It is hence quite evident that the offering of Christ in the mass is sacrilegious.

4. For it is not possible, *etc*

He confirms the former sentiment with the same reason which he had adduced before, that the blood of beasts could not cleanse souls from sin. The Jews, indeed, had in this a symbol and a pledge of the real cleansing; but it was with reference to another, even as the blood of the calf represented the blood of Christ. But the Apostle is speaking here of the efficacy of the blood of beasts in itself. He therefore justly takes away from it the power of cleansing. There is also to be understood a contrast which is not expressed, as though he had said, "It is no wonder that the ancient sacrifices were insufficient, so that they were to be offered continually, for they had nothing in them but the blood of beasts, which could not reach the conscience; but far otherwise is the power of Christ's blood: It is not then right to measure the offering which he has made by the former sacrifices."

21. And having a high priest, *etc*

Whatever he has previously said of the abrogation of the ancient priesthood, it behaves us now to bear in mind, for Christ could not be a priest without having the former priests divested of their office, as it was another order. He then intimates that all those things which Christ had changed at his coming ought to be relinquished; and God has set him over his whole house for this end – that every one who seeks a place in the Church, may submit to Christ and choose him, and no other, as his leader and ruler.

22. Let us draw near with a true heart, *etc*

As he shows that in Christ and his sacrifice there is nothing but what is spiritual or heavenly, so he would have what we bring on our part to correspond. The Jews formerly cleansed themselves by various washings to prepare themselves for the service of God. It is no wonder that the rites for cleansing were carnal, since the worship of God itself, involved in shadows, as yet partook in a manner of what was carnal. For the priest, being a mortal, was chosen from among sinners to perform for a time sacred things; he was, indeed, adorned with precious vestments, but yet they were those of this world, that he might stand in the presence of God; he only came near the work of the covenant;

sings merrily, "The Lord shall go before us, and make the crooked places straight." Foreboding, born of unbelief, cries, "The people are great and tall, and the cities walled up to heaven"; Hope already portions out the land and chooses its inheritance. But Christian hope is infinitely better and more reliable than that of the worldling. In ordinary hope there is always the element of uncertainty; it may be doomed to disillusion and disappointment; things may not turn out as we expect: and so, being the characteristic of youth, it dies down as the years advance. But Christian hope is based on the promise of God, and therefore it cannot disappoint; nay, it is the anchor of the aged soul, becoming brighter and more enduring as the years pass by, because "he is faithful that promised."

Love comes last. She is queen of all the graces of the inner life. Love is the passion of self-giving. It never stays to ask what it can afford, or what it may expect to receive; but it is ever shedding forth its perfume, breaking its alabaster boxes, and shedding its heart's blood. It will pine to death if it cannot give. It must share its possessions. It is prodigal of costliest service. Such love is in the heart of God, and should also be in us; and we may increase it materially by considering one another, and associating with our fellow-believers. Distance begets coldness and indifference. When we forsake the assembly of our fellow- Christians we are apt to wrap ourselves in the chill mantle of indifference. But when we see others in need, and help them; when we are willing to succor and save; when we discover that there is something attractive in the least lovable; when we feel the glowing sympathy of others-our own love grows by the demands made on it, and by the opportunities of manifestation.

Let us seek earnestly these best gifts; and that we may have them and abound, let us invoke the blessed indwelling of the Lord Jesus, whose entrance brings with it the whole train of sweet Christian graces.

In chapter 10 there is a threefold remonstrance. Go forward, or else you will suffer dreadful consequences (ver. 26). If a man unwittingly broke Moses' law, he was forgiven; but if he willfully despised it, he died without

mercy. What then can be expected by those who sin willfully, not against the iron obligations of Sinai, but against the gracious words which distill from the lips of the dying Savior! The heart that can turn from the love and blood-shedding of Calvary, and ignore them, and trample them ruthlessly under foot, is so hard, so hopeless, so defiant of the Holy Spirit as to expose itself to the gravest displeasure of God, and can expect no further offering for its sins. There is no sacrifice for the atonement of the sin of rejecting Calvary.

Secondly, go forward, otherwise past efforts will be nullified (ver. 32). These Hebrew Christians had suffered keenly on their first entrance into the Christian life. The martyrdom of the saintly Stephen; the great havoc wrought in the Church by Saul of Tarsus; the terrible famines that visited Jerusalem, causing widespread destitution. They had become even a gazing-stock by reproaches and afflictions. But they had taken joyfully the spoiling of their goods, not shrinking from the ordeal. To go back to Judaism now would annul the advantages which otherwise might have accrued from their bitter experience; would miss the harvest of their tears; would counterwork the respect with which they were being regarded; and would rob them of the reward which the Lord might give to them, if they only endured to the end. "Cast not away your boldness, which hath great recompense of reward."

Thirdly, go forward, for the Lord is at hand (ver. 36). Jesus was about to come in the fall of Jerusalem, as lie will come ere long to close the present age; and every sign pointed to the speedy destruction of the Jewish polity by the all-conquering might of Rome. How foolish then would it be to return to that which was on the eve of dissolution: to the Temple that would burn to the ground; to sacrifices soon to cease; to a priesthood to be speedily scattered to the winds!

There was only one alternative: not to go back to certain perdition, to the ruin of all the nobler attributes of the soul, to disgrace and disappointment and endless regret; but to go on through evil and good report, through sorrow and anxiety and blood, until the faithful servant should be vindicated by the Lord's

if any man draw back, my soul shall have no pleasure in him.

39 But we are not of them who draw back unto perdition; but of them that believe to the saving of the soul.

HEBREWS 11

1 Now faith is the substance of things hoped for, the evidence of things not seen.

2 For by it the elders obtained a good report.

3 Through faith we understand that the worlds were framed by the word of God, so that things which are seen were not made of things which do appear.

4 By faith Abel offered unto God a more excellent sacrifice than Cain, by which he obtained witness that he was righteous, God testifying of his gifts: and by it he being dead yet speaketh.

5 By faith Enoch was translated that he should not see death; and was not found, because God had translated him: for before his translation he had this testimony, that he pleased God.

6 But without faith it is impossible to please him: for he that cometh to God must believe that he is, and that he is a rewarder of them that diligently seek him.

7 By faith Noah, being warned of God of things not seen as yet, moved with fear, prepared an ark to the saving of his house; by the which he condemned the world, and became heir of the righteousness which is by faith.

8 By faith Abraham, when he was called to go out into a place which he should after receive for an inheritance, obeyed; and he went out, not knowing whither he went.

9 By faith he sojourned in the land of promise, as in a strange country, dwelling in tabernacles with Isaac and Jacob, the heirs with him of the same promise:

10 For he looked for a city which hath foundations, whose builder and maker is God.

11 Through faith also Sara herself received strength to conceive seed, and was delivered of a child when she was past age, because she judged him faithful who had promised.

and to sanctify his entrance, he borrowed for a sacrifice a brute animal either from herd or the flock. But in Christ all these things are far superior; He himself is not only pure and innocent, but is also the fountain of all holiness and righteousness, and was constituted a priest by a heavenly oracle, not for the short period of a mortal life, but perpetually. To sanction his appointment an oath was interposed. He came forth adorned with all the gifts of the Holy Spirit in the highest perfection; he propitiated God by his own blood, and reconciled him to men; he ascended up above all the heavens to appear before God as our Mediator.

HEBREWS 11

1. Now faith, *etc*

Whoever made this the beginning of the eleventh chapter, has unwisely disjointed the context; for the object of the Apostle was to prove what he had already said that there is need of patience. He had quoted the testimony of Habakkuk, who says that the just lives by faith; he now shows what remained to be proved – that faith can be no more separated from patience than from itself. The order then of what he says is this – "We shall not reach the goal of salvation except we have patience, for the Prophet declares that the just lives by faith; but faith directs us to things afar off which we do not as yet enjoy; it then necessarily includes patience." Therefore the minor proposition in the argument is this, *Faith is the substance of things hoped for*, etc. It is hence also evident, that greatly mistaken are they who think that an exact definition of faith is given here; for the Apostle does not speak here of the whole of what faith is, but selects that part of it which was suitable to his purpose, even that it has patience ever connected with it.Let us now consider the words.

He calls faith the **hypostasis**, the substance of things hoped for. We indeed know that what we hope for is not what we have as it were in hand, but what is as yet hid from us, or at least the enjoyment of which is delayed to another time. The Apostle now teaches us the same thing with what we find in Romans 8: 24; where it is said that what is hoped for is not seen, and hence the inference is drawn, that it is to be waited for in patience. So the Apostle here reminds us, that faith regards not present things, but such as are waited for. Nor is this kind of contradiction without its force and beauty: Faith, he says, is the hypostasis, the prop, or the foundation on which we plant our foot – the prop of what? Of things absent, which are so far from being really possessed by us, that they are far beyond the reach of our understanding.

The same view is to be taken of the second clause, when he calls faith the **evidence** or demonstration of things **not**

approval, and welcomed into the realms of endless blessedness.

Are we amongst those who go on to the saving of the soul? Here, as so often, the salvation of the soul is viewed as a process. True, we are in a sense saved when first we turn to the cross and trust the Crucified. But it is only as we keep in the current that streams from the cross, only as we remain in abiding fellowship with the Savior, only as we submit ourselves habitually to the gracious influences of the divine Spirit, that salvation pervades and heals our whole being. Then the soul may be said to be restored to its original type as conceived in the mind of God before he built the dust of the earth into man, and breathed into him the breath of life, and he became a living soul.

HEBREWS 11

Chapter 11 is devoted to faith and its exploits.

1. Now faith is the substance of things hoped for, the evidence of things not seen.

Society rests on the faith which man has in man. The workman, toiling through the week for the wage which he believes he will receive; the passenger, procuring a ticket for a distant town, because he believes the statements of the time-tables; the sailor, steering his bark with unerring accuracy in murky weather, because he believes in the mercantile charts and tables; the entire system of monetary credit, by which vast sums circulate from hand to hand without the use of a single coin-all these are illustrations of the immense importance of faith in the affairs of men. Nothing, therefore, is more disastrous for an individual or a community than for its credit to be impaired, or its confidence shaken.

There seem to be three necessary preliminaries in order to faith. First, some one must make an engagement or promise. Second, there must be good reason for believing in the integrity and sufficiency of the person by whom the engagement has been made. Third, there follows a comfortable assurance that it will be even so; in fact, the believer is able to count on the object promised as being not less sure than if it had already come into actual possession. And this latter frame of mind is precisely the one indicated by the writer of this Epistle, when, guided by the Holy Spirit, he affirms that faith is the assurance of things hoped for, the persuasion or conviction of things not seen. In other words, faith is the faculty of realizing the unseen.

These three conditions are fulfilled in Christian faith. The same faculty is called into action with respect to the things of God. At the outset we are sure that a Voice has spoken to man from the page of Scripture; not voices, but a Voice. Next, we are sure that this Speaker is infinitely credible. Our assurance rests on several grounds: we find that his words have ever come true in the experience of past generations; we have seen them accompanied by the introduction of miraculous phenomena, indicating in their beneficence and power the goodness and glory of the Worker; we discover in our own hearts the assent of our moral nature to their evident truth: and for all these reasons we hold that the Voice which speaks deserves our credence. And therefore, lastly, we calculate on whatever has been promised as surely as if we saw it, and may reckon on it as certainly ours.

Let us emphasize again what has been said. We look on the words which God speaks to us from the Scriptures as being altogether different from any other words which may claim our attention from the lips of men; not only because of the character of the miracles which accompany them, but because they touch us as no other words do, and elicit the spontaneous assent and consent of our moral nature, though sometimes in condemnation of ourselves. That must be the Book of God which so exactly coincides with the best emotions and intuitions of our moral nature; and not of ours only, but of the noblest and best of our race.

"The mighty God, the Lord hath spoken, and called the earth from the rising of the sun to the going down of the same." And if we are once assured of this, then there is no limit to the restful confidence, which not only counts the promise as credible, but actually begins to enjoy in anticipation the boons they offer. The maxim of human experience runs thus: Seeing is believing; but with the child of God the reverse is true: Believing is seeing. We are as

12 Therefore sprang there even of one, and him as good as dead, so many as the stars of the sky in multitude, and as the sand which is by the sea shore innumerable.

13 These all died in faith, not having received the promises, but having seen them afar off, and were persuaded of them, and embraced them, and confessed that they were strangers and pilgrims on the earth.

14 For they that say such things declare plainly that they seek a country.

15 And truly, if they had been mindful of that country from whence they came out, they might have had opportunity to have returned.

16 But now they desire a better country, that is, an heavenly: wherefore God is not ashamed to be called their God: for he hath prepared for them a city.

17 By faith Abraham, when he was tried, offered up Isaac: and he that had received the promises offered up his only begotten son,

18 Of whom it was said, That in Isaac shall thy seed be called:

19 Accounting that God was able to raise him up, even from the dead; from whence also he received him in a figure.

20 By faith Isaac blessed Jacob and Esau concerning things to come.

21 By faith Jacob, when he was a dying, blessed both the sons of Joseph; and worshipped, leaning upon the top of his staff.

22 By faith Joseph, when he died, made mention of the departing of the children of Israel; and gave commandment concerning his bones.

23 By faith Moses, when he was born, was hid three months of his parents, because they saw he was a proper child; and they were not afraid of the king's commandment.

24 By faith Moses, when he was come to years, refused to be called the son of Pharaoh's daughter;

25 Choosing rather to suffer affliction with the people of God, than to enjoy the pleasures of sin for a season;

26 Esteeming the reproach of Christ greater riches than the treasures in Egypt: for he had respect unto the recompence of the reward.

seen; for demonstration makes things to appear or to be seen; and it is commonly applied to what is subject to our senses.

Then these two things, though apparently inconsistent, do yet perfectly harmonize when we speak of faith; for the Spirit of God shows to us hidden things, the knowledge of which cannot reach our senses: Promised to us is eternal life, but it is promised to the dead; we are assured of a happy resurrection, but we are as yet involved in corruption; we are pronounced just, as yet sin dwells in us; we hear that we are happy, but we are as yet in the midst of many miseries; an abundance of all good things is promised to us, but still we often hunger and thirst; God proclaims that he will come quickly, but he seems deaf when we cry to him. What would become of us were we not supported by hope, and did not our minds emerge out of the midst of darkness above the world through the light of God's word and of his Spirit? Faith, then, is rightly said to be the subsistence or substance of things which are as yet the objects of hope and the evidence of things not seen. **Augustine** sometimes renders evidence "conviction," which I do not disapprove, for it faithfully expresses the Apostle's meaning: but I prefer "demonstration," as it is more literal.

2. For by it the elders, *etc*

He handles this subject to the end of the chapter – that the fathers obtained salvation and were accepted by God in no other way than by faith.

The Jews indeed had some reasons for paying great deference to the fathers; but a foolish admiration of the fathers had so prevailed among them, that it proved a great hindrance to a thorough surrender of themselves to Christ and to his government. It was occasioned either by ambition or superstition, or by both. For when they heard that they were the blessed and holy seed of Abraham, inflated with this distinction they fixed their eyes on men rather than on God. Then added to this was a false emulation; for they did not consider what was mainly worthy of imitation in their fathers. It thus happened that they became attached to the old ceremonies, as though the whole of religion and perfect holiness consisted in them. This error the Apostle exposes and condemns; and be shows what was the chief excellency of the fathers, in order that their posterity might understand how they might become really like them.

Let us then bear in mind that the main point and the very hinge on which the Apostle's argument turns is this – That all the fathers from the beginning of the world, were approved by God in no other way than by being united to him by faith: and this he shows, that the Jews might know that by faith alone they could be bound together in holy unity with the fathers, and that as soon as they renounced

sure of what God had promised as we would be if we saw it already before our eyes. Our vision could not make us more sure than we are that God loves us; that there is a Father's house with its many mansions; and that some day our mortality is to put on immortality, so as to live forever in a state of existence which is absolutely sinless, sorrowless, and nightless.

Such faith as this is begotten in our souls, primarily by the study of God's Word; appealing, as we have seen, to our moral consciousness, which, as it is more and more developed, is more and more satisfied with the Book which called it into being, and has done so much for its education. But sometimes faith seems to be given us in respect of some special matter which is not directly indicated in Scripture, but which we feel able to claim, yes, and as we pray and think over it we are still more able to claim it; and when we find such a conviction forming in our hearts, we may be perfectly sure of it. "Whosoever shall say to this mountain, Be thou removed, and be thou cast into the sea; and shall not doubt in his heart, but believe that those things which he saith shall come to pass, he shall have whatsoever he saith." Thus the child of God may begin to praise for blessings of which there is no outward sign; being as sure of them as though they had risen above the horizon, like the little cloud, no bigger than a man's hand, to Elijah's prayer. "We have the petitions that we desired of him."

Do you want a greater faith? then consider the promises, which are its native food! Read the story of God's mighty acts in bygone days. Open your heart to God, that he may shine in with his own revealing presence. Ask him to give you this wondrous faculty to which nothing is impossible. Put away from you aught which might clash with the growth of your heart in faith and love.

Run through this roll-call of heroes. You must admit that those whose names are mentioned stand in the first ranks of our race, shining as stars. But their claim to be thus regarded was certainly not natural genius. Enoch, for instance, and his line, being Sethites, may have been inferior to many of the family of Cain, so far as mere intellectual or artistic attainment went. But his faith lifted him out of the ranks of mediocrity to a species of primacy amongst men; and should faith become the master-principle of your life and mine, it would similarly enlarge and enrich our whole being.

Faith mightily affects our ordinary human life. With most men you can determine pretty nearly how they will act in given circumstances; you can enumerate the influences at work, and their value. But you can never be sure in the case of the Christian, because his faith is making real much of which the world around takes no thought whatever. The tyrant, anxious to save some young Christian confessor, approaches him with flatteries and promises, things that attract the young, and is surprised to find that they have no charm; he then approaches with suffering, obloquy, and death, things that sadden young hearts, and is equally astonished to discover that they cause no alarm. The cause is inexplicable, and is set down to obstinacy; but in point of fact the eyes of the young heart are opened on a world of which the tyrant has formed no conception. Faith is not careless of time, but more mindful of eternity. Faith does not underrate the power of man, but she magnifies omnipotence. Faith is not callous of present pain, but she weighs it against future joy. Against ill-gotten gains, she puts eternal treasure; against human hate the recompense of reward; against the weariness of the course, the crown of amaranth; against the tears of winter sowing, the shoutings of the autumn sheaves; against the inconvenience of the tent, the permanent city. None of these men would have lived the noble lives they did, had it not been for the recompense of reward and the gleams given them of the golden city amid the sorrows and straits of their lives.

Faith is possible for kinds of people. In this list are women as well as men. Sarah and Rahab, as well as Abraham and Joshua; the widow of Shunem, and the mighty prophet who brought her son back to life; Moses, the student of Egypt's wisdom; Gideon, the husbandman; Isaac, the grazier; Jacob, the shrewd cattle breeder; Barak, the soldier; David, the shepherd; and Samuel, the prophet. Their Occupations and circumstances varied infinitely; but there was not one of them that

27 By faith he forsook Egypt, not fearing the wrath of the king: for he endured, as seeing him who is invisible.

28 Through faith he kept the passover, and the sprinkling of blood, lest he that destroyed the firstborn should touch them.

29 By faith they passed through the Red sea as by dry land: which the Egyptians assaying to do were drowned.

30 By faith the walls of Jericho fell down, after they were compassed about seven days.

31 By faith the harlot Rahab perished not with them that believed not, when she had received the spies with peace.

32 And what shall I more say? for the time would fail me to tell of Gedeon, and of Barak, and of Samson, and of Jephthae; of David also, and Samuel, and of the prophets:

33 Who through faith subdued kingdoms, wrought righteousness, obtained promises, stopped the mouths of lions,

34 Quenched the violence of fire, escaped the edge of the sword, out of weakness were made strong, waxed valiant in fight, turned to flight the armies of the aliens.

35 Women received their dead raised to life again: and others were tortured, not accepting deliverance; that they might obtain a better resurrection:

36 And others had trial of cruel mockings and scourgings, yea, moreover of bonds and imprisonment:

37 They were stoned, they were sawn asunder, were tempted, were slain with the sword: they wandered about in sheepskins and goatskins; being destitute, afflicted, tormented;

38 (Of whom the world was not worthy:) they wandered in deserts, and in mountains, and in dens and caves of the earth.

39 And these all, having obtained a good report through faith, received not the promise:

40 God having provided some better thing for us, that they without us should not be made perfect.

HEBREWS 12

1 Wherefore seeing we also are compassed about with so great a cloud of

faith, they became banished from the Church, and that they were then no longer the legitimate children of Abraham, but a degenerate race and bastards.

3. Through, or by, faith we understand, etc

This is a most striking proof of the last verse; for we differ nothing from the brute creation, if we understand not that the world has been created by God. To what end have men been endued with understanding and reason, except that they might acknowledge their Creator? But it is by faith alone we know that it was God who created the world. No wonder then that faith shone forth in the fathers above all other virtues.

But it may be here asked, Why does the Apostle assert that what even infidels acknowledge is only understood by faith? For the very appearance of heaven and earth constrains even the ungodly to acknowledge some Maker; and hence Paul condemns all for ingratitude, because they did not, after having known God, give him the honor due to him (Romans 1: 25). And no doubt religion would not have so prevailed among all nations, had not men's minds been impressed with the convictions that God is the Creator of the world. It thus then appears that this knowledge which the Apostle ascribes to faith, exists without faith.

To this I reply – that though there has been an opinion of this kind among heathens, that the world was made by God, it was yet very evanescent, for as soon as they formed a notion of some God, they became instantly vain in their imaginations, so that they groped in the dark, having in their thoughts a mere shadow of some uncertain deity, and not the knowledge of the true God. Besides, as it was only a transient opinion that flit in their minds, it was far from being anything like knowledge. We may further add, that they assigned to fortune or chance the supremacy in the government of the world, and they made no mention of God's providence which alone rules everything. Men's minds therefore are wholly blind, so that they see not the light of nature which shines forth in created things, until being irradiated by God's Spirit, they begin to understand by faith what otherwise they cannot comprehend. Hence most correctly does the Apostle ascribe such an understanding to faith; for they who have faith do not entertain a slight opinion as to God being the Creator of the world, but they have a deep conviction fixed in their minds and behold the true God. And further, they understand the power of his word, not only as manifested instantaneously in creating the world, but also as put forth continually in its preservation; nor is it his power only that they understand, but also his goodness, and wisdom, and justice. And hence they are led to worship, love, and honor him.

did not live under the influence of this master-principle. Whatever may be a man's lawful calling, he may abide therein with God, under the influence of faith. Like the fir or pine, faith flourishes in any soil.

Faith is consistent with very different degrees of knowledge. It would be difficult to enumerate more varieties of religious knowledge than are summarized in. this catalogue of names. Abel's idea of sacrifice would differ widely from David's. The degree of acquaintance with God would be much intenser with Moses than Samson. But, notwithstanding all these differences, the same principle of faith leaped upward from each heart. And the woman who touched the hem of the garment was animated with the same spirit as that which in her sister elicited the wonder of Jesus: "o woman, great is thy faith!"

Faith can master insuperable difficulties. It is difficult to be singular; but faith enabled Abel to offer a more excellent sacrifice than Cain. It is difficult to walk constantly with God, when wickedness is great on the earth, and all flesh has corrupted its way; but it is not impossible, for Enoch walked with God on the very margin of the Flood, and obtained the testimony that he pleased him. It is difficult to lead a pilgrim life, and such difficulties would be probably as keenly felt by the patriarchs; but what faith did for them it will do for others. It is difficult, amid the cares of business or public office, to keep the heart fresh, devout, and young; but it is not impossible to faith, which maintained the spirit of patriotism and devotion in the heart of Joseph, though sorely tempted to sink into an Egyptian grandee. It is difficult to face the loss of all things, and the displeasure of the great; but Moses did both, under the spell of faith in the unseen.

There are many difficulties before us all. Stormy seas forbid our passage; frowning fortifications bar our progress; mighty kingdoms defy our power; lions roar against us; fire lights its flaming barricade in our path; the sword, the armies of the alien, mockings, scourgings, bonds, and imprisonment-all these menace our peace, darken our horizon, and try on us their power; but faith has conquered all these before, and it shall do as much again. We will laugh at impossibility; we will tread the shores of the seas, certain they must make us a way; we will enter the dens of wild beasts and the furnaces of flame, sure that they are impotent to injure us; we shall escape the edge of the sword, out of weakness become strong, turn to flight armies of aliens, and set at nought all the power of the enemy: and all because we believe in God. Reckon on God's faithfulness. Look not at the winds and waves, but at his character and will. Get alone with him, steeping your heart and mind in his precious and exceeding great promises. Be obedient to the utmost limit of your light. Walk in the Spirit, one of whose fruits is faith. So shall you be deemed worthy to join this band, whose names and exploits run over from this page into the chronicles of eternity, and to share their glorious heritage.

HEBREWS 12

Preparing for the race.

1–2. Wherefore, seeing we also are compassed about with so great a cloud of witnesses, let us lay aside every weight and the sin which doth so easily beset us, and let us run with patience the race that is set before us; looking unto Jesus, the author and finisher of our faith.

When, in his Egyptian campaign, the Emperor Napoleon was leading his troops through the neighborhood of the Pyramids, he pointed to those hoary remnants of a great antiquity, and said, "Soldiers, forty centuries look down on you! Similarly there have been summoned before our thought in the preceding chapter the good and great, the martyrs, confessors, prophets, and kings of the past. We have been led through the corridors of the divine mausoleum, and bidden to read the names and epitaphs of those of whom God was not ashamed. We have felt our faith grow stronger as we read and pondered the inspiring record; and now, by a single touch, these saintly souls are depicted as having passed from the arena into the crowded tiers, from which to observe the course which we are treading to-day. They were witnesses to the necessity, nature, and power of faith. They are witnesses also of our lives and struggles, our victories and defeats, our past and present.

witnesses, let us lay aside every weight, and the sin which doth so easily beset us, and let us run with patience the race that is set before us,

2 Looking unto Jesus the author and finisher of our faith; who for the joy that was set before him endured the cross, despising the shame, and is set down at the right hand of the throne of God.

3 For consider him that endured such contradiction of sinners against himself, lest ye be wearied and faint in your minds.

4 Ye have not yet resisted unto blood, striving against sin.

5 And ye have forgotten the exhortation which speaketh unto you as unto children, My son, despise not thou the chastening of the Lord, nor faint when thou art rebuked of him:

6 For whom the Lord loveth he chasteneth, and scourgeth every son whom he receiveth.

7 If ye endure chastening, God dealeth with you as with sons; for what son is he whom the father chasteneth not?

8 But if ye be without chastisement, whereof all are partakers, then are ye bastards, and not sons.

9 Furthermore we have had fathers of our flesh which corrected us, and we gave them reverence: shall we not much rather be in subjection unto the Father of spirits, and live?

10 For they verily for a few days chastened us after their own pleasure; but he for our profit, that we might be partakers of his holiness.

11 Now no chastening for the present seemeth to be joyous, but grievous: nevertheless afterward it yieldeth the peaceable fruit of righteousness unto them which are exercised thereby.

12 Wherefore lift up the hands which hang down, and the feeble knees;

13 And make straight paths for your feet, lest that which is lame be turned out of the way; but let it rather be healed.

14 Follow peace with all men, and holiness, without which no man shall see the Lord:

15 Looking diligently lest any man fail of the grace of God; lest any root of bitterness springing up trouble you, and thereby many be defiled;

HEBREWS 12

1. Wherefore, seeing we also, *etc*

This conclusion is, as it were, an epilogue to the former chapter, by which he shows the end for which he gave a catalogue of the saints who excelled in faith under the Law, even that every one should be prepared to imitate them; and he calls a large multitude metaphorically a cloud, for he sets what is dense in opposition to what is thinly scattered. Had they been a few in number, yet they ought to have roused us by their example; but as they were a vast throng, they ought more powerfully to stimulate us.

He says that we are so surrounded by this dense throng, that wherever we turn our eyes many examples of faith immediately meet us. The word *witnesses* I do not take in a general sense, as though he called them the martyrs of God, and I apply it to the case before us, as though he had said that faith is sufficiently proved by their testimony, so that no doubt ought to be entertained; for the virtues of the saints are so many testimonies to confirm us, that we, relying on them as our guides and associates, ought to go onward to God with more alacrity.

Let us lay aside every weight, or every burden, etc

As he refers to the likeness of a race, he bids us to be lightly equipped; for nothing more prevents haste than to be encumbered with burdens. Now there are various burdens which delay and impede our spiritual course, such as the love of this present life, the pleasures of the world, the lusts of the flesh, worldly cares, riches also and honors, and other things of this kind. Whosoever, then, would run in the course prescribed by Christ, must first disentangle himself from all these impediments, for we are already of ourselves more tardy than we ought to be, so no other causes of delay should be added.

We are not however bidden to cast away riches or other blessings of this life, except so far as they retard our course for Satan by these as by toils retains and impedes us.

Now, the metaphor of a race is often to be found in Scripture; but here it means not any kind of race, but a running contest, which is wont to call forth the greatest exertions. The import of what is said then is, that we are engaged in a contest, even in a race the most celebrated, that many witnesses stand around us, that the Son of God is the umpire who invites and exhorts us to secure the prize, and that therefore it would be most disgraceful for us to grow weary or inactive in the midst of our course. And at the same time the holy men whom he mentioned, are not only witnesses, but have been associates in the same race, who have beforehand shown the way to us; and yet he preferred calling them witnesses rather than runners, in order to intimate that they are not rivals, seeking to snatch from us the prize,

F.B. MEYER

And they are compared to a cloud. One of the finest pictures in the world is that of the Madonna de San Sisto at Dresden, which depicts the infant Savior in the arms of his mother, surrounded by clouds, which attracted no special notice until lately; but when the accumulated dust of centuries was removed, they were found to be composed of myriads of angel faces. Surely this is the thought of the inspired writer when he speaks of "so great a cloud of witnesses."

In some of the more spacious amphitheaters of olden times, the spectators rose in tier above tier to the number of forty or fifty thousand; and to the thought of the combatant as he looked around on this vast multitude of human faces, set in varied and gorgeous coloring, these vast congregations of his race must have appeared like clouds, composed of infinitesimal units, but all making up one mighty aggregate, and bathed in such hues as are cast on the clouds at sunrise or sunset by the level sun.

If before this time these Hebrew Christians had been faltering, and inclined to relinquish their earnestness, they would have been strangely stirred and quickened by the thought that they were living under the close inspection of the spirits of the mighty dead. To us also the same exhortation applies.

The speed of the Christian life. **Let us run.** We must not sit still to be carried by the stream. We must not loiter and linger as children returning from a summer's ramble. We must not even walk as men with measured step. We must run. Nor are we only to run as those who double their pace to an easy trot; we must run as men who run a race. The idea of a race is generally competition; here it is only concentration of purpose, singleness of aim, intensity.

Life in earnest – that is the idea. But how far do we seem from it! And what a contrast there is between our earnestness in all beside, and in our devotion to God and man! We are willing enough to join in the rush of business competition, in the race for wealth, in the heated discussion of politics, and in social life in the pursuit of pleasure; but, ah! how soon we slacken when it becomes a question of how much we are willing to do for God! How earnest men are around us! Newton poring over his problems till the midnight wind sweeps over his pages the ashes of his long-extinguished fire. Reynolds sitting, brush in hand, before his canvas for thirty six hours together, summoning into life forms of beauty that seemed glad to come. Dryden composing in a single fortnight his Ode for St. Cecilia's Day. Buffon dragged from his beloved slumbers to his more beloved studies. And the biographer who records these traits himself rising with the dawn to prepare for the demands of his charge.

In a world like this, and with a theme like ours, we ought not to be languid and supine; but devoted, eager, consumed with a holy love to God, and with a passion for the souls of men. Then should we make progress in the knowledge of the Word of God, and enter into the words of one of the greatest spiritual athletes that ever lived: "This one thing I do . . . I press toward the goal for the prize of the high calling in Christ Jesus."

We must run free of weights. This speed can only be maintained when we run unencumbered and free. Now, of course we would all admit the necessity of divesting ourselves of sins; but in all our lives there are weights which are not sins. A sin is that which in its very nature, and always, and by whomsoever perpetrated, is a transgression of God's law, a violation of God's will. But a weight is something which in itself or to another may be harmless, or even legitimate, but in our own case is a hindrance and an impediment.

Every believer must be left to decide what is his own special weight. We may not judge for one another. What is a weight to one is not so to all. But the Holy Spirit, if he be consulted and asked to reveal the hindrance to the earnestness and speed of the soul's progress in divine things, will not fail to indicate it swiftly and infallibly. And this is the excellence of the Holy Spirit's teaching: it is ever definite. If you have a general undefined feeling of discouragement, it is probably the work of the great enemy of souls; but if you are aware of some one hindrance and encumbrance which stays your speed, it is almost certainly the work of the divine Spirit, who is leading you to relinquish something which is slackening your

16 Lest there be any fornicator, or profane person, as Esau, who for one morsel of meat sold his birthright.

17 For ye know how that afterward, when he would have inherited the blessing, he was rejected: for he found no place of repentance, though he sought it carefully with tears.

18 For ye are not come unto the mount that might be touched, and that burned with fire, nor unto blackness, and darkness, and tempest,

19 And the sound of a trumpet, and the voice of words; which voice they that heard intreated that the word should not be spoken to them any more:

20 (For they could not endure that which was commanded, And if so much as a beast touch the mountain, it shall be stoned, or thrust through with a dart:

21 And so terrible was the sight, that Moses said, I exceedingly fear and quake:

22 But ye are come unto mount Sion, and unto the city of the living God, the heavenly Jerusalem, and to an innumerable company of angels,

23 To the general assembly and church of the firstborn, which are written in heaven, and to God the Judge of all, and to the spirits of just men made perfect,

24 And to Jesus the mediator of the new covenant, and to the blood of sprinkling, that speaketh better things than that of Abel.

25 See that ye refuse not him that speaketh. For if they escaped not who refused him that spake on earth, much more shall not we escape, if we turn away from him that speaketh from heaven:

26 Whose voice then shook the earth: but now he hath promised, saying, Yet once more I shake not the earth only, but also heaven.

27 And this word, Yet once more, signifieth the removing of those things that are shaken, as of things that are made, that those things which cannot be shaken may remain.

28 Wherefore we receiving a kingdom which cannot be moved, let us have grace, whereby we may serve God acceptably with reverence and godly fear:

29 For our God is a consuming fire.

but approves to applaud and hail our victory; and Christ also is not only the umpire, but also extends his hand to us, and supplies us with strength and energy; in short, he prepares and fits us to enter on our course, and by his power leads us on to the end of the race.

And the sin which does so easily beset us, or, **stand around us**, etc

This is the heaviest burden that impedes us. And he says that we are entangled, in order that we may know, that no one is fit to run except he has stripped off all toils and snares. He speaks not of outward, or, as they say, of actual sin, but of the very fountain, even concupiscence or lust, which so possesses every part of us, that we feel that we are on every side held by its snares.

Let us run with patience, *etc*

By this word *patience*, we are ever reminded of what the Apostle meant to be mainly regarded in faith, even that we are in spirit to seek the kingdom of God, which is invisible to the flesh, and exceeds all that our minds can comprehend; for they who are occupied in meditating on this kingdom can easily disregard all earthly things. He thus could not more effectually withdraw the Jews from their ceremonies, than by calling their attention to the real exercises of faith, by which they might learn that Christ's kingdom is spiritual, and far superior to the elements of the world.

2. Who for the joy that was set before him, *etc*

He commends to us the patience of Christ on two accounts, because he endured a most bitter death, and because he despised shame. He then mentions the glorious end of his death, that the faithful might know that all the evils which they may endure will end in their salvation and glory, provided they follow Christ. So also says James, "Ye have heard of the patience of Job, and ye know the end" (James 5: 11). Then the Apostle means that the end of our sufferings will be the same with those of Christ, according to what is said by Paul, "If we suffer with him, we shall also reign together" (Romans 8: 17).

HEBREWS 13

1. Let brotherly love, *etc*

Probably he gave this command respecting brotherly love, because a secret hatred arising from the haughtiness of the Jews was threatening to rend the Churches. But still this precept is generally very needful, for nothing flows away so easily as love; when everyone thinks of himself more than he ought, he will allow to others less than he ought; and then many offenses happen daily which cause separations.

He calls love **brotherly**, not only to teach us that we ought to be mutually united together by a peculiar and an inward feeling of love, but also that we may remember

progress in the spiritual life.

No man would think of maintaining a high speed encompassed with weights. The lads who run for a prize litter the course with garments flung away in their eager haste. There would be little difficulty in maintaining an intense and ardent spirit if we were more faithful in dealing with the habits and indulgences which cling around us and impede our steps. Thousands of Christians are like waterlogged vessels. They cannot sink; but they are so saturated with inconsistencies and worldliness and permitted evil that they can only be towed with difficulty into the celestial port.

Is there anything in your life which dissipates your energy from holy things, which disinclines you to the practice of prayer and Bible study, which rises before you in your best moments, and produces in you a general sense of uneasiness and disturbance? something which others account harmless, and permit, and in which you once saw no cause for anxiety, but which you now look on with a feeling of self-condemnation? It is likely enough a weight.

Is there anything within the circle of your consciousness concerning which you have to argue with yourself, or which you do not care to investigate, treating it as a bankrupt treats his books into which he has no desire to enter, or as a votary of pleasure treats the first symptoms of decaying vitality which he seeks to conceal from himself? We so often allow in ourselves things which we would be the first to condemn in others. We frequently find ourselves engaged in discovering ingenious reasons wily a certain course which would be wrong in others is justifiable in ourselves. All such things may be considered as weights. It may be a friendship which is too engrossing; a habit which is sapping away our energy as the tap-root the fruit bearing powers of a tree; a pursuit, an amusement, a pastime, a system of reading, a method of spending time, too fascinating and too absorbing, and therefore harmful to the soul-which is tempted to walk when it should run, and to loiter when it should haste.

But, you ask, Is it not a sign of weakness, and will it not tend to weakness, always to be relinquishing these and similar things? Surely, you cry, the life will become impoverished and barren when it is stripped in this way of its precious things. Not so. It is impossible to renounce anything at the bidding of the inner life without adding immensely to its strength; for it grows by surrender, and waxes strong by sacrifice. And for every unworthy object which is forsaken there follows an immediate enrichment of the spirit, which is the sufficient and unvarying compensation. The athlete gladly foregoes much that other men value, and which is pleasant to himself, because his mind is intent on the prize; and he considers that he will be amply repaid for all the hardships of training if he be permitted to bear it away, though it be a belt he will never wear, or a cup he will never use. How much more gladly should we be prepared to relinquish all that hinders our attainment, not of the uncertain bauble of the athlete, but the certain reward, the incorruptible crown, the smile and "well-done" of our Lord!

We must lay aside besetting sin. **Let us lay aside every weight and the sin which doth so easily beset us.** We often refer to these words; no sentence of the Bible is more often on our lips; but do we not misquote them in divorcing them from their context? We should read them as part of the great argument running through the previous chapter, and of which they are the culmination and brilliant climax. That argument has been devoted to the theme of faith. Case after case has been adduced of the exploits of the heroes of Hebrew story; and it has been shown that in each faith was the secret motive and the sufficient power. The close connection between that glowing panegyric and the opening words of the following chapter is shown by the word "Wherefore," which even defies the wanton intrusion of the division forced upon us in our English version. And surely it is most natural to hold that the sin which so closely clings to us is nothing else than the sin of unbelief, which is the opposite pole to the faith so highly eulogized.

If that be a correct exegesis, it sheds new light on unbelief. It is no longer an infirmity, it is a sin. Men sometimes carry about their doubts, as beggars a deformed or sickly child, to excite the sympathy of the benevolent. But surely there is a kind of unbelief which should

HEBREWS 13

1 Let brotherly love continue.

2 Be not forgetful to entertain strangers: for thereby some have entertained angels unawares.

3 Remember them that are in bonds, as bound with them; and them which suffer adversity, as being yourselves also in the body.

4 Marriage is honorable in all, and the bed undefiled: but whoremongers and adulterers God will judge.

5 Let your conversation be without covetousness; and be content with such things as ye have: for he hath said, I will never leave thee, nor forsake thee.

6 So that we may boldly say, The Lord is my helper, and I will not fear what man shall do unto me.

7 Remember them which have the rule over you, who have spoken unto you the word of God: whose faith follow, considering the end of their conversation.

8 Jesus Christ the same yesterday, and to day, and for ever.

9 Be not carried about with divers and strange doctrines. For it is a good thing that the heart be established with grace; not with meats, which have not profited them that have been occupied therein.

10 We have an altar, whereof they have no right to eat which serve the tabernacle.

11 For the bodies of those beasts, whose blood is brought into the sanctuary by the high priest for sin, are burned without the camp.

12 Wherefore Jesus also, that he might sanctify the people with his own blood, suffered without the gate.

13 Let us go forth therefore unto him without the camp, bearing his reproach.

14 For here have we no continuing city, but we seek one to come.

15 By him therefore let us offer the sacrifice of praise to God continually, that is, the fruit of our lips giving thanks to his name.

16 But to do good and to communicate forget not: for with such sacrifices God is well pleased.

17 Obey them that have the rule over you, and submit yourselves: for they watch for your souls, as they that must

that we cannot be Christians without being brethren; for he speaks of the love which the household of faith ought to cultivate one towards another inasmuch as the Lord has bound them closer together by the common bond of adoption. It was therefore a good custom in the primitive Church for Christians to call one another brothers; but now the name as well as the thing itself is become almost obsolete, except that the monks have appropriated to themselves the use of it when neglected by others, while at the same time they show by their discords and intestine factions that they are the children of the evil one.

2. Be not forgetful to entertain strangers, *etc*

This office of humanity has also nearly ceased to be properly observed among men; for the ancient hospitality, celebrated in histories, is unknown to us, and Inns now supply the place of accommodations for strangers. But he speaks not so much of the practice of hospitality as observed then by the rich; but he rather commends the miserable and the needy to be entertained, as at that time many were fugitives who left their homes for the name of Christ.

And that he might commend this duty the more, he adds, that angels had sometimes been entertained by those who thought that they received only men. I doubt not but that this is to be understood of Abraham and Lot; for having been in the habit of showing hospitality, they without knowing and thinking of any such thing, entertained angels; thus their houses were in no common way honored. And doubtless God proved that hospitality was especially acceptable to him, when he rendered such a reward to Abraham and to Lot. Were any one to object and say, that this rarely happened; to this the obvious answer is – That not mere angels are received, but Christ himself, when we receive the poor in his name. In the words in Greek there is a beautiful alliteration which cannot be set forth in Latin.

3. Remember them that are in bonds, *or,* Be mindful of the bound, *etc*

There is nothing that can give us a more genuine feeling of compassion than to put ourselves in the place of those who are in distress; hence he says, that we ought to think of those in bonds as though we were bound with them. What follows the first clause, *As being yourselves also in the body,* is variously explained. Some take a general view thus, "Ye are also exposed to the same evils, according to the common lot of humanity;" but others give a more restricted sense, "As though ye were in their body." Of neither can I approve, for I apply the words to the body of the Church, so that the meaning would be this, "Since ye are members of the same body, it behooves you to feel in common for each other's evils, that there may be nothing disunited among you."

not meet with sympathy, but rebuke. It is sin which needs to be repented of as sin, to be resisted as sin, and to receive as sin the cleansing of Christ.

HEBREWS 13

The unchanging Savior.

8. Jesus Christ the same yesterday and to day, and for ever.

Three times over in this chapter the sacred writer urges his readers to think kindly of those who ruled over them. The full force of the Greek word is better represented by the marginal rendering guide, than by the word rule. But in any case he referred to those who were the spiritual leaders and teachers of the flock. The three injunctions are: Remember (ver. 7); Obey (ver. 17); Salute (ver. 24).

It is a proud name for the Christian minister to be called a leader. But unless he has some other claim to it than comes from force of character, eloquence, or intellectual power, his name will be an empty sound, the sign of what he might be rather than of what he is. Those who are qualified to lead other men must be themselves close followers of Christ; so that they may be able to turn to others and say, "Be ye followers of me, even as I also am of Christ;" "Be followers together with Me."

But the Christian minister must also watch for souls (ver. 17). He is not sent to his charge to preach great sermons, to elaborate brilliant orations, or to dazzle their intellects; but to watch over their souls, as the shepherd watches over his flocks scattered upon the downs, while the light changes from the gray morning, through the deep tints of the noon, into the last delicate flush of evening far up on the loftiest cliffs. He must indeed keep careful watch, for he must give an account in the evening; of his hand every missing one will be required.

It is told of the holy Melville, that his wife would sometimes find him on his knees in the cold winter night; and on asking him to return to bed, he would reply, "I have got fifteen hundred souls in my charge, and fear that it is going ill with some of them." It is not difficult to remember or obey or salute men like that. They carry their Master's sign upon their faces. They are among Christ's most precious gifts to his Church.

But there is this sorrow connected with all human leaders and teachers. However dear and useful they are, they are not suffered to continue by reason of death. One after another they pass away into the spirit world, to enter upon their loftier service, to give in their account, to see the Master whom they have loved. The last sermon lies unfinished on the study table; but they never come there to complete it. The final word is spoken. The closing benediction is given. The ministry is done. But what a relief it is to turn from men to Christ: from the constant change in human teachers to the unchanging Master; from the under-shepherds who are here today but gone tomorrow, to the chief Shepherd and Bishop of souls who watches his sheep in the evening shadows of this era, equally as in the first bright beams of its Pentecostal morning!

This is the meaning of our writer (ver. 7).

What it implies. It implies that he is God. It implies, too, that the Gospels are a leaf out of his eternal diary, and may be taken as a true record of his present life. What he was, he is. He still sails with us in the boat; walks in the afternoon with us to Emmaus; stands in our midst at nightfall, opening to us the Scriptures. He wakes our children in the morning with his "Talitha cumi"; calls the boys to his knees; watches them at their play; and rebukes those who would forbid their Hosannas. He feeds us with bread and fish; lights fires on the sands to warm us; shows us the right side of the ship for our nets; and interests himself with the results of our toils. He takes us with him to the brow of the Transfiguration Mount, and into the glades of Gethsemane.

When we are slow to believe, he is slower still to anger. He teaches us many things, graduating his lessons, according to our ability to understand. When we cannot bear more, he shades the light. When we strive for high places, he rebukes. When soiled, he washes our feet. When in peril, he comes across the yeasty waves to our help. When weary, he leads us aside to rest.

Oh, do not read the Gospels as a record merely of the past, but as a transcript of what he is ever doing. Each miracle and parable and

give account, that they may do it with joy, and not with grief: for that is unprofitable for you.

18 Pray for us: for we trust we have a good conscience, in all things willing to live honestly.

19 But I beseech you the rather to do this, that I may be restored to you the sooner.

20 Now the God of peace, that brought again from the dead our Lord Jesus, that great shepherd of the sheep, through the blood of the everlasting covenant,

21 Make you perfect in every good work to do his will, working in you that which is wellpleasing in his sight, through Jesus Christ; to whom be glory for ever and ever. Amen.

22 And I beseech you, brethren, suffer the word of exhortation: for I have written a letter unto you in few words.

23 Know ye that our brother Timothy is set at liberty; with whom, if he come shortly, I will see you.

24 Salute all them that have the rule over you, and all the saints. They of Italy salute you.

25 Grace be with you all. Amen.

4. Marriage is honourable in all, *etc*

I am inclined to think that the Apostle sets marriage here in opposition to fornication as a remedy for that evil; and the context plainly shows that this was his meaning; for before he threatens that the Lord would punish fornicators, he first states what is the true way of escape, even if we live honourable in a state of marriage.

Let this then be the main point, that fornication will not be unpunished, for God will take vengeance on it. And doubtless as God has blessed the union of man and wife, instituted by himself, it follows that every other union different from this is by him condemned and accursed.

trait is a specimen of eternal facts, which are taking place by myriads, at every moment of the day and night; the achievements of the ever- living, ever-working Lord. No lake without that figure treading its waters. No storm without that voice mightier than its roar. No meal without that face uplifted in blessing, or that hand engaged in breaking. No grave without that tender heart touched with sorrow. No burden without those willing shoulders to share the yoke.

Oh, take me not back through the long ages to a Christ that was! He is! He lives! He is here! I can never again be alone, never grope in the dark for a hand, never be forsaken or forlorn. Never need a Guide, a Master, a Friend, or a Husband to my soul. I have him, who suffices for uncounted myriads in the dateless noon of eternity. He who was everything in the yesterday of the past, and who will be everything in the to-morrow of the future, is mine to-day; and at each present moment of my existence-here, and in all worlds.

20–21. Throughout this Epistle, the inspired writer has been appealing to man. Through successive paragraphs he has poured forth a burning stream of argument, remonstrance, or appeal; now opening the full peal of Sinai's thunders, and now the wail of Calvary's broken heart, and finally summoning the most honored names in Hebrew story to enforce his words.

All this is over now. He can say no more. The plowing and sowing and harrowing are alike complete. He must turn from earth to heaven, from man to God; and leave his converts and his work with that glorious Being whose cause he had striven so faithfully to plead, and who alone could crown his labors with success. There are many splendid outbursts of prayer beginning these Epistles; but amongst them all, it is impossible to find one more striking or beautiful than this.

The burden of the prayer is that these Hebrew Christians may be made perfect to do God's will. The word "perfect" means to set in joint, or articulate. Naturally, we are out of joint, or, at the best, work stiffly; but the ideal of Christian living is to be so perfectly "set" that God's purposes may be easily and completely realized in us.

There is no higher aim in life than to do the will of God. It was the supreme object for which our Savior lived. This brought him from heaven. This determined his every action. This fed his inner life with hidden meat. This cleared and lit up his judgment. This led him with unfaltering decision into the valley of death. This was the stay and solace of his spirit as he drank the bitter cup of agony. Throughout his mortal life his one glad shout of assurance and victory was, "I delight to do thy will, my God; yea, thy law is within my heart." And human lives climb up from the lowlands to the upland heights just in proportion as they do the will of God on earth as it is done in heaven. If every reader of these lines would resolve from this moment to do the will of God in the very smallest things-with scrupulous care, counting nothing insignificant, shrinking from no sacrifice, evading no command-life would assume entirely a new aspect. There might be a momentary experience of suffering and pain; but it would be succeeded by the light of resurrection, and the new song of heaven, stealing like morning through the chambers of the soul.

James

Introduction by John Calvin

It appears from the writings of Jerome and Eusebius, that this Epistle was not formerly received by many Churches without opposition. There are also at this day some who do not think it entitled to authority. I, however, am inclined to receive it without controversy, because I see no just cause for rejecting it. For what seems in the second chapter to be inconsistent with the doctrine of free justification, we shall easily explain in its own place. Though he seems more sparing in proclaiming the grace of Christ than it behooved an Apostle to be, it is not surely required of all to handle the same arguments. The writings of Solomon differ much from those of David; while the former was intent on forming the outward man and teaching the precepts of civil life, the latter spoke continually of the spiritual worship of God, peace of conscience, God's mercy and gratuitous promise of salvation. But this diversity should not make us to approve of one, and to condemn the other. Besides, among the evangelists themselves there is so much difference in setting forth the power of Christ, that the other three, compared with John, have hardly sparks of that full brightness which appears so conspicuous in him, and yet we commend them all alike.

It is enough to make men to receive this Epistle, that it contains nothing unworthy of an Apostle of Christ. It is indeed full of instruction on various subjects, the benefit of which extends to every part of the Christian life; for there are here remarkable passages on patience, prayer to God, the excellency and fruit of heavenly truth, humility, holy duties, the restraining of the tongue, the cultivation of peace, the repressing of lusts, the contempt of the world, and the like things, which we shall separately discuss in their own places.

But as to the author, there is somewhat more reason for doubting. It is indeed certain that he was not the Son of Zebedee, for Herod killed him shortly after our Lord's resurrection. The ancients are nearly unanimous in thinking that he was one of the disciples named Oblias and a relative of Christ, who was set over the Church at Jerusalem; and they supposed him to have been the person whom Paul mentioned with Peter and John, who he says were deemed pillars (Galatians 2: 9). But that one of the disciples was mentioned as one of the three pillars, and thus exalted above the other Apostles, does not seem to me probable. I am therefore rather inclined to the conjecture, that he of whom Paul speaks was the son of Alpheus. I do not yet deny that another was the ruler of the Church at Jerusalem, and one indeed from the college of the disciples; for the Apostles were not tied to any particular place. But whether of the two was the writer of this Epistle, it is not for me to say. That Oblias was actually a man of great authority among the Jews, appears even from this, that as he had been cruelly put to death by the faction of an ungodly chief-priest, Josephus hesitated not to impute the destruction of the city in part to his death.

The commentaries on James are by John Calvin and Albert Barnes.

JAMES 1

1 James, a servant of God and of the Lord Jesus Christ, to the twelve tribes which are scattered abroad, greeting.

2 My brethren, count it all joy when ye fall into divers temptations;

3 Knowing this, that the trying of your faith worketh patience.

4 But let patience have her perfect work, that ye may be perfect and entire, wanting nothing.

5 If any of you lack wisdom, let him ask of God, that giveth to all men liberally, and upbraideth not; and it shall be given him.

6 But let him ask in faith, nothing wavering. For he that wavereth is like a wave of the sea driven with the wind and tossed.

7 For let not that man think that he shall receive any thing of the Lord.

8 A double minded man is unstable in all his ways.

9 Let the brother of low degree rejoice in that he is exalted:

10 But the rich, in that he is made low: because as the flower of the grass he shall pass away.

11 For the sun is no sooner risen with a burning heat, but it withereth the grass, and the flower thereof falleth, and the grace of the fashion of it perisheth: so also shall the rich man fade away in his ways.

12 Blessed is the man that endureth temptation: for when he is tried, he shall receive the crown of life, which the Lord hath promised to them that love him.

13 Let no man say when he is tempted, I am tempted of God: for God cannot be tempted with evil, neither tempteth he any man:

14 But every man is tempted, when he is drawn away of his own lust, and enticed.

15 Then when lust hath conceived, it bringeth forth sin: and sin, when it is finished, bringeth forth death.

16 Do not err, my beloved brethren.

17 Every good gift and every perfect gift is from above, and cometh down from the Father of lights, with whom is no vari-

JAMES 1

1. To the twelve tribes

When the ten tribes were banished, the Assyrian king placed them in different parts. Afterwards, as it usually happens in the revolutions of kingdoms (such as then took place), it is very probable that they moved here and there in all directions. And the Jews had been scattered almost unto all quarters of the world. He then wrote and exhorted all those whom he could not personally address, because they had been scattered far and wide. But that he speaks not of the grace of Christ and of faith in him, the reason seems to be this, because he addressed those who had already been rightly taught by others; so that they had need, not so much of doctrine, as of the goads of exhortations.

2. All joy

The first exhortation is, to bear trials with a cheerful mind. And it was especially necessary at that time to comfort the Jews, almost overwhelmed as they were with troubles. For the very name of the nation was so infamous, that they were hated and despised by all people wherever they went; and their condition as Christians rendered them still more miserable, because they held their own nation as their most inveterate enemies. At the same time, this consolation was not so suited to one time, but that it is always useful to believers, whose life is a constant warfare on earth.

But that we may know more fully what he means, we must doubtless take **temptations** or *trials* as including all adverse things; and they are so called, because they are the tests of our obedience to God. He bids the faithful, while exercised with these, to rejoice; and that not only when they fall into one temptation, but into many, not only of one kind, but of various kinds. And doubtless, since they serve to mortify our flesh, as the vices of the flesh continually shoot up in us, so they must necessarily be often repeated. Besides, as we labor under diseases, so it is no wonder that different remedies are applied to remove them.

The Lord then afflicts us in various ways, because ambition, avarice, envy, gluttony, intemperance, excessive love of the world, and the innumerable lusts in which we abound, cannot be cured by the same medicine.

When he bids us to **count it all joy**, it is the same as though he had said, that temptations ought to be so deemed as gain, as to be regarded as occasions of joy. He means, in short, that there is nothing in afflictions which ought to disturb our joy. And thus, he not only commands us to bear adversities calmly, and with an even mind, but shews us that this is a reason why the faithful should rejoice when pressed down by them.

It is, indeed, certain, that all the senses of our nature are so formed, that every trial produces in us grief and sorrow;

JAMES 1

1. James, a servant of God. It is remarkable that James does not call himself an apostle; but this does not prove that the writer of the epistle was not an apostle, for the same omission occurs in the epistle of John, and in the epistle of Paul to the Philippians, to the Thessalonians, and to Philemon. It is remarkable, also, considering the relation which James is supposed to have borne to the Lord Jesus as his "brother" (Gal. 1: 19), that he did not refer to that as constituting a ground of claim to his right to address others; but this is only one instance out of many, in the New Testament, in which it is regarded as a higher honor to be the **servant of God** and to belong to his family, than to sustain any relations of blood or kindred.

2. My brethren. Not brethren as Jews, but as Christians. Compare James 2: 1. Count it all joy. Regard it as a thing to rejoice in; a matter which should afford you happiness. You are not to consider it as a punishment, a curse, or a calamity, but as a fit subject of felicitation.

3. Knowing this, that the trying of your faith worketh patience. Patience is one of the fruits of such a trial, and the grace of patience is worth the trial which it may cost to procure it. This is one of the passages which show that James was acquainted with the writings of Paul. See the Introduction to James chapter 5, James 5: 1. The sentiment expressed here is found in Rom. 5: 3.

Paul has carried the sentiment out farther, and shows that tribulation produces other effects than patience. James only asks that patience may have its perfect work, supposing that every Christian grace is implied in this.

4. But let patience have her perfect work. Let it be fairly developed. Let it produce its appropriate effects without being hindered. Let it not be obstructed in its fair influence on the soul, by murmurings, complaining, or rebellion. Patience under trials is fitted to produce important effects on the soul, and we are not to hinder them in any manner by a perspirit, or by opposition to the will of God. Every one who is afflicted should desire that the fair effects of affliction should be produced on his mind, or that there should be produced in his soul precisely the results which his trials are adapted to accomplish.

That ye may be perfect and entire. The meaning of this is explained in the following phrase – "wanting nothing;" that is, that there may be nothing lacking to complete your character. There may be the elements of a good character; there may be sound principles, but those principles may not be fully carried out so as to show what they are. Afflictions, perhaps, more than anything else, will do this; and we should therefore allow them to do all that they are adapted to do in developing what is good in us. The idea here is, that it is desirable not only to have the elements or principles of piety in the soul, but to have them fairly carried out, so as to show what is their real tendency and value.

12. Blessed is the man that endureth temptation. The apostle seems here to use the word temptation in the most general sense, as denoting anything that will try the reality of religion, whether affliction, or persecution, or a direct inducement to sin placed before the mind. The word temptation appears in this chapter to be used in two senses; and the question may arise, why the apostle so employs it. Compare James 1: 2,13. But, in fact, the word temptation is in itself of so general a character as to cover the whole usage, and to justify the manner in which it is employed. It denotes anything that will try or test the reality of our religion; and it may be applied, therefore, either to afflictions or to direct solicitations to sin – the latter being the sense in which it is now commonly employed. In another respect, also, essentially the same idea enters into both the ways in which the word is employed. Affliction, persecution, sickness, etc., may be regarded as, in a certain sense, temptations to sin; that is, the question comes before us whether we will adhere to the religion on account of which we are persecuted, or apostatize from it, and escape these sufferings; whether in sickness and losses we will be patient and submissive to that God who lays his hand upon us, or revolt and murmur. In each and every case, whether by affliction, or

ableness, neither shadow of turning.

18 Of his own will begat he us with the word of truth, that we should be a kind of firstfruits of his creatures.

19 Wherefore, my beloved brethren, let every man be swift to hear, slow to speak, slow to wrath:

20 For the wrath of man worketh not the righteousness of God.

21 Wherefore lay apart all filthiness and superfluity of naughtiness, and receive with meekness the engrafted word, which is able to save your souls.

22 But be ye doers of the word, and not hearers only, deceiving your own selves.

23 For if any be a hearer of the word, and not a doer, he is like unto a man beholding his natural face in a glass:

24 For he beholdeth himself, and goeth his way, and straightway forgetteth what manner of man he was.

25 But whoso looketh into the perfect law of liberty, and continueth therein, he being not a forgetful hearer, but a doer of the work, this man shall be blessed in his deed.

26 If any man among you seem to be religious, and bridleth not his tongue, but deceiveth his own heart, this man's religion is vain.

27 Pure religion and undefiled before God and the Father is this, To visit the fatherless and widows in their affliction, and to keep himself unspotted from the world.

JAMES 2

1 My brethren, have not the faith of our Lord Jesus Christ, the Lord of glory, with respect of persons.

2 For if there come unto your assembly a man with a gold ring, in goodly apparel, and there come in also a poor man in vile raiment;

3 And ye have respect to him that weareth the gay clothing, and say unto him, Sit thou here in a good place; and say to the poor, Stand thou there, or sit here under my footstool:

4 Are ye not then partial in yourselves, and are become judges of evil thoughts?

and no one of us can so far divest himself of his nature as not to grieve and be sorrowful whenever he feels any evil. But this does not prevent the children of God to rise, by the guidance of the Spirit, above the sorrow of the flesh. Hence it is, that in the midst of trouble they cease not to rejoice.

3. Knowing this, that the trying

We now see why he called adversities **trials** or **temptations**, even because they serve to try our faith. And there is here a reason given to confirm the last sentence. For it might, on the other hand, be objected, "How comes it, that we judge that sweet which to the sense is bitter?" He then shews by the effect that we ought to rejoice in afflictions, because they produce fruit that ought to be highly valued, even patience. If God then provides for our salvation, he affords us an occasion of rejoicing. Peter uses a similar argument at the beginning of his first Epistle, "That the trial of your faith, more precious than gold, may be," etc [1Peter 1: 7]. We certainly dread diseases, and want, and exile, and prison, and reproach, and death, because we regard them as evils; but when we understand that they are turned through God's kindness unto helps and aids to our salvation, it is ingratitude to murmur, and not willingly to submit to be thus paternally dealt with.

Paul says, in Romans 5: 3, that we are to glory in tribulations; and James says here, that we are to rejoice. "We glory," says Paul, "in tribulations, knowing that tribulation worketh patience." What immediately follows seems contrary to the words of James; for he mentions probation in the third place, as the effect of patience, which is here put first as though it were the cause. But the solution is obvious; the word there has an active, but here a passive meaning. Probation or trial is said by James to produce patience; for were not God to try us, but leave us free from trouble, there would be no patience, which is no other thing than fortitude of mind in bearing evils. But Paul means, that while by enduring we conquer evils, we experience how much God's help avails in necessities; for then the truth of God is as it were in reality manifested to us. Hence it comes that we dare to entertain more hope as to futurity; for the truth of God, known by experience, is more fully believed by us. Hence Paul teaches that by such a probation, that is, by such an experience of divine grace, hope is produced, not that hope then only begins, but that it increases and is confirmed. But both mean, that tribulation is the means by which patience is produced.

JAMES 2

This reproof seems at first sight to be hard and unreasonable; for it is one of the duties of courtesy, not to be neglected, to honor those who are elevated in the world.

by direct allurements to do wrong, the question comes before the mind whether we have religion enough to keep us, or whether we will yield to murmuring, to rebellion, and to sin. In these respects, in a general sense, all forms of trial may be regarded as temptation. Yet in the following (James 1: 13) the apostle would guard this from abuse. So far as the form of trial involved an allurement or inducement to sin, he says that no man should regard it as from God. That cannot be his design. The trial is what he aims at, not the sin. In the before us he says, that whatever may be the form of the trial, a Christian should rejoice in it, for it will furnish an evidence that he is a child of God.

For when he is tried. In any way – if he bears the trial.

20. For the wrath of man worketh not the righteousness of God. Does not produce in the life that righteousness which God requires. Its tendency is not to incline us to keep the law, but to break it; not to induce us to embrace the truth, but the opposite. The meaning of this passage is not that our wrath will make God either more or less righteous; but that its tendency is not to produce that upright course of life, and love of truth, which God requires. A man is never sure of doing right under the influence of excited feelings; he may do that which is in the highest sense wrong, and which he will regret all his life. The particular meaning of this passage is, that wrath in the mind of man will not have any tendency to make him righteous. It is only that candid state of mind which will lead him to embrace the truth which can be hoped to have such an effect.

21. Wherefore. In view of the fact that God has begotten us for his own service; in view of the fact that excited feeling tends only to wrong, let us lay aside all that is evil, and submit ourselves wholly to the influence of truth.

Lay apart all filthiness. The word here rendered filthiness, occurs nowhere else in the New Testament. It means properly filth; and then is applied to evil conduct considered as disgusting or offensive. Sin may be contemplated as a wrong thing; as a violation of law; as evil in its nature and tendency, and therefore to be avoided; or it may be contemplated

as disgusting, offensive, loathsome. To a pure mind, this is one of its most odious characteristics; for, to such a mind, sin in any form is more loathsome than the most offensive object can be to any of the senses.

And superfluity of naughtiness. Literally, "abounding of evil." It is rendered by Doddridge, "overflowing of malignity;" by Tindal, "superfluity of maliciousness;" by Benson, "superfluity of malice;" by Bloomfield, "petulance." The phrase "superfluity of naughtiness": or of evil, does not exactly express the sense, as if we were only to lay aside that which abounded, or which is superfluous, though we might retain that which does not come under this description; but the object of the apostle is to express his deep abhorrence of the thing referred to by strong and emphatic language. He had just spoken of sin in one aspect, as filthy, loathsome, detestable; here he designs to express his abhorrence of it by a still more emphatic description, and he speaks of it not merely as an evil, but as an evil abounding, overflowing; an evil in the highest degree. The thing referred to had the essence of evil in it, but it was not merely evil, it was evil that was aggravated, that was overflowing, that was eminent in degree. The particular reference in these passages is to the reception of the truth; and the doctrine taught is, that a corrupt mind, a mind full of sensuality and wickedness, is not favorable to the reception of the truth. It is not fitted to see its beauty, to appreciate its value, to understand its just claims, or to welcome it to the soul. Purity of heart is the best preparation always for seeing the force of truth. And receive with meekness. That is, open the mind and heart to instruction, and to the fair influence of truth. Meekness, gentleness, docility, are everywhere required in receiving the instructions of religion, as they are in obtaining knowledge of any kind.

JAMES 2

1. Have not the faith of our Lord Jesus Christ. Faith is the distinguishing thing in the Christian religion, for it is this by which man is justified, and hence it comes to be put for religion itself.

5 Hearken, my beloved brethren, Hath not God chosen the poor of this world rich in faith, and heirs of the kingdom which he hath promised to them that love him?

6 But ye have despised the poor. Do not rich men oppress you, and draw you before the judgment seats?

7 Do not they blaspheme that worthy name by the which ye are called?

8 If ye fulfil the royal law according to the scripture, Thou shalt love thy neighbour as thyself, ye do well:

9 But if ye have respect to persons, ye commit sin, and are convinced of the law as transgressors.

10 For whosoever shall keep the whole law, and yet offend in one point, he is guilty of all.

11 For he that said, Do not commit adultery, said also, Do not kill. Now if thou commit no adultery, yet if thou kill, thou art become a transgressor of the law.

12 So speak ye, and so do, as they that shall be judged by the law of liberty.

13 For he shall have judgment without mercy, that hath shewed no mercy; and mercy rejoiceth against judgment.

14 What doth it profit, my brethren, though a man say he hath faith, and have not works? can faith save him?

15 If a brother or sister be naked, and destitute of daily food,

16 And one of you say unto them, Depart in peace, be ye warmed and filled; notwithstanding ye give them not those things which are needful to the body; what doth it profit?

17 Even so faith, if it hath not works, is dead, being alone.

18 Yea, a man may say, Thou hast faith, and I have works: shew me thy faith without thy works, and I will shew thee my faith by my works.

19 Thou believest that there is one God; thou doest well: the devils also believe, and tremble.

20 But wilt thou know, O vain man, that faith without works is dead?

21 Was not Abraham our father justified by works, when he had offered Isaac his son upon the altar?

22 Seest thou how faith wrought with

Further, if respect of persons be vicious, servants are to be freed from all subjection; for freedom and servitude are deemed by Paul as conditions of life. The same must be thought of magistrates. But the solution of these questions is not difficult, if what James writes is not separated. For he does not simply disapprove of honor being paid to the rich, but that this should not be done in a way so as to despise or reproach the poor; and this will appear more clearly, when he proceeds to speak of the rule of love.

Let us therefore remember that the respect of persons here condemned is that by which the rich is so extolled, wrong is done to the poor, which also he shews clearly by the context and surely ambitions is that honor, and full of vanity, which is shewn to the rich to the contempt of the poor. Nor is there a doubt but that ambition reigns and vanity also, when the masks of this world are alone in high esteem. We must remember this truth, that he is to be counted among the heirs of God's kingdom, who disregards the reprobate and honors those who fear God (Psalm 15: 4).

Here then is the contrary vice condemned, that is, when from respect alone to riches, anyone honors the wicked, and as it has been said, dishonors the good. If then thou shouldest read thus, "He sins who respects the rich," the sentence would be absurd; but if as follows, "He sins who honors the rich alone and despises the poor, and treats him with contempt," it would be a pious and true doctrine.

1. Have not the faith, etc., with respect of persons
He means that the respect of persons is inconsistent with the faith of Christ, so that they cannot be united together, and rightly so; for we are by faith united into one body, in which Christ holds the primacy. When therefore the pomps of the world become preeminent so as to cover over what Christ is, it is evident that faith hath but little vigor.

In rendering t s dox s, "on account of esteem" (*ex opinione*), I have followed Erasmus; though the old interpreter cannot be blamed, who has rendered it "glory," for the word means both; and it may be fitly applied to Christ, and that according to the drift of the passage. For so great is the brightness of Christ, that it easily extinguishes all the glories of the world, if indeed it irradiates our eyes. It hence follows, that Christ is little esteemed by us, when the admiration of worldly glory lays hold on us. But the other exposition is also very suitable, for when the esteem or value of riches or of honors dazzles our eyes, the truth is suppressed, which ought alone to prevail. To sit becomingly means to sit honorably.

4. Are ye not then partial in yourselves? or, are ye not condemned in yourselves
This may be read affirmatively as well as interrogatively, but

The meaning here is, "Do not hold such views of the religion of Christ, as to lead you to manifest partiality to others on account of their difference of rank or outward circumstances."

The Lord of glory. The glorious Lord; he who is glorious himself, and who is encompassed with glory.

The design here seems to be to show that the religion of such a Lord should be in no way dishonored.

With respect of persons. That is, you are not to show respect of persons, or to evince partiality to others on account of their rank, wealth, apparel, etc. Compare Prov. 24: 23; Prov. 28: 21; Lev. 19: 15; Deut. 1: 17; Deut. 10: 17; 2 Chr. 19: 7; Ps. 40: 4.

15–17. If a brother or sister be naked, etc. The comparison in these verses is very obvious and striking. The sense is, that faith in itself, without the acts that correspond to it, and to which it would prompt, is as cold, and heartless, and unmeaning, and useless, as it would be to say to one who was destitute of the necessaries of life, "depart in peace." In itself considered, it might seem to have something that was good; but it would answer none of the purposes of faith unless it should prompt to action. In the case of one who was hungry or naked, what he wanted was not good wishes or kind words merely, but the acts to which good wishes and kind words prompt. And so in religion, what is wanted is not merely the abstract state of mind which would be indicated by faith, but the life of goodness to which it ought to lead. Good wishes and kind words, in order to make them what they should be for the welfare of the world, should be accompanied with corresponding action. So it is with faith. It is not enough for salvation without the benevolent and holy acts to which it would prompt, any more than the good wishes and kind words of the benevolent are enough to satisfy the wants of the hungry, and to clothe the naked, without correspondent action. Faith is not and cannot be shown to be genuine, unless it is accompanied with corresponding acts; as our good wishes for the poor and needy can be shown to be genuine, when we have the means of aiding them, only by actually ministering to

their necessities. In the one case, our wishes would be shown to he unmeaning and heartless; in the other, our faith would be equally so. In regard to this passage, therefore, it may be observed,

(1.) that in fact faith is of no more value, and has no more evidence of genuineness when it is unaccompanied with good works, than such empty wishes for the welfare of the poor would be when unaccompanied with the means of relieving their wants. Faith is designed to lead to good works. It is intended to produce a holy life; a life of activity in the service of the Savior. This is its very essence; it is what it always produces when it is genuine. Religion is not designed to be a cold abstraction; it is to be a living and vivifying principle.

(2.) There is a great deal of that kindness and charity in the world which is expressed by mere good wishes. If we really have not the means of relieving the poor and the needy, then the expression of a kind wish may be in itself an alleviation to their Sorrows, for even sympathy in such a case is of value, and it is much to us to know that others feel for us; but if we have the means, and the object is a worthy one, then such expressions are mere mockery, and aggravate rather than soothe the feelings of the sufferer. Such wishes will neither clothe nor feed them; and they will only make deeper the sorrows which we ought to heal. But how much of this is there in the world, when the sufferer cannot but feel that all these wishes, however kindly expressed, are hollow and false, and when he cannot but feel that relief would be easy!

(3.) In like manner there is much of this same kind of worthless faith in the world – faith that is dead; faith that produces no good works; faith that exerts no practical influence whatever on the life. The individual professes indeed to believe the truths of the gospel; he may be in the church of Christ; he would esteem it a gross calumny to be spoken of as an infidel; but as to any influence which his faith exerts over him, his life would be the same if he had never heard of the gospel. There is not one of the truths of religion which is bodied forth in his life; not a deed to which he is prompted by religion; not an act which

his works, and by works was faith made perfect?

23 And the scripture was fulfilled which saith, Abraham believed God, and it was imputed unto him for righteousness: and he was called the Friend of God.

24 Ye see then how that by works a man is justified, and not by faith only.

25 Likewise also was not Rahab the harlot justified by works, when she had received the messengers, and had sent them out another way?

26 For as the body without the spirit is dead, so faith without works is dead also.

JAMES 3

1 My brethren, be not many masters, knowing that we shall receive the greater condemnation.

2 For in many things we offend all. If any man offend not in word, the same is a perfect man, and able also to bridle the whole body.

3 Behold, we put bits in the horses' mouths, that they may obey us; and we turn about their whole body.

4 Behold also the ships, which though they be so great, and are driven of fierce winds, yet are they turned about with a very small helm, whithersoever the governor listeth.

5 Even so the tongue is a little member, and boasteth great things. Behold, how great a matter a little fire kindleth!

6 And the tongue is a fire, a world of iniquity: so is the tongue among our members, that it defileth the whole body, and setteth on fire the course of nature; and it is set on fire of hell.

7 For every kind of beasts, and of birds, and of serpents, and of things in the sea, is tamed, and hath been tamed of mankind:

8 But the tongue can no man tame; it is an unruly evil, full of deadly poison.

9 Therewith bless we God, even the Father; and therewith curse we men, which are made after the similitude of God.

10 Out of the same mouth proceedeth blessing and cursing. My brethren, these

the sense would be the same, for he amplifies the fault by this, that they took delight and indulged themselves in so great a wickedness. If it be read interrogatively, the meaning is, "Does not your own conscience hold you convicted, so that you need no other judge?" If the affirmative be preferred, it is the same as though he had said, "This evil also happens, that ye think not that ye sin, nor know that your thoughts are so wicked as they are."

JAMES 3

1. Be not many masters

The common and almost universal interpretation of this passage is, that the Apostle discourages the desire for the office of teaching, and for this reason, because it is dangerous, and exposes one to a heavier judgment, in case he transgresses: and they think that he said, **Be not many masters**, because there ought to have been some. But I take masters not to be those who performed a public duty in the Church, but such as took upon them the right of passing judgment upon others: for such reprovers sought to be accounted as masters of morals. And it has a mode of speaking usual among the Greeks as well as Latins, that they were called masters who superciliously animadverted on others.

And that he forbade them to be many, it was done for this reason, because many everywhere did thrust in themselves; for it is, as it were, an innate disease in mankind to seek reputation by blaming others. And, in this respect, a twofold vice prevails – though few excel in wisdom, yet all intrude indiscriminately into the office of masters; and then few are influenced by a right feeling, for hypocrisy and ambition stimulate them, and not a care for the salvation of their brethren. For it is to be observed, that James does not discourage those brotherly admonitions, which the Spirit so often and so much recommends to us, but that immoderate desire to condemn, which proceeds from ambition and pride, when any one exalts himself against his neighbor, slanders, carps, bites, and malignantly seeks for what he may turn to a sinister purpose: for this is usually done when impertinent censors of this kind insolently boast themselves in the work of exposing the vices of others.

From this outrage and annoyance James recalls us; and he adds a reason, because they who are thus severe towards others shall undergo a heavier judgment: for he imposes a hard law on himself, who tries the words and deeds of others according to the rule of extreme rigor; nor does he deserve pardon, who will pardon none. This truth ought to be carefully observed, that they who are too rigid towards their brethren, provoke against themselves the severity of God.

could not be accounted for on the supposition that he has no true piety. In such a case, faith may with propriety be said to be dead.

Being alone. Marg., by itself. The sense is, "being by itself;" that is, destitute of any accompanying fruits or results, it shows that it is dead. That which is alive bodies itself forth, produces effects, makes itself visible; that which is dead produces no effect, and is as if it were not.

JAMES 3

5. Even so, the tongue is a little member. Little compared with the body – as the bit or the rudder is, compared with the horse or the ship.

And boasteth great things. The design of the apostle is to illustrate the power and influence of the tongue. This may be done in a great many respects: and the apostle does it by referring to its boasting; to the effects which it produces, resembling that of fire (James 3: 6); to its untameableness, (James 3: 8–9;) and to its giving utterance to the most inconsistent and incongruous thoughts, James 3: 9–10. The particular idea here is, that the tongue seems to be conscious of its influence and power, and boasts largely of what it can do. The apostle means doubtless to convey the idea that it boasts not unjustly of its importance. It has all the influence in the world, for good or for evil, which it claims.

Behold, how great a matter a little fire kindleth! Marg., wood. The Greek word means a wood, forest, grove; and then fire-wood, fuel. This is the meaning here. The sense is, that a very little fire is sufficient to ignite a large quantity of combustible materials, and that the tongue produces effects similar to that. A spark will kindle a lofty pile; and a word spoken by the tongue may set a neighborhood or a village "in a flame."

8. But the tongue can no man tame. This does not mean that it is never brought under control, but that it is impossible effectually and certainly to subdue it. It would be possible to subdue and domesticate any kind of beasts, but this could not be done with the tongue.

It is an unruly evil. An evil without restraint, to which no certain effectual check can be applied. Of the truth of this no one can have any doubt, who looks at the condition of the world.

Full of deadly poison. That is, it acts on the happiness of man, and on the peace of society, as poison does on the human frame. The allusion here seems to be to the bite of a venomous reptile. Compare Ps. 140: 3, "They have sharpened their tongues like a serpent; adders' poison is under their lips." Rom. 3: 13, "With their tongues they have used deceit; the poison of asps is under their lips." Nothing would better describe the mischief that may be done by the tongue. There is no sting of a serpent that does so much evil in the world; there is no poison more deadly to the frame than the poison of the tongue is to the happiness of man. Who, for example, can stand before the power of the slanderer? What mischief can be done in society that can be compared with that which he, may do?

9. Therewith bless we God. We men do this; that is, all this is done by the tongue. The apostle goes not mean that the same man does this, but that all this is done by the same organ – the tongue.

Even the Father. Who sustains to us the relation of a Father. The point in the remark of the apostle is, the absurdity of employing the tongue in such contradictory uses as to bless one who has to us the relation of a Father and to curse any being, especially those who are made in his image. The word bless here is used in the sense of praise, thank, worship.

And therewith curse we men. That is, it is one by the same organ by which God is praised and honored.

Which are made after the similitude of God. After his image, Gen. 1: 26–27. As we bless God, we ought with the same organ to bless those who are like him. There is an absurdity in cursing men who are thus made, like what there would be in both blessing and cursing the Creator himself.

10. Out of the same mouth proceedeth blessing and cursing. The meaning here may be, either that out of the mouth of man two such opposite things proceed, not referring to

things ought not so to be.

11 Doth a fountain send forth at the same place sweet water and bitter?

12 Can the fig tree, my brethren, bear olive berries? either a vine, figs? so can no fountain both yield salt water and fresh.

13 Who is a wise man and endued with knowledge among you? let him shew out of a good conversation his works with meekness of wisdom.

14 But if ye have bitter envying and strife in your hearts, glory not, and lie not against the truth.

15 This wisdom descendeth not from above, but is earthly, sensual, devilish.

16 For where envying and strife is, there is confusion and every evil work.

17 But the wisdom that is from above is first pure, then peaceable, gentle, and easy to be intreated, full of mercy and good fruits, without partiality, and without hypocrisy.

18 And the fruit of righteousness is sown in peace of them that make peace.

JAMES 4

1 From whence come wars and fightings among you? come they not hence, even of your lusts that war in your members?

2 Ye lust, and have not: ye kill, and desire to have, and cannot obtain: ye fight and war, yet ye have not, because ye ask not.

3 Ye ask, and receive not, because ye ask amiss, that ye may consume it upon your lusts.

4 Ye adulterers and adulteresses, know ye not that the friendship of the world is enmity with God? whosoever therefore will be a friend of the world is the enemy of God.

5 Do ye think that the scripture saith in vain, The spirit that dwelleth in us lusteth to envy?

6 But he giveth more grace. Wherefore he saith, God resisteth the proud, but giveth grace unto the humble.

7 Submit yourselves therefore to God. Resist the devil, and he will flee from you.

17. But the wisdom which is from above

He now mentions the effects of celestial wisdom which are wholly contrary to the former effects. He says first that it is **pure**; by which term he excludes hypocrisy and ambition. He, in the second place, calls it **peaceable**, to intimate that it is not contentious. In the third place, he calls it **kind** or humane, that we may know that it is far away from that immoderate austerity which tolerates nothing in our brethren. He also calls it **gentle** or tractable; by which he means that it widely differs from pride and malignity. In the last place, he says that it is **full of mercy**, etc., while hypocrisy is inhuman and inexorable. By **good fruits** he generally refers to all those duties which benevolent men perform towards their brethren; as though he had said, it is full of benevolence. It hence follows, that they lie who glory in their cruel austerity.

But though he had sufficiently condemned hypocrisy, when he said that wisdom is **pure** or sincere; he makes it more clear by repeating the same thing at the end. We are hence reminded, that for no other reason are we beyond measure morose or austere, but this, because we too much spare ourselves, and connive at our own vices.

But what he says, **without discerning** (*sine dijudicatione,*) seems strange; for the Spirit of God does not take away the difference between good and evil; nor does he render us so senseless as to be so void of judgment as to praise vice, and regard it as virtue. To this I reply, that James here, by *discerning* or distinguishing refers to that overanxious and overscrupulous inquiry, such as is commonly carried on by hypocrites, who too minutely examine the sayings and doings of their brethren, and put on them the worst construction.

JAMES 4

1. From whence come wars

As he had spoken of peace, and had reminded them that vices are to be exterminated in such a way as to preserve peace, he now comes to their contentions, by which they created confusion among themselves; and he shews that these arose from their invidious desires and lusts, rather than from a zeal for what was just and right; for if every one observed moderation, they would not have disturbed and annoyed one another. They had their hot conflicts, because their lusts were allowed to prevail unchecked.

It hence appears, that greater peace would have been among them, had every one abstained from doing wrong to others; but the vices which prevailed among them were so many attendants armed to excite contentions. He calls our faculties **members**. He takes **lusts** as designating all

the same individual, but to different persons; or, out of the mouth of the same individual. Both of these are true; and both are equally incongruous and wrong. No organ should be devoted to uses so unlike, and the mouth should be employed in giving utterance only to that which is just, benevolent, and good. It is true, however, that the mouth is devoted to these opposite employments; and that while one part of the race employ it purposes of praise, the other employ it in uttering maledictions. It is also true of many individuals that at one time they praise their Maker, and then, with the sane organ, calumniate, and slander, and revile their fellow-men. After an act of solemn devotion in the house of God, the professed worshipper goes forth with the feelings of malice in his heart, and the language of slander, detraction, or even blasphemy on his lips.

My brethren, these things ought not so to be. They are as incongruous as it would be for the same fountain to send forth both salt water and fresh; or for the same tree to bear different kinds of fruit.

15. This wisdom descendeth not from above. The wisdom here referred to is that carnal or worldly wisdom which produces strife and contention; that kind of knowledge which leads to self-conceit, and which prompts a man to defend his opinions with overheated zeal. In the contentions which are in the world, in church and state, in neighborhoods and families, at the bar, in political life, and in theological disputes, even where there is the manifestation of enraged and irascible feeling, there is often much of a certain kind of wisdom. There is learning, shrewdness, tact, logical skill, subtle and skilful argumentation – "making the worse appear the better reason;" but all this is often connected with a spirit so narrow, bigoted, and contentious, as to show clearly that it has not its origin in heaven. The spirit which is originated there is always connected with gentleness, calmness, and a love of truth.

But is earthly. Has its origin in this world, and partakes of its spirit. It is such as men exhibit who are governed only by worldly maxims and principles.

Sensual. Marg., natural. The meaning is, that it has its origin in our sensual rather than in our intellectual and moral nature. It is that which takes counsel of our natural appetites and propensities, and not of high and spiritual influences.

Devilish. Demoniacal. Such as the demons exhibit. There may be indeed talent in it, but there is the intermingling of malignant passions, and "it leads to contentions, strifes, divisions, and "every evil work."

JAMES 4

1. From whence come wars and fightings among you? Marg., brawlings. The reference is to strifes and contentions of all kinds; and the question then, as it is now, was an important one, what was their source or origin? The answer is given in the succeeding part of the verse. Some have supposed that the apostle refers here to the contests and seditions existing among the Jews, which afterwards broke out in rebellion against the Roman authority, and which led to the overthrow of the Jewish nation. But the more probable reference is to domestic broils, and to the strifes of sects and parties; to the disputes which were carried on among the Jewish people, and which perhaps led to scenes of violence, and to popular outbreaks among themselves. When the apostle says "among you," it is not necessary to suppose that he refers to those who were members of the Christian church as actually engaged in these strifes, though he was writing to such; but he speaks of them as a part of the Jewish people, and refers to the contentions which prevailed among them as a people – contentions in which those who were Christian converts were in great danger of participating, by being drawn into their controversies, and partaking of the spirit of strife which existed among their countrymen. It is known that such a spirit of contention prevailed among the Jews at that time in an eminent degree, and it was well to put those among them who professed to be Christians on their guard against such a spirit, by stating the causes of all wars and contentious. The solution which the apostle has given of the causes of the strifes prevailing then, will apply

8 Draw nigh to God, and he will draw nigh to you. Cleanse your hands, ye sinners; and purify your hearts, ye double minded.

9 Be afflicted, and mourn, and weep: let your laughter be turned to mourning, and your joy to heaviness.

10 Humble yourselves in the sight of the Lord, and he shall lift you up.

11 Speak not evil one of another, brethren. He that speaketh evil of his brother, and judgeth his brother, speaketh evil of the law, and judgeth the law: but if thou judge the law, thou art not a doer of the law, but a judge.

12 There is one lawgiver, who is able to save and to destroy: who art thou that judgest another?

13 Go to now, ye that say, To day or to morrow we will go into such a city, and continue there a year, and buy and sell, and get gain:

14 Whereas ye know not what shall be on the morrow. For what is your life? It is even a vapor, that appeareth for a little time, and then vanisheth away.

15 For that ye ought to say, If the Lord will, we shall live, and do this, or that.

16 But now ye rejoice in your boastings: all such rejoicing is evil.

17 Therefore to him that knoweth to do good, and doeth it not, to him it is sin.

JAMES 5

1 Go to now, ye rich men, weep and howl for your miseries that shall come upon you.

2 Your riches are corrupted, and your garments are motheaten.

3 Your gold and silver is cankered; and the rust of them shall be a witness against you, and shall eat your flesh as it were fire. Ye have heaped treasure together for the last days.

4 Behold, the hire of the labourers who have reaped down your fields, which is of you kept back by fraud, crieth: and the cries of them which have reaped are entered into the ears of the Lord of sabaoth.

5 Ye have lived in pleasure on the earth, and been wanton; ye have nourished your

illicit and lustful desires or propensities which cannot be satisfied without doing injury to others.

2. Ye lust, or covet, and have not

He seems to intimate that the soul of man is insatiable, when he indulges wicked lusts; and truly it is so; for he who suffers his sinful propensities to rule uncontrolled, will know no end to his lust. Were even the world given to him, he would wish other worlds to be created for him. It thus happens, that men seek torments which exceed the cruelty of all executioners. For that saying of Horace is true: "The tyrants of Sicily found no torment greater than envy."

Some copies have *phoneuete*, "ye kill;" but I doubt not but that we ought to read, *phthoneite*, "ye envy," as I have rendered it; for the verb, to kill, does in no way suit the context.

Ye fight

He does not mean those wars and fightings, which men engage in with drawn swords, but the violent contentions which prevailed among them. They derived no benefit from contentions of this kind, for he affirms that they received the punishment of their own wickedness. God, indeed, whom they owned not as the author of blessings, justly disappointed them. For when they contended in ways so unlawful, they sought to be enriched through the favor of Satan rather than through the favor of God. One by fraud, another by violence, one by calumnies, and all by some evil or wicked arts, strove for happiness. They then sought to be happy, but not through God. It was therefore no wonder that they were frustrated in their efforts, since no success can be expected except through the blessings of God alone.

JAMES 5

1. Go to now

They are mistaken, as I think, who consider that James here exhorts the rich to repentance. It seems to me to be a simple denunciation of God's judgment, by which he meant to terrify them without giving them any hope of pardon; for all that he says tends only to despair. He, therefore, does not address them in order to invite them to repentance; but, on the contrary, he has a regard to the faithful, that they, hearing of the miserable and of the rich, might not envy their fortune, and also that knowing that God would be the avenger of the wrongs they suffered, they might with a calm and resigned mind bear them.

But he does not speak of the rich indiscriminately, but of those who, being immersed in pleasures and inflated with pride, thought of nothing but of the world, and who, like inexhaustible gulfs, devoured everything; for they, by their

substantially to all the wars which have ever existed on the earth.

Come they not hence, even of your lusts? Is not this the true source of all war and contention? The word rendered lusts is in the margin rendered pleasures. This is the usual meaning of the word, but it is commonly applied to the pleasures of sense, and thence denotes desire, appetite, lust. It may be applied to any desire of sensual gratification, and then to the indulgence of any corrupt propensity of the mind. The lust or desire of rapine, of plunder, of ambition, of fame, of a more extended dominion, would be properly embraced in the meaning of the word. The word would equally comprehend the spirit-which leads to a brawl in the street, and that which prompted to the conquests of Alexander, Caesar, or Napoleon. All this is the same spirit evinced on a larger or smaller scale.

That war in your members. The word member (*melov*) denotes, properly, a limb or member of the body; but it is used in the New Testament to denote the members of the body collectively; that is, the body itself as the seat of the desires and passions, Rom. 6: 13,19; Rom. 7: 5,23; Col. 3: 5. The word war here refers to the conflict between those passions which have their seat in the flesh, and the better principles of the mind and conscience, producing a state of agitation and conflict.

8. Draw nigh to God, and he will draw nigh to you. Compare 2 Chr. 15: 2. This declaration contains a great and important principle in religion. If we wish the favor of God, we must come to him; nor can we hope for his mercy, unless we approach him and ask him for it. We cannot come literally any nearer to God than we always are, for he is always round about us; but we may come nearer in a spiritual sense. We may address him directly in prayer; we may approach him by meditation on his character; we may draw near to him in the ordinances of religion. We can never hope for his favor while we prefer to remain at a distance from him; none who in fact draw near to him will find him unwilling to bestow on them the blessings which they need.

JAMES 5

1. Ye rich men. Not all rich men, but only that class of them who are specified as unjust and oppressive. There is no sin in merely being rich; where sin exists peculiarly among the rich, it arises from the manner in which wealth is acquired, the spirit which it tends to engender in the heart, and the way in which it is used.

Weep and howl. Gr., "Weep howling." This would be expressive of very deep distress. The language is intensive in a high degree, showing that the calamities which were coming upon them were not only such as would produce tears, but tears accompanied with loud lamentations. In the East, it is customary to give expression to deep sorrow by loud out cries. Compare Is. 13: 6; Is. 14: 31; 15: 2; 16: 7; Jer. 4: 8; Jer. 47: 2; Joel 1: 5.

For your miseries that shall come upon you. Many expositors, as Benson, Witby, Macknight, and others, suppose that this refers to the approaching destruction of Jerusalem by the Romans, and to the miseries which would be brought in the siege upon the Jewish people, in which the rich would be the peculiar objects of cupidity and vengeance. They refer to passages in Josephus, which describe particularly the sufferings to which the rich were exposed; the searching of their houses by the zealots, and the heavy calamities which came upon them and their families. But there is no reason to suppose that the apostle referred particularly to those events. The poor as well as the rich suffered in that siege, and there were no such special judgments then brought upon the rich as to show that they were the marked objects of the Divine displeasure. It is much more natural to suppose that the apostle means to say that such men as he here refers to exposed themselves always to the wrath of God, and that they had great reason to weep in the anticipation of his vengeance. The sentiments here expressed by the apostle are not applicable merely to the Jews of his time. If there is any class of men which has special reason to dread the wrath of God at all times, it is just the class of men here referred to.

2. Your riches are corrupted. The word here rendered corrupted does not occur elsewhere

hearts, as in a day of slaughter.

6 Ye have condemned and killed the just; and he doth not resist you.

7 Be patient therefore, brethren, unto the coming of the Lord. Behold, the husbandman waiteth for the precious fruit of the earth, and hath long patience for it, until he receive the early and latter rain.

8 Be ye also patient; stablish your hearts: for the coming of the Lord draweth nigh.

9 Grudge not one against another, brethren, lest ye be condemned: behold, the judge standeth before the door.

10 Take, my brethren, the prophets, who have spoken in the name of the Lord, for an example of suffering affliction, and of patience.

11 Behold, we count them happy which endure. Ye have heard of the patience of Job, and have seen the end of the Lord; that the Lord is very pitiful, and of tender mercy.

12 But above all things, my brethren, swear not, neither by heaven, neither by the earth, neither by any other oath: but let your yea be yea; and your nay, nay; lest ye fall into condemnation.

13 Is any among you afflicted? let him pray. Is any merry? let him sing psalms.

14 Is any sick among you? let him call for the elders of the church; and let them pray over him, anointing him with oil in the name of the Lord:

15 And the prayer of faith shall save the sick, and the Lord shall raise him up; and if he have committed sins, they shall be forgiven him.

16 Confess your faults one to another, and pray one for another, that ye may be healed. The effectual fervent prayer of a righteous man availeth much.

17 Elias was a man subject to like passions as we are, and he prayed earnestly that it might not rain: and it rained not on the earth by the space of three years and six months.

18 And he prayed again, and the heaven gave rain, and the earth brought forth her fruit.

19 Brethren, if any of you do err from the truth, and one convert him;

tyranny, oppressed others, as it appears from the whole passage.

Weep and howl, *or*, Lament, howling

Repentance has indeed its weeping, but being mixed with consolation, it does not proceed to howling. Then James intimates that the heaviness of God's vengeance will be so horrible and severe on the rich, that they will be constrained to break forth into howling, as though he had said briefly to them, "Woe to you!" But it is a prophetic mode of speaking: the ungodly have the punishment which awaits them set before them, and they are represented as already enduring it. As, then, they were now flattering themselves, and promising to themselves that the prosperity in which they thought themselves happy would be perpetual, he declared that the most grievous miseries were nigh at hand.

2. Your riches

The meaning may be twofold: that he ridicules their foolish confidence, because the riches in which they placed their happiness, were wholly fading, yea, that they could be reduced to nothing by one blast from God – or that he condemns as their insatiable avarice, because they heaped together wealth only for this, that they might perish without any benefit. This latter meaning is the most suitable. It is, indeed, true that those rich men are insane who glory in things so fading as garments, gold, silver, and such things, since it is nothing else than to make their glory subject to rust and moths; and well known is that saying "What is ill got is soon lost"; because the curse of God consumes it all, for it is not right that the ungodly or their heirs should enjoy riches which they have snatched, as it were, by violence from the hand of God.

But as James enumerates the vices of which the rich brought on themselves the calamity which he mentions, the context requires, as I think, that we should say, that what he condemns here is the extreme rapacity of the rich, in retaining everything they could lay hold on, that it might rot uselessly in their chests. For thus it was, that what God had created for the use of men, they destroyed, as though they were the enemies of mankind.

But it must be observed, that the vices which he mentions here do not belong to all the rich; for some of them indulge themselves in luxury, some spend much in show and display, and some pinch themselves, and live miserably in their own filth. Let us, then, know that he here reproves some vices in some, and some vices in others. However, all those are generally condemned who unjustly accumulate riches, or who foolishly abuse them. But what James now says, is not only suitable to the rich of extreme tenacity (such as Euclio of Plautus), but to those also who delight in pomp and luxury, and yet prefer to heap up riches rather

in the New Testament. It means, to cause to rot, to corrupt, to destroy. The reference here is to their hoarded treasures; and the idea is, that they had accumulated more than they needed for their own use; and that, instead of distributing them to do good to others, or employing them in any useful way, they kept them until they rotted or spoiled. It is to be remembered, that a considerable part of the treasures which a man in the East would lay up, consisted of perishable materials, as garments, grain, oil, etc. Such articles of property were often stored up, expecting that they would furnish a supply for many years, in case of the prevalence of famine or wars. Compare Luke 12: 18–19. A suitable provision for the time to come cannot be forbidden; but the reference here is to cases in which great quantities had been laid up, perhaps while the poor were suffering, and which were kept until they became worthless.

Your garments are moth-eaten. The same idea substantially is expressed here in another form. As the fashions in the East did not change as they do with us, wealth consisted much in the garments that were laid up for show or for future use.

16. Confess your faults one to another. This seems primarily to refer to those who were sick, since it is added, **that ye may be healed.** The fair interpretation is, that it might be supposed that such confession would contribute to a restoration to health. The case supposed all along here (see James 5: 15) is, that the sickness referred to had been brought upon the patient for his sins, apparently as a punishment for some particular transgressions.

In such a case, it is said that if those who were sick would make confession of their sins, it would, in connection with prayer, be an important means of restoration to health. The duty inculcated, and which is equally binding on all now, is, that if we are sick, and are conscious that we have injured any persons, to make confession to them. This indeed is a duty at all times, but in health it is often neglected, and there is a special propriety that such confession should be made when we are sick. The particular reason for doing it which is here specified is, that it would contribute to a res-

toration to health – "that ye may be healed." In the case specified, this might be supposed to contribute to a restoration to health from one of two causes:

(1.) If the sickness had been brought upon them as a special act of Divine visitation for sin, it might be hoped that when the confession was made the hand of God would be withdrawn; or

(2.) in any case, if the mind was troubled by the recollection of guilt, it might be hoped that the calmness and peace resulting from confession would be favorable to a restoration to health. The former case would of course be more applicable to the times of the apostles; the latter would pertain to all times. Disease is often greatly aggravated by the trouble of mind which arises from conscious guilt; and, in such a case, nothing will contribute more directly to recovery than the restoration of peace to the soul agitated by guilt and by the dread of a judgment to come. This may be secured by confession – confession made first to God, and then to those who are wronged. It may be added, that this is a duty to which we are prompted by the very nature of our feelings when we are sick, and by the fact that no one is willing to die with guilt on his conscience; without having done everything that he can to be at peace with all the world. This passage is one on which Roman Catholics rely to demonstrate the propriety of "auricular confession," or confession made to a priest with a view to an absolution of sin. The doctrine which is held on that point is, that it is a duty to confess to a priest, at certain seasons, all our sins, secret and open, of which we have been guilty; all our improper thoughts, desires, words, and actions; and that the priest has power to declare on such confession that the sins are forgiven. But never was any text less pertinent to prove a doctrine than this passage to demonstrate that. For,

(1.) the confession here enjoined is not to be made by a person in health, that he may obtain salvation, but by a sick person, that he may be healed.

(2.) As mutual confession is here enjoined, a priest would be as much bound to confess to the people as the people to a priest.

20 Let him know, that he which con-
verteth the sinner from the error of his
way shall save a soul from death, and
shall hide a multitude of sins.

than to employ them for necessary purposes. For such is
the malignity of some, that they grudge to others the common sun and air.

7. Be patient therefore

From this inference it is evident that what has hitherto been
said against the rich, pertains to the consolation of those
who seemed for a time to be exposed to their wrongs with
impunity. For after having mentioned the causes of those
calamities which were hanging over the rich, and having
stated this among others, that they proudly and cruelly
ruled over the poor, he immediately adds, that we who are
unjustly oppressed, have this reason to be patient, because
God would become the judge. For this is what he means
when he says, unto the coming of the Lord, that is, that
the confusion of things which is now seen in the world
will not be perpetual, because the Lord at his coming will
reduce things to order, and that therefore our minds ought
to entertain good hope; for it is not without reason that
the restoration of all things is promised to us at that day.
And though the day of the Lord is everywhere called in
the Scriptures a manifestation of his judgment and grace,
when he succors his people and chastises the ungodly, yet I
prefer to regard the expression here as referring to our final
deliverance.

(3.) No mention is made of a priest at all, or even of a minister of religion, as the one to whom the confession is to be made.

(4.) The confession referred to is for "faults" with reference to "one another," that is, where one has injured another; and nothing is said of confessing faults to those whom we have not injured at all.

(5.) There is no mention here of absolution, either by a priest or any other person.

(6.) If anything is meant by absolution that is scriptural, it may as well be pronounced by one person as another; by a layman as a clergyman. All that it can mean is, that God promises pardon to those who are truly penitent, and this fact may as well be stated by one person as another. No priest, no man whatever, is empowered to say to another either that he is truly penitent, or to forgive sin. "Who can forgive sins but God only?" None but he whose law has been violated, or who has been wronged, can pardon an offence. No third person can forgive a sin which a man has committed against a neighbor; no one but a parent can pardon the offences of which his own children have been guilty towards him; and who call put himself in the place of God, and presume to pardon the sins which his creatures have committed against him?

(7.) The practice of "auricular confession" is "evil, and only evil, and that continually." Nothing gives so much power to a priesthood as the supposition that they have the power of absolution. Nothing serves so much to pollute the soul as to keep impure thoughts before the mind long enough to make the confession, and to state them in words. Nothing gives a man so much power over a female as to have it supposed that it is required by religion, and appertains to the sacred office, that all that passes in the mind should be disclosed to him. The thought which but for the necessity of confession would have vanished at once; the image which would have departed as soon as it came before the mind but for the necessity of retaining it to make con-

fession – these are the things over which a man would seek to have control, and to which he would desire to have access, if he wished to accomplish purposes of villainy. The very thing which a seducer would desire would be the power of knowing all the thoughts of his intended victim; and if the thoughts which pass through the soul could be known, virtue would be safe nowhere. Nothing probably under the name of religion has ever done more to corrupt the morals of a community than the practice of auricular confession.

And pray one for another. One for the other; mutually. Those who have done injury, and those who are injured, should pray for each other. The apostle does not seem here, as in James 5: 14–15, to refer particularly to the prayers of the ministers of religion, or the elders of the church, but refers to it as a duty appertaining to all Christians.

That ye may be healed. Not with reference to death, and therefore not relating to "extreme unction," but in order that the sick may be restored again to health. This is said in connection with the duty of confession, as well as prayer; and it seems to be implied that both might contribute to a restoration to health. Of the way in which prayer would do this, there can be no doubt; for all healing comes from God, and it is reasonable to suppose that this might be bestowed in answer to prayer.

19. **Brethren, if any of you do err from the truth.** Either doctrinally and speculatively, by embracing error; or practically, by falling into sinful practices. Either of these may be called "erring from the truth," because they are contrary to what the truth teaches and requires. What is here said does not appear to have any connection with what precedes, but the apostle seems to have supposed that such a case might occur; and, in the conclusion of the epistle, he called their attention to the importance of endeavoring to save an erring brother, if such an instance should happen. The exhortation would be proper in addressing a letter to any church, or in publicly addressing any congregation.

1 Peter

Introduction by John Calvin

THE design of Peter in this Epistle is to exhort the faithful to a denial of the world and a contempt of it, so that being freed from carnal affections and all earthly hindrances, they might with their whole soul aspire after the celestial kingdom of Christ, that being elevated by hope, supported by patience, and fortified by courage and perseverance, they might overcome all kinds of temptations, and pursue this course and practice throughout life.

Hence at the very beginning he proclaims in express words the grace of God made known to us in Christ; and at the same time he adds, that it is received by faith and possessed by hope, so that the godly might raise up their minds and hearts above the world. Hence he exhorts them to holiness, lest they should render void the price by which they were redeemed, and lest they should suffer the incorruptible seed of the Word, by which they had been regenerated into eternal life, to be destroyed or to die. And as he had said, that they had been born again by God's Word, he makes mention of their spiritual infancy. Moreover, that their faith might not vacillate or stagger, because they saw that Christ was despised and rejected almost by the whole world, he reminds them that this was only the fulfillment of what had been written of him, that he would be the stone of stumbling. But he further teaches them that he would be a firm foundation to those who believe in him. Hence he again refers to the great honor to which God had raised them, that they might be animated by the contemplation of their former state, and by the perception of their present benefits, to devote themselves to a godly life.

He afterwards comes to particular exhortations – that they were to conduct themselves in humility and obedience under the government of princes, that servants were to be subject to their masters, that wives were to obey their husbands and to be modest and chaste, and that, on the other hand, husbands were to treat their wives with kindness. And then he commands them to observe what was just and right towards one another; and that they might do this the more willingly, he sets before them what would be the fruit – a peaceable and happy life.

As, however, it happened to Christians, that how much soever they sought peace, they were often harassed by many injuries, and had the world for no just cause inimical to them, he exhorts them calmly to bear their persecutions, which they knew would promote their salvation. For this purpose he brings forward the example of Christ. On the other hand, he reminds them what unhappy end awaits the ungodly, whilst in the meantime God wonderfully delivers his Church from death by death. He still further refers to the example of Christ to enforce the mortification of the flesh. To this exhortation he adds various and brief sentences; but shortly after he returns to the doctrine of patience, so that the faithful might mingle consolation with their evils, regarding it as good for them to be chastised by the paternal hand of God.

At the beginning of the fifth chapter he reminds the elders of their duty, that they were not to tyrannize over the Church, but to preside under Christ with moderation. He recommends to the young modesty and teachableness. At length, after a short exhortation, he closes the Epistle with a prayer.

The commentaries on 1 Peter are by John Calvin and Adam Clarke.

1 PETER 1

1 Peter, an apostle of Jesus Christ, to the strangers scattered throughout Pontus, Galatia, Cappadocia, Asia, and Bithynia,

2 Elect according to the foreknowledge of God the Father, through sanctification of the Spirit, unto obedience and sprinkling of the blood of Jesus Christ: Grace unto you, and peace, be multiplied.

3 Blessed be the God and Father of our Lord Jesus Christ, which according to his abundant mercy hath begotten us again unto a lively hope by the resurrection of Jesus Christ from the dead,

4 To an inheritance incorruptible, and undefiled, and that fadeth not away, reserved in heaven for you ,

5 Who are kept by the power of God through faith unto salvation ready to be revealed in the last time.

6 Wherein ye greatly rejoice, though now for a season, if need be, ye are in heaviness through manifold temptations:

7 That the trial of your faith, being much more precious than of gold that perisheth, though it be tried with fire, might be found unto praise and honor and glory at the appearing of Jesus Christ:

8 Whom having not seen, ye love; in whom, though now ye see him not, yet believing, ye rejoice with joy unspeakable and full of glory:

9 Receiving the end of your faith, even the salvation of your souls.

10 Of which salvation the prophets have inquired and searched diligently, who prophesied of the grace that should come unto you:

11 Searching what, or what manner of time the Spirit of Christ which was in them did signify, when it testified beforehand the sufferings of Christ, and the glory that should follow.

12 Unto whom it was revealed, that not unto themselves, but unto us they did minister the things, which are now reported unto you by them that have preached the gospel unto you with the Holy Ghost sent down from heaven; which things the angels desire to look into.

13 Wherefore gird up the loins of your mind, be sober, and hope to the end for the grace that is to be brought unto you at

1 PETER 1

1. Peter, an apostle

What in this salutation is the same with those of Paul, requires no new explanation. When Paul prayed for **grace** and **peace,** the verb is left out; but Peter adds it, and says, **be multiplied**; still the meaning is the same; for Paul did not wish to the faithful the beginning of grace and peace, but the increase of them, that is, that God would complete what he had begun.

To the elect, *or* the elected

It may be asked, how could this be found out, for the election of God is hid, and cannot be known without the special revelation of the Spirit; and as every one is made sure of his own election by the testimony of the Spirit, so he can know nothing certain of others. To this I answer, that we are not curiously to inquire about the election of our brethren, but ought on the contrary to regard their calling, so that all who are admitted by faith into the church, are to be counted as the elect; for God thus separates them from the world, which is a sign of election. It is no objection to say that many fall away, having nothing but the semblance; for it is the judgment of charity and not of faith, when we deem all those elect in whom appears the mark of God's adoption. And that he does not fetch their election from the hidden counsel of God, but gathers it from the effect, is evident from the context; for afterwards he connects it with the **sanctification of the Spirit**. As far then as they proved that they were regenerated by the Spirit of God, so far did he deem them to be the elect of God, for God does not sanctify any but those whom he has previously elected.

However, he at the same time reminds us whence that election flows, by which we are separated for salvation, that we may not perish with the world; for he says, **according to the foreknowledge of God**. This is the fountain and the first cause: God knew before the world was created whom he had elected for salvation.

But we ought wisely to consider what this precognition or foreknowledge is. For the sophists, in order to obscure the grace of God, imagine that the merits of each are foreseen by God, and that thus the reprobate are distinguished from the elect, as every one proves himself worthy of this or that lot. But Scripture everywhere sets the counsel of God, on which is founded our salvation, in opposition to our merits. Hence, when Peter calls them elect according to the precognition of God, he intimates that the cause of it depends on nothing else but on God alone, for he of his own free will has chosen us. Then the foreknowledge of God excludes every worthiness on the part of man.

As however in our election he assigns the first place to the gratuitous favor of God, so again he would have us to know

1 PETER 1

1. Peter, an apostle – Simon Peter, called also Kephas: he was a fisherman, son of Jonah, brother of Andrew, and born at Bethsaida; and one of the first disciples of our Lord.

The strangers scattered throughout – Jews first, who had believed the Gospel in the different countries here specified; and converted Gentiles also. Though the word strangers may refer to all truly religious people, see Genesis 47: 9; Psalm 39: 12, in the Septuagint, and Hebrews 11: 13, yet the inscription may have a special reference to those who were driven by persecution to seek refuge in those heathen provinces to which the influence of their persecuting brethren did not extend.

2. Elect according to the foreknowledge of God – If the apostle had directed his letter to persons elected to eternal life, no one could have received such a letter, because no one could have been sure of his election in this way till he had arrived in heaven. But the persons to whom the apostle wrote were all, with propriety, said to be elect according to the foreknowledge of God; because, agreeably to the original purpose of God, discovered in the prophetical writings, Jews and Gentiles, indiscriminately, were called to be the visible Church, and entitled to all the privileges of the people of God, on their believing the Gospel. In this sense the word elected is used in other places of Scripture; see 1 Thessalonians 1: 4.

The Rev. J. Wesley has this excellent note on this passage: "Strictly speaking, there is no foreknowledge, no more than afterknowledge, with God; but all things are known to him as present, from eternity to eternity. Election, in the scriptural sense, is God's doing any thing that our merit or power has no part in. The true predestination or foreappointment of God is,

1. He that believeth shall be saved from the guilt and power of sin.

2. He that endureth to the end shall be saved eternally.

3. They who receive the precious gift of faith thereby become the sons of God; and, being sons, they shall receive the Spirit of holiness, to walk as Christ also walked.

Throughout every part of this appointment of God, promise and duty go hand in hand. All is free gift; and yet, such is the gift, that it depends in the final issue on our future obedience to the heavenly call. But other predestination than this, either to life or death eternal, the Scripture knows not of: moreover,

1. It is cruel respect of persons; an unjust regard of one, and an unjust disregard of another: it is mere creature partiality, and not infinite justice.

2. It is not plain Scripture doctrine, (if true), but rather inconsistent with the express written word that speaks of God's universal offers of grace; his invitations, promises, threatenings, being all general.

3. We are bid to choose life, and reprehended for not doing it.

4. It is inconsistent with a state of probation in those that must be saved, or must be lost.

5. It is of fatal consequence; all men being ready, on very slight grounds, to fancy themselves of the elect number.

But the doctrine of predestination is entirely changed from what it formerly was: now it implies neither faith, peace, nor purity; it is something that will do without them all. Faith is no longer, according to the modern predestination scheme, a Divine evidence of things not seen wrought in the soul by the immediate power of the Holy Ghost; not an evidence at all, but a mere notion: neither is faith made any longer a means of holiness, but something that will do without it. Christ is no more a Savior from sin, but a defense and a countenancer of it. He is no more a fountain of spiritual life in the souls of believers, but leaves his elect inwardly dry, and outwardly unfruitful; and is made little more than a refuge from the image of the heavenly, even from righteousness, peace, and joy in the Holy Ghost."

7. That the trial of your faith, being much more precious than of gold – As by the action of fire gold is separated from all alloy and heterogeneous mixtures, and is proved to be gold by its enduring the action of the fire without losing any thing of its nature, weight, color, or any other property, so genuine faith is proved by adversities, especially such as the primitive Christians were obliged to pass through. For

the revelation of Jesus Christ;

14 As obedient children, not fashioning yourselves according to the former lusts in your ignorance:

15 But as he which hath called you is holy, so be ye holy in all manner of conversation;

16 Because it is written, Be ye holy; for I am holy.

17 And if ye call on the Father, who without respect of persons judgeth according to every man's work, pass the time of your sojourning here in fear:

18 Forasmuch as ye know that ye were not redeemed with corruptible things, as silver and gold, from your vain conversation received by tradition from your fathers;

19 But with the precious blood of Christ, as of a lamb without blemish and without spot:

20 Who verily was foreordained before the foundation of the world, but was manifest in these last times for you,

21 Who by him do believe in God, that raised him up from the dead, and gave him glory; that your faith and hope might be in God.

22 Seeing ye have purified your souls in obeying the truth through the Spirit unto unfeigned love of the brethren, see that ye love one another with a pure heart fervently:

23 Being born again, not of corruptible seed, but of incorruptible, by the word of God, which liveth and abideth for ever.

24 For all flesh is as grass, and all the glory of man as the flower of grass. The grass withereth, and the flower thereof falleth away:

25 But the word of the Lord endureth for ever. And this is the word which by the gospel is preached unto you.

1 PETER 2

1 Wherefore laying aside all malice, and all guile, and hypocrisies, and envies, and all evil speakings,

2 As newborn babes, desire the sincere milk of the word, that ye may grow thereby:

3 If so be ye have tasted that the Lord is gracious.

4 To whom coming, as unto a living

it by the effects, for there is nothing more dangerous or more preposterous than to overlook our calling and to seek for the certainty of our election in the hidden prescience of God, which is the deepest labyrinth. Therefore to obviate this danger, Peter supplies the best correction; for though in the first place he would have us to consider the counsel of God, the cause of which is alone in himself; yet he invites us to notice the effect, by which he sets forth and bears witness to our election. That effect is the sanctification of the Spirit, even effectual calling, when faith is added to the outward preaching of the gospel, which faith is begotten by the inward operation of the Spirit.

To the sojourners

They who think that all the godly are thus called, because they are strangers in the world, and are advancing towards the celestial country, are much mistaken, and this mistake is evident from the word *dispersion* which immediately follows; for this can apply only to the Jews, not only because they were banished from their own country and scattered here and there, but also because they had been driven out of that land which had been promised to them by the Lord as a perpetual inheritance. He indeed afterwards calls all the faithful sojourners, because they are pilgrims on the earth; but the reason here is different. They were sojourners, because they had been dispersed, some in Pontus, some in Galatia, and some in Bithynia. It is nothing strange that he designed this Epistle more especially for the Jews, for he knew that he was appointed in a particular manner their apostle, as Paul teaches us in Galatians 2: 8. In the countries he enumerates, he includes the whole of Asia Minor, from the Euxine to Cappadocia.

Unto obedience

He adds two things to sanctification, and seems to understand newness of life by *obedience,* and by the *sprinkling* of the blood of Christ the remission of sins. But if these be parts or *effects* of sanctification, then sanctification is to be taken here somewhat different from what it means when used by Paul, that is, more generally. God then sanctifies us by an effectual calling; and this is done when we are renewed to an obedience to his righteousness, and when we are sprinkled by the blood of Christ, and thus are cleansed from our sins. And there seems to be an implied allusion to the ancient rite of sprinkling used under the law. For as it was not then sufficient for the victim to be slain and the blood to be poured out, except the people were sprinkled; so now the blood of Christ which has been shed will avail us nothing, except our consciences are by it cleansed. There is then to be understood here a contrast, that, as formerly under the law the sprinkling of blood was made by the hand of the priest; so now the Holy Spirit sprinkles our souls with the blood of Christ for the expiation of our sins.

the word was then, "Renounce Jesus and live," "Cleave to him and die;" for every Christian was in continual danger of losing his life. He then who preferred Christianity to his life gave full proof, not only of his own sincerity, but also of the excellency of the principle by which he was influenced; as his religion put him in possession of greater blessings, and more solid comforts, than any thing the earth could afford.

Though it be tried with fire – That is: Though gold will bear the action of the fire for any given time, even millions of years, were they possible, without losing the smallest particle of weight or value, yet even gold, in process of time, will wear away by continual use; and the earth, and all its works, will be burnt up by that supernatural fire whose action nothing can resist. But on that day the faith of Christ's followers will be found brighter, and more glorious. The earth, and universal nature, shall be dissolved; but he who doeth the will of God shall abide for ever, and his faith shall then be found to the praise of God's grace, the honor of Christ, and the glory or glorification of his own soul throughout eternity. God himself will praise such faith, angels and men will hold it in honor, and Christ will crown it with glory.

24. For all flesh is as grass – Earthly seeds, earthly productions, and earthly generations, shall fail and perish like as the grass and flowers of the field; for the grass withereth, and the flower falleth off, though, in the ensuing spring and summer, they may put forth new verdure and bloom.

25. But the word of the Lord – The doctrine delivered by God concerning Christ endureth for ever, having, at all times and in all seasons, the same excellence and the same efficacy.

1 PETER 2

1. Laying aside all malice – These tempers and dispositions must have been common among the Jews, as they are frequently spoken against: Christianity can never admit of such; they show the mind, not of Christ, but of the old murderer.

2. As new-born babes – In the preceding chapter, 1 Peter 1: 23, the apostle states that they had been born again; and as the new-born infant desires that aliment which nature has provided for it, so they, being born again – born from above, should as earnestly require that heavenly nourishment which is suited to their new nature; and this the apostle calls the sincere milk of the word, or, as some translate, the rational unadulterated milk; i.e. the pure doctrines of the Gospel, as delivered in the epistles and gospels, and as preached by the apostles and their successors. The rabbins frequently express learning to know the law, etc., by the term sucking, and their disciples are often denominated those that suck the breast. The figure is very expressive: as a child newly born shows an immediate desire for that nourishment, and that only, which is its most proper food; so they, being just born of God, should show that the incorruptible seed abides in them, and that they will receive nothing that is not suited to that new nature: and, indeed, they can have no spiritual growth but by the pure doctrines of the Gospel.

3. If so be ye have tasted – Seeing ye have tasted. There could be no doubt that they had tasted the goodness of Christ who were born again, of incorruptible seed, and whose hearts were purified by the truth, and who had like precious faith with the apostles themselves.

That the Lord is gracious. This seems to refer to Psalm 34: 8: O taste and see that the Lord is good. And there is still a reference to the sucking child that, having once tasted its mother's milk, ever after desires and longs for it. As they were born of God, and had tasted his goodness, they would naturally desire the same pure unadulterated milk of the word.

4. To whom coming, as unto a living stone – This is a reference to Isaiah 28: 16: Behold, I lay in Zion for a foundation a stone, a tried stone, a precious corner stone, a sure foundation. Jesus Christ is, in both the prophet and apostle, represented as the foundation on which the Christian Church is built, and on which it must continue to rest: and the stone or foundation is called here living, to intimate that he is the source of life to all his followers,

stone, disallowed indeed of men, but chosen of God, and precious,

5 Ye also, as lively stones, are built up a spiritual house, an holy priesthood, to offer up spiritual sacrifices, acceptable to God by Jesus Christ.

6 Wherefore also it is contained in the scripture, Behold, I lay in Sion a chief corner stone, elect, precious: and he that believeth on him shall not be confounded.

7 Unto you therefore which believe he is precious: but unto them which be disobedient, the stone which the builders disallowed, the same is made the head of the corner,

8 And a stone of stumbling, and a rock of offence, even to them which stumble at the word, being disobedient: whereunto also they were appointed.

9 But ye are a chosen generation, a royal priesthood, an holy nation, a peculiar people; that ye should shew forth the praises of him who hath called you out of darkness into his marvelous light:

10 Which in time past were not a people, but are now the people of God: which had not obtained mercy, but now have obtained mercy.

11 Dearly beloved, I beseech you as strangers and pilgrims, abstain from fleshly lusts, which war against the soul;

12 Having your conversation honest among the Gentiles: that, whereas they speak against you as evildoers, they may by your good works, which they shall behold, glorify God in the day of visitation.

13 Submit yourselves to every ordinance of man for the Lord's sake: whether it be to the king, as supreme;

14 Or unto governors, as unto them that are sent by him for the punishment of evildoers, and for the praise of them that do well.

15 For so is the will of God, that with well doing ye may put to silence the ignorance of foolish men:

16 As free, and not using your liberty for a cloke of maliciousness, but as the servants of God.

17 Honor all men. Love the brotherhood. Fear God. Honor the king.

18 Servants, be subject to your masters with all fear; not only to the good and gentle, but also to the froward.

19 For this is thankworthy, if a man for

Let us now state the substance of the whole; which is, that our salvation flows from the gratuitous election of God; but that it is to be ascertained by the experience of faith, because he sanctifies us by his Spirit; and then that there are two effects or ends of our calling, even renewal into obedience and ablution by the blood of Christ; and further, that both are the work of the Holy Spirit. We hence conclude, that election is not to be separated from calling, nor the gratuitous righteousness of faith from newness of life.

1 PETER 2

After having taught the faithful that they had been regenerated by the word of God, he now exhorts them to lead a life corresponding with their birth. For if we live in the Spirit, we ought also to walk in the Spirit, as Paul says (Galatians 5: 25). It is not, then, sufficient for us to have been once called by the Lord, except we live as new creatures. This is the meaning. But as to the words, the Apostle continues the same metaphor. For as we have been born again, he requires from us a life like that of infants; by which he intimates that we are to put off the old man and his works. Hence this verse agrees with what Christ says, "Except ye become like this little child, ye shall not enter into the kingdom of God" (Matthew 18: 3).

Infancy

This is here set by Peter in opposition to the ancientness of the flesh, which leads to corruption; and under the word *milk*, he includes all the feelings of spiritual life. For there is also in part a contrast between the vices which he enumerates and the sincere milk of the word; as though he had said, "Malice and hypocrisy belong to those who are habituated to the corruptions of the world; they have imbibed these vices: what pertains to infancy is sincere simplicity, free from all guile. Men, when grown up, become imbued with envy, they learn to slander one another, they are taught the arts of mischief; in short, they become hardened in every kind of evil: infants, owing to their age, do not yet know what it is to envy, to do mischief, or the like things." He then compares the vices, in which the oldness of the flesh indulges, to strong food; and milk is called that way of living suitable to innocent nature and simple infancy.

1. All malice

There is not here a complete enumeration of all those things which we ought to lay aside; but when the Apostles speak of the old man, they lay down as examples some of those vices which mark his whole character. "Known," says Paul, "are the works of the flesh, which are these," (Galatians 5: 19;) and yet he does not enumerate them all; but in those few things, as in a mirror, we may see that immense mass

and that it is in union with him that they live, and answer the end of their regeneration; as the stones of a building are of no use but as they occupy their proper places in a building, and rest on the foundation.

Disallowed indeed of men – That is, rejected by the Jews. This is a plain reference to the prophecy, Psalm 118: 22: The stone which the builders refused is become the head stone of the corner.

Chosen of God – To be the Savior of the world, and the Founder of the Church, and the foundation on which it rests; As Christ is the choice of the Father, we need have no doubt of the efficacy and sufficiency of all that he has suffered and done for the salvation of a lost world. God can never be mistaken in his choice; therefore he that chooses Christ for his portion shall never be confounded.

Precious – Honorable. Howsoever despised and rejected by men, Jesus, as the sacrifice for a lost world, is infinitely honorable in the sight of God; and those who are united by faith to him partake of the same honor, being members of that great and glorious body of which he is the head, and stones in that superb building of which he is the foundation.

5. Ye also, as lively stones – Living stones; each being instinct with the principle of life, which proceeds from him who is the foundation, called above a living stone.

8. A stone of stumbling – Because in him all Jews and Gentiles who believe are united; and because the latter were admitted into the Church, and called by the Gospel to enjoy the same privileges which the Jews, as the peculiar people of God, had enjoyed for two thousand years before; therefore they rejected the Christian religion, they would have no partakers with themselves in the salvation of God. This was the true cause why the Jews rejected the Gospel; and they rejected Christ because he did not come as a secular prince. In the one case he was a stone of stumbling – he was poor, and affected no worldly pomp; in the other he was a rock of offense, for his Gospel called the Gentiles to be a peculiar people whom the Jews believed to be everlastingly reprobated, and utterly incapable of any spiritual good.

9. Ye are a chosen generation – The titles formerly given to the whole Jewish Church, i.e. to all the Israelites without exception, all who were in the covenant of God by circumcision, whether they were holy persons or not, are here given to Christians in general in the same way; i.e. to all who believed in Christ, whether Jews or Gentiles, and who received baptism in the name of the Father, and of the Son, and of the Holy Ghost.

The Israelites were a chosen or elected race, to be a special people unto the Lord their God, above all people that were upon the face of the earth, Deuteronomy 7: 6.

They were also a **royal priesthood**, or what Moses calls a kingdom of priests, Exodus 19: 6. For all were called to sacrifice to God; and he is represented to be the King of that people, and Father of those of whom he was king; therefore they were all royal.

They were a **holy nation**, Exodus 19: 6; for they were separated from all the people of the earth, that they might worship the one only true God, and abstain from the abominations that were in the heathen world.

They were also a **peculiar people**, a purchased people; a private property, belonging to God Almighty, Deuteronomy 7: 6; none other having any right in them, and they being under obligation to God alone. All these things the apostle applies to the Christians, to whom indeed they belong, in their spirit and essence, in such a way as they could not belong to the Hebrews of old. But they were called to this state of salvation out of darkness – idolatry, superstition, and ungodliness, into his marvelous light – the Gospel dispensation, which, in reference to the discoveries it had made of God, his nature, will, and gracious promises towards mankind, differed as much from the preceding dispensation of the Jews, as the light of the meridian sun from the faint twinkling of a star.

13. Submit yourselves to every ordinance of man – In every settled state, and under every form of political government, where the laws are not in opposition to the laws of God, it may be very soundly and rationally said: "Genuine Christians have nothing to do with the laws but to obey them." Society and civil security

conscience toward God endure grief, suffering wrongfully.

20 For what glory is it, if, when ye be buffeted for your faults, ye shall take it patiently? but if, when ye do well, and suffer for it, ye take it patiently, this is acceptable with God.

21 For even hereunto were ye called: because Christ also suffered for us, leaving us an example, that ye should follow his steps:

22 Who did no sin, neither was guile found in his mouth:

23 Who, when he was reviled, reviled not again; when he suffered, he threatened not; but committed himself to him that judgeth righteously:

24 Who his own self bare our sins in his own body on the tree, that we, being dead to sins, should live unto righteousness: by whose stripes ye were healed.

25 For ye were as sheep going astray; but are now returned unto the Shepherd and Bishop of your souls.

1 PETER 3

1 Likewise, ye wives, be in subjection to your own husbands; that, if any obey not the word, they also may without the word be won by the conversation of the wives;

2 While they behold your chaste conversation coupled with fear.

3 Whose adorning let it not be that outward adorning of plaiting the hair, and of wearing of gold, or of putting on of apparel;

4 But let it be the hidden man of the heart, in that which is not corruptible, even the ornament of a meek and quiet spirit, which is in the sight of God of great price.

5 For after this manner in the old time the holy women also, who trusted in God, adorned themselves, being in subjection unto their own husbands:

6 Even as Sara obeyed Abraham, calling him lord: whose daughters ye are, as long as ye do well, and are not afraid with any amazement.

7 Likewise, ye husbands, dwell with them according to knowledge, giving honor unto the wife, as unto the weaker vessel, and as being heirs together of

of filth which proceeds from our flesh. So also in other passages, where he refers to the new life, he touches only on a few things, by which we may understand the whole character.

What, then, he says amounts to this – "Having laid aside the works of your former life, such as malice, deceit, dissimulations, envyings, and other things of this kind, devote yourselves to things of an opposite character, cultivate kindness, honesty," etc. He, in short, urges this, that new morals ought to follow a new life.

2. The sincere milk of the word

This passage is commonly explained according to the rendering of Erasmus, "Milk not for the body but for the soul;" as though the Apostle reminded us by this expression that he spoke metaphorically. I rather think that this passage agrees with that saying of Paul, "Be ye not children in understanding, but in malice" (1 Corinthians 14: 20).

That no one might think that infancy, void of understanding and full of fatuity, was commended by him, he in due time meets this objection; so he bids them to desire milk free from guile, and yet mixed with right understanding. We now see for what purpose he joins these two words, rational and guileless (*logikon kai adolos*). For simplicity and quickness of understanding are two things apparently opposite; but they ought to be mixed together, lest simplicity should become insipid, and lest malicious craftiness should creep in for want of understanding. This mingling, well regulated, is according, to what Christ says, "Be ye wise as serpents, and harmless as doves" (Matthew 10: 16).

Paul reproves the Corinthians because they were like children, and therefore they could not take strong food, but were fed with milk (1 Corinthians 3: 1). Almost the same words are found in Hebrews 5: 12. But in these passages those are compared to children who remain always novices and ignorant scholars in the doctrine of religion, who continued in the first elements, and never penetrated into the higher knowledge of God. *Milk* is called the simpler mode of teaching, and one suitable to children, when there is no progress made beyond the first rudiments. Justly, then, does Paul charge this as a fault, as well as the author of the Epistle to the Hebrews. But milk, here, is not elementary doctrine, which one perpetually learns; and never comes to the knowledge of the truth, but a mode of living which has the savor of the new birth, when we surrender ourselves to be brought up by God. In the same manner infancy is not set in opposition to manhood, or full age in Christ, as Paul calls it in Ephesians 4: 13, but to the ancientness of the flesh and of former life. Moreover, as the infancy of the new life is perpetual, so Peter recommends milk as a perpetual aliment, for he would have those nourished by it to grow.

are in a most dangerous state when the people take it into their heads that they have a right to remodel and change the laws.

22. Who did no sin – He suffered, but not on account of any evil he had either done or said. In deed and word he was immaculate, and yet he was exposed to suffering; expect the same, and when it comes bear it in the same spirit. It is very likely that the apostle mentions guile, because those who do wrong generally strive to screen themselves by prevarication and lies. These words appear to be a quotation from Isaiah 53: 9.

25. For ye were as sheep going astray – Formerly ye were not in a better moral condition than your oppressors; ye were like stray sheep, in the wilderness of ignorance and sin, till Christ, the true and merciful Shepherd, called you back from your wanderings, by sending you the Gospel of his grace.

Bishop of your souls – Jesus Christ is the Overseer of souls; he has them continually under his eye; he knows their wants, wishes, dangers, etc., and provides for them. As their shepherd, he leads them to the best pastures, defends them from their enemies, and guides them by his eye. Jesus is the good Shepherd that laid down his life for his sheep. All human souls are inexpressibly dear to him, as they are the purchase of his blood. He is still supreme Bishop or Overseer in his Church.

1 PETER 3

7. Dwell with them according to knowledge – Give your wives, by no species of unkind carriage, any excuse for delinquency. How can a man expect his wife to be faithful to him, if he be unfaithful to her? and vice versa.

Giving honor unto the wife – Using your superior strength and experience in her behalf, and thus honoring her by becoming her protector and support. But the word honor, signifies maintenance as well as respect; – maintain, provide for the wife.

As the weaker vessel – Being more delicately, and consequently more slenderly, constructed. Roughness and strength go hand in hand; so likewise do beauty and frailty. The female has what the man wants – beauty and delicacy. The male has what the female wants – courage and strength. The one is as good in its place as the other: and by these things God has made an equality between the man and the woman, so that there is properly very little superiority on either side.

Being heirs together – Both the man and woman being equally called to eternal glory: and as prayer is one great means of obtaining a meetness for it, it is necessary that they should live together in such a manner as to prevent all family contentions, that they may not be prevented, by disputes or misunderstandings, from uniting daily in this most important duty – family and social prayer.

8. Be ye all of one mind – Unity, both in the family and in the Church, being essentially necessary to peace and salvation.

Having compassion – Being sympathetic; feeling for each other; bearing each other's burdens.

Love as brethren – Be lovers of the brethren.

Pitiful – Tender-hearted; let your bowels yearn over the distressed and afflicted.

Courteous – Be friendly-minded; acquire and cultivate a friendly disposition.

9. Not rendering evil for evil – Purposing, saying, doing nothing but good; and invariably returning good for evil.

Ye are thereunto called – This is your calling – your business in life, to do good, and to do good for evil, and to implore God's blessing even on your worst enemies. And this is not only your duty, but your interest; for in so doing you shall obtain God's blessing, even life for evermore.

10. For he that will love life – This is a quotation from Psalm 34: 12–16, as it stands in the Septuagint; only the aorist of the imperative is changed from the second into the third person, etc. He who wishes to live long and prosperously, must act as he is here directed.

1. He must refrain from evil-speaking, lying, and slandering.

2. He must avoid flattery and fair speeches, which cover hypocritical or wicked intentions.

3. He must avoid evil, keep going away, from evil.

the grace of life; that your prayers be not hindered.

8 Finally, be ye all of one mind, having compassion one of another, love as brethren, be pitiful, be courteous:

9 Not rendering evil for evil, or railing for railing: but contrariwise blessing; knowing that ye are thereunto called, that ye should inherit a blessing.

10 For he that will love life, and see good days, let him refrain his tongue from evil, and his lips that they speak no guile:

11 Let him eschew evil, and do good; let him seek peace, and ensue it.

12 For the eyes of the Lord are over the righteous, and his ears are open unto their prayers: but the face of the Lord is against them that do evil.

13 And who is he that will harm you, if ye be followers of that which is good?

14 But and if ye suffer for righteousness' sake, happy are ye: and be not afraid of their terror, neither be troubled;

15 But sanctify the Lord God in your hearts: and be ready always to give an answer to every man that asketh you a reason of the hope that is in you with meekness and fear:

16 Having a good conscience; that, whereas they speak evil of you, as of evildoers, they may be ashamed that falsely accuse your good conversation in Christ.

17 For it is better, if the will of God be so, that ye suffer for well doing, than for evil doing.

18 For Christ also hath once suffered for sins, the just for the unjust, that he might bring us to God, being put to death in the flesh, but quickened by the Spirit:

19 By which also he went and preached unto the spirits in prison;

20 Which sometime were disobedient, when once the longsuffering of God waited in the days of Noah, while the ark was a preparing, wherein few, that is, eight souls were saved by water.

21 The like figure whereunto even baptism doth also now save us (not the putting away of the filth of the flesh, but the answer of a good conscience toward God,) by the resurrection of Jesus Christ:

22 Who is gone into heaven, and is on the right hand of God; angels and authorities and powers being made subject unto him.

1 PETER 3

1. He proceeds now to another instance of subjection, and bids wives to be subject to their husbands. And as those seemed to have some pretense for shaking off the yoke, who were united to unbelieving men, he expressly reminds them of their duty, and brings forward a particular reason why they ought the more carefully to obey, even that they might by their probity allure their husbands to the faith. But if wives ought to obey ungodly husbands, with much more promptness ought they to obey, who have believing husbands.

But it may seem strange that Peter should say, that a husband might be **gained** to the Lord **without the word**; for why is it said, that "faith cometh by hearing?" Romans 10: 17. To this I reply, that Peter's words are not to be so understood as though a holy life alone could lead the unbelieving to Christ, but that it softens and pacifies their minds, so that they might have less dislike to religion; for as bad examples create offenses, so good ones afford no small help. Then Peter shews that wives by a holy and pious life could do so much as to prepare their husbands, without speaking to them on religion, to embrace the faith of Christ.

2. While they behold

For minds, however alienated from the true faith, are subdued, when they see the good conduct of believers; for as they understood not the doctrine of Christ, they form an estimate of it by our life. It cannot, then, be but that they will commend Christianity, which teaches purity and fear.

3. Whose adorning

The other part of the exhortation is, that wives are to adorn themselves sparingly and modestly: for we know that they are in this respect much more curious and ambitious than they ought to be. Then Peter does not without cause seek to correct in them this vanity. And though he reproves generally sumptuous or costly adorning, yet he points out some things in particular – that they were not artificially to curl or wreath their hair, as it was usually done by crisping-pins, or otherwise to form it according to the fashion; nor were they to set gold around their head: for these are the things in which excesses especially appear.

It may be now asked, whether the Apostle wholly condemns the use of gold in adorning the body. Were any one to urge these words, it may be said, that he prohibits precious garments no less than gold; for he immediately adds, **the putting on of apparel**, or, of clothes. But it would be an immoderate strictness wholly to forbid neatness and elegance in clothing. If the material is said to be too sumptuous, the Lord has created it; and we know that skill in art has proceeded from him. Then Peter did not intend to

4. He must do good; he must walk in the way of righteousness.

5. He must live peaceably with all men; seek peace where it has been lost; restore it where it has been broken; and pursue it where it seems to be flying away.

He who lives thus must live happy in himself. And as excess in action and passion always tends to the shortening of life, and nothing preys on the constitution more than disorderly passions, he must live not only happiest but longest who avoids them.

14. But and if ye suffer – God may permit you to be tried and persecuted for righteousness' sake, but this cannot essentially harm you; he will press even this into your service, and make it work for your good.

Happy are ye – This seems to refer to Matthew 5: 10, etc. Blessed or happy, are ye when men persecute you, etc. It is a happiness to suffer for Christ; and it is a happiness, because if a man were not holy and righteous the world would not persecute him, so he is happy in the very cause of his sufferings.

Be not afraid of their terror – Fear not their fear; see Isaiah 8: 12. Sometimes fear is put for the object of a man's religious worship; see Genesis 31: 42; Proverbs 1: 26, and the place in Isaiah just quoted. The exhortation may mean, Fear not their gods, they can do you no hurt; and supposing that they curse you by them, yet be not troubled; "He who fears God need have no other fear."

16. Having a good conscience – The testimony of God in your own soul, that in simplicity and godly sincerity you have your conversation in the world. See on the term conscience at the end of Hebrews.

Whereas they speak evil of you – See the same sentiment in 1 Peter 2: 11 and the note there.

18. Put to death in the flesh – In his human nature.

But quickened by the Spirit – That very dead body revived by the power of his Divinity.

21. The like figure whereunto, etc. There are many difficulties in this verse; but the simple meaning of the place may be easily apprehended. Noah believed in God; walked uprightly before him, and found grace in his sight; he obeyed him in building the ark, and God made it the means of his salvation from the waters of the deluge. Baptism implies a consecration and dedication of the soul and body to God, the Father, Son, and Holy Spirit. He who is faithful to his baptismal covenant, taking God through Christ, by the eternal Spirit, for his portion, is saved here from his sins; and through the resurrection of Christ from the dead, has the well-grounded hope of eternal glory. This is all plain; but was it the deluge, itself, or the ark, or the being saved by that ark from the deluge, that was the antitype of which St. Peter speaks? Noah and his family were saved by water; i.e. it was the instrument of their being saved through the good providence of God. So the water of baptism, typifying the regenerating influence of the Holy Spirit, is the means of salvation to all those who receive this Holy Spirit in its quickening, cleansing efficacy. Now as the waters of the flood could not have saved Noah and his family, had they not made use of the ark; so the water of baptism saves no man, but as it is the means of his getting his heart purified by the Holy Spirit, and typifying to him that purification. The ark was not immersed in the water; had it been so they must all have perished; but it was borne up on the water, and sprinkled with the rain that fell from heaven. This text, as far as I can see, says nothing in behalf of immersion in baptism; but is rather, from the circumstance mentioned above, in favor of sprinkling. In either case, it is not the sprinkling, washing, or cleansing the body, that can be of any avail to the salvation of the soul, but the answer of a good conscience towards God – the internal evidence and external proof that the soul is purified in the laver of regeneration, and the person enabled to walk in newness of life. We are therefore strongly cautioned here, not to rest in the letter, but to look for the substance.

22. Who is gone into heaven – Having given the fullest proof of his resurrection from the dead, and of his having accomplished the end for which he came into the world.

1 PETER 4

1 Forasmuch then as Christ hath suffered for us in the flesh, arm yourselves likewise with the same mind: for he that hath suffered in the flesh hath ceased from sin;

2 That he no longer should live the rest of his time in the flesh to the lusts of men, but to the will of God.

3 For the time past of our life may suffice us to have wrought the will of the Gentiles, when we walked in lasciviousness, lusts, excess of wine, revellings, banquetings, and abominable idolatries:

4 Wherein they think it strange that ye run not with them to the same excess of riot, speaking evil of you:

5 Who shall give account to him that is ready to judge the quick and the dead.

6 For for this cause was the gospel preached also to them that are dead, that they might be judged according to men in the flesh, but live according to God in the spirit.

7 But the end of all things is at hand: be ye therefore sober, and watch unto prayer.

8 And above all things have fervent charity among yourselves: for charity shall cover the multitude of sins.

9 Use hospitality one to another without grudging.

10 As every man hath received the gift, even so minister the same one to another, as good stewards of the manifold grace of God.

11 If any man speak, let him speak as the oracles of God; if any man minister, let him do it as of the ability which God giveth: that God in all things may be glorified through Jesus Christ, to whom be praise and dominion for ever and ever. Amen.

12 Beloved, think it not strange concerning the fiery trial which is to try you, as though some strange thing happened unto you:

13 But rejoice, inasmuch as ye are partakers of Christ's sufferings; that, when his glory shall be revealed, ye may be glad also with exceeding joy.

14 If ye be reproached for the name of Christ, happy are ye; for the spirit of glory and of God resteth upon you: on their part

condemn every sort of ornament, but the evil of vanity, to which women are subject. Two things are to be regarded in clothing, usefulness and decency; and what decency requires is moderation and modesty. Were, then, a woman to go forth with her hair wantonly curled and decked, and make an extravagant display, her vanity could not be excused. They who object and say, that to clothe one's-self in this or that manner is an indifferent thing, in which all are free to do as they please, may be easily confuted; for excessive elegance and superfluous display, in short, all excesses, arise from a corrupted mind. Besides, ambition, pride, affectation of display, and all things of this kind, are not indifferent things. Therefore they whose minds are purified from all vanity, will duly order all things, so as not to exceed moderation.

1 PETER 4

1. Forasmuch then as Christ

When he had before set forth Christ before us, he only spoke of the suffering of the cross; for sometimes the cross means mortification, because the outward man is wasted by afflictions, and our flesh is also subdued. But he now ascends higher; for he speaks of the reformation of the whole man. The Scripture recommends to us a twofold likeness to the death of Christ, that we are to be conformed to him in reproaches and troubles, and also that the old man being dead and extinct in us, we are to be renewed to a spiritual life (Philippians 3: 10; Romans 6: 4). Yet Christ is not simply to be viewed as our example, when we speak of the mortificaion of the flesh; but it is by his Spirit that we are really made conformable to his death, so that it becomes effectual to the crucifying of our flesh. In short, as Peter at the end of the last chapter exhorted us to patience after the example of Christ, because death was to him a passage to life; so now from the same death he deduces a higher doctrine, that we ought to die to the flesh and to the world, as Paul teaches us more at large in the sixth chapter of his Epistle to the Romans. He therefore says, **arm yourselves**, or **be ye armed**, intimating that we are really and effectually supplied with invincible weapons to subdue the flesh, if we partake as we ought of the efficacy of Christ's death.

For he that hath suffered

The particle hoti does not, I think, denote here the cause, but is to be taken as explanatory; for Peter sets forth what that thought or mind is with which Christ's death arms us, even that the dominion of sin ought to be abolished in us, so that God may reign in our life. Erasmus has incorrectly, as I think, rendered the word "he who did suffer" (*patiebatur*) applying it to Christ. For it is an indefinite sentence, which generally extends to all the godly, and has the same mean-

On the right hand of God – In the place of the highest dignity, honor, and influence.

Angels and authorities and powers – That is, all creatures and beings, both in the heavens and in the earth, are put under subjection to Jesus Christ. He has all power in the heavens and in the earth. He alone can save; and he alone can destroy. None need fear who put their trust in him, as he can do whatsoever he will in behalf of his followers, and has good and evil spirits under his absolute command. Well may his enemies tremble, while his friends exult and sing. He can raise the dead, and save to the uttermost all that come unto the Father through him.

1 PETER 4

1. As Christ hath suffered – He is your proper pattern; have the same disposition he had; the same forgiving spirit, with meekness, gentleness, and complete self-possession.

He that hath suffered in the flesh, hath ceased from sin – This is a general maxim, if understood literally: The man who suffers generally reflects on his ways, is humbled, fears approaching death, loathes himself because of his past iniquities, and ceases from them; for, in a state of suffering, the mind loses its relish for the sins of the flesh, because they are embittered to him through the apprehension which he has of death and judgment; and, on his application to God's mercy, he is delivered from his sin.

2. That he no longer should live – in the flesh – Governed by the base principle of giving up his faith to save his life; to the lusts of men – according to the will of his idolatrous persecutors; but to the will of God; which will of God is, that he should retain the truth, and live according to its dictates, though he should suffer for it.

9. Use hospitality – Be ever ready to divide your bread with the hungry, and to succor the stranger.

Without grudging – Without grumblings. Do nothing merely because it is commanded, but do it from love to God and man; then it will be without grumbling.

10. Hath received the gift – A gift; any blessing of providence or grace. I cannot think that the word means here the Holy Ghost, or any of his supernatural gifts or influences; it may include those, but it signifies any thing given by the mere mercy and bounty of God: but perhaps in this place it may signify some or any office in the Church; and this sense, indeed, the connection seems to require.

Stewards of the manifold grace – Whatever gifts or endowments any man may possess, they are properly speaking, not his own; they are the Lord's property, and to be employed in his work, and to promote his glory.

11. If any man speak – In order to explain or enforce God's word, and edify his neighbor, let him do it as those did to whom the living oracles were committed: they spoke as they were inspired by the Holy Ghost. Those, therefore, at Pontus, etc., who undertook to teach others, should speak by the same influence; or, if not under this immediate influence, should speak as or according to the oracles already delivered, grounding all their exhortations and doctrines on some portion of that revelation already given. This command is sent to every man upon earth in holy orders, in pretended holy orders, or pretending to holy orders. Their teaching should be what the oracles of God, the Holy Scriptures, teach and authenticate.

Of the ability which God giveth – Perhaps the ministering here may refer to the care of the poor, and the ability is the quantum of means which God may have placed in their hands; and they are to minister this as coming immediately from God, and lead the minds of the poor to consider him as their benefactor, that he in all things may be glorified through Christ Jesus. This is implied in the essence of any charitable act: the actor is not the author, God is the author; and the poor man should be taught to consider him as his immediate benefactor. Those who give any thing as from themselves, rob God; for to him the praise for all good, and the dominion over all men and things, belong for ever and ever.

19. Suffer according to the will of God – A man suffers according to the will of God who

he is evil spoken of, but on your part he is glorified.

15 But let none of you suffer as a murderer, or as a thief, or as an evildoer, or as a busybody in other men's matters.

16 Yet if any man suffer as a Christian, let him not be ashamed; but let him glorify God on this behalf.

17 For the time is come that judgment must begin at the house of God: and if it first begin at us, what shall the end be of them that obey not the gospel of God?

18 And if the righteous scarcely be saved, where shall the ungodly and the sinner appear?

19 Wherefore let them that suffer according to the will of God commit the keeping of their souls to him in well doing, as unto a faithful Creator.

1 PETER 5

1 The elders which are among you I exhort, who am also an elder, and a witness of the sufferings of Christ, and also a partaker of the glory that shall be revealed:

2 Feed the flock of God which is among you, taking the oversight thereof, not by constraint, but willingly; not for filthy lucre, but of a ready mind;

3 Neither as being lords over God's heritage, but being ensamples to the flock.

4 And when the chief Shepherd shall appear, ye shall receive a crown of glory that fadeth not away.

5 Likewise, ye younger, submit yourselves unto the elder. Yea, all of you be subject one to another, and be clothed with humility: for God resisteth the proud, and giveth grace to the humble.

6 Humble yourselves therefore under the mighty hand of God, that he may exalt you in due time:

7 Casting all your care upon him; for he careth for you.

8 Be sober, be vigilant; because your adversary the devil, as a roaring lion, walketh about, seeking whom he may devour:

9 Whom resist stedfast in the faith, knowing that the same afflictions are accomplished in your brethren that are in the world.

ing with the words of Paul in Romans 6: 7, "He who is dead is justified or freed from sin;" for both the Apostles intimate, that when we become dead to the flesh, we have no more to do with sin, that it should reign in us, and exercise its power in our life.

It may, however, be objected, that Peter here speaks unsuitably in making us to be conformable to Christ in this respect, that we suffer in the flesh; for it is certain that there was nothing sinful in Christ which required to be corrected. But the answer is obvious, that it is not necessary that a comparison should correspond in all its parts. It is then enough that we should in a measure be made conformable to the death of Christ. In the same way is also explained, not unfitly, what Paul says, that we are planted in the likeness of his death (Romans 6: 5); for the manner is not altogether the same, but that his death is become in a manner the type and pattern of our mortification.

1 PETER 5

In exhorting pastors to their duty, he points out especially three vices which are found to prevail much, even sloth, desire of gain, and lust for power. In opposition to the first vice he sets alacrity or a willing attention; to the second, liberality; to the third, moderation and meekness, by which they are to keep themselves in their own rank.

He then says that pastors ought not to exercise care over the flock of the Lord, as far only as they are constrained; for they who seek to do no more than what constraint compels them, do their work formally and negligently. Hence he would have them to do willingly what they do, as those who are really devoted to their work. To correct avarice, he bids them to perform their office with a ready mind; for whosoever has not this end in view, to spend himself and his labor disinterestedly and gladly in behalf of the Church, is not a minister of Christ, but a slave to his own stomach and his purse. The third vice which he condemns is a lust for exercising power or dominion. But it may be asked, what kind of power does he mean? This, as it seems to me, may be gathered from the opposite clause, in which he bids them to be examples to the flock. It is the same as though he had said that they are to preside for this end, to be eminent in holiness, which cannot be, except they humbly subject themselves and their life to the same common rule. What stands opposed to this virtue is tyrannical pride, when the pastor exempts himself from all subjection, and tyrannizes over the Church. Ezekiel condemned the false prophets for this, that *they ruled cruelly and tyrannically* (Ezekiel 34: 4). Christ condemned the Pharisees, because they laid intolerable burdens on the shoulders of the people which they would not touch, *no, not with a finger* (Matthew

suffers for righteousness' sake; and who, being reviled, reviles not again.

Commit the keeping of their souls – Place their lives confidently in his hand, who, being their Creator, will also be their preserver, and keep that safely which is committed to his trust. God is here represented as faithful, because he will always fulfill his promises, and withhold no good thing from them that walk uprightly.

1 PETER 5

1. The elders which are among you – In this place the term elders or presbyters is the name of an office. They were as pastors or shepherds of the flock of God, the Christian people among whom they lived. They were the same as bishops, presidents, teachers and deacons, Acts 14: 23; 1 Timothy 5: 17. And that these were the same as bishops the next verse proves.

Who am also an elder – A fellow elder; one on a level with yourselves.

A witness of the sufferings of Christ – He was with Christ in the garden; he was with him when he was apprehended. and he was with him in the high priest's hall. Whether he followed him to the cross we know not; probably he did not, for in the hall of the high priest he had denied him most shamefully; and, having been deeply convinced of the greatness of his crime, it is likely he withdrew to some private place, to humble himself before God, and to implore mercy. He could, however, with the strictest propriety, say, from the above circumstances, that he was a witness of the sufferings of Christ.

A partaker of the glory – He had a right to it through the blood of the Lamb; he had a blessed anticipation of it by the power of the Holy Ghost; and he had the promise from his Lord and Master that he should be with him in heaven, to behold his glory; John 17: 21,24.

4. When the chief Shepherd – That is, the Lord Jesus Christ, whose is the flock, and who provides the pasture, and from whom, if ye are legally called to the most awful work of preaching the Gospel, ye have received your commission; when he shall appear to judge the world in righteousness, ye who have fed

his flock, who have taken the superintendency of it, not by constraint, nor for filthy lucre's sake, not as lords over the heritage, but with a ready mind, employing body, soul, spirit, time and talents, in endeavoring to pluck sinners as brands from eternal burnings, and build up the Church of Christ on its most holy faith; ye shall receive a crown of glory that fadeth not away, an eternal nearness and intimacy with the ineffably glorious God; so that ye who have turned many to righteousness shall shine, not merely as stars, but as suns in the kingdom of your Father! O ye heavenly-minded, diligent, self-denying pastors after God's own heart, whether ye be in the Church established by the state, or in those divisions widely separated from, or nearly connected with it, take courage; preach Jesus; press through all difficulties in the faith of your God; fear no evil while meditating nothing but good. Ye are stars in the right hand of Jesus, who walks among your golden candlesticks, and has lighted that lamp of life which ye are appointed to trim; fear not, your labor in the Lord cannot be in vain! Never, never can ye preach one sermon in the spirit of your office, which the God of all grace shall permit to be unfruitful; ye carry and sow the seed of the kingdom by the command and on the authority of your God; ye sow it, and the heavens shall drop down dew upon it. Ye may go forth weeping, though bearing this precious seed; but ye shall doubtless come again with rejoicing, bringing your sheaves with you. Amen, even so, Lord Jesus!

6. Humble yourselves – Those who submit patiently to the dispensations of God's providence he lifts up; those who lift themselves up, God thrusts down.

If we humble not ourselves under God's grace, he will humble us under his judgments. Those who patiently submit to him, he exalts in due time; if his hand be mighty to depress, it is also mighty to exalt.

7. Casting all your care – Your anxiety, your distracting care, on him, for he careth for you, for he meddles or concerns himself, with the things that interest you. Whatever things concern a follower of God, whether they be spiritual or temporal, or whether in themselves

10 But the God of all grace, who hath called us unto his eternal glory by Christ Jesus, after that ye have suffered a while, make you perfect, stablish, strengthen, settle you.

11 To him be glory and dominion for ever and ever. Amen.

12 By Silvanus, a faithful brother unto you, as I suppose, I have written briefly, exhorting, and testifying that this is the true grace of God wherein ye stand.

13 The church that is at Babylon, elected together with you, saluteth you; and so doth Marcus my son.

14 Greet ye one another with a kiss of charity. Peace be with you all that are in Christ Jesus. Amen.

23: 4). This imperious rigour, then, which ungodly pastors exercise over the Church, cannot be corrected, except their authority be restrained, so that they may rule in such a way as to afford an example of a godly life.

1. The elders

By this name he designates pastors and all those who are appointed for the government of the Church. But they called them presbyters or elders for honor's sake, not because they were all old in age, but because they were principally chosen from the aged, for old age for the most part has more prudence, gravity, and experience. But as sometimes hoariness is not wisdom, according to a Greek proverb, and as young men are found more fit, such as Timothy, these were also usually called presbyters, after having been chosen into that order. Since Peter calls himself in like manner a presbyter, it appears that it was a common name. Moreover, by this title he secured for himself more authority, as though he had said that he had a right to admonish pastors, because he was one of themselves, for there ought to be mutual liberty between colleagues. But if he had the right of primacy he would have claimed it; and this would have been most suitable on the present occasion. But though he was an Apostle, he yet knew that authority was by no means delegated to him over his colleagues, but that on the contrary he was joined with the rest in the participation of the same office.

great or small, God concerns himself with them; what affects them affects him; in all their afflictions he is afflicted. He who knows that God cares for him, need have no anxious cares about himself. This is a plain reference to Psalm 55: 22: Cast thy burden upon the Lord, and he will sustain thee. He will bear both thee and thy burden.

8. Be sober – Avoid drunkenness of your senses, and drunkenness in your souls; be not overcharged with the concerns of the world.

Be vigilant – Awake, and keep awake; be always watchful; never be off your guard; your enemies are alert, they are never off theirs.

Your adversary the devil – This is the reason why ye should be sober and vigilant; ye have an ever active, implacable, subtle enemy to contend with. He walketh about – he has access to you everywhere; he knows your feelings and your propensities, and informs himself of all your circumstances; only God can know more and do more than he, therefore your care must be cast upon God.

As a roaring lion – Satan tempts under three forms:

1. The subtle serpent; to beguile our senses, pervert our judgment, and enchant our imagination.

2. As an angel of light; to deceive us with false views of spiritual things, refinements in religion, and presumption on the providence and grace of God.

3. As a roaring lion; to bear us down, and destroy us by violent opposition, persecution, and death. Thus he was acting towards the followers of God at Pontus, etc., who were now suffering a grievous persecution.

Walketh about – Traversing the earth; a plain reference to Job 2: 2, which see.

Seeking whom he may devour – Whom he may gulp down. It is not every one that he can swallow down: those who are sober and vigilant are proof against him, these he MAY NOT swallow down; those who are drunken with the cares of this world, etc., and are unwatchful, these he MAY swallow down.

14. Peace be with you all – May all prosperity, spiritual and temporal, be with all that are in Christ Jesus – at are truly converted to him, and live in his Spirit obedient to his will.

2 Peter

Introduction by John Calvin

THE doubts respecting this Epistle mentioned by Eusebius, ought not to keep us from reading it. For if the doubts rested on the authority of men, whose names he does not give, we ought to pay no more regard to it than to that of unknown men. And he afterwards adds, that it was everywhere received without any dispute. What Jerome writes influences me somewhat more, that some, induced by a difference in the style, did not think that Peter was the author. For though some affinity may be traced, yet I confess that there is that manifest difference which distinguishes different writers. There are also other probable conjectures by which we may conclude that it was written by another rather than by Peter. At the same time, according to the consent of all, it has nothing unworthy of Peter, as it shews everywhere the power and the grace of an apostolic spirit. If it be received as canonical, we must allow Peter to be the author, since it has his name inscribed, and he also testifies that he had lived with Christ: and it would have been a fiction unworthy of a minister of Christ, to have personated another individual. So then I conclude, that if the Epistle be deemed worthy of credit, it must have proceeded from Peter; not that he himself wrote it, but that some one of his disciples set forth in writing, by his command, those things which the necessity of the times required. For it is probable that he was now in extreme old age, for he says, that he was near his end. And it may have been that at the request of the godly, he allowed this testimony of his mind to be recorded shortly before his death, because it might have somewhat availed, when he was dead, to support the good, and to repress the wicked. Doubtless, as in every part of the Epistle the majesty of the Spirit of Christ appears, to repudiate it is what I dread, though I do not here recognize the language of Peter. But since it is not quite evident as to the author, I shall allow myself the liberty of using the word Peter or Apostle indiscriminately.

I shall now come to the argument, which may be briefly stated.

The *design* is to shew, that those who have once professed the true faith of Christ, ought to respond to their calling to the last. After having then extolled, in high terms, the grace of God, he recommends to them holiness of life, because God usually punishes in hypocrites a false profession of his name, with dreadful blindness, and on the other hand he increases his gifts to those who truly and from the heart embrace the doctrine of religion. He, therefore, exhorts them to prove their calling by a holy life. And, to give a greater weight to his admonitions, he says that he is already near his end, and at the same time, excuses himself that he so often repeated the same things, his object being that they who should remain alive on the earth after his death, might have what he, when alive, wrote, more deeply fixed in their minds.

And as the foundation of true religion is the certainty or the truth of the gospel, he shews, first, how indubitable is its truth by this fact – that he himself had been an eyewitness of all things which it contains, and especially that he had heard Christ proclaimed from heaven to be the Son of God; and, in the second place, it was God's will that it should be borne witness to, and approved by the oracles of the prophets.

He, however, predicts, at the same time, that

danger was approaching from false teachers, who would spread impious inventions, as well as from the despisers of God, who would mock all religion; and he did this, that the faithful might learn to be watchful, and that they might be fortified. And he seems to have spoken thus designedly, lest they expected that the course of truth in the kingdom of Christ would be tranquil and peaceable, and free from all contention. He afterwards, as on a tablet, describes the character and manners of those who would, by their corruptions, pollute Christianity. But the description which he presents, especially suits the present age, as it will be more evident by a comparison. For he especially draws his pen against Lucianic men, who abandon themselves to every wickedness, and take a profane license to shew contempt to God, yea, and treat with ridicule the hope of a better life; and at this day we see that the world is everywhere full of such rabble.

He further exhorts the faithful, not only to look always for the coming of Christ with suspended and expectant minds, but also to regard that day as present before their eyes, and in the meantime to keep themselves unpolluted for the Lord: in which doctrine he makes Paul as his associate and approver; and to defend his writings from the calumnies of the ungodly, he severely reproves all those who pervert them.

The commentaries on 2 Peter are by John Calvin and Adam Clarke.

2 PETER 1

1 Simon Peter, a servant and an apostle of Jesus Christ, to them that have obtained like precious faith with us through the righteousness of God and our Savior Jesus Christ:

2 Grace and peace be multiplied unto you through the knowledge of God, and of Jesus our Lord,

3 According as his divine power hath given unto us all things that pertain unto life and godliness, through the knowledge of him that hath called us to glory and virtue:

4 Whereby are given unto us exceeding great and precious promises: that by these ye might be partakers of the divine nature, having escaped the corruption that is in the world through lust.

5 And beside this, giving all diligence, add to your faith virtue; and to virtue knowledge;

6 And to knowledge temperance; and to temperance patience; and to patience godliness;

7 And to godliness brotherly kindness; and to brotherly kindness charity.

8 For if these things be in you, and abound, they make you that ye shall neither be barren nor unfruitful in the knowledge of our Lord Jesus Christ.

9 But he that lacketh these things is blind, and cannot see afar off, and hath forgotten that he was purged from his old sins.

10 Wherefore the rather, brethren, give diligence to make your calling and election sure: for if ye do these things, ye shall never fall:

11 For so an entrance shall be ministered unto you abundantly into the everlasting kingdom of our Lord and Savior Jesus Christ.

12 Wherefore I will not be negligent to put you always in remembrance of these things, though ye know them, and be established in the present truth.

13 Yea, I think it meet, as long as I am in this tabernacle, to stir you up by putting you in remembrance;

14 Knowing that shortly I must put off this my tabernacle, even as our Lord Jesus Christ hath shewed me.

15 Moreover I will endeavor that ye

2 PETER 1

1. Simon Peter

Prayer takes the first place at the beginning of this Epistle, and then follows thanksgiving, by which he excites the Jews to gratitude, lest they should forget what great benefits they had already received from God's hand. Why he called himself the **servant and an apostle of Jesus Christ**, we have elsewhere stated, even because no one is to be heard in the Church, except he speaks as from the mouth of Christ. But the word **servant** has a more general meaning, because it includes all the ministers of Christ, who sustain any public office in the Church. There was in the apostleship a higher rank of honor. He then intimates, that he was not one from the rank of ministers, but was made by the Lord an apostle, and therefore superior to them.

Like precious faith

This is a commendation of the grace which God had indiscriminately shewed to all his elect people; for it was no common gift, that they had all been called to one and the same faith, since faith is the special and chief good of man. But he calls it *like* or equally *precious*, not that it is equal in all, but because all possess by faith the same Christ with his righteousness, and the same salvation. Though then the measure is different, that does not prevent the knowledge of God from being common to all, and the fruit which proceeds from it. Thus we have a real fellowship of faith with Peter and the Apostles.

He adds, **through the righteousness of God**, in order that they might know that they did not obtain faith through their own efforts or strength, but through God's favor alone. For these things stand opposed the one to the other, the righteousness of God (in the sense in which it is taken here) and the merit of man. For the efficient cause of faith is called God's righteousness for this reason, because no one is capable of conferring it on himself. So the righteousness that is to be understood, is not that which remains in God, but that which he imparts to men, as in Romans 3: 22. Besides, he ascribes this righteousness in common to God and to Christ, because it flows from God, and through Christ it flows down to us.

2. Grace and peace

By grace is designated God's paternal favor towards us. We have indeed been once for all reconciled to God by the death of Christ, and by faith we come to the possession of this so great a benefit; but as we perceive the grace of God according to the measure of our faith, it is said to increase according to our perception when it becomes more fully known to us.

Peace is added; for as the beginning of our happiness is when God receives us into favor; so the more he confirms

2 PETER 1

2. Grace – God's favor; **peace** – the effects of that favor in the communication of spiritual and temporal blessings.

Through the knowledge of God – By the acknowledging of God, and of Jesus our Lord. For those who acknowledge him in all their ways, he will direct their steps. Those who know Christ; and do not acknowledge him before men, can get no multiplication of grace and peace.

3. As his Divine power – His power, which no power can resist, because it is Divine – that which properly belongs to the infinite Godhead.

Hath given unto us – Hath endowed us with the gifts; or, hath gifted us. It refers to the gifts which the Holy Spirit communicated to the apostles, to enable them to bring men to life and godliness; which were,

1. A complete knowledge of the doctrines of the Gospel.

2. Power to preach and defend their doctrines in suitable language, which their adversaries were not able to gainsay or resist.

3. Wisdom to direct them how to behave in all cases, where and when to labor; and the matter suitable to all different cases, and every variety of persons.

4. Miraculous powers, so that on all proper and necessary occasions they could work miracles for the confirmation of their doctrines and mission.

By **life and godliness** we may understand,

1. a godly life; or,

2. eternal life as the end, and godliness the way to it; or,

3. what was essentially necessary for the present life, food, raiment, etc., and what was requisite for the life to come.

7. Brotherly kindness – Love of the brotherhood – the strongest attachment to Christ's flock; feeling each as a member of your own body.

Charity – Love to the whole human race, even to your persecutors: love to God and the brethren they had; love to all mankind they must also have. True religion is neither selfish nor insulated; where the love of God is, bigotry cannot exist. Narrow, selfish people, and people of a party, who scarcely have any hope of the salvation of those who do not believe as they believe, and who do not follow with them, have scarcely any religion, though in their own apprehension none is so truly orthodox or religious as themselves.

13. As long as I am in this tabernacle – By tabernacle we are to understand his body. Peter's mode of speaking is very remarkable: as long as I am in this tabernacle, so then the body was not Peter, but Peter dwelt in that body. Is not this a proof that St. Peter believed his soul to be very distinct from his body? As a man's house is the place where he dwells, so the body is the house where the soul dwells.

14. Knowing that shortly I must put off – St. Peter plainly refers to the conversation between our Lord and himself, related John 21: 18–19. And it is likely that he had now a particular intimation that he was shortly to seal the truth with his blood. But as our Lord told him that his death would take place when he should be old, being aged now he might on this ground fairly suppose that his departure was at hand.

16. Cunningly devised fables – I think, with Macknight and others, from the apostle's using **eyewitnesses**, or rather beholders, in the end of the verse, it is probable that he means those cunningly devised fables among the heathens, concerning the appearance of their gods on earth in human form. And to gain the greater credit to these fables, the priests and statesmen instituted what they called the mysteries of the gods, in which the fabulous appearance of the gods was represented in mystic shows. But one particular show none but the fully initiated were permitted to behold; hence they were entitled beholders. This show was probably some resplendent image of the god, imitating life, which, by its glory, dazzled the eyes of the beholders, while their ears were ravished by hymns sung in its praise; to this it was natural enough for St. Peter to allude, when speaking about the transfiguration of Christ. Here the indescribably resplendent majesty of the great God was manifested, as far as it could be, in conjunction with that human

may be able after my decease to have these things always in remembrance.

16 For we have not followed cunningly devised fables, when we made known unto you the power and coming of our Lord Jesus Christ, but were eyewitnesses of his majesty.

17 For he received from God the Father honor and glory, when there came such a voice to him from the excellent glory, This is my beloved Son, in whom I am well pleased.

18 And this voice which came from heaven we heard, when we were with him in the holy mount.

19 We have also a more sure word of prophecy; whereunto ye do well that ye take heed, as unto a light that shineth in a dark place, until the day dawn, and the day star arise in your hearts:

20 Knowing this first, that no prophecy of the scripture is of any private interpretation.

21 For the prophecy came not in old time by the will of man: but holy men of God spake as they were moved by the Holy Ghost.

2 PETER 2

1 But there were false prophets also among the people, even as there shall be false teachers among you, who privily shall bring in damnable heresies, even denying the Lord that bought them, and bring upon themselves swift destruction.

2 And many shall follow their pernicious ways; by reason of whom the way of truth shall be evil spoken of.

3 And through covetousness shall they with feigned words make merchandise of you: whose judgment now of a long time lingereth not, and their damnation slumbereth not.

4 For if God spared not the angels that sinned, but cast them down to hell, and delivered them into chains of darkness, to be reserved unto judgment;

5 And spared not the old world, but saved Noah the eighth person, a preacher of righteousness, bringing in the flood upon the world of the ungodly;

6 And turning the cities of Sodom and Gomorrha into ashes condemned them with an overthrow, making them an en-

his love in our hearts, the richer blessing he confers on us, so that we become happy and prosperous in all things, **Through the knowledge**, literally, in the knowledge; but the preposition *en* often means "through" or "with: " yet both senses may suit the context. I am, however, more disposed to adopt the former. For the more any one advances in the knowledge of God, every kind of blessing increases also equally with the sense of divine love. Whosoever then aspires to the full fruition of the blessed life which is mentioned by Peter, must remember to observe the right way. He connects together at the same time the knowledge of God and of Christ; because God cannot be rightly known except in Christ, according to that saying, "No one knoweth the Father but the Son, and he to whom the Son will reveal him" (Matthew 11: 27).

3. According as his divine power

He refers to the infinite goodness of God which they had already experienced, that they might more fully understand it for the future. For he continues the course of his benevolence perpetually to the end, except when we ourselves break it off by our unbelief; for he possesses exhaustless power and an equal will to do good. Hence the Apostle justly animates the faithful to entertain good hope by the consideration of the former benefits of God. For the same purpose is the amplification which he makes; for he might have spoken more simply, "As he has freely given us all things." But by mentioning "divine power," he rises higher, that is, that God has copiously unfolded the immense resources of his power. But the latter clause may be referred to Christ as well as to the Father, but both are suitable. It may however be more fitly applied to Christ, as though he had said, that the grace which is conveyed to us by him, is an evidence of divinity, because it could not have done by humanity.

2 PETER 2

1. But there were

As weak consciences are usually very grievously and dangerously shaken, when false teachers arise, who either corrupt or mutilate the doctrine of faith, it was necessary for the Apostle, while seeking to encourage the faithful to persevere, to remove out of the way an offense of this kind. He, moreover, comforted those to whom he was writing, and confirmed them by this argument, that God has always tried and proved his Church by such a temptation as this, in order that novelty might not disturb their hearts. "Not different," he says, "will be the condition of the Church under the gospel, from what it was formerly under the law; false prophets disturbed the ancient Church; the same thing must also be expected by us."

body in which the fullness of the Divinity dwelt. And we, says the apostle, were beholders, of his own majesty. Here was no trick, no feigned show; we saw him in his glory whom thousands saw before and afterwards; and we have made known to you the power and coming, the appearance and presence, of our Lord Jesus; and we call you to feel the exceeding greatness of this power in your conversion, and the glory of this appearance in his revelation by the power of his Spirit to your souls. These things we have witnessed, and these things ye have experienced: and therefore we can confidently say that neither you nor we have followed cunningly devised fables, but that blessed Gospel which is the power of God to the salvation of every one that believes.

20. Knowing this first – Considering this as a first principle, that no prophecy of the Scripture, whether that referred to above, or any other, is of any private interpretation – proceeds from the prophet's own knowledge or invention, or was the offspring of calculation or conjecture.

21. For the prophecy came not in old time – That is, in any former time, by the will of man – by a man's own searching, conjecture, or calculation; but holy men of God – persons separated from the world, and devoted to God's service, spake, moved by the Holy Ghost. So far were they from inventing these prophetic declarations concerning Christ, or any future event, that they were carried away, out of themselves and out of the whole region, as it were, of human knowledge and conjecture, by the Holy Ghost, who, without their knowing any thing of the matter, dictated to them what to speak, and what to write; and so far above their knowledge were the words of the prophecy, that they did not even know the intent of those words, but searched what, or what manner of time the Spirit of Christ which was in them did signify, when it testified beforehand the sufferings of Christ, and the glory that should follow.

2 PETER 2

1. But there were false prophets – There were not only holy men of God among the Jews,

who prophesied by Divine inspiration, but there were also false prophets, whose prophecies were from their own imagination, and perverted many.

As there shall be false teachers among you – At a very early period of the Christian Church many heresies sprung up; but the chief were those of the Ebionites, Cerinthians, Nicolaitans, Menandrians, and Gnostics, of whom many strange things have been spoken by the primitive fathers, and of whose opinions it is difficult to form any satisfactory view. They were, no doubt, bad enough, and their opponents in general have doubtless made them worse. By what name those were called of whom the apostle here speaks, we cannot tell. They were probably some sort of apostate Jews, or those called the Nicolaitans.

Damnable heresies – Heresies of destruction; such as, if followed, would lead a man to perdition. And these they will bring in privately – cunningly, without making much noise, and as covertly as possible. It would be better to translate destructive heresies than damnable.

Denying the Lord that bought them – It is not certain whether God the Father be intended here, or our Lord Jesus Christ; for God is said to have purchased the Israelites, Exodus 15: 16, and to be the Father that had bought them, Deuteronomy 32: 6, and the words may refer to these or such like passages; or they may point out Jesus Christ, who had bought them with his blood; and the heresies, or dangerous opinions, may mean such as opposed the Divinity of our Lord, or his meritorious and sacrificial death, or such opinions as bring upon those who hold them swift destruction. It seems, however, more natural to understand the Lord that bought them as applying to Christ, than otherwise; and if so, this is another proof, among many,

1. That none can be saved but by Jesus Christ.

2. That through their own wickedness some may perish for whom Christ died.

4. For if God spared not the angels – The angels were originally placed in a state of probation; some having fallen and some having stood proves this. How long that probation was

sample unto those that after should live ungodly;

7 And delivered just Lot, vexed with the filthy conversation of the wicked:

8 (For that righteous man dwelling among them, in seeing and hearing, vexed his righteous soul from day to day with their unlawful deeds;)

9 The Lord knoweth how to deliver the godly out of temptations, and to reserve the unjust unto the day of judgment to be punished:

10 But chiefly them that walk after the flesh in the lust of uncleanness, and despise government. Presumptuous are they, selfwilled, they are not afraid to speak evil of dignities.

11 Whereas angels, which are greater in power and might, bring not railing accusation against them before the Lord.

12 But these, as natural brute beasts, made to be taken and destroyed, speak evil of the things that they understand not; and shall utterly perish in their own corruption;

13 And shall receive the reward of unrighteousness, as they that count it pleasure to riot in the day time. Spots they are and blemishes, sporting themselves with their own deceivings while they feast with you;

14 Having eyes full of adultery, and that cannot cease from sin; beguiling unstable souls: an heart they have exercised with covetous practices; cursed children:

15 Which have forsaken the right way, and are gone astray, following the way of Balaam the son of Bosor, who loved the wages of unrighteousness;

16 But was rebuked for his iniquity: the dumb ass speaking with man's voice forbad the madness of the prophet.

17 These are wells without water, clouds that are carried with a tempest; to whom the mist of darkness is reserved for ever.

18 For when they speak great swelling words of vanity, they allure through the lusts of the flesh, through much wantonness, those that were clean escaped from them who live in error.

19 While they promise them liberty, they themselves are the servants of corruption: for of whom a man is overcome, of the same is he brought in bondage.

It was necessary expressly to shew this, because many imagined that the Church would enjoy tranquillity under the rein of Christ; for as the prophets had promised that at his coming there would be real peace, the highest degree of heavenly wisdom, and the full restoration of all things, they thought that the Church would be no more exposed to any contests. Let us then remember that the Spirit of God hath once for all declared, that the Church shall never be free from this intestine evil; and let this likeness be always borne in mind, that the trial of our faith is to be similar to that of the fathers, and for the same reason – that in this way it may be made evident, whether we really love God, as we find it written in Deuteronomy 13: 3.

But it is not necessary here to refer to every example of this kind; it is enough, in short, to know that, like the fathers, we must contend against false doctrines, that our faith ought by no means to be shaken on account of discords and sects, because the truth of God shall remain unshaken notwithstanding the violent agitations by which Satan strives often to upset all things.

Observe also, that no one time in particular is mentioned by Peter, when he says **there shall be false teachers**, but that all ages are included; for he makes here a comparison between Christians and the ancient people. We ought, then, to apply this truth to our own time, lest, when we see false teachers rising up to oppose the truth of God, this trial should break us down. But the Spirit reminds us, in order that we may take the more heed; and to the same purpose is the whole description which follows.

He does not, indeed, paint each sect in its own colors, but particularly refers to profane men who manifested contempt towards God. The advice, indeed, is general, that we ought to beware of false teachers; but, at the same time, he selected one kind of such from whom the greater danger arose. What is said here will hereafter become more evident from the words of Jude [Jude 1: 4], who treats exactly of the same subject.

Who privily shall bring in

By these words he points out the craftiness of Satan, and of all the ungodly who militate under his banner, that they would creep in by oblique turnings, as through burrows under ground. The more watchful, then, ought the godly to be, so that they may escape their hidden frauds: for however they may insinuate themselves, they cannot circumvent those who are carefully vigilant.

He calls them **opinions of perdition**, or *destructive opinions*, that every one, solicitous for his salvation, might dread such opinions as the most noxious pests. As to the word *opinions* or heresies, it has not, without reason, been always deemed infamous and hateful by the children of God; for the bond of holy unity is the simple truth. As soon as we

to last to them, and what was the particular test of their fidelity, we know not; nor indeed do we know what was their sin; nor when nor how they fell. St. Jude says they kept not their first estate, but left their own habitation; which seems to indicate that they got discontented with their lot, and aspired to higher honors, or perhaps to celestial domination. The tradition of their fall is in all countries and in all religions, but the accounts given are various and contradictory; and no wonder, for we have no direct revelation on the subject. They kept not their first estate, and they sinned, is the sum of what we know on the subject; and here curiosity and conjecture are useless.

14. Having eyes full of adultery – Of an adulteress; being ever bent on the gratification of their sensual desires, so that they are represented as having an adulteress constantly before their eyes, and that their eyes can take in no other object but her. Having eyes full of adultery and incessant sin. The images of sinful acts were continually floating before their disordered and impure fancy.

Beguiling unstable souls – The metaphor is taken from adulterers seducing unwary, inexperienced, and light, trifling women; so do those false teachers seduce those who are not established in righteousness.

Exercised with covetous practices – The metaphor is taken from the agonistae in the Grecian games, who exercised themselves in those feats, such as wrestling, boxing, running, etc., in which they proposed to contend in the public games. These persons had their hearts schooled in nefarious practices; they had exercised themselves till they were perfectly expert in all the arts of seduction, overreaching, and every kind of fraud.

Cursed children – Such not only live under God's curse here, but they are heirs to it hereafter.

15. Which have forsaken the right way – As Balaam did, who, although God showed him the right way, took one contrary to it, preferring the reward offered him by Balak to the approbation and blessing of God.

The way of Balaam – Is the counsel of Balaam. He counseled the Moabites to give their most beautiful young women to the Israelitish youth, that they might be enticed by them to commit idolatry.

17. These are wells without water – Persons who, by their profession, should furnish the water of life to souls athirst for salvation; but they have not this water; they are teachers without ability to instruct; they are sowers, and have no seed in their basket. Nothing is more cheering in the deserts of the east than to meet with a well of water; and nothing more distressing, when parched with thirst, than to meet with a well that contains no water.

Clouds that are carried with a tempest – In a time of great drought, to see clouds beginning to cover the face of the heavens raises the expectation of rain; but to see these carried off by a sudden tempest is a dreary disappointment. These false teachers were equally as unprofitable as the empty well, or the light, dissipated cloud.

To whom the mist of darkness is reserved – That is, an eternal separation from the presence of God, and the glory of his power. They shall be thrust into outer darkness, Matthew 8: 12; into the utmost degrees of misery and despair. False and corrupt teachers will be sent into the lowest hell; and be "the most downcast, underfoot vassals of perdition."

18. They speak great swelling words of vanity – The word **swelling** signifies things of great magnitude, grand, superb, sublime; it sometimes signifies inflated, tumid, bombastic. These false teachers spoke of great and high things, and no doubt promised their disciples the greatest privileges, as they themselves pretended to a high degree of illumination; but they were all false and vain, though they tickled the fancy and excited the desires of the flesh; and indeed this appears to have been their object.

Those that were clean escaped – Those who, through hearing the doctrines of the Gospel, had been converted, were perverted by those false teachers.

21. For it had been better for them not to have known – For the reasons assigned above; because they have sinned against more mercy, are capable of more sin, and are liable

20 For if after they have escaped the pollutions of the world through the knowledge of the Lord and Savior Jesus Christ, they are again entangled therein, and overcome, the latter end is worse with them than the beginning.

21 For it had been better for them not to have known the way of righteousness, than, after they have known it, to turn from the holy commandment delivered unto them.

22 But it is happened unto them according to the true proverb, The dog is turned to his own vomit again; and the sow that was washed to her wallowing in the mire.

2 PETER 3

1 This second epistle, beloved, I now write unto you; in both which I stir up your pure minds by way of remembrance:

2 That ye may be mindful of the words which were spoken before by the holy prophets, and of the commandment of us the apostles of the Lord and Savior:

3 Knowing this first, that there shall come in the last days scoffers, walking after their own lusts,

4 And saying, Where is the promise of his coming? for since the fathers fell asleep, all things continue as they were from the beginning of the creation.

5 For this they willingly are ignorant of, that by the word of God the heavens were of old, and the earth standing out of the water and in the water:

6 Whereby the world that then was, being overflowed with water, perished:

7 But the heavens and the earth, which are now, by the same word are kept in store, reserved unto fire against the day of judgment and perdition of ungodly men.

8 But, beloved, be not ignorant of this one thing, that one day is with the Lord as a thousand years, and a thousand years as one day.

9 The Lord is not slack concerning his promise, as some men count slackness; but is longsuffering to us-ward, not willing that any should perish, but that all should come to repentance.

10 But the day of the Lord will come as a thief in the night; in the which the heavens shall pass away with a great noise,

depart from that, nothing remains but dreadful discord.

Even denying the Lord that bought them

Though Christ may be denied in various ways, yet Peter, as I think, refers here to what is expressed by Jude, that is, when the grace of God is turned into lasciviousness; for Christ redeemed us, that he might have a people separated from all the pollutions of the world, and devoted to holiness and innocency. They, then, who throw off the bridle, and give themselves up to all kinds of licentiousness, are not unjustly said to deny Christ by whom they have been redeemed. Hence, that the doctrine of the gospel may remain whole and complete among us, let this be fixed in our minds, that we have been redeemed by Christ, that he may be the Lord of our life and of our death, and that our main object ought to be, to live to him and to die to him. He then says, that their **swift destruction** was at hand, lest others should be ensnared by them.

2. And many shall follow

It is, indeed, no slight offense to the weak, when they see that false doctrines are received by the common consent of the world, that a large number of men are led astray, so that few continue in true obedience to Christ. So, at this day, there is nothing that more violently disturbs pious minds than such a defection. For hardly one in ten of those who have once made a profession of Christ, retains the purity of faith to the end. Almost all turn aside into corruptions, and being deluded by the teachers of licentiousness, they become profane. Lest this should make our faith to falter, Peter comes to our help, and in due time foretells that this very thing would be, that is, that false teachers would draw many to perdition.

But there is a double reading even in the Greek copies; for some read, "lasciviousness," and others, "perdition." I have, however, followed what has been mostly approved.

By reason of whom the way of truth

This I consider to have been said for this reason, because as religion is adorned when men are taught to fear God, to maintain uprightness of life, a chaste and virtuous conduct, or when at least the mouth of the wicked is closed, that they do not speak evil of the gospel; so when the reins are let loose, and every kind of licentiousness is practiced, the name and the doctrine of Christ are exposed to the reproaches of the ungodly. Others give a different explanation – that these false teachers, like filthy dogs, barked at sound doctrine. But the words of Peter appear to me on the contrary to intimate, that these would give occasion to enemies insolently to assail the truth of God. Though then they would not themselves assail the Christian faith with calumnies, yet they would arm others with the means of reproaching it.

to greater punishment.

The holy commandment – The whole religion of Christ is contained in this one commandment, "Thou shalt love the Lord thy God with all thy heart, with all thy soul, with all thy mind, and with all thy strength; and thy neighbor as thyself." He who obeys this great commandment, and this by the grace of Christ is possible to every man, is saved from sinning either against his God or against his neighbor. Nothing less than this does the religion of Christ require.

22. According to the true proverb – This seems to be a reference to Proverbs 26: 11.

Here is a sad proof of the possibility of falling from grace, and from very high degrees of it too. These had escaped from the contagion that was in the world; they had had true repentance, and cast up "their soursweet morsel of sin;" they had been washed from all their filthiness, and this must have been through the blood of the Lamb; yet, after all, they went back, got entangled with their old sins, swallowed down their formerly rejected lusts, and rewallowed in the mire of corruption. It is no wonder that God should say, the latter end is worse with them than the beginning: reason and nature say it must be so; and Divine justice says it ought to be so; and the person himself must confess that it is right that it should be so. But how dreadful is this state! How dangerous when the person has abandoned himself to his old sins! Yet it is not said that it is impossible for him to return to his Maker; though his case be deplorable, it is not utterly hopeless; the leper may yet be made clean, and the dead may be raised. Reader, is thy backsliding a grief and burden to thee? Then thou art not far from the kingdom of God; believe on the Lord Jesus, and thou shalt be saved.

2 PETER 3

1. This second epistle – In order to guard them against the seductions of false teachers, he calls to their remembrance the doctrine of the ancient prophets, and the commands or instructions of the apostles, all founded on the same basis.

He possibly refers to the prophecies of Enoch, as mentioned by Jude, Jude 14, 15; of David, Psalm 1: 1, etc.; and of Daniel, Daniel 12: 2, relative to the coming of our Lord to judgment: and he brings in the instructions of the apostles of Christ, by which they were directed how to prepare to meet their God.

3. Knowing this first – Considering this in an especial manner, that those prophets predicted the coming of false teachers: and their being now in the Church proved how clearly they were known to God, and showed the Christians at Pontus the necessity of having no intercourse or connection with them.

There shall come – scoffers – Persons who shall endeavor to turn all religion into ridicule, as this is the most likely way to depreciate truth in the sight of the giddy multitude.

Walking after their own lusts – Here is the true source of all infidelity. The Gospel of Jesus is pure and holy, and requires a holy heart and holy life. They wish to follow their own lusts, and consequently cannot brook the restraints of the Gospel: therefore they labor to prove that it is not true, that they may get rid of its injunctions, and at last succeed in persuading themselves that it is a forgery; and then throw the reins on the neck of their evil propensities. Thus their opposition to revealed truth began and ended in their own lusts.

7. But the heavens and the earth, which are now – The present earth and its atmosphere, which are liable to the same destruction, because the same means still exist, (for there is still water enough to drown the earth, and there is iniquity enough to induce God to destroy it and its inhabitants), are nevertheless kept in store, treasured up, kept in God's storehouse, to be destroyed, not by water, but by fire at the day of judgment.

From all this it appears that those mockers affected to be ignorant of the Mosaic account of the formation of the earth, and of its destruction by the waters of the deluge; and indeed this is implied in their stating that all things continued as they were from the creation. But St. Peter calls them back to the Mosaic account, to prove that this was false; for the earth, etc., which were then formed, had perished by the flood; and that the present earth,

and the elements shall melt with fervent heat, the earth also and the works that are therein shall be burned up.

11 Seeing then that all these things shall be dissolved, what manner of persons ought ye to be in all holy conversation and godliness,

12 Looking for and hasting unto the coming of the day of God, wherein the heavens being on fire shall be dissolved, and the elements shall melt with fervent heat?

13 Nevertheless we, according to his promise, look for new heavens and a new earth, wherein dwelleth righteousness.

14 Wherefore, beloved, seeing that ye look for such things, be diligent that ye may be found of him in peace, without spot, and blameless.

15 And account that the longsuffering of our Lord is salvation; even as our beloved brother Paul also according to the wisdom given unto him hath written unto you;

16 As also in all his epistles, speaking in them of these things; in which are some things hard to be understood, which they that are unlearned and unstable wrest, as they do also the other scriptures, unto their own destruction.

17 Ye therefore, beloved, seeing ye know these things before, beware lest ye also, being led away with the error of the wicked, fall from your own stedfastness.

18 But grow in grace, and in the knowledge of our Lord and Savior Jesus Christ. To him be glory both now and for ever. Amen.

2 PETER 3

1. Lest they should be wearied with the Second Epistle as though the first was sufficient, he says that it was not written in vain, because they stood in need of being often stirred up. To make this more evident, he shews that they could not be beyond danger, except they were well fortified, because they would have to contend with desperate men, who would not only corrupt the purity of the faith, by false opinions, but do what they could to subvert entirely the whole faith.

By saying, **I stir up your pure mind**, he means the same as though he had said, "I wish to awaken you to a sincerity of mind." And the words ought to be thus explained, "I stir up your mind that it may be pure and bright." For the meaning is, that the minds of the godly become dim, and as it were contract rust, when admonitions cease. But we also hence learn, that men even endued with learning, become, in a manner, drowsy, except they are stirred up by constant warnings.

It now appears what is the use of admonitions, and how necessary they are; for the sloth of the flesh smothers the truth once received, and renders it inefficient, except the goads of warnings come to its aid. It is not then enough, that men should be taught to know what they ought to be, but there is need of godly teachers, to do this second part, deeply to impress the truth on the memory of their hearers. And as men are, by nature, for the most part, fond of novelty and thus inclined to be fastidious, it is useful for us to bear in mind what Peter says, so that we may not only willingly suffer ourselves to be admonished by others, but that every one may also exercise himself in calling to mind continually the truth, so that our minds may become resplendent with the pure and clear knowledge of it.

2. That ye may be mindful

By these words he intimates that we have enough in the writings of the prophets, and in the gospel, to stir us up, provided we be as diligent as it behoves us, in meditating on them; and that our minds sometimes contract a rust, or become bedimmed through darkness, is owing to our sloth. That God may then continually shine upon us, we must devote ourselves to that study: let our faith at the same time acquiesce in witnesses so certain and credible. For when we have the prophets and apostles agreeing with us, nay, as the ministers of our faith, and God as the author, and angels as approvers, there is no reason that the ungodly, all united, should move us from our position. By the **commandment of the apostles** he means the whole doctrine in which they had instructed the faithful.

etc., which were formed out of the preceding, should, at the day of judgment, perish by the fire of God's wrath.

8. Be not ignorant – Though they are willfully ignorant, neglect not ye the means of instruction.

One day is with the Lord as a thousand years – That is: All time is as nothing before him, because in the presence as in the nature of God all is eternity; therefore nothing is long, nothing short, before him; no lapse of ages impairs his purposes, nor need he wait to find convenience to execute those purposes. And when the longest period of time has passed by, it is but as a moment or indivisible point in comparison of eternity.

10. The heavens shall pass away with a great noise – As the heavens mean here, and in the passages above, the whole atmosphere, in which all the terrestrial vapors are lodged; and as water itself is composed of two gases, eighty-five parts in weight of oxygen, and fifteen of hydrogen, or two parts in volume of the latter, and one of the former; (for if these quantities be put together, and several electric sparks passed through them, a chemical union takes place, and water is the product; and, vice versa, if the galvanic spark be made to pass through water, a portion of the fluid is immediately decomposed into its two constituent gases, oxygen and hydrogen); and as the electric or ethereal fire is that which, in all likelihood, God will use in the general conflagration; the noise occasioned by the application of this fire to such an immense congeries of aqueous particles as float in the atmosphere, must be terrible in the extreme. Put a drop of water on an anvil, place over it a piece of iron red hot, strike the iron with a hammer on the part above the drop of water, and the report will be as loud as a musket; when, then, the whole strength of those opposite agents is brought together into a state of conflict, the noise, the thunderings, the innumerable explosions, (till every particle of water on the earth and in the atmosphere is, by the action of the fire, reduced into its component gaseous parts), will be frequent, loud, confounding, and terrific, beyond every comprehension but that of God himself.

18. But grow in grace – Increase in the image and favor of God; every grace and Divine influence which ye have received is a seed, a heavenly seed, which, if it be watered with the dew of heaven from above, will endlessly increase and multiply itself. He who continues to believe, love, and obey, will grow in grace, and continually increase in the knowledge of Jesus Christ, as his sacrifice, sanctifier, counselor, preserver, and final Savior. The life of a Christian is a growth; he is at first born of God, and is a little child; becomes a young man, and a father in Christ. Every father was once an infant; and had he not grown, he would have never been a man. Those who content themselves with the grace they received when converted to God, are, at best, in a continual state of infancy: but we find, in the order of nature, that the infant that does not grow, and grow daily, too, is sickly and soon dies; so, in the order of grace, those who do not grow up into Jesus Christ are sickly, and will soon die, die to all sense and influence of heavenly things.

There are many who boast of the grace of their conversion; persons who were never more than babes, and have long since lost even that grace, because they did not grow in it. Let him that readeth understand.

1 John

Introduction by John Calvin

THIS Epistle is altogether worthy of the spirit of that disciple who, above others, was loved by Christ, that he might exhibit him as a friend to us. But it contains doctrines mixed with exhortations; for he speaks of the eternal Deity of Christ, and at the same time of the incomparable grace which he brought with him when he appeared in the world, and generally of all his blessings; and he especially commends and extols the inestimable grace of divine adoption.

On these truths he grounds his exhortations; and at one time he admonishes us in general to lead a pious and holy life, and at another time he expressly enjoins love. But he does none of these things in a regular order; for he everywhere mixes teaching with exhortation. But he particularly urges brotherly love: he also briefly touches on other things, such as to beware of impostors, and similar things. But each particular shall be noticed in its own place.

The commentaries on 1 John are by John Calvin and John Gill.

1 JOHN 1

1 That which was from the beginning, which we have heard, which we have seen with our eyes, which we have looked upon, and our hands have handled, of the Word of life;

2 (For the life was manifested, and we have seen it, and bear witness, and shew unto you that eternal life, which was with the Father, and was manifested unto us;)

3 That which we have seen and heard declare we unto you, that ye also may have fellowship with us: and truly our fellowship is with the Father, and with his Son Jesus Christ.

4 And these things write we unto you, that your joy may be full.

5 This then is the message which we have heard of him, and declare unto you, that God is light, and in him is no darkness at all.

6 If we say that we have fellowship with him, and walk in darkness, we lie, and do not the truth:

7 But if we walk in the light, as he is in the light, we have fellowship one with another, and the blood of Jesus Christ his Son cleanseth us from all sin.

8 If we say that we have no sin, we deceive ourselves, and the truth is not in us.

9 If we confess our sins, he is faithful and just to forgive us our sins, and to cleanse us from all unrighteousness.

10 If we say that we have not sinned, we make him a liar, and his word is not in us.

1 JOHN 2

1 My little children, these things write I unto you, that ye sin not. And if any man sin, we have an advocate with the Father, Jesus Christ the righteous:

2 And he is the propitiation for our sins: and not for ours only, but also for the sins of the whole world.

3 And hereby we do know that we know him, if we keep his commandments.

4 He that saith, I know him, and keepeth not his commandments, is a liar, and the truth is not in him.

5 But whoso keepeth his word, in him verily is the love of God perfected: hereby

1 JOHN 1

He shows, first, that life has been exhibited to us in Christ; which, as it is an incomparable good, ought to rouse and inflame all our powers with a marvelous desire for it, and with the love of it. It is said, indeed, in a few and plain words, that life is manifested; but if we consider how miserable and horrible a condition death is, and also what is the kingdom and the glory of immortality, we shall perceive that there is something here more magnificent than what can be expressed in any words.

Then the Apostle's object, in setting before us the vast good, yea, the chief and only true happiness which God has conferred on us, in his own Son, is to raise our thoughts above; but as the greatness of the subject requires that the truth should be certain, and fully proved, this is what is here much dwelt upon. For these words, **What we have seen, what we have heard, what we have looked on**, serve to strengthen our faith in the gospel. Nor does he, indeed, without reason, make so many asseverations; for since our salvation depends on the gospel, its certainty is in the highest degree necessary; and how difficult it is for us to believe, every one of us knows too well by his own experience. To believe is not lightly to form an opinion, or to assent only to what is said, but a firm, undoubting conviction, so that we may dare to subscribe to the truth as fully proved. It is for this reason that the Apostle heaps together so many things in confirmation of the gospel.

1. That which was from the beginning

As the passage is abrupt and involved, that the sense may be made clearer, the words may be thus arranged; "We announce to you the word of life, which was from the beginning and really testified to us in all manner of ways, that life has been manifested in him;" or, if you prefer, the meaning may be thus given, "What we announce to you respecting the word of life, has been from the beginning, and has been openly shewed to us, that life was manifested in him." But the words, **That which was from the beginning**, refer doubtless to the divinity of Christ, for God manifested in the flesh was not from the beginning; but he who always was life and the eternal Word of God, appeared in the fullness of time as man. Again, what follows as to the looking on and the handling of the hands, refers to his human nature. But as the two natures constitute but one person, and Christ is one, because he came forth from the Father that he might put on our flesh, the Apostle rightly declares that he is the same, and had been invisible, and afterwards became visible.

Hereby the senseless cavil of Servetus is disproved, that the nature and essence of Deity became one with the flesh, and that thus the Word was transformed into flesh, because the life-giving Word was seen in the flesh.

1 JOHN 1

1. That which was from the beginning. By which is meant not the Gospel, as if the apostle's design was to assert the antiquity of that, and clear it from the charge of novelty; for though that is called the word, and the word of life, and is the Spirit which gives life, and is the means of quickening dead sinners, and brings the report of eternal life and salvation by Christ, yet the seeing of it with bodily eyes, and handling it with corporeal hands, do not agree with that; but Jesus Christ is here intended, who in his divine nature was, really existed as a divine person, as the everlasting Jehovah, the eternal I AM, which is, and was, and is to come, and existed "from the beginning"; not from the beginning of the preaching of the Gospel by John only, for he was before the Gospel was preached, being the first preacher of it himself, and before John was; yea, before the prophets, before Abraham, and before Adam, and before all creatures, from the beginning of time, and of the creation of the world, being the Maker of all things, even from everlasting; for otherwise he could not have been set up in an office capacity so early, or God's elect be chosen in him before the foundation of the world, and they have grace and blessings given them in him before the world began, or an everlasting covenant be made with him; see John 1: 1.

8. If we say that we have no sin. Notwithstanding believers are cleansed from their sins by the blood of Christ, yet they are not without sin; no man is without sin: this is not only true of all men, as they come into the world, being conceived in sin, and shapen in iniquity, and of all that are in a state of unregeneracy, and of God's elect, while in such a state, but even of all regenerated and sanctified persons in this life; as appears by the ingenuous confessions of sin made by the saints in all ages; by their complaints concerning it, and groans under it; by the continual war in them between flesh and spirit; and by their prayers for the discoveries of pardoning grace, and for the fresh application of Christ's blood for cleansing; by their remissness in the discharge of duty, and by their frequent slips and falls, and often backslidings: and though their sins are all pardoned, and they are justified from all things by the righteousness of Christ, yet they are not without sin; though they are freed from the guilt of sin, and are under no obligation to punishment on account of it, yet not from the being of it; their sins were indeed transferred from them to Christ, and he has bore them, and took them and put them away, and they are redeemed from them, and are acquitted, discharged, and pardoned, so that sin is not imputed to them, and God sees no iniquity in them in the article of justification; and also, their iniquities are caused to pass from them, as to the guilt of them, and are taken out of their sight, and they have no more conscience of them, having their hearts sprinkled and purged by the blood of Jesus, and are clear of all condemnation, the curse of the law, the wrath of God, or the second death, by reason of them; yet pardon of sin, and justification from it, though they take away the guilt of sin, and free from obligation to punishment, yet they do not take out the being of sin, or cause it to cease to act, or do not make sins cease to be sins, or change the nature of actions, of sinful ones, to make them harmless, innocent, or indifferent; the sins of believers are equally sins with other persons, are of the same kind and nature, and equally transgressions of the law, and many of them are attended with more aggravating circumstances, and are taken notice of by God, and resented by him, and for which he chastises his people in love: now though a believer may say that he has not this or that particular sin, or is not guilty of this or that sin, for he has the seeds of all sin in him, yet he cannot say he has no sin; and though he may truly say he shall have no sin, for in the other state the being and principle of sin will be removed, and the saints will be perfectly holy in themselves, yet he cannot, in this present life, say that he is without it.

1 JOHN 2

1. My little children. The apostle may address the saints under this character, on account of their regeneration by the Spirit and grace of God, in which they were as newborn babes;

know we that we are in him.

6 He that saith he abideth in him ought himself also so to walk, even as he walked.

7 Brethren, I write no new commandment unto you, but an old commandment which ye had from the beginning. The old commandment is the word which ye have heard from the beginning.

8 Again, a new commandment I write unto you, which thing is true in him and in you: because the darkness is past, and the true light now shineth.

9 He that saith he is in the light, and hateth his brother, is in darkness even until now.

10 He that loveth his brother abideth in the light, and there is none occasion of stumbling in him.

11 But he that hateth his brother is in darkness, and walketh in darkness, and knoweth not whither he goeth, because that darkness hath blinded his eyes.

12 I write unto you, little children, because your sins are forgiven you for his name's sake.

13 I write unto you, fathers, because ye have known him that is from the beginning. I write unto you, young men, because ye have overcome the wicked one. I write unto you, little children, because ye have known the Father.

14 I have written unto you, fathers, because ye have known him that is from the beginning. I have written unto you, young men, because ye are strong, and the word of God abideth in you, and ye have overcome the wicked one.

15 Love not the world, neither the things that are in the world. If any man love the world, the love of the Father is not in him.

16 For all that is in the world, the lust of the flesh, and the lust of the eyes, and the pride of life, is not of the Father, but is of the world.

17 And the world passeth away, and the lust thereof: but he that doeth the will of God abideth for ever.

18 Little children, it is the last time: and as ye have heard that antichrist shall come, even now are there many antichrists; whereby we know that it is the last time.

19 They went out from us, but they

1 JOHN 2

1. My little children

It is not only the sum and substance of the preceding doctrine, but the meaning of almost the whole gospel, that we are to depart from sin; and yet, though we are always exposed to God's judgment, we are certain that Christ so intercedes by the sacrifice of his death, that the Father is propitious to us. In the meantime, he also anticipates an objection, lest any one should think that he gave license to sin when he spoke of God's mercy, and shewed that it is presented to us all. He then joins together two parts of the gospel, which unreasonable men separate, and thus lacerate and mutilate. Besides, the doctrine of grace has always been calumniated by the ungodly. When the expiation of sins by Christ is set forth, they boastingly say that a license is given to sin.

To obviate these calumnies, the Apostle testifies first that the design of his doctrine was to keep men from sinning; for when he says, **that ye sin not**, his meaning only is, that they, according to the measure of human infirmity, should abstain from sins. And to the same purpose is what I have already said respecting fellowship with God, that we are to be conformable to him. He is not, however, silent as to the gratuitous remission of sins; for though heaven should fall and all things be confounded, yet this part of truth ought never to be omitted; but, on the contrary, what Christ is ought to be preached clearly and distinctly.

So ought we also to do at this day. As the flesh is inclined to wantonness, men ought to be carefully warned, that righteousness and salvation are provided in Christ for this end, that we may become the holy possession of God. Yet whenever it happens that men wantonly abuse the mercy of God, there are many snarlish men who load us with calumny, as though we gave loose reins to vices. We ought still boldly to go on and proclaim the grace of Christ, in which especially shines forth the glory of God, and in which consists the whole salvation of men. These barkings of the ungodly ought, I repeat it, to be wholly disregarded; for we see that the apostles were also by these barkings assailed.

For this reason he immediately adds the second clause, that when we sin we **have an advocate**. By these words he confirms what we have already said, that we are very far from being perfectly righteous, nay, that we contract new guilt daily, and that yet there is a remedy for reconciling us to God, if we flee to Christ; and this is alone that in which consciences call acquiesce, in which is included the righteousness of men, in which is founded the hope of salvation.

The conditional particle, **if**, ought to be viewed as causal; for it cannot be but that we sin. In short, John means, that

and on account of his being the instrument of their conversion, and so was their spiritual father, and therefore calls them his own children; and he might the rather use such a way of speaking, because of his advanced age, being now in his old age, and John the elder in age as well as in office; as well as to show his paternal affection for them, and care of them, and that what he had wrote, or should write, was not from any disrespect, but from pure love to them; and it might serve to put them in mind of their weakness in faith, in knowledge, and spiritual strength, that they might not entertain high notions of themselves, as if they were perfect and without infirmities; and it is easy to observe, that this is one of Christ's expressions, John 13: 33, from whose lips the apostle took it, whose words and phrases he greatly delighted in, as he seems to do in this, by his frequent use of it; see 1 John 2: 18.

These things write I unto you; concerning the purity and holiness of God, who is light itself; concerning fellowship with him, which no one that lives in sin can have; concerning pardon and cleansing from sin by the blood of Christ, and concerning sin being in them, and they not without it.

that ye sin not; not that he thought they could be entirely without it, either without the being of it, or the commission of it, in thought, word, or deed, for this would be to suppose that which is contrary to his own words, in 1 John 1: 8; but he suggests that the end of his writing on these subjects was, that they might not live in sin, and indulge themselves in a vicious course of living, give up themselves to it, and walk in it, and work it with all greediness: and nothing could be more suitably adapted to such an end than the consideration of the holiness of God, who calls by his grace; and of the necessity of light and grace and holiness in men to communion with him; and of the pardoning grace of God and cleansing blood of Christ, which, when savingly applied, sets men against sin, and makes them zealous of good works; and of the indwelling of sin in the saints, which puts them upon their guard against it.

10. He that loveth his brother. As such, and because he is his brother in Christ, and that

cordially and sincerely, without hypocrisy and dissimulation, and by love serves him, both in things temporal and spiritual, and so observes the new, and yet old commandment.

abideth in the light: it is a plain case, that such a man is in the light of grace, and continues in it; for though it is not his love to the brethren which is the cause of his light, of his being and continuing in it, for that is owing to the spirit of light and knowledge, but on the contrary, light is the cause of his love; yet it is an evidence of it, that by which it is known, as the cause is known by the effect; see John 3: 14.

and there is none occasion of stumbling in him, or "there is no scandal" or "offence in him"; he gives no offence to his brother, or at least, as much as in him lies, he takes care that he gives none; he avoids, as much as can be, putting a stumblingblock, or an occasion to fall, in his brother's way, by the use of things indifferent, or by any other action; nor will he easily take offence at what is said or done unto him, for charity or love is not easily provoked, it suffers long, and bears all things; see 1 Corinthians 13: 4; nor does he so much and so frequently transgress the laws of God, and particularly those which regard his neighbor or his brother, and so easily fall into the snares of Satan, because he is in the light, and walks in the light, and sees his way, and what lies in his way, and, so shuns and avoids occasion of stumbling and falling. There is not in him that wrath, and malice, and envy, which lead on to the commission of other sins; for love works no ill, but fulfils the law, and will not suffer him to commit adultery, to kill, to steal, or bear false witness against his neighbor, friend, and brother; see Romans 13: 9; and such an one enjoys great peace, tranquility, and happiness; he has much comfort in himself, and pleasure in the saints, and delight in their company; he walks inoffensively, and in an harmless manner, without hurting himself, or any other, Psalm 119: 165.

16. For all that [is] in the world. This is the sum of the evil things in the world; or these following are the objects of sin in the world, or about which wicked men are conversant; even such as are carnal or grateful to the flesh,

were not of us; for if they had been of us, they would no doubt have continued with us: but they went out, that they might be made manifest that they were not all of us.

20 But ye have an unction from the Holy One, and ye know all things.

21 I have not written unto you because ye know not the truth, but because ye know it, and that no lie is of the truth.

22 Who is a liar but he that denieth that Jesus is the Christ? He is antichrist, that denieth the Father and the Son.

23 Whosoever denieth the Son, the same hath not the Father: (but) he that acknowledgeth the Son hath the Father also.

24 Let that therefore abide in you, which ye have heard from the beginning. If that which ye have heard from the beginning shall remain in you, ye also shall continue in the Son, and in the Father.

25 And this is the promise that he hath promised us, even eternal life.

26 These things have I written unto you concerning them that seduce you.

27 But the anointing which ye have received of him abideth in you, and ye need not that any man teach you: but as the same anointing teacheth you of all things, and is truth, and is no lie, and even as it hath taught you, ye shall abide in him.

28 And now, little children, abide in him; that, when he shall appear, we may have confidence, and not be ashamed before him at his coming.

29 If ye know that he is righteous, ye know that every one that doeth righteousness is born of him.

1 JOHN 3

1 Behold, what manner of love the Father hath bestowed upon us, that we should be called the sons of God: therefore the world knoweth us not, because it knew him not.

2 Beloved, now are we the sons of God, and it doth not yet appear what we shall be: but we know that, when he shall appear, we shall be like him; for we shall see him as he is.

3 And every man that hath this hope in him purifieth himself, even as he is pure.

4 Whosoever committeth sin trans-

we are not only called away from sin by the gospel, because God invites us to himself, and offers to us the Spirit of regeneration, but that a provision is made for miserable sinners, that they may have God always propitious to them, and that the sins by which they are entangled, do not prevent them from becoming just, because they have a Mediator to reconcile them to God. But in order to shew how we return into favor with God, he says that Christ is our advocate; for he appears before God for this end, that he may exercise towards us the power and efficacy of his sacrifice. That this may be better understood, I will speak more homely. The intercession of Christ is a continual application of his death for our salvation. That God then does not impute to us our sins, this comes to us, because he has regard to Christ as intercessor.

But the two names, by which he afterwards signalizes Christ, properly belong to the subject of this passage. He calls him *just* and *a propitiation*. It is necessary for him to be both, that he might sustain the office and person of an Advocate; for who that is a sinner could reconcile God to us? For we are excluded from access to him, because no one is pure and free from sin. Hence no one is fit to be a high priest, except he is innocent and separated from sinners, as it is also declared in Hebrews 7: 26.

Propitiation is added, because no one fit to be a high priest without a sacrifice. Hence, under the Law, no priest entered the sanctuary without blood; and a sacrifice, as a usual seal, was wont, according to God's appointment, to accompany prayers. By this symbol it was God's design to shew, that whosoever obtains favor for us, must be furnished with a sacrifice; for when God is offended, in order to pacify him a satisfaction is required. It hence follows, that all the saints who have ever been and shall be, have need of an advocate, and that no one except Christ is equal to undertake this office. And doubtless John ascribed these two things to Christ, to shew that he is the only true advocate.

Now, as no small consolation comes to us, when we hear that Christ not only died for us to reconcile us to the Father, but that he continually intercedes for us, so that an access in his name is open to us, that our prayers may be heard; so we ought especially to beware, lest this honor, which belongs peculiarly to him, should be transferred to another.

1 JOHN 3

1. Behold

The second argument is from the dignity and excellency of our calling; for it was not common honor, he says, that the heavenly Father bestowed on us, when he adopted us as his children. This being so great a favor, the desire for

visible to the eye, and belong to this vain life, or serve to fill with pride and vanity; or these are the main things, which men that love the world most highly value and esteem.

the lust of the flesh; by which is meant, not lust in general, or concupiscence, the corruption of nature, which is the fountain of all sin, or indwelling sin, the flesh, or that corrupt principle which lusts against the Spirit; nor the various lusts of the flesh, fleshly lusts, which war against the soul, and which are many, and are also called worldly lusts; but some particular one, "a lust of the body," as the SyriAct version reads; either the lust of uncleanness, which includes all unchaste desires, thoughts, words, and actions, fornication, adultery, rape, incest, sodomy, and all unnatural lusts; and which make up a considerable part of the all that is in the world: or else intemperance in eating and drinking, gluttony and drunkenness, excess of wine, surfeitings, rioting, and revellings, and all the sensual pleasures of life, by which the carnal mind, and the lusts of it, are gratified; whereby the soul is destroyed, the body is dishonored, and a wound, dishonor, and reproach brought on the character, not to be removed; for which reasons the world, and the things of it, are not to be loved.

the lust of the eyes: after unlawful objects, and may design unchaste and lascivious looks, eyes full of adultery, and whereby adultery is committed; see Matthew 5: 28; but then this falls in with the other, unless that be confined to intemperance; rather then this may intend a sinful curiosity of seeing vain sights, and shows, with which the eye of man is never satisfied, Ecclesiastes 1: 8; and against which the psalmist prays, Psalm 119: 37, or rather the sin of covetousness is here designed, the objects of which are visible things, as gold, silver, houses, lands, and possessions, with which riches the eyes of men are never satisfied, and which sin is drawn forth and cherished by the eyes; and indeed a covetous man has little more satisfaction than the beholding his substance with his eyes, and in which he takes much sinful pleasure; see Ecclesiastes 4: 8; and what a poor vain empty thing is this! therefore, love not the world, since this is a principal thing in it.

the pride of life; by which seems to be meant, ambition of honor, of chief places and high titles, as in the Scribes and Pharisees, Matthew 23: 6, or of grand living, for the word signifies not so much life as living; living in a sumptuous, gay, luxurious, and pompous manner, in rich diet, costly apparel, having fine seats, palaces, and stately buildings, and numerous attendance; all which is but vanity and vexation of spirit; see Ecclesiastes 2: 1. The SyriAct and Arabic versions read, "the pride of the age"; and every age has some peculiar things in which the pride of it appears.

1 JOHN 3

1. Behold what manner of love. See, take notice, consider, look by faith, with wonder and astonishment, and observe how great a favor, what an instance of matchless love, what a wonderful blessing of grace.

the Father hath bestowed upon us: the Father of Christ, and the Father of us in Christ, who hath adopted us into his family, and regenerated us by his grace, and hath freely given us the new name:

that we should be called the sons of God. The Alexandrian copy, and some others, and the Vulgate Latin version, add, "and we are," or "be"; and the Ethiopic version, "and have been"; for it is not a mere name that is bestowed, but the thing itself in reality; and in the Hebrew language, "to be called," and "to be," are terms synonymous.

3. And every man that hath this hope in him. Or on him, Jesus Christ; for a true hope of that eternal happiness, which lies in likeness to Christ, and in the vision of him, is only founded on his person, blood, righteousness, and sacrifice: and this hope every man has not, only he who is born again; for this grace is implanted in regeneration, when men are of abundant mercy begotten unto it, and have it bestowed upon them as a free grace gift; and which is of great service to them both in life and in death; and among the rest it has this influence and effect upon them, that every such person that has it.

purifieth himself even as he is pure; not that any man can purify or cleanse himself

gresseth also the law: for sin is the transgression of the law.

5 And ye know that he was manifested to take away our sins; and in him is no sin.

6 Whosoever abideth in him sinneth not: whosoever sinneth hath not seen him, neither known him.

7 Little children, let no man deceive you: he that doeth righteousness is righteous, even as he is righteous.

8 He that committeth sin is of the devil; for the devil sinneth from the beginning. For this purpose the Son of God was manifested, that he might destroy the works of the devil.

9 Whosoever is born of God doth not commit sin; for his seed remaineth in him: and he cannot sin, because he is born of God.

10 In this the children of God are manifest, and the children of the devil: whosoever doeth not righteousness is not of God, neither he that loveth not his brother.

11 For this is the message that ye heard from the beginning, that we should love one another.

12 Not as Cain, who was of that wicked one, and slew his brother. And wherefore slew he him? Because his own works were evil, and his brother's righteous.

13 Marvel not, my brethren, if the world hate you.

14 We know that we have passed from death unto life, because we love the brethren. He that loveth not his brother abideth in death.

15 Whosoever hateth his brother is a murderer: and ye know that no murderer hath eternal life abiding in him.

16 Hereby perceive we the love of God, because he laid down his life for us: and we ought to lay down our lives for the brethren.

17 But whoso hath this world's good, and seeth his brother have need, and shutteth up his bowels of compassion from him, how dwelleth the love of God in him?

18 My little children, let us not love in word, neither in tongue; but in deed and in truth.

19 And hereby we know that we are of the truth, and shall assure our hearts

purity ought to be kindled in us, so as to be conformed to his image; nor, indeed, can it be otherwise, but that he who acknowledges himself to be one of God's children should purify himself. And to make this exhortation more forcible, he amplifies the favor of God; for when he says, that **love has been bestowed**, he means that it is from mere bounty and benevolence that God makes us his children; for whence comes to us such a dignity, except from the love of God? Love, then, is declared here to be gratuitous. There is, indeed, an impropriety in the language; but the Apostle preferred speaking thus rather than not to express what was necessary to be known. He, in short, means that the more abundantly God's goodness has been manifested towards us, the greater are our obligations to him, according to the teaching of Paul, when he besought the Romans by the mercies of God to present themselves as pure sacrifices to him (Romans 12: 1). We are at the same time taught, as I have said, that the adoption of all the godly is gratuitous, and does not depend on any regard to works.

What the sophists say, that God foresees those who are worthy to be adopted, is plainly refuted by these words, for, in this way the gift would not be gratuitous. It behooves us especially to understand this doctrine; for since the only cause of our salvation is adoption, and since the Apostle testifies that this flows from the mere love of God alone, there is nothing left to our worthiness or to the merits of works. For why are we sons? Even because God began to love us freely, when we deserved hatred rather than love. And as the Spirit is a pledge of our adoption, it hence follows, that if there be any good in us, it ought not to be set up in opposition to the grace of God, but, on the contrary, to be ascribed to him.

When he says that we are *called*, or *named*, the expression is not without its meaning; for it is God who with his own mouth declares us to be sons, as he gave a name to Abraham according to what he was.

Therefore the world

It is a trial that grievously assaults our faith, that we are not so much regarded as God's children, or that no mark of so great an excellency appears in us, but that, on the contrary, almost the whole world treats us with ridicule and contempt. Hence it can hardly be inferred from our present state that God is a Father to us, for the devil so contrives all things as to obscure this benefit. He obviates this offense by saying that we are not as yet acknowledged to be such as we are, because the world knows not God: a remarkable example of this very thing is found in Isaac and Jacob; for though both were chosen by God, yet Ishmael persecuted the former with laughter and taunts; and Esau, the latter with threats and the sword. However, then, we may be oppressed by the world, still our salvation remains safe and secure.

from sin, this is only owing to the grace of God and blood of Christ; nor that any man can be so pure and holy as Christ is, who is free from all sin, both original and actual; but this must be understood either of a man that has faith and hope in Christ, dealing by these with the blood of Christ for purity and cleansing, with whom and which these graces are conversant for such purposes; or of such a person's imitating of Christ in the holiness of his life and conversation, making him his pattern and example, studying to walk as he walked; to which he is the more excited and stimulated by the hope he has of being a Son of God, a dear child of his, and therefore ought to be a follower of him, and walk as Christ walked, in humility; love, patience, and in other acts of holiness; and by the hope he has of being like unto him, and with him in the other world to all eternity: but then this "as" is only expressive of some degree of likeness and similitude, and not perfect equality, which is not to be expected in this, or in the world to come; believers indeed, who have faith and hope in the justifying righteousness of Christ, may, and should consider themselves pure and righteous, and free from sin, as Christ is; being clothed upon with his robe of righteousness, in which they stand without fault before the throne, without spot or wrinkle, or any such thing; but this does not seem to be the sense of the place here, the argument being to engage the saints to purity and holiness of life and conversation, from the consideration of the great love of God bestowed upon them in their adoption, and from their hope of eternal happiness, as the context shows.

9. Whosoever is born of God. In a figurative and spiritual sense; who are regenerated, or born from above; who are quickened by the grace of God, and have Christ formed in them; who are made partakers of the divine nature, and new creatures in Christ; which spiritual birth is not owing to men, to the power and will of men, but to the grace of God; and is sometimes ascribed to the Father, who of his own will and abundant mercy begets souls again to a lively hope, and saves them by the washing of regeneration; and sometimes to Christ, who quickens whom he will, whose

grace is implanted, and image stamped in it, and by whose resurrection from the dead men are begotten again; and chiefly, to the Spirit of God, who is the author of regeneration, and of the whole of sanctification: and such as are born of him are alive through him, the spirit of life entering into them, and live to God and upon Christ, and breathe after divine and spiritual things, and have their senses to discern them; they see, hear, feel, taste, and savor them; and desire the sincere milk of the word, for their nourishment and growth; and have every grace implanted in them, as faith, hope, and love.

doth not commit sin; does not make it his trade and business; it is not the constant course of his life; he does not live and walk in sin, or give up himself to it; he is not without the being of it in him, or free from acts of sin in his life and conversation, but he does not so commit it as to be the servant of it, a slave unto it, or to continue in it.

for his seed remaineth in him; not the word of God, or the Gospel, though that is a seed which is sown by the ministers of it, and blessed by God, and by which he regenerates his people; and which having a place in their hearts, becomes the ingrafted word, and there abides, nor can it be rooted out; where it powerfully teaches to avoid sin, is an antidote against it, and a preservative from it: nor the Holy Spirit of God, though he is the author of the new birth, and the principle of all grace; and where he once is, he always abides; and through the power of his grace believers prevail against sin, and mortify the deeds of the body, and live: but rather the grace of the Spirit, the internal principle of grace in the soul, the new nature, or new man formed in the soul, is meant; which seminally contains all grace in it, and which, like seed, springs up and gradually increases, and always abides; and is pure and incorruptible, and neither sins itself, nor encourages sin, but opposes, checks, and prevents it.

and he cannot sin; not that it is impossible for such a man to do acts of sin, or that it is possible for him to live without sin; for the words are not to be understood in the sense of those who plead for perfection in this life; for though

before him.

20 For if our heart condemn us, God is greater than our heart, and knoweth all things.

21 Beloved, if our heart condemn us not, then have we confidence toward God.

22 And whatsoever we ask, we receive of him, because we keep his commandments, and do those things that are pleasing in his sight.

23 And this is his commandment, That we should believe on the name of his Son Jesus Christ, and love one another, as he gave us commandment.

24 And he that keepeth his commandments dwelleth in him, and he in him. And hereby we know that he abideth in us, by the Spirit which he hath given us.

1 JOHN 4

1 Beloved, believe not every spirit, but try the spirits whether they are of God: because many false prophets are gone out into the world.

2 Hereby know ye the Spirit of God: Every spirit that confesseth that Jesus Christ is come in the flesh is of God:

3 And every spirit that confesseth not that Jesus Christ is come in the flesh is not of God: and this is that spirit of antichrist, whereof ye have heard that it should come; and even now already is it in the world.

4 Ye are of God, little children, and have overcome them: because greater is he that is in you, than he that is in the world.

5 They are of the world: therefore speak they of the world, and the world heareth them.

6 We are of God: he that knoweth God heareth us; he that is not of God heareth not us. Hereby know we the spirit of truth, and the spirit of error.

7 Beloved, let us love one another: for love is of God; and every one that loveth is born of God, and knoweth God.

8 He that loveth not knoweth not God; for God is love.

9 In this was manifested the love of God toward us, because that God sent his only begotten Son into the world, that we might live through him.

2. Now are we the sons of God

He comes now to what every one knows and feels himself; for though the ungodly may not entice us to give up our hope, yet our present condition is very short of the glow of God's children; for as to our body we are dust and a shadow, and death is always before our eyes; we are also subject to thousand miseries, and the soul is exposed to innumerable evils; so that we find always a hell within us. The more necessary it is that all our thoughts should be withdrawn from the present view of things, lest the miseries by which we are on every side surrounded and almost overwhelmed, should shake our faith in that felicity which as yet lies hid. For the Apostle's meaning is this, that we act very foolishly when we estimate what God has bestowed on us according to the present state of things, but that we ought with undoubting faith to hold to that which does not yet appear.

1 JOHN 4

He returns to his former doctrine, which he had touched upon in the second chapter; for many (as it is usual in new things) abused the name of Christ for the purpose of serving their own errors. Some made a half profession of Christ; and when they obtained a place among his friends, they had more opportunity to injure his cause. Satan took occasion to disturb the Church, especially through Christ himself; for he is the stone of offense, against whom all necessarily stumble who keep not on the right way, as shewn to us by God.

But what the Apostle says consists of three parts. He first shews an evil dangerous to the faithful; and therefore he exhorts them to beware. He *prescribes* how they were to beware, that is, by making a distinction between the spirits; and this is the second part. In the third place, he points out a particular error, the most dangerous to them, he therefore forbids them to hear those who denied that the Son of God appeared in the flesh. We shall now consider each in order.

But though in the passage this reason is added, that many false prophets had gone forth into the world, yet it is convenient to begin with it. The announcement contains a useful admonition; for if Satan had then already seduced many, who under the name of Christ scattered their impostures, similar instances at this day ought not to terrify us. For it is the case perpetually with the Gospel, that Satan attempts to pollute and corrupt its purity by variety of errors. This our age has brought forth some horrible and monstrous sects; and for this reason many stand amazed; and not knowing where to turn, they cast aside every care for religion; for they find no more summary way for extricating themselves from the danger of errors. They thus, indeed, act most foolishly; for by shunning the light of truth, they

the saints have perfection in Christ, yet not in themselves; they are not impeccable, they are not free from sin, neither from the being nor actings of it; sin is in them, lives in them, dwells in them, hinders all the good, and does all the mischief it can: or in such sense, as if the sins of believers were not sins; for though they are pardoned and expiated, and they are justified from them, yet they do not cease to be sins; they are equally contrary to the nature, will, and law of God, as well as the sins of others; and are oftentimes attended with more aggravated circumstances, and which God in a fatherly way takes notice of, and chastises for, and on the account of which he hides his face from them: nor does the phrase intend any particular single sin, which cannot be committed; though there are such, as sinning willfully after receiving the knowledge of the truth, or denying Christ to be the Savior of sinners, and a sacrifice for sin, and hatred of a Christian brother as such, and sinning the sin unto death, or the unpardonable sin; neither of which can be committed by a regenerate man: nor is the meaning only, though it is a sense that will very well bear, and agrees with the context, that such persons cannot sin as unregenerate men do; that is, live in a continued course of sinning, and with pleasure, and without reluctance, and so as to lie in it, as the whole world does: but rather the meaning is, he that is born of God, as he is born of God, or that which is born of God in him, the new man, or new creature, cannot sin; for that is pure and holy; there is nothing sinful in it, nor can anything that is sinful come out of it, or be done by it; it is the workmanship of the Holy Spirit of God; it is a good work, and well pleasing: in the sight of God.

because he is born of God: for that which is born of God in him, does, under the influence of the Spirit, power, and grace of God, preserve him from the temptations of Satan, the pollutions of the world, and the corruptions of his own heart; see 1 John 5: 18; which the Vulgate Latin version there renders, "the generation of God," meaning regeneration, or that which is born of God, "preserveth him": this furnishes out a considerable argument for the perseverance of the saints.

1 JOHN 4

1. Beloved, believe not every spirit. The apostle having mentioned the word "spirit" in the latter part of the preceding chapter, takes an occasion from thence to return to what he had been suggesting in the "second" chapter, concerning the many antichrists that then were, and whom he points out, and here cautions against. By "every spirit" he means, either every doctrine that is pretended to come from the Spirit of God, or every teacher, who professes to be qualified and sent by him, and to have his light, knowledge, and doctrine from him. Every true minister of the Gospel has the Spirit, and the gifts of the Spirit, more or less, to qualify him for his work; he is separated, and called to it by him, and receives his spiritual light find knowledge from him; it is he that teaches him sound doctrine, and leads him into all truth, as it is in Jesus, and brings every necessary truth to his remembrance; and who succeeds his ministrations to the good of souls: but there are some who call themselves the ministers of the Gospel, who, though they may have some natural abilities, and a share of human learning, and a notional knowledge of things, yet have never received either grace or gifts from the Spirit; nor have they been ever called by him; nor are their ministrations according to that divine word which is inspired by him, nor attended with his demonstration and power; wherefore, though some professing to have the Spirit of Christ are to be believed, yet not everyone; and though the Spirit is not to be quenched in any, nor prophesying to be despised, yet care should be taken what is heard and received: some persons are so obstinate and incredulous as not to believe anything that is declared, be the evidence what it will; as the Jews would not believe Christ and his apostles, though what they said agreed with Moses and the prophets, and was confirmed by miracles; and others are too credulous; at once receive every teacher, and embrace every upstart doctrine.

but try the spirits whether they are of God; not by human reason, especially as carnal and unsanctified; for though the doctrines of the Gospel are not contrary to true reason, they are above it, and not to be judged of by it,

10 Herein is love, not that we loved God, but that he loved us, and sent his Son to be the propitiation for our sins.

11 Beloved, if God so loved us, we ought also to love one another.

12 No man hath seen God at any time. If we love one another, God dwelleth in us, and his love is perfected in us.

13 Hereby know we that we dwell in him, and he in us, because he hath given us of his Spirit.

14 And we have seen and do testify that the Father sent the Son to be the Savior of the world.

15 Whosoever shall confess that Jesus is the Son of God, God dwelleth in him, and he in God.

16 And we have known and believed the love that God hath to us. God is love; and he that dwelleth in love dwelleth in God, and God in him.

17 Herein is our love made perfect, that we may have boldness in the day of judgment: because as he is, so are we in this world.

18 There is no fear in love; but perfect love casteth out fear: because fear hath torment. He that feareth is not made perfect in love.

19 We love him, because he first loved us.

20 If a man say, I love God, and hateth his brother, he is a liar: for he that loveth not his brother whom he hath seen, how can he love God whom he hath not seen?

21 And this commandment have we from him, That he who loveth God love his brother also.

1 JOHN 5

1 Whosoever believeth that Jesus is the Christ is born of God: and every one that loveth him that begat loveth him also that is begotten of him.

2 By this we know that we love the children of God, when we love God, and keep his commandments.

3 For this is the love of God, that we keep his commandments: and his commandments are not grievous.

4 For whatsoever is born of God overcometh the world: and this is the victory that overcometh the world, even our faith.

cast themselves into the darkness of errors. Let, therefore, this fact remain fixed in our minds, that from the time the Gospel began to be preached, false prophets immediately appeared; and the fact will fortify us against such offenses.

The antiquity of errors keeps many, as it were, fast bound, so that they dare not emerge from them. But John points out here all intestine evil which was then in the Church. Now, if there were impostors mixed then with the Apostles and other faithful teachers, what wonder is it, that the doctrine of the Gospel has been long ago suppressed, and that many corruptions have prevailed in the world? There is, then, no reason why antiquity should hinder us to exercise our liberty in distinguishing between truth and falsehood.

1. Believe not every spirit

When the Church is disturbed by discords and contentions, many, as it has been said, being frightened, depart from the Gospel. But the Spirit prescribes to us a far different remedy, that is, that the faithful should not receive any doctrine thoughtlessly and without discrimination. We ought, then, to take heed lest, being offended at the variety of opinions, we should discard teachers, and, together with them, the word of God. But this precaution is sufficient, that all are not to be heard indiscriminately.

The word *spirit* I take metonymically, as signifying him who boasts that he is endowed with the gift of the Spirit to perform his office as a prophet. For as it was not permitted to any one to speak in his own name, nor was credit given to speakers but as far as they were the organs of the Holy Spirit, in order that prophets might have more authority, God honored them with this name, as though he had separated them from mankind in general. Those, then, were called spirits, who, giving only a language to the oracles of the Holy Spirit, in a manner represented him. They brought nothing of their own, nor came they forth in their own name, but the design of this honorable title was, that God's word should not lose the respect due to it through the humble condition of the minister. For God would have his word to be always received from the mouth of man no otherwise than if he himself had appeared from heaven.

Here Satan interposed, and having sent false teachers to adulterate God's word, he gave them also this name, that they might more easily deceive. Thus false prophets have always been wont superciliously and boldly to claim for themselves whatever honor God had bestowed on his own servants. But the Apostle designedly made use of this name, lest they who falsely pretend God's name should deceive us by their masks.

and are disapproved of and rejected by carnal reason; but by the word of God, which is the standard of all doctrine; and whatever agrees with that is to be received, and what does not should be rejected. And so to do is very commendable, as appears from the instance of the Beraeans, who on this account are said to be more noble than those of Thessalonica, Acts 17: 11; and from the commendation of the church at Ephesus, Rev. 2: 2. And this is what every believer, every private Christian should do; to them it belongs to read and search the Scriptures, and prove all things, and judge for themselves of the truth of doctrine; and to such a probation or trial of the spirits, spiritual light, knowledge, judgment, sense, experience, and divine guidance are necessary, which should be asked of God, and an increase thereof; and all such diligent searchers, and humble inquirers, are capable of making judgment of persons and doctrines, whether they are from the Spirit of God or not, for the Spirit of God never speaks contrary to his word.

because many false prophets are gone out into the world: such who pretended either to a revelation of future things, and to foretell things to come; or rather to a gift of prophesying, or preaching in Christ's name, to be "prophets" and spiritual men, and ministers of the word, but were "false" ones; who either predicted what did not come to pass, or rather preached false doctrine, by corrupting the word, and handling it deceitfully, and so imposed upon and ruined the souls of others, as well as deceived their own.

15. Whosoever shall confess that Jesus is the Son of God. The only begotten of the Father; that he is not a mere man, as the Jews, and Ebion and Cerinthus said, but a divine person, equal with the Father; which contains all that relates to the dignity of his person, and his fitness for his office as a Savior, and which was the test of faith in those times, and the grand article of belief: not that a bare assent to this had what followed annexed to it; for the devils believed and owned that Jesus was the Son of God; and so might, and did, unregenerate persons, as the centurion at the cross of Christ, who know nothing what communion with God is; but this confession is such as is

attended with a believing in Christ from the heart unto righteousness, life, and salvation, and a cheerful obedience to his ordinances and commands, from a principle of love to him, and faith in him, things not to be found in devils and carnal men; see Rom. 10: 9.

1 JOHN 5

3. For this is the love of God, that we keep his commandments. Keeping of the commandments of God is an evidence of love to God; this shows that love is not in word and tongue, in profession only, but in deed and in truth; and that such persons have a sense of the love of God upon their souls, under the influence of which they act; and such shall have, and may expect to have, greater manifestations of the love of God unto them.

and his commandments are not grievous; heavy, burdensome, and disagreeable; by which are meant, not so much the precepts of the moral law, which through the weakness of the flesh are hard to be kept, and cannot be perfectly fulfilled; though believers indeed, being freed from the rigorous exaction, curse, and condemnation of the law, delight in it after the inward man, and serve it cheerfully with their spirit; and still less the commands of the ceremonial law, which were now abolished, and were grievous to be borne; but rather those of faith in Christ, and love to the saints, 1 John 3: 23; or it may be the ordinances of the Gospel, baptism, and the Lord's supper, with others, which though disagreeable to unregenerate persons, who do not care to be under the yoke of Christ, however easy and light it is, yet are not heavy and burdensome to regenerate ones; and especially when they have the love of God shed abroad in them, the presence of God with them, communion with Jesus Christ, and a supply of grace and strength from him; then are these ways ways of pleasantness, and paths of peace, and the tabernacles of the Lord are amiable and lovely.

12. He that hath the Son. Has a spiritual and experimental knowledge of him, true faith in him; who has him dwelling in his heart, and living in him.

hath life: not only spiritual life, being

5 Who is he that overcometh the world, but he that believeth that Jesus is the Son of God?

6 This is he that came by water and blood, even Jesus Christ; not by water only, but by water and blood. And it is the Spirit that beareth witness, because the Spirit is truth.

7 For there are three that bear record in heaven, the Father, the Word, and the Holy Ghost: and these three are one.

8 And there are three that bear witness in earth, the spirit, and the water, and the blood: and these three agree in one.

9 If we receive the witness of men, the witness of God is greater: for this is the witness of God which he hath testified of his Son.

10 He that believeth on the Son of God hath the witness in himself: he that believeth not God hath made him a liar; because he believeth not the record that God gave of his Son.

11 And this is the record, that God hath given to us eternal life, and this life is in his Son.

12 He that hath the Son hath life; and he that hath not the Son of God hath not life.

13 These things have I written unto you that believe on the name of the Son of God; that ye may know that ye have eternal life, and that ye may believe on the name of the Son of God.

14 And this is the confidence that we have in him, that, if we ask any thing according to his will, he heareth us:

15 And if we know that he hear us, whatsoever we ask, we know that we have the petitions that we desired of him.

16 If any man see his brother sin a sin which is not unto death, he shall ask, and he shall give him life for them that sin not unto death. There is a sin unto death: I do not say that he shall pray for it.

17 All unrighteousness is sin: and there is a sin not unto death.

18 We know that whosoever is born of God sinneth not; but he that is begotten of God keepeth himself, and that wicked one toucheth him not.

19 And we know that we are of God, and the whole world lieth in wickedness.

20 And we know that the Son of God is come, and hath given us an understand-

1 JOHN 5

20. And we know that the Son of God is come

As the children of God are assailed on every side, he, as we have said, encourages and exhorts them to persevere in resisting their enemies, and for this reason, because they fight under the banner of God, and certainly know that they are ruled by his Spirit; but he now reminds them where this knowledge is especially to be found.

He then says that God has been so made known to us, that now there is no reason for doubting. The Apostle does not without reason dwell on this point; for except our faith is really founded on God, we shall never stand firm in the contest. For this purpose the Apostle shews that we have obtained through Christ a sure knowledge of the true God, so that we may not fluctuate in uncertainty.

By **true God** he does not mean one who tells the truth, but him who is really God; and he so calls him to distinguishing him from all idols. Thus true is in opposition to what is fictitious; for it is *alethinos*, and not *alethes*. A similar passage is in John "This is eternal life, to know thee, the only true God, and him whom thou hast sent, Jesus Christ." (John 17: 3) And he justly ascribes to Christ this office of illuminating our minds as to the knowledge of God. For, as he is the only true image of the invisible God, as he is the only interpreter of the Father, as he is the only guide of life, yea, as he is the life and light of the world and the truth, as soon as we depart from him, we necessarily become vain in our own devices.

And Christ is said to have **given us an understanding**, not only because he shews us in the gospel what sort of being is the true God, and also illuminates us by his Spirit; but because in Christ himself we have God manifested in the flesh, as Paul says, since *in him dwells all the fullness of the Deity, and are hid all the treasures of knowledge and wisdom* (Colossians 2: 9). Thus it is that the face of God in a manner appears to us in Christ; not that there was no knowledge, or a doubtful knowledge of God, before the coming of Christ,, but that now he manifests himself more fully and more clearly. And this is what Paul says in 2 Corinthians 4: 6, that "God, who formerly commanded light to shine out of darkness at the creation of the world, hath now shone in our hearts through the brightness of the knowledge of his glory in the face of Christ."

And it must be observed, that this gift is peculiar to the elect. Christ, indeed, kindles for all indiscriminately the torch of his gospel; but all have not the eyes of their minds opened to see it, but on the contrary Satan spreads the veil of blindness over many. Then the Apostle means the light which Christ kindles within in the hearts of his people, and which when once kindled, is never extinguished, though in

quickened by him, and living by faith on him, but eternal life; the knowledge he has of him is eternal life; he has it in faith and hope, and has a right unto it, and the earnest of it, as well as has it in Christ his representative, whom he has, and in whom this life is.

[and] he that hath not the Son of God; no knowledge of him, nor faith in him, nor enjoyment of him:

hath not life; he is dead in sin, he is alienated from the life of God, has no title to eternal life, nor meetness for it, nor shall enjoy it, but shall die the second death.

13. These things have I written unto you. Which are contained in the epistle in general, and particularly what is written in the context, concerning the victory of the world, being ascribed to him who believes that Christ is the Son of God; and concerning the six witnesses of his sonship, and the record bore by God, that the gift of eternal life is in him.

that believe on the name of the Son of God; who not only believed that Christ is the Son of God, which this six fold testimony would confirm them in, but also believed in his name for righteousness, life, and salvation; in which name there is all this, and in no other; and who also professed their faith in him, and were baptized in his name, and continued believing in him, and holding fast their profession of him.

that ye may know that ye have eternal life; that there is such a thing as eternal life; that this is in Christ; that believers have it in him, and the beginning of it in themselves; and that they have a right unto it, and meetness for it, and shall certainly enjoy it; the knowledge of which is had by faith, under the testimony of the Spirit of God, and particularly what is above written concerning eternal life, being a free grace gift of God; and this being in Christ, and the assurance of it, that such who have him, or believe in him, have that which might serve to communicate, cultivate, and increase such knowledge.

and that ye may believe on the name of the Son of God; which they had done already, and still did; the sense is, the above things were written to them concerning the Son of God, that they might be encouraged to continue believing in him, as such; to hold fast the faith of him and go on believing in him to the end; and that their faith in him might be increased; for faith is imperfect and is capable of increasing, and growing exceedingly: and nothing more tends unto, or is a more proper means of it, than the sacred writings, the reading and hearing them explained, and especially that part of them which respects the person, office, and grace of Christ.

17. All unrighteousness is sin. All unrighteousness against God or man is a sin against the law of God, and the wrath of God is revealed against it, and it is deserving of death; yet all unrighteousness is not unto death, as the sins of David, which were unrighteousness both to God and man, and yet they were put away, and he died not; Peter sinned very foully, and did great injustice to his dear Lord, and yet his sin was not unto death; he had repentance unto life given him, and a fresh application of pardoning grace.

and there is a sin not unto death; this is added for the relief of weak believers, who hearing of a sin unto death, not to be prayed for, might fear that theirs were of that kind, whereas none of them are; for though they are guilty of many unrighteousnesses, yet God is merciful to them and forgives, Heb 8: 12, and so they are not unto death.

19. [And] we know that we are of God. The sons of God, and regenerated by him; this is known by the Spirit of God, which witnesses to the spirits of the saints that they are the children of God; and by the fruits and effects of regenerating grace, as love to the brethren, and the like.

and the whole world lies in wickedness; that is, the men of the world, the greater part of the inhabitants of it, who are as they were when they came into it, not being born of God; these are addicted to sin and, wickedness; the bias of their minds is to it, they are set upon it, and give themselves up to it, are immersed in it, and are under the power of it: or "in the wicked one"; Satan, the god of this world; they are under his influence, and led according to

ing, that we may know him that is true, and we are in him that is true, even in his Son Jesus Christ. This is the true God, and eternal life.

21 Little children, keep yourselves from idols. Amen.

some it may for a time be smothered.

We are in him that is true

By these words he reminds us how efficacious is that knowledge which he mentions, even because by it we are united to Christ; and become one with God; for it has a living root, fixed in the heart, by which it comes that God lives in us and we in him. As he says, without a copulative, that: **we are in him that is true, in his Son**, he seems to express the manner of our union with God, as though he had said, that we are in God through Christ.

This is the true God

Though the Arians have attempted to elude this passage, and some agree with them at this day, yet we have here a remarkable testimony to the divinity of Christ. The Arians apply this passage to the Father, as though the Apostle should again repeat that he is the true God. But nothing could be more frigid than such a repetition. It has already twice testified that the true God is he who has been made known to us in Christ, why should he again add, This is the true God? It applies, indeed, most suitably to Christ; for after having taught us that Christ is the guide by whose hand we are led to God, he now, by way of amplifying, affirms that Christ is that God, lest we should think that we are to seek further; and he confirms this view by what is added, **and eternal life**.

his will, and they are governed by him, and are at his beck and command; and this is known, by sad experience.

21. Little children, keep yourselves from idols. Amen. From Heathen idols and idolatry, into which the saints in those times might be liable to be drawn, by reason of their dwelling among Heathen idolaters, and being related to them, and by the too great freedom used in eating things sacrificed to idols in their temples; and from all other idols that might be introduced by some who went by the name of Christians, as the Gnostics, who worshipped the images of Simon and Helena; and the passage may be an antidote against the worshipping of images, afterwards introduced by the Papists. Moreover, errors and false doctrines, which are the figments of men's minds, and what they are fond of, may be called idols, and should be guarded against, and abstained from; as also the lusts of men's hearts, and all the evil things that are in the world, which are adored by the men of it; and even every creature that is loved too much is an idol; hence covetousness is called idolatry; nor should any creature or thing be loved more than God or Christ: the one only living and true God, Father, Son, and Spirit, he is only to be worshipped, feared, and loved.

2 John and 3 John

Introductions by John Gill

THOUGH 2 John epistle was called in question and gainsaid by some as authentic, as Eusebius says, yet there is no room to doubt of the authority of it; it was very early received into the canon of the Scripture, and is cited as such, and also as the Apostle John's, by Irenaeus, who was a disciple of Polycarp, and an hearer of Papias, who were both disciples of the Apostle John; nor need there be any question as to his being the author of it. Eusebius indeed does say, it was a doubt whether it was the Apostle John's or another of the same name; and some have since asserted, that it was written not by John the Evangelist, but by John the Presbyter of Ephesus, after the apostle; and this is thought to have some confirmation from the author of it being called an elder, or presbyter, which is judged not so agreeable to the Apostle John; though it should be observed, that Peter an apostle styles himself an elder, as John here does, 1 Pet. 5: 1, moreover, the above ancient writer, Irenaeus, expressly ascribes this epistle to John, the disciple of the Lord; and whoever compares some passages in this epistle with the former, particularly 2 John 1: 5, with 1 John 2: 7, will easily conclude, from the likeness of style and matter, that it is a genuine epistle of the Apostle John: the design of which is to exhort and encourage the lady he writes to, to continue in the truth and faith of the Gospel, and in love to God and his people, and to avoid false teachers and their doctrines.

3 John was written by the Apostle John, who calls himself an "elder", as in the preceding, and is inscribed to a friend of his, whom he mentions by name, and expresses a very great affection for, on account of his steady adherence to the truths of the Gospel, 3 John 1: 1; he wishes him bodily health equal to that prosperity of soul he was indulged with, 3 John 1: 2; congratulates him upon the testimony the brethren that came from him gave him of the truth being in him, and of his walking in it, and upon hearing that his children also trod in the same path, 3 John 1: 3; commends him for his hospitality and charity, of which testimonies were given before the church; and encourages him to go on doing the same acts of beneficence, since it was to such persons that went forth for the sake of Christ, and preaching in his name, and had nothing of the Gentiles for so doing; wherefore they ought to be received, and entertained by those of ability, that they might be fellow helpers to the truth with them, 3 John 1: 5. He complains of Diotrephes as a proud, haughty, and overbearing man in the church, where Gaius was a member, who would neither receive the letters the apostle sent, nor the brethren that came with them; nay, forbid them that would, and cast them out of the church for it, and prated against them with malicious words, whom he threatens to remember when he himself should come thither, 3 John 1: 9; wherefore he exhorts Gaius not to follow such an ill example, but that which is good in any person; since he that does good appears to be of God, and he that does evil, it looks as if he had never known him, 3 John 1: 11. And particularly he recommends Demetrius, who had a good report of all men, and of the truth itself, and had a testimony from the apostle, and those that were with him, which was known to be a true one, 3 John 1: 12. But though he had many things to say, both of one, and of the other, he determines to write

no more at present, hoping he should shortly see him, and personally converse together; and closes the epistle with his own good wish, and with mutual salutations of friends, 3 John 1: 13.

The commentaries on 2 John and 3 John are by A. R. Fausset and John Gill.

2 JOHN

1 The elder unto the elect lady and her children, whom I love in the truth; and not I only, but also all they that have known the truth;

2 For the truth's sake, which dwelleth in us, and shall be with us for ever.

3 Grace be with you, mercy, and peace, from God the Father, and from the Lord Jesus Christ, the Son of the Father, in truth and love.

4 I rejoiced greatly that I found of thy children walking in truth, as we have received a commandment from the Father.

5 And now I beseech thee, lady, not as though I wrote a new commandment unto thee, but that which we had from the beginning, that we love one another.

6 And this is love, that we walk after his commandments. This is the commandment, That, as ye have heard from the beginning, ye should walk in it.

7 For many deceivers are entered into the world, who confess not that Jesus Christ is come in the flesh. This is a deceiver and an antichrist.

8 Look to yourselves, that we lose not those things which we have wrought, but that we receive a full reward.

9 Whosoever transgresseth, and abideth not in the doctrine of Christ, hath not God. He that abideth in the doctrine of Christ, he hath both the Father and the Son.

10 If there come any unto you, and bring not this doctrine, receive him not into your house, neither bid him God speed:

11 For he that biddeth him God speed is partaker of his evil deeds.

12 Having many things to write unto you, I would not write with paper and ink: but I trust to come unto you, and speak face to face, that our joy may be full.

13 The children of thy elect sister greet thee. Amen.

2 JOHN

ADDRESS: GREETING: THANKSGIVING FOR THE ELECT LADY'S FAITHFULNESS IN THE TRUTH: ENJOINS LOVE: WARNS AGAINST DECEIVERS, LEST WE LOSE OUR REWARD: CONCLUSION.

1. The elder

In a familiar letter John gives himself a less authoritative designation than "apostle"; so 1 Pet 5: 1.

lady – Bengel takes the *Greek* as a proper name *Kyria,* answering to the *Hebrew* "Martha." Being a person of influence, "deceivers" (2 John 7) were insinuating themselves into her family to seduce her and her children from the faith [Tirinus], whence John felt it necessary to write a warning to her. A particular *Church,* probably that at Babylon, was intended. "Church" is derived from *Greek* "Kuriake" akin to *Kuria,* or *Kyria* here; the latter word among the Romans and Athenians means the same as *ecclesia,* the term appropriated to designate the *Church assembly.*

2. For the truth's sake – joined with "I love," 2 John 1. "They who love *in* the truth, also love *on account of the truth.*"

3. Grace be with you – one of the oldest manuscripts and several versions have "us" for *you.* The *Greek* is literally, "Grace *shall be* with us," that is, with both *you and me.* A prayer, however, is implied besides a confident affirmation. **grace ... mercy ... peace**

"*Grace*" covers the sins of men; "mercy," their miseries. *Grace* must first do away with man's guilt before his misery can be relieved by *mercy.* Therefore *grace* stands before *mercy. Peace* is the result of both, and therefore stands third in order. Casting all our care on the Lord, with thanksgiving, maintains this peace.

8. Look to yourselves – amidst the widespread prevalence of deception so many being led astray. So Christ's warning, Matt. 24: 4–5, 24.

a full reward – of grace not of debt. *Fully* consummated glory. If "which YE have wrought" be read with very old authorities, the reward meant is that of their "work (of faith) and labor of love." There are degrees of heavenly reward proportioned to the degrees of capability of receiving heavenly blessedness. Each vessel of glory hanging on Jesus shall be fully happy. But the larger the vessel, the greater will be its capacity for receiving heavenly bliss. He who with one pound made ten, received authority over ten cities. He who made five pounds received five cities; each according to his capacity of rule, and in proportion to his faithfulness. Compare 1 Cor. 15: 41. "There is no half reward of the saints. It is either lost altogether, or received *in full; in full* communion with God" [Bengel]. Still no service of

2 JOHN

1. The elder unto the elect lady and her children. By the **elder** is meant the writer of this epistle, the Apostle John, who so calls himself either on account of his age, he being now near an hundred years of age, having outlived all the apostles: or on account of his office, being a bishop or overseer, not only of the church at Ephesus, but of all the Asiatic churches.

whom I love in the truth; either as being in the truth and faith of the Gospel; for though all men are to be loved as men, and to be done well to, yet they that are of the household of faith, or are in the faith, are in and especial manner to be loved and respected; see Gal. 6: 10; or the sense is, that the apostle loved this lady and her children sincerely and heartily, without dissimulation; not in word and in tongue, but in deed and in truth, 1 John 3: 18:

and not I only, but also all they that have known the truth; either the Lord Jesus Christ, who is the truth; not with a notional knowledge, but with the knowledge of approbation and affection; with a fiducial and appropriating one: or the Gospel, the word of truth; not with a speculative, but with a spiritual and experimental knowledge of it: and this is not to be understood of every individual person then living, which had such a knowledge of the truth; for it cannot be reasonably thought that every individual person should know this lady and her children; but of all such persons who had any knowledge of them; for such who are born again by the word of truth, love not only him that begot them, but all those who are begotten of him.

6. And this is love, that we walk after his commandments. By observing them as a rule of conversation, in so doing love is shown to God; and such may expect the fresh discoveries of the love of God to, them.

7. For many deceivers are entered into the world. By whom are meant false teachers, who are described by their quality, "deceivers", deceitful workers, pretending to be ministers of Christ, to have a: value for truth, a love for souls, and a view to the glory of God, but lie in wait to deceive, and handle the word of God deceitfully.

who confess not that Jesus Christ is come in the flesh; these were not the Jews who denied that Jesus was the Christ, though they would not allow that Christ was come in the flesh; but these were some who bore the Christian name, and professed to believe in Jesus Christ, but would not own that he was really incarnate, or assumed a true human nature, only in appearance; and denied that he took true and real flesh of the virgin, but only seemed to do so; and these are confuted by the apostle, 1 John 1: 1; and upon everyone of these he justly fixes the following character.

This is a deceiver and an antichrist; one of the deceivers that were come into the world, and one of the antichrists that were already in it; and who were the forerunners of the man of sin, and in whom the mystery of iniquity already began to work; for antichrist does not design anyone particular individual person, but a set of men, that are contrary to Christ, and opposers of him.

12. Having many things to write unto you. Either on a civil, or on a religious account, concerning the state of the churches of Asia, and particularly Ephesus, and of private families and persons, and concerning the truths and doctrines of the Gospel; not that he had any new one, or any other than what they had heard from the beginning, to communicate to them, by word of mouth, for this he denies, 2 John 1: 5.

I would not [write] with paper and ink; any more than what was written: but I trust to come unto you; where they were, but where that was is not known; very likely in some parts of Asia, and it may be not far from Ephesus, since any long journey would not have been fit for the apostle to have taken in this his old age.

3 JOHN

1. The elder unto the well beloved Gaius. The elder is the writer of the epistle, the Apostle John, who so styles himself on account of his age, and office, as in the preceding epistle. The person to whom he writes is "the well beloved Gaius"; not that Gaius, who was the Apostle Paul's host, Rom. 16: 23, for though

3 JOHN

1 The elder unto the wellbeloved Gaius, whom I love in the truth.

2 Beloved, I wish above all things that thou mayest prosper and be in health, even as thy soul prospereth.

3 For I rejoiced greatly, when the brethren came and testified of the truth that is in thee, even as thou walkest in the truth.

4 I have no greater joy than to hear that my children walk in truth.

5 Beloved, thou doest faithfully whatsoever thou doest to the brethren, and to strangers;

6 Which have borne witness of thy charity before the church: whom if thou bring forward on their journey after a godly sort, thou shalt do well:

7 Because that for his name's sake they went forth, taking nothing of the Gentiles.

8 We therefore ought to receive such, that we might be fellowhelpers to the truth.

9 I wrote unto the church: but Diotrephes, who loveth to have the preeminence among them, receiveth us not.

10 Wherefore, if I come, I will remember his deeds which he doeth, prating against us with malicious words: and not content therewith, neither doth he himself receive the brethren, and forbiddeth them that would, and casteth them out of the church.

11 Beloved, follow not that which is evil, but that which is good. He that doeth good is of God: but he that doeth evil hath not seen God.

12 Demetrius hath good report of all men, and of the truth itself: yea, and we also bear record; and ye know that our record is true.

13 I had many things to write, but I will not with ink and pen write unto thee:

14 But I trust I shall shortly see thee, and we shall speak face to face. Peace be to thee. Our friends salute thee. Greet the friends by name.

minister or people shall fail to receive its reward.

9. The *loss* **(2 John 8) meant is here explained: the** *not having God,* **which results from** *abiding not in the doctrine of Christ.*

10. If there come any – as a teacher or brother. The *Greek* is indicative, not subjunctive; implying that such persons *do actually come,* and *are sure to come;* when any comes, as there will. True love is combined with hearty renunciation and separation from all that is false, whether persons or doctrines.

12. I would not write – A heart full of love pours itself out more freely face to face, than by letter.

paper – made of Egyptian papyrus. Pens were then reeds split.

ink – made of soot and water, thickened with gum. Parchment was used for the permanent manuscripts in which the Epistles were preserved. Writing *tablets* were used merely for temporary purposes, as our slates.

3 JOHN

ADDRESS: WISH FOR GAIUS' PROSPERITY: JOY AT HIS WALK-ING IN THE TRUTH. HOSPITALITY TO THE BRETHREN AND STRANGERS THE FRUIT OF LOVE. DIOTREPHES' OPPOSITION AND AMBITION. PRAISE OF DEMETRIUS. CONCLUSION.

1. love in the truth – (2 John 1). "Beloved" is repeated often in this Epistle, indicating strong affection (3 John 1–2,5,11).

4. my children – members of the Church: confirming the view that the "elect lady" is a Church.

5. faithfully – an act becoming a faithful man.

6. borne witness of thy charity before the church—to stimulate others by the good example. The brethren so entertained by Gaius were missionary evangelists (3 John 7); and, probably, in the course of narrating their missionary labors for the edification of the Church where John then was, incidentally mentioned the loving hospitality shown them by Gaius.

14. face to face – *Greek,* "mouth to mouth."

Peace – peace inward of conscience, peace fraternal of friendship, peace supernal of glory [Lyra].

friends – a title seldom used in the New Testament, as it is absorbed in the higher titles of "brother, brethren."

their characters agree, being both hospitable men, yet neither the place nor time in which they lived. The Apostle Paul's Gaius lived at Corinth, this is in some place near to Ephesus, for the apostle in his old age purposed to come and see him shortly; the other was contemporary with Paul, this with John; there were thirty or forty years difference between them: besides, the Corinthian Gaius was baptized by Paul, and was doubtless one of his spiritual children, or converts, whereas this Gaius was one of the Apostle John's spiritual children, 3 John 1: 4; nor does he seem to be the same with Gaius of Macedonia, Acts 19: 29, or with Gaius of Derbe, Acts 20: 4, who seem to be two different persons by their country, though both companions in travel of the Apostle Paul; for which reason, as well as the time of their living, neither of them can be this Gaius, who was a settled housekeeper, and resided at some certain place. His name is a Roman name, and the same with Caius, though he seems to have been a Jew, as he might, it being usual with the Jews in other countries to take Gentile names. His character is, that he was "well beloved"; that is, of God, as it appears he was from the grace bestowed on him, from the prosperous estate of his soul, and from the truth that was in him, and his walking in it; and of the Lord Jesus Christ, for the same reasons; and also of all the brethren and saints that knew him; he being a person not only truly gracious, and of faithfulness and integrity, but of great liberality and beneficence, which must gain him much love and esteem among them; and he was well beloved by the Apostle John.

11. Beloved, follow not that which is evil. Follow not evil in general, it being hateful to God, contrary to his nature and will, and bad in itself, as well as pernicious in its consequences; and particularly follow not, or do not imitate the particular evil or evils in Diotrephes; as his pride, ambition, love of preeminence, and tyrannical government in the church, and especially his hard heartedness, cruelty, and inhospitality to the poor saints; and so the Arabic version reads, "do not imitate him in evil"; the examples of persons in office and authority have great influence, especially in cases of charity, when men can be excused thereby, and save their money, or be freed from an expense:

but that which is good; follow and imitate that, be a follower of God, imitate him in acts of kindness and beneficence, be merciful as he is; copy the deeds of Jesus Christ, who went about doing good, and declared it to be more blessed to give than to receive; and tread in the steps of those good men, who have shown love to the name of Christ, by ministering to his saints; for though the apostle may mean everything that is good, which is to be followed and imitated in any, yet he chiefly designs acts of kindness and beneficence to poor saints and ministers.

he that doeth good is of God; he is a child of God, he appears to be so, in that he is like to his heavenly Father, who is kind and merciful; he is born of God, he is passed from death to life, which his love to the brethren shows; he has the grace of God, and strength from Christ, and the assistance of the Spirit, without either of which he could not do that which is good.

but he that doeth evil hath not seen God; has had no spiritual saving sight of God in Christ; for if he had, he would abhor that which is evil, and, with Job, abhor himself for it, and reckon himself, with Isaiah, as undone, Job 42: 6, for such effects has the sight of God on the souls of men; such an one knows not God, nor what it is to have communion with him: for those who live in sin, in whom it is a governing principle, cannot have fellowship with God; nor has such an one ever felt the love of God in his soul, or been made a partaker of his grace, which would teach and constrain him to act otherwise.

Jude

Introduction by John Calvin

THOUGH there was a dispute among the ancients respecting this Epistle, yet as the reading of it is useful, and as it contains nothing inconsistent with the purity of apostolic doctrine, and was received as authentic formerly, by some of the best, I willingly add it to the others. Its brevity, moreover, does not require a long statement of its contents; and almost the whole of it is nearly the same with the second chapter of the last Epistle.

As unprincipled men, under the name of Christians, had crept in, whose chief object was to lead the unstable and weak to a profane contempt of God, Jude first shews, that the faithful ought not to have been moved by agents of this kind, by which the Church has always been assailed; and yet he exhorts them carefully to beware of such pests. And to render them more hateful and detestable, he denounces on them the approaching vengeance of God, such as their impiety deserved. Now, if we consider what Satan has attempted in our age, from the commencement of the revived gospel, and what arts he still busily employs to subvert the faith, and the fear of God, what was a useful warning in the time of Jude, is more than necessary in our age. But this will appear more fully as we proceed in reading the Epistle.

The commentaries on Jude are by John Calvin and Adam Clarke.

JUDE

1 Jude, the servant of Jesus Christ, and brother of James, to them that are sanctified by God the Father, and preserved in Jesus Christ, and called:

2 Mercy unto you, and peace, and love, be multiplied.

3 Beloved, when I gave all diligence to write unto you of the common salvation, it was needful for me to write unto you, and exhort you that ye should earnestly contend for the faith which was once delivered unto the saints.

4 For there are certain men crept in unawares, who were before of old ordained to this condemnation, ungodly men, turning the grace of our God into lasciviousness, and denying the only Lord God, and our Lord Jesus Christ.

5 I will therefore put you in remembrance, though ye once knew this, how that the Lord, having saved the people out of the land of Egypt, afterward destroyed them that believed not.

6 And the angels which kept not their first estate, but left their own habitation, he hath reserved in everlasting chains under darkness unto the judgment of the great day.

7 Even as Sodom and Gomorrha, and the cities about them in like manner, giving themselves over to fornication, and going after strange flesh, are set forth for an example, suffering the vengeance of eternal fire.

8 Likewise also these filthy dreamers defile the flesh, despise dominion, and speak evil of dignities.

9 Yet Michael the archangel, when contending with the devil he disputed about the body of Moses, durst not bring against him a railing accusation, but said, The Lord rebuke thee.

10 But these speak evil of those things which they know not: but what they know naturally, as brute beasts, in those things they corrupt themselves.

11 Woe unto them! for they have gone in the way of Cain, and ran greedily after the error of Balaam for reward, and perished in the gainsaying of Core.

12 These are spots in your feasts of charity, when they feast with you, feeding themselves without fear: clouds they

JUDE

1. Jude the servant of Jesus Christ

He calls himself the servant of Christ, not as the name applies to all the godly, but with respect to his apostleship; for they were deemed peculiarly the servants of Christ, who had some public office committed to them. And we know why the apostles were wont to give themselves this honorable name. Whosoever is not called, arrogates to himself presumptuously the right and authority of teaching. Then their calling was an evidence to the apostles, that they did not thrust themselves into their office through their own will. It was not, however, of itself sufficient to be appointed to their office, except they faithfully discharged it. And, no doubt, he who declares himself to be the servant of God, includes both these things, that is, that God is the bestower of the office which he exercises, and that he faithfully performs what has been committed to him. Many act falsely, and falsely boast to be what they are very far from being: we ought always to examine whether the reality corresponds with the profession.

And brother of James

He mentions a name more celebrated than his own, and more known to the churches. For though faithfulness of doctrine and authority do not depend on the names of mortal men, yet it is a confirmation to the faith, when the integrity of the man who undertakes the office of a teacher is made certain to us. Besides, the authority of James is not here brought forward as that of a private individual, but because he was counted by all the Church as one of the chief apostles of Christ. He was the son of Alpheus, as I have said elsewhere. Nay, this very passage is a sufficient proof to me against Eusebius and others, who say, that he was a disciple, named Oblias [James], mentioned by Luke, in Acts 15: 13; Acts 21: 18, who was more eminent than the apostles in the Church. But there is no doubt but that Jude mentions here his own brother, because he was eminent among the apostles. It is, then, probable, that he was the person to whom the chief honor was conceded by the rest, according to what Luke relates.

To them that are sanctified by God the Father, or, to the called who are sanctified, etc

By this expression "the called" he denotes all the faithful, because the Lord has separated them for himself. But as calling is nothing else but the effect of eternal election, it is sometimes taken for it. In this place it makes but little difference in which way you take it; for he, no doubt, commends the grace of God, by which he has been pleased to choose them as his peculiar treasure. And he intimates that men do not anticipate God, and that they never come to him until he draws them.

JUDE

1. Jude, the servant of Jesus Christ – Probably Jude the apostle, who was surnamed Thaddeus and Lebbeus, was son to Alpheus, and brother to James the less, Joses, and Simon. See Matthew 10: 3, and collate with Luke 6: 16; Matthew 13: 55.

Brother of James – Supposed to be James the less, bishop of Jerusalem, mentioned here, because he was an eminent person in the Church. See the preface to St. James.

To them that are sanctified by God – Sanctified signifies here consecrated to God through faith in Christ.

Preserved in (or by) Jesus Christ – Signifies those who continued unshaken in the Christian faith; and implies also, that none can be preserved in the faith that do not continue in union with Christ, by whose grace alone they can be preserved and called. This should be read consecutively with the other epithets, and should be rather, in a translation, read first than last, to the saints in God the Father, called and preserved by Christ Jesus. Saints is the same as Christians; to become such they were called to believe in Christ by the preaching of the Gospel, and having believed, were preserved by the grace of Christ in the life and practice of piety.

4. For there are certain men crept in unawares – They had got into the Church under specious pretences; and, when in, began to sow their bad seed.

10. Speak evil of those things which they know not – They do not understand the origin and utility of civil government; they revile that which ever protects their own persons and their property. This is true in most insurrections and seditions.

But what they know naturally – They are destitute of reflection; their minds are uncultivated; they follow mere natural instinct, and are slaves to their animal propensities.

As brute beasts – Like the irrational animals; but, in the indulgence of their animal propensities, they corrupt themselves, beyond the example of the brute beasts. A fearful description; and true of many in the present day.

11. They have gone in the way of Cain – They are haters of their brethren, and they that are such are murderers; and by their false doctrine they corrupt and destroy the souls of the people.

The error of Balaam – For the sake of gain they corrupt the word of God and refine away its meaning, and let it down so as to suit the passions of the profligate. This was literally true of the Nicolaitans, who taught most impure doctrines, and followed the most lascivious practices.

Gainsaying of Core – See the account of the rebellion of Korah, Dathan, and Abiram, and their company, in Num. 22. It appears that these persons opposed the authority of the apostles of our Lord, as Korah and his associates did that of Moses and Aaron; and St. Jude predicts them a similar punishment. In this verse he accuses them of murder, covetousness, and rebellion against the authority of God.

12. Spots in your feasts of charity – It appears that these persons, unholy and impure as they were, still continued to have outward fellowship with the Church! This is strange: but it is very likely that their power and influence in that place had swallowed up, or set aside, the power and authority of the real ministers of Christ; a very common case when worldly, time-serving men get into the Church.

Clouds – without water – The doctrine of God is compared to the rain, Deuteronomy 32: 2, and clouds are the instruments by which the rain is distilled upon the earth. In arid or parched countries the very appearance of a cloud is delightful, because it is a token of refreshing showers; but when sudden winds arise, and disperse these clouds, the hope of the husbandman and shepherd is cut off. These false teachers are represented as clouds; they have the form and office of the teachers of righteousness, and from such appearances pure doctrine may be naturally expected: but these are clouds without water – they distil no refreshing showers, because they have none; they are carried away and about by their passions, as those light fleecy clouds are carried by the winds.

Twice dead – First, naturally and practically

are without water, carried about of winds; trees whose fruit withereth, without fruit, twice dead, plucked up by the roots;

13 Raging waves of the sea, foaming out their own shame; wandering stars, to whom is reserved the blackness of darkness for ever.

14 And Enoch also, the seventh from Adam, prophesied of these, saying, Behold, the Lord cometh with ten thousands of his saints,

15 To execute judgment upon all, and to convince all that are ungodly among them of all their ungodly deeds which they have ungodly committed, and of all their hard speeches which ungodly sinners have spoken against him.

16 These are murmurers, complainers, walking after their own lusts; and their mouth speaketh great swelling words, having men's persons in admiration because of advantage.

17 But, beloved, remember ye the words which were spoken before of the apostles of our Lord Jesus Christ;

18 How that they told you there should be mockers in the last time, who should walk after their own ungodly lusts.

19 These be they who separate themselves, sensual, having not the Spirit.

20 But ye, beloved, building up yourselves on your most holy faith, praying in the Holy Ghost,

21 Keep yourselves in the love of God, looking for the mercy of our Lord Jesus Christ unto eternal life.

22 And of some have compassion, making a difference:

23 And others save with fear, pulling them out of the fire; hating even the garment spotted by the flesh.

24 Now unto him that is able to keep you from falling, and to present you faultless before the presence of his glory with exceeding joy,

25 To the only wise God our Savior, be glory and majesty, dominion and power, both now and ever. Amen.

Of the same he says that they were **sanctified in God the Father**, which may be rendered, "by God the Father." I have, however, retained the very form of the expression, that readers may exercise their own judgment. For it may be, that this is the sense – that being profane in themselves, they had their holiness in God. But the way in which God sanctifies is, by regenerating us by his Spirit.

Another reading, which the Vulgate has followed, is somewhat harsh, "To the beloved (*egapemenois*) in God the Father." I therefore regard it as corrupt; and it is, indeed, found but in a few copies.

He further adds, that they were **preserved in Jesus Christ**. For we should be always in danger of death through Satan, and he might take us at any moment as an easy prey, were we not safe under the protection of Christ, whom the Father has given to be our guardian, so that none of those whom he has received under his care and shelter should perish.

Jude then mentions here a threefold blessing, or favor of God, with regard to all the godly – that he has made them by his calling partakers of the gospel; that he has regenerated them, by his Spirit, unto newness of life; and that he has preserved them by the hand of Christ, so that they might not fall away from salvation.

21. Keep yourselves in the love of God.

He has made love as it were the guardian and the ruler of our life; not that he might set it in opposition to the grace of God, but that it is the right course of our calling, when we make progress in love. But as many things entice us to apostasy, so that it is difficult to keep us faithful to God to the end, he calls the attention of the faithful to the last day. For the hope of that alone ought to sustain us, so that we may at no time despond; otherwise we must necessarily fail every moment.

But it ought to be noticed that he would not have us to hope for eternal life, except through the mercy of Christ: for he will in such a manner be our judge, as to have no other rule in judging us than that gratuitous benefit of redemption obtained by himself.

22. And of some have compassion

He adds another exhortation, shewing how the faithful ought to act in reproving their brethren, in order to restore them to the Lord. He reminds them that such ought to be treated in different ways, every one according to his disposition: for to the meek and teachable we ought to use kindness; but others, who are hard and perverse, must be subdued by terror. This is the **difference** which he mentions.

ADAM CLARKE

dead in sin, from which they had been revived by the preaching and grace of the Gospel. Secondly, dead by backsliding or apostasy from the true faith, by which they lost the grace they had before received; and now likely to continue in that death, because plucked up from the roots, their roots of faith and love being no longer fixed in Christ Jesus. Perhaps the aorist is taken here for the future: They SHALL BE plucked up from the roots – God will exterminate them from the earth.

16. These are murmurers – Grudging and grumbling at all men, and at all things; complainers of their fate or destiny – finding fault with God and all his providential dispensations, making and governing worlds in their own way; persons whom neither God nor man can please.

Walking after their own lusts – Taking their wild, disorderly, and impure passions for the rule of their conduct, and not the writings of the prophets and apostles.

Having men's persons in admiration – Time-servers and flatterers; persons who pretend to be astonished at the greatness, goodness, sagacity, learning, wisdom; etc., of rich and great men, hoping thereby to acquire money, influence, power, friends, and the like.

Because of advantage – For the sake of lucre. All the flatterers of the rich are of this kind; and especially those who profess to be ministers of the Gospel, and who, for the sake of a more advantageous settlement or living, will soothe the rich even in their sins. With such persons a rich man is every thing; and if he have but a grain of grace, his piety is extolled to the skies! I have known several ministers of this character, and wish them all to read the sixteenth verse of Jude.

17. Remember – the words – Instead of following those teachers and their corrupt doctrine,

remember what Christ and his apostles have said; for they foretold the coming of such false teachers and impostors.

21 Keep yourselves in the love of God – By building up yourselves on your most holy faith, and praying in the Holy Ghost; for without this we shall soon lose the love of God.

Looking for the mercy of our Lord – For although they were to build themselves up, and to pray in the Holy Ghost, and keep themselves in the love of God, yet this building, praying, and keeping, cannot merit heaven; for, after all their diligence, earnestness, self-denial, watching, obedience, etc., they must look for the MERCY of the Lord Jesus Christ, to bring them to ETERNAL LIFE.

25 To the only wise God – Who alone can teach, who alone has declared the truth; that truth in which ye now stand.

Our Savior – Who has by his blood washed us from our sins, and made us kings and priests unto God the Father.

Be glory – Be ascribed all light, excellence, and splendor.

Majesty – All power, authority, and pre-eminence.

Dominion – All rule and government in the world and in the Church, in earth and in heaven.

And power – All energy and operation to every thing that is wise, great, good, holy, and excellent.

Both now – In the present state of life and things.

And ever – To the end of all states, places, dispensations, and worlds; and to a state which knows no termination, being that ETERNITY in which this glory, majesty, dominion, and power ineffably and incomprehensibly dwell.

Amen – So let it be, so ought it to be, and so it shall be.

Revelation

Introduction by A.R. Faussett

AUTHENTICITY – The author calls himself John (Rev. 1: 1,4,9; 2: 8). JUSTIN MARTYR [*Dialogue with Trypho*, p. 308] (AD 139–161) quotes from the Apocalypse, as *John the apostle's* work, the prophecy of the millennium of the saints, to be followed by the general resurrection and judgment. This testimony of JUSTIN is referred to also by EUSEBIUS [*Ecclesiastical History*, 4.18]. JUSTIN MARTYR, in the early part of the second century, held his controversy with TRYPHO, a learned Jew, at *Ephesus*, where John had been living thirty or thirty-five years before: he says that "the Revelation had been given to John, one of the twelve apostles of Christ." MELITO, bishop of *Sardis* (about AD 171), *one of the seven churches addressed*, a successor, therefore, of one of the seven angels, is said by EUSEBIUS [*Ecclesiastical History*, 4.26] to have written treatises on the Apocalypse *of John*. The testimony of the bishop of Sardis is the more impartial, as Sardis is one of the churches severely reproved (Rev. 3: 1).

The personal notices of John in the Apocalypse occur Rev. 1: 1,4,9; Rev. 22: 8. Moreover, the writer's addresses to the churches of Proconsular *Asia* (Rev. 2: 1) accord with the concurrent tradition, that after John's return from his exile in Patmos, at the death of Domitian, under Nerva, he resided for long, and died at last in Ephesus, in the time of Trajan [EUSEBIUS, *Ecclesiastical History*, 3.20,23]. If the Apocalypse were not the inspired work of John, purporting as it does to be an address from their superior to the seven churches of Proconsular Asia, it would have assuredly been rejected *in that region;* whereas the earliest testimonies *in those churches* are all in its favor. One person

alone was entitled to use language of authority such as is addressed to the seven angels of the churches – namely, John, as the last surviving apostle and superintendent of all the churches. Also, it accords with John's manner to assert the accuracy of his testimony both at the beginning and end of his book (compare Rev. 1: 2–3, and 22: 8, with John 1: 14; 21: 24; 1 John 1: 1,2). Again, it accords with the view of the writer being an *inspired apostle* that he addresses the angels or presidents of the several churches in the tone of a *superior* addressing inferiors. Also, he commends the Church of Ephesus for trying and convicting "them which *say they are apostles,* and are not," by which he implies his own undoubted claim to apostolic inspiration (Rev. 2: 2), as declaring in the seven epistles Christ's will revealed through him.

As to the difference of style, as compared with the Gospel and Epistle, the *difference of subject* in part accounts for it, the visions of the seer, transported as he was above the region of sense, appropriately taking a form of expression abrupt, and unbound by the grammatical laws which governed his writings of a calmer and more deliberate character. Moreover, as being a Galilean Hebrew, John, in writing a Revelation akin to the Old Testament prophecies, naturally reverted to their Hebraistic style.

PLACE AND TIME OF WRITING – The best authorities among the Fathers state that John was exiled under Domitian (IRENÆUS [*Against Heresies*, 5; 30]; CLEMENT OF ALEXANDRIA; EUSEBIUS [*Ecclesiastical History*, 3.20]). VICTORINUS says that he had to labor in the mines of Patmos. At Domitian's death, AD 95, he returned to Ephesus under the Emperor Nerva.

Probably it was immediately after his return that he wrote, under divine inspiration, the account of the visions vouchsafed to him in Patmos (Rev. 1: 2,9).

To what readers addressed – The inscription states that it is addressed to the seven churches of Asia, that is, Proconsular Asia. John's reason for fixing on the number *seven* (for there were more than seven churches in the region meant by "Asia," for instance, Magnesia and Tralles) was doubtless because *seven* is the sacred number implying totality and universality: so it is implied that John, through the medium of the seven churches, addresses in the Spirit the Church of all places and ages. The Church in its various states of spiritual life or deadness, in all ages and places, is represented by the seven churches, and is addressed with words of consolation or warning accordingly. Smyrna and Philadelphia alone of the seven are honored with unmixed praise, as faithful in tribulation and rich in good works. Heresies of a decided kind had by this time arisen in the churches of Asia, and the love of many had waxed cold, while others had advanced to greater zeal, and one had sealed his testimony with his blood.

Object – It begins with admonitory addresses to the seven churches from the divine Son of man, whom John saw in vision, after a brief introduction which sets forth the main subject of the book, namely, to "show unto His servants things which must shortly come to pass" (the first through third chapters). From the fourth chapter to the end is mainly prophecy, with practical exhortations and consolations, however, interspersed, similar to those addressed to the seven churches (the representatives of the universal Church of every age), and so connecting the body of the book with its beginning, which therefore forms its appropriate introduction. Three schools of interpreters exist: (1) The Preterists, who hold that almost the whole has been fulfilled. (2) The Historical Interpreters, who hold that it comprises the history of the Church from John's time to the end of the world, the seals being *chronologically* succeeded, by the trumpets and the trumpets by the vials. (3) The Futurists, who consider almost the whole as yet future, and to be fulfilled immediately before Christ's second coming. The first theory was not held by any of the earliest Fathers, and is only held now by Rationalists, who limit John's vision to things within his own horizon, pagan Rome's persecutions of Christians, and its consequently anticipated destruction. The Futurist school is open to this great objection: it would leave the Church of Christ unprovided with prophetical guidance or support under her fiery trials for 1700 or 1800 years. Now God has said, "Surely He will do nothing, but He revealeth His secrets unto His servants the prophets" (Amos 3: 7). The Jews had a succession of prophets who guided them with the light of prophecy: what their prophets were to them, that the apocalyptic Scriptures have been, and are, to us.

The commentaries on Revelation are by A. R. Faussett and Albert Barnes.

REVELATION 1

1 The Revelation of Jesus Christ, which God gave unto him, to shew unto his servants things which must shortly come to pass; and he sent and signified it by his angel unto his servant John:

2 Who bare record of the word of God, and of the testimony of Jesus Christ, and of all things that he saw.

3 Blessed is he that readeth, and they that hear the words of this prophecy, and keep those things which are written therein: for the time is at hand.

4 John to the seven churches which are in Asia: Grace be unto you, and peace, from him which is, and which was, and which is to come; and from the seven Spirits which are before his throne;

5 And from Jesus Christ, who is the faithful witness, and the first begotten of the dead, and the prince of the kings of the earth. Unto him that loved us, and washed us from our sins in his own blood,

6 And hath made us kings and priests unto God and his Father; to him be glory and dominion for ever and ever. Amen.

7 Behold, he cometh with clouds; and every eye shall see him, and they also which pierced him: and all kindreds of the earth shall wail because of him. Even so, Amen.

8 I am Alpha and Omega, the beginning and the ending, saith the Lord, which is, and which was, and which is to come, the Almighty.

9 I John, who also am your brother, and companion in tribulation, and in the kingdom and patience of Jesus Christ, was in the isle that is called Patmos, for the word of God, and for the testimony of Jesus Christ.

10 I was in the Spirit on the Lord's day, and heard behind me a great voice, as of a trumpet,

11 Saying, I am Alpha and Omega, the first and the last: and, What thou seest, write in a book, and send it unto the seven churches which are in Asia; unto Ephesus, and unto Smyrna, and unto Pergamos, and unto Thyatira, and unto Sardis, and unto Philadelphia, and unto Laodicea.

12 And I turned to see the voice that spake with me. And being turned, I saw seven golden candlesticks;

13 And in the midst of the seven candlesticks one like unto the Son of

REVELATION 1

Rev. 1:1–20. TITLE: SOURCE AND OBJECT OF THIS REVELATION: BLESSING ON THE READER AND KEEPER OF IT, AS THE TIME IS NEAR: INSCRIPTION TO THE SEVEN CHURCHES: APOSTOLIC GREETING: KEYNOTE, "BEHOLD HE COMETH" (Compare at the close, Rev. 22: 20, "Surely I come quickly"): INTRODUCTORY VISION OF THE SON OF MAN IN GLORY, AMIDST THE SEVEN CANDLESTICKS, WITH SEVEN STARS IN HIS RIGHT HAND.

1. Revelation – an apocalypse or *unveiling* of those things which had been veiled. A *manifesto* of the kingdom of Christ. The travelling manual of the Church for the Gentile Christian times. Not a *detailed history* of the future, but a representation of the great epochs and chief powers in developing the kingdom of God in relation to the world. The "Church-*historical*" view goes counter to the great principle that Scripture interprets itself. Revelation is to teach us to understand the times, not the times to interpret to us the Apocalypse, although it is in the nature of the case that a reflex influence is exerted here and is understood by the prudent [Auberlen]. The book is in a series of parallel groups, not in chronological succession. Still there is an organic historical development of the kingdom of God. In this book all the other books of the Bible end and meet: in it is the consummation of all previous prophecy. Daniel foretells as to Christ and the Roman destruction of Jerusalem, and the last Antichrist. But John's Revelation fills up the intermediate period, and describes the millennium and final state beyond Antichrist. Daniel, as a godly statesman, views the history of God's people in relation to the *four world kingdoms*. John, as an apostle, views history from the *Christian Church aspect*. The term *Apocalypse* is applied to no Old Testament book. Daniel is the nearest approach to it; but what Daniel was told to *seal* and *shut up till the time of the end*, John, now that *the time is at hand* (Rev. 1: 3), is directed to *reveal*.

of Jesus Christ – coming *from* Him. Jesus Christ, not John the writer, is the Author of the Apocalypse. Christ taught many things before His departure; but those which were unsuitable for announcement at that time He brought together into the Apocalypse [Bengel]. Compare His promise, John 15: 15, "All things that I have heard of My Father, I have made known unto you"; also, John 16: 13, "The Spirit of truth *will show* you things to come." The Gospels and Acts are the books, respectively, of His first advent, in the flesh, and in the Spirit; the Epistles are the inspired comment on them. The Apocalypse is the book of His second advent and the events preliminary to it.

which God gave unto him – The Father reveals Himself and His will in, and by, His Son.

REVELATION 1

Chapter one contains a general introduction to the whole book, and comprises the following parts:

I. The announcement that the object of the book is to record a revelation which the Lord Jesus Christ had made of important events which were shortly to occur, and which were signified by an angel to the author, John, Rev. 1: 1–3. A blessing is pronounced on him who should read and understand the book, and special attention is directed to it because the time was st hand when the predicted events would occur.

II. Salutation to the seven churches of Asia, Rev. 1: 4–8. To those churches, it. would seem from this, the book was originally dedicated or addressed, and two of the chapters (2 and 3) refer exclusively to them. Among them evidently the author had resided (Rev. 1: 9), and the whole book was doubtless sent to them, and committed to their keeping. In this salutation, the author wishes for them grace, mercy, and peace from "him which is, and which was, and which is to come" – the original fountain of all light and truth – referring to more sublime.

1. The Revelation of Jesus Christ. This is evidently a title or caption of the whole book, and is designed to comprise the substance of the whole; for all that the book contains would be embraced in the general declaration that it is a Revelation of Jesus Christ. The word rendered Revelation – from which we have derived our word Apocalypse – means properly an uncovering; that is, nakedness. It would apply to anything which had been covered up so as to be hidden from the view – as by a veil; by darkness; in an ark or chest – and then made manifest by removing the covering. It comes then to be used in the sense of disclosing or revealing by removing the veil of darkness or ignorance. "There is nothing covered that shall not be revealed." It may be applied to the disclosing or manifesting of anything which was before obscure or unknown.

2. Who bare record of the word of God. Who bore witness to, or testified of the word of God. He regarded himself merely as a witness of what he had seen, and claimed only to make a fair and faithful record of it.

3. Blessed is he that readeth. That is, it is to be regarded as a privilege attended with many blessings, to be permitted to mark the disclosures to be made in this book; the important revelations respecting future times.

And hear the words of this prophecy. As they shall be declared or repeated by others; or perhaps the word hear is used in a sense that is not uncommon, that of giving attention to; taking heed to. The general sense is, that they were to be regarded as highly favored who became acquainted in any way with what is here communicated.

8. I am Alpha and Omega. These are the first and the last letters of the Greek alphabet, and denote properly the first and the last. So in Rev. 22: 13, when the two expressions are united, "I am Alpha and Omega, the beginning and the end, the first and the last." So in Rev. 1: 17, the speaker says of himself, "I am the first and the last." Among the Jewish Rabbins, it was common to use the first and the last letters of the Hebrew alphabet to denote the whole of anything, from beginning to end.

9. I John, who also am your brother. Your Christian brother; who am a fellow-Christian with you. The reference here is doubtless to the members of the seven churches in Asia, to whom the epistles in the following chapters were addressed, and to whom the whole book seems to have been sent. In the previous verse, the writer had closed the salutation, and he here commences a description of the Circumstances under which the vision appeared to him. He was in a lonely island, to which he had been banished on account of his attachment to religion; he was in a state of high spiritual enjoyment on the day devoted to the sacred remembrance of the Redeemer; he suddenly heard a voice behind him, and turning saw the Son of man himself in glorious form in the midst of seven golden lamps, and fell at his feet as dead.

13. And in the midst of the seven candlesticks. Standing among them, so as to be

man, clothed with a garment down to the foot, and girt about the paps with a golden girdle.

14 His head and his hairs were white like wool, as white as snow; and his eyes were as a flame of fire;

15 And his feet like unto fine brass, as if they burned in a furnace; and his voice as the sound of many waters.

16 And he had in his right hand seven stars: and out of his mouth went a sharp twoedged sword: and his countenance was as the sun shineth in his strength.

17 And when I saw him, I fell at his feet as dead. And he laid his right hand upon me, saying unto me, Fear not; I am the first and the last:

18 I am he that liveth, and was dead; and, behold, I am alive for evermore, Amen; and have the keys of hell and of death.

19 Write the things which thou hast seen, and the things which are, and the things which shall be hereafter;

20 The mystery of the seven stars which thou sawest in my right hand, and the seven golden candlesticks. The seven stars are the angels of the seven churches: and the seven candlesticks which thou sawest are the seven churches.

REVELATION 2

1 Unto the angel of the church of Ephesus write; These things saith he that holdeth the seven stars in his right hand, who walketh in the midst of the seven golden candlesticks;

2 I know thy works, and thy labour, and thy patience, and how thou canst not bear them which are evil: and thou hast tried them which say they are apostles, and are not, and hast found them liars:

3 And hast borne, and hast patience, and for my name's sake hast laboured, and hast not fainted.

4 Nevertheless I have somewhat against thee, because thou hast left thy first love.

5 Remember therefore from whence thou art fallen, and repent, and do the first works; or else I will come unto thee quickly, and will remove thy candlestick out of his place, except thou repent.

6 But this thou hast, that thou hatest the deeds of the Nicolaitans, which I also hate.

to show – The word recurs in Rev. 22: 6: so entirely have the parts of Revelation reference to one another. It is its peculiar excellence that it comprises in a perfect compendium future things, and these widely differing: things close at hand, far off, and between the two; great and little; destroying and saving; repeated from old prophecies and new; long and short, and these interwoven with one another, opposed and mutually agreeing; mutually involving and evolving one another; so that in no book more than in this would the addition, or taking away, of a single word or clause (Rev. 22: 18–19), have the effect of marring the sense of the context and the comparison of passages together [Bengel].

his servants – not merely to "His servant John," but to *all* His servants (compare Rev. 22: 3).

shortly – *Greek,* "speedily"; literally, "in," or "with speed." Compare "the time is at hand," Rev. 1: 3; 22: 6, "shortly"; Rev. 22: 7, "Behold, I come *quickly.*" Not that the things prophesied were according to man's computation near; but this word "shortly" implies a corrective of our estimate of worldly events and periods. Though a "thousand years" (Rev. 20: 1–15) at least are included, the time is declared to be *at hand.* Luke 18: 8, "speedily." The Israelite Church hastened eagerly to the predicted end, which premature eagerness prophecy restrains (compare Dan. 9: 1–27). The Gentile Church needs to be reminded of the transitoriness of the world (which it is apt to make its home) and the nearness of Christ's advent. On the one hand Revelation says, "the time is at hand"; on the other, the succession of seals, &c., show that many intermediate events must first elapse.

he sent – Jesus Christ sent.

by his angel – joined with "sent." The angel does not come forward to "signify" things to John until Rev. 17: 1; 19: 9–10. Previous to that John receives information from others. Jesus Christ opens the Revelation, Rev. 1: 10–11; 4: 1; in Rev. 6: 1 one of the four living creatures acts as his informant; in Rev. 7: 13, one of the elders; in Rev. 10: 8–9, the Lord and His angel who stood on the sea and earth. Only at the end (Rev. 17: 1) does the one angel stand by Him (compare Dan. 8: 16; 9: 21; Zech. 1: 19).

REVELATION 2

Rev. 2: 1–29. Epistles to Ephesus, Smyrna, Pergamos, Thyatira.

Each of the seven epistles in this and the third chapter, commences with, "I know thy works." Each contains a promise from Christ, "To him that overcometh." Each ends with, "He that hath an ear, let him hear what the Spirit saith unto the churches." The title of our Lord in each case accords with the nature of the address, and is mainly taken from the im-

encircled within them. This shows that the representation could not have been like that of the vision of Zechariah (Zech. 4: 2), where the prophet sees "a candlestick all of gold with a bowl upon the top of it, and his seven lamps thereon." In the vision as it appeared to John, there was not one lamp-bearer with seven lamps or branches, but there were seven lamp-bearers so arranged that one in the likeness of the Son of man could stand in the midst of them.

One like unto the Son of man. This was evidently the Lord Jesus Christ himself, elsewhere so often called "the Son of man." That it was the Savior himself is apparent from Rev. 1: 18. The expression rendered "like unto the Son of man," should have been "like unto a son of man;" that is, like a man – a human being, or in a human form.

Clothed with a garment down to the foot. A robe reaching down to the feet, or to the ankles, yet so as to leave the feet themselves visible. The allusion here, doubtless, is to a long, loose, flowing robe, such as was worn by kings.

17. And when I saw him, I fell at his feet as dead. As if I were dead; deprived of sense and consciousness. He was overwhelmed with the suddenness of the vision; he saw that this was a Divine being; but he did not as yet know that it was the Savior. It is not probable that in this vision he would immediately recognize any of the familiar features of the Lord Jesus as he had been accustomed to see him some sixty years before; and if he did, the effect would have been quite as overpowering as is here described. But the subsequent revelations of this Divine personage would rather seem to imply that John did not at once recognize him as the Lord Jesus. The effect here described is one that often occurred to those who had a vision of God. See Dan. 8: 18, "Now as he was speaking with me, I was in a deep sleep on my face toward the ground: but he touched me, and set me upright." Dan. 8: 27, "And I Daniel fainted, and was sick certain days; afterward I rose up, and did the king's business."

And he laid his right hand upon me. For the purpose of raising him up. Compare Dan. 8: 18, "He touched me, and set me upright."

We usually stretch out the right hand to raise up one who is fallen.

Saying unto me, Fear not. Compare Matt. 14: 27, "It is I; be not afraid." The fact that it was the Savior, though he appeared in this form of overpowering majesty, was a reason why John should not be afraid.

REVELATION 2

This chapter comprises four of the seven epistles addressed to the seven churches: those addressed to Ephesus, Smyrna, Pergamos, and Thyatira.

1–7. The contents of the epistle to the church at Ephesus – the first addressed – are these:

(1.) The attribute of the Savior referred to is, that he "holds the stars in his right hand, and walks in the midst of the golden candlesticks," Rev. 2: 1.

(2.) He commends them for their patience, and for their opposition to those who are evil, and for their zeal and fidelity in carefully examining into the character of some who claimed to be apostles, but who were in fact impostors; for their perseverance in bearing up under trial, and not fainting in his cause, and for their opposition to the Nicolaitanes, whom he says he hates, Rev. 2: 2–3,6.

(3.) He reproves them for having left their first love to him, Rev. 2: 4.

(4.) He admonishes them to remember whence they had fallen, to repent, and to do their first works, Rev. 2: 5.

(5.) He threatens them that if they do not repent he will come and remove the candlestick out of its place, Rev. 2: 5; and

(6.) he assures them and all others that whosoever overcomes, he will "give him to eat of the tree of life which is in the midst of the paradise of God," Rev. 2: 7.

8. And unto the angel of the church in Smyrna write. . . . Which was dead, and is alive. The idea is, that he is a living Savior; and there was a propriety in referring to that fact here from the nature of the promise which he was about to make to the church at Smyrna: "He that overcometh shall not be hurt of the second death," Rev. 2: 11. As he had himself triumphed over death in all its forms, and was

7 He that hath an ear, let him hear what the Spirit saith unto the churches; To him that overcometh will I give to eat of the tree of life, which is in the midst of the paradise of God.

8 And unto the angel of the church in Smyrna write; These things saith the first and the last, which was dead, and is alive;

9 I know thy works, and tribulation, and poverty, (but thou art rich) and I know the blasphemy of them which say they are Jews, and are not, but are the synagogue of Satan.

10 Fear none of those things which thou shalt suffer: behold, the devil shall cast some of you into prison, that ye may be tried; and ye shall have tribulation ten days: be thou faithful unto death, and I will give thee a crown of life.

11 He that hath an ear, let him hear what the Spirit saith unto the churches; He that overcometh shall not be hurt of the second death.

12 And to the angel of the church in Pergamos write; These things saith he which hath the sharp sword with two edges;

13 I know thy works, and where thou dwellest, even where Satan's seat is: and thou holdest fast my name, and hast not denied my faith, even in those days wherein Antipas was my faithful martyr, who was slain among you, where Satan dwelleth.

14 But I have a few things against thee, because thou hast there them that hold the doctrine of Balaam, who taught Balac to cast a stumblingblock before the children of Israel, to eat things sacrificed unto idols, and to commit fornication.

15 So hast thou also them that hold the doctrine of the Nicolaitans, which thing I hate.

16 Repent; or else I will come unto thee quickly, and will fight against them with the sword of my mouth.

17 He that hath an ear, let him hear what the Spirit saith unto the churches; To him that overcometh will I give to eat of the hidden manna, and will give him a white stone, and in the stone a new name written, which no man knoweth saving he that receiveth it.

18 And unto the angel of the church in Thyatira write; These things saith the Son of God, who hath his eyes like unto

agery of the vision, Rev. 1: 12–16. Each address has a threat or a promise, and most of the addresses have both. Their order seems to be ecclesiastical, civil, and geographical: Ephesus first, as being the Asiatic metropolis (termed "the light of Asia," and "first city of Asia"), the nearest to Patmos, where John received the epistle to the seven churches, and also as being that Church with which John was especially connected; then the churches on the west coast of Asia; then those in the interior. Smyrna and Philadelphia alone receive unmixed praise. Sardis and Laodicea receive almost solely censure. In Ephesus, Pergamos, and Thyatira, there are some things to praise, others to condemn, the latter element preponderating in one case (Ephesus), the former in the two others (Pergamos and Thyatira). Thus the main characteristics of the different states of different churches, in all times and places, are portrayed, and they are suitably encouraged or warned.

1. Ephesus – famed for the temple of Diana, one of the seven wonders of the world. For three years Paul labored there. He subsequently ordained Timothy superintending overseer or bishop there: probably his charge was but of a temporary nature. John, towards the close of his life, took it as the center from which he superintended the province.

holdeth – Greek, "holdeth fast," as in Rev. 2: 25; Rev. 3: 11; compare John 10: 28–29. The title of Christ here as "holding fast the seven stars (from Rev. 1: 16: only that, for *having* is substituted *holding fast* in His grasp), and walking in the midst of the seven candlesticks," accords with the beginning of His address to the *seven* churches representing the universal Church. *Walking* expresses His unwearied activity in the Church, guarding her from internal and external evils, as the high priest moved to and fro in the sanctuary.

2. I know thy works – expressing His omniscience. Not merely "thy professions, desires, good resolutions" (Rev. 14: 13, end).

patience – persevering *endurance*.

bear – *evil men* are a *burden* which the Ephesian Church regarded as intolerable. We are to "*bear* (the same Greek, Gal. 6: 2) one another's burdens" in the case of *weak* brethren; but not to bear *false brethren*.

tried – by experiment; not the *Greek* for "test," as 1 John 4: 1. The apostolical churches had the miraculous gift of *discerning spirits*. Compare Acts 20: 28–30, wherein Paul presciently warned the *Ephesian* elders of the coming false teachers, as also in writing to Timothy at Ephesus. Tertullian [*On Baptism*, 17], and Jerome [*On Illustrious Men*, in Lucca 7], record of John, that when a writing, professing to be a canonical history of the acts of Paul, had been composed by a presbyter of Ephesus, John convicted the author and condemned the work. So on one occasion he would not remain under

now alive for ever, it was appropriate that he should promise to his true friends the same protection from the second death. He who was wholly beyond the reach of death could give the assurance that they who put their trust in him should come off victorious.

9. I know thy works. The uniform method of introducing these epistles, implying a most intimate acquaintance with all that pertained to the church.

And tribulation. This word is of a general signification, and probably includes all that they suffered in any form, whether from persecution, poverty, or the blasphemy of opposers.

And poverty. It would seem that this church, at that time, was eminently poor, for this is not specified in regard to any one of the others. No reason is suggested why they were particularly poor.

But thou art rich. Not in this world's goods, but in a more important respect – in the grace and favor of God. These things are not unfrequently united. Poverty is no hindrance to the favor of God, and there are some things in it favorable to the promotion of a right spirit towards God which are not found where there is abundant wealth. The Savior was eminently poor, and not a few of his most devoted and useful followers have had as little of this world's goods as he had. The poor should always be cheerful and happy, if they can hear their Savior saying unto them, "I know thy poverty – but thou art rich." However keen the feeling arising from the reflection "I am a poor man," the edge of the sorrow is taken off if the mind can be turned to a brighter image – "but thou art rich."

10. Fear none of those things which thou shalt suffer. He did not promise them exemption from suffering. He saw that they were about to suffer, and he specifies the manner in which their affliction would occur. But he entreats and commands them not to be afraid. They were to look to the "crown of life," and to be comforted with the assurance that if they were faithful unto death, that would be theirs. We need not dread suffering if we can hear the voice of the Redeemer encouraging us, and if

he assures us that in a little while we shall have the crown of life.

12. And to the angel of the church in Pergamos. These things saith he which hath the sharp sword etc. As he was about to reprove the church at Pergamos, there was a propriety in referring to this power of the Savior. Reproof cuts deep; and this is the idea represented here.

13. And where thou dwellest. That is, I know all the temptations to which you are exposed; all the allurements to sin by which you are surrounded; all the apologies which might be made for what has occurred arising from those circumstances; and all that could be said in commendation of you for having been as faithful as you have been. The sense of the passage is, that it does much to enable us to judge of character to know where men live. It is much more easy to be virtuous and pious in some circumstances than in others; and in order to determine how much credit is due to a man for his virtues, it is necessary to understand how much he has been called to resist, how many temptations he has encountered, what easily-besetting sins he may have, or what allurements may have been presented to his mind to draw him from the path of virtue and religion.

14. But I have a few things against thee. As against the church at Ephesus, Rev. 2: 4. The charge against this church, however, is somewhat different from that against the church at Ephesus. The charge there was, that they had "left their first love;" but it is spoken in commendation of them that they "hated the deeds of the Nicolaitanes," Rev. 2: 6. Here the charge is, that they tolerated that sect among them, and that they had among them also those who held the doctrine of Balaam. Their general Course had been such that the Savior could approve it; he did not approve, however, of their tolerating those who held to pernicious practical error – error that tended to sap the very foundation of morals.

18. These things saith the Son of God. This is the first time, in these epistles, that the name of the speaker is referred to. In each

a flame of fire, and his feet are like fine brass;

19 I know thy works, and charity, and service, and faith, and thy patience, and thy works; and the last to be more than the first.

20 Notwithstanding I have a few things against thee, because thou sufferest that woman Jezebel, which calleth herself a prophetess, to teach and to seduce my servants to commit fornication, and to eat things sacrificed unto idols.

21 And I gave her space to repent of her fornication; and she repented not.

22 Behold, I will cast her into a bed, and them that commit adultery with her into great tribulation, except they repent of their deeds.

23 And I will kill her children with death; and all the churches shall know that I am he which searcheth the reins and hearts: and I will give unto every one of you according to your works.

24 But unto you I say, and unto the rest in Thyatira, as many as have not this doctrine, and which have not known the depths of Satan, as they speak; I will put upon you none other burden.

25 But that which ye have already hold fast till I come.

26 And he that overcometh, and keepeth my works unto the end, to him will I give power over the nations:

27 And he shall rule them with a rod of iron; as the vessels of a potter shall they be broken to shivers: even as I received of my Father.

28 And I will give him the morning star.

29 He that hath an ear, let him hear what the Spirit saith unto the churches.

REVELATION 3

1 And unto the angel of the church in Sardis write; These things saith he that hath the seven Spirits of God, and the seven stars; I know thy works, that thou hast a name that thou livest, and art dead.

2 Be watchful, and strengthen the things which remain, that are ready to die: for I have not found thy works perfect before God.

3 Remember therefore how thou hast received and heard, and hold fast, and repent. If therefore thou shalt not watch,

the same roof with Cerinthus the heretic.

say they are apostles – probably Judaizers. Ignatius [*Epistle to the Ephesians*, 6], says subsequently, "Onesimus praises exceedingly your good discipline that no heresy dwells among you"; and [*Epistle to the Ephesians*, 9], "Ye did not permit those having evil doctrine to sow their seed among you, but closed your ears."

3. borne … patience – The oldest manuscripts transpose these words. Then translate as *Greek,* "persevering endurance … borne." "Thou hast borne" My reproach, but "thou canst not bear the evil" (Rev. 2: 2). A beautiful antithesis.

4. somewhat … because – Translate, "I have against thee (this) *that,*" &c. It is not a mere somewhat"; it is everything. How characteristic of our gracious Lord, that He puts foremost all He can find to approve, and only after this notes the shortcomings!

left thy first love – to Christ. Compare 1 Tim. 5: 12, "cast off their first faith." See the Ephesians' first *love,* Eph. 1: 15. This epistle was written under Domitian, when thirty years had elapsed since Paul had written his Epistle to them. Their warmth of love had given place to a lifeless orthodoxy. Compare Paul's view of faith so called without love, 1 Cor. 13: 2.

5. whence – from what a height.

do the first works – the *works* which flowed from thy *first love.* Not merely "feel thy first feelings," but do works flowing from the same principle as formerly, "faith which worketh by love."

I will come – *Greek,* "I am coming" in special judgment on thee.

remove thy candlestick out of his place – I will take away the Church from Ephesus and remove it elsewhere. "It is removal of the candlestick, not extinction of the candle, which is threatened here; judgment for some, but that very judgment the occasion of mercy for others. So it has been. The seat of the Church has been changed, but the Church itself survives. What the East has lost, the West has gained. One who lately visited Ephesus found only three Christians there, and these so ignorant as scarcely to have heard the names of St. Paul or St. John" [Trench].

REVELATION 3

Rev. 3: 1–22. THE EPISTLES TO SARDIS, PHILADELPHIA, AND LAODICEA.

1. Sardis – the ancient capital of Lydia, the kingdom of wealthy Croesus, on the river Pactolus. The address to this Church is full of rebuke. It does not seem to have been in vain; for Melito, bishop of Sardis in the second century, was

other instance, there is merely some attribute of the Savior mentioned. Perhaps the severity of the rebuke contemplated here made it proper that there should be a more impressive reference to the authority of the speaker; and hence he is introduced as the "Son of God." It is not a reference to him as the "Son of man" – the common appellation which he gave to himself when on earth – for that might have suggested his humanity only, and would not have conveyed the same impression in regard to his authority; but it is to himself as sustaining the rank, and having the authority of the Son of God – one who, therefore, has a right to speak, and a right to demand that what he says shall be heard.

Before the glance of his eye all is light, and nothing can be concealed from his view. Nothing would be better fitted to inspire awe then, as nothing should be now, than such a reference to the Son of God as being able to penetrate the secret recesses of the heart.

21. And I gave her space to repent of her fornication. Probably after some direct and solemn warning of the evil of her course. The error and sin had been of long standing, but he now resolved to bear with it no longer. It is true of almost every great sinner, that sufficient time is given for repentance, and that vengeance is delayed after crime is committed. But it cannot always be deferred, for the period must arrive when no reason shall exist for longer delay, and when punishment must come upon the offender.

And she repented not. As she did not do it; as she showed no disposition to abandon her course; as all plea of having had no time to repent would now be taken away, it was proper that he should rise in his anger and cut her down.

28. And I will give him the morning star. The "morning star" is that bright planet – Venus – which at some seasons of the year appears so beautifully in the east, leading on the morning – the harbinger of the day. It is one of the most beautiful objects in nature, and is susceptible of a great variety of uses for illustration. It appears as the darkness passes away; it is an indication that the morning comes; it is inter-

mingled with the first rays of the light of the sun; it seems to be a herald to announce the coming of that glorious luminary; it is a pledge of the faithfulness of God. The idea seems to be, that the Savior would give him something that would resemble that morning planet in beauty and splendor – perhaps meaning that it would be placed as a gem in his diadem, and would sparkle on his brow – bearing some such relation to him who is called "the Sun of Righteousness," as the morning star does to the glorious sun on his rising. If so, the meaning would be, that he would receive a beautiful ornament, bearing a near relation to the Redeemer himself as a bright sun – a pledge that the darkness was past – but one whose beams would melt away into the superior light of the Redeemer himself, as the beams of the morning star are lost in the superior glory of the sun.

REVELATION 3

1–6. The contents of the epistle to the church at Sardis (Rev. 3: 1–6) are:

(1.) The usual salutation to the angel of the church, Rev. 3: 1.

(2.) The usual reference to the attributes of the Savior – those referred to here being that he had the seven Spirits of God, and the seven stars, Rev. 3: 1.

(3.) The assurance that he knew their works, Rev. 3: 1.

(4.) The statement of the peculiarity of the church, or what he saw in it – that it had a name to live and was dead, Rev. 3: 1.

(5.) A solemn direction to the members of the church, arising from their character and circumstances, to be watchful, and to strengthen the things which remained, but which were ready to die; to remember what they had received, and to hold fast that Which had been communicated to them, and to repent of all their sins, Rev. 3: 2–3.

(6.) A threat that if they did not do this, he would come suddenly upon them, at an hour which they could not anticipate, Rev. 3: 3.

(7.) A commendation of the church as far as it could be done, for there were still a few among theta who had not defiled their garments, and a promise that they should walk before him in

I will come on thee as a thief, and thou shalt not know what hour I will come upon thee.

4 Thou hast a few names even in Sardis which have not defiled their garments; and they shall walk with me in white: for they are worthy.

5 He that overcometh, the same shall be clothed in white raiment; and I will not blot out his name out of the book of life, but I will confess his name before my Father, and before his angels.

6 He that hath an ear, let him hear what the Spirit saith unto the churches.

7 And to the angel of the church in Philadelphia write; These things saith he that is holy, he that is true, he that hath the key of David, he that openeth, and no man shutteth; and shutteth, and no man openeth;

8 I know thy works: behold, I have set before thee an open door, and no man can shut it: for thou hast a little strength, and hast kept my word, and hast not denied my name.

9 Behold, I will make them of the synagogue of Satan, which say they are Jews, and are not, but do lie; behold, I will make them to come and worship before thy feet, and to know that I have loved thee.

10 Because thou hast kept the word of my patience, I also will keep thee from the hour of temptation, which shall come upon all the world, to try them that dwell upon the earth.

11 Behold, I come quickly: hold that fast which thou hast, that no man take thy crown.

12 Him that overcometh will I make a pillar in the temple of my God, and he shall go no more out: and I will write upon him the name of my God, and the name of the city of my God, which is new Jerusalem, which cometh down out of heaven from my God: and I will write upon him my new name.

13 He that hath an ear, let him hear what the Spirit saith unto the churches.

14 And unto the angel of the church of the Laodiceans write; These things saith the Amen, the faithful and true witness, the beginning of the creation of God;

15 I know thy works, that thou art neither cold nor hot: I would thou wert cold or hot.

16 So then because thou art lukewarm, and neither cold nor hot, I will spue

eminent for piety and learning. He visited Palestine to assure himself and his flock as to the Old Testament canon and wrote an epistle on the subject [EUSEBIUS *Ecclesiastical History*, **4.26**]; he also wrote a commentary on the Apocalypse [EUSEBIUS, *Ecclesiastical History*, 4.26; JEROME, *On Illustrious Men*, 24].

he that hath the seven Spirits of God – that is, He who hath all the fulness of the Spirit (Rev. 1: 4; 4: 5; 5: 6, with which compare Zech. 3: 9; 4: 10, proving His Godhead). This attribute implies His infinite power by the Spirit to convict of sin and of a hollow profession.

and the seven stars – (Rev. 1: 16,20). His *having the seven stars,* or presiding ministers, flows, as a consequence, from His *having the seven Spirits,* or the fulness of the Holy Spirit. The human ministry is the fruit of Christ's sending down the gifts of the Spirit. *Stars* imply brilliancy and glory; the fulness of the Spirit, and the fulness of brilliant light in Him, form a designed contrast to the formality which He reproves.

name ... livest ... dead – (1 Tim. 5: 6; 2 Tim. 3: 5; Titus 1: 16; compare Eph. 2:1,5; 5:14). "A name," that is, a reputation. Sardis was famed among the churches for spiritual *vitality;* yet the Heart-searcher, who seeth not as man seeth, pronounces her *dead;* how great searchings of heart should her case create among even the best of us! Laodicea deceived herself as to her true state (Rev. 3: 17), but it is not written that she had a high *name* among the other churches, as Sardis had.

2. Be – *Greek.* "Become," what thou art not, "watchful," or "wakeful," literally, "waking."

the things which remain – Strengthen those thy remaining few graces, which, in thy spiritual deadly slumber, are not yet quite extinct [Alford]. "The things that remain" can hardly mean "the PERSONS that are not yet dead, but *are ready to die*"; for Rev. 3: 4 implies that the "few" faithful ones at Sardis were not "ready to die," but were full of life.

perfect – literally, "filled up in full complement"; Translate, "complete." Weighed in the balance of Him who requires living faith as the motive of works, and found wanting.

3. how thou hast received – (Col. 2: 6; 1 Thess. 4: 1; 1 Tim. 6: 20). What Sardis is to "remember" is, not *how* joyfully she had received originally the Gospel message, but how the precious deposit was committed to her originally, so that she could not say, she had not "received and heard" it. The *Greek* is not aorist (as in Rev. 2: 4, as to Ephesus, "Thou *didst leave* thy first love"), but "thou hast received" (perfect), and still hast the permanent deposit of doctrine committed to thee. The word "keep" (so the *Greek* is for *English Version,* "hold fast") which follows, accords with this sense. "Keep" or observe the commandment which thou hast received

white, Rev. 3: 4.

(8.) A promise, as usual, to him that should be victorious. The promise here is, that he should walk before him in white; that his name should not be blotted out Of the book of life; that he should be acknowledged before the Father, and before the angels, Rev. 3: 5.

(9.) The usual call on all persons to hear what the Spirit said to the churches.

7. **These things saith he that is holy.** This refers undoubtedly to the Lord Jesus. The appellation holy, or the holy one, is one that befits him, and is not unfrequently given to him in the New Testament Luke 1: 35 Acts 2: 27, 3: 14.

He that hath the key of David. This expression is manifestly taken from Is. 22: 22, "And the key of the house of David will I lay upon his shoulder." The language is that which properly denotes authority or control – as when one has the key of a house, and has unlimited access to it; and the meaning here is, that as David is represented as the king of Israel residing in a palace, so he who had the key to that palace had regal authority.

He that openeth, and no man shutteth, etc. He has free and unrestrained access to the house; the power of admitting any one, or of excluding any one. Applied here to the Savior, as king in Zion, this means that in his kingdom he has the absolute control in regard to the admission or exclusion of any one. He can prescribe the terms; he can invite whom he chooses; he can exclude those whom he judges should not be admitted. A reference to this absolute control was every way proper when he was addressing a church, and is every way proper for us to reflect on when we think of the subject of our personal salvation.

And no man can shut it. No one has the power of preventing this, for he who has control over all things concedes these privileges to you.

For thou hast a little strength. This would imply that they had not great vigor, but still that, notwithstanding there were so many obstacles to their doing good, and so many temptations to evil, there still remained with them some degree of energy. They were not wholly dead; and, as long as that was the case,

the door was still open for them to do good. The words "little strength" may refer either to the smallness of the number – meaning that they were few; or it may refer to the spiritual life and energy of the church – meaning that, though feeble, their vital energy was not wholly gone. The more natural interpretation seems to be to refer it to the latter; and the sense is, that although they had not the highest degree of energy, or had not all that the Savior desired they should have, they were not wholly dead. The Savior saw among them the evidences of spiritual life; and in view of that he says he had set before them an open door, and there was abundant opportunity to employ all the energy and zeal which they had.

14. **And unto the angel of the church of the Laodiceans write. These things saith the Amen.** Referring, as is the case in every epistle, to some attribute of the speaker adapted to impress their minds, or to give peculiar force to what he was about to say to that particular church. Laodicea was characterized by lukewarmness, and the reference to the fact that he who was about to address them was the "Amen" – that is, was characterized by the simple earnestness and sincerity denoted by that word – was eminently fitted to make an impression on the minds of such a people. The word Amen means true, certain, faithful; and, as used here, it means that he to whom it is applied is eminently true and faithful. What he affirms is true; what he promises or threatens is certain. Himself characterized by sincerity and truth, he can look with approbation only on the same thing in others: and hence he looks with displeasure on the lukewarmness which, from its very nature, always approximates insincerity. This was an attribute, therefore, every way appropriate to be referred to in addressing a lukewarm church.

The faithful and true witness. This is presenting the idea implied in the word Amen in a more complete form, but substantially the same thing is referred to. He is a witness for God and his truth, and he can approve of nothing which the God of truth would not approve.

The beginning of the creation of God. This

thee out of my mouth.

17 Because thou sayest, I am rich, and increased with goods, and have need of nothing; and knowest not that thou art wretched, and miserable, and poor, and blind, and naked:

18 I counsel thee to buy of me gold tried in the fire, that thou mayest be rich; and white raiment, that thou mayest be clothed, and that the shame of thy nakedness do not appear; and anoint thine eyes with eyesalve, that thou mayest see.

19 As many as I love, I rebuke and chasten: be zealous therefore, and repent.

20 Behold, I stand at the door, and knock: if any man hear my voice, and open the door, I will come in to him, and will sup with him, and he with me.

21 To him that overcometh will I grant to sit with me in my throne, even as I also overcame, and am set down with my Father in his throne.

22 He that hath an ear, let him hear what the Spirit saith unto the churches.

REVELATION 4

1 After this I looked, and, behold, a door was opened in heaven: and the first voice which I heard was as it were of a trumpet talking with me; which said, Come up hither, and I will shew thee things which must be hereafter.

2 And immediately I was in the spirit: and, behold, a throne was set in heaven, and one sat on the throne.

3 And he that sat was to look upon like a jasper and a sardine stone: and there was a rainbow round about the throne, in sight like unto an emerald.

4 And round about the throne were four and twenty seats: and upon the seats I saw four and twenty elders sitting, clothed in white raiment; and they had on their heads crowns of gold.

5 And out of the throne proceeded lightnings and thunderings and voices: and there were seven lamps of fire burning before the throne, which are the seven Spirits of God.

6 And before the throne there was a sea of glass like unto crystal: and in the midst of the throne, and round about the throne, were four beasts full of eyes before and behind.

7 And the first beast was like a lion,

and didst hear.

heard – *Greek* aorist, "didst hear," namely, when the Gospel doctrine was committed to thee. Trench explains "how," *with what demonstration of the Spirit and power* from Christ's ambassadors the truth came to you, and how heartily and zealously you at first received it.

come on thee as a thief – in special judgment on thee as a Church, with the same stealthiness and as unexpectedly as shall be My visible second coming. As *the thief* gives no notice of his approach. Christ applies the language which in its fullest sense describes His second coming, to describe His coming in special judgments on churches and states (as Jerusalem, Matt. 24: 4–28) these special judgments being anticipatory earnests of that great last coming. "The last day is hidden from us, that every day may be observed by us" [Augustine]. Twice Christ in the days of His flesh spake the same words (Matt. 24: 42–43; Luke 12: 39–40); and so deeply had His words been engraven on the minds of the apostles that they are often repeated in their writings (Rev. 16: 15; 1 Thess. 5: 2,4,6; 2 Pet. 3: 10). The Greek proverb was that "the feet of the avenging deities are shod with wool," expressing the noiseless approach of the divine judgments, and their possible nearness at the moment when they were supposed the farthest off [Trench].

4. names – persons *named* in the book of life (Rev. 3: 5) known by name by the Lord as His own. These had the reality corresponding to their name; not a mere *name* among men as *living*, while really *dead* (Rev. 3: 1). The gracious Lord does not overlook any exceptional cases of real saints in the midst of unreal professors.

not defiled their garments – namely, the garments of their Christian profession, of which baptism is the initiatory seal, whence the candidates for baptism used in the ancient Church to be arrayed in white. Compare also Eph. 5: 27, as to the spotlessness of the Church when she shall be presented to Christ; and Rev. 19: 8, as to the "fine linen, clean and white, the righteousness of the saints," in which it shall be granted to her to be arrayed; and "the wedding garment." Meanwhile she is not to sully her Christian profession with any defilement of flesh or spirit, but to "keep her garments." For no defilement shall enter the heavenly city. Not that any keep themselves here wholly free from defilement; but, as compared with hollow professors, the godly *keep themselves unspotted from the world;* and when they do contract it, they wash it away, so as to have their "robes white in the blood of the Lamb" (Rev. 7: 14). The *Greek* is not "to stain" (*Greek,* "*miainein*"), but to "defile," or besmear (*Greek,* "*molunein*"), Song 5: 3.

expression is a very important one in regard to the rank and dignity of the Savior, and, like all similar expressions respecting him.

20. Behold, I stand at the door, and knock. Intimating that, though they had erred, the way of repentance and hope was not closed against them. He was still willing to be gracious, though their conduct had been such as to be loathsome, Rev. 3: 16. To see the real force of this language, we must remember how disgusting and offensive their conduct had been to him. And yet he was willing, notwithstanding this, to receive them to his favor; nay more, he stood and pleaded with them that he might be received with the hospitality that would be shown to a friend or stranger. The language here is so plain that it scarcely needs explanation. It is taken from an act when we approach a dwelling, and, by a well-understood sign – knocking – announce our presence, and ask for admission. The act of knocking implies two things:

(a) that we desire admittance; and

(b) that we recognize the right of him who dwells in the house to open the door to us or not, as he shall please. We would not obtrude upon him; we would not force his door; and if, after we are sure that we are heard, we are not admitted, we turn quietly away. Both of these things are implied here by the language used by the Savior when he approaches man as represented under the image of knocking at the door: that he desires to be admitted to our friendship; and that he recognizes our freedom in the matter. He does not obtrude himself upon us, nor does he employ force to find admission to the heart. If admitted, he comes and dwells with us; if rejected, he turns quietly away – perhaps to return and knock again, perhaps never to come back. The language here used, also, may be understood as applicable to all persons, and to all the methods by which the Savior seeks to come into the heart of a sinner. It would properly refer to anything which would announce his presence: his word; his Spirit; the solemn events of his Providence; the invitations of his gospel. In these and in other methods he comes to man; and the manner in which these invitations ought to be estimated would be seen by

supposing that he came to us personally and solicited our friendship, and proposed to be our Redeemer. It may be added here, that this expression proves that the attempt at reconciliation begins with the Savior. It is not that the sinner goes out to meet him, or to seek for him; it is that the Savior presents himself at the door of the heart as if he were desirous to enjoy the friendship of man. This is in accordance with the uniform language of the New Testament, that "God so loved the world as to give his only-begotten Son;" that "Christ came to seek and to save the lost;" that the Savior says, "Come unto me, all ye that labor and are heavy laden," etc. Salvation, in the Scriptures, is never represented as originated by man.

REVELATION 4

Chapter 4 properly commences the series of visions respecting future events, and introduces those remarkable symbolical descriptions which were designed to cheer the hearts of those to whom the book was first sent, in their trials, and the hearts of all believers in all ages, with the assurance of the final triumph of the gospel.

1. After this. Gr., "after these things;" that is, after what he had seen, and after what he had been directed to record in the preceding chapters, How long after these things this occurred, he does not say – whether on the same day, or at some subsequent time; and conjecture would be useless. The scene, however, is changed. Instead of seeing the Savior standing before him, (chapter 1) the scene is transferred to heaven, and he is permitted to look in upon the throne of God, and upon the worshippers there.

I looked. Gr., I saw. Our word look would rather indicate purpose or intention, as if he had designedly directed his attention to heaven, to see what could be discovered there. The meaning, however, is simply that he saw a new vision, without intimating whether there was any design on his part, and without saying how his thoughts came to be directed to heaven.

A door was opened. That is, there was apparently an opening in the sky, like a door,

and the second beast like a calf, and the third beast had a face as a man, and the fourth beast was like a flying eagle.

8 And the four beasts had each of them six wings about him; and they were full of eyes within: and they rest not day and night, saying, Holy, holy, holy, Lord God Almighty, which was, and is, and is to come.

9 And when those beasts give glory and honor and thanks to him that sat on the throne, who liveth for ever and ever,

10 The four and twenty elders fall down before him that sat on the throne, and worship him that liveth for ever and ever, and cast their crowns before the throne, saying,

11 Thou art worthy, O Lord, to receive glory and honor and power: for thou hast created all things, and for thy pleasure they are and were created.

REVELATION 5

1 And I saw in the right hand of him that sat on the throne a book written within and on the backside, sealed with seven seals.

2 And I saw a strong angel proclaiming with a loud voice, Who is worthy to open the book, and to loose the seals thereof?

3 And no man in heaven, nor in earth, neither under the earth, was able to open the book, neither to look thereon.

4 And I wept much, because no man was found worthy to open and to read the book, neither to look thereon.

5 And one of the elders saith unto me, Weep not: behold, the Lion of the tribe of Juda, the Root of David, hath prevailed to open the book, and to loose the seven seals thereof.

6 And I beheld, and, lo, in the midst of the throne and of the four beasts, and in the midst of the elders, stood a Lamb as it had been slain, having seven horns and seven eyes, which are the seven Spirits of God sent forth into all the earth.

7 And he came and took the book out of the right hand of him that sat upon the throne.

8 And when he had taken the book, the four beasts and four and twenty elders fell down before the Lamb, having every one of them harps, and golden vials full of odors, which are the prayers of saints.

9 And they sung a new song, saying,

REVELATION 4

Rev. 4:1–11. Vision of God's Throne in Heaven; the Four and Twenty Elders; the Four Living Creatures.

Here begins the Revelation proper; and first, the fourth and fifth chapters set before us the heavenly scenery of the succeeding visions, and God on His throne, as the *covenant God of His Church,* the Revealer of them to His apostle through Jesus Christ. The first great portion comprises the opening of the seals and the sounding of the trumpets (fourth to eleventh chapters). As the communication respecting the seven churches opened with a suitable vision of the Lord Jesus as Head of the Church, so the second part opens with a vision suitable to the matter to be revealed. The scene is changed from earth to *heaven.*

1. After this – *Greek,* "After these things," marking the opening of the next vision in the succession. Here is the transition from "the things which are" (Rev. 1: 19), the existing state of the seven churches, as a type of the Church in general, in John's time, to "the things which shall be hereafter," namely, in relation to the time when John wrote.

opened – "standing open"; not as though John saw it in the act of being opened. Compare Ezek. 1: 1; Matt. 3: 16; Acts 7: 56; 10: 11. But in those visions the heavens opened, disclosing the visions to those below on earth. Whereas here, heaven, the temple of God, remains closed to those on earth, but John is transported in vision through an open door up into heaven, whence he can see things passing on earth or in heaven, according as the scenes of the several visions require.

the first voice which I heard – the voice which I heard at first, namely, in Rev. 1: 10; *the former voice.*

2. one sat on the throne – the Eternal Father: the Creator (Rev. 4: 11): also compare Rev. 4: 8 with Rev. 1: 4, where also the Father is designated, "which is, and was, and is to come." When the Son, "the Lamb," is introduced, Rev. 5: 5–9, a *new* song is sung which distinguishes *the Sitter on the throne* from *the Lamb,* "Thou hast redeemed us to God," and Rev. 5: 13, "Unto Him that sitteth upon the throne, and unto the Lamb." So also in Rev. 5: 7, as in Dan. 7: 13, the *Son of man* brought before *the Ancient of days* is distinguished from Him. The Father in essence is invisible, but in Scripture at times is represented as assuming a visible form.

3. rainbow round about the throne – forming a complete circle (type of God's perfection and eternity: not a half circle as the earthly rainbow) surrounding the throne vertically. Its various colors, which combined form one pure solar ray, symbolize the varied aspects of God's providential dealings uniting in one harmonious whole.

so that he could look into heaven.

In heaven. Or, rather, in the expanse above – in the visible heavens as they appear to spread out over the earth. So Ezek. 1: 1, "The heavens were opened, and I saw visions of God." The Hebrews spoke of the sky above as a solid expanse; or as a curtain stretched out; or as an extended arch above the earth – describing it as it appears to the eye. In that expanse, or arch, the stars are set at gems, through apertures or windows in that expanse the rain comes down, Gen. 7: 11; and that is opened when a heavenly messenger comes down to the earth, Matt. 3: 16. Compare Luke 3: 21 Acts 7: 56; 10: 11.

Of course, all this is figurative, but it is such language as all men naturally use. The simple meaning here is, that John had a vision of what is in heaven as if there had been such an opening made through the sky, and he had been permitted to look into the world above.

And the first voice which I heard. That is, the first sound which he heard was a command to come up and see the glories of that world. He afterwards heard other sounds – the sounds of praise; but the first notes that fell on his ear were a direction to come up there and to receive a revelation respecting future things.

Was as it were of a trumpet. It resembled the sound of a trumpet, Rev. 1: 10.

Talking with me. As of a trumpet that seemed to speak directly to me.

Come up hither. To the place whence the voice seemed to proceed – heaven.

And I will shew thee things which must be hereafter. Gr., "after these things." The reference is to future events; and the meaning is, that there would be disclosed to him events that were to occur at some future period. There is no intimation here when they would occur, or what would be embraced in the period referred to. All that the words would properly convey would be, that there would be a disclosure of things that were to occur in some future time.

11. Thou art worthy, Lord. In thy character, perfections, and government, there is that which makes it proper that universal praise should be rendered. The feeling of all true wor-

shippers is, that God is worthy of the praise that is ascribed to him. No man worships him aright who does not feel that there is that in his nature and his doings which makes it proper that he should receive universal adoration.

To receive glory. To have praise or glory ascribed to thee.

And honor. To be honored; that is, to be approached and adored as worthy of honor.

And power. To have power ascribed to thee, or to be regarded as having infinite power. Man can confer no power on God, but he may acknowledge that which he has, and adore him for its exertion in his behalf and in the government of the world.

REVELATION 5

Chapter 5 introduces the disclosure of future events. It is done in a manner eminently fitted to impress the mind with a sense of the importance of the revelations about to be made. The proper state of mind for appreciating this chapter is that when we look on the future and are sensible that important events are about to occur; when we feel that that future is wholly impenetrable to us; and when the efforts of the highest created minds fail to lift the mysterious veil which hides those events from our view. It is in accordance with our nature that the mind should be impressed with solemn awe under such circumstances; it is not a violation of the laws of our nature that one who had an earnest desire to penetrate that future, and who saw the volume before him which contained the mysterious revelation, and who yet felt that there was no one in heaven or earth who could break the seals, and disclose what was to come, should weep. Rev. 5: 4. The design of the whole chapter is evidently to honor the Lamb of God, by showing that the power was entrusted to him which was confided to no one else in heaven or earth, of disclosing what is to come. Nothing else would better illustrate this than the fact that he alone could break the mysterious seals which barred out the knowledge of the future from all created eyes; and nothing would be better adapted to impress this on the mind than the representation in this chapter – the

Thou art worthy to take the book, and to open the seals thereof: for thou wast slain, and hast redeemed us to God by thy blood out of every kindred, and tongue, and people, and nation;

10 And hast made us unto our God kings and priests: and we shall reign on the earth.

11 And I beheld, and I heard the voice of many angels round about the throne and the beasts and the elders: and the number of them was ten thousand times ten thousand, and thousands of thousands;

12 Saying with a loud voice, Worthy is the Lamb that was slain to receive power, and riches, and wisdom, and strength, and honor, and glory, and blessing.

13 And every creature which is in heaven, and on the earth, and under the earth, and such as are in the sea, and all that are in them, heard I saying, Blessing, and honor, and glory, and power, be unto him that sitteth upon the throne, and unto the Lamb for ever and ever.

14 And the four beasts said, Amen. And the four and twenty elders fell down and worshipped him that liveth for ever and ever.

REVELATION 6

1 And I saw when the Lamb opened one of the seals, and I heard, as it were the noise of thunder, one of the four beasts saying, Come and see.

2 And I saw, and behold a white horse: and he that sat on him had a bow; and a crown was given unto him: and he went forth conquering, and to conquer.

3 And when he had opened the second seal, I heard the second beast say, Come and see.

4 And there went out another horse that was red: and power was given to him that sat thereon to take peace from the earth, and that they should kill one another: and there was given unto him a great sword.

5 And when he had opened the third seal, I heard the third beast say, Come and see. And I beheld, and lo a black horse; and he that sat on him had a pair of balances in his hand.

6 And I heard a voice in the midst of the four beasts say, A measure of wheat for a penny, and three measures of barley

REVELATION 5

Rev. 5:1–14. THE BOOK WITH SEVEN SEALS: NONE WORTHY TO OPEN IT BUT THE LAMB: HE TAKES IT AMIDST THE PRAISES OF THE REDEEMED, AND OF THE WHOLE HEAVENLY HOST.

1. book – rather, as accords with the ancient form of books, and with the *writing on the backside*, "a roll." The *writing on the back* implies fulness and completeness, so that nothing more needs to be added (Rev. 22: 18). The roll, or book, appears from the context to be "*the title-deed of man's inheritance*" [Deut. Burgh] redeemed by Christ, and contains the successive steps by which He shall recover it from its usurper and obtain actual possession of the kingdom already "purchased" for Himself and His elect saints. However, no portion of the roll is said to be *unfolded* and *read*; but simply the *seals* are successively *opened*, giving final access to its contents being read as a perfect whole, which shall not be until the events symbolized by the seals shall have been past, when Eph. 3: 10 shall receive its *complete* accomplishment, and the Lamb shall reveal God's providential plans in redemption in all their manifold beauties. Thus the opening of the seals will mean the successive steps by which God in Christ clears the way for the final opening and reading of the book at the visible setting up of the kingdom of Christ. Compare, at the grand consummation, Rev. 20: 12, "Another book was opened … the book of life"; Rev. 22: 19. None is worthy to do so save the Lamb, for He alone as such has redeemed man's forfeited inheritance, of which *the book is the title-deed*. The question (Rev. 5: 2) is not (as commonly supposed), Who should reveal the destinies of the Church (for this any inspired prophet would be competent to do)? but, Who has the WORTH *to give man a new title to his lost inheritance?* [Deut. Burgh].

REVELATION 6

Rev. 6: 1–17. THE OPENING OF THE FIRST SIX OF THE SEVEN SEALS.

2. Evidently Christ, whether in person, or by His angel, preparatory to His coming again, as appears from Rev. 19: 11–12.

crown – Greek, "*stephanos*," the garland or wreath of a *conqueror*, which is also implied by His *white horse*, white being the emblem of victory. In Rev. 19: 11–12 the last step in His victorious progress is represented; accordingly there He wears *many diadems* (Greek, "*diademata*"; not merely Greek, "*stephanoi*," "crowns" or "wreaths"), and is personally attended by the hosts of heaven. Compare Zech. 1: 7–17; 6: 1–8; especially Rev. 6: 10 below, with Zech. 1: 12; also compare the colors of the four horses.

exhibition of a mysterious book in the hand of God; the proclamation of the angel, calling on any who could do it to open the book; the fact that no one in heaven or earth could do it; the tears shed by John when it was found that no one could do it; the assurance of one of the elders that the Lion of the tribe of Judah had power to do it; and the profound adoration of all in heaven and in earth and under the earth, in view of the power entrusted to him of breaking these mysterious seals.

1. And I saw in the right hand of him that sat on the throne. His form is not described there, nor is there any intimation of it here except the mention of his "right hand." The book or roll seems to have been so held in his hand that John could see its shape, and see distinctly how it was written and sealed.

4. And I wept much, because no man was found worthy, etc. Gr., as in Rev. 5: 3, no one. It would seem as if there was a pause to see if there were any response to the proclamation of the angel. There being none, John gave way to his deep emotions in a flood of tears. The tears of the apostle here may be regarded as an illustration of two things which are occurring constantly in the minds of men:

(1.) The strong desire to penetrate the future; to lift the mysterious veil which shrouds that which is to come; to find some way to pierce the dark wall which seems to stand up before us, and which shuts from our view that which is to be hereafter.

(2.) The weeping of the apostle may be regarded as an instance of the deep grief which men often experience when all efforts to penetrate the future fail, and they feel that after all they are left completely in the dark. Often is the soul overpowered with grief, and often are the eyes filled with sadness at the reflection that there is an absolute limit to the human powers; that all that man can arrive at by his own efforts is uncertain conjecture, and that there is no way possible by which he can make nature speak out and disclose what is to come.

14. And the four beasts said, Amen. The voice of universal praise came to them from abroad, and they accorded with it, and ascribed honor to God.

REVELATION 6

1. And I saw. Or, I looked. He fixed his eye attentively on what was passing, as promising important disclosures. No one had been found in the universe who could open the seals but the Lamb of God, (Rev. 5: 2–4) and it was natural for John, therefore, to look upon the transaction with profound interest.

When the Lamb opened one of the seals. This was the first or outermost of the seals, and its being broken would permit a certain portion of the volume to be unrolled and read.

The representation in this place is, therefore, that of a volume with a small portion unrolled, and written on both sides of the parchment.

And I heard, as it were the noise of thunder. One of the four living creatures speaking as with a voice of thunder, or with a loud voice.

2. And behold a white horse. In order to any definite understanding of what was denoted by these symbols, it is proper to form in our minds, in the first place, a clear conception of what the symbol properly represents, or an idea of what it would naturally convey. It may be assumed that the symbol was significant, and that there was some reason why that was used rather than another; why, for instance, a horse was employed rather than an eagle or a lion; why a white horse was employed in one case, and a red one, a black one, a pale one in the others; why in this case a bow was in the hand of the rider, and a crown was placed on his head. Each one of these particulars enters into the constitution of the symbol; and we must find something in the event which fairly corresponds with each – for the symbol is made up of all these things grouped together. It may be farther observed, that where the general symbol is the same – as in the opening of the first four seals – it may be assumed that the same object or class of objects is referred to; and the particular things denoted, or the diversity in the general application, is to be found in the variety in the representation – the color, etc., of the horse, and the arms, apparel, etc., of the rider. The specifications under the first seal are four:

for a penny; and see thou hurt not the oil and the wine.

7 And when he had opened the fourth seal, I heard the voice of the fourth beast say, Come and see.

8 And I looked, and behold a pale horse: and his name that sat on him was Death, and Hell followed with him. And power was given unto them over the fourth part of the earth, to kill with sword, and with hunger, and with death, and with the beasts of the earth.

9 And when he had opened the fifth seal, I saw under the altar the souls of them that were slain for the word of God, and for the testimony which they held:

10 And they cried with a loud voice, saying, How long, O Lord, holy and true, dost thou not judge and avenge our blood on them that dwell on the earth?

11 And white robes were given unto every one of them; and it was said unto them, that they should rest yet for a little season, until their fellowservants also and their brethren, that should be killed as they were, should be fulfilled.

12 And I beheld when he had opened the sixth seal, and, lo, there was a great earthquake; and the sun became black as sackcloth of hair, and the moon became as blood;

13 And the stars of heaven fell unto the earth, even as a fig tree casteth her untimely figs, when she is shaken of a mighty wind.

14 And the heaven departed as a scroll when it is rolled together; and every mountain and island were moved out of their places.

15 And the kings of the earth, and the great men, and the rich men, and the chief captains, and the mighty men, and every bondman, and every free man, hid themselves in the dens and in the rocks of the mountains;

16 And said to the mountains and rocks, Fall on us, and hide us from the face of him that sitteth on the throne, and from the wrath of the Lamb:

17 For the great day of his wrath is come; and who shall be able to stand?

REVELATION 7

1 And after these things I saw four angels standing on the four corners of the earth, holding the four winds of the

and to conquer – that is, so as to gain a lasting victory. All four seals usher in *judgments* on the earth, as the power which opposes the reign of Himself and His Church. This, rather than the work of conversion and conviction, is primarily meant, though doubtless, secondarily, the elect will be gathered out through His word and His judgments.

4. red – the color of *blood*. The color of the horse in each case answers to the mission of the rider. Compare Matt. 10: 24–36, "Think not I am come to send *peace* on earth; I came not to send *peace*, but a *sword*." The *white* horse of Christ's bloodless victories is soon followed, through man's perversion of the Gospel, by the *red* horse of bloodshed; but this is overruled to the clearing away of the obstacles to Christ's coming kingdom. The patient *ox* is the emblem of the second *living creature* who, at the opening of this seal, saith, "Come." The saints amidst judgments on the earth in patience "endure to the end."

5. black – implying *sadness* and *want*.
a pair of balances – the symbol of scarcity of provisions, the bread being doled out by weight.

6. A measure – "A chœnix." While making food scarce, do not make it so much so that a chœnix (about a day's provision of wheat, variously estimated at two or three pints) shall be obtainable "for a penny" (*denarius*, eight and a half pence of our money, probably the day's wages of a laborer). *Famine* generally follows the *sword*. Ordinarily, from sixteen to twenty measures were given for a denarius. The *sword, famine, noisome beasts,* and the *pestilence,* are God's four judgments on the earth. A spiritual famine, too, may be included in the judgment. The "Come," in the case of this third seal, is said by the third of the four living creatures, whose likeness is *a man* indicative of sympathy and human compassion for the sufferers. God in it tempers judgment with mercy. Compare Matt. 24: 7, which indicates the very calamities foretold in these seals, *nation rising against nation* (the sword), *famines, pestilences* (Rev. 6: 8), and *earthquakes* (Rev. 6: 12).

three measures of barley for a penny – the cheaper and less nutritious grain, bought by the laborer who could not buy enough wheat for his family with his day's wages, a denarius, and, therefore, buys barley.

REVELATION 7

Rev. 7: 1–17. Sealing of the Elect of Israel. The Countless Multitude of the Gentile Elect.

1. The two visions in this chapter come in as an episode *after* the sixth seal, and before the seventh seal. It is clear that, though "Israel" may elsewhere designate the spiritual

(1) the general symbol of the horse – common to the first four seals;

(2) the color of the horse;

(3) the fact that he that sat on him had a bow; and

(4) that a crown was given him by some one as indicative of victory. The question now is, what these symbols would naturally denote.

4. And there went out another horse. The color of the horse: another horse that was **red.** This symbol cannot be mistaken. As the white horse denoted prosperity, triumph, and happiness, so this would denote carnage, discord, bloodshed. This is clear, not only from the nature of the emblem, but from the explanation immediately added: **And power was given to him that sat thereon to take peace from the earth, and that they should kill one another.**

5. And I beheld, and lo, a black horse. Black, in the Scriptures, is the image of fear, of famine, of death. Lam. 5: 10: "Our skin was black like an oven, because of the terrible famine." Jer. 14: 2: "Because of the drought Judah mourneth, and tile gates thereof languish; they are in deep mourning [literally, black] for the land." Joel 2: 6: "All faces shall gather blackness." Nah. 2: 10: "The knees smite together, and there is great pain in all loins, and the faces of them all gather blackness." Compare Rev. 6: 12 Ezek. 32: 7. Famine, pestilence, oppression, heavy taxation, tyranny, invasion – any of these might be denoted by the color of the horse.

8. And I looked, and behold a pale horse. The peculiarity of this emblem consists in the color of the horse, the rider, and the power that was given unto him. In these there is entire harmony, and there can be comparatively little difficulty in the explanation and application. The color here would be an appropriate one to denote the reign of Death – as one of the most striking effects of death is paleness – and, of course, of death produced by any cause, famine, pestilence, or the sword. From this portion of the symbol, if it stood with nothing to limit and define it, we should naturally look for some condition of things in which death would prevail in a remarkable manner, or in which multitudes of human beings would be

swept away. And yet, perhaps, from the very nature of this part of the symbol, we should look for the prevalence of death in some such peaceful manner as by famine or disease. The red color would more naturally denote the ravages of death in war; the black, the ravages of death by sudden calamity; the pale would more obviously suggest famine or wasting disease.

13. The falling of the stars: **And the stars of heaven fell unto the earth.** This language is derived from the poetic idea that the sky seems to be a solid concave in which the stars are set, and that, when any convulsion takes place, that concave will be shaken, and the stars will be loosened and fall from their places.

Even as a fig-tree casteth her untimely figs. This word properly denotes winter-figs, or such as grow under the leaves, and do not ripen at the proper season, but hang upon the trees during the winter. A violent wind shaking a plantation of fig-trees would of course cast many such figs to the ground. The point of the comparison is, the ease with which the stars would seem to be shaken from their places, and hence the ease with which, in these commotions, princes would be dethroned.

REVELATION 7

1. And after these things. After the vision of the things referred to in the opening of the sixth seal. The natural interpretation would be, that what is here said of the angels and the winds occurred after those things which are described in the previous chapter. The exact chronology may not be always observed in these symbolical representations, but doubtless there is a general order which is observed.

I saw four angels. He does not describe their forms, but merely mentions their agency. This is, of course, a symbolical representation. We are not to suppose that it would be literally fulfilled, or that, at the time referred to by the vision, four celestial beings would be stationed in the four quarters of the world, for the purpose of checking and restraining the winds that blow from the four points of the compass. The meaning is, that events would occur which would be properly represented by four angels

earth, that the wind should not blow on the earth, nor on the sea, nor on any tree.

2 And I saw another angel ascending from the east, having the seal of the living God: and he cried with a loud voice to the four angels, to whom it was given to hurt the earth and the sea,

3 Saying, Hurt not the earth, neither the sea, nor the trees, till we have sealed the servants of our God in their foreheads.

4 And I heard the number of them which were sealed: and there were sealed an hundred and forty and four thousand of all the tribes of the children of Israel.

5 Of the tribe of Juda were sealed twelve thousand. Of the tribe of Reuben were sealed twelve thousand. Of the tribe of Gad were sealed twelve thousand.

6 Of the tribe of Aser were sealed twelve thousand. Of the tribe of Nephalim were sealed twelve thousand. Of the tribe of Manasses were sealed twelve thousand.

7 Of the tribe of Simeon were sealed twelve thousand. Of the tribe of Levi were sealed twelve thousand. Of the tribe of Issachar were sealed twelve thousand.

8 Of the tribe of Zabulon were sealed twelve thousand. Of the tribe of Joseph were sealed twelve thousand. Of the tribe of Benjamin were sealed twelve thousand.

9 After this I beheld, and, lo, a great multitude, which no man could number, of all nations, and kindreds, and people, and tongues, stood before the throne, and before the Lamb, clothed with white robes, and palms in their hands;

10 And cried with a loud voice, saying, Salvation to our God which sitteth upon the throne, and unto the Lamb.

11 And all the angels stood round about the throne, and about the elders and the four beasts, and fell before the throne on their faces, and worshipped God,

12 Saying, Amen: Blessing, and glory, and wisdom, and thanksgiving, and honor, and power, and might, be unto our God for ever and ever. Amen.

13 And one of the elders answered, saying unto me, What are these which are arrayed in white robes? and whence came they?

14 And I said unto him, Sir, thou knowest. And he said to me, These are they which came out of great tribulation, and have washed their robes, and made them

Israel, "the elect (Church) on earth" [Alford], here, where the names of the tribes one by one are specified, these names cannot have any but the literal meaning. The second advent will be the time of *the restoration of the kingdom to Israel*, when *the times of the Gentiles shall have been fulfilled*, and the Jews shall at last say, "Blessed is He that cometh in the name of the Lord." The period of the Lord's absence has been a blank in the history of the Jews as a nation. As then Revelation is the Book of the Second Advent [Deut. Burgh], naturally mention of God's restored favor to Israel occurs among the events that usher in Christ's advent.

earth … sea … tree – The judgments to descend on these are in answer to the martyrs' prayer under the *fifth* seal. Compare the same judgments under the *fifth* trumpet, the sealed being exempt (Rev. 9: 4).

on any tree – *Greek,* "*against* any tree" (*Greek,* "*epi ti dendron*": but "*on* the earth," *Greek,* "*epi tees gees*").

2. from the east – *Greek,* "**the rising of the sun.**" The quarter from which God's glory oftenest manifests itself.

3. Hurt not – by letting loose the destructive winds. till we have sealed the servants of our God – parallel to Matt. 24: 31, "His angels … shall gather together His elect from the four winds." God's love is such, that He *cannot do anything* in the way of judgment, till His people are secured from hurt (Gen. 19: 22). Israel, at the eve of the Lord's coming, shall be found re-embodied as a nation; for its tribes are distinctly specified (Joseph, however, being substituted for Dan; whether because Antichrist is to come from Dan, or because Dan is to be Antichrist's especial tool [Aretas, tenth century], compare Gen. 49: 17; Jer. 8: 16; Amos 8: 14; just as there was a Judas among the Twelve). Out of these tribes *a believing remnant* will be preserved from the judgments which shall destroy all the Antichristian confederacy (Rev. 6: 12–17), and *shall be transfigured with the elect Church of all nations*, namely, 144,000 (or whatever number is meant by this symbolical number), who shall faithfully resist the seductions of Antichrist, while the rest of the nation, restored to Palestine in unbelief, are his dupes, and at last his victims. Previously to the Lord's judgments on Antichrist and his hosts, these latter shall destroy *two-thirds* of the nation, *one-third* escaping, and, by the Spirit's operation through affliction, turning to the Lord, which remnant shall form the nucleus on earth of the Israelite nation that is from this time to stand at the head of the millennial nations of the world. Israel's spiritual resurrection shall be "as life from the dead" to all the nations. As now a regeneration goes on here and there of individuals, so there shall then be a regeneration of nations universally, and this in connection with Christ's coming. Matt. 24: 34; "this generation (the Jewish nation) shall not pass till all these

standing in the four quarters of the world, and having power over the winds.

Standing on the four corners of the earth. This language is, of course, accommodated to the prevailing mode of speaking of the earth among the Hebrews. It was a common method among them to describe it as a vast plain, having four corners, those corners being the prominent points – north, south, east, and west. So we speak now of the four winds, the four quarters of the world, etc. The Hebrews spoke of the earth, as we do of the rising and setting of the sun, and of the motions of the heavenly bodies, according to appearances, and without aiming at philosophical exactness.

4. And I heard the number of them which were sealed. He does not say where he heard that, or by whom it was communicated to him, or when it was done. The material point is, that he heard it; he did not see it done. Either by the angel, or by some direct communication from God, he was told of the number that would be sealed, and of the distribution of the whole number into twelve equal parts, represented by the tribes of the children of Israel.

And there were sealed an hundred and forty and four thousand of all the tribes of the children of Israel. In regard to this number, the first and the main question is, whether it is meant that this was to be the literal number, or whether it was symbolical; and, if the latter, of what it is a symbol.

I. As to the first of these inquiries, there does not appear to be any good reason for doubt. The fair interpretation seems to require that it should be understood as symbolical, or as designed not to be literally taken; for
(a) the whole scene is symbolical – the winds, the angels, the sealing.
(b) It cannot be supposed that this number will include all who will be sealed and saved. In whatever way this is interpreted, and whatever we may suppose it to refer to, we cannot but suppose that more than this number will be saved.
(c) The number is too exact and artificial to suppose that it is literal. It is inconceivable that exactly the same number – precisely

twelve thousand – should be selected from each tribe of the children of Israel.
(d) If literal, it is necessary to suppose that this refers to the twelve tribes of the children of Israel. But on every supposition this is absurd. Ten of their tribes had been long before carried away, and the distinction of the tribes was lost, no more to be recovered, and the Hebrew people never have been, since the time of John, in circumstances to which the description here could be applicable. These considerations make it clear that the description here is symbolical. But,

II. Of what is it symbolical? Is it of a large number, or of a small number? Is it of those who would be saved from among the Jews, or of all who would be saved in the Christian church – represented as the "tribes of the children of Israel?" To these inquiries we may answer,

(1.) that the representation seems to be rather that of a comparatively small number than a large one, for these reasons:
(a) The number of itself is not large.
(b) The number is not large as compared with those who must have constituted the tribes here referred to – the number twelve thousand, for example, as compared with the whole number of the tribe of Judah, of the tribe of Reuben, etc.
(c) It would seem from the language that there would be some selection from a much greater number.
The phrase, then, would properly denote those taken out of some other and greater number – as a portion of a tribe, and not the whole tribe. If the reference here is to the church, it would seem to denote that a portion only of that church would be sealed.

(2.) To the other inquiry – whether this refers to those who would be sealed and saved among the Jews, or to those in the Christian church – we may answer,
(a) that there are strong reasons for supposing the latter to be the correct opinion. Long before the time of John all these distinctions of tribe were abolished. The ten tribes had been carried away and scattered in distant lands, never more to be restored; and it cannot be supposed that there was any such lit-

white in the blood of the Lamb.

15 Therefore are they before the throne of God, and serve him day and night in his temple: and he that sitteth on the throne shall dwell among them.

16 They shall hunger no more, neither thirst any more; neither shall the sun light on them, nor any heat.

17 For the Lamb which is in the midst of the throne shall feed them, and shall lead them unto living fountains of waters: and God shall wipe away all tears from their eyes.

REVELATION 8

1 And when he had opened the seventh seal, there was silence in heaven about the space of half an hour.

2 And I saw the seven angels which stood before God; and to them were given seven trumpets.

3 And another angel came and stood at the altar, having a golden censer; and there was given unto him much incense, that he should offer it with the prayers of all saints upon the golden altar which was before the throne.

4 And the smoke of the incense, which came with the prayers of the saints, ascended up before God out of the angel's hand.

5 And the angel took the censer, and filled it with fire of the altar, and cast it into the earth: and there were voices, and thunderings, and lightnings, and an earthquake.

6 And the seven angels which had the seven trumpets prepared themselves to sound.

7 The first angel sounded, and there followed hail and fire mingled with blood, and they were cast upon the earth: and the third part of trees was burnt up, and all green grass was burnt up.

8 And the second angel sounded, and as it were a great mountain burning with fire was cast into the sea: and the third part of the sea became blood;

9 And the third part of the creatures which were in the sea, and had life, died; and the third part of the ships were destroyed.

10 And the third angel sounded, and there fell a great star from heaven, burning as it were a lamp, and it fell upon the third part of the rivers, and upon the foun-

things be fulfilled," which implies that Israel can no more *pass away* before Christ's advent, than Christ's own *words* can *pass away* (the same *Greek*), Matt. 24: 35. So exactly Zech. 13: 8–9; 14: 2–4,9–21; compare Zech. 12: 2–14; 13: 1–2. So also Ezek. 8: 17–18; 9: 1–7, especially Ezek. 9: 4. Compare also Ezek. 10: 2 with Rev. 8: 5, where the final judgments actually fall on the earth, with the same accompaniment, *the fire of the altar cast into the earth,* including the *fire scattered over the city.* So again, Rev. 14: 1, the same 144,000 appear on Zion with the Father's name in their forehead, at the close of the section, the twelfth through fourteenth chapters, concerning the Church and her foes. Not that the saints are exempt from trial: Rev. 7: 14 proves the contrary; but their trials are distinct from the *destroying* judgments that fall on the world; from these they are exempted, as Israel was from the plagues of Egypt, especially from the last, the Israelite doors having the protecting seal of the blood-mark.

REVELATION 8

Rev. 8: 1–13. Seventh Seal. Preparation for the Seven Trumpets. The First Four and the Consequent Plagues.

1. was – *Greek, "came to pass"; "began to be."*
silence in heaven about … half an hour – The last seal having been broken open, the book of God's eternal plan of redemption is opened for the Lamb to read to the blessed ones in heaven. The *half hour's silence* contrasts with the previous jubilant songs of *the great multitude,* taken up by the *angels* (Rev. 7: 9–11). It is the solemn introduction to the employments and enjoyments of the eternal Sabbath-rest of the people of God, commencing with the Lamb's reading the book heretofore sealed up, and which we cannot know till then. In Rev. 10: 4, similarly at the eve of the sounding of the seventh trumpet, when the seven thunders uttered their voices, John is forbidden to write them. The seventh trumpet (Rev. 11: 15–19) winds up God's vast plan of providence and grace in redemption, just as the seventh seal brings it to the same consummation. So also the seventh vial, Rev. 16: 17. Not that the seven seals, the seven trumpets, and the seven vials, though parallel, are repetitions. They each trace the course of divine action up to the grand consummation in which they all meet, under a different aspect. *Thunders, lightnings, an earthquake,* and *voices* close the seven thunders and the seven seals alike (compare Rev. 8: 5, with Rev. 11: 19). Compare at the seventh vial, the voices, thunders, lightnings, and earthquake, Rev. 16: 18. *The half-hour silence* is the brief pause GIVEN TO John between the preceding vision and the following one, implying, on the one hand, the solemn introduction to the eternal sabbatism which is to follow the seventh seal; and, on the other, the

eral selection from the twelve tribes as is here spoken of, or any such designation of twelve thousand from each. There was no occasion – either when Jerusalem was destroyed, or at any other time – on which there were such transactions as are here referred to occurring in reference to the children of Israel.

(b) The language is such as a Christian, who had been by birth and education a Hebrew, would naturally use if he wished to designate the church.

17. And shall lead them unto living fountains of waters. Living fountains refer to running streams, as contrasted with standing water and stagnant pools. The allusion is undoubtedly to the happiness of heaven, represented as fresh and ever-flowing, like streams in the desert. No image of happiness, perhaps, is more vivid, or would be more striking to an Oriental, than that of such fountains flowing in sandy and burning wastes. The word living here must refer to the fact that that happiness will be perennial. These fountains will always bubble; these streams will never dry up. The thirst for salvation will always be gratified; the soul will always be made happy.

And God shall wipe away all tears from their eyes. This is a new image of happiness taken from another place in Isaiah, (Is. 25: 8) "The Lord God will wipe away tears from off all faces." The expression is one of exquisite tenderness and beauty. The poet Burns said that he could never read this without being affected to weeping. Of all the negative descriptions of heaven, there is no one perhaps that would be better adapted to produce consolation than this. This is a world of weeping – a vale of tears. Philosophers have sought a brief definition of man, and have sought in vain. Would there be any better description of him, as representing the reality of his condition here, than to say that he is one who weeps? Who is there of the human family that has not shed a tear? Who that has not wept over the grave of a friend; over his own losses and cares; over his disappointments; over the treatment he has received from others; over his sins; over the follies, vices, and woes of his fellow-men? And what a change would it make in our world if it could be said that hence forward not

another tear would be shed; not a head would ever be bowed again in grief! Yet this is to be the condition of heaven. In that world there is to be no pain, no disappointment, no bereavement. No friend is to lie in dreadful agony on a sick bed; no grave is to be opened to receive a parent, a wife, a child; no gloomy prospect of death is to draw tears of sorrow from the eyes. To that blessed world, when our eyes run down with tears, are we permitted to look forward; and the prospect of such a world should contribute to wipe away our tears here – for all our sorrows will soon be over.

REVELATION 8

1. There was silence in heaven. The whole scene of the vision is laid in heaven, (chapter 4) and John represents things as they seem to be passing there. The meaning here is, that on the opening of this seal, instead of voices, thunderings, tempests, as perhaps was expected from the character of the sixth seal, (Rev. 6: 12, seq.,) and which seemed only to have been suspended for a time, (chapter 7) there was an awful stillness, as if all heaven was reverently waiting for the development. Of course, this is a symbolical representation, and is designed not to represent a pause in the events themselves, but only the impressive and fearful nature of the events which are now to be disclosed.

4. And the smoke of the incense, etc. The smoke caused by the burning incense. John, as he saw this, naturally interpreted it of the prayers of the saints. The meaning of the whole symbol, thus explained, is that, at the time referred to, the anxiety of the church in regard to the events which were about to occur would naturally lead to much prayer. It is not necessary to attempt to verify this by any distinct historical facts, for no one can doubt that, in a time of such impending calamities, the church would be earnestly engaged in devotion. Such has always been the case in times of danger; and it may always be assumed to be true, that when danger threatens, whether it be to the church at large or to an individual Christian, there will be a resort to the throne of grace.

13. And I beheld. My attention was attracted

tains of waters;

11 And the name of the star is called Wormwood: and the third part of the waters became wormwood; and many men died of the waters, because they were made bitter.

12 And the fourth angel sounded, and the third part of the sun was smitten, and the third part of the moon, and the third part of the stars; so as the third part of them was darkened, and the day shone not for a third part of it, and the night likewise.

13 And I beheld, and heard an angel flying through the midst of heaven, saying with a loud voice, Woe, woe, woe, to the inhabiters of the earth by reason of the other voices of the trumpet of the three angels, which are yet to sound!

REVELATION 9

1 And the fifth angel sounded, and I saw a star fall from heaven unto the earth: and to him was given the key of the bottomless pit.

2 And he opened the bottomless pit; and there arose a smoke out of the pit, as the smoke of a great furnace; and the sun and the air were darkened by reason of the smoke of the pit.

3 And there came out of the smoke locusts upon the earth: and unto them was given power, as the scorpions of the earth have power.

4 And it was commanded them that they should not hurt the grass of the earth, neither any green thing, neither any tree; but only those men which have not the seal of God in their foreheads.

5 And to them it was given that they should not kill them, but that they should be tormented five months: and their torment was as the torment of a scorpion, when he striketh a man.

6 And in those days shall men seek death, and shall not find it; and shall desire to die, and death shall flee from them.

7 And the shapes of the locusts were like unto horses prepared unto battle; and on their heads were as it were crowns like gold, and their faces were as the faces of men.

8 And they had hair as the hair of women, and their teeth were as the teeth of lions.

silence which continued during the incense-accompanied prayers which usher in the first of the seven trumpets (Rev. 8: 3–5). In the Jewish temple, musical instruments and singing resounded during the whole time of the offering of the sacrifices, which formed the first part of the service. But at the offering of incense, solemn silence was kept ("My soul *waiteth* upon God," Ps. 62: 1; "is silent," *Margin*; Ps. 65: 1, *Margin*), the people praying secretly all the time. The *half-hour* stillness implies, too, the earnest adoring expectation with which the blessed spirits and the angels await the succeeding unfolding of God's judgments. A *short* space is implied; for even an *hour* is so used (Rev. 17: 12; 18: 10,19).

REVELATION 9

Rev. 9: 1–21. THE FIFTH TRUMPET: THE FALLEN STAR OPENS THE ABYSS WHENCE ISSUE LOCUSTS. THE SIXTH TRUMPET. FOUR ANGELS AT THE EUPHRATES LOOSED.

1. The last three trumpets of the seven are called, from Rev. 8: 13, *the woe-trumpets.*

fall – rather as *Greek,* "fallen." When John saw it, it was not in the act of *falling,* but had *fallen* already. This is a connecting link of this fifth trumpet with Rev. 12: 8–9,12, *"Woe to the inhabiters of the earth,* for the *devil* is *come down,"* &c. Compare Is. 14: 12, "How art thou *fallen from heaven,* Lucifer, son of the morning!"

the bottomless pit – *Greek,* "the pit of the abyss"; *the orifice of the hell* where Satan and his demons dwell.

3. as the scorpions of the earth – as contrasted with the "locusts" which come up *from hell,* and are not "of the earth."

have power – namely, to sting.

4. not hurt the grass … neither … green thing … neither … tree – the food on which they ordinarily prey. Therefore, not natural and ordinary locusts. Their natural instinct is supernaturally restrained to mark the judgment as altogether divine.

in, &c – *Greek,* "*upon* their forehead." Thus this fifth trumpet is proved to follow the *sealing* in Rev. 7: 1–8, under the sixth seal. None of the saints are hurt by these locusts.

5. five months – the ordinary time in the year during which locusts continue their ravages.

their torment – the torment of the sufferers. This fifth verse and Rev. 9: 6 cannot refer to an invading army. For an army would *kill,* and not merely *torment.*

6. shall flee. In Rev. 6: 16, which is at a later stage of God's judgments, the ungodly seek annihilation, not from the torment of their suffering, but from fear of the face of the

by a new vision.

And heard an angel flying, etc. I heard the voice of an angel making this proclamation.

Woe, woe, woe. That is, there will be great woe. The repetition of the word is intensive, and the idea is, that the sounding of the three remaining trumpets would indicate great and fearful calamities. These three are grouped together, as if they pertained to a similar series of events, as the first four had been. The two classes are separated from each other by this interval and by this proclamation – implying that the first series had been completed, and that there would be some interval, either of space or time, before the other series would come upon the world. All that is fairly implied here would be fulfilled by the supposition that the former referred to the West, and that the latter pertained to the East, and were to follow when those should have been completed.

REVELATION 9

2. And he opened the bottomless pit. It is represented before as wholly confined, so that not even the smoke or vapor could escape.

And there arose a smoke out of the pit. Compare Rev. 14: 11. The meaning here is, that the pit, as a place of punishment, or as the abode of the wicked, was filled with burning sulfur, and consequently that it emitted smoke and vapor as soon as opened. The common image of the place of punishment, in the Scriptures, is that of a "lake that burns with fire and brimstone." Compare Rev. 14: 10.

It is not improbable that this image was taken from the destruction of Sodom and Gomorrah, Gen. 19: 24. Such burning sulfur would produce, of course, a dense smoke or vapor; and the idea here is, that the pit had been closed, and that as soon as the door was opened, a dense column escaped that darkened the heavens. The purpose of this is, probably, to indicate the origin of the plague that was about to come upon the world. It would be of such a character that it would appear as if it had been emitted from hell; as if the inmates of that dark world had broke loose upon the earth.

As the smoke of a great furnace. So in Gen. 19: 28, whence probably this image is taken:

"And he looked towards Sodom and Gomorrah, and all the land of the plain, and beheld, and lo, the smoke of the country went up as the smoke of a furnace."

And the sun and the air were darkened, etc. As will be the case when a smoke ascends from a furnace. The meaning here is, that an effect would be produced as if a dense and dark vapor should ascend from the under-world. We are not, of course, to understand this literally.

3. And there came out of the smoke locusts upon the earth. That is, they escaped from the pit with the smoke. At first they were mingled with the smoke so that they were not distinctly seen, but when the smoke cleared away, they appeared in great numbers. The idea seems to be, that the bottomless pit was filled with vapor and with those creatures, and that as soon as the gate was opened the whole contents expanded and burst forth upon the earth. The sun was immediately darkened and the air was full, but the smoke soon cleared away, so that the locusts became distinctly visible. The appearance of these locusts is described in another part of the chapter, Rev. 9: 7, seq. The locust is a voracious insect belonging to the grasshopper or grylli genus, and is a great scourge in Oriental countries. There are ten Hebrew words to denote the locust, and there are numerous references to the destructive habits of the insect in the Scriptures. In fact, from their numbers, and their destructive habits, there was scarcely any other plague that was so much dreaded in the East.

7. And the shapes of the locusts were like unto horses prepared for battle. The resemblance between the locust and the horse, dissimilar as they are in most respects, has been often remarked.

And their faces were as the faces of men. They had a human countenance. This would indicate that, after all, they were human beings that the symbol described, though they had come up from the bottomless pit. Horsemen, in strange apparel, with a strange head-dress, would be all that would be properly denoted by this.

9 And they had breastplates, as it were breastplates of iron; and the sound of their wings was as the sound of chariots of many horses running to battle.

10 And they had tails like unto scorpions, and there were stings in their tails: and their power was to hurt men five months.

11 And they had a king over them, which is the angel of the bottomless pit, whose name in the Hebrew tongue is Abaddon, but in the Greek tongue hath his name Apollyon.

12 One woe is past; and, behold, there come two woes more hereafter.

13 And the sixth angel sounded, and I heard a voice from the four horns of the golden altar which is before God,

14 Saying to the sixth angel which had the trumpet, Loose the four angels which are bound in the great river Euphrates.

15 And the four angels were loosed, which were prepared for an hour, and a day, and a month, and a year, for to slay the third part of men.

16 And the number of the army of the horsemen were two hundred thousand thousand: and I heard the number of them.

17 And thus I saw the horses in the vision, and them that sat on them, having breastplates of fire, and of jacinth, and brimstone: and the heads of the horses were as the heads of lions; and out of their mouths issued fire and smoke and brimstone.

18 By these three was the third part of men killed, by the fire, and by the smoke, and by the brimstone, which issued out of their mouths.

19 For their power is in their mouth, and in their tails: for their tails were like unto serpents, and had heads, and with them they do hurt.

20 And the rest of the men which were not killed by these plagues yet repented not of the works of their hands, that they should not worship devils, and idols of gold, and silver, and brass, and stone, and of wood: which neither can see, nor hear, nor walk:

21 Neither repented they of their murders, nor of their sorceries, nor of their fornication, nor of their thefts.

Lamb before whom they have to stand.

7. crowns – (Nah. 3: 17). Elliott explains this of the *turbans* of Mohammedans. But how could turbans be "like gold?" Alford understands it of the head of the locusts actually ending in a crown-shaped fillet which resembled gold in its material.

as the faces of men – The "as" seems to imply the locusts here do not mean *men*. At the same time they are not natural locusts, for these do not sting *men* (Rev. 9: 5). They must be supernatural.

8. hair of women – long and flowing. An Arabic proverb compares the antlers of locusts to the hair of girls. Ewald in Alford understands the allusion to be to the hair on the legs or bodies of the locusts: compare "rough caterpillars," Jer. 51: 27.

9. as it were breastplates of iron – not such as forms the thorax of the natural locust.

11. Abaddon – that is, *perdition* or *destruction* (Job 26: 6; Prov. 27: 20). The locusts are supernatural instruments in the hands of Satan to torment, and yet not kill, the ungodly, under this fifth trumpet. Just as in the case of godly Job, Satan was allowed to torment with elephantiasis, but not to touch his *life*. In Rev. 9: 20, these two woe-trumpets are expressly called "plagues." Andreas of Cæsarea, ad 500, held, in his *Commentary on Revelation*, that the locusts mean *evil spirits* again permitted to come forth on earth and afflict men with various plagues.

12. hereafter – Greek, "after these things." I agree with Alford and Deut. Burgh, that these *locusts from the abyss* refer to judgments about to fall on the ungodly immediately before Christ's second advent. None of the interpretations which regard them as past, are satisfactory. Joel 1: 2–7; 2: 1–11, is strictly parallel and expressly refers (Joel 2: 11) to THE DAY OF THE Lord great and very terrible: Joel 2: 10 gives the portents accompanying the day of the Lord's coming, *the earth quaking, the heavens trembling, the sun, moon, and stars, withdrawing their shining*: Joel 2: 18,31–32, also point to the immediately succeeding deliverance of Jerusalem: compare also, the previous last conflict in the valley of Jehoshaphat, and the dwelling of God thenceforth in Zion, blessing Judah. Deut. Burgh confines the locust judgment to *the Israelite land*, even as the sealed in Rev. 7: 1–8 are Israelites: not that there are not others sealed as elect in *the earth;* but that, the judgment being confined to *Palestine*, the sealed of *Israel alone* needed to be expressly excepted from the visitation. Therefore, he translates throughout, "the land" (that is, of Israel and Judah), instead of "the earth." I incline to agree with him.

12. One woe is past. The woe referred to in Rev. 9: 1–11. In Rev. 8: 13, three woes are mentioned which were to occur successively, and which were to embrace the whole of the period comprised in the seven seals and the seven trumpets. Under the last of the seals, we have considered four successive periods, referring to events connected with the downfall of the Western empire; and then we have found one important event, worthy of a place in noticing the things which would permanently affect the destiny of the world – the rise, the character, and the conquests of the Saracens. This was referred to by the first woe-trumpet. We enter now on the consideration of the second. This occupies the remainder of the chapter, and in illustrating it the same method will be pursued as heretofore: first, to explain the literal meaning of the words, phrases, and symbols; and then to inquire what events in history, if any, succeeding the former, occurred, which would correspond with the language used.

And, behold, there come two woes more hereafter. Two momentous and important events that will be attended with sorrow to mankind. It cannot be intended that there would be no other evils that would visit mankind; but the eye, in glancing along the future, rested on these as having a special preeminence in affecting the destiny of the church and the world.

19. For their power is in their mouth. That is, as described, in the fire, smoke, and brimstone that proceeded out of their mouths. What struck the seer as remarkable on looking on the symbol was, that this immense destruction seemed to proceed out of their mouths. It was not that they trampled down their enemies; nor that they destroyed them with the sword, the bow, or the spear: it was some new and remarkable power in warfare – in which the destruction seemed to proceed from fire and smoke and sulfur issuing from the mouths of the horses themselves.

And in their tails. The tails of the horses. This, of course, was something unusual and remarkable in horses, for naturally they have no power there. The power of a fish, or a scorpion, or a wasp, may be said to be in their tails, for their strength or their means of defense or of injury are there, but we never think of speaking in this way of horses: It is not necessary, in the interpretation of this, to suppose that the reference is literally to the tails of the horses, any more than it is to suppose that the smoke and fire and brimstone literally proceeded from their mouths. John describes things as they appeared to him in looking at them from a considerable distance. From their mouths the horses belched forth fire, and smoke, and sulfur, and even their tails seemed to be armed for the work of death.

For their tails were like unto serpents. Not like the tails of serpents, but like serpents themselves.

And had heads. That is, there was something remarkable in the position and appearance of their heads. All serpents, of course, have heads; but John saw something unusual in this – or something so peculiar in their heads as to attract special attention. It would seem most probable that the heads of these serpents appeared to extend in every direction – as if the hairs of the horses' tails had been converted into snakes, presenting a most fearful and destructive image.

REVELATION 10

1. And I saw. I had a vision of. The meaning is, that he saw this subsequently to the vision in the previous chapter. The attention is now arrested by a new vision – as if some new dispensation or economy was about to occur in the world.

Another mighty angel. He had before seen the seven angels who were to blow the seven trumpets, (Rev. 8: 2) he had seen six of them successively blow the trumpet; he now sees another angel, different from them, and apparently having no connection with them, coming from heaven to accomplish some important purpose before the seventh angel should give the final blast. The angel is here characterized as a "mighty" angel – *iscuron* – one of strength and power; implying that the work to be accomplished by his mission demanded the interposition of one of the higher orders of the heavenly inhabitants. The coming of an angel at all was indicative of some Divine interposition in human affairs; the fact that he was one

REVELATION 10

1 And I saw another mighty angel come down from heaven, clothed with a cloud: and a rainbow was upon his head, and his face was as it were the sun, and his feet as pillars of fire:

2 And he had in his hand a little book open: and he set his right foot upon the sea, and his left foot on the earth,

3 And cried with a loud voice, as when a lion roareth: and when he had cried, seven thunders uttered their voices.

4 And when the seven thunders had uttered their voices, I was about to write: and I heard a voice from heaven saying unto me, Seal up those things which the seven thunders uttered, and write them not.

5 And the angel which I saw stand upon the sea and upon the earth lifted up his hand to heaven,

6 And sware by him that liveth for ever and ever, who created heaven, and the things that therein are, and the earth, and the things that therein are, and the sea, and the things which are therein, that there should be time no longer:

7 But in the days of the voice of the seventh angel, when he shall begin to sound, the mystery of God should be finished, as he hath declared to his servants the prophets.

8 And the voice which I heard from heaven spake unto me again, and said, Go and take the little book which is open in the hand of the angel which standeth upon the sea and upon the earth.

9 And I went unto the angel, and said unto him, Give me the little book. And he said unto me, Take it, and eat it up; and it shall make thy belly bitter, but it shall be in thy mouth sweet as honey.

10 And I took the little book out of the angel's hand, and ate it up; and it was in my mouth sweet as honey: and as soon as I had eaten it, my belly was bitter.

11 And he said unto me, Thou must prophesy again before many peoples, and nations, and tongues, and kings.

REVELATION 11

1 And there was given me a reed like unto a rod: and the angel stood, saying, Rise, and measure the temple of God, and the altar, and them that worship therein.

2 But the court which is without the

REVELATION 10

Rev. 10: 1–11. VISION OF THE LITTLE BOOK.

As an episode was introduced between the sixth and seventh seals, so there is one here (Rev. 10: 1–11: 14) after the sixth and introductory to the seventh trumpet (Rev. 11: 15, which forms the grand consummation). The Church and her fortunes are the subject of this episode: as the judgments on the unbelieving *inhabiters of the earth* (Rev. 8: 13) were the exclusive subject of the fifth and sixth woe-trumpets. Rev. 6: 11 is plainly referred to in Rev. 10: 6 below; in Rev. 6: 11 the martyrs crying to be avenged were told they must "rest yet for a little season" or *time*: in Rev. 10: 6 here they are assured, "There shall be no longer (any interval of) time"; their prayer shall have no longer to wait, but (Rev. 10: 7) *at the trumpet sounding of the seventh angel* shall be consummated, and *the mystery of God* (His mighty plan heretofore hidden, but then to be revealed) *shall be finished*. The *little open book* (Rev. 10: 2,9–10) is given to John by the angel, with a charge (Rev. 10: 11) that he *must prophesy again concerning* (so the *Greek) peoples, nations, tongues, and kings:* which prophecy (as appears from Rev. 11: 15–19) affects those *peoples, nations, tongues, and kings* only in relation to Israel and the Church, who form the main object of the prophecy.

1. another mighty angel – as distinguished from the *mighty angel* who asked as to the former and more comprehensive book (Rev. 5: 2), "Who is worthy to open the book?"

clothed with a cloud – the emblem of God coming in judgment.

rainbow upon his head – the emblem of covenant mercy to God's people, amidst judgments on God's foes.

feet as pillars of fire – (Rev. 1: 15; Ezek. 1: 7). The angel, as representative of Christ, reflects His glory and bears the insignia attributed in Rev. 1: 15–16; 4: 3, to Christ Himself. The *pillar of fire* by night led Israel through the wilderness, and was the symbol of God's presence.

REVELATION 11

Rev. 11: 1–19. MEASUREMENT OF THE TEMPLE. THE TWO WITNESSES' TESTIMONY: THEIR DEATH, RESURRECTION, AND ASCENSION: THE EARTHQUAKE: THE THIRD WOE: THE SEVENTH TRUMPET USHERS IN CHRIST'S KINGDOM. THANKSGIVING OF THE TWENTY-FOUR ELDERS.

This eleventh chapter is a compendious summary of, and introduction to, the more detailed prophecies of the same events to come in the twelfth through twentieth chapters. Hence we find *anticipatory* allusions to the subsequent prophecies; compare Rev. 11: 7, "the beast that ascendeth out of the bottomless pit" (not mentioned before), with the

of exalted rank, or endowed with vast power, indicated the nature of the work to be done – that it was a work to the execution of which great obstacles existed, and where great power would be needed.

Clothed with a cloud. Encompassed with a cloud, or enveloped in a cloud. This was a symbol of majesty and glory, and is often represented as accompanying the Divine presence, Ex. 16: 9–10. The Savior also ascended in a cloud, Acts 1: 9; and he will again descend in clouds to judge the world, Matt. 24: 30.

Nothing can be argued here as to the purpose for which the angel appeared, from his being encompassed with a cloud; nor can anything be argued from it in respect to the question who this angel was. The fair interpretation is, that this was one of the angels now represented as sent forth on an errand of mercy to man, and coming with appropriate majesty, as the messenger of God.

And a rainbow was upon his head. In Rev. 4: 3, the throne in heaven is represented as encircled by a rainbow.

The rainbow is properly an emblem of peace. Here the symbol would mean that the angel came not for wrath, but for purposes of peace; that he looked with a benign aspect on men, and that the effect of his coming would be like that of sunshine after a storm.

And his face was as it were the sun. Bright like the sun, that is, he looked upon men with (a) an intelligent aspect – as the sun is the source of light; and (b) with benignity – not covered with clouds, or darkened by wrath. The brightness is probably the main idea, but the appearance of the angel would as here represented, naturally suggest the ideas just referred to. As an emblem or symbol, we should regard his appearing as that which was to be followed by knowledge and by prosperity.

In this symbol, then, we have the following things:

(a) An angel – as the messenger of God, indicating that some new communication was to be brought to mankind, or that there would be some interposition in human affairs which might be well represented by the coming of an angel;

(b) the fact that he was "mighty" – indicating that the work to be done required power beyond human strength;

(c) the fact that he came in a cloud – an embassage so grand and magnificent as to make this symbol of majesty proper;

(d) the fact that he was encircled by a rainbow – that the visitation was to be one of peace to mankind; and

(e) the fact that his coming was like the sun – or would diffuse light and peace.

11. Thou must prophesy. The word "prophesy" here is evidently used in the large sense of making known Divine truth in general; not in the comparatively narrow and limited sense in which it is commonly used, as referring merely to the foretelling of future events.

The meaning is, that, as a consequence of becoming possessed of the little volume and its contents, he would be called to proclaim Divine truth, or to make the message of God known to mankind. The direct address is to John himself; but it is evidently not to be understood of him personally. He is represented as seeing the angel; as hearkening to his voice; as listening to the solemn oath which he took; as receiving and eating the volume; and then as prophesying to many people: but the reference is undoubtedly to the far-distant future. If the allusion is to the times of the Reformation, the meaning is, that the end of the world was not, as would be expected, about to occur, but that there was to be an interval long enough to permit the gospel to be proclaimed before "nations, and tongues, and kings;" that in consequence of coming into possession of the "little book," the word of God, the truth was yet to be proclaimed far and wide on the earth.

REVELATION 11

1. And there was given me. He does not say by whom, but the connection would seem to imply that it was by the angel. All this is of course to be regarded as symbolical. The representation undoubtedly pertains to a future age, but the language is such as would be properly addressed to one who had been a Jew, and the imagery employed is such as he would be

temple leave out, and measure it not; for it is given unto the Gentiles: and the holy city shall they tread under foot forty and two months.

3 And I will give power unto my two witnesses, and they shall prophesy a thousand two hundred and threescore days, clothed in sackcloth.

4 These are the two olive trees, and the two candlesticks standing before the God of the earth.

5 And if any man will hurt them, fire proceedeth out of their mouth, and devoureth their enemies: and if any man will hurt them, he must in this manner be killed.

6 These have power to shut heaven, that it rain not in the days of their prophecy: and have power over waters to turn them to blood, and to smite the earth with all plagues, as often as they will.

7 And when they shall have finished their testimony, the beast that ascendeth out of the bottomless pit shall make war against them, and shall overcome them, and kill them.

8 And their dead bodies shall lie in the street of the great city, which spiritually is called Sodom and Egypt, where also our Lord was crucified.

9 And they of the people and kindreds and tongues and nations shall see their dead bodies three days and an half, and shall not suffer their dead bodies to be put in graves.

10 And they that dwell upon the earth shall rejoice over them, and make merry, and shall send gifts one to another; because these two prophets tormented them that dwelt on the earth.

11 And after three days and an half the Spirit of life from God entered into them, and they stood upon their feet; and great fear fell upon them which saw them.

12 And they heard a great voice from heaven saying unto them, Come up hither. And they ascended up to heaven in a cloud; and their enemies beheld them.

13 And the same hour was there a great earthquake, and the tenth part of the city fell, and in the earthquake were slain of men seven thousand: and the remnant were affrighted, and gave glory to the God of heaven.

14 The second woe is past; and, behold, the third woe cometh quickly.

15 And the seventh angel sounded;

detailed accounts, Rev. 13: 1,11; 17: 8; also Rev. 11: 8, "the great city," with Rev. 14: 8; 17: 1,5; 18: 10.

1. the temple – Greek, *"naon"* (**as distinguished from the** Greek, *"hieron,"* **or temple in general**), **the Holy Place,** *"the sanctuary."*

the altar – of incense; for it alone was in "the sanctuary." (*Greek, "naos"*). The measurement of the Holy place seems to me to stand parallel to the sealing of the elect of Israel under the sixth seal. God's elect are symbolized by the sanctuary at Jerusalem (1 Cor. 3: 16–17, where the same Greek word, *"naos,"* occurs for "temple," as here). Literal Israel in Jerusalem, and with the temple restored (Ezek. 40: 3,5, where also the temple is measured with the measuring reed, the forty-first, forty-second, forty-third, and forty-fourth chapters), shall stand at the head of the elect Church. The measuring implies at once the exactness of the proportions of the temple to be restored, and the definite completeness (not one being wanting) of the numbers of the Israelite and of the Gentile elections. The literal temple at Jerusalem shall be the typical forerunner of the heavenly Jerusalem, in which there shall be all temple, and *no* portion exclusively set apart as *temple*. John's accurately drawing the distinction in subsequent chapters between God's servants and those who bear the mark of the beast, is the way whereby he fulfils the direction here given him *to measure the temple*. The fact that the *temple* is distinguished from *them that worship therein,* favors the view that the spiritual temple, the Jewish and Christian Church, is not exclusively meant, but that the literal temple must also be meant. It shall be rebuilt on the return of the Jews to their land. Antichrist shall there put forward his blasphemous claims. The sealed elect of Israel, the head of the elect Church, alone shall refuse his claims. These shall constitute the true sanctuary which is here measured, that is, accurately marked and kept by God, whereas the rest shall yield to his pretensions.

2. unto the Gentiles – In the wider sense, there are meant here "the times of the Gentiles," wherein Jerusalem is *"trodden* down of the Gentiles," as the parallel, Luke 21: 24, proves; for the same word is used here [*Greek, "patein"*], "tread under foot." Compare also Ps. 79: 1; Is. 63: 18.

forty ... two months—(Rev. 13: 5). The same period as Daniel's "time, times, and half" (Rev. 12: 14); and Rev. 11: 3, and Rev. 12: 6, the woman a fugitive in the wilderness "a thousand two hundred and threescore days." In the wider sense, we may either adopt the year-day theory of 1260 years (on which, and the papal rule of 1260 years), or rather, regard the 2300 days (Dan. 8: 14), 1335 days (Dan. 12: 11–12). 1290 days, and 1260 days, as symbolical of the long period of the Gentile times, whether dating from the subversion of the Jewish theocracy at the Babylonian captivity (the

more likely to understand than any other. The language and the imagery are, therefore, taken from the temple, but there is no reason to suppose that it had any literal reference to the temple, or even that John would so understand it. Nor does the language here used prove that the temple was standing at the time when the book was written; for as it is symbolical, it is what would be employed whether the temple were standing or not, and would be as likely to be used in the one case as in the other. It is such language as John, educated as a Jew, and familiar with the temple worship, would be likely to employ if he designed to make a representation pertaining to the church.

A reed. This word properly denotes a plant with a jointed hollow stalk, growing in wet grounds. Then it refers to the stalk as cut for use, as a measuring-stick, as in this place; or a mock scepter, Matt. 27: 29–30; or a pen for writing, 3 John 1: 13. Here it means merely a stick that could be used for measuring.

Like unto a rod. This word means properly a rod, wand, staff, used either for scourging, 1 Cor. 4: 21; or for leaning upon in walking, Matt. 10: 10; or for a scepter, Heb. 1: 8. Here the meaning is, that the reed that was put into his hands was like such a rod or staff in respect to size, and was therefore convenient for handling. The word rod also is used to denote a measuring-pole, Ps. 74: 2; Jer. 10: 16.

3. And I will give power unto my two witnesses. The word "power" is not in the original. The Greek is simply, "I will give;" that is, I will grant to my two witnesses the right, or the power, of prophesying, during the time specified – correctly expressed in the margin, "give unto my two witnesses that they may prophesy." The meaning is not that he would send two witnesses to prophesy, but rather that these were in fact such "witnesses," and that he would during that time permit them to exercise their prophetic gifts, or give them the privilege and the strength to enunciate the truth which they were commissioned to communicate as his "witnesses" to mankind. Some word, then, like power, privilege, opportunity, or boldness, it is necessary to supply in order to complete the sense.

Unto my two witnesses. The word "two"

evidently denotes that the number would be small; and yet it is not necessary to confine it literally to two persons, or to two societies or communities. Perhaps the meaning is, that as, under the law, two witnesses were required, and were enough, to establish any fact, such a number would, during those times, be preserved from apostasy, as would be sufficient to keep up the evidence of truth; to testify against the prevailing abominations, errors, and corruptions; to show what was the real church, and to bear a faithful witness against the wickedness of the world. The law of Moses required that there should be two witnesses on a trial, and this, under that law, was deemed a competent number. See Num. 35: 30.

The essential meaning of this passage then is, that there would be a competent number of witnesses in the case; that is, as many as would be regarded as sufficient to establish the points concerning which they would testify, with perhaps the additional idea that the number would be small. There is no reason for limiting it strictly to two persons, or for supposing that they would appear in pairs, two and two; nor is it necessary to suppose that it refers particularly to two people or nations. The word rendered witnesses – *martuv* that from which we have derived the word martyr. It means properly one who bears testimony, either in a judicial sense, or one who can in any way testify to the truth of what he has seen and known, Luke 24: 48.

11. The Spirit of life from God. The living, or life-giving Spirit that proceeds from God entered into them.

There is evidently allusion here to Gen. 2: 7, where God is spoken of as the Author of life. The meaning is, that they would seem to come to life again, or that effects would follow as if the dead were restored to life. If, when they had been-compelled to cease from prophesying, they should, after the interval here denoted by three days and a half, again prophesy, or their testimony should be again borne to the truth as it had been before, this would evidently be all that would be implied in the language here employed.

Entered into them. Seemed to animate them again.

and there were great voices in heaven, saying, The kingdoms of this world are become the kingdoms of our Lord, and of his Christ; and he shall reign for ever and ever.

16 And the four and twenty elders, which sat before God on their seats, fell upon their faces, and worshipped God,

17 Saying, We give thee thanks, O Lord God Almighty, which art, and wast, and art to come; because thou hast taken to thee thy great power, and hast reigned.

18 And the nations were angry, and thy wrath is come, and the time of the dead, that they should be judged, and that thou shouldest give reward unto thy servants the prophets, and to the saints, and them that fear thy name, small and great; and shouldest destroy them which destroy the earth.

19 And the temple of God was opened in heaven, and there was seen in his temple the ark of his testament: and there were lightnings, and voices, and thunderings, and an earthquake, and great hail.

REVELATION 12

1 And there appeared a great wonder in heaven; a woman clothed with the sun, and the moon under her feet, and upon her head a crown of twelve stars:

2 And she being with child cried, travailing in birth, and pained to be delivered.

3 And there appeared another wonder in heaven; and behold a great red dragon, having seven heads and ten horns, and seven crowns upon his heads.

4 And his tail drew the third part of the stars of heaven, and did cast them to the earth: and the dragon stood before the woman which was ready to be delivered, for to devour her child as soon as it was born.

5 And she brought forth a man child, who was to rule all nations with a rod of iron: and her child was caught up unto God, and to his throne.

6 And the woman fled into the wilderness, where she hath a place prepared of God, that they should feed her there a thousand two hundred and threescore days.

7 And there was war in heaven: Michael and his angels fought against the dragon; and the dragon fought and his angels,

kingdom having been never since restored to Israel), or from the last destruction of Jerusalem under Titus, and extending to the restoration of the theocracy at the coming of Him "whose right it is"; the different epochs marked by the 2300, 1335, 1290, and 1260 days, will not be fully cleared up till the grand consummation; but, meanwhile, our duty and privilege urge us to investigate them. Some one of the epochs assigned by many may be right but as yet it is uncertain. The times of the Gentile monarchies during Israel's *seven times* punishment, will probably, in the narrower sense (Rev. 11: 2), be succeeded by the much more restricted times of the personal Antichrist's tyranny in the Holy Land.

3. I will give power – There is no "power" in the *Greek*, so that "give" must mean "give *commission*," or some such word.

my two witnesses – *Greek*, "*the* two witnesses of me." The article implies that the two were well known at least to John.

prophesy – preach under the inspiration of the Spirit, denouncing judgments against the apostate. They are described by symbol as "the two olive trees" and "the two candlesticks," or *lamp-stands*, "standing before the God of the earth." The reference is to Zech. 4: 3,12, where two *individuals* are meant, Joshua and Zerubbabel, who ministered to the Jewish Church, just as the two olive trees emptied the oil out of themselves into the bowl of the candlestick. So in the final apostasy God will raise up two inspired witnesses to minister encouragement to the afflicted, though sealed, remnant.

REVELATION 12

Rev. 12: 1–17. VISION OF THE WOMAN, HER CHILD, AND THE PERSECUTING DRAGON.

1. This episode (Rev. 12: 1–15: 8) describes *in detail* the persecution of Israel and the elect Church by the beast, which had been *summarily* noticed, Rev. 11: 7–10, and the triumph of the faithful, and torment of the unfaithful. So also the sixteenth through twentieth chapters are the description in detail of the judgment on the beast, &c., summarily noticed in Rev. 11: 13,18. The beast in Rev. 12: 3, &c., is shown not to be alone, but to be the instrument in the hand of a greater power of darkness, Satan. That this is so, appears from the time of the eleventh chapter being the period also in which the events of the twelfth and thirteenth chapters take place, namely, 1260 days (Rev. 12: 6,14; Rev. 13: 5; compare Rev. 11: 2–3).

great – in size and significance.

wonder – *Greek*, "sign": significant of momentous truths.

woman clothed with the sun ... moon under her feet

And they stood upon their feet. As if they had come to life again.

And great fear fell upon them which saw them. This would be true if those who were dead should be literally restored to life; and this would be the effect if those who had given great annoyance by their doctrines, and who had been silenced, and who seemed to be dead, should again, as if animated anew by a Divine power, begin to prophesy, or to proclaim their doctrines to the world. The statement in the symbol is, that those who had put them to death had been greatly troubled by these "witnesses;" that they had sought to silence them, and in order to this had put them to death; that they then greatly rejoiced, as if they would no more be annoyed by them. The fact that they seemed to come to life again would, therefore, fill them with consternation, for they would anticipate a renewal of their troubles, and they would see in this fact evidence of the Divine favor towards those whom they persecuted, and reason to apprehend Divine vengeance on themselves.

19. And the temple of God was opened in heaven. The temple of God at Jerusalem was a pattern of the heavenly one, or of heaven, Heb. 8: 1–5. In that temple God was supposed to reside by the visible symbol of his presence – the Shekinah – in the holy of holies.

Thus God dwells in heaven, as in a holy temple, of which that on earth was the emblem. When it is said that that was "opened in heaven," the meaning is, that John was permitted, as it were, to look into heaven, the abode of God, and to see him in his glory.

And there was seen in his temple the ark of his testament. That is, the very interior of heaven was laid open, and John was permitted to witness what was transacted in its obscurest recesses, and what were its most hidden mysteries. It will be remembered, as an illustration of the correctness of this view of the meaning of the verse, and of its proper place in the divisions of the book – assigning it as the opening verse of a new series of visions – that in the first series of visions we have a statement remarkably similar to this, Rev. 4: 1: "After this I looked, and, behold, a door was opened in heaven;" that is, there was,

as it were, an opening made into heaven, so that John was permitted to look in and see what was occurring there. The same idea is expressed substantially here, by saying that the very interior of the sacred temple where God resides was "opened in heaven," so that John was permitted to look in and see what was transacted in his very presence.

REVELATION 12

3. And there appeared another wonder in heaven. And behold a great red dragon. The word rendered dragon occurs, in the New Testament, only in the book of Revelation, where it is uniformly rendered as here – dragon: Rev. 12: 3–4,7,9,13,16–17; 13: 2,4,11; Rev. 16: 13; 20: 2.

In all these places there is reference to the same thing. The word properly means a large serpent; and the allusion in the word commonly is to some serpent, perhaps such as the anaconda, that resides in a desert or wilderness. Two special characteristics are stated by John in the general description of the dragon: one is, its red color; the other, that it was great. In regard to the former, the dragon was supposed to be black, red, yellow, or ashy. There was doubtless a reason why the one seen by John should be represented as red. As to the other characteristic – great – the idea is, that it was a huge monster, and this would properly refer to some mighty, terrible power which would be properly symbolized by such a monster.

Having seven heads. It was not unusual to attribute many heads to monsters, especially to fabulous monsters, and these greatly increased the terror of the animal. The seven heads would somehow denote power, or seats of power. Such a number of heads increase the terribleness, and, as it were, the vitality of the monster. What is here represented would be as terrible and formidable as such a monster; or such a monster would appropriately represent what was designed to be symbolized here. The number seven may be used here "as a perfect number," or merely to heighten the terror of the image; but it is more natural to suppose that there would be something in what is here represented which would lay the foundation

8 And prevailed not; neither was their place found any more in heaven.

9 And the great dragon was cast out, that old serpent, called the Devil, and Satan, which deceiveth the whole world: he was cast out into the earth, and his angels were cast out with him.

10 And I heard a loud voice saying in heaven, Now is come salvation, and strength, and the kingdom of our God, and the power of his Christ: for the accuser of our brethren is cast down, which accused them before our God day and night.

11 And they overcame him by the blood of the Lamb, and by the word of their testimony; and they loved not their lives unto the death.

12 Therefore rejoice, ye heavens, and ye that dwell in them. Woe to the inhabiters of the earth and of the sea! for the devil is come down unto you, having great wrath, because he knoweth that he hath but a short time.

13 And when the dragon saw that he was cast unto the earth, he persecuted the woman which brought forth the man child.

14 And to the woman were given two wings of a great eagle, that she might fly into the wilderness, into her place, where she is nourished for a time, and times, and half a time, from the face of the serpent.

15 And the serpent cast out of his mouth water as a flood after the woman, that he might cause her to be carried away of the flood.

16 And the earth helped the woman, and the earth opened her mouth, and swallowed up the flood which the dragon cast out of his mouth.

17 And the dragon was wroth with the woman, and went to make war with the remnant of her seed, which keep the commandments of God, and have the testimony of Jesus Christ.

REVELATION 13

1 And I stood upon the sand of the sea, and saw a beast rise up out of the sea, having seven heads and ten horns, and upon his horns ten crowns, and upon his heads the name of blasphemy.

2 And the beast which I saw was like unto a leopard, and his feet were as the feet of a bear, and his mouth as the mouth

– the Church, Israel first, and then the Gentile Church; clothed with Christ, "the Sun of righteousness." "Fair as the moon, clear as the sun." Clothed with the Sun, the Church is the bearer of divine supernatural light in the world. So the seven churches (that is, the Church universal, the woman) are represented as light-bearing *candlesticks* (Rev. 1: 12,20). On the other hand, the *moon*, though standing above the sea and earth, is altogether connected with them and is an earthly light: *sea, earth*, and *moon* represent the worldly element, in opposition to the kingdom of God – heaven, the sun. The moon cannot disperse the darkness and change it into-day: thus she represents the world religion (heathenism) in relation to the supernatural world. The Church has the moon, therefore, under her feet; but the stars, as heavenly lights, on her head. The devil directs his efforts against the stars, the angels of the churches, about hereafter to shine for ever. The twelve stars, the crown around her head, are the twelve tribes of Israel [Auberlen]. The allusions to *Israel* before accord with this: compare Rev. 11: 19, "the temple of God"; "the ark of His testament." The ark lost at the Babylonian captivity, and never since found, is seen in the "temple of God opened in heaven," signifying that God now enters again into covenant with His ancient people. The woman cannot mean, literally, the virgin mother of Jesus, for she did not flee into the wilderness and stay there for 1260 days, while the dragon persecuted the remnant of her seed (Rev. 12: 13–17) [Deut. Burgh]. The *sun, moon,* and *twelve stars,* are emblematical of Jacob, Leah, or else Rachel, and the twelve patriarchs, that is, the Jewish Church: secondarily, the Church universal, having *under her feet*, in due subordination, the ever changing moon, which shines with a borrowed light, emblem of *the Jewish dispensation,* which is now in a position of inferiority, though supporting the woman, and also of the changeful things of this world, and having on her head the crown of twelve stars, the twelve apostles, who, however, are related closely to Israel's twelve tribes. The Church, in passing over into the Gentile world, is (1) persecuted; (2) then seduced, as heathenism begins to react on her. This is the key to the meaning of the symbolic woman, beast, harlot, and false prophet.

REVELATION 13

Rev. 13: 1–18. VISION OF THE BEAST THAT CAME OUT OF THE SEA: THE SECOND BEAST, OUT OF THE EARTH, EXERCISING THE POWER OF THE FIRST BEAST, AND CAUSING THE EARTH TO WORSHIP HIM.

1. upon the sand of the sea – where *the four winds* were to be seen *striving upon the great sea* (Dan. 7: 2).

beast – *Greek,* "wild beast." Man becomes "brutish" when he severs himself from God, the archetype and true ideal,

for the use of this number. There would be something either in the origin of the power; or in the union of various powers now combined in the one represented by the dragon; or in the seat of the power, which this would properly symbolize.

And ten horns. Emblems of power, denoting that, in some respects, there were ten powers combined in this one.

There can be little doubt that John had passages of Daniel (Dan. 7: 7–8,20,24) in his eye, and perhaps as little that the reference is to the same thing. The meaning is, that, in some respects, there would be a tenfold origin or division of the power represented by the dragon.

And seven crowns upon his heads. There is a reference here to some kingly power, and doubtless John had some kingdom or sovereignty in his eye that would be properly symbolized in this manner. The method in which these heads and horns were arranged on the dragon is not stated, and is not material. All that is necessary in the explanation is, that there was something in the power referred to that would be properly represented by the seven heads, and something by the ten horns.

11. And they overcame him. That is, he was foiled in his attempt thus to destroy the church. The reference here, undoubtedly, is primarily to the martyr age, and to the martyr spirit; and the meaning is, that religion had not become extinct by these accusations, as Satan hoped it would be, but lived and triumphed. By their holy lives; by their faithful testimony; by their patient sufferings, they showed that all these accusations were false, and that the religion which they professed was from God, and thus in fact gained a victory over their accuser. Instead of being themselves subdued, Satan himself was vanquished, and the world was constrained to acknowledge that the persecuted religion had a heavenly origin. No design was ever more ineffectual than that of crushing the church by persecution; no victory was ever more signal than that which was gained when it could be said that "the blood of the martyrs is the seed of the church."

By the blood of the Lamb. The Lord Jesus – the Lamb of God.

The blood of Christ was that by which they were redeemed, and it was in virtue of the efficacy of the atonement that they were enabled to achieve the victory.

Christ himself achieved a victory over Satan by his death, and it is in virtue of the victory which he thus achieved that we are now able to triumph over our great foe.

And by the word of their testimony. The faithful testimony which they bore to the truth. That is, they adhered to the truth in their sufferings; they declared their belief in it, even in the pains of martyrdom, and it was by this that they overcame the great enemy; that is, by this that the belief in the gospel was established and maintained in the world. The reference here is to the effects of persecution, and to the efforts of Satan to drive religion from the world by persecution. John says that the result, as he saw it in vision, was that the persecuted church bore a faithful testimony to the truth, and that the great enemy was overcome.

And they loved not their lives unto the death. They did not so love their lives that they were unwilling to die as martyrs. They did not shrink back when threatened with death, but remained firm in their attachment to their Savior, and left their dying testimony to the truth and power of religion. It was by these means that Christianity was established in the world, and John, in the scene before us, saw it thus triumphant, and saw the angels and the redeemed in heaven celebrating the triumph. The result of the attempts to destroy the Christian religion by persecution demonstrated that it was to triumph. No more mighty power could be employed to crush it than was employed by the Roman emperors; and when it was seen that Christianity could survive those efforts to crush it, it was certain that it was destined to live for ever.

REVELATION 13

1. And saw a beast. Daniel saw four in succession, (Dan. 7: 3–7,) all different, yet succeeding each other; John saw two in succession, yet strongly resembling each other, Rev. 13: 1,11. The beast here is evidently a symbol of some power or kingdom that would arise in future times.

of a lion: and the dragon gave him his power, and his seat, and great authority.

3 And I saw one of his heads as it were wounded to death; and his deadly wound was healed: and all the world wondered after the beast.

4 And they worshipped the dragon which gave power unto the beast: and they worshipped the beast, saying, Who is like unto the beast? who is able to make war with him?

5 And there was given unto him a mouth speaking great things and blasphemies; and power was given unto him to continue forty and two months.

6 And he opened his mouth in blasphemy against God, to blaspheme his name, and his tabernacle, and them that dwell in heaven.

7 And it was given unto him to make war with the saints, and to overcome them: and power was given him over all kindreds, and tongues, and nations.

8 And all that dwell upon the earth shall worship him, whose names are not written in the book of life of the Lamb slain from the foundation of the world.

9 If any man have an ear, let him hear.

10 He that leadeth into captivity shall go into captivity: he that killeth with the sword must be killed with the sword. Here is the patience and the faith of the saints.

11 And I beheld another beast coming up out of the earth; and he had two horns like a lamb, and he spake as a dragon.

12 And he exerciseth all the power of the first beast before him, and causeth the earth and them which dwell therein to worship the first beast, whose deadly wound was healed.

13 And he doeth great wonders, so that he maketh fire come down from heaven on the earth in the sight of men,

14 And deceiveth them that dwell on the earth by the means of those miracles which he had power to do in the sight of the beast; saying to them that dwell on the earth, that they should make an image to the beast, which had the wound by a sword, and did live.

15 And he had power to give life unto the image of the beast, that the image of the beast should both speak, and cause that as many as would not worship the image of the beast should be killed.

16 And he causeth all, both small and great, rich and poor, free and bond, to

in whose image he was first made, which ideal is realized by the man Christ Jesus. Hence, the world powers seeking their own glory, and not God's, are represented as *beasts*; and Nebuchadnezzar, when in self-deification he forgot that "the Most High ruleth in the kingdom of men," was driven among the beasts. In Dan. 7: 4–7 there are *four* beasts: here the *one* beast expresses the sum-total of the God-opposed world power viewed in its universal development, not restricted to one manifestation alone, as Rome. This first beast expresses the world power attacking the Church more from without; the second, which is a revival of, and minister to, the first, is the world power as *the false prophet* corrupting and destroying the Church from within.

out of the sea – out of the troubled waves of *peoples, multitudes, nations, and tongues*. The *earth* (Rev. 13: 11), on the other hand, means the consolidated, ordered world of nations, with its culture and learning.

2. leopard ... bear ... lion – This beast unites in itself the God-opposed characteristics of the three preceding kingdoms, resembling respectively the *leopard, bear,* and *lion*. It rises up out *of the sea*, as Daniel's four beasts, and has *ten horns*, as Daniel's fourth beast, *and seven heads*, as Daniel's four beasts had in all, namely, one on the first, one on the second, four on the third, and one on the fourth. Thus it represents comprehensively in one figure *the world power* (which in Daniel is represented by four) *of all times and places*, not merely of one period and one locality, viewed as opposed to God; just as the *woman* is the Church of all ages. This view is favored also by the fact, that the beast is the vicarious representative of Satan, who similarly has *seven heads* and *ten horns*: a general description of his universal power in all ages and places of the world. Satan appears as a serpent, as being the archetype of the beast nature (Rev. 12: 9). "If the seven heads meant merely seven Roman emperors, one cannot understand why they alone should be mentioned in the original image of Satan, whereas it is perfectly intelligible if we suppose them to represent Satan's power on earth viewed collectively" [Auberlen].

3. wounded ... healed – twice again repeated emphatically (Rev. 13: 12,14); compare Rev. 17: 8,11, "the beast that *was, and is not, and shall ascend* out of the bottomless pit" (compare Rev. 13: 11); the Germanic empire, the seventh head (revived in *the eighth*), as yet future in John's time (Rev. 17: 10). Contrast the change whereby Nebuchadnezzar, being humbled from his self-deifying pride, was converted from his *beast-*like form and character to MAN'S form and true position towards God; symbolized by his *eagle wings being plucked,* and himself made to stand upon his feet as a *man* (Dan. 7: 4). Here, on the contrary, the *beast's* head is not changed into a *human* head, but receives a deadly wound, that is, the world

Having seven heads. So also the dragon is represented in Rev. 12: 3.

The representation there is of Satan, as the source of all the power lodged in the two beasts that John subsequently saw. In Rev. 17: 9, referring substantially to the same vision, it is said that "the seven heads are seven mountains;" and that there can be no difficulty, therefore, in referring this to the seven hills on which the city of Rome was built, and consequently this must be regarded as designed, in some way, to be a representation of Rome.

11. And I beheld another beast. This was so distinct from the first that its characteristics could be described, though, there was, in many points, a strong resemblance between them.

And he spake as a dragon. The meaning here is, that he spake in a harsh, haughty, proud, arrogant tone – as we should suppose a dragon would if he had the power of utterance. The general sense is, that while this "beast" had, in one respect – in its resemblance to a lamb – the appearance of great gentleness, meekness, and kindness, it had, in another respect, a haughty, imperious, and arrogant spirit.

13. And he doeth great wonders. Signs – the word commonly employed to denote miracles. The representation here is, that the power referred to by the second beast would found its claim on pretended miracles, and would accomplish an effect on the world as if it actually did work miracles.

That he maketh fire come down from heaven on the earth in the sight of men. That is, he pretends to do this; he accomplishes an effect as if he did it. It is not necessary to suppose that he actually did this, any more than it is to suppose that he actually performed the other pretended miracles referred to in other places. John describes him as he saw him in the vision; and he saw him laying claim to this power, and actually producing an effect as if by a miracle he actually made fire descend from heaven upon the earth. This is to be understood as included in what the apostle Paul (2 Thess. 2: 9) calls "signs and lying wonders," as among the things by which the "man of sin and the son of perdition" would be character-

ized, and by which he would be sustained.

Why this particular pretended miracle is specified here is not certain. It may be because this would be among the most striking and impressive of the pretended miracles wrought – as if lying beyond all human power – as Elijah made fire come down from heaven to consume the sacrifice (1 Kgs. 18: 37–38), and as the apostles proposed to do on the Samaritans (Luke 9: 54), as if fire were called down on them from heaven. The phrase "in the sight of men" implies that this would be done publicly, and is such language as would be used of pretended miracles designed for purposes of ostentation.

15. And he had power to give life unto the image of the beast. That is, that image of the beast would be naturally powerless, or would have no life in itself. The second beast, however, had power to impart life to it, so that it would be invested with authority, and would exercise that authority in the manner specified.

That the image of the beast should both speak. Should give signs of life; should issue authoritative commands. The speaking here referred to pertains to that which is immediately specified, in issuing a command that they who "would not worship the image of the beast should be killed."

And cause that as many as would not worship the image of the beast. Would not honor it, or acknowledge its authority.

16. And he caused all. He claims jurisdiction, in the matters here referred to, over all classes of persons, and compels them to do his will.

Both small and great. All these expressions are designed to denote universality – referring to various divisions into which the human family may be regarded as divided. One of those divisions is into "small and great;" that is, into young and old; those small in stature and those large in stature; those of humble, and those of elevated rank.

Rich and poor. Another way of dividing the human race, and denoting here, as in the former case, all – for it is a common method, in speaking of mankind, to describe them as "the rich and poor."

receive a mark in their right hand, or in their foreheads:

17 And that no man might buy or sell, save he that had the mark, or the name of the beast, or the number of his name.

18 Here is wisdom. Let him that hath understanding count the number of the beast: for it is the number of a man; and his number is Six hundred threescore and six.

REVELATION 14

1 And I looked, and, lo, a Lamb stood on the mount Sion, and with him an hundred forty and four thousand, having his Father's name written in their foreheads.

2 And I heard a voice from heaven, as the voice of many waters, and as the voice of a great thunder: and I heard the voice of harpers harping with their harps:

3 And they sung as it were a new song before the throne, and before the four beasts, and the elders: and no man could learn that song but the hundred and forty and four thousand, which were redeemed from the earth.

4 These are they which were not defiled with women; for they are virgins. These are they which follow the Lamb whithersoever he goeth. These were redeemed from among men, being the firstfruits unto God and to the Lamb.

5 And in their mouth was found no guile: for they are without fault before the throne of God.

6 And I saw another angel fly in the midst of heaven, having the everlasting gospel to preach unto them that dwell on the earth, and to every nation, and kindred, and tongue, and people,

7 Saying with a loud voice, Fear God, and give glory to him; for the hour of his judgment is come: and worship him that made heaven, and earth, and the sea, and the fountains of waters.

8 And there followed another angel, saying, Babylon is fallen, is fallen, that great city, because she made all nations drink of the wine of the wrath of her fornication.

9 And the third angel followed them, saying with a loud voice, If any man worship the beast and his image, and receive his mark in his forehead, or in his hand,

10 The same shall drink of the wine of the wrath of God, which is poured

kingdom which this head represents does not truly turn to God, but for a time its God-opposed character remains paralyzed ("as it were slain"; the very words marking the beast's outward resemblance to the Lamb, "as it were slain". Compare also the second beast's resemblance to the *Lamb*, Rev. 13: 11). Though seemingly *slain* (*Greek* for "wounded"), it remains the beast still, to rise again in another form (Rev. 13: 11).

REVELATION 14

Rev. 14: 1–20. THE LAMB SEEN ON ZION WITH THE 144,000. THEIR SONG. THE GOSPEL PROCLAIMED BEFORE THE END BY ONE ANGEL: THE FALL OF BABYLON, BY ANOTHER: THE DOOM OF THE BEAST WORSHIPPERS, BY A THIRD. THE BLESSEDNESS OF THE DEAD IN THE LORD. THE HARVEST. THE VINTAGE.

In contrast to the beast, false prophet, and apostate Church (Rev. 13: 1–18) and introductory to the announcement of judgments about to descend on them and the world (Rev. 14: 8–11, anticipatory of Rev. 18: 2–6), stand here the redeemed, "the divine kernel of humanity, the positive fruits of the history of the world and the Church" [Auberlen]. The fourteenth through sixteenth chapters describe the preparations for the Messianic judgment. As the fourteenth chapter begins with *the* 144,000 *of Israel* (compare Rev. 7: 4–8, no longer exposed to trial as then, but now triumphant), so the fifteenth chapter begins with those who have *overcome* from among the Gentiles (compare Rev. 15: 1–5 with Rev. 7: 9–17); the two classes of elect forming together the whole company of transfigured saints who shall reign with Christ.

1. Lamb ... on ... Sion – having left His position "in the midst of the throne," and now taking His stand *on Sion.*
in – *Greek,* "upon." God's and Christ's *name* here answers to the *seal* "upon their foreheads" in Rev. 7: 3. As the 144,000 of Israel are "the first-fruits" (Rev. 14: 4), so "the harvest" (Rev. 14: 15) is the general assembly of Gentile saints to be translated by Christ as His first act in assuming His kingdom, prior to His judgment (Rev. 16: 17–21, the last seven vials) on the Antichristian world, in executing which His saints shall share. As Noah and Lot were taken seasonably out of the *judgment,* but exposed to the *trial* to the last moment [Deut. Burgh], so those who shall reign with Christ shall first suffer with Him, being delivered out of the *judgments,* but not out of the *trials.* The Jews are meant by "the saints of the Most High": against them Antichrist makes war, *changing their times and laws;* for true Israelites cannot join in the idolatry of the beast, any more than true Christians. The common affliction will draw closely together, in opposing the beast's

Free and bond. Another method still of dividing the human race embracing all – for all the dwellers upon the earth are either free or bond. These various forms of expression, therefore, are designed merely to denote, in an emphatic manner, universality. The idea is, that, in the matter referred to, none were exempt, either on account of their exalted rank, or on account of their humble condition; either because they were so mighty as to be beyond control, or so mean and humble as to be beneath notice.

18. Here is wisdom. That is, in what is stated respecting the name and the number of the name of the beast. The idea is, either that there would be need of peculiar sagacity in determining what the "number" of the "beast" or of his "name" was, or that peculiar "wisdom" was shown by the fact that the number could be thus expressed. The language used in the verse would lead the reader to suppose that the attempt to make out the "number" was not absolutely hopeless, but that the number was so far enigmatical as to require much skill in determining its meaning. It may also be implied that, for some reason, there was true "wisdom" in designating the name by this number, either because a more direct and explicit statement might expose him who made it to persecution, and it showed practical wisdom thus to guard against this danger; or because there was "wisdom" or skill shown in the fact that a number could be found which would thus correspond with the name.

Count the number of the beast. The word here means compute; that is, ascertain the exact import of the number, so as to identify the beast. The "number" is that which is immediately specified, "six hundred threescore and six" – 666. The phrase "the number of the beast" means, that somehow this number was so connected with the beast, or would so represent its name or character, that the "beast" would be identified by its proper application. The mention in Rev. 13: 17 of "the name of the beast," and "the number of his name," shows that this "number" was somehow connected with his proper designation, so that by this he would be identified. The plain meaning is, that the number 666 would be so connected with

his name, or with that which would properly designate him, that it could be determined who was meant by finding that number in his name or in his proper designation. This is the exercise of the skill or wisdom to which the writer here refers: substantially that which is required in the solution of a riddle or a conundrum.

REVELATION 14

1 And I looked. My attention was drawn to a new vision. The eye was turned away from the beast and his image to the heavenly world – the Mount Zion above.

Stood on the mount Sion. That is, in heaven.

Zion, literally the southern hill in the city of Jerusalem, was a name also given to the whole city; and, as that was the seat of the Divine worship on earth, it became an emblem of heaven – the dwelling-place of God. The scene of the vision here is laid in heaven, for it is a vision of the ultimate triumph of the redeemed, designed to sustain the church in view of the trials that had already come upon it, and of those which were yet to come.

And with him an hundred forty and four thousand. These are evidently the same persons that were seen in the vision recorded in Rev. 7: 3–8, and the representation is made for the same purpose – to sustain the church in trial, with the certainty of its future glory.

Having his Father's name written in their foreheads. Showing that they were his. In Rev. 7: 3, it is merely said that they were "sealed in their foreheads" The passage here shows how they were sealed. They had the name of God so stamped or marked on their foreheads as to show that they belonged to him.

10. The same shall drink of the wine of the wrath of God. The **wine of the wrath of God** is the cup in the hand of the Lord, which when drunk makes them reel and fall. The image would seem to have been taken from the act of holding out a cup of poison to a condemned man that he might drink and die.

Which is poured out without mixture. Without being diluted with water; that is, in its full strength. In other words, there would

out without mixture into the cup of his indignation; and he shall be tormented with fire and brimstone in the presence of the holy angels, and in the presence of the Lamb:

11 And the smoke of their torment ascendeth up for ever and ever: and they have no rest day nor night, who worship the beast and his image, and whosoever receiveth the mark of his name.

12 Here is the patience of the saints: here are they that keep the commandments of God, and the faith of Jesus.

13 And I heard a voice from heaven saying unto me, Write, Blessed are the dead which die in the Lord from henceforth: Yea, saith the Spirit, that they may rest from their labours; and their works do follow them.

14 And I looked, and behold a white cloud, and upon the cloud one sat like unto the Son of man, having on his head a golden crown, and in his hand a sharp sickle.

15 And another angel came out of the temple, crying with a loud voice to him that sat on the cloud, Thrust in thy sickle, and reap: for the time is come for thee to reap; for the harvest of the earth is ripe.

16 And he that sat on the cloud thrust in his sickle on the earth; and the earth was reaped.

17 And another angel came out of the temple which is in heaven, he also having a sharp sickle.

18 And another angel came out from the altar, which had power over fire; and cried with a loud cry to him that had the sharp sickle, saying, Thrust in thy sharp sickle, and gather the clusters of the vine of the earth; for her grapes are fully ripe.

19 And the angel thrust in his sickle into the earth, and gathered the vine of the earth, and cast it into the great winepress of the wrath of God.

20 And the winepress was trodden without the city, and blood came out of the winepress, even unto the horse bridles, by the space of a thousand and six hundred furlongs.

REVELATION 15

1 And I saw another sign in heaven, great and marvelous, seven angels having the seven last plagues; for in them is filled up the wrath of God.

worship, the Old Testament and New Testament people of God. Thus the way is paved for Israel's conversion. This last utter *scattering of the holy people's power* leads them, under the Spirit, to seek Messiah, and to cry at His approach, "Blessed is He that cometh in the name of the Lord."

2. voice of many waters – as is the voice of Himself, such also is the voice of His people.

3. new song – (Rev. 5: 9–10). The song is that of victory after conflict with the dragon, beast, and false prophet: never sung before, for such a conflict had never been fought before; therefore *new*: till now the kingdom of *Christ* on earth had been usurped; they sing the new song in anticipation of His blood-bought kingdom with His saints.

four beasts – rather, as *Greek*, "four living creatures." The harpers and singers evidently include the 144,000: so the parallel proves (Rev. 15: 2–3), where the same act is attributed to *the general company of the saints*, the *harvest* (Rev. 14: 15) from all nations.

redeemed – literally, "purchased." Not even the angels can learn that song, for they know not *experimentally* what it is to have "come out of the great tribulation, and washed their robes white in the blood of the Lamb" (Rev. 7: 14).

4. virgins – spiritually (Matt. 25: 1); in contrast to the apostate Church, Babylon (Rev. 14: 8), spiritually "a harlot" (Rev. 17: 1–5; Is.a 1: 21; contrast 2 Cor. 11: 2; Eph. 5: 25–27). Their not being *defiled with women* means they were not led astray from Christian faithfulness by the tempters who jointly constitute the spiritual "harlot."

follow the Lamb whithersoever he goeth – in glory, being especially near His person; the fitting reward of their following Him so fully on earth.

5. without fault – *Greek*, "blameless": in respect to the sincerity of their fidelity to Him. Not absolutely, and in themselves *blameless*; but regarded as such on the ground of His righteousness in whom alone they trusted, and whom they faithfully served by His Spirit in them. The allusion seems to be to Ps. 15: 1–2. Compare Rev. 14: 1, "*stood on* Mount Sion."

REVELATION 15

Rev. 15: 1–8. THE LAST SEVEN VIALS OF PLAGUES: SONG OF THE VICTORS OVER THE BEAST.

1. the seven last plagues – *Greek*, "seven plagues which are the last."

is filled up – literally, "was finished," or "consummated": the prophetical past for the future, the future being to God as though it were past, so sure of accomplishment is His word. This verse is the summary of the vision that follows:

be no mitigation of the punishment.

Into the cup of his indignation. The cup held in his hand and given them to drink. This is expressive of his indignation, as it causes them to reel and fall. The sentiment here is substantially the same, though in another form, as that which is expressed in 2 Thess. 2: 12.

And he shall be tormented. Shall be punished in a manner that would be well represented by being burned with fire and brimstone.

With fire and brimstone. As if with burning sulfur. The imagery is taken from the destruction of Sodom and Gomorrah, Gen. 19: 24. The common representation of the punishment of the wicked is, that it will be in the manner here represented, Matt. 5: 22.

20. **And the wine-press was trodden without the city.** The representation was made as if it were outside of the city; that is, the city of Jerusalem, for that is represented as the abode of the holy. The word trodden refers to the manner in which wine was usually prepared, by being trodden by the feet of men.

The wine-press was usually in the vineyard – not in a city – and this is the representation here. As appearing to the eye of John, it was not within the walls of any city, but standing without. And blood came out of the wine-press. The representation is, that there would be a great destruction which would be well represented by the juice flowing from a wine-press.

Even unto the horse-bridles. Deep – as blood would be in a field of slaughter where it would come up to the very bridles of the horses. The idea is, that there would be a great slaughter.

By the space of a thousand and six hundred furlongs. That is, two hundred miles; covering a space of two hundred miles square – a lake of blood. This is designed to represent a great slaughter.

REVELATION 15

1. **And I saw another sign in heaven.** Another wonder or extraordinary symbol. The word sign here is the same which in Rev. 12: 1,3; 13:

13, is rendered wonder and wonders, and in Rev. 13: 14; 16: 14; 19: 20, miracles. The word is not elsewhere found in the book of Revelation, though it is of frequent occurrence in other parts of the New Testament.

Here it is used to denote something wonderful or marvelous. This is represented as appearing in heaven, for the judgments that were to fall upon the world were to come thence.

Great and marvelous. Great and wonderful, or fitted to excite admiration – *yaumaston*. The subsequent statements fully justify this, and show that the vision was one of portentous character, and that was fitted to hold the mind in astonishment.

Having the seven last plagues. The article here, "the seven last plagues," would seem to imply that the plagues referred to had been before specified, or that it would be at once understood what is referred to. These plagues, however, have not been mentioned before, and the reason why the article is used here seems to be this: the destruction of this great Antichristian power had been distinctly mentioned, Revelation 14. That might be spoken of as a thing now well known, and the mention of it would demand the article; and as that was well known, and would demand the article, so any allusion to it, or description of it, might be spoken of in the same manner, as a thing that was definite and fixed, and hence the mention of the plagues by which it was to be accomplished would be referred to in the same manner. The word plagues means properly a wound caused by a stripe or blow, and is frequently rendered stripe and stripes, Luke 12: 48; Acts 16: 23,33; 2 Cor. 6: 5; 11: 23.

It does not elsewhere occur in the New Testament except in the book of Revelation. In this book it is rendered wound in Rev. 13: 3,12,14; and plagues in Rev. 9: 20; 11: 6; 15: 1,6,8; 16: 9,21; 18: 4,8; 21: 9; 22: 18.

It does not occur elsewhere. The secondary meaning of the word, and the meaning in the passage before us, is a stripe or blow inflicted by God; calamity or punishment. The word "last" means those under which the order of things here referred to would terminate; the winding up of the affairs respecting the beast

2 And I saw as it were a sea of glass mingled with fire: and them that had gotten the victory over the beast, and over his image, and over his mark, and over the number of his name, stand on the sea of glass, having the harps of God.

3 And they sing the song of Moses the servant of God, and the song of the Lamb, saying, Great and marvelous are thy works, Lord God Almighty; just and true are thy ways, thou King of saints.

4 Who shall not fear thee, O Lord, and glorify thy name? for thou only art holy: for all nations shall come and worship before thee; for thy judgments are made manifest.

5 And after that I looked, and, behold, the temple of the tabernacle of the testimony in heaven was opened:

6 And the seven angels came out of the temple, having the seven plagues, clothed in pure and white linen, and having their breasts girded with golden girdles.

7 And one of the four beasts gave unto the seven angels seven golden vials full of the wrath of God, who liveth for ever and ever.

8 And the temple was filled with smoke from the glory of God, and from his power; and no man was able to enter into the temple, till the seven plagues of the seven angels were fulfilled.

REVELATION 16

1 And I heard a great voice out of the temple saying to the seven angels, Go your ways, and pour out the vials of the wrath of God upon the earth.

2 And the first went, and poured out his vial upon the earth; and there fell a noisome and grievous sore upon the men which had the mark of the beast, and upon them which worshipped his image.

3 And the second angel poured out his vial upon the sea; and it became as the blood of a dead man: and every living soul died in the sea.

4 And the third angel poured out his vial upon the rivers and fountains of waters; and they became blood.

5 And I heard the angel of the waters say, Thou art righteous, O Lord, which art, and wast, and shalt be, because thou hast judged thus.

6 For they have shed the blood of saints and prophets, and thou hast given

the angels do not actually receive the vials till Rev. 15: 7; but here, in Rev. 15: 1, by anticipation they are spoken of as *having* them. There are no more plagues after these until the Lord's coming in judgment. The destruction of Babylon (Rev. 18: 2) is the last: then in Rev. 19: 11–16 He appears.

2. sea of glass – Answering to the molten sea or great brazen laver before the mercy seat of the earthly temple, for the purification of the priests; typifying the baptism of water and the Spirit of all who are made kings and priests unto God.

mingled with fire – answering to the *baptism* on earth *with fire*, that is, fiery trial, as well as with the Holy Ghost, which Christ's people undergo to purify them, as gold is purified of its dross in the furnace.

harps of God – in the hands of these heavenly *virgins*, infinitely surpassing the timbrels of Miriam and the Israelitesses.

3. song of Moses ... and ... the Lamb – The New Testament song of the Lamb (that is, the song which the Lamb shall lead, as being "the Captain of our salvation," just as Moses was leader of the Israelites, the song in which those who conquer through Him [Rom. 8: 37] shall join, Rev. 12: 11) is the antitype to the triumphant Old Testament song of Moses and the Israelites at the Red Sea (Ex. 15: 1–21). The Churches of the Old and New Testament are essentially one in their conflicts and triumphs.

REVELATION 16

Rev. 16: 1–21. THE SEVEN VIALS AND THE CONSEQUENT PLAGUES.

The trumpets shook the world kingdoms in a longer process; the vials destroy with a swift and sudden overthrow the kingdom of "the beast" in particular who had invested himself with the world kingdom. The Hebrews thought the Egyptian plagues to have been inflicted with but an interval of a month between them severally [Bengel, referring to Seder Olam]. As Moses took ashes from an earthly common furnace, so angels, as priestly ministers in the heavenly temple, take holy fire in sacred vials or bowls, from the heavenly altar to pour down (compare Rev. 8: 5). The same heavenly altar which would have kindled the sweet incense of prayer bringing down blessing upon earth, by man's sin kindles the fiery descending curse. Just as the river Nile, which ordinarily is the source of Egypt's fertility, became blood and a curse through Egypt's sin.

1. a great voice – namely, God's. These seven vials (the detailed expansion of *the vintage*, Rev. 14: 18–20) being called "the last," must belong to the period just when the term of

and his image – not necessarily the closing of the affairs of the world. Important events were to occur subsequent to the destruction of this Antichristian power, but these were the plagues which would come finally upon the beast and his image, and which would terminate the existence of this formidable enemy.

For in them is filled up the wrath of God. That is, in regard to the beast and his image. All the expressions of the Divine indignation towards that oppressive and persecuting power will be completed or exhausted by the pouring out of the contents of these vials.

2. And I saw as it were a sea of glass. In Rev. 4: 6, a similar vision is recorded – "And before the throne there was a sea of glass, like unto a crystal."

The sea of glass here means a sea, clear, pellucid, like glass: an expanse that seemed to be made of glass. There it was entirely clear; here it is mingled with fire.

Mingled with fire. That is, a portion of the sea was red like fire. It was not all clear and pellucid, as in Rev. 4: 6, but it was, as it were, a tesselated expanse, composed in part of what seemed to be glass, and in part of a material of a red or fiery color. In the former case (Rev. 4: 6), the emblem was designed to represent the pure worship of heaven without reference to any other symbolic design, and hence the sea is wholly clear and pellucid; here, in connection with the purpose of furnishing an appropriate symbol of the Divine Majesty, there is united the idea of punishment on the foes of God, represented by the fiery or red color. If it is proper, from conjecture, to suggest the meaning of this as an emblem, it would be that the foundation – the main element – of all the Divine dealings is justice or holiness – represented by the portion of the sea that seemed to be glass; and that there was, in this case, intermingled with that, the image of wrath or anger – represented by the portion that was fiery or red. The very sight of the pavement, therefore, on which they stood when worshipping God, would keep before their minds impressive views of his character and dealings. And them that had gotten the victory over the beast. Rev. 13: 11. That is, they who had gained a victory in times of persecution and tempta-

tion; or they whom the "beast" had not been able, by arts or arms, to subdue.

REVELATION 16

1. And I heard a great voice out of the temple. A loud voice out of the temple as seen in heaven, and that came, therefore, from the very presence of God.

Saying to the seven angels. That had the seven vials of wrath.

Go your ways. Your respective ways, to the fulfillment of the task assigned to each.

And pour out the vials of the wrath of God. Empty those vials; cause to come upon the earth the plagues indicated by their contents. The order in which this was to be done is not intimated. It seems to be supposed that that would be understood by each.

Upon the earth. The particular part of the earth is not here specified, but it should not be inferred that it was to be upon the earth in general, or that there were any calamities in consequence of this pouring out of the vials of wrath, to spread over the whole world. The subsequent statements show what parts of the earth were particularly to be affected.

2. And the first went. Went forth from heaven, where the seat of the vision was laid.

And poured out his vial upon the earth. That is, upon the land, in contradistinction from the sea, the rivers, the air, the seat of the beast, the sun, as represented in the other vials. In Rev. 16: 1, the word earth is used in the general sense to denote this world as distinguished from heaven; in this verse it is used in the specific sense, to denote land as distinguished from other things.

In many respects there is a strong resemblance between the pouring out of these seven vials, and the sounding of the seven trumpets, in chapters 8 and 9, though they refer to different events. In the sounding of the first trumpet (Rev. 8: 7), it was the earth that was particularly affected, in contradistinction from the sea, the fountains, and the sun: "The first angel sounded, and there followed hail and fire mingled with blood, and they were east upon the earth." Compare Rev. 8: 8,10,12.

And there fell a noisome and grievous

them blood to drink; for they are worthy.

7 And I heard another out of the altar say, Even so, Lord God Almighty, true and righteous are thy judgments.

8 And the fourth angel poured out his vial upon the sun; and power was given unto him to scorch men with fire.

9 And men were scorched with great heat, and blasphemed the name of God, which hath power over these plagues: and they repented not to give him glory.

10 And the fifth angel poured out his vial upon the seat of the beast; and his kingdom was full of darkness; and they gnawed their tongues for pain,

11 And blasphemed the God of heaven because of their pains and their sores, and repented not of their deeds.

12 And the sixth angel poured out his vial upon the great river Euphrates; and the water thereof was dried up, that the way of the kings of the east might be prepared.

13 And I saw three unclean spirits like frogs come out of the mouth of the dragon, and out of the mouth of the beast, and out of the mouth of the false prophet.

14 For they are the spirits of devils, working miracles, which go forth unto the kings of the earth and of the whole world, to gather them to the battle of that great day of God Almighty.

15 Behold, I come as a thief. Blessed is he that watcheth, and keepeth his garments, lest he walk naked, and they see his shame.

16 And he gathered them together into a place called in the Hebrew tongue Armageddon.

17 And the seventh angel poured out his vial into the air; and there came a great voice out of the temple of heaven, from the throne, saying, It is done.

18 And there were voices, and thunders, and lightnings; and there was a great earthquake, such as was not since men were upon the earth, so mighty an earthquake, and so great.

19 And the great city was divided into three parts, and the cities of the nations fell: and great Babylon came in remembrance before God, to give unto her the cup of the wine of the fierceness of his wrath.

20 And every island fled away, and the mountains were not found.

21 And there fell upon men a great

the beast's power has expired (whence reference is made in them all to the worshippers of the beast as the objects of the judgments), close to the end or coming of the Son of man. The first four are distinguished from the last three, just as in the case of the seven seals and the seven trumpets. The first four are more general, affecting the earth, the sea, springs, and the sun, not merely a portion of these natural bodies, as in the case of the trumpets, but the whole of them; the last three are more particular, affecting the throne of the beast, the Euphrates, and the grand consummation. Some of these particular judgments are set forth in detail in the seventeenth through twentieth chapters.

2. poured out – So the angel cast fire into the earth previous to the series of trumpets (Rev. 8: 5).

grievous – distressing to the sufferers.

which had the mark of the beast – Therefore this first vial is subsequent to the period of the beast's rule.

5. angel of the waters – that is, presiding over the waters.

8. sun – Whereas by the fourth trumpet the sun is darkened (Rev. 8: 12) in a third part, here by the fourth vial the sun's bright scorching power is intensified.

9. repented not to give him glory – (Rev. 9: 20). Affliction, if it does not melt, hardens the sinner. Compare the better result on others, Rev. 11: 13; 14: 7; 15: 4.

10. seat – Greek, "*throne* of the beast": set up in arrogant mimicry of God's throne; the dragon gave his throne to the beast (Rev. 13: 2).

darkness – parallel to the Egyptian plague of darkness, Pharaoh being the type of Antichrist.

13. unclean spirits like frogs – the antitype to the plague of frogs sent on Egypt. The presence of the "unclean spirit" in the land (Palestine) is foretold, Zech. 13: 2, in connection with idolatrous *prophets*. Beginning with infidelity as to Jesus Christ's coming in the flesh, men shall end in the grossest idolatry of the beast, the incarnation of all that is self-deifying and God-opposed in the world powers of all ages; having rejected Him that came in the Father's name, they shall worship one that comes in his own, though really the devil's representative; as frogs croak by night in marshes and quagmires, so these unclean spirits in the darkness of error teach lies amidst the mire of filthy lusts. They talk of *liberty*, but it is not Gospel liberty, but license for lust.

REVELATION 17

Rev. 17: 1–18. THE HARLOT BABYLON'S GAUD: THE BEAST ON WHICH SHE RIDES, HAVING SEVEN HEADS AND TEN

sore. The judgment here is specifically different from that inflicted under the first trumpet, Rev. 8: 7. There it is said to have been that "the third part of trees was burnt up, and all green grass was burnt up." Here it is that there fell upon men a noisome and grievous sore." The two, therefore, are designed to refer to different events, and to different forms of punishment.

Which had the mark of the beast. This determines the portion of the earth that was to be afflicted. It was not the whole world; it was only that part of it where the "beast" was honored.

7. And I heard another. Evidently another angel, though this is not specified.

Out of the altar. Either the angel of the altar – that is, who presided over the altar, or an angel whose voice seemed to come from the altar. The sense is essentially the same. The writer seemed to hear a voice coming from the altar responding to what had just been said in regard to the judgment of God, or to his righteousness in bringing the judgment upon men, Rev. 16: 5. This was evidently the voice of some one who was interested in what was occurring, or to whom these things particularly appertained; that is, one who was particularly connected with the martyrs referred to, whose blood was now, as it were, to be avenged. We are naturally reminded by this of the martyr-scene in Rev. 6: 9–11, in the opening of the fifth seal, though it cannot be supposed that the same events are referred to. There "the souls of those that had been slain for the word of God" are represented as being "under the altar," and as crying to God to "avenge their blood on them who dwelt on the earth." Here a voice is heard with reference to martyrs, as of one interested in them, ascribing praise to God for having brought a righteous judgment on those who had shed the blood of the saints. They are both, for similar reasons, connected with the "altar," and the voice is heard proceeding from the same source.

True and righteous are thy judgments. Responding to what is said in Rev. 16: 5. That is, God is "true" or faithful to his promises made to his people, and "righteous" in the judgments which he has now inflicted. These judgments had come upon those who had shed the blood of the martyrs, and they were just.

In regard to the application of this, there are several things to be said. The following points are clear:

(a) That this judgment would succeed the first mentioned, and apparently at a period not remote.

(b) It would occur in a region where there had been much persecution.

(c) It would be in a Country of streams, and rivers, and fountains.

(d) It would be a just retribution for the bloody persecutions which had occurred there.

20. And every island fled away. Expressive of great and terrible judgments, as if the very earth were convulsed, and everything were moved out of its place.

And the mountains were not found. The same image occurs in Rev. 6: 14.

21. And there fell upon men a great hail out of heaven. Perhaps this is an allusion to one of the plagues of Egypt, Ex. 9: 22–26.

Because of the plague of the hail. Using the word plague in allusion to the plagues of Egypt.

For the plague thereof was exceeding great. The calamity was great and terrible. The design of the whole is to show that the destruction would be complete and awful.

This finishes the summary statement of the final destruction of this formidable Antichristian power. The details and the consequences of that overthrow are more fully stated in the subsequent chapters. The fulfillment of what is here stated will be found, according to the method of interpretation proposed, in the ultimate overthrow of the Papacy. The process described in this chapter is that of successive calamities that would weaken it and prepare it for its fall; then a rallying of its dying strength; and then some tremendous judgment that is compared with a storm of hail, accompanied with lightning, and thunder, and an earthquake, that would completely overthrow all that was connected with it. We are not, indeed, to suppose that this will literally occur; but the fair interpretation of prophecy leads us to suppose that that formidable power will, at no

hail out of heaven, every stone about the weight of a talent: and men blasphemed God because of the plague of the hail; for the plague thereof was exceeding great.

REVELATION 17

1 And there came one of the seven angels which had the seven vials, and talked with me, saying unto me, Come hither; I will shew unto thee the judgment of the great whore that sitteth upon many waters:

2 With whom the kings of the earth have committed fornication, and the inhabitants of the earth have been made drunk with the wine of her fornication.

3 So he carried me away in the spirit into the wilderness: and I saw a woman sit upon a scarlet colored beast, full of names of blasphemy, having seven heads and ten horns.

4 And the woman was arrayed in purple and scarlet color, and decked with gold and precious stones and pearls, having a golden cup in her hand full of abominations and filthiness of her fornication.

5 And upon her forehead was a name written, MYSTERY, BABYLON THE GREAT, THE MOTHER OF HARLOTS AND ABOMINATIONS OF THE EARTH.

6 And I saw the woman drunken with the blood of the saints, and with the blood of the martyrs of Jesus: and when I saw her, I wondered with great admiration.

7 And the angel said unto me, Wherefore didst thou marvel? I will tell thee the mystery of the woman, and of the beast that carrieth her, which hath the seven heads and ten horns.

8 The beast that thou sawest was, and is not; and shall ascend out of the bottomless pit, and go into perdition: and they that dwell on the earth shall wonder, whose names were not written in the book of life from the foundation of the world, when they behold the beast that was, and is not, and yet is.

9 And here is the mind which hath wisdom. The seven heads are seven mountains, on which the woman sitteth.

10 And there are seven kings: five are fallen, and one is, and the other is not yet come; and when he cometh, he must continue a short space.

11 And the beast that was, and is not, even he is the eighth, and is of the seven,

HORNS, SHALL BE THE INSTRUMENT OF JUDGMENT ON HER.

As Rev. 16: 12 stated generally the vial judgment about to be poured on *the harlot*, Babylon's power, as the seventeenth and eighteen chapters give the same in detail, so the nineteenth chapter gives in detail the judgment on the *beast* and the *false prophet*, summarily alluded to in Rev. 16: 13–15, in connection with the Lord's *coming*.

3. the wilderness – Contrast her in Rev. 12: 6,14, having *a place in the wilderness*-world, but not a home; a sojourner here, looking for the city to come. Now, on the contrary, she is contented to have her portion in this moral wilderness.

5. upon … forehead … name – as harlots usually had. What a contrast to "Holiness to the Lord," inscribed on the miter *on* the high priest's *forehead!*
mystery – implying a spiritual fact heretofore hidden, and incapable of discovery by mere reason, but now revealed. As the union of Christ and the Church is a "great mystery" (a spiritual truth of momentous interest, once hidden, now revealed, Eph. 5: 31–32), so the Church conforming to the world and thereby becoming a harlot is a counter "mystery" (or spiritual truth, symbolically now revealed).

6. martyrs – witnesses.
I wondered with great admiration – As the *Greek* is the same in the verb and the noun, translate the latter "wonder." John certainly did not *admire* her in the modern English sense. Elsewhere (Rev. 17: 8; 13: 3), all the earthly-minded ("they that dwell on the earth") *wonder* in admiration of the beast. Here only is John's *wonder* called forth; not the *beast*, but the woman sunken into the harlot, the Church become a world-loving apostate, moves his sorrowful astonishment at so awful a change. That the world should be beastly is natural, but that the faithful bride should become the whore is monstrous, and excites the same amazement in him as the same awful change in Israel excited in Isaiah and Jeremiah. "Horrible thing" in them answers to "abominations" here.

9. Compare Rev. 13: 18; Dan.. 12: 10, where similarly spiritual discernment is put forward as needed in order to understand the symbolical prophecy.

14. These shall … war with the Lamb – in league with the beast. This is a summary anticipation of Rev. 19: 19. This shall not be till *after* they have first executed judgment on the harlot (Rev. 17: 15–16).

18. reigneth – literally, "*hath kingship* over the kings." The harlot cannot be a mere *city* literally, but is called so in a

very distant period, be overthrown in a manner that would be well represented by such a fearful storm.

REVELATION 17

1. And there came one of the seven angels which had the seven vials. Reference is again made to these angels in the same manner in Rev. 21: 9, where one of them says that he would show to John "the bride, the Lamb's wife." No particular one is specified. The general idea seems to be, that to those seven angels was entrusted the execution of the last things, or the winding up of affairs introductory to the reign of God, and that the communications respecting those last events were properly made through them. It is clearly quite immaterial by which of these it is done. The expression "which had the seven vials" would seem to imply that though they had emptied the vials in the manner stated in the previous chapter, they still retained them in their hands.

And talked with me. Spake to me. The word talk would imply a more protracted conversation than occurred here.

Come hither. This is a word merely calling the attention, as we should say now "here." It does not imply that John was to leave the place where he was.

I will show thee. Partly by symbols, and partly by express statements: for this is the way in which, in fact, he showed him.

The judgment. The condemnation and calamity that will come upon her.

Of the great whore. It is not uncommon in the Scriptures to represent a city under the image of a woman – a pure and holy city under the image of a virgin or chaste female; a corrupt, idolatrous, and wicked city under the image of an abandoned or lewd woman.

That sitteth upon many waters. An image drawn either from Babylon, situated on the Euphrates, and encompassed by the many artificial rivers which had been made to irrigate the country, or Rome, situated on the Tiber. In Rev. 16: 15, these waters are said to represent the peoples, multitudes, nations, and tongues over which the government symbolized by the woman ruled. Waters are often used to symbolize nations.

5. And upon her forehead. In a circlet around her forehead. That is, it was made prominent and public, as if written on the forehead in blazing capitals. In Rev. 13: 1, it is said that "the name of blasphemy" was written on the "heads" of the beast. The meaning in both places is substantially the same, that it was prominent and unmistakable.

Was a name written. A title, or something that would properly indicate her character.

Mystery. It is proper to remark that there is nothing in the original as written by John, so far as now known, that corresponded with what is implied in placing this inscription in capital letters.

Here it seems to be used to denote that there was something hidden, obscure, or enigmatical under the title adopted; that is, the word Babylon, and the word mother, were symbolical. Our translators have printed and pointed the word mystery as if it were part of the inscription. It would probably be better to regard it as referring to the inscription thus: "a name was written – a mysterious name, to wit, Babylon," etc. Or, "a name was written mysteriously." According to this it would mean, not that there was any wonderful "mystery" about the thing itself, whatever might be true on that point, but that the name was enigmatical or symbolical; or that there was something hidden or concealed under the name. It was not to be literally understood.

The mother of harlots.

(a) Of that spiritual apostasy from God which in the language of the prophets might be called adultery;

(b) the promoter of lewdness by her institutions.

In both these senses, there never was a more expressive or appropriate title than the one here employed.

And abominations of the earth. Abominable things that prevail on the earth, Rev. 17: 4.

10. And there are seven kings. That is, seven in all, as they are enumerated in this verse and the next. An eighth is mentioned in Rev. 17: 11, but it is at the same time said that this one so pertains to the seven, or is so properly in one

and goeth into perdition.

12 And the ten horns which thou sawest are ten kings, which have received no kingdom as yet; but receive power as kings one hour with the beast.

13 These have one mind, and shall give their power and strength unto the beast.

14 These shall make war with the Lamb, and the Lamb shall overcome them: for he is Lord of lords, and King of kings: and they that are with him are called, and chosen, and faithful.

15 And he saith unto me, The waters which thou sawest, where the whore sitteth, are peoples, and multitudes, and nations, and tongues.

16 And the ten horns which thou sawest upon the beast, these shall hate the whore, and shall make her desolate and naked, and shall eat her flesh, and burn her with fire.

17 For God hath put in their hearts to fulfil his will, and to agree, and give their kingdom unto the beast, until the words of God shall be fulfilled.

18 And the woman which thou sawest is that great city, which reigneth over the kings of the earth.

REVELATION 18

1 And after these things I saw another angel come down from heaven, having great power; and the earth was lightened with his glory.

2 And he cried mightily with a strong voice, saying, Babylon the great is fallen, is fallen, and is become the habitation of devils, and the hold of every foul spirit, and a cage of every unclean and hateful bird.

3 For all nations have drunk of the wine of the wrath of her fornication, and the kings of the earth have committed fornication with her, and the merchants of the earth are waxed rich through the abundance of her delicacies.

4 And I heard another voice from heaven, saying, Come out of her, my people, that ye be not partakers of her sins, and that ye receive not of her plagues.

5 For her sins have reached unto heaven, and God hath remembered her iniquities.

6 Reward her even as she rewarded you, and double unto her double accord-

spiritual sense (Rev. 11: 8). Also the beast cannot represent a spiritual power, but a world power. In this verse the harlot is presented before us ripe for judgment. The eighteenth chapter details that judgment.

REVELATION 18

Rev. 18: 1–24. BABYLON'S FALL: GOD'S PEOPLE CALLED OUT OF HER: THE KINGS AND MERCHANTS OF THE EARTH MOURN, WHILE THE SAINTS REJOICE AT HER FALL.

6. Addressed to the executioners of God's wrath.

double – of sorrow. Contrast with this the *double* of joy which Jerusalem shall receive for her past suffering (Is. 61: 7; Zech. 9: 12); even as she has received *double* punishment for her sins (Is. 40: 2).

13. cinnamon – designed by God for better purposes: being an ingredient in the holy anointing oil, and a plant in the garden of the Beloved (Song 4: 14); but desecrated to vile uses by the adulteress (Prov. 7: 17).

odours – of incense.

frankincense – Contrast the true "incense" which God loves (Ps. 141: 2; Mal. 1: 11).

18. What city is like – Compare the similar beast as to *the beast*, Rev. 13: 4: so closely do the harlot and beast approximate one another. Contrast the attribution of this praise to God, to whom alone it is due, by *His* servants (Ex. 15: 11). Martial says of Rome, "Nothing is equal to her;" and Athenæus, "She is the epitome of the world."

19. costliness – her costly treasures: abstract for concrete.

20. avenged you on her – *Greek*, "judged your judgment on (literally, exacting it *from*) her." "There is more joy in heaven at the harlot's downfall than at that of the two beasts. For the most heinous of all sin is the sin of those who know God's word of grace, and keep it not. The worldliness of the Church is the most worldly of all worldliness. Hence, Babylon, in Revelation, has not only Israel's sins, but also the sins of the heathen; and John dwells longer on the abominations and judgments of the harlot than on those of the beast. The term 'harlot' describes the false Church's essential character. She retains her human shape as the *woman*, does not become a *beast*: she has the form of godliness, but denies its power. Her rightful lord and husband, Jehovah-Christ, and the joys and goods of His house, are no longer her all in all, but she runs after the visible and vain things of the world, in its manifold forms. The fullest form of her whoredom is, where the Church wishes to be itself a worldly power, uses politics and diplomacy, makes flesh her arm, uses unholy means for holy ends, spreads her dominion by sword or money, fascinates men by sensual ritualism, becomes

sense of the number seven, though in another sense to be regarded as an eighth, that it may be properly reckoned as the seventh. The word kings here may be understood, so far as the meaning of the word is concerned,

(a) literally as denoting a king, or one who exercises royal authority;

(b) in a more general sense as denoting one of distinguished honor – a viceroy, prince, leader, chief, Matt. 2: 1,3,9; Luke 1: 5; Acts 12: 1

(c) in a still larger sense as denoting a dynasty, a form of government, a mode of administration – as that which in fact rules.

17. For God hath put in their hearts to fulfill his will. That is, in regard to the destruction of this mighty power. They would be employed as his agents in bringing about his designs. Kings and princes are under the control of God, and, whatever may be their own designs, they are in fact employed to accomplish his purposes, and are instruments in his hands.

And to agree. See Rev. 17: 13. That is, they act harmoniously in their support of this power, and so they will in its final destruction.

Until the words of God shall be fulfilled. Not for ever; not as a permanent arrangement. God has fixed a limit to the existence of this power. When his purposes are accomplished, these kingdoms will withdraw their support, and this mighty power will fall to rise no more.

REVELATION 18

1. And after these things. After the vision referred to in the previous chapter.

I saw another angel come down from heaven. Different from the one that had last appeared, and therefore coming to make a new communication to him. It is not unusual in this book that different communications should be entrusted to different angels.

Having great power. That is, he was one of the higher rank or order of angels.

And the earth was lightened with his glory. The usual representation respecting the heavenly beings.

5. For her sins have reached unto heaven. So in Jer. 51: 9, speaking of Babylon, it is said, "For her judgment reacheth unto heaven, and

is lifted up even to the skies." The meaning is not that the sins of this mystical Babylon were like a mass or pile so high as to reach to heaven, but that it had become so prominent as to attract the attention of God. Compare Gen. 4: 10, "The voice of thy brother's blood crieth unto me from the ground." See also Gen. 18: 20.

And God hath remembered, her iniquities. He had seemed to forget them, or not to notice them, but now he acted as if they had come to his recollection.

6. Reward her even as she rewarded you. It is not said to whom this command is addressed, but it would seem to be to those who had been persecuted and wronged. Applied to mystical Babylon, it would seem to be a call on the nations that had been so long under her sway, and among whom, from time to time, so much blood had been shed by her, to arise now in their might, and to inflict deserved vengeance.

And double unto her double according to her works. That is, bring upon her double the amount of calamity which she has brought upon others; take ample vengeance upon her. Compare, for similar language, Is. 40: 2, "She hath received of the Lord's hand double for all her sins." Is. 61: 7, "For your shame ye shall have double."

In the cup which she hath filled. To bring wrath on others.

Fill to her double. Let her drink abundantly of the wine of the wrath of God – double that which she has dealt out to others. That is, either let the quantity administered to her be doubled, or let the ingredients in the cup be doubled in intensity.

14. And the fruits that thy soul lusted after. Literally, "The fruits of the desire of thy soul." The word rendered fruits properly means, late summer. In the East, this is the season when the fruits ripen, and hence the word comes to denote fruit. The reference is to any kind of fruit that would be brought for traffic into a great city, and that would be regarded as an article of luxury.

Are departed from thee. That is, they are no more brought for sale into the city.

ing to her works: in the cup which she hath filled fill to her double.

7 How much she hath glorified herself, and lived deliciously, so much torment and sorrow give her: for she saith in her heart, I sit a queen, and am no widow, and shall see no sorrow.

8 Therefore shall her plagues come in one day, death, and mourning, and famine; and she shall be utterly burned with fire: for strong is the Lord God who judgeth her.

9 And the kings of the earth, who have committed fornication and lived deliciously with her, shall bewail her, and lament for her, when they shall see the smoke of her burning,

10 Standing afar off for the fear of her torment, saying, Alas, alas, that great city Babylon, that mighty city! for in one hour is thy judgment come.

11 And the merchants of the earth shall weep and mourn over her; for no man buyeth their merchandise any more:

12 The merchandise of gold, and silver, and precious stones, and of pearls, and fine linen, and purple, and silk, and scarlet, and all thyine wood, and all manner vessels of ivory, and all manner vessels of most precious wood, and of brass, and iron, and marble,

13 And cinnamon, and odors, and ointments, and frankincense, and wine, and oil, and fine flour, and wheat, and beasts, and sheep, and horses, and chariots, and slaves, and souls of men.

14 And the fruits that thy soul lusted after are departed from thee, and all things which were dainty and goodly are departed from thee, and thou shalt find them no more at all.

15 The merchants of these things, which were made rich by her, shall stand afar off for the fear of her torment, weeping and wailing,

16 And saying, Alas, alas, that great city, that was clothed in fine linen, and purple, and scarlet, and decked with gold, and precious stones, and pearls!

17 For in one hour so great riches is come to nought. And every shipmaster, and all the company in ships, and sailors, and as many as trade by sea, stood afar off,

18 And cried when they saw the smoke of her burning, saying, What city is like unto this great city!

'mistress of ceremonies' to the dignitaries of the world, flatters prince or people, and like Israel, seeks the help of one world power against the danger threatening from another" [Auberlen]. *Judgment*, therefore, *begins with* the harlot, as in privileges *the house of God.*

21. millstone – Compare the judgment on the Egyptian hosts at the Red Sea, Ex. 15: 5, 10; Neh. 9: 11, and the foretold doom of Babylon, the world power, Jer. 51: 63–64.

with violence – *Greek,* "with impetus." This verse shows that this prophecy is regarded as still to be fulfilled.

22. pipers – flute players. "Musicians," painters and sculptors, have desecrated their art to lend fascination to the sensuous worship of corrupt Christendom.

23. What a blessed contrast is Rev. 22: 5, respecting the city of God: "They need *no candle* (just as Babylon shall *no more* have *the light of a candle,* but for a widely different reason), for the Lord God giveth them light."

candle – Translate as *Greek,* "lamp."

bridegroom ... bride ... no more ... in thee – Contrast the heavenly city, with its *Bridegroom, Bride,* and blessed *marriage supper* (Rev. 19: 7,9; 21: 2,9; Is. 62: 4–5).

24. Applied by Christ (Matt. 23: 35) to apostate Jerusalem, which proves that not merely the literal city Rome, and the Church of Rome (though the *chief* representative of the apostasy), but the WHOLE of the faithless Church of both the Old and New Testament is meant by Babylon the harlot; just as the whole Church (Old and New Testament) is meant by "the woman" (Rev. 12: 1).

REVELATION 19

Rev. 19: 1–21. THE CHURCH'S THANKSGIVING IN HEAVEN FOR THE JUDGMENT ON THE HARLOT. THE MARRIAGE OF THE LAMB: THE SUPPER: THE BRIDE'S PREPARATION: JOHN IS FORBIDDEN TO WORSHIP THE ANGEL: THE LORD AND HIS HOSTS COME FORTH FOR WAR: THE BEAST AND THE FALSE PROPHET CAST INTO THE LAKE OF FIRE: THE KINGS AND THEIR FOLLOWERS SLAIN BY THE SWORD OUT OF CHRIST'S MOUTH.

1. As in the case of the opening of the prophecy, Rev. 4: 8; 5: 9, &c.; so now, at one of the great closing events seen in vision, the judgment on the harlot (described in Rev. 18: 1–24), there is a song of praise in heaven to God: compare Rev. 7: 10, &c., toward the close of the seals, and Rev. 11: 15–18, at the close of the trumpets: Rev. 15: 3, at the saints' victory over the beast.

Alleluia – *Hebrew,* "Praise ye Jah," or Jehovah: here first used in Revelation, whence Ellicott infers the *Jews* bear a prominent part in this thanksgiving. Jah is not a contraction of

And all things which were dainty and goodly. These words "characterize all kinds of furniture and clothing which were gilt, or plated, or embroidered, and therefore were bright or splendid." – Prof. Stuart.

And thou shalt find them no more at all. The address here is decidedly to the city itself. The meaning is, that they would no more be found there.

15. The merchants of these things. Who trafficked in these things, and who supplied the city with them, Rev. 18: 11.

Which were made rich by her. By traffic with her.

Shall stand afar off. Rev. 18: 10.

For fear of her torment. Struck with terror by her torment, so that they did not dare to approach her, Rev. 18: 10.

16. That was clothed in fine linen. In the previous description (Rev. 18: 12–13), these are mentioned as articles of traffic; here the city, under the image of a female is represented as clothed in the most rich and gay of these articles.

17. For in one hour. In a very brief period – so short that it seemed to them to be but one hour. In the prediction (Rev. 18: 8) it is said that it would be "in one day," (see Barnes on "Rev. 18: 8") here it is said, that to the lookers-on it seemed to be but an hour. There is no inconsistency, therefore, between the two statements.

So great riches is come to nought. All the accumulated wealth of so great and rich a city. This should have been united with Rev. 18: 16, as it is a part of the lamentation of the merchants, and as the lamentation of the mariners commences in the other part of the verse. It is so divided in the Greek Testaments.

And every ship-master. This introduces the lamentation of the mariners, who would, of course, be deeply interested in the destruction of a city with which they had been accustomed to trade, and by carrying merchandise to which they had been enriched. The word ship-master means, properly, a governor; then a governor of a ship – the steersman, or pilot, Acts 27: 11.

And as many as trade by sea. In any kind of craft, whether employed in a near or a remote trade.

18. And cried, etc. That is, as they had a deep interest in it, they would, on their own account, as well as hers, lift up the voice of lamentation.

What city is like unto this great city? In her destruction. What calamity has ever come upon a city like this?

19. And they east dust on their heads. A common sign of lamentation and mourning among the Orientals.

By reason of her costliness. The word rendered costliness means, properly, preciousness, costliness; then magnificence, costly merchandise. The luxury of a great city enriches many individuals, however much it may impoverish itself.

For in one hour is she made desolate. So it seemed to them.

20. Rejoice over her. Over her ruin. There is a strong contrast between this language and that which precedes. Kings, merchants, and seamen, who had been countenanced and sustained by her in the indulgence of corrupt passions, or who had been enriched by traffic with her, would have occasion to mourn. But not so they who had been persecuted by her. Not so the church of the redeemed. Not so heaven itself. The great oppressor of the church, and the corrupter of the world, was now destroyed; the grand hindrance to the spread of the gospel was now removed, and all the holy in heaven and on earth would have occasion to rejoice. This is not the language of vengeance, but it is the language of exultation and rejoicing in view of the fact that the cause of truth might now spread without hindrance through the earth.

Thou heaven. The inhabitants of heaven. The meaning here is, that the dwellers in heaven – the holy angels and the redeemed – had occasion to rejoice over the downfall of the great enemy of the church.

And ye holy apostles. Professor Stuart renders this, "Ye saints, and apostles, and prophets." In the common Greek text it is, as in our version, "holy apostles and prophets." In the text of Griesbach, Hahn, and Tittman, the word and is interposed between the world "holy" and "apostle." This is, doubtless, the

19 And they cast dust on their heads, and cried, weeping and wailing, saying, Alas, alas, that great city, wherein were made rich all that had ships in the sea by reason of her costliness! for in one hour is she made desolate.

20 Rejoice over her, thou heaven, and ye holy apostles and prophets; for God hath avenged you on her.

21 And a mighty angel took up a stone like a great millstone, and cast it into the sea, saying, Thus with violence shall that great city Babylon be thrown down, and shall be found no more at all.

22 And the voice of harpers, and musicians, and of pipers, and trumpeters, shall be heard no more at all in thee; and no craftsman, of whatsoever craft he be, shall be found any more in thee; and the sound of a millstone shall be heard no more at all in thee;

23 And the light of a candle shall shine no more at all in thee; and the voice of the bridegroom and of the bride shall be heard no more at all in thee: for thy merchants were the great men of the earth; for by thy sorceries were all nations deceived.

24 And in her was found the blood of prophets, and of saints, and of all that were slain upon the earth.

REVELATION 19

1 And after these things I heard a great voice of much people in heaven, saying, Alleluia; Salvation, and glory, and honor, and power, unto the Lord our God:

2 For true and righteous are his judgments: for he hath judged the great whore, which did corrupt the earth with her fornication, and hath avenged the blood of his servants at her hand.

3 And again they said, Alleluia. And her smoke rose up for ever and ever.

4 And the four and twenty elders and the four beasts fell down and worshipped God that sat on the throne, saying, Amen; Alleluia.

5 And a voice came out of the throne, saying, Praise our God, all ye his servants, and ye that fear him, both small and great.

6 And I heard as it were the voice of a great multitude, and as the voice of many waters, and as the voice of mighty thunderings, saying, Alleluia: for the Lord God omnipotent reigneth.

"Jehovah," as it sometimes occurs jointly with the latter. It means "He who Is": whereas Jehovah is "He who will be, is, and was." It implies God experienced as a PRESENT help; so that "Hallelujah," says Kimchi in Bengel, is found first in the Psalms *on the destruction of the ungodly.* "Hallelu-Jah" occurs four times in this passage. Compare Ps. 149: 4–9, which is plainly parallel, and indeed identical in many of the phrases, as well as the general idea. Israel, especially, will join in the Hallelujah, when "her warfare is accomplished" and her foe destroyed.

2. which did corrupt the earth – *Greek,* "*used* to corrupt" continually. "Instead of opposing and lessening, she promoted the sinful life and decay of the world by her own earthliness, allowing the salt to lose its savor" [Auberlen].

avenged – *Greek,* "exacted in retribution." A particular application of the principle (Gen. 9: 5).

blood of his servants – literally shed by the Old Testament adulterous Church, and by the New Testament apostate Church; also virtually, though not literally, by all who, though called Christians, hate their brother, or love not the brethren of Christ, but shrink from the reproach of the cross, and show unkindness towards those who bear it.

3. again – *Greek,* "a second time."

rose up – *Greek,* "goeth up."

for ever and ever – *Greek,* "to the ages of the ages."

4. beasts – rather, **"living creatures."**

sat – *Greek,* "sitteth."

5. Praise our God – Compare the solemn act of praise performed by the Levites, 1 Chr. 16: 36; 23: 5, especially when the house of God was filled with the divine glory (2 Chr. 5: 13).

6. many waters – Contrast the "many waters" on which the whore sitteth (Rev. 17: 1). This verse is the hearty response to the stirring call, "Alleluia! Praise our God" (Rev. 19: 4–5).

the Lord God omnipotent – *Greek,* "*the* Omnipotent."

reigneth – literally, "reigned": hence *reigneth once for all.* His reign is a fact already established. Babylon, the harlot, was one great hindrance to His reign being recognized. Her overthrow now clears the way for His advent to reign; therefore, not merely Rome, but the whole of Christendom in so far as it is carnal and compromised Christ for the world, is comprehended in the term "harlot." The beast hardly arises when he at once "goeth into perdition": so that Christ is prophetically considered as already reigning, so soon does His advent follow the judgment on the harlot.

7. glad ... rejoice – *Greek,* "rejoice ... exult."

the marriage of the Lamb is come – The *full* and *final* consummation is at Rev. 21: 2–9, &c. Previously there must

true reading. The meaning then is, that the saints in heaven are called on to rejoice over the fall of the mystical Babylon.

Apostles. The twelve who were chosen by the Savior to be his witnesses on earth.

The word is commonly limited to the twelve, but in a larger sense it is applied to other distinguished teachers and preachers of the gospel. There is no impropriety, however, in supposing that the apostles are referred to here as such, since they would have occasion to rejoice that the great obstacle to the reign of the Redeemer was now taken away, and that that cause in which they had suffered and died was now to be triumphant.

And prophets. Prophets of the Old Testament, and distinguished teachers of the New. All these would have occasion to rejoice in the prospect of the final triumph of the true religion.

For God hath avenged you on her. Has taken vengeance on her for her treatment of you. That is, as she had persecuted the church as such, they all might be regarded as interested in it, and affected by it. All the redeemed, therefore, in earth and in heaven, are interested in whatever tends to retard or to promote the cause of truth. All have occasion to mourn when the enemies of the truth triumph; to rejoice when they fall.

21. Took up a stone like a great millstone. And cast it into the sea. As an emblem of the utter ruin of the city; an indication that the city would be as completely destroyed as that stone was covered by the waters.

Saying, Thus with violence. With force – as the stone was thrown into the sea. The idea is, that it would not be by a gentle and natural decline, but by the application of foreign power.

REVELATION 19

THIS chapter, as well as the last, is an episode, delaying the final catastrophe, and describing more fully the effect of the destruction of the mystical Babylon. The chapter consists of the following parts:

I. A hymn of the heavenly hosts in view of the destruction of the mystical Babylon, Rev. 19: 1–7.

(a) A voice is heard in heaven shouting Hallelujah, in view of the fact that God had judged the great harlot that had corrupted the earth, Rev. 19: 1–2.

(b) The sound is echoed and repeated as the smoke of her torment ascends, Rev. 19: 3.

(c) The four and twenty elders, and the four living creatures, as interested in all that pertains to the church, unite in that shout of Hallelujah, Rev. 19: 4.

(d) A voice is heard from the throne commanding them to praise God, Rev. 19: 5; and

(e) the mighty shout of Hallelujah is echoed and repeated from unnumbered hosts, Rev. 19: 6,7.

II. The marriage of the Lamb, Rev. 19: 8–9. The Lamb of God is united to his bride – the church – never more to be separated; and after all the persecutions, conflicts, and embarrassments which had existed, this long-desired union is consummated, and the glorious triumph of the church is described under the image of a joyous wedding ceremony.

III. John is so overcome with this representation, that in his transports of feeling he prostrates himself before the angel, who shows him all this, ready to worship one who discloses such bright and glorious scenes, Rev. 19: 10. He is gently rebuked for allowing himself to be so overcome that he would render Divine homage to any creature, and is told that he who communicates this to him is but a fellow-servant, and that God only is to be worshipped.

IV. The final conquest over the beast and the false prophet, and the subjugation of all the foes of the church, Rev. 9: 11–21.

(a) A description of the conqueror – the Son of God, Rev. 9: 11–16. He appears on a white horse – emblem of victory. He has on his head many crowns; wears a vesture dipped in blood; is followed by the armies of heaven on white horses; from his mouth goes a sharp sword; and his name is prominently written on his vesture and his thigh – all emblematic of certain victory.

(b) An angel is seen standing in the sun, calling

7 Let us be glad and rejoice, and give honor to him: for the marriage of the Lamb is come, and his wife hath made herself ready.

8 And to her was granted that she should be arrayed in fine linen, clean and white: for the fine linen is the righteousness of saints.

9 And he saith unto me, Write, Blessed are they which are called unto the marriage supper of the Lamb. And he saith unto me, These are the true sayings of God.

10 And I fell at his feet to worship him. And he said unto me, See thou do it not: I am thy fellowservant, and of thy brethren that have the testimony of Jesus: worship God: for the testimony of Jesus is the spirit of prophecy.

11 And I saw heaven opened, and behold a white horse; and he that sat upon him was called Faithful and True, and in righteousness he doth judge and make war.

12 His eyes were as a flame of fire, and on his head were many crowns; and he had a name written, that no man knew, but he himself.

13 And he was clothed with a vesture dipped in blood: and his name is called The Word of God.

14 And the armies which were in heaven followed him upon white horses, clothed in fine linen, white and clean.

15 And out of his mouth goeth a sharp sword, that with it he should smite the nations: and he shall rule them with a rod of iron: and he treadeth the winepress of the fierceness and wrath of Almighty God.

16 And he hath on his vesture and on his thigh a name written, KING OF KINGS, AND LORD OF LORDS.

17 And I saw an angel standing in the sun; and he cried with a loud voice, saying to all the fowls that fly in the midst of heaven, Come and gather yourselves together unto the supper of the great God;

18 That ye may eat the flesh of kings, and the flesh of captains, and the flesh of mighty men, and the flesh of horses, and of them that sit on them, and the flesh of all men, both free and bond, both small and great.

19 And I saw the beast, and the kings of the earth, and their armies, gathered together to make war against him that sat on the horse, and against his army.

20 And the beast was taken, and

be the overthrow of the beast, &c., at the Lord's coming, the binding of Satan, the millennial reign, the loosing of Satan and his last overthrow, and the general judgment. The elect-Church, the heavenly Bride, soon after the destruction of the harlot, is transfigured at the Lord's coming, and joins with Him in His triumph over the beast. On the emblem of the heavenly Bridegroom and Bride, compare Matt. 22: 2; 25: 6,10; 2 Cor. 11: 2. Perfect union with Him personally, and participation in His holiness; joy, glory, and kingdom, are included in this symbol of "marriage"; compare Song of Solomon everywhere. Besides the *heavenly* Bride, the transfigured, translated, and risen Church, reigning *over* the earth with Christ, there is also the *earthly* bride, Israel, in the flesh, never yet *divorced*, though for a time separated, from her divine husband, who shall then be reunited to the Lord, and be the mother Church of the millennial earth, Christianized through her. Note, we ought, as Scripture does, restrict the language drawn from marriage-love to *the Bride*, the Church *as a whole*; not use it as individuals in our relation to Christ, which Rome does in the case of her nuns. Individually, believers are effectually-*called guests*; collectively, they constitute *the bride*. The harlot divides her affections among many lovers: the bride gives hers exclusively to Christ.

8. granted – Though in one sense *she* "made herself ready," having by the Spirit's work in her put on "the wedding garment," yet in the fullest sense it is not she, but her Lord, who makes her ready by "*granting* to her that she be arrayed in fine linen." It is He who, by *giving Himself for* her, *presents her to Himself a glorious Church, not having spot, but holy and without blemish*. It is He also who sanctifies her, naturally vile and without beauty, *with the washing of water by the word, and puts His own comeliness on her*, which thus becomes hers.

righteousness – *Greek*, "righteousnesses"; distributively used. *Each* saint must have this righteousness: not merely be justified, as if the righteousness belonged to the Church *in the aggregate*; the saints together have *righteousnesses*; namely, He is *accounted as* "the Lord our righteousness" to each saint on his believing, their robes being made *white in the blood of the Lamb*.

11. behold a white horse; and he that sat upon him – identical with Rev. 6: 2. Here as there he comes forth "conquering and to conquer." Compare the *ass*-colt on which He rode into Jerusalem (Matt. 21: 1–7). The *horse* was used for war: and here He is going forth to war with the beast. The *ass* is for peace. His riding on it into Jerusalem is an earnest of His reign in Jerusalem over the earth, as the *Prince of peace*, after all hostile powers have been overthrown. When the security of the world power, and the distress of the people of God, have reached the highest point, the Lord

on all the fowls of heaven to come to the great feast prepared for them in the destruction of the enemies of God – as if there were a great slaughter sufficient to supply all the fowls that feed on flesh, Rev. 19: 17–18.

(c) The final war, Rev. 19: 19,21. The beast, and the kings of the earth, and their armies are gathered together for battle; the beast and the false prophet are taken, and are cast into the lake that burns with fire and brimstone; and all that remain of the enemies of God are slain, and the fowls are satisfied with their flesh. The last obstacle that prevented the dawn of the millennial morning is taken away, and the church is triumphant.

16. And he hath on his vesture. That is, this name was conspicuously written on his garment – probably his military robe.

And on his thigh. The robe or military cloak may be conceived of as open and flowing, so as to expose the limbs of the rider; and the idea is, that the name was conspicuously written not only on the flowing robe, but on the other parts of his dress, so that it must be conspicuous whether his military cloak were wrapped closely around him, or whether it was open to the breeze. Grotius supposes that this name was on the edge or hilt of the sword which depended from his thigh.

A name written. Or a title descriptive of his character.

King of kings, and Lord of lords. As in Rev. 17: 5, so here, there is nothing in the original to denote that this should be distinguished as it is by capital letters. As a conspicuous title, however, it is not improper. It means that he is, in fact, the sovereign over the kings of the earth, and that all nobles and princes are under his control – a rank that properly belongs to the Son of God.

The custom here alluded to of inscribing the name or rank of distinguished individuals on their garments, so that they might be readily recognized, was not uncommon in ancient times.

17. And I saw an angel standing in the sun. A different angel evidently from the one which had before appeared to him. The number of angels that appeared to John, as referred to in this book, was very great, and each one came on a new errand, or with a new message. Every one must be struck with the image here. The description is as simple as it can be; and yet as sublime. The fewest words possible are used; and yet the image is distinct and clear. A heavenly being stands in the blaze of the brightest of the orbs that God permits us here to see – yet not consumed, and himself so bright that he can be distinctly seen amidst the dazzling splendors of that luminary. It is difficult to conceive of an image more sublime than this. Why he has his place in the sun is not stated, for there does not appear to be anything more intended by this than to give grandeur and impressiveness to the scene.

And he cried with a loud voice. So that all the fowls of heaven could hear.

Saying to all the fowls that fly in the midst of heaven. That is, to all the birds of prey – all that feed on flesh – such as hover over a battle-field.

Come and gather yourselves together. All this imagery is taken from the idea that there would be a great slaughter, and that the bodies of the dead would be left unburied to the birds of prey.

Unto the supper of the great God. As if the great God were about to give you a feast: to wit, the carcasses of those slain. It is called "his supper" because he gives it; and the image is merely that there would be a great slaughter of his foes, as is specified in the following verse.

18. That ye may eat the flesh of kings. Of the kings under the control of the beast and the false prophet, Rev. 16: 14; 17: 12–14.

And the flesh of captains. Of those subordinate to kings in command.

And the flesh of mighty men. The word here means strong, and the reference is to the robust soldiery – rank and file in the army.

And the flesh of horses, and of them that sit on them. Cavalry – for most armies are composed in part of horsemen.

And the flesh of all men, both free and bond. Freemen and slaves. It is not uncommon that freemen and slaves are mingled in the same army. This was the case in the American Revolution, and is common in the East.

with him the false prophet that wrought miracles before him, with which he deceived them that had received the mark of the beast, and them that worshipped his image. These both were cast alive into a lake of fire burning with brimstone.

21 And the remnant were slain with the sword of him that sat upon the horse, which sword proceeded out of his mouth: and all the fowls were filled with their flesh.

REVELATION 20

1 And I saw an angel come down from heaven, having the key of the bottomless pit and a great chain in his hand.

2 And he laid hold on the dragon, that old serpent, which is the Devil, and Satan, and bound him a thousand years,

3 And cast him into the bottomless pit, and shut him up, and set a seal upon him, that he should deceive the nations no more, till the thousand years should be fulfilled: and after that he must be loosed a little season.

4 And I saw thrones, and they sat upon them, and judgment was given unto them: and I saw the souls of them that were beheaded for the witness of Jesus, and for the word of God, and which had not worshipped the beast, neither his image, neither had received his mark upon their foreheads, or in their hands; and they lived and reigned with Christ a thousand years.

5 But the rest of the dead lived not again until the thousand years were finished. This is the first resurrection.

6 Blessed and holy is he that hath part in the first resurrection: on such the second death hath no power, but they shall be priests of God and of Christ, and shall reign with him a thousand years.

7 And when the thousand years are expired, Satan shall be loosed out of his prison,

8 And shall go out to deceive the nations which are in the four quarters of the earth, Gog and Magog, to gather them together to battle: the number of whom is as the sand of the sea.

9 And they went up on the breadth of the earth, and compassed the camp of the saints about, and the beloved city: and fire came down from God out of heaven, and devoured them.

10 And the devil that deceived them

Jesus shall appear visibly from heaven to put an end to the whole course of the world, and establish His kingdom of glory. He comes to judge with vengeance the world power, and to bring to the Church redemption, transfiguration, and power over the world. Distinguish between this *coming* (Matt. 24: 27,29,37,39; *Greek*, "*parousia*") and *the end*, or final judgment (Matt. 25: 31; 1 Cor. 15: 23). Powerful natural phenomena shall accompany His advent [Auberlen].

REVELATION 20

Rev. 20: 1–15. Satan Bound, and the First-Risen Saints Reign with Christ, a Thousand Years; Satan Loosed, Gathers the Nations, Gog and Magog, Round the Camp of the Saints, and Is Finally Consigned to the Lake of Fire; the General Resurrection and Last Judgment.

1. The destruction of his representatives, the beast and the false prophet, to whom he had given his *power, throne*, and *authority*, is followed by the binding of Satan himself for a thousand years.

the key of the bottomless pit – now transferred from Satan's hands, who had heretofore been permitted by God to use it in letting loose plagues on the earth; he is now to be made to feel himself the torment which he had inflicted on men, but his full torment is not until he is cast into "the lake of fire" (Rev. 20: 10).

2. thousand years – As *seven* mystically implies universality, so a *thousand* implies *perfection*, whether in good or evil [Aquinas on ch. 11]. *Thousand* symbolizes that the world is perfectly leavened and pervaded by the divine; since *thousand* is *ten*, the number of the world, raised to the *third* power, *three* being the number of God [Auberlen]. It may denote *literally* also a *thousand years*.

3. set a seal upon him – *Greek*, "over him," that is, sealed up the door of the abyss over his head. A surer seal to keep him from getting out than his seal over Jesus in the tomb of Joseph, which was burst on the resurrection morn. Satan's binding at' this juncture is not arbitrary, but is the necessary consequence of the events (Rev. 19: 20); just as Satan's being cast out of heaven, where he had previously been the accuser of the brethren, was the legitimate judgment which passed on him through the death, resurrection, and ascension of Christ (Rev. 12: 7–10). Satan imagined that he had overcome Christ on Golgotha, and that his power was secure for ever, but the Lord in death overcame him, and by His ascension as our righteous Advocate cast out Satan, the accuser from heaven. Time was given on earth to make the beast and harlot powerful, and then to concentrate all his power in Antichrist. The Antichristian kingdom, his last effort, being utterly destroyed by Christ's mere appearing,

Both small and great. Young and old; of small size and of great size; of those of humble, and those of exalted rank. The later armies of Napoleon were composed in great part of conscripts, many of whom were only about eighteen years of age, and to this circumstance many of his later defeats are to be traced. In the army that was raised after the invasion of Russia, no less than one hundred and fifty thousand of the conscripts were between eighteen and nineteen years of age.

REVELATION 20

This chapter, like chapters 16: 12–21; 17, 18, and 19 pertains to the future, and discloses things which are yet to occur. It is not to be wondered at, therefore, that much obscurity should hang over it, nor that it is difficult to explain it so as to remove all obscurity. The statement in this chapter, however, is distinct and clear in its general characteristics, and time will make all its particular statements free from ambiguity.

In the previous chapter, an account is given of the final destruction of two of the most formidable enemies of the church, and consequently the removal of two of the hindrances to the universal spread of the gospel – the beast and the false prophet. But one obstacle remains to be removed – the power of Satan as concentrated and manifested in the form of Pagan power. These three powers it was said Rev. 16: 13–14 would concentrate their forces as the time of the final triumph of Christianity drew on; and with these the last great battle was to be fought. Two of these have been subdued; the conquest over the other remains, and Satan is to be arrested and bound for a thousand years. He is then to be released for a time, and afterwards finally destroyed, and at that period the end will come.

The chapter comprises the following parts:

I. The binding of Satan, Rev. 20: 1–3. An angel comes down from heaven, with the key of the bottomless pit, and a great chain in his hand, and seizes upon the dragon, and casts him into the pit, that for a thousand years he should deceive the nations no more. The great enemy of God and his cause is thus made a prisoner, and is restrained from making war in any form against the church. The way is thus prepared for the peace and triumph which follow.

II. The millennium, Rev. 20: 4–6. John sees thrones, and persons sitting on them; he sees the souls of those who were beheaded for the witness of Jesus, and for the word of God – those who had not worshipped the beast nor his image – living and reigning with Christ during the thousand years: the spirits of the martyrs revived, and becoming again the reigning spirit on earth. This he calls the first resurrection; and on all such he says the second death has no power. Temporal death they might experience – for such the martyrs had experienced – but over them the second death has no dominion, for they live and reign with the Savior. This is properly the millennium – the long period when the principles of true religion will have the ascendency on the earth, as if the martyrs and confessors – the most devoted and eminent Christians of other times – should appear again upon the earth, and as if their spirit should become the reigning and pervading spirit of all who professed the Christian name.

III. The release of Satan, Rev. 20: 7,8. After the thousand years of peace and triumph shall have expired, Satan will be released from his prison, and will be permitted to go out and deceive the nations which are in the four quarters of the earth, and gather them together to battle; that is, a state of things will exist as if Satan were then released. There will be again an outbreak of sin on the earth, and a conflict with the principles of religion, as if an innumerable multitude of opposers should be marshaled for the conflict by the great author of all evil.

IV. The final subjugation of Satan, and destruction of his power on the earth, Rev. 20: 9–10. After the temporary and partial outbreak of evil (Rev. 20: 7–8), Satan and his hosts will be entirely destroyed. The destruction will be as if fire should come down from heaven to devour the assembled hosts (Rev. 20: 9), and as if Satan, the great leader of evil, should be cast into the same lake where the beast and false prophet are, to be tormented for ever. Then the church will be delivered from all its

was cast into the lake of fire and brimstone, where the beast and the false prophet are, and shall be tormented day and night for ever and ever.

11 And I saw a great white throne, and him that sat on it, from whose face the earth and the heaven fled away; and there was found no place for them.

12 And I saw the dead, small and great, stand before God; and the books were opened: and another book was opened, which is the book of life: and the dead were judged out of those things which were written in the books, according to their works.

13 And the sea gave up the dead which were in it; and death and hell delivered up the dead which were in them: and they were judged every man according to their works.

14 And death and hell were cast into the lake of fire. This is the second death.

15 And whosoever was not found written in the book of life was cast into the lake of fire.

REVELATION 21

1 And I saw a new heaven and a new earth: for the first heaven and the first earth were passed away; and there was no more sea.

2 And I John saw the holy city, new Jerusalem, coming down from God out of heaven, prepared as a bride adorned for her husband.

3 And I heard a great voice out of heaven saying, Behold, the tabernacle of God is with men, and he will dwell with them, and they shall be his people, and God himself shall be with them, and be their God.

4 And God shall wipe away all tears from their eyes; and there shall be no more death, neither sorrow, nor crying, neither shall there be any more pain: for the former things are passed away.

5 And he that sat upon the throne said, Behold, I make all things new. And he said unto me, Write: for these words are true and faithful.

6 And he said unto me, It is done. I am Alpha and Omega, the beginning and the end. I will give unto him that is athirst of the fountain of the water of life freely.

7 He that overcometh shall inherit all things; and I will be his God, and he shall

his power on earth is at an end. He had thought to destroy God's people on earth by Antichristian persecutions (just as he had thought previously to destroy Christ); but the Church is not destroyed from the earth but is raised to rule over it, and Satan himself is shut up for a thousand years in the "abyss" (*Greek* for "bottomless pit"), the preparatory prison to the "lake of fire," his final doom.

REVELATION 21

Rev. 21: 1–27. The New Heaven and Earth: New Jerusalem Out of Heaven.

The remaining two chapters describe the eternal and consummated kingdom of God and the saints on the new earth. As the world of nations is to be pervaded by divine influence in the millennium, so the world of nature shall be, not annihilated, but transfigured universally in the eternal state which follows it. The earth was cursed for man's sake; but is redeemed by the second Adam. *Now* is the Church; in the millennium shall be the kingdom; and after that shall be the new world wherein God shall be all in all. The "day of the Lord" and the conflagration of the earth are in 2 Pet. 3: 10–11 spoken of as if connected together, from which many argue against a millennial interval between His coming and the general conflagration of the old earth, preparatory to the new; but "day" is used often of a whole period comprising events intimately connected together, as are the Lord's second advent, the millennium, and the general conflagration and judgment. Compare Gen. 2: 4 as to the wide use of "day." Man's *soul* is redeemed by regeneration through the Holy Spirit now; man's *body* shall be redeemed at the resurrection; man's *dwelling-place*, His inheritance, the earth, shall be redeemed perfectly at the creation of the new heaven and earth, which shall exceed in glory the first Paradise, as much as the second Adam exceeds in glory the first Adam before the fall, and as man regenerated in body and soul shall exceed man as he was at creation.

1. no more sea – The sea is the type of perpetual unrest. Hence our Lord rebukes it as an unruly hostile troubler of His people. It symbolized the political tumults out of which "the beast" arose, Rev. 13: 1. As the physical corresponds to the spiritual and moral world, so the absence of *sea*, after the metamorphosis of the earth by *fire*, answers to the unruffled state of solid peace which shall then prevail. The *sea*, though severing lands from one another, is now, by God's eliciting of good from evil, made the medium of communication between countries through navigation. Then man shall possess inherent powers which shall make the sea no longer necessary, but an element which would detract from a perfect state. A "river" and "water" are spoken of in Rev.

enemies, and religion henceforward will be triumphant. How long the interval will be between this state and that next disclosed, (Rev. 20: 11–15) – the final judgment – is not stated. The eye of the seer glances from one to the other, but there is nothing to forbid the supposition, that, according to the laws of prophetic vision, there may be a long interval in which righteousness shall reign upon the earth.

V. The final judgment, Rev. 20: 11–15. This closes the earthly scene. Henceforward (chapters 21 and 22) the scene is transferred to heaven – the abode of the redeemed. The last judgment is the winding up of the earthly affairs. The enemies of the church are all long since destroyed; the world has experienced, perhaps for a long series of ages, the full influence of the gospel; countless millions have been, we may suppose, brought under its power; and then at last, in the winding up of human affairs, comes the judgment of the great day, when the dead, small and great, shall stand before God; when the sea shall give up its dead; when death and hell shall give up the dead that are in them; when the records of human actions shall be opened, and all shall be judged according to their works, and when all who are not found written in the book of life shall be cast into the lake of fire. This is the earthly consummation; henceforward the saints shall reign in glory – the New Jerusalem above, chapters 21 and 22.

REVELATION 21

1. And I saw a new heaven and a new earth. Such a heaven and earth that they might properly be called new; such transformations, and such changes in their appearance, that they seemed to be just created, He does not say that they were created now, or anew; that the old heavens and earth were annihilated; – but all that he says is that there were such changes that they seemed to be new. If the earth is to be renovated by fire, such a renovation will give an appearance to the globe as if it were created anew, and might be attended with such an apparent change in the heavens that they might be said to be new. The description

here (Rev. 21: 1) relates to scenes after the general resurrection and the judgment – for those events are detailed in the close of the previous chapter.

For the first heaven and the first earth were passed away. They had passed away by being changed, and a renovated universe had taken their place.

And there was no more sea. This change struck John more forcibly, it would appear, than anything else. Now, the seas and oceans occupy about three-fourths of the surface of the globe, and of course to that extent prevent the world from being occupied by men – except by the comparatively small number that are mariners. There, the idea of John seems to be, the whole world will be inhabitable, and no part will be given up to the wastes of oceans. In the present state of things, these vast oceans are necessary to render the world a fit abode for human beings, as well as to give life and happiness to the numberless tribes of animals that find their homes in the waters. In the future state, it would seem, the present arrangement will be unnecessary; and if man dwells upon the earth at all, or if he visits it as a temporary abode, these vast wastes of water will be needless. It should be remembered that the earth, in its changes, according to the teachings of geology, has undergone many revolutions quite as remarkable as it would be if all the lakes, and seas, and oceans of the earth should disappear. Still, it is not certain that it was intended that this language should be understood literally as applied to the material globe. The object is to describe the future blessedness of the righteous; and the idea is, that that will be a world where there will be no such wastes as those produced by oceans.

2. And I John saw the holy city, new Jerusalem, coming down from God out of heaven. Here it refers to the residence of the redeemed, the heavenly world, of which Jerusalem was the type and symbol. It is here represented as "coming down from God out of heaven." This, of course, does not mean that this great city was literally to descend upon the earth, and to occupy any one part of the renovated world; but it is a symbolical or figurative representation, designed to show that the abode of the

be my son.

8 But the fearful, and unbelieving, and the abominable, and murderers, and whoremongers, and sorcerers, and idolaters, and all liars, shall have their part in the lake which burneth with fire and brimstone: which is the second death.

9 And there came unto me one of the seven angels which had the seven vials full of the seven last plagues, and talked with me, saying, Come hither, I will shew thee the bride, the Lamb's wife.

10 And he carried me away in the spirit to a great and high mountain, and shewed me that great city, the holy Jerusalem, descending out of heaven from God,

11 Having the glory of God: and her light was like unto a stone most precious, even like a jasper stone, clear as crystal;

12 And had a wall great and high, and had twelve gates, and at the gates twelve angels, and names written thereon, which are the names of the twelve tribes of the children of Israel:

13 On the east three gates; on the north three gates; on the south three gates; and on the west three gates.

14 And the wall of the city had twelve foundations, and in them the names of the twelve apostles of the Lamb.

15 And he that talked with me had a golden reed to measure the city, and the gates thereof, and the wall thereof.

16 And the city lieth foursquare, and the length is as large as the breadth: and he measured the city with the reed, twelve thousand furlongs. The length and the breadth and the height of it are equal.

17 And he measured the wall thereof, an hundred and forty and four cubits, according to the measure of a man, that is, of the angel.

18 And the building of the wall of it was of jasper: and the city was pure gold, like unto clear glass.

19 And the foundations of the wall of the city were garnished with all manner of precious stones. The first foundation was jasper; the second, sapphire; the third, a chalcedony; the fourth, an emerald;

20 The fifth, sardonyx; the sixth, sardius; the seventh, chrysolite; the eighth, beryl; the ninth, a topaz; the tenth, a chrysoprasus; the eleventh, a jacinth; the twelfth, an amethyst.

21 And the twelve gates were twelve pearls; every several gate was of one

22: 1–2, probably literal (that is, with such changes of the natural properties of water, as correspond analogically to man's own transfigured body), as well as symbolical. The sea was once the element of the world's destruction, and is still the source of death to thousands, whence after the millennium, at the general judgment, it is specially said, "The *sea* gave up the dead … in it." Then it shall cease to destroy, or disturb, being removed altogether on account of its past destructions.

2. bride – made up of the blessed citizens of "the holy city." There is no longer merely a Paradise as in Eden (though there is that also, Rev. 2: 7), no longer a mere garden, but now *the city of* God on earth, costlier, statelier, and more glorious, but at the same time the result of labor and pains such as had not to be expended by man in dressing the primitive garden of Eden. "The lively stones" were severally in time laboriously chiselled into shape, after the pattern of "the Chief corner-stone," to prepare them for the place which they shall everlastingly fill in the heavenly Jerusalem.

3. the tabernacle – alluding to the tabernacle of God in the wilderness (wherein many signs of His presence were given): of which this is the antitype, having previously been in heaven: Rev. 11: 19; 15: 5, "the temple of the tabernacle of the testimony in heaven"; also Rev. 13: 6. Compare the contrast in Heb. 9: 23, 14, between "the patterns" and "the heavenly things themselves," between "the figures" and "the true." The earnest of the true and heavenly tabernacle was afforded in the Jerusalem temple described in Ezek. 40: 1–42: 20, as about to be, namely, during the millennium.

dwell with them – literally, "*tabernacle* with them"; the same *Greek* word as is used of the divine Son "*tabernacling* among us." Then He was in the weakness of the *flesh*: but at the new creation of heaven and earth He shall tabernacle among us in the glory of His manifested Godhead (Rev. 22: 4).

God himself … with them – realizing fully His name Immanuel.

4. all tears – *Greek,* "every tear."

no more death – *Greek,* "death shall be no more." Therefore it is not the millennium, for in the latter there is *death* (Is. 65: 20; 1 Cor. 15: 26, 54, "the *last* enemy … destroyed is *death,*" Rev. 20: 14, *after* the millennium).

REVELATION 22

Rev. 22: 1–21. The River of Life: The Tree of Life: The Other Blessednesses of the Redeemed. John Forbidden to Worship the Angel. Nearness of Christ's Coming to Fix Man's Eternal State. Testimony of Jesus, His Spirit, and the Bride, Any Addition to Which,

righteous will be splendid and glorious. The idea of a city literally descending from heaven, and being set upon the earth with such proportions – three hundred and seventy miles high (Rev. 21: 16), made of gold, and with single pearls for gates, and single gems for the foundations – is absurd. No man can suppose that this is literally true, and hence this must be regarded as a figurative or emblematic description. It is a representation of the heavenly state under the image of a beautiful city, of which Jerusalem was, in many respects, a natural and striking emblem.

Prepared as a bride adorned for her husband. The purpose here is, to represent it as exceedingly beautiful. The comparison of the church with a bride, or a wife, is common in the Scriptures.

It is also common in the Scriptures to compare a city with a beautiful woman, and these images here seem to be combined. It is a beautiful city that seems to descend, and this city is itself compared with a richly attired bride prepared for her husband.

4. And God shall wipe away all tears from their eyes. This will be one of the characteristics of that blessed state, that not a tear shall ever be shed there. How different will that be from the condition here – for who is there here who has not learned to weep?

And there shall be no more death. In all that future world of glory, not one shall ever die; not a grave shall ever be dug! What a view do we begin to get of heaven, when we are told there shall be no death there! How different from earth, where death is so common; where it spares no one; where our best friends die; where the wise, the good, the useful, the lovely, die; where fathers, mothers, wives, husbands, sons, daughters, all die; where we habitually feel that we must die. Assuredly we have here a view of heaven most glorious and animating to those who dwell in a world like this, and to whom nothing is more common than death. In all their endless and glorious career, the redeemed will never see death again; they will never themselves die. They will never follow a friend to the tomb, nor fear that an absent friend is dead. The slow funeral procession will never be witnessed there; nor will the soil ever open its bosom to furnish a grave.

Neither sorrow. The word sorrow here denotes sorrow or grief of any kind; sorrow for the loss of property or friends; sorrow for disappointment, persecution, or care; sorrow over our sins, or sorrow that we love God so little, and serve him so unfaithfully; sorrow that we are sick, or that we must die. How innumerable are the sources of sorrow here; how constant is it on the earth! Since the fall of man there has not been a day, an hour, a moment, in which this has not been a sorrowful world; there has not been a nation, a tribe – a city or a village – nay, not a family where there has not been grief. There has been no individual who has been always perfectly happy. No one rises in the morning with any certainty that he may not end the day in grief; no one lies down at night with any assurance that it may not be a night of sorrow. How different would this world be if it were announced that hence forward there would be no sorrow! How different, therefore, will heaven be when we shall have the assurance that henceforward grief shall be at an end!

Nor crying. This word properly denotes a cry, an outcry, as in giving a public notice; a cry in a tumult – a clamor, Acts 23: 9; and then a cry of sorrow, or wailing. This is evidently its meaning here, and it refers to all the outbursts of grief arising from affliction, from oppression, from violence. The sense is, that as none of these causes of wailing will be known in the future state, all such wailing will cease. This, too, will make the future state vastly different from our condition here; for what a change would it produce on the earth if the cry of grief were never to be heard again!

Neither shall there be any more pain. There will be no sickness, and no calamity; and there will be no mental sorrow arising from remorse, from disappointment, or from the evil conduct of friends. And what a change would this produce – for how full of pain is the world now! How many lie on beds of languishing; how many are suffering under incurable diseases; how many are undergoing severe surgical operations; how many are pained by the loss of property or friends, or subjected to acuter anguish by the misconduct of those

pearl: and the street of the city was pure gold, as it were transparent glass.

22 And I saw no temple therein: for the Lord God Almighty and the Lamb are the temple of it.

23 And the city had no need of the sun, neither of the moon, to shine in it: for the glory of God did lighten it, and the Lamb is the light thereof.

24 And the nations of them which are saved shall walk in the light of it: and the kings of the earth do bring their glory and honor into it.

25 And the gates of it shall not be shut at all by day: for there shall be no night there.

26 And they shall bring the glory and honor of the nations into it.

27 And there shall in no wise enter into it any thing that defileth, neither whatsoever worketh abomination, or maketh a lie: but they which are written in the Lamb's book of life.

REVELATION 22

1 And he shewed me a pure river of water of life, clear as crystal, proceeding out of the throne of God and of the Lamb.

2 In the midst of the street of it, and on either side of the river, was there the tree of life, which bare twelve manner of fruits, and yielded her fruit every month: and the leaves of the tree were for the healing of the nations.

3 And there shall be no more curse: but the throne of God and of the Lamb shall be in it; and his servants shall serve him:

4 And they shall see his face; and his name shall be in their foreheads.

5 And there shall be no night there; and they need no candle, neither light of the sun; for the Lord God giveth them light: and they shall reign for ever and ever.

6 And he said unto me, These sayings are faithful and true: and the Lord God of the holy prophets sent his angel to shew unto his servants the things which must shortly be done.

7 Behold, I come quickly: blessed is he that keepeth the sayings of the prophecy of this book.

8 And I John saw these things, and heard them. And when I had heard and seen, I fell down to worship before the

OR SUBTRACTION FROM WHICH, SHALL BE ETERNALLY PUNISHED. CLOSING BENEDICTION.

1. – infinitely superior to the typical waters in the first Paradise (Gen. 2: 10–14); and even superior to those figurative ones in the millennial Jerusalem (Ezek. 47: 1,12; Zech. 14: 8), as the matured fruit is superior to the flower. The millennial waters represent full Gospel grace; these waters of new Jerusalem represent Gospel glory perfected. Their continuous flow from God, the Fountain of life, symbolizes the uninterrupted continuance of life derived by the saints, ever fresh, from Him: life in fulness of joy, as well as perpetual vitality. Like pure crystal, it is free from every taint: compare Rev. 4: 6, "before the throne a sea of glass, like crystal."

4. see his face – revealed in divine glory, *in Christ Jesus*. They shall see and know Him with intuitive knowledge of Him, *even as they are known by Him* (1 Cor. 13: 9–12), and face to face. Compare 1 Tim. 6: 16, with John 14: 9. God the Father can only be seen in Christ.

in – Greek, "*on* their foreheads." Not only shall they personally and in secret (Rev. 3: 17) know their sonship, but they shall be known as sons of God to all the citizens of the new Jerusalem, so that the free flow of mutual love among the members of Christ's family will not be checked by suspicion as here.

5. reign – with a glory probably transcending that of their reign in heaven with Christ over the millennial nations in the flesh described in Rev. 20: 4,6; that reign was but for a limited time, "a thousand years"; this final reign is "unto the ages of the ages."

6. These sayings are true – thrice repeated (Rev. 19: 9; 21: 5). For we are slow to believe that God is as good as He is. The news seems to us, habituated as we are to the misery of this fallen world, too good to be true [Nangle]. They are no dreams of a visionary, but the realities of God's sure word.

8. Both here and in Rev. 19: 9–10, the apostle's falling at the feet of the angel is preceded by a glorious promise to the Church, accompanied with the assurance, that "These are the true sayings of God," and that those are "blessed" who keep them. Rapturous emotion, gratitude, and adoration, at the prospect of the Church's future glory transport him out of himself, so as all but to fall into an unjustifiable act; contrast his opposite feeling at the prospect of the Church's deep fall.

13. I am Alpha – Greek, "… *the* Alpha and *the* Omega." At the winding up of the whole scheme of revelation He announces Himself as the One *before whom and after whom there is no God.*

who are loved! How different would this world be, if all pain were to cease for ever; how different, therefore, must the future state of the blessed be from the present!

For the former things are passed away. The world as it was before the judgment.

26. And they shall bring, etc. That blessed world shall be made up of all that was truly valuable and pure on the earth.

REVELATION 22

1. And he showed me a pure river of water of life. In the New Jerusalem; the happy abode of the redeemed. The phrase "water of life," means living or running water, like a spring or fountain, as contrasted with a stagnant pool.

The allusion here is doubtless to the first Eden, where a river watered the garden (Gen. 2: 10, seq.), and as this is a description of Eden recovered, or Paradise regained, it was natural to introduce a river of water also, yet in such a way as to accord with the general description of that future abode of the redeemed. It does not spring up, therefore, from the ground, but flows from the throne of God and the Lamb. Perhaps, also, the writer had in his eye the description in Ezek. 47: 1–12, where a stream issues from under the temple, and is parted in different directions.

Proceeding out of the throne of God and of the Lamb. Flowing from the foot of the throne. Compare Rev. 4: 6. This idea is strictly in accordance with Oriental imagery. In the East, fountains and running streams constituted an essential part of the image of enjoyment and prosperity, and such fountains were common in the courts of Oriental houses. Here, the river is an emblem of peace, happiness, plenty; and the essential thought in its flowing from the throne is, that all the happiness of heaven proceeds from God.

4. And they shall see his face. They would be constantly in his presence, and be permitted continually to behold his glory.

And his name shall be in their foreheads. They shall be designated as his.

5. And they need no candle. No lamp; no artificial light, as in a world where there is night and darkness.

And they shall reign for ever and ever. That is, with God; they shall be as kings.

Analysis of 22: 6–20

This portion of the book of Revelation is properly the epilogue, or conclusion. The main purposes of the vision are accomplished; the enemies of the church are quelled; the church is triumphant; the affairs of the world are wound up; the redeemed are received to their blissful, eternal abode; the wicked are cut off; the earth is purified, and the affairs of the universe are fixed on their permanent foundation. A few miscellaneous matters, therefore, close the book.

(1.) A solemn affirmation on the part of him who had made these revelations, that they are true, and that they will be speedily accomplished, and that he will be blessed or happy who shall keep the sayings of the book, Rev. 22: 6–7.

(2.) The effect of all these things on John himself, leading him, as in a former case, Rev. 19: 10 to a disposition to worship him who had been the medium in making to him such extraordinary communications, Rev. 22: 8,9.

(3.) A command not to seal up what had been revealed, since the time was near. These things would soon have their fulfillment, and it was proper that the prophecies should be unsealed, or open, both that the events might be compared with the predictions, and that a persecuted church might be able to see what would be the result of all these things, and to find consolation in the assurance of the final triumph of the Son of God, Rev. 22: 10.

(4.) The fixed and unchangeable state of the righteous and the wicked, Rev. 22: 11–13.

(5.) The blessedness of those who keep the commandments of God, and who enter into the New Jerusalem, Rev. 22: 14–15.

(6.) Jesus, the root and the offspring of David, and the bright and morning star, proclaims himself to be the Author of all these revelations by the instrumentality of an angel, Rev. 22: 16.

(7.) The universal invitation of the gospel – the language of Jesus himself – giving utterance to his strong desire for the salvation of men, Rev. 22: 17.

feet of the angel which shewed me these things.

9 Then saith he unto me, See thou do it not: for I am thy fellowservant, and of thy brethren the prophets, and of them which keep the sayings of this book: worship God.

10 And he saith unto me, Seal not the sayings of the prophecy of this book: for the time is at hand.

11 He that is unjust, let him be unjust still: and he which is filthy, let him be filthy still: and he that is righteous, let him be righteous still: and he that is holy, let him be holy still.

12 And, behold, I come quickly; and my reward is with me, to give every man according as his work shall be.

13 I am Alpha and Omega, the beginning and the end, the first and the last.

14 Blessed are they that do his commandments, that they may have right to the tree of life, and may enter in through the gates into the city.

15 For without are dogs, and sorcerers, and whoremongers, and murderers, and idolaters, and whosoever loveth and maketh a lie.

16 I Jesus have sent mine angel to testify unto you these things in the churches. I am the root and the offspring of David, and the bright and morning star.

17 And the Spirit and the bride say, Come. And let him that heareth say, Come. And let him that is athirst come. And whosoever will, let him take the water of life freely.

18 For I testify unto every man that heareth the words of the prophecy of this book, If any man shall add unto these things, God shall add unto him the plagues that are written in this book:

19 And if any man shall take away from the words of the book of this prophecy, God shall take away his part out of the book of life, and out of the holy city, and from the things which are written in this book.

20 He which testifieth these things saith, Surely I come quickly. Amen. Even so, come, Lord Jesus.

15. dogs – *Greek*, "the dogs"; the impure, filthy (Rev. 22: 11; compare Phil. 3: 2).

16. mine angel – **f**or Jesus is Lord of the angels.

unto you – ministers and people in the seven representative churches, and, through you, to testify to Christians of all times and places.

root … offspring of David – appropriate title here where assuring His Church of "the sure mercies of David," secured to Israel first, and through Israel to the Gentiles. *Root* of David, as being Jehovah; the offspring of David as man. David's Lord, yet David's son (Matt. 22: 42–45).

the morning star – that ushered in the day of grace in the beginning of this dispensation and that shall usher in the everlasting day of glory at its close.

17. Reply of the spiritual Church and John to Christ's words (Rev. 22: 7,12,16).

the Spirit – in the churches and in the prophets.

the bride – not here called "wife," as that title applies to her only when the full number constituting the Church shall have been completed. The invitation, "Come," only holds good while the Church is still but an affianced *Bride,* and not the actually wedded *wife.* However, "Come" may rather be the prayer of the Spirit in the Church and in believers in reply to Christ's "I come quickly," crying, Even so, "Come" (Rev. 22: 7,12); Rev. 22: 20 confirms this view. The whole question of your salvation hinges on this, that you be able to hear with joy Christ's announcement, "I come," and to reply, "Come" [Bengel]. Come to fully glorify Thy Bride.

20. Amen. Even so, come – The Song of Solomon (Song 8: 14) closes with the same yearning prayer for Christ's coming.

Amen – May the Blessed Lord who has caused all holy Scriptures to be written for our learning, bless this humble effort to make Scripture expound itself, and make it an instrument towards the conversion of sinners and the edification of saints, to the glory of His great name and the hastening of His kingdom! Amen.

(8.) A solemn command not to change anything that had been revealed in this book, either by adding to it or by taking from it, Rev. 22: 18–19.

(9.) The assurance that he who had made these revelations would come quickly, and the joyous assent of John to this, and prayer that his advent might soon occur, Rev. 22: 20.

(10.) The benediction, Rev. 22: 21.

19. And if any man shall take away from the words of the book of this prophecy. If he shall reject the book altogether; if he shall, in transcribing it, designedly strike any part of it out. It is conceivable that, from the remarkable nature of the communications made in this book, and the fact that they seemed to be unintelligible, John supposed there might be those who would be inclined to omit some portions as improbable, or that he apprehended that when the portions which describe Antichrist were fulfilled in distant ages, those to whom those portions applied would be disposed to strike them from the sacred volume, or to corrupt them. He thought proper to guard against this by this solemn declaration of the consequence which would follow such an act. The whole book was to be received – with all its fearful truths – as a revelation from God;

and however obscure it might seem, in due time it would be made plain; however faithfully it might depict a fearful apostasy, it was important, both to show the truth of Divine inspiration and to save the church, that these disclosures should be in their native purity in the possession of the people of God.

God shall take away his part out of the book of life. Perhaps there is here an intimation that this would be most likely to be done by those who professed to be Christians, and who supposed that their names were in the book of life. In fact, most of the corruptions of the sacred Scriptures have been attempted by those who have professed some form of Christianity. Infidels have but little interest in attempting such changes, and but little influence to make them received by the church. It is most convenient for them, as it is most agreeable to their feelings, to reject the Bible altogether. When it said here that "God would take away his part out of the book of life," the meaning is not that his name had been written in that book, but that he would take away the part which he might have had, or which he professed to have in that book. Such corruption of the Divine oracles would show that they had no true religion, and would be excluded from heaven.